# REVEL for *The Necessary Shakespeare*

REVEL is Pearson's newest way of delivering our respected content. Fully digital and highly engaging, REVEL offers an immersive learning experience designed for the way today's students read, think, and learn. Enlivening course content with media interactives and assessments, REVEL empowers educators to increase engagement with the course and to connect better with students.

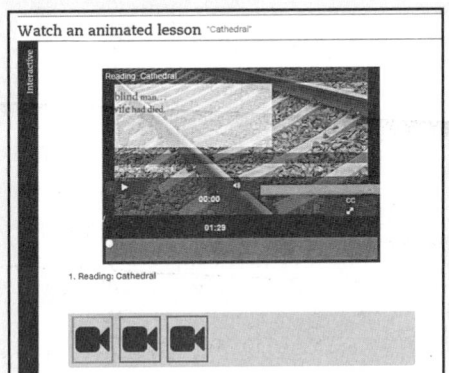

## Video and Rich Multimedia Content

Videos, audio recordings, animations, and multimedia instruction provide context that enables students to engage with the text in a more meaningful way.

## Interactive Readings and Exercises

Students explore readings through interactive texts. Robust annotation tools allow students to take notes, and post-reading assignments let instructors monitor their students' completion of readings before class begins.

## Just-in-Time Context

Just-in-time context—encompassing biographical, historical, and social insights—is incorporated throughout, giving students a deeper understanding of what they read.

## Integrated Writing Assignments

Minimal-stakes, low-stakes, and high-stakes writing tasks allow students multiple opportunities to interact with the ideas presented in the reading assignments, ensuring that they come to class better prepared.

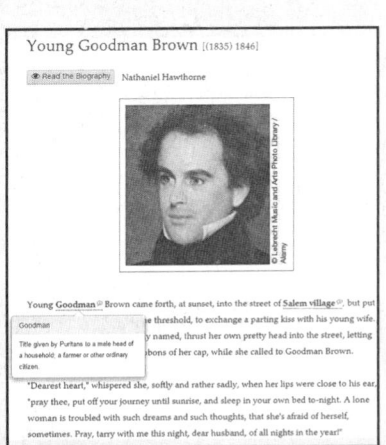

**Visit www.pearsonhighered.com revel for more information.**

# The Necessary Shakespeare

# The
# Necessary
# Shakespeare

### Fifth Edition

Edited by

## *David Bevington*

The University of Chicago

Boston   Columbus   Indianapolis   New York   San Francisco   Amsterdam
Cape Town   Dubai   London   Madrid   Milan   Munich   Paris   Montréal   Toronto   Delhi
Mexico City   São Paulo   Sydney   Hong Kong   Seoul   Singapore   Taipei   Tokyo

Senior Acquisitions Editor: Brad Potthoff
Program Manager: Katharine Glynn
Product Marketing Manager: Ali Arnold
Digital Editor: Tracy Cunningham
Media Producer: Alex Brown
Content Specialist: Julia Pomann
Project Manager: Shannon Kobran
Project Coordination, Text Design, and Electronic Page Makeup: Integra
Program Design Lead: Heather Scott
Cover Designer: Studio Montage
Cover Art: Claudio Divizia/Shutterstock
Senior Manufacturing Buyer: Roy L. Pickering, Jr.
Printer/Binder: Manufactured in the United States by RR Donnelley
Insert Printer: Phoenix Color/Hagerstown

Acknowledgments of third-party content appear below appear on the appropriate page within text. Diagram from Swan Theatre by Van Buchell (van Buchell/DeWitt) on pages 1, 269, 459, 801, and 879: Van Buchell/Utrecht University

**Library of Congress Cataloging-in-Publication Data Is Available On Request**

1 2 3 4 5 6 7 8 9 10—V011—19 18 17 16

www.pearsonhighered.com

Student ISBN 10:      0-13-413988-7
Student ISBN 13: 978-0-13-413988-3
A la Carte ISBN-10:      0-13-431092-6
A la Carte ISBN-13: 978-0-13-431092-3

# CONTENTS

**Preface**    viii
*Shakespeare's World:* **A Visual Portfolio**    **following page I-22**

# PREFACE

*The Necessary Shakespeare* distills the best, the oftenest read, the most often produced of Shakespeare's great plays. By publishing this selection in a compact paperback edition, my hope is to expose a new broader student audience to the work of perhaps the greatest author in the history of the English language.

Of the thirty-eight or so plays and various poems written by or attributed to Shakespeare, this collection offers twenty plays and the sonnets. I have made these selections based on the response of Shakespeare instructors across the country who indicated which works are truly "necessary" in the undergraduate classroom. I have also tried to select plays that are frequently performed or widely available on film or video.

I include seven romantic comedies, four English history plays, seven of the great tragedies, and two romances. Cutting is always a thankless task, and I have omitted some works that some readers will miss: *Troilus and Cressida, The Second Part of King Henry the Fourth, Coriolanus,* and *Cymbeline* might well be on such a list. Even so, I hope that this collection does represent the best and best known of his work. It covers Shakespeare's favorite genres; it shows his development from the early *The Taming of the Shrew* and *Richard the Third* to the late *The Tempest;* it shows him as an amazing poet as well as dramatist. My hope is that such a volume will find a real use in personal libraries and classrooms.

The arrangement of the plays in this volume under the categories of comedies, histories, tragedies, and romances is close to that of the First Folio of 1623, in which Shakespeare's plays were grouped under three categories of comedies, histories, and tragedies (the romances were included under "comedies"). They were published posthumously by two of his erstwhile colleagues in the acting company known as the King's Men. The poems and sonnets were published separately.

My edition of *The Complete Works of Shakespeare* (seventh edition, Pearson, 2014) is available for more complete coverage. Over the course of its publishing history, I have profited greatly from the consultation of various friends and colleagues at colleges and universities all over the world. In each case I showed the consultant all the materials I had prepared—the Shakespeare text, the commentary notes, the textual notes, the introduction—and sought that person's aid in revision. These friends have aided me through progressive reconsiderations of the work. Other colleagues helped me with the plays and poems omitted from this present volume. I want to extend my warmest thanks to all.

In this present edition, I have also selected from the front matter and appendices of the 2014 edition of *The Complete Works of Shakespeare.* The choices here are an attempt to respond to the desires of representative readers and users of the volume. They helped me decide that we should keep the introductory material on life in Shakespeare's England, the drama before Shakespeare, London theatres and dramatic companies, Shakespeare's life and work, how to read Shakespeare, Shakespeare's language, and Shakespeare criticism. All of these sections have been brought up to date, especially the materials on Shakespeare criticism. I have added substantially to the bibliography, to make it as up-to-date as possible.

In the appendices, I have kept the material on Canon, Dates, and Early Texts, and on sources. An essay on "Shakespeare in Performance," by Professor Lois Potter of the University of Delaware, brings performance history up to date with an emphasis on film and television. An updated Appendix on Films and Videos as a Guide to the Study of Shakespeare provides an extensive filmography or film biography, listing the best and most available of films or videos for each play in this edition. I have revised the bibliographies to focus on the works contained in this edition. I have recast the index. Readers and teachers seem to appreciate having an index, although many editions do not include one. I have kept this as part of the volume.

# KEY FEATURES OF THE FIFTH EDITION

- **"Reading Shakespeare in the Twenty-First Century,"** an updated essay that opens the general introduction, poses questions about the relevance and difficulty of Shakespeare for contemporary students and offers practical strategies for readers new to Shakespeare.
- A new section in the General Introduction, **"Shakespeare on Family Life and Women,"** describes how Shakespeare's views about families and women can be discerned from what we know of his personal life. The section also discusses what we can learn from a study of the the many memorable female characters portrayed in his plays.
- To help both instructors and students with usability, the General Introduction is numbered with Arabic numbers instead of Roman numerals.
- **"Shakespeare's Language,"** in the general introduction, has been completely rewritten in order to better introduce Shakespeare's idioms and vocabulary to novice readers.
- **"Films and Videos as a Guide to the Study of Shakespeare,"** is an updated appendix for the fifth edition, offering an annotated filmography and advice on how to use films and videos to study a play.

- **"Thoroughly revised and updated notes and glosses** provide contemporary readers the support they need to understand Elizabethan language and idioms in accessible and clear modern language, line by line.
- **A richly illustrated general introduction** provides readers with the historical and cultural background required to understand Shakespeare's works in context.
- **"Shakespeare's World: A Visual Portfolio"** provides 16 pages of full-color illustrations to help readers visualize Renaissance life and culture and to trace the history of significant performances on stage and screen. Nearly one-third of these color images are new to this edition and are drawn from Shakespeare productions from around the globe.
- Woodcuts and other illustrations throughout the volume from the sixteenth and seventeenth centuries, depicting famous persons, animals, social customs, pastimes, hobbies, costuming conventions, themes, myths, and the like from the world that Shakespeare knew.

# SUPPLEMENTS

The following supplements are available free when ordered with this text. Please consult your local Pearson representative if you would like to set up a value pack.

*Evaluating a Performance,* **by Mike Greenwald,** informs students about stage and theatrical performance and helps them to become more critical viewers of dramatic productions (ISBN 0-321-09541-3).

*Screening Shakespeare: Using Film to Understand the Plays,* **by Michael Greer,** is a brief, practical guide to select feature films of the most commonly taught plays (ISBN 0-321-19479-9).

David Bevington
2016

# GENERAL INTRODUCTION

## READING SHAKESPEARE IN THE TWENTY-FIRST CENTURY

Why read Shakespeare today? He lived some four centuries ago. He wrote in an earlier form of English that needs getting used to. His vocabulary is daunting. He and his audiences lived in a world that was remarkably different from ours: a world of religious wars between Catholic and Protestant, of competing monarchies, and of extreme contrasts between the wealth of a tiny wealthy ruling elite and the poverty of a huge underclass composed largely of agricultural laborers. Travel was unsafe and sanitation conditions were rudimentary. Shakespeare dramatizes the lives of ancient kings and personages that are not an immediate part of our own history. He is familiar with old myths and legends that are no longer current today. Given these circumstances, how can Shakespeare hope to be relevant?

Until recently, Shakespeare was more a required subject in schools and colleges than is the case today. As a mandatory subject, he was resisted like any inflexible requirement. Why study something simply because it is a traditional part of the curriculum? Isn't that boring? In an age when we are inclined to be wary of dead European white male authors, isn't Shakespeare a prime candidate for dismissal? He is all of those things: dead, European, white, and male.

Yet Shakespeare lives, despite these hazards, in the theater, in film and video, and in the classroom. The evidence is all around us. Enrollments are up in colleges and universities, largely on a voluntary basis. And Shakespeare has enjoyed a remarkable revival in film and video. See Appendix 4 at the back of this volume for an extensive account of plays available in films and video, along with a selective play-by-play filmography giving dates, directors, and leading actors.

Here we might name some of the greatest Shakespeare films of the twentieth and twenty-first centuries, to make the point of Shakespeare's great popularity on screen. Mary Pickford and Douglas Fairbanks Sr. starred as Kate and Petruchio in the first full-length talking film of a Shakespeare play, *The Taming of the Shrew*, 1929. Max Reinhardt's *A Midsummer Night's Dream*, 1935, starred Mickey Rooney as Puck and James Cagney as Bottom the Weaver, along with some other Hollywood celebrities. Franco Zeffirelli cast Richard Burton and Elizabeth Taylor as Petruchio and Kate in his *The Taming of the Shrew* (1967), Leonard Whiting and Olivia Hussey as the title characters in his *Romeo and Juliet* (1968), and Mel Gibson as the protagonist in his *Hamlet* (1990), along with Glenn Close as Gertrude, Helena Bonham Carter as Ophelia, Ian Holm as Polonius, Alan Bates as Claudius, and Paul Scofield as the Ghost.

Laurence Olivier achieved great success in 1944 with his full-length color film of *Henry V*, produced during World War II to encourage patriotic support for the war effort against Germany. Olivier's *Hamlet*, 1948, *Richard III*, 1955, and *Othello*, 1965, were no less popular.

Orson Welles's *Macbeth*, 1948, and *Othello*, 1952, were conscious attempts to show that the United States could match the British film industry in Shakespearean high art. Welles's *Chimes at Midnight* (1965), with himself in the role of Falstaff, combined elements of *1* and *2 Henry IV* and bits of *The Merry Wives of Windsor* to produce a moving account of Prince Hal's friendship with, and ultimate rejection of, Falstaff.

Another wave of Shakespeare films began in 1989 with Kenneth Branagh's highly successful *Henry V*, challenging the patriotism of Olivier's 1944 version with a more matter-of-fact appraisal of warmaking. *Much Ado About Nothing* followed in 1993 with Branagh as Benedick and his then wife Emma Thompson as Beatrice, along with Denzel Washington as Don Pedro, Keanu Reeves as Don John, and Michael Keaton as Dogberry. Branagh repeated the surefire stratagem of employing star actors in his four-hour *Hamlet*, 1996, with himself as Hamlet, Julie Christie as Gertrude, Kate Winslet as Ophelia, Derek Jacobi as Claudius, and a host of cameo appearances by Jack Lemmon (Marcellus), Gérard Depardieu (Reynaldo), Robin Williams (Osric), Billy Crystal (the Gravedigger), and Charlton Heston (the Player King). More recent have been Branagh's *Love's Labour's Lost* (2000) and *As You Like It* (2006).

Other famous directors on the Shakespeare scene have included Akira Kurosawa, with his *Throne of Blood*, 1957, based on *Macbeth*, and his *Ran*, 1985, based on *King Lear*; Grigori Kozintsev, with two notable Russian films, *Hamlet*, 1964, and *King Lear*, 1970; Peter Brook, directing *King Lear* in 1971 with Paul Scofield in the lead role; Trevor Nunn, directing *Antony and Cleopatra* (1974), *The Comedy of Errors* (1978), *Macbeth* (1979), *Othello* (1990), and *Twelfth Night* (1996); Peter Hall, directing *A Midsummer Night's Dream* (1969); Roman Polanski, directing *Macbeth* (1971); Julie Taymor, directing *Titus Andronicus* (1999) and *The Tempest* (2010), with Helen Mirren as a female protagonist named Prospera; Baz Luhrmann, directing *Romeo + Juliet* (1996); Michael Almeyerda, directing *Hamlet* (2000); Michael Radford, directing Al Pacino, Jeremy Irons, and others in *The Merchant of Venice* (2004), based on a Broadway production; Gregory Doran, directing *Macbeth* (2004), with Antony Sher in the title role; Gregory Doran, directing David Tennant, Patrick Stewart, and others in a TV film version of *Hamlet* based on a stage production for the Royal Shakespeare Company (2009); Trevor Nunn, directing *King Lear* (2009), with Ian McKellen as King Lear; Nicholas Hytner, directing *Hamlet* (2010), with Rory Kinnear in the title role; Ralph Fiennes, directing *Coriolanus* (2011), with Fiennes himself in the title role; and still others.

Film adaptations are a sure sign of Shakespeare's popularity today. Along with the films of Akira Kurosawa listed above, one thinks immediately of *West Side Story*, 1961, based on *Romeo and Juliet*; *Kiss Me, Kate*, 1953, based on *The Taming of the Shrew*; Gil Junger's *10 Things I Hate About You*, 1999, based on the same play; Tim Blake Nelson's *O*, 2001, based on *Othello*; and *Shakespeare in Love*, 1998, containing some fine scenes from *Romeo and Juliet*. Again, there are many others.

Recent stage productions of Shakespeare's plays have also enjoyed as great a success, albeit necessarily for less-global audiences. Ian McKellen in *King Lear* (2007) has toured intercontinentally to positive reviews. Greg Doran had great success at the Swan Theatre in Stratford-upon-Avon with his *Othello* (2004), starring Antony Sher as Iago. Sher was no less astonishing as Richard III at Stratford-upon-Avon in 1984 and as Falstaff in 2014. Equally wonderful in the same role were Ian McKellen at London's National Theatre in 1990 and Simon Russell Beale at Stratford in 1992. Patrick Stewart has been very well received in *Macbeth* (London, 2007). Some of the best film versions we have began as stage productions, including Olivier's *Richard III*, Branagh's *Henry V*, McKellen and Dench in *Macbeth*, McKellen and Willard White in *Othello*, *West Side Story*, *Kiss Me, Kate*, and still others. *Much Ado About Nothing* was produced by Joseph Papp and directed by A. J. Antoon at the New York Shakespeare Festival in Delacorte Theatre in 1972 before it was telecast the following year. The enduring popularity of outdoor summer performances in New York's Central Park is confirmed by the fact that fans will wait in line for hours to see the productions. Other festivals and repertory Shakespeare companies at Stratford in Canada, Stratford-upon-Avon in England; Ashland, Oregon; Washington, D.C.; Chicago; and many others are no less a mark of tribute to Shakespeare as a preeminently successful writer for the stage. Shakespeare has become big business.

Seeing one or more productions of a Shakespeare play is often a very good way to start. Films are easily rented or otherwise obtained in video, and watching a film is something we all generally enjoy. Seeing a play in the theater can certainly be no less engrossing, but the opportunities come far less often, so the thing to do is to take advantage of film or video. A common experience today is for viewers, in the theater or watching a screen, to be surprised with how clear the story can be and how good acting can really help with interpretation. Watching a play, even for the first time, one scarcely notices how some forms of expression might seem a little archaic or unfamiliar. Fine actors deliver the lines with their own well-trained comprehension, so that what they say to each other or in soliloquy sounds intelligible and persuasive.

When one reads a play for the first time, probably the best thing to do is to ignore the notes for the moment and try to hear voices saying the lines as they would in a performance. We can take advantage of the notes in a subsequent reading, as we retrace our steps and stop to reflect on the meanings of unfamiliar terms. Reading a play, by Shakespeare or anyone else, is a challenging and exciting assignment, because as readers our task is in effect to produce and direct the play in our heads. We need to imagine the setting, whether indoors or outdoors, with scenic effects and furniture as needed. We need to clothe the actors in appropriate garb and give them the hand props called for in the script. We need to decide what age the actors are and what they look like. As Shakespeare says to his spectators in the opening chorus of Henry V:

> Piece out our imperfections with your thoughts.
> Into a thousand parts divide one man,
> And make imaginary puissance.
> Think, when we talk of horses, that you see them
> Printing their proud hoofs i'th' receiving earth.

Shakespeare asks us to adorn the actors with our thoughts and "Carry them here and there, jumping o'er times." We are in charge of the show. Classroom discussion can be invaluable, of course. But one needs to take individual initiative and be an active, imaginative reader. One needs to ask questions all the time: why is a character saying what he or she is saying to another character? Where are the changes in tempo or "beat" in a scene? What happens when someone else enters or exits? What are the characters trying to do in a particular scene? What are they after? How do they change under the pressure of observation and conversation?

Why read Shakespeare, when some more modern dramatist or novelist or poet or short story writer might seem more available and relevant? Each reader or viewer must answer this for him- or herself, of course, but the general view down through the centuries is that Shakespeare is an extraordinary poet and that he excels in the breadth and incisiveness of his depictions of human experience. As a poet he commands an extraordinary range of vocabulary and image-making. His vocabulary is roughly twice that of his nearest competitor in English and American literature. He has a formidable talent in his use of verse forms, from blank verse to rhymed couplets to the fourteen-line sonnet to various lyric stanzas. His prose is admirably flexible, especially for comedy. He thinks in images, as all great poets do. He says things so well that countless utterances of his have become proverbial: "Neither a borrower nor a lender be," "The apparel oft proclaims the man," "Frailty, thy name is woman," "The time is out of joint," "Brevity is the soul of wit," "To be or not to be, that is the question," "Thus conscience doth make cowards of us all," "Get thee to a nunnery," "There's a divinity that shapes our ends, rough-hew them how we will," and on and on. All these are chosen from *Hamlet*; the list could be substantially extended just in this one play. Shakespeare is an important architect of the English language as we have come to know it.

Then, too, we have in Shakespeare's writings a remarkable breadth of human experience, analyzed and depicted with acumen and compassionate understanding. His characters fall in love, experience jealousy and rivalry, cope with parental obtuseness, learn what it is like to challenge the authority of a parent, experience frustration in personal ambitions, suffer neglect and misunderstanding. As they grow older, they often encounter religious doubt, go through the dark night of skeptical uncertainty and loss of faith, know what it is to become middle-aged and fearful of a decline in sexual potency and physical strength, and discover to their horror their own capacity for evil, even to the point of killing another human being. They sometimes experience the total disillusionment of misanthropy and misogyny, feel shame and the need to be forgiven, and worry about retirement from the world. One beautiful thing about this richly complex portrait of human striving is that it paints a chronological portrait of the life of the human being from childhood to middle years and then to a decline toward death, all of this brilliantly laid out by Shakespeare as his plays and poems move from early to late. The plays and poems are the biography of what it is to be human.

The fact that Shakespeare's world is very different from ours ought to be an added incentive for wanting to read him, not a detraction. We all need to know more about other cultures and other value systems, in our world today and in the past. Strangeness can give us a perspective on ourselves. It can give us the chance to question our values by comparing them with what other peoples in other eras have believed in.

This is only a sketch of the author from whom we can hope to learn so much about ourselves. The place to begin, perhaps, is to locate Shakespeare in the England and the London in which he lived and worked. What was England like in the late sixteenth and early seventeenth centuries, while he was alive, from 1564 to 1616? In what ways did it differ from our modern world? What insights into his work can we derive by seeing him in the context of his personal environment?

## LIFE IN SHAKESPEARE'S ENGLAND

England during Shakespeare's lifetime (1564–1616) was a proud nation with a strong sense of national identity, but it was also a small nation by modern standards. Probably not more than five million people lived in the whole of England, considerably fewer than now live in London. England's territories in France were no longer extensive, as they had been during the fourteenth century and earlier; in fact, by the end of Queen Elizabeth's reign (1558–1603), England had virtually retired from the territories she had previously controlled on the Continent, especially in France. Wales was a conquered principality. England's overseas empire in America had scarcely begun, with the Virginia settlement established in the 1580s. Scotland was not yet a part of Great Britain; union with Scotland would not take place until 1707,

*"Enclosure" was a problem throughout the sixteenth century in England. Croplands were converted into pasture. The livelihood of the plowman was threatened by the pasturing of sheep and the growing production of wool.*

despite the fact that King James VI of Scotland assumed the English throne in 1603 as James I of England. Ireland, although declared a kingdom under English rule in 1541, was more a source of trouble than of economic strength. The last years of Elizabeth's reign, especially from 1597 to 1601, were plagued by the rebellion of the Irish under Hugh O'Neill, Earl of Tyrone. Thus, England of the sixteenth and early seventeenth centuries was both small and isolated.

## THE SOCIAL AND ECONOMIC BACKGROUND

By and large, England was a rural land. Much of the kingdom was still wooded, though timber was being used increasingly in manufacturing and shipbuilding. The area of the Midlands, today heavily industrialized, was at that time still a region of great trees, green fields, and clear streams. England's chief means of livelihood was agriculture. This part of the economy was generally in a bad way, however, and people who lived off the land did not share in the prosperity of many Londoners. A problem throughout the sixteenth century was that of "enclosure": the conversion by rich landowners of croplands into pasturage. Farmers and peasants complained bitterly that they were being dispossessed and starved for the benefit of livestock. Rural uprisings and food riots were common, to the dismay of the authorities. Some Oxfordshire peasants arose in 1596, threatening to massacre the gentry and march on London; other riots had occurred in 1586 and 1591. There were thirteen riots in Kent alone during Elizabeth's reign. Unrest continued into the reign of James I, notably the Midlands' rising of 1607. Although the

*Sixteenth-century London was a city teeming with activity. Pedestrians were often forced to make way for the livestock being driven through the streets.*

government did what it could to inhibit enclosure, the economic forces at work were too massive and too inadequately understood to be curbed by governmental fiat. The absence of effective bureaucracies or agencies of coercion compounded the difficulty of governmental control. Pasture used large areas with greater efficiency than crop farming and required far less labor. The wool produced by the pasturing of sheep was needed in ever increasing amounts for the manufacture of cloth.

The wool industry also experienced occasional economic difficulties, to be sure; overexpansion in the early years of the sixteenth century created a glutted market that collapsed disastrously in 1551, producing widespread unemployment. Despite such fluctuations and reversals, however, the wool industry at least provided handsome profits for some landowners and middlemen. Mining and manufacture in coal, iron, tin, copper, and lead, although insignificant by modern standards, also were expanding at a significant rate. Trading companies exploited the rich new resources of the Americas, as well as of eastern Europe and the Orient. Queen Elizabeth aided economic development by keeping England out of war with her continental enemies as long as possible, despite provocations from those powers and despite the eagerness of some of her advisers to retaliate.

Certainly England's economic condition was better than the economic condition of the rest of the Continent; an Italian called England "the land of comforts." Yet although some prosperity did exist, it was not evenly distributed. Especially during Shakespeare's first years in London, in the late 1580s and the 1590s, the gap between rich and poor grew more and more extreme. Elizabeth's efforts at peacemaking were no longer able to prevent years of war with the Catholic powers of the Continent. Taxation grew heavier, and inflation proceeded at an unusually rapid rate during this period. A succession of bad harvests compounded the miseries of those who dwelled on the land. When the hostilities on the Continent ceased for a time in about 1597, a wave of returning veterans added to unemployment and crime. The rising prosperity experienced by Shakespeare and other fortunate Londoners was undeniably real, but it was not universal. Nowhere was the contrast between rich and poor more visible than in London.

*This detail from a 1572 map of London shows closely packed buildings intersected with throroughfares, with gardens and open spaces on the outskirts.*

COURTESY, GUILDHALL LIBRARY, CORPORATION OF LONDON

*London Bridge, lined with shops, houses, and severed heads on poles, provided a colorful route for those traveling between the north and south banks of the Thames. A number of Elizabethan theaters, including the Globe, were located on the south bank.*

BY PERMISSION OF THE FOLGER SHAKESPEARE LIBRARY

*The taverns of Cheapside in London were popular and occasionally rowdy.*

## London

Sixteenth-century London was at once more attractive and less attractive than twenty-first-century London. It was full of trees and gardens; meadows and cultivated lands reached in some places to its very walls. Today we can perhaps imagine the way in which it bordered clear streams and green fields when we approach from a distance some noncommercial provincial city such as Lincoln, York, or Hereford. Partly surrounded by its ancient wall, London was by no means a large metropolis. With 190,000 to 200,000 inhabitants in the city proper and its suburbs, it was nonetheless the largest city of Europe, and its dominance among English cities was even more striking; in 1543–1544, London paid thirty times the subsidy of Norwich, then the second-largest city in the kingdom (15,000 inhabitants). Although London's population had expanded into the surrounding area in all directions, the city proper stretched along the north bank of the Thames River from the old Tower of London on the east to St. Paul's Cathedral and the Fleet Ditch on the west—a distance of little more than a mile. Visitors approaching London from the south bank of the Thames (the Bankside) and crossing London Bridge could see virtually all of this exciting city lying before them. London Bridge itself was one of the major

attractions of the city, lined with shops and richly decorated on occasion for the triumphal entry of a king or queen.

Yet London had its grim and ugly side as well. On London Bridge could sometimes be seen the heads of executed traitors. The city's houses were generally small and crowded; its streets were often narrow and filthy. In the absence of sewers, open ditches in the streets served to collect and carry off refuse. Frequent epidemics of the bubonic plague were the inevitable result of unsanitary conditions and medical ignorance. Lighting of the streets at night was generally nonexistent, and the constabulary was notoriously unreliable. Shakespeare gives us unforgettable satires of night watchmen and bumbling police officials in *Much Ado About Nothing* (Dogberry and the night watch) and *Measure for Measure* (Constable Elbow). Prostitution thrived in the suburbs, conveniently located, although beyond the reach of the London authorities. Again, we are indebted to Shakespeare for a memorable portrayal in *Measure for Measure* of just such a demimonde (Mistress Overdone the bawd, Pompey her pimp, and various customers). Houses of prostitution were often found in the vicinity of the public theaters, since the theaters also took advantage of suburban locations to escape the stringent regulations imposed by London's

Lord Mayor and Council of Aldermen. The famous Globe Theatre, for example, was on the south bank of the Thames, a short distance west of London Bridge. Another theatrical building (called simply "The Theatre"), used earlier by Shakespeare and the Lord Chamberlain's players, was located in Finsbury Fields, a short distance across Moorfields from London's northeast corner. The suburbs also housed various con games and illegal operations, some of them brilliantly illustrated (and no doubt exaggerated) in Ben Jonson's *The Alchemist* (1610).

Roughly half of London's total population, perhaps 100,000 people, lived within its walls, and as many more in the suburbs. The royal palace of Whitehall, Westminster Abbey (then known as the Abbey Church of St. Peter), the Parliament House, and Westminster Hall were well outside London, two miles or so to the west on the Thames River. They remain today in the same location, in Westminster, although the metropolis of London has long since surrounded these official buildings.

## Travel

Travel was still extremely painful and slow because of the poor condition of the roads. Highway robbers were a constant threat. (The celebrated highway robbery in Shakespeare's *1 Henry IV* takes place at Gads Hill, on the main road between London and Canterbury.) English inns seem to have been good, however, and certainly much better than the inns of the Continent. Travel on horseback was the most common method of transportation, and probably the most comfortable, since coach building was a new and imperfect art. Coaches of state, some of which we see in prints and pictures of the era, were lumbering affairs, no doubt handsome enough in processions, but springless, unwieldly, and hard to pull. Carts and wagons were used for carrying merchandise, but packsaddles were safer and quicker. Under such difficulties, no metropolitan area such as London could possibly have thrived in the interior. London depended for its commercial greatness upon the Thames River and its access to the North Sea.

## Commerce

When Elizabeth came to the English throne in 1558, England's chief foreign trade was with Antwerp, Bruges, and other Belgian cities. Antwerp was an especially important market for England's export of wool cloth. This market was seriously threatened, however, since the Low Countries were under the domination of the Catholic King of Spain, Philip II. When Philip undertook to punish his Protestant subjects in the Low Countries for their religious heresy, many of Elizabeth's counselors and subjects urged her to come to the defense of England's Protestant neighbors and trading allies. Elizabeth held back. Philip's armies attacked Antwerp in 1576 and again in 1585,

putting an end to the commercial ascendancy of that great northern European metropolis. Perhaps as many as one-third of Antwerp's merchants and artisans settled in London, bringing with them their expert knowledge of commerce and manufacture. The influx of so many skilled workers and merchants into London produced problems of unemployment and overcrowding but contributed nevertheless to London's emergence as a leading port of trade.

English ships assumed a dominant position in Mediterranean trade, formerly carried on mainly by the Venetians. In the Baltic Sea, England competed successfully in trade that had previously been controlled by the Hanseatic League. Bristol thrived on commerce with Ireland and subsequently on trade with the Western Hemisphere. Boston and Hull increased their business with Scandinavian ports. The Russia Company was founded in 1555; the Levant Company became the famous East India Company in 1600; and the Virginia Company opened up trade with the New World in the Western Hemisphere. Fisheries were developed in the North Sea, in the waters north of Ireland, and off the banks of Newfoundland. Elizabeth and her ministers encouraged this commercial expansion.

## The Poor Laws and Apprenticeship

Despite the new prosperity experienced by many Elizabethans, especially in London, unemployment remained a serious problem. The suppresssion of the monasteries in 1536–1539, as part of Henry VIII's reformation of the Catholic Church, had dispossessed a large class of persons who were not easily reemployed. Other causes of unemployment, such as the periodic collapse of the wool trade, dispossession of farm workers by enclosure of land, the sudden influx of skilled artisans from Antwerp, and the

*Although some Elizabethans rose to great wealth, poverty and unemployment were widespread.*

return of army veterans, have already been mentioned. Elizabethan parliaments attempted to cope with the problem of unemployment but did so in ways that seem unduly harsh today. Several laws were passed between 1531, when the distinction between those poor needing charity and those unwilling to work first became law, and 1597–1598. The harshest of the laws was that of 1547, providing that vagabonds be branded and enslaved for two years; escape was punishable by death or life enslavement. This act was repealed in 1549, but subsequent acts of 1572 and 1576 designated ten classes of vagrants and required municipal authorities to provide work for the healthy unemployed of each town or parish. This localization of responsibility laid the basis for what has been known historically as the "poor rate" (a local tax levied for the support of the poor) and for that sinister institution, the workhouse. The provisions of this act remained in force for centuries. The most comprehensive laws were those of the Parliament of 1597–1598, which repeated many provisions of earlier acts and added harsh, punitive penalties intended to send vagabonds back to the parishes in which they had been born or had last worked. After 1597, no begging was permitted; the poor were supposed to be provided for by the "poor rate" already established.

Regulations for apprentices were no less strict. An act of Parliament of 1563, known as the Statute of Artificers, gave the craft trades of England—still organized as medieval guilds—virtually complete authority over the young persons apprenticed to a trade. The law severely limited access to apprenticeship to sons of families with estates worth at least forty shillings of income. Apprenticeship usually began between the ages of fourteen and seventeen and lasted for a period of not less than seven years. During this time, the young worker lived with the family of the employer. Without such an extensive apprenticeship, entry into the skilled crafts was virtually impossible. Apprenticeships were not open, however, in all guilds, and the law courts subsequently ruled that apprenticeship rules did not apply to crafts developed after 1563, so that exceptions did exist. All able-bodied workers not bound to crafts were supposed to work in agriculture. Acting companies, such as the company Shakespeare joined, were not technically organized as guilds, though the boys who played women's parts were in some cases at least bound by the terms of apprenticeship; a number of the adult actors belonged to one London guild or another and could use that status to apprentice boys. We do not know whether Shakespeare actually served such an indenture before becoming a full member of his acting company.

## Social Change

The opportunities for rapid economic advance in Elizabethan England, though limited almost entirely to those who were already prosperous, did produce social change

and a quality of restlessness in English society. "New men" at court were an increasing phenomenon under the Tudor monarchs, especially Henry VII and Henry VIII, who tended to rely on loyal counselors of humble origin rather than on the once-too-powerful nobility. Cardinal Wolsey, for example, rose from obscurity to become the most mighty subject of Henry VIII's realm, with a newly built residence (Hampton Court) rivaling the splendor of the King's own palaces. He was detested as an upstart by old aristocrats, such as the Duke of Norfolk, and his sudden fall was as spectacular as had been his rise to power. The Earl of Leicester, Queen Elizabeth's first favorite, was a descendant of the Edmund Dudley who had risen from unpretentious beginnings to great eminence under Henry VII, Queen Elizabeth's grandfather. Although Queen Elizabeth did not contribute substantially to the new aristocracy—she created only three peers from 1573 onward—new and influential families were numerous throughout the century. Conversely, the ancient families discovered that they were no longer entrusted with positions of highest authority. To be sure, the aristocracy remained at the apex of England's social structure. New aspirants to power emulated the aristocracy by purchasing land and building splendid residences, rather than defining themselves as a rich new "middle class." Bourgeois status was something the new men put behind them as quickly as they could. Moreover, social mobility could work in both directions: upward and downward. Many men were quickly ruined by the costly and competitive business of seeking favor at the Tudor court. The poor, in a vast majority, enjoyed virtually no rights at all. Nonetheless, the Elizabethan era was one of greater opportunity for rapid social and economic advancement among persons of wealth than England had heretofore known.

Increased economic contacts with the outside world inevitably led to the importation of new styles of living. Such new fashions, together with the rapid changes now possible in social position, produced a reaction of dismay from those who feared the destruction of traditional English values. Attitudes toward Italy veered erratically between condemnation and admiration: on the one hand, Italy was the home of the Catholic Church and originator of many supposedly decadent fashions, whereas, on the other hand, Italy was the cradle of humanism and the country famed for Venice's experiment in republican government. To many conservative Englishmen, the word *Italianate* connoted a whole range of villainous practices, including diabolical methods of torture and revenge: poisoned books of devotion that would kill the unsuspecting victims who kissed them, ingeniously contrived chairs that would close upon the person who sat in them, and the like. The revenge plays of Shakespeare's contemporaries, such as *Antonio's Revenge* by John Marston, *The Revenger's Tragedy* by Thomas Middleton, and *The White Devil* by John Webster, offer spectacular caricatures of the so-called

*This brothel scene, featuring gambling or dicing, illustrates some of the vices that were attributed to the corrupting influence from abroad.*

Italianate style in murder. The name of Italy was also associated with licentiousness, immorality, and outlandish fashions in clothes. France, too, was accused of encouraging such extravagances in dress as ornamented headdresses, stiffly pleated ruffs, padded doublets, puffed or double sleeves, and richly decorated hose. Rapid changes in fashion added to the costliness of being up to date and thereby increased the outcry against vanity in dress. Fencing, dicing, the use of cosmetics, the smoking of tobacco, the drinking of imported wines, and almost every vice known to humanity were attributed by angry moralists to the corrupting influence from abroad.

Not all Englishmen deplored continental fashion, of course. Persons of advanced taste saw the importation of European styles as a culturally liberating process. Fashion thus became a subject of debate between moral traditionalists and those who welcomed the new styles. The controversy was a bitter one, with religious overtones, in which the reformers' angry accusations became increasingly extreme. This attack on changing fashion was, in fact, an integral part of the Puritan movement. It therefore stressed the sinfulness, not only of extravagance in clothing, but also of the costliness in building great houses and other such worldly pursuits. Those whose sympathies were Puritan became more and more disaffected with the cultural values represented by the court, and thus English society drifted further and further toward irreconcilable conflict.

Shakespeare's personal views on this controversy are hard to determine and do not bear importantly on his achievement as an artist. Generally, however, we can observe that his many references to changes in fashion cater neither to the avant-garde nor to reactionary traditionalists. Shakespeare's audience was, after all, a broadly national one. It included many well-informed Londoners who viewed "Italianate" fashion neither with enthusiasm nor with alarm, but with satiric laughter. Such spectators would certainly have seen the point, for example, in Mercutio's witty diatribe at the expense of the new French style in fencing. The object of his scorn is Tybalt, who, according to Mercutio, "fights as you sing prick song" and fancies himself to be "the very butcher of a silk button." "Is not this a lamentable thing," asks Mercutio rhetorically, "that we should be thus afflicted with these strange flies, these fashionmongers, these pardon-me's, who stand so much on the new form that they cannot sit at ease on the old bench?" (*Romeo and Juliet*, 2.4.20–35). In a similar vein, Shakespeare's audience would have appreciated the joking in *The Merchant of Venice* about England's servile imitation of continental styles in clothes. "What say you, then, to Falconbridge, the young baron of England?" asks Nerissa of her mistress Portia concerning one of Portia's many suitors. Portia replies, "How oddly he is suited! I think he bought his doublet in Italy, his round hose in France, his bonnet in Germany, and his behavior everywhere" (1.2.64–74). Court butterflies in Shakespeare's plays who bow and scrape and fondle their plumed headgear, like Le Beau in *As You Like It* and Osric in *Hamlet*, are the objects of ridicule. Hotspur in *1 Henry IV*, proud northern aristocrat that he is, has nothing but contempt for an effeminate courtier, "perfumèd like a milliner," who has come from King Henry to discuss the question of prisoners (1.3.36). Throughout Shakespeare's plays, the use of cosmetics generally has the negative connotation of artificial beauty used to conceal inward corruption, as in Claudius's reference to "the harlot's cheek, beautied with plast'ring art" (*Hamlet*, 3.1.52). Yet Shakespeare's treatment of newness in fashion is never shrill in tone. Nor does he fail in his dramas to give an honorable place to the ceremonial use of wealth and splendid costuming. His plays thus avoid both extremes in the controversy over changing fashions, though they give plentiful evidence as to the liveliness and currency of the topic.

Shakespeare also reflects a contemporary interest in the problem of usury, especially in *The Merchant of Venice*. Although usury was becoming more and more of a necessity, emotional attitudes toward it changed only slowly. The traditional moral view condemned usury as forbidden by Christian teaching; on the other hand, European governments of the sixteenth century found themselves increasingly obliged to borrow large sums of money. The laws against usury were alternatively relaxed and enforced, according to the economic exigencies of the moment. Shakespeare's plays capture the Elizabethan ambivalence of attitude toward this feared but necessary practice (see Introduction to *The Merchant of Venice*). Similarly, most Englishmen had contradictory attitudes toward what we today would call the law of supply and demand in the marketplace. Conservative moralists complained bitterly when merchants exploited the scarcity of some commodity by forcing up prices; the practice was denounced as excessive profit taking and declared to be sinful, like usury. In economic policy, then, as in matters of changing fashion or increased social mobility, many Englishmen were ambivalent about the perennial conflict between the old order and the new.

## Elizabethan Houses

Those fortunate Englishmen who grew wealthy in the reign of Elizabeth took special pleasure in building themselves fine new houses with furnishings to match. Chimneys were increasingly common, so that smoke no longer had to escape through a hole in the roof. Pewter, or even silver, dishes took the place of the wooden spoon and trencher. Beds, and even pillows, became common. Carpets were replacing rushes as covering for the floors; wainscoting, tapestries or hangings, and pictures appeared on the walls; and glass began to be used extensively for windows.

Despite the warnings of those moralists who preached against the vanity of worldly acquisition, domestic comfort made considerable progress in Elizabethan England. Many splendid Tudor mansions stand today, testifying to the important social changes that had taken place between the strife-torn fifteenth century and the era of relative peace under Elizabeth. The battlement, the moat, the fortified gate, and the narrow window used for archery or firearms generally disappeared in favor of handsome gardens and terraces. At the lower end of the social scale, the agricultural laborers who constituted the great mass of the English population were generally poor, malnourished, and uneducated, but they seem to have enjoyed greater physical security than did their ancestors

*Tudor mansions were often splendid, with impressive gardens and terraces. Shown here is Little Moreton Hall, in Cheshire, built in 1559.*

in the fifteenth century and no longer needed to bring their cows, pigs, and poultry into their dwellings at night in order to protect them from thieves. City houses, of which many exist today, were often large and imposing structures, three or four stories in height, and framed usually of strong oak, with the walls filled in with brick and plaster. Although the frontage on the streets of London was usually narrow, many houses had trees and handsome gardens at the rear. Of course London also had its plentiful share of tenements for the urban poor.

With the finer houses owned by the fortunate elite came features of privacy that had been virtually unknown to previous generations. Life in the household of a medieval lord had generally focused on the great hall, which could serve variously as the kitchen, dining hall, and sitting room for the entire family and its retainers. The men drank in the hall in the evenings and slept there at night. The new dwellings of prosperous Elizabethans, on the other hand, featured private chambers into which the family and the chief guests could retire.

The Elizabethans built well. Not only do we still admire their houses, but also we can see from their oriel windows and stained glass, their broad staircases, their jewels, and their costumes that they treasured the new beauty of their lives made possible by the culture of the Renaissance. Although the graphic and plastic arts did not thrive in England to the same extent as in Italy, France, and the Low Countries, England made lasting achievements in architecture, as well as in music, drama, and all forms of literature.

## THE POLITICAL AND RELIGIOUS BACKGROUND

England under the Tudors suffered from almost unceasing religious conflict. The battle over religion affected every aspect of life and none more so than politics. At the very beginning of the Tudor reign, to be sure, England's problem was not religious but dynastic. Henry VII, the first of the Tudor kings, brought an end to the devastating civil wars of the fifteenth century with his overthrow

*On Sundays crowds gathered to listen to the sermon at St. Paul's Cathedral, the subject of this anonymous painting dated 1616.*

*The Knights of the Garter belonged to the highest order of knighthood; many were influential courtiers and favorites of Queen Elizabeth. A masterful politician, Elizabeth remained unmarried throughout her life. A marriage would have upset the political balance and would have committed her to one foreign nation or to one constituency at home.*

of Richard III at the battle of Bosworth Field in 1485. The civil wars thus ended were the so-called Wars of the Roses, between the Lancastrian House of Henry VI (symbolized by the red rose) and the Yorkist House of Edward IV (symbolized by the white rose). Shakespeare chose these eventful struggles as the subject for his first series of English history plays, from *Henry VI* in three parts to *Richard III*. The House of Lancaster drew its title from John of Gaunt, Duke of Lancaster, father of Henry IV and great-grandfather of Henry VI; the House of York drew its title from Edmund Langley, Duke of York, great-grandfather of Edward IV and Richard III. Because John of Gaunt and Edmund Langley had been brothers, virtually all the noble contestants in this War of the Roses were cousins, caught in a remorseless dynastic struggle for control of the English crown. Many of them lost their lives in the fighting. By 1485, England was exhausted from civil conflict. Although Henry VII's own dynastic claim to the throne was weak, he managed to suppress factional opposition and to give England the respite from war so desperately needed. His son, Henry VIII, inherited a throne in 1509 that was more secure than it had been in nearly a century.

Henry VIII's notorious marital difficulties, however, soon brought an end to dynastic security and civil accord. Moreover, religious conflict within the Catholic Church was growing to the extent that a break with Rome appeared inevitable. Henry's marriage troubles precipitated that momentous event. Because he divorced his first wife, Katharine of Aragon, in 1530 without the consent of Rome, he was excommunicated by the pope. His response in 1534 was to have himself proclaimed "Protector and only Supreme Head of the Church and Clergy of England." This decisive act signaled the beginning of the Reformation in England, not many years after Martin Luther's momentous break with the papacy in 1517 and the consequent beginning of Lutheran Protestantism on the Continent. In England, Henry's act of defiance split the Church and the nation. Many persons chose Sir Thomas More's path of martyrdom rather than submit to Henry's new title as supreme head of the English church. Henry's later years did witness a period of retrenchment in religion, after the downfall of Thomas Cromwell in 1540, and indeed Henry's break with Rome had had its origin in political and marital strife as well as in matters of dogma and liturgy. Nevertheless, the establishment of an English church was now an accomplished fact. The accession of Henry's ten-year-old son Edward VI in 1547 gave reformers an opportunity to bring about rapid changes in English Protestantism. Archbishop Cranmer's forty-two articles of religion (1551) and his prayer book laid the basis for the Anglican Church of the sixteenth century.

The death of the sickly Edward VI in 1553 brought with it an intense crisis in religious politics and a temporary reversal of England's religious orientation. The Duke of Northumberland, Protector and virtual ruler of England in Edward's last years, attempted to secure a Protestant succession and his own power by marrying his son to Lady Jane Grey, a granddaughter of Henry VII, whom Edward had named heir to the throne, but the proclamation of Lady Jane as Queen ended in failure. She was executed, as were her husband and father-in-law. For five years, England returned to Catholicism under the rule of Edward's elder sister Mary, daughter of the Catholic Queen Katharine of Aragon. The crisis accompanying such changes of government during this midcentury period was greatly exacerbated by the fact that all three of Henry VIII's living children were considered illegitimate by one faction or another of the English people. In Protestant eyes, Mary was the daughter of the divorced Queen Katharine, whose marriage to Henry had never been valid because she had previously been the spouse of Henry VIII's older brother Arthur. This Arthur had died at a young age, in 1502, shortly after his state marriage to the Spanish princess. If, as the Protestants insisted, Arthur had consummated the marriage, then Katharine's subsequent union with her deceased husband's brother was invalid, and Henry was free, instead, to marry Anne Boleyn—the mother-to-be of Elizabeth. In Catholic eyes, however, both Elizabeth and her brother Edward VI (son of Jane Seymour, Henry VIII's

third wife) were the bastard issue of Henry's bigamous marriages; Henry's one and only true marriage in the Catholic faith was that to Katharine of Aragon. Edward and Elizabeth were regarded by many Catholics, at home and abroad, not only as illegitimate children, but also as illegitimate rulers, to be disobeyed and even overthrown by force. Thus, dynastic and marital conflicts became matters of grave political consequence.

Because of these struggles, Elizabeth's accession to the throne in 1558 remained an uncertainty until the last moment. Once she actually became ruler, England returned once more to the Protestant faith. Even then, tact and moderation were required to prevent open religious war. Elizabeth's genius at compromise prompted her to seek a middle position for her church, one that combined an episcopal form of church government (owing no allegiance to the pope) with an essentially traditional form of liturgy and dogma. As much as was practicable, she left matters up to individual conscience; she drew the line, however, where matters of conscience tended to "exceed their bounds and grow to be matter of faction." In practice, this meant that she did not tolerate avowed Catholics on the religious right or Protestant sects who denied the doctrine of the Trinity on the religious left. The foundation for this so-called Elizabethan compromise was the thirty-nine articles, adopted in 1563 and based in many respects upon Cranmer's forty-two articles of 1551. The compromise did not please everyone, of course, but it did achieve a remarkable degree of consensus during Elizabeth's long reign.

## Queen Elizabeth and Tudor Absolutism

Elizabeth had to cope with a religiously divided nation and with extremists of both the right and the left who wished her downfall. She was a woman, in an age openly skeptical of women's ability or right to rule. Her success in dealing with such formidable odds was in large measure the result of her personal style as a monarch. Her combination of imperious will and femininity and her brilliant handling of her many contending male admirers have become legendary. She remained unmarried throughout her life, in part, at least, because marriage would have upset the delicate balance she maintained among rival groups, both foreign and domestic. Marriage would have committed her irretrievably to either one foreign nation or one constituency at home. She chose instead to bestow her favor on certain courtiers, notably Robert Dudley (whom she elevated to be the Earl of Leicester) and, after Leicester's death in 1588, Robert Devereux, second Earl of Essex. Her relationship with these men, despite her partiality to them, was marked by her outbursts of tempestuous jealousy. In addition, she relied on the staid counsel of her hard-working ministers: Lord Burghley, Sir Francis Walsingham, Burghley's son Robert Cecil, and a few others.

In her personal style as monarch, Elizabeth availed herself of the theory of absolute supremacy. Under all the Tudors, England was, nominally at least, an absolute monarchy in an age when many of England's greatest rivals—France, Spain, the Holy Roman Empire—were also under absolutist rule. "Absolutism" meant that the monarch served for life, could not legally be removed from office, and was normally succeeded by his eldest son—all of this bolstered by claims of divine sanction, though the claims were frequently contested. The rise of absolutism throughout Renaissance Europe was the result of an increase of centralized national power and a corresponding decrease in autonomous baronial influence. Henry VII's strong assertion of his royal authority at the expense of the feudal lords corresponded roughly in time with the ascendancy of Francis I of France (1515) and Charles V of the Holy Roman Empire (1519). Yet England had long enjoyed a tradition of rule by consensus. When Elizabeth came to the throne, England was already in some ways a "limited" monarchy. Parliament, and especially the members of the House of Commons, claimed prerogatives of their own and were steadily gaining in both experience and power. In the mid-1560s, for example, the Commons made repeated attempts to use parliamentary tax-levying authority as a means of obliging Elizabeth to name a Protestant successor to the throne. The attempt, despite its failure to achieve its immediate goal, was significant; the Commons had shown that they

were a force to be reckoned with. Even though Elizabeth made skillful rhetorical use of the theory of absolutism, portraying herself as God's appointed deputy on earth, her idea of absolutism should not be confused with despotism. To be sure, Elizabeth learned to avoid parliamentary interference in her affairs whenever possible; there were only thirteen sessions of Parliament in her forty-five years of rule. Still, Parliament claimed the right to establish law and to levy taxes on which the monarchy had to depend. Elizabeth needed all her considerable diplomatic skills in dealing with her parliaments and with the English people, who were self-reliant and proud of their reputation for independence. Elizabeth had more direct authority over her Privy Council, since she could appoint its members herself, yet even here she consulted faithfully with them on virtually everything she did. Nor were her closest advisers reluctant to offer her advice. Many vocal leaders in her government, including Walsingham and Leicester, urged the Queen during the 1570s and 1580s to undertake a more active military role on the Continent against the Catholic powers. So did her later favorite, the Earl of Essex. With remarkable tact, she managed to retain the loyalty of her militant and sometimes exasperated counselors and yet keep England out of war with Spain until that country actually launched an invasion attempt in 1588 (the Great Armada).

## Catholic Opposition

During her early years, Elizabeth sought through her religious compromise to ease the divisions of her kingdom and attempted to placate her enemies abroad (notably Philip II of Spain) rather than involve England in a costly war. For about twelve years, while England's economy gained much-needed strength, this policy of temporizing succeeded. Yet Elizabeth's more extreme Catholic opponents at home and abroad could never be reconciled to the daughter of that Protestant "whore," Anne Boleyn. England's period of relative accommodation came to an end in 1569 and 1570, with Catholic uprisings in the north and with papal excommunication of the English Queen. As a declared heretic, Elizabeth's very life was in danger; her Catholic subjects were encouraged by Rome to disobey her and to seek means for her violent overthrow.

Conspirators did, in fact, make attempts on the Queen's life, notably in the so-called Babington conspiracy of 1586, named for one of the chief participants. This plot, brought to light by Secretary of State Walsingham, sought to place Mary, Queen of Scots, on the English throne in Elizabeth's stead. Mary was Elizabeth's kinswoman; Mary's grandmother, sister to Henry VIII, had been married to James IV of Scotland. So long as Elizabeth remained childless, Mary was a prominent heir to the English throne. Catholics pinned their hopes on her succession, by force if necessary; Protestant leaders

*Along with the defeat of the Spanish Armada in 1588, the 1587 beheading of Mary, Queen of Scots, shown holding a crucifix and surrounded by official witnesses in this contemporary illustration, virtually ended any serious Catholic challenge to Elizabeth's throne.*

urged Elizabeth to marry and give birth to a Protestant heir or at least to name a Protestant successor. Mary had abdicated the Scottish throne in 1567 after the sensational murder of her Catholic counselor, David Rizzio; the murder of Mary's husband, the Earl of Darnley (in which Mary was widely suspected to have taken part); and her subsequent marriage to Darnley's slayer, the Earl of Bothwell. Taking refuge in England, Mary remained a political prisoner and the inevitable focus of Catholic plotting against Elizabeth for approximately two decades. She, in fact, assented in writing to Babington's plot against Elizabeth. All that long while, Elizabeth resisted demands from her Protestant advisers that she execute her kinswoman and thereby end a constant threat to the throne; Elizabeth was reluctant to kill a fellow monarch and agreed fully with Mary's son James that "anointing by God cannot be defiled by man." Nonetheless, Mary's clear involvement in the Babington conspiracy led to the so-called Bond of Association, in which thousands of Englishmen pledged to prevent the succession of any person plotting Elizabeth's death, and then at last to Mary's execution in 1587. By that time, Spain was mounting an invasion against England, the Great Armada of 1588, and Elizabeth's temporizing tactics were no longer feasible. The long years of peace had done their work, however, and England was considerably stronger and more resolute than thirty years before. With Elizabeth's tacit approval, Sir Francis Drake

and other naval commanders carried the fighting to Spain's very shore and to her American colonies. The war with Spain continued from 1588 until about 1597.

Elizabeth's great compromise dealt not only with the political dangers of opposition, but also with the more central theological issues. England was sorely divided, as was much of Europe, on such matters as whether Christ's body was transubstantially present in the Mass, as Catholic faith maintained; whether good works were efficacious in salvation or whether people could be saved by God's grace alone, as the Reformers insisted; whether a portion of humankind was predeterminately damned, as the Calvinists believed; and the like. During the turbulent years of the Reformation, many people died for their faith. In general, the Elizabethan compromise insisted on allegiance to the English throne, church, and ecclesiastical hierarchy but allowed some latitude in matters of faith. The degree of elaboration in vestments and ritual was also an explosive issue on which the English church attempted to steer a central and pragmatic course, although conflicts inevitably arose within the church itself.

### Protestant Opposition

The threat from the Protestant left was no less worrisome than that from the Catholic right. Protestant reformers had experienced their first taste of power at the time of

Henry VIII's break with Rome in 1534. Under Thomas Cromwell, Cardinal Wolsey's successor as the King's chief minister, the monasteries were suppressed and William Tyndale's English Bible was authorized. The execution of Cromwell in 1540 introduced a period of conservative retrenchment, but the accession of Edward VI in 1547 brought reform once more into prominence. Thereafter, Mary's Catholic reign drove most of the reformers into exile on the Continent. When they returned after 1558, many had been made more radical by their continental experience.

To be sure, reform covered a wide spectrum, from moderation to radicalism. Some preferred to work within the existing hierarchical structure of church and state, whereas others were religious separatists. Only the more radical groups, such as the Brownists and Anabaptists, endorsed ideas of equality and communal living. The abusive epithet "Puritan," applied indiscriminately to all reformers, tended to obscure the wide range of difference in the reform movement. The reformers were, to some extent, united by a dislike for formal ritual and ecclesiastical garments, by a preference for a simple and pious manner of living, and by a belief in the literal word of the Bible rather than the traditional teachings of the church fathers. They stressed personal responsibility in religion and were Calvinist in their emphasis on human depravity and the need for grace through election. Yet at first only the more radical were involved in a movement to separate entirely from the established English church.

The radicals on the religious left, even if they represented at first only a minority of the reformers, posed a serious threat to Elizabeth's government. Their program bore an ironic resemblance to that of the Catholic opposition on the religious right. In their theoretical writings, the extreme reformers justified overthrow of what they considered to be tyrannical rule, just as Catholic spokesmen had absolved Elizabeth's subjects of obedience to her on the grounds that she was illegitimate. Both extremes appealed to disobedience in the name of a higher religious law, as enunciated in Romans 13:1–2: "For there is no power but of God." Among the reforming theoreticians was John Ponet, whose *Short Treatise of Politic Power* (1556) argued that a monarch is subject to a social contract and must rule according to laws that are equally subscribed to by Parliament, the clergy, and the people.

## The Doctrine of Passive Obedience

Elizabeth's government countered such assaults on its authority, from both the right and the left, with many arguments, of which perhaps the most central was that of passive obedience. This doctrine condemned rebellion under virtually all circumstances. Its basic assumption was that the king or queen is God's appointed deputy on earth. To depose such a monarch must therefore be an act of disobedience against God's will. Since God is all-wise and all-powerful, his placing of an evil ruler in power must proceed from some divine intention, such as the punishment of a wayward people. Rebellion against God's "scourge" merely displays further disobedience to God's will. A people suffering under a tyrant must wait patiently for God to remove the burden, which he will surely do when the proper time arrives.

This doctrine was included in the official book of homilies of the Church of England and was read from the pulpit at regular intervals. The best-known such homily, entitled *Against Disobedience and Willful Rebellion,* had been preceded by such tracts as William Tyndale's *Obedience of a Christian Man* (1528); a book of homilies, published in 1547, including an "Exhortation Concerning Good Order and Obedience"; Thomas Cranmer's *Notes for a Sermon on the Rebellion of 1549;* and Hugh Latimer's *Sermon on the Lord's Prayer* (1552). Shakespeare heard such homilies often, and he expresses their ideas through several of his characters, such as John of Gaunt and the Bishop of Carlisle in *Richard II* (1.2.37–41, 4.1.115–50). This is not to say that he endorses such ideas, for he sets them in dramatic opposition to other and more heterodox concepts. We can say, nevertheless, that Shakespeare's audience would have recognized in Gaunt's speeches a clear expression of a familiar and officially correct position.

## The Political Ideas of Machiavelli

The orthodoxies of the Elizabethan establishment were under attack, not only from the Catholic right and the Protestant left, but also from a new and revolutionary point of view that set aside all criteria of religious morality. Tudor defense of order was based, as we have seen, on the assumption that the monarch rules in accord with a divine plan, a higher Law of Nature to which every just ruler is attuned. Political morality must be at one with religious morality. Catholic and Protestant critiques of the Tudor establishment made similar assumptions, even though they appealed to revolution in the name of that religious morality. To Niccolò Machiavelli, on the other hand, politics was a manipulative science best governed by the dictates of social expediency. His philosophy did not, as many accusingly charged, lead necessarily to the cynical promotion of mere self-interest. Nevertheless, he did argue, in his *Discourses* and *The Prince,* that survival and political stability are the first obligations of any ruler. Machiavelli regarded religion as a tool of the enlightened ruler rather than as a morally absolute guide. He extolled in his ideal leader the quality of *virtù*—a mixture of cunning and forcefulness. He saw history as a subject offering practical lessons in the kind of pragmatic statecraft he proposed.

Machiavelli was a hated name in England, and most of his works were never available in an English printed edition during Shakespeare's lifetime. (The *Florentine History* was translated in 1595; *The Prince* was not translated until 1640.) Nevertheless, his writings were available in Italian, French, and Latin editions and in manuscript English translations. His ideas certainly had a profound impact on the England of the 1590s. Marlowe caricatures the Italian writer in his *The Jew of Malta,* but he clearly was fascinated by what Machiavelli had to say. Shakespeare, too, reveals a complex awareness. However much he may lampoon the Machiavellian type of conscienceless villain in *Richard III,* he shows us more-plausible pragmatists in *Richard II* and *1 Henry IV.* Conservative theories of the divine right of kings are set in debate with the more heterodox ambitions of Henry Bolingbroke (who then adopts the most orthodox of political vocabularies once he is king). Bolingbroke is not a very attractive figure, but he does succeed politically where Richard has failed.

Shakespeare thus reveals himself as less a defender of the established order than as a great dramatist able to give sympathetic expression to the aspirations of all sides in a tense political struggle. His history plays have been variously interpreted either as defenses of monarchy or as subtle pleas for rebellion, but the consensus today is that the plays use political conflict as a way of probing the motivations of social behavior. To be sure, the plays do stress the painful consequences of disorder and present, on the whole, an admiring view of monarchy (especially in *Henry V*), despite the manifest limitations of that institution. Certainly, we can sense that Shakespeare's history plays were written for a generation of Englishmen who had experienced political crisis and who could perceive issues of statecraft in Shakespeare's plays that were relevant to England's struggles in the 1580s and the 1590s. The play of *King John,* for example, deals with a king whose uncertain claim to the throne is challenged by France and the papacy in the name of John's nephew, Arthur; Elizabeth faced a similar situation in her dilemma over her kinswoman, Mary, Queen of Scots. Elizabeth also bitterly acknowledged the cogency of a popular analogy comparing her reign with that of King Richard II. And when Shakespeare's play about Bolingbroke's overthrow of Richard was apparently revived for political purposes shortly before the Earl of Essex's abortive rebellion against Elizabeth in 1601, Shakespeare's acting company had some explaining to do to the authorities (see Introduction to *Richard II*). Nevertheless, Shakespeare's attitudes toward the issues of his own day are ultimately unknowable and unimportant, since his main concern seems to have been with the dramatization of political conflict rather than with the urging of a polemical position.

## Shakespeare on Religion

Our impressions of Shakespeare's personal sympathies in religion are similarly obscured by his refusal to use his art for polemical purposes. To be sure, members of his moth-er's family in Warwickshire seem to have remained loyal to Catholicism, and his father, John Shakespeare, may conceivably have undergone financial and other difficulties in Stratford for reasons of faith. (See "Shakespeare's Family" below, in the section on Shakespeare's Life and Work.) Certainly Shakespeare himself displays a familiarity with some Catholic practices and theology, as when the Ghost of Hamlet's father speaks of being "Unhousled, disappointed, unaneled" (i.e., not having received last rites) at the time of his murder (*Hamlet,* 1.5.78). Nonetheless, we see in his plays a spectrum of religious attitudes portrayed with an extraordinary range of insight. In matters of doctrine, his characters are at various times acquainted with Catholic theology or with the controversy concerning salvation by faith or good works (see *Measure for Measure,* 1.2.24–5), and yet a consistent polemical bias is absent. Some Catholic prelates are schemers, like Pandulph in *King John.* Ordinarily, however, Shakespeare's satirical digs at ecclesiastical pomposity and hypocrisy have little to do with the Catholic question. Cardinal Beaufort in *1 Henry VI* is a political maneuverer, but so are many of his secular rivals. Cardinal Wolsey in *Henry VIII* is motivated by personal ambition rather than by any sinister conspiracy of the international church. Many of Shakespeare's nominally Catholic clerics, such as Friar Laurence in *Romeo and Juliet* or Friar Francis in *Much Ado About Nothing,* are gentle and well-intentioned people, even if occasionally bumbling. We can certainly say that Shakespeare consistently avoids the chauvinistic anti-Catholic baiting so often found in the plays of his contemporaries.

The same avoidance of extremes can be seen in his portrayal of Protestant reformers, though the instances in this case are few. Malvolio in *Twelfth Night* is fleetingly compared with a "Puritan" (2.3.139–46), although Shakespeare insists that no extensive analogy can be made. Angelo in *Measure for Measure* is sometimes thought to be a critical portrait of the Puritan temperament. Even if this were so, Shakespeare's satire is extremely indirect compared with the lampoons written by his contemporaries Ben Jonson and Thomas Dekker.

## Stuart Absolutism

Queen Elizabeth's successor, James I of the Scottish House of Stuarts, reigned from 1603 to 1625. Even more than Elizabeth, he was a strong believer in the divinely appointed authority of kings; whereas she had insisted on divine sanction, James and his successor, Charles, called it a divine right. Although James succeeded easily to the throne in 1603, since he was Protestant, with a legitimate claim of descent from Henry VIII, the English people did not take to this foreigner from the north. James was eccentric in his personal habits, and the English were always inclined to be suspicious of the Scots in any case. As a result, James was less successful in dealing with the heterogeneous and antagonistic forces that Elizabeth had kept in precarious balance. At the Hampton Court Conference of 1604, relations quickly broke down between James and the Puritan wing of the church, so that even its more moderate adherents joined forces with the separatists. James had similar difficulties with an increasingly radical group in the House of Commons. In the widening rift between the absolutists and those who defended the supremacy of Parliament, James's court moved toward the right. Catholic sympathies at court became common. Civil war was still a long way off and by no means inevitable; the beheading of King Charles I (James's son) would not occur until 1649. Still, throughout James's reign, the estrangement between the right and the left was becoming more and more uncomfortable. The infamous Gunpowder Plot of 1605, in which Guy Fawkes and other Catholic conspirators were accused of having plotted to blow up the houses of Parliament, raised hysteria to a new intensity. Penal laws against papists were harshly enforced. The Parliament of 1614 included in its membership John Pym, Thomas Wentworth, and John Eliot—men who were to become turbulent spokesmen against taxes imposed without parliamentary grant, imprisonment without the stating of specific criminal charges, and other purported abuses of royal power. The polarization of English society naturally affected the London theaters. Popular London audiences (generally sympathetic with religious reform) eventually grew disaffected with the stage, while even the popular acting companies came under the increasing domination of the court. Shakespeare's late plays reflect the increasing influence of a courtly audience.

## THE INTELLECTUAL BACKGROUND

### Renaissance Cosmology

In learning, as in politics and religion, Shakespeare's England was a time of conflict and excitement. Medieval ideas of a hierarchical and ordered creation were under attack but were still widely prevalent and were used to justify a hierarchical order in society itself. According to the so-called Ptolemaic system of the universe, formulated by Ptolemy of Alexandria in the second century A.D., the earth stood at the center of creation. Around it moved, in nine concentric spheres, the heavenly bodies of the visible universe, in order as follows (from the earth outward): the moon, Mercury, Venus, the sun, Mars, Jupiter, Saturn, the fixed stars on a single plane, and lastly the *primum mobile*, imparting motion to the whole system. (See the accompanying illustration.) Some commentators proposed alternate arrangements or speculated as to the existence of one or two additional spheres, in particular a "crystalline sphere" between the fixed stars and the *primum mobile*. These additional spheres were needed to

cope with matters not adequately explained in Ptolemaic astronomy, such as the precession of the equinoxes. More troublesomely, the seemingly erratic retrograde motion of the planets—that is, the refusal of Mars and other planets to move around the earth in steady orbit—called forth increasingly ingenious theories, such as Tycho Brahe's scheme of epicycles. Still, the conservative appeal of the earth-centered cosmos remained very strong. How could one suppose that the earth was not at the center of the universe?

The *primum mobile* was thought to turn the entire universe around the earth once every twenty-four hours. Simultaneously, the individual heavenly bodies moved more slowly around the earth on their individual spheres, constantly changing position with respect to the fixed stars. The moon, being the only heavenly body that seemed subject to change in its monthly waxing and waning, was thought to represent the boundary between the unchanging universe and the incessantly changing world. Beneath the moon, in the "sublunary" sphere, all creation was subject to death as a result of Adam's fall from grace; beyond the moon lay perfection. Hell was imagined to exist deep within the earth, as in Dante's *Inferno*, or else outside the *primum mobile* and far below the created universe in the realm of chaos, as in Milton's *Paradise Lost*.

Heaven, or the Empyrean, stood, according to most Ptolemaic systems, at the top of the universe. Between heaven and earth dwelled the nine angelic orders, each associated with one of the nine concentric spheres. According to a work attributed to Dionysius the Areopagite, *On the Heavenly Hierarchy* (fifth century A.D.), the nine angelic orders consisted of three hierarchies. Closest to God were the contemplative orders of Seraphim, Cherubim, and Thrones; next, the intermediate orders of Dominions, Powers, and Virtues; and finally the active orders of Principalities, Archangels, and Angels. These last served as God's messengers and intervened from time to time in the affairs of mortals. Ordered life among humans, although manifestly imperfect when compared with the eternal bliss of the angelic orders, still modeled itself on that platonic idea of perfect harmony. Thus the state, the church, and the family all resembled one another because they resembled (however distantly) the kingdom of God. Richard Hooker, in his *Of the Laws of Ecclesiastical Polity* (1594–1597), defends the established Church of England in terms that emanate from a comparable idea of a divine, creative, and ordering law of nature "Whose seat is the bosom of God, whose voice the harmony of the world."

The devils of hell were fallen angels, with Satan as their leader. Such evil spirits might assume any number of shapes, such as demons, goblins, wizards, or witches. Believers in evil spirits generally made no distinction between orthodox Christian explanations of evil and the more primitive folklore of witchcraft. Belief in witchcraft was widespread indeed; King James I took the matter

*Ptolemy's earth-centered system of the universe (top) was chal-lenged by the sun-centered system of Copernicus (bottom) with the publishing of* De revolutionibus orbium coelestium *in 1543. Shakespeare, like other major poets of the English Renaissance, poet-ically represents the universe in cosmic terms as described by Ptole-my, but also reflects uncertainties generated by the new cosmology.*

very seriously. So did Reginald Scot's *The Discovery of Witchcraft* (1584), though its author also attempted to confute what he regarded as ignorant superstition and charlatanism. Throughout Shakespeare's lifetime, belief and skepticism about such matters existed side by side.

A similar ambiguity pertained to belief in the Ptolema-ic universe itself. All major poets of the Renaissance, including Shakespeare, Spenser, and Milton (who com-pleted *Paradise Lost* after 1660), represented the universe in cosmic terms essentially as described by Ptolemy. Yet Nicolaus Copernicus's revolutionary theory of a sun-centered solar system (*De revolutionibus orbium coelestium*, published on the Continent in 1543) and the discovery of a new star in Cassiopeia in 1572 stimulated much new thought. Galileo Galilei, born in the same year as Shake-speare (1564), published in 1610 the results of his tele-scopic examinations of Jupiter's moons, thereby further confirming Copernicus's hypothesis. Although the news of Galileo's astounding discovery came too late to affect any but the latest of Shakespeare's plays, a sense of excite-ment and dislocation was apparent throughout most of the years of his writing career. Thomas Nashe, in 1595, referred familiarly to Copernicus as the author "who held that the sun remains immobile in the center of the world, and that the earth is moved about the sun" (Nashe, *Works*, ed. R. B. McKerrow, 1904–1910, 3.94). John Donne lament-ed in 1611–1612 that the "new philosophy" (i.e., the new science) "calls all in doubt." Skeptical uncertainty about the cosmos was on the rise. The poetic affirmations in Renaissance art of traditional ideas of the cosmos can best be understood as a response to uncertainty—a statement of faith in an age of increasing skepticism.

### Alchemy and Medicine

In all areas of Renaissance learning, the new and the old science were juxtaposed. Alchemy, for example, made important contributions to learning, despite its supersti-tious character. Its chief goal was the transformation of base metals into gold, on the assumption that all metals were ranked on a hierarchical scale and could be raised from lower to higher positions on that scale by means of certain alchemical techniques. Other aims of alchemy included the discovery of a universal cure for diseases and of a means for preserving life indefinitely. Such aims encouraged quackery and prompted various exposés, such as Chaucer's "The Canon's Yeoman's Tale" (late fourteenth century) and Jonson's *The Alchemist* (1610). Yet many of the procedures used in alchemy were essen-tially chemical procedures, and the science of chemistry received a valuable impetus from constant experimenta-tion. Queen Elizabeth was seriously interested in alche-my throughout her life.

In physics, medicine, and psychology, as well, older concepts vied with new. Traditional learning apportioned

*Alchemists employed relatively sophisticated equipment in their futile search for the "philosopher's stone," a reputed substance supposed to possess the property of changing other metals into gold and silver.*

all physical matter into four elements: earth, air, fire, and water. Each of these was thought to be a different combination of the four "qualities" of the universe: hot, cold, moist, and dry. Earth combined cold and dry; air, hot and moist; fire, hot and dry; and water, cold and moist. Earth and water were the baser or lower elements, confined to the physical world; fire and air were aspiring elements, tending upward. Humans, as a microcosm of the larger universe, contained in themselves the four elements. The individual's temperament, or "humor" or "complexion," depended on which "humor" predominated in that person. The four humors in humans corresponded to the four elements of physical matter. The blood was hot and moist, like air; yellow bile, or choler, was hot and dry, like fire; phlegm was cold and moist, like water; and black bile was cold and dry, like earth. A predominance of blood in an individual created a sanguine or cheerful temperament (or humor), yellow bile produced a choleric or irascible temperament, phlegm produced a phlegmatic or stolid temperament, and black bile produced a melancholic temperament. Diet could affect the balance among these humors, since an excess of a particular food would stimulate overproduction of one humor. The stomach and the liver, which converted food into humors, were regarded as the seat of human passions. The spleen was thought to be the seat of laughter, sudden impulse, or caprice, and also melancholy. (Hotspur, in *1 Henry IV*, is said to be "governed by a spleen," 5.2.19.) Strong emotional reactions could be explained in terms of the physiology of the humors: in anger, the blood rushed to the head and thereby produced a flush of red color and staring eyes; in fear, the blood migrated to the heart and thus left the face and liver pale, and so on. Sighs supposedly cost the heart a drop of blood, while wine could refortify it (as Falstaff insists in *2 Henry IV*, 4.3.90–123). The signs of youth were

warmth and moisture, as in Desdemona's "hot and moist" hand (*Othello*, 3.4.39); those of age were "a moist eye, a dry hand, a yellow cheek, a white beard, a decreasing leg, an increasing belly" (*2 Henry IV*, 1.2.179–81). A common remedy for illness was to let blood and thereby purge the body of unwanted humors.

The name traditionally associated with such theories was that of Galen, the most celebrated of ancient writers on medicine (c. 130 A.D.). A more revolutionary name was that of Paracelsus, a famous German physician (c. 1493–1541) who attacked the traditional medical learning of his time and urged a more unfettered, pragmatic research into pharmacy and medicine. Such experimentalism bore fruit in the anatomical research of Vesalius (1514–1564) and in William Harvey's investigations of the circulation of the blood (c. 1616). Nevertheless, the practice of medicine in Renaissance times remained under the influence of the "humors" theory until quite late, and its ideas are found throughout Shakespeare's writings.

*The four humors of black bile, blood, yellow bile (or choler), and phlegm, as shown in this illustration from an illuminated manuscript, were believed to govern the human personality by producing a disposition toward melancholic, sanguine, choleric, or phlegmatic temperaments.*

## Learning

In learning generally, and in theories of education, new ideas conflicted with old. The curriculum of schools and colleges in the Renaissance was inherited largely from the Middle Ages and displayed many traditional characteristics. The curriculum consisted of the seven Liberal Arts: a lower division, called the trivium, composed of grammar, rhetoric, and logic; and an upper division, called the quadrivium, composed of arithmetic, geometry, astronomy, and music. In addition, there were the philosophical studies associated chiefly with Aristotle: natural philosophy, ethics, and metaphysics.

Aristotle's name had a towering influence in medieval times and remained important to the Renaissance as well. Even among his Renaissance admirers, however, Aristotle proved more compelling in practical matters than in the abstract scholastic reasoning associated with his name in the Middle Ages. The Italian Aristotelians whose work made its way into England were interested primarily in the science of human behavior. Aristotelian ethics was for them a practical subject, telling people how to live usefully and well and how to govern themselves politically. Rhetoric was the science of persuasion, enabling people to use eloquence for socially useful goals. Poetry was a kind of rhetoric, a language of persuasion that dramatists, too, might use for morally pragmatic ends.

At the same time, new thinkers were daring to attack Aristotle by name as a symbol of traditional medieval thought. The attack was not always fair to Aristotle himself, whose work had been bent to the *a priori* purposes of much medieval scholasticism. Nevertheless, his name had assumed such symbolic importance that he had to be confronted directly. The Huguenot logician Petrus Ramus (1515–1572), defiantly proclaiming that "everything that Aristotle taught is false," argued for rules of logic as derived from observation. He urged, for example, that his students learn about rhetoric from observing in detail Cicero's effect on his listeners, rather than by the rote practice of syllogism. Actually, Ramus's thought was less revolutionary in its concepts of logic than in the tremendous ferment of opinion caused by his iconoclastic teaching.

A basic issue at stake in the anti-Aristotelian movement was that of traditional authority versus independent observation. How do people best acquire true knowledge—through the teachings of their predecessors or through their own discovery? The issue had profound implications for religious truth as well: should individuals heed the collective wisdom of the earthly church or read the Bible with their individual perceptions as their guide? Is "reason" an accretive wisdom handed down by authority or a quality of the individual soul? Obviously, a middle ground exists between the two extremes, and no new thinker of the Renaissance professed to abandon entirely the use of ancient author-

ity. For men like Henricus Agrippa (1486–1535) and Sir Francis Bacon (1561–1626), however, scholastic tradition had exerted its oppressive influence far too long. Authority needed to be examined critically and scientifically. Bacon, in his *The Advancement of Learning* (1605), fought against the blind acceptance of ancient wisdom and argued that "knowledge derived from Aristotle, and exempted from liberty of examination, will not rise again higher than the knowledge of Aristotle." Sir Walter Ralegh and others joined in the exciting new search for what human "reason" could discover when set free from scholastic restraint. Such belief in the perfectibility of human reason owed some of its inspiration to Italian Neoplatonic humanists like Giovanni Pico della Mirandola (1463–1494), who, in his *Oration on the Dignity of Man*, celebrated a human race "constrained by no limits," in accordance with the potential of its own free will. The new learning did not seem to trouble these men in their religious faith, although a tension between scientific observation and faith in miracles was to become plentifully evident in the seventeenth century.

## The Nature of Humankind

Medieval thought generally assigned to humankind a uniquely superior place in the order of creation on earth. That assumption of superiority rested on biblical and patristic teachings about the hierarchy of creation, in which humanity stood at the apex of physical creation nearest God and the angels. Humankind was thus supreme on earth in the so-called chain of being. Human reason, though subject to error because of sinfulness, enabled humans to aspire toward divinity. Humans were, in the view of medieval philosophers, the great amphibians, as well as the microcosm of the universe, part bestial and part immortal, doomed by Adam's fall to misery and death in this life but promised eternal salvation through Christ's atonement. Right reason, properly employed, could lead to the truths of revealed Christianity and thus give humankind a glimpse of the heavenly perfection one day to be ours. Renaissance Neoplatonism, as expounded, for example, in the writings of Marsilio Ficino, Pico della Mirandola, and Baldassare Castiglione (in *The Courtier*, translated by Sir Thomas Hoby in 1561), offered humanity a vision of a platonic ladder, extending from the perception of physical beauty to contemplation of the platonic idea of beauty and finally to the experiencing of God's transcendent love.

Protestant thought of the Renaissance did not wholly disagree with this formulation, but it did place a major new emphasis on human reprobation. The idea was not new, for Saint Augustine (354–430) had insisted on human depravity and our total dependence on God's inscrutable grace, but, in the years of the Reformation, this theology took on a new urgency. Martin Luther

(1483–1540), by rejecting veneration of the Virgin Mary and the saints and by taking away the sacraments of confession and penance, by which individual Christians could seek the institutional comforts of the Catholic Church, exposed the individual sinner to agonies of conscience that could result in a sense of alienation and loss. The rewards were great for those who found new faith in God's infinite goodness, but the hazards of predestinate damnation were fearsome to those who were less sure of their spiritual welfare. Luther's God was inscrutable, majestic, and infallible. Luther's God decreed salvation for the elect and damnation for all others, and His will could not be challenged or questioned. The individual was to blame for sin, even though God hardened the hearts of the reprobate. John Calvin (1509–1564) placed even greater stress on predestinate good and evil and insisted that the grace of salvation was founded on God's freely given mercy that humans could not possibly deserve. Salvation was God's to give or withhold as He wished; humans might not repine that in His incomprehensible wisdom God has "barred the door of life to those whom He has given over to damnation." Faced with such

a view of human spiritual destiny, the individual Christian's lot was one of potential tragedy. The human soul was a battleground of good and evil.

Michel de Montaigne (1533–1592), Shakespeare's great French contemporary, provided a very different and heterodox way of thinking about human imperfection. In his "Apology for Raymond Sebond" and other essays, Montaigne questioned the assumption of humanity's superiority to the animal kingdom, and in doing so gave Shakespeare a fundamentally different way to consider the nature of humankind—a way that reflects itself, for example, in Hamlet's observations on humans as "quintessence of dust." Montaigne stressed humans' arrogance, vanity, and frailty. He was unconvinced of humanity's purported moral superiority to the animals and argued that animals are no less endowed with a soul. Montaigne undermined, in other words, the hierarchy in which the human race was the unquestioned master of the physical world, just as Copernican science overturned the earth-centered cosmos and Machiavelli's political system dismissed as an improbable fiction the divinely constituted hierarchy of the state. Montaigne's very choice of

*This guide, graphically setting forth the ideals to which every English gentlewoman and gentleman should aspire, illustrates the Renaissance concept that outward deportment and accomplishments should correctly and invariably mirror a person's inner nature.*

# *Shakespeare's World*
## A Visual Portfolio

**PLATE 1. The Seventeenth-Century World.** *Dutch cartographer Willem Janszoon Blaeu (1571–1638) produced this map in 1635. Around the border are panels depicting the four elements, the seven known planets, the four seasons, and the seven wonders of the world. While the establishment of English settlements in North America expanded the scope of the early seventeenth-century world, England in Shakespeare's day still remained both small and isolated.*

**PLATE 2. London in Shakespeare's Time.** *In this anonymous seventeenth-century painting, the theaters of Southwark are clearly visible in the left foreground, flags flying. London Bridge crosses the River Thames into the city, where St Paul's Cathedral dominates the central skyline. The Tower of London is visible on the right. The many boats on the Thames are evidence of the vital role the river played in the city's emerging importance in national and international trade.*

**Plate 4. Queen Elizabeth I.** *Few monarchs have ever influenced an age so pervasively and left their stamp on it so permanently as did Elizabeth I during her reign from 1558–1603. Elizabeth is celebrated in this portrait that commemorates the English defeat of the Spanish Armada in 1588. A mythology developed around the Queen, linked to her virginity and devotion to her people. With her right hand on the globe, she is shown here in all her glory as the empress of the world.*

**PLATE 5. King James I.** *James I, King of England from 1603–1625, was the first of the Stuart dynasty. His name is linked to one of the most creative periods in the history of the theater: that of the Jacobean drama. "Jacobean" is derived from* Jacobus, *the Latin word for James.*

**PLATE 6. Social Class in Shakespeare's Time.** *Social classes and fashions in Shakespeare's day were clearly defined. People were required by English law to dress according to their social status. Shown here are a workman (top), carrying his tools; "a presumptuous woman" (center), gaudily attired beyond her appointed station; and a "gentleman" (bottom), privileged to wear his apparel.*

**PLATE 7. Ben Jonson.** *Chief dramatic rival for public acclaim during Shakespeare's later years was Ben Jonson (1572–1637). Jonson, a poet, playwright, and literary critic, was a noted scholar of classical literature and a good friend of Shakespeare. The First Folio of 1623 contains a poetic eulogy of Shakespeare written by Jonson.*

**PLATE 8. Edward Alleyn.** *Edward Alleyn (1566–1626) won great acclaim in the roles of Tamburlaine and Doctor Faustus, among many others. As leading player of Lord Strange's Men and then the Lord Admiral's Men, he became a prominent rival of Richard Burbage of the Lord Chamberlain's Men. This was the company in which Shakespeare served as actor-sharer and playwright, starting in 1594. Alleyn was also the founder of Dulwich College.*

**PLATE 9. Falstaff and Crew.** *William Hogarth's painting, "Falstaff Examining His Recruits from Henry IV," dates from 1730. Sir John Falstaff was one of Shakespeare's most popular characters, appearing in parts 1 and 2 of* Henry IV *as well as* The Merry Wives of Windsor. *Falstaff, in the red jacket and feathered hat, here reviews his ragged recruits in a scene from* 2 Henry IV *(3.2).*

**PLATE 10.** *A Midsummer Night's Dream. Peter Brook's brilliantly revisionary stage production for the Royal Shakespeare Company in 1970 set* A Midsummer Night's Dream *in a brightly lit white box peopled with jugglers and athletic trapeze artists who tumbled and dashed about after one another with abandon. Here, Titania, under the spell of a love potion, embraces the weaver, Bottom, whom Puck has mischievously given an ass's ears and a clown nose. (The clown nose is Brook's invention; Shakespeare's script calls for an ass's head.)*

**PLATE 11.** *Kenneth Branagh (right) stars as King Henry V, with Christopher Ravenscroft (left) as Mountjoy, in this 1989 film adaptation of* Henry V, *directed by Branagh.*

**PLATE 12.** *Kevin Kline as Bottom and Michelle Pfeiffer as Titania star in this 1999 film adaptation of* A Midsummer Night's Dream *directed by Michael Hoffman and set in the Tuscan hills of Italy at the turn of the 20th century.*

**PLATE 13.** *Much Ado About Nothing. This 2010 Parisian adaption titled* Beaucoup de Bruit Pour Rien *featured Vincent Caire and Gael Collins along with Theatre du Ranalagh company actors.*

**PLATE 14.** *Directed by Baz Luhrmann, this 1996 adaptation of* Romeo & Juliet *features Leonardo DiCaprio and Claire Danes in the title roles.*

**PLATE 15.** *Hamlet. David Tennant plays the leading role in a 2008 film version of* Hamlet, *based on the Royal Shakespeare's production directed by Gregory Doran at the Courtyard Theatre, Stratford-upon-Avon*

**PLATE 16.** *King Lear. Kazunori Akitaya as Gloucester shown after being brutally blinded in this 1991 Tokyo Globe Company production.*

**PLATE 17.** *King Lear.*
*Written and directed by Akira Kurosawa, the 1985 film* Ran *is a retelling of* King Lear *transposing the plot into 16th century Japanese life, culture, and images. Stars include Tatsuya Nakadi and Akira Terao.*

**PLATE 18.** *The Tempest. Jasper Britton played Caliban in this 2000 production staged at Shakespeare's Globe Theatre. Britton's legendary performance included such actions as spitting fish-heads into the audience.*

**PLATE 19.** *The Tempest.*

**PLATE 20.** *Macbeth.*
*Umabatha Theatre Company as they rehearse The Zulu Macbeth, a reimagining of Shakespeare's play. It was performed at the London Globe Theatre in 2001.*

**PLATE 21.** *Measure for Measure.* The 2012 production was performed by the Umabatha Theatre Company in Taiwan.

**PLATE 22.** *Richard III.* Ian McKellan stars in the 1995 film directed by Richard Loncraine. Others actors who appeared in the film include Annette Bening, Jim Broadbent, Robert Downey Jr., Nigel Hawthorne, Kristin Scott Thomas, Maggie Smith, John Wood and Dominic West. The film changes the play's setting to 1930s Britain under a fascist regime.

**PLATE 23.** *Twelfth Night.* Ben Kingsley as Feste in director Trevor Nunn's 1996 film. The film cast includes Helena Bonham Carter, Richard E. Grant, and Imogen Stubbs.

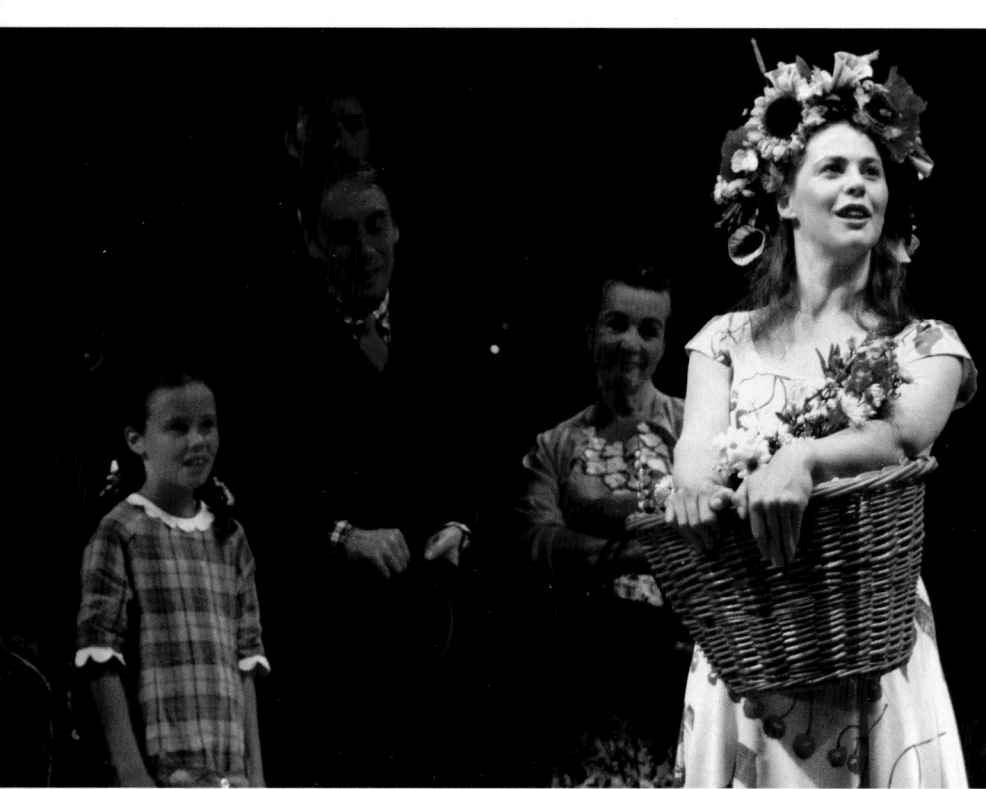

**PLATE 24.** *The Winter's Tale.* Phyllida Hancock appeared as Perdita in a Royal Shakespeare Company 1992 production held at the Barbican Theatre in London. Regarded as a landmark production, it was hailed by critics and played to packed houses both in Stratford and London.

I-23 appears at top

the essay as his favorite literary form bespeaks his commitment to attempts and explorations, rather than to definite solutions; etymologically, the very word "essay" signifies an exploration or inquiry. Montaigne was not alone in his skepticism about human nature; his ideas had much in common with Bernardino Telesio's *De Rerum Natura* and with the writings of the Italian Giordano Bruno. Montaigne was followed in the seventeenth century by that overpowering iconoclast, Thomas Hobbes, who extended the concept of mechanical laws governing human society and human psychology. Hobbes postdates Shakespeare, to be sure, but one has only to consider Iago's philosophy of the assertive individual will (in *Othello*) or Edmund's contempt for his father Gloucester's astrological pieties (in *King Lear*) to see the enormous impact on Shakespeare of the new heterodoxies of his age. Shakespeare makes us aware that skeptical thought can be used by dangerous men like Iago, Edmund, and Richard III to promote their own villainies in a world no longer held together by the certitudes of traditional faith, but he also shows us the gullibility of some traditionalists and the abuses of power that can be perpetrated in the name of ancient and divine privilege by a king like Richard II. Above all, Shakespeare delights in the play of mind among competing ideas, inviting us to wonder, for example, if Caliban in *The Tempest* is not invested with natural qualities that Prospero, his Christian colonizer, does not sufficiently understand and whether some of the other supposedly civilized Europeans who come to Caliban's island do not have a great deal to learn from its uncivilized beauty.

# THE DRAMA BEFORE SHAKESPEARE

When William Shakespeare made his first acquaintance with the professions of acting and playwriting in the late 1580s, the English theater was already a flourishing institution with a long and complex history. In order to understand what opportunities it offered Shakespeare, we need to look briefly at that history.

## *The Liturgical Drama*

The sixth-century Catholic Church had been largely responsible for closing down the late Roman theater, with its bloody gladiatorial contests and its pervasive moral decadence. Thereafter, for about four centuries, the theater officially did not exist in western Europe. Paradoxically, it was the Church in the tenth century that sponsored the beginnings of a new dramatic form within the liturgy (the prescribed form of worship) of the Church itself. This dramatic activity perhaps began as an insertion into the regular service of a "trope" or musical composition designed to be sung antiphonally by members of a monastic community. The earliest of these may have been composed for Easter morning, at the supremely important moment of Christ's Resurrection. The Mass itself had long displayed semidramatic characteristics, and the first Easter expansions must not have seemed particularly revolutionary to anyone involved. The simplest of the early tropes (though perhaps not the first), composed at St. Gall in Switzerland some time early in the tenth century, consists merely of a chanted interrogation, "*Quem quaeritis in sepulchro, Christicolae?*" ("Whom do you seek in the sepulcher, O followers of Christ?"), and a chanted response, "*Jesum Nazarenum crucifixum, o caelicolae*" ("Jesus of Nazareth who was crucified, O heaven-dwellers"), followed by an announcement that Christ is risen as He had predicted. From other early texts of this sort, we can guess that this simple antiphon was accompanied by some stylized semidramatic assignment of roles to members of the religious community as the three Marys visiting Christ's tomb and as the angels guarding the tomb. At any rate, tenth-century tropes of Easter soon included use of simple costumes, physical movement toward the tomb, and appropriate gestures.

Other actions were appropriate to such a dramatic representation of the Resurrection: the visit of the disciples to the sepulchre, the appearance of Christ as a gardener to Mary Magdalene, and his appearance to the disciples on the road to Emmaus. Moreover, other seasons of the year afforded similar opportunities, especially Christmas; the crèche was already a venerable custom, and Christmas tropes may have originated as early as Easter tropes or possibly even earlier.

In any event, Christmas liturgical dramatic activity grew apace, perhaps more rapidly than at Easter because of the sacred inhibitions associated with the Resurrection. By the twelfth century, Christmas liturgical drama had become lengthy and complex, including not only the visit of the shepherds and the Magi, but also the slaughter of the innocents and the flight into Egypt. Simultaneously, liturgical plays were developed for other festivals in the liturgical calendar. Some were in the vernacular: by the end of the twelfth century, an Anglo-Norman poet had written a play of Adam featuring the creation of humankind, the expulsion from the garden of Eden, the slaughter of Abel by Cain, and a lengthy procession of prophets announcing the advent of Christ. Such early vernacular plays may well have influenced the development of Latin liturgical drama. The twelfth century also saw a play about Daniel in the lions' den, various Saint Nicholas plays in which that popular saint performed miracles, a play at Tegernsee about the Antichrist, a play about the conversion of Saint Paul, and many others. In other words, by 1200 or thereabouts, the liturgical drama had produced plays of considerable length and complexity for numerous religious festivals throughout the year. Montecassino in Italy had a complex Passion play by this date. The late twelfth or early thirteenth century saw the performance at Benediktbeuren in Germany of the impressive "Carmina Burana" plays for Easter and Christmas.

## The Corpus Christi Play

Although one might suppose that these liturgical plays would be gathered together into larger cycles of the divine history of the world, compilations of this sort do not seem generally to have taken place. Liturgical plays continued to be performed individually at appropriate times in the Church calendar. Most religious communities owned and produced one or two such plays year after year, but no communities owned or produced very many such plays. The plays were numerous but scattered throughout western Europe.

What appears to have happened instead of the forming of liturgical plays into a cycle is that the various craft guilds of certain towns, especially in England, banded together with the ecclesiastical authorities to produce a summer festival that would be both civic and religious in nature. One impetus was the institution of the feast of Corpus Christi in the early fourteenth century. The feast was designed to honor the Eucharist (the sacrament of the Lord's Supper) in a joyous mood, uninhibited by the somber reflections on Christ's crucifixion that are appropriate to Passion Week. The date chosen, the Thursday after Trinity Sunday, came during a slack period in the liturgical calendar in very late spring. In May or June the days of the year are longest, and the English weather is generally cooperative. The cycles that thus originated were performed on other festivals of the early summer season besides Corpus Christi day, but that festival has given its name to the genre.

V & A IMAGES, LONDON / ART RESOURCE, NY

*Corpus Christi plays were often performed either in procession on moving pageant wagons or in arena theaters with scaffolds located around the acting area. This illustration shows a procession around a square in Brussels in 1615, using staging methods perhaps not unlike those in use in England during the fifteenth and sixteenth centuries.*

The feast of Corpus Christi regularly featured elaborate processions through town, and, indeed, these processions may have preceded the plays themselves. Various guilds were usually assigned events in the divine history of the world, for which they undertook to present dramatized renditions. The plays written for such guilds had to be numerous in most towns, since there were many guilds: the York cycle, for example, had forty-eight plays; the so-called Towneley cycle (probably misnamed, perhaps acted at Wakefield), thirty-two; the so-called N-Town or *Ludus Coventriae* cycle (perhaps acted in the vicinity of Lincoln), forty-three. The texts were evidently not translations from the Latin liturgical drama, but were English compositions often based on medieval narrative accounts of the divine history of the world. Such versions contained much patristic and legendary material, as well as straightforward biblical narrative; for example, the account of Christ's harrowing of hell, based on the apocryphal Gospel of Saint Thomas rather than on the Bible itself, had become an accepted part of the story. More noncanonical still are accounts of Mary's childhood and of her marriage to Joseph. The cycles varied somewhat as to content, but they tended to choose many of the same traditional stories embodied in Church liturgy. The main figures in these favorite stories—Abel, Noah, Abraham, and Isaac—were often seen as "typological," that is, prefiguring by their piety and suffering the advent of Christ himself.

The common core of most cycles included the following: the creation, the fall of Adam and expulsion from Paradise, Cain's slaying of Abel, Noah's flood, Abraham and Isaac, Moses, the prophets, the Annunciation, the visit of the shepherds and the Magi, the flight into Egypt, the slaughter of the innocents, the baptism, the temptation in the wilderness, the raising of Lazarus, the entry into Jerusalem and the entire Passion sequence, the burial, the harrowing of hell, the Resurrection, Christ's appearances to the disciples, his Ascension, and the day of doom. Other subjects were often added, such as the story of Pentecost, the assumption of the blessed Virgin Mary, and the coming of Antichrist.

Sometimes these medieval "pageants" were acted by individual craft guilds on pageant wagons before a series of audiences gathered at fixed locales throughout the town. Recent investigations have shown, however, the formidable difficulties involved in performing a complete cycle of plays in narrow streets, with each pageant having to wait in line until the preceding pageant had finished. Street processions remained common but may, in some cases, have involved displays in *tableau vivant* rather than a full performance of each play. Certainly, in some towns the plays themselves were acted not on pageant wagons but in the round, in arena theaters with several scaffolds on the periphery or even in the center of the acting area. Scaffolds variously represented heaven and hell, Pilate's judgment hall, the house of the Last Supper, and the like.

In the marketplace or in the cathedral close, the pageants may have been ranged in order about the open space so that the spectators themselves could move from scene to scene. Multiple-place staging certainly existed in London and in the south of England and was the regular form of the mystery-play stage on the Continent. (The Corpus Christi plays are sometimes called "mystery" plays, since they were acted by the "mystery" or trade guilds.)

As many as twenty full-scope plays, mostly of the Corpus Christi type, may have existed at one time in England, though the complete texts of only four have been preserved. The York, Towneley, and N-Town cycles have already been mentioned; a fourth extant cycle was acted at Chester. In addition, two fragments exist of a cycle acted at Coventry, one each from Norwich and Newcastle-on-Tyne, and several other single scenes from places not located. A Cornish cycle, written in Celtic, presents some Old Testament episodes and a Passion sequence more like certain continental religious dramas than the English plays we have been discussing.

Shakespeare probably saw Corpus Christi plays in his youth, before they were suppressed by Protestant authorities, and he appears to recollect them at times in his plays. When Hamlet says disparagingly of bombastic acting that "it out-herods Herod" (*Hamlet*, 3.2.14), he is thinking of the stage bully of the slaughter of the innocents who, in the Coventry version, "ragis in the pagond [pageant] and in the strete also." Herod was indeed legendary for his rant. The Porter in *Macbeth* is surely alluding to Christ's harrowing of hell when he complains, "But this place is too cold for hell. / I'll devil-porter it no further" (2.3.16–17). The medieval heritage adds a remarkable dimension to this scene: Macbeth's castle becomes a kind of hell, as the Porter jokingly observes, and Macduff's arrival takes on an aspect of deliverance through which Macbeth and his "fiendlike queen" (5.8.70) will be brought to account. Henry V has Herod in mind again in his speech to the beleaguered citizens of Harfleur, when he bids them surrender lest they see their naked infants "spitted upon pikes" and the childrens' mothers howling in grief "as did the wives of Jewry / At Herod's bloody-hunting slaughtermen" (3.3.38–41). More broadly, the cosmic structure of the cycle plays, bound together in their many episodes by an overarching narrative of divine history, offered a model of construction that Shakespeare would apply in modified form to his writing of English history plays.

## Saints' Plays and Morality Plays

Saints' plays were also widely current in England, although few examples survive today. These dramas resembled the Corpus Christi cycles in their staging and their panoramic religious spectacle, but they differed from the cycles in that they told about the lives and miracles of individual saints and martyrs rather than, as in the cycles, telling the entire divine history of the human race as incorporated chiefly in the Old and New Testaments. Some particular cases, to be sure, incorporated features of both saints' lives and Corpus Christi drama. The story of Mary Magdalene, for example, was derived in part from the biblical accounts of her meetings with Christ, but the narrative had been enormously expanded to include legendary reports of her travels and miraculous deeds as a saint. St. Paul was another biblical figure whose sudden conversion and subsequent travels gave to his story the characteristics of a typical saint's life. As a group, however, saints' plays offered more emphasis on miraculous conversion from sin to grace and on the wondrous intervention of saints in the lives of ordinary people than did the Corpus Christi cycles.

Allegorical characters in the morality play Hickescorner *were Contemplation, Pity, Free Will, Imagination, Hickescorner, and Perseverance.*

Shakespeare's debt to saints' plays is indirect and hard to demonstrate. Some of his history plays reveal a pattern of conversion followed by glorious acts, as in the saga of Henry V, but this story was inherent in the myth of Henry V that Shakespeare inherited. Comedies of repentance, such as *Measure for Measure* and *The Winter's Tale,* show us a pattern of redemptive sorrow and renewal in which the protagonist is given an almost miraculous second chance. Shakespeare's late romances are especially illuminated by this tradition of conversion narratives. We cannot be sure, however, that he encountered such stories through saints' plays (which were suppressed by the English Reformation), since nondramatic sources, such as the Legenda Aurea (or Golden Legend) of the lives of the saints, were more immediately available to him.

Shakespeare's awareness of the morality play is easier to prove. Indeed, this genre had survived well enough into the late sixteenth century to make a significant impact on the plays of Shakespeare, Ben Jonson, and others. The morality play chose as its distinctive mode the allegorical rendition of humanity's spiritual journey through life to an eventual preparation for death and judgment before God. Allegory was not unknown in the cycles or in the saints' plays, but it became the staple of the morality play. The earliest texts, from the sixteenth century, include *The Castle of Perseverance, Mankind,* and *Everyman.* Although the last of these focuses atypically on the moment of death, more-typical early morality plays tell a story of spiritual struggle and eventual triumph over sin. This simple plot had an advantage over the cycles and saints' plays in that it could be adapted to the religious and social controversies of the era. The Corpus Christi cycles and saints' plays were, after all, tied to biblical or legendary events; when Reformation authorities sought to suppress the "idolatrous" representation of God on stage or banned worship of the Virgin Mary and the saints, the cycles and saints' plays were doomed. Even though they were occasionally staged late enough in the sixteenth century for Shakespeare to have seen performances, they belonged chiefly to an earlier, pre-Reformation era. The morality play, on the other hand, thrived on controversy. Its plot of soul struggle between the forces of good and evil for the allegiance of Mankind or Everyman, and his wavering progress toward eventual salvation, could and did frequently serve as a vehicle for portraying many social phenomena of the sixteenth century.

In John Skelton's political morality play called *Magnificence* (1515–1518), for example, the protagonist is a representative king figure who must choose between evil counselors urging fiscal extravagance on the one hand and wise counselors urging fiscal prudence on the other hand. The plot, telling of the King's temptation and his choosing of the wrong path before he is finally awakened to his folly, is essentially that of nonpolitical morality plays—such as *Hickescorner*, or *Youth* (c. 1513–1520), in which the human protagonist inevitably succumbs to temptation but is eventually rescued through divine guidance. The issues in Skelton's play have embraced secular as well as spiritual concerns, while the simple story line and the dramatic structure have remained virtually unchanged. The study of a "historical" type, in this case a king, enables such a play to comment on contemporary history and yet appeal simultaneously to a universal moral pattern. Skelton's play may allude indirectly to the fiscal recklessness of Henry VIII under Cardinal Wolsey's persuasive tutelage, but it discusses fiscal responsibility in general terms that also apply to any king—or to any human. Shakespeare's English history plays, especially the early plays about Henry VI and Richard III, owe an important debt to the tradition of the political morality, as exemplified by *Magnificence.*

Shakespeare's history play *King John* studies a king who had actually been the protagonist of the first play to represent an English monarch, *King Johan*, by John Bale (1538, later revised). Although Shakespeare may not have consulted Bale's play directly, Bale still had made an impressive contribution to the English history play by demonstrating how the morality structure could be used in the analysis of political crises. His play is an avowedly Protestant tract in the guise of a morality play, depicting its historical protagonist as a victim of Catholic duplicity and hence an example of what sixteenth-century England had to fear from its Catholic enemies. Later popular plays, combining a morality structure with a passionate interest in history and contemporary political theory, include Thomas Preston's *Cambises* (1560–1561) and John Pickering's *Horestes* (1567).

During the Reformation, the morality play was used polemically by both the Protestants and the Catholics. Dramatists were often commissioned by governmental authorities to write plays for public performance by touring actors, as weapons of ideological persuasion. In Protestant plays, such as *Lusty Juventus* (c. 1547–1553) or *New Custom* (c. 1570), the villainous Vices were depicted as Catholic tempters; in Catholic plays, such as *Respublica* (1553, during the reign of Queen Mary), the Vices were Protestant. The protean flexibility of the morality formula enabled it to adapt itself to many different situations in this way. Polemical drama put ideology ahead of artistic concern, to be sure, but constant experimentation with new forms provided the popular drama of midcentury England with much-needed practical experience. One permutation of the Reformation morality play, for example, proved of considerable importance to the development of English tragedy. In some Protestant morality plays that Calvinistically stress humankind's innate depravity—such as William Wager's *Enough Is as Good as a Feast* (c. 1559–1570) and Nathaniel Woodes's *The Conflict of Conscience* (1570–1581)—spiritual struggle ends in failure rather than in triumph for the human protagonist. Among the great English tragedies of the late sixteenth century, Christopher Marlowe's *Doctor Faustus* (c. 1588) is most obviously indebted to such dramatic renditions of spiritual despair, but Shakespeare's *Macbeth* and other plays may also have learned something from a native homiletic tradition in tragedy.

In staging and acting, as well, the morality play served as an important transition from late medieval religious drama to the drama of the late sixteenth century. In its origins, as seen, for example, in *The Castle of Perseverance* (early fifteenth century), the morality play had been staged like many of the cycles or saints' plays, such as *Mary Magdalene*, that is, in the round, with an open acting area surrounded by acting scaffolds on the periphery. The morality play developed great flexibility in its staging, however, just as it had developed flexibility in its approach to contemporary political or social issues. *Mankind* (c. 1471) required only an acting platform, raised probably on trestles to a height of four or five feet, and a curtain backdrop through which the actors could enter and exit. A stage of this simplicity could be carried anywhere in England and set up at a moment's notice—on a village green, in a town hall, or in the banqueting hall of a lord's manor. The troupe acting *Mankind* was vastly more efficient and transportable than the company of twenty-two or more actors required for *The Castle of Perseverance; Mankind* required only six actors.

Troupes of four or five men and one boy apprentice (for women's roles) were quite standard in early Tudor England. Similar or even smaller troupes enacted folk plays and miracle plays, the texts of which are regrettably not as extensively preserved as those of morality plays. Such troupes traveled the length and breadth of the country and dominated the field of popular entertainment from the late fifteenth century until Shakespeare's day. They were, in fact, the professional ancestors of the Shakespearean acting company. Under the direction of their leading player, who often acted the part of Vice since it was usually the choice role of the morality play, the actors were organized as repertory companies able to perform a number of plays on short notice and to present a remarkably large number of roles by the doubling of parts. They grew slowly in size as they prospered, but they retained their traditional organization. The best of the troupes gravitated to London, where, in 1576, a troupe of perhaps six or eight men and two boys founded England's first permanent theater. Shakespeare's company, the Lord Chamberlain's Men, founded in 1594 and renamed the King's Men in 1603, was only slightly larger than this, with perhaps ten actors who were partners or "sharers" in the company, two or more boys, and a few hired hands. Shakespeare's early plays, moreover, were sometimes structured for presentation by just such a company, much as earlier popular plays had been structured, with considerable doubling of

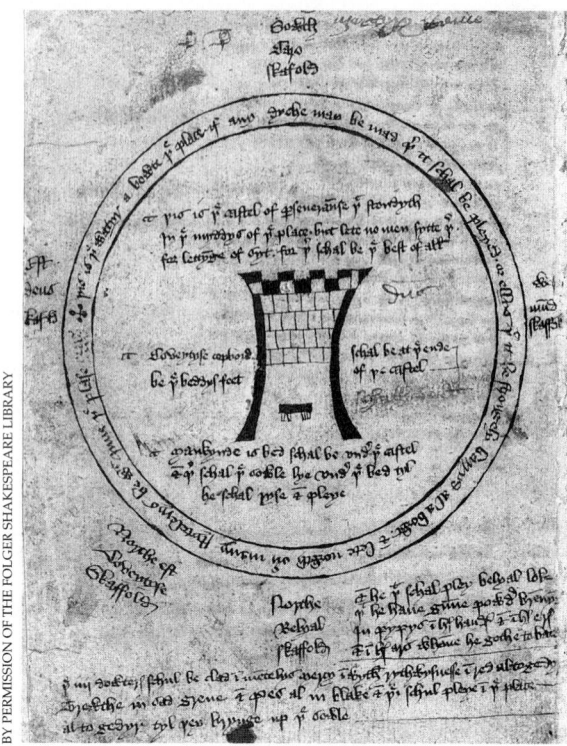

*A fifteenth-century diagram for the presentation of* The Castle of Perseverance *shows the scaffolds surrounding the open acting area with the castle in the center.*

parts and with a multiplicity of episodes allowing for the sequential presentation of numerous minor roles. The early history plays about Henry VI and Richard III are especially illustrative of this structural tradition.

Shakespeare's references to morality drama suggest a real familiarity. Prince Hal jestingly caricatures Falstaff as "that roasted Manningtree ox with the pudding in his belly, that reverend Vice, that grey iniquity, that father ruffian, that vanity in years … that old white-bearded Satan" (*1 Henry IV*, 2.4.447–58). Manningtree, in Essex, appears to have been renowned for its annual fair at which plays were acted and great-sized oxen were roasted; the Vice, as we have seen, was the chief comic tempter of most morality plays. Falstaff himself refers to the Vice's traditional dagger of lath in his contemptuous remarks about Justice Shallow: "And now is this Vice's dagger become a squire" (*2 Henry IV*, 3.2.317–18). Feste, in *Twelfth Night*, exits at one point with a promise to the audience that he will return soon "Like to the old Vice," with his "dagger of lath" and "his rage and his wrath" (4.2.121–32). Kent, in *King Lear*, speaks of Goneril as having taken "Vanity the puppet's part against the royalty of her father" (2.2.36–7), as though she were a personified representation of Pride in a morality play. The evocation of that

genre strengthens our perception that good and evil are indeed battling over Lear's destiny on a cosmic scale. Richard III explicitly compares himself to "the formal Vice, Iniquity" in his use of sinister double entendres and his boasting to the audience of his cleverness (3.1.82–3).

Shakespeare's specific references to late medieval drama are less important, however, than his larger indebtedness to it. His use of a structural tradition of episodic multiplicity and of alternation between seriousness and comedy is especially evident in the early history plays. Of equal significance is his indebtedness to the Vice, the comic tempter of the morality play whose sinister but fascinating techniques of evil persuasion had become an enduring part of Tudor popular drama. The Vice's boastful and chortling brand of villainy is still clearly recognizable, though transmuted into superb poetry, in the insinuations of Richard III, Aaron the Moor (in *Titus Andronicus*), Iago (in *Othello*), and Edmund (in *King Lear*). As Bernard Spivack has argued, in his *Shakespeare and the Allegory of Evil*, Shakespeare's secular vision of the contest between good and evil for human souls owes much to the morality tradition and to other forms of medieval drama.

### Early Tudor Humanist Drama

The development of the morality play and of other medieval drama, briefly sketched in the preceding sections, tells only one part of the story of sixteenth-century drama. The trend we have observed in morality drama, toward the depiction of contemporary English life, manifested itself also in other kinds of plays that were not so plainly derived from the religious drama of the Middle Ages. A relatively new influence was that of classical and neoclassical drama, from the ancient classical world and from Renaissance Europe. Important, too, were the secular kinds of dramatic entertainment that had flourished in the English court even before the advent of neoclassicism. Early Tudor drama for courtly and well-educated audiences was heterogeneous because it reflected so many diverse impulses: the intensified renewal of classical learning that had come about through the activities of the new humanists, the ferment of ideologies introduced by the Reformation, the increase in social mobility in the Tudor court, and the like. In varying proportions, the courtly and intellectual drama of the period borrowed from the English morality play, from courtly pastimes such as the "disguising" (a kind of masque) and the dialogue or *débat*, from secular farce and romance, from classical and neoclassical literature, and even from the Corpus Christi cycles and saints' plays. The mixture, experimental and often uneven, was nonetheless stimulating because it attempted to fuse English culture with the thought of neoclassical Europe. This drama was usually staged in courtly surroundings, such as the banqueting halls of the aristocracy. (See "The

Tudor Hall" below, in the section on London Theaters and Dramatic Companies.)

Especially important in the development of this early Tudor drama were the humanists who associated themselves with Sir Thomas More and his patron Cardinal Morton. These men were, like their counterparts in Italy and elsewhere on the Continent, intensely devoted to the revival of classical learning in all its aspects—art, architecture, literary texts, historical knowledge, and politics—and thus to the enhancement of the human spirit. Their shared ideals can be seen in the plays that they wrote or sponsored. Henry Medwall, chaplain to Cardinal Morton, wrote a morality play called *Nature* (c. 1490–1501) that reveals an interest in Aristotelian ethics, as well as in traditional Christian ideas of salvation. Medwall also wrote *Fulgens and Lucrece* (c. 1490–1500), the earliest extant play in England to use an ancient Roman setting and a secular romantic love plot. The heroine, Lucrece, chooses the love of a virtuous but untitled "new" man at court in preference to a haughty and degenerate aristocrat. This *débat* was derived from *De Vera Nobilitate* by Buonaccorso of Pistoia, an ardent Italian humanist. Despite its ancient setting and romantic plot, it is also unmistakably relevant to the struggle between "new" men and old aristocrats in the court of Henry VII. Both of Medwall's plays were printed by John Rastell, another humanist in the service of Cardinal Morton. Rastell, who married More's sister, wrote a humanist interlude called *The Nature of the Four Elements* (c. 1517–1518), in which he excitedly discussed the latest scientific theories concerning the roundness of the world and other such new ideas. He is probably the author of *Of Gentleness and Nobility* (c. 1527–1530) as well, a play that iconoclastically asks whether monarchy and the inheritance of property are not social evils that ideally ought to be abolished. The influence of Thomas More's *Utopia* on this play is unmistakable.

John Heywood, son-in-law of John Rastell, was the most important and versatile dramatist of the humanist group. All his plays, except *Witty and Witless*, which has been preserved only in manuscript, were printed by John Rastell or his son, William Rastell. Heywood's plays fall into two groups: the courtly disputations, such as *The Play of Love, The Play of the Weather*, and *Witty and Witless* (c. 1525–1533), and the more popular farces that may have been intended for popular audiences as well, such as *The Pardoner and the Friar, The Four PP*, and *John John the Husband* (c. 1513–1533). In the first group, *Weather* reveals a characteristic attention to humanist and courtly themes. In an obvious analogy to the Tudor concept of an absolutist yet benevolent monarchy, the various petitioners of the play complain to Jupiter about the weather but are finally persuaded to be grateful for the mixed weather that is provided them. Heywood is suggesting, in other words, that the English monarchy must bestow its favors impartially on all classes of persons and that all subjects

ought to recognize the essential soundness of the social order as it presently exists. Heywood's second group of plays, on the other hand, eschews such courtly and political themes for a broader slapstick comedy, in the vein of Chaucerian fabliau and French farce.

In addition to these humanist plays written by members of the Sir Thomas More circle, the learned drama of early Tudor England included many plays written for schoolboys or for the choristers attached to royal and noble households. The plays written under such auspices tended to reveal a much stronger interest in classical and neoclassical drama than did the plays written for popular audiences. Schoolmasters wrote dramatic texts derived from the classics for educational purposes; at court, sophisticated audiences were interested in the latest dramatic fashions from Italy or France. Ancient Greek drama did not receive nearly so much attention, however, as did the Latin drama of Terence (c. 186–159 B.C.), Plautus (c. 254–184 B.C.), and Seneca (c. 4 B.C. –65 A.D.). These Latin authors had long been used as schoolboys' texts, though they were frequently expurgated or allegorized into the terms of Christian morality in order to render them suitable for schoolboys' sensibilities. This academic tradition, on the Continent and in England, produced a number of imitative plays that could be acted by boys as part of their training in classical languages. Some plays, such as John Palsgrave's *Acolastus* (1540), were intended to be read rather than acted. Many others were Latin biblical plays in classical guise, such as Thomas Watson's *Absalom* (c. 1535–1544) and George Buchanan's *Jephthes* (1540–1545).

At court and in noble households, choristers were becoming noted for their acting ability. They performed chiefly during seasons of revels, such as in the Christmas season. They did not appear commercially before public audiences during the early Tudor period, as did the players of moralities and popular interludes. The Children of the Royal Chapel are known to have presented plays as early as 1506. The boys of St. Paul's School acted before King Henry VIII in 1528. Later, in the 1570s and 1580s, these children's groups were organized into professional acting companies. Children's plays were generally written by schoolmasters or choirmasters. The plays were heavily influenced by continental traditions and often depicted themes, such as that of the Prodigal Son, that were congenial to boys of school age. *Nice Wanton* (1547–1553) offers an instance of this sort. Biblical themes were common and were sometimes used to urge a political lesson in the presence of a courtly audience. *Godly Queen Hester* (1525–1529), for example, seems to defend the cause of Katharine of Aragon and to denounce the machinations of Cardinal Wolsey. *Jacob and Esau* (1547–1553) draws an unflattering comparison between the unregenerate Esau and those who refuse to abandon the Catholic faith. Classical subjects were, of course, much in

*Early Tudor drama employed the talents of boy actors on stage such as this company, the Children of the Royal Chapel.*

demand as a way of educating youth, as in *Appius and Virginia* (1559–1567) and in Richard Edwards's *Damon and Pythias* (c. 1565).

## Early Comedy

Schoolboys' drama was also vitally important in the development of classical or "regular" comedy on the English stage. Native morality drama was often highly comic, to be sure, especially in its depiction of the resourceful and scheming Vice; but English drama still had much to learn from classical examples about play construction and about the presentation of various types of characters. Perhaps the two best-known early English "regular" comedies were *Ralph Roister Doister* and *Gammer Gurton's Needle*.

*Ralph Roister Doister,* by Nicholas Udall, at one time headmaster of Eton, was acted probably between 1552 and 1554 by boy actors. Its staging is essentially that of neoclassical comedy, with two houses facing onto a street. The play employs a classical five-act structure and preserves the unities of time and place. (According to classical and neoclassical theory, a play's action should be limited to one location—a city, for example—and to a single day.) Stock comic types include the *miles gloriosus,* or braggart soldier, and the parasite. At the same time, Udall has transformed his heroine, usually a courtesan in Plautus's racy comedies, into a winsomely pious Englishwoman named Christian Custance. Ralph Roister Doister, the braggardly type for whom the play is named, is foiled in his mean-spirited determination to win Christian Custance away from her true love, Gawin Goodluck. Almost all the characters virtuously conspire to expose Ralph for his effrontery and pretended bravery; even Matthew Merrygreek, the fun-loving parasite, proves ultimately to be on the side of decency and fair play. Throughout, Udall has adapted Roman comedy to English customs and mores.

*Gammer Gurton's Needle*, written by William Stevenson, fellow of Christ's College, Cambridge, at about the same time as *Ralph Roister Doister,* is similarly designed for student acting. Stock Roman characters are transformed into hearty English types. Diccon the Bedlam, who engineers the farcical action of the lost needle, resembles not only the Roman parasite but also the English natural fool or zany. To some extent, he also reminds us of the mischievous and inventive Vice of the morality play. Other characters are even less purely Roman in their origin: Hodge, the clownish servant; Dame Chat, the shrewish neighbor; and Dr. Rat, the impoverished and ill-trained clergyman who spends most of his time drinking and complaining about his wretched lot. The play is an educated college man's indulgent laugh at his country neighbors. Yet the play is, like *Ralph Roister Doister,* classically structured into five acts, with a single stage setting that preserves the unities of time and place.

In 1566, the members of Gray's Inn saw a production of George Gascoigne's *Supposes,* translated from the Italian of Ariosto (1509). Because it was a translation and not an English adaptation, this play preserves essentially in their original form the stock character types of neoclassical comedy: the parasite, the pantaloon or miserly aged rival in love, the overly watchful father, the clever servant, the bawdy nurse, and so on. The heroine, though no longer a Roman courtesan as in the comedies of the much-imitated Latin dramatist Plautus, is nonetheless a self-possessed and sophisticated young woman who conducts a secret affair for some time without being detected by her father. The mores of this continental play must have seemed challengingly cosmopolitan to its fashionable courtly and intellectual audience. Just as importantly, the play offered graceful prose language as its medium, rather than the homely English verse of *Ralph Roister Doister* and *Gammer Gurton's Needle. Supposes* provided a new model for neoclassical comedy and was to become (with some of its continental morality anglicized) a source for Shakespeare's *The Taming of the Shrew.* Indeed, Shakespeare learned much about play construction, dialogue, and characterization from neoclassical comedies of this sort; perhaps his earliest comedy, *The Comedy of Errors,* owes a great deal to Plautus and to neoclassical imitators of that Latin comic writer. Another early Italian comedy in English, *The Bugbears,* was adapted from Grazzini's *La Spiritata* and acted in about 1563–1565 by boy actors.

## Early Tragedy

In early English tragedy, as in early comedy, native and neoclassical traditions coalesced and sometimes clashed. Native conceptions of tragedy had partly originated in two great medieval commonplaces: the "wheel of fortune" and the "fall of princes." Both were incorporated in Chaucer's "The Monk's Tale" and its source, Boccaccio's *De Casibus Virorum Illustrium,* which presented moral examples from the lives of famous men. Chaucer had defined "tragedy" as the story of a great person "that stood in greet prosperitee, / And is yfallen out of heigh degree / Into myserie, and endeth wrecchedly." His examples, taken from Boccaccio, included Lucifer, Adam, Samson, Hercules, Julius Caesar, and others. These were men or evil beings who had either fallen through sinful pride or had been brought low through the inevitable turn of fortune's wheel. Both types of tragedy illustrated to the medieval mind the folly of trusting to worldly expectations. The "fall of princes" tradition was extended into Elizabethan times through John Lydgate's Chaucerian imitation, *The Fall of Princes,* and its Tudor sequel, *The Mirror for Magistrates* (1559, with many subsequent revisions and enlargements). The morality play contributed a pattern similar to that of Satan's tragic fall through pride; and, although the mankind figure of early morality plays invariably was recovered to God's grace by the end of the play, some early Elizabethan Calvinistic moralities (such as *Enough Is as Good as a Feast* or *The Longer Thou Livest the More Fool Thou Art*) featured human protagonists who were eternally damned. As we have already seen, Elizabethan moralities of this sort anticipated the tragic pattern of Marlowe's *Doctor Faustus.*

Native traditions of tragedy evolved quite independent of classical tragic drama and were, in some ways, strikingly different from it. Christian morality often served as a major explanation of the cause of tragic fall in medieval tragedy. Moreover, the focus was broad and cosmic, as in *Doctor Faustus.* Scenes of comic depravity often alternated with scenes of tragic seriousness, especially in the morality plays. Classical tragedy, on the other hand, usually focused on a moment of crisis in the protagonist's life and presented this crisis in its full, tragic intensity, without the undercutting of comic effect. In classical tragedy generally, narrative interest was subordinated to dramatic or lyrical interest. Unity of action, as understood by Renaissance theorists of drama, necessarily included unity of time and place. Thus, the gap between native and classical tragedy was potentially vast.

Perhaps the earliest tragedy based on classical models in England was Thomas Norton and Thomas Sackville's *Gorboduc,* presented before Queen Elizabeth at Whitehall on January 18, 1562. The play attempted to offer Queen Elizabeth political advice on the need for naming a Protestant successor, by way of a cautionary example in the fratricidal strife between Gorboduc's two sons. Although Sir Philip Sidney later complained about the play's violation of the unities in the fifth act, he praised it otherwise as "an exact model of all tragedies." To be sure, native concepts of tragedy are observable in *Gorboduc,* especially in its use of an ancient British setting and in its moral and Christian explanations of the causes of tragedy. Nevertheless, the classical element predominates.

This classical element is basically Senecan. Ancient Greek tragedy was relatively unknown to Elizabethan England except through Seneca's Roman adaptations. Seneca's ten plays were all translated into English by 1581 and had long been read in the schools as models of rhetoric (just as Terence and Plautus were also read). Seneca's plays were, in fact, closet dramas, intended to be recited rather than acted. Seneca provided *Gorboduc* with a model for its long declamatory speeches, its occasional passages of stichomythia (rapid one-line exchange of dialogue), its five-act structure punctuated by dumb shows, and its supernatural agents prognosticating doom. Moreover, *Gorboduc's* blank verse, created to approximate the Latin meters of Seneca, set a style for blank verse tragedy that dominated the English stage throughout Shakespeare's career. (Blank verse had been used shortly before *Gorboduc* by the Earl of Surrey in his translations from Virgil's *Aeneid,* but never before in drama.) *Gorboduc* also made an important contribution to the English history play by its use of chronicle materials in a tragic setting.

Other Senecan plays followed, written at first for gentlemanly audiences of the universities and the Inns of Court, rather than for the popular stage. One such was George Gascoigne's *Jocasta* (1566). In 1588, eight gentlemen of Gray's Inn, including Thomas Hughes and Francis Bacon, presented before the Queen a drama similar in form to *Gorboduc,* called *The Misfortunes of Arthur.* This tragedy borrows from Seneca not only chorus, messengers, and machinery, but also ideas, sentiments, and heightened language. Like *Gorboduc, The Misfortunes of Arthur* is somewhat free with the classical unities. Also, it is based upon the chronicle history of Britain, which was to become one of the chief sources of subject matter for English tragedy.

Another principal source for tragic writers was the Italian short story, which, because it was also impassioned and serious, offered many themes to writers of tragedy. *Gismond of Salerne* dramatizes a well-known Italian tale and, like *Gorboduc* and *The Misfortunes of Arthur,* is Senecan in form and nature. It was acted before the Queen in 1566 or 1568. In the same storehouse of narrative,

Shakespeare was later to find his source for *Othello*, as well as for such comedies as *The Merchant of Venice* and *Measure for Measure*. *Romeo and Juliet* was based on a English poem which in turn drew from an Italian source.

## *Sir Philip Sidney as Dramatic Critic*

The kind of tragedy that Shakespeare and other popular dramatists wrote in the late sixteenth and early seventeenth centuries is not rigorously classical. It preserves many of the elements of English tragedy already enumerated: a broad narrative focus, frequent violations or total ignoring of the classical unities of time and place, the inclusion of comedy, and the like. Tragedy of this sort might never have developed in England to so high a point or might never have been accepted as the prevailing form of tragedy but for two things: in the first place, few Elizabethan dramatists learned their craft by studying the classical rules; in the second place, the Elizabethan audience, with a taste for native English drama, demanded new, varied, and sensational plots, accompanied by vaudeville clownery and songs. Such popular drama was often condemned by those critics who were familiar with classical literature, but to have made English tragedy conform with classical rules would have meant changing its nature. In France, where in Shakespeare's time the drama came under the control of the court and the learned classes, tragedy developed according to classical rules into the drama of Corneille and Racine; in England, on the other hand, Shakespeare and his contemporaries created a kind of tragedy particularly their own.

The most famous neoclassical critic of the age, Sir Philip Sidney, took vigorous exception to the kind of tragedy in vogue during the 1580s. His views are set forth in *The Defence of Poesy*, written in 1581 or slightly later:

Our tragedies and comedies not without cause cried out against, observing rules neither of honest civility nor skillful poetry, excepting *Gorboduc*—again I say of those that I have seen. Which notwithstanding as it is full of stately speeches and well-sounding phrases, climbing to the height of Seneca his style, and as full of notable morality, which it doth most delightfully teach, and so obtain the very end of poesy, yet in truth it is very defective in the circumstances, which grieves me, because it might not remain as an exact model of all tragedies. For it is faulty both in place and time, the two necessary companions of all corporal actions. For where the stage should alway represent but one place, and the uttermost time presupposed in it should be, both by Aristotle's precept and common reason, but one day, there is both many days and many places inartificially imagined.

But if it be so in *Gorboduc*, how much more in all the rest? where you shall have Asia of the one side and Afric of the other, and so many other under-kingdoms, that the player, when he comes in, must ever begin with telling where he is, or else the tale will not be conceived. Now you shall have three ladies walk to gather flowers, and then we must believe the stage to be a gar-

den. By and by we hear news of shipwreck in the same place; then we are to blame if we accept it not for a rock. Upon the back of that comes out a hideous monster with fire and smoke, and then the miserable beholders are bound to take it for a cave. While in the meantime two armies fly in, represented with four swords and bucklers, and then what hard heart will not receive it for a pitched field?

Now of time they are much more liberal. For ordinary it is that two young princes fall in love; after many traverses she is got with child, delivered of a fair boy; he is lost, groweth a man, falleth in love, and is ready to get another child,—and all this in two hours space; which how absurd it is in sense even sense may imagine, and art hath taught, and all ancient examples justified, and at this day the ordinary players in Italy will not err in....

Later he tells us that English plays are "neither right tragedies nor right comedies"; instead, they mingle clowns and kings with "neither decency nor discretion."

To be sure, Sidney's criticism is not narrowly classical; in the essay as a whole, he affirms the power of the artist to range freely in the world of wit and imagination and to create artifacts that are more universally "true" than either philosophy or history. At the same time, his strictures against the contemporary English stage do invoke classical ideals of unity that many dramatists and audiences ignored. Popular audiences of the time seem to have had no more difficulty imagining the lapse of twenty years than the lapse of two hours. Nor were they troubled by scenic shifts from one continent to another, or by shifts in tone from the comic to the pathetic, the grotesque, or the tragic. Because native English drama had never paid much attention to classical precept, it worked out its own sense of cohesion according to different criteria of multiplicity, alternating effects, sudden juxtapositions, typological recurrence, and the like.

## *John Lyly, George Peele, and Robert Greene*

In facing the problem of understanding just what Elizabethan drama was and how it became what it was, we must recognize that the classification of drama into comedy and tragedy by the ancients does not tell the whole story. Even when we add the history or chronicle play to these two divisions of drama, we have, at best, a rough classification that leaves out a great deal and implies that these three forms were sharply discriminated. In fact, Elizabethan drama is, generally speaking, a blend of many elements. Nearly all Elizabethan tragedies have in them comic scenes and by-plots; most comedies have in them serious issues that might conceivably result in disaster; and history plays are often capable of being classified as comedies or as tragedies. To appreciate further this protean quality of genre in early Elizabethan drama, we might consider the varied works of a number of dramatists whose practice was successful on the stage and who influenced Shakespeare and his immediate contemporaries. Of these, John Lyly is one of the most important.

John Lyly (1554?–1606), grandson of the grammarian William Lyly or Lilly, educated at Oxford and Cambridge, first acquired fame not as a dramatist, but as a writer of prose. His *Euphues, The Anatomy of Wit*, published in 1578, and its sequel, *Euphues and His England* (1580), stand as the most sensational and brilliant effort in the struggle of English Renaissance prose to acquire a conscious artistic manner. The style is, to a remarkable extent, composed of rhetorical devices: antithesis, personification, rhetorical question, metaphor, simile, and, above all, balance reinforced by alliteration. Recondite tidbits and fanciful legends about natural history are garnered from Plutarch, Pliny, and many other writers. The overall result is a kind of handbook for the courtier, the lover, the traveler, and the statesman. Lyly's deliberately outrageous style was imitated by dozens of other writers, including Robert Greene and Thomas Lodge, and seems to have set a new fashion of smart speech in the court of Queen Elizabeth. "Euphuism" itself had a vast influence on the style of the drama and other literature, both in poetry and in prose. Shakespeare is one of those who imitated and also ridiculed euphuistic speech. (For amusing examples of Shakespeare's parodying of the euphuistic style, see Falstaff's speech in *1 Henry IV*, 2.4.396 ff., beginning "for though the camomile, the more it is trodden on the faster it grows, yet youth, the more it is wasted the sooner it wears," or Don Armado's love letter in *Love's Labor's Lost*, 4.1.61 ff.: "Shall I command thy love? I may. Shall I enforce thy love? I could. Shall I entreat thy love? I will," and so on.)

Lyly was also the author of at least eight comedies, written to suit the taste of the court and possibly all acted before the Queen by the children of the Chapel Royal or of St. Paul's School. The plays are often courtly debates in the tradition of Medwall's *Fulgens and Lucrece*, with much combat of wits and philosophical argument. These comedies are also sufficiently modeled on Plautus or Terence to indicate that the characteristic features of Latin comedy by this time (1580–1590) had become naturalized on the English stage. *Mother Bombie*, for example, is an adaptation of Latin comedy, containing such stock figures as the pedant, the rascally servant, the duped parent, the parasite, and the aged lover, although, as usual, in Lyly the clownery has an English flavor as well.

Indeed, however much Lyly may recall classical Latin comedy, he is most important as the inventor of a fanciful type of love comedy to which Shakespeare was significantly indebted in several of his plays. Lyly's *Sappho and Phao, Endymion*, and *Midas* have romantic plots derived from Ovidian mythology. *Galatea* uses a pastoral setting for its love story and male disguises for the heroines, as in *As You Like It*. *Love's Metamorphosis* and *The Woman in the Moon* are also pastoral comedies. *Campaspe*, like *The Merchant of Venice*, portrays conflicts of love and friendship. Lyly's flattery of Queen Elizabeth through topical allegory and his appeal to a courtly clientele are, to be sure, modes that Shakespeare does not generally adopt. On the other hand, Shakespeare learned a good deal from Lyly's sensitive portrayal of the psychology of love. The depiction is often wryly comic: Lyly's men abase themselves before women, vacillate between idealization and misogyny, and not infrequently fail as wooers—much as the young lords do in Shakespeare's most Lylyan play, *Love's Labor's Lost*. Shakespeare's lovers generally work toward a more successful and realistic completion of romantic expectations, but Shakespeare's interest in love comedy began, in part, with what Lyly had achieved.

George Peele (1558?–1597) was also active as a dramatist around the time that Shakespeare first came to London. Peele's *The Arraignment of Paris* (1581) offers a quality of blank verse not previously seen in comedy and shows how classical legend could be adapted to a thoroughly English celebration of the nation and its Queen. *The Old Wives' Tale* (c. 1588–1594) is a seemingly naive but actually skillful medley of folk legends in the spirit of popular romance. *David and Bethsabe* (c. 1581–1594) dramatizes a familar biblical narrative in terms of erotic love and kingly power. Peele also contributed importantly to the new and burgeoning genre of the English history play with his *Edward I* (1590–1593); it is, like other history plays of the Armada era, jingoistically anti-Spanish and features a popular folk-hero king who understands and respects the proud local customs of his people. *The Battle of Alcazar* (1588–1589), another play of the Armada era, revels in the exotic world of Africa and the Middle East, in the vaunting heroic vein of Christopher Marlowe's *Tamburlaine*. Peele also devised two London civic pageants.

Robert Greene (1558–1592), more than any other dramatist, opened up for Shakespeare the world of Greek romance—the kind of fiction ultimately derived from Heliodorus, Achilles Tatius, and other protonovelists of the Mediterranean world in the second through fourth centuries. The Greeks of that era were the merchants, traders, sailors, and schoolmasters of the Roman Empire, and the early form of prose romance they created was a reflection of the adventurous life they lived. This romantic fiction reveled in strange and improbable encounters, piracies, the exposure of infant children to the elements and their eventual restoration as grown-ups to their aging parents, the separation and reunion of indistinguishable twins, and many other plot devices rendered familiar to us in the writings of Renaissance authors for whom this kind of sensationalism was every bit as interesting and worthy of imitation as the classics of Virgil and Ovid. Stories of the Greek kind, translated into various languages and ultimately into English, were to serve as models for a number of Shakespeare's late romances, especially *Pericles, The Winter's Tale*, and *Cymbeline*. Indeed, the plot of *The Winter's Tale* came to Shakespeare by way of Greene's prose romance, *Pandosto.*

From Greek romantic fiction, Greene devised a type of plucky romantic heroine for his plays and novels that Shakespeare was to develop further in his comedies. The society depicted by Greek romance gave women great liberty, and, like them, Greene's heroines are independent, witty, and resourceful, though at the same time feminine. Greene's dramas are almost the first modern productions in which women are in any degree represented as assuming a relatively dignified station in a mutually supportive love relationship with a man.

Greene also borrowed from Greek romantic fiction, and from other sources, especially for pastoral fiction. His plays, particularly *James IV* and *Friar Bacon and Friar Bungay* (c. 1589–1592), give us that blend of the pastoral and the romantic which the world has enjoyed in *As You Like It* and *Love's Labor's Lost*. *Friar Bacon* is particularly noteworthy for its multiple plot, its resourceful heroine, and its embracing of serious issues in a comic world. Greene must be regarded as the first great master of plot in English comedy.

Greene may also have written *George a Greene, the Pinner of Wakefield* (1587–1593), a play that exalts the virtues of England's yeoman class in defiance of the aristocracy and all foreign foes. The hero, George, is a patriot, a scorner of hereditary titles, and a representative of the common people against vested interests. As a new breed of English folk hero, he is so invincible that even Robin Hood must yield to his authority. The appeal of this dream of power to the artisans and yeomen in Greene's popular audiences must have been heady indeed.

Shortly before he fell victim to the notorious debaucheries of his bohemian existence (he was reported to have died from a surfeit of pickled herring and Rhenish wine), Greene wrote many pamphlets, some about London roguery, some about his own hard usage at the hands of the world. In one of the latter, *Greene's Groatsworth of Wit Bought with a Million of Repentance* (1592), he gave us our first personal reference to Shakespeare. (See "The Only Shake-scene in a Country" in the biographical account of Shakespeare's life and work, below.) Shakespeare was, of course, not the only dramatist to be influenced by Greene; Anthony Munday, Thomas Dekker, and most of the popular dramatists of the next decade were similarly indebted to Greene's example.

### Thomas Kyd and Christopher Marlowe

While romantic comedy was being shaped and developed in the hands of Lyly, Peele, and Greene, Senecan tragedy was also finding its proponents on the English stage. Lucius Annaeus Seneca (c. 4 B.C.–65 A.D.), a Roman statesman and stoic philosopher during the reign of the emperor Nero, wrote tragedies of a severely formal cast based on the tragedies of Aeschylus, Sophocles, and Euripides. Although never performed in Seneca's lifetime and indeed written as "closet" dramas, they became immensely influential on dramatists of later generations, especially during the Renaissance on the Continent and in England. The greatest genius in adapting Senecan action to the English theater was Thomas Kyd (1558–1594). His influence on his contemporaries and on later dramatists was immense; *The Spanish Tragedy* (c. 1583–1587) was probably acted more times during the sixteenth century than any other English play and became a pattern for subsequent revenge drama. Although Senecan tradition by no means accounts for all of the play's successful qualities, it remains a central part. Kyd catches the unabashed brutality and horror of the Senecan story and reveals it openly. Instead of having the action reported as taking place off the stage, as in Seneca and in most classical tragedy, he presents it directly. For tales of Greek mythology, he substitutes a modern story of love,

*Thomas Kyd's* The Spanish Tragedy *was perhaps the most popular play of the sixteenth century; it may have been performed more often than any other English drama of the time.* The Spanish Tragedy *served as a pattern and influenced subsequent revenge drama—including Shakespeare's* Hamlet.

conspiracy, murder, and political intrigue. He retains the Senecan ghost, the revenge motive, the spirit of stoicism, and a modified form of the chorus. The play deals both seriously and sensationally with the conflicting codes of revenge and Christian faith in God's providence. The protagonist Hieronimo, confronted with his son's murder and seemingly unable to obtain justice through the state, finds his pleas to the heavens unanswered and turns instead to a revenge that hardens his spirit and requires his own violent death as payment. The action is presided over by the spirit of Revenge, a chorus-like figure whose aims share nothing in common with Christian views of justice and mercy. *The Spanish Tragedy* is also noteworthy for a style that is a tour de force of rhetorical figures, such as anaphora and oxymoron—an achievement both imitated and mocked by later dramatists. Probably Kyd is also the author of an early lost dramatic version of the story of Hamlet.

Kyd's work gave rise to a series of revenge plays, not only in his own time, but also later, in 1600 and the years following, when the revenge tragedy again became fashionable. Moreover, Kyd seems to have had a shaping influence on Greene and on Marlowe. For example, Marlowe's *The Jew of Malta* (c. 1589), in its verbal extravagance and sensational intrigue, seems particularly indebted to *The Spanish Tragedy*.

Nevertheless, however much Kyd may have contributed in matters of style and form, Marlowe remains the leader in the great English type of Elizabethan tragedy. He shaped the genre that subsequently was perfected by Shakespeare. His achievement is all the more remarkable when we consider that he was born in the same year as Shakespeare (1564) and died in 1593, when Shakespeare had written no more than six or seven of his earliest plays. Marlowe's great contribution to English drama was a type of protagonist expressing something of the aspiration of the very Renaissance itself. Tamburlaine thirsts for world conquest; Dr. Faustus would go to the utmost bounds of knowledge and the power which knowledge gives; and Barabas in *The Jew of Malta* sets no limit to his longing for wealth.

Structurally, *Tamburlaine* (1587–1588) is a good deal closer to the English popular morality play than to classical drama. Each of the play's two parts consists of a linear sequence of conquests by the humbly born but seemingly invincible Tamburlaine, until at last death ends his glory. Because many characters appear in one episode only, the cast is large and yet within the capacities of an Elizabethan acting company. Doubling of parts, as in Shakespeare's early history plays, is both common and necessary. Structural unity is achieved through thematic repetition rather than through a narrowing of the narrative focus. At the same time, the language of *Tamburlaine* is rich and new in its vibrant appeal to limitless human aspiration. The Elizabethan playgoer is invited to forget moral considerations in evaluating the play's ruthless hero and to revel instead in the intoxicating spectacle of a baseborn shepherd "threat'ning the world with high astounding terms."

A profound ambivalence permeates all of Marlowe's plays and gives them a restless, brilliant energy that is characteristic of the times for which they were written. Tamburlaine is both a remorseless butcher of his enemies and a superhuman quester. He is fierce, mysterious, oriental, exotic, unknowable; as the projection of a universal human dream of aspiration, he is to be both admired and feared. Barabas in *The Jew of Malta* is at once colossally rich and colossally evil. Similarly, the protagonist of *Doctor Faustus* (c. 1588–1589) is both a sinner who falls from grace and a noble but doomed Overreacher (as Harry Levin describes him), daring like Icarus to fly toward the sun. In medieval and Christian orthodox terms, Faustus is guilty of pride, the deadliest of the Deadly Sins; but in Renaissance terms he at least fleetingly resembles Prometheus, challenging the hierarchy of an oppressive and outmoded universe. In its free mixture of comedy and tragedy and its wholesale disregard of the classical unities, *Doctor Faustus* brilliantly demonstrates

*The title page of the 1616 edition of Christopher Marlowe's* Doctor Faustus *shows Faustus's conjuration of the devil. The play illustrates native rather than classical traditions of tragedy in its disregard of the unities and its free use of comedy.*

what the native and homiletic tradition of tragedy had to offer Shakespeare.

*Edward II*, perhaps Marlowe's last play (1591–1593), is ambivalent toward its paired central figures, Edward and Mortimer Junior. At first, the effeminate King seems chiefly in the wrong, while his baronial opponents lament England's decline. Toward the end of the play, however, the King becomes the sympathetic victim of a power-mad and Machiavellian Mortimer. Queen Isabella also changes radically from a long-suffering, neglected wife into a scheming adulteress. This shift in sympathy from the barons to King Edward is structurally much like that of Shakespeare's *Richard II*, and, unquestionably, Marlowe's history play had a profound effect on Shakespeare. Yet Marlowe's tone, as in his other plays, remains one of naturalistic amorality. He wryly regards England's political struggles as one more manifestation of the restlessness and ambition afflicting all mortal endeavors. His world is one of constant turmoil in which persons of insatiable will assert themselves and rise to the top, at whatever cost to themselves and to society. Shakespeare's world is basically different, even though he learned a great deal from Marlowe's tragic vision.

Marlowe first gave to English tragedy its realization of character and, still more, its dignity and seriousness. He endowed English drama with a spirit of aspiration. His enthusiasm for beauty of language, shared by Spenser, Greene, Peele, and others, provided a rich heritage for the young Shakespeare. Not the least among Marlowe's gifts to English drama was a new and more flexible blank-verse style. In the following prologue to *Tamburlaine the Great*, Part I, Marlowe does not treat each blank-verse line as a separate unit but runs the sense on from line to line in order to produce what might be described as a blank-verse paragraph, a thing most necessary to drama if it is to represent widely varying emotions, thoughts, and characters:

> From jigging veins of rhyming mother-wits,
> And such conceits as clownage keeps in pay,
> We'll lead you to the stately tent of war,
> Where you shall hear the Scythian Tamburlaine
> Threat'ning the world with high astounding terms,
> And scourging kingdoms with his conquering sword.
> View but his picture in this tragic glass,
> And then applaud his fortunes as you please.

This is not only a manifesto of tragic seriousness; it is also, in spite of its elevated style, one of the first examples in English tragedy of vigorous, natural, straightforward expression. Tamburlaine in his utterances is a typical Renaissance poet on the themes of both love and war, as can be seen in the following evocation of the aspiring mind:

> If all the pens that ever poets held
> Had fed the feeling of their masters' thoughts,
> And every sweetness that inspired their hearts,
> Their minds, and muses on admirèd themes;
> If all the heavenly quintessence they still
> From their immortal flowers of poesy,
> Wherein, as in a mirror, we perceive
> The highest reaches of a human wit;
> If these had made one poem's period,
> And all combined in beauty's worthiness,
> Yet should there hover in their restless heads
> One thought, one grace, one wonder, at the least,
> Which into words no virtue can digest.

> —*Tamburlaine*, Pt. I, 5.1.161–73

## Shakespeare's Dramatic Heritage

Shakespearean tragedy began, roughly speaking, with marked indebtedness to the tragic writing of Marlowe and Kyd: poetry, character, and style from Marlowe; motive, plot, and tragic intensity from Kyd. No evidence suggests that Shakespeare was ever particularly aware of, or influenced by, Aristotelian theories of tragedy. His wish was to hold "the mirror up to nature" and show "virtue her feature, scorn her own image, and the very age and body of the time his form and pressure" (*Hamlet*, 3.2.22–4). Sometimes he approximated Aristotelian ideals in his plays (most nearly, perhaps, in *Othello, Macbeth*, and *Coriolanus*), but not by conscious design. Nor was he a slavish borrower from Marlowe and Kyd, even in his early tragedies, such as *Titus Andronicus*. Greene and many others sought to imitate Marlowe in tragedy, with but indifferent success. Shakespeare, Marlowe's only successful imitator, soon outdistanced Marlowe in those very qualities for which he was indebted to him.

Similarly, the elements of Shakespearean comedy are, in part, derived from Lyly, Peele, and Greene. The contributions of Lyly and Peele were those of style, setting, and movement. Greene, primarily a writer of romance, an adapter of Greek romantic fiction, furnished the element of love and adventure that makes so many Elizabethan plays delightful merely as stories. He also put upon the stage the witty, independent-minded woman, often in boy's clothes, who gives point and naturalness to love intrigue whether in serious drama or in comedy. Not only did Shakespeare, who was a far greater genius than any of them, combine the elements of the comedies of these men and better the instruction, but, as his career went on, he realized on a broad scale the possibilities of the comic point of view in the representation of human life and character.

In the English history play, though he may have learned much from Marlowe, Peele, and others, Shakespeare was clearly an innovator as well. His early history plays on the reigns of Henry VI and Richard III were among the earliest such plays seen in London and were (at least some of them) enormous stage successes. Even here, however, we can see how much Shakespeare learned from such earlier plays as *Gorboduc* and *The Troublesome Reign of King John*.

# LONDON THEATERS AND DRAMATIC COMPANIES

Throughout Shakespeare's life, the propriety of acting any plays at all was a matter of bitter controversy. Indeed, when one considers the power and earnestness of the opposition, one is surprised that such a wealth of dramatic excellence could come into being and that Shakespeare's plays should reflect so little the anger and hostility generated by this continuing conflict.

## *Religious and Moral Opposition to the Theater*

From the 1570s onward, and even earlier, the city fathers of London revealed an ever-increasing distrust of the public performance of plays. They fretted about the dangers of plague and of riotous assembly. They objected to the fact that apprentices idly wasted their time instead of working in their shops. And always the municipal authorities suspected immorality. Thus, by an order of the Common Council of London, dated December 6, 1574, the players were put under severe restrictions.

The order cites the reasons. The players, it was charged, had been acting in the innyards of the city, which in consequence were haunted by great multitudes of people, especially youths. These gatherings had been the occasions of frays and quarrels, "evil practices of incontinency in great inns"; the players published "uncomely and unshamefast speeches and doings," withdrew the Queen's subjects from divine service on Sundays and holidays, wasted the money of "poor and fond persons," gave opportunity to pickpockets, uttered "busy and seditious matters," and injured and maimed people by the falling of their scaffolds and by weapons and powder used in plays. The order goes on to state the Common Council's fear that if the plays, which had been forbidden on account of the plague, should be resumed, God's wrath would manifest itself by an increase of the infection. Therefore, no innkeeper, tavernkeeper, or other person might cause or suffer to be openly played "any play, interlude, comedy, tragedy, matter, or show" which had not been first licensed by the mayor and the Court of Aldermen.

The mayor and aldermen did not always state their case plainly, because Queen Elizabeth was a patron of the players, and because the players had friends and patrons in the Privy Council and among the nobility; sometimes, however, they did so quite boldly. One sees the case against plays stated syllogistically in the following words of Thomas White, a preacher at Paul's Cross in 1577:

Look but upon the common plays of London, and see the multitude that flocketh to them and followeth them! Behold the sumptuous theater houses, a continual monument of London prodigality and folly! But I understand they are now forbidden because of the plague. I like the policy well if it hold still, for a disease is but botched and patched up that is not cured in the cause, and the cause of plagues is sin, if you look to it well, and the cause of sin are plays. Therefore the cause of plagues are plays. (From *A Sermon preached at Paul's Cross…in the Time of the Plague*, 1578.)

Moved, no doubt, by the prohibition of the Common Council, James Burbage, with a company of actors under the patronage of the Earl of Leicester, leased a site in Shoreditch, a London suburb in Middlesex, beyond the immediate jurisdiction of the official enemies in the Common Council, whose authority extended only to the city limits. By 1576, he had completed the Theatre. Perhaps he called it "the Theatre" because it had no competitor (other than the Red Lion, established in 1567 and used seemingly as a playing place for feasts and festival days in the performance style of Corpus Christi and saints' plays). Burbage erected what may have been England's first permanent commercial theatrical building. In general, the building combined features of the innyard and the animal-baiting house, having a central and probably paved courtyard open to the sky (like an innyard) and surrounding galleries on all sides (like an animal-baiting house). Burbage erected a stage at one side of the circular arena and put dressing rooms behind it to form the "tiring house," or backstage area for the actors; the facade of this "tiring house" served as a visible backdrop to the stage itself. Burbage's Theatre became the model for other public playhouses, such as the Curtain, the Swan, and the Globe, which were constructed later.

By building his playhouse in Shoreditch, Burbage gained immunity from the London authorities. The city fathers could not suppress plays or control them with perfect success if they were performed in Middlesex, or in the "liberty" of Blackfriars and similar districts exempted by charters from London's civic authority (see "London's Private Theaters," below), or (in the case of later playhouses) on the Bankside across the Thames in Surrey. In order to get at them in these suburban regions, the city authorities had to petition the Queen's Privy Council to give orders to the magistrates and officers of the law in these counties. The Queen's Privy Council, although always on the most polite terms with the Lord Mayor and his brethren of the city and always open to the argument that the assemblage of crowds caused the spread of the plague, was to a much less degree in sympathy with the moral scruples of the city. Current arguments for the plays, derived from the works

ANDREW SALTER/NATIONAL TRUST PHOTOGRAPHIC LIBRARY

*The George Inn of Southwark, England, London's only surviving galleried inn, was destroyed by fire in 1676 but rebuilt the following year with two galleries instead of the original three. Despite these changes, the George Inn gives us the best picture we have of the kind of space in which traveling companies could mount their plays on bare platform stages.*

of scholars, poets, and playwrights, were numerous and often heard: namely, that classical antiquity gave precedent for dramatic spectacles; that by drawing a true picture of both the bad and the good in life, plays enabled people to choose the good; that people should have wholesome amusement; and that plays provided livelihood for loyal subjects of the Queen.

Of these arguments, to be sure, the Privy Council made little use, resting the case for plays instead on what was, no doubt, an unanswerable argument: that since the players might appear before Her Majesty, especially during the Christmas/Shrovetide period, the players needed practice in order to prepare themselves to please the royal taste. A good deal of politic fencing ensued, and, so far as orders, complaints, and denunciations were concerned, the reforming opposition had much the better of it. The preachers thundered against plays. Pamphleteers denounced all matters pertaining to the stage: Stephen Gosson in *The School of Abuse, Containing a Pleasant Invective Against Poets, Pipers, Players, Jesters and Suchlike Caterpillars of a Commonwealth* (1579) and other works; Philip Stubbes in *The Anatomy of Abuses* (1583); and finally and most furiously of all, William Prynne in *Histrio-Mastix:*

*The Players' Scourge or Actor's Tragedy* (1633). Gosson spoke of plays as "the inventions of the devil, the offerings of idolatry, the pomp of worldlings, the blossoms of vanity, the root of apostacy, food of iniquity, riot and adultery." "Detest them," he warned. "Players are masters of vice, teachers of wantonness, spurs to impurity, the sons of idleness."

At first, such diatribes represented an extreme reforming opinion obviously not shared by a majority of London viewers. They kept coming to plays, and the flourishing public theaters attracted the talents of the age's leading dramatists. An ominous note of polarization was sounded, however, early in the reign of James I (1603–1625), when the rift between the Puritans and the court broke into open antagonism. After about 1604, when James alienated the Puritans at the Hampton Court Conference, the split between popular audiences and the best drama of the age became increasingly evident. Shakespeare's company, now the King's Men, gravitated, whether through choice or necessity, toward the precinct of the court. Although the public theater, with its capacity for large audiences, continued to serve as a lively center of theatrical activity, Puritan opposition to the stage gathered momentum. Many dramatists, in turn, grew more satirical of London customs and more attuned to courtly tastes. Eventually, Puritan hostility to the theater was at least part of the motive behind Parliament's order to close the theaters in 1642.

## The Public Theaters

A year or more after Burbage built the Theatre in 1576, the Curtain was put up near it by Philip Henslowe, or possibly by Henry Laneman, or Lanman. About ten years later, Philip Henslowe built the Rose, the first playhouse on the Bankside (the southern bank of the Thames River). In 1599, James Burbage's sons Richard and Cuthbert dismantled the Theatre because of trouble about the lease of the land and rebuilt it as the Globe on the Bankside. This Globe playhouse burned on June 29, 1613, from the discharge of cannon backstage during a performance of *All Is True*, a play thought to be identical with Shakespeare's *Henry VIII*. The Globe was rebuilt, probably in its original polygonal form—that is, essentially round, with a large number of sides. In 1600, Henslowe built the Fortune as a theater for the Lord Admiral's Men, who were chief rivals to the Lord Chamberlain's Men. The companies were differently organized, in that the Lord Chamberlain's Men were joint sharers in their own enterprise and owners of their own theatrical building, whereas Henslowe owned the Fortune (and the Rose before it) and served as landlord to the Admiral's Men—no doubt profiting handsomely from their activities.

Various records of these theatrical buildings have survived. One such record is the Fortune contract, preserved at Dulwich College among other invaluable papers of

Philip Henslowe, theatrical entrepreneur and father-in-law of the famous Edward Alleyn of the Lord Admiral's Men. The contract for building the Fortune was let to the same contractor who had built the new Globe, and, since the specifications required that the Fortune should be like the Globe in all its main features, except that it was to be square instead of polygonal, we may gain from these specifications an idea of the Globe. A second documentary record is a drawing of the Swan, a Bankside theater, accompanying a description of the playhouse by Johannes De Witt, who visited London in 1596. The drawing, which was discovered in the University Library at Utrecht, is the work of one Van Buchell and may be based on drawings by De Witt himself. Besides the Fortune contract and the Swan drawing, we have two or three little pictures of the Elizabethan public stage on the title pages of published plays, the most important being that on the title page of William Alabaster's *Roxana* (1632). Just recently, in 1989, the discovery and excavation of the foundations of the Rose playhouse and partial excavation of the Globe playhouse foundations in Southwark, together with the construction of a modern replica of the Globe playhouse near the site of these two theaters, have

*This drawing of an Elizabethan public stage appeared on the title page of the published version of William Alabaster's play* Roxana *(1632).*

added invaluable archeological information about the dimensions of that acting arena.

## The London Public Stage

From these documents and pictures and from scattered references to the theaters, as well as from extended studies of stage directions and scenic conditions in plays themselves, we have a fairly clear idea of the public stage in London. Its features are these: a pit about seventy feet in diameter, usually circular and open to the sky; surrounding this, galleries in three tiers, containing the most expensive seats; and a rectangular stage, about forty-three by twenty-seven feet, wider than it was deep, raised about five and one-half feet above the surface of the yard, sometimes built on trestles so that it could be removed if the house was also customarily used for bear-baiting and bullbaiting. The flat, open stage usually contained one trapdoor. Part of the stage was afforded some protection from the weather by a brightly decorated wooden roof supported by posts, constituting the "heavens." Above this roof was a "hut," perhaps containing suspension gear for ascents and descents. (The Rose appears originally to have been generally smaller than what is described here, with a stage that tapered toward the front to a width of only twenty-five feet or so. The building was somewhat expanded in 1592 but was still small compared with other theaters. The original building shows no certain evidence of a roof over the stage supported by pillars, but the later building appears to have had roof pillars at the front of the stage.)

At the back of the stage was a partition wall, the "tiring-house facade," with at least two doors in it connecting the stage with the actors' dressing rooms or "tiring house." In the Rose, the tiring-house facade seems to have curved with the polygonal shape of the theater building, but in the DeWitt drawing the Swan facade looks perfectly straight across. Some theaters appear to have had no more than two doors, left and right, as shown in the Swan drawing; other theaters may have had a third door in the center. The arrangement of the Globe playhouse in this important matter cannot be finally determined, although some particular scenes from Shakespeare's plays seem to demand a third door. In any case, the so-called inner stage, long supposed to have stood at the rear of the Elizabeth stage, almost certainly did not exist. A more modest "discovery space" could be provided at one of the curtained doors when needed, as for example in *The Tempest* when Ferdinand and Miranda are suddenly "discovered" at their game of chess by Prospero. Such scenes never called for extensive action within the discovery space, however, and, indeed, the number of such discoveries in Elizabethan plays is very few. Well-to-do spectators who may have been seated in the gallery above the rear of the stage could not see into the discovery

*This diagram of the Swan Theatre (left) by Van Buchell (c. 1596), based on the observations of Johannes De Witt, shows features of the public playhouse shared by James Burbage's Theatre and the Globe. To the right, a modern rendition of a typical Elizabethan playhouse shows the acting platform with spectators standing around three sides of it in the "yard," and a roofed hut above the acting area. Like the Globe and other open theaters, the design of the Swan seems to resemble the Elizabethan innyard with an added stage.*

space. Accordingly, it was used sparingly and only for brief visual effects. Otherwise, the actors performed virtually all their scenes on the open stage. Sometimes curtains were hung over the tiring-house facade between the doors to facilitate scenes of concealment, as when Polonius and Claudius eavesdrop on Hamlet and Ophelia.

An upper station was sometimes used as an acting space, but not nearly so often as was once supposed. The gallery seats above the stage, sometimes known as the "Lord's room," were normally sold to well-to-do spectators. (We can see such spectators in the Swan drawing and in Alabaster's *Roxana*.) Occasionally, these box seats could be used by the actors, as when Juliet appears at her window (it is never called a balcony). In military sequences, as in the *Henry VI* plays, the tiring-house facade could represent the walls of a besieged city, with the city's defenders appearing "on the walls" (i.e., in the gallery above the stage) in order to parley with the besieging enemy standing below on the main stage. Such scenes were relatively infrequent, however, and usually required only a small number of persons to be aloft. A music room, when needed, could be located in one of the gallery boxes over the stage, but public theaters did not emulate the private stages with music rooms and music between the acts until some time around 1609.

The use of scenery was largely unknown on the Elizabethan public stage, although we do find occasional hints of the use of labels to designate a certain door or area as a fixed location (as, perhaps, in *The Comedy of Errors*). For the most part, the scene was unlimited and the concept of space was fluid. No proscenium arch or curtain stood between the actors and the audience, and so the action could not be easily interrupted. Only belatedly did the public companies adopt the private-theater practice of entr'acte music, as we have seen. Most popular Elizabethan plays were written to be performed nonstop. Five-act structure had little currency, especially at first, and the occasional act divisions in the published versions of Shakespeare's plays may be nonauthorial. Acting tempo was brisk. The Prologue of *Romeo and Juliet* speaks of "the two hours' traffic of our stage." Plays were performed in the afternoons and had to be completed by dark in order to allow the audience to return safely to London. During the winter season, playing time was severely restricted. Outbreaks of plague often occasioned the closing of the theaters, especially in warm weather.

A capacity audience for the popular theaters came to about 2,000 to 3,000 persons. (The recently excavated Rose playhouse foundations suggest an audience there of around 2,000.) For the most part, the audience was

*Elizabethan dancers, shown above, perform on a stage below a gallery of musicians. Imported stage designs from Italy made more use of perspective scenery than did the commercial theaters.*

affluent, consisting chiefly of the gentry and of London's substantial mercantile citizenry who paid two to three pence or more for gallery seats or the "Lord's room," but the ample pit or yard also provided room for small shop-keepers and artisans who stood for a penny. The spectators were lively, demanding, and intelligent. Although Shakespeare does allow Hamlet to refer disparagingly on one occasion to the "groundlings" who "for the most part are capable of nothing but inexplicable dumbshows and noise" (*Hamlet*, 3.2.11–12), Shakespeare appealed to the keenest understanding of his whole audience, thereby achieving a breadth of vision seldom found in continental courtly drama of the same period. The vitality and financial success of the Elizabethan public theater is without parallel in English history. The city of London itself, in 1600 or so, had only about 100,000 inhabitants, yet throughout Shakespeare's career several companies were

competing simultaneously for this audience and constantly producing new plays. Most new plays ran for only a few performances, so that the acting companies were always in rehearsal with new shows. The actors needed phenomenal memories and a gift of improvisation as well. Their acting seems to have been of a high caliber, despite the speed with which they worked. Among other things, many of them were expert fencers and singers.

The London public stage inherited many of its practices from native and medieval traditions. The fluid, open stage, with spectators on four sides, recalled the arena staging of many early Corpus Christi cycles, saints' plays, and morality plays. The adult professional companies were, as we have seen, descended from the itinerant troupes that had acted their plays throughout England in guildhalls, private residences, monastic houses and schools, and perhaps occasionally outdoors on booth stages (though the evidence for this last possible venue is scarce). The Elizabethan tiring-house facade and platform stage may have owed much to the kinds of theatrical space that touring actors had known, and perhaps to the arrangement of a booth stage and a trestle platform set up against one wall of an innyard, where the guests of the inn could enjoy a performance, along with standing spectators in the yard. When the itinerant actors had set up their plays in noblemen's banqueting halls or at court, at any rate, they encountered another space that had an important influence on their concept of a theater: the Tudor hall. We must next examine the significance of this indoor theatrical setting.

## The Tudor Hall

The Tudor banqueting hall played a major part in the staging of much early Tudor drama. Medwall's *Fulgens and Lucrece*, one of the earliest such plays, was written to be performed during the intervals of a state banquet. The patrician guests were seated at tables, while servingmen bustled to and fro or stood crowded together at the doors in the hall "screen." This screen or partition traversed the lower end of the rectangular hall, providing a passageway to the kitchens and to the outside. Its doors—often two, sometimes three—were normally curtained to prevent drafts. This arrangement of the doors bears an interesting resemblance to that of many playhouses in late Elizabethan England, both public and private. Moreover, hall screens and passageways were normally surmounted by a gallery, where musicians could play—an archi-

tectural feature markedly resembling the upper galleries of late Elizabethan theaters. Could the Tudor hall screen provide a natural facade for dramatic action? Perhaps it did, although records from Shakespeare's era only rarely document an actual performance in front of the screen, whereas performances were common at the upper end of the hall in front of the dais or in the midst of the hall, where the persons of highest social rank sitting on the dais would have had the best view. The actors of *Fulgens and Lucrece* clearly made use of the doorways in the hall screen, sometimes joking with the servingmen as the actors pushed their way into the hall, but they probably acted in the center, among the spectators' tables. John Heywood's *Play of the Weather* calls for a similar *mise en scène*. Although this ready-made "stage" sufficed for most Tudor plays, the actors sometimes provided additional stage structures; *Weather,* for example, calls for a throne room into which Jupiter can retire without leaving the hall. Similar structures could represent a shop, an orchard, a mountain, or what have you.

Guild and town halls, where players on tour performed before the mayor and council (and sometimes a wider public), provided a similar physical environment, except that we cannot be sure that such spaces had galleries in the sixteenth century. Since the gallery is not necessary for many Tudor plays, the players may well have gained experience in halls of this kind that influenced their techniques of staging once they had gravitated to London.

Although both medieval and continental drama offered traditions of multiple staging, in which a series of simultaneously visible and adjacent structures would

The Tudor banqueting hall provided a place to "stage" much early Tudor drama. The actors performed on the floor, among the tables of the guests. The Middle Temple Hall, shown here, later served as the location for a performance of Shakespeare's Twelfth Night *on February 2, 1602. The Middle Temple is one of the Inns of Court, where young men studied law and occasionally relaxed by staging dramatic entertainments.*

represent as fixed locations all the playing areas needed for the performance of a play, Tudor indoor staging seems to have made less use of this method than was once supposed. Nor did the various indoor theaters of Tudor England make extensive use of neoclassical staging from Italy, with its street scene in perspective created by means of lath-and-canvas stage "houses." Italian scenery of this sort came into use sooner in the court masque than in regular drama. Nevertheless, we do find in the Tudor indoor theater a neoclassical tendency toward a fixed locale, in preference to the unlimited open stage. *Gammer Gurton's Needle*, for example, acted probably in a university hall, seems to have used one stage structure, or possibly one door, to represent Gammer's house throughout the action, and another to represent Dame Chat's house. Shakespeare may have been influenced by this kind of fixed-locale staging in *The Comedy of Errors*. (Alan Nelson's *Early Cambridge Theaters*, 1994, is an important resource for school staging.)

### The Private Stage

Despite such influences on the public stage, the most significant contribution of the Tudor hall and its hall screen was to the so-called private stage of the late Elizabethan period—"private" in the sense of being intended for a more select and courtly audience than that which frequented the "public" theaters. In the 1570s, choir boys began performing professionally to courtly and intellectual audiences in London. The choir boys had long performed plays for the royal and noble households to which they were attached, but in the 1570s they were, in effect, organized into professional acting companies. Sebastian

*A reconstruction of the Second Blackfriars, featuring a rectangular stage, a tiring house with three doors, and a gallery.*

Westcote and the Children of Paul's may have originated this enterprise. Their theater was apparently some indoor hall in the vicinity of St. Paul's in London, outfitted much like the typical domestic Tudor hall to which the boys had grown accustomed. Comparable indoor "private" theaters soon followed at Blackfriars and Whitefriars.

At some point, a low stage was constructed in front of the hall screen, and seats were provided for all the spectators. Many of these seats were in the "pit," or what we would call the "orchestra," facing toward the stage at one end of the rectangular room. Other seats were in galleries along both sides of the room; these were quite elaborate in the so-called Second Blackfriars of 1596 and provided two or three tiers of seats. Elegant box seats stood at either side of the stage itself. The Second Blackfriars had a permanently built tiring house to the rear of the stage, with probably three doors. Above it was a gallery used variously as a lord's room, a music room, and an upper station for occasional acting.

The private theater flourished during the 1580s and again after 1598–1599, having been closed down during most of the 1590s because of its satirical activities. Although it was a commercial theater, it was "private" in its clientele, because its high price of admission (sixpence) excluded those who could stand in the yards of the "public" theaters for a penny (roughly the equivalent of an hour's wage for a skilled worker). Plays written for the more select audiences of the "private" theaters tended to be more satirical and oriented to courtly values than those written for the "public" theaters, although the distinction is by no means absolute.

### London Private Theaters

The important private theaters of Shakespeare's London were two in the precinct, or "liberty," of Blackfriars, an early one in Whitefriars about which little is known, a later one there, and a theater at Paul's, the exact location and nature of which is not known. In the thirteenth century, the mother house of the Dominican friars, or Blackfriars, was established on the sloping ground between St. Paul's Cathedral and the river. It was a sizable institution, ultimately covering about five acres of ground. It stood on the very border of the city and, after the custom of the time, was made a liberty; that is to say, it had its own local government and was removed from the immediate jurisdiction of the city of London. After the suppression of the friary and the confiscation of its lands, the jealousy existing between the Privy Council, representing the crown, and the mayor and aldermen, representing the city and probably also the rights of property holders, prevented the district of the Blackfriars from losing its political independence of the municipality. It was still a liberty and therefore attractive to players and other persons wishing to avoid the London authorities. At the same time, aristocrats residing in the area required protection, and the Crown had certain rights still in its control.

From 1576 to 1584, the Children of the Queen's Chapel, one of the two most important companies of boy actors, had used a hall in the precinct of Blackfriars in which to act their plays. Here were acted at least some of John Lyly's plays. In 1596, James Burbage purchased property in this precinct and seems to have spent a good deal of money in adapting it for use as an indoor theater (the so-called Second Blackfriars). He probably appreciated its advantages over Cripplegate or the Bankside of greater proximity to London and of protection against the elements, particularly for use in winter. But the aristocratic residents of the Blackfriars, by petition to the Privy Council, prevented him from making use of his theater. Plays within the city proper had only recently been finally and successfully prohibited, and the petitioners no doubt objected to their intrusion into Blackfriars, on the grounds that the plays and their crowds were a nuisance.

Burbage's new indoor theater may have lain idle from the time of its preparation until 1600; but, in any case, in that year it became the scene of many plays. It was let by lease for the use of the Children of the Chapel, who in 1604 became the Children of the Queen's Revels. Their theater managers brought into their service a number of new dramatists—Ben Jonson, John Marston, George Chapman, and later John Webster. The vogue of the plays acted by the Children of the Chapel was so great as to damage the patronage of the established companies and to compel them to go on the road. Out of this rivalry between the children and the adult actors arose that open competition alluded to in *Hamlet* (2.2.328–362) and sometimes referred to today as the "War of the Theaters." The skirmishes were relatively brief, arising in part from a clash of personalities among Jonson, Marston, and Thomas Dekker, but the debate between public and private acting companies was significant as an indication of whether London drama would continue to play to large popular audiences or would increasingly turn to a more courtly clientele. In 1608, the Burbage interests secured the evacuation of the lease, so that the theater in Blackfriars became the winter playhouse of Shakespeare's company from that time forward.

## System of Patronage

In 1572, common players of interludes, along with minstrels, bearwards, and fencers, were included within the hard terms of the act for the punishment of vagabonds, provided that such common players were not enrolled as the servants of a baron of the realm or of some honorable person of greater degree. The result was a system of patronage of theatrical companies in Elizabethan and Jacobean times, according to which players became the "servants" of some nobleman or of some member of the royal family.

By the time Shakespeare came to London in the late 1580s, many of these companies were already in existence, some of which long antedated the passage of the act of 1572. Provincial records of the visits of players, to be sure, sometimes failed to distinguish actors from acrobats or other public performers who were similarly organized. Nonetheless, we have evidence that various companies of players performed in London and elsewhere in the late 1580s, under the patronage of the Queen, the Earl of Worcester, the Earl of Leicester, the Earl of Oxford, the Earl of Sussex, the Lord Admiral, and Charles, Lord Howard of Effingham. These companies were eventually much reduced in number; usually only three adult companies acted at any given time in London during Shakespeare's prime. In addition, the children's companies, privately controlled, acted intermittently but at times very successfully. The most important of these were the Children of the Chapel and Queen's Revels and the Children of Paul's, but there were also boy players of Windsor, Eton College, the Merchant Taylors, Westminster, and other schools.

## Shakespeare and the London Theatrical Companies

We know that by 1592 Shakespeare had arrived in London and had achieved sufficient notice as a young playwright to arouse the resentment of a rival dramatist, Robert Greene. In that year, shortly before he died, Greene—or possibly his editor after Greene's death—lashed out at an "upstart crow, beautified with our feathers," who had had the audacity to fancy himself "the only Shake-scene in a country" (*Groats-worth of Wit*). This petulant outburst was plainly directed at Shakespeare, since Greene included in his remarks a parody of some lines from *3 Henry VI*. As a university man and an established dramatist, Greene seems to have resented the intrusion into his profession of a mere player who was not university trained. This "upstart crow" was achieving a very real success on the London stage. Shakespeare had probably already written *The Comedy of Errors, Love's Labor's Lost, The Two Gentlemen of Verona*, the *Henry VI* plays, and *Titus Andronicus*, and perhaps also *Richard III* and *The Taming of the Shrew*.

For which acting company or companies had he written these plays, however? By 1594, we know that Shakespeare was an established member of the Lord Chamberlain's company, important enough, in fact, to have been named, along with Will Kempe and Richard Burbage, as payee for court performances on December 26 and 28 of 1594. But when had he joined the Chamberlain's Men, and for whom had he written and acted previously? These are the problems of the so-called dark years, during which Shakespeare came to London (perhaps as early as 1587) and got started on his career.

One prestigious acting company he could have joined was the Earl of Leicester's company, led by James Burbage, father of Shakespeare's later colleague, Richard Burbage.

Leicester was a favorite minister of Queen Elizabeth until his death in 1588, and his company of actors received from the Queen in 1574 an extraordinary patent to perform plays anywhere in England, despite all local prohibitions, provided that the plays were approved beforehand by the master of the Queen's Revels. Since an act of 1572 had outlawed all unlicensed troupes, Leicester's Men and similar companies attached to important noblemen were given a virtual monopoly over public acting. In 1576, Burbage built the Theatre for his company in the northeast suburbs of London. This group also toured the provinces: Leicester's company visited Stratford-upon-Avon in 1587. Conceivably, Shakespeare served an apprenticeship in this company, though no evidence exists to prove a connection. Leicester's company had lost some of its prominence in 1583, when several of its best men joined the newly formed Queen's Men, with Richard Tarlton as its most famous actor. The remaining members of Leicester's company disbanded in 1588 upon the death of the Earl, and many of its principal actors ultimately became part of Lord Strange's company. These probably included George Bryan, Will Kempe, and Thomas Pope, all of whom subsequently went on to become Lord Chamberlain's Men.

### Lord Strange's (The Earl of Derby's) Men

The Queen's Men gained an extraordinary prominence in the 1580s, as Scott McMillin and Sally-Beth MacLean have shown in the *Queen's Men and Their Plays* (1998). This acting group was assembled under royal sponsorship, as an instrument of furthering the Protestant Reformation through its performances of plays, and did so with notable success, although it then declined rapidly in the early 1590s, chiefly because as a touring company it was unprepared to compete with the new companies that learned how to succeed in the metropolis by staging a wide variety of plays in a fixed London theater. Prominent among the acting companies to which Shakespeare could have belonged when he came to London, probably in the late 1580s, were Lord Strange's Men, the Lord Admiral's Men, the Earl of Pembroke's Men, and the Earl of Sussex's Men. Scholars have long speculated that Shakespeare may have joined the company of Ferdinando Stanley, Lord Strange (who in 1593 became the Earl of Derby). The names of George Bryan, Will Kempe, and Thomas Pope appear on a roster of Strange's company in 1593, along with those of John Heminges and Augustine Phillips. All of these men later became part of the Lord Chamberlain's company, most of them when it was first formed in 1594. Shakespeare's name does not appear on the 1593 Lord Strange's list (which was a license for touring in the provinces), but he may possibly have stayed in London to attend to his writing while the company toured. Certainly, an important number of his later associates belonged to this group.

*Clowns were enormously popular on the Elizabethan stage. Of the many Elizabethan clowns whose names are known to us, Richard Tarlton is one of the most famous. (Will Kempe, in Shakespeare's company, the Lord Chamberlain's Men, is another; see pp. I-62 and I-63.) Tarlton is shown here inside an elaborate letter T, dancing a jig with his pipe and tabor. Such jigs were often used at the conclusion of a play.*

During the years from 1590 to 1594, some of Lord Strange's Men appear to have joined forces on occasion with Edward Alleyn and others of the Admiral's Men. This impressive combination of talents enjoyed a successful season in 1591–1592, with six performances at court. Alleyn's father-in-law, Philip Henslowe, recorded in his *Diary* the performances of the combined players in early 1592, probably at the Rose Theatre. Their repertory included a *Harey the vj* and a *Titus & Vespacia*. The latter play is, however, no longer thought to have any connection with Shakespeare's *Titus Andronicus;* and the *Harey the vj* may or may not have been Shakespeare's, since *3 Henry VI* was (according to its 1595 title page) acted by Pembroke's Men rather than Lord Strange's Men. If Shakespeare was a member of the Strange-Admiral's combination in 1591–1592, we are at a loss to explain why Henslowe's 1592 list records so many performances of plays by Marlowe, Greene, Kyd, and others, but none that are certainly by Shakespeare. On the other hand, the *Harey the vj* may be his, and the title page of the 1594 quarto of *Titus Andronicus* does list the Earl of Derby's Men as performers of the play, in addition to the Earl of Pembroke's and the Earl of Sussex's Men. (Lord Strange's Men became officially known as the Earl of Derby's Men when Lord Strange was made an earl in September 1593.) At any rate, the company disbanded when the Earl died in April 1594, leaving them without a patron. The connection with the Admiral's Men was discontinued, with Alleyn returning to the Admiral's Men and the rest of the group forming a new company under the patronage of Henry Carey, first Lord Hunsdon, the Lord Chamberlain.

### The Earl of Pembroke's Men

The other company to which Shakespeare is most likely to have belonged prior to 1594 is the Earl of Pembroke's company. This group came to grief in 1593–1594, evidently as a result of virulent outbursts of the plague, which had kept the theaters closed during most of 1592 and 1593. Pembroke's Men were forced to tour the provinces and then to sell a number of their best plays to the booksellers. Henslowe wrote to Alleyn in September 1593 of the extreme financial plight of Pembroke's company: "As for my lord of Pembroke's [Men], which you desire to know where they be, they are all at home and has been this five or six weeks, for they cannot save their charges [expenses] with travel, as I hear, and were fain to pawn their parell [apparel] for their charge." Soon thereafter this company disbanded.

Pembroke's Men were associated with a significant number of Shakespeare's early plays. Among the playbooks they evidently sold in 1593–1594 were *The Taming of a Shrew* and *The True Tragedy of Richard Duke of York*. The first of these was published in 1594 with the assertion that it had been "sundry times acted by the Right Honorable the Earle of Pembroke his Servants." Although the text of this quarto is not Shakespeare's play as we know it but, instead, an anonymous version, most scholars now feel certain that it was an imitation of Shakespeare's play and that the work performed by Pembroke's Men was, in fact, Shakespeare's. The same conclusion pertains to a performance in 1594 of "*the Tamynge of a Shrowe*" at Newington Butts, a playhouse south of London Bridge. Henslowe's *Diary* informs us that the actors on this occasion were either the Lord Chamberlain's or the Lord Admiral's Men. The probability, then, is that Shakespeare's *The Taming of the Shrew* passed from Pembroke's Men to the Chamberlain's Men when Pembroke's company collapsed in 1593–1594.

*The True Tragedy of Richard Duke of York,* published in 1595, was a seemingly unauthorized quarto of Shakespeare's *3 Henry VI.* Its title page declared that it had been "sundry times acted by the Right Honorable the Earl of Pembroke his Servants." Probably they acted *2 Henry VI* as well, to which part three was a sequel. In addition, the 1594 quarto of *Titus Andronicus* mentions on its title page the Earl of Pembroke's Servants, although the Earl of Derby's and the Earl of Sussex's Men are named there as well. Thus, Pembroke's Men performed as many as four of Shakespeare's early plays—more than we can assign to any other known company. Nevertheless, their claim to Shakespeare remains uncertain. We simply do not know who acted several of Shakespeare's earliest plays, such as *The Comedy of Errors, Love's Labor's Lost,* and *The Two Gentlemen of Verona.* Lord Strange's (Derby's) men, as we have seen, did act something called *Harey the vj* and are named on the 1594 title page of *Titus Andronicus.* Sussex's Men may conceivably have owned for a time some early Shakespearean plays that later went to the Lord Chamberlain's Men, such as *Titus Andronicus.* The Queen's Men, although associated with no known Shakespeare play, other than the old *King Lear* (acted jointly with Sussex's Men in 1593), were a leading company during the years in question. All we can say for sure is that the difficulties of 1592–1593 with the plague and the death of the Earl of Derby in 1594 led to a major reshuffling of the London acting companies. From this reshuffling emerged in 1594 the Lord Chamberlain's company, with Shakespeare and Richard Burbage (whose earlier history is also difficult to trace) as two of its earliest and most prominent members.

*The earliest written reference to William Shakespeare is this record of his christening in the register of Holy Trinity Church at Stratford, April 26, 1564. The entry reads, "Gulielmus filius Johannes Shakspere."*

1. Greenhill Street, or Moor Town's End.
2. Henley Lane.
3. Rother Market.
4. Henley Street.
5. Meer Pool Lane.
6. Wood Street.
7. Ely Street, or Swine Street.
8. Scholar's Lane, or Tinker's Lane.
9. Bull Lane.
10. Old Town, where John Hall lived.
11. Church Street.
12. Chapel Street.
13. High Street.
14. Market Cross.
15. *Town Hall*—a post-Shakespearean building.
16. New Place, Shakespeare's House.

17. Guild Chapel, Grammar School and Guild Hall.
18. Shakespeare's birth-place.
19. Back Bridge Street.
20. Bridge, or Fore Bridge Street.
21. Sheep Street.
22. Chapel Lane.
23. Buildings known as Waterside.
24. Southam's Lane.
25. *Dissenters' Meeting House* (post-Shakespearean.)
26. *White Lion* (post-Shakespearean).

[The Mill and Mill Bridge are indicated on the river at the left-hand corner of the map. Bridge Town lies in the right-hand corner. The Great Western Railway's modern station at Stratford is built on ground to the right of the road "to Alcester."]

*The town of Stratford-upon-Avon as Shakespeare knew it. The house in which he is considered to have been born is on Henley Street (number 2); the larger house he purchased in 1597, New Place, is on Chapel Street (number 16).*

# SHAKESPEARE'S LIFE AND WORK

## THE EARLY YEARS, 1564–C. 1594

### Stratford-upon-Avon

About Shakespeare's place of birth, Stratford-upon-Avon, there is no doubt. He spent his childhood there and returned periodically throughout his life. During most or all of his long professional career in London, his wife and children lived in Stratford. He acquired property and took some interest in local affairs. He retired to Stratford and chose to be buried there. Its Warwickshire surroundings lived in his poetic imagination.

The Stratford of Shakespeare's day was a "handsome small market town" (as described by William Camden) of perhaps 1,500 inhabitants, with fairly broad streets and half-timbered houses roofed with thatch. It could boast of a long history and an attractive setting on the river Avon. A bridge of fourteen arches, built in 1496 by Sir Hugh Clopton, Lord Mayor of London, spanned the river. Beside the Avon stood Trinity Church, built on the site of a Saxon monastery. The chapel of the Guild of the

Holy Trinity, dating from the thirteenth century, and an old King Edward VI grammar school were buildings of note. Stratford had maintained a grammar school at least since 1424 and probably long before that. It was a town without the domination of clergy, aristocracy, or great wealth. It lay in a rich agricultural region, in the county of Warwickshire. To the north of Stratford lay the Forest of Arden.

### Shakespeare's Family

The family that bore the name of Shakespeare was well distributed throughout England, but was especially numerous in Warwickshire. A name "Saquespee," in various spellings, is found in Normandy at an early date. It means, according to J. Q. Adams, "to draw out the sword quickly." That name, in the form "Sakspee," with many variants, is found in England; also the name "Saksper," varying gradually to the form "Shakespeare." It may have been wrought into that form by the obvious military meaning of "one who shakes the spear."

Our first substantial records of the family begin with Richard Shakespeare, who was, in all probability, Shakespeare's grandfather, a farmer living in the village of

*This house on Henley Street in Stratford is considered to have been the birthplace of Shakespeare. Its considerable size shows what must have been an important house of business. Shakespeare's father dealt chiefly in leather goods, though he also traded in wool, grain, and other farm produce.*

Snitterfield four miles from Stratford. He was a tenant on the property of Robert Arden of Wilmcote, a wealthy man with the social status of gentleman. Richard Shakespeare died about 1561, possessed of an estate valued at the very respectable sum of thirty-eight pounds and seventeen shillings.

His son John made a great step forward in the world by his marriage with Mary Arden, daughter of his father's landlord. John Shakespeare had some property of his own and through his wife acquired a good deal more. He moved from Snitterfield to Stratford at some date before 1552. He rose to great local importance in Stratford and bought several houses, among which was the one on Henley Street traditionally identified as Shakespeare's birthplace. William Shakespeare was born in 1564 and was baptized on April 26. The exact date of his birth is not known, but traditionally we celebrate it on April 23, the feast day of St. George, England's patron saint. (The date is at least plausible in view of the practice of baptizing infants shortly after birth.) The house in which Shakespeare was probably born, though almost entirely rebuilt and changed in various and unknown ways during the years that have intervened since Shakespeare's birth, still stands. It is of considerable size, having four rooms on the ground floor, and must, therefore, have been an important business house in the Stratford of those days. John Shakespeare's occupation seems to

have been that of a tanner and glover; that is, he cured skins, made gloves and some other leather goods, and sold them in his shop. He was also a dealer in wool, grain, malt, and other farm produce.

The long story, beginning in 1552, of John Shakespeare's success and misfortunes in Stratford is attested to by many borough records. He held various city offices. He was ale taster (inspector of bread and malt), burgess (petty constable), affeeror (assessor of fines), city chamberlain (treasurer), alderman, and high bailiff of the town—the highest municipal office in Stratford. At some time around 1576, he applied to the Herald's office for the right to bear arms and style himself a gentleman. This petition was later to be renewed and successfully carried through to completion by his famous son. In 1577 or 1578, however, when William was as yet only thirteen or fourteen years old, John Shakespeare's fortunes began a sudden and mysterious decline. He absented himself from council meetings. He had to mortgage his wife's property and showed other signs of being in financial difficulty. He became involved in serious litigation and was assessed heavy fines. Although he kept his position on the corporation council until 1586 or 1587, he was finally replaced as alderman because of his failure to attend. Conceivably, John Shakespeare's sudden difficulties were the result of persecution for his Catholic faith, since John's wife's family had remained loyal to Catholicism, and the old faith

*The interior of the Stratford grammar school: a late and not very reliable tradition claims that Shakespeare's desk was third from the front on the left-hand side.*

was being attacked with new vigor in the Warwickshire region in 1577 and afterward. This hypothesis is unsubstantial, however, especially in view of the fact that some Catholics and Puritans seem to have held posts of trust and to have remained prosperous in Stratford during this period. In the last analysis, we have little evidence as to John Shakespeare's religious faith or as to the reasons for his sudden reversal of fortune.

The family of Shakespeare's mother could trace its ancestry back to the time of William the Conqueror, and Shakespeare's father, in spite of his troubles, was a citizen of importance. John Shakespeare made his mark, instead of writing his name, but so did other men of the time who we know could read and write. His offices, particularly that of chamberlain, and the various public functions he discharged indicate that he must have had some education.

### Shakespeare in School

Nicholas Rowe, who published in 1709 the first extensive biographical account of Shakespeare, reports the tradition that Shakespeare studied "for some time at a Free-School." Although the list of students who actually attended the King's New School at Stratford-upon-Avon in the late sixteenth century has not survived, we cannot doubt that Rowe is reporting accurately. Shakespeare's father, as a leading citizen of Stratford, would scarcely have spurned the benefits of one of Stratford's most prized institutions. The town had had a free school since the thirteenth century, at first under the auspices of the Church. During the reign of King Edward VI (1547–1553), the Church lands were expropriated by the Crown, and the town of Stratford was granted a corporate charter. At this time, the school was reorganized as the King's New School, named in honor of the reigning monarch. It prospered. Its teachers, or "masters," regularly held degrees from Oxford during Shakespeare's childhood and received salaries that were superior to those of most comparable schools.

Much has been learned about the curriculum of such a school. A child would first learn the rudiments of reading and writing English by spending two or three years in a "petty" or elementary school. The child learned to

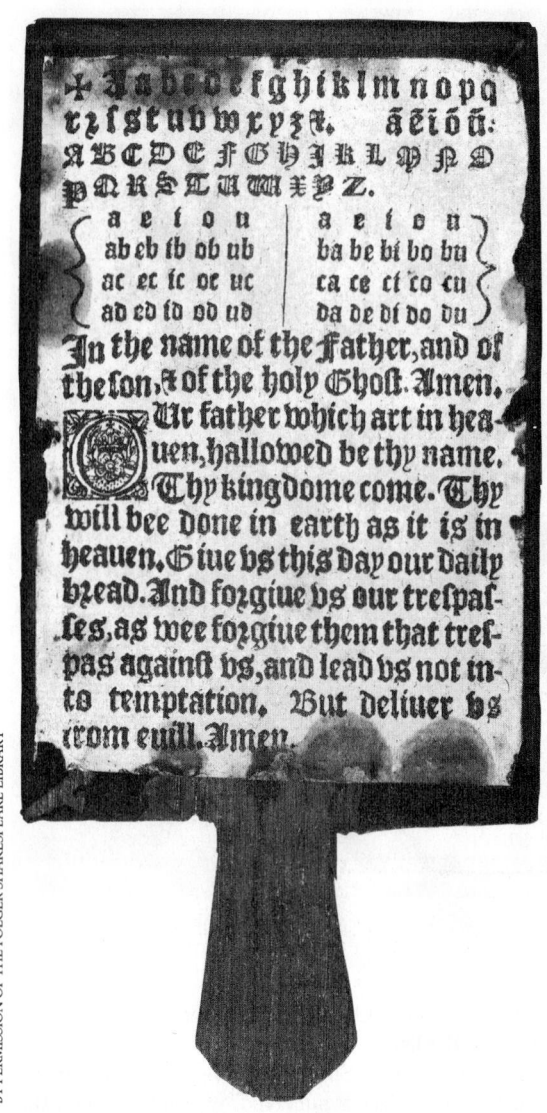

*The hornbook pictured here—showing the alphabet and the Lord's Prayer—was part of a child's education in Shakespeare's time.*

Latin formed the basis of the grammar school curriculum. The scholars studied grammar, read ancient writers, recited, and learned to write in Latin. A standard text was the *Grammatica Latina* by William Lilly or Lyly, grandfather of the later Elizabethan dramatist John Lyly. The scholars also became familiar with the *Disticha de Moribus* (moral proverbs) attributed to Cato, *Aesop's Fables,* the *Eclogues* of Baptista Spagnuoli Mantuanus or Mantuan (alluded to in *Love's Labor's Lost*), the *Eclogues* and *Aeneid* of Virgil, the comedies of Plautus or Terence (sometimes performed in Latin by the children), Ovid's *Metamorphoses* and other of his works, and possibly some Horace and Seneca.

Shakespeare plentifully reveals in his dramatic writings an awareness of many of these authors, especially Plautus (in *The Comedy of Errors*), Ovid (in *A Midsummer Night's Dream* and elsewhere), and Seneca (in *Titus Andronicus*). Although he often consulted translations of these authors, he seems to have known the originals as well. He had, in Ben Jonson's learned estimation, "small Latin and less Greek"; the tone is condescending, but the statement does concede that Shakespeare had some of both. He would have acquired some Greek in the last years of his grammar schooling. By twentieth-century standards, Shakespeare had a fairly comprehensive amount of training in the ancient classics, certainly enough to account for the general, if unscholarly, references we find in the plays.

### Shakespeare's Marriage

When Shakespeare was eighteen years old, he married Anne Hathaway, a woman eight years his senior. (The inscription on her grave states that she was sixty-seven when she died in August 1623.) The bishop's register of Worcester, the central city of the diocese, shows for November 27, 1582, the issue of a bishop's license for the marriage of William Shakespeare and Anne "Whately"; the bond of sureties issued next day refers to her as "Hathaway." She has been identified with all reasonable probability as Agnes (or Anne) Hathaway, daughter of the then recently deceased Richard Hathaway of the hamlet of Shottery, a short distance from Stratford.

The obtaining of a license was not normally required for a marriage. William Shakespeare and Anne Hathaway seem to have applied for a license on this occasion because they wished to be married after only one reading of the banns rather than the usual three. (The reading of the banns, or announcement in church of a forthcoming marriage, usually on three successive Sundays, enabled any party to object to the marriage if he or she knew of any legal impediment.) Since the reading of all banns was suspended for long periods during Advent (before Christmas) and Lent (before Easter), a couple intending to marry shortly before Christmas might have had to wait until April before the banns could be read thrice. Accordingly, the bishop not uncommonly granted a license permitting

read from a "hornbook," a single sheet of paper mounted on a board and protected by a thin transparent layer of horn, on which was usually printed the alphabet in small and capital letters and the Lord's Prayer. The child would also practice an ABC book with catechism. When the child had demonstrated the ability to read satisfactorily, the child was admitted, at about the age of seven, to the grammar school proper. Here the day was a rigorous one, usually extending from 6 A.M. in the summer or 7 A.M. in the winter until 5 P.M. Intervals for food or brief recreation came at midmorning, noon, and midafternoon. Holidays occurred at Christmas, Easter, and Whitsuntide (usually late May and June), comprising perhaps forty days in all through the year. Discipline was strict, and physical punishment was common.

*A schoolroom in Tudor England.*

couples to marry during the winter season with only one reading of the banns. To obtain such a license, two friends of the bride's family had to sign a bond obligating themselves to pay the bishop up to forty pounds, should any impediment to the marriage result in a legal action against the bishop for having issued the license.

The actual record of the marriage in a parish register has not survived, but presumably the couple were married shortly after obtaining the license. They may have been married in Temple Grafton, where Anne had relatives. The couple took up residence in Stratford. Anne was already pregnant at the time of the marriage, for she

*The substantial farmhouse owned by the Hathaways of Shottery, originally known as "Hewland" but now almost universally famous as Anne Hathaway's Cottage.*

gave birth to a daughter, Susanna, baptized on May 26, 1583. The birth of a child six months after the wedding may explain the need for haste the previous November. These circumstances, and Anne's considerable seniority in age to William, have given rise to much speculation about matters that can never be satisfactorily resolved. We do know that a formal betrothal in the presence of witnesses could legally validate a binding relationship, enabling a couple to consummate their love without social stigma. We know also that Shakespeare dramatized the issue of premarital contract and pregnancy in *Measure for Measure*. Whether Shakespeare entered into such a formal relationship with Anne is, however, undiscoverable.

On February 2, 1585, Shakespeare's only other children, the twins Hamnet and Judith, were baptized in Stratford Church. The twins seem to have been named after Shakespeare's friends and neighbors, Hamnet Sadler, a baker, and his wife, Judith.

## The Seven "Dark" Years

From 1585, the year in which his twins were baptized, until 1592, when he was first referred to as an actor and dramatist of growing importance in London, Shakespeare's activities are wholly unknown. Presumably, at some time during this period he made his way to London and entered its theatrical world, but otherwise we can only record traditions and guesses as to what he did between the ages of 21 and 28.

One of the oldest and most intriguing suggestions comes from John Aubrey, who, in collecting information in the late seventeenth century about actors and dramatists for his "Minutes of Lives," sought the help of one William Beeston. John Dryden believed Beeston to be "the chronicle of the stage," and Aubrey seems also to have had a high opinion of Beeston's theatrical knowledge. In his manuscript, Aubrey made a note to himself: "W. Shakespeare—quaere [i.e., inquire of] Mr. Beeston, who knows most of him." Aubrey then cites Beeston as his authority for this tradition about Shakespeare:

Though, as Ben Jonson says of him, that he had but little Latin and less Greek, he understood Latin pretty well, for he had been in his younger years a schoolmaster in the country.

Beeston had been a theatrical manager all his life. He was the son of the actor Christopher Beeston, who had been a member of Shakespeare's company, probably from 1596 until 1602, and who therefore had occasion to know Shakespeare well.

Shakespeare's own grammar school education would not have qualified him to be the master of a school, but he could have served as "usher" or assistant to the master. The idea that Shakespeare may have taught in this way is not unattractive. Although, as we have seen, he had some acquaintance with Plautus, Ovid, and other classical writers through his own grammar school reading, a stint as schoolmaster would have made these authors more familiar and readily accessible to him when he began writing his plays and nondramatic poems. His earliest works—*The Comedy of Errors, Love's Labor's Lost, Titus Andronicus, Venus and Adonis, The Rape of Lucrece*—show most steadily and directly the effect of his classical reading. Schoolteaching experience might have encouraged his ambitions to be a writer, like Marlowe or Greene, who went to London not to be actors but to try their hands at poetry and playwriting. All in all, however, it seems more probable that Shakespeare became a young actor rather than a schoolteacher.

Another tradition about the years from 1585 to 1592 asserts that Shakespeare served part of an apprenticeship in Stratford. This suggestion comes to us from one John Dowdall, who, traveling through Warwickshire in 1693, heard the story from an old parish clerk who was showing him around the town of Stratford. According to this parish clerk, Shakespeare had been bound as apprentice to a butcher but ran away from his master to London, where he was received into a playhouse as "servitor." John Aubrey records a similar tradition: "When he [Shakespeare] was a boy he exercised his father's trade." Aubrey believed this trade to have been that of a butcher. Moreover, says Aubrey, "When he killed a calf, he would do it in a high style, and make a speech." No other evidence confirms, however, that Shakespeare was a runaway apprentice. The allusion to "killing a calf" may, instead, refer to an ancient rural amusement in which the slaughter of a calf was staged behind a curtain for the entertainment of visitors at county fairs. Conceivably, Shakespeare's participation in such a game during his youth may have given rise to the tradition that he had been a butcher's apprentice.

Another legend, that of Shakespeare's deer stealing, has enjoyed wide currency. We are indebted for this story to the Reverend Richard Davies, who, some time between 1688 and 1709, jotted down some gossipy interpolations in the manuscripts of the Reverend William Fulman. (Fulman himself was an antiquarian who had collected a number of notes about Shakespeare and Stratford.) According to Davies, Shakespeare was "much given to all unluckiness in stealing venison and rabbits, particularly from Sir———Lucy, who had him oft whipped and sometimes imprisoned and at last made him fly his native country, to his great advancement." This tradition has led to speculation by Nicholas Rowe that Justice Shallow of *2 Henry IV* and *The Merry Wives of Windsor* is a satirical portrait of Sir Thomas Lucy of Charlecote Hall and that Shakespeare even composed an irreverent ballad about Lucy that added to the urgency of Shakespeare's departure for London. In fact, however, there is no compelling reason to believe that Shallow is based on Lucy, on Justice William Gardiner of Surrey (as Leslie Hotson insists), or on any live Elizabethan. We don't know that Shakespeare ever drew contemporary portraits in his plays, as is sometimes alleged; is Polonius in *Hamlet* Lord Burghley, for example, or is he Shakespeare's original portrait of a minister of state who is also a busybody? Nor do we know if the deer-slaying incident took place at all. It makes interesting fiction but unreliable biography.

## Shakespeare's Arrival in London

Because of the total absence of reliable information concerning the seven years from 1585 to 1592, we do not know how Shakespeare got his start in the theatrical world. He may have joined one of the touring companies that came to Stratford and then accompanied the players to London. Edmund Malone offered the unsupported statement (in 1780) that Shakespeare's "first office in the theater was that of prompter's attendant." Presumably, a young man from the country would have had to begin at the bottom. Shakespeare's later work certainly reveals an intimate and practical acquaintance with technical matters of stagecraft. In any case, his rise to eminence as an actor and a writer seems to have been rapid. He was fortunate also in having at least one prosperous acquaintance in London, Richard Field, formerly of Stratford and the son of an associate of Shakespeare's father. Field was a printer, and in 1593 and 1594 he published two handsome editions of Shakespeare's first serious poems, *Venus and Adonis* and *The Rape of Lucrece*.

## "The Only Shake-scene in a Country"

The first allusion to Shakespeare after his Stratford days is a vitriolic attack on him. It occurs in *Greene's Groatsworth of Wit Bought with a Million of Repentance,* written by Robert Greene during the last months of his wretched existence (he died in poverty in September 1592). A famous passage in this work lashes out at the actors of the public theaters for having deserted Greene and for bestowing their favor instead on a certain upstart dramatist. The passage warns three fellow dramatists and University Wits, Christopher Marlowe, Thomas Nashe, and George Peele, to abandon the writing of plays before they fall prey to a similar ingratitude. The diatribe runs as follows:

… Base minded men all three of you, if by my misery you be not warned. For unto none of you (like me) sought those burs to cleave—those puppets, I mean, that spake from our mouths, those antics garnished in our colors. Is it not strange that I, to whom they all have been beholding, is it not like that you, to whom they all have been beholding, shall (were ye in that case as I am now) be both at once of them forsaken? Yes, trust them not. For there is an upstart crow, beautified with our feathers, that with his "Tiger's heart wrapped in a player's hide" supposes he is as well able to bombast out a blank verse as the best of you, and, being an absolute *Johannes Factotum,* is in his own conceit the only Shake-scene in a country.

The "burs" here referred to are those who have forsaken Greene in his poverty for the rival playwright "Shake-scene"—an obvious hit at Shakespeare. The sneer at a *"Johannes Factotum"* suggests another dig at Shakespeare for being a jack-of-all-trades—actor, playwright, poet, and theatrical handyman in the directing and producing of plays. The most unmistakable reference to Shakespeare, however, is to be found in the burlesque line, "Tiger's heart wrapped in a player's hide," modeled after "Oh, tiger's heart wrapped in a woman's hide!" from *3 Henry VI* (1.4.137). Shakespeare's success as a dramatist had led to an envious outburst from an older, disappointed rival. (Did Shakespeare possibly have this attack in mind some years later when he has Polonius object, in *Hamlet,* 2.2.111–12, "'beautified' is a vile phrase"?)

Soon after Greene's death, Henry Chettle, who had seen the manuscript through the press (and who today some believe to have written the attack himself), issued an apology in his *Kind-Heart's Dream* that may refer to Shakespeare. The apology begins with a disclaimer of all personal responsibility for the incident and with Chettle's insistence that he has neither known nor wishes to know Marlowe (whom Greene's pamphlet had accused of atheism). Toward another unidentified playwright, on the other hand, Chettle expresses genuine concern and regret that Chettle had not done more to soften the acerbity of Greene's vitriol:

The other, whom at that time I did not so much spare as since I wish I had, for that, as I have moderated the heat of living writers and might have used my own discretion (especially in such a case, the author being dead), that I did not I am as sorry as if the original fault had been my fault; because myself have seen his demeanor no less civil than he excellent in the quality he professes. Besides, divers of worship have reported his uprightness of dealing, which argues his honesty and his facetious grace in writing that approves his art.

If the unnamed person here is to be understood as Shakespeare, it represents him in a most attractive light. Chettle freely admits to having been impressed by this person's civility. He praises the dramatist as "excellent in the quality he professes," that is, excellent as an actor. Chettle notes with approval that the man he is describing enjoys the favor of certain persons of importance, some of whom have borne witness to his uprightness in dealing. *Greene's Groatsworth of Wit*, then, with its rancorous attack on Shakespeare, has paradoxically led to the plausible inference (though not certain in its identification) that in 1592 Shakespeare was regarded as a man of pleasant demeanor, honest reputation, and acknowledged skill as an actor and writer.

## Dramatic Apprenticeship

By the end of the year 1594, when after the long plague the theatrical companies were again permitted to act before London audiences, we find Shakespeare as a member of the Lord Chamberlain's company. Probably he had already written *The Comedy of Errors, Love's Labor's Lost, The Two Gentlemen of Verona, the Henry VI* plays, and *Titus Andronicus.* (*A Love's Labor's Won,* mentioned by Francis Meres in 1598, is possibly either a lost play or an alternate title for one of the extant comedies.) He may also have completed *The Taming of the Shrew, A Midsummer Night's Dream, Richard III, King John,* and *Romeo and Juliet.* Although some scholars still question his authorship in part or all of *Titus* and the *Henry VI* plays, no one questions that they are from the period around 1590.

Shakespeare's early development is hard to follow because of difficulties in exact dating of the early plays and because some of the texts (such as *Love's Labor's Lost*) may have been later revised. As a learner making rapid progress in the skill of his art, Shakespeare was also subjected to outside influences that can only partly be determined. Among these influences, we may be sure, were the plays of his contemporary dramatists. If we could define these influences and form an idea of the kinds of plays acceptable on the stage during Shakespeare's early period, we could better understand the milieu in which he began his work.

Fortunately, we know a fair amount concerning the dramatic repertory in London during Shakespeare's early years. Henslowe's *Diary,* for example, records the daily performances of plays by the Lord Strange's Men, in conjunction with the Admiral's Men, from February 19, 1592, to June 22, 1592. Many of their plays unfortunately are lost, but enough of them are preserved to indicate the sorts of drama then in vogue. The Strange-Admiral's repertory included Christopher Marlowe's *The Jew of Malta,* Robert Greene's *Orlando Furioso* and *Friar Bacon and Friar Bungay,* Robert Greene and Thomas Lodge's *A Looking Glass for London and England,* Thomas Kyd's *The Spanish Tragedy,* the anonymous *A Knack to Know a Knave,* and possibly George Peele's *The Battle of Alcazar* and Shakespeare's *1 Henry VI.* We find, in other words, a tragedy with a villain as hero, a romantic comedy masquerading as a heroic play, a love comedy featuring a lot of magic, a biblical moral, England's first great revenge tragedy, a popular satiric comedy aimed at dissolute courtiers and usurers, a history play about Portugal's African empire, and an English history play. The titles of other works now lost suggest a similar amalgam of widely differing genres.

Comparatively few plays may have been written during the period when plays were forbidden because of the long plague of 1592–1594. When the Lord Chamberlain's Men and the Lord Admiral's Men acted under Henslowe's management at the suburban theater of Newington Butts from June 3–13, 1594, their repertories seem to have consisted largely of old plays. In this brief period, they are thought to have acted *Titus Andronicus,*

*Hamlet* (the pre-Shakespearean version), *The Taming of a Shrew* (quite possibly Shakespeare's version), *The Jew of Malta,* a lost play called *Hester and Ahasuerus,* and others.

The Lord Admiral's Men probably moved soon afterwards in 1594 to the Rose on the Bankside, across the River Thames from the city of London, where they continued to play under Henslowe's management until 1603. During the years 1594–1597, Henslowe kept in his *Diary* a careful record of their plays and of the sums of money taken in. This circumstance enables us to know a great deal more about the repertory of Shakespeare's rival company than we can ever know about his own. When the Lord Admiral's Men began again in 1594, they had five of Marlowe's plays. They seem also to have had Peele's *Edward I,* Kyd's *The Spanish Tragedy,* and a Henry V play. They may also have had plays by both Greene and Peele (Henslowe's chaotic spelling makes it hard to determine), although some of the principal dramas of these two authors had probably ceased to be acted.

We do not know as much about the repertory of the Lord Chamberlain's company as we do about that of the Lord Admiral's Men. We know enough, however, to be sure that in 1594 both companies were acting the same sorts of plays that had been on the boards in 1592. We have, therefore, grounds for assuming that, in spite of the loss of many plays (some of which may have been important), the chief contemporary influences upon Shakespeare during his early period were those of Marlowe, Greene, Peele, and Kyd. As an actor possibly in Lord Strange's company or the Earl of Pembroke's company, he would have been familiar with their plays.

Shakespeare learned also from Lyly, though perhaps more from reading Lyly's plays than from actually seeing or performing in them. The boy actors for whom Lyly wrote were forced by the authorities to suspend acting in about 1591 because of their tendency toward controversial satire, and a number of Lyly's plays were printed at that time. As a theatrical figure, therefore, Lyly belonged really to the previous decade.

## The Early Plays

Although Shakespeare's genius manifests itself in his early work, his indebtedness to contemporary dramatists and to classical writers is also more plainly evident than in his later writings. His first tragedy, *Titus Andronicus* (c. 1589–1592), is more laden with quotations and classical references than any other tragedy he wrote. Its genre owes much to the revenge play that had been made so popular by Thomas Kyd. Like Kyd, Shakespeare turns to Seneca but also reveals on stage a considerable amount of sensational violence in a manner that is distinctly not classical. For his first villain, Aaron the Moor, Shakespeare borrows some motifs from the morality play and its gleefully sinister tempter, the Vice. Shakespeare may also

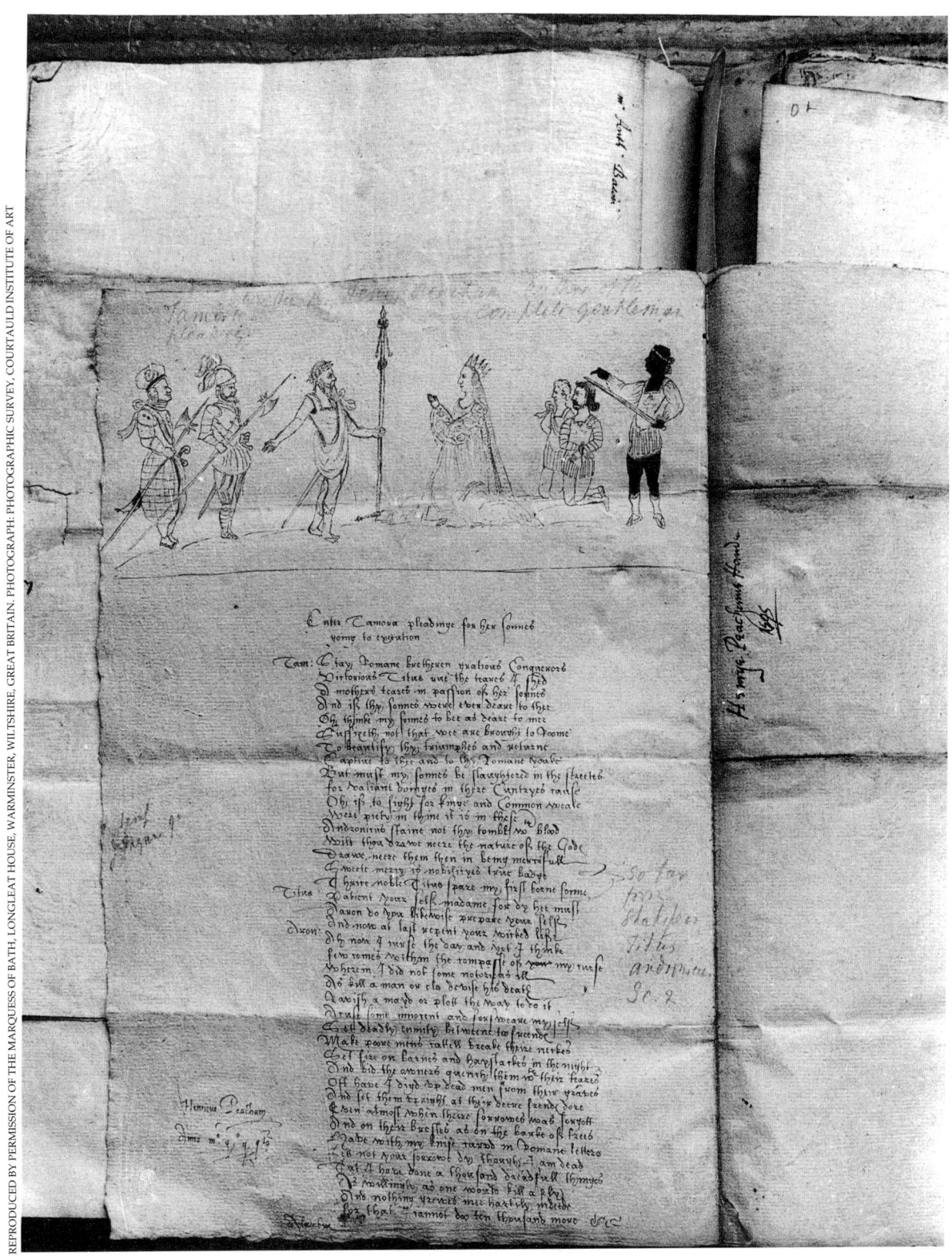

*A contemporary illustration of* Titus Andronicus, *the earliest of Shakespeare's tragedies. Shakespeare's early plays demonstrated that he was more than a slavish imitator of predecessors such as Kyd and Marlowe.*

THE  GREAT  POND  AT  ELVETHAM
arranged for the Second Day's Entertainment.

A. Her Majestie's presence seate and traine.   B. Nereus and his followers.   C. The pinnace of Neæra and her musicke.   D. The Ship-ile.
E. A boate with musicke, attending on the pinnace of Neæra.   F. The Fort-mount.   G. The Snaile-mount.   H. The Roome of Estate.
I. Her Majestie's Court.   K. Her Majestie's Wardrop.   L. The place whence Silvanus and his companie issued.

*An entertainment presented by the Earl of Hertford to Queen Elizabeth during her visit to Elvetham in 1591 is seemingly referred to by Shakespeare in* A Midsummer Night's Dream, *2.1.157–64. The scene shows an elaborate water pageant in honor of the Queen, who appears enthroned at the left of the picture.*

have had in mind the boastful antics of Marlowe's Vice-like Barabas, in *The Jew of Malta.* Certainly, Shakespeare reveals an extensive debt in his early works to Ovid and to the vogue of Ovidian narrative poetry in the early 1590s, as, for example, in his repeated allusions to the story of Philomela and Tereus (in *Titus Andronicus*) and in his Ovidian poems, *Venus and Adonis* and *The Rape of Lucrece* (1593, 1594).

Shakespeare was still questing for a suitable mode in tragedy and was discovering that the English drama of the 1590s offered no single, clear model. His only other early tragedy, *Romeo and Juliet* (c. 1594–1596), proved to be as different a tragedy from *Titus Andronicus* as could be imagined. Revenge is still prominent in *Romeo and Juliet* but is ultimately far less compelling a theme than the brevity of love and the sacrifice the lovers make of themselves to one another. Shakespeare's source is not the

revenge drama of Seneca or Kyd, but a romantic love narrative derived from the fiction of Renaissance Italy. Elements of comedy so predominate in the play's first half that one senses a closer affinity to *A Midsummer Night's Dream* than to *The Spanish Tragedy.*

Shakespeare discovered his true bent more quickly in comedy than in tragedy. Again, however, he experimented with a wide range of models and genres. *The Comedy of Errors* (c. 1589–1594) brings together elements of two plots from the Latin drama of Plautus. The character types and situations are partly derivative, but Shakespeare still reveals an impressive skill in plot construction. *Love's Labor's Lost* (c. 1588–1597) is Shakespeare's most Lylyan early comedy, with its witty debates and its amicable, if brittle, war between the sexes. The play also features an array of humorous characters, including a clownish bumpkin, a country slut, a fantastic courtier, a pedant, a country curate, and the like, whose mannerisms and wordplay add to the rich feast of language in a play that centers its attention on proper and improper styles. *The Two Gentlemen of Verona* (c. 1590–1594) and *The Taming of the Shrew* (c. 1590–1593) are derived from Italianate romantic fiction and comedy. In both, Shakespeare skillfully combines simultaneous plots that offer contrasting views on love and friendship. (*The Taming of the Shrew* makes effective use of a "frame" plot involving a group of characters who serve as audience for the rest of the play.) *A Midsummer Night's Dream* (c. 1595), with its four brilliantly interwoven actions involving court figures, lovers, fairies, and Athenian tradesmen, shows us Shakespeare already at the height of his powers in play construction, even though the comic emphasis on love's irrationality in this play is still in keeping with Shakespeare's early style. The early comedies do not ignore conflict and danger, as we see in the threatened execution of Egeon in *The Comedy of Errors* and the failure of courtships in *Love's Labor's Lost,* but these plays do not as yet fully explore the social dilemmas of *The Merchant of Venice,* the narrowly averted catastrophe of *Much Ado About Nothing,* or the melancholy vein of *As You Like It* and *Twelfth Night.* On stage, early comedies such as *The Comedy of Errors* and *The Taming of the Shrew* are as hilariously funny as anything Shakespeare ever wrote.

Shakespeare's early history plays show a marked affinity with those of Marlowe, Peele, and Greene. Yet today Shakespeare is given more credit for pioneering in the genre of the English history play than he once was. If all the *Henry VI* plays (c. 1589–1592) are basically his, as scholars now often allow, he had more imitators in this genre than predecessors. He scored a huge early success with the heroic character of Lord Talbot in *1 Henry VI,* and by the time Richard Duke of Gloucester had emerged from the *Henry VI* plays to become King Richard III, Shakespeare's fame as a dramatist was assured. He had, of course, learned much from Marlowe's "mighty line" in *Tamburlaine* (1587–1588) and perhaps from Peele's *The Battle of Alcazar* (1588–1589). The anonymous *Famous Victories of Henry V* (1583–1588) must have preceded and influenced his work. Even so, Shakespeare had done much more than simply "beautify" himself with the "feathers" of earlier dramatists, as Greene (or Chettle) enviously charged. Even in his earliest work, Shakespeare already displayed an extraordinary ability to transcend the models from which he learned.

### SHAKESPEARE IN THE THEATER, C. 1594–1601

By the year 1594, Shakespeare had already achieved a considerable reputation as a poet and dramatist. We should not be surprised that many of his contemporaries thought of his nondramatic writing as his most significant literary achievement. Throughout his lifetime, in fact, his contemporary fame rested, to a remarkable degree, on his non-dramatic poems, *Venus and Adonis, The Rape of Lucrece,* and the *Sonnets* (which were circulated in manuscript prior to their unauthorized publication in 1609). One of the earliest tributes suggesting the importance of the poems is found in an anonymous commendatory verse prefixed to Henry Willobie's *Willobie His Avisa* (1594). It summarizes the plot and theme of *The Rape of Lucrece:*

> Though *Collatine* have dearly bought,
> To high renown, a lasting life,
> And found—that most in vain have sought—
> To have a fair and constant wife,
>      Yet Tarquin plucked his glistering grape,
>      And Shakespeare paints poor Lucrece' rape.

Richard Barnfield, in his *Poems in Divers Humors* (1598), praised the "honey-flowing vein" of Shakespeare's *Venus and Adonis* and *The Rape of Lucrece.*

Yet Shakespeare's plays were also highly regarded by his contemporaries, even if those plays were generally accorded a literary status below that given to the narrative and lyrical poems. Francis Meres insisted, in 1598, that Shakespeare deserved to be compared not only with Ovid for his verse, but also with Plautus and Seneca for his comedies and tragedies:

> As the soul of Euphorbus was thought to live in Pythagoras, so the sweet, witty soul of Ovid lives in mellifluous and honey-tongued Shakespeare: witness his *Venus and Adonis,* his *Lucrece,* his sugared sonnets among his private friends, etc.
>
> As Plautus and Seneca are accounted the best for comedy and tragedy among the Latins, so Shakespeare among the English is the most excellent in both kinds for the stage: for comedy, witness his *Gentlemen of Verona,* his *Errors,* his *Love's Labor's Lost,* his *Love's Labor's Won,* his *Midsummer Night's Dream,* and his *Merchant of Venice;* for tragedy, his *Richard the II, Richard the III, Henry the IV, King John, Titus Andronicus,* and his *Romeo and Juliet.*

Comedy and tragedy were, after all, literary forms sanctioned by classical precept. By calling some of Shakespeare's English history plays "tragedies," Meres endowed them with the respectability of an ancient literary tradition, recognizing, too, that many of Shakespeare's historical plays culminate in the death of an English king.

John Weever, too, in his epigram *Ad Gulielmum Shakespeare* in *Epigrams in the Oldest Cut and Newest Fashion* (1599), mentioned not only the ever-popular narrative poems, but also *Romeo and Juliet* and a history play about one of the Richards:

> Honey-tongued Shakespeare! When I saw thine issue,
> I swore Apollo got them and none other:
> Their rosy-tainted features clothed in tissue,
> Some heaven-born goddess said to be their mother;
> Rose-cheeked Adonis, with his amber tresses,
> Fair fire-hot Venus, charming him to love her;

*Falstaff and Mistress Quickly are shown here in a composite theatrical illustration of about 1662. The engraving, used as the frontispiece to Francis Kirkman's* The Wits, or Sport upon Sport, *also shows other theatrical types. Visible are candelabras and footlights for stage lighting and a curtained area used perhaps for "discoveries." Spectators are visible in the gallery above, as they are also in the De Witt drawing of the Swan Theatre on p. xlviii and in Alabaster's* Roxana *on p. xlvii.*

Chaste Lucretia virgin-like her dresses,
Proud lust-stung Tarquin seeking still to prove her;
*Romeo, Richard*—more whose names I know not.
Their sugared tongues and power-attractive beauty
Say they are saints, although that saints they show not,
For thousands vows to them subjective duty;
They burn in love thy children. Shakespeare het them.
Go, woo thy muse more nymphish brood beget them.

Even Gabriel Harvey, an esteemed classical scholar and friend of Edmund Spenser, considered Shakespeare's play *Hamlet* to be worthy of no less praise than the best of the Ovidian poems. Harvey's comments are to be found in a marginal note to a copy of Speght's *Chaucer,* written down some time between 1598 and 1601:

The younger sort takes much delight in Shakespeare's *Venus and Adonis,* but his *Lucrece* and his tragedy of *Hamlet, Prince of Denmark* have it in them to please the wiser sort.

Shakespeare's growing fame was even such that his dramatic characters began to enter into the intellectual life of the time. The name of Falstaff became a byword almost as soon as he made his appearance on the stage. The references were not always friendly. A play written to be performed by the rival Admiral's company in answer to *1 Henry IV,* called *Sir John Oldcastle* (1599), took Falstaff to task for being a "pampered glutton" and an "aged counsellor to youthful sin." Evidently, the authors of this attack were offended by the fact that Falstaff had been named "Oldcastle" in an early version of *1 Henry IV,*

thereby dishonoring the name of one whom many Puritans regarded as a martyr to their cause (see the Introduction to *1 Henry IV*). Generally, however, the references during this period to Falstaff and his cronies were fond. In a letter to a friend in London, for example, Sir Charles Percy fretted jocosely that his prolonged stay in the country among his rustic neighbors might cause him to "be taken for Justice Silence or Justice Shallow" (1600). In another letter, from the Countess of Southampton to her husband (written seemingly in 1599), Falstaff's name had become so familiar that it was used apparently as a privately understood substitute for the name of some real person in an item of court gossip:

All the news I can send you, that I think will make you merry, is that I read in a letter from London that Sir John Falstaff is by his Mistress Dame Pintpot made father of a godly miller's thumb, a boy that's all head and very little body; but this is a secret.

Shakespeare's immense popularity as a dramatist was bound to invite some resentment. One irreverent reaction is found in the so-called *Parnassus* trilogy (1598–1603). The three plays in this series consist of *The Pilgrimage to Parnassus* and *The Return from Parnassus,* in two parts, all of which were acted by the students of St. John's College, Cambridge.

These *Parnassus* plays take a mordantly satirical view of English life around 1600, from the point of view of university graduates attempting to find gainful employment. The graduates discover, to their vocal dismay, that they must seek the patronage of fashion-mongering courtiers,

*Henry Fuseli's nineteenth-century interpretation of Falstaff shows him in the tavern in Eastcheap with Doll Tearsheet on his lap while Prince Hal and Poins, disguised as tapsters, enter from behind. Falstaff is perhaps saying, "Peace, good Doll, do not speak like a death's-head" (2 Henry IV, 2.4.233–4).*

complacent justices of the peace, professional acting companies who offer them pitifully small wages, and the like. One especially foolish patron, to whom the witty Ingenioso applies for a position, is a poetaster named Gullio. This courtly fop aspires to be a fashionable poet himself, and agrees to hire Ingenioso if the latter will help him with his verse writing. In fact, however, as Ingenioso scornfully observes in a series of asides, Gullio's verses are "nothing but pure Shakespeare and shreds of poetry that he hath gathered at the theaters." Most of all, Gullio loves to plagiarize from *Venus and Adonis* and *Romeo and Juliet*. With unparalleled presumption, he actually requests Ingenioso to compose poems "in two or three divers veins, in Chaucer's, Gower's and Spenser's and Mr. Shakespeare's," which Gullio will then pass off as his own inspiration. When Ingenioso does so extempore, producing, among other things, a fine parody of *Venus and Adonis*, Gullio is as delighted as a child. Although he admires Spenser, Chaucer, and Gower, Gullio confesses that Shakespeare is his favorite; he longs to hang Shakespeare's portrait "in my study at the court" and vows he will sleep with *Venus and Adonis* under his pillow (*The Return from Parnassus*, Part I, 1009–1217). Later on (lines 1875–1880), some university graduates trying out as actors in Shakespeare's company are requested to recite a few famous lines from the beginning of *Richard III*—lines that, in the satirical context of this play, sound both stereotyped and bombastic. Shakespeare's fame made him an easy target for university "wits" who regarded the theater of London as lowbrow. Still, the portrait throughout is more satirical of those who plagiarize and idolize Shakespeare than of the dramatist's own work. In their backhanded tribute, the *Parnassus* authors make plain that Shakespeare was a household name even at the universities.

## Shakespeare's Career and Private Life

During the years from 1594 to 1601, Shakespeare seems to have prospered as an actor and writer for the Lord Chamberlain's Men. Whether he had previously belonged to Lord Strange's company or to the Earl of Pembroke's company, or possibly to some other group, is uncertain, but we know that he took part in 1594 in the general reorganization of the companies, out of which emerged the Lord Chamberlain's company. In 1595, his name appeared, for the first time, in the accounts of the Treasurer of the Royal Chamber as a member of the Chamberlain's company of players, which had presented two comedies before Queen Elizabeth at Greenwich in the Christmas season of 1594. This company usually performed at the Theatre, northeast of London, from 1594 until 1599, when they moved to the Globe playhouse south of the Thames. They seem to have been the victors in the intense economic rivalry between themselves and the Lord Admiral's company at the Rose playhouse, under Philip Henslowe's management. Fortunately for all the adult companies, the boys' private theatrical companies were shut down during most of the 1590s. Shakespeare's company enjoyed a phenomenal success, and in a short time it became the most successful theatrical organization in England.

The nucleus of the Chamberlain's company in 1594 was the family of Burbage. James Burbage, the father, was owner of the Theatre, Cuthbert Burbage was a manager, and Richard Burbage became the principal actor of the troupe. Together the Burbages owned five "shares" in the

*First among the actors in Shakespeare's company was Richard Burbage (1567–1619). He played Hamlet, Othello, King Lear, and presumably other major roles including Macbeth, Antony, Coriolanus, and Prospero.*

company, entitling them to half the profits. Shakespeare and four other principal actors—John Heminges, Thomas Pope, Augustine Phillips, and Will Kempe—owned one share each. Not only was Shakespeare a full sharing actor, but he was also the principal playwright of the company. He was named as a chief actor in the 1616 edition of Ben Jonson's *Every Man in His Humor,* performed by the Chamberlain's company in 1598. Later tradition reports, with questionable reliability, that Shakespeare specialized in "kingly parts" or in the roles of older men, such as Adam in *As You Like It* and the Ghost in *Hamlet.* Shakespeare was more celebrated as a playwright than as an actor, and his acting responsibilities may well have diminished as his writing reputation grew. The last occasion on which he is known to have acted was in Jonson's *Sejanus* in 1603.

His prosperity appears in the first record of his residence in London. The tax returns, or Subsidy Rolls, of a parliamentary subsidy granted to Queen Elizabeth for the year 1596 show that Shakespeare was a resident in the parish of St. Helen's, Bishopsgate, near the Theatre, and was assessed at the respectable sum of five pounds. By the next year, Shakespeare had evidently moved to Southwark, near the Bear Garden, for the returns from Bishopsgate show his taxes delinquent. He was later located and the taxes paid.

In 1596, Shakespeare suffered a serious personal loss: the death of his only son Hamnet, at the age of eleven. Hamnet was buried at Stratford in August.

Shakespeare acquired property in Stratford during these years, as well as in London. In 1597 he purchased New Place, a house of importance and one of the two largest in Stratford. Shakespeare's family entered the house as residents shortly after the purchase and contin-

ued to live there until long after Shakespeare's death. The last of his family, his granddaughter, Lady Bernard, died in 1670, and New Place was sold.

Shakespeare was also interested in the purchase of land at Shottery in 1598. He was listed among the chief holders of corn and malt in Stratford that same year and sold a load of stone to the Stratford corporation in 1599.

No less suggestive of Shakespeare's rapid rise in the world is his acquisition of the right to bear arms, or, in other words, his establishment in the rank and title of gentleman. The Herald's College in London preserves two drafts of a grant of arms to Shakespeare's father, devised by one William Dethick and dated October 20, 1596. Although we may certainly believe that the application was put forward by William Shakespeare, John Shakespeare was still living, and the grant was drawn up in the father's name. The device for Shakespeare's coat of arms makes a somewhat easy use of the meaning of his name:

Gold on a bend sables, a spear of the first steeled argent. And for his crest of cognizance a falcon, his wings displayed argent, standing on a wreath of his colors, supporting a spear, gold steeled as aforesaid, set upon a helmet with mantles and tassels, as hath been accustomed and doth more plainly appear depicted on this margent.

According to one of the documents in the grant, John Shakespeare, at the height of his prosperity as a Stratford burgher, had applied twenty years before to the Herald's College for authority to bear arms. The family may not have been able to meet the expense of seeing the application through, however, until William Shakespeare had made his fortune. The grant of heraldic honors to John Shakespeare was confirmed in 1599.

*This recreation of what New Place purportedly looked like during Shakespeare's ownership suggests that it must have indeed been an imposing structure. It was warmed by ten fireplaces and had surrounding grounds that included two gardens and two barns.*

A lawsuit during this period gives us a rather baffling glimpse into Shakespeare's life in the theater. From a writ discovered by Leslie Hotson (*Shakespeare Versus Shallow,* 1931) in the records of the Court of the Queen's Bench, Michaelmas term 1596, we learn that a person named William Wayte sought "for fear of death" to have William Shakespeare, Francis Langley, and two unknown women bound over to keep the peace. Earlier in the same term, moreover, Francis Langley had sworn out a similar writ against this same William Wayte and his stepfather William Gardiner, a justice of the peace in Surrey. Langley was owner of the Swan playhouse on the bankside, near the later-built Globe. His quarrel with Gardiner and Wayte appears to have jeopardized all the acting companies that performed plays south of the Thames, for William Gardiner's jurisdiction included the Bankside theater district. Gardiner and Wayte vengefully tried to drive the theaters out of the area. Possibly Shakespeare's company acted occasionally at the Swan in 1596. Hotson speculates that Shakespeare retaliated by immortalizing Gardiner and Wayte as Shallow and Slender in *The Merry Wives of Windsor.* The date of 1596 is too early for that play, and we do not know that Shakespeare drew contemporary portraits in his drama, but we can wonder if lawsuits of this sort gave him no very high opinion of the law's delay and the insolence of office.

During this period Shakespeare's plays began to appear occasionally in print. His name was becoming such a drawing card that it appeared on the title pages of the second and third quartos of *Richard II* (1598), the second quarto of *Richard III* (1598), *Love's Labor's Lost* (1598), and the second quarto of *1 Henry IV* (1599).

In 1599, the printer William Jaggard sought to capitalize unscrupulously on Shakespeare's growing reputation by bringing out a slender volume of twenty or twenty-one poems called *The Passionate Pilgrim,* attributed to Shakespeare. In fact, only five of the poems were assuredly his, and none of them was newly composed for the occasion. Three came from *Love's Labor's Lost* (published in 1598) and two from Shakespeare's as yet unpublished sonnet sequence.

## Contemporary Drama

Shakespeare was without doubt the leading dramatist of the period from 1594 to 1601, not only in our view, but also in that of his contemporaries. The earlier group of dramatists from whom he had learned so much—Lyly, Greene, Marlowe, Peele, Kyd, Nashe—were either dead or no longer writing plays. The group of dramatists who were to rival him in the 1600s and eventually surpass him in contemporary popularity had not yet become well known.

Ben Jonson's early career is obscure. He may have written an early version of his *A Tale of a Tub* in 1596 and *The Case Is Altered* in 1597, though both were later revised. Unquestionably, his first major play was *Every Man in His Humor* (1598), in which Shakespeare acted. This comedy did much to establish the new vogue of comedy of humors, a realistic and satirical kind of drama featuring "humors" characters whose personalities are dominated by some exaggerated trait. We are invited to laugh at the country simpleton, the jealous husband, the overly careful father, the cowardly braggart soldier, the poetaster, and the like. Shakespeare responded to the vogue of humors comedy in his *Henry IV* plays and *The Merry Wives.* Jonson followed his great success with *Every Man Out of His Humor* (1599), an even more biting vision of human folly. George Chapman also deserves important credit for the establishment of humors comedy, with his *The Blind Beggar of Alexandria* (1596) and *An Humorous Day's Mirth* (1597).

Despite the emergence of humors comedy, however, with its important anticipations of Jacobean and even Restoration comedy of manners, the prevailing comedy to be seen on the London stage between 1595 and 1601 was romantic comedy. William Haughton wrote *Englishmen for My Money* in 1598. Thomas Dekker's *Old Fortunatus,* the dramatization of a German folktale, appeared in 1599. Dekker's *The Shoemaker's Holiday* (1599), despite its seemingly realistic touches of life among the apprentices of London, is a thoroughly romanticized saga of rags to riches. A young aristocrat disguises himself as a shoemaker to woo a mayor's daughter; love conquers social rank, and the King himself sentimentally blesses the union. Thomas Heywood wrote heroical romances and comedies, perhaps including *Godfrey of Boulogne* (1594), although most of his early works have disappeared. The boys' private theaters were closed during most of the 1590s, until 1598–1599, and thus the child actors could not perform the satirical comedies at which they were so adept.

Patriotic history drama also continued to flourish on the public stage during those years when Shakespeare wrote his best history plays. Heywood wrote the two parts of *Edward IV* between 1592 and 1599. The anonymous *Edward III* appeared in 1595 or earlier, enough in the vein of Shakespeare's histories that it is sometimes attributed (albeit on uncertain and impressionistic grounds) to him. *Sir Thomas More,* by Munday, Dekker, Chettle, and perhaps Heywood, was written sometime in the later 1590s and very probably revised by Shakespeare himself. Chettle and Munday wrote a trilogy of plays about *Robert, Earl of Huntingdon,* or Robin Hood (1598–1599), on themes that remind us of Shakespeare's *As You Like It.* These plays were performed by the Admiral's Men, who also produced the two parts of *Sir John Oldcastle* (1599–1600) by Drayton, Hathway, Munday, and others, in rivalry with Shakespeare's *Henry IV* plays.

## Shakespeare's Work

Shakespeare thus wrote his greatest history plays for an audience that knew the genre well. The history play had first become popular just at the start of Shakespeare's career, during the patriotic aftermath of the defeat of the Spanish Armada (1588). Shakespeare himself did much to establish the genre. He wrote first his four-play series dealing with the Lancastrian wars of the fifteenth century, and then went backwards in historical time to King John's reign and to the famous reigns of Henry IV and Henry V.

His romantic comedies were also written for audiences that knew what to expect from the genre. From the comedies of Greene, Peele, Munday, and the rest, as well as Shakespeare himself, Elizabethan audiences were thoroughly familiar with such conventions as fairy charms, improbable adventures in forests, heroines disguised as young men, shipwrecks, love overcoming differences in social rank, and the like. Yet the conventions also demanded more than mere horseplay or foolish antics. Plays of this sort customarily affirmed "wholesome" moral values and appealed to generosity and decency. They were written, like the history plays, for a socially diversified, though generally intelligent and well-to-do, audience.

Several critical terms have been used to suggest the special quality of Shakespeare's comedies during this period of the later 1590s. "Romantic comedy" implies first of all a story in which the main action is about love, but it can also imply elements of the improbable and the miraculous. (The difference between the "romantic comedies" of the later 1590s and the "romances" of Shakespeare's last years, 1606–1613, is that, in part at least, romantic comedy seeks to "make wonder familiar," whereas the romances seek to make the familiar wonderful.) "Philosophical comedy" emphasizes the moral, and sometimes Christian idealism, underlying many of these comedies of the 1590s: the quest for deep and honest understanding between men and women in *Much Ado About Nothing*, the awareness of an eternal and spiritual dimension to love in *The Merchant of Venice*, and the theme of love as a mysterious force able to regenerate a

corrupted social world from which it has been banished in *As You Like It*. "Love-game comedy" pays particular attention to the witty battle of the sexes that we find in several of these plays. "Festive comedy" urges the celebratory nature of comedy, especially in *Twelfth Night* and the *Henry IV* plays, in which Saturnalian revelry must contend against grim and disapproving forces of sobriety. "Comedy of forgiveness," although applicable to only a limited number of plays of this period (especially *Much Ado*), stresses the unexpected second chance that the world of comedy extends to even the most undeserving of heroes; Claudio is forgiven his ill treatment of Hero, although the play's villain, Don John, is not.

## SHAKESPEARE IN THE THEATER, C. 1601–1608

When the Globe, the most famous of the London public playhouses, was built in 1599, one-half interest in the property was assigned to the Burbage family, especially to the brothers Cuthbert and Richard Burbage. The other half was divided among five actor-sharers: Shakespeare, Will Kempe, Thomas Pope, Augustine Phillips, and John Heminges. Kempe left the company, however, in 1599 and subsequently became a member of the Earl of Worcester's Men. His place as leading comic actor was taken by Robert Armin, an experienced man of the theater and occasional author, whose comic specialty was the role of the wise fool. We can observe in Shakespeare's plays the effects of Kempe's departure and of Armin's arrival. Kempe had apparently specialized in clownish and rustic parts, such as those of Dogberry in *Much Ado*, Lancelot Gobbo in *The Merchant of Venice*, and Bottom in *A Midsummer Night's Dream*. (We know that he played Dogberry because his name appears in the early quarto, derived from the play manuscript; similar evidence links his name to the role of Peter in *Romeo and Juliet*.) For Armin, on the other hand,

*Among the members of Shakespeare's acting company were John Lowin, William Sly, and Nathaniel Field.*

BY PERMISSION OF THE FOLGER SHAKESPEARE LIBRARY

HUNTINGTON LIBRARY/SUPERSTOCK

*Will Kempe (above), for whom Shakespeare created several clownish roles, was a member of the Lord Chamberlain's Men and a noted Elizabethan comic. Kempe left the company in 1599 and was replaced by Robert Armin (right), an accomplished actor who specialized in fool's roles.*

Shakespeare evidently created such roles as Touchstone in *As You Like It*, Feste in *Twelfth Night*, Lavatch in *All's Well That Ends Well*, and the Fool in *King Lear*.

Other shifts in personnel can sometimes be traced in Shakespeare's plays, especially changes in the number and ability of the boy actors (whose voices would suddenly start to crack at puberty). Shakespeare makes an amusing point about the relative size of two boy actors, for example, in *A Midsummer Night's Dream* and in *As You Like It*; this option may have been available to him only at certain times. On the other hand, not all changes in the company roster can be related meaningfully to Shakespeare's dramatic development. Augustine Phillips, who died in 1605, was a full actor-sharer of long standing in the company, but his "type" of role was probably not sharply differentiated from that of several of his associates. Shakespeare's plays, after all, involve many important supporting roles, and versatility in the undertaking of such parts must have been more common than specialization. (Phillips is remembered also for his last will and testament: he left a bequest of "a thirty shillings piece in gold" to "my fellow, William Shakespeare," and similar bequests to other members of the troupe.)

With the reopening of the boys' acting companies in 1598–1599, a serious economic rivalry sprang up between them and the adult companies. The Children of the Chapel Royal occupied the theater in Blackfriars, and the Children of Paul's probably acted in their own singing school in St. Paul's churchyard. Their plays exploited a new vogue for satire. The satiric laughter was often directed at the city of London and its bourgeois inhabitants: socially ambitious tradesmen's wives, Puritan zealots, and the like. Other favorite targets included parvenu knights at court, would-be poets, and hysterical governmental officials. The price of admission at the private theaters was considerably higher than at the Globe or Rose, so the clientele tended to be more fashionable. Sophisticated authors like Ben Jonson, George Chapman, and John Marston tended to find writing for the boy actors more rewarding literarily than writing for the adult players.

One manifestation of the rivalry between public and private theaters was the so-called War of the Theaters, or Poetomachia. In part, this was a personal quarrel between Jonson on one side and Marston and Thomas Dekker on the other. Underlying this quarrel, however, was a serious hostility between a public theater and one that catered more to the elite. Dekker, with Marston's encouragement, attacked Jonson as a literary dictator and snob—one who subverted public decency. Jonson replied with a fervent defense of the artist's right to criticize everything that the artist sees wrong. The major plays in the exchange (1600–1601) were Jonson's *Cynthia's Revels*, Dekker and Marston's *Satiromastix*, and Jonson's *The Poetaster*.

Shakespeare allows Hamlet to comment on the theatrical rivalry (2.2.330–62), with seeming regret for the fact that the boys have been overly successful and that many adult troupes have been obliged to tour the provinces. Most of all, though, Hamlet's remarks deplore the needless bitterness on both sides. The tone of kindly remonstrance makes it seem unlikely that Shakespeare took an active part in the fracas. To be sure, in the Cambridge play *2 Return from Parnassus* (1601–1603), the character called

Will Kempe does assert that his fellow actor, Shakespeare, had put down the famous Ben Jonson:

Why, here's our fellow Shakespeare puts them all down, ay, and Ben Jonson, too. Oh, that Ben Jonson is a pestilent fellow! He brought up Horace giving the poets a pill, but our fellow Shakespeare hath given him a purge that made him bewray his credit (lines 1809–1813).

Perhaps Shakespeare did offer a riposte to Jonson in *Troilus and Cressida*, where the portraits of Ajax and Achilles collectively display the arrogance, shaggy appearance, and large girth that were notoriously characteristic of Jonson himself.

Upon the death of Queen Elizabeth in 1603 and the accession to the throne of King James I, Shakespeare's company added an important new success to their already great prosperity. According to a document of instruction from King James to his Keeper of the Privy Seal, dated May 19, 1603, and endorsed as "The Players' Privilege," the acting company that had formerly been the Lord Chamberlain's Men now became the King's company. The document names Shakespeare, Richard Burbage, Augustine Phillips, John Heminges, Henry Condell, Will Sly, Robert Armin, Richard Cowley, and Lawrence Fletcher—the last, an actor who had played before the King and the Scottish court in 1599 and 1601. These players are accorded the usual privileges of exercising their art anywhere within the kingdom and are henceforth to be known as the King's company. The principal members of the troupe also were appointed to the honorary rank of Grooms of the Royal Chamber. We therefore find them duly recorded in the Accounts of the Master of the Wardrobe on March 15, 1604, as recipients of the customary grants of red cloth, so that they, dressed in the royal livery, might take part in the approaching coronation procession of King James. The same men are mentioned in these grants as in the Players' Privilege. Shakespeare's name stands second in the former document and first in the latter. In a somewhat similar manner, the King's players, as Grooms of the Royal Chamber, were called in attendance on the Spanish ambassador at Somerset House in August 1604.

The Revels Accounts of performances at court during the winter season of 1604–1605 contain an unusually full entry, listing several of Shakespeare's plays. The list includes *Othello, The Merry Wives of Windsor, Measure for Measure*, "The play of Errors," *Love's Labor's Lost, Henry V*, and *The Merchant of Venice*. The last play was "again commanded by the King's majesty," and so was performed a second time. This list also sporadically notes the names of "the poets which made the plays," ascribing three of these works to "Shaxberd." (Probably the final *d* is an error for *e*, since the two characters are easily confused in Elizabethan handwriting; the word represents "Shaxbere" or "Shaxpere.") The entire entry

was once called into question as a possible forgery but is now generally regarded as authentic.

A number of records during this period show us glimpses of Shakespeare as a man of property. On May 1, 1602, John and William Combe conveyed to Shakespeare one hundred and seven acres of arable land, plus twenty acres of pasture in the parish of Old Stratford, for the sizable payment of three hundred and twenty pounds. The deed was delivered to Shakespeare's brother Gilbert and not to the poet, who was probably at that time occupied in London. On September 28 of the same year, Shakespeare acquired the title to "one cottage and one garden by estimation a quarter of an acre," located opposite his home (New Place) in Stratford.

Shakespeare made still other real-estate investments in his hometown. In 1605 he purchased an interest in the tithes of Stratford and adjacent villages from one Ralph Hubaud for the considerable sum of four hundred and forty pounds. The purchasing of tithes was a common financial transaction in Shakespeare's time, though unknown today. Tithes were originally intended for the support of the Church but had, in many cases, become privately owned and hence negotiable. The owners of tithes paid a fixed rental sum for the right to collect as many of these taxes as they could, up to the total amount due under the law. Shakespeare seems, on this occasion in 1605, to have bought from Ralph Hubaud a one-half interest, or "moiety," in certain tithes of Stratford and vicinity. Later, probably in 1609, Shakespeare was one of those who brought a bill of complaint before the Lord Chancellor, requesting that certain other titheholders be required to come into the High Court of Chancery and make answer to the complaints alleged, namely, that they had not paid their proportional part of an annual rental of twenty-seven pounds, thirteen shillings, and four pence on the whole property in the tithes to one Henry Barker. This Barker had the theoretical right to foreclose on the entire property if any one of the forty-two titheholders failed to contribute his share of the annual fee. The suit was, in effect, a friendly one, designed to ensure that all those who were supposed to contribute did so on an equitable and businesslike basis.

We learn from the Stratford Registers of baptism, marriage, and burial of the changes in Shakespeare's family during this period. His father died in 1601, his brother Edmund in 1607, and his mother in 1608. On June 5, 1607, his daughter Susanna was married to Dr. John Hall in Holy Trinity Church, Stratford. Their first child, and Shakespeare's first grandchild, Elizabeth, was christened in the same church on February 21, 1608.

## Shakespeare's Reputation, 1601–1608

Allusions to Shakespeare are frequent during this period of his life. One amusing reference is not literary but professes to tell about Shakespeare's prowess as a lover and rival of his good friend and theatrical colleague, Richard Burbage. Perhaps the joke was just a good bawdy story and should not be taken too seriously, but it is nonetheless one of the few anecdotes that date from Shakespeare's lifetime. Our informant is John Manningham, a young law student, who notes in his commonplace book in 1602 the following:

13 March 1601 [1602] … Upon a time, when Burbage played Richard III there was a citizen grew so far in liking with him that, before she went to the play, she appointed him to come that night unto her by the name of Richard the Third. Shakespeare, overhearing their conclusion, went before, was entertained and at his game ere Burbage came. Then message being brought that Richard the Third was at the door, Shakespeare caused return to be made that William the Conqueror was before Richard the Third. Shakespeare's name William.

Other allusions of the time are more literary. Shakespeare's greatness is, by this time, taken for granted. Anthony Scoloker, for example, in his epistle prefatory to *Diaphantus, or the Passions of Love* (1604), attempts to describe an excellent literary work in this way:

It should be like the never-too-well read Arcadia … or to come home to the vulgar's element, like friendly Shakespeare's tragedies, where the comedian rides, when the tragedian stands on tip-toe. Faith, it should please all, like Prince Hamlet.

The antiquarian William Camden includes Shakespeare's name among his list of England's greatest writers in his *Remains of a Greater Work Concerning Britain* (1605):

These may suffice for some poetical descriptions of our ancient poets. If I would come to our time, what a world could I present to you out of Sir Philip Sidney, Edmund Spenser, Samuel Daniel, Hugh Holland, Ben Jonson, Thomas Campion, Michael Drayton, George Chapman, John Marston, William Shakespeare, and other most pregnant wits of these our times, whom succeeding ages may justly admire.

An attempt to use one of Shakespeare's plays for political purposes had some potentially serious repercussions. Two days before the abortive rebellion of the Earl of Essex on February 7, 1601, Shakespeare's company was commissioned to perform a well-known play in its repertory about King Richard II. This play must almost surely have been Shakespeare's. Evidently, the purpose of this extraordinary performance was to awaken public sympathy for Essex by suggesting that Queen Elizabeth was another Richard II, surrounded by corrupt favorites and deaf to the pleas of her subjects. Essex's avowed intention was to remove from positions of influence those men whom he considered his political enemies. Fortunately, Shakespeare's company was later exonerated of any blame in the affair (see the Introduction to *Richard II*).

Perhaps no other allusion to Shakespeare during this period can suggest so well as the following quotation the extent to which Shakespeare's plays had become familiar to English citizens everywhere. The quotation is taken from the notes of a certain Captain Keeling, commander of the East India Company's ship *Dragon*, off Sierra Leone, in the years 1607 and 1608:

1607, Sept. 5. I sent the interpreter, according to his desire, aboard the *Hector*, where he broke fast, and after came aboard me, where we gave the tragedy of *Hamlet*.

30. Captain Hawkins dined with me, where my companions acted *King Richard the Second*.

[March 31.] I invited Captain Hawkins to a fish dinner and had *Hamlet* acted aboard me, which I permit to keep my people from idleness and unlawful games or sleep.

## Other Drama of the Period

Even without Shakespeare, the early Jacobean drama in England would rank as one of the most creative periods in the history of all theater. (The word *Jacobean* is derived from *Jacobus*, the Latin form of the name of King James I.) Shakespeare's earlier contemporaries—Lyly, Greene, Marlowe, Peele, Kyd—were dead or silent, but another generation of playwrights was at hand. George Chapman, John Marston, and Ben Jonson all began writing plays shortly before 1600. So did Thomas Dekker and Thomas Heywood, whose dramatic output, often in collaboration, would prove to be considerable. Francis Beaumont, John Fletcher, Cyril Tourneur, and Thomas Middleton emerged into prominence in about 1606 or 1607. John Webster collaborated with Dekker and others in such plays as *Westward Ho* and *Sir Thomas Wyatt* around 1604, although he did not write his great tragedies until 1609–1614. Lesser talents, such as Henry Chettle, Anthony Munday, Henry Porter, John Day, and William Haughton, continued to pour forth an abundant supply of workmanlike plays. As Shakespeare's career developed, therefore, he enjoyed the fellowship and, no doubt, the rivalry of a remarkably gifted and diverse group of practicing dramatists.

Early Jacobean drama is, on the whole, characteristically different from the late Elizabethan drama that had preceded it. Other dramatists besides Shakespeare mirror his shift of focus from romantic comedies and patriotic histories to "problem" plays and tragedies. The boys' companies, reopening in 1598–1599 after virtually a decade of silence, did much to set the new tone. They avoided almost entirely the English history play, with its muscularly heroic style, so unsuited for the acting capabilities of boys. Besides, sophisticated audiences were sated with jingoistic fare, and even in the public theaters the genre had pretty well run its course. The fashion of the moment turned instead to revenge tragedy and satiric comedy.

The Jacobean revenge play owed much of its original inspiration to Thomas Kyd's *The Spanish Tragedy* (c. 1587), with its influential conventions: the intervention of supernatural forces, the feigned madness of the avenger, his difficulty in ascertaining the true facts of the murder, his morbid awareness of the conflict between human injustice and divine justice, his devising of a play within the play, and his invention of ingenious methods of slaughter in the play's gory ending. Kyd may also have written an early version of *Hamlet* featuring similar motifs. Shakespeare confronted cosmic issues of justice and human depravity in his revenge tragedy, *Hamlet* (c. 1599–1601), as indeed Kyd had done, but most followers of Kyd preferred to revel in the sensationalism of the genre. Some private-theater dramatists, such as Marston, subjected the conventions of the genre to caricature. Marston's revenge plays, written chiefly for Paul's boys and (after 1604) for the Children of the Queen's Revels, include *Antonio's Revenge* (1599–1601) and *The Malcontent* (1600–1604). These dramas are marked by flamboyantly overstated cynicism and are, in many ways, as close to satire as they are to tragedy. Marston had, in fact, made his first reputation as a nondramatic satirist, with *The Metamorphosis of Pygmalion's Image* and *The Scourge of Villainy* in 1598. His plays represent a continuation in dramatic form of the techniques of the Roman satirist. The typical Marstonian avenger, such as Malevole in *The Malcontent,* is an exaggeratedly unattractive authorial spokesman, pouring forth venomous hatred upon the loathsome and degenerate court in which he finds himself.

Similar in their exaggerated pursuit of the grotesque and the morbid are Cyril Tourneur's *The Atheist's Tragedy* (1607–1611) and a play formerly attributed to Tourneur but probably by Thomas Middleton, *The Revenger's Tragedy* (1606–1607). These plays are brilliant in the plotting of impossible situations and in the invention of cunning Italianate forms of torture and murder. Any sympathetic identification with the characters of these plays is sacrificed in the interests of technical virtuosity. As a result, the plays are more ironic than cathartic in their effect; we are overwhelmed by life's dark absurdities rather than ennobled by a vision of humanity's tragic grandeur. *The Tragedy of Hoffman, or A Revenge for a Father* by Henry Chettle (Admiral's Men, 1602) is similarly grotesque and lacking in sympathy for its revenger hero. To be sure, George Chapman's *Bussy D'Ambois* (1600–1604) and its sequel, *The Revenge of Bussy D'Ambois* (1607–1612), are thoughtful plays about human aspiration, in the vein of Marlowe's *Tamburlaine,* but even these plays employ a good deal of Senecan bloody melodrama.

The revenge play enjoyed a great popularity on the public stage and (in a caricatured form) on the private stage. The public theater did, however, cater also to its Puritan-leaning audiences, with more pious and moral tragedy. *Arden of Feversham* (c. 1591) is a good early example of what has come to be called domestic or homiletic tragedy. In the studiously plain style of a broadside ballad, it sets forth the facts of an actual murder that had occurred in 1551 and had been reported in Holinshed's *Chronicles.* The play interprets those events earnestly and providen-

tially. The most famous play in the genre of domestic tragedy is Thomas Heywood's *A Woman Killed with Kindness* (1603). It tells, not of a murder, but of an adultery, for which the goodhearted but offending wife must be perpetually banished by her grieving husband. The play succeeds in elevating the private sorrows of its ordinary characters to tragic stature. The moral stances appear to be unambiguous: adultery is a heinous offense but can be transcended by Christian forgiveness; dueling is evil. Still, a mix of sympathies is perhaps reflective of shifting public attitudes toward the role of women in marriage. Other plays in the vein of domestic tragedy include *A Yorkshire Tragedy* (1605–1608), *The Miseries of Enforced Marriage* (1605–1606), and *Two Lamentable Tragedies* (c. 1594–1598).

In comedy, the greatest writer of the period besides Shakespeare was Ben Jonson. His predilection was toward the private theater, though he continued to write occasionally for the public stage as well. To an ever-increasing extent, he fixed his satirical gaze on those values and institutions which Thomas Heywood cherished: the city of London, its bourgeois citizens, its traditional approach to morality, and its religious zeal. *Every Man Out of His Humor* (1599), written for the Chamberlain's Men, features a foolish, uxorious citizen, his socially aspiring wife, and her fashionmongering lover—humors types that were to appear again and again in the genre of satirical comedy known as "city comedy." (See Brian Gibbons, *Jacobean City Comedy,* 1968.) *Volpone* (1605–1606), though technically not a London city comedy, since it purportedly takes place in Venice, castigates greed among lawyers, businessmen, and other professional types. *The Alchemist* (1610) ridicules the affectations of petty shopkeepers, lawyers' clerks, Puritan divines, and others. *Bartholomew Fair* (1614) and *The Alchemist* give us Jonson's most memorable indictment of the Puritans.

Numerous other writers contributed to humors comedy and city comedy. George Chapman probably deserves more credit than he usually receives for having helped determine the shape of humors comedy in his *The Blind Beggar of Alexandria* (1596), *An Humorous Day's Mirth* (1597), *All Fools* (1599–1604), *May-Day* (1601–1609), *The Gentleman Usher* (1602–1604), and others. Francis Beaumont, assisted perhaps by John Fletcher, ridicules London grocers and apprentices for their naive tastes in romantic chivalry in *The Knight of the Burning Pestle* (1607–1610). Some satire in this vein, to be sure, is reasonably good-humored. *Eastward Ho!* (1605), by Chapman, Jonson, and Marston, is genially sympathetic toward the lifestyle of the small shopkeeper, even though the play contains a good deal of satire directed at social climbing and sharp business practices. Thomas Dekker's collaboration with Thomas Middleton on *The Honest Whore* (Part I, 1604) gives us an amused and yet warm portrayal of a linen draper who succeeds in business by insisting that the customer is always right. Dekker often shows a wry but generous appreciation of bourgeois ethics, as in *The Shoe-maker's Holiday* (1599). Yet even he turns against the Puritans in *If This Be Not a Good Play, the Devil Is in It* (1611–1612).

Marston shows his talent for city comedy in *The Dutch Courtesan* (1603–1605). Perhaps the most ingratiating and truly funny of the writers of city comedy, however, is Middleton. His *A Trick to Catch the Old One* (1604–1607) illustrates the tendency of Jacobean comedy to move away both from Shakespeare's romantic vein and Jonson's morally satirical vein toward a more lighthearted comedy of manners, anticipating the style of Restoration comedy. One of Middleton's most hilarious and philosophically unpretentious plays, though plotted with great ingenuity of situation, is *A Mad World, My Masters* (1604–1607). *Michaelmas Term*, written about the same time, exposes the sharp practices of usurers and lawyers. All these Middleton plays were written for Paul's boys.

Romantic comedy, though overshadowed by humors and city comedy during the 1600s, still held forth at the public theaters. A leading exponent was Thomas Heywood, in such plays as *The Fair Maid of the West,* or *A Girl Worth Gold* (1597–1610). Heywood also wrote English history plays designed to prove the sturdiness and historical importance of the London citizenry he so loved, as in *Edward IV* (1597–1599), *The Four Prentices of London* (c. 1600), and *If You Know Not Me You Know Nobody* (1605). Classical tragedy also continued to be written, despite the vogue of revenge tragedy. Ben Jonson rather dogmatically illustrated his classical theories of tragedy in *Sejanus* (1603) and *Catiline* (1611). Samuel Daniel wrote *Philotas* in 1604 and a revision of his *Cleopatra* in 1607. Heywood's *The Rape of Lucrece* appeared in 1606–1608. These are not, however, the immortal tragedies for which the Jacobean period is remembered.

## Shakespeare's Work, 1601–1608

Shakespeare's plays of this period are characteristically Jacobean in their fascination with the dark complexities of sexual jealousy, betrayal, revenge, and social conflict. The comedies are few in number and lack the joyous affirmation we associate with *Twelfth Night* and earlier plays. *Measure for Measure*, for example, is not about young men and women happily in love, but about pre-marital sex and the insoluble problems that arise when vice-prone men attempt to legislate morality for their fellow mortals. Angelo, self-hating and out of emotional control, is a tragic hero providentially rescued from his own worst self. The Duke and Isabella must use ethically dubious means—the bed trick—to effect their virtuous aims. Comedy in the play deals darkly in terms of prostitution, slander, and police inefficiency.

*All's Well That Ends Well*, though less grim than *Measure for Measure* in its confrontation of human degeneracy, does apply a similar bed trick as its central plot device. Just as important, the obstacles to love are internal and psychological, rather than external; that is, the happy union of Bertram and Helena is delayed, not by parental objections or by accident (as in *Romeo and Juliet* and *A Midsummer Night's Dream*), but by Bertram's unreadiness for the demands of a mature marital relationship. *Troilus and Cressida* is a play in which love is paralyzed by a combination of external and internal forces. Troilus must hand Cressida over to the Greeks because his code of honor bids him put his country's cause before his own, and yet that code of "honor" is based on Paris's rape of Helen. Cressida simply gives herself up to Diomedes, knowing she is not strong enough to stand alone in a moral wilderness. The combatants in

*Raphael Holinshed's* Chronicles of England, Scotland, and Ireland, *which was published (1577, 2nd edition in 1587) before Shakespeare's career began, served as principal historic source for many plays, including* Macbeth, King Lear, *and* Cymbeline, *as well as the history plays. Here, in a woodcut from the* Chronicles, Macbeth *and Banquo are shown encountering the three weird sisters.*

the greatest war in all history turn out to be petty bickerers who play nasty games on one another and sulk when their reputations are impugned. The cause for which both sides fight is squalid and senseless.

In *Hamlet*, Shakespeare explores similar dilemmas posed by human carnality. Women, in Hamlet's misogynistic angst, are too often frail; men are too often importunate and brutal. How is a thoughtful person to justify his or her own existence? Should one struggle actively against injustice and personal wrong? How can one know what is really true or foresee the complex results of action? How, in *Othello*, can the protagonist resist temptation and inner weakness, prompting him to destroy the very thing on which his happiness depends? Is Macbeth tempted to sin by the weird sisters and his wife, or is the choice to murder Duncan ultimately his? To what extent is humanity responsible for its tragic fate? Most of all, in *King Lear*, are the heavens themselves indifferent to human bestiality? Must Cordelia die? Yet, despite these overwhelmingly pessimistic questions, and the tragic consequences they imply for all human life, Shakespeare's "great" tragedies affirm at least the nobility of humanity's striving to know itself, and the redeeming fact that human goodness does exist (in Desdemona, Duncan, Cordelia), even if those who practice goodness are often slaughtered.

The Roman or classical tragedies are something apart from the "great" tragedies. They are more ironic in tone, more dispiriting, though they, too, affirm an essential nobility in humanity. Brutus misguidedly leads a revolution against Caesar but dies loyal to his great principles. Timon of Athens proves the appalling ingratitude of his fellow creature and resolutely cuts himself off from all human contact. Coriolanus proclaims himself an enemy of the Roman people and seeks to destroy them for their ingratitude, though he is compromised and destroyed at last by his promptings of human feeling. Antony, too, is pulled apart by an irreconcilable conflict. Yet, in this play at least, Shakespeare achieves, partly through the greatness of Cleopatra, a triumph over defeat that seems to offer a new resolution of humanity's tragic dilemma.

## THE LATE YEARS: 1608–1616

In the summer of 1608, Shakespeare's acting company signed a twenty-one-year lease for the use of the Blackfriars playhouse, an indoor and rather intimate, artificially lighted theater inside the city of London, close to the site of St. Paul's Cathedral. A private theater had existed on this spot since 1576, when the Children of the Chapel and then Paul's boys began acting their courtly plays for paying spectators in a building that had once belonged to the Dominicans, or Black Friars. James Burbage had begun construction in 1596 of the so-called Second Blackfriars theater in the same building. Although James encountered opposition from the residents of the area and died before

he could complete the work, James's son Richard did succeed in opening the new theater in 1600. At first, he leased it (for twenty-one years) to a children's company, but when that company was suppressed in 1608 for offending the French ambassador in a play by George Chapman, Burbage seized the opportunity to take back the unexpired lease and to set up Blackfriars as the winter playhouse for his adult company, the King's Men. By this time, the adult troupes could plainly see that they needed to cater more directly to courtly audiences than they once had done. Their popular audiences were becoming increasingly disenchanted with the drama. Puritan fulminations against the stage gained in effect, especially when many playwrights refused to disguise their satirical hostility toward Puritans and the London bourgeoisie.

Several of Shakespeare's late plays may have been acted both at the Globe and at Blackfriars. The plays he wrote after 1608–1609—*Cymbeline, The Winter's Tale*, and *The Tempest*—all show the distinct influence of the dramaturgy of the private theaters. Also, we know that an increasing number of Shakespeare's plays were acted at the court of King James. *Othello, King Lear*, and *The Tempest* are named in court revels accounts, and *Macbeth* dramatizes Scottish history with a seemingly explicit reference to King James as the descendant of Banquo, who bears the "twofold balls and treble scepters" (4.1.121); James had received a double coronation as King of England and Scotland, and took seriously his assumed title as King of Great Britain, France, and Ireland. On the other hand, Shakespeare's plays certainly continued to be acted at the Globe to the very end of his career. The 1609 quarto of *Pericles* advertises that it was acted "by his Majesty's Servants, at the Globe on the Bankside." The 1608 quarto of *King Lear* mentions a performance at court and assigns the play to "His Majesty's servants playing usually at the Globe on the Bankside." Simon Forman saw *Macbeth, Cymbeline*, and *The Winter's Tale* at the Globe. Finally, a performance of *Henry VIII* on June 29, 1613, resulted in the burning of the Globe to the ground, though afterwards it soon was rebuilt.

Shakespeare's last plays, written with a view to Blackfriars and the court as well as to the Globe, are now usually called "romances" or "tragicomedies," or sometimes both. Although they were not known by these terms in Shakespeare's day—they were grouped with the comedies in the First Folio of 1623, except for *Cymbeline*, which was placed among the tragedies—the very ambiguity about the genre in this arrangement is suggestive of an uncertainty as to whether they were seen as predominantly comic or tragic. The term "romance" suggests a return to the kind of story Robert Greene had derived from Greek romance: tales of adventure, long separation, and tearful reunion, involving shipwreck, capture by pirates, riddling prophecies, children set adrift in boats or abandoned on foreign shores, the illusion of death and subsequent restoration to life, the revelation of the identity of long-lost children by birthmarks, and

*This section of Wenceslaus Hollar's "Long View" of London dates from 1647, some years after Shakespeare's death, but gives nonetheless a fine view of two theater buildings on the south bank of the Thames River, across from the city. The two labels of "The Globe" and "Beere bayting" should in fact be reversed; the Globe (rebuilt in 1613) appears to the left and below the bearbaiting arena.*

the like. The term "tragicomedy" suggests a play in which the protagonist commits a seemingly fatal error or crime, or (as in *Pericles*) suffers an extraordinarily adverse fortune to test his patience; in either event, he must experience agonies of contrition and bereavement until he is providentially delivered from his tribulations. The tone is deeply melancholic and resigned, although suffused also with a sense of gratitude for the harmonies that are mysteriously restored.

The appropriateness of such plays to the elegant atmosphere of Blackfriars and the court is subtle but real. Although one might suppose at first that old-fashioned naiveté would seem out of place in a sophisticated milieu, the naiveté is only superficial. Tragicomedy and pastoral romance were, in the period from 1606 to 1610, beginning to enjoy a fashionable courtly revival. The leading practitioners of the new genre were Beaumont and Fletcher, though Shakespeare made a highly significant contribution. Perhaps sophisticated audiences responded to pastoral and romantic drama as the nostalgic evocation of an idealized past, a chivalric "golden world" fleetingly recovered through an artistic journey back to naiveté and inno-

cence. The evocation of such a world demands the kind of studied but informal artifice we find in many tragicomic plays of the period: the elaborate masques and allegorical shows, the descents of enthroned gods from the heavens (as in *Cymbeline*), the use of quaint Chorus figures like Old Gower or Time (in *Pericles* and *The Winter's Tale*), and the quasi-operatic blend of music and spectacle. At their best, such plays powerfully compel belief in the artistic world thus artificially created. The very improbability of the story becomes, paradoxically, part of the means by which an audience must "awake its faith" in a mysterious truth.

Shakespeare did not merely ape the new fashion in tragicomedy and romance. In fact, he may have done much to establish it. His *Pericles,* written seemingly in about 1606–1608 for the public stage before Shakespeare's company acquired Blackfriars, anticipated many important features, not only of Shakespeare's own later romances, but also of Beaumont and Fletcher's *The Maid's Tragedy* and *Philaster* (c. 1608–1611). Still, Shakespeare was on the verge of retirement, and the future belonged to Beaumont and Fletcher. Gradually, Shakespeare disengaged himself, spending more and more time in Stratford. His last-known stint as an actor was in Jonson's *Sejanus* in 1603. Some time in 1611 or 1612, he probably gave up his lodgings in London, though he still may have returned for such occasions as the opening performance of *Henry VIII* in 1613. He continued to be one of the proprietors of the newly rebuilt Globe, but his involvement in its day-to-day operations dwindled.

## Shakespeare's Reputation, 1608–1616

Shakespeare's reputation among his contemporaries was undiminished in his late years, even though Beaumont and Fletcher were the new rage at the Globe and Blackfriars. Among those who apostrophized Shakespeare was John Davies of Hereford in *The Scourge of Folly* (entered in the Stationers' Register in 1610):

> To our English Terence, Mr. Will Shakespeare.
>
> Some say, good Will, which I, in sport, do sing:
> Hadst thou not played some kingly parts in sport,
> Thou hadst been a companion for a king,
> And been a king among the meaner sort.
> Some others rail. But, rail as they think fit,
> Thou hast no railing, but a reigning, wit.
> And honesty thou sow'st, which they do reap,
> So to increase their stock which they do keep.

The following sonnet is from *Run and a Great Cast* (1614) by Thomas Freeman:

> To Master W. Shakespeare.
>
> Shakespeare, that nimble Mercury thy brain
> Lulls many hundred Argus-eyes asleep,
> So fit, for all thou fashionest thy vein,

At th' horse-foot fountain thou hast drunk full deep.
Virtue's or vice's theme to thee all one is.
Who loves chaste life, there's *Lucrece* for a teacher;
Who list read lust, there's *Venus and Adonis,*
True model of a most lascivious lecher.
Besides, in plays thy wit winds like Meander,
Whence needy new composers borrow more
Than Terence doth from Plautus or Menander.
But to praise thee aright, I want thy store.
   Then let thine own works thine own worth upraise,
   And help t' adorn thee with deservèd bays.

Ben Jonson took a more critical view, though he also admired Shakespeare greatly. In the Induction to his *Bartholomew Fair* (1631 edition), Jonson compared the imaginary world he presented in his play with the more improbable fantasies of romantic drama:

If there be never a servant-monster i' the fair, who can help it? He [the author, Jonson] says; nor a nest of antics? He is loath to make Nature afraid in his plays, like those that beget tales, Tempests, and suchlike drolleries to mix his head with other men's heels.

From this, one judges that Jonson had in mind not only *The Tempest*, but also Shakespeare's other late romances. He similarly protested in the Prologue to his 1616 edition of *Every Man in His Humor* that his own playwriting was free of the usual romantic claptrap:

Where neither Chorus wafts you o'er the seas,
Nor creaking throne comes down the boys to please,
Nor nimble squib is seen to make afeard
The gentlewomen, nor rolled bullet heard
To say it thunders, nor tempestuous drum
Rumbles to tell you when the storm doth come.

Still, Shakespeare's reputation was assured. John Webster paid due homage, in his note To the Reader accompanying *The White Devil* (1612): to "the right happy and copious industry of M. *Shakespeare,* M. *Dekker,* & M. *Heywood,*" along with Chapman, Jonson, Beaumont, and Fletcher.

### Records of the Late Years

Shakespeare's last recorded investment in real estate was the purchase of a house in Blackfriars, London, in 1613. There is no indication he lived there, for he had retired to Stratford. He did not pay the full purchase price of one hundred and forty pounds, and the mortgage deed executed for the unpaid balance furnishes one of the six unquestioned examples of his signature.

John Combe, a wealthy bachelor of Stratford and Shakespeare's friend, left him a legacy of five pounds in his will at the time of Combe's death in 1613. At about the same time, John's kinsman William Combe began a controversial attempt to enclose Welcombe Common, that is, to convert narrow strips of arable land to pasture.

Presumably, Combe was interested in a more efficient means of using the land. Enclosure was, however, an explosive issue, since many people feared they would lose the right to farm the land and would be evicted to make room for cattle and sheep. Combe attempted to guarantee Shakespeare and other titheholders that they would lose no money. He offered similar assurances to the Stratford Council, but the townspeople were adamantly opposed. Shakespeare was consulted by letter as a leading titheholder. The letter is lost, but, presumably, it set forth the Council's reasons for objecting to enclosure. Shakespeare's views on the controversy remain unknown. Eventually, the case went to the Privy Council, where Combe was ordered to restore the land to its original use.

One of the most interesting documents from these years consists of the records of a lawsuit entered into in 1612 by Stephen Belott against his father-in-law, Christopher Mountjoy, a Huguenot maker of women's ornamental headdresses who resided on Silver Street, St. Olave's parish, London. Belott sought to secure the payment of a dower promised him at the time of his marriage to Mountjoy's daughter. In this suit, Shakespeare was summoned as a witness and made deposition on five interrogatories. From this document we learn that Shakespeare was a lodger in Mountjoy's house at the time of the marriage in 1604 and probably for some time before that, since he states in his testimony that he had known Mountjoy for more than ten years. Shakespeare admitted that, at the solicitation of Mountjoy's wife, he had acted as an intermediary in the arrangement of the marriage between Belott and Mountjoy's daughter. Shakespeare declared himself unable, however, to recall the exact amount of the portion or the date on which it was to have been paid. Shakespeare's signature to his deposition is authentic and one of the best samples of his handwriting that we have.

In January 1616, Shakespeare drew up his last will and testament with the assistance of his lawyer Francis Collins, who had aided him earlier in some of his transactions in real estate. On March 25, 1616, Shakespeare revised his will in order to provide for the marriage of his daughter Judith and Thomas Quiney in that same year. Shakespeare's three quavering signatures, one on each page of this document, suggest that he was in failing health. The cause of his death on April 23 is not known. An intriguing bit of Stratford gossip is reported by John Ward, vicar of Holy Trinity in Stratford from 1662 to 1689, in his diary: "Shakespeare, Drayton, and Ben Jonson had a merry meeting, and it seems drank too hard, for Shakespeare died of a fever there contracted." The report comes fifty years after Shakespeare's death, however, and is hardly an expert medical opinion.

The will disposes of all the property of which Shakespeare is known to have died possessing, the greater share of it going to his daughter Susanna. His recently married daughter, Judith, received a dowry, a provision for any children that might be born of her marriage, and other gifts. Ten pounds went to the poor of Stratford; Shakespeare's sword went to Mr. Thomas Combe; twenty-six shillings and eight pence apiece went to Shakespeare's fellow actors Heminges, Burbage, and Condell to buy them mourning rings; and other small bequests went to various other friends and relatives.

An interlineation contains the bequest of Shakespeare's "second best bed with the furniture" that is, the hangings, to his wife. Anne's name appears nowhere else in the will. Some scholars, beginning with Edmund Malone, have taken this reference as proof of an unhappy marriage, confirming earlier indications, such as the hasty wedding to a woman who was William's senior by eight years and his prolonged residence in London for twenty years or more, seemingly without his family. The evidence is inconclusive, however. Shakespeare certainly supported his family handsomely, acquired much property in Stratford, and retired there when he might have remained still in London. Although he showed no great solicitude for Anne's well-being in the will, her rights were protected by law; a third of her husband's estate went to her without having to be mentioned in the will. New Place was to be the home of Shakespeare's favorite daughter, Susanna, wife of the distinguished Dr. John Hall. Anne Shakespeare would make her home with her

*As with so many other things in his life, the curious terms of Shakespeare's will have led to endless and provocative conjecture.*

daughter and, with her dower rights secured by law, would be quite as wealthy as she would need to be.

The date of Shakespeare's death (April 23, 1616) and his age (his fifty-third year) are inscribed on his monument. This elaborate structure, still standing in the chancel of Trinity Church, Stratford, was erected some time before 1623 by the London stonecutting firm of Gheerart Janssen and his sons. Janssen's shop was in Southwark, near the Globe, and may have been familiar to the actors. The bust of Shakespeare is a conventional sort of statuary for its time. Still, it is one of the only two contemporary likenesses we have. The other is the Droeshout engraving of Shakespeare in the Folio of 1623.

The epitaph on the monument reads as follows:

> *Iudicio Pylium, genio Socratem, arte Maronem;*
> *Terra tegit, populus maeret, Olympus habet.*
> Stay, passenger. Why goest thou by so fast?
> Read, if thou canst, whom envious Death hath placed
> Within this monument: Shakespeare, with whom
> Quick Nature died, whose name doth deck this tomb
> Far more than cost, sith all that he hath writ
> Leaves living art but page to serve his wit.
>
> *Obiit anno domini 1616,*
> *Aetatis 53, die 23 April.*

These lines, of which the beginning Latin couplet compares Shakespeare with Nestor (King of Pylos) for wise judgment, Socrates for genius, and Virgil (Maro) for poetic art, and avers that the earth covers him, people grieve for him, and Mount Olympus (that is, heaven) has him, indicate the high reputation he enjoyed at the time of his death. More widely known, perhaps, are the four lines inscribed over Shakespeare's grave near the north wall of the chancel. A local tradition assigns them to Shakespeare himself and implies that he wrote them "to suit the capacity of clerks and sextons," whom he wished apparently to frighten out of the idea of opening the grave to make room for a new occupant:

> Good friend, for Jesus' sake forbear
> To dig the dust enclosèd here.
> Blest be the man that spares these stones,
> And curst be he that moves my bones.

Whether Shakespeare actually wrote these lines cannot, however, be determined.

## Other Dramatists

The most significant new development in the drama of the period from about 1608 to 1616, apart from Shakespeare's new interest in romance and tragicomedy, was the emergence of the famous literary partners Francis Beaumont and John Fletcher. Beaumont, the son of a distinguished lawyer, studied for a while at Oxford and then at the Inner Temple before drifting into a literary career. In 1613, he married an heiress and retired almost completely from the theater. John Fletcher was the son of Richard Fletcher, Queen Elizabeth's chaplain and later Bishop of London. The young man probably studied at Cambridge. The father died in 1596 heavily in debt, leaving the young Fletcher to support a family of eight children. Fletcher became a professional writer, earning his living as chief dramatist for the King's Men. He was Shakespeare's successor. Fletcher's cousins, Giles and Phineas Fletcher, gained some reputation as poets. Beaumont and Fletcher, who were close friends, regarded themselves also as poets and as members of the "tribe of Ben"—the disciples of the great Ben Jonson who often gathered together at the Mermaid Tavern for an evening of witty literary conversation.

> What things have we seen
> Done at the Mermaid! heard words that have been
> So nimble, and so full of subtle flame,
> As if that every one from whence they came
> Had meant to put his whole wit in a jest,
> And had resolved to live a fool the rest
> Of his dull life!
>
> (Master Francis Beaumont's Letter to Ben Jonson)

Beaumont and Fletcher actually collaborated on only about seven plays: *The Woman Hater,* a comedy (1606); *The Maid's Tragedy*, a tragedy (1608–1611); *Philaster,* a tragicomedy (1608–1610); *Cupid's Revenge,* a tragedy (c. 1607–1612); *The Coxcomb,* a comedy (1608–1610); *A King and No King*, a tragicomedy (1611); *The Scornful Lady,* a tragicomedy (1613–1616); and perhaps one or two others. They may have collaborated on *The Knight of the Burning Pestle* (c. 1607–1610), though it was chiefly Beaumont's. Beaumont also wrote *Mask of the Inner Temple and Gray's Inn* (1613). Fletcher unassisted wrote *The Faithful Shepherdess* (1608–1609), *The Night Walker* (c. 1611), *Bonduca* (1611–1614), *Valentinian* (1610–1614), and others. He also collaborated with several other writers, including Massinger, Middleton, Field, and Rowley. Importantly, he seems to have collaborated with Shakespeare on *The Two Noble Kinsmen* (1613–1616) and, probably, on *Henry VIII*. Eventually, most of these various dramatic enterprises were gathered together in 1647 as the works of Beaumont and Fletcher. They have remained coupled in this fashion ever since, partly because the original collaboration of these two men did so much to set a new style in coterie drama.

The plays they wrote together, such as *The Maid's Tragedy* and *Philaster,* offer an interesting comparison with Shakespeare's contemporary writing in a similar genre. Beaumont and Fletcher often employ exotic settings, like Rhodes or Sicily. In such an environment, refined aristocratic characters are caught in dynastic struggles or in a rarified conflict between love and honor. They must cope with stereotyped villains, such as tyrants or shamelessly lustful courtiers. The sentiments are lofty, the rhetoric is mannered; elaborately contrived situations are offered with no pretense of verisimilitude. The characters live according to lofty chivalric codes and despise ill breeding above all else. In the plotting of the tragicomic reversal, the audience is sometimes deliberately deceived into believing something that is not true, so that the sudden happy outcome arrives as a theatrically contrived surprise. Disguising and masking are common motifs. The audience is deliberately made aware throughout of the play's theatrical artifice, statuesque scene building, and titillating sensationalism.

Although Shakespeare wrote no tragedies after *Coriolanus,* great tragedy did continue to appear on the Jacobean stage. John Webster wrote his two most splendid plays, *The White Devil* and *The Duchess of Malfi,* between 1609 and 1614. Both contain elements of the still-popular revenge tradition. They also manage to achieve a vision of triumphant human dignity in defeat that merits comparison with Shakespeare's greatest tragic achievement. Still to come were *The Changeling* (1622) by Thomas Middleton and William Rowley, *Women Beware Women* (c. 1620–1627) by Middleton, *'Tis Pity She's a Whore* (1629?–1633) by John Ford, and others. Although these tragedies are more concerned with the grotesque than are Shakespeare's great tragedies, and more obsessed with abnormal human psychology (incest, werewolfism, and the like), they are nonetheless sublime achievements in art. The genius of the age for tragedy did not die with Shakespeare. During Shakespeare's last years, George Chapman was also writing his best tragedies, including *Charles Duke of Byron* in 1608, *The Revenge of Bussy D'Ambois* in about 1610, and *Chabot, Admiral of France* between 1611 and 1622. Ben Jonson's *Catiline His Conspiracy,* a classical tragedy, appeared in 1611; Marston's *The Insatiate Countess,* in about 1610.

## The Anti-Stratfordian Movement

What we know of Shakespeare's life is really quite considerable. The information we have is just the kind one would expect. It hangs together and refers to one man and one career. Though lacking in the personal details we should like to have, it is both adequate and plausible. Yet the past hundred years or so have seen the growth of a tendency to doubt Shakespeare's authorship of the plays and poems ascribed to him. The phenomenon is sometimes called the "anti-Stratfordian" movement, since its attack is leveled at the literary credentials of the man who was born in Stratford and later became an actor in London. Although based on no reliable evidence, the movement has persisted long enough to become a kind of myth. It also has the appeal of a mystery thriller: who really wrote Shakespeare's plays? A brief account must be made here of the origins of the anti-Stratfordian movement.

Beginning in the late eighteenth century, and especially in the mid-nineteenth century, a few admirers of

Shakespeare began to be troubled by the scantiness of information about England's greatest author. As we have already seen, good reasons exist for the scarcity: the great London fire of 1666 that destroyed many records, the relatively low social esteem accorded to popular dramatists during the Elizabethan period, and the like. Also, we do actually know more about Shakespeare than about most of his contemporaries in the theater, despite the difficulties imposed by the passage of time. Still, some nineteenth-century readers saw only that they knew far less about Shakespeare than about many authors of more recent date.

Moreover, the impressions of the man did not seem to square with his unparalleled literary greatness. William Shakespeare had been brought up in a small country town; were his parents cultured folk or even literate? No record of his schooling has been preserved; was Shakespeare himself able to read and write, much less write immortal plays and poems? The anti-Stratfordians do not deny the existence of a man called Shakespeare from Stratford-upon-Avon, but they find it incredible that such a person should be connected with the works ascribed to him. Mark Twain, himself an anti-Stratfordian, was fond of joking that the plays were not by Shakespeare but by another person of the same name. Beneath the humor in this remark lies a deep-seated mistrust: how could a country boy have written so knowledgeably and eloquently about the lives of kings and queens? Where could such a person have learned so much about the law, about medicine, about the art of war, about heraldry? The puzzle seemed a genuine one, even though no one until the late eighteenth century had thought to question Shakespeare's authorship of the plays—least of all his colleagues and friends, such as Ben Jonson, who admitted that Shakespeare's classical learning was "small" but insisted that Shakespeare was an incomparable genius.

The first candidate put forward in the anti-Stratfordian cause as the "real" author of the plays was Sir Francis Bacon, a reputable Elizabethan writer with connections at court and considerable cultural attainments. Yet the ascription of the plays to Bacon was based on no documentary evidence. It relied, instead, on the essentially snobbish argument that Bacon was better born and purportedly better educated than Shakespeare—an argument that appealed strongly to the nineteenth century in which a university education was becoming more and more a distinctive mark of the cultivated person. The assertion of Bacon's authorship was also based on a conspiratorial theory of history; that is, its believers had to assume the existence of a mammoth conspiracy in Elizabethan times, in which Shakespeare would allow his name to be used by Bacon as a *nom de plume* and in which Shakespeare's friends, such as Ben Jonson, would take part. (Jonson knew Shakespeare too well, after all, to have been duped for a period of almost twenty years.) The motive for such an arrangement, presumably, was that Bacon did not

deign to lend his dignified name to the writing of popular plays (since they were considered subliterary) and so chose a common actor named Shakespeare to serve as his alter ego. This theory of an elaborate hoax involving England's greatest literary giant has proved powerfully attractive to modern writers like Mark Twain, who have sometimes thought of themselves as rebels against the cultural "Establishment" of their own times.

The claim that Bacon wrote Shakespeare's works was soon challenged in the name of other prominent Elizabethans: the Earl of Oxford, the Earl of Southampton, Anthony Bacon, the Earl of Rutland, the Earl of Devonshire, Christopher Marlowe, and others. Since documentary claims as to Bacon's authorship of the Shakespearen canon were nonexistent, other Elizabethans could be proposed to fill his role just as satisfactorily as Bacon himself. The anti-Stratfordian movement gained momentum and came to include several prominent persons, such as Delia Bacon and Sigmund Freud, as well as Mark Twain. One of the appeals of the anti-Stratfordian movement in recent years has proved to be a kind of amateur sleuthing or scholarship, carried on by professional lawyers, doctors, and the like, who have explored Shakespeare's interest in law and medicine as a hobby and have convinced themselves that Shakespeare's wisdom in these subjects entitles him to claim a better birth than that of a glover's son from Stratford. Ingenious efforts at "deciphering" hidden meanings in the works have been adduced to prove one authorship claim or another. The academic "Establishments" of modern universities have been accused of perpetuating Shakespeare's name out of mere vested self-interest: Shakespeare scholarship is an industry, and its busy workers need to preserve their source of income.

We must ask in all seriousness, however, whether such assertions are not offering answers to nonexistent questions. Responsible scholarship has admirably dispelled the seeming mystery of Shakespeare's humble beginnings. T. W. Baldwin, for example, in *William Shakspere's Petty School* (1943) and *William Shakspere's Small Latine and Lesse Greeke* (1944), has shown just what sort of classical training Shakespeare almost surely received in the free grammar school of Stratford. It is precisely the sort of training that would have enabled him to use classical authors as he does, with the familiarity of one who likes to read. His Latin and Greek were passable but not strong; he often consulted modern translations, as well as classical originals. Just as importantly, Shakespeare's social background was, in fact, typical of many of the greatest writers of the English Renaissance. He earned his living by his writing, and thus had one of the strongest of motives for success. So did his contemporaries Marlowe (who came from a shoemaker's family) and Jonson (whose stepfather was a brickmason). Greene, Peele, Nashe, and many others sold plays and other writings for a livelihood. Although a few wellborn persons, such as

Bacon and Sir Philip Sidney, also made exceptional contributions to literature, and although a number of courtiers emulated Henry VIII and Elizabeth as gifted amateurs in the arts, the court was not the direct or major source of England's literary greatness. Most courtiers were not professional writers. A man like Bacon lacked Shakespeare's connection with a commercial acting company. Surely the theater was a more relevant "university" for Shakespeare than Oxford or Cambridge, where most of his studies would have been in ancient languages and in divinity.

## Shakespeare on Family Life and Women

We have seen how Shakespeare married Anne Hathaway when he was eighteen in 1582, and how she bore him a daughter, Susanna, some six months later, followed by the twins, Hamnet and Judith, in early 1585. During his many years as an actor and dramatist in London, roughly 1590 to 1611–12, he left his family in Stratford. He provided comfortably for them, and presumably paid visits home when he could; he may even have partly retired to Stratford a little earlier than 1611–12, continuing to write while no longer in residence with his acting company.

Scholars to this day disagree as to whether the sparse records of Shakespeare's personal life point to a happy marriage or to one in which the husband chose to live apart from his wife and family for personal reasons. Divorce was in effect legally impossible. Did Shakespeare marry a women eight years his senior, since he had conceived a child by her in 1582, and then prefer to be on his own, or was the arrangement dictated by the practicalities of a busy career? He does lie buried beside her and other members of the family in Holy Trinity Church in Stratford. He bought real estate there, including a large house in town. But then why did he mention Anne so briefly and perhaps even curtly in his will when he died in 1616?

The puzzle points to larger questions of Shakespeare's treatment of love and marriage in his plays and poems. Generally, in the romantic comedies of the 1590s, he celebrates marriage as the happy conclusion of love and courtship, even when courtship itself is fraught with misunderstandings and threats that can prove nearly fatal. Granted, in the early *Love's Labor's Lost*, the three lovelorn gentlemen are told by the young women they love that they will have to spend a year in penitential austerity before they can hope to wed, but even here the clear assumption is they will at last be rewarded with marital bliss. Elsewhere, *The Taming of the Shrew* concludes with a wedding feast for Petruchio and his erstwhile shrewish Katharine, accompanied by the marriages of Lucentio with his Bianca and Hortensio with a widow. Antipholus of Syracuse happily marries Luciana in *The Comedy of Errors*, while old Egeon is reunited with his long-lost Emilia. Valentine is united with his beloved Silvia in *The Two Gentlemen of Verona*, while the inconstant Proteus

finally returns to his faithful and longsuffering Julia. *A Midsummer Night's Dream* ends with wedding festivities for Duke Theseus and Hippolyta along with Lysander and Hermia, and Demetrius and Helena. Oberon, the Fairy King, is reconciled with his Queen Titania. In *The Merchant of Venice*, Bassanio is rewarded in his quest for Portia to be his bride, while Gratiano is united with Nerissa and Lorenzo with Jessica. *Much Ado About Nothing* celebrates the successful courtship of Benedick and Beatrice, while Claudio is at last reconciled with the innocent Hero whom he has wrongly suspected of infidelity. Rosalind marries her Orlando in *As You Like It*, while Rosalind's cousin Celia is united with Orlando's brother Oliver. Viola in *Twelfth Night* becomes the bride of her beloved master Orsino, while Viola's long-lost brother Sebastian marries the Countess Olivia; even Sir Toby couples with Maria. *The Merry Wives of Windsor*, largely concerned with reconciling marital jealousies, similarly ends with the marriage of young Master Fenton to Anne Page.

The tests that courtship must undergo are, to be sure, genuinely threatening. The young women in *A Midsummer Night's Dream* feel abandoned and unloved, while the young men are driven by imagined sexual rivalries to try to kill each other. Kate, in *The Taming of the Shrew*, is forced to undergo humiliation at the hands of Petruchio designed to break her of her shrewish ways. Hero's undeserved humiliation in *Much Ado About Nothing* is so horrendous that she is threatened with death or a cloistered life for the duration of her existence. And so it goes in other comedies as well.

In the English history plays that Shakespeare wrote in the 1590s, the vindication of women is less clear. Queen Margaret, consort of Henry VI, is an adulterous wife who domineers over her husband in ways that bode ill for England in a century of civil war. Edward IV's lust-prompted marriage to the widow of a Lancastrian officer against the urgings of his family leads to venomous rivalries at court. Yet the marriage of the newly crowned Henry VII to Elizabeth of York in *Richard III* brings Shakespeare's first historical tetralogy to a triumphant conclusion by initiating a new Tudor dynasty that will provide England with its famous virgin monarch, Elizabeth I. Similarly, In Shakespeare's second historical tetralogy the marriage of the Princess Katherine of France at the conclusion of *Henry V* signals an end, however temporary, to the wars of England and France.

Some time around 1600, roughly at the midpoint of Shakespeare's writing career, the upbeat account of love and marriage takes a turn toward the problematic. In the so-called Dark Lady sonnets, written perhaps in these years, the poet agonizes over a guilty and adulterous relationship in which the woman he compulsively desires becomes the mistress of the poet's dear friend. *Troilus and Cressida, c.* 1601, tells of Cressida's desertion of Troilus; even if the circumstances of this desertion lay the blame on the Trojan war more than on her, the infidelity is now real rather than illusory as it was in *Much Ado About Nothing*, for example. The protagonist of *Hamlet, c.* 1600–1601, broods misogynistically over his mother's overhasty marriage to the hated Claudius. Hamlet is no less bitterly disappointed by Ophelia's returning his love letters to him at the behest of her father, Polonius. "Frailty, thy name is woman!" he exclaims (1.2.146). In the tragedies that follow in quick succession, male unhappiness with women grows in intensity. Desdemona in *Othello* is guiltless of the accusations of adultery aimed at her by her jealous husband, but that accusation nonetheless leads to her violent death and Othello's suicide. In *King Lear*, the King's wicked daughters, Goneril and Regan, compete adulterously for the sexual company of the villainous Edmund. Lady Macbeth, though faithful to her husband, tempts him toward an act of regicide that destroys all hope of happiness; she herself commits suicide. The mother of the protagonist in *Coriolanus*, Volumnia, is an overbearing parent who drives her son into self-destruction.

Importantly, *Antony and Cleopatra* (c. 1606–1607) does offer, at least glimpsingly, a more redeeming view of sexuality. Cleopatra has slept with many men, and her tempestuous love affair with Antony undoes the career of a brave military officer and statesman, but in the world of poetic imagination at least these famous lovers triumph, though death, over the Machiavellian world of Octavius Caesar. And in the plays that follow, the so-called late romances, happiness is belatedly and magically restored to the marriages of Pericles and Thaisa, Posthumus Leonatus and Imogen (in *Cymbeline*), and Leontes and Hermione (in *The Winter's Tale*). Ferdinand and Miranda marry happily in *The Tempest*. Prospero's wife has no role in that play, but Prospero finds immense consolation in his love for his daughter Miranda, as also is true of Pericles in his loving reunion with Marina, King Cymbeline with Imogen, and Leontes with Perdita. Many scholars wonder if these happy endings bear a significant resemblance to Shakespeare's own retirement to Stratford and his seemingly nurturing relationship with his daughter Susanna and her husband John Hall. Whether the absence of Prospero's wife in *The Tempest* reflects any dissatisfaction at last with Shakespeare's own marriage is a matter of vigorous debate. See the section above on Shakespeare's Life and Work for further details.

Throughout his work, Shakespeare seems fascinated by courtship, love, and marriage, both when love is successfully enduring and when it encounters painful difficulties. In courtship, the young women tend to be more constant and aware of who they are; the young men are often frenetically inconstant and desperately in need of the reassurance and instruction that the young women can provide. When the young women are suspected of disloyalty, more often than not the problem lies in men's morbid suspicions. Men in Shakespeare tend to project their own

insecurities onto the women; fearful of their own inadequacies, men are too prone to suspect that the women they love have turned to rival wooers. The tribulations of courtship generally arise out of the young men's tendency to expect the worst. The women are patient and forgiving. They are better than the young men deserve, but the young women are content to take the men back despite their having wandered from the true path.

The young women are apt also to accept their dependent place in a tradition of hierarchical male authority. Kate, in *The Taming of the Shrew*, famously rebels against sexism, and for good reasons at least in part, but she seemingly learns the contentment of acknowledging Petruchio's role as master of the household. She can be interpreted this way, at any rate, though modern sensibilities can ask if she is simply brainwashed, or has chosen to conform with ironic detachment to what her husband demands, in the interests of keeping the peace. Whatever the case may be, Shakespeare revisits a similar relationship in *Much Ado About Nothing*, where Benedick and Beatrice arrive at an equality of relationship that seems much more in line with an ideal of companionate marriage. The Anglican church of Shakespeare's day urged this on husbands, asking them to use their authority sparingly and generously over their wives and children. Patriarchal authority remains the order of the day, but with forbearance.

Wives and young women are often seen as wise counselors to their wooers or husbands. Portia in *The Merchant of Venice*, Juliet in *Romeo and Juliet*, Rosalind in *As You Like It*, and Viola in *Twelfth Night*, among others, enable the men they love to reach for a mature and mutual relationship that is far superior to the adolescent posturing and romantic idealizations of women to which those young man are far too prone. In more tragic circumstances, woman are ready to offer sane advice that the men ignore to their peril. Hotspur in *I Henry IV* refuses to listen to his sprightly wife Kate, and marches accordingly to his death at the Battle of Shrewsbury. Calpurnia, the wife of Julius Caesar, fruitlessly warns her husband not to go the Senate House on the fatal Ides of March. Portia, in the same play, cannot persuade her husband Brutus to share with her his knowledge of a plot to assassinate Caesar. Hector brusquely orders his wife Andromache to be silent when she attempts to dissuade him from venturing into battle in *Troilus and Cressida*.

Women thus often embody a quality that is precious and nearly divine in its selfless generosity and love. Desdemona forgives the enraged husband who kills her in *Othello*, to the extraordinary extent of trying to take the blame on herself. When King Lear says to his daughter Cordelia, whom he has banished, that she has cause not to love him, she replies with stunning simplicity, "No cause, no cause" (*King Lear*, 4. 7.81). Cleopatra forgives Antony his mad rages and attempts to kill her. Imogen forgives her father in *Cymbeline*, as does Marina in *Pericles*

I-76    GENERAL INTRODUCTION

and Perdita in *The Winter's Tale*. Such forgiveness, all the more precious for being undeserved, redeems situations that would otherwise end in bitter negation and disaster. To be sure, frightening women like Queen Margaret in the Henry VI plays, or Lady Macbeth, or Volumnia in *Coriolanus* remind us that the male vision of women is often deeply ambivalent: women can be both the source of life and the destroyer of that life. Still, at his generous best, Shakespeare sounds apologetic for his own gender and grateful for help without which men would proceed to their own undoing.

# HOW TO READ SHAKESPEARE

In the short essay on "Reading Shakespeare in the Twenty-First Century" at the head of the General Introduction to this book, I have suggested that anyone newly coming on Shakespeare, and finding the language difficult, might do well to adopt several strategies. One is to see the play that interests you, or is assigned for class study, in performance. Many excellent film interpretations are available on film or in video, and are discussed in Appendix 4 at the end of this volume. Good actors can make a Shakespeare play seem entirely intelligible and moving.

Another approach is to read the play to oneself, or aloud with friends, without at first consulting the notes, taking the play it as it comes, as a script for performance. Hear Shakespeare's words in your head. Ask, as you read, why the characters are saying what they say, to one another or to themselves. What is motivating their arguments, their pleadings with one another, their boasts, their anxieties? Shakespeare is wonderful at creating character. Listen for verbal traits that distinguish them one from another. How do Romeo's vocabulary and images differ from those of Juliet? In what ways does Juliet's father, old Capulet, create such a distinctive impression of who he is by the way he goes about determining that his only daughter will marry a young man of his choice? In what ways does Hermia's father, old Egeus, define himself for us in *A Midsummer Night's Dream* by his equally stubborn insistence that Hermia marry his choice, Demetrius, rather than the young man she loves, Lysander? How is King Claudius, in *Hamlet*, revealed to us by his suave explanations as to why he has so quickly married his widowed sister-in-law after the unexpected and sudden death of her husband, Claudius's older brother?

Because Shakespeare's characters live so vividly in the ways they speak, our job as readers of his plays is to stage a given play in our minds as we read. Imagine yourself as director, coaching the actors as to whether they should at various times speak tenderly, or ironically, or angrily, or in a sullen whisper or defiant outburst. In your imagination as you read, try to hear what characters are arguing about. What is at issue? Why do things matter to them? What is Juliet thinking about when she gives such evasive answers to her father about his plans for her to marry Count Paris? What is Romeo thinking about when he has slain Juliet's cousin Tybalt in a street quarrel and must now face the certainty of his being punished for that homicide? How does Shakespeare go about portraying through the spoken word the anguish of a young man who knows that he has betrayed his vows of undying loyalty to Juliet?

Such questions prompt others that we must think about as we read. What is it that has prompted Romeo to refuse to fight the angry Tybalt at first but then to challenge Tybalt to a duel in revenge for Tybalt's having slain Romeo's dear friend Mercutio? The emotional necessity of avenging that deed, Romeo's wish to show himself manly in a quarrel—how are these considerations balanced off against his promises to Juliet?

Shakespeare loves hard questions. Is misfortune partly to blame for the tragic outcome of *Romeo and Juliet*, particularly when the letter written by Friar Laurence to Romeo in banishment fails to reach him in time, or is the tragedy centered around Romeo's ill-considered killing of Tybalt, or is the tragic cause to be found more in the long-standing quarrel setting Capulets against Montagues? Shakespeare not only loves hard questions, he refuses to give simple answers. Does Hamlet hesitate to avenge his father's murder because he is emotionally confused or because the very nature of action requires careful deliberation? Why is Claudius, in *Hamlet*, unable to pray that he be forgiven for having murdered his own brother? Did Queen Gertrude have any foreknowledge of this crime before it was committed?

Hard questions like these require careful reading, but they also should add real excitement to the adventure of reading Shakespeare. He challenges us at every turn. The rewards are that we are invited by Shakespeare into consideration of issues that matter deeply to us as human beings: love, friendship, physical attraction, marriage, jealousy, self-betrayal, inconstancy, forgiveness, fear of death, renunciation, affirmation, and so much else.

When Shakespeare wrote his plays and poems, some four centuries ago, the English language was in transition from the Middle English of Geoffrey Chaucer to the modern English we speak and read today. Chaucer's English is notably different from ours, though still recognizably the same language. The opening of *The Canterbury Tales* reads as follows:

Whan that Aprill with his shoures soote
The droghte of March hath perced to the roote,

that is to say,

When April with its sweet showers
Has pierced to the root the drought of March.

Shakespeare's English, sometimes called Early Modern English, is more familiar than that, and is assisted too by the fact that Shakespeare editions today generally modernize spellings and pronunciation. This present edition does so. We can modernize Shakespeare in a way that isn't quite possible with Chaucer, because Shakespeare is closer to modern English.

Still, differences are marked. Shakespeare regularly uses "he hath" and "she hath" for "he has" and "she has." He uses a personal form in the second-person singular that we have lost: "thou art" for "you are," "I would thou wert" for "I wish you were," "How camest thou" for "How did you come." Many European languages, including French, Italian, Spanish, and German, retain the personal form here, as an intimate form of address among family and friends, and Quakers do so still in English, but the rest of us have lost that personal form of address. In so doing, we have lost a nuance of language that can be eloquently meaningful; expressions of tender feeling are marked as such by the personal pronoun.

What's more, Elizabethan language can express power relationships this way: parents address their children as "thee" and "thou," while children show their respect for parents by using the more formal "you." Addressing someone who is not a family member or intimate friend as "thou" can be terribly insulting. When Tybalt says to Mercutio, in Act 3, scene 1 of *Romeo and Juliet*, "Mercutio, thou consortest with Romeo" (line 44), Mercutio correctly interprets this as offensive and so a fight begins. And when Romeo, now married to Tybalt's cousin Juliet, though without Tybalt's knowledge, uses the personal pronoun to Tybalt as a kinsman by marriage ("Tybalt, the reason that I have to love thee," etc., lines 61 ff.), Tybalt misinterprets this as an insult. "Boy," he shouts back, "this shall not excuse the injuries / That thou hast done me," etc., lines 65 ff.). "Boy" is deeply insulting, too. As readers of Shakespeare, we need to learn to read these linguistic signals.

Colloquial expressions change rapidly in any language, and for that reason the colloquialisms in Shakespeare are apt to sound unfamiliar. "Marry, come up, I trow," says the Nurse in *Romeo and Juliet* (2.5.62), meaning something like "Goodness gracious, what's all this fuss about?" It is an exclamation of impatient reproof, occasioned by what Juliet has just said to the Nurse. "Marry" is a common mild oath, originally meaning "By the Virgin Mary." "Go to" is a familiar expostulation, as when Capulet rebukes his nephew Tybalt for creating dissension over Romeo's having crashed the dance at the Capulets' house. "Go to, go to," says Capulet, "You are a saucy boy" (1.5.83–4). The Nurse's speech is full of colloquialisms: "by the rood" ("by Christ's cross"), "by my halidom" ("by all things holy," but confused popularly with "by my Holy Dame"), "now by my maidenhead at twelve year old" ("now by the virginity I still had when I was twelve"), "Nay, I do bear a brain" ("My memory is as keen as can be"), and much more (1.3.1–44). These colorful speech patterns help characterize the Nurse as of

lower social station than the Capulets whom she serves. The commentary notes and glossary can help with unfamiliar speech patterns of this sort.

Shakespeare's impressively large vocabulary contains many words no longer current in English, and, to complicate matters still further, sometimes look familiar but with a different meaning in Shakespeare's day. *An* and *An if* can both mean "if." *Wherefore* means "why." *Withal* usually simply means "with." Sometimes words convey their modern meaning along with others that are lost. *Brave* can mean "gallant, full of courage," but it more commonly means "elegantly dressed, decked out in finery," or simply "splendid." *Fond* can be tricky for us today: "fond of" can mean having a fond feeling for someone or something, but "fond" is more likely to mean "foolish, doting." *Travel* often suggests both "journey" and "hard labor, travail"; the common early spelling, "trauaile," captures the fruitful ambiguity. *Large* can mean "large" in our sense; it also suggests "liberal, bounteous, lavish." *Liberal* has a similar multiplicity of meanings: "genteel, wellborn, refined, free of speech, unrestrained, licentious." *Front* can mean "forehead." A *humor* is a mood, fancy, temperament, cast of mind; it can also be one of the four "humors" of the body that determine temperament. *Like* can mean "likely," as in Juliet's "If he be marrièd, / My grave is like to be my wedding bed" (1.5.135–6). The notes and glossary are helpful here, buttressed by an awareness on the part of the reader that terms can mean something quite apart from their normal meaning today.

Shakespeare often writes in verse, though he is also a master of prose. Verse takes getting used to. Shakespeare's favorite verse form by far is the so-called blank-verse line, in iambic pentameter. That means that each line has essentially five "feet," or metrical units. "Penta" means five, from the Latin. The "feet" in this verse form have two syllables each, normally with no stress on the first syllable and a stress on the second. Words like "todáy," "remárk," "imménse," and "suppóse" are all naturally iambic; we stress the second syllables of these words when we talk. Iambic pentameter is a verse form that more closely approximates the rhythms of English speech than other verse forms; that is presumably why it is so often used by English poets and dramatists.

Shakespeare's blank verse, then, normally has ten syllables per line, with five stresses interspersed with unaccented syllables. Here is an example from Romeo's first speech as he enters the garden below Juliet's window in Act 2, scene 2 of *Romeo and Juliet*. He is alone on stage:

> But sóft, what líght through yónder wíndow bréaks?
> It ís the éast, and Júliet ís the sún.
> Aríse, fair sún, and kíll the énvious móon,
> Who ís alréady síck and pále with gríef
> That thóu her máid art fár more fáir than shé.

We can observe here that words of more than one syllable are placed so that the stress falls on the right syllable: yónder wíndow, Júliet, Aríse, énvious, alréady. Actually, two of these words have three syllables of which the third is an added unaccented syllable: Júliet, énvious, both spoken almost as in two syllables. A certain delicate variation in the pattern of unstressed/ stressed can help prevent a sing-song effect. Then we note that the important words are stressed: sóft, líght, bréaks, ís, éast, sún, kíll, móon, síck, pále, gríef, thóu, máid, fár, fáir, shé. These words are nouns, pronouns, verbs, and adjectives. Left generally unstressed are functional words such as prepositions and conjunctions: through, and, with.

# SHAKESPEARE'S LANGUAGE

How are we as readers to proceed, in view of these unfamiliar qualities of Shakespeare's English? As we've already suggested, watching a film or video can be a good place to start, along with a reading to oneself or with friends that continually asks the questions, who are these characters that speak, and why are they speaking as they do? What are they arguing about? Other questions need to be considered as well. Again, it can be helpful to imagine oneself as a director of a production. We as readers have to stage the play in our imaginations.

Where is the action taking place in any given scene, and why are the characters here? Shakespeare is wonderfully helpful at giving us the information we need, if we read carefully; everything is to be found in what the characters say. Why does Shakespeare begin *Hamlet* with two guardsmen nervously talking to each other about their relieving of the watch? We learn shortly that it is midnight, and that the weather is very cold; the actors tell us this. Why are they so apprehensive? What is about to happen? A ghost suddenly appears. Whose spirit is this, and why is it walking in Denmark in the dead of night? What does the Ghost look like? What is it wearing? We learn shortly that it appears "in the same figure like the King that's dead." What King? How did he die? The men on watch, now joined by Hamlet's friend Horatio, agree that the resemblance of this Ghost to the dead king is striking. But why will the Ghost not answer Horatio's asking the Ghost why it has thus appeared in such a frightening shape? Why is it important that Horatio is a "scholar" if he is to speak to this Ghost?

The play thus begins with many unanswered questions, creating a sense of mystery and dread. But as we read, the conversation of the men on watch provides some answers. The dead Danish king, Hamlet's father, had fought and won a duel with the King of Norway, thereby obliging Norway to become a client state of Denmark; now that the Danish king has suddenly died, the Norwegian King's nephew, Fortinbras, is bent on invading Denmark to recover Norway's lost rights. Denmark is busy arming itself to resist that invasion. If as readers we concentrate on what we are learning that is necessary to the plot, the difficulties of language should fall into place.

What props are needed for this scene? We are not actually putting together a production as we read, so that we need not worry about practicalities that would be considered in the shop creating costumes and props, but we need to bring the scene alive in our imaginations as we read. What weapons are the guards carrying as they challenge one another and then the Ghost? The weapon is called a "partisan" in line 144; a note in the edition will explain that this is a long-handled spear, much like the halberd or battle-axe with a sharp pike that is mentioned elsewhere in Shakespeare. The particular weapon matters less than how it is deployed. Why is it that the guards' attempts to strike at it with their partisans are ineffectual? Presumably the Ghost is a disembodied spirit. The actors can easily mime an action of swinging at the Ghost, missing him but in such a way that the visual impression for the audience is one of invulnerability.

What does it mean when we learn, in scene 2, that the Ghost "wore his beaver up" and that he bore a countenance "more in sorrow than in anger"? Why are we told that "His beard was grizzled," that is, "A sable silvered," just as when old King Hamlet was still alive? These are telling details to which we want to pay attention as we read. They suggest here that the Ghost's face was indeed visible to the audience and to the Guard in scene 1, because the visor of his helmet was in its upright position, allowing the wearer to be seen. The details help confirm that this was indeed the ghost of the dead king. The very fact of the Ghost's having appeared in armor was presumably a signal of the warlike state of Denmark as well as pointing to Hamlet senior's warlike valor and armed might. All these details are revealing as we read.

Horatio presumably is not dressed like the ordinary guardsmen on duty, even if he is probably cloaked against the cold. Horatio is a gentleman. Class differences were visibly marked by costume in Shakespeare's day, and, as we read, we would do well to be sensitive to such differences. In the play's second scene, we should note that Hamlet is dressed in mourning black, whereas evidently the courtiers and their new king and queen have set aside black for something more colorful. As the new king has said to them, it has befitted the court to mourn a royal death for a time, but the time has come to move toward something more normal and even festive, mixing "mirth in funeral" and "dirge in marriage." These signals are eloquent testimonials to the haste with which Claudius has married his brother's widow. To Hamlet, such haste is unseemly, even outrageous; to the King and his court, the time has come to move on. As readers, we must be attuned to these visible distinctions. Costuming can at once enable an audience to distinguish a king from a Franciscan friar or a soothsayer or an apothecary or a fairy. We as readers must supply these staging requirements with our thoughts if we are to savor properly the gradations of rank that were so integral a part of courtly life in the Elizabethan era.

Reading a play differs in these matters from reading a short story or a novel. In such prose genres, the author has ample opportunity to spell out for the readers exactly how persons are dressed, where they live, what personal habits they practice, and the rest. Drama, and especially the highly poetic drama of an author like Shakespeare, must convey the story through dialogue. Stage directions can be provided, of course, although they tend to be sparse in the drama of Shakespeare because he was an actor in the company for which he wrote, and was thus at hand to help with blocking, gesture, inflections of speech, and the like. Reading today these scripts that were written for an acting company some 400 years ago invites us to write our own stage directions, in effect.

When the Chorus of *Henry V* opens the play with an appeal to his audience, his words are wonderfully pertinent to us as attentive readers. This is part of what he says:

> On your imaginary forces work.
> Suppose within the girdles of these walls
> Are now contained two mighty monarchies,
> Whose high upreared and abutting fronts
> The perilous narrow ocean parts asunder.
> Piece out our imperfections with your thoughts:
> Into a thousand parts divide one man,
> And make imaginary puissance.
> Think, when we talk of horses, that you see them
> Printing their proud hoofs i'th' receiving earth.
> For 'tis your thoughts that now must deck our kings,
> Carry them here and there, jumping o'er times,
> Turning the accomplishments of many years
> Into an hourglass.

This is precisely what we must do as readers. Theatrical performance, in Shakespeare's view, is a kind of shorthand, a set of clues that we as readers (or viewers in the theater) much augment with our imaginative reconstruction of how the whole thing is to look and sound and take on meaning. We must visualize horses when they are talked about. We must suppose a world of human action that can encompass a battle between two kingdoms, or between two families, or indeed between the elemental forces of good and evil. We must "piece out" the imperfections of a stage presentation or the dramatist's script with our thoughts, making "imaginary puissance." We must understand that actions of several years can be compressed "into an hourglass"—a shorthand expression for the time needed for performance. Our sense of place must be equally flexible, as we move from Venice to Cyprus in *Othello* or from the royal court to Scotland and thence to England's southwest counties and finally to Dover cliffs in the course of *King Lear*.

Once you have read through the play in this way of bringing it to life as a theatrical experience, and have (if possible) supplemented that journey by savoring the play in a good performance in film or video (or, best of all, on stage if a production is available), you will then be in a good position to go back through the play with the assistance of the notes and commentary, including the Introduction. The information here can be invaluable, and will, we hope, enrich and test the perceptions you have already begun to form in your first reading. The reason I am suggesting that you postpone the notes to this second stage is that you should first try to enjoy the play as performance, just as you would if you were seeing it on stage or in film, even if seeing it for the first time. Let it roll over you as you react to its power, its humor, its brilliant insights. Shakespeare's plays work splendidly for those who encounter them for the first time in performance. Do what you can to give yourself that pleasure. For now, when the language seems difficult, go right on and listen to what is being said.

For a more detailed essay on the topic we have been discussing here, with illustrations from *A Midsummer Night's Dream, Romeo and Juliet, 1 Henry IV, Hamlet, King Lear*, and *The Tempest*, you might want to take a look at my *How to Read a Shakespeare Play* (Oxford: Blackwell Publishing, 2006). If you are interested in a further discussion of Shakespeare's style as it develops from his early to his late work, the pronunciation of Shakespeare's language in its own day, his conventions of grammar and rhetoric, and his vocabulary, I can refer you to earlier editions of *The Complete Works of Shakespeare* (seventh edition, 2014); this present, shorter account of Shakespeare's English takes the place of those more specialized analyses. Similarly, the section in previous editions on "Editions and Editors of Shakespeare" is omitted here as of specialized interest; it too is available in those earlier editions.

## SHAKESPEARE CRITICISM

In his own time, Shakespeare achieved a reputation for immortal greatness that is astonishing when we consider the low regard in which playwrights were then generally held. Francis Meres compared him to Ovid, Plautus, and Seneca, and proclaimed Shakespeare to be England's most excellent writer in both comedy and tragedy. John Weever spoke of "honey-tongued Shakespeare." The number of such praising allusions is high. Even Ben Jonson, a learned writer strongly influenced by the classical tradition, lauded Shakespeare as "a monument without a tomb," England's best poet, exceeding

Chaucer, Spenser, Beaumont, Kyd, and Marlowe. In tragedy, Jonson compared Shakespeare with Aeschylus, Euripides, and Sophocles; in comedy, he insisted Shakespeare had no rival even in "insolent Greece or haughty Rome." This tribute appeared in Jonson's commendatory poem written for the Shakespeare First Folio of 1623.

To be sure, Jonson had more critical things to say about Shakespeare. Even in the Folio commendatory poem, Jonson could not resist a dig at Shakespeare's "small Latin, and less Greek." To William Drummond of Hawthornden, he objected that Shakespeare "wanted art" because in a play (*The Winter's Tale*) he "brought in a number of men saying they had suffered shipwreck in Bohemia, where there is no sea near by some hundred miles." In *Timber, or Discoveries*, Jonson chided Shakespeare for his unrestrained facility in writing. "The players have often mentioned it as an honor to Shakespeare, that in his writing, whatsoever he penned he never blotted out [a] line. My answer hath been, would he had blotted a thousand." In a prologue to his own play, *Every Man in His Humor* (1616 edition), Jonson satirized English history plays (such as Shakespeare's) that "with three rusty swords, / And help of some few foot-and-half-foot words, / Fight over York and Lancaster's long jars, / And in the tiring-house bring wounds to scars." He also jeered at plays lacking unity of time in which children grow to the age of sixty or older and at nonsensical romantic plays featuring fireworks, thunder, and a chorus that "wafts you o'er the seas."

These criticisms are all of a piece. As a classicist himself, Jonson held in high regard the classical unities. He deplored much English popular drama, including some of Shakespeare's plays, for their undisciplined mixture of comedy and tragedy. Measured against his cherished ideals of classical decorum and refinement of language, Shakespeare's histories and the late romances—*Pericles, Cymbeline, The Winter's Tale*, and *The Tempest*—seemed irritatingly naive and loose-jointed. Yet Jonson knew that Shakespeare had an incomparable genius, superior even to his own. Jonson's affection and respect for Shakespeare seem to have been quite unforced. In the midst of his critical remarks in *Timber*, he freely conceded that "I loved the man, and do honor his memory (on this side idolatry) as much as any. He was indeed honest, and of an open and free nature, had an excellent fantasy, brave notions, and gentle expressions."

## The Age of Dryden and Pope

Jonson's attitude toward Shakespeare lived on into the Restoration period of the late seventeenth century. A commonplace of that age held it proper to "admire" Ben Jonson but to "love" Shakespeare. Jonson was the more correct poet, the better model for imitation. Shakespeare often had to be rewritten according to the sophisticated tastes of the Restoration (see Appendix 3 for an account of Restoration stage adaptations of Shakespeare), but he

was also regarded as a natural genius. Dryden reflected this view in his *Essay of Dramatic Poesy* (1668) and his *Essay on the Dramatic Poetry of the Last Age* (1672). Dryden condemned *The Winter's Tale, Pericles,* and several other late romances for "the lameness of their plots" and for their "ridiculous incoherent story" which is usually "grounded on impossibilities." Not only Shakespeare, he charged, but several of his contemporaries "neither understood correct plotting nor that which they call *the decorum of the stage.*" Had Shakespeare lived in the Restoration, Dryden believed, he would doubtless have written "more correctly" under the influence of a language that had become more "courtly" and a wit that had grown more "refined." Shakespeare, he thought, had limitless "fancy" but sometimes lacked "judgment." Dryden regretted that Shakespeare had been forced to write in "ignorant" times and for audiences who "knew no better." Like Jonson, nevertheless, Dryden had the magnanimity to perceive that Shakespeare transcended his limitations. Shakespeare, said Dryden, was "the man who of all modern and perhaps ancient poets had the largest and most comprehensive soul." From a classical writer, this was high praise indeed.

Alexander Pope's edition of Shakespeare (1725) was based upon a similar estimate of Shakespeare as an untutored genius. Pope freely "improved" Shakespeare's language, rewriting lines and excising those parts he considered vulgar, in order to rescue Shakespeare from the barbaric circumstances of his Elizabethan milieu. Other critics of the Restoration and early eighteenth century who stressed Shakespeare's "natural" genius and imaginative powers were John Dennis, Joseph Addison, and the editors Nicholas Rowe and Lewis Theobald.

## The Age of Johnson

Shakespeare was not without his detractors during the late seventeenth and early eighteenth centuries; after all, classical criticism tended to distrust imagination and fancy. Notable among the harsher critics of the Restoration period was Thomas Rymer, whose *Short View of Tragedy* (1692) included a famous attack on *Othello* for making too much out of Desdemona's handkerchief. In the eighteenth century, Voltaire spoke out sharply against Shakespeare's violation of the classical unities, though Voltaire also had some admiring things to say.

The most considered answer to such criticism in the later eighteenth century was that of Dr. Samuel Johnson, in his edition of Shakespeare's plays and its great preface (1765). Shakespeare, said Johnson, is the poet of nature who "holds up to his readers a faithful mirror of manners and of life. His characters are not modified by the customs of particular places, unpracticed by the rest of the world. … In the writings of other poets a character is too often an individual; in those of Shakespeare it is commonly a species." Johnson's attitudes were essentially classical in that he praised Shakespeare for being universal, for having provided a "just representation of general nature," and for having stood the test of time. Yet Johnson also magnanimously praised Shakespeare for having transcended the classical rules. Johnson triumphantly vindicated the mixture of comedy and tragedy in Shakespeare's plays and the supposed indecorum of his characters.

Of course, Johnson did not praise everything he saw. He objected to Shakespeare's loose construction of plot, careless huddling together of the ends of his plays, licentious humor, and, above all, the punning wordplay. He deplored Shakespeare's failure to satisfy the demands of poetic justice, especially in *King Lear,* and he regretted that Shakespeare seemed more anxious to please than to instruct. Still, Johnson did much to free Shakespeare from the constraint of an overly restrictive classical approach to criticism.

## The Age of Coleridge

With the beginning of the Romantic period, in England and on the Continent, Shakespeare criticism increasingly turned away from classical precept in favor of a more spontaneous and enthusiastic approach to Shakespeare's creative genius. The new Shakespeare became indeed a rallying cry for those who now deplored such "regular" dramatic poets as Racine and Corneille. Shakespeare became a seer, a bard with mystic powers of insight into the human condition. Goethe, in *Wilhelm Meister* (1796), conceived of Hamlet as the archetypal "Romantic" poet: melancholic, delicate, and unable to act.

Critical trends in England moved toward similar conclusions. Maurice Morgann, in his *Essay on the Dramatic Character of Sir John Falstaff* (1777), glorified Falstaff into a rare individual of courage, dignity, and—yes—honor. To do so, Morgann; had to suppress much evidence as to Falstaff's overall function in the *Henry IV* plays. Dramatic structure, in fact, did not interest Morgann; his passion was "character," and his study of Falstaff reflected a new Romantic preoccupation with character analysis. Like other character critics who followed him, Morgann tended to move away from the play itself and into a world where the dramatic personage being considered might lead an independent existence. What would it have been like to know Falstaff as a real person? How would he have behaved on occasions other than those reported by Shakespeare? Such questions fascinated Morgann and others because they led into grand speculations about human psychology and philosophy. Shakespeare's incomparably penetrating insights into character prompted further investigations of the human psyche.

Other late eighteenth-century works devoted to the study of character included Lord Kames's *Elements of Criticism* (1762), Thomas Whately's *Remarks on Some of the Characters of Shakespeare* (1785), William Richardson's *Philosophical Analysis and Illustration of Some of Shakespeare's Remarkable Characters* (1774), and William Jackson's *Thirty Letters on Various Subjects* (1782). Morgann spoke for this school of critics when he insisted, "It may be fit to consider them [Shakespeare's characters] rather as historic than dramatic beings; and, when occasion requires, to account for their conduct from the whole of character, from general principles, from latent motives, and from policies not avowed."

Samuel Taylor Coleridge, the greatest of the English Romantic critics, was profoundly influenced by character criticism, both English and continental. He himself made important contributions to the study of character. His conception of Hamlet, derived in part from Goethe and Hegel, as one who "vacillates from sensibility, and procrastinates from thought, and loses the power of action in the energy of resolve," was to dominate nineteenth-century interpretations of Hamlet. His insight into Iago's evil nature—"the motive-hunting of a motiveless malignity"— was also influential.

Nevertheless, Coleridge did not succumb to the temptation, as did so many character critics, of ignoring the unity of an entire play. Quite to the contrary, he affirmed in Shakespeare an "organic form" or "innate" sense of shape, developed from within, that gave new meaning to Shakespeare's fusion of comedy and tragedy, his seeming anachronisms, his improbable fictions, and his supposedly rambling plots. Coleridge heaped scorn on the eighteenth-century idea of Shakespeare as a "natural" but untaught genius. He praised Shakespeare not for having mirrored life, as Dr. Johnson had said, but for having created an imaginative world attuned to its own internal harmonies. He saw Shakespeare as an inspired but deliberate artist who fitted together the parts of his imaginative world with consummate skill. "The judgment of Shakespeare is commensurate with his genius."

In all this, Coleridge was remarkably close to his German contemporary and rival, August Wilhelm Schlegel, who insisted that Shakespeare was "a profound artist, and not a blind and wildly luxuriant genius." In Shakespeare's plays, said Schlegel, "The fancy lays claim to be considered as an independent mental power governed according to its own laws." Between them, Coleridge and Schlegel utterly inverted the critical values of the previous age, substituting "sublimity" and "imagination" for universality and trueness to nature.

Other Romantic critics included William Hazlitt (*Characters of Shakespear's Plays,* 1817), Charles Lamb (*On the Tragedies of Shakespeare,* 1811), and Thomas De Quincey (*On the Knocking at the Gate in Macbeth,* 1823). Hazlitt reveals a political liberalism characteristic of a number of Romantic writers in his skeptical view of Henry V's absolutism and his imperialist war against the French. John

Keats has some penetrating things to say in his letters about Shakespeare's "negative capability," or his ability to see into characters' lives with an extraordinary self-effacing sympathy. As a whole, the Romantics were enthusiasts of Shakespeare, and sometimes even idolaters. Yet they consistently refused to recognize him as a man of the theater. Lamb wrote, "It may seem a paradox, but I cannot help being of the opinion that the plays of Shakespeare are less calculated for performance on a stage than those of almost any other dramatist whatever." Hazlitt similarly observed: "We do not like to see our author's plays acted, and least of all, *Hamlet*. There is no play that suffers so much in being transferred to the stage." These hostile attitudes toward the theater reflected, in part, the condition of the stage in nineteenth-century England. In part, however, these attitudes were the inevitable result of character criticism, or what Lamb called the desire "to know the internal workings and movements of a great mind, of an Othello or a Hamlet for instance, the *when* and the *why* and the *how far* they should be moved." This fascination with character swept everything before it during the Romantic period.

## A. C. Bradley and the Turn of the Century

The tendency of nineteenth-century criticism, then, was to exalt Shakespeare as a poet and a philosopher rather than as a playwright, and as a creator of immortal characters whose "lives" might be studied as though existing independent of a dramatic text. Not infrequently, this critical approach led to a biographical interpretation of Shakespeare through his plays, on the assumption that what he wrote was his own spiritual autobiography and a key to his own fascinating character. Perhaps the most famous critical study in this line was Edward Dowden's *Shakspere: A Critical Study of His Mind and Art* (1875), in which he traced a progression from Shakespeare's early exuberance and passionate involvement through brooding pessimism to a final philosophical calm.

At the same time, the nineteenth century also saw the rise of a more factual and methodological scholarship, especially in the German universities. Dowden, in fact, reflected this trend as well, for one of the achievements of philological study was to establish with some accuracy the dating of Shakespeare's plays and thus make possible an analysis of his artistic development. Hermann Ulrici's *Über Shakespeares dramatische Kunst* (1839) and Gottfried Gervinus's edition of 1849 were among the earliest studies to interest themselves in Shakespeare's chronological development.

The critic who best summed up the achievement of nineteenth-century Shakespeare criticism was A. C. Bradley, in his *Shakespearean Tragedy* (1904) and other studies. *Shakespearean Tragedy* dealt with the four "great" tragedies: *Hamlet*, *Othello*, *King Lear*, and *Macbeth*. Brad-

ley revealed his Romantic tendencies in his focus on psychological analysis of character, but he also brought to his work a scholarly awareness of the text that had been missing in some earlier character critics. His work continues to have considerable influence today, despite modern tendencies to rebel against nineteenth-century idealism. To Bradley, Shakespeare's tragic world was ultimately explicable and profoundly moral. Despite the overwhelming impression of tragic waste in *King Lear*, he argued, we as audience experience a sense of compensation and completion that implies an ultimate pattern in human life. "Good, in the widest sense, seems thus to be the principle of life and health in the world; evil, at least in these worst forms, to be a poison. The world reacts against it violently, and, in the struggle to expel it, is driven to devastate itself." Humanity must suffer because of its fatal tendency to pursue some extreme passion, but humanity learns through suffering about itself and the nature of its world. We as audience are reconciled to our existence through purgative release; we smile through our tears. Cordelia is wantonly destroyed, but the fact of her transcendent goodness is eternal. Although in one sense she fails, said Bradley, she is "in another sense superior to the world in which [she] appears; is, in some way which we do not seek to define, untouched by the doom that overtakes [her]; and is rather set free from life than deprived of it."

## Historical Criticism

The first major twentieth-century reaction against character criticism was that of the so-called historical critics. (On the later critical movement known as the New Historicism, see below, following "Jan Kott and the Theater of the Absurd.") These critics insisted on a more hardheaded and skeptical appraisal of Shakespeare through better understanding of his historical milieu: his theater, his audience, and his political and social environment. In good part, this movement was the result of a new professionalism of Shakespearean studies in the twentieth century. Whereas earlier critics—Dryden, Pope, Johnson, and Coleridge—had generally been literary amateurs in the best sense, early twentieth-century criticism became increasingly the province of those who taught in universities. Historical research became a professional activity. Bradley himself was Professor of English Literature at Liverpool and Oxford, and did much to legitimize the incorporation of Shakespeare into the humanities curriculum. German scholarship produced the first regular periodical devoted to Shakespeare studies, *Shakespeare-Jahrbuch*, to be followed in due course in England and America by *Shakespeare Survey* (beginning in 1948), *Shakespeare Quarterly* (1950), and *Shakespeare Studies* (1965).

From the start, historical criticism took a new look at Shakespeare as a man of the theater. Sir Walter Raleigh

(Professor of English Literature at Oxford, not to be confused with his Elizabethan namesake) rejected the Romantic absorption in psychology and turned his attention instead to the artistic methods by which plays affect theater-going spectators. The poet Robert Bridges insisted that Shakespeare had often sacrificed consistency and logic for primitive theatrical effects designed to please his vulgar audience. Bridges's objections were often based on a serious lack of information about Shakespeare's stage, but they had a healthy iconoclastic effect nonetheless on the scholarship of his time. In Germany, Levin Schücking pursued a similar line of reasoning in his *Character Problems in Shakespeare's Plays* (1917, translated into English in 1922). Schücking argued that Shakespeare had disregarded coherent structure and had striven instead for vivid dramatic effect ("episodic intensification") in his particular scenes. Schücking's *The Meaning of Hamlet* (1937) explained the strange contradictions of that play as resulting from primitive and brutal Germanic source materials which Shakespeare had not fully assimilated.

A keynote for historical critics of the early twentieth century was the concept of artifice or convention in the construction of a play. Perhaps the leading spokesman for this approach was E. E. Stoll, a student of G. L. Kittredge of Harvard University, himself a leading force in historical scholarship in America. Stoll vigorously insisted, in such works as *Othello: An Historical and Comparative Study* (1915), *Hamlet: An Historical and Comparative Study* (1919), and *Art and Artifice in Shakespeare* (1933), that a critic must never be sidetracked by moral, psychological, or biographical interpretations. A play, he argued, is an artifice arising out of its historical milieu. Its conventions are implicit agreements between playwright and spectator. They alter with time, and a modern reader who is ignorant of Elizabethan conventions is all too apt to be misled by his own post-Romantic preconceptions. For example, a calumniator like Iago in *Othello* is conventionally supposed to be believed by the other characters on stage. We do not need to speculate about the "realities" of Othello's being duped, and, in fact, we are likely to be led astray by such Romantic speculations. Stoll went so far as to affirm, in fact, that Shakespearean drama intentionally distorts reality through its theatrical conventions, in order to fulfill its own existence as artifice. *Hamlet* is not a play about delay, but a revenge story of a certain length, containing many conventional revenge motifs, such as the ghost and the "mousetrap" scheme used to test the villain, and deriving many of its circumstances from Shakespeare's sources; delay is a conventional device needed to continue the story to its conclusion.

Stoll's zeal led to excessive claims for historical criticism, as one might expect in the early years of a pioneering movement. At its extreme, historical criticism came close to implying that Shakespeare was a mere

product of his environment. Indeed, the movement owed many of its evolutionist assumptions to the supposedly scientific "social Darwinism" of Thomas Huxley and other late nineteenth-century social philosophers. In more recent years, however, the crusading spirit has given way to a more moderate historical criticism that continues to be an important part of Shakespearean scholarship.

Alfred Harbage, for example, in *As They Liked It* (1947) and *Shakespeare and the Rival Traditions* (1952), has analyzed the audience for which Shakespeare wrote and the rivalry between popular and elite theaters in the London of his day. Harbage sees Shakespeare as a popular dramatist writing for a highly intelligent, enthusiastic, and socially diversified audience. More recently, in *The Privileged Playgoers of Shakespeare's London, 1576–1642* (1981), Ann Jennalie Cook has qualified Harbage's view, arguing that Shakespeare's audience was, for the most part, affluent and well connected. G. E. Bentley has amassed an invaluable storehouse of information about *The Jacobean and Caroline Stage* (1941–1968), just as E. K. Chambers earlier had collected documents and data on *The Elizabethan Stage* (1923). Other studies by historical scholars include Chambers's *William Shakespeare: A Study of Facts and Problems* (1930), and Bentley's *Shakespeare and His Theatre* (1964) and *The Profession of Dramatist in Shakespeare's Time* (1971). T. W. Baldwin exemplifies the historical scholar who, like Stoll, claims too much for the method; nevertheless, much information on Shakespeare's schooling, reading, and professional theatrical life is available in such works as *William Shakspere's Small Latine and Lesse Greeke* (1944) and *The Organization and Personnel of the Shakespearean Company* (1927). Hardin Craig uses historical method in *An Interpretation of Shakespeare* (1948).

Historical criticism has contributed greatly to our knowledge of the staging of Shakespeare's plays. George Pierce Baker, in *The Development of Shakespeare as a Dramatist* (1907), continued the line of investigation begun by Walter Raleigh. Harley Granville-Barker brought to his *Prefaces to Shakespeare* (1930, 1946) a wealth of professional theatrical experience of his own. Ever since his time, the new theatrical method of interpreting Shakespeare has been based to an ever increasing extent on a genuine revival of interest in Shakespearean production. John Dover Wilson shows an awareness of the stage in *What Happens in Hamlet* (1935) and *The Fortunes of Falstaff* (1943). At its best, as in John Russell Brown's *Shakespeare's Plays in Performance* (1966), in John Styan's *Shakespeare's Stagecraft* (1967), in Michael Goldman's *Shakespeare and the Energies of Drama* (1972), and in Alan Dessen's *Elizabethan Drama and the Viewer's Eye* (1977) and his *Recovering Shakespeare's Theatrical Vocabulary* (1995), this critical method reveals many insights into the text that are hard to obtain without an awareness of theatrical technique.

Supporting this theatrical criticism, historical research has learned a great deal about the physical nature of Shakespeare's stage. J. C. Adams's well-known model of the Globe Playhouse, as presented in Irwin Smith's *Shakespeare's Globe Playhouse: A Modern Reconstruction* (1956), is now generally discredited in favor of a simpler building, as reconstructed by C. Walter Hodges (*The Globe Restored*, 1953, 2nd edition, 1968), Bernard Beckerman (*Shakespeare at the Globe*, 1962, 2nd edition, 1967), Richard Hosley ("The Playhouses and the Stage" in *A New Companion to Shakespeare Studies*, edited by K. Muir and S. Schoenbaum, 1971, and several other good essays), T. J. King (*Shakespearean Staging, 1599–1642*, 1971), and others. Information on the private theaters, such as the Blackfriars, where Shakespeare's plays were also performed, appears in William Armstrong, *The Elizabethan Private Theatres* (1958); Richard Hosley, "A Reconstruction of the Second Blackfriars" (*The Elizabethan Theatre*, 1969); Glynne Wickham, *Early English Stages* (1959–1972); and others. For further information on innyard theaters and on courtly or private theaters, see the contributions of Herbert Berry, D. F. Rowan, W. Reavley Gair, and others cited in the bibliography at the end of this volume.

A related pursuit of historical criticism has been the better understanding of Shakespeare through his dramatic predecessors and contemporaries. Willard Farnham, in *The Medieval Heritage of Elizabethan Tragedy* (1936), traces the evolution of native English tragedy through the morality plays of the early Tudor period. J. M. R. Margeson's *The Origins of English Tragedy* (1967) broadens the pattern to include still other sources for Elizabethan ideas on dramatic tragedy. Bernard Spivack, in *Shakespeare and the Allegory of Evil* (1958), sees Iago, Edmund, Richard III, and other boasting villains in Shakespeare as descendants of the morality Vice. In *Shakespeare and the Idea of the Play* (1962), Anne Righter (Barton) traces the device of the play-within-the-play and the metaphor of the world as a stage back to medieval and classical ideas of dramatic illusion. Irving Ribner's *The English History Play in the Age of Shakespeare* (1959, revised 1965) examines Shakespeare's plays on English history in the context of the popular Elizabethan genre to which they belonged. Robert Weimann's *Shakespeare and the Popular Tradition in the Theatre* (translated from the German in 1978) is a Marxist study in the social dimension of dramatic form and function. Many other studies of this sort could be cited, including Glynne Wickham's *Shakespeare's Dramatic Heritage* (1969), Oscar J. Campbell's *Shakespeare's Satire* (1943), M. C. Bradbrook's *Themes and Conventions of Elizabethan Tragedy* (1935), and S. L. Bethell's *Shakespeare and the Popular Dramatic Tradition* (1944).

Another important concern of historical criticism has been the relationship between Shakespeare and the ideas of his age—cosmological, philosophical, and political.

Among the first scholars to study Elizabethan cosmology were Hardin Craig in *The Enchanted Glass* (1936) and A. O. Lovejoy in *The Great Chain of Being* (1936). As their successor, E. M. W. Tillyard provided in *The Elizabethan World Picture* (1943) a definitive view of the conservative and hierarchical values that Elizabethans were supposed to have espoused. In *Shakespeare's History Plays* (1944), Tillyard extended his essentially conservative view of Shakespeare's philosophical outlook to the histories, arguing that they embody a "Tudor myth" and thereby lend support to the Tudor state. Increasingly, however, critics have disputed the extent to which Shakespeare in fact endorsed the "establishment" values of the Elizabethan world picture. Theodore Spencer, in *Shakespeare and the Nature of Man* (1942), discusses the impact on Shakespeare of radical new thinkers like Machiavelli, Montaigne, and Copernicus. In political matters, Henry A. Kelly's *Divine Providence in the England of Shakespeare's Histories* (1970) has challenged the existence of a single "Tudor myth" and has argued that Shakespeare's history plays reflect contrasting political philosophies set dramatically in conflict with one another. M. M. Reese's *The Cease of Majesty* (1961) also offers a graceful corrective to Tillyard's lucid but occasionally one-sided interpretations. Revisions in this direction continue in the work of the so-called new historicists and cultural materialists, to be discussed below.

Historical criticism has also yielded many profitable specialized studies, in which Shakespeare is illuminated by a better understanding of various sciences of his day. Lily Bess Campbell approaches Shakespearean tragedy through Renaissance psychology in *Shakespeare's Tragic Heroes: Slaves of Passion* (1930). Paul Jorgensen uses Elizabethan documents on the arts of war and generalship in his study *Shakespeare's Military World* (1956). Many similar studies examine Shakespeare in relation to law, medicine, and other professions.

## *"New" Criticism*

As we have seen, historical criticism is still an important part of Shakespeare criticism; for better or worse, it is the stuff of some research-oriented universities and their Ph.D. programs. Since its beginning, however, historical criticism has had to face a critical reaction, generated, in part, by its own utilitarian and fact-gathering tendencies. The suggestions urged by Stoll and others that Shakespeare was the product of his cultural and theatrical environment tended to obscure his achievement as a poet. Amassing of information about Shakespeare's reading or his theatrical company often seemed to inhibit the scholar from responding to the power of words and images.

Such at any rate was the rallying cry of the *Scrutiny* group in England, centered on F. R. Leavis, L. C. Knights, and Derek Traversi, and the "new" critics in America, such as Cleanth Brooks. The new critics demanded close attention to the poetry without the encumbrance of historical research. Especially at first, the new critics were openly hostile to any criticism distracting readers from the text. The satirical force of the movement can perhaps best be savored in L. C. Knights's "How Many Children Had Lady Macbeth?" (1933), prompted by the learned appendices in Bradley's *Shakespearean Tragedy*: "When was the murder of Duncan first plotted? Did Lady Macbeth really faint? Duration of the action in *Macbeth*. Macbeth's age. 'He has no children.'"

In part, the new critical movement was (and still is) a pedagogical movement, a protest against the potential dryness of historical footnoting and an insistence that classroom study of Shakespeare ought to focus on a response to his language. Cleanth Brooks's "The Naked Babe and the Cloak of Manliness" (in *The Well Wrought Urn*, 1947) offers to the teacher a model of close reading that focuses on imagery and yet attempts to see a whole vision of the play through its language. G. Wilson Knight concentrates on imagery and verbal texture, sometimes to the exclusion of the play as a whole, in his *The Wheel of Fire* (1930), *The Imperial Theme* (1931), *The Shakespearian Tempest* (1932), *The Crown of Life* (1947), and others. William Empson is best known for his *Seven Types of Ambiguity* (1930) and *Some Versions of Pastoral* (1935). Derek Traversi's works include *An Approach to Shakespeare* (1938), *Shakespeare: The Last Phase* (1954), *Shakespeare: From Richard II to Henry V* (1957), and *Shakespeare: The Roman Plays* (1963). Perhaps the greatest critic of this school has been L. C. Knights, whose books include *Explorations* (1946), *Some Shakespearean Themes* (1959), *An Approach to Hamlet* (1960), and *Further Explorations* (1965). T. S. Eliot's perceptive and controversial observations have also had an important influence on critics of this school. Other studies making good use of the new critical method include Robert Heilman's *This Great Stage* (1948) and *Magic in the Web* (1956). Many of these critics are concerned not only with language, but also with the larger moral and structural implications of Shakespeare's plays as discovered through a sensitive reading of the text.

More specialized studies of Shakespearean imagery and language include Caroline Spurgeon's *Shakespeare's Imagery and What It Tells Us* (1935). Its classifications are now recognized to be overly statistical and restricted in definition, but the work has nonetheless prompted valuable further study. Among later works are Sister Miriam Joseph's *Shakespeare's Use of the Arts of Language* (1947, partly reprinted in *Rhetoric in Shakespeare's Time*, 1962), Wolfgang Clemen's *The Development of Shakespeare's Imagery* (1951), and M. M. Mahood's *Shakespeare's Wordplay* (1957). The study of prose has not received as much attention as that of poetry, although Brian Vickers's *The Artistry of Shakespeare's Prose* (1968) and Milton Crane's *Shakespeare's Prose* (1951) make significant contributions.

See also Edward Armstrong's *Shakespeare's Imagination* (1963) and Kirby Farrell's *Shakespeare's Creation: The Language of Magic and Play* (1975).

A more recent development in studies of Shakespeare's imagery has led to the examination of visual images in the theater as part of Shakespeare's art. Reginald Foakes ("Suggestions for a New Approach to Shakespeare's Imagery," *Shakespeare Survey*, 5, 1952, 81–92) and Maurice Charney (*Shakespeare's Roman Plays: The Function of Imagery in the Drama*, 1961) were among the first to notice that Caroline Spurgeon and other "new" critics usually excluded stage picture in their focus on verbal image patterns. Yet Shakespeare's extensive involvement with the practicalities of theatrical production might well lead one to suspect that he arranges his stage with care and that the plays are full of hints as to how he communicates through visual means. Costume, properties, the theater building, the blocking of actors in visual patterns onstage, expression, movement—all of these contribute to the play's artistic whole. Francis Fergusson analyzes the way in which the Elizabethan theatrical building provides *Hamlet* with an eloquently expressive idea of order and hierarchy, against which are ironically juxtaposed Claudius's acts of killing a king and marrying his widow (*The Idea of a Theater*, 1949). Other studies of stage imagery include Ann Pasternak Slater's *Shakespeare the Director* (1982) and David Bevington's *Action Is Eloquence: Shakespeare's Language of Gesture* (1984).

Another call for expansion of the occasionally narrow limits of "new" criticism comes from the so-called Chicago school of criticism, centered on R. S. Crane, Richard McKeon, Elder Olson, Bernard Weinberg, and others, who, in the 1950s and 1960s, espoused a formal or structural approach to criticism, using Aristotle as its point of departure. Crane was reacting to the new critics who, in his view, restricted the kinds of answers they could obtain by limiting themselves to one methodology. Critics hostile to the Chicago school have responded, to be sure, that Crane's own approach tends to produce its own dogmatism. Formalist analyses of Shakespeare plays are to be found, for example, in the work of W. R. Keast, Wayne Booth, and Norman Maclean; see *Critics and Criticism*, edited by R. S. Crane (1952) and the bibliography at the back of this book.

## Psychological Criticism

In a sense, Freudian and other psychological criticism continues the "character" criticism of the nineteenth century. Freudian critics sometimes follow a character into a world outside the text, analyzing Hamlet (for instance) as though he were a real person whose childhood traumas can be inferred from the symptoms he displays. The most famous work in this vein is *Hamlet and Oedipus* (1910, revised 1949), by Freud's disciple, Ernest Jones, who develops Freud's own idea that Hamlet's delay is caused by an oedipal trauma. Hamlet's uncle, Claudius, has done exactly what Hamlet himself incestuously and subconsciously wished to do: kill his father and marry his mother. Because he cannot articulate these forbidden impulses to himself, Hamlet is paralyzed into inactivity. This critical analysis thus assumes, as did such Romantic critics as Coleridge, that the central problem of *Hamlet* is one of character and motivation: why does Hamlet delay? Many modern critics would deny that this is a problem or would insist, at least, that by setting such a problem, Jones has limited the number of possible answers. Avi Erlich proposes an entirely different psychological reading of the play in *Hamlet's Absent Father*, 1977. Psychological criticism sometimes also reveals its affinities with nineteenth-century character criticism in its attempt to analyze Shakespeare's personality through his plays, as though the works constituted a spiritual autobiography. The terminology of psychological criticism is suspect to some readers because it is at least superficially anachronistic when dealing with a Renaissance writer. The terminology is also sometimes overburdened with technical jargon.

Nonetheless, psychological criticism has afforded many insights into Shakespeare not readily available through other modes of perception. Jones's book makes clear the intensity of Hamlet's revulsion toward women as a result of his mother's inconstancy. At a mythic level, Hamlet's story certainly resembles that of Oedipus, and Freudian criticism is often at its best when it shows us this universal aspect of the human psyche. Freudian terminology need not be anachronistic when it deals with timeless truths. Psychological criticism can reveal to us Shakespeare's preoccupation with certain types of women in his plays, such as the domineering and threatening masculine type (Joan of Arc, Margaret of Anjou) or, conversely, the long-suffering and patient heroine (Helena in *All's Well,* Hermione in *The Winter's Tale*). Psychological criticism is perhaps most useful in studying family relationships in Shakespeare. It also has much to say about the psychic or sexual connotations of symbols. Influential books include Norman O. Brown's *Life Against Death: The Psychoanalytical Meaning of History* (1959) and Norman Holland's *Psychoanalysis and Shakespeare* (1966) and *The Shakespearean Imagination* (1964).

Richard Wheeler's *Turn and Counter-Turn: Shakespeare's Development and the Problem Comedies* (1981) applies psychoanalytic method to a study of Shakespeare's development, in which, as Wheeler sees it, the sonnets and the problem plays are pivotal as Shakespeare turns from the safely contained worlds of romantic comedy (with non-threatening heroines) and the English history play (in which women are generally denied anything more than a marginal role in state affairs) to the tragedies, in which sexual conflict is shown in all its potentially terrifying destructiveness. Wheeler's completion of C. L. Barber's

*The Whole Journey: Shakespeare's Power of Development* (1986) continues the study of Shakespeare's development in the late plays. The dichotomies of gender and genre urged in these studies and continued by Linda Bamber (*Comic Women, Tragic Men: A Study of Gender and Genre in Shakespeare,* 1982), among others, have been challenged by Jonathan Goldberg in his essay, "Shakespearean Inscriptions: The Voicing of Power," in *Shakespeare and the Question of Theory* (edited by Patricia Parker and Geoffrey Hartman, 1985). A collection of essays under the editorship of Murray Schwartz and Coppélia Kahn, *Representing Shakespeare* (1980), affords a sample of work by Janet Adelman, David Wilbern, Meredith Skura, David Sundelson, Madelon Gohlke Sprengnether, Joel Fineman, and others.

Much psychoanalytic criticism of the 1980s has sought to displace Freud's emphasis upon the relation of son and father in the oedipal triangle in favor of attention to the mother and child preoedipal relation; a model here is the work of Karen Horney (e.g., *Neurosis and Human Growth: The Struggle Toward Self-Realization*, 1950). Jacques Lacan (*Écrits,* translated by Alan Sheridan, 1977) and Erik Erikson (*Childhood and Selfhood,* 1978) are also prominent theorists in the post-Freudian era. Despite such changes, the psychoanalytic critic still attempts to discover in the language of the play the means by which he or she can reconstruct an early stage in the development of one or more of the dramatic characters.

## Mythological Criticism

Related to psychological criticism is the search for archetypal myth in literature, as an expression of the "collective unconscious" of the human race. Behind such an approach lie the anthropological and psychological assumptions of Carl Jung and his followers. One of the earliest studies of this sort was Gilbert Murray's *Hamlet and Orestes* (1914), analyzing the archetype of revenge for a murdered father. Clearly this custom goes far back into tribal prehistory and emerges in varying but interrelated forms in many different societies. This anthropological universality enables us to look at Hamlet as the heightened manifestation of an incredibly basic story. *Hamlet* gives shape to urgings that are a part of our innermost social being. The struggle between the civilized and the primitive goes on in us as in the play *Hamlet*.

The vast interdisciplinary character of mythological criticism leaves it vulnerable to charges of speculativeness and glib theorizing. At its best, however, mythological criticism can illuminate the nature of our responses as audience to a work of art. Northrop Frye argues, in *A Natural Perspective* (1965), that we respond to mythic patterns by imagining ourselves participating in them communally. The Greek drama emerged, after all, from Dionysiac ritual. All drama celebrates in one form or another the primal myths of vegetation, from the death of the year to the renewal or resurrection of life. In his most influential book, *Anatomy of Criticism* (1957), Frye argues that mythic criticism presents a universal scheme for the investigation of all literature, or all art, since art is itself the ordering of our most primal stirrings. Frye sees in drama (as in other literature) a fourfold correspondence to the cyclical pattern of the year: comedy is associated with spring, romance with summer, tragedy with autumn, and satire with winter. Historically, civilization moves through a recurrent cycle from newness to decadence and decay; this cycle expresses itself culturally in a progression from epic and romance to tragedy, to social realism, and, finally, to irony and satire before the cycle renews itself. Thus, according to Frye, the genres of dramatic literature (and of other literary forms as well) have an absolute and timeless relationship to myth and cultural history. That is why we as audience respond so deeply to form and meaning as contained in genre. C. L. Barber, in *Shakespeare's Festive Comedy* (1959), makes a similar argument: our enjoyment of comedy arises from our intuitive appreciation of such "primitive" social customs as Saturnalian revels, May games, and fertility rites. John Holloway offers an anthropological study of Shakespeare's tragedies in *The Story of the Night* (1961).

Frye's critical system has not been without its detractors. For example, Frederick Crews (*Psychoanalysis and Literary Process,* 1970) argues that Frye's system is too self-contained in its ivory tower and too much an abstract artifact of the critical mind to be "relevant" to the social purposes of art. Nevertheless, Frye continues to be one of the most influential critics of the late twentieth century.

## Typological Criticism

Another controversy of the later twentieth century has to do with the Christian interpretation of Shakespeare. Do the images and allusions of Shakespeare's plays show him to be deeply immersed in a Christian culture inherited from the Middle Ages? Does he reveal a typological cast of mind, so common in medieval literature, whereby a story can suggest through analogy a universal religious archetype? For example, does the mysterious Duke in *Measure for Measure* suggest to us a God figure, hovering unseen throughout the play to test human will and then to present humanity with an omniscient but merciful judgment? Is the wanton slaughter of the good Cordelia in *King Lear* reminiscent of the Passion of Christ? Can Portia in *The Merchant of Venice* be seen as an angelic figure descending from Belmont into the fallen human world of Venice? Often the operative question we must ask is: "How far should such analogy be pursued?" Richard II unquestionably likens himself to Christ betrayed by the disciples, and at times the play evokes images of Adam banished from Paradise, but do these allusions coalesce into a sustained analogy?

Among the most enthusiastic searchers after Christian meaning are J. A. Bryant, in *Hippolyta's View* (1961); Roy Battenhouse, in *Shakespearean Tragedy: Its Art and Christian Premises* (1969); and R. Chris Hassel, in *Renaissance Drama and the English Church* (1979) and *Faith and Folly in Shakespeare: Romantic Comedies* (1980). Their efforts have encountered stern opposition, however. One notable dissenter is Roland M. Frye, whose *Shakespeare and Christian Doctrine* (1963) argues that Shakespeare cannot be shown to have known much Renaissance theology and that, in any case, his plays are concerned with human drama rather than with otherworldly questions of damnation or salvation. Frye's argument stresses the incompatibility of Christianity and tragedy, as does also D. G. James's *The Dream of Learning* (1951) and Clifford Leech's *Shakespeare's Tragedies and Other Studies in Seventeenth-Century Drama* (1950). Virgil Whitaker's *The Mirror Up to Nature* (1965) sees religion as an essential element in Shakespeare's plays but argues that Shakespeare uses the religious knowledge of his audience as a shortcut to characterization and meaning, rather than as an ideological weapon. The controversy will doubtless long continue, even though the typological critics have had to assume a defensive posture.

## Jan Kott and the Theater of the Absurd

At an opposite extreme from the Christian idealism of most typological critics is the iconoclasm of those who have been disillusioned by recent events in history. One who brilliantly epitomizes political disillusionment in the aftermath of World War II, especially in Eastern Europe, is Jan Kott. The evocative debunking of romantic idealism set forth in his *Shakespeare Our Contemporary* (1964, translated from the Polish) has enjoyed enormous influence since the 1960s, especially in the theater. Kott sees Shakespeare as a dramatist of the absurd and the grotesque. In this view, Shakespearean plays are often close to "black" comedy or comedy of the absurd, as defined by Antonin Artaud (*The Theatre and Its Double,* 1958) and Jerzy Grotowski (*Towards a Poor Theatre,* 1968). Indeed, Kott has inspired productions that expose traditional values to skepticism and ridicule. Portia and Bassanio in *The Merchant of Venice* become scheming adventurers; Henry V becomes a priggish warmonger. History is for Kott a nightmare associated with his country's experience in World War II, and Shakespeare's modernity can be seen in his sardonic portrayal of political opportunism and violence. Even *A Midsummer Night's Dream* is a play of disturbingly erotic brutality, Kott argues. Here is an interpretation of Shakespeare that was bound to have an enormous appeal in a world confronted by the assassinations of the Kennedys and Martin Luther King Jr.; by incessant war in the Middle East, Southeast Asia, and much of the third world; by the threat of nuclear annihilation and ecological disaster; and by political leadership generally perceived as interested only in the public-relations techniques of self-preservation. An essentially ironic view of politics and, more broadly, of human nature has informed a good deal of criticism since Kott's day and has led to the dethronement of E. M. W. Tillyard and his essentially positive view of English patriotism and heroism in the history plays.

## New Historicism and Cultural Materialism

A more recent way of investigating Shakespeare through the demystifying perspective of modern experience—the so-called new historicism— has focused on the themes of political self-fashioning and role playing in terms of power and subversion. This critical school has paid close attention to historians and cultural anthropologists like Lawrence Stone (*The Crisis of the Aristocracy, 1558–1641*, 1965) and Clifford Geertz (*Negara: The Theatre State in Nineteenth-Century Bali*, 1980), who explore new ways of looking at the relationship between historical change and the myths generated to bring it about or to retain power. Geertz analyzes the way in which the ceremonies and myths of political rule can, in effect, become a self-fulfilling reality; kings and other leaders, acting out their roles in ceremonials designed to encapsulate the myth of their greatness and divine origin, essentially become what they have created in their impersonations of power. Such a view of political authority is an inherently skeptical one, seeing government as a process of manipulating illusions. When Shakespeare's English history plays—or indeed any plays dealing with conflicts of authority—are analyzed in these terms, subversion and containment become important issues. Do the plays of Shakespeare and other Renaissance dramatists celebrate the power of the Tudor monarchs, or do they question and undermine assumptions of hierarchy? Did Elizabethan drama serve to increase skepticism and pressure for change, or was it, conversely, a way of easing that pressure so that the power structure could remain in force?

The "new historicism" is a name applied to a kind of literary criticism practiced in America, prominently by Stephen Greenblatt. Especially influential have been his *Renaissance Self-Fashioning* (1980), *Shakespearean Negotiations* (1988), and his editing of the journal *Representations*. Those who pursue similar concerns, including Louis Montrose, Stephen Orgel, Richard Helgerson, Don E. Wayne, Frank Whigham, Richard Strier, Jonathan Goldberg, David Scott Kastan, and Steven Mullaney, share Greenblatt's goals to a greater or lesser extent and think of themselves only with important reservations as "new historicists"; the term is misleadingly categorical, and Greenblatt, among others, is eager to enlarge the parameters of the method rather than to allow it to harden into an orthodoxy. (Greenblatt, in fact, prefers the term "poetics of culture" to "new historicism," even though the latter phrase remains better known.) Still, these critics do generally share a number of common con-

cerns. Among the ways in which new historicists seek to separate themselves from earlier historical critics is by denying that the work of art is a unified and self-contained product of an independent creator in masterful control of the meaning of the work. Instead, the new historicists represent the work as shot through with the multiple and contradictory discourses of its time. New historicists also deny the notion that art merely "reflects" its historical milieu; instead, they argue that art is caught up in, and contributes to, the social practices of its time. Although the boundary between new and old historical criticism is often hard to draw, in general the new historicists are apt to be skeptical of the accepted canon of literary texts and are drawn to a markedly politicized reading of Renaissance plays. One finds everywhere in the new historicism a deep ambivalence toward political authority.

Mikhail Bakhtin's provocative ideas on carnival (*L'Oeuvre de François Rabelais et la Culture Populaire du Moyen Age*, 1970) have had an important influence in new historical circles, as reflected, for example, in the work of Michael Bristol (*Carnival and Theatre: Plebeian Culture and the Structure of Authority in Renaissance England*, 1985), Peter Stallybrass, Gail Paster, and others. Like new historicism, this critical approach looks at so-called high cultural entertainment, including Shakespeare, in relation to the practices of popular culture, thereby breaking down the distinction between "high" and "popular." Literary and nonliterary texts are subjected to the same kind of serious scrutiny. Popular origins of the theater receive new attention, as in Robert Weimann's *Shakespeare and the Popular Tradition in the Theater: Studies in the Social Dimension of Dramatic Form and Function* (published in German in 1967 and in English translation in 1978).

Cultural materialism, in Britain, takes an analogous approach to the dethroning of canonical texts and the emphasis on art as deeply implicated in the social practices of its time, but differs from American new historicism on the issue of change. New historicism is sometimes criticized for its lack of a model for change and for its reluctant belief, instead (in Greenblatt's formulation especially), that all attempts at subversion through art are destined to be contained by power structures in society; art permits the expression of heterodox points of view, but only as a way of letting off steam, as it were, and thereby easing the pressures for actual radical change. British cultural materialism, in contrast, is more avowedly committed not only to radical political interpretation, but also to rapid political change, partly in response to what are perceived to be more deeply rooted class differences than are found in America. Jonathan Dollimore's *Radical Tragedy* (1984) and *Political Shakespeare* (1985), edited by Dollimore and Alan Sinfield, enlist the dramatist on the side of class struggle. So do *Alternative Shakespeares*, edited by John Drakakis (1985), and Terry Eagleton's *Shakespeare and Society* (1967) and *William Shakespeare* (1986). Raymond Williams, not himself a Shakespearean critic, is an acknowledged godfather of the movement.

## Feminist Criticism

Feminist criticism is such an important and diverse field that it has necessarily and productively reached into a number of related disciplines, such as cultural anthropology and its wealth of information about family structures. In his *The Elementary Structures of Kinship* (1949, translated 1969) and other books, Claude Lévi-Strauss analyzes the way in which men, as fathers and as husbands, control the transfer of women from one family to another in an "exogamous" marital system designed to strengthen commercial and other ties among men. Recent feminist criticism has had a lot to say about patriarchal structures in the plays and poems of Shakespeare, some of it building upon Lévi-Strauss's analysis of patriarchy; see, for example, Karen Newman, "Portia's Ring: Unruly Women and Structures of Exchange in *The Merchant of Venice,*" *Shakespeare Quarterly,* 38 (1987), 10–33, and Lynda Boose, "The Father and the Bride in Shakespeare," *PMLA,* 97 (1982), 325–47. Coppélia Kahn has examined the ideology of rape in *The Rape of Lucrece,* showing how the raped woman is devalued by the shame that attaches to her husband even though she is innocent (*Shakespeare Studies,* 9, 1976, 45–72).

Another important source of insight for feminist criticism is the anthropological work on rites of passage by Arnold Van Gennep (*The Rites of Passage,* translated by M. B. Vizedom and G. L. Caffee, 1960) and Victor Turner (*The Ritual Process,* 1969), among others. The focus here is on the dangers of transition at times of birth, puberty, marriage, death, and other turning points of human life. Feminist criticism, in dealing with such crises of transition, concerns itself not only with women's roles, but also more broadly with gender relations, with family structures, and with the problems that males encounter in their quest for mature sexual identity. Coppélia Kahn's *Man's Estate; Masculine Identity in Shakespeare* (1981) looks particularly at the difficulty of the male in confronting the hazards of maturity. Robert Watson's *Shakespeare and the Hazards of Ambition* (1984) also looks at the male in the political context of career and self-fashioning. Marjorie Garber's *Coming of Age in Shakespeare* (1981) takes a broad look at maturation.

As these titles suggest, the models are often psychological, as well as anthropological. One focus of feminist criticism is the role of women in love and marriage. Feminist critics disagree among themselves as to whether the portrait depicted by Shakespeare and other Elizabethan dramatists is a hopeful one, as argued, for example, by Juliet Dusinberre in *Shakespeare and the Nature of Women* (1975, 1996), or repressive, as argued by Lisa Jardine in *Still Harping on Daughters: Women and Drama in the Age of Shakespeare* (1983). Recent historians add an important perspective, especially Lawrence Stone in his *The Family, Sex, and Marriage in England, 1500–1800* (1977). Did the Protestant emphasis on marriage as a morally elevated and reciprocal relationship have the paradoxical effect of arousing in men an increased hostility and wariness toward women and a resulting increase in repression and violence? Or, as David Underdown suggests, should we look to economic explanations of hostility and wariness toward women in the Renaissance? His studies indicate that repression of women is greatest in regions of the country where their place in the economy offers the possibility of their having some control over family finances. (See *Revel, Riot, and Rebellion: Popular Culture in England, 1603–1660,* 1985, pp. 73–105, especially p. 99.)

Certainly, recent criticism has paid a lot of attention to male anxieties about women in Shakespeare's plays, as various male protagonists resolve to teach women a lesson (*The Taming of the Shrew*), succumb to dark fantasies of female unfaithfulness (*Much Ado About Nothing, Othello*), or are overwhelmed by misogynistic revulsion (*Hamlet, King Lear*). It is as though Shakespeare, in his plays and poems, works through the problems that men experience throughout their lives in their relationships with women, from the insecurities of courtship to the desire for possession and control in marriage, and from jealous fears of betrayal to the longing for escape into middle-age sexual adventure (as in *Antony and Cleopatra*). The late plays show us the preoccupation of the aging male with the marriages of his daughters (another form of betrayal) and with the approach of death.

Recently, feminist criticism has begun to increase its historical consciousness. Critics such as Gail Paster, Jean Howard, Phyllis Rackin, Dympna Callaghan, Lorraine Helms, Jyotsna Singh, Alison Findlay, Lisa Jardine, and Karen Newman focus on the construction of gender in early modern England in terms of social and material conditions, abandoning the nonhistorical psychological model of earlier feminist criticism. See the bibliography at the end of this book for feminist studies by these and other feminist critics, including Catherine Belsey, Carol Neely, Peter Erickson, Meredith Skura, Marianne Novy, Margo Hendricks, Kim Hall, Philippa Berry, Frances Dolan, Mary Beth Rose, Valerie Traub, Susan Zimmerman, Lynda Boose, and Ania Loomba. Gender studies concerned with issues of same-sex relationships have made important contributions in recent years, in the work of Bruce Smith, Laurie Shannon, Jonathan Goldberg, Stephen Orgel, Leonard Barkan, Mario DiGangi, and others.

## Poststructuralism and Deconstruction

A major influence today in Shakespeare criticism, as in virtually all literary criticism of recent date, is the school of analysis known as poststructuralism or deconstruction; the terms, though not identical, significantly overlap. This school derives its inspiration originally from the work of certain French philosophers and critics, chief among whom are Ferdinand de Saussure, a specialist in linguistics, Michel Foucault, a historian of systems of discourse, and Jacques Derrida, perhaps the most highly visible exponent and practitioner of deconstruction. The ideas of these men were first introduced into American literary criticism by scholars at Yale such as Geoffrey Hartman, J. Hillis Miller, and Paul De Man. The ideas are controversial and difficult.

Poststructuralism and deconstruction begin with an insistence that language is a system of difference—one in which the signifiers (such as words and gestures) are essentially arbitrary to the extent that "meaning" and "authorial intention" are virtually impossible to fix precisely; that is, language enjoys a potentially infinite subjectivity. To an extent, this approach to the subjectivity of meaning in a work of art resembles "new" criticism in its mistrust of "message" in literature, but the new method goes further. It resists all attempts at paraphrase, for example, insisting that the words of a text cannot be translated into other words without altering something vital; indeed, there is no way of knowing if an author's words will strike any two readers or listeners in the same way. The very concept of an author has been challenged by Michel Foucault ("What Is an Author?" in *Language, Counter-Memory, Practice,* edited by Donald F. Bouchard, 1977). Deconstruction proclaims that there is no single identifiable author in the traditional sense; instead of a single text, we have a potentially infinite number of texts.

Both the theory and practice of deconstruction remain highly controversial. Although poststructuralism and deconstruction owe a debt to the general philosophical theory of signs and symbols known as semiotics, in which the function of linguistic signs is perceived to be artificially constructed, the new method also calls into question the very distinctions on which the discipline of semiotics is based. Derrida builds upon the work of Saussure and yet goes well beyond him in an insistence that words (signifiers) be left in play rather than attached to their alleged meaning (signifieds). Frank Lentricchia (*After the New Criticism,* 1980) takes the Yale school critics to task for interpreting Derrida in too formalist and apolitical a sense. Despite disagreements among theorists, nevertheless, the approach has deeply influenced Shakespeare criticism as a whole by urging critics to consider the suppleness with which signifiers (words) in the Shakespearean text are converted by listeners and readers into some approximation of meaning.

The ramifications of poststructuralism and deconstruction are increasingly felt in other forms of criticism, even those at least nominally at odds with poststructuralist assumptions. Some radical textual critics, for example, are fascinated by the unsettling prospects of the deconstructed text. What does one edit and how does one go about editing when words are to be left in play, to the infinite regress of meaning? The problems are acutely examined in a collection of essays called *The Division of the Kingdom,* edited by Gary Taylor and Michael Warren, on the two early and divergent texts of *King Lear* (1983). The method of linguistic analysis known as "speech-act theory," developed by the philosopher J. L. Austin as a way of exploring how we perform certain linguistic acts when we swear oaths or make asseverations and the like, is sharply at variance with deconstruction in its premises about a correlation between speech and intended meaning, and yet it, too, can help us understand the instability of spoken or written language in Shakespeare. Joseph Porter's *The Drama of Speech Acts* (1979), for example, looks at ways in which Shakespeare's characters in the plays about Henry IV and Henry V reveal, through their language of oath making and oath breaking, asseveration, and the like, their linguistic adaptability or lack of adaptability to historical change. Richard II resists historical change in the very way he speaks; Prince Hal embraces it. A third related field of analysis that is interested in the instability of meaning in Shakespeare's texts is metadramatic criticism, where the focus is on ways in which dramatic texts essentially talk about the drama itself, about artistic expression, and about the artist's quest for immortality in art. James Calderwood's *Shakespearean Metadrama* (1971) is an influential example.

At its extreme, then, deconstructive criticism comes close to undermining all kinds of "meaningfulness" in artistic utterance and to being thus at war with other methods of interpretation. Still, deconstruction continues to remain influential, because it also usefully challenges complacent formulations of meaning and because it promotes such a subtle view of linguistic complexity.

At its best, late twentieth-century criticism transcends the splintering effect of a heterogeneous critical tradition to achieve a synthesis that is at once unified and multiform in its vision. The pluralistic approach aims at overall balance and a reinforcement of one critical approach through the methodology of another. Many of the works already cited in this introduction refuse to be constricted by methodological boundaries. The best historical criticism makes use of close explication of the text where appropriate; image patterns can certainly reinforce mythological patterns; typological interpretation, when sensibly applied, serves the cause of image study. Some fine books are so eclectic in their method that one hesitates to apply the label of any one critical school. Among such works are Maynard Mack's *King Lear in Our Time* (1965), David Young's *Something of Great Constancy: The Art of A Midsummer Night's Dream* (1966), R. G. Hunter's *Shakespeare and the Comedy of Forgiveness* (1965), Janet Adelman's *The Common Liar: An Essay on "Antony and Cleopatra"* (1973), Stanley Cavell's "The Avoidance of Love: A Reading of King Lear," in *Must We Mean What We Say?* (1969, reprinted in *Disowning Knowledge in Seven Plays of Shakespeare,* 2003), and Paul Jorgensen's *Our Naked Frailties: Sensational Art and Meaning in Macbeth* (1971).

## Into the Twenty-First Century

The sense of where we are in the twenty-first century in Shakespeare criticism reflects the uncertainties and guardedly hopeful expectations of the academic profession as a whole. The period of the 1970s and 1980s, described previously, was one of extraordinary ferment, brought on by a host of developments: the Vietnam War and its aftermath, the assassinations of the Kennedys and Martin Luther King Jr., the impact of French linguistic and philosophical thought on American intellectual writing, the frustrations of many academics with Reaganomics and their consequent fascination with British Marxism, emerging demands on behalf of minorities and women, a revolution in social and sexual mores accompanied by a backlash in the name of "family values," conflict over American foreign policy in the Middle East, terrorism, global warming, and much more. The result was what must be regarded as a genuine revolution in methods of critical analysis and reading. The literary text became multivalent, ambiguous, deconstructed, dethroned as a unique artifact, and was seen, instead, as a product of and contributing to its social and intellectual environment. The author became a construction of criticism and of a new kind of literary history.

Shakespeare studies have taken a lead in all of this new exploration. Although one of the postmodern demands has been for a recanonizing of literature in favor of newer literature, works by women and minorities, and works from countries other than Britain and the United States instead of the traditional canon of dead white European males, Shakespeare not only has survived this recanonization but also has become more prominent than ever. Other Renaissance writers such as Ben Jonson, John Webster, Thomas Dekker, Thomas Nashe, John Lyly, Edmund Spenser, and even Christopher Marlowe, John Milton, and John Donne have been the victims of declining enrollments in classes generally, but Shakespeare triumphs. Why?

One compelling answer is that Shakespeare is simply indispensable to postmodern critical inquiry. His texts are so extraordinarily responsive that new questions put to them—about the changing role of women, about cynicism in the political process, about the protean near-indeterminacy of meaning in language—evoke insights that are hard to duplicate in other literary texts. Shakespeare does not seem out of date. The very impulse of so much recent criticism to claim Shakespeare as "our contemporary," attuned to our own skepticisms and disillusionment and even despair (as in the writings of Jan Kott, for example), attests to his unparalleled engagement with the issues about which we care so deeply. Even those who argue that Shakespeare exhibits the male hang-ups of a patriarchal society and that he is a social snob who glorifies aristocracy and warfare do not

see Shakespeare as a writer who is out of touch with the values of our contemporary society but, rather, as one who gives eloquent testimonial to structures that were alive in our cultural past and with which we sense a continuum today even if outward circumstances have changed. The best scholarship does not condemn Shakespeare for believing in kingship or for sometimes showing men as victorious in the battle of the sexes; instead, that criticism is interested in the whole process of the literary text's participation in the creation of culture. Even when recent scholarship is concerned with examining class and gender issues to clarify some of the systematic oppressiveness of early modern culture, it does so generally in an attempt to negotiate the relationship of the present to the past, rather than assuming a superiority in our modern world's approaches to issues of class, gender, and ethnicity.

To be sure, a number of Shakespeare's plays are in trouble today because they make us uncomfortable about these issues. *The Merchant of Venice* is, in the eyes of many, almost unproduceable, because the anti-Semitic emotions it explores are so distasteful. It is less often assigned now in classrooms than it once was, even though, when it is taught or produced onstage, it can lead to extraordinarily searching discussions of painful but real issues. The same is true of *The Taming of the Shrew,* which is being taken from the shelves of more than a few libraries because of its apparent flaunting of sexist behavior toward women. *Othello* offends some readers and viewers because of its racist language and, in the view of some, racial stereotypes. Yet, the power of Shakespeare's language continues to exert its spell despite, and in part because of, these troubling conflicts over the role of dramatic art in modern society.

The world of Shakespeare criticism today, after two decades or so of revolution, is seemingly one of consolidation. At a March 1995 meeting of the Shakespeare Association of America in Chicago, many conferees wondered: Where is the profession going? What are the hot new issues? Who are the new critics that no one wants to miss? And, in fact, there seemed to be little dramatic excitement of this sort, little agreement as to any discernible new trend. To some, this is frustrating. Where does one turn for real creativity after a thoroughgoing revolution such as we have experienced?

To others, a time of stocktaking is potentially healthy. There seems to be relatively little interest in turning the clock back; postmodernism and indeterminacy have changed the critical landscape for better and for worse. Now that this new landscape begins to seem familiar, however, new members of the profession seem less anxious to resolve their own identity crises in terms of affiliating with some critical school or other. The critical challenges are there, not so stridently new as they were ten years ago, and adaptable to various uses.

The result is increasing variety in the kinds of critical work being done. Some of it is recognizably traditional, dealing with stage history and conditions of performance during Shakespeare's lifetime, as, for example, in T. J. King, *Casting Shakespeare's Plays: London Actors and Their Roles* (1992); William Ingram, *The Business of Playing: The Beginnings of the Adult Professional Theater in Elizabethan London* (1992); David Bradley, *From Text to Performance in the Elizabethan Theatre: Preparing the Play for the Stage* (1992); David Mann, *The Elizabethan Player: Contemporary Stage Representation* (1991); John H. Astington, ed., *The Development of Shakespeare's Theater* (1992); Andrew Gurr, *Playgoing in Shakespeare's London* (1987, 2nd edition, 1996) and *The Shakespearian Playing Companies* (1996); and Roslyn Lander Knutson, *The Repertory of Shakespeare's Company, 1594–1613* (1991). Background and historical studies of the conditions that helped produce Shakespeare's theater can sometimes be informatively revisionist in the sense of toppling cherished older notions without at the same time being postmodern in approach. Examples here might include Richard Dutton, *Mastering the Revels: The Regulation and Censorship of English Renaissance Drama* (1991); Scott McMillin and Sally-Beth MacLean, *The Queen's Men and Their Plays* (1998); and Leeds Barroll, *Politics, Plague, and Shakespeare's Theater: The Stuart Years* (1991).

Other studies are more openly revisionist in a postmodern vein, sometimes in dealing with hypotheses about bibliography and textual studies, as in Margreta de Grazia, *Shakespeare Verbatim: The Reproduction of Authenticity and the 1790 Apparatus* (1991), and Grace Ioppolo, *Revising Shakespeare* (1991). The New Folger Library Shakespeare, edited by Barbara Mowat and Paul Werstine (1992—), gives a more measured approach. The Arden Shakespeare is currently bringing out new critical editions of all the plays in individual volumes (Arden 3), as are the New Cambridge Shakespeare and the Oxford Shakespeare. Occasionally a conservative counterblast is heard, as in Brian Vickers's entertaining, learned, and feisty polemic, *Appropriating Shakespeare: Contemporary Critical Quarrels* (1993). A forum of essays edited by Ivo Kamps, called *Shakespeare Left and Right* (1999), gives us a chance to weigh arguments from various sides.

What the contemporary critical scene does best is to free critics to be who they are and to write without paying dues to any particular affiliation. The results are refreshingly diverse. Among the books of the 1990s that show this spread of critical approaches are Karen Newman, *Fashioning Femininity and the English Renaissance Drama* (1991); Bruce R. Smith, *Homosexual Desire in Shakespeare's England* (1991); Janet Adelman, *Suffocating Mothers: Fantasies of Maternal Origin in Shakespeare's Plays, "Hamlet" to "The Tempest"* (1992); Alan Sinfield, *Faultlines: Cultural Materialism and the Politics of Dissident Reading* (1992); Valerie Traub, *Desire and Anxiety: Circulations of Sexuality in Shakespearean Drama* (1992); Richard Burt, *Licensed by Authority: Ben Jonson and the Discourses of Censorship* (1993); Linda Charnes, *Notorious Identity: Materializing the Subject in Shakespeare* (1993); Lars Engle, *Shakespearean Pragmatism: Market of His Time* (1993); Gail Kern Paster, *The Body Embarrassed: Drama and the Disciplines of Shame in Early Modern England* (1993); Meredith Anne Skura, *Shakespeare the Actor and the Purposes of Playing* (1993); Frances E. Dolan, *Dangerous Familiars: Representations of Domestic Crime in England, 1550–1700* (1994); Kim F. Hall, *Things of Darkness: Economies of Race and Gender in Early Modern England* (1994); Jean Howard, *The Stage and Social Struggle in Early Modern England* (1994); Robert Watson, *The Rest Is Silence: Death as Annihilation in the English Renaissance* (1994); Katharine Eisaman Maus, *Inwardness and Theatre in the English Renaissance Drama* (1995); Louis Montrose, *The Purpose of Playing: Shakespeare and the Cultural Politics of the Elizabethan Theatre* (1996); Patricia Parker, *Shakespeare from the Margins: Language, Culture, Context* (1996); Jean E. Howard and Phyllis Rackin, *Engendering a Nation: A Feminist Account of Shakespeare's English Histories* (1997); and David Scott Kastan, ed., *A Companion to Shakespeare* (1999).

These same qualities of excellence in diverse critical approaches can be sampled in many studies of Shakespeare in the two decades of the twenty-first century, as for example in Stephen Greenblatt, *Hamlet in Purgatory* (2001); Anthony B. Dawson and Paul Yachnin, *The Culture of Playgoing in Shakespeare's England* (2001); David Scott Kastan, *Shakespeare and the Book* (2001); Mary Beth Rose, *Gender and Heroism in Early Modern Literature* (2002); Stephen Orgel, *The Authentic Shakespeare* (2002); Ania Loomba, *Shakespeare, Race, and Colonialism* (2002); Laurie Shannon, *Sovereign Amity: Figures of Friendship in Shakespeare's Contexts* (2002); Richard Dutton and Jean E. Howard, eds., *A Companion to Shakespeare's Works*, in 4 vols. (2003); B. J. and Mary Sokol, *Shakespeare, Law, and Marriage* (2003); Stephen Orgel, *Imagining Shakespeare* (2003); Stanley Wells, *Shakespeare: For All Time* (2003); Stephen Greenblatt, *Will in the World: How Shakespeare Became Shakespeare* (2004); Marjorie Garber, *Shakespeare After All* (2004); Andrew Gurr, *The Shakespeare Company, 1594–1642* (2004); Gale Paster, *Humoring the Body: Emotions and the Renaissance Stage* (2004); James S. Shapiro, *A Year in the Life of William Shakespeare, 1599* (2005); Phyllis Rackin, *Shakespeare and Women* (2005); Robin Headlam Wells, *Shakespeare's Humanism* (2005); William M. Hamlin, *Tragedy and Scepticism in Shakespeare's England* (2005); Arthur F. Kinney, *Shakespeare and cognition: Aristotle's Legacy and Shakespearean Drama* (2006); Peter Holland, *Shakespeare, Memory, and Performance* (2006); Kenneth Gross, *Shylock is Shakespeare* (2006); Eric Scott Mallin, *Godless Shakespeare* (2007); A. D. Nutall, *Shakespeare the Thinker* (2007); Charlotte Scott, *Shakespeare and the Idea of the Book* (2007); Tzachi Zamir, *Double Vision: Moral Philosophy* and *Shakespearean Drama* (2007); Margreta De Grazia, *"Hamlet" without Hamlet* (2007); Gordon McMullan, *Shakespeare and the Idea of Late Writing: Authorship in the Proximity of Death* (2007); David Schalkwyk, *Shakespeare, Love and Service* (2008); Michael Witmore, *Shakespearean Metaphysics* (2008); Janet Adelman, *Blood Relations: Christian and Jew in "The Merchant of Venice"* (2008); Jonathan Bate, *Soul of the Age: A Biography of the Mind of William Shakespeare* (2009); James Shapiro, *Contested Will: Who Wrote Shakespeare?* (2010); Jonathan Gil Harris, *Shakespeare and Literary Theory* (2010); Joel B. Altman, *The Improbability of Othello: Rhetorical Anthropology and* *Shakespearean Selfhood* (2010); Julia Reinhard Lupton, *Thinking with Shakespeare: Essays on Politics and Life* (2011); Catherine Richardson, *Shakespeare and Material Culture* (2011); Richard Strier, *The Unrepentant Renaissance: From Petrarch to Shakespeare to Milton* (2011); Ayanna Thompson, *Passing Strange: Shakespeare, Race, and Contemporary America* (2011); Margaret Litvin, *Hamlet's Arab Journey: Shakespeare's Prince and Nasser's Ghost* (2011); Colin Burrow, *Shakespeare and Classical Antiquity* (2013); Richard C. McCoy, *Faith in Shakespeare* (2013); and Andrew Cutrofello, *All for Nothing: Hamlet's Negativity* (2014).

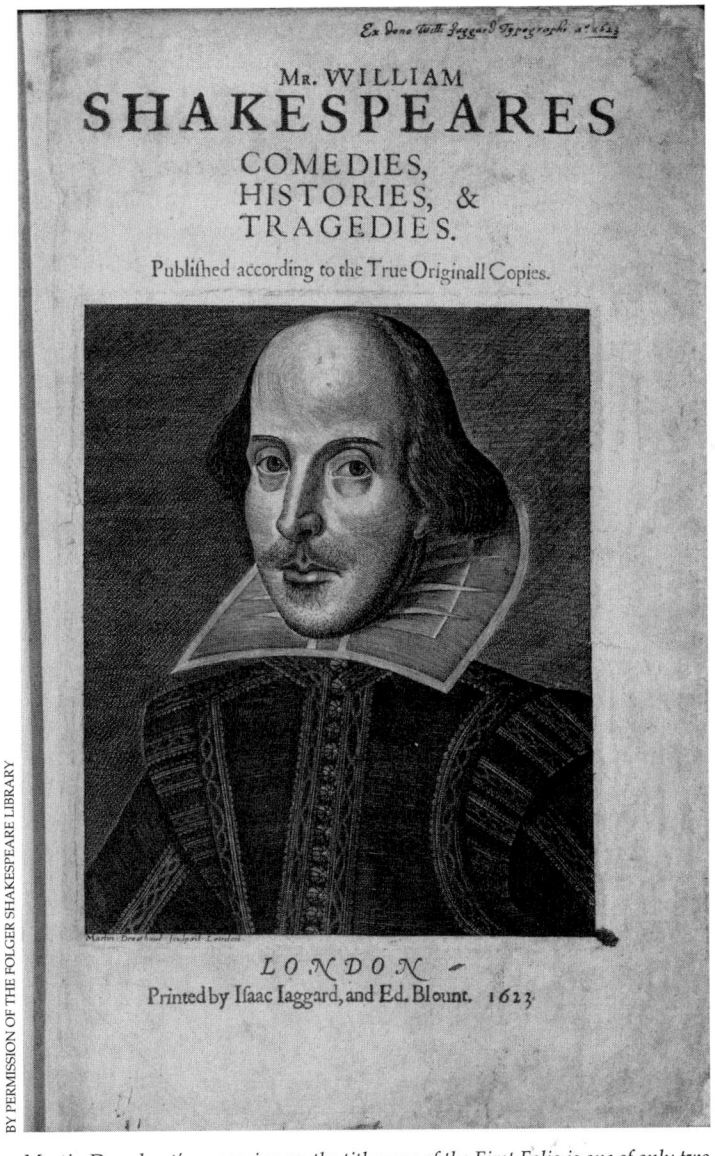

*Martin Droeshout's engraving on the title page of the First Folio is one of only two authentic likenesses of Shakespeare in existence.*

# A CATALOGVE

of the seuerall Comedies, Histories, and Tragedies contained in this Volume.

## COMEDIES.

## HISTORIES.

## TRAGEDIES.

*John Heminges and Henry Condell, Shakespeare's fellow actors, gathered contents for the First Folio, published in 1623. They collected thirty-six plays in the volume, omitting* Pericles *and* The Two Noble Kinsmen. Troilus and Cressida *is included in most copies of the First Folio but is not listed here in the contents.*

# The Comedies

# The Taming of the Shrew

For all its comic brilliance, *The Taming of the Shrew* (c. 1592–1594) is a troublesome play in our contemporary world. The very idea of teaching a wife unquestioning obedience to her husband is so objectionable today that many acting companies find ways to refute the play's premise, or take the play out of their repertories. Some libraries remove the play from their shelves. Yet the play can be seen as part of an ongoing debate in Shakespearean comedy concerning the battle of the sexes, with *Taming* at one extreme and later comedies like *Much Ado About Nothing* offering a more temperate and balanced view. *Taming* shares with other romantic comedies a delight in the device of mistaken identities. It inverts appearance and reality, dreaming and waking, and the master-servant relationship in order to create a transformed Saturnalian world anticipating that of *A Midsummer Night's Dream* and *Twelfth Night*.

The induction sets up the theme of illusion, using an old motif known as "The Sleeper Awakened" (as found, for example, in *The Arabian Nights*). This device frames the main action of the play, giving to it an added perspective. *The Taming of the Shrew* purports, in fact, to be a play within a play, an entertainment devised by a witty nobleman as a practical joke on a drunken tinker, Christopher Sly. The jest is to convince Sly that he is not Sly at all, but an aristocrat suffering delusions. Outlandishly dressed in new finery, Sly is invited to witness a play from the gallery over the stage. In a rendition called *The Taming of a Shrew* (printed in 1594 and now generally thought to be taken from an earlier version of Shakespeare's play, employing a good deal of conscious originality along with some literary borrowing and even plagiarism), the framing plot concludes by actually putting Sly back out on the street in front of the alehouse where he was found. He awakes, recalls the play as a dream, and proposes to put the vision to good use by taming his own wife. Whether this ending reflects an epilogue now lost from the text of Shakespeare's play cannot be said, but it does reinforce the idea of the play as Sly's fantasy. Like Puck at the end of *A Midsummer Night's Dream*, urging us to dismiss what we have seen as the product of our own slumbering, Sly continually reminds us that the play is only an illusion or shadow.

With repeated daring, Shakespeare calls attention to the contrived nature of his artifact, the play. When, for example, Sly is finally convinced that he is, in fact, a noble lord recovering from madness and lustily proposes to hasten off to bed with his long-neglected wife, we are comically aware that the "wife" is an impostor, a young page in disguise. Yet this counterfeiting of roles is no more unreal than the employment of Elizabethan boy-actors for the parts of Katharina and Bianca in the "real" play. As we watch Sly watching a play, levels of meaning intersect in this evocative fashion. Again, the paintings offered to Sly by his new attendants call attention to art's ability to confound illusion and reality. In one painting, Cytherea is hidden by reeds "Which seem to move and wanton with her breath, / Even as the waving sedges play wi'th'wind," and, in another painting, Io appears "As lively painted as the deed was done" (Induction, 2.50–6). Sly's function, then, is that of the naive observer who inverts illusion and reality in his mind, concluding that his whole previous life of tinkers and alehouses and Cicely Hackets has been unreal. As his attendants explain to him, "These fifteen years you have been in a dream, / Or when you waked, so waked as if you slept." We as audience laugh at Sly's naiveté, and yet we, too, are moved and even transformed by an artistic vision that we know to be illusory.

Like Sly, many characters in the main action of the play are persuaded, or contrive, to be what they are not. Lucentio and Tranio exchange roles of master and servant. Bianca's supposed tutors are, in fact, her wooers, using their lessons to disguise messages of love. Katharina is prevailed upon by her husband, Petruchio, to declare that the sun is the moon and that an old gentleman (Vincentio) is a fair young maiden. Vincentio is publicly informed that he is an impostor and that the "real" Vincentio (the Pedant) is at that very moment looking at him out of the window of his son Lucentio's house. This last ruse does not fool the real Vincentio, but it nearly succeeds in fooling everyone else. Baptista Minola is about to commit Vincentio to jail for the infamous slander of asserting that the supposed Lucentio is only a servant in disguise. Vincentio, as the newly arrived stranger, is able to see matters as they really are, but the dwellers of Padua have grown so accustomed to the mad and improbable fictions of their life that they are not easily awakened to reality.

Such illusions have the effect of challenging the norms of social order. If a servant can playact at being the master so successfully that no one can tell the difference, are we to understand that social distinctions are mere arbitrary constructions? If Sly can become a lord by wearing the right clothes and speaking blank verse (as in the Induction, 2.68 and following), might audience members similarly raise their status? The theater promotes such skeptical questions, since it is in the business of dressing actors up as persons of whatever rank the playwright chooses. Surely one of the pleasures of theatrical performance for Elizabethan audiences was that of dreaming of social advancement or social control. At the same time, this theater treats such a liberating experience as holiday or farcical nightmare, and as Saturnalian escape; we realize as audience that we will return to the norms of our daily lives after having visited an imagined space where anything is possible.

Shakespeare multiplies his devices of illusion by combining two entirely distinct plots, each concerned, at least in part, with the comic inversion of appearance and reality: the shrew-taming plot involving Petruchio and Kate, and the more conventional romantic plot involving Lucentio and Bianca. The latter plot is derived from the *Supposes* of George Gascoigne, a play first presented at Gray's Inn (one of the Inns of Court) in 1566, as translated from Ariosto's neoclassical comedy, *I Suppositi*, 1509. (Ariosto's work, in turn, was based upon Terence's *Eunuchus* and Plautus's *Captivi*.) The "Supposes" are mistaken identities or misunderstandings, the kind of hilarious farcical mix-ups with which Shakespeare had already experimented in *The Comedy of Errors*. Shakespeare has, as usual, both romanticized his source and moralized it in a characteristically English way. The heroine, who in the Roman comedy of Plautus and Terence would have been a courtesan, and who in *Supposes* is made pregnant by her clandestine lover, remains thoroughly chaste in Shakespeare's comedy. Consequently, she has no need for a pander, or go-between, such as the bawdy Duenna or Nurse of *Supposes*. The satire directed at the heroine's unwelcome old wooer Gremio is far less savage than in *Supposes*, where the "pantaloon," Dr. Cleander, is a villainously corrupt lawyer epitomizing the depravity of "respectable" society. Despite Shakespeare's modifications, however, the basic plot remains an effort to foil parental authority. The young lovers, choosing each other for romantic reasons, must fend off the materialistic calculations of their parents.

In a stock situation of this sort, the character types are also conventional. Gremio, the aged wealthy wooer, is actually labeled a "pantaloon" in the text (3.1.36–7) to stress his neoclassical ancestry. (Lean and foolish old wooers of this sort were customarily dressed in pantaloons, slippers, and spectacles on the Italian stage.) Gremio is typically "the graybeard," and Baptista Minola is "the narrow-prying father" (3.2.145–6). Even though Shakespeare renders these characters far less unattractive than in *Supposes*, their worldly behavior still invites reprisal from the young. Since Baptista Minola insists on selling his daughter Bianca to the highest bidder, it is fitting that her wealthiest suitor (the supposed Lucentio) should turn out in the end to be a penniless servant (Tranio) disguised as a man of affluence and position. In his traditional role as the clever servant of neoclassical comedy, Tranio skillfully apes the mannerisms of respectable society. He can deal in the mere surfaces—clothes or reputation—out of which a man's social importance is created, and can even furnish himself with a rich father. Gremio and Baptista deserve to be foiled, because they accept the illusion of respectability as real.

Even the romantic lovers of this borrowed plot are largely conventional. To be sure, Shakespeare emphasizes their virtuous qualities and their sincerity. He adds Hortensio (not in *Supposes*) to provide Lucentio with a genuine, if foolish, rival and Bianca with two wooers closer to her age than old Gremio. Lucentio and Bianca deserve their romantic triumph; they are self-possessed, witty, and steadfast to each other. Yet we know very little about them, nor have they seen deeply into each other. Lucentio's love talk is laden with conventional images in praise of Bianca's dark eyes and scarlet lips. At the play's end, he discovers, to his surprise, that she can be willful, even disobedient. Has her appearance of virtue concealed something from him and from us? Because the relationship between these lovers is superficial, they are appropriately destined to a superficial marriage as well. The passive Bianca becomes the proud and defiant wife.

By contrast, Petruchio and Kate are the more interesting lovers, whose courtship involves mutual self-discovery. Admittedly, we must not overstate the case. Especially at first, these lovers are also stock types: the shrew tamer and his proverbially shrewish wife. (The word *shrew*, originally signifying a wicked or malignant man, often applied to the devil or to a malignant planet, had come to mean a scolding or turbulent wife.) Although Shakespeare seems not to have used any single source for this plot, he was well acquainted with crude, misogynistic stories demonstrating the need for putting women in their place. In a ballad called *A Merry Jest of a Shrewd and Curst Wife, Lapped in Morel's Skin* (printed c. 1550), for example, the husband tames his shrewish wife by flaying her bloody with birch rods and then wrapping her in the freshly salted skin of a plow horse named Morel. (This shrewish wife, like Kate, has an obedient and gentle younger sister who is their father's favorite.) Other features of Shakespeare's plot can be found in similar tales: the tailor scolded for devising a gown of outlandish fashion (Gerard Legh's *Accidence of Armory*, 1562), the wife obliged to agree with her husband's assertion of some patent falsehood (Don Juan Manuel's *El Conde Lucanor*, c. 1335), and the three husbands' wager on their wives' obedience (*The Book of the Knight of La Tour-Landry*, printed 1484). In the raw spirit of this sexist tradition, so unlike the refined Italianate sentiment of his other plot, Shakespeare introduces Petruchio as a man of reckless bravado who is ready to marry the ugliest or sharpest-tongued woman alive so long as she is rich. However much he may be later attracted by Kate's fiery spirit, his first attraction to her is crassly financial. Kate is, moreover, a troublesomely defiant young woman at first, described by the men who know her as "intolerable curst / And shrewd and froward," and aggressive in her bullying of Bianca. She and Petruchio meet as grotesque comic counterparts.

At the play's end, the traditional pattern of male dominance and female acquiescence is still prominent. Kate is allowed food, sleep, and sex only when she yields to a socially ordained patriarchal framework in which a husband is the princely ruler of his wife. Kate is not like the young heroines of many other Shakespearean comedies (Portia in *The Merchant of Venice* and Rosalind in *As You Like It*, for example) who wittily guide their immature and overly romantic young men toward a pragmatic view of love and marriage; in this play, Kate is the one who must be mastered by the self-assured male. Her shrewishness is an open threat to male control in the marital bond, and, accordingly, the play's comic finale celebrates containment of this threat in her, along with a sharp reminder of the resistance to be endured by other husbands who have failed to tame their shrews.

Within this male-oriented frame of reference, however, Petruchio and Kate are surprisingly like Benedick and Beatrice of *Much Ado About Nothing*. Petruchio, for all his rant, is increasingly drawn to Kate by her spirit. As wit-combatants, they are worthy of one another's enmity— or love. No one else in the play is a fit match for either of them. Kate, too, is attracted to Petruchio, despite her war of words. Her anger is part defensive protection, part testing of his sincerity. If she is contemptuous of the wooers she has seen till now, she has good reason to be. We share her condescension toward the aged Gremio or the laughably inept Hortensio. She rightly fears that her father wishes to dispose of her so that he may auction off Bianca to the wealthiest competitor. Kate's jaded view of such marriage brokering is entirely defensible. Not surprisingly, she first views Petruchio, whose professed intentions are far from reassuring, as another mere adventurer in love. She is impressed by his "line" in wooing her but needs to test his constancy and sincerity.

Marriage for her would be a serious step, since social convention allows a dominant role for the husband; can she hope that she and Petruchio will arrive at some sort of understanding in which her role as wife and partner will be an honorable one? She puts down most men with a shrewish manner that challenges their very masculinity; Petruchio is the first man to counter her wit and energy with his own. Can she learn to live with this man?

Kate's rejection of men has not left her very happy, however genuine her disdain is for most of those who have come to woo. Petruchio's "schooling" can be seen as addressing that unhappiness, even if his purpose is unremittingly masculine in its assumption that a rebellious wife has to be "tamed" as one would tame a hawk. Having wooed and partly won her, Petruchio tests her with his late arrival at the marriage, his unconventional dress, and his crossing all her desires. Like the hawk-tamer, Petruchio uses harsh physical means, including deprivation of food and drink. He treats Kate as his chattel, and never wavers in his certainty that he is right to do so. Other males applaud his success and wish only to follow his example. The resolution is in these terms manifestly more sexist than in *Much Ado About Nothing*; it is as though Shakespeare works his way through the problems of sexual conflict from this early, very masculine play to a more complex and mutual accommodation in his later comedies.

At the same time, it is possible to see *The Taming of the Shrew* as a play in which a genuine accommodation is reached, even if it is on the man's terms with the woman being given no choice. The play can be interpreted as suggesting that Petruchio's treatment of Kate, no matter how temporarily harsh, is ultimately benign in its intent. Petruchio, by his outlandish behavior of overturning tables and scolding servants, shows Kate an ugly picture of what her refractoriness is like. He succeeds by insisting on what, arguably, she may desire too: a well-defined relationship tempered by mutual respect and love. In this interpretation, Kate may gain something by the play's end. Her closing speech, with its fine blend of irony and self-conscious hyperbole, together with its seriousness of concern, can be read as expressing the way in which her independence of spirit and her newfound acceptance of a domestic rule are successfully fused, enabling her to gain widespread applause instead of opprobrium.

This is by no means the only way of reading the final scene, as modern productions often make clear: Kate emerges in various stage productions as more or less contented, or as simply resigned, or as cruelly brainwashed, or as only playing the role of obedient wife to get what she wants. The uncertainty of interpretation is one of the great pleasures and challenges today, in a world for which ideas about marriage have manifestly shifted since Shakespeare wrote. Even so, the play offers common ground in its appreciation for the seriousness of the issue and in its wonderful transparency as a text that offers itself up for rival interpretations.

# The Taming of the Shrew

[*Dramatis Personae*

CHRISTOPHER SLY, *a tinker and beggar,*
HOSTESS *of an alehouse,*
A LORD,
A PAGE, SERVANTS, HUNTSMEN,
PLAYERS,

} *Persons in the Induction*

BAPTISTA, *a rich gentleman of Padua*
KATHARINA, *the shrew, also called Katharine and Kate, Baptista's elder daughter*
BIANCA, *Baptista's younger daughter*

PETRUCHIO, *a gentleman of Verona, suitor to Katharina*
GRUMIO, *Petruchio's servant*
CURTIS, NATHANIEL, PHILIP, JOSEPH, NICHOLAS, PETER, *and other servants of Petruchio*

GREMIO, *elderly suitor to Bianca*
HORTENSIO, *suitor to Bianca*
LUCENTIO, *son of Vincentio, in love with Bianca*
TRANIO, *Lucentio's servant*
BIONDELLO, *Lucentio's servant*
VINCENTIO, *a gentleman of Pisa*
A PEDANT *(or Merchant) of Mantua*
A WIDOW, *courted by Hortensio*

A TAILOR
A HABERDASHER
AN OFFICER
*Other Servants of Baptista and Lucentio*

SCENE: *Padua, and Petruchio's country house in Italy; the Induction is located in the countryside and at a Lord's house in England*]

## [Induction.1]

*Enter Beggar (Christopher Sly) and Hostess.*

SLY  I'll feeze you, in faith.  1
HOSTESS  A pair of stocks, you rogue!  2
SLY  You're a baggage. The Slys are no rogues. Look in  3
the chronicles; we came in with Richard Conqueror.  4
Therefore *paucas pallabris*, let the world slide. Sessa!  5
HOSTESS  You will not pay for the glasses you have
burst?
SLY  No, not a denier. Go by, Saint Jeronimy, go to thy  8
cold bed and warm thee.  9

HOSTESS  I know my remedy; I must go fetch the third-  10
borough.  [*Exit.*]  11
SLY  Third, or fourth, or fifth borough, I'll answer him  12
by law. I'll not budge an inch, boy. Let him come, and  13
kindly.  *Falls asleep.*  14

*Wind horns [within]. Enter a Lord from hunting,
with his train.*

LORD
Huntsman, I charge thee, tender well my hounds.  15
Breathe Merriman—the poor cur is embossed—  16
And couple Clowder with the deep-mouthed brach.  17
Saw'st thou not, boy, how Silver made it good  18
At the hedge corner, in the coldest fault?  19

---

I would not lose the dog for twenty pound.

FIRST HUNTSMAN
Why, Bellman is as good as he, my lord.
He cried upon it at the merest loss,                                    22
And twice today picked out the dullest scent.
Trust me, I take him for the better dog.

LORD
Thou art a fool. If Echo were as fleet,
I would esteem him worth a dozen such.
But sup them well and look unto them all.                               27
Tomorrow I intend to hunt again.

FIRST HUNTSMAN   I will, my lord.

LORD [seeing Sly]
What's here? One dead, or drunk? See, doth he
    breathe?

SECOND HUNTSMAN [examining Sly]
He breathes, my lord. Were he not warmed with ale,
This were a bed but cold to sleep so soundly.

LORD
Oh, monstrous beast, how like a swine he lies!
Grim death, how foul and loathsome is thine image!                     34
Sirs, I will practice on this drunken man.                             35
What think you, if he were conveyed to bed,
Wrapped in sweet clothes, rings put upon his fingers,                  37
A most delicious banquet by his bed,                                   38
And brave attendants near him when he wakes,                           39
Would not the beggar then forget himself?

FIRST HUNTSMAN
Believe me, lord, I think he cannot choose.                            41

SECOND HUNTSMAN
It would seem strange unto him when he waked.

LORD
Even as a flatt'ring dream or worthless fancy.                         43
Then take him up, and manage well the jest.
Carry him gently to my fairest chamber,
And hang it round with all my wanton pictures.
Balm his foul head in warm distillèd waters,                           47
And burn sweet wood to make the lodging sweet.
Procure me music ready when he wakes,
To make a dulcet and a heavenly sound.                                 50
And if he chance to speak, be ready straight,                          51
And with a low submissive reverence                                    52
Say, "What is it Your Honor will command?"
Let one attend him with a silver basin
Full of rosewater and bestrewed with flowers;
Another bear the ewer, the third a diaper,                             56
And say, "Will 't please Your Lordship cool your
    hands?"
Someone be ready with a costly suit,
And ask him what apparel he will wear;
Another tell him of his hounds and horse,                              60
And that his lady mourns at his disease.                               61

Persuade him that he hath been lunatic,
And when he says he is, say that he dreams,                            63
For he is nothing but a mighty lord.
This do, and do it kindly, gentle sirs.                                65
It will be pastime passing excellent,                                  66
If it be husbanded with modesty.                                       67

FIRST HUNTSMAN
My lord, I warrant you we will play our part
As he shall think by our true diligence                                69
He is no less than what we say he is.

LORD
Take him up gently, and to bed with him,
And each one to his office when he wakes.                              72
        [Some bear out Sly.] Sound trumpets [within].
Sirrah, go see what trumpet 'tis that sounds.                          73
                            [Exit a Servingman.]
Belike some noble gentleman that means,                                74
Traveling some journey, to repose him here.

            Enter [a] Servingman.

How now? Who is it?

SERVINGMAN   An't please Your Honor, players               76
That offer service to Your Lordship.

            Enter Players.

LORD
Bid them come near.—Now, fellows, you are welcome.

PLAYERS   We thank Your Honor.

LORD
Do you intend to stay with me tonight?

FIRST PLAYER
So please Your Lordship to accept our duty.                81

LORD
With all my heart. This fellow I remember
Since once he played a farmer's eldest son.—
'Twas where you wooed the gentlewoman so well.
I have forgot your name, but sure that part
Was aptly fitted and naturally performed.

SECOND PLAYER
I think 'twas Soto that Your Honor means.

LORD
'Tis very true. Thou didst it excellent.
Well, you are come to me in happy time,                    89
The rather for I have some sport in hand                   90
Wherein your cunning can assist me much.                   91
There is a lord will hear you play tonight.
But I am doubtful of your modesties,                       93
Lest, overeyeing of his odd behavior—                      94
For yet His Honor never heard a play—
You break into some merry passion                          96

---

22 **cried . . . loss** bayed to signal his recovery of the scent after it had been
completely lost   27 **sup them well** feed them a good supper
34 **image** likeness (since sleep was regarded as a likeness of death).
35 **practice on** play a joke on   37 **sweet** perfumed   38 **banquet** light
repast   39 **brave** finely arrayed   41 **cannot choose** is bound to.
43 **fancy** flight of imagination.   47 **Balm** Bathe, anoint   50 **dulcet** melodious   51 **straight** at once   52 **reverence** bow   56 **ewer** jug, pitcher.
**diaper** towel   60 **horse** horses   61 **disease** i.e., mental derangement.

63 **when . . . is** i.e., when he says he must be mad indeed. (The *is* is
stressed.)   65 **kindly** naturally (and thus persuasively).   **gentle** kind
66 **passing** surpassingly   67 **husbanded with modesty** managed
with decorum.   69 **As** so that.   **by** as a result of   72 **office** duty
73 **Sirrah** (Usual form of address to inferiors.)   74 **Belike** Perhaps
76 **An't** If it   81 **So please** If it please.   **duty** expression of respect
and dutiful service.   89 **happy** opportune   90 **The rather for** the
more so since   91 **cunning** professional skill   93 **doubtful** apprehensive.   **modesties** discretion, self-control   94 **overeyeing of** witnessing   96 **merry passion** outburst of laughter

And so offend him; for I tell you, sirs,
If you should smile, he grows impatient.

FIRST PLAYER
Fear not, my lord, we can contain ourselves,
Were he the veriest antic in the world.    100

LORD [to a Servingman]
Go, sirrah, take them to the buttery,    101
And give them friendly welcome every one.
Let them want nothing that my house affords.    103
                              *Exit one with the Players.*
Sirrah, go you to Barthol'mew my page,
And see him dressed in all suits like a lady.    105
That done, conduct him to the drunkard's chamber,
And call him "madam," do him obeisance.    107
Tell him from me, as he will win my love,    108
He bear himself with honorable action
Such as he hath observed in noble ladies
Unto their lords by them accomplishèd.    111
Such duty to the drunkard let him do
With soft low tongue and lowly courtesy,
And say, "What is't Your Honor will command,
Wherein your lady and your humble wife
May show her duty and make known her love?"
And then with kind embracements, tempting kisses,
And with declining head into his bosom,
Bid him shed tears, as being overjoyed
To see her noble lord restored to health,
Who for this seven years hath esteemèd him    121
No better than a poor and loathsome beggar.
And if the boy have not a woman's gift
To rain a shower of commanded tears,
An onion will do well for such a shift,    125
Which in a napkin being close conveyed    126
Shall in despite enforce a watery eye.    127
See this dispatched with all the haste thou canst.
Anon I'll give thee more instructions.    129
                              *Exit a Servingman.*
I know the boy will well usurp the grace,    130
Voice, gait, and action of a gentlewoman.
I long to hear him call the drunkard husband,
And how my men will stay themselves from laughter    133
When they do homage to this simple peasant.
I'll in to counsel them. Haply my presence    135
May well abate the overmerry spleen    136
Which otherwise would grow into extremes.
                              [*Exeunt.*]

❧

# [Induction.2]

*Enter aloft the drunkard [Sly], with attendants;*
*some with apparel, basin, and ewer and other*
*appurtenances; and Lord.*

SLY    For God's sake, a pot of small ale.    1
FIRST SERVINGMAN
Will't please Your Lordship drink a cup of sack?    2
SECOND SERVINGMAN
Will't please Your Honor taste of these conserves?    3
THIRD SERVINGMAN
What raiment will Your Honor wear today?
SLY    I am Christophero Sly. Call not me "Honor" nor
"Lordship." I ne'er drank sack in my life; and if you
give me any conserves, give me conserves of beef.    7
Ne'er ask me what raiment I'll wear, for I have no
more doublets than backs, no more stockings than    9
legs, nor no more shoes than feet—nay, sometimes
more feet than shoes, or such shoes as my toes look    11
through the overleather.    12
LORD
Heaven cease this idle humor in Your Honor!    13
Oh, that a mighty man of such descent,
Of such possessions and so high esteem,
Should be infusèd with so foul a spirit!
SLY    What, would you make me mad? Am not I Christo-
pher Sly, old Sly's son of Burton-heath, by birth a    18
peddler, by education a cardmaker, by transmutation    19
a bearherd, and now by present profession a tinker?    20
Ask Marian Hacket, the fat alewife of Wincot, if she    21
know me not. If she say I am not fourteen pence on    22
the score for sheer ale, score me up for the lyingest    23
knave in Christendom. What, I am not bestraught:    24
here's—
THIRD SERVINGMAN
Oh, this it is that makes your lady mourn!
SECOND SERVINGMAN
Oh, this is it that makes your servants droop!
LORD
Hence comes it that your kindred shuns your house,
As beaten hence by your strange lunacy.    29
Oh, noble lord, bethink thee of thy birth.
Call home thy ancient thoughts from banishment,    31
And banish hence these abject lowly dreams.
Look how thy servants do attend on thee,
Each in his office ready at thy beck.    34

---

100 **veriest antic** oddest buffoon or eccentric    101 **buttery** pantry, or
a room for storing liquor (in butts) and other provisions    103 **want**
lack    105 **in all suits** in every detail. (With a pun on *suits* of clothes.)
107 **do him obeisance** show him dutiful respect.    108 **him** i.e., the
page Bartholomew.    **as he will** if he wishes to    111 **by them accomplishèd** performed by the ladies.    121 **him** himself    125 **shift** purpose    126 **napkin** handkerchief.    **close** secretly    127 **in despite** i.e.,
notwithstanding a natural inclination to laugh rather than cry
129 **Anon** Soon    130 **usurp** assume    133 **And how** i.e., and to see
how    135 **I'll in** I'll go in    136 **spleen** mood. (The spleen was the
supposed seat of laughter and anger.)

**Induction.2. Location: A bedchamber in the Lord's house.**
**0.1** *aloft* i.e., in the gallery over the rear facade of the stage    **1 small**
weak (and therefore cheap)    **2 sack** sweet Spanish wine (suited for a
gentleman to drink).    **3 conserves** candied fruit.    **7 conserves of**
**beef** preserved (salted) beef.    **9 doublets** men's jackets    **11 as that**
**12 overleather** upper leather of the shoe.    **13 idle humor** foolish
whim    **18 Burton-heath** (Perhaps Barton on the Heath, about sixteen
miles from Stratford, the home of Shakespeare's aunt.)    **19 card-**
**maker** maker of cards or combs used to prepare wool for spinning
**20 bearherd** keeper of a performing bear.    **tinker** pot mender.
**21 alewife** woman who keeps an alehouse.    **Wincot** small village about
four miles from Stratford. (The parish register shows that there were
Hackets living there in 1591.)    **22–3 on the score** in debt (since such
reckonings were originally notched or scored on a stick)    **23 sheer**
nothing but.    **score me up for** reckon me to be    **24 bestraught** distracted    **29 As** as if    **31 ancient** former    **34 beck** nod.

Wilt thou have music? Hark, Apollo plays,    *Music.*    35
And twenty cagèd nightingales do sing.
Or wilt thou sleep? We'll have thee to a couch,
Softer and sweeter than the lustful bed
On purpose trimmed up for Semiramis.    39
Say thou wilt walk; we will bestrew the ground.    40
Or wilt thou ride? Thy horses shall be trapped,    41
Their harness studded all with gold and pearl.
Dost thou love hawking? Thou hast hawks will soar
Above the morning lark. Or wilt thou hunt?
Thy hounds shall make the welkin answer them    45
And fetch shrill echoes from the hollow earth.

FIRST SERVINGMAN
Say thou wilt course, thy greyhounds are as swift    47
As breathèd stags, ay, fleeter than the roe.    48

SECOND SERVINGMAN
Dost thou love pictures? We will fetch thee straight
Adonis painted by a running brook,    50
And Cytherea all in sedges hid,    51
Which seem to move and wanton with her breath,    52
Even as the waving sedges play wi'th'wind.

LORD
We'll show thee Io as she was a maid,    54
And how she was beguilèd and surprised,
As lively painted as the deed was done.    56

THIRD SERVINGMAN
Or Daphne roaming through a thorny wood,    57
Scratching her legs that one shall swear she bleeds,
And at that sight shall sad Apollo weep,
So workmanly the blood and tears are drawn.    60

LORD
Thou art a lord, and nothing but a lord.
Thou hast a lady far more beautiful
Than any woman in this waning age.    63

FIRST SERVINGMAN
And till the tears that she hath shed for thee
Like envious floods o'errun her lovely face,    65
She was the fairest creature in the world;
And yet she is inferior to none.    67

SLY
Am I a lord? And have I such a lady?
Or do I dream? Or have I dreamed till now?
I do not sleep: I see, I hear, I speak,
I smell sweet savors, and I feel soft things.
Upon my life, I am a lord indeed,
And not a tinker nor Christopher Sly.
Well, bring our lady hither to our sight,

And once again a pot o'th' smallest ale.

SECOND SERVINGMAN
Will 't please Your Mightiness to wash your hands?
Oh, how we joy to see your wit restored!    77
Oh, that once more you knew but what you are!    78
These fifteen years you have been in a dream,
Or when you waked, so waked as if you slept.

SLY
These fifteen years! By my fay, a goodly nap.    81
But did I never speak of all that time?    82

FIRST SERVINGMAN
Oh, yes, my lord, but very idle words;
For though you lay here in this goodly chamber,
Yet would you say ye were beaten out of door,
And rail upon the hostess of the house,    86
And say you would present her at the leet    87
Because she brought stone jugs and no sealed quarts.    88
Sometimes you would call out for Cicely Hacket.

SLY
Ay, the woman's maid of the house.

THIRD SERVINGMAN
Why, sir, you know no house, nor no such maid,
Nor no such men as you have reckoned up,
As Stephen Sly, and old John Naps of Greet,    93
And Peter Turf, and Henry Pimpernel,
And twenty more such names and men as these,
Which never were, nor no man ever saw.

SLY
Now Lord be thankèd for my good amends!    97

ALL
Amen.

*Enter [the Page as a] lady, with Attendants.*

SLY        I thank thee. Thou shalt not lose by it.    98

PAGE
How fares my noble lord?

SLY                    Marry, I fare well,    99
For here is cheer enough. Where is my wife?

PAGE
Here, noble lord. What is thy will with her?

SLY
Are you my wife, and will not call me husband?
My men should call me "lord"; I am your goodman.    103

PAGE
My husband and my lord, my lord and husband;
I am your wife in all obedience.

SLY
I know it well.—What must I call her?

LORD                                Madam.

---

35 **Apollo** i.e., as god of music    39 **Semiramis** legendary queen of Assyria, famous for her voluptuousness.    40 **bestrew** i.e., scatter rushes on    41 **trapped** adorned    45 **welkin** sky, heavens    47 **course** hunt the hare    48 **breathèd** in good physical condition, with good wind.    **roe** small, swift deer.    50 **Adonis** a young huntsman with whom Venus is vainly in love. (See Ovid's *Metamorphoses*, Book 10, and Shakespeare's poem *Venus and Adonis*.)    51 **Cytherea** one of the names for Venus (because of her association with the island of Cythera).    **sedges** grassy marsh plants    52 **wanton** play seductively 54 **Io** a woman who, according to Ovid, was seduced by Jove concealed in a mist and afterwards transformed into a heifer    56 **as** as if    57 **Daphne** a wood nymph beloved by Apollo, changed by Diana into a laurel tree to preserve her from Apollo's assault (*Metamorphoses*, Book 1)    60 **workmanly** skillfully    63 **waning** degenerate    65 **envious** spiteful    67 **yet** even today

77 **wit** mental faculties    78 **knew but** only knew    81 **fay** faith    82 **of** during    86 **house** tavern    87 **present** bring accusation against.    **leet** manorial court    88 **sealed quarts** quart containers officially stamped as a guarantee of that capacity. (The irregular stoneware quarts might be used to cheat customers.)    93 **Stephen . . . Greet** (A Stephen Sly lived in Stratford during Shakespeare's day. *Greet* is a Gloucestershire hamlet not far from Stratford. The Folio reading, "Greece," is an easy misreading if Shakespeare wrote "Greete.")    97 **amends** recovery.    98 **Thou . . . it** i.e., I will reward your solicitude toward me.    99 **Marry** (A mild oath, derived from "by Mary.")    **fare well** (1) am fine (2) have plenty of good *cheer* (line 100), refreshment    103 **goodman** (A homely term for "husband.")

SLY   Al'ce madam, or Joan madam?

LORD
Madam, and nothing else. So lords call ladies.

SLY
Madam wife, they say that I have dreamed
And slept above some fifteen year or more.

PAGE
Ay, and the time seems thirty unto me,
Being all this time abandoned from your bed.        112

SLY
'Tis much.—Servants, leave me and her alone.—
Madam, undress you and come now to bed.

PAGE
Thrice-noble lord, let me entreat of you
To pardon me yet for a night or two,
Or, if not so, until the sun be set.
For your physicians have expressly charged,
In peril to incur your former malady,
That I should yet absent me from your bed.
I hope this reason stands for my excuse.

SLY   Ay, it stands so that I may hardly tarry so long. But 122
I would be loath to fall into my dreams again. I will
therefore tarry in despite of the flesh and the blood.

*Enter a [Servingman as] messenger.*

SERVINGMAN
Your Honor's players, hearing your amendment,
Are come to play a pleasant comedy,
For so your doctors hold it very meet,        127
Seeing too much sadness hath congealed your blood,
And melancholy is the nurse of frenzy.
Therefore they thought it good you hear a play
And frame your mind to mirth and merriment,
Which bars a thousand harms and lengthens life.

SLY   Marry, I will let them play it. Is not a comonty a 133
Christmas gambold or a tumbling-trick?        134

PAGE
No, my good lord, it is more pleasing stuff.

SLY   What, household stuff?        136

PAGE   It is a kind of history.        137

SLY   Well, we'll see 't. Come, madam wife, sit by my side
and let the world slip; we shall ne'er be younger.        139
*[They sit over the stage.] Flourish.*

## 1.1

*Enter Lucentio and his man, Tranio.*

LUCENTIO
Tranio, since for the great desire I had
To see fair Padua, nursery of arts,        2
I am arrived fore fruitful Lombardy,        3
The pleasant garden of great Italy,
And by my father's love and leave am armed
With his good will and thy good company,
My trusty servant, well approved in all,        7
Here let us breathe and haply institute        8
A course of learning and ingenious studies.        9
Pisa, renownèd for grave citizens,
Gave me my being, and my father first—        11
A merchant of great traffic through the world,        12
Vincentio, come of the Bentivolii.        13
Vincentio's son, brought up in Florence,        14
It shall become to serve all hopes conceived        15
To deck his fortune with his virtuous deeds.        16
And therefore, Tranio, for the time I study,        17
Virtue and that part of philosophy
Will I apply that treats of happiness        19
By virtue specially to be achieved.
Tell me thy mind, for I have Pisa left
And am to Padua come as he that leaves
A shallow plash to plunge him in the deep,        23
And with satiety seeks to quench his thirst.

TRANIO
*Mi perdonate,* gentle master mine.        25
I am in all affected as yourself,        26
Glad that you thus continue your resolve
To suck the sweets of sweet philosophy.
Only, good master, while we do admire
This virtue and this moral discipline,
Let's be no stoics nor no stocks, I pray,        31
Or so devote to Aristotle's checks        32
As Ovid be an outcast quite abjured.        33
Balk logic with acquaintance that you have,        34
And practice rhetoric in your common talk.        35
Music and poesy use to quicken you;        36

112 **abandoned** banished   122 **stands** (1) is the case (2) punningly, "is giving me an erection." The joke picks up on *stands*, meaning "serves," in line 121.   127 **meet** suitable   133 **Marry . . . play it** (Perhaps the Folio punctuation should be emended to "Marry, I will. Let them play it.")   **comonty** (Sly's approximation of "comedy.")   134 **gambold** (Sly's version of "gambol," frolicsome merry-making and leaping about.)   136 **household stuff** i.e., domestic doings.   137 **history** story.   139.1 *They sit over the stage* (Possibly the Lord and some servingmen exeunt here or at line 113. At 1.1.249 ff., a servingman, the Page, and Sly speak, while the Lord is no longer heard from.)

**1.1 Location: Padua. A street before Baptista's house.**
**2 Padua . . . arts** (Padua's was one of the most renowned of universities during Shakespeare's time.)   **3 am arrived fore** have arrived at, or at the gates of, before. (Padua is not in Lombardy, but imprecise maps may have allowed Shakespeare to think of Lombardy as comprising all of northern Italy.)   **7 approved** tested and proved trustworthy   **8 breathe** pause, settle down.   **haply institute** begin, as circumstances permit   **9 ingenious** i.e., liberal, befitting a wellborn person   **11 first** i.e., before me   **12 of great traffic** involved in extensive trade   **13 come of** descended from   **14–16 Vincentio's . . . deeds** It will befit Vincentio's son, brought up in Florence, to fulfill all the hopes of his family by adding virtuous deeds to what fortune has bestowed on him.   **17 for . . . study** for my term of study   **19 apply** study.   treats of discusses, concerns   **23 plash** pool   **25 *Mi perdonate*** Pardon me   **26 affected** disposed   **31 stocks** persons devoid of feeling, like wooden posts. (With a play on *stoics.*)   **32 devote** devoted.   **checks** restraints   **33 As** so that.   **Ovid** Latin love poet. (Used here to typify amorous light entertainment, as contrasted with the constraining philosophic study of Aristotle.)   **34 Balk logic** Argue, bandy words.   **acquaintance** acquaintances   **35 common talk** ordinary conversation.   **36 Music . . . you** Use music and poetry to refresh yourself

The mathematics and the metaphysics,
Fall to them as you find your stomach serves you.        38
No profit grows where is no pleasure ta'en.
In brief, sir, study what you most affect.               40

LUCENTIO
Gramercies, Tranio, well dost thou advise.               41
If, Biondello, thou wert come ashore,                    42
We could at once put us in readiness
And take a lodging fit to entertain
Such friends as time in Padua shall beget.
But stay awhile, what company is this?

TRANIO
Master, some show to welcome us to town.                 47

*Enter Baptista with his two daughters, Katha-*
*rina and Bianca; Gremio, a pantaloon; [and]*
*Hortensio, suitor to Bianca. Lucentio [and]*
*Tranio stand by.*

BAPTISTA
Gentlemen, importune me no farther,
For how I firmly am resolved you know:
That is, not to bestow my youngest daughter
Before I have a husband for the elder.
If either of you both love Katharina,
Because I know you well and love you well,
Leave shall you have to court her at your pleasure.

GREMIO
To cart her rather. She's too rough for me.              55
There, there, Hortensio, will you any wife?

KATHARINA [*to Baptista*]
I pray you, sir, is it your will
To make a stale of me amongst these mates?               58

HORTENSIO
"Mates," maid? How mean you that? No mates for
    you,
Unless you were of gentler, milder mold.

KATHARINA
I'faith, sir, you shall never need to fear;
Iwis it is not halfway to her heart.                     62
But if it were, doubt not her care should be             63
To comb your noddle with a three-legged stool,           64
And paint your face, and use you like a fool.            65

HORTENSIO
From all such devils, good Lord deliver us!

GREMIO    And me too, good Lord!

TRANIO [*aside to Lucentio*]
Husht, master, here's some good pastime toward.          68

That wench is stark mad or wonderful froward.            69

LUCENTIO [*aside to Tranio*]
But in the other's silence do I see
Maid's mild behavior and sobriety.
Peace, Tranio!

TRANIO [*aside to Lucentio*]
Well said, master. Mum, and gaze your fill.

BAPTISTA
Gentlemen, that I may soon make good
What I have said—Bianca, get you in.
And let it not displease thee, good Bianca,
For I will love thee ne'er the less, my girl.

KATHARINA    A pretty peat! It is best                   78
Put finger in the eye, an she knew why.                  79

BIANCA
Sister, content you in my discontent.—
Sir, to your pleasure humbly I subscribe.                81
My books and instruments shall be my company,
On them to look and practice by myself.

LUCENTIO [*aside to Tranio*]
Hark, Tranio, thou mayst hear Minerva speak.             84

HORTENSIO
Signor Baptista, will you be so strange?                 85
Sorry am I that our good will effects                    86
Bianca's grief.

GREMIO              Why will you mew her up,              87
Signor Baptista, for this fiend of hell,                 88
And make her bear the penance of her tongue?             89

BAPTISTA
Gentlemen, content ye. I am resolved.
Go in, Bianca.                    [*Exit Bianca.*]
And for I know she taketh most delight                   92
In music, instruments, and poetry,
Schoolmasters will I keep within my house
Fit to instruct her youth. If you, Hortensio,
Or, Signor Gremio, you know any such,
Prefer them hither; for to cunning men                   97
I will be very kind, and liberal
To mine own children in good bringing up.
And so farewell.—Katharina, you may stay,
For I have more to commune with Bianca.    *Exit.* 101

KATHARINA
Why, and I trust I may go too, may I not?
What, shall I be appointed hours,                        103
As though, belike, I knew not what to take,              104
And what to leave? Ha!                    *Exit.* 105

GREMIO    You may go to the devil's dam. Your gifts are 106
so good, here's none will hold you.—Their love is not 107

so great, Hortensio, but we may blow our nails together 108
and fast it fairly out. Our cake's dough on both 109
sides. Farewell. Yet, for the love I bear my sweet 110
Bianca, if I can by any means light on a fit man to teach
her that wherein she delights, I will wish him to 112
her father.

HORTENSIO   So will I, Signor Gremio. But a word, I pray.
Though the nature of our quarrel yet never brooked 115
parle, know now, upon advice, it toucheth us both, 116
that we may yet again have access to our fair mistress
and be happy rivals in Bianca's love, to labor and
effect one thing specially.

GREMIO   What's that, I pray?

HORTENSIO   Marry, sir, to get a husband for her sister.

GREMIO   A husband? A devil.

HORTENSIO   I say a husband.

GREMIO   I say a devil. Think'st thou, Hortensio, though
her father be very rich, any man is so very a fool to be 125
married to hell?

HORTENSIO   Tush, Gremio, though it pass your patience 127
and mine to endure her loud alarums, why, man, there 128
be good fellows in the world, an a man could light on 129
them, would take her with all faults, and money 130
enough.

GREMIO   I cannot tell. But I had as lief take her dowry 132
with this condition: to be whipped at the high cross 133
every morning.

HORTENSIO   Faith, as you say, there's small choice in
rotten apples. But come, since this bar in law makes us 136
friends, it shall be so far forth friendly maintained till
by helping Baptista's eldest daughter to a husband we
set his youngest free for a husband, and then have to't 139
afresh. Sweet Bianca! Happy man be his dole! He that 140
runs fastest gets the ring. How say you, Signor 141
Gremio?

GREMIO   I am agreed, and would I had given him the
best horse in Padua to begin his wooing that would
thor-oughly woo her, wed her, and bed her and rid
the house of her! Come on.         *Exeunt ambo. Manent* 146
                                  *Tranio and Lucentio.*

TRANIO
I pray, sir, tell me, is it possible
That love should of a sudden take such hold?

LUCENTIO
Oh, Tranio, till I found it to be true,
I never thought it possible or likely.
But see, while idly I stood looking on,

I found the effect of love in idleness,                     152
And now in plainness do confess to thee,
That art to me as secret and as dear                         154
As Anna to the Queen of Carthage was,                        155
Tranio, I burn, I pine, I perish, Tranio,
If I achieve not this young modest girl.
Counsel me, Tranio, for I know thou canst;
Assist me, Tranio, for I know thou wilt.

TRANIO
Master, it is no time to chide you now.
Affection is not rated from the heart.                       161
If love have touched you, naught remains but so,
*"Redime te captum quam queas minimo."*                      163

LUCENTIO
Gramercies, lad. Go forward. This contents;                  164
The rest will comfort, for thy counsel's sound.              165

TRANIO
Master, you looked so longly on the maid,                    166
Perhaps you marked not what's the pith of all.               167

LUCENTIO
Oh, yes, I saw sweet beauty in her face,
Such as the daughter of Agenor had,                          169
That made great Jove to humble him to her hand,              170
When with his knees he kissed the Cretan strand.             171

TRANIO
Saw you no more? Marked you not how her sister
Began to scold and raise up such a storm
That mortal ears might hardly endure the din?

LUCENTIO
Tranio, I saw her coral lips to move,
And with her breath she did perfume the air.
Sacred and sweet was all I saw in her.

TRANIO [*aside*]
Nay, then, 'tis time to stir him from his trance.—
I pray, awake, sir. If you love the maid,
Bend thoughts and wits to achieve her. Thus it stands:
Her elder sister is so curst and shrewd                      181
That till the father rid his hands of her,
Master, your love must live a maid at home,                  183
And therefore has he closely mewed her up,                   184
Because she will not be annoyed with suitors.                185

LUCENTIO
Ah, Tranio, what a cruel father's he!
But art thou not advised he took some care                   187
To get her cunning schoolmasters to instruct her?           188

TRANIO
Ay, marry, am I, sir; and now 'tis plotted.

---

**108 blow . . . together** i.e., twiddle our thumbs, wait patiently
**109 fast . . . out** abstain as best we can.   **109–10 Our cake's . . . sides**
i.e., We're both out of luck, getting nowhere.   **112 wish** commend
**115-16 brooked parle** tolerated conference   **116 advice** reflection.
**toucheth** concerns   **125 very a** utterly a   **127 pass** exceed
**128 alarums** i.e., loud, startling noises. (In military terms, a call to
arms.)   **129 an** if   **130 would** who would   **132 I cannot tell** i.e., I
don't know about that, don't know what to say.   **had as lief** would
as willingly   **133 high cross** cross set on a pedestal in a marketplace
or center of a town   **136 bar in law** legal impediment, i.e., Baptista's
refusal to receive suitors for Bianca   **139 have to't** renew combat
**140 Happy . . . dole!** i.e., May happiness be the reward of him who
wins! (Proverbial.)   **141 the ring** (An allusion to the sport of riding at
the ring, with quibble on "wedding ring" and also sexual sense, "vul-
var ring.")   **146 s.d. ambo** both.   *Manent* They remain on stage

**152 love in idleness** i.e., (1) desire bred by idleness (2) a popular name
for the pansy, thought to induce love   **154 secret** trusted, intimate
**155 Anna** confidante of her sister Dido, Queen of Carthage, beloved of
Aeneas   **161 rated** driven away by chiding   **163 Redime . . . minimo**
Buy yourself out of bondage for as little as you can. (From Terence's
*Eunuchus* as quoted in William Lilly's *Latin Grammar*.)   **164 Gramercies** Thanks   **165 The rest** the rest of what you have to say   **166 so
longly** (1) for such a long time (2) so longingly   **167 marked** noted.
**pith** core, essence   **169 daughter of Agenor** Europa, beloved of Jove;
Jove took the form of a bull in order to abduct her   **170 him** himself
**171 kissed** i.e., knelt on   **181 curst and shrewd** shrewish and ill-
natured   **183 must . . . home** must remain unattached, unmated
**184 mewed** cooped   **185 Because** so that   **187 advised** aware
(that)   **188 cunning** expert

LUCENTIO
I have it, Tranio.
TRANIO                    Master, for my hand,                    190
Both our inventions meet and jump in one.                        191
LUCENTIO
Tell me thine first.
TRANIO                    You will be schoolmaster
And undertake the teaching of the maid:
That's your device.
LUCENTIO                It is. May it be done?
TRANIO
Not possible; for who shall bear your part
And be in Padua here Vincentio's son,
Keep house and ply his book, welcome his friends,    197
Visit his countrymen, and banquet them?
LUCENTIO
*Basta*, content thee, for I have it full.    199
We have not yet been seen in any house,
Nor can we be distinguished by our faces
For man or master. Then it follows thus:
Thou shalt be master, Tranio, in my stead,
Keep house, and port, and servants, as I should.    204
I will some other be, some Florentine,
Some Neapolitan, or meaner man of Pisa.    206
'Tis hatched and shall be so. Tranio, at once
Uncase thee. Take my colored hat and cloak.    208
When Biondello comes, he waits on thee,
But I will charm him first to keep his tongue.    210
TRANIO    So had you need.
In brief, sir, sith it your pleasure is,    212
And I am tied to be obedient—
For so your father charged me at our parting,
"Be serviceable to my son," quoth he,
Although I think 'twas in another sense—
I am content to be Lucentio,
Because so well I love Lucentio.
                    [*They exchange clothes.*]
LUCENTIO
Tranio, be so, because Lucentio loves.
And let me be a slave t'achieve that maid
Whose sudden sight hath thralled my wounded eye.    221

        *Enter Biondello.*

Here comes the rogue.—Sirrah, where have you been?
BIONDELLO
Where have I been? Nay, how now, where are you?
Master, has my fellow Tranio stol'n your clothes?
Or you stol'n his? Or both? Pray, what's the news?
LUCENTIO
Sirrah, come hither. 'Tis no time to jest,
And therefore frame your manners to the time.    227
Your fellow Tranio here, to save my life,
Puts my apparel and my countenance on,    229

And I for my escape have put on his;
For in a quarrel since I came ashore,
I killed a man, and fear I was descried.    232
Wait you on him, I charge you, as becomes,    233
While I make way from hence to save my life.
You understand me?
BIONDELLO                    I, sir?—Ne'er a whit.    235
LUCENTIO
And not a jot of Tranio in your mouth.
Tranio is changed into Lucentio.
BIONDELLO
The better for him. Would I were so, too!
TRANIO
So could I, faith, boy, to have the next wish after,
That Lucentio indeed had Baptista's youngest
    daughter.
But, sirrah, not for my sake, but your master's, I advise
You use your manners discreetly in all kind of com-
    panies.
When I am alone, why, then I am Tranio,
But in all places else your master Lucentio.
LUCENTIO    Tranio, let's go.
One thing more rests, that thyself execute:    246
To make one among these wooers. If thou ask me
    why,    247
Sufficeth my reasons are both good and weighty.    248
                    *Exeunt.*

        *The presenters above speak.*

FIRST SERVINGMAN
My lord, you nod. You do not mind the play.    249
SLY    Yes, by Saint Anne, do I. A good matter, surely.
Comes there any more of it?
PAGE [*as lady*]    My lord, 'tis but begun.
SLY    'Tis a very excellent piece of work, madam lady.
Would 'twere done!                    *They sit and mark.*    254

                    ❧

# [1.2]

        *Enter Petruchio and his man, Grumio.*

PETRUCHIO
Verona, for a while I take my leave
To see my friends in Padua, but of all    2
My best belovèd and approvèd friend,
Hortensio; and I trow this is his house.    4
Here, sirrah Grumio, knock, I say.
GRUMIO    Knock, sir? Whom should I knock? Is there any
man has rebused Your Worship?    7
PETRUCHIO    Villain, I say, knock me here soundly.    8

---

**190 for my hand** (A mild oath.)    **191 inventions** plans.    **jump** tally,
agree    **197 Keep . . . book** entertain guests and pursue his studies
**199 *Basta*** Enough.    **full** i.e., fully thought out.    **204 port** state, style
of living    **206 meaner** of a lower social class    **208 Uncase thee**
remove your outer garments.    **210 charm** i.e., command, persuade
**212 sith** since    **221 Whose . . . thralled** the sudden sight of whom has
captured    **227 frame** adapt, suit    **229 countenance** bearing, manner

**232 descried** observed.    **233 as becomes** as is suitable    **235 I, sir**
(Lucentio may hear this as "Ay, sir.")    **Ne'er a whit** Not in the least.
**246 rests** remains to be done    **247 make one** join in    **248 Sufficeth**
it suffices that    **248.2 *presenters*** characters of the Induction,
whose role it is to "present" the play proper    **249 mind** attend to
**254 s.d. *mark*** observe.
**1.2. Location: Padua. Before Hortensio's house.**
**2 of all** above all    **4 trow** believe    **7 rebused** (A blunder for "abused.")
**8 Villain** i.e., Wretch. (A term of abuse.)    **me** i.e., for me.
(But Grumio, perhaps intentionally, misunderstands.)

GRUMIO  Knock you here, sir? Why, sir, what am I, sir, that I should knock you here, sir?

PETRUCHIO
Villain, I say, knock me at this gate,  11
And rap me well, or I'll knock your knave's pate.

GRUMIO
My master is grown quarrelsome. I should knock you first,  13
And then I know after who comes by the worst.  14

PETRUCHIO  Will it not be?  15
Faith, sirrah, an you'll not knock, I'll ring it.  16
I'll try how you can *sol fa* and sing it.  17
*He wrings him by the ears.*

GRUMIO
Help, masters, help! My master is mad.  18

PETRUCHIO
Now knock when I bid you, sirrah villain.

*Enter Hortensio.*

HORTENSIO  How now, what's the matter? My old friend Grumio and my good friend Petruchio? How do you all at Verona?

PETRUCHIO
Signor Hortensio, come you to part the fray?
*Con tutto il cuore ben trovato,* may I say.  24

HORTENSIO
*Alla nostra casa ben venuto,*  25
*Molto onorato signor mio Petruchio.*—  26
Rise, Grumio, rise. We will compound this quarrel.  27

GRUMIO  Nay, 'tis no matter, sir, what he 'leges in Latin.  28 If this be not a lawful cause for me to leave his service! Look you, sir: he bid me knock him and rap him soundly, sir. Well, was it fit for a servant to use his master so, being perhaps, for aught I see, two-and-  32 thirty, a pip out?  33
Whom would to God I had well knocked at first! Then had not Grumio come by the worst.

PETRUCHIO
A senseless villain! Good Hortensio,
I bade the rascal knock upon your gate,
And could not get him for my heart to do it.  38

GRUMIO  Knock at the gate? Oh, heavens! Spake you not these words plain, "Sirrah, knock me here, rap me here, knock me well, and knock me soundly"? And come you now with "knocking at the gate"?  42

PETRUCHIO
Sirrah, begone, or talk not, I advise you.

HORTENSIO
Petruchio, patience. I am Grumio's pledge.  44
Why, this's a heavy chance twixt him and you,  45
Your ancient, trusty, pleasant servant Grumio.  46
And tell me now, sweet friend, what happy gale
Blows you to Padua here from old Verona?

PETRUCHIO
Such wind as scatters young men through the world
To seek their fortunes farther than at home,
Where small experience grows. But in a few,  51
Signor Hortensio, thus it stands with me:
Antonio, my father, is deceased,
And I have thrust myself into this maze,
Happily to wive and thrive as best I may.  55
Crowns in my purse I have, and goods at home,  56
And so am come abroad to see the world.

HORTENSIO
Petruchio, shall I then come roundly to thee  58
And wish thee to a shrewd, ill-favored wife?  59
Thou'dst thank me but a little for my counsel.
And yet I'll promise thee she shall be rich,
And very rich. But thou'rt too much my friend,
And I'll not wish thee to her.

PETRUCHIO
Signor Hortensio, twixt such friends as we
Few words suffice. And therefore, if thou know
One rich enough to be Petruchio's wife—
As wealth is burden of my wooing dance—  67
Be she as foul as was Florentius' love,  68
As old as Sibyl, and as curst and shrewd  69
As Socrates' Xanthippe, or a worse,  70
She moves me not, or not removes, at least,  71
Affection's edge in me, were she as rough  72
As are the swelling Adriatic seas.
I come to wive it wealthily in Padua;
If wealthily, then happily in Padua.

GRUMIO  Nay, look you, sir, he tells you flatly what his mind is. Why, give him gold enough and marry him to a puppet or an aglet-baby, or an old trot with ne'er  78 a tooth in her head, though she have as many diseases as two-and-fifty horses. Why, nothing comes amiss,  80 so money comes withal.  81

**HORTENSIO**
Petruchio, since we are stepped thus far in,
I will continue that I broached in jest. 83
I can, Petruchio, help thee to a wife
With wealth enough, and young and beauteous,
Brought up as best becomes a gentlewoman.
Her only fault, and that is faults enough,
Is that she is intolerable curst 88
And shrewd, and froward, so beyond all measure 89
That, were my state far worser than it is, 90
I would not wed her for a mine of gold.
**PETRUCHIO**
Hortensio, peace! Thou know'st not gold's effect.
Tell me her father's name and 'tis enough;
For I will board her, though she chide as loud 94
As thunder when the clouds in autumn crack. 95
**HORTENSIO**
Her father is Baptista Minola,
An affable and courteous gentleman.
Her name is Katharina Minola,
Renowned in Padua for her scolding tongue.
**PETRUCHIO**
I know her father, though I know not her,
And he knew my deceasèd father well.
I will not sleep, Hortensio, till I see her;
And therefore let me be thus bold with you
To give you over at this first encounter, 104
Unless you will accompany me thither.
**GRUMIO** [to Hortensio]  I pray you, sir, let him go while
the humor lasts. O' my word, an she knew him as well 107
as I do, she would think scolding would do little good
upon him. She may perhaps call him half a score 109
knaves or so. Why, that's nothing; an he begin once,
he'll rail in his rope tricks. I'll tell you what, sir: an she 111
stand him but a little, he will throw a figure in her face 112
and so disfigure her with it that she shall have no more 113
eyes to see withal than a cat. You know him not, sir. 114
**HORTENSIO**
Tarry, Petruchio, I must go with thee,
For in Baptista's keep my treasure is. 116
He hath the jewel of my life in hold, 117
His youngest daughter, beautiful Bianca,
And her withholds from me and other more, 119
Suitors to her and rivals in my love,
Supposing it a thing impossible,
For those defects I have before rehearsed, 122
That ever Katharina will be wooed.
Therefore this order hath Baptista ta'en, 124
That none shall have access unto Bianca

Till Katharine the curst have got a husband.
**GRUMIO**  Katharine the curst!
A title for a maid of all titles the worst.
**HORTENSIO**
Now shall my friend Petruchio do me grace, 129
And offer me disguised in sober robes
To old Baptista as a schoolmaster
Well seen in music, to instruct Bianca, 132
That so I may by this device at least
Have leave and leisure to make love to her, 134
And unsuspected court her by herself.

*Enter Gremio [with a paper], and Lucentio disguised [as a schoolmaster].*

**GRUMIO**  Here's no knavery! See, to beguile the old 136
folks, how the young folks lay their heads together!
Master, master, look about you. Who goes there, ha?
**HORTENSIO**
Peace, Grumio, it is the rival of my love.
Petruchio, stand by awhile.  [*They stand aside.*]
**GRUMIO** [aside]
A proper stripling and an amorous! 141
**GREMIO** [to Lucentio]
Oh, very well, I have perused the note. 142
Hark you, sir, I'll have them very fairly bound—
All books of love, see that at any hand— 144
And see you read no other lectures to her. 145
You understand me. Over and beside
Signor Baptista's liberality,
I'll mend it with a largess. Take your paper too, 148
[*giving Lucentio the note*]
And let me have them very well perfumed, 149
For she is sweeter than perfume itself
To whom they go to. What will you read to her?
**LUCENTIO**
Whate'er I read to her, I'll plead for you
As for my patron, stand you so assured, 153
As firmly as yourself were still in place— 154
Yea, and perhaps with more successful words
Than you, unless you were a scholar, sir.
**GREMIO**
Oh, this learning, what a thing it is!
**GRUMIO** [aside]
Oh, this woodcock, what an ass it is! 158
**PETRUCHIO**  Peace, sirrah!
**HORTENSIO** [coming forward]
Grumio, mum!—God save you, Signor Gremio.
**GREMIO**
And you are well met, Signor Hortensio. 161
Trow you whither I am going? To Baptista Minola. 162

**83 that I broached** what I began  **88–9 intolerable . . . froward** intolerably ill-natured and willful  **90 state** estate  **94 board** woo aggressively, accost, have intercourse with  **95 crack** make a thunderous noise.  **104 give you over** leave you  **107 humor** whim.  **O' my word, an** On my word, if  **109 half a score** ten  **111 he'll . . . tricks** i.e., he has tricks up his sleeve to answer her scolding.  **111–12 an . . . little** if she stands up to him no matter how slightly  **112–14 he will . . . cat** i.e., he will utterly dazzle and disable her with his rhetorical tricks. (A *figure* is a figure of speech.)  **116 keep** (1) place to store treasure (2) keeping  **117 in hold** (1) in his custody (2) in his stronghold  **119 And . . . more** and witholds her from me and others besides  **122 rehearsed** related, described  **124 this order . . . ta'en** Baptista has laid down the following terms

**129 grace** a favor  **132 seen** skilled  **134 make love to** woo  **136 Here's no knavery!** (Said sarcastically.)  **141 proper stripling** handsome young fellow. (Said ironically, in reference to Gremio.)  **142 note** (Evidently, a list of books for Bianca's tutoring.)  **144 see** see to.  **at any hand** in any case  **145 read . . . lectures** teach no other lessons  **148 mend** improve, increase.  **largess** gift of money.  **149 them** i.e., the books  **153 stand . . . assured** be you assured of that  **154 as** as if.  **still in place** present all the time  **158 woodcock** (A bird easily caught; proverbially stupid.)  **161 you are well met** i.e., how opportune to meet you just now  **162 Trow** Know

I promised to inquire carefully
About a schoolmaster for the fair Bianca,
And by good fortune I have lighted well     165
On this young man, for learning and behavior
Fit for her turn, well read in poetry     167
And other books—good ones, I warrant ye.

HORTENSIO
'Tis well. And I have met a gentleman
Hath promised me to help me to another,     170
A fine musician to instruct our mistress.
So shall I no whit be behind in duty     172
To fair Bianca, so beloved of me.

GREMIO
Beloved of me, and that my deeds shall prove.

GRUMIO [aside]   And that his bags shall prove.     175

HORTENSIO
Gremio, 'tis now no time to vent our love.     176
Listen to me, and if you speak me fair,     177
I'll tell you news indifferent good for either.     178
Here is a gentleman whom by chance I met,
Upon agreement from us to his liking,     180
Will undertake to woo curst Katharine,
Yea, and to marry her, if her dowry please.

GREMIO   So said, so done, is well.     183
Hortensio, have you told him all her faults?

PETRUCHIO
I know she is an irksome brawling scold.
If that be all, masters, I hear no harm.     186

GREMIO
No? Say'st me so, friend? What countryman?

PETRUCHIO
Born in Verona, old Antonio's son.
My father dead, his fortune lives for me,
And I do hope good days and long to see.     190

GREMIO
Oh, sir, such a life with such a wife were strange.     191
But if you have a stomach, to't, i' God's name.     192
You shall have me assisting you in all.
But will you woo this wildcat?

PETRUCHIO                      Will I live?

GRUMIO
Will he woo her? Ay, or I'll hang her.

PETRUCHIO
Why came I hither but to that intent?
Think you a little din can daunt mine ears?
Have I not in my time heard lions roar?
Have I not heard the sea, puffed up with winds,
Rage like an angry boar chafèd with sweat?
Have I not heard great ordnance in the field,     201
And heaven's artillery thunder in the skies?

Have I not in a pitchèd battle heard     203
Loud 'larums, neighing steeds, and trumpets' clang?     204
And do you tell me of a woman's tongue,
That gives not half so great a blow to hear
As will a chestnut in a farmer's fire?     207
Tush, tush! Fear boys with bugs.

GRUMIO                      For he fears none.     208

GREMIO   Hortensio, hark.
This gentleman is happily arrived,     210
My mind presumes, for his own good and ours.

HORTENSIO
I promised we would be contributors
And bear his charge of wooing, whatsoe'er.     213

GREMIO
And so we will, provided that he win her.

GRUMIO
I would I were as sure of a good dinner.     215

*Enter Tranio, brave [as Lucentio], and
Biondello.*

TRANIO
Gentlemen, God save you. If I may be bold,
Tell me, I beseech you, which is the readiest way
To the house of Signor Baptista Minola?

BIONDELLO   He that has the two fair daughters, is't he
you mean?

TRANIO   Even he, Biondello.     221

GREMIO
Hark you, sir, you mean not her to—

TRANIO
Perhaps him and her, sir. What have you to do?     223

PETRUCHIO
Not her that chides, sir, at any hand, I pray.     224

TRANIO
I love no chiders, sir.—Biondello, let's away.

LUCENTIO [aside]
Well begun, Tranio.

HORTENSIO               Sir, a word ere you go.
Are you a suitor to the maid you talk of, yea or no?

TRANIO
An if I be, sir, is it any offense?

GREMIO
No, if without more words you will get you hence.

TRANIO
Why, sir, I pray, are not the streets as free
For me as for you?

GREMIO               But so is not she.

TRANIO
For what reason, I beseech you?

GREMIO                      For this reason, if you'll know,
That she's the choice love of Signor Gremio.

---

**165 lighted** alighted   **167 Fit for her turn** suited to her needs. (Something that is true in more ways than Gremio realizes.)   **170 Hath . . . another** who has promised to help me to obtain another   **172 no whit** not in the slightest   **175 bags** moneybags   **176 vent** express   **177 speak me fair** deal with me courteously   **178 indifferent** equally   **180 Upon . . . liking** who, if we agree to terms satisfactory to him   **183 So . . . is well** i.e., That's all very well, when his deeds match his words (which may not be soon).   **186 masters** good sirs   **190 And . . . see** and I hope to see many happy days and long life.   **191 were** would be   **192 a stomach** an appetite, inclination   **201 ordnance** artillery.   **field** battlefield

**203 a pitchèd battle** a planned battle set in orderly array (not just a skirmish)   **204 'larums** calls to arms   **207 chestnut** (Chestnuts roasted will pop open or explode with a loud report.)   **208 Fear . . . bugs.** Frighten children with bugbears, bogeymen.   **210 happily** fortunately, just when needed   **213 charge** expense   **215.1 brave** elegantly dressed   **221 Even he** Yes, precisely, he   **223 Perhaps . . . do?** i.e., Perhaps I mean to woo both Baptista Minola and Katharina, sir. What's that to you?   **224 at any hand** on any account

HORTENSIO
  That she's the chosen of Signor Hortensio.
TRANIO
  Softly, my masters! If you be gentlemen,
  Do me this right: hear me with patience.
  Baptista is a noble gentleman,
  To whom my father is not all unknown;                          238
  And were his daughter fairer than she is,
  She may more suitors have, and me for one.
  Fair Leda's daughter had a thousand wooers;                    241
  Then well one more may fair Bianca have,
  And so she shall. Lucentio shall make one,
  Though Paris came in hope to speed alone.                      244
GREMIO
  What, this gentleman will out-talk us all!
LUCENTIO
  Sir, give him head. I know he'll prove a jade.                 246
PETRUCHIO
  Hortensio, to what end are all these words?
HORTENSIO [to Tranio]
  Sir, let me be so bold as ask you,                             248
  Did you yet ever see Baptista's daughter?
TRANIO
  No, sir, but hear I do that he hath two,
  The one as famous for a scolding tongue
  As is the other for beauteous modesty.
PETRUCHIO
  Sir, sir, the first's for me. Let her go by.                   253
GREMIO
  Yea, leave that labor to great Hercules,
  And let it be more than Alcides' twelve.                       255
PETRUCHIO
  Sir, understand you this of me, in sooth:                      256
  The youngest daughter, whom you hearken for,                   257
  Her father keeps from all access of suitors,
  And will not promise her to any man
  Until the elder sister first be wed.
  The younger then is free, and not before.
TRANIO
  If it be so, sir, that you are the man
  Must stead us all, and me amongst the rest;                    263
  And if you break the ice and do this feat,
  Achieve the elder, set the younger free
  For our access, whose hap shall be to have her                 266
  Will not so graceless be to be ingrate.                        267
HORTENSIO
  Sir, you say well, and well you do conceive.                   268
  And since you do profess to be a suitor,
  You must, as we do, gratify this gentleman,                    270

To whom we all rest generally beholding.                         271
TRANIO
  Sir, I shall not be slack. In sign whereof,
  Please ye we may contrive this afternoon,                      273
  And quaff carouses to our mistress' health,                    274
  And do as adversaries do in law—                               275
  Strive mightily, but eat and drink as friends.
GRUMIO, BIONDELLO
  Oh, excellent motion! Fellows, let's be gone.                  277
HORTENSIO
  The motion's good indeed, and be it so.
  Petruchio, I shall be your *ben venuto*.         *Exeunt.*     279

❧

# [2.1]

*Enter Katharina and Bianca [with her hands tied].*

BIANCA
  Good sister, wrong me not, nor wrong yourself,
  To make a bondmaid and a slave of me.
  That I disdain. But for these other goods,                       3
  Unbind my hands, I'll pull them off myself,                      4
  Yea, all my raiment, to my petticoat,
  Or what you will command me will I do,
  So well I know my duty to my elders.
KATHARINA
  Of all thy suitors here I charge thee tell
  Whom thou lov'st best. See thou dissemble not.
BIANCA
  Believe me, sister, of all the men alive
  I never yet beheld that special face
  Which I could fancy more than any other.
KATHARINA
  Minion, thou liest. Is't not Hortensio?                         13
BIANCA
  If you affect him, sister, here I swear                         14
  I'll plead for you myself but you shall have him.               15
KATHARINA
  Oh, then belike you fancy riches more.                          16
  You will have Gremio to keep you fair.                          17
BIANCA
  Is it for him you do envy me so?
  Nay, then, you jest, and now I well perceive
  You have but jested with me all this while.
  I prithee, sister Kate, untie my hands.
KATHARINA ( *strikes her*)
If that be jest, then all the rest was so.

*Enter Baptista.*

---

238 all entirely   241 Leda's daughter Helen of Troy   244 Though . . .
alone even if Paris (who abducted Helen from her husband,
Menelaus) were to come in hopes of succeeding above all others.
246 Sir . . . jade Sir, give him a loose bridle; i.e., let him talk freely. I
know he'll prove to be a worthless horse, soon tired.   248 as ask as
to ask   253 Let her go by Pass over her.   255 And . . . twelve (Hercules, called *Alcides* because he was the reputed grandson of Alcaeus,
had to perform twelve huge labors.)   256 of me from me.   sooth
truth   257 hearken for seek to win   263 Must stead who must help
266 whose hap he whose good fortune   267 to be ingrate as to be
ungrateful.   268 conceive understand.   270 gratify this gentleman
reward Petruchio

271 beholding beholden, indebted.   273 contrive manage our affairs,
pass the time   274 quaff carouses drink toasts   275 adversaries
opposing lawyers   277 motion suggestion.   279 ben venuto welcome, i.e., host.

2.1. Location: Padua. Baptista's house.
3 for as for.   goods i.e., clothes, jewels, love tokens   4 Unbind if you
will unbind   13 Minion Hussy   14 affect love   15 but . . . him if
necessary for you to win him.   16 belike perhaps   17 fair resplendent with finery.

**BAPTISTA**
Why, how now, dame, whence grows this
   insolence?—
Bianca, stand aside. Poor girl, she weeps.
Go ply thy needle, meddle not with her.— 25
For shame, thou hilding of a devilish spirit, 26
Why dost thou wrong her that did ne'er wrong thee?
When did she cross thee with a bitter word? 28

**KATHARINA**
Her silence flouts me, and I'll be revenged. 29
               *[She] flies after Bianca.*

**BAPTISTA**
What, in my sight? Bianca, get thee in.   *Exit [Bianca].*

**KATHARINA**
What, will you not suffer me? Nay, now I see 31
She is your treasure, she must have a husband;
I must dance barefoot on her wedding day, 33
And for your love to her lead apes in hell. 34
Talk not to me. I will go sit and weep
Till I can find occasion of revenge.   *[Exit.]*

**BAPTISTA**
Was ever gentleman thus grieved as I?
But who comes here? 38

*Enter Gremio, Lucentio [as a schoolmaster] in the
habit of a mean man, Petruchio, with [Hortensio as
a musician, and] Tranio [as Lucentio] with his boy
[Biondello] bearing a lute and books.*

**GREMIO**   Good morrow, neighbor Baptista.
**BAPTISTA**   Good morrow, neighbor Gremio. God save
you, gentlemen.
**PETRUCHIO**
And you, good sir. Pray, have you not a daughter
Called Katharina, fair and virtuous?
**BAPTISTA**
I have a daughter, sir, called Katharina.
**GREMIO**
You are too blunt. Go to it orderly. 45
**PETRUCHIO**
You wrong me, Signor Gremio; give me leave.— 46
I am a gentleman of Verona, sir,
That, hearing of her beauty and her wit,
Her affability and bashful modesty,
Her wondrous qualities and mild behavior,
Am bold to show myself a forward guest
Within your house, to make mine eye the witness
Of that report which I so oft have heard.
And, for an entrance to my entertainment, 54
I do present you with a man of mine,
            *[presenting Hortensio]*
Cunning in music and the mathematics, 56

To instruct her fully in those sciences, 57
Whereof I know she is not ignorant.
Accept of him, or else you do me wrong. 59
His name is Litio, born in Mantua.
**BAPTISTA**
You're welcome, sir, and he, for your good sake.
But for my daughter Katharine, this I know, 62
She is not for your turn, the more my grief.
**PETRUCHIO**
I see you do not mean to part with her,
Or else you like not of my company. 65
**BAPTISTA**
Mistake me not, I speak but as I find.
Whence are you, sir? What may I call your name?
**PETRUCHIO**
Petruchio is my name, Antonio's son,
A man well known throughout all Italy.
**BAPTISTA**
I know him well. You are welcome for his sake. 70
**GREMIO**
Saving your tale, Petruchio, I pray, 71
Let us that are poor petitioners speak too.
*Bacare!* You are marvelous forward. 73
**PETRUCHIO**
Oh, pardon me, Signor Gremio, I would fain be doing. 74
**GREMIO**
I doubt it not, sir, but you will curse your wooing.—
Neighbors, this is a gift very grateful, I am sure of 76
it. *[To Baptista]* To express the like kindness, my-
self, that have been more kindly beholding to you
than any, freely give unto you this young scholar
*[presenting Lucentio]*, that hath been long studying at
Rheims, as cunning in Greek, Latin, and other
languages as the other in music and mathematics. His 82
name is Cambio. Pray, accept his service. 83
**BAPTISTA**   A thousand thanks, Signor Gremio.—
Welcome, good Cambio. *[To Tranio]* But, gentle sir,
methinks you walk like a stranger. May I be so bold
to know the cause of your coming?
**TRANIO**
Pardon me, sir, the boldness is mine own,
That, being a stranger in this city here,
Do make myself a suitor to your daughter,
Unto Bianca, fair and virtuous.
Nor is your firm resolve unknown to me
In the preferment of the eldest sister. 93
This liberty is all that I request,
That, upon knowledge of my parentage, 95
I may have welcome 'mongst the rest that woo,
And free access and favor as the rest. 97

---

25 **meddle not with** have nothing to do with   26 **hilding** vicious (hence worthless) beast   28 **cross** contradict, thwart   29 **flouts** mocks, insults   31 **suffer me** let me have my own way.   33, 34 **dance . . . day, lead . . . hell** (Popularly supposed to be the fate of old maids.)   38.2 *habit* dress.   *mean* of low social station. (Said here of a schoolmaster.)   45 **orderly** in a properly orderly manner.   46 **give me leave** excuse me, let me do this my way.   54 **entrance** entrance fee.   **entertainment** reception   56 **Cunning** skillful

57 **sciences** subjects, branches of knowledge   59 **Accept of** Accept   62 **for** as for   65 **like not of** do not like   70 **know** know of. (See also lines 104–5.)   71 **Saving** With all due respect for   73 *Bacare!* Stand back!   74 **fain** gladly.   **doing** getting on with the business. (With sexual suggestion.)   76 **grateful** pleasing   82 **the other** i.e., Hortensio   83 **Cambio** (In Italian, appropriately, the word means "change" or "exchange.")   93 **In the preferment of** in the precedence you give to   95 **upon knowledge of** when you know about   97 **favor** leave, permission

And toward the education of your daughters
I here bestow a simple instrument,
And this small packet of Greek and Latin books.
If you accept them, then their worth is great.
    [*Biondello brings forward the lute and books.*]

BAPTISTA
Lucentio is your name? Of whence, I pray?  102

TRANIO
Of Pisa, sir, son to Vincentio.

BAPTISTA
A mighty man of Pisa. By report
I know him well. You are very welcome, sir.
[*To Hortensio*] Take you the lute, [*to Lucentio*] and
  you the set of books;
You shall go see your pupils presently.—
Holla, within!

    *Enter a Servant.*

    Sirrah, lead these gentlemen
To my daughters, and tell them both
These are their tutors. Bid them use them well.
    [*Exit Servant, with Lucentio and Hortensio.*]
We will go walk a little in the orchard,
And then to dinner. You are passing welcome,  112
And so I pray you all to think yourselves.

PETRUCHIO
Signor Baptista, my business asketh haste,
And every day I cannot come to woo.
You knew my father well, and in him me,
Left solely heir to all his lands and goods,
Which I have bettered rather than decreased.
Then tell me, if I get your daughter's love,
What dowry shall I have with her to wife?

BAPTISTA
After my death the one half of my lands,
And in possession twenty thousand crowns.  122

PETRUCHIO
And for that dowry I'll assure her of  123
Her widowhood, be it that she survive me,  124
In all my lands and leases whatsoever.
Let specialties be therefore drawn between us,  126
That covenants may be kept on either hand.

BAPTISTA
Ay, when the special thing is well obtained,
That is, her love; for that is all in all.

PETRUCHIO
Why, that is nothing, for I tell you, father,  130
I am as peremptory as she proud-minded;
And where two raging fires meet together,
They do consume the thing that feeds their fury.
Though little fire grows great with little wind,
Yet extreme gusts will blow out fire and all.
So I to her, and so she yields to me,  136

For I am rough and woo not like a babe.

BAPTISTA
Well mayst thou woo, and happy be thy speed!  138
But be thou armed for some unhappy words.

PETRUCHIO
Ay, to the proof, as mountains are for winds,  140
That shakes not, though they blow perpetually.  141

   *Enter Hortensio* [*as Litio*], *with his head broke.*

BAPTISTA
How now, my friend, why dost thou look so pale?

HORTENSIO
For fear, I promise you, if I look pale.  143

BAPTISTA
What, will my daughter prove a good musician?

HORTENSIO
I think she'll sooner prove a soldier.  145
Iron may hold with her, but never lutes.  146

BAPTISTA
Why then, thou canst not break her to the lute?  147

HORTENSIO
Why, no, for she hath broke the lute to me.
I did but tell her she mistook her frets,  149
And bowed her hand to teach her fingering,
When, with a most impatient devilish spirit,
"Frets, call you these?" quoth she, "I'll fume with
  them."
And with that word she struck me on the head,
And through the instrument my pate made way;
And there I stood amazèd for a while,  155
As on a pillory, looking through the lute,  156
While she did call me rascal fiddler
And twangling Jack, with twenty such vile terms,  158
As had she studied to misuse me so.  159

PETRUCHIO
Now, by the world, it is a lusty wench!  160
I love her ten times more than e'er I did.
Oh, how I long to have some chat with her!

BAPTISTA [*to Hortensio*]
Well, go with me, and be not so discomfited.
Proceed in practice with my younger daughter;  164
She's apt to learn and thankful for good turns.—
Signor Petruchio, will you go with us,
Or shall I send my daughter Kate to you?

PETRUCHIO
I pray you, do.    *Exeunt. Manet Petruchio.*
    I'll attend her here,  168
And woo her with some spirit when she comes.

---

102 **Lucentio . . . name?** (Baptista may have learned this information from a note accompanying the books and lute.) 112 **passing** exceedingly 122 **in possession** in immediate possession 123 **for** in exchange for 124 **widowhood** i.e., widow's share of the estate. **be it that** she if she should 126 **specialties** terms of contract 130 **father** father-in-law 136 **So I** i.e., So I behave, like an extreme gust of wind

138 **happy . . . speed!** may fortune give you success! 140 **to the proof** i.e., in armor, proof against her shrewishness 141 **shakes** shake 141.1 **broke** with a bleeding cut. (Hortensio usually appears on stage with his head emerging through a broken lute.)
143 **promise** assure 145 **I think . . . soldier** i.e., She's better suited for the manly career of soldiering. 146 **hold with** hold out against 147 **break** train. (With pun in the next line.) 149 **frets** ridges or bars on the fingerboard of the lute. (But Kate puns on the sense of "fume," "be indignant.") 155 **amazèd** bewildered 156 **As on a pillory** as if with my head in a wooden collar used as punishment 158 **Jack** knave 159 **As . . . so** as if she had practiced how to abuse me so.
160 **lusty** lively 164 **practice** instruction 168 s.d. *Manet* He remains on stage

Say that she rail, why then I'll tell her plain
She sings as sweetly as a nightingale.
Say that she frown, I'll say she looks as clear          172
As morning roses newly washed with dew.
Say she be mute and will not speak a word,
Then I'll commend her volubility
And say she uttereth piercing eloquence.                 176
If she do bid me pack, I'll give her thanks,             177
As though she bid me stay by her a week.
If she deny to wed, I'll crave the day                   179
When I shall ask the banns and when be married.          180
But here she comes; and now, Petruchio, speak.

  *Enter Katharina.*

Good morrow, Kate, for that's your name, I hear.
KATHARINA
Well have you heard, but something hard of hearing.      183
They call me Katharine that do talk of me.
PETRUCHIO
You lie, in faith, for you are called plain Kate,
And bonny Kate, and sometimes Kate the curst;
But Kate, the prettiest Kate in Christendom,
Kate of Kate Hall, my superdainty Kate,
For dainties are all Kates, and therefore, Kate,         189
Take this of me, Kate of my consolation:                 190
Hearing thy mildness praised in every town,
Thy virtues spoke of, and thy beauty sounded,            192
Yet not so deeply as to thee belongs,
Myself am moved to woo thee for my wife.                 194
KATHARINA
Moved? In good time! Let him that moved you hither       195
Remove you hence. I knew you at the first
You were a movable.
PETRUCHIO     Why, what's a movable?       197
KATHARINA
A joint stool.
PETRUCHIO    Thou hast hit it. Come, sit on me.  198
KATHARINA
Asses are made to bear, and so are you.                  199
PETRUCHIO
Women are made to bear, and so are you.
KATHARINA
No such jade as you, if me you mean.                     201
PETRUCHIO
Alas, good Kate, I will not burden thee,                 202

For knowing thee to be but young and light.              203
KATHARINA
Too light for such a swain as you to catch,              204
And yet as heavy as my weight should be.
PETRUCHIO
Should be? Should—buzz!
KATHARINA      Well ta'en, and like a buzzard. 206
PETRUCHIO
Oh, slow-winged turtle, shall a buzzard take thee?
KATHARINA
Ay, for a turtle, as he takes a buzzard.
PETRUCHIO
Come, come, you wasp, i'faith you are too angry.         209
KATHARINA
If I be waspish, best beware my sting.
PETRUCHIO
My remedy is then to pluck it out.
KATHARINA
Ay, if the fool could find it where it lies.
PETRUCHIO
Who knows not where a wasp does wear his sting?
In his tail.
KATHARINA    In his tongue.
PETRUCHIO    Whose tongue?
KATHARINA
Yours, if you talk of tales, and so farewell.            217
PETRUCHIO
What, with my tongue in your tail? Nay, come again.
Good Kate, I am a gentleman—
KATHARINA      That I'll try.
          *She strikes him.*
PETRUCHIO
I swear I'll cuff you if you strike again.
KATHARINA    So may you lose your arms.
If you strike me, you are no gentleman,
And if no gentleman, why then no arms.                   223
PETRUCHIO
A herald, Kate? Oh, put me in thy books!                 224
KATHARINA    What is your crest, a coxcomb?     225
PETRUCHIO
A combless cock, so Kate will be my hen.                 226
KATHARINA
No cock of mine. You crow too like a craven.             227

---

172 **clear** serene 176 **piercing** moving 177 **pack** begone 179 **deny** refuse. **crave the day** ask her to name the day 180 **ask the banns** have a reading of the required announcement in church of a forth-coming marriage 183 **heard, hard** (Pronounced nearly alike.) 189 **all Kates** (With a quibble on "cates," confections, delicacies.) 190 **of me** from me. **consolation** comfort 192 **sounded** proclaimed. (With a quibble on "plumbed," as indicated by *deeply* in the next line.) 194 **moved** impelled. (Followed by wordplay on the more literal meaning of *move* and *remove*.) 195 **In good time!** Forsooth! Indeed! 197 **movable** (1) one easily changed or dissuaded (2) an article of furniture. 198 **A joint stool** a well-fitted stool made by an expert crafts-man. 199 **bear** carry. (With puns in the following lines suggesting "bear children" and "support a man during sexual intercourse.") 201 **jade** an ill-conditioned horse 202 **burden** (1) oppress with a heavy load—a term appropriate to *asses* and *bear* in line 199, since asses are beasts of *burden* (2) lie on during sexual intercourse, impreg-nate. (See notes on lines 199 and 203.)

203 **For knowing** because I know. **light** (1) of delicate stature (2) las-civious (3) lacking a *burden* (see previous line) in the musical sense of lacking a bass undersong or accompaniment (4) elusive (in the fol-lowing line). 204 **swain** young rustic in love 206 **Should . . . buzz!** (Petruchio puns on *be* and "bee," and uses *buzz* in perhaps three senses: [1] an interjection of impatience or contempt [2] a bee's sound [3] a rumor being buzzed about, to which, he implies, Kate had better listen.) **buzzard** (1) figuratively, a fool (2) in the next line, an inferior kind of hawk, fit only to overtake a slow-winged *turtle* or turtledove, as Petruchio might overtake Kate (3) a buzzing insect, caught by a turtledove. 209 **wasp** i.e., waspish, scolding woman. (But suggested by *buzzard*, buzzing insect.) 217 **talk of tales** i.e., idly tell stories. (With pun on "tail.") 223 **no arms** no coat of arms. (With pun on *arms* as limbs of the body.) 224 **books** (1) books of heraldry, heraldic registers (2) grace, favor. 225 **crest** (1) armorial device (2) a rooster's comb, setting up the joke on *coxcomb*, the cap of the court fool 226 **A combless cock** i.e., A gentle rooster. (With suggestion of the male sexual organ.) **so** provided that 227 **a craven** a cock that is not "game" or willing to fight.

PETRUCHIO
Nay, come, Kate, come. You must not look so sour.
KATHARINA
It is my fashion when I see a crab.                                    229
PETRUCHIO
Why, here's no crab, and therefore look not sour.
KATHARINA    There is, there is.
PETRUCHIO
Then show it me.
KATHARINA              Had I a glass, I would.
PETRUCHIO    What, you mean my face?
KATHARINA    Well aimed of such a young one.              234
PETRUCHIO
Now, by Saint George, I am too young for you.
KATHARINA
Yet you are withered.
PETRUCHIO                      'Tis with cares.
KATHARINA                              I care not.
PETRUCHIO
Nay, hear you, Kate. In sooth, you scape not so.     237
KATHARINA
I chafe you if I tarry. Let me go.                         238
PETRUCHIO
No, not a whit. I find you passing gentle.             239
'Twas told me you were rough, and coy, and sullen,  240
And now I find report a very liar,                          241
For thou art pleasant, gamesome, passing courteous, 242
But slow in speech, yet sweet as springtime flowers. 243
Thou canst not frown, thou canst not look askance,  244
Nor bite the lip, as angry wenches will,
Nor hast thou pleasure to be cross in talk;          246
But thou with mildness entertain'st thy wooers,     247
With gentle conference, soft and affable.            248
Why does the world report that Kate doth limp?
Oh, sland'rous world! Kate like the hazel twig
Is straight and slender, and as brown in hue
As hazelnuts, and sweeter than the kernels.
Oh, let me see thee walk. Thou dost not halt.        253
KATHARINA
Go, fool, and whom thou keep'st command.          254
PETRUCHIO
Did ever Dian so become a grove                        255
As Kate this chamber with her princely gait?
Oh, be thou Dian, and let her be Kate,
And then let Kate be chaste and Dian sportful!     258
KATHARINA
Where did you study all this goodly speech?        259
PETRUCHIO
It is extempore, from my mother wit.                   260

KATHARINA
A witty mother! Witless else her son.                 261
PETRUCHIO    Am I not wise?                             262
KATHARINA    Yes, keep you warm.                     263
PETRUCHIO
Marry, so I mean, sweet Katharine, in thy bed.
And therefore, setting all this chat aside,
Thus in plain terms: your father hath consented
That you shall be my wife; your dowry 'greed on;
And will you, nill you, I will marry you.            268
Now, Kate, I am a husband for your turn,            269
For by this light, whereby I see thy beauty—
Thy beauty that doth make me like thee well—
Thou must be married to no man but me.

    *Enter Baptista, Gremio, [and] Tranio [as
    Lucentio].*

For I am he am born to tame you, Kate,
And bring you from a wild Kate to a Kate          274
Conformable as other household Kates.              275
Here comes your father. Never make denial;
I must and will have Katharine to my wife.
BAPTISTA
Now, Signor Petruchio, how speed you with my
    daughter?                                             278
PETRUCHIO
How but well, sir, how but well?
It were impossible I should speed amiss.
BAPTISTA
Why, how now, daughter Katharine, in your dumps? 281
KATHARINA
Call you me daughter? Now, I promise you,         282
You have showed a tender fatherly regard,
To wish me wed to one half-lunatic,
A madcap ruffian and a swearing Jack,              285
That thinks with oaths to face the matter out.     286
PETRUCHIO
Father, 'tis thus: yourself and all the world
That talked of her have talked amiss of her.
If she be curst, it is for policy,                        289
For she's not froward, but modest as the dove.    290
She is not hot, but temperate as the morn.
For patience she will prove a second Grissel,      292
And Roman Lucrece for her chastity.               293
And to conclude, we have 'greed so well together
That upon Sunday is the wedding day.

---

**229 crab** crab apple.   **234 aimed of** guessed for.   **young** i.e., inexperienced. (But Petruchio picks up the word in the sense of "strong," "virile.")   **237 scape** escape   **238 chafe** irritate, arouse   **239 passing** very. (Also in line 242.)   **240 coy** disdainful   **241 a very** an utter   **242 pleasant, gamesome** merry, spirited   **243 But slow** never anything but slow   **244 askance** scornfully   **246 cross in talk** always contradicting   **247 entertain'st** receive   **248 conference** conversation   **253 halt** limp.   **254 whom thou keep'st command** i.e., order about those whom you employ, your servants, not me.   **255 Dian** Diana, goddess of the hunt and of chastity.   **become** adorn   **258 sportful** amorous.   **259 study** memorize   **260 mother wit** native intelligence.

**261 Witless . . . son** i.e., Without the intelligence inherited from her, he would have none at all.   **262–3 wise . . . warm** (An allusion to the proverbial phrase "enough wit to keep oneself warm.")   **268 will you, nill you** whether you're willing or not   **269 for your turn** to suit you   **274 wild Kate** (With a quibble on "wildcat.")   **275 Conformable** compliant   **278 speed** fare, get on   **281 in your dumps** in low spirits.   **282 promise** assure   **285 Jack** ill-mannered fellow   **286 face** brazen   **289 policy** cunning, ulterior motive   **290 froward** willful, perverse   **292 Grissel** patient Griselda, the epitome of wifely patience and devotion (whose story was told by Chaucer in "The Clerk's Tale" of *The Canterbury Tales* and earlier by Boccaccio and Petrarch)   **293 Roman Lucrece** Lucretia, a Roman lady who took her own life after her chastity had been violated by the Tarquin prince, Sextus. (Shakespeare tells the story in *The Rape of Lucrece*.)

KATHARINA
I'll see thee hanged on Sunday first.

GREMIO    Hark, Petruchio, she says she'll see thee
hanged first.

TRANIO
Is this your speeding? Nay then, good night our part!    299

PETRUCHIO
Be patient, gentlemen. I choose her for myself.
If she and I be pleased, what's that to you?
'Tis bargained twixt us twain, being alone,
That she shall still be curst in company.
I tell you, 'tis incredible to believe
How much she loves me. Oh, the kindest Kate!
She hung about my neck, and kiss on kiss
She vied so fast, protesting oath on oath,    307
That in a twink she won me to her love.
Oh, you are novices! 'Tis a world to see    309
How tame, when men and women are alone,    310
A meacock wretch can make the curstest shrew.—    311
Give me thy hand, Kate. I will unto Venice
To buy apparel gainst the wedding day.—    313
Provide the feast, father, and bid the guests.
I will be sure my Katharine shall be fine.    315

BAPTISTA
I know not what to say. But give me your hands.
God send you joy, Petruchio! 'Tis a match.

GREMIO, TRANIO
Amen, say we. We will be witnesses.

PETRUCHIO
Father, and wife, and gentlemen, adieu.
I will to Venice. Sunday comes apace.
We will have rings, and things, and fine array;
And kiss me, Kate. We will be married o'Sunday.    322
                    *Exeunt Petruchio and Katharine [separately].*

GREMIO
Was ever match clapped up so suddenly?    323

BAPTISTA
Faith, gentlemen, now I play a merchant's part,    324
And venture madly on a desperate mart.    325

TRANIO
'Twas a commodity lay fretting by you;    326
'Twill bring you gain, or perish on the seas.

BAPTISTA
The gain I seek is quiet in the match.

GREMIO
No doubt but he hath got a quiet catch.    329
But now, Baptista, to your younger daughter.
Now is the day we long have looked for.
I am your neighbor, and was suitor first.

TRANIO
And I am one that love Bianca more
Than words can witness, or your thoughts can guess.

GREMIO
Youngling, thou canst not love so dear as I.

TRANIO
Graybeard, thy love doth freeze.

GREMIO                            But thine doth fry.
Skipper, stand back. 'Tis age that nourisheth.    337

TRANIO
But youth in ladies' eyes that flourisheth.

BAPTISTA
Content you, gentlemen, I will compound this strife.    339
'Tis deeds must win the prize, and he of both    340
That can assure my daughter greatest dower    341
Shall have my Bianca's love.
Say, Signor Gremio, what can you assure her?

GREMIO
First, as you know, my house within the city
Is richly furnishèd with plate and gold,    345
Basins and ewers to lave her dainty hands;    346
My hangings all of Tyrian tapestry;    347
In ivory coffers I have stuffed my crowns;    348
In cypress chests my arras counterpoints,    349
Costly apparel, tents, and canopies,    350
Fine linen, Turkey cushions bossed with pearl,    351
Valance of Venice gold in needlework,    352
Pewter and brass, and all things that belongs
To house or housekeeping. Then at my farm
I have a hundred milch kine to the pail,    355
Sixscore fat oxen standing in my stalls,
And all things answerable to this portion.    357
Myself am struck in years, I must confess,    358
And if I die tomorrow, this is hers,
If whilst I live she will be only mine.

TRANIO
That "only" came well in.—Sir, list to me:
I am my father's heir and only son.
If I may have your daughter to my wife,
I'll leave her houses three or four as good,
Within rich Pisa walls, as any one
Old Signor Gremio has in Padua,
Besides two thousand ducats by the year    367
Of fruitful land, all which shall be her jointure.—    368
What, have I pinched you, Signor Gremio?

GREMIO
Two thousand ducats by the year of land!
[*Aside*] My land amounts not to so much in all.—
That she shall have, besides an argosy    372

---

299 **speeding** success.  **good night our part** good-bye to what we
hoped to get.  307 **vied** went me one better, kiss for kiss
309–11 **'Tis . . . shrew** i.e., It's a sight to behold how even the most
cowardly of men, when no one is watching, can tame the most
execrable scold that ever lived.  313 **gainst** in anticipation of
315 **fine** elegantly dressed.  322 **kiss me** (Petruchio probably kisses
her.)  323 **clapped up** settled (by a shaking of hands)  324 **Faith**
In faith  325 **desperate mart** risky venture.  326 **lay fretting**
i.e., which lay in storage being destroyed by moths, weevils,
or spoilage. (With a pun on "chafing.")  329 **quiet catch** (Said
ironically; Gremio is sure that Kate will be anything but quiet.)

337 **Skipper . . . nourisheth** Stand aside, you whippersnapper. It's
age that provides the comforts of a good life.  339 **compound** settle
340 **deeds** (1) actions (2) legal deeds.  **he of both** the one of you
two  341 **dower** portion of a husband's estate settled on his wife in
his will. (Also at line 387 and 4.4.45.)  345 **plate** silver utensils
346 **ewers to lave** pitchers to wash  347 **hangings** draperies hung on
beds and walls.  **Tyrian** dark red or purple  348 **crowns** five-shilling
coins  349 **arras counterpoints** counterpanes of tapestry
350 **tents** bed curtains  351 **Turkey** Turkish.  **bossed** embossed
352 **Valance** fringes of drapery around the canopy or bed frame
355 **milch kine to the pail** dairy cattle  357 **answerable to** on the
same scale as  358 **struck** advanced  367 **ducats** gold coins
368 **Of** from.  **jointure** marriage settlement.  372 **argosy** merchant
vessel of the largest size

That now is lying in Marseilles road. 373
[*To Tranio*] What, have I choked you with an argosy?
TRANIO
Gremio, 'tis known my father hath no less
Than three great argosies, besides two galliases 376
And twelve tight galleys. These I will assure her, 377
And twice as much, whate'er thou off'rest next.
GREMIO
Nay, I have offered all. I have no more,
And she can have no more than all I have.
[*To Baptista*] If you like me, she shall have me and
    mine.
TRANIO
Why then, the maid is mine from all the world,
By your firm promise. Gremio is outvied. 383
BAPTISTA
I must confess your offer is the best;
And, let your father make her the assurance, 385
She is your own; else, you must pardon me.
If you should die before him, where's her dower?
TRANIO
That's but a cavil. He is old, I young. 388
GREMIO
And may not young men die, as well as old?
BAPTISTA
Well, gentlemen, I am thus resolved:
On Sunday next, you know
My daughter Katharine is to be married.
Now, on the Sunday following shall Bianca
Be bride [*to Tranio*] to you, if you make this assurance;
If not, to Signor Gremio.
And so I take my leave, and thank you both.    *Exit.*
GREMIO
Adieu, good neighbor.—Now I fear thee not.
Sirrah, young gamester, your father were a fool
To give thee all, and in his waning age
Set foot under thy table. Tut, a toy! 400
An old Italian fox is not so kind, my boy.    *Exit.*
TRANIO
A vengeance on your crafty withered hide!
Yet I have faced it with a card of ten. 403
'Tis in my head to do my master good.
I see no reason but supposed Lucentio
Must get a father, called supposed Vincentio—
And that's a wonder. Fathers commonly
Do get their children; but in this case of wooing, 408
A child shall get a sire, if I fail not of my cunning.
    *Exit.*

❧

## [3.1]

*Enter Lucentio [as Cambio], Hortensio [as Litio], and Bianca.*

LUCENTIO
Fiddler, forbear. You grow too forward, sir.
Have you so soon forgot the entertainment
Her sister Katharine welcomed you withal?
HORTENSIO
But, wrangling pedant, this is
The patroness of heavenly harmony. 4
Then give me leave to have prerogative, 6
And when in music we have spent an hour,
Your lecture shall have leisure for as much. 8
LUCENTIO
Preposterous ass, that never read so far
To know the cause why music was ordained! 10
Was it not to refresh the mind of man
After his studies or his usual pain? 12
Then give me leave to read philosophy, 13
And, while I pause, serve in your harmony. 14
HORTENSIO
Sirrah, I will not bear these braves of thine. 15
BIANCA
Why, gentlemen, you do me double wrong
To strive for that which resteth in my choice.
I am no breeching scholar in the schools; 18
I'll not be tied to hours nor 'pointed times,
But learn my lessons as I please myself.
And, to cut off all strife, here sit we down.
[*To Hortensio*] Take you your instrument, play you the
    whiles; 22
His lecture will be done ere you have tuned.
HORTENSIO
You'll leave his lecture when I am in tune?
LUCENTIO
That will be never. Tune your instrument.
        [*Hortensio moves aside and tunes.*]
BIANCA    Where left we last?
LUCENTIO    Here, madam. [*He reads.*]
    "Hic ibat Simois; hic est Sigeia tellus; 28
    Hic steterat Priami regia celsa senis." 29
BIANCA    Conster them. 30
LUCENTIO    "Hic ibat," as I told you before, "Simois," I
am Lucentio, "hic est," son unto Vincentio of Pisa,"
Sigeia tellus," disguised thus to get your love; "Hic
steterat," and that Lucentio that comes a-wooing,
"Priami," is my man Tranio, "regia," bearing my port, 35
"celsa senis," that we might beguile the old panta- 36
loon. 37

373 **road** roadstead, harbor.  376 **galliases** heavy, low-built vessels  377 **tight** watertight  383 **outvied** outbidden.  385 **let** provided  388 **but a cavil** merely a frivolous objection.  400 **Set . . . toy!** i.e., become a dependent in your household. Tut, nonsense!  403 **faced . . . ten** brazened it out with only a ten-spot of cards.  408 **get** beget. (With a play on *get*, "obtain," in line 406.)

3.1. Location: The same.
4 **this** i.e., Bianca  6 **prerogative** precedence  8 **lecture** lesson  10 **To know** as to know  12 **usual pain** regular labors.  13 **read** teach  14 **serve in** present, serve up  15 **braves** insults  18 **breeching scholar** i.e., schoolboy liable to be whipped  22 **the whiles** meantime  28–9 *Hic . . . senis* Here flowed the river Simois; here is the Sigeian land; here stood the lofty palace of old Priam. (Ovid, *Heroides*, 1.33–4.)  30 **Conster** Construe  35 **bearing my port** i.e., pretending to be me  36–7 **pantaloon** foolish old man, i.e., Gremio.

HORTENSIO    Madam, my instrument's in tune.
BIANCA    Let's hear. [*He plays.*] Oh, fie! The treble jars.
LUCENTIO    Spit in the hole, man, and tune again.    40
                                        [*Hortensio moves aside.*]
BIANCA    Now let me see if I can conster it: *"Hic ibat
    Simois,"* I know you not, *"hic est Sigeia tellus,"* I trust
    you not; *"Hic steterat Priami,"* take heed he hear us not,
    *"regia,"* presume not, *"celsa senis,"* despair not.
HORTENSIO
    Madam, 'tis now in tune.                [*He plays again.*]
LUCENTIO                        All but the bass.
HORTENSIO
    The bass is right, 'tis the base knave that jars.
    [*Aside*] How fiery and forward our pedant is!
    Now, for my life, the knave doth court my love.
    *Pedascule*, I'll watch you better yet.    49
BIANCA [*to Lucentio*]
    In time I may believe, yet I mistrust.
LUCENTIO
    Mistrust it not, for, sure, Aeacides    51
    Was Ajax, called so from his grandfather.
BIANCA
    I must believe my master; else, I promise you,
    I should be arguing still upon that doubt.
    But let it rest.—Now, Litio, to you:
    Good master, take it not unkindly, pray,
    That I have been thus pleasant with you both.    57
HORTENSIO [*to Lucentio*]
    You may go walk, and give me leave awhile.
    My lessons make no music in three parts.
LUCENTIO
    Are you so formal, sir? Well, I must wait.    60
    [*Aside*] And watch withal; for, but I be deceived,    61
    Our fine musician groweth amorous.
                                        [*He moves aside.*]
HORTENSIO
    Madam, before you touch the instrument,
    To learn the order of my fingering,    64
    I must begin with rudiments of art,
    To teach you gamut in a briefer sort,    66
    More pleasant, pithy, and effectual
    Than hath been taught by any of my trade.
    And there it is in writing, fairly drawn.    69
                                        [*He gives her a paper.*]
BIANCA
    Why, I am past my gamut long ago.

HORTENSIO
    Yet read the gamut of Hortensio.
BIANCA [*reads*]
    " *Gamut* I am, the ground of all accord,    72
    *A re*, to plead Hortensio's passion;
    *B mi*, Bianca, take him for thy lord,    74
    *C fa ut*, that loves with all affection.    75
    *D sol re*, one clef, two notes have I;    76
    *E la mi*, show pity, or I die."    77
    Call you this gamut? Tut, I like it not.
    Old fashions please me best; I am not so nice    79
    To change true rules for odd inventions.

                *Enter a* [*Servant as*] *messenger.*

SERVANT
    Mistress, your father prays you leave your books
    And help to dress your sister's chamber up.
    You know tomorrow is the wedding day.
BIANCA
    Farewell, sweet masters both. I must be gone.
LUCENTIO
    Faith, mistress, then I have no cause to stay.
                [*Exeunt Bianca, Servant, and Lucentio.*]
HORTENSIO
    But I have cause to pry into this pedant.
    Methinks he looks as though he were in love.
    Yet if thy thoughts, Bianca, be so humble
    To cast thy wandering eyes on every stale,    89
    Seize thee that list. If once I find thee ranging,    90
    Hortensio will be quit with thee by changing.    *Exit.*    91

                                        ❖

# [3.2]

                *Enter Baptista, Gremio, Tranio* [*as Lucentio*],
                *Katharine, Bianca,* [*Lucentio as Cambio*], *and
                others, attendants.*

BAPTISTA [*to Tranio*]
    Signor Lucentio, this is the 'pointed day
    That Katharine and Petruchio should be married,    2
    And yet we hear not of our son-in-law.
    What will be said? What mockery will it be,    4
    To want the bridegroom when the priest attends    5
    To speak the ceremonial rites of marriage?
    What says Lucentio to this shame of ours?

---

40 **Spit in the hole** i.e., to make the peg stick    49 *Pedascule* (A word contemptuously coined by Hortensio, presumably the vocative of an invented Latinism, *pedasculus*, "little pedant.")    51 **Mistrust** (Lucentio plays upon Bianca's *mistrust* in line 50, in which she expresses skepticism about his secret wooing; his answer seeks to reassure her, while at the same time in "Litio's" hearing he seems to emphasize the truth of his instruction as he goes on with his lesson from the *Heroides*. Her reply is ambiguous in the same way.)    **Aeacides** descendant of Aeacus, King of Aegina, father of Telamon and grandfather of Ajax    57 **pleasant** merry    60 **formal** precise    61 **but** unless    64 **order** method    66 **gamut** the scale, from the alphabet name (*gamma*) of the first note plus *ut*, its syllable name, now commonly called *do*. (The *gamut* of Hortensio begins on G instead of on C.)    69 **drawn** set out, copied.

72 **ground** bass note, foundation.    **accord** harmony    74 *B mi* (With a suggestion of "be my.")    75 *fa ut* (The note C is the fourth note, or *fa*, of a scale based on G but is the first note, *ut*, or *do*, of the more universal major scale based on C. Similarly, D is the fifth note, or *sol*, in the G scale but is the second, or *re*, in the C scale; similarly, with E as sixth and third.)    76 **two notes** (Hinting at Hortensio's disguise.)    77 *E la mi* (Suggesting "Ill am I.")    79 **nice** capricious    89 **stale** ridiculous rival    90 **Seize . . . list** let him who wants you have you.    **ranging** inconstant. (The metaphor is that of a straying hawk.)    91 **be quit** get even.    **changing** loving another.
3.2. **Location:** Padua. Before Baptista's house.
2 **should be** are to be    4 **What . . . said?** What will people say?
5 **want** lack

KATHARINA
No shame but mine. I must, forsooth, be forced
To give my hand opposed against my heart
Unto a mad-brain rudesby full of spleen,       10
Who wooed in haste and means to wed at leisure.
I told you, I, he was a frantic fool,
Hiding his bitter jests in blunt behavior.
And, to be noted for a merry man,              14
He'll woo a thousand, 'point the day of marriage,
Make friends, invite, and proclaim the banns,  16
Yet never means to wed where he hath wooed.
Now must the world point at poor Katharine
And say, "Lo, there is mad Petruchio's wife,
If it would please him come and marry her!"

TRANIO
Patience, good Katharine, and Baptista, too.
Upon my life, Petruchio means but well,
Whatever fortune stays him from his word.       23
Though he be blunt, I know him passing wise;    24
Though he be merry, yet withal he's honest.     25

KATHARINA
Would Katharine had never seen him, though!
                              *Exit weeping.*

BAPTISTA
Go, girl, I cannot blame thee now to weep,
For such an injury would vex a very saint,
Much more a shrew of thy impatient humor.

                *Enter Biondello.*

BIONDELLO   Master, master! News, and such old news   30
as you never heard of!
BAPTISTA   Is it new and old too? How may that be?
BIONDELLO   Why, is it not news to hear of Petruchio's
coming?
BAPTISTA   Is he come?
BIONDELLO   Why, no, sir.
BAPTISTA   What, then?
BIONDELLO   He is coming.
BAPTISTA   When will he be here?
BIONDELLO   When he stands where I am and sees you
there.
TRANIO   But say, what to thine old news?            42
BIONDELLO   Why, Petruchio is coming in a new hat and
an old jerkin; a pair of old breeches thrice turned;   44
a pair of boots that have been candle-cases, one buckled,  45
another laced; an old rusty sword ta'en out of the town
armory, with a broken hilt, and chapeless; with two   47
broken points; his horse hipped, with an old mothy   48

saddle and stirrups of no kindred; besides, possessed   49
with the glanders and like to mose in the chine, troubled   50
with the lampass, infected with the fashions, full   51
of windgalls, sped with spavins, rayed with the yel-   52
lows, past cure of the fives, stark spoiled with the stag-   53
gers, begnawn with the bots, swayed in the back and   54
shoulder-shotten; near-legged before, and with a half-   55
cheeked bit and a headstall of sheep's leather which,   56
being restrained to keep him from stumbling, hath   57
been often burst and now repaired with knots; one
girth six times pieced, and a woman's crupper of   59
velour, which hath two letters for her name fairly   60
set down in studs, and here and there pieced
with packthread.                                   62
BAPTISTA   Who comes with him?
BIONDELLO   Oh, sir, his lackey, for all the world capari-   64
soned like the horse; with a linen stock on one leg and   65
a kersey boot-hose on the other, gartered with a red   66
and blue list; an old hat, and the humor of forty fan-   67
cies pricked in 't for a feather—a monster, a very mon-   68
ster in apparel, and not like a Christian footboy or a
gentleman's lackey.
TRANIO
'Tis some odd humor pricks him to this fashion;   71
Yet oftentimes he goes but mean-appareled.        72
BAPTISTA   I am glad he's come, howsoe'er he comes.
BIONDELLO   Why, sir, he comes not.
BAPTISTA   Didst thou not say he comes?
BIONDELLO   Who? That Petruchio came?
BAPTISTA   Ay, that Petruchio came.
BIONDELLO   No, sir, I say his horse comes, with him on
his back.
BAPTISTA   Why, that's all one.                      80
BIONDELLO
Nay, by Saint Jamy,

---

**10 rudesby** unmannerly fellow.   **spleen** i.e., changeable temper
**14 to be noted for** in order to get a reputation as   **16 banns** wedding
announcement   **23 Whatever . . . word** whatever accident keeps him
from fulfilling his promise.   **24 passing** exceedingly   **25 merry**
given to joking   **30 old** rare; and referring to Petruchio's old clothes
**42 to** about   **44 jerkin** man's jacket.   **turned** i.e., with the material
reversed to get more wear   **45 candle-cases** i.e., discarded boots,
used only as a receptacle for candle ends   **47 chapeless** without the
chape, the metal plate or mounting of a scabbard, especially that
which covers the point   **48 points** tagged laces for attaching hose to
doublet.   **hipped** lamed in the hip. (Almost all the diseases here
named are described in Gervase Markham's *How to Choose, Ride,
Train, and Diet both Hunting Horses and Running Horses . . . Also a Discourse of Horsemanship*, probably first published in 1593.)

**49 of no kindred** that don't match   **50 glanders** contagious disease in
horses causing swelling beneath the jaw and mucous discharge from
the nostrils.   **mose in the chine** suffer from glanders   **51 lampass** a
thick, spongy flesh growing over a horse's upper teeth and hindering
his eating.   **fashions** i.e., farcins, or farcy, a disease like glanders
**52 windgalls** soft tumors or swellings generally found on the fetlock
joint, so called from having been supposed to contain air.   **sped** far
gone.   **spavins** a disease of the hock, marked by a small bony enlargement inside the leg.   **rayed** bespattered, defiled   **52–3 yellows** jaundice   **53 fives** avives, a glandular disease causing swelling behind the
ear   **53–4 stark . . . staggers** completely destroyed by a disease causing
palsylike staggering   **54 bots** parasitic worms   **55 shoulder-shotten**
with sprained or dislocated shoulder.   **near-legged before** with knock-
kneed forelegs   **55–6 half-cheeked bit** one to which the bridle is
attached halfway up the cheek or sidepiece and thus not giving sufficient control over the horse   **56 headstall** part of the bridle over the
head.   **sheep's leather** (i.e., of inferior quality; pigskin was used for
strongest harness)   **57 restrained** drawn back   **59 girth** saddle-strap
passing under the horse's belly.   **pieced** mended.   **crupper** leather
loop passing under the horse's tail and fastened to the saddle
**60 velour** velvet.   **two . . . name** her initials   **62 packthread** twine for
securing parcels.   **64–5 for . . . caparisoned** in all respects outfitted
**65 stock** stocking   **66 kersey boot-hose** overstocking of coarse material
for wearing under boots   **67 list** strip of cloth   **67–8 the humor . . .
feather** a trite motto incised in it instead of a feather   **68 pricked**
pinned.   **for** in place of   **71 humor pricks** whim that spurs   **72 mean-
appareled** poorly dressed.   **80 all one** the same thing.

I hold you a penny,
A horse and a man
Is more than one,
And yet not many.                                                          82

*Enter Petruchio and Grumio.*

PETRUCHIO
Come, where be these gallants? Who's at home?
BAPTISTA    You are welcome, sir.
PETRUCHIO    And yet I come not well.                                       88
BAPTISTA    And yet you halt not.                                           89
TRANIO
Not so well appareled as I wish you were.
PETRUCHIO
Were it better, I should rush in thus.                                      91
But where is Kate? Where is my lovely bride?
How does my father? Gentles, methinks you frown.
And wherefore gaze this goodly company,
As if they saw some wondrous monument,                                      95
Some comet, or unusual prodigy?                                             96
BAPTISTA
Why, sir, you know this is your wedding day.
First were we sad, fearing you would not come,
Now sadder that you come so unprovided.                                     99
Fie, doff this habit, shame to your estate,                                 100
An eyesore to our solemn festival!
TRANIO
And tell us, what occasion of import
Hath all so long detained you from your wife
And sent you hither so unlike yourself?
PETRUCHIO
Tedious it were to tell, and harsh to hear.
Sufficeth I am come to keep my word,                                        106
Though in some part enforcèd to digress,                                    107
Which at more leisure I will so excuse
As you shall well be satisfied withal.
But where is Kate? I stay too long from her.
The morning wears; 'tis time we were at church.                             111
TRANIO
See not your bride in these unreverent robes.
Go to my chamber. Put on clothes of mine.
PETRUCHIO
Not I, believe me. Thus I'll visit her.
BAPTISTA
But thus, I trust, you will not marry her.
PETRUCHIO
Good sooth, even thus. Therefore ha' done with
    words.                                                                  116
To me she's married, not unto my clothes.
Could I repair what she will wear in me                                     118
As I can change these poor accoutrements,
'Twere well for Kate and better for myself.

But what a fool am I to chat with you,
When I should bid good morrow to my bride
And seal the title with a lovely kiss!            *Exit.*  123
TRANIO
He hath some meaning in his mad attire.
We will persuade him, be it possible,
To put on better ere he go to church.
BAPTISTA
I'll after him, and see the event of this.                                 127
*Exit [with all but Tranio and Lucentio].*
TRANIO
But, sir, to love concerneth us to add                                     128
Her father's liking, which to bring to pass,
As I before imparted to Your Worship,                                      130
I am to get a man—whate'er he be
It skills not much, we'll fit him to our turn—                             132
And he shall be Vincentio of Pisa
And make assurance here in Padua
Of greater sums than I have promisèd.
So shall you quietly enjoy your hope
And marry sweet Bianca with consent.
LUCENTIO
Were it not that my fellow schoolmaster
Doth watch Bianca's steps so narrowly,
'Twere good, methinks, to steal our marriage,                              140
Which once performed, let all the world say no,
I'll keep mine own, despite of all the world.
TRANIO
That by degrees we mean to look into,
And watch our vantage in this business.                                    144
We'll overreach the graybeard, Gremio,
The narrow-prying father, Minola,                                          146
The quaint musician, amorous Litio,                                        147
All for my master's sake, Lucentio.

*Enter Gremio.*

Signor Gremio, came you from the church?
GREMIO
As willingly as e'er I came from school.
TRANIO
And is the bride and bridegroom coming home?
GREMIO
A bridegroom, say you? 'Tis a groom indeed,                                152
A grumbling groom, and that the girl shall find.
TRANIO
Curster than she? Why, 'tis impossible.
GREMIO
Why, he 's a devil, a devil, a very fiend.
TRANIO
Why, she's a devil, a devil, the devil's dam.                              156

---

**82 hold** wager    **88 I come not well** i.e., I am not made to feel welcome; or, I come admittedly not well appareled.    **89 halt** limp, move slowly    **91 Were it** Even if it (my apparel) were.    **rush** come quickly. (Referring to *halt not* in line 89.)    **95 monument** portent    **96 prodigy** omen.    **99 unprovided** ill equipped.    **100 habit** outfit.    **estate** position, station    **106 Sufficeth** It is enough that    **107 digress** i.e., deviate    **111 wears** is going by quickly    **116 Good sooth** i.e., Yes, indeed    **118 Could . . . me** If I could amend in my character what she'll have to put up with

**123 lovely** loving    **127 event** outcome    **128 to love . . . add** besides obtaining the love of the lady, it behooves us to add    **130 to Your Worship** (Tranio privately drops the fiction that he is Lucentio's master.)    **132 skills** matters    **140 steal our marriage** elope    **144 watch our vantage** look out for our best opportunity, advantage    **146 narrow-prying** suspicious, watchful    **147 quaint** skillful    **152 'Tis a groom indeed** A fine bridegroom he is. (Said ironically, with pun on the sense of "servant," "rough fellow.")    **156 dam** mother.

GREMIO
Tut, she's a lamb, a dove, a fool to him.                              157
I'll tell you, Sir Lucentio. When the priest
Should ask if Katharine should be his wife,                            159
"Ay, by Gog's wouns," quoth he, and swore so loud                      160
That all amazed the priest let fall the book,
And as he stooped again to take it up,
This mad-brained bridegroom took him such a cuff                       163
That down fell priest and book, and book and priest.
"Now take them up," quoth he, "if any list."                           165
TRANIO
What said the wench when he rose again?
GREMIO
Trembled and shook, forwhy he stamped and swore                        167
As if the vicar meant to cozen him.                                    168
But after many ceremonies done
He calls for wine. "A health!" quoth he, as if
He had been aboard, carousing to his mates                             171
After a storm; quaffed off the muscatel
And threw the sops all in the sexton's face,                           173
Having no other reason
But that his beard grew thin and hungerly                              175
And seemed to ask him sops as he was drinking.                         176
This done, he took the bride about the neck
And kissed her lips with such a clamorous smack
That at the parting all the church did echo.
And I seeing this came thence for very shame,
And after me, I know, the rout is coming.                              181
Such a mad marriage never was before.    *Music plays.*
Hark, hark! I hear the minstrels play.

*Enter Petruchio, Kate, Bianca, Hortensio [as Litio],*
*Baptista, [with Grumio, and train].*

PETRUCHIO
Gentlemen and friends, I thank you for your pains.
I know you think to dine with me today,
And have prepared great store of wedding cheer;
But so it is my haste doth call me hence,
And therefore here I mean to take my leave.
BAPTISTA
Is't possible you will away tonight?
PETRUCHIO
I must away today, before night come.
Make it no wonder. If you knew my business,                            191
You would entreat me rather go than stay.
And, honest company, I thank you all                                   193
That have beheld me give away myself
To this most patient, sweet, and virtuous wife.
Dine with my father, drink a health to me,
For I must hence; and farewell to you all.

TRANIO
Let us entreat you stay till after dinner.
PETRUCHIO
It may not be.
GREMIO                Let me entreat you.
PETRUCHIO
It cannot be.
KATHARINA    Let me entreat you.
PETRUCHIO
I am content.
KATHARINA        Are you content to stay?
PETRUCHIO
I am content you shall entreat me stay;
But yet not stay, entreat me how you can.
KATHARINA
Now, if you love me, stay.
PETRUCHIO                Grumio, my horse.        204
GRUMIO    Ay, sir, they be ready. The oats have eaten the   205
horses.                                                      206
KATHARINA    Nay, then,
Do what thou canst, I will not go today,
No, nor tomorrow—not till I please myself.
The door is open, sir; there lies your way.
You may be jogging whiles your boots are green.             211
For me, I'll not be gone till I please myself.              212
'Tis like you'll prove a jolly, surly groom,                213
That take it on you at the first so roundly.                214
PETRUCHIO
Oh, Kate, content thee. Prithee, be not angry.
KATHARINA
I will be angry. What hast thou to do?—                     216
Father, be quiet. He shall stay my leisure.                 217
GREMIO
Ay, marry, sir, now it begins to work.                      218
KATHARINA
Gentlemen, forward to the bridal dinner.
I see a woman may be made a fool
If she had not a spirit to resist.
PETRUCHIO
They shall go forward, Kate, at thy command.—
Obey the bride, you that attend on her.
Go to the feast, revel and domineer,                        224
Carouse full measure to her maidenhead,                     225
Be mad and merry, or go hang yourselves.
But for my bonny Kate, she must with me.                     227
Nay, look not big, nor stamp, nor stare, nor fret;          228
I will be master of what is mine own.
She is my goods, my chattels; she is my house,
My household stuff, my field, my barn,
My horse, my ox, my ass, my anything;                       232
And here she stands, touch her whoever dare.

---

157 **a fool to** i.e., a pitiable weak creature compared with
159 **Should ask** came to the point (in the service) where he is directed
to ask    160 **Gog's wouns** God's (Christ's) wounds    163 **took** gave,
struck    165 **list** choose.    167 **forwhy** for    168 **cozen** cheat
171 **aboard** aboard ship    173 **sops** cakes or bread soaked in the wine
175 **hungerly** hungry looking, having a starved or famished look
176 **And . . . drinking** and seemed to invite the throwing in his face of
what Petruchio was drinking.    181 **rout** crowd, wedding party
191 **Make it no wonder** Don't be surprised.    193 **honest** worthy, kind

204 **horse** horses.    205–6 **oats . . . horses** (A comic inversion.)
211 **be . . . green** (Proverbial for "getting an early start," with a sarcastic allusion to his unseemly attire.)    **green** fresh, new.    212 **For** As
for    213 **like** likely.    **jolly** (Said sarcastically.)    214 **take it on you**
i.e., throw your weight around.    **roundly** unceremoniously.
216 **What . . . do?** What business is it of yours?    217 **stay my leisure**
wait until I am ready.    218 **now . . . work** now it starts.    224 **domi-**
**neer** feast riotously    225 **to her maidenhead** to her loss of virginity
227 **for** as for    228 **big** threatening    232 **ox . . . anything** (This catalogue of a man's possessions is from the Tenth Commandment.)

I'll bring mine action on the proudest he                    234
That stops my way in Padua.—Grumio,
Draw forth thy weapon. We are beset with thieves.    236
Rescue thy mistress, if thou be a man.—
Fear not, sweet wench, they shall not touch thee, Kate!
I'll buckler thee against a million.                         239
        *Exeunt Petruchio, Katharina, [and Grumio].*

BAPTISTA
Nay, let them go—a couple of quiet ones!

GREMIO
Went they not quickly, I should die with laughing.

TRANIO
Of all mad matches never was the like.

LUCENTIO
Mistress, what's your opinion of your sister?

BIANCA
That, being mad herself, she's madly mated.

GREMIO
I warrant him, Petruchio is Kated.                           245

BAPTISTA
Neighbors and friends, though bride and bridegroom
   wants                                       246
For to supply the places at the table,                       247
You know there wants no junkets at the feast.                248
Lucentio, you shall supply the bridegroom's place,
And let Bianca take her sister's room.

TRANIO
Shall sweet Bianca practice how to bride it?                 251

BAPTISTA
She shall, Lucentio.—Come, gentlemen, let's go.
        *Exeunt.*

❖

# [4.1]

*Enter Grumio.*

GRUMIO    Fie, fie on all tired jades, on all mad masters,    1
and all foul ways! Was ever man so beaten? Was ever    2
man so rayed? Was ever man so weary? I am sent be-    3
fore to make a fire, and they are coming after to warm
them. Now, were not I a little pot and soon hot, my    5
very lips might freeze to my teeth, my tongue to the
roof of my mouth, my heart in my belly, ere I should
come by a fire to thaw me. But I with blowing the fire    8
shall warm myself; for, considering the weather, a    9
taller man than I will take cold.—Holla, ho! Curtis!    10

*Enter Curtis.*

CURTIS    Who is that calls so coldly?

GRUMIO    A piece of ice. If thou doubt it, thou mayst
slide from my shoulder to my heel with no greater
a run but my head and my neck. A fire, good Curtis!    14

CURTIS    Is my master and his wife coming, Grumio?

GRUMIO    Oh, ay, Curtis, ay, and therefore fire, fire! Cast    16
no no water.    17

CURTIS    Is she so hot a shrew as she's reported?

GRUMIO    She was, good Curtis, before this frost. But,
thou know'st, winter tames man, woman, and beast;
for it hath tamed my old master and my new mistress
and myself, fellow Curtis.

CURTIS    Away, you three-inch fool! I am no beast.    23

GRUMIO    Am I but three inches? Why, thy horn is a foot,    24
and so long am I, at the least. But wilt thou make a fire,    25
or shall I complain on thee to our mistress, whose
hand—she being now at hand—thou shalt soon feel,
to thy cold comfort, for being slow in thy hot office?    28

CURTIS    I prithee, good Grumio, tell me, how goes the
world?

GRUMIO    A cold world, Curtis, in every office but thine,
and therefore fire. Do thy duty, and have thy duty, for    32
my master and mistress are almost frozen to death.

CURTIS    There's fire ready, and therefore, good Grumio,
the news.

GRUMIO    Why, "Jack boy, ho, boy!" and as much news    36
as wilt thou.

CURTIS    Come, you are so full of coney-catching.    38

GRUMIO    Why, therefore fire, for I have caught extreme
cold. Where's the cook? Is supper ready, the house
trimmed, rushes strewed, cobwebs swept, the serving-    41
men in their new fustian, the white stockings, and    42
every officer his wedding garment on? Be the Jacks    43
fair within, the Jills fair without, the carpets laid, and    44
everything in order?

CURTIS    All ready; and therefore, I pray thee, news.

GRUMIO    First, know my horse is tired, my master and
mistress fallen out.    48

CURTIS    How?

GRUMIO    Out of their saddles into the dirt—and thereby    50
hangs a tale.    51

---

234 **action** (1) lawsuit (2) attack    236 **Draw** (Perhaps Petruchio and Grumio actually draw their swords.)    239 **buckler** shield, defend    245 **Kated** (Gremio's invention for "mated and matched with Kate.")    246–7 **wants For to supply** are not present to fill    248 **there wants no junkets** there is no lack of sweetmeats    251 **bride it** play the bride.

**4.1. Location:** Petruchio's country house. A table is set out, with seats.

1 **jades** ill-conditioned horses    2 **ways** roads.    3 **rayed** bespattered.    5 **a little ... hot** (Proverbial expression for a person of small stature soon angered.)    8 **come by** find.    **blowing the fire** i.e., to make it burn hotter    9–10 **a taller** even a taller. (With play on the meaning "better," "finer.")

14 **run** running start    16–17 **Cast ... water** (Alludes to the round "Scotland's burning," in which the phrase "Fire, fire!" is followed by "Pour on water, pour on water.")    23 **three-inch fool** (Another reference to Grumio's small size.)    **I am no beast** (Curtis protests being called *fellow* by Grumio, since Grumio in line 20 has paralleled himself with *beast*.)    24–5 **Why ... least** (Grumio hints that Curtis is a beast with a prominent *horn*, and hence a cuckold; suggesting too that Grumio's *horn*, i.e., *penis*, is as long as Curtis's or longer.)    28 **hot office** i.e., duty of providing a fire.    32 **have thy duty** have what's coming to you, your due    36 **Jack ... boy** (The first line of another round or catch.)    38 **coney-catching** cheating, trickery. (With wordplay on *catch*, or round, like "Jack boy, ho, boy" in line 36.)    41 **rushes** (Used to cover the floor.)    42 **fustian** coarse cloth of cotton and flax    43 **officer** household servant.    **Jacks** (1) servingmen (2) drinking vessels, usually of leather and hence needing to be clean *within*    44 **Jills** (1) maidservants (2) "gills," drinking vessels holding a quarter pint, often of metal and hence in need of polishing *without*. (Grumio may joke that the maidservants cannot be expected to be clean *within*.)    48 **fallen out** quarreling. (But with a pun on the literal sense in line 50.)    50–1 **thereby hangs a tale** there's quite a story to tell about that. (But with a risible suggestion of hanging by one's tail.)

CURTIS   Let's ha 't, good Grumio.                                    52
GRUMIO   Lend thine ear.
CURTIS   Here.
GRUMIO   There.                              [*He cuffs Curtis.*]
CURTIS   This 'tis to feel a tale, not to hear a tale.
GRUMIO   And therefore 'tis called a sensible tale, and    57
this cuff was but to knock at your ear and beseech
listening. Now I begin: Imprimis, we came down a   59
foul hill, my master riding behind my mistress—    60
CURTIS   Both of one horse?                                    61
GRUMIO   What's that to thee?
CURTIS   Why, a horse.
GRUMIO   Tell thou the tale. But hadst thou not crossed   64
me, thou shouldst have heard how her horse fell and
she under her horse; thou shouldst have heard in how
miry a place, how she was bemoiled, how he left her   67
with the horse upon her, how he beat me because her
horse stumbled, how she waded through the dirt to
pluck him off me, how he swore, how she prayed that   70
never prayed before, how I cried, how the horses
ran away, how her bridle was burst, how I lost my
crupper, with many things of worthy memory, which   73
now shall die in oblivion and thou return unexperi-
enced to thy grave.
CURTIS   By this reckoning he is more shrew than she.
GRUMIO   Ay, and that thou and the proudest of you all
shall find when he comes home. But what talk I of   78
this? Call forth Nathaniel, Joseph, Nicholas, Philip,
Walter, Sugarsop, and the rest. Let their heads be
sleekly combed, their blue coats brushed, and their   81
garters of an indifferent knit; let them curtsy with their   82
left legs, and not presume to touch a hair of my
master's horsetail till they kiss their hands. Are they
all ready?
CURTIS   They are.
GRUMIO   Call them forth.
CURTIS   [*calling*]   Do you hear, ho? You must meet my
master to countenance my mistress.                          89
GRUMIO   Why, she hath a face of her own.
CURTIS   Who knows not that?
GRUMIO   Thou, it seems, that calls for company to
countenance her.
CURTIS   I call them forth to credit her.                      94

*Enter four or five Servingmen.*

GRUMIO   Why, she comes to borrow nothing of them.
NATHANIEL   Welcome home, Grumio!
PHILIP   How now, Grumio?
JOSEPH   What, Grumio!
NICHOLAS   Fellow Grumio!
NATHANIEL   How now, old lad?

GRUMIO   Welcome, you; how now, you; what, you;
fellow, you—and thus much for greeting. Now, my
spruce companions, is all ready, and all things neat?   103
NATHANIEL   All things is ready. How near is our
master?
GRUMIO   E'en at hand, alighted by this; and therefore
be not—Cock's passion, silence! I hear my master.   107

*Enter Petruchio and Kate.*

PETRUCHIO
Where be these knaves? What, no man at door
To hold my stirrup nor to take my horse?                  109
Where is Nathaniel, Gregory, Philip?
ALL SERVANTS   Here, here, sir, here, sir.
PETRUCHIO
Here, sir! Here, sir! Here, sir! Here, sir!
You loggerheaded and unpolished grooms!
What, no attendance? No regard? No duty?
Where is the foolish knave I sent before?                  115
GRUMIO
Here, sir, as foolish as I was before.
PETRUCHIO
You peasant swain, you whoreson, malt-horse
drudge!                                                        117
Did I not bid thee meet me in the park
And bring along these rascal knaves with thee?
GRUMIO
Nathaniel's coat, sir, was not fully made,
And Gabriel's pumps were all unpinked i'the heel.   121
There was no link to color Peter's hat,                     122
And Walter's dagger was not come from sheathing.   123
There were none fine but Adam, Ralph, and Gregory;   124
The rest were ragged, old, and beggarly.
Yet, as they are, here are they come to meet you.
PETRUCHIO
Go, rascals, go and fetch my supper in.
                                          *Exeunt Servants.*
[*He sings.*] "Where is the life that late I led?           128
Where are those—" Sit down, Kate, and welcome.—   129
                                       [*They sit at table.*]
Soud, soud, soud, soud!                                        130

*Enter Servants with supper.*

Why, when, I say?—Nay, good sweet Kate, be
merry.—                                                        131
Off with my boots, you rogues! You villains, when?
                     [*A Servant takes off Petruchio's boots.*]
[*He sings.*] "It was the friar of orders gray,              133
            As he forth walkèd on his way—"               134

---

52 **ha 't** have it   57 **sensible** (1) capable of being felt (2) showing good sense   59 **Imprimis** In the first place   60 **foul** muddy   61 **of** on   64 **crossed** thwarted, interrupted   67 **bemoiled** befouled with mire   70 **him** Petruchio   73 **crupper** (See 3.2.59.)   **of worthy** worthy of   78 **what** why   81 **blue coats** (Usual dress for servingmen.)   82 **indifferent** well-matched, identical   89 **countenance** pay respects to. (With a following pun on the meaning "face.")   94 **credit** pay respects to. (With another pun following, on "extend financial credit.")

103 **spruce** lively, trim in appearance   107 **Cock's passion** By God's (Christ's) suffering   109 **hold my stirrup** i.e., help me dismount   115 **before** ahead. (With pun in next line on "previously.")   117 **swain** rustic.   **whoreson . . . drudge** worthless plodding work animal, such as would be used on a treadmill to grind malt.   121 **pumps** low-cut shoes.   **unpinked** lacking in eyelets or in ornamental tracing in the leather   122 **link** blacking made from burnt "links" or torches   123 **sheathing** being fitted with a sheath.   124 **fine** well clothed   128–9 **Where . . . those** (A fragment of a lost ballad, probably lamenting the man's loss of freedom in marriage.)   130 **Soud** (A nonsense song, or expression of impatience, or perhaps "food!")   131 **when** (An exclamation of impatience.)   133–4 **"It . . . way"** (A fragment of a lost ballad, probably bawdy.)

Out, you rogue! You pluck my foot awry.     135
               [*He kicks the Servant.*]
Take that, and mend the plucking of the other.—     136
Be merry, Kate.—Some water, here. What, ho!

*Enter one with water.*

Where's my spaniel Troilus? Sirrah, get you hence,
And bid my cousin Ferdinand come hither—
                    [*Exit Servant.*]
One, Kate, that you must kiss and be acquainted with.
Where are my slippers? Shall I have some water?
Come, Kate, and wash, and welcome heartily.
       [*A Servant offers water, but spills some.*]
You whoreson villain, will you let it fall?
                  [*He strikes the Servant.*]

KATHARINA
Patience, I pray you, 'twas a fault unwilling.     144

PETRUCHIO
A whoreson, beetleheaded, flap-eared knave!—     145
Come, Kate, sit down. I know you have a stomach.     146
Will you give thanks, sweet Kate, or else shall I?—     147
What's this? Mutton?

FIRST SERVANT          Ay.

PETRUCHIO             Who brought it?

PETER                        I.

PETRUCHIO
'Tis burnt, and so is all the meat.
What dogs are these? Where is the rascal cook?
How durst you, villains, bring it from the dresser     151
And serve it thus to me that love it not?
There, take it to you, trenchers, cups, and all.     153
           [*He throws the meat, etc., at them.*]
You heedless jolt-heads and unmannered slaves!     154
What, do you grumble? I'll be with you straight.     155
                    [*They run out.*]

KATHARINA
I pray you, husband, be not so disquiet.
The meat was well, if you were so contented.     157

PETRUCHIO
I tell thee, Kate, 'twas burnt and dried away,
And I expressly am forbid to touch it;
For it engenders choler, planteth anger,     160
And better 'twere that both of us did fast,
Since, of ourselves, ourselves are choleric,     162
Than feed it with such overroasted flesh.
Be patient. Tomorrow 't shall be mended,
And for this night we'll fast for company.     165
Come, I will bring thee to thy bridal chamber.     166
                         *Exeunt.*

*Enter Servants severally.*

NATHANIEL    Peter, didst ever see the like?
PETER    He kills her in her own humor.     168

*Enter Curtis.*

GRUMIO    Where is he?
CURTIS    In her chamber,
Making a sermon of continency to her,     171
And rails, and swears, and rates, that she, poor soul,     172
Knows not which way to stand, to look, to speak,
And sits as one new risen from a dream.
Away, away! For he is coming hither.       [*Exeunt.*]

*Enter Petruchio.*

PETRUCHIO
Thus have I politicly begun my reign,     176
And 'tis my hope to end successfully.
My falcon now is sharp and passing empty,     178
And till she stoop she must not be full-gorged,     179
For then she never looks upon her lure.
Another way I have to man my haggard,     181
To make her come and know her keeper's call:
That is, to watch her, as we watch these kites     183
That bate and beat and will not be obedient.     184
She ate no meat today, nor none shall eat.
Last night she slept not, nor tonight she shall not.
As with the meat, some undeservèd fault
I'll find about the making of the bed,
And here I'll fling the pillow, there the bolster,
This way the coverlet, another way the sheets.
Ay, and amid this hurly I intend     191
That all is done in reverent care of her.
And in conclusion she shall watch all night,     193
And if she chance to nod I'll rail and brawl,
And with the clamor keep her still awake.
This is a way to kill a wife with kindness;
And thus I'll curb her mad and headstrong humor.     197
He that knows better how to tame a shrew,
Now let him speak. 'Tis charity to show.     *Exit.* 199

                        ❧

## [4.2]

*Enter Tranio [as Lucentio] and Hortensio
[as Litio].*

TRANIO
Is't possible, friend Litio, that Mistress Bianca
Doth fancy any other but Lucentio?
I tell you, sir, she bears me fair in hand.     3

---

**135 Out** (Exclamation of anger or reproach.)   **136 mend the plucking of** do a better job of pulling off   **144 unwilling** not intentional.
**145 beetleheaded** i.e., blockheaded (since a *beetle* is a pounding tool)
**146 stomach** appetite. (With a suggestion also of "temper.")
**147 give thanks** say grace   **151 dresser** one who "dresses" or prepares the food; or, sideboard   **153 trenchers** wooden dishes or plates
**154 jolt-heads** blockheads   **155 with you straight** after you at once (to get even for this).   **157 if . . . contented** if you had chosen to be pleased with it.   **160 choler** the humor or bodily fluid, hot and dry in character, that supposedly produced ill temper and was thought to be aggravated by the eating of roast meat   **162 of ourselves** by our natures   **165 for company** together.   **166.2** *severally* separately.

**168 He . . . humor** He subdues her shrewishness with his own greater shrewishness.   **171 sermon of continency** lecture on self-restraint
**172 rates** scolds.   **that** so that   **176 politicly** with skillful calculation
**178 sharp** hungry.   **passing** very   **179 stoop** fly down to the lure
**181 man** tame, assert masculine authority over.   **haggard** wild female hawk; hence, an intractable woman   **183 watch her** keep her watching, i.e., awake.   **kites** a kind of hawk. (With a pun on *Kate*.)
**184 bate and beat** beat the wings impatiently and flutter away from the hand or perch   **191 hurly** commotion.   **intend** pretend
**193 watch** stay awake   **197 humor** disposition.   **199 'Tis charity to show** This is to perform an act of Christian benevolence. (On the rhyme with *shrew*, see also the play's final lines.)
**4.2. Location:** Padua. Before Baptista's house.
**3 bears . . . hand** gives me encouragement, leads me on.

HORTENSIO
Sir, to satisfy you in what I have said,                           4
Stand by and mark the manner of his teaching.
                            [*They stand aside.*]

*Enter Bianca [and Lucentio as Cambio].*

LUCENTIO
Now, mistress, profit you in what you read?        6
BIANCA
What, master, read you? First resolve me that.     7
LUCENTIO
I read that I profess, *The Art to Love.*           8
BIANCA
And may you prove, sir, master of your art!
LUCENTIO
While you, sweet dear, prove mistress of my heart!
                    [*They move aside and court each other.*]
HORTENSIO [*to Tranio, coming forward*]
Quick proceeders, marry! Now, tell me, I pray,    11
You that durst swear that your mistress Bianca
Loved none in the world so well as Lucentio.
TRANIO
Oh, despiteful love! Unconstant womankind!        14
I tell thee, Litio, this is wonderful.            15
HORTENSIO
Mistake no more. I am not Litio,
Nor a musician, as I seem to be,
But one that scorn to live in this disguise        18
For such a one as leaves a gentleman               19
And makes a god of such a cullion.                 20
Know, sir, that I am called Hortensio.
TRANIO
Signor Hortensio, I have often heard
Of your entire affection to Bianca;                23
And since mine eyes are witness of her lightness,  24
I will with you, if you be so contented,
Forswear Bianca and her love forever.
HORTENSIO
See how they kiss and court! Signor Lucentio,
Here is my hand, and here I firmly vow
                            [*giving his hand*]
Never to woo her more, but do forswear her,
As one unworthy all the former favors
That I have fondly flattered her withal.           31
TRANIO
And here I take the like unfeignèd oath,
Never to marry with her though she would entreat.
Fie on her, see how beastly she doth court him!
HORTENSIO
Would all the world but he had quite forsworn!     35

For me, that I may surely keep mine oath,          36
I will be married to a wealthy widow,
Ere three days pass, which hath as long loved me
As I have loved this proud disdainful haggard.     39
And so farewell, Signor Lucentio.
Kindness in women, not their beauteous looks,
Shall win my love. And so I take my leave,
In resolution as I swore before.          [*Exit.*] 43
TRANIO [*as Lucentio and Bianca come forward again*]
Mistress Bianca, bless you with such grace
As 'longeth to a lover's blessèd case!             45
Nay, I have ta'en you napping, gentle love,        46
And have forsworn you with Hortensio.
BIANCA
Tranio, you jest. But have you both forsworn me?
TRANIO
Mistress, we have.
LUCENTIO              Then we are rid of Litio.
TRANIO
I' faith, he'll have a lusty widow now,            50
That shall be wooed and wedded in a day.
BIANCA    God give him joy!
TRANIO    Ay, and he'll tame her.
BIANCA    He says so, Tranio?
TRANIO
Faith, he is gone unto the taming-school.
BIANCA
The taming-school! What, is there such a place?
TRANIO
Ay, mistress, and Petruchio is the master,
That teacheth tricks eleven-and-twenty long        58
To tame a shrew and charm her chattering tongue.

*Enter Biondello.*

BIONDELLO
Oh, master, master, I have watched so long
That I am dog-weary, but at last I spied
An ancient angel coming down the hill             62
Will serve the turn.
TRANIO              What is he, Biondello?        63
BIONDELLO
Master, a marcant, or a pedant,                   64
I know not what, but formal in apparel,
In gait and countenance surely like a father.
LUCENTIO    And what of him, Tranio?
TRANIO
If he be credulous and trust my tale,
I'll make him glad to seem Vincentio,              69
And give assurance to Baptista Minola

---

4 **satisfy** convince   6 **read** (Evidently, both Bianca and "Cambio"
carry books.)   7 **resolve** answer   8 **I read . . .** *Love* I read what I
practice, Ovid's *Ars Amatoria.*   11 **proceeders** (1) workers, doers
(2) candidates for academic degrees (as suggested by the phrase
*master of your art* in line 9)   14 **despiteful** cruel   15 **wonderful** cause
for wonder.   18 **scorn** scorns   19 **such a one** i.e., Bianca   20 **cullion**
base fellow. (Referring to "Cambio"; literally, *cullion* means "testicle.")
23 **entire** unwavering   24 **lightness** wantonness   31 **fondly** foolishly   35 **Would . . . forsworn!** i.e., May everyone in the world
forsake her except the penniless "Cambio," and may she thus get
what she deserves!

36 **For** As for   39 **haggard** wild hawk.   43 **In resolution** determined
45 **'longeth** belongs   46 **ta'en you napping** i.e., done something
while you were not paying attention   50 **lusty** merry, lively
58 **eleven . . . long** i.e., right on the money. (Alluding to the card
game called "one-and-thirty" referred to at 1.2.32–3.)   62 **ancient
angel** i.e., old man who can save us in our urgent necessity. (Literally,
an "angel" or gold coin bearing the stamp of the archangel Michael
and thus distinguishable from more recent debased coinage.)
63 **Will . . . turn** who will serve our purposes.   64 **marcant**
merchant.   **pedant** schoolmaster. (Though at lines 90–1 he speaks
more like a merchant.)   69 **seem** pretend to be

As if he were the right Vincentio.
Take in your love, and then let me alone.     72
[*Exeunt Lucentio and Bianca.*]

*Enter a Pedant.*

PEDANT
God save you, sir!
TRANIO                    And you sir! You are welcome.
Travel you farre on, or are you at the farthest?     74
PEDANT
Sir, at the farthest for a week or two,
But then up farther, and as far as Rome,
And so to Tripoli, if God lend me life.
TRANIO
What countryman, I pray?
PEDANT                    Of Mantua.
TRANIO
Of Mantua, sir? Marry, God forbid!
And come to Padua, careless of your life?
PEDANT
My life, sir? How, I pray? For that goes hard.     81
TRANIO
'Tis death for anyone in Mantua
To come to Padua. Know you not the cause?
Your ships are stayed at Venice, and the Duke,     84
For private quarrel twixt your Duke and him,
Hath published and proclaimed it openly.
'Tis marvel, but that you are but newly come,
You might have heard it else proclaimed about.
PEDANT
Alas, sir, it is worse for me than so,     89
For I have bills for money by exchange     90
From Florence, and must here deliver them.
TRANIO
Well, sir, to do you courtesy,
This will I do, and this I will advise you—
First, tell me, have you ever been at Pisa?
PEDANT
Ay, sir, in Pisa have I often been,
Pisa renownèd for grave citizens.
TRANIO
Among them know you one Vincentio?
PEDANT
I know him not, but I have heard of him;
A merchant of incomparable wealth.
TRANIO
He is my father, sir, and, sooth to say,
In count'nance somewhat doth resemble you.
BIONDELLO [*aside*]   As much as an apple doth an oy-
ster, and all one.     103
TRANIO
To save your life in this extremity,
This favor will I do you for his sake;
And think it not the worst of all your fortunes
That you are like to Sir Vincentio.

His name and credit shall you undertake,     108
And in my house you shall be friendly lodged.
Look that you take upon you as you should.     110
You understand me, sir. So shall you stay
Till you have done your business in the city.
If this be courtesy, sir, accept of it.
PEDANT
Oh, sir, I do, and will repute you ever     114
The patron of my life and liberty.
TRANIO
Then go with me to make the matter good.     116
This, by the way, I let you understand:
My father is here looked for every day
To pass assurance of a dower in marriage     119
Twixt me and one Baptista's daughter here.
In all these circumstances I'll instruct you.
Go with me to clothe you as becomes you.
                                        *Exeunt.*

❦

# [4.3]

*Enter Katharina and Grumio.*

GRUMIO
No, no, forsooth, I dare not for my life.
KATHARINA
The more my wrong, the more his spite appears.     2
What, did he marry me to famish me?
Beggars that come unto my father's door
Upon entreaty have a present alms;     5
If not, elsewhere they meet with charity.
But I, who never knew how to entreat,
Nor never needed that I should entreat,
Am starved for meat, giddy for lack of sleep,
With oaths kept waking, and with brawling fed.
And that which spites me more than all these wants,
He does it under name of perfect love,
As who should say, if I should sleep or eat     13
'Twere deadly sickness or else present death.
I prithee, go and get me some repast,
I care not what, so it be wholesome food.     16
GRUMIO   What say you to a neat's foot?     17
KATHARINA
'Tis passing good. I prithee, let me have it.     18
GRUMIO
I fear it is too choleric a meat.
How say you to a fat tripe finely broiled?
KATHARINA
I like it well. Good Grumio, fetch it me.
GRUMIO
I cannot tell. I fear 'tis choleric.     22
What say you to a piece of beef and mustard?

72 **let me alone** leave things to me.   74 **farre** farther   81 **goes hard** is serious indeed.   84 **stayed** detained   89 **than so** than that   90 **bills ... exchange** promissory notes   103 **all one** no matter.

108 **credit** reputation   110 **Look ... upon you** See to it that you play your part   114 **repute you** regard you as   116 **make ... good** carry out the plan.   119 **pass assurance** convey a legal guarantee
4.3. Location: Petruchio's house. A table is set out, with seats.
2 **my wrong** the wrong done to me   5 **present** immediate. (As in line 14.)   13 **As who** as if one   16 **so** so long as   17 **neat's** ox's   18 **passing** extremely   22 **I cannot tell** I don't know what to say.

KATHARINA
A dish that I do love to feed upon.

GRUMIO
Ay, but the mustard is too hot a little.

KATHARINA
Why then, the beef, and let the mustard rest. 26

GRUMIO
Nay then, I will not. You shall have the mustard,
Or else you get no beef of Grumio.

KATHARINA
Then both, or one, or anything thou wilt.

GRUMIO
Why then, the mustard without the beef.

KATHARINA
Go, get thee gone, thou false, deluding slave,
                                    [*She*] *beats him.*
That feed'st me with the very name of meat!          32
Sorrow on thee and all the pack of you,
That triumph thus upon my misery!
Go, get thee gone, I say.

            *Enter Petruchio and Hortensio with meat.*

PETRUCHIO
How fares my Kate? What, sweeting, all amort?        36

HORTENSIO
Mistress, what cheer?

KATHARINA                    Faith, as cold as can be.

PETRUCHIO
Pluck up thy spirits; look cheerfully upon me.
Here, love, thou see'st how diligent I am
To dress thy meat myself and bring it thee.          40
I am sure, sweet Kate, this kindness merits thanks.
What, not a word? Nay, then thou lov'st it not,
And all my pains is sorted to no proof.—             43
Here, take away this dish.

KATHARINA                      I pray you, let it stand.

PETRUCHIO
The poorest service is repaid with thanks,
And so shall mine before you touch the meat.

KATHARINA    I thank you, sir.

HORTENSIO
Signor Petruchio, fie, you are to blame.
Come, Mistress Kate, I'll bear you company.

PETRUCHIO [*aside to Hortensio*]
Eat it up all, Hortensio, if thou lovest me.—
Much good do it unto thy gentle heart!
Kate, eat apace. And now, my honey love,
Will we return unto thy father's house
And revel it as bravely as the best,                 54
With silken coats and caps and golden rings,
With ruffs, and cuffs, and farthingales, and things, 56
With scarves, and fans, and double change of brav'ry, 57
With amber bracelets, beads, and all this knav'ry.

What, hast thou dined? The tailor stays thy leisure,   59
To deck thy body with his ruffling treasure.           60

            *Enter Tailor* [*with a gown*].

Come, tailor, let us see these ornaments.
Lay forth the gown.

            *Enter Haberdasher* [*with a cap*].

                    What news with you, sir?

HABERDASHER
Here is the cap Your Worship did bespeak.              63

PETRUCHIO
Why, this was molded on a porringer—                   64
A velvet dish. Fie, fie, 'tis lewd and filthy.         65
Why, 'tis a cockle or a walnut shell,                  66
A knack, a toy, a trick, a baby's cap.                 67
Away with it! Come, let me have a bigger.

KATHARINA
I'll have no bigger. This doth fit the time,           69
And gentlewomen wear such caps as these.

PETRUCHIO
When you are gentle, you shall have one too,           71
And not till then.

HORTENSIO [*aside*]    That will not be in haste.

KATHARINA
Why, sir, I trust I may have leave to speak,
And speak I will. I am no child, no babe.
Your betters have endured me say my mind,              75
And if you cannot, best you stop your ears.
My tongue will tell the anger of my heart,
Or else my heart, concealing it, will break.
And rather than it shall, I will be free
Even to the uttermost, as I please, in words.

PETRUCHIO
Why, thou say'st true. It is a paltry cap,
A custard-coffin, a bauble, a silken pie.              82
I love thee well in that thou lik'st it not.

KATHARINA
Love me or love me not, I like the cap,
And it I will have, or I will have none.

                            [*Exit Haberdasher.*]

PETRUCHIO
Thy gown? Why, ay. Come, tailor, let us see't.
Oh, mercy, God, what masquing stuff is here?           87
What's this, a sleeve? 'Tis like a demicannon.         88
What, up and down carved like an apple tart?           89
Here's snip, and nip, and cut, and slish and slash,
Like to a censer in a barber's shop.                   91
Why, what i' devil's name, tailor, call'st thou this?

---

**26 let . . . rest** i.e., forget about the mustard. **32 very** mere **36 all amort** dejected, dispirited. **40 dress** prepare **43 is . . . proof** have proved to be to no purpose. **54 bravely** splendidly **56 farthingales** hooped petticoats **57 brav'ry** finery

**59 stays** awaits **60 ruffling treasure** finery trimmed with ruffles. **63 bespeak** order. **64 porringer** porridge bowl **65 lewd** vile **66 cockle** cockleshell **67 trick** trifle **69 fit the time** suit the current fashion **71 gentle** mild. (Petruchio plays on Kate's *gentlewomen*, line 70, i.e., women of high social station.) **75 endured me say** suffered me to say **82 custard-coffin** pastry crust for a custard **87 masquing** i.e., suited only for a masque **88 demicannon** large cannon. **89 What . . . tart?** What, carved from one end to the other with slits like those in the crust of an apple tart? (Such slits in gowns were designed to reveal the fabric underneath.) **91 censer** perfuming pan having an ornamental lid

HORTENSIO [*aside*]
    I see she's like to have neither cap nor gown.    93
TAILOR
    You bid me make it orderly and well,
    According to the fashion and the time.
PETRUCHIO
    Marry, and did. But if you be remembered,    96
    I did not bid you mar it to the time.
    Go hop me over every kennel home,    98
    For you shall hop without my custom, sir.
    I'll none of it. Hence, make your best of it.
KATHARINA
    I never saw a better fashioned gown,
    More quaint, more pleasing, nor more
        commendable.    102
    Belike you mean to make a puppet of me.    103
PETRUCHIO
    Why, true, he means to make a puppet of thee.
TAILOR
    She says Your Worship means to make a puppet of her.
PETRUCHIO
    Oh, monstrous arrogance! Thou liest, thou thread,
        thou thimble,    106
    Thou yard, three-quarters, half-yard, quarter, nail!    107
    Thou flea, thou nit, thou winter cricket, thou!    108
    Braved in mine own house with a skein of thread?    109
    Away, thou rag, thou quantity, thou remnant,    110
    Or I shall so be-mete thee with thy yard    111
    As thou shalt think on prating whilst thou liv'st!    112
    I tell thee, I, that thou hast marred her gown.
TAILOR
    Your Worship is deceived. The gown is made
    Just as my master had direction.
    Grumio gave order how it should be done.
GRUMIO    I gave him no order. I gave him the stuff.    117
TAILOR
    But how did you desire it should be made?
GRUMIO    Marry, sir, with needle and thread.
TAILOR
    But did you not request to have it cut?
GRUMIO    Thou hast faced many things.    121
TAILOR    I have.
GRUMIO    Face not me. Thou hast braved many men;    123
    brave not me. I will neither be faced nor braved. I say    124
    unto thee, I bid thy master cut out the gown, but I did
    not bid him cut it to pieces. Ergo, thou liest.    126
TAILOR    Why, here is the note of the fashion to testify.
                                    [*He displays his bill.*]

PETRUCHIO    Read it.

GRUMIO    The note lies in 's throat if he say I said so.    129
TAILOR [*reads*]    "Imprimis, a loose-bodied gown—"    130
GRUMIO    Master, if ever I said loose-bodied gown,    131
    sew me in the skirts of it and beat me to death with a
    bottom of brown thread. I said a gown    133
PETRUCHIO    Proceed.
TAILOR [*reads*]    "With a small compassed cape—"    135
GRUMIO    I confess the cape.
TAILOR [*reads*]    "With a trunk sleeve—"    137
GRUMIO    I confess two sleeves.
TAILOR [*reads*]    "The sleeves curiously cut."    139
PETRUCHIO    Ay, there's the villainy.
GRUMIO    Error i'the bill, sir, error i'the bill. I commanded
    the sleeves should be cut out and sewed up again, and
    that I'll prove upon thee, though thy little finger be    143
    armed in a thimble.
TAILOR    This is true that I say. An I had thee in place    145
    where, thou shouldst know it.    146
GRUMIO    I am for thee straight. Take thou the bill, give    147
    me thy mete-yard, and spare not me.    148
HORTENSIO    God-a-mercy, Grumio, then he shall have    149
    no odds.    150
PETRUCHIO    Well, sir, in brief, the gown is not for me.
GRUMIO    You are i'the right, sir, 'tis for my mistress.
PETRUCHIO    Go, take it up unto thy master's use.    153
GRUMIO [*to the Tailor*]    Villain, not for thy life! Take up
    my mistress' gown for thy master's use!
PETRUCHIO    Why sir, what's your conceit in that?    156
GRUMIO
    Oh, sir, the conceit is deeper than you think for:    157
    Take up my mistress' gown to his master's use!
    Oh, fie, fie, fie!
PETRUCHIO [*aside to Hortensio*]
    Hortensio, say thou wilt see the tailor paid.
    [*To Tailor*] Go, take it hence. Begone, and say no more.
HORTENSIO [*aside to the Tailor*]
    Tailor, I'll pay thee for thy gown tomorrow.
    Take no unkindness of his hasty words.
    Away, I say. Commend me to thy master.
                                    *Exit Tailor.*

PETRUCHIO
    Well, come, my Kate. We will unto your father's
    Even in these honest, mean habiliments.    166
    Our purses shall be proud, our garments poor,
    For 'tis the mind that makes the body rich;
    And as the sun breaks through the darkest clouds,

93 **like** likely    96 **Marry . . . remembered** I did indeed. But if you recollect    98 **hop . . . home** hop on home over every street gutter    102 **quaint** elegant    103 **Belike** Perhaps    106–10 **thou thread . . . remnant** Petruchio attacks the tailor's proverbial thinness and effeminacy using metaphors from tailoring.    107 **nail** a measure of length for cloth: 2 ¼ inches.    108 **nit** louse egg    109 **Braved** Defied.    **with** by    110 **quantity** fragment    111 **be-mete** measure, i.e., thrash.    **yard** yardstick    112 **think on prating** i.e., remember this thrashing and think twice before talking so again    117 **stuff** material.    121 **faced** trimmed, decked    123 **Face** Bully.    **braved** dressed finely    124 **brave** defy    126 **Ergo** Therefore

129 **lies in 's throat** i.e., lies utterly    130 **Imprimis** First    131 **loose-bodied gown** (Grumio plays on *loose*, "wanton"; a gown fit for a prostitute.)    133 **bottom** i.e., ball or skein. (A weaver's term for the bobbin.)    135 **compassed** flared, cut on the bias so as to fall in a circle    137 **trunk** full, wide    139 **curiously** elaborately    143 **prove upon thee** prove by fighting you    145–6 **in place where** in a suitable place    147 **bill** (1) the note ordering the gown (2) a weapon, a halberd    148 **mete-yard** measuring stick    149 **God-a-mercy** Thanks    150 **no odds** no advantage. (The contest between Grumio and the Tailor will be evenly matched.)    153 **take it up** take it away.    **use** i.e., whatever use he can make of it. (But Grumio deliberately misinterprets both expressions in a bawdy sense.)    156 **conceit** idea    157 **deeper** more serious. (But continuing the sexual idea of lifting up the dress and entering for sexual "use," as in lines 155 and 158.)    166 **honest, mean habiliments** respectable, plain clothes.

So honor peereth in the meanest habit.                      170
What, is the jay more precious than the lark
Because his feathers are more beautiful?
Or is the adder better than the eel
Because his painted skin contents the eye?                  174
Oh, no, good Kate; neither art thou the worse
For this poor furniture and mean array.                     176
If thou account'st it shame, lay it on me.
And therefore frolic; we will hence forthwith,
To feast and sport us at thy father's house.
[*To Grumio*] Go call my men, and let us straight
    to him;
And bring our horses unto Long Lane end.
There will we mount, and thither walk on foot.
Let's see, I think 'tis now some seven o'clock,
And well we may come there by dinnertime.                   184

KATHARINA
I dare assure you, sir, 'tis almost two,
And 'twill be suppertime ere you come there.

PETRUCHIO
It shall be seven ere I go to horse.
Look what I speak, or do, or think to do,                   188
You are still crossing it.—Sirs, let 't alone.             189
I will not go today, and ere I do,
It shall be what o'clock I say it is.

HORTENSIO [*aside*]
Why, so this gallant will command the sun.                  192
                                              [*Exeunt.*]

❧

## [4.4]

*Enter Tranio [as Lucentio], and the Pedant
dressed like Vincentio [booted].*

TRANIO
Sir, this is the house. Please it you that I call?

PEDANT
Ay, what else? And but I be deceived,                       2
Signor Baptista may remember me,                            3
Near twenty years ago, in Genoa—                            4

TRANIO
Where we were lodgers at the Pegasus.—                     5
'Tis well; and hold your own in any case                    6
With such austerity as 'longeth to a father.                7

*Enter Biondello.*

PEDANT
I warrant you. But, sir, here comes your boy.
'Twere good he were schooled.                               9

TRANIO
Fear you not him.—Sirrah Biondello,                         10
Now do your duty throughly, I advise you.                   11
Imagine 'twere the right Vincentio.                         12

BIONDELLO   Tut, fear not me.                               13

TRANIO
But hast thou done thy errand to Baptista?

BIONDELLO
I told him that your father was at Venice
And that you looked for him this day in Padua.

TRANIO [*giving money*]
Thou'rt a tall fellow. Hold thee that to drink.             17
Here comes Baptista. Set your countenance, sir.            18

*Enter Baptista, and Lucentio [as Cambio].
[The] Pedant [stands] bareheaded.*

Signor Baptista, you are happily met.                       19
[*To the Pedant*] Sir, this is the gentleman I told you of.
I pray you, stand good father to me now;
Give me Bianca for my patrimony.

PEDANT   Soft, son!—                                        23
Sir, by your leave, having come to Padua
To gather in some debts, my son Lucentio
Made me acquainted with a weighty cause
Of love between your daughter and himself;
And, for the good report I hear of you                      28
And for the love he beareth to your daughter
And she to him, to stay him not too long,                   30
I am content, in a good father's care,
To have him matched. And if you please to like             32
No worse than I, upon some agreement
Me shall you find ready and willing
With one consent to have her so bestowed;                   35
For curious I cannot be with you,                           36
Signor Baptista, of whom I hear so well.

BAPTISTA
Sir, pardon me in what I have to say.
Your plainness and your shortness please me well.
Right true it is your son Lucentio here
Doth love my daughter, and she loveth him,
Or both dissemble deeply their affections.
And therefore, if you say no more than this,
That like a father you will deal with him
And pass my daughter a sufficient dower,                    45
The match is made, and all is done.
Your son shall have my daughter with consent.

TRANIO
I thank you, sir. Where then do you know best              48
We be affied and such assurance ta'en                       49
As shall with either part's agreement stand?               50

---

170 **peereth . . . habit** peeps through the humblest attire.
174 **painted** colorfully patterned   176 **furniture** furnishings of attire
184 **dinnertime** i.e., about noon.   188 **Look what** Whatever
189 **still crossing** always contradicting or defying   192 **so** at this rate
**4.4. Location: Padua. Before Baptista's house.**
0.2 *booted* (signifying travel)   2 **but** unless   3–4 **Signor . . . Genoa**
(The Pedant rehearses what he is to say.)   5 **Where . . . Pegasus**
(Tranio is coaching the Pedant in further details of his story.)   **the
Pegasus** i.e., an inn, so named after the famous winged horse of classical myth.   6 **hold your own** play your part   7 **'longeth** belongs
9 **'Twere** It would be   **schooled** i.e., rehearsed in his part.

10 **Fear . . . him** Don't you worry about Biondello.   11 **throughly**
thoroughly   12 **right** real   13 **fear not me** don't worry about my
doing my part.   17 **tall** fine.   **Hold . . . drink** Take that and buy a
drink.   18 **Set your countenance** i.e., Put on the expression of an austere father (line 7).   19 **happily** fortunately   23 **Soft** i.e., Steady, take
it easy   28 **for** because of   30 **to stay him not** not to keep him waiting   32 **like** i.e., approve of the match   35 **one** i.e., firm   36 **curious**
overly particular   45 **pass** settle on, give   48–50 **Where . . . stand?**
Where in your view is the best place for us to be betrothed and for
legal assurances to be made that will confirm an agreement satisfactory to both parties?

**BAPTISTA**
Not in my house, Lucentio, for you know
Pitchers have ears, and I have many servants.    52
Besides, old Gremio is heark'ning still,    53
And happily we might be interrupted.    54

**TRANIO**
Then at my lodging, an it like you.    55
There doth my father lie, and there this night    56
We'll pass the business privately and well.    57
Send for your daughter by your servant here.
        [*He indicates Lucentio, and winks at him.*]
My boy shall fetch the scrivener presently.    59
The worst is this, that at so slender warning
You are like to have a thin and slender pittance.    61

**BAPTISTA**
It likes me well. Cambio, hie you home,
And bid Bianca make her ready straight.
And if you will, tell what hath happened:
Lucentio's father is arrived in Padua,
And how she's like to be Lucentio's wife.
        [*Exit Lucentio.*]

**BIONDELLO**
I pray the gods she may with all my heart!

**TRANIO**
Dally not with the gods, but get thee gone.
        *Exit* [*Biondello*].
Signor Baptista, shall I lead the way?
Welcome! One mess is like to be your cheer.    70
Come, sir, we will better it in Pisa.    71

**BAPTISTA**    I follow you.    72
        *Exeunt* [*Tranio, Pedant, and Baptista*].

*Enter Lucentio* [*as Cambio*] *and Biondello.*

**BIONDELLO**    Cambio!
**LUCENTIO**    What say'st thou, Biondello?
**BIONDELLO**    You saw my master wink and laugh upon you?
**LUCENTIO**    Biondello, what of that?
**BIONDELLO**    Faith, nothing; but he's left me here behind to expound the meaning or moral of his signs and to-    79 kens.
**LUCENTIO**    I pray thee, moralize them.    81
**BIONDELLO**    Then thus. Baptista is safe, talking with    82 the deceiving father of a deceitful son.
**LUCENTIO**    And what of him?
**BIONDELLO**    His daughter is to be brought by you to the supper.
**LUCENTIO**    And then?
**BIONDELLO**    The old priest at Saint Luke's church is at your command at all hours.
**LUCENTIO**    And what of all this?

**BIONDELLO**    I cannot tell, except they are busied about a    91 counterfeit assurance. Take you assurance of her    92 *cum privilegio ad imprimendum solum.* To th'    93 church take the priest, clerk, and some sufficient hon-    94 est witnesses.
If this be not that you look for, I have no more to say,    96 But bid Bianca farewell forever and a day.
        [*Biondello starts to leave.*]
**LUCENTIO**    Hear'st thou, Biondello?
**BIONDELLO**    I cannot tarry. I knew a wench married in an afternoon as she went to the garden for parsley to stuff a rabbit, and so may you, sir. And so, adieu, sir. My master hath appointed me to go to Saint Luke's, to bid the priest be ready to come against you come with    103 your appendix.    *Exit.*    104
**LUCENTIO**
I may, and will, if she be so contented.
She will be pleased; then wherefore should I doubt?
Hap what hap may, I'll roundly go about her.    107
It shall go hard if Cambio go without her.    *Exit.*    108

# [4.5]

*Enter Petruchio, Kate,* [*and*] *Hortensio.*

**PETRUCHIO**
Come on, i'God's name, once more toward our father's.    1
Good Lord, how bright and goodly shines the moon!
**KATHARINA**
The moon? The sun. It is not moonlight now.
**PETRUCHIO**
I say it is the moon that shines so bright.
**KATHARINA**
I know it is the sun that shines so bright.
**PETRUCHIO**
Now, by my mother's son, and that's myself,
It shall be moon, or star, or what I list    7
Or ere I journey to your father's house.—    8
Go on, and fetch our horses back again—
Evermore crossed and crossed, nothing but crossed!
**HORTENSIO** [*to Katharina*]
Say as he says, or we shall never go.
**KATHARINA**
Forward, I pray, since we have come so far,
And be it moon, or sun, or what you please;
An if you please to call it a rush candle,    14

---

52 **Pitchers have ears** i.e., One can't be too careful to avoid being over-heard. (Proverbial.)    53 **heark'ning still** continually listening    54 **happily** haply    55 **an it like** if it please    56 **lie** lodge    57 **pass** transact    59 **scrivener** notary, one to draw up contracts.    **presently** at once.    61 **like** likely.    **slender pittance** i.e., scanty banquet.    70 **mess** dish.    **cheer** entertainment.    71 **better it** serve a finer banquet    72.1 *Exeunt* (Technically, the cleared stage may mark a new scene, but the conversation of Lucentio and Biondello suggests that they come creeping back on stage as the others leave rather than doing the errands Baptista and Tranio bid them.)    79 **moral** hidden meaning    81 **moralize** elucidate    82 **safe** i.e., safely out of the way

91 **except** unless    92 **counterfeit assurance** pretended betrothal agreement.    **Take . . . of her** Legalize your claim to her (by marriage)    93 *cum . . . solum* with exclusive printing rights. (A copyright formula often appearing on the title pages of books, here jokingly applied to the marriage and to procreation as an act of imprinting.)    94 **sufficient** meeting the legal requirement in number and social standing    96 **that you look for** what you are looking for    103 **against you come** in anticipation of your arrival    104 **appendix** something appended, i.e., the bride. (Continuing the metaphor of printing.)    107–8 **Hap . . . without her** i.e., No matter what happens, I'm determined to have her. (With a sexual pun: *go hard,* have an erection.)    **4.5. Location:** A road on the way to Padua.    1 **our father's** our father's house.    7 **list** please    8 **Or ere** before    14 **a rush candle** a rush dipped into tallow; hence a very feeble light

Henceforth I vow it shall be so for me.

PETRUCHIO
I say it is the moon.

KATHARINA                    I know it is the moon.

PETRUCHIO
Nay, then you lie. It is the blessèd sun.

KATHARINA
Then, God be blessed, it is the blessèd sun.
But sun it is not, when you say it is not,
And the moon changes even as your mind.
What you will have it named, even that it is,
And so it shall be so for Katharine.                    22

HORTENSIO
Petruchio, go thy ways. The field is won.                    23

PETRUCHIO
Well, forward, forward. Thus the bowl should run,
And not unluckily against the bias.                    25
But soft! Company is coming here.

                    *Enter Vincentio.*

[*To Vincentio*] Good morrow, gentle mistress. Where
    away?—                    27
Tell me, sweet Kate, and tell me truly too,
Hast thou beheld a fresher gentlewoman?
Such war of white and red within her cheeks!
What stars do spangle heaven with such beauty
As those two eyes become that heavenly face?—
Fair lovely maid, once more good day to thee.—
Sweet Kate, embrace her for her beauty's sake.

HORTENSIO [*aside*]
'A will make the man mad, to make a woman of him.    35

KATHARINA [*embracing Vincentio*]
Young budding virgin, fair, and fresh, and sweet,
Whither away, or where is thy abode?
Happy the parents of so fair a child!
Happier the man whom favorable stars
Allots thee for his lovely bedfellow!                    40

PETRUCHIO
Why, how now, Kate? I hope thou art not mad.
This is a man, old, wrinkled, faded, withered,
And not a maiden, as thou say'st he is.

KATHARINA
Pardon, old father, my mistaking eyes,
That have been so bedazzled with the sun
That everything I look on seemeth green.                    46
Now I perceive thou art a reverend father.
Pardon, I pray thee, for my mad mistaking.

PETRUCHIO
Do, good old grandsire, and withal make known          49
Which way thou travelest—if along with us,
We shall be joyful of thy company.

VINCENTIO
Fair sir, and you, my merry mistress,
That with your strange encounter much amazed me,

My name is called Vincentio, my dwelling Pisa,
And bound I am to Padua, there to visit
A son of mine, which long I have not seen.

PETRUCHIO
What is his name?

VINCENTIO                    Lucentio, gentle sir.

PETRUCHIO
Happily met, the happier for thy son.
And now by law as well as reverend age
I may entitle thee my loving father.
The sister to my wife, this gentlewoman,
Thy son by this hath married. Wonder not,          62
Nor be not grieved. She is of good esteem,          63
Her dowry wealthy, and of worthy birth;
Besides, so qualified as may beseem                    65
The spouse of any noble gentleman.
Let me embrace with old Vincentio,
And wander we to see thy honest son,          68
Who will of thy arrival be full joyous.
                    [*He embraces Vincentio.*]

VINCENTIO
But is this true? Or is it else your pleasure,
Like pleasant travelers, to break a jest          71
Upon the company you overtake?

HORTENSIO
I do assure thee, father, so it is.

PETRUCHIO
Come, go along, and see the truth hereof,
For our first merriment hath made thee jealous.          75
                    *Exeunt [all but Hortensio].*

HORTENSIO
Well, Petruchio, this has put me in heart.          76
Have to my widow! And if she be froward,          77
Then hast thou taught Hortensio to be untoward.          78
                    *Exit.*

                    ❧

# [5.1]

*Enter Biondello, Lucentio [no longer disguised],
and Bianca. Gremio is out before [and stands
aside].*

BIONDELLO    Softly and swiftly, sir, for the priest is
ready.

LUCENTIO    I fly, Biondello. But they may chance to need
thee at home; therefore leave us.

BIONDELLO    Nay, faith, I'll see the church a' your back,          5
and then come back to my master's as soon as I can.
                    [*Exeunt Lucentio, Bianca, and Biondello.*]

---

**62 by this** by this time    **63 esteem** reputation    **65 so qualified** having
such qualities.    **beseem** befit    **68 wander** go (having changed plans)
**71 pleasant** humorous, jocular.    **break a jest** play a practical joke
**75 jealous** suspicious.    **76 put me in heart** given me courage.
**77 Have to** i.e., Now for.    **froward** perverse    **78 untoward**
unmannerly.
**5.1. Location:** Padua. Before Lucentio's house.
**0.2 out before** i.e., onstage first. (Gremio does not see Biondello,
Lucentio, and Bianca as they steal to church, or else he does not
recognize Lucentio in his own person.)    **5 a' your back** at your back,
behind you. (Biondello first wants to see them in church and safely
married.)

**22 for Katharine** as far as Katherine is concerned.    **23 go thy ways**
i.e., well done, carry on.    **25 against the bias** off its proper course.
(The *bias* is an off-center weight in a bowling ball enabling the bowler
to roll the ball in an oblique or curving path.)    **27 Where away?**
Where are you going?    **35 'A** He    **40 Allots** allot    **46 green** young
and fresh.    **49 withal** in addition

GREMIO
    I marvel Cambio comes not all this while.

*Enter Petruchio, Kate, Vincentio, Grumio, with attendants.*

PETRUCHIO
    Sir, here's the door. This is Lucentio's house.
    My father's bears more toward the marketplace;      9
    Thither must I, and here I leave you, sir.
VINCENTIO
    You shall not choose but drink before you go.      11
    I think I shall command your welcome here,
    And by all likelihood some cheer is toward.      *Knock.*   13
GREMIO *[advancing]*  They're busy within. You were   14
    best knock louder.   15

*Pedant looks out of the window.*

PEDANT   What's he that knocks as he would beat down   16
    the gate?
VINCENTIO   Is Signor Lucentio within, sir?
PEDANT   He's within, sir, but not to be spoken withal.   19
VINCENTIO   What if a man bring him a hundred pound
    or two to make merry withal?
PEDANT   Keep your hundred pounds to yourself. He
    shall need none, so long as I live.
PETRUCHIO *[to Vincentio]*  Nay, I told you your son was
    well beloved in Padua.—Do you hear, sir? To leave
    frivolous circumstances, I pray you, tell Signor Lucen-   26
    tio that his father is come from Pisa and is here at the
    door to speak with him.
PEDANT   Thou liest. His father is come from Padua and   29
    here looking out at the window.
VINCENTIO   Art thou his father?
PEDANT   Ay, sir, so his mother says, if I may believe
    her.
PETRUCHIO *[to Vincentio]*  Why, how now, gentleman!
    Why, this is flat knavery, to take upon you another   35
    man's name.
PEDANT   Lay hands on the villain. I believe 'a means to
    cozen somebody in this city under my countenance.   38

*Enter Biondello.*

BIONDELLO *[aside]*  I have seen them in the church
    together, God send 'em good shipping! But who is   40
    here? Mine old master Vincentio! Now we are undone
    and brought to nothing.
VINCENTIO *[seeing Biondello]*   Come hither, crackhemp.   43
BIONDELLO   I hope I may choose, sir.   44

VINCENTIO   Come hither, you rogue. What, have you
    forgot me?
BIONDELLO   Forgot you? No, sir. I could not forget you,
    for I never saw you before in all my life.
VINCENTIO   What, you notorious villain, didst thou
    never see thy master's father, Vincentio?
BIONDELLO   What, my old worshipful old master? Yes,
    marry, sir, see where he looks out of the window.
VINCENTIO   Is't so, indeed?      *He beats Biondello.*
BIONDELLO   Help, help, help! Here's a madman will
    murder me.      *[Exit.]*
PEDANT   Help, son! Help, Signor Baptista!
      *[Exit from the window.]*
PETRUCHIO   Prithee, Kate, let's stand aside and see the
    end of this controversy.      *[They stand aside.]*

*Enter [below] Pedant with servants, Baptista, [and] Tranio [as Lucentio].*

TRANIO   Sir, what are you that offer to beat my servant?   59
VINCENTIO   What am I, sir? Nay, what are you, sir? O
    immortal gods! Oh, fine villain! A silken doublet, a vel-
    vet hose, a scarlet cloak, and a copintank hat! Oh, I am   62
    undone, I am undone! While I play the good husband   63
    at home, my son and my servant spend all at the uni-
    versity.
TRANIO   How now, what's the matter?
BAPTISTA   What, is the man lunatic?
TRANIO   Sir, you seem a sober ancient gentleman by
    your habit, but your words show you a madman.   69
    Why, sir, what 'cerns it you if I wear pearl and gold?   70
    I thank my good father, I am able to maintain it.   71
VINCENTIO   Thy father! Oh, villain, he is a sailmaker in
    Bergamo.
BAPTISTA   You mistake, sir, you mistake, sir. Pray, what
    do you think is his name?
VINCENTIO   His name! As if I knew not his name! I have
    brought him up ever since he was three years old, and
    his name is Tranio.
PEDANT   Away, away, mad ass! His name is Lucentio,
    and he is mine only son, and heir to the lands of me,
    Signor Vincentio.
VINCENTIO   Lucentio! Oh, he hath murdered his master!
    Lay hold on him, I charge you, in the Duke's name.
    Oh, my son, my son! Tell me, thou villain, where is my
    son Lucentio?
TRANIO   Call forth an officer.

*[Enter an Officer.]*

    Carry this mad knave to the jail. Father Baptista, I
    charge you see that he be forthcoming.   88
VINCENTIO   Carry me to the jail?
GREMIO   Stay, officer, he shall not go to prison.
BAPTISTA   Talk not, Signor Gremio. I say he shall go to
    prison.

GREMIO    Take heed, Signor Baptista, lest you be coney-  93
catched in this business. I dare swear this is the right  94
Vincentio.

PEDANT    Swear, if thou dar'st.

GREMIO    Nay, I dare not swear it.

TRANIO    Then thou wert best say that I am not Lucentio.  98

GREMIO    Yes, I know thee to be Signor Lucentio.

BAPTISTA    Away with the dotard! To the jail with him!

*Enter Biondello, Lucentio, and Bianca.*

VINCENTIO    Thus strangers may be haled and abused.  101
—Oh, monstrous villain!

BIONDELLO    Oh! We are spoiled and—yonder he is.  103
Deny him, forswear him, or else we are all undone.
                    *Exeunt Biondello, Tranio, and Pedant as fast as
                    may be. [Lucentio and Bianca] kneel.*

LUCENTIO
Pardon, sweet father.

VINCENTIO                            Lives my sweet son?

BIANCA
Pardon, dear father.

BAPTISTA                        How hast thou offended?
Where is Lucentio?

LUCENTIO                    Here's Lucentio,
Right son to the right Vincentio,
That have by marriage made thy daughter mine,
While counterfeit supposes bleared thine eyne.  110

GREMIO
Here's packing, with a witness, to deceive us all!  111

VINCENTIO
Where is that damnèd villain Tranio,
That faced and braved me in this matter so?  113

BAPTISTA
Why, tell me, is not this my Cambio?

BIANCA
Cambio is changed into Lucentio.  115

LUCENTIO
Love wrought these miracles. Bianca's love
Made me exchange my state with Tranio,  117
While he did bear my countenance in the town,  118
And happily I have arrivèd at the last
Unto the wishèd haven of my bliss.
What Tranio did, myself enforced him to;
Then pardon him, sweet father, for my sake.

VINCENTIO    I'll slit the villain's nose, that would have
sent me to the jail.

BAPTISTA    [*to Lucentio*]    But do you hear, sir? Have you
married my daughter without asking my good will?

VINCENTIO    Fear not, Baptista, we will content you. Go  127
to. But I will in, to be revenged for this villainy.  128
                                            *Exit.*

BAPTISTA    And I, to sound the depth of this knavery.
                                            *Exit.*

LUCENTIO    Look not pale, Bianca. Thy father will not
frown.                    *Exeunt [Lucentio and Bianca].*

GREMIO
My cake is dough, but I'll in among the rest,  132
Out of hope of all but my share of the feast.    [*Exit.*]  133

KATHARINA    Husband, let's follow, to see the end of
this ado.

PETRUCHIO    First kiss me, Kate, and we will.

KATHARINA    What, in the midst of the street?

PETRUCHIO    What, art thou ashamed of me?

KATHARINA    No, sir, God forbid, but ashamed to kiss.

PETRUCHIO
Why, then let's home again. [*To Grumio*] Come, sirrah,
let's away.

KATHARINA
Nay, I will give thee a kiss. [*She kisses him.*] Now pray
thee, love, stay.

PETRUCHIO
Is not this well? Come, my sweet Kate.
Better once than never, for never too late.    *Exeunt.*  143

## [5.2]

*Enter Baptista, Vincentio, Gremio, the Pedant,
Lucentio, and Bianca; [Petruchio, Kate, Hortensio,] Tranio, Biondello, Grumio, and [the]
Widow; the servingmen with Tranio bringing
in a banquet.*

LUCENTIO
At last, though long, our jarring notes agree,  1
And time it is, when raging war is done,
To smile at scapes and perils overblown.  3
My fair Bianca, bid my father welcome,
While I with selfsame kindness welcome thine.
Brother Petruchio, sister Katharina,
And thou, Hortensio, with thy loving widow,
Feast with the best, and welcome to my house.
My banquet is to close our stomachs up  9
After our great good cheer. Pray you, sit down,  10
For now we sit to chat as well as eat.    [*They sit.*]

PETRUCHIO
Nothing but sit and sit, and eat and eat!

BAPTISTA
Padua affords this kindness, son Petruchio.

PETRUCHIO
Padua affords nothing but what is kind.

---

**93–4 coney-catched** tricked    **98 wert best** might as well
**101 haled** hauled about, maltreated    **103 spoiled** ruined
**110 supposes** suppositions, false appearances. (With an allusion to
Gascoigne's *Supposes*, an adaptation of *I Suppositi* by Ariosto, from
which Shakespeare took the Lucentio-Bianca plot of intrigue.)
**eyne** eyes.    **111 Here's ... all!** Here's evidence of a conspiracy, no
mistake about it!    **113 faced and braved** stood up to and defied
**115 Cambio is changed** (A pun. *Cambio* in Italian means "change"
or "exchange.")    **117 state** social station    **118 countenance** appearance, identity

**127–8 Go to** i.e., Don't worry. (An expression of impatience or annoyance.)    **132 My ... dough** i.e., I'm out of luck, I failed    **133 Out ...
but** having hope for nothing other than    **143 once** at some time.
(Compare with "better late than never.")
**5.2. Location: Padua. Lucentio's house.**
**1 long** after long time    **3 scapes** close calls    **9 stomachs** (1) appetites
(2) quarrels    **10 cheer** i.e., wedding feast.

HORTENSIO
For both our sakes, I would that word were true.
PETRUCHIO
Now, for my life, Hortensio fears his widow.    16
WIDOW
Then never trust me if I be afeard.    17
PETRUCHIO
You are very sensible, and yet you miss my sense:
I mean Hortensio is afeard of you.
WIDOW
He that is giddy thinks the world turns round.
PETRUCHIO
Roundly replied.
KATHARINA    Mistress, how mean you that?    21
WIDOW    Thus I conceive by him.    22
PETRUCHIO
Conceives by me! How likes Hortensio that?
HORTENSIO
My widow says, thus she conceives her tale.    24
PETRUCHIO
Very well mended. Kiss him for that, good widow.
KATHARINA
"He that is giddy thinks the world turns round":
I pray you, tell me what you meant by that.
WIDOW
Your husband, being troubled with a shrew,
Measures my husband's sorrow by his woe.    29
And now you know my meaning.
KATHARINA
A very mean meaning.
WIDOW    Right, I mean you.    31
KATHARINA
And I am mean indeed, respecting you.    32
PETRUCHIO    To her, Kate!    33
HORTENSIO    To her, widow!
PETRUCHIO
A hundred marks, my Kate does put her down.    35
HORTENSIO    That's my office.
PETRUCHIO
Spoke like an officer. Ha' to thee, lad!    37
                    [He] drinks to Hortensio.
BAPTISTA
How likes Gremio these quick-witted folks?
GREMIO
Believe me, sir, they butt together well.    39
BIANCA
Head, and butt! An hasty-witted body    40
Would say your head and butt were head and horn.    41

VINCENTIO
Ay, mistress bride, hath that awakened you?
BIANCA
Ay, but not frighted me. Therefore I'll sleep again.
PETRUCHIO
Nay, that you shall not. Since you have begun,
Have at you for a bitter jest or two!    45
BIANCA
Am I your bird? I mean to shift my bush;    46
And then pursue me as you draw your bow.
You are welcome all.
                    Exit Bianca [with Katharina and the Widow].
PETRUCHIO
She hath prevented me. Here, Signor Tranio,    49
This bird you aimed at, though you hit her not.    50
Therefore a health to all that shot and missed.    51
                    [He offers a toast.]
TRANIO
Oh, sir, Lucentio slipped me like his greyhound,    52
Which runs himself and catches for his master.
PETRUCHIO
A good swift simile, but something currish.    54
TRANIO
'Tis well, sir, that you hunted for yourself.
'Tis thought your deer does hold you at a bay.    56
BAPTISTA
Oho, Petruchio! Tranio hits you now.
LUCENTIO
I thank thee for that gird, good Tranio.    58
HORTENSIO
Confess, confess, hath he not hit you here?
PETRUCHIO
'A has a little galled me, I confess;    60
And as the jest did glance away from me,
'Tis ten to one it maimed you two outright.
BAPTISTA
Now, in good sadness, son Petruchio,    63
I think thou hast the veriest shrew of all.
PETRUCHIO
Well, I say no. And therefore for assurance    65
Let's each one send unto his wife;
And he whose wife is most obedient
To come at first when he doth send for her
Shall win the wager which we will propose.
HORTENSIO
Content. What's the wager?
LUCENTIO    Twenty crowns.
PETRUCHIO    Twenty crowns!
I'll venture so much of my hawk or hound,    72
But twenty times so much upon my wife.

16 **for my life** upon my life.   **fears** is afraid of   17 **afeard** frightened
(by Hortensio).   21 **Roundly** Boldly, bluntly   22 **Thus . . . him** i.e.,
That's what I think of him, Petruchio. (But Petruchio takes up
*conceives* in the sense of "is made pregnant.")   24 **conceives** intends,
interprets. (With a possible pun on *tale* and "tail.")   29 **his** his own
31 **very mean** contemptible. (But the Widow takes up *mean* in the
sense of "have in mind," and Kate replies in the sense of "moderate in
shrewishness.")   32 **respecting** compared to   33 **To her** (A cry used
to egg on fighting roosters.)   35 **marks** coins worth thirteen shillings
four pence.   **put her down** overcome her. (But Hortensio takes up the
phrase in a bawdy sense.)   37 **officer** (playing on Hortensio's speaking of his *office* or function).   **Ha'** Have, i.e., Here's   39 **butt** butt heads
40 **An hasty-witted body** A quick-witted person   41 **head and horn**
(Alluding to the familiar joke about cuckolds' horns.)

45 **Have at you for** Here comes   46 **Am . . . bush** i.e., If you mean to
shoot your barbs at me, I intend to move out of the way, as a bird
would fly to another bush. (With a possible bawdy double meaning;
*bush* can suggest pubic hair.)   49 **prevented** forestalled   50 **This bird**
i.e., Bianca, whom Tranio courted (*aimed at*) in his disguise as Lucentio   51 **a health** a toast   52 **slipped** unleashed   54 **swift** (1) quick-
witted (2) concerning swiftness.   **currish** (1) ignoble (2) concerning
dogs.   56 **deer** (Punning on "dear.")   **does . . . bay** turns on you like
a cornered animal and holds you at a distance.   58 **gird** sharp, biting
jest   60 **galled** scratched, chafed   63 **sadness** seriousness   65 **assurance** proof   72 **of** on

LUCENTIO   A hundred then.
HORTENSIO   Content.
PETRUCHIO   A match. 'Tis done.
HORTENSIO   Who shall begin?
LUCENTIO   That will I.
      Go, Biondello, bid your mistress come to me.
BIONDELLO   I go.                                              *Exit.*
BAPTISTA
      Son, I'll be your half Bianca comes.                          81
LUCENTIO
      I'll have no halves; I'll bear it all myself.

            *Enter Biondello.*

      How now, what news?
BIONDELLO
      Sir, my mistress sends you word
      That she is busy and she cannot come.
PETRUCHIO
      How? She's busy and she cannot come?
      Is that an answer?
GREMIO                        Ay, and a kind one too.
      Pray God, sir, your wife send you not a worse.
PETRUCHIO   I hope better.
HORTENSIO
      Sirrah Biondello, go and entreat my wife
      To come to me forthwith.          *Exit Biondello.*
PETRUCHIO                        Oho, entreat her!
      Nay, then she must needs come.
HORTENSIO                        I am afraid, sir,        92
      Do what you can, yours will not be entreated.

            *Enter Biondello.*

      Now, where's my wife?
BIONDELLO
      She says you have some goodly jest in hand.
      She will not come. She bids you come to her.
PETRUCHIO
      Worse and worse. She will not come!
      Oh, vile, intolerable, not to be endured!—
      Sirrah Grumio, go to your mistress.
      Say I command her come to me.       *Exit [Grumio].*
HORTENSIO
      I know her answer.
PETRUCHIO            What?
HORTENSIO                        She will not.
PETRUCHIO
      The fouler fortune mine, and there an end.    ·    102

            *Enter Katharina.*

BAPTISTA
      Now, by my halidom, here comes Katharina!       103
KATHARINA
      What is your will, sir, that you send for me?
PETRUCHIO
      Where is your sister, and Hortensio's wife?

KATHARINA
      They sit conferring by the parlor fire.
PETRUCHIO
      Go fetch them hither. If they deny to come,
      Swinge me them soundly forth unto their husbands.   108
      Away, I say, and bring them hither straight.
                              *[Exit Katharina.]*
LUCENTIO
      Here is a wonder, if you talk of a wonder.
HORTENSIO
      And so it is. I wonder what it bodes.
PETRUCHIO
      Marry, peace it bodes, and love, and quiet life,
      An aweful rule, and right supremacy,             113
      And, to be short, what not that's sweet and happy.
BAPTISTA
      Now, fair befall thee, good Petruchio!           115
      The wager thou hast won, and I will add
      Unto their losses twenty thousand crowns,
      Another dowry to another daughter,
      For she is changed, as she had never been.       119
PETRUCHIO
      Nay, I will win my wager better yet,
      And show more sign of her obedience,
      Her new-built virtue and obedience.

            *Enter Kate, Bianca, and [the] Widow.*

      See where she comes and brings your froward wives   123
      As prisoners to her womanly persuasion.—
      Katharine, that cap of yours becomes you not.
      Off with that bauble. Throw it underfoot.        126
                              *[She obeys.]*
WIDOW
      Lord, let me never have a cause to sigh
      Till I be brought to such a silly pass!          128
BIANCA
      Fie, what a foolish duty call you this?
LUCENTIO
      I would your duty were as foolish, too.
      The wisdom of your duty, fair Bianca,
      Hath cost me a hundred crowns since suppertime.
BIANCA
      The more fool you, for laying on my duty.        133
PETRUCHIO
      Katharine, I charge thee tell these headstrong women
      What duty they do owe their lords and husbands.
WIDOW
      Come, come, you're mocking. We will have no telling.
PETRUCHIO
      Come on, I say, and first begin with her.
WIDOW   She shall not.
PETRUCHIO
      I say she shall—and first begin with her.

---

81 **be your half** take half your bet   92 **must needs come** will have to
come, whether she wants to or not. (Said sardonically.)   102 **there
an end** that's that.   103 **by my halidom** (Originally an oath by the
holy relics, but confused with an oath to the Virgin Mary.)

108 **Swinge** thrash.   **me** i.e., at my behest. (*Me* is used colloquially.)
113 **aweful rule** authority commanding awe or respect   115 **fair
befall thee** good luck to you, and congratulations   119 **as ... been** as
if she had never existed, i.e., she is totally changed.   123 **froward**
willful, contrary   126 **bauble** showy trifle.   128 **pass** state of
affairs.   133 **laying** wagering

KATHARINA

  Fie, fie! Unknit that threatening, unkind brow,

  And dart not scornful glances from those eyes

  To wound thy lord, thy king, thy governor.

  It blots thy beauty as frosts do bite the meads,    143

  Confounds thy fame as whirlwinds shake fair buds,   144

  And in no sense is meet or amiable.

  A woman moved is like a fountain troubled,    146

  Muddy, ill-seeming, thick, bereft of beauty;

  And while it is so, none so dry or thirsty    148

  Will deign to sip or touch one drop of it.

  Thy husband is thy lord, thy life, thy keeper,

  Thy head, thy sovereign; one that cares for thee,

  And for thy maintenance commits his body

  To painful labor both by sea and land,    153

  To watch the night in storms, the day in cold,    154

  Whilst thou liest warm at home, secure and safe;

  And craves no other tribute at thy hands

  But love, fair looks, and true obedience—

  Too little payment for so great a debt.

  Such duty as the subject owes the prince,

  Even such a woman oweth to her husband;

  And when she is froward, peevish, sullen, sour,    161

  And not obedient to his honest will,    162

  What is she but a foul contending rebel

  And graceless traitor to her loving lord?

  I am ashamed that women are so simple    165

  To offer war where they should kneel for peace,

  Or seek for rule, supremacy, and sway,

  When they are bound to serve, love, and obey.

  Why are our bodies soft, and weak, and smooth,

  Unapt to toil and trouble in the world,    170

  But that our soft conditions and our hearts    171

  Should well agree with our external parts?

  Come, come, you froward and unable worms!    173

  My mind hath been as big as one of yours,    174

  My heart as great, my reason haply more,

  To bandy word for word and frown for frown;

  But now I see our lances are but straws,

  Our strength as weak, our weakness past compare,   178

  That seeming to be most which we indeed least are.   179

  Then vail your stomachs, for it is no boot,    180

  And place your hands below your husband's foot,

  In token of which duty, if he please,

  My hand is ready; may it do him ease.    183

PETRUCHIO

  Why, there's a wench! Come on, and kiss me, Kate.

                               *[They kiss.]*

LUCENTIO

  Well, go thy ways, old lad, for thou shalt ha 't.    185

VINCENTIO

  'Tis a good hearing when children are toward.    186

LUCENTIO

  But a harsh hearing when women are froward.

PETRUCHIO    Come, Kate, we'll to bed.

  We three are married, but you two are sped.    189

  *[To Lucentio]* 'Twas I won the wager, though you hit

    the white,    190

  And, being a winner, God give you good night!    191

                    *Exit Petruchio [with Katharina].*

HORTENSIO

  Now go thy ways. Thou hast tamed a curst shrew.    192

LUCENTIO

  'Tis a wonder, by your leave, she will be tamed so.

                                 *[Exeunt.]*

---

**143 meads** meadows   **144 Confounds thy fame** ruins your reputation   **146 moved** angry   **148 none . . . thirsty** there is no one so thirsty that he   **153 painful** onerous   **154 watch** stay awake throughout   **161 peevish** obstinate   **162 to his honest will** (Kate may suggest that she will be obedient when his will is decent and virtuous, not that his will is always so.)   **165 simple** foolish   **170 Unapt to** unfit for   **171 conditions** qualities

**173 unable worms** i.e., poor feeble creatures.   **174 big** haughty   **178 as weak** i.e., as weak as straws   **179 That seeming to be** seeming to be that   **180 Then . . . boot** Then lower your pride, for it is no use striving   **183 do him ease** give him pleasure.   **185 go thy ways** well done.   **ha 't** have it, the prize.   **186 'Tis . . . toward** i.e., One likes to hear when children are obedient.   **189 We . . . sped** i.e., All we three men have taken wives, but you two are done for (*sped*) through disobedient wives.   **190 the white** the center of the target. (With quibble on the name of Bianca, which in Italian means "white.")   **191 being** since I am   **192 shrew** pronounced "shrow" (and thus spelled in the Folio). See also 4.1.198 and 5.2.28.

# A Midsummer Night's Dream

One of the many astonishing achievements in *A Midsummer Night's Dream* (c. 1594–1595) is its development of the motif of love as an imaginative journey from a world of social conflict into a fantasy world created by the artist, ending in a return to a reality that has itself been partly transformed by the experience of the journey. As the lovers in this play flee from the Athenian law to lose themselves in the forest, they reveal and discover in themselves the simultaneously hilarious and horrifying effects of sexual desire. Moreover, their journey suggests the extent to which love or desire is itself an act of imagination, not unlike the imagination that underlies the creation of art. The fifth act especially invites us to see theatrical experience as like a dream, at times nightmarish but at its best an emancipating foray into an imagined space wholly beyond the realm of ordinary human happenings. Shakespeare gives us an earlier hint of an imaginary sylvan landscape in *The Two Gentlemen of Verona*, but not until *A Midsummer Night's Dream* is the idea fully realized. The motif of contrasting worlds, one of social convention and the other of visionary fantasy, will remain an enduring preoccupation of Shakespeare to the very last. This visionary world brings with it some of the most poetic passages of the entire Shakespeare canon, from Titania's evocation of her bond of affection with her votaress "in the spicèd Indian air by night" (2.1.123–37) to Oberon's memory of a mermaid singing on a dolphin's back (2.1.150–4). Containing the highest percentage of rhymed verse in all of Shakespeare's plays, *A Midsummer Night's Dream* calls attention to the seemingly magical capacity of words to weave spells not only on the characters but on the audience as well.

In construction, *A Midsummer Night's Dream* is a skillful interweaving of four plots involving four groups of characters: the court party of Theseus, the four young lovers, the fairies, and the "rude mechanicals" or would-be actors. Felix Mendelssohn's incidental music for the play evokes the contrasting textures of the various groups: Theseus's hunting horns and ceremonial wedding marches, the lovers' soaring and throbbing melodies, the fairies' pianissimo staccato, the tradesmen's clownish bassoon. Moreover, each plot is derived from its own set of source materials. The action involving Theseus and Hippolyta, for example, owes several details to Thomas North's translation (1579) of Plutarch's *Lives of the Noble Grecians and Romans*, to Chaucer's *Knight's Tale* and perhaps to his *Legend of Good Women*, and to Ovid's *Metamorphoses* (in the Latin text or in Arthur Golding's popular Elizabethan translation). The lovers' story, meanwhile, is Italianate and Ovidian in tone and also, in the broadest sense, follows the conventions of plot in Plautus's and Terence's Roman comedies, although no particular source is known. Shakespeare's rich fairy lore, by contrast, is part folk tradition and part learned. For some of his material he seems to have turned to written sources, such as the French romance *Huon of Bordeaux* (translated into English by 1540), Robert Greene's play *James IV* (c. 1591), and Edmund Spenser's *The Faerie Queene*, II.i.8 (1590). Similarly, he may have taken Titania's name from the *Metamorphoses*, where it is used as an epithet for both Diana and Circe. At the same time, in his creation of Mustardseed, Cobweb, Mote, and Peaseblossom, Shakespeare also pays homage to a rich body of unwritten sources that are, for the most part, no longer accessible. Changeling children, mortals kidnapped by fairy queens, men transformed to beasts by evil spells: these were the stuff of oral tales circulated by firesides on winter nights. Finally, for Bottom the weaver and company, Shakespeare's primary inspiration was doubtless his own theatrical experience, although even here he is indebted to Ovid for the story of Pyramus and Thisbe, and probably to Apuleius's *Golden Ass* (translated by William Adlington, 1566) for Bottom's transformation.

Each of the four main plots in *A Midsummer Night's Dream* contains one or more pairs of lovers whose happiness has been frustrated by misunderstanding or parental opposition. Theseus and Hippolyta, once enemies in battle, become husband and wife; their court marriage, constituting the overplot of the play, provides a framework for other dramatic actions that similarly oscillate between conflict and harmony. In fact, Theseus's actions are instrumental in setting in motion and finally resolving the tribulations of the other characters. In the beginning of the play, for example, the lovers flee from Theseus's Athenian law; at the end, they are awakened by him from their dream. As the king and queen of fairies come to Athens to celebrate Theseus's wedding, they exchange jealous accusations: Oberon accuses his queen of being overly partial to Theseus, while she is critical of Oberon's attentions to Hippolyta. These plots of the Athenian and the fairy monarchs are drawn even more closely together by the common practice in today's theater of doubling the parts of Theseus and Oberon, Hippolyta and Titania (also, frequently, Philostrate and Puck). The broadly comic action of Bottom the Weaver and his companions is drawn into the overall design by means of their deciding to use the forest of Athens as the place where they will rehearse their performance of "Pyramus and Thisbe" in anticipation of the wedding festivities.

The tragic love story of Pyramus and Thisbe, although it seems absurdly ill suited to a wedding, reminds us of the discord and potentially fatal misunderstandings that threaten even the best of relationships between men and women. For all his graceful bearing and princely authority, Theseus is a conquering male who freely admits that he has won the love of Hippolyta with his sword, doing her "injuries" (1.1.17). He never questions that the accord between them should now be stated in terms of male ascendancy over the female. The Amazonian Hippolyta may accept with good grace the marriage she previously resisted with all her might, like Kate in *The Taming of the Shrew*, and yet, in many recent stage productions, the actress playing Hippolyta has found it easy to cast doubt on the presumed tranquility of this forthcoming marriage by a display of feminist impatience at Theseus's urbanely patriarchal ways. The reconciliation of Oberon and Titania, meanwhile, reinforces the hierarchy of male over female in no uncertain terms. Having taught Titania a lesson for trying to keep a changeling boy from him, Oberon relents and eventually frees Titania from her debasing enchantment. She does not reproach him with so much as a word when she is awakened from her "vision." Even so, the very existence of the abundantly female space of Titania's bower where, surrounded by her attendants, she has acted out desires that she thought were her own, poses an alternative to patriarchy. The four young lovers end up happily paired, but only after they have experienced rejection, rivalry, hatred, and the desire to kill; the final resolution of this plot would not be possible if Demetrius were not left under the spell of the fairy love-

juice. Thus, Theseus's wedding provides a ceremonial occasion of harmony and reconciliation but in such a way as to highlight the difficulties that have beset the drama's various couples.

Despite Theseus's cheerful preoccupation with marriage, his court embodies at first a stern attitude toward young love. As administrator of the law, Theseus must accede to the remorseless demands of Hermia's father, Egeus. The inflexible Athenian law sides with parentage, age, male dominance, wealth, and position against youth and romantic choice in love. The penalties are harsh: death or perpetual virginity—and virginity is presented in this comedy (despite the nobly chaste examples of Christ, St. Paul, and Queen Elizabeth) as a fate worse than death. Egeus is a familiar type, the interfering parent found in the Roman comedy of Plautus and Terence (and in Shakespeare's *Romeo and Juliet*). Indeed, the lovers' story is distantly derived from Roman comedy, which conventionally celebrated the triumph of young love over the machinations of age and wealth. Lysander reminds us that "the course of true love never did run smooth," and he sees its enemies as being chiefly external: the conflicting interests of parents or friends; mismating with respect to years and blood, war, death, or sickness (1.1.134–42). This description clearly applies to "Pyramus and Thisbe," and it is tested by the action of *A Midsummer Night's Dream* as a whole (as well as by other early Shakespearean plays, such as *Romeo and Juliet*). The archetypal story, whether ending happily or sadly, is an evocation of love's difficulties in the face of social hostility and indifference.

While Shakespeare uses several elements of Roman comedy in setting up the basic conflicts of his drama, he also introduces important modifications from the beginning. For example, he discards one conventional confrontation of classical and neoclassical comedy, in which the heroine must choose between an old, wealthy suitor supported by her family and the young but impecunious darling of her heart. Lysander is equal to his rival in social position, income, and attractiveness. Egeus's demand, therefore—that Hermia marry Demetrius rather than Lysander—seems simply arbitrary and unjust. Shakespeare emphasizes in this way the irrationality of Egeus's harsh insistence on being obeyed and of Theseus's rather complacent acceptance of the law's inequity. Spurned by an unfeeling social order, Lysander and Hermia are compelled to elope. To be sure, in the end Egeus proves to be no formidable threat; even he must admit the logic of permitting the lovers to couple as they ultimately desire. Thus, the obstacles to love are seen from the start as fundamentally superficial and indeed almost whimsical. Egeus is as heavy a villain as we are likely to find in this *jeu d'esprit*. Moreover, the very irrationality of his position prepares the way for an ultimate resolution of the conflict. Nevertheless, by the end of the first act, the supposedly rational world of conformity and duty, by its customary insensitivity to youthful happiness, has set in motion a temporary escape to a fantasy world where the law cannot reach.

In the forest, all the lovers—including Titania and Bottom—undergo a transforming experience engineered by the mischievous Puck. This experience demonstrates the universal power of love, which can overcome the queen of fairies as readily as the lowliest of humans. It also suggests the irrational nature of love and its affinity to enchantment, witchcraft, and even madness. Love is seen as an affliction taken in through the frail senses, particularly the eyes. When it strikes, the victim cannot choose but to embrace the object of his or her infatuation. By his amusing miscalculations, Puck shuffles the four lovers through various permutations with mathematical predictability. First, two gentlemen compete for one lady, leaving the second lady sadly unrequited in love; then everything is at cross-purposes, with each gentleman pursuing the lady who is in love with the other man; then the two gentlemen compete for the lady they both previously ignored. Finally, of course, Jack shall have his Jill—whom else should he have? The couples are properly united, as they evidently were at some time prior to the commencement of the play, when Demetrius had been romantically attached to Helena and Lysander to Hermia.

Their experience in the forest is an unsettling one for the four young lovers. Although some of them seek out the forest as a refuge from the Athenian law, the place rapidly takes on the darker aspect of a nightmare. Hermia awakens from sleep to find Lysander gone and soon discovers that her dream of a serpent eating her heart away while Lysander watches smiling (2.2.155–6) is all too prophetically true. The forest is a place of testing of the lovers, and the test appears at first to show how they are all their own worst enemies. Helena, having been rejected by Demetrius, can only suppose that she is being mocked when Lysander and Demetrius both pay court to her. Next, it occurs to her that Hermia must be part of their conspiracy, too. Even though Hermia and Helena recall to each other the selfless devotion they have known as young friends, they become hated rivals in their present mood of self-pity and injured self-regard. The threshold of sexual awakening, it would seem, confronts them with a hazardous rite of passage—one that is especially threatening to the nonsexual friendship of their adolescent years. The two young men respond to similar conflicts by turning on one another in characteristically aggressive male ways. Puck allows them to playact their intended mayhem in a way that cannot harm them and then brings all four lovers together where they can awaken from their nightmare of imagined persecution. How much do they remember? Have they been changed by their journey in the forest? The lovers convey a sense of confusion, of an unreconciled dissonance of perspective in which "everything seems double" (4.1.189). As the

lovers return to the daylight world of Athens and the court, their experiences assume the unreality of a remembered dream, like "far-off mountains turnèd into clouds" (4.1.187). When they thus awaken and return to the daylight world of Athens and the court, their renewed love and friendship are presumably deepened by their perception of how narrowly they have escaped from their own self-destructive imaginings. Their new happiness, they see, is better than they have deserved.

We sense that Puck is by no means unhappy about his knavish errors and manipulations: "Lord, what fools these mortals be!" (3.2.115). Along with the other fairies in this play, Puck takes his being and his complex motivation from many denizens of the invisible world. As the agent of all-powerful love, Puck compares himself to Cupid. The love juice he administers comes from Cupid's flower, "love-in-idleness." Like Cupid, Puck acts at the behest of the gods, and yet he wields a power that the chiefest of the gods themselves cannot resist. Essentially, however, Puck is less a classical love deity than a prankish folk spirit, such as we find everywhere in folklore: gremlin, leprechaun, hobgoblin, and the like. Titania's fairies recognize Puck as the folk figure Robin Goodfellow, able to deprive a beer barrel of its yeast so that it spoils rather than ferments. Puck characterizes himself as a practical joker, pulling stools out from under old ladies.

Folk wisdom imagines the inexplicable and unaccountable events in life to be caused by invisible spirits who laugh at mortals' discomfiture and mock them for mere sport. Puck is related to these mysterious spirits dwelling in nature, who must be placated with gifts and ceremonies. Although Shakespeare restricts Puck to a benign sportive role in dealing with the lovers or with Titania, the actual folk legends about Puck mentioned in this play are frequently disquieting. Puck is known to "mislead night wanderers, laughing at their harm" (2.1.39); indeed, he demonstrates as much with Demetrius and Lysander, leading them on through the forest to the point of exhaustion, even though we perceive the sportful intent. At the play's end, Puck links himself and his fellows with the ghoulish apparitions of death and night: wolves howling at the moon, screech owls, shrouds, gaping graves. Associations of this sort go beyond mere sportiveness to the witchcraft and demonology involving spirits rising from the dead. Even Oberon's assurance that the fairies will bless all the marriages of this play, shielding their progeny against mole, harelip, or other birth defects, carries the implication that such misfortunes can be caused by offended spirits. The magic of this play is thus explicitly related to deep irrational powers and forces capable of doing great harm, although, to be sure, the spirit of comedy keeps such veiled threats safely at a distance in A Midsummer Night's Dream.

Oberon and Titania, in their view of the relationship between gods and humans, reflect yet another aspect of the fairies' spiritual ancestry. The king and queen of fairies assert that, because they are immortal, their regal quarrels in love must inevitably have dire consequences on earth, either in the love relationship of Theseus and Hippolyta or in the management of the weather. Floods, storms, diseases, and sterility abound, "And this same progeny of evils comes / From our debate, from our dissension. / We are their parents and original" (2.1.115–17). This motif of the gods' quarreling over human affairs reminds us of Homer and Virgil. At the same time, in this lighthearted play the motif is more nearly mock-epic than truly epic. The consequences of the gods' anger are simply mirth-provoking, most of all in Titania's love affair with Bottom the weaver.

The story of Bottom and Titania is simultaneously classical and folk in nature. In a playfully classical mode, this love affair between a god and an earthy creature underscores humanity's double nature. Bottom himself becomes half man and half beast, even if he is more ludicrously comic than the centaurs, satyrs, griffins, sphinxes, and other amphibious beings of classical mythology. Some ballads of the early modern period tell of humans transformed into beasts, or of mortals kidnapped by a fairy queen; see, for example, "Tam Lin" and "Thomas Rhymer." Bottom is an especially comic example of metamorphosis because he reverses the usual pattern of a human head and an animal body: instead, his head is animal, his body human. His very name suggests the solid nature of his fleshly being (*bottom* is appropriately also a weaving term). He and Titania represent the opposites of flesh and spirit, miraculously yoked for a time in a twofold vision of humankind's absurd and ethereal nature.

A play bringing together fairies and mortals inevitably raises questions of illusion and reality. These questions reach their greatest intensity in the presentation of "Pyramus and Thisbe." This play within a play focuses our attention on the familiarly Shakespearean metaphor of art as illusion and of the world itself as a stage on which men and women are merely players. As Theseus observes, apologizing for the ineptness of the tradesmen's performance, "the best in this kind are but shadows" (5.1.210); that is, Shakespeare's own play is of the same order of reality as Bottom's play. Puck too, in his epilogue, invites any spectator offended by Shakespeare's play to dismiss it as a mere dream—as, indeed, the play's very title suggests. Theseus goes even further, linking dream to the essence of imaginative art, although he does so in a clearly critical and rather patronizing way. The artist, he says, is like the maniac or the lover in his or her frenzy of inspiration, giving "to airy nothing / A local habitation and a name" (5.1.16–17). Artistic achievements are too unsubstantial for Theseus; from his point of view they are the products of mere fantasy and irrationality, mere myths or fairy stories or old wives' tales. Behind this critical persona defending the "real" world of his court, however,

we can hear Shakespeare's characteristically self-effacing defense of "dreaming."

"Pyramus and Thisbe," like the larger play surrounding it, attempts to body forth "the forms of things unknown." The play within the play gives us personified moonshine, a speaking wall, and an apologetic lion. Of course, it is an absurdly bad play, full of lame epithets, bombastic alliteration, and bathos. In part, Shakespeare here is satirizing the abuses of a theater he had helped reform. The players' chosen method of portraying imaginative matters is ridiculous and calls forth deliciously wry comments from the courtly spectators on stage: "Would you desire lime and hair to speak better?" (5.1.164–5). At the same time, those spectators on stage are actors in our play. Their sarcasms render them less sympathetic in our eyes; we see that their kind of sophistication is as restrictive as it is illuminating. Bottom and his friends have conceived moonshine and lion as they did because these simple men are so responsive to the terrifying power of art. A lion might frighten the ladies and get the men hanged. Theirs is a primitive faith, naive but strong, and in this sense it contrasts favorably with the jaded rationality of the court party. Theseus's valuable reminder that all art is only "illusion" is thus juxtaposed with Bottom's insistence that imaginative art has a reality of its own.

Theseus above all embodies the sophistication of the court in his description of art as a frenzy of seething brains. Ironically, Theseus's genial scoffing at "These antique fables" and "these fairy toys" (5.1.3) would seem to efface his own identity as the figure of legend. Limited by his own skepticism, Theseus seems to have forgotten his own forest wanderings, led by Titania through the "glimmering night" (2.1.77). Bottom, contrastingly, has experienced "a most rare vision," such a dream as is "past the wit of man to say what dream it was" (4.1.203–5). He alone can claim to have been the lover of the queen of fairies; and, although his language cannot adequately describe the experience, Bottom will see it made into a ballad called "Bottom's Dream." Shakespeare leaves the status of his fantasy world deliberately complex; Theseus's lofty denial of dreaming is too abrupt. Even if the Athenian forest world can be made only momentarily substantial in the artifact of Shakespeare's play, we as audience respond to its tantalizing vision. We emerge back into our lives wondering if the fairies were "real"; that is, we are puzzled by the relationship of these artistic symbols to the tangible concreteness of our daily existence. Unless our perceptions have been thus enlarged by sharing in the author's dream, we have not surrendered to the imaginative experience.

Recent performances of this enduringly popular play suggest how open it is to varying interpretation and especially to postmodern views of love and politics as thoroughly unsettling in their irrationality. Nineteenth-century staging generally preferred to see the play as a gossamer delight of diminutive gilded-winged fairies and prankish hobgoblins, all underscored by the romantic strains of Mendelssohn's incidental music. More recently, and especially after World War II, theater and film versions have responded to a darker view. Inspired by Jan Kott's *Shakespeare Our Contemporary* (1964), a book written from the perspective of Soviet-dominated eastern Europe of the Cold War, Peter Brook's brilliantly revisionary stage version for the Royal Shakespeare Theater in 1970 set the play in a brightly lit white box peopled with jugglers and athletic trapeze artists who tumbled and dashed about after one another with abandon. A fisted arm thrust between the legs of Bottom the Weaver as he was carried off stage from his rendezvous with Queen Titania suggested a triumphant phallus.

Brook's avowed aim of freeing the play from what he saw as an oppressive tradition has proved to be immensely influential. Ever since, the young lovers have learned to express their sexual energies through vigorous pursuit and physical contact. Feminist insights have enriched the role of Queen Hippolyta: formerly a captive queen resigned to her marriage to Theseus, she has become in many productions a champion of Hermia's right to resist her father's patriarchal insistence on his will. Puck, in many a recent production, is the denizen of a drug culture, with the love potion as the weed he gleefully distributes. The experience of the forest becomes a drug-induced "high," for audiences as for the actors. The fairies, sometimes played by adult and hairy males, can exhibit a steak of cruelty. The doubling of some central roles, notably Theseus/Oberon, Hippolyta/Titania, and Philostrate/Puck, has given ironic emphasis to parallels between human society and fairyland. Throughout, modern productions have tended to exploit disenchantment with traditional social structures and the surging energy of sexual self-discovery. These modern interpretations are arguably neither more nor less "true" to Shakespeare's text than earlier or more "traditional" versions. What they do demonstrate is the play's remarkable permeability and openness to differing views.

# A Midsummer Night's Dream

[*Dramatis Personae*

THESEUS, *Duke of Athens*

HIPPOLYTA, *Queen of the Amazons, betrothed to Theseus*
PHILOSTRATE, *Master of the Revels*
EGEUS, *father of Hermia*

HERMIA, *daughter of Egeus, in love with Lysander*
LYSANDER, *in love with Hermia*
DEMETRIUS, *in love with Hermia and favored by Egeus*
HELENA, *in love with Demetrius*

OBERON, *King of the Fairies*
TITANIA, *Queen of the Fairies*
PUCK, *or* ROBIN GOODFELLOW

PEASEBLOSSOM,
COBWEB,
MOTE,          } *fairies attending Titania*
MUSTARDSEED,
Other FAIRIES *attending*

PETER QUINCE, *a carpenter,*                          PROLOGUE
NICK BOTTOM, *a weaver,*                              PYRAMUS
FRANCIS FLUTE, *a bellows*
   *mender,*                        *repre-*          THISBE
TOM SNOUT, *a tinker,*              *senting*         WALL
SNUG, *a joiner,*                                     LION
ROBIN STARVELING, *a tailor,*                         MOONSHINE

*Lords and Attendants on Theseus and Hippolyta*

SCENE: *Athens, and a wood near it*]

# [1.1]

*Enter Theseus, Hippolyta, [and Philostrate,]
with others.*

THESEUS

Now, fair Hippolyta, our nuptial hour
Draws on apace. Four happy days bring in
Another moon; but, oh,- methinks, how slow
This old moon wanes! She lingers my desires,                    4
Like to a stepdame or a dowager                                 5
Long withering out a young man's revenue.                       6

HIPPOLYTA

Four days will quickly steep themselves in night;               7
Four nights will quickly dream away the time;
And then the moon, like to a silver bow
New bent in heaven, shall behold the night
Of our solemnities.

THESEUS                        Go, Philostrate,                 11
Stir up the Athenian youth to merriments.
Awake the pert and nimble spirit of mirth.
Turn melancholy forth to funerals;
The pale companion is not for our pomp.                         15
                                   [Exit Philostrate.]
Hippolyta, I wooed thee with my sword                           16
And won thy love doing thee injuries;
But I will wed thee in another key,
With pomp, with triumph, and with reveling.                     19

*Enter Egeus and his daughter Hermia, and
Lysander, and Demetrius.*

EGEUS

Happy be Theseus, our renownèd duke!

THESEUS

Thanks, good Egeus. What's the news with thee?

EGEUS    Full of vexation come I, with complaint
Against my child, my daughter Hermia.—
Stand forth, Demetrius.—My noble lord,
This man hath my consent to marry her.—
Stand forth, Lysander.—And, my gracious Duke,
This man hath bewitched the bosom of my child.—
Thou, thou Lysander, thou hast given her rhymes
And interchanged love tokens with my child.
Thou hast by moonlight at her window sung
With feigning voice verses of feigning love,                    31
And stol'n the impression of her fantasy                        32
With bracelets of thy hair, rings, gauds, conceits,             33

Knacks, trifles, nosegays, sweetmeats—messengers                34
Of strong prevailment in unhardened youth.                      35
With cunning hast thou filched my daughter's heart,
Turned her obedience, which is due to me,
To stubborn harshness. And, my gracious Duke,
Be it so she will not here before Your Grace                    39
Consent to marry with Demetrius,
I beg the ancient privilege of Athens:
As she is mine, I may dispose of her,
Which shall be either to this gentleman
Or to her death, according to our law
Immediately provided in that case.                              45

THESEUS

What say you, Hermia? Be advised, fair maid.
To you your father should be as a god—
One that composed your beauties, yea, and one                   48
To whom you are but as a form in wax                            49
By him imprinted, and within his power                          50
To leave the figure or disfigure it.                            51
Demetrius is a worthy gentleman.

HERMIA

So is Lysander.

THESEUS            In himself he is;
But in this kind, wanting your father's voice,                  54
The other must be held the worthier.

HERMIA

I would my father looked but with my eyes.

THESEUS

Rather your eyes must with his judgment look.

HERMIA

I do entreat Your Grace to pardon me.
I know not by what power I am made bold,
Nor how it may concern my modesty
In such a presence here to plead my thoughts;
But I beseech Your Grace that I may know
The worst that may befall me in this case
If I refuse to wed Demetrius.

THESEUS

Either to die the death or to abjure                            65
Forever the society of men.
Therefore, fair Hermia, question your desires,
Know of your youth, examine well your blood,                    68
Whether, if you yield not to your father's choice,
You can endure the livery of a nun,                             70
For aye to be in shady cloister mewed,                          71
To live a barren sister all your life,
Chanting faint hymns to the cold fruitless moon.
Thrice blessèd they that master so their blood
To undergo such maiden pilgrimage;
But earthlier happy is the rose distilled                       76
Than that which, withering on the virgin thorn,
Grows, lives, and dies in single blessedness.

---

**1.1. Location: Athens. Theseus's court.**
**4 lingers** frustrates   **5 stepdame** stepmother.   **a dowager** i.e., a
widow (whose right of inheritance from her dead husband is eating
into her son's estate)   **6 withering out** causing to dwindle
**7 Four . . . night** (The image is of the day sinking into the ocean as
night comes on.)   **11 solemnities** festive ceremonies of marriage.
**15 companion** fellow. (A pale complexion is linked to melancholy.)
**pomp** ceremonial magnificence.   **16 with my sword** i.e., in a military
engagement against the Amazons, when Hippolyta was taken captive
**19 triumph** public festivity   **31 feigning** (1) counterfeiting
(2) faining, desirous   **32 And . . . fantasy** and made her fall in love
with you (imprinting your image on her imagination) by stealthy and
dishonest means   **33 gauds, conceits** playthings, fanciful trifles

**34 Knacks . . . sweetmeats** knicknacks, trinkets, bouquets, candies
**35 prevailment in** influence on   **39 Be it so** if   **45 Immediately**
directly, with nothing intervening   **48–50 One . . . imprinted** (Men
were thought to be the creative force in engendering a child; the
mother's body was the passive carrier of what the male had given
shape to.)   **51 leave** i.e., leave unaltered   **54 kind** respect.   **wanting**
lacking.   **voice** approval   **65 die the death** be executed by legal
process   **68 blood** passions   **70 livery** habit, costume   **71 aye**
ever.   **mewed** shut in. (Said of a hawk, poultry, etc.)   **76 earthlier**
**happy** happier as respects this world.   **distilled** i.e., to make perfume

**HERMIA**

So will I grow, so live, so die, my lord,
Ere I will yield my virgin patent up                           80
Unto His Lordship, whose unwishèd yoke
My soul consents not to give sovereignty.

**THESEUS**

Take time to pause, and by the next new moon—
The sealing day betwixt my love and me
For everlasting bond of fellowship—
Upon that day either prepare to die
For disobedience to your father's will,
Or else to wed Demetrius, as he would,
Or on Diana's altar to protest                                 89
For aye austerity and single life.

**DEMETRIUS**

Relent, sweet Hermia, and, Lysander, yield
Thy crazèd title to my certain right.                          92

**LYSANDER**

You have her father's love, Demetrius;
Let me have Hermia's. Do you marry him.

**EGEUS**

Scornful Lysander! True, he hath my love,
And what is mine my love shall render him.
And she is mine, and all my right of her
I do estate unto Demetrius.                                    98

**LYSANDER**

I am, my lord, as well derived as he,                          99
As well possessed; my love is more than his;                  100
My fortunes every way as fairly ranked,                        101
If not with vantage, as Demetrius';                            102
And, which is more than all these boasts can be,
I am beloved of beauteous Hermia.
Why should not I then prosecute my right?
Demetrius, I'll avouch it to his head,                         106
Made love to Nedar's daughter, Helena,
And won her soul; and she, sweet lady, dotes,
Devoutly dotes, dotes in idolatry
Upon this spotted and inconstant man.                          110

**THESEUS**

I must confess that I have heard so much,
And with Demetrius thought to have spoke thereof;
But, being overfull of self-affairs,                           113
My mind did lose it. But, Demetrius, come,
And come, Egeus, you shall go with me;
I have some private schooling for you both.                    116
For you, fair Hermia, look you arm yourself                    117
To fit your fancies to your father's will,                     118
Or else the law of Athens yields you up—
Which by no means we may extenuate—                            120
To death or to a vow of single life.
Come, my Hippolyta. What cheer, my love?
Demetrius and Egeus, go along.                                 123

I must employ you in some business
Against our nuptial, and confer with you                       125
Of something nearly that concerns yourselves.                  126

**EGEUS**

With duty and desire we follow you.
                    *Exeunt [all but Lysander and Hermia].*

**LYSANDER**

How now, my love, why is your cheek so pale?
How chance the roses there do fade so fast?

**HERMIA**

Belike for want of rain, which I could well                    130
Beteem them from the tempest of my eyes.                       131

**LYSANDER**

Ay me! For aught that I could ever read,
Could ever hear by tale or history,
The course of true love never did run smooth;
But either it was different in blood—                          135

**HERMIA**

Oh, cross! Too high to be enthralled to low.                   136

**LYSANDER**

Or else misgrafted in respect of years—                        137

**HERMIA**

Oh, spite! Too old to be engaged to young.                     138

**LYSANDER**

Or else it stood upon the choice of friends—                   139

**HERMIA**

Oh, hell, to choose love by another's eyes!

**LYSANDER**

Or if there were a sympathy in choice,                         141
War, death, or sickness did lay siege to it,
Making it momentany as a sound,                                143
Swift as a shadow, short as any dream,
Brief as the lightning in the collied night                    145
That in a spleen unfolds both heaven and earth,                146
And ere a man hath power to say "Behold!"
The jaws of darkness do devour it up.
So quick bright things come to confusion.                      149

**HERMIA**

If then true lovers have been ever crossed,                    150
It stands as an edict in destiny.
Then let us teach our trial patience,                          152
Because it is a customary cross,
As due to love as thoughts, and dreams, and sighs,
Wishes, and tears, poor fancy's followers.                     155

**LYSANDER**

A good persuasion. Therefore, hear me, Hermia:                 156
I have a widow aunt, a dowager
Of great revenue, and she hath no child.
From Athens is her house remote seven leagues;                 159
And she respects me as her only son.                           160

---

**80 my virgin patent** my right to remain a virgin    **89 Diana's altar**
Diana was the Roman goddess of the hunt, of the moon, of chastity,
and of giving birth.    **protest** vow    **92 crazèd** cracked, unsound
**98 estate unto** settle or bestow upon    **99 as well derived** as well born
and descended    **100 possessed** endowed with wealth    **101 fairly**
handsomely    **102 vantage** superiority    **106 head** i.e., face    **110 spotted**
i.e., morally stained    **113 self-affairs** my own concerns    **116 schooling**
admonition    **117 For** As for.    **look you arm** take care you prepare
**118 fancies** likings, thoughts of love    **120 extenuate** mitigate, relax
**123 go** i.e., come

**125 Against** in preparation for    **126 nearly that** that closely    **130 Belike**
Very likely    **131 Beteem** grant, afford    **135 blood** hereditary rank
**136 cross** vexation.    **Too . . . low** i.e., Too exalted a thing to be forced to conform to base worldly considerations.    **137 misgrafted** ill grafted, badly
matched    **138 Too old . . . young** i.e., Too old a wooer to be forced
upon a young woman.    **139 friends** relatives    **141 sympathy** agreement
**143 momentany** lasting but a moment    **145 collied** blackened (as with
coal dust), darkened    **146 in a spleen** in a swift impulse, in a violent flash.
**unfolds** reveals    **149 confusion** ruin.    **150 ever crossed** always thwarted
**152 teach . . . patience** i.e., teach ourselves patience in this trial    **155 fancy's**
amorous passion's    **156 persuasion** doctrine.    **159 seven leagues**
about 21 miles    **160 respects** regards

There, gentle Hermia, may I marry thee,
And to that place the sharp Athenian law
Cannot pursue us. If thou lovest me, then,
Steal forth thy father's house tomorrow night;
And in the wood, a league without the town,                    165
Where I did meet thee once with Helena
To do observance to a morn of May,                             167
There will I stay for thee.

HERMIA                              My good Lysander!
I swear to thee, by Cupid's strongest bow,
By his best arrow with the golden head,                        170
By the simplicity of Venus' doves,                             171
By that which knitteth souls and prospers loves,
And by that fire which burned the Carthage queen               173
When the false Trojan under sail was seen,                     174
By all the vows that ever men have broke,
In number more than ever women spoke,
In that same place thou hast appointed me
Tomorrow truly will I meet with thee.

LYSANDER
Keep promise, love. Look, here comes Helena.

            *Enter Helena.*

HERMIA
God speed, fair Helena! Whither away?                          180

HELENA
Call you me fair? That "fair" again unsay.
Demetrius loves your fair. Oh, happy fair!                     182
Your eyes are lodestars, and your tongue's sweet air          183
More tunable than lark to shepherd's ear                       184
When wheat is green, when hawthorn buds appear.                185
Sickness is catching. Oh, were favor so,                       186
Yours would I catch, fair Hermia, ere I go;
My ear should catch your voice, my eye your eye,
My tongue should catch your tongue's sweet melody.
Were the world mine, Demetrius being bated,                    190
The rest I'd give to be to you translated.                     191
Oh, teach me how you look and with what art
You sway the motion of Demetrius' heart.                       193

HERMIA
I frown upon him, yet he loves me still.

HELENA
Oh, that your frowns would teach my smiles such
     skill!

HERMIA
I give him curses, yet he gives me love.

HELENA
Oh, that my prayers could such affection move!                 197

HERMIA
The more I hate, the more he follows me.

HELENA
The more I love, the more he hateth me.

HERMIA
His folly, Helena, is no fault of mine.

HELENA
None, but your beauty. Would that fault were mine!

HERMIA
Take comfort. He no more shall see my face.
Lysander and myself will fly this place.
Before the time I did Lysander see                             204
Seemed Athens as a paradise to me.                             205
Oh, then, what graces in my love do dwell,
That he hath turned a heaven unto a hell?

LYSANDER
Helen, to you our minds we will unfold.
Tomorrow night, when Phoebe doth behold                        209
Her silver visage in the watery glass,                         210
Decking with liquid pearl the bladed grass,                    211
A time that lovers' flights doth still conceal,                212
Through Athens' gates have we devised to steal.

HERMIA
And in the wood, where often you and I
Upon faint primrose beds were wont to lie,                     215
Emptying our bosoms of their counsel sweet,                    216
There my Lysander and myself shall meet,
And thence from Athens turn away our eyes
To seek new friends and stranger companies.                    219
Farewell, sweet playfellow. Pray thou for us,
And good luck grant thee thy Demetrius!
Keep word, Lysander. We must starve our sight
From lovers' food till morrow deep midnight.

LYSANDER
I will, my Hermia.                            *Exit Hermia.*
                    Helena, adieu!
As you on him, Demetrius dote on you!
                                      *Exit Lysander.*

HELENA
How happy some o'er other some can be!                         226
Through Athens I am thought as fair as she.
But what of that? Demetrius thinks not so;
He will not know what all but he do know.                      229
And as he errs, doting on Hermia's eyes,
So I, admiring of his qualities.                               231
Things base and vile, holding no quantity,                     232
Love can transpose to form and dignity.
Love looks not with the eyes, but with the mind,
And therefore is winged Cupid painted blind.

**165 without** outside   **167 To do . . . May** to perform the ceremonies
of May Day   **170 best arrow** (Cupid's best gold-pointed arrows
were supposed to induce love; his blunt leaden arrows, aversion.)
**171 simplicity** innocence.   **doves** i.e., those that drew Venus's chariot
**173, 174 Carthage queen, false Trojan** (Dido, Queen of Carthage,
immolated herself on a funeral pyre after having been deserted by the
Trojan hero Aeneas.)   **180 fair** fair-complexioned. (Generally
regarded by the Elizabethans as more beautiful than a dark complexion.)
**182 your fair** your beauty (even though Hermia is dark complexioned).
**happy fair** lucky fair one.   **183 lodestars** guiding stars.   **air** music
**184 tunable** tuneful, melodious   **185 green** of springtime color, not
yet ripe   **186 favor** appearance, looks   **190–1 Were . . . translated**
i.e., If all the world were mine, I'd give it all—except my dear Demetrius—
in return for my being transformed into a woman as beautiful as
you.   **193 sway the motion** control the impulses

**197 Oh, that . . . move!** Would that my prayers could arouse such desire!
**204–5 Before . . . to me** (Hermia's falling in love with Lysander has led
to such complications and jealousies that Athens no longer seems a
paradise to her.)   **209 Phoebe** Diana, the moon   **210 glass** reflecting
surface (of a lake, etc.)   **211 liquid pearl** i.e., dew   **212 still** always
**215 faint** pale   **216 counsel** secret thought   **219 stranger companies**
the company of strangers.   **226 o'er . . . can be** can be in comparison
to some others.   **229 He . . . know** Demetrius stubbornly refuses to
acknowledge what seems so clear to everyone else (that he and Helena
belong to each other).   **231 So I . . . qualities** i.e., I too dote foolishly,
in that I long for Demetrius when he has found someone else.
**232 holding no quantity** i.e., unsubstantial, unshapely

Nor hath Love's mind of any judgment taste;            236
Wings and no eyes figure unheedy haste.                237
And therefore is Love said to be a child,
Because in choice he is so oft beguiled.               239
As waggish boys in game themselves forswear,           240
So the boy Love is perjured everywhere.
For ere Demetrius looked on Hermia's eyne,             242
He hailed down oaths that he was only mine;
And when this hail some heat from Hermia felt,         244
So he dissolved, and showers of oaths did melt.        245
I will go tell him of fair Hermia's flight.
Then to the wood will he tomorrow night
Pursue her; and for this intelligence                  248
If I have thanks, it is a dear expense.                249
But herein mean I to enrich my pain,
To have his sight thither and back again.      *Exit.*

♣

## [1.2]

*Enter Quince the carpenter, and Snug the
joiner, and Bottom the weaver, and Flute the
bellows mender, and Snout the tinker, and
Starveling the tailor.*

QUINCE   Is all our company here?
BOTTOM   You were best to call them generally, man by    2
man, according to the scrip.                             3
QUINCE   Here is the scroll of every man's name which
is thought fit, through all Athens, to play in our inter-  5
lude before the Duke and the Duchess on his wedding       6
day at night.
BOTTOM   First, good Peter Quince, say what the play
treats on, then read the names of the actors, and so
grow to a point.                                          10
QUINCE   Marry, our play is "The most lamentable com-    11
edy and most cruel death of Pyramus and Thisbe."
BOTTOM   A very good piece of work, I assure you, and
a merry. Now, good Peter Quince, call forth your
actors by the scroll. Masters, spread yourselves.
QUINCE   Answer as I call you. Nick Bottom, the weaver.  16
BOTTOM   Ready. Name what part I am for, and proceed.
QUINCE   You, Nick Bottom, are set down for Pyramus.
BOTTOM   What is Pyramus? A lover or a tyrant?
QUINCE   A lover, that kills himself most gallant for love.
BOTTOM   That will ask some tears in the true performing
of it. If I do it, let the audience look to their eyes. I will
move storms; I will condole in some measure. To the     23
rest—yet my chief humor is for a tyrant. I could play    24

**236 Nor . . . taste** i.e., Nor has Love, which dwells in the fancy or imagination, any least bit of judgment or reason   **237 figure** signify   **239 in
choice** in choosing.   **beguiled** self-deluded, making unaccountable
choices.   **240 As . . . forswear** Just as mischievous boys forswear themselves (by cheating, tricking, etc.) in their childish games   **242 eyne** eyes.
(Old form of plural.)   **244–5 And when . . . melt** i.e., but when he saw
Hermia, the heat of that encounter melted the oaths he had professed to
me as if they where so much hail or frozen drops of water. (With a pun
on *hailed* and *hail*.)   **248 intelligence** information   **249 a dear expense**
i.e., a trouble worth taking on my part.
**1.2. Location: Athens.**   **2 generally** (Bottom's blunder for "individually.")
**3 scrip** script.   **5–6 interlude** play   **10 grow to** come to   **11 Marry**
(A mild oath; originally the name of the Virgin Mary.)   **16 Bottom** (As a
weaver's term, a *bottom* was an object around which thread was wound.)
**23 condole** lament, arouse pity   **24 humor** inclination

Ercles rarely, or a part to tear a cat in, to make all split.  25
   "The raging rocks
   And shivering shocks
   Shall break the locks
      Of prison gates;
   And Phibbus' car                                            30
   Shall shine from far
   And make and mar
      The foolish Fates."
This was lofty! Now name the rest of the players. This is
Ercles' vein, a tyrant's vein. A lover is more condoling.
QUINCE   Francis Flute, the bellows mender.
FLUTE   Here, Peter Quince.
QUINCE   Flute, you must take Thisbe on you.
FLUTE   What is Thisbe? A wandering knight?
QUINCE   It is the lady that Pyramus must love.
FLUTE   Nay, faith, let not me play a woman. I have a
beard coming.
QUINCE   That's all one. You shall play it in a mask, and   43
you may speak as small as you will.                         44
BOTTOM   An I may hide my face, let me play Thisbe too.     45
I'll speak in a monstrous little voice: "Thisne, Thisne!"
"Ah, Pyramus, my lover dear! Thy Thisbe dear, and
lady dear!"
QUINCE   No, no, you must play Pyramus, and Flute, you
Thisbe.
BOTTOM   Well, proceed.
QUINCE   Robin Starveling, the tailor.
STARVELING   Here, Peter Quince.
QUINCE   Robin Starveling, you must play Thisbe's
mother. Tom Snout, the tinker.
SNOUT   Here, Peter Quince.
QUINCE   You, Pyramus' father; myself, Thisbe's father;
Snug, the joiner, you, the lion's part; and I hope here is
a play fitted.
SNUG   Have you the lion's part written? Pray you, if it
be, give it me, for I am slow of study.
QUINCE   You may do it extempore, for it is nothing but   62
roaring.
BOTTOM   Let me play the lion too. I will roar that I will
do any man's heart good to hear me. I will roar that I
will make the Duke say, "Let him roar again, let him
roar again."
QUINCE   An you should do it too terribly, you would
fright the Duchess and the ladies, that they would
shriek; and that were enough to hang us all.
ALL   That would hang us, every mother's son.
BOTTOM   I grant you, friends, if you should fright the
ladies out of their wits, they would have no more discretion but to hang us; but I will aggravate my voice    74
so that I will roar you as gently as any sucking dove; I   75
will roar you an 'twere any nightingale.                   76

**25 Ercles** Hercules. (The tradition of ranting came from Seneca's *Hercules Furens*.)   **tear a cat** i.e., rant.   **make all split** i.e., cause a stir, bring
the house down.   **30 Phibbus' car** Phoebus's, the sun god's, chariot
**43 That's all one** It makes no difference.   **44 small** high-pitched
**45 An** If. (Also at line 68.)   **62 extempore** without a text.
**74 aggravate** (Bottom's blunder for "moderate.")   **75 roar you** i.e.,
roar for you.   **sucking dove** (Bottom conflates *sitting dove* and *sucking
lamb*, two proverbial images of innocence.)   **76 an 'twere** as if it were

QUINCE    You can play no part but Pyramus; for Pyramus is a sweet-faced man, a proper man as one shall   78
see in a summer's day, a most lovely gentlemanlike
man. Therefore you must needs play Pyramus.

BOTTOM    Well, I will undertake it. What beard were I
best to play it in?

QUINCE    Why, what you will.

BOTTOM    I will discharge it in either your straw-color   84
beard, your orange-tawny beard, your purple-in-grain   85
beard, or your French-crown-color beard, your perfect   86
yellow.

QUINCE    Some of your French crowns have no hair at all,   88
and then you will play barefaced. But, masters, here
are your parts. [*He distributes parts.*] And I am to
entreat you, request you, and desire you to con them   91
by tomorrow night, and meet me in the palace wood,
a mile without the town, by moonlight. There will we
rehearse; for if we meet in the city, we shall be dogged
with company, and our devices known. In the mean-   95
time I will draw a bill of properties, such as our play   96
wants. I pray you, fail me not.

BOTTOM    We will meet, and there we may rehearse most
obscenely and courageously. Take pains, be perfect.   99
Adieu.

QUINCE    At the Duke's oak we meet.

BOTTOM    Enough. Hold, or cut bowstrings.    *Exeunt.*  102

❧

# [2.1]

*Enter a Fairy at one door, and Robin Goodfellow
[Puck] at another.*

PUCK
    How now, spirit, whither wander you?

FAIRY
    Over hill, over dale,
        Thorough bush, thorough brier,            3
    Over park, over pale,                          4
        Thorough flood, thorough fire,
    I do wander everywhere,
    Swifter than the moon's sphere;           7
    And I serve the Fairy Queen,
    To dew her orbs upon the green.          9
    The cowslips tall her pensioners be.      10
    In their gold coats spots you see;

    Those be rubies, fairy favors;          12
        In those freckles live their savors.    13
  I must go seek some dewdrops here
  And hang a pearl in every cowslip's ear.
  Farewell, thou lob of spirits; I'll be gone.    16
  Our Queen and all her elves come here anon.  17

PUCK
  The King doth keep his revels here tonight.
  Take heed the Queen come not within his sight.
  For Oberon is passing fell and wrath,        20
  Because that she as her attendant hath      21
  A lovely boy, stolen from an Indian king;
  She never had so sweet a changeling.      23
  And jealous Oberon would have the child
  Knight of his train, to trace the forests wild.  25
  But she perforce withholds the lovèd boy,    26
  Crowns him with flowers, and makes him all her joy.
  And now they never meet in grove or green,
  By fountain clear, or spangled starlight sheen,  29
  But they do square, that all their elves for fear  30
  Creep into acorn cups and hide them there.

FAIRY
  Either I mistake your shape and making quite,
  Or else you are that shrewd and knavish sprite  33
  Called Robin Goodfellow. Are not you he
  That frights the maidens of the villagery,     35
  Skim milk, and sometimes labor in the quern,  36
  And bootless make the breathless huswife churn,  37
  And sometimes make the drink to bear no barm,  38
  Mislead night wanderers, laughing at their harm?  39
  Those that "Hobgoblin" call you, and "Sweet Puck,"  40
  You do their work, and they shall have good luck.
  Are you not he?

PUCK                Thou speakest aright;
  I am that merry wanderer of the night.
  I jest to Oberon and make him smile
  When I a fat and bean-fed horse beguile,     45
  Neighing in likeness of a filly foal;       46
  And sometimes lurk I in a gossip's bowl     47
  In very likeness of a roasted crab,        48
  And when she drinks, against her lips I bob
  And on her withered dewlap pour the ale.    50
  The wisest aunt, telling the saddest tale,    51

---

**78 proper** handsome    **84 discharge** perform.    **your** i.e., you know
the kind I mean    **85 purple-in-grain** dyed a very deep red. (From
*grain,* the name applied to the dried insect used to make the dye.)
**86 French-crown-color** i.e., color of a French crown, a gold coin
**88 crowns** heads bald from syphilis, the "French disease"    **91 con**
memorize    **95 devices** plans    **96 draw a bill** draw up a list
**99 obscenely** (An unintentionally funny blunder, whatever Bottom
meant to say.)    **perfect** i.e., letter-perfect in memorizing your parts.
**102 Hold . . . bowstrings** (An archers' expression, not definitely
explained, but probably meaning here "keep your promises, or give
up the play.")

**2 .1. Location: A wood near Athens.**
**3 Thorough** through    **4 pale** enclosure    **7 sphere** orbit    **9 dew**
sprinkle with dew.    **orbs** circles, i.e., fairy rings (circular bands of
grass, darker than the surrounding area, caused by fungi enriching
the soil)    **10 pensioners** retainers, members of the royal bodyguard

**12 favors** love tokens    **13 savors** sweet smells.    **16 lob** country
bumpkin    **17 anon** at once.    **20 passing fell** exceedingly angry.
**wrath** wrathful    **21 Because that** because    **23 changeling** child
exchanged for another by the fairies.    **25 trace** range through
**26 perforce** forcibly    **29 fountain** spring.    **starlight sheen** shining
starlight    **30 square** quarrel    **33 shrewd** mischievous.    **sprite**
spirit    **35 villagery** village population    **36 Skim milk** i.e., steal the
cream.    **quern** hand mill (where Puck presumably hampers the
grinding of grain)    **37 bootless** in vain. (Puck prevents the cream
from turning to butter.)    **huswife** housewife    **38 barm** head on the ale.
(Puck prevents the barm or yeast from producing fermentation.)
**39 Mislead night wanderers** i.e., mislead with false fire those who
walk abroad at night (hence earning Puck his other names of Jack o'
Lantern and Will o' the Wisp)    **40 Those . . . Puck** i.e., Those who
call you by the names you favor rather than those denoting the mischief you do    **45 bean-fed** full of beans    **46 a filly foal** a mare (in
heat)    **47 gossip's** old woman's    **48 crab** crab apple    **50 dewlap**
loose skin on neck    **51 aunt** old woman.    **saddest** most serious

Sometime for three-foot stool mistaketh me;
Then slip I from her bum, down topples she,
And "Tailor" cries, and falls into a cough;                                    54
And then the whole choir hold their hips and laugh,                            55
And waxen in their mirth, and neeze, and swear                                 56
A merrier hour was never wasted there.                                         57
But, room, fairy! Here comes Oberon.                                           58

FAIRY
And here my mistress. Would that he were gone!

*Enter [Oberon] the King of Fairies at one door,
with his train, and [Titania] the Queen at
another, with hers.*

OBERON
Ill met by moonlight, proud Titania.

TITANIA
What, jealous Oberon? Fairies, skip hence.
I have forsworn his bed and company.

OBERON
Tarry, rash wanton. Am not I thy lord?                                         63

TITANIA
Then I must be thy lady; but I know
When thou hast stolen away from Fairyland
And in the shape of Corin sat all day,                                         66
Playing on pipes of corn and versing love                                      67
To amorous Phillida. Why art thou here                                         68
Come from the farthest step of India,                                          69
But that, forsooth, the bouncing Amazon,
Your buskined mistress and your warrior love,                                  71
To Theseus must be wedded, and you come
To give their bed joy and prosperity.

OBERON
How canst thou thus for shame, Titania,
Glance at my credit with Hippolyta,                                            75
Knowing I know thy love to Theseus?
Didst not thou lead him through the glimmering
    night
From Perigenia, whom he ravishèd?                                              78
And make him with fair Aegles break his faith,                                 79
With Ariadne and Antiopa?                                                      80

TITANIA
These are the forgeries of jealousy;
And never, since the middle summer's spring,                                   82
Met we on hill, in dale, forest, or mead,                                      83

By pavèd fountain or by rushy brook,                                           84
Or in the beachèd margent of the sea,                                          85
To dance our ringlets to the whistling wind,                                   86
But with thy brawls thou hast disturbed our sport.
Therefore the winds, piping to us in vain,
As in revenge, have sucked up from the sea
Contagious fogs which, falling in the land,                                    90
Hath every pelting river made so proud                                         91
That they have overborne their continents.                                     92
The ox hath therefore stretched his yoke in vain,                             93
The plowman lost his sweat, and the green corn                                 94
Hath rotted ere his youth attained a beard;
The fold stands empty in the drownèd field,                                    96
And crows are fatted with the murrain flock;                                   97
The nine-men's morris is filled up with mud,                                   98
And the quaint mazes in the wanton green                                       99
For lack of tread are undistinguishable.
The human mortals want their winter here;                                      101
No night is now with hymn or carol blessed.
Therefore the moon, the governess of floods,                                   103
Pale in her anger, washes all the air,                                         104
That rheumatic diseases do abound.                                             105
And thorough this distemperature we see                                        106
The seasons alter: hoary-headed frosts
Fall in the fresh lap of the crimson rose,
And on old Hiems' thin and icy crown                                           109
An odorous chaplet of sweet summer buds
Is, as in mockery, set. The spring, the summer,
The childing autumn, angry winter, change                                      112
Their wonted liveries, and the mazèd world                                     113
By their increase now knows not which is which.                                114
And this same progeny of evils comes
From our debate, from our dissension.                                          116
We are their parents and original.                                             117

OBERON
Do you amend it, then. It lies in you.
Why should Titania cross her Oberon?
I do but beg a little changeling boy
To be my henchman.

TITANIA                        Set your heart at rest.                         121
The fairy land buys not the child of me.
His mother was a vot'ress of my order,                                         123

---

**54 "Tailor"** (Seemingly a cry of distress or embarrassment.)    **55 choir** company    **56 waxen** increase.    **neeze** sneeze    **57 wasted** spent **58 room** stand aside, make room    **63 wanton** headstrong creature. **66 , 68 Corin, Phillida** (Conventional names of pastoral lovers.) **67 corn** (Here, oat stalks.)    **versing love** writing love verses    **69 step** farthest limit of travel, or, perhaps, *steppe*, vast flat treeless tract **71 buskined** wearing half-boots called buskins    **75 Glance . . . Hippolyta** make insinuations about my favored relationship with Hippolyta **78 Perigenia** i.e., Perigouna, one of Theseus's conquests. (This and the following women are named in Thomas North's translation of Plutarch's "Life of Theseus.")    **79 Aegles** i.e., Aegle, for whom Theseus deserted Ariadne according to some accounts    **80 Ariadne** the daughter of Minos, King of Crete, who helped Theseus to escape the labyrinth after killing the Minotaur; later she was abandoned by Theseus.    **Antiopa** Queen of the Amazons and wife of Theseus; elsewhere identified with Hippolyta, but here thought of as a separate woman.    **82 middle summer's spring** beginning of midsummer **83 mead** meadow

**84 pavèd** with pebbled bottom.    **rushy** bordered with rushes **85 in** on.    **margent** edge, border    **86 ringlets** dances in a ring. (See *orbs* in line 9.)    **to** to the sound of    **90 Contagious** noxious **91 pelting** paltry    **92 continents** banks that contain them. **93 stretched his yoke** i.e., pulled at his yoke in plowing    **94 corn** grain of any kind    **96 fold** pen for sheep or cattle    **97 murrain** having died of the plague    **98 nine-men's morris** i.e., portion of the village green marked out in a square for a game played with nine pebbles or pegs    **99 quaint mazes** i.e., intricate paths marked out on the village green to be followed rapidly on foot as a kind of contest.    **wanton** luxuriant    **101 want** lack.    **winter** i.e., regular winter season; or, proper observances of winter, such as the *hymn* or *carol* in the next line (?)    **103 Therefore** i.e., As a result of our quarrel **104 washes** saturates with moisture    **105 rheumatic diseases** colds, flu, and other respiratory infections    **106 distemperature** disturbance in nature    **109 Hiems'** the winter god's    **112 childing** fruitful, pregnant    **113 wonted liveries** usual apparel.    **mazèd** bewildered **114 their increase** the increasing pace of change; or, their produce **116 debate** quarrel    **117 original** origin.    **121 henchman** attendant, page.    **123 was . . . order** had taken a vow to serve me

And in the spicèd Indian air by night
Full often hath she gossiped by my side
And sat with me on Neptune's yellow sands,
Marking th'embarkèd traders on the flood,      127
When we have laughed to see the sails conceive
And grow big-bellied with the wanton wind;      129
Which she, with pretty and with swimming gait,      130
Following—her womb then rich with my young
    squire—
Would imitate, and sail upon the land
To fetch me trifles, and return again
As from a voyage, rich with merchandise.
But she, being mortal, of that boy did die;
And for her sake do I rear up her boy,
And for her sake I will not part with him.

OBERON
How long within this wood intend you stay?

TITANIA
Perchance till after Theseus' wedding day.
If you will patiently dance in our round      140
And see our moonlight revels, go with us;
If not, shun me, and I will spare your haunts.      142

OBERON
Give me that boy, and I will go with thee.

TITANIA
Not for thy fairy kingdom. Fairies, away!
We shall chide downright, if I longer stay.
                *Exeunt* [*Titania with her train*].

OBERON
Well, go thy way. Thou shalt not from this grove      146
Till I torment thee for this injury.
My gentle Puck, come hither. Thou rememb'rest
Since once I sat upon a promontory,      149
And heard a mermaid on a dolphin's back
Uttering such dulcet and harmonious breath      151
That the rude sea grew civil at her song,      152
And certain stars shot madly from their spheres
To hear the sea-maid's music?

PUCK                      I remember.

OBERON
That very time I saw, but thou couldst not,
Flying between the cold moon and the earth
Cupid, all armed. A certain aim he took      157
At a fair vestal thronèd by the west,      158
And loosed his love shaft smartly from his bow      159
As it should pierce a hundred thousand hearts;      160
But I might see young Cupid's fiery shaft      161
Quenched in the chaste beams of the wat'ry moon,
And the imperial vot'ress passèd on,
In maiden meditation, fancy-free.      164
Yet marked I where the bolt of Cupid fell:      165

It fell upon a little western flower,
Before milk-white, now purple with love's wound,
And maidens call it love-in-idleness.      168
Fetch me that flower; the herb I showed thee once.
The juice of it on sleeping eyelids laid
Will make or man or woman madly dote      171
Upon the next live creature that it sees.
Fetch me this herb, and be thou here again
Ere the leviathan can swim a league.      174

PUCK
I'll put a girdle round about the earth
In forty minutes.                        [*Exit.*]

OBERON                 Having once this juice,
I'll watch Titania when she is asleep
And drop the liquor of it in her eyes.
The next thing then she waking looks upon,
Be it on lion, bear, or wolf, or bull,
On meddling monkey, or on busy ape,
She shall pursue it with the soul of love.
And ere I take this charm from off her sight,
As I can take it with another herb,
I'll make her render up her page to me.
But who comes here? I am invisible,
And I will overhear their conference.

                           [*He stands aside.*]

         *Enter Demetrius, Helena following him.*

DEMETRIUS
I love thee not; therefore pursue me not.
Where is Lysander and fair Hermia?
The one I'll slay; the other slayeth me.
Thou told'st me they were stol'n unto this wood;
And here am I, and wood within this wood      192
Because I cannot meet my Hermia.
Hence, get thee gone, and follow me no more.

HELENA
You draw me, you hardhearted adamant!      195
But yet you draw not iron, for my heart
Is true as steel. Leave you your power to draw,      197
And I shall have no power to follow you.

DEMETRIUS
Do I entice you? Do I speak you fair?      199
Or rather do I not in plainest truth
Tell you I do not nor I cannot love you?

HELENA
And even for that do I love you the more.
I am your spaniel; and, Demetrius,
The more you beat me I will fawn on you.
Use me but as your spaniel, spurn me, strike me,
Neglect me, lose me; only give me leave,
Unworthy as I am, to follow you.
What worser place can I beg in your love—
And yet a place of high respect with me—
Than to be usèd as you use your dog?

---

127 **traders** trading vessels. **flood** tide, sea   129 **wanton** (1) playful (2) amorous   130 **swimming** smooth, gliding   140 **round** circular dance   142 **spare your haunts** shun your terrain.   146 **from** go from   149 **Since** when   151 **dulcet** sweet. **breath** voice, song   152 **rude** rough   157 **all** fully. **certain** sure   158 **vestal** vestal virgin. (Contains a complimentary allusion to Queen Elizabeth as a votaress of Diana and probably refers to an actual entertainment in her honor at Elvetham in 1591.)   **by** in the region of   159 **loosed** released 160 **As** as if   161 **might** could   164 **fancy-free** free of love's spell. 165 **bolt** arrow

168 **love-in-idleness** pansy, heartsease.   171 **or man** either man 174 **leviathan** sea monster, whale   192 **wood . . . wood** frantically mad within this wood. (With an obvious wordplay on *wood*, meaning "woods.")   195 **adamant** lodestone, magnet. (With pun on *hardhearted*, since adamant was also thought to be the hardest of all stones and was confused with the diamond.)   197 **Leave you** Give up 199 **speak you fair** speak courteously to you.

DEMETRIUS
    Tempt not too much the hatred of my spirit,
    For I am sick when I do look on thee.

HELENA
    And I am sick when I look not on you.

DEMETRIUS
    You do impeach your modesty too much                214
    To leave the city and commit yourself              215
    Into the hands of one that loves you not,
    To trust the opportunity of night
    And the ill counsel of a desert place              218
    With the rich worth of your virginity.

HELENA
    Your virtue is my privilege. For that               220
    It is not night when I do see your face,
    Therefore I think I am not in the night;
    Nor doth this wood lack worlds of company,
    For you, in my respect, are all the world.          224
    Then how can it be said I am alone
    When all the world is here to look on me?

DEMETRIUS
    I'll run from thee and hide me in the brakes,       227
    And leave thee to the mercy of wild beasts.

HELENA
    The wildest hath not such a heart as you.
    Run when you will. The story shall be changed:
    Apollo flies and Daphne holds the chase,            231
    The dove pursues the griffin, the mild hind         232
    Makes speed to catch the tiger—bootless speed,      233
    When cowardice pursues and valor flies!

DEMETRIUS
    I will not stay thy questions. Let me go!           235
    Or if thou follow me, do not believe
    But I shall do thee mischief in the wood.

HELENA
    Ay, in the temple, in the town, the field,
    You do me mischief. Fie, Demetrius!
    Your wrongs do set a scandal on my sex.             240
    We cannot fight for love, as men may do;
    We should be wooed and were not made to woo.
                                      [Exit Demetrius.]
    I'll follow thee and make a heaven of hell,
    To die upon the hand I love so well.    [Exit.] 244

OBERON
    Fare thee well, nymph. Ere he do leave this grove
    Thou shalt fly him, and he shall seek thy love.

            Enter Puck.

    Hast thou the flower there? Welcome, wanderer.

PUCK
    Ay, there it is.                  [He offers the flower.]
OBERON          I pray thee, give it me.
    I know a bank where the wild thyme blows,           249
    Where oxlips and the nodding violet grows,          250
    Quite overcanopied with luscious woodbine,          251
    With sweet muskroses and with eglantine.            252
    There sleeps Titania sometime of the night,         253
    Lulled in these flowers with dances and delight;
    And there the snake throws her enameled skin,       255
    Weed wide enough to wrap a fairy in.                256
    And with the juice of this I'll streak her eyes     257
    And make her full of hateful fantasies.
    Take thou some of it, and seek through this grove.
                                     [He gives some love juice.]
    A sweet Athenian lady is in love
    With a disdainful youth. Anoint his eyes,
    But do it when the next thing he espies
    May be the lady. Thou shalt know the man
    By the Athenian garments he hath on.
    Effect it with some care, that he may prove         265
    More fond on her than she upon her love;            266
    And look thou meet me ere the first cock crow.      267

PUCK
    Fear not, my lord, your servant shall do so.
                                 Exeunt [separately].


                        ❧


# [2.2]

        *Enter Titania, Queen of Fairies, with her train.*

TITANIA
    Come, now a roundel and a fairy song;                1
    Then, for the third part of a minute, hence—
    Some to kill cankers in the muskrose buds,           3
    Some war with reremice for their leathern wings      4
    To make my small elves coats, and some keep back
    The clamorous owl, that nightly hoots and wonders
    At our quaint spirits. Sing me now asleep.           7
    Then to your offices, and let me rest.

        *Fairies sing.*

FIRST FAIRY
    You spotted snakes with double tongue,               9
        Thorny hedgehogs, be not seen;
    Newts and blindworms, do no wrong;                  11
        Come not near our Fairy Queen.

---

214 **impeach** call into question, cast an imputation upon   215 **To leave** by leaving   218 **desert** deserted   220 **privilege** safeguard, warrant.   **For that** Because   224 **in my respect** in my estimation   227 **brakes** thickets   231 **Apollo . . . chase** (In the ancient myth, Daphne fled from Apollo and was saved from rape by being transformed into a laurel tree; here it is the female who *holds the chase*, or pursues, instead of the male.)   232 **griffin** a fabulous monster with the head and wings of an eagle and the body of a lion.   **hind** female deer   233 **bootless** fruitless   235 **stay** wait for, put up with.   **questions** talk or argument.   240 **Your . . . sex** i.e., The wrongs that you do me cause me to act in a manner that disgraces my sex.   244 **upon** by

249 **blows** blooms   250 **oxlips** flowers resembling cowslip and primrose   251 **woodbine** honeysuckle   252 **muskroses** a kind of large, sweet-scented rose.   **eglantine** sweetbrier, another kind of rose.   253 **sometime of** for part of   255 **throws** sloughs off, sheds   256 **Weed** garment   257 **streak** anoint, touch gently   265 **prove** prove to be   266 **fond on** doting on   267 **look** see to it that

**2.2. Location: The wood.**
1 **roundel** dance in a ring   3 **cankers** cankerworms (i.e., caterpillars or grubs)   4 **reremice** bats   7 **quaint** dainty   9 **double** forked
11 **Newts** water lizards. (Considered poisonous, as were *blindworms*—small snakes with tiny eyes—and spiders.)

CHORUS [*dancing*]

>Philomel, with melody                13
>Sing in our sweet lullaby;
>Lulla, lulla, lullaby, lulla, lulla, lullaby.
>Never harm
>Nor spell nor charm
>Come our lovely lady nigh.
>So good night, with lullaby.

FIRST FAIRY

>Weaving spiders, come not here;
>Hence, you long-legged spinners, hence!
>Beetles black, approach not near;
>Worm nor snail, do no offense.        23

CHORUS [*dancing*]

>Philomel, with melody
>Sing in our sweet lullaby;
>Lulla, lulla, lullaby, lulla, lulla, lullaby.
>Never harm
>Nor spell nor charm
>Come our lovely lady nigh.
>So good night, with lullaby.        [*Titania sleeps.*]

SECOND FAIRY

>Hence, away! Now all is well.
>One aloof stand sentinel.        32

>>[*Exeunt Fairies, leaving one sentinel.*]

>*Enter Oberon [and squeezes the flower on*
>*Titania's eyelids].*

OBERON

>What thou see'st when thou dost wake,
>Do it for thy true love take;
>Love and languish for his sake.
>Be it ounce, or cat, or bear,        36
>Pard, or boar with bristled hair,        37
>In thy eye that shall appear
>When thou wak'st, it is thy dear.
>Wake when some vile thing is near.        [*Exit.*]

>*Enter Lysander and Hermia.*

LYSANDER

>Fair love, you faint with wand'ring in the wood;
>And to speak truth, I have forgot our way.
>We'll rest us, Hermia, if you think it good,
>And tarry for the comfort of the day.

HERMIA

>Be it so, Lysander. Find you out a bed,
>For I upon this bank will rest my head.

LYSANDER

>One turf shall serve as pillow for us both;
>One heart, one bed, two bosoms, and one troth.        48

HERMIA

>Nay, good Lysander, for my sake, my dear,
>Lie further off yet. Do not lie so near.

LYSANDER

>Oh, take the sense, sweet, of my innocence!        51
>Love takes the meaning in love's conference.        52
>I mean that my heart unto yours is knit,
>So that but one heart we can make of it;
>Two bosoms interchainèd with an oath—
>So then two bosoms and a single troth.
>Then by your side no bed-room me deny,
>For lying so, Hermia, I do not lie.        58

HERMIA

>Lysander riddles very prettily.
>Now much beshrew my manners and my pride        60
>If Hermia meant to say Lysander lied.
>But, gentle friend, for love and courtesy
>Lie further off, in human modesty.
>Such separation as may well be said
>Becomes a virtuous bachelor and a maid,
>So far be distant; and, good night, sweet friend.
>Thy love ne'er alter till thy sweet life end!

LYSANDER

>Amen, amen, to that fair prayer, say I,
>And then end life when I end loyalty!
>Here is my bed. Sleep give thee all his rest!

HERMIA

>With half that wish the wisher's eyes be pressed!        71

>>[*They sleep, separated by a short distance.*]

>*Enter Puck.*

PUCK

>Through the forest have I gone,
>But Athenian found I none
>On whose eyes I might approve        74
>This flower's force in stirring love.
>Night and silence.—Who is here?
>Weeds of Athens he doth wear.        77
>This is he, my master said,
>Despisèd the Athenian maid;
>And here the maiden, sleeping sound,
>On the dank and dirty ground.
>Pretty soul, she durst not lie
>Near this lack-love, this kill-courtesy.
>Churl, upon thy eyes I throw
>All the power this charm doth owe.        85

>>[*He applies the love juice.*]

>When thou wak'st, let love forbid        86
>Sleep his seat on thy eyelid.        87
>So awake when I am gone,
>For I must now to Oberon.        *Exit.*

>*Enter Demetrius and Helena, running.*

HELENA

>Stay, though thou kill me, sweet Demetrius!

---

**13 Philomel** the nightingale. (Philomela, daughter of King Pandion, was transformed into a nightingale, according to Ovid's *Metamorphoses* 6, after she had been raped by her sister Procne's husband, Tereus.) **23 offense** harm.    **32 sentinel** (Presumably Oberon is able to outwit or intimidate this guard.)    **36 ounce** lynx    **37 Pard** leopard    **48 troth** faith, trothplight.

**51–2 take . . . conference** take my meaning in an innocent sense, with generosity and sympathy! True lovers do so when they converse. **58 lie** tell a falsehood. (With a riddling pun on *lie,* "recline.") **60 beshrew** (A mild oath.)    **71 With . . . pressed!** i.e., I return half that wish, so that you, the wisher, may sleep well too (instead of Sleep giving all his rest to me)!    **74 approve** test    **77 Weeds** Garments **85 owe** own, possess.    **86–7 let . . . eyelid** may love, heretofore denied, be enthroned in your eyes.

DEMETRIUS
  I charge thee, hence, and do not haunt me thus.
HELENA
  Oh, wilt thou darkling leave me? Do not so.                    92
DEMETRIUS
  Stay, on thy peril! I alone will go.               [Exit.]  93
HELENA
  Oh, I am out of breath in this fond chase!                    94
  The more my prayer, the lesser is my grace.                   95
  Happy is Hermia, wheresoe'er she lies,                        96
  For she hath blessèd and attractive eyes.
  How came her eyes so bright? Not with salt tears;
  If so, my eyes are oft'ner washed than hers.
  No, no, I am as ugly as a bear,
  For beasts that meet me run away for fear.
  Therefore no marvel though Demetrius                         102
  Do, as a monster, fly my presence thus.                      103
  What wicked and dissembling glass of mine                    104
  Made me compare with Hermia's sphery eyne?                   105
  But who is here? Lysander, on the ground?
  Dead, or asleep? I see no blood, no wound.
  Lysander, if you live, good sir, awake.
LYSANDER [awaking]
  And run through fire I will for thy sweet sake.
  Transparent Helena! Nature shows art,                        110
  That through thy bosom makes me see thy heart.
  Where is Demetrius? Oh, how fit a word
  Is that vile name to perish on my sword!
HELENA
  Do not say so, Lysander; say not so.
  What though he love your Hermia? Lord, what
     though?
  Yet Hermia still loves you. Then be content.
LYSANDER
  Content with Hermia? No! I do repent
  The tedious minutes I with her have spent.
  Not Hermia but Helena I love.
  Who will not change a raven for a dove?
  The will of man is by his reason swayed,                     121
  And reason says you are the worthier maid.
  Things growing are not ripe until their season;
  So I, being young, till now ripe not to reason.              124
  And, touching now the point of human skill,                  125
  Reason becomes the marshal to my will
  And leads me to your eyes, where I o'erlook                  127
  Love's stories written in love's richest book.
HELENA
  Wherefore was I to this keen mockery born?                   129
  When at your hands did I deserve this scorn?
  Is't not enough, is't not enough, young man,
  That I did never—no, nor never can—
  Deserve a sweet look from Demetrius' eye,

  But you must flout my insufficiency?
  Good troth, you do me wrong, good sooth, you do,   135
  In such disdainful manner me to woo.
  But fare you well. Perforce I must confess
  I thought you lord of more true gentleness.          138
  Oh, that a lady, of one man refused,                 139
  Should of another therefore be abused!       Exit.  140
LYSANDER
  She sees not Hermia. Hermia, sleep thou there,
  And never mayst thou come Lysander near!
  For as a surfeit of the sweetest things
  The deepest loathing to the stomach brings,
  Or as the heresies that men do leave                 145
  Are hated most of those they did deceive,            146
  So thou, my surfeit and my heresy,
  Of all be hated, but the most of me!                 148
  And, all my powers, address your love and might      149
  To honor Helen and to be her knight!        Exit.
HERMIA [awaking]
  Help me, Lysander, help me! Do thy best
  To pluck this crawling serpent from my breast!
  Ay me, for pity! What a dream was here!
  Lysander, look how I do quake with fear.
  Methought a serpent ate my heart away,
  And you sat smiling at his cruel prey.               156
  Lysander! What, removed? Lysander! Lord!
  What, out of hearing? Gone? No sound, no word?
  Alack, where are you? Speak, an if you hear;         159
  Speak, of all loves! I swoon almost with fear.       160
  No? Then I well perceive you are not nigh.
  Either death, or you, I'll find immediately.
              Exit. [The sleeping Titania remains.]

                          ❧

## [3.1]

*Enter the clowns [Quince, Snug, Bottom, Flute,*
*Snout, and Starveling].*

BOTTOM   Are we all met?
QUINCE   Pat, pat; and here's a marvelous convenient   2
  place for our rehearsal. This green plot shall be our
  stage, this hawthorn brake our tiring-house, and we   4
  will do it in action as we will do it before the Duke.
BOTTOM   Peter Quince?
QUINCE   What sayest thou, bully Bottom?                 7
BOTTOM   There are things in this comedy of Pyramus
  and Thisbe that will never please. First, Pyramus must
  draw a sword to kill himself, which the ladies cannot
  abide. How answer you that?
SNOUT   By'r lakin, a parlous fear.                     12

92 **darkling** in the dark   93 **on thy peril** i.e., on pain of reprisal if you don't obey me and stay.   94 **fond** doting   95 **my grace** the favor I obtain.   96 **lies** dwells   102–3 **no marvel . . . thus** i.e., no wonder that Demetrius flies from me as from a monster.   104 **glass** mirror   105 **compare** compare myself.   **sphery eyne** eyes as bright as stars in their spheres.   110 **Transparent** Radiant, pure.   **art** skill, magic power   121 **will** desire   124 **ripe not** have not ripened   125 **touching . . . skill** reaching now the age of mature judgment   127 **o'erlook** read over   129 **Wherefore** Why

135 **Good troth, good sooth** i.e., Indeed, truly   138 **lord of** i.e., possessor of.   **gentleness** courtesy.   139 **of** by   140 **abused** ill treated.
145–6 **as . . . deceive** as renounced heresies are hated most by those persons who formerly were deceived by them   148 **Of . . . of** by . . . by   149 **address** direct, apply   156 **prey** act of preying.   159 **an if** if   160 **of all loves** for love's sake.
**3.1. Location: The action is continuous.**
0.1 *clowns* rustics   2 **Pat** On the dot, punctually   4 **brake** thicket.   **tiring-house** attiring area, hence backstage   7 **bully** i.e., worthy, jolly, fine fellow   12 **By'r lakin** By our ladykin, i.e., the Virgin Mary.   **parlous** perilous, alarming

STARVELING   I believe we must leave the killing out, when all is done.    14

BOTTOM   Not a whit. I have a device to make all well. Write me a prologue, and let the prologue seem to say, we will do no harm with our swords, and that Pyramus is not killed indeed; and for the more better assurance, tell them that I, Pyramus, am not Pyramus but Bottom the weaver. This will put them out of fear.    16

QUINCE   Well, we will have such a prologue, and it shall be written in eight and six.    22

BOTTOM   No, make it two more: let it be written in eight and eight.

SNOUT   Will not the ladies be afeard of the lion?

STARVELING   I fear it, I promise you.

BOTTOM   Masters, you ought to consider with yourself, to bring in—God shield us!—a lion among ladies is a most dreadful thing. For there is not a more fearful wildfowl than your lion living, and we ought to look to 't.    28   29

SNOUT   Therefore another prologue must tell he is not a lion.

BOTTOM   Nay, you must name his name, and half his face must be seen through the lion's neck, and he himself must speak through, saying thus or to the same defect: "Ladies," or "Fair ladies, I would wish you," or "I would request you," or "I would entreat you, not to fear, not to tremble; my life for yours. If you think I come hither as a lion, it were pity of my life. No, I am no such thing; I am a man as other men are." And there indeed let him name his name, and tell them plainly he is Snug the joiner.    37   39   40   43

QUINCE   Well, it shall be so. But there is two hard things: that is, to bring the moonlight into a chamber; for, you know, Pyramus and Thisbe meet by moonlight.

SNOUT   Doth the moon shine that night we play our play?

BOTTOM   A calendar, a calendar! Look in the almanac. Find out moonshine, find out moonshine.

*[They consult an almanac.]*

QUINCE   Yes, it doth shine that night.

BOTTOM   Why then may you leave a casement of the great chamber window where we play open, and the moon may shine in at the casement.    52

QUINCE   Ay; or else one must come in with a bush of thorns and a lantern and say he comes to disfigure, or to present, the person of Moonshine. Then there is another thing: we must have a wall in the great    55   56

chamber; for Pyramus and Thisbe, says the story, did talk through the chink of a wall.

SNOUT   You can never bring in a wall. What say you, Bottom?

BOTTOM   Some man or other must present Wall. And let him have some plaster, or some loam, or some roughcast about him, to signify wall; or let him hold his fingers thus, and through that cranny shall Pyramus and Thisbe whisper.    64   65

QUINCE   If that may be, then all is well. Come, sit down, every mother's son, and rehearse your parts. Pyramus, you begin. When you have spoken your speech, enter into that brake, and so everyone according to his cue.

*Enter Robin [Puck].*

PUCK *[aside]*
What hempen homespuns have we swagg'ring here    72
So near the cradle of the Fairy Queen?    73
What, a play toward? I'll be an auditor;    74
An actor, too, perhaps, if I see cause.

QUINCE   Speak, Pyramus. Thisbe, stand forth.

BOTTOM *[as Pyramus]*
"Thisbe, the flowers of odious savors sweet—"

QUINCE   Odors, odors.

BOTTOM   "—Odors savors sweet;
    So hath thy breath, my dearest Thisbe dear.
But hark, a voice! Stay thou but here awhile,
    And by and by I will to thee appear."    *Exit.*

PUCK   A stranger Pyramus than e'er played here. *[Exit.]*    83

FLUTE   Must I speak now?

QUINCE   Ay, marry, must you; for you must understand he goes but to see a noise that he heard, and is to come again.

FLUTE *[as Thisbe]*
"Most radiant Pyramus, most lily-white of hue,
    Of color like the red rose on triumphant brier,    89
Most brisky juvenal and eke most lovely Jew,    90
    As true as truest horse that yet would never tire.
I'll meet thee, Pyramus, at Ninny's tomb."

QUINCE   "Ninus' tomb," man. Why, you must not speak that yet. That you answer to Pyramus. You speak all your part at once, cues and all. Pyramus, enter. Your cue is past; it is "never tire."    93   95

FLUTE
Oh—"As true as truest horse that yet would never tire."    97

*[Enter Puck, and Bottom as Pyramus with the ass head.]*

---

**14 when all is done** i.e., when all is said and done.   **16 Write me** i.e., Write at my suggestion. (*Me* is used colloquially.)   **22 eight and six** alternating lines of eight and six syllables, a common ballad measure.   **28 lion among ladies** (A contemporary pamphlet tells how, at the christening in 1594 of Prince Henry, eldest son of King James VI of Scotland, later James I of England, a "blackamoor" instead of a lion drew the triumphal chariot, since the lion's presence might have "brought some fear to the nearest.")   **29 fearful** fear-inspiring   **37 defect** (Bottom's blunder for "effect.")   **39 my life for yours** i.e., I pledge my life to make your lives safe.   **40 it were . . . life** i.e., I should be sorry, by my life; or, my life would be endangered.   **43 joiner** expert carpenter.   **52 casement** hinged window   **55–6 bush of thorns** bundle of thornbush fagots. (Part of the accoutrements of the man in the moon, according to the popular notions of the time, along with his lantern and his dog.)   **56 disfigure** (Quince's blunder for "figure," "represent.")

**64–5 roughcast** a mixture of lime and gravel used to plaster the outside of buildings   **72 hempen homespuns** i.e., rustics dressed in homespun fabric made from hemp   **73 cradle** i.e., Titania's bower   **74 toward** about to take place.   **83 A stranger . . . here** The strangest Pyramus you ever saw.   **89 triumphant** magnificent   **90 brisky juvenal** lively youth. **eke** also. **Jew** (A desperate attempt to rhyme with *hue*, inspired perhaps by the first syllable of *juvenal*.)   **93 Ninus'** Ninus was the mythical founder of Nineveh (whose wife, Semiramis, was supposed to have built the walls of Babylon where the story of Pyramus and Thisbe takes place)   **95 part** (An actor's *part* was a script consisting only of his speeches and their cues.)   **97.1–2 with the ass head** (This stage direction, taken from the Folio, presumably refers to a standard stage property.)

BOTTOM
"If I were fair, Thisbe, I were only thine."                    98
QUINCE    Oh, monstrous! Oh, strange! We are haunted.
Pray, masters! Fly, masters! Help!

[*Exeunt Quince, Snug, Flute,*
*Snout, and Starveling.*]

PUCK
I'll follow you: I'll lead you about a round,           101
    Through bog, through bush, through brake,
        through brier.
Sometimes a horse I'll be, sometimes a hound,
    A hog, a headless bear, sometimes a fire;           104
And neigh, and bark, and grunt, and roar, and burn,
Like horse, hound, hog, bear, fire, at every turn.  *Exit.*
BOTTOM    Why do they run away? This is a knavery of
them to make me afeard.

*Enter Snout.*

SNOUT    Oh, Bottom, thou art changed! What do I see on
thee?
BOTTOM    What do you see? You see an ass head of your
own, do you?                          [*Exit Snout.*]

*Enter Quince.*

QUINCE    Bless thee, Bottom, bless thee! Thou art trans-  113
lated.                                          *Exit.* 114
BOTTOM    I see their knavery. This is to make an ass of
me, to fright me, if they could. But I will not stir from
this place, do what they can. I will walk up and down
here, and I will sing, that they shall hear I am not
afraid.                                     [*He sings.*]
    The ouzel cock so black of hue,                     120
        With orange-tawny bill,
    The throstle with his note so true,                 122
        The wren with little quill—                     123
TITANIA [*awaking*]
What angel wakes me from my flow'ry bed?
BOTTOM [*sings*]
    The finch, the sparrow, and the lark,
        The plainsong cuckoo gray,                      126
    Whose note full many a man doth mark,
        And dares not answer nay—                       128
For indeed, who would set his wit to so foolish a bird?  129
Who would give a bird the lie, though he cry "cuckoo"  130
never so?                                            131
TITANIA
I pray thee, gentle mortal, sing again.
Mine ear is much enamored of thy note;
So is mine eye enthrallèd to thy shape;
And thy fair virtue's force perforce doth move me     135
On the first view to say, to swear, I love thee.

BOTTOM    Methinks, mistress, you should have little reason for that. And yet, to say the truth, reason and love
keep little company together nowadays—the more the
pity that some honest neighbors will not make them
friends. Nay, I can gleek upon occasion.             141
TITANIA
Thou art as wise as thou art beautiful.
BOTTOM    Not so, neither. But if I had wit enough to get
out of this wood, I have enough to serve mine own   144
turn.                                                145
TITANIA
Out of this wood do not desire to go.
Thou shalt remain here, whether thou wilt or no.
I am a spirit of no common rate.                     148
The summer still doth tend upon my state,            149
And I do love thee. Therefore, go with me.
I'll give thee fairies to attend on thee,
And they shall fetch thee jewels from the deep,
And sing while thou on pressèd flowers dost sleep.
And I will purge thy mortal grossness so
That thou shalt like an airy spirit go.—
Peaseblossom, Cobweb, Mote, and Mustardseed!         156

*Enter four Fairies [Peaseblossom, Cobweb,*
*Mote, and Mustardseed].*

PEASEBLOSSOM    Ready.
COBWEB
And I.
MOTE    And I.
MUSTARDSEED And I.
ALL                         Where shall we go?
TITANIA
Be kind and courteous to this gentleman.
Hop in his walks and gambol in his eyes;             160
Feed him with apricots and dewberries,               161
    With purple grapes, green figs, and mulberries;
The honey bags steal from the humble-bees,
And for night tapers crop their waxen thighs,        164
And light them at the fiery glowworms' eyes,         165
To have my love to bed and to arise;
And pluck the wings from painted butterflies
To fan the moonbeams from his sleeping eyes.
Nod to him, elves, and do him courtesies.
PEASEBLOSSOM    Hail, mortal!
COBWEB    Hail!
MOTE    Hail!
MUSTARDSEED    Hail!
BOTTOM    I cry Your Worships mercy, heartily. I beseech  174
Your Worship's name.
COBWEB    Cobweb.

---

98 **If** Even if.  **fair** handsome.  **were** would be   101 **about a round**
roundabout   104 **fire** will-o'-the-wisp   113–14 **translated** transformed.
120 **ouzel cock** male blackbird   122 **throstle** song thrush   123 **with**
**little quill** with small pipe, i.e., high-pitched note; or else with small
feathers   126 **plainsong** singing a melody without variations
128 **dares . . . nay** i.e., cannot deny that he is a cuckold   129 **set his**
**wit to** employ his intelligence to answer   130 **give . . . lie** call the bird
a liar   131 **never so** ever so much.   135 **thy . . . force** the power of
your unblemished excellence

141 **gleek** jest   144–5 **serve . . . turn** answer my purpose.   148 **rate**
rank, value.   149 **still . . . state** always waits upon me as a part of my
royal retinue   156 **Mote** i.e., speck. (The two words *moth* and *mote*
were pronounced alike, and both meanings may be present.)
160 **gambol in his eyes** jump about playfully in his sight (i.e., before
him)   161 **dewberries** blackberries   164 **And . . . thighs** i.e., and crop
off the waxen thighs of bumblebees to serve as wax candles in the
night   165 **eyes** (In fact, the light is emitted by the abdomen. *Eyes*
may be metaphorical.)   174 **I cry . . . mercy** I beg pardon of Your
Worships (for presuming to ask a question)

BOTTOM   I shall desire you of more acquaintance, good 177
Master Cobweb. If I cut my finger, I shall make bold 178
with you.—Your name, honest gentleman? 179

PEASEBLOSSOM   Peaseblossom.

BOTTOM   I pray you, commend me to Mistress Squash, 181
your mother, and to Master Peascod, your father. 182
Good Master Peaseblossom, I shall desire you of more
acquaintance too.—Your name, I beseech you, sir?

MUSTARDSEED   Mustardseed.

BOTTOM   Good Master Mustardseed, I know your 186
patience well. That same cowardly, giantlike ox-beef 187
hath devoured many a gentleman of your house. I
promise you, your kindred hath made my eyes water 189
ere now. I desire you of more acquaintance, good
Master Mustardseed.

TITANIA
Come wait upon him; lead him to my bower.
    The moon methinks looks with a wat'ry eye;
And when she weeps, weeps every little flower, 194
    Lamenting some enforcèd chastity. 195
    Tie up my lover's tongue; bring him silently. 196

                                        *Exeunt.*

# [3.2]

*Enter [Oberon,] King of Fairies.*

OBERON
I wonder if Titania be awaked;
Then, what it was that next came in her eye,
Which she must dote on in extremity.

*[Enter] Robin Goodfellow [Puck].*

Here comes my messenger. How now, mad spirit?
What night-rule now about this haunted grove? 5

PUCK
My mistress with a monster is in love.
Near to her close and consecrated bower, 7
While she was in her dull and sleeping hour, 8
A crew of patches, rude mechanicals, 9
That work for bread upon Athenian stalls, 10
Were met together to rehearse a play
Intended for great Theseus' nuptial day.
The shallowest thickskin of that barren sort, 13
Who Pyramus presented, in their sport 14
Forsook his scene and entered in a brake. 15
When I did him at this advantage take,

An ass's noll I fixèd on his head. 17
Anon his Thisbe must be answerèd,
And forth my mimic comes. When they him spy, 19
As wild geese that the creeping fowler eye, 20
Or russet-pated choughs, many in sort, 21
Rising and cawing at the gun's report,
Sever themselves and madly sweep the sky, 23
So, at his sight, away his fellows fly;
And, at our stamp, here o'er and o'er one falls;
He "Murder!" cries and help from Athens calls.
Their sense thus weak, lost with their fears thus
    strong, 27
Made senseless things begin to do them wrong, 28
For briers and thorns at their apparel snatch;
Some, sleeves—some, hats; from yielders all things
    catch. 30
I led them on in this distracted fear
And left sweet Pyramus translated there,
When in that moment, so it came to pass,
Titania waked and straightway loved an ass.

OBERON
This falls out better than I could devise.
But hast thou yet latched the Athenian's eyes 36
With the love juice, as I did bid thee do?

PUCK
I took him sleeping—that is finished too—
And the Athenian woman by his side,
That, when he waked, of force she must be eyed. 40

*Enter Demetrius and Hermia.*

OBERON
Stand close. This is the same Athenian.

PUCK
This is the woman, but not this the man.

                        *[They stand aside.]*

DEMETRIUS
Oh, why rebuke you him that loves you so?
Lay breath so bitter on your bitter foe.

HERMIA
Now I but chide; but I should use thee worse,
For thou, I fear, hast given me cause to curse.
If thou hast slain Lysander in his sleep,
Being o'er shoes in blood, plunge in the deep, 48
And kill me too.
The sun was not so true unto the day
As he to me. Would he have stolen away
From sleeping Hermia? I'll believe as soon
This whole earth may be bored, and that the moon 53
May through the center creep, and so displease
Her brother's noontide with th'Antipodes. 55

177 I . . . acquaintance I crave to be better acquainted with you
178–9 If . . . you (Cobwebs were used to stanch bleeding.)   179 honest
worthy   181 Squash unripe pea pod   182 Peascod ripe pea pod
186–7 your patience what you have endured. (Mustard is eaten with
beef.)   189 water (1) weep for sympathy (2) smart, sting   194 And . . .
flower (Dew was thought to fall from the heavens in greater proportion
as the moon shown fully.)   195 enforcèd violated. (The moon is associated throughout the play with the goddess Diana and chastity.)
196 Tie . . . tongue (Presumably Bottom is braying like an ass.)
3.2. Location: The wood.
5 night-rule diversion or misrule for the night   7 close secret   8 dull
drowsy   9 patches clowns, fools.  rude mechanicals ignorant artisans   10 stalls market booths   13 barren sort stupid company or
crew   14 presented acted   15 scene playing area

17 noll noddle, head   19 mimic actor   20 fowler hunter of game
birds   21 russet-pated choughs reddish brown or gray-headed
jackdaws.  in sort in a flock   23 Sever themselves i.e., scatter
27–8 Their . . . wrong Their weakened physical senses, disabled by
their strong fears, made it seem to them as though inanimate things
in the forest were attacking them   30 from . . . catch the forest
snatches away everything from those who yield to it.   36 latched
anointed   40 of force perforce   48 Being o'er shoes having waded
in so far   53 whole solid   55 Her . . . Antipodes i.e., the sun's noon-
time on the opposite side of the earth, among the people who live
there, the Antipodes.

It cannot be but thou hast murdered him;
So should a murderer look, so dead, so grim.                      57

DEMETRIUS
So should the murdered look, and so should I,
Pierced through the heart with your stern cruelty.
Yet you, the murderer, look as bright, as clear
As yonder Venus in her glimmering sphere.

HERMIA
What's this to my Lysander? Where is he?                          62
Ah, good Demetrius, wilt thou give him me?

DEMETRIUS
I had rather give his carcass to my hounds.

HERMIA
Out, dog! Out, cur! Thou driv'st me past the bounds
Of maiden's patience. Hast thou slain him, then?
Henceforth be never numbered among men.
Oh, once tell true, tell true, even for my sake:                 68
Durst thou have looked upon him being awake?                     69
And hast thou killed him sleeping? Oh, brave touch!              70
Could not a worm, an adder, do so much?                          71
An adder did it; for with doubler tongue                         72
Than thine, thou serpent, never adder stung.

DEMETRIUS
You spend your passion on a misprised mood.                      74
I am not guilty of Lysander's blood,
Nor is he dead, for aught that I can tell.

HERMIA
I pray thee, tell me then that he is well.

DEMETRIUS
And if I could, what should I get therefor?                      78

HERMIA
A privilege never to see me more.
And from thy hated presence part I so.
See me no more, whether he be dead or no.          *Exit.*

DEMETRIUS
There is no following her in this fierce vein.
Here therefore for a while I will remain.
So sorrow's heaviness doth heavier grow                          84
For debt that bankrupt sleep doth sorrow owe,                    85
Which now in some slight measure it will pay,                    86
If for his tender here I make some stay.                         87
                         *[He] lie[s] down [and sleeps].*

OBERON
What hast thou done? Thou hast mistaken quite
And laid the love juice on some true love's sight.
Of thy misprision must perforce ensue                            90
Some true love turned, and not a false turned true.

PUCK
Then fate o'errules, that, one man holding troth,                92
A million fail, confounding oath on oath.                        93

OBERON
About the wood go swifter than the wind,
And Helena of Athens look thou find.
All fancy-sick she is and pale of cheer                           96
With sighs of love, that cost the fresh blood dear.               97
By some illusion see thou bring her here.
I'll charm his eyes against she do appear.                        99

PUCK
I go, I go, look how I go,
Swifter than arrow from the Tartar's bow.        *[Exit.]*       101

OBERON *[applying love juice to Demetrius's eyes]*
Flower of this purple dye,
Hit with Cupid's archery,                                        103
Sink in apple of his eye.                                        104
When his love he doth espy,                                      105
Let her shine as gloriously
As the Venus of the sky.
When thou wak'st, if she be by,
Beg of her for remedy.

                         *Enter Puck.*

PUCK
Captain of our fairy band,
Helena is here at hand,
And the youth, mistook by me,
Pleading for a lover's fee.                                      113
Shall we their fond pageant see?                                 114
Lord, what fools these mortals be!

OBERON
Stand aside. The noise they make
Will cause Demetrius to awake.

PUCK
Then will two at once woo one;
That must needs be sport alone.                                  119
And those things do best please me
That befall preposterously.                                      121
                         *[They stand aside.]*

                *Enter Lysander and Helena.*

LYSANDER
Why should you think that I should woo in scorn?
Scorn and derision never come in tears.
Look when I vow, I weep; and vows so born,                       124
In their nativity all truth appears.                             125
How can these things in me seem scorn to you,
Bearing the badge of faith to prove them true?

HELENA
You do advance your cunning more and more.                       128
When truth kills truth, oh, devilish-holy fray!                  129
These vows are Hermia's. Will you give her o'er?
Weigh oath with oath, and you will nothing weigh;

---

**57 dead** deadly, or deathly pale   **62 to** to do with   **68 once** once and for all   **69 being awake** when he was awake   **70 brave touch!** fine stroke! (Said ironically.)   **71 worm** serpent   **72 doubler** (1) more forked (2) more deceitful   **74 You ... mood** Your anger is misdirected.   **78 therefor** in return for that.   **84–7 So ... stay** The heaviness of sorrow grows still heavier when sleepiness adds to the weariness caused by sorrow, which debt to sleepiness I will now repay in part if I can stop here and accept what sleep has to offer. **90 misprision** mistake   **92–3 Then ... oath** If so, then fate prevails; for each male who is able to keep true faith in love, a million will fail, breaking oath on oath.

**96 fancy-sick** lovesick.   **cheer** complexion   **97 sighs ... dear** (Each sigh was supposed to cost the heart a drop of blood.)   **99 against ... appear** in anticipation of her coming.   **101 Tartar's bow** (Tartars were famed for their skill with the bow.)   **103 Hit ... archery** (See 2.1. 157–68.)   **104 apple** pupil   **105 his love** Helena   **113 fee** privilege, reward.   **114 fond pageant** foolish spectacle   **119 alone** unequaled. **121 preposterously** out of the natural order.   **124 Look when** Whenever   **124–5 vows ... appears** i.e., vows made by one who is weeping give evidence thereby of their sincerity.   **128 advance** carry forward, display   **129 When ... truth** i.e., When one of your vows cancels the other

Your vows to her and me, put in two scales,
Will even weigh, and both as light as tales.          133

LYSANDER
I had no judgment when to her I swore.

HELENA
Nor none, in my mind, now you give her o'er.

LYSANDER
Demetrius loves her, and he loves not you.

DEMETRIUS [*awaking*]
O Helen, goddess, nymph, perfect, divine!
To what, my love, shall I compare thine eyne?
Crystal is muddy. Oh, how ripe in show          139
Thy lips, those kissing cherries, tempting grow!
That pure congealèd white, high Taurus' snow,          141
Fanned with the eastern wind, turns to a crow          142
When thou hold'st up thy hand. Oh, let me kiss
This princess of pure white, this seal of bliss!          144

HELENA
Oh, spite! Oh, hell! I see you all are bent
To set against me for your merriment.          146
If you were civil and knew courtesy,
You would not do me thus much injury.
Can you not hate me, as I know you do,
But you must join in souls to mock me too?          150
If you were men, as men you are in show,
You would not use a gentle lady so—
To vow, and swear, and superpraise my parts,          153
When I am sure you hate me with your hearts.
You both are rivals, and love Hermia,
And now both rivals to mock Helena.
A trim exploit, a manly enterprise,          157
To conjure tears up in a poor maid's eyes
With your derision! None of noble sort          159
Would so offend a virgin and extort          160
A poor soul's patience, all to make you sport.

LYSANDER
You are unkind, Demetrius. Be not so.
For you love Hermia; this you know I know.
And here, with all good will, with all my heart,
In Hermia's love I yield you up my part;
And yours of Helena to me bequeath,
Whom I do love, and will do till my death.

HELENA
Never did mockers waste more idle breath.

DEMETRIUS
Lysander, keep thy Hermia; I will none.          169
If e'er I loved her, all that love is gone.
My heart to her but as guestwise sojourned,          171
And now to Helen is it home returned,
There to remain.

LYSANDER          Helen, it is not so.

DEMETRIUS
Disparage not the faith thou dost not know,
Lest, to thy peril, thou aby it dear.          175
Look where thy love comes; yonder is thy dear.

*Enter Hermia.*

HERMIA
Dark night, that from the eye his function takes,          177
The ear more quick of apprehension makes          178
Wherein it doth impair the seeing sense,
It pays the hearing double recompense.
Thou art not by mine eye, Lysander, found;
Mine ear, I thank it, brought me to thy sound.
But why unkindly didst thou leave me so?

LYSANDER
Why should he stay, whom love doth press to go?

HERMIA
What love could press Lysander from my side?

LYSANDER
Lysander's love, that would not let him bide—
Fair Helena, who more engilds the night
Than all yon fiery oes and eyes of light.          188
Why seek'st thou me? Could not this make thee know
The hate I bear thee made me leave thee so?

HERMIA
You speak not as you think. It cannot be.

HELENA
Lo, she is one of this confederacy!
Now I perceive they have conjoined all three
To fashion this false sport, in spite of me.          194
Injurious Hermia, most ungrateful maid!
Have you conspired, have you with these contrived
To bait me with this foul derision?          197
Is all the counsel that we two have shared—          198
The sisters' vows, the hours that we have spent
When we have chid the hasty-footed time
For parting us—oh, is all forgot?          201
All schooldays' friendship, childhood innocence?
We, Hermia, like two artificial gods          203
Have with our needles created both one flower,
Both on one sampler, sitting on one cushion,
Both warbling of one song, both in one key,
As if our hands, our sides, voices, and minds
Had been incorporate. So we grew together,          208
Like to a double cherry, seeming parted,
But yet an union in partition,
Two lovely berries molded on one stem;
So, with two seeming bodies but one heart,
Two of the first, like coats in heraldry,          213
Due but to one and crownèd with one crest.          214
And will you rend our ancient love asunder,
To join with men in scorning your poor friend?
It is not friendly, 'tis not maidenly.

---

133 **Will even weigh** will weigh exactly the same.   **tales** lies.
139 **show** appearance   141 **Taurus'** Taurus was a lofty mountain
range in Asia Minor   142 **turns to a crow** i.e., seems black by contrast
144 **seal** pledge   146 **set against** attack   150 **in souls** i.e., heart and
soul   153 **superpraise** overpraise.   **parts** qualities   157 **trim** pretty,
fine. (Said ironically.)   159 **sort** character, quality   160 **extort** twist,
torture   169 **will none** want no part of her.   171 **to . . . sojourned**
only visited with her

175 **aby** pay for   177 **his** its   178 **The ear . . . makes** makes the ear
more quick to hear and understand   188 **oes** spangles (here, stars)
194 **in spite of me** to vex me.   197 **bait** torment, as one sets on dogs
to bait a bear   198 **counsel** confidential talk   201 **For parting us** for
not allowing us to be together longer   203 **artificial** skilled in art or
creation   208 **incorporate** of one body.   213–14 **Two . . . crest** i.e., we,
having two separate bodies, just as a coat of arms in heraldry can be
represented twice on a shield but surmounted by a single crest.

Our sex, as well as I, may chide you for it,
Though I alone do feel the injury.

HERMIA
I am amazèd at your passionate words.
I scorn you not. It seems that you scorn me.

HELENA
Have you not set Lysander, as in scorn,
To follow me and praise my eyes and face?
And made your other love, Demetrius,
Who even but now did spurn me with his foot,
To call me goddess, nymph, divine, and rare,
Precious, celestial? Wherefore speaks he this
To her he hates? And wherefore doth Lysander
Deny your love, so rich within his soul,
And tender me, forsooth, affection,                              230
But by your setting on, by your consent?
What though I be not so in grace as you,                         232
So hung upon with love, so fortunate,                            233
But miserable most, to love unloved?                             234
This you should pity rather than despise.

HERMIA
I understand not what you mean by this.

HELENA
Ay, do! Persever, counterfeit sad looks,                         237
Make mouths upon me when I turn my back,                         238
Wink each at other, hold the sweet jest up.                      239
This sport, well carried, shall be chronicled                    240
If you have any pity, grace, or manners,
You would not make me such an argument.                          242
But fare ye well. 'Tis partly my own fault,
Which death, or absence, soon shall remedy.

LYSANDER
Stay, gentle Helena; hear my excuse,
My love, my life, my soul, fair Helena!

HELENA
Oh, excellent!

HERMIA [to Lysander]    Sweet, do not scorn her so.

DEMETRIUS [to Lysander]
If she cannot entreat, I can compel.                             248

LYSANDER
Thou canst compel no more than she entreat.
Thy threats have no more strength than her weak
     prayers.—
Helen, I love thee, by my life, I do!
I swear by that which I will lose for thee,                      252
To prove him false that says I love thee not.

DEMETRIUS [to Helena]
I say I love thee more than he can do.

LYSANDER
If thou say so, withdraw, and prove it too.                      255

DEMETRIUS
Quick, come!

HERMIA            Lysander, whereto tends all this?

LYSANDER
Away, you Ethiope!
                    [He tries to break away from Hermia.]

DEMETRIUS            No, no; he'll                                257
Seem to break loose; take on as you would follow,               258
But yet come not. You are a tame man. Go!

LYSANDER [to Hermia]
Hang off, thou cat, thou burr! Vile thing, let loose,           260
Or I will shake thee from me like a serpent!

HERMIA
Why are you grown so rude? What change is this,
Sweet love?

LYSANDER            Thy love? Out, tawny Tartar, out!
Out, loathèd med'cine! O hated potion, hence!                   264

HERMIA
Do you not jest?

HELENA            Yes, sooth, and so do you.                     265

LYSANDER
Demetrius, I will keep my word with thee.

DEMETRIUS
I would I had your bond, for I perceive
A weak bond holds you. I'll not trust your word.                268

LYSANDER
What, should I hurt her, strike her, kill her dead?
Although I hate her, I'll not harm her so.

HERMIA
What, can you do me greater harm than hate?
Hate me? Wherefore? Oh, me, what news, my love?                 272
Am not I Hermia? Are not you Lysander?
I am as fair now as I was erewhile.                             274
Since night you loved me; yet since night you left me.
Why, then you left me—oh, the gods forbid!—
In earnest, shall I say?

LYSANDER            Ay, by my life!
And never did desire to see thee more.
Therefore be out of hope, of question, of doubt;
Be certain, nothing truer. 'Tis no jest
That I do hate thee and love Helena.

HERMIA [to Helena]
Oh, me! You juggler! You cankerblossom!                          282
You thief of love! What, have you come by night
And stol'n my love's heart from him?

HELENA                          Fine, i'faith!
Have you no modesty, no maiden shame,
No touch of bashfulness? What, will you tear
Impatient answers from my gentle tongue?
Fie, fie! You counterfeit, you puppet, you!                      288

HERMIA
"Puppet"? Why, so! Ay, that way goes the game.
Now I perceive that she hath made compare
Between our statures; she hath urged her height,
And with her personage, her tall personage,

---

230 **tender** offer    232 **grace** favor    233 **So . . . love** so favored with wooers who hang upon one so persistently    234 **But . . . unloved** but instead to be the most miserable of persons, loving where my love is not reciprocated.    237 **sad** grave, serious    238 **mouths** i.e., mows, faces, grimaces.    **upon** at    239 **hold . . . up** keep up the joke.    240 **carried** carried out.    **shall be chronicled** deserves to be set down in the chronicles as a supreme example of duplicitous love rivalry.    242 **argument** subject for a jest.    248 **entreat** i.e., succeed by entreaty    252 **I swear . . . for thee** I swear by my life, which I would willingly sacrifice to do you service    255 **withdraw . . . too** i.e., withdraw with me and prove your claim in a duel. (The two gentlemen are armed.)

257 **Ethiope** (Referring to Hermia's relatively dark hair and complexion; see also *tawny Tartar* six lines later.)    258 **take on as** act as if, make a fuss as if    260 **Hang off** Let go    264 **med'cine** i.e., poison    265 **sooth** truly    268 **weak bond** i.e., Hermia's arm. (With a pun on *bond*, "oath," in the previous line.)    272 **what news** what is the matter    274 **erewhile** just now.    282 **cankerblossom** worm that destroys the flower bud, or wild rose.    288 **puppet** (1) counterfeit (2) dwarfish woman (in reference to Hermia's smaller stature)

Her height, forsooth, she hath prevailed with him.
And are you grown so high in his esteem
Because I am so dwarfish and so low?
How low am I, thou painted maypole? Speak!
How low am I? I am not yet so low
But that my nails can reach unto thine eyes.

[*She flails at Helena but is restrained.*]

HELENA
I pray you, though you mock me, gentlemen,
Let her not hurt me. I was never curst;                    300
I have no gift at all in shrewishness;
I am a right maid for my cowardice.                        302
Let her not strike me. You perhaps may think,
Because she is something lower than myself,                304
That I can match her.

HERMIA                    Lower? Hark, again!

HELENA
Good Hermia, do not be so bitter with me.
I evermore did love you, Hermia,
Did ever keep your counsels, never wronged you,
Save that, in love unto Demetrius,
I told him of your stealth unto this wood.                 310
He followed you; for love I followed him.
But he hath chid me hence and threatened me               312
To strike me, spurn me, nay, to kill me too.              313
And now, so you will let me quiet go,                      314
To Athens will I bear my folly back
And follow you no further. Let me go.
You see how simple and how fond I am.                      317

HERMIA
Why, get you gone. Who is't that hinders you?

HELENA
A foolish heart, that I leave here behind.

HERMIA
What, with Lysander?

HELENA                    With Demetrius.

LYSANDER
Be not afraid; she shall not harm thee, Helena.

DEMETRIUS
No, sir, she shall not, though you take her part.

HELENA
Oh, when she is angry, she is keen and shrewd.            323
She was a vixen when she went to school;
And though she be but little, she is fierce.

HERMIA
"Little" again? Nothing but "low" and "little"?—
Why will you suffer her to flout me thus?
Let me come to her.

LYSANDER                    Get you gone, you dwarf!
You minimus, of hind'ring knotgrass made!                 329
You bead, you acorn!

DEMETRIUS                    You are too officious
In her behalf that scorns your services.
Let her alone. Speak not of Helena;

Take not her part. For, if thou dost intend              333
Never so little show of love to her,
Thou shalt aby it.

LYSANDER                    Now she holds me not.        335
Now follow, if thou dar'st, to try whose right,
Of thine or mine, is most in Helena.          [*Exit.*]

DEMETRIUS
Follow? Nay, I'll go with thee, cheek by jowl.           338

[*Exit, following Lysander.*]

HERMIA
You, mistress, all this coil is 'long of you.            339
Nay, go not back.

HELENA                    I will not trust you, I,       340
Nor longer stay in your curst company.
Your hands than mine are quicker for a fray;
My legs are longer, though, to run away.        [*Exit.*]

HERMIA
I am amazed and know not what to say.          *Exit.*

[*Oberon and Puck come forward.*]

OBERON
This is thy negligence. Still thou mistak'st,
Or else commit'st thy knaveries willfully.

PUCK
Believe me, king of shadows, I mistook.
Did not you tell me I should know the man
By the Athenian garments he had on?
And so far blameless proves my enterprise
That I have 'nointed an Athenian's eyes;
And so far am I glad it so did sort,                      352
As this their jangling I esteem a sport.                  353

OBERON
Thou see'st these lovers seek a place to fight.
Hie therefore, Robin, overcast the night;                355
The starry welkin cover thou anon                         356
With drooping fog as black as Acheron,                    357
And lead these testy rivals so astray
As one come not within another's way.                     359
Like to Lysander sometimes frame thy tongue,             360
Then stir Demetrius up with bitter wrong;                 361
And sometimes rail thou like Demetrius.
And from each other look thou lead them thus,
Till o'er their brows death-counterfeiting sleep
With leaden legs and batty wings doth creep.             365
Then crush this herb into Lysander's eye,                366

[*giving herb*]

Whose liquor hath this virtuous property,                367
To take from thence all error with his might             368
And make his eyeballs roll with wonted sight.            369
When they next wake, all this derision                    370
Shall seem a dream and fruitless vision,

---

**300 curst** shrewish   **302 right** true.   **for** for all   **304 something** somewhat   **310 stealth** stealing away   **312 chid me hence** driven me away with his scolding   **313 spurn** kick   **314 so** if only   **317 fond** foolish   **323 keen and shrewd** fierce and shrewish.   **329 minimus** diminutive creature.   **knotgrass** a weed, an infusion of which was thought to stunt the growth

**333 intend** give sign of   **335 aby** pay for   **338 cheek by jowl** i.e., side by side.   **339 coil** turmoil, dissension.   **'long of** on account of   **340 go not back** i.e., don't retreat. (Hermia is again proposing a fight.)   **352 so far** at least to this extent.   **sort** turn out   **353 As** in that   **355 Hie** Hasten   **356 welkin** sky   **357 Acheron** river of Hades (here representing Hades itself)   **359 As** that   **360 frame thy tongue** fashion your speech   **361 wrong** insults   **365 batty** batlike   **366 this herb** i.e., the antidote (mentioned in 2.1.184) to love-in-idleness   **367 virtuous** efficacious   **368 his** its   **369 wonted** accustomed   **370 derision** laughable business

And back to Athens shall the lovers wend
With league whose date till death shall never end.   373
Whiles I in this affair do thee employ,
I'll to my queen and beg her Indian boy;
And then I will her charmèd eye release
From monster's view, and all things shall be peace.

PUCK
My fairy lord, this must be done with haste,
For night's swift dragons cut the clouds full fast,   379
And yonder shines Aurora's harbinger,   380
At whose approach ghosts, wand'ring here and there,
Troop home to churchyards. Damnèd spirits all,
That in crossways and floods have burial,   383
Already to their wormy beds are gone.
For fear lest day should look their shames upon,
They willfully themselves exile from light
And must for aye consort with black-browed night.   387

OBERON
But we are spirits of another sort.
I with the Morning's love have oft made sport,   389
And, like a forester, the groves may tread   390
Even till the eastern gate, all fiery red,
Opening on Neptune with fair blessèd beams,   392
Turns into yellow gold his salt green streams.
But notwithstanding, haste, make no delay.
We may effect this business yet ere day.   [*Exit.*]

PUCK
Up and down, up and down,
I will lead them up and down.
I am feared in field and town.
Goblin, lead them up and down.   399
Here comes one.

*Enter Lysander.*

LYSANDER
Where art thou, proud Demetrius? Speak thou now.
PUCK   [*mimicking Demetrius*]
Here, villain, drawn and ready. Where art thou?   402
LYSANDER
I will be with thee straight.
PUCK                    Follow me, then,   403
To plainer ground.
   [*Lysander wanders about, following the voice.*]

*Enter Demetrius.*

DEMETRIUS            Lysander! Speak again!   404
Thou runaway, thou coward, art thou fled?
Speak! In some bush? Where dost thou hide thy head?

PUCK   [*mimicking Lysander*]
Thou coward, art thou bragging to the stars,
Telling the bushes that thou look'st for wars,
And wilt not come? Come, recreant; come, thou child,   409
I'll whip thee with a rod. He is defiled   410
That draws a sword on thee.
DEMETRIUS               Yea, art thou there?   411
PUCK
Follow my voice. We'll try no manhood here.   412
                                   *Exeunt.*

[*Lysander returns.*]

LYSANDER
He goes before me and still dares me on.
When I come where he calls, then he is gone.
The villain is much lighter-heeled than I.
I followed fast, but faster he did fly,
That fallen am I in dark uneven way,
And here will rest me. [*He lies down.*] Come, thou
   gentle day!
For if but once thou show me thy gray light,
I'll find Demetrius and revenge this spite. [*He sleeps.*]

[*Enter*] Robin [*Puck*] *and Demetrius.*

PUCK
Ho, ho, ho! Coward, why com'st thou not?
DEMETRIUS
Abide me, if thou dar'st; for well I wot   422
Thou runn'st before me, shifting every place,
And dar'st not stand nor look me in the face.
Where art thou now?
PUCK               Come hither. I am here.
DEMETRIUS
Nay, then, thou mock'st me. Thou shalt buy this dear,   426
If ever I thy face by daylight see.
Now go thy way. Faintness constraineth me
To measure out my length on this cold bed.
By day's approach look to be visited.
                      [*He lies down and sleeps.*]

*Enter Helena.*

HELENA
O weary night, O long and tedious night,
   Abate thy hours! Shine comforts from the east,   432
That I may back to Athens by daylight
   From these that my poor company detest;
And sleep, that sometimes shuts up sorrow's eye,
Steal me awhile from mine own company!
                      [*She lies down and*] sleep[*s*].

PUCK
Yet but three? Come one more;
Two of both kinds makes up four.
Here she comes, curst and sad.   439
Cupid is a knavish lad,
Thus to make poor females mad.

[*Enter Hermia.*]

---

373 **league** covenant.   **date** duration   379 **dragons** (Supposed here to be yoked to the car of the goddess of night or the moon.)
380 **Aurora's harbinger** the morning star, precursor of dawn
383 **crossways . . . burial** (Those who had committed suicide were buried at crossways, with a stake driven through them; those who intentionally or accidentally drowned [in *floods* or deep water] would be condemned to wander disconsolately for lack of burial rites.)
387 **for aye** forever   389 **the Morning's love** Cephalus, a beautiful youth beloved by Aurora; or perhaps the goddess of the dawn herself
390 **forester** keeper of a royal forest   392 **Neptune** i.e., the sea
399 **Goblin** Hobgoblin. (Puck refers to himself.)   402 **drawn** with drawn sword   403 **straight** immediately.   404 **plainer** more open.   s.d. *Lysander wanders about* (Lysander may exit here, but perhaps not; neither exit nor reentrance is indicated in the early texts.)

409 **recreant** cowardly wretch   410–11 **He is . . . on thee** i.e., A gentleman would be dishonored to draw on so pusillanimous a coward.   412 **We'll . . . here** This is no place for a manly battle of swords; let's look for something better suited.   422 **Abide** Confront, face.   **wot** know   426 **buy this dear** pay for this dearly   432 **Abate** lessen, shorten   439 **curst** ill-tempered

**HERMIA**

Never so weary, never so in woe,
  Bedabbled with the dew and torn with briers,
I can no further crawl, no further go;
  My legs can keep no pace with my desires.
Here will I rest me till the break of day.
Heavens shield Lysander, if they mean a fray!
                          [*She lies down and sleeps.*]

**PUCK**

          On the ground
          Sleep sound.
          I'll apply
          To your eye,
      Gentle lover, remedy.
              [*He squeezes the juice on Lysander's eyes.*]
          When thou wak'st,
          Thou tak'st
          True delight
          In the sight
      Of thy former lady's eye;
      And the country proverb known,
      That every man should take his own,
      In your waking shall be shown:
          Jack shall have Jill;                    461
          Naught shall go ill;
      The man shall have his mare again, and all shall
          be well.   [*Exit. The four sleeping lovers remain.*]

❧

# [4.1]

*Enter [Titania,] Queen of Fairies, and [Bottom
the] clown, and Fairies; and [Oberon,] the King,
behind them.*

**TITANIA**

Come, sit thee down upon this flow'ry bed,
  While I thy amiable cheeks do coy,                    2
And stick muskroses in thy sleek smooth head,          3
  And kiss thy fair large ears, my gentle joy.
                                    [*They recline.*]

**BOTTOM**   Where's Peaseblossom?

**PEASEBLOSSOM**   Ready.

**BOTTOM**   Scratch my head, Peaseblossom. Where's
Monsieur Cobweb?

**COBWEB**   Ready.

**BOTTOM**   Monsieur Cobweb, good monsieur, get you
your weapons in your hand, and kill me a red-hipped
humble-bee on the top of a thistle; and, good monsieur, bring me the honey bag. Do not fret yourself too
much in the action, monsieur; and, good monsieur,
have a care the honey bag break not. I would be loath
to have you overflown with a honey bag, signor.
                                    [*Exit Cobweb.*]
Where's Monsieur Mustardseed?

**MUSTARDSEED**   Ready.

**BOTTOM**   Give me your neaf, Monsieur Mustardseed.   19
Pray you, leave your courtesy, good monsieur.          20

**MUSTARDSEED**   What's your will?

**BOTTOM**   Nothing, good monsieur, but to help Cavalery   22
Cobweb to scratch. I must to the barber's, monsieur,   23
for methinks I am marvelous hairy about the face; and
I am such a tender ass, if my hair do but tickle me I
must scratch.

**TITANIA**

What, wilt thou hear some music, my sweet love?

**BOTTOM**   I have a reasonable good ear in music. Let's
have the tongs and the bones.                          29
                          [*Music: tongs, rural music.*]

**TITANIA**

Or say, sweet love, what thou desirest to eat.

**BOTTOM**   Truly, a peck of provender. I could munch    31
your good dry oats. Methinks I have a great desire to   32
a bottle of hay. Good hay, sweet hay, hath no fellow.   33

**TITANIA**

I have a venturous fairy that shall seek
The squirrel's hoard, and fetch thee new nuts.

**BOTTOM**   I had rather have a handful or two of dried
peas. But, I pray you, let none of your people stir me.  37
I have an exposition of sleep come upon me.            38

**TITANIA**

Sleep thou, and I will wind thee in my arms.—
Fairies, begone, and be all ways away.                 40
                                    [*Exeunt Fairies.*]
So doth the woodbine the sweet honeysuckle             41
Gently entwist; the female ivy so
Enrings the barky fingers of the elm.
Oh, how I love thee! How I dote on thee!
                                    [*They sleep.*]

*Enter Robin Goodfellow [Puck].*

**OBERON** [*coming forward*]

Welcome, good Robin. See'st thou this sweet sight?
Her dotage now I do begin to pity.
For, meeting her of late behind the wood
Seeking sweet favors for this hateful fool,            48
I did upbraid her and fall out with her.               49
For she his hairy temples then had rounded
With coronet of fresh and fragrant flowers;
And that same dew, which sometime on the buds          52
Was wont to swell like round and orient pearls,        53
Stood now within the pretty flowerets' eyes
Like tears that did their own disgrace bewail.         55
When I had at my pleasure taunted her,

---

**461 Jack shall have Jill** (Proverbial for "boy gets girl.")
**4.1. Location: The action is continuous. The four lovers are still
asleep on stage. (Compare with the Folio stage direction: "*They sleep
all the act.*")**
**2 amiable** lovely.   **coy** caress   **3 head** hair

**19 neaf** fist   **20 leave your courtesy** i.e., stop bowing, or put on your
hat   **22 Cavalery** Cavalier. (Form of address for a gentleman.)
**23 Cobweb** (Seemingly an error, since Cobweb has been sent to bring
honey, while Peaseblossom has been asked to scratch.)   **29 tongs . . .
bones** instruments for rustic music. (The tongs were played like a triangle, whereas the bones were held between the fingers and used as clap-
pers.)   **29.1 Music . . . music** (This stage direction is added from the
Folio.)   **31 peck of provender** one-quarter bushel of grain.   **32 your
good dry oats** the kind of good oats that people talk about. (The "your"
is not personal.)   **33 bottle** bundle.   **fellow** equal.   **37 stir** disturb
**38 exposition of** (Bottom's phrase for "disposition to.")   **40 all ways** in
all directions   **41 woodbine** bindweed, a climbing plant   **48 favors** i.e.,
gifts of flowers   **49 fall out** quarrel   **52 sometime** formerly   **53 orient**
lustrous   **55 Like . . . bewail** like tears bewailing the flowers' disgrace of
having been plucked and woven into a garland for the foolish Bottom.

And she in mild terms begged my patience,
I then did ask of her her changeling child,
Which straight she gave me, and her fairy sent
To bear him to my bower in Fairyland.
And, now I have the boy, I will undo                              61
This hateful imperfection of her eyes.
And, gentle Puck, take this transformèd scalp
From off the head of this Athenian swain,
That he, awaking when the other do,                              65
May all to Athens back again repair,                             66
And think no more of this night's accidents
But as the fierce vexation of a dream.
But first I will release the Fairy Queen.
                    [*He squeezes an herb on her eyes.*]
        Be as thou wast wont to be;
        See as thou wast wont to see.
        Dian's bud o'er Cupid's flower                           72
        Hath such force and blessèd power.
Now, my Titania, wake you, my sweet queen.
TITANIA [*awaking*]
My Oberon! What visions have I seen!
Methought I was enamored of an ass.
OBERON
There lies your love.
TITANIA                        How came these things to pass?
Oh, how mine eyes do loathe his visage now!
OBERON
Silence awhile. Robin, take off this head.
Titania, music call, and strike more dead                       80
Than common sleep of all these five the sense.                  81
TITANIA
Music, ho! Music, such as charmeth sleep!    [*Music.*]  82
PUCK [*removing the ass head*]
Now, when thou wak'st, with thine own fool's eyes
    peep.
OBERON
Sound, music! Come, my queen, take hands with me,
And rock the ground whereon these sleepers be.
                                    [*They dance.*]
Now thou and I are new in amity,
And will tomorrow midnight solemnly                              87
Dance in Duke Theseus' house triumphantly,
And bless it to all fair prosperity.
There shall the pairs of faithful lovers be
Wedded, with Theseus, all in jollity.
PUCK
        Fairy King, attend, and mark:
        I do hear the morning lark.
OBERON
        Then, my queen, in silence sad,                          94
        Trip we after night's shade.
        We the globe can compass soon,                           96
        Swifter than the wand'ring moon.

TITANIA
Come, my lord, and in our flight
Tell me how it came this night
That I sleeping here was found
With these mortals on the ground.
            *Exeunt* [*Oberon, Titania, and Puck*].
                    *Wind horn* [*within*].

*Enter Theseus and all his train;* [*Hippolyta,
Egeus*].

THESEUS
Go, one of you, find out the forester,
For now our observation is performed;                           103
And since we have the vaward of the day,                        104
My love shall hear the music of my hounds.
Uncouple in the western valley; let them go.                    106
Dispatch, I say, and find the forester.
                            [*Exit an Attendant.*]
We will, fair queen, up to the mountain's top
And mark the musical confusion
Of hounds and echo in conjunction.
HIPPOLYTA
I was with Hercules and Cadmus once                             111
When in a wood of Crete they bayed the bear                     112
With hounds of Sparta. Never did I hear                         113
Such gallant chiding; for, besides the groves,                 114
The skies, the fountains, every region near
Seemed all one mutual cry. I never heard
So musical a discord, such sweet thunder.
THESEUS
My hounds are bred out of the Spartan kind,                     118
So flewed, so sanded; and their heads are hung                  119
With ears that sweep away the morning dew;
Crook-kneed, and dewlapped like Thessalian bulls;               121
Slow in pursuit, but matched in mouth like bells,               122
Each under each. A cry more tunable                             123
Was never holloed to nor cheered with horn                      124
In Crete, in Sparta, nor in Thessaly.
Judge when you hear. [*He sees the sleepers.*] But soft!
    What nymphs are these?                                      126
EGEUS
My lord, this is my daughter here asleep,
And this Lysander; this Demetrius is;
This Helena, old Nedar's Helena.
I wonder of their being here together.                          130
THESEUS
No doubt they rose up early to observe
The rite of May, and hearing our intent,

61 now I have now that I have   65 other others   66 repair return
72 Dian's bud (Perhaps the flower of the *agnus castus* or chaste-tree,
supposed to preserve chastity; or perhaps referring simply to Oberon's
herb by which he can undo the effects of "Cupid's flower," the love-
in-idleness of 2.1.166–8.)   80–1 and strike . . . sense and strike the
senses of these five (the four lovers and Bottom, all lying asleep on
stage) to awaken them from a sleep more deathlike than is common.
82 such as charmeth sleep i.e., of the sort that can awaken the lovers
and Bottom from something more magical than ordinary sleep.
(See the previous two lines and note.)   87 solemnly ceremoniously
94 sad solemn   96 compass encompass, circumnavigate

103 observation i.e., observance to a morn of May (1.1.167)
104 vaward vanguard, i.e., earliest part   106 Uncouple Set free
for the hunt   111 Cadmus mythical founder of Thebes. (This
story about him is unknown.)   112 bayed brought to bay
113 hounds of Sparta (A breed famous in antiquity for their hunting
skill.)   114 chiding i.e., yelping   118 kind strain, breed   119 So
flewed similarly having large hanging chaps or fleshy covering
of the jaw.   sanded of sandy color   121 dewlapped having
pendulous folds of skin under the neck.   Thessalian from Thessaly,
in Greece   122–3 matched . . . each i.e., harmoniously matched
in their various cries like a set of bells, from treble down to bass.
123 cry pack of hounds.   tunable well tuned, melodious
124 cheered encouraged   126 soft i.e., gently, wait a minute.
130 of at

Came here in grace of our solemnity.     133
But speak, Egeus. Is not this the day
That Hermia should give answer of her choice?

EGEUS   It is, my lord.

THESEUS
Go bid the huntsmen wake them with their horns.   137
                                *[Exit an Attendant.]*

*Shout within. Wind horns. They all start up.*

Good morrow, friends. Saint Valentine is past.   138
Begin these woodbirds but to couple now?

LYSANDER
Pardon, my lord.                       *[They kneel.]*

THESEUS         I pray you all, stand up.
                                  *[They stand.]*

I know you two are rival enemies;
How comes this gentle concord in the world,
That hatred is so far from jealousy
To sleep by hate and fear no enmity?

LYSANDER
My lord, I shall reply amazedly,
Half sleep, half waking; but as yet, I swear,
I cannot truly say how I came here.
But, as I think—for truly would I speak,
And now I do bethink me, so it is—
I came with Hermia hither. Our intent
Was to be gone from Athens, where we might,
Without the peril of the Athenian law—

EGEUS
Enough, enough, my lord; you have enough.
I beg the law, the law, upon his head.
They would have stol'n away; they would, Demetrius,
Thereby to have defeated you and me,
You of your wife and me of my consent,
Of my consent that she should be your wife.

DEMETRIUS
My lord, fair Helen told me of their stealth,
Of this their purpose hither to this wood,
And I in fury hither followed them,
Fair Helena in fancy following me.     162
But, my good lord, I wot not by what power—
But by some power it is—my love to Hermia,
Melted as the snow, seems to me now
As the remembrance of an idle gaud     166
Which in my childhood I did dote upon;
And all the faith, the virtue of my heart,     168
The object and the pleasure of mine eye,
Is only Helena. To her, my lord,
Was I betrothed ere I saw Hermia,
But like a sickness did I loathe this food;
But, as in health, come to my natural taste,
Now I do wish it, love it, long for it,
And will forevermore be true to it.

THESEUS
Fair lovers, you are fortunately met.
Of this discourse we more will hear anon.

Egeus, I will overbear your will;
For in the temple, by and by, with us
These couples shall eternally be knit.
And, for the morning now is something worn,   181
Our purposed hunting shall be set aside.
Away with us to Athens. Three and three,   183
We'll hold a feast in great solemnity.   184
Come, Hippolyta.
      *[Exeunt Theseus, Hippolyta, Egeus, and train.]*

DEMETRIUS
These things seem small and undistinguishable,
Like far-off mountains turnèd into clouds.

HERMIA
Methinks I see these things with parted eye,   188
When everything seems double.

HELENA                 So methinks;
And I have found Demetrius like a jewel,   190
Mine own, and not mine own.

DEMETRIUS              Are you sure   191
That we are awake? It seems to me
That yet we sleep, we dream. Do not you think
The Duke was here, and bid us follow him?

HERMIA
Yea, and my father.

HELENA                And Hippolyta.

LYSANDER
And he did bid us follow to the temple.

DEMETRIUS
Why, then, we are awake. Let's follow him,
And by the way let us recount our dreams.
                        *[Exeunt the lovers.]*

BOTTOM *[awaking]*   When my cue comes, call me, and I
will answer. My next is "Most fair Pyramus." Heigh-
ho! Peter Quince! Flute, the bellows mender! Snout,
the tinker! Starveling! God's my life, stolen hence and   202
left me asleep! I have had a most rare vision. I have
had a dream, past the wit of man to say what dream it
was. Man is but an ass if he go about to expound this   205
dream. Methought I was—there is no man can tell
what. Methought I was—and methought I had—but
man is but a patched fool if he will offer to say what   208
methought I had. The eye of man hath not heard, the   209
ear of man hath not seen, man's hand is not able to   210
taste, his tongue to conceive, nor his heart to report,   211
what my dream was. I will get Peter Quince to write
a ballad of this dream. It shall be called "Bottom's   213
Dream," because it hath no bottom; and I will sing it   214
in the latter end of a play, before the Duke. Peradventure, to make it the more gracious, I shall sing it at her   216
death.                                      *[Exit.]*

---

**133 in . . . solemnity** in honor of our wedding ceremony.   **137 s.d.2 *Wind horns*** Sound hunting horns.   **138 Saint Valentine** (Birds were supposed to choose their mates on Saint Valentine's Day.)   **162 in fancy** driven by love   **166 idle gaud** worthless trinket   **168 virtue** vigor

**181 for** since.   **something** somewhat   **183 Three and three** Three couples: Theseus/Oberon, Lysander/Hermia, and Demetrius/Helena   **184 in great solemnity** with great ceremony.   **188 parted** i.e., improperly focused   **190–1 like . . . own** i.e., something precious that seems mine and yet so mysteriously found that I can hardly believe it is mine.   **202 God's** May God save   **205 go about** attempt   **208 patched** wearing motley, i.e., a dress of various colors.   **offer** venture   **209–11 The eye . . . report** (Bottom garbles 1 Corinthians 2:9.)   **213 ballad** (The proper medium for relating sensational stories and preposterous events.)   **214 hath no bottom** is unfathomable   **216 her** Thisbe's (?) Queen Elizabeth's (?)

# [4.2]

*Enter Quince, Flute, [Snout, and Starveling].*

QUINCE  Have you sent to Bottom's house? Is he come home yet?

STARVELING  He cannot be heard of. Out of doubt he is transported. 4

FLUTE  If he come not, then the play is marred. It goes not forward. Doth it?

QUINCE  It is not possible. You have not a man in all Athens able to discharge Pyramus but he. 8

FLUTE  No, he hath simply the best wit of any handicraft 9 man in Athens.

QUINCE  Yea, and the best person too, and he is a very 11 paramour for a sweet voice.

FLUTE  You must say "paragon." A paramour is, God bless us, a thing of naught. 14

*Enter Snug the joiner.*

SNUG  Masters, the Duke is coming from the temple, and there is two or three lords and ladies more married. If our sport had gone forward, we had all been 17 made men. 18

FLUTE  Oh, sweet bully Bottom! Thus hath he lost 19 sixpence a day during his life; he could not have 20 scaped sixpence a day. An the Duke had not given him sixpence a day for playing Pyramus, I'll be hanged. He would have deserved it. Sixpence a day in Pyramus, or nothing.

*Enter Bottom.*

BOTTOM  Where are these lads? Where are these hearts? 25

QUINCE  Bottom! Oh, most courageous day! Oh, most happy hour!

BOTTOM  Masters, I am to discourse wonders. But ask 28 me not what; for if I tell you, I am no true Athenian. I will tell you everything, right as it fell out. 30

QUINCE  Let us hear, sweet Bottom.

BOTTOM  Not a word of me. All that I will tell you is 32 that the Duke hath dined. Get your apparel together, good strings to your beards, new ribbons to your 34 pumps; meet presently at the palace; every man look 35 o'er his part; for the short and the long is, our play is preferred. In any case, let Thisbe have clean linen; and 37 let not him that plays the lion pare his nails, for they shall hang out for the lion's claws. And, most dear actors, eat no onions nor garlic, for we are to utter sweet breath; and I do not doubt but to hear them say it is a sweet comedy. No more words. Away! Go, away!

*[Exeunt.]*

**4.2. Location: Athens.**
**4 transported** carried off by fairies; or, transformed.   **8 discharge** perform   **9 wit** intellect   **11 person** appearance   **14 a . . . naught** a shameful thing.   **17–18 we . . . men** i.e., we would have had our fortunes made.   **19 bully** i.e., fine fellow. (Compare "Bully for you!" meaning "Jolly well done"!)   **20 sixpence a day** i.e., as a royal pension   **25 hearts** good fellows.   **28 am . . . wonders** have wonders to relate.   **30 fell out** took place.   **32 of** out of   **34 strings** (to attach the beards)   **35 pumps** light shoes or slippers   **37 preferred** selected for consideration.

# [5.1]

*Enter Theseus, Hippolyta, and Philostrate, [lords, and attendants].*

HIPPOLYTA
'Tis strange, my Theseus, that these lovers speak of. 1

THESEUS
More strange than true. I never may believe 2
These antique fables nor these fairy toys. 3
Lovers and madmen have such seething brains,
Such shaping fantasies, that apprehend 5
More than cool reason ever comprehends. 6
The lunatic, the lover, and the poet
Are of imagination all compact. 8
One sees more devils than vast hell can hold;
That is the madman. The lover, all as frantic,
Sees Helen's beauty in a brow of Egypt. 11
The poet's eye, in a fine frenzy rolling,
Doth glance from heaven to earth, from earth to heaven;
And as imagination bodies forth
The forms of things unknown, the poet's pen
Turns them to shapes and gives to airy nothing
A local habitation and a name.
Such tricks hath strong imagination
That, if it would but apprehend some joy, 19
It comprehends some bringer of that joy; 20
Or in the night, imagining some fear, 21
How easy is a bush supposed a bear!

HIPPOLYTA
But all the story of the night told over,
And all their minds transfigured so together,
More witnesseth than fancy's images 25
And grows to something of great constancy; 26
But, howsoever, strange and admirable. 27

*Enter lovers: Lysander, Demetrius, Hermia, and Helena.*

THESEUS
Here come the lovers, full of joy and mirth.
Joy, gentle friends! Joy and fresh days of love
Accompany your hearts!

LYSANDER                    More than to us
Wait in your royal walks, your board, your bed!

THESEUS
Come now, what masques, what dances shall we have, 32
To wear away this long age of three hours
Between our after-supper and bedtime?
Where is our usual manager of mirth?

**5 .1. Location: Athens. The palace of Theseus.**
**1 that** that which   **2 may** can   **3 antique** old-fashioned. (Punning, too, on *antic*, "strange," "grotesque.")   **fairy toys** trifling stories about fairies.   **5 fantasies** imaginations.   **apprehend** conceive, imagine **6 comprehends** understands.   **8 all compact** composed alike.
**11 Helen's** i.e., of Helen of Troy, pattern of beauty.   **brow of Egypt** i.e., face of a gypsy.   **19 apprehend** experience   **20 comprehends** grasps mentally, understands, conceives.   **bringer** i.e., source   **21 fear** object of fear   **25 More . . . images** testifies to something more substantial than mere imaginings   **26 constancy** certainty   **27 howsoever** in any case.   **admirable** a source of wonder.   **32 masques** courtly entertainments

What revels are in hand? Is there no play
To ease the anguish of a torturing hour?
Call Philostrate.
PHILOSTRATE    Here, mighty Theseus.
THESEUS
Say, what abridgment have you for this evening?    39
What masque? What music? How shall we beguile
The lazy time, if not with some delight?
PHILOSTRATE [giving him a paper]
There is a brief how many sports are ripe.    42
Make choice of which Your Highness will see first.
THESEUS [reads]
"The battle with the Centaurs, to be sung    44
By an Athenian eunuch to the harp"?
We'll none of that. That have I told my love,
In glory of my kinsman Hercules.    47
[He reads.] "The riot of the tipsy Bacchanals,    48
Tearing the Thracian singer in their rage"?    49
That is an old device; and it was played    50
When I from Thebes came last a conqueror.
[He reads.] "The thrice three Muses mourning for the
    death    52
Of Learning, late deceased in beggary"?    53
That is some satire, keen and critical,
Not sorting with a nuptial ceremony.    55
[He reads.] "A tedious brief scene of young Pyramus
And his love Thisbe; very tragical mirth"?
Merry and tragical? Tedious and brief?
That is, hot ice and wondrous strange snow.    59
How shall we find the concord of this discord?
PHILOSTRATE
A play there is, my lord, some ten words long,
Which is as brief as I have known a play;
But by ten words, my lord, it is too long,
Which makes it tedious. For in all the play
There is not one word apt, one player fitted.
And tragical, my noble lord, it is,
For Pyramus therein doth kill himself.
Which, when I saw rehearsed, I must confess,
Made mine eyes water; but more merry tears
The passion of loud laughter never shed.
THESEUS    What are they that do play it?
PHILOSTRATE
Hardhanded men that work in Athens here,
Which never labored in their minds till now,
And now have toiled their unbreathed memories    74

With this same play, against your nuptial.    75
THESEUS
And we will hear it.
PHILOSTRATE    No, my noble lord,
It is not for you. I have heard it over,
And it is nothing, nothing in the world;
Unless you can find sport in their intents,
Extremely stretched and conned with cruel pain    80
To do you service.
THESEUS    I will hear that play;
For never anything can be amiss
When simpleness and duty tender it.
Go, bring them in; and take your places, ladies.
        [Philostrate goes to summon the players.]
HIPPOLYTA
I love not to see wretchedness o'ercharged,    85
And duty in his service perishing.    86
THESEUS
Why, gentle sweet, you shall see no such thing.
HIPPOLYTA
He says they can do nothing in this kind.    88
THESEUS
The kinder we, to give them thanks for nothing.
Our sport shall be to take what they mistake;
And what poor duty cannot do, noble respect    91
Takes it in might, not merit.    92
Where I have come, great clerks have purposèd    93
To greet me with premeditated welcomes;
Where I have seen them shiver and look pale,
Make periods in the midst of sentences,
Throttle their practiced accent in their fears,    97
And in conclusion dumbly have broke off,
Not paying me a welcome. Trust me, sweet,
Out of this silence yet I picked a welcome;
And in the modesty of fearful duty
I read as much as from the rattling tongue
Of saucy and audacious eloquence.
Love, therefore, and tongue-tied simplicity
In least speak most, to my capacity.    105

        [Philostrate returns.]

PHILOSTRATE
So please Your Grace, the Prologue is addressed.    106
THESEUS    Let him approach.    [A flourish of trumpets.]

        Enter the Prologue [Quince].

PROLOGUE
If we offend, it is with our good will.
    That you should think, we come not to offend,
But with good will. To show our simple skill,
    That is the true beginning of our end.

39 abridgment pastime (to abridge or shorten the evening)    42 brief summary    44 battle . . . Centaurs (Probably refers to the battle of the Centaurs and the Lapithae, when the Centaurs attempted to carry off Hippodamia, bride of Theseus's friend Pirothous. The story is told in Ovid's Metamorphoses 12.)    47 kinsman (Plutarch's "Life of Theseus" states that Hercules and Theseus were near kinsmen. Theseus is referring to a version of the battle of the Centaurs in which Hercules was said to be present.)    48–9 The riot . . . rage (This was the story of the death of Orpheus, as told in Metamorphoses 11.)    50 device show, performance    52–3 The thrice . . . beggary (Possibly an allusion to Spenser's Teares of the Muses, 1591, though "satires" deploring the neglect of learning and the creative arts were commonplace.)    55 sorting with befitting    59 strange (Sometimes emended to an adjective that would contrast with snow, just as hot contrasts with ice.)    74 toiled taxed.    unbreathed unexercised

75 against in preparation for    80 conned memorized    85 wretchedness o'ercharged social or intellectual inferiority overburdened    86 his service its attempt to serve    88 kind kind of thing.    91–2 noble . . . merit noble consideration values it for the effort made rather than for the actual worth.    93 clerks learned men    97 practiced accent i.e., rehearsed speech; or, usual way of speaking    105 least i.e., saying least.    to my capacity in my judgment and understanding.    106 Prologue speaker of the prologue.    addressed ready.

Consider, then, we come but in despite.
    We do not come, as minding to content you,     113
Our true intent is. All for your delight
    We are not here. That you should here repent you,
The actors are at hand; and, by their show,
You shall know all that you are like to know.
THESEUS     This fellow doth not stand upon points.     118
LYSANDER     He hath rid his prologue like a rough colt; he     119
knows not the stop. A good moral, my lord: it is not     120
enough to speak, but to speak true.
HIPPOLYTA     Indeed, he hath played on his prologue like
a child on a recorder: a sound, but not in government.     123
THESEUS     His speech was like a tangled chain: nothing     124
impaired, but all disordered. Who is next?

    *Enter Pyramus [Bottom], and Thisbe [Flute],*
    *and Wall [Snout], and Moonshine [Starveling],*
    *and Lion [Snug].*

PROLOGUE
Gentles, perchance you wonder at this show;
    But wonder on, till truth make all things plain.
This man is Pyramus, if you would know;
    This beauteous lady Thisbe is, certain.
This man with lime and roughcast doth present
    Wall, that vile wall which did these lovers sunder;
And through Wall's chink, poor souls, they are content
    To whisper. At the which let no man wonder.
This man with lantern, dog, and bush of thorn
    Presenteth Moonshine; for, if you will know,
By moonshine did these lovers think no scorn     136
    To meet at Ninus' tomb, there, there to woo.
This grisly beast, which Lion hight by name,     138
The trusty Thisbe coming first by night
Did scare away, or rather did affright;
And as she fled, her mantle she did fall,     141
    Which Lion vile with bloody mouth did stain.
Anon comes Pyramus, sweet youth and tall,     143
    And finds his trusty Thisbe's mantle slain;
Whereat, with blade, with bloody, blameful blade,
    He bravely broached his boiling bloody breast.     146
And Thisbe, tarrying in mulberry shade,
    His dagger drew, and died. For all the rest,     148
Let Lion, Moonshine, Wall, and lovers twain
At large discourse, while here they do remain.     150
           *Exeunt Lion, Thisbe, and Moonshine.*
THESEUS     I wonder if the lion be to speak.
DEMETRIUS     No wonder, my lord. One lion may, when
many asses do.
WALL
In this same interlude it doth befall     154
That I, one Snout by name, present a wall;
And such a wall as I would have you think

That had in it a crannied hole or chink,
Through which the lovers, Pyramus and Thisbe,
Did whisper often, very secretly.
This loam, this roughcast, and this stone doth show
That I am that same wall; the truth is so.
And this the cranny is, right and sinister,     162
Through which the fearful lovers are to whisper.
THESEUS     Would you desire lime and hair to speak
better?
DEMETRIUS     It is the wittiest partition that ever I heard     166
discourse, my lord.

    *[Pyramus comes forward.]*

THESEUS     Pyramus draws near the wall. Silence!
PYRAMUS
O grim-looked night! O night with hue so black!     169
    O night, which ever art when day is not!
O night, O night! Alack, alack, alack,
    I fear my Thisbe's promise is forgot.
And thou, O wall, O sweet, O lovely wall,
    That stand'st between her father's ground and
        mine,
Thou wall, O wall, O sweet and lovely wall,
    Show me thy chink, to blink through with mine
        eyne.          *[Wall makes a chink with his fingers.]*
Thanks, courteous wall. Jove shield thee well for
    this.
    But what see I? No Thisbe do I see.
O wicked wall, through whom I see no bliss!
    Cursed be thy stones for thus deceiving me!
THESEUS     The wall, methinks, being sensible, should     181
curse again.     182
PYRAMUS     No, in truth, sir, he should not. "Deceiving
me" is Thisbe's cue: she is to enter now, and I am to
spy her through the wall. You shall see, it will fall pat     185
as I told you. Yonder she comes.

    *Enter Thisbe.*

THISBE
O wall, full often hast thou heard my moans
    For parting my fair Pyramus and me.
My cherry lips have often kissed thy stones,
    Thy stones with lime and hair knit up in thee.
PYRAMUS
I see a voice. Now will I to the chink,
    To spy an I can hear my Thisbe's face.     192
Thisbe!
THISBE     My love! Thou art my love, I think.
PYRAMUS
    Think what thou wilt, I am thy lover's grace,     194
And like Limander am I trusty still.     195
THISBE
And I like Helen, till the Fates me kill.     196

---

**113 minding** intending     **118 stand upon points** (1) heed niceties or
small points (2) pay attention to punctuation in his reading. (The
humor of Quince's speech is in the blunders of its punctuation.)
**119 rid** ridden.     **rough** unbroken     **120 stop** (1) stopping of a colt by
reining it in (2) punctuation mark.     **123 recorder** wind instrument
like a flute.     **government** control.     **124 nothing** not at all     **136 think
no scorn** think it no disgraceful matter     **138 hight** is called     **141 fall**
let fall     **143 tall** brave and handsome     **146 broached** stabbed
**148 For** As for     **150 At large** in full, at length     **154 interlude** play

**162 right and sinister** from right to left     **166 partition** (1) wall
(2) section of a learned treatise or oration     **169 grim-looked** grim-
looking     **181 sensible** capable of feeling     **182 again** in return.
**185 pat** exactly     **192 an** if     **194 lover's grace** i.e., gracious lover
**195, 196 Limander, Helen** (Blunders for "Leander" and "Hero.")

PYRAMUS
  Not Shafalus to Procrus was so true.                          197
THISBE
  As Shafalus to Procrus, I to you.
PYRAMUS
  Oh, kiss me through the hole of this vile wall!
THISBE
  I kiss the wall's hole, not your lips at all.
PYRAMUS
  Wilt thou at Ninny's tomb meet me straightway?
THISBE
  'Tide life, 'tide death, I come without delay.             202
                              [*Exeunt Pyramus and Thisbe.*]
WALL
  Thus have I, Wall, my part dischargèd so;
  And, being done, thus Wall away doth go.          [*Exit.*]
THESEUS    Now is the mural down between the two
  neighbors.
DEMETRIUS    No remedy, my lord, when walls are so
  willful to hear without warning.                          208
HIPPOLYTA    This is the silliest stuff that ever I heard.
THESEUS    The best in this kind are but shadows; and the   210
  worst are no worse, if imagination amend them.
HIPPOLYTA    It must be your imagination then, and not
  theirs.
THESEUS    If we imagine no worse of them than they of
  themselves, they may pass for excellent men. Here
  come two noble beasts in, a man and a lion.

              *Enter Lion and Moonshine.*

LION
  You, ladies, you, whose gentle hearts do fear
    The smallest monstrous mouse that creeps on
      floor,
  May now perchance both quake and tremble here,
    When lion rough in wildest rage doth roar.
  Then know that I, as Snug the joiner, am             221
  A lion fell, nor else no lion's dam;                 222
  For, if I should as lion come in strife
  Into this place, 'twere pity on my life.
THESEUS    A very gentle beast, and of a good conscience.
DEMETRIUS    The very best at a beast, my lord, that e'er I
  saw.
LYSANDER    This lion is a very fox for his valor.        228
THESEUS    True; and a goose for his discretion.          229
DEMETRIUS    Not so, my lord, for his valor cannot carry
  his discretion, and the fox carries the goose.
THESEUS    His discretion, I am sure, cannot carry his
  valor; for the goose carries not the fox. It is well. Leave
  it to his discretion, and let us listen to the moon.

MOON
  This lanthorn doth the hornèd moon present—            235
DEMETRIUS    He should have worn the horns on his      236
  head.                                                   237
THESEUS    He is no crescent, and his horns are invisible  238
  within the circumference.                                239
MOON
  This lanthorn doth the hornèd moon present;
  Myself the man i'th' moon do seem to be.
THESEUS    This is the greatest error of all the rest. The
  man should be put into the lanthorn. How is it else the
  man i'th' moon?
DEMETRIUS    He dares not come there for the candle, for  245
  you see it is already in snuff.                          246
HIPPOLYTA    I am aweary of this moon. Would he would
  change!
THESEUS    It appears, by his small light of discretion, that
  he is in the wane; but yet, in courtesy, in all reason, we
  must stay the time.
LYSANDER    Proceed, Moon.
MOON    All that I have to say is to tell you that the lanthorn is the moon, I, the man i'th' moon, this thornbush my thornbush, and this dog my dog.
DEMETRIUS    Why, all these should be in the lanthorn,
  for all these are in the moon. But silence! Here comes
  Thisbe.

              *Enter Thisbe.*

THISBE
  This is old Ninny's tomb. Where is my love?
LION [*roaring*]    Oh!
DEMETRIUS    Well roared, Lion.
                  [*Thisbe runs off, dropping her mantle.*]
THESEUS    Well run, Thisbe.
HIPPOLYTA    Well shone, Moon. Truly, the moon shines
  with a good grace.
                  [*The Lion worries Thisbe's mantle.*]
THESEUS    Well moused, Lion.                             265

              *Enter Pyramus.*          [*Exit Lion.*]

DEMETRIUS    And then came Pyramus.
LYSANDER    And so the lion vanished.
PYRAMUS
  Sweet Moon, I thank thee for thy sunny beams;
    I thank thee, Moon, for shining now so bright;
  For, by thy gracious, golden, glittering gleams,
    I trust to take of truest Thisbe sight.
        But stay, oh, spite!
        But mark, poor knight,
  What dreadful dole is here?                            274
        Eyes, do you see?
        How can it be?

---

197 **Shafalus, Procrus** (Blunders for "Cephalus" and "Procris," also
famous lovers.)    202 **'Tide** Betide, come    208 **willful** willing.
**without warning** i.e., without warning the parents. (Demetrius
makes a joke on the proverb "Walls have ears.")    210 **in this kind**
of this sort.    **shadows** likenesses, representations    221–2 **am . . . dam**
enact the part of a fierce lion, but otherwise am not really a lion. (*Dam*
means "mother"; in Shakespeare's source the beast is a lioness.)
228 **is . . . valor** i.e., his valor consists of craftiness and discretion.
229 **a goose . . . discretion** i.e., as discreet as a goose, that is, more
foolish than discreet.

235 **lanthorn** (This original spelling, "lanthorne," may suggest a play
on the *horn* of which lanterns were made and also on a cuckold's
horns; however, the spelling "lanthorne" is not used consistently for
comic effect in this play or elsewhere. At 5.1.134, for example, the
word is "lanterne" in the original.)    236–7 **on his head** (As a sign
of cuckoldry.)    238 **crescent** a waxing moon    238–9 **and his . . .
circumference** (Cuckold's horns, generally thought to be imaginary,
would not be visible in the circumference of a full moon.)    245 **for
the** because of the, for fear of the    246 **in snuff** (1) offended (2) in
need of snuffing or trimming.    265 **moused** shaken, torn, bitten
274 **dole** grievous event

Oh, dainty duck! Oh, dear!
    Thy mantle good,
    What, stained with blood?
    Approach, ye Furies fell!                                   280
      O Fates, come, come,                                   281
      Cut thread and thrum;                                   282
    Quail, crush, conclude, and quell!                           283

THESEUS    This passion, and the death of a dear friend, 284
would go near to make a man look sad.                               285

HIPPOLYTA    Beshrew my heart, but I pity the man.                  286

PYRAMUS
    Oh, wherefore, Nature, didst thou lions frame?               287
    Since lion vile hath here deflowered my dear,
    Which is—no, no, which was—the fairest dame
    That lived, that loved, that liked, that looked with
      cheer.                                                 290
      Come, tears, confound,
      Out, sword, and wound
    The pap of Pyramus;                                          293
      Ay, that left pap,
      Where heart doth hop.         [He stabs himself.]
    Thus die I, thus, thus, thus.
      Now am I dead,
      Now am I fled;
    My soul is in the sky.
      Tongue, lose thy light;
      Moon, take thy flight.        [Exit Moonshine.]
    Now die, die, die, die, die.           [Pyramus dies.]

DEMETRIUS    No die, but an ace, for him; for he is   303
but one.                                                           304

LYSANDER    Less than an ace, man; for he is dead, he is
nothing.

THESEUS    With the help of a surgeon he might yet
recover, and yet prove an ass.                                     308

HIPPOLYTA    How chance Moonshine is gone before
Thisbe comes back and finds her lover?

THESEUS    She will find him by starlight.

        [Enter Thisbe.]

Here she comes; and her passion ends the play.

HIPPOLYTA    Methinks she should not use a long one for
such a Pyramus. I hope she will be brief.

DEMETRIUS    A mote will turn the balance, which Pyra-  315
mus, which Thisbe, is the better: he for a man, God   316
warrant us; she for a woman, God bless us.                         317

LYSANDER    She hath spied him already with those sweet
eyes.

DEMETRIUS    And thus she means, videlicet:                        320
THISBE
    Asleep, my love?
    What, dead, my dove?
    O Pyramus, arise!
      Speak, speak. Quite dumb?
      Dead, dead? A tomb
    Must cover thy sweet eyes.
      These lily lips,
      This cherry nose,
    These yellow cowslip cheeks,
      Are gone, are gone!
      Lovers, make moan.
    His eyes were green as leeks.
      O Sisters Three,                                       333
      Come, come to me,
    With hands as pale as milk;
      Lay them in gore,
      Since you have shore                                   337
    With shears his thread of silk.
      Tongue, not a word.
      Come, trusty sword,
    Come, blade, my breast imbrue!                               341
               [She stabs herself.]
      And farewell, friends.
      Thus Thisbe ends.
      Adieu, adieu, adieu.          [She dies.]

THESEUS    Moonshine and Lion are left to bury the dead.
DEMETRIUS    Ay, and Wall too.
BOTTOM [starting up, as Flute does also]    No, I assure you,
the wall is down that parted their fathers. Will it please
you to see the epilogue, or to hear a Bergomask dance 349
between two of our company?

      [The other players enter.]

THESEUS    No epilogue, I pray you; for your play needs
no excuse. Never excuse; for when the players are all
dead, there need none to be blamed. Marry, if he that
writ it had played Pyramus and hanged himself in
Thisbe's garter, it would have been a fine tragedy; and
so it is, truly, and very notably discharged. But, come,
your Bergomask. Let your epilogue alone. [A dance.]
The iron tongue of midnight hath told twelve.                      358
Lovers, to bed, 'tis almost fairy time.
I fear we shall outsleep the coming morn
As much as we this night have overwatched.                         361
This palpable-gross play hath well beguiled                        362
The heavy gait of night. Sweet friends, to bed.                    363
A fortnight hold we this solemnity,
In nightly revels and new jollity.            [Exeunt.]

      Enter Puck [carrying a broom].

---

280 **Furies fell** fierce avenging goddesses of Greek myth.   281 **Fates** the three goddesses (Clotho, Lachesis, Atropos) of Greek myth who spun, drew, and cut the thread of human life   282 **thread and thrum** i.e., everything—the good and bad alike; literally, the warp in weaving and the loose end of the warp   283 **Quail** overpower.   **quell** kill, destroy.   284–5 **This . . . sad** i.e., If one had other reason to grieve, one might be sad, but not from this absurd portrayal of passion.   286 **Beshrew** Curse. (A mild curse.)   287 **frame** create.   290 **cheer** countenance.   293 **pap** breast   303 **ace** the side of the die featuring the single pip, or spot. (The pun is on *die* as a singular of *dice*; Bottom's performance is not worth a whole *die* but rather one single face of it, one small portion.)   304 **one** (1) an individual person (2) unique.   308 **ass** (With a pun on *ace*.)   315 **mote** small particle   315–16 **which . . . which** whether . . . or   316–17 **God warrant us** may God justify and protect us

320 **means** moans, laments. (With a pun on the meaning, "lodge a formal complaint.")   **videlicet** to wit   333 **Sisters Three** the Fates   337 **shore** shorn   341 **imbrue** stain with blood.   349 **Bergomask dance** a rustic dance named from Bergamo, a province in the state of Venice   358 **iron tongue** i.e., of a bell.   **told** counted, struck ("tolled")   361 **overwatched** stayed up too late.   362 **palpable-gross** palpably gross, obviously crude   363 **heavy gait** melancholy tread

PUCK

Now the hungry lion roars,
    And the wolf behowls the moon,
Whilst the heavy plowman snores,                    368
    All with weary task fordone.                    369
Now the wasted brands do glow,                      370
    Whilst the screech owl, screeching loud,
Puts the wretch that lies in woe
    In remembrance of a shroud.
Now it is the time of night
    That the graves, all gaping wide,
Every one lets forth his sprite,                    376
    In the churchway paths to glide.
And we fairies, that do run
    By the triple Hecate's team.                    379
From the presence of the sun,
    Following darkness like a dream,
Now are frolic. Not a mouse                         382
    Shall disturb this hallowed house.
I am sent with broom before,
To sweep the dust behind the door.                  385

*Enter* [*Oberon and Titania,*] *King and Queen of*
*Fairies, with all their train.*

OBERON

Through the house give glimmering light,            386
    By the dead and drowsy fire;                    387
Every elf and fairy sprite
    Hop as light as bird from brier;
And this ditty, after me,
Sing, and dance it trippingly.

TITANIA

First, rehearse your song by rote,                  392
To each word a warbling note.
Hand in hand, with fairy grace,
Will we sing, and bless this place.

                    [*Song and dance.*]

OBERON

Now, until the break of day,
Through this house each fairy stray.
To the best bride-bed will we,
Which by us shall blessèd be;
And the issue there create                          400
Ever shall be fortunate.
So shall all the couples three
Ever true in loving be;
And the blots of Nature's hand
Shall not in their issue stand;
Never mole, harelip, nor scar,
Nor mark prodigious, such as are                    407
Despisèd in nativity,
Shall upon their children be.
With this field dew consecrate,                     410
Every fairy take his gait,                          411
And each several chamber bless,                     412
Through this palace, with sweet peace;
And the owner of it blest
Ever shall in safety rest.
Trip away; make no stay;
Meet me all by break of day.
            *Exeunt* [*Oberon, Titania, and train*].

PUCK [*to the audience*]

If we shadows have offended,
Think but this, and all is mended,
That you have but slumbered here                    420
While these visions did appear.
And this weak and idle theme,
No more yielding but a dream,                       423
Gentles, do not reprehend.
If you pardon, we will mend.                         425
And, as I am an honest Puck,
If we have unearnèd luck
Now to scape the serpent's tongue,                  428
We will make amends ere long;
Else the Puck a liar call.
So, good night unto you all.
Give me your hands, if we be friends,               432
And Robin shall restore amends.     [*Exit.*] 433

---

**368 heavy** tired   **369 fordone** exhausted.   **370 wasted brands**
burned-out logs   **376 Every . . . sprite** every grave lets forth its
ghost   **379 triple Hecate's** (Hecate ruled in three capacities: as
Luna or Cynthia in heaven, as Diana on earth, and as Proserpina
in hell.)   **382 frolic** merry.   **385 behind** from behind, or else like
sweeping the dirt under the carpet. (Robin Goodfellow was a household spirit who helped good housemaids and punished lazy ones,
but he could, of course, be mischievous.)   **386–7 Through . . . fire**
(The elves and sprites are bidden to take brands from the dying fire
in order to give "glimmering light" to the rooms in the palace.)
**392 rehearse** recite

**400 issue** offspring.   **create** engendered   **407 prodigious** monstrous,
unnatural   **410 consecrate** consecrated   **411 take his gait** go his
way   **412 several** separate   **420 That . . . here** i.e., that it is a "midsummer night's dream"   **423 No . . . but** yielding no more than
**425 mend** improve.   **428 serpent's tongue** i.e., hissing   **432 Give . . .
hands** Applaud   **433 restore amends** give satisfaction in return.

# The Merchant of Venice

Although Shylock is the most prominent character in *The Merchant of Venice*, he takes part in neither the beginning nor the ending of the play. And, although the play's title might seem to suggest that he is the "merchant" of Venice, Shylock is, strictly speaking, a moneylender whose usury is portrayed as the very opposite of true commerce. His vengeful struggle to obtain a pound of flesh from Antonio contrasts with the various romantic episodes woven together in this play: Bassanio's choosing of Portia by means of the caskets, Gratiano's wooing of Nerissa, Jessica's elopement with Lorenzo, Lancelot Gobbo's changing of masters, and the episode of the rings. In all these stories, a Christian ethic of generosity, love, and risk-taking friendship is set in pointed contrast with a non-Christian ethic that is seen, from a Christian point of view, as grudging, resentful, and self-calculating. Yet this contrasting vision is made problematic by the deplorable behavior of some Christians. In stage productions today, Belmont and its inhabitants are apt to seem frivolous, pleasure-loving, hedonistic, and above all racist in their insular preference for their own economically and culturally privileged position. The play invites us to question the motives of Shylock's enemies. It makes us (today, at least, after the terrors of the German Holocaust) uncomfortable at the insularity of a Venetian ethic that has no genuine place for non-Christians or cultural outsiders. The most painful question of all, for us, is to wonder whether the play assumes for its own dramatic purposes a Christian point of view, however much it sees a genuine and understandable motive in Shylock's desire for revenge. The problem of divided sympathies is exacerbated because Shylock's structural function in the play is essentially that of the villain in a love comedy. His remorseless pursuit of Antonio darkens the mood of the play, and his overthrow signals the providential triumph of love and friendship, even though that triumph is not without its undercurrent of wry melancholy. Before we examine the painful issue of anti-Semitism more closely, we need to establish the structural context of this love comedy as a whole.

Like many of Shakespeare's philosophical and festive comedies, *The Merchant of Venice* presents two contrasting worlds—one fantasy-like and the other marked by conflict and anxiety. To an extent, these contrasting worlds can be identified with the locations of Belmont and Venice. Belmont, to which the various happy lovers and their friends eventually retire, is a place of magic and romance. As its name implies, it is on a mountain, and it is reached by a journey across water. As often happens in fairy stories, on this mountain dwells a princess who must be won by means of a riddling contest. We usually see Belmont at night. Music surrounds it, and women preside over it. Even its caskets, houses, and rings are essentially feminine symbols. Venice, on the other hand, is a place of bustle and economic competition, seen most characteristically in the heat of the day. It lies low and flat, at a point where rivers reach the sea. Men preside over its contentious marketplace and its haggling law courts. Actually, the opposition of Venice and Belmont is not quite so clear-cut: Venice contains much compassionate friendship, whereas Belmont is subject to the arbitrary command of Portia's dead father. (Portia somewhat resembles Jessica in being imprisoned by her father's will.) Even though Portia descends to Venice in the angelic role of mercy giver, she also remains very human: sharp-tongued and even venomous in caricaturing her unwelcome wooers, crafty in her legal maneuvering, saucily prankish in her torturing of Bassanio about the rings. For all its warmth and generosity, Belmont is also the embodiment of an insular Christian culture that makes room for outsiders only when they convert to Christian mores. The traits that Shylock carries to an unpleasant extreme are needed in moderation by the Venetians, notably thrift, promise-keeping, and prudent self-interest; only when the Christians temper their penchant for reckless extravagance, legal sophistry or even theft, and risk-taking is a happy resolution possible. Nevertheless, the polarity of two contrasting localities and two groups of characters is vividly real in this play.

The play's opening scene, from which Shylock is excluded, sets forth the interrelated themes of friendship, romantic love, and risk or "hazard." The merchant who seemingly fulfills the title role, Antonio, is the victim of a mysterious melancholy. He is wealthy enough and surrounded by friends, but something is missing from his life. He assures his solicitous companions that he has no financial worries, for he has been too careful to trust all his cargoes to one sea vessel. Antonio, in fact, has no idea why he is so sad. The question is haunting. What is the matter? Perhaps the answer is to be found in a paradox: those who strive to prosper in the world's terms are doomed to frustration, not because prosperity will necessarily elude them, but because it will not satisfy the spirit. "You have too much respect upon the world," argues the carefree Gratiano. "They lose it that do buy it with much care" (1.1.74–5). Portia and Jessica, too, are at first afflicted by a melancholy that stems from the incompleteness of living isolated lives, with insufficient opportunities for love and sacrifice. They must learn, as Antonio learns with the help of his dear friend Bassanio, to seek happiness by daring to risk everything for friendship. Antonio's risk is most extreme: only when he has thrown away concern for his life can he discover what there is to live for.

At first, Bassanio's request for assistance seems just as materialistic as the worldliness from which Antonio suffers. Bassanio proposes to marry a rich young lady, Portia, in order to recoup his fortune lost through prodigality, and he needs money from Antonio so that he may woo Portia in proper fashion. She is "richly left," the heiress of a dead father, a golden fleece for whom this new Jason will make a quest. Bassanio's adventure is partly commercial. Yet his pilgrimage for Portia is magnanimous as well. The occasional modern practice of playing Bassanio and Portia as cynical antiheroes of a "black" comedy points up the problematic character of their materialism and calculation, but it gives only one aspect of the portrayal. Bassanio has lost his previous fortune through the amiable faults of reckless generosity and a lack of concern for financial prudence. The money he must now borrow, and the fortune he hopes to acquire, are to him no more than a means to carefree happiness. Although Portia's rich dowry is a strong consideration, he describes her also as "fair and, fairer than that word, / Of wondrous virtues" (1.1.162–3). Moreover, he enjoys the element of risk in wooing her. It is like shooting a second arrow in order to recover one that has been lost—double or nothing. This gamble, or "hazard," involves risk for Antonio as well as for Bassanio, and it ultimately brings a double reward to them both— spiritual as well as financial. Unless one recognizes these

aspects of Bassanio's quest, as well as the clear fairy-tale quality with which Shakespeare deliberately invests this part of the plot, one cannot properly assess Bassanio's role in this romantic comedy.

Bassanio's quest for Portia can, in fact, never succeed until he disavows the very financial considerations that brought him to Belmont in the first place. This is the paradox of the riddle of the three caskets, an ancient parable stressing the need for choosing by true substance rather than by outward show. To choose "what many men desire," as the Prince of Morocco does, is to pin one's hopes on worldly wealth; to believe that one "deserves" good fortune, as the Prince of Aragon does, is to reveal a fatal pride in one's own merit. Bassanio perceives that, in order to win true love, he must "give and hazard all he hath" (2.7.9). He is not "deceived with ornament" (3.2.74). Just as Antonio must risk all for friendship, and just as Bassanio himself must later be willing to risk losing Portia for the sake of true friendship (in the episode of the rings), Bassanio must renounce worldly ambition and beauty before he can be rewarded with success. Paradoxically, only those who learn to subdue such worldly desires may then legitimately enjoy the world's pleasures. Only they have acknowledged the hierarchical subservience of the flesh to the spirit. These are the philosophical truisms of Renaissance Neoplatonism, depicting love as a chain or ladder from the basest carnality to the supreme love of God for humanity. On this ladder, perfect friendship and spiritual union are more sublimely Godlike than sexual fulfillment. This idealism may seem a strange doctrine for Bassanio the fortune hunter, but, actually, its conventional wisdom simply confirms his role as romantic hero. He and Portia are not denied worldly happiness or erotic pleasure; they are merely asked to give first thought to their Christian duty in marriage.

For Portia, marriage represents both a gain and a loss. She can choose only by her dead father's will; the patriarchal system, according to which a woman is given in marriage by her father to a younger man, is seemingly able to extend its control even beyond the grave. The prospect of marrying the Prince of Morocco or the Prince of Aragon dismays her, and yet she persists in her vow of obedience and is eventually rewarded by the man of her choice. It is as though the benign father knew how to set the terms of choice in such a way that the "lottery" of the caskets would turn out right for her. When she accepts Bassanio, too, she must make a difficult choice, for in legal terms she makes Bassanio master over everything she owns. Portia is at once spirited and submissive, able to straighten out Venice's legal tangles when all the men have failed and yet ready to call Bassanio her lord. Her teasing him about the ring is a sign that she will make demands of him in marriage, but it is a testing that cannot produce lasting disharmony so long as Bassanio is truly loyal. Portia is, from Bassanio's male point of view, the perfect woman: humanly attainable and yet never seriously threatening. Guided by her, Bassanio makes the potentially hazardous transition from the male-oriented friendships of Venice (especially with Antonio) to heterosexual union. Portia is more fortunate than Jessica, who must break with her faith and her father in order to find marital happiness. The two women are alike, however, in that they experience the play's central paradox of losing the world in order to gain the world. Through them, we see that this paradox illuminates the casket episode, the struggle for the pound of flesh, the elopement of Jessica, the ring episode, and even the comic foolery of Lancelot Gobbo.

Shylock, in his quest for the pound of flesh, represents, as seen from a Christian point of view, a denial of all the paradoxical truths just described. As a usurer, he refuses to lend money interest-free in the name of friendship. Instead of taking risks, he insists on his bond. He spurns mercy and demands strict justice. By calculating all his chances too craftily, he appears to win at first but must eventually lose all. He has "too much respect upon the world" (1.1.74). His God is the Old Testament God of Moses, the God of wrath, the God of the Ten Commandments, with their forbidding emphasis on "Thou shalt not." (This oversimplified contrast between Judaism and Christianity was commonplace in Shakespeare's time.) Shylock abhors stealing but admires equivocation as a means of out-maneuvering a competitor; he approvingly cites Jacob's ruse to deprive Laban of his sheep (1.3.69–88). Any tactic is permissible so long as it falls within the realm of legality and contract.

Shylock's ethical outlook, then, justifies both usury and the old dispensation of the Jewish law. The two are philosophically combined, just as usury and Judaism had become equated in the popular imagination of Renaissance Europe. Even though lending at interest was becoming increasingly necessary and common, old prejudices against it still persisted. Angry moralists pointed out that the New Testament had condemned usury and that Aristotle had described money as barren. To breed money was therefore regarded as unnatural. Usury was considered sinful because it did not involve the usual risks of commerce; the lender was assured against loss of his principal by the posting of collateral and, at the same time, was sure to earn a handsome interest. The usurer seemed to be getting something for nothing. For these reasons, usury was sometimes declared illegal. Its practitioners were viewed as corrupt and grasping, hated as misers. In some European countries, Jews were permitted to practice this un-Christian living (and permitted to do very little else) and then, hypocritically, were detested for performing un-Christian deeds. Ironically, the moneylenders of England were Christians, and few Jews were to be found in any professions. Nominally excluded since Edward I's reign, the Jews had returned in small numbers

to London but did not practice their Judaism openly. They attended Anglican services as required by law and then worshiped in private, relatively undisturbed by the authorities. Shylock may not be based on observation from London life. He is derived from continental tradition and reflects a widespread conviction that Jews and usurers were alike in being un-Christian and sinister.

Shylock is unquestionably sinister, even if he also invites sympathy. He bears an "ancient grudge" against Antonio simply because Antonio is "a Christian." We recognize in Shylock the archetype of the supposed Jew who wishes to kill a Christian and obtain his flesh. In early medieval anti-Semitic legends of this sort, the flesh thus obtained was imagined to be eaten ritually during Passover. Because some Jews had once persecuted Christ, all were unfairly presumed to be implacable enemies of all Christians. These anti-Semitic superstitions were likely to erupt into hysteria at any time, as in 1594 when Dr. Roderigo Lopez, a Portuguese Jewish physician, was accused of having plotted against the life of Queen Elizabeth and of Don Antonio, pretender to the Portuguese throne. Christopher Marlowe's *The Jew of Malta* was revived for this occasion, enjoying an unusually successful run of fifteen performances, and scholars have often wondered if Shakespeare's play was not written under the same impetus. On this score, the evidence is inconclusive, and the play might have been written any time between 1594 and 1598 (when it is mentioned by Francis Meres), but, in any case, Shakespeare has made no attempt to avoid the anti-Semitic nature of his story.

To offset the portrayal of Jewish villainy, however, the play also dramatizes the possibility of conversion to Christianity, suggesting that Judaism is more a matter of benighted faith than of ethnic origin. Converted Jews were not new on the stage: they had appeared in medieval cycle drama, in the Croxton *Play of the Sacrament* (late fifteenth century), and more recently in *The Jew of Malta*, in which Barabas' daughter Abigail falls in love with a Christian and eventually becomes a nun. Shylock's daughter Jessica similarly embraces Christianity as Lorenzo's wife and is received into the happy comradeship of Belmont. Shylock is forced to accept Christianity, presumably for the benefit of his eternal soul (though today we find this deeply offensive, and it is sometimes cut from stage productions). Earlier in the play, Antonio repeatedly indicates his willingness to befriend Shylock if the latter will only give up usury, and he is even cautiously hopeful when Shylock offers him an interest-free loan: "The Hebrew will turn Christian; he grows kind" (1.3.177). To be sure, Antonio's denunciation of Shylock's usurious Judaism has been vehement and personal; we learn that he has spat on Shylock's gaberdine and kicked him as one would kick a dog. This violent disapproval offers no opportunity for the toleration of cultural and religious differences that we expect today from people of good will, but at least Antonio is prepared to accept Shylock if Shylock will embrace the Christian faith and its ethical responsibilities. Whether the play itself endorses Antonio's Christian point of view as normative or insists on a darker reading by making us uneasy with intolerance is a matter of unceasing critical debate. Quite possibly, the play's power to disturb emanates—at least in part—from the dramatic conflict of irreconcilable sets of values.

To Antonio, then, as well as to other Venetians, true Christianity is both an absolute good from which no deviation is possible without evil and a state of faith to which aliens may turn by abjuring the benighted creeds of their ancestors. By this token, the Prince of Morocco is condemned to failure in his quest for Portia, not so much because he is black as because he is an infidel, one who worships "blind fortune" and therefore chooses a worldly rather than a spiritual reward. Although Portia pertly dismisses him with "Let all of his complexion choose me so" (2.7.79), she professes earlier to find him handsome and agrees that he should not be judged by his complexion (2.1.13–22). Unless she is merely being hypocritical, she means by her later remark that black-skinned people are generally infidels, just as Jews are as a group un-Christian. Such pejorative thinking about persons as types is no doubt distressing and suggests—at least to a modern audience—the cultural limitation of Portia's view, but, in any case, it shows her to be no less well disposed toward black suitors than toward others who are also alien. She is glad not to be won by the Prince of Aragon because he, too, though nominally a Christian, is too self-satisfied and proud. All persons, therefore, may aspire to truly virtuous conduct, and those who choose virtue are equally blessed; however, the terms of defining that ideal in this play are essentially Christian. Jews and Blacks may rise spiritually only by abandoning their pagan creeds for the new dispensation of charity and forgiveness.

The superiority of Christian teaching to the older Jewish dispensation was, of course, a widely accepted notion of Shakespeare's time. After all, these were the years when people fought and died to maintain their religious beliefs. Today, the notion of a single true church is less widely held, and we have difficulty understanding why anyone would wish to force conversion on Shylock. Modern productions find it tempting to portray Shylock as a victim of bigotry and to put great stress on his heart-rending assertions of his humanity: "Hath not a Jew eyes? . . . If you prick us, do we not bleed?" (3.1.56–62). Shylock does indeed suffer from his enemies, and his sufferings add a tortured complexity to this play—even, one suspects, for an Elizabethan audience. Those who profess Christianity must surely examine their own motives and conduct. Is it right to steal treasure from Shylock's house along with his eloped daughter? Is it considerate of Jessica and Lorenzo to squander Shylock's turquoise ring, the gift of his wife Leah, on a monkey? Does Shylock's

vengeful insistence on law justify the quibbling countermeasures devised by Portia even as she piously declaims about mercy? Do Shylock's misfortunes deserve the mirthful parodies of Solanio ("My daughter! Oh, my ducats!") or the hostile jeering of Gratiano at the conclusion of the trial? Because he stands outside Christian faith, Shylock can provide a perspective whereby we see the hypocrisies of those who profess a higher ethical code. Nevertheless, Shylock's compulsive desire for vengeance according to an Old Testament code of an eye for an eye cannot be justified by the wrongdoings of any particular Christian. In the play's control of an ethical point of view, such deeds condemn the doer rather than undermine the Christian standards of true virtue as ideally expressed. Shakespeare humanizes Shylock by portraying him as a believable and sensitive man, and he shows much that is to be regretted in Shylock's Christian antagonists, but he also allows Shylock to place himself in the wrong by his refusal to forgive his enemies.

Shylock thus loses everything through his effort to win everything on his own terms. His daughter, Jessica, by her elopement, follows an opposite course. She characterizes her father's home as "hell," and she resents being locked up behind closed windows. Shylock detests music and the sounds of merriment; Jessica's new life in Belmont is immersed in music. He is old, suspicious, miserly; she is young, loving, adventurous. Most important, she seems to be at least part Christian when we first see her. As Lancelot jests half in earnest, "If a Christian did not play the knave and get thee, I am much deceived" (2.3.11–12). Her removal from Shylock's house involves theft, and her running from Venice is, she confesses, an "unthrift love." Paradoxically, however, she sees this recklessness as of more blessed effect than her father's legalistic caution. As she says, "I shall be saved by my husband. He hath made me a Christian" (3.5.17–18).

Lancelot Gobbo's clowning offers a similarly paradoxical comment on the tragedy of Shylock. Lancelot debates whether or not to leave Shylock's service in terms of a soul struggle between his conscience and the devil (2.2.1–29). Conscience bids him stay, for service is a debt, a bond, an obligation, whereas abandonment of one's indenture is a kind of rebellion or stealing away. Yet Shylock's house is "hell" to Lancelot as it is to Jessica. Comparing his new master with his old, Lancelot observes to Bassanio, "You have the grace of God, sir, and he hath enough." Service with Bassanio involves imprudent risks, since Bassanio is a spendthrift. The miserly Shylock rejoices to see the ever hungry Lancelot, this "huge feeder," wasting the substance of a hated Christian. Once again, however, Shylock will lose everything in his grasping quest for security. Another spiritual renewal occurs when Lancelot encounters his old and nearly blind father (2.2). In a scene echoing the biblical stories of the Prodigal Son and of Jacob and Esau, Lancelot teases the old man with false rumors of Lancelot's own death in order to make their reunion seem all the more unexpected and precious. The illusion of loss gives way to joy: Lancelot is, in language adapted from the liturgy, "your boy that was, your son that is, your child that shall be."

In the episode of the rings, we encounter a final playful variation on the paradox of winning through losing. Portia and Nerissa cleverly present their new husbands with a cruel choice: disguised as a doctor of law and his clerk, who have just saved the life of Antonio from Shylock's wrath, the two wives ask nothing more for their services than the rings they see on the fingers of Bassanio and Gratiano. The two husbands, who have vowed never to part with these wedding rings, must therefore choose between love and friendship. Portia knows well enough that Bassanio's obedience to the Neoplatonic ideal of disinterested friendship is an essential part of his virtue. Just as he previously renounced beauty and riches before he could deserve Portia, he must now risk losing her for friendship's sake. The testing of the husbands' constancy does border at times on gratuitous harshness and exercise of power, for it deals with the oldest of masculine nightmares: cuckoldry. Wives are not without weapons in the struggle for control in marriage, and Portia and Nerissa enjoy trapping their new husbands in a no-win situation. Still, the threat is easily resolved by the dispelling of farcically mistaken identities. The young men have been tricked into bestowing their rings on their wives for a second time in the name of perfect friendship, thereby confirming a relationship that is both platonic and fleshly. As Gratiano bawdily points out in the play's last line, the ring is both a spiritual and a sexual symbol of marriage. The resolution of this illusory quarrel also brings to an end the merry battle of the sexes between wives and husbands. Having hinted at the sorts of misunderstandings that afflict even the best of human relationships and having proved themselves wittily able to torture and deceive their husbands, Portia and Nerissa submit at last to the patriarchal norms of their age and to the authority of Bassanio and Gratiano.

Bassanio's marriage to Portia represents a heterosexual fulfillment of their courtship that leaves Antonio without a partner at the play's end. He is, to be sure, included in the camaraderie of Belmont, but a part of the sacrifice he has made for Bassanio is to give that young man the freedom and means to marry as he chooses. Antonio's attachment for Bassanio is a deeply loving one, and is sometimes portrayed as homosexual in modern productions. The force of Antonio's attachment to Bassanio should not be underestimated. At the same time, he does appear to be truly willing for the young man to marry. In this sense, the marriage represents a completion in which friendship and love are fully complementary. Heterosexual union is, in this play and in Shakespearean comedy generally, a dominant and

theatrically conventional resolution; but it is so without denying that there are other forms of human happiness. Whether or not Antonio is entirely content with his final role as a kind of benign older friend we cannot be sure, but his pronouncements in the final act are all aimed at encouraging the harmony between husband and wife that he has risked his life to enable.

As defined by the accepted notions of gender relations in Shakespeare's time, then, all appears to be in harmony in Belmont. The disorders of Venice have been left far behind, however imperfectly they may have been resolved. Jessica and Lorenzo contrast their present happiness with the sufferings of less fortunate lovers of long ago: Troilus and Cressida, Pyramus and Thisbe, Aeneas and Dido, Jason and Medea. The tranquil joy found in Belmont is attuned to the music of the spheres, the singing of the "young-eyed cherubins" (5.1.62), although with a proper Christian humility the lovers also realize that the harmony of immortal souls is infinitely beyond their comprehension. Bound in by the grossness of the flesh, "this muddy vesture of decay" (5.1.64), they can only reach toward the bliss of eternity through music and the perfect friendship of true love. Even in their final joy, accordingly, the lovers find an incompleteness that lends a wistful and slightly melancholy reflective tone to the play's ending. That sense of imperfection is accentuated for us by our awareness that the play's serious problems of gender relations, friendship, and anti-Semitism have by no means been fully resolved; the final concord is one that arises out of discord. Even so, this concluding sense of the unavoidable incompleteness of all human life is of a very different order from that earlier melancholy of isolation and lack of commitment experienced by Portia, Jessica, Antonio, and others.

In performance, the play has prompted both hostile and genuinely sympathetic responses for Shylock. The traditional anti-Semitic interpretation in early stage history manifested itself, for instance, in the performance of George Frederick Cooke in 1803–1804, "bent with age and ugly with mental deformity, grinning with deadly malice, with the venom of his heart congealed in the expression of his countenance, sullen, morose, gloomy, inflexible" (these are William Hazlitt's words). Still other renditions made use of the red wig and hooked nose of the stereotypical stage Jew that associated Shylock with Judas Iscariot. Conversely, Edmund Kean, in 1814, evoked such sympathy as to make the Christians in the play seem hypocrites by comparison. Henry Irving in 1879, and Beerbohm Tree in 1908, combined a kind of ancient dignity with pathos. George C. Scott, at the New York Shakespeare Festival in 1962, acted Shylock as a persecuted and desperate man surrounded by powerful enemies. Laurence Olivier's anguished Shylock (1970, subsequently televised) showed up the Christians as complacent members of a bigoted Venetian social world of privilege and exclusivity. A production in Weimar, Germany, in 1995, commemorating the fiftieth anniversary of the liberation of the concentration camp at nearby Buchenwald, captured what is so horrendously problematic in the play by imagining what it would be like if enacted by German officers and guards amusing themselves with amateur theatricals during wartime and assigning three Jewish inmates to the roles of Shylock, Tubal, and Jessica. Perhaps no Shakespeare play raises more painful issues today for us to think hard about than *The Merchant of Venice*.

# *The Merchant of Venice*

[*Dramatis Personae*

THE DUKE OF VENICE
ANTONIO, *a merchant of Venice*
BASSANIO, *his friend, suitor to Portia*
GRATIANO, *a follower of Bassanio, in love with Nerissa*
SOLANIO, ⎫ *friends to Antonio*
SALERIO, ⎭ *and Bassanio*
LORENZO, *in love with Jessica*
LEONARDO, *servant to Bassanio*

PORTIA, *a rich heiress of Belmont*
NERISSA, *her waiting-gentlewoman*
BALTHASAR, *servant to Portia*
STEPHANO, *servant to Portia*

THE PRINCE OF MOROCCO, *suitor to Portia*
THE PRINCE OF ARAGON, *suitor to Portia*
A MESSENGER *to Portia*

SHYLOCK, *a rich Jew*
JESSICA, *his daughter*
TUBAL, *a Jew, Shylock's friend*
LANCELOT GOBBO, *a clown, servant to Shylock and then to Bassanio*
OLD GOBBO, *Lancelot's father*

*Magnificoes of Venice, Officers of the Court of Justice, Jailor, Servants to Portia, and other Attendants*

SCENE: *Partly at Venice and partly at Belmont, the seat of Portia*]

# [1.1]

*Enter Antonio, Salerio, and Solanio.*

ANTONIO
  In sooth, I know not why I am so sad.                    1
  It wearies me, you say it wearies you;
  But how I caught it, found it, or came by it,
  What stuff 'tis made of, whereof it is born,
  I am to learn;                    5
  And such a want-wit sadness makes of me                    6
  That I have much ado to know myself.

SALERIO
  Your mind is tossing on the ocean,
  There where your argosies with portly sail,                    9
  Like signors and rich burghers on the flood,                    10
  Or as it were the pageants of the sea,                    11
  Do overpeer the petty traffickers                    12
  That curtsy to them, do them reverence,                    13
  As they fly by them with their woven wings.                    14
SOLANIO
  Believe me, sir, had I such venture forth,                    15
  The better part of my affections would

---

**1.1. Location: A street in Venice.**
**1 In sooth** Truly.   **sad** morose, dismal-looking.   **5 am to learn** have yet to learn   **6 such . . . of me** such sadness makes me so distracted, lacking in good sense

**9 argosies** large merchant ships. (So named from *Ragusa*, the modern city of Dubrovnik.)   **portly** majestic   **10 signors** gentlemen.   **flood** sea   **11 pageants** mobile stages used in plays or processions **12 overpeer** look down upon   **13 curtsy** i.e., bob up and down, or lower topsails in token of respect (*reverence*)   **14 woven wings** canvas sails.   **15 venture forth** investment at risk

Be with my hopes abroad. I should be still
Plucking the grass to know where sits the wind,                        17
Peering in maps for ports and piers and roads;                         19
And every object that might make me fear
Misfortune to my ventures, out of doubt
Would make me sad.

SALERIO                          My wind cooling my broth
Would blow me to an ague when I thought                                23
What harm a wind too great might do at sea.
I should not see the sandy hourglass run
But I should think of shallows and of flats,                           26
And see my wealthy *Andrew* docked in sand,                            27
Vailing her high-top lower than her ribs                               28
To kiss her burial. Should I go to church                              29
And see the holy edifice of stone
And not bethink me straight of dangerous rocks                         31
Which, touching but my gentle vessel's side,
Would scatter all her spices on the stream,
Enrobe the roaring waters with my silks,
And, in a word, but even now worth this,                               35
And now worth nothing? Shall I have the thought
To think on this, and shall I lack the thought
That such a thing bechanced would make me sad?                         38
But tell not me. I know Antonio
Is sad to think upon his merchandise.

ANTONIO
Believe me, no. I thank my fortune for it,
My ventures are not in one bottom trusted,                             42
Nor to one place; nor is my whole estate
Upon the fortune of this present year.                                 44
Therefore my merchandise makes me not sad.

SOLANIO
Why then, you are in love.

ANTONIO                                  Fie, fie!

SOLANIO
Not in love neither? Then let us say you are sad
Because you are not merry; and 'twere as easy
For you to laugh and leap, and say you are merry
Because you are not sad. Now, by two-headed
    Janus,                                                             50
Nature hath framed strange fellows in her time:                        51
Some that will evermore peep through their eyes                        52
And laugh like parrots at a bagpiper,                                  53
And other of such vinegar aspect                                       54
That they'll not show their teeth in way of smile
Though Nestor swear the jest be laughable.                             56

        *Enter Bassanio, Lorenzo, and Gratiano.*

Here comes Bassanio, your most noble kinsman,
Gratiano, and Lorenzo. Fare ye well.
We leave you now with better company.

SALERIO
I would have stayed till I had made you merry,
If worthier friends had not prevented me.                              61

ANTONIO
Your worth is very dear in my regard.
I take it your own business calls on you,
And you embrace th'occasion to depart.                                 64

SALERIO    Good morrow, my good lords.

BASSANIO
Good signors both, when shall we laugh? Say,
    when?                                                              66
You grow exceeding strange. Must it be so?                             67

SALERIO
We'll make our leisures to attend on yours.                            68
            *Exeunt Salerio and Solanio.*

LORENZO
My lord Bassanio, since you have found Antonio,
We two will leave you, but at dinnertime,
I pray you, have in mind where we must meet.

BASSANIO    I will not fail you.

GRATIANO
You look not well, Signor Antonio.
You have too much respect upon the world.                              74
They lose it that do buy it with much care.
Believe me, you are marvelously changed.

ANTONIO
I hold the world but as the world, Gratiano—
A stage where every man must play a part,
And mine a sad one.

GRATIANO                   Let me play the fool.
With mirth and laughter let old wrinkles come,
And let my liver rather heat with wine                                 81
Than my heart cool with mortifying groans.                             82
Why should a man whose blood is warm within
Sit like his grandsire cut in alabaster?                               84
Sleep when he wakes, and creep into the jaundice                       85
By being peevish? I tell thee what, Antonio—
I love thee, and 'tis my love that speaks—
There are a sort of men whose visages
Do cream and mantle like a standing pond,                              89
And do a willful stillness entertain                                   90
With purpose to be dressed in an opinion                               91
Of wisdom, gravity, profound conceit,                                  92
As who should say, "I am Sir Oracle,                                   93

---

**17 still** continually   **19 roads** anchorages, open harbors   **23 blow . . .
ague** i.e., start me shivering   **26 flats** shoals   **27 *Andrew*** name of a
ship. (Perhaps after the *St. Andrew*, a Spanish galleon captured at
Cadiz in 1596.)   **28 Vailing** lowering. (Usually as a sign of submission.)   **high-top** topmast   **29 burial** burial place.   **31 bethink me
straight** be put in mind immediately   **35 even now** a short while
ago.   **this** i.e., the cargo of spices and silks   **38 bechanced** having
happened   **42 bottom** ship's hold   **44 Upon . . . year** i.e., risked
upon the chance of the present year.   **50 two-headed Janus** a Roman
god of all beginnings, represented by a figure with two faces
**51 framed** fashioned   **52 peep . . . eyes** i.e., look with eyes narrowed
by laughter   **53 at a bagpiper** i.e., even at a bagpiper, whose music
was regarded as melancholic   **54 other** others.   **vinegar aspect** sour,
sullen looks   **56 Nestor** venerable senior officer in the *Iliad*, noted
for gravity

**61 prevented** forestalled   **64 th'occasion** the opportunity   **66 laugh**
i.e., be merry together.   **67 strange** distant.   **Must it be so?** Must
you go? or, Must you show reserve?   **68 We'll . . . yours** We'll adjust
our spare time to accommodate your schedule.   **74 respect . . . world**
concern for worldly affairs of business.   **81 heat with wine** (The liver
was regarded as the seat of the passions and wine as an agency for
inflaming them.)   **82 mortifying** penitential and deadly. (Sighs were
thought to cost the heart a drop of blood.)   **84 in alabaster** i.e., in a
stone effigy upon a tomb.   **85 jaundice** (Regarded as arising from the
effects of too much choler or yellow bile, one of the four humors, in
the blood.)   **89 cream and mantle** become covered with scum, i.e.,
acquire a lifeless, stiff expression.   **standing** stagnant   **90–2 And . . .
conceit** and who maintain a willful silence in order to acquire a reputation for gravity and deep thought   **93 As . . . say** as if to say

And when I ope my lips let no dog bark!"                              94
Oh, my Antonio, I do know of these
That therefore only are reputed wise
For saying nothing, when, I am very sure,
If they should speak, would almost damn those ears   98
Which, hearing them, would call their brothers
    fools.                                        99
I'll tell thee more of this another time.
But fish not with this melancholy bait               101
For this fool gudgeon, this opinion.—                102
Come, good Lorenzo.—Fare ye well awhile.
I'll end my exhortation after dinner.

LORENZO [*to Antonio and Bassanio*]
Well, we will leave you then till dinnertime.
I must be one of these same dumb wise men,           106
For Gratiano never lets me speak.

GRATIANO
Well, keep me company but two years more,            108
Thou shalt not know the sound of thine own
    tongue.

ANTONIO
Fare you well. I'll grow a talker for this gear.     110

GRATIANO
Thanks, i'faith, for silence is only commendable
In a neat's tongue dried and a maid not vendible.    112
         *Exeunt [Gratiano and Lorenzo].*

ANTONIO    Is that anything now?                      113

BASSANIO    Gratiano speaks an infinite deal of nothing,
more than any man in all Venice. His reasons are as  115
two grains of wheat hid in two bushels of chaff; you
shall seek all day ere you find them, and when you
have them they are not worth the search.

ANTONIO
Well, tell me now what lady is the same              119
To whom you swore a secret pilgrimage,
That you today promised to tell me of.

BASSANIO
'Tis not unknown to you, Antonio,
How much I have disabled mine estate
By something showing a more swelling port            124
Than my faint means would grant continuance.         125
Nor do I now make moan to be abridged                126
From such a noble rate; but my chief care            127
Is to come fairly off from the great debts           128
Wherein my time, something too prodigal,             129
Hath left me gaged. To you, Antonio,                 130
I owe the most, in money and in love,

And from your love I have a warranty                 132
To unburden all my plots and purposes                133
How to get clear of all the debts I owe.

ANTONIO
I pray you, good Bassanio, let me know it;
And if it stand, as you yourself still do,           136
Within the eye of honor, be assured                  137
My purse, my person, my extremest means
Lie all unlocked to your occasions.

BASSANIO
In my schooldays, when I had lost one shaft,         140
I shot his fellow of the selfsame flight             141
The selfsame way with more advisèd watch             142
To find the other forth, and by adventuring both     143
I oft found both. I urge this childhood proof
Because what follows is pure innocence.              145
I owe you much, and, like a willful youth,
That which I owe is lost; but if you please
To shoot another arrow that self way                 148
Which you did shoot the first, I do not doubt,
As I will watch the aim, or to find both             150
Or bring your latter hazard back again               151
And thankfully rest debtor for the first.            152

ANTONIO
You know me well, and herein spend but time          153
To wind about my love with circumstance,             154
And out of doubt you do me now more wrong
In making question of my uttermost                    156
Than if you had made waste of all I have.            157
Then do but say to me what I should do
That in your knowledge may by me be done,            159
And I am prest unto it. Therefore speak.             160

BASSANIO
In Belmont is a lady richly left;                    161
And she is fair and, fairer than that word,
Of wondrous virtues. Sometimes from her eyes         163
I did receive fair speechless messages.
Her name is Portia, nothing undervalued              165
To Cato's daughter, Brutus' Portia.                  166
Nor is the wide world ignorant of her worth,
For the four winds blow in from every coast
Renownèd suitors, and her sunny locks
Hang on her temples like a golden fleece,
Which makes her seat of Belmont Colchis' strand,     171
And many Jasons come in quest of her.
Oh, my Antonio, had I but the means
To hold a rival place with one of them,

---

**94 let . . . bark** i.e., let no creature dare to interrupt me.   **98–9 would . . . fools** i.e., would almost provoke the hearers into damning themselves by calling the speaker a fool. (Compare Matthew 5:22, in which anyone calling another a fool is threatened with damnation.) **101–2 fish . . . opinion** i.e., don't go fishing for a reputation of being wise, using your melancholy silence as the bait to fool people. (*Gudgeon*, a small fish, was thought of as a type of gullibility.) **106 dumb** mute, speechless   **108 keep** if you keep   **110 for this gear** in view of what you say.   **112 neat's** ox's.   **a maid not vendible** i.e., a maiden judged unmarriageable (whose silence might then be a virtue outweighing her other disadvantages).   **113 Is . . . now?** i.e., Was all that talk about anything?   **115 reasons** reasonable ideas **119 the same** i.e., the one   **124 By . . . port** by showing a somewhat more lavish style of living   **125 grant continuance** allow to continue. **126–7 make . . . rate** complain at being cut back from such a high style of living   **128 to . . . off** honorably to extricate myself   **129 time** youthful inclinations   **130 gaged** pledged, in pawn.

**132 warranty** authorization   **133 unburden** disclose   **136–7 if . . . honor** if it looks honorable, as your conduct has always done   **140 shaft** arrow **141 his** its.   **selfsame flight** same capacity and range   **142 advisèd** careful   **143 forth** out.   **adventuring** risking   **145 innocence** ingenuousness, sincerity.   **148 self** same   **150 or** either   **151–2 Or . . . first** or at least bring back what you will have risked on me this time and gratefully acknowledge myself in debt to you for what you lent before. **153 spend but time** only waste time   **154 To wind . . . circumstance** to use such roundabout language in appealing to the love you know I feel for you. (*Circumstance* here means "circumlocution.")   **156 In . . . uttermost** in showing any doubt of my intention to do all I can   **157 made waste of** spent recklessly   **159 in your knowledge** as you understand the situation **160 prest** ready   **161 richly left** left a large fortune (by her father's will) **163 Sometimes** Once   **165–6 nothing undervalued To** of no less worth than   **166 Portia** (The same Portia as in Shakespeare's *Julius Caesar*.) **171 Which . . . strand** i.e., which has the effect of transforming her estate at Belmont into something like the land of Colchis, on the Black Sea coast, to which Jason adventured in pursuit of the golden fleece.   **strand** shore

I have a mind presages me such thrift                    175
That I should questionless be fortunate.
ANTONIO
Thou know'st that all my fortunes are at sea;
Neither have I money nor commodity                       178
To raise a present sum. Therefore go forth.             179
Try what my credit can in Venice do;
That shall be racked even to the uttermost              181
To furnish thee to Belmont, to fair Portia.
Go presently inquire, and so will I,                    183
Where money is, and I no question make                  184
To have it of my trust or for my sake.      *Exeunt.* 185

❧

# [1.2]

*Enter Portia with her waiting woman, Nerissa.*

PORTIA    By my troth, Nerissa, my little body is aweary    1
of this great world.
NERISSA    You would be, sweet madam, if your miseries      3
were in the same abundance as your good fortunes
are; and yet, for aught I see, they are as sick that surfeit  5
with too much as they that starve with nothing. It is
no mean happiness, therefore, to be seated in the         7
mean. Superfluity comes sooner by white hairs, but        8
competency lives longer.                                  9
PORTIA    Good sentences, and well pronounced.             10
NERISSA    They would be better if well followed.
PORTIA    If to do were as easy as to know what were
good to do, chapels had been churches and poor
men's cottages princes' palaces. It is a good divine that  14
follows his own instructions. I can easier teach twenty
what were good to be done than to be one of the
twenty to follow mine own teaching. The brain may
devise laws for the blood, but a hot temper leaps o'er    18
a cold decree; such a hare is madness, the youth, to
skip o'er the meshes of good counsel, the cripple. But    20
this reasoning is not in the fashion to choose me a       21
husband. Oh, me, the word "choose"! I may neither        22
choose who I would nor refuse who I dislike; so is the
will of a living daughter curbed by the will of a dead    24
father. Is it not hard, Nerissa, that I cannot choose one
nor refuse none?
NERISSA    Your father was ever virtuous, and holy men
at their death have good inspirations; therefore the

lottery that he hath devised in these three chests of
gold, silver, and lead, whereof who chooses his mean-     30
ing chooses you, will no doubt never be chosen by
any rightly but one who you shall rightly love. But       32
what warmth is there in your affection towards any of
these princely suitors that are already come?
PORTIA    I pray thee, overname them, and as thou nam-     35
est them I will describe them; and according to my
description level at my affection.                        37
NERISSA    First, there is the Neapolitan prince.           44
PORTIA    Ay, that's a colt indeed, for he doth nothing but  39
talk of his horse, and he makes it a great appropriation  40
to his own good parts that he can shoe him him-           41
self. I am much afeard my lady his mother played
false with a smith.                                       43
NERISSA    Then is there the County Palatine.              44
PORTIA    He doth nothing but frown, as who should say,    45
"An you will not have me, choose." He hears merry         46
tales and smiles not. I fear he will prove the weeping    47
philosopher when he grows old, being so full of          48
unmannerly sadness in his youth. I had rather be married  49
to a death's-head with a bone in his mouth than to
either of these. God defend me from these two!
NERISSA    How say you by the French lord, Monsieur        52
Le Bon?
PORTIA    God made him, and therefore let him pass for a
man. In truth, I know it is a sin to be a mocker, but
he! Why, he hath a horse better than the Neapolitan's,
a better bad habit of frowning than the Count Palatine; he is every man in no man. If a throstle sing, he   58
falls straight a-capering. He will fence with his own     59
shadow. If I should marry him, I should marry twenty
husbands. If he would despise me, I would forgive
him, for if he love me to madness, I shall never re-      62
quite him.
NERISSA    What say you, then, to Falconbridge, the        64
young baron of England?
PORTIA    You know I say nothing to him, for he understands not me, nor I him. He hath neither Latin,
French, nor Italian, and you will come into the court     68
and swear that I have a poor pennyworth in the English.   69
He is a proper man's picture, but alas, who can           70
converse with a dumb show? How oddly he is suited!        71
I think he bought his doublet in Italy, his round hose    72

in France, his bonnet in Germany, and his behavior  73
everywhere.

NERISSA    What think you of the Scottish lord, his
neighbor?

PORTIA    That he hath a neighborly charity in him, for he
borrowed a box of the ear of the Englishman and swore  78
he would pay him again when he was able. I think the
Frenchman became his surety and sealed under for an-  80
other.  81

NERISSA    How like you the young German, the Duke of
Saxony's nephew?

PORTIA    Very vilely in the morning, when he is sober,
and most vilely in the afternoon, when he is drunk.
When he is best he is a little worse than a man, and
when he is worst he is little better than a beast. An  87
the worst fall that ever fell, I hope I shall make shift to  88
go without him.

NERISSA    If he should offer to choose, and choose the  90
right casket, you should refuse to perform your father's
will if you should refuse to accept him.

PORTIA    Therefore, for fear of the worst, I pray thee, set
a deep glass of Rhenish wine on the contrary casket,  94
for if the devil be within and that temptation without,  95
I know he will choose it. I will do anything, Nerissa,  96
ere I will be married to a sponge.

NERISSA    You need not fear, lady, the having any of
these lords. They have acquainted me with their de-
terminations, which is indeed to return to their home
and to trouble you with no more suit, unless you may
be won by some other sort than your father's imposi-  102
tion depending on the caskets.  103

PORTIA    If I live to be as old as Sibylla, I will die as chaste  104
as Diana, unless I be obtained by the manner of my  105
father's will. I am glad this parcel of wooers are so rea-  106
sonable, for there is not one among them but I dote
on his very absence, and I pray God grant them a fair
departure.

NERISSA    Do you not remember, lady, in your father's
time, a Venetian, a scholar and a soldier, that came
hither in company of the Marquess of Montferrat?

PORTIA    Yes, yes, it was Bassanio—as I think, so was
he called.

NERISSA    True, madam. He, of all the men that ever my
foolish eyes looked upon was the best deserving a fair
lady.

PORTIA    I remember him well, and I remember him
worthy of thy praise.

*Enter a Servingman.*

How now, what news?

SERVINGMAN    The four strangers seek for you, madam,  121
to take their leave; and there is a forerunner come from  122
a fifth, the Prince of Morocco, who brings word the
Prince his master will be here tonight.

PORTIA    If I could bid the fifth welcome with so good
heart as I can bid the other four farewell, I should be
glad of his approach. If he have the condition of a saint  127
and the complexion of a devil, I had rather he should  128
shrive me than wive me.  129
Come, Nerissa. [*To Servingman*] Sirrah, go before.  130
Whiles we shut the gate upon one wooer, another
knocks at the door.  *Exeunt.*

# [1.3]

*Enter Bassanio with Shylock the Jew.*

SHYLOCK    Three thousand ducats, well.  1

BASSANIO    Ay, sir, for three months.

SHYLOCK    For three months, well.

BASSANIO    For the which, as I told you, Antonio shall
be bound.

SHYLOCK    Antonio shall become bound, well.

BASSANIO    May you stead me? Will you pleasure me?  7
Shall I know your answer?

SHYLOCK    Three thousand ducats for three months and
Antonio bound.

BASSANIO    Your answer to that.

SHYLOCK    Antonio is a good man.  12

BASSANIO    Have you heard any imputation to the
contrary?

SHYLOCK    Ho, no, no, no, no! My meaning in saying he
is a good man is to have you understand me that he is
sufficient. Yet his means are in supposition. He hath an  17
argosy bound to Tripolis, another to the Indies. I understand, moreover, upon the Rialto, he hath a third  19
at Mexico, a fourth for England, and other ventures
he hath squandered abroad. But ships are but boards,  21
sailors but men. There be land rats and water rats,
water thieves and land thieves—I mean pirates—and
then there is the peril of waters, winds, and rocks. The
man is, notwithstanding, sufficient. Three thousand
ducats. I think I may take his bond.

BASSANIO    Be assured you may.  27

SHYLOCK    I will be assured I may; and that I may be  28
assured, I will bethink me. May I speak with Antonio?

---

**121 four** (Nerissa actually names six suitors; possibly a sign of revision or the author's early draft.)    **122 forerunner** herald
**127 condition** disposition, character    **128 complexion of a devil** (Devils were thought to be black; but *complexion* can also mean "temperament," "disposition.")    **129 shrive me** pardon me, excuse me from having to be wooed. (Literally, act as my confessor and give absolution.)    **130 Sirrah** (Form of address to social inferior.)
**1.3. Location: Venice. A public place.**
**1 ducats** gold coins    **7 stead** supply, assist.    **pleasure** oblige    **12 good** (Shylock means "solvent," a good credit risk; Bassanio interprets it in the moral sense.)    **17 sufficient** i.e., a good security.    **in supposition** doubtful, uncertain.    **19 the Rialto** the merchants' exchange in Venice and the center of commercial activity    **21 squandered** scattered    **27, 28 assured** (Bassanio means that Shylock may trust Antonio, whereas Shylock means that he will obtain legal assurances.)

**73 bonnet** hat    **78 borrowed** received. (But with a play on the idea of something that must be repaid.)    **80–1 became . . . another** offered to back up the Scottish lord and promised (with as solemn a vow as if he were signing and sealing a document) to add a blow of his own. (An allusion to the age-old alliance of the French and the Scots against the English.)    **87–8 An . . . fell** If worst should come to worst.    **88 make shift** manage    **90 offer** undertake    **94 Rhenish wine** a German white wine from the Rhine Valley.    **contrary** i.e., wrong    **95 if** even if    **96 it** i.e., the tempting red wine.    **102 sort** means. (With perhaps a suggestion too of "casting or drawing of lots.")    **102–3 imposition** command, charge    **104 Sibylla** the Cumaean Sibyl, to whom Apollo gave as many years as there were grains in her handful of sand    **105 Diana** goddess of chastity and of the hunt    **106 parcel** assembly, group

BASSANIO    If it please you to dine with us.

SHYLOCK    Yes, to smell pork, to eat of the habitation
which your prophet the Nazarite conjured the devil    32
into. I will buy with you, sell with you, talk with you,
walk with you, and so following, but I will not eat    34
with you, drink with you, nor pray with you. What
news on the Rialto? Who is he comes here?

*Enter Antonio.*

BASSANIO    This is Signor Antonio.

SHYLOCK [*aside*]
How like a fawning publican he looks!    38
I hate him for he is a Christian,    39
But more for that in low simplicity    40
He lends out money gratis and brings down    41
The rate of usance here with us in Venice.    42
If I can catch him once upon the hip,    43
I will feed fat the ancient grudge I bear him.    44
He hates our sacred nation, and he rails,    45
Even there where merchants most do congregate,
On me, my bargains, and my well-won thrift,
Which he calls interest. Cursèd be my tribe
If I forgive him!

BASSANIO            Shylock, do you hear?

SHYLOCK    I am debating of my present store,    50
And, by the near guess of my memory,
I cannot instantly raise up the gross    52
Of full three thousand ducats. What of that?
Tubal, a wealthy Hebrew of my tribe,
Will furnish me. But soft, how many months    55
Do you desire? [*To Antonio*] Rest you fair, good
signor!
Your Worship was the last man in our mouths.    57

ANTONIO
Shylock, albeit I neither lend nor borrow
By taking nor by giving of excess,    59
Yet, to supply the ripe wants of my friend,    60
I'll break a custom. [*To Bassanio*] Is he yet possessed    61
How much ye would?    62

SHYLOCK    Ay, ay, three thousand ducats.

ANTONIO    And for three months.

SHYLOCK
I had forgot—three months, you told me so.
Well then, your bond. And let me see—but hear
you,
Methought you said you neither lend nor borrow
Upon advantage.

ANTONIO            I do never use it.    68

SHYLOCK
When Jacob grazed his uncle Laban's sheep—    69
This Jacob from our holy Abram was,    70
As his wise mother wrought in his behalf,
The third possessor; ay, he was the third—    72

ANTONIO
And what of him? Did he take interest?

SHYLOCK
No, not take interest, not as you would say
Directly interest. Mark what Jacob did.
When Laban and himself were compromised    76
That all the eanlings which were streaked and pied    77
Should fall as Jacob's hire, the ewes, being rank,    78
In end of autumn turnèd to the rams,
And when the work of generation was    80
Between these woolly breeders in the act,
The skillful shepherd peeled me certain wands,    82
And in the doing of the deed of kind    83
He stuck them up before the fulsome ewes,    84
Who then conceiving did in eaning time    85
Fall parti-colored lambs, and those were Jacob's.    86
This was a way to thrive, and he was blest;
And thrift is blessing, if men steal it not.    88

ANTONIO
This was a venture, sir, that Jacob served for,    89
A thing not in his power to bring to pass,
But swayed and fashioned by the hand of heaven.
Was this inserted to make interest good?    92
Or is your gold and silver ewes and rams?

SHYLOCK
I cannot tell. I make it breed as fast.    94
But note me, signor—

ANTONIO            Mark you this, Bassanio,
The devil can cite Scripture for his purpose.    96
An evil soul producing holy witness
Is like a villain with a smiling cheek,
A goodly apple rotten at the heart.
Oh, what a goodly outside falsehood hath!

SHYLOCK
Three thousand ducats. 'Tis a good round sum.
Three months from twelve, then let me see, the rate—

ANTONIO
Well, Shylock, shall we be beholding to you?    103

SHYLOCK
Signor Antonio, many a time and oft
In the Rialto you have rated me    105
About my moneys and my usances.
Still have I borne it with a patient shrug,

---

**32 Nazarite** Nazarene. (For the reference to Christ's casting evil spirits into a herd of swine, see Matthew 8:30–2, Mark 5:1–13, and Luke 8:32–3.)    **34 so following** so forth    **38 publican** Roman tax gatherer (a term of opprobrium; see Luke 18:9–14); or, innkeeper    **39 for** because    **40 low simplicity** humble foolishness    **41 gratis** without charging interest    **42 usance** usury, interest    **43 upon the hip** i.e., at my mercy. (A figure of speech from wrestling; see Genesis 32:24–9.)    **44 feed fat** gorge myself on    **45 our sacred nation** i.e., the Hebrew people    **50 I am . . . store** I am considering my current supply of money    **52 gross** total    **55 soft** i.e., wait a minute    **57 Your . . . mouths** i.e., We were just speaking of you. (But with ominous connotation of devouring; compare line 44.)    **59 excess** interest    **60 ripe wants** pressing needs    **61 possessed** informed    **62 ye would** you want.    **68 advantage** interest.

**69 Jacob** (See Genesis 27, 30:25–43.)    **70 Abram** Abraham    **72 third** i.e., after Abraham and Isaac.    **possessor** i.e., of the birthright of which, with the help of Rebecca, he was able to cheat Esau, his elder brother    **76 compromised** agreed    **77 eanlings** young lambs or kids.    **pied** spotted    **78 hire** wages, share.    **rank** in heat    **80 work of generation** mating    **82 peeled . . . wands** i.e., partly stripped the bark of some sticks. (*Me* is used colloquially.)    **83 deed of kind** i.e., copulation    **84 fulsome** in heat    **85 eaning** lambing    **86 Fall** give birth to    **88 thrift** thriving, profit    **89 venture . . . for** uncertain commercial venture on which Jacob risked his wages    **92 inserted . . . good** brought in to justify the practice of usury.    **94 I cannot tell** i.e., I don't know about that.    **96 devil . . . Scripture** (See Matthew 4:6.)    **103 beholding** beholden, indebted    **105 rated** berated, rebuked

For sufferance is the badge of all our tribe.                    108
You call me misbeliever, cutthroat dog,
And spit upon my Jewish gaberdine,                               110
And all for use of that which is mine own.
Well then, it now appears you need my help.
Go to, then. You come to me and you say,                         113
"Shylock, we would have moneys"—you say so,
You, that did void your rheum upon my beard                      115
And foot me as you spurn a stranger cur                          116
Over your threshold. Moneys is your suit.                        117
What should I say to you? Should I not say,
"Hath a dog money? Is it possible
A cur can lend three thousand ducats?" Or
Shall I bend low, and in a bondman's key,                        121
With bated breath and whispering humbleness,                     122
Say this:
"Fair sir, you spit on me on Wednesday last,
You spurned me such a day, another time
You called me dog, and for these courtesies
I'll lend you thus much moneys"?
ANTONIO
    I am as like to call thee so again,                          128
    To spit on thee again, to spurn thee too.
    If thou wilt lend this money, lend it not
    As to thy friends, for when did friendship take
    A breed for barren metal of his friend?                      132
    But lend it rather to thine enemy,                           133
    Who, if he break, thou mayst with better face                134
    Exact the penalty.
SHYLOCK                    Why, look you how you storm!
    I would be friends with you and have your love,
    Forget the shames that you have stained me with,
    Supply your present wants, and take no doit                  138
    Of usance for my moneys, and you'll not hear me.
    This is kind I offer.                                        140
BASSANIO    This were kindness.                                  141
SHYLOCK    This kindness will I show.
    Go with me to a notary, seal me there
    Your single bond; and, in a merry sport,                     144
    If you repay me not on such a day,
    In such a place, such sum or sums as are
    Expressed in the condition, let the forfeit
    Be nominated for an equal pound                              148
    Of your fair flesh, to be cut off and taken
    In what part of your body pleaseth me.
ANTONIO
    Content, in faith. I'll seal to such a bond
    And say there is much kindness in the Jew.

BASSANIO                                                         
    You shall not seal to such a bond for me!
    I'll rather dwell in my necessity.                           154
ANTONIO
    Why, fear not, man, I will not forfeit it.
    Within these two months—that's a month before
    This bond expires—I do expect return
    Of thrice three times the value of this bond.
SHYLOCK
    O father Abram, what these Christians are,
    Whose own hard dealings teaches them suspect
    The thoughts of others! Pray you, tell me this:
    If he should break his day, what should I gain
    By the exaction of the forfeiture?
    A pound of man's flesh taken from a man
    Is not so estimable, profitable neither,                     165
    As flesh of muttons, beefs, or goats. I say
    To buy his favor I extend this friendship.
    If he will take it, so; if not, adieu.                       168
    And for my love, I pray you, wrong me not.                   169
ANTONIO
    Yes, Shylock, I will seal unto this bond.
SHYLOCK
    Then meet me forthwith at the notary's.
    Give him direction for this merry bond,
    And I will go and purse the ducats straight,
    See to my house, left in the fearful guard                   174
    Of an unthrifty knave, and presently
    I'll be with you.                              Exit.
ANTONIO               Hie thee, gentle Jew.—                     176
    The Hebrew will turn Christian; he grows kind.
BASSANIO
    I like not fair terms and a villain's mind.
ANTONIO
    Come on. In this there can be no dismay;
    My ships come home a month before the day.
                                            [Exeunt.]

                            ❖

## [2.1]

[Flourish of cornets.] Enter [the Prince of]
Morocco, a tawny Moor all in white, and three
or four followers accordingly, with Portia, Nerissa, and their train.

MOROCCO
    Mislike me not for my complexion,
    The shadowed livery of the burnished sun,                    2
    To whom I am a neighbor and near bred.                       3
    Bring me the fairest creature northward born,
    Where Phoebus' fire scarce thaws the icicles,                5
    And let us make incision for your love

108 **sufferance** patience    110 **gaberdine** loose outer garment like a
cape or mantle, worn especially by Jews    113 **Go to** (An exclamation
of impatience or annoyance.)    115 **void your rheum** spit    116 **spurn**
kick    117 **suit** request.    121 **bondman's key** serf's tone of voice
122 **bated** subdued    128 **like** likely    132 **A breed . . . metal** offspring
from money, which cannot naturally breed. (One of the oldest
arguments against usury was that it was thereby "unnatural.")
**of** from    133 **to** as if to    134 **Who** from whom.    **break** fail to pay on
time    138 **doit** a Dutch coin of very small value    140 **kind** kindly;
kindness    141 **were** would be (if seriously offered)    144 **single bond**
bond signed alone without other security; unconditional. (Shylock
pretends the *condition,* line 147, is only a joke.)    148 **nominated for**
named, specified as.    **equal** exact

154 **dwell** remain    165 **estimable** valuable    168 **so** well and
good    169 **wrong me not** do not think evil of me.    174 **fearful**
untrustworthy    176 **gentle** gracious, courteous. (With a play on
"gentile.")
**2.1. Location:** Belmont. Portia's house.
0.3 *accordingly* similarly (i.e., dressed in white and dark-skinned like
Morocco)    2 **shadowed livery** i.e., dark complexion, worn as though
it were a costume of the sun's servants    3 **near bred** closely
related.    5 **Phoebus'** i.e., the sun's

To prove whose blood is reddest, his or mine.                    7
I tell thee, lady, this aspect of mine                           8
Hath feared the valiant. By my love I swear,                     9
The best-regarded virgins of our clime
Have loved it too. I would not change this hue,
Except to steal your thoughts, my gentle queen.

PORTIA
In terms of choice I am not solely led
By nice direction of a maiden's eyes;                            14
Besides, the lott'ry of my destiny
Bars me the right of voluntary choosing.
But if my father had not scanted me,                            17
And hedged me by his wit to yield myself                        18
His wife who wins me by that means I told you,                  19
Yourself, renownèd prince, then stood as fair                   20
As any comer I have looked on yet
For my affection.

MOROCCO                    Even for that I thank you.           22
Therefore, I pray you, lead me to the caskets
To try my fortune. By this scimitar
That slew the Sophy and a Persian prince,                       25
That won three fields of Sultan Solyman,                        26
I would o'erstare the sternest eyes that look,                  27
Outbrave the heart most daring on the earth,                    28
Pluck the young sucking cubs from the she-bear,
Yea, mock the lion when 'a roars for prey,                      30
To win thee, lady. But alas the while!
If Hercules and Lichas play at dice                             32
Which is the better man, the greater throw
May turn by fortune from the weaker hand.
So is Alcides beaten by his page,
And so may I, blind Fortune leading me,
Miss that which one unworthier may attain,
And die with grieving.

PORTIA                          You must take your chance,
And either not attempt to choose at all
Or swear before you choose, if you choose wrong
Never to speak to lady afterward
In way of marriage. Therefore be advised.                       42

MOROCCO
Nor will not. Come, bring me unto my chance.                    43

PORTIA
First, forward to the temple. After dinner                      44
Your hazard shall be made.

MOROCCO                          Good fortune then!
To make me blest or cursed'st among men.
                              [*Cornets, and*] *Exeunt.*

7 **reddest** (Red blood was regarded as a sign of courage.)    8 **aspect**
visage   9 **feared** frightened   14 **nice direction** careful guidance
17 **scanted** limited   18 **wit** wisdom   18–19 **yield . . . who** give myself
to be the wife of him who   20 **then . . . fair** would then have looked
as attractive and stood as fair a chance. (With a play on "fair-
skinned.")   22 **For my** of gaining my   25 **Sophy** Shah of Persia
26 **fields** battles.   **Solyman** a Turkish sultan ruling from 1520 to
1566   27 **o'erstare** outstare   28 **Outbrave . . . earth** outboast the most
daring brave-hearted person alive   30 **'a** he   32 **Lichas** a page of
Hercules (Alcides). See the note for 3.2.55.   42 **be advised** take warning, consider.   43 **Nor will not** i.e., Nor indeed will I violate the oath.
44 **to the temple** i.e., in order to take the oaths.

## [2.2]

*Enter* [*Lancelot*] *the clown, alone.*

LANCELOT   Certainly my conscience will serve me to        1
run from this Jew my master. The fiend is at mine
elbow and tempts me, saying to me, "Gobbo, Lancelot
Gobbo, good Lancelot," or "Good Gobbo," or "Good
Lancelot Gobbo, use your legs, take the start, run
away." My conscience says, "No, take heed, honest
Lancelot, take heed, honest Gobbo," or, as aforesaid,
"Honest Lancelot Gobbo, do not run; scorn running
with thy heels." Well, the most courageous fiend bids   9
me pack. " Fia!" says the fiend."Away!" says the fiend.  10
 "For the heavens, rouse up a brave mind," says the     11
fiend, "and run." Well, my conscience, hanging about    12
the neck of my heart, says very wisely to me,"My hon-   13
est friend Lancelot, being an honest man's son," or
rather an honest woman's son—for indeed my father
did something smack, something grow to, he had a        16
kind of taste—well, my conscience says, "Lancelot,      17
budge not." "Budge," says the fiend "Budge not,"
says my conscience. "Conscience," say I, "you counsel
well." "Fiend," say I, "you counsel well." To be ruled by
my conscience, I should stay with the Jew my master,
who, God bless the mark, is a kind of devil; and to run  22
away from the Jew, I should be ruled by the fiend, who,
saving your reverence, is the devil himself. Certainly
the Jew is the very devil incarnation; and, in my con-  25
science, my conscience is but a kind of hard conscience
to offer to counsel me to stay with the Jew. The fiend
gives the more friendly counsel. I will run, fiend. My
heels are at your commandment. I will run.

*Enter Old Gobbo, with a basket.*

GOBBO   Master young man, you, I pray you, which is       30
the way to master Jew's?

LANCELOT   [*aside*] Oh, heavens, this is my true-
begotten father, who, being more than sand-blind,       33
high-gravel-blind, knows me not. I will try confusions   34
with him.

GOBBO   Master young gentleman, I pray you, which is
the way to master Jew's?

LANCELOT   Turn up on your right hand at the next
turning, but at the next turning of all on your left;
marry, at the very next turning, turn of no hand, but   40
turn down indirectly to the Jew's house.

**2.2. Location: Venice. A street.**
**0.1** *clown* (1) country bumpkin (2) comic type in an Elizabethan
acting company   **1 serve** permit   **9 with thy heels** i.e., emphatically.
(With a pun on the literal sense.)   **10 pack** begone.   **Fia!** i.e., Via,
away!   **11 For the heavens** i.e., In heaven's name   **12–13 hanging . . .
heart** i.e., timidly   **16–17 did something . . . taste** i.e., had a tendency to
lechery   **22 God . . . mark** (An expression by way of apology for
introducing something potentially offensive, as also in *saving your
reverence* in line 24.)   **25 incarnation** (Lancelot means "incarnate.")
**30 you** (Gobbo uses the formal *you* but switches to the familiar *thou*,
line 88, when he accepts Lancelot as his son.)   **33–4 sand-blind** dim-
sighted   **33–4 high-gravel-blind** blinder than sand-blind. (A term
seemingly invented by Lancelot.)   **34 try confusions** (Lancelot's blunder
for "try conclusions," i.e., experiment, though his error is comically
apt.)   **40 marry** i.e., by the Virgin Mary, indeed. (A mild
interjection.)   **of no hand** neither right nor left

GOBBO   By God's sonties, 'twill be a hard way to hit.  42
Can you tell me whether one Lancelot, that dwells
with him, dwell with him or no?

LANCELOT   Talk you of young Master Lancelot? [*Aside*]
Mark me now; now will I raise the waters.—Talk you  46
of young Master Lancelot?

GOBBO   No master, sir, but a poor man's son. His father,  48
though I say't, is an honest exceeding poor man and,
God be thanked, well to live.  50

LANCELOT   Well, let his father be what 'a will, we talk  51
of young Master Lancelot.

GOBBO   Your Worship's friend, and Lancelot, sir.  53

LANCELOT   But I pray you, ergo, old man, ergo, I be-  54
seech you, talk you of young Master Lancelot?

GOBBO   Of Lancelot, an't please Your Mastership.

LANCELOT   Ergo, Master Lancelot. Talk not of Master
Lancelot, father, for the young gentleman, according  58
to Fates and Destinies and such odd sayings, the Sis-  59
ters Three and such branches of learning, is indeed  60
deceased, or, as you would say in plain terms, gone to
heaven.

GOBBO   Marry, God forbid! The boy was the very staff
of my age, my very prop.

LANCELOT   Do I look like a cudgel or a hovel post, a  65
staff, or a prop? Do you know me, father?

GOBBO   Alack the day, I know you not, young gentleman. But I pray you, tell me, is my boy, God rest his
soul, alive or dead?

LANCELOT   Do you not know me, father?

GOBBO   Alack, sir, I am sand-blind. I know you not.

LANCELOT   Nay, indeed, if you had your eyes you
might fail of the knowing me; it is a wise father that  73
knows his own child. Well, old man, I will tell you  74
news of your son. [*He kneels.*] Give me your blessing.
Truth will come to light; murder cannot be hid long; a
man's son may, but in the end truth will out.

GOBBO   Pray you, sir, stand up. I am sure you are not
Lancelot, my boy.

LANCELOT   Pray you, let's have no more fooling about
it, but give me your blessing. I am Lancelot, your  81
boy that was, your son that is, your child that shall be.  82

GOBBO   I cannot think you are my son.

LANCELOT   I know not what I shall think of that; but I
am Lancelot, the Jew's man, and I am sure Margery
your wife is my mother.

GOBBO   Her name is Margery indeed. I'll be sworn, if
thou be Lancelot, thou art mine own flesh and blood.
Lord worshiped might he be, what a beard hast thou  89
got! Thou hast got more hair on thy chin than Dobbin
my fill horse has on his tail.  91

LANCELOT   [*rising*] It should seem then that Dobbin's
tail grows backward. I am sure he had more hair of  93
his tail than I have of my face when I last saw him.  94

GOBBO   Lord, how art thou changed! How dost thou and
thy master agree? I have brought him a present. How
'gree you now?

LANCELOT   Well, well; but for mine own part, as I have
set up my rest to run away, so I will not rest till I have  99
run some ground. My master's a very Jew. Give him  100
a present? Give him a halter! I am famished in his ser-  101
vice; you may tell every finger I have with my ribs.  102
Father, I am glad you are come. Give me your present  103
to one Master Bassanio, who indeed gives rare new  104
liveries. If I serve not him, I will run as far as God has  105
any ground. Oh, rare fortune! Here comes the man. To
him, father, for I am a Jew if I serve the Jew any longer.  107

*Enter Bassanio, with* [*Leonardo and*] *a follower
or two.*

BASSANIO   You may do so, but let it be so hasted that  108
supper be ready at the farthest by five of the clock. See  109
these letters delivered, put the liveries to making, and
desire Gratiano to come anon to my lodging.
[*Exit a Servant.*]

LANCELOT   To him, father.

GOBBO   [*advancing*] God bless Your Worship!

BASSANIO   Gramercy. Wouldst thou aught with me?  114

GOBBO   Here's my son, sir, a poor boy—  115

LANCELOT   Not a poor boy, sir, but the rich Jew's man,
that would, sir, as my father shall specify—

GOBBO   He hath a great infection, sir, as one would say,  118
to serve—

LANCELOT   Indeed, the short and the long is, I serve the
Jew, and have a desire, as my father shall specify—

GOBBO   His master and he, saving Your Worship's
reverence, are scarce cater-cousins—  123

LANCELOT   To be brief, the very truth is that the Jew,
having done me wrong, doth cause me, as my father,
being, I hope, an old man, shall frutify unto you—  126

GOBBO   I have here a dish of doves that I would bestow
upon Your Worship, and my suit is—

LANCELOT   In very brief, the suit is impertinent to  129
myself, as Your Worship shall know by this honest old
man, and, though I say it, though old man, yet poor
man, my father.

---

**42 sonties** little saints   **46 raise the waters** i.e., start tears.   **48 master**
(The title was applied to gentlefolk only.)   **50 well to live** prospering,
in good health.   **51 'a** he   **53 Your . . . Lancelot** (Again, Old Gobbo
denies that Lancelot is entitled to be called "Master.")   **54 ergo** therefore. (But Lancelot may use this Latin word with no particular meaning
in mind.)   **58 father** (1) old man (2) father   **59–60 the Sisters Three**
the three Fates   **65 hovel post** post holding up a hovel or open
shed   **73–4 it is . . . child** (Reverses the proverb "It is a wise child that
knows his own father.")   **81–2 your . . . shall be** (Echoes the *Gloria*
from the Book of Common Prayer: "As it was in the beginning, is now,
and ever shall be.")   **89 beard** (Stage tradition has Old Gobbo mistaking Lancelot's long hair for a beard.)   **91 fill horse** cart horse

**93 grows backward** grows at the wrong end.   **94 of** on   **99 set up my
rest** determined to risk all. (A metaphor from the card game *primero*, in
which a final wager is made, with a pun also on *rest* as "place of
residence.")   **not rest** i.e., not stop running. (More punning on *rest*.)
**100 very** veritable.   **Jew** (1) Hebrew (2) grasping old usurer.   **101
halter** hangman's noose.   **102 tell** count.   **tell . . . ribs** (Comically
reverses the usual saying of counting one's ribs with one's fingers.)
**103 Give me** Give. (*Me* suggests "on my behalf.")   **104 rare** splendid
**105 liveries** uniforms or costumes for servants.   **107 a Jew** i.e., a villain.
(Punning on the literal sense in *the Jew*. Compare with line 100.)
**108 hasted** hastened, hurried   **109 farthest** latest   **114 Gramercy**
Many thanks.   **aught** anything   **115 poor** (1) unfortunate (2) penniless (contrasted with *rich* in the next line)   **118 infection** (Blunder for
"affection" or "inclination.")   **123 cater-cousins** good friends
**126 frutify** (Lancelot may be trying to say "fructify," but he means
"certify" or "notify.")   **129 impertinent** (Blunder for "pertinent.")

BASSANIO   One speak for both. What would you?
LANCELOT   Serve you, sir.
GOBBO   That is the very defect of the matter, sir.                    135
BASSANIO
  I know thee well; thou hast obtained thy suit.
  Shylock thy master spoke with me this day,
  And hath preferred thee, if it be preferment                    138
  To leave a rich Jew's service to become
  The follower of so poor a gentleman.
LANCELOT   The old proverb is very well parted 141
  between my master Shylock and you, sir: you have
  the grace of God, sir, and he hath enough.
BASSANIO
  Thou speak'st it well. Go, father, with thy son.
  Take leave of thy old master, and inquire
  My lodging out. [*To a Servant*] Give him a livery
  More guarded than his fellows'. See it done.                    147
LANCELOT   Father, in. I cannot get a service, no! I have
  ne'er a tongue in my head, well! [*He looks at his palm.*]
  If any man in Italy have a fairer table which doth offer 150
  to swear upon a book, I shall have good fortune. Go 151
  to, here's a simple line of life. Here's a small trifle of 152
  wives! Alas, fifteen wives is nothing. Eleven widows
  and nine maids is a simple coming-in for one man.   154
  And then to scape drowning thrice, and to be in peril
  of my life with the edge of a feather bed! Here are 156
  simple scapes. Well, if Fortune be a woman, she's a 157
  good wench for this gear. Father, come. I'll take my 158
  leave of the Jew in the twinkling.
                    *Exit clown* [*Lancelot, with Old Gobbo*].
BASSANIO [*giving Leonardo a list*]
  I pray thee, good Leonardo, think on this:
  These things being bought and orderly bestowed,   161
  Return in haste, for I do feast tonight              162
  My best-esteemed acquaintance. Hie thee, go.
LEONARDO
  My best endeavors shall be done herein.
                    [*He starts to leave.*]

                    *Enter Gratiano.*

GRATIANO [*to Leonardo*]
  Where's your master?
LEONARDO                    Yonder, sir, he walks.

                    *Exit Leonardo.*

GRATIANO   Signor Bassanio!
BASSANIO   Gratiano!

GRATIANO
  I have a suit to you.
BASSANIO                    You have obtained it.
GRATIANO   You must not deny me. I must go with you
  to Belmont.
BASSANIO
  Why, then you must. But hear thee, Gratiano;
  Thou art too wild, too rude and bold of voice—
  Parts that become thee happily enough,                    173
  And in such eyes as ours appear not faults,
  But where thou art not known, why, there they show
  Something too liberal. Pray thee, take pain               176
  To allay with some cold drops of modesty                    177
  Thy skipping spirit, lest through thy wild behavior
  I be misconstered in the place I go to                    179
  And lose my hopes.
GRATIANO                    Signor Bassanio, hear me:
  If I do not put on a sober habit,                    181
  Talk with respect and swear but now and then,
  Wear prayer books in my pocket, look demurely,
  Nay more, while grace is saying, hood mine eyes               184
  Thus with my hat, and sigh and say "amen,"
  Use all the observance of civility,
  Like one well studied in a sad ostent                    187
  To please his grandam, never trust me more.              188
BASSANIO   Well, we shall see your bearing.
GRATIANO
  Nay, but I bar tonight. You shall not gauge me
  By what we do tonight.
BASSANIO                    No, that were pity.
  I would entreat you rather to put on
  Your boldest suit of mirth, for we have friends
  That purpose merriment. But fare you well;
  I have some business.
GRATIANO
  And I must to Lorenzo and the rest,
  But we will visit you at suppertime.              *Exeunt.*

# [2.3]

                    *Enter Jessica and [Lancelot] the clown.*

JESSICA
  I am sorry thou wilt leave my father so.
  Our house is hell, and thou, a merry devil,
  Didst rob it of some taste of tediousness.
  But fare thee well. There is a ducat for thee.
                    [*Giving money.*]
  And, Lancelot, soon at supper shalt thou see
  Lorenzo, who is thy new master's guest.
  Give him this letter; do it secretly.     [*Giving a letter.*]
  And so farewell. I would not have my father
  See me in talk with thee.

135 **defect** (Blunder for "effect," i.e., "purport.")   138 **preferred** recommended   141 **proverb** i.e., "He who has the grace of God has enough."   **parted** divided   147 **guarded** trimmed with braided ornament   150 **table** palm of the hand. (Lancelot now reads the lines of his palm.)   151 **book** i.e., Bible. (The image is of a hand being laid on the Bible to take an oath.)   151–2 **Go to** (An expression of impatience.)   152 **simple** unremarkable. (Said ironically.)   **line of life** curved line at the base of the thumb.   154 **simple coming-in** modest beginning or income. (With sexual suggestion.)   156 **feather bed** (Suggesting marriage bed or love bed; Lancelot sees sexual adventure and the dangers of marriage in his palm reading.)   157 **scapes** 1) adventures (2) transgressions.   **Fortune . . . woman** (Fortune was personified as a goddess.)   158 **gear** matter.   161 **bestowed** i.e., stowed on board ship   162 **feast tonight** give a feast tonight for

173 **Parts** qualities   176 **liberal** free of manner. (Often with sexual connotation.)   177 **allay** temper, moderate.   **modesty** decorum   179 **misconstered** misconstrued   181 **habit** demeanor. (With a suggestion of "clothes.")   184 **saying** being said   187 **sad ostent** grave appearance   188 **grandam** grandmother
2.3. **Location: Venice. Shylock's house.**

LANCELOT   Adieu! Tears exhibit my tongue. Most   10
beautiful pagan, most sweet Jew! If a Christian did not
play the knave and get thee, I am much deceived. But,   12
adieu! These foolish drops do something drown my
manly spirit. Adieu!

JESSICA   Farewell, good Lancelot.        [Exit Lancelot.]
Alack, what heinous sin is it in me
To be ashamed to be my father's child!
But though I am a daughter to his blood,
I am not to his manners. O Lorenzo,
If thou keep promise, I shall end this strife,
Become a Christian and thy loving wife.        Exit.

❖

# [2.4]

*Enter Gratiano, Lorenzo, Salerio, and Solanio.*

LORENZO
Nay, we will slink away in suppertime,   1
Disguise us at my lodging, and return
All in an hour.

GRATIANO
We have not made good preparation.

SALERIO
We have not spoke us yet of torchbearers.   5

SOLANIO
'Tis vile, unless it may be quaintly ordered,   6
And better in my mind not undertook.

LORENZO
'Tis now but four o'clock. We have two hours
To furnish us.

*Enter Lancelot [with a letter].*

Friend Lancelot, what's the news?

LANCELOT   An it shall please you to break up this, it   10
shall seem to signify.        [Giving the letter.]

LORENZO
I know the hand. In faith, 'tis a fair hand,
And whiter than the paper it writ on
Is the fair hand that writ.

GRATIANO                  Love news, in faith.

LANCELOT   By your leave, sir.        [He starts to leave.]

LORENZO   Whither goest thou?

LANCELOT   Marry, sir, to bid my old master the Jew to
sup tonight with my new master the Christian.

LORENZO
Hold here, take this. [He gives money.] Tell gentle
   Jessica
I will not fail her. Speak it privately.
                        Exit clown [Lancelot].
Go, gentlemen,
Will you prepare you for this masque tonight?
I am provided of a torchbearer.

SALERIO
Ay, marry, I'll be gone about it straight.   24

SOLANIO
And so will I.

LORENZO          Meet me and Gratiano.
At Gratiano's lodging some hour hence.   26

SALERIO   'Tis good we do so.        Exit [with Solanio].

GRATIANO
Was not that letter from fair Jessica?

LORENZO
I must needs tell thee all. She hath directed   29
How I shall take her from her father's house,
What gold and jewels she is furnished with,
What page's suit she hath in readiness.
If e'er the Jew her father come to heaven,
It will be for his gentle daughter's sake;   34
And never dare misfortune cross her foot,   35
Unless she do it under this excuse,   36
That she is issue to a faithless Jew.   37
Come, go with me. Peruse this as thou goest.
                  [He gives Gratiano the letter.]
Fair Jessica shall be my torchbearer.        Exeunt.

❖

# [2.5]

*Enter [Shylock the] Jew and [Lancelot,] his man
that was, the clown.*

SHYLOCK
Well, thou shalt see, thy eyes shall be thy judge,
The difference of old Shylock and Bassanio.—   2
What, Jessica!—Thou shalt not gormandize,   3
As thou hast done with me—What, Jessica!—
And sleep and snore, and rend apparel out—   5
Why, Jessica, I say!

LANCELOT   Why, Jessica!

SHYLOCK
Who bids thee call? I do not bid thee call.

LANCELOT   Your Worship was wont to tell me I could
do nothing without bidding.

*Enter Jessica.*

JESSICA   Call you? What is your will?

SHYLOCK
I am bid forth to supper, Jessica.
There are my keys. But wherefore should I go?   13
I am not bid for love—they flatter me—
But yet I'll go in hate, to feed upon
The prodigal Christian. Jessica, my girl,
Look to my house. I am right loath to go.   17
There is some ill a-brewing towards my rest,
For I did dream of moneybags tonight.   19

LANCELOT   I beseech you, sir, go. My young master
doth expect your reproach.   21

10 **exhibit** (Blunder for "inhibit," "restrain.")   12 **get** beget
**2.4. Location: Venice. A street.**
1 **in** during   5 **spoke . . . of** yet bespoken, ordered   6 **quaintly
ordered** skillfully and tastefully managed   10 **An** If.   **break up this**
unseal the letter   24 **straight** at once.

26 **some hour** about an hour   29 **must needs** must   34 **gentle** (With
pun on "gentile"?)   35 **foot** footpath   36 **she** i.e., Misfortune
37 **she is issue** i.e., Jessica is daughter.   **faithless** pagan
**2.5. Location: Venice. Before Shylock's house.**
2 **of** between   3 **gormandize** eat gluttonously   5 **rend apparel out**
i.e., wear out your clothes   13 **wherefore** why   17 **right loath** reluctant   19 **tonight** last night.   21 **reproach** (Lancelot's blunder for
"approach." Shylock takes it in grim humor.)

SHYLOCK    So do I his.

LANCELOT    And they have conspired together. I will not say you shall see a masque, but if you do, then it was not for nothing that my nose fell a-bleeding on Black Monday last at six o'clock i'th' morning, falling    26 out that year on Ash Wednesday was four year in th'afternoon.

SHYLOCK
What, are there masques? Hear you me, Jessica:
Lock up my doors, and when you hear the drum
And the vile squealing of the wry-necked fife,    31
Clamber not you up to the casements then,
Nor thrust your head into the public street
To gaze on Christian fools with varnished faces,    34
But stop my house's ears—I mean my casements.
Let not the sound of shallow fopp'ry enter
My sober house. By Jacob's staff I swear    37
I have no mind of feasting forth tonight.
But I will go.—Go you before me, sirrah.
Say I will come.

LANCELOT    I will go before, sir. [Aside to Jessica] Mistress, look out at window, for all this;
                    There will come a Christian by,
                    Will be worth a Jewess' eye.    [Exit.]

SHYLOCK
What says that fool of Hagar's offspring, ha?    45

JESSICA
His words were "Farewell, mistress," nothing else.

SHYLOCK
The patch is kind enough, but a huge feeder,    47
Snail-slow in profit, and he sleeps by day    48
More than the wildcat. Drones hive not with me;
Therefore I part with him, and part with him
To one that I would have him help to waste
His borrowed purse. Well, Jessica, go in.
Perhaps I will return immediately.
Do as I bid you. Shut doors after you.
Fast bind, fast find—    55
A proverb never stale in thrifty mind.    Exit.

JESSICA
Farewell, and if my fortune be not crossed,
I have a father, you a daughter, lost.    Exit.

❖

# [2.6]

*Enter the masquers, Gratiano and Salerio.*

GRATIANO
This is the penthouse under which Lorenzo    1

Desired us to make stand.

SALERIO    His hour is almost past.

GRATIANO
And it is marvel he outdwells his hour,    4
For lovers ever run before the clock.

SALERIO
Oh, ten times faster Venus' pigeons fly    6
To seal love's bonds new-made than they are wont    7
To keep obligèd faith unforfeited.    8

GRATIANO
That ever holds. Who riseth from a feast    9
With that keen appetite that he sits down?
Where is the horse that doth untread again    11
His tedious measures with the unbated fire    12
That he did pace them first? All things that are
Are with more spirit chasèd than enjoyed.
How like a younger or a prodigal    15
The scarfèd bark puts from her native bay,    16
Hugged and embracèd by the strumpet wind!    17
How like the prodigal doth she return,
With overweathered ribs and ragged sails,    19
Lean, rent, and beggared by the strumpet wind!    20

*Enter Lorenzo.*

SALERIO
Here comes Lorenzo. More of this hereafter.

LORENZO
Sweet friends, your patience for my long abode;    22
Not I, but my affairs, have made you wait.
When you shall please to play the thieves for wives,
I'll watch as long for you then. Approach;    25
Here dwells my father Jew.—Ho! Who's within?    26

*[Enter] Jessica, above [in boys' clothes].*

JESSICA
Who are you? Tell me for more certainty,
Albeit I'll swear that I do know your tongue.

LORENZO    Lorenzo, and thy love.

JESSICA
Lorenzo, certain, and my love indeed,
For who love I so much? And now who knows
But you, Lorenzo, whether I am yours?    32

LORENZO
Heaven and thy thoughts are witness that thou art.

JESSICA [throwing down a casket]
Here, catch this casket. It is worth the pains.
I am glad 'tis night, you do not look on me,

---

26 **Black Monday** Easter Monday. (Lancelot's talk of omens is perhaps intentional gibberish, a parody of Shylock's fears.)    31 **wry-necked** i.e., played with the musician's head awry; or possibly comparing the fife's *vile squealing* to the call of the wryneck, a bird with a high-pitched call and a writhing movement of head and neck    34 **varnished faces** i.e., painted masks    37 **Jacob's staff** (See Genesis 32:10 and Hebrews 11:21.)    45 **Hagar's offspring** (Hagar, a gentile and Abraham's servant, gave birth to Ishmael; both mother and son were cast out after the birth of Isaac.)    47 **patch** fool    48 **profit** profitable labor    55 **Fast . . . find** i.e., Keep your property secure and you will always know where it is. (Proverbial.)
**2.6. Location:** Before Shylock's house, as in 2.5.
1 **penthouse** projecting roof or upper story of a house

4 **it . . . hour** i.e., it is surprising that he is late    6–8 **Oh, ten . . . unforfeited** i.e., Oh, lovers are ten times more alacritous in their first pledge of love than in keeping faith in a long-term commitment. (*Venus' pigeons* are the doves that draw her chariot.)    9 **ever holds** always holds true.    11 **untread** retrace    12 **measures** paces    15 **younger** i.e., younger son, as in the parable of the Prodigal Son (Luke 15). (Often emended to *younker*, youth.)    16 **scarfèd bark** sailing vessel festooned with flags or streamers    17 **strumpet** i.e., inconsistent, variable. (Likened metaphorically to the harlots with whom the Prodigal Son wasted his fortune.)    19 **overweathered ribs** i.e., weather-beaten and leaking timbers    20 **rent** torn    22 **your patience** i.e., I beg your patience.    **abode** delay    25 **watch** keep watch    26 **father** i.e., father-in-law    32 **But you** better than you

For I am much ashamed of my exchange.                    36
But love is blind, and lovers cannot see
The pretty follies that themselves commit,               38
For if they could, Cupid himself would blush
To see me thus transformèd to a boy.

LORENZO
Descend, for you must be my torchbearer.

JESSICA
What, must I hold a candle to my shames?                 42
They in themselves, good sooth, are too too light.       43
Why, 'tis an office of discovery, love,                  44
And I should be obscured.

LORENZO                      So are you, sweet,
Even in the lovely garnish of a boy.                     46
But come at once,
For the close night doth play the runaway,               48
And we are stayed for at Bassanio's feast.               49

JESSICA
I will make fast the doors, and gild myself              50
With some more ducats, and be with you straight.
                                   [Exit above.]

GRATIANO
Now, by my hood, a gentle and no Jew.                    52

LORENZO
Beshrew me but I love her heartily,                      53
For she is wise, if I can judge of her,
And fair she is, if that mine eyes be true,
And true she is, as she hath proved herself;
And therefore, like herself, wise, fair, and true,
Shall she be placèd in my constant soul.

        Enter Jessica [below].

What, art thou come? On, gentlemen, away!
Our masquing mates by this time for us stay.             60
               Exit [with Jessica and Salerio;
               Gratiano is about to follow them].

        Enter Antonio.

ANTONIO   Who's there?
GRATIANO   Signor Antonio?
ANTONIO
Fie, fie, Gratiano! Where are all the rest?
'Tis nine o'clock; our friends all stay for you.
No masque tonight. The wind is come about;
Bassanio presently will go aboard.
I have sent twenty out to seek for you.

GRATIANO
I am glad on 't. I desire no more delight
Than to be under sail and gone tonight.      Exeunt.

                ❧

36 exchange change of clothes.   38 pretty ingenious, artful   42 hold a candle i.e., stand by and witness. (With a play on the idea of acting as torchbearer.)   43 light (1) immodest (2) illuminated.   44 'tis ... discovery i.e., torchbearing is intended to shed light on matters   46 garnish outfit, trimmings   48 close dark, secretive.   doth ... runaway i.e., is quickly passing, just as we are about to elope   49 stayed waited   50 gild adorn. (Literally, cover with gold.)   52 by my hood (An asseveration.)   gentle gracious person. (With pun on "gentile," as at 2.4.34.)   53 Beshrew i.e., A mischief on. (A mild oath.)   60 stay wait. (Also in line 64.)

## [2.7]

[Flourish of cornets.] Enter Portia, with [the Prince of] Morocco, and both their trains.

PORTIA
Go, draw aside the curtains and discover                 1
The several caskets to this noble prince.                2
Now make your choice.        [The curtains are drawn.]

MOROCCO
The first, of gold, who this inscription bears,          4
"Who chooseth me shall gain what many men desire";
The second, silver, which this promise carries,
"Who chooseth me shall get as much as he deserves";
This third, dull lead, with warning all as blunt,        8
"Who chooseth me must give and hazard all he hath."
How shall I know if I do choose the right?

PORTIA
The one of them contains my picture, Prince.
If you choose that, then I am yours withal.              12

MOROCCO
Some god direct my judgment! Let me see,
I will survey th'inscriptions back again.
What says this leaden casket?
"Who chooseth me must give and hazard all he hath."
Must give—for what? For lead? Hazard for lead?
This casket threatens. Men that hazard all
Do it in hope of fair advantages.
A golden mind stoops not to shows of dross.              20
I'll then nor give nor hazard aught for lead.            21
What says the silver with her virgin hue?
"Who chooseth me shall get as much as he deserves."
As much as he deserves! Pause there, Morocco,
And weigh thy value with an even hand.                   25
If thou be'st rated by thy estimation,                   26
Thou dost deserve enough; and yet enough
May not extend so far as to the lady;
And yet to be afeard of my deserving
Were but a weak disabling of myself.                     30
As much as I deserve? Why, that's the lady.
I do in birth deserve her, and in fortunes,
In graces, and in qualities of breeding;
But more than these, in love I do deserve.
What if I strayed no farther, but chose here?
Let's see once more this saying graved in gold:          36
"Who chooseth me shall gain what many men desire."
Why, that's the lady; all the world desires her.
From the four corners of the earth they come
To kiss this shrine, this mortal breathing saint.        40
The Hyrcanian deserts and the vasty wilds                41
Of wide Arabia are as throughfares now
For princes to come view fair Portia.

2.7. Location: Belmont. Portia's house.
0.2 trains followers   1 discover reveal   2 several different, various   4 who which   8 dull (1) dull-colored (2) blunt.   all as blunt as blunt as lead   12 withal with it.   20 dross worthless matter. (Literally, the impurities cast off in the melting down of metals.)   21 nor give neither give   25 even impartial   26 estimation worth   30 disabling underrating   36 graved engraved   40 mortal breathing living   41 Hyrcanian (Hyrcania was the country south of the Caspian Sea celebrated for its wildness.)   vasty vast

The watery kingdom, whose ambitious head
Spits in the face of heaven, is no bar                                    45
To stop the foreign spirits, but they come,                              46
As o'er a brook, to see fair Portia.
One of these three contains her heavenly picture.
Is't like that lead contains her? 'Twere damnation     49
To think so base a thought; it were too gross          50
To rib her cerecloth in the obscure grave.             51
Or shall I think in silver she's immured,              52
Being ten times undervalued to tried gold?             53
Oh, sinful thought! Never so rich a gem
Was set in worse than gold. They have in England       55
A coin that bears the figure of an angel               56
Stamped in gold, but that's insculped upon;            57
But here an angel in a golden bed
Lies all within. Deliver me the key.
Here do I choose, and thrive I as I may!

PORTIA
There, take it, Prince; and if my form lie there,      61
Then I am yours.
                            [*He unlocks the golden casket.*]

MOROCCO          Oh, hell! What have we here?
A carrion Death, within whose empty eye                63
There is a written scroll! I'll read the writing.
[*He reads.*]
        "All that glisters is not gold;
        Often have you heard that told.
        Many a man his life hath sold
        But my outside to behold.                      68
        Gilded tombs do worms infold.
        Had you been as wise as bold,
        Young in limbs, in judgment old,
        Your answer had not been inscrolled.           72
        Fare you well; your suit is cold."
    Cold, indeed, and labor lost.
    Then, farewell, heat, and welcome, frost!
Portia, adieu. I have too grieved a heart
To take a tedious leave. Thus losers part.             77
                    *Exit* [*with his train. Flourish of cornets.*]

PORTIA
A gentle riddance. Draw the curtains, go.
Let all of his complexion choose me so.                79
            [*The curtains are closed, and*] *Exeunt.*

❖

## [2.8]

*Enter Salerio and Solanio.*

SALERIO
Why, man, I saw Bassanio under sail.
With him is Gratiano gone along,
And in their ship I am sure Lorenzo is not.

SOLANIO
The villain Jew with outcries raised the Duke,         4
Who went with him to search Bassanio's ship.

SALERIO
He came too late. The ship was under sail.
But there the Duke was given to understand
That in a gondola were seen together
Lorenzo and his amorous Jessica.
Besides, Antonio certified the Duke
They were not with Bassanio in his ship.

SOLANIO
I never heard a passion so confused,                   12
So strange, outrageous, and so variable
As the dog Jew did utter in the streets:
"My daughter! Oh, my ducats! Oh, my daughter!
Fled with a Christian! Oh, my Christian ducats!
Justice! The law! My ducats, and my daughter!
A sealèd bag, two sealèd bags of ducats,
Of double ducats, stol'n from me by my daughter!
And jewels, two stones, two rich and precious
   stones,
Stol'n by my daughter! Justice! Find the girl!
She hath the stones upon her, and the ducats."

SALERIO
Why, all the boys in Venice follow him,
Crying his stones, his daughter, and his ducats.        24

SOLANIO
Let good Antonio look he keep his day,                  25
Or he shall pay for this.

SALERIO                        Marry, well remembered.
I reasoned with a Frenchman yesterday,                  27
Who told me, in the narrow seas that part              28
The French and English, there miscarrièd
A vessel of our country richly fraught.                 30
I thought upon Antonio when he told me,
And wished in silence that it were not his.

SOLANIO
You were best to tell Antonio what you hear.
Yet do not suddenly, for it may grieve him.

SALERIO
A kinder gentleman treads not the earth.
I saw Bassanio and Antonio part.
Bassanio told him he would make some speed
Of his return; he answered, "Do not so.
Slubber not business for my sake, Bassanio,             39
But stay the very riping of the time;                   40

45 Spits (The image is of huge waves breaking at sea.)   46 spirits i.e.,
men of courage   49 like likely   50 base (1) ignoble (2) low in the
natural scale, as with lead, a *base* metal   50–1 it were . . . grave i.e., it
would be too gross an insult to inter her, as it were, wrapped in a
waxed cloth, in a lead casket.   52 immured enclosed, confined
53 Being . . . gold which has only one-tenth the value of assayed and
purified gold.   55 Was . . . gold was given a frame or setting in anything less precious than gold.   56 coin i.e., the gold coin known as
the *angel*, which bore the device of the archangel Michael treading on
the dragon   57 insculped upon merely engraved upon the surface
61 form image   63 carrion Death death's-head   68 But only
72 inscrolled i.e., written on this scroll.   77 part depart.
79 complexion temperament (not merely skin color)

2.8. Location: Venice. A street.
4 raised roused   12 passion passionate outburst   24 stones (In the boys'
jeering cry, the *two stones* suggest testicles; see line 20.)   25 look . . . day
see to it that he repays his loan on time   27 reasoned talked   28 narrow
seas English Channel   30 fraught freighted.   39 Slubber not business Don't do the business hastily and badly   40 But stay . . . time
i.e., but pursue your business at Belmont until it is brought to completion

And for the Jew's bond which he hath of me,　　41
Let it not enter in your mind of love.　　42
Be merry, and employ your chiefest thoughts
To courtship and such fair ostents of love　　44
As shall conveniently become you there."
And even there, his eye being big with tears,　　46
Turning his face, he put his hand behind him,　　47
And with affection wondrous sensible　　48
He wrung Bassanio's hand; and so they parted.

SOLANIO
I think he only loves the world for him.　　50
I pray thee, let us go and find him out
And quicken his embracèd heaviness　　52
With some delight or other.

SALERIO　　　　　　　　　　Do we so.　　　*Exeunt.*

❖

# [2.9]

*Enter Nerissa and a Servitor.*

NERISSA
Quick, quick, I pray thee, draw the curtain straight.　　1
The Prince of Aragon hath ta'en his oath,
And comes to his election presently.　　3
　　　　　　　　　　[*The curtains are drawn back.*]

[*Flourish of cornets.*] *Enter* [*the Prince of*]
*Aragon, his train, and Portia.*

PORTIA
Behold, there stand the caskets, noble Prince.
If you choose that wherein I am contained,
Straight shall our nuptial rites be solemnized;
But if you fail, without more speech, my lord,
You must be gone from hence immediately.

ARAGON
I am enjoined by oath to observe three things:
First, never to unfold to anyone　　10
Which casket 'twas I chose; next, if I fail
Of the right casket, never in my life
To woo a maid in way of marriage;
Lastly,
If I do fail in fortune of my choice,
Immediately to leave you and be gone.

PORTIA
To these injunctions everyone doth swear
That comes to hazard for my worthless self.

ARAGON
And so have I addressed me. Fortune now　　19
To my heart's hope! Gold, silver, and base lead.
"Who chooseth me must give and hazard all he hath."

You shall look fairer ere I give or hazard.
What says the golden chest? Ha, let me see:
"Who chooseth me shall gain what many men desire."
What many men desire! That "many" may be meant
By the fool multitude, that choose by show,　　26
Not learning more than the fond eye doth teach,　　27
Which pries not to th'interior, but like the martlet　　28
Builds in the weather on the outward wall,　　29
Even in the force and road of casualty.　　30
I will not choose what many men desire,
Because I will not jump with common spirits　　32
And rank me with the barbarous multitudes.
Why then, to thee, thou silver treasure-house!
Tell me once more what title thou dost bear:
"Who chooseth me shall get as much as he deserves."
And well said too; for who shall go about
To cozen fortune, and be honorable　　38
Without the stamp of merit? Let none presume　　39
To wear an undeservèd dignity.
Oh, that estates, degrees, and offices　　41
Were not derived corruptly, and that clear honor
Were purchased by the merit of the wearer!
How many then should cover that stand bare?　　44
How many be commanded that command?　　45
How much low peasantry would then be gleaned　　46
From the true seed of honor, and how much honor　　47
Picked from the chaff and ruin of the times
To be new-varnished? Well, but to my choice:　　49
"Who chooseth me shall get as much as he deserves."
I will assume desert. Give me a key for this,
And instantly unlock my fortunes here.
　　　　　　　　　　[*He opens the silver casket.*]

PORTIA
Too long a pause for that which you find there.

ARAGON
What's here? The portrait of a blinking idiot,
Presenting me a schedule! I will read it.　　55
How much unlike art thou to Portia!
How much unlike my hopes and my deservings!
"Who chooseth me shall have as much as he
　　deserves."
Did I deserve no more than a fool's head?
Is that my prize? Are my deserts no better?

PORTIA
To offend and judge are distinct offices　　61
And of opposèd natures.

ARAGON　　　　　　　　　What is here?　　62

41 **for** as for　42 **of** preoccupied with　44 **ostents** expressions, shows
46 **there** thereupon, then　47 **behind him** (Antonio turns away in
tears while extending his hand back to Bassanio.)　48 **affection
wondrous sensible** wondrously sensitive and keen emotion
50 **he . . . him** i.e., Bassanio is all he lives for.　52 **quicken . . . heaviness**
lighten the sorrow he has embraced
**2.9. Location: Belmont. Portia's house.**
0.1 *Servitor* servant.　1 **straight** at once.　3 **election presently** choice
immediately.　10 **unfold** disclose　19 **addressed me** prepared
myself (by this swearing).

26 **By** for, to signify　27 **fond** foolish　28 **martlet** swift　29 **in** exposed
to　30 **force . . . casualty** power and path of mischance.　32 **jump**
agree　38 **cozen** cheat　39 **stamp** seal of approval　41 **estates,
degrees** status, social rank　44 **cover . . . bare** i.e., wear hats (of
authority) who now stand bareheaded.　45 **How . . . command?** How
many then should be servants that are now masters?　46 **gleaned**
culled out and discarded　47 **the true seed of honor** i.e., persons of
noble descent　49 **new-varnished** i.e., having the luster of their true
nobility restored to them.　55 **schedule** written paper.　61–2 **To
offend . . . natures** i.e., You have no right, having submitted your case
to judgment, to attempt to judge your own case; or, it is not for me to
say, since I've been the indirect cause of your discomfiture.

[*He reads.*]"The fire seven times tried this;                       63
              Seven times tried that judgment is
              That did never choose amiss.
              Some there be that shadows kiss;                        66
              Such have but a shadow's bliss.
              There be fools alive, iwis,                             68
              Silvered o'er, and so was this.                         69
              Take what wife you will to bed;
              I will ever be your head.                               71
              So begone; you are sped."                               72

Still more fool I shall appear                                        73
By the time I linger here.                                           74
With one fool's head I came to woo,
But I go away with two.
Sweet, adieu. I'll keep my oath,
Patiently to bear my wroth.                                          78
                    [*Exeunt Aragon and train.*]

PORTIA
Thus hath the candle singed the moth.
Oh, these deliberate fools! When they do choose,                    80
They have the wisdom by their wit to lose.                          81
NERISSA
The ancient saying is no heresy:
Hanging and wiving goes by destiny.
PORTIA    Come, draw the curtain, Nerissa.
                    [*The curtains are closed.*]

              *Enter Messenger.*

MESSENGER
Where is my lady?
PORTIA                        Here. What would my lord?              85
MESSENGER
Madam, there is alighted at your gate
A young Venetian, one that comes before
To signify th'approaching of his lord,
From whom he bringeth sensible regreets,                            89
To wit, besides commends and courteous breath,                     90
Gifts of rich value. Yet I have not seen                           91
So likely an ambassador of love.
A day in April never came so sweet,
To show how costly summer was at hand,                             94
As this fore-spurrer comes before his lord.                        95
PORTIA
No more, I pray thee. I am half afeard
Thou wilt say anon he is some kin to thee,
Thou spend'st such high-day wit in praising him.                   98
Come, come, Nerissa, for I long to see
Quick Cupid's post that comes so mannerly.                        100

NERISSA
Bassanio, Lord Love, if thy will it be!          *Exeunt.* 101

## [3.1]

              [*Enter*] *Solanio and Salerio.*

SOLANIO    Now, what news on the Rialto?
SALERIO    Why, yet it lives there unchecked that Anto-nio          2
hath a ship of rich lading wrecked on the narrow                    3
seas—the Goodwins, I think they call the place, a                   4
very dangerous flat, and fatal, where the carcasses of             5
many a tall ship lie buried, as they say, if my gossip             6
Report be an honest woman of her word.                              7
SOLANIO    I would she were as lying a gossip in that as
ever knapped ginger or made her neighbors believe                  9
she wept for the death of a third husband. But it is
true, without any slips of prolixity or crossing the              11
plain highway of talk, that the good Antonio, the                 12
honest Antonio—oh, that I had a title good enough
to keep his name company!—
SALERIO    Come, the full stop.                                    15
SOLANIO    Ha, what sayest thou? Why, the end is, he
hath lost a ship.
SALERIO    I would it might prove the end of his losses.
SOLANIO    Let me say "amen" betimes, lest the devil             19
cross my prayer, for here he comes in the likeness of            20
a Jew.

              *Enter Shylock.*

How now, Shylock, what news among the merchants?
SHYLOCK    You knew, none so well, none so well as
you, of my daughter's flight.
SALERIO    That's certain. I for my part knew the tailor
that made the wings she flew withal.                               26
SOLANIO    And Shylock for his own part knew the bird
was fledge, and then it is the complexion of them all             28
to leave the dam.                                                 29
SHYLOCK    She is damned for it.
SALERIO    That's certain, if the devil may be her judge.
SHYLOCK    My own flesh and blood to rebel!
SOLANIO    Out upon it, old carrion! Rebels it at these          33
years?                                                            34
SHYLOCK    I say my daughter is my flesh and my blood.

---

**63 The fire . . . this** This silver has been seven times tested and purified
**66 shadows** illusions   **68 iwis** certainly   **69 Silvered o'er** i.e., with silver
hair and so apparently wise   **71 I . . . head** i.e., you will always have a
fool's head, be a fool.   **72 sped** done for.   **73–4 Still . . . here** i.e., I shall
seem all the greater fool for wasting any more time here.   **78 wroth**
sorrow, unhappy lot (a variant of *ruth*); or, anger.   **80 deliberate** reasoning, calculating   **81 They . . . lose** i.e., Fools of this deliberating sort
paradoxically lose by the exercise of what they believe to be their wise
wit.   **85 my lord** (A jesting response to "my lady." At the same time,
Portia's wit unconsciously anticipates what she has been longing for, the
arrival of an ideal suitor who will become her lord.)   **89 sensible regreets**
tangible gifts, greetings   **90 commends** greetings.   **breath** speech
**91 Yet** Heretofore   **94 costly** lavish, rich   **95 fore-spurrer** herald,
harbinger   **98 high-day** holiday (i.e., extravagant)   **100 post** messenger

**101 Lord Love** Cupid
**3.1. Location: Venice. A street.**
**2 yet . . . unchecked** i.e., a rumor is spreading undenied   **3 lading**
freight, cargo   **3–4 the narrow seas** the English Channel, as at
2.8.28   **4 Goodwins** Goodwin Sands, off the Kentish coast near the
Thames estuary   **5 flat** shoal, sandbank   **6 tall** gallant   **6-7 gossip
Report** i.e., Dame Rumor   **9 knapped** nibbled   **11 slips of prolixity**
lapses into long-windedness; or, long-winded lies. *Slips* may be the
cuttings or offshoots of tediousness.   **11–12 crossing . . . talk** deviating from honest, plain speech   **15 Come . . . stop** Finish your sentence; rein in your tongue as a horse is checked in its manage.   **19
betimes** while there is yet time   **20 cross** thwart; make the sign of the
cross following   **26 the wings . . . withal** i.e., the disguise she
escaped in. (With a play on *wings* or ornamented shoulder flaps sewn
on garments.)   **28 fledge** ready to fly.   **complexion** natural disposition, as at 2.7.79   **29 dam** mother.   **33–4 Rebels . . . years?** (Solanio
pretends to interpret Shylock's cry about the rebellion of his own flesh
and blood as referring to his own carnal desires, his own erection.)

SALERIO   There is more difference between thy flesh and
hers than between jet and ivory, more between your  37
bloods than there is between red wine and Rhenish.  38
But tell us, do you hear whether Antonio have had any
loss at sea or no?

SHYLOCK   There I have another bad match! A bankrupt,  41
a prodigal, who dare scarce show his head on the
Rialto; a beggar, that was used to come so smug upon
the mart! Let him look to his bond. He was wont to  44
call me usurer. Let him look to his bond. He was wont
to lend money for a Christian courtesy. Let him look
tohis bond.

SALERIO   Why, I am sure, if he forfeit, thou wilt not take
his flesh. What's that good for?

SHYLOCK   To bait fish withal. If it will feed nothing else,
it will feed my revenge. He hath disgraced me, and
hindered me half a million, laughed at my losses,
mocked at my gains, scorned my nation, thwarted my  53
bargains, cooled my friends, heated mine enemies;
and what's his reason? I am a Jew. Hath not a Jew
eyes? Hath not a Jew hands, organs, dimensions, senses, affections, passions? Fed with the same food, hurt
with the same weapons, subject to the same diseases,
healed by the same means, warmed and cooled by the
same winter and summer, as a Christian is? If you
prick us, do we not bleed? If you tickle us, do we not
laugh? If you poison us, do we not die? And if you
wrong us, shall we not revenge? If we are like you in
the rest, we will resemble you in that. If a Jew wrong
a Christian, what is his humility? Revenge. If a  65
Christian wrong a Jew, what should his sufferance be  66
by Christian example? Why, revenge. The villainy you
teach me I will execute, and it shall go hard but I will  68
better the instruction.

*Enter a Man from Antonio.*

MAN   Gentlemen, my master Antonio is at his house
and desires to speak with you both.

SALERIO   We have been up and down to seek him.  72

*Enter Tubal.*

SOLANIO   Here comes another of the tribe. A third
cannot be matched, unless the devil himself turn Jew.  74
            *Exeunt gentlemen [Solanio, Salerio, with Man].*

SHYLOCK   How now, Tubal, what news from Genoa?
Hast thou found my daughter?

TUBAL   I often came where I did hear of her, but cannot
find her.

SHYLOCK   Why, there, there, there, there! A diamond
gone, cost me two thousand ducats in Frankfort! The  80
curse never fell upon our nation till now; I never felt it  81

---

till now. Two thousand ducats in that, and other
precious, precious jewels. I would my daughter were
dead at my foot, and the jewels in her ear! Would she
were hearsed at my foot, and the ducats in her coffin!  85
No news of them? Why, so—and I know not what's
spent in the search. Why, thou loss upon loss! The
thief gone with so much, and so much to find the
thief, and no satisfaction, no revenge! Nor no ill luck
stirring but what lights o' my shoulders, no sighs but
o' my breathing, no tears but o' my shedding.

TUBAL   Yes, other men have ill luck too. Antonio, as I
heard in Genoa—

SHYLOCK   What, what, what? Ill luck, ill luck?

TUBAL   Hath an argosy cast away, coming from Tripolis.  95

SHYLCOK   I thank God, I thank God. Is it true, is it true?

TUBAL   I spoke with some of the sailors that escaped the
wreck.

SHYLOCK   I thank thee, good Tubal. Good news, good
news! Ha, ha! Heard in Genoa?

TUBAL   Your daughter spent in Genoa, as I heard, one
night fourscore ducats.

SHYLOCK   Thou stick'st a dagger in me. I shall never see
my gold again. Fourscore ducats at a sitting? Fourscore ducats?

TUBAL   There came divers of Antonio's creditors in my
company to Venice that swear he cannot choose but  107
break.  108

SHYLOCK   I am very glad of it. I'll plague him, I'll torture
him. I am glad of it.

TUBAL   One of them showed me a ring that he had of
your daughter for a monkey.

SHYLOCK   Out upon her! Thou torturest me, Tubal. It
was my turquoise; I had it of Leah when I was a  114
bachelor. I would not have given it for a wilderness
of monkeys.

TUBAL   But Antonio is certainly undone.

SHYLOCK   Nay, that's true, that's very true. Go, Tubal,
fee me an officer; bespeak him a fortnight before. I will  119
have the heart of him if he forfeit, for were he out of
Venice I can make what merchandise I will. Go, Tubal,  121
and meet me at our synagogue. Go, good Tubal; at our
synagogue, Tubal.          *Exeunt [separately].*

# [3.2]

*Enter Bassanio, Portia, Gratiano, [Nerissa,]
and all their trains.*

PORTIA
I pray you, tarry. Pause a day or two
Before you hazard, for in choosing wrong  2
I lose your company. Therefore forbear awhile.
There's something tells me—but it is not love—
I would not lose you; and you know yourself
Hate counsels not in such a quality.  6

---

37 **jet** a black, hard mineral, here contrasted with the whiteness of
ivory and Jessica's fair complexion    38 **Rhenish** i.e., a German white
wine from the Rhine valley. (Salerio seems to prefer the white wine
as more refined than the red.)    41 **match** bargain.    44 **mart** marketplace, Rialto.    53 **nation** ethnic community    65 **what . . . Revenge**
i.e., in what spirit does the Christian receive the injury, that of
Christian humility? No, he seeks revenge.    66 **his sufferance** the
Jew's patient endurance    68 **it shall . . . but** i.e., you can count on
this; nothing can stop me    72 **up and down** i.e., everywhere    74
**matched** i.e., found to match them    80–1 **The curse** God's curse
(such as the plagues visited upon Egypt in Exodus 7–12)

85 **hearsed** coffined    95 **cast away** shipwrecked    107–8 **cannot . . .
break** can't escape going bankrupt.    114 **Leah** Shylock's wife
119 **fee** hire.  **officer** bailiff.  **bespeak** engage    121 **make . . . I will**
drive whatever bargains I please.
**3.2. Location:** Belmont. Portia's house.
2 **in choosing** if you choose    6 **quality** way, manner.

But lest you should not understand me well—
And yet a maiden hath no tongue but thought—
I would detain you here some month or two
Before you venture for me. I could teach you
How to choose right, but then I am forsworn.
So will I never be. So may you miss me.                    12
But if you do, you'll make me wish a sin,
That I had been forsworn. Beshrew your eyes,
They have o'erlooked me and divided me!                    15
One half of me is yours, the other half yours—
Mine own, I would say; but if mine, then yours,
And so all yours. Oh, these naughty times                  18
Puts bars between the owners and their rights!             19
And so, though yours, not yours. Prove it so,             20
Let Fortune go to hell for it, not I.                      21
I speak too long, but 'tis to peise the time,            22
To eke it and to draw it out in length,                   23
To stay you from election.

BASSANIO                                Let me choose,      24
For as I am, I live upon the rack.

PORTIA
Upon the rack, Bassanio? Then confess                      26
What treason there is mingled with your love.             27

BASSANIO
None but that ugly treason of mistrust,                    28
Which makes me fear th'enjoying of my love.               29
There may as well be amity and life
'Tween snow and fire, as treason and my love.             31

PORTIA
Ay, but I fear you speak upon the rack,
Where men enforcèd do speak anything.

BASSANIO
Promise me life, and I'll confess the truth.

PORTIA
Well then, confess and live.

BASSANIO                          "Confess and love"
Had been the very sum of my confession.
Oh, happy torment, when my torturer
Doth teach me answers for deliverance!
But let me to my fortune and the caskets.                  39

PORTIA
Away, then! I am locked in one of them.
If you do love me, you will find me out.
Nerissa and the rest, stand all aloof.                     42
Let music sound while he doth make his choice;
Then, if he lose, he makes a swanlike end,                 44
Fading in music. That the comparison
May stand more proper, my eye shall be the stream          46

And wat'ry deathbed for him. He may win;                   47
And what is music then? Then music is
Even as the flourish when true subjects bow                49
To a new-crownèd monarch. Such it is
As are those dulcet sounds in break of day
That creep into the dreaming bridegroom's ear
And summon him to marriage. Now he goes,
With no less presence, but with much more love,            54
Than young Alcides when he did redeem                      55
The virgin tribute paid by howling Troy                    56
To the sea monster. I stand for sacrifice;                 57
The rest aloof are the Dardanian wives,                    58
With blearèd visages, come forth to view                   59
The issue of th'exploit. Go, Hercules!                     60
Live thou, I live. With much, much more dismay             61
I view the fight than thou that mak'st the fray.

*A song, the whilst Bassanio comments on the
caskets to himself.*

Tell me where is fancy bred,                               63
Or in the heart or in the head?                            64
How begot, how nourishèd?
      Reply, reply.
It is engendered in the eyes,                              67
With gazing fed, and fancy dies
In the cradle where it lies.                               69
      Let us all ring fancy's knell.
      I'll begin it—Ding, dong, bell.

ALL     Ding, dong, bell.

BASSANIO
So may the outward shows be least themselves;             73
The world is still deceived with ornament.                74
In law, what plea so tainted and corrupt
But, being seasoned with a gracious voice,
Obscures the show of evil? In religion,
What damnèd error but some sober brow                      78
Will bless it and approve it with a text,                 79
Hiding the grossness with fair ornament?
There is no vice so simple but assumes                     81
Some mark of virtue on his outward parts.                 82
How many cowards, whose hearts are all as false
As stairs of sand, wear yet upon their chins               84
The beards of Hercules and frowning Mars,
Who, inward searched, have livers white as milk?           86
And these assume but valor's excrement                     87

---

12 **So** i.e., Forsworn. **So may . . . me** That being the case, you may fail to win me. **15 o'erlooked** bewitched **18 naughty** wicked **19 bars** barriers **20 though yours, not yours** (I am) yours by right but not by actual possession. **20–1 Prove . . . not I** i.e., If it turn out thus (that you are cheated of what is justly yours, i.e., of me), let Fortune be blamed for it, not I, for I will not be forsworn. **22 peise** retard (by hanging on of weights) **23 eke it** stretch it out, make it last **24 election** choice. **26–7 confess What treason** (The rack was used to force traitors to confess.) **28 mistrust** misapprehension **29 fear** fearful about **31 as** as between **39 fortune . . . caskets** (Presumably the curtains are drawn at about this point, as in the previous "casket" scenes, revealing the three caskets.) **42 aloof** apart, at a distance. **44 swanlike** (Swans were believed to sing when they came to die.) **46–7 my eye . . . him** i.e., I will weep.

49 **flourish** sounding of trumpets **54 presence** noble bearing **55 Alcides** Hercules (called *Alcides,* as at 2.1.32–5, because he was the grandson of Alcaeus) rescued Hesione, daughter of the Trojan king Laomedon, from a monster to which, by command of Neptune, she was about to be sacrificed. Hercules was rewarded, however, not with the lady's love, but with a famous pair of horses. **56 howling** lamenting **57 stand for sacrifice** represent the sacrificial victim **58 The rest aloof** i.e., Nerissa and attendants standing by. **Dardanian** Trojan **59 blearèd** tear-stained **60 issue** outcome **61 Live thou** If you live **63 fancy** love **64 Or** either **67 eyes** (Love entered the heart especially through the eyes.) **69 In the cradle** i.e., in its infancy, in the eyes **73 be least themselves** least represent the inner reality **74 still** ever **78 sober brow** i.e., solemn-faced clergyman **79 approve** confirm **81 simple** unadulterated **82 his** its **84 stairs** steps **86 searched** surgically probed. **livers** (The liver was thought to be the seat of courage; for it to be deserted by the blood would be the condition of cowardice.) **87 excrement** outgrowth, here a beard

To render them redoubted. Look on beauty,                                88
And you shall see 'tis purchased by the weight,                          89
Which therein works a miracle in nature,
Making them lightest that wear most of it.                               91
So are those crispèd, snaky, golden locks,                               92
Which maketh such wanton gambols with the wind
Upon supposèd fairness, often known                                      94
To be the dowry of a second head,                                        95
The skull that bred them in the sepulcher.                               96
Thus ornament is but the guilèd shore                                    97
To a most dangerous sea, the beauteous scarf
Veiling an Indian beauty; in a word,                                     99
The seeming truth which cunning times put on
To entrap the wisest. Therefore, thou gaudy gold,
Hard food for Midas, I will none of thee;                                102
Nor none of thee, thou pale and common drudge                           103
'Tween man and man. But thou, thou meager lead,                         104
Which rather threaten'st than dost promise aught,
Thy paleness moves me more than eloquence;
And here choose I. Joy be the consequence!

PORTIA [aside]
How all the other passions fleet to air,
As doubtful thoughts, and rash-embraced despair,                         109
And shuddering fear, and green-eyed jealousy!
O love, be moderate, allay thy ecstasy,
In measure rain thy joy, scant this excess!                              112
I feel too much thy blessing. Make it less,
For fear I surfeit.

BASSANIO [opening the leaden casket]
                    What find I here?
Fair Portia's counterfeit! What demigod                                  115
Hath come so near creation? Move these eyes?
Or whether, riding on the balls of mine,
Seem they in motion? Here are severed lips,
Parted with sugar breath; so sweet a bar                                 119
Should sunder such sweet friends. Here in her hairs                      120
The painter plays the spider, and hath woven
A golden mesh t'entrap the hearts of men
Faster than gnats in cobwebs. But her eyes—                              123
How could he see to do them? Having made one,
Methinks it should have power to steal both his
And leave itself unfurnished. Yet look how far                           126
The substance of my praise doth wrong this shadow                        127
In underprizing it, so far this shadow                                   128
Doth limp behind the substance. Here's the scroll,                       129

The continent and summary of my fortune.                                 130
[He reads.] "You that choose not by the view
            Chance as fair, and choose as true.                          132
      Since this fortune falls to you,
      Be content and seek no new.
      If you be well pleased with this,
      And hold your fortune for your bliss,
      Turn you where your lady is
      And claim her with a loving kiss."
A gentle scroll. Fair lady, by your leave,
I come by note, to give and to receive.                                  140
Like one of two contending in a prize,                                   141
That thinks he hath done well in people's eyes,
Hearing applause and universal shout,
Giddy in spirit, still gazing in a doubt
Whether those peals of praise be his or no,                              145
So, thrice-fair lady, stand I, even so,
As doubtful whether what I see be true,
Until confirmed, signed, ratified by you.

PORTIA
You see me, Lord Bassanio, where I stand,
Such as I am. Though for myself alone
I would not be ambitious in my wish
To wish myself much better, yet for you
I would be trebled twenty times myself,
A thousand times more fair, ten thousand times
      more rich,
That only to stand high in your account                                 155
I might in virtues, beauties, livings, friends,                          156
Exceed account. But the full sum of me                                   157
Is sum of something, which, to term in gross,                            158
Is an unlessoned girl, unschooled, unpracticèd;
Happy in this, she is not yet so old
But she may learn; happier than this,
She is not bred so dull but she can learn;
Happiest of all is that her gentle spirit
Commits itself to yours to be directed
As from her lord, her governor, her king.
Myself and what is mine to you and yours
Is now converted. But now I was the lord                                 167
Of this fair mansion, master of my servants,
Queen o'er myself; and even now, but now,
This house, these servants, and this same myself
Are yours, my lord's. I give them with this ring,
Which when you part from, lose, or give away,
Let it presage the ruin of your love
And be my vantage to exclaim on you.                                     174
                              [She puts a ring on his finger.]

BASSANIO
Madam, you have bereft me of all words.
Only my blood speaks to you in my veins,

---

**88 redoubted** feared.   **89 purchased by the weight** bought (as cosmetics) at so much per ounce   **91 lightest** most frivolous or lascivious. (With pun on the sense of "least heavy.")   **92 crispèd** curly   **94 Upon supposèd fairness** i.e., on a woman supposed beautiful and fair-haired   **95–6 To . . . sepulcher** i.e., to be a wig of hair taken from a woman now dead.   **97 guilèd** treacherous   **99 Indian** i.e., swarthy, not fair   **102 Midas** the Phrygian king whose touch turned everything to gold, including his food   **103–4 pale . . . man** i.e., silver, used in commerce.   **104 meager** wanting in richness   **109 As** such as   **112 rain** rain down, or perhaps "rein."   **scant** lessen   **115 counterfeit** portrait.   **demigod** i.e., the painter as creator   **119–20 so . . . friends** i.e., only so sweet a barrier as her mouth and breath should be allowed to part such sweet friends as her two lips.   **123 Faster** (1) more tightly (2) quicker   **126 unfurnished** i.e., without a companion.   **look how far** however far   **127 shadow** painting, semblance   **128 underprizing it** failing to do it justice.   **so far** to a similar extent   **129 the substance** the subject, i.e., Portia.

**130 continent** container   **132 Chance as fair** take your chances fortunately   **140 by note** by a bill of dues (i.e., the scroll). The commercial metaphor continues in *confirmed, signed, ratified* (line 148), *account* (155), *sum* (157), *term in gross* (158), etc.   **141 prize** competition   **145 his** for him   **155 account** estimation   **156 livings** possessions   **157 account** calculation. (Playing on *account*, estimation, in line 155.)   **157–8 But . . . something** i.e., But the full sum of my worth can only be the sum of whatever I am   **158 term in gross** denote in full   **167 But now** A moment ago   **174 vantage to exclaim on** opportunity to reproach

And there is such confusion in my powers
As, after some oration fairly spoke
By a belovèd prince, there doth appear
Among the buzzing pleasèd multitude,
Where every something being blent together    181
Turns to a wild of nothing save of joy    182
Expressed and not expressed. But when this ring    183
Parts from this finger, then parts life from hence.
Oh, then be bold to say Bassanio's dead!

NERISSA
My lord and lady, it is now our time,
That have stood by and seen our wishes prosper,    187
To cry, "good joy." Good joy, my lord and lady!

GRATIANO
My lord Bassanio and my gentle lady,
I wish you all the joy that you can wish—
For I am sure you can wish none from me.    191
And when Your Honors mean to solemnize
The bargain of your faith, I do beseech you
Even at that time I may be married too.

BASSANIO
With all my heart, so thou canst get a wife.    195

GRATIANO
I thank Your Lordship, you have got me one.
My eyes, my lord, can look as swift as yours.
You saw the mistress, I beheld the maid;    198
You loved, I loved; for intermission    199
No more pertains to me, my lord, than you.
Your fortune stood upon the caskets there,
And so did mine too, as the matter falls;    202
For wooing here until I sweat again,    203
And swearing till my very roof was dry    204
With oaths of love, at last, if promise last,    205
I got a promise of this fair one here
To have her love, provided that your fortune
Achieved her mistress.

PORTIA                              Is this true, Nerissa?

NERISSA
Madam, it is, so you stand pleased withal.    209

BASSANIO
And do you, Gratiano, mean good faith?

GRATIANO    Yes, faith, my lord.

BASSANIO
Our feast shall be much honored in your marriage.

GRATIANO    We'll play with them the first boy for a thou-    213
sand ducats.

NERISSA    What, and stake down?    215

GRATIANO    No, we shall ne'er win at that sport, and    177
stake down.

*Enter Lorenzo, Jessica, and Salerio, a messenger
from Venice.*

But who comes here? Lorenzo and his infidel?
What, and my old Venetian friend Salerio?

BASSANIO
Lorenzo and Salerio, welcome hither,
If that the youth of my new interest here    221
Have power to bid you welcome.—By your leave,
I bid my very friends and countrymen,    223
Sweet Portia, welcome.

PORTIA    So do I, my lord.
They are entirely welcome.

LORENZO
I thank Your Honor. For my part, my lord,
My purpose was not to have seen you here,
But, meeting with Salerio by the way,
He did entreat me, past all saying nay,
To come with him along.

SALERIO                          I did, my lord,
And I have reason for it. Signor Antonio
Commends him to you.    [*He gives Bassanio a letter.*]

BASSANIO                          Ere I ope his letter,    232
I pray you tell me how my good friend doth.

SALERIO
Not sick, my lord, unless it be in mind,
Nor well, unless in mind. His letter there
Will show you his estate.    [*Bassanio*] open[*s*] *the letter.*    236

GRATIANO [*indicating Jessica*]
Nerissa, cheer yond stranger, bid her welcome.    237
Your hand, Salerio. What's the news from Venice?
How doth that royal merchant, good Antonio?    239
I know he will be glad of our success.
We are the Jasons; we have won the fleece.    241

SALERIO
I would you had won the fleece that he hath lost.

PORTIA
There are some shrewd contents in yond same paper    243
That steals the color from Bassanio's cheek—
Some dear friend dead, else nothing in the world
Could turn so much the constitution
Of any constant man. What, worse and worse?    247
With leave, Bassanio; I am half yourself,    248
And I must freely have the half of anything
That this same paper brings you.

BASSANIO                          O sweet Portia,
Here are a few of the unpleasant'st words
That ever blotted paper! Gentle lady,
When I did first impart my love to you,
I freely told you all the wealth I had
Ran in my veins, I was a gentleman;
And then I told you true. And yet, dear lady,

---

**177 powers** faculties    **181–3 Where . . . expressed** i.e., in which every individual utterance, being blended and confused, turns into a hubbub of joy.    **187 That** we who    **191 For . . . me** i.e., I'm sure I can't wish you any more joy than you could wish for yourselves, or, I'm sure your wishes for happiness cannot take away from my happiness.    **195 so** provided    **198 maid** (Nerissa is a lady-in-waiting, not a house servant.)    **199 intermission** delay (in loving)    **202 falls** falls out, happens    **203 sweat again** sweated repeatedly    **204 roof** roof of my mouth    **205 if promise last** i.e., if Nerissa's promise should last, hold out. (With a play on *last* and *at last*, "finally.")    **209 so** provided    **213 We'll . . . boy** We'll wager with them to see who has the first male heir    **215 stake down** cash placed in advance. (But Gratiano, in his reply, turns the phrase into a bawdy joke; *stake down* to him suggests a non-erect phallus.)

**221 youth . . . interest** i.e., newness of my household authority    **223 very** true    **232 Commends him** desires to be remembered    **236 estate** situation.    **237 stranger** alien    **239 royal merchant** i.e., chief among merchants    **241 Jasons . . . fleece** (Compare with 1.1.170–2.)    **243 shrewd** cursed, grievous    **247 constant** settled, not swayed by passion    **248 With leave** With your permission

Rating myself at nothing, you shall see
How much I was a braggart. When I told you
My state was nothing, I should then have told you    259
That I was worse than nothing; for indeed
I have engaged myself to a dear friend,
Engaged my friend to his mere enemy,    262
To feed my means. Here is a letter, lady,
The paper as the body of my friend,
And every word in it a gaping wound
Issuing lifeblood. But is it true, Salerio?
Hath all his ventures failed? What, not one hit?    267
From Tripolis, from Mexico, and England,
From Lisbon, Barbary, and India,
And not one vessel scape the dreadful touch
Of merchant-marring rocks?

SALERIO             Not one, my lord.    271
Besides, it should appear that if he had
The present money to discharge the Jew    273
He would not take it. Never did I know    274
A creature that did bear the shape of man
So keen and greedy to confound a man.    276
He plies the Duke at morning and at night,
And doth impeach the freedom of the state    278
If they deny him justice. Twenty merchants,
The Duke himself, and the magnificoes    280
Of greatest port have all persuaded with him,    281
But none can drive him from the envious plea    282
Of forfeiture, of justice, and his bond.

JESSICA
When I was with him I have heard him swear
To Tubal and to Chus, his countrymen,    285
That he would rather have Antonio's flesh
Than twenty times the value of the sum
That he did owe him; and I know, my lord,
If law, authority, and power deny not,
It will go hard with poor Antonio.

PORTIA [to Bassanio]
Is it your dear friend that is thus in trouble?

BASSANIO
The dearest friend to me, the kindest man,
The best-conditioned and unwearied spirit    293
In doing courtesies, and one in whom
The ancient Roman honor more appears
Than any that draws breath in Italy.

PORTIA    What sum owes he the Jew?

BASSANIO
For me, three thousand ducats.

PORTIA            What, no more?
Pay him six thousand, and deface the bond;    299
Double six thousand, and then treble that,

Before a friend of this description
Shall lose a hair through Bassanio's fault.
First go with me to church and call me wife,
And then away to Venice to your friend;
For never shall you lie by Portia's side
With an unquiet soul. You shall have gold
To pay the petty debt twenty times over.
When it is paid, bring your true friend along.
My maid Nerissa and myself meantime
Will live as maids and widows. Come, away!
For you shall hence upon your wedding day.
Bid your friends welcome, show a merry cheer;    312
Since you are dear bought, I will love you dear.    313
But let me hear the letter of your friend.

BASSANIO [reads] "Sweet Bassanio, my ships have all miscarried, my creditors grow cruel, my estate is very low, my bond to the Jew is forfeit; and since in paying it, it is impossible I should live, all debts are cleared between you and I if I might but see you at my death. Notwithstanding, use your pleasure. If your love do not persuade you to come, let not my letter."

PORTIA
O love, dispatch all business, and begone!

BASSANIO
Since I have your good leave to go away,
I will make haste; but till I come again
No bed shall e'er be guilty of my stay,
Nor rest be interposer twixt us twain.    *Exeunt.*

❧

## [3.3]

*Enter [Shylock] the Jew and Solanio and Antonio and the Jailer.*

SHYLOCK
Jailer, look to him. Tell not me of mercy.
This is the fool that lent out money gratis.    2
Jailer, look to him.

ANTONIO           Hear me yet, good Shylock.

SHYLOCK
I'll have my bond. Speak not against my bond.
I have sworn an oath that I will have my bond.
Thou called'st me dog before thou hadst a cause,
But since I am a dog, beware my fangs.
The Duke shall grant me justice. I do wonder,
Thou naughty jailer, that thou art so fond    9
To come abroad with him at his request.    10

ANTONIO    I pray thee, hear me speak.

SHYLOCK
I'll have my bond. I will not hear thee speak.
I'll have my bond, and therefore speak no more.
I'll not be made a soft and dull-eyed fool,    14
To shake the head, relent, and sigh, and yield
To Christian intercessors. Follow not.
I'll have no speaking. I will have my bond.    *Exit Jew.*

259 **state** estate    262 **mere** absolute    267 **hit** success.    271 **merchant-marring** capable of damaging a merchant ship    273 **present** available. **discharge** pay off    274 **He** i.e., Shylock    276 **confound** destroy    278 **doth . . . state** i.e., calls in question the ability of Venice to defend legally the freedom of commerce of its citizens    280 **magnificoes** chief men of Venice    281 **port** dignity. **persuaded** argued    282 **envious** malicious    285 **Chus** the Bishops' Bible spelling of *Cush*, son of Ham and grandson of Noah. *Tubal* was son of Japheth and grandson of Noah (Genesis 10:2, 6).    293 **best-conditioned** best-natured    299 **deface** erase

312 **cheer** countenance    313 **dear . . . dear** at great cost . . . dearly. **3.3. Location: Venice. A street.** 2 **gratis** free (of interest).    9 **naughty** worthless, wicked.    **fond** foolish 10 **abroad** outside    14 **dull-eyed** easily duped

SOLANIO
　It is the most impenetrable cur
　That ever kept with men.
ANTONIO　　　　　　　　　　Let him alone.  19
　I'll follow him no more with bootless prayers.  20
　He seeks my life. His reason well I know:
　I oft delivered from his forfeitures
　Many that have at times made moan to me;
　Therefore he hates me.
SOLANIO　　　　　　　　I am sure the Duke
　Will never grant this forfeiture to hold.
ANTONIO
　The Duke cannot deny the course of law;
　For the commodity that strangers have  27
　With us in Venice, if it be denied,
　Will much impeach the justice of the state,
　Since that the trade and profit of the city  30
　Consisteth of all nations. Therefore go.
　These griefs and losses have so bated me  32
　That I shall hardly spare a pound of flesh
　Tomorrow to my bloody creditor.—
　Well, jailer, on. Pray God Bassanio come
　To see me pay his debt, and then I care not.    *Exeunt.*

❖

## [3.4]

*Enter Portia, Nerissa, Lorenzo, Jessica, and
[Balthasar,] a man of Portia's.*

LORENZO
　Madam, although I speak it in your presence,
　You have a noble and a true conceit  2
　Of godlike amity, which appears most strongly  3
　In bearing thus the absence of your lord.
　But if you knew to whom you show this honor,  5
　How true a gentleman you send relief,
　How dear a lover of my lord your husband,  7
　I know you would be prouder of the work
　Than customary bounty can enforce you.  9
PORTIA
　I never did repent for doing good,
　Nor shall not now; for in companions
　That do converse and waste the time together,  12
　Whose souls do bear an equal yoke of love,
　There must be needs a like proportion  14
　Of lineaments, of manners, and of spirit;  15
　Which makes me think that this Antonio,
　Being the bosom lover of my lord,  17
　Must needs be like my lord. If it be so,
　How little is the cost I have bestowed
　In purchasing the semblance of my soul  20

　From out the state of hellish cruelty!  21
　This comes too near the praising of myself;
　Therefore no more of it. Hear other things:
　Lorenzo, I commit into your hands
　The husbandry and manage of my house  25
　Until my lord's return. For mine own part,
　I have toward heaven breathed a secret vow
　To live in prayer and contemplation,
　Only attended by Nerissa here,
　Until her husband and my lord's return.
　There is a monastery two miles off,
　And there we will abide. I do desire you
　Not to deny this imposition,  33
　The which my love and some necessity
　Now lays upon you.
LORENZO　　　　　　　Madam, with all my heart,
　I shall obey you in all fair commands.
PORTIA
　My people do already know my mind,  37
　And will acknowledge you and Jessica
　In place of Lord Bassanio and myself.
　So fare you well till we shall meet again.
LORENZO
　Fair thoughts and happy hours attend on you!
JESSICA
　I wish Your Ladyship all heart's content.
PORTIA
　I thank you for your wish and am well pleased
　To wish it back on you. Fare you well, Jessica.
　　　　　　　*Exeunt [Jessica and Lorenzo].*
　Now, Balthasar,
　As I have ever found thee honest-true,
　So let me find thee still. Take this same letter,
　　　　　　　　*[giving a letter]*
　And use thou all th'endeavor of a man
　In speed to Padua. See thou render this
　Into my cousin's hands, Doctor Bellario;
　And look what notes and garments he doth give thee,  51
　Bring them, I pray thee, with imagined speed  52
　Unto the traject, to the common ferry  53
　Which trades to Venice. Waste no time in words,  54
　But get thee gone. I shall be there before thee.  55
BALTHASAR
　Madam, I go with all convenient speed.    *[Exit.]*
PORTIA
　Come on, Nerissa, I have work in hand
　That you yet know not of. We'll see our husbands
　Before they think of us.
NERISSA　　　　　　　　Shall they see us?
PORTIA
　They shall, Nerissa, but in such a habit  60
　That they shall think we are accomplishèd  61
　With that we lack. I'll hold thee any wager,  62

19 **kept** associated, dwelt　**20 bootless** unavailing　**27 commodity** facilities or privileges for trading.　**strangers** noncitizens, including Jews　**30 Since that** since　**32 bated** reduced
**3.4. Location:** Belmont. Portia's house.
**2 conceit** understanding　**3 amity** friendship and love　**5 to whom . . . honor** i.e., Antonio, who you honor by sending money to relieve him　**7 lover** friend　**9 Than . . . you** than ordinary benevolence can make you.　**12 waste** spend　**14 must be needs** must be　**15 lineaments** physical features　**17 bosom lover** dear friend　**20 the semblance of my soul** i.e., Antonio, so like my Bassanio

21 **From . . . cruelty** from the cruel state in which he presently stands.　**25 husbandry and manage** care and management　**33 deny this imposition** refuse this charge imposed　**37 people** servants　**51 look what** whatever　**52 imagined** all imaginable　**53 traject** ferry. (Italian *traghetto*.)　**common** public　**54 trades** plies back and forth　**55 I shall . . . thee** If you don't hurry, I will get there first.　**60 habit** apparel, garb　**61 accomplishèd** supplied　**62 that** that which. (With the bawdy suggestion of a penis.)

When we are both accoutered like young men
I'll prove the prettier fellow of the two,
And wear my dagger with the braver grace,
And speak between the change of man and boy    66
With a reed voice, and turn two mincing steps    67
Into a manly stride, and speak of frays
Like a fine bragging youth, and tell quaint lies,    69
How honorable ladies sought my love,
Which I denying, they fell sick and died—
I could not do withal! Then I'll repent,    72
And wish, for all that, that I had not killed them;
And twenty of these puny lies I'll tell,    74
That men shall swear I have discontinued school    75
Above a twelvemonth. I have within my mind    76
A thousand raw tricks of these bragging Jacks,    77
Which I will practice.
NERISSA                        Why, shall we turn to men?    78
PORTIA    Fie, what a question's that,
If thou wert near a lewd interpreter!
But come, I'll tell thee all my whole device    81
When I am in my coach, which stays for us
At the park gate; and therefore haste away,
For we must measure twenty miles today.    *Exeunt.*    84

❖

## [3.5]

*Enter [Lancelot the] clown and Jessica.*

LANCELOT    Yes, truly, for look you, the sins of the father are to be laid upon the children; therefore, I prom-    2
ise you, I fear you. I was always plain with you, and    3
so now I speak my agitation of the matter. Therefore    4
be o' good cheer, for truly I think you are damned.
There is but one hope in it that can do you any good,
and that is but a kind of bastard hope, neither.    7
JESSICA    And what hope is that, I pray thee?
LANCELOT    Marry, you may partly hope that your father got you not, that you are not the Jew's daughter.    10
JESSICA    That were a kind of bastard hope, indeed! So
the sins of my mother should be visited upon me.
LANCELOT    Truly, then, I fear you are damned both by
father and mother. Thus when I shun Scylla, your    14
father, I fall into Charybdis, your mother. Well, you    15
are gone both ways.    16
JESSICA    I shall be saved by my husband. He hath made    17
me a Christian.

LANCELOT    Truly, the more to blame he! We were    19
Christians enough before, e'en as many as could well    20
live one by another. This making of Christians will    21
raise the price of hogs. If we grow all to be pork eaters,
we shall not shortly have a rasher on the coals for    23
money.    24

*Enter Lorenzo.*

JESSICA    I'll tell my husband, Lancelot, what you say.
Here he comes.
LORENZO    I shall grow jealous of you shortly, Lancelot,
if you thus get my wife into corners.
JESSICA    Nay, you need not fear us, Lorenzo. Lancelot
and I are out. He tells me flatly there's no mercy for me    30
in heaven because I am a Jew's daughter; and he says
you are no good member of the commonwealth, for
in converting Jews to Christians you raise the price
of pork.
LORENZO    [*to Lancelot*] I shall answer that better to the
commonwealth than you can the getting up of the
Negro's belly. The Moor is with child by you, Lancelot.    37
LANCELOT    It is much that the Moor should be more    38
than reason; but if she be less than an honest woman,    39
she is indeed more than I took her for.    40
LORENZO    How every fool can play upon the word!
I think the best grace of wit will shortly turn into    42
silence, and discourse grow commendable in none
only but parrots. Go in, sirrah, bid them prepare for
dinner.
LANCELOT    That is done, sir. They have all stomachs.    46
LORENZO    Goodly Lord, what a wit-snapper are you!
Then bid them prepare dinner.
LANCELOT    That is done too, sir, only "cover" is the    49
word.
LORENZO    Will you cover then, sir?    51
LANCELOT    Not so, sir, neither. I know my duty.    52
LORENZO    Yet more quarreling with occasion! Wilt thou    53
show the whole wealth of thy wit in an instant? I pray
thee, understand a plain man in his plain meaning: go
to thy fellows, bid them cover the table, serve in the
meat, and we will come in to dinner.    57
LANCELOT    For the table, sir, it shall be served in; for    58
the meat, sir, it shall be covered; for your coming in to    59

**19–20 We . . . enough** There were enough of us Christians    **21 one by another** (1) as neighbors (2) off one another.    **23 rasher** i.e., of bacon    **23–4 for money** even for ready money, at any price.    **30 are out** have fallen out.    **37 The Moor** (Lancelot has evidently impregnated some woman of the household, who, being of African heritage, is referred to as both "Negro" and "Moor.")    **38–40 It is . . . for** i.e., It is a matter of concern that the Moor is larger (being pregnant) than usual, larger than she should be; but if it turns out that she is less than perfectly chaste, she is something more than I originally supposed. (Lancelot professes to be surprised by what has happened. With wordplay on *less/more* and *more/Moor*.)    **42 the best . . . wit** true wittiness    **46 They . . . stomachs** The guests all have appetites, and are prepared in that sense. (Lancelot quibbles with Lorenzo's meaning that the cooks and servants should be told to get dinner ready.)    **49, 51 cover** spread the table for the meal. (But in line 52 Lancelot uses the word to mean "put on one's hat.")    **52 my duty** i.e., my duty to remain bareheaded.    **53 Yet . . . occasion!** i.e., Still quibbling at every opportunity!    **57 meat** food    **58 For** As for.    **table** (Here Lancelot quibblingly takes the word to mean the food itself.)    **59 covered** (Here used in the sense of providing a cover for each separate dish.)

**66–7 And speak . . . voice** and speak with the voice of an adolescent youth changing awkwardly from treble to manly bass    **69 quaint** elaborate, clever    **72 do withal** help it.    **74 puny** childish    **75–6 I . . . twelvemonth** that I am scarcely more than a year out of my pre-adolescence.    **76 Above** more than    **77 Jacks** fellows    **78 turn to** turn into. (But Portia sees the occasion for a bawdy quibble on the idea of "turning toward, lying next to.")    **81 device** plan    **84 measure** traverse
**3.5. Location: Belmont. Outside Portia's house.**
**2–3 promise** assure    **3 fear you** fear for you.    **4 my agitation of** my sense of agitation about    **7 bastard** i.e., unfounded. (But also anticipating the usual meaning in lines 9–10.)    **neither** i.e., to be sure.    **10 got** begot    **14, 15 Scylla, Charybdis** twin dangers of the *Odyssey*, 12.255, a monster and a whirlpool guarding the straits presumably between Italy and Sicily. (*Fall into* plays on the idea of entering the female sexual anatomy.)    **16 gone** done for    **17 I . . . husband** (Compare 1 Corinthians 7:14: "the unbelieving wife is sanctified by the husband.")

dinner, sir, why, let it be as humors and conceits shall    60
govern.                              *Exit [Lancelot the] clown.*

LORENZO
Oh, dear discretion, how his words are suited!              62
The fool hath planted in his memory
An army of good words; and I do know
A many fools, that stand in better place,                   65
Garnished like him, that for a tricksy word                 66
Defy the matter. How cheer'st thou, Jessica?               67
And now, good sweet, say thy opinion:
How dost thou like the Lord Bassanio's wife?

JESSICA
Past all expressing. It is very meet                        70
The Lord Bassanio live an upright life,
For, having such a blessing in his lady,
He finds the joys of heaven here on earth;
And if on earth he do not merit it,
In reason he should never come to heaven.                   75
Why, if two gods should play some heavenly match
And on the wager lay two earthly women,                     77
And Portia one, there must be something else                78
Pawned with the other, for the poor rude world              79
Hath not her fellow.

LORENZO                      Even such a husband              80
Hast thou of me as she is for a wife.

JESSICA
Nay, but ask my opinion too of that!

LORENZO
I will anon. First let us go to dinner.

JESSICA
Nay, let me praise you while I have a stomach.              84

LORENZO
No, pray thee, let it serve for table talk;
Then, howsome'er thou speak'st, 'mong other things
I shall digest it.

JESSICA                      Well, I'll set you forth.    *Exeunt.* 87

❖

# [4.1]

*Enter the Duke, the Magnificoes, Antonio, Bas-*
*sanio, [Salerio,] and Gratiano [with others. The*
*judges take their places.]*

DUKE    What, is Antonio here?
ANTONIO    Ready, so please Your Grace.

DUKE
I am sorry for thee. Thou art come to answer               3
A stony adversary, an inhuman wretch
Uncapable of pity, void and empty
From any dram of mercy.

ANTONIO                          I have heard               6
Your Grace hath ta'en great pains to qualify               7
His rigorous course; but since he stands obdurate
And that no lawful means can carry me
Out of his envy's reach, I do oppose                        10
My patience to his fury and am armed
To suffer with a quietness of spirit
The very tyranny and rage of his.                           13

DUKE
Go one, and call the Jew into the court.

SALERIO
He is ready at the door. He comes, my lord.

*Enter Shylock.*

DUKE
Make room, and let him stand before our face.—            16
Shylock, the world thinks, and I think so too,
That thou but leadest this fashion of thy malice          18
To the last hour of act, and then 'tis thought            19
Thou'lt show thy mercy and remorse more strange           20
Than is thy strange apparent cruelty;                     21
And where thou now exacts the penalty,
Which is a pound of this poor merchant's flesh,
Thou wilt not only loose the forfeiture,                  24
But, touched with human gentleness and love,
Forgive a moiety of the principal,                        26
Glancing an eye of pity on his losses
That have of late so huddled on his back—
Enough to press a royal merchant down
And pluck commiseration of his state                      30
From brassy bosoms and rough hearts of flint,             31
From stubborn Turks and Tartars never trained
To offices of tender courtesy.
We all expect a gentle answer, Jew.

SHYLOCK
I have possessed Your Grace of what I purpose,            35
And by our holy Sabaoth have I sworn                      36
To have the due and forfeit of my bond.
If you deny it, let the danger light                      38
Upon your charter and your city's freedom!                39
You'll ask me why I rather choose to have
A weight of carrion flesh than to receive
Three thousand ducats. I'll not answer that,
But say it is my humor. Is it answered?                   43
What if my house be troubled with a rat
And I be pleased to give ten thousand ducats

**60 humors and conceits** whims and fancies    **62 Oh, dear discretion**
Oh, what precious discrimination.    **suited** suited to the occasion    **65
A many** many.    **better place** higher social station    **66 Garnished**
i.e., furnished with words, or with garments    **66–7 that . . . matter**
who for the sake of ingenious wordplay torture the plain meaning.
**67 How cheer'st thou**, What cheer, how are you doing    **70 meet**
fitting    **75 In reason** it stands to reason. (Jessica jokes that for
Bassanio to receive unmerited bliss on earth—unmerited because no
person can earn bliss through his or her own deserving—is to run the
risk of eternal damnation.)    **77 lay** stake    **78 else** more    **79 Pawned**
staked, wagered    **80 fellow** equal.    **84 stomach** (1) appetite
(2) inclination.    **87 digest** (1) ponder, analyze (2) "swallow," put up
with. (With a play also on the gastronomic sense.)    **set you forth**
(1) serve you up, as at a feast (2) set forth your praises.
**4.1. Location:** Venice. A court of justice. Benches, etc., are provided
for the justices.
**0.1 *Magnificoes*** noblemen of the Venetian republic

**3 answer** defend yourself against. (A legal term.)    **6 dram** sixty
grains apothecaries' weight, a tiny quantity    **7 qualify** moderate
**10 envy's** malice's    **13 tyranny** cruelty    **16 our** (The royal plural.)
**18 That . . . fashion** that you only maintain this pretense or form
**19 the last . . . act** the brink of action    **20 remorse** pity.    **strange**
remarkable    **21 strange** unnatural, foreign.    **apparent** (1) manifest,
overt (2) seeming    **24 loose** release, waive    **26 moiety** part, portion
**30 of** for    **31 brassy** unfeeling, hard like brass    **35 possessed**
informed    **36 Sabaoth** Lord of Hosts    **38 danger** injury
**39 Upon . . . freedom** (See 3.2.278.)    **43 humor** whim.

To have it baned? What, are you answered yet? 46
Some men there are love not a gaping pig, 47
Some that are mad if they behold a cat,
And others, when the bagpipe sings i'th' nose,
Cannot contain their urine; for affection, 50
Mistress of passion, sways it to the mood
Of what it likes or loathes. Now, for your answer:
As there is no firm reason to be rendered
Why he cannot abide a gaping pig, 54
Why he a harmless necessary cat, 55
Why he a woolen bagpipe, but of force 56
Must yield to such inevitable shame
As to offend, himself being offended,
So can I give no reason, nor I will not,
More than a lodged hate and a certain loathing 60
I bear Antonio, that I follow thus
A losing suit against him. Are you answered? 62
BASSANIO
This is no answer, thou unfeeling man,
To excuse the current of thy cruelty. 64
SHYLOCK
I am not bound to please thee with my answers.
BASSANIO
Do all men kill the things they do not love?
SHYLOCK
Hates any man the thing he would not kill?
BASSANIO
Every offense is not a hate at first.
SHYLOCK
What, wouldst thou have a serpent sting thee twice?
ANTONIO
I pray you, think you question with the Jew. 70
You may as well go stand upon the beach
And bid the main flood bate his usual height; 72
You may as well use question with the wolf 73
Why he hath made the ewe bleat for the lamb;
You may as well forbid the mountain pines
To wag their high tops and to make no noise
When they are fretten with the gusts of heaven; 77
You may as well do anything most hard
As seek to soften that—than which what's harder?—
His Jewish heart. Therefore, I do beseech you,
Make no more offers, use no farther means,
But with all brief and plain conveniency
Let me have judgment, and the Jew his will.
BASSANIO [to Shylock]
For thy three thousand ducats here is six.
SHYLOCK
If every ducat in six thousand ducats
Were in six parts, and every part a ducat,
I would not draw them. I would have my bond. 87

DUKE
How shalt thou hope for mercy, rendering none?
SHYLOCK
What judgment shall I dread, doing no wrong? 89
You have among you many a purchased slave,
Which, like your asses and your dogs and mules,
You use in abject and in slavish parts, 92
Because you bought them. Shall I say to you,
"Let them be free, marry them to your heirs!
Why sweat they under burdens? Let their beds
Be made as soft as yours, and let their palates
Be seasoned with such viands"? You will answer 97
"The slaves are ours." So do I answer you:
The pound of flesh which I demand of him
Is dearly bought, is mine, and I will have it.
If you deny me, fie upon your law!
There is no force in the decrees of Venice.
I stand for judgment. Answer: shall I have it?
DUKE
Upon my power I may dismiss this court, 104
Unless Bellario, a learnèd doctor, 105
Whom I have sent for to determine this, 106
Come here today.
SALERIO          My lord, here stays without 107
A messenger with letters from the doctor,
New come from Padua.
DUKE
Bring us the letters. Call the messenger. [Exit one.]
BASSANIO
Good cheer, Antonio. What, man, courage yet!
The Jew shall have my flesh, blood, bones, and all,
Ere thou shalt lose for me one drop of blood.
ANTONIO
I am a tainted wether of the flock, 114
Meetest for death. The weakest kind of fruit 115
Drops earliest to the ground, and so let me.
You cannot better be employed, Bassanio,
Than to live still and write mine epitaph.

Enter Nerissa [dressed like a lawyer's clerk].

DUKE
Came you from Padua, from Bellario?
NERISSA
From both, my lord. Bellario greets Your Grace.
[She presents a letter. Shylock whets his knife on his shoe.]
BASSANIO
Why dost thou whet thy knife so earnestly?
SHYLOCK
To cut the forfeiture from that bankrupt there.
GRATIANO
Not on thy sole, but on thy soul, harsh Jew,
Thou mak'st thy knife keen; but no metal can,
No, not the hangman's ax, bear half the keenness 125
Of thy sharp envy. Can no prayers pierce thee? 126

46 baned poisoned.   47 love who love.  gaping pig pig roasted whole with its mouth open   50 affection feeling, desire   54, 55, 56 he, he, he one person, another, yet another   55 necessary i.e., useful for catching rats and mice   56 woolen i.e., with flannel-covered bag   60 lodged settled, steadfast.  certain unwavering, fixed   62 losing unprofitable   64 current flow, tendency   70 think bear in mind.  question argue   72 And . . . height and bid the ocean put an end to its usual high tide   73 use question with interrogate   77 fretten fretted, i.e., disturbed, ruffled   87 draw them receive them, as in drawing money out of a bank.

89 wrong legal wrong.   92 parts duties, capacities   97 such viands food such as you eat.   104 Upon In accordance with   105 doctor person of learning. (Here, of law.)   106 determine this resolve this legal dispute   107 stays without waits outside   114 wether ram, especially a castrated ram   115 Meetest fittest   125 hangman's executioner's.  keenness (1) sharpness (2) savagery   126 envy malice.

SHYLOCK
No, none that thou hast wit enough to make.

GRATIANO
Oh, be thou damned, inexecrable dog,            128
And for thy life let Justice be accused!         129
Thou almost mak'st me waver in my faith
To hold opinion with Pythagoras                  131
That souls of animals infuse themselves
Into the trunks of men. Thy currish spirit
Governed a wolf who, hanged for human slaughter, 134
Even from the gallows did his fell soul fleet,   135
And, whilst thou layest in thy unhallowed dam,   136
Infused itself in thee; for thy desires
Are wolvish, bloody, starved, and ravenous.

SHYLOCK
Till thou canst rail the seal from off my bond,  139
Thou but offend'st thy lungs to speak so loud.   140
Repair thy wit, good youth, or it will fall
To cureless ruin. I stand here for law.          142

DUKE
This letter from Bellario doth commend
A young and learnèd doctor to our court.
Where is he?

NERISSA          He attendeth here hard by
To know your answer, whether you'll admit him.

DUKE
With all my heart. Some three or four of you
Go give him courteous conduct to this place.
                              [Exeunt some.]
Meantime the court shall hear Bellario's letter.
[He reads.] "Your Grace shall understand that at the 150
receipt of your letter I am very sick; but in the instant
that your messenger came, in loving visitation was
with me a young doctor of Rome. His name is Balthasar. I acquainted him with the cause in controversy
between the Jew and Antonio the merchant. We
turned o'er many books together. He is furnished with
my opinion, which, bettered with his own learning,
the greatness whereof I cannot enough commend,
comes with him, at my importunity, to fill up Your 159
Grace's request in my stead. I beseech you, let his lack
of years be no impediment to let him lack a reverend 161
estimation, for I never knew so young a body with so
old a head. I leave him to your gracious acceptance,
whose trial shall better publish his commendation." 164

Enter Portia for Balthasar [dressed like a doctor
of laws, escorted].

You hear the learn'd Bellario, what he writes;
And here, I take it, is the doctor come.—
Give me your hand. Come you from old Bellario?

PORTIA
I did, my lord.

DUKE          You are welcome. Take your place.
                    [Portia takes her place.]
Are you acquainted with the difference           169
That holds this present question in the court?

PORTIA
I am informèd throughly of the cause.            171
Which is the merchant here, and which the Jew?

DUKE
Antonio and old Shylock, both stand forth.
              [Antonio and Shylock stand forth.]

PORTIA
Is your name Shylock?

SHYLOCK                Shylock is my name.

PORTIA
Of a strange nature is the suit you follow,
Yet in such rule that the Venetian law           176
Cannot impugn you as you do proceed.—            177
You stand within his danger, do you not?

ANTONIO
Ay, so he says.

PORTIA          Do you confess the bond?

ANTONIO
I do.

PORTIA    Then must the Jew be merciful.

SHYLOCK
On what compulsion must I? Tell me that.

PORTIA
The quality of mercy is not strained.            182
It droppeth as the gentle rain from heaven
Upon the place beneath. It is twice blest:       184
It blesseth him that gives and him that takes.
'Tis mightiest in the mightiest; it becomes
The thronèd monarch better than his crown.
His scepter shows the force of temporal power,   188
The attribute to awe and majesty,                189
Wherein doth sit the dread and fear of kings.
But mercy is above this sceptered sway;
It is enthronèd in the hearts of kings,
It is an attribute to God himself;
And earthly power doth then show likest God's
When mercy seasons justice. Therefore, Jew,
Though justice be thy plea, consider this,
That in the course of justice none of us         197
Should see salvation. We do pray for mercy,
And that same prayer doth teach us all to render
The deeds of mercy. I have spoke thus much
To mitigate the justice of thy plea,             201
Which if thou follow, this strict court of Venice
Must needs give sentence 'gainst the merchant there.

128 inexecrable thoroughly execrable   129 And . . . accused! and may Justice herself be accused for allowing you to live!   131 Pythagoras ancient Greek philosopher who argued for the transmigration of souls   134 hanged for human slaughter (A possible allusion to the Elizabethan practice of trying and hanging animals for various crimes.)   135 fell fierce, cruel.   fleet flit, i.e., pass from the body   136 whilst . . . dam while you lay unborn in your evil mother's womb   139 rail remove by your abusive language   140 Thou but offend'st you merely injure   142 cureless incurable   150 [He reads.] (In many modern editions, the reading of the letter is assigned to a clerk, but the original text gives no such indication.)   159 comes with him accompanies him in the form of my learned opinion.   importunity insistence   161 to let him lack such as would deprive him of   164 whose . . . commendation the demonstration of whose excellence will proclaim what is commendable in him better than my letter can.   164.1 for i.e., disguised as

169 difference argument   171 throughly thoroughly.   cause case.   176 rule order   177 impugn find fault with   182 strained forced, constrained.   184 is twice blest grants a double blessing   188 His i.e., The monarch's   189 attribute to symbol of   197 justice divine justice   201 To . . . plea i.e., to show the way in which your call for justice needs to be mitigated or reduced in severity

THE MERCHANT OF VENICE: 4.1    105

**SHYLOCK**
My deeds upon my head! I crave the law,                    204
The penalty and forfeit of my bond.

**PORTIA**
Is he not able to discharge the money?

**BASSANIO**
Yes, here I tender it for him in the court,
Yea, twice the sum. If that will not suffice,
I will be bound to pay it ten times o'er,
On forfeit of my hands, my head, my heart.
If this will not suffice, it must appear
That malice bears down truth. And I beseech you,    212
Wrest once the law to your authority.              213
To do a great right, do a little wrong,
And curb this cruel devil of his will.

**PORTIA**
It must not be. There is no power in Venice
Can alter a decree establishèd.
'Twill be recorded for a precedent,
And many an error by the same example
Will rush into the state. It cannot be.

**SHYLOCK**
A Daniel come to judgment! Yea, a Daniel!          221
O wise young judge, how I do honor thee!

**PORTIA**
I pray you, let me look upon the bond.

SHYLOCK [*giving the bond*]
Here 'tis, most reverend doctor, here it is.

**PORTIA**
Shylock, there's thrice thy money offered thee.

**SHYLOCK**
An oath, an oath! I have an oath in heaven.
Shall I lay perjury upon my soul?
No, not for Venice.

**PORTIA**                    Why, this bond is forfeit,
And lawfully by this the Jew may claim
A pound of flesh, to be by him cut off
Nearest the merchant's heart.—Be merciful.
Take thrice thy money; bid me tear the bond.

**SHYLOCK**
When it is paid according to the tenor.            233
It doth appear you are a worthy judge.
You know the law. Your exposition
Hath been most sound. I charge you by the law,
Whereof you are a well-deserving pillar,
Proceed to judgment. By my soul I swear
There is no power in the tongue of man
To alter me. I stay here on my bond.               240

**ANTONIO**
Most heartily I do beseech the court
To give the judgment.

**PORTIA**                    Why then, thus it is:
You must prepare your bosom for his knife.

**SHYLOCK**
O noble judge! O excellent young man!

**PORTIA**
For the intent and purpose of the law
Hath full relation to the penalty                  246
Which here appeareth due upon the bond.

**SHYLOCK**
'Tis very true. O wise and upright judge!
How much more elder art thou than thy looks!

**PORTIA**
Therefore lay bare your bosom.

**SHYLOCK**                    Ay, his breast.
So says the bond, doth it not, noble judge?
"Nearest his heart," those are the very words.

**PORTIA**
It is so. Are there balance here                   253
To weigh the flesh?

**SHYLOCK**                    I have them ready.

**PORTIA**
Have by some surgeon, Shylock, on your charge,     255
To stop his wounds, lest he do bleed to death.

**SHYLOCK**
Is it so nominated in the bond?

**PORTIA**
It is not so expressed, but what of that?
'Twere good you do so much for charity.

**SHYLOCK**
I cannot find it. 'Tis not in the bond.

**PORTIA**
You, merchant, have you anything to say?

**ANTONIO**
But little. I am armed and well prepared.—         262
Give me your hand, Bassanio; fare you well!
Grieve not that I am fall'n to this for you,
For herein Fortune shows herself more kind
Than is her custom. It is still her use            266
To let the wretched man outlive his wealth
To view with hollow eye and wrinkled brow
An age of poverty; from which ling'ring penance
Of such misery doth she cut me off.
Commend me to your honorable wife.
Tell her the process of Antonio's end,             272
Say how I loved you, speak me fair in death;       273
And, when the tale is told, bid her be judge
Whether Bassanio had not once a love.              275
Repent but you that you shall lose your friend,    276
And he repents not that he pays your debt.
For if the Jew do cut but deep enough,
I'll pay it instantly with all my heart.           279

**BASSANIO**
Antonio, I am married to a wife,
Which is as dear to me as life itself;
But life itself, my wife, and all the world

---

**204 My . . . head!** (Compare the cry of the crowd at Jesus' crucifixion: "His blood be on us, and on our children," Matthew 27:25.) **212 bears down truth** overwhelms righteousness. **213 Wrest once** for once, forcibly subject **221 Daniel** (In the Apocrypha's story of Susannah and the Elders, Daniel is the young man who rescues Susannah from her false accusers.) **233 tenor** conditions. **240 stay** stand, insist

**246 Hath . . . to** is fully in accord with **253 balance** scales **255 Have by** Have ready at hand. **on your charge** at your personal expense **262 armed** i.e., fortified in spirit **266 still her use** i.e., commonly Fortune's practice **272 process** story, manner **273 speak me fair** speak well of me **275 a love** a friend's love. **276 Repent but you** Grieve only **279 with . . . heart** (1) wholeheartedly (2) literally, with my heart's blood.

Are not with me esteemed above thy life.
I would lose all, ay, sacrifice them all
Here to this devil, to deliver you.

PORTIA
Your wife would give you little thanks for that,
If she were by to hear you make the offer.    287

GRATIANO
I have a wife who, I protest, I love;
I would she were in heaven, so she could
Entreat some power to change this currish Jew.

NERISSA
'Tis well you offer it behind her back;
The wish would make else an unquiet house.

SHYLOCK
These be the Christian husbands. I have a daughter;    293
Would any of the stock of Barabbas    294
Had been her husband rather than a Christian!—
We trifle time. I pray thee, pursue sentence.    296

PORTIA
A pound of that same merchant's flesh is thine.
The court awards it, and the law doth give it.

SHYLOCK    Most rightful judge!

PORTIA
And you must cut this flesh from off his breast.
The law allows it, and the court awards it.

SHYLOCK
Most learnèd judge! A sentence!—Come, prepare.

PORTIA
Tarry a little; there is something else.
This bond doth give thee here no jot of blood;
The words expressly are "a pound of flesh."
Take then thy bond, take thou thy pound of flesh,
But in the cutting it if thou dost shed
One drop of Christian blood, thy lands and goods
Are by the laws of Venice confiscate
Unto the state of Venice.

GRATIANO
O upright judge! Mark, Jew. O learnèd judge!

SHYLOCK
Is that the law?

PORTIA                Thyself shalt see the act;
For, as thou urgest justice, be assured
Thou shalt have justice, more than thou desir'st.

GRATIANO
O learnèd judge! Mark, Jew, a learnèd judge!

SHYLOCK
I take this offer, then. Pay the bond thrice
And let the Christian go.

BASSANIO                        Here is the money.

PORTIA    Soft!    318
The Jew shall have all justice. Soft, no haste.    319
He shall have nothing but the penalty.

GRATIANO
O Jew! An upright judge, a learnèd judge!

PORTIA
Therefore prepare thee to cut off the flesh.
Shed thou no blood, nor cut thou less nor more
But just a pound of flesh. If thou tak'st more
Or less than a just pound, be it but so much
As makes it light or heavy in the substance    326
Or the division of the twentieth part    327
Of one poor scruple, nay, if the scale do turn    328
But in the estimation of a hair,
Thou diest, and all thy goods are confiscate.

GRATIANO
A second Daniel, a Daniel, Jew!    331
Now, infidel, I have you on the hip.    332

PORTIA
Why doth the Jew pause? Take thy forfeiture.

SHYLOCK
Give me my principal, and let me go.

BASSANIO
I have it ready for thee. Here it is.

PORTIA
He hath refused it in the open court.
He shall have merely justice and his bond.

GRATIANO
A Daniel, still say I, a second Daniel!
I thank thee, Jew, for teaching me that word.

SHYLOCK
Shall I not have barely my principal?

PORTIA
Thou shalt have nothing but the forfeiture,
To be so taken at thy peril, Jew.

SHYLOCK
Why, then the devil give him good of it!
I'll stay no longer question.                [He starts to go.]

PORTIA                        Tarry, Jew!    344
The law hath yet another hold on you.
It is enacted in the laws of Venice,
If it be proved against an alien
That by direct or indirect attempts
He seek the life of any citizen,
The party 'gainst the which he doth contrive
Shall seize one half his goods; the other half
Comes to the privy coffer of the state,    352
And the offender's life lies in the mercy    353
Of the Duke only, 'gainst all other voice.    354
In which predicament, I say, thou stand'st;
For it appears, by manifest proceeding,
That indirectly and directly too
Thou hast contrived against the very life
Of the defendant; and thou hast incurred
The danger formerly by me rehearsed.    360
Down therefore, and beg mercy of the Duke.    361

287 by nearby    293 These . . . husbands i.e., These Christians are
showing what I suppose they mean by Christian charity.    294 Would
. . . Barabbas I would prefer that any Jew, any Jew at all. (Barabbas is
the name of the thief whom Pontius Pilate set free instead of Christ in
response to the people's demand in Mark 15; also, the villainous protagonist in Marlowe's *The Jew of Malta*.)    296 trifle waste.    pursue
proceed with    318 Soft! i.e., Not so fast!    319 all justice precisely
what the law provides.

326 substance mass or gross weight    327 division fraction
328 scruple twenty grains apothecaries' weight, a small quantity
331 Daniel (See line 221 above and note.)    332 on the hip i.e., at a
disadvantage. (A phrase from wrestling.)    344 I'll . . . question I'll
stay no further pursuing of the case.    352 privy coffer private treasury    353 lies in lies at    354 'gainst . . . voice without appeal
360 The danger . . . rehearsed the penalty already cited by me.
361 Down Down on your knees

**GRATIANO**
Beg that thou mayst have leave to hang thyself!
And yet, thy wealth being forfeit to the state,
Thou hast not left the value of a cord;
Therefore thou must be hanged at the state's charge.   365

**DUKE**
That thou shalt see the difference of our spirit,
I pardon thee thy life before thou ask it.
For half thy wealth, it is Antonio's;   368
The other half comes to the general state,
Which humbleness may drive unto a fine.   370

**PORTIA**
Ay, for the state, not for Antonio.   371

**SHYLOCK**
Nay, take my life and all! Pardon not that!
You take my house when you do take the prop
That doth sustain my house. You take my life
When you do take the means whereby I live.

**PORTIA**
What mercy can you render him, Antonio?

**GRATIANO**
A halter gratis! Nothing else, for God's sake.   377

**ANTONIO**
So please my lord the Duke and all the court
To quit the fine for one half of his goods,   379
I am content, so he will let me have   380
The other half in use, to render it,   381
Upon his death, unto the gentleman
That lately stole his daughter.
Two things provided more: that for this favor
He presently become a Christian;   385
The other, that he do record a gift
Here in the court of all he dies possessed   387
Unto his son Lorenzo and his daughter.

**DUKE**
He shall do this, or else I do recant
The pardon that I late pronouncèd here.   389

**PORTIA**
Art thou contented, Jew? What dost thou say?

**SHYLOCK**
I am content.

**PORTIA**               Clerk, draw a deed of gift.

**SHYLOCK**
I pray you, give me leave to go from hence;
I am not well. Send the deed after me,
And I will sign it.

**DUKE**               Get thee gone, but do it.

**GRATIANO**
In christening shalt thou have two godfathers.
Had I been judge, thou shouldst have had ten more,   397

To bring thee to the gallows, not the font.
                                        *Exit [Shylock].*

**DUKE** [*to Portia*]
Sir, I entreat you home with me to dinner.

**PORTIA**
I humbly do desire Your Grace of pardon.
I must away this night toward Padua,
And it is meet I presently set forth.   402

**DUKE**
I am sorry that your leisure serves you not.
Antonio, gratify this gentleman,   404
For in my mind you are much bound to him.
                        *Exeunt Duke and his train.*

**BASSANIO** [*to Portia*]
Most worthy gentleman, I and my friend
Have by your wisdom been this day acquitted
Of grievous penalties, in lieu whereof,   408
Three thousand ducats due unto the Jew
We freely cope your courteous pains withal.   410
                                        [*He offers money.*]

**ANTONIO**
And stand indebted over and above
In love and service to you evermore.

**PORTIA**
He is well paid that is well satisfied,   413
And I, delivering you, am satisfied,
And therein do account myself well paid.
My mind was never yet more mercenary.
I pray you, know me when we meet again.   417
I wish you well, and so I take my leave.
                                        [*She starts to leave.*]

**BASSANIO**
Dear sir, of force I must attempt you further.   419
Take some remembrance of us as a tribute,
Not as fee. Grant me two things, I pray you:
Not to deny me, and to pardon me.   422

**PORTIA**
You press me far, and therefore I will yield.
Give me your gloves, I'll wear them for your sake.   424
And, for your love, I'll take this ring from you.   425
Do not draw back your hand; I'll take no more,
And you in love shall not deny me this.

**BASSANIO**
This ring, good sir? Alas, it is a trifle!
I will not shame myself to give you this.

**PORTIA**
I will have nothing else but only this;
And now, methinks, I have a mind to it.

**BASSANIO**
There's more depends on this than on the value.

---

**365 charge** expense.   **368 For** As for   **370 Which . . . fine** i.e., which penitence on your part may persuade me to reduce to a fine.
**371 Ay . . . Antonio** i.e., Yes, the state's half may be reduced to a fine, but not Antonio's half.   **377 halter** hangman's noose   **379 To . . . goods** i.e., to cancel the fine of one-half of Shylock's estate owed to the state of Venice (line 352)   **380 so** provided that   **381 in use** in trust (until Shylock's death)   **385 presently** at once   **387 of . . . possessed** i.e., what remains of the portion not placed under Antonio's trust (which will also go to Lorenzo and Jessica)   **389 late** lately, just now   **397 ten more** i.e., to make up a jury of twelve. (Jurors were colloquially termed *godfathers.*)

**402 meet** necessary, suitable   **404 gratify** reward   **408 in lieu whereof** in return for which   **410 cope** requite   **413 He** Any person   **417 know . . . again** i.e., consider our acquaintance well established. (But punning on *know* in the sense of "recognize" and "have sexual relations with"—meanings that are hidden from Bassanio by Portia's disguise.)   **419 of force** of necessity.   **attempt** urge   **422 pardon me** i.e., pardon my presumption in pressing the matter.   **424 gloves** (Perhaps Bassanio removes his gloves, thereby revealing the ring that "Balthasar" asks of him.)   **425 for your love** i.e., for friendship's sake—a polite phrase, but with ironic double meaning as applied to husband and wife

The dearest ring in Venice will I give you,                          433
And find it out by proclamation.
Only for this, I pray you, pardon me.

PORTIA
I see, sir, you are liberal in offers.                               436
You taught me first to beg, and now, methinks,
You teach me how a beggar should be answered.

BASSANIO
Good sir, this ring was given me by my wife,
And when she put it on she made me vow
That I should neither sell nor give nor lose it.

PORTIA
That 'scuse serves many men to save their gifts.
An if your wife be not a madwoman,                                  443
And know how well I have deserved this ring,
She would not hold out enemy forever
For giving it to me. Well, peace be with you!
                              *Exeunt [Portia and Nerissa].*

ANTONIO
My lord Bassanio, let him have the ring.
Let his deservings and my love withal
Be valued 'gainst your wife's commandement.                          449

BASSANIO
Go, Gratiano, run and overtake him;
Give him the ring, and bring him, if thou canst,
Unto Antonio's house. Away, make haste!
                              *Exit Gratiano [with the ring].*
Come, you and I will thither presently,
And in the morning early will we both
Fly toward Belmont. Come, Antonio.         *Exeunt.*

❖

# [4.2]

*Enter [Portia and] Nerissa [still disguised].*

PORTIA *[giving a deed to Nerissa]*
Inquire the Jew's house out; give him this deed            1
And let him sign it. We'll away tonight
And be a day before our husbands home.
This deed will be well welcome to Lorenzo.

*Enter Gratiano.*

GRATIANO    Fair sir, you are well o'erta'en.              5
My lord Bassanio upon more advice                          6
Hath sent you here this ring and doth entreat
Your company at dinner.          *[He gives a ring.]*
PORTIA                    That cannot be.
His ring I do accept most thankfully,
And so, I pray you, tell him. Furthermore,
I pray you, show my youth old Shylock's house.
GRATIANO
That will I do.
NERISSA              Sir, I would speak with you.
*[Aside to Portia]* I'll see if I can get my husband's
   ring,
Which I did make him swear to keep forever.

PORTIA *[aside to Nerissa]*
Thou mayst, I warrant. We shall have old swearing   15
That they did give the rings away to men;
But we'll outface them, and outswear them too.—    17
Away, make haste! Thou know'st where I will tarry.
NERISSA *[to Gratiano]*
Come, good sir, will you show me to this house?
                *[Exeunt, Portia separately from the others.]*

❖

# [5.1]

*Enter Lorenzo and Jessica.*

LORENZO
The moon shines bright. In such a night as this,
When the sweet wind did gently kiss the trees
And they did make no noise, in such a night
Troilus methinks mounted the Trojan walls          4
And sighed his soul toward the Grecian tents
Where Cressid lay that night.
JESSICA                    In such a night
Did Thisbe fearfully o'ertrip the dew,             7
And saw the lion's shadow ere himself,
And ran dismayed away.
LORENZO                  In such a night
Stood Dido with a willow in her hand               10
Upon the wild sea banks, and waft her love         11
To come again to Carthage.
JESSICA                    In such a night
Medea gathered the enchanted herbs                 13
That did renew old Aeson.
LORENZO                  In such a night
Did Jessica steal from the wealthy Jew             15
And with an unthrift love did run from Venice      16
As far as Belmont.
JESSICA              In such a night
Did young Lorenzo swear he loved her well,
Stealing her soul with many vows of faith,
And ne'er a true one.
LORENZO              In such a night
Did pretty Jessica, like a little shrew,
Slander her love, and he forgave it her.
JESSICA
I would out-night you, did nobody come.            23
But hark, I hear the footing of a man.             24

*Enter [Stephano,] a messenger.*

LORENZO
Who comes so fast in silence of the night?

---

433 **dearest** most expensive    436 **liberal** generous    443 **An if** If
449 **commandement** (Pronounced in four syllables.)
**4.2. Location: Venice. A street.**
1 **this deed** i.e., the deed of gift    5 **you . . . o'erta'en** I'm happy to
have caught up with you.    6 **advice** consideration

15 **old** plenty of    17 **outface** boldly contradict
**5.1. Location: Belmont. Outside Portia's house.**
4 **Troilus** Trojan prince deserted by his beloved, Cressida, after she had
been transferred to the Greek camp    7 **Thisbe** beloved of Pyramus
who, arranging to meet him by night, was frightened by a lion and fled;
the tragic misunderstanding of her absence led to the suicides of both
lovers. (See *A Midsummer Night's Dream*, Act 5.)    10 **Dido** Queen of
Carthage, deserted by Aeneas.    **willow** (A symbol of forsaken love.)
11 **waft** wafted, beckoned    13 **Medea** famous sorceress of Colchis
who, after falling in love with Jason and helping him to gain the
Golden Fleece, used her magic to restore youth to Aeson, Jason's father
15 **steal** (1) escape (2) rob    16 **unthrift** prodigal    23 **out-night** i.e.,
outdo in the verbal games we've been playing    24 **footing** footsteps

**STEPHANO**    A friend.

**LORENZO**

A friend? What friend? Your name, I pray you,
    friend?

**STEPHANO**

Stephano is my name, and I bring word
My mistress will before the break of day
Be here at Belmont. She doth stray about
By holy crosses, where she kneels and prays            31
For happy wedlock hours.

**LORENZO**                    Who comes with her?

**STEPHANO**

None but a holy hermit and her maid.
I pray you, is my master yet returned?

**LORENZO**

He is not, nor we have not heard from him.
But go we in, I pray thee, Jessica,
And ceremoniously let us prepare
Some welcome for the mistress of the house.

*Enter [Lancelot, the] clown.*

**LANCELOT**    Sola, sola! Wo ha, ho! Sola, sola!            39

**LORENZO**    Who calls?

**LANCELOT**    Sola! Did you see Master Lorenzo? Master
    Lorenzo, sola, sola!

**LORENZO**    Leave holloing, man! Here.

**LANCELOT**    Sola! Where, where?

**LORENZO**    Here.

**LANCELOT**    Tell him there's a post come from my mas-    46
    ter, with his horn full of good news: my master will be   47
    here ere morning.                    *[Exit.]*

**LORENZO**

Sweet soul, let's in, and there expect their coming.    49
And yet no matter. Why should we go in?
My friend Stephano, signify, I pray you,            51
Within the house, your mistress is at hand,
And bring your music forth into the air.
                    *[Exit Stephano.]*
How sweet the moonlight sleeps upon this bank!
Here will we sit and let the sounds of music
Creep in our ears. Soft stillness and the night
Become the touches of sweet harmony.            57
Sit, Jessica. *[They sit.]* Look how the floor of heaven
Is thick inlaid with patens of bright gold.        59
There's not the smallest orb which thou behold'st
But in his motion like an angel sings,
Still choiring to the young-eyed cherubins.        62
Such harmony is in immortal souls,
But whilst this muddy vesture of decay            64
Doth grossly close it in, we cannot hear it.        65

*[Enter musicians.]*

Come, ho, and wake Diana with a hymn!            66
With sweetest touches pierce your mistress' ear
And draw her home with music.            *Play music.*

**JESSICA**

I am never merry when I hear sweet music.

**LORENZO**

The reason is, your spirits are attentive.        70
For do but note a wild and wanton herd,
Or race of youthful and unhandled colts,        72
Fetching mad bounds, bellowing and neighing loud,
Which is the hot condition of their blood;
If they but hear perchance a trumpet sound,
Or any air of music touch their ears,
You shall perceive them make a mutual stand,        77
Their savage eyes turned to a modest gaze
By the sweet power of music. Therefore the poet    79
Did feign that Orpheus drew trees, stones, and
    floods,                            80
Since naught so stockish, hard, and full of rage    81
But music for the time doth change his nature.    82
The man that hath no music in himself,
Nor is not moved with concord of sweet sounds,
Is fit for treasons, stratagems, and spoils;        85
The motions of his spirit are dull as night
And his affections dark as Erebus.                87
Let no such man be trusted. Mark the music.

*Enter Portia and Nerissa.*

**PORTIA**

That light we see is burning in my hall.
How far that little candle throws his beams!
So shines a good deed in a naughty world.        91

**NERISSA**

When the moon shone, we did not see the candle.

**PORTIA**

So doth the greater glory dim the less.
A substitute shines brightly as a king
Until a king be by, and then his state            95
Empties itself, as doth an inland brook
Into the main of waters. Music! Hark!            97

**NERISSA**

It is your music, madam, of the house.

**PORTIA**

Nothing is good, I see, without respect.        99
Methinks it sounds much sweeter than by day.

**NERISSA**

Silence bestows that virtue on it, madam.

**PORTIA**

The crow doth sing as sweetly as the lark
When neither is attended; and I think            103
The nightingale, if she should sing by day,

---

**31 holy crosses** wayside shrines    **39 Sola** (Imitation of a post horn.)
**46 post** courier    **47 horn** (Lancelot jestingly compares the courier's
post horn to a cornucopia; perhaps too with a glance at the frayed jest
about cuckolds' horns.)    **49 expect** await    **51 signify** make known
**57 Become** suit.    **touches** strains, notes (produced by the fingering
of an instrument)    **59 patens** thin, circular plates of metal    **62 Still
choiring** continually singing.    **young-eyed** eternally clear-sighted.
(In Ezekiel 10:12, the bodies and wings of cherubim are "full of eyes
round about.")    **64 muddy . . . decay** i.e., mortal flesh    **65 close it in**
i.e., enclose the soul.    **hear it** i.e., hear the music of the spheres.

**66 Diana** (Here, goddess of the moon; compare with 1.2.105.)
**70 spirits are attentive** (The spirits would be in motion within the
body in merriment, whereas in sadness they would be drawn to the
heart and, as it were, busy listening.)    **72 race** herd    **77 mutual** common or simultaneous    **79 poet** perhaps Ovid, with whom the story
of Orpheus was a favorite theme    **80 Orpheus** legendary musician.
**drew** attracted, charmed.    **floods** rivers    **81 stockish** unfeeling
**82 his** its (a tree, a stone, etc.)    **85 spoils** acts of pillage    **87 Erebus** a
place of primeval darkness on the way to Hades.    **91 naughty**
wicked    **95 his** i.e., the substitute's    **97 main of waters** sea.
**99 respect** comparison, context.    **103 attended** listened to

When every goose is cackling, would be thought
No better a musician than the wren.
How many things by season seasoned are        107
To their right praise and true perfection!
Peace, ho! The moon sleeps with Endymion       109
And would not be awaked.        [*The music ceases.*]
LORENZO                        That is the voice,
Or I am much deceived, of Portia.
PORTIA
He knows me as the blind man knows the cuckoo,
By the bad voice.
LORENZO        Dear lady, welcome home.
PORTIA
We have been praying for our husbands' welfare,
Which speed, we hope, the better for our words.    115
Are they returned?
LORENZO        Madam, they are not yet;
But there is come a messenger before,
To signify their coming.
PORTIA                Go in, Nerissa.
Give order to my servants that they take
No note at all of our being absent hence;
Nor you, Lorenzo; Jessica, nor you. [*A tucket sounds.*] 121
LORENZO
Your husband is at hand. I hear his trumpet.
We are no telltales, madam, fear you not.
PORTIA
This night, methinks, is but the daylight sick;    124
It looks a little paler. 'Tis a day
Such as the day is when the sun is hid.

    *Enter Bassanio, Antonio, Gratiano, and their*
    *followers.*

BASSANIO
We should hold day with the Antipodes,       127
If you would walk in absence of the sun.      128
PORTIA
Let me give light, but let me not be light;    129
For a light wife doth make a heavy husband,    130
And never be Bassanio so for me.
But God sort all! You are welcome home, my lord.   132
BASSANIO
I thank you, madam. Give welcome to my friend.
This is the man, this is Antonio,
To whom I am so infinitely bound.
PORTIA
You should in all sense be much bound to him,     136
For, as I hear, he was much bound for you.        137

**107 season** fit occasion. (But playing on the idea of seasoning, spices.) **109 Endymion** a shepherd loved by the moon goddess, who caused him to sleep a perennial sleep in a cave on Mount Latmos where she could visit him **115 Which . . . words** who prosper and return speedily, we hope, because we prayed for them. **121 s.d.** *tucket* flourish on a trumpet **124 sick** i.e., made pale by the approach of dawn **127–8 We . . . sun** i.e., If you, Portia, like a second sun, would always walk about during the sun's absence, we should never have night but would enjoy daylight even when the Antipodes, those who dwell on the opposite side of the globe, enjoy daylight. **129 be light** be wanton, unchaste **130 heavy** sad. (With wordplay on the antithesis of *light* and *heavy*.) **132 sort** decide, dispose **136 in all sense** in every way, with every reason **136–7 bound . . . bound** Portia plays on (1) obligated (2) indebted and imprisoned.

ANTONIO
No more than I am well acquitted of.       138
PORTIA
Sir, you are very welcome to our house.
It must appear in other ways than words;
Therefore I scant this breathing courtesy.    141
GRATIANO [*to Nerissa*]
By yonder moon I swear you do me wrong!
In faith, I gave it to the judge's clerk.
Would he were gelt that had it, for my part,   144
Since you do take it, love, so much at heart.
PORTIA
A quarrel, ho, already? What's the matter?
GRATIANO
About a hoop of gold, a paltry ring
That she did give me, whose posy was         148
For all the world like cutler's poetry
Upon a knife, "Love me, and leave me not."
NERISSA
What talk you of the posy or the value?
You swore to me, when I did give it you,
That you would wear it till your hour of death
And that it should lie with you in your grave.
Though not for me, yet for your vehement oaths
You should have been respective and have kept it.  156
Gave it a judge's clerk! No, God's my judge,
The clerk will ne'er wear hair on 's face that had it.
GRATIANO
He will, an if he live to be a man.          159
NERISSA
Ay, if a woman live to be a man.
GRATIANO
Now, by this hand, I gave it to a youth,
A kind of boy, a little scrubbèd boy         162
No higher than thyself, the judge's clerk,
A prating boy, that begged it as a fee.      164
I could not for my heart deny it him.
PORTIA
You were to blame—I must be plain with you—
To part so slightly with your wife's first gift,
A thing stuck on with oaths upon your finger,
And so riveted with faith unto your flesh.
I gave my love a ring and made him swear
Never to part with it; and here he stands.
I dare be sworn for him he would not leave it,
Nor pluck it from his finger, for the wealth
That the world masters. Now, in faith, Gratiano,   174
You give your wife too unkind a cause of grief.
An 'twere to me, I should be mad at it.      176
BASSANIO [*aside*]
Why, I were best to cut my left hand off
And swear I lost the ring defending it.
GRATIANO
My lord Bassanio gave his ring away

**138 acquitted of** freed from and amply repaid (by thanks and love). **141 scant . . . courtesy** make brief these empty (i.e., merely verbal) compliments. **144 gelt** gelded, castrated. **for my part** as far as I'm concerned **148 posy** a motto on a ring **156 respective** mindful, careful **159 an if** if **162 scrubbèd** diminutive **164 prating** chattering **174 masters** owns. **176 An** If. **mad** beside myself

Unto the judge that begged it and indeed
Deserved it too; and then the boy, his clerk,
That took some pains in writing, he begged mine;
And neither man nor master would take aught                183
But the two rings.
PORTIA [to Bassanio]    What ring gave you, my lord?
Not that, I hope, which you received of me.

BASSANIO
If I could add a lie unto a fault,
I would deny it; but you see my finger
Hath not the ring upon it. It is gone.

PORTIA
Even so void is your false heart of truth.
By heaven, I will ne'er come in your bed
Until I see the ring!

NERISSA [to Gratiano]    Nor I in yours
Till I again see mine.

BASSANIO                    Sweet Portia,
If you did know to whom I gave the ring,
If you did know for whom I gave the ring,
And would conceive for what I gave the ring,
And how unwillingly I left the ring,
When naught would be accepted but the ring,
You would abate the strength of your displeasure.

PORTIA
If you had known the virtue of the ring,                  199
Or half her worthiness that gave the ring,
Or your own honor to contain the ring,                    201
You would not then have parted with the ring.
What man is there so much unreasonable,
If you had pleased to have defended it
With any terms of zeal, wanted the modesty                205
To urge the thing held as a ceremony?                     206
Nerissa teaches me what to believe:
I'll die for't but some woman had the ring.

BASSANIO
No, by my honor, madam! By my soul,
No woman had it, but a civil doctor,                       210
Which did refuse three thousand ducats of me
And begged the ring, the which I did deny him
And suffered him to go displeased away—                   213
Even he that had held up the very life
Of my dear friend. What should I say, sweet lady?
I was enforced to send it after him.
I was beset with shame and courtesy.
My honor would not let ingratitude
So much besmear it. Pardon me, good lady!                 219
For by these blessèd candles of the night,                220
Had you been there, I think you would have begged
The ring of me to give the worthy doctor.

PORTIA
Let not that doctor e'er come near my house.
Since he hath got the jewel that I loved,
And that which you did swear to keep for me,
I will become as liberal as you:                          226

I'll not deny him anything I have,
No, not my body nor my husband's bed.
Know him I shall, I am well sure of it.                   229
Lie not a night from home. Watch me like Argus;          230
If you do not, if I be left alone,
Now, by mine honor, which is yet mine own,                232
I'll have that doctor for my bedfellow.

NERISSA
And I his clerk; therefore be well advised                234
How you do leave me to mine own protection.

GRATIANO
Well, do you so. Let not me take him, then!               236
For if I do, I'll mar the young clerk's pen.              237

ANTONIO
I am th'unhappy subject of these quarrels.

PORTIA
Sir, grieve not you; you are welcome notwithstanding.

BASSANIO
Portia, forgive me this enforcèd wrong,
And in the hearing of these many friends
I swear to thee, even by thine own fair eyes
Wherein I see myself—

PORTIA                    Mark you but that!
In both my eyes he doubly sees himself;
In each eye, one. Swear by your double self,              245
And there's an oath of credit.

BASSANIO                    Nay, but hear me.              246
Pardon this fault, and by my soul I swear
I never more will break an oath with thee.

ANTONIO
I once did lend my body for his wealth,                   249
Which, but for him that had your husband's ring,
Had quite miscarried. I dare be bound again,
My soul upon the forfeit, that your lord                  252
Will nevermore break faith advisedly.                     253

PORTIA
Then you shall be his surety. Give him this,              254
And bid him keep it better than the other.
    [She gives the ring to Antonio, who gives it to Bassanio.]

ANTONIO
Here, Lord Bassanio. Swear to keep this ring.

BASSANIO
By heaven, it is the same I gave the doctor!

PORTIA
I had it of him. Pardon me, Bassanio,
For by this ring the doctor lay with me.

NERISSA
And pardon me, my gentle Gratiano,
For that same scrubbèd boy, the doctor's clerk,
In lieu of this last night did lie with me.               262
                              [Presenting her ring.]

183 aught anything   199 virtue moral efficacy   201 contain keep safe   205 wanted the modesty who would have been so lacking in consideration as   206 urge insist upon receiving.   ceremony something sacred.   210 civil doctor i.e., doctor of civil law   213 suffered allowed   219 it i.e., my honor.   220 blessèd . . . night i.e., stars   226 liberal generous (sexually as well as otherwise)

229 Know (With the suggestion of carnal knowledge.)   230 from away from.   Argus mythological monster with a hundred eyes   232 honor (1) honorable name (2) chastity   234 be well advised take care   236 take apprehend   237 pen (With sexual suggestion of castration.)   245 double i.e., deceitful   246 of credit worthy to be believed. (Said mockingly.)   249 wealth welfare   252 My . . . forfeit at the risk of eternal damnation   253 advisedly intentionally.   254 surety guarantor.   262 In lieu of in return for

GRATIANO
    Why, this is like the mending of highways
    In summer, where the ways are fair enough.                264
    What, are we cuckolds ere we have deserved it?            265
PORTIA
    Speak not so grossly. You are all amazed.
    Here is a letter; read it at your leisure.
                                        [*She gives a letter.*]
    It comes from Padua, from Bellario.
    There you shall find that Portia was the doctor,
    Nerissa there her clerk. Lorenzo here
    Shall witness I set forth as soon as you,
    And even but now returned; I have not yet
    Entered my house. Antonio, you are welcome,
    And I have better news in store for you
    Than you expect. Unseal this letter soon.
                                    [*She gives him a letter.*]
    There you shall find three of your argosies
    Are richly come to harbor suddenly.
    You shall not know by what strange accident
    I chancèd on this letter.
ANTONIO                        I am dumb.                     279
BASSANIO [*to Portia*]
    Were you the doctor and I knew you not?
GRATIANO [*to Nerissa*]
    Were you the clerk that is to make me cuckold?
NERISSA
    Ay, but the clerk that never means to do it,
    Unless he live until he be a man.
BASSANIO
    Sweet doctor, you shall be my bedfellow.

When I am absent, then lie with my wife.
ANTONIO
    Sweet lady, you have given me life and living;
    For here I read for certain that my ships
    Are safely come to road.
PORTIA                        How now, Lorenzo?               288
    My clerk hath some good comforts too for you.
NERISSA
    Ay, and I'll give them him without a fee.
                                        [*She gives a deed.*]
    There do I give to you and Jessica,
    From the rich Jew, a special deed of gift,
    After his death, of all he dies possessed of.
LORENZO
    Fair ladies, you drop manna in the way                   294
    Of starvèd people.
PORTIA                        It is almost morning,
    And yet I am sure you are not satisfied
    Of these events at full. Let us go in;
    And charge us there upon inter'gatories,                 298
    And we will answer all things faithfully.
GRATIANO
    Let it be so. The first inter'gatory
    That my Nerissa shall be sworn on is
    Whether till the next night she had rather stay          302
    Or go to bed now, being two hours to day.
    But were the day come, I should wish it dark
    Till I were couching with the doctor's clerk.            305
    Well, while I live I'll fear no other thing
    So sore as keeping safe Nerissa's ring.     *Exeunt.* 307

**288 road** anchorage.   **294 manna** the food from heaven that was miraculously supplied to the Israelites in the wilderness (Exodus 16) **298 And . . . inter'gatories** and put questions to us (as in a court of law)   **302 stay** wait   **305 couching** going to bed   **307 ring** (With sexual suggestion.)

**264 are fair enough** i.e., are not in need of repair.   **265 cuckolds** husbands whose wives are unfaithful   **279 dumb** dumbfounded.

# Much Ado About Nothing

*M*uch Ado About Nothing belongs to a group of Shakespeare's most mature romantic comedies, linked by similar titles, that also includes *As You Like It* and *Twelfth Night* (subtitled *What You Will*). All date from the period 1598 to 1600. These plays are the culmination of Shakespeare's exuberant, philosophical, and festive vein in comedy, interwoven with darker themes of estrangement, jealous rivalry, and betrayal. They parallel the culmination of Shakespeare's writing of history plays, in *Henry IV* and *V*.

*Much Ado* excels in combative wit and in swift, colloquial prose. It differs from several other comedies (including *A Midsummer Night's Dream* and *The Merchant of Venice*) in that it features no journey of the lovers, no heroine disguised as a man, no envious court or city contrasted with an idealized landscape of the artist's imagination. Instead, the prevailing motif is that of the mask. Prominent scenes include a masked ball (2.1), a charade offstage in which the villainous Borachio misrepresents himself as the lover of Hero (actually Margaret in disguise), and a marriage ceremony with the supposedly dead bride masking as her own cousin (5.3). The word *Nothing* in the play's title, pronounced rather like *noting* in the English of Elizabethan London and vicinity, suggests a pun on the idea of overhearing as well as of musical notation; it also has a bawdy connotation, as when Hamlet wryly suggests to Ophelia that "Nothing" is "a fair thought to lie between maids' legs" (*Hamlet*, 3.2.116–18; see also *Othello*, 3.3.317, where Iago responds to his wife's "I have a thing for you" with a degrading sexual insult). Overhearings are constant and are essential to the process of both misunderstanding (as in the false rumor of Don Pedro's wooing Hero for himself) and clarification (as in the discovery by the night watch of the slander done to Hero's reputation, or in the revelation to Beatrice and Benedick of each other's true state of mind). The masks, or roles, that the characters incessantly assume are, for the most part, defensive and inimical to mutual understanding. How can they be dispelled? It is the search for candor and self-awareness in relationships with others, the quest for honesty and respect beneath conventional outward appearances, that provides the journey in this play.

Structurally, the play contrasts two pairs of lovers. The ladies, Beatrice and Hero, are cousins and close friends. The gentlemen, Benedick and Claudio, Italian gentlemen and fellow officers under the command of Don Pedro, have returned from the war, in which they have fought bravely. These similarities chiefly serve, however, to accentuate the differences between the two couples. Hero is modest, retiring, usually silent, and obedient to her father's will. Claudio appears ideally suited to her, since he is also respectful and decorous. They are conventional lovers in the roles of romantic hero and naive heroine. Beatrice and Benedick, on the other hand, are renowned for "a kind of merry war" between them. Although obviously destined to come together, they are seemingly too independent and skeptical of convention to be tolerant and accepting in love. They scoff so at romantic sentimentality that they cannot permit themselves to drop their satirical masks. Yet, paradoxically, their relationship is ultimately more surefooted because of their refusal to settle for the illusory cliches of many young wooers.

As in some of his other comic double plots (*The Taming of the Shrew*, for example), Shakespeare has linked together two stories of diverse origins and contrasting tones in order to set off one against the other. The Hero-Claudio plot is Italianate in flavor and origin, sensational, melodramatic, and potentially tragic. In fact, the often told story of the maiden falsely slandered did frequently end in disaster—as, for example, in Edmund Spenser's *Faerie Queene*, 2.4 (1590). Spenser was apparently indebted to Ariosto's *Orlando Furioso* (translated into English by Sir John Harington, 1591), as were Peter Beverly in *The Historie of Ariodanto and Ieneura* (1566) and Richard Mulcaster in his play *Ariodante and Genevora* (1583).

Shakespeare seems to have relied more on the Italian version by Matteo Bandello (Lucca, 1554) and its French translation by Belleforest, *Histoires Tragiques* (1569). Still other versions have been discovered, both nondramatic and dramatic, although it cannot be established that Shakespeare was reworking an old play. Various factual inconsistencies in Shakespeare's text (such as Leonato's wife Innogen and a "kinsman" who are named briefly in both quarto and Folio but have no roles in the play) can perhaps be explained by Shakespeare's having worked quickly from more than one source.

Shakespeare's other plot, of Benedick and Beatrice, is much more English and his own. The battle of the sexes is a staple of English medieval humor (Chaucer's Wife of Bath, the Wakefield play of *Noah*) and of Shakespeare's own early comedy: Berowne and Rosaline in *Love's Labor's Lost*, Petruchio and Katharina in *The Taming of the Shrew*. The merry war of Benedick and Beatrice is Shakespeare's finest achievement in this vein and was to become a rich legacy in the later English comedy of William Congreve, Oscar Wilde, and George Bernard Shaw. The tone is lighthearted, bantering, and reassuring, in contrast with the Italianate mood of vengeance and duplicity in the Claudio-Hero plot. No less English are the clownish antics of Dogberry and his crew, representing still another group of characters although not a separate plot. Like Constable Dull in *Love's Labor's Lost* or the tradesmen of *A Midsummer Night's Dream*, the buffoons of *Much Ado* function in a nominally Mediterranean setting but are nonetheless recognizable London types. Their preposterous antics not only puncture the ominous mood threatening our enjoyment of the main plot but also, absurdly enough, even help to abort a potential crime. When Dogberry comes, laughter cannot be far behind.

The two plots provide contrasting perspectives on the nature of love. Because it is sensational and melodramatic, the Claudio-Hero plot stresses situation at the expense of character. The conspiracy that nearly overwhelms the lovers is an engrossing story, but they themselves remain one-dimensional. They interest us more as conventional types, and hence as foils to Benedick and Beatrice, than as lovers in their own right. Benedick and Beatrice, on the other hand, are psychologically complex. Clearly, they are fascinated with each other. Beatrice's questions in the first scene, although abusive in tone, betray her concern for Benedick's welfare. Has he safely returned from the wars? How did he bear himself in battle? Who are his companions? She tests his moral character by high standards, suspecting that he will fail because she demands so much. We are not surprised when she lectures her docile cousin, Hero, on the folly of submitting to parental choice in marriage: "It is my cousin's duty to make curtsy and say, 'Father, as it please you.' But yet for all that, cousin, let him be a handsome fellow, or else

make another curtsy and say, 'Father, as it please me' " (2.1.49–52). Beatrice remains single not from love of spinsterhood but from insistence on a nearly perfect mate. Paradoxically, she who is the inveterate scoffer is the true idealist. And we know from her unceasing fascination with Benedick that he, of all the men in her acquaintance, comes closest to her mark. The only fear preventing the revelation of her love—a not unnatural fear, in view of the insults she and Benedick exchange—is that he will prove faithless and jest at her weakness.

Benedick is similarly hemmed in by his posturing as "a professed tyrant to their sex." Despite his reputation as a perennial bachelor and his wry amusement at Claudio's newfound passion, Benedick confesses in soliloquy (2.3.8–34) that he could be won to affection by the ideal woman. Again, his criteria are chiefly those of temperament and moral character, although he by no means spurns wealth, beauty, and social position; the happiest couples are those well matched in fortune's gifts. "Rich she shall be, that's certain; wise, or I'll none; virtuous, or I'll never cheapen her; fair, or I'll never look on her; mild, or come not near me; noble, or not I for an angel; of good discourse, an excellent musician, and her hair shall be of what color it please God." This last self-mocking concession indicates that Benedick is aware of how impossibly much he is asking. Still, there is one woman, Beatrice, who may well possess all of these qualities except mildness. Even her sharp wit is part of her admirable intelligence. She is a match for Benedick, and he is a man who would never tolerate the submissive conventionality of someone like Hero. All that appears to be lacking, in fact, is any sign of fondness on Beatrice's part. For him to make overtures would be to invite her withering scorn—not to mention the I-told-you-so mockery of his friends.

Benedick and Beatrice have been playing the game of verbal abuse for so long that they scarcely remember how it started—perhaps as a squaring-off between the only two intelligences worthy of contending with each other, perhaps as a more profoundly defensive reaction of two sensitive persons not willing to part lightly with their independence. They seem to have had a prior relationsip with each other that ended unhappily. They know that intimate involvement with another person is a complex matter—one that can cause heartache. Yet the masks they wear with each other are scarcely satisfactory. At the masked ball (2.1), we see how hurtful the "merry war" has become. Benedick, attempting to pass himself off as a stranger in a mask, abuses Beatrice by telling her of her reputation for disdain; but she, perceiving who he is, retaliates by telling him as a purported stranger what she "really" thinks of Benedick. These devices cut deeply and confirm the worst fears of each. Ironically, these fears can be dispelled only by the virtuous deceptions practiced on them by their friends. Once Benedick is assured that Beatrice secretly loves him, masking her affection with scorn, he acquires the confidence he needs to make a commitment, and vice versa in her case. The beauty of the virtuous deceptions, moreover, is that they are so plausible—because, indeed, they are essentially true. Benedick overhears himself described as a person so satirical that Beatrice dare not reveal her affection, for fear of being repulsed (2.3). Beatrice learns that she is indeed called disdainful by her friends (3.1). Both lovers respond generously to these revelations, accepting the accusations as richly deserved and placing no blame on the other. As Beatrice proclaims to herself, "Contempt, farewell, and maiden pride, adieu!" The relief afforded by this honesty is genuine and lasting.

Because Claudio knows so little about Hero and is content with superficial expectations, he is vulnerable to a far uglier sort of deception. Claudio's first questions about Hero betray his romantically stereotyped attitudes and his willingness to let Don Pedro and Hero's father, Leonato, arrange a financially advantageous match. Claudio treasures Hero's outward reputation for modesty, an appearance easily besmirched. When a false rumor suggests that Don Pedro is wooing the lady for himself, Claudio's response is predictably cliché-ridden: all's fair in love and war, you can't trust friends in an affair of the heart, and so farewell Hero. The rumor has a superficial plausibility about it, especially when the villainous Don John steps into the situation. Motivated in part by pure malice and the sport of ruining others' happiness, Don John speaks to the masked Claudio at the ball (2.1) as though he were speaking to Benedick and, in this guise, pretends to reveal the secret "fact" of Don Pedro's duplicity in love. (The device is precisely that used by Beatrice to put down Benedick in the same scene.) With this specious confirmation, Claudio leaps to a wrong conclusion, thereby judging both his friend and mistress to be false. He gives them no chance to speak in their own defense. To be sure, Hero's father and uncle have also believed in the false report and have welcomed the prospect of Don Pedro as Hero's husband. She herself raises no objection to the prospect of marriage with the older man. Don Pedro is, after all, a prince of presumably enormous wealth, power, and social status, well above that of Leonato and his well-to-do but bourgeois family; when he asks (perhaps as a pleasantry) if Beatrice will have him as her husband, her polite refusal seems tinged with a note of regret (2.1.303–21). These attractive features in Don Pedro tend to excuse the general willingness to accept the idea of him as a splendidly suitable husband for Hero. Even so, Claudio has revealed a lack of faith resulting from his slender knowledge of Hero and of himself.

The nearly tragic "demonstration" of Hero's infidelity follows the same course, because Claudio has not learned from his first experience. Once again, the villainous Don John first implants the insidious suggestion in Claudio's mind, then creates an illusion entirely plausible to the senses, and finally confirms it with Borachio's testimony. What Claudio and Don Pedro have actually seen is Margaret wooed at Hero's window, shrouded in the dark of night and seen from "afar off in the orchard." The power of suggestion is enough to do the rest. Don John's method, and his pleasure in evil, are much like those of his later counterparts, Iago in *Othello* and Edmund in *King Lear*. Indeed, John is compared with the devil, who has power over mortals' frail senses but must rely on their complicity and acquiescence in evil. Claudio is once again led to denounce faithlessly the virtuous woman whose loyalty he no longer deserves. Yet his fault is typically human and is shared by Don Pedro. Providence gives him a second chance, through the ludicrous and bumbling intervention of Dogberry's night watch. These men overhear the plot of Don John as soon as it is announced to us, so that we know justice will eventually prevail, even though it will also be farcically delayed. Once again, misunderstanding has become "much ado about nothing," an escalating of recriminations based on a purely chimerical assumption that must eventually be deflated. The painful experience is not without value, for it tests the characters' spiritual worth in a crisis. Beatrice, like Friar Francis, shows herself to be a person of unshakable faith in goodness. Benedick, though puzzled and torn in his loyalties, also passes the test and proves himself worthy of Beatrice. Claudio is found wanting, and indeed is judged by many modern readers and audiences to be wholly inadequate, but Hero forgives and accepts him anyway. In her role as the granter of a merciful second chance, she foreshadows the beatifically symbolic nature of many of Shakespeare's later heroines.

*Much Ado* comes perhaps closer to potentially tragic action than Shakespeare's other festive comedies, though *The Merchant of Venice* is another, and so are late romances like *Cymbeline* and *The Winter's Tale* that *Much Ado* can be said to anticipate in the serious matter of slander against a virtuous heroine. Most strikingly, Claudio's failure is unnervingly like that of Othello. The fact that both men are too easily persuaded to reject and humiliate the innocent women they love suggests a deep inadequacy in each. The tempters (Don John, Iago) cannot alone be blamed; the male lovers themselves are too prone to believe the worst of women. In Claudio we can see a vulnerability in the very way he looks at courtship and marriage. As Benedick jests, Claudio talks almost as though he wants to buy Hero (1.1.172). Certainly his attitude is acquisitive and superficial; as the conquering hero returned from the wars, he is ready to settle down into married respectability, and he needs a socially eligible wife. He desires Hero for her beauty, for her wealth and family connections, and above all for her modesty and her reputation for virginal purity. These are attributes easily impugned by false apearances, and in his too-quick rejection of Hero we see in Claudio a deep cynicism about women. He fears the betrayal and loss of masculine self-esteem that a woman can inflict on him by sexual infidelity. To Claudio, Hero is a saint one moment and a whore the next.

Nor is he the only man to demean her (and women) thus. Don Pedro, his patron and older friend, is no less ready to believe Don John's lies, even though Don Pedro has been deceived by his brother before and should know better. Hero's father collapses in shame when he hears his daughter publicly accused of promiscuity, for Leonato's own reputation is on the line: as a father in a patriarchal society, his responsibility is to guarantee the chastity of his daughter to the younger man who proposes to receive her. Leonato's first assumption is that she must be guilty if other men say so; even he is altogether ready to believe the worst of women. Virtually the whole male world of Messina is victimized by its own fear of womanly perfidy—a fear that seems to arise from male lack of self-assurance and a deep inner conviction of being unloved. Benedick is much to be commended for his skepticism about the slanderous attacks on Hero; in no way does he better prove his worthiness of being Beatrice's husband than in his defense of a traduced and innocent woman. Yet Benedick, too, suffers to such a degree from his own male insecurity that he nearly gives up Beatrice at the very end of the play, even as she is nearly ready to give up him. Despite their self-awareness, these lovers must be rescued from their autonomous self-defensiveness by one more intervention on the part of their friends. Benedick and Beatrice are not wholly unlike Claudio and Hero after all. Both pairs of lovers are saved from their own worst selves by a harmonizing force that works its will through strange and improbable means—even through Constable Dogberry and his watch.

Performance history has abundantly illustrated the durable quality of this remarkable play. Perhaps no other comedy by Shakespeare has been as influential as *Much Ado*, providing as it does a model for wit combat and comedy of manners in William Congreve's *The Way of the World*, Oscar Wilde's *The Importance of Being Earnest*, George Bernard Shaw's *Man and Superman*, Noel Coward's *Private Lives*, Tom Stoppard's *The Real Thing*, and many others. Onstage the play has always been a favorite in the repertory, featuring such couples as Hannah Pritchard and David Garrick, Ellen Terry and Henry Irving, Peggy Ashcroft and John Gielgud, Diana Wynyard and Anthony Quayle, Janet Suzman and Alan Howard, Maggie Smith and Robert Stephens, Judi Dench and Donald Sinden, Sinead Cusack and Derek Jacobi, and many more. A commercial television production by A. J. Antoon, originating in New York's Delacorte Theater in 1972, was witnessed by more viewers on that occasion than had seen the play in its entire stage history. Kenneth Branagh's 1993 film, with Emma Thompson and Branagh in the leading roles, along with Denzel Washington as Don Pedro and Michael Keaton as Dogberry, capitalized on a gorgeous Italian villa and its star-laden cast to produce one of the most popular of Shakespeare cinemas. Emma Thompson shows us a Beatrice who is strong, independent, not easily fooled, undaunted by men, and willing to marry Benedick (Branagh) only after she has tested him and made clear the mutuality of respect that she demands. In recent years the play has been located in a wide variety of updated settings: frontier Texas, small-town America right after the Spanish-American War, Victorian India of the British Raj, Regency England, the Edwardian era, mafiosa Sicily, and still more. The incessant updating testifies paradoxically to the play's engaging timelessness; it works anywhere and any time. The play continues to succeed because it is so genuinely open to such interpretations.

# *Much Ado About Nothing*

[*Dramatis Personae*

DON PEDRO, *Prince of Aragon*
LEONATO, *Governor of Messina*
ANTONIO, *his brother*

BENEDICK, *a young lord of Padua*
BEATRICE, *Leonato's niece*
CLAUDIO, *a young lord of Florence*
HERO, *Leonato's daughter*
MARGARET,
URSULA, } *gentlewomen attending Hero*

DON JOHN, *Don Pedro's bastard brother*
BORACHIO,
CONRADE, } *followers of Don John*

DOGBERRY, *Constable in charge of the Watch*
VERGES, *the Headborough, or parish constable, Dogberry's partner*
A SEXTON (FRANCIS SEACOAL)
FIRST WATCHMAN
SECOND WATCHMAN (GEORGE SEACOAL)

BALTHASAR, *a singer attending Don Pedro*
FRIAR FRANCIS
A BOY
MESSENGER *to Leonato*
*Another* MESSENGER

*Attendants, Musicians, Members of the Watch, Antonio's Son, and other Kinsmen*

SCENE: *Messina*]

## [1.1]

*Enter Leonato, Governor of Messina, Hero his daughter, and Beatrice his niece, with a Messenger.*

LEONATO [*holding a letter*]   I learn in this letter that Don Pedro of Aragon comes this night to Messina.

MESSENGER   He is very near by this. He was not three 3
leagues off when I left him. 4

LEONATO   How many gentlemen have you lost in this action? 6

MESSENGER   But few of any sort and none of name. 7

LEONATO   A victory is twice itself when the achiever brings home full numbers. I find here that Don Pedro hath bestowed much honor on a young Florentine 10
called Claudio.

MESSENGER   Much deserved on his part and equally remembered by Don Pedro. He hath borne himself 13
beyond the promise of his age, doing in the figure of a lamb the feats of a lion. He hath indeed better bettered expectation than you must expect of me to tell 16
you how.

LEONATO   He hath an uncle here in Messina will be 18
very much glad of it.

MESSENGER   I have already delivered him letters, and there appears much joy in him, even so much that joy 21
could not show itself modest enough without a badge 22
of bitterness. 23

LEONATO   Did he break out into tears?

MESSENGER   In great measure.

LEONATO   A kind overflow of kindness. There are no 26
faces truer than those that are so washed. How much better is it to weep at joy than to joy at weeping!

BEATRICE   I pray you, is Signor Mountanto returned 29
from the wars or no?

MESSENGER   I know none of that name, lady. There was none such in the army of any sort.

LEONATO   What is he that you ask for, niece?

---

1.1. Location: Messina., Sicily Before, Leonato's house.
**3 by this** by this time.   **4 leagues** units of about three miles
**6 action** battle.   **7 sort** rank.   **name** reputation, or noble name.
**10 Florentine** resident of Florence   **13 remembered** rewarded

**16 bettered** surpassed   **18 will** who will   **21–3 joy . . . bitterness** joy could show a decorous moderation only by weeping at the same time.   **26 kind** natural   **29 Mountanto** montanto, an upward blow or thrust in fencing, here used as a satirical name

HERO   My cousin means Signor Benedick of Padua.

MESSENGER   Oh, he's returned, and as pleasant as ever 35
he was.

BEATRICE   He set up his bills here in Messina and chal- 37
lenged Cupid at the flight; and my uncle's fool, reading 38
the challenge, subscribed for Cupid and challenged 39
him at the bird-bolt. I pray you, how many hath he 40
killed and eaten in these wars? But how many hath he
killed? For indeed I promised to eat all of his killing.

LEONATO   Faith, niece, you tax Signor Benedick too 43
much, but he'll be meet with you, I doubt it not. 44

MESSENGER   He hath done good service, lady, in these
wars.

BEATRICE   You had musty victual, and he hath help to 47
eat it. He is a very valiant trencherman; he hath an 48
excellent stomach. 49

MESSENGER   And a good soldier too, lady.

BEATRICE   And a good soldier to a lady, but what is he 51
to a lord? 52

MESSENGER   A lord to a lord, a man to a man, stuffed 53
with all honorable virtues.

BEATRICE   It is so, indeed, he is no less than a stuffed 55
man. But for the stuffing—well, we are all mortal. 56

LEONATO   You must not, sir, mistake my niece. There is
a kind of merry war betwixt Signor Benedick and her.
They never meet but there's a skirmish of wit between
them.

BEATRICE   Alas! He gets nothing by that. In our last
conflict, four of his five wits went halting off, and now 62
is the whole man governed with one; so that if he have 63
wit enough to keep himself warm, let him bear it for a
difference between himself and his horse, for it is all 65
the wealth that he hath left to be known a reasonable 66
creature. Who is his companion now? He hath every 67
month a new sworn brother. 68

MESSENGER   Is't possible?

BEATRICE   Very easily possible. He wears his faith but as 70
the fashion of his hat; it ever changes with the next
block. 72

MESSENGER   I see, lady, the gentleman is not in your 73
books. 74

BEATRICE   No. An he were, I would burn my study. But 75
I pray you, who is his companion? Is there no young
squarer now that will make a voyage with him to the 77
devil?

MESSENGER   He is most in the company of the right
noble Claudio.

BEATRICE   Oh, Lord, he will hang upon him like a 81
disease! He is sooner caught than the pestilence, and
the taker runs presently mad. God help the noble 83
Claudio! If he have caught the Benedick, it will cost 84
him a thousand pound ere 'a be cured. 85

MESSENGER   I will hold friends with you, lady. 86

BEATRICE   Do, good friend.

LEONATO   You will never run mad, niece. 88

BEATRICE   No, not till a hot January. 89

MESSENGER   Don Pedro is approached.

*Enter Don Pedro, Claudio, Benedick, Balthasar,
and [Don] John the Bastard.*

DON PEDRO   Good Signor Leonato, are you come to
meet your trouble? The fashion of the world is to 92
avoid cost, and you encounter it. 93

LEONATO   Never came trouble to my house in the
likeness of Your Grace. For trouble being gone,
comfort should remain; but when you depart from
me, sorrow abides and happiness takes his leave.

DON PEDRO   You embrace your charge too willingly.—I 98
think this is your daughter.

*[Presenting himself to Hero.]*

LEONATO   Her mother hath many times told me so.

BENEDICK   Were you in doubt, sir, that you asked her?

LEONATO   Signor Benedick, no; for then were you a
child.

DON PEDRO   You have it full, Benedick. We may guess 104
by this what you are, being a man. Truly, the lady
fathers herself. Be happy, lady, for you are like an 106
honorable father.

BENEDICK   If Signor Leonato be her father, she would
not have his head on her shoulders for all Messina, as 109
like him as she is.   *[Don Pedro and Leonato talk aside.]*

BEATRICE   I wonder that you will still be talking, Signor
Benedick. Nobody marks you.

BENEDICK   What, my dear Lady Disdain! Are you yet
living?

BEATRICE   Is it possible disdain should die while she
hath such meet food to feed it as Signor Benedick? 116

---

**35 pleasant** jocular   **37 bills** placards, advertisements   **38 at the flight** to a long-distance archery contest. (Beatrice mocks Benedick's pretentions as a lady killer.)   **my uncle's fool** (Perhaps a professional fool in her uncle's service.)   **39 subscribed for** accepted on behalf of   **40 bird-bolt** a blunt-headed arrow used for fowling. (Sometimes used by children because of its relative harmlessness and thus conventionally appropriate to Cupid.)   **43 tax** disparage   **44 meet** even, quits   **47 musty victual** stale food.   **holp** helped   **48 valiant trencherman** great eater   **49 stomach** appetite. (With a mocking suggestion also of "courage.")   **51 soldier to a lady** lady killer. (With a play on *to/too*.)   **52 to** compared to   **53 stuffed** amply supplied   **55–6 a stuffed man** i.e., a figure stuffed to resemble a man.   **56 the stuffing** i.e., what he's truly made of.   **well . . . mortal** i.e., well, we all have our faults.   **62 five wits** i.e., not the five senses, but the five faculties: memory, imagination, judgment, fantasy, common sense.   **halting** limping   **63 with one** i.e., with nothing more than the kind of simple wit that prompts him to stay warm; this instinctive and self-protective wit, says Beatrice, is all that Benedick has to distinguish him from the horse he rides.   **65 difference** heraldic feature distinguishing a junior member or branch of a family. (With a play on the usual sense.)   **65–7 it is . . . creature** i.e., his feeble wit is all he has left to identify him as rationally human.   **68 sworn brother** brother in arms (*frater juratus*, an allusion to the ancient practice of swearing brotherhood).   **70 faith** allegiance, or fidelity   **72 block** mold for shaping hats.

**73–4 in your books** in favor with you, in your good books. (But Beatrice, in her reply, takes *books* in the literal sense of something to be found in a library.)   **75 An** If. (Also in lines 131, 183, and 192.)   **77 squarer** quarreler   **81 he** i.e., Benedick   **83 presently** immediately   **84 the Benedick** i.e., as if this were a disease   **85 'a** he   **86 hold friends** keep on friendly terms (so as not to earn your enmity)   **88 run mad** i.e., "catch the Benedick"   **89 not . . . January** i.e., not any time soon.   **92 your trouble** i.e., the expense of entertaining me and my retinue.   **93 encounter** go to meet   **98 charge** social responsibility and expense   **104 have it full** are well answered   **106 fathers herself** shows by appearance who her father is.   **109 his head** i.e., with Leonato's white beard and signs of age   **116 meet** suitable. (With a pun on "meat.")

Courtesy itself must convert to disdain, if you come in 117
her presence.

BENEDICK   Then is courtesy a turncoat. But it is certain
I am loved of all ladies, only you excepted; and I
would I could find in my heart that I had not a hard
heart, for truly I love none.

BEATRICE   A dear happiness to women! They would 123
else have been troubled with a pernicious suitor. I 124
thank God and my cold blood I am of your humor for 125
that. I had rather hear my dog bark at a crow than a 126
man swear he loves me.

BENEDICK   God keep Your Ladyship still in that mind!
So some gentleman or other shall scape a predestinate 129
scratched face.

BEATRICE   Scratching could not make it worse, an 'twere
such a face as yours were.                                                    132

BENEDICK   Well, you are a rare parrot-teacher.                   133

BEATRICE   A bird of my tongue is better than a beast of 134
yours.                                                                              135

BENEDICK   I would my horse had the speed of your
tongue and so good a continuer. But keep your way, 137
i'God's name; I have done.

BEATRICE   You always end with a jade's trick. I know 139
you of old.

DON PEDRO   That is the sum of all, Leonato. Signor 141
Claudio and Signor Benedick, my dear friend Leonato
hath invited you all. I tell him we shall stay here at the
least a month, and he heartily prays some occasion
may detain us longer. I dare swear he is no hypocrite,
but prays from his heart.

LEONATO   If you swear, my lord, you shall not be forsworn. [To Don John] Let me bid you welcome, my
lord, being reconciled to the Prince your brother. I owe 149
you all duty.

DON JOHN   I thank you. I am not of many words, but I
thank you.

LEONATO   Please it Your Grace lead on?                           153

DON PEDRO   Your hand, Leonato. We will go together. 154
          *Exeunt. Manent Benedick and Claudio.*

CLAUDIO   Benedick, didst thou note the daughter of
Signor Leonato?

BENEDICK   I noted her not, but I looked on her.              157

CLAUDIO   Is she not a modest young lady?

BENEDICK   Do you question me as an honest man
should do, for my simple true judgment? Or would

you have me speak after my custom, as being a
professed tyrant to their sex?                                           162

CLAUDIO   No, I pray thee, speak in sober judgment.

BENEDICK   Why, i'faith, methinks she's too low for a 164
high praise, too brown for a fair praise, and too little 165
for a great praise. Only this commendation I can afford
her, that were she other than she is, she were unhand- 167
some, and being no other but as she is, I do not like 168
her.

CLAUDIO   Thou thinkest I am in sport. I pray thee, tell
me truly how thou lik'st her.

BENEDICK   Would you buy her, that you inquire after
her?

CLAUDIO   Can the world buy such a jewel?

BENEDICK   Yea, and a case to put it into. But speak you 175
this with a sad brow? Or do you play the flouting Jack, 176
to tell us Cupid is a good hare-finder and Vulcan a rare 177
carpenter? Come, in what key shall a man take you, to 178
go in the song?                                                               179

CLAUDIO   In mine eye she is the sweetest lady that ever
I looked on.

BENEDICK   I can see yet without spectacles, and I see no
such matter. There's her cousin, an she were not possessed with a fury, exceeds her as much in beauty as the 184
first of May doth the last of December. But I hope you
have no intent to turn husband, have you?

CLAUDIO   I would scarce trust myself, though I had
sworn the contrary, if Hero would be my wife.

BENEDICK   Is't come to this? In faith, hath not the world 189
one man but he will wear his cap with suspicion? Shall 190
I never see a bachelor of threescore again? Go to, 191
i'faith; an thou wilt needs thrust thy neck into a yoke,
wear the print of it and sigh away Sundays. Look, Don 193
Pedro is returned to seek you.

          *Enter Don Pedro.*

DON PEDRO   What secret hath held you here, that you
followed not to Leonato's?

BENEDICK   I would Your Grace would constrain me to 197
tell.

DON PEDRO   I charge thee on thy allegiance.

BENEDICK   You hear, Count Claudio. I can be secret as a
dumb man—I would have you think so—but on my
allegiance, mark you this, on my allegiance! He is in
love. With who? Now that is Your Grace's part. Mark 203
how short his answer is: with Hero, Leonato's short
daughter.

**117 convert** change   **123 dear happiness** precious piece of luck
**124 else** otherwise   **125–6 I am . . . that** I am of the same disposition
in that matter, i.e., of loving no one.   **129 scape** escape.   **predestinate**
inevitable (for any man who should woo Beatrice)   **132 were** i.e., is.
**133 rare** outstanding.   **parrot-teacher** i.e., one who would teach a parrot well, because you merely "parrot" my lines.   **134 of my tongue**
taught to speak like me, i.e., incessantly   **134–5 of yours** taught to
speak like you.   **137 and . . . continuer** i.e., and as much staying
power in running as you have in talking.   **139 a jade's trick** i.e., an ill-
tempered horse's habit of slipping its head out of the collar or stopping
suddenly (just as Benedick proposes to abandon this exchange
of witticisms when he thinks he has had the last word).   **141 sum of
all** (Don Pedro and Leonato have been conversing apart on other
matters.)   **149 being** since you are   **153 Please it** May it please
**154 go together** i.e., go arm in arm (thus avoiding the question of
precedence in order of leaving).   **154.1 *Manent*** They remain onstage
**157 noted her not** gave her no special attention

**162 tyrant** one who is cruel or pitiless in attitude   **164 low** short
**165 brown** dark-complected   **167–8 were she . . . unhandsome** if Hero's looks
were different from the way she looks now, she would be less attractive. (A roundabout way of complimenting Hero's beauty.)   **175 case**
(1) jewel case who is (2) clothing, outer garments. (There is also a
bawdy play on the meaning "female pudenda.")   **176 sad** serious.
**flouting Jack** i.e., mocking rascal   **177–8 to tell . . . carpenter?** i.e., are
you mocking us with nonsense? (Cupid was blind, not sharp-eyed like
a hunter, and Vulcan was a blacksmith, not a carpenter.)   **178–9 to . . .
song** as the song expresses it. (Alluding perhaps to some popular
song.)   **184 with a fury** by an avenging, infernal spirit   **189–90 hath . . .
suspicion?** i.e., isn't there a man left alive who will regard marriage
with a jaundiced eye? (A cap might be used, unsuccessfully perhaps,
in an attempt to hide a cuckold's horns.)   **191 threescore** sixty.   **Go to**
(An expression of impatience.)   **193 wear . . . Sundays** i.e., display
the marks of your domestic enslavement resignedly.   **197 constrain**
compel   **203 part** speaking part. (I.e., to say, "With who?")

CLAUDIO    If this were so, so were it uttered.    206

BENEDICK    Like the old tale, my lord: "It is not so, nor 207 'twas not so, but indeed, God forbid it should be so."

CLAUDIO    If my passion change not shortly, God forbid it should be otherwise.

DON PEDRO    Amen, if you love her, for the lady is very well worthy.

CLAUDIO    You speak this to fetch me in, my lord.    213

DON PEDRO    By my troth, I speak my thought.    214

CLAUDIO    And in faith, my lord, I spoke mine.

BENEDICK    And by my two faiths and troths, my lord, I 216 spoke mine.

CLAUDIO    That I love her, I feel.

DON PEDRO    That she is worthy, I know.

BENEDICK    That I neither feel how she should be loved nor know how she should be worthy is the opinion that fire cannot melt out of me. I will die in it at the stake.

DON PEDRO    Thou wast ever an obstinate heretic in the despite of beauty.    225

CLAUDIO    And never could maintain his part but in the 226 force of his will.    227

BENEDICK    That a woman conceived me, I thank her; that she brought me up, I likewise give her most humble thanks. But that I will have a recheat winded in my 230 forehead or hang my bugle in an invisible baldrick, all 231 women shall pardon me. Because I will not do them 232 the wrong to mistrust any, I will do myself the right to trust none; and the fine is, for the which I may go the 234 finer, I will live a bachelor.    235

DON PEDRO    I shall see thee, ere I die, look pale with love.

BENEDICK    With anger, with sickness, or with hunger, my lord, not with love. Prove that ever I lose more 239 blood with love than I will get again with drinking, 240 pick out mine eyes with a ballad-maker's pen and 241 hang me up at the door of a brothel house for the sign 242 of blind Cupid.

DON PEDRO    Well, if ever thou dost fall from this faith, thou wilt prove a notable argument.    245

BENEDICK    If I do, hang me in a bottle like a cat and 246 shoot at me, and he that hits me, let him be clapped on the shoulder and called Adam.    248

DON PEDRO    Well, as time shall try:
"In time the savage bull doth bear the yoke."    250

BENEDICK    The savage bull may; but if ever the sensible Benedick bear it, pluck off the bull's horns and set them in my forehead, and let me be vilely painted, and in such great letters as they write, "Here is good horse to hire," let them signify under my sign, "Here you may see Benedick the married man."

CLAUDIO    If this should ever happen, thou wouldst be horn-mad.    258

DON PEDRO    Nay, if Cupid have not spent all his quiver in Venice, thou wilt quake for this shortly.    260

BENEDICK    I look for an earthquake too, then.    261

DON PEDRO    Well, you will temporize with the hours. In 262 the meantime, good Signor Benedick, repair to Leonato's. Commend me to him, and tell him I will not fail him at supper, for indeed he hath made great preparation.

BENEDICK    I have almost matter enough in me for such 267 an embassage; and so I commit you—    268

CLAUDIO    To the tuition of God. From my house, if I had 269 it—

DON PEDRO    The sixth of July. Your loving friend, Benedick.

BENEDICK    Nay, mock not, mock not. The body of your discourse is sometime guarded with fragments, and 274 the guards are but slightly basted on neither. Ere you 275 flout old ends any further, examine your conscience. 276 And so I leave you.                                *Exit.*

CLAUDIO
My liege, Your Highness now may do me good.    278

DON PEDRO
My love is thine to teach. Teach it but how,
And thou shalt see how apt it is to learn
Any hard lesson that may do thee good.

CLAUDIO
Hath Leonato any son, my lord?

DON PEDRO
No child but Hero; she's his only heir.
Dost thou affect her, Claudio?

CLAUDIO                                    O my lord,    284

---

**206 If . . . uttered** If this were true, it might be told in words to this effect.    **207 old tale** (In the English fairy tale known as "Mr. Fox," a murderous wooer, discovered in his crimes by the lady he seeks to marry and victimize, repeatedly disclaims her recital of what she has seen by the refrain here set in quotations. The story is a variant of the theme known as "the Robber Bridegroom." Benedick uses it mockingly here to characterize Claudio's reluctance to admit his "crime" of falling in love.)    **213 fetch me in** get me to confess    **214 By my troth** By my faith, upon my word. (A mild oath.)    **216 by . . . troths** as it were, by my loyalty to you both    **225 despite** contempt    **226–7 in . . . will** by mere obstinacy (which, as defined by the Schoolmen, was the state of the heretic).    **230–2 But that . . . me** i.e., Women must pardon me for refusing to have a horn placed on my head as if I were a cuckold. (A *recheat* is a hunting call sounded [*winded*] on a horn to assemble the hounds; a *baldrick* is a strap that supports the horn, here *invisible* because the horn is the metaphorical one of cuckoldry.)    **234 fine** conclusion    **234–5 go the finer** be more finely dressed (since without a wife I will have more money to spend on clothing)    **239 Prove** If you can prove    **239–40 lose . . . drinking** (According to Elizabethan theory, each sigh cost the heart a drop of blood, whereas blood was replenished by wine.)    **241 ballad-maker's pen** i.e., such as would be used to write love ballads or satires    **242 sign** painted sign, such as hung over inns and shops    **245 notable argument** notorious subject for conversation, example.

**246 bottle** wicker or leather basket (to hold the cat sometimes used as an archery target)    **248 Adam** (Probably refers to Adam Bell, archer outlaw of the ballads.)    **250 In . . . yoke** (Proverbial.)    **258 horn-mad** stark mad. (From the fury of horned beasts; with allusion to cuckoldry.)    **260 Venice** (A city noted for licentiousness.)    **quake** (With a pun on *quiver* in the previous line.)    **261 I . . . then** i.e., My falling in love will be at least as rare as an earthquake.    **262 temporize . . . hours** come to terms, or become milder, in time. (With perhaps a bawdy pun on *hours,* "whores," pronounced something like "hoors.")    **267 matter** wit, intelligence    **268 embassage** mission.    **and so . . . you** (A conventional close, which Claudio and Don Pedro mockingly play with as though it were the complimentary close of a letter.)    **269 tuition** protection    **274 guarded** ornamented, trimmed    **275 guards . . . neither** trimmings are tenuously stitched on at best, have only the flimsiest connection.    **276 flout old ends** quote or recite mockingly proverbial tags of wisdom (as well as fragments of cloth, or the *ends* of letters that Claudio and Don Pedro have been parodying).    **examine your conscience** look to your own behavior or speech.    **278 do me good** do me some good, help me.    **284 affect** love

When you went onward on this ended action,    285
I looked upon her with a soldier's eye,
That liked, but had a rougher task in hand
Than to drive liking to the name of love.    288
But now I am returned and that war thoughts    289
Have left their places vacant, in their rooms
Come thronging soft and delicate desires,
All prompting me how fair young Hero is,
Saying, I liked her ere I went to wars.

DON PEDRO
Thou wilt be like a lover presently
And tire the hearer with a book of words.
If thou dost love fair Hero, cherish it,
And I will break with her and with her father,    297
And thou shalt have her. Was't not to this end
That thou began'st to twist so fine a story?    299

CLAUDIO
How sweetly you do minister to love,
That know love's grief by his complexion!    301
But lest my liking might too sudden seem,
I would have salved it with a longer treatise.    303

DON PEDRO
What need the bridge much broader than the flood?    304
The fairest grant is the necessity.    305
Look what will serve is fit. 'Tis once: thou lovest,    306
And I will fit thee with the remedy.
I know we shall have reveling tonight;
I will assume thy part in some disguise
And tell fair Hero I am Claudio,
And in her bosom I'll unclasp my heart
And take her hearing prisoner with the force
And strong encounter of my amorous tale.
Then after to her father will I break,
And the conclusion is, she shall be thine.
In practice let us put it presently.    *Exeunt.* 316

## [1.2]

*Enter Leonato and an old man [Antonio],*
*brother to Leonato, [meeting].*

LEONATO    How now, brother, where is my cousin,    1
your son? Hath he provided this music?

ANTONIO    He is very busy about it. But brother, I can
tell you strange news that you yet dreamt not of.

LEONATO    Are they good?    5

ANTONIO    As the event stamps them, but they have a    6
good cover; they show well outward. The Prince and    7

Count Claudio, walking in a thick-pleached alley in    8
mine orchard, were thus much overheard by a man of    9
mine: the Prince discovered to Claudio that he loved    10
my niece your daughter and meant to acknowledge it
this night in a dance, and if he found her accordant, he    12
meant to take the present time by the top and instantly    13
break with you of it.

LEONATO    Hath the fellow any wit that told you this?    15

ANTONIO    A good sharp fellow. I will send for him, and
question him yourself.

LEONATO    No, no; we will hold it as a dream till it
appear itself. But I will acquaint my daughter withal,
that she may be the better prepared for an answer, if
peradventure this be true. Go you and tell her of it.

*[Enter Antonio's Son, with a musician and*
*others.]*

Cousins, you know what you have to do.—Oh, I cry    22
you mercy, friend; go you with me, and I will use your    23
skill.—Good cousin, have a care this busy time.

*Exeunt.*

## [1.3]

*Enter Sir [Don] John the Bastard and Conrade,*
*his companion.*

CONRADE    What the goodyear, my lord! Why are you    1
thus out of measure sad?    2

DON JOHN    There is no measure in the occasion that
breeds; therefore the sadness is without limit.

CONRADE    You should hear reason.    5

DON JOHN    And when I have heard it, what blessing
brings it?

CONRADE    If not a present remedy, at least a patient
sufferance.    9

DON JOHN    I wonder that thou, being, as thou say'st
thou art, born under Saturn, goest about to apply a    11
moral medicine to a mortifying mischief. I cannot hide    12
what I am: I must be sad when I have cause and smile
at no man's jests, eat when I have stomach and wait    14
for no man's leisure, sleep when I am drowsy and
tend on no man's business, laugh when I am merry    16
and claw no man in his humor.    17

CONRADE    Yea, but you must not make the full show of
this till you may do it without controlment. You have    19
of late stood out against your brother, and he hath    20
ta'en you newly into his grace, where it is impossible    21
you should take true root but by the fair weather that

---

285 **ended action** military action now ended    288 **Than . . . love**
than to pursue my liking Hero to the point of being in love with her.
289 **now** now that    297 **break** open the subject. (As also in line 314.)
299 **twist** draw out the thread of    301 **his complexion** its outward
appearance.    303 **salved** soothed, eased the way for    304 **What need**
Why need be.    **flood** river.    305 **The fairest . . . necessity** The best
thing to do is simply what is necessary.    306 **Look what** Whatever.
**'Tis once** In short, once and for all. (This speech of Don Pedro's is
overheard by a servant of Antonio's, as we learn in the next scene.)
316 **presently** at once.
**1.2. Location: Leonato's house.**
1 **cousin** kinsman    5 **they** i.e., the news. (Often treated as a
plural noun, as at 2.1.167.)    6 **event** outcome    6–7 **they . . . cover**
(The image is of a printed book, promising well by its cover.)

8 **thick-pleached alley** walk lined with dense hedges of intertwined
shrubs    9 **orchard** garden.    **man** servant    10 **discovered** disclosed
12 **accordant** agreeing, consenting    13 **take . . . top** i.e., seize the
opportunity. (Proverbially, Occasion was imagined bald in the back
of the head but with a forelock hair in the front that opportunistically
could be grabbed.)    15 **wit** sense, intelligence    22–3 **cry you mercy**
beg your pardon    23 **friend** (Addressed perhaps to the musician.)
**1.3. Location: Leonato's house.**
1 **What the goodyear** i.e., What the deuce    2 **out of measure** immoderately    5 **hear** listen to    9 **sufferance** endurance.    11 **under Saturn**
(Hence, of a morose disposition.)    11–12 **goest . . . mischief** endeavor
to cure with moral commonplaces a deadly disease.    14 **stomach**
appetite    16 **tend on** attend to    17 **claw** flatter.    **humor** whim.
19 **controlment** restraint.    20 **stood out** rebelled    21 **grace** favor

you make yourself. It is needful that you frame the 23
season for your own harvest.

DON JOHN   I had rather be a canker in a hedge than a 25
rose in his grace, and it better fits my blood to be dis- 26
dained of all than to fashion a carriage to rob love from 27
any. In this, though I cannot be said to be a flattering
honest man, it must not be denied but I am a plain-
dealing villain. I am trusted with a muzzle and 30
enfranchised with a clog; therefore I have decreed not 31
to sing in my cage. If I had my mouth, I would bite; if
I had my liberty, I would do my liking. In the
meantime let me be that I am, and seek not to alter me.

CONRADE   Can you make no use of your discontent?

DON JOHN   I make all use of it, for I use it only. Who 36
comes here?

*Enter Borachio.*

What news, Borachio?

BORACHIO   I came yonder from a great supper. The
Prince your brother is royally entertained by Leonato,
and I can give you intelligence of an intended mar- 41
riage.

DON JOHN   Will it serve for any model to build mischief
on? What is he for a fool that betroths himself to 44
unquietness?

BORACHIO   Marry, it is your brother's right hand. 46

DON JOHN   Who, the most exquisite Claudio?

BORACHIO   Even he.

DON JOHN   A proper squire! And who, and who? Which 49
way looks he?

BORACHIO   Marry, one Hero, the daughter and heir of
Leonato.

DON JOHN   A very forward March chick! How came 53
you to this?

BORACHIO   Being entertained for a perfumer, as I was 55
smoking a musty room, comes me the Prince and 56
Claudio, hand in hand, in sad conference. I whipped 57
me behind the arras, and there heard it agreed upon 58
that the Prince should woo Hero for himself and,
having obtained her, give her to Count Claudio.

DON JOHN   Come, come, let us thither. This may prove
food to my displeasure. That young start-up hath all 62
the glory of my overthrow. If I can cross him any way, 63
I bless myself every way. You are both sure, and will 64
assist me?

CONRADE   To the death, my lord.

DON JOHN   Let us to the great supper. Their cheer is the
greater that I am subdued. Would the cook were o' my 68
mind! Shall we go prove what's to be done? 69

BORACHIO   We'll wait upon Your Lordship.   *Exeunt.*

# [2.1]

*Enter Leonato, his brother [Antonio], Hero his
daughter, and Beatrice his niece [with Margaret
and Ursula].*

LEONATO   Was not Count John here at supper?

ANTONIO   I saw him not.

BEATRICE   How tartly that gentleman looks! I never can 3
see him but I am heartburned an hour after. 4

HERO   He is of a very melancholy disposition.

BEATRICE   He were an excellent man that were made 6
just in the midway between him and Benedick. The
one is too like an image and says nothing, and the 8
other too like my lady's eldest son, evermore tattling. 9

LEONATO   Then half Signor Benedick's tongue in Count
John's mouth, and half Count John's melancholy in
Signor Benedick's face—

BEATRICE   With a good leg and a good foot, uncle, and
money enough in his purse, such a man would win
any woman in the world, if 'a could get her good will. 15

LEONATO   By my troth, niece, thou wilt never get thee a
husband if thou be so shrewd of thy tongue. 17

ANTONIO   In faith, she's too curst. 18

BEATRICE   Too curst is more than curst. I shall lessen 19
God's sending that way; for it is said, "God sends a 20
curst cow short horns," but to a cow too curst he sends 21
none.

LEONATO   So, by being too curst, God will send you no
horns.

BEATRICE   Just, if he send me no husband, for the which 25
blessing I am at him upon my knees every morning
and evening. Lord, I could not endure a husband with
a beard on his face! I had rather lie in the woolen. 28

LEONATO   You may light on a husband that hath no
beard.

BEATRICE   What should I do with him? Dress him in my
apparel and make him my waiting-gentlewoman? He
that hath a beard is more than a youth, and he that
hath no beard is less than a man; and he that is more
than a youth is not for me, and he that is less than
a man, I am not for him. Therefore I will even take

23 **frame** fashion   25 **canker** dog rose, one that grows wild rather
than being cultivated in formal gardens   26 **blood** mood, disposition   27 **fashion . . . love** counterfeit a behavior to gain undeserved
attention   30–1 **I . . . clog** I am trusted only with my muzzle on and
am allowed freedom only to the extent of being hampered by a heavy
wooden block   31 **decreed** determined   36 **I . . . only** Discontent is
my only resource, and I cultivate it alone.   41 **intelligence** news
44 **What . . . fool** What kind of fool is he   46 **Marry** By the Virgin
Mary, i.e., indeed   49 **proper squire** fine young man. (Said contemptuously.)   53 **forward March chick** precocious young thing (like a
chick hatched early).   55 **entertained for** hired as   56 **smoking**
sweetening the air of (with aromatic smoke).   **comes me** comes. (*Me*
is used colloquially, as also in line 58.)   57 **sad** serious   58 **arras**
tapestry, wall hanging   62 **start-up** upstart   63 **cross** thwart
64 **sure** trustworthy

68–9 **o' my mind** i.e., of a mind to poison the food.   69 **prove** try out
**2.1. Location: Leonato's house.**
3 **tartly** sour of disposition   4 **heartburned** afflicted with heartburn or
indigestion   6 **He were** A man would be   8 **image** statue   9 **my . . . son**
i.e., a spoiled child.   **tattling** chattering.   15 **'a** he   17 **shrewd** shrewish,
sharp-tongued   18 **curst** shrewish.   19 **more** better. (Beatrice jokes that
she would rather be known as too curst (very shrewish) than just ordinarily shrewish, since then she will not be troubled with a husband,
just as a too-curst cow is given no horn.)   20 **that way** in that respect
21 **curst** i.e., savage, vicious. (God proverbially takes care that the
vicious creatures are limited in their ability to do harm.)   25 **Just** Right,
exactly so.   **no husband** If Beatrice has no husband, there can be no prospect of cuckold's horns. (She may also be jesting about a short penis here
and in lines 20–2.)   28 **in the woolen** between blankets, without sheets.

sixpence in earnest of the bearward, and lead his apes 37
into hell. 38

LEONATO  Well, then, go you into hell?

BEATRICE  No, but to the gate; and there will the devil
meet me, like an old cuckold, with horns on his head,
and say, "Get you to heaven, Beatrice, get you to
heaven, here's no place for you maids." So deliver I up
my apes, and away to Saint Peter, for the heavens; he 44
shows me where the bachelors sit, and there live we 45
as merry as the day is long.

ANTONIO [to Hero]  Well, niece, I trust you will be ruled
by your father.

BEATRICE  Yes, faith, it is my cousin's duty to make
curtsy and say, "Father, as it please you." But yet for
all that, cousin, let him be a handsome fellow, or else
make another curtsy and say, "Father, as it please me."

LEONATO  Well, niece, I hope to see you one day fitted
with a husband.

BEATRICE  Not till God make men of some other metal 55
than earth. Would it not grieve a woman to be over-
mastered with a piece of valiant dust? To make an
account of her life to a clod of wayward marl? No, 58
uncle, I'll none. Adam's sons are my brethren, and 59
truly I hold it a sin to match in my kindred. 60

LEONATO [to Hero]  Daughter, remember what I told
you. If the Prince do solicit you in that kind, you know 62
your answer.

BEATRICE  The fault will be in the music, cousin, if you
be not wooed in good time. If the Prince be too 65
important, tell him there is measure in everything, 66
and so dance out the answer. For, hear me, Hero:
wooing, wedding, and repenting is as a Scotch jig, a 68
measure, and a cinquepace. The first suit is hot and 69
hasty, like a Scotch jig, and full as fantastical; the
wedding, mannerly-modest, as a measure, full of state 71
and ancientry; and then comes Repentance, and with 72
his bad legs falls into the cinquepace faster and faster
till he sink into his grave.

LEONATO  Cousin, you apprehend passing shrewdly. 75

BEATRICE  I have a good eye, uncle; I can see a church by 76
daylight. 77

LEONATO  The revelers are entering, brother. Make good
room.                              [The men put on their masks.]

Enter [as maskers] Prince [Don] Pedro, Claudio, and Benedick, and Balthasar, [Borachio,]
and Don John.

DON PEDRO  Lady, will you walk a bout with your 80
friend?            [The couples pair off for the dance.] 81

HERO  So you walk softly and look sweetly and say 82
nothing, I am yours for the walk, and especially when
I walk away.

DON PEDRO  With me in your company?

HERO  I may say so, when I please.

DON PEDRO  And when please you to say so?

HERO  When I like your favor, for God defend the lute 88
should be like the case! 89

DON PEDRO  My visor is Philemon's roof; within the 90
house is Jove.

HERO  Why, then, your visor should be thatched. 92

DON PEDRO  Speak low, if you speak love. 93
                              [They dance to one side.]

BALTHASAR  Well, I would you did like me. 94

MARGARET  So would not I for your own sake, for I have
many ill qualities.

BALTHASAR  Which is one?

MARGARET  I say my prayers aloud.

BALTHASAR  I love you the better. The hearers may cry
Amen.

MARGARET  God match me with a good dancer!

BALTHASAR  Amen.

MARGARET  And God keep him out of my sight when
the dance is done! Answer, clerk. 104

BALTHASAR  No more words. The clerk is answered. 105
                              [They dance to one side.]

URSULA  I know you well enough. You are Signor
Antonio.

ANTONIO  At a word, I am not. 108

URSULA  I know you by the waggling of your head.

ANTONIO  To tell you true, I counterfeit him.

URSULA  You could never do him so ill-well unless you 111
were the very man. Here's his dry hand up and down. 112
You are he, you are he.

ANTONIO  At a word, I am not.

URSULA  Come, come, do you think I do not know you
by your excellent wit? Can virtue hide itself? Go to,
mum, you are he. Graces will appear, and there's an 117
end.                              [They dance to one side.] 118

---

**37 in earnest** in token advance payment for.  **bearward** one who
keeps and exhibits a bear (and sometimes apes)  **37–8 lead . . . hell**
(An ancient proverb says, "Such as die maids do all lead apes in
hell.")  **44 for the heavens** (A common interjection, like "Good
heavens!" but here also carrying its literal meaning, i.e., bound for
heaven.)  **45 bachelors** unmarried persons of either sex  **55 metal**
substance. (With play on "mettle.")  **58 marl** clay, earth (such as
was used by God to make Adam in Genesis 2).  **59–60 Adam's . . .
kindred** (Beatrice jests that since men and women are all descended
from Adam, it would be incestuous for her to marry a man.)  **62 in
that kind** to that effect (i.e., to marriage)  **65 in good time** (1) soon
(2) in time to the music, rhythmically.  **66 important** importunate,
urgent.  **measure** (1) moderation (2) rhythm, dance  **68–9 a measure**
a formal dance  **69 cinquepace** five-step lively dance, galliard.
(The pun on "sink apace," as it was pronounced, is evident in lines
72–4: repentance will *sink faster and faster,* with a suggestion of
detumescence.)  **71–2 state and ancientry** dignity and traditional
stateliness  **75 apprehend passing shrewdly** understand with
unusual perspicacity.  **76–7 see . . . daylight** i.e., see something as
plain as the nose on your face.

**80 walk a bout** take a turn, join in a section of a dance. (Here probably
a slow, stately pavane.)  **81 friend** wooer.  **82 So** Provided  **88 favor**
face  **88–9 God . . . case!** i.e., God forbid the face within should be as
unhandsome as its cover, your visor!  **90–3 My . . . love** (A fourteen-
syllable rhymed couplet, the verse form of Arthur Golding's translation
of the *Metamorphoses*, 1567.)  **90 Philemon's roof** i.e., the humble
cottage in which the peasants Philemon and Baucis entertained Jove,
or Jupiter, unawares. (See Ovid, *Metamorphoses*, 8.)  **92 visor** mask.
**thatched** i.e., whiskered, to resemble the thatch of a humble cottage.
**94–105 BALTHASAR** (The speech prefixes in the quarto text for Balthasar's
lines read *Bene.* and *Balth.* Some editors speculate that *Borachio* is
intended.)  **104 clerk** (So addressed because of Balthasar's repeatedly
answering "Amen" like the parish clerk saying the responses.)
**108 At a word** In short  **111 do . . . ill-well** imitate his imperfections
so perfectly  **112 dry hand** (A sign of age.)  **up and down** exactly.
**117 mum** be silent  **117–18 an end** no more to be said.

BEATRICE    Will you not tell me who told you so?

BENEDICK    No, you shall pardon me.     120

BEATRICE    Nor will you not tell me who you are?

BENEDICK    Not now.

BEATRICE    That I was disdainful and that I had my good wit out of the *Hundred Merry Tales*—well, this was 124 Signor Benedick that said so.

BENEDICK    What's he?

BEATRICE    I am sure you know him well enough.

BENEDICK    Not I, believe me.

BEATRICE    Did he never make you laugh?

BENEDICK    I pray you, what is he?

BEATRICE    Why, he is the Prince's jester, a very dull fool. Only his gift is in devising impossible slanders. None 132 but libertines delight in him, and the commendation 133 is not in his wit but in his villainy, for he both pleases 134 men and angers them, and then they laugh at him and 135 beat him. I am sure he is in the fleet. I would he had 136 boarded me.     137

BENEDICK    When I know the gentleman, I'll tell him 138 what you say.

BEATRICE    Do, do. He'll but break a comparison or two 140 on me, which peradventure not marked or not laughed 141 at strikes him into melancholy; and then there's a par- tridge wing saved, for the fool will eat no supper that night. [*Music.*] We must follow the leaders.     144

BENEDICK    In every good thing.

BEATRICE    Nay, if they lead to any ill, I will leave them at the next turning.     147

     *Dance. Exeunt [all except Don John, Borachio, and Claudio. Don John and Borachio are unmasked.]*

DON JOHN  [*to Borachio*]    Sure my brother is amorous on Hero and hath withdrawn her father to break with him about it. The ladies follow her, and but one visor remains.

BORACHIO    And that is Claudio. I know him by his bearing.

DON JOHN  [*advancing to Claudio*]    Are not you Signor Benedick?

CLAUDIO    You know me well. I am he.

DON JOHN    Signor, you are very near my brother in his 157 love. He is enamored on Hero. I pray you, dissuade 158 him from her; she is no equal for his birth. You may do 159 the part of an honest man in it.

CLAUDIO    How know you he loves her?

DON JOHN    I heard him swear his affection.

BORACHIO    So did I, too, and he swore he would marry her tonight.

DON JOHN    Come, let us to the banquet.     165

     *Exeunt. Manet Claudio.*

CLAUDIO

Thus answer I in name of Benedick,
But hear these ill news with the ears of Claudio.
'Tis certain so. The Prince woos for himself.
Friendship is constant in all other things
Save in the office and affairs of love;
Therefore all hearts in love use their own tongues.
Let every eye negotiate for itself
And trust no agent; for beauty is a witch
Against whose charms faith melteth into blood.     174
This is an accident of hourly proof,     175
Which I mistrusted not. Farewell therefore Hero!     176

     *Enter Benedick [unmasked].*

BENEDICK    Count Claudio?

CLAUDIO    Yea, the same.

BENEDICK    Come, will you go with me?

CLAUDIO    Whither?

BENEDICK    Even to the next willow, about your own 181 business, County. What fashion will you wear the gar- 182 land of? About your neck, like an usurer's chain? Or 183 under your arm, like a lieutenant's scarf? You must 184 wear it one way, for the Prince hath got your Hero.     185

CLAUDIO    I wish him joy of her.

BENEDICK    Why, that's spoken like an honest drover; so 187 they sell bullocks. But did you think the Prince would 188 have served you thus?

CLAUDIO    I pray you, leave me.

BENEDICK    Ho, now you strike like the blind man. 'Twas 191 the boy that stole your meat, and you'll beat the post.     192

CLAUDIO    If it will not be, I'll leave you.     *Exit.* 193

BENEDICK    Alas, poor hurt fowl! Now will he creep into 194 sedges. But that my Lady Beatrice should know me, 195 and not know me! The Prince's fool! Ha? It may be I 196 go under that title because I am merry. Yea, but so I am apt to do myself wrong. I am not so reputed. It is the 198 base, though bitter, disposition of Beatrice that puts the 199 world into her person and so gives me out. Well, I'll be 200 revenged as I may.

     *Enter the Prince [Don Pedro], Hero, [and] Leonato. [All are unmasked.]*

---

**120 you shall pardon me** please excuse me if I don't answer.
**124** *Hundred Merry Tales* (A popular collection of anecdotes first published by John Rastell in 1526.)   **132 Only his gift** His only talent. **impossible** unbelievable   **133 libertines** i.e., those who disregard conventional moral laws   **134 villainy** i.e., mocking, raillery; also, clownishness   **134–5 pleases . . . angers them** i.e., amuses some with his rudeness and angers others with his slanders   **136 fleet** i.e., crowd, company sailing past in the dance.   **137 boarded** i.e., accosted. (Continuing the nautical metaphor begun in *fleet*.) **138 know** become acquainted with   **140 break a comparison** i.e., make a scornful simile (as if he were tilting with lances) **141 peradventure** if it is   **144 leaders** i.e., of the dance.   **147 turning** turning figure in the dance.   **157–8 near . . . love** close to my brother. **159 birth** aristocratic rank.

**165 banquet** light repast of fruit, wine, and dessert.   **165.1** *Manet* He remains on stage   **174 faith . . . blood** loyalty gives way to passion. **175 accident** occurrence   **176 mistrusted** suspected   **181 willow** (A tree emblematic of disappointed love, from which a rejected wooer might then take branches to fashion himself a garland or to whip himself, see lines 208–10 below.)   **182 County** count. **182–3 garland** i.e., of willow   **183 usurer's chain** heavy gold chain, worn by rich men as if it were a badge of office.   **184 scarf** sling.   **185 one way** one way or the other   **187 drover** cattle dealer   **188 bullocks** oxen.   **191 strike . . . man** lash out blindly in every direction.   **191–2 'Twas . . . post** i.e., You're ready to blame anything but the true cause of your distress. (Benedick seemingly alludes to some fable about a boy and an innocent postman that demonstrates this object lesson.)   **193 If . . . be** i.e., If you won't leave me as I asked   **194–5 creep into sedges** i.e., hide himself away, as wounded fowl creep into rushes along the river.   **195–6 know me, and not know me** i.e., be of my long acquaintance, and yet misjudge me so cruelly.   **198–200 It is . . . out** It is Beatrice's low and harsh disposition to assume that she speaks for everyone when she characterizes me this way.

DON PEDRO   Now, signor, where's the Count? Did you see him?

BENEDICK   Troth, my lord, I have played the part of Lady 204 Fame. I found him here as melancholy as a lodge in a 205 warren. I told him, and I think I told him true, that 206 Your Grace had got the good will of this young lady, and I offered him my company to a willow tree, either 208 to make him a garland, as being forsaken, or to bind 209 him up a rod, as being worthy to be whipped 210

DON PEDRO   To be whipped! What's his fault?

BENEDICK   The flat transgression of a schoolboy, who, 212 being overjoyed with finding a bird's nest, shows it his companion, and he steals it.

DON PEDRO   Wilt thou make a trust a transgression? The 215 transgression is in the stealer. 216

BENEDICK   Yet it had not been amiss the rod had been made, and the garland too; for the garland he might have worn himself, and the rod he might have 219 bestowed on you, who, as I take it, have stolen his 220 bird's nest.

DON PEDRO   I will but teach them to sing and restore 222 them to the owner. 223

BENEDICK   If their singing answer your saying, by my 224 faith, you say honestly.

DON PEDRO   The Lady Beatrice hath a quarrel to you. 226 The gentleman that danced with her told her she is much wronged by you.

BENEDICK   Oh, she misused me past the endurance of a block! An oak but with one green leaf on it would have 230 answered her. My very visor began to assume life and 231 scold with her. She told me, not thinking I had been myself, that I was the Prince's jester, that I was duller than a great thaw; huddling jest upon jest with such 234 impossible conveyance upon me that I stood like a 235 man at a mark, with a whole army shooting at me. She 236 speaks poniards, and every word stabs. If her breath 237 were as terrible as her terminations, there were no liv- 238 ing near her; she would infect to the North Star. I 239 would not marry her, though she were endowed with all that Adam had left him before he transgressed. She 241 would have made Hercules have turned spit, yea, and 242 have cleft his club to make the fire, too. Come, talk not 243 of her. You shall find her the infernal Ate in good 244 apparel. I would to God some scholar would conjure 245 her, for certainly, while she is here, a man may live as 246 quiet in hell as in a sanctuary, and people sin upon purpose because they would go thither; so indeed all 248 disquiet, horror, and perturbation follows her.

*Enter Claudio and Beatrice.*

DON PEDRO   Look, here she comes.

BENEDICK   Will Your Grace command me any service to the world's end? I will go on the slightest errand now to the Antipodes that you can devise to send me on; I 253 will fetch you a toothpicker now from the furthest inch 254 of Asia, bring you the length of Prester John's foot, 255 fetch you a hair off the great Cham's beard, do you any 256 embassage to the Pygmies, rather than hold three 257 words' conference with this harpy. You have no 258 employment for me?

DON PEDRO   None but to desire your good company.

BENEDICK   Oh, God, sir, here's a dish I love not! I cannot endure my Lady Tongue.                                    *Exit.*

DON PEDRO   Come, lady, come, you have lost the heart of Signor Benedick.

BEATRICE   Indeed, my lord, he lent it me awhile, and I 265 gave him use for it, a double heart for his single one. 266 Marry, once before he won it of me with false dice; 267 therefore Your Grace may well say I have lost it.

DON PEDRO   You have put him down, lady, you have 269 put him down.

BEATRICE   So I would not he should do me, my lord, lest I should prove the mother of fools. I have brought Count Claudio, whom you sent me to seek.

DON PEDRO   Why, how now, Count? Wherefore are you sad?

CLAUDIO   Not sad, my lord.

DON PEDRO   How then? Sick?

CLAUDIO   Neither, my lord.

BEATRICE   The Count is neither sad, nor sick, nor merry, nor well; but civil count, civil as an orange, and some- 280 thing of that jealous complexion. 281

DON PEDRO   I'faith, lady, I think your blazon to be true, 282 though I'll be sworn, if he be so, his conceit is false. 283 Here, Claudio, I have wooed in thy name, and fair

**204 Troth** By my faith   **204–5 Lady Fame** Dame Rumor.   **205–6 lodge in a warren** isolated gamekeeper's hut in a large game preserve.   **208 offered . . . to** offered to accompany him to   **209–10 bind . . . rod** tie several willow switches into a scourge for him   **212 flat** plain   **215 a trust** a trusted assignment (here, the Prince's having taken in trust the wooing of Hero for Claudio, not himself.)   **215–16 The transgression . . . stealer** i.e., This would have been a transgression only if I had in fact stolen Hero away from Claudio.   **219–20 the rod . . . on you** he could have used the willow branches to give you a whipping   **222–3 I will . . . owner** I will merely teach the fledglings to sing of their love and will restore them to the parent bird, i.e., I'll arrange for the lovers to marry with her father's blessing.   **224 answer your saying** correspond to what you say   **226 to** with   **230–1 An oak . . . her** i.e., No one could possibly have refrained from answering the things she said.   **234 great thaw** i.e., time when roads are muddy and impassable, obliging one to stay dully at home.   **huddling** piling, heaping up   **235 impossible conveyance** incredible dexterity   **236 at a mark** at a shooting target   **237 poniards** daggers   **238 terminations** terms, expressions   **239 to the North Star** i.e., to the farthest limit possible.   **241 all . . . him** i.e., Paradise before the fall of man   **242 Hercules . . . spit** (The Amazon Omphale forced the captive Hercules to wear women's clothing and spin; turning the spit would be an even more menial kitchen duty.)   **243 cleft . . . fire** chopped up Hercules's mighty club into firewood   **244 Ate** goddess of discord

**245 scholar . . . conjure** (Scholars were supposed to be able to conjure evil spirits back into hell by addressing them in Latin.)   **246 here** i.e., on earth. (As long as Beatrice is on earth, hell will seem like a place of refuge.)   **248 because** so that   **253 Antipodes** people and region on the opposite side of the earth   **254 toothpicker** toothpick   **255 Prester John** a legendary Christian king of the Far East   **256 great Cham** the Khan of Tartary, ruler of the Mongols   **257 Pygmies** legendary small race thought to live in India   **258 harpy** legendary creature with a woman's face and body and a bird's wings and claws.   **265–7 he . . . dice** (Beatrice refers seemingly to a previous courtship in which she feels that Benedick prevailed over her unfairly, in return for which she now has paid him back with *use* or interest, two to one.)   **269 put him down** got the better of him. (But Beatrice plays with the phrase in its literal and sexual sense.)   **280 civil** serious, grave. (Punning on *Seville* for the city in Spain whence came bitter-tasting oranges.)   **280–1 something** somewhat   **281 jealous complexion**, i.e., yellow, associated with melancholy and symbolic of jealousy.   **282 blazon** description. (A heraldic term.)   **283 if he be so** if Claudio is jealous.   **conceit** (1) notion, idea (2) heraldic device. (Continuing the metaphor of *blazon*.)

Hero is won. I have broke with her father and his good 285
will obtained. Name the day of marriage, and God
give thee joy!

LEONATO   Count, take of me my daughter and with her
my fortunes. His Grace hath made the match, and all 289
grace say Amen to it.                                        290

BEATRICE   Speak, Count, 'tis your cue.

CLAUDIO   Silence is the perfectest herald of joy. I were 292
but little happy if I could say how much!—Lady, as 293
you are mine, I am yours. I give away myself for you
and dote upon the exchange.

BEATRICE   Speak, cousin, or if you cannot, stop his
mouth with a kiss, and let not him speak neither.
                        [*Claudio and Hero kiss.*]

DON PEDRO   In faith, lady, you have a merry heart.

BEATRICE   Yea, my lord; I thank it, poor fool, it keeps on
the windy side of care. My cousin tells him in his ear 300
that he is in her heart.

CLAUDIO   And so she doth, cousin.

BEATRICE   Good Lord, for alliance! Thus goes everyone 303
to the world but I, and I am sunburnt. I may sit in a 304
corner and cry, "Heigh-ho for a husband!"              305

DON PEDRO   Lady Beatrice, I will get you one.

BEATRICE   I would rather have one of your father's
getting. Hath Your Grace ne'er a brother like you? 308
Your father got excellent husbands, if a maid could come
by them.

DON PEDRO   Will you have me, lady?

BEATRICE   No, my lord, unless I might have another for
working days. Your Grace is too costly to wear every
day. But I beseech Your Grace, pardon me. I was born
to speak all mirth and no matter.                      315

DON PEDRO   Your silence most offends me, and to be
merry best becomes you, for out o' question you were
born in a merry hour.

BEATRICE   No, sure, my lord, my mother cried; but then
there was a star danced, and under that was I born.
Cousins, God give you joy!

LEONATO   Niece, will you look to those things I told you
of?

BEATRICE   I cry you mercy, uncle. [*To Don Pedro*] By Your 324
Grace's pardon.                         *Exit Beatrice.* 325

DON PEDRO   By my troth, a pleasant-spirited lady.

LEONATO   There's little of the melancholy element in 327
her, my lord. She is never sad but when she sleeps, and
not ever sad then; for I have heard my daughter say 329
she hath often dreamt of unhappiness and waked 330
herself with laughing.

DON PEDRO   She cannot endure to hear tell of a husband.

LEONATO   Oh, by no means. She mocks all her wooers 333
out of suit.                                             334

DON PEDRO   She were an excellent wife for Benedick.

LEONATO   Oh, Lord, my lord, if they were but a week
married they would talk themselves mad.

DON PEDRO   County Claudio, when mean you to go to
church?

CLAUDIO   Tomorrow, my lord. Time goes on crutches till
Love have all his rites.

LEONATO   Not till Monday, my dear son, which is hence
a just sevennight and a time too brief, too, to have all 343
things answer my mind.                                  344

DON PEDRO   Come, you shake the head at so long a
breathing, but I warrant thee, Claudio, the time shall 346
not go dully by us. I will in the interim undertake one
of Hercules' labors, which is to bring Signor Benedick 348
and the Lady Beatrice into a mountain of affection
th'one with th'other. I would fain have it a match, and 350
I doubt not but to fashion it, if you three will but
minister such assistance as I shall give you direction. 352

LEONATO   My lord, I am for you, though it cost me ten
nights' watchings.                                      354

CLAUDIO   And I, my lord.

DON PEDRO   And you too, gentle Hero?

HERO   I will do any modest office, my lord, to help my 357
cousin to a good husband.

DON PEDRO   And Benedick is not the unhopefullest hus- 359
band that I know. Thus far can I praise him: he is of a
noble strain, of approved valor and confirmed honesty. 361
I will teach you how to humor your cousin, that she
shall fall in love with Benedick; and I, with your two
helps, will so practice on Benedick that, in despite of
his quick wit and his queasy stomach, he shall fall in 365
love with Beatrice. If we can do this, Cupid is no longer
an archer; his glory shall be ours, for we are the
only love gods. Go in with me, and I will tell you my
drift.                                       *Exeunt.* 369

## [2.2]

*Enter [Don] John and Borachio.*

DON JOHN   It is so. The Count Claudio shall marry the  1
daughter of Leonato.

BORACHIO   Yea, my lord, but I can cross it.             3

DON JOHN   Any bar, any cross, any impediment will be  4
medicinable to me. I am sick in displeasure to him,    5

**285 broke** spoken   **289–90 all . . . to it** i.e., let us all thank God for this union.   **292–3 I were . . . much** i.e., Words could not convey a sense of my happiness.   **300 windy** windward, safe. (In sailing, the ship to windward has the advantage.)   **303 alliance** relationship by marriage. (Claudio has just called her "cousin.")   **303–4 goes . . . world** i.e., gets married   **304 sunburnt** (The Renaissance considered dark complexions unattractive.)   **305 Heigh-ho . . . husband!** (The title of a ballad.)   **308 getting** begetting. (Playing on *get*, "procure," in the previous speech.)   **315 matter** substance.   **324 cry you mercy** beg your pardon (for not having obeyed earlier)   **324–5 By . . . pardon** i.e., I beg you to excuse my departure.   **327 melancholy element** i.e., earth, associated with the humor of melancholy in the old physiology   **329 ever** always   **330 unhappiness** misfortune

**333–4 She . . . suit** She discomfits and discourages all her wooers.   **343 a just sevennight** exactly a week   **344 answer my mind** suit my wishes.   **346 breathing** pause, interval   **348 Hercules' labors** The twelve labors assigned to Hercules included the slaying of the Nemean lion, the Lernean Hydra, the Erymanthian Boar, the Stymphalian Birds, etc.   **350 fain** gladly   **352 minister** furnish, supply   **354 watchings** staying awake.   **357 do . . . office** play any seemly role   **359 unhopefullest** most unpromising   **361 strain** ancestry.   **approved** tested.   **honesty** honor.   **365 queasy** squeamish, delicate (about marriage)   **369 drift** purpose.
**2.2. Location:** Leonato's house.
**1 shall** is going to   **3 cross** thwart. (Also in line 7.)   **4 bar** obstacle   **5 medicinable** medicinal.   **in displeasure to** with dislike of

and whatsoever comes athwart his affection ranges
evenly with mine. How canst thou cross this mar- ⁷
riage?

BORACHIO    Not honestly, my lord, but so covertly that
no dishonesty shall appear in me.

DON JOHN    Show me briefly how.

BORACHIO    I think I told Your Lordship, a year since, ¹²
how much I am in the favor of Margaret, the waiting
gentlewoman to Hero.

DON JOHN    I remember.

BORACHIO    I can, at any unseasonable instant of the ¹⁶
night, appoint her to look out at her lady's chamber
window.

DON JOHN    What life is in that, to be the death of this
marriage?

BORACHIO    The poison of that lies in you to temper. Go ²¹
you to the Prince your brother; spare not to tell him
that he hath wronged his honor in marrying the renowned Claudio—whose estimation do you mightily ²⁴
hold up—to a contaminated stale, such a one as Hero. ²⁵

DON JOHN    What proof shall I make of that?

BORACHIO    Proof enough to misuse the Prince, to vex ²⁷
Claudio, to undo Hero, and kill Leonato. Look you for
any other issue? ²⁹

DON JOHN    Only to despite them I will endeavor any- ³⁰
thing.

BORACHIO    Go, then, find me a meet hour to draw Don ³²
Pedro and the Count Claudio alone. Tell them that you
know that Hero loves me. Intend a kind of zeal both to ³⁴
the Prince and Claudio, as—in love of your brother's ³⁵
honor, who hath made this match, and his friend's
reputation, who is thus like to be cozened with the ³⁷
semblance of a maid—that you have discovered thus. ³⁸
They will scarcely believe this without trial. Offer
them instances, which shall bear no less likelihood ⁴⁰
than to see me at her chamber window, hear me call
Margaret Hero, hear Margaret term me Claudio; and ⁴²
bring them to see this the very night before the
intended wedding—for in the meantime I will so
fashion the matter that Hero shall be absent—and
there shall appear such seeming truth of Hero's
disloyalty that jealousy shall be called assurance and ⁴⁷
all the preparation overthrown. ⁴⁸

DON JOHN    Grow this to what adverse issue it can, I will ⁴⁹
put it in practice. Be cunning in the working this, and
thy fee is a thousand ducats. ⁵¹

BORACHIO    Be you constant in the accusation, and my
cunning shall not shame me.

DON JOHN    I will presently go learn their day of mar- ⁵⁴
riage.                                    *Exit [with Borachio].*

# [2.3]

*Enter Benedick alone.*

BENEDICK    Boy!

*[Enter Boy.]*

BOY    Signor?

BENEDICK    In my chamber window lies a book. Bring it
hither to me in the orchard. ⁴

BOY    I am here already, sir. ⁵

BENEDICK    I know that, but I would have thee hence and
here again.                                    *Exit [Boy].*
I do much wonder that one man, seeing how much
another man is a fool when he dedicates his behaviors
to love, will, after he hath laughed at such shallow follies in others, become the argument of his own scorn ¹¹
by falling in love; and such a man is Claudio. I have
known when there was no music with him but the ¹³
drum and the fife, and now had he rather hear the ¹⁴
tabor and the pipe. I have known when he would have ¹⁵
walked ten mile afoot to see a good armor, and now ¹⁶
will he lie ten nights awake carving the fashion of a ¹⁷
new doublet. He was wont to speak plain and to the ¹⁸
purpose, like an honest man and a soldier, and now is
he turned orthography—his words are a very fantas- ²⁰
tical banquet, just so many strange dishes. May I be so
converted and see with these eyes? I cannot tell; I think
not. I will not be sworn but Love may transform me to
an oyster, but I'll take my oath on it, till he have made
an oyster of me, he shall never make me such a fool.
One woman is fair, yet I am well; another is wise, yet
I am well; another virtuous, yet I am well; but till all
graces be in one woman, one woman shall not come
in my grace. Rich she shall be, that's certain; wise, or
I'll none; virtuous, or I'll never cheapen her; fair, or I'll ³⁰
never look on her; mild, or come not near me; noble, ³¹
or not I for an angel; of good discourse, an excellent ³²
musician, and her hair shall be of what color it please
God. Ha! The Prince and Monsieur Love. I will hide
me in the arbor.                                    *[He hides.]*

*Enter Prince [Don Pedro], Leonato, Claudio.*

DON PEDRO    Come, shall we hear this music?

---

6–7 **whatsoever . . . mine** whatever crosses his inclination runs parallel
with mine.    **12 since** ago    **16 unseasonable** unsuitable, unseemly
**21 lies in** rests with.    **temper** mix, compound.    **24–5 whose . . . up** and
emphasize how much you admire Claudio's reputation    **25 stale** prostitute
**27 misuse** abuse, deceive    **29 issue** outcome. (With a pun on children as
the product of marriage; cf. 4.1.132.)    **30 despite** torture, injure    **32 meet**
suitable    **34 Intend** Pretend    **35 as** i.e., saying as follows. (The words
between the dashes are to be understood as instructions to Don John as
to what he is to say.)    **37 like** likely.    **cozened** deceived, cheated
**38 semblance** semblance only, outward appearance.    **discovered** revealed
**40 instances** proofs    **42 hear . . . Claudio** (Many editors read *Borachio* for
*Claudio*. The present reading may be defended if one imagines that, by
arrangement with Margaret, Borachio is playing the part of Claudio,
but the reading may also be an inconsistency.)    **47 jealousy** suspicion.
**assurance** certainty    **48 preparation** i.e., for marriage    **49 Grow this**
Let this ripen    **51 ducats** gold coins.

**54 presently** immediately.
**2.3. Location: Leonato's garden.**
**4 orchard** garden.    **5 I . . . already** i.e., I will be so quick as to use no
time at all. (But Benedick quibbles on the literal sense.)    **11 argument**
subject    **13–14 there was . . . fife** i.e., his only commitment was to
soldiering    **15 tabor . . . pipe** (Symbols of peaceful merriment and
wooing.)    **16 armor** suit of armor    **17 carving** planning    **18 doublet**
jacket.    **20 turned orthography** become fastidious and fashionable in
his choice of language    **30 I'll none** I'll have none of her.    **cheapen**
make a bid for. (The idea of lessening her value by using her may also
be suggested, though historically it is a later meaning.)    **31, 32 noble,
angel** (Each of these words involves a pun on the meaning "a coin," a
noble being worth six shillings eightpence and an angel, ten shillings.)

CLAUDIO
Yea, my good lord. How still the evening is,
As hushed on purpose to grace harmony!                              38
DON PEDRO [*apart to them*]
See you where Benedick hath hid himself?
CLAUDIO [*apart in reply*]
Oh, very well, my lord. The music ended,                           40
We'll fit the kid-fox with a pennyworth.                            41

*Enter Balthasar with music.*

DON PEDRO
Come, Balthasar, we'll hear that song again.
BALTHASAR
Oh, good my lord, tax not so bad a voice                            43
To slander music any more than once.
DON PEDRO
It is the witness still of excellency                               45
To put a strange face on his own perfection.                        46
I pray thee, sing, and let me woo no more.                          47
BALTHASAR
Because you talk of wooing, I will sing,                            48
Since many a wooer doth commence his suit                           49
To her he thinks not worthy, yet he woos,                           50
Yet will he swear he loves.
DON PEDRO                        Nay, pray thee, come,              51
Or if thou wilt hold longer argument,
Do it in notes.
BALTHASAR          Note this before my notes:                       53
There's not a note of mine that's worth the noting.
DON PEDRO
Why, these are very crotchets that he speaks!                       55
Note, notes, forsooth, and nothing.          [*Music.*]             56
BENEDICK [*aside*]   Now, divine air! Now is his soul rav-          57
ished! Is it not strange that sheeps' guts should hale              58
souls out of men's bodies? Well, a horn for my money,              59
when all's done.

*The Song.*

BALTHASAR
Sigh no more, ladies, sigh no more.
Men were deceivers ever,
One foot in sea and one on shore,
To one thing constant never.

Then sigh not so, but let them go,
And be you blithe and bonny,                                        66
Converting all your sounds of woe
Into Hey nonny, nonny.                                              68

Sing no more ditties, sing no moe,                                  69
Of dumps so dull and heavy;                                         70
The fraud of men was ever so,
Since summer first was leavy.                                       72
Then sigh not so, but let them go,
And be you blithe and bonny,
Converting all your sounds of woe
Into Hey nonny, nonny.

DON PEDRO    By my troth, a good song.
BALTHASAR    And an ill singer, my lord.
DON PEDRO    Ha, no, no, faith, thou sing'st well enough
for a shift.                                                        80
BENEDICK [*aside*]   An he had been a dog that should              81
have howled thus, they would have hanged him, and
I pray God his bad voice bode no mischief. I has as
lief have heard the night raven, come what plague                   84
could have come after it.
DON PEDRO    Yea, marry, dost thou hear, Balthasar? I              86
pray thee, get us some excellent music, for tomorrow
night we would have it at the Lady Hero's chamber
window.
BALTHASAR    The best I can, my lord.
DON PEDRO    Do so. Farewell.          *Exit Balthasar.*
Come hither, Leonato. What was it you told me of
today, that your niece Beatrice was in love with Signor
Benedick?
CLAUDIO    Oh, ay! [*Aside to Pedro*] Stalk on, stalk on; the     95
fowl sits.—I did never think that lady would have             96
loved any man.
LEONATO    No, nor I neither, but most wonderful that she
should so dote on Signor Benedick, whom she hath in
all outward behaviors seemed ever to abhor.
BENEDICK [*aside*]   Is't possible? Sits the wind in that        101
corner?                                                            102
LEONATO    By my troth, my lord, I cannot tell what to
think of it but that she loves him with an enraged            104
affection; it is past the infinite of thought.                    105
DON PEDRO    Maybe she doth but counterfeit.
CLAUDIO    Faith, like enough.                                    107
LEONATO    Oh, God, counterfeit? There was never counterfeit of passion came so near the life of passion as
she discovers it.                                                  110
DON PEDRO    Why, what effects of passion shows she?
CLAUDIO [*aside to them*]   Bait the hook well; this fish will
bite.

---

38 As as if.   grace harmony do honor to music.   40 The music ended
When the music is over   41 We'll . . . pennyworth i.e., we'll give our
sly victim more than he bargained for. (A *kid-fox* is presumably a
young fox, as in beast fable; *kid*, i.e., young goat, also suggests one
whom they are stalking as their quarry. Claudio may be referring to
some children's game.)   43 tax task   45–6 It . . . perfection It is
always characteristic of excellence to pretend not to know its own
skill.   47 woo entreat   48–51 Because . . . he loves (Balthasar modestly claims to be unworthy of being *wooed*, i.e., entreated, but will
comply, since he knows Don Pedro speaks with the hyperbole all
wooers use in addressing women they actually consider unworthy.)   53 notes music.   55 crotchets (1) whims, fancies (2) musical
notes of brief duration   56 nothing (With a pun on *noting*; the two
words were pronounced alike. Compare the same pun in the title
of the play, where *Nothing* suggests "noting," or eavesdropping.)
57 air melody.   58 sheeps' guts strings on musical instruments.
hale draw   59 a horn a hunting horn, a more masculine instrument
than a lute. (But with a perhaps unconscious allusion to a cuckold's
horns.)

66 blithe and bonny cheerful and carefree   68 Hey nonny, nonny
(A nonsense refrain.)   69 moe more   70 dumps mournful songs; also,
dances   72 leavy leafy.   80 for a shift in a pinch.   81 An If. (Also in
line 161.)   84 lief willingly.   night raven a bird of night, portending
disaster   86 Yea, marry (A continuation of Don Pedro's speech preceding Benedick's aside.)   95–6 Stalk . . . sits i.e., Proceed stealthily;
the hunted bird is hiding in the bush.   101–2 Sits . . . corner? Is that
the way the wind is blowing?   104 enraged maddened with passion
105 infinite farthest reach. (It's unbelievable but true.)   107 like
likely   110 discovers betrays

LEONATO    What effects, my lord? She will sit you—you 114
heard my daughter tell you how.

CLAUDIO    She did indeed.

DON PEDRO    How, how, I pray you? You amaze me. I
would have thought her spirit had been invincible
against all assaults of affection.

LEONATO    I would have sworn it had, my lord—especially against Benedick.

BENEDICK [aside]    I should think this a gull but that the 122
white-bearded fellow speaks it. Knavery cannot, sure,
hide himself in such reverence.

CLAUDIO [apart to them]    He hath ta'en th'infection.
Hold it up.                                              126

DON PEDRO    Hath she made her affection known to
Benedick?

LEONATO    No, and swears she never will. That's her
torment.

CLAUDIO    'Tis true, indeed. So your daughter says.
"Shall I," says she, "that have so oft encountered him 132
with scorn, write to him that I love him?"

LEONATO    This says she now when she is beginning to
write to him, for she'll be up twenty times a night, and
there will she sit in her smock till she have writ a sheet 136
of paper. My daughter tells us all.

CLAUDIO    Now you talk of a sheet of paper, I remember
a pretty jest your daughter told us of.

LEONATO    Oh, when she had writ it and was reading it
over, she found "Benedick" and "Beatrice" between
the sheet?

CLAUDIO    That.                                        143

LEONATO    Oh, she tore the letter into a thousand half- 144
pence; railed at herself, that she should be so immod- 145
est to write to one that she knew would flout her. "I 146
measure him," says she, "by my own spirit, for I
should flout him if he writ to me. Yea, though I love
him, I should."

CLAUDIO    Then down upon her knees she falls, weeps,
sobs, beats her heart, tears her hair, prays, curses: "O
sweet Benedick! God give me patience!"

LEONATO    She doth indeed; my daughter says so. And
the ecstasy hath so much overborne her that my 154
daughter is sometime afeard she will do a desperate
outrage to herself. It is very true.

DON PEDRO    It were good that Benedick knew of it by
some other, if she will not discover it.                158

CLAUDIO    To what end? He would make but a sport of
it and torment the poor lady worse.

DON PEDRO    An he should, it were an alms to hang him. 161
She's an excellent sweet lady, and, out of all suspicion, 162
she is virtuous.

CLAUDIO    And she is exceeding wise.

DON PEDRO    In everything but in loving Benedick.

LEONATO    O my lord, wisdom and blood combating in 166

so tender a body, we have ten proofs to one that blood
hath the victory. I am sorry for her, as I have just
cause, being her uncle and her guardian.

DON PEDRO    I would she had bestowed this dotage on 170
me. I would have doffed all other respects and made 171
her half myself. I pray you, tell Benedick of it, and hear 172
what 'a will say.

LEONATO    Were it good, think you?

CLAUDIO    Hero thinks surely she will die; for she says
she will die if he love her not, and she will die ere she
make her love known, and she will die if he woo her,
rather than she will bate one breath of her accustomed 178
crossness.                                              179

DON PEDRO    She doth well. If she should make tender 180
of her love, 'tis very possible he'll scorn it; for the man,
as you know all, hath a contemptible spirit.            182

CLAUDIO    He is a very proper man.                     183

DON PEDRO    He hath indeed a good outward happiness. 184

CLAUDIO    Before God, and in my mind, very wise.      185

DON PEDRO    He doth indeed show some sparks that are
like wit.

CLAUDIO    And I take him to be valiant.

DON PEDRO    As Hector, I assure you; and in the manag- 189
ing of quarrels you may say he is wise, for either he
avoids them with great discretion or undertakes them
with a most Christian-like fear.

LEONATO    If he do fear God, 'a must necessarily keep
peace. If he break the peace, he ought to enter into a
quarrel with fear and trembling.

DON PEDRO    And so will he do, for the man doth fear
God, howsoever it seems not in him by some large 197
jests he will make. Well, I am sorry for your niece. Shall
we go seek Benedick and tell him of her love?

CLAUDIO    Never tell him, my lord. Let her wear it out 200
with good counsel.                                      201

LEONATO    Nay, that's impossible. She may wear her
heart out first.

DON PEDRO    Well, we will hear further of it by your
daughter. Let it cool the while. I love Benedick well,
and I could wish he would modestly examine himself,
to see how much he is unworthy so good a lady.

LEONATO    My lord, will you walk? Dinner is ready.

[They walk aside.]

CLAUDIO    If he do not dote on her upon this, I will never 209
trust my expectation.

DON PEDRO    Let there be the same net spread for her;
and that must your daughter and her gentlewomen
carry. The sport will be when they hold one an opinion 213
of another's dotage, and no such matter; that's the 214

---

114 **sit you** i.e., sit. (*You* is used idiomatically.)    122 **gull** trick, deception.
**but** except for the fact    126 **Hold it up** Keep up the jest.    132 **she** i.e.,
Beatrice    136 **smock** chemise    143 **That** i.e., That's it.    144–5 **halfpence** i.e., small pieces    145 **railed at** scolded    146 **flout** mock
154 **overborne** overwhelmed    158 **other** other person.    **discover**
reveal    161 **were an alms** would be a good deed. (Hanging would be
too good for him.)    162 **out of** beyond    166 **blood** amorous desire

170 **dotage** doting affection    171 **doffed** put or turned aside.
**respects** considerations    172 **half myself** i.e., my wife.    178 **bate**
abate    179 **crossness** perversity, contrariety.    180 **tender** offer
182 **contemptible** contemptuous    183 **proper** handsome    184 **outward happiness** fortune in his good looks.    185 **Before God** i.e.,
By God, you're absolutely right    189 **Hector** the mightiest of the
Trojans    197 **by** to judge by.    **large** broad, indelicate    200 **wear
it out** eradicate it    201 **counsel** advice, deliberation    209 **upon**
as a result of, after    213 **carry** carry out.    213–14 **they . . . dotage**
each believes the other to be in love    214 **no such matter** the reality is
quite otherwise

scene that I would see, which will be merely a dumb 215
show. Let us send her to call him in to dinner.    216

[*Exeunt Don Pedro, Claudio, and Leonato.*]

BENEDICK [*coming forward*]    This can be no trick. The
conference was sadly borne. They have the truth of 218
this from Hero. They seem to pity the lady. It seems
her affections have their full bent. Love me? Why, it 220
must be requited. I hear how I am censured. They say
I will bear myself proudly if I perceive the love come
from her; they say too that she will rather die than give
any sign of affection. I did never think to marry. I must
not seem proud; happy are they that hear their detrac- 225
tions and can put them to mending. They say the lady 226
is fair; 'tis a truth, I can bear them witness; and virtuous; 'tis so, I cannot reprove it; and wise but for loving 228
me; by my troth, it is no addition to her wit, nor no
great argument of her folly, for I will be horribly in
love with her. I may chance have some odd quirks and 231
remnants of wit broken on me, because I have railed
so long against marriage. But doth not the appetite
alter? A man loves the meat in his youth that he cannot endure in his age. Shall quips and sentences and 235
these paper bullets of the brain awe a man from the 236
career of his humor? No, the world must be peopled. 237
When I said I would die a bachelor, I did not think I
should live till I were married. Here comes Beatrice.
By this day, she's a fair lady! I do spy some marks of
love in her.

*Enter Beatrice.*

BEATRICE    Against my will I am sent to bid you come in
to dinner.
BENEDICK    Fair Beatrice, I thank you for your pains.
BEATRICE    I took no more pains for those thanks than
you take pains to thank me. If it had been painful I
would not have come.
BENEDICK    You take pleasure then in the message?
BEATRICE    Yea, just so much as you may take upon a 249
knife's point and choke a daw withal. You have no 250
stomach, signor. Fare you well.                *Exit.* 251
BENEDICK    Ha! "Against my will I am sent to bid you
come in to dinner." There's a double meaning in that.
"I took no more pains for those thanks than you took
pains to thank me." That's as much as to say, "Any
pains that I take for you is as easy as thanks." If I do
not take pity of her, I am a villain; if I do not love her,
I am a Jew. I will go get her picture.            *Exit.* 258

# [3.1]

*Enter Hero and two gentlewomen, Margaret
and Ursula.*

HERO
  Good Margaret, run thee to the parlor.
  There shalt thou find my cousin Beatrice
  Proposing with the Prince and Claudio.            3
  Whisper her ear and tell her I and Ursley          4
  Walk in the orchard, and our whole discourse
  Is all of her. Say that thou overheard'st us,
  And bid her steal into the pleachèd bower,          7
  Where honeysuckles, ripened by the sun,
  Forbid the sun to enter, like favorites,
  Made proud by princes, that advance their pride    10
  Against that power that bred it. There will she hide
    her,                                             11
  To listen our propose. This is thy office.         12
  Bear thee well in it and leave us alone.           13
MARGARET
  I'll make her come, I warrant you, presently.    [*Exit.*] 14
HERO
  Now, Ursula, when Beatrice doth come,
  As we do trace this alley up and down,             16
  Our talk must only be of Benedick.
  When I do name him, let it be thy part
  To praise him more than ever man did merit.
  My talk to thee must be how Benedick
  Is sick in love with Beatrice. Of this matter
  Is little Cupid's crafty arrow made,
  That only wounds by hearsay.

*Enter Beatrice [behind].*

                          Now begin,                 23
  For look where Beatrice, like a lapwing, runs      24
  Close by the ground, to hear our conference.
URSULA [*to Hero*]
  The pleasant'st angling is to see the fish
  Cut with her golden oars the silver stream         27
  And greedily devour the treacherous bait.
  So angle we for Beatrice, who even now
  Is couchèd in the woodbine coverture.              30
  Fear you not my part of the dialogue.              31
HERO [*to Ursula*]
  Then go we near her, that her ear lose nothing
  Of the false sweet bait that we lay for it.
                          [*They approach the bower.*]
  No, truly, Ursula, she is too disdainful;
  I know her spirits are as coy and wild             35
  As haggards of the rock.
URSULA                    But are you sure            36

---

**215–16 dumb show** pantomime (lacking their usual banter)
**218 sadly borne** soberly conducted.    **220 have . . . bent** i.e., are fully
engaged. (The image is of a bow pulled taut.)    **225–6 that . . . mending**
that can hear themselves criticized and undertake to remedy the
defect.    **228 reprove** refute    **231 quirks** witty conceits or jokes
**235 sentences** saws, maxims    **236 paper bullets** i.e., words
**237 career of his humor** pursuit of his inclination. (In horsemanship,
a *career* is a short gallop.)    **249–50 just . . . withal** i.e., very little.
(A daw or jackdaw is a common blackbird, smaller than a crow.)
**251 stomach** appetite    **258 I am a Jew.** (A common defamatory
comparison.)

**3.1. Location:** Leonato's garden.
**3 Proposing** conversing    **4 Ursley** (A nickname for *Ursula.*)
**7 pleachèd** formed by densely interwoven branches    **10–11 that . . . it**
i.e., who dare set themselves up against the very princes who advanced
them.    **12 listen our propose** listen to our conversation.    **office** responsibility.    **13 leave us alone** leave the rest to us.    **14 presently** immediately.    **16 trace** walk    **23 only . . . hearsay** wounds by mere report.
**24 lapwing** bird of the plover family    **27 oars** i.e., fins    **30 Is . . . coverture** is hid in the honeysuckle bower.    **31 Fear . . . dialogue** Don't worry
about my not holding up my part in the conversation.    **35 coy** disdainful
**36 As . . . rock** as untamed female hawks in mountainous terrain.

That Benedick loves Beatrice so entirely?

HERO
So says the Prince and my new-trothèd lord.

URSULA
And did they bid you tell her of it, madam?

HERO
They did entreat me to acquaint her of it;
But I persuaded them, if they loved Benedick,
To wish him wrestle with affection
And never to let Beatrice know of it.

URSULA
Why did you so? Doth not the gentleman
Deserve as full as fortunate a bed    45
As ever Beatrice shall couch upon?    46

HERO
O god of love! I know he doth deserve
As much as may be yielded to a man;
But Nature never framed a woman's heart
Of prouder stuff than that of Beatrice.
Disdain and scorn ride sparkling in her eyes,
Misprizing what they look on, and her wit    52
Values itself so highly that to her
All matter else seems weak. She cannot love,    54
Nor take no shape nor project of affection,    55
She is so self-endearèd.

URSULA      Sure I think so,    56
And therefore certainly it were not good
She knew his love, lest she'll make sport at it.

HERO
Why, you speak truth. I never yet saw man,
How wise, how noble, young, how rarely featured,    60
But she would spell him backward. If fair-faced,    61
She would swear the gentleman should be her
    sister;
If black, why, Nature, drawing of an antic,    63
Made a foul blot; if tall, a lance ill-headed;
If low, an agate very vilely cut;    65
If speaking, why, a vane blown with all winds;
If silent, why, a block movèd with none.
So turns she every man the wrong side out
And never gives to truth and virtue that
Which simpleness and merit purchaseth.    70

URSULA
Sure, sure, such carping is not commendable.

HERO
No, not to be so odd and from all fashions    72
As Beatrice is cannot be commendable.
But who dare tell her so? If I should speak,
She would mock me into air; oh, she would laugh me    75
Out of myself, press me to death with wit.    76

Therefore let Benedick, like covered fire,
Consume away in sighs, waste inwardly.    78
It were a better death than die with mocks,
Which is as bad as die with tickling.

URSULA
Yet tell her of it. Hear what she will say.

HERO
No, rather I will go to Benedick
And counsel him to fight against his passion.
And truly, I'll devise some honest slanders    84
To stain my cousin with. One doth not know
How much an ill word may empoison liking.

URSULA
Oh, do not do your cousin such a wrong!
She cannot be so much without true judgment—
Having so swift and excellent a wit
As she is prized to have—as to refuse    90
So rare a gentleman as Signor Benedick.

HERO
He is the only man of Italy,
Always excepted my dear Claudio.

URSULA
I pray you, be not angry with me, madam,
Speaking my fancy: Signor Benedick,
For shape, for bearing, argument, and valor,    96
Goes foremost in report through Italy.

HERO
Indeed, he hath an excellent good name.

URSULA
His excellence did earn it ere he had it.
When are you married, madam?

HERO
Why, every day, tomorrow. Come, go in.    101
I'll show thee some attires and have thy counsel
Which is the best to furnish me tomorrow.
                    [*They walk away.*]

URSULA [*to Hero*]
She's limed, I warrant you. We have caught her,
    madam.    104

HERO [*to Ursula*]
If it prove so, then loving goes by haps;    105
Some Cupid kills with arrows, some with traps.    106
             [*Exeunt Hero and Ursula.*]

BEATRICE [*coming forward*]
What fire is in mine ears? Can this be true?    107
    Stand I condemned for pride and scorn so much?
Contempt, farewell, and maiden pride, adieu!
    No glory lives behind the back of such.    110
And Benedick, love on; I will requite thee,
    Taming my wild heart to thy loving hand.    112

---

45–6 as full . . . upon i.e., as good a wife as Beatrice. 52 Misprizing undervaluing, despising 54 weak unimportant. 55 project conception, idea 56 self-endeared full of self-love. 60 How however. rarely excellently 61 spell him backward i.e., speak contrarily of him by characterizing his virtues as vices. 63 black dark. antic buffoon, grotesque figure 65 agate i.e., diminutive person. (Alluding to the small figures cut in agate for rings.) 70 simpleness integrity, plainness. purchaseth earn, deserve. 72 from contrary to 75–6 she . . . myself she would mockingly put me down 76 press me to death (Pressing to death with weights was the usual punishment for those accused of crimes who refused to plead either guilty or not guilty.)

78 Consume . . . sighs (An allusion to the belief that each sigh cost the heart a drop of blood.) 84 honest slanders i.e., slanders that do not involve her virtue 90 prized esteemed 96 argument skill in discourse 101 every day, tomorrow tomorrow and every day thereafter. 104 limed caught, like a bird in birdlime, a sticky substance spread on branches to trap the birds that perch on them 105 by haps by chance 106 Some Cupid kills Cupid kills some 107 What . . . ears? (An allusion to the old saying that a person's ears burn when one is being discussed in one's absence.) 110 No . . . such Nothing is gained by hiding behind such defenses. 112 Taming . . . hand (A figure derived from the taming of the hawk by the hand of the falconer.)

If thou dost love, my kindness shall incite thee
   To bind our loves up in a holy band;                    114
For others say thou dost deserve, and I
Believe it better than reportingly.                    *Exit.* 116

❖

## [3.2]

*Enter Prince [Don Pedro], Claudio, Benedick,*
*and Leonato.*

DON PEDRO   I do but stay till your marriage be con-   1
summate, and then go I toward Aragon.                    2
CLAUDIO   I'll bring you thither, my lord, if you'll   3
vouchsafe me.                    4
DON PEDRO   Nay, that would be as great a soil in the   5
new gloss of your marriage as to show a child his new
coat and forbid him to wear it. I will only be bold with   7
Benedick for his company, for from the crown of his
head to the sole of his foot he is all mirth. He hath
twice or thrice cut Cupid's bowstring, and the little
hangman dare not shoot at him. He hath a heart as   11
sound as a bell, and his tongue is the clapper, for what
his heart thinks his tongue speaks.
BENEDICK   Gallants, I am not as I have been.
LEONATO   So say I. Methinks you are sadder.   15
CLAUDIO   I hope he be in love.
DON PEDRO   Hang him, truant! There's no true drop of   17
blood in him, to be truly touched with love. If he be
sad, he wants money.   19
BENEDICK   I have the toothache.   20
DON PEDRO   Draw it.   21
BENEDICK   Hang it!   22
CLAUDIO   You must hang it first and draw it after-
wards.
DON PEDRO   What, sigh for the toothache?
LEONATO   Where is but a humor or a worm.   26
BENEDICK   Well, everyone can master a grief but he that   27
has it.
CLAUDIO   Yet say I, he is in love.
DON PEDRO   There is no appearance of fancy in him,   30
unless it be a fancy that he hath to strange disguises;   31
as, to be a Dutchman today, a Frenchman tomorrow,
or in the shape of two countries at once, as, a German
from the waist downward, all slops, and a Spaniard   34
from the hip upward, no doublet. Unless he have a   35

fancy to this foolery, as it appears he hath, he is no fool   36
for fancy, as you would have it appear he is.   37
CLAUDIO   If he be not in love with some woman, there
is no believing old signs. 'A brushes his hat o'
mornings. What should that bode?
DON PEDRO   Hath any man seen him at the barber's?
CLAUDIO   No, but the barber's man hath been seen with
him, and the old ornament of his cheek hath already   43
stuffed tennis balls.   44
LEONATO   Indeed he looks younger than he did by the
loss of a beard.
DON PEDRO   Nay, 'a rubs himself with civet. Can you   47
smell him out by that?   48
CLAUDIO   That's as much as to say the sweet youth's in
love.
DON PEDRO   The greatest note of it is his melancholy.   51
CLAUDIO   And when was he wont to wash his face?   52
DON PEDRO   Yea, or to paint himself? For the which I   53
hear what they say of him.   54
CLAUDIO   Nay, but his jesting spirit, which is now crept
into a lute string and now governed by stops.   56
DON PEDRO   Indeed, that tells a heavy tale for him.
Conclude, conclude he is in love.
CLAUDIO   Nay, but I know who loves him.
DON PEDRO   That would I know too. I warrant, one that
knows him not.
CLAUDIO   Yes, and his ill conditions; and, in despite of   62
all, dies for him.
DON PEDRO   She shall be buried with her face upwards.   64
BENEDICK   Yet is this no charm for the toothache. Old
signor, walk aside with me. I have studied eight or
nine wise words to speak to you, which these hobby-   67
horses must not hear.   *[Exeunt Benedick and Leonato.]*   68
DON PEDRO   For my life, to break with him about   69
Beatrice.
CLAUDIO   'Tis even so. Hero and Margaret have by this   71
played their parts with Beatrice, and then the two
bears will not bite one another when they meet.

*Enter [Don] John the Bastard.*

DON JOHN   My lord and brother, God save you!
DON PEDRO   Good e'en, brother.   75
DON JOHN   If your leisure served, I would speak with
you.
DON PEDRO   In private?

---

**114 band** bond   **116 better than reportingly** on better evidence than mere report.
**3.2. Location:** Leonato's house.
**1–2 consummate** consummated   **3 bring** escort   **4 vouchsafe** allow   **5 soil** stain   **7 be bold with** ask   **11 hangman** executioner; rogue. (Playfully applied to Cupid.)   **15 sadder** more serious.
**17 truant** i.e., from love.   **19 wants** lacks   **20 toothache** (Thought to be a common ailment of lovers.)   **21 Draw** Extract. (But Claudio jokes on the method of executing traitors, who were hanged first and then cut down alive and drawn, i.e., disemboweled, and finally quartered.)   **22 Hang it!** Confound it!   **26 Where** Where there.   **humor or a worm** (A toothache was ascribed to "humors," or unhealthy secretions, and to actual worms in the teeth.)   **27 grief** pain.   **but** except   **30 fancy** love   **31 fancy** whim, liking   **34 slops** loose breeches   **35 no doublet** i.e., with a hip-length cloak in place of, or covering, the close-fitting doublet.

**36–7 fool for fancy** i.e., lover   **43–4 the old . . . tennis balls** i.e., Benedick's beard has gone to stuff tennis balls. (He appears on stage beardless in this scene for the first time.)   **47 civet** perfume derived from the civet cat.   **48 smell him out** (1) discern his secret (2) smell him coming   **51 note** mark   **52 wont** accustomed.   **wash** i.e., with cosmetics; similarly with *paint* in the next line   **53–4 For . . . him** That's what I hear people saying about him.   **56 stops** (1) frets on the fingerboard (2) restraints.   **62 ill conditions** bad qualities   **64 She . . . upwards** (Suicides were buried face downwards; Beatrice, conversely, is comically imagined to die as a martyr to love. Dying here suggests sexual orgasm, continuing the idea that she "dies for him," line 63.)   **67–8 hobbyhorses** i.e., buffoons. (Originally, figures in a morris dance made to resemble a horse and rider.)   **69 For** Upon.   **break** speak   **71 Margaret** (Ursula joined Hero in playing the trick on Beatrice, but Margaret has been in on it.)   **75 e'en** evening, i.e., afternoon

DON JOHN   If it please you. Yet Count Claudio may hear, for what I would speak of concerns him.

DON PEDRO   What's the matter?

DON JOHN   [*to Claudio*]   Means Your Lordship to be married tomorrow?

DON PEDRO   You know he does.

DON JOHN   I know not that, when he knows what I know.

CLAUDIO   If there be any impediment, I pray you discover it.   88

DON JOHN   You may think I love you not. Let that appear hereafter, and aim better at me by that I now 90 will manifest. For my brother, I think he holds you 91 well and in dearness of heart hath holp to effect your 92 ensuing marriage—surely suit ill spent and labor ill bestowed.

DON PEDRO   Why, what's the matter?

DON JOHN   I came hither to tell you, and, circumstances 96 shortened—for she has been too long a-talking of— 97 the lady is disloyal.   98

CLAUDIO   Who, Hero?

DON JOHN   Even she—Leonato's Hero, your Hero, every man's Hero.

CLAUDIO   Disloyal?

DON JOHN   The word is too good to paint out her 103 wickedness. I could say she were worse; think you of a worse title, and I will fit her to it. Wonder not till fur- 105 ther warrant. Go but with me tonight, you shall see her 106 chamber window entered, even the night before her wedding day. If you love her then, tomorrow wed her; but it would better fit your honor to change your mind.

CLAUDIO   May this be so?

DON PEDRO   I will not think it.

DON JOHN   If you dare not trust that you see, confess not 113 that you know. If you will follow me, I will show you 114 enough; and when you have seen more and heard more, proceed accordingly.

CLAUDIO   If I see anything tonight why I should not marry her, tomorrow in the congregation, where I should wed, there will I shame her.

DON PEDRO   And, as I wooed for thee to obtain her, I will join with thee to disgrace her.

DON JOHN   I will disparage her no farther till you are my witnesses. Bear it coldly but till midnight, and let the 123 issue show itself.   124

DON PEDRO   O day untowardly turned!   125

CLAUDIO   O mischief strangely thwarting!

DON JOHN   O plague right well prevented! So will you say when you have seen the sequel.   [*Exeunt.*]

❧

88 **discover** reveal   90 **aim better at** judge better of.   **that** that which   91–2 **holds you well** thinks well of you   92 **holp** helped   96–7 **circumstances shortened** without unnecessary details   97 **a-talking of** under discussion (by us)   98 **disloyal** unfaithful.   103 **paint out** portray in full   105–6 **till further warrant** till further proof appears.   113–14 **If . . . know** i.e., If you are unwilling to believe what you see, then don't claim to know the truth.   123 **coldly** calmly   124 **issue** outcome   125 **untowardly turned** wretchedly altered.

# [3.3]

*Enter Dogberry and his compartner [*Verges*] with the Watch.*

DOGBERRY   Are you good men and true?

VERGES   Yea, or else it were pity but they should suffer salvation, body and soul.   3

DOGBERRY   Nay, that were a punishment too good for them, if they should have any allegiance in them, 5 being chosen for the Prince's watch.

VERGES   Well, give them their charge, neighbor Dog- 7 berry.

DOGBERRY   First, who think you the most desartless 9 man to be constable?

FIRST WATCH   Hugh Oatcake, sir, or George Seacoal, for they can write and read.

DOGBERRY   Come hither, neighbor Seacoal. [*Seacoal, or Second Watch, steps forward.*] God hath blessed you with a good name. To be a well-favored man is the gift 15 of fortune, but to write and read comes by nature.

SEACOAL   Both which, Master Constable—

DOGBERRY   You have. I knew it would be your answer. Well, for your favor, sir, why, give God thanks, and 19 make no boast of it; and for your writing and reading, let that appear when there is no need of such vanity. You are thought here to be the most senseless and fit 22 man for the constable of the watch; therefore bear you the lantern. This is your charge: you shall comprehend 24 all vagrom men; you are to bid any man stand, in the 25 Prince's name.

SEACOAL   How if 'a will not stand?

DOGBERRY   Why, then, take no note of him, but let him go, and presently call the rest of the watch together and thank God you are rid of a knave.

VERGES   If he will not stand when he is bidden, he is none of the Prince's subjects.

DOGBERRY   True, and they are to meddle with none but the Prince's subjects. You shall also make no noise in the streets; for, for the watch to babble and to talk is most tolerable and not to be endured.   36

WATCH   We will rather sleep than talk. We know what belongs to a watch.   38

DOGBERRY   Why, you speak like an ancient and most 39 quiet watchman, for I cannot see how sleeping should offend. Only have a care that your bills be not stolen. 41 Well, you are to call at all the alehouses and bid those that are drunk get them to bed.

WATCH   How if they will not?

**3.3. Location: A street.**
**3 salvation** (A blunder for "damnation.")   **5 allegiance** (For "treachery.")   **7 charge** instructions   **9 desartless** (For "deserving.")   **15 a good name** (Sea coal was high-grade coal shipped from New-castle, not the charcoal usually sold by London colliers.)   **well-favored** good-looking   **19 favor** good looks   **22 senseless** (For "sensible.")   **24 comprehend** (For "apprehend.")   **25 vagrom** vagrant.   **stand** stand still, stop   **36 tolerable** (For "intolerable.")   **38 Watch** (Here and at lines 44, 48, 53, and 66 Shakespeare's text does not specify which watchman speaks. These lines are sometimes assigned to the Second Watch, Seacoal, but could be spoken by others of the watch.)   **38 belongs to** are the duties of   **39 ancient** venerable, experienced   **41 bills** pikes, with axes fixed to long poles

DOGBERRY   Why, then, let them alone till they are sober. If they make you not then the better answer, you may say they are not the men you took them for.

WATCH   Well, sir.

DOGBERRY   If you meet a thief, you may suspect him, by virtue of your office, to be no true man; and for such 50 kind of men, the less you meddle or make with them, 51 why, the more is for your honesty. 52

WATCH   If we know him to be a thief, shall we not lay hands on him?

DOGBERRY   Truly, by your office you may, but I think they that touch pitch will be defiled. The most 56 peaceable way for you, if you do take a thief, is to let him show himself what he is and steal out of your company.

VERGES   You have been always called a merciful man, partner.

DOGBERRY   Truly, I would not hang a dog by my will, much more a man who hath any honesty in him.

VERGES   If you hear a child cry in the night, you must call to the nurse and bid her still it.

WATCH   How if the nurse be asleep and will not hear us?

DOGBERRY   Why, then, depart in peace and let the child wake her with crying, for the ewe that will not hear her lamb when it baas will never answer a calf when 70 he bleats.

VERGES   'Tis very true.

DOGBERRY   This is the end of the charge: you, Constable, are to present the Prince's own person. If you meet 74 the Prince in the night, you may stay him.

VERGES   Nay, by'r Lady, that I think 'a cannot. 76

DOGBERRY   Five shillings to one on't, with any man that knows the statutes, he may stay him; marry, not without the Prince be willing, for indeed the watch ought to offend no man, and it is an offense to stay a man against his will.

VERGES   By'r Lady, I think it be so.

DOGBERRY   Ha, ah ha! Well, masters, good night. An 83 there be any matter of weight chances, call up me. 84 Keep your fellows' counsels and your own, and good 85 night. Come, neighbor. [*He starts to leave with Verges.*]

SEACOAL   Well, masters, we hear our charge. Let us go 87 sit here upon the church bench till two, and then all to bed.

DOGBERRY   One word more, honest neighbors. I pray you, watch about Signor Leonato's door, for the wedding being there tomorrow, there is a great coil 92 tonight. Adieu. Be vigitant, I beseech you. 93

*Exeunt* [*Dogberry and Verges*].

*Enter Borachio and Conrade.*

BORACHIO   What, Conrade!

SEACOAL [*aside*]   Peace! Stir not.

BORACHIO   Conrade, I say!

CONRADE   Here, man. I am at thy elbow.

BORACHIO   Mass, and my elbow itched; I thought there 98 would a scab follow. 99

CONRADE   I will owe thee an answer for that. And now, 100 forward with thy tale.

BORACHIO   Stand thee close, then, under this penthouse, 102 for it drizzles rain, and I will, like a true drunkard, 103 utter all to thee.

SEACOAL [*aside*]   Some treason, masters. Yet stand 105 close. 106

BORACHIO   Therefore know I have earned of Don John a thousand ducats.

CONRADE   Is it possible that any villainy should be so dear? 110

BORACHIO   Thou shouldst rather ask if it were possible any villainy should be so rich; for when rich villains 112 have need of poor ones, poor ones may make what price they will.

CONRADE   I wonder at it.

BORACHIO   That shows thou art unconfirmed. Thou 116 knowest that the fashion of a doublet, or a hat, or a cloak, is nothing to a man. 118

CONRADE   Yes, it is apparel.

BORACHIO   I mean, the fashion. 120

CONRADE   Yes, the fashion is the fashion.

BORACHIO   Tush, I may as well say the fool's the fool. But see'st thou not what a deformed thief this fashion 123 is?

SEACOAL [*aside*]   I know that Deformed. 'A has been a vile thief this seven year; 'a goes up and down like a 126 gentleman. I remember his name.

BORACHIO   Didst thou not hear somebody?

CONRADE   No, 'twas the vane on the house.

BORACHIO   See'st thou not, I say, what a deformed thief this fashion is, how giddily 'a turns about all the hot bloods between fourteen and five-and-thirty, sometimes fashioning them like Pharaoh's soldiers in the reechy painting, sometime like god Bel's priests in the 134 old church-window, sometime like the shaven 135 Hercules in the smirched worm-eaten tapestry, where 136 his codpiece seems as massy as his club? 137

---

**98 Mass** i.e., By the Mass.   **my elbow itched** (Proverbially, a warning against questionable companions.)   **99 scab** i.e., scoundrel. (With play on literal meaning.)   **100 owe thee an answer** answer later   **102 penthouse** overhanging structure   **103 true drunkard** (Alludes to the commonplace that the drunkard tells all; Borachio's name in Spanish means "drunkard.")   **105–6 stand close** stay hidden.   **110 dear** expensive.   **112 rich** well-paid   **116 unconfirmed** inexperienced.   **118 is ... man** does not make the man. (But Conrade plays on the phrase in the sense of "means nothing to a man.")   **120 I ... fashion** i.e., My emphasis was on the mere fashion, not on the apparel itself. (But Conrade wittily refuses to allow the difference.)   **123 deformed thief** i.e., so called because fashion takes such varied and extreme shapes and because it impoverishes those who follow fashion   **126 'a goes up and down** he struts here and there   **134 reechy** dirty, grimy. (Perhaps this painting is of the Israelites passing through the Red Sea.)   **god Bel's priests** (Probably alludes to the story of Bel and the Dragon, from the apocryphal Book of Daniel, depicted in a stained-glass window.)   **135–6 shaven Hercules** (A reference either to young Hercules at the crossroads, choosing between virtue and vice, or in the service of Omphale—see 2.1.242, note—or, confusedly, to the story of Samson.)   **137 codpiece** decorative pouch at the front of a man's breeches (indelicately conspicuous in this tapestry)

---

**50 true** honest   **51 meddle or make** have to do   **52 is** it is   **56 they ... defiled** (A commonplace, derived from Ecclesiasticus 13:1.)   **70 calf** (1) immature cow (2) blockhead   **74 present** represent   **76 by'r Lady** i.e., by Our Lady. (A mild oath.)   **83–4 An ... chances** If anything significant occurs   **85 keep ... own** i.e., keep everything to yourselves   **87 masters** sirs   **92 coil** to-do   **93 vigitant** (For "vigilant.")

CONRADE   All this I see, and I see that the fashion wears 138
out more apparel than the man. But art not thou 139
thyself giddy with the fashion, too, that thou hast
shifted out of thy tale into telling me of the fashion?

BORACHIO   Not so, neither. But know that I have tonight
wooed Margaret, the Lady Hero's gentlewoman, by
the name of Hero. She leans me out at her mistress' 144
chamber window, bids me a thousand times good
night—I tell this tale vilely; I should first tell thee how
the Prince, Claudio, and my master, planted and
placed and possessed by my master Don John, saw 148
afar off in the orchard this amiable encounter. 149

CONRADE   And thought they Margaret was Hero?

BORACHIO   Two of them did, the Prince and Claudio,
but the devil my master knew she was Margaret; and
partly by his oaths, which first possessed them, partly
by the dark night, which did deceive them, but chiefly
by my villainy, which did confirm any slander that
Don John had made, away went Claudio enraged;
swore he would meet her, as he was appointed, next
morning at the temple, and there, before the whole
congregation, shame her with what he saw o'ernight
and send her home again without a husband.

SEACOAL   We charge you, in the Prince's name, stand!

FIRST WATCH   Call up the Right Master Constable. We 162
have here recovered the most dangerous piece of 163
lechery that ever was known in the commonwealth. 164

SEACOAL   And one Deformed is one of them. I know
him; 'a wears a lock. 166

CONRADE   Masters, masters—

FIRST WATCH   You'll be made bring Deformed forth, I 168
warrant you.

CONRADE   Masters—

SEACOAL   Never speak, we charge you. Let us obey you 171
to go with us.

BORACHIO   We are like to prove a goodly commodity, 173
being taken up of these men's bills. 174

CONRADE   A commodity in question, I warrant you. 175
Come, we'll obey you.                    *Exeunt.*

# [3.4]

*Enter Hero, and Margaret and Ursula.*

HERO   Good Ursula, wake my cousin Beatrice, and
desire her to rise.

URSULA   I will, lady.

HERO   And bid her come hither.

URSULA   Well.                    [*Exit.*]  5

MARGARET   Troth, I think your other rabato were better.  6

HERO   No, pray thee, good Meg, I'll wear this.

MARGARET   By my troth, 's not so good, and I warrant 8
your cousin will say so.

HERO   My cousin's a fool, and thou art another. I'll wear
none but this.

MARGARET   I like the new tire within excellently, if the 12
hair were a thought browner; and your gown's a most 13
rare fashion, i'faith. I saw the Duchess of Milan's gown
that they praise so.

HERO   Oh, that exceeds, they say. 16

MARGARET   By my troth, 's but a nightgown in respect 17
of yours: cloth o' gold, and cuts, and laced with silver, 18
set with pearls, down sleeves, side sleeves, and skirts, 19
round underborne with a bluish tinsel. But for a fine, 20
quaint, graceful, and excellent fashion, yours is worth 21
ten on't. 22

HERO   God give me joy to wear it! For my heart is
exceeding heavy.

MARGARET   'Twill be heavier soon by the weight of a
man.

HERO   Fie upon thee! Art not ashamed?

MARGARET   Of what, lady? Of speaking honorably? Is
not marriage honorable in a beggar? Is not your lord 29
honorable without marriage? I think you would have
me say, "saving your reverence, a husband." An bad 31
thinking do not wrest true speaking, I'll offend 32
nobody. Is there any harm in "the heavier for a husband"? None, I think, an it be the right husband and
the right wife; otherwise 'tis light, and not heavy. Ask 35
my Lady Beatrice else. Here she comes.

*Enter Beatrice.*

HERO   Good morrow, coz.

BEATRICE   Good morrow, sweet Hero.

HERO   Why, how now? Do you speak in the sick tune? 39

BEATRICE   I am out of all other tune, methinks.

MARGARET   Clap 's into "Light o' love." That goes 41
without a burden; do you sing it, and I'll dance it. 42

BEATRICE   Ye light o' love with your heels! Then, if your 43
husband have stables enough, you'll see he shall lack
no barns. 45

MARGARET   Oh, illegitimate construction! I scorn that 46
with my heels. 47

138–9 fashion . . . man i.e., fashion prompts the discarding of clothes
faster than honest use.   144 leans me leans. (*Me* is an emphatic
marker.)   148 possessed (misleadingly) informed; also, perhaps,
possessed, as by the devil   149 amiable amorous   162 Right Master
Constable (A comically exaggerated title on the pattern of "Right
Worshipful," etc.)   163 recovered (For "discovered.")   164 lechery
(For "treachery.")   166 lock lock of hair hanging down on the left
shoulder; the lovelock.   168 made bring ordered to bring   171 obey
(For "oblige," "command.")   173 like likely   173–4 goodly . . . bills
(1) valuable asset for the constabulary, having been arrested by these
watchmen armed with pikes (2) valuable goods having been acquired
on credit by means of *bills* or bonds given as security.   175 in question
(1) subject to judicial examination (2) of doubtful value
3.4. Location: Leonato's house.
5 Well Very well, as you wish.

6 rabato tall collar supporting a ruff, stiffened with wire or starch
8 troth, 's faith, it is   12 tire within headdress in the inner room
13 hair hairpiece attached to the *tire* (line 12)   16 exceeds i.e., goes
beyond comparison   17 nightgown dressing gown   17–18 in respect
of compared to   18 cuts . . . silver slashes in a garment revealing the
underlying fabic, and laced with silver thread   19 down sleeves
tight-fitting sleeves to the wrist.   side sleeves secondary ornamental
sleeves hanging from the shoulder   20 round underborne with a
lining around the edge of the skirt.   tinsel cloth, usually silk, interwoven with threads of silver or gold.   21 quaint elegant   22 on't of it.
29 in even in   31 saving . . . husband (By this apologetic formula,
Margaret suggests that Hero is too prudish even to hear the word
*husband* mentioned.)   An bad If bawdy   32 wrest misinterpret
35 light harmless. (With a play on the meaning "wanton.")   39 tune
i.e., mood.   41 Clap 's Let's sing.   Light o' love. (A popular song.)
42 burden bass accompaniment. (With play on the idea of "the
weight of a man.")   43 Ye . . . heels! i.e., You're light-heeled, wanton!   45 barns (With pun on "bairns," children.)   46 illegitimate
construction false inference. (But with a play on the idea of bastard
"bairns.")   47 with my heels (A proverbial expression of scorn.)

BEATRICE    'Tis almost five o'clock, cousin; 'tis time you
were ready. By my troth, I am exceeding ill. Heigh-ho!
MARGARET    For a hawk, a horse, or a husband?    50
BEATRICE    For the letter that begins them all, H.    51
MARGARET    Well, an you be not turned Turk, there's no    52
more sailing by the star.    53
BEATRICE    What means the fool, trow?    54
MARGARET    Nothing, I; but God send everyone their
heart's desire!
HERO    These gloves the Count sent me, they are an
excellent perfume.    58
BEATRICE    I am stuffed, cousin. I cannot smell.    59
MARGARET    A maid, and stuffed! There's goodly catch-
ing of cold.
BEATRICE    Oh, God help me, God help me! How long
have you professed apprehension?    63
MARGARET    Ever since you left it. Doth not my wit    64
become me rarely?    65
BEATRICE    It is not seen enough; you should wear it in    66
your cap. By my troth, I am sick.    67
MARGARET    Get you some of this distilled *carduus bene-*    68
*dictus*, and lay it to your heart. It is the only thing for a    69
qualm.    70
HERO    There thou prick'st her with a thistle.
BEATRICE    *Benedictus!* Why *benedictus?* You have some
moral in this *benedictus*.    73
MARGARET    Moral? No, by my troth, I have no moral
meaning, I meant plain holy thistle. You may think    75
perchance that I think you are in love. Nay, by'r Lady,
I am not such a fool to think what I list, nor I list not to    77
think what I can, nor indeed I cannot think, if I would
think my heart out of thinking, that you are in love or    79
that you will be in love or that you can be in love. Yet
Benedick was such another, and now is he become a    81
man. He swore he would never marry, and yet now,    82
in despite of his heart, he eats his meat without grudging;    83
and how you may be converted I know not, but    84
methinks you look with your eyes as other women do.
BEATRICE    What pace is this that thy tongue keeps?
MARGARET    Not a false gallop.    87

*Enter Ursula.*

URSULA    Madam, withdraw. The Prince, the Count,
Signor Benedick, Don John, and all the gallants of the
town are come to fetch you to church.
HERO    Help to dress me, good coz, good Meg, good    91
Ursula.    [*Exeunt.*]

# [3.5]

*Enter Leonato and the Constable [Dogberry]*
*and the Headborough [Verges].*

LEONATO    What would you with me, honest neighbor?    1
DOGBERRY    Marry, sir, I would have some confidence    2
with you that decerns you nearly.    3
LEONATO    Brief, I pray you, for you see it is a busy time
with me.
DOGBERRY    Marry, this it is, sir.
VERGES    Yes, in truth it is, sir.
LEONATO    What is it, my good friends?
DOGBERRY    Goodman Verges, sir, speaks a little off the    9
matter—an old man, sir, and his wits are not so blunt    10
as, God help, I would desire they were, but, in faith,
honest as the skin between his brows.    12
VERGES    Yes, I thank God I am as honest as any man living that is an old man and no honester than I.
DOGBERRY    Comparisons are odorous. *Palabras*, neigh-    15
bor Verges.
LEONATO    Neighbors, you are tedious.
DOGBERRY    It pleases Your Worship to say so, but we
are the poor Duke's officers. But truly, for mine own    19
part, if I were as tedious as a king, I could find in my    20
heart to bestow it all of Your Worship.    21
LEONATO    All thy tediousness on me, ah?
DOGBERRY    Yea, an 'twere a thousand pound more than
'tis; for I hear as good exclamation on Your Worship    24
as of any man in the city, and though I be but a poor
man, I am glad to hear it.
VERGES    And so am I.
LEONATO    I would fain know what you have to say.    28
VERGES    Marry, sir, our watch tonight, excepting Your    29
Worship's presence, ha' ta'en a couple of as arrant    30
knaves as any in Messina.
DOGBERRY    A good old man, sir; he will be talking. As
they say, when the age is in, the wit is out. God help    33
us, it is a world to see! Well said, i'faith, neighbor    34

---

**50 For . . . husband?** (*Heigh-ho* might be a cry of encouragement in the
hunt or else "Heigh-ho for a husband!" as at 2.1.305.)    **51 H** (With a
pun on "ache," pronounced "aitch." Beatrice complains of aching
with a cold.)    **52 turned Turk** i.e., turned apostate to the true faith (by
violating your oath not to become a lover)    **52–3 no . . . star** no more
navigating by the North Star, i.e., no certain truth in which to trust.
**54 trow** I wonder.    **58 perfume** (Gloves were often perfumed.)
**59 stuffed** i.e., stuffed up with a cold. (But Margaret takes it in a
bawdy sense.)    **63 professed apprehension** made claim to be witty.
**64 left it** gave it up. (Margaret gibes at Beatrice's pretending not to
know what the joking is all about.)    **65 rarely** excellently.    **66–7 wear
. . . cap** i.e., wear it prominently visible, as a fool wears his coxcomb.
(Beatrice jokes that Margaret's supposed wit is imperceptible.)
**68–9 carduus benedictus** the blessed thistle, noted for medicinal
properties. (With a pun on "Benedick.")    **69–70 a qualm** an attack of
nausea (or misgiving).    **73 moral** hidden meaning    **75 holy thistle**
the blessed thistle or *carduus benedictus* of 68–9.    **77 list** please
**79 think . . . thinking** i.e., rack my brains    **81 such another** i.e., seemingly proof against love    **81–2 a man** i.e., like other men.    **83 eats . . .
grudging** i.e., is content to be like other men, to be in love    **87 Not . . .
gallop** i.e., I'm not speaking at a false pace, at a canter; I speak the truth.

**91 coz** cousin
**3.5. Location: Leonato's house.**
**0.2** *Headborough* local constable    **1 honest** worthy    **2 confidence**
(A blunder for "conference.")    **3 decerns** (For "concerns.")
**9 Goodman** (Title of a person under the social rank of gentleman.)
**10 blunt** (He means "sharp.")    **12 honest . . . brows** (Proverbial
expression of honesty.)    **15 odorous** (For "odious.")    *Palabras* (For
*pocas palabras*, "few words" in Spanish.)    **19 poor Duke's officers**
(For "Duke's poor officers.")    **20 tedious** (Dogberry evidently thinks
*tedious* means "rich.")    **21 of** on    **24 exclamation** (Possibly for
"acclamation.")    **28 fain** glad    **29 tonight** last night    **29–30 excepting . . . presence** (The normal meaning, "with the exception of your
honored self," comically implies that Leonato is an even more
arrant knave than the men arrested. Verges probably means,
"begging Your Worship's pardon.")    **30 ha' ta'en** have arrested
**33 when . . . out** (An adaptation of the proverb, "When ale is in, wit
is out.")    **34 a world** i.e., wonderful. (Proverbial.)

Verges. Well, God's a good man. An two men ride     35
of a horse, one must ride behind. An honest soul,     36
i'faith, sir, by my troth he is, as ever broke bread. But, God
is to be worshiped, all men are not alike, alas, good
neighbor!

LEONATO   Indeed, neighbor, he comes too short of you.

DOGBERRY   Gifts that God gives.

LEONATO   I must leave you.

DOGBERRY   One word, sir. Our watch, sir, have indeed
comprehended two aspicious persons, and we would     44
have them this morning examined before Your Worship.

LEONATO   Take their examination yourself and bring
it me. I am now in great haste, as it may appear
unto you.

DOGBERRY   It shall be suffigance.     50

LEONATO   Drink some wine ere you go. Fare you well.

[Enter a Messenger.]

MESSENGER   My lord, they stay for you to give your
daughter to her husband.

LEONATO   I'll wait upon them. I am ready.     54
                         [Exeunt Leonato and Messenger.]

DOGBERRY   Go, good partner, go, get you to Francis Sea-     55
coal. Bid him bring his pen and inkhorn to the jail. We     56
are now to examination these men.     57

VERGES   And we must do it wisely.

DOGBERRY   We will spare for no wit, I warrant you.
Here's that shall drive some of them to a noncome.     60
Only get the learned writer to set down our excom-     61
munication, and meet me at the jail.     [Exeunt.]     62

# [4.1]

*Enter Prince [Don Pedro], [Don John the]*
*Bastard, Leonato, Friar [Francis], Claudio,*
*Benedick, Hero, and Beatrice [with attendants].*

LEONATO   Come, Friar Francis, be brief—only to the
plain form of marriage, and you shall recount their
particular duties afterwards.

FRIAR   You come hither, my lord, to marry this lady?

CLAUDIO   No.

LEONATO   To be married to her. Friar, you come to
marry her.

FRIAR   Lady, you come hither to be married to this
Count?

HERO   I do.

FRIAR   If either of you know any inward impediment     11

why you should not be conjoined, I charge you on
your souls to utter it.

CLAUDIO   Know you any, Hero?

HERO   None, my lord.

FRIAR   Know you any, Count?

LEONATO   I dare make his answer: none.

CLAUDIO   Oh, what men dare do! What men may do!
What men daily do, not knowing what they do!

BENEDICK   How now? Interjections? Why, then, some be     20
of laughing, as, ah, ha, he!     21

CLAUDIO
Stand thee by, Friar.—Father, by your leave,     22
Will you with free and unconstrainèd soul
Give me this maid, your daughter?

LEONATO
As freely, son, as God did give her me.

CLAUDIO
And what have I to give you back, whose worth
May counterpoise this rich and precious gift?     27

DON PEDRO
Nothing, unless you render her again.

CLAUDIO
Sweet Prince, you learn me noble thankfulness.     29
                    [He hands Hero to Leonato.]
There, Leonato, take her back again.
Give not this rotten orange to your friend;
She's but the sign and semblance of her honor.     32
Behold how like a maid she blushes here!
Oh, what authority and show of truth
Can cunning sin cover itself withal!
Comes not that blood as modest evidence     36
To witness simple virtue? Would you not swear,     37
All you that see her, that she were a maid,
By these exterior shows? But she is none:
She knows the heat of a luxurious bed.     40
Her blush is guiltiness, not modesty.

LEONATO
What do you mean, my lord?

CLAUDIO                           Not to be married,     42
Not to knit my soul to an approvèd wanton.     43

LEONATO
Dear my lord, if you, in your own proof,     44
Have vanquished the resistance of her youth,
And made defeat of her virginity—

CLAUDIO
I know what you would say: if I have known her,     47
You will say, she did embrace me as a husband,
And so extenuate the forehand sin.     49
No, Leonato,
I never tempted her with word too large,     51

---

35 **God's . . . man** i.e., God is good. (A proverbial saying.)   **36 of** on
44 **comprehended** (For "apprehended.")   **aspicious** (For "suspicious.")
50 **suffigance** (For "sufficient.")   54 **wait upon** attend   55–6 **Francis
Seacoal** i.e., the Sexton of 4.2, not George, the member of the watch
in 3.3.   57 **examination** (For "examine.")   60 **that** that which.   **noncome**
(Probably an unintended contraction for *non compos mentis*, "not of
sound mind," but Dogberry may have intended "nonplus.")
61–2 **excommunication** (For "examination" or "communication.")
**4.1. Location:** A church.
11 **inward** secret

20–1 **some . . . he** (Benedick quotes from Lilly's Latin grammar on the
subject of interjections; according to Lilly, these are to be classified
as laughing interjections.)   22 **Stand thee by** Stand aside   27 **counterpoise** balance, be equivalent to   29 **learn** teach   32 **sign and
semblance** pretense and outward show   36 **blood** i.e., blush.   **modest
evidence** evidence of modesty   37 **witness** bear witness to
40 **luxurious** lascivious, lustful   42 **mean** imply, suggest. (But
Claudio bitterly replies in the sense of "intend.")   43 **approved**
proven   44 **in . . . proof** in making trial of her yourself   47 **known
her** i.e., known her sexually   49 **extenuate** excuse, lessen.   **forehand
sin** sin of anticipating (marriage).   51 **large** broad, immodest

But, as a brother to his sister, showed
Bashful sincerity and comely love.

HERO
And seemed I ever otherwise to you?

CLAUDIO
Out on thee, seeming! I will write against it.                    55
You seem to me as Dian in her orb,                                56
As chaste as is the bud ere it be blown;                          57
But you are more intemperate in your blood
Than Venus, or those pampered animals                             59
That rage in savage sensuality.

HERO
Is my lord well, that he doth speak so wide?                      61

LEONATO
Sweet Prince, why speak not you?

DON PEDRO                                    What should I speak?
I stand dishonored, that have gone about                          63
To link my dear friend to a common stale.                         64

LEONATO
Are these things spoken, or do I but dream?

DON JOHN
Sir, they are spoken, and these things are true.

BENEDICK    This looks not like a nuptial.

HERO    "True"! Oh, God!                                          68

CLAUDIO    Leonato, stand I here?
Is this the Prince? Is this the Prince's brother?
Is this face Hero's? Are our eyes our own?

LEONATO
All this is so. But what of this, my lord?

CLAUDIO
Let me but move one question to your daughter,                    73
And by that fatherly and kindly power                             74
That you have in her, bid her answer truly.

LEONATO [to Hero]
I charge thee do so, as thou art my child.

HERO
Oh, God defend me, how am I beset!
What kind of catechizing call you this?                           78

CLAUDIO
To make you answer truly to your name.

HERO
Is it not Hero? Who can blot that name
With any just reproach?

CLAUDIO                            Marry, that can Hero!
Hero itself can blot out Hero's virtue.                           82
What man was he talked with you yesternight
Out at your window betwixt twelve and one?
Now, if you are a maid, answer to this.

HERO
I talked with no man at that hour, my lord.

DON PEDRO
Why, then are you no maiden. Leonato,
I am sorry you must hear. Upon mine honor,
Myself, my brother, and this grievèd Count                        89
Did see her, hear her, at that hour last night
Talk with a ruffian at her chamber window,
Who hath indeed, most like a liberal villain,                     92
Confessed the vile encounters they have had
A thousand times in secret.

DON JOHN
Fie, fie, they are not to be named, my lord,
Not to be spoke of!
There is not chastity enough in language
Without offense to utter them. Thus, pretty lady,
I am sorry for thy much misgovernment.                            99

CLAUDIO
O Hero, what a Hero hadst thou been
If half thy outward graces had been placed                        101
About thy thoughts and counsels of thy heart!                     102
But fare thee well, most foul, most fair! Farewell,
Thou pure impiety and impious purity!
For thee I'll lock up all the gates of love,                      105
And on my eyelids shall conjecture hang,                          106
To turn all beauty into thoughts of harm,
And never shall it more be gracious.                              108

LEONATO
Hath no man's dagger here a point for me?
                                              [Hero swoons.]

BEATRICE
Why, how now, cousin, wherefore sink you down?                    110

DON JOHN
Come, let us go. These things, come thus to light,
Smother her spirits up.
                  [Exeunt Don Pedro, Don John, and Claudio.]

BENEDICK
How doth the lady?

BEATRICE                          Dead, I think. Help, uncle!
Hero, why, Hero! Uncle! Signor Benedick! Friar!

LEONATO
O Fate, take not away thy heavy hand!
Death is the fairest cover for her shame
That may be wished for.

BEATRICE    How now, cousin Hero?

FRIAR    Have comfort, lady.

LEONATO
Dost thou look up?

FRIAR                          Yea, wherefore should she not?       119

LEONATO
Wherefore? Why, doth not every earthly thing
Cry shame upon her? Could she here deny
The story that is printed in her blood?                           122
Do not live, Hero, do not ope thine eyes;
For, did I think thou wouldst not quickly die,
Thought I thy spirits were stronger than thy shames, 125

---

55 Out . . . seeming! i.e., Shame on you, you mere semblance of
good!   56 Dian . . . orb i.e., Diana, goddess of chastity, enthroned in
the moon   57 blown open, flowering   59 pampered crammed
with rich food   61 wide wide of the mark.   63 gone about undertaken   64 stale whore.   68 "True!" (A response to Don John's use of
the term.)   73 move put   74 kindly natural   78 catechizing formal
questioning used by the Church to teach the principles of faith. The
first question in the Church of England's catechism is, "What is your
name?"   82 Hero itself The very name of Hero (who, in the story of
Hero and Leander, is the faithful tragic heroine)

89 grievèd (1) aggrieved, wronged (2) struck with grief
92 liberal licentious   99 much misgovernment gross misconduct.
101–2 had . . . heart had enclosed inward thoughts as pure as your
exterior beauty would suggest.   105 For thee Because of you
106 conjecture evil suspicion   108 be gracious seem attractive, graceful.   110, 119 wherefore why   122 blood i.e., blushes.   125 spirits
life-giving energies, vital powers

Myself would, on the rearward of reproaches,            126
Strike at thy life. Grieved I I had but one?
Chid I for that at frugal nature's frame?               128
Oh, one too much by thee! Why had I one?
Why ever wast thou lovely in my eyes?
Why had I not with charitable hand
Took up a beggar's issue at my gates,                   132
Who, smirchèd thus and mired with infamy,
I might have said, "No part of it is mine;
This shame derives itself from unknown loins"?
But mine, and mine I loved, and mine I praised,         136
And mine that I was proud on, mine so much
That I myself was to myself not mine,                   138
Valuing of her—why, she, oh, she, is fallen             139
Into a pit of ink, that the wide sea                    140
Hath drops too few to wash her clean again
And salt too little which may season give               142
To her foul-tainted flesh!
BENEDICK                        Sir, sir, be patient.
For my part, I am so attired in wonder,
I know not what to say.
BEATRICE
Oh, on my soul, my cousin is belied!
BENEDICK
Lady, were you her bedfellow last night?
BEATRICE
No, truly, not; although, until last night,
I have this twelvemonth been her bedfellow.
LEONATO
Confirmed, confirmed! Oh, that is stronger made
Which was before barred up with ribs of iron!          151
Would the two princes lie and Claudio lie,
Who loved her so that, speaking of her foulness,
Washed it with tears? Hence from her! Let her die.
FRIAR     Hear me a little;
For I have only been silent so long
And given way unto this course of fortune              157
By noting of the lady. I have marked
A thousand blushing apparitions
To start into her face, a thousand innocent shames
In angel whiteness beat away those blushes,
And in her eye there hath appeared a fire
To burn the errors that these princes hold
Against her maiden truth. Call me a fool;
Trust not my reading nor my observations,
Which with experimental seal doth warrant              166
The tenor of my book; trust not my age,                167
My reverence, calling, nor divinity,
If this sweet lady lie not guiltless here
Under some biting error.
LEONATO                         Friar, it cannot be.
Thou see'st that all the grace that she hath left
Is that she will not add to her damnation

A sin of perjury; she not denies it.
Why seek'st thou then to cover with excuse
That which appears in proper nakedness?                175
FRIAR
Lady, what man is he you are accused of?
HERO
They know that do accuse me; I know none.
If I know more of any man alive
Than that which maiden modesty doth warrant,           179
Let all my sins lack mercy! O my father,
Prove you that any man with me conversed               181
At hours unmeet or that I yesternight                  182
Maintained the change of words with any creature,     183
Refuse me, hate me, torture me to death!               184
FRIAR
There is some strange misprision in the princes.       185
BENEDICK
Two of them have the very bent of honor;               186
And if their wisdoms be misled in this,
The practice of it lives in John the Bastard,          188
Whose spirits toil in frame of villainies.             189
LEONATO
I know not. If they speak but truth of her,
These hands shall tear her; if they wrong her honor,
The proudest of them shall well hear of it.
Time hath not yet so dried this blood of mine,
Nor age so eat up my invention,                        194
Nor fortune made such havoc of my means,
Nor my bad life reft me so much of friends,            196
But they shall find, awaked in such a kind,            197
Both strength of limb and policy of mind,              198
Ability in means, and choice of friends,
To quit me of them throughly.
FRIAR                           Pause awhile,         200
And let my counsel sway you in this case.
Your daughter here the princes left for dead,          202
Let her awhile be secretly kept in,                    203
And publish it that she is dead indeed.
Maintain a mourning ostentation,                       205
And on your family's old monument                      206
Hang mournful epitaphs, and do all rites
That appertain unto a burial.
LEONATO
What shall become of this? What will this do?          209
FRIAR
Marry, this, well carried, shall on her behalf         210
Change slander to remorse. That is some good.
But not for that dream I on this strange course,       212

126 on . . . reproaches following this public disgrace   128 Chid Chided.
frame plan, order.   132 Took . . . issue taken up a beggar's child
136 mine i.e., my own daughter   138–9 That . . . her i.e., that I set no value
on myself in caring so much for her   140 that such that   142 season
preservative   151 before already   157 given . . . fortune yielded to this
turn of events   166–7 Which . . . book i.e., by means of which observations and experience I have confirmed what I learned from books

175 proper true   179 warrant sanction, permit   181 Prove you if you
prove   182 unmeet improper   183 Maintained the change held
exchange   184 Refuse disown   185 misprision mistake, misunderstanding   186 Two . . . honor i.e., Don Pedro and Claudio are wholly
honorable   188 practice scheming   189 frame contriving   194 eat
eaten. (Pronounced "et.")   invention power to plan (vengeance)
196 reft robbed   197 kind manner   198 policy shrewdness
200 quit . . . throughly settle accounts with them thoroughly.
202 the princes i.e., (whom) Don Pedro and Claudio   203 in in
hiding, at home   205 Maintain . . . ostentation Perform all the outward signs of mourning   206 monument burial vault   209 become
of result from   210 carried managed   212 not for that not for that
reason alone

But on this travail look for greater birth. 213
She—dying, as it must be so maintained,
Upon the instant that she was accused—
Shall be lamented, pitied, and excused
Of every hearer; for it so falls out 217
That what we have we prize not to the worth 218
Whiles we enjoy it, but, being lacked and lost,
Why then we rack the value, then we find 220
The virtue that possession would not show us
Whiles it was ours. So will it fare with Claudio.
When he shall hear she died upon his words, 223
Th'idea of her life shall sweetly creep
Into his study of imagination, 225
And every lovely organ of her life 226
Shall come appareled in more precious habit, 227
More moving-delicate, and full of life,
Into the eye and prospect of his soul, 229
Than when she lived indeed. Then shall he mourn,
If ever love had interest in his liver, 231
And wish he had not so accusèd her,
No, though he thought his accusation true. 233
Let this be so, and doubt not but success 234
Will fashion the event in better shape 235
Than I can lay it down in likelihood. 236
But if all aim but this be leveled false, 237
The supposition of the lady's death
Will quench the wonder of her infamy.
And if it sort not well, you may conceal her, 240
As best befits her wounded reputation,
In some reclusive and religious life, 242
Out of all eyes, tongues, minds, and injuries. 243

BENEDICK
Signor Leonato, let the Friar advise you.
And though you know my inwardness and love 245
Is very much unto the Prince and Claudio,
Yet, by mine honor, I will deal in this
As secretly and justly as your soul 248
Should with your body.

LEONATO                   Being that I flow in grief, 249
The smallest twine may lead me.

FRIAR
'Tis well consented. Presently away; 251
For to strange sores strangely they strain the cure. 252
Come, lady, die to live. This wedding day
Perhaps is but prolonged. Have patience, and
endure. 254

                    *Exit [with all but Benedick and Beatrice].*
BENEDICK   Lady Beatrice, have you wept all this while?

---

BEATRICE   Yea, and I will weep a while longer.
BENEDICK   I will not desire that.
BEATRICE   You have no reason. I do it freely. 258
BENEDICK   Surely I do believe your fair cousin is
wronged.
BEATRICE   Ah, how much might the man deserve of me
that would right her!
BENEDICK   Is there any way to show such friendship?
BEATRICE   A very even way, but no such friend. 264
BENEDICK   May a man do it?
BEATRICE   It is a man's office, but not yours. 266
BENEDICK   I do love nothing in the world so well as you.
Is not that strange?
BEATRICE   As strange as the thing I know not. It were as
possible for me to say I loved nothing so well as you.
But believe me not; and yet I lie not. I confess nothing,
nor I deny nothing. I am sorry for my cousin.
BENEDICK   By my sword, Beatrice, thou lovest me.
BEATRICE   Do not swear and eat it. 274
BENEDICK   I will swear by it that you love me, and I will
make him eat it that says I love not you. 276
BEATRICE   Will you not eat your word?
BENEDICK   With no sauce that can be devised to it. I
protest I love thee. 279
BEATRICE   Why, then, God forgive me!
BENEDICK   What offense, sweet Beatrice?
BEATRICE   You have stayed me in a happy hour. I was 282
about to protest I loved you.
BENEDICK   And do it with all thy heart.
BEATRICE   I love you with so much of my heart that
none is left to protest. 286
BENEDICK   Come, bid me do anything for thee.
BEATRICE   Kill Claudio.
BENEDICK   Ha! Not for the wide world.
BEATRICE   You kill me to deny it. Farewell.   [*Going.*]
BENEDICK   Tarry, sweet Beatrice.
BEATRICE   I am gone, though I am here. There is no love 292
in you. Nay, I pray you, let me go.
BENEDICK   Beatrice—
BEATRICE   In faith, I will go.
BENEDICK   We'll be friends first.
BEATRICE   You dare easier be friends with me than fight
with mine enemy.
BENEDICK   Is Claudio thine enemy?
BEATRICE   Is 'a not approved in the height a villain, that 300
hath slandered, scorned, dishonored my kinswoman?
Oh, that I were a man! What, bear her in hand until 302
they come to take hands, and then, with public accu-
sation, uncovered slander, unmitigated rancor—Oh, 304
God, that I were a man! I would eat his heart in the
marketplace.

---

213 **on this travail** from this effort (which is metaphorically like the
*travail,* or labor, of childbirth)   217 **Of** by.   **for . . . out** for it generally
happens   218 **to the worth** as fully as it deserves   220 **rack** stretch,
extend   223 **upon** in consequence of   225 **Into . . . imagination** into
his thoughts   226 **organ . . . life** aspect of her when she was alive
227 **habit** apparel   229 **prospect** range of vision   231 **interest in** claim
upon.   **liver** (The supposed seat of the passion of love.)   233 **though** even
though   234 **success** i.e., what succeeds or happens in time as my plan
unfolds   235 **event** outcome   236 **lay . . . likelihood** anticipate its
probable course.   237 **if . . . false** i.e., if every other aim miscarry   240 **sort**
turn out   242 **reclusive** cloistered   243 **injuries** insults.   245 **inwardness
and love** close friendship   248–9 **as your soul . . . your body** as one's soul
should deal with one's body.   249 **Being . . . grief** Since I overflow in
grief   251 **Presently** Immediately   252 **For . . . cure** for strange diseases
require strange and desperate cures.   254 **prolonged** deferred.

258 **You . . . reason** (Beatrice twists Benedick's "I wish you weren't so
unhappy," line 257, into "There's no need for you to bid me stop
weeping.")   264 **even** direct, straightforward   266 **office** duty
274 **eat it** i.e., eat your words.   276 **eat it** i.e., eat my sword, be
stabbed by it   279 **protest** affirm. (Also in line 283.)   282 **stayed**
stopped.   **in . . . hour** at an appropriate moment.   286 **protest** object.
(With a play on the sense of "affirm" in 279 and 283.)   292 **gone** i.e.,
in spirit   300 **approved in the height** proved in the highest degree
302 **bear her in hand** delude Hero with false hopes   304 **uncovered**
open, unconcealed

BENEDICK    Hear me, Beatrice—

BEATRICE    Talk with a man out at a window! A proper 308
saying!                                                         309

BENEDICK    Nay, but Beatrice—

BEATRICE    Sweet Hero! She is wronged, she is slandered,
she is undone.

BENEDICK    Beat—

BEATRICE    Princes and counties! Surely, a princely testi- 314
mony, a goodly count, Count Comfect; a sweet gallant, 315
surely! Oh, that I were a man for his sake! Or that I had
any friend would be a man for my sake! But manhood
is melted into curtsies, valor into compliment, and 318
men are only turned into tongue, and trim ones too. 319
He is now as valiant as Hercules that only tells a lie 320
and swears it. I cannot be a man with wishing, there- 321
fore I will die a woman with grieving.

BENEDICK    Tarry, good Beatrice. By this hand, I love
thee.

BEATRICE    Use it for my love some other way than
swearing by it.

BENEDICK    Think you in your soul the Count Claudio
hath wronged Hero?

BEATRICE    Yea, as sure as I have a thought or a soul.

BENEDICK    Enough, I am engaged. I will challenge him. 330
I will kiss your hand, and so I leave you. By this hand,
Claudio shall render me a dear account. As you hear 332
of me, so think of me. Go comfort your cousin. I must
say she is dead. And so, farewell.    [*Exeunt separately.*]

❖

## [4.2]

*Enter the Constables [Dogberry and Verges]
and the Town Clerk [Sexton] in gowns, Borachio, [Conrade, and Watch].*

DOGBERRY    Is our whole dissembly appeared?        1

VERGES    Oh, a stool and a cushion for the sexton.
[*Stool and cushion are brought. The Sexton sits.*]

SEXTON    Which be the malefactors?

DOGBERRY    Marry, that am I and my partner.        4

VERGES    Nay, that's certain; we have the exhibition to 5
examine.

SEXTON    But which are the offenders that are to be
examined? Let them come before Master Constable.

DOGBERRY    Yea, marry, let them come before me. [*The
prisoners are brought forward.*] What is your name,
friend?

BORACHIO    Borachio.

DOGBERRY    Pray, write down Borachio.—Yours, sirrah? 13

CONRADE    I am a gentleman, sir, and my name is
Conrade.

DOGBERRY    Write down Master Gentleman Conrade.
Masters, do you serve God?

CONRADE, BORACHIO    Yea, sir, we hope.

DOGBERRY    Write down that they hope they serve God;
and write God first, for God defend but God should 20
go before such villains! Masters, it is proved already
that you are little better than false knaves, and it will
go near to be thought so shortly. How answer you for
yourselves?

CONRADE    Marry, sir, we say we are none.

DOGBERRY    A marvelous witty fellow, I assure you, but 26
I will go about with him. [*To Borachio*] Come you 27
hither, sirrah. A word in your ear. Sir, I say to you, it
is thought you are false knaves.

BORACHIO    Sir, I say to you we are none.

DOGBERRY    Well, stand aside. 'Fore God, they are both 31
in a tale. Have you writ down that they are none?      32

SEXTON    Master Constable, you go not the way to
examine. You must call forth the watch that are their
accusers.

DOGBERRY    Yea, marry, that's the eftest way. Let the 36
watch come forth.—Masters, I charge you in the
Prince's name accuse these men.

SEACOAL    This man said, sir, that Don John, the Prince's
brother, was a villain.

DOGBERRY    Write down Prince John a villain. Why, this
is flat perjury, to call a prince's brother villain.       42

BORACHIO    Master Constable—

DOGBERRY    Pray thee, fellow, peace. I do not like thy
look, I promise thee.

SEXTON    What heard you him say else?

FIRST WATCH    Marry, that he had received a thousand
ducats of Don John for accusing the Lady Hero
wrongfully.

DOGBERRY    Flat burglary as ever was committed.

VERGES    Yea, by Mass, that it is.                    51

SEXTON    What else, fellow?

SEACOAL    And that Count Claudio did mean, upon his 53
words, to disgrace Hero before the whole assembly, 54
and not marry her.

DOGBERRY    Oh, villain! Thou wilt be condemned into
everlasting redemption for this.                       57

SEXTON    What else?

WATCH    This is all.                                  59

SEXTON    And this is more, masters, than you can deny:
Prince John is this morning secretly stolen away.
Hero was in this manner accused, in this very manner refused, and upon the grief of this suddenly
died.—Master Constable, let these men be bound and
brought to Leonato's. I will go before and show him
their examination.                          [*Exit.*]

308–9 proper saying likely story.   314 counties counts.   315 count
(1) the title (2) declaration of complaint in an indictment (3) account.
Comfect candy or sweetmeat   318 compliment polite courtly chatter
319 are . . . tongue have become mere (flattering) voices.   trim nice,
elegant, fine. (Used ironically.)   320–1 He . . . swears it A man need
only tell lies and swear they are true to gain a reputation for bravery
nowadays.   330 I am engaged I pledge myself.   332 dear costly
4.2. Location: The jail.
1 dissembly (A blunder for "assembly.")   4 that am I (Dogberry
evidently understands *malefactors* to mean "factors," agents.)
5 exhibition (Possibly for "commission.")   13 sirrah (Used to
address inferiors; Conrade objects.)

20 defend forbid   26 witty clever, cunning   27 go about with get
the better of, deal with   31 'Fore God i.e., As God is my witness.
(A mild oath.)   32 in a tale in agreement.   36 eftest (Some sort of
invention for "easiest" or "deftest.")   42 perjury (Dogberry means
"slander.")   51 by Mass by the Mass   53–4 And . . . Hero And the
intent of the villains was that Claudio, upon hearing Borachio's false
allegation, would disgrace Hero on the basis of Borachio's testimony
57 redemption (Dogberry means "damnation.")   59 WATCH (Perhaps
both Seacoal and his partner speak.)

DOGBERRY   Come, let them be opinioned.                                    67
VERGES   Let them be in the hands—
CONRADE   Off, coxcomb!                                                    69
DOGBERRY   God's my life, where's the sexton? Let him   70
  write down the Prince's officer coxcomb. Come, bind
  them. Thou naughty varlet!                                               72
CONRADE   Away! You are an ass, you are an ass.
DOGBERRY   Dost thou not suspect my place? Dost thou   74
  not suspect my years? Oh, that he were here to write   75
  me down an ass! But masters, remember that I am an
  ass; though it be not written down, yet forget not that
  I am an ass. No, thou villain, thou art full of piety, as   78
  shall be proved upon thee by good witness. I am a
  wise fellow, and, which is more, an officer, and, which
  is more, a householder, and, which is more, as pretty a
  piece of flesh as any is in Messina, and one that knows
  the law, go to, and a rich fellow enough, go to, and
  a fellow that hath had losses, and one that hath two
  gowns and everything handsome about him.—Bring
  him away. Oh, that I had been writ down an ass!

                                                        *Exeunt.*

                            ❖

## [5.1]

            *Enter Leonato and his brother [Antonio].*

ANTONIO
  If you go on thus, you will kill yourself;
  And 'tis not wisdom thus to second grief                                 2
  Against yourself.
LEONATO              I pray thee, cease thy counsel,
  Which falls into mine ears as profitless
  As water in a sieve. Give not me counsel,
  Nor let no comforter delight mine ear
  But such a one whose wrongs do suit with mine.                           7
  Bring me a father that so loved his child,
  Whose joy of her is overwhelmed like mine,
  And bid him speak of patience;
  Measure his woe the length and breadth of mine,                         11
  And let it answer every strain for strain,                              12
  As thus for thus, and such a grief for such,
  In every lineament, branch, shape, and form;
  If such a one will smile and stroke his beard,
  Bid sorrow wag, cry "hem!" when he should groan,                        16
  Patch grief with proverbs, make misfortune drunk                        17
  With candle wasters, bring him yet to me,                               18
  And I of him will gather patience.
  But there is no such man. For, brother, men
  Can counsel and speak comfort to that grief
  Which they themselves not feel; but tasting it,

67 **opinioned** (For "pinioned.")   69 **coxcomb** fop, conceited fool.
70 **God's** May God save   72 **naughty** wicked   74 **suspect** (For
"respect.")   75 **my years** (With an unconscious suggestion of
"my ears," i.e., ass's ears.)   78 **piety** (For "impiety.")
**5.1. Location:** Near Leonato's house.
2 **second** assist, encourage   7 **suit with** match   11 **Measure his woe**
let his woe equal in scope   12 **answer . . . for strain** correspond, pang
for pang. (With a musical sense also of echoing a refrain.)   16 **wag** be
off.   **cry "hem"** i.e., clear the throat as before some wordy speech
17 **drunk** i.e., insensible to pain   18 **candle wasters** those who waste
candles by late study, bookworms, moral philosophers

Their counsel turns to passion, which before
Would give preceptial medicine to rage,                                   24
Fetter strong madness in a silken thread,
Charm ache with air and agony with words.                                 26
No, no, 'tis all men's office to speak patience                          27
To those that wring under the load of sorrow,                             28
But no man's virtue nor sufficiency                                       29
To be so moral when he shall endure                                       30
The like himself. Therefore give me no counsel.
My griefs cry louder than advertisement.                                  32
ANTONIO
  Therein do men from children nothing differ.                            33
LEONATO
  I pray thee, peace. I will be flesh and blood;
  For there was never yet philosopher
  That could endure the toothache patiently,
  However they have writ the style of gods                                37
  And made a push at chance and sufferance.                               38
ANTONIO
  Yet bend not all the harm upon yourself.
  Make those that do offend you suffer, too.
LEONATO
  There thou speak'st reason. Nay, I will do so.
  My soul doth tell me Hero is belied,
  And that shall Claudio know; so shall the Prince
  And all of them that thus dishonor her.

            *Enter Prince [Don Pedro] and Claudio.*

ANTONIO
  Here comes the Prince and Claudio hastily.
DON PEDRO
  Good e'en, good e'en.
CLAUDIO                         Good day to both of you.
LEONATO
  Hear you, my lords—
DON PEDRO                  We have some haste, Leonato.
LEONATO
  Some haste, my lord! Well, fare you well, my lord.
  Are you so hasty now? Well, all is one.                                 49
DON PEDRO
  Nay, do not quarrel with us, good old man.
ANTONIO
  If he could right himself with quarreling,                             51
  Some of us would lie low.
CLAUDIO                     Who wrongs him?                               52
LEONATO
  Marry, thou dost wrong me, thou dissembler, thou!                      53
  Nay, never lay thy hand upon thy sword;
  I fear thee not.
CLAUDIO              Marry, beshrew my hand                              55
  If it should give your age such cause of fear.

24 **preceptial** consisting of precepts   26 **air** mere breath, words
27 **office** duty   28 **wring** writhe   29 **sufficiency** ability, power
30 **moral** prone to moralizing   32 **advertisement** advice, counsel.
33 **Therein . . . differ** i.e., It is childish to be so inconsolable.   37 **writ . . .
gods** uttered godlike wisdom   38 **made . . . sufferance** scoffed at misfortune and suffering.   49 **all is one** i.e., it makes no difference.   51 **he** i.e.,
Leonato   52 **Some of us** i.e., Don Pedro and Claudio   53 **thou** (Used
contemptuously instead of the more polite *you*.)   55 **beshrew** curse

In faith, my hand meant nothing to my sword.                           57

LEONATO
Tush, tush, man, never fleer and jest at me.                           58
I speak not like a dotard nor a fool,
As under privilege of age to brag
What I have done being young or what would do
Were I not old. Know, Claudio, to thy head,                            62
Thou hast so wronged mine innocent child and me
That I am forced to lay my reverence by,                               64
And with gray hairs and bruise of many days
Do challenge thee to trial of a man.                                   66
I say thou hast belied mine innocent child.
Thy slander hath gone through and through her
   heart,
And she lies buried with her ancestors—
Oh, in a tomb where never scandal slept,
Save this of hers, framed by thy villainy!                             71

CLAUDIO
My villainy?

LEONATO            Thine, Claudio, thine, I say.

DON PEDRO
You say not right, old man.

LEONATO                        My lord, my lord,
I'll prove it on his body if he dare,
Despite his nice fence and his active practice,                        75
His May of youth and bloom of lustihood.                               76

CLAUDIO
Away! I will not have to do with you.

LEONATO
Canst thou so daff me? Thou hast killed my child.                      78
If thou kill'st me, boy, thou shalt kill a man.

ANTONIO
He shall kill two of us, and men indeed.
But that's no matter; let him kill one first.
Win me and wear me! Let him answer me.                                 82
Come follow me, boy. Come, sir boy, come follow me,
Sir boy, I'll whip you from your foining fence!                        84
Nay, as I am a gentleman, I will.

LEONATO        Brother—

ANTONIO
Content yourself. God knows I loved my niece,                          87
And she is dead, slandered to death by villains
That dare as well answer a man indeed
As I dare take a serpent by the tongue.
Boys, apes, braggarts, jacks, milksops!

LEONATO        Brother Antony—

ANTONIO
Hold you content. What, man! I know them, yea,
And what they weigh, even to the utmost scruple—                       94
Scambling, outfacing, fashionmonging boys,                             95

That lie and cog and flout, deprave and slander,                       96
Go anticly, show outward hideousness,                                  97
And speak off half a dozen dangerous words                             98
How they might hurt their enemies, if they durst,
And this is all.

LEONATO
But brother Antony—

ANTONIO                  Come, 'tis no matter.
Do not you meddle; let me deal in this.

DON PEDRO
Gentlemen both, we will not wake your patience.                        103
My heart is sorry for your daughter's death;
But, on my honor, she was charged with nothing
But what was true and very full of proof.

LEONATO    My lord, my lord—

DON PEDRO    I will not hear you.

LEONATO
No? Come, brother, away! I will be heard.

ANTONIO
And shall, or some of us will smart for it.                            110
                    *Exeunt ambo* [*Leonato and Antonio*].

        *Enter Benedick.*

DON PEDRO
See, see, here comes the man we went to seek.

CLAUDIO    Now, signor, what news?

BENEDICK    Good day, my lord.

DON PEDRO    Welcome, signor. You are almost come to
part almost a fray.

CLAUDIO    We had like to have had our two noses           116
snapped off with two old men without teeth.                117

DON PEDRO    Leonato and his brother. What think'st
thou? Had we fought, I doubt we should have been           119
too young for them.

BENEDICK    In a false quarrel there is no true valor. I came
to seek you both.

CLAUDIO    We have been up and down to seek thee, for
we are high-proof melancholy and would fain have it        124
beaten away. Wilt thou use thy wit?

BENEDICK    It is in my scabbard. Shall I draw it?

DON PEDRO    Dost thou wear thy wit by thy side?

CLAUDIO    Never any did so, though very many have
been beside their wit. I will bid thee draw as we do the   129
minstrels, draw to pleasure us.                            130

DON PEDRO    As I am an honest man, he looks pale. Art
thou sick, or angry?

CLAUDIO    What, courage, man! What though care killed
a cat, thou hast mettle enough in thee to kill care.

BENEDICK    Sir, I shall meet your wit in the career, an you   135
charge it against me. I pray you, choose another subject.      136

---

57 **my . . . sword** I had no intention of using my sword.    58 **fleer** sneer,
jeer    62 **head** i.e., face    64 **my reverence** i.e., the reverence due old
age    66 **trial of a man** manly contest, i.e., duel.    71 **framed** devised
75 **nice fence** dexterous swordsmanship. (Said contemptuously.)
76 **lustihood** bodily vigor.    78 **daff** doff, brush aside    82 **Win . . .
me!** (A proverbial expression, used as a challenge, meaning he'll have
to overcome me before he can claim me as a prize.)    **answer me** i.e., in
a duel.    84 **foining** thrusting    87 **Content yourself** i.e., Don't try to
stop me.    94 **scruple** small measure of weight    95 **Scambling . . .
boys** contentious, swaggering, dandified boys

96 **cog** cheat.    **deprave** defame, traduce    97 **anticly** fantastically
dressed.    **hideousness** frightening appearance    98 **dangerous**
threatening, haughty    103 **wake your patience** put your patience to
any further test.    110.1 *ambo* both    116 **We had . . . had** We almost
had    117 **with** by    119 **doubt** fear, suspect. (Said ironically.)
124 **high-proof** to the highest degree.    **fain** gladly    129 **beside their
wit** out of their wits. (Playing on *by thy side* in line 127.)    130 **draw**
(1) draw your weapon (2) draw a bow across a musical instrument
135 **career** short gallop at full speed (as in a tourney).    **an** if
136 **charge** level (as a weapon)

CLAUDIO    Nay, then, give him another staff. This last 138
was broke cross. 139

DON PEDRO    By this light, he changes more and more. I
think he be angry indeed.

CLAUDIO    If he be, he knows how to turn his girdle. 142

BENEDICK    Shall I speak a word in your ear?

CLAUDIO    God bless me from a challenge!

BENEDICK [aside to Claudio]    You are a villain. I jest not. I
will make it good how you dare, with what you dare,
and when you dare. Do me right, or I will protest your 147
cowardice. You have killed a sweet lady, and her death
shall fall heavy on you. Let me hear from you.

CLAUDIO    Well, I will meet you, so I may have good
cheer. 151

DON PEDRO    What, a feast, a feast?

CLAUDIO    I'faith, I thank him, he hath bid me to a calf's 153
head and a capon, the which if I do not carve most 154
curiously, say my knife's naught. Shall I not find a 155
woodcock too? 156

BENEDICK    Sir, your wit ambles well; it goes easily. 157

DON PEDRO    I'll tell thee how Beatrice praised thy wit
the other day. I said thou hadst a fine wit. "True,"
said she, "a fine little one." "No," said I, "a great wit."
"Right," says she, "a great gross one." "Nay," said I, "a
good wit." "Just," said she, "it hurts nobody." "Nay," 162
said I, "the gentleman is wise." "Certain," said she,
"a wise gentleman." "Nay," said I, "he hath the 164
tongues." "That I believe," said she, "for he swore a 165
thing to me on Monday night which he forswore on
Tuesday morning. There's a double tongue; there's
two tongues." Thus did she, an hour together, trans- 168
shape thy particular virtues. Yet at last she concluded 169
with a sigh, thou wast the proper'st man in Italy. 170

CLAUDIO    For the which she wept heartily and said she
cared not.

DON PEDRO    Yea, that she did. But yet for all that, an if
she did not hate him deadly, she would love him
dearly. The old man's daughter told us all. 175

CLAUDIO    All, all. And, moreover, God saw him when 176
he was hid in the garden. 177

DON PEDRO    But when shall we set the savage bull's
horns on the sensible Benedick's head?

CLAUDIO    Yea, and text underneath, "Here dwells 180
Benedick, the married man"?

BENEDICK    Fare you well, boy. You know my mind. I
will leave you now to your gossiplike humor. You
break jests as braggarts do their blades, which, God be 184
thanked, hurt not.—My lord, for your many courtesies I thank you. I must discontinue your company.
Your brother the bastard is fled from Messina. You
have among you killed a sweet and innocent lady. For
my Lord Lackbeard there, he and I shall meet, and till
then peace be with him.                              [Exit.]

DON PEDRO    He is in earnest.

CLAUDIO    In most profound earnest, and, I'll warrant
you, for the love of Beatrice.

DON PEDRO    And hath challenged thee?

CLAUDIO    Most sincerely.

DON PEDRO    What a pretty thing man is when he goes 196
in his doublet and hose and leaves off his wit! 197

CLAUDIO    He is then a giant to an ape; but then is an ape 198
a doctor to such a man. 199

DON PEDRO    But, soft you, let me be. Pluck up, my heart, 200
and be sad. Did he not say my brother was fled? 201

*Enter Constables, [Dogberry and Verges, and
the Watch, with] Conrade and Borachio.*

DOGBERRY    Come you, sir. If Justice cannot tame you,
she shall ne'er weigh more reasons in her balance. 203
Nay, an you be a cursing hypocrite once, you must be 204
looked to.

DON PEDRO    How now, two of my brother's men
bound? Borachio one!

CLAUDIO    Hearken after their offense, my lord. 208

DON PEDRO    Officers, what offense have these men
done?

DOGBERRY    Marry, sir, they have committed false report;
moreover, they have spoken untruths; secondarily,
they are slanders; sixth and lastly, they have belied a 213
lady; thirdly, they have verified unjust things; and to
conclude, they are lying knaves.

DON PEDRO    First, I ask thee what they have done;
thirdly, I ask thee what's their offense; sixth and lastly,
why they are committed; and to conclude, what you
lay to their charge.

CLAUDIO    Rightly reasoned, and in his own division; 220
and, by my troth, there's one meaning well suited. 221

DON PEDRO    Who have you offended, masters, that you
are thus bound to your answer? This learned consta- 223
ble is too cunning to be understood. What's your
offense?

---

138 staff spear shaft.    139 broke cross i.e., broken by clumsily allowing the spear to break crosswise against the opponent's shield. (In
other words, Claudio accuses Benedick of having failed in his sally of
wit.)    142 turn his girdle i.e., turn his sword belt around so that
he's ready to fight. (A proverbial expression of uncertain meaning.)
147 Do me right Give me satisfaction.    protest proclaim before witnesses
151 cheer entertainment. (Claudio is ready to fight, he says, for the
pleasant diversion it should offer.)    153–6 calf's head, capon, woodcock (In the proposed feast of dueling, Claudio plans to carve various
dishes connoting foolishness, effeminate cowardice, and stupidity.)
155 curiously daintily.    naught good for nothing.    157 ambles
i.e., minces along    162 good (1) keen (2) harmless.    Just Exactly
164 a wise gentleman i.e., an old fool.    164–5 hath the tongues masters several languages.    168–9 trans-shape distort, turn the wrong
side out    170 proper'st handsomest    175 old man's daughter i.e.,
Hero    176–7 God . . . garden (Alluding to the trick played on Benedick
to love Beatrice, and also to Genesis 3:8.)    180 text (In 1.1.251–6, Benedick
vowed that, if he were ever to fall in love, his friends might set a bull's
horns on his head and label him "Benedick the married man.")

184 as . . . blades i.e., as braggarts furtively damage their blades to
make it appear they have been fighting fiercely    196–7 goes . . . wit
goes about fully dressed like a rational creature but forgets to equip
himself with good sense.    198–9 He . . . man i.e., Such a man looks
like a hero in a fool's eyes, but actually the fool is a wise man compared to him.    200–1 soft . . . be sad wait a minute, not so fast; let me
think. Rouse yourself, my heart, and be serious.    201.1–2 (The quarto
placement of this stage direction after line 197 suggests that Dogberry
is visible, strutting and fussing with his prisoners, before he speaks.)
203 she . . . balance i.e., Justice will never find weightier reasons for
prosecuting crimnal behavior, weighing the case in her balance scales.
(With a pun on reasons and raisins.)    204 cursing accursed.    once
in a word    208 Hearken after Inquire into    213 slanders (For
"slanderers.")    220 his own division its own logical arrangement.
(Said ironically.)    221 well suited nicely dressed up in the trappings
of language.    223 bound (Playing on the meanings "pinioned"
and "headed for a destination.")    answer trial, account.

BORACHIO    Sweet Prince, let me go no farther to mine answer. Do you hear me, and let this count kill me. I have deceived even your very eyes. What your wisdoms could not discover, these shallow fools have brought to light, who in the night overheard me confessing to this man how Don John your brother incensed me to slander the Lady Hero, how you were 232 brought into the orchard and saw me court Margaret in Hero's garments, how you disgraced her when you should marry her. My villainy they have upon record, which I had rather seal with my death than repeat over to my shame. The lady is dead upon mine and 237 my master's false accusation; and, briefly, I desire nothing but the reward of a villain.

DON PEDRO [*to Claudio*]
Runs not this speech like iron through your blood?

CLAUDIO
I have drunk poison whiles he uttered it.

DON PEDRO [*to Borachio*]
But did my brother set thee on to this?

BORACHIO    Yea, and paid me richly for the practice of it. 243

DON PEDRO
He is composed and framed of treachery,
And fled he is upon this villainy.                                    245

CLAUDIO
Sweet Hero! Now thy image doth appear
In the rare semblance that I loved it first.                           247

DOGBERRY    Come, bring away the plaintiffs. By this time 248 our sexton hath reformed Signor Leonato of the 249 matter. And masters, do not forget to specify, when 250 time and place shall serve, that I am an ass.

VERGES    Here, here comes Master Signor Leonato, and the sexton, too.

*Enter Leonato, his brother [Antonio], and the Sexton.*

LEONATO
Which is the villain? Let me see his eyes,
That when I note another man like him,
I may avoid him. Which of these is he?

BORACHIO
If you would know your wronger, look on me.

LEONATO
Art thou the slave that with thy breath hast killed
Mine innocent child?

BORACHIO                        Yea, even I alone.

LEONATO
No, not so, villain, thou beliest thyself.
Here stand a pair of honorable men—                                   261
A third is fled—that had a hand in it.
I thank you, princes, for my daughter's death.
Record it with your high and worthy deeds.
'Twas bravely done, if you bethink you of it.

CLAUDIO
I know not how to pray your patience,
Yet I must speak. Choose your revenge yourself;

Impose me to what penance your invention             268
Can lay upon my sin. Yet sinned I not
But in mistaking.

DON PEDRO               By my soul, nor I.
And yet, to satisfy this good old man,
I would bend under any heavy weight
That he'll enjoin me to.

LEONATO
I cannot bid you bid my daughter live—
That were impossible—but, I pray you both,
Possess the people in Messina here                   276
How innocent she died; and if your love
Can labor aught in sad invention,                    278
Hang her an epitaph upon her tomb,
And sing it to her bones; sing it tonight.
Tomorrow morning come you to my house,
And since you could not be my son-in-law,
Be yet my nephew. My brother hath a daughter,
Almost the copy of my child that's dead,
And she alone is heir to both of us.                 285
Give her the right you should have giv'n her cousin, 286
And so dies my revenge.

CLAUDIO                   O noble sir,
Your overkindness doth wring tears from me!
I do embrace your offer; and dispose                 289
For henceforth of poor Claudio.                      290

LEONATO
Tomorrow then I will expect your coming;
Tonight I take my leave. This naughty man            292
Shall face to face be brought to Margaret,
Who I believe was packed in all this wrong,          294
Hired to it by your brother.

BORACHIO    No, by my soul, she was not,
Nor knew not what she did when she spoke to me,
But always hath been just and virtuous
In anything that I do know by her.                   299

DOGBERRY    Moreover, sir, which indeed is not under 300 white and black, this plaintiff here, the offender, did 301 call me ass. I beseech you, let it be remembered in his punishment. And also the watch heard them talk of one Deformed. They say he wears a key in his ear and 304 a lock hanging by it and borrows money in God's 305 name, the which he hath used so long and never paid 306 that now men grow hardhearted and will lend nothing for God's sake. Pray you, examine him upon that point.

LEONATO    I thank thee for thy care and honest pains.

DOGBERRY    Your Worship speaks like a most thankful and reverend youth, and I praise God for you.

LEONATO    There's for thy pains.    [*He gives money.*]

DOGBERRY    God save the foundation!                 314

---

268 **Impose me to** impose on me    276 **Possess** inform    278 **aught** to any extent    285 **heir to both** (Leonato overlooks Antonio's son mentioned in 1.2.2.)    286 **right** equitable treatment. (Quibbling on "rite," "ceremony.")    289 **dispose** you may dispose    290 **For henceforth** for the future    292 **naughty** wicked    294 **packed** involved as an accomplice    299 **by** concerning    300–1 **under . . . black** written down in black and white    304–5 **key . . . by it** (This is what Dogberry has made out of the lovelock mentioned in 3.3.166.)    305–6 **in God's name** (A phrase of the professional beggar.)    314 **God . . . foundation!** (A formula of those who received alms at religious houses or charitable foundations.)

---

232 **incensed** incited    237 **upon** in consequence of    243 **practice** cunning execution    245 **upon** i.e., having committed    247 **rare semblance** splendid likeness    248 **plaintiffs** (For "defendants.")    249 **reformed** (For "informed.")    250 **specify** (For "testify"?)    261 **honorable men** i.e., Don Pedro and Claudio, men of rank

LEONATO    Go, I discharge thee of thy prisoner, and I thank thee.

DOGBERRY    I leave an arrant knave with Your Worship, which I beseech Your Worship to correct yourself, for the example of others. God keep Your Worship! I wish Your Worship well. God restore you to health! I humbly give you leave to depart; and if a merry meet- 321 ing may be wished, God prohibit it! Come, neighbor. 322
                                     [*Exeunt Dogberry and Verges.*]

LEONATO    Until tomorrow morning, lords, farewell.

ANTONIO    Farewell, my lords. We look for you tomorrow.

DON PEDRO    We will not fail.

CLAUDIO              Tonight I'll mourn with Hero.

LEONATO [*to the Watch*]
    Bring you these fellows on.—We'll talk with Margaret,
    How her acquaintance grew with this lewd fellow.    327
                                     *Exeunt [separately]*.

## [5.2]

*Enter Benedick and Margaret, [meeting].*

BENEDICK    Pray thee, sweet Mistress Margaret, deserve well at my hands by helping me to the speech of 2 Beatrice.

MARGARET    Will you then write me a sonnet in praise of my beauty?

BENEDICK    In so high a style, Margaret, that no man 6 living shall come over it, for in most comely truth thou 7 deservest it.

MARGARET    To have no man come over me! Why, shall I always keep below stairs?    10

BENEDICK    Thy wit is as quick as the greyhound's mouth; it catches.

MARGARET    And yours as blunt as the fencer's foils, which hit but hurt not.

BENEDICK    A most manly wit, Margaret; it will not hurt a woman. And so, I pray thee, call Beatrice. I give thee 16 the bucklers.    17

MARGARET    Give us the swords. We have bucklers of our own.

BENEDICK    If you use them, Margaret, you must put in the pikes with a vice, and they are dangerous weapons 21 for maids.

MARGARET    Well, I will call Beatrice to you, who I think hath legs.    *Exit Margaret.*

BENEDICK    And therefore will come.
    [*He sings.*] "The god of love,    26
                    That sits above,
                    And knows me, and knows me,
                    How pitiful I deserve—"    29
    I mean in singing; but in loving, Leander the good 30 swimmer, Troilus the first employer of panders, and a 31 whole bookful of these quondam carpetmongers, 32 whose names yet run smoothly in the even road of a blank verse, why, they were never so truly turned over 34 and over as my poor self in love. Marry, I cannot show 35 it in rhyme. I have tried. I can find out no rhyme to "lady" but "baby," an innocent rhyme; for "scorn," 37 "horn," a hard rhyme; for "school," "fool," a babbling 38 rhyme; very ominous endings. No, I was not born under a rhyming planet, nor I cannot woo in festival terms.

*Enter Beatrice.*

Sweet Beatrice, wouldst thou come when I called thee?

BEATRICE    Yea, signor, and depart when you bid me.

BENEDICK    Oh, stay but till then!    [*She starts to leave.*]

BEATRICE    "Then" is spoken; fare you well now. And yet, ere I go, let me go with that I came, which is, with 46 knowing what hath passed between you and Claudio.

BENEDICK    Only foul words; and thereupon I will kiss thee.

BEATRICE    Foul words is but foul wind, and foul wind is but foul breath, and foul breath is noisome; there- 51 fore I will depart unkissed.

BENEDICK    Thou hast frighted the word out of his right 53 sense, so forcible is thy wit. But I must tell thee plainly, Claudio undergoes my challenge; and either I must shortly hear from him, or I will subscribe him a 56 coward. And I pray thee now tell me, for which of my bad parts didst thou first fall in love with me?

BEATRICE    For them all together, which maintained so politic a state of evil that they will not admit any good 60 part to intermingle with them. But for which of my good parts did you first suffer love for me?    62

BENEDICK    Suffer love! A good epithet. I do suffer love 63 indeed, for I love thee against my will.

BEATRICE    In spite of your heart, I think. Alas, poor heart, if you spite it for my sake I will spite it for yours, for I will never love that which my friend hates.

BENEDICK    Thou and I are too wise to woo peaceably.

321 give you leave (For "ask your leave.")   322 prohibit (For "permit.") 327 lewd wicked, worthless
5 .2. Location: Leonato's garden (? At the scene's end, Leonato's house is some distance away.)
2 to the speech of to speak with   6 style (1) poetic style (2) stile, stairs over a fence   7 come over (1) excel beyond (2) traverse, as one would cross a stile (3) in Margaret's next speech, the phrase is taken to mean "mount sexually."   comely good. (With an allusion to Margaret's beauty.)   10 keep below stairs dwell in the servants' quarters. 16 –17 I . . . bucklers i.e., I acknowledge myself beaten (in repartee). (Bucklers are shields with spikes [pikes] in their centers. Margaret uses the word in a bawdy sense in her reply.)   21 pikes spikes in the center of a shield.   vice screw. (Benedick's bawdy sense continues Margaret's jest.)

26 –9 The god . . . deserve (The beginning of an old song by William Elderton.)   29 How . . . deserve how I deserve pity. (But Benedick uses the phrase to mean "how little I deserve.")   30 Leander lover of Hero of Sestos; he swam the Hellespont nightly to see her until he drowned   31 Troilus lover of Cressida, whose affair was assisted by her uncle Pandarus   32 quondam carpetmongers ladies' men of old, such as one might find in the carpeted boudoirs of the women they woo   34 –5 over and over i.e., head over heels   37 innocent childish   38 hard (1) exact (2) unpleasant, because of the association with cuckold's horns   46 that I came what I came for   51 noisome noxious   53 his its   56 subscribe formally proclaim in writing 60 politic prudently governed   62 suffer (1) experience (2) feel the pain of   63 epithet expression.

BEATRICE    It appears not in this confession. There's not 69
one wise man among twenty that will praise himself.
BENEDICK    An old, an old instance, Beatrice, that lived 71
in the time of good neighbors. If a man do not erect in 72
this age his own tomb ere he dies, he shall live no 73
longer in monument than the bell rings and the 74
widow weeps. 75
BEATRICE    And how long is that, think you?
BENEDICK    Question: why, an hour in clamor and a 77
quarter in rheum. Therefore is it most expedient for 78
the wise, if Don Worm, his conscience, find no imped- 79
iment to the contrary, to be the trumpet of his own
virtues, as I am to myself. So much for praising myself,
who, I myself will bear witness, is praiseworthy. And
now tell me, how doth your cousin?
BEATRICE    Very ill.
BENEDICK    And how do you?
BEATRICE    Very ill too.
BENEDICK    Serve God, love me, and mend. There will I
leave you too, for here comes one in haste.

*Enter Ursula.*

URSULA    Madam, you must come to your uncle. Yonder's old coil at home. It is proved my lady Hero hath 90
been falsely accused, the Prince and Claudio mightily
abused, and Don John is the author of all, who is fled 92
and gone. Will you come presently? 93
BEATRICE    Will you go hear this news, signor?
BENEDICK    I will live in thy heart, die in thy lap, and be 95
buried in thy eyes; and moreover I will go with thee
to thy uncle's.                                      *Exeunt.*

## [5.3]

*Enter Claudio, Prince [Don Pedro, Balthasar],
and three or four with tapers.*

CLAUDIO    Is this the monument of Leonato?
A LORD    It is, my lord.
CLAUDIO    [*reading from a scroll*]

*Epitaph.*

"Done to death by slanderous tongues
Was the Hero that here lies.
Death, in guerdon of her wrongs,                         5
Gives her fame which never dies.
So the life that died with shame
Lives in death with glorious fame."

Hang thou there upon the tomb,
Praising her when I am dumb.                              10
                        [*He hangs up the scroll.*]
Now, music, sound, and sing your solemn hymn.

                    *Song.*

BALTHASAR
Pardon, goddess of the night,                            12
Those that slew thy virgin knight;                       13
For the which, with songs of woe,
Round about her tomb they go.
    Midnight, assist our moan;
    Help us to sigh and groan,
        Heavily, heavily.
Graves, yawn and yield your dead,                        19
Till death be utterèd,                                   20
    Heavily, heavily.

CLAUDIO
Now, unto thy bones good night!
Yearly will I do this rite.
DON PEDRO
Good morrow, masters. Put your torches out.
    The wolves have preyed; and look, the gentle day, 25
Before the wheels of Phoebus, round about               26
    Dapples the drowsy east with spots of gray.
Thanks to you all, and leave us. Fare you well.
CLAUDIO
Good morrow, masters. Each his several way.             29
DON PEDRO
Come, let us hence, and put on other weeds,             30
    And then to Leonato's we will go.
CLAUDIO
And Hymen now with luckier issue speed's               32
Than this for whom we rendered up this woe.            33
                                      *Exeunt.*

## [5.4]

*Enter Leonato, Benedick, [Beatrice], Margaret,
Ursula, old man [Antonio], Friar [Francis, and]
Hero.*

FRIAR
Did I not tell you she was innocent?
LEONATO
So are the Prince and Claudio, who accused her
Upon the error that you heard debated.                   3
But Margaret was in some fault for this,
Although against her will, as it appears                 5
In the true course of all the question.                 6

---

**69 It . . . confession** i.e., You don't show wisdom in praising yourself
for being wise.    **71 instance** proverb (i.e., "He has ill neighbors that is
fain to praise himself")    **72 time . . . neighbors** good old times (when
one's neighbors spoke well of one)    **73–5 he shall . . . weeps** i.e., he
will be memorialized only during the (brief) time of the funeral service
and the official mourning.    **77 Question** i.e., An easy question, which
I will answer as follows.    **clamor** noise (of the bell)    **78 rheum** tears
(of the widow).    **79 Don . . . conscience** (The action of the conscience
was traditionally described as the gnawing of a worm; compare with
Mark 9:44–8.)    **90 old coil** great confusion    **92 abused** deceived
**93 presently** immediately.    **95 die** (With the common connotation
of "experience sexual climax.")
**5.3. Location:** A churchyard.
**5 guerdon** recompense

**10 dumb** speechless (in death).    **12 goddess of the night** i.e., Diana,
moon goddess, patroness of chastity    **13 knight** i.e., follower    **19 yawn**
open wide    **20 utterèd** fully expressed    **25 have preyed** i.e., have done
their preying. (Wolves howl and hunt by night.)    **26 Before . . . about** in
front of the chariot of the sun god, on every side    **29 several** separate
**30 weeds** garments    **32 And . . . speed's** And may the god of marriage
favor us with better fortune    **33 Than this** Hero
**5.4. Location:** Leonato's house.
**3 Upon** on the basis of    **5 against her will** unintentionally    **6 question**
investigation.

**ANTONIO**
Well, I am glad that all things sorts so well.                    7
**BENEDICK**
And so am I, being else by faith enforced                    8
To call young Claudio to a reckoning for it.
**LEONATO**
Well, daughter, and you gentlewomen all,
Withdraw into a chamber by yourselves,
And when I send for you, come hither masked.
The Prince and Claudio promised by this hour
To visit me. You know your office, brother:
You must be father to your brother's daughter,
And give her to young Claudio.          *Exeunt ladies.*
**ANTONIO**
Which I will do with confirmed countenance.                    17
**BENEDICK**
Friar, I must entreat your pains, I think.                    18
**FRIAR**   To do what, signor?
**BENEDICK**
To bind me or undo me—one of them.                    20
Signor Leonato, truth it is, good signor,
Your niece regards me with an eye of favor.
**LEONATO**
That eye my daughter lent her. 'Tis most true.                    23
**BENEDICK**
And I do with an eye of love requite her.
**LEONATO**
The sight whereof I think you had from me,                    25
From Claudio, and the Prince. But what's your will?                    26
**BENEDICK**
Your answer, sir, is enigmatical.
But, for my will, my will is your good will                    28
May stand with ours, this day to be conjoined
In the state of honorable marriage,
In which, good Friar, I shall desire your help.
**LEONATO**
My heart is with your liking.
**FRIAR**                          And my help.
Here comes the Prince and Claudio.

          *Enter Prince [Don Pedro] and Claudio, and
          two or three other.*

**DON PEDRO**
Good morrow to this fair assembly.
**LEONATO**
Good morrow, Prince. Good morrow, Claudio.
We here attend you. Are you yet determined                    36
Today to marry with my brother's daughter?
**CLAUDIO**
I'll hold my mind, were she an Ethiope.
**LEONATO**
Call her forth, brother. Here's the Friar ready.
                              [*Exit Antonio.*]

**DON PEDRO**
Good morrow, Benedick. Why, what's the matter,
That you have such a February face,
So full of frost, of storm, and cloudiness?
**CLAUDIO**
I think he thinks upon the savage bull.                    43
Tush, fear not, man! We'll tip thy horns with gold,
And all Europa shall rejoice at thee,                    45
As once Europa did at lusty Jove                    46
When he would play the noble beast in love.
**BENEDICK**
Bull Jove, sir, had an amiable low,
And some such strange bull leapt your father's cow
And got a calf in that same noble feat
Much like to you, for you have just his bleat.

          *Enter [Leonato's] brother [Antonio], Hero,
          Beatrice, Margaret, [and] Ursula, [the ladies
          masked].*

**CLAUDIO**
For this I owe you. Here comes other reckonings.                    52
Which is the lady I must seize upon?
**ANTONIO**
This same is she, and I do give you her.
**CLAUDIO**
Why then, she's mine. Sweet, let me see your face.
**LEONATO**
No, that you shall not, till you take her hand
Before this friar and swear to marry her.
**CLAUDIO**
Give me your hand before this holy friar.
I am your husband, if you like of me.                    59
**HERO** [*unmasking*]
And when I lived, I was your other wife;
And when you loved, you were my other husband.
**CLAUDIO**
Another Hero!
**HERO**                          Nothing certainer.
One Hero died defiled, but I do live,
And surely as I live, I am a maid.
**DON PEDRO**
The former Hero! Hero that is dead!
**LEONATO**
She died, my lord, but whiles her slander lived.                    66
**FRIAR**
All this amazement can I qualify,                    67
When, after that the holy rites are ended,
I'll tell you largely of fair Hero's death.                    69
Meantime let wonder seem familiar,                    70
And to the chapel let us presently.                    71
**BENEDICK**
Soft and fair, Friar. Which is Beatrice?                    72

---

**7 sorts** turn out   **8 being ... enforced** since otherwise I would be enforced by my promise to Beatrice   **17 confirmed countenance** straight face.   **18 entreat your pains** beg your help   **20 undo** (1) ruin (2) untie, unbind   **23 That ... her** (Alludes to Hero's role in tricking Beatrice into confessing her love for Benedick.)   **25–6 The sight ... Prince** (Alludes to their role in tricking Benedick into confessing his love for Beatrice.)   **28 for** as for.   **is** is that   **36 yet** still

**43 I ... bull** (A jocular reminiscence of the conversation in 1.1.250 ff.) **45 Europa** Europe   **46 Europa** a princess whom Jove approached in the form of a white bull and bore on his back through the sea to Crete **52 I owe you** i.e., I'll pay you back later (for calling me a calf and a bastard).   **other reckonings** i.e., other matters to be settled first. **59 like of** care for   **66 but whiles** only while   **67 qualify** moderate **69 largely** at large, in full   **70 let ... familiar** treat these marvels as ordinary matters   **71 let us presently** let us go at once.   **72 Soft and fair** i.e., Wait a minute

BEATRICE [*unmasking*]
 I answer to that name. What is your will?
BENEDICK
 Do not you love me?
BEATRICE                    Why, no, no more than reason.
BENEDICK
 Why, then your uncle and the Prince and Claudio
 Have been deceived. They swore you did.
BEATRICE
 Do not you love me?
BENEDICK                    Troth, no, no more than reason.
BEATRICE
 Why, then my cousin, Margaret, and Ursula          78
 Are much deceived, for they did swear you did.
BENEDICK
 They swore that you were almost sick for me.
BEATRICE
 They swore that you were well-nigh dead for me.
BENEDICK
 'Tis no such matter. Then you do not love me?
BEATRICE
 No, truly, but in friendly recompense.
LEONATO
 Come, cousin, I am sure you love the gentleman.    84
CLAUDIO
 And I'll be sworn upon't that he loves her;
 For here's a paper written in his hand,
 A halting sonnet of his own pure brain,            87
 Fashioned to Beatrice.          [*He shows a paper.*]
HERO                         And here's another
 Writ in my cousin's hand, stol'n from her pocket,
 Containing her affection unto Benedick.
                          [*She shows another paper.*]
BENEDICK   A miracle! Here's our own hands against our  91
 hearts. Come, I will have thee, but by this light I take  92
 thee for pity.
BEATRICE   I would not deny you, but by this good day,
 I yield upon great persuasion, and partly to save your
 life, for I was told you were in a consumption.   96

BENEDICK   Peace! I will stop your mouth. [*Kissing her.*]
DON PEDRO   How dost thou, Benedick, the married
 man?
BENEDICK   I'll tell thee what, Prince: a college of wit-  100
 crackers cannot flout me out of my humor. Dost thou
 think I care for a satire or an epigram? No. If a man   102
 will be beaten with brains, 'a shall wear nothing hand-  103
 some about him. In brief, since I do purpose to marry,  104
 I will think nothing to any purpose that the world can
 say against it; and therefore never flout at me for what  106
 I have said against it; for man is a giddy thing, and this
 is my conclusion. For thy part, Claudio, I did think to
 have beaten thee, but in that thou art like to be my   109
 kinsman, live unbruised, and love my cousin.
CLAUDIO   I had well hoped thou wouldst have denied
 Beatrice, that I might have cudgeled thee out of thy
 single life, to make thee a double-dealer, which out of  113
 question thou wilt be, if my cousin do not look   114
 exceeding narrowly to thee.                      115
BENEDICK   Come, come, we are friends. Let's have a
 dance ere we are married, that we may lighten our
 own hearts and our wives' heels.
LEONATO   We'll have dancing afterward.
BENEDICK   First, of my word! Therefore play, music.  120
 Prince, thou art sad. Get thee a wife, get thee a wife.
 There is no staff more reverend than one tipped with  122
 horn.                                          123

           *Enter Messenger.*

MESSENGER
 My lord, your brother John is ta'en in flight
 And brought with armèd men back to Messina.     125
BENEDICK   Think not on him till tomorrow. I'll devise
 thee brave punishments for him. Strike up, pipers!  127
                            *Dance.* [*Exeunt.*]

---

**78 my cousin** i.e., Hero   **84 cousin** i.e., niece   **87 halting** limping.
**his own pure** purely his own   **91–2 against our hearts** i.e., to prove
our hearts guilty as charged.   **96 in a consumption** i.e., wasting
away in sighs.

**100 college** assembly   **102–4 If . . . him** i.e., If a man allows himself
to be cowed by ridicule, he'll never dare dress handsomely or do anything conspicuous that will draw attention.   **106 flout** mock   **109 in
that** in view of the fact that.   **like** likely   **113 a double-dealer** (1) a
married man (2) a deceiver, adulterer   **114–15 look . . . narrowly to**
keep close watch over   **120 of** on   **122–3 tipped with horn** (Alludes
to the usual joke about cuckolds, as at line 44.)   **125 with** by
**127 brave** fine

# As You Like It

*A*s You Like It represents, together with *Much Ado About Nothing* and *Twelfth Night,* the summation of Shakespeare's achievement in festive, happy comedy during the years 1598–1601. contains several motifs found in other Shakespearean comedies: the journey from a jaded court into a transforming sylvan environment and back to a revitalized court (as in *A Midsummer Night's Dream*); hence, a contrasting of two worlds in the play—one presided over by a virtuous but exiled older brother and the other, by a usurping younger brother (as in *The Tempest*); the heroine disguised as a man (as in *The Merchant of Venice, The Two Gentlemen of Verona, Cymbeline, and Twelfth Night*); and a structure of multiple plotting in which numerous groups of characters are thematically played off against one another (as in several of Shakespeare's comedies). What chiefly distinguishes this play from the others, however, is the nature and function of its pastoral setting—the Forest of Arden.

The Forest of Arden is seen in many perspectives. As a natural wilderness, it is probably most like the real forest Shakespeare knew near Stratford-upon-Avon in Warwickshire—a place capable of producing the folk wisdom of an honest shepard like Corin, the vulgarity of an Audrey, or the bumptuous clowning of a William. The forest bears the name of Shakespeare's mother, Mary Arden, the daughter of a prosperous Warwickshire farmer. Its name also owes something to the forest in Shakespeare's source, *Rosalynde,* based in turn on the forest of Ardennes in France. No less vividly, the place recalls for us Nottinghamshire and the Sherwood Forest of Robin Hood, where persons in retreat from a society seemingly beyond repair find refuge in a mythic folk world purged of social injustice. As the "golden world" (1.1.114), the forest evokes an even deeper longing for a mythological past age of innocence and plenty, when humans shared some attributes of the giants and the gods. This myth has its parallel in the biblical Garden of Eden, before the human race experienced "the penalty of Adam" (2.1.5). Finally, in another of its aspects, the forest is Arcadia, a pastoral landscape embodied in an ancient and sophisticated literary tradition and peopled by the likes of Silvius and Phoebe.

Most of these Ardens, compared and contrasted with one another, involve some idealization, not only of nature and the natural landscape, but also of the human condition. They place our real life in a complex perspective and force us to a fresh appraisal of our own ordinary existence. Duke Senior, for example, describes the forest environment as a corrective for the evils of society. He addresses his followers in the forest as "my co-mates and brothers in exile" (2.1.1), suggesting a kind of social equality that he could never know in the cramped formality of his previous official existence. The banished Duke Senior and his followers have had to leave behind their lands and revenues in the grip of the usurping Duke Frederick. No longer rich, though adequately provided with life's necessities, the Duke and his "merry men" live "like the old Robin Hood of England" and "fleet the time carelessly as they did in the golden world" (1.1.111–14). In this friendly society, a strong communal sense replaces the necessity for individual proprietorship. All comers are welcome, with food for all.

Even though the forest provides no luxuries, its spare existence does afford relief from the decadence of courtly life. "Sweet are the uses of adversity" (2.1.12), insists Duke Senior. He welcomes the cold of winter because it teaches him the true condition of humanity and of himself. The forest is serenely impartial: neither malicious nor compassionate. Death, and even killing for food, are an inevitable part of forest existence. The Duke concedes that his presence in the forest means the slaughter of deer, who were the original inhabitants; Orlando and Adam find that death through starvation in the forest is all too real a possibility. The forest is never guilty of the degrading perversity of humans at their worst, but it is also incapable of charity and forgiveness.

Shakespeare's sources reflect the complexity of his vision of Arden. The original of the Orlando story, which Shakespeare may not have used directly, is *The Cook's Tale of Gamelyn,* found in a number of manuscripts of *The Canterbury Tales* and wrongly attributed to Chaucer. This hearty English romance glorifies the rebellious and even violent spirit of its Robin Hood hero, the neglected youngest son Gamelyn, who, aided by faithful old Adam the Spencer, evades his wicked eldest brother in a cunning and bloody escape. As king of the outlaws in Sherwood Forest, Gamelyn eventually triumphs over his eldest brother (now the sheriff) and sees him hanged. Here, then, originates the motif of refuge from social injustice in Arden, even though most of the actual violence has been omitted from Shakespeare's version. (A trio of Robin Hood plays on a similar theme, beginning in 1598 with Anthony Munday's *The Downfall of Robert Earl of Huntingdon After Called Robin Hood*, was being performed with great success by the Admiral's company, chief rivals of the Lord Chamberlain's company to which Shakespeare belonged.)

*As You Like It* is clearly indebted to Thomas Lodge's *Rosalynde: Euphues' Golden Legacy* (published in 1590), a prose narrative version of the Gamelyn story in the ornate Euphuistic style of the 1580s. (Lodge's Epistle to the Gentleman Readers, casually inviting them to be pleased with this story if they are so inclined—"*If you like it, so*"—probably gave Shakespeare a hint for the name of his play.) Lodge accentuated the love story with its courtship in masquerade, provided some charming songs, and introduced the pastoral love motif involving Corin, Silvius, Phoebe, and Ganymede. Shakespeare's ordering of episode is generally close to that of Lodge. Pastoral literature, which had become a literary rage in the 1580s and early 1590s, owing particularly to Edmund Spenser's *Shepheardes Calendar* (1579) and Philip Sidney's *Arcadia* (1590), traced its ancestry through such Renaissance continental writers as Jorge de Montemayor, Jacopo Sannazaro, and Giovanni Battista Guarini to the so-called Greek romances, and finally back to the eclogues of Virgil, Theocritus, and Bion. A literary mode that had begun originally as a realistic evocation of difficult country life had become, in the Renaissance, an elegant vehicle for the loftiest and most patrician sentiments in love, for philosophic debate, and even for extensive political analysis and satire of the clergy.

Shakespeare's alterations and additions give us insight into his method of construction and his thematic focus. Whereas Lodge cheerfully accepts the pastoral conventions of his day, Shakespeare exposes those conventions to some criticism and considerable irony. Alongside the mannered and literary Silvius and Phoebe, he places William and Audrey, as peasantlike a couple as ever drew milk from a cow's teat. The juxtaposition holds up to critical perspective the rival claims of the literary and natural worlds by examining the defects of each in relation to the strengths of the other. William and Audrey are Shakespeare's own creation, based presumably on observation and also on the dramatic convention of the rustic clown and wench, as exemplified earlier in his Costard and Jaquenetta (*Love's Labor's Lost*).

Equally original, and essential to the many-sided debate concerning the virtues of the court versus those of the country, are Touchstone and Jaques. Touchstone is a professional court fool, dressed in motley, a new comic type in Shakespeare, created apparently in response to the recent addition to the Lord Chamberlain's company of the brilliant actor Robert Armin. Jaques is also a new type, the malcontent satirist, reflecting the very latest literary vogue in the nondramatic poetry and in drama of George Chapman, John Marston, and Ben Jonson. (The so-called private theaters, featuring boy actors, reopened in 1598–1599 after nearly a decade of enforced silence and proceeded at once to specialize in satirical drama; the public theaters like the Globe, the Rose, and the Swan sometimes joined in.) Touchstone and Jaques complement one another as critics and observers—one laughing at human folly with quizzical comic detachment and the other satirizing it with self-righteous scorn. Once we have been exposed to this assortment of newly created characters, we can no longer view either pastoral life or pastoral love as simply as Lodge and some other writers of the period portray them.

When *As You Like It* is compared with its chief source, Shakespeare can also be seen to have altered and considerably softened the characters of the wicked brothers Oliver and Frederick. Whereas Lodge's Saladyne is motivated by a greedy desire to seize his younger brother Rosader's property, Shakespeare's Oliver is envious of Orlando's natural goodness and popularity. As Oliver confesses in soliloquy, Orlando is "so much in the heart of the world and especially of my own people . . . that I am altogether misprized" (1.1.159–61). In his warped way, Oliver desires to be more like Orlando, and in the enchanted forest of Arden he eventually becomes so. Duke Frederick, too, is plainly envious of goodness. Trying to persuade his daughter Celia of the need for banishing Rosalind, he argues, "thou wilt show more bright and seem more virtuous / When she is gone" (1.3.79–80). In spite of his obsession with the mere "seeming" of virtue, Duke Frederick acknowledges the power of a goodness that will eventually convert him along with the rest. Penitence and conciliation replace the vengeful conclusion of Lodge's novel, in which the nobles of France finally overthrow and execute the usurping king. Although Shakespeare's resolutions are sudden, like all miracles they attest to the inexplicable power of goodness.

The court of Duke Frederick is "the envious court," identified by this fixed epithet. In it, brothers turn unnaturally against brothers: the younger Frederick usurps his older brother's throne, while the older Oliver denies the younger Orlando his birthright of education. In still another parallel, both Rosalind and Orlando find themselves mistrusted as the children of Frederick's political enemies, Duke Senior and Sir Rowland de Boys. A daughter and a son are held to be guilty by association. "Thou art thy father's daughter. There's enough" (1.3.56), Frederick curtly retorts in explaining Rosalind's exile. And to Orlando, triumphant in wrestling with Charles, Frederick asserts, "I would thou hadst been son to some man else" (1.2.214). Here again, Frederick plaintively reveals his envy of goodness, even if at present any potential for goodness in him is thwarted by tyrannous whim. Many of Frederick's entourage might also be better persons if they only knew how to escape the insincerities of their courtly life. Charles the wrestler, for example, places himself at Oliver's service, and yet he would happily avoid breaking Orlando's neck if to do so were consistent with self-interest. Even Le Beau, the giddy fop so delighted at first with the cruel sport of wrestling, takes Orlando aside at some personal risk to warn him of Duke Frederick's foul humor. Ideally, Le Beau would prefer to be a companion of Orlando's "in a better world than this" (1.2.275). The vision of a regenerative Utopia secretly abides in the heart of this courtly creature.

It is easier to anatomize the defects of a social order than to propound solutions. As have other creators of visionary landscapes (including Thomas More in his Utopia), Shakespeare uses playful debate to elicit complicated responses on the part of his audience. Which is preferable, the court or the country? Jaques and Touchstone are adept gadflies, incessantly pointing out contradictions and ironies. Jaques, the malcontent railer derived from literary satire, takes delight in being out of step with everyone. Seemingly, his chief reason for having joined the others in the forest is to jibe at their motives for being there. To their song about the rejection of courtly ambition he mockingly supplies another verse, charging them with having left their wealth and ease out of mere willfulness (2.5.46–54). With ironic appropriateness, Jaques eventually decides to remain in the forest in the company of Frederick; Jaques cannot thrive on resolution and harmony. His humor is "melancholy," from which, as he observes, he draws consolation as a weasel sucks eggs (2.5.11–12). The others treat him as a sort of profane jester whose soured conceits add relish to their enjoyment of the forest life.

Despite his affectation, however, Jaques is serious and even excited in his defense of satire as a curative form of laughter (2.7.47–87). The appearance of Touchstone in the forest has reaffirmed in Jaques his profound commitment to a view of life as an absurd process of decay governed by inexorable time. His function in such a life is to be mordant, unsparing. As literary satirist, he

must be free to awaken people's minds to their own folly. To Duke Senior's protestation that the satirist is merely self-indulgent and licentious, Jaques counters with a thoughtful and classically Horatian defense of satire as an art form devoted not to libelous attacks on individuals but to exposing types of folly. Any observer who feels individually portrayed merely condemns himself or herself by confessing his or her resemblance to the type. This particular debate between Duke Senior and Jaques ends, appropriately, in a draw. The Duke's point is well taken, for Jaques's famous "Seven Ages of Man" speech, so often read out of context, occurs in a scene that also witnesses the sacrifices and brave deeds that Orlando and Adam are prepared to undertake for each other. The feeling bond between the generations that they share refutes Jaques's wry narrative of isolated self-interest. As though in answer to Jaques's acid depiction of covetous old age, we see old Adam's self-sacrifice and trust in Providence. Instead of "mere oblivion," we see charitable compassion prompting Duke Senior to aid Orlando and Orlando to aid Adam. Perhaps this vision seems of a higher spiritual order than that of Jaques. Nonetheless, without him the forest would lack a satirical perspective that continually requires us to reexamine our romantic assumptions about human happiness.

Touchstone's name suggests that he similarly offers a multiplicity of viewpoints. (A touchstone is a kind of stone used to test for gold and silver.) He shares with Jaques a skeptical view of life, but for Touchstone the inconsistency and absurdity of life are occasions for wit and humor rather than melancholy and cynicism. As a professional fool, he observes that many supposedly sane men are more foolish than he—as, for example, in their elaborate dueling code of the Retort Courteous and the Reply Churlish, leading finally to the Lie Circumstantial and the Lie Direct (5.4.89–102). He is fascinated by the games people make of their lives and is amused by their inability to be content with what they already have. Of the shepherd's life, he comments, "In respect that it is solitary, I like it very well; but in respect that it is private, it is a very vile life" (3.2.15–16). This paradox, though nonsensical, captures the restlessness of human striving for a life that can somehow combine the peaceful solitude of nature with the convenience and excitement of city life. Although Touchstone marries, even his marriage is a spoof of the institution rather than a serious attempt at commitment. Like all fools, who in Renaissance times were regarded as a breed apart, Touchstone exists outside the realm of ordinary human responses. There he can comment disinterestedly on human folly. He is prevented, however, from sharing fully in the human love and conciliation with which the play ends. He and Jaques are not touched by the play's regenerative magic;

Jaques will remain in the forest, and Touchstone will remain forever a childlike entertainer.

The regenerative power of Arden, as we have seen, is not the forest's alone. What saves Orlando is the human charity practiced by him and by Duke Senior, who, for all his love of the forest, longs to rejoin that human society where he has "with holy bell been knolled to church" (2.7.120). Civilization at its best is no less necessary to the human spirit than is the natural order of the forest. In love, also, perception and wisdom must be combined with nature's gifts. Orlando, when we first see him, is a young man of the finest natural qualities but admittedly lacking experience in the nuances of complex human relationships. Nowhere does his lack of sophistication betray him more unhappily than in his first encounter with Rosalind, following the wrestling match. In response to her unmistakable hints of favor, he stands ox-like, tongue-tied. Later, in the forest, his first attempts at self-education in love lead him into an opposite danger: an excess of platitudinous manners parading in the guise of Petrarchism. (The Italian sonneteer Francis Petrarch has given to the language a name for the stereotypical literary mannerisms we associate with courtly love: the sighing and self-abasement of the young man, the chaste denial of love by the woman whom he worships, and the like.) Orlando's newfound self-abasement and idealization of his absent mistress are as unsatisfactory as his former naiveté. The sonnets he hangs on trees are deserving of the delicious parody they get from Touchstone. Orlando must learn from Rosalind that a quest for true understanding in love avoids the extreme of pretentious mannerism as well as that of mere artlessness. Orlando as Petrarchan lover too much resembles Silvius, the lovesick young man, cowering before the imperious will of his coy mistress Phoebe. This stereotyped relationship, taken from the pages of fashionable pastoral romance, represents a posturing that Rosalind hopes to cure in Silvius and Phoebe even as she will also cure Orlando.

Rosalind is, above all, the realistic one, the plucky Shakespearean heroine showing her mettle in the world of men, emotionally more mature than her lover. Her concern is with a working and clear-sighted relationship in love, and to that end she daringly insists that Orlando learn something of woman's changeable mood. Above all, she must disabuse him of the dangerously misleading clichés of the Petrarchan love myth. When he protests he would die for love of Rosalind, she lectures him mockingly in her guise of Ganymede: "No, faith, die by attorney. The poor world is almost six thousand years old, and in all this time there was not any man died in his own person, videlicet, in a love cause." She debunks the legends of Troilus and Leander, youths supposed to have died for love who, if they had ever really existed, would no doubt have met with more prosaic ends. "But

these are all lies. Men have died from time to time, and worms have eaten them, but not for love" (4.1.89–102). Rosalind wants Orlando to know that women are not goddesses but frail human beings who can be giddy, jealous, infatuated with novelty, irritatingly talkative, peremptory, and hysterical (4.1.142–9), though she is circumspect as to whether women can also be unfaithful. Orlando must be taught that love is a madness (3.2.390), and he must be cured, not of loving Rosalind, but of worshiping her with unrealistic expectations that can lead only to disillusionment. Rosalind teases him, as Portia does Bassanio in *The Merchant of Venice*, but she does not seriously threaten him with wantonness. Her disguise as Ganymede provides for her the perfect role in Orlando's approach to sexual manhood: he can learn to love "Ganymede" as a friend and then make the transition to heterosexual union in his blessed discovery that the friend is also the lover. Rosalind's own rite of passage is easier; for all her reliance on her loving friendship with Celia, or "Aliena," she is ready to exclaim, "But what talk we of fathers, when there is such a man as Orlando?" (3.4.36–7). She is spiritedly independent, even more so than Portia; whereas Portia's choice of husband is controlled by her father from his grave, Rosalind picks for herself. To be sure, Duke Senior is certainly happy that she marries Orlando, and she is glad to be reunited with her father, but her choice in marriage is very much her own. The forest is indeed a place where she can encounter her father "man to man," as it were, and be liberated from him while coming to terms with a patriarchal world. She is ready to give herself to Orlando, but she must educate him first. When Orlando has been sufficiently tested as to patience, loyalty, and understanding, she unmasks herself to him and simultaneously unravels the plot of ridiculous love we have come to associate with Silvius and Phoebe.

Rosalind's disguise name, Ganymede, has connotations that suggest ways in which human sexuality can be partly understood as socially constructed. If Rosalind in disguise as Ganymede wins the affection and eventually the love of Orlando, while her father and the other forest dwellers are equally taken in by the disguise, are maleness and femaleness chiefly matters of sartorial convention and superficial appearance? When Phoebe falls in love with Ganymede, is not her infatuation a way of showing that the roles of the sexes can be put on and off? Theatrically, the device of having a young male actor play Rosalind who then disguises him/herself as a young man adds to the witty confusion of sexual identities by introducing homoerotic possibilities. Not only can the roles of the sexes be put on and off, sexual desire itself is unstable, attaching itself to effeminate or sexually indeterminate young men like Rosalind/Ganymede, who is described as being "Of female favor" and "Like a ripe sister"

(4.3.87–8; compare *Twelfth Night*, 1.4.31–4, where Orsino says of "Cesario" that "all is semblative a woman's part"). Both Phoebe and Orlando are in some ways attracted to Ganymede; when Rosalind says of Orlando that "his kissing is as full of sanctity as the touch of holy bread" (3.4.13–14), she seems to suggest that Orlando has kissed her in her male disguise. Mythologically Ganymede is Zeus's or Jupiter's young male lover as well as cupbearer. The very role of boy actors in an all-male acting company must have struck some viewers as homoerotically suggestive.

At the same time, the motif of disguise enables the play to pursue a serious point about love and friendship. Orlando can speak frankly and personally to "Ganymede" as a perfect friend, one who can enable him as a young man still faced with the uncertainties and hazards of courtship to traverse the potentially difficult transition from male-to-male friendship into adult heterosexuality. The relationship closely anticipates that of "Cesario" and Orsino in *Twelfth Night*, where once again a powerful and loving attraction to a sexually ambiguous young man/woman ripens into mature love when the older man has been educated by the experience of loving friendship. Both plays depict heterosexual courtship as full of dangers for the male. In *As You Like It*, Rosalind is at pains to coach Orlando in what to expect from unruly women; and indeed, Rosalind's very readiness to wear male apparel bespeaks her daring intrusion into a man's world, even if Shakespeare carefully hedges this threat by insisting on Rosalind's hesitancy in being so bold. Rosalind is thus, like Portia in *The Merchant of Venice*, both spirited and eventually ready to comply with the mores of a male-dominated world.

By becoming Orlando's teacher, Rosalind is able to claim a strong position in their friendship and in our estimate of her remarkable worthiness. Posing as Ganymede, Rosalind can observe and test Orlando and thereby learn the truth about his capability for lifelong fidelity as only another man would have the opportunity to do. Once a loving friendship has grown strong between them, the unmasking of Rosalind's sexual identity makes possible a physical union between them to confirm and express the spiritual. In these terms, the play's happy ending affirms marriage as an institution, not simply as the expected denouement. The procession to the altar is synchronous with the return to civilization's other institutions, made whole again not solely by the forest but by the power of goodness embodied in Rosalind, Orlando, Duke Senior, and the others who persevere.

# As You Like It

[*Dramatis Personae*

DUKE SENIOR, *a banished duke*
DUKE FREDERICK, *his usurping brother*
ROSALIND, *daughter of Duke Senior, later disguised as*
   GANYMEDE
CELIA, *daughter of Duke Frederick, later disguised as* ALIENA

OLIVER,
JAQUES, } *sons of Sir Rowland de Boys*
ORLANDO,

AMIENS,
JAQUES, } *lords attending Duke Senior*

LE BEAU, *a courtier attending Duke Frederick*
CHARLES, *a wrestler in the court of Duke Frederick*

ADAM, *an aged servant of Oliver and then Orlando*
DENNIS, *a servant of Oliver*

TOUCHSTONE, *the* CLOWN *or* FOOL

CORIN, *an old shepherd*
SILVIUS, *a young shepherd, in love with Phoebe*
PHOEBE, *a shepherdess*
WILLIAM, *a country youth, in love with Audrey*
AUDREY, *a country wench*
SIR OLIVER MAR-TEXT, *a country vicar*

HYMEN, *god of marriage*

*Lords and Attendants waiting on Duke Frederick and Duke*
  *Senior*

SCENE: *Oliver's house; Duke Frederick's court; and the Forest of Arden*]

## 1.1

*Enter Orlando and Adam.*

ORLANDO   As I remember, Adam, it was upon this fash- 1
ion bequeathed me by will but poor a thousand 2
crowns and, as thou say'st, charged my brother on his 3
blessing to breed me well; and there begins my 4
sadness. My brother Jaques he keeps at school, and 5
report speaks goldenly of his profit. For my part, he 6
keeps me rustically at home—or, to speak more
properly, stays me here at home unkept; for call you 8
that "keeping" for a gentleman of my birth, that
differs not from the stalling of an ox? His horses are 10
bred better, for, besides that they are fair with their 11
feeding, they are taught their manage, and to that end 12

**1.1. Location: The garden of Oliver's house.**
**1–3 it was . . . crowns** it was in this way that I was left, by the terms of
my father's will, a mere thousand crowns or £250   **3 crowns** coins
worth five shillings.   **3–4 charged . . . well** my brother was
instructed as a condition of my father's blessing to educate me
well   **5 My . . . school** My oldest brother Oliver maintains my other
brother, Jaques, at university   **6 profit** progress.   **8 stays**
detains.   **unkept** poorly supported   **10 the stalling of** accommodation provided for   **11–12 fair . . . feeding** kept well groomed with
good diet   **12 manage** manège, paces and maneuvers in the art of
horsemanship

riders dearly hired. But I, his brother, gain nothing 13
under him but growth, for the which his animals on
his dunghills are as much bound to him as I. Besides
this nothing that he so plentifully gives me, the
something that nature gave me his countenance 17
seems to take from me. He lets me feed with his
hinds, bars me the place of a brother, and as much as 19
in him lies, mines my gentility with my education. 20
This is it, Adam, that grieves me; and the spirit of my
father, which I think is within me, begins to mutiny
against this servitude. I will no longer endure it,
though yet I know no wise remedy how to avoid it.

*Enter Oliver.*

ADAM   Yonder comes my master, your brother.
ORLANDO   Go apart, Adam, and thou shalt hear how 26
he will shake me up.      [*Adam stands aside.*] 27
OLIVER   Now, sir, what make you here? 28

**13 riders** trainers.   **dearly** expensively   **17 countenance** behavior;
(neglectful) patronage   **19 hinds** farm hands.   **bars me** excludes me
from   **19–20 as much . . . education** with all the authority at his disposal, undermines my right to be educated as a gentleman.   **26 Go
apart** Stand aside   **27 shake me up** abuse me.   **28 make** do. (But
Orlando takes it in the more usual sense.)

ORLANDO    Nothing. I am not taught to make anything.

OLIVER    What mar you then, sir?    30

ORLANDO    Marry, sir, I am helping you to mar that 31 which God made, a poor unworthy brother of yours, with idleness.

OLIVER    Marry, sir, be better employed, and be naught 34 awhile.    35

ORLANDO    Shall I keep your hogs and eat husks with 36 them? What prodigal portion have I spent, that I 37 should come to such penury?    38

OLIVER    Know you where you are, sir?    39

ORLANDO    Oh, sir, very well: here in your orchard.    40

OLIVER    Know you before whom, sir?

ORLANDO    Ay, better than him I am before knows me. I know you are my eldest brother, and in the gentle 43 condition of blood you should so know me. The cour- 44 tesy of nations allows you my better, in that you are 45 the firstborn, but the same tradition takes not away my blood, were there twenty brothers betwixt us. I 47 have as much of my father in me as you, albeit I con- fess your coming before me is nearer to his reverence. 49

OLIVER    What, boy!                    [He strikes Orlando.]

ORLANDO    Come, come, elder brother, you are too young in this.            [He seizes Oliver by the throat.] 52

OLIVER    Wilt thou lay hands on me, villain?    53

ORLANDO    I am no villain. I am the youngest son of Sir Rowland de Boys. He was my father, and he is thrice 55 a villain that says such a father begot villains. Wert thou not my brother, I would not take this hand from thy throat till this other had pulled out thy tongue for saying so. Thou hast railed on thyself.    59

ADAM    Sweet masters, be patient! For your father's 60 remembrance, be at accord.    61

OLIVER    Let me go, I say.

ORLANDO    I will not till I please. You shall hear me. My father charged you in his will to give me good educa- tion. You have trained me like a peasant, obscuring and hiding from me all gentlemanlike qualities. The 66 spirit of my father grows strong in me, and I will no longer endure it; therefore allow me such exercises as 68 may become a gentleman, or give me the poor allotery 69 my father left me by testament. With that I will go buy my fortunes.            [He releases Oliver.]

OLIVER    And what wilt thou do? Beg when that is spent? Well, sir, get you in. I will not long be troubled with you; you shall have some part of your will. I pray 74 you, leave me.

ORLANDO    I will no further offend you than becomes me for my good.

OLIVER    [to Adam]    Get you with him, you old dog.

ADAM    Is "old dog" my reward? Most true, I have lost my teeth in your service. God be with my old master! He would not have spoke such a word.
                    Exeunt Orlando [and] Adam.

OLIVER    Is it even so? Begin you to grow upon me? I will 82 physic your rankness and yet give no thousand 83 crowns neither.—Holla, Dennis!    84

                Enter Dennis.

DENNIS    Calls Your Worship?

OLIVER    Was not Charles, the Duke's wrestler, here to speak with me?

DENNIS    So please you, he is here at the door and 88 importunes access to you.    89

OLIVER    Call him in.                    [Exit Dennis.]
'Twill be a good way; and tomorrow the wrestling is.

                Enter Charles.

CHARLES    Good morrow to Your Worship.    92

OLIVER    Good Monsieur Charles, what's the new news at the new court?

CHARLES    There's no news at the court, sir, but the old news: that is, the old Duke is banished by his younger brother the new Duke, and three or four loving lords have put themselves into voluntary exile with him, whose lands and revenues enrich the new Duke; 99 therefore he gives them good leave to wander.    100

OLIVER    Can you tell if Rosalind, the Duke's daughter, be banished with her father?

CHARLES    Oh, no; for the Duke's daughter, her cousin, so loves her, being ever from their cradles bred together, 104 that she would have followed her exile or have died to 105 stay behind her. She is at the court and no less beloved 106 of her uncle than his own daughter, and never two ladies loved as they do.

OLIVER    Where will the old Duke live?

CHARLES    They say he is already in the Forest of Arden, and a many merry men with him; and there they live 111 like the old Robin Hood of England. They say many young gentlemen flock to him every day and fleet the 113 time carelessly as they did in the golden world.    114

OLIVER    What, you wrestle tomorrow before the new Duke?

---

30 mar ("To make or mar" is a commonplace antithesis.)    31 Marry i.e., Indeed. (Originally an oath by the Virgin Mary.)    34–5 be naught awhile i.e., stay in your place, don't grumble.    36–8 Shall . . . penury? (Alluding to the story of the Prodigal Son, in Luke 15:11–32, who, hav- ing wasted his "portion" or inheritance, had to tend swine and eat with them.)    39 where in whose presence. (But Orlando sarcastically takes the more literal meaning.)    40 orchard garden.    43–4 in . . . know me you should acknowledge that I share with you the condition of being well-born.    44–5 courtesy of nations recognized custom (of primogeniture, whereby the eldest son inherits all the land)    47 blood (1) gentlemanly lineage (2) spirit    49 is nearer . . . reverence is closer to his position of authority (as head of family).    52 young inexperi- enced (at fighting)    53 villain i.e., wicked fellow. (But Orlando plays on the literal meaning of "bondman" or "serf," as well as Oliver's meaning.)    55 he is anyone is    59 railed on thyself insulted your own blood.    60–1 your father's remembrance the sake of your father's memory    66 qualities (1) characteristics (2) accomplishments. 68 exercises activities, employments    69 allottery portion

74 will (1) desire (2) portion from your father's will (3) willfulness (i.e., you'll get what is coming to you).    82 grow upon me take liberties with me; grow too big for your breeches.    83 physic your rankness apply medicine to your overweening    84 neither either.    88 So please you If you please    89 importunes begs    92 Good morrow Good morning 99 whose all of whose    100 good leave full permission    104 being they being    105–6 died to stay died from being forced to stay    111 a many many    113 fleet pass    114 carelessly free from care.    golden world the primal age of innocence and ease from which humankind was thought to have degenerated. (See Ovid, Metamorphoses 1.)

CHARLES   Marry, do I, sir; and I came to acquaint you with a matter. I am given, sir, secretly to understand that your younger brother Orlando hath a disposition to come in disguised against me to try a fall. Tomor- 120 row, sir, I wrestle for my credit, and he that escapes 121 me without some broken limb shall acquit him well. 122 Your brother is but young and tender, and for your love I would be loath to foil him, as I must for my 124 own honor if he come in. Therefore, out of my love to you, I came hither to acquaint you withal, that either 126 you might stay him from his intendment or brook 127 such disgrace well as he shall run into, in that it is a thing of his own search and altogether against my will. 129

OLIVER   Charles, I thank thee for thy love to me, which thou shalt find I will most kindly requite. I had myself notice of my brother's purpose herein and have by underhand means labored to dissuade him from it, but 133 he is resolute. I'll tell thee, Charles, it is the stubbornest young fellow of France, full of ambition, an envious 135 emulator of every man's good parts, a secret and 136 villainous contriver against me his natural brother. 137 Therefore use thy discretion. I had as lief thou didst 138 break his neck as his finger. And thou wert best look 139 to't; for if thou dost him any slight disgrace, or if he 140 do not mightily grace himself on thee, he will practice 141 against thee by poison, entrap thee by some treacher- ous device, and never leave thee till he hath ta'en thy life by some indirect means or other; for I assure thee, and almost with tears I speak it, there is not one so 145 young and so villainous this day living. I speak but brotherly of him, but should I anatomize him to thee as 147 he is, I must blush and weep, and thou must look pale 148 and wonder.

CHARLES   I am heartily glad I came hither to you. If he come tomorrow, I'll give him his payment. If ever he go alone again, I'll never wrestle for prize more. And 152 so God keep Your Worship!

OLIVER   Farewell, good Charles.                    Exit [Charles]. Now will I stir this gamester. I hope I shall see an end of 155 him; for my soul, yet I know not why, hates nothing more than he. Yet he's gentle, never schooled and yet 157 learned, full of noble device, of all sorts enchantingly 158 beloved, and indeed so much in the heart of the world and especially of my own people, who best know him, 160 that I am altogether misprized. But it shall not be so 161

long; this wrestler shall clear all. Nothing remains but 162 that I kindle the boy thither, which now I'll go about. 163
                                                            *Exit.*

## 1.2

*Enter Rosalind and Celia.*

CELIA   I pray thee, Rosalind, sweet my coz, be merry.   1

ROSALIND   Dear Celia, I show more mirth than I am mistress of, and would you yet I were merrier? Unless you could teach me to forget a banished father, you must not learn me how to remember any extraordi- 5 nary pleasure.

CELIA   Herein I see thou lov'st me not with the full weight that I love thee. If my uncle, thy banished 8 father, had banished thy uncle, the Duke my father, so thou hadst been still with me, I could have taught 10 my love to take thy father for mine. So wouldst thou, 11 if the truth of thy love to me were so righteously tem- 12 pered as mine is to thee. 13

ROSALIND   Well, I will forget the condition of my estate 14 to rejoice in yours.

CELIA   You know my father hath no child but I, nor none is like to have. And truly, when he dies thou 17 shalt be his heir, for what he hath taken away from thy father perforce I will render thee again in affection. By 19 mine honor, I will, and when I break that oath, let me turn monster. Therefore, my sweet Rose, my dear Rose, be merry.

ROSALIND   From henceforth I will, coz, and devise sports. Let me see, what think you of falling in love?

CELIA   Marry, I prithee, do, to make sport withal. But 25 love no man in good earnest, nor no further in sport neither than with safety of a pure blush thou mayst in 27 honor come off again. 28

ROSALIND   What shall be our sport, then?

CELIA   Let us sit and mock the good huswife Fortune 30 from her wheel, that her gifts may henceforth be be- stowed equally.

ROSALIND   I would we could do so, for her benefits are mightily misplaced, and the bountiful blind woman 34 doth most mistake in her gifts to women.

CELIA   'Tis true, for those that she makes fair she scarce 36 makes honest, and those that she makes honest she 37 makes very ill-favoredly. 38

**162 clear all** solve everything.   **163 kindle . . . thither** inflame Orlando with desire to go to the wrestling match
**1.2. Location: Duke Frederick's court. A place suitable for wrestling.**
**1 sweet my coz** my sweet cousin   **5 learn** teach   **8 that** with which   **10 so** provided that   **10–11 I could . . . for mine** i.e., I would have been content to live here, loving your father as if he were my father also.   **11 So wouldst thou** i.e., If you truly loved me, you would do the same, i.e., love my father (Duke Frederick) as your father also   **12–13 righteously tempered** harmoniously composed   **14 condition of my estate** state of my fortunes   **17 like** likely   **19 perforce** by force   **25 sport** pastimes   **27 pure** (1) mere (2) innocent   **28 come off** retire, leave   **30 huswife** one who manages household affairs and operates the spinning wheel—here the wheel of Fortune, on which that capricious goddess arbitrarily lifts people up and throws them down. *Huswife* is used derogatorily here, with a suggestion of "hussy."
**34 bountiful blind woman** i.e., Fortune   **36 scarce** rarely   **37 honest** chaste   **38 ill-favoredly** ugly.

**120 a fall** a bout of wrestling.   **121 credit** reputation   **122 shall . . . well** (1) must exert himself very skillfully (2) will be lucky indeed.
**124 foil** defeat   **126 withal** with this   **127 stay . . . intendment** restrain him from his intent.   **brook** endure   **129 search** seeking
**133 underhand** unobtrusive, subtle   **135–6 envious emulator** malicious disparager   **136 parts** qualities   **137 contriver** plotter.
**natural** blood   **138 lief** willingly   **139–40 thou . . . to't** you'd better beware   **140–1 if he . . . on thee** if he fails to distinguish himself at your expense   **141 practice** plot   **145 not one** no person   **147 brotherly** as a brother should.   **anatomize** analyze   **147–8 as he is** as he truly is   **152 go alone** walk unassisted   **155 gamester** playboy, gamesome youth. (Said sardonically.)   **157 gentle** gentlemanly, gracious, noble-spirited   **158 noble device** lofty aspiration.   **sorts** classes of people.
**enchantingly** as if they were under his spell   **160 people** servants
**161 misprized** undervalued, scorned.

ROSALIND    Nay, now thou goest from Fortune's office to
Nature's. Fortune reigns in gifts of the world, not in   40
the lineaments of Nature.                                41

*Enter [Touchstone the] Clown.*

CELIA    No; when Nature hath made a fair creature, may
she not by Fortune fall into the fire? Though Nature   43
hath given us wit to flout at Fortune, hath not Fortune   44
sent in this fool to cut off the argument?

ROSALIND    Indeed, there is Fortune too hard for Nature,   46
when Fortune makes Nature's natural the cutter-off of   47
Nature's wit.                                            48

CELIA    Peradventure this is not Fortune's work neither   49
but Nature's, who perceiveth our natural wits too dull
to reason of such goddesses and hath sent this natural   51
for our whetstone; for always the dullness of the fool   52
is the whetstone of the wits.—How now, wit, whither   53
wander you?                                              54

TOUCHSTONE    Mistress, you must come away to your
father.

CELIA    Were you made the messenger?

TOUCHSTONE    No, by mine honor, but I was bid to
come for you.

ROSALIND    Where learned you that oath, Fool?

TOUCHSTONE    Of a certain knight that swore by his
honor they were good pancakes and swore by his   62
honor the mustard was naught. Now I'll stand to it the   63
pancakes were naught and the mustard was good,
and yet was not the knight forsworn.                     65

CELIA    How prove you that in the great heap of your
knowledge?

ROSALIND    Ay, marry, now unmuzzle your wisdom.

TOUCHSTONE    Stand you both forth now. Stroke your
chins, and swear by your beards that I am a knave.

CELIA    By our beards, if we had them, thou art.

TOUCHSTONE    By my knavery, if I had it, then I were;
but if you swear by that that is not, you are not
forsworn. No more was this knight, swearing by his
honor, for he never had any; or if he had, he had
sworn it away before ever he saw those pancakes or
that mustard.

CELIA    Prithee, who is't that thou mean'st?

TOUCHSTONE    One that old Frederick, your father,
loves.

CELIA    My father's love is enough to honor him enough.
Speak no more of him; you'll be whipped for taxation   81
one of these days.

TOUCHSTONE    The more pity that fools may not speak
wisely what wise men do foolishly.

CELIA    By my troth, thou sayest true; for since the little   85
wit that fools have was silenced, the little foolery that   86
wise men have makes a great show. Here comes
Monsieur Le Beau.

*Enter Le Beau.*

ROSALIND    With his mouth full of news.

CELIA    Which he will put on us as pigeons feed their   90
young.

ROSALIND    Then shall we be news-crammed.

CELIA    All the better; we shall be the more mar-   93
ketable.—*Bonjour*, Monsieur Le Beau. What's the   94
news?

LE BEAU    Fair princess, you have lost much good sport.

CELIA    Sport? Of what color?                           97

LE BEAU    What color, madam? How shall I answer you?

ROSALIND    As wit and fortune will.

TOUCHSTONE    Or as the Destinies decrees.

CELIA    Well said. That was laid on with a trowel.   101

TOUCHSTONE    Nay, if I keep not my rank—        102

ROSALIND    Thou loosest thy old smell.

LE BEAU    You amaze me, ladies. I would have told you   104
of good wrestling, which you have lost the sight of.

ROSALIND    Yet tell us the manner of the wrestling.

LE BEAU    I will tell you the beginning, and if it please
Your Ladyships you may see the end, for the best is yet   108
to do, and here, where you are, they are coming to   109
perform it.

CELIA    Well, the beginning, that is dead and buried.   111

LE BEAU    There comes an old man and his three sons—

CELIA    I could match this beginning with an old tale.   113

LE BEAU    Three proper young men, of excellent growth   114
and presence—

ROSALIND    With bills on their necks, "Be it known unto   116
all men by these presents."                              117

LE BEAU    The eldest of the three wrestled with Charles,
the Duke's wrestler, which Charles in a moment threw
him and broke three of his ribs, that there is little hope
of life in him. So he served the second, and so the   121
third. Yonder they lie, the poor old man their father
making such pitiful dole over them that all the beholders   123
take his part with weeping.

ROSALIND    Alas!

TOUCHSTONE    But what is the sport, monsieur, that the
ladies have lost?

LE BEAU    Why, this that I speak of.

**40 gifts of the world** e.g., riches and power   **41 the lineaments of
Nature** the features that Nature provides (like beauty or ugliness).
**41.1** *Touchstone* a stone used to test for gold and silver   **43 she** the
woman whom Nature has made beautiful   **44 flout** scoff   **46 there** in
that instance   **47–8 when . . . wit** i.e., when Fortune makes this natural
half-wit (Touchstone) the cutter-off of witty dialogue that our natural
gifts enable us to engage in. (A *natural* here means a born idiot; also in
line 51.)   **49 Peradventure** Perhaps   **51 to reason . . . goddesses** to
engage in debate about Reason and Nature   **52 whetstone** grinding
stone against which to sharpen things (in this case, wit)   **52–3 the
dullness . . . wits** i.e., the mindless things said by an idiot serve as
material on which to sharpen our wits.   **53–4 whither wander you**
(An allusion to the expression "wandering wits.")   **62 pancakes** fritters
(which might be made of meat and so require mustard)   **63 naught**
worthless.   **stand to it** maintain, argue   **65 forsworn** perjured.
**81 taxation** censure, slander

**85–6 since . . . silenced** (Perhaps refers specifically to the Bishops'
order of June 1599 banning satirical books.)   **90 put on** force
upon   **93–4 marketable** i.e., like animals that have been crammed
with food before being sent to market.   **97 color** kind.   **101 with a
trowel** i.e., thick.   **102 rank** i.e., status as a wit. (But Rosalind plays on
the sense of "stench.")   **104 amaze** bewilder   **108–9 yet to do** still to
come   **111 the beginning** tell us what has already occurred
**113 I could . . . tale** i.e, Many an old tale begins like that.   **114 proper**
handsome   **116 bills** proclamations   **117 these presents** the present
document. (Rosalind uses this legal phrase to pun on *presence* in line
115.)   **121 So** Similarly   **123 dole** lamentation

TOUCHSTONE   Thus men may grow wiser every day. It is the first time that ever I heard breaking of ribs was sport for ladies.

CELIA   Or I, I promise thee.                                    132

ROSALIND   But is there any else longs to see this broken music in his sides? Is there yet another dotes upon rib breaking?—Shall we see this wrestling, cousin?    133 / 134

LE BEAU   You must if you stay here, for here is the place appointed for the wrestling, and they are ready to perform it.

CELIA   Yonder, sure, they are coming. Let us now stay and see it.                                    140

*Flourish. Enter Duke [Frederick], Lords, Orlando, Charles, and attendants.*

DUKE FREDERICK   Come on. Since the youth will not be entreated, his own peril on his forwardness.    142

ROSALIND   [*to Le Beau*]   Is yonder the man?

LE BEAU   Even he, madam.

CELIA   Alas, he is too young! Yet he looks successfully.    145

DUKE FREDERICK   How now, daughter and cousin? Are you crept hither to see the wrestling?    146

ROSALIND   Ay, my liege, so please you give us leave.    148

DUKE FREDERICK   You will take little delight in it, I can tell you, there is such odds in the man. In pity of the challenger's youth I would fain dissuade him, but he will not be entreated. Speak to him, ladies; see if you can move him.    150 / 151

CELIA   Call him hither, good Monsieur Le Beau.

DUKE FREDERICK   Do so. I'll not be by. [*He steps aside.*]

LE BEAU   [*to Orlando*]   Monsieur the challenger, the princess calls for you.

ORLANDO   [*approaching the ladies*]   I attend them with all respect and duty.

ROSALIND   Young man, have you challenged Charles the wrestler?

ORLANDO   No, fair princess. He is the general challenger. I come but in, as others do, to try with him the strength of my youth.    162 / 163

CELIA   Young gentleman, your spirits are too bold for your years. You have seen cruel proof of this man's strength. If you saw yourself with your eyes or knew yourself with your judgment, the fear of your adventure would counsel you to a more equal enterprise. We pray you, for your own sake, to embrace your own safety and give over this attempt.    167 / 168 / 169 / 171

ROSALIND   Do, young sir. Your reputation shall not therefore be misprized. We will make it our suit to the Duke that the wrestling might not go forward.    173

ORLANDO   I beseech you, punish me not with your hard thoughts, wherein I confess me much guilty to deny so fair and excellent ladies anything. But let your fair eyes and gentle wishes go with me to my trial, wherein if I be foiled, there is but one shamed that was never gracious, if killed, but one dead that is willing to be so. I shall do my friends no wrong, for I have none to lament me; the world no injury, for in it I have nothing. Only in the world I fill up a place which may be better supplied when I have made it empty.    176 / 179 / 180 / 183

ROSALIND   The little strength that I have, I would it were with you.

CELIA   And mine, to eke out hers.

ROSALIND   Fare you well. Pray heaven I be deceived in you!    188 / 189

CELIA   Your heart's desires be with you!

CHARLES   Come, where is this young gallant that is so desirous to lie with his mother earth?

ORLANDO   Ready, sir, but his will hath in it a more modest working.    194

DUKE FREDERICK   You shall try but one fall.

CHARLES   No, I warrant Your Grace, you shall not entreat him to a second, that have so mightily persuaded him from a first.

ORLANDO   You mean to mock me after; you should not have mocked me before. But come your ways.    200

ROSALIND   Now Hercules be thy speed, young man!    201

CELIA   I would I were invisible, to catch the strong fellow by the leg.    [*Orlando and Charles*] *wrestle.*

ROSALIND   Oh, excellent young man!

CELIA   If I had a thunderbolt in mine eye, I can tell who should down.    *Shout. [Charles is thrown.]*    205 / 206

DUKE FREDERICK   No more, no more.

ORLANDO   Yes, I beseech Your Grace. I am not yet well breathed.    208 / 209

DUKE FREDERICK   How dost thou, Charles?

LE BEAU   He cannot speak, my lord.

DUKE FREDERICK   Bear him away.—What is thy name, young man?    [*Charles is borne out.*]

ORLANDO   Orlando, my liege, the youngest son of Sir Rowland de Boys.

DUKE FREDERICK
I would thou hadst been son to some man else.
The world esteemed thy father honorable,
But I did find him still mine enemy.
Thou shouldst have better pleased me with this deed
Hadst thou descended from another house.
But fare thee well; thou art a gallant youth.
I would thou hadst told me of another father.
*Exit Duke [with train, and others. Rosalind and Celia remain; Orlando stands apart from them.]*

132 **promise** assure   133 **any else** anyone else who   133–4 **broken music** literally, music arranged in parts for different instruments; here applied to the breaking of ribs   134 **another who** young man who   140.1 *Flourish* a trumpet fanfare announcing the entrance of an important person.   142 **entreated ... forwardness** i.e., entreated to desist, let the risk be blamed upon his own rashness.   145 **successfully** i.e., as if he would be successful.   146 **cousin** i.e., niece.   148 **so ... leave** if you will permit us.   150 **there ... man** Charles is such an odds-on favorite to win.   151 **fain** willingly   162 **the general challenger** the one who is ready to take on all comers. (Orlando is the challenger in a more limited sense.)   167–8 **If ... judgment** If you saw yourself objectively   169 **equal** i.e., where the odds are more equal   171 **give over** give up   173 **misprized** despised, undervalued.

176 **wherein** though.   **to deny** in denying   179 **foiled** overthrown   180 **gracious** looked upon with favor   183 **Only ... I** In the world I merely   188–9 **deceived in you** i.e., mistaken in fearing you will lose.   194 **modest working** decorous endeavor (than to lie with one's mother earth. For a man to lie with his mother is to commit incest.)   200 **come your ways** come on.   201 **Hercules be thy speed** may Hercules help you   205 **If ... eye** i.e., If I were Zeus or Jupiter   206 **down** fall.   208–9 **well breathed** warmed up.

CELIA [*to Rosalind*]
  Were I my father, coz, would I do this?
ORLANDO [*to no one in particular*]
  I am more proud to be Sir Rowland's son,
  His youngest son, and would not change that calling 223
  To be adopted heir to Frederick.
ROSALIND [*to Celia*]
  My father loved Sir Rowland as his soul,
  And all the world was of my father's mind.
  Had I before known this young man his son,
  I should have given him tears unto entreaties 228
  Ere he should thus have ventured.
CELIA [*to Rosalind*]                    Gentle cousin,
  Let us go thank him and encourage him.
  My father's rough and envious disposition
  Sticks me at heart.—Sir, you have well deserved. 232
  If you do keep your promises in love
  But justly as you have exceeded all promise, 234
  Your mistress shall be happy.
ROSALIND [*giving him a chain from her neck*]  Gentleman, 235
  Wear this for me, one out of suits with fortune, 236
  That could give more, but that her hand lacks means. 237
  [*To Celia*] Shall we go, coz?
CELIA                    Ay.—Fare you well, fair gentleman.
                    [*Rosalind and Celia start to leave.*]
ORLANDO [*aside*]
  Can I not say, "I thank you"? My better parts
  Are all thrown down, and that which here stands up
  Is but a quintain, a mere lifeless block. 241
ROSALIND [*to Celia*]
  He calls us back. My pride fell with my fortunes;
  I'll ask him what he would.—Did you call, sir? 243
  Sir, you have wrestled well and overthrown
  More than your enemies.
CELIA  Will you go, coz?
ROSALIND  Have with you.—Fare you well. 247
                    *Exit [with Celia].*
ORLANDO
  What passion hangs these weights upon my tongue?
  I cannot speak to her, yet she urged conference. 249
  O poor Orlando, thou art overthrown!
  Or Charles or something weaker masters thee. 251

    *Enter Le Beau.*

LE BEAU
  Good sir, I do in friendship counsel you
  To leave this place. Albeit you have deserved
  High commendation, true applause, and love,
  Yet such is now the Duke's condition 255
  That he misconsters all that you have done. 256
  The Duke is humorous. What he is indeed 257
  More suits you to conceive than I to speak of. 258

ORLANDO
  I thank you, sir. And, pray you, tell me this:
  Which of the two was daughter of the Duke
  That here was at the wrestling?
LE BEAU
  Neither his daughter, if we judge by manners,
  But yet indeed the taller is his daughter. 263
  The other is daughter to the banished Duke,
  And here detained by her usurping uncle
  To keep his daughter company, whose loves
  Are dearer than the natural bond of sisters.
  But I can tell you that of late this Duke
  Hath ta'en displeasure gainst his gentle niece,
  Grounded upon no other argument 270
  But that the people praise her for her virtues
  And pity her for her good father's sake;
  And, on my life, his malice gainst the lady 273
  Will suddenly break forth. Sir, fare you well.
  Hereafter, in a better world than this, 275
  I shall desire more love and knowledge of you.
ORLANDO
  I rest much bounden to you. Fare you well. 277
                    [*Exit Le Beau.*]
  Thus must I from the smoke into the smother, 278
  From tyrant Duke unto a tyrant brother. 279
  But heavenly Rosalind!                    *Exit.*

❖

## 1.3

    *Enter Celia and Rosalind.*

CELIA  Why, cousin, why, Rosalind! Cupid have mercy!
  Not a word?
ROSALIND  Not one to throw at a dog.
CELIA  No, thy words are too precious to be cast away
  upon curs. Throw some of them at me. Come, lame 5
  me with reasons. 6
ROSALIND  Then there were two cousins laid up, when
  the one should be lamed with reasons and the other
  mad without any.
CELIA  But is all this for your father?
ROSALIND  No, some of it is for my child's father. Oh, 11
  how full of briers is this working-day world!
CELIA  They are but burrs, cousin, thrown upon thee in 13
  holiday foolery. If we walk not in the trodden paths, 14
  our very petticoats will catch them. 15
ROSALIND  I could shake them off my coat. These burrs
  are in my heart.

223 change that calling exchange that name and vocation 228 unto in addition to 232 Sticks stabs 234 But justly exactly 235 s.d. chain (See 3.2.178, where Celia speaks of a chain given to Orlando by Rosalind.) 236 out . . . fortune (1) whose petitions to Fortune are rejected (2) not wearing the livery of Fortune, not in her service 237 could would 241 quintain wooden figure used as a target in tilting 243 would wants. 247 Have with you I'll go with you. 249 urged conference invited conversation. 251 Or Either 255 condition disposition 256 misconsters misconstrues 257 humorous capricious. 258 conceive imagine, understand

263 taller (Perhaps a textual error for *smaller* or *lesser*, or else an inconsistency on Shakespeare's part; at 1.3.113, Rosalind is shown to be the taller.) 270 argument reason 273 on my life as I value my life. (A mild oath.) 275 in . . . world in better times 277 bounden indebted 278 from . . . smother i.e., out of the frying pan into the fire. (*Smother* means "a dense suffocating smoke.") 279 a tyrant brother i.e., Oliver (not Duke Senior).
1.3. Location: Duke Frederick's court.
5–6 lame . . . reasons throw some explanations (for your silence) at me. 11 my child's father one who might father my children, i.e., Orlando. 13–15 They . . . them i.e., You are making too much of minor difficulties; one catches such burrs on one's clothes constantly if one strays from the path of propriety (by falling into the folly of love). (*Holiday* and *working-day*, lines 12 and 14, form a crucial comic binary in this play.)

**CELIA**  Hem them away. 18

**ROSALIND**  I would try, if I could cry "hem" and have 19
him.

**CELIA**  Come, come, wrestle with thy affections.

**ROSALIND**  Oh, they take the part of a better wrestler than
myself.

**CELIA**  Oh, a good wish upon you! You will try in time, 24
in despite of a fall. But, turning these jests out of 25
service, let us talk in good earnest. Is it possible, on 26
such a sudden, you should fall into so strong a liking
with old Sir Rowland's youngest son?

**ROSALIND**  The Duke my father loved his father dearly.

**CELIA**  Doth it therefore ensue that you should love his
son dearly? By this kind of chase, I should hate him, 31
for my father hated his father dearly; yet I hate not 32
Orlando.

**ROSALIND**  No, faith, hate him not, for my sake. 34

**CELIA**  Why should I not? Doth he not deserve well? 35

*Enter Duke [Frederick], with Lords.*

**ROSALIND**  Let me love him for that, and do you love
him because I do.—Look, here comes the Duke.

**CELIA**  With his eyes full of anger.

**DUKE FREDERICK** [*to Rosalind*]
Mistress, dispatch you with your safest haste
And get you from our court.

**ROSALIND**           Me, uncle?

**DUKE FREDERICK**         You, cousin. 40
Within these ten days if that thou be'st found
So near our public court as twenty miles,
Thou diest for it.

**ROSALIND**        I do beseech Your Grace
Let me the knowledge of my fault bear with me.
If with myself I hold intelligence 45
Or have acquaintance with mine own desires,
If that I do not dream or be not frantic— 47
As I do trust I am not—then, dear uncle,
Never so much as in a thought unborn
Did I offend Your Highness.

**DUKE FREDERICK**       Thus do all traitors.
If their purgation did consist in words, 51
They are as innocent as grace itself.
Let it suffice thee that I trust thee not.

**ROSALIND**
Yet your mistrust cannot make me a traitor.
Tell me whereon the likelihood depends.

**DUKE FREDERICK**
Thou art thy father's daughter. There's enough. 56

**ROSALIND**
So was I when Your Highness took his dukedom;
So was I when Your Highness banished him.
Treason is not inherited, my lord;
Or, if we did derive it from our friends, 60
What's that to me? My father was no traitor.
Then, good my liege, mistake me not so much
To think my poverty is treacherous. 63

**CELIA**  Dear sovereign, hear me speak.

**DUKE FREDERICK**
Ay, Celia, we stayed her for your sake, 65
Else had she with her father ranged along. 66

**CELIA**
I did not then entreat to have her stay;
It was your pleasure and your own remorse. 68
I was too young that time to value her, 69
But now I know her. If she be a traitor,
Why, so am I. We still have slept together, 71
Rose at an instant, learned, played, eat together, 72
And wheresoe'er we went, like Juno's swans 73
Still we went coupled and inseparable.

**DUKE FREDERICK**
She is too subtle for thee; and her smoothness,
Her very silence, and her patience
Speak to the people, and they pity her.
Thou art a fool. She robs thee of thy name, 78
And thou wilt show more bright and seem more
virtuous
When she is gone. Then open not thy lips.
Firm and irrevocable is my doom 81
Which I have passed upon her; she is banished.

**CELIA**
Pronounce that sentence then on me, my liege!
I cannot live out of her company.

**DUKE FREDERICK**
You are a fool.—You, niece, provide yourself. 85
If you outstay the time, upon mine honor,
And in the greatness of my word, you die. 87

           *Exit Duke [with Lords].*

**CELIA**
O my poor Rosalind, whither wilt thou go?
Wilt thou change fathers? I will give thee mine. 89
I charge thee, be not thou more grieved than I am.

**ROSALIND**
I have more cause.

**CELIA**         Thou hast not, cousin.
Prithee, be cheerful. Know'st thou not the Duke
Hath banished me, his daughter?

**ROSALIND**         That he hath not.

---

**18 Hem** (1) Tuck (2) Cough (since you say they are in the chest). A *bur* can be something that sticks in the throat. **19 cry "hem"** attract Orlando's attention by coughing. (But with the suggestion too of a bawd's warning cry to the lovers whose secrecy is being guarded. With a pun on *"hem"* and *him*.) **24–5 Oh . . . fall** i.e., Good luck to you; you'll undertake to wrestle with Orlando sooner or later, despite the danger of your being thrown down. (With sexual suggestion.) **25–6 turning . . . service** i.e., dismissing this banter **31 By . . . chase** To pursue this line of reasoning **32 dearly** intensely **34 faith** in truth **35 Why . . . not?** Why shouldn't I hate him, i.e., love him? (Celia has just argued by chop-logic, in lines 30-2, that to love is to hate and vice versa.) **40 cousin** i.e., niece. **45 if . . . intelligence** If I understand my own feelings **47 If that** if. **frantic** insane **51 purgation** clearing of guilt. (A medical, legal, and theological metaphor.)

**56 There's enough** That's reason enough. **60 friends** relatives **63 To think** as to think **65 stayed** kept **66 ranged** roamed **68 remorse** compassion. **69 that time** at that time **71 still** continually **72 at an instant** at the same time. **eat** ate **73 Juno's swans** i.e., yoked together. (Though according to Ovid it was Venus, not Juno, who used swans to draw her chariot.) **78 name** reputation **81 doom** sentence **85 provide yourself** get ready. **87 in . . . word** upon my authority as Duke **89 change** exchange

**CELIA**
No, hath not? Rosalind lacks then the love
Which teacheth thee that thou and I am one.
Shall we be sundered? Shall we part, sweet girl?
No, let my father seek another heir.
Therefore devise with me how we may fly,
Whither to go, and what to bear with us.
And do not seek to take your change upon you,   100
To bear your griefs yourself and leave me out;
For, by this heaven, now at our sorrows pale,   102
Say what thou canst, I'll go along with thee.
**ROSALIND**   Why, whither shall we go?
**CELIA**
To seek my uncle in the Forest of Arden.
**ROSALIND**
Alas, what danger will it be to us,
Maids as we are, to travel forth so far!
Beauty provoketh thieves sooner than gold.
**CELIA**
I'll put myself in poor and mean attire   109
And with a kind of umber smirch my face;   110
The like do you. So shall we pass along
And never stir assailants.
**ROSALIND**                    Were it not better,
Because that I am more than common tall,
That I did suit me all points like a man?   114
A gallant curtal ax upon my thigh,   115
A boar spear in my hand, and—in my heart
Lie there what hidden woman's fear there will—
We'll have a swashing and a martial outside,   118
As many other mannish cowards have
That do outface it with their semblances.   120
**CELIA**
What shall I call thee when thou art a man?
**ROSALIND**
I'll have no worse a name than Jove's own page,
And therefore look you call me Ganymede.   123
But what will you be called?
**CELIA**
Something that hath a reference to my state:
No longer Celia, but Aliena.   126
**ROSALIND**
But, cousin, what if we assayed to steal   127
The clownish fool out of your father's court?
Would he not be a comfort to our travel?   129
**CELIA**
He'll go along o'er the wide world with me.
Leave me alone to woo him. Let's away,   131
And get our jewels and our wealth together,
Devise the fittest time and safest way
To hide us from pursuit that will be made

After my flight. Now go we in content   135
To liberty, and not to banishment.   *Exeunt.*

❖

# 2.1

*Enter Duke Senior, Amiens, and two or three*
*Lords, [dressed] like foresters.*

**DUKE SENIOR**
Now, my co-mates and brothers in exile,
Hath not old custom made this life more sweet   2
Than that of painted pomp? Are not these woods
More free from peril than the envious court?
Here feel we not the penalty of Adam,   5
The seasons' difference, as the icy fang   6
And churlish chiding of the winter's wind,
Which when it bites and blows upon my body
Even till I shrink with cold, I smile and say
"This is no flattery; these are counselors
That feelingly persuade me what I am."
Sweet are the uses of adversity,
Which, like the toad, ugly and venomous,   13
Wears yet a precious jewel in his head;   14
And this our life, exempt from public haunt,   15
Finds tongues in trees, books in the running brooks,
Sermons in stones, and good in everything.
**AMIENS**
I would not change it. Happy is Your Grace
That can translate the stubbornness of fortune
Into so quiet and so sweet a style.
**DUKE SENIOR**
Come, shall we go and kill us venison?
And yet it irks me the poor dappled fools,   22
Being native burghers of this desert city,   23
Should in their own confines with forkèd heads   24
Have their round haunches gored.   25
**FIRST LORD**                    Indeed, my lord,
The melancholy Jaques grieves at that,
And in that kind swears you do more usurp   27
Than doth your brother that hath banished you.
Today my lord of Amiens and myself
Did steal behind him as he lay along   30
Under an oak whose antique root peeps out   31
Upon the brook that brawls along this wood,   32
To the which place a poor sequestered stag   33
That from the hunter's aim had ta'en a hurt
Did come to languish. And indeed, my lord,
The wretched animal heaved forth such groans

---

100 **change** change of fortune   102 **pale** (Heaven is pale in sympathy with their plight.)   109 **mean** lowly   110 **umber** yellow-brown pigment (to give a tanned appearance appropriate to countrywomen) 114 **suit me all points** outfit myself in all ways   115 **curtal ax** broad cutting sword   118 **swashing** swaggering   120 **outface . . . semblances** bluff their way through with mere appearances.   123 **Ganymede** Jupiter's cupbearer. (The name used for disguise also in Lodge's *Rosalynde*.)   126 **Aliena** the estranged one.   127 **assayed** undertook   129 **travel** (1) movement from place to place (2) labor, hardship (*travail*).   131 **Leave . . . him** Leave it to me to persuade him.

135 **content** contentment
**2.1. Location: The Forest of Arden.**
2 **old custom** long experience   5–6 **feel . . . difference** we don't mind the consequences of Adam's original sin—the hardship of the seasons. (*Not* is often emended to *but*.)   6 **as** such as   13–14 **like . . . head** (Alludes to the widespread belief that the toad was a poisonous creature but with a jewel embedded in its head that worked as an antidote.)   15 **exempt** cut off.   **haunt** society   22 **fools** innocents   23 **burghers** citizens.   **desert city** uninhabited place 24 **forkèd heads** barbed hunting arrows, but also suggesting antlers 25 **round** plump   27 **kind** regard   30 **along** stretched out 31 **antique** (1) ancient or (2) *antic*, "gnarled"   32 **brawls** noisily flows   33 **sequestered** separated (from the herd)

That their discharge did stretch his leathern coat
Almost to bursting, and the big round tears
Coursed one another down his innocent nose    39
In piteous chase. And thus the hairy fool,
Much markèd of the melancholy Jaques,    41
Stood on th'extremest verge of the swift brook,    42
Augmenting it with tears.

DUKE SENIOR                    But what said Jaques?
Did he not moralize this spectacle?    44

FIRST LORD
Oh, yes, into a thousand similes.
First, for his weeping into the needless stream:    46
"Poor deer," quoth he, "thou mak'st a testament    47
As worldings do, giving thy sum of more    48
To that which had too much." Then, being there alone,    49
Left and abandoned of his velvet friends:    50
"'Tis right," quoth he, "thus misery doth part    51
The flux of company." Anon a careless herd,    52
Full of the pasture, jumps along by him    53
And never stays to greet him. "Ay," quoth Jaques,
"Sweep on, you fat and greasy citizens;    55
'Tis just the fashion. Wherefore do you look    56
Upon that poor and broken bankrupt there?"    57
Thus most invectively he pierceth through    58
The body of the country, city, court,
Yea, and of this our life, swearing that we
Are mere usurpers, tyrants, and what's worse,    61
To fright the animals and to kill them up    62
In their assigned and native dwelling place.

DUKE SENIOR
And did you leave him in this contemplation?

SECOND LORD
We did, my lord, weeping and commenting
Upon the sobbing deer.

DUKE SENIOR                    Show me the place.
I love to cope him in these sullen fits,    67
For then he's full of matter.    68

FIRST LORD    I'll bring you to him straight.    *Exeunt.*    69

❖

## 2.2

*Enter Duke [Frederick], with Lords.*

DUKE FREDERICK
Can it be possible that no man saw them?
It cannot be. Some villains of my court
Are of consent and sufferance in this.    3

FIRST LORD
I cannot hear of any that did see her.    4
The ladies, her attendants of her chamber,
Saw her abed, and in the morning early
They found the bed untreasured of their mistress.

SECOND LORD
My lord, the roynish clown, at whom so oft    8
Your Grace was wont to laugh, is also missing.
Hisperia, the princess' gentlewoman,
Confesses that she secretly o'erheard
Your daughter and her cousin much commend
The parts and graces of the wrestler    13
That did but lately foil the sinewy Charles,    14
And she believes wherever they are gone
That youth is surely in their company.

DUKE FREDERICK
Send to his brother. Fetch that gallant hither.    17
If he be absent, bring his brother to me;    18
I'll make him find him. Do this suddenly,    19
And let not search and inquisition quail    20
To bring again these foolish runaways.    *Exeunt.*    21

❖

## 2.3

*Enter Orlando and Adam, [meeting].*

ORLANDO    Who's there?

ADAM
What, my young master? Oh, my gentle master,
Oh, my sweet master, oh, you memory    3
Of old Sir Rowland! Why, what make you here?    4
Why are you virtuous? Why do people love you?
And wherefore are you gentle, strong, and valiant?
Why would you be so fond to overcome    7
The bonny prizer of the humorous Duke?    8
Your praise is come too swiftly home before you.    9
Know you not, master, to some kind of men
Their graces serve them but as enemies?    11
No more do yours. Your virtues, gentle master,    12
Are sanctified and holy traitors to you.

39 **Coursed** chased    41 **markèd of** observed by    42 **th'extremest verge** the very edge    44 **moralize** draw out the hidden meaning of    46 **needless** having no need of more water. (Weeping deer are common in literature.)    47 **testament** will    48 **worldings** worldly men    48–9 **giving . . . much** bequeathing your superabundance of wealth to heirs who are already too wealthy.    49 **being** the deer being    50 **of** by.    **velvet** i.e., prosperous. (Velvet was an appropriately rich dress for a courtier; the term also alludes here to the deers' velvety coat or to the covering of their antlers during rapid growth.)    51 **'Tis right** i.e., That's how it goes    51–2 **thus . . . company** thus the miserable are separated from and forgotten by the herd.    52 **careless** (1) carefree (2) uncaring    53 **the pasture** i.e., good food    55 **greasy** fat and unctuously prosperous, like rich burghers or *citizens*    56–7 **Wherefore . . . there?** Why do you even bother to glance at that poor physically shattered deer there? (*Broken* also hints at a financial ruin appropriate to *citizens* in line 55.)    58 **invectively** in the most bitter terms    61 **what's worse** whatever is worse than these    62 **up** off, utterly    67 **cope** encounter    68 **matter** substance, morally edifying discourse.    69 **straight** at once.

**2.2. Location:** Duke Frederick's court.
3 **Are . . . this** have conspired in and permitted this.    4 **her** Celia.
8 **roynish** scurvy, rascally. (Literally, covered with scale or scurf.)
13 **parts** good qualities    14 **foil** defeat    17 **Send . . . hither** i.e., Send word to Oliver to bring Orlando here.    18 **he** i.e., Orlando.    **his brother** i.e., Oliver. (Or possibly referring to Jaques de Boys, the other brother.)    19 **suddenly** speedily    20 **inquisition quail** investigation falter and fail    21 **again** back
**2.3. Location:** Before Oliver's house.
3 **memory** likeness, reminder    4 **what make you** what are you doing    7 **fond to** foolish as to    8 **bonny prizer** sturdy prizefighter.    **humorous** temperamental    9 **Your . . . you** i.e., The praise you won at wrestling is turning out to be a threat to you, since it has come all too quickly to the ear of the envious Oliver.    11 **graces** best qualities.
12 **No . . . yours** Your fine qualities serve you no better than that.

Oh, what a world is this, when what is comely
Envenoms him that bears it!

ORLANDO
Why, what's the matter?

ADAM                                    O unhappy youth,
Come not within these doors! Within this roof
The enemy of all your graces lives.
Your brother—no, no brother; yet the son—
Yet not the son, I will not call him son
Of him I was about to call his father—
Hath heard your praises, and this night he means    22
To burn the lodging where you use to lie    23
And you within it. If he fail of that,
He will have other means to cut you off.
I overheard him and his practices.    26
This is no place, this house is but a butchery.    27
Abhor it, fear it, do not enter it.

ORLANDO
Why, whither, Adam, wouldst thou have me go?

ADAM
No matter whither, so you come not here.    30

ORLANDO
What, wouldst thou have me go and beg my food?
Or with a base and boist'rous sword enforce    32
A thievish living on the common road?
This I must do or know not what to do;
Yet this I will not do, do how I can.
I rather will subject me to the malice
Of a diverted blood and bloody brother.    37

ADAM
But do not so. I have five hundred crowns,
The thrifty hire I saved under your father,    39
Which I did store to be my foster nurse
When service should in my old limbs lie lame    41
And unregarded age in corners thrown.    42
Take that, and He that doth the ravens feed,    43
Yea, providently caters for the sparrow,    44
Be comfort to my age! Here is the gold; [offering gold]
All this I give you. Let me be your servant.
Though I look old, yet I am strong and lusty,    47
For in my youth I never did apply
Hot and rebellious liquors in my blood,
Nor did not with unbashful forehead woo
The means of weakness and debility;    50
Therefore my age is as a lusty winter,    51
Frosty but kindly. Let me go with you.
I'll do the service of a younger man
In all your business and necessities.    53

ORLANDO
Oh, good old man, how well in thee appears
The constant service of the antique world,    57
When service sweat for duty, not for meed!    58
Thou art not for the fashion of these times,
Where none will sweat but for promotion,
And having that do choke their service up    61
Even with the having. It is not so with thee.    62
But, poor old man, thou prun'st a rotten tree,
That cannot so much as a blossom yield
In lieu of all thy pains and husbandry.    65
But come thy ways. We'll go along together,
And ere we have thy youthful wages spent,
We'll light upon some settled low content.    68

ADAM
Master, go on, and I will follow thee
To the last gasp, with truth and loyalty.
From seventeen years till now almost fourscore    71
Here livèd I, but now live here no more.
At seventeen years many their fortunes seek,
But at fourscore it is too late a week;    74
Yet fortune cannot recompense me better
Than to die well and not my master's debtor.    76

*Exeunt.*

❖

## 2.4

*Enter Rosalind for Ganymede, Celia for Aliena,
and Clown, alias Touchstone.*

ROSALIND    Oh, Jupiter, how weary are my spirits!
TOUCHSTONE    I care not for my spirits, if my legs were
not weary.
ROSALIND    I could find in my heart to disgrace my man's
apparel and to cry like a woman; but I must comfort    5
the weaker vessel, as doublet and hose ought to show    6
itself courageous to petticoat. Therefore courage, good    7
Aliena!
CELIA    I pray you, bear with me. I cannot go no further.
TOUCHSTONE    For my part, I had rather bear with you
than bear you; yet I should bear no cross if I did bear    11
you, for I think you have no money in your purse.
ROSALIND    Well, this is the Forest of Arden.
TOUCHSTONE    Ay, now am I in Arden; the more fool I.
When I was at home I was in a better place, but
travelers must be content.

*Enter Corin and Silvius.*

22 **your praises** people's praise of you    23 **use** are accustomed
26 **practices** plots.    27 **place** place for you    30 **so** provided that
32 **boist'rous** rough    37 **diverted blood** kinship diverted from the
natural source    39 **thrifty . . . saved** wages I thriftily saved    41 **lie
lame** i.e., be performed only lamely    42 **And . . . thrown** and when I
will be neglected and thrown aside because of my old age.    43–4 **and
He . . . sparrow** i.e., and may God, who guards over all His creatures
(see Luke 12:6, 22-4, Psalms 147:9, etc.)    47 **lusty** vigorous    50–1 **Nor
. . . debility** nor did I with shameless countenance chase after pleasures that would have weakened and disabled me    53 **Frosty** i.e.,
white-haired

57 **constant** faithful.    **antique** ancient (as in the Golden Age)
58 **sweat** sweated.    **meed** reward.    61–2 **do choke . . . having** i.e.,
cease serving once they have gained promotion.    65 **lieu of** return
for.    **husbandry** careful management.    68 **low content** lowly contented state.    71 **fourscore** eighty    74 **too . . . week** i.e., too late in life
76 **not . . . debtor** i.e., not indebted to my master.
2.4 **Location: The Forest of Arden.**
0.1. *for* i.e., disguised as    5–6 **comfort the weaker vessel** (The First
Epistle of Peter 3:7, bids husbands give honor to their wives "as unto
the weaker vessel.")    6 **doublet and hose** close-fitting jacket and
breeches; typical male attire    7 **petticoat** i.e., women.    11 **cross** (1)
burden (2) coin having on it a figure of a cross

ROSALIND    Ay, be so, good Touchstone.—Look you
who comes here, a young man and an old in solemn
talk.                                    [*They stand aside and listen.*]

CORIN
That is the way to make her scorn you still.

SILVIUS
Oh, Corin, that thou knew'st how I do love her!

CORIN
I partly guess, for I have loved ere now.

SILVIUS
No, Corin, being old, thou canst not guess,
Though in thy youth thou wast as true a lover
As ever sighed upon a midnight pillow.
But if thy love were ever like to mine—
As sure I think did never man love so—
How many actions most ridiculous
Hast thou been drawn to by thy fantasy?              29

CORIN
Into a thousand that I have forgotten.

SILVIUS
Oh, thou didst then never love so heartily!
If thou remember'st not the slightest folly
That ever love did make thee run into,
Thou hast not loved.
Or if thou hast not sat as I do now,
Wearing thy hearer in thy mistress' praise,          36
Thou hast not loved.
Or if thou hast not broke from company
Abruptly, as my passion now makes me,
Thou has not loved.
O Phoebe, Phoebe, Phoebe!                      *Exit.*

ROSALIND
Alas, poor shepherd! Searching of thy wound,        42
I have by hard adventure found mine own.            43

TOUCHSTONE    And I mine. I remember, when I was in
love I broke my sword upon a stone and bid him take  45
that for coming a-night to Jane Smile; and I remember 46
the kissing of her batler and the cow's dugs that her 47
pretty chapped hands had milked; and I remember     48
the wooing of a peascod instead of her, from whom I  49
took two cods and, giving her them again, said with  50
weeping tears, "Wear these for my sake." We that are 51
true lovers run into strange capers; but as all is mortal 52
in nature, so is all nature in love mortal in folly.   53

ROSALIND    Thou speak'st wiser than thou art ware of.  54

TOUCHSTONE    Nay, I shall ne'er be ware of mine own  55
wit till I break my shins against it.                56

ROSALIND
Jove, Jove! This shepherd's passion
Is much upon my fashion.                        58

TOUCHSTONE
And mine, but it grows something stale with me.     59

CELIA
I pray you, one of you question yond man
If he for gold will give us any food.
I faint almost to death.

TOUCHSTONE [*to Corin*]    Holla: you, clown!        62

ROSALIND
Peace, Fool! He's not thy kinsman.

CORIN                                  Who calls?

TOUCHSTONE
Your betters, sir.

CORIN                        Else are they very wretched.  64

ROSALIND
Peace, I say.—Good even to you, friend.             65

CORIN
And to you, gentle sir, and to you all.

ROSALIND
I prithee, shepherd, if that love or gold            67
Can in this desert place buy entertainment,          68
Bring us where we may rest ourselves and feed.
Here's a young maid with travel much oppressed,
And faints for succor.

CORIN                     Fair sir, I pity her          71
And wish, for her sake more than for mine own,
My fortunes were more able to relieve her;
But I am shepherd to another man
And do not shear the fleeces that I graze.           75
My master is of churlish disposition                 76
And little recks to find the way to heaven           77
By doing deeds of hospitality.
Besides, his cote, his flocks, and bounds of feed    79
Are now on sale, and at our sheepcote now,           80
By reason of his absence, there is nothing
That you will feed on. But what is, come see,        82
And in my voice most welcome shall you be.           83

ROSALIND
What is he that shall buy his flock and pasture?     84

CORIN
That young swain that you saw here but erewhile,     85
That little cares for buying anything.

ROSALIND
I pray thee, if it stand with honesty,               87
Buy thou the cottage, pasture, and the flock,
And thou shalt have to pay for it of us.             89

---

**29 fantasy** love imaginings.   **36 Wearing** wearing out.   **in . . . praise** in praise of the young woman you love. (*Mistress* here does not convey the modern meaning of "unmarried sexual partner"; Phoebe is the woman that Silvius serves and adores, entirely without sexual reward.)   **42 Searching of** Probing   **43 hard adventure** painful experience   **45–6 I broke . . . Smile** (In his parody of a distraught lover, Touchstone imagines himself attacking a stone as if it were his rival for a country maiden named Jane Smile. *A-night* means "by night.")   **47 batler** club for beating clothes in process of washing.   **dugs** udder   **48–51 and I . . . sake** (Touchstone absurdly imagines himself courting a pea plant as though it were Jane Smile and exchanging pea pods with her by way of love tokens.)   **52 mortal** subject to death   **53 mortal** typically human, frail   **54 ware** aware   **55–6 Nay . . . against it** (Touchstone, as a professional fool, laughs at the idea of stumbling on or discovering his own capacity for saying something wise. His use of *ware* plays on [1] aware [2] wary.)

**58 much upon** very similar to   **59 something** somewhat   **62 clown** yokel. (But Rosalind then alludes to the word as it applies to Touchstone as a court fool or clown.)   **64 Else . . . wretched** i.e., If the people you mean aren't at least somewhat better off than myself, who am a poor shepherd to a churlish master, they are poor indeed.   **65 even** evening, i.e., afternoon   **67 if that** if   **68 desert** uninhabited.   **entertainment** hospitality, provision   **71 for succor** for lack of food.   **75 do . . . graze** i.e., do not enjoy the landowner's profits in wool; I merely tend to the sheep.   **76 churlish** miserly   **77 recks** reckons   **79 cote** cottage.   **bounds of feed** range of pasture   **80 sheepcote** pen for sheep (here probably part of a cottage)   **82 That . . . feed on** suitable for your refined tastes.   **83 in my voice** insofar as I have authority to speak   **84 What** Who   **85 but erewhile** just now   **87 stand** be consistent   **89 have to pay** have the money

CELIA
>     And we will mend thy wages. I like this place          90
>     And willingly could waste my time in it.               91

CORIN
>     Assuredly the thing is to be sold.
>     Go with me. If you like upon report
>     The soil, the profit, and this kind of life,
>     I will your very faithful feeder be                     95
>     And buy it with your gold right suddenly.   *Exeunt.*   96

❖

## 2.5

*Enter Amiens, Jaques, and others. [A table is set out.]*

*Song.*

AMIENS [*sings*]
>         Under the greenwood tree
>         Who loves to lie with me,                            2
>         And turn his merry note                              3
>         Unto the sweet bird's throat,                        4
>       Come hither, come hither, come hither.
>         Here shall he see
>         No enemy
>       But winter and rough weather.

JAQUES   More, more, I prithee, more.
AMIENS   It will make you melancholy, Monsieur Jaques.
JAQUES   I thank it. More, I prithee, more. I can suck melancholy out of a song as a weasel sucks eggs. More, I prithee, more.
AMIENS   My voice is ragged. I know I cannot please you.   14
JAQUES   I do not desire you to please me, I do desire you to sing. Come, more, another stanzo. Call you   16 'em "stanzos"?
AMIENS   What you will, Monsieur Jaques.
JAQUES   Nay, I care not for their names; they owe me   19 nothing. Will you sing?   20
AMIENS   More at your request than to please myself.
JAQUES   Well then, if ever I thank any man, I'll thank you; but that they call "compliment" is like th'en-counter   23 of two dog-apes, and when a man thanks me   24 heartily, methinks I have given him a penny and he renders me the beggarly thanks. Come, sing; and   26 you that will not, hold your tongues.
AMIENS   Well, I'll end the song.—Sirs, cover the while;   28 the Duke will drink under this tree.—He hath been all this day to look you.   [*Food and drink are set out.*]   30

JAQUES   And I have been all this day to avoid him. He is too disputable for my company. I think of as many   32 matters as he, but I give heaven thanks and make no boast of them. Come, warble, come.

*Song.*

AMIENS [*sings*]
>         Who doth ambition shun
>         And loves to live i'th' sun,                         36
>         Seeking the food he eats                             37
>         And pleased with what he gets,
>                              *All together here.*
>       Come hither, come hither, come hither.
>         Here shall he see
>         No enemy
>       But winter and rough weather.

JAQUES   I'll give you a verse to this note that I made   43 yesterday in despite of my invention.   44
AMIENS   And I'll sing it.
JAQUES   Thus it goes:

>         If it do come to pass
>         That any man turn ass,
>         Leaving his wealth and ease,
>         A stubborn will to please,
>       Ducdame, ducdame, ducdame.   51
>         Here shall he see
>         Gross fools as he,
>       An if he will come to me.

AMIENS   What's that "ducdame"?
JAQUES   'Tis a Greek invocation, to call fools into a circle. I'll go sleep, if I can; if I cannot, I'll rail against all the firstborn of Egypt.   58
AMIENS   And I'll go seek the Duke. His banquet is pre-   59 pared.   *Exeunt [separately].*

❖

## 2.6

*Enter Orlando and Adam.*

ADAM   Dear master, I can go no further. Oh, I die for food! Here lie I down and measure out my grave. Farewell, kind master.   [*He lies down.*]

---

90 **mend** improve   91 **waste** spend   95 **feeder** dependent, servant   96 **right suddenly** without delay.
**2.5. Location: The forest.**
2 **Who** anyone who.   **lie** dwell   3–4 **And . . . throat** and tune his song to the bird's voice   14 **ragged** hoarse.   16 **stanzo** (The word *stanza*, variously spelled, was newfangled and therefore of ironic interest to Jaques.)   19–20 **they owe me nothing** (Jaques speaks of names as of something valuable only when written as signatures to a bond of indebtedness.)   23 **that** what.   **"compliment"** courtesy   24 **dog-apes** dog-faced baboons   26 **beggarly** effusive, like the thanks of a beggar   28 **cover the while** set the table for a meal meanwhile   30 **to look** looking for

32 **disputable** inclined to dispute   36 **live i'th' sun** dwell in the open air, without the cares of the court   37 **Seeking** hunting for   43 **note** tune   44 **in . . . invention** i.e., without needing to make use of my powerful rhetorical skills. (The nonsense that follows will make a mockery of true invention.)   51 **Ducdame** (Probably a nonsense term devised to puzzle Jaques's hearers, although with intriguing resemblances to phrases in Romany, *dukrà me*, "I foretell," or Welsh *Dewch da mi*, "Come with (or to) me," or dog-Latin *Duc ad me*, "Lead him to me," or simply "Duke damn me.")   58 **firstborn of Egypt** (In Exodus 12:28–33, the firstborn of Egypt are slain by the Lord as the enemies of Moses and the Israelites, who, like the Duke and his followers, are in exile.)   59 **banquet** wine and dessert after dinner. (This repast, now prepared on stage, seemingly is to remain there during the short following scene.)
**2.6. Location: The forest. The scene is continuous. By convention we understand that Adam and Orlando are in a different part of the forest and do not "see" the table remaining on stage.**

ORLANDO    Why, how now, Adam? No greater heart in
thee? Live a little, comfort a little, cheer thyself a little.   5
If this uncouth forest yield anything savage, I will   6
either be food for it or bring it for food to thee. Thy   7
conceit is nearer death than thy powers. For my sake   8
be comfortable; hold death awhile at the arm's end. I   9
will here be with thee presently, and if I bring thee not
something to eat, I will give thee leave to die; but if
thou diest before I come, thou art a mocker of my
labor. Well said! Thou look'st cheerly, and I'll be with   13
thee quickly. Yet thou liest in the bleak air. Come, I
will bear thee to some shelter; and thou shalt not die
for lack of a dinner, if there live anything in this desert.
[*He picks up Adam.*] Cheerly, good Adam!     *Exeunt.*

❧

## 2.7

*Enter Duke Senior and Lords, like outlaws.*

DUKE SENIOR
I think he be transformed into a beast,
For I can nowhere find him like a man.

FIRST LORD
My lord, he is but even now gone hence.
Here was he merry, hearing of a song.

DUKE SENIOR
If he, compact of jars, grow musical,   5
We shall have shortly discord in the spheres.   6
Go seek him. Tell him I would speak with him.

*Enter Jaques.*

FIRST LORD
He saves my labor by his own approach.

DUKE SENIOR
Why, how now, monsieur, what a life is this,
That your poor friends must woo your company!
What, you look merrily.

JAQUES
A fool, a fool! I met a fool i'th' forest,
A motley fool. A miserable world!   13
As I do live by food, I met a fool,
Who laid him down and basked him in the sun,
And railed on Lady Fortune in good terms,
In good set terms, and yet a motley fool.   17
"Good morrow, Fool," quoth I. "No, sir," quoth he,
"Call me not fool till heaven hath sent me fortune."   19
And then he drew a dial from his poke   20
And, looking on it with lackluster eye,
Says very wisely, "It is ten o'clock.

Thus we may see," quoth he, "how the world wags.   23
'Tis but an hour ago since it was nine,
And after one hour more 'twill be eleven;
And so from hour to hour we ripe and ripe,
And then from hour to hour we rot and rot,
And thereby hangs a tale." When I did hear
The motley fool thus moral on the time,   29
My lungs began to crow like Chanticleer,   30
That fools should be so deep-contemplative,
And I did laugh sans intermission   32
An hour by his dial. Oh, noble fool!
A worthy fool! Motley's the only wear.   34

DUKE SENIOR    What fool is this?

JAQUES
Oh, worthy fool! One that hath been a courtier,
And says, if ladies be but young and fair,
They have the gift to know it. And in his brain,   38
Which is as dry as the remainder biscuit   39
After a voyage, he hath strange places crammed   40
With observation, the which he vents   41
In mangled forms. Oh, that I were a fool!
I am ambitious for a motley coat.

DUKE SENIOR
Thou shalt have one.

JAQUES        It is my only suit,   44
Provided that you weed your better judgments
Of all opinion that grows rank in them   46
That I am wise. I must have liberty
Withal, as large a charter as the wind,   48
To blow on whom I please, for so fools have.
And they that are most gallèd with my folly,   50
They most must laugh. And why, sir, must they so?
The "why" is plain as way to parish church:
He that a fool doth very wisely hit   53
Doth very foolishly, although he smart,   54
Not to seem senseless of the bob. If not,   55
The wise man's folly is anatomized   56
Even by the squand'ring glances of the fool.   57
Invest me in my motley; give me leave   58
To speak my mind, and I will through and through
Cleanse the foul body of th'infected world,   60
If they will patiently receive my medicine.

DUKE SENIOR
Fie on thee! I can tell what thou wouldst do.

JAQUES
What, for a counter, would I do but good?   63

---

**5 comfort** comfort yourself   **6 uncouth** strange, wild   **7–8 Thy conceit . . . powers** You imagine you are nearer death than you really are.   **9 comfortable** comforted   **13 Well said!** Well done!   **2.7. Location:** The forest; the scene is continuous. (A repast, set out for the Duke in 2.5, has remained onstage during 2.6.)   **5 compact of jars** composed of discords   **6 the spheres** the concentric spheres of the old Ptolemaic solar system (which, by their movement, were thought to produce harmonious music).   **13 motley** wearing motley, the parti-colored dress of the professional jester   **17 set** carefully composed   **19 Call . . . fortune** Fortune proverbially favors fools. In Jaques's ironic view, those who are favored with fortune are fools by definition.   **20 dial** pocket sundial or watch. **poke** pouch or pocket

**23 wags** goes.   **29 moral** moralize   **30 crow** i.e., laugh merrily. **Chanticleer** a rooster   **32 sans** without   **34 only wear** only thing worth wearing.   **38 know it** i.e., put their beauty to advantage.   **39 dry** (According to Elizabethan physiology, a dry brain was marked by a strong memory but a slowness of apprehension.) **remainder** left over   **40 places** (1) nooks and corners (2) rhetorical topics   **41 vents** utters   **44 suit** (1) request (2) suit of clothes   **46 rank** vigorously; coarsely   **48 Withal** in addition. **charter** license, privilege   **50 gallèd** rubbed sore   **53–5 He . . . bob** He whom a fool wittily attacks behaves very foolishly, no matter how much he feels the sting, unless he pretends to be unaware of the taunt.   **55–7 If not . . . fool** Otherwise, the folly of even a wise person is dissected and laid open by the variously directed shots of wit made by the fool.   **58 Invest** Array   **60 Cleanse** purge. (A medical metaphor.)   **63 counter** (1) thing of no intrinsic value, a metal disk used in counting (2) parry

DUKE SENIOR
  Most mischievous foul sin, in chiding sin.
  For thou thyself hast been a libertine,
  As sensual as the brutish sting itself;
  And all th'embossèd sores and headed evils    66
  That thou with license of free foot hast caught    67
  Wouldst thou disgorge into the general world.    68
                                                   69
JAQUES    Why, who cries out on pride    70
  That can therein tax any private party?    71
  Doth it not flow as hugely as the sea,    72
  Till that the weary very means do ebb?    73
  What woman in the city do I name,
  When I say the city woman bears    75
  The cost of princes on unworthy shoulders?    76
  Who can come in and say that I mean her,    77
  When such a one as she, such is her neighbor?    78
  Or what is he of basest function    79
  That says his bravery is not on my cost,    80
  Thinking that I mean him, but therein suits    81
  His folly to the mettle of my speech?    82
  There then, how then? What then? Let me see
     wherein
  My tongue hath wronged him. If it do him right,    84
  Then he hath wronged himself. If he be free,    85
  Why then my taxing like a wild goose flies,    86
  Unclaimed of any man.—But who comes here?    87

        *Enter Orlando [with his sword drawn].*

ORLANDO
  Forbear, and eat no more!
JAQUES                        Why, I have eat none yet.    88
ORLANDO
  Nor shalt not, till necessity be served.
JAQUES
  Of what kind should this cock come of?    90
DUKE SENIOR
  Art thou thus boldened, man, by thy distress,
  Or else a rude despiser of good manners,
  That in civility thou seem'st so empty?
ORLANDO
  You touched my vein at first. The thorny point    94
  Of bare distress hath ta'en from me the show
  Of smooth civility; yet am I inland bred    96

  And know some nurture. But forbear, I say.    97
  He dies that touches any of this fruit
  Till I and my affairs are answerèd.    99
JAQUES
  An you will not be answered with reason, I must die.    100
DUKE SENIOR
  What would you have? Your gentleness shall force
  More than your force move us to gentleness.
ORLANDO
  I almost die for food, and let me have it!
DUKE SENIOR
  Sit down and feed, and welcome to our table.
ORLANDO
  Speak you so gently? Pardon me, I pray you.
  I thought that all things had been savage here,
  And therefore put I on the countenance
  Of stern commandment. But whate'er you are
  That in this desert inaccessible,    109
  Under the shade of melancholy boughs,    110
  Lose and neglect the creeping hours of time;
  If ever you have looked on better days,
  If ever been where bells have knolled to church,    113
  If ever sat at any good man's feast,
  If ever from your eyelids wiped a tear
  And know what 'tis to pity and be pitied,
  Let gentleness my strong enforcement be,
  In the which hope I blush and hide my sword.
                              *[He sheathes his sword.]*
DUKE SENIOR
  True is it that we have seen better days,
  And have with holy bell been knolled to church,
  And sat at good men's feasts, and wiped our eyes
  Of drops that sacred pity hath engendered.
  And therefore sit you down in gentleness,
  And take upon command what help we have    124
  That to your wanting may be ministered.    125
ORLANDO
  Then but forbear your food a little while,
  Whiles, like a doe, I go to find my fawn
  And give it food. There is an old poor man
  Who after me hath many a weary step
  Limped in pure love. Till he be first sufficed,
  Oppressed with two weak evils, age and hunger,    131
  I will not touch a bit.
DUKE SENIOR                    Go find him out,
  And we will nothing waste till you return.    133
ORLANDO
  I thank ye; and be blest for your good comfort!
                                          *[Exit.]*
DUKE SENIOR
  Thou see'st we are not all alone unhappy.
  This wide and universal theater
  Presents more woeful pageants than the scene
  Wherein we play in.
JAQUES                        All the world's a stage,

66 **brutish sting** carnal impulse    67 **th'embossèd** the swollen.    **headed evils** sores that have come to a head    68 **license . . . foot** the licentious freedom of a libertine    69 **disgorge** vomit    70–1 **who . . . party?** what true satirist inveighs against extravagance in dress with only some private individual in mind?    72–3 **Doth . . . ebb?** Is not pride as universal as the sea, overflowing everywhere until it finally ebbs like the tide, having exhausted what it fed upon?    75–6 **When . . . shoulders?** when I characterize the typical citizen's wife as dressing herself in finery that is costly enough to adorn a prince?    77 **come in** i.e., come into court as a complainant.    **her** some particular women    78 **When . . . neighbor?** when I am describing satirically a type of female vanity that applies fully as much to her neighbor as to her.    79–82 **Or . . . speech?** Or who is he of whatever social standing who says that my satire of extravagance in dress cannot apply specifically to himself, supposing I have him in mind, when his own foolish behavior condemns him to be a perfect example of the kind of folly I am talking about?    84–7 **If . . . man** If my satirical sketch fits him, then he condemns himself by resembling my portrait of folly. If he does not resemble my sketch, my criticism does him no harm.    88 **have eat** have eaten. (Pronounced "et.")    90 **Of? . . . of?** What sort of fighting cock is this?    94 **You . . . first** Your first supposition is correct.    96 **inland bred** i.e., raised in a center of civilization rather than on the outskirts

97 **nurture** education, breeding.    99 **answerèd** satisfied.    100 **An** If.    **reason** (A pun on "raisin" plays upon *fruit* in line 98.)    109 **desert** (Here, a large, wild, sparsely inhabited area, forested and with brooks and rivers.)    110 **melancholy** dark, shadowy    113 **knolled** knelled, rung    124 **upon command** for the asking    125 **wanting** need    131 **weak evils** disabilities causing weakness    133 **waste** consume

And all the men and women merely players. 139
They have their exits and their entrances,
And one man in his time plays many parts,
His acts being seven ages. At first the infant,
Mewling and puking in the nurse's arms. 143
Then the whining schoolboy, with his satchel
And shining morning face, creeping like snail
Unwillingly to school. And then the lover,
Sighing like furnace, with a woeful ballad
Made to his mistress' eyebrow. Then a soldier,
Full of strange oaths and bearded like the pard, 149
Jealous in honor, sudden, and quick in quarrel, 150
Seeking the bubble reputation
Even in the cannon's mouth. And then the justice,
In fair round belly with good capon lined, 153
With eyes severe and beard of formal cut,
Full of wise saws and modern instances; 155
And so he plays his part. The sixth age shifts
Into the lean and slippered pantaloon, 157
With spectacles on nose and pouch on side,
His youthful hose, well saved, a world too wide
For his shrunk shank; and his big manly voice, 160
Turning again toward childish treble, pipes
And whistles in his sound. Last scene of all, 162
That ends this strange, eventful history,
Is second childishness and mere oblivion, 164
Sans teeth, sans eyes, sans taste, sans everything. 165

*Enter Orlando, with Adam.*

DUKE SENIOR
Welcome. Set down your venerable burden
And let him feed.
ORLANDO    I thank you most for him.
                    [*He sets down Adam.*]
ADAM    So had you need.
I scarce can speak to thank you for myself.
DUKE SENIOR
Welcome. Fall to. I will not trouble you
As yet to question you about your fortunes.—
Give us some music, and, good cousin, sing. 173
          [*They eat, while Orlando and Duke Senior
                              converse apart.*]

*Song.*

AMIENS [*sings*]
          Blow, blow, thou winter wind.
          Thou art not so unkind
               As man's ingratitude.
          Thy tooth is not so keen,
          Because thou art not seen,
               Although thy breath be rude. 179

Heigh-ho, sing heigh-ho, unto the green holly. 180
Most friendship is feigning, most loving mere
     folly.
          Then heigh-ho, the holly!
               This life is most jolly.
     Freeze, freeze, thou bitter sky,
     That dost not bite so nigh 185
          As benefits forgot.
     Though thou the waters warp, 187
     Thy sting is not so sharp
          As friend remembered not.
Heigh-ho, sing heigh-ho, unto the green holly.
Most friendship is feigning, most loving mere
     folly.
          Then heigh-ho, the holly!
               This life is most jolly.

DUKE SENIOR [*to Orlando*]
If that you were the good Sir Rowland's son, 194
As you have whispered faithfully you were 195
And as mine eye doth his effigies witness 196
Most truly limned and living in your face, 197
Be truly welcome hither. I am the Duke
That loved your father. The residue of your fortune, 199
Go to my cave and tell me.—Good old man,
Thou art right welcome as thy master is.—
Support him by the arm. Give me your hand,
And let me all your fortunes understand.     *Exeunt.* 203

❧

# 3.1

*Enter Duke [Frederick], Lords, and Oliver.*

DUKE FREDERICK
Not see him since? Sir, sir, that cannot be. 1
But were I not the better part made mercy, 2
I should not seek an absent argument 3
Of my revenge, thou present. But look to it: 4
Find out thy brother, wheresoe'er he is.
Seek him with candle. Bring him dead or living 6
Within this twelvemonth, or turn thou no more 7
To seek a living in our territory.
Thy lands and all things that thou dost call thine
Worth seizure do we seize into our hands, 10
Till thou canst quit thee by thy brother's mouth 11
Of what we think against thee.

---

**180 holly** (An emblem of Christmastime and holiday cheer, as in "the holly and the ivy.")    **185 nigh** deeply, near (to the heart)    **187 warp** freeze so that the surface of the ice cracks and forces up ridges    **194 If that** If    **195 faithfully** persuasively and honestly    **196–7 doth . . . face** bears witness to the likeness between yourself and the dead Sir Rowland    **197 limned** painted    **199 The . . . fortune** The rest of your adventure    **203 s.d. *Exeunt*** (The table must be removed at this point.)
**3.1. Location: Duke Frederick's court.**
**1 Not . . . since?** i.e., You mean to tell me you claim not to have seen Orlando since the disappearance of Celia and Rosalind?    **2 were . . . mercy** i.e., if I were not a merciful man. (Literally, if I were not composed mostly of mercy.)    **3–4 I . . . present** i.e., I would seek revenge not on the absent Orlando, but on you, who are right here.    **6 Seek . . . candle** i.e., Look for him everywhere, even in the darkest corners. (See Luke 15:8.)    **7 turn** return    **10 we . . . our** (The royal plural.)    **11 quit . . . mouth** acquit yourself by the direct testimony of Orlando. (The Duke suspects that Oliver has murdered Orlando.)

---

**139 players** actors.    **143 Mewling** crying with a catlike noise    **149 bearded . . . pard** having bristling mustaches like the leopard's    **150 Jealous in honor** quick to anger in matters of honor    **153 capon** rooster castrated to make the flesh more tender for eating (and often presented to judges as a bribe)    **155 saws** sayings.    **modern instances** commonplace illustrations    **157 pantaloon** baggy trousers, signifying the stock character type of the ridiculous and enfeebled old man regularly featured in Italian *commedia dell'arte*    **160 shank** calf    **162 his** its    **164 mere oblivion** total forgetfulness    **165 Sans** without    **173 cousin** (A term used by sovereigns to address their nobility.)    **179 rude** rough.

OLIVER
Oh, that Your Highness knew my heart in this!
I never loved my brother in my life.

DUKE FREDERICK
More villain thou.—Well, push him out of doors,
And let my officers of such a nature                    16
Make an extent upon his house and lands.                17
Do this expediently, and turn him going.    *Exeunt.*   18

♣

## 3.2

*Enter Orlando [with a paper].*

ORLANDO
Hang there, my verse, in witness of my love;
    And thou, thrice-crownèd queen of night, survey   2
With thy chaste eye, from thy pale sphere above,
    Thy huntress' name that my full life doth sway.   4
O Rosalind! These trees shall be my books,
    And in their barks my thoughts I'll character,    6
That every eye which in this forest looks
    Shall see thy virtue witnessed everywhere.
Run, run, Orlando, carve on every tree
The fair, the chaste, and unexpressive she.   *Exit.* 10

*Enter Corin and [Touchstone the] Clown.*

CORIN    And how like you this shepherd's life, Master
Touchstone?
TOUCHSTONE    Truly, shepherd, in respect of itself, it is a   13
good life; but in respect that it is a shepherd's life, it is
naught. In respect that it is solitary, I like it very well;   15
but in respect that it is private, it is a very vile life.
Now in respect it is in the fields, it pleaseth me well;
but in respect it is not in the court, it is tedious. As it
is a spare life, look you, it fits my humor well; but as   19
there is no more plenty in it, it goes much against my
stomach. Hast any philosophy in thee, shepherd?
CORIN    No more but that I know the more one sickens
the worse at ease he is; and that he that wants money,   23
means, and content is without three good friends; that
the property of rain is to wet and fire to burn; that
good pasture makes fat sheep and that a great cause
of the night is lack of the sun; that he that hath learned
no wit by nature nor art may complain of good   28
breeding or comes of a very dull kindred.
TOUCHSTONE    Such a one is a natural philosopher.
Wast ever in court, shepherd?
CORIN    No, truly.

TOUCHSTONE    Then thou art damned.
CORIN    Nay, I hope.                                          34
TOUCHSTONE    Truly, thou art damned, like an ill-
roasted egg, all on one side.
CORIN    For not being at court? Your reason.
TOUCHSTONE    Why, if thou never wast at court, thou
never saw'st good manners; if thou never saw'st good   39
manners, then thy manners must be wicked; and   40
wickedness is sin, and sin is damnation. Thou art in
a parlous state, shepherd.                                    42
CORIN    Not a whit, Touchstone. Those that are good
manners at the court are as ridiculous in the country
as the behavior of the country is most mockable at the
court. You told me you salute not at the court but you   46
kiss your hands; that courtesy would be uncleanly, if   47
courtiers were shepherds.
TOUCHSTONE    Instance, briefly; come, instance.            49
CORIN    Why, we are still handling our ewes, and their   50
fells you know are greasy.                                    51
TOUCHSTONE    Why, do not your courtier's hands sweat?  52
And is not the grease of a mutton as wholesome as the   53
sweat of a man? Shallow, shallow. A better instance, I   54
say. Come.
CORIN    Besides, our hands are hard.
TOUCHSTONE    Your lips will feel them the sooner.
Shallow again. A more sounder instance. Come.
CORIN    And they are often tarred over with the surgery   59
of our sheep; and would you have us kiss tar? The
courtier's hands are perfumed with civet.                   61
TOUCHSTONE    Most shallow man! Thou worms' meat, in   62
respect of a good piece of flesh indeed! Learn of the   63
wise, and perpend: civet is of a baser birth than tar,   64
the very uncleanly flux of a cat. Mend the instance,   65
shepherd.
CORIN    You have too courtly a wit for me. I'll rest.
TOUCHSTONE    Wilt thou rest damned? God help thee,
shallow man! God make incision in thee! Thou art   69
raw.                                                          70
CORIN    Sir, I am a true laborer: I earn that I eat, get that   71
I wear, owe no man hate, envy no man's happiness,   72
glad of other men's good, content with my harm, and   73
the greatest of my pride is to see my ewes graze and
my lambs suck.
TOUCHSTONE    That is another simple sin in you, to bring   76
the ewes and the rams together and to offer to get your   77

---

16 **of such a nature** who attend to such duties    17 **extent** writ of
seizure    18 **expediently** expeditiously.    **turn him going** send him
packing.
**3.2. Location: The forest.**
2 **thrice-crownèd . . . night** i.e., Diana in the three aspects of her
divinity: as Luna or Cynthia, goddess of the moon; as Diana, goddess
on earth; and as Hecate or Proserpina, goddess in the lower world
4 **Thy huntress'** i.e., Rosalind's, who is here thought of as accompanying Diana, patroness of the hunt and of chastity.    **sway** control.
6 **character** inscribe    10 **unexpressive** inexpressible    13 **in respect of
itself** considered in and for itself    15 **naught** vile, of no social consequence.    19 **spare** frugal.    **humor** temperament    23 **wants**
lacks    28 **wit** wisdom.    **art** study.    **complain of** lament the lack of

34 **hope** i.e., hope not.    39 **manners** etiquette    40 **manners** morals    42 **parlous** perilous    46 **salute** greet    46–7 **but . . . hands** without kissing the other person's hands    49 **Instance** Proof    50 **still**
constantly    51 **fells** skins with the wool, or fleeces    52 **your courtier's** your typical courtier's    53–4 **And . . . man?** (Human sweat was
thought to be fat oozing from the pores.)    59 **tarred over** anointed
with tar on their cuts and sores    61 **civet** a musky perfume derived
from glands in the anal pouch of the civet cat. (As Touchstone points
out.)    62–3 **Thou . . . indeed!** You miserable creature (literally, you
food for worms, subject to the decay of death), if we compare you
with any worthy sample of humankind!    64 **perpend** consider
65 **flux** secretion.    **Mend** Improve    69 **incision** a cut, perhaps for the
purpose of letting blood (here, to let out folly); or for seasoning as
raw meat is scored and salted before cooking    70 **raw** (1) wet behind
the ears (2) uncooked (3) afflicted with a raw wound.    71 **earn . . . eat**
earn my living    71–2 **get . . . wear** wear homemade garments
73 **content . . . harm** patient with my ill fortune    76 **simple sin** sin
arising from simplicity    77 **offer** undertake

living by the copulation of cattle; to be bawd to a bell-  78
wether,  and to betray a she-lamb of a twelvemonth to  79
a crooked-pated old cuckoldly ram, out of all reasonable  80
match. If thou be'st not damned for this, the devil him-  81
self will have no shepherds; I cannot see else how thou  82
shouldst scape.  83

CORIN   Here comes young Master Ganymede, my new
mistress's brother.

*Enter Rosalind [with a paper, reading].*

ROSALIND
    "From the east to western Ind,  86
    No jewel is like Rosalind.
    Her worth, being mounted on the wind,  88
    Through all the world bears Rosalind.  89
    All the pictures fairest lined  90
    Are but black to Rosalind.  91
    Let no face be kept in mind
    But the fair of Rosalind."  93
TOUCHSTONE   I'll rhyme you so eight years together,  94
dinners and suppers and sleeping hours excepted. It  95
is the right butter-women's rank to market.  96
ROSALIND   Out, fool!  97
TOUCHSTONE   For a taste:
    If a hart do lack a hind,  99
    Let him seek out Rosalind.
    If the cat will after kind,  101
    So, be sure, will Rosalind.
    Wintered garments must be lined,  103
    So must slender Rosalind.
    They that reap must sheaf and bind;  105
    Then to cart with Rosalind.  106
    Sweetest nut hath sourest rind;
    Such a nut is Rosalind.
    He that sweetest rose will find
    Must find love's prick and Rosalind.  110

This is the very false gallop of verses. Why do you  111
infect yourself with them?
ROSALIND   Peace, you dull fool! I found them on a tree.
TOUCHSTONE   Truly, the tree yields bad fruit.

ROSALIND   I'll graft it with you, and then I shall graft it  115
with a medlar. Then it will be the earliest fruit i'th'  116
country; for you'll be rotten ere you be half ripe, and
that's the right virtue of the medlar.  118
TOUCHSTONE   You have said; but whether wisely or no,
let the forest judge.

*Enter Celia, with a writing.*

ROSALIND   Peace! Here comes my sister, reading. Stand
aside.
CELIA *[reads]*
    "Why should this a desert be?
      For it is unpeopled? No.  124
    Tongues I'll hang on every tree,
      That shall civil sayings show:  126
    Some, how brief the life of man
      Runs his erring pilgrimage,  128
    That the stretching of a span  129
      Buckles in his sum of age;  130
    Some, of violated vows
      Twixt the souls of friend and friend;
    But upon the fairest boughs,
      Or at every sentence end,
    Will I 'Rosalinda' write,
      Teaching all that read to know
    The quintessence of every sprite  137
      Heaven would in little show.  138
    Therefore heaven Nature charged  139
      That one body should be filled
    With all graces wide-enlarged.  141
      Nature presently distilled
    Helen's cheek, but not her heart,  143
      Cleopatra's majesty,
    Atalanta's better part,  145
      Sad Lucretia's modesty.  146
    Thus Rosalind of many parts
      By heavenly synod was devised  148
    Of many faces, eyes, and hearts
      To have the touches dearest prized.  150
    Heaven would that she these gifts should have,  151
    And I to live and die her slave."  152

---

**78 cattle** livestock   **78–9 bellwether** the leading male sheep
of a flock, wearing a bell   **80 crooked-pated** with crooked
horns.   **cuckoldly** i.e., horned like a cuckold (husband of an unfaithful wife).   **out of** contrary to   **81–2 If . . . shepherds** i.e., Your only
possible escape from damnation would be if the devil should find
shepherds too objectionable to have in hell under any circumstances   **83 scape** escape.   **86 Ind** Indies   **88–9 Her . . . Rosalind**
The fame of Rosalind will be carried throughout the world as if by
the wind, or even literally so as the wind blows Orlando's verses
hither and yon.   **90 lined** drawn   **91 black to** dark-complexioned
and hence ugly compared to   **93 fair** beauty   **94 together** without
stop   **95–6 It is . . . market** i.e., The rhymes, all alike, follow each
other precisely like a line of butter women or dairy women jogging
along to market.   **97 Out** (An exclamation here denoting comic
indignation.)   **99 If . . . hind** If a male deer longs for a female deer.
(Touchstone wryly suggests in his verses that Rosalind is the responsive object of male desire.)   **101 after kind** follow its natural
instinct   **103 Wintered** Old, worn; used in winter.   **lined** (1) given a
winter lining (2) stuffed. (The term was sometimes used for the copulating of dogs.)   **105 sheaf and bind** tie in a bundle   **106 to cart** (1)
onto the harvest cart (2) onto the cart used to carry prostitutes
through the streets, exposing them to public ridicule   **110 prick**
thorn. (With bawdy suggestion.)   **111 false gallop** canter

**115 you** (With a pun on "yew.")   **116 medlar** a fruit like a small
brown-skinned apple that is eaten when it starts to decay. (With a
pun on "meddler.")   **118 right virtue** true quality   **124 For**
Because   **126 civil sayings** maxims of civilized life   **128 his erring** its
wandering   **129–30 That . . . age** i.e., so that a very brief span encom-
passes his whole life. (A *span* is a handbreadth. See Psalm 39:5.)
**137 quintessence** highest perfection. (Literally, the fifth essence or
element of the medieval alchemists, purer even than fire.)   **sprite**
spirit   **138 Heaven . . . show** that heaven wishes to show in one small
person, Rosalind (who, in microcosm, embodies the supreme essence
of the heavens, or macrocosm).   **139 heaven . . . charged** heaven commanded Nature   **141 wide-enlarged** all-encompassing.   **143 Helen's
. . . heart** i.e., the beauty of Helen of Troy but not her false heart
**145 Atalanta's better part** i.e., her beauty or her fleetness of foot, not
her scornfulness and greed. (She refused to marry any man who was
unable to defeat her in a foot race and, when challenged by Hippomenes, lost to him because Hippomenes dropped in her way three
golden apples of the Hesperides.)   **146 Lucretia's** Lucretia was an
honorable Roman lady raped by Tarquin (whose story Shakespeare
tells in *The Rape of Lucrece*)   **148 synod** assembly   **150 touches**
traits   **151 would** decree   **152 And I to** and that I should

ROSALIND   Oh, most gentle Jupiter, what tedious homily 153
of love have you wearied your parishioners withal,
and never cried, "Have patience, good people!"

CELIA   How now? Back, friends. Shepherd, go off a 156
little. [*To Touchstone*] Go with him, sirrah. 157

TOUCHSTONE   Come, shepherd, let us make an honorable retreat, though not with bag and baggage, yet 159
with scrip and scrippage.           *Exit* [*with Corin*]. 160

CELIA   Didst thou hear these verses?

ROSALIND   Oh, yes, I heard them all, and more, too, for
some of them had in them more feet than the verses
would bear.

CELIA   That's no matter. The feet might bear the verses.

ROSALIND   Ay, but the feet were lame and could not
bear themselves without the verse and therefore stood 167
lamely in the verse.

CELIA   But didst thou hear without wondering how thy
name should be hanged and carved upon these trees?

ROSALIND   I was seven of the nine days out of the 171
wonder before you came; for look here what I found 172
on a palm tree. I was never so berhymed since
Pythagoras' time, that I was an Irish rat, which I can 174
hardly remember.

CELIA   Trow you who hath done this? 176

ROSALIND   Is it a man?

CELIA   And a chain that you once wore about his neck. 178
Change you color?

ROSALIND   I prithee, who?

CELIA   Oh, Lord, Lord, it is a hard matter for  friends 181
to meet; but mountains may be removed with earth- 182
quakes  and so encounter. 183

ROSALIND   Nay, but who is it?

CELIA   Is it possible? 185

ROSALIND   Nay, I prithee now with most petitionary
vehemence, tell me who it is.

CELIA   Oh, wonderful, wonderful, and most wonderful-
wonderful! And yet again wonderful, and after that,
out of all whooping! 190

ROSALIND   Good my complexion! Dost thou think, 191
though I am caparisoned like a man, I have a doublet 192
and hose in my disposition? One inch of delay more 193
is a South Sea of discovery. I prithee, tell me who is it 194
quickly, and speak apace. I would thou couldst stam-

mer, that thou mightst pour this concealed man out of
thy mouth as wine comes out of a narrow-mouthed
bottle, either too much at once or none at all. I prithee,
take the cork out of thy mouth that I may drink thy
tidings.

CELIA   So you may put a man in your belly. 201

ROSALIND   Is he of God's making? What manner of 202
man? Is his head worth a hat, or his chin worth a
beard?

CELIA   Nay, he hath but a little beard.

ROSALIND   Why, God will send more, if the man will be
thankful. Let me stay the growth of his beard, if thou 207
delay me not the knowledge of his chin. 208

CELIA   It is young Orlando, that tripped up the wrestler's
heels and your heart both in an instant.

ROSALIND   Nay, but the devil take mocking. Speak sad 211
brow and true maid. 212

CELIA   I'faith, coz, 'tis he.

ROSALIND   Orlando?

CELIA   Orlando.

ROSALIND   Alas the day, what shall I do with my
doublet and hose? What did he when thou saw'st him?
What said he? How looked he? Wherein went he? 218
What makes he here? Did he ask for me? Where 219
remains he? How parted he with thee? And when 220
shalt thou see him again? Answer me in one word.

CELIA   You must borrow me Gargantua's mouth first; 222
'tis a word too great for any mouth of this age's size.
To say ay and no to these particulars is more than to 224
answer in a catechism. 225

ROSALIND   But doth he know that I am in this forest
and in man's apparel? Looks he as freshly as he did
the day he wrestled?

CELIA   It is as easy to count atomies as to resolve the 229
propositions of a lover. But take a taste of my finding 230
him, and relish it with good observance. I found him 231
under a tree, like a dropped acorn.

ROSALIND   It may well be called Jove's tree, when it 233
drops forth such fruit.

CELIA   Give me audience, good madam. 235

ROSALIND   Proceed.

CELIA   There lay he, stretched along, like a wounded
knight.

ROSALIND   Though it be pity to see such a sight, it well
becomes the ground. 240

CELIA   Cry "holla" to thy tongue, I prithee; it curvets 241
unseasonably. He was furnished like a hunter. 242

---

153 **Jupiter** (Often emended to "pulpiter.")    156 **Back** i.e., Move back,
away. (Addressed to Corin and Touchstone.)    157 **sirrah** A form of
address to inferiors (here, Touchstone).    159 **bag and baggage** i.e.,
equipment appropriate to a retreating army    160 **scrip and scrippage**
shepherd's pouch and its contents.    167 **without** (1) without the help
of (2) outside    171–2 **seven . . . wonder** (A reference to the common
phrase "a nine days' wonder.")    174 **Pythagoras** Greek philosopher
credited with the doctrine of the transmigration of souls.    **that**
when.    **Irish rat** (Refers to a current belief that Irish enchanters could
rhyme rats and other animals to death.)    **which** a thing which
176 **Trow you** Have you any idea    178 **And a chain** And with a
chain    181–3 **it is . . . encounter** (A playful inversion of the proverb,
"Friends may meet, but mountains never greet." Celia appears to be
teasing Rosalind's eagerness to meet Orlando.)    **removed with** moved
by    185 **possible** i.e., possible you don't know.    190 **out . . . whooping** beyond all power to utter.    191 **Good my complexion!** Oh, my
(feminine) temperament, my woman's curiosity!    192 **caparisoned**
bedecked. (Usually said of a horse.)    192–3 **I have . . . disposition?**
i.e., that I have a man's patience?    194 **a South Sea of discovery** i.e.,
as tedious as a long exploratory voyage to the South Pacific Ocean.

201 **belly** (1) stomach (2) womb.    202 **of God's making** i.e., a real man,
not a fantasy.    207 **stay** wait for    207–8 **if . . . chin** i.e., if you will please
tell me whom you are talking about.    211–12 **Speak . . . maid** i.e., Speak
seriously and truthfully.    218 **Wherein went he?** In what clothes was
he dressed?    219 **makes** does    220 **remains** dwells    222 **Gargantua's
mouth** (Gargantua is the giant of popular literature who, in Rabelais'
novel, swallowed five pilgrims in a salad.)    224–5 **To . . . catechism** To
give even yes and no answers to these questions would take longer
than to go through the catechism (i.e., the formal questioning used in
the Church to teach the principles of faith).    229 **atomies** motes, specks
of dirt    230 **propositions** questions    231 **relish it** heighten its pleasant
taste.    **observance** attention.    233 **Jove's tree** the oak    235 **Give me
audience** Pay attention    240 **becomes** adorns    241 **holla** stop.
**curvets** prances    242 **furnished** equipped, dressed

ROSALIND   Oh, ominous! He comes to kill my heart.   243

CELIA   I would sing my song without a burden. Thou   244
bring'st me out of tune.   245

ROSALIND   Do you not know I am a woman? When I
think, I must speak. Sweet, say on.

*Enter Orlando and Jaques.*

CELIA   You bring me out.—Soft, comes he not here?   248

ROSALIND   'Tis he. Slink by, and note him.
                                   [*They stand aside and listen.*]

JAQUES   [*to Orlando*]   I thank you for your company,
but, good faith, I had as lief have been myself alone.   251

ORLANDO   And so had I; but yet, for fashion sake, I   252
thank you too for your society.

JAQUES   God b'wi'you. Let's meet as little as we can.   254

ORLANDO   I do desire we may be better strangers.

JAQUES   I pray you, mar no more trees with writing
love songs in their barks.

ORLANDO   I pray you, mar no more of my verses with
reading them ill-favoredly.   259

JAQUES   Rosalind is your love's name?

ORLANDO   Yes, just.   261

JAQUES   I do not like her name.

ORLANDO   There was no thought of pleasing you when
she was christened.

JAQUES   What stature is she of?

ORLANDO   Just as high as my heart.

JAQUES   You are full of pretty answers. Have you not
been acquainted with goldsmiths' wives, and conned   268
them out of rings?   269

ORLANDO   Not so; but I answer you right painted cloth,   270
from whence you have studied your questions.   271

JAQUES   You have a nimble wit; I think 'twas made of
Atalanta's heels. Will you sit down with me? And we   273
two will rail against our mistress the world and all our
misery.

ORLANDO   I will chide no breather in the world but   276
myself, against whom I know most faults.

JAQUES   The worst fault you have is to be in love.

ORLANDO   'Tis a fault I will not change for your best
virtue. I am weary of you.

JAQUES   By my troth, I was seeking for a fool when I
found you.

ORLANDO   He is drowned in the brook. Look but in,
and you shall see him.

JAQUES   There I shall see mine own figure.   285

ORLANDO   Which I take to be either a fool or a cipher.   286

JAQUES   I'll tarry no longer with you. Farewell, good
Seigneur Love.

ORLANDO   I am glad of your departure. Adieu, good
Monsieur Melancholy.                     [*Exit Jaques.*]

ROSALIND   [*aside to Celia*]   I will speak to him like a
saucy lackey and under that habit play the knave   292
with him.—Do you hear, forester?

ORLANDO   Very well. What would you?

ROSALIND   I pray you, what is't o'clock?

ORLANDO   You should ask me what time o' day.
There's no clock in the forest.

ROSALIND   Then there is no true lover in the forest, else
sighing every minute and groaning every hour would
detect the lazy foot of Time as well as a clock.   300

ORLANDO   And why not the swift foot of Time? Had
not that been as proper?

ROSALIND   By no means, sir. Time travels in divers
paces with divers persons. I'll tell you who Time
ambles withal, who Time trots withal, who Time   305
gallops withal, and who he stands still withal.

ORLANDO   I prithee, who doth he trot withal?

ROSALIND   Marry, he trots hard with a young maid
between the contract of her marriage and the day it is
solemnized. If the interim be but a se'nnight, Time's   310
pace is so hard that it seems the length of seven year.

ORLANDO   Who ambles Time withal?

ROSALIND   With a priest that lacks Latin and a rich man
that hath not the gout, for the one sleeps easily
because he cannot study and the other lives merrily
because he feels no pain, the one lacking the burden of
lean and wasteful learning, the other knowing no   317
burden of heavy tedious penury. These Time ambles
withal.

ORLANDO   Who doth he gallop withal?

ROSALIND   With a thief to the gallows, for though he go
as softly as foot can fall, he thinks himself too soon
there.

ORLANDO   Who stays it still withal?

ROSALIND   With lawyers in the vacation; for they sleep
between term and term, and then they perceive not   326
how Time moves.

ORLANDO   Where dwell you, pretty youth?

ROSALIND   With this shepherdess, my sister, here in the
skirts of the forest, like fringe upon a petticoat.

ORLANDO   Are you native of this place?

ROSALIND   As the coney that you see dwell where she is   332
kindled.   333

ORLANDO   Your accent is something finer than you   334
could purchase in so removed a dwelling.   334

ROSALIND   I have been told so of many. But indeed an
old religious uncle of mine taught me to speak, who   337
was in his youth an inland man, one that knew   338
courtship too well, for there he fell in love. I have   339

---

**243 heart** (With pun on "hart.")   **244 burden** refrain, or bass
part.   **244–5 Thou bring'st** You put   **248 Soft** i.e., Wait a minute,
or, stop talking   **251 I had as lief** I would just as soon   **252 fashion**
fashion's   **254 God b'wi'you** God be with you, good-bye.
**259 ill-favoredly** unsympathetically.   **261 just** just so.   **268 conned**
memorized   **269 rings** (Verses or "posies" were often inscribed in
rings.)   **270 right painted cloth** in the true spirit of a painted cloth
decorated with commonplace pictures and cliché mottoes (frequently
mythological or scriptural)   **271 studied** learned   **273 Atalanta's
heels** (See above, the note for line 145.)   **276 breather** living
being   **285 figure** reflection. (Narcissus fell in love with his own
reflection in a pool.)   **286 cipher** nonentity, zero.

**292 and under . . . knave** and in that disguise (1) pose as a boy (2)
deal mischievously   **300 detect** reveal.   **the lazy foot** i.e., the slow
passing   **305 withal** with   **310 se'nnight** week   **317 lean** unremu-
nerative.   **wasteful** making one waste away   **326 term** court session   **332 coney** rabbit   **333 kindled** littered, born.   **334 something**
somewhat   **335 purchase** acquire.   **removed** remote   **337 religious**
i.e., belonging to a religious order   **338 inland** from a center of civilization   **339 courtship** (1) wooing (2) knowledge of courtly manners

heard him read many lectures against it, and I thank 340
God I am not a woman, to be touched with so many 341
giddy offenses as he hath generally taxed their whole 342
sex withal. 343

ORLANDO    Can you remember any of the principal evils
that he laid to the charge of women?

ROSALIND    There were none principal; they were all like
one another as halfpence are, every one fault seeming
monstrous till his fellow fault came to match it. 348

ORLANDO    I prithee, recount some of them.

ROSALIND    No, I will not cast away my physic but on 350
those that are sick. There is a man haunts the forest
that abuses our young plants with carving "Rosalind"
on their barks, hangs odes upon hawthorns and
elegies on brambles, all, forsooth, deifying the name of
Rosalind. If I could meet that fancy-monger, I would 355
give him some good counsel, for he seems to have the
quotidian of love upon him. 357

ORLANDO    I am he that is so love-shaked. I pray you,
tell me your remedy.

ROSALIND    There is none of my uncle's marks upon you.
He taught me how to know a man in love, in which
cage of rushes I am sure you are not prisoner. 362

ORLANDO    What were his marks?

ROSALIND    A lean cheek, which you have not; a blue eye 364
and sunken, which you have not; an unquestionable 365
spirit, which you have not; a beard neglected, which
you have not—but I pardon you for that, for simply 367
your having in beard is a younger brother's revenue. 368
Then your hose should be ungartered, your bonnet un- 369
banded, your sleeve unbuttoned, your shoe untied, 370
and everything about you demonstrating a careless
desolation. But you are no such man. You are rather
point-device in your accoutrements, as loving your- 373
self, than seeming the lover of any other. 374

ORLANDO    Fair youth, I would I could make thee believe
I love.

ROSALIND    Me believe it? You may as soon make her
that you love believe it, which I warrant she is apter to
do than to confess she does. That is one of the points
in the which women still give the lie to their con- 380
sciences. But in good sooth, are you he that hangs the 381
verses on the trees, wherein Rosalind is so
admired?

ORLANDO    I swear to thee, youth, by the white hand of
Rosalind, I am that he, that unfortunate he.

ROSALIND    But are you so much in love as your rhymes
speak?

ORLANDO    Neither rhyme nor reason can express how
much.

ROSALIND    Love is merely a madness and, I tell you, 390
deserves as well a dark house and a whip as madmen 391
do; and the reason why they are not so punished and
cured is that the lunacy is so ordinary that the
whippers are in love too. Yet I profess curing it by 394
counsel.

ORLANDO    Did you ever cure any so?

ROSALIND    Yes, one, and in this manner. He was to
imagine me his love, his mistress; and I set him every
day to woo me. At which time would I, being but a
moonish youth, grieve, be effeminate, changeable, 400
longing and liking, proud, fantastical, apish, shallow,
inconstant, full of tears, full of smiles; for every passion
something and for no passion truly anything, as boys
and women are for the most part cattle of this color;
would now like him, now loathe him; then entertain 405
him, then forswear him; now weep for him, then spit
at him; that I drave my suitor from his mad humor of 407
love to a living humor of madness, which was to for- 408
swear the full stream of the world and to live in a nook
merely monastic. And thus I cured him; and this way 410
will I take upon me to wash your liver as clean as a 411
sound sheep's heart, that there shall not be one spot of
love in't.

ORLANDO    I would not be cured, youth.

ROSALIND    I would cure you, if you would but call me
Rosalind and come every day to my cote and woo me. 416

ORLANDO    Now by the faith of my love, I will. Tell me
where it is.

ROSALIND    Go with me to it, and I'll show it you; and
by the way you shall tell me where in the forest you 420
live. Will you go?

ORLANDO    With all my heart, good youth.

ROSALIND    Nay, you must call me Rosalind.—Come,
sister, will you go?                                    *Exeunt.*

❖

## 3.3

*Enter [Touchstone the] Clown, Audrey; and Jaques
[apart].*

TOUCHSTONE    Come apace, good Audrey. I will fetch up 1
your goats, Audrey. And how, Audrey, am I the man 2
yet? Doth my simple feature content you? 3

AUDREY    Your features, Lord warrant us! What features? 4

TOUCHSTONE    I am here with thee and thy goats, as the
most capricious poet, honest Ovid, was among the 6
Goths. 7

---

340 **read many lectures** deliver many admonitory speeches
341 **touched** tainted    342–3 **taxed . . . withal** accused all women
of.    348 **his** its    350 **physic** medicine    355 **fancy-monger** love peddler    357 **quotidian** fever recurring daily. (See *love-shaked*, line
358.)    362 **cage of rushes** i.e., flimsy prison    364 **blue eye** i.e., having
dark circles    365 **unquestionable** unwilling to be conversed
with    367–8 **simply . . . revenue** what beard you have is like a
younger brother's inheritance (i.e., small).    369 **hose** leggings
369–70 **bonnet unbanded** hat lacking a band around the crown
373 **point-device** meticulous.    **accoutrements** items of dress
373–4 **as loving yourself** (Rosalind suggests that Orlando is somewhat obsessed with his appearance and wishes to appear nattily
dressed.)    380 **still** continually    381 **good sooth** honest truth

390 **merely** utterly    391 **dark . . . whip** (The common treatment of
lunatics.)    394 **profess** am expert in    400 **moonish** changeable
405 **entertain** receive cordially    407 **that** with the result that.    **drave**
drove    407–8 **mad . . . madness** mad fancy of love to a real madness    410 **merely** utterly    411 **liver** (Supposed seat of the
emotions, especially love.)    416 **cote** cottage    420 **by** on
3.3. Location: The forest.
1 **apace** quickly    2 **And how** i.e., What do you say    3 **simple feature**
plain appearance. (But Audrey, in her answer, may have her mind on
*features* as "parts of the body.")    4 **warrant** protect    6 **capricious**
witty, fanciful. (Derived from the Latin *caper,* "male goat"; hence,
"goatish, lascivious.")    **honest** worthy    7 **Goths** Ovid was exiled,
much against his will, from Rome to the western shore of the Black
Sea, in present-day Romania, a region imagined by Touchstone to be
inhabited by barbarian Goths. (With a pun on "goats"; the two words
were pronounced alike.)

JAQUES [*aside*]  Oh, knowledge ill-inhabited, worse than  8
Jove in a thatched house!  9

TOUCHSTONE  When a man's verses cannot be under-  10
stood, nor a man's good wit seconded with the  11
forward child, understanding, it strikes a man more  12
dead than a great reckoning in a little room. Truly, I  13
would the gods had made thee poetical.

AUDREY  I do not know what "poetical" is. Is it honest
in deed and word? Is it a true thing?

TOUCHSTONE  No, truly; for the truest poetry is the most
feigning, and lovers are given to poetry, and what  18
they swear in poetry may be said as lovers they do  19
feign.  20

AUDREY  Do you wish then that the gods had made me
poetical?

TOUCHSTONE  I do, truly; for thou swear'st to me thou
art honest. Now, if thou wert a poet, I might have  24
some hope thou didst feign.  25

AUDREY  Would you not have me honest?

TOUCHSTONE  No, truly, unless thou wert hard-  27
favored; for honesty coupled to beauty is to have  28
honey a sauce to sugar.

JAQUES [*aside*]  A material fool!  30

AUDREY  Well, I am not fair, and therefore I pray the
gods make me honest.

TOUCHSTONE  Truly, and to cast away honesty upon a
foul slut were to put good meat into an unclean dish.  34

AUDREY  I am not a slut, though I thank the gods I am  35
foul.  36

TOUCHSTONE  Well, praised be the gods for thy foulness!
Sluttishness may come hereafter. But be it as it
may be, I will marry thee, and to that end I have been
with Sir Oliver Mar-text, the vicar of the next village,  40
who hath promised to meet me in this place of the
forest and to couple us.

JAQUES [*aside*]  I would fain see this meeting.  43

AUDREY  Well, the gods give us joy!

TOUCHSTONE  Amen. A man may, if he were of a
fearful heart, stagger in this attempt; for here we have  46
no temple but the wood, no assembly but horn-beasts.  47

But what though? Courage! As horns are odious, they  48
are necessary. It is said, "Many a man knows no end  49
of his goods." Right! Many a man has good horns and  50
knows no end of them. Well, that is the dowry of his  51
wife; 'tis none of his own getting. Horns? Even so.  52
Poor men alone? No, no, the noblest deer hath them  53
as huge as the rascal. Is the single man therefore  54
blessed? No. As a walled town is more worthier than
a village, so is the forehead of a married man more
honorable than the bare brow of a bachelor; and by
how much defense is better than no skill, by so much  58
is a horn more precious than to want.  59

*Enter Sir Oliver Mar-text.*

Here comes Sir Oliver.—Sir Oliver Mar-text, you are
well met. Will you dispatch us here under this tree, or  61
shall we go with you to your chapel?

SIR OLIVER  Is there none here to give the woman?  63

TOUCHSTONE  I will not take her on gift of any man.

SIR OLIVER  Truly, she must be given, or the marriage is
not lawful.

JAQUES [*advancing*]  Proceed, proceed. I'll give her.

TOUCHSTONE  Good even, good Master What-ye-call-'t.  68
How do you, sir? You are very well met. God 'ild you  69
for your last company. I am very glad to see you. Even  70
a toy in hand here, sir.—Nay, pray be covered.  71

JAQUES  Will you be married, motley?

TOUCHSTONE  As the ox hath his bow, sir, the horse his  73
curb, and the falcon her bells, so man hath his desires;  74
and as pigeons bill, so wedlock would be nibbling.  75

JAQUES  And will you, being a man of your breeding,
be married under a bush like a beggar? Get you to  77
church, and have a good priest that can tell you what  78
marriage is. This fellow will but join you together as  79
they join wainscot; then one of you will prove a
shrunk panel and, like green timber, warp, warp.  81

---

**48 what though** what though it be so.  **As** Though  **49 necessary** (1) useful to horned animals (2) unavoidable to cuckolds.  **49–50 knows . . . goods** is endlessly well provided.  **51 knows . . . them** i.e., is endlessly supplied with cuckold's horns. (A sardonic interpretation of the proverb in lines 49–50.)  **dowry** marriage gift  **52 getting** (1) obtaining (2) begetting (in the sense that his wife's children will not be his).  **Even so** That's just how it is.  **53 Poor men alone?** i.e., Are lower-class men the only ones to suffer the indignity of wearing the horns of cuckoldry?  **deer** (1) horned animal (2) dear husband  **54 rascal** (1) young deer that are lean and out of season (2) poor ordinary husband.  **single** unmarried  **58 defense** (1) fortifications (including a type known as "hornwork") (2) the art of self-defense  **59 than to want** i.e., than to be without a horn. (Recalling the "horn of plenty," which is indeed precious.)  **61 dispatch us** finish off our business  **63 give the woman** give away the bride; conventionally, the bride's father answered the question, "Who giveth this woman to be married to this man?"  **68 What-ye-call-'t** (Probably joking on *Jakes* as "outhouse.")  **69 'ild you** yield you, reward you  **70 last** most recent  **71 a toy in hand** a trifle to be attended to, or literally by the hand.  **be covered** put on your hat, i.e., no need to show respect; or, cover up your bosom. (Said to Audrey, or perhaps to Jaques, who may have removed his hat in sardonic deference to the ceremony.)  **73 bow** yoke  **74 curb** chain or strap attached to the horse's bit and used to control it.  **bells** (Attached to a falcon's leg during training.)  **75 bill** stroke bill with bill  **77 under a bush** i.e., by a "hedge-priest," an uneducated clergyman  **78–9 tell . . . is** expound the obligations of marriage.  **81 warp** (1) shrivel and fit badly together (2) stray from the true path.

---

**8 ill-inhabited** ill-lodged  **9 Jove . . . house!** (An allusion to Ovid's *Metamorphoses* 8, containing the story of Jupiter and Mercury lodging disguised in the humble cottage of Baucis and Philemon.)  **10–11 verses . . . understood** (Ovid's verses were misunderstood by the barbaric Goths, among whom he lived in exile, just as Touchstone's wit is misunderstood by Audrey.)  **11–12 nor . . . understanding** (Wisdom, understanding, and memory were thought to occupy three main ventricles in the brain, and to be interconnected in the process of thought. *Forward* means "precocious.")  **13 great . . . room** exorbitant charge for refreshment or lodging in a cramped tavern room. (Some scholars see in this passage an allusion to the death of Christopher Marlowe, who was stabbed by Ingram Frysar at an inn in Deptford in a quarrel over a tavern reckoning, May 30, 1593.)  **18 feigning** inventive, imaginative. (But Touchstone plays on the sense of "false, lying.")  **19 may be said** i.e., it may be said  **20 feign** (With a further play on "desire.")  **24 honest** chaste.  **25 feign** (1) pretend (2) desire.  **27–8 hard-favored** ugly  **28 honesty** chastity  **30 material** full of pithy matter  **34 foul** ugly  **35–6 I thank . . . foul** i.e., my unattractive looks are what destiny has allotted to me.  **40 Sir** (Courtesy title for a clergyman.)  **next** nearest  **43 fain** gladly  **46 stagger** hesitate  **47 horn-beasts** antlered animals like deer and cattle, and therefore resembling cuckolded men with their cuckolds' horns.

TOUCHSTONE    I am not in the mind but I were better 82
to be married of him than of another, for he is not 83
like to marry me well; and not being well married, 84
it will be a good excuse for me hereafter to leave my
wife.

JAQUES    Go thou with me, and let me counsel thee.

TOUCHSTONE
Come, sweet Audrey.
We must be married, or we must live in bawdry. 89
Farewell, good Master Oliver; not
    "O sweet Oliver, 91
    O brave Oliver, 92
  Leave me not behind thee";
but
    "Wind away, 95
    Begone, I say,
  I will not to wedding with thee." 97
        [*Exeunt Jaques, Touchstone, and Audrey.*]

SIR OLIVER    'Tis no matter. Ne'er a fantastical knave of 98
them all shall flout me out of my calling.    *Exit.*

## 3.4

*Enter Rosalind and Celia.*

ROSALIND    Never talk to me. I will weep.

CELIA    Do, I prithee, but yet have the grace to consider
that tears do not become a man.

ROSALIND    But have I not cause to weep?

CELIA    As good cause as one would desire; therefore
weep.

ROSALIND    His very hair is of the dissembling color. 7

CELIA    Something browner than Judas's. Marry, his 8
kisses are Judas's own children. 9

ROSALIND    I'faith, his hair is of a good color.

CELIA    An excellent color. Your chestnut was ever the 11
only color. 12

ROSALIND    And his kissing is as full of sanctity as the
touch of holy bread. 14

CELIA    He hath bought a pair of cast lips of Diana. A 15
nun of winter's sisterhood kisses not more religiously; 16
the very ice of chastity is in them.

---

**82 I am . . . better** I do not know but that it would be better for me.
(Touchstone may be speaking aside here to Jaques.)    **83 of** by
**84 like** likely.    **well** (1) suitably (2) legally    **89 married** i.e., properly
married, as Jaques suggests, not by a hedge-priest. (Having been
found out, Touchstone wryly defers matters for the present.)
**91–7 "O . . . thee."** (Phrases from a current ballad.)    **92 brave**
worthy    **95 Wind** Wend, go    **98 fantastical** affected
**3.4. Location: The forest.**
**7 the dissembling color** i.e., reddish, traditionally the color of Judas's
hair.    **8 Something** Somewhat    **9 Judas's own children** i.e., as false
and betraying as the kiss given by Judas to Jesus when he betrayed
him to the high priests.    **11 Your chestnut** i.e., This chestnut color
that people talk about    **12 only** only fashionable    **14 holy bread**
either the unleavened bread of the Eucharist or ordinary leavened
bread that was blessed after the Eucharist and distributed to those
who had not received communion.    **15 cast . . . Diana** lips taken
from or modeled on a statue of Diana, goddess of chastity; such
stone lips would be severely cold and chaste. (Celia is puckishly
satirizing Rosalind's anxiety about Orlando's being late to his
appointment with her. Rosalind, she muses, certainly has found a
reticent lover!)    **16 of winter's sisterhood** i.e., devoted to barrenness
and cold

---

ROSALIND    But why did he swear he would come this
morning, and comes not?

CELIA    Nay, certainly, there is no truth in him.

ROSALIND    Do you think so?

CELIA    Yes. I think he is not a pickpurse nor a horse-
stealer, but for his verity in love, I do think him as
concave as a covered goblet or a worm-eaten nut. 24

ROSALIND    Not true in love?

CELIA    Yes, when he is in, but I think he is not in.

ROSALIND    You have heard him swear downright he
was.

CELIA    "Was" is not "is." Besides, the oath of a lover is
no stronger than the word of a tapster; they are both
the confirmer of false reckonings. He attends here in 31
the forest on the Duke your father.

ROSALIND    I met the Duke yesterday and had much
question with him. He asked me of what parentage I 34
was. I told him, of as good as he; so he laughed and let
me go. But what talk we of fathers, when there is such 36
a man as Orlando?

CELIA    Oh, that's a brave man! He writes brave verses, 38
speaks brave words, swears brave oaths, and breaks
them bravely, quite traverse, athwart the heart of his 40
lover, as a puny tilter, that spurs his horse but on 41
one side, breaks his staff like a noble goose. But all's 42
brave that youth mounts and folly guides. Who comes 43
here?

*Enter Corin.*

CORIN
Mistress and master, you have oft inquired
After the shepherd that complained of love, 46
Who you saw sitting by me on the turf,
Praising the proud disdainful shepherdess
That was his mistress.

CELIA                            Well, and what of him?

CORIN
If you will see a pageant truly played
Between the pale complexion of true love 51
And the red glow of scorn and proud disdain,
Go hence a little, and I shall conduct you,
If you will mark it.

ROSALIND                  Oh, come, let us remove! 54
The sight of lovers feedeth those in love.
Bring us to this sight, and you shall say
I'll prove a busy actor in their play.    *Exeunt.*

---

**24 concave** hollow, i.e., insincere    **31 false reckonings** (Tapsters, or
barkeeps, were notorious for inflating bills.)    **34 question** conversation    **36 what** why    **38 brave** fine, excellent    **40 traverse** across,
awry. (A term from medieval jousting or tilting; hence *tilter*, line 41.)
**41 puny** inexperienced. (Literally, junior.)    **but** only    **42 a noble
goose** i.e., a goose-headed young gallant.    **42–3 But . . . guides** But
everything is admirable that youth undertakes under the influence
of folly. (Said sardonically.)    **46 complained of** uttered a lament
against    **51 pale complexion** (Sighing was believed to draw blood
from the heart.)    **54 will mark** wish to observe.    **remove** leave
here and go.

# 3.5

*Enter Silvius and Phoebe.*

SILVIUS
Sweet Phoebe, do not scorn me, do not, Phoebe!
Say that you love me not, but say not so
In bitterness. The common executioner,
Whose heart th'accustomed sight of death makes hard,
Falls not the ax upon the humbled neck                    5
But first begs pardon. Will you sterner be                6
Than he that dies and lives by bloody drops?              7

*Enter Rosalind, Celia, and Corin [behind].*

PHOEBE
I would not be thy executioner;
I fly thee, for I would not injure thee.
Thou tell'st me there is murder in mine eye.
'Tis pretty, sure, and very probable,                     11
That eyes, that are the frail'st and softest things,
Who shut their coward gates on atomies,                   13
Should be called tyrants, butchers, murderers!
Now I do frown on thee with all my heart,
And if mine eyes can wound, now let them kill thee.
Now counterfeit to swoon; why, now fall down,            17
Or if thou canst not, oh, for shame, for shame,
Lie not, to say mine eyes are murderers!                  19
Now show the wound mine eye hath made in thee.
Scratch thee but with a pin, and there remains
Some scar of it; lean upon a rush,                        22
The cicatrice and capable impressure                      23
Thy palm some moment keeps; but now mine eyes,           24
Which I have darted at thee, hurt thee not,
Nor, I am sure, there is no force in eyes
That can do hurt.
SILVIUS                          O dear Phoebe,
If ever—as that "ever" may be near—
You meet in some fresh cheek the power of fancy,          29
Then shall you know the wounds invisible
That love's keen arrows make.
PHOEBE                              But till that time
Come not thou near me; and when that time comes,
Afflict me with thy mocks; pity me not,
As till that time I shall not pity thee.                  34
ROSALIND *[advancing]*
And why, I pray you? Who might be your mother,            35
That you insult, exult, and all at once,                  36
Over the wretched? What though you have no beauty—        37
As, by my faith, I see no more in you                     38
Than without candle may go dark to bed—                   39
Must you be therefore proud and pitiless?
Why, what means this? Why do you look on me?
I see no more in you than in the ordinary                 42
Of nature's sale-work. 'Od's my little life,              43
I think she means to tangle my eyes too!                  44
No, faith, proud mistress, hope not after it.             45
'Tis not your inky brows, your black silk hair,
Your bugle eyeballs, nor your cheek of cream              47
That can entame my spirits to your worship.               48
*[To Silvius]* You foolish shepherd, wherefore do you follow her,
Like foggy south, puffing with wind and rain?             50
You are a thousand times a properer man                   51
Than she a woman. 'Tis such fools as you
That makes the world full of ill-favored children.        53
'Tis not her glass, but you, that flatters her,           54
And out of you she sees herself more proper                55
Than any of her lineaments can show her.—                 56
But, mistress, know yourself. Down on your knees,
And thank heaven, fasting, for a good man's love!
For I must tell you friendly in your ear,
Sell when you can. You are not for all markets.
Cry the man mercy, love him, take his offer;              61
Foul is most foul, being foul to be a scoffer.—           62
So take her to thee, shepherd. Fare you well.
PHOEBE
Sweet youth, I pray you, chide a year together.           64
I had rather hear you chide than this man woo.
ROSALIND *[to Phoebe]*   He's fallen in love with your foulness, *[to Silvius]* and she'll fall in love with my anger. If it be so, as fast as she answers thee with frowning looks, I'll sauce her with bitter words. *[To* 69 *Phoebe]* Why look you so upon me?
PHOEBE    For no ill will I bear you.
ROSALIND
I pray you, do not fall in love with me,
For I am falser than vows made in wine.                   73
Besides, I like you not. *[To Silvius]* If you will know my house,
'Tis at the tuft of olives here hard by.—
Will you go, sister?—Shepherd, ply her hard.—             76

---

**3.5. Location: The forest.**
**5 Falls** lets fall   **6 But first begs pardon** without first begging pardon (as executioners did in Elizabethan times).   **7 dies . . . drops** makes his living by the deaths of others. (Stated as an oxymoron.)   **11 sure** to be sure. (Phoebe speaks ironically.)   **13 Who . . . atomies** i.e., that shut their sensitive eyelids against specks of dirt   **17 counterfeit to swoon** pretend that you are fainting   **19 to say** by saying   **22 lean upon a rush** press your hand against a reed   **23–4 The cicatrice . . . keeps** the scarlike and perceptible impression is retained by one's palm for a moment   **29 You . . . fancy** you yourself feel the powerful spell of love for some new face   **34 As** since   **35 Who . . . mother** (1) What human mother could have produced so inhuman a daughter (2) From what sort of a mother did you learn such scorn   **36 insult** exult scornfully.   **all at once** all at the same time

**37 have no beauty** are not particularly beautiful   **38–9 I see . . . bed** i.e., I see nothing in your beauty that might not go entirely unnoticed, nothing to distinguish you from other young women   **42 ordinary** common run   **43 sale-work** ready-made products, not of the best quality, not distinctive.   **'Od's** May God save   **44 tangle** ensnare   **45 faith** in faith. (A mild oath.)   **47 bugle** beadlike, black and glassy   **48 to your worship** (1) to the worship of you (2) to adore Your Worship (as if such beauty deserved an honorific title).   **50 south** south wind (from which came fog and rain; hence, Silvius's sighs and tears)   **51 properer** better-looking (since handsome is as handsome does)   **53 ill-favored** ugly   **54 glass** mirror   **55 out of you** i.e., with you as her mirror   **56 lineaments** features   **61 Cry . . . mercy** Beg the man's pardon   **62 Foul . . . scoffer** i.e., unattractive behavior like yours is at its most foul when it consists of scoffing. (Plays on two meanings of *foul*.)   **64 together** without intermission.   **69 sauce** rebuke   **73 in wine** while drunk.   **76 ply her hard** woo her energetically.

Come, sister.—Shepherdess, look on him better,
And be not proud. Though all the world could see, 78
None could be so abused in sight as he.— 79
Come, to our flock.          *Exit [with Celia and Corin].*

PHOEBE
Dead shepherd, now I find thy saw of might, 81
"Who ever loved that loved not at first sight?" 82

SILVIUS
Sweet Phoebe—

PHOEBE          Ha, what say'st thou, Silvius?

SILVIUS   Sweet Phoebe, pity me.

PHOEBE
Why, I am sorry for thee, gentle Silvius.

SILVIUS
Wherever sorrow is, relief would be. 86
If you do sorrow at my grief in love,
By giving love, your sorrow and my grief
Were both extermined. 89

PHOEBE
Thou hast my love. Is not that neighborly? 90

SILVIUS
I would have you.

PHOEBE          Why, that were covetousness. 91
Silvius, the time was that I hated thee,
And yet it is not that I bear thee love; 93
But since that thou canst talk of love so well, 94
Thy company, which erst was irksome to me, 95
I will endure, and I'll employ thee too.
But do not look for further recompense
Than thine own gladness that thou art employed.

SILVIUS
So holy and so perfect is my love,
And I in such a poverty of grace, 100
That I shall think it a most plenteous crop
To glean the broken ears after the man 102
That the main harvest reaps. Loose now and then 103
A scattered smile, and that I'll live upon. 104

PHOEBE
Know'st thou the youth that spoke to me erewhile? 105

SILVIUS
Not very well, but I have met him oft,
And he hath bought the cottage and the bounds 107
That the old carlot once was master of. 108

PHOEBE
Think not I love him, though I ask for him.
'Tis but a peevish boy—yet he talks well—
But what care I for words? Yet words do well

When he that speaks them pleases those that hear.
It is a pretty youth—not very pretty—
But sure he's proud—and yet his pride becomes him.
He'll make a proper man. The best thing in him 115
Is his complexion; and faster than his tongue
Did make offense, his eye did heal it up.
He is not very tall—yet for his years he's tall.
His leg is but so-so—and yet 'tis well.
There was a pretty redness in his lip,
A little riper and more lusty red
Than that mixed in his cheek; 'twas just the difference
Betwixt the constant red and mingled damask. 123
There be some women, Silvius, had they marked him
In parcels as I did, would have gone near 125
To fall in love with him; but for my part, 126
I love him not nor hate him not; and yet
I have more cause to hate him than to love him.
For what had he to do to chide at me? 129
He said mine eyes were black and my hair black,
And, now I am remembered, scorned at me. 131
I marvel why I answered not again. 132
But that's all one; omittance is no quittance. 133
I'll write to him a very taunting letter,
And thou shalt bear it. Wilt thou, Silvius?

SILVIUS
Phoebe, with all my heart.

PHOEBE          I'll write it straight; 136
The matter's in my head and in my heart.
I will be bitter with him and passing short. 138
Go with me, Silvius.          *Exeunt.*

❖

## 4.1

*Enter Rosalind and Celia, and Jaques.*

JAQUES   I prithee, pretty youth, let me be better acquainted with thee.

ROSALIND   They say you are a melancholy fellow.

JAQUES   I am so. I do love it better than laughing.

ROSALIND   Those that are in extremity of either are 5
abominable fellows and betray themselves to every
modern censure worse than drunkards. 7

JAQUES   Why, 'tis good to be sad and say nothing.

ROSALIND   Why then, 'tis good to be a post.

JAQUES   I have neither the scholar's melancholy, which
is emulation, nor the musician's, which is fantastical, 11
nor the courtier's, which is proud, nor the soldier's,
which is ambitious, nor the lawyer's, which is politic, 13
nor the lady's, which is nice, nor the lover's, which is 14

---

**78 could see** could look at you   **79 abused in sight** deceived through the eyes   **81 Dead shepherd** i.e., Christopher Marlowe, who died in 1593.   **saw** saying.   **of might** forceful, convincing   **82 Who . . . sight?** (From Marlowe's *Hero and Leander*, Sestiad 1, 176, first published in 1598.)   **86 Wherever . . . be** Sorrow cries out for relief.   **89 Were both extermined** would both be exterminated, ended.   **90 Is . . . neighborly?** i.e., May not I love you in the sense of loving one's neighbor as oneself?   **91 covetousness** (The tenth commandment forbids coveting anything that is one's neighbor's.)   **93 yet it is not** the time has not yet come   **94 since that** since   **95 erst** formerly   **100 poverty of grace** lack of reciprocated affection   **102 To glean . . . ears** to gather up the scattered fragments of grain   **103 Loose** Release, send forth   **104 scattered** thrown negligently, as in the gleanings of the harvest   **105 erewhile** just now.   **107 bounds** pastures   **108 carlot** churl, countryman

**115 proper** handsome   **123 mingled damask** mingled red and white, the color of the damask rose.   **125 In parcels** bit by bit   **125–6 gone . . . fall** been on the point of falling   **129 what . . . do** what business had he   **131 am remembered** remember   **132 again** back.   **133 But . . . quittance** i.e., But just the same, my failure to answer him doesn't mean I won't do so later.   **136 straight** immediately   **138 passing short** exceedingly curt.
**4.1. Location: The forest.**
**5 are in . . . of** go to extremes in   **7 modern censure** common judgment   **11 emulation** envy (of a fellow scholar).   **fantastical** extravagantly fanciful   **13 politic** grave and diplomatic, calculated   **14 nice** fastidious

all these; but it is a melancholy of mine own, com- 15
pounded of many simples, extracted from many 16
objects, and indeed the sundry contemplation of my 17
travels, in which my often rumination wraps me in a 18
most humorous sadness. 19

ROSALIND    A traveler! By my faith, you have great
reason to be sad. I fear you have sold your own lands
to see other men's. Then to have seen much and to
have nothing is to have rich eyes and poor hands.

JAQUES    Yes, I have gained my experience.

*Enter Orlando.*

ROSALIND    And your experience makes you sad. I had
rather have a fool to make me merry than experience
to make me sad—and to travel for it too! 27

ORLANDO    Good day and happiness, dear Rosalind!

JAQUES    Nay, then, God b'wi'you, an you talk in blank 29
verse.

ROSALIND    Farewell, Monsieur Traveler. Look you lisp 31
and wear strange suits, disable all the benefits of your 32
own country, be out of love with your nativity, and 33
almost chide God for making you that countenance
you are, or I will scarce think you have swam in a 35
gondola. *[Exit Jaques.]* 36
Why, how now, Orlando, where have you been all this
while? You a lover? An you serve me such another
trick, never come in my sight more.

ORLANDO    My fair Rosalind, I come within an hour of
my promise.

ROSALIND    Break an hour's promise in love? He that will
divide a minute into a thousand parts and break but
a part of the thousandth part of a minute in the affairs
of love, it may be said of him that Cupid hath clapped 45
him o'th' shoulder, but I'll warrant him heart-whole. 46

ORLANDO    Pardon me, dear Rosalind.

ROSALIND    Nay, an you be so tardy, come no more in
my sight. I had as lief be wooed of a snail. 49

ORLANDO    Of a snail?

ROSALIND    Ay, of a snail; for though he comes slowly,
he carries his house on his head—a better jointure, I 52
think, than you make a woman. Besides, he brings his 53
destiny with him.

ORLANDO    What's that?

ROSALIND    Why, horns, which such as you are fain to 56
be beholding to your wives for. But he comes armed in 57

his fortune and prevents the slander of his wife. 58

ORLANDO    Virtue is no horn-maker, and my Rosalind is
virtuous.

ROSALIND    And I am your Rosalind.

CELIA    It pleases him to call you so; but he hath a Rosalind of a better leer than you. 63

ROSALIND    Come, woo me, woo me, for now I am in a
holiday humor and like enough to consent. What
would you say to me now, an I were your very, very
Rosalind?

ORLANDO    I would kiss before I spoke.

ROSALIND    Nay, you were better speak first, and when
you were graveled for lack of matter, you might take 70
occasion to kiss. Very good orators, when they are out, 71
they will spit; and for lovers lacking—God warrant 72
us!—matter, the cleanliest shift is to kiss. 73

ORLANDO    How if the kiss be denied?

ROSALIND    Then she puts you to entreaty, and there
begins new matter.

ORLANDO    Who could be out, being before his beloved
mistress?

ROSALIND    Marry, that should you, if I were your
mistress, or I should think my honesty ranker than 80
my wit.

ORLANDO    What, of my suit? 82

ROSALIND    Not out of your apparel, and yet out of your
suit. Am not I your Rosalind?

ORLANDO    I take some joy to say you are, because I
would be talking of her.

ROSALIND    Well, in her person I say I will not have you.

ORLANDO    Then in mine own person, I die.

ROSALIND    No, faith, die by attorney. The poor world is 89
almost six thousand years old, and in all this time 90
there was not any man died in his own person, 91
videlicet, in a love cause. Troilus had his brains 92
dashed out with a Grecian club, yet he did what he 93
could to die before, and he is one of the patterns of
love. Leander, he would have lived many a fair year 95
though Hero had turned nun, if it had not been for a
hot midsummer night; for, good youth, he went but
forth to wash him in the Hellespont and being taken
with the cramp was drowned; and the foolish chron-

---

15–19 **compounded . . . sadness** made up of many ingredients, extracted from the many objects of my observation and, indeed, from the diversified considerations of my travels, my frequent rumination upon which wraps me in a most whimsical and moody sadness. 27 **travel** (Meaning also "travail," labor.) 29 **an** if 31 **Look** Be sure, see to it. (Said ironically.) **lisp** i.e., affect a foreign accent 32 **disable** disparage. **benefits** attractive features 33 **nativity** country of birth 35 **are** i.e., have 35–6 **swam . . . gondola** floated in a gondola, i.e., been in Venice, where almost all travelers go. 45–6 **Cupid . . . heart-whole** Cupid may have tried to arrest him, but I'm sure his heart remains unengaged. (Arresting officers customarily grasped the culprit by the shoulder.) 49 **lief** willingly. **of** by 52 **jointure** marriage settlement 53 **than . . . woman** than you, Orlando, are able to settle on your prospective wife. 56 **horns** (1) snails' horns (2) cuckold's horns, signs of an unfaithful wife. **fain** obliged 57 **beholding** beholden, indebted

57–8 **But . . . fortune** The snail comes already provided with the horns that are his nature and his destiny, thereby forestalling the scandal that would otherwise attach to his wife. (Since a snail is naturally horned, no scandal can be adduced from them.) 63 **leer** appearance, color 70 **graveled** stuck. (Literally, run aground on a shoal.) 71 **out** at a loss for words 72 **warrant** defend 73 **shift** tactic 80 **honesty ranker** chastity more corrupt. (Rosalind would rely on her wit to keep her lover off balance and thus defend her chastity. She may use Orlando's *out*, line 77, in a sexual sense of not being admitted.) 82 **of my suit** (Orlando means "out of my suit," at a loss for words in my wooing; but Rosalind puns on the meaning "suit of clothes"; to be out of apparel would be to be undressed.) 89 **attorney** proxy. 90 **six . . . old** (A common figure in biblical calculation.) 91 **died** who died 92 **videlicet** namely. **Troilus** hero of the story of Troilus and Cressida, in which he remains faithful to her, but she is faithless to him 92–3 **had . . . club** (Troilus was slain by Achilles with sword or spear in more traditional accounts. Rosalind's version is calculatedly unromantic.) 95 **Leander** the hero of the story of Hero and Leander, who lost his life swimming the Hellespont to visit his sweetheart. (Rosalind's account of the cramp again undercuts romantic idealism.)

iclers of that age found it was—Hero of Sestos. But 100
these are all lies. Men have died from time to time,
and worms have eaten them, but not for love.

ORLANDO   I would not have my right Rosalind of this 103
mind, for I protest her frown might kill me.          104

ROSALIND   By this hand, it will not kill a fly. But come,
now I will be your Rosalind in a more coming-on 106
disposition; and ask me what you will, I will grant it.

ORLANDO   Then love me, Rosalind.

ROSALIND   Yes, faith, will I, Fridays and Saturdays 109
and all.

ORLANDO   And wilt thou have me?

ROSALIND   Ay, and twenty such.

ORLANDO   What sayest thou?

ROSALIND   Are you not good?

ORLANDO   I hope so.

ROSALIND   Why then, can one desire too much of a
good thing?—Come, sister, you shall be the priest
and marry us.—Give me your hand, Orlando.—
What do you say, sister?

ORLANDO   Pray thee, marry us.

CELIA   I cannot say the words.                        121

ROSALIND   You must begin, "Will you, Orlando—"

CELIA   Go to. Will you, Orlando, have to wife this 123
Rosalind?

ORLANDO   I will.

ROSALIND   Ay, but when?

ORLANDO   Why now, as fast as she can marry us.      127

ROSALIND   Then you must say, "I take thee, Rosalind,
for wife."                                             129

ORLANDO   I take thee, Rosalind, for wife.

ROSALIND   I might ask you for your commission; but I 131
do take thee, Orlando, for my husband. There's a girl
goes before the priest, and certainly a woman's 133
thought runs before her actions.                      134

ORLANDO   So do all thoughts; they are winged.

ROSALIND   Now tell me how long you would have her
after you have possessed her.

ORLANDO   For ever and a day.

ROSALIND   Say "a day," without the "ever." No, no, Orlando, men are April when they woo, December when
they wed. Maids are May when they are maids, but
the sky changes when they are wives. I will be more
jealous of thee than a Barbary cock-pigeon over his 143
hen, more clamorous than a parrot against rain, more 144
newfangled than an ape, more giddy in my desires 145
than a monkey. I will weep for nothing, like Diana in 146

the fountain, and I will do that when you are disposed 147
to be merry; I will laugh like a hyena, and that when
thou art inclined to sleep.

ORLANDO   But will my Rosalind do so?

ROSALIND   By my life, she will do as I do.

ORLANDO   Oh, but she is wise.

ROSALIND   Or else she could not have the wit to do this.
The wiser, the waywarder. Make the doors upon a 154
woman's wit, and it will out at the casement; shut 155
that, and 'twill out at the keyhole; stop that, 'twill fly
with the smoke out at the chimney.

ORLANDO   A man that had a wife with such a wit, he
might say, "Wit, whither wilt?"                        159

ROSALIND   Nay, you might keep that check for it till 160
you met your wife's wit going to your neighbor's bed.

ORLANDO   And what wit could wit have to excuse that? 162

ROSALIND   Marry, to say she came to seek you there. 163
You shall never take her without her answer unless 164
you take her without her tongue. Oh, that woman that
cannot make her fault her husband's occasion, let her 166
never nurse her child herself, for she will breed it like 167
a fool!

ORLANDO   For these two hours, Rosalind, I will leave
thee.

ROSALIND   Alas, dear love, I cannot lack thee two
hours!

ORLANDO   I must attend the Duke at dinner. By two
o'clock I will be with thee again.

ROSALIND   Ay, go your ways, go your ways. I knew
what you would prove. My friends told me as much,
and I thought no less. That flattering tongue of yours
won me. 'Tis but one cast away, and so, come, death! 177
Two o'clock is your hour?

ORLANDO   Ay, sweet Rosalind.

ROSALIND   By my troth, and in good earnest, and so
God mend me, and by all pretty oaths that are not
dangerous, if you break one jot of your promise or 182
come one minute behind your hour, I will think you
the most pathetical break-promise, and the most 184
hollow lover, and the most unworthy of her you call
Rosalind, that may be chosen out of the gross band of 186
the unfaithful. Therefore beware my censure, and
keep your promise.

ORLANDO   With no less religion than if thou wert 189
indeed my Rosalind. So adieu.

**100 found it was** arrived at the verdict that the cause (of his death) was   **103 right** real   **104 protest** insist, proclaim   **106 coming-on** compliant   **109 faith** in faith. (A mild oath.)   **121 I . . . words** i.e., I don't know the proper words for the marriage service.   **123 Go to** (An exclamation of mild impatience.)   **have to wife** take to you as your wife   **127 she** Celia   **129 for wife** as my wife.   **131 ask . . . commission** ask you what authority you have for taking her (since no one is here to give the bride away and since she herself has not yet consented)   **133 goes . . . priest** who anticipates before the "priest" has even asked the question   **134 runs . . . actions** i.e., goes flightily on, outstripping sane conduct.   **143 Barbary cock-pigeon** an ornamental pigeon actually from the orient, not the Barbary (north) coast of Africa. (Following Pliny, the cock-pigeon's jealousy was often contrasted with the mildness of the hen.)   **144 against** in anticipation of   **145 newfangled** infatuated with novelty   **146 for nothing** for no apparent reason

**146–7 Diana in the fountain** (Diana frequently appeared as the centerpiece of fountains. John Stowe's *Survey of London* describes the setting up of a fountain with a Diana in green marble in the year 1596.)   **154 The wiser, the waywarder** i.e., The more experienced in the war of the sexes, the more a woman can insist on having her own way.   **Make** Make fast, shut   **155 casement** hinged window   **159 Wit, whither wilt?** Wit, where are you going? (A common Elizabethan expression implying that the person addressed is talking fantastically, with a wildly wandering wit.)   **160 check for it** retort for your wife's conduct   **162 And . . . that?** And what witty wife would have the presence of mind to explain how she happened to be climbing into your neighbor's bed?   **163 Marry** i.e., Truly   **164 take her** catch her unawares. (With wordplay on *take her*, i.e., find her speechless, in the next line.)   **166 make . . . occasion** i.e., turn a defense of her own conduct into an accusation against her husband   **167 breed it** bring it up   **177 'Tis . . . away** i.e., It's only another a sad instance of a woman being jilted. (Rosalind feigns hysterics.)   **182 dangerous** i.e., blasphemous. (Rosalind's oaths are decorous.)   **184 pathetical** awful, miserable   **186 gross band** whole troop   **189 religion** strict fidelity

ROSALIND    Well, Time is the old justice that examines all such offenders, and let Time try. Adieu. 192

*Exit [Orlando].*

CELIA    You have simply misused our sex in your love 193 prate. We must have your doublet and hose plucked 194 over your head and show the world what the bird 195 hath done to her own nest. 196

ROSALIND    Oh, coz, coz, coz, my pretty little coz, that thou didst know how many fathom deep I am in love! But it cannot be sounded; my affection hath an unknown 199 bottom, like the Bay of Portugal.

CELIA    Or rather, bottomless, that as fast as you pour 201 affection in, it runs out.

ROSALIND    No, that same wicked bastard of Venus, that 203 was begot of thought, conceived of spleen, and born of 204 madness, that blind rascally boy that abuses everyone's 205 eyes because his own are out, let him be judge 206 how deep I am in love. I'll tell thee, Aliena, I cannot be out of the sight of Orlando. I'll go find a shadow and 208 sigh till he come.

CELIA    And I'll sleep.    *Exeunt.*

❖

## 4.2

*Enter Jaques and Lords [dressed as] foresters.*

JAQUES    Which is he that killed the deer?

FIRST LORD    Sir, it was I.

JAQUES    Let's present him to the Duke, like a Roman conqueror, and it would do well to set the deer's horns upon his head for a branch of victory. Have you no 5 song, Forester, for this purpose?

SECOND LORD    Yes, sir.

JAQUES    Sing it. 'Tis no matter how it be in tune, so it 8 make noise enough.    *Music.*

*Song.*

SECOND LORD *[sings]*
What shall he have that killed the deer?
His leather skin and horns to wear.
Then sing him home; the rest shall bear    12
    This burden.    13
Take thou no scorn to wear the horn;    14
It was a crest ere thou wast born.
    Thy father's father wore it,
    And thy father bore it.
The horn, the horn, the lusty horn
Is not a thing to laugh to scorn.    *Exeunt.*

❖

## 4.3

*Enter Rosalind and Celia.*

ROSALIND How say you now? Is it not past two o'clock? And here much Orlando!    2

CELIA    I warrant you, with pure love and troubled brain 3 he hath ta'en his bow and arrows and is gone forth—to sleep.

*Enter Silvius [with a letter].*

Look who comes here.

SILVIUS *[to Rosalind]*
My errand is to you, fair youth.
My gentle Phoebe bid me give you this.
    *[He gives the letter.]*
I know not the contents, but as I guess,
By the stern brow and waspish action
Which she did use as she was writing of it,
It bears an angry tenor. Pardon me;
I am but as a guiltless messenger.

ROSALIND *[examining the letter]*
Patience herself would startle at this letter    14
And play the swaggerer. Bear this, bear all!    15
She says I am not fair, that I lack manners;    16
She calls me proud, and that she could not love me
Were man as rare as phoenix. 'Od's my will!    18
Her love is not the hare that I do hunt.    19
Why writes she so to me? Well, shepherd, well,
This is a letter of your own device.

SILVIUS
No, I protest, I know not the contents.
Phoebe did write it.

ROSALIND                Come, come, you are a fool,
And turned into the extremity of love.    24
I saw her hand; she has a leathern hand,    25
A freestone-colored hand. I verily did think    26
That her old gloves were on, but 'twas her hands;
She has a huswife's hand—but that's no matter.    28
I say she never did invent this letter;
This is a man's invention and his hand.

SILVIUS    Sure it is hers.

ROSALIND
Why, 'tis a boisterous and a cruel style,
A style for challengers. Why, she defies me,    33
Like Turk to Christian. Women's gentle brain
Could not drop forth such giant-rude invention,

192 **try** determine, judge.    193 **simply misused** absolutely slandered
**194–6 We . . . nest** i.e., We must expose you for what you are, a woman, and show everyone how a woman has defamed her own kind just as an unclean bird proverbially fouls its own nest.    199 **sounded** measured for depth    201 **that** so that    203 **bastard of Venus** i.e., Cupid, son of Venus and Mercury (or Zeus) rather than Vulcan, Venus's husband    204 **thought** fancy.    **spleen** i.e., impulse    205 **abuses** deceives    206 **out** blinded    208 **shadow** shady spot
**4.2. Location: The forest.**
5 **branch** wreath    8 **so** provided that    **12–13 bear This burden** (1) sing this refrain (2) wear the horns that all cuckolds must wear.
**14 Take . . . scorn** Be not ashamed. (Alludes to joke about cuckold's horns.)

**4.3. Location: The forest.**
**2 much Orlando** (Said ironically: A fat lot we see of Orlando!)
**3 warrant** assure    **14–15 Patience . . . all!** Patience herself would be startled into a violent display by this letter. If one were to put up with such a missive, one would have to accept any insult!    **16 fair** handsome    **18 phoenix** a fabulous bird of Arabia, the only one of its kind, which lived five hundred years, died in flames, and was reborn of its own ashes.    **'Od's my will!** (An oath: "May God's will be done!")
**19 Her . . . hunt** i.e., I am not seeking her love.    **24 turned** transformed
**25 leathern** leathery (Said of the handwriting and the hand itself.)
**26 freestone-colored** sandstone-colored, brownish-yellow
**28 huswife's hand** (Suggesting "dishpan hands")    **33 challengers** those who issue challenges to a duel.

Such Ethiop words, blacker in their effect    36
Than in their countenance. Will you hear the letter?    37

SILVIUS
So please you, for I never heard it yet;
Yet, heard too much of Phoebe's cruelty.

ROSALIND
She Phoebes me. Mark how the tyrant writes.    40
    (*Read*) "Art thou god to shepherd turned,
    That a maiden's heart hath burned?"
Can a woman rail thus?

SILVIUS    Call you this railing?

ROSALIND
    (*Read*) "Why, thy godhead laid apart,    45
    War'st thou with a woman's heart?"    46
Did you ever hear such railing?    47
    "Whiles the eye of man did woo me,    48
    That could do no vengeance to me."—    49
Meaning me a beast.    50
    "If the scorn of your bright eyne    51
    Have power to raise such love in mine,
    Alack, in me what strange effect    53
    Would they work in mild aspect!    54
    Whiles you chid me, I did love;    55
    How then might your prayers move!    56
    He that brings this love to thee    57
    Little knows this love in me;    58
    And by him seal up thy mind,    59
    Whether that thy youth and kind    60
    Will the faithful offer take
    Of me and all that I can make,    62
    Or else by him my love deny,
    And then I'll study how to die."    64

SILVIUS    Call you this chiding?
CELIA    Alas, poor shepherd!
ROSALIND    Do you pity him? No, he deserves no pity.—
Wilt thou love such a woman? What, to make thee an    68
instrument and play false strains upon thee? Not to be    69
endured! Well, go your way to her, for I see love hath
made thee a tame snake, and say this to her: that if she    71
love me, I charge her to love thee; if she will not, I will
never have her unless thou entreat for her. If you be a
true lover, hence, and not a word; for here comes
more company.    *Exit Silvius.*

    *Enter Oliver.*

OLIVER
    Good morrow, fair ones. Pray you, if you know,

Where in the purlieus of this forest stands    77
A sheepcote fenced about with olive trees?

CELIA
West of this place, down in the neighbor bottom;    79
The rank of osiers by the murmuring stream    80
Left on your right hand brings you to the place.    81
But at this hour the house doth keep itself;
There's none within.

OLIVER
If that an eye may profit by a tongue,
Then should I know you by description,
Such garments and such years: "The boy is fair,
Of female favor, and bestows himself    87
Like a ripe sister; the woman, low    88
And browner than her brother." Are not you
The owner of the house I did inquire for?

CELIA
It is no boast, being asked, to say we are.

OLIVER
Orlando doth commend him to you both,    92
And to that youth he calls his Rosalind
He sends this bloody napkin. Are you he?    94
    [*He produces a bloody handkerchief.*]

ROSALIND
I am. What must we understand by this?

OLIVER
Some of my shame, if you will know of me
What man I am, and how, and why, and where
This handkerchief was stained.

CELIA                        I pray you, tell it.

OLIVER
When last the young Orlando parted from you
He left a promise to return again
Within an hour, and, pacing through the forest,
Chewing the food of sweet and bitter fancy,    102
Lo, what befell! He threw his eye aside,
And mark what object did present itself:
Under an old oak, whose boughs were mossed with
    age
And high top bald with dry antiquity,
A wretched, ragged man, o'ergrown with hair,
Lay sleeping on his back. About his neck
A green and gilded snake had wreathed itself,
Who with her head, nimble in threats, approached
The opening of his mouth; but suddenly,
Seeing Orlando, it unlinked itself    112
And with indented glides did slip away    113
Into a bush, under which bush's shade
A lioness, with udders all drawn dry,    115
Lay couching, head on ground, with catlike watch,
When that the sleeping man should stir; for 'tis    117

---

36 **Ethiop** i.e., black    36–7 **blacker . . . countenance** even blacker in what they say than in their black appearance on the page.    40 **Phoebes me** i.e., addresses me in her cruel style.    45 **thy . . . apart** having laid aside your godhead (for human shape)    46 **War'st thou** warrest thou, do you make war    47 **railing** scolding.    48 **Whiles . . . woo me** While any other man did woo me    49 **vengeance** mischief, harm    50 **Meaning me** i.e., Implying that I am    51 **eyne** eyes    53–4 **Alack . . . aspect!** Alas, what powerful effect would your eyes have on me if you were to speak mildly rather than scornfully! (With a suggestion in *aspect* of astrological influence.)    55 **chid** chided    56 **then** i.e., if you were to speak kindly to me    57 **He** Silvius.    **this love** the love expressed in this letter    58 **Little . . . me** has no personal experience of the love I feel    59 **by . . . mind** i.e., send your thoughts in a letter via Silvius    60 **Whether . . . kind** if your youthful nature    62 **make** make offer of    64 **study** practice    68–9 **to make . . . instrument** to make an instrument (i.e., messenger) of you. (With a suggestion of making a person into a musical instrument; cf. *Hamlet*, 3.2.363, "You would play upon me," etc.)    69 **strains** parts of a piece of music    71 **tame snake** i.e., pathetic wretch

77 **purlieus** borders, boundaries    79 **neighbor bottom** neighboring dell    80 **rank of osiers** row of willows    81 **Left** left behind, passed    87 **favor** features.    **bestows** comports    88 **ripe** mature or elder    92 **doth commend him** sends his greetings    94 **napkin** handkerchief.    102 **Chewing . . . fancy** ruminating on the bittersweet nature of love    112 **unlinked** uncoiled    113 **indented** zigzag    115 **with . . . dry** (It would therefore be fierce with hunger.)    117 **When** for the moment

The royal disposition of that beast
To prey on nothing that doth seem as dead.
This seen, Orlando did approach the man
And found it was his brother, his elder brother.

CELIA
Oh, I have heard him speak of that same brother,
And he did render him the most unnatural          123
That lived amongst men.

OLIVER                                 And well he might so do,
For well I know he was unnatural.

ROSALIND
But to Orlando: did he leave him there,
Food to the sucked and hungry lioness?

OLIVER
Twice did he turn his back and purposed so;
But kindness, nobler ever than revenge,
And nature, stronger than his just occasion,      130
Made him give battle to the lioness,
Who quickly fell before him; in which hurtling    132
From miserable slumber I awaked.

CELIA
Are you his brother?

ROSALIND                          Was't you he rescued?

CELIA
Was't you that did so oft contrive to kill him?

OLIVER
'Twas I, but 'tis not I. I do not shame            136
To tell you what I was, since my conversion
So sweetly tastes, being the thing I am.

ROSALIND
But for the bloody napkin?

OLIVER                            By and by.            139
When from the first to last betwixt us two
Tears our recountments had most kindly bathed,     141
As how I came into that desert place,
In brief, he led me to the gentle Duke,
Who gave me fresh array and entertainment,         144
Committing me unto my brother's love;
Who led me instantly unto his cave,
There stripped himself, and here upon his arm
The lioness had torn some flesh away,
Which all this while had bled; and now he fainted
And cried, in fainting, upon Rosalind.
Brief, I recovered him, bound up his wound,        151
And after some small space, being strong at heart,
He sent me hither, stranger as I am,
To tell this story, that you might excuse
His broken promise, and to give this napkin
Dyed in his blood unto the shepherd youth
That he in sport doth call his Rosalind.
                                    [*Rosalind swoons.*]

CELIA
Why, how now, Ganymede, sweet Ganymede!

OLIVER
Many will swoon when they do look on blood.

CELIA
There is more in it.—Cousin Ganymede!              160

OLIVER   Look, he recovers.

ROSALIND   I would I were at home.

CELIA   We'll lead you thither.—
I pray you, will you take him by the arm?
                            [*They help Rosalind up.*]

OLIVER   Be of good cheer, youth. You a man? You lack
a man's heart.

ROSALIND   I do so, I confess it. Ah, sirrah, a body would  167
think this was well counterfeited. I pray you, tell your
brother how well I counterfeited. Heigh-ho!

OLIVER   This was not counterfeit. There is too great testimony in your complexion that it was a passion of   171
earnest.                                             172

ROSALIND   Counterfeit, I assure you.

OLIVER   Well then, take a good heart and counterfeit to   174
be a man.                                            175

ROSALIND   So I do; but, i'faith, I should have been a
woman by right.

CELIA   Come, you look paler and paler. Pray you, draw
homewards.—Good sir, go with us.

OLIVER
That will I, for I must bear answer back
How you excuse my brother, Rosalind.

ROSALIND   I shall devise something. But, I pray you,
commend my counterfeiting to him. Will you go?
                                            *Exeunt.*

## 5.1

*Enter* [*Touchstone the*] *Clown and Audrey.*

TOUCHSTONE   We shall find a time, Audrey. Patience,
gentle Audrey.

AUDREY   Faith, the priest was good enough, for all the   3
old gentleman's saying.                              4

TOUCHSTONE   A most wicked Sir Oliver, Audrey, a most
vile Mar-text. But Audrey, there is a youth here in the
forest lays claim to you.

AUDREY   Ay, I know who 'tis. He hath no interest in me   8
in the world. Here comes the man you mean.

*Enter William.*

TOUCHSTONE   It is meat and drink to me to see a clown.   10
By my troth, we that have good wits have much to     11
answer for. We shall be flouting; we cannot hold.    12

WILLIAM   Good even, Audrey.

AUDREY   God gi' good even, William.                 14

WILLIAM   And good even to you, sir.
                            [*He removes his hat.*]

**160 There is more in it** There is more to it than that.   **Cousin** i.e.,
kinsperson, a term appropriate to brother and sister. (In reality,
Rosalind is Celia's cousin.)   **167 a body** anybody   **171–2 a passion of
earnest** a genuine swoon.   **174–5 counterfeit . . . man** i.e., be a man.
(With wordplay on *counterfeit*, pretend.)
**5.1. Location: The forest.**
**3–4 the old gentleman's** i.e., Jaques's   **8 interest in** claim to
**10 clown** i.e., country yokel.   **11–12 we . . . hold** i.e., we professional
fools have much to answer for in providing a model of folly that
yokels like William are too apt to imitate. We fools are always scoffing; we can't restrain ourselves.   **14 God gi' good even** God give you
good evening. (Here, afternoon.)

**123 render him** describe him as   **130 just occasion** just opportunity
and motive (for revenge)   **132 hurtling** conflict, tumult   **136 do not
shame** am not ashamed   **139 for** as regards   **141 recountments**
relating of events (to one another)   **144 array** attire.   **entertainment**
hospitality, provision   **151 Brief** In brief.   **recovered** revived

TOUCHSTONE    Good even, gentle friend. Cover thy head, cover thy head. Nay, prithee be covered. How old are you, friend?

WILLIAM    Five-and-twenty, sir.

TOUCHSTONE    A ripe age. Is thy name William?

WILLIAM    William, sir.

TOUCHSTONE    A fair name. Wast born i'th' forest here?

WILLIAM    Ay, sir, I thank God.

TOUCHSTONE    "Thank God"—a good answer. Art rich?

WILLIAM    Faith, sir, so-so.

TOUCHSTONE    "So-so" is good, very good, very excellent good; and yet it is not, it is but so-so. Art thou wise?

WILLIAM    Ay, sir, I have a pretty wit.

TOUCHSTONE    Why, thou say'st well. I do now remember a saying, "The fool doth think he is wise, but the wise man knows himself to be a fool." The heathen 32 philosopher, when he had a desire to eat a grape, 33 would open his lips when he put it into his mouth, 34 meaning thereby that grapes were made to eat and 35 lips to open. You do love this maid? 36

WILLIAM    I do, sir.

TOUCHSTONE    Give me your hand. Art thou learned?

WILLIAM    No, sir.

TOUCHSTONE    Then learn this of me: to have is to have. For it is a figure in rhetoric that drink, being poured 41 out of a cup into a glass, by filling the one doth empty 42 the other. For all your writers do consent that *ipse* is 43 he. Now, you are not ipse, for I am he. 44

WILLIAM    Which he, sir?

TOUCHSTONE    He, sir, that must marry this woman. Therefore, you clown, abandon—which is in the 47 vulgar "leave"—the society—which in the boorish is 48 "company"—of this female—which in the common is "woman"; which together is, abandon the society of this female, or, clown, thou perishest; or, to thy better understanding, diest; or, to wit, I kill thee, make thee 52 away, translate thy life into death, thy liberty into bondage. I will deal in poison with thee, or in basti- 54 nado, or in steel; I will bandy with thee in faction, I 55 will o'errun thee with policy; I will kill thee a hundred 56 and fifty ways. Therefore tremble, and depart.

AUDREY    Do, good William.

WILLIAM    God rest you merry, sir.                    *Exit*. 59

*Enter Corin.*

CORIN    Our master and mistress seeks you. Come, away, away!

TOUCHSTONE    Trip, Audrey, trip, Audrey!—I attend, I 62 attend.                                                    *Exeunt*.

❖

## 5.2

*Enter Orlando [with his wounded arm in a sling] and Oliver.*

ORLANDO    Is't possible that on so little acquaintance you should like her? That but seeing, you should love her? And loving, woo? And, wooing, she should grant? And will you persevere to enjoy her?

OLIVER    Neither call the giddiness of it in question, the 5 poverty of her, the small acquaintance, my sudden wooing, nor her sudden consenting; but say with me, "I love Aliena"; say with her that she loves me; consent with both that we may enjoy each other. It shall be to your good; for my father's house and all the revenue that was old Sir Rowland's will I estate upon 11 you, and here live and die a shepherd.

*Enter Rosalind.*

ORLANDO    You have my consent. Let your wedding be tomorrow. Thither will I invite the Duke and all 's 14 contented followers. Go you and prepare Aliena; for look you, here comes my Rosalind. 16

ROSALIND    God save you, brother. 17

OLIVER    And you, fair sister.                    [*Exit*.] 18

ROSALIND    O my dear Orlando, how it grieves me to see thee wear thy heart in a scarf! 20

ORLANDO    It is my arm.

ROSALIND    I thought thy heart had been wounded with the claws of a lion.

ORLANDO    Wounded it is, but with the eyes of a lady.

ROSALIND    Did your brother tell you how I counterfeited to swoon when he showed me your handkerchief?

ORLANDO    Ay, and greater wonders than that.

ROSALIND    Oh, I know where you are. Nay, 'tis true. 28 There was never anything so sudden but the fight of two rams and Caesar's thrasonical brag of "I came, 30 saw, and overcame." For your brother and my sister 31 no sooner met but they looked, no sooner looked but they loved, no sooner loved but they sighed, no sooner sighed but they asked one another the reason, no sooner knew the reason but they sought the remedy; and in these degrees have they made a pair of 36

---

**32–6 The heathen . . . open** (This bit of fatuously self-evident wisdom parodies the logical proofs of the ancient philosophers. William, whose mouth is no doubt gaping like a rustic's, is invited to consider the consequences of his desire.)    **41 figure** figure of speech, trope    **41–3 drink . . . other** i.e., both Touchstone and William cannot possess Audrey.    **43–4 For . . . am he** For all the ancient authorities concur that the word *ipse* in Latin means "he." But you are not *ipse*, i.e., the man of the hour, the one destined to win Audrey, for I am that man. (By "your writers," Touchstone means "these writers that people talk about," not writers that William can lay personal claim to.)    **47–8 the vulgar** common colloquial speech. ("The boorish" and "the common" have the same meaning in Touchstone's continuing speech.)    **52 to wit** in other words    **54–5 or in bastinado** either in beating with a cudgel    **55 bandy** contend.    **in faction** factiously    **56 o'errun . . . policy** overwhelm you with craft, cunning    **59 God . . . merry** (A common salutation at parting.)

**62 Trip** Go nimbly
**5.2. Location: The forest.**
**5 giddiness** sudden speed    **11 estate** settle as an estate, bestow    **14 all's** all his    **16 look you** look    **17 brother** i.e., brother-in-law to be.    **18 sister** (Rosalind is still dressed as a man, but Oliver evidently adopts the fiction that "Ganymede" is Orlando's Rosalind. See 4.3.92 ff.)    **20 scarf** sling.    **28 where you are** i.e., what you mean.    **30 thrasonical** boastful. (From Thraso, the boaster in Terence's *Eunuchus*.)    **30–1 "I came . . . overcame"** (Julius Caesar's famous pronouncement, *Veni, vidi, vici*, on the occasion of his victory over Pharnaces at Zela in 47 B.C.)    **36 degrees** (Plays on the original meaning, "steps," and also on the rhetorical figure of climax illustrated by Rosalind's sentence as it moves from one step to the next by linked words, *looked, loved, sighed*, etc.)    **pair** flight

stairs to marriage which they will climb incontinent, or 37
else be incontinent before marriage. They are in the
very wrath of love, and they will together. Clubs 39
cannot part them.

ORLANDO   They shall be married tomorrow, and I will
bid the Duke to the nuptial. But oh, how bitter a thing
it is to look into happiness through another man's
eyes! By so much the more shall I tomorrow be at the
height of heart-heaviness, by how much I shall think
my brother happy in having what he wishes for.

ROSALIND   Why, then, tomorrow I cannot serve your
turn for Rosalind?

ORLANDO   I can live no longer by thinking.

ROSALIND   I will weary you then no longer with idle
talking. Know of me then—for now I speak to some
purpose—that I know you are a gentleman of good con- 52
ceit. I speak not this that you should bear a good opin- 53
ion of my knowledge, insomuch I say I know you are; 54
neither do I labor for a greater esteem than may in 55
some little measure draw a belief from you to do 56
yourself good, and not to grace me. Believe then, if you 57
please, that I can do strange things. I have, since I was
three year old, conversed with a magician, most 59
profound in his art and yet not damnable. If you do 60
love Rosalind so near the heart as your gesture cries it 61
out, when your brother marries Aliena shall you 62
marry her. I know into what straits of fortune she is 63
driven; and it is not impossible to me, if it appear not
inconvenient to you, to set her before your eyes 65
tomorrow, human as she is, and without any danger. 66

ORLANDO   Speak'st thou in sober meanings? 67

ROSALIND   By my life, I do, which I tender dearly, 68
though I say I am a magician. Therefore, put you in 69
your best array; bid your friends; for if you will be 70
married tomorrow, you shall, and to Rosalind, if you
will.

*Enter Silvius and Phoebe.*

Look, here comes a lover of mine and a lover of hers. 73

PHOEBE [*to Rosalind*]
Youth, you have done me much ungentleness, 74
To show the letter that I writ to you.

ROSALIND
I care not if I have. It is my study 76
To seem despiteful and ungentle to you.
You are there followed by a faithful shepherd.
Look upon him; love him. He worships you.

PHOEBE [*to Silvius*]
Good shepherd, tell this youth what 'tis to love.

SILVIUS
It is to be all made of sighs and tears;
And so am I for Phoebe.

PHOEBE   And I for Ganymede.

ORLANDO   And I for Rosalind.

ROSALIND   And I for no woman.

SILVIUS
It is to be all made of faith and service;
And so am I for Phoebe.

PHOEBE   And I for Ganymede.

ORLANDO   And I for Rosalind.

ROSALIND   And I for no woman.

SILVIUS
It is to be all made of fantasy, 91
All made of passion and all made of wishes,
All adoration, duty, and observance, 93
All humbleness, all patience and impatience,
All purity, all trial, all observance; 95
And so am I for Phoebe.

PHOEBE   And so am I for Ganymede.

ORLANDO   And so am I for Rosalind.

ROSALIND   And so am I for no woman.

PHOEBE [*to Rosalind*]
If this be so, why blame you me to love you? 100

SILVIUS [*to Phoebe*]
If this be so, why blame you me to love you?

ORLANDO
If this be so, why blame you me to love you?

ROSALIND   Why do you speak too, "Why blame you me
to love you?"

ORLANDO   To her that is not here, nor doth not hear.

ROSALIND   Pray you, no more of this; 'tis like the
howling of Irish wolves against the moon. [*To Silvius*]
I will help you, if I can. [*To Phoebe*] I would love you, if
I could.—Tomorrow meet me all together. [*To Phoebe*] I
will marry you, if ever I marry woman, and I'll be
married tomorrow. [*To Orlando*] I will satisfy you, if
ever I satisfied man, and you shall be married
tomorrow. [*To Silvius*] I will content you, if what
pleases you contents you, and you shall be married
tomorrow. [*To Orlando*] As you love Rosalind, meet.
[*To Silvius*] As you love Phoebe, meet. And as I love
no woman, I'll meet. So fare you well. I have left you
commands.

SILVIUS   I'll not fail, if I live.

PHOEBE   Nor I.

ORLANDO   Nor I.                    *Exeunt [separately].*

37 **incontinent** immediately. (Followed by a pun on the meaning
"unchaste or sexually unrestrained.")   39 **wrath** impetuosity,
ardor.   **Clubs** i.e., Physical force, such as that employed by night-
watchmen armed with clubs   52–3 **conceit** intelligence, understanding.   53 **that** in order that   54 **insomuch . . . are** granted that I do
freely admit you are intelligent   55–7 **neither . . . grace me** nor am
I interested in winning approval except insofar as it may, by inspiring
your confidence in my ability, prompt you to do something for your
own benefit; it is not intended to bring favor on myself.   59 **conversed**
associated   60 **not damnable** not a practicer of forbidden or black
magic, worthy of execution and damnation.   61–2 **gesture cries it out**
bearing and behavior proclaim   63 **she** Rosalind   65 **inconvenient**
inappropriate   66 **human** i.e., the real Rosalind, not a phantom.
**danger** i.e., the danger to the soul from involvement in magic or
witchcraft.   67 **in sober meanings** seriously.   68 **tender dearly**
value highly   69 **though . . . magician** (According to Elizabethan
antiwitchcraft statutes, some forms of witchcraft were punishable
by death; Rosalind thus endangers her life by what she has said.)
70 **bid** invite.   **friends** family and friends.   **will be** wish to be
73 **a lover of mine . . . hers** i.e., Phoebe, who is in love with me
(Rosalind), and Silvius, who is in love with Phoebe.   74 **ungentleness**
discourtesy

76 **study** conscious endeavor   91 **fantasy** fancy, imagination
93 **observance** devotion, respect   95 **observance** (Perhaps a compositor's error, repeated from two lines previous; many editors emend it
to *obedience*.)   100 **to love you** for loving you.

## 5.3

*Enter [Touchstone the] Clown and Audrey.*

TOUCHSTONE    Tomorrow is the joyful day, Audrey;
tomorrow will we be married.

AUDREY    I do desire it with all my heart; and I hope it
is no dishonest desire to desire to be a woman of the          4
world. Here come two of the banished Duke's pages.          5

*Enter two Pages.*

FIRST PAGE    Well met, honest gentleman.          6

TOUCHSTONE    By my troth, well met. Come, sit, sit,
and a song.                                        *[They sit.]*

SECOND PAGE    We are for you. Sit i'th' middle.          9

FIRST PAGE    Shall we clap into't roundly, without hawk-    10
ing or spitting or saying we are hoarse, which are the       11
only prologues to a bad voice?                               12

SECOND PAGE    I'faith, i'faith, and both in a tune, like    13
two gypsies on a horse.                                      14

*Song.*

BOTH PAGES

It was a lover and his lass,
    With a hey, and a ho, and a hey-nonny-no,
That o'er the green cornfield did pass          17
    In springtime, the only pretty ring time,          18
When birds do sing, hey ding a ding, ding,
Sweet lovers love the spring.

Between the acres of the rye,          21
    With a hey, and a ho, and a hey-nonny-no,
These pretty country folks would lie
    In springtime, the only pretty ring time,
When birds do sing, hey ding a ding, ding,
Sweet lovers love the spring.

This carol they began that hour,
    With a hey, and a ho, and hey-nonny-no,
How that a life was but a flower
    In springtime, the only pretty ring time,
When birds do sing, hey ding a ding, ding,
Sweet lovers love the spring.

And therefore take the present time,
    With a hey, and a ho, and a hey-nonny-no,
For love is crownèd with the prime          35
    In springtime, the only pretty ring time,
When birds do sing, hey ding a ding, ding,
Sweet lovers love the spring.

TOUCHSTONE    Truly, young gentlemen, though there
was no great matter in the ditty, yet the note was very      40
untunable.                                                   41

---

**5.3. Location: The forest.**
**4 dishonest** immodest    **4–5 woman of the world** married woman;
also, one who advances herself socially.    **6 honest** worthy
**9 We are for you** i.e., Fine, we're ready.    **10 clap . . . roundly** begin
briskly and with spirit    **10–11 hawking** clearing the throat    **12 only**
customary    **13 in a tune** (1) in unison (2) keeping time    **14 on a** on
one    **17 cornfield** field of grain    **18 ring time** time most apt for marriage    **21 Between the acres** On unplowed strips between the
fields    **35 prime** (1) height of perfection (2) spring    **40 matter** sense,
meaning.    **note** music    **41 untunable** discordant.

FIRST PAGE    You are deceived, sir. We kept time, we lost    42
not our time.

TOUCHSTONE    By my troth, yes; I count it but time lost
to hear such a foolish song. God b'wi'you, and God
mend your voices! Come, Audrey. *Exeunt [separately].*

❖

## 5.4

*Enter Duke Senior, Amiens, Jaques, Orlando,
Oliver, [and] Celia.*

DUKE SENIOR
Dost thou believe, Orlando, that the boy
Can do all this that he hath promisèd?

ORLANDO
I sometimes do believe, and sometimes do not,
As those that fear they hope and know they fear.          4

*Enter Rosalind, Silvius, and Phoebe.*

ROSALIND
Patience once more, whiles our compact is urged.          5
[*To the Duke*] You say, if I bring in your Rosalind
You will bestow her on Orlando here?

DUKE SENIOR
That would I, had I kingdoms to give with her.

ROSALIND [*to Orlando*]
And you say you will have her when I bring her?

ORLANDO
That would I, were I of all kingdoms king.

ROSALIND [*to Phoebe*]
You say you'll marry me if I be willing?

PHOEBE
That will I, should I die the hour after.

ROSALIND
But if you do refuse to marry me
You'll give yourself to this most faithful shepherd?

PHOEBE    So is the bargain.

ROSALIND [*to Silvius*]
You say that you'll have Phoebe if she will?

SILVIUS
Though to have her and death were both one thing.

ROSALIND
I have promised to make all this matter even.          18
Keep you your word, O Duke, to give your daughter;
You yours, Orlando, to receive his daughter;
Keep you your word, Phoebe, that you'll marry me,
Or else, refusing me, to wed this shepherd;
Keep your word, Silvius, that you'll marry her
If she refuse me; and from hence I go,
To make these doubts all even.
                              *Exeunt Rosalind and Celia.*

DUKE SENIOR
I do remember in this shepherd boy
Some lively touches of my daughter's favor.          27

---

**42 deceived** mistaken
**5.4. Location: The forest.**
**4 they hope** i.e., that they merely hope    **5 urged** put forward.
**18 make . . . even** set all this to rights, square accounts.    **27 lively**
lifelike.    **favor** appearance.

ORLANDO
My lord, the first time that I ever saw him
Methought he was a brother to your daughter.
But, my good lord, this boy is forest-born
And hath been tutored in the rudiments
Of many desperate studies by his uncle,          32
Whom he reports to be a great magician,
Obscurèd in the circle of this forest.           34

*Enter [Touchstone the] Clown and Audrey.*

JAQUES     There is, sure, another flood toward, and these   35
couples are coming to the ark. Here comes a pair of   36
very strange beasts, which in all tongues are called
fools.

TOUCHSTONE     Salutation and greeting to you all!

JAQUES [*to the Duke*]     Good my lord, bid him welcome.
This is the motley-minded gentleman that I have so often
met in the forest. He hath been a courtier, he swears.

TOUCHSTONE     If any man doubt that, let him put me to
my purgation. I have trod a measure; I have flattered a   44
lady; I have been politic with my friend, smooth with   45
mine enemy; I have undone three tailors; I have had   46
four quarrels and like to have fought one.               47

JAQUES     And how was that ta'en up?                    48

TOUCHSTONE     Faith, we met and found the quarrel was
upon the seventh cause.

JAQUES     How seventh cause?—Good my lord, like this
fellow.

DUKE SENIOR     I like him very well.

TOUCHSTONE     God 'ild you, sir, I desire you of the like.   54
I press in here, sir, amongst the rest of the country   55
copulatives, to swear and to forswear, according as   56
marriage binds and blood breaks. A poor virgin, sir,   57
an ill-favored thing, sir, but mine own; a poor humor   58
of mine, sir, to take that that no man else will. Rich
honesty dwells like a miser, sir, in a poor house, as   60
your pearl in your foul oyster.                          61

DUKE SENIOR     By my faith, he is very swift and sen-   62
tentious.                                                63

TOUCHSTONE     According to the fool's bolt, sir, and such   64
dulcet diseases.                                         65

JAQUES     But for the seventh cause. How did you find
the quarrel on the seventh cause?

TOUCHSTONE     Upon a lie seven times removed—bear
your body more seeming, Audrey—as thus, sir. I did   69
dislike the cut of a certain courtier's beard. He sent me   70
word if I said his beard was not cut well, he was in
the mind it was: this is called the Retort Courteous. If I
sent him word again it was not well cut, he would
send me word he cut it to please himself: this is called
the Quip Modest. If again it was not well cut, he dis-   75
abled my judgment: this is called the Reply Churlish. If   76
again it was not well cut, he would answer I spake
not true: this is called the Reproof Valiant. If again it
was not well cut, he would say I lie: this is called the
Countercheck Quarrelsome. And so to the Lie Cir-   80
cumstantial and the Lie Direct.

JAQUES     And how oft did you say his beard was not well
cut?

TOUCHSTONE     I durst go no further than the Lie Circumstantial, nor he durst not give me the Lie Direct;
and so we measured swords and parted.                    86

JAQUES     Can you nominate in order now the degrees of
the lie?

TOUCHSTONE     Oh, sir, we quarrel in print, by the book, as   89
you have books for good manners. I will name you the
degrees. The first, the Retort Courteous; the second,
the Quip Modest; the third, the Reply Churlish; the
fourth, the Reproof Valiant; the fifth, the Countercheck
Quarrelsome; the sixth, the Lie with Circumstance;
the seventh, the Lie Direct. All these you may
avoid but the Lie Direct; and you may avoid that, too,
with an If. I knew when seven justices could not take   97
up a quarrel, but when the parties were met them-   98
selves, one of them thought but of an If, as, "If you
said so, then I said so"; and they shook hands and
swore brothers. Your If is the only peacemaker; much   101
virtue in If.

JAQUES     Is not this a rare fellow, my lord? He's as good   103
at anything and yet a fool.

DUKE SENIOR     He uses his folly like a stalking-horse,   105
and under the presentation of that he shoots his wit.   106

*Enter Hymen, Rosalind, and Celia. Still music.
[Rosalind and Celia are no longer disguised.]*

HYMEN
Then is there mirth in heaven,                           107
When earthly things made even                           108
    Atone together.                                      109
Good Duke, receive thy daughter;
Hymen from heaven brought her,
    Yea, brought her hither,

32 **desperate** dangerous   34 **Obscurèd** hidden.   **circle** compass,
boundaries. (With a possible allusion to the magic circle that protected the magician from the devil during incantation.)   35 **toward**
coming on   36 **a pair** (In Genesis 7:2, God commands Noah to take
on board every "clean" beast by sevens, but those that are not clean,
by twos.)   44 **purgation** proof, trial.   **measure** slow, stately
dance   45 **politic** cunning, Machiavellian.   **smooth** insinuating
46 **undone** bankrupted (by refusing to pay debts owed them)
47 **like** came close   48 **ta'en up** settled, made up.   54 **'ild** yield,
reward.   **I . . . like** I wish the same to you. (A polite phrase used to
reply to a compliment.)   55–6 **country copulatives** country couples
about to marry and with sex on their minds   56 **to swear . . . forswear**
to pronounce the marriage vows and then to violate them   57 **blood
breaks** as illicit desire fractures the marriage bond.   58 **ill-favored**
ugly.   **humor** whim   60 **honesty** chastity   61 **your pearl** i.e., the
pearl that one hears about   62–3 **swift and sententious** quick-witted
and good at aphorisms.   64 **fool's bolt** (Alluding to the proverb "A
fool's bolt [arrow] is soon shot.")   65 **dulcet diseases** pleasant afflictions, entertaining yet sharp. (Touchstone wryly agrees with the
Duke's assessment of the Fool as swift and sententious.)

69 **seeming** seemly   70 **dislike** express dislike of   75–6 **disabled** dis-
paraged   80 **Countercheck** Rebuff   86 **measured swords** i.e., as in
the mere preliminary to a duel   89 **in . . . book** in a precise way.
(Touchstone is travestying books on the general subject of honor and
arms, which dealt with occasions and circumstances of the
duel.)   97–8 **take up** settle   101 **swore brothers** became sworn
brothers.   103 **rare** excellent   105 **stalking-horse** a real or artificial
horse under cover of which the hunter approached his game
106 **presentation** semblance   106.1 *Hymen* Roman god of faithful
marriage. *Still* Soft   107 **mirth** joy   108 **made even** set straight
109 **Atone** are at one

That thou mightst join her hand with his
Whose heart within his bosom is.                                    114

ROSALIND [*to the Duke*]
To you I give myself, for I am yours.
[*To Orlando*] To you I give myself, for I am yours.
DUKE SENIOR
If there be truth in sight, you are my daughter.
ORLANDO
If there be truth in sight, you are my Rosalind.
PHOEBE
If sight and shape be true,
Why then, my love adieu!
ROSALIND [*to the Duke*]
I'll have no father, if you be not he.
[*To Orlando*] I'll have no husband, if you be not he.
[*To Phoebe*] Nor ne'er wed woman, if you be not she.
HYMEN
Peace, ho! I bar confusion.
'Tis I must make conclusion
    Of these most strange events.
Here's eight that must take hands
To join in Hymen's bands,
    If truth holds true contents.                                  129
[*To Orlando and Rosalind*]
You and you no cross shall part.                                    130
[*To Oliver and Celia*]
You and you are heart in heart.
[*To Phoebe*]
You to his love must accord                                        132
Or have a woman to your lord.                                      133
[*To Touchstone and Audrey*]
You and you are sure together,                                     134
As the winter to foul weather.
[*To all*]
Whiles a wedlock hymn we sing,
Feed yourselves with questioning,                                  137
That reason wonder may diminish                                    138
How thus we met, and these things finish.

*Song.*

Wedding is great Juno's crown,                                     140
    O blessèd bond of board and bed!                               141
'Tis Hymen peoples every town;
    High wedlock then be honorèd.                                  143
Honor, high honor and renown
To Hymen, god of every town!

DUKE SENIOR [*to Celia*]
O my dear niece, welcome thou art to me!
Even daughter, welcome, in no less degree.                         147

PHOEBE [*to Silvius*]
I will not eat my word, now thou art mine;
Thy faith my fancy to thee doth combine.                           149

*Enter Second Brother [Jaques de Boys].*

JAQUES DE BOYS
Let me have audience for a word or two.
I am the second son of old Sir Rowland,
That bring these tidings to this fair assembly.
Duke Frederick, hearing how that every day
Men of great worth resorted to this forest,
Addressed a mighty power, which were on foot                       155
In his own conduct, purposely to take                              156
His brother here and put him to the sword;
And to the skirts of this wild wood he came,
Where, meeting with an old religious man,
After some question with him, was converted                        160
Both from his enterprise and from the world,
His crown bequeathing to his banished brother,
And all their lands restored to them again
That were with him exiled. This to be true
I do engage my life.
DUKE SENIOR                     Welcome, young man.                 165
Thou offer'st fairly to thy brothers' wedding:                     166
To one his lands withheld and to the other                         167
A land itself at large, a potent dukedom.                          168
First, in this forest let us do those ends                         169
That here were well begun and well begot;                          170
And after, every of this happy number                              171
That have endured shrewd days and nights with us                   172
Shall share the good of our returnèd fortune
According to the measure of their states.                          174
Meantime, forget this new-fall'n dignity,                          175
And fall into our rustic revelry.
Play, music! And you, brides and bridegrooms all,
With measure heaped in joy, to th' measures fall.                  178
JAQUES
Sir, by your patience.—If I heard you rightly,                     179
The Duke hath put on a religious life                              180
And thrown into neglect the pompous court.                         181
JAQUES DE BOYS    He hath.
JAQUES
To him will I. Out of these convertites                            183
There is much matter to be heard and learned.                      184
[*To the Duke*] You to your former honor I bequeath;
Your patience and your virtue well deserves it.
[*To Orlando*] You to a love that your true faith doth
    merit;

114 **Whose** (Refers to Rosalind.)  129 **If . . . contents** if the newly revealed truths are indeed true and bring true contentment. 130 **cross** vexation, mischance  132 **his** i.e., Silvius's.  **accord** agree  133 **to your lord** for your husband.  134 **sure** closely united  137 **Feed** satisfy  138 **That . . . diminish** that understanding may lessen your wonder  140 **Juno's** (Juno was the Roman queen of the gods, presiding, in the Renaissance view, over faithful wedlock.)  141 **board and bed** the food table and the marriage bed, symbolic of the marital household.  143 **High** solemn  147 **Even . . . degree** You are as welcome to me as if you were my own daughter.

149 **Thy faith . . . combine** your faithful love for me ties my love to you.  155 **Addressed** prepared.  **power** army  156 **In . . . conduct** under his own command  160 **question** conversation  165 **engage** pledge  166 **Thou offer'st fairly** You contribute handsomely  167 **To one** to Oliver  167–8 **to the other . . . large** to Orlando an entire dukedom (since, as husband of Rosalind, Orlando will eventually inherit as duke).  169 **do those ends** accomplish those purposes  170 **begot** conceived  171 **every** every one  172 **shrewd** hard, trying  174 **According . . . states** according to their degrees.  175 **new-fall'n** newly acquired  178 **With . . . fall** with an overflowing measure of joy, fall to dancing. (With wordplay on *measure* and *measures*, "dances.")  179 **by your patience** by your leave, i.e., let the music wait a moment.  180 **The Duke** Duke Frederick  181 **pompous** ceremonious  183 **convertites** converts  184 **matter** sound sense

[*To Oliver*] You to your land and love and great allies; 188
[*To Silvius*] You to a long and well-deservèd bed;
[*To Touchstone*] And you to wrangling, for thy loving
   voyage
Is but for two months victualed. So, to your pleasures. 191
I am for other than for dancing measures. 192

DUKE SENIOR    Stay, Jaques, stay.

JAQUES
To see no pastime I. What you would have
I'll stay to know at your abandoned cave. *Exit.*

DUKE SENIOR
Proceed, proceed. We'll begin these rites,
As we do trust they'll end, in true delights.
         [*They dance.*] *Exeunt* [*all but Rosalind*].

# [Epilogue]

ROSALIND
It is not the fashion to see the lady the epilogue;
but it is no more unhandsome than to see the 2

lord the prologue. If it be true that good wine needs 3
no bush, 'tis true that a good play needs no epilogue. 4
Yet to good wine they do use good bushes, and good
plays prove the better by the help of good epilogues.
What a case am I in then, that am neither a good epilogue nor cannot insinuate with you in the behalf of a 8
good play! I am not furnished like a beggar; therefore 9
to beg will not become me. My way is to conjure you, 10
and I'll begin with the women. I charge you, O
women, for the love you bear to men, to like as much
of this play as please you; and I charge you, O men,
for the love you bear to women—as I perceive by your
simpering, none of you hates them—that between
you and the women the play may please. If I were a 16
woman I would kiss as many of you as had beards 17
that pleased me, complexions that liked me, and 18
breaths that I defied not; and I am sure as many as 19
have good beards or good faces or sweet breaths will,
for my kind offer, when I make curtsy, bid me fare- 21
well.                                    *Exit.* 22

188 allies kinfolk   191 victualed provisioned.
192 dancing measures dancing steps.
Epilogue
2 unhandsome in bad taste

3–4 good . . . bush (A proverb derived from the custom of displaying a piece of ivy or holly at the tavern door to denote that wine was for sale there.)   8 insinuate ingratiate myself   9 furnished equipped, decked out   10 conjure adjure, earnestly charge   16–17 If . . . woman (Womens's parts on the Elizabethan stage were played by boys in feminine costume.)   18 liked pleased   19 defied rejected, disdained   21–2 bid me farewell i.e., applaud me (and the acting company and the play).

# *Twelfth Night; or, What You Will*

*welfth Night* is possibly the latest of the three festive comedies, including *Much Ado About Nothing* and *As You Like It,* with which Shakespeare climaxed his distinctively philosophical and joyous vein of comic writing. Performed on February 2, 1602, at the Middle Temple and written possibly as early as 1599, *Twelfth Night* is usually dated 1600 or 1601. This play is indeed the most festive of the lot. Its keynote is Saturnalian release and the carnival pursuit of love and mirth. Along with such familiar motifs as the plucky heroine disguised as a man (found earlier in *The Two Gentlemen of Verona, As You Like It,* and *The Merchant of Venice*), *Twelfth Night* also returns to the more farcical routines of mistaken identity found in Shakespeare's early comedy. As a witness of the 1602 performance, John Manningham, observes, the play is "much like the *Comedy of Errors,* or *Menaechmi* in Plautus, but most like and near to that in Italian called *Inganni.*"

The carnival atmosphere is appropriate to the season designated in the play's title: the twelfth night of Christmas, January 6, the Feast of Epiphany. (The prologue to *Gl'Ingannati,* perhaps the Italian play referred to by Manningham, speaks of "La Notte di Beffania," Epiphany night.) Along with its primary Christian significance as the Feast of the Magi, Epiphany was also in Renaissance times the last day of the Christmas revels. Over a twelve-day period, from Christmas until January 6, noble households sponsored numerous performances of plays, masques, banquets, and every kind of festivity. (Leslie Hotson argues, in fact, that *Twelfth Night* was first performed on twelfth night in early 1601, in the presence of Queen Elizabeth.) Students left schools for vacations, celebrating release from study with plays and revels of their own. The stern rigors of a rule-bound society gave way temporarily to playful inversions of authority. The reign of the Boy Bishop and the Feast of Fools, for example, gave choristers and minor church functionaries the cherished opportunity to boss the hierarchy around, mock the

liturgy with outrageous lampooning, and generally let off steam. Although such customs occasionally got out of hand, the idea was to channel potentially destructive insubordination into playacting and thereby promote harmony. Behind these Elizabethan midwinter customs lies the Roman Saturnalia, with its pagan spirit of gift giving, sensual indulgence, and satirical hostility to those who would curb merriment. Shakespeare's play captures the medieval and Renaissance spirit of Epiphany by its often playful allusions to religious practice: Feste's disguise as "Sir Topas," the priest, Feste's joke about living by the church (3.1.3–7), Sir Toby's defense of "cakes and ale," Feste's swearing by Saint Anne, mother of the Virgin Mary (2.3.115–16), Feste's joking about "clerestories" (4.2.38), and the like. Shakespeare lovingly evokes a tradition of festivals and ceremonies that incorporates self-mockery into its celebration of renewal at Christmas time.

Shakespeare's choice of sources for *Twelfth Night* underscores his commitment to mirth. Renaissance literature offered numerous instances of mistaken identity among twins and of the disguised heroine serving as page to her beloved. Among those in English were the anonymous play *Sir Clyomon and Sir Clamydes* (c. 1570–1583), Sir Philip Sidney's *Arcadia* (1590), and the prose romance *Parismus* by Emmanuel Forde (1598), featuring both a shipwreck and two characters with the names of Olivia and Violetta. Of particular significance, though partly for negative reasons, is Barnabe Riche's tale of "Apollonius and Silla" in *Riche His Farewell to Military Profession* (1581), which was based on François de Belleforest's 1571 French version of Matteo Bandello's *Novelle* (1554). Here we find most of the requisite plot elements: the shipwreck; Silla's disguise as a page in Duke Apollonius's court; her office as ambassador of love from Apollonius to the lady Julina, who thereupon falls in love with Silla; and the arrival of Silla's twin brother Silvio and his consequent success in winning Julina's affection. To Riche, however, this tale is merely a long warning against the enervating power of infatuation. Silvio gets Julina with child and disappears forthwith, making his belated reappearance almost too late to save the wrongly accused Silla. Riche's moralizing puts the blame on the gross and drunken appetite of carnal love. The total mismatching of affection with which the story begins, and the sudden realignments of desire based on mere outward resemblances, are seen as proofs of love's unreasonableness. Shakespeare, of course, retains and capitalizes on the irrational quality of love, as in *A Midsummer Night's Dream*, but in doing so he minimizes the harm done (Olivia is not made pregnant) and repudiates any negative moral judgments. The added subplot, with its rebuking of Malvolio's censoriousness, may have been conceived as a further answer to Riche, Fenton, and their sober school.

Shakespeare's festive spirit owes much, as Manningham observed, to Plautus and to neoclassical Italian comic writers. At least three Italian comedies called *Gl'Inganni* ("The Frauds") employ the motif of mistaken identity, and one of them, by Curzio Gonzaga (1592), supplies Viola's assumed name of "Cesare," or Cesario. Another play with the same title appeared in 1562. More useful is *Gl'Ingannati* ("The Deceived"), performed in 1531 and translated into French in 1543. Besides a plot line generally similar to *Twelfth Night* and the reference to La Notte di Beffania (Epiphany), this play offers the suggestive name *Malevolti*, "evil-faced," and *Fabio* (which resembles "Fabian"). It also contains possible hints for Malvolio, Sir Toby, and company, although the plot of the counterfeit letter is original with Shakespeare. Essentially, Shakespeare combines his own plot with an Italianate novella plot, as he did in *The Taming of the Shrew* and *Much Ado About Nothing*. And it is in the Malvolio story that Shakespeare most pointedly defends merriment. Feste the professional fool, an original stage type for Shakespeare in *Twelfth Night* and in *As You Like It*, also reinforces the theme of seizing the moment of mirth.

This great lesson, of savoring life's pleasures while one is still young, is something that Orsino and Olivia have not yet learned when the play commences. Although suited to one another in rank, wealth, and attractiveness, they are unable to overcome their own willful posturing in the elaborate charade of courtship. Like Silvius in *As You Like It*, Orsino is the conventional wooer trapped in the courtly artifice of love's rules. He opens the play on a cloying note of self-pity. He is fascinated with his own degradation as a rejected suitor and bores his listeners with his changeable moods and fondness for poetical "conceits." He sees himself as a hart pursued by his desires "like fell and cruel hounds," reminding us that enervating lovesickness has, in fact, robbed him of his manly occupation, hunting. He sends ornately contrived messages to Olivia but has not seen her in so long that his passion has become unreal and fantastical, feeding on itself.

Olivia plays the opposite role of chaste, denying womanhood. She explains her retirement from the world as mourning for a dead brother (whose name we never learn), but this withdrawal from life is another unreal vision. Olivia's practice of mourning, whereby she will "water once a day her chamber round / With eye-offending brine" (1.1.28–9), is a lifeless ritual. As others view the matter, she is senselessly wasting her beauty and affection on the dead. "What a plague means my niece to take the death of her brother thus?" Sir Toby expostulates (1.3.1–2). Viola, though she, too, has seemingly lost a brother, is an important foil in this regard, for she continues to hope for her brother's safety, trusts his soul is in heaven if he is dead, and refuses to give up her commitment to life in any case. We suspect that Olivia takes a willful pleasure in self-denial not unlike Orsino's self-congratulatory suffering. She appears to derive satisfaction from the power she holds over Orsino, a power of refusal. And she must know that she looks stunning in black.

Olivia's household reflects, in part, her mood of self-denial. She keeps Malvolio as steward because he, too, dresses somberly, insists on quiet as befits a house in mourning, and maintains order. Yet Olivia also retains a fool, Feste, who is Malvolio's opposite in every way. Hard-pressed to defend his mirthful function in a household so given over to melancholy, Feste must find some way of persuading his mistress that her very gravity is itself the essence of folly. This is a paradox, because sobriety and order appeal to the conventional wisdom of the world. Malvolio, sensing that his devotion to propriety is being challenged by the fool's prating, chides Olivia for taking "delight in such a barren rascal" (1.5.80–1).

Feste must argue for an inversion of appearance and reality whereby many of the world's ordinary pursuits can be seen to be ridiculous. As he observes, in his habitually elliptical manner of speech, *"Cucullus non facit monachum* [the cowl doesn't make the monk]; that's as much to say as I wear not motley in my brain" (1.5.52–4). Feste wins his case by making Olivia laugh at her own illogic in grieving for a brother whose soul she assumes to be in heaven. By extension, Olivia has indeed been a fool for allowing herself to be deprived of happiness in love by her brother's death ("there is no true cuckold but calamity") and for failing to consider the brevity of youth ("beauty's a flower"). Yet, paradoxically, only one who professes to be a fool can point this out, enabled by his detachment and innocence to perceive simple but profound truths denied to supposedly rational persons. This vision of the fool as naturally wise, and of society as self-indulgently insane, fascinated Renaissance writers, from Erasmus's *In Praise of Folly* and Cervantes's *Don Quixote* to Shakespeare's *King Lear*.

Viola, although not dressed in motley, aligns herself with Feste's rejection of self-denial. Refreshingly, even comically, she challenges the staid artifice of Orsino's and Olivia's lives. She is an ocean traveler, like many of Shakespeare's later heroines (Marina in *Pericles,* Perdita in *The Winter's Tale),* arriving on Illyria's shore plucky and determined. On her first embassy to Olivia from Orsino, she exposes with disarming candor the willfully ritualistic quality of Olivia's existence. Viola discards the flowery set speech she had prepared and memorized at Orsino's behest; despite her charmingly conceited assertion that the speech has been "excellently well penned," she senses that its elegant but empty rhetoric is all too familiar to the disdainful Olivia. Instead, Viola departs from her text to urge seizing the moment of happiness. "You do usurp yourself," she lectures Olivia, "for what is yours to bestow is not yours to reserve" (1.5.183–4). Beauty is a gift of nature, and failure to use it is a sin against nature. Or, again, "Lady, you are the cruel'st she alive / If you will lead these graces [Olivia's beauty] to the grave / And leave the world no copy" (lines 236–8). An essential argument in favor of love, as in Shakespeare's sonnets, is the necessity of marriage and childbearing in order to perpetuate beauty. This approach is new to Olivia and catches her wholly by surprise. In part, she reacts, like Phoebe in *As You Like It,* with perverse logic, rejecting a too-willing wooer for one who is hard to get. Yet Olivia is also attracted by a new note of sincerity, prompting her to reenter life and accept maturely both the risks and rewards of romantic involvement. Her longing for "Cesario" is, of course, sexually misdirected, but the appearance of Viola's identical twin, Sebastian, soon puts all to rights.

The motifs of Olivia's attraction for another woman (both actors would have been boys) and of Orsino's deep fondness for a seeming young man ("Cesario"), which matures into sexual love, raise delicate suggestions of love between members of the same sex, as in *As You Like It.* Once again, the ambiguities of disguise point toward the socially constructed nature of sexual difference. Viola as "Cesario" strikes those who meet her as almost sexually indeterminate. Orsino puts the matter well, in conversing with "Cesario," when he observes, "they shall yet belie thy happy years / That say thou art a man. Diana's lip / Is not more smooth and rubious; thy small pipe / Is as the maiden's organ, shrill and sound, / And all is semblative a woman's part" (1.4.30–4). Male adolescence and femininity are seen as virtually indistinguishable—a point that is wittily reinforced in the theater by the fact that a boy actor is playing Viola disguised as "Cesario."

At the same time, this playful confusion of sexual difference becomes the vehicle for a serious exploration of love and friendship. Like Rosalind in *As You Like It,* Viola uses her male attire to win Orsino's pure affection in a friendship nominally devoid of sexual interest, since both seemingly are men. Friendship must come first; the Renaissance generally accorded a higher value to friendship than to erotic passion. Yet Shakespeare also insists, as did many of his contemporaries (including Montaigne), that friendship is not only possible between men and women but also that such a relationship, formalized in marriage, offers the best of all worlds; hence, the importance of Viola's male disguise. As "Cesario," she can teach Orsino about the conventions of love in relaxed and frank conversations that would not be possible if she were known to be a woman. She teaches him to avoid the beguiling but misleading myths of Petrarchan love (named after the Italian sonneteer Francis Petrarch, whose poems embody the idealization of courtly love) and so prepares him for the realities of marriage. Comparing men and women in love, she confides, "We men may say more, swear more, but indeed / Our shows are more than will; for still we prove / Much in our vows, but little in our love" (2.4.116–18). Once she and Orsino have achieved an instinctive rapport—all the more remarkable for their talking so often at cross-purposes—Viola's unmasking can make possible a physical communion as well. Orsino, no longer trapped in the futile worship of a seemingly unapproachable goddess, can come to terms with his sexuality as part of a unified and loving human relationship.

The friendship of Sebastian and Antonio, meanwhile, sorely tested by the mix-ups of the mistaken identity plot, similarly places Sebastian in a love-and-friendship triangle like that involving Bassanio, Portia, and Antonio in *The Merchant of Venice.* Sebastian and Antonio are loving friends, so much so that Antonio willingly risks his life to be with Sebastian in a country where Antonio has many enemies. Antonio's expressions of fondness for Sebastian are extraordinarily warm. "If you will not murder me for my love, let me be your servant," he pleads. "I do adore thee so / That danger shall seem sport, and I will go" (2.1.33–4, 45–6). A desire "More sharp than filèd steel" spurs Antonio to seek out his friend, despite the manifest danger (3.3.4–5). "A witchcraft" draws him to Sebastian (5.1.72). Whether the attachment is homosexual, as it is often played on the modern stage, is debatable; expressions of warmth between men seem to have been more common in Elizabethan times than today, and centuries of intervening time have no doubt altered our understanding of same-sex relationships; the term *homosexual* is of much later date. What remains true for the play is that this portrayal of emotional and loving closeness between two men gives way to the marriage of one of them to a woman (as in *The Merchant of Venice*). The depiction of love and friendship between two men is a repeated motif in the play, embodied most of all in the loving relationship of Orsino and "Cesario." Shakespeare chooses to resolve his plot by defining heterosexual marriage as the completion of relationships begun in friendship and incorporating that friendship in a union that finally offers heterosexual fulfillment as well.

The below-stairs characters of the subplot, Sir Toby and the rest, share with Feste and Viola a commitment to joy. As Sir Toby proclaims in his first speech, "care's an enemy to life" (1.3.2–3). Even the simpleton Sir Andrew, although gulled by Sir Toby into spending his money on a hopeless pursuit of Olivia, seems none the worse for his treatment; he loves to drink in Sir Toby's company and can afford to pay for his entertainment. Sir Toby gives us some of the richly inventive humor of Falstaff, another lovable fat roguish knight. In this subplot, however, the confrontations between merriment and sobriety are more harshly drawn than in the main plot. Whereas the gracious Olivia is won away from her folly, the obdurate Malvolio can only be exposed to ridicule. He is chiefly to blame for the polarization of attitudes, for he insists on rebuking the mirth of others. His name (*Mal-volio*, the "ill-wisher") implies a self-satisfied determination to impose his rigid moral code on others. As Sir Toby taunts him, "Dost thou think, because thou art virtuous, there shall be no more cakes and ale?" (2.3.114–15). Malvolio's inflexible hostility provokes a desire for comic vengeance. The method is satiric: the clever manipulators, Maria and Sir Toby, invent a scheme to entrap Malvolio in his own self-deceit. The punishment fits the crime, for he has long dreamed of himself as "Count Malvolio," rich, powerful, and in a position to demolish Sir Toby and the rest. Without Malvolio's infatuated predisposition to believe that Olivia could actually love him and write such a letter as he finds, Maria's scheme would have no hope of success. He tortures the text to make it yield a suitable meaning, much in the style of Puritan theologizing. His conviction that Jove is with him (2.5.169) reminds us of the Puritan belief that prosperity of the "elect" is a sign of God's grace.

Indeed, Malvolio in some ways does resemble a Puritan, as Maria observes (2.3.139–47), even though she qualifies the assertion by saying that he is not a religious fanatic but a "time-pleaser." She directs her observation not at a religious group but at all who would be killjoys;

if the Puritans are like that, she intimates, so much the worse for them. This uncharacteristic lack of charity gives a sharp tone to the vengeance practiced on Malvolio, evoking from Olivia a protest that "he hath been most notoriously abused" (5.1.379). The belated attempt to make a reconciliation with him seems, however, doomed to failure, in light of his grim resolve to "be revenged on the whole pack of you" (5.1.378). This ominous threat had serious implications for the time when Shakespeare wrote *Twelfth Night*: the Puritans, with their influential role in London's civic affairs, were increasingly dismayed by the popularity of the theater, and did what they could to suppress or at least restrain that theater's commitment to merriment and "license." As C. L. Barber has pointed out, the Puritans were to gain their revenge in 1642, when a Puritan-dominated Parliament closed all theaters, imposing a total ban on such entertainments that was to remain in force until the restoration of the monarchy in 1660.

Meantime, in 1600–1, the threat to the theater implicitly posed by Malvolio's desire to suppress hedonistic pleasure is dealt a severe blow by the merrymakers' plot to subject Malvolio to the satirical exposure and punishment it deserves. At the height of his discomfiture, he has been tricked into doing the two things he hates most: smiling affably and wearing sportive attire. The appearance of merriment is so grossly unsuited to him that he is declared mad and put into safekeeping. The apostle of sobriety in this play thus comes before us as a declared madman, while the fool Feste offers him sage comment in the guise of a priest. Wisdom and folly have changed places. The upside-down character of the play is epitomized in Malvolio's plaintive remark to Feste (no longer posing as the priest): "I am as well in my wits, Fool, as thou art" (4.2.88). Malvolio's comeuppance is richly deserved, but the severity of vengeance and countervengeance suggests that the triumph of festival will not last long. This brevity is, of course, inherent in the nature of such holiday release from responsibility. As Feste sings, "What's to come is still unsure. / In delay there lies no plenty" (2.3.49–50).

# *Twelfth Night; or, What You Will*

[*Dramatis Personae*

ORSINO, *Duke (sometimes called Count) of Illyria*
VALENTINE, *gentleman attending on Orsino*
CURIO, *gentleman attending on Orsino*

VIOLA, *a shipwrecked lady, later disguised as Cesario*
SEBASTIAN, *twin brother of Viola*
ANTONIO, *a sea captain, friend to Sebastian*
CAPTAIN *of the shipwrecked vessel*

OLIVIA, *a rich countess of Illyria*
MARIA, *gentlewoman in Olivia's household*

SCENE: Illyria]

SIR TOBY BELCH, *Olivia's uncle*
SIR ANDREW AGUECHEEK, *a companion of Sir Toby*
MALVOLIO, *steward of Olivia's household*
FABIAN, *a member of Olivia's household*
FESTE, *a clown, also called* FOOL, *Olivia's jester*

A PRIEST
FIRST OFFICER
SECOND OFFICER

*Lords, Sailors, Musicians, and other Attendants*

## 1.1

*Enter Orsino Duke of Illyria, Curio, and other lords [with musicians].*

ORSINO
If music be the food of love, play on;
Give me excess of it, that surfeiting,
The appetite may sicken and so die.
That strain again! It had a dying fall; 4
Oh, it came o'er my ear like the sweet sound
That breathes upon a bank of violets,
Stealing and giving odor. Enough, no more.
'Tis not so sweet now as it was before.
O spirit of love, how quick and fresh art thou, 9
That, notwithstanding thy capacity 10
Receiveth as the sea, naught enters there, 11
Of what validity and pitch soe'er, 12
But falls into abatement and low price 13
Even in a minute! So full of shapes is fancy 14
That it alone is high fantastical. 15

CURIO
Will you go hunt, my lord?
ORSINO                    What, Curio?
CURIO                              The hart.
ORSINO
Why, so I do, the noblest that I have. 17
Oh, when mine eyes did see Olivia first,
Methought she purged the air of pestilence.
That instant was I turned into a hart,
And my desires, like fell and cruel hounds, 21
E'er since pursue me.

*Enter Valentine.*

                    How now, what news from her? 22
VALENTINE
So please my lord, I might not be admitted,
But from her handmaid do return this answer:
The element itself, till seven years' heat, 25
Shall not behold her face at ample view;
But like a cloistress she will veilèd walk, 27
And water once a day her chamber round
With eye-offending brine—all this to season 29

---

**1.1. Location: Orsino's court** in Illyria, nominally on the east coast of the Adriatic Sea, but with a suggestion also of "illusion" and "delirium." **4 fall** cadence   **9 quick and fresh** keen and hungry   **10–11 notwithstanding . . . sea** i.e., not withstanding the fact that love appears to have a capacity as vast as the sea   **12 validity** value.   **pitch** superiority. (Literally, the highest point of a falcon's flight.)   **13 abatement** depreciation. (The lover's brain entertains innumerable fantasies but soon tires of them all.)   **14 shapes** imagined forms.   **fancy** love   **15 it . . . fantastical** it surpasses everything else in imaginative power and craziness.

**17 the noblest . . . have** i.e., my noblest part, my heart. (Punning on *hart*.)   **21 fell** fierce   **22 pursue me** (Alludes to the story in Ovid of Actaeon, who, having seen Diana bathing, was transformed into a stag and killed by his own hounds.)   **25 element** sky.   **seven years' heat** seven summers   **27 cloistress** nun secluded in a religious community   **29 season** keep fresh. (Playing on the idea of the salt in her tears.)

A brother's dead love, which she would keep fresh          30
And lasting in her sad remembrance.

ORSINO
Oh, she that hath a heart of that fine frame          32
To pay this debt of love but to a brother,
How will she love, when the rich golden shaft          34
Hath killed the flock of all affections else          35
That live in her; when liver, brain, and heart,          36
These sovereign thrones, are all supplied, and filled          37
Her sweet perfections, with one self king!          38
Away before me to sweet beds of flowers.
Love-thoughts lie rich when canopied with bowers.
                                                                         *Exeunt.*

# 1.2

*Enter Viola, a Captain, and sailors.*

VIOLA     What country, friends, is this?
CAPTAIN     This is Illyria, lady.
VIOLA
And what should I do in Illyria?
My brother he is in Elysium.          4
Perchance he is not drowned. What think you, sailors?          5
CAPTAIN
It is perchance that you yourself were saved.          6
VIOLA
Oh, my poor brother! And so perchance may he be.          7
CAPTAIN
True, madam, and to comfort you with chance,          8
Assure yourself, after our ship did split,
When you and those poor number saved with you
Hung on our driving boat, I saw your brother,          11
Most provident in peril, bind himself,
Courage and hope both teaching him the practice,
To a strong mast that lived upon the sea;          14
Where, like Arion on the dolphin's back,          15
I saw him hold acquaintance with the waves
So long as I could see.
VIOLA     For saying so, there's gold. [*She gives money.*]
Mine own escape unfoldeth to my hope,          19
Whereto thy speech serves for authority,          20
The like of him. Know'st thou this country?          21

CAPTAIN
Ay, madam, well, for I was bred and born
Not three hours' travel from this very place.
VIOLA     Who governs here?
CAPTAIN     A noble duke, in nature as in name.
VIOLA     What is his name?
CAPTAIN     Orsino.
VIOLA
Orsino! I have heard my father name him.
He was a bachelor then.
CAPTAIN
And so is now, or was so very late;          30
For but a month ago I went from hence,
And then 'twas fresh in murmur—as, you know,          32
What great ones do the less will prattle of—          33
That he did seek the love of fair Olivia.
VIOLA     What's she?
CAPTAIN
A virtuous maid, the daughter of a count
That died some twelvemonth since, then leaving her
In the protection of his son, her brother,
Who shortly also died; for whose dear love,
They say, she hath abjured the sight
And company of men.
VIOLA                         Oh, that I served that lady,
And might not be delivered to the world          42
Till I had made mine own occasion mellow,          43
What my estate is!
CAPTAIN                         That were hard to compass,          44
Because she will admit no kind of suit,
No, not the Duke's.          46
VIOLA
There is a fair behavior in thee, Captain,
And though that nature with a beauteous wall          48
Doth oft close in pollution, yet of thee
I will believe thou hast a mind that suits
With this thy fair and outward character.          51
I prithee, and I'll pay thee bounteously,
Conceal me what I am, and be my aid
For such disguise as haply shall become          54
The form of my intent. I'll serve this duke.          55
Thou shalt present me as an eunuch to him.          56
It may be worth thy pains, for I can sing
And speak to him in many sorts of music
That will allow me very worth his service.          59
What else may hap, to time I will commit;
Only shape thou thy silence to my wit.          61
CAPTAIN
Be you his eunuch, and your mute I'll be;          62
When my tongue blabs, then let mine eyes not see.
VIOLA     I thank thee. Lead me on.          *Exeunt.*

30 **A brother's dead love** her love for her dead brother and the memory of his love for her     32 **frame** construction     34 **golden shaft** Cupid's golden-tipped arrow, causing love. (His lead-tipped arrow causes aversion.)     35 **affections else** other feelings     36–8 **when . . . king** i.e., when passion, thought, and feeling all sit in majesty in their proper thrones (liver, brain, and heart), and her sweet perfections are brought to completion by her union with a single lord and husband.
**1.2. Location: The seacoast.**
4 **Elysium** classical abode of the blessed dead.     5–7 **Perchance . . . perchance** Perhaps . . . by mere chance . . . with any luck     8 **chance** i.e., what one may hope that chance will bring about     11 **driving** drifting, driven by the seas     14 **lived** i.e., kept afloat     15 **Arion** a Greek poet who so charmed the dolphins with his lyre that they saved him when he leaped into the sea to escape murderous sailors     19–21 **unfoldeth . . . him** offers a hopeful example that he may have escaped similarly, to which hope your speech provides support.

30 **late** lately     32 **murmur** rumor     33 **less** social inferiors     42 **delivered** revealed, made known. (With suggestion of "born.")     43 **Till . . . mellow** until the time is ripe for my purpose     44 **estate** social rank.     **were** would be.     **compass** encompass, bring about     46 **not** not even     48 **though that** though     51 **character** face or features as indicating moral qualities.     54–5 **as haply . . . intent** as may suit the nature of my purpose.     56 **eunuch** castrato, high-voiced singer     59 **allow** prove     61 **wit** plan, invention.     62 **mute** silent attendant. (Sometimes used of nonspeaking actors.)

# 1.3

*Enter Sir Toby [Belch] and Maria.*

SIR TOBY   What a plague means my niece to take the   1
death of her brother thus? I am sure care's an enemy   2
to life.

MARIA   By my troth, Sir Toby, you must come in earlier
o'nights. Your cousin, my lady, takes great exceptions   5
to your ill hours.

SIR TOBY   Why, let her except before excepted.   7

MARIA   Ay, but you must confine yourself within the
modest limits of order.   9

SIR TOBY   Confine? I'll confine myself no finer than I am.   10
These clothes are good enough to drink in, and so be
these boots too. An they be not, let them hang them-   12
selves in their own straps.

MARIA   That quaffing and drinking will undo you. I
heard my lady talk of it yesterday, and of a foolish
knight that you brought in one night here to be her
wooer.

SIR TOBY   Who, Sir Andrew Aguecheek?

MARIA   Ay, he.

SIR TOBY   He's as tall a man as any's in Illyria.   20

MARIA   What's that to th' purpose?

SIR TOBY   Why, he has three thousand ducats a year.   22

MARIA   Ay, but he'll have but a year in all these ducats.   23
He's a very fool and a prodigal.

SIR TOBY   Fie, that you'll say so! He plays o'th' viol-de-   25
gamboys, and speaks three or four languages word   26
for word without book, and hath all the good gifts of   27
nature.

MARIA   He hath indeed, almost natural, for, besides that   29
he's a fool, he's a great quarreler, and but that he hath   30
the gift of a coward to allay the gust he hath in quarreling,   31
'tis thought among the prudent he would quickly
have the gift of a grave.

SIR TOBY   By this hand, they are scoundrels and sub-   34
stractors that say so of him. Who are they?   35

MARIA   They that add, moreover, he's drunk nightly in
your company.

SIR TOBY   With drinking healths to my niece. I'll drink
to her as long as there is a passage in my throat and
drink in Illyria. He's a coward and a coistrel that will   40
not drink to my niece till his brains turn o'th' toe like   41

a parish top. What, wench? *Castiliano vulgo!* For here   42
comes Sir Andrew Agueface.   43

*Enter Sir Andrew [Aguecheek].*

SIR ANDREW   Sir Toby Belch! How now, Sir Toby Belch?

SIR TOBY   Sweet Sir Andrew!

SIR ANDREW   [*to Maria*]   Bless you, fair shrew.   46

MARIA   And you too, sir.

SIR TOBY   Accost, Sir Andrew, accost.   48

SIR ANDREW   What's that?

SIR TOBY   My niece's chambermaid.   50

SIR ANDREW   Good Mistress Accost, I desire better
acquaintance.

MARIA   My name is Mary, sir.

SIR ANDREW   Good Mistress Mary Accost—

SIR TOBY   You mistake, knight. "Accost" is front her,   55
board her, woo her, assail her.   56

SIR ANDREW   By my troth, I would not undertake her in   57
this company. Is that the meaning of "accost"?

MARIA   Fare you well, gentlemen.   [*Going.*]

SIR TOBY   An thou let part so, Sir Andrew, would thou   60
mightst never draw sword again.

SIR ANDREW   An you part so, mistress, I would I might
never draw sword again. Fair lady, do you think you
have fools in hand?   64

MARIA   Sir, I have not you by th' hand.

SIR ANDREW   Marry, but you shall have, and here's my   66
hand.   [*He gives her his hand.*]

MARIA   Now, sir, thought is free. I pray you, bring your   68
hand to th' buttery-bar, and let it drink.   69

SIR ANDREW   Wherefore, sweetheart? What's your
metaphor?

MARIA   It's dry, sir.   72

SIR ANDREW   Why, I think so. I am not such an ass but
I can keep my hand dry. But what's your jest?

MARIA   A dry jest, sir.   75

SIR ANDREW   Are you full of them?

MARIA   Ay, sir, I have them at my fingers' ends. Marry,   77
now I let go your hand, I am barren.   78

[*She lets go his hand.*] *Exit Maria.*

---

**1.3. Location: Olivia's house.**
**1 What a plague** i.e., What the devil   **2 care's** sorrow is   **5 cousin**
kinswoman   **7 let . . . excepted** i.e., let her take exception to my conduct all she wants; I don't care. (Plays on the legal phrase *exceptis exci-
piendis,* "with the exceptions before named.")   **9 modest** moderate
**10 I'll . . . finer** (1) I'll constrain myself no more rigorously (2) I'll
dress myself no more finely   **12 An** If   **20 tall** brave. (But Maria pretends to take the word in the common sense.)   **22 ducats** coins worth
about four or five shillings   **23 he'll . . . ducats** he'll spend all his
money within a year.   **25–6 viol-de-gamboys** viola da gamba, leg-
viol, bass viol   **27 without book** by heart   **29 natural** (With a play
on the sense "born idiot.")   **30 a great quarreler** one who delights in
issuing and answering challenges to a duel; or, simply one who takes
pleasure in being quarrelsome.   **but that** were it not that   **31 gift**
natural ability. (But shifted to mean "present" in line 33.)   **allay the
gust** moderate the taste   **34–5 substractors** detractors   **40 coistrel**
horse-groom, base fellow   **41 turn o'th' toe** spin about drunkenly

**42 parish top** a large top provided by the parish to be spun by whipping, apparently for exercise.   *Castiliano vulgo* ! (Of uncertain
meaning. Possibly Sir Toby is saying "Speak of the devil!" Castiliano
is the name adopted by a devil in Haughton's *Grim the Collier of Croy-
don.*)   **43 Agueface** (Like *Aguecheek,* this name betokens the thin, pale
countenance of one suffering from an ague or fever.)   **46 shrew** i.e.,
diminutive creature. (But with probably unintended suggestion of
shrewishness.)   **48 Accost** Go alongside (a nautical term), i.e., greet
her, address her   **50 chambermaid** lady-in-waiting (a gentlewoman,
not one who would do menial tasks).   **55 front** confront, come alongside   **56 board** greet, approach (as though preparing to board in a
naval encounter)   **57 undertake** have to do with. (Here with unintended sexual suggestion, to which Maria mirthfully replies with her
jokes about *dry jests, barren,* and *buttery-bar.*)   **60 An . . . so** If you will
let her leave thus   **64 have . . . hand** i.e., have to deal with fools. (But
Maria puns on the literal sense.)   **66 Marry** i.e., Indeed. (Originally,
"By the Virgin Mary.")   **68 thought is free** i.e., I may think what I
like. (Proverbial; replying to *do you think . . . in hand,* above.)   **69 buttery-bar** ledge on top of the half-door to the buttery or the wine cellar. (Maria's language is sexually suggestive, though Sir Andrew
seems oblivious to that.)   **72 dry** thirsty; also dried up, a sign of age
and sexual debility   **75 dry** (1) ironic (2) dull, barren. (Referring to
Sir Andrew.)   **77 at my fingers' ends** (1) at the ready (2) by the
hand.   **78 barren** i.e., empty of jests and of Sir Andrew's hand.

SIR TOBY　Oh, knight, thou lack'st a cup of canary! When 79
did I see thee so put down?

SIR ANDREW　Never in your life, I think, unless you see
canary put me down. Methinks sometimes I have no 82
more wit than a Christian or an ordinary man has. But
I am a great eater of beef, and I believe that does harm
to my wit.

SIR TOBY　No question.

SIR ANDREW　An I thought that, I'd forswear it. I'll ride
home tomorrow, Sir Toby.

SIR TOBY　*Pourquoi*, my dear knight? 89

SIR ANDREW　What is "*pourquoi*"? Do or not do? I would
I had bestowed that time in the tongues that I 91
have in fencing, dancing, and bearbaiting. Oh, had I 92
but followed the arts! 93

SIR TOBY　Then hadst thou had an excellent head of hair.

SIR ANDREW　Why, would that have mended my hair? 95

SIR TOBY　Past question, for thou see'st it will not curl by
nature.

SIR ANDREW　But it becomes me well enough, does't
not?

SIR TOBY　Excellent. It hangs like flax on a distaff; and I 100
hope to see a huswife take thee between her legs and
spin it off. 102

SIR ANDREW　Faith, I'll home tomorrow, Sir Toby. Your
niece will not be seen, or if she be, it's four to one
she'll none of me. The Count himself here hard by 105
woos her.

SIR TOBY　She'll none o'th' Count. She'll not match
above her degree, neither in estate, years, nor wit; I 108
have heard her swear't. Tut, there's life in't, man. 109

SIR ANDREW　I'll stay a month longer. I am a fellow o'th'
strangest mind i'th' world; I delight in masques and
revels sometimes altogether.

SIR TOBY　Art thou good at these kickshawses, knight? 113

SIR ANDREW　As any man in Illyria, whatsoever he be,
under the degree of my betters, and yet I will not com- 115
pare with an old man. 116

SIR TOBY　What is thy excellence in a galliard, knight? 117

SIR ANDREW　Faith, I can cut a caper. 118

SIR TOBY　And I can cut the mutton to't.

SIR ANDREW　And I think I have the back-trick simply 120
as strong as any man in Illyria.

SIR TOBY　Wherefore are these things hid? Wherefore
have these gifts a curtain before 'em? Are they like to 123
take dust, like Mistress Mall's picture? Why dost thou 124
not go to church in a galliard and come home in a
coranto? My very walk should be a jig; I would not so 126
much as make water but in a sink-a-pace. What dost 127
thou mean? Is it a world to hide virtues in? I did think, 128
by the excellent constitution of thy leg, it was formed
under the star of a galliard. 130

SIR ANDREW　Ay, 'tis strong, and it does indifferent well 131
in a dun-colored stock. Shall we set about some 132
revels?

SIR TOBY　What shall we do else? Were we not born
under Taurus? 135

SIR ANDREW　Taurus? That's sides and heart.

SIR TOBY　No, sir, it is legs and thighs. Let me see thee
caper. [*Sir Andrew capers.*] Ha, higher! Ha, ha, excellent!　　　　　　　　　　　　　　　　　　　　　*Exeunt.*

# 1.4

*Enter Valentine, and Viola in man's attire.*

VALENTINE　If the Duke continue these favors towards
you, Cesario, you are like to be much advanced. He 2
hath known you but three days, and already you are
no stranger.

VIOLA　You either fear his humor or my negligence, that 5
you call in question the continuance of his love. Is he
inconstant, sir, in his favors?

VALENTINE　No, believe me.

*Enter Duke [Orsino], Curio, and attendants.*

VIOLA　I thank you. Here comes the Count.

ORSINO　Who saw Cesario, ho?

VIOLA　On your attendance, my lord, here. 11

ORSINO
Stand you awhile aloof. [*The others stand aside.*]
Cesario, 12
Thou know'st no less but all. I have unclasped
To thee the book even of my secret soul.
Therefore, good youth, address thy gait unto her; 15
Be not denied access, stand at her doors,

---

79 **thou . . . canary** i.e., you look as if you need a drink. (*Canary* is a sweet wine from the Canary Islands.)　82 **put me down** (1) baffle my wits (2) lay me out flat.　89 *Pourquoi* Why　91 **tongues** languages. (Sir Toby then puns on "tongs," curling irons.)　92 **bearbaiting** the sport of setting dogs on a chained bear.　93 **the arts** the liberal arts, learning. (But Sir Toby plays on the phrase as meaning "artifice," the antithesis of *nature*.)　95 **mended** improved　100 **distaff** a staff for holding the flax, tow, or wool in spinning　102 **spin it off** i.e., (1) treat your flaxen hair as though it were flax on a distaff to be spun (2) cause you to lose hair as a result of venereal disease (3) make you ejaculate. (*Huswife* suggests "hussy," "whore.")　105 **Count** i.e., Duke Orsino, sometimes referred to as Count.　**hard by** near by　108 **degree** social position.　**estate** fortune, social position　109 **there's life in't** i.e., while there's life there's hope　113 **kickshawses** delicacies, fancy trifles. (From the French, *quelque chose*.)　115 **under . . . betters** excepting those who are above me　115–16 **I will not . . . old man** i.e., I will not presume to compare myself as a reveler with anyone old enough to have more experience in such matters.　117 **galliard** lively dance in triple time　118 **Faith** In faith. (A mild oath.)　**cut a caper** make a lively leap. (But Sir Toby puns on the *caper* used to make a sauce served with mutton. *Mutton*, in turn, suggests "whore.")

120 **back-trick** backward step in the galliard. (With sexual innuendo; the back was associated with sexual vigor.)　123–4 **like to take** likely to collect　124 **Mistress Mall's picture** i.e., perhaps the portrait of some woman protected from light and dust, as many pictures were, by curtains. (*Mall* is a diminutive of *Mary*.)　126 **coranto** lively running dance.　127 **sink-a-pace** dance like the galliard. (French *cinquepace. Sink* also suggests a cesspool into which one might urinate.)　128 **virtues** talents　130 **under . . . galliard** i.e., under a star favorable to dancing.　131 **indifferent well** well enough. (Said complacently.)　132 **dun-colored stock** mouse-colored stocking.　135 **Taurus** zodiacal sign. (Sir Andrew is mistaken, since Leo governed sides and hearts in medical astrology. Taurus governed legs and thighs, as Toby insists, or, more commonly, neck and throat.)
**1.4. Location: Orsino's court.**
2 **like** likely　5 **humor** changeableness　11 **On your attendance** Ready to do you service　12 **aloof** aside.　15 **address thy gait** go

And tell them, there thy fixèd foot shall grow
Till thou have audience.                                    17

VIOLA                              Sure, my noble lord,    18
If she be so abandoned to her sorrow
As it is spoke, she never will admit me.

ORSINO
Be clamorous and leap all civil bounds              21
Rather than make unprofited return.

VIOLA
Say I do speak with her, my lord, what then?    23

ORSINO
Oh, then unfold the passion of my love;
Surprise her with discourse of my dear faith.    25
It shall become thee well to act my woes;       26
She will attend it better in thy youth
Than in a nuncio's of more grave aspect.       28

VIOLA
I think not so, my lord.

ORSINO                        Dear lad, believe it;
For they shall yet belie thy happy years
That say thou art a man. Diana's lip
Is not more smooth and rubious; thy small pipe  32
Is as the maiden's organ, shrill and sound,    33
And all is semblative a woman's part.        34
I know thy constellation is right apt         35
For this affair.—Some four or five attend him.
All, if you will, for I myself am best
When least in company.—Prosper well in this,
And thou shalt live as freely as thy lord,
To call his fortunes thine.

VIOLA                        I'll do my best
To woo your lady. [*Aside*] Yet a barful strife!  41
Whoe'er I woo, myself would be his wife.    *Exeunt.*

✤

## 1.5

*Enter Maria and Clown [Feste].*

MARIA    Nay, either tell me where thou hast been, or I will not open my lips so wide as a bristle may enter in way of thy excuse. My lady will hang thee for thy absence.

FESTE    Let her hang me. He that is well hanged in this world needs to fear no colors.    6

MARIA    Make that good.    7

FESTE    He shall see none to fear.    8

MARIA    A good Lenten answer. I can tell thee where that saying was born, of "I fear no colors."    9

FESTE    Where, good Mistress Mary?

MARIA    In the wars, and that may you be bold to say in your foolery.    12 / 13

FESTE    Well, God give them wisdom that have it; and those that are fools, let them use their talents.    15

MARIA    Yet you will be hanged for being so long absent; or to be turned away, is not that as good as a hanging to you?    17

FESTE    Many a good hanging prevents a bad marriage; and for turning away, let summer bear it out.    19 / 20

MARIA    You are resolute, then?

FESTE    Not so, neither, but I am resolved on two points.    23

MARIA    That if one break, the other will hold; or if both break, your gaskins fall.    25

FESTE    Apt, in good faith, very apt. Well, go thy way. If Sir Toby would leave drinking, thou wert as witty a piece of Eve's flesh as any in Illyria.    27 / 28

MARIA    Peace, you rogue, no more o' that. Here comes my lady. Make your excuse wisely, you were best.    30

                                    [*Exit.*]

*Enter Lady Olivia with Malvolio, [and attendants].*

FESTE    [*aside*]    Wit, an't be thy will, put me into good fooling! Those wits that think they have thee do very oft prove fools, and I that am sure I lack thee may pass for a wise man. For what says Quinapalus? "Better a witty fool than a foolish wit."—God bless thee, lady!    31 / 34

OLIVIA    [*to attendants*]    Take the fool away.

FESTE    Do you not hear, fellows? Take away the lady.

OLIVIA    Go to, you're a dry fool. I'll no more of you. Besides, you grow dishonest.    38

FESTE    Two faults, madonna, that drink and good counsel will amend. For give the dry fool drink, then is the fool not dry. Bid the dishonest man mend himself; if he mend, he is no longer dishonest; if he cannot, let the botcher mend him. Anything that's mended is but patched; virtue that transgresses is but patched with sin, and sin that amends is but patched with virtue. If that this simple syllogism will serve, so; if it will not, what remedy? As there is no true cuckold but calamity, so beauty's a flower. The lady bade take    40 / 44 / 45 / 47 / 48 / 49

---

**17 them** i.e., Olivia's servants  **18 audience** admittance.  **21 civil bounds** bounds of civility  **23 Say** Supposing  **25 Surprise** Take by storm. (A military term.)  **dear** heartfelt  **26 become** suit  **28 nuncio's** messenger's  **32 rubious** ruby red.  **pipe** voice, throat  **33 shrill and sound** high and clear, uncracked  **34 semblative** resembling, like  **35 constellation** i.e., nature as determined by your horoscope  **41 barful strife** endeavor full of impediments.

**1.5. Location: Olivia's house.**

**6 fear no colors** i.e., fear no foe, fear nothing. (With pun on *colors*, worldly deceptions, and "collars," halters or nooses.)  **7 Make that good** Explain that.  **8 He . . . fear** i.e., The hanged man will be dead and unable to see anything.  **9 Lenten** meager, scanty (like Lenten fare), and morbid

**12 In the wars** (Where *colors* would mean "military standards, enemy flags"—the literal meaning of the proverb.)  **12–13 that . . . foolery** that's an answer you may be bold to use in your fool's conundrums. (*Colors* here refer to military banners and insignia used to align rows of fighting men in battle.)  **15 talents** abilities. (Also alluding to the parable of the talents, Matthew 25:14–29, and to "talons," claws.)  **17 turned away** dismissed. (Possibly also meaning "turned off," "hanged.")  **19 good hanging** (With possible bawdy pun on "being well hung.")  **20 for** as for.  **let . . . out** i.e., let mild weather make dismissal endurable.  **23 points** (Maria, in lines 24–5, plays on the meaning "laces used to hold up hose or breeches.")  **25 gaskins** wide breeches  **27–8 thou . . . Illyria** (Feste may be hinting that Maria would be a suitable mate for Sir Toby.)  **30 you were best** it would be best for you.  **31 an't** if it  **34 Quinapalus** (Feste's invented authority.)  **38 Go to** (An expression of annoyance or expostulation.)  **dry** dull  **40 madonna** my lady  **44 botcher** mender of old clothes and shoes. (Playing on two senses of *mend:* "reform" and "repair.")  **44–5 Anything . . . patched** i.e., Life is patched or parti-colored like the Fool's garment, a mix of good and bad  **47 so** well and good  **48–9 As . . . flower** (Nonsense, yet with a suggestion that Olivia has wedded calamity but should not be faithful to it, for the natural course is to seize the moment of youth and beauty before we lose it.)

away the fool; therefore I say again, take her away.

OLIVIA  Sir, I bade them take away you.

FESTE  Misprision in the highest degree! Lady, *cucullus* 52
*non facit monachum;* that's as much to say as I wear not 53
motley in my brain. Good madonna, give me leave to 54
prove you a fool.

OLIVIA  Can you do it?

FESTE  Dexteriously, good madonna.

OLIVIA  Make your proof.

FESTE  I must catechize you for it, madonna. Good my 59
mouse of virtue, answer me. 60

OLIVIA  Well, sir, for want of other idleness, I'll bide 61
your proof.

FESTE  Good madonna, why mourn'st thou?

OLIVIA  Good fool, for my brother's death.

FESTE  I think his soul is in hell, madonna.

OLIVIA  I know his soul is in heaven, fool.

FESTE  The more fool, madonna, to mourn for your
brother's soul, being in heaven.—Take away the fool,
gentlemen.

OLIVIA  What think you of this fool, Malvolio? Doth he
not mend? 71

MALVOLIO  Yes, and shall do till the pangs of death
shake him. Infirmity, that decays the wise, doth ever 73
make the better fool. 74

FESTE  God send you, sir, a speedy infirmity for the
better increasing your folly! Sir Toby will be sworn
that I am no fox, but he will not pass his word for 77
twopence that you are no fool.

OLIVIA  How say you to that, Malvolio?

MALVOLIO  I marvel Your Ladyship takes delight in such
a barren rascal. I saw him put down the other day
with an ordinary fool that has no more brain than a 82
stone. Look you now, he's out of his guard already. 83
Unless you laugh and minister occasion to him, he is 84
gagged. I protest I take these wise men that crow so at 85
these set kind of fools no better than the fools' zanies. 86

OLIVIA  Oh, you are sick of self-love, Malvolio, and taste
with a distempered appetite. To be generous, guiltless, 88
and of free disposition is to take those things for bird- 89
bolts that you deem cannon bullets. There is no slan- 90
der in an allowed fool, though he do nothing but rail; 91
nor no railing in a known discreet man, though he do 92
nothing but reprove. 93

**52 Misprision** Mistake, misunderstanding. (A legal term meaning a wrongful action or misdemeanor.)  **52–3 cucullus . . . monachum** the cowl does not make the monk  **54 motley** the many-colored garment of jesters  **59 catechize** put you to your catechism, a religious exercise of question and answer designed to instruct neophytes in the elements of Christian faith  **59–60 Good . . . virtue** My good, virtuous mouse. (A term of endearment.)  **61 want** lack.  **idleness** pastime.  **bide** submit myself to  **71 mend** i.e., improve, grow more amusing. (But Malvolio uses the word to mean "grow more like a fool.")  **73-4 Infirmity . . . fool** i.e., Infirmity, the inevitable consequence of aging, makes foolish old people even more foolish than they were before.  **77 pass** give  **82 with** by  **83 out of his guard** defenseless, unprovided with a witty answer  **84 minister occasion** provide opportunity (for his fooling)  **85 protest** avow, declare.  **crow** laugh stridently  **86 set** artificial, stereotyped.  **zanies** assistants, aping attendants.  **88 distempered** diseased.  **generous** noble-minded  **89 free** magnanimous  **89–90 bird-bolts** blunt arrows for shooting small birds  **90–3 There . . . reprove** Both a fool who is licensed to speak freely and a man known for discretion can criticize freely without being accused of slander in the first instance or railing in the second. (In rebuking Malvolio here, Olivia implies that he is not behaving like a "known discreet man.")

FESTE  Now Mercury endue thee with leasing, for thou 94
speak'st well of fools!

*Enter Maria.*

MARIA  Madam, there is at the gate a young gentleman
much desires to speak with you. 97

OLIVIA  From the Count Orsino, is it?

MARIA  I know not, madam. 'Tis a fair young man, and
well attended.

OLIVIA  Who of my people hold him in delay?

MARIA  Sir Toby, madam, your kinsman.

OLIVIA  Fetch him off, I pray you. He speaks nothing
but madman. Fie on him!          [*Exit Maria.*] 104
Go you, Malvolio. If it be a suit from the Count, I am
sick or not at home; what you will, to dismiss it.
*Exit Malvolio.*
Now you see, sir, how your fooling grows old, and 107
people dislike it.

FESTE  Thou hast spoke for us, madonna, as if thy eldest
son should be a fool; whose skull Jove cram with
brains, for—here he comes—

*Enter Sir Toby.*

one of thy kin has a most weak *pia mater.* 112

OLIVIA  By mine honor, half drunk.—What is he at the
gate, cousin?

SIR TOBY  A gentleman.

OLIVIA  A gentleman? What gentleman?

SIR TOBY  'Tis a gentleman here—[*He belches.*] A plague
o' these pickle-herring! [*To Feste*] How now, sot? 118

FESTE  Good Sir Toby.

OLIVIA  Cousin, cousin, how have you come so early by 120
this lethargy?

SIR TOBY  Lechery? I defy lechery. There's one at the
gate.

OLIVIA  Ay, marry, what is he?

SIR TOBY  Let him be the devil an he will, I care not.
Give me faith, say I. Well, it's all one.        *Exit.* 126

OLIVIA  What's a drunken man like, Fool?

FESTE  Like a drowned man, a fool, and a madman.
One draft above heat makes him a fool, the second 129
mads him, and a third drowns him.

OLIVIA  Go thou and seek the crowner, and let him sit 131
o' my coz; for he's in the third degree of drink, he's 132
drowned. Go, look after him.

FESTE  He is but mad yet, madonna; and the fool shall
look to the madman.          [*Exit.*]

*Enter Malvolio.*

MALVOLIO  Madam, yond young fellow swears he will
speak with you. I told him you were sick; he takes on
him to understand so much, and therefore comes to
speak with you. I told him you were asleep; he seems

**94 Now . . . leasing** i.e., May Mercury, the god of deception, make you a skillful liar  **97 much** who much  **104 madman** i.e., the words of madness.  **107 old** stale  **112 pia mater** i.e., brain. (Actually the soft membrane enclosing the brain.)  **118 sot** (1) fool (2) drunkard.  **120 Cousin** Kinsman. (Here, uncle.)  **126 Give me faith** i.e., to resist the devil.  **it's all one** it doesn't matter.  **129 draft above heat** helping of drink raising his temperature above normal bodily warmth  **131 crowner** coroner, an official responsible for investigating deaths  **131–2 sit o' my coz** hold an inquest on my kinsman (Sir Toby) to have a foreknowledge of that too, and therefore comes to speak with you. What is to be said to him, lady? He's fortified against any denial.

OLIVIA     Tell him he shall not speak with me.

MALVOLIO     He's been told so; and he says he'll stand at your door like a sheriff's post, and be the supporter to 145 a bench, but he'll speak with you.

OLIVIA     What kind o' man is he?

MALVOLIO     Why, of mankind.

OLIVIA     What manner of man?

MALVOLIO     Of very ill manner. He'll speak with you, will you or no.

OLIVIA     Of what personage and years is he?

MALVOLIO     Not yet old enough for a man, nor young enough for a boy; as a squash is before 'tis a peascod, 154 or a codling when 'tis almost an apple. 'Tis with him in 155 standing water between boy and man. He is very 156 well-favored, and he speaks very shrewishly. One 157 would think his mother's milk were scarce out of him.

OLIVIA     Let him approach. Call in my gentlewoman.

MALVOLIO     Gentlewoman, my lady calls.          *Exit.*

*Enter Maria.*

OLIVIA
Give me my veil. Come, throw it o'er my face.
We'll once more hear Orsino's embassy. [*Olivia veils.*]

*Enter Viola.*

VIOLA     The honorable lady of the house, which is she?

OLIVIA     Speak to me; I shall answer for her. Your will?

VIOLA     Most radiant, exquisite, and unmatchable beauty—I pray you, tell me if this be the lady of the house, for I never saw her. I would be loath to cast away my speech; for besides that it is excellently well penned, I have taken great pains to con it. Good 170 beauties, let me sustain no scorn; I am very comptible, 171 even to the least sinister usage. 172

OLIVIA     Whence came you, sir?

VIOLA     I can say little more than I have studied, and that question's out of my part. Good gentle one, give me modest assurance if you be the lady of the house, 176 that I may proceed in my speech.

OLIVIA     Are you a comedian? 178

VIOLA     No, my profound heart; and yet, by the very 179 fangs of malice, I swear I am not that I play. Are you 180 the lady of the house?

OLIVIA     If I do not usurp myself, I am. 182

VIOLA     Most certain, if you are she, you do usurp your- 183 self; for what is yours to bestow is not yours to reserve. 184

But this is from my commission. I will on with my 185 speech in your praise, and then show you the heart of my message.

OLIVIA     Come to what is important in't. I forgive you 188 the praise.

VIOLA     Alas, I took great pains to study it, and 'tis 190 poetical.

OLIVIA     It is the more like to be feigned. I pray you, 192 keep it in. I heard you were saucy at my gates, and allowed your approach rather to wonder at you than to hear you. If you be not mad, begone; if you have 195 reason, be brief. 'Tis not that time of moon with me to 196 make one in so skipping a dialogue. 197

MARIA     Will you hoist sail, sir? Here lies your way.

VIOLA     No, good swabber, I am to hull here a little 199 longer.—Some mollification for your giant, sweet 200 lady. Tell me your mind; I am a messenger.

OLIVIA     Sure you have some hideous matter to deliver, when the courtesy of it is so fearful. Speak your office. 203

VIOLA     It alone concerns your ear. I bring no overture of 204 war, no taxation of homage. I hold the olive in my 205 hand; my words are as full of peace as matter. 206

OLIVIA     Yet you began rudely. What are you? What 207 would you?

VIOLA     The rudeness that hath appeared in me have I learned from my entertainment. What I am and what 210 I would are as secret as maidenhead—to your ears, 211 divinity; to any other's, profanation. 212

OLIVIA [*to the others*]     Give us the place here alone. We will hear this divinity. [*Exeunt Maria and attendants.*] Now, sir, what is your text?

VIOLA     Most sweet lady—

OLIVIA     A comfortable doctrine, and much may be said 217 of it. Where lies your text?

VIOLA     In Orsino's bosom.

OLIVIA     In his bosom? In what chapter of his bosom?

VIOLA     To answer by the method, in the first of his 221 heart.

OLIVIA     Oh, I have read it. It is heresy. Have you no more to say?

VIOLA     Good madam, let me see your face.

OLIVIA     Have you any commission from your lord to negotiate with my face? You are now out of your text. 227 But we will draw the curtain and show you the

145 **sheriff's post** post before the sheriff's door to mark a residence of authority, often elaborately carved and decorated.   **supporter prop**   154 **squash** unripe pea pod.   **peascod** ripe pea pod. (The image suggests that the boy's testicles have not yet dropped.)   155 **codling** unripe apple   155–6 **in standing water** at the turn of the tide   157 **well-favored** good-looking.   **shrewishly** sharply.   170 **con** memorize   171 **comptible** susceptible, sensitive   172 **least sinister** slightest discourteous   176 **modest** reasonable   178 **comedian** actor.   179 **my profound heart** my most wise lady; or, in all sincerity   179–80 **and yet . . . I play** and yet, despite what the malicious might say of me, I am not what I impersonate. (The audience knows this to be true.)   182 **do . . . myself** am not an impostor   183–4 **usurp yourself** i.e., misappropriate yourself, by withholding yourself from love and marriage

185 **from** outside of   188 **forgive you** excuse you from reciting   190 **study** memorize   192 **like** likely   195 **not mad** i.e., not altogether mad   196 **reason** sanity.   **moon** (The moon was thought to affect lunatics according to its changing phases.)   197 **make one** take part   199 **swabber** one in charge of scrubbing the decks. (A nautical retort to *hoist sail.*)   **hull** lie with sails furled   200 **Some . . . for** i.e., Please mollify, pacify.   **giant** i.e., the diminutive Maria who, like many giants in medieval romances, is guarding the lady   203 **courtesy** i.e., complimentary, "poetical" introduction. (Or Olivia may refer to Cesario's importunate manner at her gate, as reported by Malvolio.)   **office** commission, business.   204 **overture** declaration. (Literally, opening.)   205 **taxation of homage** demand for tribute.   **olive** olive-branch (signifying peace)   206 **matter** substance.   207 **Yet . . . rudely** i.e., Yet you were saucy at my gates.   210 **entertainment** reception.   211 **maidenhead** virginity   212 **divinity** sacred discourse   217 **comfortable** comforting   221 **To . . . method** i.e., To continue the metaphor of delivering a sermon, begun with *divinity* and *what is your text* and continued in *doctrine, heresy,* etc.   227 **out of** straying from

picture. [*Unveiling.*] Look you, sir, such a one I was 229
this present. Is't not well done? 230

VIOLA   Excellently done, if God did all.

OLIVIA   'Tis in grain, sir; 'twill endure wind and 232
weather.

VIOLA
'Tis beauty truly blent, whose red and white 234
Nature's own sweet and cunning hand laid on. 235
Lady, you are the cruel'st she alive
If you will lead these graces to the grave
And leave the world no copy. 238

OLIVIA   Oh, sir, I will not be so hardhearted. I will give
out divers schedules of my beauty. It shall be invento- 240
ried, and every particle and utensil labeled to my 241
will: as, item, two lips, indifferent red; item, two gray 242
eyes, with lids to them; item, one neck, one chin, and
so forth. Were you sent hither to praise me? 244

VIOLA
I see you what you are: you are too proud.
But, if you were the devil, you are fair. 246
My lord and master loves you. Oh, such love 247
Could be but recompensed, though you were
  crowned 248
The nonpareil of beauty!

OLIVIA                    How does he love me? 249

VIOLA
With adorations, fertile tears, 250
With groans that thunder love, with sighs of fire.

OLIVIA
Your lord does know my mind; I cannot love him.
Yet I suppose him virtuous, know him noble,
Of great estate, of fresh and stainless youth, 254
In voices well divulged, free, learned, and valiant, 255
And in dimension and the shape of nature 256
A gracious person. But yet I cannot love him. 257
He might have took his answer long ago.

VIOLA
If I did love you in my master's flame, 259
With such a suff'ring, such a deadly life, 260
In your denial I would find no sense;
I would not understand it.

OLIVIA                    Why, what would you?

VIOLA
Make me a willow cabin at your gate 263
And call upon my soul within the house; 264
Write loyal cantons of contemnèd love 265

And sing them loud even in the dead of night;
Hallow your name to the reverberate hills, 267
And make the babbling gossip of the air 268
Cry out "Olivia!" Oh, you should not rest
Between the elements of air and earth 270
But you should pity me!

OLIVIA                You might do much.
What is your parentage?

VIOLA
Above my fortunes, yet my state is well: 273
I am a gentleman.

OLIVIA            Get you to your lord.
I cannot love him. Let him send no more—
Unless, perchance, you come to me again
To tell me how he takes it. Fare you well.
I thank you for your pains. Spend this for me. 278
[*She offers a purse.*]

VIOLA
I am no fee'd post, lady. Keep your purse. 279
My master, not myself, lacks recompense.
Love make his heart of flint that you shall love, 281
And let your fervor, like my master's, be
Placed in contempt! Farewell, fair cruelty.   *Exit.*

OLIVIA   "What is your parentage?"
"Above my fortunes, yet my state is well:
I am a gentleman." I'll be sworn thou art!
Thy tongue, thy face, thy limbs, actions, and spirit
Do give thee fivefold blazon. Not too fast! Soft, soft! 288
Unless the master were the man. How now? 289
Even so quickly may one catch the plague?
Methinks I feel this youth's perfections
With an invisible and subtle stealth
To creep in at mine eyes. Well, let it be.—
What ho, Malvolio!

*Enter Malvolio.*

MALVOLIO            Here, madam, at your service.

OLIVIA
Run after that same peevish messenger,
The County's man. He left this ring behind him, 296
[*giving a ring*]
Would I or not. Tell him I'll none of it. 297
Desire him not to flatter with his lord, 298
Nor hold him up with hopes; I am not for him. 299
If that the youth will come this way tomorrow, 300
I'll give him reasons for't. Hie thee, Malvolio. 301

MALVOLIO   Madam, I will.                    *Exit.*

OLIVIA
I do I know not what, and fear to find
Mine eye too great a flatterer for my mind. 304

229–30 such . . . present this is a recent portrait of me. (Since it was customary to hang curtains in front of pictures, Olivia in unveiling speaks as if she were displaying a picture of herself.)   232 in grain fast dyed   234 blent blended   235 cunning skillful   238 copy i.e., a child. (But Olivia uses the word to mean "transcript.")   240 schedules inventories   241 utensil article, item.   labeled added as a codicil   242 item . . . item first item in the inventory . . . second item, etc.   indifferent somewhat   244 praise (With pun on "appraise.")   246 if even if   247–9 Oh . . . beauty! i.e., Even if you were the most beautiful woman alive, that beauty could do no more than repay my master's love for you!   250 fertile copious   254 estate wealth, property   255 In . . . divulged well spoken of.   free generous   256 in . . . nature in his physical form   257 gracious graceful, attractive   259 flame passion   260 With . . . life with suffering so intense as to be a kind of living death   263 willow cabin shelter, hut. (Willow was a symbol of unrequited love.)   264 my soul i.e., Olivia   265 cantons songs.   contemnèd rejected

267 Hallow (1) halloo (2) bless   268 babbling . . . air echo   270 Between . . . earth i.e., anywhere   273 state social standing   278 pains troubles, efforts.   279 fee'd post messenger to be tipped   281 Love . . . love May Cupid make the heart of the man you love as hard as flint   288 Do . . . blazon proclaim you as would a coat of arms bearing five insignia.   Soft Wait a minute. (Said to herself.)   289 Unless . . . man i.e., Unless Cesario and Orsino changed places.   296 County's Count's, i.e., Duke's   297 Would I or not whether I wanted it or not.   298 flatter with encourage   299 Nor . . . hopes nor hold up hope to him   300 If that If   301 Hie thee Hasten   304 Mine . . . mind i.e., that my eyes (through which love enters the soul) have deceived my reason.

Fate, show thy force. Ourselves we do not owe.                    305
What is decreed must be; and be this so.         [*Exit.*]

❧

## 2.1

*Enter Antonio and Sebastian.*

ANTONIO   Will you stay no longer? Nor will you not      1
that I go with you?

SEBASTIAN   By your patience, no. My stars shine darkly    3
over me. The malignancy of my fate might perhaps      4
distemper yours; therefore I shall crave of you your    5
leave that I may bear my evils alone. It were a bad      6
recompense for your love to lay any of them on you.

ANTONIO   Let me yet know of you whither you are
bound.

SEBASTIAN   No, sooth, sir; my determinate voyage is    10
mere extravagancy. But I perceive in you so excellent    11
a touch of modesty that you will not extort from me
what I am willing to keep in; therefore it charges me in    13
manners the rather to express myself. You must know    14
of me then, Antonio, my name is Sebastian, which I
called Roderigo. My father was that Sebastian of
Messaline whom I know you have heard of. He left    17
behind him myself and a sister, both born in an hour.    18
If the heavens had been pleased, would we had so    19
ended! But you, sir, altered that, for some hour before    20
you took me from the breach of the sea was my sister    21
drowned.

ANTONIO   Alas the day!

SEBASTIAN   A lady, sir, though it was said she much resembled me, was yet of many accounted beautiful. But
though I could not with such estimable wonder overfar    26
believe that, yet thus far I will boldly publish her:    27
she bore a mind that envy could not but call fair. She    28
is drowned already, sir, with salt water, though I seem
to drown her remembrance again with more.    30

ANTONIO   Pardon me, sir, your bad entertainment.    31

SEBASTIAN   O good Antonio, forgive me your trouble.    32

ANTONIO   If you will not murder me for my love, let me    33
be your servant.

SEBASTIAN   If you will not undo what you have done,
that is, kill him whom you have recovered, desire it    36
not. Fare ye well at once. My bosom is full of

kindness, and I am yet so near the manners of my    38
mother that upon the least occasion more mine eyes    39
will tell tales of me. I am bound to the Count Orsino's    40
court. Farewell.                                    *Exit.*

ANTONIO
The gentleness of all the gods go with thee!
I have many enemies in Orsino's court,
Else would I very shortly see thee there.
But come what may, I do adore thee so
That danger shall seem sport, and I will go.       *Exit.*

❧

## 2.2

*Enter Viola and Malvolio, at several doors.*

MALVOLIO   Were not you ev'n now with the Countess
Olivia?

VIOLA   Even now, sir. On a moderate pace I have since
arrived but hither.

MALVOLIO   She returns this ring to you, sir. You might
have saved me my pains, to have taken it away    6
yourself. She adds, moreover, that you should put
your lord into a desperate assurance she will none of    8
him. And one thing more: that you be never so hardy    9
to come again in his affairs, unless it be to report your    10
lord's taking of this. Receive it so.    [*Offering the ring*]

VIOLA   She took the ring of me. I'll none of it.    12

MALVOLIO   Come, sir, you peevishly threw it to her,
and her will is it should be so returned.    [*He throws
down the ring.*] If it be worth stooping for, there it lies,
in your eye; if not, be it his that finds it.    *Exit.*   16

VIOLA [*picking up the ring*]
I left no ring with her. What means this lady?
Fortune forbid my outside have not charmed her!    18
She made good view of me, indeed so much
That sure methought her eyes had lost her tongue,    20
For she did speak in starts, distractedly.
She loves me, sure! The cunning of her passion
Invites me in this churlish messenger.    23
None of my lord's ring? Why, he sent her none.    24
I am the man. If it be so—as 'tis—    25
Poor lady, she were better love a dream.
Disguise, I see, thou art a wickedness
Wherein the pregnant enemy does much.    28
How easy is it for the proper false    29
In women's waxen hearts to set their forms!    30
Alas, our frailty is the cause, not we,    31
For such as we are made of, such we be.    32

---

**305 owe** own, control.
**2.1. Location: Somewhere in Illyria.**
**1 Nor will you not** Do you not wish   **3 patience** leave, permission
**4 malignancy** malevolence (of the stars; also in a medical sense)
**5 distemper** infect   **6 leave** permission.   **It were** It would be
**10 sooth** truly.   **determinate** intended, determined upon   **11 extrav-**
**agancy** aimless wandering.   **13 am willing . . . in** wish to keep secret
**13-14 it charges . . . manners** good manners require   **14 express**
reveal   **17 Messaline** possibly Messina, or, more likely, Massila (the
modern Marseilles). In Plautus's *Menaechmi*, Massilians and Illyrians
are mentioned together.   **18 in an hour** in the same hour, as twins.
**19 If . . . pleased** If the heavens had willed it so   **20 some hour** about
an hour   **21 breach of the sea** surf   **26 estimable wonder** admiring
judgment   **27 publish** proclaim   **28 envy** even malice   **30 with**
**more** i.e., with salt tears.   **31 Pardon . . . entertainment** i.e., I am
sorry that you have had such an unfortunate reception here in Illyria.
**32 your trouble** the trouble I put you to.   **33 murder . . . love** i.e.,
cause me to die from lacking your love   **36 recovered** rescued

**38 kindness** emotion, affection   **38–9 manners of my mother**
i.e., womanly inclination to weep   **40 tell . . . me** betray my secret.
**2.2. Location: Near Olivia's house.**
**0.1 *several*** different   **6 to have taken** by taking   **8 desperate** without
hope   **9–10 so hardy to come** so bold as to come   **12 She . . . it** (Viola
tells a quick and friendly lie to shield Olivia.)   **16 in your eye** in plain
sight   **18 charmed** enchanted   **20 her eyes . . . tongue** i.e., the sight of
me had deprived her of speech   **23 Invites me in** issues to me a loving
invitation through the agency of   **24 he** Orsino   **25 the man** the man
of her choice.   **28 the pregnant enemy** the resourceful enemy (either
Satan or Cupid)   **29 the proper false** deceptively handsome men
**30 waxen** i.e., malleable, impressionable.   **set their forms** stamp their
images (as of a seal).   **31–2 our . . . be** i.e., the fault lies not in our true
selves but in the susceptibility to love that we share with other women.

How will this fadge? My master loves her dearly,      33
And I, poor monster, fond as much on him;             34
And she, mistaken, seems to dote on me.
What will become of this? As I am man,
My state is desperate for my master's love;
As I am woman—now, alas the day!—
What thriftless sighs shall poor Olivia breathe!      39
O Time, thou must untangle this, not I;
It is too hard a knot for me t'untie.          [*Exit.*]

❖

## 2.3

*Enter Sir Toby and Sir Andrew.*

SIR TOBY   Approach, Sir Andrew. Not to be abed after
midnight is to be up betimes; and *diluculo surgere,*   2
thou know'st—

SIR ANDREW   Nay, by my troth, I know not, but I know
to be up late is to be up late.

SIR TOBY   A false conclusion. I hate it as an unfilled
can. To be up after midnight and to go to bed then,    7
is early; so that to go to bed after midnight is to go
to bed betimes. Does not our lives consist of the four  9
elements?                                              10

SIR ANDREW   Faith, so they say, but I think it rather consists of eating and drinking.

SIR TOBY   Thou'rt a scholar; let us therefore eat and
drink.—Marian, I say, a stoup of wine!                 14

*Enter Clown [Feste].*

SIR ANDREW   Here comes the Fool, i'faith.

FESTE   How now, my hearts! Did you never see the
picture of "we three"?                                 17

SIR TOBY   Welcome, ass. Now let's have a catch.       18

SIR ANDREW   By my troth, the Fool has an excellent
breast. I had rather than forty shillings I had such a  20
leg, and so sweet a breath to sing, as the Fool has. In 21
sooth, thou wast in very gracious fooling last night,
when thou spok'st of Pigrogromitus, of the Vapians    23
passing the equinoctial of Queubus. 'Twas very good,   24
i'faith. I sent thee sixpence for thy leman. Hadst it? 25

FESTE   I did impeticos thy gratillity; for Malvolio's nose  26
is no whipstock. My lady has a white hand, and the    27
Myrmidons are no bottle-ale houses.                    28

SIR ANDREW   Excellent! Why, this is the best fooling,
when all is done. Now, a song.                         30

SIR TOBY   Come on, there is sixpence for you. [*He gives
money.*] Let's have a song.

SIR ANDREW   There's a testril of me too. [*He gives money.*]  33
If one knight give a—

FESTE   Would you have a love song, or a song of good   35
life?                                                  36

SIR TOBY   A love song, a love song.

SIR ANDREW   Ay, ay, I care not for good life.

FESTE (*sings*)
          O mistress mine, where are you roaming?
          Oh, stay and hear, your true love 's coming,
              That can sing both high and low.
          Trip no further, pretty sweeting;
          Journeys end in lovers' meeting,
              Every wise man's son doth know.

SIR ANDREW   Excellent good, i'faith.

SIR TOBY   Good, good.

FESTE [*sings*]
          What is love? 'Tis not hereafter;
          Present mirth hath present laughter;
              What's to come is still unsure.           49
          In delay there lies no plenty.
          Then come kiss me, sweet and twenty;          51
              Youth's stuff will not endure.

SIR ANDREW   A mellifluous voice, as I am true knight.

SIR TOBY   A contagious breath.                        54

SIR ANDREW   Very sweet and contagious, i'faith.

SIR TOBY   To hear by the nose, it is dulcet in contagion.  56
But shall we make the welkin dance indeed? Shall we    57
rouse the night owl in a catch that will draw three    58
souls out of one weaver? Shall we do that?             59

SIR ANDREW   An you love me, let's do't. I am dog at a  60
catch.                                                 61

FESTE   By'r Lady, sir, and some dogs will catch well.  62

SIR ANDREW   Most certain. Let our catch be "Thou      63
knave."                                                64

FESTE   "Hold thy peace, thou knave," knight? I shall be  65
constrained in't to call thee knave, knight.           66

SIR ANDREW   'Tis not the first time I have constrained
one to call me knave. Begin, Fool. It begins, "Hold thy
peace."

---

**33 fadge** turn out   **34 monster** i.e., being both man and woman.
**fond** dote   **39 thriftless** unprofitable
**2.3. Location:** Olivia's house.
**2 betimes** early.   *diluculo surgere* i.e., *diluculo surgere saluberrimum est,*
to rise early is very healthful. (A sentence from Lilly's *Latin Grammar.*)
**7 can** tankard.   **9–10 four elements** i.e., fire, air, water, and earth, the
elements that were thought to make up all matter.   **14 stoup** drinking
vessel   **17 picture of "we three"** picture of two fools or asses inscribed
"we three," the spectator being the third.   **18 catch** round.
**20 breast** voice.   **21 leg** (for dancing)   **23–4 Pigrogromitus . . . Queubus**
(Feste's mock erudition.)   **25 leman** sweetheart.   **26 impeticos thy
gratillity** (Suggests "impetticoat, or pocket up, thy gratuity.")
**27 is no whipstock** is no whip-handle. (More nonsense, but perhaps
suggesting that Malvolio's nose for smelling out faults does not give
him the right to punish, so that he need not be feared.)   **has a white
hand** i.e., is lady-like. (But Feste's speech may be mere nonsense.)
**28 Myrmidons** followers of Achilles.   **bottle-ale houses** (Used contemptuously of taverns because they sold low-class drink.)

**30 when all is done** when all is said.   **33 testril** tester, a coin worth
sixpence   **35–6 good life** virtuous living. (Or perhaps Feste means
simply "life's pleasures," but is misunderstood by Sir Andrew to
mean "virtuous living.")   **49 still** always   **51 sweet and twenty** i.e.,
sweet and twenty times sweet, or twenty years old   **54 contagious**
infectiously delightful   **56 To . . . contagion** i.e., If we were to
describe hearing in olfactory terms, we could say it is sweet in stench.
**57 make . . . dance** i.e., drink till the sky seems to turn around
**58–9 draw three souls** (Refers to the threefold nature of the soul—
vegetal, sensible, and intellectual—or to the three singers of the three-
part catch; or, just a comic exaggeration.)   **59 weaver** (Weavers were
often associated with psalm singing.)   **60 dog at** very clever at. (But
Feste uses the word literally.)   **61 catch** round. (But Feste uses it to
mean "seize.")   **62 By 'r Lady** (An oath, originally, "by the Virgin
Mary.")   **63–4 "Thou knave"** (This popular round is arranged so
that the three singers repeatedly accost one another with "Thou
knave.")   **65–6 "Hold . . . knight** ("Knight and knave" is a common
antithesis, like "rich and poor.")

FESTE   I shall never begin if I hold my peace.   70
SIR ANDREW   Good, i'faith. Come, begin.   *Catch sung.*   71

*Enter Maria.*

MARIA   What a caterwauling do you keep here! If my   72
lady have not called up her steward Malvolio and bid
him turn you out of doors, never trust me.   74
SIR TOBY   My lady's a Cataian, we are politicians,   75
Malvolio's a Peg-o'-Ramsey, and [*he sings*] "Three   76
merry men be we." Am not I consanguineous? Am I   77
not of her blood? Tillyvally! Lady! [*He sings.*] "There   78
dwelt a man in Babylon, lady, lady."   79
FESTE   Beshrew me, the knight's in admirable fooling.   80
SIR ANDREW   Ay, he does well enough if he be disposed,
and so do I too. He does it with a better grace,
but I do it more natural.   83
SIR TOBY   [*sings*]
"O' the twelfth day of December"—   84
MARIA   For the love o' God, peace!

*Enter Malvolio.*

MALVOLIO   My masters, are you mad? Or what are you?
Have you no wit, manners, nor honesty but to gabble   87
like tinkers at this time of night? Do ye make an alehouse of my lady's house, that ye squeak out your coz-   89
iers' catches without any mitigation or remorse of   90
voice? Is there no respect of place, persons, nor time in
you?
SIR TOBY   We did keep time, sir, in our catches. Sneck   93
up!   94
MALVOLIO   Sir Toby, I must be round with you. My   95
lady bade me tell you that though she harbors you as
her kinsman, she's nothing allied to your disorders. If
you can separate yourself and your misdemeanors,
you are welcome to the house; if not, an it would
please you to take leave of her, she is very willing to
bid you farewell.
SIR TOBY   [*sings*]
"Farewell, dear heart, since I must needs be gone."   102
MARIA   Nay, good Sir Toby.
FESTE   [*sings*]
"His eyes do show his days are almost done."
MALVOLIO   Is't even so?
SIR TOBY   [*sings*]
"But I will never die."
FESTE
"Sir Toby, there you lie."

MALVOLIO   This is much credit to you.
SIR TOBY   [*sings*]
"Shall I bid him go?"
FESTE   [*sings*]
"What an if you do?"
SIR TOBY   [*sings*]
"Shall I bid him go, and spare not?"
FESTE   [*sings*]
"Oh, no, no, no, no, you dare not."
SIR TOBY   Out o' tune, sir? Ye lie. Art any more than a   113
steward? Dost thou think, because thou art virtuous,
there shall be no more cakes and ale?
FESTE   Yes, by Saint Anne, and ginger shall be hot i'th'   116
mouth, too.
SIR TOBY   Thou'rt i'the right.—Go, sir, rub your chain   118
with crumbs.—A stoup of wine, Maria!   119
MALVOLIO   Mistress Mary, if you prized my lady's
favor at anything more than contempt, you would not
give means for this uncivil rule. She shall know of it,   122
by this hand.   *Exit.*
MARIA   Go shake your ears.   124
SIR ANDREW   'Twere as good a deed as to drink when a   125
man's a-hungry to challenge him the field and then to   126
break promise with him and make a fool of him.
SIR TOBY   Do't, knight. I'll write thee a challenge, or I'll
deliver thy indignation to him by word of mouth.
MARIA   Sweet Sir Toby, be patient for tonight. Since the
youth of the Count's was today with my lady, she is
much out of quiet. For Monsieur Malvolio, let me   132
alone with him. If I do not gull him into a nayword   133
and make him a common recreation, do not think I   134
have wit enough to lie straight in my bed. I know I can
do it.
SIR TOBY   Possess us, possess us. Tell us something of   137
him.
MARIA   Marry, sir, sometimes he is a kind of Puritan.   139
SIR ANDREW   Oh, if I thought that, I'd beat him like a
dog.
SIR TOBY   What, for being a Puritan? Thy exquisite   142
reason, dear knight?
SIR ANDREW   I have no exquisite reason for't, but I
have reason good enough.

---

**70 if . . . peace** if I keep silent.   **71 Good, i'faith** (Sir Andrew appreci-
ates Feste's play on words.)   **72 keep** keep up   **74 never trust me**
don't believe me ever again.   **75 Cataian** Cathayan, i.e., Chinese, a
trickster or inscrutable; or, just nonsense.   **politicians** schemers,
intriguers   **76 Peg-o'-Ramsey** character in a popular song. (Used
here contemptuously.)   **76–7 "Three . . . we"** (A snatch of an old
song.)   **77 consanguineous** i.e., a blood relative of Olivia.   **78 Tillyvally!** Nonsense, fiddle-faddle!   **78–9 "There . . . lady"** (The first line
of a ballad, "The Constancy of Susanna," together with the refrain,
"Lady, lady.")   **80 Beshrew** i.e., The devil take. (A mild curse.)
**83 natural** naturally. (But unconsciously suggesting idiocy.)   **84 "O' . . .
December"** (Possibly part of a ballad about the Battle of Musselburgh
Field, or Toby's error for the "twelfth day of Christmas," i.e., Twelfth
Night.)   **87 wit** common sense.   **honesty** decency   **89–90 coziers'
catches** cobblers' rounds   **90 mitigation or remorse** i.e., considerate
lowering   **93–4 Sneck up!** Go hang!   **95 round** blunt   **102 "Farewell . . .
gone"** (From the ballad "Corydon's Farewell to Phyllis.")

**113 Out o' tune** (Perhaps a quibbling reply—"We did too keep time in
our tune"—to Malvolio's accusation of having no respect for place or
time, line 91. Often emended to *Out o' time*, easily misread in secretary
hand.)   **116 Saint Anne** mother of the Virgin Mary. (Her cult was
derided in the Reformation, much as Puritan reformers also derided the
tradition of *cakes and ale* at church feasts.)   **ginger** (Commonly used to
spice ale.)   **118–19 rub . . . crumbs** i.e., scour or polish your steward's
chain; attend to your own business and remember your station.
**119 stoup** drinking vessel (as at line 14)   **122 give means for** allow,
abet.   **rule** conduct.   **124 your ears** i.e., your ass's ears.   **125 'Twere . . .
to drink** i.e., It would be a fine jest. (Sir Andrew is trying to think of
some comeuppance they could administer to Malvolio.)   **126 the field**
i.e., to a duel   **132 For** As for   **132–3 let . . . him** leave him to me.
**133 gull** trick.   **nayword** byword. (Maria hopes to make Malvolio's
name a synonym for "gull.")   **134 recreation** sport   **137 Possess**
Inform   **139 puritan** (Maria's point is that Malvolio is sometimes a *kind*
of Puritan, insofar as he is precise about moral conduct and censorious
of others for immoral conduct, but that he is nothing consistently except
a time-server. He is not, then, simply a satirical type of the Puritan sect.
The extent of the resemblance is left unstated.)   **142 exquisite** elegant

**MARIA**  The devil a Puritan that he is, or anything con- 146
stantly, but a time-pleaser; an affectioned ass, that cons 147
state without book and utters it by great swaths; the 148
best persuaded of himself, so crammed, as he thinks, 149
with excellencies, that it is his grounds of faith that all 150
that look on him love him; and on that vice in him
will my revenge find notable cause to work.

**SIR TOBY**  What wilt thou do?

**MARIA**  I will drop in his way some obscure epistles of 154
love, wherein by the color of his beard, the shape of
his leg, the manner of his gait, the expressure of his 156
eye, forehead, and complexion, he shall find himself
most feelingly personated. I can write very like my 158
lady your niece; on a forgotten matter we can  hardly 159
make distinction of our hands. 160

**SIR TOBY**  Excellent! I smell a device.

**SIR ANDREW**  I have't in my nose too.

**SIR TOBY**  He shall think, by the letters that thou wilt
drop, that they come from my niece, and that she's in
love with him.

**MARIA**  My purpose is indeed a horse of that color.

**SIR ANDREW**  And your horse now would make him an
ass.

**MARIA**  Ass, I doubt not. 169

**SIR ANDREW**  Oh, 'twill be admirable!

**MARIA**  Sport royal, I warrant you. I know my physic 171
will work with him. I will plant you two, and let the
Fool make a third, where he shall find the letter. Observe his construction of it. For this night, to bed, 174
and dream on the event. Farewell. *Exit.* 175

**SIR TOBY**  Good night, Penthesilea. 176

**SIR ANDREW**  Before me, she's a good wench. 177

**SIR TOBY**  She's a beagle true-bred and one that adores 178
me. What o'that?

**SIR ANDREW**  I was adored once, too.

**SIR TOBY**  Let's to bed, knight. Thou hadst need send
for more money.

**SIR ANDREW**  If I cannot recover your niece, I am a foul 183
way out. 184

**SIR TOBY**  Send for money, knight. If thou hast her not
i'th' end, call me cut. 186

**SIR ANDREW**  If I do not, never trust me, take it how
you will.

**SIR TOBY**  Come, come, I'll go burn some sack. 'Tis too 189
late to go to bed now. Come, knight; come, knight. 190
*Exeunt.*

## 2.4

*Enter Duke [Orsino], Viola, Curio, and others.*

**ORSINO**
Give me some music. Now, good morrow, friends. 1
Now, good Cesario, but that piece of song, 2
That old and antique song we heard last night. 3
Methought it did relieve my passion much,
More than light airs and recollected terms 5
Of these most brisk and giddy-pacèd times.
Come, but one verse.

**CURIO**  He is not here, so please Your Lordship, that
should sing it.

**ORSINO**  Who was it?

**CURIO**  Feste the jester, my lord, a fool that the Lady
Olivia's father took much delight in. He is about the
house.

**ORSINO**
Seek him out, and play the tune the while. 14
                              *[Exit Curio.] Music plays.*
*[To Viola]* Come hither, boy. If ever thou shalt love,
In the sweet pangs of it remember me;
For such as I am, all true lovers are,
Unstaid and skittish in all motions else 18
Save in the constant image of the creature
That is beloved. How dost thou like this tune?

**VIOLA**
It gives a very echo to the seat 21
Where Love is throned.

**ORSINO**                    Thou dost speak masterly.
My life upon't, young though thou art, thine eye
Hath stayed upon some favor that it loves. 24
Hath it not, boy?

**VIOLA**                    A little, by your favor. 25

**ORSINO**
What kind of woman is't?

**VIOLA**                    Of your complexion.

**ORSINO**
She is not worth thee, then. What years, i'faith?

**VIOLA**  About your years, my lord.

**ORSINO**
Too old, by heaven. Let still the woman take 29
An elder than herself. So wears she to him; 30
So sways she level in her husband's heart. 31
For, boy, however we do praise ourselves,

Our fancies are more giddy and unfirm,
More longing, wavering, sooner lost and worn, 34
Than women's are.

VIOLA                    I think it well, my lord.

ORSINO
Then let thy love be younger than thyself,
Or thy affection cannot hold the bent; 37
For women are as roses, whose fair flower
Being once displayed, doth fall that very hour. 39

VIOLA
And so they are. Alas that they are so,
To die even when they to perfection grow! 41

*Enter Curio and Clown [Feste].*

ORSINO
Oh, fellow, come, the song we had last night.
Mark it, Cesario, it is old and plain;
The spinsters and the knitters in the sun, 44
And the free maids that weave their thread with
   bones, 45
Do use to chant it. It is silly sooth, 46
And dallies with the innocence of love, 47
Like the old age. 48

FESTE    Are you ready, sir?

ORSINO    Ay, prithee, sing.                    *Music.*

The Song.

FESTE [*sings*]
       Come away, come away, death, 51
          And in sad cypress let me be laid. 52
       Fly away, fly away, breath;
          I am slain by a fair cruel maid.
       My shroud of white, stuck all with yew, 55
          Oh, prepare it!
       My part of death, no one so true 57
          Did share it. 58

       Not a flower, not a flower sweet
          On my black coffin let there be strown; 60
       Not a friend, not a friend greet
          My poor corpse, where my bones shall be
             thrown.
       A thousand thousand sighs to save,
          Lay me, oh, where
       Sad true lover never find my grave,
          To weep there!

ORSINO [*offering money*]    There's for thy pains.
FESTE    No pains, sir. I take pleasure in singing, sir.
ORSINO    I'll pay thy pleasure then.

FESTE    Truly, sir, and pleasure will be paid, one time 70
   or another. 71
ORSINO    Give me now leave to leave thee. 72
FESTE    Now, the melancholy god protect thee, and the 73
   tailor make thy doublet of changeable taffeta, for thy 74
   mind is a very opal. I would have men of such con- 75
   stancy put to sea, that their business might be every- 76
   thing and their intent everywhere, for that's it that 77
   always makes a good voyage of nothing. Farewell. 78

                                        *Exit.*

ORSINO
Let all the rest give place.

          [*Curio and attendants withdraw.*]
             Once more, Cesario, 79
Get thee to yond same sovereign cruelty. 80
Tell her, my love, more noble than the world,
Prizes not quantity of dirty lands; 82
The parts that fortune hath bestowed upon her, 83
Tell her, I hold as giddily as fortune; 84
But 'tis that miracle and queen of gems 85
That nature pranks her in attracts my soul. 86

VIOLA    But if she cannot love you, sir?

ORSINO
I cannot be so answered.

VIOLA                    Sooth, but you must. 88
Say that some lady—as perhaps there is—
Hath for your love as great a pang of heart
As you have for Olivia. You cannot love her;
You tell her so. Must she not then be answered? 92

ORSINO    There is no woman's sides
Can bide the beating of so strong a passion 94
As love doth give my heart; no woman's heart
So big, to hold so much. They lack retention. 96
Alas, their love may be called appetite,
No motion of the liver, but the palate, 98
That suffer surfeit, cloyment, and revolt; 99
But mine is all as hungry as the sea,
And can digest as much. Make no compare 101
Between that love a woman can bear me
And that I owe Olivia.

VIOLA                    Ay, but I know— 103

ORSINO    What dost thou know?

34 **worn** exhausted. (Sometimes emended to *won*.)    37 **hold the bent** hold steady, keep the intensity (like the tension of a bow)    39 **displayed** full blown    41 **even when** just as    44 **spinsters** spinners    45 **free** carefree, innocent.    **bones** bobbins on which bone-lace was made    46 **Do use** are accustomed.    **silly sooth** simple truth    47 **dallies with** dwells lovingly on, sports with    48 **Like . . . age** as in the good old times.    51 **Come away** Come hither    52 **cypress** i.e., a coffin of cypress wood, or bier strewn with sprigs of cypress    55 **yew** yew sprigs. (Emblematic of mourning, like cypress.)    57–8 **My . . . it** No one died for love so true to love as I.    60 **strown** strewn

70–1 **pleasure . . . another** sooner or later one must pay for indulgence.    72 **leave to leave** permission to take leave of, dismiss    73 **the melancholy god** i.e., Saturn, whose planet was thought to control the melancholy temperament    74 **doublet** close-fitting jacket.    **changeable taffeta** a silk so woven of various-colored threads that its color shifts with changing perspective    75 **opal** an iridescent precious stone that changes color when seen from various angles or in different lights.    76–7 **that . . . everywhere** i.e., so that they could there find everchanging business and locale attuned to the constant flux of the sea    77–8 **for . . . nothing** because that's the quality that is satisfied with an aimless voyage.    79 **give place** withdraw.    80 **sovereign cruelty** cruel tyrant ruling my heart.    82 **dirty lands** i.e., mere acreage.    83 **parts** attributes such as wealth or rank    84 **I . . . fortune** I esteem as carelessly as I do fortune, that fickle goddess    85 **that miracle . . . gems** i.e., her beauty    86 **pranks** adorns.    **attracts** that attracts    88 **Sooth** In truth    92 **be answered** be satisfied with your answer.    94 **Can bide** that can withstand    96 **to hold** as to contain.    **retention** constancy, the power of retaining.    98 **motion** impulse.    **liver . . . palate** (Real love is a passion of the liver, whereas fancy, light love, is born in the eye and nourished in the palate.)    99 **cloyment** satiety.    **revolt** revulsion    101 **compare** comparison    103 **owe** have for

**VIOLA**
Too well what love women to men may owe.
In faith, they are as true of heart as we.
My father had a daughter loved a man
As it might be, perhaps, were I a woman,
I should Your Lordship.

**ORSINO**                    And what's her history?

**VIOLA**
A blank, my lord. She never told her love,
But let concealment, like a worm i'th' bud,
Feed on her damask cheek. She pined in thought,          112
And with a green and yellow melancholy;                  113
She sat like Patience on a monument,                     114
Smiling at grief. Was not this love indeed?
We men may say more, swear more, but indeed
Our shows are more than will; for still we prove         117
Much in our vows, but little in our love.

**ORSINO**
But died thy sister of her love, my boy?

**VIOLA**
I am all the daughters of my father's house,
And all the brothers too—and yet I know not.
Sir, shall I to this lady?

**ORSINO**                    Ay, that's the theme.
To her in haste; give her this jewel. [*He gives a jewel.*]
    Say
My love can give no place, bide no denay.                124
                              *Exeunt* [*separately*].

❖

## 2.5

*Enter Sir Toby, Sir Andrew, and Fabian.*

**SIR TOBY**    Come thy ways, Signor Fabian.             1
**FABIAN**    Nay, I'll come. If I lose a scruple of this sport,   2
let me be boiled to death with melancholy.               3
**SIR TOBY**    Wouldst thou not be glad to have the niggardly rascally sheep-biter come by some notable         5
shame?
**FABIAN**    I would exult, man. You know he brought me
out o'favor with my lady about a bearbaiting here.       8
**SIR TOBY**    To anger him we'll have the bear again, and
we will fool him black and blue. Shall we not, Sir An-   10
drew?
**SIR ANDREW**    An we do not, it is pity of our lives.  12

*Enter Maria [with a letter].*

**SIR TOBY**    Here comes the little villain.—How now, my   13
metal of India!                                          14
**MARIA**    Get ye all three into the boxtree. Malvolio's   15
coming down this walk. He has been yonder i'the sun
practicing behavior to his own shadow this half hour.
Observe him, for the love of mockery, for I know this
letter will make a contemplative idiot of him. Close, in   19
the name of jesting! [*The others hide.*] Lie thou there
[*throwing down a letter*]; for here comes the trout that
must be caught with tickling.                *Exit.*     22

*Enter Malvolio.*

**MALVOLIO**    'Tis but fortune; all is fortune. Maria once
told me she did affect me; and I have heard herself      24
come thus near, that should she fancy, it should be      25
one of my complexion. Besides, she uses me with a
more exalted respect than anyone else that follows       27
her. What should I think on't?
**SIR TOBY**    Here's an overweening rogue!
**FABIAN**    Oh, peace! Contemplation makes a rare turkey-   30
cock of him. How he jets under his advanced plumes!      31
**SIR ANDREW**    'Slight, I could so beat the rogue!    32
**SIR TOBY**    Peace, I say.
**MALVOLIO**    To be Count Malvolio.
**SIR TOBY**    Ah, rogue!
**SIR ANDREW**    Pistol him, pistol him.                36
**SIR TOBY**    Peace, peace!
**MALVOLIO**    There is example for't. The lady of the Stra-   38
chy married the yeoman of the wardrobe.                  39
**SIR ANDREW**    Fie on him, Jezebel!                   40
**FABIAN**    Oh, peace! Now he's deeply in. Look how imag-
ination blows him.                                       42
**MALVOLIO**    Having been three months married to her,
sitting in my state—                                     44
**SIR TOBY**    Oh, for a stone-bow, to hit him in the eye!   45
**MALVOLIO**    Calling my officers about me, in my
branched velvet gown; having come from a daybed,         47
where I have left Olivia sleeping—
**SIR TOBY**    Fire and brimstone!
**FABIAN**    Oh, peace, peace!
**MALVOLIO**    And then to have the humor of state; and   51
after a demure travel of regard, telling them I know     52
my place as I would they should do theirs, to ask for
my kinsman Toby.                                         54
**SIR TOBY**    Bolts and shackles!
**FABIAN**    Oh, peace, peace, peace! Now, now.

---

**112 damask** pink and white like the damask rose   **113 green and yellow** pale and sallow   **114 on a monument** carved in statuary on a tomb   **117 shows** displays of passion.   **more than will** greater than our determination.   **still** always   **124 can . . . denay** cannot yield or endure denial.
**2.5. Location:** Olivia's garden.
**1 Come thy ways** Come along   **2 a scruple** the least bit   **3 boiled** (With a pun on "biled"; black bile was the "humor" of melancholy and was thought to be a cold humor.)   **5 sheep-biter** a dog that bites sheep, i.e., a scoundrel (here meaning Malvolio)   **8 bearbaiting** a blood sport in which dogs were unleashed against a chained bear. (A special target of Puritan disapproval.)   **10 fool . . . blue** mock him until he is figuratively black and blue.   **12 An** If.   **pity of our lives** a pity we should live.

**13 villain** (Here, a term of endearment.)   **14 metal** gold, i.e., priceless one   **15 boxtree** an evergreen shrub, often shaped into a hedge.   **19 contemplative** one who is meditating   **22 tickling** (1) stroking gently about the gills—an actual method of fishing (2) deception.   **24 she** Olivia.   **affect** have fondness for   **25 fancy** fall in love   **27 follows** serves   **30 rare** extraordinary   **31 jets** struts.   **advanced** prominent   **32 'Slight** By His (God's) light   **36 Pistol him** Beat him with a pistol.   **38 example** precedent   **38–9 lady of the Strachy** (Apparently a lady who had married below her station; no certain identification.)   **40 Jezebel** the proud queen of Ahab, King of Israel.   **42 blows** puffs up   **44 state** chair of state   **45 stone-bow** crossbow that shoots stones   **47 branched** adorned with a figured pattern suggesting branched leaves or flowers.   **daybed** sofa, couch   **51 have . . . state** adopt the imperious manner of authority   **52 demure . . . regard** grave survey of the company   **54 Toby** (Malvolio omits the title *Sir*.)

MALVOLIO   Seven of my people, with an obedient start, make out for him. I frown the while, and perchance wind up my watch, or play with my—some rich 59 jewel. Toby approaches; curtsies there to me— 60

SIR TOBY   Shall this fellow live?

FABIAN   Though our silence be drawn from us with 62 cars, yet peace. 63

MALVOLIO   I extend my hand to him thus, quenching my familiar smile with an austere regard of control— 65

SIR TOBY   And does not Toby take you a blow o'the lips 66 then?

MALVOLIO   Saying, "Cousin Toby, my fortunes having cast me on your niece give me this prerogative of speech—"

SIR TOBY   What, what?

MALVOLIO   "You must amend your drunkenness."

SIR TOBY   Out, scab! 73

FABIAN   Nay, patience, or we break the sinews of our 74 plot.

MALVOLIO   "Besides, you waste the treasure of your time with a foolish knight—"

SIR ANDREW   That's me, I warrant you.

MALVOLIO   "One Sir Andrew."

SIR ANDREW   I knew 'twas I, for many do call me fool.

MALVOLIO   What employment have we here? 81
                                    [*Taking up the letter.*]

FABIAN   Now is the woodcock near the gin. 82

SIR TOBY   Oh, peace, and the spirit of humors intimate 83 reading aloud to him! 84

MALVOLIO   By my life, this is my lady's hand. These be her very c's, her u's, and her t's; and thus makes she 86 her great P's. It is in contempt of question her hand. 87

SIR ANDREW   Her c's, her u's, and her t's. Why that?

MALVOLIO [*reads*]   "To the unknown beloved, this, and my good wishes."—Her very phrases! By your 90 leave, wax. Soft! And the impressure her Lucrece, 91 with which she uses to seal. 'Tis my lady. To whom 92 should this be?                        [*He opens the letter.*]

FABIAN   This wins him, liver and all. 94

MALVOLIO [*reads*]
      "Jove knows I love,
            But who?
      Lips, do not move;
            No man must know."

"No man must know." What follows? The numbers 99 altered! "No man must know." If this should be thee, 100 Malvolio?

SIR TOBY   Marry, hang thee, brock! 102

MALVOLIO [*reads*]
      "I may command where I adore,
            But silence, like a Lucrece knife, 104
      With bloodless stroke my heart doth gore; 105
            M.O.A.I. doth sway my life."

FABIAN   A fustian riddle! 107

SIR TOBY   Excellent wench, say I.

MALVOLIO   "M.O.A.I. doth sway my life." Nay, but first, let me see, let me see, let me see.

FABIAN   What dish o'poison has she dressed him! 111

SIR TOBY   And with what wing the staniel checks 112 at it! 113

MALVOLIO   "I may command where I adore." Why, she may command me; I serve her, she is my lady. Why, this is evident to any formal capacity. There is no 116 obstruction in this. And the end—what should that alphabetical position portend? If I could make that 118 resemble something in me! Softly! "M.O.A.I."—

SIR TOBY   Oh, ay, make up that. He is now at a cold scent. 120

FABIAN   Sowter will cry upon't for all this, though it be 121 as rank as a fox. 122

MALVOLIO   "M"—Malvolio. "M"! Why, that begins my name!

FABIAN   Did not I say he would work it out? The cur is excellent at faults. 126

MALVOLIO   "M"—But then there is no consonancy in the 127 sequel that suffers under probation: "A" should fol- 128 low, but "O" does.

FABIAN   And "O" shall end, I hope. 130

SIR TOBY   Ay, or I'll cudgel him, and make him cry "Oh!"

MALVOLIO   And then "I" comes behind.

FABIAN   Ay, an you had any eye behind you, you 133 might see more detraction at your heels than fortunes 134 before you.

MALVOLIO   "M.O.A.I." This simulation is not as the 136 former. And yet, to crush this a little, it would bow to me, for every one of these letters are in my name. Soft! Here follows prose.

---

**59 play with my** (Malvolio perhaps means his steward's chain but checks himself in time; as "Count Malvolio," he would not be wearing it. A bawdy meaning of playing with himself is also suggested.) **60 curtsies** bows   **62–3 with cars** with chariots, i.e., pulling apart by force   **65 familiar** (1) customary (2) friendly.   **regard of control** look of authority   **66 take** deliver   **73 scab** scurvy fellow.   **74 break . . . of** hamstring, disable   **81 employment** business   **82 woodcock** (A bird proverbial for its stupidity.)   **gin** snare.   **83-4 the spirit . . . to him** may his own whimsical nature suggest to him that he read the letter out loud.   **86 c's . . . t's** i.e., *cut,* slang for the female pudenda   **87 great** (1) uppercase (2) copious. (*P* suggests "pee.") **in contempt of** beyond   **90–1 By . . . wax** (Addressed to the seal on the letter.)   **91 Soft** Softly, not so fast.   **impressure** device imprinted on the seal.   **Lucrece** Lucretia, chaste matron who, ravished by Tarquin, committed suicide   **92 uses** is accustomed   **94 liver** i.e., the seat of passion   **99–100 The numbers altered!** More verses, in a different meter!

**102 brock** badger. (Used contemptuously.)   **104 like . . . knife** like the knife that Lucretia silently used to commit suicide; see note 91 above **105 gore** pierce, stab   **107 fustian** bombastic, ridiculously pompous **111 What** What a.   **dressed** prepared for   **112 wing** speed.   **staniel** kestrel, a sparrow hawk. (The word is used contemptuously because of the uselessness of the staniel for falconry.)   **112–13 checks at it** turns to fly at it.   **116 formal capacity** normal understanding. **118 position** arrangement   **120 Oh, ay** (Playing on *O.I.* of *M.O.A.I.*) **make up** work out   **121–2 Sowter . . . fox** The hound Sowter (literally, "Cobbler") will bay triumphantly at picking up this false scent, even though the smell is as rank as a fox. ("M.O.A.I." is a false lead that reeks.)   **126 at faults** i.e., at maneuvering his way past breaks in the line of scent—in this case, on a false trail.   **127–8 no consonancy . . . probation** no pattern in the following letters that stands up under examination. (In fact, the letters "M.O.A.I." represent the first, last, second, and next to last letters of Malvolio's name.)   **130 "O" shall end** (1) "O" ends Malvolio's name (2) *omega* ends the Greek alphabet and is thus a symbol for the ending of the world, *alpha* to *omega* (3) Malvolio's cry of pain will end the matter, as Sir Toby suggests in the next line.   **133 eye** (punning on the "I" of "Oh, ay" and "M.O.A.I.")   **134 detraction . . . heels** defamation pursuing you **136 simulation** disguise, riddle

[*He reads.*] "If this fall into thy hand, revolve. In my 140
stars I am above thee, but be not afraid of greatness. 141
Some are born great, some achieve greatness, and
some have greatness thrust upon 'em. Thy Fates open 143
their hands; let thy blood and spirit embrace them; 144
and, to inure thyself to what thou art like to be, cast 145
thy humble slough and appear fresh. Be opposite with 146
a kinsman, surly with servants. Let thy tongue tang 147
arguments of state; put thyself into the trick of 148
singularity. She thus advises thee that sighs for thee. 149
Remember who commended thy yellow stockings,
and wished to see thee ever cross-gartered. I say, 151
remember. Go to, thou art made, if thou desir'st to be 152
so. If not, let me see thee a steward still, the fellow of
servants, and not worthy to touch Fortune's fingers.
Farewell. She that would alter services with thee, 155
                          The Fortunate-Unhappy."
Daylight and champaign discovers not more! This is 157
open. I will be proud, I will read politic authors, I will 158
baffle Sir Toby, I will wash off gross acquaintance, I 159
will be point-devise the very man. I do not now fool 160
myself, to let imagination jade me; for every reason 161
excites to this, that my lady loves me. She did com- 162
mend my yellow stockings of late, she did praise my
leg being cross-gartered; and in this she manifests her- 164
self to my love, and with a kind of injunction drives
me to these habits of her liking. I thank my stars, I am 166
happy. I will be strange, stout, in yellow stockings 167
and cross-gartered, even with the swiftness of putting
on. Jove and my stars be praised! Here is yet a postscript. [*He reads.*] "Thou canst not choose but know who
I am. If thou entertain'st my love, let it appear in thy 171
smiling; thy smiles become thee well. Therefore in my
presence still smile, dear my sweet, I prithee." 173
Jove, I thank thee. I will smile; I will do everything that
thou wilt have me.                                    *Exit.*

[*Sir Toby, Sir Andrew, and Fabian come from hiding.*]

FABIAN    I will not give my part of this sport for a
pension of thousands to be paid from the Sophy. 177
SIR TOBY    I could marry this wench for this device.
SIR ANDREW    So could I too.
SIR TOBY    And ask no other dowry with her but such
another jest.

*Enter Maria.*

SIR ANDREW    Nor I neither.
FABIAN    Here comes my noble gull-catcher. 183
SIR TOBY    Wilt thou set thy foot o' my neck? 184
SIR ANDREW    Or o' mine either?
SIR TOBY    Shall I play my freedom at tray-trip, and 186
become thy bondslave?
SIR ANDREW    I'faith, or I either?
SIR TOBY    Why, thou hast put him in such a dream that
when the image of it leaves him he must run mad.
MARIA    Nay, but say true, does it work upon him?
SIR TOBY    Like aqua vitae with a midwife. 192
MARIA    If you will then see the fruits of the sport, mark
his first approach before my lady. He will come to her
in yellow stockings, and 'tis a color she abhors, and
cross-gartered, a fashion she detests; and he will smile
upon her, which will now be so unsuitable to her
disposition, being addicted to a melancholy as she is,
that it cannot but turn him into a notable contempt. If 199
you will see it, follow me.
SIR TOBY    To the gates of Tartar, thou most excellent 201
devil of wit!
SIR ANDREW    I'll make one too.                  *Exeunt.* 203

❖

## 3.1

*Enter Viola, and Clown* [*Feste, playing his pipe
and tabor*].

VIOLA    Save thee, friend, and thy music. Dost thou live 1
by thy tabor? 2
FESTE    No, sir, I live by the church.
VIOLA    Art thou a churchman?
FESTE    No such matter, sir. I do live by the church, for
I do live at my house, and my house doth stand by
the church.
VIOLA    So thou mayst say the king lies by a beggar if 8
a beggar dwell near him, or the church stands by thy 9
tabor if thy tabor stand by the church. 10
FESTE    You have said, sir. To see this age! A sentence is 11
but a cheveril glove to a good wit. How quickly the 12
wrong side may be turned outward!
VIOLA    Nay, that's certain. They that dally nicely with 14
words may quickly make them wanton. 15
FESTE    I would therefore my sister had had no name,
sir.
VIOLA    Why, man?

140 **revolve** consider.  **141 stars** fortune  **143–4 open their hands**
offer their bounty  **145 inure** accustom.  **like** likely.  **cast** cast off
146 **slough** skin of a snake; hence, former demeanor of humbleness.
**opposite** contradictory  **147 tang** sound loud with  **148 state** politics,
statecraft  **148–9 trick of singularity** eccentricity of manner.
**151 cross-gartered** wearing garters above and below the knee so as
to cross behind it.  **152 Go to** (An expression of remonstrance.)
**155 alter services** i.e., exchange place of mistress and servant
**157 champaign** open country.  **discovers** discloses  **158 politic**
dealing with state affairs  **159 baffle** deride, degrade. (A technical chivalric term used to describe the disgrace of a perjured knight.)  **gross**
base  **160 point-devise** correct to the letter  **161 to let** by letting.
**jade me** trick me, make me look ridiculous (as an unruly horse might
do)  **162 excites to this** prompts this conclusion  **164 this** this letter
**166 these habits** this attire  **167 happy** fortunate.  **strange, stout**
aloof, haughty  **171 thou entertain'st** you accept  **173 still** continually
**177 Sophy** Shah of Persia.

183 **gull-catcher** tricker of *gulls* or dupes.  **184 set . . . neck?** i.e., make
me your slave?  **186 play** gamble.  **tray-trip** a game of dice, success
in which depended on throwing a three (*tray*). (Sir Toby extravagantly
offers to gamble away his freedom to become a slave of Maria.)
**192 aqua vitae** brandy or other distilled liquor  **199 notable contempt**
notorious object of contempt.  **201 Tartar** Tartarus, the infernal
regions  **203 make one** i.e., tag along
**3.1. Location: Olivia's garden.**
**1 Save** God save  **1–2 live by** earn your living with. (But Feste uses
the phrase to mean "dwell near.")  **2 tabor** small drum.  **8 lies by**
(1) lies sexually with (2) dwells near  **9–10 stands by . . . stand by** is
maintained by . . . is placed near  **11 You have said** You've had your
little joke.  **sentence** maxim, judgment, opinion  **12 cheveril** kidskin
**14 dally nicely** (1) play subtly (2) toy amorously  **15 wanton**
(1) equivocal (2) licentious, unchaste. (Feste then "dallies" with the
word in its sexual sense; see line 20.)

FESTE    Why, sir, her name's a word, and to dally with
that word might make my sister wanton. But indeed,
words are very rascals since bonds disgraced them.    21
VIOLA    Thy reason, man?
FESTE    Troth, sir, I can yield you none without words,
and words are grown so false I am loath to prove
reason with them.
VIOLA    I warrant thou art a merry fellow and car'st for    26
nothing.    27
FESTE    Not so, sir, I do care for something; but in my
conscience, sir, I do not care for you. If that be to care
for nothing, sir, I would it would make you invisible.    30
VIOLA    Art not thou the Lady Olivia's fool?
FESTE    No indeed, sir. The Lady Olivia has no folly. She
will keep no fool, sir, till she be married, and fools are
as like husbands as pilchers are to herrings—the    34
husband's the bigger. I am indeed not her fool but    35
her corrupter of words.
VIOLA    I saw thee late at the Count Orsino's.    37
FESTE    Foolery, sir, does walk about the orb like the    38
sun; it shines everywhere. I would be sorry, sir, but    39
the fool should be as oft with your master as with my    40
mistress. I think I saw Your Wisdom there.    41
VIOLA    Nay, an thou pass upon me, I'll no more with    42
thee. Hold, there's expenses for thee.    43
                    [She gives a coin.]
FESTE    Now Jove, in his next commodity of hair, send    44
thee a beard!
VIOLA    By my troth, I'll tell thee, I am almost sick for    46
one—[aside] though I would not have it grow on my    47
chin.—Is thy lady within?    48
FESTE    Would not a pair of these have bred, sir?
VIOLA    Yes, being kept together and put to use.    50
FESTE    I would play Lord Pandarus of Phrygia, sir, to    51
bring a Cressida to this Troilus.
VIOLA    I understand you, sir. 'Tis well begged.
                    [She gives another coin.]
FESTE    The matter, I hope, is not great, sir, begging    54
but a beggar; Cressida was a beggar. My lady is    55
within, sir. I will conster to them whence you come.    56
Who you are and what you would are out of my
welkin—I might say "element," but the word is    58
overworn.                            Exit.

VIOLA
This fellow is wise enough to play the fool,
And to do that well craves a kind of wit.
He must observe their mood on whom he jests,
The quality of persons, and the time,    63
Not, like the haggard, check at every feather    64
That comes before his eye. This is a practice    65
As full of labor as a wise man's art;
For folly that he wisely shows is fit,    67
But wise men, folly-fall'n, quite taint their wit.    68

            Enter Sir Toby and [Sir] Andrew.

SIR TOBY    Save you, gentleman.
VIOLA    And you, sir.
SIR ANDREW    Dieu vous garde, monsieur.    71
VIOLA    Et vous aussi; votre serviteur.    72
SIR ANDREW    I hope, sir, you are, and I am yours.
SIR TOBY    Will you encounter the house? My niece is    74
desirous you should enter, if your trade be to her.    75
VIOLA    I am bound to your niece, sir; I mean, she is the    76
list of my voyage.    77
SIR TOBY    Taste your legs, sir. Put them to motion.    78
VIOLA    My legs do better understand me, sir, than I un-    79
derstand what you mean by bidding me taste my legs.
SIR TOBY    I mean, to go, sir, to enter.
VIOLA    I will answer you with gait and entrance.—But    82
we are prevented.    83

            Enter Olivia and gentlewoman [Maria].

Most excellent accomplished lady, the heavens rain
odors on you!
SIR ANDREW    [to Sir Toby]    That youth's a rare courtier.
"Rain odors"—well.
VIOLA    [to Olivia]    My matter hath no voice, lady, but to    88
your own most pregnant and vouchsafed ear.    89
SIR ANDREW    [to Sir Toby]    "Odors," "pregnant," and
"vouchsafed." I'll get 'em all three all ready.    91
OLIVIA    Let the garden door be shut, and leave me to
my hearing. [Exeunt Sir Toby, Sir Andrew, and Maria.]
Give me your hand, sir.
VIOLA
My duty, madam, and most humble service.
OLIVIA    What is your name?
VIOLA
Cesario is your servant's name, fair princess.

---

21 since . . . them i.e., since bonds have been needed to make sworn
statements good. (Words cannot be relied on since not even contractual
promises are reliable.)    26–7 car'st for nothing are without any worries. (But Feste puns on care for in lines 29–30 in the sense of "like.")
30 invisible i.e., nothing; absent.    34 pilchers pilchards, fish resembling herring but smaller    35 the bigger (1) the larger (2) the bigger
fool.    37 late recently    38 orb earth    39–41 I would . . . mistress
(1) I should be sorry not to visit Orsino's house often (2) It would be a
shame if folly were no less common there than in Olivia's household.
41 Your Wisdom i.e., you. (A title of mock courtesy.)    42 an . . . me if
you fence (verbally) with me, pass judgment on me    43 expenses i.e.,
a little tip for you to buy something.    44 commodity supply    46–7
sick for one (1) eager to have a beard (2) in love with a bearded man
47–8 on my chin Viola emphasizes my: I long for a beard that grows on
someone else's chin, i.e., Orsino's.    50 put to use put out at interest.
51 Pandarus the go-between in the love story of Troilus and Cressida;
uncle to Cressida    54–5 begging . . . was a beggar (A reference to Henryson's Testament of Cresseid in which Cressida became a leper and a
beggar. Feste desires another coin to be the mate of the one he has, just
as Cressida, the beggar, was mate to Troilus.)    56 conster to them construe to Olivia and her household    58 welkin sky, element. (The common phrase "out of my element" means "beyond my scope.")

63 quality character, rank    64 haggard untrained adult hawk, hence
unmanageable    64–5 check . . . eye strike at every bird it sees, i.e.,
dart from subject to subject.    65 practice exercise of skill    67–8 For
. . . wit for the folly that the fool judiciously displays is appropriate
and clever, whereas when wise men fall into folly they utterly corrupt
their own intelligence.    71 Dieu . . . monsieur God keep you, sir.
72 Et . . . serviteur And you, too; (I am) your servant. (Sir Andrew is
not quite up to a reply in French.)    74 encounter (High-sounding
word to express "approach.")    75 trade business. (Suggesting also a
commercial venture.)    76 I am bound (1) I am on a journey. (Continuing Sir Toby's metaphor in trade.) (2) I am confined, obligated
77 list limit, destination    78 Taste Try    79 understand stand under,
support    82 gait and entrance going and entering. (With a pun on
gate: [1] stride [2] entryway.)    83 prevented anticipated.    88 hath no
voice cannot be uttered    89 pregnant and vouchsafed receptive and
attentive    91 all ready committed to memory for future use.

OLIVIA
My servant, sir? 'Twas never merry world          98
Since lowly feigning was called compliment.       99
You're servant to the Count Orsino, youth.

VIOLA
And he is yours, and his must needs be yours;     101
Your servant's servant is your servant, madam.

OLIVIA
For him, I think not on him. For his thoughts,    103
Would they were blanks, rather than filled with me!

VIOLA
Madam, I come to whet your gentle thoughts
On his behalf.

OLIVIA          Oh, by your leave, I pray you.    106
I bade you never speak again of him.
But, would you undertake another suit,
I had rather hear you to solicit that
Than music from the spheres.

VIOLA                          Dear lady—         110

OLIVIA
Give me leave, beseech you. I did send,
After the last enchantment you did here,
A ring in chase of you; so did I abuse            113
Myself, my servant, and, I fear me, you.
Under your hard construction must I sit,          115
To force that on you in a shameful cunning        116
Which you knew none of yours. What might you
    think?
Have you not set mine honor at the stake          118
And baited it with all th'unmuzzled thoughts      119
That tyrannous heart can think? To one of your
    receiving                                     120
Enough is shown; a cypress, not a bosom,          121
Hides my heart. So, let me hear you speak.        122

VIOLA
I pity you.

OLIVIA          That's a degree to love.

VIOLA
No, not a grece; for 'tis a vulgar proof          124
That very oft we pity enemies.

OLIVIA
Why then, methinks 'tis time to smile again.      126
Oh, world, how apt the poor are to be proud!      127
If one should be a prey, how much the better

To fall before the lion than the wolf!   *Clock strikes.* 129
The clock upbraids me with the waste of time.
Be not afraid, good youth, I will not have you;
And yet, when wit and youth is come to harvest
Your wife is like to reap a proper man.           133
There lies your way, due west.

VIOLA                    Then westward ho!         134
Grace and good disposition attend Your Ladyship.  135
You'll nothing, madam, to my lord by me?

OLIVIA   Stay.
I prithee, tell me what thou think'st of me.

VIOLA
That you do think you are not what you are.       139

OLIVIA
If I think so, I think the same of you.           140

VIOLA
Then think you right. I am not what I am.

OLIVIA
I would you were as I would have you be!

VIOLA
Would it be better, madam, than I am?
I wish it might, for now I am your fool.           144

OLIVIA [*aside*]
Oh, what a deal of scorn looks beautiful
In the contempt and anger of his lip!
A murderous guilt shows not itself more soon
Than love that would seem hid; love's night is noon.— 148
Cesario, by the roses of the spring,
By maidhood, honor, truth, and everything,
I love thee so that, maugre all thy pride,        151
Nor wit nor reason can my passion hide.           152
Do not extort thy reasons from this clause,       153
For that I woo, thou therefore hast no cause.     154
But rather reason thus with reason fetter:        155
Love sought is good, but given unsought is better.

VIOLA
By innocence I swear, and by my youth,
I have one heart, one bosom, and one truth,
And that no woman has, nor never none
Shall mistress be of it save I alone.
And so adieu, good madam. Nevermore
Will I my master's tears to you deplore.          162

OLIVIA
Yet come again, for thou perhaps mayst move
That heart, which now abhors, to like his love.
                        *Exeunt [separately].*

❧

**98–9 'Twas . . . compliment** Things have never been the same since affected humility (like calling oneself another's servant) began to be mistaken for courtesy.   **101 is yours** is your servant.   **his** those belonging to him   **103 For** As for   **106 by your leave** i.e., allow me to interrupt   **110 music from the spheres** (The heavenly bodies were thought to be fixed in hollow concentric spheres that revolved one about the other, producing a harmony too exquisite to be heard by human ears.)   **113 abuse** wrong, mislead   **115 hard construction** harsh interpretation   **116 To force that** for forcing the ring   **118 at the stake** (The figure is from bearbaiting.)   **119 baited** harassed. (Literally, set the unmuzzled dogs on to bite the bear.)   **120 receiving** capacity, intelligence   **121–2 a cypress . . . heart** i.e., I have shown my heart to you, veiled only with thin, gauzelike cypress cloth rather than the opaque flesh of my bosom.   **124 grece** step. (Synonymous with *degree* in the preceding line.)   **vulgar proof** common experience   **126 smile** i.e., cast off love's melancholy   **127 how . . . proud!** how ready the unfortunate and rejected (like myself) are to find something to be proud of in their distress! Or, how apt are persons of comparatively low social station like yourself to show pride in rejecting love!

**129 To fall . . . wolf!** i.e., to fall before a noble adversary rather than to a person like you who attacks me thus!   **133 like** likely.   **proper** handsome, worthy   **134 westward ho** (The cry of Thames watermen to attract westward-bound passengers.)   **135 Grace . . . Ladyship** May you enjoy God's blessing and a happy frame of mind.   **139 That . . . are** i.e., That you think you are in love with a man, and you are mistaken.   **140 If . . . you** (Olivia may interpret Viola's cryptic statement as suggesting that Olivia "does not know herself," i.e., is distracted with passion; she may also hint at her suspicion that "Cesario" is higher born than he admits.)   **144 fool** butt.   **148 love's . . . noon** i.e., love, despite its attempt to be secret, reveals itself as plain as day.   **151 maugre** in spite of   **152 Nor** neither   **153–4 Do . . . cause** Do not rationalize your indifference along these lines, that because I am the wooer you have no cause to reciprocate.   **155 But . . . fetter** But instead control your reasoning with the following reason   **162 deplore** beweep.

## 3.2

*Enter Sir Toby, Sir Andrew, and Fabian.*

SIR ANDREW   No, faith, I'll not stay a jot longer.

SIR TOBY   Thy reason, dear venom, give thy reason.   2

FABIAN   You must needs yield your reason, Sir Andrew.

SIR ANDREW   Marry, I saw your niece do more favors to the Count's servingman than ever she bestowed upon me. I saw't i'th' orchard.   6

SIR TOBY   Did she see thee the while, old boy? Tell me that.

SIR ANDREW   As plain as I see you now.

FABIAN   This was a great argument of love in her toward you.   10

SIR ANDREW   'Slight, will you make an ass o'me?   12

FABIAN   I will prove it legitimate, sir, upon the oaths of judgment and reason.   13

SIR TOBY   And they have been grand-jurymen since before Noah was a sailor.   15 16

FABIAN   She did show favor to the youth in your sight only to exasperate you, to awake your dormouse valor, to put fire in your heart and brimstone in your liver. You should then have accosted her, and with some excellent jests, fire-new from the mint, you should have banged the youth into dumbness. This was looked for at your hand, and this was balked. The double gilt of this opportunity you let time wash off, and you are now sailed into the north of my lady's opinion, where you will hang like an icicle on a Dutchman's beard unless you do redeem it by some laudable attempt either of valor or policy.   18 19 21 22 23 24 25 26 27 28

SIR ANDREW   An't be any way, it must be with valor, for policy I hate. I had as lief be a Brownist as a politician.   30 31

SIR TOBY   Why, then, build me thy fortunes upon the basis of valor. Challenge me the Count's youth to fight with him; hurt him in eleven places. My niece shall take note of it; and assure thyself, there is no love-broker in the world can more prevail in man's commendation with woman than report of valor.   32 33 36

FABIAN   There is no way but this, Sir Andrew.

SIR ANDREW   Will either of you bear me a challenge to him?

SIR TOBY   Go, write it in a martial hand. Be curst and brief; it is no matter how witty, so it be eloquent and full of invention. Taunt him with the license of ink. If   41 43

thou "thou"-est him some thrice, it shall not be amiss; and as many lies as will lie in thy sheet of paper, although the sheet were big enough for the bed of Ware in England, set 'em down. Go, about it. Let there be gall enough in thy ink, though thou write with a goose pen, no matter. About it.   44 45 46 47 48 49

SIR ANDREW   Where shall I find you?

SIR TOBY   We'll call thee at the cubiculo. Go.   51

*Exit Sir Andrew.*

FABIAN   This is a dear manikin to you, Sir Toby.   52

SIR TOBY   I have been dear to him, lad, some two thousand strong or so.   53 54

FABIAN   We shall have a rare letter from him; but you'll not deliver't?   55 56

SIR TOBY   Never trust me, then; and by all means stir on the youth to an answer. I think oxen and wainropes cannot hale them together. For Andrew, if he were opened and you find so much blood in his liver as will clog the foot of a flea, I'll eat the rest of th'anatomy.   57 58 59 60 61

FABIAN   And his opposite, the youth, bears in his visage no great presage of cruelty.   62 63

*Enter Maria.*

SIR TOBY   Look where the youngest wren of nine comes.   64

MARIA   If you desire the spleen, and will laugh yourselves into stitches, follow me. Yond gull Malvolio is turned heathen, a very renegado; for there is no Christian that means to be saved by believing rightly can ever believe such impossible passages of grossness. He's in yellow stockings.   66 68 70 71

SIR TOBY   And cross-gartered?

MARIA   Most villainously, like a pedant that keeps a school i'th' church. I have dogged him like his murderer. He does obey every point of the letter that I dropped to betray him. He does smile his face into more lines than is in the new map with the augmentation of the Indies. You have not seen such a thing as 'tis. I can hardly forbear hurling things at him. I know my lady will strike him. If she do, he'll smile and take't for a great favor.   73 77 78

SIR TOBY   Come, bring us, bring us where he is.

*Exeunt omnes.*

---

**3.2. Location:** Olivia's house.
**2 venom** i.e., person filled with venomous anger   **6 orchard** garden.
**10 argument** proof   **12 'Slight** By his (God's) light   **13 it** my contention.
**oaths** i.e., testimony under oath   **15–16 And . . . sailor** i.e., Judgment and reason have been mighty factors in such disputes since the very beginning of time.   **18 dormouse** i.e., sleepy and timid   **19 brimstone** sulfur   **21 fire-new . . . mint** newly coined   **22 banged** struck
**23 balked** missed, neglected.   **23–4 double gilt** thick layer of gold, i.e., rare worth   **25 into . . . opinion** i.e., out of the warmth and sunshine of Olivia's favor   **26–7 icicle . . . beard** (Alludes to the arctic voyage of William Barents in 1596–1597.)   **28 policy** stratagem.
**30 Brownist** (An early name of the Congregationalists, from the name of the founder, Robert Browne.)   **30–1 politician** intriguer. (Sir Andrew gives a Machiavellian twist to Fabian's more neutral use of *policy*, "clever stratagem.")   **32–3 build me . . . Challenge me** build . . . Challenge. ("Me" is idiomatic.)   **36 love-broker** agent between lovers
**41 curst** fierce   **43 with . . . ink** i.e., with an insulting frankness that can be expressed more effectively in writing than in conversation.

**44 "thou"-est** ("Thou" was used only between friends or to inferiors.)
**45 lies** charges of lying   **46–7 bed of Ware** a famous bedstead capable of holding twelve persons, about eleven feet square, said to have been at the Stag Inn in Ware, Hertfordshire   **48 gall** (1) bitterness, rancor (2) a growth found on certain oaks, used as an ingredient of ink
**49 goose pen** (1) goose quill (2) foolish style   **51 call thee** call for you.
**cubiculo** little chamber, bedchamber.   **52 manikin** puppet   **53 dear** expensive. (Playing on *dear*, "fond," in the previous speech.)   **53–4 two thousand** i.e., £2000   **55 rare** extraordinary   **57 then** if I do   **58 wainropes** wagon ropes   **59 hale** haul.   **For** As for   **60 liver** (A pale `and bloodless liver was a sign of cowardice.)   **61 th'anatomy** the cadaver.
**62 opposite** adversary   **63 presage** prediction   **64 youngest . . . nine** the last hatched and smallest of a nest of wrens   **66 the spleen** a laughing fit. (The spleen was thought to be the seat of immoderate laughter.)   **68 renegado** renegade, deserter of his religion   **70–1 impossible . . . grossness** gross impossibilities (i.e., in the letter).   **73 villainously** i.e., abominably.
**pedant** schoolmaster.   **keeps** conducts   **77–8 the new . . . Indies** (Probably a reference to a map made by Emmeric Mollineux in 1599–1600 to be printed in Hakluyt's *Voyages*, showing more of the East Indies, including Japan, than had ever been mapped before.)

## 3.3

*Enter Sebastian and Antonio.*

SEBASTIAN
I would not by my will have troubled you,                    1
But since you make your pleasure of your pains,              2
I will no further chide you.

ANTONIO
I could not stay behind you. My desire,
More sharp than filèd steel, did spur me forth,
And not all love to see you—though so much                   6
As might have drawn one to a longer voyage—
But jealousy what might befall your travel,                  8
Being skilless in these parts, which to a stranger,          9
Unguided and unfriended, often prove
Rough and unhospitable. My willing love,
The rather by these arguments of fear,                       12
Set forth in your pursuit.

SEBASTIAN                        My kind Antonio,
I can no other answer make but thanks,
And thanks; and ever oft good turns                          15
Are shuffled off with such uncurrent pay.                    16
But were my worth, as is my conscience, firm,                17
You should find better dealing. What's to do?                18
Shall we go see the relics of this town?                     19

ANTONIO
Tomorrow, sir. Best first go see your lodging.

SEBASTIAN
I am not weary, and 'tis long to night.
I pray you, let us satisfy our eyes
With the memorials and the things of fame
That do renown this city.

ANTONIO                          Would you'd pardon me.      24
I do not without danger walk these streets.
Once in a sea fight 'gainst the Count his galleys            26
I did some service, of such note indeed
That were I ta'en here it would scarce be answered.          28

SEBASTIAN
Belike you slew great number of his people?                  29

ANTONIO
Th'offense is not of such a bloody nature,
Albeit the quality of the time and quarrel
Might well have given us bloody argument.                    32
It might have since been answered in repaying                33
What we took from them, which for traffic's sake             34
Most of our city did. Only myself stood out,                 35
For which, if I be lapsèd in this place,                     36
I shall pay dear.

SEBASTIAN                  Do not then walk too open.

ANTONIO
It doth not fit me. Hold, sir, here's my purse.              38
*[He gives his purse.]*
In the south suburbs, at the Elephant,                       39
Is best to lodge. I will bespeak our diet,                   40
Whiles you beguile the time and feed your knowl-
edge
With viewing of the town. There shall you have me.           42

SEBASTIAN   Why I your purse?

ANTONIO
Haply your eye shall light upon some toy                     44
You have desire to purchase; and your store                  45
I think is not for idle markets, sir.                        46

SEBASTIAN
I'll be your purse-bearer and leave you
For an hour.

ANTONIO             To th'Elephant.

SEBASTIAN                      I do remember.
*Exeunt [separately].*

❧

## 3.4

*Enter Olivia and Maria.*

OLIVIA *[aside]*
I have sent after him; he says he'll come.                   1
How shall I feast him? What bestow of him?                   2
For youth is bought more oft than begged or
borrowed.                                                    3
I speak too loud.—
Where's Malvolio? He is sad and civil,                       5
And suits well for a servant with my fortunes.
Where is Malvolio?

MARIA   He's coming, madam, but in very strange
manner. He is, sure, possessed, madam.                       9

OLIVIA   Why, what's the matter? Does he rave?

MARIA   No, madam, he does nothing but smile. Your
Ladyship were best to have some guard about you if he        12
come, for sure the man is tainted in's wits                  13

OLIVIA
Go call him hither. *[Maria summons Malvolio.]* I am as
mad as he,
If sad and merry madness equal be.                           15

*Enter Malvolio, [cross-gartered and in yellow
stockings].*

How now, Malvolio?

MALVOLIO   Sweet lady, ho, ho!

OLIVIA   Smil'st thou? I sent for thee upon a sad            18
occasion.

---

**3.3. Location: A street.**
**1 by my will** willingly   **2 since . . . pains** since you take pleasure in doing something painful and dangerous   **6 all** only, merely.   **so much** i.e., that was great enough   **8 jealousy** anxiety   **9 skilless in** unacquainted with   **12 The rather** made all the more willing   **15 And . . . turns** (This probably corrupt line is usually read to read, "And thanks and ever thanks; and oft good turns.")   **16 shuffled off** turned aside. **uncurrent** worthless (such as mere thanks)   **17 worth** wealth.   **conscience** i.e., moral inclination to assist   **18 dealing** treatment, payment.   **19 relics** antiquities   **24 renown** make famous   **26 Count his** Count's, i.e., Duke's   **28 it . . . answered** I'd be hard put to offer a defense.   **29 Belike** Perhaps **32 bloody argument** cause for bloodshed.   **33 answered** compensated **34 traffic's** trade's   **35 our city** those fellow-citizens who fought on Antonio's side.   **Only . . . out** I alone did not return what I took from the Illyrians in that sea fight.   **36 lapsèd** caught off guard, surprised

**38 It . . . me** It would not be wise for me to do so.   **39 Elephant** the name of an inn   **40 bespeak our diet** order our food   **42 have** find   **44 Haply** Perhaps.   **toy** trifle   **45 store** store of money **46 is not . . . markets** cannot afford luxuries
**3.4. Location: Olivia's garden.**
**1 he . . . come** i.e., suppose he says he'll come.   **2 of** on   **3 For . . . borrowed** For young men are more easily won by gifts than by anything less substantial.   **5 sad and civil** sober and decorous   **9 possessed** (1) possessed with an evil spirit (2) mad   **12 were best** would do best **13 in's** in his   **15 If . . . equal be** i.e., if love melancholy and smiling madness are essentially alike. (Love melancholy was regarded as a kind of madness.)   **18 sad** serious

MALVOLIO    Sad, lady? I could be sad. This does make   20
some obstruction in the blood, this cross-gartering,
but what of that? If it please the eye of one, it is with
me as the very true sonnet is, "Please one and please   23
all."   24

OLIVIA    Why, how dost thou, man? What is the matter
with thee?

MALVOLIO    Not black in my mind, though yellow in my   27
legs. It did come to his hands, and commands shall be   28
executed. I think we do know the sweet roman hand.   29

OLIVIA    Wilt thou go to bed, Malvolio?   30

MALVOLIO    To bed! "Ay, sweetheart, and I'll come to   31
thee."   32

OLIVIA    God comfort thee! Why dost thou smile so and
kiss thy hand so oft?

MARIA    How do you, Malvolio?

MALVOLIO    At your request? Yes, nightingales answer   36
daws.   37

MARIA    Why appear you with this ridiculous boldness
before my lady?

MALVOLIO    "Be not afraid of greatness." 'Twas well writ.

OLIVIA    What mean'st thou by that, Malvolio?

MALVOLIO    "Some are born great—"

OLIVIA    Ha?

MALVOLIO    "Some achieve greatness—"

OLIVIA    What say'st thou?

MALVOLIO    "And some have greatness thrust upon them."

OLIVIA    Heaven restore thee!

MALVOLIO    "Remember who commended thy yellow
stockings—"

OLIVIA    Thy yellow stockings?

MALVOLIO    "And wished to see thee cross-gartered."

OLIVIA    Cross-gartered?

MALVOLIO    "Go to, thou art made, if thou desir'st to
be so—"

OLIVIA    Am I made?

MALVOLIO    "If not, let me see thee a servant still."

OLIVIA    Why, this is very midsummer madness.   57

*Enter Servant.*

SERVANT    Madam, the young gentleman of the Count
Orsino's is returned. I could hardly entreat him back.
He attends Your Ladyship's pleasure.

OLIVIA    I'll come to him.                          [*Exit Servant.*]
Good Maria, let this fellow be looked to. Where's my
cousin Toby? Let some of my people have a special

care of him. I would not have him miscarry for the half   64
of my dowry.

*Exeunt [Olivia and Maria, different ways].*

MALVOLIO    Oho, do you come near me now? No worse   66
man than Sir Toby to look to me! This concurs directly
with the letter. She sends him on purpose that I may
appear stubborn to him, for she incites me to that in
the letter. "Cast thy humble slough," says she; "be opposite with a kinsman, surly with servants; let thy
tongue tang with arguments of state; put thyself into
the trick of singularity." And consequently sets down   73
the manner how: as, a sad face, a reverend carriage, a   74
slow tongue, in the habit of some sir of note, and so   75
forth. I have limed her, but it is Jove's doing, and Jove   76
make me thankful! And when she went away now,
"Let this fellow be looked to." "Fellow!" Not "Malvo-   78
lio," nor after my degree, but "fellow." Why, every-   79
thing adheres together, that no dram of a scruple, no   80
scruple of a scruple, no obstacle, no incredulous or un-   81
safe circumstance—what can be said?—nothing that   82
can be can come between me and the full prospect of
my hopes. Well, Jove, not I, is the doer of this, and he
is to be thanked.

*Enter [Sir] Toby, Fabian, and Maria.*

SIR TOBY    Which way is he, in the name of sanctity? If
all the devils of hell be drawn in little, and Legion him-   87
self possessed him, yet I'll speak to him.

FABIAN    Here he is, here he is.—How is't with you,
sir? How is't with you, man?

MALVOLIO    Go off. I discard you. Let me enjoy my
private. Go off.   92

MARIA    Lo, how hollow the fiend speaks within him!
Did not I tell you? Sir Toby, my lady prays you to
have a care of him.

MALVOLIO    Aha, does she so?

SIR TOBY    Go to, go to! Peace, peace, we must deal
gently with him. Let me alone.—How do you,   98
Malvolio? How is't with you? What, man, defy the   99
devil! Consider, he's an enemy to mankind.

MALVOLIO    Do you know what you say?

MARIA    La you, an you speak ill of the devil, how he   102
takes it at heart! Pray God he be not bewitched!

FABIAN    Carry his water to th' wise woman.   104

MARIA    Marry, and it shall be done tomorrow morning,
if I live. My lady would not lose him for more than
I'll say.

MALVOLIO    How now, mistress?

---

20 **sad** (1) serious (2) melancholy.   23 **sonnet** song, ballad
23–4 **"Please . . . all"** "To please one special person is as good as to
please everybody." (The refrain of a ballad.)   27 **black** i.e., melancholic
28 **It** i.e., The letter.   **his** Malvolio's   29 **roman hand** fashionable
italic or Italian style of handwriting rather than English "secretary"
handwriting.   30 **go to bed** i.e., try to sleep off your mental distress.
(But Malvolio misinterprets as a sexual invitation.)   31–2 **"Ay . . .
thee"** (Malvolio quotes from a popular song of the day.)   36–7 **nightingales answer daws** i.e. (to Maria), do you suppose a fine fellow like
me would answer a lowly creature (a *daw*, a "jackdaw") like you?
57 **midsummer madness** (A proverbial phrase; the midsummer
moon was supposed to cause madness.)

64 **miscarry** come to harm    66 **do you . . . now?** i.e., do you begin to
understand my situation?   73–5 **And . . . note** And thereafter she
specifies how I am to conduct myself, with a serious demeanor, a dignified bearing, carefully measured speech, and dressed as a person
of importance   76 **limed** caught like a bird with birdlime (a sticky
substance spread on branches)   78 **Fellow** (Malvolio takes the basic
meaning, "companion.")   79 **after my degree** according to my
position   80 **dram** (Literally, one-eighth of a fluid ounce.)   **scruple**
(Literally, one-third of a dram.)   81 **incredulous** incredible
81–2 **unsafe** uncertain, unreliable   87 **drawn in little** (1) portrayed in
miniature (2) gathered into a small space.   **Legion** an unclean spirit.
("My name is Legion, for we are many," Mark 5:9.)   92 **private**
privacy.   98 **Let me alone** Leave him to me.   99 **defy** renounce
102 **La you** Look you   104 **water** urine (for medical analysis).   **wise
woman** a woman skilled in charms, sorcery, fortune-telling, etc.

MARIA   Oh, Lord!

SIR TOBY   Prithee, hold thy peace; this is not the way. Do you not see you move him? Let me alone with him. [111]

FABIAN   No way but gentleness, gently, gently. The fiend is rough, and will not be roughly used.

SIR TOBY   Why, how now, my bawcock! How dost thou, chuck? [115] [116]

MALVOLIO   Sir!

SIR TOBY   Ay, biddy, come with me. What, man, 'tis not for gravity to play at cherry-pit with Satan. Hang him, foul collier! [118] [119] [120]

MARIA   Get him to say his prayers, good Sir Toby, get him to pray.

MALVOLIO   My prayers, minx?

MARIA   No, I warrant you, he will not hear of godliness.

MALVOLIO   Go hang yourselves all! You are idle, shallow things; I am not of your element. You shall know more hereafter.                                          *Exit.* [125] [126] [127]

SIR TOBY   Is't possible?

FABIAN   If this were played upon a stage, now, I could condemn it as an improbable fiction.

SIR TOBY   His very genius hath taken the infection of the device, man. [131]

MARIA   Nay, pursue him now, lest the device take air and taint. [133] [134]

FABIAN   Why, we shall make him mad indeed.

MARIA   The house will be the quieter.

SIR TOBY   Come, we'll have him in a dark room and bound. My niece is already in the belief that he's mad. We may carry it thus for our pleasure and his penance till our very pastime, tired out of breath, prompt us to have mercy on him, at which time we will bring the device to the bar and crown thee for a finder of madmen. But see, but see! [137] [138] [139] [142] [143]

*Enter Sir Andrew [with a letter].*

FABIAN   More matter for a May morning. [144]

SIR ANDREW   Here's the challenge. Read it. I warrant there's vinegar and pepper in't.

FABIAN   Is't so saucy? [147]

SIR ANDREW   Ay, is't, I warrant him. Do but read. [148]

SIR TOBY   Give me. [*He reads.*] "Youth, whatsoever thou art, thou art but a scurvy fellow."

FABIAN   Good, and valiant.

SIR TOBY   [*reads*]   "Wonder not, nor admire not in thy mind, why I do call thee so, for I will show thee no reason for't." [152]

FABIAN   A good note, that keeps you from the blow of the law. [155]

SIR TOBY   [*reads*]   "Thou com'st to the Lady Olivia, and in my sight she uses thee kindly. But thou liest in thy throat; that is not the matter I challenge thee for."

FABIAN   Very brief, and to exceeding good sense—less.

SIR TOBY   [*reads*]   "I will waylay thee going home, where if it be thy chance to kill me—"

FABIAN   Good.

SIR TOBY   [*reads*]   "Thou kill'st me like a rogue and a villain."

FABIAN   Still you keep o' th' windy side of the law. Good. [166]

SIR TOBY   [*reads*]   "Fare thee well, and God have mercy upon one of our souls! He may have mercy upon mine, but my hope is better, and so look to thyself. Thy friend, as thou usest him, and thy sworn enemy, [170]
                                                              Andrew Aguecheek."
If this letter move him not, his legs cannot. I'll give't him. [173]

MARIA   You may have very fit occasion for't. He is now in some commerce with my lady, and will by and by depart. [176]

SIR TOBY   Go, Sir Andrew. Scout me for him at the corner of the orchard like a bum-baily. So soon as ever thou see'st him, draw, and as thou draw'st, swear horrible; for it comes to pass oft that a terrible oath, with a swaggering accent sharply twanged off, gives manhood more approbation than ever proof itself would have earned him. Away! [178] [179] [180] [181] [183]

SIR ANDREW   Nay, let me alone for swearing.   *Exit.* [185]

SIR TOBY   Now will not I deliver his letter, for the behavior of the young gentleman gives him out to be of good capacity and breeding; his employment between his lord and my niece confirms no less. Therefore this letter, being so excellently ignorant, will breed no terror in the youth. He will find it comes from a clodpoll. But, sir, I will deliver his challenge by word of mouth, set upon Aguecheek a notable report of valor, and drive the gentleman—as I know his youth will aptly receive it—into a most hideous opinion of his rage, skill, fury, and impetuosity. This will so fright them both that they will kill one another by the look, like cockatrices. [191] [194] [195] [198]

*Enter Olivia and Viola.*

FABIAN   Here he comes with your niece. Give them way till he take leave, and presently after him. [199] [200]

---

111 **move** upset, excite   115 **bawcock** fine fellow. (From the French *beau-coq*.)   116 **chuck** (A form of "chick," term of endearment.) 118 **biddy** chicken   119 **for gravity** suitable for a man of your dignity.   **cherry-pit** a children's game consisting of throwing cherry stones into a little hole   120 **collier** i.e., Satan. (Literally, a coal vendor.)   125 **idle** foolish   126 **element** sphere.   126–7 **know more** i.e., hear about this   131 **genius** i.e., soul, spirit   133–4 **take . . . taint** become exposed to air (i.e., become known) and thus spoil. 137–8 **have . . . bound** (The standard treatment for insanity at this time.)   139 **carry** manage   142 **bar** i.e., bar of judgment   142–3 **finder of madmen** member of a jury changed with "finding" if the accused is insane.   144 **matter . . . morning** sport for Mayday plays or games.   147 **saucy** (1) spicy (2) insolent.   148 **him** it. 152 **admire** marvel

155 **note** observation, remark   166 **windy** windward, i.e., safe, where one is less likely to be driven onto legal rocks and shoals   170 **my hope is better** (Sir Andrew's comically inept way of saying he hopes to be the survivor; instead, he seems to say, "May I be damned.") 173 **move** (1) stir up (2) set in motion   176 **commerce** transaction 178 **Scout me** Keep watch   179 **bum-baily** minor sheriff's officer employed in making arrests.   180–1 **horrible** horribly   183 **approbation** reputation (for courage).   **proof** performance   185 **let . . . swearing** don't worry about my ability in swearing.   191 **clodpoll** blockhead.   194–5 **his youth . . . receive it** his inexperience will make him all the more ready to believe it   **his rage** Sir Andrew's rage 198 **cockatrices** basilisks, fabulous serpents reputed to be able to kill by a mere look.   199 **Give them way** Stay out of their way 200 **presently** immediately

SIR TOBY    I will meditate the while upon some horrid 201
message for a challenge.
[*Exeunt Sir Toby, Fabian, and Maria.*]

OLIVIA
I have said too much unto a heart of stone
And laid mine honor too unchary on't.                    204
There's something in me that reproves my fault,          205
But such a headstrong potent fault it is                  206
That it but mocks reproof.                                207

VIOLA
With the same havior that your passion bears              208
Goes on my master's griefs.                               209

OLIVIA [*giving a locket*]
Here, wear this jewel for me. 'Tis my picture.
Refuse it not; it hath no tongue to vex you.
And I beseech you come again tomorrow.
What shall you ask of me that I'll deny,
That honor, saved, may upon asking give?                 214

VIOLA
Nothing but this: your true love for my master.

OLIVIA
How with mine honor may I give him that
Which I have given to you?

VIOLA                                I will acquit you.      217

OLIVIA
Well, come again tomorrow. Fare thee well.
A fiend like thee might bear my soul to hell.   [*Exit.*] 219

*Enter [Sir] Toby and Fabian.*

SIR TOBY    Gentleman, God save thee.

VIOLA    And you, sir.

SIR TOBY    That defense thou hast, betake thee to't. Of 222
what nature the wrongs are thou hast done him, I
know not, but thy intercepter, full of despite, bloody 224
as the hunter, attends thee at the orchard end.          225
Dismount thy tuck, be yare in thy preparation, for thy 226
assailant is quick, skillful, and deadly.

VIOLA    You mistake sir. I am sure no man hath any
quarrel to me. My remembrance is very free and clear 229
from any image of offense done to any man.

SIR TOBY    You'll find it otherwise, I assure you. Therefore, if you hold your life at any price, betake you to 232
your guard, for your opposite hath in him what youth, 233
strength, skill, and wrath can furnish man withal.       234

VIOLA    I pray you, sir, what is he?

SIR TOBY    He is knight, dubbed with unhatched rapier 236

and on carpet consideration, but he is a devil in 237
private brawl. Souls and bodies hath he divorced
three, and his incensement at this moment is so implacable that satisfaction can be none but by pangs of
death and sepulchre. Hob, nob is his word; give't or 241
take't.

VIOLA    I will return again into the house and desire
some conduct of the lady. I am no fighter. I have heard 244
of some kind of men that put quarrels purposely
on others, to taste their valor. Belike this   is a 246
man of that quirk.                                         247

SIR TOBY    Sir, no. His indignation derives itself out of a
very competent injury; therefore, get you on and give 249
him his desire. Back you shall not to the house unless
you undertake that with me which with as much
safety you might answer him. Therefore, on, or strip 252
your sword stark naked; for meddle you must, that's 253
certain, or forswear to wear iron about you.             254

VIOLA    This is as uncivil as strange. I beseech you, do
me this courteous office as to know of the  knight what 256
my offense to him is. It is something of my negligence, 257
nothing of my purpose.                                     258

SIR TOBY    I will do so.—Signor Fabian, stay you by this
gentleman till my return.                *Exit [Sir] Toby.*

VIOLA    Pray you, sir, do you know of this matter?

FABIAN    I know the knight is incensed against you,
even to a mortal arbitrament, but nothing of the 263
circumstance more.

VIOLA    I beseech you, what manner of man is he?

FABIAN    Nothing of that  wonderful promise, to read 266
him by his form, as you are like to find  him in the 267
proof of his valor. He is, indeed, sir, the most skillful,
bloody, and fatal opposite that you could possibly
have found in any part of Illyria. Will you walk 270
towards him, I will make your peace with him if I can.

VIOLA    I shall be much bound to you for't. I am one
that had rather go with Sir Priest than Sir Knight. I 273
care not who knows so much of my mettle.    *Exeunt.*

*Enter [Sir] Toby and [Sir] Andrew.*

SIR TOBY    Why, man, he's a very devil; I have not seen
such a firago. I had a pass with him, rapier, scabbard, 276
and all, and he gives me the stuck-in with such a 277
mortal motion that it is inevitable; and on the answer, 278
he pays you as surely as your feet hits the ground they
step on. They say he has been fencer to the Sophy. 280

SIR ANDREW    Pox on't, I'll not meddle with him.

---

**201 the while** meanwhile.   **horrid** i.e., bristling, terrifying.   **204 laid** hazarded.   **unchary on't** recklessly on it.   **205–7 There's . . . reproof** Part of me tells me that I am foolish for declaring my love to you, but my passion is so insistent that it merely scoffs at being corrected. **208–9 With . . . griefs** i.e., Orsino's sufferings in love are as reckless and uncontrollable as your feelings.   **214 That . . . give?** that can be granted without compromising my chaste virtue?   **217 acquit you** release you of your promise.   **219 A fiend . . . hell** i.e., You are my torment. (*Like thee* means "in your likeness.")   **222 That . . . to't** Get ready to deploy whatever skill you have in fencing.   **224 intercepter** he who lies in wait. **despite** defiance, ill will   **224–5 bloody as the hunter** bloodthirsty as a hunting dog   **226 Dismount thy tuck** Draw your rapier.   **yare** ready, nimble   **229 to** with   **232-3 betake . . . guard** put yourself on guard **233 opposite** opponent.   **what** whatsoever   **234 withal** with. **236 unhatched** unhacked, unused in battle

**237 carpet consideration** (A carpet knight was one whose title was obtained, not in battle, but through connections at court.)   **241 Hob, nob** Have or have not, i.e., give it or take it, kill or be killed.   **word** motto   **244 conduct** safe-conduct, escort   **246 taste** test, prove   **Belike** Probably   **247 quirk** peculiar humor.   **249 competent** sufficient **252-3 strip . . . naked** draw your sword from its sheath   **253 meddle** engage (in conflict)   **254 forswear . . . iron** give up your right to wear a sword   **256 know of** inquire from   **257–8 It is . . . purpose** It is the result of some oversight, not anything I intended.   **263 mortal arbitrament** trial to the death   **266–7 read . . . form** judge him by his appearance   **267 like** likely   **270 Will you** If you will   **273 go with** associate with.   **Sir Priest** (*Sir* was a courtesy title for priests.)   **276 firago** virago, a person of strength and spirit. (Often applied to shrewish women.)   **pass** bout **277 stuck-in** stoccado, a thrust in fencing   **278 answer** return hit **280 to the Sophy** in the service of the Shah of Persia.

SIR TOBY    Ay, but he will not now be pacified. Fabian
can scarce hold him yonder.                                                283

SIR ANDREW    Plague on't, an I thought he had been    284
valiant and so cunning in fence, I'd have seen him
damned ere I'd have challenged him. Let him let the
matter slip and I'll give him my horse, gray Capilet.    287

SIR TOBY    I'll make the motion. Stand here, make a    288
good show on't. This shall end without the perdition    289
of souls. [*Aside, as he crosses to meet Fabian*] Marry, I'll    290
ride your horse as well as I ride you.

       *Enter Fabian and Viola.*

[*Aside to Fabian*] I have his horse to take up the    292
quarrel. I have persuaded him the youth's a devil.

FABIAN    He is as horribly conceited of him, and pants    294
and looks pale as if a bear were at his heels.

SIR TOBY [*to Viola*]    There's no remedy, sir, he will
fight with you for's oath's sake. Marry, he hath    297
better bethought him of his quarrel, and he finds    298
that now scarce to be worth talking of. Therefore
draw, for the supportance of his vow; he protests he    300
will not hurt you.

VIOLA [*aside*]    Pray God defend me! A little thing    302
would make me tell them how much I lack of a man.    303

FABIAN    Give ground, if you see him furious.

SIR TOBY [*crossing to Sir Andrew*]    Come, Sir Andrew,
there's no remedy. The gentleman will, for his
honor's sake, have one bout with you. He cannot by
the *duello* avoid it. But he has promised me, as he is    308
a gentleman and a soldier, he will not hurt you.
Come on, to't.

SIR ANDREW    Pray God he keep his oath!

       *Enter Antonio.*

VIOLA [*to Fabian*]    I do assure you, 'tis against my will.
                           [*They draw.*]

ANTONIO [*drawing, to Sir Andrew*]
    Put up your sword. If this young gentleman
    Have done offense, I take the fault on me;
    If you offend him, I for him defy you.

SIR TOBY    You, sir? Why, what are you?

ANTONIO
    One, sir, that for his love dares yet do more
    Than you have heard him brag to you he will.

SIR TOBY [*drawing*]
    Nay, if you be an undertaker, I am for you.    319

       *Enter Officers.*

FABIAN    Oh, good Sir Toby, hold! Here come the officers.

SIR TOBY [*to Antonio*]    I'll be with you anon.

VIOLA [*to Sir Andrew*]    Pray, sir, put your sword up, if
you please.

SIR ANDREW    Marry, will I, sir; and for that I promised    324
you, I'll be as good as my word. He will bear you    325
easily, and reins well.

FIRST OFFICER    This is the man. Do thy office.

SECOND OFFICER
    Antonio, I arrest thee at the suit
    Of Count Orsino.

ANTONIO              You do mistake me, sir.

FIRST OFFICER
    No, sir, no jot. I know your favor well,    330
    Though now you have no sea-cap on your head.—
    Take him away. He knows I know him well.

ANTONIO
    I must obey. [*To Viola*] This comes with seeking you.
    But there's no remedy; I shall answer it.    334
    What will you do, now my necessity
    Makes me to ask you for my purse? It grieves me
    Much more for what I cannot do for you
    Than what befalls myself. You stand amazed,    338
    But be of comfort.

SECOND OFFICER    Come, sir, away.

ANTONIO [*to Viola*]
    I must entreat of you some of that money.

VIOLA    What money, sir?
    For the fair kindness you have showed me here,
    And part being prompted by your present trouble,    343
    Out of my lean and low ability
    I'll lend you something. My having is not much;    345
    I'll make division of my present with you.    346
    Hold, there's half my coffer.    [*She offers money.*]    347

ANTONIO    Will you deny me now?
    Is't possible that my deserts to you    349
    Can lack persuasion? Do not tempt my misery,    350
    Lest that it make me so unsound a man    351
    As to upbraid you with those kindnesses
    That I have done for you.

VIOLA              I know of none,
    Nor know I you by voice or any feature.
    I hate ingratitude more in a man
    Than lying, vainness, babbling drunkenness,    356
    Or any taint of vice whose strong corruption
    Inhabits our frail blood.

ANTONIO    Oh, heavens themselves!

SECOND OFFICER    Come, sir, I pray you, go.

ANTONIO
    Let me speak a little. This youth that you see here
    I snatched one half out of the jaws of death,
    Relieved him with such sanctity of love,    363
    And to his image, which methought did promise    364
    Most venerable worth, did I devotion.    365

---

**283 scarce** scarcely    **284 Plague on't** (A common oath.)    **287 Capilet**
i.e., "little horse." (From "capel," a nag.)    **288 motion** offer.    **289–90**
**perdition of souls** i.e., loss of lives.    **292 take up** settle, make up
**294 He . . . him** i.e., Cesario has as horrible a conception of Sir Andrew
**297 for oath's sake** merely because he swore an oath to do so.
**298 bethought him of** reconsidered    **300 supportance** upholding
**302–3 A little . . . man** (With bawdy suggestion of the penis.)
**308** *duello* dueling code    **319 undertaker** one who takes upon himself a task or business; here, a challenger.    **for you** ready for you.

**324 for that** as for what    **325 He** i.e., The horse    **330 no jot** not a bit.
**favor** face    **334 answer it** stand trial and make reparation for it.
**338 befalls** happens to    **343 part** partly    **345 having** wealth
**346 present** present store    **347 coffer** purse. (Literally, strongbox.)
**349–50 deserts . . . persuasion** claims on you can fail to persuade you to
help me.    **350 tempt** try too severely    **351 Lest that** lest.    **unsound**
morally weak, lacking in self-control    **356 vainness** vaingloriousness
**363 such . . . love** i.e., such veneration as is due to a sacred relic
**364 image** what he appeared to be. (Playing on the idea of a religious icon
to be venerated.)    **365 venerable worth** worthiness of being venerated

FIRST OFFICER
What's that to us? The time goes by. Away!

ANTONIO
But, oh, how vile an idol proves this god!
Thou hast, Sebastian, done good feature shame.    368
In nature there's no blemish but the mind;
None can be called deformed but the unkind.    370
Virtue is beauty, but the beauteous evil    371
Are empty trunks o'erflourished by the devil.    372

FIRST OFFICER
The man grows mad. Away with him! Come, come,
sir.

ANTONIO    Lead me on.    *Exit [with Officers].*

VIOLA [*aside*]
Methinks his words do from such passion fly
That he believes himself. So do not I.    376
Prove true, imagination, oh, prove true,
That I, dear brother, be now ta'en for you!

SIR TOBY    Come hither, knight. Come hither, Fabian.
We'll whisper o'er a couplet or two of most sage saws.    380
    [*They gather apart from Viola.*]

VIOLA
He named Sebastian. I my brother know    381
Yet living in my glass; even such and so    382
In favor was my brother, and he went    383
Still in this fashion, color, ornament,    384
For him I imitate. Oh, if it prove,    385
Tempests are kind, and salt waves fresh in love!
    [*Exit.*]

SIR TOBY    A very dishonest paltry boy, and more a    387
coward than a hare. His dishonesty appears in leaving    388
his friend here in necessity and denying him; and for    389
his cowardship, ask Fabian.

FABIAN    A coward, a most devout coward, religious in it.    391

SIR ANDREW    'Slid, I'll after him again and beat him.    392

SIR TOBY    Do, cuff him soundly, but never draw thy
sword.

SIR ANDREW    An I do not—    [*Exit.*]

FABIAN    Come, let's see the event.    396

SIR TOBY    I dare lay any money 'twill be nothing yet.    397
    *Exeunt.*

❖

# 4.1

*Enter Sebastian and Clown [Feste].*

FESTE    Will you make me believe that I am not sent for
you?

SEBASTIAN    Go to, go to, thou art a foolish fellow. Let
me be clear of thee.

FESTE    Well held out, i'faith! No, I do not know you,    5
nor I am not sent to you by my lady to bid you come
speak with her, nor your name is not Master Cesario,
nor this is not my nose, neither. Nothing that is so is so.

SEBASTIAN    I prithee, vent thy folly somewhere else.    9
Thou know'st not me.

FESTE    Vent my folly! He has heard that word of some    11
great man, and now applies it to a fool. Vent my folly!
I am afraid this great lubber, the world, will prove a    13
cockney. I prithee now, ungird thy strangeness and    14
tell me what I shall vent to my lady. Shall I vent to her
that thou art coming?

SEBASTIAN    I prithee, foolish Greek, depart from me.    17
There's money for thee. [*He gives money.*] If you tarry
longer, I shall give worse payment.

FESTE    By my troth, thou hast an open hand. These wise    20
men that give fools money get themselves a good
report—after fourteen years' purchase.    22

*Enter [Sir] Andrew, [Sir] Toby, and Fabian.*

SIR ANDREW    Now, sir, have I met you again? There's
for you!    [*He strikes Sebastian.*]

SEBASTIAN    Why, there's for thee, and there, and there!
    [*He beats Sir Andrew with the hilt of his dagger.*]
Are all the people mad?

SIR TOBY    Hold, sir, or I'll throw your dagger o'er the
house.

FESTE    This will I tell my lady straight. I would not be in    29
some of your coats for twopence.    [*Exit.*]    30

SIR TOBY    Come on, sir, hold!    [*He grips Sebastian.*]

SIR ANDREW    Nay, let him alone. I'll go another way to
work with him. I'll have an action of battery against    33
him, if there be any law in Illyria. Though I struck him
first, yet it's no matter for that.

SEBASTIAN    Let go thy hand!

SIR TOBY    Come, sir, I will not let you go. Come, my
young soldier, put up your iron. You are well fleshed.    38
Come on.

SEBASTIAN
I will be free from thee. [*He breaks free and draws his
    sword.*] What wouldst thou now?
If thou dar'st tempt me further, draw thy sword.    41

SIR TOBY    What, what? Nay, then I must have an ounce
or two of this malapert blood from you.    [*He draws.*]    43

*Enter Olivia.*

---

368 **Thou . . . shame** i.e., You have shamed physical beauty by showing that it does not always reflect inner beauty.    370 **unkind** ungrateful, unnatural.    371 **beauteous evil** those who are outwardly beautiful but evil within    372 **trunks** (1) chests (2) bodies.    **o'erflourished** (1) covered with ornamental carvings (2) made outwardly beautiful    376 **So . . . I** i.e., I do not believe myself (in the hope that has arisen in me).    380 **We'll . . . saws** i.e., Let's converse privately. (*Saws* are sayings.)    381–2 **I . . . glass** i.e., I know that my brother's likeness lives in me    383 **favor** appearance    384 **Still** always    385 **prove** prove true    387 **dishonest** dishonorable    388 **dishonesty** dishonor    389 **denying** refusing to acknowledge    391 **religious in it** making a religion of cowardice.    392 **'Slid** By his (God's) eyelid    396 **event** outcome.    397 **lay** wager.    **yet** nevertheless, after all.
**4.1. Location: Before Olivia's house.**

5 **held out** kept up    9 **vent** (1) utter (2) void, excrete, get rid of    11 **of** from, suited to the diction of; or, with reference to    13 **lubber** lout    14 **cockney** effeminate or foppish fellow. (Feste comically despairs of finding common sense anywhere if people start using affected phrases like those Sebastian uses.)    **ungird thy strangeness** put off your affectation of being a stranger. (Feste apes the kind of high-flown speech he has just deplored.)    17 **Greek** (1) one who speaks gibberish (as in "It's all Greek to me") (2) buffoon (as in "merry Greek")    20 **open** generous. (With money or with blows.)    22 **report** reputation.    **after . . . purchase** i.e., at great cost and after long delays. (Land was ordinarily valued at the price of twelve years' rental; the Fool adds two years to this figure.)    29 **straight** at once.    29–30 **in . . . coats** i.e., in your shoes    33 **action of battery** lawsuit for physical assault    38 **iron** sword.    **fleshed** initiated into battle.    41 **tempt** make trial of    43 **malapert** saucy, impudent

OLIVIA
Hold, Toby! On thy life I charge thee, hold!
SIR TOBY    Madam—
OLIVIA
Will it be ever thus? Ungracious wretch,
Fit for the mountains and the barbarous caves,
Where manners ne'er were preached! Out of my
    sight!—
Be not offended, dear Cesario.—
Rudesby, begone!
        [*Exeunt Sir Toby, Sir Andrew, and Fabian.*]
            I prithee, gentle friend,    50
Let thy fair wisdom, not thy passion, sway
In this uncivil and unjust extent    52
Against thy peace. Go with me to my house,
And hear thou there how many fruitless pranks
This ruffian hath botched up, that thou thereby    55
Mayst smile at this. Thou shalt not choose but go.    56
Do not deny. Beshrew his soul for me!    57
He started one poor heart of mine, in thee.    58
SEBASTIAN [*aside*]
What relish is in this? How runs the stream?    59
Or I am mad, or else this is a dream.    60
Let fancy still my sense in Lethe steep;    61
If it be thus to dream, still let me sleep!
OLIVIA
Nay, come, I prithee. Would thou'dst be ruled by me!
SEBASTIAN
Madam, I will.
OLIVIA        Oh, say so, and so be!    *Exeunt.*

❖

# 4.2

*Enter Maria [carrying a gown and a false beard], and Clown [Feste].*

MARIA    Nay, I prithee, put on this gown and this beard;
make him believe thou art Sir Topas the curate. Do it    2
quickly. I'll call Sir Toby the whilst.    [*Exit.*]    3
FESTE    Well, I'll put it on, and I will dissemble myself    4
in't, and I would I were the first that ever dissembled
in such a gown. [*He disguises himself in gown and
beard.*] I am not tall enough to become the function    7
well, nor lean enough to be thought a good student;    8

but to be said an honest man and a good housekeeper    9
goes as fairly as to say a careful man  and a great    10
scholar. The competitors enter.    11

*Enter [Sir] Toby [and Maria].*

SIR TOBY    Jove bless thee, Master Parson.
FESTE    *Bonos dies*, Sir Toby. For, as the old  hermit of    13
Prague, that never saw pen and ink, very  wittily said    14
to a niece of King Gorboduc, "That that is, is"; so I,    15
being Master Parson, am Master Parson; for what is
"that" but "that," and "is" but "is"?
SIR TOBY    To him, Sir Topas.
FESTE    What, ho, I say! Peace in this prison!
        [*He approaches the door
        behind which Malvolio is confined.*]
SIR TOBY    The knave counterfeits well; a good knave.    20
MALVOLIO    (*within*) Who calls there?
FESTE    Sir Topas the curate, who comes to visit Malvolio
the lunatic.
MALVOLIO    Sir Topas, Sir Topas, good Sir Topas, go to
my lady—
FESTE    Out, hyperbolical fiend! How vexest thou this    26
man! Talkest thou nothing but of ladies?
SIR TOBY    Well said, Master Parson.
MALVOLIO    Sir Topas, never was man thus wronged.
Good Sir Topas, do not think I am mad. They have
laid me here in hideous darkness.
FESTE    Fie, thou dishonest Satan! I call thee by the most
modest terms, for I am one of those gentle ones that    33
will use the devil himself with courtesy. Say'st thou
that house is dark?    35
MALVOLIO    As hell, Sir Topas.
FESTE    Why, it hath bay windows transparent as barri-    37
cadoes, and the clerestories toward the south north    38
are as lustrous as ebony; and yet complainest thou of
obstruction?
MALVOLIO    I am not mad, Sir Topas. I say to you this
house is dark.
FESTE    Madman, thou errest. I say there is no darkness
but ignorance, in which thou art more puzzled than
the Egyptians in their fog.    45
MALVOLIO    I say this house is as dark as ignorance,
though ignorance were as dark as hell; and I say there
was never man thus abused. I am no more mad than
you are. Make the trial of it in any constant question.    49

---

**50 Rudesby** Ruffian    **52 extent** attack    **55 botched up** clumsily contrived    **56 Thou . . . go** I insist on your going with me.    **57 deny**
refuse.    **Beshrew** Curse. (A mild oath.)    **for me** for my part.
**58 He . . . thee** i.e., He alarmed that part of my heart which lies in
your bosom. (To *start* is also to drive an animal such as a *hart* [*heart*]
from its cover.)    **59 What . . . this?** i.e., What am I to make of this?
(*Relish* means "taste.")    **60 Or** Either    **61 Let . . . steep** i.e., Let this
fantasy continue to steep my senses in forgetfulness. (*Lethe* is the
river of forgetfulness in the underworld.)
**4.2. Location: Olivia's house.**
**2 Sir** (An honorific title for priests.)    **Topas** (A name perhaps derived
from Chaucer's comic knight in the "Rime of Sir Thopas" or from a
similar character in Lyly's *Endymion*. Topaz, a semiprecious stone,
was believed to be a cure for lunacy.)    **3 the whilst** in the meantime.
**4 dissemble** disguise. (With a play on "feign.")    **7 become the function** adorn the priestly office    **8 lean** (Scholars were proverbially
sparing of diet.)    **student** scholar (in divinity)

**9–11 to be . . . scholar** a reputation for honesty and hospitality is as
becoming to ordinary men as carefulness and learning are to scholars.
(Feste suggests that honesty and charity are found as often in ordinary men as in clerics.)    **11 competitors** associates, partners (in this
plot)    **13 *Bonos dies*** Good day    **13–14 hermit of Prague** (Probably
another invented authority.)    **14 that . . . ink** who was no scholar
**15 King Gorboduc** a legendary king of ancient Britain, protagonist in
the English tragedy *Gorboduc* (1562)    **"That . . . is"** (Feste parades this
self-evident piece of nonsense as suited to his new role as a learned
divine.)    **20 knave** rascal    **26 hyperbolical** vehement, boisterous.
**fiend** i.e., the devil supposedly possessing Malvolio.    **33 modest**
moderate    **35 house** i.e., room    **37–8 barricadoes** barricades. (Which
are opaque. Feste speaks comically in impossible paradoxes, but
Malvolio seems not to notice.)    **38 clerestories** windows in an upper
wall    **45 Egyptians . . . fog** (Alluding to the darkness brought upon
Egypt by Moses; see Exodus 10:21–3.)    **49 constant question**
problem that requires consecutive reasoning.

FESTE    What is the opinion of Pythagoras concerning 50
wildfowl? 51

MALVOLIO    That the soul of our grandam might haply 52
inhabit a bird.

FESTE    What think'st thou of his opinion?

MALVOLIO    I think nobly of the soul, and no way
approve his opinion.

FESTE    Fare thee well. Remain thou still in darkness.
Thou shalt hold th'opinion of Pythagoras ere I will
allow of thy wits, and fear to kill a woodcock lest thou 59
dispossess the soul of thy grandam. Fare thee well.
             [He moves away from Malvolio's prison.]

MALVOLIO    Sir Topas, Sir Topas!

SIR TOBY    My most exquisite Sir Topas!

FESTE    Nay, I am for all waters. 63

MARIA    Thou mightst have done this without thy beard
and gown. He sees thee not.

SIR TOBY    To him in thine own voice, and bring me 66
word how thou find'st him.—I would we were well rid
of this knavery. If he may be conveniently delivered, I 68
would he were, for I am now so far in offense with my
niece that I cannot pursue with any safety this sport to
the upshot. Come by and by to my chamber. 71
                              Exit [with Maria].

FESTE [singing as he approaches Malvolio's prison]
    "Hey, Robin, jolly Robin, 72
    Tell me how thy lady does." 73

MALVOLIO    Fool!

FESTE    "My lady is unkind, pardie." 75

MALVOLIO    Fool!

FESTE    "Alas, why is she so?"

MALVOLIO    Fool, I say!

FESTE    "She loves another—" Who calls, ha?

MALVOLIO    Good Fool, as ever thou wilt deserve well at 80
my hand, help me to a candle, and pen, ink, and
paper. As I am a gentleman, I will live to be thankful
to thee for't.

FESTE    Master Malvolio?

MALVOLIO    Ay, good Fool.

FESTE    Alas, sir, how fell you besides your five wits? 86

MALVOLIO    Fool, there was never man so notoriously 87
abused. I am as well in my wits, Fool, as thou art. 88

FESTE    But as well? Then you are mad indeed, if you be 89
no better in your wits than a fool.

MALVOLIO    They have here propertied me, keep me in 91
darkness, send ministers to me—asses—and do all
they can to face me out of my wits. 93

FESTE    Advise you what you say. The minister is here. 94
[He speaks as Sir Topas.] Malvolio, Malvolio, thy wits
the heavens restore! Endeavor thyself to sleep, and
leave thy vain bibble-babble.

MALVOLIO    Sir Topas!

FESTE [in Sir Topas's voice]    Maintain no words with
him, good fellow. [In his own voice] Who, I, sir? Not
I, sir. God b'wi'you, good Sir Topas. [In Sir Topas's
voice] Marry, amen. [In his own voice] I will, sir, I will.

MALVOLIO    Fool! Fool! Fool, I say!

FESTE    Alas, sir, be patient. What say you, sir? I am
shent for speaking to you. 105

MALVOLIO    Good Fool, help me to some light and some
paper. I tell thee I am as well in my wits as any man in
Illyria.

FESTE    Welladay that you were, sir! 109

MALVOLIO    By this hand, I am. Good Fool, some ink, 110
paper, and light; and convey what I will set down to
my lady. It shall advantage thee more than ever the
bearing of letter did.

FESTE    I will help you to't. But tell me true, are you
not mad indeed, or do you but counterfeit?

MALVOLIO    Believe me, I am not. I tell thee true.

FESTE    Nay, I'll ne'er believe a madman till I see his
brains. I will fetch you light and paper and ink.

MALVOLIO    Fool, I'll requite it in the highest degree. I
prithee, begone.

FESTE [sings]
    I am gone, sir,
    And anon, sir,
I'll be with you again,
    In a trice,
    Like to the old Vice, 125
Your need to sustain;

    Who, with dagger of lath, 127
    In his rage and his wrath,
Cries, "Aha!" to the devil;
    Like a mad lad,
    "Pare thy nails, dad? 131
Adieu, goodman devil!"                        Exit. 132

                    ❦

## 4.3

*Enter Sebastian [with a pearl].*

SEBASTIAN
This is the air; that is the glorious sun;

---

**50–1 Pythagoras . . . wildfowl** (An opening for the discussion of
transmigration of souls, a doctrine held by Pythagoras.)    **52 haply**
perhaps    **59 allow of thy wits** certify your sanity.    **woodcock** (A
proverbially stupid bird, easily caught.)    **63 Nay . . . waters** i.e., Indeed,
I can turn my hand to anything.    **66 To him** Speak to him    **68 delivered** i.e., delivered from prison    **71 upshot** conclusion.    **72–3 "Hey,
Robin . . . does"** (Another fragment of an old song, a version of which
is attributed to Sir Thomas Wyatt.)    **75 pardie** i.e., by God, certainly.
**80 as** if    **86 besides** out of.    **five wits** The intellectual faculties,
usually listed as common wit, imagination, fantasy, judgment, and
memory.    **87–8 notoriously abused** egregiously ill treated.    **89 But**
Only    **91 propertied me** i.e., treated me as property and thrown me
into the lumber-room    **93 face . . . wits** brazenly represent me as
having lost my wits.

**94 Advise you** Take care    **105 shent** scolded, rebuked    **109 Welladay**
Alas, would that    **110 By this hand** (A mild oath.)    **125 Vice** comic
tempter of the "old" morality plays    **127 dagger of lath** comic weapon
of the Vice in at least some morality plays    **131 Pare thy nails** (This
may allude to the belief that evil spirits could use nail parings to get
control of their victims; cf. Dromio of Syracuse in *The Comedy of Errors*,
4.3.69, "Some devils ask but the parings of one's nail," and the Boy's
characterization of Pistol in *Henry V*, 4.4.72–3, as "this roaring devil i'th'
old play, that everyone may pare his nails with a wooden dagger.")
**132 goodman** title for a person of substance but not of gentle birth.
(This line could be Feste's farewell to Malvolio and his "devil.")
**4.3. Location: Olivia's garden.**

This pearl she gave me, I do feel't and see't;
And though 'tis wonder that enwraps me thus,
Yet 'tis not madness. Where's Antonio, then?
I could not find him at the Elephant;
Yet there he was, and there I found this credit,   6
That he did range the town to seek me out.
His counsel now might do me golden service;
For though my soul disputes well with my sense   9
That this may be some error, but no madness,   10
Yet doth this accident and flood of fortune   11
So far exceed all instance, all discourse,   12
That I am ready to distrust mine eyes
And wrangle with my reason that persuades me
To any other trust but that I am mad,   15
Or else the lady's mad. Yet if 'twere so,
She could not sway her house, command her
    followers,   17
Take and give back affairs and their dispatch   18
With such a smooth, discreet, and stable bearing
As I perceive she does. There's something in't
That is deceivable. But here the lady comes.   21

*Enter Olivia and Priest.*

OLIVIA
Blame not this haste of mine. If you mean well,
Now go with me and with this holy man
Into the chantry by. There, before him,   24
And underneath that consecrated roof,
Plight me the full assurance of your faith,
That my most jealous and too doubtful soul   27
May live at peace. He shall conceal it
Whiles you are willing it shall come to note,   29
What time we will our celebration keep   30
According to my birth. What do you say?   31

SEBASTIAN
I'll follow this good man, and go with you,
And having sworn truth, ever will be true.

OLIVIA
Then lead the way, good father, and heavens so shine
That they may fairly note this act of mine!    *Exeunt.*   35

# 5.1

*Enter Clown [Feste] and Fabian.*

FABIAN    Now, as thou lov'st me, let me see his letter.
FESTE    Good Master Fabian, grant me another request.
FABIAN    Anything.

FESTE    Do not desire to see this letter.
FABIAN    This is to give a dog and in recompense desire   5
my dog again.   6

*Enter Duke [Orsino], Viola, Curio, and lords.*

ORSINO    Belong you to the Lady Olivia, friends?
FESTE    Ay, sir, we are some of her trappings.   8
ORSINO    I know thee well. How dost thou, my good fellow?
FESTE    Truly, sir, the better for my foes and the worse   10
for my friends.   11
ORSINO    Just the contrary—the better for thy friends.
FESTE    No, sir, the worse.
ORSINO    How can that be?
FESTE    Marry, sir, they praise me, and make an ass of   15
me. Now my foes tell me plainly I am an ass, so that   16
by my foes, sir, I profit in the knowledge of myself,
and by my friends I am abused; so that, conclusions   18
to be as kisses, if your four negatives make your two   19
affirmatives, why then the worse for my friends and   20
the better for my foes.
ORSINO    Why, this is excellent.
FESTE    By my troth, sir, no, though it please you to be   23
one of my friends.   24
ORSINO    Thou shalt not be the worse for me. There's gold.
    *[He gives a coin.]*
FESTE    But that it would be double-dealing, sir, I would   26
you could make it another.
ORSINO    Oh, you give me ill counsel.
FESTE    Put your grace in your pocket, sir, for this once,   29
and let your flesh and blood obey it.   30
ORSINO    Well, I will be so much a sinner to be a   31
double-dealer. There's another. *[He gives another coin.]*
FESTE    *Primo, secundo, tertio*, is a good play, and the old   33
saying is, the third pays for all. The triplex, sir, is a   34
good tripping measure; or the bells of Saint Bennet,   35
sir, may put you in mind—one, two, three.   36
ORSINO    You can fool no more money out of me at this
throw. If you will let your lady know I am here to   38
speak with her, and bring her along with you, it may
awake my bounty further.
FESTE    Marry, sir, lullaby to your bounty till I come
again. I go, sir, but I would not have you to think that

---

**6 was** was previously.   **credit** report   **9–10 For . . . madness** for though my reason argues that my amazing experience just now with Olivia must be the result of some strange misunderstanding, to my physical senses the encounter appears as something totally weird and inexplicable   **11 accident** unexpected event   **12 instance** precedent. **discourse** reason   **15 trust** belief   **17 sway** rule   **18 Take . . . dispatch** receive reports on matters of household business and see to their execution   **21 deceivable** deceptive.   **24 chantry by** private endowed chapel nearby.   **27 jealous** anxious, mistrustful.   **doubtful** full of doubts   **29 Whiles** until.   **come to note** become known   **30 What time** at which time.   **our celebration** i.e., the actual marriage. (What they are about to perform is a binding betrothal.)   **31 birth** social position.   **35 fairly note** look upon with favor
**5.1. Location: Before Olivia's house.**

**5–6 This . . . again** (Apparently a reference to a well-known reply of Dr. Bulleyn when Queen Elizabeth asked for his dog and promised a gift of his choosing in return; he asked to have his dog back.) **8 trappings** ornaments, decorations.   **10–11 the better . . . friends** i.e., I am the better for having foes, and the worse for having friends. (Feste explains his paradox in lines 15–20.)   **15–16 they . . . of me** i.e., my friends flatter me into foolishly thinking well of myself.   **18 abused** flatteringly deceived   **18–20 conclusions . . . affirmatives** i.e., as when a young lady, asked for a kiss, says "no, no" really meaning "yes"; or, as in grammar, where two negatives make an affirmative   **23 though** even though   **24 friends** i.e., those who, according to Feste's syllogism, flatter him.   **26 But** Except for the fact.   **double-dealing** (1) giving twice (2) deceit, practicing duplicity   **29 Put . . . pocket** (1) Pay no attention to your honor, put it away (2) Reach in your pocket or purse and show your customary grace or munificence. (*Your Grace* is also the formal way of addressing a duke.)   **30 it** i.e., my "ill counsel." **31 to be** as to be   **33 Primo . . . tertio** Latin ordinals: first, second, third.   **play** (Perhaps a mathematical game or game of dice.)   **34 the third . . . all** the third time is lucky. (Proverbial.)   **triplex** triple time in music   **35 Saint Bennet** church of St. Benedict   **36 put . . . three** remind you of things in threes, when the church bells ring thrice in succession.   **38 throw** (1) time (2) throw of the dice.

my desire of having is the sin of covetousness. But as 43
you say, sir, let your bounty take a nap. I will awake
it anon.        *Exit.*

*Enter Antonio and Officers.*

**VIOLA**
Here comes the man, sir, that did rescue me.

**ORSINO**
That face of his I do remember well,
Yet when I saw it last it was besmeared
As black as Vulcan in the smoke of war. 49
A baubling vessel was he captain of, 50
For shallow draft and bulk unprizable, 51
With which such scatheful grapple did he make 52
With the most noble bottom of our fleet 53
That very envy and the tongue of loss 54
Cried fame and honor on him. What's the matter? 55

**FIRST OFFICER**
Orsino, this is that Antonio
That took the *Phoenix* and her freight from Candy, 57
And this is he that did the *Tiger* board
When your young nephew Titus lost his leg.
Here in the streets, desperate of shame and state, 60
In private brabble did we apprehend him. 61

**VIOLA**
He did me kindness, sir, drew on my side,
But in conclusion put strange speech upon me. 63
I know not what 'twas but distraction. 64

**ORSINO**
Notable pirate, thou saltwater thief, 65
What foolish boldness brought thee to their mercies
Whom thou in terms so bloody and so dear 67
Hast made thine enemies?

**ANTONIO**      Orsino, noble sir,
Be pleased that I shake off these names you give me. 69
Antonio never yet was thief or pirate,
Though, I confess, on base and ground enough 71
Orsino's enemy. A witchcraft drew me hither.
That most ingrateful boy there by your side
From the rude sea's enraged and foamy mouth
Did I redeem; a wreck past hope he was. 75
His life I gave him, and did thereto add
My love, without retention or restraint, 77
All his in dedication. For his sake 78
Did I expose myself—pure for his love— 79
Into the danger of this adverse town, 80
Drew to defend him when he was beset;

Where being apprehended, his false cunning, 82
Not meaning to partake with me in danger,
Taught him to face me out of his acquaintance 84
And grew a twenty years' removèd thing 85
While one would wink; denied me mine own purse, 86
Which I had recommended to his use 87
Not half an hour before.

**VIOLA**   How can this be?

**ORSINO**   When came he to this town?

**ANTONIO**
Today, my lord; and for three months before,
No interim, not a minute's vacancy,
Both day and night did we keep company.

*Enter Olivia and attendants.*

**ORSINO**
Here comes the Countess. Now heaven walks on
  earth.
But for thee, fellow—fellow, thy words are madness. 95
Three months this youth hath tended upon me;
But more of that anon.—Take him aside.

**OLIVIA** [*to Orsino*]
What would my lord—but that he may not have— 98
Wherein Olivia may seem serviceable?—
Cesario, you do not keep promise with me.

**VIOLA**   Madam?

**ORSINO**   Gracious Olivia—

**OLIVIA**
What do you say, Cesario?—Good my lord— 103

**VIOLA**
My lord would speak. My duty hushes me.

**OLIVIA**
If it be aught to the old tune, my lord,
It is as fat and fulsome to mine ear 106
As howling after music.

**ORSINO**   Still so cruel?

**OLIVIA**   Still so constant, lord.

**ORSINO**
What, to perverseness? You uncivil lady,
To whose ingrate and unauspicious altars 111
My soul the faithfull'st off'rings have breathed out 112
That e'er devotion tendered! What shall I do? 113

**OLIVIA**
Even what it please my lord that shall become him. 114

**ORSINO**
Why should I not, had I the heart to do it,
Like to th'Egyptian thief at point of death 116
Kill what I love?—a savage jealousy
That sometime savors nobly. But hear me this: 118

---

**43 desire . . . covetousness** (Feste hopes he is not guilty of an inordinate desire for possessions, which i s indeed covetousness, one of the Seven Deadly Sins.)   **49 Vulcan** Roman god of fire and smith to the other gods; his face was blackened by the fire   **50 baubling** insignificant, trifling   **51–5 For . . . on him** a sailing vessel of shallow depth in the water and too small to be worth taking as a prize, with which he nevertheless managed to grapple destructively the mightiest ship of our fleet, thereby earning praise even from those who had the most reason to envy and hate him.   **57 from Candy** on her return from Candia, or Crete   **60 desperate . . . state** recklessly disregarding the disgrace and danger to himself   **61 brabble** brawl   **63 put . . . me** spoke to me strangely.   **64 but distraction** unless (it was) madness.   **65 Notable** Notorious   **67 in terms . . . dear** in so bloodthirsty and costly a manner   **69 Be pleased that I** Allow me to   **71 base and ground** solid grounds   **75 redeem** rescue.   **wreck** shipwrecked person   **77 retention** reservation   **78 All . . . dedication** devoted wholly to him.   **79 pure** entirely, purely   **80 Into** unto.   **adverse** hostile

**82 being** I being   **84 face . . . acquaintance** brazenly deny he knew me   **85–6 grew . . . wink** in the twinkling of an eye acted as though we had been estranged for twenty years   **87 recommended** consigned   **95 for** as for   **98 but . . . have** except that which he may not have—i.e., my love   **103 What . . . my lord** (Olivia first addresses Cesario/Viola, who spoke to her in line 101, and then turns to Orsino, who spoke to her in line 102.)   **106 fat and fulsome** gross and offensive   **111–13 To . . . tendered** to whose unresponsive altars my soul has uttered the most faithful professions of love that ever were offered by a devoted worshipper.   **114 become** suit   **116 th'Egyptian thief** (An allusion to the story of Theagenes and Chariclea in the *Ethiopica,* a Greek romance by Heliodorus. The robber chief, Thyamis of Memphis, having captured Chariclea and fallen in love with her, is attacked by a larger band of robbers; threatened with death, he attempts to slay her first.)   **118 savors nobly** is not without nobility.

Since you to nonregardance cast my faith,                              119
And that I partly know the instrument                                  120
That screws me from my true place in your favor,                       121
Live you the marble-breasted tyrant still.
But this your minion, whom I know you love,                            123
And whom, by heaven I swear, I tender dearly,                          124
Him will I tear out of that cruel eye                                  125
Where he sits crownèd in his master's spite.—                          126
Come, boy, with me. My thoughts are ripe in
  mischief.
I'll sacrifice the lamb that I do love,                                128
To spite a raven's heart within a dove.          [*Going.*]  129

VIOLA
And I, most jocund, apt, and willingly,                                130
To do you rest, a thousand deaths would die.                           131
                                                 [*Going.*]

OLIVIA
Where goes Cesario?

VIOLA                        After him I love
More than I love these eyes, more than my life,
More by all mores than e'er I shall love wife.                         134
If I do feign, you witnesses above                                     135
Punish my life for tainting of my love!                                136

OLIVIA
Ay me, detested! How am I beguiled!                                    137

VIOLA
Who does beguile you? Who does do you wrong?

OLIVIA
Hast thou forgot thyself? Is it so long?
Call forth the holy father.          [*Exit an attendant.*]

ORSINO [*to Viola*]          Come, away!

OLIVIA
Whither, my lord?—Cesario, husband, stay.

ORSINO
Husband?

OLIVIA          Ay, husband. Can he that deny?

ORSINO [*to Viola*]
Her husband, sirrah?

VIOLA                        No, my lord, not I.         143

OLIVIA
Alas, it is the baseness of thy fear
That makes thee strangle thy propriety.                                145
Fear not, Cesario, take thy fortunes up;                               146
Be that thou know'st thou art, and then thou art                       147
As great as that thou fear'st.

          *Enter Priest.*

                    Oh, welcome, father!                               148
Father, I charge thee by thy reverence

Here to unfold—though lately we intended
To keep in darkness what occasion now                                  151
Reveals before 'tis ripe—what thou dost know
Hath newly passed between this youth and me.

PRIEST
A contract of eternal bond of love,
Confirmed by mutual joinder of your hands,                             155
Attested by the holy close of lips,                                    156
Strengthened by interchangement of your rings,
And all the ceremony of this compact
Sealed in my function, by my testimony;                                159
Since when, my watch hath told me, toward my
  grave
I have traveled but two hours.

ORSINO [*to Viola*]
Oh, thou dissembling cub! What wilt thou be
When time hath sowed a grizzle on thy case?                            163
Or will not else thy craft so quickly grow
That thine own trip shall be thine overthrow?                          165
Farewell, and take her, but direct thy feet
Where thou and I henceforth may never meet.

VIOLA
My Lord, I do protest—

OLIVIA                Oh, do not swear!
Hold little faith, though thou hast too much fear.                     169

          *Enter Sir Andrew.*

SIR ANDREW   For the love of God, a surgeon! Send one
  presently to Sir Toby.                                               171

OLIVIA   What's the matter?

SIR ANDREW   He's broke my head across, and has given       173
  Sir Toby a bloody coxcomb too.  For the love of God,      174
  your help! I had rather than forty pound I were at
  home.

OLIVIA   Who has done this, Sir Andrew?

SIR ANDREW   The Count's gentleman, one Cesario. We
  took him for a coward, but he's the very devil
  incarnate.                                                           180

ORSINO   My gentleman, Cesario?

SIR ANDREW   'Od's lifelings, here he is!—You broke my      182
  head for nothing, and that that I did I was set on to
  do't by Sir Toby.

VIOLA
Why do you speak to me? I never hurt you.
You drew your sword upon me without cause,
But I bespake you fair, and hurt you not.                              187

SIR ANDREW   If a bloody coxcomb be a hurt, you have
  hurt me. I think you set nothing by a bloody cox-         189
  comb.

          *Enter [Sir] Toby and Clown [Feste].*

---

**119 nonregardance** neglect   **120 that** since.   **the instrument** i.e.,
Cesario/Viola   **121 screws** pries, forces   **123 minion** darling, favorite
**124 tender** regard   **125–6 Him . . . spite** I will tear Cesario away from
Olivia, in whose cruel eye he sits like a king to spite me, his true master.   **128–9 I'll . . . dove** i.e., I'll kill Cesario, whom I love, to revenge
myself on this seemingly gracious but black-hearted lady.   **130 apt**
readily   **131 do you rest** give you ease   **134 by all mores** by all such
comparisons   **135 witnesses** gods   **136 Punish . . . love!** punish me
with death for being disloyal to the one I love!   **137 detested** hated
and denounced by the one I love.   **143 sirrah** (The normal way of
addressing an inferior.)   **145 strangle thy propriety** i.e., deny what is
properly yours, disavow your marriage to me.   **146 take . . . up**
embrace your good fortune, that of being my husband   **147 that** that
which   **148 as that thou fear'st** as him you fear, i.e., Orsino.

**151 occasion** necessity   **155 joinder** joining   **156 close** meeting
**159 Sealed . . . function** ratified through my carrying out of my
priestly office   **163 a grizzle** a beard, or perhaps a scattering of grey
hair.   **case** skin.   **165 trip** wrestling trick used to throw an opponent.
(You'll get overclever and trip yourself up.)   **169 Hold . . . fear** Keep
to your oath as well as you can, even if you are frightened by Orsino's
threats.   **171 presently** immediately   **173 broke** broken the skin,
cut   **174 coxcomb** fool's cap resembling the crest of a cock; here,
head   **180 incarnate** (For "incarnate.")   **182 'Od's lifelings** By
God's little lives   **187 bespake you fair** addressed you courteously
**189 set nothing by** regard as insignificant

Here comes Sir Toby, halting. You shall hear more.  191
But if he had not been in drink, he would have tickled
you othergates than he did.  193

ORSINO   How now, gentleman? How is't with you?

SIR TOBY   That's all one. He's hurt me, and there's  195
th'end on't.—Sot, didst see Dick surgeon, sot?  196

FESTE   Oh, he's drunk, Sir Toby, an hour agone; his eyes  197
were set at eight i'th' morning.  198

SIR TOBY   Then he's a rogue, and a passy measures  199
pavane. I hate a drunken rogue.  200

OLIVIA   Away with him! Who hath made this havoc
with them?

SIR ANDREW   I'll help you, Sir Toby, because we'll be  203
dressed together.  204

SIR TOBY   Will you help? An ass-head and a coxcomb
and a knave, a thin-faced knave, a gull!

OLIVIA
Get him to bed, and let his hurt be looked to.

[*Exeunt Feste, Fabian, Sir Toby, and Sir Andrew.*]

*Enter Sebastian.*

SEBASTIAN
I am sorry, madam, I have hurt your kinsman;
But, had it been the brother of my blood,  209
I must have done no less with wit and safety.—  210
You throw a strange regard upon me, and by that  211
I do perceive it hath offended you.
Pardon me, sweet one, even for the vows
We made each other but so late ago.

ORSINO
One face, one voice, one habit, and two persons,  215
A natural perspective, that is and is not!  216

SEBASTIAN
Antonio, O my dear Antonio!
How have the hours racked and tortured me  218
Since I have lost thee!

ANTONIO   Sebastian are you?

SEBASTIAN   Fear'st thou that, Antonio?  221

ANTONIO
How have you made division of yourself?
An apple cleft in two is not more twin
Than these two creatures. Which is Sebastian?

OLIVIA   Most wonderful!

SEBASTIAN [*seeing Viola*]
Do I stand there? I never had a brother;
Nor can there be that deity in my nature
Of here and everywhere. I had a sister,  228
Whom the blind waves and surges have devoured.  229
Of charity, what kin are you to me?  230

What countryman? What name? What parentage?

VIOLA
Of Messaline. Sebastian was my father.
Such a Sebastian was my brother, too.
So went he suited to his watery tomb.  234
If spirits can assume both form and suit,  235
You come to fright us.

SEBASTIAN                A spirit I am indeed,  236
But am in that dimension grossly clad  237
Which from the womb I did participate.  238
Were you a woman, as the rest goes even,  239
I should my tears let fall upon your cheek
And say, "Thrice welcome, drownèd Viola!"

VIOLA
My father had a mole upon his brow.

SEBASTIAN   And so had mine.

VIOLA
And died that day when Viola from her birth
Had numbered thirteen years.

SEBASTIAN
Oh, that record is lively in my soul!  246
He finishèd indeed his mortal act  247
That day that made my sister thirteen years.

VIOLA
If nothing lets to make us happy both  249
But this my masculine usurped attire,  250
Do not embrace me till each circumstance
Of place, time, fortune, do cohere and jump  252
That I am Viola—which to confirm
I'll bring you to a captain in this town
Where lie my maiden weeds, by whose gentle help  255
I was preserved to serve this noble count.
All the occurrence of my fortune since
Hath been between this lady and this lord.

SEBASTIAN [*to Olivia*]
So comes it, lady, you have been mistook.
But nature to her bias drew in that.  260
You would have been contracted to a maid,
Nor are you therein, by my life, deceived.
You are betrothed both to a maid and man.  263

ORSINO [*to Olivia*]
Be not amazed; right noble is his blood.
If this be so, as yet the glass seems true,  265
I shall have share in this most happy wreck.  266
[*To Viola*] Boy, thou hast said to me a thousand times
Thou never shouldst love woman like to me.  268

VIOLA
And all those sayings will I over swear,  269
And all those swearings keep as true in soul

---

191 **halting** limping.   193 **othergates** otherwise   195 **That's all one** It doesn't matter; never mind.   195–6 **there's . . . on't** that's all there is to it.   196 **Sot** (1) Fool (2) Drunkard   197 **agone** ago   198 **set** fixed or closed   199–200 **passy measures pavane** passe-measure pavane, a slow-moving, stately dance. (Suggesting Sir Toby's impatience to have his wounds dressed.)   203–4 **be dressed** have our wounds surgically dressed   209 **the brother . . . blood** my own brother   210 **with wit and safety** with intelligent concern for my own safety.   211 **You . . . me** You look strangely at me   215 **habit** dress   216 **A natural perspective** an optical device or illusion created in this instance by nature   218 **racked** tortured   221 **Fear'st thou that** Do you doubt that   228 **here and everywhere** omnipresence.   229 **blind** heedless, indiscriminate   230 **Of charity** (Tell me) in kindness

234 **suited** dressed; clad in human form   235 **form and suit** physical appearance and dress   236 **A spirit . . . indeed** i.e., I am a living creature endowed with a soul   237 **in . . . clad** clothed in that fleshly shape   238 **participate** possess in common with all humanity.   239 **as . . . even** since everything else agrees   246 **record** recollection   247 **his mortal act** his life   249 **lets** hinders   250 **usurped** assumed under false pretenses   252 **jump** coincide, fit exactly   255 **weeds** clothes   260 **nature . . . that** nature followed her bent in that. (The metaphor is from the game of bowls.)   263 **a maid and man** a man who has not yet slept with a woman.   265 **the glass** i.e., the *natural perspective* of line 216   266 **wreck** shipwreck, accident.   268 **Thou . . . to me** (See 2.4.26–8, where Viola/Cesario riddlingly tells Orsino that she has loved a woman of his complexion and age.)   269 **over swear** swear again

As doth that orbèd continent the fire                          271
That severs day from night.

ORSINO                                           Give me thy hand,
And let me see thee in thy woman's weeds.

VIOLA
The captain that did bring me first on shore
Hath my maid's garments. He upon some action      275
Is now in durance, at Malvolio's suit,             276
A gentleman and follower of my lady's.

OLIVIA
He shall enlarge him. Fetch Malvolio hither.       278
And yet, alas, now I remember me,
They say, poor gentleman, he's much distract.

*Enter Clown [Feste] with a letter, and Fabian.*

A most extracting frenzy of mine own               281
From my remembrance clearly banished his.          282
How does he, sirrah?

FESTE   Truly, madam, he holds Beelzebub at the stave's  284
end as well as a man in his case may do. He's here  285
writ a letter to you; I should have given't you today  286
morning. But as a madman's epistles are no gospels,  287
so it skills not much when they are delivered.      288

OLIVIA   Open't and read it.

FESTE   Look then to be well edified when the fool
delivers the madman. [*He reads loudly.*] "By the Lord,  291
madam—"

OLIVIA   How now, art thou mad?

FESTE   No, madam, I do but read madness. An Your
Ladyship will have it as it ought to be, you must allow
vox.                                                296

OLIVIA   Prithee, read i'thy right wits.

FESTE   So I do, madonna; but to read his right wits is to  298
read thus. Therefore perpend, my princess, and give  299
ear.

OLIVIA [*to Fabian*]   Read it you, sirrah.

FABIAN (*reads*)   "By the Lord, madam, you wrong me,
and the world shall know it. Though you have put me
into darkness and given your drunken cousin rule
over me, yet have I the benefit of my senses as well
as Your Ladyship. I have your own letter that induced
me to the semblance I put on, with the which I  307
doubt not but to do myself much right or you much
shame. Think of me as you please. I leave my duty  309
a little unthought of, and speak out of my injury.  310
                          The madly used Malvolio."

OLIVIA   Did he write this?

FESTE   Ay, madam.

ORSINO   This savors not much of distraction.

OLIVIA
See him delivered, Fabian. Bring him hither.       315
                              [*Exit Fabian.*]
My lord, so please you, these things further thought
on,                                                 316
To think me as well a sister as a wife,             317
One day shall crown th'alliance on't, so please you,  318
Here at my house and at my proper cost.             319

ORSINO
Madam, I am most apt t'embrace your offer.          320
[*To Viola*] Your master quits you; and for your
service done him,                                   321
So much against the mettle of your sex,             322
So far beneath your soft and tender breeding,
And since you called me master for so long,
Here is my hand. You shall from this time be
Your master's mistress.

OLIVIA                       A sister! You are she.

*Enter [Fabian, with] Malvolio.*

ORSINO
Is this the madman?

OLIVIA                       Ay, my lord, this same.
How now, Malvolio?

MALVOLIO                    Madam, you have done me wrong,
Notorious wrong.

OLIVIA             Have I, Malvolio? No.

MALVOLIO [*showing a letter*]
Lady, you have. Pray you, peruse that letter.
You must not now deny it is your hand.
Write from it, if you can, in hand or phrase,       332
Or say 'tis not your seal, not your invention.      333
You can say none of this. Well, grant it then,
And tell me, in the modesty of honor,               335
Why you have given me such clear lights of favor,   336
Bade me come smiling and cross-gartered to you,
To put on yellow stockings, and to frown
Upon Sir Toby and the lighter people?               339
And, acting this in an obedient hope,               340
Why have you suffered me to be imprisoned,
Kept in a dark house, visited by the priest,        342
And made the most notorious geck and gull           343
That e'er invention played on? Tell me why?         344

OLIVIA
Alas, Malvolio, this is not my writing,
Though, I confess, much like the character;         346

---

271 **As . . . fire** i.e., as the sun maintains the fire   275 **action** legal
charge   276 **in durance** imprisoned   278 **enlarge** release   281
**extracting** distracting   282 **his** Malvolio's madness.   284–5 **holds . . .
end** i.e., keeps the devil at a safe distance. (The metaphor is of fighting with quarterstaffs or long poles.)   286–7 **today morning** this
morning.   287 **a madman's . . . gospels** i.e., there is no truth in a
madman's letters. (An allusion to readings in the church service of
selected passages from the epistles and the gospels.)   288 **skills**
matters.   **delivered** (1) delivered to their recipient (2) read aloud.
291 **delivers** speaks the words of   296 **vox** voice, i.e., an appropriately loud voice.   298 **to read . . . wits** to express his true state of mind
299 **perpend** consider, attend. (A deliberately lofty word.)   307 **semblance** visual appearance.   **with the which** with which letter
309–10 **I leave . . . injury** I leave unsaid the expressions of duty with
which I would normally conclude, and convey instead my sense of
having been wronged.

315 **delivered** released   316 **so . . . on** if you are pleased on further
consideration of all that has happened   317 **To . . . wife** to regard me
as favorably as a sister-in-law as you had hoped to regard me as a
wife   318 **crown . . . on't** i.e., serve as occasion for two marriages
confirming our new relationships   319 **proper** own   320 **apt** ready
321 **quits** releases   322 **mettle** natural disposition   332 **from it** differently   333 **invention** composition.   335 **in . . . honor** in the name
of all that is decent and honorable   336 **clear lights** evident signs
339 **lighter** lesser   340 **acting . . . hope** when I acted thus out of obedience to you and in hope of your favor   342 **priest** i.e., Feste
343 **geck** dupe   344 **That . . . played on** that ever a practical joke
played trick with.   346 **the character** my handwriting

But out of question 'tis Maria's hand.                                   347
And now I do bethink me, it was she
First told me thou wast mad; then cam'st in smiling,      349
And in such forms which here were presupposed         350
Upon thee in the letter. Prithee, be content.
This practice hath most shrewdly passed upon thee;     352
But when we know the grounds and authors of it,
Thou shalt be both the plaintiff and the judge
Of thine own cause.
FABIAN                          Good madam, hear me speak,
And let no quarrel nor no brawl to come                   356
Taint the condition of this present hour,                    357
Which I have wondered at. In hope it shall not,
Most freely I confess, myself and Toby
Set this device against Malvolio here,
Upon some stubborn and uncourteous parts              361
We had conceived against him. Maria writ                  362
The letter at Sir Toby's great importance,                  363
In recompense whereof he hath married her.
How with a sportful malice it was followed               365
May rather pluck on laughter than revenge,                366
If that the injuries be justly weighed                         367
That have on both sides passed.
OLIVIA [to Malvolio]
Alas, poor fool, how have they baffled thee!             369
FESTE   Why, "Some are born great, some achieve
greatness, and some have greatness thrown upon
them." I was one, sir, in this interlude, one Sir Topas,   372
sir, but that's all one. "By the Lord, fool, I am not      373
mad." But do you remember? "Madam, why laugh       374
you at such a barren rascal? An you smile not, he's      375
gagged." And thus the whirligig of time brings in his    376
revenges.
MALVOLIO   I'll be revenged on the whole pack of you!
[Exit.]

OLIVIA
He hath been most notoriously abused.
ORSINO
Pursue him, and entreat him to a peace.
He hath not told us of the captain yet.
When that is known, and golden time convents,         382
A solemn combination shall be made
Of our dear souls. Meantime, sweet sister,
We will not part from hence. Cesario, come—
For so you shall be, while you are a man;
But when in other habits you are seen,                      387
Orsino's mistress and his fancy's queen.                    388
                          Exeunt [all, except Feste].
FESTE (sings)
When that I was and a little tiny boy,                        389
     With hey, ho, the wind and the rain,
A foolish thing was but a toy,                                 391
     For the rain it raineth every day.

But when I came to man's estate,
     With hey, ho, the wind and the rain,
'Gainst knaves and thieves men shut their gate,
     For the rain it raineth every day.

But when I came, alas, to wive,
     With hey, ho, the wind and the rain,
By swaggering could I never thrive,
     For the rain it raineth every day.

But when I came unto my beds,                              401
     With hey, ho, the wind and the rain,
With tosspots still had drunken heads,                     403
     For the rain it raineth every day.

A great while ago the world begun,
     With hey, ho, the wind and the rain,
But that's all one, our play is done,
     And we'll strive to please you every day.
                                             [Exit.]

347 **out of** beyond   349 **cam'st** you came   350 **presupposed** specified beforehand   352 **practice** plot.   **shrewdly passed** mischievously
been perpetrated   356 **to come** in the future   357 **condition** (happy)
nature   361–2 **Upon . . . him** because of a certain stubbornness and
lack of courtesy we had held against him.   363 **importance** importunity
365 **followed** carried out   366 **pluck on** induce   367 **If that** if
369 **baffled** disgraced, quelled   372 **interlude** little play   373 **that's
all one** no matter for that.   374–6 **Madam . . . gagged** (Feste quotes
Malvolio at 1.5.80–5.)   376 **whirligig** spinning top

382 **convents** (1) summons, calls together (2) suits   387 **habits**
attire   388 **fancy's** love's   389 **and a little** a little   391 **toy** trifle
401 **unto my beds** i.e., (1) drunk to bed, or, perhaps, (2) in the evening of life   403 **tosspots** drunkards

# Measure for Measure

❦

**"A** play Caled Mesur for Mesur" by "Shax-berd" was performed at court, for the new King James I, by "his Maiesties plaiers" on December 26, 1604. Probably it had been composed that same year or in late 1603. The play dates from the very height of Shakespeare's tragic period, three years or so after *Hamlet*, contemporary with *Othello*, shortly before *King Lear* and *Macbeth*. This period includes very little comedy of any sort, and what there is differs markedly from the festive comedy of the 1590s. *Troilus and Cressida* (c. 1601–1602), hovering between satire and tragedy, bleakly portrays a hopeless love affair caught in the toils of a pointless and stalemated war. *All's Well That Ends Well* (c. 1601–1604) resembles *Measure for Measure* in its portrayal of an undeserving protagonist who must be deceived into marriage by the ethically ambiguous trick of substituting one woman for another in the protagonist's bed. *Measure for Measure*, perhaps the last such comedy from the tragic period, illustrates most clearly of all what critics usually mean by "problem comedy" or "problem play."

Its chief concern is not with the triumphs of love, as in the happy comedies, but with moral and social problems: "filthy vices" arising from sexual desire and the abuses of political authority. Images of disease abound in this play. We see corruption in Vienna "boil and bubble / Till it o'errun the stew" (5.1.326–7). The protagonist, Angelo, is for most of the play a deeply torn character, abhorring his own perverse sinfulness, compulsively driven to an attempted murder in order to cover up his lust for the heroine, Isabella. His soliloquies are introspective, tortured, focused on the psychological horror of an intelligent mind succumbing to criminal desire. The disguised Duke Vincentio, witnessing this fall into depravity and despair, can offer Angelo's intended victims no better philosophical counsel than Christian renunciation of the world and all its vain hopes. Tragedy is averted only by providential intervention and by the harsh trickery of "Craft against vice" (3.2.270), in which the Duke becomes involved as chief manipulator and stage manager. Of the concluding marriages, two are foisted on the bridegrooms (Angelo and Lucio) against their wills, whereas that of the Duke and Isabella jars oddly with his stoical teachings and with her previous determination to be a nun. The ending thus seems problematic; both justice and romantic happiness are so perilously achieved in this play that they seem inconsistent with the injustice and lechery that have prevailed until the last.

Yet the very improbability of the ending and the sense of tragedy narrowly averted are perhaps intentional. These features are appropriate, not only for problem comedy, but also for tragicomedy or comedy of forgiveness, overlapping genres toward which Shakespeare gravitated in his late romances. Angelo is, like Leontes in *The Winter's Tale* (or like Bertram in *All's Well That Ends Well* and Claudio in *Much Ado About Nothing*), an erring protagonist forgiven in excess of his deserving, spared by a benign, overseeing providence from destroying that which is most precious to him.

That providence is partly ascribed to divine intervention, as when the disguised Duke, at a loss for a means of saving Claudio from imminent death, and learning that a prisoner named Ragozine has just died and is enough like Claudio physically that his head can be substituted for that of Claudio as proof that an execution has taken place, exclaims, "Oh, 'tis an accident that heaven provides!" (4.3.77). Yet most of the "providential" oversight in this play is essentially theatrical and humanly devised. It is engineered by "the old fantastical Duke of dark corners" (4.3.156–7), the resourceful Vincentio. Indeed, this mysterious Duke becomes a kind of embodiment of the manipulations and sleights of hand through which this dark comedy achieves its improbable ends.

The play's title, *Measure for Measure*, introduces a paradox of human justice which this "problem" play cannot wholly resolve. How are fallible humans to judge the sins of their fellow mortals and still obey Christ's injunction of the Sermon on the Mount: "Judge not that ye be not judged"? Three positions emerge from the debate: absolute justice at one extreme, mercy at the other, and equity as a middle ground. Isabella speaks for mercy, and her words ring with biblical authority. Since all humanity would be condemned to eternal darkness were God not merciful as well as just, should not humans also be merciful? The difficulty, however, is that Vienna shows all too clearly the effects of leniency under the indulgent Duke. Vice is rampant; stern measures are needed. Though he has not wished to crack the whip himself, the Duke firmly endorses "strict statutes and most biting laws, / The needful bits and curbs to headstrong steeds" (1.3.19–20). To carry out necessary reform, the Duke has chosen Angelo, spokesman for absolute justice, to represent him. Angelo's position is cold but consistent. Only by a literal and impartial administering of the statutes, he maintains, can the law deter potential offenders. If the judge is found guilty, he must pay the penalty as well. One difficulty here, however, is that literal enforcement of the statute on fornication seems ironically to catch the wrong culprits. Claudio and Juliet, who are about to be married and are already joined by a "true contract" of betrothal, are sentenced to the severest limit of the law, whereas the pimps and whores of Vienna's suburbs manage at first to evade punishment entirely. Angelo's deputy, Escalus, can only shake his head in dismay at this unjust result of strict justice. Angelo has not remembered fully the terms of his commission from the Duke: to practice both "Mortality and mercy" in Vienna, to "enforce or qualify the laws / As to your soul seems good." The attributes of a ruler, like those of God, must include "terror" but also "love" (1.1.20–67).

Escalus's compassionate and pragmatic approach to law illustrates equity or the flexible application of the law to particular cases. Because Claudio is only technically guilty (though still guilty), Escalus would pronounce for him a light sentence. Pompey and Mistress Overdone, on the other hand, require vigorous prosecution. The problem of policing vice is compounded by the law's inefficiency, as well as by erring human nature, which will never be wholly tamed. Constable Elbow, like Dogberry in *Much Ado,* is a pompous user of mala-propisms, less clever by far than the criminals he would arrest. His evidence against Pompey is so absurdly circumstantial that Escalus is first obliged to let off this engaging pimp with a stern warning. Yet Escalus patiently and tenaciously attends to such proceedings, unlike Angelo, whose interest in the law is too theoretical. Escalus deals with day-to-day problems effectively. He orders reforms of the system by which constables are selected, instructs Elbow in the rudiments of his office, and so proceeds, ultimately, to an effective arrest. Vice is not eliminated; as Pompey defiantly points out, unless someone plans to "geld and splay all the youth of the city," they "will to't

then" (2.1.229–33). Still, vice is held in check. Law can shape the outer person and hope for some inner reform. Even Pompey is taught a trade, albeit a grisly one, as an apprentice hangman. The law must use both "correction" and "instruction."

The solutions arrived at in the comic subplot do not fit the case of Angelo, for he is powerful enough to be above the Viennese law. Indeed, he tries finally to brazen it out, pitting his authority against that of the seemingly friendless Isabella, much like the biblical Elders (in the Apocryphal Book of Daniel and Susanna) when justly accused of immorality by the innocent Susanna. Society is on Angelo's side—even the well-meaning Escalus; only a seeming providence can rescue the defenseless. The Duke of Vienna, hovering in the background and seeing all that happens, intervenes just at those points when tragedy threatens to become irreversible. Moreover, the Duke is testing those he observes. As he says to Friar Thomas, explaining why he has delegated his power to Angelo: "Hence shall we see, / If power change purpose, what our seemers be" (1.3.53–4). The Duke obviously expects Angelo to fall. Indeed, he has known all along that Angelo had dishonorably repudiated his solemn contract to Mariana when her marriage dowry disappeared at sea (3.1.215–25). Like an all-seeing deity who keeps a reckoning of humanity's good and evil deeds, the Duke has found out Angelo's great weakness. As Angelo confesses, "I perceive Your Grace, like power divine, / Hath looked upon my passes" (5.1.377–8). Paradoxically, this seemingly tragic story of temptation and fall yields precious benefits of remorse and humility. Angelo is rescued from his self-made nightmare of seduction, murder, and tyranny. Knowing now that he is prone like other mortals to fleshly weakness, he knows also that he needs spiritual assistance and that, as judge, he ought to use mercy. Seen in retrospect, his panic, despair, and humiliation are curative.

The Duke is no less a problematic character than Angelo, Isabella, and the rest. Vienna's deep corruption is, in part, the result of his unwillingness to bear down on vice, and yet, rather than undertake to remedy the failure himself, this strange monarch elects to leave the business to one he suspects will make matters worse. The Duke has a great deal to learn about his own dislike of crowds, his complacent tolerance of human weakness, and his naive supposition that all his subjects speak well of him. He is a highly manipulative character, the one most responsible in the play for the ethically dubious solutions through which craft must be employed against vice. The comforting words of spiritual counsel he offers Claudio, Juliet, and the rest are spoken by a secular ruler fraudulently disguised as a friar. Certainly, the Duke is no allegorized god-figure, for all his omniscience and final role as both punisher and forgiver. As *deux ex machina* of this problem comedy, the Duke is human, frail, and vulnerable—as indeed he ought to be in a play that explores with such rich complexity the ironic distance between divine and human justice.

Yet, for all his manifest and even comic weaknesses, the Duke is finally the authority figure who must attempt to bring order to the imperfect world of Vienna. The devices he employs, including the bed trick, seem morally questionable and yet are palpable comic fictions that unmistakably notify us what genre we are watching. If the Duke's role is more that of artist than ruler or diety, his being so is appropriate to the artistically contrived and theatrical world that Shakespeare presents to us. Within the world of this play, the disguised Duke's chief function is to test the other characters and to mislead them intentionally into expecting the worst, in order to try their resolve. On a comic level, he exposes the amiable but loose-tongued Lucio as a slanderer against the Duke himself and devises for Lucio a suitably satirical exposure and witty punishment. More seriously, as confessor to Juliet, he assures her that her beloved Claudio must die on the morrow. As she ought, she penitentially accepts "shame with joy" and so is cleansed (2.3.37). Because the Duke is not really a friar, he does not have the spiritual authority to do this, and the ruse strikes us as theatrical, employing devices of illusion that actors and dramatists use. Even so, it provides real comfort for Juliet. The very theatricality of the illusion, by reminding us that we are in the theater, enables us to see the Duke as a kind of morally persuasive playwright who can change the lives of his characters for the better.

Similarly, the counsel of Christian renunciation offered to Claudio by the bogus friar (3.1) is at once illusory and comforting. The Duke's poignant reflection on the vanity of human striving is made ironic but not invalid by our awareness that we are viewing a deception with a seemingly benign purpose—that of persuading Claudio to see matters in their cosmic perspective. The Duke characterizes life as a breath, a dreamlike "after-dinner's sleep," a fever of inconstancy in which timorous humans long fretfully for what they do not have and spurn those things they have. Claudio responds as he ought, resolving to "find life" by "seeking death" (3.1.5–43). He achieves this calm, however, in the face of certain execution; ironically, what he must then learn to overmaster is the desperate hope of living by means of his sister's dishonor. Claudio is broken by this test and perversely begs for a few years of guilty life at the cost of eternal shame for himself and Isabella. From this harrowing experience, he emerges at length with a better understanding of his own weakness and a greater compassion toward the weakness of others.

The searing encounter between Claudio and Isabella puts her to the test as well, and her response seems hysterical and no doubt prudish to modern audiences. She has much to learn about the complexities of human behavior. Although she is sincere in protesting that she would lay down her life for her brother and is correct, in the play's terms, to prefer virtue to mere existence, her tone is too strident. Like other major characters, she must be humbled before she can rise. She and Claudio must heed the Duke's essential admonition: "Do not satisfy your resolution with hopes that are fallible" (3.1.170–1). Only then, paradoxically, can Isabella and Claudio go on to achieve earthly happiness.

Isabella and Angelo are paradoxically alike. Both have retreated from the world of carnal pleasure into havens they regard as safe but that turn out not to work in the way they had hoped. Isabella longs for the restraints of the sisterhood into which she is about to enter. Her suspicions about human frailty can be seen in her testing of her brother; she fears he will fail her by begging life at the cost of her eternal shame, and when he does just that, she reacts with shrill condemnation and even hatred. This is a dark moment for Isabella, and she needs the spiritual counsel of the disguised Duke to enable her to forgive not only her brother but also herself. Angelo, meanwhile, has attempted to put down the rebellion of the flesh by suppressing and denying all such feeling in himself. We see him at first as the workaholic official who is not hesitant to condemn in others what he believes he is free of personally. He cherishes restraint as much as Isabella does, and that is why he is so terrified when the apparent absence of his only superior, the Duke, opens up to him the abyss of his own licentiousness. Once his word is law, Angelo perceives that he can play the tyrant and seducer without check. He is horrified to discover not only that he has ungovernable sexual longings within him but also that they perversely direct themselves toward a woman who is virginal and saintly. Why does he yearn to "raze the sanctuary" thus (2.2.178)? The revelation to him of his own innate evil is virtually tragic in the intensity of his self-loathing, and yet, in this strange comedy, this revelation is a first step toward coming to terms with his reprobate self. Until Angelo acknowledges the carnal within, he cannot begin looking for a way to understand and accept this frailty. The Duke's test provides the means of self-discovery that Angelo cannot fashion on his own.

In her final testing, Isabella shows greatness of spirit. Here, Shakespeare significantly alters his chief sources, George Whetstone's *Promos and Cassandra* (1578), Giovanni Baptista Giraldi Cinthio's *Hecatommithi*, and Whetstone's *Heptameron of Civil Discourses*. In all these versions, the character corresponding to Angelo does actually ravish the heroine, and in the *Hecatommithi* he also murders her brother. Shakespeare, by withholding these irreversible acts, not only gives to Angelo a technical innocence, but also allows the Duke, as *deus ex machina*, to practice virtuous deception on Isabella one more time. Can she forgive the supposed murderer of her brother? Her affirmative answer confutes the Old Testament ethic of "An Angelo for Claudio, death for death" whereby "Like doth quit like, and measure still for measure" (5.1.417–19). Although Angelo concedes that he deserves to die for what he intended, the forfeit need not be paid so long as humanity can reveal itself capable of Isabella's godlike mercy.

With its apparently unsuitable marriages and its improbable plotting, *Measure for Measure* does end by dealing directly with the problems of human nature confronted in the earlier scenes. The bed trick (switching Mariana for Isabella) may seem a legalistic and contrived way to bring Angelo to terms with his own carnality, but it is instructive not only to him but also to Isabella; she, like Angelo, must learn to accept the realities of the human condition. By helping Mariana to achieve her legitimate desire to couple and marry, Isabella sees into her own need. Her begging for Angelo's life is not merely an act of forgiveness to an enemy; it is a gift of continued marriage to Mariana. This realization helps to prepare Isabella herself for a marriage that, although dramatically surprising on stage (and even rejected by her in some modern productions), may be intended to demonstrate her having given up the cloistered life for all that marriage signifies. *Measure for Measure* is thus essentially comic (unlike *Troilus and Cressida*), despite its harrowing scenes of conflict and its awareness of vice everywhere in human nature. The play celebrates the *felix culpa* of human nature, the fall from grace that is an integral part of humanity's rise to happiness and self-knowledge. Throughout, in the play's finest scenes, poignancy is tempered by a wit and humor that are ultimately gracious. The formal and substantive emphasis on marriage stresses not just the benefits of remorse and humility but also the real possibility of psychic and spiritual growth: Isabella can acknowledge that she is a woman, Angelo can be genuinely freed from repression, and Claudio can value life more intensely because he has confronted death. All these recognitions affirm the acceptance and proper use of the physical and sexual side of human nature, and yet they are achieved only through charity and forgiveness. Humanity can learn, however slowly and painfully, that the talents entrusted to it by providence are to be used wisely.

The guardedly hopeful reading of the play offered here is, to be sure, not the only way in which it can be understood. The stage history of *Measure for Measure* highlights much that is problematic and troubling about it. For virtually all of the seventeenth, eighteenth, and nineteenth centuries, after its initial production, the play disappeared from the theater, other than in a heavily rewritten adaptation of the Restoration period and an even more radically recast nineteenth-century operatic version by Richard Wagner called *Das Liebesverbot* ("Forbidden Love"). The play was, it seems, too disagreeable for audiences in those centuries, too given over to vice and moral ambiguity. Readers were sometimes warned away from it. The twentieth and twenty-first centuries, conversely, have found in *Measure for Measure* a persuasive and even devastating dramatization of human imperfection. In an age that has learned to distrust authority figures, Duke Vincentio can come across as officious and sadistic in his manipulation of human lives, rather than ultimately benign. The director Keith Hack, at Stratford-upon-Avon in 1974, saw the Duke as devious, hypocritical, deeply implicated in the corruption of his city, and bitterly resented by the characters whose lives are intrusively managed by him. Some productions have asked if Lucio is justified in his suspicions that the Duke is really a fleshmonger after all. Isabella's longing for the cloistered life of the convent is sometimes seen today as psychologically driven by a fear of sexuality more than by religious faith. Some stage productions revel in the tawdriness of the bordello world of a corrupted Vienna, as for example in Michael Bogdanov's production at Stratford, Canada, in 1985. To Keith Hack, in 1974, the play was a fable of social impression in the vein of Bertolt Brecht. The marriages with which the play ends are often held up to skeptical scrutiny. Is Angelo chastised by his searing experience into resolving to be a good husband to Mariana, or does he snarl at her when he is led off with her to be married? Most significantly, perhaps, does Isabella accept the surprising offer of marriage from the Duke who has protected her but also deceived her into believing that her brother was dead? Today, beginning with Estelle Kohler in John Barton's production at Stratford-upon-Avon in 1970, actresses and directors get to choose; since Isabella is given no lines indicating her acceptance, the actress may simply act bewildered or may decide, with a gesture of defiance or indifference, to have nothing to do with men. The range of options is extraordinary, and helps demonstrate the way in which Shakespeare provides such an unsettling challenge to actors, directors, and audiences alike.

# Measure for Measure

## The Names of All the Actors

VINCENTIO, *the Duke*
ANGELO, *the deputy*
ESCALUS, *an ancient lord*
CLAUDIO, *a young gentleman*
LUCIO, *a fantastic*
*Two other like* GENTLEMEN
PROVOST
THOMAS, ⎫
PETER,  ⎬ *two friars*
[A JUSTICE]
[VARRIUS, *a friend of the Duke*]

ELBOW, *a simple constable*
FROTH, *a foolish gentleman*
CLOWN [POMPEY, *a servant to Mistress Overdone*]

ABHORSON, *an executioner*
BARNARDINE, *a dissolute prisoner*

ISABELLA, *sister to Claudio*
MARIANA, *betrothed to Angelo*
JULIET, *beloved of Claudio*
FRANCISCA, *a nun*
MISTRESS OVERDONE, *a bawd*

[A SERVANT *of Angelo*
BOY *singer*
A MESSENGER *from Angelo*

*Lords, Officers, Citizens, Servants, and other Attendants*]

THE SCENE: *Vienna*

## 1.1

*Enter Duke, Escalus, lords, [and attendants].*

DUKE  Escalus.
ESCALUS   My lord.
DUKE

Of government the properties to unfold                    3
Would seem in me t'affect speech and discourse,          4
Since I am put to know that your own science             5
Exceeds, in that, the lists of all advice                6
My strength can give you. Then no more remains           7
But that to your sufficiency . . . . .                    8
. . . . . . . . . . . . . . . . . . . . . . . as your worth is able,   9
And let them work. The nature of our people,            10

Our city's institutions, and the terms                  11
For common justice, you're as pregnant in               12
As art and practice hath enrichèd any                    13
That we remember. There is our commission,
                              [*giving a paper*]
From which we would not have you warp.—Call
  hither,                                                15
I say, bid come before us Angelo.        [*Exit one.*]
What figure of us think you he will bear?                17
For you must know, we have with special soul             18
Elected him our absence to supply,                       19
Lent him our terror, dressed him with our love,          20
And given his deputation all the organs                  21
Of our own power. What think you of it?                  22
ESCALUS

If any in Vienna be of worth
To undergo such ample grace and honor,                   24

---

**1.1. Location: Vienna. The court of Duke Vincentio.**
**3–4 Of . . . discourse** For me to deliver a disquisition on the qualities needed in governing well would make me seem enamored of my own pomposity   **5–7 Since . . . you** since I am obliged to admit that your knowledge exceeds, in such matters, the limited wisdom that my intellect could provide you.   **8–10 But . . . work** (Evidently the Duke wishes to entrust the affairs of government to Angelo to the extent of his worthiness. The passage appears in the Folio as a single line. Several attempts at emendation have been made, but the most plausible explanation is that something has been deleted or inadvertently omitted.)

**11 terms** law court terms, or, modes of procedure   **12 pregnant** well-informed   **13 art** learning, theory   **15 warp** deviate.   **17 What . . . bear?** i.e., How do you think he will do as my substitute?   **18 special soul** all the powers of the mind; whole heart   **19 Elected** chosen. **supply** fill, make up for   **20 terror** power to inspire awe and fear **21 his deputation** him as deputy.   **organs** instruments   **22 our** (The royal plural.)   **24 undergo** bear the weight of

It is Lord Angelo.

*Enter Angelo.*

DUKE                      Look where he comes.

ANGELO
Always obedient to Your Grace's will,
I come to know your pleasure.

DUKE                                        Angelo,
There is a kind of character in thy life
That to th'observer doth thy history
Fully unfold. Thyself and thy belongings            30
Are not thine own so proper as to waste             31
Thyself upon thy virtues, they on thee.             32
Heaven doth with us as we with torches do,          33
Not light them for themselves; for if our virtues
Did not go forth of us, 'twere all alike            35
As if we had them not. Spirits are not finely touched  36
But to fine issues, nor Nature never lends          37
The smallest scruple of her excellence              38
But, like a thrifty goddess, she determines         39
Herself the glory of a creditor,                    40
Both thanks and use. But I do bend my speech        41
To one that can my part in him advertise.           42
Hold, therefore, Angelo:
In our remove be thou at full ourself.              44
Mortality and mercy in Vienna                       45
Live in thy tongue and heart. Old Escalus,
Though first in question, is thy secondary.         47
Take thy commission.            [*He gives a paper.*]

ANGELO                        Now, good my lord,
Let there be some more test made of my mettle       49
Before so noble and so great a figure
Be stamped upon it.

DUKE                            No more evasion.
We have with a leavened and preparèd choice         52
Proceeded to you; therefore take your honors.
Our haste from hence is of so quick condition       54
That it prefers itself and leaves unquestioned      55
Matters of needful value. We shall write to you,
As time and our concernings shall importune,        57
How it goes with us, and do look to know            58

What doth befall you here. So, fare you well.
To th' hopeful execution do I leave you             60
Of your commissions.

ANGELO                        Yet give leave, my lord,    61
That we may bring you something on the way.          62

DUKE    My haste may not admit it;                   63
Nor need you, on mine honor, have to do              64
With any scruple. Your scope is as mine own,         65
So to enforce or qualify the laws
As to your soul seems good. Give me your hand.
I'll privily away. I love the people                 68
But do not like to stage me to their eyes;           69
Though it do well, I do not relish well              70
Their loud applause and "aves" vehement,             71
Nor do I think the man of safe discretion            72
That does affect it. Once more, fare you well.       73

ANGELO
The heavens give safety to your purposes!

ESCALUS
Lead forth and bring you back in happiness!          75

DUKE    I thank you. Fare you well.            *Exit.*

ESCALUS
I shall desire you, sir, to give me leave
To have free speech with you; and it concerns me     78
To look into the bottom of my place.                 79
A power I have, but of what strength and nature
I am not yet instructed.

ANGELO
'Tis so with me. Let us withdraw together,
And we may soon our satisfaction have
Touching that point.

ESCALUS                      I'll wait upon Your Honor.     84

*Exeunt.*

❖

## 1.2

*Enter Lucio and two other Gentlemen.*

LUCIO    If the Duke with the other dukes come not to
composition with the King of Hungary, why then all   2
the dukes fall upon the King.                         3

FIRST GENTLEMAN    Heaven grant us its peace, but not
the King of Hungary's!

SECOND GENTLEMAN    Amen.

LUCIO    Thou conclud'st like the sanctimonious pirate
that went to sea with the Ten Commandments but
scraped one out of the table.                         9

SECOND GENTLEMAN    "Thou shalt not steal"?

LUCIO    Ay, that he razed.                            11

30 **belongings** attributes, endowments   31 **proper** exclusively
31–2 **as to . . . thee** that you can expend all your efforts developing
your own talents or use them solely for your own advantage.
33 **torches** (Compare Jesus' command that we not hide our light
under a bushel, Matthew 5:14–16.)   35 **forth of us** out of us and into
the world.   **'twere all alike** it would be exactly the same   36–7 **Spirits . . . issues** Souls are not deeply moved unless for noble purposes
38 **scruple** bit. (Literally, a small weight.)   39–41 **But . . . use** unless,
like a thrifty goddess, she gathers to herself the glory due to a creditor, gaining both thanks from her debtor and interest on the loan.
41 **bend** direct   42 **that . . . advertise** who understands and can
explain to others the authority that I am delegating to him as my substitute.   44 **In . . . ourself** During my absence be in every respect my
deputy. (The royal plural.)   45 **Mortality** The full rigor of the law,
the death sentence   47 **first in question** senior and first
appointed   49 **mettle** worth, quality. (With play on "metal," a common variant spelling, continued in the coining imagery of lines
50–1.)   52 **leavened** i.e., carefully considered (just as yeast is given
time to leaven dough)   54–5 **Our . . . itself** The cause for my hasty
departure is so urgent that it takes precedence over all other matters   55 **unquestioned** not yet considered   57 **concernings**
affairs.   **importune** urge   58 **look to know** expect to be informed

60–1 **To . . . commissions** to the carrying out of your assignments with
all hope of success.   61 **leave** permission   62 **bring you something**
accompany you for a short distance   63 **admit** permit   64–5 **have . . .
scruple** have the least doubt or hesitation about what is to be done.
68 **I'll privily away** I'll go away secretly.   69 **stage me** make a show of
myself   70 **do well** i.e., serves a political purpose   71 **aves** hails of
acclamation   72 **the man** any man.   **safe** sound   73 **affect** desire, court
75 **Lead** May the heavens conduct you   78 **free** frank   79 **the bottom of
my place** the extent of my commission.   84 **Touching** regarding
1.2. Location. A public place.
2 **composition** agreement   3 **fall upon** will attack   9 **table** tablet.
11 **razed** scraped out. (The word may also suggest *rased*, "erased.")

FIRST GENTLEMAN   Why, 'twas a commandment to command the captain and all the rest from their function; they put forth to steal. There's not a soldier of us all that, in the thanksgiving before meat, do relish the petition well that prays for peace. [14] [15]

SECOND GENTLEMAN   I never heard any soldier dislike it.

LUCIO   I believe thee, for I think thou never wast where grace was said.

SECOND GENTLEMAN   No? A dozen times at least.

FIRST GENTLEMAN   What, in meter?

LUCIO   In any proportion or in any language. [22]

FIRST GENTLEMAN   I think, or in any religion.

LUCIO   Ay, why not? Grace is grace, despite of all controversy; as, for example, thou thyself art a wicked villain, despite of all grace. [24] [25]

FIRST GENTLEMAN   Well, there went but a pair of shears between us. [27] [28]

LUCIO   I grant; as there may between the lists and the velvet. Thou art the list. [29] [30]

FIRST GENTLEMAN   And thou the velvet. Thou art good velvet; thou'rt a three-piled piece, I warrant thee. I had as lief be a list of an English kersey as be piled, as thou art piled, for a French velvet. Do I speak feelingly now? [32] [33] [34]

LUCIO   I think thou dost, and indeed with most painful feeling of thy speech. I will, out of thine own confession, learn to begin thy health, but, whilst I live, forget to drink after thee. [37] [38]

FIRST GENTLEMAN   I think I have done myself wrong, have I not? [39]

SECOND GENTLEMAN   Yes, that thou hast, whether thou art tainted or free. [42]

*Enter bawd [Mistress Overdone].*

LUCIO   Behold, behold, where Madam Mitigation comes! I have purchased as many diseases under her roof as come to— [43]

SECOND GENTLEMAN   To what, I pray?

LUCIO   Judge. [47]

SECOND GENTLEMAN   To three thousand dolors a year. [48]

FIRST GENTLEMAN   Ay, and more.

LUCIO   A French crown more. [50]

FIRST GENTLEMAN   Thou art always figuring diseases in me, but thou art full of error. I am sound. [51]

LUCIO   Nay, not, as one would say, healthy, but so sound as things that are hollow. Thy bones are hollow; impiety has made a feast of thee. [54] [55]

FIRST GENTLEMAN   [*to Mistress Overdone*]   How now, which of your hips has the most profound sciatica? [57]

MISTRESS OVERDONE   Well, well; there's one yonder arrested and carried to prison was worth five thousand of you all.

SECOND GENTLEMAN   Who's that, I pray thee?

MISTRESS OVERDONE   Marry, sir, that's Claudio, Signor Claudio. [62]

FIRST GENTLEMAN   Claudio to prison? 'Tis not so.

MISTRESS OVERDONE   Nay, but I know 'tis so. I saw him arrested, saw him carried away; and, which is more, within these three days his head to be chopped off. [66]

LUCIO   But, after all this fooling, I would not have it so. Art thou sure of this? [68]

MISTRESS OVERDONE   I am too sure of it; and it is for getting Madam Julietta with child.

LUCIO   Believe me, this may be. He promised to meet me two hours since, and he was ever precise in promise-keeping. [73]

SECOND GENTLEMAN   Besides, you know, it draws something near to the speech we had to such a purpose. [75] [76] [77]

FIRST GENTLEMAN   But most of all agreeing with the proclamation.

LUCIO   Away! Let's go learn the truth of it.
*Exit [Lucio with the Gentlemen].*

MISTRESS OVERDONE   Thus, what with the war, what with the sweat, what with the gallows, and what with poverty, I am custom-shrunk. [82] [83]

*Enter Clown [Pompey].*

How now, what's the news with you?

POMPEY   Yonder man is carried to prison.

MISTRESS OVERDONE   Well, what has he done? [86]

POMPEY   A woman.

MISTRESS OVERDONE   But what's his offense?

POMPEY   Groping for trouts in a peculiar river. [89]

---

**14 put forth** set out to sea   **15 thanksgiving before meat** saying of grace before a meal. (As in line 19.)   **22 proportion** form   **24–5 Grace . . . controversy** (Refers to the Catholic-Protestant *controversy*, line 25, as to whether humanity can be saved by works or by grace alone; with punning on *grace* as "thanks for a meal," line 19, and "gracefulness" or "becomingness," line 26.)   **27–8 there . . . between us** i.e., we're cut from the same cloth.   **29–30 as . . . list** (Lucio jokes that the shears might also cut between, i.e., distinguish between, the mere *lists* or selvages, edges of a woven fabric, and the *velvet* betokening a true gentlemen. Lucio wittily asserts himself to be a true gentleman; the other speaker, not.)   **32 three-piled** having a threefold pile or nap, the best grade. (Velvet patches might be used to conceal syphilitic sores or scars.)   **33 as lief** as soon, rather.   **kersey** a coarse woolen fabric. (The First Gentleman turns the joke on Lucio by saying he would rather be a plain, homespun Englishman than a Frenchified velvet gentleman in decay and threadbare. *Velvet* suggests prostitutes and venereal disease, as in the following notes.)   **be piled** (1) have a cloth nap (2) suffer from hemorrhoids (3) be pilled or peeled, i.e., hairless, bald, as a result of mercury treatment for syphilis (known as the "French disease"; see *French velvet* in the next line and *French crown*, line 50)   **34 feelingly** to the purpose, so as to hit home. (But Lucio's reply quibbles on "painfully," meaning the Gentleman's mouth is affected by the French disease; hence, Lucio will not drink from the same cup after him.)   **37 begin thy health** drink to your health   **37–8 forget . . . thee** take care not to drink from your cup.   **39 done myself wrong** i.e., asked for that   **42 tainted** infected   **43 Mitigation** (So called because her function is to relieve desire.)

**47 Judge** Guess.   **48 dolors** (Quibbling on *dollars*; spelled "Dollours" in the Folio.)   **50 French crown** (1) gold coin (2) bald head incurred through syphilis, the "French disease"   **51 figuring** (1) imagining (2) reckoning. (Recalling the monetary puns of lines 48 and 50.)   **54 sound** (1) healthy (2) resounding (because of hollow bones caused by syphilis)   **55 impiety** wickedness   **57 sciatica** a disease affecting the sciatic nerve in the hip and thigh, thought to be a symptom of syphilis.   **62 Marry** i.e., By the Virgin Mary   **66 which** what   **68 after** notwithstanding   **73 ever** always   **75–6 draws . . . near to** approaches, sounds somewhat like   **76–7 to . . . purpose** on that topic.   **82 sweat** sweating sickness (often fatal), or the plague; also, the sweating tub, a treatment for syphilis   **83 custom-shrunk** having fewer customers.   **86 done** (Pompey quibbles in line 87 on a sexual sense of the word, present also in Mistress Overdone's name.)   **89 peculiar** privately owned. (With bawdy suggestion.)

MISTRESS OVERDONE    What? Is there a maid with child
  by him?

POMPEY    No, but there's a woman with maid by him.    92
  You have not heard of the proclamation, have you?

MISTRESS OVERDONE    What proclamation, man?

POMPEY    All houses in the suburbs of Vienna must be    95
  plucked down.

MISTRESS OVERDONE    And what shall become of those
  in the city?

POMPEY    They shall stand for seed. They had gone    99
  down too, but that a wise burgher put in for them.    100

MISTRESS OVERDONE    But shall all our houses of resort
  in the suburbs be pulled down?

POMPEY    To the ground, mistress.

MISTRESS OVERDONE    Why, here's a change indeed in
  the commonwealth! What shall become of me?

POMPEY    Come, fear not you. Good counselors lack no    106
  clients. Though you change your place, you need not    107
  change your trade; I'll be your tapster still. Courage!    108
  There will be pity taken on you. You that have worn    109
  your eyes almost out in the service, you will be con-    110
  sidered.

MISTRESS OVERDONE    What's to do here, Thomas Tapster? Let's withdraw.

POMPEY    Here comes Signor Claudio, led by the Pro-    114
  vost to prison; and there's Madam Juliet.    *Exeunt.*    115

  *Enter Provost, Claudio, Juliet, Officers; Lucio*
  *and two Gentlemen [follow].*

CLAUDIO [*to the Provost*]
  Fellow, why dost thou show me thus to the world?
  Bear me to prison, where I am committed.

PROVOST
  I do it not in evil disposition,
  But from Lord Angelo by special charge.

CLAUDIO
  Thus can the demigod Authority
  Make us pay down for our offense, by weight,    121
  The words of heaven. On whom it will, it will;    122
  On whom it will not, so; yet still 'tis just.    123

LUCIO
  Why, how now, Claudio? Whence comes this
  restraint?

CLAUDIO
  From too much liberty, my Lucio, liberty.

As surfeit is the father of much fast,    126
So every scope, by the immoderate use,    127
Turns to restraint. Our natures do pursue,
Like rats that ravin down their proper bane,    129
A thirsty evil, and when we drink we die.

LUCIO    If I could speak so wisely under an arrest, I    131
  would send for certain of my creditors. And yet, to say    132
  the truth, I had as lief have the foppery of freedom as    133
  the morality of imprisonment. What's thy offense,
  Claudio?

CLAUDIO
  What but to speak of would offend again.

LUCIO
  What, is't murder?

CLAUDIO                        No.

LUCIO                                Lechery?

CLAUDIO
  Call it so.

PROVOST    Away, sir, you must go.

CLAUDIO
  One word, good friend.—Lucio, a word with you.

LUCIO
  A hundred, if they'll do you any good.
  Is lechery so looked after?    141

CLAUDIO
  Thus stands it with me: upon a true contract    142
  I got possession of Julietta's bed.
  You know the lady; she is fast my wife,    144
  Save that we do the denunciation lack    145
  Of outward order. This we came not to,    146
  Only for propagation of a dower    147
  Remaining in the coffer of her friends,    148
  From whom we thought it meet to hide our love    149
  Till time had made them for us. But it chances    150
  The stealth of our most mutual entertainment
  With character too gross is writ on Juliet.    152

LUCIO
  With child, perhaps?

CLAUDIO                        Unhappily, even so.
  And the new deputy now for the Duke—
  Whether it be the fault and glimpse of newness,    155
  Or whether that the body public be
  A horse whereon the governor doth ride,
  Who, newly in the seat, that it may know
  He can command, lets it straight feel the spur;    159

---

92 **woman with maid** (Pompey playfully corrects Mistress Overdone's use of the word "maid," joking that a pregnant woman cannot
be a virgin [maid] though the child she carries is one.)    95 **houses** i.e.,
brothels.    **suburbs** (Location of the brothels in Shakespeare's London, as in other walled cities.)    99 **for seed** to preserve the species.
(*Seed* also suggests "sperm.")    100 **burgher** citizen.    **put . . . them**
interceded on their behalf, offered to acquire them.    106–7 **Good . . .
clients** Good lawyers (and, by implication, pimps and bawds) are
never at a loss for clients.    108 **tapster** one who serves beer in an
alehouse    109–10 **worn . . . out** i.e., worked so hard. (Perhaps with an
ironic reference to the traditional image of the blind Cupid, often
depicted on signs hung at the doors of brothels.)    114–15 **Provost**
officer charged with apprehension, custody, and punishment of
offenders    121–2 **Make . . . heaven** make us pay the full penalty for
our offenses in obedience to divine command.    122–3 **On whom . . .
'tis just** (Compare Romans 9:18: "Therefore hath he [God] mercy on
whom he will have mercy, and whom he will he hardeneth.")

126 **As . . . fast** Just as excessive indulgence inevitably leads to revulsion and abstinence    127 **scope** liberty, license    129 **ravin . . . bane**
greedily devour what is poisonous to them    131–2 **If . . . creditors** If
imprisonment would gain me such wisdom, I would send for those
to whom I owe money and thus be arrested for debt. (But then Lucio
concedes that he cherishes his licentious freedom too much to do any
such thing as willingly submit to arrest.)    133 **lief** willingly.    **foppery**
folly    141 **looked after** kept under observation.    142 **a true contract**
i.e., one made in the presence of witnesses, though without a religious
ceremony. (Such a precontract was binding but, in the eyes of the
Church, did not confer the right of sexual consummation before the
nuptials.)    144 **fast my wife** my wife in all but as formalized by religious ritual    145 **denunciation** formal declaration    146 **outward order**
public ceremony.    147 **propagation** increase, begetting    148 **friends**
relatives    149 **meet** fitting, necessary    150 **made . . . us** disposed them
in our favor.    152 **character too gross** writing too evident    155 **the
fault . . . newness** the excessive zeal that sometimes is shown by persons newly in a place of authority    159 **straight** at once

Whether the tyranny be in his place,                    160
Or in his eminence that fills it up,                     161
I stagger in—but this new governor                       162
Awakes me all the enrollèd penalties                     163
Which have, like unscoured armor, hung by the wall
So long that nineteen zodiacs have gone round            165
And none of them been worn; and for a name               166
Now puts the drowsy and neglected act
Freshly on me. 'Tis surely for a name.

LUCIO    I warrant it is, and thy head stands so tickle on   169
thy shoulders that a milkmaid, if she be in love, may
sigh it off. Send after the Duke and appeal to him.

CLAUDIO
I have done so, but he's not to be found.
I prithee, Lucio, do me this kind service:
This day my sister should the cloister enter             174
And there receive her approbation.                       175
Acquaint her with the danger of my state;
Implore her, in my voice, that she make friends          177
To the strict deputy; bid herself assay him.             178
I have great hope in that, for in her youth
There is a prone and speechless dialect                  180
Such as move men; beside, she hath prosperous art        181
When she will play with reason and discourse,            182
And well she can persuade.                               183

LUCIO    I pray she may, as well for the encouragement of   184
the like, which else would stand under grievous impo-    185
sition, as for the enjoying of thy life, who I would     186
be sorry should be thus foolishly lost at a game of tick-  187
tack. I'll to her.                                       188

CLAUDIO    I thank you, good friend Lucio.

LUCIO    Within two hours.

CLAUDIO    Come, officer, away!                *Exeunt.*

❧

# [1.3]

*Enter Duke and Friar Thomas.*

DUKE
No, holy Father, throw away that thought;
Believe not that the dribbling dart of love              2
Can pierce a complete bosom. Why I desire thee           3
To give me secret harbor hath a purpose                  4
More grave and wrinkled than the aims and ends           5
Of burning youth.

FRIAR THOMAS            May Your Grace speak of it?

DUKE
My holy sir, none better knows than you
How I have ever loved the life removed                   8
And held in idle price to haunt assemblies               9
Where youth and cost witless bravery keeps.              10
I have delivered to Lord Angelo,
A man of stricture and firm abstinence,                  12
My absolute power and place here in Vienna,
And he supposes me traveled to Poland;
For so I have strewed it in the common ear,
And so it is received. Now, pious sir,
You will demand of me why I do this.

FRIAR THOMAS    Gladly, my lord.

DUKE
We have strict statutes and most biting laws,
The needful bits and curbs to headstrong steeds,         20
Which for this fourteen years we have let slip,          21
Even like an o'ergrown lion in a cave                    22
That goes not out to prey. Now, as fond fathers,         23
Having bound up the threat'ning twigs of birch
Only to stick it in their children's sight
For terror, not to use, in time the rod
Becomes more mocked than feared, so our decrees,
Dead to infliction, to themselves are dead;              28
And liberty plucks justice by the nose,                  29
The baby beats the nurse, and quite athwart              30
Goes all decorum.

FRIAR THOMAS            It rested in Your Grace            31
To unloose this tied-up justice when you pleased;
And it in you more dreadful would have seemed
Than in Lord Angelo.

DUKE                    I do fear, too dreadful.
Sith 'twas my fault to give the people scope,            35
'Twould be my tyranny to strike and gall them            36
For what I bid them do; for we bid this be done          37
When evil deeds have their permissive pass               38
And not the punishment. Therefore indeed, my father,
I have on Angelo imposed the office,                     40
Who may in th'ambush of my name strike home,             41
And yet my nature never in the fight                     42
To do in slander. And to behold his sway                 43
I will, as 'twere a brother of your order,
Visit both prince and people. Therefore, I prithee,
Supply me with the habit, and instruct me                46
How I may formally in person bear                        47

---

160 **in his place** inherent in the office    161 **his eminence** the eminence of him    162 **I stagger in** I am uncertain    163 **Awakes me** i.e.,
awakes, activates. (*Me* is used colloquially.)    **enrollèd** written on a
roll or deed    165 **zodiacs** i.e., years    166 **for a name** in order to gain a
reputation for severity    169 **tickle** uncertain, unstable    174 **cloister** i.e.,
convent    175 **approbation** novitiate, period of probation.    177 **in my
voice** on my behalf    178 **To** with.    **assay** try, test    180 **prone** eager,
apt, supplicating.    **dialect** language    181–3 **she . . . persuade** she has
great skill when she undertakes to use the arts of reasonable discourse
and rhetorical persuasion.    184–6 **I pray . . . life** i.e., I pray she
may be persuasive both in encouraging lax enforcement of Vienna's
anti-fornication laws, which would otherwise subject us all to grievous
penalties, and in pleading for your life    187–8 **tick-tack** a form of back-
gammon in which pegs were fitted into holes. (Here applied bawdily.)
**1.3. Location: A friary.**
2 **dribbling** falling short or wide of the mark    3 **complete** perfect,
whole, strong    4 **harbor** concealment    5 **wrinkled** i.e., mature

8 **removed** retired    9 **held . . . price** held it unprofitable    10 **Where
. . . keeps** where youth and costly expenditure put themselves foolishly on display.    12 **stricture** strictness    20 **steeds** (The Folio reading, "weedes," is possible in the sense of "lawless and uncontrolled
impulses.")    21 **fourteen** (Claudio mentions nineteen years at
1.2.165; possibly the compositor confused *xiv* and *xix*.)    22 **o'ergrown**
too old and large    23 **fond** doting    28 **Dead to infliction** dead in
that they are not enforced    29 **liberty** license    30 **athwart** wrongly,
awry    31 **decorum** social order.    **It rested . . . Grace** It lay in your
ducal authority, was incumbent on you    35 **Sith** Since    36 **gall**
chafe, injure    37 **we . . . done** i.e., we virtually order a crime to be
committed    38 **pass** sanction    40 **office** duty    41 **Who . . . home**
who may, under cover of my ducal authority, strike to the heart of
the matter    42 **nature** i.e., personal identity (as distinguished from
official capacity)    43 **do in slander** act so as to invite slander (for
being too repressive).    **sway** rule    46 **habit** garment (of a friar)
47 **formally** in outward appearance.    **bear** bear myself

Like a true friar. More reasons for this action
At our more leisure shall I render you.                                    49
Only this one: Lord Angelo is precise,                                     50
Stands at a guard with envy, scarce confesses                              51
That his blood flows or that his appetite                                  52
Is more to bread than stone. Hence shall we see,                           53
If power change purpose, what our seemers be.
*Exeunt.*

❦

# [1.4]

*Enter Isabella and Francisca, a nun.*

**ISABELLA**
And have you nuns no farther privileges?
**FRANCISCA**    Are not these large enough?
**ISABELLA**
Yes, truly. I speak not as desiring more,
But rather wishing a more strict restraint
Upon the sisterhood, the votarists of Saint Clare.                          5
**LUCIO**    (*within*)
Ho! Peace be in this place!
**ISABELLA**                            Who's that which calls?
**FRANCISCA**
It is a man's voice. Gentle Isabella,
Turn you the key, and know his business of him.
You may, I may not; you are yet unsworn.                                     9
When you have vowed, you must not speak with men
But in the presence of the prioress;
Then if you speak you must not show your face,
Or if you show your face you must not speak.
He calls again. I pray you, answer him.             [*Exit.*]
**ISABELLA**
Peace and prosperity! Who is 't that calls?

[*She opens the door. Enter Lucio.*]

**LUCIO**
Hail, virgin, if you be, as those cheek roses              16
Proclaim you are no less. Can you so stead me             17
As bring me to the sight of Isabella,                     18
A novice of this place, and the fair sister              19
To her unhappy brother Claudio?                          20
**ISABELLA**
Why "her unhappy brother"? Let me ask,
The rather for I now must make you know                    22
I am that Isabella, and his sister.
**LUCIO**
Gentle and fair, your brother kindly greets you.
Not to be weary with you, he's in prison.                 25

49 **more** greater   50 **precise** strict, puritanical   51 **Stands . . . envy**
guards himself severely against calumny   52–3 **or . . . stone** or that
he has an appetite for bread (i.e., food or physical pleasure) any more
than if it were stone. (See Matthew 4.3, where the devil tempts Jesus
to turn stone into bread.)
**1.4. Location: A convent.**
5 **votarists of Saint Clare** An order founded in 1212 by Saint Francis
of Assisi and Saint Clare; its members were enjoined to a life of poverty, service, and contemplation.   9 **you . . . unsworn** i.e., you have
not yet taken your formal vows to enter the convent.   16 **cheek**
**roses** i.e., blushes   17 **stead** help   18 **As** as to   19 **fair** beautiful
20 **unhappy** unfortunate   22 **The rather for** the more so because
25 **weary** tedious

**ISABELLA**    Woe me! For what?
**LUCIO**
For that which, if myself might be his judge,
He should receive his punishment in thanks:
He hath got his friend with child.
**ISABELLA**
Sir, make me not your story.
**LUCIO**                            'Tis true.                              30
I would not—though 'tis my familiar sin                   31
With maids to seem the lapwing, and to jest,              32
Tongue far from heart—play with all virgins so.
I hold you as a thing enskied and sainted                 34
By your renouncement, an immortal spirit
And to be talked with in sincerity
As with a saint.
**ISABELLA**
You do blaspheme the good in mocking me.                   38
**LUCIO**
Do not believe it. Fewness and truth, 'tis thus:          39
Your brother and his lover have embraced.
As those that feed grow full, as blossoming time          41
That from the seedness the bare fallow brings             42
To teeming foison, even so her plenteous womb             43
Expresseth his full tilth and husbandry.                  44
**ISABELLA**
Someone with child by him? My cousin Juliet?
**LUCIO**    Is she your cousin?
**ISABELLA**
Adoptedly, as schoolmaids change their names              47
By vain though apt affection.
**LUCIO**                            She it is.                             48
**ISABELLA**
Oh, let him marry her.
**LUCIO**                            This is the point.
The Duke is very strangely gone from hence;
Bore many gentlemen, myself being one,                    51
In hand and hope of action; but we do learn,              52
By those that know the very nerves of state,
His givings-out were of an infinite distance              54
From his true-meant design. Upon his place,               55
And with full line of his authority,                      56
Governs Lord Angelo, a man whose blood
Is very snow broth; one who never feels                   58
The wanton stings and motions of the sense,               59
But doth rebate and blunt his natural edge                60

30 **story** subject for mirth.   31 **familiar** customary; cheeky   32 **lapwing**
peewit or plover. (The lapwing runs away from its nest in order to
draw away enemies from its young, much as Lucio throws up smoke-
screens in his seductive talk with young women.)   34 **enskied** placed
in heaven   38 **You . . . me** You blaspheme goodness itself when you
mockingly praise me, unworthy as I am, for saintliness.   39 **it** i.e.,
that I am mocking.   **Fewness and truth** In few words and truly
41–3 **As . . . foison** Just as the season of blossoming brings the sowing
of the bare untilled land to teeming fruitfulness   44 **Expresseth . . .**
**husbandry** makes plainly visible Claudio's tilling of the crop, i.e., his
plowing and fertilizing Juliet's body.   47 **change** exchange   48 **vain**
**though apt** girlish though natural and suitable   51–2 **Bore . . . action**
i.e., he misleadingly kept us in expectation of some military action
54 **givings-out** public statements   55 **Upon** In   56 **line** extent
58 **snow broth** melted snow (i.e., ice water)   59 **motions . . . sense**
promptings of sexual desire   60 **But . . . edge** but dulls and blunts
the sharp desire of sexuality

With profits of the mind, study, and fast.
He—to give fear to use and liberty, 62
Which have for long run by the hideous law 63
As mice by lions—hath picked out an act,
Under whose heavy sense your brother's life 65
Falls into forfeit. He arrests him on it
And follows close the rigor of the statute
To make him an example. All hope is gone,
Unless you have the grace by your fair prayer
To soften Angelo. And that's my pith of business 70
Twixt you and your poor brother.

ISABELLA                   Doth he so
Seek his life?

LUCIO          He's censured him already, 72
And, as I hear, the Provost hath a warrant
For 's execution.

ISABELLA         Alas, what poor
Ability's in me to do him good?

LUCIO    Assay the power you have. 76

ISABELLA
My power? Alas, I doubt.

LUCIO              Our doubts are traitors,
And makes us lose the good we oft might win, 78
By fearing to attempt. Go to Lord Angelo,
And let him learn to know, when maidens sue
Men give like gods, but when they weep and kneel,
All their petitions are as freely theirs 82
As they themselves would owe them. 83

ISABELLA    I'll see what I can do.

LUCIO    But speedily.

ISABELLA    I will about it straight,
No longer staying but to give the Mother 87
Notice of my affair. I humbly thank you. 88
Commend me to my brother. Soon at night 89
I'll send him certain word of my success. 90

LUCIO
I take my leave of you.

ISABELLA          Good sir, adieu.

                       *Exeunt [separately].*

❖

# 2.1

*Enter Angelo, Escalus, and servants, [a] Justice.*

ANGELO
We must not make a scarecrow of the law,
Setting it up to fear the birds of prey, 2
And let it keep one shape till custom make it 3
Their perch and not their terror.

ESCALUS           Ay, but yet
Let us be keen and rather cut a little 5

---

Than fall and bruise to death. Alas, this gentleman 6
Whom I would save had a most noble father!
Let but Your Honor know, 8
Whom I believe to be most strait in virtue, 9
That, in the working of your own affections, 10
Had time cohered with place, or place with wishing,
Or that the resolute acting of your blood 12
Could have attained th'effect of your own purpose, 13
Whether you had not sometime in your life 14
Erred in this point which now you censure him, 15
And pulled the law upon you.

ANGELO
'Tis one thing to be tempted, Escalus,
Another thing to fall. I not deny
The jury, passing on the prisoner's life,
May in the sworn twelve have a thief or two
Guiltier than him they try. What's open made to
    justice, 21
That justice seizes. What knows the laws 22
That thieves do pass on thieves? 'Tis very pregnant, 23
The jewel that we find, we stoop and take't
Because we see it; but what we do not see
We tread upon and never think of it.
You may not so extenuate his offense
For I have had such faults; but rather tell me, 28
When I that censure him do so offend,
Let mine own judgment pattern out my death 30
And nothing come in partial. Sir, he must die. 31

*Enter Provost.*

ESCALUS
Be it as your wisdom will.

ANGELO           Where is the Provost?

PROVOST
Here, if it like Your Honor.

ANGELO         See that Claudio 33
Be executed by nine tomorrow morning.
Bring him his confessor; let him be prepared.
For that's the utmost of his pilgrimage. 36

                    *[Exit Provost.]*

ESCALUS
Well, heaven forgive him, and forgive us all!
Some rise by sin, and some by virtue fall; 38
Some run from breaks of ice and answer none, 39
And some condemnèd for a fault alone. 40

*Enter Elbow, Froth, Clown [Pompey], officers.*

---

62 **use and liberty** habitual licentiousness   63 **run by** run around or away from   65 **heavy sense** severe interpretation   70 **my pith of business** the essence of my business   72 **censured** sentenced   76 **Assay** Try   78 **makes** make   82 **their petitions** i.e., the things the maidens ask for   83 **As . . . them** as they themselves would wish to have them. 87 **but** than.   **Mother** Mother Superior, prioress   88 **affair** business. 89 **Soon at night** Early tonight   90 **my success** how I have succeeded. 2.1. **Location: A court of justice.** 2 **fear** frighten   3 **And . . . shape** and let it remain motionless, like a scarecrow that ceases to frighten crows because it is so inert   5 **keen** sharp

6 **fall** let fall heavily.   **bruise** i.e., crush   8 **know** consider   9 **strait** strict   10 **affections** desires   12–13 **Or . . . purpose** or if the passionate strength of your sexual longing could have led you to achieve the fulfillment of that desire   14 **had** would have.   **sometime** on some occasion   15 **censure him** sentence Claudio for   21–2 **What's . . . seizes** The law concerns itself specifically with the issues that are brought before it.   22–3 **What knows . . . thieves?** i.e., Why should we waste time wondering what laws thieves would pass upon other thieves? That is not what law is for.   23 **pregnant** clear   28 **For** because   30–1 **Let . . . partial** let the sentence I have imposed serve as a model in sentencing me if I commit a crime, no partiality or extenuating circumstances being admitted.   33 **like** please   36 **that's . . . pilgrimage** that's the furthest point of his life's journey.   38 **Some . . . fall** Sometimes sinners prosper while the virtuous suffer   39 **Some . . . none** some break the ice repeatedly (i.e., commit serious infractions of the law) and yet escape punishment. (A famous crux; the Folio reads "brakes of Ice.")   40 **a fault alone** one single minor infraction.

ELBOW   Come, bring them away. If these be good 41
people in a commonweal that do nothing but use their 42
abuses in common houses, I know no law. Bring them 43
away.

ANGELO   How now, sir, what's your name? And what's
the matter?

ELBOW   If it please Your Honor, I am the poor Duke's 47
constable, and my name is Elbow. I do lean upon 48
justice, sir, and do bring in here before Your good Honor
two notorious benefactors.

ANGELO   Benefactors? Well, what benefactors are they?
Are they not malefactors?

ELBOW   If it please Your Honor, I know not well what
they are; but precise villains they are, that I am sure of, 54
and void of all profanation in the world that good 55
Christians ought to have.

ESCALUS   [*to Angelo*]   This comes off well. Here's a
wise officer.

ANGELO   Go to. What quality are they of?—Elbow is 59
your name? Why dost thou not speak, Elbow?

POMPEY   He cannot, sir; he's out at elbow. 61

ANGELO   What are you, sir?

ELBOW   He, sir? A tapster, sir, parcel-bawd, one that 63
serves a bad woman, whose house, sir, was, as they
say, plucked down in the suburbs; and now she
professes a hothouse, which I think is a very ill house 66
too.

ESCALUS   How know you that?

ELBOW   My wife, sir, whom I detest before heaven and 69
Your Honor—

ESCALUS   How? Thy wife?

ELBOW   Ay, sir; whom I thank heaven is an honest
woman—

ESCALUS   Dost thou detest her therefore?

ELBOW   I say, sir, I will detest myself also, as well as
she, that this house, if it be not a bawd's house, it is
pity of her life, for it is a naughty house. 77

ESCALUS   How dost thou know that, Constable?

ELBOW   Marry, sir, by my wife, who, if she had been a
woman cardinally given, might have been accused in 80
fornication, adultery, and all uncleanliness there.

ESCALUS   By the woman's means?

ELBOW   Ay, sir, by Mistress Overdone's means; but
as she spit in his face, so she defied him. 84

POMPEY   Sir, if it please Your Honor, this is not so.

ELBOW   Prove it before these varlets here, thou honor- 86
able man, prove it. 87

ESCALUS   [*to Angelo*]   Do you hear how he misplaces?

POMPEY   Sir, she came in great with child, and longing,
saving Your Honor's reverence, for stewed prunes. Sir, 90
we had but two in the house, which at that very
distant time stood, as it were, in a fruit dish, a 92
dish of some threepence. Your Honors have seen
such dishes; they are not China dishes, but very good
dishes—

ESCALUS   Go to, go to. No matter for the dish, sir.

POMPEY   No, indeed, sir, not of a pin; you are therein 97
in the right. But to the point. As I say, this Mistress
Elbow, being, as I say, with child, and being great-
bellied, and longing, as I said, for prunes; and having
but two in the dish, as I said, Master Froth here, this
very man, having eaten the rest, as I said, and, as I
say, paying for them very honestly—for, as you
know, Master Froth, I could not give you threepence
again. 105

FROTH   No, indeed.

POMPEY   Very well. You being then, if you be
remembered, cracking the stones of the foresaid 108
prunes—

FROTH   Ay, so I did indeed.

POMPEY   Why, very well; I telling you then, if you be
remembered, that such a one and such a one were
past cure of the thing you wot of, unless they kept 113
very good diet, as I told you— 114

FROTH   All this is true.

POMPEY   Why, very well, then—

ESCALUS   Come, you are a tedious fool. To the purpose.
What was done to Elbow's wife, that he hath cause to
complain of? Come me to what was done to her. 119

POMPEY   Sir, Your Honor cannot come to that yet.

ESCALUS   No, sir, nor I mean it not.

POMPEY   Sir, but you shall come to it, by Your Honor's
leave. And, I beseech you, look into Master Froth here,
sir, a man of fourscore pound a year, whose father 124
died at Hallowmas.—Was 't not at Hallowmas, Mas- 125
ter Froth?

FROTH   All-hallond eve. 127

POMPEY   Why, very well. I hope here be truths. He, sir,
sitting, as I say, in a lower chair, sir—'twas in the 129
Bunch of Grapes, where indeed you have a delight to 130
sit, have you not?

---

**41 away** along.   **42–3 use . . . houses** practice their vices in bawdy
houses   **47 poor Duke's** i.e., Duke's poor   **48 lean upon** rely on,
appeal to. (With an unintended comic reference to the idea of leaning
on one's elbow.)   **54 precise** complete. (Or perhaps a blunder for
"precious." *Precise* unintentionally recalls the description of Angelo
as *precise*, i.e., strict or puritanical, at 1.3.50.)   **55 profanation** (A
blunder for "profession," or a word meaning "irreverence" where
Elbow intends "reverence." Elbow already has used several mala-
propisms, including *lean upon, benefactors,* and *precise.*)   **59 Go to** An
expression of impatience or reproof.   **quality** social standing, occupation   **61 out at elbow** (1) impoverished, threadbare, hence without
any ideas (2) missing his cue, i.e., at a loss for words after being called
by his name.   **63 parcel-bawd** part-time bawd (and part-time tapster)   **66 professes a hothouse** professes to run a bathhouse
**69 detest** (For "protest.")   **77 pity of her life** a great pity.   **naughty**
wicked   **80 cardinally** (For "carnally.")   **given** inclined   **84 she spit
. . . face** Elbow's wife spat in the face of Pompey (who, as pimp, was
acting as Mistress Overdone's *means,* line 83).

**86–7 varlets . . . honorable** (Elbow reverses or *misplaces* these epithets.)   **90 saving . . . reverence** i.e., begging your pardon for what
I'm about to say.   **stewed prunes** (Commonly served in houses of
prostitution, or *stews,* and therefore suggesting prostitutes. The dialogue throughout is sexually suggestive.)   **92 distant** (Blunder for
"instant"?)   **97 a pin** i.e., an insignificant trifle   **105 again** back.
**108 stones** pits. (With suggestion also of "testicles.")   **113 the thing . . .
of** you know what I mean (i.e., venereal disease)   **114 diet** strict regimen prescribed for medical treatment   **119 Come me** i.e., Come. (*Me*
is used colloquially. Pompey makes a vulgar joke on the words *come*
and *done;* see note at line 140.)   **124 of . . . year** i.e., well off
**125 Hallowmas** All Saints' Day, November 1   **127 All-hallond eve**
Halloween, October 31.   **129 a lower chair** i.e., an easy chair (?)
**130 Bunch of Grapes** (It was not uncommon to designate particular
rooms in inns by such names.)

FROTH    I have so, because it is an open room and good 132
for winter.

POMPEY    Why, very well, then. I hope here be truths.

ANGELO
This will last out a night in Russia,
When nights are longest there. I'll take my leave
And leave you to the hearing of the cause,                           137
Hoping you'll find good cause to whip them all.

ESCALUS
I think no less. Good morrow to Your Lordship.                       139
                                                    Exit [Angelo].
Now, sir, come on. What was done to Elbow's wife,                    140
once more?

POMPEY    Once, sir? There was nothing done to her
once.                                                                143

ELBOW    I beseech you, sir, ask him what this man did
to my wife.

POMPEY    I beseech Your Honor, ask me.

ESCALUS    Well, sir, what did this gentleman to her?

POMPEY    I beseech you, sir, look in this gentleman's
face. Good Master Froth, look upon His Honor; 'tis for
a good purpose. Doth Your Honor mark his face?                       150

ESCALUS    Ay, sir, very well.

POMPEY    Nay, I beseech you, mark it well.

ESCALUS    Well, I do so.

POMPEY    Doth Your Honor see any harm in his face?

ESCALUS    Why, no.

POMPEY    I'll be supposed upon a book, his face is the 156
worst thing about him. Good, then; if his face be the
worst thing about him, how could Master Froth do the
Constable's wife any harm? I would know that of Your
Honor.

ESCALUS    He's in the right, Constable. What say you
to it?

ELBOW    First, an it like you, the house is a respected 163
house; next, this is a respected fellow; and his mistress
is a respected woman.

POMPEY    By this hand, sir, his wife is a more respected
person than any of us all.

ELBOW    Varlet, thou liest! Thou liest, wicked varlet! The
time is yet to come that she was ever respected with
man, woman, or child.

POMPEY    Sir, she was respected with him before he
married with her.

ESCALUS    Which is the wiser here, Justice or Iniquity?— 173
Is this true?

ELBOW    O thou caitiff! O thou varlet! O thou wicked 175
Hannibal! I respected with her before I was married 176
to her?—If ever I was respected with her, or she with
me, let not Your Worship think me the poor Duke's

officer.—Prove this, thou wicked Hannibal, or I'll
have mine action of battery on thee.                                 180

ESCALUS    If he took you a box o'th'ear, you might have 181
your action of slander too.

ELBOW    Marry, I thank Your good Worship for it. What
is't Your Worship's pleasure I shall do with this
wicked caitiff?

ESCALUS    Truly, officer, because he hath some offenses
in him that thou wouldst discover if thou couldst, let 187
him continue in his courses till thou know'st what 188
they are.

ELBOW    Marry, I thank Your Worship for it.—Thou see'st,
thou wicked varlet, now, what's come upon thee: thou
art to continue now, thou varlet, thou art to continue. 192

ESCALUS    [to Froth]    Where were you born, friend?

FROTH    Here in Vienna, sir.

ESCALUS    Are you of fourscore pounds a year?                       195

FROTH    Yes, an't please you, sir.

ESCALUS    So. [To Pompey] What trade are you of, sir?

POMPEY    A tapster, a poor widow's tapster.

ESCALUS    Your mistress' name?

POMPEY    Mistress Overdone.

ESCALUS    Hath she had any more than one husband?

POMPEY    Nine, sir. Overdone by the last.                          202

ESCALUS    Nine?—Come hither to me, Master Froth.
Master Froth, I would not have you acquainted with
tapsters. They will draw you, Master Froth, and you 205
will hang them. Get you gone, and let me hear no 206
more of you.

FROTH    I thank Your Worship. For mine own part, I
never come into any room in a taphouse but I am 209
drawn in.                                                            210

ESCALUS    Well, no more of it, Master Froth. Farewell.
                                                    [Exit Froth.]
Come you hither to me, Master Tapster. What's your
name, Master Tapster?

POMPEY    Pompey.

ESCALUS    What else?

POMPEY    Bum, sir.

ESCALUS    Troth, and your bum is the greatest thing
about you, so that in the beastliest sense you are Pompey the Great. Pompey, you are partly a bawd, Pompey, howsoever you color it in being a tapster, are you 220
not? Come, tell me true. It shall be the better for you.

POMPEY    Truly, sir, I am a poor fellow that would live.

ESCALUS    How would you live, Pompey? By being a 223
bawd? What do you think of the trade, Pompey? Is
it a lawful trade?

POMPEY    If the law would allow it, sir.

---

132 **open** public    137 **cause** case. (With word play on *cause*, "reason,"
in the next line. See also the play on *leave* in 136–7.)    139 **I . . . less** I
think so, too.    140 **done** (Pompey, in his answer, uses *done* in a sexual
sense.)    143 **once** only once. (Pompey replies wittily to Escalus's *once
more* in 141, meaning "once again.")    150 **mark** observe    156 **supposed**
(A malapropism for "deposed," i.e., sworn.)    **book** i.e., Bible
163 **an it like** if it please.    **respected** (For "suspected.")    173 **Justice
or Iniquity** (Personified characters in a morality play.)    175 **caitiff**
knave, villain.    176 **Hannibal** (A blunder for "cannibal," perhaps
also suggested by the fact that Hannibal and Pompey were both
famous generals in the classical world.)

180 **battery** (An error for "slander," as Escalus amusedly points
out.)    181 **took** gave.    **o'** on    187 **discover** (1) detect (2) reveal
188 **courses** courses of action    192 **continue** (Elbow may confuse the
word with its opposite.)    195 **of** possessed of    202 **Overdone . . . last**
(1) Her name, Overdone, was given her by her last husband (2) She
has been worn out (*overdone*) by the last one.    205 **draw** (1) cheat,
take in (2) empty, deplete. (With a pun on the tapster's trade of drawing liquor from a barrel, and on Froth's name.) (3) disembowel, or
drag to execution    206 **will hang them** will be the cause of their
hanging.    209 **taphouse** alehouse    210 **drawn in** enticed. (Still
another meaning of *draw,* line 205.)    220 **color** disguise    223 **live**
make a living

ESCALUS   But the law will not allow it, Pompey; nor it shall not be allowed in Vienna.

POMPEY   Does Your Worship mean to geld and splay all 229 the youth of the city?

ESCALUS   No, Pompey.

POMPEY   Truly, sir, in my poor opinion they will to't then. If Your Worship will take order for the drabs and 233 the knaves, you need not to fear the bawds.

ESCALUS   There is pretty orders beginning, I can tell you. It is but heading and hanging. 236

POMPEY   If you head and hang all that offend that way but for ten year together, you'll be glad to give out a 238 commission for more heads. If this law hold in Vienna 239 ten year, I'll rent the fairest house in it after threepence 240 a bay. If you live to see this come to pass, say Pompey 241 told you so.

ESCALUS   Thank you, good Pompey. And, in requital of 243 your prophecy, hark you: I advise you let me not find you before me again upon any complaint whatsoever; no, not for dwelling where you do. If I do, Pompey, I shall beat you to your tent and prove a shrewd Caesar 247 to you; in plain dealing, Pompey, I shall have you whipped. So for this time, Pompey, fare you well.

POMPEY   I thank Your Worship for your good counsel. [*Aside*] But I shall follow it as the flesh and fortune shall better determine.

Whip me? No, no, let carman whip his jade. 253
The valiant heart's not whipped out of his trade. 254

                             *Exit.*

ESCALUS   Come hither to me, Master Elbow; come hither, Master Constable. How long have you been in this place of constable?

ELBOW   Seven year and a half, sir.

ESCALUS   I thought, by the readiness in the office, you 259 had continued in it some time. You say, seven years together?

ELBOW   And a half, sir.

ESCALUS   Alas, it hath been great pains to you. They do you wrong to put you so oft upon't. Are there not 264 men in your ward sufficient to serve it? 265

ELBOW   Faith, sir, few of any wit in such matters. As they are chosen, they are glad to choose me for them. 267 I do it for some piece of money and go through with 268 all. 269

ESCALUS   Look you bring me in the names of some six 270 or seven, the most sufficient of your parish.

ELBOW   To Your Worship's house, sir?

ESCALUS   To my house. Fare you well.    [*Exit Elbow.*]
What's o'clock, think you?

JUSTICE   Eleven, sir.

ESCALUS   I pray you home to dinner with me. 276

JUSTICE   I humbly thank you.

ESCALUS
It grieves me for the death of Claudio;
But there's no remedy.

JUSTICE   Lord Angelo is severe.

ESCALUS                           It is but needful.
Mercy is not itself, that oft looks so; 281
Pardon is still the nurse of second woe. 282
But yet—poor Claudio! There is no remedy.
Come, sir.                          *Exeunt.*

❖

## 2.2

*Enter Provost [and a] Servant.*

SERVANT
He's hearing of a cause; he will come straight. 1
I'll tell him of you.

PROVOST          Pray you, do.     [*Exit Servant.*]
                         I'll know 2
His pleasure; maybe he will relent. Alas, 3
He hath but as offended in a dream! 4
All sects, all ages smack of this vice—and he 5
To die for't!

      *Enter Angelo.*

ANGELO       Now, what's the matter, Provost?

PROVOST
Is it your will Claudio shall die tomorrow?

ANGELO
Did not I tell thee yea? Hadst thou not order?
Why dost thou ask again?

PROVOST   Lest I might be too rash.
Under your good correction, I have seen 11
When, after execution, judgment hath
Repented o'er his doom. 13

ANGELO   Go to; let that be mine. 14
Do you your office, or give up your place,
And you shall well be spared. 16

PROVOST   I crave Your Honor's pardon.
What shall be done, sir, with the groaning Juliet? 18
She's very near her hour.

ANGELO          Dispose of her 19
To some more fitter place, and that with speed.

      [*Enter a Servant.*]

---

229 **splay** spay   233 **take order** take measures.  **drabs** prostitutes 236 **It . . . hanging** Beheading and hanging are the order of the day.  238 **year together** years at a stretch  239 **commission** order.  **hold** remain in force  240 **fairest** handsomest.  **after** at the rate of  241 **bay** division of a house included under one gable.  243 **requital of** return for  247 **shrewd** harsh, severe.  **Caesar** (Julius Caesar defeated Pompey the Great at Pharsalia in 48 B.C.)  253 **carman** cart driver.  **jade** broken-down horse.  254 **The valiant . . . trade** A valiant young man cannot be deterred from an occupation like pimping merely by fear of a whipping.  259 **readiness** proficiency, alacrity 264 **to put . . . upon't** to impose this task on you so many times. 265 **sufficient** able  267 **for them** i.e., to take their place.  268–9 **go . . . all** i.e., perform my duties thoroughly.  270 **Look** See to it that

276 **dinner** (Dinner was customarily eaten just before midday.) 281 **Mercy . . . so** i.e., What seems merciful may not really be so (since it may encourage crime and hence lead to more punishment) 282 **Pardon . . . woe** i.e., pardon continually nurtures and encourages a repetition of offenses and hence of punishment.
**2.2. Location: Adjacent to the court of justice, perhaps at Angelo's official residence.**
1 **hearing . . . cause** listening to a case.  **straight** immediately. 2–3 **I'll know . . . pleasure** I'll see what he wants to do.  **4 He . . . dream** i.e., Claudio offended without intending harm.  **5 All sects . . . smack** All classes of people of all ages (and in all past history) partake  **11 Under . . . correction** i.e., Allow me to say  **13 doom** sentence.  **14 mine** my business.  **16 well be spared** easily be done without.  **18 groaning** (with labor pains)  **19 hour** time of delivery.

SERVANT
    Here is the sister of the man condemned
    Desires access to you.
ANGELO                              Hath he a sister?                    22
PROVOST
    Ay, my good lord, a very virtuous maid,
    And to be shortly of a sisterhood,
    If not already.
ANGELO            Well, let her be admitted.
                                    [*Exit Servant.*]
    See you the fornicatress be removed.
    Let her have needful but not lavish means.
    There shall be order for't.

    *Enter Lucio and Isabella.*

PROVOST                  Save Your Honor!                    28
ANGELO [*to Provost*]
    Stay a little while. [*To Isabella*] You're welcome.
        What's your will?
ISABELLA
    I am a woeful suitor to Your Honor,
    Please but Your Honor hear me.
ANGELO                          Well, what's your suit?   31
ISABELLA
    There is a vice that most I do abhor,
    And most desire should meet the blow of justice,
    For which I would not plead, but that I must;
    For which I must not plead, but that I am
    At war twixt will and will not.
ANGELO                          Well, the matter?
ISABELLA
    I have a brother is condemned to die.
    I do beseech you, let it be his fault,                    38
    And not my brother.
PROVOST [*aside*]        Heaven give thee moving graces!
ANGELO
    Condemn the fault, and not the actor of it?
    Why, every fault's condemned ere it be done.
    Mine were the very cipher of a function,
    To fine the faults, whose fine stands in record,         43
    And let go by the actor.
ISABELLA   Oh, just but severe law!
    I had a brother, then. Heaven keep your honor!
LUCIO [*aside to Isabella*]
    Give't not o'er so. To him again, entreat him!          47
    Kneel down before him; hang upon his gown.
    You are too cold. If you should need a pin,             49
    You could not with more tame a tongue desire it.
    To him, I say!
ISABELLA [*to Angelo*]
    Must he needs die?
ANGELO              Maiden, no remedy.
ISABELLA
    Yes, I do think that you might pardon him,
    And neither heaven nor man grieve at the mercy.

ANGELO
    I will not do't.
ISABELLA              But can you, if you would?
ANGELO
    Look what I will not, that I cannot do.                  56
ISABELLA
    But might you do't, and do the world no wrong,
    If so your heart were touched with that remorse         58
    As mine is to him?
ANGELO    He's sentenced. 'Tis too late.
LUCIO [*aside to Isabella*]   You are too cold.
ISABELLA
    Too late? Why, no; I that do speak a word
    May call it back again. Well, believe this:
    No ceremony that to great ones 'longs,                  64
    Not the king's crown, nor the deputed sword,            65
    The marshal's truncheon, nor the judge's robe           66
    Become them with one half so good a grace
    As mercy does.
    If he had been as you, and you as he,
    You would have slipped like him; but he, like you,      70
    Would not have been so stern.
ANGELO                      Pray you, begone.
ISABELLA
    I would to heaven I had your potency,
    And you were Isabel. Should it then be thus?
    No, I would tell what 'twere to be a judge              74
    And what a prisoner.
LUCIO [*aside to Isabella*]   Ay, touch him; there's the vein.   75
ANGELO
    Your brother is a forfeit of the law,                   76
    And you but waste your words.
ISABELLA                      Alas, alas!
    Why, all the souls that were were forfeit once,         78
    And He that might the vantage best have took            79
    Found out the remedy. How would you be,                 80
    If He, which is the top of judgment, should             81
    But judge you as you are? Oh, think on that,
    And mercy then will breathe within your lips,
    Like man new-made.
ANGELO              Be you content, fair maid.             84
    It is the law, not I, condemn your brother.
    Were he my kinsman, brother, or my son,
    It should be thus with him. He must die tomorrow.
ISABELLA
    Tomorrow! Oh, that's sudden! Spare him, spare him!
    He's not prepared for death. Even for our kitchens
    We kill the fowl of season. Shall we serve heaven       90
    With less respect than we do minister

**56 Look what** Whatever   **58 remorse** pity   **64 'longs** is fitting,
belongs   **65 deputed sword** sword of justice entrusted to the ruler
**66 truncheon** staff borne by military officers   **70 like you** in your situation   **74 tell** make known   **75 there's the vein** i.e., that's the right
approach. (*Vein* means "lode to be profitably mined," or perhaps
"vein for bloodletting.")   **76 a forfeit** one who must incur the
penalty   **78–80 Why . . . remedy** (A reference to God's redemption of
sinful humanity when He would have been justified in destroying
humankind.)   **81 top of judgment** supreme judge   **84 new-made**
i.e., created new by salvation, born again.   **90 of season** that is in season and properly mature.

**22 Desires** who desires   **28 Save** May God save   **31 Please . . . me** if
Your Honor will please hear me.   **38 let . . . fault** i.e., let the fault die,
be condemned   **43 To fine . . . record** to punish only the faults, for
which the penalty stands in the statute books   **47 Give't . . . so** Don't
give up so soon.   **49 need a pin** i.e., ask for the smallest trifle

To our gross selves? Good, good my lord, bethink
    you:
Who is it that hath died for this offense?
There's many have committed it.
LUCIO [*aside to Isabella*]                    Ay, well said.
ANGELO
The law hath not been dead, though it hath slept.
Those many had not dared to do that evil
If the first that did th'edict infringe
Had answered for his deed. Now 'tis awake,                    98
Takes note of what is done, and like a prophet
Looks in a glass that shows what future evils,                    100
Either now, or by remissness new-conceived                    101
And so in progress to be hatched and born,                    102
Are now to have no successive degrees,                    103
But ere they live, to end.
ISABELLA                    Yet show some pity.                    104
ANGELO
.I show it most of all when I show justice;
For then I pity those I do not know,
Which a dismissed offense would after gall,                    107
And do him right that, answering one foul wrong,                    108
Lives not to act another. Be satisfied;
Your brother dies tomorrow. Be content.
ISABELLA
So you must be the first that gives this sentence,
And he that suffers. Oh, it is excellent
To have a giant's strength, but it is tyrannous
To use it like a giant.
LUCIO [*aside to Isabella*]    That's well said.
ISABELLA    Could great men thunder
As Jove himself does, Jove would never be quiet,                    116
For every pelting, petty officer                    117
Would use his heaven for thunder,
Nothing but thunder. Merciful heaven,
Thou rather with thy sharp and sulfurous bolt                    120
Splits the unwedgeable and gnarlèd oak                    121
Than the soft myrtle; but man, proud man,
Dressed in a little brief authority,
Most ignorant of what he's most assured,                    124
His glassy essence, like an angry ape                    125
Plays such fantastic tricks before high heaven
As makes the angels weep; who, with our spleens,                    127
Would all themselves laugh mortal.                    128

LUCIO [*aside to Isabella*]
Oh, to him, to him, wench! He will relent.
He's coming, I perceive't.
PROVOST [*aside*]                    Pray heaven she win him!                    130
ISABELLA
We cannot weigh our brother with ourself.                    131
Great men may jest with saints; 'tis wit in them,                    132
But in the less, foul profanation.                    133
LUCIO [*aside to Isabella*]
Thou'rt i'th' right, girl. More o' that.
ISABELLA
That in the captain's but a choleric word                    135
Which in the soldier is flat blasphemy.
LUCIO [*aside to Isabella*]    Art advised o' that? More on't.                    137
ANGELO
Why do you put these sayings upon me?                    138
ISABELLA
Because authority, though it err like others,                    139
Hath yet a kind of medicine in itself                    140
That skins the vice o'th' top. Go to your bosom;                    141
Knock there, and ask your heart what it doth know
That's like my brother's fault. If it confess
A natural guiltiness such as is his,
Let it not sound a thought upon your tongue                    145
Against my brother's life.                    146
ANGELO [*aside*]    She speaks, and 'tis such sense                    147
That my sense breeds with it.—Fare you well.                    148
    [*He starts to go.*]
ISABELLA    Gentle my lord, turn back.                    149
ANGELO
I will bethink me. Come again tomorrow.                    150
ISABELLA
Hark how I'll bribe you. Good my lord, turn back.
ANGELO    How? Bribe me?
ISABELLA
Ay, with such gifts that heaven shall share with you.                    153
LUCIO [*aside to Isabella*]    You had marred all else.                    154
ISABELLA
Not with fond sicles of the tested gold,                    155
Or stones whose rate are either rich or poor                    156
As fancy values them, but with true prayers                    157
That shall be up at heaven and enter there
Ere sunrise—prayers from preservèd souls,                    159

98 answered suffered the penalty    100 glass magic crystal
101 Either . . . new-conceived i.e., both evils already hatched and
those that would be encouraged by continued laxity of enforcement
102 in progress in the course of time    103 no successive degrees no
successors or future stages. (Future evils are to be aborted before they
are born and propogate.)    104 ere they live i.e., before they can be
committed    107 Which . . . gall whom a forgiven offense would give
trouble to later on    108 do . . . answering do justice to that person
who, by paying the penalty for    116 be quiet (1) have any quiet, or
(2) cease thundering    117 pelting paltry    120 bolt thunderbolt
121 unwedgeable unsplittable    124–5 Most . . . essence i.e., most
ignorant of what religion teaches him to know, his spiritual nature;
or, most ignorant of that which is most certainly his natural frailty
125 angry ape i.e., ludicrous buffoon    127–8 who . . . mortal who, if
they had the organs of laughter that we have, would laugh themselves mortal, becoming like us. (The spleen was thought to be the
seat of laughter.)

130 coming coming around    131–3 We . . . profanation We cannot
judge our fellow mortals by the same standards we use in judging
ourselves. Persons of great authority are allowed liberties that in
lesser persons would be condemned as blasphemies. (Lines 135–6
make much the same point.)    135 That . . . word i.e., We treat the
abusive language a commanding officer uses in anger merely as an
outburst; we are indulgent toward the failings of great men. (As in
lines 131–3, Isabella's point seems to be that our judgments are biased
by our inordinate regard for authority.)    137 advised informed,
aware.  on't of it.    138 put . . . me apply these sayings to me.
139–41 Because . . . top Because authority, though like all humankind in
being prone to sinfulness, has a way of seeming to heal itself by covering
over the boil with a film of skin, leaving the sore unhealed.    145–6 Let
. . . life let not your heart prompt your tongue to condemn my brother to
death.    147–8 sense . . . sense import . . . sensuality  149 Gentle my lord
My noble lord    150 bethink me think it over.    153 that as    154 else
otherwise.    155 Not . . . gold Not with foolishly valued shekels of pure
gold. (Shekels are Hebrew coins.)    156–7 Or . . . them or jewels the value
of which is merely subjective and transitory    159 preservèd souls
devout religious who have withdrawn from the world

From fasting maids whose minds are dedicate     160
To nothing temporal.

ANGELO     Well, come to me tomorrow.

LUCIO [*aside to Isabella*]     Go to, 'tis well. Away!

ISABELLA
Heaven keep Your Honor safe!

ANGELO [*aside*]     Amen!
For I am that way going to temptation,
Where prayers cross.

ISABELLA     At what hour tomorrow     165
Shall I attend Your Lordship?

ANGELO     At any time 'fore noon.

ISABELLA     Save Your Honor!     168
          [*Exeunt Isabella, Lucio, and Provost.*]

ANGELO     From thee, even from thy virtue!
What's this, what's this? Is this her fault or mine?
The tempter or the tempted, who sins most, ha?
Not she, nor doth she tempt; but it is I
That, lying by the violet in the sun,
Do, as the carrion does, not as the flower,     174
Corrupt with virtuous season. Can it be     175
That modesty may more betray our sense     176
Than woman's lightness? Having waste ground
     enough,     177
Shall we desire to raze the sanctuary
And pitch our evils there? Oh, fie, fie, fie!     179
What dost thou, or what art thou, Angelo?
Dost thou desire her foully for those things
That make her good? Oh, let her brother live!
Thieves for their robbery have authority
When judges steal themselves. What, do I love her,
That I desire to hear her speak again
And feast upon her eyes? What is't I dream on?
Oh, cunning enemy that, to catch a saint,     187
With saints dost bait thy hook! Most dangerous
Is that temptation that doth goad us on
To sin in loving virtue. Never could the strumpet,
With all her double vigor—art and nature—     191
Once stir my temper; but this virtuous maid     192
Subdues me quite. Ever till now,
When men were fond, I smiled and wondered how.     194
          *Exit.*

❖

## 2.3

*Enter, [meeting,] Duke [disguised as a friar]
and Provost.*

DUKE
Hail to you, Provost—so I think you are.

---

160 **fasting maids** i.e., nuns.  **dedicate** dedicated     165 **cross** are at
cross purposes.     168 **Save** May God save     174 **carrion** decaying
flesh     175 **Corrupt . . . season** i.e., putrefy while all else flourishes.
(The warmth of flowering time causes the violet, Isabella, to blossom
but causes the carrion lying beside it, Angelo, to rot.)     176 **modesty**
virtue, chastity.  **sense** sensual nature     177 **lightness** immodesty,
lust.     179 **pitch our evils there** i.e., erect a privy, not on *waste ground*
(line 177), but on sanctified ground. (*Evils* also has the more common
meaning of "wickedness.")     187 **enemy** i.e., Satan     191 **double . . .
nature** twofold power (of alluring men) through artifice and a sensu-
ous nature     192 **temper** temperament     194 **fond** foolishly in love
**2.3. Location: A prison.**

---

PROVOST
I am the Provost. What's your will, good Friar?

DUKE
Bound by my charity and my blest order,
I come to visit the afflicted spirits
Here in the prison. Do me the common right     5
To let me see them and to make me know
The nature of their crimes, that I may minister
To them accordingly.

PROVOST
I would do more than that, if more were needful.

          *Enter Juliet.*

Look, here comes one: a gentlewoman of mine,
Who, falling in the flaws of her own youth,     11
Hath blistered her report. She is with child,     12
And he that got it, sentenced—a young man     13
More fit to do another such offense
Than die for this.

DUKE
When must he die?

PROVOST     As I do think, tomorrow.
[*To Juliet*] I have provided for you. Stay awhile,     17
And you shall be conducted.     18

DUKE
Repent you, fair one, of the sin you carry?

JULIET
I do, and bear the shame most patiently.

DUKE
I'll teach you how you shall arraign your conscience,     21
And try your penitence, if it be sound     22
Or hollowly put on.     23

JULIET     I'll gladly learn.

DUKE     Love you the man that wronged you?

JULIET
Yes, as I love the woman that wronged him.

DUKE
So then it seems your most offenseful act
Was mutually committed?

JULIET     Mutually.

DUKE
Then was your sin of heavier kind than his.

JULIET
I do confess it and repent it, Father.

DUKE
'Tis meet so, daughter. But lest you do repent     31
As that the sin hath brought you to this shame,     32
Which sorrow is always toward ourselves, not heaven,     33
Showing we would not spare heaven as we love it,     34
But as we stand in fear—

JULIET
I do repent me as it is an evil,

---

5 **common right** i.e., right extended to all clerics     11 **flaws** (1) weaknesses, fissures (2) sudden gusts (of passion)     12 **blistered her report**
marred her reputation.     13 **got** begot     17 **provided** provided a place
to stay     18 **conducted** taken there.     21 **arraign** accuse     22 **try** test
23 **hollowly** falsely     31 **'Tis meet so** It is fitting that you do so
32 **As that** merely because     33 **toward ourselves** i.e., narrowly self-
concerned rather than loving virtue for its own sake     34 **Showing . . .
it** showing that we wish to avoid offending heaven not out of sheer
love of goodness

And take the shame with joy.

DUKE                                        There rest.                37
Your partner, as I hear, must die tomorrow,
And I am going with instruction to him.
Grace go with you. *Benedicite!*            *Exit.*        40

JULIET
Must die tomorrow? O injurious law,                       41
That respites me a life whose very comfort                42
Is still a dying horror!

PROVOST                              'Tis pity of him.    *Exeunt.*   43

❖

## 2.4

*Enter Angelo.*

ANGELO
When I would pray and think, I think and pray
To several subjects. Heaven hath my empty words,        2
Whilst my invention, hearing not my tongue,             3
Anchors on Isabel; Heaven in my mouth,
As if I did but only chew His name,                     5
And in my heart the strong and swelling evil
Of my conception. The state, whereon I studied,         7
Is like a good thing, being often read,
Grown sere and tedious. Yea, my gravity,                9
Wherein—let no man hear me—I take pride,
Could I with boot change for an idle plume,            11
Which the air beats for vain. O place, O form,         12
How often dost thou with thy case, thy habit,          13
Wrench awe from fools and tie the wiser souls          14
To thy false seeming! Blood, thou art blood.           15
Let's write "good angel" on the devil's horn,          16
'Tis not the devil's crest.

*Enter Servant.*

                            How now? Who's there?       17
SERVANT
One Isabel, a sister, desires access to you.
ANGELO    Teach her the way.          *[Exit Servant.]*
                            Oh, heavens!                 19
Why does my blood thus muster to my heart,              20

Making both it unable for itself                        21
And dispossessing all my other parts
Of necessary fitness?
So play the foolish throngs with one that swoons,       24
Come all to help him, and so stop the air
By which he should revive; and even so
The general subject to a well-wished king               27
Quit their own part and in obsequious fondness          28
Crowd to his presence, where their untaught love        29
Must needs appear offense.

*Enter Isabella.*

                            How now, fair maid?          30
ISABELLA    I am come to know your pleasure.
ANGELO
That you might know it would much better please me      32
Than to demand what 'tis. Your brother cannot live.     33
ISABELLA
Even so. Heaven keep Your Honor!                         34
                            *[She turns to leave.]*
ANGELO
Yet may he live awhile; and, it may be,
As long as you or I. Yet he must die.
ISABELLA    Under your sentence?
ANGELO    Yea.
ISABELLA
When, I beseech you? That in his reprieve,
Longer or shorter, he may be so fitted                   40
That his soul sicken not.
ANGELO
Ha? Fie, these filthy vices! It were as good            42
To pardon him that hath from nature stolen              43
A man already made, as to remit                          44
Their saucy sweetness that do coin heaven's image       45
In stamps that are forbid. 'Tis all as easy             46
Falsely to take away a life true made
As to put metal in restrainèd means                     48
To make a false one.
ISABELLA
'Tis set down so in heaven, but not in earth.            50
ANGELO
Say you so? Then I shall pose you quickly:               51
Which had you rather, that the most just law
Now took your brother's life, or, to redeem him,
Give up your body to such sweet uncleanness

---

**37 There rest.** Hold fast to that truth.   **40** *Benedicite!* Blessings on you!
**41–3 O . . . horror!** O injurious law (the Folio reads "Loue") that saves me
from the death penalty (owing to my pregnancy), thereby granting me a
life whose best comfort is like the horror of death itself! (Pregnancy
could save a woman from being executed.)   **43 'Tis pity of him** It's a
pity about Claudio.
**2.4 Location:** Angelo's official residence.
**2 several** separate   **3 invention** imagination   **5 His** i.e., heaven's,
God's   **7 conception** thought.   **The state** Statecraft   **9 sere** withered,
old   **11–12 Could . . . vain** I could willingly exchange (my gravity) for
the frivolity of a pleasure-loving gallant, sporting a feather that seems
to beat the air in its vanity (or, perhaps, is beaten by the air in reproof
of its vanity).   **12 O place, O form** O authority of high position, O ceremonial dignity of office   **13 thy case . . . habit** your mere outward
appearance and garb   **14–15 Wrench . . . seeming** intimidate ordinary
foolish men and subjugate even the wise to the seeming virtue of
authority.   **15 Blood . . . blood** i.e., No position of authority or birth,
no matter how lofty, can protect a person from his own lustful
appetites.   **16–17 Let's . . . crest** i.e., No matter how hard we try to
disguise evil under the semblance of good, it remains recognizably
evil still. (In heraldic terms, the devil is known by his baleful horns;
the heraldic crest on his coat of arms does not alter his true identity.)
**19 Teach** Show   **20 muster to** assemble like soldiers in

**21 unable** ineffectual   **24 play** behave   **27 general subject** i.e., commoners, subjects.   **well-wished** attended by good wishes   **28 Quit
. . . part** abandon their proper function and (politely distant) place
**29 untaught** ignorant, unmannerly   **30 Must needs** will necessarily
**32–3 That . . . 'tis** i.e., I wish you could know the nature of my desire
without your asking and my having to be explicit. (*Know* suggests
carnal knowledge.)   **34 Even so** So be it.   **40 fitted** prepared
**42–6 It were . . . forbid** One might as well pardon the murderer of a
living man as pardon the wanton pleasures of those persons
who produce illegitimate offspring, like counterfeit coiners.
(*Heaven's image* is humankind, made in God's likeness; Genesis 1:27.)
**48 metal** i.e., the metal used in coining (lines 45–6), with a play on
*mettle*, natural vigor or spirit.   **restrainèd** prohibited, illicit (both in
counterfeiting coinage and in begetting illegitimate children)
**50 'Tis . . . earth** i.e., Equating murder and bastardizing accords with
divine law but not with human law, according to which murder is
more heinous.   **51 pose you** put a perplexing question to you

As she that he hath stained?

**ISABELLA**                              Sir, believe this,
I had rather give my body than my soul.                    56

**ANGELO**
I talk not of your soul. Our compelled sins                57
Stand more for number than for account.

**ISABELLA**                              How say you?     58

**ANGELO**
Nay, I'll not warrant that, for I can speak                59
Against the thing I say. Answer to this:
I, now the voice of the recorded law,
Pronounce a sentence on your brother's life;
Might there not be a charity in sin
To save this brother's life?

**ISABELLA**                    Please you to do't,         64
I'll take it as a peril to my soul;                        65
It is no sin at all, but charity.

**ANGELO**
Pleased you to do't at peril of your soul                  67
Were equal poise of sin and charity.                       68

**ISABELLA**
That I do beg his life, if it be sin,
Heaven let me bear it! You granting of my suit,
If that be sin, I'll make it my morn prayer
To have it added to the faults of mine,
And nothing of your answer.

**ANGELO**                        Nay, but hear me.         73
Your sense pursues not mine. Either you are ignorant
Or seem so craftily; and that's not good.

**ISABELLA**
Let me be ignorant, and in nothing good,
But graciously to know I am no better.                     77

**ANGELO**
Thus wisdom wishes to appear most bright
When it doth tax itself, as these black masks              79
Proclaim an enshield beauty ten times louder              80
Than beauty could, displayed. But mark me.
To be receivèd plain, I'll speak more gross:               82
Your brother is to die.

**ISABELLA**  So.

**ANGELO**
And his offense is so, as it appears,
Accountant to the law upon that pain.                      86

**ISABELLA**  True.

**ANGELO**
Admit no other way to save his life—                       88
As I subscribe not that, nor any other,                    89
But in the loss of question—that you, his sister,          90

Finding yourself desired of such a person                  91
Whose credit with the judge, or own great place,
Could fetch your brother from the manacles
Of the all-binding law; and that there were
No earthly means to save him, but that either
You must lay down the treasures of your body
To this supposed, or else to let him suffer.               97
What would you do?

**ISABELLA**
As much for my poor brother as myself:
That is, were I under the terms of death,                  100
Th'impression of keen whips I'd wear as rubies,            101
And strip myself to death as to a bed
That longing have been sick for, ere I'd yield             103
My body up to shame.

**ANGELO**  Then must your brother die.

**ISABELLA**  And 'twere the cheaper way.
Better it were a brother died at once                      107
Than that a sister, by redeeming him,
Should die forever.

**ANGELO**
Were not you then as cruel as the sentence
That you have slandered so?

**ISABELLA**
Ignomy in ransom and free pardon                           112
Are of two houses. Lawful mercy                            113
Is nothing kin to foul redemption.                         114

**ANGELO**
You seemed of late to make the law a tyrant,               115
And rather proved the sliding of your brother              116
A merriment than a vice.

**ISABELLA**
Oh, pardon me, my lord. It oft falls out,
To have what we would have, we speak not what
    we mean.
I something do excuse the thing I hate                     120
For his advantage that I dearly love.

**ANGELO**
We are all frail.

**ISABELLA**          Else let my brother die,
If not a fedary but only he                                123
Owe and succeed thy weakness.                              124

**ANGELO**  Nay, women are frail too.

**ISABELLA**
Ay, as the glasses where they view themselves,            126
Which are as easy broke as they make forms.               127

---

56 **give** i.e., give to death or punishment. (Isabella avoids or does not understand the drift of the question.)   57–8 **Our . . . account** Our sins committed under compulsion are recorded but not charged to our spiritual account.   59 **I'll . . . that** i.e., I'm not necessarily endorsing the view I just expressed   64 **Please you** If you please   65 **take** accept   67 **Pleased** If it pleased   68 **Were equal poise** there would be equal balance   73 **of your answer** to which you will have to answer.   77 **graciously** through divine grace   79 **tax itself** accuse itself (of ignorance).   **these** (Generically referring to any.)   80 **enshield** shielded, protected from view behind the black masks   82 **receivèd plain** plainly understood.   **gross** (1) openly (2) offensively   86 **Accountant** accountable.   **pain** penalty.   88 **Admit** Suppose   89–90 **As . . . question** since I will admit no alternative possibility in our discussion. (*Loss of question* means "forfeiting the terms of our debate.")

91 **of** by   97 **supposed** hypothetical person.   **him** i.e., Claudio   100 **terms** sentence   101 **Th'impression of keen whips** the cruel stripes laid on my body   103 **That . . . for** i.e., that I have been sick with longing for. (Isabella's images are of love, death, and flagellation.)   107 **died at once** should die once for all, rather than *die forever* (line 109) in the death of the soul through sin   112–14 **Ignomy . . . redemption** Being ransomed under ignominious circumstances and being released without conditions are two entirely different things. Mercy under law bears no relation to being spared under foul stipulations.   115 **of late** in what you just argued   116 **proved . . . brother** argued that your brother's fleshly sin was more   120 **something** to some extent   123 **fedary** confederate, companion who is equally guilty   124 **Owe . . . weakness** possess and inherit the weakness you speak of, or the weakness to which all men as a class are prone. (Isabella argues that Claudio should die only if he is the only man who is frail.)   126 **glasses** mirrors   127 **forms** (1) images (2) copies of themselves, i.e., children

Women? Help, heaven! Men their creation mar          128
In profiting by them. Nay, call us ten times frail,     129
For we are soft as our complexions are,                 130
And credulous to false prints.

ANGELO                          I think it well.           131
And from this testimony of your own sex—                132
Since I suppose we are made to be no stronger           133
Than faults may shake our frames—let me be bold.        134
I do arrest your words. Be that you are,                135
That is, a woman; if you be more, you're none.          136
If you be one, as you are well expressed                137
By all external warrants, show it now                   138
By putting on the destined livery.                      139

ISABELLA
I have no tongue but one. Gentle my lord,               140
Let me entreat you speak the former language.           141

ANGELO    Plainly conceive, I love you.

ISABELLA    My brother did love Juliet,
And you tell me that he shall die for't.

ANGELO
He shall not, Isabel, if you give me love.

ISABELLA
I know your virtue hath a license in't,                 146
Which seems a little fouler than it is                  147
To pluck on others.

ANGELO                     Believe me, on mine honor,     148
My words express my purpose.

ISABELLA
Ha! Little honor to be much believed,
And most pernicious purpose! Seeming, seeming!
I will proclaim thee, Angelo, look for't!
Sign me a present pardon for my brother,                153
Or with an outstretched throat I'll tell the world
    aloud
What man thou art.

ANGELO                    Who will believe thee, Isabel?
My unsoiled name, th'austereness of my life,
My vouch against you, and my place i'th' state          157
Will so your accusation overweigh
That you shall stifle in your own report
And smell of calumny. I have begun,                     160
And now I give my sensual race the rein.                161
Fit thy consent to my sharp appetite;
Lay by all nicety and prolixious blushes                163
That banish what they sue for. Redeem thy brother       164

By yielding up thy body to my will,
Or else he must not only die the death,                 166
But thy unkindness shall his death draw out
To ling'ring sufferance. Answer me tomorrow,            168
Or, by the affection that now guides me most,           169
I'll prove a tyrant to him. As for you,
Say what you can, my false o'erweighs your true.        171
                                               Exit.

ISABELLA
To whom should I complain? Did I tell this,             172
Who would believe me? O perilous mouths,                173
That bear in them one and the selfsame tongue,          174
Either of condemnation or approof,                      175
Bidding the law make curtsy to their will,              176
Hooking both right and wrong to th'appetite,            177
To follow as it draws! I'll to my brother.              178
Though he hath fall'n by prompture of the blood,        179
Yet hath he in him such a mind of honor
That, had he twenty heads to tender down                181
On twenty bloody blocks, he'd yield them up
Before his sister should her body stoop
To such abhorred pollution.
Then, Isabel, live chaste, and, brother, die;
More than our brother is our chastity.                  186
I'll tell him yet of Angelo's request,
And fit his mind to death, for his soul's rest.   Exit.

❖

## 3.1

*Enter Duke [disguised as before], Claudio, and Provost.*

DUKE
So then you hope of pardon from Lord Angelo?

CLAUDIO
The miserable have no other medicine
But only hope.
I have hope to live and am prepared to die.

DUKE
Be absolute for death. Either death or life
Shall thereby be the sweeter. Reason thus with life:
If I do lose thee, I do lose a thing
That none but fools would keep. A breath thou art,
Servile to all the skyey influences                     9
That dost this habitation where thou keep'st            10
Hourly afflict. Merely, thou art death's fool,          11
For him thou labor'st by thy flight to shun,
And yet run'st toward him still. Thou art not noble,    13

128–9 Men . . . them Men mar their creation in God's likeness by taking advantage of women.   130 complexions constitutions, appearance
131 credulous . . . prints susceptible to false impressions. (The metaphor is from the stamping of coins and other metal.)   132 of about
133–4 we . . . frames we human beings are not so strong but that our sins may threaten us   135 arrest your words take what you have said and hold you to it.   that what   136 if . . . none i.e., if you insist on remaining a virgin and free of fleshly desire, you are no woman as we have defined the term—that is, frail and susceptible.   137–8 expressed
. . . warrants shown to be by your physical beauty   139 putting . . . livery i.e., assuming the characteristic frailty that all women possess.
140 tongue language   141 speak . . . language speak to be understood, in the language I understand.   146–8 I know . . . others i.e., I am sure that you, out of virtuous motives, are speaking licentiously (and with the license of authority) in order to put me to the test.   153 present immediate   157 vouch allegation   160 calumny slander.   161 I give
. . . rein I give free rein to my sensual desires.   163–4 Lay . . . sue for Set aside all the coyness and time-wasting blushes that make a pretense of repulsing the embrace they actually beg for.

166 die the death be put to death   168 sufferance torture.
169 affection passion   171 my false . . . true my false declaration of innocence will prevail over your telling the truth.   172 Did I tell If I told   173–8 O perilous . . . draws! O dangerous voices of authority, able with one tongue either to condemn or approve, forcing both right and wrong to obey the willful appetite!   179 prompture prompting, suggestion   181 tender down lay down in payment
186 More Of more spiritual worth
3.1. Location: The prison.
9 skyey influences influence of the stars   10 this habitation i.e., the earth (and the body as well).   keep'st dwell   11 Merely Utterly, only
13 still continually.

For all th'accommodations that thou bear'st                14
Are nursed by baseness. Thou'rt by no means valiant,       15
For thou dost fear the soft and tender fork                16
Of a poor worm. Thy best of rest is sleep,                 17
And that thou oft provok'st, yet grossly fear'st           18
Thy death, which is no more. Thou art not thyself,
For thou exists on many a thousand grains
That issue out of dust. Happy thou art not,
For what thou hast not, still thou striv'st to get,
And what thou hast, forget'st. Thou art not certain,       23
For thy complexion shifts to strange effects,              24
After the moon. If thou art rich, thou'rt poor,            25
For, like an ass whose back with ingots bows,              26
Thou bear'st thy heavy riches but a journey,
And death unloads thee. Friend hast thou none,
For thine own bowels which do call thee sire,              29
The mere effusion of thy proper loins,                     30
Do curse the gout, serpigo, and the rheum                  31
For ending thee no sooner. Thou hast nor youth
    nor age,                            32
But as it were an after-dinner's sleep                     33
Dreaming on both, for all thy blessèd youth                34
Becomes as agèd and doth beg the alms                      35
Of palsied eld; and, when thou art old and rich,          36
Thou hast neither heat, affection, limb, nor beauty       37
To make thy riches pleasant. What's yet in this
That bears the name of life? Yet in this life
Lie hid more thousand deaths; yet death we fear,
That makes these odds all even.

CLAUDIO                          I humbly thank you.       41
To sue to live, I find I seek to die,                      42
And, seeking death, find life. Let it come on.

    *Enter Isabella.*

ISABELLA
What, ho! Peace here; grace and good company!             44
PROVOST
Who's there? Come in. The wish deserves a welcome.
                        *[He goes to greet her.]*
DUKE *[to Claudio]*
Dear sir, ere long I'll visit you again.
CLAUDIO   Most holy sir, I thank you.
ISABELLA
My business is a word or two with Claudio.
PROVOST
And very welcome.—Look, signor, here's your sister.
DUKE *[aside to the Provost]*   Provost, a word with you.

PROVOST     As many as you please.
DUKE
Bring me to hear them speak, where I may be
Concealed.          *[The Duke and the Provost withdraw.]*
CLAUDIO          Now, sister, what's the comfort?
ISABELLA                                            Why,
As all comforts are: most good, most good indeed.
Lord Angelo, having affairs to heaven,
Intends you for his swift ambassador,
Where you shall be an everlasting leiger.                 57
Therefore your best appointment make with speed;         58
Tomorrow you set on.
CLAUDIO                    Is there no remedy?            59
ISABELLA
None but such remedy as, to save a head,
To cleave a heart in twain.
CLAUDIO     But is there any?
ISABELLA     Yes, brother, you may live.
There is a devilish mercy in the judge,
If you'll implore it, that will free your life
But fetter you till death.
CLAUDIO                    Perpetual durance?            66
ISABELLA
Ay, just; perpetual durance, a restraint,               67
Though all the world's vastidity you had,               68
To a determined scope.
CLAUDIO                    But in what nature?           69
ISABELLA
In such a one as, you consenting to't,
Would bark your honor from that trunk you bear          71
And leave you naked.
CLAUDIO                    Let me know the point.
ISABELLA
Oh, I do fear thee, Claudio, and I quake                73
Lest thou a feverous life shouldst entertain,           74
And six or seven winters more respect                   75
Than a perpetual honor. Dar'st thou die?
The sense of death is most in apprehension,             77
And the poor beetle that we tread upon
In corporal sufferance finds a pang as great
As when a giant dies.
CLAUDIO   Why give you me this shame?
Think you I can a resolution fetch                      82
From flow'ry tenderness? If I must die,                 83
I will encounter darkness as a bride
And hug it in mine arms.
ISABELLA
There spake my brother! There my father's grave
Did utter forth a voice. Yes, thou must die.
Thou art too noble to conserve a life

---

**14 accommodations . . . bear'st** conveniences and civilized comforts that you enjoy   **15 nursed by baseness** nurtured by ignoble means.   **16 fork** forked tongue   **17 worm** (1) snake (2) grave worm.   **18 thou oft provok'st** you often pray for   **23 certain** steadfast   **24–5 For . . . moon** since your constitution seeks incessantly for newness and strangeness, changing like the inconstant moon.   **26 like . . . bows** like an ass bowed down by a heavy burden of wood   **29 bowels** i.e., offspring   **30 mere** very.   **proper** own   **31 serpigo** a skin eruption.   **rheum** catarrh   **32 nor youth** neither youth   **33 after-dinner's** i.e., afternoon's   **34–6 all . . . eld** your happy youth must decline all too soon into old age and become like a beggar, pleading for the little comfort that palsied infirmity can provide. (Youth is penniless and dependent on the aged, whereas the old lack the physical capacity of youth.)   **37 heat, affection** vigor, passion   **41 That . . . even** i.e., that evens the score by putting an end to all suffering.   **42 To sue** Suing, petitioning   **44 grace** God's grace

**57 leiger** resident ambassador.   **58 appointment** preparation   **59 set on** set forward.   **66 durance** imprisonment.   **67–9 Ay, just . . . scope** i.e., Yes, exactly so, a confinement to the eternal bounds of damnation and to inescapable guilt and perpetual remorse for the sinful bargain to which you agreed, a confinement so limitless as to extend beyond the entire vastness of the world.   **71 bark** strip off (as one strips bark from a tree *trunk*)   **73 fear** fear for   **74 feverous** feverish.   **entertain** desire   **75 respect** value   **77 apprehension** anticipation   **82–3 Think . . . tenderness?** Do you think I can find the courage to face death in your flowery rhetoric?

In base appliances. This outward-sainted deputy, 89
Whose settled visage and deliberate word 90
Nips youth i'th' head, and follies doth enew 91
As falcon doth the fowl, is yet a devil; 92
His filth within being cast, he would appear 93
A pond as deep as hell.

CLAUDIO                    The prenzie Angelo? 94

ISABELLA
Oh, 'tis the cunning livery of hell, 95
The damned'st body to invest and cover 96
In prenzie guards! Dost thou think, Claudio: 97
If I would yield him my virginity,
Thou mightst be freed!

CLAUDIO                    Oh, heavens, it cannot be.

ISABELLA
Yes, he would give't thee, from this rank offense, 100
So to offend him still. This night's the time 101
That I should do what I abhor to name,
Or else thou diest tomorrow.

CLAUDIO   Thou shalt not do't.

ISABELLA   Oh, were it but my life,
I'd throw it down for your deliverance
As frankly as a pin.

CLAUDIO                    Thanks, dear Isabel. 107

ISABELLA
Be ready, Claudio, for your death tomorrow.

CLAUDIO
Yes. Has he affections in him, 109
That thus can make him bite the law by th' nose 110
When he would force it? Sure it is no sin, 111
Or of the deadly seven it is the least. 112

ISABELLA   Which is the least?

CLAUDIO
If it were damnable, he being so wise,
Why would he for the momentary trick 115
Be perdurably fined? Oh, Isabel! 116

ISABELLA
What says my brother?

CLAUDIO                    Death is a fearful thing.

ISABELLA   And shamèd life a hateful.

CLAUDIO
Ay, but to die, and go we know not where,
To lie in cold obstruction and to rot, 120
This sensible warm motion to become 121

A kneaded clod, and the delighted spirit 122
To bathe in fiery floods, or to reside
In thrilling region of thick-ribbèd ice; 124
To be imprisoned in the viewless winds 125
And blown with restless violence round about
The pendent world; or to be worse than worst 127
Of those that lawless and incertain thought 128
Imagine howling—'tis too horrible!
The weariest and most loathèd worldly life
That age, ache, penury, and imprisonment
Can lay on nature is a paradise
To what we fear of death. 133

ISABELLA   Alas, alas!

CLAUDIO   Sweet sister, let me live.
What sin you do to save a brother's life,
Nature dispenses with the deed so far 137
That it becomes a virtue.

ISABELLA                    Oh, you beast!
Oh, faithless coward! Oh, dishonest wretch! 139
Wilt thou be made a man out of my vice?
Is't not a kind of incest, to take life
From thine own sister's shame? What should I think?
Heaven shield my mother played my father fair! 143
For such a warpèd slip of wilderness 144
Ne'er issued from his blood. Take my defiance,
Die, perish! Might but my bending down 146
Reprieve thee from thy fate, it should proceed.
I'll pray a thousand prayers for thy death,
No word to save thee.

CLAUDIO
Nay, hear me, Isabel.

ISABELLA                    Oh, fie, fie, fie!
Thy sin's not accidental, but a trade. 151
Mercy to thee would prove itself a bawd; 152
'Tis best that thou diest quickly.

CLAUDIO   Oh, hear me, Isabella!

[The Duke comes forward.]

DUKE
Vouchsafe a word, young sister, but one word. 155

ISABELLA   What is your will?

DUKE   Might you dispense with your leisure, I would 157
by and by have some speech with you. The satisfaction I would require is likewise your own benefit. 159

ISABELLA   I have no superfluous leisure—my stay
must be stolen out of other affairs—but I will attend 161
you awhile.                                    [She walks apart.]

DUKE   Son, I have overheard what hath passed between
you and your sister. Angelo had never the purpose to

---

**89 In base appliances** by means of ignoble devices, remedies.
**89–92 This ... fowl** This outwardly holy deputy, who with composed features and judiciously chosen words swoops down on youth
like a falcon and drives his prey into covert. (To *enew* is to drive prey
down into the water or into hiding.)   **93 cast** dug out; diagnosed,
sounded; vomited (?)   **94 prenzie** (A word unknown elsewhere,
perhaps meaning "princely" or "precise.")   **95–7 'tis ... guards** it is
the cunning ruse of the devil to clothe and conceal the wickedest man
imaginable in decorously proper trimmings.   **97 Dost thou think**
i.e., Would you believe   **100–1 he would ... still** he would grant you
license, in return for the committing of this foul crime, to continue
with your sinful life.   **107 frankly** freely   **109 affections** passions
**110 bite ... nose** i.e., flout the law   **111 force** enforce. (Claudio wonders that lust can drive Angelo to make a mockery of the law even
while purporting to enforce it.)   **112 Or ... least** (Claudio tries to
exonerate himself and beg Isabella to sacrifice her virginity by reflecting that Lechery conventionally appears last in the catalogue of the
Seven Deadly Sins: Pride, Wrath, Envy, Covetousness, Gluttony,
Sloth, and Lechery.)   **115 trick** trifle   **116 perdurably fined** everlastingly punished.   **120 obstruction** cessation of vital functions
**121 sensible** endowed with feeling.   **motion** organism

**122 kneaded clod** shapeless lump of earth.   **delighted spirit** spirit
that is now attended with delight, or capable of being so
**124 thrilling** piercingly cold   **125 viewless** invisible   **127 pendent**
hanging in space. (A Ptolemaic concept.)   **128 lawless ... thought**
i.e., wild conjecture   **133 To** compared to   **137 dispenses with**
grants a dispensation for, excuses   **139 dishonest** dishonorable
**143 Heaven ... fair** i.e., Heaven forbid that my mother cheated on
her husband by giving him a bastard child, namely, you, Claudio.
**144 warpèd ... wilderness** perverse, licentious scion, one that reverts
to the original wild stock   **146 but** merely   **151 accidental** happening by chance.   **trade** long-practiced mode of living.   **152 prove ...
bawd** i.e., provide opportunity for sexual license   **155 Vouchsafe**
Allow   **157 Might ... leisure** If you have a moment   **159 require**
ask.   **is ... benefit** will also benefit you.   **161 attend** await; listen to

corrupt her; only he hath made an assay of her virtue 165
to practice his judgment with the disposition of na- 166
tures. She, having the truth of honor in her, hath made 167
him that gracious denial which he is most glad to re- 168
ceive. I am confessor to Angelo, and I know this to be
true; therefore prepare yourself to death. Do not satisfy
your resolution with hopes that are fallible. Tomorrow
you must die. Go to your knees and make ready.

CLAUDIO    Let me ask my sister pardon. I am so out of
love with life that I will sue to be rid of it.    174

DUKE    Hold you there. Farewell.    [Claudio retires.] 175
Provost, a word with you.

[The Provost comes forward.]

PROVOST    What's your will, Father?

DUKE    That now you are come, you will be gone. Leave
me awhile with the maid. My mind promises with my 179
habit no loss shall touch her by my company.    180

PROVOST    In good time.    Exit [Provost with Claudio]. 181

[Isabella comes forward.]

DUKE    The hand that hath made you fair hath made you 182
good. The goodness that is cheap in beauty makes 183
beauty brief in goodness; but grace, being the soul of 184
your complexion, shall keep the body of it ever fair. 185
The assault that Angelo hath made to you, fortune
hath conveyed to my understanding; and, but that 187
frailty hath examples for his falling, I should wonder 188
at Angelo. How will you do to content this substitute 189
and to save your brother?

ISABELLA    I am now going to resolve him. I had rather 191
my brother die by the law than my son should be
unlawfully born. But, oh, how much is the good Duke
deceived in Angelo! If ever he return and I can speak
to him, I will open my lips in vain, or discover his 195
government.    196

DUKE    That shall not be much amiss. Yet, as the matter
now stands, he will avoid your accusation; he made 198
trial of you only. Therefore fasten your ear on my
advisings. To the love I have in doing good a remedy
presents itself. I do make myself believe that you may
most uprighteously do a poor wronged lady a merited
benefit, redeem your brother from the angry law, do
no stain to your own gracious person, and much
please the absent Duke, if peradventure he shall ever
return to have hearing of this business.

ISABELLA    Let me hear you speak farther. I have spirit 207
to do anything that appears not foul in the truth of my 208
spirit.    209

DUKE    Virtue is bold, and goodness never fearful. Have
you not heard speak of Mariana, the sister of Frederick, the great soldier who miscarried at sea?    212

ISABELLA    I have heard of the lady, and good words
went with her name.

DUKE    She should this Angelo have married, was 215
affianced to her by oath, and the nuptial appointed;
between which time of the contract and limit of the 217
solemnity, her brother Frederick was wrecked at sea, 218
having in that perished vessel the dowry of his sister.
But mark how heavily this befell to the poor gentlewoman. There she lost a noble and renowned brother,
in his love toward her ever most kind and natural;
with him, the portion and sinew of her fortune, her 223
marriage dowry; with both, her combinate husband, 224
this well-seeming Angelo.

ISABELLA    Can this be so? Did Angelo so leave her?

DUKE    Left her in her tears, and dried not one of them
with his comfort; swallowed his vows whole, pretend- 228
ing in her discoveries of dishonor; in few, bestowed 229
her on her own lamentation, which she yet wears for 230
his sake; and he, a marble to her tears, is washed with 231
them but relents not.

ISABELLA    What a merit were it in death to take this 233
poor maid from the world! What corruption in this 234
life, that it will let this man live! But how out of this can
she avail?    236

DUKE    It is a rupture that you may easily heal, and the
cure of it not only saves your brother but keeps you
from dishonor in doing it.

ISABELLA    Show me how, good Father.

DUKE    This forenamed maid hath yet in her the continuance of her first affection; his unjust unkindness, that
in all reason should have quenched her love, hath, like
an impediment in the current, made it more violent
and unruly. Go you to Angelo; answer his requiring
with a plausible obedience; agree with his demands to 246
the point. Only refer yourself to this advantage: first, 247
that your stay with him may not be long, that the time
may have all shadow and silence in it, and the place 249
answer to convenience. This being granted in
course—and now follows all—we shall advise this
wronged maid to stead up your appointment, go in 252
your place. If the encounter acknowledge itself here- 253
after, it may compel him to her recompense. And here, 254
by this, is your brother saved, your honor untainted,
the poor Mariana advantaged, and the corrupt deputy
scaled. The maid will I frame and make fit for his at- 257

---

165 **only he hath** he has only.    **assay** test    166–7 **his judgment . . . natures** his ability to judge people's characters.    167 **truth** essence, highest degree    168 **gracious** virtuous    174 **sue** beg    175 **Hold you there** Hold fast to that resolution.    179–80 **with my habit** as well as my priestly garb (that)    181 **In good time** i.e., Very well.    182 **The hand** The hand of God    183–4 **The goodness . . . in goodness** i.e., The physical attractions that come easily with beauty make beauty soon cease to be morally good    185 **complexion** character and appearance    187 **but that** were it not that    188 **examples** precedents    189 **this substitute** i.e., the deputy, Angelo    191 **resolve him** set his mind at rest.    195–6 **discover his government** expose Angelo's miscon- duct.    198 **avoid** evade, refute.    **he made** i.e., he will say that he made    207 **spirit** courage    208 **truth** righteousness    209 **spirit** soul.

212 **miscarried** suffered misfortune    215 **She . . . married** Angelo was supposed to have married her.    **was** i.e., he was    217–18 **limit . . . solemnity** date set for the ceremony    223 **the portion and sinew** i.e., the mainstay    224 **combinate husband** i.e., betrothed    228–9 **pretend- ing . . . dishonor** falsely alleging to have found evidence of unchastity in her    229–30 **in few . . . lamentation** in short, left her to her grief. (With quibble on *bestowed,* meaning "gave in marriage.")    230 **wears** i.e., carries in her heart    231 **a marble to** i.e., unmoved by    233–4 **What . . . world!** What a relief it would be for this poor maid if she were to die!    236 **avail** benefit.    246–7 **to the point** precisely. 247 **refer . . . advantage** obtain these conditions    249 **shadow** darkness, secrecy    252 **stead . . . appointment** go in your stead    253–4 **If the . . . hereafter** i.e., If she should become pregnant    254 **to her recompense** to recompense her by marrying her.    257 **scaled** weighed in the scales of justice (and found wanting).    **frame** prepare

tempt. If you think well to carry this as you may, the
doubleness of the benefit defends the deceit from reproof. What think you of it?

ISABELLA   The image of it gives me content already,
and I trust it will grow to a most prosperous perfection.

DUKE   It lies much in your holding up. Haste you speed-   264
ily to Angelo. If for this night he entreat you to his
bed, give him promise of satisfaction. I will presently   266
to Saint Luke's; there, at the moated grange, resides   267
this dejected Mariana. At that place call upon me; and
dispatch with Angelo, that it may be quickly.   269

ISABELLA   I thank you for this comfort. Fare you well,
good Father.                              *Exit.* [*The Duke remains.*]

## [3.2]

*Enter [to the Duke] Elbow, Clown [Pompey, and]
officers.*

ELBOW   Nay, if there be no remedy for it but that you
will needs buy and sell men and women like beasts,
we shall have all the world drink brown and white
bastard.                                                    4

DUKE [*aside*]   Oh, heavens, what stuff is here?

POMPEY   'Twas never merry world since, of two usur-   6
ies, the merriest was put down, and the worser al-   7
lowed by order of law a furred gown to keep him   8
warm, and furred with fox on lambskins too, to signify that craft, being richer than innocency, stands   10
for the facing.   11

ELBOW   Come your way, sir.—Bless you, good Father
Friar.

DUKE   And you, good Brother Father. What offense hath   14
this man made you, sir?

ELBOW   Marry, sir, he hath offended the law; and, sir,
we take him to be a thief too, sir, for we have found
upon him, sir, a strange picklock, which we have sent   18
to the deputy.

DUKE [*to Pompey*]
Fie, sirrah, a bawd, a wicked bawd!
The evil that thou causest to be done,
That is thy means to live. Do thou but think
What 'tis to cram a maw or clothe a back   23
From such a filthy vice; say to thyself,
From their abominable and beastly touches   25
I drink, I eat, array myself, and live.

Canst thou believe thy living is a life,
So stinkingly depending? Go mend, go mend.   28

POMPEY   Indeed, it does stink in some sort, sir. But yet,
sir, I would prove—   30

DUKE
Nay, if the devil have given thee proofs for sin,   31
Thou wilt prove his.—Take him to prison, officer.   32
Correction and instruction must both work
Ere this rude beast will profit.

ELBOW   He must before the deputy, sir; he has given   35
him warning. The deputy cannot abide a whoremaster. If he be a whoremonger and comes before him, he   37
were as good go a mile on his errand.   38

DUKE
That we were all, as some would seem to be,   39
From our faults, as faults from seeming, free!   40

*Enter Lucio.*

ELBOW   His neck will come to your waist—a cord, sir.   41

POMPEY   I spy comfort, I cry bail. Here's a gentleman
and a friend of mine.

LUCIO   How now, noble Pompey? What, at the wheels
of Caesar? Art thou led in triumph? What, is there   45
none of Pygmalion's images, newly made woman, to   46
be had now, for putting the hand in the pocket and
extracting it clutched? What reply, ha? What say'st thou   48
to this tune, matter, and method? Is 't not drowned i' th'   49
last rain, ha? What say'st thou, trot? Is the world as   50
it was, man? Which is the way? Is it sad, and few   51
words? Or how? The trick of it?   52

DUKE   Still thus, and thus; still worse!

LUCIO   How doth my dear morsel, thy mistress? Pro-   54
cures she still, ha?   55

POMPEY   Troth, sir, she hath eaten up all her beef, and   56
she is herself in the tub.   57

LUCIO   Why, 'tis good. It is the right of it, it must be so.   58
Ever your fresh whore and your powdered bawd; an   59
unshunned consequence, it must be so. Art going to   60
prison, Pompey?

POMPEY   Yes, faith, sir.                                                            62

LUCIO   Why, 'tis not amiss, Pompey. Farewell. Go, say I sent thee thither. For debt, Pompey? Or how?

ELBOW   For being a bawd, for being a bawd.

LUCIO   Well, then, imprison him. If imprisonment be the due of a bawd, why, 'tis his right. Bawd is he doubtless, and of antiquity too; bawd-born. Farewell,    68
good Pompey. Commend me to the prison, Pompey. You will turn good husband now, Pompey; you will    70
keep the house.                                                                       71

POMPEY   I hope, sir, Your good Worship will be my bail.

LUCIO   No, indeed, will I not, Pompey; it is not the wear. I will pray, Pompey, to increase your bondage.    74
If you take it not patiently, why, your mettle is the    75
more. Adieu, trusty Pompey.—Bless you, Friar.    76

DUKE   And you.

LUCIO   Does Bridget paint still, Pompey, ha?    78

ELBOW   [to Pompey]   Come your ways, sir, come.    79

POMPEY   [to Lucio]   You will not bail me, then, sir?

LUCIO   Then, Pompey, nor now.—What news abroad,    81
Friar? What news?

ELBOW   Come your ways, sir, come.

LUCIO   Go to kennel, Pompey, go.
                   [Exeunt Elbow, Pompey, and Officers.]
What news, Friar, of the Duke?

DUKE   I know none. Can you tell me of any?

LUCIO   Some say he is with the Emperor of Russia; other    87
some, he is in Rome. But where is he, think you?    88

DUKE   I know not where; but wheresoever, I wish him well.

LUCIO   It was a mad fantastical trick of him to steal from    91
the state and usurp the beggary he was never born to.    92
Lord Angelo dukes it well in his absence; he puts    93
transgression to't.    94

DUKE   He does well in't.

LUCIO   A little more lenity to lechery would do no harm in him. Something too crabbed that way, Friar.    97

DUKE   It is too general a vice, and severity must cure it.

LUCIO   Yes, in good sooth, the vice is of a great kindred;    99
it is well allied. But it is impossible to extirp it quite,    100
Friar, till eating and drinking be put down. They say this Angelo was not made by man and woman after    102
this downright way of creation. Is it true, think you?    103

DUKE   How should he be made, then?

LUCIO   Some report a sea maid spawned him; some,    105
that he was begot between two stockfishes. But it is    106

certain that when he makes water his urine is congealed ice; that I know to be true. And he is a motion    108
ungenerative; that's infallible.    109

DUKE   You are pleasant, sir, and speak apace.    110

LUCIO   Why, what a ruthless thing is this in him, for the rebellion of a codpiece to take away the life of a man!    112
Would the Duke that is absent have done this? Ere he would have hanged a man for the getting a hundred bastards, he would have paid for the nursing a thousand. He had some feeling of the sport; he knew the service, and that instructed him to mercy.    117

DUKE   I never heard the absent Duke much detected for    118
women. He was not inclined that way.

LUCIO   Oh, sir, you are deceived.

DUKE   'Tis not possible.

LUCIO   Who, not the Duke? Yes, your beggar of fifty; and his use was to put a ducat in her clack-dish. The    123
Duke had crotchets in him. He would be drunk too, that let me inform you.

DUKE   You do him wrong, surely.

LUCIO   Sir, I was an inward of his. A shy fellow was    127
the Duke, and I believe I know the cause of his withdrawing.

DUKE   What, I prithee, might be the cause?

LUCIO   No, pardon. 'Tis a secret must be locked within the teeth and the lips. But this I can let you understand: the greater file of the subject held the Duke to    133
be wise.

DUKE   Wise? Why, no question but he was.

LUCIO   A very superficial, ignorant, unweighing fellow.    136

DUKE   Either this is envy in you, folly, or mistaking. The    137
very stream of his life and the business he hath helmed    138
must, upon a warranted need, give him a better proc-    139
lamation. Let him be but testimonied in his own    140
bringings-forth, and he shall appear to the envious a    141
scholar, a statesman, and a soldier. Therefore you speak unskillfully; or, if your knowledge be more, it is    143
much darkened in your malice.

LUCIO   Sir, I know him, and I love him.

DUKE   Love talks with better knowledge, and knowledge with dearer love.

LUCIO   Come, sir, I know what I know.

DUKE   I can hardly believe that, since you know not what you speak. But if ever the Duke return, as our prayers are he may, let me desire you to make your answer before him. If it be honest you have spoke, you have courage to maintain it. I am bound to call upon you; and, I pray you, your name?

---

62 **faith** in good faith. (A mild oath.)   68 **antiquity** long continuance. **bawd-born** a born bawd and born of a bawd.   70 **good husband** thrifty manager   71 **keep the house** stay indoors. (With pun on the pimp's function as doorkeeper.)   74 **wear** fashion.   75–6 **your . . . more** (1) your spirit is revealed all the more (2) your shackles will be made heavier. (Playing on *mettle/metal*.)   78 **paint** use cosmetics   79 **Come your ways** Come along   81 **Then** Neither then.   **abroad** about town   87–8 **other some** some others say   91 **steal** steal away   92 **beggary** i.e., status of a wanderer or traveler. (With unconscious ironic appropriateness; Lucio clearly does not see through the Duke's disguise as a mendicant friar.)   93–4 **puts . . . to't** puts lawbreaking under severe restraint.   97 **Something too crabbed** Somewhat too harsh   99 **in good sooth** truly.   **kindred** i.e., family, numerous and well connected   100 **extirp** eradicate   102 **after** in accordance with   103 **downright** straightforward, usual   105 **sea maid** mermaid   106 **stockfishes** dried codfish.

108–9 **motion ungenerative** masculine puppet, without sexual potency   110 **pleasant** jocose.   **apace** fast and idly.   112 **codpiece** an appendage to the front of close-fitting hose or breeches worn by men, often ornamented and indelicately conspicuous; hence, slang for "penis"   117 **the service** i.e., prostitution   118 **detected** accused   123 **his . . . clack-dish** his custom was to put a coin in her wooden beggar's bowl, with its lid that was "clacked" to attract attention. (Lucio hints that the Duke had sex with her.)   127 **inward** intimate   133 **the greater . . . subject** most of his subjects   136 **unweighing** injudicious   137 **envy** malice   138 **helmed** steered   139 **upon . . . need** if a warrant were needed   139–40 **give . . . proclamation** proclaim him better (than you assert).   140–1 **in . . . bringings-forth** by his own public actions   141 **to the envious** even to the malicious   143 **unskillfully** in ignorance

LUCIO   Sir, my name is Lucio, well known to the Duke.

DUKE   He shall know you better, sir, if I may live to report you.

LUCIO   I fear you not.

DUKE   Oh, you hope the Duke will return no more, or you imagine me too unhurtful an opposite. But indeed 160 I can do you little harm; you'll forswear this again. 161

LUCIO   I'll be hanged first. Thou art deceived in me, Friar. But no more of this. Canst thou tell if Claudio die tomorrow or no?

DUKE   Why should he die, sir?

LUCIO   Why? For filling a bottle with a tundish. I would 166 the Duke we talk of were returned again. This ungeni- 167 tured agent will unpeople the province with conti- 168 nency. Sparrows must not build in his house eaves, 169 because they are lecherous. The Duke yet would have dark deeds darkly answered; he would never bring 171 them to light. Would he were returned! Marry, this Claudio is condemned for untrussing. Farewell, good 173 Friar. I prithee, pray for me. The Duke, I say to thee again, would eat mutton on Fridays. He's now past it, 175 yet, and I say to thee, he would mouth with a beggar, 176 though she smelt brown bread and garlic. Say that I 177 said so. Farewell.                           *Exit.*

DUKE

No might nor greatness in mortality                          179
Can censure scape; back-wounding calumny                    180
The whitest virtue strikes. What king so strong             181
Can tie the gall up in the slanderous tongue?               182
But who comes here?

*Enter Escalus, Provost, and [officers with] bawd
[Mistress Overdone].*

ESCALUS   Go, away with her to prison.

MISTRESS OVERDONE   Good my lord, be good to me. Your Honor is accounted a merciful man. Good my lord.

ESCALUS   Double and treble admonition, and still forfeit 188 in the same kind! This would make mercy swear and 189 play the tyrant.

PROVOST   A bawd of eleven years' continuance, may it please Your Honor.

MISTRESS OVERDONE   My lord, this is one Lucio's infor- 193 mation against me. Mistress Kate Keepdown was with 194 child by him in the Duke's time; he promised her mar-

riage. His child is a year and a quarter old, come Philip 196 and Jacob. I have kept it myself; and see how he goes 197 about to abuse me! 198

ESCALUS   That fellow is a fellow of much license. Let him be called before us. Away with her to prison! Go to, no more words.        [*Exeunt Officers with Mistress Overdone.*]

Provost, my brother Angelo will not be al- 202 tered; Claudio must die tomorrow. Let him be fur- nished with divines and have all charitable 204 preparation. If my brother wrought by my pity, it 205 should not be so with him.

PROVOST   So please you, this friar hath been with him, and advised him for th'entertainment of death.          208

ESCALUS   Good even, good Father.

DUKE   Bliss and goodness on you!

ESCALUS   Of whence are you?

DUKE

Not of this country, though my chance is now           212
To use it for my time. I am a brother                  213
Of gracious order, late come from the See              214
In special business from His Holiness.

ESCALUS   What news abroad i'th' world?

DUKE   None but that there is so great a fever on good- ness that the dissolution of it must cure it. Novelty is 218 only in request, and, as it is, as dangerous to be aged 219 in any kind of course as it is virtuous to be constant 220 in any undertaking. There is scarce truth enough alive 221 to make societies secure, but security enough to make 222 fellowships accursed. Much upon this riddle runs the 223 wisdom of the world. This news is old enough, yet it is every day's news. I pray you, sir, of what disposi- tion was the Duke?

ESCALUS   One that, above all other strifes, contended 227 especially to know himself.

DUKE   What pleasure was he given to?

ESCALUS   Rather rejoicing to see another merry than merry at anything which professed to make him re- 231 joice—a gentleman of all temperance. But leave we him to his events, with a prayer they may prove pros- 233 perous, and let me desire to know how you find Clau- dio prepared. I am made to understand that you have lent him visitation. 236

**196–7 Philip and Jacob** the Feast of Saint Philip and Saint James (*Jacobus* in Latin), May 1.   **197–8 goes about** busies himself   **202 brother** i.e., fellow officer of state   **204 divines** clergymen (to offer spiritual counsel and administer last rites)   **205 wrought . . . pity** acted in accord with my impulses of pity   **208 th'entertainment** the reception, acceptance   **212 chance** fortune   **213 To . . . time** to dwell here for my present purposes.   **214 the See** Rome   **218 the dissolution . . . cure it** i.e., only by dying can goodness be rid of the disease.   **218–19 is only in request** is the only thing people seek   **219–21 as it . . . undertaking** as things currently stand, (it is) as dangerous to be constant in any undertaking as it is virtuous to be thus constant.   **221–3 There . . . accursed** i.e., There is hardly enough integrity extant to establish secure and trusting associations among men, but binding contractual obligations enough to be the curse of friendship. (The Duke thus puns on *security* [1] a sense of trust [2] financial pledge required to borrow money, and on *fellowship* [1] friendship [2] corporations formed for trading ventures.)   **223 upon this riddle** in this riddling fashion   **227 strifes** endeavors   **231 professed** attempted   **233 his events** his affairs and their outcome   **236 lent him visitation** paid him a priestly visit.

**160 too . . . opposite** too harmless an adversary.   **161 forswear this again** deny another time what you have said under oath.   **166 tundish** funnel. (Here representing the penis.)   **167–8 ungeni- tured agent** sexless deputy   **169 Sparrows** (Proverbially lecherous birds.)   **171 darkly** secretly   **173 untrussing** undressing. (Specifi- cally, untying the points used to fasten hose to doublet.)   **175 eat . . . Fridays** i.e., frequent loose women in flagrant disregard of the law. (Literally, violate religious observance by eating meat on fast days.)   **past it** beyond the age for sex   **176 mouth** kiss   **177 smelt brown bread** smelled of coarse bran bread   **179 mortality** humankind; human life   **180–1 Can . . . strikes** can escape censure; backbiting slander strikes even the purest of virtues.   **181 so** be he never so   **182 gall** effrontery, spleen, malice (believed in humors theory to be the product of the gallbladder)   **188–9 Double . . . kind!** Behavior thrice deserving admonition and forfeiture at law!   **189 mercy** i.e., mercy itself   **193–4 information** accusation

DUKE   He professes to have received no sinister measure 237
from his judge, but most willingly humbles himself to
the determination of justice; yet had he framed to him- 239
self, by the instruction of his frailty, many deceiving 240
promises of life, which I, by my good leisure, have
discredited to him, and now is he resolved to die.

ESCALUS   You have paid the heavens your function, and
the prisoner the very debt of your calling. I have la- 244
bored for the poor gentleman to the extremest shore of 245
my modesty, but my brother justice have I found so 246
severe that he hath forced me to tell him he is indeed
Justice.                                                 248

DUKE   If his own life answer the straitness of his 249
proceeding, it shall become him well; wherein if he
chance to fail, he hath sentenced himself.

ESCALUS   I am going to visit the prisoner. Fare you well.

DUKE   Peace be with you!
                              [*Exeunt Escalus and Provost.*]
He who the sword of heaven will bear
Should be as holy as severe;
Pattern in himself to know,                              256
Grace to stand, and virtue go;                           257
More nor less to others paying                           258
Than by self-offenses weighing.                          259
Shame to him whose cruel striking
Kills for faults of his own liking!
Twice treble shame on Angelo,
To weed my vice and let his grow!                        263
Oh, what may man within him hide,
Though angel on the outward side!
How may likeness made in crimes,                         266
Making practice on the times,                            267
To draw with idle spiders' strings                       268
Most ponderous and substantial things!                   269
Craft against vice I must apply.
With Angelo tonight shall lie
His old betrothèd but despisèd;
So disguise shall, by the disguisèd,                     273
Pay with falsehood false exacting                        274
And perform an old contracting.       *Exit.*            275

❧

## 4.1

*Enter Mariana, and Boy singing.*

                    Song.
BOY
Take, oh, take those lips away,
    That so sweetly were forsworn,
And those eyes, the break of day,
    Lights that do mislead the morn;                     4
But my kisses bring again, bring again,                  5
Seals of love, but sealed in vain, sealed in vain.       6

    *Enter Duke [disguised as before].*

MARIANA
Break off thy song, and haste thee quick away.
Here comes a man of comfort, whose advice
Hath often stilled my brawling discontent. [*Exit Boy.*] 9
I cry you mercy, sir, and well could wish                10
You had not found me here so musical.
Let me excuse me, and believe me so,
My mirth it much displeased, but pleased my woe.         13
DUKE
'Tis good; though music oft hath such a charm
To make bad good, and good provoke to harm.              15
I pray you, tell me, hath anybody inquired for me here
today? Much upon this time have I promised here          17
to meet.
MARIANA   You have not been inquired after. I have sat
here all day.

    *Enter Isabella.*

DUKE   I do constantly believe you. The time is come     21
even now. I shall crave your forbearance a little. May-  22
be I will call upon you anon, for some advantage to      23
yourself.
MARIANA   I am always bound to you.          *Exit.*
DUKE   Very well met, and welcome.
What is the news from this good deputy?
ISABELLA
He hath a garden circummured with brick,                 28
Whose western side is with a vineyard backed;
And to that vineyard is a planchèd gate,                 30
That makes his opening with this bigger key.             31
                              [*She shows keys.*]

237 **no sinister measure** no unfair treatment meted out to him
**239–40 framed to himself** formulated in his mind   **240 by . . . frailty**
at the prompting of his natural human weakness   **244 the
prisoner . . . calling** what your calling as a friar obliges you to give
the prisoner, i.e., the comforts of spiritual counsel.   **245–6 shore . . .
modesty** limit of propriety   **248 Justice** i.e., the full rigor of justice
untempered by mercy.   **249 straitness** strictness   **256–9 Pattern . . .
weighing** he must know himself and be a pattern for others to emulate, with the grace to stand firm and the virtue to guide himself in the
straight path, judging and punishing others with neither more nor
less severity than he applies to his own offenses.   **263 my vice** i.e.,
vice in everyone except Angelo. (The Duke speaks chorically on
behalf of everyone generally.)   **266–9 How . . . things!** How may false
seeming of a criminal sort, practicing deception on the world, make
weighty and substantial matters seem as illusory and unsubstantial as
spider webs!   **273–5 So . . . contracting** so shall disguise, employed
by those in disguise (i.e., Mariana and the Duke himself), use a kind
of (virtuous) falsehood to pay back what was exacted through deception (by Angelo), and thereby fulfill an old contract.

**4.1. Location:** The moated grange at Saint Luke's.
**4 Lights . . . morn** eyes that mislead the morning (the goddess of
dawn, Eos or Aurora) into taking them for the rising sun   **5 again**
back   **6 Seals** confirmations, pledges   **9 brawling** clamorous
**10 cry you mercy** beg your pardon   **13 My . . . woe** i.e., it suited not a
merry but a melancholy mood.   **15 bad good** i.e., bad seem good,
attractive. (The Duke, echoing Renaissance conceptions of the psychological effects of music, warns that music can sometimes lend a
pleasing aura to sin and lead virtue into harm.)   **17 Much upon**
Pretty nearly about   **21 constantly** confidently   **22 crave . . . little**
i.e., ask you to withdraw briefly.   **23 anon** presently   **28 circummured** walled about   **30 planchèd** made of boards, planks
**31 his** its

This other doth command a little door
Which from the vineyard to the garden leads;
There have I made my promise, upon the                          34
Heavy middle of the night, to call upon him.

**DUKE**
But shall you on your knowledge find this way?

**ISABELLA**
I have ta'en a due and wary note upon't.
With whispering and most guilty diligence,
In action all of precept, he did show me                        39
The way twice o'er.

**DUKE**                          Are there no other tokens
Between you 'greed concerning her observance?                   41

**ISABELLA**
No, none, but only a repair i'th' dark,                         42
And that I have possessed him my most stay                      43
Can be but brief; for I have made him know
I have a servant comes with me along,                           45
That stays upon me, whose persuasion is                         46
I come about my brother.

**DUKE**                           'Tis well borne up.          47
I have not yet made known to Mariana
A word of this.—What, ho, within! Come forth!

*Enter Mariana.*

I pray you, be acquainted with this maid;
She comes to do you good.

**ISABELLA**                        I do desire the like.

**DUKE**
Do you persuade yourself that I respect you?                    52

**MARIANA**
Good Friar, I know you do, and have found it.                   53

**DUKE**
Take then this your companion by the hand,
Who hath a story ready for your ear.
I shall attend your leisure. But make haste;
The vaporous night approaches.

**MARIANA**    Will't please you walk aside?

*Exit [with Isabella].*

**DUKE**
O place and greatness! Millions of false eyes
Are stuck upon thee. Volumes of report                          60
Run with these false and most contrarious quests               61
Upon thy doings; thousand escapes of wit                        62
Make thee the father of their idle dream                        63
And rack thee in their fancies.

*Enter Mariana and Isabella.*

Welcome. How agreed?                                            64

**ISABELLA**
She'll take the enterprise upon her, Father,
If you advise it.

**DUKE**                    It is not my consent,                66
But my entreaty too.

**ISABELLA**                    Little have you to say           67
When you depart from him but, soft and low,
"Remember now my brother."

**MARIANA**                         Fear me not.                 69

**DUKE**
Nor, gentle daughter, fear you not at all.
He is your husband on a precontract;                            71
To bring you thus together, 'tis no sin,
Sith that the justice of your title to him                      73
Doth flourish the deceit. Come, let us go.                      74
Our corn's to reap, for yet our tithe's to sow.   *Exeunt.*     75

❧

# 4.2

*Enter Provost and Clown [Pompey].*

**PROVOST**    Come hither, sirrah. Can you cut off a man's       1
head?

**POMPEY**    If the man be a bachelor, sir, I can; but if he be
a married man, he's his wife's head, and I can never            4
cut off a woman's head.                                         5

**PROVOST**    Come, sir, leave me your snatches, and yield      6
me a direct answer. Tomorrow morning are to die
Claudio and Barnardine. Here is in our prison a com-            8
mon executioner, who in his office lacks a helper. If           9
you will take it on you to assist him, it shall redeem
you from your gyves; if not, you shall have your full           11
time of imprisonment and your deliverance with an
unpitied whipping, for you have been a notorious
bawd.

**POMPEY**    Sir, I have been an unlawful bawd time out of
mind, but yet I will be content to be a lawful hangman.
I would be glad to receive some instruction from
my fellow partner.

**PROVOST** [*calling*]    What, ho, Abhorson! Where's Abhorson, there?

*Enter Abhorson.*

**ABHORSON**    Do you call, sir?

**PROVOST**    Sirrah, here's a fellow will help you tomorrow    22
in your execution. If you think it meet, compound               23
with him by the year, and let him abide here with
you; if not, use him for the present and dismiss him.

---

34 **upon** during, at   39 **In action . . . precept** i.e., teaching by demonstration   41 **her observance** what she is supposed to do.   42 **repair** act of going or coming to a place   43 **possessed** informed.   **my most stay** my stay at the longest   45 **comes** who comes   46 **stays upon** waits for.   **persuasion** understanding   47 **borne up** sustained, carried out.   52 **respect you** are concerned for your welfare.   53 **found it** found it to be true.   60 **stuck** fastened   60–2 **Volumes . . . doings** Innumerable rumors follow a false scent and hunt counter in pursuing your activities   62 **escapes** sallies   63 **Make . . . dream** credit you with being the source of their fantasies   64 **rack** stretch as on the rack, distort

66 **not** not only   67 **Little . . . say** Say little   69 **Fear me not** i.e., Don't worry about my carrying out my part.   71 **precontract** legally binding agreement entered into before any church ceremony. (Compare Claudio's and Juliet's *true contract* at 1.2.142.)   73 **Sith that** since   74 **flourish** adorn, make fair   75 **Our corn's . . . sow** We must first sow grain before we can expect to reap a harvest; i.e., we must get started.   **tithe** grain sown for tithe dues; or, an error for "tilth"
4.2. Location: The prison.
1 **sirrah** (Form of address to a social inferior.)   4 **he's . . . head** (Compare Ephesians 5:23: "The husband is the head of the wife.")   5 **head** (With wordplay on "maidenhead.")   6 **leave . . . snatches** leave off your quibbles   8–9 **common** public   11 **gyves** fetters, shackles
22 **will** that will   23 **meet** fitting.   **compound** make an agreement

He cannot plead his estimation with you; he hath   26
been a bawd.

ABHORSON   A bawd, sir? Fie upon him! He will discredit our mystery.   29

PROVOST   Go to, sir, you weigh equally; a feather will   30
turn the scale.   *Exit.*   31

POMPEY   Pray, sir, by your good favor—for surely, sir,   32
a good favor you have, but that you have a hanging   33
look—do you call, sir, your occupation a mystery?   34

ABHORSON   Ay, sir, a mystery.

POMPEY   Painting, sir, I have heard say, is a mystery,   36
and your whores, sir, being members of my occupation, using painting, do prove my occupation a
mystery. But what mystery there should be in hanging, if I should be hanged, I cannot imagine.

ABHORSON   Sir, it is a mystery.

POMPEY   Proof?

ABHORSON   Every true man's apparel fits your thief. If it   43
be too little for your thief, your true man thinks it big   44
enough; if it be too big for your thief, your thief thinks   45
it little enough. So every true man's apparel fits your   46
thief.   47

*Enter Provost.*

PROVOST   Are you agreed?

POMPEY   Sir, I will serve him, for I do find your hangman is a more penitent trade than your bawd: he doth   50
oftener ask forgiveness.   51

PROVOST   You, sirrah, provide your block and your ax
tomorrow four o'clock.

ABHORSON   Come on, bawd. I will instruct thee in my
trade. Follow!

POMPEY   I do desire to learn, sir; and I hope, if you have
occasion to use me for your own turn, you shall find   57
me yare. For truly, sir, for your kindness I owe you a   58
good turn.

PROVOST
Call hither Barnardine and Claudio.
                              *Exit [Pompey, with Abhorson].*
Th'one has my pity; not a jot the other,
Being a murderer, though he were my brother.

*Enter Claudio.*

Look, here's the warrant, Claudio, for thy death.
'Tis now dead midnight, and by eight tomorrow
Thou must be made immortal. Where's Barnardine?   65

CLAUDIO
As fast locked up in sleep as guiltless labor   66
When it lies starkly in the traveler's bones.   67
He will not wake.

PROVOST            Who can do good on him?
Well, go, prepare yourself. [*Knocking within.*] But hark,
what noise?
Heaven give your spirits comfort!   [*Exit Claudio.*]
                              [*calling*] By and by—
I hope it is some pardon or reprieve
For the most gentle Claudio.

*Enter Duke [disguised as before].*

                              Welcome, Father.

DUKE
The best and wholesom'st spirits of the night
Envelop you, good Provost! Who called here of late?

PROVOST   None since the curfew rung.

DUKE
Not Isabel?

PROVOST            No.

DUKE            They will, then, ere't be long.

PROVOST   What comfort is for Claudio?

DUKE
There's some in hope.

PROVOST            It is a bitter deputy.

DUKE
Not so, not so. His life is paralleled   79
Even with the stroke and line of his great justice.   80
He doth with holy abstinence subdue
That in himself which he spurs on his power   82
To qualify in others. Were he mealed with that   83
Which he corrects, then were he tyrannous;   84
But this being so, he's just. [*Knocking within.*] Now
are they come.   [*The Provost goes to the door.*]   85
This is a gentle provost; seldom when   86
The steelèd jailer is the friend of men.   87
                              [*Knocking within.*]
How now? What noise? That spirit's possessed with
haste
That wounds th'unsisting postern with these strokes.   89

PROVOST [*speaking at the door*]
There he must stay until the officer
Arise to let him in. He is called up.
                              [*He returns to the Duke.*]

DUKE
Have you no countermand for Claudio yet,
But he must die tomorrow?

PROVOST            None, sir, none.

DUKE
As near the dawning, Provost, as it is,

---

**26 plead his estimation** claim any respect on account of his reputation   **29 mystery** craft, occupation.   **30 Go to** (An exclamation of impatience or protest.)   **30–1 a feather . . . scale** a feather added to one side of a balance scales will tip the balance to that side.   **32 favor** leave, permission   **33 favor** face   **33–4 hanging look** (1) downcast look (2) look of a hangman   **36 Painting** (1) Painting of pictures (2) Applying cosmetics   **43–7 Every . . . thief** (Abhorson alludes to the custom of giving to the hangman the garments of the executed criminal. Like a thief, a hangman takes from all sorts of men; Death is the great thief. The hangman's occupation is to settle all scores.)   **44–5 big enough** i.e., enough of a loss   **46 little enough** little enough for his efforts.   **50–1 he doth . . . forgiveness** (The executioner perfunctorily asked forgiveness of those whose lives he was about to take. Pompey comically sees penitence as well suited to him as a perpetual offender.)   **57 for . . . turn** (1) as a pimp to provide for your sexual needs (2) as your hangman when it is your turn to be hanged or "turned off" the ladder   **58 yare** ready, alacritous.   **65 made immortal** i.e., executed.

**66 fast** firmly, soundly.   **guiltless labor** (A personification of the well-earned weariness that tires the innocent laborer.)   **67 starkly** stiffly.   **traveler's bones** bones of one who travails or labors or journeys.   **79–80 His . . . justice** His life runs parallel and in exact conformity with the straight line and precise execution of the justice he carries out. (With a hidden irony: Angelo's life is precisely equal to the corrupt justice he practices.)   **82–3 which . . . others** which he then powerfully seeks to restrain in others.   **83 mealed** spotted, stained   **84 were he** he would be   **85 But . . . so** But since Angelo is not stained with the sin he corrects in others; or, conditionally, if this were so   **86 seldom when** i.e., it is seldom that   **87 steelèd** hardened   **89 unsisting** unyielding, unresting, or unresisting (?).   **postern** small door

You shall hear more ere morning.

PROVOST                                        Happily    95
You something know, yet I believe there comes
No countermand. No such example have we;    97
Besides, upon the very siege of justice    98
Lord Angelo hath to the public ear
Professed the contrary.

*Enter a Messenger.*

This is His Lordship's man.

DUKE
And here comes Claudio's pardon.

MESSENGER [*giving a paper*]  My lord hath sent you
this note, and by me this further charge, that you
swerve not from the smallest article of it, neither in
time, matter, or other circumstance. Good morrow;
for, as I take it, it is almost day.

PROVOST  I shall obey him.                *[Exit Messenger.]*

DUKE [*aside*]
This is his pardon, purchased by such sin
For which the pardoner himself is in.    109
Hence hath offense his quick celerity,    110
When it is borne in high authority.    111
When vice makes mercy, mercy's so extended    112
That for the fault's love is th'offender friended.—    113
Now, sir, what news?

PROVOST  I told you. Lord Angelo, belike thinking me    115
remiss in mine office, awakens me with this un-    116
wonted putting-on—methinks strangely, for he hath    117
not used it before.

DUKE  Pray you, let's hear.

PROVOST [*reads*] *the letter*  "Whatsoever you may hear
to the contrary, let Claudio be executed by four of
the clock, and in the afternoon Barnardine. For my
better satisfaction, let me have Claudio's head sent    123
me by five. Let this be duly performed, with a
thought that more depends on it than we must yet
deliver. Thus fail not to do your office, as you will    126
answer it at your peril." What say you to this, sir?

DUKE  What is that Barnardine who is to be executed in
th'afternoon?

PROVOST  A Bohemian born, but here nursed up and    131
bred; one that is a prisoner nine years old.    132

DUKE  How came it that the absent Duke had not either
delivered him to his liberty or executed him? I have
heard it was ever his manner to do so.

PROVOST  His friends still wrought reprieves for him;    136
and indeed his fact, till now in the government of Lord    137
Angelo, came not to an undoubtful proof.

DUKE  It is now apparent?

PROVOST  Most manifest, and not denied by himself.

DUKE  Hath he borne himself penitently in prison? How
seems he to be touched?    142

PROVOST  A man that apprehends death no more dread-    143
fully but as a drunken sleep—careless, reckless, and    144
fearless of what's past, present, or to come; insensible    145
of mortality, and desperately mortal.    146

DUKE  He wants advice.    147

PROVOST  He will hear none. He hath evermore had the    148
liberty of the prison; give him leave to escape hence,    149
he would not. Drunk many times a day, if not many
days entirely drunk. We have very oft awaked him,
as if to carry him to execution, and showed him a
seeming warrant for it; it hath not moved him at all.

DUKE  More of him anon. There is written in your brow,
Provost, honesty and constancy; if I read it not truly,
my ancient skill beguiles me, but, in the boldness of my    156
cunning, I will lay myself in hazard. Claudio, whom    157
here you have warrant to execute, is no greater forfeit to the law than Angelo who hath sentenced him.
To make you understand this in a manifested effect, I    160
crave but four days' respite, for the which you are to
do me both a present and a dangerous courtesy.    162

PROVOST  Pray, sir, in what?

DUKE  In the delaying death.

PROVOST  Alack, how may I do it, having the hour
limited, and an express command, under penalty, to    166
deliver his head in the view of Angelo? I may make
my case as Claudio's, to cross this in the smallest.

DUKE  By the vow of mine order I warrant you, if my
instructions may be your guide. Let this Barnardine
be this morning executed, and his head borne to
Angelo.

PROVOST  Angelo hath seen them both and will discover    173
the favor.    174

DUKE  Oh, death's a great disguiser, and you may add
to it. Shave the head, and tie the beard, and say it was    176
the desire of the penitent to be so bared before his
death. You know the course is common. If anything    178
fall to you upon this more than thanks and good    179
fortune, by the saint whom I profess, I will plead    180
against it with my life.

PROVOST  Pardon me, good Father, it is against my oath.

DUKE  Were you sworn to the Duke or to the deputy?

PROVOST  To him, and to his substitutes.

DUKE  You will think you have made no offense if the
Duke avouch the justice of your dealing?    186

PROVOST  But what likelihood is in that?

DUKE  Not a resemblance, but a certainty. Yet since I see
you fearful, that neither my coat, integrity, nor    189

---

95 **Happily** Haply, perhaps  97 **example** precedent  98 **siege** seat
109 **in** engaged.  110–11 **Hence . . . authority** Hence it is that criminal
behavior in high places has its (*his*) own quick way of covering its
tracks.  112–13 **When . . . friended** When criminality acts to save a
life, as in this case, mercy is so strangely broadened in definition that
the offender (here, Claudio) is spared for the fault committed by the
person in authority.  115 **belike** perchance  116–17 **unwonted
putting-on** unaccustomed urging  123 **better satisfaction** greater
assurance  126 **deliver** make known.  131 **here** i.e., in Vienna
132 **a prisoner . . . old** nine years a prisoner.  136 **His friends**
Barnardine's friends  137 **fact** crime.  **in the government of** in
a case assigned to

142 **touched** affected, touched by remorse.  143–4 **no more dreadfully but** with no more dread than  145–6 **insensible . . . mortal**
incapable of comprehending the meaning of death, and incorrigible.
147 **wants advice** needs spiritual counsel.  148 **evermore** constantly
148–9 **the liberty . . . prison** freedom to go anywhere within the
prison  149 **give him** if you were to give him  156–7 **in the . . .
hazard** confident in my knowledge (of human character), I will put
myself at risk.  160 **in . . . effect** by means of concrete proof
162 **present** immediate  166 **limited** fixed, set  173–4 **discover the
favor** recognize the face.  176 **tie** tie up, tidy up  178 **course** practice
179 **fall to** befall  180 **the saint . . . profess** i.e., St. Benedict, whose
example I follow  186 **avouch** confirm  189 **coat** clerical garment

persuasion can with ease attempt you, I will go further 190
than I meant, to pluck all fears out of you. Look you,
sir, here is the hand and seal of the Duke. [*He shows a
letter.*] You know the character, I doubt not, and the 193
signet is not strange to you. 194

PROVOST    I know them both.

DUKE    The contents of this is the return of the Duke.
You shall anon overread it at your pleasure, where
you shall find within these two days he will be here.
This is a thing that Angelo knows not, for he this very
day receives letters of strange tenor, perchance of the
Duke's death, perchance entering into some monas- 201
tery, but by chance nothing of what is writ. Look, th'un- 202
folding star calls up the shepherd. Put not yourself 203
into amazement how these things should be; all difficulties are but easy when they are known. Call your
executioner, and off with Barnardine's head. I will
give him a present shrift and advise him for a better 207
place. Yet you are amazed, but this shall absolutely 208
resolve you. Come away; it is almost clear dawn. 209

*Exit [with Provost].*

## 4.3

*Enter Clown [Pompey].*

POMPEY    I am as well acquainted here as I was in our 1
house of profession. One would think it were Mistress
Overdone's own house, for here be many of her old
customers. First, here's young Master Rash; he's in for 4
a commodity of brown paper and old ginger, nine- 5
score and seventeen pounds, of which he made five 6
marks, ready money. Marry, then ginger was not 7
much in request, for the old women were all dead. 8
Then is there here one Master Caper, at the suit of Mas- 9
ter Three-pile the mercer, for some four suits of peach- 10
colored satin, which now peaches him a beggar. 11
Then have we here young Dizzy, and young 12
Master Deep-vow, and Master Copper-spur, and 13

Master Starve-lackey the rapier and dagger man, and 14
young Drop-heir that killed lusty Pudding, and Mas- 15
ter Forthlight the tilter, and brave Master Shoe-tie the 16
great traveler, and wild Half-can that stabbed Pots, 17
and I think forty more, all great doers in our trade, and
are now "for the Lord's sake." 19

*Enter Abhorson.*

ABHORSON    Sirrah, bring Barnardine hither.

POMPEY [*calling*]    Master Barnardine! You must rise and
be hanged, Master Barnardine! 22

ABHORSON    What, ho, Barnardine!

BARNARDINE    (*within*)A pox o' your throats! Who 24
makes that noise there? What are you?

POMPEY    Your friends, sir, the hangman. You must be
so good, sir, to rise and be put to death.

BARNARDINE [*within*]    Away, you rogue, away! I am
sleepy.

ABHORSON    Tell him he must awake, and that quickly,
too.

POMPEY    Pray, Master Barnardine, awake till you are executed, and sleep afterwards.

ABHORSON    Go in to him, and fetch him out.

POMPEY    He is coming, sir, he is coming. I hear his
straw rustle.

*Enter Barnardine.*

ABHORSON    Is the ax upon the block, sirrah?

POMPEY    Very ready, sir.

BARNARDINE    How now, Abhorson? What's the news
with you?

ABHORSON    Truly, sir, I would desire you to clap into 41
your prayers; for, look you, the warrant's come.

BARNARDINE    You rogue, I have been drinking all
night. I am not fitted for't.

POMPEY    Oh, the better, sir, for he that drinks all night
and is hanged betimes in the morning may sleep the 46
sounder all the next day.

*Enter Duke [disguised as before].*

ABHORSON    Look you, sir, here comes your ghostly 48
father. Do we jest now, think you?

DUKE    Sir, induced by my charity, and hearing how
hastily you are to depart, I am come to advise you,
comfort you, and pray with you.

BARNARDINE    Friar, not I. I have been drinking hard all
night, and I will have more time to prepare me, or

---

190 **attempt** win, persuade    193 **character** handwriting    194 **strange**
unknown    201 **entering** of his entering    202 **writ** i.e., written here.
202-3 **unfolding star** i.e., morning star, Venus, which bids the shepherd lead his sheep from the fold    207 **present shrift** immediate
absolution for sins (after confession)    207–8 **advise . . . place** counsel
him on the comforts of heaven.    208 **Yet** Still    209 **resolve you** dispel
your uncertainties.
**4.3. Location: The prison.**
1 **well** widely    4 **Rash** (All the names mentioned by Pompey apparently glance at contemporary social affectations and defects. *Rash*
means "reckless.")    5–8 **a commodity . . . dead** (To circumvent the
laws against excessive rates of interest, moneylenders often advanced
cheap commodities to gullible borrowers in lieu of cash. Master Rash,
having agreed to a valuation of 197 pounds for such merchandise,
has been able to resell it for only five marks, each mark worth about
two-thirds of a pound, and has been thrown into prison for debt. The
ginger has not fetched a good price, owing to lack of customers, since
the old women who are proverbially fond of ginger are no longer
alive.)    9 **Caper** (To *caper* was to dance or leap gracefully.)
10 **Three-pile** the thickest nap and most expensive grade of velvet.
**mercer** cloth merchant.    **suits** (With a play on *suit*, line 9.)
11 **peaches him** denounces him as. (With a play on *peach*.)    12 **Dizzy**
i.e., giddy, foolish    13 **Deep-vow** one who swears earnestly and
often.    **Copper-spur** (Copper was often used fraudulently to simu-
late gold.)

14 **Starve-lackey** (Spendthrift gallants often virtually starved their
pages.)    **the rapier . . . man** one who fights with rapier and dagger
15 **Drop-heir** (Perhaps referring to those who disinherited or preyed
on unsuspecting heirs; or else *Drop-hair*, losing hair from syphilis.)    **lusty** vigorous.    **Pudding** i.e., sausage    16 **Forthlight**
(Unexplained; perhaps an error for *Forthright*, referring to a style of
tilting.)    **tilter** jouster.    **brave** showy, splendidly dressed.    **Shoe-tie**
(Evidently a nickname for travelers and others who affected the foreign fashion of elaborate rosettes on the tie of the shoe.)    17 **Half-can**
i.e., a small drinking tankard.    **Pots** i.e., ale pots    19 **"for . . . sake"**
(The cry of prisoners from jail grates to passers-by to give them food
or alms.)    22 **be hanged** (with wordplay on the common imprecation,
"Be hanged." Compare "Go to the devil.")    24 **A pox** i.e., A curse on
you. ("Pox" refers to syphilis or any pockmarking disease.)
41 **clap into** quickly begin    46 **betimes** early    48 **ghostly** spiritual

they shall beat out my brains with billets. I will not    55
consent to die this day, that's certain.

DUKE
Oh, sir, you must, and therefore I beseech you
Look forward on the journey you shall go.

BARNARDINE    I swear I will not die today for any man's
persuasion.

DUKE    But hear you—

BARNARDINE    Not a word. If you have anything to say
to me, come to my ward, for thence will not I today.    63
                                                    *Exit.*

*Enter Provost.*

DUKE
Unfit to live or die. Oh, gravel heart!                    64
After him, fellows. Bring him to the block.
                        [*Exeunt Abhorson and Pompey.*]

PROVOST
Now, sir, how do you find the prisoner?

DUKE
A creature unprepared, unmeet for death;                  67
And to transport him in the mind he is                    68
Were damnable.

PROVOST              Here in the prison, Father,           69
There died this morning of a cruel fever
One Ragozine, a most notorious pirate,
A man of Claudio's years, his beard and head
Just of his color. What if we do omit                      73
This reprobate till he were well inclined,                 74
And satisfy the deputy with the visage
Of Ragozine, more like to Claudio?

DUKE
Oh, 'tis an accident that heaven provides!
Dispatch it presently; the hour draws on                   78
Prefixed by Angelo. See this be done,                      79
And sent according to command, whiles I
Persuade this rude wretch willingly to die.               81

PROVOST
This shall be done, good Father, presently.
But Barnardine must die this afternoon.
And how shall we continue Claudio,                         84
To save me from the danger that might come
If he were known alive?

DUKE                       Let this be done:
Put them in secret holds, both Barnardine and
    Claudio.
Ere twice the sun hath made his journal greeting           87
To yond generation, you shall find                         88
Your safety manifested.                                    89

PROVOST    I am your free dependent.                       91

DUKE
Quick, dispatch, and send the head to Angelo.
                                        *Exit* [*Provost*].
Now will I write letters to Varrius—                       93
The Provost, he shall bear them—whose contents
Shall witness to him I am near at home,
And that, by great injunctions, I am bound                 96
To enter publicly. Him I'll desire
To meet me at the consecrated fount                        98
A league below the city; and from thence,                  99
By cold gradation and well-balanced form,                 100
We shall proceed with Angelo.

*Enter Provost* [*with Ragozine's head*].

PROVOST
Here is the head. I'll carry it myself.

DUKE
Convenient is it. Make a swift return,                    103
For I would commune with you of such things              104
That want no ear but yours.

PROVOST                        I'll make all speed.    *Exit.* 105

ISABELLA (*within*) Peace, ho, be here!

DUKE
The tongue of Isabel. She's come to know
If yet her brother's pardon be come hither.
But I will keep her ignorant of her good,
To make her heavenly comforts of despair                  110
When it is least expected.

*Enter Isabella.*

ISABELLA                     Ho, by your leave!

DUKE
Good morning to you, fair and gracious daughter.

ISABELLA
The better, given me by so holy a man.
Hath yet the deputy sent my brother's pardon?

DUKE
He hath released him, Isabel, from the world.
His head is off and sent to Angelo.

ISABELLA
Nay, but it is not so!

DUKE                      It is no other.
Show your wisdom, daughter, in your close patience.       118

ISABELLA
Oh, I will to him and pluck out his eyes!

DUKE
You shall not be admitted to his sight.

ISABELLA
Unhappy Claudio! Wretched Isabel!
Injurious world! Most damnèd Angelo!

---

**55 they . . . billets** they will have to beat me to death with cudgels or blocks of wood.    **63 ward** cell.    **thence** from there    **64 gravel** stony    **67 unmeet** unready, unfit    **68 transport him** i.e., send him to his doom.    **he is** he is in    **69 Were** would be    **73 omit** ignore, overlook    **74 This reprobate** i.e., Barnardine    **78 presently** immediately. (As also in line 82.)    **79 Prefixed** appointed beforehand, stipulated    **81 rude** uncivilized    **84 continue Claudio** keep Claudio in concealment    **87 holds** cells, dungeons    **88 journal** daily    **89 yond** i.e., beyond these walls, outside the perpetually dark prison (?). Sometimes it is emended to *th' under*, the people of the Antipodes, on the opposite side of the earth, or, people under the sun, the human race.    **91 free dependent** willing servant.

**93 to Varrius** (The Folio reads "to Angelo," but see line 99 below and 4.5.12–14; evidently, the Duke's plan is to meet Varrius "a league below the city" and then proceed to the rendezvous with Angelo.)    **96 by great injunctions** by powerful precedent or for compelling reasons    **98 fount** spring    **99 league** (A measure of varying length but usually about three miles.)    **100 cold . . . form** i.e., moving deliberately and with proper observance of all formalities    **103 Convenient** Timely, fitting    **104 commune** converse    **105 want** require    **110 To . . . despair** to transform her despair into heavenly comforts    **118 close patience** silent enduring.

DUKE
This nor hurts him nor profits you a jot. 123
Forbear it therefore; give your cause to heaven.
Mark what I say, which you shall find
By every syllable a faithful verity. 126
The Duke comes home tomorrow. Nay, dry your eyes;
One of our convent, and his confessor,
Gives me this instance. Already he hath carried 129
Notice to Escalus and Angelo,
Who do prepare to meet him at the gates,
There to give up their pow'r. If you can, pace your
   wisdom 132
In that good path that I would wish it go,
And you shall have your bosom on this wretch, 134
Grace of the Duke, revenges to your heart, 135
And general honor.

ISABELLA          I am directed by you.

DUKE
This letter, then, to Friar Peter give.
                         *[He gives her a letter.]*
'Tis that he sent me of the Duke's return. 138
Say, by this token, I desire his company
At Mariana's house tonight. Her cause and yours
I'll perfect him withal, and he shall bring you 141
Before the Duke, and to the head of Angelo 142
Accuse him home and home. For my poor self, 143
I am combinèd by a sacred vow, 144
And shall be absent. Wend you with this letter.
Command these fretting waters from your eyes 146
With a light heart. Trust not my holy order
If I pervert your course. Who's here?

*Enter Lucio.*

LUCIO    Good even. Friar, where's the Provost?
DUKE    Not within, sir.
LUCIO    Oh, pretty Isabella, I am pale at mine heart to see 151
thine eyes so red. Thou must be patient. I am fain to 152
dine and sup with water and bran; I dare not for my 153
head fill my belly; one fruitful meal would set me 154
to't. But they say the Duke will be here tomorrow. 155
By my troth, Isabel, I loved thy brother. If the old fantastical Duke of dark corners had been at home, he
had lived.                   *[Exit Isabella.]*
DUKE    Sir, the Duke is marvelous little beholding to 159
your reports; but the best is, he lives not in them. 160
LUCIO    Friar, thou knowest not the Duke so well as I
do. He's a better woodman than thou tak'st him for. 162

DUKE    Well, you'll answer this one day. Fare ye well.
                                *[He starts to go.]*
LUCIO    Nay, tarry, I'll go along with thee. I can tell thee
pretty tales of the Duke.
DUKE    You have told me too many of him already, sir, if
they be true; if not true, none were enough.
LUCIO    I was once before him for getting a wench with
child.
DUKE    Did you such a thing?
LUCIO    Yes, marry, did I, but I was fain to forswear it.
They would else have married me to the rotten medlar. 172
DUKE    Sir, your company is fairer than honest. Rest you 173
well.
LUCIO    By my troth, I'll go with thee to the lane's end. 175
If bawdy talk offend you, we'll have very little of it.
Nay, Friar, I am a kind of burr; I shall stick.   *Exeunt.*

## 4.4

*Enter Angelo and Escalus, [reading letters].*

ESCALUS    Every letter he hath writ hath disvouched 1
other.
ANGELO    In most uneven and distracted manner. His
actions show much like to madness. Pray heaven his
wisdom be not tainted! And why meet him at the 5
gates and redeliver our authorities there?
ESCALUS    I guess not. 7
ANGELO    And why should we proclaim it in an hour be- 8
fore his entering, that if any crave redress of injustice,
they should exhibit their petitions in the street? 10
ESCALUS    He shows his reason for that: to have a
dispatch of complaints, and to deliver us from devices 12
hereafter, which shall then have no power to stand
against us.
ANGELO    Well, I beseech you, let it be proclaimed.
Betimes i'th' morn I'll call you at your house. Give 16
notice to such men of sort and suit as are to meet him. 17
ESCALUS    I shall, sir. Fare you well.
ANGELO    Good night.             *Exit [Escalus].*
This deed unshapes me quite, makes me unpregnant 20
And dull to all proceedings. A deflowered maid,
And by an eminent body that enforced 22
The law against it! But that her tender shame 23
Will not proclaim against her maiden loss,
How might she tongue me! Yet reason dares her no, 25
For my authority bears of a credent bulk 26
That no particular scandal once can touch
But it confounds the breather. He should have lived, 28

---

**123 nor hurts** neither hurts   **126 By** in   **129 instance** proof.
**132 pace** teach to move in response to your will, as with a horse
**134 bosom** heart's desire   **135 Grace of** manifestation of favor
from.   **to your heart** to your heart's content   **138 that** that
which.   **of** concerning   **141 perfect** acquaint completely.   **withal**
with   **142 head** i.e., face   **143 home and home** thoroughly.   **For** As
for   **144 combinèd** bound   **146 fretting** corroding   **151 pale ...
heart** i.e., pale from sighing (since sighs cost the heart loss of
blood)   **152 fain** compelled. (As also in line 171.)   **153–4 for my
head** i.e., on my life   **154 fruitful** abundant   **154–5 set me to't** i.e.,
awaken my lust and thus place me in danger of Angelo's edict.
**159 marvelous** marvelously.   **beholding** beholden   **160 he ... them**
i.e., he is not accurately described by them.   **162 woodman** i.e.,
hunter (of women)

**172 medlar** a fruit that was eaten after it had begun to rot; here, signifying a prostitute.   **173 fairer** i.e., more enjoyable   **175 to ... end** i.e.,
anywhere.
**4.4. Location: In Vienna.**
**1 disvouched** contradicted   **5 tainted** diseased.   **7 guess not** cannot
guess.   **8 in an hour** i.e., a full hour   **10 exhibit** present   **12 dispatch**
prompt settlement.   **devices** contrived complaints   **16 Betimes**
Early   **17 men ... suit** men of rank with a retinue   **20 unpregnant**
unapt   **22–3 body ... it** i.e., person (Angelo himself) whose duty it
was to enforce the laws against sexual license.   **23 But that** Were it
not that   **25 tongue** i.e., reproach, accuse.   **dares her no** i.e., frightens
her to say nothing   **26 bears ... bulk** bears such a huge credibility
**28 But ... breather** without its confuting the person who speaks.

Save that his riotous youth, with dangerous sense,　29
Might in the times to come have ta'en revenge
By so receiving a dishonored life　31
With ransom of such shame. Would yet he had lived!
Alack, when once our grace we have forgot,
Nothing goes right; we would, and we would not.　34

　　　　　　　　　　　　　　　　　　　*Exit.*

♣

## 4.5

*Enter Duke [in his own habit] and Friar Peter.*

DUKE

These letters at fit time deliver me.　　[*Giving letters.*]　1
The Provost knows our purpose and our plot.
The matter being afoot, keep your instruction,　3
And hold you ever to our special drift,　4
Though sometimes you do blench from this to that　5
As cause doth minister. Go call at Flavius' house,　6
And tell him where I stay. Give the like notice
To Valencius, Rowland, and to Crassus,
And bid them bring the trumpets to the gate;　9
But send me Flavius first.

FRIAR PETER　　It shall be speeded well.　　[*Exit.*]　11

*Enter Varrius.*

DUKE

I thank thee, Varrius. Thou hast made good haste.
Come, we will walk. There's other of our friends
Will greet us here anon. My gentle Varrius!　*Exeunt.*　14

♣

## 4.6

*Enter Isabella and Mariana.*

ISABELLA

To speak so indirectly I am loath.
I would say the truth, but to accuse him so,
That is your part. Yet I am advised to do it,
He says, to veil full purpose.

MARIANA　　　　　　　　Be ruled by him.　4

ISABELLA

Besides, he tells me that if peradventure　5
He speak against me on the adverse side,
I should not think it strange, for 'tis a physic　7
That's bitter to sweet end.

　　　　*Enter [Friar] Peter.*

MARIANA

I would Friar Peter—

ISABELLA　　　　　　Oh, peace, the Friar is come.

FRIAR PETER

Come, I have found you out a stand most fit,　10
Where you may have such vantage on the Duke
He shall not pass you. Twice have the trumpets
　sounded.
The generous and gravest citizens　13
Have hent the gates, and very near upon　14
The Duke is entering. Therefore hence, away!

　　　　　　　　　　　　　　　　　　　*Exeunt.*

♣

## 5.1

*Enter Duke, Varrius, lords, Angelo, Escalus,
Lucio, [Provost, officers, and] citizens at several
doors.*

DUKE

My very worthy cousin, fairly met!　1
Our old and faithful friend, we are glad to see you.　2

ANGELO, ESCALUS

Happy return be to Your royal Grace!

DUKE

Many and hearty thankings to you both.
We have made inquiry of you, and we hear
Such goodness of your justice that our soul
Cannot but yield you forth to public thanks,　7
Forerunning more requital.　8

ANGELO　　You make my bonds still greater.　9

DUKE

Oh, your desert speaks loud, and I should wrong it
To lock it in the wards of covert bosom,　11
When it deserves with characters of brass　12
A forted residence 'gainst the tooth of time　13
And razure of oblivion. Give me your hand,　14
And let the subject see, to make them know　15
That outward courtesies would fain proclaim　16
Favors that keep within. Come, Escalus,　17
You must walk by us on our other hand,
And good supporters are you.

　　　　*Enter [Friar] Peter and Isabella.*

FRIAR PETER [*to Isabella*]

Now is your time. Speak loud, and kneel before him.

ISABELLA [*kneeling*]

Justice, O royal Duke! Vail your regard　21
Upon a wronged—I would fain have said a maid.
O worthy prince, dishonor not your eye
By throwing it on any other object
Till you have heard me in my true complaint
And given me justice, justice, justice, justice!

**29 Save that** were it not that.　**sense** passion, intention
**31 By** because of　**34 we would . . . not** i.e., we don't know which
way to turn.
**4.5. Location: Outside the city.**
**1 me** for me.　**3 keep** keep to　**4 drift** plot　**5 blench . . . that** swerve
from one expedient to another　**6 minister** prompt, provide occasion.
**9 trumpets** trumpeters　**11 speeded** accomplished, expedited
**14 Will** who will
**4.6. Location: Near the city gate.**
**4 veil full purpose** conceal our plan.　**5 peradventure** perhaps
**7 physic** medicine, remedy

**10 stand** place to stand　**13 generous** highborn　**14 hent** reached,
occupied.　**very near upon** almost immediately now
**5.1. Location: The city gate.**
**0.2** *several* separate　**1 cousin** fellow nobleman. (Addressed to
Angelo.)　**2 friend** i.e., Escalus　**7 yield . . . to** call you forth to give
you　**8 Forerunning . . . requital** anticipating further reward.
**9 bonds** obligations　**11 To lock . . . bosom** i.e., to keep it locked up
in my heart　**12 characters of brass** words carved in eternal brass
**13 forted** fortified　**14 razure** effacement　**15 the subject** those who
are subjects　**16–17 That . . . within** that public ceremonies serve as
outward manifestations of the approval my heart feels for you.
**21 Vail your regard** Look down

DUKE
Relate your wrongs. In what? By whom? Be brief.
Here is Lord Angelo shall give you justice.    28
Reveal yourself to him.

ISABELLA         O worthy Duke,
You bid me seek redemption of the devil.
Hear me yourself; for that which I must speak
Must either punish me, not being believed,    32
Or wring redress from you.
Hear me, oh, hear me, hear!

ANGELO
My lord, her wits, I fear me, are not firm.
She hath been a suitor to me for her brother
Cut off by course of justice.

ISABELLA [standing]        By course of justice!

ANGELO
And she will speak most bitterly and strange.    38

ISABELLA
Most strange, but yet most truly, will I speak.
That Angelo's forsworn, is it not strange?
That Angelo's a murderer, is 't not strange?
That Angelo is an adulterous thief,
An hypocrite, a virgin-violator,
Is it not strange, and strange?

DUKE    Nay, it is ten times strange.

ISABELLA
It is not truer he is Angelo
Than this is all as true as it is strange.    47
Nay, it is ten times true, for truth is truth
To th'end of reck'ning.

DUKE        Away with her! Poor soul,    49
She speaks this in th'infirmity of sense.    50

ISABELLA
O prince, I conjure thee, as thou believ'st
There is another comfort than this world,
That thou neglect me not with that opinion    53
That I am touched with madness. Make not
impossible    54
That which but seems unlike. 'Tis not impossible    55
But one, the wicked'st caitiff on the ground,    56
May seem as shy, as grave, as just, as absolute    57
As Angelo; even so may Angelo,
In all his dressings, characts, titles, forms,    59
Be an archvillain. Believe it, royal prince,
If he be less, he's nothing; but he's more,    61
Had I more name for badness.

DUKE        By mine honesty,
If she be mad—as I believe no other—
Her madness hath the oddest frame of sense,    64
Such a dependency of thing on thing,    65

As e'er I heard in madness.

ISABELLA        O gracious Duke,
Harp not on that, nor do not banish reason    67
For inequality, but let your reason serve    68
To make the truth appear where it seems hid,
And hide the false seems true.    70

DUKE    Many that are not mad
Have, sure, more lack of reason. What would
you say?

ISABELLA
I am the sister of one Claudio,
Condemned upon the act of fornication
To lose his head, condemned by Angelo.
I, in probation of a sisterhood,    76
Was sent to by my brother; one Lucio
As then the messenger—

LUCIO       That's I, an't like Your Grace.    78
I came to her from Claudio and desired her
To try her gracious fortune with Lord Angelo
For her poor brother's pardon.

ISABELLA        That's he indeed.

DUKE [to Lucio]
You were not bid to speak.

LUCIO        No, my good lord,
Nor wished to hold my peace.

DUKE        I wish you now, then.
Pray you, take note of it. And when you have
A business for yourself, pray heaven you then
Be perfect.    86

LUCIO    I warrant Your Honor.    87

DUKE
The warrant's for yourself. Take heed to 't.

ISABELLA
This gentleman told somewhat of my tale—

LUCIO    Right.

DUKE
It may be right, but you are i'the wrong
To speak before your time.—Proceed.

ISABELLA        I went
To this pernicious caitiff deputy—

DUKE
That's somewhat madly spoken.

ISABELLA        Pardon it;
The phrase is to the matter.    95

DUKE    Mended again. The matter; proceed.    96

ISABELLA
In brief, to set the needless process by,    97
How I persuaded, how I prayed and kneeled,
How he refelled me, and how I replied—    99
For this was of much length—the vile conclusion

---

28 **shall** who shall   32 **not being** if I am not   38 **strange** strangely.
47 **Than** than that   49 **To . . . reck'ning** to the end of time and Day of
Judgment, always.   50 **in . . . sense** out of a sick mind, out of the
weakness of passion.   53 **with that opinion** out of a supposition
54 **Make not** Do not consider as   55 **unlike** unlikely.   56 **But** but
that.   **ground** earth   57 **shy** quietly dignified.   **absolute** flawless
59 **dressings, characts** ceremonial robes, insignia of office   61 **If . . .
more** i.e., even if he deserves to be called less than an archvillain, he
is still insignificant and vile, but he is worse than that   64 **frame of
sense** form of reason   65 **dependency . . . on thing** coherence

67–8 **do . . . inequality** i.e., do not assume lack of reason on my part
because of the inconsistency between my story and Angelo's refutation, or because of the inequality in our reputations   70 **hide** put out
of sight, remove from consideration.   **seems** that seems   76 **in probation** i.e., a novice   78 **As then** being at that time.   **an't like** if it
please   86 **perfect** prepared.   87 **warrant** assure. (The Duke, however, quibbles in line 88 on the meaning "judicial writ.")   95 **to the
matter** to the purpose.   96 **Mended . . . proceed** That sets things
right. Proceed to the main point.   97 **to set . . . by** not to dwell on
unnecessary details in the story   99 **refelled** refuted, repelled

I now begin with grief and shame to utter.
He would not, but by gift of my chaste body
To his concupiscible intemperate lust,                              103
Release my brother; and after much debatement          104
My sisterly remorse confutes mine honor,                      105
And I did yield to him. But the next morn betimes,      106
His purpose surfeiting, he sends a warrant               107
For my poor brother's head.

DUKE                              This is most likely!

ISABELLA
Oh, that it were as like as it is true!                              109

DUKE
By heaven, fond wretch, thou know'st not what thou
   speak'st,                                                                    110
Or else thou art suborned against his honor            111
In hateful practice. First, his integrity                  112
Stands without blemish. Next, it imports no reason    113
That with such vehemency he should pursue            114
Faults proper to himself. If he had so offended,      115
He would have weighed thy brother by himself        116
And not have cut him off. Someone hath set you on.
Confess the truth, and say by whose advice
Thou cam'st here to complain.

ISABELLA                              And is this all?
Then, O you blessèd ministers above,
Keep me in patience, and with ripened time
Unfold the evil which is here wrapped up               122
In countenance! Heaven shield Your Grace from woe,  123
As I thus wronged hence unbelievèd go!

                                   [She starts to leave.]

DUKE
I know you'd fain be gone.—An officer!                  125
To prison with her. Shall we thus permit
A blasting and a scandalous breath to fall              127
On him so near us? This needs must be a practice.  128
Who knew of your intent and coming hither?

ISABELLA
One that I would were here, Friar Lodowick.          130

DUKE
A ghostly father, belike. Who knows that Lodowick?  131

LUCIO
My lord, I know him; 'tis a meddling friar.
I do not like the man. Had he been lay, my lord,      133
For certain words he spake against Your Grace
In your retirement, I had swinged him soundly.      135

DUKE
Words against me? This' a good friar, belike!          136
And to set on this wretched woman here

Against our substitute! Let this friar be found.

                                   [Exit one or more attendants.]

LUCIO
But yesternight, my lord, she and that friar,
I saw them at the prison. A saucy friar,
A very scurvy fellow.

FRIAR PETER   Blessed be Your royal Grace!
I have stood by, my lord, and I have heard
Your royal ear abused. First, hath this woman
Most wrongfully accused your substitute,
Who is as free from touch or soil with her
As she from one ungot.                                              147

DUKE   We did believe no less.
Know you that Friar Lodowick that she speaks of?

FRIAR PETER
I know him for a man divine and holy,
Not scurvy, nor a temporary meddler,                     151
As he's reported by this gentleman;
And, on my trust, a man that never yet
Did, as he vouches, misreport Your Grace.

LUCIO
My lord, most villainously, believe it.

FRIAR PETER
Well, he in time may come to clear himself;
But at this instant he is sick, my lord,
Of a strange fever. Upon his mere request,            158
Being come to knowledge that there was complaint  159
Intended 'gainst Lord Angelo, came I hither,
To speak, as from his mouth, what he doth know
Is true and false, and what he with his oath
And all probation will make up full clear,                163
Whensoever he's convented. First, for this woman,  164
To justify this worthy nobleman,                            165
So vulgarly and personally accused,                       166
Her shall you hear disprovèd to her eyes,             167
Till she herself confess it.        [Exit Isabella, guarded.]

DUKE                              Good Friar, let's hear it.     168
                    [Friar Peter goes to bring in Mariana.]
Do you not smile at this, Lord Angelo?
Oh, heaven, the vanity of wretched fools!             170
Give us some seats.              [Seats are provided.]
                                   Come, cousin Angelo,
In this I'll be impartial. Be you judge
Of your own cause.            [The Duke and Angelo sit.]

   Enter Mariana, [veiled, with Friar Peter].

                                   Is this the witness, Friar?
First, let her show her face, and after speak.

MARIANA
Pardon, my lord, I will not show my face
Until my husband bid me.

---

103 **concupiscible** lustful   104 **debatement** argument, debate
105 **remorse** pity.  **confutes** confounds, silences   106 **betimes** early
107 **surfeiting** being satiated   109 **like** likely   110 **fond** foolish
111 **suborned** induced to give false testimony   112 **practice** machination, conspiracy.   113 **imports no reason** i.e., makes no sense
114 **pursue** persecute   115 **proper to himself** of which he himself is
guilty.   116 **weighed** judged   122 **Unfold** disclose   122–3 **wrapped
. . . countenance** concealed by the privilege of authority.   125 **fain**
gladly   127 **blasting** blighting   128 **needs . . . practice** must be a plot.
130 **would** wish   131 **A ghostly . . . belike** A cleric, apparently.
133 **lay** not a cleric   135 **In your retirement** during your absence.
**had swinged** would have beaten   136 **This'** This is.  **belike** no
doubt, fosooth.

147 **ungot** unbegotten.   151 **temporary meddler** meddler in temporal
affairs   158 **Upon . . . request** Solely at his request   159 **Being . . .
knowledge** having learned   163 **probation** proof   164 **convented**
summoned.  **for** as for   165 **this worthy gentleman** Angelo
166 **vulgarly** publicly   167 **to her eyes** i.e., to her face   168 s.d. *Exit
Isbella, guarded* (Isabella seemingly must leave the stage here or
soon afterwards. She is described as "gone" at line 250, and is
summoned at line 278. The phrase "to her eyes" in line 167 may
mean "incontrovertibly.")   170 **vanity** folly

DUKE  What, are you married?

MARIANA  No, my lord.

DUKE  Are you a maid?

MARIANA  No, my lord.

DUKE  A widow, then?

MARIANA  Neither, my lord.

DUKE  Why, you are nothing then, neither maid,
  widow, nor wife?

LUCIO  My lord, she may be a punk, for many of them  185
  are neither maid, widow, nor wife.

DUKE
  Silence that fellow. I would he had some cause
  To prattle for himself.                       188

LUCIO  Well, my lord.

MARIANA
  My lord, I do confess I ne'er was married,
  And I confess besides I am no maid.
  I have known my husband, yet my husband     192
  Knows not that ever he knew me.

LUCIO  He was drunk then, my lord; it can be no better.  194

DUKE  For the benefit of silence, would thou wert so too!

LUCIO  Well, my lord.

DUKE
  This is no witness for Lord Angelo.          197

MARIANA  Now I come to 't, my lord.
  She that accuses him of fornication
  In selfsame manner doth accuse my husband,
  And charges him, my lord, with such a time     201
  When, I'll depose, I had him in mine arms     202
  With all th'effect of love.                203

ANGELO  Charges she more than me?        204

MARIANA  Not that I know.

DUKE  No? You say your husband?

MARIANA
  Why, just, my lord, and that is Angelo,     207
  Who thinks he knows that he ne'er knew my body,
  But knows he thinks that he knows Isabel's.   209

ANGELO
  This is a strange abuse. Let's see thy face.   210

MARIANA
  My husband bids me. Now I will unmask.
                             [She unveils.]
  This is that face, thou cruel Angelo,
  Which once thou swor'st was worth the looking on;
  This is the hand which, with a vowed contract,
  Was fast belocked in thine; this is the body   215
  That took away the match from Isabel,     216
  And did supply thee at thy garden house
  In her imagined person.

DUKE [to Angelo]  Know you this woman?

LUCIO  Carnally, she says.

DUKE  Sirrah, no more!

LUCIO  Enough, my lord.

ANGELO
  My lord, I must confess I know this woman,
  And five years since there was some speech of
    marriage
  Betwixt myself and her, which was broke off,
  Partly for that her promisèd proportions     226
  Came short of composition, but in chief     227
  For that her reputation was disvalued     228
  In levity. Since which time of five years     229
  I never spake with her, saw her, nor heard from her,
  Upon my faith and honor.

MARIANA [kneeling]         Noble prince,
  As there comes light from heaven and words from
    breath,
  As there is sense in truth and truth in virtue,
  I am affianced this man's wife as strongly
  As words could make up vows; and, my good lord,
  But Tuesday night last gone in's garden house   237
  He knew me as a wife. As this is true,
  Let me in safety raise me from my knees,
  Or else forever be confixèd here,         239
  A marble monument!

ANGELO  I did but smile till now.
  Now, good my lord, give me the scope of justice.   242
  My patience here is touched. I do perceive     243
  These poor informal women are no more     244
  But instruments of some more mightier member   245
  That sets them on. Let me have way, my lord,
  To find this practice out.

DUKE                Ay, with my heart,
  And punish them to your height of pleasure.—
  Thou foolish friar, and thou pernicious woman,
  Compact with her that's gone, think'st thou thy oaths,  250
  Though they would swear down each particular saint,  251
  Were testimonies against his worth and credit   252
  That's sealed in approbation?—You, Lord Escalus,   253
  Sit with my cousin; lend him your kind pains
  To find out this abuse, whence 'tis derived.
  There is another friar that set them on;
  Let him be sent for.
            [The Duke rises; Escalus takes his chair.]

FRIAR PETER
  Would he were here, my lord! For he indeed
  Hath set the women on to this complaint.
  Your Provost knows the place where he abides,
  And he may fetch him.

DUKE             Go do it instantly.
                      [Exit Provost.]
  And you, my noble and well-warranted cousin,   262
  Whom it concerns to hear this matter forth,   263
  Do with your injuries as seems you best,   264

---

**185 punk** harlot   **188 To . . . himself** to speak in his own defense. (The Duke hints that there may well be charges pending against Lucio.) **192 known** had sexual intercourse with   **194 it . . . better** i.e., that's bound to be the case: it's just what you'd expect.   **197 This . . . Angelo** This has no bearing on the matter of the accusation against Angelo. **201 with . . . time** with doing the deed at just the same time   **202 depose** testify under oath   **203 With . . . love** i.e., with sexual fulfillment. **204 Charges . . . me?** Does she (Isabella) bring charges against persons besides myself?   **207 just** just so   **209 But . . . Isabel's** but Angelo thinks (incorrectly) that he enjoyed Isabel's body.   **210 abuse** deception.   **215 fast belocked** firmly locked   **216 match** assignation

**226 for that** because.   **proportions** dowry   **227 composition** the agreed amount   **228–9 disvalued In levity** discredited for lightness.   **237 But** only.   **gone** ago   **239 confixèd** firmly fixed   **242 scope** full authority   **243 touched** injured, affected.   **244 informal** rash, distracted **245 But** than   **250 Compact . . . gone** i.e., in collusion with Isabella **251 swear . . . saint** call down to witness every single saint   **252 Were** would be   **253 sealed in approbation** ratified by proof, like weights and measures being given a stamp or seal to attest to their genuineness. **262 well-warranted** highly regarded   **263 forth** through   **264 Do . . . best** respond to the wrongs done you as seems best to you

In any chastisement. I for a while
Will leave you; but stir not you till you have
Well determined upon these slanderers.                                267

ESCALUS    My lord, we'll do it throughly.    *Exit [Duke].* 268
Signor Lucio, did not you say you knew that Friar
Lodowick to be a dishonest person?

LUCIO    *Cucullus non facit monachum;* honest in nothing 271
but in his clothes, and one that hath spoke most
villainous speeches of the Duke.

ESCALUS    We shall entreat you to abide here till he come,
and enforce them against him. We shall find this friar 275
a notable fellow.                                                           276

LUCIO    As any in Vienna, on my word.

ESCALUS    Call that same Isabel here once again. I would
speak with her.                        *[Exit an Attendant.]*
Pray you, my lord, give me leave to question. You shall
see how I'll handle her.

LUCIO    Not better than he, by her own report.        282

ESCALUS    Say you?

LUCIO    Marry, sir, I think, if you handled her privately, 284
she would sooner confess; perchance publicly she'll
be ashamed.

ESCALUS    I will go darkly to work with her.        287

LUCIO    That's the way, for women are light at midnight. 288

*Enter Duke [disguised as a friar], Provost, Isabella,
[and officers].*

ESCALUS    Come on, mistress. Here's a gentlewoman
denies all that you have said.

LUCIO    My lord, here comes the rascal I spoke of, here
with the Provost.

ESCALUS    In very good time. Speak not you to him till
we call upon you.

LUCIO    Mum.

ESCALUS    Come, sir, did you set these women on to
slander Lord Angelo? They have confessed you did.

DUKE    'Tis false.

ESCALUS    How? Know you where you are?

DUKE
Respect to your great place! And let the devil        300
Be sometime honored for his burning throne!        301
Where is the Duke? 'Tis he should hear me speak.

ESCALUS
The Duke's in us, and we will hear you speak.
Look you speak justly.

DUKE
Boldly, at least. But oh, poor souls,
Come you to seek the lamb here of the fox?
Good night to your redress! Is the Duke gone?
Then is your cause gone too. The Duke's unjust,
Thus to retort your manifest appeal,                        309

And put your trial in the villain's mouth
Which here you come to accuse.

LUCIO
This is the rascal. This is he I spoke of.

ESCALUS
Why, thou unreverend and unhallowed friar,
Is't not enough thou hast suborned these women
To accuse this worthy man, but, in foul mouth
And in the witness of his proper ear,                        316
To call him villain? And then to glance from him
To th'Duke himself, to tax him with injustice?—        318
Take him hence. To th' rack with him!—We'll touse
    you                                                                   319
Joint by joint, but we will know his purpose.        320
What, "unjust"?

DUKE                                    Be not so hot. The Duke
Dare no more stretch this finger of mine than he
Dare rack his own. His subject am I not,
Nor here provincial. My business in this state        324
Made me a looker-on here in Vienna,
Where I have seen corruption boil and bubble
Till it o'errun the stew; laws for all faults,        327
But faults so countenanced that the strong statutes 328
Stand like the forfeits in a barber's shop,        329
As much in mock as mark.

ESCALUS                                    Slander to th' state!        330
Away with him to prison.

ANGELO
What can you vouch against him, Signor Lucio?
Is this the man that you did tell us of?

LUCIO    'Tis he, my lord.—Come hither, Goodman 334
Baldpate. Do you know me?                                    335

DUKE    I remember you, sir, by the sound of your voice.
I met you at the prison, in the absence of the Duke.

LUCIO    Oh, did you so? And do you remember what you
said of the Duke?

DUKE    Most notedly, sir.                                       340

LUCIO    Do you so, sir? And was the Duke a fleshmonger, a fool, and a coward, as you then reported him to be?

DUKE    You must, sir, change persons with me ere you 344
make that my report. You indeed spoke so of him, and
much more, much worse.

LUCIO    Oh, thou damnable fellow! Did not I pluck thee by
the nose for thy speeches?

DUKE    I protest I love the Duke as I love myself.

ANGELO    Hark how the villain would close now, after 350
his treasonable abuses!

---

267 **determined** reached judgment    268 **throughly** thoroughly.
271 *Cucullus . . . monachum* A cowl doesn't make a monk.
275 **enforce them** forcefully urge your charges    276 **notable** notorious    282 **Not . . . report** (Lucio salaciously turns Escalus's *handle her*
into a sexual slur: You, Escalus, will do no better at "handling" Isabella than did Angelo, according to Isabella's testimony.)    284 **if . . .
privately** (Lucio continues his sexual joke about "handling.")
287 **darkly** subtly, slyly    288 **light** wanton, unchaste    300–1 **let . . .
throne** i.e., may all authority be respected, even the devil's. (Said
sardonically.)    309 **retort** turn back.    **manifest** obviously just

316 **in . . . ear** within his own hearing    318 **tax him with** accuse him
of    319 **touse** tear    320 **but we will** i.e., if necessary; until we
324 **provincial** subject to the religious authority of this province or
state.    327 **stew** (1) stewpot (2) brothel    328 **countenanced** tolerated
and protected by corrupt authority    329 **forfeits** cautionary displays,
or lists of rules and fines for handling razors, etc., which barbers
(who also acted as dentists and surgeons) hung in their shops
330 **As . . . mark** as often flouted as observed.    334–5 **Goodman
Baldpate** (Lucio refers to the tonsure that he assumes the Duke must
have under his hood, though the Duke is clearly hooded at this
point.)    340 **notedly** particularly    344 **change** exchange    350 **close**
come to terms, compromise

ESCALUS   Such a fellow is not to be talked withal. Away   352
with him to prison! Where is the Provost? Away with
him to prison! Lay bolts enough upon him. Let him   354
speak no more. Away with those giglots too, and with   355
the other confederate companion!   356

                         *[The Provost lays hands on the Duke.]*

DUKE *[to Provost]*   Stay, sir, stay awhile.

ANGELO   What, resists he? Help him, Lucio.

LUCIO   Come, sir, come, sir, come, sir; foh, sir! Why,
you bald-pated, lying rascal, you must be hooded,
must you? Show your knave's visage, with a pox to
you! Show your sheep-biting face, and be hanged an   362
hour! Will't not off?   363

             *[He pulls off the friar's hood, and discovers*
                 *the Duke. Angelo and Escalus rise.]*

DUKE

Thou art the first knave that e'er mad'st a duke.
First, Provost, let me bail these gentle three.   365
*[To Lucio]* Sneak not away, sir, for the Friar and you
Must have a word anon.—Lay hold on him.

LUCIO   This may prove worse than hanging.

DUKE *[to Escalus]*

What you have spoke I pardon. Sit you down.
We'll borrow place of him. *[To Angelo]* Sir, by your
   leave.      *[He takes Angelo's seat. Escalus also sits.]*
Hast thou or word, or wit, or impudence,   371
That yet can do thee office? If thou hast,   372
Rely upon it till my tale be heard,
And hold no longer out.

ANGELO *[kneeling]*        O my dread lord,   374
I should be guiltier than my guiltiness
To think I can be undiscernible,
When I perceive Your Grace, like power divine,
Hath looked upon my passes. Then, good prince,   378
No longer session hold upon my shame,
But let my trial be mine own confession.
Immediate sentence then and sequent death   381
Is all the grace I beg.

DUKE                Come hither, Mariana.—
Say, wast thou e'er contracted to this woman?

ANGELO   I was, my lord.

DUKE

Go take her hence and marry her instantly.
Do you the office, Friar, which consummate,   386
Return him here again. Go with him, Provost.

            *Exit [Angelo, with Mariana, Friar Peter, and*
                          *Provost].*

ESCALUS

My lord, I am more amazed at his dishonor
Than at the strangeness of it.

DUKE                  Come hither, Isabel.
Your friar is now your prince. As I was then

Advertising and holy to your business,   391
Not changing heart with habit, I am still   392
Attorneyed at your service.

ISABELLA           Oh, give me pardon,   393
That I, your vassal, have employed and pained   394
Your unknown sovereignty!

DUKE              You are pardoned, Isabel.
And now, dear maid, be you as free to us.   396
Your brother's death, I know, sits at your heart;
And you may marvel why I obscured myself,
Laboring to save his life, and would not rather
Make rash remonstrance of my hidden power   400
Than let him so be lost. O most kind maid,
It was the swift celerity of his death,
Which I did think with slower foot came on,
That brained my purpose. But peace be with him!   404
That life is better life past fearing death
Than that which lives to fear. Make it your comfort,
So happy is your brother.

      *Enter Angelo, Mariana, [Friar] Peter, [and]*
      *Provost.*

ISABELLA             I do, my lord.   407

DUKE

For this new-married man approaching here,   408
Whose salt imagination yet hath wronged   409
Your well-defended honor, you must pardon
For Mariana's sake. But as he adjudged your
   brother—
Being criminal, in double violation
Of sacred chastity and of promise-breach   413
Thereon dependent, for your brother's life—   414
The very mercy of the law cries out   415
Most audible, even from his proper tongue,   416
"An Angelo for Claudio, death for death!"
Haste still pays haste, and leisure answers leisure;   418
Like doth quit like, and measure still for measure.   419
Then, Angelo, thy fault's thus manifested,
Which, though thou wouldst deny, denies thee
   vantage.   421
We do condemn thee to the very block
Where Claudio stooped to death, and with like haste.
Away with him!

MARIANA        O my most gracious lord,
I hope you will not mock me with a husband!

DUKE

It is your husband mocked you with a husband.
Consenting to the safeguard of your honor,
I thought your marriage fit; else imputation,   428
For that he knew you, might reproach your life   429

---

352 **withal** with.  354 **bolts** iron fetters  355 **giglots** wanton women
356 **confederate companion** i.e., Friar Peter.  362 **sheep-biting** knavish. (From the action of wolves or dogs that prey on sheep.)
362–3 **hanged an hour** (A sardonic way of saying "hanged.")
365 **gentle three** i.e., Mariana, Isabella, and Friar Peter.  371 **or word**
either word  372 **office** service.  374 **hold . . . out** then persist no
longer.  378 **passes** actions, trespasses.  381 **sequent** subsequent
386 **Do . . . office** Please perform the service.  **consummate** being
completed

391 **Advertising and holy** attentive and wholly dedicated (in my
priestly role)  392 **Not . . . with habit** still devoted to you in my heart
though changed in my attire  393 **Attorneyed . . . service** i.e.,
devoted to serve you.  394 **pained** put to trouble  396 **as free to us**
i.e., as generous in pardoning me.  400 **rash remonstrance** sudden
manifestation  404 **brained** dashed, defeated  407 **So** thus  408 **For**
As for  409 **salt** lecherous  413–14 **promise-breach . . . dependent**
i.e., breaking his promise made in return for the yielding up of chastity  415 **The very . . . law** i.e., even mercy itself  416 **his proper** its
own  418 **still** always  419 **quit** requite  421 **though** even if.
**vantage** i.e., any advantage. (Angelo must suffer the same penalty as
Claudio.)  428 **fit** appropriate.  **imputation** accusation, slander
429 **For that he knew you** since he knew you sexually

And choke your good to come. For his possessions,    430
Although by confiscation they are ours,
We do instate and widow you withal,    432
To buy you a better husband.

MARIANA                            O my dear lord,
I crave no other, nor no better man.

DUKE
Never crave him; we are definitive.    435

MARIANA [kneeling]
Gentle my liege—

DUKE                            You do but lose your labor.—
Away with him to death! [To Lucio] Now, sir, to you.

MARIANA
O my good lord!—Sweet Isabel, take my part!
Lend me your knees, and all my life to come
I'll lend you all my life to do you service.

DUKE
Against all sense you do importune her.
Should she kneel down in mercy of this fact,    442
Her brother's ghost his pavèd bed would break,    443
And take her hence in horror.

MARIANA                            Isabel,
Sweet Isabel, do yet but kneel by me!
Hold up your hands, say nothing; I'll speak all.
They say best men are molded out of faults,    447
And, for the most, become much more the better    448
For being a little bad. So may my husband.
O Isabel, will you not lend a knee?

DUKE
He dies for Claudio's death.

ISABELLA [kneeling]                            Most bounteous sir,
Look, if it please you, on this man condemned
As if my brother lived. I partly think
A due sincerity governed his deeds,
Till he did look on me. Since it is so,
Let him not die. My brother had but justice,
In that he did the thing for which he died.
For Angelo,    458
His act did not o'ertake his bad intent,    459
And must be buried but as an intent    460
That perished by the way. Thoughts are no subjects,    461
Intents but merely thoughts.

MARIANA                            Merely, my lord.

DUKE
Your suit's unprofitable. Stand up, I say.

[They stand.]

I have bethought me of another fault.
Provost, how came it Claudio was beheaded
At an unusual hour?

PROVOST    It was commanded so.

DUKE
Had you a special warrant for the deed?

PROVOST
No, my good lord, it was by private message.

DUKE
For which I do discharge you of your office.
Give up your keys.

PROVOST                            Pardon me, noble lord.
I thought it was a fault, but knew it not,    472
Yet did repent me after more advice;    473
For testimony whereof, one in the prison,
That should by private order else have died,
I have reserved alive.

DUKE    What's he?

PROVOST    His name is Barnardine.

DUKE
I would thou hadst done so by Claudio.
Go fetch him hither. Let me look upon him.

[Exit Provost.]

ESCALUS
I am sorry one so learnèd and so wise
As you, Lord Angelo, have still appeared,    482
Should slip so grossly, both in the heat of blood
And lack of tempered judgment afterward.

ANGELO
I am sorry that such sorrow I procure,    485
And so deep sticks it in my penitent heart
That I crave death more willingly than mercy.
'Tis my deserving, and I do entreat it.    488

Enter Barnardine and Provost, Claudio [muffled],
[and] Juliet.

DUKE
Which is that Barnardine?

PROVOST                            This, my lord.

DUKE
There was a friar told me of this man.—
Sirrah, thou art said to have a stubborn soul
That apprehends no further than this world,
And squar'st thy life according. Thou'rt condemned;    493
But, for those earthly faults, I quit them all,    494
And pray thee take this mercy to provide
For better times to come.—Friar, advise him;
I leave him to your hand.—What muffled fellow's
    that?

PROVOST
This is another prisoner that I saved,
Who should have died when Claudio lost his head,
As like almost to Claudio as himself.

[He unmuffles Claudio.]

DUKE [to Isabella]
If he be like your brother, for his sake
Is he pardoned, and for your lovely sake,
Give me your hand and say you will be mine;
He is my brother too. But fitter time for that.
By this Lord Angelo perceives he's safe;
Methinks I see a quick'ning in his eye.
Well, Angelo, your evil quits you well.    507
Look that you love your wife, her worth worth yours.    508

---

430 For As for    432 widow endow with a widow's rights
435 definitive firmly resolved.    442 in . . . fact pleading mercy for
this crime    443 pavèd bed grave covered with a stone slab    447 best
men even the best of men    448 most most part    458 For As for
459 His . . . intent his sexual act did not in fact accomplish what he
had intended, the seduction of Isabel.    460 buried i.e., forgotten    461 no subjects i.e., not subject to the state's authority

472 knew it not was not sure    473 advice consideration    482 still always    485 procure cause, prompt    488.1 muffled wrapped up so as to
conceal identity. (As also in line 497.)    493 squar'st regulates    494 for
as for.    quit pardon    507 quits rewards, requites    508 her . . . yours
her worthiness richly deserving your love and worthy of your estate.

I find an apt remission in myself;                              509
And yet here's one in place I cannot pardon.                    510
[*To Lucio*] You, sirrah, that knew me for a fool,
   a coward,
One all of luxury, an ass, a madman—                            512
Wherein have I so deserved of you
That you extol me thus?

LUCIO    Faith, my lord, I spoke it but according to the
   trick. If you will hang me for it, you may; but I had       516
   rather it would please you I might be whipped.

DUKE
Whipped first, sir, and hanged after.—
Proclaim it, Provost, round about the city,
If any woman wronged by this lewd fellow—
As I have heard him swear himself there's one
Whom he begot with child—let her appear,
And he shall marry her. The nuptial finished,
Let him be whipped and hanged.

LUCIO    I beseech Your Highness, do not marry me to a
   whore. Your Highness said even now I made you a            526
   duke; good my lord, do not recompense me in making me a cuckold.

DUKE
Upon mine honor, thou shalt marry her.
Thy slanders I forgive and therewithal                          530
Remit thy other forfeits.—Take him to prison,                  531

And see our pleasure herein executed.                           532

LUCIO    Marrying a punk, my lord, is pressing to death,       533
   whipping, and hanging.

DUKE
Slandering a prince deserves it.
                        [*Exeunt officers with Lucio.*]
She, Claudio, that you wronged, look you restore.               536
Joy to you, Mariana! Love her, Angelo.
I have confessed her, and I know her virtue.
Thanks, good friend Escalus, for thy much goodness;
There's more behind that is more gratulate.                     540
Thanks, Provost, for thy care and secrecy;
We shall employ thee in a worthier place.
Forgive him, Angelo, that brought you home
The head of Ragozine for Claudio's;
Th'offense pardons itself. Dear Isabel,
I have a motion much imports your good,                          546
Whereto if you'll a willing ear incline,
What's mine is yours, and what is yours is mine.—              548
So, bring us to our palace, where we'll show                    549
What's yet behind, that's meet you all should know.            550
                                    [*Exeunt.*]

---

509 apt remission readiness to show mercy   510 in place present
512 luxury lechery   516 trick fashion.   526 even just   530–1 and
therewithal . . . forfeits i.e., and in addition to that I will not have
you whipped and hanged.

---

532 see . . . executed i.e., see that my order be carried out that Lucio
marry Kate Keepdown (see 3.2.194–6).   533 pressing to death i.e., by
having heavy weights placed on the chest. (A standard form of executing those who refused to plead to a felony charge.) Lucio wryly
complains that marrying a whore is as bad as death by torture.
536 She . . . restore i.e., See to it that you marry Juliet.   540 behind in
store, to come.   gratulate gratifying.   546 motion proposal (which)
548 What's . . . is mine i.e., we will give ourselves and all that we
own to each other in the perfect union of marriage.   549 bring escort
550 What's yet behind what is still to be told

# The Histories

# The Tragedy of King Richard the Third

The fascinating evil ruler for whom *Richard III* is named has already made his appearance in the third part of *Henry VI*, in the four-play sequence that makes up Shakespeare's first foray into English history. In the final installment in this tetralogy, Richard, Duke of Gloucester, stands fully revealed as the evil genius of England's prolonged crisis of civil war. With a bold stroke, Shakespeare opens *Richard III* with his arresting soliloquy; Richard takes over the stage in a way that has held audiences spellbound ever since Richard Burbage first performed the role. Richard announces his determination to "prove a villain," both defying and fulfilling Nature, which made his body deformed. In fact, he has already begun his treacherous course, and we see at once how his plot against Clarence, founded on something so trivial as the letter G, has manipulated the King and has ensnared Clarence. Then, with outrageous hypocrisy, he "comforts" Clarence. Within less than a hundred lines, Shakespeare makes us feel how brilliant, cynical, charming, and dangerous Richard of Gloucester is. Richard proceeds to dominate the other characters—and the whole play—to an extraordinary degree.

By organizing this play firmly around Richard, Shakespeare solved the problems of giving form to his drama and of concluding the series of plays about the dynastic rivalry of York and Lancaster. *Richard III* begins and ends with a peace, yet the recent peace of the Yorkist King Edward is scorned and sabotaged by Richard as soon as it is introduced. It is vulnerable to factions at court and is bitterly denounced by that living embodiment of the cruel and violent past, Queen Margaret. There can be no peace in England while Richard lives to undermine it. Still, as the plot moves through Richard's exhilarating rise to the throne and the events of his tragic fall—when his conscience, the spirits of those he murdered, and the Earl of Richmond punish and defeat him—we see that his career is part of a larger order, a seemingly providential plan of retribution for wickedness and injustice and for reconciling England's divisions. For all its specific reminders of past warfare and atrocity on both Yorkist and Lancastrian sides, *Richard III* dramatizes an archetypal struggle between good and evil, personified in Richard the villain-hero and Richmond his opponent, who plays the role of the righteous agent of divine and poetic justice.

Dramatically, Richmond, like Queen Margaret, is more a symbol than a fully developed character. It is Richard who is the exciting figure as he deceives and manipulates others and finally faces the chillingly isolated condition into which he has brought himself by being so truly a villain. He climbs to power by deceit, and so he is constantly acting a part. Richard's ability as an actor is seemingly limitless. He has already boasted, in 3 Henry VI, that he can deceive more slyly than Ulysses, Sinon, or Machiavelli and can put on more false shapes than Proteus. To us as audience, he is cynically candid and boastful, setting us up in advance to watch his unbelievable performances. In an instant, before our eyes, he is the concerned younger brother of Clarence, sharing a hatred of Queen Elizabeth and her kindred; he is the jocular uncle of the little princes; or he is the pious recluse studying divinity with his clerical teachers, reluctant to accept the responsibilities of state that are thrust upon him by his importunate subjects (i.e., by Catesby and Buckingham, who are also actors in this staged scene).

None of these bravura performances, however, matches the wooing of Lady Anne. Richard himself sees it as the great test of his powers and is suitably impressed by his victory. The wooing scene, to some critics, challenges credibility. One key to credibility must lie in superb acting. The actor who plays Richard must transform himself from the gloating villain we know in soliloquy to the grief-stricken lover. Richard's argument is, after all, speciously plausible: that he has killed Anne's husband and father-in-law out of desperate love for her. The argument appeals to vanity, that most fatal of human weaknesses. What power Anne suddenly appears to have over

Richard! She can kill him or spare his life. Richard shrewdly judges her as one who is not able to kill, and so he risks offering her his sword. As stage manager, he has altered her role from that of sincere mourner to the stereotype of the proud woman worshiped by her groveling servant in love. With superb irony, Richard has inverted the appearance and the reality of control in this struggle between man and woman, winning mastery by flattering Anne that she has such power over his emotions and his life. From his amazing success, Richard concludes that ordinary men and women can be made to believe anything and to betray their own instincts by "the plain devil and dissembling looks" (1.2.239). Richard is indeed devil-like; his role as actor stems in part from that of the Vice in the morality play, brilliantly comic and sinister. Yet even the devil can prevail over his victims only when they acquiesce in evil. The devil can deceive the senses, but acceptance of evil is still an act of the perverted will. Anne is guilty, however much we can appreciate the mesmerizing power of Richard's personality. By the end of the scene, she has violated everything she holds sacred.

The image of Richard as devil or Vice raises questions of motivation and of symbolic meaning, and suggests two seemingly disparate ways of reading the play, one psychological and the other providential. Is Richard a human character, propelled toward the throne by his insatiable ambition, like Macbeth? Is there a clue to his behavior in his ugliness and misanthropy? One might argue that he compensates for his ugliness and unlovability by resolving to domineer. Feeling unwanted, he despises all humans and undertakes to prove them weak and corrupt in order to affirm himself. He expresses a universal human penchant for cruelty and senseless domination. Yet the proposition that Richard is evil because he was born ugly logically can be reversed as well: he was born ugly because he is evil. In providential terms, Richard can be seen as the result of a divine plan in which evil ironically has a place in a larger scheme of things that is ultimately benign.

This latter concept, owing much to Renaissance notions of platonic correspondence between outer appearances and inner qualities, is grounded on the idea of a vast struggle in the cosmos between the forces of absolute good and the forces of absolute evil, one in which every event in human life has divine meaning and cause. Richard's birth is, according to this theory, a physical manifestation of that divine meaning. Providential destiny, having determined the need for a genius of evil at this point in English history, decrees that Richard shall be born. The teeth and hunched back merely give evidence of what is already predetermined. In the apt words of the choric Queen Margaret, Richard was "sealed in thy nativity / The slave of nature and the son of hell" (1.3.229–30). Though he devotes himself to selfish ambition and evildoing, Richard ultimately serves the righteous purpose of divine Providence in human affairs. He functions, in this interpretation, as a scourge of God, whose tyrannous plotting is permitted in order to bring just retribution upon offenders of the moral law. He is fundamentally unlike Shakespeare's more human villains, such as Macbeth or Claudius, but belongs, instead, to a special group of villains, including Iago in Othello and Edmund in King Lear. Like them, Richard is driven both by human motivation and by his preexistent evil genius; he displays the "motiveless malignity" ascribed by Coleridge to Iago.

Such a reading is only one approach to an understanding of Richard's character and function; he is also a human being involved in a struggle for power, motivated by ambition and hatred. The two readings, one psychological and the other providential, are complementary and need not contradict each other. The psychological reading seems more intelligible to us today, based as it is on character and motivation. The providential reading, more traditional in its ideology, helps explain not only Richard's delight in evil but also the necessity for so much evil and suffering in England's civil wars. This theory of history owes much to Edward Hall's *Union of the Two Noble and Illustre Families of Lancaster and York* (1542), Shakespeare's chief source, along with Raphael Holinshed's *Chronicles* (1578), for his *Henry VI* plays. Shakespeare's treatment of Richard is ultimately indebted to Polydore Vergil's *Anglica Historia* (1534) and especially to *The History of King Richard the Third*, attributed to Sir Thomas More (published 1557). This latter work, adopted in turn by Edward Hall, Richard Grafton, and Raphael Holinshed, purposefully blackens Richard's character. He becomes a study in the nature of tyranny, an object lesson to future rulers and their subjects. He is, moreover, a result of the curse placed by God on the English people for their sinful disobedience.

Richmond, in this Tudor explanation, becomes God's minister, chosen to destroy the scourge and thereafter to fulfill a new and happy covenant between God and humanity as King Henry VII. Thus, the play hardly touches on the sensitive matter of his somewhat remote Lancastrian claim to the crown. His victory at Bosworth is not one more turn of Fortune's wheel raising or deposing Lancastrian or Yorkist kings, but the end of a long cycle of unnatural violence, and his marriage to the Yorkist Princess Elizabeth is the restoration and the symbol of unity and peace in England's fair land. Although modern historians more impartially regard the defeat of Richard III at Bosworth Field in 1485 as a political overthrow not unlike Henry IV's overthrow of Richard II, and stress that Richard III was a talented administrator guilty of no worse political crimes than those of his more fortunate successor, Elizabethan audiences (under the constant promptings of the Tudor state) could not have found sufficient meaning in such a neutral interpretation. They were taught to see history as revealing God's intention and to view Henry VII's accession not as a parallel to the deposing of Richard II by Henry IV but, instead, as a divinely sanctioned deliverance of the English nation, to which Elizabeth's subjects were the happy heirs. Accordingly, the Tudor myth stressed the tyrannical nature of Richard III's seizure of power and conversely minimized the political and Machiavellian elements in Henry VII's takeover. Bosworth Field was seen as an act of God, a rising up of some irresistible force, and under no circumstances as a precedent for future rebellion.

In the *Henry VI* plays, Shakespeare puts considerable distance between himself and the Tudor orthodox reading of history, allowing the grim realities of civil war to speak for themselves. In *Richard III*, however, the pattern shown in the chronicles provides Shakespeare with an essential structural device. Viewing the civil wars in retrospect, *Richard III* potentially manifests a cohesive sense in which England's suffering has fulfilled a necessary plan of fall from innocence, leading through sin and penitence to regeneration. Evil is seen at last as something through which good triumphs, in English history, as in the story of humankind's fall and a restoration by divine grace.

This providential scheme imposes a double irony on *Richard III*. In the short run, Richard appears to be complete master over his victims. "Your imprisonment shall not be long," Richard assures his brother Clarence. "I will deliver you, or else lie for you" (1.1.114–15). The audience, already let in on the secret, can shiver at the grisly humor of these double entendres. Clarence will indeed soon be delivered—to his death. Richard's henchmen are fond of such jokes, too. When Lord Hastings is on his way to the Tower, where he plans to stay for midday dinner, Buckingham observes aside, "And supper too, although thou know'st it not" (3.2.122). Buckingham, knowing that Hastings is about to be arrested in the Tower and executed for treason, chillingly suggests that Hastings will soon be a feast for worms. Shortly before, Catesby has assured Hastings of Richard's and Buckingham's favor: "The princes both make high account of you—/[*Aside*] For they account his head upon the Bridge" (3.2.69–70). That is to say, Hastings's severed head will soon be raised on a pole on London Bridge as a grim warning to those who run afoul of the new regime. Richard has a phrase for such wit: "Thus, like the formal Vice, Iniquity, /I moralize two meanings in one word" (3.1.82–3). The point of such ironies is always the same: the scheming villain is cleverer than his victims, deceiving them through equivocation and triumphing in their spriritual blindness.

The delayed irony of the play, however, ultimately offers another possible explanation for the seemingly nihilistic conclusions of the early scenes; that is, there may be a larger plan at work, of which Richard is unconscious and in which he plays a role quite unlike the one he creates for himself. In this interpretive view,

Shakespeare's Richard fulfills a plan of which he is unaware, as in the chronicles of Edward Hall and others, even in the process of what he gloatingly regards as his own self-aggrandizement.

Providential plans are always complex, inscrutable to the minds of mortals, and understood least by those who unwittingly execute them. In attempting to prove his own contention that human nature is bestial and that a Machiavellian man of utter self-confidence can force his way to the top, flouting all conventions of morality, Richard succeeds in demonstrating the opposite. From the moment he takes the throne, he feels it insecure beneath him; opposition and betrayal spring up from every quarter, and, in his last moments, a mere horse is worth his whole kingdom. With sardonic comedy and poetic justice, Richard becomes the proverbial beguiler who is beguiled.

Even if this is not the only way to interpret Richard's character, the play does offer for our consideration a theory of divine causality in which virtually all of Richard's victims deserve their fate because they have offended God. Prophecies and dreams give structure to the sequence of retributive actions and keep grim score. As the choric Margaret observes, a Yorkist must pay for a Lancastrian, eye for an eye: Edward IV for Henry VI, young Edward V for Henry VI's son Edward. Thus, the Yorkist princes, though guiltless, die for their family's sins. The Yorkist Queen Elizabeth, like the Lancastrian Margaret, must outlive her husband into impotent old age, bewailing her children's cruel deaths. Clarence sees his death as punishment for breaking his oath at the battle of Tewkesbury and for his part in murdering Henry VI's son, Prince Edward. The Queen's kindred have been guilty of ambition, and Lord Hastings, in turn, is vulnerable because he has been willing to plot with Richard against the Queen's kindred. Margaret's curses serve both to warn the characters of their fates (a warning they blindly ignore) and to invite each person to curse himself or herself unwittingly but with ironic appropriateness. Lady Anne wishes unhappiness on any woman so insane as to marry Richard. Buckingham protests in a most sacred oath that whenever he turns again on the Queen's kindred, he will deserve to be punished by the treachery of his dearest friend (i.e., Richard). Dreams serve the same purpose of divine warning, giving Clarence a grotesque intimation of his death by drowning (in a butt of malmsey wine) and warning Hastings (through Stanley's dream) that the boar, Richard, will cut off his head. Thus, the English court punishes itself through Richard. He is the essence of the courtiers' factionalism, able to succeed as he does only because they forswear their most holy vows and conspire to destroy one another. They deserve to be outwitted at their own dismal game. Yet their falls are curative as well; Richard's victims acknowledge the justice of their undoings and penitently implore divine forgiveness. Richard contrastingly finds conscience a torment, rather than a voice of comfort and wisdom.

*Richard III* is not without its ironies and historical anxieties. Richard's own successful career of evil through much of the play demonstrates how rhetoric and theater can be used to dupe and to corrupt. The political process seems endlessly prone to cynical manipulation, and triumph comes chiefly to those who know how to use rhetoric to calculated effect. The Lord Mayor and his London associates are as pliable as the aristocracy. For all the belated assurances of providential meaning in Richard's rise to power and overthrow, we are allowed to speculate uncomfortably about the pragmatic action of history and its seeming ability to thrust forward into prominence an evil king or a good one, as individual temperament happens to dictate. Finally, there is the question of how Richard is supplanted. Whatever the reasons for Richard's baleful emergence, the process of his overthrow requires human agency and a rebellion against established (even if tyrannical) royal authority. To thoughtful observers in the sixteenth century, including Queen Elizabeth, any such rebellion, no matter how seemingly necessary, established a disturbing precedent and a threat to Tudor monarchical stability. If *Richard III* finds reassuring answers in the victory of Henry Tudor, Earl of Richmond, it does so in the face of pressing and troublesome circumstances.

The pattern of reciprocity and retaliation is much more than a way of demonstrating an ultimate divine purpose in human affairs; it is also a theatrically effective way of structuring a drama so as to make history coherent and entertaining. Shakespeare strikes us as above all a man of the theater, an artist and entertainer who senses masterfully what his audiences want. The shape of *Richard III*, as it moves through the anxieties of Richard's seemingly unstoppable rise to power to an eventual affirmation that brings closure not only to this play but to the entire four-play cycle of the three parts of Henry VI and Richard III, is immensely satisfying as theatrical experience. Modern audiences, with no ideological commitment to the propagandistic view that God chose Henry VII as the savior of England, can respond warmly to the play's artistic and theatrical depiction of coherence and pattern. That pattern allows us to enjoy Richard's villainies as theatrical performance while perceiving that those villainies are contained and disarmed by a larger structure.

Good eventually triumphs over evil in Richard III, if only because some Englishmen have the patience and common sense to endure a presumably deserved punishment and wait for deliverance. As in 3 Henry VI, the common people have little to do with the action of the play. They are choric spokesmen and bystanders, virtuous in their attitude (except for the two suborned murderers of Clarence). In their plain folk wisdom, they see the folly and evil their betters ignore: "Oh, full of danger is the Duke of Gloucester, / And the Queen's sons and brothers haught and proud" (2.3.28–9). And, although they accept Richard as ruler, they do so most reluctantly; Buckingham's first attempt to persuade the people to this course meets with apathy and silence. Their wisdom is to "leave it all to God" (line 46). In the fullness of time, this faith in goodness brings its just reward.

*Richard III* compresses historical time. It begins where *3 Henry VI* has left off, with the return of Edward IV to the throne in 1471, and ends with the defeat of Richard III, the last Yorkist king, at the battle of Bosworth (1485). Because of its close relation in subject to passages in *3 Henry VI* and its similar Senecan style, the play appears to have been written soon after its predecessors, sometime between 1591 and 1594. It greatly condenses events of fourteen years, particularly at the beginning, when King Henry VI's funeral rites (1471), Richard's courtship of Lady Anne (1472), Clarence's murder in the Tower (1478), and Edward's death (1483) are made to take place in rapid succession. Similarly, Buckingham's rebellion (1483), Richmond's thwarted sailing (1483), and his landing at Milford Haven (1485) are also compressed. Queen Margaret's role is a nonhistorical addition to the play, for the widowed Queen never left France after her ransom in 1475 by Louis XI.

*Richard III* is irresistible in performance. However much Richard reveals himself to be a conscienceless villain, his versatility as a performer and his taking us into his confidence invite a kind of complicity between actor and audience that is the stuff of dramatic excitement. These qualities are brilliantly on display in two film versions, that of Laurence Olivier in 1955 and Richard Loncraine in 1995. The first shows Richard's protean skills in deception as he soliloquizes candidly to us as his confidants, then transforms himself into the devoted brother of George Clarence (John Gielgud) and then the heartstricken wooer of the Lady Anne (Claire Bloom), seemingly at the mercy of the lady he worships. Loncraine transfers the play to the era of an imagined English civil war in the 1930s in which the ruthless, Nazi-like Richard (Ian McKellen) claws his way to the top. His thirst for mayhem is psychotic, but is not without its esthetic dimension as well; he murders with style, and savors the results by examining photographs of his dead victims. His teamwork with Buckingham (Jim Broadbent) in bamboozling the citizens of London is a thing of beauty. Closeups focus on McKellen's creased visage as he contemplates his next move. Al Pacino's *Looking for Richard* (1996) explores the play in rehearsal with an all-star cast including Winona Ryder, Kevin Spacey, Alec Baldwin, and Aidan Quinn. Many other great actors have excelled in the quintessentially theatrical role of Richard, including Marius Goring, Brian Bedford, Ian Holm, Antony Sher, Kevin Kline, and Simon Russell Beale.

# The Tragedy of King Richard the Third

[*Dramatis Personae*

KING EDWARD THE FOURTH
QUEEN ELIZABETH, *wife of King Edward*
EDWARD, PRINCE OF WALES, } *sons of Edward and*
RICHARD, DUKE OF YORK, } *Elizabeth*
GEORGE, DUKE OF CLARENCE,
RICHARD, DUKE OF GLOUCESTER, } *brothers of the King*
  *later King Richard III,*
DUCHESS OF YORK, *mother of Edward IV,*
  *Clarence, and Richard, Duke of Gloucester*
LADY ANNE, *widow of Edward, Prince of Wales*
  *(son of Henry VI); later wife of Richard, Duke of*
  *Gloucester*
MARGARET, *widow of King Henry VI*
BOY, *son of Clarence (Edward Plantagenet, Earl of*
  *Warwick)*
GIRL, *daughter of Clarence (Margaret Plantagenet,*
  *Countess of Salisbury)*

ANTHONY WOODVILLE, EARL RIVERS, *brother of*
  *Queen Elizabeth*
MARQUESS OF DORSET, } *sons of Queen*
LORD GREY, } *Elizabeth*
SIR THOMAS VAUGHAN, *executed with Rivers and*
  *Grey*

WILLIAM, LORD HASTINGS, *the Lord Chamberlain*
DUKE OF BUCKINGHAM, *Richard's supporter, later*
  *in opposition*
SIR WILLIAM CATESBY,
SIR RICHARD RATCLIFFE, } *Richard's supporters*
LORD LOVELL, } *and henchmen*
SIR JAMES TYRREL,
DUKE OF NORFOLK, } *Richard's generals*
EARL OF SURREY, }

HENRY, EARL OF RICHMOND, *later King Henry VII*

SCENE: *England.*]

LORD STANLEY, EARL OF DERBY,
EARL OF OXFORD,
SIR JAMES BLUNT, } *supporters of*
SIR WALTER HERBERT, } *Richmond*
SIR WILLIAM BRANDON,
CHRISTOPHER URSWICK, *a priest,*

CARDINAL BOURCHIER, *Archbishop of Canterbury*
ARCHBISHOP OF YORK (*Thomas Rotherham*)
BISHOP OF ELY (*John Morton*)
GHOSTS *of King Henry VI, Edward Prince of*
  *Wales, and others murdered by Richard*
  *(Clarence, Rivers, Grey, Vaughan, Hastings, the*
  *two young princes, Anne, and Buckingham)*
SIR ROBERT BRACKENBURY, *Lieutenant of the Tower*
TRESSEL,
BERKELEY, } *attending the*
HALBERDIER, } *Lady Anne*
GENTLEMAN,
*Two* MURDERERS
KEEPER *in the Tower*
*Three* CITIZENS
MESSENGER *to Queen Elizabeth*
LORD MAYOR OF LONDON
MESSENGER *to Lord Hastings*
PURSUIVANT
PRIEST
SCRIVENER
*Two* BISHOPS
PAGE *to Richard III*
*Four* MESSENGERS *to Richard III*
SHERIFF OF WILTSHIRE

*Lords, Attendants, Aldermen, Citizens, Councilors,*
  *Soldiers*

## 1.1

*Enter Richard, Duke of Gloucester, solus.*

RICHARD
Now is the winter of our discontent
Made glorious summer by this son of York,                    2
And all the clouds that loured upon our house                3
In the deep bosom of the ocean buried.
Now are our brows bound with victorious wreaths,             5
Our bruisèd arms hung up for monuments,                      6
Our stern alarums changed to merry meetings,                 7
Our dreadful marches to delightful measures.                 8
Grim-visaged War hath smoothed his wrinkled
    front;                                                   9
And now, instead of mounting barbèd steeds                   10
To fright the souls of fearful adversaries,
He capers nimbly in a lady's chamber
To the lascivious pleasing of a lute.
But I, that am not shaped for sportive tricks,               14
Nor made to court an amorous looking glass;
I, that am rudely stamped, and want love's majesty           16
To strut before a wanton ambling nymph;                      17
I, that am curtailed of this fair proportion,                18
Cheated of feature by dissembling Nature,                    19
Deformed, unfinished, sent before my time
Into this breathing world scarce half made up,
And that so lamely and unfashionable                         22
That dogs bark at me as I halt by them—                      23
Why, I, in this weak piping time of peace,                   24
Have no delight to pass away the time,
Unless to see my shadow in the sun
And descant on mine own deformity.                           27
And therefore, since I cannot prove a lover
To entertain these fair well-spoken days,                    29
I am determinèd to prove a villain
And hate the idle pleasures of these days.
Plots have I laid, inductions dangerous,                     32
By drunken prophecies, libels, and dreams,
To set my brother Clarence and the King
In deadly hate the one against the other;
And if King Edward be as true and just

As I am subtle, false, and treacherous,
This day should Clarence closely be mewed up                 38
About a prophecy, which says that G                          39
Of Edward's heirs the murderer shall be.
Dive, thoughts, down to my soul; here Clarence
    comes.

*Enter Clarence, guarded, and Brackenbury,*
*[Lieutenant of the Tower].*

Brother, good day. What means this armèd guard
That waits upon Your Grace?
CLARENCE                               His Majesty,           43
Tend'ring my person's safety, hath appointed                 44
This conduct to convey me to the Tower.                      45
RICHARD
Upon what cause?
CLARENCE                         Because my name is George.
RICHARD
Alack, my lord, that fault is none of yours.
He should, for that, commit your godfathers.
Oh, belike His Majesty hath some intent                      49
That you should be new christened in the Tower.              50
But what's the matter, Clarence, may I know?                 51
CLARENCE
Yea, Richard, when I know; for I protest
As yet I do not. But, as I can learn,
He hearkens after prophecies and dreams,
And from the crossrow plucks the letter G,                   55
And says a wizard told him that by G
His issue disinherited should be;                            57
And, for my name of George begins with G,                    58
It follows in his thought that I am he.
These, as I learn, and suchlike toys as these                60
Hath moved His Highness to commit me now.                    61
RICHARD
Why, this it is when men are ruled by women.
'Tis not the King that sends you to the Tower;
My Lady Grey his wife, Clarence, 'tis she                    64
That tempers him to this extremity.                          65
Was it not she, and that good man of worship,                66
Anthony Woodville, her brother there,                        67

---

1.1. **Location: London. Near the Tower.**
**0.1** *solus* alone.   **2 son** Edward IV was the son of Richard, Duke of York. (With a pun on "sun"; Edward IV used the sun on his badge.)   **3 loured** looked threateningly   **5 brows** foreheads   **6 arms** armor.   **monuments** trophies   **7 alarums** calls to arms, or assaults   **8 dreadful** formidable, awe-inspiring.   **measures** stately dances.   **9 wrinkled front** furrowed forehead   **10 barbèd** armored   **14 sportive** amorous   **16 rudely stamped** roughly fashioned, coined.   **want** lack   **17 ambling** walking affectedly, wantonly   **18 curtailed** cut short, denied.   **proportion** shape   **19 feature** shapeliness of body   **22 unfashionable** badly fashioned   **23 halt** limp   **24 piping time** i.e., a time when the music heard is that of pipes and not fifes and drums   **27 descant** compose variations, comment on   **29 entertain** pass away pleasurably.   **well-spoken** refined, elegant   **32 inductions** preparations

**38 mewed up** confined (like a hawk)   **39 prophecy . . . G** (The prophecy is mentioned in the chronicles; the quibble is that *G* stands for *Gloucester* and not for *George*, the given name of the Duke of Clarence.)   **43 waits** attends   **44 Tend'ring** having care for   **45 conduct** escort   **49 belike** probably   **50 new christened** (Anticipates, ironically, Clarence's death by drowning in 1.4.)   **51 matter** reason, cause   **55 crossrow** Christ-crossrow, or alphabet (so called from the cross printed before the alphabet in the hornbook)   **57 issue** offspring   **58 for** because   **60 toys** trifles   **61 commit** arrest   **64 My Lady Grey** (A disrespectful reference to the Queen, whose maiden name was Elizabeth Woodville and who, when the King married her, was the widow of Sir John Grey.)   **65 tempers** governs, directs   **66 worship** honor. (Said ironically.)   **67 Woodville** i.e., Earl Rivers (whom Richard also disrespectfully refers to by his family name rather than by his recently acquired title)

That made him send Lord Hastings to the Tower,
From whence this present day he is delivered?
We are not safe, Clarence, we are not safe.

CLARENCE
By heaven, I think there is no man secure
But the Queen's kindred and night-walking heralds     72
That trudge betwixt the King and Mistress Shore.      73
Heard you not what an humble suppliant
Lord Hastings was to her for his delivery?            75

RICHARD
Humbly complaining to Her Deity                       76
Got my Lord Chamberlain his liberty.                  77
I'll tell you what: I think it is our way,            78
If we will keep in favor with the King,
To be her men and wear her livery.                    80
The jealous, o'erworn widow and herself,              81
Since that our brother dubbed them gentlewomen,       82
Are mighty gossips in our monarchy.                   83

BRACKENBURY
I beseech Your Graces both to pardon me:
His Majesty hath straitly given in charge             85
That no man shall have private conference,
Of what degree soever, with your brother.             87

RICHARD
Even so? An't please Your Worship, Brackenbury,       88
You may partake of anything we say.
We speak no treason, man. We say the King
Is wise and virtuous, and his noble queen
Well struck in years, fair, and not jealous.          92
We say that Shore's wife hath a pretty foot,
A cherry lip, a bonny eye, a passing pleasing tongue;  94
And that the Queen's kindred are made gentlefolks.
How say you, sir? Can you deny all this?

BRACKENBURY
With this, my lord, myself have naught to do.

RICHARD
Naught to do with Mistress Shore? I tell thee, fellow,  98
He that doth naught with her, excepting one,          99
Were best to do it secretly, alone.

BRACKENBURY     What one, my lord?

RICHARD
Her husband, knave. Wouldst thou betray me?           102

BRACKENBURY
I beseech Your Grace to pardon me, and withal         103
Forbear your conference with the noble Duke.

CLARENCE
We know thy charge, Brackenbury, and will obey.

RICHARD
We are the Queen's abjects, and must obey.            106
Brother, farewell. I will unto the King;
And whatsoe'er you will employ me in,
Were it to call King Edward's widow sister,           109
I will perform it to enfranchise you.                 110
Meantime, this deep disgrace in brotherhood
Touches me deeper than you can imagine.               112

CLARENCE
I know it pleaseth neither of us well.

RICHARD
Well, your imprisonment shall not be long;            114
I will deliver you, or else lie for you.              115
Meantime, have patience.

CLARENCE                    I must perforce. Farewell.  116
                    Exit Clarence [with Brackenbury and guard].

RICHARD
Go tread the path that thou shalt ne'er return.
Simple, plain Clarence, I do love thee so
That I will shortly send thy soul to heaven,
If heaven will take the present at our hands.
But who comes here? The new-delivered Hastings?       121

                    Enter Lord Hastings.

HASTINGS
Good time of day unto my gracious lord.

RICHARD
As much unto my good Lord Chamberlain.
Well are you welcome to the open air.
How hath Your Lordship brooked imprisonment?          125

HASTINGS
With patience, noble lord, as prisoners must.
But I shall live, my lord, to give them thanks        127
That were the cause of my imprisonment.

RICHARD
No doubt, no doubt; and so shall Clarence too,
For they that were your enemies are his,
And have prevailed as much on him as you.

HASTINGS
More pity that the eagles should be mewed,            132
Whiles kites and buzzards prey at liberty.            133

RICHARD     What news abroad?                          134

HASTINGS
No news so bad abroad as this at home:

---

72 **night-walking heralds** i.e., secret messengers for an assignation
73 **Mistress Shore** Jane Shore, the King's mistress, and wife of a gold-
smith in Lombard Street. (The title *Mistress* is a respectful form of
address for any woman, married or unmarried.)   75 **to her . . . delivery** i.e., to Jane Shore, petitioning her to urge Lord Hastings' release
from the Tower. (A risky business; Hastings seeks help from the very
woman with whom he is having an affair, Jane Shore, the King's mistress.)   76 **Her Deity** (A mock title for Jane Shore, suggesting she is
even more elevated than "Her Grace" or "Her Majesty.")   77 **Lord
Chamberlain** i.e., Lord Hastings   78 **our way** i.e., our only way (to
succeed)   80 **To be her men** to devote our service to Jane Shore
81 **widow** i.e., Queen Elizabeth. (See the note for line 64.)   **herself**
i.e., Jane Shore   82 **Since that** since.   **gentlewomen** (A sneer at the
Queen's family, which was gentle but not noble until after her
marriage with the King; Jane Shore was, of course, neither gentle nor
noble.)   83 **mighty gossips** i.e., influential busybodies   85 **straitly . . .
charge** strictly ordered   87 **degree** rank   88 **An't** If it   92 **Well struck**
i.e., well along.   **not jealous** (Implies there are things she might be
jealous about.)   94 **passing** surpassingly   98 **Naught** (Richard quibbles on the meanings "nothing" and "naughtiness," "betokening the
sexual act.")   99 **excepting one** except her husband   102 **betray me**
i.e., trick me into naming either the King or Lord Hastings, or both, as
persons who do "naught" with Mistress Shore.

103 **withal** furthermore   106 **abjects** abjectly servile subjects. (With
wordplay: "abjects/subjects.")   109 **King Edward's widow** i.e., the
widow whom Edward has made queen   110 **enfranchise** release
from imprisonment   112 **Touches . . . imagine** (1) distresses me more
than can be imagined (2) concerns me (in my personal ambition)
more than you could possibly guess   114 **shall not be long** (for
sinister reasons that we hear but Clarence does not)   115 **lie for you**
(1) take your place in prison (2) tell lies about you.   116 **perforce**
necessarily.   121 **new-delivered** recently released   125 **brooked**
endured   127 **give them thanks** i.e., pay them back. (Said ironically.)
132 **mewed** confined, caged   133 **kites** scavengers of the hawk
family   134 **abroad** at large, circulating.

The King is sickly, weak, and melancholy,
And his physicians fear him mightily.                                    137

RICHARD
Now, by Saint John, that news is bad indeed!
Oh, he hath kept an evil diet long                                        139
And overmuch consumed his royal person.
'Tis very grievous to be thought upon.
Where is he, in his bed?

HASTINGS   He is.

RICHARD
Go you before, and I will follow you.     *Exit Hastings.*
He cannot live, I hope, and must not die
Till George be packed with post-horse up to heaven.    146
I'll in, to urge his hatred more to Clarence            147
With lies well steeled with weighty arguments;          148
And, if I fail not in my deep intent,
Clarence hath not another day to live.
Which done, God take King Edward to his mercy
And leave the world for me to bustle in!
For then I'll marry Warwick's youngest daughter.        153
What though I killed her husband and her father?        154
The readiest way to make the wench amends
Is to become her husband and her father,
The which will I; not all so much for love
As for another secret close intent                      158
By marrying her which I must reach unto.
But yet I run before my horse to market.
Clarence still breathes, Edward still lives and reigns;
When they are gone, then must I count my gains.
                                                  *Exit.*

❖

# 1.2

*Enter the corpse of [King] Henry the Sixth,*
*with Halberds to guard it; Lady Anne being the*
*mourner [attended by Tressel and Berkeley].*

ANNE
Set down, set down your honorable load—
If honor may be shrouded in a hearse—                   2
Whilst I awhile obsequiously lament                     3
Th'untimely fall of virtuous Lancaster.                 4
               *[The bearers set down the coffin.]*
Poor key-cold figure of a holy king,                    5
Pale ashes of the house of Lancaster,
Thou bloodless remnant of that royal blood,
Be it lawful that I invocate thy ghost                  8
To hear the lamentations of poor Anne,

Wife to thy Edward, to thy slaughtered son,
Stabbed by the selfsame hand that made these wounds!    11
Lo, in these windows that let forth thy life            12
I pour the helpless balm of my poor eyes.               13
Oh, cursèd be the hand that made these holes!
Cursèd the heart that had the heart to do it!
Cursèd the blood that let this blood from hence!
More direful hap betide that hated wretch               17
That makes us wretched by the death of thee
Than I can wish to wolves, to spiders, toads,
Or any creeping venomed thing that lives!
If ever he have child, abortive be it,                  21
Prodigious, and untimely brought to light,              22
Whose ugly and unnatural aspect                         23
May fright the hopeful mother at the view,              24
And that be heir to his unhappiness!                    25
If ever he have wife, let her be made
More miserable by the life of him
Than I am made by my young lord and thee!—              28
Come now towards Chertsey with your holy load,          29
Taken from Paul's to be interrèd there.                 30
               *[The bearers take up the hearse.]*
And still as you are weary of this weight,              31
Rest you, whiles I lament King Henry's corpse.

*Enter Richard, Duke of Gloucester.*

RICHARD
Stay, you that bear the corpse, and set it down.

ANNE
What black magician conjures up this fiend
To stop devoted charitable deeds?                       35

RICHARD
Villains, set down the corpse, or, by Saint Paul,
I'll make a corpse of him that disobeys.

HALBERDIER *[advancing with his halberd lowered]*
My lord, stand back, and let the coffin pass.

RICHARD
Unmannered dog, stand thou when I command!              39
Advance thy halberd higher than my breast,              40
Or, by Saint Paul, I'll strike thee to my foot
And spurn upon thee, beggar, for thy boldness.          42
               *[The bearers set down the hearse.]*

ANNE
What do you tremble? Are you all afraid?                43
Alas, I blame you not, for you are mortal,
And mortal eyes cannot endure the devil.—
Avaunt, thou dreadful minister of hell!                 46
Thou hadst but power over his mortal body;
His soul thou canst not have. Therefore, begone.

---

**137 fear** fear for   **139 diet** course of life, regimen   **146 with post-horse** by post-horses, i.e., by swiftest possible means   **147 I'll . . . Clarence** I'll go visit the King to urge on his hatred for Clarence (as a result of Clarence's havi ng temporarily changed his loyalty to the Lancastrian side during the wars)   **148 steeled** reinforced   **153 Warwick's youngest daughter** the Lady Anne Neville, widow of Edward, Prince of Wales, son of King Henry VI.   **154 father** i.e., father-in-law (Henry VI).   **158 intent** design (i.e., Richard hopes to ally himself with the house of Lancaster to bolster his claim to the throne)   **1.2. Location: London. A street.**   **0.2** *Halberds* halberdiers, guards with halberds, or long poleaxes   **2 hearse** (Probably here an open coffin on a bier.)   **3 obsequiously** as befits a funeral, mournfully   **4 Lancaster** King Henry VI had been the head of the house of Lancaster.   **5 key-cold** extremely cold, cold as a metal key. (Proverbial.)   **8 Be it** Let it be.   **invocate** invoke

**11 the selfsame hand** i.e., the hand of Richard, Duke of Glouces-ter   **12 windows** i.e., wounds   **13 helpless** useless, unavailing   **17 hap betide** fortune befall   **21 abortive** misshapen, premature   **22 Prodigious** monstrous, unnatural   **23 aspect** appearance   **24 the hopeful mother** any mother expecting a baby   **25 And . . . unhappi-ness!** and may that be the legacy of his evil nature!   **28 by . . . thee** i.e., by the deaths of Prince Edward and King Henry VI.   **29 Chert-sey** monastery in Surrey, near London, where King Henry's body is to be buried   **30 Paul's** Saint Paul's Cathedral in London   **31 still as** as often as   **35 devoted** holy   **39 stand** halt   **40 Advance . . . breast** Raise your halberd upright (rather than pointing it at me)   **42 spurn** kick, trample   **43 What** Why   **46 Avaunt** Begone

RICHARD
  Sweet saint, for charity, be not so curst.                                    49
ANNE
  Foul devil, for God's sake hence and trouble us not,                          50
  For thou hast made the happy earth thy hell,
  Filled it with cursing cries and deep exclaims.                               52
  If thou delight to view thy heinous deeds,
  Behold this pattern of thy butcheries.                                        54
                                    [*She uncovers the corpse.*]
  Oh, gentlemen, see, see dead Henry's wounds
  Open their congealed mouths and bleed afresh!                                 56
  Blush, blush, thou lump of foul deformity!
  For 'tis thy presence that exhales this blood                                 58
  From cold and empty veins where no blood dwells.
  Thy deeds inhuman and unnatural
  Provokes this deluge most unnatural.                                          61
  O God, which this blood mad'st, revenge his death!                            62
  O earth, which this blood drink'st, revenge his death!
  Either heav'n with lightning strike the murd'rer dead,
  Or earth gape open wide and eat him quick,                                    65
  As thou dost swallow up this good king's blood,
  Which his hell-governed arm hath butcherèd!
RICHARD
  Lady, you know no rules of charity,
  Which renders good for bad, blessings for curses.
ANNE
  Villain, thou know'st nor law of God nor man.                                 70
  No beast so fierce but knows some touch of pity.                              71
RICHARD
  But I know none, and therefore am no beast.
ANNE
  Oh, wonderful, when devils tell the truth!                                    73
RICHARD
  More wonderful, when angels are so angry.
  Vouchsafe, divine perfection of a woman,                                      75
  Of these supposèd crimes to give me leave
  By circumstance but to acquit myself.                                         77
ANNE
  Vouchsafe, defused infection of a man,                                        78
  Of these known evils but to give me leave
  By circumstance t'accuse thy cursèd self.
RICHARD
  Fairer than tongue can name thee, let me have                                 81
  Some patient leisure to excuse myself.
ANNE
  Fouler than heart can think thee, thou canst make
  No excuse current but to hang thyself.                                        84
RICHARD
  By such despair I should accuse myself.                                       85

ANNE
  And by despairing shalt thou stand excused                                    86
  For doing worthy vengeance on thyself
  That didst unworthy slaughter upon others.
RICHARD   Say that I slew them not?
ANNE   Then say they were not slain.
  But dead they are, and, devilish slave, by thee.
RICHARD   I did not kill your husband.
ANNE   Why, then he is alive.
RICHARD
  Nay, he is dead, and slain by Edward's hand.                                  94
ANNE
  In thy foul throat thou liest! Queen Margaret saw
  Thy murd'rous falchion smoking in his blood,                                  96
  The which thou once didst bend against her breast,                            97
  But that thy brothers beat aside the point.
RICHARD
  I was provokèd by her sland'rous tongue,
  That laid their guilt upon my guiltless shoulders.                            100
ANNE
  Thou wast provokèd by thy bloody mind,
  That never dream'st on aught but butcheries.                                  102
  Didst thou not kill this king?
RICHARD                                    I grant ye.
ANNE
  Dost grant me, hedgehog? Then God grant me too                                104
  Thou mayst be damnèd for that wicked deed!
  Oh, he was gentle, mild, and virtuous!
RICHARD
  The better for the King of Heaven that hath him.
ANNE
  He is in heaven, where thou shalt never come.
RICHARD
  Let him thank me that holp to send him thither;                               109
  For he was fitter for that place than earth.
ANNE
  And thou unfit for any place but hell.
RICHARD
  Yes, one place else, if you will hear me name it.
ANNE   Some dungeon.
RICHARD   Your bedchamber.
ANNE
  Ill rest betide the chamber where thou liest!                                 115
RICHARD
  So will it, madam, till I lie with you.
ANNE
  I hope so.
RICHARD   I know so. But, gentle Lady Anne,
  To leave this keen encounter of our wits
  And fall something into a slower method,                                      119
  Is not the causer of the timeless deaths                                      120
  Of these Plantagenets, Henry and Edward,
  As blameful as the executioner?

**49 curst** spiteful, shrewish.   **50 hence** go hence, depart   **52 exclaims** exclamations.   **54 pattern** example   **56 bleed afresh** (A phenomenon popularly supposed to occur in the presence of the murderer.)   **58 exhales** draws out   **61 deluge** ample flow (of blood)   **62 O God . . . mad'st** O God, who made King Henry VI (since all humans are made in God's image)   **65 quick** alive   **70 nor . . . nor** neither . . . nor   **71 so fierce but knows** is so savage that it has not   **73 Oh . . . truth** (Anne bitterly reinterprets Richard's *am no beast*, "am not beastly," to mean that he is neither man nor beast, but devil.)   **75 Vouchsafe** Deign, consent   **77 circumstance** detailed argument   **78 defused** diffused, disordered, shapeless; *defused infection* means "spreading plague"   **81 Fairer** More beautiful   **84 current** genuine, acceptable (as in coinage)   **85 By . . . myself** i.e., If I were to commit suicide I should in effect plead guilty to the most heinous of sins.

**86 stand excused** be justified   **94 Edward's** Edward IV's   **96 falchion** curved sword   **97 bend** direct, aim   **100 their guilt** the guilt of my brothers, Edward IV and Clarence   **102 aught** anything   **104 hedgehog** (Richard's heraldic emblem featured a boar or wild hog.)   **109 holp** helped   **115 betide** befall   **119 something into a** into a somewhat   **120 timeless** untimely

ANNE
Thou wast the cause and most accurst effect. 123
RICHARD
Your beauty was the cause of that effect— 124
Your beauty, that did haunt me in my sleep
To undertake the death of all the world,
So I might live one hour in your sweet bosom.
ANNE
If I thought that, I tell thee, homicide, 128
These nails should rend that beauty from my cheeks. 129
RICHARD
These eyes could not endure that beauty's wrack; 130
You should not blemish it, if I stood by.
As all the world is cheerèd by the sun,
So I by that. It is my day, my life.
ANNE
Black night o'ershade thy day, and death thy life!
RICHARD
Curse not thyself, fair creature—thou art both. 135
ANNE
I would I were, to be revenged on thee. 136
RICHARD
It is a quarrel most unnatural
To be revenged on him that loveth thee.
ANNE
It is a quarrel just and reasonable
To be revenged on him that killed my husband.
RICHARD
He that bereft thee, lady, of thy husband
Did it to help thee to a better husband.
ANNE
His better doth not breathe upon the earth.
RICHARD
He lives that loves thee better than he could. 144
ANNE
Name him.
RICHARD                Plantagenet.
ANNE                                Why, that was he. 145
RICHARD
The selfsame name, but one of better nature.
ANNE
Where is he?
RICHARD        Here.                [*She*] *spits at him.*
Why dost thou spit at me?
ANNE
Would it were mortal poison for thy sake!
RICHARD
Never came poison from so sweet a place.
ANNE
Never hung poison on a fouler toad. 150

Out of my sight! Thou dost infect mine eyes.
RICHARD
Thine eyes, sweet lady, have infected mine. 152
ANNE
Would they were basilisks, to strike thee dead! 153
RICHARD
I would they were, that I might die at once;
For now they kill me with a living death.
Those eyes of thine from mine have drawn salt tears,
Shamed their aspects with store of childish drops; 157
These eyes, which never shed remorseful tear—
No, when my father York and Edward wept
To hear the piteous moan that Rutland made 160
When black-faced Clifford shook his sword at him; 161
Nor when thy warlike father, like a child, 162
Told the sad story of my father's death
And twenty times made pause to sob and weep,
That all the standers-by had wet their cheeks 165
Like trees bedashed with rain—in that sad time
My manly eyes did scorn an humble tear;
And what these sorrows could not thence exhale, 168
Thy beauty hath, and made them blind with weeping.
I never sued to friend nor enemy; 170
My tongue could never learn sweet smoothing words; 171
But now thy beauty is proposed my fee, 172
My proud heart sues and prompts my tongue to speak.
                                *She looks scornfully at him.*
Teach not thy lip such scorn, for it was made
For kissing, lady, not for such contempt.
If thy revengeful heart cannot forgive,
Lo, here I lend thee this sharp-pointed sword,
Which if thou please to hide in this true breast
And let the soul forth that adoreth thee,
I lay it naked to the deadly stroke
And humbly beg the death upon my knee. 181
            *He [kneels and] lays his breast open; she offers at [it]*
                                            *with his sword.*
Nay, do not pause; for I did kill King Henry—
But 'twas thy beauty that provokèd me.
Nay, now dispatch; 'twas I that stabbed young Edward—
But 'twas thy heavenly face that set me on. 185
                                *She falls the sword.*
Take up the sword again, or take up me.
ANNE
Arise, dissembler. Though I wish thy death,
I will not be thy executioner.
RICHARD [*rising*]
Then bid me kill myself, and I will do it.

---

123 **effect** fulfillment.   124 **effect** result   128 **homicide** murderer   129 **rend** tear   130 **wrack** destruction   135 **thou art both** i.e., you are my black night and my death, if you deny me love; or, you are my life and my death.   136 **I would I were** (If Anne were truly both Richard's day and his life, she could terminate both.)   144 **He lives** i.e., There is a man.   **he** i.e., Prince Edward   145 **Plantagenet** (Richard's father, the Duke of York, adopted this name when he made his claim to the English throne—see *1 Henry VI*, 2.4.36—but the name had been in the family of England's Angevin rulers since the time of Henry II and thus could also be claimed by Henry VI and his son, Prince Edward.)   150 **poison . . . toad** (Toads were popularly regarded as poisonous.)

152 **infected** i.e., with love (since love was thought to enter through the eyes)   153 **basilisks** mythical reptiles reputed to kill by their looks   157 **aspects** appearance   160 **Rutland** second son of Richard, Duke of York. (See *3 Henry VI*, 1.3, for his death scene.)   161 **black-faced** i.e., foreboding in appearance   162 **thy warlike father** i.e., the Earl of Warwick   165 **That** so that   168 **exhale** draw out   170 **sued** supplicated, appealed   171 **smoothing** flattering   172 **now** now that.   **proposed my fee** proposed as my reward   181 **the death** death after sentencing   181.1 *offers* aims   185.1 *falls* lets fall

ANNE
   I have already.
RICHARD         That was in thy rage.
   Speak it again, and even with the word
   This hand, which for thy love did kill thy love,
   Shall for thy love kill a far truer love.
   To both their deaths shalt thou be accessory.
ANNE    I would I knew thy heart.             195
RICHARD    'Tis figured in my tongue.       196
ANNE    I fear me both are false.
RICHARD    Then never man was true.
ANNE    Well, well, put up your sword.
RICHARD    Say, then, my peace is made.
ANNE    That shalt thou know hereafter.
RICHARD    But shall I live in hope?
ANNE    All men, I hope, live so.           203
RICHARD    Vouchsafe to wear this ring.      204
ANNE    To take is not to give.           205
                 *[He slips the ring on her finger.]*
RICHARD
   Look how my ring encompasseth thy finger,     206
   Even so thy breast encloseth my poor heart;
   Wear both of them, for both of them are thine.
   And if thy poor devoted servant may        209
   But beg one favor at thy gracious hand,
   Thou dost confirm his happiness forever.
ANNE    What is it?
RICHARD
   That it may please you leave these sad designs    213
   To him that hath most cause to be a mourner,
   And presently repair to Crosby House,      215
   Where, after I have solemnly interred
   At Chertsey monast'ry this noble king
   And wet his grave with my repentant tears,
   I will with all expedient duty see you.      219
   For divers unknown reasons, I beseech you,    220
   Grant me this boon.
ANNE
   With all my heart, and much it joys me, too,
   To see you are become so penitent.—
   Tressel and Berkeley, go along with me.
RICHARD
   Bid me farewell.
ANNE             'Tis more than you deserve;
   But since you teach me how to flatter you,
   Imagine I have said farewell already.
             *Exeunt two [Tressel and Berkeley] with Anne.*
RICHARD
   Sirs, take up the corpse.
GENTLEMAN           Towards Chertsey, noble lord?
RICHARD
   No, to Whitefriars. There attend my coming.    229
                *Exeunt [bearers with] corpse.*

Was ever woman in this humor wooed?      230
Was ever woman in this humor won?       231
I'll have her, but I will not keep her long.
What? I, that killed her husband and his father,
To take her in her heart's extremest hate,
With curses in her mouth, tears in her eyes,
The bleeding witness of my hatred by,
Having God, her conscience, and these bars against me, 237
And I no friends to back my suit withal
But the plain devil and dissembling looks?
And yet to win her! All the world to nothing!    240
Ha!
Hath she forgot already that brave prince,
Edward, her lord, whom I, some three months since,
Stabbed in my angry mood at Tewkesbury?
A sweeter and a lovelier gentleman,
Framed in the prodigality of nature,       246
Young, valiant, wise, and, no doubt, right royal,
The spacious world cannot again afford.     248
And will she yet abase her eyes on me,     249
That cropped the golden prime of this sweet prince  250
And made her widow to a woeful bed?
On me, whose all not equals Edward's moiety?   252
On me, that halts and am misshapen thus?    253
My dukedom to a beggarly denier,       254
I do mistake my person all this while.
Upon my life, she finds, although I cannot,
Myself to be a marv'lous proper man.     257
I'll be at charges for a looking glass      258
And entertain a score or two of tailors     259
To study fashions to adorn my body.
Since I am crept in favor with myself,
I will maintain it with some little cost.
But first I'll turn yon fellow in his grave,    263
And then return lamenting to my love.
Shine out, fair sun, till I have bought a glass,   265
That I may see my shadow as I pass.    *Exit.*

                    ❧

## 1.3

*Enter the Queen Mother [Elizabeth], Lord Rivers,*
*[Marquess of Dorset,] and Lord Grey.*

RIVERS
   Have patience, madam. There's no doubt His Majesty
   Will soon recover his accustomed health.
GREY
   In that you brook it ill, it makes him worse.    3
   Therefore, for God's sake, entertain good comfort,  4
   And cheer His Grace with quick and merry eyes.

---

**195 would** wish   **196 figured** portrayed   **203 All ... so** (Anne replies to Richard's plea for hope in his love suit with a central thesis of Christian faith: all humans live in hope of salvation.)   **204 Vouchsafe** Consent   **205 To take ... give** i.e., I accept the ring but I make no promises.   **206 Look how** Just as   **209 servant** i.e., male admirer, one whom she may command   **213 these sad designs** these solemn ceremonial duties   **215 presently repair** go right away.   **Crosby House** (One of Richard's London dwellings; built originally by Sir John Crosby.)   **219 expedient** expeditious   **220 unknown** secret   **229 Whitefriars** the Carmelite priory in London.   **attend** await

**230, 231 humor** whimsical frame of mind   **237 bars** obstacles   **240 All ... nothing** i.e., Against infinite odds.   **246 Framed ... nature** i.e., formed in nature's most lavish mood   **248 The spacious ... afford** Nature, having been so prodigal in her gifts when she created young Edward, can scarcely afford another such.   **249 abase her eyes** degrade herself by looking favorably   **250 cropped** cut short.   **prime** springtime, early manhood   **252 Edward's moiety** half of Edward's worth.   **253 halts** limps   **254 denier** small copper coin, the twelfth part of a sou   **257 proper** handsome   **258 be ... for** undertake the expense of   **259 entertain** retain, employ   **263 in** into   **265 glass** mirror
**1.3. Location:** London. The royal court.
**3 brook** endure   **4 entertain ... comfort** cheer up

**QUEEN ELIZABETH**
If he were dead, what would betide on me?                        6

**GREY**
No other harm but loss of such a lord.

**QUEEN ELIZABETH**
The loss of such a lord includes all harms.

**GREY**
The heavens have blessed you with a goodly son
To be your comforter when he is gone.

**QUEEN ELIZABETH**
Ah, he is young, and his minority                                11
Is put unto the trust of Richard Gloucester,                     12
A man that loves not me, nor none of you.

**RIVERS**
Is it concluded he shall be Protector?

**QUEEN ELIZABETH**
It is determined, not concluded yet;                             15
But so it must be, if the King miscarry.                         16

*Enter Buckingham and [Lord Stanley Earl of] Derby.*

**GREY**
Here come the lords of Buckingham and Derby.

**BUCKINGHAM**
Good time of day unto Your Royal Grace!

**STANLEY**
God make Your Majesty joyful, as you have been!

**QUEEN ELIZABETH**
The Countess Richmond, good my lord of Derby,                    20
To your good prayer will scarcely say amen.
Yet, Derby, notwithstanding she's your wife
And loves not me, be you, good lord, assured
I hate not you for her proud arrogance.                          24

**STANLEY**
I do beseech you, either not believe
The envious slanders of her false accusers,                      26
Or, if she be accused on true report,                            27
Bear with her weakness, which I think proceeds
From wayward sickness and no grounded malice.                    29

**QUEEN ELIZABETH**
Saw you the King today, my lord of Derby?

**STANLEY**
But now the Duke of Buckingham and I                             31
Are come from visiting His Majesty.

**QUEEN ELIZABETH**
What likelihood of his amendment, lords?                         33

**BUCKINGHAM**
Madam, good hope; His Grace speaks cheerfully.

**QUEEN ELIZABETH**
God grant him health! Did you confer with him?

**BUCKINGHAM**
Ay, madam. He desires to make atonement                          36
Between the Duke of Gloucester and your brothers,                37
And between them and my Lord Chamberlain,                        38
And sent to warn them to his royal presence.                     39

**QUEEN ELIZABETH**
Would all were well! But that will never be.
I fear our happiness is at the height.

*Enter Richard [Duke of Gloucester, and Lord Hastings].*

**RICHARD**
They do me wrong, and I will not endure it!
Who is it that complains unto the King
That I, forsooth, am stern and love them not?
By holy Paul, they love His Grace but lightly
That fill his ears with such dissentious rumors.                 46
Because I cannot flatter and look fair,                          47
Smile in men's faces, smooth, deceive, and cog,                  48
Duck with French nods and apish courtesy,                        49
I must be held a rancorous enemy.
Cannot a plain man live and think no harm,
But thus his simple truth must be abused
With silken, sly, insinuating Jacks?                             53

**GREY**
To whom in all this presence speaks Your Grace?                  54

**RICHARD**
To thee, that hast nor honesty nor grace.                        55
When have I injured thee? When done thee wrong?
Or thee? Or thee? Or any of your faction?                        57
A plague upon you all! His Royal Grace—
Whom God preserve better than you would wish!—
Cannot be quiet scarce a breathing while                         60
But you must trouble him with lewd complaints.                   61

**QUEEN ELIZABETH**
Brother of Gloucester, you mistake the matter.                   62
The King, on his own royal disposition,                          63
And not provoked by any suitor else,
Aiming, belike, at your interior hatred,                         65
That in your outward action shows itself
Against my children, brothers, and myself,
Makes him to send, that he may learn the ground                  68
Of your ill will, and thereby to remove it.

**RICHARD**
I cannot tell. The world is grown so bad                         70
That wrens make prey where eagles dare not perch.

---

6 **betide on** become of   11–12 **his minority / Is put** until he comes of age, he is put   15 **determined, not concluded** i.e., decided though not officially passed   16 **miscarry** perish.   20 **The Countess Richmond** i.e., Margaret Beaufort (1443–1509), who married, successively, Edmund Tudor (Earl of Richmond), Lord Henry Stafford, and Thomas Lord Stanley (here called the Earl of Derby), to whom she is currently married. By the Earl of Richmond, she was mother of the future Henry VII.   24 **arrogance** i.e., ambition for her son.   26 **envious** malicious   27 **Or . . . report** or, if what people say about the Countess of Richmond is true   29 **wayward** not yielding readily to treatment.   **grounded** firmly fixed   31 **But now** Just now   33 **amendment** recovery

36 **atonement** reconciliation   37 **brothers** (Only one brother, Earl Rivers, is mentioned in the play, though historically Elizabeth had others; Shakespeare may be thinking of other kinsmen, including her sons, whom she helped to advance.)   38 **Lord Chamberlain** Hastings   39 **warn** summon   46 **dissentious** quarrelsome, discordant   47 **look fair** put on a pleasing appearance   48 **smooth** flatter.   **cog** deceive   49 **Duck . . . nods** i.e., bow affectedly   53 **With silken** by smooth.   **Jacks** lowbred persons.   54 **presence** company   55 **nor . . . grace** neither honesty nor a sense of duty or propriety. (Playing upon *Your Grace* in the preceding line.)   57 **Or thee? Or thee?** (Richard turns accusingly to Lord Rivers, the Queen's brother, and Lord Grey, her son.)   60 **breathing while** i.e., brief time   61 **lewd** vile, base   62 **Brother** (Richard is the Queen's brother-in-law.)   63 **disposition** inclination   65 **Aiming** guessing.   **belike** probably   68 **Makes him** causes him. (The implied subject is "The King's own disposition.")   **ground** cause   70 **I cannot tell** i.e., I don't know what to think. (Richard plays the role of the exasperated moralist.)

Since every Jack became a gentleman,
There's many a gentle person made a Jack.

QUEEN ELIZABETH
Come, come, we know your meaning, brother Gloucester;
You envy my advancement and my friends'.          75
God grant we never may have need of you!

RICHARD
Meantime, God grants that I have need of you.
Our brother is imprisoned by your means,          78
Myself disgraced, and the nobility
Held in contempt, while great promotions
Are daily given to ennoble those
That scarce some two days since were worth a noble.   82

QUEEN ELIZABETH
By Him that raised me to this careful height       83
From that contented hap which I enjoyed,           84
I never did incense His Majesty
Against the Duke of Clarence, but have been
An earnest advocate to plead for him.
My lord, you do me shameful injury
Falsely to draw me in these vile suspects.         89

RICHARD
You may deny that you were not the mean            90
Of my Lord Hastings' late imprisonment.            91

RIVERS   She may, my lord, for—

RICHARD
She may, Lord Rivers! Why, who knows not so?
She may do more, sir, than denying that:
She may help you to many fair preferments,         95
And then deny her aiding hand therein,
And lay those honors on your high desert.          97
What may she not? She may, ay, marry, may she—     98

RIVERS   What, marry, may she?

RICHARD
What, marry, may she? Marry with a king,           100
A bachelor, and a handsome stripling too!          101
Iwis your grandam had a worser match.              102

QUEEN ELIZABETH
My lord of Gloucester, I have too long borne
Your blunt upbraidings and your bitter scoffs.
By heaven, I will acquaint His Majesty
Of those gross taunts that oft I have endured.
I had rather be a country servant maid
Than a great queen with this condition,
To be so baited, scorned, and stormèd at.          109

*Enter old Queen Margaret [behind].*

Small joy have I in being England's queen.

QUEEN MARGARET [*aside*]
And lessened be that small, God I beseech him!     111
Thy honor, state, and seat is due to me.           112

RICHARD
What? Threat you me with telling of the King?      113
Tell him, and spare not. Look what I have said     114
I will avouch 't in presence of the King.
I dare adventure to be sent to the Tower.          116
'Tis time to speak; my pains are quite forgot.     117

QUEEN MARGARET [*aside*]
Out, devil! I do remember them too well:           118
Thou killed'st my husband Henry in the Tower,
And Edward, my poor son, at Tewkesbury.

RICHARD
Ere you were queen, ay, or your husband king,
I was a packhorse in his great affairs,            122
A weeder-out of his proud adversaries,
A liberal rewarder of his friends.
To royalize his blood I spent mine own.

QUEEN MARGARET [*aside*]
Ay, and much better blood than his or thine.       126

RICHARD
In all which time you and your husband Grey
Were factious for the house of Lancaster;          128
And, Rivers, so were you. Was not your husband     129
In Margaret's battle at Saint Albans slain?
Let me put in your minds, if you forget,
What you have been ere this, and what you are;
Withal, what I have been, and what I am.           133

QUEEN MARGARET [*aside*]
A murd'rous villain, and so still thou art.

RICHARD
Poor Clarence did forsake his father, Warwick,     135
Ay, and forswore himself—which Jesu pardon!—

QUEEN MARGARET [*aside*]   Which God revenge!

RICHARD
To fight on Edward's party for the crown;
And for his meed, poor lord, he is mewed up.       139
I would to God my heart were flint, like Edward's,
Or Edward's soft and pitiful, like mine.
I am too childish-foolish for this world.

QUEEN MARGARET [*aside*]
Hie thee to hell for shame, and leave this world,  143
Thou cacodemon! There thy kingdom is.              144

RIVERS
My lord of Gloucester, in those busy days
Which here you urge to prove us enemies,           146

---

**75 friends'** i.e., kinsmen's.   **78 Our brother** i.e., Clarence   **82 noble** (1) gold coin worth six shillings eight pence (2) nobleman.   **83 careful** full of cares   **84 hap** fortune   **89 in** into.   **suspects** suspicions.   **90 mean** means   **91 late** recent   **95 preferments** advancements, promotions   **97 lay . . . desert** attribute these high honors to your supposedly rich deservings.   **98 marry** i.e., indeed. (A mild oath, literally, "by the Virgin Mary.")   **100 Marry with** Wed. (Punning on *marry*, indeed, in line 98.)   **101 stripling** young man   **102 Iwis** (1) Certainly (2) *I wis*, I know.   **your grandam** your grandmother. (Richard sarcastically suggests that Lord Rivers is descended from such a politically calculated marriage. Richard regards the Queen's kindred as social climbers.)   **109 baited** harassed, as in bearbaiting   **109.1 Queen Margaret** (Historically, the widow of Henry VI was held prisoner in England for five years following the battle of Tewkesbury in 1471 and then was sent to France; see the note to line 167 below.)

**111 And . . . him** I beseech God that Queen Elizabeth's small joy may be even smaller.   **112 state** degree, high rank.   **seat** throne   **113 Threat** Threaten.   **of** to   **114 Look what** Whatever   **116 adventure to be** risk being   **117 pains** efforts (in King Edward's behalf)   **118 Out** (An exclamation of anger.)   **122 packhorse** workhorse, beast of burden   **126 much . . . thine** you have spilt much finer (i.e., Lancastrian) blood than Edward IV's or Queen Elizabeth's.   **128 Were factious for** fought factiously on the side of   **129 husband** (Queen Elizabeth's first husband, Sir John Grey, fell fighting on the Lancastrian side at Saint Albans.)   **133 Withal** in addition   **135 father** i.e., father-in-law. (See *3 Henry VI*, 4.1, when Clarence deserted his brothers to marry Warwick's daughter Isabella and supported the Lancastrian cause for a time; thereafter, he forswore his oath to Warwick by returning to fight on Edward's *party* [line 138] or side.)   **139 meed** reward.   **mewed** caged (like a hawk)   **143 Hie** Hasten   **144 cacodemon** evil spirit.   **146 urge** cite

We followed then our lord, our sovereign king.
So should we you, if you should be our king.

RICHARD
If I should be? I had rather be a peddler.
Far be it from my heart, the thought thereof!

QUEEN ELIZABETH
As little joy, my lord, as you suppose
You should enjoy were you this country's king,
As little joy you may suppose in me
That I enjoy, being the queen thereof.

QUEEN MARGARET [aside]
Ah, little joy enjoys the queen thereof,
For I am she, and altogether joyless.
I can no longer hold me patient.    [Advancing.]
Hear me, you wrangling pirates, that fall out
In sharing that which you have pilled from me!  159
Which of you trembles not that looks on me?
If not, that I am queen, you bow like subjects,  161
Yet that, by you deposed, you quake like rebels?  162
[To Richard] Ah, gentle villain, do not turn away!  163

RICHARD
Foul wrinkled witch, what mak'st thou in my sight?  164

QUEEN MARGARET
But repetition of what thou hast marred;  165
That will I make before I let thee go.  166

RICHARD
Wert thou not banishèd on pain of death?  167

QUEEN MARGARET
I was; but I do find more pain in banishment
Than death can yield me here by my abode.  169
A husband and a son thou ow'st to me,  170
And thou a kingdom; all of you allegiance.  171
This sorrow that I have by right is yours,
And all the pleasures you usurp are mine.

RICHARD
The curse my noble father laid on thee  174
When thou didst crown his warlike brows with paper
And with thy scorns drew'st rivers from his eyes,  176
And then, to dry them, gav'st the Duke a clout  177
Steeped in the faultless blood of pretty Rutland—  178
His curses then, from bitterness of soul
Denounced against thee, are all fall'n upon thee;  180
And God, not we, hath plagued thy bloody deed.

QUEEN ELIZABETH
So just is God, to right the innocent.  182

HASTINGS
Oh, 'twas the foulest deed to slay that babe,  183
And the most merciless, that e'er was heard of!

RIVERS
Tyrants themselves wept when it was reported.  185

DORSET
No man but prophesied revenge for it.  186

BUCKINGHAM
Northumberland, then present, wept to see it.

QUEEN MARGARET
What? Were you snarling all before I came,
Ready to catch each other by the throat,
And turn you all your hatred now on me?
Did York's dread curse prevail so much with heaven  191
That Henry's death, my lovely Edward's death,
Their kingdom's loss, my woeful banishment,
Should all but answer for that peevish brat?  194
Can curses pierce the clouds and enter heaven?
Why, then, give way, dull clouds, to my quick curses!  196
Though not by war, by surfeit die your king,  197
As ours by murder, to make him a king!
Edward thy son, that now is Prince of Wales,
For Edward our son, that was Prince of Wales,
Die in his youth by like untimely violence!
Thyself a queen, for me that was a queen,
Outlive thy glory, like my wretched self!
Long mayst thou live to wail thy children's death
And see another, as I see thee now,
Decked in thy rights, as thou art stalled in mine!  206
Long die thy happy days before thy death,
And, after many lengthened hours of grief,
Die neither mother, wife, nor England's queen!
Rivers and Dorset, you were standers-by,  210
And so wast thou, Lord Hastings, when my son  211
Was stabbed with bloody daggers: God, I pray him,
That none of you may live his natural age,  213
But by some unlooked accident cut off!  214

RICHARD
Have done thy charm, thou hateful withered hag!  215

QUEEN MARGARET
And leave out thee? Stay, dog, for thou shalt hear me.
If heaven have any grievous plague in store
Exceeding those that I can wish upon thee,
Oh, let them keep it till thy sins be ripe,  219
And then hurl down their indignation
On thee, the troubler of the poor world's peace!
The worm of conscience still begnaw thy soul!  222
Thy friends suspect for traitors while thou liv'st,
And take deep traitors for thy dearest friends!
No sleep close up that deadly eye of thine,
Unless it be while some tormenting dream
Affrights thee with a hell of ugly devils!
Thou elvish-marked, abortive, rooting hog,  228

**159 pilled** pillaged, robbed **161–2 If . . . rebels** i.e., Even if you do not bow low to me as your queen, you quake as rebels who have deposed me. **163 gentle** nobly born. *Gentle villain* is an oxymoron, since *villain* can mean "one ignobly born." **164 mak'st thou** are you doing **165 But . . . marred** Only reciting your crimes **166 That** that repetition or recital **167 banishèd** (Margaret was banished in 1464, returned to England in 1471, and after the Battle of Tewkesbury was confined in the Tower until 1476, when she returned to France, dying there in 1482, one year before the historical time of this scene.)
**169 Than . . . abode** than my death can provide me here where I am to live until I die. **170 thou** i.e., Richard **171 thou** i.e., Elizabeth
**174 The curse** (See *3 Henry VI*, 1.4.164–6.) **176 rivers** i.e., copious tears
**177 clout** cloth, handkerchief **178 faultless** innocent **180 Denounced** proclaimed vengefully **182 right** defend, vindicate **183 that babe** i.e., Rutland (who historically was an older brother of Richard)

**185 Tyrants** Even pitiless men **186 No . . . prophesied** There was no one who did not prophesy **191 York's** Richard Duke of York's
**194 but answer for** merely atone for, equal. **peevish** silly, senseless **196 quick** lively, piercing **197 surfeit** dissipated living **206 Decked** dressed. **stalled** installed **210–11 Rivers, Dorset, Hastings** (Not present in Shakespeare's dramatization of the event in *3 Henry VI*, 5.5, but named in the chronicles as having been present.) **213 natural age** full course of life **214 unlooked** unexpected **215 charm** magic curse, pronounced by a witch
**219 them** i.e., the heavens, heaven **222 still begnaw** continually gnaw **228 elvish-marked** marked by elves at birth. **hog** (Alludes to Richard's badge, the wild boar.)

Thou that wast sealed in thy nativity                                  229
The slave of nature and the son of hell!                               230
Thou slander of thy heavy mother's womb,                               231
Thou loathèd issue of thy father's loins,                              232
Thou rag of honor, thou detested—                                      233

RICHARD
Margaret.

QUEEN MARGARET   Richard!

RICHARD                                  Ha?

QUEEN MARGARET                                   I call thee not.

RICHARD
I cry thee mercy then, for I did think                                 235
That thou hadst called me all these bitter names.

QUEEN MARGARET
Why, so I did, but looked for no reply.
Oh, let me make the period to my curse!                                238

RICHARD
'Tis done by me, and ends in "Margaret."

QUEEN ELIZABETH [to Queen Margaret]
Thus have you breathed your curse against yourself.

QUEEN MARGARET
Poor painted queen, vain flourish of my fortune!                       241
Why strew'st thou sugar on that bottled spider,                        242
Whose deadly web ensnareth thee about?
Fool, fool, thou whet'st a knife to kill thyself.
The day will come that thou shalt wish for me
To help thee curse this poisonous bunch-backed toad.  246

HASTINGS
False-boding woman, end thy frantic curse,                             247
Lest to thy harm thou move our patience.

QUEEN MARGARET
Foul shame upon you! You have all moved mine.

RIVERS
Were you well served, you would be taught your duty.  250

QUEEN MARGARET
To serve me well, you all should do me duty,                           251
Teach me to be your queen, and you my subjects.                        252
Oh, serve me well, and teach yourselves that duty!

DORSET
Dispute not with her. She is lunatic.

QUEEN MARGARET
Peace, Master Marquess, you are malapert.                              255
Your fire-new stamp of honor is scarce current.                        256
Oh, that your young nobility could judge
What 'twere to lose it and be miserable!
They that stand high have many blasts to shake them,  259
And if they fall, they dash themselves to pieces.

RICHARD
Good counsel, marry! Learn it, learn it, Marquess.

DORSET
It touches you, my lord, as much as me.                                262

RICHARD
Ay, and much more; but I was born so high.                             263
Our aerie buildeth in the cedar's top,                                 264
And dallies with the wind and scorns the sun.

QUEEN MARGARET
And turns the sun to shade; alas, alas!                                266
Witness my son, now in the shade of death,
Whose bright outshining beams thy cloudy wrath
Hath in eternal darkness folded up.
Your aerie buildeth in our aerie's nest.                               270
O God, that see'st it, do not suffer it!                               271
As it is won with blood, lost be it so!

BUCKINGHAM
Peace, peace, for shame, if not for charity!

QUEEN MARGARET
Urge neither charity nor shame to me.
                                   [Turning to the others.]
Uncharitably with me have you dealt,
And shamefully my hopes by you are butchered.
My charity is outrage, life my shame,                                  277
And in that shame still live my sorrow's rage!

BUCKINGHAM   Have done, have done.

QUEEN MARGARET
O princely Buckingham, I'll kiss thy hand
In sign of league and amity with thee.
Now fair befall thee and thy noble house!                              282
Thy garments are not spotted with our blood,
Nor thou within the compass of my curse.                               284

BUCKINGHAM
Nor no one here; for curses never pass                                 285
The lips of those that breathe them in the air.

QUEEN MARGARET
I will not think but they ascend the sky                               287
And there awake God's gentle-sleeping peace.
O Buckingham, take heed of yonder dog!
Look when he fawns, he bites; and when he bites,       290
His venom tooth will rankle to the death.              291
Have not to do with him, beware of him;
Sin, death, and hell have set their marks on him,
And all their ministers attend on him.

RICHARD
What doth she say, my lord of Buckingham?

BUCKINGHAM
Nothing that I respect, my gracious lord.              296

QUEEN MARGARET
What, dost thou scorn me for my gentle counsel?        297

229 sealed stamped   230 slave of nature i.e., wretch made by the malignancy of nature (as seen in his deformity)   231 heavy (1) sorrowful (2) weighted down in pregnancy   232 issue offspring, child   233 rag tattered remnant   235 cry thee mercy beg your pardon. (Said sarcastically.)   238 period conclusion   241 painted counterfeit. vain . . . fortune i.e., mere ornament of a position that is mine by right.   242 bottled bottle-shaped, swollen   246 bunch-backed hunch-backed   247 False-boding Falsely prophesying   250 well served treated as you deserve. (But Margaret turns the phrase around to mean "served as befitting one of royal rank.")   your duty your place (i.e., to be obedient).   251 duty reverence   252 Teach me i.e., show by your obedience what is my role   255 Master (A title for a boy of good family, used insultingly here.)   malapert impudent.   256 fire-new newly coined.   current genuine as legal tender.   259 blasts strong gusts of wind

262 touches concerns   263 born so high i.e., born noble—unlike you.   264 Our . . . top i.e., We are like eagles, building our nest in the top of the noble cedar   266 sun (With a play on son in the next line.)   270 Your . . . nest i.e., You Yorkists' nest usurps the high place that rightly belongs to us Lancastrians.   271 suffer allow   277 My . . . shame i.e., Instead of charity I receive outrage, and the only life given me is one of shame; or, outrage is all the charity I feel, and shame is my only life   282 fair befall good luck to   284 compass scope   285 pass get any further than   287 I . . . but I must believe that   290 Look when (1) Whenever (2) Expect that when   291 venom envenomed.   rankle cause a festering wound   296 respect heed   297 gentle well-meaning

And soothe the devil that I warn thee from?    298
Oh, but remember this another day,
When he shall split thy very heart with sorrow,
And say poor Margaret was a prophetess!
Live each of you the subjects to his hate,    302
And he to yours, and all of you to God's!    *Exit.* 303

BUCKINGHAM
My hair doth stand on end to hear her curses.

RIVERS
And so doth mine. I muse why she's at liberty.    305

RICHARD
I cannot blame her. By God's holy mother,
She hath had too much wrong, and I repent
My part thereof that I have done to her.

QUEEN ELIZABETH
I never did her any, to my knowledge.

RICHARD
Yet you have all the vantage of her wrong.    310
I was too hot to do somebody good    311
That is too cold in thinking of it now.    312
Marry, as for Clarence, he is well repaid;
He is franked up to fatting for his pains—    314
God pardon them that are the cause thereof!

RIVERS
A virtuous and a Christian-like conclusion,
To pray for them that have done scathe to us.    317

RICHARD
So do I ever—(*speaks to himself*) being well advised.    318
For had I cursed now, I had cursed myself.

*Enter Catesby.*

CATESBY
Madam, His Majesty doth call for you,
And for Your Grace, and yours, my gracious lord.

QUEEN ELIZABETH
Catesby, I come.—Lords, will you go with me?

RIVERS
We wait upon Your Grace.    323
         *Exeunt all but [Richard Duke of] Gloucester.*

RICHARD
I do the wrong, and first begin to brawl.
The secret mischiefs that I set abroach    325
I lay unto the grievous charge of others.    326
Clarence, who I indeed have cast in darkness,
I do beweep to many simple gulls—    328
Namely, to Derby, Hastings, Buckingham—
And tell them 'tis the Queen and her allies
That stir the King against the Duke my brother.
Now they believe it, and withal whet me    332
To be revenged on Rivers, Dorset, Grey.
But then I sigh and, with a piece of Scripture,

Tell them that God bids us do good for evil.    335
And thus I clothe my naked villainy
With odd old ends stol'n forth of Holy Writ,    337
And seem a saint when most I play the devil.

*Enter two Murderers.*

But soft! Here come my executioners.—    339
How now, my hardy, stout, resolvèd mates,    340
Are you now going to dispatch this thing?

FIRST MURDERER
We are, my lord, and come to have the warrant
That we may be admitted where he is.

RICHARD
Well thought upon. I have it here about me.
                     *[He gives the warrant.]*
When you have done, repair to Crosby Place.    345
But sirs, be sudden in the execution,
Withal obdurate; do not hear him plead;    347
For Clarence is well-spoken, and perhaps
May move your hearts to pity if you mark him.    349

FIRST MURDERER
Tut, tut, my lord, we will not stand to prate;    350
Talkers are no good doers. Be assured
We go to use our hands and not our tongues.

RICHARD
Your eyes drop millstones when fools' eyes fall tears.   353
I like you, lads. About your business straight.
Go, go, dispatch.

FIRST MURDERER    We will, my noble lord.    [*Exeunt.*]

❧

# 1.4

*Enter Clarence and Keeper.*

KEEPER
Why looks Your Grace so heavily today?    1

CLARENCE
Oh, I have passed a miserable night,
So full of fearful dreams, of ugly sights,
That, as I am a Christian faithful man,
I would not spend another such a night
Though 'twere to buy a world of happy days,
So full of dismal terror was the time!

KEEPER
What was your dream, my lord? I pray you, tell me.

CLARENCE
Methoughts that I had broken from the Tower    9
And was embarked to cross to Burgundy,    10
And in my company my brother Gloucester,
Who from my cabin tempted me to walk

---

298 **soothe** flatter   302 **the subjects to** subjugated to   303 **he . . . God's** he will be the subjects of your hatred, and God will hate you all.   305 **muse** wonder   310 **vantage of her wrong** benefits derived from the wrongs she has suffered.   311 **too hot . . . good** i.e., too eager in helping Edward to the throne   312 **That . . . cold** who is too ungrateful   314 **franked . . . fatting** shut up in a frank or sty to be fattened for slaughter   317 **scathe** harm   318 **well advised** cautious.   323 **wait upon** attend   325 **set abroach** set flowing   326 **lay . . . of** impute as a serious accusation against   328 **gulls** credulous persons   332 **withal** furthermore.   **whet** urge, incite

335 **for** in return for   337 **ends** fragments, tags   339 **soft** gently; wait a minute.   340 **stout . . . mates** bold, resolute fellows   345 **repair** betake yourselves   347 **Withal** at the same time   349 **mark** pay attention to   350 **prate** prattle   353 **millstones** heavy stone disks used for grinding. (To *drop millstones* was proverbially to show signs of hardheartedness.)   **fall** let fall
**1.4. Location: London. The Tower.**
1 **heavily** sad   9 **Methoughts** It seemed to me   10 **Burgundy** (Clarence and Richard, according to the chronicles, had been sent to Burgundy for protection following their father's death.)

Upon the hatches. Thence we looked toward England  13
And cited up a thousand heavy times,  14
During the wars of York and Lancaster,
That had befall'n us. As we paced along
Upon the giddy footing of the hatches,  17
Methought that Gloucester stumbled, and in falling
Struck me, that thought to stay him, overboard  19
Into the tumbling billows of the main.  20
Oh, Lord, methought what pain it was to drown!
What dreadful noise of waters in my ears!
What sights of ugly death within my eyes!
Methought I saw a thousand fearful wracks;  24
Ten thousand men that fishes gnawed upon;
Wedges of gold, great anchors, heaps of pearl,  26
Inestimable stones, unvalued jewels,  27
All scattered in the bottom of the sea.
Some lay in dead men's skulls, and in the holes
Where eyes did once inhabit there were crept,
As 'twere in scorn of eyes, reflecting gems,  31
That wooed the slimy bottom of the deep  32
And mocked the dead bones that lay scattered by.

KEEPER
Had you such leisure in the time of death
To gaze upon these secrets of the deep?

CLARENCE
Methought I had, and often did I strive
To yield the ghost; but still the envious flood  37
Stopped in my soul and would not let it forth  38
To seek the empty, vast, and wand'ring air,
But smothered it within my panting bulk,  40
Which almost burst to belch it in the sea.

KEEPER
Awaked you not in this sore agony?

CLARENCE
No, no, my dream was lengthened after life.
Oh, then began the tempest to my soul!
I passed, methought, the melancholy flood,  45
With that sour ferryman which poets write of,  46
Unto the kingdom of perpetual night.
The first that there did greet my stranger soul  48
Was my great father-in-law, renownèd Warwick,
Who spake aloud, "What scourge for perjury
Can this dark monarchy afford false Clarence?"
And so he vanished. Then came wand'ring by
A shadow like an angel, with bright hair  53
Dabbled in blood, and he shrieked out aloud,
"Clarence is come—false, fleeting, perjured Clarence,  55
That stabbed me in the field by Tewkesbury.
Seize on him, Furies, take him unto torment!"
With that, methought, a legion of foul fiends

Environed me and howlèd in mine ears
Such hideous cries that with the very noise
I trembling waked, and for a season after  61
Could not believe but that I was in hell,
Such terrible impression made my dream.

KEEPER
No marvel, my lord, though it affrighted you.
I am afraid, methinks, to hear you tell it.

CLARENCE
Ah, keeper, keeper, I have done these things,
That now give evidence against my soul,
For Edward's sake, and see how he requites me!  68
O God! If my deep prayers cannot appease thee,
But thou wilt be avenged on my misdeeds,
Yet execute thy wrath in me alone!
Oh, spare my guiltless wife and my poor children!
Keeper, I prithee, sit by me awhile.
My soul is heavy, and I fain would sleep.  74

KEEPER
I will, my lord. God give Your Grace good rest!

[Clarence sleeps.]

Enter Brackenbury, the Lieutenant.

BRACKENBURY
Sorrow breaks seasons and reposing hours,  76
Makes the night morning and the noontide night.
Princes have but their titles for their glories,
An outward honor for an inward toil,  79
And, for unfelt imaginations,  80
They often feel a world of restless cares;
So that between their titles and low name  82
There's nothing differs but the outward fame.  83

Enter two Murderers.

FIRST MURDERER  Ho! Who's here?
BRACKENBURY
What would'st thou, fellow, and how cam'st thou hither?
SECOND MURDERER  I would speak with Clarence, and I
came hither on my legs.
BRACKENBURY  What, so brief?
FIRST MURDERER  'Tis better, sir, than to be tedious.—
Let him see our commission, and talk no more.

[Brackenbury] reads [it].
BRACKENBURY
I am in this commanded to deliver
The noble Duke of Clarence to your hands.
I will not reason what is meant hereby,
Because I will be guiltless from the meaning.  94
There lies the Duke asleep, and there the keys.

[He gives keys.]
I'll to the King and signify to him
That thus I have resigned to you my charge.

13 hatches movable planks forming a deck.  14 cited up recalled.  heavy troublesome  17 giddy unsteady  19 thought to stay him tried to steady him  20 main sea.  24 wracks shipwrecked vessels  26 Wedges ingots  27 Inestimable precious and innumerable.  unvalued priceless  31 As . . . eyes as if mockingly taking the place of eyes  32 wooed (These lifeless eyes have nothing to flirt with but the murky depths.)  37 To . . . ghost to give my soul to death.  envious flood malicious water  38 Stopped held  40 bulk body  45 melancholy flood i.e., River Styx  46 ferryman i.e., Charon, who ferried souls to Hades, the kingdom of perpetual night (line 47)  48 stranger i.e., newly arrived  53 shadow i.e., ghost of Edward, Prince of Wales, son of Henry VI  55 fleeting fickle, deceitful

61 season time  68 requites repays  74 fain willingly  76 breaks . . . hours disrupts the normal rhythms of life and hours properly devoted to sleep  79 for in return for  80 for unfelt imaginations in return for glories that are merely illusory  82 low name i.e., the lowly position of ordinary men  83 fame reputation.  94 will be wish to be

FIRST MURDERER    You may, sir; 'tis a point of wisdom. Fare you well.                    *Exit [Brackenbury with Keeper]*.

SECOND MURDERER    What, shall I stab him as he sleeps?

FIRST MURDERER    No. He'll say 'twas done cowardly, when he wakes.

SECOND MURDERER    Why, he shall never wake until the great Judgment Day.

FIRST MURDERER    Why, then he'll say we stabbed him sleeping.

SECOND MURDERER    The urging of that word "judgment" hath bred a kind of remorse in me.

FIRST MURDERER    What, art thou afraid?

SECOND MURDERER    Not to kill him, having a warrant, but to be damned for killing him, from the which no warrant can defend me.

FIRST MURDERER    I thought thou hadst been resolute.

SECOND MURDERER    So I am—to let him live.

FIRST MURDERER    I'll back to the Duke of Gloucester and tell him so.

SECOND MURDERER    Nay, I prithee, stay a little. I hope this passionate humor of mine will change. It was 119 wont to hold me but while one tells twenty. 120

FIRST MURDERER    How dost thou feel thyself now?

SECOND MURDERER    Faith, some certain dregs of conscience are yet within me.

FIRST MURDERER    Remember our reward when the deed 's done.

SECOND MURDERER    Zounds, he dies! I had forgot the 126 reward.

FIRST MURDERER    Where's thy conscience now?

SECOND MURDERER    Oh, in the Duke of Gloucester's purse.

FIRST MURDERER    When he opens his purse to give us our reward, thy conscience flies out.

SECOND MURDERER    'Tis no matter; let it go. There's few or none will entertain it. 134

FIRST MURDERER    What if it come to thee again?

SECOND MURDERER    I'll not meddle with it; it makes a man a coward. A man cannot steal but it accuseth him; a man cannot swear but it checks him; a man cannot 138 lie with his neighbor's wife but it detects him. 'Tis a blushing, shamefaced spirit that mutinies in a man's bosom. It fills a man full of obstacles. It made me once restore a purse of gold that by chance I found. It beggars any man that keeps it. It is turned out of 143 towns and cities for a dangerous thing, and every man that means to live well endeavors to trust to himself and live without it.

FIRST MURDERER    Zounds, 'tis even now at my elbow, persuading me not to kill the Duke.

SECOND MURDERER    Take the devil in thy mind, and 149 believe him not. He would insinuate with thee but to 150 make thee sigh. 151

FIRST MURDERER    Tut, I am strong-framed; he cannot prevail with me.

SECOND MURDERER    Spoke like a tall man that respects 154 thy reputation. Come, shall we fall to work? 155

FIRST MURDERER    Take him on the costard with the hilts 156 of thy sword, and then throw him into the malmsey 157 butt in the next room. 158

SECOND MURDERER    Oh, excellent device! And make a sop of him. 159

FIRST MURDERER    Soft, he wakes.

SECOND MURDERER    Strike!

FIRST MURDERER    No, we'll reason with him. 163

CLARENCE  [*waking*]
    Where art thou, keeper? Give me a cup of wine.

SECOND MURDERER
    You shall have wine enough, my lord, anon.

CLARENCE    In God's name, what art thou?

FIRST MURDERER    A man, as you are.

CLARENCE    But not, as I am, royal.

FIRST MURDERER    Nor you, as we are, loyal.

CLARENCE
    Thy voice is thunder, but thy looks are humble.

FIRST MURDERER
    My voice is now the King's, my looks mine own.

CLARENCE
    How darkly and how deadly dost thou speak! 172
    Your eyes do menace me. Why look you pale?
    Who sent you hither? Wherefore do you come? 174

SECOND MURDERER    To, to, to—

CLARENCE    To murder me?

BOTH    Ay, ay.

CLARENCE
    You scarcely have the hearts to tell me so,
    And therefore cannot have the hearts to do it.
    Wherein, my friends, have I offended you?

FIRST MURDERER
    Offended us you have not, but the King.

CLARENCE
    I shall be reconciled to him again.

SECOND MURDERER
    Never, my lord; therefore prepare to die.

CLARENCE
    Are you drawn forth among a world of men 184
    To slay the innocent? What is my offense?
    Where is the evidence that doth accuse me?
    What lawful quest have given their verdict up 187
    Unto the frowning judge? Or who pronounced
    The bitter sentence of poor Clarence' death
    Before I be convict by course of law? 190
    To threaten me with death is most unlawful.
    I charge you, as you hope to have redemption
    By Christ's dear blood shed for our grievous sins,
    That you depart and lay no hands on me.
    The deed you undertake is damnable.

---

119 **passionate humor** compassionate mood    120 **wont** accustomed. **tells** counts    126 **Zounds** i.e., By God's (Christ's) wounds    134 **entertain it** receive it, give it welcome. (Not many people pay heed to their consciences.)    138 **checks** reproves, stops    143 **turned out of** banished from    149–50 **Take ... not** i.e., Listen to the devil and pay no heed to conscience.    150–1 **He ... sigh** Your conscience would ingratiate itself with you merely for the purpose of making you unhappy.

154 **tall** brave    155 **thy reputation** your reputation for bravery.    156 **Take** Strike.  **costard** head. (Literally, a kind of apple.)    157–8 **malmsey butt** wine barrel. (Malmsey is a sweet wine.)    159 **sop** bread or cake soaked in wine    163 **reason** talk    172 **darkly** ominously    174 **Wherefore** Why    184 **drawn ... men** especially selected from the whole human race    187 **quest** inquest, i.e., jury    190 **convict** convicted

FIRST MURDERER
    What we will do, we do upon command.
SECOND MURDERER
    And he that hath commanded is our king.
CLARENCE
    Erroneous vassals! The great King of kings                      198
    Hath in the table of His law commanded                          199
    That thou shalt do no murder. Will you then
    Spurn at His edict and fulfill a man's?
    Take heed; for He holds vengeance in His hand
    To hurl upon their heads that break His law.
SECOND MURDERER
    And that same vengeance doth He hurl on thee
    For false forswearing and for murder, too.
    Thou didst receive the Sacrament to fight                       206
    In quarrel of the house of Lancaster.
FIRST MURDERER
    And, like a traitor to the name of God,
    Didst break that vow, and with thy treacherous blade
    Unripped'st the bowels of thy sovereign's son.                  210
SECOND MURDERER
    Whom thou wast sworn to cherish and defend.
FIRST MURDERER
    How canst thou urge God's dreadful law to us
    When thou hast broke it in such dear degree?                    213
CLARENCE
    Alas! For whose sake did I that ill deed?
    For Edward, for my brother, for his sake.
    He sends you not to murder me for this,
    For in that sin he is as deep as I.
    If God will be avengèd for the deed,
    Oh, know you yet he doth it publicly!
    Take not the quarrel from His powerful arm.
    He needs no indirect or lawless course
    To cut off those that have offended Him.
FIRST MURDERER
    Who made thee, then, a bloody minister                          223
    When gallant-springing brave Plantagenet,                       224
    That princely novice, was struck dead by thee?                  225
CLARENCE
    My brother's love, the devil, and my rage.                      226
FIRST MURDERER
    Thy brother's love, our duty, and thy faults                    227
    Provoke us hither now to slaughter thee.
CLARENCE
    If you do love my brother, hate not me!
    I am his brother, and I love him well.
    If you are hired for meed, go back again,                       231
    And I will send you to my brother Gloucester,
    Who shall reward you better for my life
    Than Edward will for tidings of my death.

SECOND MURDERER
    You are deceived. Your brother Gloucester hates you.
CLARENCE
    Oh, no, he loves me, and he holds me dear.
    Go you to him from me.
FIRST MURDERER                      Ay, so we will.                 237
CLARENCE
    Tell him, when that our princely father York                    238
    Blessed his three sons with his victorious arm
    And charged us from his soul to love each other,
    He little thought of this divided friendship.
    Bid Gloucester think of this, and he will weep.
FIRST MURDERER
    Ay, millstones, as he lessoned us to weep.                      243
CLARENCE
    Oh, do not slander him, for he is kind.
FIRST MURDERER
    Right, as snow in harvest. Come, you deceive
        yourself.                                                   245
    'Tis he that sends us to destroy you here.
CLARENCE
    It cannot be, for he bewept my fortune,
    And hugged me in his arms, and swore with sobs
    That he would labor my delivery.                                249
FIRST MURDERER
    Why, so he doth, when he delivers you
    From this earth's thralldom to the joys of heaven.              251
SECOND MURDERER
    Make peace with God, for you must die, my lord.
CLARENCE
    Have you that holy feeling in your souls
    To counsel me to make my peace with God,
    And are you yet to your own souls so blind
    That you will war with God by murd'ring me?
    Oh, sirs, consider, they that set you on
    To do this deed will hate you for the deed.
SECOND MURDERER [to First Murderer]
    What shall we do?
CLARENCE                        Relent, and save your souls.
    Which of you, if you were a prince's son,
    Being pent from liberty, as I am now,                           261
    If two such murderers as yourselves came to you,
    Would not entreat for life?
FIRST MURDERER
    Relent? No. 'Tis cowardly and womanish.
CLARENCE
    Not to relent is beastly, savage, devilish.
    [To Second Murderer] My friend, I spy some pity in thy looks.
    Oh, if thine eye be not a flatterer,
    Come thou on my side, and entreat for me,
    As you would beg, were you in my distress.
    A begging prince what beggar pities not?                        270
SECOND MURDERER    Look behind you, my lord.

198 Erroneous vassals! Sinful and mistaken wretches!  199 table tablet (the Ten Commandments)  206 receive the Sacrament i.e., swear
upon the Sacrament  210 sovereign's son i.e., Prince Edward, son of
Henry VI.  213 dear grievous, costly  223 minister agent of God
224 gallant-springing i.e., gallant and sprightly, aspiring.
Plantagenet i.e., the Lancastrian Prince Edward, killed in 3 Henry VI,
5.5. (See the note at 1.2.145 on Edward's claim to this name.)
225 novice youth  226 My brother's love i.e., My love for my
brother  227 Thy brother's love i.e., our love and duty owed to
Richard Duke of Gloucester. (But Clarence understands the First
Murderer to mean "our duty owed to King Edward IV.")  231 meed
financial reward

237 Ay . . . will i.e., Sure, we'll be going to Gloucester all right, to collect our reward for killing you. (Said with grim humor.)  238 when
that when  243 millstones (The First Murderer, with grim amusement, recalls what Richard said to them at 1.3.353 about hard millstones taking the place of merciful tears.)  lessoned taught
245 Right . . . harvest i.e., He's just as kind and natural—that is, both
affectionate and with the natural feelings of a brother—as is snow
at harvest time.  249 labor my delivery work for my release.
251 thralldom bondage, captivity  261 pent shut up  270 A begging
. . . not? What beggar would not pity a prince begging mercy?

FIRST MURDERER
Take that, and that! (*Stabs him.*) If all this will not do,
I'll drown you in the malmsey butt within.
                                            *Exit [with the body].*

SECOND MURDERER
A bloody deed, and desperately dispatched!
How fain, like Pilate, would I wash my hands          275
Of this most grievous murder!

            *Enter First Murderer.*

FIRST MURDERER
How now? What mean'st thou that thou help'st me not?
By heaven, the Duke shall know how slack you
      have been.

SECOND MURDERER
I would he knew that I had saved his brother!
Take thou the fee, and tell him what I say,
For I repent me that the Duke is slain.              *Exit.*

FIRST MURDERER
So do not I. Go, coward as thou art.—
Well, I'll go hide his body in some hole
Till that the Duke give order for his burial;         284
And when I have my meed, I will away,                 285
For this will out, and then I must not stay.      *Exit.* 286

## 2.1

        *Flourish. Enter the King [Edward], sick, the*
        *Queen [Elizabeth], Lord Marquess Dorset, [Grey,]*
        *Rivers, Hastings, Catesby, Buckingham, [and*
        *others].*

KING EDWARD
Why, so. Now have I done a good day's work.
You peers, continue this united league.
I every day expect an embassage
From my Redeemer to redeem me hence;
And more in peace my soul shall part to heaven,
Since I have made my friends at peace on earth.
Rivers and Hastings, take each other's hand;
Dissemble not your hatred, swear your love.            8

RIVERS [*taking Hastings' hand*]
By heaven, my soul is purged from grudging hate,
And with my hand I seal my true heart's love.

HASTINGS
So thrive I, as I truly swear the like!

KING EDWARD
Take heed you dally not before your king,              12
Lest he that is the supreme King of kings
Confound your hidden falsehood, and award             14
Either of you to be the other's end.                   15

HASTINGS
So prosper I, as I swear perfect love!

RIVERS
And I, as I love Hastings with my heart!

KING EDWARD
Madam, yourself is not exempt from this,
Nor you, son Dorset, Buckingham, nor you;             19
You have been factious one against the other.         20
Wife, love Lord Hastings; let him kiss your hand;
And what you do, do it unfeignedly.

QUEEN ELIZABETH
There, Hastings, I will never more remember
Our former hatred, so thrive I and mine!              24
                          [*Hastings kisses her hand.*]

KING EDWARD
Dorset, embrace him. Hastings, love Lord Marquess.

DORSET
This interchange of love, I here protest,             26
Upon my part shall be inviolable.

HASTINGS   And so swear I.          [*They embrace.*]

KING EDWARD
Now, princely Buckingham, seal thou this league
With thy embracements to my wife's allies,            30
And make me happy in your unity.

BUCKINGHAM [*to the Queen*]
Whenever Buckingham doth turn his hate
Upon Your Grace, but with all duteous love            33
Doth cherish you and yours, God punish me
With hate in those where I expect most love!
When I have most need to employ a friend,
And most assurèd that he is a friend,
Deep, hollow, treacherous, and full of guile          38
Be he unto me! This do I beg of God,
When I am cold in love to you or yours.
                              [*They*] embrace.

KING EDWARD
A pleasing cordial, princely Buckingham,              41
Is this thy vow unto my sickly heart.
There wanteth now our brother Gloucester here         43
To make the blessèd period of this peace.             44

BUCKINGHAM   And, in good time,
Here comes Sir Richard Ratcliffe and the Duke.

      *Enter Ratcliffe and [Richard Duke of] Gloucester.*

RICHARD
Good morrow to my sovereign king and queen;
And, princely peers, a happy time of day!

KING EDWARD
Happy, indeed, as we have spent the day.
Gloucester, we have done deeds of charity,
Made peace of enmity, fair love of hate,
Between these swelling wrong-incensèd peers.          52

---

275 **fain** gladly.   **Pilate** The Roman governor of Judaea who ordered the crucifixion of Jesus at the behest of the chief priests but symbolically washed his hands of the business (Matthew 27:24).   **284 Till that** until   285 **meed** reward   286 **this will out** this will become known. ("Murder will out" was a proverbial saying.)
**2.1. Location:** London. The royal court.
**0.1** *Flourish* Trumpet call to announce the arrival of a distinguished person.   **8 Dissemble** conceal, disguise (under a false appearance of love)   **12 dally** trifle   **14 Confound** defeat   **15 Either . . . end** each of you to be the agent of death of the other.

19 **son** stepson   20 **factious** quarrelsome   24 **mine** my family and children.   26 **protest** declare   30 **allies** kindred   33 **but** and does not   38 **Deep** subtle, crafty   41 **cordial** restorative   43 **wanteth** is lacking   44 **period** conclusion   52 **swelling** i.e., with anger or rivalry

RICHARD
A blessèd labor, my most sovereign lord.
Among this princely heap, if any here,                               54
By false intelligence, or wrong surmise,                             55
Hold me a foe;
If I unwittingly, or in my rage,
Have aught committed that is hardly borne                            58
By any in this presence, I desire
To reconcile me to his friendly peace.
'Tis death to me to be at enmity;
I hate it, and desire all good men's love.
First, madam, I entreat true peace of you,                           63
Which I will purchase with my duteous service;
Of you, my noble cousin Buckingham,
If ever any grudge were lodged between us;
Of you and you, Lord Rivers, and of Dorset,
That all without desert have frowned on me;                          68
Dukes, earls, lords, gentlemen—indeed, of all.
I do not know that Englishman alive
With whom my soul is any jot at odds
More than the infant that is born tonight.                           72
I thank my God for my humility.

QUEEN ELIZABETH
A holy day shall this be kept hereafter.
I would to God all strifes were well compounded.                     75
My sovereign lord, I do beseech Your Highness
To take our brother Clarence to your grace.                          77

RICHARD
Why, madam, have I offered love for this,
To be so flouted in this royal presence?                             79
Who knows not that the gentle Duke is dead?                          80
                                          They all start.
You do him injury to scorn his corpse.

KING EDWARD
Who knows not he is dead? Who knows he is?

QUEEN ELIZABETH
All-seeing heaven, what a world is this!

BUCKINGHAM
Look I so pale, Lord Dorset, as the rest?

DORSET
Ay, my good lord, and no man in the presence                         85
But his red color hath forsook his cheeks.

KING EDWARD
Is Clarence dead? The order was reversed.

RICHARD
But he, poor man, by your first order died,
And that a wingèd Mercury did bear;                                  89
Some tardy cripple bare the countermand,                             90
That came too lag to see him buried.                                 91

God grant that some, less noble and less loyal,                      92
Nearer in bloody thoughts but not in blood,                          93
Deserve not worse than wretched Clarence did,                        94
And yet go current from suspicion!                                   95

           Enter [Lord Stanley] Earl of Derby.

STANLEY [kneeling]
A boon, my sovereign, for my service done!                           96
KING EDWARD
I prithee, peace. My soul is full of sorrow.
STANLEY
I will not rise unless Your Highness hear me.
KING EDWARD
Then say at once what is it thou requests.
STANLEY
The forfeit, sovereign, of my servant's life,                        100
Who slew today a riotous gentleman
Lately attendant on the Duke of Norfolk.
KING EDWARD
Have I a tongue to doom my brother's death,                          103
And shall that tongue give pardon to a slave?                        104
My brother killed no man; his fault was thought,
And yet his punishment was bitter death.
Who sued to me for him? Who, in my wrath,
Kneeled at my feet, and bid me be advised?                           108
Who spoke of brotherhood? Who spoke of love?
Who told me how the poor soul did forsake
The mighty Warwick and did fight for me?
Who told me, in the field at Tewkesbury,
When Oxford had me down, he rescued me                               113
And said, "Dear brother, live, and be a king"?
Who told me, when we both lay in the field
Frozen almost to death, how he did lap me                            116
Even in his garments, and did give himself,
All thin and naked, to the numb-cold night?                          118
All this from my remembrance brutish wrath
Sinfully plucked, and not a man of you
Had so much grace to put it in my mind.
But when your carters or your waiting vassals                        122
Have done a drunken slaughter and defaced                            123
The precious image of our dear Redeemer,                             124
You straight are on your knees for pardon, pardon;                   125
And I, unjustly too, must grant it you.
                                       [Stanley rises.]
But for my brother not a man would speak,
Nor I, ungracious, speak unto myself
For him, poor soul. The proudest of you all
Have been beholding to him in his life;                              130

54 heap assembly   55 false intelligence having been misinformed   58 hardly borne taken amiss, deeply resented   63 madam Queen Elizabeth   68 all without desert wholly without my having deserved it   72 More than the infant i.e., more than is that infant's soul   75 compounded settled.   77 To . . . grace to pardon Clarence, your brother and my brother-in-law.   79 flouted mocked   80 gentle noble   85 presence i.e., royal presence   89 Mercury messenger of the classical gods   90 tardy cripple (Richard privately shares with the audience a jest on his own role in this.)   bare bore   91 lag late

92–5 God . . . suspicion! i.e., (ironically) Pray God there be not persons who deserve worse than Clarence got, persons less noble or related by blood to the King than he, although closely involved in bloody plots, who yet go undetected! (Richard means the Queen and her kindred.)   95 go current are accepted at face value (like legal currency).   from free from   96 A boon (I crave) a favor   100 The forfeit i.e., The remission of the forfeit   103 doom decree   104 slave servant, wretch.   108 be advised consider carefully.   113 Oxford (See 3 Henry VI, 5.5.2; this episode has no historical basis.)   116 lap wrap   118 thin thinly clad   122 your carters . . . vassals your cart drivers or your attendants   123–4 defaced . . . Redeemer i.e., killed a man. (God made humanity in his own image; Genesis 1:27.)   125 straight at once   130 beholding beholden

Yet none of you would once beg for his life.
O God, I fear thy justice will take hold
On me and you, and mine and yours, for this!
Come, Hastings, help me to my closet. Ah, poor Clarence! 134
                          *Exeunt some with King and Queen.*

RICHARD
This is the fruits of rashness. Marked you not
How that the guilty kindred of the Queen
Looked pale when they did hear of Clarence' death?
Oh, they did urge it still unto the King.                   138
God will revenge it. Come, lords, will you go
To comfort Edward with our company?
BUCKINGHAM    We wait upon Your Grace.        *Exeunt.*

## 2.2

*Enter the old Duchess of York, with the two
children of Clarence, [Edward and Margaret
Plantagenet].*

BOY
Good grandam, tell us, is our father dead?               1
DUCHESS    No, boy.
GIRL
Why do you weep so oft, and beat your breast,
And cry, "O Clarence, my unhappy son"?
BOY
Why do you look on us, and shake your head,
And call us orphans, wretches, castaways,
If that our noble father were alive?                       7
DUCHESS
My pretty cousins, you mistake me both.                    8
I do lament the sickness of the King,
As loath to lose him, not your father's death;           10
It were lost sorrow to wail one that's lost.
BOY
Then, you conclude, my grandam, he is dead.
The King mine uncle is to blame for it.
God will revenge it, whom I will importune               14
With earnest prayers all to that effect.
GIRL    And so will I.
DUCHESS
Peace, children, peace! The King doth love you well.
Incapable and shallow innocents,                          18
You cannot guess who caused your father's death.
BOY
Grandam, we can; for my good uncle Gloucester
Told me the King, provoked to it by the Queen,
Devised impeachments to imprison him;                    22
And when my uncle told me so, he wept,
And pitied me, and kindly kissed my cheek;
Bade me rely on him as on my father,
And he would love me dearly as his child.

DUCHESS
Ah, that deceit should steal such gentle shape,
And with a virtuous visor hide deep vice!                 28
He is my son—ay, and therein my shame;
Yet from my dugs he drew not this deceit.                 30
BOY
Think you my uncle did dissemble, grandam?
DUCHESS    Ay, boy.
BOY
I cannot think it. Hark, what noise is this?              33

*Enter the Queen [Elizabeth], with her hair about
her ears; Rivers and Dorset after her.*

QUEEN ELIZABETH
Ah, who shall hinder me to wail and weep,
To chide my fortune and torment myself?
I'll join with black despair against my soul,
And to myself become an enemy.
DUCHESS
What means this scene of rude impatience?                 38
QUEEN ELIZABETH
To make an act of tragic violence.                        39
Edward, my lord, thy son, our king, is dead!              40
Why grow the branches when the root is gone?
Why wither not the leaves that want their sap?            42
If you will live, lament; if die, be brief,               43
That our swift-wingèd souls may catch the King's,
Or, like obedient subjects, follow him
To his new kingdom of ne'er-changing night.
DUCHESS
Ah, so much interest have I in thy sorrow
As I had title in thy noble husband!                      48
I have bewept a worthy husband's death
And lived with looking on his images;                     50
But now two mirrors of his princely semblance            51
Are cracked in pieces by malignant death,
And I for comfort have but one false glass,               53
That grieves me when I see my shame in him.               54
Thou art a widow; yet thou art a mother,
And hast the comfort of thy children left;
But death hath snatched my husband from mine arms
And plucked two crutches from my feeble hands,
Clarence and Edward. Oh, what cause have I,               59
Thine being but a moiety of my moan,                      60
To overgo thy woes and drown thy cries!                   61
BOY
Ah, aunt! You wept not for our father's death.            62
How can we aid you with our kindred tears?                63

134 **closet** private chambers.   138 **still** continually
2.2. Location: London. The royal court.
1 **grandam** grandmother   7 **If that** if   8 **cousins** kinfolks   10 **As
loath** being reluctant   14 **importune** solicit, beg   18 **Incapable**
Unable to understand   22 **impeachments** accusations

28 **visor** mask   30 **dugs** breasts   33.1–2 *with her ... ears* (A conventional sign of grief.)   38 **rude impatience** violent unwillingness to
accept misfortune.   39 **make** perform. (Continues the theatrical metaphor in the previous line.)   40 **Edward ... dead** (Clarence's death,
February 1478, and Edward IV's death, April 1483, are treated as if
they had occurred nearly together.)   42 **want** lack   43 **brief** quick
48 **title** i.e., as mother of the King   50 **images** likenesses; here, children   51 **two mirrors** i.e., Edward and Clarence. (The Duchess does
not count Rutland.)   53 **false glass** i.e., Richard   54 **my ... him** a
son of whom to be ashamed   59 **what ... I** what a cause I have
60 **Thine ... moan** since your grief is only half of my grief   61 **To ...
cries** to exceed your weeping so loudly that yours are scarcely heard.
62–3 **You ... tears?** i.e., How can we be expected to mourn as kinsfolk
for your losses when you don't weep for Clarence's death?

GIRL
　Our fatherless distress was left unmoaned;
　Your widow-dolor likewise be unwept!　　　　　　　　65
QUEEN ELIZABETH
　Give me no help in lamentation;
　I am not barren to bring forth complaints.　　　　　　67
　All springs reduce their currents to mine eyes,　　　68
　That I, being governed by the watery moon,　　　　　69
　May send forth plenteous tears to drown the world!
　Ah, for my husband, for my dear lord Edward!
CHILDREN
　Ah, for our father, for our dear lord Clarence!
DUCHESS
　Alas for both, both mine, Edward and Clarence!
QUEEN ELIZABETH
　What stay had I but Edward? And he's gone.　　　　74
CHILDREN
　What stay had we but Clarence? And he's gone.
DUCHESS
　What stays had I but they? And they are gone.
QUEEN ELIZABETH
　Was never widow had so dear a loss!　　　　　　　　77
CHILDREN
　Were never orphans had so dear a loss!
DUCHESS
　Was never mother had so dear a loss!
　Alas, I am the mother of these griefs;
　Their woes are parceled, mine is general.　　　　　　81
　She for an Edward weeps, and so do I;　　　　　　　　82
　I for a Clarence weep, so doth not she.
　These babes for Clarence weep, and so do I;
　I for an Edward weep, so do not they.
　Alas, you three, on me, threefold distressed,
　Pour all your tears! I am your sorrow's nurse,　　　87
　And I will pamper it with lamentation.　　　　　　　88
DORSET [to Queen Elizabeth]
　Comfort, dear mother. God is much displeased
　That you take with unthankfulness His doing.
　In common worldly things 'tis called ungrateful
　With dull unwillingness to repay a debt　　　　　　　92
　Which with a bounteous hand was kindly lent;　　93
　Much more to be thus opposite with heaven　　　　94
　For it requires the royal debt it lent you.　　　　　　95
RIVERS
　Madam, bethink you like a careful mother　　　　　96
　Of the young Prince your son. Send straight for him;　97
　Let him be crowned. In him your comfort lives.
　Drown desperate sorrow in dead Edward's grave

And plant your joys in living Edward's throne.

　　*Enter Richard [Duke of Gloucester], Buckingham,*
　　*[Lord Stanley Earl of] Derby, Hastings, and*
　　*Ratcliffe.*

RICHARD [to Queen Elizabeth]
　Sister, have comfort. All of us have cause　　　　101
　To wail the dimming of our shining star,
　But none can help our harms by wailing them.—
　Madam, my mother, I do cry you mercy;　　　　　104
　I did not see Your Grace. Humbly on my knee
　I crave your blessing.　　　　　　　[He kneels.]
DUCHESS
　God bless thee, and put meekness in thy breast,
　Love, charity, obedience, and true duty!
RICHARD
　Amen! [Aside] And make me die a good old man!
　That is the butt end of a mother's blessing;　　　110
　I marvel that Her Grace did leave it out.
BUCKINGHAM
　You cloudy princes and heart-sorrowing peers,　112
　That bear this heavy mutual load of moan,　　　113
　Now cheer each other in each other's love.
　Though we have spent our harvest of this king,
　We are to reap the harvest of his son.
　The broken rancor of your high-swoll'n hates,
　But lately splintered, knit, and joined together,　118
　Must gently be preserved, cherished, and kept.　119
　Me seemeth good that with some little train　　120
　Forthwith from Ludlow the young Prince be fet　121
　Hither to London, to be crowned our king.
RIVERS
　Why with some little train, my lord of Buckingham?
BUCKINGHAM
　Marry, my lord, lest by a multitude　　　　　　　124
　The new-healed wound of malice should break out,
　Which would be so much the more dangerous
　By how much the estate is green and yet ungoverned.　127
　Where every horse bears his commanding rein　128
　And may direct his course as please himself,　　129
　As well the fear of harm, as harm apparent,　　130
　In my opinion, ought to be prevented.
RICHARD
　I hope the King made peace with all of us;
　And the compact is firm and true in me.
RIVERS
　And so in me, and so, I think, in all.
　Yet since it is but green, it should be put
　To no apparent likelihood of breach,

---

**65 Your widow-dolor** may your widow's grief　**67 barren to** i.e., unable to. (She is pregnant with grief.)　**68 All . . . eyes** Let all springs be concentrated in my eyes　**69 I . . . moon** (Her grief is now a sea, fed by springs and her tides governed by the moon.)　**74 stay** support　**77 dear** costly, grievous　**81 Their . . . general** the woes of Queen Elizabeth and these children are particular to each of them, mine is all-embracing.　**82 She** Queen Elizabeth　**87 nurse** source　**88 pamper** feed luxuriously, nourish　**92 dull** sluggish　**93 Which with** with which　**94 opposite** stubborn, ungrateful　**95 For it requires** because it calls back　**96 bethink you** call to mind　**97 the young Prince your son** Edward, son of Edward IV and Queen Elizabeth, now king from the moment of his father's death though not yet crowned.　**straight** at once

**101 Sister** Sister-in-law　**104 cry you mercy** beg your pardon　**110 butt end** concluding portion. (The *butt* is the end of a spear shaft.)　**112 cloudy** clouded with grief　**113 moan** lamentation　**118 But lately splintered** only recently bound together (as with a splint)　**119 Must . . . preserved** i.e., the recent mending of differences must be preserved　**120 Me seemeth** It seems to me.　**train** entourage　**121 Ludlow** royal castle in Shropshire, near the Welsh border.　**fet** fetched　**124 multitude** i.e., large train or entourage　**127 estate** state, government.　**green** unripe, i.e., newly established　**128 bears . . . rein** controls the reins that ought to control it　**129 as please** as it pleases　**130 As . . . apparent** both the fear of trouble and the actual manifestation of it

Which haply by much company might be urged.                    137
Therefore I say with noble Buckingham
That it is meet so few should fetch the Prince.                 139

HASTINGS    And so say I.

RICHARD
Then be it so; and go we to determine
Who they shall be that straight shall post to Ludlow.          142
Madam, and you, my sister, will you go
To give your censures in this business?                        144

QUEEN ELIZABETH, DUCHESS    With all our hearts.              145

*Exeunt. Manent Buckingham and Richard.*

BUCKINGHAM
My lord, whoever journeys to the Prince,
For God's sake let not us two stay at home;
For by the way I'll sort occasion,                             148
As index to the story we late talked of,                       149
To part the Queen's proud kindred from the Prince.

RICHARD
My other self, my counsel's consistory,                        151
My oracle, my prophet! My dear cousin,
I, as a child, will go by thy direction.
Toward Ludlow then, for we'll not stay behind.

*Exeunt.*

❖

## 2.3

*Enter one Citizen at one door, and another at the
other.*

FIRST CITIZEN
Good morrow, neighbor. Whither away so fast?

SECOND CITIZEN
I promise you, I scarcely know myself.                          2
Hear you the news abroad?

FIRST CITIZEN    Yes, that the King is dead.

SECOND CITIZEN
Ill news, by'r Lady; seldom comes the better.                   5
I fear, I fear 'twill prove a giddy world.                      6

*Enter another Citizen.*

THIRD CITIZEN
Neighbors, God speed!

FIRST CITIZEN                Give you good morrow, sir.

THIRD CITIZEN
Doth the news hold of good King Edward's death?                 8

SECOND CITIZEN
Ay, sir, it is too true, God help the while!

THIRD CITIZEN
Then, masters, look to see a troublous world.                  10

FIRST CITIZEN
No, no; by God's good grace his son shall reign.

THIRD CITIZEN
Woe to that land that's governed by a child!                   12

SECOND CITIZEN
In him there is a hope of government,
Which in his nonage, council under him,                        14
And in his full and ripened years, himself,
No doubt shall then, and till then, govern well.

FIRST CITIZEN
So stood the state when Henry the Sixth
Was crowned in Paris but at nine months old.

THIRD CITIZEN
Stood the state so? No, no, good friends, God wot,             19
For then this land was famously enriched
With politic, grave counsel; then the King                     21
Had virtuous uncles to protect His Grace.

FIRST CITIZEN
Why, so hath this, both by his father and mother.

THIRD CITIZEN
Better it were they all came by his father,
Or by his father there were none at all;
For emulation who shall now be nearest                         26
Will touch us all too near, if God prevent not.                27
Oh, full of danger is the Duke of Gloucester,
And the Queen's sons and brothers haught and proud!            29
And were they to be ruled, and not to rule,
This sickly land might solace as before.                       31

FIRST CITIZEN
Come, come, we fear the worst. All will be well.

THIRD CITIZEN
When clouds are seen, wise men put on their cloaks;
When great leaves fall, then winter is at hand;
When the sun sets, who doth not look for night?
Untimely storms makes men expect a dearth.                     36
All may be well; but if God sort it so,                        37
'Tis more than we deserve or I expect.

SECOND CITIZEN
Truly, the hearts of men are full of fear.
You cannot reason almost with a man                            40
That looks not heavily and full of dread.                      41

THIRD CITIZEN
Before the days of change, still is it so.                     42
By a divine instinct men's minds mistrust                      43
Ensuing danger; as, by proof, we see                           44
The water swell before a boist'rous storm.
But leave it all to God. Whither away?

SECOND CITIZEN
Marry, we were sent for to the justices.

THIRD CITIZEN
And so was I. I'll bear you company.            *Exeunt.*

❖

---

137 **haply** perhaps.    **urged** encouraged, provoked.    **139 meet**
fitting    **142 Who . . . Ludlow** who the persons are that are to be
appointed to hasten immediately to Ludlow Castle.    **144 censures**
judgments    **145.1** *Manent* They remain on stage    **148 by** on.    **sort**
find, contrive    **149 index** prologue.    **late** lately    **151 my counsel's
consistory** the person whom I trust to give me private advice as a
special counselor
**2.3. Location: London. A street.**
**2 promise** assure    **5 Ill . . . better** Ill news, by Our Lady. Good news
comes seldom; most news is bad news. Seldom does one find a better
king than Edward IV.    **6 giddy** mad    **8 Doth the news hold** Is the
news true    **10 masters** good sirs.    **troublous** troubled, disorderly

12 **Woe . . . child!** (Compare with Ecclesiastes 10:16: "Woe to thee,
O land, when thy king is a child.")    **14 nonage** minority.    **council
under him** i.e., with the Privy Council governing in his name
**19 wot** knows    **21 politic** sagacious    **26 emulation** ambitious rivalry
**27 touch** affect    **29 haught** haughty    **31 solace** be happy, have comfort    **36 dearth** i.e., scarcity of food.    **37 sort** dispose    **40 You . . .
man** There is scarcely anyone with whom you can talk    **41 heavily**
sad    **42 still** ever    **43 mistrust** suspect, fear    **44 proof** experience

## 2.4

*Enter [the] Archbishop [of York], [the] young*
*[Duke of] York, the Queen [Elizabeth], and the*
*Duchess [of York].*

ARCHBISHOP
   Last night, I hear, they lay at Stony Stratford,                    1
   And at Northampton they do rest tonight.                            2
   Tomorrow, or next day, they will be here.
DUCHESS
   I long with all my heart to see the Prince.
   I hope he is much grown since last I saw him.
QUEEN ELIZABETH
   But I hear, no; they say my son of York
   Has almost overta'en him in his growth.
YORK
   Ay, mother, but I would not have it so.
DUCHESS
   Why, my young cousin? It is good to grow.
YORK
   Grandam, one night as we did sit at supper,
   My uncle Rivers talked how I did grow
   More than my brother. "Ay," quoth my uncle Gloucester,
   "Small herbs have grace; great weeds do grow apace."          13
   And since, methinks, I would not grow so fast,                14
   Because sweet flow'rs are slow and weeds make haste.
DUCHESS
   Good faith, good faith, the saying did not hold               16
   In him that did object the same to thee.                      17
   He was the wretched'st thing when he was young,
   So long a-growing and so leisurely,
   That, if his rule were true, he should be gracious.           20
ARCHBISHOP
   And so no doubt he is, my gracious madam.
DUCHESS
   I hope he is, but yet let mothers doubt.
YORK
   Now, by my troth, if I had been remembered,                   23
   I could have given my uncle's Grace a flout                   24
   To touch his growth nearer than he touched mine.             25
DUCHESS
   How, my young York? I prithee, let me hear it.
YORK
   Marry, they say my uncle grew so fast
   That he could gnaw a crust at two hours old;
   'Twas full two years ere I could get a tooth.
   Grandam, this would have been a biting jest.                  30

DUCHESS
   I prithee, pretty York, who told thee this?
YORK   Grandam, his nurse.
DUCHESS
   His nurse? Why, she was dead ere thou wast born.
YORK
   If 'twere not she, I cannot tell who told me.
QUEEN ELIZABETH
   A parlous boy! Go to, you are too shrewd.                     35
DUCHESS
   Good madam, be not angry with the child.
QUEEN ELIZABETH   Pitchers have ears.                             37

*Enter a Messenger.*

ARCHBISHOP
   Here comes a messenger.—What news?
MESSENGER
   Such news, my lord, as grieves me to report.
QUEEN ELIZABETH
   How doth the Prince?
MESSENGER                  Well, madam, and in health.
DUCHESS   What is thy news?
MESSENGER
   Lord Rivers and Lord Grey are sent to Pomfret,               42
   And with them Sir Thomas Vaughan, prisoners.
DUCHESS
   Who hath committed them?
MESSENGER                        The mighty dukes
   Gloucester and Buckingham.
ARCHBISHOP                        For what offense?
MESSENGER
   The sum of all I can, I have disclosed.
   Why or for what the nobles were committed
   Is all unknown to me, my gracious lord.
QUEEN ELIZABETH
   Ay me, I see the ruin of my house!
   The tiger now hath seized the gentle hind;                    50
   Insulting tyranny begins to jut                               51
   Upon the innocent and aweless throne.                         52
   Welcome, destruction, blood, and massacre!
   I see, as in a map, the end of all.                           54
DUCHESS
   Accursèd and unquiet wrangling days,
   How many of you have mine eyes beheld!
   My husband lost his life to get the crown,
   And often up and down my sons were tossed                     58
   For me to joy and weep their gain and loss;
   And being seated, and domestic broils                         60
   Clean overblown, themselves the conquerors                    61
   Make war upon themselves, brother to brother,
   Blood to blood, self against self. O preposterous             63

---

**2.4. Location: London. The royal court.**
**1 Stony Stratford** village in Buckinghamshire   **2 Northampton** town in Northamptonshire and hence farther from London than Stony Stratford. The Prince was taken back to Northampton after the arrest of Rivers, Grey, and Vaughan. The Archbishop does not yet know of that arrest, but the Folio version of his speech, followed here, is based misleadingly on historical information of subsequent events. (The quartos reverse the order in which the two towns are named.)
**13 grace** virtuous qualities.   **apace** rapidly.   **14 since** ever since
**16–17 the saying . . . thee** i.e., this saying did not at all apply to Richard of Gloucester, the person who applied the proverb to you (in line 13).   **20 if . . . true** if Richard's proverb were true   **23 troth** truth, faith.   **had been remembered** had recollected   **24–5 I . . . mine** I could have teased him about his growth more tellingly than he teased me.   **30 biting** (With a play on the idea of teething.)

**35 parlous** cunning, precocious.   **Go to** (An expression of remonstrance.)   **shrewd** sharp-tongued.   **37 Pitchers have ears** Little pitchers have large ears. (Proverbial.)   **42 Pomfret** the castle at Pontefract in Yorkshire   **50 hind** doe   **51 Insulting** scornfully triumphing.   **jut** encroach   **52 aweless** inspiring no awe (because of the youth of the King)   **54 map** i.e., of future events   **58 up . . . tossed** i.e., my sons were raised and then lowered on fortune's wheel   **60 seated** i.e., on the throne   **61 Clean overblown** entirely finished   **63 preposterous** monstrous, perverse

And frantic outrage, end thy damnèd spleen,     64
Or let me die, to look on death no more!

QUEEN ELIZABETH
Come, come, my boy, we will to sanctuary.     66
Madam, farewell.

DUCHESS           Stay, I will go with you.

QUEEN ELIZABETH
You have no cause.

ARCHBISHOP [*to the Queen*]    My gracious lady, go,
And thither bear your treasure and your goods.
For my part, I'll resign unto Your Grace
The seal I keep; and so betide to me     71
As well I tender you and all of yours!     72
Go, I'll conduct you to the sanctuary.        *Exeunt.*

# 3.1

*The trumpets sound. Enter [the] young Prince
[Edward], the Dukes of Gloucester and
Buckingham, [Lord] Cardinal [Bourchier, Catesby],
etc.*

BUCKINGHAM
Welcome, sweet Prince, to London, to your chamber.    1

RICHARD
Welcome, dear cousin, my thoughts' sovereign!    2
The weary way hath made you melancholy.

PRINCE EDWARD
No, uncle, but our crosses on the way     4
Have made it tedious, wearisome, and heavy.
I want more uncles here to welcome me.     6

RICHARD
Sweet Prince, the untainted virtue of your years
Hath not yet dived into the world's deceit.
Nor more can you distinguish of a man
Than of his outward show—which, God he knows,
Seldom or never jumpeth with the heart.     11
Those uncles which you want were dangerous.
Your Grace attended to their sugared words
But looked not on the poison of their hearts.
God keep you from them, and from such false
    friends!

PRINCE EDWARD
God keep me from false friends! But they were none.

RICHARD
My lord, the Mayor of London comes to greet you.

*Enter [the] Lord Mayor [and his train].*

MAYOR
God bless Your Grace with health and happy days!

PRINCE EDWARD
I thank you, good my lord, and thank you all.
        [*The Mayor and his train stand aside.*]
I thought my mother and my brother York
Would long ere this have met us on the way.
Fie, what a slug is Hastings, that he comes not     22
To tell us whether they will come or no!

*Enter Lord Hastings.*

BUCKINGHAM
And, in good time, here comes the sweating lord.

PRINCE EDWARD
Welcome, my lord. What, will our mother come?

HASTINGS
On what occasion God he knows, not I,     26
The Queen your mother and your brother York
Have taken sanctuary. The tender Prince
Would fain have come with me to meet Your Grace,   29
But by his mother was perforce withheld.     30

BUCKINGHAM
Fie, what an indirect and peevish course     31
Is this of hers!—Lord Cardinal, will Your Grace
Persuade the Queen to send the Duke of York
Unto his princely brother presently?     34
If she deny, Lord Hastings, go with him,
And from her jealous arms pluck him perforce.     36

CARDINAL
My lord of Buckingham, if my weak oratory
Can from his mother win the Duke of York,
Anon expect him here; but if she be obdurate     39
To mild entreaties, God in heaven forbid
We should infringe the holy privilege
Of blessèd sanctuary! Not for all this land
Would I be guilty of so deep a sin.

BUCKINGHAM
You are too senseless-obstinate, my lord,
Too ceremonious and traditional.     45
Weigh it but with the grossness of this age,     46
You break not sanctuary in seizing him.
The benefit thereof is always granted
To those whose dealings have deserved the place
And those who have the wit to claim the place.
This prince hath neither claimed it nor deserved it,
And therefore, in mine opinion, cannot have it.
Then, taking him from thence that is not there,     53
You break no privilege nor charter there.
Oft have I heard of sanctuary men,
But sanctuary children never till now.

CARDINAL
My lord, you shall o'errule my mind for once.
Come on, Lord Hastings, will you go with me?

---

64 **spleen** i.e., malice, hatred   66 **sanctuary** (Queen Elizabeth, with her son, daughters, and kinsmen, lodged in the precincts of Westminster Abbey, which served as a legal refuge for criminals and persons in danger of their lives.)   71 **seal** seal of office, i.e., the Great Seal of England. (The Archbishop's giving the Great Seal to Elizabeth is an unusual and extralegal action.)   71–2 **so . . . you** may my fortunes be measured by the care I take of you
**3.1. Location:** London. A street.
1 **chamber** (London was called the *camera regis*, or King's chamber.)   2 **cousin** i.e., nephew   4 **crosses** vexations (i.e., the arrests of the Queen's kindred)   6 **want** (1) lack (2) wish   11 **jumpeth** agrees

22 **slug** sluggard   26 **On what occasion** For what reason   29 **fain** willingly   30 **perforce** forcibly   31 **peevish** perverse   34 **presently** at once   36 **jealous** vigilant, solicitous, suspicious   39 **Anon** shortly   45 **ceremonious** bound by formalities   46 **grossness** lack of moral refinement   53 **taking . . . there** i.e., taking the Prince from a place that cannot properly be called a sanctuary in his case

HASTINGS   I go, my lord.

PRINCE EDWARD
Good lords, make all the speedy haste you may.
[*Exeunt Cardinal and Hastings.*]
Say, uncle Gloucester, if our brother come,
Where shall we sojourn till our coronation?    62

RICHARD
Where it seems best unto your royal self.
If I may counsel you, some day or two
Your Highness shall repose you at the Tower;    65
Then where you please, and shall be thought most fit
For your best health and recreation.

PRINCE EDWARD
I do not like the Tower, of any place.    68
Did Julius Caesar build that place, my lord?

BUCKINGHAM
He did, my gracious lord, begin that place,
Which, since, succeeding ages have re-edified.    71

PRINCE EDWARD
Is it upon record, or else reported    72
Successively from age to age, he built it?

BUCKINGHAM   Upon record, my gracious lord.

PRINCE EDWARD
But say, my lord, it were not registered,    75
Methinks the truth should live from age to age,
As 'twere retailed to all posterity,    77
Even to the general all-ending day.    78

RICHARD [*aside*]
So wise so young, they say, do never live long.

PRINCE EDWARD   What say you, uncle?

RICHARD
I say, without characters fame lives long.    81
[*Aside*] Thus, like the formal Vice, Iniquity,    82
I moralize two meanings in one word.    83

PRINCE EDWARD
That Julius Caesar was a famous man;
With what his valor did enrich his wit,    85
His wit set down to make his valor live.    86
Death makes no conquest of this conqueror,
For now he lives in fame, though not in life.
I'll tell you what, my cousin Buckingham—

BUCKINGHAM   What, my gracious lord?

PRINCE EDWARD
An if I live until I be a man,    91
I'll win our ancient right in France again
Or die a soldier, as I lived a king.

RICHARD [*aside*]
Short summers lightly have a forward spring.    94

*Enter young York, Hastings, [and the] Cardinal.*

BUCKINGHAM
Now, in good time, here comes the Duke of York.

PRINCE EDWARD
Richard of York, how fares our loving brother?    96

YORK
Well, my dread lord—so must I call you now.    97

PRINCE EDWARD
Ay, brother, to our grief, as it is yours.
Too late he died that might have kept that title,    99
Which by his death hath lost much majesty.    100

RICHARD
How fares our cousin, noble lord of York?    101

YORK
I thank you, gentle uncle. Oh, my lord,    102
You said that idle weeds are fast in growth;    103
The Prince my brother hath outgrown me far.

RICHARD
He hath, my lord.

YORK             And therefore is he idle?

RICHARD
Oh, my fair cousin, I must not say so.

YORK
Then he is more beholding to you than I.    107

RICHARD
He may command me as my sovereign,
But you have power in me as in a kinsman.

YORK
I pray you, uncle, give me this dagger.

RICHARD
My dagger, little cousin? With all my heart.    111

PRINCE EDWARD   A beggar, brother?

YORK
Of my kind uncle, that I know will give;    113
And being but a toy, which is no grief to give.    114

RICHARD
A greater gift than that I'll give my cousin.

YORK
A greater gift? Oh, that's the sword to it.

RICHARD
Ay, gentle cousin, were it light enough.

YORK
Oh, then I see you will part but with light gifts.    118
In weightier things you'll say a beggar nay.    119

RICHARD
It is too heavy for Your Grace to wear.

YORK
I weigh it lightly, were it heavier.    121

---

**62 sojourn** reside   **65 Tower** (Although in the fifteenth century—the historical time this play represents—the Tower of London was a royal palace, by Shakespeare's day it had acquired a sinister reputation.) **68 of any place** of all places.   **71 re-edified** rebuilt.   **72 upon record** in the written record.   **reported** i.e., by oral tradition   **75 say** suppose. **registered** written down   **77 retailed** repeated, handed down from one to another   **78 general . . . day** Day of Judgment.   **81 without characters** even lacking written records   **82 formal Vice** i.e., the conventional Vice figure of the morality play, a comic tempter to evil, who would habitually *moralize two meanings in one word,* that is, play on double meanings in a single phrase, as Richard does in the phrase *live long*   **83 moralize** interpret, illustrate   **85–6 With . . . live** having improved his understanding through his military achievements, he used his understanding to set down in writing an account (the *Gallic Wars*) that would make his valor immortal.   **91 An if** If

**94 lightly** commonly, often.   **forward** early. (Alludes to Edward's precociousness.)   **96 our** i.e., my. (The royal "we.")   **97 dread** inspiring reverential fear (as king)   **99 late** lately   **100 Which . . . majesty** the institution of kingship has lost much dignity and grandeur by the death of King Edward IV.   **101 cousin** nephew   **102 gentle** noble **103 idle** worthless   **107 beholding** beholden   **111 With . . . heart** Willingly. (Richard combines in one phrase an overt generosity and a hidden threat.)   **113 that** who   **114 toy** trifle   **118 light** trivial **119 say . . . nay** say no to a beggar.   **121 I weigh . . . heavier** I consider it a trifle (playing on the literal meanings of "light" and "heavy") and would do so even if it were heavier.

RICHARD
What, would you have my weapon, little lord?

YORK
I would, that I might thank you as you call me.

RICHARD   How?

YORK   Little.                                                      125

PRINCE EDWARD
My lord of York will still be cross in talk.                        126
Uncle, Your Grace knows how to bear with him.

YORK
You mean, to bear me, not to bear with me.
Uncle, my brother mocks both you and me:
Because that I am little, like an ape,
He thinks that you should bear me on your shoulders. 131

BUCKINGHAM [aside to Hastings]
With what a sharp-provided wit he reasons!                          132
To mitigate the scorn he gives his uncle,
He prettily and aptly taunts himself.
So cunning and so young is wonderful.

RICHARD [to the Prince]
My lord, will't please you pass along?
Myself and my good cousin Buckingham
Will to your mother, to entreat of her
To meet you at the Tower and welcome you.

YORK [to the Prince]
What, will you go unto the Tower, my lord?

PRINCE EDWARD
My Lord Protector needs will have it so.

YORK
I shall not sleep in quiet at the Tower.

RICHARD   Why, what should you fear?

YORK
Marry, my uncle Clarence' angry ghost.
My grandam told me he was murdered there.

PRINCE EDWARD   I fear no uncles dead.

RICHARD   Nor none that live, I hope.

PRINCE EDWARD
An if they live, I hope I need not fear.                            148
But come, my lord; with a heavy heart,
Thinking on them, go I unto the Tower.                               150
            [A sennet.] Exeunt Prince, York,
        Hastings, [Cardinal, and others]. Manent
            Richard, Buckingham, [and Catesby].

BUCKINGHAM
Think you, my lord, this little prating York                        151
Was not incensèd by his subtle mother                               152
To taunt and scorn you thus opprobriously?

RICHARD
No doubt, no doubt. Oh, 'tis a parlous boy,                         154
Bold, quick, ingenious, forward, capable.
He is all the mother's, from the top to toe.

BUCKINGHAM
Well, let them rest.—Come hither, Catesby.                          157
Thou art sworn as deeply to effect what we intend
As closely to conceal what we impart.                               159
Thou know'st our reasons urged upon the way.                        160
What think'st thou? Is it not an easy matter
To make William Lord Hastings of our mind
For the installment of this noble Duke
In the seat royal of this famous isle?

CATESBY
He for his father's sake so loves the Prince                        165
That he will not be won to aught against him.

BUCKINGHAM
What think'st thou, then, of Stanley? Will not he?

CATESBY
He will do all in all as Hastings doth.

BUCKINGHAM
Well, then, no more but this: go, gentle Catesby,
And, as it were far off, sound thou Lord Hastings                   170
How he doth stand affected to our purpose,                          171
And summon him tomorrow to the Tower
To sit about the coronation.                                        173
If thou dost find him tractable to us,
Encourage him, and tell him all our reasons.
If he be leaden, icy, cold, unwilling,
Be thou so too; and so break off the talk,
And give us notice of his inclination.
For we tomorrow hold divided councils,                              179
Wherein thyself shalt highly be employed.

RICHARD
Commend me to Lord William. Tell him, Catesby,                      181
His ancient knot of dangerous adversaries                           182
Tomorrow are let blood at Pomfret Castle;                           183
And bid my lord, for joy of this good news,
Give Mistress Shore one gentle kiss the more.                       185

BUCKINGHAM
Good Catesby, go, effect this business soundly.                     186

CATESBY
My good lords both, with all the heed I can.                        187

RICHARD
Shall we hear from you, Catesby, ere we sleep?

CATESBY   You shall, my lord.

RICHARD
At Crosby House, there shall you find us both.
                                          Exit Catesby.

---

125 Little (York saucily suggests that he would give little thanks for such a "light" gift. York also dares to make fun of his uncle Richard's size. See next two notes.)   126 My . . . talk i.e., My younger brother is always twisting words in his wittily perverse but annoying way.   131 bear me . . . shoulders (At fairs, the bear commonly carried an ape on his back. The speech is doubtless an allusion to Richard's hump and puns triply on *bear with*, "put up with," *bear*, "carry," and *bear*, "an animal.")   132 sharp-provided nimble and ready   148 An if If. they i.e., Rivers and Grey. (Grey was, in fact, Edward's stepbrother, not his uncle. See the note to 1.3.37.)   150.1 *sennet* trumpet call to announce the approach or departure of processions.   150.2 *Manent* They remain on stage   151 prating chattering, prattling   152 incensèd incited

154 parlous clever, but also dangerous   157 let them rest leave them for the moment.   159 closely secretly   160 the way i.e., the journey to London from Ludlow.   165 He . . . sake i.e., Hastings for King Edward IV's sake   170 sound sound out   171 doth stand affected is disposed   173 sit sit in council   179 divided councils (While the regular Council meets about the coronation, Richard plans also to have his own private consultation at Crosby House.)   181 Lord William i.e., Hastings.   182 knot group   183 are let blood will be bled, i.e., executed   185 Mistress Shore (According to Thomas More, Jane Shore had become the mistress of Hastings after the death of Edward IV.)   186 soundly thoroughly.   187 heed attention, care

BUCKINGHAM
Now, my lord, what shall we do if we perceive
Lord Hastings will not yield to our complots?    192
RICHARD
Chop off his head. Something we will determine.
And look when I am king, claim thou of me    194
The earldom of Hereford and all the movables    195
Whereof the King my brother was possessed.
BUCKINGHAM
I'll claim that promise at Your Grace's hand.
RICHARD
And look to have it yielded with all kindness.
Come, let us sup betimes, that afterwards    199
We may digest our complots in some form.    *Exeunt.* 200

## 3.2

*Enter a Messenger to the door of Hastings.*

MESSENGER    My lord! My lord!
HASTINGS [*within*]    Who knocks?
MESSENGER    One from the Lord Stanley.
HASTINGS [*within*]    What is't o'clock?    4
MESSENGER    Upon the stroke of four.

*Enter Lord Hastings.*

HASTINGS
Cannot my Lord Stanley sleep these tedious nights?
MESSENGER
So it appears by that I have to say.
First, he commends him to your noble self.
HASTINGS    What then?
MESSENGER
Then certifies Your Lordship that this night    10
He dreamt the boar had razèd off his helm.    11
Besides, he says there are two councils kept,
And that may be determined at the one
Which may make you and him to rue at th'other.    14
Therefore he sends to know Your Lordship's pleasure,
If you will presently take horse with him    16
And with all speed post with him toward the north,    17
To shun the danger that his soul divines.    18
HASTINGS
Go, fellow, go, return unto thy lord.
Bid him not fear the separated councils.
His Honor and myself are at the one,    21
And at the other is my good friend Catesby,
Where nothing can proceed that toucheth us
Whereof I shall not have intelligence.    24
Tell him his fears are shallow, without instance.    25

And for his dreams, I wonder he's so simple    26
To trust the mock'ry of unquiet slumbers.
To fly the boar before the boar pursues    28
Were to incense the boar to follow us,
And make pursuit where he did mean no chase.
Go, bid thy master rise and come to me,
And we will both together to the Tower,
Where he shall see the boar will use us kindly.
MESSENGER
I'll go, my lord, and tell him what you say.    *Exit.*

*Enter Catesby.*

CATESBY
Many good morrows to my noble lord!
HASTINGS
Good morrow, Catesby. You are early stirring.
What news, what news, in this our tott'ring state?
CATESBY
It is a reeling world, indeed, my lord,
And I believe will never stand upright
Till Richard wear the garland of the realm.
HASTINGS
How? Wear the garland? Dost thou mean the crown?
CATESBY    Ay, my good lord.
HASTINGS
I'll have this crown of mine cut from my shoulders    43
Before I'll see the crown so foul misplaced.
But canst thou guess that he doth aim at it?
CATESBY
Ay, on my life, and hopes to find you forward    46
Upon his party for the gain thereof;    47
And thereupon he sends you this good news,
That this same very day your enemies,
The kindred of the Queen, must die at Pomfret.
HASTINGS
Indeed, I am no mourner for that news,
Because they have been still my adversaries.    52
But that I'll give my voice on Richard's side
To bar my master's heirs in true descent,
God knows I will not do it, to the death.    55
CATESBY
God keep Your Lordship in that gracious mind!
HASTINGS
But I shall laugh at this a twelvemonth hence,
That they which brought me in my master's hate,    58
I live to look upon their tragedy.    59
Well, Catesby, ere a fortnight make me older,
I'll send some packing that yet think not on't.
CATESBY
'Tis a vile thing to die, my gracious lord,
When men are unprepared and look not for it.

---

**192 complots** conspiracies.    **194 look when** as soon as
**195 movables** personal property, other than real estate    **199 betimes**
early, soon    **200 digest** arrange, perfect.    **form** good order.
**3.2. Location:** Before Lord Hastings's house.
**4 What is't o'clock?** What time is it?    **10 certifies** informs    **11 boar**
i.e., Richard.    **razèd** torn, slashed    **14 th'other** i.e., the regular Council meeting in the Tower, in which Hastings and Stanley will participate.    **16 presently** immediately    **17 post** hasten (literally, by means
of post horses)    **18 divines** foretells and fears.    **21 His Honor** Lord
Stanley    **24 intelligence** information.    **25 instance** grounds.

**26 for** as for.    **simple** simpleminded (as)    **28 fly** flee    **43 crown** i.e.,
head. (Recalls Stanley's dream in line 11 and anticipates Hastings's
execution by beheading.)    **46 forward** inclined    **47 Upon his party**
on his side    **52 still** always    **55 to the death** i.e., though I lose my
life. (A common asseveration, but here with ironic meaning.)
**58–9 That . . . tragedy** that I will live to see the fatal end of those
who brought me out of favor with King Edward IV.

HASTINGS
Oh, monstrous, monstrous! And so falls it out 64
With Rivers, Vaughan, Grey; and so 'twill do
With some men else, that think themselves as safe
As thou and I—who, as thou know'st, are dear
To princely Richard and to Buckingham.
CATESBY
The princes both make high account of you— 69
[*Aside*] For they account his head upon the Bridge. 70
HASTINGS
I know they do, and I have well deserved it.

*Enter Lord Stanley [Earl of Derby].*

Come on, come on, where is your boar spear, man?
Fear you the boar, and go so unprovided?
STANLEY
My lord, good morrow. Good morrow, Catesby.
You may jest on, but, by the Holy Rood, 75
I do not like these several councils, I. 76
HASTINGS   My lord,
I hold my life as dear as you do yours,
And never in my days, I do protest,
Was it so precious to me as 'tis now.
Think you, but that I know our state secure, 81
I would be so triumphant as I am?
STANLEY
The lords at Pomfret, when they rode from London, 83
Were jocund and supposed their states were sure, 84
And they indeed had no cause to mistrust;
But yet you see how soon the day o'ercast. 86
This sudden stab of rancor I misdoubt. 87
Pray God, I say, I prove a needless coward!
What, shall we toward the Tower? The day is spent. 89
HASTINGS
Come, come, have with you. Wot you what, my lord? 90
Today the lords you talk of are beheaded.
STANLEY
They, for their truth, might better wear their heads 92
Than some that have accused them wear their hats. 93
But come, my lord, let's away. 94

*Enter a Pursuivant.*

HASTINGS
Go on before. I'll talk with this good fellow.
*Exit Lord Stanley [Earl of Derby] and Catesby.*

How now, sirrah? How goes the world with thee? 96
PURSUIVANT
The better that Your Lordship please to ask.
HASTINGS
I tell thee, man, 'tis better with me now
Than when thou met'st me last where now we meet.
Then was I going prisoner to the Tower,
By the suggestion of the Queen's allies; 101
But now, I tell thee—keep it to thyself—
This day those enemies are put to death,
And I in better state than e'er I was.
PURSUIVANT
God hold it, to Your Honor's good content! 105
HASTINGS
Gramercy, fellow. There, drink that for me. 106
*Throws him his purse.*
PURSUIVANT   I thank Your Honor.   *Exit Pursuivant.*

*Enter a Priest.*

PRIEST
Well met, my lord. I am glad to see Your Honor.
HASTINGS
I thank thee, good Sir John, with all my heart. 109
I am in your debt for your last exercise; 110
Come the next Sabbath, and I will content you. 111
*[He whispers in his ear.]*
PRIEST   I'll wait upon Your Lordship.

*Enter Buckingham.*

BUCKINGHAM
What, talking with a priest, Lord Chamberlain?
Your friends at Pomfret, they do need the priest;
Your Honor hath no shriving work in hand. 115
HASTINGS
Good faith, and when I met this holy man,
The men you talk of came into my mind.
What, go you toward the Tower?
BUCKINGHAM
I do, my lord, but long I cannot stay there.
I shall return before Your Lordship thence.
HASTINGS
Nay, like enough, for I stay dinner there. 121
BUCKINGHAM [*aside*]
And supper too, although thou know'st it not.— 122
Come, will you go?
HASTINGS   I'll wait upon Your Lordship.
*Exeunt.*

**64 so . . . out** so it has happened   **69 high account** great estimation. (The quibble on *high* appears in the next line.)   **70 account** expect, reckon. (Punning on *account* in the previous line.)   **the Bridge** London Bridge, on a tower of which the heads of traitors were exposed.   **75 Rood** cross   **76 several** separate   **81 our state** the positions we (Stanley and Hastings) occupy   **83 London** (An error for "Ludlow"?)   **84 jocund** merry   **86 o'ercast** became overcast. **87 This . . . misdoubt** This sudden rancorous vengeance (against Rivers, Vaughan, and Grey) makes me uneasy.   **89 spent** i.e., well advanced (although the scene began at 4:00 A.M.).   **90 have with you** let's go together.   **Wot** Know   **92–3 They . . . hats** They, for their honest loyalty (to King Edward and now his son), might more justly be allowed to keep their heads than some of their accusers wear their hats of office.   **94.1 *Pursuivant*** attendant on a herald with authority to serve warrants.

**96 sirrah** (Form of address to inferiors.)   **101 By the suggestion** at the instigation   **105 hold it** continue it (i.e., the better state)   **106 Gramercy** Many thanks.   **drink that for me** i.e., here's a tip to enable you to wet your whistle.   **109 Sir** (Common title for addressing any priest.)   **110 exercise** sermon or devotional exercise   **111 content** compensate   **115 shriving work** confession and absolution   **121 like** likely.   **stay** stay for   **122 And supper . . . not** i.e., You won't be leaving as soon as you think. (Also suggesting that Hastings will be a feast for worms.)

## 3.3

*Enter Sir Richard Ratcliffe, with Halberds, carrying
the nobles [Rivers, Grey, and Vaughan] to death
at Pomfret.*

RATCLIFFE    Come, bring forth the prisoners.

RIVERS
Sir Richard Ratcliffe, let me tell thee this:
Today shalt thou behold a subject die
For truth, for duty, and for loyalty.

GREY
God bless the Prince from all the pack of you!    5
A knot you are of damnèd bloodsuckers.    6

VAUGHAN
You live that shall cry woe for this hereafter.

RATCLIFFE
Dispatch. The limit of your lives is out.    8

RIVERS
O Pomfret, Pomfret! O thou bloody prison,
Fatal and ominous to noble peers!
Within the guilty closure of thy walls    11
Richard the Second here was hacked to death;
And, for more slander to thy dismal seat,    13
We give to thee our guiltless blood to drink.

GREY
Now Margaret's curse is fall'n upon our heads,
When she exclaimed on Hastings, you, and I,
For standing by when Richard stabbed her son.

RIVERS
Then cursed she Richard, then cursed she Buckingham,
Then cursed she Hastings. Oh, remember, God,
To hear her prayer for them, as now for us!
And for my sister and her princely sons,    21
Be satisfied, dear God, with our true blood,
Which, as thou know'st, unjustly must be spilt.

RATCLIFFE
Make haste. The hour of death is expiate.    24

RIVERS
Come, Grey, come, Vaughan, let us here embrace.
*[They embrace.]*
Farewell, until we meet again in heaven.    *Exeunt.*

## 3.4

*Enter Buckingham, [Lord Stanley Earl of] Derby,
Hastings, Bishop of Ely, Norfolk, Ratcliffe, Lovell,
with others, at a table.*

HASTINGS
Now, noble peers, the cause why we are met
Is to determine of the coronation.
In God's name, speak. When is the royal day?    2

BUCKINGHAM
Is all things ready for the royal time?

STANLEY
It is, and wants but nomination.    5

ELY
Tomorrow, then, I judge a happy day.    6

BUCKINGHAM
Who knows the Lord Protector's mind herein?
Who is most inward with the noble Duke?    8

ELY
Your Grace, methinks, should soonest know his mind.

BUCKINGHAM
We know each other's faces; for our hearts,    10
He knows no more of mine than I of yours,
Or I of his, my lord, than you of mine.
Lord Hastings, you and he are near in love.

HASTINGS
I thank His Grace, I know he loves me well;
But, for his purpose in the coronation,
I have not sounded him, nor he delivered
His gracious pleasure any way therein.
But you, my honorable lords, may name the time,
And in the Duke's behalf I'll give my voice,    19
Which I presume he'll take in gentle part.    20

*Enter [Richard Duke of] Gloucester.*

ELY
In happy time, here comes the Duke himself.

RICHARD
My noble lords and cousins all, good morrow.    22
I have been long a sleeper; but I trust
My absence doth neglect no great design    24
Which by my presence might have been concluded.

BUCKINGHAM
Had you not come upon your cue, my lord,
William Lord Hastings had pronounced your part,
I mean your voice for crowning of the King.

RICHARD
Than my Lord Hastings no man might be bolder.
His Lordship knows me well, and loves me well.—
My lord of Ely, when I was last in Holborn,    31
I saw good strawberries in your garden there.
I do beseech you send for some of them.

ELY
Marry, and will, my lord, with all my heart.
*Exit Bishop.*

RICHARD
Cousin of Buckingham, a word with you.
*[Drawing him aside.]*
Catesby hath sounded Hastings in our business,
And finds the testy gentleman so hot
That he will lose his head ere give consent
His master's child, as worshipfully he terms it,    39
Shall lose the royalty of England's throne.

---

3.3. Location: Pomfret (Pontefract) Castle.
5 pack gang    6 knot group    8 Dispatch Hurry.    is out has been
reached.    11 closure enclosure    13 for . . . seat i.e., to add further to
the evil reputation of this place    21 for as for    24 expiate fully come.
3.4. Location: London. The Tower.
2 determine of decide upon

5 wants but nomination lacks only naming of the day.    6 happy
favorable    8 inward intimate    10 for as for    19 voice vote    20 in
gentle part with gracious acceptance.    22 cousins i.e., peers
24 neglect cause the neglect of    31 Holborn (location of the Bishop's
London palace)    39 worshipfully reverently. (Said contemptuously.)

BUCKINGHAM
Withdraw yourself awhile. I'll go with you.
*Exeunt [Richard and Buckingham].*

STANLEY
We have not yet set down this day of triumph.
Tomorrow, in my judgment, is too sudden,
For I myself am not so well provided                    44
As else I would be, were the day prolonged.             45

*Enter the Bishop of Ely.*

ELY
Where is my lord the Duke of Gloucester?
I have sent for these strawberries.

HASTINGS
His Grace looks cheerfully and smooth this morning;     48
There's some conceit or other likes him well            49
When that he bids good morrow with such spirit.         50
I think there's never a man in Christendom
Can lesser hide his love or hate than he,
For by his face straight shall you know his heart.      53

STANLEY
What of his heart perceive you in his face
By any likelihood he showed today?

HASTINGS
Marry, that with no man here he is offended;
For, were he, he had shown it in his looks.

STANLEY    I pray God he be not, I say.

*Enter Richard and Buckingham.*

RICHARD
I pray you all, tell me what they deserve
That do conspire my death with devilish plots
Of damnèd witchcraft, and that have prevailed
Upon my body with their hellish charms?

HASTINGS
The tender love I bear Your Grace, my lord,             63
Makes me most forward in this princely presence
To doom th'offenders, whosoe'er they be:
I say, my lord, they have deservèd death.

RICHARD
Then be your eyes the witness of their evil.
                              *[He bares his arm.]*
Look how I am bewitched! Behold, mine arm
Is like a blasted sapling withered up.                  69
And this is Edward's wife, that monstrous witch,        70
Consorted with that harlot strumpet Shore,              71
That by their witchcraft thus have markèd me.

HASTINGS
If they have done this deed, my noble lord—

RICHARD
If? Thou protector of this damnèd strumpet,             74
Talk'st thou to me of "ifs"? Thou art a traitor.—
Off with his head! Now, by Saint Paul I swear,
I will not dine until I see the same.
Lovell and Ratcliffe, look that it be done.             78

The rest that love me, rise and follow me.              79
          *Exeunt. Manent Lovell and Ratcliffe, with the Lord
                                                Hastings.*

HASTINGS
Woe, woe for England! Not a whit for me,
For I, too fond, might have prevented this.             81
Stanley did dream the boar did raze our helms,
And I did scorn it and disdain to fly.                  83
Three times today my footcloth horse did stumble,      84
And started, when he looked upon the Tower,
As loath to bear me to the slaughterhouse.
Oh, now I need the priest that spake to me!
I now repent I told the pursuivant,                     88
As too triumphing, how mine enemies
Today at Pomfret bloodily were butchered,
And I myself secure in grace and favor.
O Margaret, Margaret, now thy heavy curse
Is lighted on poor Hastings' wretched head!

RATCLIFFE
Come, come, dispatch. The Duke would be at
    dinner.
Make a short shrift. He longs to see your head.         95

HASTINGS
Oh, momentary grace of mortal men,                      96
Which we more hunt for than the grace of God!
Who builds his hope in air of your good looks           98
Lives like a drunken sailor on a mast,
Ready with every nod to tumble down
Into the fatal bowels of the deep.

LOVELL
Come, come, dispatch. 'Tis bootless to exclaim.         102

HASTINGS
Oh, bloody Richard! Miserable England!
I prophesy the fearful'st time to thee
That ever wretched age hath looked upon.
Come, lead me to the block; bear him my head.
They smile at me who shortly shall be dead.
                                        *Exeunt.*

❖

# [3.5]

*Enter Richard [Duke of Gloucester] and
Buckingham in rotten armor, marvelous
ill-favored.*

RICHARD
Come, cousin, canst thou quake and change thy color,
Murder thy breath in middle of a word,                  2
And then again begin, and stop again,
As if thou wert distraught and mad with terror?

44 **provided** equipped   45 **prolonged** postponed.   48 **smooth** pleasant   49 **conceit** fancy, idea.   **likes** pleases   50 **When that** when   53 **straight** straightway, at once   63 **tender** dear   69 **blasted** shriveled   70–1 **And . . . Shore** (Richard alleges, most outlandishly, that the widowed Queen Elizabeth is conspiring with Jane Shore, the mistress of her dead husband and of Hastings.)   71 **Consorted** who associated, conspired   74 **Thou . . . strumpet** You who are protecting the woman who is notoriously your mistress   78 **look** see to it

79.1 *Manent* They remain on stage   81 **fond** foolish.   **prevented** anticipated   83 **fly** flee.   84 **footcloth** large, richly ornamented cloth laid over the back of a horse and hanging to the ground on each side.   **stumble** (An omen of misfortune.)   88 **pursuivant** (See note at 3.2.94.1.)   95 **shrift** confession.   96 **grace** favor, fortune   98 **Who** Anyone who.   **in . . . looks** on the insubstantial foundation of your favor   102 **bootless** useless
**3.5. Location: London. The Tower.**
**0.2** *rotten* rusty   **0.2–3** *marvelous ill-favored* remarkably unattractive.
**2 Murder** i.e., stop, catch

**BUCKINGHAM**
Tut, I can counterfeit the deep tragedian,
Speak and look back, and pry on every side,    6
Tremble and start at wagging of a straw;
Intending deep suspicion, ghastly looks    8
Are at my service, like enforcèd smiles;
And both are ready in their offices,    10
At any time, to grace my stratagems.
But what, is Catesby gone?

**RICHARD**
He is; and, see, he brings the Mayor along.

*Enter the Mayor and Catesby.*

**BUCKINGHAM**    Lord Mayor—
**RICHARD**    Look to the drawbridge there!
**BUCKINGHAM**    Hark, a drum!
**RICHARD**    Catesby, o'erlook the walls.    [*Exit Catesby.*]   17

**BUCKINGHAM**
Lord Mayor, the reason we have sent—

**RICHARD**
Look back, defend thee, here are enemies!

**BUCKINGHAM**
God and our innocence defend and guard us!

*Enter Lovell and Ratcliffe, with Hastings' head.*

**RICHARD**
Be patient. They are friends, Ratcliffe and Lovell.

**LOVELL**
Here is the head of that ignoble traitor,
The dangerous and unsuspected Hastings.

**RICHARD**
So dear I loved the man that I must weep.
I took him for the plainest harmless creature
That breathed upon the earth a Christian,
Made him my book wherein my soul recorded    27
The history of all her secret thoughts.
So smooth he daubed his vice with show of virtue
That, his apparent open guilt omitted—    30
I mean, his conversation with Shore's wife—    31
He lived from all attainder of suspects.    32

**BUCKINGHAM**
Well, well, he was the covert'st sheltered traitor    33
That ever lived. Look ye, my Lord Mayor,
Would you imagine, or almost believe,    35
Were't not that by great preservation    36
We live to tell it, that the subtle traitor
This day had plotted, in the Council House,
To murder me and my good lord of Gloucester?

**MAYOR**    Had he done so?    40

**RICHARD**
What, think you we are Turks or infidels?
Or that we would, against the form of law,

Proceed thus rashly in the villain's death,
But that the extreme peril of the case,
The peace of England, and our persons' safety,
Enforced us to this execution?

**MAYOR**
Now fair befall you! He deserved his death,    47
And Your good Graces both have well proceeded    48
To warn false traitors from the like attempts.

**BUCKINGHAM**
I never looked for better at his hands
After he once fell in with Mistress Shore.
Yet had we not determined he should die    52
Until Your Lordship came to see his end,
Which now the loving haste of these our friends,
Something against our meanings, have prevented;    55
Because, my lord, we would have had you hear    56
The traitor speak and timorously confess
The manner and the purpose of his treasons,
That you might well have signified the same
Unto the citizens, who haply may    60
Misconster us in him and wail his death.    61

**MAYOR**
But, my good lord, Your Grace's words shall serve
As well as I had seen and heard him speak.    63
And do not doubt, right noble princes both,
But I'll acquaint our duteous citizens
With all your just proceedings in this cause.

**RICHARD**
And to that end we wished Your Lordship here,
T'avoid the censures of the carping world.

**BUCKINGHAM**
Which, since you come too late of our intent,    69
Yet witness what you hear we did intend.    70
And so, my good Lord Mayor, we bid farewell.

*Exit Mayor.*

**RICHARD**
Go, after, after, cousin Buckingham.
The Mayor towards Guildhall hies him in all post.    73
There, at your meet'st advantage of the time,    74
Infer the bastardy of Edward's children.    75
Tell them how Edward put to death a citizen
Only for saying he would make his son
Heir to the Crown—meaning indeed his house,    78
Which, by the sign thereof, was termèd so.    79
Moreover, urge his hateful luxury    80

---

**6 back** over my shoulder.  **pry** peer  **8 Intending** pretending
**10 offices** uses, functions  **17 o'erlook** inspect  **27 book** i.e., table
book or diary  **30 his . . . omitted** apart from his manifest open guilt
**31 conversation** sexual intimacy  **32 from . . . suspects** free from all
stain of suspicion.  **33 covert'st sheltered** most secret, hidden
**35 almost** even  **36 great preservation** providential protection
**40 Had he** Would he have

**47 fair** good fortune  **48 Your . . . proceeded** Your Graces (the Dukes
of Gloucester and Buckingham) have done well  **52 had we . . . die**
we had determined he should not die  **55 Something . . . meanings**
somewhat contrary to our intent  **56 we . . . hear** we would have
wished you to have heard  **60 haply** perhaps  **61 Misconster . . . him**
i.e., misconstrue our intentions regarding him  **63 as** as if  **69 of** to
accord with  **70 witness** bear witness to  **73 Guildhall** central hall
for municipal affairs.  **hies . . . post** hurries with all possible speed.
**74 meet'st advantage** most suitable opportunity  **75 Infer** allege,
adduce  **78 the Crown** i.e., a tavern in Cheapside identified by the
sign of the Crown. (King Edward is portrayed as having been so sensitive to possible rivals that he put to death a man merely for naming
his son heir to "the Crown," even though the poor fellow innocently
meant nothing more than his own tavern. The story is from Sir
Thomas More's *History of King Richard III.*)  **house** tavern  **79 sign**
tavern or shop sign displayed over the door  **80 luxury** lechery

And bestial appetite in change of lust,                              81
Which stretched unto their servants, daughters, wives,   82
Even where his raging eye or savage heart,
Without control, lusted to make a prey.
Nay, for a need, thus far come near my person:           85
Tell them, when that my mother went with child           86
Of that insatiate Edward, noble York                     87
My princely father then had wars in France,
And by true computation of the time
Found that the issue was not his begot—
Which well appearèd in his lineaments,                   91
Being nothing like the noble duke my father.
Yet touch this sparingly, as 'twere far off,
Because, my lord, you know my mother lives.

BUCKINGHAM
Doubt not, my lord, I'll play the orator
As if the golden fee for which I plead                   96
Were for myself. And so, my lord, adieu.

RICHARD
If you thrive well, bring them to Baynard's Castle,      98
Where you shall find me well accompanied
With reverend fathers and well-learnèd bishops.

BUCKINGHAM
I go; and towards three or four o'clock
Look for the news that the Guildhall affords.            102
                              *Exit Buckingham.*

RICHARD
Go, Lovell, with all speed to Doctor Shaw.               103
[*To Ratcliffe*] Go thou to Friar Penker. Bid them both  104
Meet me within this hour at Baynard's Castle.
                              *Exeunt [all but Richard].*
Now will I go to take some privy order                   106
To draw the brats of Clarence out of sight,
And to give order that no manner person                  108
Have any time recourse unto the princes.      *Exit.* 109

❧

## [3.6]

*Enter a Scrivener [with a paper in his hand].*

SCRIVENER
Here is the indictment of the good Lord Hastings,
Which in a set hand fairly is engrossed                  2
That it may be today read o'er in Paul's.                3
And mark how well the sequel hangs together:             4

Eleven hours I have spent to write it over,
For yesternight by Catesby was it sent me;
The precedent was full as long a-doing.                  7
And yet within these five hours Hastings lived,
Untainted, unexamined, free, at liberty.                 9
Here's a good world the while! Who is so gross           10
That cannot see this palpable device?
Yet who so bold but says he sees it not?
Bad is the world, and all will come to naught
When such ill dealing must be seen in thought.           14
                              *Exit.*

## [3.7]

*Enter Richard [Duke of Gloucester] and
Buckingham, at several doors.*

RICHARD
How now, how now, what say the citizens?
BUCKINGHAM
Now, by the holy mother of our Lord,
The citizens are mum, say not a word.
RICHARD
Touched you the bastardy of Edward's children?          4
BUCKINGHAM
I did; with his contract with Lady Lucy                 5
And his contract by deputy in France;                   6
Th'insatiate greediness of his desire                   7
And his enforcement of the city wives;                  8
His tyranny for trifles; his own bastardy,              9
As being got, your father then in France,               10
And his resemblance, being not like the Duke.          11
Withal I did infer your lineaments,                     12
Being the right idea of your father                     13
Both in your form and nobleness of mind;
Laid open all your victories in Scotland,               15
Your discipline in war, wisdom in peace,                16
Your bounty, virtue, fair humility;
Indeed, left nothing fitting for your purpose
Untouched or slightly handled in discourse.
And when mine oratory drew toward end,
I bid them that did love their country's good
Cry, "God save Richard, England's royal king!"
RICHARD    And did they so?

81 in . . . lust i.e., constantly desiring new mistresses   82 their i.e., the citizens'   85 for a need if necessary   86–7 when . . . Of when my mother was pregnant with   91 his lineaments Edward's features   96 golden fee i.e., crown   98 Baynard's Castle Richard's residence on the north bank of the Thames. It was founded by Baynard, a nobleman in the time of the Conquest, and had belonged to Richard's father.   102 the Guildhall (See 3.5.73 and note. That is where Buckingham is going to bamboozle the Mayor and citizens into endorsing Richard's candidacy for the crown.)   103, 104 Doctor Shaw, Friar Penker (Well-known divines who delivered sermons in Richard's favor.)   106 take . . . order give some secret instruction   108 no manner person no one at all   109 Have . . . recourse have access at any time   3.6. Location: London. A street.
2 in . . . engrossed is written out in a style of script used for legal documents   3 read . . . Paul's posted and read publicly in St. Paul's Cathedral.   4 the sequel what follows

7 precedent prologue, indictment   9 Untainted, unexamined not yet accused or interrogated   10 Here's . . . while! Here's a fine state of affairs!   gross dull, stupid   14 seen in thought i.e., perceived in silence.
3.7. Location: The courtyard of Baynard's Castle.
0.2 several separate   4 Touched you Did you deal with, touch upon, discuss   5 contract betrothal.   Lady Lucy Elizabeth Lucy (by whom Edward had a child, though there was no formal contract of betrothal)   6 deputy (See 3 Henry VI, 3.3.49 ff., where Warwick, as deputy, contracts with Louis XI of France for the marriage of King Edward to Lady Bona, sister of the French queen.)   7 precedent prologue, indictment   8 enforcement forcible seduction   9 tyranny for trifles harsh punishment of minor offenses, or cruel behavior over trifles   10 got begot.   your father Richard Duke of York   11 And . . . Duke and he, Edward, not physically resembling his putative father, Richard Duke of York.   12 Withal . . . lineaments Besides that, I pointed to your features   13 right idea true image   15 Laid . . . Scotland I elaborated on your successful expedition against Scotland in 1482   16 discipline skill, training

BUCKINGHAM
No, so God help me, they spake not a word,
But, like dumb statues or breathing stones,
Stared each on other and looked deadly pale.
Which when I saw, I reprehended them,
And asked the Mayor what meant this willful silence.
His answer was, the people were not used
To be spoke to but by the Recorder.                              30
Then he was urged to tell my tale again:                         31
"Thus saith the Duke, thus hath the Duke inferred"—             32
But nothing spake in warrant from himself.                       33
When he had done, some followers of mine own,
At lower end of the hall, hurled up their caps,
And some ten voices cried, "God save King Richard!"
And thus I took the vantage of those few:                        37
"Thanks, gentle citizens and friends," quoth I,
"This general applause and cheerful shout
Argues your wisdoms and your love to Richard"—
And even here brake off and came away.                           41
RICHARD
What tongueless blocks were they! Would they not speak?
BUCKINGHAM   No, by my troth, my lord.
RICHARD
Will not the Mayor, then, and his brethren come?                 44
BUCKINGHAM
The Mayor is here at hand. Intend some fear;                     45
Be not you spoke with but by mighty suit.                        46
And look you get a prayer book in your hand,                     47
And stand between two churchmen, good my lord,
For on that ground I'll make a holy descant;                     49
And be not easily won to our requests.
Play the maid's part: still answer nay and take it.
RICHARD
I go; and if you plead as well for them
As I can say nay to thee for myself,
No doubt we'll bring it to a happy issue.                        54
BUCKINGHAM
Go, go, up to the leads. The Lord Mayor knocks.                  55
                                    [Exit Richard.]

        Enter the Mayor, [aldermen,] and citizens.

Welcome, my lord. I dance attendance here;                       56
I think the Duke will not be spoke withal.                       57

        Enter Catesby.

Now, Catesby, what says your lord to my request?
CATESBY
He doth entreat Your Grace, my noble lord,
To visit him tomorrow or next day.
He is within, with two right reverend fathers,                   61
Divinely bent to meditation,

And in no worldly suits would he be moved
To draw him from his holy exercise.
BUCKINGHAM
Return, good Catesby, to the gracious Duke.
Tell him myself, the Mayor and aldermen,
In deep designs, in matter of great moment,                      67
No less importing than our general good,                         68
Are come to have some conference with His Grace.
CATESBY
I'll signify so much unto him straight.          Exit.
BUCKINGHAM
Aha, my lord, this prince is not an Edward!
He is not lolling on a lewd love bed
But on his knees at meditation;
Not dallying with a brace of courtesans                          74
But meditating with two deep divines;                            75
Not sleeping, to engross his idle body,                          76
But praying, to enrich his watchful soul.
Happy were England, would this virtuous prince
Take on His Grace the sovereignty thereof;
But sure I fear we shall not win him to it.
MAYOR
Marry, God defend His Grace should say us nay!                   81
BUCKINGHAM
I fear he will.—Here Catesby comes again.

        Enter Catesby.

Now, Catesby, what says His Grace?
CATESBY                                    My lord,
He wonders to what end you have assembled
Such troops of citizens to come to him,
His Grace not being warned thereof before.
He fears, my lord, you mean no good to him.
BUCKINGHAM
Sorry I am my noble cousin should
Suspect me that I mean no good to him.
By heaven, we come to him in perfect love,
And so once more return and tell His Grace.
                                    Exit [Catesby].
When holy and devout religious men
Are at their beads, 'tis much to draw them thence,               93
So sweet is zealous contemplation.                               94

        Enter Richard aloft, between two bishops. [Catesby
        returns to the main stage.]

MAYOR
See where His Grace stands, 'tween two clergymen!
BUCKINGHAM
Two props of virtue for a Christian prince,
To stay him from the fall of vanity.                             97
And, see, a book of prayer in his hand,
True ornaments to know a holy man.—                              99
Famous Plantagenet, most gracious prince,

Lend favorable ear to our requests,
And pardon us the interruption
Of thy devotion and right Christian zeal.

**RICHARD**
My lord, there needs no such apology.
I do beseech Your Grace to pardon me,
Who, earnest in the service of my God,
Deferred the visitation of my friends.
But, leaving this, what is Your Grace's pleasure?

**BUCKINGHAM**
Even that, I hope, which pleaseth God above,
And all good men of this ungoverned isle.

**RICHARD**
I do suspect I have done some offense
That seems disgracious in the city's eye,     112
And that you come to reprehend my ignorance.

**BUCKINGHAM**
You have, my lord. Would it might please Your Grace,
On our entreaties, to amend your fault!

**RICHARD**
Else wherefore breathe I in a Christian land?    116

**BUCKINGHAM**
Know then, it is your fault that you resign
The supreme seat, the throne majestical,
The sceptered office of your ancestors,
Your state of fortune and your due of birth,     120
The lineal glory of your royal house,        121
To the corruption of a blemished stock;      122
While, in the mildness of your sleepy thoughts,   123
Which here we waken to our country's good,
The noble isle doth want her proper limbs;     125
Her face defaced with scars of infamy,
Her royal stock graft with ignoble plants,      127
And almost shouldered in the swallowing gulf   128
Of dark forgetfulness and deep oblivion.
Which to recure, we heartily solicit         130
Your gracious self to take on you the charge
And kingly government of this your land—
Not as protector, steward, substitute,
Or lowly factor for another's gain,          134
But as successively from blood to blood,      135
Your right of birth, your empery, your own.    136
For this, consorted with the citizens,        137
Your very worshipful and loving friends,      138
And by their vehement instigation,
In this just cause come I to move Your Grace.   140

**RICHARD**
I cannot tell if to depart in silence
Or bitterly to speak in your reproof

Best fitteth my degree or your condition.     143
If not to answer, you might haply think       144
Tongue-tied ambition, not replying, yielded    145
To bear the golden yoke of sovereignty,
Which fondly you would here impose on me.    147
If to reprove you for this suit of yours,
So seasoned with your faithful love to me,     149
Then on the other side I checked my friends.    150
Therefore, to speak, and to avoid the first,
And then, in speaking, not to incur the last,
Definitively thus I answer you.          153
Your love deserves my thanks, but my desert   154
Unmeritable shuns your high request.        155
First, if all obstacles were cut away,
And that my path were even to the crown     157
As the ripe revenue and due of birth,        158
Yet so much is my poverty of spirit,
So mighty and so many my defects,
That I would rather hide me from my greatness—   161
Being a bark to brook no mighty sea—      162
Than in my greatness covet to be hid        163
And in the vapor of my glory smothered.
But, God be thanked, there is no need of me,
And much I need to help you, were there need.   166
The royal tree hath left us royal fruit,
Which, mellowed by the stealing hours of time,   168
Will well become the seat of majesty       169
And make, no doubt, us happy by his reign.
On him I lay that you would lay on me,      171
The right and fortune of his happy stars,      172
Which God defend that I should wring from him!   173

**BUCKINGHAM**
My lord, this argues conscience in Your Grace;
But the respects thereof are nice and trivial,    175
All circumstances well considerèd.
You say that Edward is your brother's son.
So say we too, but not by Edward's wife;
For first was he contract to Lady Lucy—     179
Your mother lives a witness to his vow—     180
And afterward by substitute betrothed       181
To Bona, sister to the King of France.       182
These both put off, a poor petitioner,
A care-crazed mother to a many sons,        184

---

**143 Best . . . condition** is more appropriate to my rank (as Duke and Protector) and your status as citizens.   **144 haply** perhaps   **145 Tongue-tied** silent. (Silence gives consent.)   **yielded** consented   **147 fondly** foolishly   **149 seasoned** i.e., made agreeable or palatable   **150 checked** rebuked, i.e., would have rebuked   **153 Definitively** once and for all   **154–5 my desert . . . request** my unworthiness means that I should reject a request of such high importance.   **157 even** smooth   **158 ripe revenue** possession ready to be inherited   **161 my greatness** i.e., my claim to the throne   **162 bark** ship.   **brook** endure   **163 Than . . . hid** than wish to be enveloped in and overwhelmed by my greatness, i.e., the throne   **166 I need** I lack the requisite ability   **168 stealing** stealthily moving   **169 become** suit   **171 On him** on young Edward, son of Edward IV.   **that** that which   **172 happy** fortunate   **173 defend** forbid   **175 respects thereof** considerations by which you support your argument.   **nice** overscrupulous   **179 contract** contracted   **180 Your . . . vow** (According to the chronicles, Richard's mother, in opposing Edward's intention of marrying Lady Grey because it was interfering with the negotiations for his marriage to Lady Bona of Savoy, asserted that Lady Elizabeth Lucy was already Edward's trothplight wife. Compare with 3.5.75 and 3.7.6.)   **181 substitute** proxy   **182 sister** i.e., sister-in-law, the Queen's sister   **184 A care-crazed mother** Lady Elizabeth Grey, then a widow of John Grey of Groby, a Lancastrian officer who died at the battle of St Albans in 1461

**112 disgracious** unbecoming, displeasing   **116 Else . . . land?** i.e., How could I call myself a Christian if I am not prepared to amend my faults?   **120 state of fortune** position to which fortune entitles you   **121 lineal** inherited from your ancestors   **122 blemished** i.e., through bastardy; see lines 177–91 below   **123 sleepy** passive   **125 want her proper limbs** lack its own limbs, is crippled   **127 graft . . . plants** engrafted with illegitimate offspring   **128 shouldered in** jostled into, or immersed up to the shoulders in   **130 recure** restore, make whole   **134 factor** agent   **135 successively** in order of succession   **136 empery** empire   **137 consorted** associated, leagued   **138 worshipful** respectful   **140 move** persuade

A beauty-waning and distressèd widow,
Even in the afternoon of her best days,
Made prize and purchase of his wanton eye,     187
Seduced the pitch and height of his degree     188
To base declension and loathèd bigamy.     189
By her, in his unlawful bed, he got
This Edward, whom our manners call the Prince.     191
More bitterly could I expostulate,     192
Save that, for reverence to some alive,     193
I give a sparing limit to my tongue.
Then, good my lord, take to your royal self     195
This proffered benefit of dignity,
If not to bless us and the land withal,
Yet to draw forth your noble ancestry     198
From the corruption of abusing times
Unto a lineal true-derivèd course.

MAYOR
    Do, good my lord. Your citizens entreat you.

BUCKINGHAM
    Refuse not, mighty lord, this proffered love.

CATESBY
    Oh, make them joyful. Grant their lawful suit!

RICHARD
    Alas, why would you heap this care on me?
    I am unfit for state and majesty.
    I do beseech you, take it not amiss;
    I cannot nor I will not yield to you.

BUCKINGHAM
    If you refuse it—as, in love and zeal,     208
    Loath to depose the child, your brother's son,
    As well we know your tenderness of heart     210
    And gentle, kind, effeminate remorse,     211
    Which we have noted in you to your kindred
    And equally indeed to all estates—     213
    Yet know, whe'er you accept our suit or no,     214
    Your brother's son shall never reign our king,
    But we will plant some other in the throne
    To the disgrace and downfall of your house.
    And in this resolution here we leave you.—
    Come, citizens. Zounds! I'll entreat no more.     219

RICHARD
    Oh, do not swear, my lord of Buckingham.

            *Exeunt [Buckingham,*
            *Mayor, aldermen, and the citizens].*

CATESBY
    Call him again, sweet prince. Accept their suit.
    If you deny them, all the land will rue it.

RICHARD
    Will you enforce me to a world of cares?
    Call them again. I am not made of stone,
    But penetrable to your kind entreaties,
    Albeit against my conscience and my soul.

        *Enter Buckingham and the rest.*

    Cousin of Buckingham, and sage, grave men,
    Since you will buckle fortune on my back,
    To bear her burden, whe'er I will or no,
    I must have patience to endure the load.
    But if black scandal or foul-faced reproach
    Attend the sequel of your imposition,     232
    Your mere enforcement shall acquittance me     233
    From all the impure blots and stains thereof;
    For God doth know, and you may partly see,
    How far I am from the desire of this.

MAYOR
    God bless Your Grace! We see it and will say it.

RICHARD
    In saying so, you shall but say the truth.

BUCKINGHAM
    Then I salute you with this royal title:
    Long live Richard, England's worthy king!

MAYOR AND CITIZENS    Amen.

BUCKINGHAM
    Tomorrow may it please you to be crowned?

RICHARD
    Even when you please, for you will have it so.

BUCKINGHAM
    Tomorrow, then, we will attend Your Grace.
    And so most joyfully we take our leave.

RICHARD [*to the Bishops*]
    Come, let us to our holy work again.—
    Farewell, my cousin. Farewell, gentle friends. *Exeunt.*

# 4.1

        *Enter [at one door] the Queen [Elizabeth], the*
        *Duchess of York, and Marquess [of] Dorset; [at*
        *another door] Anne, Duchess of Gloucester,*
        *[leading Lady Margaret Plantagenet, Clarence's*
        *young daughter].*

DUCHESS
    Who meets us here? My niece Plantagenet     1
    Led in the hand of her kind aunt of Gloucester?     2
    Now, for my life, she's wand'ring to the Tower,     3
    On pure heart's love to greet the tender Prince.     4
    Daughter, well met.

ANNE                 God give Your Graces both     5
    A happy and a joyful time of day!

QUEEN ELIZABETH
    As much to you, good sister. Whither away?     7

---

187 **purchase** booty    **188–9 Seduced . . . declension** i.e., seduced him away from his high rank to ignoble decline. (*Pitch* is the highest point in a falcon's flight.)    **189 bigamy** (Edward was not only bound by previous contracts, as indicated in lines 178–82 above, but also, by marrying a widow, entered into a union that was widely regarded as bigamous.)    **191 manners** sense of politeness    **192 expostulate** discuss, dilate    **193 some alive** i.e., the Duchess of York. (See 3.5.93–4.) **195 good my lord** my good lord    **198 draw forth** rescue    **208 as** from being    **210 As . . . know** since we know well    **211 kind, effeminate remorse** natural, tender pity    **213 estates** ranks. (Buckingham argues that this virtue of pity is found in Richard's treatment of everyone.)    **214 whe'er** whether    **219 Zounds!** By His (God's) wounds!

232 **Attend . . . imposition** should follow as a result of your laying this duty upon me    **233 Your . . . acquittance me** the mere fact of your insistence will exonerate me
**4.1. Location:** London. Before the Tower.
**1 niece** i.e., granddaughter Margaret Plantagenet    **2 aunt of Gloucester** the Lady Anne, now Duchess of Gloucester, Richard's wife.    **3 for** on    **4 On** out of.    **tender** young    **5 Daughter** i.e., Daughter-in-law    **7 sister** i.e., sister-in-law.

ANNE
No farther than the Tower, and, as I guess,
Upon the like devotion as yourselves,                              9
To gratulate the gentle princes there.                            10
QUEEN ELIZABETH
Kind sister, thanks. We'll enter all together.

*Enter [Brackenbury] the Lieutenant.*

And, in good time, here the Lieutenant comes.—
Master Lieutenant, pray you, by your leave,
How doth the Prince and my young son of York?
BRACKENBURY
Right well, dear madam. By your patience,
I may not suffer you to visit them;                                16
The King hath strictly charged the contrary.
QUEEN ELIZABETH
The King! Who's that?
BRACKENBURY                        I mean the Lord Protector.
QUEEN ELIZABETH
The Lord protect him from that kingly title!
Hath he set bounds between their love and me?                     20
I am their mother; who shall bar me from them?
DUCHESS
I am their father's mother; I will see them.
ANNE
Their aunt I am in law, in love their mother;
Then bring me to their sights. I'll bear thy blame
And take thy office from thee, on my peril.                       25
BRACKENBURY
No, madam, no; I may not leave it so.
I am bound by oath, and therefore pardon me.
                                          *Exit Lieutenant.*

*Enter [Lord] Stanley [Earl of Derby].*

STANLEY
Let me but meet you, ladies, one hour hence,
And I'll salute Your Grace of York as mother,                     29
And reverend looker-on, of two fair queens.                       30
[*To Anne*] Come, madam, you must straight to
    Westminster,
There to be crownèd Richard's royal queen.
QUEEN ELIZABETH    Ah, cut my lace asunder,                        33
That my pent heart may have some scope to beat,
Or else I swoon with this dead-killing news!
ANNE
Despiteful tidings! Oh, unpleasing news!
DORSET
Be of good cheer. Mother, how fares Your Grace?
QUEEN ELIZABETH
Oh, Dorset, speak not to me. Get thee gone!
Death and destruction dogs thee at thy heels;
Thy mother's name is ominous to children.
If thou wilt outstrip death, go cross the seas

And live with Richmond, from the reach of hell.                   42
Go, hie thee, hie thee from this slaughterhouse,                  43
Lest thou increase the number of the dead
And make me die the thrall of Margaret's curse,                   45
Nor mother, wife, nor England's counted queen.                    46
STANLEY
Full of wise care is this your counsel, madam.
[*To Dorset*] Take all the swift advantage of the hours.
You shall have letters from me to my son                          49
In your behalf, to meet you on the way.                           50
Be not ta'en tardy by unwise delay.                               51
DUCHESS
Oh, ill-dispersing wind of misery!                                52
Oh, my accursèd womb, the bed of death!
A cockatrice hast thou hatched to the world,                      54
Whose unavoided eye is murderous.                                 55
STANLEY [*to Anne*]
Come, madam, come. I in all haste was sent.
ANNE
And I with all unwillingness will go.
Oh, would to God that the inclusive verge                         58
Of golden metal that must round my brow
Were red-hot steel, to sear me to the brains!
Anointed let me be with deadly venom                              61
And die ere men can say, "God save the Queen!"
QUEEN ELIZABETH
Go, go, poor soul. I envy not thy glory.
To feed my humor, wish thyself no harm.                           64
ANNE
No? Why? When he that is my husband now
Came to me, as I followed Henry's corpse,
When scarce the blood was well washed from his hands
Which issued from my other angel husband                          68
And that dear saint which then I weeping followed—                69
Oh, when, I say, I looked on Richard's face,
This was my wish: "Be thou," quoth I, "accurst
For making me, so young, so old a widow!                          72
And, when thou wed'st, let sorrow haunt thy bed;                  73
And be thy wife—if any be so mad—                                 74
More miserable by the life of thee                                75
Than thou hast made me by my dear lord's death!"                  76
Lo, ere I can repeat this curse again,
Within so small a time, my woman's heart
Grossly grew captive to his honey words                           79
And proved the subject of mine own soul's curse,

42 **with Richmond** i.e., with Henry Tudor, Earl of Richmond, at this
time in Brittany   43 **hie** hasten   45 **thrall** subject, victim.   **Margaret's
curse** (See 1.3.202-9.)   46 **Nor** neither.   **counted** accepted, esteemed
49–50 **You . . . way** i.e., I will arrange to have a letter catch up with
you on your journey, recommending you to my stepson, the Earl
of Richmond. (Lord Stanley's own son, George Stanley, may also
be involved in this rapid negotiation; see 4.4.494-6 ff. below.)
51 **ta'en** taken, caught   52 **ill-dispersing** evil-spreading   54 **cockatrice**
basilisk. (See the note for 1.2.153.)   55 **unavoided** unavoidable
58 **inclusive verge** enclosing circle, i.e., the crown, here likened to
an instrument of torture used to punish regicides or other criminals
61 **Anointed** (Anne desires to be anointed with poison rather than
with holy oil, as in the ceremony of coronation.)   64 **To . . . harm**
Do not curse yourself (or, possibly, I do not wish you harm) just to
satisfy my vengeful mood.   68 **angel husband** Edward, son of Henry
VI   69 **saint** Henry VI   72 **so old a widow** i.e., prematurely old as a
widow.   73–6 **And . . . death!"** (For Anne's cursing herself, see
1.2.26–8.)   79 **Grossly** stupidly

9 **like devotion** same devout errand   10 **gratulate** greet, salute
16 **suffer** permit   20 **bounds** barriers   25 **take . . . thee** i.e., relieve
you of the responsibility   29 **mother** i.e., mother-in-law (of Elizabeth
as widow of Edward and of Anne as wife of King Richard)
30 **looker-on** beholder.   **two fair queens** i.e., Elizabeth and Anne,
since Anne's husband, Richard, is about to be crowned.   33 **lace** cord
used to lace the bodice

Which hitherto hath held mine eyes from rest;                        81
For never yet one hour in his bed
Did I enjoy the golden dew of sleep,
But with his timorous dreams was still awaked.                       84
Besides, he hates me for my father Warwick,                          85
And will, no doubt, shortly be rid of me.

QUEEN ELIZABETH
Poor heart, adieu! I pity thy complaining.

ANNE
No more than with my soul I mourn for yours.

DORSET
Farewell, thou woeful welcomer of glory!                             89

ANNE
Adieu, poor soul, that tak'st thy leave of it!                       90

DUCHESS [to Dorset]
Go thou to Richmond, and good fortune guide thee!
[To Anne] Go thou to Richard, and good angels tend thee!
[To Queen Elizabeth] Go thou to sanctuary, and good
    thoughts possess thee!
I to my grave, where peace and rest lie with me!
Eighty-odd years of sorrow have I seen,
And each hour's joy wracked with a week of teen.                     96
                                              [They start to go.]

QUEEN ELIZABETH
Stay, yet look back with me unto the Tower.
Pity, you ancient stones, those tender babes
Whom envy hath immured within your walls—                            99
Rough cradle for such little pretty ones!
Rude ragged nurse, old sullen playfellow                             101
For tender princes, use my babies well!
So foolish sorrows bids your stones farewell.   Exeunt.

## 4.2

*Sound a sennet. Enter Richard, in pomp;
Buckingham, Catesby, Ratcliffe, Lovell, [a Page,
and others].*

KING RICHARD
Stand all apart. Cousin of Buckingham!                               1
                [The others stand aside, out of earshot.]

BUCKINGHAM    My gracious sovereign?

KING RICHARD
Give me thy hand.
                *Sound [trumpets. Here he ascends the throne.]*
                      Thus high, by thy advice
And thy assistance, is King Richard seated.
But shall we wear these glories for a day?
Or shall they last, and we rejoice in them?

BUCKINGHAM
Still live they, and forever let them last!

KING RICHARD
Ah, Buckingham, now do I play the touch,                             8
To try if thou be current gold indeed:                               9
Young Edward lives. Think now what I would speak.

BUCKINGHAM    Say on, my loving lord.

KING RICHARD
Why, Buckingham, I say I would be king.

BUCKINGHAM
Why, so you are, my thrice-renownèd lord.

KING RICHARD
Ha! Am I king? 'Tis so. But Edward lives.

BUCKINGHAM
True, noble prince.

KING RICHARD            Oh, bitter consequence,                       15
That Edward still should live "true, noble prince"!                  16
Cousin, thou wast not wont to be so dull.                            17
Shall I be plain? I wish the bastards dead,
And I would have it suddenly performed.                              19
What say'st thou now? Speak suddenly; be brief.

BUCKINGHAM    Your Grace may do your pleasure.

KING RICHARD
Tut, tut, thou art all ice; thy kindness freezes.
Say, have I thy consent that they shall die?

BUCKINGHAM
Give me some little breath, some pause, dear lord,
Before I positively speak in this.
I will resolve you herein presently.    *Exit Buckingham.*           26

CATESBY [to those standing aside]
The King is angry. See, he gnaws his lip.

KING RICHARD [aside]
I will converse with iron-witted fools                               28
And unrespective boys. None are for me                               29
That look into me with considerate eyes.                             30
High-reaching Buckingham grows circumspect.—                         31
Boy!

PAGE [approaching]    My lord?

KING RICHARD
Know'st thou not any whom corrupting gold
Will tempt unto a close exploit of death?                            35

PAGE
My lord, I know a discontented gentleman
Whose humble means match not his haughty spirit.                     37
Gold were as good as twenty orators,
And will, no doubt, tempt him to anything.

KING RICHARD
What is his name?

PAGE                      His name, my lord, is Tyrrel.

KING RICHARD
I partly know the man. Go call him hither, boy.
                                              *Exit [Page].*

---

81 **hitherto** until now   84 **timorous** full of fears.   **still** continually
85 **Warwick** the Earl of Warwick, a Lancastrian leader in *3 Henry VI*
89 **glory** i.e., the rank of queen—*woeful* because it involves marriage
to Richard.   90 **poor . . . of it** Queen Elizabeth, who wretchedly
bids farewell to her authority as queen.   96 **wracked** destroyed, or,
*racked*, tortured.   **teen** woe.   99 **envy** malice.   **immured** walled up
101 **Rude** Rough
**4.2. Location:** London. The royal court.
1 **apart** aside.

8 **play the touch** play the part of a touchstone (to test the quality of
gold)   9 **current** sterling, genuine   15 **bitter consequence** i.e., intolerable answer to my words, and an intolerable fact   16 **"true, noble
prince"** (Richard mockingly repeats Buckingham's evasive reply in
line 15 and applies it to the irritating fact that young Edward still
lives and is a noble prince.)   17 **wast not wont** used not   19 **suddenly** swiftly   26 **resolve** answer   28–31 **I will . . . circumspect** i.e.,
Apparently I have no choice but to communicate my intentions to
dim-witted fools and inattentive boys. I will have nothing more to do
with men who look into my thoughts too searchingly. Ambitious
Buckingham grows wary.   35 **close** secret   37 **humble means**
meager source of livelihood

[*Aside*] The deep-revolving, witty Buckingham 42
No more shall be the neighbor to my counsels.
Hath he so long held out with me untired,
And stops he now for breath? Well, be it so.

*Enter [Lord] Stanley [Earl of Derby].*

How now, Lord Stanley? What's the news?
STANLEY    Know, my loving lord,
The Marquess Dorset, as I hear, is fled
To Richmond, in the parts where he abides. 49
[*He stands apart.*]
KING RICHARD
Come hither, Catesby. Rumor it abroad
That Anne my wife is very grievous sick;
I will take order for her keeping close. 52
Inquire me out some mean poor gentleman, 53
Whom I will marry straight to Clarence' daughter.
The boy is foolish, and I fear not him. 55
Look how thou dream'st! I say again, give out
That Anne my queen is sick and like to die. 57
About it, for it stands me much upon 58
To stop all hopes whose growth may damage me. 59
[*Exit Catesby.*]
I must be married to my brother's daughter, 60
Or else my kingdom stands on brittle glass.
Murder her brothers, and then marry her—
Uncertain way of gain! But I am in
So far in blood that sin will pluck on sin. 64
Tear-falling pity dwells not in this eye. 65

*Enter [Page, with] Tyrrel.*

Is thy name Tyrrel?
TYRREL
James Tyrrel, and your most obedient subject.
KING RICHARD
Art thou, indeed?
TYRREL                        Prove me, my gracious lord. 68
KING RICHARD
Dar'st thou resolve to kill a friend of mine?
TYRREL    Please you; 70
But I had rather kill two enemies.
KING RICHARD
Why, there thou hast it: two deep enemies,
Foes to my rest and my sweet sleep's disturbers
Are they that I would have thee deal upon— 74
Tyrrel, I mean those bastards in the Tower.
TYRREL
Let me have open means to come to them, 76
And soon I'll rid you from the fear of them.

KING RICHARD
Thou sing'st sweet music. Hark, come hither, Tyrrel.
Go, by this token. [*He gives him a token.*] Rise, and lend
thine ear.                        *Whispers.*
There is no more but so. Say it is done,
And I will love thee and prefer thee for it. 81
TYRREL    I will dispatch it straight.        *Exit.*

*Enter Buckingham.*

BUCKINGHAM
My lord, I have considered in my mind
The late request that you did sound me in. 84
KING RICHARD
Well, let that rest. Dorset is fled to Richmond.
BUCKINGHAM    I hear the news, my lord.
KING RICHARD
Stanley, he is your wife's son. Well, look to it. 87
BUCKINGHAM
My lord, I claim the gift, my due by promise,
For which your honor and your faith is pawned: 89
Th'earldom of Hereford and the movables 90
Which you have promisèd I shall possess.
KING RICHARD
Stanley, look to your wife. If she convey
Letters to Richmond, you shall answer it. 93
BUCKINGHAM
What says Your Highness to my just request?
KING RICHARD
I do remember me, Henry the Sixth
Did prophesy that Richmond should be king,
When Richmond was a little peevish boy.
A king! Perhaps, perhaps—
BUCKINGHAM    My lord!
KING RICHARD
How chance the prophet could not at that time 100
Have told me, I being by, that I should kill him? 101
BUCKINGHAM
My lord, your promise for the earldom!
KING RICHARD
Richmond! When last I was at Exeter,
The Mayor in courtesy showed me the castle
And called it Rougemont, at which name I started, 105
Because a bard of Ireland told me once
I should not live long after I saw Richmond.
BUCKINGHAM    My lord!
KING RICHARD    Ay, what's o'clock? 109
BUCKINGHAM
I am thus bold to put Your Grace in mind
Of what you promised me.
KING RICHARD    Well, but what's o'clock?
BUCKINGHAM    Upon the stroke of ten.
KING RICHARD    Well, let it strike.
BUCKINGHAM    Why let it strike?

42 **deep-revolving** deeply scheming.  **witty** cunning  49 **in . . . abides** in the part of England where he dwells. (Richmond is now in the westerly part of greater London, upstream on the River Thames.) 52 **I will . . . close** I will give orders for her close confinement. 53 **mean** of humble station  55 **boy** i.e., Clarence's eldest son, Edward Plantagenet, Earl of Warwick  57 **like** likely  58 **stands . . . upon** is a matter of the utmost importance to me  59 **To . . . me** i.e., to cut off all potential claimants to the throne, who might challenge my claim in time.  60 **brother's daughter** i.e., Elizabeth of York, daughter to Edward IV, who will, in fact, later become the queen of Henry VII; see 4.5.7–9 and 5.5.29–31  64 **pluck on** draw on  65 **Tear-falling** Tear-dropping  68 **Prove** Test  70 **Please** If it please  74 **deal upon** proceed against  76 **open** unhampered

81 **prefer** promote, advance  84 **late** recent.  **sound me in** ask me about.  87 **he** i.e., Richmond  89 **pawned** pledged  90 **movables** personal property; see 3.1.194–5, where Richard has made this promise.  93 **answer it** pay for it.  100 **the prophet** i.e., Henry VI  101 **by** nearby.  **him** (The word applies to Richmond and Henry VI.)  105 **Rougemont** i.e., Red Hill. (With a play on "Richmond.")  109 **what's o'clock?** what time is it?

KING RICHARD
    Because that, like a jack, thou keep'st the stroke     116
    Betwixt thy begging and my meditation.
    I am not in the giving vein today.     118
BUCKINGHAM
    May it please you to resolve me in my suit.     119
KING RICHARD
    Thou troublest me. I am not in the vein.
                              *Exit [with all but Buckingham].*
BUCKINGHAM
    And is it thus? Repays he my deep service
    With such contempt? Made I him king for this?
    Oh, let me think on Hastings, and be gone
    To Brecknock, while my fearful head is on!     *Exit.* 124

                              ❧

## [4.3]

                    *Enter Tyrrel.*

TYRREL
    The tyrannous and bloody act is done,
    The most arch deed of piteous massacre     2
    That ever yet this land was guilty of.
    Dighton and Forrest, whom I did suborn     4
    To do this piece of ruthless butchery,
    Albeit they were fleshed villains, bloody dogs,     6
    Melted with tenderness and mild compassion,
    Wept like to children in their deaths' sad story.     8
    "Oh, thus," quoth Dighton, "lay the gentle babes."
    "Thus, thus," quoth Forrest, "girdling one another
    Within their alabaster innocent arms.     11
    Their lips were four red roses on a stalk,
    Which in their summer beauty kissed each other.     13
    A book of prayers on their pillow lay,
    Which once," quoth Forrest, "almost changed my mind;
    But oh, the devil!"—there the villain stopped;
    When Dighton thus told on: "We smotherèd
    The most replenishèd sweet work of Nature     18
    That from the prime creation e'er she framed."     19
    Hence both are gone; with conscience and remorse     20
    They could not speak; and so I left them both,
    To bear this tidings to the bloody king.

                    *Enter [King] Richard.*

    And here he comes.—All health, my sovereign lord!
KING RICHARD
    Kind Tyrrel, am I happy in thy news?

TYRREL
    If to have done the thing you gave in charge     25
    Beget your happiness, be happy then,
    For it is done.
KING RICHARD     But didst thou see them dead?
TYRREL
    I did, my lord.
KING RICHARD     And buried, gentle Tyrrel?
TYRREL
    The chaplain of the Tower hath buried them;
    But where, to say the truth, I do not know.
KING RICHARD
    Come to me, Tyrrel, soon at after-supper,     31
    When thou shalt tell the process of their death.     32
    Meantime, but think how I may do thee good,
    And be inheritor of thy desire.     34
    Farewell till then.
TYRREL                    I humbly take my leave.     [*Exit.*]
KING RICHARD
    The son of Clarence have I pent up close,     36
    His daughter meanly have I matched in marriage,     37
    The sons of Edward sleep in Abraham's bosom,     38
    And Anne my wife hath bid this world good night.
    Now, for I know the Breton Richmond aims     40
    At young Elizabeth, my brother's daughter,     41
    And by that knot looks proudly on the crown,     42
    To her go I, a jolly thriving wooer.

                    *Enter Ratcliffe.*

RATCLIFFE    My lord!
KING RICHARD
    Good or bad news, that thou com'st in so bluntly?
RATCLIFFE
    Bad news, my lord. Morton is fled to Richmond,     46
    And Buckingham, backed with the hardy Welshmen,     47
    Is in the field, and still his power increaseth.     48
KING RICHARD
    Ely with Richmond troubles me more near     49
    Than Buckingham and his rash-levied strength.     50
    Come, I have learned that fearful commenting     51
    Is leaden servitor to dull delay;     52
    Delay leads impotent and snail-paced beggary.     53
    Then fiery expedition be my wing,     54
    Jove's Mercury, and herald for a king!     55

---

116 **jack** the figure of a man that strikes the bell on the outside of a clock. (With a play on the meaning "lowbred fellow." Richard's complaint is that Buckingham, like the jack of a clock, being on the point of striking the hour—i.e., speaking his request—breaks the continuity of Richard's reflections.)   118 **vein** mood   119 **resolve me** give me a final answer   124 **Brecknock** i.e., Brecon, Buckingham's family seat in Wales.   **fearful** full of fears
**4.3. Location:** London. The royal court.
2 **arch deed** i.e., chief or notorious act   4 **suborn** bribe or otherwise induce a person to commit a crime   6 **fleshed** experienced in bloodshed   8 **in their . . . story** in telling the story of the childrens' deaths   11 **alabaster** i.e., white and marble-like, as in statues or ornaments   13 **summer beauty** the beauty of youth   18 **replenishèd** complete, perfect   19 **prime** first   20 **both are gone** Dighton and Forrest have fled

25 **gave in charge** ordered, commanded   31 **after-supper** dessert after supper   32 **process** story   34 **be . . . desire** expect to get what you ask.   36 **pent up close** strictly confined   37 **His . . . marriage** (Margaret Plantagenet was about twelve years old when Richard died. Shakespeare may have confused her with Lady Cicely, a daughter of Edward IV, whom Richard, according to Holinshed, intended to marry to "a man found in a cloud, and of an unknown lineage and family.")   38 **in Abraham's bosom** i.e., in heaven. (See Luke 16.22.)   40 **for** because.   **Breton** currently located in Brittany   41 **my brother's** Edward's   42 **by that knot** by virtue of that alliance   46 **Morton** i.e., John Morton, Bishop of Ely, who had been kept prisoner at Brecknock (or Brecon) Castle; he is the Ely of 3.4   47 **the hardy Welshmen** i.e., the men of Brecknock, Buckingham's family seat, in Wales; see 4. 2.124 and note   48 **power** army   49 **near** deeply   50 **rash-levied** hastily recruited   51–2 **fearful . . . delay** timorous talk serves the purposes of sluggish delay   53 **leads** leads to.   **beggary** ruin.   54 **expedition** speed   55 **Mercury** messenger of the gods

Go muster men. My counsel is my shield;    56
We must be brief when traitors brave the field.    57

*Exeunt.*

❖

# [4.4]

*Enter old Queen Margaret.*

QUEEN MARGARET
So now prosperity begins to mellow    1
And drop into the rotten mouth of death.
Here in these confines slyly have I lurked    3
To watch the waning of mine enemies.
A dire induction am I witness to,    5
And will to France, hoping the consequence    6
Will prove as bitter, black, and tragical.
Withdraw thee, wretched Margaret. Who comes here?
    *[She steps aside.]*

*Enter Duchess [of York] and Queen [Elizabeth].*

QUEEN ELIZABETH
Ah, my poor princes! Ah, my tender babes!
My unblown flowers, new-appearing sweets!    10
If yet your gentle souls fly in the air
And be not fixed in doom perpetual,    12
Hover about me with your airy wings
And hear your mother's lamentation!

QUEEN MARGARET *[aside]*
Hover about her; say that right for right    15
Hath dimmed your infant morn to agèd night.    16

DUCHESS
So many miseries have crazed my voice    17
That my woe-wearied tongue is still and mute.
Edward Plantagenet, why art thou dead?    19

QUEEN MARGARET *[aside]*
Plantagenet doth quit Plantagenet.    20
Edward for Edward pays a dying debt.    21

QUEEN ELIZABETH
Wilt thou, O God, fly from such gentle lambs    22
And throw them in the entrails of the wolf?
When didst thou sleep when such a deed was done?    24

QUEEN MARGARET *[aside]*
When holy Harry died, and my sweet son.    25

DUCHESS
Dead life, blind sight, poor mortal-living ghost,    26

Woe's scene, world's shame, grave's due by life usurped,    27
Brief abstract and record of tedious days,    28
Rest thy unrest on England's lawful earth,    29
    *[sitting down]*
Unlawfully made drunk with innocent blood!    30

QUEEN ELIZABETH
Ah, that thou wouldst as soon afford a grave    31
As thou canst yield a melancholy seat!
Then would I hide my bones, not rest them here.
Ah, who hath any cause to mourn but we?
    *[Sitting down by her.]*

QUEEN MARGARET *[coming forward]*
If ancient sorrow be most reverend,    35
Give mine the benefit of seniory    36
And let my griefs frown on the upper hand.    37
If sorrow can admit society,    *[sitting down with them]*
Tell o'er your woes again by viewing mine:
I had an Edward, till a Richard killed him;    40
I had a Harry, till a Richard killed him:    41
Thou hadst an Edward, till a Richard killed him;    42
Thou hadst a Richard, till a Richard killed him.    43

DUCHESS
I had a Richard too, and thou didst kill him;    44
I had a Rutland too, thou holp'st to kill him.    45

QUEEN MARGARET
Thou hadst a Clarence too, and Richard killed him.    46
From forth the kennel of thy womb hath crept
A hellhound that doth hunt us all to death.
That dog, that had his teeth before his eyes    49
To worry lambs and lap their gentle blood,    50
That foul defacer of God's handiwork,
That excellent grand tyrant of the earth,    52
That reigns in gallèd eyes of weeping souls,    53
Thy womb let loose, to chase us to our graves.
O upright, just, and true-disposing God,
How do I thank thee that this carnal cur    56
Preys on the issue of his mother's body    57
And makes her pew-fellow with others' moan!    58

DUCHESS
O Harry's wife, triumph not in my woes!
God witness with me, I have wept for thine.

QUEEN MARGARET
Bear with me. I am hungry for revenge,
And now I cloy me with beholding it.    62

---

**56 My . . . shield** i.e., I will take counsel by arming myself and trust no adviser other than my own weapons    **57 brave** challenge
**4.4. Location:** London. Near the royal court.
**1 mellow** mature    **3 Here . . . confines** here where I am.    **slyly** stealthily
**5 induction** prologue (as to a play)    **6 will** will go.    **the consequence** what follows, the sequel and conclusion (as in a play)    **10 unblown** unopened.    **sweets** flowers.    **12 fixed . . . perpetual** confined to the eternal destiny of your souls    **15 right for right** i.e., a just punishment for an offense against justice    **16 dimmed . . . night** i.e., brought the youthful promise of your children to ruin and death.    **17 crazed** cracked
**19 Edward Plantagenet** the Duchess's son, the dead King Edward IV; or, his son Edward V    **20 quit** requite    **21 Edward for . . . debt** Edward V, the young son of Edward IV and Elizabeth, as requital for Edward, son of Henry VI and Margaret.    **dying debt** debt paid through death.
**22 fly . . . lambs** i.e., abandon my two sons    **24 When** i.e., Whenever till now    **25 holy Harry** i.e., Henry VI.    **my sweet son** Edward Prince of Wales, son of Henry VI and Margaret.    **26 Dead . . . ghost** (The Duchess laments her own sad condition as one whose life is a living death, whose eyes cannot see, and who is thus a ghost among the living.)

**27 Woe's . . . usurped** (The Duchess continues her litany of grief: she is the embodiment of woe, is shamed by the world, and whose continued wretched existence merely deprives the grave of its due.)
**28 Brief . . . days** (Hers is the sad epitome and chronicle of a tedious life.)    **29 Rest thy unrest** rest your restless body and soul
**30 Unlawfully . . . blood** (England's earth, not the Duchess herself, is unlawfully made thus drunk with innocent blood.)    **31 that thou** would that you, England's earth    **35 reverend** worthy of respect
**36 seniory** seniority of age    **37 on . . . hand** i.e., from a place of precedence.    **40 Edward** i.e., my son, the former Prince of Wales
**41 Harry** i.e., my husband, King Henry VI    **42 Thou** i.e., Queen Elizabeth.    **Edward** i.e., Edward V    **43 Thou . . . Richard** You, Queen Elizabeth, had a son, the young Duke of York    **44 Richard** i.e., Duke of York, the Duchess's husband and father of Richard III, killed by Margaret's army at the Battle of Wakefield in 1460    **45 Rutland** i.e., Edmund, son of the Duke of York, also killed at Wakefield
**46 Clarence** Duke of Clarence    **49 teeth** (Richard was supposedly born with teeth.)    **50 worry** bite on the throat, tear to pieces.    **lap** drink, lap up    **52 excellent** unparalleled    **53 gallèd** sore with weeping    **56 carnal** flesh-eating    **57 issue** offspring    **58 pew-fellow** i.e., fellow sufferer    **62 cloy me** gorge myself

Thy Edward he is dead that killed my Edward;    63
Thy other Edward dead, to quit my Edward;    64
Young York he is but boot, because both they    65
Matched not the high perfection of my loss.
Thy Clarence he is dead that stabbed my Edward;
And the beholders of this frantic play,    68
Th'adulterate Hastings, Rivers, Vaughan, Grey,    69
Untimely smothered in their dusky graves.    70
Richard yet lives, hell's black intelligencer,    71
Only reserved their factor to buy souls    72
And send them thither; but at hand, at hand    73
Ensues his piteous and unpitied end.    74
Earth gapes, hell burns, fiends roar, saints pray,
To have him suddenly conveyed from hence.
Cancel his bond of life, dear God, I pray,
That I may live and say, "The dog is dead!"

QUEEN ELIZABETH
Oh, thou didst prophesy the time would come
That I should wish for thee to help me curse
That bottled spider, that foul bunch-backed toad!    81

QUEEN MARGARET
I called thee then vain flourish of my fortune;    82
I called thee then poor shadow, painted queen,
The presentation of but what I was,    84
The flattering index of a direful pageant,    85
One heaved a-high to be hurled down below,
A mother only mocked with two fair babes,    87
A dream of what thou wast, a garish flag    88
To be the aim of every dangerous shot;    89
A sign of dignity, a breath, a bubble,    90
A queen in jest, only to fill the scene.
Where is thy husband now? Where be thy brothers?
Where be thy two sons? Wherein dost thou joy?
Who sues and kneels and says, "God save the Queen"?
Where be the bending peers that flattered thee?    95
Where be the thronging troops that followed thee?    96
Decline all this, and see what now thou art:    97
For happy wife, a most distressèd widow;
For joyful mother, one that wails the name;
For one being sued to, one that humbly sues;
For queen, a very caitiff crowned with care;    101
For she that scorned at me, now scorned of me;    102
For she being feared of all, now fearing one;    103
For she commanding all, obeyed of none.
Thus hath the course of justice whirled about

And left thee but a very prey to time,    106
Having no more but thought of what thou wast    107
To torture thee the more, being what thou art.
Thou didst usurp my place, and dost thou not
Usurp the just proportion of my sorrow?    110
Now thy proud neck bears half my burdened yoke,    111
From which even here I slip my weary head
And leave the burden of it all on thee.
Farewell, York's wife, and queen of sad mischance!
These English woes shall make me smile in France.
     [*She starts to leave.*]

QUEEN ELIZABETH
O thou well skilled in curses, stay awhile,
And teach me how to curse mine enemies!

QUEEN MARGARET
Forbear to sleep the nights, and fast the days;
Compare dead happiness with living woe;
Think that thy babes were sweeter than they were
And he that slew them fouler than he is.
Bett'ring thy loss makes the bad causer worse;    122
Revolving this will teach thee how to curse.    123

QUEEN ELIZABETH
My words are dull. Oh, quicken them with thine!    124

QUEEN MARGARET
Thy woes will make them sharp, and pierce like mine.
     *Exit Margaret.*

DUCHESS
Why should calamity be full of words?

QUEEN ELIZABETH
Windy attorneys to their client's woes,    127
Airy succeeders of intestate joys,    128
Poor breathing orators of miseries,    129
Let them have scope! Though what they will impart
Help nothing else, yet do they ease the heart.

DUCHESS
If so, then be not tongue-tied. Go with me,
And in the breath of bitter words let's smother
My damnèd son that thy two sweet sons smothered.
     [*Sound trumpet.*]
The trumpet sounds. Be copious in exclaims.    135

     *Enter King Richard and his train [marching, with drums and trumpets].*

KING RICHARD
Who intercepts me in my expedition?    136

DUCHESS
Oh, she that might have intercepted thee,
By strangling thee in her accursèd womb,
From all the slaughters, wretch, that thou hast done!

QUEEN ELIZABETH
Hid'st thou that forehead with a golden crown
Where should be branded, if that right were right,

---

**63 Thy Edward** Edward IV.   **my Edward** the son of Henry VI **64 other Edward** Edward V.   **to quit my Edward** to answer for the killing of my son. (Margaret claims two Yorkist deaths to compensate for the death of her son, as she explains in lines 65–6.)   **65 Young York** Richard, Duke of York, the younger of the princes murdered in the Tower.   **but boot** merely into the bargain   **68 frantic** frenzied, insane **69 Th'adulterate** the adulterous   **70 smothered** buried   **71 intelligencer** agent, go-between, spy   **72 Only ... factor** chosen above all others as their (hell's) agent, and sent to earth for no other purpose   **73 thither** to their graves   **74 his piteous** Richard's deplorable   **81 bottled** bottle-shaped, swollen (as at 1.3.242).   **bunch-backed** hunchbacked   **82 flourish** mere ornament, embellishment. (See 1.3.241.)   **84 presentation** representation, semblance   **85 index** argument, preface, prologue. **pageant** spectacular entertainment   **87 only ... babes** given two lovely babies only to be mocked by painful destiny when they are destroyed   **88–9 garish ... shot** i.e., standard-bearer, conspicuous in appearance, and thus the target of enemy fire   **90 sign** mere token **95 bending** bowing   **96 troops** supporters, followers   **97 Decline** Go through in order. (A grammatical metaphor.)   **101 caitiff** wretch, slave   **102 of** by. (Also in lines 103 and 104.)   **103 one** i.e., Richard

**106 very** utter   **107 no ... thought** only the memory   **110 the just proportion** the equal quantity   **111 burdened** burdensome **122 Bett'ring** Magnifying   **123 Revolving** meditating on **124 quicken** put life into   **127 Windy ... woes** i.e., Words, which are airy pleaders on behalf of one who is suffering   **128 Airy ... joys** insubstantial words, all that is left of joys that died unfulfilled. (Literally, having died without anything to bequeath.)   **129 breathing** speaking   **135 exclaims** exclamations.   **136 expedition** (1) haste (2) military undertaking.

The slaughter of the prince that owed that crown  142
And the dire death of my poor sons and brothers?
Tell me, thou villain slave, where are my children?

**DUCHESS**
Thou toad, thou toad, where is thy brother Clarence?
And little Ned Plantagenet, his son?  146

**QUEEN ELIZABETH**
Where is the gentle Rivers, Vaughan, Grey?

**DUCHESS**  Where is kind Hastings?

**KING RICHARD**
A flourish, trumpets! Strike alarum, drums!  149
Let not the heavens hear these telltale women  150
Rail on the Lord's anointed. Strike, I say!
                    *Flourish. Alarums.*
Either be patient and entreat me fair,  152
Or with the clamorous report of war  153
Thus will I drown your exclamations.

**DUCHESS**  Art thou my son?

**KING RICHARD**
Ay, I thank God, my father, and yourself.

**DUCHESS**
Then patiently hear my impatience.

**KING RICHARD**
Madam, I have a touch of your condition,  158
That cannot brook the accent of reproof.  159

**DUCHESS**
Oh, let me speak!

**KING RICHARD**      Do then, but I'll not hear.

**DUCHESS**
I will be mild and gentle in my words.

**KING RICHARD**
And brief, good mother, for I am in haste.

**DUCHESS**
Art thou so hasty? I have stayed for thee,  163
God knows, in torment and in agony.  164

**KING RICHARD**
And came I not at last to comfort you?

**DUCHESS**
No, by the Holy Rood, thou know'st it well,  166
Thou cam'st on earth to make the earth my hell.
A grievous burden was thy birth to me;
Tetchy and wayward was thy infancy;  169
Thy schooldays frightful, desp'rate, wild, and furious;
Thy prime of manhood daring, bold, and venturous;
Thy age confirmed, proud, subtle, sly, and bloody,  172
More mild, but yet more harmful—kind in hatred.  173
What comfortable hour canst thou name
That ever graced me with thy company?

**KING RICHARD**
Faith, none, but Humphrey Hour, that called Your Grace  176

To breakfast once forth of my company.  177
If I be so disgracious in your eye,  178
Let me march on and not offend you, madam.—
Strike up the drum.

**DUCHESS**      I prithee, hear me speak.

**KING RICHARD**
You speak too bitterly.

**DUCHESS**      Hear me a word,
For I shall never speak to thee again.

**KING RICHARD**  So.

**DUCHESS**
Either thou wilt die by God's just ordinance
Ere from this war thou turn a conqueror,  185
Or I with grief and extreme age shall perish
And nevermore behold thy face again.
Therefore take with thee my most grievous curse,
Which in the day of battle tire thee more
Than all the complete armor that thou wear'st!
My prayers on the adverse party fight,  191
And there the little souls of Edward's children
Whisper the spirits of thine enemies  193
And promise them success and victory!
Bloody thou art, bloody will be thy end;
Shame serves thy life and doth thy death attend.  196
                    *Exit.*

**QUEEN ELIZABETH**
Though far more cause, yet much less spirit to curse
Abides in me; I say amen to her.

**KING RICHARD**
Stay, madam. I must talk a word with you.

**QUEEN ELIZABETH**
I have no more sons of the royal blood
For thee to slaughter. For my daughters, Richard,  201
They shall be praying nuns, not weeping queens,  202
And therefore level not to hit their lives.  203

**KING RICHARD**
You have a daughter called Elizabeth,
Virtuous and fair, royal and gracious.

**QUEEN ELIZABETH**
And must she die for this? Oh, let her live,
And I'll corrupt her manners, stain her beauty,  207
Slander myself as false to Edward's bed,
Throw over her the veil of infamy;
So she may live unscarred of bleeding slaughter,  210
I will confess she was not Edward's daughter.

**KING RICHARD**
Wrong not her birth. She is a royal princess.

**QUEEN ELIZABETH**
To save her life, I'll say she is not so.

**KING RICHARD**
Her life is safest only in her birth.  214

**QUEEN ELIZABETH**
And only in that safety died her brothers.

---

142 **owed** owned   146 **Ned Plantagenet** (See 4.3.36.)   **149 flourish** fanfare.   **alarum** call to arms   150 **telltale** tattling, gabbling   152 **entreat me fair** treat me with courtesy   153 **report** noise   158 **condition** disposition   159 **brook** tolerate   163 **stayed** waited   164 **in agony** i.e., in childbirth.   166 **Holy Rood** Christ's cross   169 **Tetchy** fretful, peevish   172 **age confirmed** riper manhood   173 **kind in hatred** concealing hatred under pretense of kindness.   176 **Humphrey Hour** (To "dine with Duke Humphrey" was to go hungry; hence, Richard flippantly suggests, he was saved from a spare breakfast. The passage is obscure.)

177 **forth of** away from   178 **disgracious** unpleasing, disliked   185 **turn** return   191 **party** side   193 **Whisper** whisper to   196 **serves** accompanies   201 **For my** As for my   202 **They . . . queens** i.e., I will put my daughters in a convent rather than expose them to the cruelties of life at court   203 **level** aim   207 **manners** morals   210 **So** provided.   **of** by   214 **Her . . . birth** Her best guarantee of personal safety is her high birth.

**KING RICHARD**
Lo, at their birth good stars were opposite.                                    216

**QUEEN ELIZABETH**
No, to their lives ill friends were contrary.                                   217

**KING RICHARD**
All unavoided is the doom of destiny.                                           218

**QUEEN ELIZABETH**
True, when avoided grace makes destiny.                                         219
My babes were destined to a fairer death,
If grace had blessed thee with a fairer life.

**KING RICHARD**
You speak as if that I had slain my cousins.                                    222

**QUEEN ELIZABETH**
Cousins, indeed, and by their uncle cozened                                     223
Of comfort, kingdom, kindred, freedom, life.
Whose hand soever lanced their tender hearts,                                   225
Thy head, all indirectly, gave direction.                                       226
No doubt the murd'rous knife was dull and blunt
Till it was whetted on thy stone-hard heart,
To revel in the entrails of my lambs.
But that still use of grief makes wild grief tame,                              230
My tongue should to thy ears not name my boys
Till that my nails were anchored in thine eyes;                                 232
And I, in such a desp'rate bay of death,                                        233
Like a poor bark of sails and tackling reft,                                    234
Rush all to pieces on thy rocky bosom.

**KING RICHARD**
Madam, so thrive I in my enterprise                                             236
And dangerous success of bloody wars                                            237
As I intend more good to you and yours                                          238
Than ever you or yours by me were harmed!                                       239

**QUEEN ELIZABETH**
What good is covered with the face of heaven,                                   240
To be discovered, that can do me good?

**KING RICHARD**
Th'advancement of your children, gentle lady.

**QUEEN ELIZABETH**
Up to some scaffold, there to lose their heads.

**KING RICHARD**
Unto the dignity and height of fortune,
The high imperial type of this earth's glory.                                   245

**QUEEN ELIZABETH**
Flatter my sorrow with report of it;
Tell me what state, what dignity, what honor,
Canst thou demise to any child of mine?                                         248

**KING RICHARD**
Even all I have—ay, and myself and all—
Will I withal endow a child of thine,
So in the Lethe of thy angry soul                                               251

Thou drown the sad remembrance of those wrongs
Which thou supposest I have done to thee.

**QUEEN ELIZABETH**
Be brief, lest that the process of thy kindness                                 254
Last longer telling than thy kindness' date.                                    255

**KING RICHARD**
Then know that from my soul I love thy daughter.                                256

**QUEEN ELIZABETH**
My daughter's mother thinks it with her soul.

**KING RICHARD**   What do you think?

**QUEEN ELIZABETH**
That thou dost love my daughter from thy soul.
So from thy soul's love didst thou love her brothers,                           260
And from my heart's love I do thank thee for it.                                261

**KING RICHARD**
Be not so hasty to confound my meaning.                                         262
I mean that with my soul I love thy daughter
And do intend to make her Queen of England.

**QUEEN ELIZABETH**
Well then, who dost thou mean shall be her king?

**KING RICHARD**
Even he that makes her queen. Who else should be?

**QUEEN ELIZABETH**
What, thou?

**KING RICHARD**   Even so. How think you of it?

**QUEEN ELIZABETH**
How canst thou woo her?

**KING RICHARD**                       That would I learn of you,
As one being best acquainted with her humor.                                    269

**QUEEN ELIZABETH**
And wilt thou learn of me?

**KING RICHARD**                       Madam, with all my heart.

**QUEEN ELIZABETH**
Send to her, by the man that slew her brothers,
A pair of bleeding hearts; thereon engrave
"Edward" and "York"; then haply will she weep.                                  273
Therefore present to her—as sometime Margaret                                   274
Did to thy father, steeped in Rutland's blood—
A handkerchief, which, say to her, did drain
The purple sap from her sweet brother's body;
And bid her wipe her weeping eyes withal.
If this inducement move her not to love,
Send her a letter of thy noble deeds.
Tell her thou mad'st away her uncle Clarence,
Her uncle Rivers, ay, and for her sake
Mad'st quick conveyance with her good aunt Anne.                                283

**KING RICHARD**
You mock me, madam. This is not the way
To win your daughter.

**QUEEN ELIZABETH**                       There is no other way,
Unless thou couldst put on some other shape
And not be Richard that hath done all this.

---

**216 opposite** hostile.   **217 contrary** opposed.   **218 unavoided** unavoidable   **219 avoided grace** i.e., Richard, in whom grace is void or lacking   **222 as if that** as if   **223 cozened** cheated. (With a bitter pun on *Cousins/cozened*.)   **225 Whose hand soever** Whoever it was whose hand   **226 all indirectly** by indirect means, and wrongly   **230 But . . . tame** Were it not that constant grieving exhausts the wildness of my grief   **232 Till that** until   **233 bay** (1) inlet (2) position of a hunted animal turning to face the hounds   **234 bark** sailing vessel. **reft** bereft   **236–9 so thrive . . . harmed!** i.e., may my success in war thrive only to the extent that I wish more good to you and your kindred than the harm you have suffered at my hands!   **240 covered with** hidden by (and therefore not yet revealed to humanity)   **245 imperial type** symbol of rule   **248 demise** convey   **251 Lethe** underworld river of forgetfulness

**254 process** story   **255 date** duration.   **256 from** from the very depths of (But Queen Elizabeth, in lines 259–61, sarcastically uses the word in the sense "apart from," "at variance with.")   **260–1 So . . . for it** (Queen Elizabeth bitterly interprets Richard's "from my soul" in line 256 to mean that Richard's love for Elizabeth must be just about as reassuring as the murderous love he bore for her two brothers.)   **262 confound** deliberately misconstrue   **269 humor** temperament.   **273 haply** perhaps   **274 sometime** once.   **Margaret** Queen Margaret, who killed the Yorkist Earl of Rutland, young brother of Richard, Edward IV, and Clarence, and then presented to their father, the Duke of York, a handkerchief stained with Rutland's blood. (See *3 Henry VI*, 1.4.79–83.)   **283 conveyance with** disposal of

KING RICHARD
Say that I did all this for love of her.
QUEEN ELIZABETH
Nay, then indeed she cannot choose but hate thee,
Having bought love with such a bloody spoil.                                    290
KING RICHARD
Look what is done cannot be now amended.                                        291
Men shall deal unadvisedly sometimes,                                           292
Which after-hours gives leisure to repent.
If I did take the kingdom from your sons,
To make amends I'll give it to your daughter.
If I have killed the issue of your womb,
To quicken your increase I will beget                                           297
Mine issue of your blood upon your daughter.
A grandam's name is little less in love
Than is the doting title of a mother;
They are as children but one step below,
Even of your metal, of your very blood,                                         302
Of all one pain, save for a night of groans                                     303
Endured of her for whom you bid like sorrow.                                    304
Your children were vexation to your youth,
But mine shall be a comfort to your age.
The loss you have is but a son being king,
And by that loss your daughter is made queen.
I cannot make you what amends I would;
Therefore accept such kindness as I can.                                        310
Dorset your son, that with a fearful soul
Leads discontented steps in foreign soil,
This fair alliance quickly shall call home
To high promotions and great dignity.
The king that calls your beauteous daughter wife
Familiarly shall call thy Dorset brother;                                       316
Again shall you be mother to a king,
And all the ruins of distressful times
Repaired with double riches of content.
What? We have many goodly days to see.
The liquid drops of tears that you have shed
Shall come again, transformed to orient pearl,                                  322
Advantaging their love with interest                                            323
Of ten times double gain of happiness.                                          324
Go then, my mother, to thy daughter go.
Make bold her bashful years with your experience;                              326
Prepare her ears to hear a wooer's tale;
Put in her tender heart th'aspiring flame                                       328
Of golden sovereignty; acquaint the Princess                                    329
With the sweet silent hours of marriage joys.
And when this arm of mine hath chastisèd
The petty rebel, dull-brained Buckingham,
Bound with triumphant garlands will I come
And lead thy daughter to a conqueror's bed;
To whom I will retail my conquest won,                                          335
And she shall be sole victoress, Caesar's Caesar.

QUEEN ELIZABETH
What were I best to say? Her father's brother
Would be her lord? Or shall I say her uncle?
Or, he that slew her brothers and her uncles?
Under what title shall I woo for thee
That God, the law, my honor, and her love
Can make seem pleasing to her tender years?
KING RICHARD
Infer fair England's peace by this alliance.                                    343
QUEEN ELIZABETH
Which she shall purchase with still-lasting war.                                344
KING RICHARD
Tell her the King, that may command, entreats.
QUEEN ELIZABETH
That at her hands which the King's King forbids.                                346
KING RICHARD
Say she shall be a high and mighty queen.
QUEEN ELIZABETH
To vail the title, as her mother doth.                                          348
KING RICHARD
Say I will love her everlastingly.
QUEEN ELIZABETH
But how long shall that title "ever" last?
KING RICHARD
Sweetly in force unto her fair life's end.
QUEEN ELIZABETH
But how long fairly shall her sweet life last?                                  352
KING RICHARD
As long as heaven and nature lengthens it.
QUEEN ELIZABETH
As long as hell and Richard likes of it.
KING RICHARD
Say I, her sovereign, am her subject low.
QUEEN ELIZABETH
But she, your subject, loathes such sovereignty.
KING RICHARD
Be eloquent in my behalf to her.
QUEEN ELIZABETH
An honest tale speeds best being plainly told.                                  358
KING RICHARD
Then plainly to her tell my loving tale.
QUEEN ELIZABETH
Plain and not honest is too harsh a style.
KING RICHARD
Your reasons are too shallow and too quick.                                     361
QUEEN ELIZABETH
Oh, no, my reasons are too deep and dead—
Too deep and dead, poor infants, in their graves.
KING RICHARD
Harp not on that string, madam. That is past.
QUEEN ELIZABETH
Harp on it still shall I till heartstrings break.

---

290 **spoil** slaughter. (A hunting term.)   291 **Look what** Whatever
292 **shall deal** cannot but act   297 **quicken your increase** give new life
to your progeny   302 **metal** substance. (With a suggestion also of *mettle*, "spirit." The Folio reads "mettall.")   303–4 **Of . . . sorrow** i.e., linked
in human suffering, with the exception of the night of labor pains to be
endured by her (young Elizabeth) at whose birth you suffered the same
happy pain of labor and childbirth.   310 **can** am able (to give).
316 **Familiarly** familially   322 **orient** bright, shining   323–4 **Advantaging . . . happiness** i.e., repaying the love shown by your tears with
tenfold increase of happiness.   326 **Make . . . experience** teach her
how to conquer her shyness with a boldness learned by what you can

relate to her of your own experience in love   328–9 **th'aspiring . . .
sovereignty** aspirations for the authority of a sovereign's consort
335 **retail** relate   343 **Infer** Allege, adduce (as a reason)   344 **still-
lasting war** i.e., perpetual domestic strife.   346 **forbids** (*The Book of
Common Prayer*, echoing the injunctions of Leviticus 18, prohibits the
marriage of a man with his brother's daughter.)   348 **vail** yield;
lower or abase as a sign of submission   352 **fairly** without foul
play   358 **speeds** succeeds   361 **quick** hasty. (With a pun on the
meaning "alive," contrasted with *dead* in the next line, just as *shallow*
is punningly contrasted with *deep*.)

KING RICHARD
    Now, by my George, my Garter, and my crown—                366
QUEEN ELIZABETH
    Profaned, dishonored, and the third usurped.
KING RICHARD
    I swear—
QUEEN ELIZABETH    By nothing, for this is no oath.
    Thy George, profaned, hath lost his lordly honor;                369
    Thy Garter, blemished, pawned his knightly virtue;
    Thy crown, usurped, disgraced his kingly glory.
    If something thou wouldst swear to be believed,
    Swear then by something that thou hast not wronged.
KING RICHARD
    Then, by myself—
QUEEN ELIZABETH    Thyself is self-misused.
KING RICHARD
    Now, by the world—
QUEEN ELIZABETH    'Tis full of thy foul wrongs.
KING RICHARD
    My father's death—
QUEEN ELIZABETH    Thy life hath it dishonored.
KING RICHARD
    Why then, by God—
QUEEN ELIZABETH    God's wrong is most of all.
    If thou didst fear to break an oath with Him,
    The unity the King my husband made                369
    Thou hadst not broken, nor my brothers died.
    If thou hadst feared to break an oath by Him,
    Th'imperial metal circling now thy head
    Had graced the tender temples of my child,
    And both the princes had been breathing here,                384
    Which now, two tender bedfellows for dust,
    Thy broken faith hath made the prey for worms.
    What canst thou swear by now?
KING RICHARD                The time to come.
QUEEN ELIZABETH
    That thou hast wrongèd in the time o'erpast;
    For I myself have many tears to wash                389
    Hereafter time, for time past wronged by thee.                390
    The children live whose fathers thou hast slaughtered,
    Ungoverned youth, to wail it in their age;                392
    The parents live whose children thou hast butchered,
    Old barren plants, to wail it with their age.                394
    Swear not by time to come, for that thou hast
    Misused ere used, by times ill-used o'erpast.                396
KING RICHARD
    As I intend to prosper and repent,                397
    So thrive I in my dangerous affairs
    Of hostile arms! Myself myself confound!                399

Heaven and fortune bar me happy hours!
Day, yield me not thy light, nor, night, thy rest!
Be opposite all planets of good luck                402
To my proceeding if, with dear heart's love,
Immaculate devotion, holy thoughts,
I tender not thy beauteous, princely daughter!                405
In her consists my happiness and thine;
Without her follows to myself and thee,
Herself, the land, and many a Christian soul,
Death, desolation, ruin, and decay.
It cannot be avoided but by this;
It will not be avoided but by this.
Therefore, dear mother—I must call you so—
Be the attorney of my love to her.
Plead what I will be, not what I have been,
Not my deserts, but what I will deserve.
Urge the necessity and state of times,                416
And be not peevish-fond in great designs.                417
QUEEN ELIZABETH
    Shall I be tempted of the devil thus?
KING RICHARD
    Ay, if the devil tempt you to do good.
QUEEN ELIZABETH
    Shall I forget myself to be myself?                420
KING RICHARD
    Ay, if yourself's remembrance wrong yourself.                421
QUEEN ELIZABETH
    Yet thou didst kill my children.
KING RICHARD
    But in your daughter's womb I bury them,
    Where in that nest of spicery they will breed                424
    Selves of themselves, to your recomfiture.                425
QUEEN ELIZABETH
    Shall I go win my daughter to thy will?
KING RICHARD
    And be a happy mother by the deed.
QUEEN ELIZABETH
    I go. Write to me very shortly,
    And you shall understand from me her mind.
KING RICHARD
    Bear her my true love's kiss; and so, farewell.
                        Exit Queen [Elizabeth].
    Relenting fool, and shallow, changing woman!

    Enter Ratcliffe; [Catesby following].

    How now, what news?
RATCLIFFE
    Most mighty sovereign, on the western coast
    Rideth a puissant navy; to our shores                434
    Throng many doubtful, hollow-hearted friends,                435

366 George . . . Garter (The George, a badge showing Saint George slaying the dragon, was not added to the insignia of the Order of the Garter until the reign of Henry VII or Henry VIII.)    369 his its (as also in lines 370, 371)    379 The unity . . . made i.e., the reconciliation fashioned by the dying Edward IV between Queen Elizabeth and her enemies; see 2.1.1–44    384 breathing here alive today    389–90 to wash . . . by thee to cleanse the time to come, as a remedy for the past times that you have wronged.    392 Ungoverned . . . age i.e., children deprived of a father's guidance, left to wail their misfortune as they grow old    394 Old barren plants i.e., aging parents, no longer able to have children (to replace those whom Richard has butchered)    396 Misused . . . o'erpast misused even before it came time to be used, by your ill use of past times.    397 As . . . repent i.e., I swear that as I hope to thrive and intend to repent    399 Myself . . . confound! May I destroy myself!

402 opposite opposed, adverse    405 I tender not I fail to show a tender regard for    416 state of times urgent political need    417 And . . . designs and do not stand by, childishly foolish as great plans are afoot.    420 Shall . . . myself? i.e., Shall I, in order to be queen mother, forget that I am the person you have wronged?    421 wrong yourself i.e., interferes with what is to your advantage.    424 nest of spicery (The fabled phoenix arose anew from the nest of spices, its funeral pyre.)    425 Selves of themselves new selves out of their former selves.    recomfiture comfort, consolation.    434 puissant powerful    435 doubtful apprehensive; not to be trusted

Unarmed and unresolved to beat them back.
'Tis thought that Richmond is their admiral;    437
And there they hull, expecting but the aid    438
Of Buckingham to welcome them ashore.

KING RICHARD
Some light-foot friend post to the Duke of Norfolk:    440
Ratcliffe, thyself, or Catesby; where is he?

CATESBY
Here, my good lord.

KING RICHARD            Catesby, fly to the Duke.

CATESBY
I will, my lord, with all convenient haste.    443

KING RICHARD
Ratcliffe, come hither. Post to Salisbury.
When thou com'st thither—[*To Catesby*] Dull, unmindful
     villain,
Why stay'st thou here, and go'st not to the Duke?

CATESBY
First, mighty liege, tell me Your Highness' pleasure,
What from Your Grace I shall deliver to him.

KING RICHARD
Oh, true, good Catesby. Bid him levy straight
The greatest strength and power that he can make,    450
And meet me suddenly at Salisbury.    451

CATESBY   I go.                             *Exit.*

RATCLIFFE
What, may it please you, shall I do at Salisbury?

KING RICHARD
Why, what wouldst thou do there before I go?

RATCLIFFE
Your Highness told me I should post before.    455

KING RICHARD
My mind is changed.

*Enter Lord Stanley [Earl of Derby].*

              Stanley, what news with you?

STANLEY
None good, my liege, to please you with the hearing,
Nor none so bad but well may be reported.

KING RICHARD
Hoyday, a riddle! Neither good nor bad!    459
What need'st thou run so many miles about,
When thou mayst tell thy tale the nearest way?    461
Once more, what news?

STANLEY           Richmond is on the seas.

KING RICHARD
There let him sink, and be the seas on him!
White-livered runagate, what doth he there?    464

STANLEY
I know not, mighty sovereign, but by guess.

KING RICHARD    Well, as you guess?

STANLEY
Stirred up by Dorset, Buckingham, and Morton,

He makes for England, here to claim the crown.

KING RICHARD
Is the chair empty? Is the sword unswayed?    469
Is the King dead? The empire unpossessed?    470
What heir of York is there alive but we?
And who is England's king but great York's heir?
Then tell me, what makes he upon the seas?    473

STANLEY
Unless for that, my liege, I cannot guess.

KING RICHARD
Unless for that he comes to be your liege,    475
You cannot guess wherefore the Welshman comes.    476
Thou wilt revolt and fly to him, I fear.

STANLEY
No, my good lord; therefore mistrust me not.

KING RICHARD
Where is thy power, then, to beat him back?    479
Where be thy tenants and thy followers?
Are they not now upon the western shore,
Safe-conducting the rebels from their ships?

STANLEY
No, my good lord, my friends are in the north.

KING RICHARD
Cold friends to me! What do they in the north
When they should serve their sovereign in the west?

STANLEY
They have not been commanded, mighty King.
Pleaseth Your Majesty to give me leave,    487
I'll muster up my friends and meet Your Grace
Where and what time Your Majesty shall please.

KING RICHARD
Ay, thou wouldst be gone to join with Richmond.
But I'll not trust thee.

STANLEY           Most mighty sovereign,
You have no cause to hold my friendship doubtful.
I never was nor never will be false.

KING RICHARD
Go then and muster men, but leave behind
Your son, George Stanley. Look your heart be firm,
Or else his head's assurance is but frail.    496

STANLEY
So deal with him as I prove true to you.
                *Exit Stanley [Earl of Derby].*

*Enter a Messenger.*

FIRST MESSENGER
My gracious sovereign, now in Devonshire,
As I by friends am well advisèd,    499
Sir Edward Courtney and the haughty prelate,
Bishop of Exeter, his elder brother,    501
With many more confederates, are in arms.

*Enter another Messenger.*

---

**437 their admiral** i.e., of the *puissant navy* named three lines earlier, not of the fainthearted soldiers who are mustering in Richard's army   **438 hull** drift with the sails furled   **440 light-foot** swift-footed. **post** hasten   **443 convenient** appropriate, suitable   **450 make** raise   **451 suddenly** swiftly   **455 post** hasten **459 Hoyday** Heyday. (Expressing mock wonderment.)   **461 the nearest way** directly, simply.   **464 White-livered runagate** Cowardly renegade, vagabond

**469 chair** throne. **unswayed** unwielded.   **470 empire** kingdom **473 makes he** is he doing   **475 for that** because (playing on *for that*, for that purpose, in the previous line)   **476 Welshman** (Richmond was the grandson of Owen Tudor, a Welshman of Anglesea, who fathered three sons and a daughter by Katharine of Valois, widow of Henry V.)   **479 power** army   **487 Pleaseth** May it please **496 assurance** safety   **499 advisèd** informed   **501 brother** (Actually, a cousin.)

**SECOND MESSENGER**
In Kent, my liege, the Guildfords are in arms,
And every hour more competitors                                  504
Flock to the rebels, and their power grows strong.

*Enter another Messenger.*

**THIRD MESSENGER**
My lord, the army of great Buckingham—
**KING RICHARD**
Out on ye, owls! Nothing but songs of death?                     507
                            *He striketh him.*
There, take thou that, till thou bring better news.
**THIRD MESSENGER**
The news I have to tell Your Majesty
Is that by sudden floods and fall of waters
Buckingham's army is dispersed and scattered,
And he himself wandered away alone,
No man knows whither.
**KING RICHARD**                    I cry thee mercy.            513
There is my purse to cure that blow of thine.
                            *[He gives money.]*
Hath any well-advisèd friend proclaimed                          515
Reward to him that brings the traitor in?
**THIRD MESSENGER**
Such proclamation hath been made, my lord.

*Enter another Messenger.*

**FOURTH MESSENGER**
Sir Thomas Lovell and Lord Marquess Dorset,                      518
'Tis said, my liege, in Yorkshire are in arms.
But this good comfort bring I to Your Highness:
The Breton navy is dispersed by tempest.
Richmond, in Dorsetshire, sent out a boat
Unto the shore, to ask those on the banks
If they were his assistants, yea or no,
Who answered him they came from Buckingham
Upon his party. He, mistrusting them,
Hoised sail and made his course again for Brittany.              527
**KING RICHARD**
March on, march on, since we are up in arms,
If not to fight with foreign enemies,
Yet to beat down these rebels here at home.

*Enter Catesby.*

**CATESBY**
My liege, the Duke of Buckingham is taken!
That is the best news. That the Earl of Richmond
Is with a mighty power landed at Milford              533
Is colder tidings, yet they must be told.
**KING RICHARD**
Away towards Salisbury! While we reason here,        535

A royal battle might be won and lost.
Someone take order Buckingham be brought             537
To Salisbury. The rest march on with me.
                            *Flourish. Exeunt.*

❖

# [4.5]

*Enter [Lord Stanley Earl of ] Derby and Sir
Christopher [Urswick, a priest].*

**STANLEY**
Sir Christopher, tell Richmond this from me:
That in the sty of the most deadly boar
My son George Stanley is franked up in hold.        3
If I revolt, off goes young George's head;
The fear of that holds off my present aid.
So get thee gone; commend me to thy lord.           6
Withal say that the Queen hath heartily consented   7
He should espouse Elizabeth her daughter.
But tell me, where is princely Richmond now?
**CHRISTOPHER**
At Pembroke, or at Ha'rfordwest, in Wales.          10
**STANLEY**    What men of name resort to him?      11
**CHRISTOPHER**
Sir Walter Herbert, a renownèd soldier,
Sir Gilbert Talbot, Sir William Stanley,
Oxford, redoubted Pembroke, Sir James Blunt,        14
And Rice ap Thomas, with a valiant crew,
And many other of great name and worth;
And towards London do they bend their power,        17
If by the way they be not fought withal.            18
**STANLEY**
Well, hie thee to thy lord; I kiss his hand.        19
My letter will resolve him of my mind.              20
                            *[He gives a letter.]*
Farewell.                            *Exeunt.*

❖

# 5.1

*Enter Buckingham, with [Sheriff and] halberds,
led to execution.*

**BUCKINGHAM**
Will not King Richard let me speak with him?
**SHERIFF**
No, my good lord. Therefore be patient.
**BUCKINGHAM**
Hastings, and Edward's children, Grey, and Rivers,
Holy King Henry, and thy fair son Edward,           4
Vaughan, and all that have miscarrièd               5

---

**504 competitors** confederates   **507 owls** (The cry of the owl was
thought to portend death.)   **513 I cry thee mercy** I beg your pardon.   **515 well-advisèd** judicious, well informed   **518 Sir Thomas
Lovell** (Not the Lovell of 3.4 and 3.5, who was historically Sir Francis
Lovell, Richard's Lord Chamberlain, but perhaps related to
him.)   **527 Hoised** hoisted   **533 Milford** Milford Haven on the coast
of Wales in the county of Pembroke. (A gap of two years is bridged
here. Richmond's first fruitless expedition was in October 1483; his
landing at Milford was in August 1485.)   **535 reason** talk

**537 take order** see to it that
**4.5. Location: London. The house of Lord Stanley, Earl of Derby.**
**0.1 Sir** (Honorific title for a clergyman.)   **3 franked up in hold** shut
up in custody, as in a pigpen.   **6 commend me** convey my greetings
**7 Withal** In addition   **10 Ha'rfordwest** Haverfordwest, in Wales
**11 name** rank   **14 redoubted Pembroke** awe-inspiring Jasper Tudor,
Earl of Pembroke (uncle to Richmond)   **17 bend their power** direct
their forces   **18 withal** with.   **19 hie** hasten   **20 resolve him of**
inform him concerning
**5.1. Location: Salisbury. An open place.**
**4 thy** i.e., Henry VI's   **5 miscarrièd** perished

By underhand corrupted foul injustice:
If that your moody, discontented souls
Do through the clouds behold this present hour,
Even for revenge mock my destruction!                                        7
This is All Souls' Day, fellow, is it not?                                   10

SHERIFF  It is, my lord.

BUCKINGHAM
Why, then All Souls' Day is my body's doomsday.
This is the day which, in King Edward's time,                                13
I wished might fall on me when I was found
False to his children and his wife's allies;
This is the day wherein I wished to fall
By the false faith of him whom most I trusted;
This, this All Souls' Day to my fearful soul
Is the determined respite of my wrongs.                                      19
That high All-Seer which I dallied with
Hath turned my feignèd prayer on my head
And given in earnest what I begged in jest.
Thus doth He force the swords of wicked men
To turn their own points in their masters' bosoms.
Thus Margaret's curse falls heavy on my neck:
"When he," quoth she, "shall split thy heart with sorrow,                    26
Remember Margaret was a prophetess."
Come lead me, officers, to the block of shame.
Wrong hath but wrong, and blame the due of blame.

*Exeunt Buckingham with officers.*

❧

## 5.2

*Enter Richmond, Oxford, [Sir James] Blunt, [Sir
Walter] Herbert, and others, with drum and
colors.*

RICHMOND
Fellows in arms, and my most loving friends
Bruised underneath the yoke of tyranny,
Thus far into the bowels of the land                                         3
Have we marched on without impediment;
And here receive we from our father Stanley                                  5
Lines of fair comfort and encouragement.
The wretched, bloody, and usurping boar,
That spoiled your summer fields and fruitful vines,                          8
Swills your warm blood like wash, and makes his trough                       9
In your emboweled bosoms, this foul swine                                    10
Is now even in the center of this isle,
Near to the town of Leicester, as we learn.
From Tamworth thither is but one day's march.
In God's name, cheerly on, courageous friends,                              14
To reap the harvest of perpetual peace
By this one bloody trial of sharp war.

OXFORD
Every man's conscience is a thousand swords
To fight against this guilty homicide.

HERBERT
I doubt not but his friends will turn to us.

BLUNT
He hath no friends but what are friends for fear,                           20
Which in his dearest need will fly from him.                                21

RICHMOND
All for our vantage. Then, in God's name, march!
True hope is swift and flies with swallow's wings;
Kings it makes gods and meaner creatures kings.                             24

*Exeunt omnes.*

## [5.3]

*Enter King Richard in arms, with Norfolk,
Ratcliffe, and the Earl of Surrey [and others].*

KING RICHARD
Here pitch our tent, even here in Bosworth Field.
My lord of Surrey, why look you so sad?

SURREY
My heart is ten times lighter than my looks.

KING RICHARD
My lord of Norfolk—

NORFOLK                     Here, most gracious liege.

KING RICHARD
Norfolk, we must have knocks; ha! Must we not?                               5

NORFOLK
We must both give and take, my loving lord.

KING RICHARD
Up with my tent! Here will I lie tonight.
          *[Soldiers begin to set up King Richard's tent.]*
But where tomorrow? Well, all's one for that.                               8
Who hath descried the number of the traitors?                               9

NORFOLK
Six or seven thousand is their utmost power.

KING RICHARD
Why, our battalia trebles that account.                                     11
Besides, the King's name is a tower of strength,
Which they upon the adverse faction want.                                   13
Up with the tent! Come, noble gentlemen,
Let us survey the vantage of the ground.                                    15
Call for some men of sound direction.                                       16
Let's lack no discipline, make no delay,
For, lords, tomorrow is a busy day.          *Exeunt.*

*Enter [on the other side of the stage] Richmond,
Sir William Brandon, Oxford, and Dorset, [Blunt,
Herbert, and others. Some of the soldiers pitch
Richmond's tent.]*

**7 If that** if.   **moody, discounted** angry, vengeance-seeking   **10 All
Souls' Day** November 2, the day on which the Church intercedes for
all Christian souls   **13 This is the day** (The following passage, lines
13–27, recalls in detail what Buckingham said at 2.1.32–8.)   **19 the
determined . . . wrongs** the ordained date to which the punishment
of my evil practices was respited or postponed.   **26 he** Richard
**5.2. Location: A camp near Tamworth.**
**3 bowels** interior   **5 father** stepfather, Lord Stanley, Earl of Derby
**8 spoiled** despoiled   **9 Swills** gulps.   **wash** hogwash, swill
**10 emboweled** disemboweled   **14 cheerly** cheerily, heartily

**20 for fear** i.e., out of fearing Richard   **21 dearest** direst   **24 meaner**
of lower degree.   **24.1 omnes** all.
**5.3. Location: Bosworth Field.**
**5 knocks** blows   **8 all's . . . that** be that as it may.   **9 descried**
reconnoitred   **11 battalia** army   **13 Which . . . want** which they of
the opposite army lack.   **15 vantage of the ground** i.e., way in which
the field can best be used for tactical advantage.   **16 direction** judgment, military skill.

RICHMOND
　The weary sun hath made a golden set,
　And, by the bright track of his fiery car,                    20
　Gives token of a goodly day tomorrow.
　Sir William Brandon, you shall bear my standard.              22
　Give me some ink and paper in my tent.
　I'll draw the form and model of our battle,
　Limit each leader to his several charge,                      25
　And part in just proportion our small power.                  26
　My lord of Oxford, you, Sir William Brandon,
　And you, Sir Walter Herbert, stay with me.
　The Earl of Pembroke keeps his regiment;                      29
　Good Captain Blunt, bear my good-night to him,
　And by the second hour in the morning
　Desire the Earl to see me in my tent.
　Yet one thing more, good Captain, do for me:
　Where is Lord Stanley quartered, do you know?
BLUNT
　Unless I have mista'en his colors much,
　Which well I am assured I have not done,
　His regiment lies half a mile at least
　South from the mighty power of the King.                      38
RICHMOND
　If without peril it be possible,
　Sweet Blunt, make some good means to speak with him,
　And give him from me this most needful note.
　　　　　　　　　　　　　　　　　　　　　　[He gives a letter.]
BLUNT
　Upon my life, my lord, I'll undertake it.
　And so, God give you quiet rest tonight!
RICHMOND
　Good night, good Captain Blunt.          [Exit Blunt.]
　　　　　　　　　　　　　Come, gentlemen,
　Let us consult upon tomorrow's business.
　Into my tent; the dew is raw and cold.
　　　　　　　　　　　　　They withdraw into the tent.

　　　　　　　Enter [to his tent, King] Richard, Ratcliffe,
　　　　　　　Norfolk, and Catesby.

KING RICHARD
　What is't o'clock?
CATESBY　　　　　　　　It's suppertime, my lord;
　It's nine o'clock.
KING RICHARD　　　I will not sup tonight.
　Give me some ink and paper.
　What, is my beaver easier than it was,                        50
　And all my armor laid into my tent?
CATESBY
　It is, my liege, and all things are in readiness.
KING RICHARD
　Good Norfolk, hie thee to thy charge.
　Use careful watch; choose trusty sentinels.
NORFOLK　　I go, my lord.

KING RICHARD
　Stir with the lark tomorrow, gentle Norfolk.
NORFOLK　　I warrant you, my lord.          [Exit.]   57
KING RICHARD　　Catesby!
CATESBY
　My lord?
KING RICHARD　　Send out a pursuivant at arms           59
　To Stanley's regiment. Bid him bring his power            60
　Before sunrising, lest his son George fall
　Into the blind cave of eternal night.      [Exit Catesby.]
　Fill me a bowl of wine. Give me a watch.                      63
　Saddle white Surrey for the field tomorrow.                   64
　Look that my staves be sound and not too heavy.               65
　Ratcliffe!
RATCLIFFE　　My lord?
KING RICHARD
　Saw'st thou the melancholy Lord Northumberland?
RATCLIFFE
　Thomas the Earl of Surrey and himself,
　Much about cockshut time, from troop to troop              70
　Went through the army, cheering up the soldiers.
KING RICHARD
　So, I am satisfied. Give me a bowl of wine.
　I have not that alacrity of spirit
　Nor cheer of mind that I was wont to have.                    74
　　　　　　　　　　　　　　　　　　　[Wine is brought.]
　Set it down. Is ink and paper ready?
RATCLIFFE
　It is, my lord.
KING RICHARD　　Bid my guard watch. Leave me.
　Ratcliffe, about the mid of night come to my tent
　And help to arm me. Leave me, I say.
　　　　　　　　　　Exit Ratcliffe. [Richard sleeps.]

　　　　　　　Enter [Lord Stanley Earl of] Derby, to Richmond
　　　　　　　in his tent, [lords and others attending].

STANLEY
　Fortune and victory sit on thy helm!                          79
RICHMOND
　All comfort that the dark night can afford
　Be to thy person, noble father-in-law!                        81
　Tell me, how fares our loving mother?
STANLEY
　I, by attorney, bless thee from thy mother,                   83
　Who prays continually for Richmond's good.
　So much for that. The silent hours steal on,
　And flaky darkness breaks within the east.                    86
　In brief—for so the season bids us be—                        87
　Prepare thy battle early in the morning,                      88
　And put thy fortune to the arbitrament                        89

---

57 **warrant** guarantee　59 **pursuivant at arms** junior officer acting as messenger　60 **power** forces　63 **watch** watch light, candle marked into equal divisions to show time; or, perhaps, sentinel.　64 **white Surrey** (The name seems to be Shakespeare's invention. The chroniclers say that Richard was mounted on a "great white courser.")　65 **staves** lance shafts　70 **cockshut time** evening twilight; possibly, the time at which the poultry are shut up　74 **was wont** used　79 **helm** helmet.　81 **father-in-law** stepfather.　83 **by attorney** as proxy　86 **flaky** streaked with light　87 **season** time　88 **battle** troops　89 **arbitrament** arbitration

---

20 **car** chariot (of Phoebus)　22 **standard** flag.　25 **Limit** appoint. **several charge** individual command　26 **And . . . power** and divide proportionately our small army.　29 **keeps** i.e., is with　38 **power** army　50 **beaver** face-guard or visor of helmet.　**easier** looser, better fitting

Of bloody strokes and mortal-staring war.    90
I, as I may—that which I would I cannot—    91
With best advantage will deceive the time    92
And aid thee in this doubtful shock of arms.    93
But on thy side I may not be too forward,    94
Lest, being seen, thy brother, tender George,    95
Be executed in his father's sight.
Farewell. The leisure and the fearful time    97
Cuts off the ceremonious vows of love
And ample interchange of sweet discourse
Which so-long-sundered friends should dwell upon.
God give us leisure for these rites of love!
Once more, adieu. Be valiant, and speed well!    102

RICHMOND
Good lords, conduct him to his regiment.
I'll strive with troubled thoughts to take a nap,
Lest leaden slumber peise me down tomorrow,    105
When I should mount with wings of victory.
Once more, good night, kind lords and gentlemen.
                 *Exeunt.* [*Richmond remains.*]
O Thou whose captain I account myself,
Look on my forces with a gracious eye;
Put in their hands Thy bruising irons of wrath,
That they may crush down with a heavy fall
The usurping helmets of our adversaries!
Make us Thy ministers of chastisement,
That we may praise Thee in the victory!
To thee I do commend my watchful soul
Ere I let fall the windows of mine eyes.    116
Sleeping and waking, oh, defend me still!    117
                     [*He sleeps.*]

*Enter the Ghost of young Prince Edward, son* [*of*]
*Harry the Sixth, to Richard.*

GHOST (*to Richard*)
Let me sit heavy on thy soul tomorrow!    118
Think, how thou stabbed'st me in my prime of youth
At Tewkesbury. Despair therefore and die!
(*To Richmond*) Be cheerful, Richmond, for the wrongèd souls
Of butchered princes fight in thy behalf.
King Henry's issue, Richmond, comforts thee.   [*Exit.*] 123

*Enter the Ghost of Henry the Sixth.*

GHOST (*to Richard*)
When I was mortal, my anointed body    124
By thee was punchèd full of deadly holes.
Think on the Tower and me. Despair and die!    126
Harry the Sixth bids thee despair and die!
(*To Richmond*) Virtuous and holy, be thou conqueror!

Harry, that prophesied thou shouldst be king,    129
Doth comfort thee in thy sleep. Live and flourish!
                     [*Exit.*]

*Enter the Ghost of Clarence.*

GHOST [*to Richard*]
Let me sit heavy in thy soul tomorrow,
I, that was washed to death with fulsome wine,    132
Poor Clarence, by thy guile betrayed to death!
Tomorrow in the battle think on me,
And fall thy edgeless sword. Despair and die!    135
(*To Richmond*) Thou offspring of the house of Lancaster,
The wrongèd heirs of York do pray for thee.
Good angels guard thy battle! Live and flourish!    138
                     [*Exit.*]

*Enter the Ghosts of Rivers, Grey,* [*and*] *Vaughan.*

GHOST OF RIVERS [*to Richard*]
Let me sit heavy in thy soul tomorrow,
Rivers that died at Pomfret! Despair and die!
GHOST OF GREY [*to Richard*]
Think upon Grey, and let thy soul despair!
GHOST OF VAUGHAN [*to Richard*]
Think upon Vaughan, and, with guilty fear,
Let fall thy lance. Despair and die!
ALL (*to Richmond*)
Awake, and think our wrongs in Richard's bosom
Will conquer him! Awake, and win the day!
                     [*Exeunt Ghosts.*]

*Enter the Ghost of Hastings.*

GHOST [*to Richard*]
Bloody and guilty, guiltily awake
And in a bloody battle end thy days!
Think on Lord Hastings. Despair and die!
(*To Richmond*) Quiet untroubled soul, awake, awake!
Arm, fight, and conquer for fair England's sake!
                     [*Exit.*]

*Enter the Ghosts of the two young Princes.*

GHOSTS (*to Richard*)
Dream on thy cousins smothered in the Tower.    151
Let us be lead within thy bosom, Richard,
And weigh thee down to ruin, shame, and death!
Thy nephews' souls bid thee despair and die!
(*To Richmond*) Sleep, Richmond, sleep in peace, and
     wake in joy.
Good angels guard thee from the boar's annoy!    156
Live, and beget a happy race of kings!
Edward's unhappy sons do bid thee flourish.
                     [*Exeunt Ghosts.*]

*Enter the Ghost of Lady Anne, his wife.*

GHOST [*to Richard*]
Richard, thy wife, that wretched Anne thy wife,
That never slept a quiet hour with thee,

---

**90 mortal-staring** fatal-visaged   **91 that . . . cannot** i.e., I cannot fight openly on your side, though I want to   **92 With . . . time** as best I can I will work for your side without seeming to do so   **93 shock** encounter   **94 forward** zealous   **95 brother** i.e., stepbrother. **tender** young, of tender years   **97 leisure** i.e., brief time allowed   **102 speed well** may you succeed.   **105 peise** weigh   **116 windows** i.e., eyelids **117 still** continually.   **118 sit heavy on** be oppressive to   **123 issue** son   **124 anointed** i.e., with the sacred oil used in the coronation ceremony; compare with 4.4.151   **126 Tower** (Where Henry VI was supposed to have been murdered.)

**129 prophesied** (See *3 Henry VI*, 4.6.68 ff.)   **132 washed to death** i.e., drowned in a butt of malmsey. **fulsome** cloying   **135 fall** let fall. **edgeless** blunt, useless   **138 battle** troops.   **151 cousins** i.e., nephews   **156 the boar's annoy** i.e., Richard's attack.

Now fills thy sleep with perturbations.
Tomorrow in the battle think on me,
And fall thy edgeless sword. Despair and die!
(*To Richmond*) Thou quiet soul, sleep thou a quiet sleep;
Dream of success and happy victory!
Thy adversary's wife doth pray for thee.          [*Exit.*]

*Enter the Ghost of Buckingham.*

GHOST [*to Richard*]
The first was I that helped thee to the crown;
The last was I that felt thy tyranny.
Oh, in the battle think on Buckingham,
And die in terror of thy guiltiness!
Dream on, dream on of bloody deeds and death;
Fainting, despair; despairing, yield thy breath!          172
(*To Richmond*) I died for hope ere I could lend thee aid,     173
But cheer thy heart, and be thou not dismayed.
God and good angels fight on Richmond's side,
And Richard fall in height of all his pride!          [*Exit.*]  176
                     *Richard starteth up out of a dream.*

KING RICHARD
Give me another horse! Bind up my wounds!
Have mercy, Jesu!—Soft, I did but dream.
O coward conscience, how dost thou afflict me!
The lights burn blue. It is now dead midnight.          180
Cold fearful drops stand on my trembling flesh.
What do I fear? Myself? There's none else by.
Richard loves Richard; that is, I am I.          183
Is there a murderer here? No. Yes, I am.
Then fly. What, from myself? Great reason why:          185
Lest I revenge. What, myself upon myself?
Alack, I love myself. Wherefore? For any good          187
That I myself have done unto myself?
Oh, no! Alas, I rather hate myself
For hateful deeds committed by myself!
I am a villain. Yet I lie, I am not.
Fool, of thyself speak well. Fool, do not flatter.
My conscience hath a thousand several tongues,          193
And every tongue brings in a several tale,
And every tale condemns me for a villain.
Perjury, perjury, in the highest degree,
Murder, stern murder, in the direst degree,
All several sins, all used in each degree,          198
Throng to the bar, crying all, "Guilty! Guilty!"          199
I shall despair. There is no creature loves me,          200
And if I die no soul will pity me.
And wherefore should they, since that I myself
Find in myself no pity to myself?
Methought the souls of all that I had murdered

Came to my tent, and every one did threat
Tomorrow's vengeance on the head of Richard.

*Enter Ratcliffe.*

RATCLIFFE   My lord!
KING RICHARD   Zounds! Who is there?
RATCLIFFE
My lord, 'tis I. The early village cock
Hath twice done salutation to the morn.
Your friends are up and buckle on their armor.
KING RICHARD
Oh, Ratcliffe, I have dreamed a fearful dream!
What think'st thou, will our friends prove all true?
RATCLIFFE
No doubt, my lord.
KING RICHARD          Oh, Ratcliffe, I fear, I fear!
RATCLIFFE
Nay, good my lord, be not afraid of shadows.
KING RICHARD
By the apostle Paul, shadows tonight
Have struck more terror to the soul of Richard
Than can the substance of ten thousand soldiers
Armèd in proof and led by shallow Richmond.          219
'Tis not yet near day. Come, go with me;
Under our tents I'll play the eavesdropper,          221
To see if any mean to shrink from me.
                     *Exeunt* [*Richard and Ratcliffe*].

*Enter the Lords to Richmond, [sitting in his tent].*

LORDS   Good morrow, Richmond!
RICHMOND
Cry mercy, lords and watchful gentlemen,          224
That you have ta'en a tardy sluggard here.
A LORD   How have you slept, my lord?
RICHMOND
The sweetest sleep and fairest-boding dreams
That ever entered in a drowsy head
Have I since your departure had, my lords.
Methought their souls whose bodies Richard murdered
Came to my tent and cried on victory.          231
I promise you, my soul is very jocund          232
In the remembrance of so fair a dream.
How far into the morning is it, lords?
A LORD   Upon the stroke of four.
RICHMOND
Why, then 'tis time to arm and give direction.

*His oration to his soldiers.*

More than I have said, loving countrymen,          237
The leisure and enforcement of the time          238
Forbids to dwell upon. Yet remember this:
God and our good cause fight upon our side.
The prayers of holy saints and wrongèd souls,
Like high-reared bulwarks, stand before our faces.

---

172 **Fainting** losing heart   173 **for hope** i.e., for hoping to support you, or for want of hope, hoping in vain to help   176 **Richard fall** may Richard fall   180 **lights burn blue** (Superstitiously regarded as evidence of the presence of ghosts.)   183 **I am I** (A blasphemy of God's "*ego sum.*")   185 **fly** flee.   187 **Wherefore?** Why?   193 **several** different, separate   198 **used ... degree** committed in every degree of infamy, from bad to worst   199 **bar** i.e., bar of justice   200 **despair** (Considered the only unforgivable sin.)

219 **proof** armor   221 **Under our tents** concealing myself among the tents   224 **Cry mercy** I beg your pardon   231 **cried on victory** invoked victory, cried out to it.   232 **promise** assure.   **jocund** cheerful   237 **have said** have already said before   238 **leisure** i.e., brief time allowed

Richard except, those whom we fight against                    243
Had rather have us win than him they follow.
For what is he they follow? Truly, gentlemen,
A bloody tyrant and a homicide;
One raised in blood, and one in blood established;          247
One that made means to come by what he hath,               248
And slaughtered those that were the means to help him;
A base, foul stone, made precious by the foil              250
Of England's chair, where he is falsely set;              251
One that hath ever been God's enemy.
Then if you fight against God's enemy,
God will in justice ward you as his soldiers;              254
If you do sweat to put a tyrant down,
You sleep in peace, the tyrant being slain;
If you do fight against your country's foes,
Your country's fat shall pay your pains the hire;          258
If you do fight in safeguard of your wives,
Your wives shall welcome home the conquerors;
If you do free your children from the sword,
Your children's children quits it in your age.             262
Then, in the name of God and all these rights,
Advance your standards! Draw your willing swords!          264
For me, the ransom of my bold attempt                      265
Shall be this cold corpse on the earth's cold face;        266
But if I thrive, the gain of my attempt
The least of you shall share his part thereof.
Sound drums and trumpets boldly and cheerfully;
God and Saint George! Richmond and victory!
                                              [*Exeunt.*]

*Enter King Richard, Ratcliffe, [attendants and
forces].*

KING RICHARD
   What said Northumberland as touching Richmond?          271
RATCLIFFE
   That he was never trainèd up in arms.
KING RICHARD
   He said the truth. And what said Surrey then?
RATCLIFFE
   He smiled and said, "The better for our purpose."
KING RICHARD
   He was in the right, and so indeed it is.
                                   *The clock striketh.*
   Tell the clock there. Give me a calendar.               276
   Who saw the sun today?          [*He takes an almanac.*]
RATCLIFFE                  Not I, my lord.
KING RICHARD
   Then he disdains to shine, for by the book              278
   He should have braved the east an hour ago.             279
   A black day will it be to somebody.

Ratcliffe!
RATCLIFFE
   My lord?
KING RICHARD    The sun will not be seen today;
   The sky doth frown and lour upon our army.              283
   I would these dewy tears were from the ground.
   Not shine today? Why, what is that to me
   More than to Richmond? For the selfsame heaven
   That frowns on me looks sadly upon him.

           *Enter Norfolk.*

NORFOLK
   Arm, arm, my lord, the foe vaunts in the field!         288
KING RICHARD
   Come, bustle, bustle! Caparison my horse.               289
   Call up Lord Stanley; bid him bring his power.
   I will lead forth my soldiers to the plain,
   And thus my battle shall be orderèd:                    292
   My foreward shall be drawn out all in length,           293
   Consisting equally of horse and foot;
   Our archers shall be placèd in the midst.
   John Duke of Norfolk, Thomas Earl of Surrey,
   Shall have the leading of this foot and horse.
   They thus directed, we will follow                      298
   In the main battle, whose puissance on either side      299
   Shall be well wingèd with our chiefest horse.           300
   This, and Saint George to boot! What think'st thou,
   Norfolk?                                                301
NORFOLK
   A good direction, warlike sovereign.
   This found I on my tent this morning.
                               *He showeth him a paper.*
KING RICHARD [*reads*]
   "Jockey of Norfolk, be not so bold,                     304
   For Dickon thy master is bought and sold."              305
   A thing devisèd by the enemy.
   Go, gentlemen, every man unto his charge.
   Let not our babbling dreams affright our souls;
   Conscience is but a word that cowards use,
   Devised at first to keep the strong in awe.
   Our strong arms be our conscience, swords our law!
   March on, join bravely! Let us to it pell-mell;         312
   If not to heaven, then hand in hand to hell.

       *His oration to his army.*

   What shall I say more than I have inferred?             314
   Remember whom you are to cope withal:
   A sort of vagabonds, rascals, and runaways,             316
   A scum of Bretons and base lackey peasants,             317
   Whom their o'ercloyèd country vomits forth              318
   To desperate adventures and assured destruction.

---

243 **except** excepted  247 **in blood** by bloodshed  248 **made means**
i.e., has taken advantage, created opportunity  250 **foil** a thin leaf of
metal placed under a gem to set it off to advantage  251 **chair**
throne.  **set** (1) seated (2) set like a jewel  254 **ward** protect
258 **Your . . . hire** England's prosperity will reward your efforts
262 **Your . . . age** your grandchildren will requite it when you are
old.  264 **Advance** raise  265–6 **the ransom . . . face** i.e., if I fail, there
will be no question of ransom, but only death  271 **as touching**
regarding  276 **Tell** Count the strokes of.  **calendar** almanac.
278 **the book** i.e., the almanac  279 **braved** made resplendent

283 **lour** look threateningly  288 **vaunts** boasts his strength
289 **Caparison** Put on the battle trappings of  292 **battle** troops
293 **foreward** vanguard  298 **directed** deployed  299 **main battle**
main body of troops.  **puissance** strength  300 **wingèd** flanked.
**horse** cavalry.  301 **to boot** i.e., to give us aid in addition.
304 **Jockey** i.e., Jack, John  305 **Dickon** i.e., Dick, Richard.  **bought
and sold** done for, finished.  312 **join** join battle.  **pell-mell**
headlong, hand to hand  314 **inferred** alleged.  316 **sort** gang
317 **lackey** servile  318 **o'ercloyèd** satiated, glutted

You sleeping safe, they bring to you unrest;
You having lands, and blest with beauteous wives,
They would restrain the one, distain the other.          322
And who doth lead them but a paltry fellow,
Long kept in Brittany at our mother's cost?          324
A milksop, one that never in his life
Felt so much cold as over shoes in snow?          326
Let's whip these stragglers o'er the seas again.
Lash hence these overweening rags of France,          328
These famished beggars, weary of their lives,
Who, but for dreaming on this fond exploit,          330
For want of means, poor rats, had hanged themselves.          331
If we be conquered, let men conquer us,
And not these bastard Bretons, whom our fathers
Have in their own land beaten, bobbed, and thumped,          334
And in record left them the heirs of shame.          335
Shall these enjoy our lands? Lie with our wives?
Ravish our daughters? [*Drum afar off.*] Hark! I hear
    their drum.
Fight, gentlemen of England! Fight, bold yeomen!
Draw, archers, draw your arrows to the head!          339
Spur your proud horses hard, and ride in blood;
Amaze the welkin with your broken staves!          341

[*Enter a Messenger.*]

What says Lord Stanley? Will he bring his power?
MESSENGER    My lord, he doth deny to come.
KING RICHARD    Off with his son George's head!
NORFOLK
My lord, the enemy is past the marsh.
After the battle let George Stanley die.
KING RICHARD
A thousand hearts are great within my bosom.
Advance our standards! Set upon our foes!          348
Our ancient word of courage, fair Saint George,          349
Inspire us with the spleen of fiery dragons!          350
Upon them! Victory sits on our helms!          *Exeunt.*

✿

## [5.4]

*Alarum. Excursions. [Norfolk and forces continue
to make forays, entering and exiting.] Enter [in
the melee] Catesby.*

CATESBY
Rescue, my lord of Norfolk, rescue, rescue!
The King enacts more wonders than a man,          2
Daring an opposite to every danger.          3
His horse is slain, and all on foot he fights,
Seeking for Richmond in the throat of death.
Rescue, fair lord, or else the day is lost!

[*Alarums.*] *Enter* [*King*] *Richard.*

KING RICHARD
A horse! A horse! My kingdom for a horse!
CATESBY
Withdraw, my lord. I'll help you to a horse.
KING RICHARD
Slave, I have set my life upon a cast,          9
And I will stand the hazard of the die.          10
I think there be six Richmonds in the field;          11
Five have I slain today instead of him.
A horse! A horse! My kingdom for a horse!    [*Exeunt.*]

## [5.5]

*Alarum. Enter Richard and Richmond; they fight.
Richard is slain. [Exit Richmond.] Then, retreat
being sounded, [flourish, and] enter Richmond,
[Lord Stanley Earl of] Derby bearing the crown,
with other lords, etc.*

RICHMOND
God and your arms be praised, victorious friends!
The day is ours; the bloody dog is dead.
STANLEY [*offering him the crown*]
Courageous Richmond, well hast thou acquit thee.
Lo, here this long-usurpèd royalty          4
From the dead temples of this bloody wretch
Have I plucked off, to grace thy brows withal.          6
Wear it, enjoy it, and make much of it.
RICHMOND
Great God of heaven, say amen to all!
But, tell me, is young George Stanley living?
STANLEY
He is, my lord, and safe in Leicester town,
Whither, if it please you, we may now withdraw us.
RICHMOND
What men of name are slain on either side?          12
STANLEY
John Duke of Norfolk, Walter Lord Ferrers,
Sir Robert Brackenbury, and Sir William Brandon.
RICHMOND
Inter their bodies as becomes their births.          15
Proclaim a pardon to the soldiers fled

---

**322 restrain** deprive you of.   **distain** defile, sully   **324 our mother's**
(Richmond's mother was not Richard's. This error occurs in the
second edition of Holinshed's *Chronicles*. The first edition reads
"brothers," the reference being to the fact that Richmond had been
supported at the court of the Duke of Brittany at the cost of Charles,
Duke of Burgundy, Richard's brother-in-law.)   **326 over shoes** i.e.,
over his shoe-tops   **328 rags** ragged fellows   **330 fond** foolish
**331 want of means** lack of the means (i.e., rope) to hang themselves
**334 bobbed** thrashed   **335 And . . . shame** and left them with nothing
but the promise of a shameful record in history.   **339 draw your . . .
head** i.e., draw the bow taut by pulling the arrow all the way back.
**341 Amaze the welkin** frighten the skies   **348 Advance our standards!** Raise our flags!   **349 word of courage** battle cry
**350 dragons** (Richard ironically identifies with the dragon slain by
Saint George.)
**5.4. Location: Bosworth Field, as before; the action is continuous.**
**0.1 *Excursions*** Sorties.

**2 than a man** than seems possible for a human being   **3 Daring . . .
danger** boldly facing every danger in battle.   **9 cast** throw of the
dice   **10 stand the hazard** accept the fortune.   **die** (Singular of *dice*.)
**11 six Richmonds** i.e., Richmond himself and five men dressed like
him as a safety precaution
**5.5. Location: Action continues at Bosworth Field.**
**0.2 *retreat*** trumpet signal to withdraw, cease the attack   **4 royalty**
i.e., the royal crown   **6 withal** with.   **12 of name** of title
**15 becomes** suits

That in submission will return to us,
And then, as we have ta'en the Sacrament,                    18
We will unite the white rose and the red.
Smile heaven upon this fair conjunction,                     20
That long have frowned upon their enmity!
What traitor hears me and says not amen?
England hath long been mad, and scarred herself;
The brother blindly shed the brother's blood,
The father rashly slaughtered his own son,
The son, compelled, been butcher to the sire.
All this divided York and Lancaster,
Divided in their dire division.

Oh, now let Richmond and Elizabeth,
The true succeeders of each royal house,
By God's fair ordinance conjoin together!                    31
And let their heirs, God, if thy will be so,
Enrich the time to come with smooth-faced peace,
With smiling plenty, and fair prosperous days!
Abate the edge of traitors, gracious Lord,                   35
That would reduce these bloody days again                    36
And make poor England weep in streams of blood!
Let them not live to taste this land's increase             38
That would with treason wound this fair land's peace!
Now civil wounds are stopped, peace lives again.            40
That she may long live here, God say amen! [*Exeunt.*]      41

**18 ta'en the Sacrament** sworn a sacred oath on the Sacrament (to marry Princess Elizabeth, daughter of Edward IV, thereby uniting the houses of York and of Lancaster, white rose and red rose) **20 conjunction** union. (An astrological metaphor.)

**31 ordinance** decree   **35 Abate the edge** Blunt and render ineffective the sword's edge   **36 reduce** bring back   **38 taste** enjoy   **40 stopped** closed up   **41 she** peace

# The Tragedy of King Richard the Second

*R*ichard II (c. 1595–1596) is the first play in Shakespeare's great four-play historical saga, or tetralogy, that continues with the two parts of *Henry IV* (c. 1596–1598) and concludes with *Henry V* (1599). In this, his second, tetralogy, Shakespeare dramatizes the beginnings of the great conflict called the Wars of the Roses, having already dramatized the conclusion of that civil war in his earlier tetralogy on Henry VI and Richard III (c. 1589–1594). Both sequences move from an outbreak of civil faction to the eventual triumph of political stability. Together, they comprise the story of England's long century of political turmoil from the 1390s until Henry Tudor's victory over Richard III in 1485. Yet Shakespeare chose to tell the two halves of this chronicle in reverse order. His culminating statement about kingship in *Henry V* focuses on the earlier historical period, on the education and kingly success of Prince Hal.

With *Richard II,* then, Shakespeare turns to the events that had launched England's century of crisis. These events were still fresh and relevant to Elizabethan minds. Richard and Bolingbroke's contest for the English crown provided a sobering example of political wrongdoing and, at least by implication, a rule for political right conduct. One prominent reason for studying history, to an Elizabethan, was to avoid the errors of the past. The relevance of such historical analogy was, in fact, vividly underscored some six years after Shakespeare wrote the play: in 1601, followers of the Earl of Essex commissioned Shakespeare's acting company to perform a revived play about Richard II on the eve of what was to be an abortive rebellion, perhaps with the intention of inciting a riot. Whether the play was Shakespeare's is not certain, but it seems likely. The acting company was ultimately exonerated, but not before Queen Elizabeth concluded that she was being compared to Richard II. When he wrote the play, Shakespeare presumably did not know that it would be used for such a purpose, but he must have known that the overthrow of Richard II was,

in any case, a controversial subject because of its potential use as a precedent for rebellion. The scene of Richard's deposition (4.1) was considered so provocative by Elizabeth's government that it was censored in the printed quartos of Shakespeare's play during the Queen's lifetime.

In view of the startling relevance of this piece of history to Shakespeare's own times, then, what are the rights and wrongs of Richard's deposition, and to what extent can political lessons be drawn from Shakespeare's presentation?

To begin with, we should not underestimate Richard's attractive qualities, as a man and even as a king. Throughout the play, Richard is consistently more impressive and majestic in appearance than his rival, Bolingbroke. Richard fascinates us with his verbal sensitivity, his poetic insight, and his dramatic self-consciousness. He eloquently expounds a sacramental view of kingship, according to which "Not all the water in the rough rude sea / Can wash the balm off from an anointed king" (3.2.54–5). Bolingbroke can depose Richard but can never capture the aura of majesty Richard possesses; Bolingbroke may succeed politically but only at the expense of desecrating an idea. Richard is much more interesting to us as a man than Bolingbroke, more capable of grief, more tender in his personal relationships, and more in need of being understood. Indeed, a major factor in Richard's tragedy is the conflict between his public role (wherein he sees himself as divinely appointed, almost superhuman) and his private role (wherein he is emotionally dependent and easily hurt). He confuses what the medieval and Renaissance world knew as the king's "two bodies," the sacramental body of kingship, which is eternal, and the human body of a single occupant of the throne, whose frail mortal condition is subject to time and fortune. Richard's failure to perceive and to act wisely on this difference is part of his tragic predicament, but his increasing insight, through suffering, into the truth of the distinction is also part of his spiritual growth. His dilemma, however poignantly individual, lies at the heart of kingship. Richard is thus very much a king. Although he sometimes indulges in childish sentimentality, at his best he is superbly refined, perceptive, and poetic.

These qualities notwithstanding, Richard is an incompetent ruler, compared with the man who supplants him. Richard himself confesses to the prodigal expense of "too great a court." In order to raise funds, he has been obliged to "farm our royal realm"; that is, to sell for ready cash the right of collecting taxes to individual courtiers, who are then free to extort what the market will bear (1.4.43–5). Similarly, Richard proposes to issue "blank charters" (line 48) to his minions, who will then be authorized to fill in the amount of tax to be paid by any hapless subject. These abuses were infamous to Elizabethan audiences as symbols of autocratic misgovernment. No less heinous is Richard's seizure of the dukedom of Lancaster from his cousin Bolingbroke. Although Richard does receive the consent of his Council to banish Bolingbroke because of the divisiveness of the quarrel between him and Mowbray, the King violates the very idea of inheritance of property when he takes away Bolingbroke's title and lands. And, as his uncle the Duke of York remonstrates, Richard's own right to the throne depends on that idea of due inheritance. By offending against the most sacred concepts of order and degree, he teaches others to rebel.

Richard's behavior even prior to the commencement of the play arouses suspicion. The nature of his complicity in the death of his uncle Thomas of Woodstock, Duke of Gloucester, is perhaps never entirely clear, and Gloucester may have given provocation. Indeed, one can sympathize with the predicament of a young ruler prematurely thrust into the center of power by the untimely death of his father, the crown prince, now having to cope with an array of worldly-wise, advice-giving uncles. Nevertheless, Richard is unambiguously guilty of murder in the eyes of Gloucester's widow, while her brother-in-law John of Gaunt, Duke of Lancaster, assumes that Richard has caused Gloucester's death, "the which if wrongfully / Let heaven revenge" (1.2.39–40). Apparently, too, Gaunt's son Bolingbroke believes Richard to be a murderer, and he brings accusation against Thomas Mowbray, Duke of Norfolk, partly as a means of embarrassing the King, whom he cannot accuse directly. Mowbray's lot is an unenviable one: he was in command at Calais when Gloucester was executed there, and he hints that Richard ordered the execution (even though Mowbray alleges that he himself did not carry out the order). For his part, Richard is only too glad to banish the man suspected of having been his agent in murder. Mowbray is a convenient scapegoat.

The polished, ceremonial tone of the play's opening is vitiated, then, by our growing awareness of hidden violence and factionalism going on behind the scene. Our first impression of Richard is of a king devoted to the public display of conciliatory even-handedness. He listens to the rival claims of Bolingbroke and Mowbray, and, when he cannot reconcile them peacefully, he orders a trial by combat. This trial (1.3) is replete with ceremonial repetition and ritual. The combatants are duly sworn in the justice of their cause, and God is to decide the quarrel by awarding victory to the champion who speaks the truth. Richard, the presiding officer, assumes the role of God's anointed deputy on earth. Yet it becomes evident in due course that Richard is a major perpetrator of injustice rather than an impartial judge, that Bolingbroke is after greater objectives than he acknowledges even to himself, and that Richard's refusal to let the trial by combat take place and his banishment of the two contenders are his desperate ways of burying a problem he cannot deal with forthrightly. His uncles reluctantly consent to the banishment only because they, too, see that disaffection has reached alarming proportions.

Bolingbroke's motivation in these opening scenes is perhaps even more obscure than Richard's. Our first impression of Bolingbroke is of forthrightness, moral indignation, and patriotic zeal. In fact, we never really question the earnestness of his outrage at Richard's misgovernance, his longing to avenge a family murder (for Gloucester was his uncle, too), or his bitter disappointment at being banished. Yet we are prompted to ask further: what is the essential cause of the enmity between Bolingbroke and Richard? If Mowbray is only a stalking-horse, is not Gloucester's death also the excuse for pursuing a preexistent animosity? Richard, for one, appears to think so. His portrayal of Bolingbroke as a scheming politician, who curries favor with the populace in order to build a widely based alliance against the King himself, is telling and prophetic. Bolingbroke, says Richard, acts "As were our England in reversion his, / And he our subjects' next degree in hope" (1.4.35–6). This unflattering appraisal might be ascribed to malicious envy on Richard's part, were it not proved by subsequent events to be at least partly accurate.

Paradoxically, Richard is far the more prescient of the two contenders for the English throne. It is he, in fact, who perceives from the start that the conflict between them is irreconcilable. He banishes Bolingbroke as his chief rival and does not doubt what motives will call Bolingbroke home again. Meanwhile, Bolingbroke disclaims any motive for his return other than love of country and hatred of injustice. Although born with a political canniness that Richard lacks, Bolingbroke does not reflect (out loud, at least) upon the consequences of his own acts. As a man of action, he lives in the present.

Richard, conversely, a person of exquisite contemplative powers and poetic imagination, does not deign to cope with the practical. He both envies and despises Bolingbroke's easy way with the commoners. Richard cherishes kingship for the majesty and the royal prerogative it confers, not for the power to govern wisely. Thus it is that, despite his perception of what will follow, Richard habitually indulges his worst instincts, buying a moment of giddy pleasure at the expense of future disaster.

Granted Richard's incompetence as a ruler, is Bolingbroke justified in armed rebellion against him? According to Bolingbroke's uncle, the Duke of York (who later, to be sure, shifts his allegiance), and to the Bishop of Carlisle, Bolingbroke is not justified in the rebellion. The attitude of these men can be summed up by the phrase "passive obedience." And, although Bolingbroke's own father, John of Gaunt, dies before his son returns to England to seize power, Gaunt, too, is opposed to such human defiances of the sacred institution of kingship. "God's is the quarrel," he insists (1.2.37). Because Richard is God's anointed deputy on earth, as Gaunt sees the matter, only God may punish the King's wrongdoing. Gaunt may not question Richard's guilt, but neither does he question God's ability to avenge. Gaunt sees human intervention in God's affair as blasphemous: "for I may never lift / An angry arm against His minister" (1.2.40–1). To be sure, Gaunt does acknowledge a solemn duty to offer frank advice to extremists of both sides, and he does so unsparingly. He consents to the banishment of his son, and he rebukes Richard with his dying breath.

This doctrine of passive obedience was familiar to Elizabethans, for they heard it in church periodically in official homilies against rebellion. It was the Tudor state's answer to those who asserted a right to overthrow reputedly evil kings. The argument was logically ingenious. Why are evil rulers permitted to govern from time to time? Presumably, because God wishes to test a people or to punish them for waywardness. Any king performing such chastisement is a divine scourge. Accordingly, the worst thing a people can do is to rebel against God's scourge, thereby manifesting more waywardness. Instead, they must attempt to remedy the insolence in their hearts, advise the King to mend his ways, and patiently await God's pardon. If they do so, they will not long be disappointed. The doctrine is essentially conservative, defending the status quo. It is reinforced in this play by the Bishop of Carlisle's prophecy that God will avenge through civil war the deposition of his anointed (4.1.126–50); an Elizabethan audience would have appreciated the irony of the prophecy's having come true and having been the subject of Shakespeare's first historical tetralogy. Moreover, in *Richard II* the doctrine of passive obedience is a moderate position between the extremes of tyranny and rebellion, and is expressed by thoughtful,

selfless characters. We might be tempted to label it Shakespeare's view if we did not also perceive that the doctrine is continually placed in ironic conflict with harsh political realities. The character who most reflects the ironies and even ludicrous incongruities of the position is the Duke of York.

York is to an extent a choric character, that is, one who helps direct our viewpoint, because his transfer of loyalties from Richard to Bolingbroke structurally delineates the decline of Richard's fortunes and the concurrent rise of Bolingbroke's. At first York shares his brother Gaunt's unwillingness to act, despite their dismay at Richard's willfulness. It is only when Richard seizes the dukedom of Lancaster that York can no longer hold his tongue. His condemnation is as bitter as that of Gaunt, hinting even at loss of allegiance (2.1.200–8). Still, he accepts the responsibility, so cavalierly bestowed by Richard, of governing England in the King's absence. He musters what force he can to oppose Bolingbroke's advance and lectures against this rebellion with the same vehemence he had used against Richard's despotism. Yet, when faced with Bolingbroke's overwhelming military superiority, he accedes rather than fight on behalf of a lost cause. However much this may resemble cowardice or mere expediency, it also displays a pragmatic logic. Once Bolingbroke has become de facto king, in York's view, he must be acknowledged and obeyed. By a kind of analogy to the doctrine of passive obedience (which more rigorous theorists would never allow), York accepts the status quo as inevitable. He is vigorously ready to defend the new regime, just as he earlier defended Richard's de jure rule. York's inconsistent loyalty helps define the structure of the play.

When, however, this conclusion brings York to the point of turning in his own son, Aumerle, for a traitor and quarreling with his wife as to whether their son shall live, the ironic absurdity is apparent. Bolingbroke, now King Henry, himself is amused, in one of the play's rare lighthearted moments (5.3.79–80). At the same time, the comedy deals with serious issues, especially the conflict between public responsibility urged by York and private or emotional satisfaction urged by his Duchess—a conflict seen earlier, for example, in the debate between Gaunt and his sister-in-law, the widowed Duchess of Gloucester (1.2). When a family and a kingdom are divided against one another, there can be no really satisfactory resolution.

We are never entirely convinced that all the fine old medieval theories surrounding kingship—divine right, passive obedience, trial by combat, and the like—can ever wholly explain or remedy the complex and nasty political situation afflicting England. The one man capable of decisive action, in fact, is he who never theorizes at all: Bolingbroke. As we have seen, his avowed motive for opposing Mowbray—simple patriotic indignation—is uttered with such earnestness that we wonder if indeed Bolingbroke has examined those political ambitions in himself that are so plainly visible to Richard and others. This same discrepancy between surface and depth applies to Bolingbroke's motives in returning to England. We cannot be sure at what time he begins to plot that return; the conspiracy announced by Northumberland (2.1.224–300) follows so closely after Richard's violation of Bolingbroke's hereditary rights and is already so well advanced that we gain the impression of an already existing plot, though some of this impression may be simply owing to Shakespeare's characteristic compression of historic time. When Bolingbroke arrives in England, in any case, he protests to York with seemingly passionate sincerity that he comes only for his dukedom of Lancaster (2.3.113–36). If so, why does he set about executing Richard's followers without legal authority and otherwise establishing his own claim to power? Why does he indulge in homophobic slurs against Richard, insinuating that Richard's favorites have "Broke the possession of a royal bed" (3.1.13), when, as far as we can see from the devotion Richard shows to his queen, the charges are trumped up and untrue? Does Bolingbroke seriously think he can reclaim his dukedom by force and then yield to Richard without either maintaining Richard as a puppet king or placing himself in intolerable jeopardy? And can he suppose that his allies, Northumberland and the rest, who have now openly defied the King, will countenance the return to power of one who would never trust them again? It is in this context that York protests, "Well, well, I see the issue of these arms" (2.3.152). The deposition of Richard and then Richard's death are unavoidable conclusions once Bolingbroke has succeeded in an armed rebellion. There can be no turning back. Yet Bolingbroke simply will not think in these terms. He permits Northumberland to proceed with almost sadistic harshness in the arrest and impeachment of Richard and then admonishes Northumberland in public for acting so harshly; the dirty work goes forward, with Northumberland taking the blame, while Bolingbroke assumes a statesmanlike pose. When the new King Henry discovers—to his surprise, evidently—that Richard's life is now a burden to the state, he ponders aloud, "Have I no friend will rid me of this living fear?" (5.4.2) and then rebukes Exton for proceeding on cue.

Bolingbroke's pragmatic spirit and new mode of governing are the embodiment of de facto rule. Ultimately, the justification for his authority is the very fact of its existence, its functioning. Bolingbroke is the man of the hour. To apply William Butler Yeats's striking contrast, the Lancastrian usurpers, Bolingbroke and his son, are vessels of clay, whereas Richard is a vessel of porcelain. One is durable and utilitarian, yet unattractive; the other is exquisite, fragile, and impractical. The comparison does not force us to prefer one to the other, even though Yeats himself characteristically sided with beauty against politics. Rather, Shakespeare gives us our choice, allowing us to see in ourselves an inclination toward political and social stability or toward artistic temperament.

The paradox may suggest that the qualities of a good administrator are not those of a sensitive, thoughtful man. However hopeless as a king, Richard stands before us increasingly as an introspective and fascinating person. The contradictions of his character are aptly focused in the business of breaking a mirror during his deposition: it is at once symbolic of a narcissistic, shallow concern for appearances and a quest for a deeper, inward truth, so that the smashing of the mirror is an act both of self-destruction and of self-discovery. When Richard's power crumbles, his spirit is enhanced, as though loss of power and royal identity were necessary for the discovery of true values.

In this we can see a faint anticipation of King Lear's self-learning, fearfully and preciously bought. The trace is only slight here, because in good part *Richard II* is a political history play rather than a tragedy and because Richard's self-realization is imperfect. Nevertheless, when Richard faces deposition and separation from his queen, and especially when he is alone in prison expecting to die, he strives to understand his life and through it the general condition of humanity. He gains our sympathy in the wonderfully humane interchange between this deposed king and the poor groom of his stable, who once took care of Richard's horse, roan Barbary, now the possession of the new monarch (5.5.67–94). Richard perceives a contradiction in heaven's assurances about salvation: Christ promises to receive all God's children, and yet He also warns that it is as hard for a rich man to enter heaven as for a camel to be threaded through a needle's eye (5.5.16–17). The paradox echoes the Beatitudes: the last shall be first, the meek shall inherit the earth. Richard, now one of the downtrodden, gropes for an understanding of the vanity of human achievement whereby he can aspire to the victory Christ promised. At his death, that victory seems to him assured: his soul will mount to its seat on high "Whilst my gross flesh sinks downward, here to die" (line 112).

In this triumph of spirit over flesh, the long downward motion of Richard's worldly fortune is crucially reversed. By the same token, the worldly success of Bolingbroke is shown to be no more than that: worldly success. His archetype is Cain, the primal murderer of a brother. To the extent that the play is a history, Bolingbroke's de facto success is a matter of political relevance; but, in the belated movement toward Richard's personal tragedy, we experience a profound countermovement that partly achieves a purgative sense of atonement and reassurance. Whatever Richard may have lost, his gain is also great.

Balance and symmetry are unusually important in *Richard II*. The play begins and ends with elaborate ritual obeisance to the concept of social and monarchic order, and yet, in both cases, a note of personal disorder refuses to be subdued by the public ceremonial. Shakespeare keeps our response to both Richard and Bolingbroke ambivalent by clouding their respective responsibilities for murder. Just as Richard's role in Gloucester's death remains unclear, so Bolingbroke's role in the assassination of Richard remains equally unclear. Mowbray and Exton, as scapegoats, are in some respects parallel. Because Richard and Bolingbroke are both implicated in the deaths of near kinsmen, both are associated with Cain's murder of Abel. As Bolingbroke rises in worldly fortune, Richard falls; as Richard finds insight and release through suffering, Bolingbroke finds guilt and remorse through distasteful political necessity. Verbally and structurally, the play explores the rhetorical figure of chiasmus, or the pairing of opposites in an inverted and diagonal pattern whereby one goes down as the other goes up and vice versa. Again and again, the ritual effects of staging and style draw our attention to the balanced conflicts between the two men and within Richard. Symmetry helps to focus these conflicts in visual and aural ways. In particular, the deposition scene, with its spectacle of a coronation in reverse, brings the sacramental and human sides of the central figure into poignant dramatic relationship.

Women play a subsidiary role in this play about male struggles for power, and yet the brief scenes in which women take part—the Duchess of Gloucester with Gaunt (1.2), Richard's queen with his courtiers and gardeners and then with Richard himself (2.2, 3.4, 5.1), the Duchess of York with her husband and son and King Henry (5.2–5.3)—highlight for us important thematic contrasts between the public and private spheres, power and powerlessness, political struggle and humane sensitivity, the state and the family. The women, excluded from roles of practical authority, offer, nonetheless, an invaluable critical perspective on the fateful and often self-consuming political games that men play among themselves. As in *Julius Caesar* and *Troilus and Cressida*, the men of *Richard II* ignore women's warnings and insights to their own peril and to the discomfiting of the body politic.

The imagery of *Richard II* reinforces structure and meaning. The play is unlike the history plays that follow in its extensive use of blank verse and rhyme and in its interwoven sets of recurring images; *Richard II* is, in this respect, more typical of the so-called lyric period (c. 1594–1596) that also produced *Romeo and Juliet* and *A Midsummer Night's Dream*. Image patterns locate the play in our imaginations as a kind of lost Eden. England is a garden mismanaged by her royal gardener, so that weeds and caterpillars (e.g., Bushy, Bagot, and Green) flourish. The "garden" scene (3.4), located near the center of the play, offering a momentary haven of allegorical reflection on the play's hectic events, is central in the development of the garden metaphor. England is also a sick body, ill-tended by her royal physician, and a family divided against itself, yielding abortive and sterile progeny. Her political ills are attested to by disorders in the cosmos: comets, shooting stars, withered bay trees, and weeping rains. Night owls, associated with death, prevail over the larks of morning. The sun, royally associated at first with Richard, deserts him for Bolingbroke and leaves Richard as the Phaëthon who has mishandled the sun-god's chariot and so scorched the earth. Linked to the sun image is the prevalent leitmotif of ascent and descent. And, touching on all these, a cluster of biblical images sees England as a despoiled garden of Eden witnessing a second fall of humanity. Richard repeatedly brands his enemies and deserters as Judases and Pilates—not always fairly; nonetheless, in his last agony, he finds genuine consolation in Christ's example. For a man so self-absorbed in the drama of his existence, this poetic method is intensely suitable. Language and stage action have combined perfectly to express the conflict between a sensitive but flawed king and his efficient but unlovable successor.

In performance, the play belongs to Richard. However much he ends up the loser, his role calls for a kind of royal charisma that Bolingbroke never achieves. Such was the effect, at any rate, in Brian Bedford's enactment of the role at Stratford, Canada, in 1983; his appearance on the walls of Flint Castle in 3.3, splendidly attired in white robes with gold trim, embodied a regal image of kingship that was then forced to humble itself before Bolingbroke's brute might. John Gielgud, Alec Guinness, Michael Redgrave, Paul Scofield, John Neville, Ian McKellen, Ian Richardson, Richard Pasco, Derek Jacobi, Alan Howard, Jeremy Irons, Ralph Fiennes, the actress Fiona Shaw, and still other leading performers of their day have found the role one in which they could enthrall audiences with the nuanced cadences of Richard's speeches. The role has also afforded a wide range of interpretations; Guinness saw him as unhappily neurotic, Gielgud as kindly, Redgrave as effeminate, Scofield as cerebral and remote, McKellen as one who is convinced of his semi-divine nature. The play has also become a vehicle for spectacle and striking visual effects emphasizing the symmetries of the text's attention to poetic symbolism and social ritual; glittering pageantry and fading splendor vie for our interest and our loyalties.

# The Tragedy of King Richard the Second

[*Dramatis Personae*

KING RICHARD THE SECOND
QUEEN, *Richard's wife*
JOHN OF GAUNT, *Duke of Lancaster, King Richard's uncle*
HENRY BOLINGBROKE, *John of Gaunt's son, Duke of Hereford and claimant to his father's dukedom of Lancaster, later King Henry IV*
DUKE OF YORK, *Edmund of Langley, King Richard's uncle*
DUCHESS OF YORK
DUKE OF AUMERLE, *York's son and the Earl of Rutland*
DUCHESS OF GLOUCESTER, *widow of Thomas of Woodstock, Duke of Gloucester (King Richard's uncle)*

THOMAS MOWBRAY, *Duke of Norfolk,*
EARL OF SALISBURY,
LORD BERKELEY,
DUKE OF SURREY,
BISHOP OF CARLISLE,
SIR STEPHEN SCROOP,
ABBOT OF WESTMINSTER,
BUSHY,
BAGOT,    *favorites of King Richard,*
GREEN,
CAPTAIN *of the Welsh Army,*
} *supporters of King Richard*

EARL OF NORTHUMBERLAND,
HARRY PERCY, *Northumberland's son,*
LORD ROSS,
LORD WILLOUGHBY,
LORD FITZWATER,
SIR PIERCE OF EXTON,
*Another* LORD,
} *supporters of Bolingbroke*

LORD MARSHAL
*Two* HERALDS
GARDENER
GARDENER'S MAN
LADY *attending the Queen*
KEEPER *of the prison*
A MAN *attending Exton*

SERVINGMAN *to York*
GROOM *of the stable*

*Lords, Officers, Soldiers, Attendants, Ladies attending the Queen*

scene: England and Wales]

## [1.1]

*Enter King Richard, John of Gaunt, with other nobles and attendants.*

KING RICHARD
Old John of Gaunt, time-honored Lancaster,          1
Hast thou according to thy oath and bond
Brought hither Henry Hereford, thy bold son,          3
Here to make good the boist'rous late appeal,          4
Which then our leisure would not let us hear,          5
Against the Duke of Norfolk, Thomas Mowbray?
GAUNT    I have, my liege.          7
KING RICHARD
Tell me, moreover, hast thou sounded him          8

---

1.1. Location: A room of state. (Holinshed's *Chronicles* places this scene at Windsor, in 1398.)
1 **Old John of Gaunt** (Born in 1340 at Ghent; hence the surname *Gaunt.* In 1398 he was fifty-eight years old.)

**3 Henry Hereford** Henry Bolingbroke, Duke of Hereford    **4 late** recent.    **appeal** accusation, formal challenge or impeachment that the accuser was obliged to maintain in combat    **5 our, us** (The royal plural.)    **leisure** i.e., lack of leisure    **7 liege** i.e., sovereign.    **8 sounded** inquired of

331

If he appeal the Duke on ancient malice,                                    9
Or worthily, as a good subject should,
On some known ground of treachery in him?

GAUNT
As near as I could sift him on that argument,                               12
On some apparent danger seen in him                                         13
Aimed at Your Highness, no inveterate malice.

KING RICHARD
Then call them to our presence.        [*Exit an attendant.*]
                                Face to face,
And frowning brow to brow, ourselves will hear                              16
The accuser and the accusèd freely speak.
High-stomached are they both, and full of ire;                              18
In rage, deaf as the sea, hasty as fire.                                    19

*Enter Bolingbroke and Mowbray.*

BOLINGBROKE
Many years of happy days befall
My gracious sovereign, my most loving liege!

MOWBRAY
Each day still better others' happiness,                                    22
Until the heavens, envying earth's good hap,                                23
Add an immortal title to your crown!                                        24

KING RICHARD
We thank you both. Yet one but flatters us,
As well appeareth by the cause you come:                                    26
Namely, to appeal each other of high treason.                               27
Cousin of Hereford, what dost thou object                                   28
Against the Duke of Norfolk, Thomas Mowbray?

BOLINGBROKE
First—heaven be the record to my speech!—                                   30
In the devotion of a subject's love,
Tend'ring the precious safety of my prince,                                 32
And free from other misbegotten hate,
Come I appellant to this princely presence.                                 34
Now, Thomas Mowbray, do I turn to thee;
And mark my greeting well, for what I speak
My body shall make good upon this earth
Or my divine soul answer it in heaven.                                      38
Thou art a traitor and a miscreant,                                         39
Too good to be so and too bad to live,                                      40
Since the more fair and crystal is the sky,                                 41
The uglier seem the clouds that in it fly.
Once more, the more to aggravate the note,                                  43
With a foul traitor's name stuff I thy throat,
And wish, so please my sovereign, ere I move,                               45
What my tongue speaks my right-drawn sword may prove.  46

MOWBRAY
Let not my cold words here accuse my zeal.                                  47
'Tis not the trial of a woman's war,                                        48
The bitter clamor of two eager tongues,                                     49
Can arbitrate this cause betwixt us twain;                                  50
The blood is hot that must be cooled for this.
Yet can I not of such tame patience boast
As to be hushed and naught at all to say.
First, the fair reverence of Your Highness curbs me
From giving reins and spurs to my free speech,
Which else would post until it had returned                                56
These terms of treason doubled down his throat.
Setting aside his high blood's royalty,                                     58
And let him be no kinsman to my liege,                                      59
I do defy him, and I spit at him,
Call him a slanderous coward and a villain;
Which to maintain I would allow him odds
And meet him, were I tied to run afoot                                      63
Even to the frozen ridges of the Alps
Or any other ground inhabitable                                            65
Wherever Englishman durst set his foot.
Meantime, let this defend my loyalty:
By all my hopes, most falsely doth he lie.

BOLINGBROKE [*throwing down his gage*]
Pale trembling coward, there I throw my gage,                               69
Disclaiming here the kindred of the King,                                   70
And lay aside my high blood's royalty,
Which fear, not reverence, makes thee to except.                           72
If guilty dread have left thee so much strength
As to take up mine honor's pawn, then stoop.                               74
By that, and all the rites of knighthood else,
Will I make good against thee, arm to arm,
What I have spoke or thou canst worse devise.                              77

MOWBRAY [*taking up the gage*]
I take it up; and by that sword I swear
Which gently laid my knighthood on my shoulder,                            79
I'll answer thee in any fair degree
Or chivalrous design of knightly trial;
And when I mount, alive may I not light                                    82
If I be traitor or unjustly fight!

KING RICHARD
What doth our cousin lay to Mowbray's charge?
It must be great that can inherit us                                       85
So much as of a thought of ill in him.

BOLINGBROKE
Look what I speak, my life shall prove it true:                            87
That Mowbray hath received eight thousand nobles                           88
In name of lendings for Your Highness' soldiers,                           89

---

**9 appeal** accuse.   **on . . . malice** on the grounds of a long-standing enmity   **12 sift** discover by questioning.   **argument** subject   **13 apparent** obvious, manifest   **16 ourselves** I myself. (The royal plural.)   **18 High-stomached** Haughty   **19 In . . . sea** i.e., raging so loudly, like a stormy sea, as to be deafening   **22 Each . . . happiness** May each day improve on the happiness of other past days   **23 hap** fortune   **24 Add . . . crown** i.e., take you up to heaven in glory at the time of your death.   **26 you come** for which you come   **27 appeal** accuse   **28 what . . . object** what accusation do you bring   **30 record** witness   **32 Tend'ring** watching over, holding dear   **34 appellant** as the accuser   **38 answer** answer for   **39 miscreant** irreligious villain   **40 good** i.e., noble, high-born   **41 crystal** clear. (The image alludes to the crystal spheres in which, according to the Ptolemaic conception of the universe, the heavenly bodies were fixed.)   **43 aggravate the note** emphasize the stigma, i.e., the charge of treason   **45 so please** if it please   **46 right-drawn** justly drawn

**47 accuse my zeal** cast doubt on my zeal or loyalty.   **48 woman's war** i.e., war of words   **49 eager** sharp, biting   **50 Can** that can   **56 post** ride at high speed (like a messenger riding relays of horses)   **58 Setting . . . royalty** Disregarding Bolingbroke's royal blood (as grandson of Edward III)   **59 let him be** suppose him to be   **63 tied** obliged   **65 inhabitable** uninhabitable   **69 gage** a pledge to combat (usually a glove or gauntlet, i.e., a mailed or armored glove)   **70 Disclaiming . . . King** setting aside for the moment my kinship with King Richard (as Mowbray proposed in line 58)   **72 except** exempt, set aside.   **74 pawn** i.e., the gage   **77 or . . . devise** or anything else worse you can propose.   **79 on my shoulder** (The ceremony of conferring knighthood involved laying a sword on a shoulder of the candidate.)   **82 when** once.   **light** alight, dismount   **85 inherit us** put me in possession of, make me have   **87 Look what** Whatever   **88 nobles** gold coins worth six shillings eight pence   **89 lendings** advances on pay

The which he hath detained for lewd employments,    90
Like a false traitor and injurious villain.
Besides I say, and will in battle prove
Or here or elsewhere to the furthest verge    93
That ever was surveyed by English eye,
That all the treasons for these eighteen years    95
Complotted and contrivèd in this land    96
Fetch from false Mowbray their first head and
    spring.    97
Further I say, and further will maintain
Upon his bad life to make all this good,    99
That he did plot the Duke of Gloucester's death,    100
Suggest his soon-believing adversaries,    101
And consequently, like a traitor coward,    102
Sluiced out his innocent soul through streams of
    blood—    103
Which blood, like sacrificing Abel's, cries    104
Even from the tongueless caverns of the earth    105
To me for justice and rough chastisement.
And, by the glorious worth of my descent,    107
This arm shall do it or this life be spent.

KING RICHARD
How high a pitch his resolution soars!    109
Thomas of Norfolk, what say'st thou to this?

MOWBRAY
Oh, let my sovereign turn away his face
And bid his ears a little while be deaf,
Till I have told this slander of his blood    113
How God and good men hate so foul a liar!

KING RICHARD
Mowbray, impartial are our eyes and ears.
Were he my brother, nay, my kingdom's heir,
As he is but my father's brother's son,
Now, by my scepter's awe I make a vow,    118
Such neighbor nearness to our sacred blood
Should nothing privilege him nor partialize    120
The unstooping firmness of my upright soul.
He is our subject, Mowbray; so art thou.
Free speech and fearless I to thee allow.

MOWBRAY
Then, Bolingbroke, as low as to thy heart
Through the false passage of thy throat thou liest!
Three parts of that receipt I had for Calais    126
Disbursed I duly to His Highness' soldiers;

The other part reserved I by consent,
For that my sovereign liege was in my debt    129
Upon remainder of a dear account    130
Since last I went to France to fetch his queen.    131
Now swallow down that lie. For Gloucester's death,    132
I slew him not, but to my own disgrace    133
Neglected my sworn duty in that case.    134
[To Gaunt] For you, my noble lord of Lancaster,
The honorable father to my foe,
Once did I lay an ambush for your life,
A trespass that doth vex my grievèd soul;
But ere I last received the Sacrament
I did confess it, and exactly begged    140
Your Grace's pardon, and I hope I had it.
This is my fault. As for the rest appealed,    142
It issues from the rancor of a villain,
A recreant and most degenerate traitor,    144
Which in myself I boldly will defend,    145
And interchangeably hurl down my gage    146
Upon this overweening traitor's foot,    147
To prove myself a loyal gentleman
Even in the best blood chambered in his bosom.    149
    [He throws down his gage. Bolingbroke picks it up.]
In haste whereof most heartily I pray    150
Your Highness to assign our trial day.

KING RICHARD
Wrath-kindled gentlemen, be ruled by me;
Let's purge this choler without letting blood.    153
This we prescribe, though no physician;
Deep malice makes too deep incision.
Forget, forgive; conclude and be agreed;    156
Our doctors say this is no month to bleed.—    157
Good uncle, let this end where it begun;
We'll calm the Duke of Norfolk, you your son.

GAUNT
To be a make-peace shall become my age.
Throw down, my son, the Duke of Norfolk's gage.

KING RICHARD
And Norfolk, throw down his.

GAUNT                        When, Harry, when?
Obedience bids I should not bid again.

KING RICHARD
Norfolk, throw down, we bid; there is no boot.    164

---

90 **lewd** vile, base    93 **Or** either    95 **these eighteen years** i.e., ever since the Peasants' Revolt of 1381    96 **Complotted** plotted in a conspiracy    97 **Fetch** derive.    **head and spring** (Synonymous words meaning "origin.")    99 **Upon . . . good** to prove all this to be true of this man who has lived so unworthily    100 **Duke of Gloucester's death** (Thomas of Woodstock, Duke of Gloucester, a younger son of Edward III and brother of John of Gaunt, was murdered at Calais in September 1397, while in Mowbray's custody.)    101 **Suggest . . . adversaries** did prompt Gloucester's easily persuaded enemies (to believe him guilty of treason)    102 **consequently** afterward    103 **Sluiced out** let flow (as by the opening of a sluice, or valve)    104 **Abel's** (For the story of Cain's murder of his brother Abel, the first such murder on earth and the archetype of the killing of a kinsman, see Genesis 4:3–12.)    105 **tongueless** resonant but without articulate speech; echoing    107 **my descent** my noble lineage    109 **pitch** highest reach of a falcon's flight    113 **this slander . . . blood** this disgrace to the royal family    118 **my scepter's awe** the reverence due my scepter    120 **nothing** not at all.    **partialize** make partial, bias    126 **receipt** money received

129 **For that** because    130 **Upon . . . account** for the balance of a heavy debt    131 **Since . . . queen** (Mowbray went in 1395 to France to negotiate the King's marriage to Isabella, daughter of the French King Charles VI, but Richard himself escorted her to England.)    132–4 **For . . . case** (Mowbray speaks guardedly but seems to imply that he postponed the execution of Gloucester that he was ordered by Richard to carry out.)    132 **For** As for    140 **exactly** (1) explicitly (2) fully    142 **appealed** of which I am charged    144 **recreant** cowardly; or, coward (used as a noun)    145 **Which** which charge.    **in myself** in my own person    146 **interchangeably** in exchange, reciprocally    147 **overweening** arrogant, proud    149 **Even in** by shedding    150 **In haste whereof** To hasten which proof of my innocence    153 **Let's . . . blood** let's treat this wrath (caused by an excess of bile or choler) by purging (vomiting or evacuation) rather than by medical bloodletting. (With a play on "bloodshed in combat.")    156 **conclude** come to a final agreement    157 **no month to bleed** (Learned authorities often differed as to which months or seasons were best for medicinal bloodletting.)    164 **boot** help for it.

MOWBRAY [*kneeling*]
    Myself I throw, dread sovereign, at thy foot.                165
    My life thou shalt command, but not my shame.
    The one my duty owes; but my fair name,                      167
    Despite of death that lives upon my grave,                   168
    To dark dishonor's use thou shalt not have.                  169
    I am disgraced, impeached, and baffled here,                 170
    Pierced to the soul with slander's venomed spear,
    The which no balm can cure but his heart-blood               172
    Which breathed this poison.
KING RICHARD                        Rage must be withstood.      173
    Give me his gage. Lions make leopards tame.                  174
MOWBRAY
    Yea, but not change his spots. Take but my shame,            175
    And I resign my gage. My dear dear lord,
    The purest treasure mortal times afford                      177
    Is spotless reputation; that away,
    Men are but gilded loam or painted clay.
    A jewel in a ten-times-barred-up chest
    Is a bold spirit in a loyal breast.
    Mine honor is my life; both grow in one;                     182
    Take honor from me, and my life is done.
    Then, dear my liege, mine honor let me try;                  184
    In that I live, and for that will I die.
KING RICHARD [*to Bolingbroke*]
    Cousin, throw up your gage; do you begin.                    186
BOLINGBROKE
    Oh, God defend my soul from such deep sin!
    Shall I seem crestfallen in my father's sight?
    Or with pale beggar-fear impeach my height                   189
    Before this out-dared dastard? Ere my tongue                 190
    Shall wound my honor with such feeble wrong,                 191
    Or sound so base a parle, my teeth shall tear                192
    The slavish motive of recanting fear                         193
    And spit it bleeding in his high disgrace,                   194
    Where shame doth harbor, even in Mowbray's face.             195
                                            [*Exit Gaunt.*]
KING RICHARD
    We were not born to sue but to command;                     196
    Which since we cannot do to make you friends,
    Be ready, as your lives shall answer it,
    At Coventry upon Saint Lambert's day.                        199

165 **Myself I throw** i.e., I throw myself, instead of my gage   167 **The
one . . . owes** My duty requires that I owe my life to you; it is at your
service   168 **Despite . . . grave** that will live in the epitaph on my
grave in spite of devouring Death   169 **To . . . have** you may not have
my name to dishonor it.   170 **impeached** accused.   **baffled** publicly
dishonored   172–3 **but . . . poison** but the heart's blood of him who
uttered this poisonous slander.   174 **Lions . . . tame** (The royal arms
showed a lion rampant; Mowbray's emblem was a leopard.)
175 **spots** (1) leopard spots (2) stains of dishonor.   177 **mortal times**
our earthly lives   182 **in one** inseparably   184 **let me try** let me put
my honor to the test (by fighting this contest)   186 **throw . . . gage**
i.e., surrender your gage up to me, thereby ending the quarrel.
(Richard is probably seated on a raised throne, as in scene 3.)
189 **impeach my height** discredit my high rank   190 **out-dared**
dared down, cowed.   **dastard** coward.   191 **feeble wrong** dishonorable submission   192 **Or . . . parle** or enter into so dishonorable a
negotiation   192–5 **my teeth . . . face** my teeth will bite off my tongue
as a craven instrument of cowardly capitulation and spit it out bleeding, to its (the tongue's) great disgrace, into Mowbray's face, where
shame abides perpetually.   195.1 *Exit Gaunt* (A stage direction
from the Folio, adopted by most editors so that Gaunt will not be
required to exit at the end of scene 1 and then immediately reenter.)
196 **sue** beg   199 **Saint Lambert's day** September 17.

---

    There shall your swords and lances arbitrate
    The swelling difference of your settled hate.
    Since we cannot atone you, we shall see                      202
    Justice design the victor's chivalry.                        203
    Lord Marshal, command our officers at arms
    Be ready to direct these home alarms.                        205
                                            *Exeunt.*

## [1.2]

*Enter John of Gaunt with the Duchess of
Gloucester.*

GAUNT
    Alas, the part I had in Woodstock's blood                    1
    Doth more solicit me than your exclaims                      2
    To stir against the butchers of his life!                    3
    But since correction lieth in those hands                    4
    Which made the fault that we cannot correct,
    Put we our quarrel to the will of heaven,
    Who, when they see the hours ripe on earth,
    Will rain hot vengeance on offenders' heads.
DUCHESS
    Finds brotherhood in thee no sharper spur?
    Hath love in thy old blood no living fire?
    Edward's seven sons, whereof thyself art one,               11
    Were as seven vials of his sacred blood
    Or seven fair branches springing from one root.
    Some of those seven are dried by nature's course,           14
    Some of those branches by the Destinies cut;                15
    But Thomas, my dear lord, my life, my Gloucester,
    One vial full of Edward's sacred blood,
    One flourishing branch of his most royal root,
    Is cracked, and all the precious liquor spilt,
    Is hacked down, and his summer leaves all faded,
    By envy's hand and murder's bloody ax.                       21
    Ah, Gaunt, his blood was thine! That bed, that womb,
    That metal, that self mold that fashioned thee,             23
    Made him a man; and though thou livest and
        breathest,
    Yet art thou slain in him. Thou dost consent                 25
    In some large measure to thy father's death
    In that thou see'st thy wretched brother die,
    Who was the model of thy father's life.                      28
    Call it not patience, Gaunt; it is despair.
    In suff'ring thus thy brother to be slaughtered,
    Thou showest the naked pathway to thy life,                  31

202–3 **we shall . . . chivalry** we shall let the outcome of this fight
determine who is in the right.   205 **home alarms** domestic conflicts.
**1.2. Location:** John of Gaunt's house (? No place is specified, and
the scene is not in Holinshed.)
1 **the part . . . blood** my kinship with my (older) brother, Thomas of
Woodstock, Duke of Gloucester   2 **exclaims** exclamations   3 **stir**
take action   4 **those hands** i.e., Richard's (whom Gaunt charges with
responsibility for Gloucester's death)   11 **Edward's** Edward
III's   14–15 **are dried . . . cut** are ended by natural deaths or by the
decrees of Destiny   21 **envy's** malice's   23 **metal** substance out
of which a person or a thing is made. (With a sense too of *mettle*,
"temperament, disposition.")   **self** selfsame   25 **consent** acquiesce   28 **model** likeness, copy   31 **naked** i.e., undefended

Teaching stern murder how to butcher thee.
That which in mean men we entitle patience
Is pale cold cowardice in noble breasts.                                    33
What shall I say? To safeguard thine own life
The best way is to venge my Gloucester's death.

GAUNT
God's is the quarrel; for God's substitute,                                 37
His deputy anointed in His sight,
Hath caused his death; the which if wrongfully                              39
Let heaven revenge, for I may never lift
An angry arm against His minister.

DUCHESS
Where then, alas, may I complain myself?                                     42

GAUNT
To God, the widow's champion and defense.

DUCHESS
Why, then, I will. Farewell, old Gaunt.
Thou goest to Coventry, there to behold
Our cousin Hereford and fell Mowbray fight.                                 46
Oh, sit my husband's wrongs on Hereford's spear,                           47
That it may enter butcher Mowbray's breast!
Or if misfortune miss the first career,                                     49
Be Mowbray's sins so heavy in his bosom
That they may break his foaming courser's back                             51
And throw the rider headlong in the lists,                                 52
A caitiff recreant to my cousin Hereford!                                  53
Farewell, old Gaunt. Thy sometimes brother's wife                          54
With her companion, Grief, must end her life.

GAUNT
Sister, farewell. I must to Coventry.
As much good stay with thee as go with me!                                 57

DUCHESS
Yet one word more. Grief boundeth where it falls,                          58
Not with the empty hollowness, but weight.                                 59
I take my leave before I have begun,                                       60
For sorrow ends not when it seemeth done.                                  61
Commend me to thy brother, Edmund York.                                    62
Lo, this is all. Nay, yet depart not so!
Though this be all, do not so quickly go;
I shall remember more. Bid him—ah, what?—
With all good speed at Pleshey visit me.                                   66
Alack, and what shall good old York there see
But empty lodgings and unfurnished walls,                                  68
Unpeopled offices, untrodden stones,                                       69
And what hear there for welcome but my groans?
Therefore commend me; let him not come there

To seek out sorrow that dwells everywhere.
Desolate, desolate, will I hence and die.
The last leave of thee takes my weeping eye.    *Exeunt.*

# [1.3]

*Enter Lord Marshal and the Duke [of] Aumerle.*

MARSHAL
My Lord Aumerle, is Harry Hereford armed?

AUMERLE
Yea, at all points, and longs to enter in.                                  2

MARSHAL
The Duke of Norfolk, sprightfully and bold,                                 3
Stays but the summons of the appellant's trumpet.                           4

AUMERLE
Why then the champions are prepared, and stay
For nothing but His Majesty's approach.

*The trumpets sound, and the King enters with his
nobles [Gaunt, Bushy, Bagot, Green, and others].
When they are set, enter [Mowbray] the Duke of
Norfolk in arms, defendant, [with a herald].*

KING RICHARD
Marshal, demand of yonder champion
The cause of his arrival here in arms.
Ask him his name, and orderly proceed                                       9
To swear him in the justice of his cause.

MARSHAL [*to Mowbray*]
In God's name and the King's, say who thou art
And why thou comest thus knightly clad in arms,
Against what man thou com'st, and what thy quarrel.    13
Speak truly on thy knighthood and thy oath,
As so defend thee heaven and thy valor!

MOWBRAY
My name is Thomas Mowbray, Duke of Norfolk,
Who hither come engagèd by my oath—
Which God defend a knight should violate!—              18
Both to defend my loyalty and truth
To God, my king, and my succeeding issue               20
Against the Duke of Hereford that appeals me,          21
And by the grace of God and this mine arm
To prove him, in defending of myself,
A traitor to my God, my king, and me;
And as I truly fight, defend me heaven!

*The trumpets sound. Enter [Bolingbroke,] Duke of
Hereford, appellant, in armor, [with a herald].*

KING RICHARD
Marshal, ask yonder knight in arms

33 **mean** lowly   37 **God's substitute** i.e., the King, God's deputy on earth   39 **his** i.e., Gloucester's   42 **complain myself** lodge my complaint.   46 **cousin** kinsman.   **fell** cruel   47 **sit . . . wrongs** may my husband's wrongs sit   49 **misfortune** i.e., the overthrow of Mowbray.   **career** charge of the horse in a tourney or combat   51 **courser's** horse's   52 **lists** barriers enclosing the tournament area   53 **caitiff** base, cowardly.   **to** compared to   54 **sometimes** late   57 **As . . . me** i.e., may good fortune reside with us both. **58–9 Grief . . . weight** i.e., Grief insistently repeats itself like a bouncing ball, not out of emptiness but because of its own heaviness of sorrow.   **60–1 I take . . . done** Even though I must leave, I have not yet begun to utter my sorrow; my sorrow may seem to have ended but in fact is unending.   **62 Commend me** Convey my greetings. (Also in line 71.)   **Edmund York** Edmund of Langley, fifth son of Edward III.   **66 Pleshey** Gloucester's country seat, in Essex **68 unfurnished** bare   **69 offices** service quarters, workrooms

**1.3. Location:** The lists at Coventry. Scaffolds or raised seats are provided for the King and his nobles, and chairs are provided for the combatants.
**2 at all points** completely.   **in** i.e., into the lists, the space designed for combat.   **3 sprightfully** with high spirit   **4 Stays but** awaits only   **9 orderly** according to the rules   **13 quarrel** complaint. **18 defend** forbid   **20 my succeeding issue** all my descendants **21 appeals** accuses

Both who he is and why he cometh hither
Thus plated in habiliments of war;                                    28
And formally, according to our law,
Depose him in the justice of his cause.                               30

MARSHAL [to Bolingbroke]
What is thy name? And wherefore com'st thou hither,
Before King Richard in his royal lists?
Against whom comest thou? And what's thy quarrel?
Speak like a true knight, so defend thee heaven!

BOLINGBROKE
Harry of Hereford, Lancaster, and Derby
Am I, who ready here do stand in arms
To prove, by God's grace and my body's valor,
In lists, on Thomas Mowbray, Duke of Norfolk,
That he is a traitor foul and dangerous
To God of heaven, King Richard, and to me;
And as I truly fight, defend me heaven!

MARSHAL
On pain of death, no person be so bold
Or daring-hardy as to touch the lists,                                43
Except the Marshal and such officers
Appointed to direct these fair designs.

BOLINGBROKE
Lord Marshal, let me kiss my sovereign's hand
And bow my knee before His Majesty;                                   47
For Mowbray and myself are like two men
That vow a long and weary pilgrimage.
Then let us take a ceremonious leave
And loving farewell of our several friends.                           51

MARSHAL [to King Richard]
The appellant in all duty greets Your Highness
And craves to kiss your hand and take his leave.

KING RICHARD [coming down]
We will descend and fold him in our arms.
                              [He embraces Bolingbroke.]
Cousin of Hereford, as thy cause is right,                            55
So be thy fortune in this royal fight!                                56
Farewell, my blood—which if today thou shed,
Lament we may, but not revenge thee dead.

BOLINGBROKE
Oh, let no noble eye profane a tear                                   59
For me if I be gored with Mowbray's spear.                            60
As confident as is the falcon's flight
Against a bird do I with Mowbray fight.
[To the King] My loving lord, I take my leave of you;
[To Aumerle] Of you, my noble cousin, Lord Aumerle;
Not sick, although I have to do with death,
But lusty, young, and cheerly drawing breath.                         66
Lo, as at English feasts, so I regreet                                67
The daintiest last, to make the end most sweet.                       68

[To Gaunt] O thou, the earthly author of my blood,
Whose youthful spirit, in me regenerate,                              70
Doth with a twofold vigor lift me up                                  71
To reach at victory above my head,
Add proof unto mine armor with thy prayers,                           73
And with thy blessings steel my lance's point
That it may enter Mowbray's waxen coat                                75
And furbish new the name of John o' Gaunt                             76
Even in the lusty havior of his son.                                  77

GAUNT
God in thy good cause make thee prosperous!
Be swift like lightning in the execution,
And let thy blows, doubly redoubled,
Fall like amazing thunder on the casque                               81
Of thy adverse pernicious enemy.
Rouse up thy youthful blood, be valiant, and live.

BOLINGBROKE
Mine innocence and Saint George to thrive!                            84

MOWBRAY
However God or fortune cast my lot,
There lives or dies, true to King Richard's throne,
A loyal, just, and upright gentleman.
Never did captive with a freer heart
Cast off his chains of bondage and embrace
His golden uncontrolled enfranchisement                               90
More than my dancing soul doth celebrate
This feast of battle with mine adversary.
Most mighty liege, and my companion peers,
Take from my mouth the wish of happy years.                           94
As gentle and as jocund as to jest                                    95
Go I to fight. Truth hath a quiet breast.                             96

KING RICHARD
Farewell, my lord. Securely I espy                                    97
Virtue with valor couchèd in thine eye.—                              98
Order the trial, Marshal, and begin.

MARSHAL
Harry of Hereford, Lancaster, and Derby,
Receive thy lance; and God defend the right!
                              [A lance is given to Bolingbroke.]

BOLINGBROKE
Strong as a tower in hope, I cry "Amen!"                             102

MARSHAL [to an officer]
Go bear this lance to Thomas, Duke of Norfolk.
                              [A lance is given to Mowbray.]

FIRST HERALD
Harry of Hereford, Lancaster, and Derby
Stands here for God, his sovereign, and himself,
On pain to be found false and recreant,
To prove the Duke of Norfolk, Thomas Mowbray,

28 plated armored.   habiliments the attire   30 Depose him take his
sworn deposition   43 daring-hardy daringly bold, reckless.   touch
i.e., interfere in   47 bow my knee (Presumably Bolingbroke kneels to
Richard and, at about line 69, to Gaunt.)   51 several various   55 as
insofar as   56 royal fight i.e., a fight taking place in the presence of
the King.   59–60 profane . . . For me misuse tears by weeping for
me   66 lusty full of vigor.   cheerly cheerfully   67 regreet greet,
salute   68 The daintiest i.e., the most tasty, the finest. (Bolingbroke
refers to the custom of ending banquets with a sweet dessert.)

70 regenerate born anew   71 twofold i.e., of father and son
73 proof invulnerability   75 enter . . . coat pierce Mowbray's armor
as though it were made of wax   76 furbish polish   77 lusty havior
vigorous behavior, deportment   81 amazing bewildering.   casque
helmet   84 Mine . . . thrive! May my innocence and the protector-
ship of Saint George bring me victory!   90 enfranchisement freedom
94 Take . . . years take from me the wish that you may enjoy many
happy years.   95 gentle unperturbed in spirit.   to jest i.e., to a
play or entertainment   96 quiet calm   97 Securely Confidently
98 couchèd lodged, expressed, leveled in readiness (as with a lance)
102 Strong . . . hope (Alludes to Psalm 61:3: "for thou hast been my
hope, and a strong tower for me against the face of the enemy.")

A traitor to his God, his king, and him,                               108
And dares him to set forward to the fight.

SECOND HERALD
Here standeth Thomas Mowbray, Duke of Norfolk,
On pain to be found false and recreant,
Both to defend himself and to approve                                  112
Henry of Hereford, Lancaster, and Derby,
To God, his sovereign, and to him disloyal,                            114
Courageously and with a free desire
Attending but the signal to begin.                                     116

MARSHAL
Sound, trumpets, and set forward, combatants!
            [A charge is sounded. Richard throws
                              down his baton.]
Stay! The King hath thrown his warder down.                            118

KING RICHARD
Let them lay by their helmets and their spears,
And both return back to their chairs again.
[To his counselors] Withdraw with us, and let the trumpets
     sound
While we return these dukes what we decree.                            122
            [A long flourish. Richard consults apart with
                              Gaunt and others.]
Draw near,
And list what with our council we have done.                           124
For that our kingdom's earth should not be soiled                      125
With that dear blood which it hath fostered;
And for our eyes do hate the dire aspect                               127
Of civil wounds plowed up with neighbors' sword;
And for we think the eagle-winged pride
Of sky-aspiring and ambitious thoughts,
With rival-hating envy, set on you                                     131
To wake our peace, which in our country's cradle
Draws the sweet infant breath of gentle sleep,
Which, so roused up with boist'rous untuned drums,   134
With harsh-resounding trumpets' dreadful bray
And grating shock of wrathful iron arms,
Might from our quiet confines fright fair peace
And make us wade even in our kindred's blood:
Therefore we banish you our territories.
You, cousin Hereford, upon pain of life,                               140
Till twice five summers have enriched our fields,
Shall not regreet our fair dominions,
But tread the stranger paths of banishment.                            143

BOLINGBROKE
Your will be done. This must my comfort be:
That sun that warms you here shall shine on me,
And those his golden beams to you here lent
Shall point on me and gild my banishment.

KING RICHARD
Norfolk, for thee remains a heavier doom,                              148

Which I with some unwillingness pronounce:
The sly slow hours shall not determinate                               150
The dateless limit of thy dear exile.                                  151
The hopeless word of "never to return"
Breathe I against thee, upon pain of life.

MOWBRAY
A heavy sentence, my most sovereign liege,
And all unlooked-for from Your Highness' mouth.
A dearer merit, not so deep a maim                                     156
As to be cast forth in the common air,
Have I deservèd at Your Highness' hands.
The language I have learned these forty years,
My native English, now I must forgo;
And now my tongue's use is to me no more
Than an unstringèd viol or a harp,                                     162
Or like a cunning instrument cased up,                                 163
Or, being open, put into his hands                                     164
That knows no touch to tune the harmony.
Within my mouth you have enjailed my tongue,
Doubly portcullised with my teeth and lips,                            167
And dull unfeeling barren ignorance
Is made my jailer to attend on me.
I am too old to fawn upon a nurse,
Too far in years to be a pupil now.
What is thy sentence then but speechless death,
Which robs my tongue from breathing native breath?   173

KING RICHARD
It boots thee not to be compassionate.                                 174
After our sentence plaining comes too late.                            175

MOWBRAY
Then thus I turn me from my country's light,
To dwell in solemn shades of endless night.
                              [He starts to leave.]

KING RICHARD
Return again, and take an oath with thee.
Lay on our royal sword your banished hands.
            [They place their hands on Richard's sword.]
Swear by the duty that you owe to God—
Our part therein we banish with yourselves—                            181
To keep the oath that we administer:
You never shall, so help you truth and God,
Embrace each other's love in banishment,
Nor never look upon each other's face,
Nor never write, regreet, nor reconcile                                186
This louring tempest of your homebred hate;                            187
Nor never by advisèd purpose meet                                      188
To plot, contrive, or complot any ill                                  189
'Gainst us, our state, our subjects, or our land.

BOLINGBROKE    I swear.

108 him himself, Bolingbroke. (See line 40.)   112 approve prove
114 him i.e., Mowbray. (See line 24.)   116 Attending awaiting
118 warder staff or truncheon borne by the King when presiding over
a trial by combat   122 we return I inform   122.1 flourish fanfare.
124 list hear   125 For that In order that   127 for because (also in
line 129)   131 envy enmity.   set on you set you on   134 Which
i.e., which enmity, disturbance of the peace. (Although, in literal
terms, the antecedent of Which is peace in line 132.)   140 life i.e., loss
of life   143 stranger alien   148 doom sentence

150 sly stealthy.   determinate put to an end   151 dateless limit
unlimited term.   dear grievous   156 dearer merit better
reward.   maim injury   162 viol a six-stringed instrument, related
to the modern violin, played with a curved bow   163 cunning
skillfully made   164 open taken from its case.   his that person's
167 portcullised shut in by a portcullis, an iron grating over a
gateway that can be raised and lowered   173 breathing . . . breath
speaking English.   174 boots avails.   compassionate full of
laments.   175 plaining complaining   181 Our part therein i.e.,
the duty you owe me as King   186 regreet greet   187 louring
threatening, scowling   188 advisèd deliberate, premeditated
189 complot plot together

MOWBRAY    And I, to keep all this.
BOLINGBROKE
　　Norfolk, so far as to mine enemy:                        193
　　By this time, had the King permitted us,
　　One of our souls had wandered in the air,
　　Banished this frail sepulchre of our flesh,            196
　　As now our flesh is banished from this land.
　　Confess thy treasons ere thou fly the realm.
　　Since thou hast far to go, bear not along
　　The clogging burden of a guilty soul.                   200
MOWBRAY
　　No, Bolingbroke. If ever I were traitor,
　　My name be blotted from the book of life,
　　And I from heaven banished as from hence!
　　But what thou art, God, thou, and I do know,
　　And all too soon, I fear, the King shall rue.—
　　Farewell, my liege. Now no way can I stray;             206
　　Save back to England, all the world's my way.    *Exit.*
KING RICHARD [*to Gaunt*]
　　Uncle, even in the glasses of thine eyes               208
　　I see thy grievèd heart. Thy sad aspect
　　Hath from the number of his banished years
　　Plucked four away. [*To Bolingbroke*] Six frozen winters
　　　　spent,
　　Return with welcome home from banishment.
BOLINGBROKE
　　How long a time lies in one little word!
　　Four lagging winters and four wanton springs          214
　　End in a word; such is the breath of kings.
GAUNT
　　I thank my liege that in regard of me
　　He shortens four years of my son's exile.
　　But little vantage shall I reap thereby;
　　For, ere the six years that he hath to spend
　　Can change their moons and bring their times about,
　　My oil-dried lamp and time-bewasted light             221
　　Shall be extinct with age and endless night;
　　My inch of taper will be burnt and done,              223
　　And blindfold Death not let me see my son.            224
KING RICHARD
　　Why, uncle, thou hast many years to live.
GAUNT
　　But not a minute, King, that thou canst give.
　　Shorten my days thou canst with sullen sorrow,
　　And pluck nights from me, but not lend a morrow;
　　Thou canst help Time to furrow me with age,
　　But stop no wrinkle in his pilgrimage;                230
　　Thy word is current with him for my death,            231
　　But dead, thy kingdom cannot buy my breath.           232

KING RICHARD
　　Thy son is banished upon good advice,
　　Whereto thy tongue a party verdict gave.              234
　　Why at our justice seem'st thou then to lour?
GAUNT
　　Things sweet to taste prove in digestion sour.
　　You urged me as a judge, but I had rather
　　You would have bid me argue like a father.
　　Oh, had it been a stranger, not my child,
　　To smooth his fault I should have been more mild.     240
　　A partial slander sought I to avoid                    241
　　And in the sentence my own life destroyed.
　　Alas, I looked when some of you should say            243
　　I was too strict, to make mine own away;              244
　　But you gave leave to my unwilling tongue
　　Against my will to do myself this wrong.
KING RICHARD
　　Cousin, farewell; and, uncle, bid him so.
　　Six years we banish him, and he shall go.
　　　　　　　[*Flourish. Exit King Richard with his train.*]
AUMERLE [*to Bolingbroke*]
　　Cousin, farewell. What presence must not know,        249
　　From where you do remain let paper show.    [*Exit.*] 250
MARSHAL [*to Bolingbroke*]
　　My lord, no leave take I, for I will ride,            251
　　As far as land will let me, by your side.

　　　　　[*Bolingbroke makes no answer. The Lord Marshal
　　　　　　　　　　　　　　　　stands aside.*]

GAUNT [*to Bolingbroke*]
　　Oh, to what purpose dost thou hoard thy words,
　　That thou returnest no greeting to thy friends?
BOLINGBROKE
　　I have too few to take my leave of you,
　　When the tongue's office should be prodigal           256
　　To breathe the abundant dolor of the heart.           257
GAUNT
　　Thy grief is but thy absence for a time.              258
BOLINGBROKE
　　Joy absent, grief is present for that time.           259
GAUNT
　　What is six winters? They are quickly gone.
BOLINGBROKE
　　To men in joy; but grief makes one hour ten.
GAUNT
　　Call it a travel that thou tak'st for pleasure.       262
BOLINGBROKE
　　My heart will sigh when I miscall it so,
　　Which finds it an enforcèd pilgrimage.
GAUNT
　　The sullen passage of thy weary steps                 265

193 **so far** let me say this much    196 **sepulchre of our flesh** i.e., body, the temple of the soul    200 **clogging** (A clog was a wooden block attached to the leg to hinder movement.)    206 **stray** take the wrong road    208 **glasses** mirrors (here glistening with tears)    214 **wanton** luxuriant    221 **oil-dried** empty of oil    223 **taper** candle    224 **blindfold Death** i.e., *blindfold* because *Death* deprives its victims of their sight and because it is often pictured as an eyeless skull    230 **in his pilgrimage** brought about in time's journey    231 **current with him** i.e., as good as current coin, valid with Death    232 **dead** i.e., once I am dead.    **buy** i.e., restore with a payment

234 **a party verdict** one person's share in a joint verdict    240 **smooth** extenuate    241 **partial slander** accusation of partiality (on behalf of my son)    243 **looked when** expected that, awaited the point at which    244 **to . . . away** in punishing my own (son)    249 **What . . . know** What I cannot learn from you in person    250 **paper** your letters    **s.d.** *Exit* (The exit is uncertain; see 1.4.1–4.)    251 **no leave take I** i.e., I will not take my leave of you, my lord; I will not say goodbye    256 **office** function.    **prodigal** lavish    257 **To breathe** in uttering    258 **grief** grievance    259 **grief** unhappiness    262 **travel** (The quarto spelling, "trauaile," suggests an interchangeable meaning of "travel" and "labor.")    265 **sullen** (1) melancholy (2) dull

Esteem as foil wherein thou art to set                                266
The precious jewel of thy home return.

BOLINGBROKE
Nay, rather every tedious stride I make
Will but remember me what a deal of world                             269
I wander from the jewels that I love.
Must I not serve a long apprenticehood
To foreign passages, and in the end,                                  272
Having my freedom, boast of nothing else                              273
But that I was a journeyman to grief?                                 274

GAUNT
All places that the eye of heaven visits                              275
Are to a wise man ports and happy havens.
Teach thy necessity to reason thus:
There is no virtue like necessity.
Think not the King did banish thee,
But thou the King. Woe doth the heavier sit                           280
Where it perceives it is but faintly borne.                           281
Go, say I sent thee forth to purchase honor,                          282
And not the King exiled thee; or suppose
Devouring pestilence hangs in our air
And thou art flying to a fresher clime.
Look what thy soul holds dear, imagine it                             286
To lie that way thou goest, not whence thou com'st.
Suppose the singing birds musicians,
The grass whereon thou tread'st the presence strewed,   289
The flowers fair ladies, and thy steps no more
Than a delightful measure or a dance;                                 291
For gnarling sorrow hath less power to bite                           292
The man that mocks at it and sets it light.                           293

BOLINGBROKE
Oh, who can hold a fire in his hand
By thinking on the frosty Caucasus?                                   295
Or cloy the hungry edge of appetite
By bare imagination of a feast?
Or wallow naked in December snow
By thinking on fantastic summer's heat?                               299
Oh, no, the apprehension of the good
Gives but the greater feeling to the worse.
Fell Sorrow's tooth doth never rankle more                            302
Than when he bites but lanceth not the sore.                          303

GAUNT
Come, come, my son, I'll bring thee on thy way.          304
Had I thy youth and cause, I would not stay.             305

BOLINGBROKE
Then, England's ground, farewell. Sweet soil, adieu,
My mother and my nurse that bears me yet!
Where'er I wander, boast of this I can:
Though banished, yet a trueborn Englishman.

*Exeunt.*

# [1.4]

*Enter the King, with Bagot, [Green,] etc. at one
door, and the Lord Aumerle at another.*

KING RICHARD
We did observe.—Cousin Aumerle,                                        1
How far brought you high Hereford on his way?                          2

AUMERLE
I brought high Hereford, if you call him so,
But to the next highway, and there I left him.                         4

KING RICHARD
And say, what store of parting tears were shed?

AUMERLE
Faith, none for me, except the northeast wind,                         6
Which then blew bitterly against our faces,
Awaked the sleeping rheum and so by chance                             8
Did grace our hollow parting with a tear.                              9

KING RICHARD
What said our cousin when you parted with him?

AUMERLE    "Farewell!"
And, for my heart disdainèd that my tongue                            12
Should so profane the word, that taught me craft                      13
To counterfeit oppression of such grief
That words seemed buried in my sorrow's grave.
Marry, would the word "farewell" have lengthened
    hours                                                             16
And added years to his short banishment,
He should have had a volume of farewells;
But since it would not, he had none of me.                            19

KING RICHARD
He is our cousin, cousin; but 'tis doubt,                             20
When time shall call him home from banishment,
Whether our kinsman come to see his friends.                          22
Ourself and Bushy, Bagot here, and Green
Observed his courtship to the common people,
How he did seem to dive into their hearts
With humble and familiar courtesy,
What reverence he did throw away on slaves,                           27
Wooing poor craftsmen with the craft of smiles

266 **foil** thin metal leaf set behind gems to show off their luster;
hence, that which sets something off to advantage   269 **remember**
remind.  **a deal of world** a great distance   272 **passages** wanderings, experiences   273 **Having my freedom** (1) having completed my
apprenticeship (2) having been allowed to return home   274 **journeyman** (Literally, one who labors for day wages as a fully qualified
craftsman—with a hint also of one who makes a journey. Bolingbroke
will be proficient only in grief.)   275 **the eye of heaven** the sun
280 **But . . . King** i.e., but suppose that you are banishing the King to
the moral wilderness his crimes deserve.   280–1 **Woe . . . borne**
Woe is all the more oppressive when it perceives that the sufferer is
heavy.   282 **purchase** acquire, win   286 **Look what** Whatever
289 **the presence strewed** the royal presence chamber strewn with
rushes   291 **measure** stately, formal dance   292 **gnarling** twisting,
knotted   293 **sets it light** regards it lightly.   295 **Caucasus** mountain
range between the Black and Caspian seas.   299 **fantastic**
imagined   302 **Fell** Fierce.   **rankle** cause irritation and festering
303 **lanceth . . . sore** does not open the wound (to permit the release
of the infection; Bolingbroke's point is that sorrow should be openly
confronted, not rationalized or covered over and thus allowed to
fester)

304 **bring** escort   305 **stay** linger.
**1.4. Location:** The court.
1 **We did observe** (The scene begins in the midst of a conversation.)   2 **high** noble. (But Aumerle plays with the word in lines 3–4.)
4 **next** nearest   6 **for me** on my part.   **except** except that   8 **rheum**
watery discharge (i.e., tears)   9 **hollow** insincere   12 **for** because
13 **that** i.e., my disdain. (Aumerle says he pretended to be overcome
by grief in order to avoid saying an insincere "Farewell" to Bolingbroke.)   16 **Marry** Indeed. (From the oath, "by the Virgin Mary.")
19 **of** from   20 **cousin, cousin** (Both Bolingbroke and Aumerle are
first cousins of the King.)   22 **friends** kinsmen, i.e., us, his cousins.
27 **slaves** lower-class people.

And patient underbearing of his fortune,  29
As 'twere to banish their affects with him.  30
Off goes his bonnet to an oyster wench;  31
A brace of draymen bid God speed him well  32
And had the tribute of his supple knee,
With "Thanks, my countrymen, my loving friends,"
As were our England in reversion his,  35
And he our subjects' next degree in hope.  36

GREEN
Well, he is gone, and with him go these thoughts.  37
Now for the rebels which stand out in Ireland,  38
Expedient manage must be made, my liege,  39
Ere further leisure yield them further means
For their advantage and Your Highness' loss.

KING RICHARD
We will ourself in person to this war.
And, for our coffers with too great a court  43
And liberal largess are grown somewhat light,  44
We are enforced to farm our royal realm,  45
The revenue whereof shall furnish us
For our affairs in hand. If that come short,
Our substitutes at home shall have blank charters,  48
Whereto, when they shall know what men are rich,
They shall subscribe them for large sums of gold  50
And send them after to supply our wants;  51
For we will make for Ireland presently.  52

*Enter Bushy.*

Bushy, what news?

BUSHY
Old John of Gaunt is grievous sick, my lord,
Suddenly taken, and hath sent posthaste
To entreat Your Majesty to visit him.

KING RICHARD    Where lies he?

BUSHY    At Ely House.  58

KING RICHARD
Now put it, God, in the physician's mind
To help him to his grave immediately!
The lining of his coffers shall make coats  61
To deck our soldiers for these Irish wars.
Come, gentlemen, let's all go visit him.
Pray God we may make haste and come too late!

ALL    Amen.    *Exeunt.*

# [2.1]

*Enter John of Gaunt sick, with the Duke of York,*
*etc.*

GAUNT
Will the King come, that I may breathe my last
In wholesome counsel to his unstaid youth?  2

YORK
Vex not yourself, nor strive not with your breath,  3
For all in vain comes counsel to his ear.

GAUNT
Oh, but they say the tongues of dying men
Enforce attention like deep harmony.
Where words are scarce, they are seldom spent in vain,
For they breathe truth that breathe their words in pain.  8
He that no more must say is listened more  9
    Than they whom youth and ease have taught to glose.  10
More are men's ends marked than their lives before.  11
    The setting sun, and music at the close,
As the last taste of sweets, is sweetest last,  13
Writ in remembrance more than things long past.  14
Though Richard my life's counsel would not hear,  15
My death's sad tale may yet undeaf his ear.  16

YORK
No, it is stopped with other, flattering sounds,
As praises, of whose taste the wise are fond;  18
Lascivious meters, to whose venom sound  19
The open ear of youth doth always listen;
Report of fashions in proud Italy,  21
Whose manners still our tardy-apish nation  22
Limps after in base imitation.
Where doth the world thrust forth a vanity—
So it be new, there's no respect how vile—  25
That is not quickly buzzed into his ears?
Then all too late comes counsel to be heard
Where will doth mutiny with wit's regard.  28
Direct not him whose way himself will choose.  29
'Tis breath thou lack'st, and that breath wilt thou lose.  30

GAUNT
Methinks I am a prophet new inspired,
And thus expiring do foretell of him:
His rash fierce blaze of riot cannot last,  33
For violent fires soon burn out themselves;
Small showers last long, but sudden storms are short;

---

29 **underbearing** bearing, endurance    30 **banish . . . him** take their affections with him into banishment.    31 **bonnet** hat.    **oyster wench** woman who sells oysters etc.    32 **brace of draymen** pair of cart drivers    35 **As . . . his** i.e., as if my England were to revert to him as true owner after my death    36 **our . . . hope** i.e., the heir presumptive to the throne and favorite choice of the people.    37 **go** let go    38 **for** as for.    **stand out** hold out, resist    39 **Expedient manage** speedy arrangements    43 **for** because.    **too great a court** i.e., too great an extravagance at court    44 **liberal largess** extravagant generosity    45 **farm** lease the right of collecting taxes, for a present cash payment, to the highest bidder    48 **substitutes** deputies.    **blank charters** writs authorizing the collection of revenues or forced loans to the crown, blank spaces being left for the names of the parties and the sums they were to provide    50 **subscribe them** put down their names    51 **them** i.e., the sums collected    52 **presently** at once.    58 **Ely House** (Palace of the Bishop of Ely in Holborn, a London district.)    61 **lining** contents. (With pun on lining for coats.)    **coats** coats of mail, armor

**2.1. Location: Ely House.**
**0.1 *Enter John of Gaunt sick*** (Presumably he is leaning on a cane or is carried in by servants in a chair.)    **2 unstaid** unsteady, unruly    **3 strive . . . breath** i.e., don't waste your breath    **8 they breathe truth** those persons speak truth    **9 He . . . listened more** He who will soon be silenced by death is listened to more    **10 glose** flatter, deceive in speech.    **11 marked** noticed    **13 is sweetest last** i.e., is most memorable and delightful for being the thing said last    **14 Writ in remembrance** written down in the memory    **15 my life's counsel** my advice while I lived    **16 My . . . tale** my grave dying speech    **18 As . . . fond** such as praises, which even wise men are foolishly inclined to hear    **19 meters** verses.    **venom** poisonous    **21 proud Italy** (Roger Ascham, John Lyly, and other sixteenth-century writers complained of the growing influence of Italian luxury.)    **22 still** always.    **tardy-apish** belatedly imitative    **25 So** so long as.    **there's no respect** it makes no difference    **28 Where . . . regard** where willfulness rebels against what reason esteems.    **29 Direct . . . choose** Don't try to offer advice to one who insists on going his own way.    **30 'Tis . . . lose** i.e., You're about to lose all breath owing to the approach of death, and you'll just be losing your breath if you try to advise Richard.    **33 riot** profligacy

He tires betimes that spurs too fast betimes;                     36
With eager feeding food doth choke the feeder;
Light vanity, insatiate cormorant,                                38
Consuming means, soon preys upon itself.                          39
This royal throne of kings, this sceptered isle,
This earth of majesty, this seat of Mars,                         41
This other Eden, demi-paradise,
This fortress built by Nature for herself
Against infection and the hand of war,                            44
This happy breed of men, this little world,                       45
This precious stone set in the silver sea,
Which serves it in the office of a wall                           47
Or as a moat defensive to a house,
Against the envy of less happier lands,                           49
This blessed plot, this earth, this realm, this England,
This nurse, this teeming womb of royal kings,                     51
Feared by their breed and famous by their birth,                 52
Renownèd for their deeds as far from home
For Christian service and true chivalry
As is the sepulcher in stubborn Jewry                             55
Of the world's ransom, blessèd Mary's son,
This land of such dear souls, this dear dear land,
Dear for her reputation through the world,
Is now leased out—I die pronouncing it—
Like to a tenement or pelting farm.                               60
England, bound in with the triumphant sea,                        61
Whose rocky shore beats back the envious siege
Of wat'ry Neptune, is now bound in with shame,                    63
With inky blots and rotten parchment bonds.                       64
That England that was wont to conquer others                      65
Hath made a shameful conquest of itself.
Ah, would the scandal vanish with my life,
How happy then were my ensuing death!                             68

*Enter King [Richard] and Queen, [Aumerle,*
*Bushy, Green, Bagot, Ross, and Willoughby,] etc.*

YORK
The King is come. Deal mildly with his youth,
For young hot colts being reined do rage the more.
QUEEN
How fares our noble uncle Lancaster?
KING RICHARD
What comfort, man? How is't with agèd Gaunt?
GAUNT
Oh, how that name befits my composition!                          73
Old Gaunt indeed, and gaunt in being old.
Within me grief hath kept a tedious fast,
And who abstains from meat that is not gaunt?                     76
For sleeping England long time have I watched;                    77

Watching breeds leanness, leanness is all gaunt.
The pleasure that some fathers feed upon
Is my strict fast—I mean, my children's looks—                   80
And, therein fasting, hast thou made me gaunt.                    81
Gaunt am I for the grave, gaunt as a grave,
Whose hollow womb inherits naught but bones.                      83
KING RICHARD
Can sick men play so nicely with their names?                     84
GAUNT
No, misery makes sport to mock itself.                            85
Since thou dost seek to kill my name in me,                       86
I mock my name, great King, to flatter thee.                      87
KING RICHARD
Should dying men flatter with those that live?                    88
GAUNT
No, no, men living flatter those that die.                        89
KING RICHARD
Thou, now a-dying, sayest thou flatterest me.
GAUNT
Oh, no, thou diest, though I the sicker be.
KING RICHARD
I am in health, I breathe, and see thee ill.
GAUNT
Now He that made me knows I see thee ill;
Ill in myself to see, and in thee seeing ill.                     94
Thy deathbed is no lesser than thy land,
Wherein thou liest in reputation sick;
And thou, too careless patient as thou art,
Commit'st thy anointed body to the cure
Of those physicians that first wounded thee.                      99
A thousand flatterers sit within thy crown,
Whose compass is no bigger than thy head,                         101
And yet, encagèd in so small a verge,                             102
The waste is no whit lesser than thy land.                        103
Oh, had thy grandsire with a prophet's eye                        104
Seen how his son's son should destroy his sons,                   105
From forth thy reach he would have laid thy shame,                106
Deposing thee before thou wert possessed,                         107
Which art possessed now to depose thyself.                        108
Why, cousin, wert thou regent of the world,                       109
It were a shame to let this land by lease;                        110

---

36 **betimes** soon, early    38 **Light vanity** frivolous dissipation.
**cormorant** glutton. (Literally, a voracious seabird.)    39 **means** i.e.,
means of sustenance    41 **earth of majesty** land fit for kings.    **seat of
Mars** residence of the god of war    44 **infection** (1) plague (2) moral
pollution    45 **happy breed** fortunate race    47 **office** function
49 **envy** malice    51 **teeming** fruitful    52 **by their breed** for their
ancestral reputation for prowess    55 **stubborn Jewry** i.e., Judea,
called stubborn because it resisted Christianity    60 **tenement** land or
property held by a tenant.    **pelting** paltry    61 **bound in** bordered,
surrounded    63 **bound in** legally constrained    64 **blots . . . bonds**
i.e., the blank charters.    65 **wont** accustomed    68 **were . . . death**
would be my approaching death.    73 **composition** constitution.
76 **meat** food    77 **watched** kept watch at night, been vigilant

80 **Is . . . fast** is something I must forgo    81 **And . . . fasting** and, by
starving me of that pleasure (by banishing my son Bolingbroke)
83 **inherits** possesses, will receive    84 **nicely** (1) ingeniously (2) tri-
flingly    85 **to mock** by mocking    86–7 **Since . . . thee** Since you seek
to destroy my family name (by banishing my son), I mock my name
to please you and flatter your greatness.    88 **flatter with** try to
please    89 **flatter** i.e., are attentive to, offer comfort to    94 **Ill . . . ill**
seeing myself to be physically ill, and seeing the illness in you of
abusing your royal authority.    99 **physicians** i.e., the King's favorites
101 **compass** circle, circumference    102 **verge** (1) circle, ring (2) the
compass about the King's court, which extended for twelve miles
103 **waste** (1) waist, circumference (2) that which is destroyed. (With
a quibble on the legal meaning of *waste*, "damage done to property
by a tenant.")    **whit** bit, speck    104 **grandsire** i.e., Edward III
105 **destroy his sons** (1) destroy Edward III's sons, Richard's uncles
(2) destroy Richard's own heritage    106 **From . . . shame** he would
have put the matter you have shamefully handled out of your reach
107 **Deposing** dispossessing.    **possessed** put in possession of the
crown    108 **Which . . . thyself** you who are now seized with an
obsessive desire to give away your authority (by leasing the realm to
favorites).    109 **cousin** kinsman, nephew.    **regent** ruler    110 **to
let . . . lease** to lease out this land

But, for thy world enjoying but this land, 111
Is it not more than shame to shame it so? 112
Landlord of England art thou now, not king. 113
Thy state of law is bondslave to the law, 114
And thou—
KING RICHARD   A lunatic lean-witted fool,
Presuming on an ague's privilege, 116
Darest with thy frozen admonition 117
Make pale our cheek, chasing the royal blood
With fury from his native residence. 119
Now, by my seat's right royal majesty, 120
Wert thou not brother to great Edward's son, 121
This tongue that runs so roundly in thy head 122
Should run thy head from thy unreverent shoulders. 123
GAUNT
Oh, spare me not, my brother Edward's son,
For that I was his father Edward's son! 125
That blood already, like the pelican, 126
Hast thou tapped out and drunkenly caroused. 127
My brother Gloucester, plain well-meaning soul—
Whom fair befall in heaven 'mongst happy souls!— 129
May be a precedent and witness good
That thou respect'st not spilling Edward's blood. 131
Join with the present sickness that I have, 132
And thy unkindness be like crooked age 133
To crop at once a too-long-withered flower!— 134
Live in thy shame, but die not shame with thee! 135
These words hereafter thy tormentors be!—
Convey me to my bed, then to my grave.
Love they to live that love and honor have. 138
                    *Exit* [*borne off by his attendants*].
KING RICHARD
And let them die that age and sullens have, 139
For both hast thou, and both become the grave. 140
YORK
I do beseech Your Majesty, impute his words
To wayward sickliness and age in him.
He loves you, on my life, and holds you dear
As Harry Duke of Hereford, were he here. 144

KING RICHARD
Right, you say true. As Hereford's love, so his; 145
As theirs, so mine; and all be as it is.

[*Enter Northumberland.*]

NORTHUMBERLAND
My liege, old Gaunt commends him to Your Majesty.
KING RICHARD
What says he?
NORTHUMBERLAND   Nay, nothing, all is said.
His tongue is now a stringless instrument;
Words, life, and all, old Lancaster hath spent.
YORK
Be York the next that must be bankrupt so!
Though death be poor, it ends a mortal woe. 152
KING RICHARD
The ripest fruit first falls, and so doth he;
His time is spent, our pilgrimage must be. 154
So much for that. Now for our Irish wars:
We must supplant those rough rug-headed kerns, 156
Which live like venom where no venom else 157
But only they have privilege to live. 158
And, for these great affairs do ask some charge, 159
Towards our assistance we do seize to us
The plate, coin, revenues, and movables 161
Whereof our uncle Gaunt did stand possessed.
YORK
How long shall I be patient? Ah, how long
Shall tender duty make me suffer wrong?
Not Gloucester's death, nor Hereford's banishment,
Nor Gaunt's rebukes, nor England's private wrongs, 166
Nor the prevention of poor Bolingbroke 167
About his marriage, nor my own disgrace, 168
Have ever made me sour my patient cheek
Or bend one wrinkle on my sovereign's face. 170
I am the last of noble Edward's sons,
Of whom thy father, Prince of Wales, was first. 172
In war was never lion raged more fierce, 173
In peace was never gentle lamb more mild,
Than was that young and princely gentleman.
His face thou hast, for even so looked he,
Accomplished with the number of thy hours; 177
But when he frowned, it was against the French
And not against his friends. His noble hand 179

111 **But . . . land** i.e., but since you enjoy as your domain only this land of England (rather than the whole world)   112 **Is it . . . so?** isn't it all the more shameful to lease it in this shameful way?   113 **Landlord** i.e., One who leases out property   114 **Thy . . . to the law** i.e., Your legal status as King is now subservient to and at the mercy of the law governing contracts, such as blank charters   116 **an ague's privilege** i.e., a sick person's right to be testy   117 **frozen** (1) chilly (2) caused by a chill   119 **his** its   120 **seat's** throne's   121 **great Edward's son** Edward the Black Prince, Richard's father   122–3 **runs . . . run** runs on, talks . . . drive, chase   122 **roundly** unceremoniously, bluntly   123 **unreverent** irreverent, disrespectful   125 **For that** simply because   126 **pelican** (The pelican was thought to feed its ungrateful and murderous young with its own blood.)   127 **tapped out** drawn as from a tapped barrel.   **caroused** gulped, quaffed.   129 **Whom fair befall** to whom may good come   131 **thou respect'st not** you care nothing about   132–4 **Join . . . flower!** May your unnatural behavior act in concert with my present illness and my advanced years to cut down my life like a too-long-withered flower! (*Unkindness* means both cruelty and behavior contrary to the natural bond that should exist in blood ties.)   135 **die . . . thee** i.e., may your shame live after you.   138 **Love they** Let them desire   139 **sullens** sullenness, melancholy   140 **become** suit   144 **As** i.e., as he would love. (But see the next note.)

145 **Right . . . his** (Richard deliberately takes the opposite of what York had intended to say; Richard gibes that Gaunt is as little fond of the King as is Hereford.)   152 **Though . . . woe** Though death is the privation of life, it does end the misery of human existence which is itself a kind of death in life.   154 **our . . . be** i.e., our journey through life is yet to be completed but will also end.   156–8 **We . . . live** We must expel these shaggy-haired light-armed Irish foot soldiers, who live there like poisonous snakes where no others are allowed to exist. (Richard alludes to the freedom of Ireland from snakes, traditionally ascribed to Saint Patrick.)   159 **for** because.   **ask some charge** require some expenditure   161 **plate** tableware, etc., made of precious metals; also in line 210.   **movables** personal property   166 **Nor . . . wrongs** nor the rebukes given to Gaunt, nor wrongs inflicted on private English subjects   167–8 **prevention . . . marriage** (Holinshed's *Chronicles* report that Richard had forestalled Bolingbroke's intended marriage with the Duke de Berri's daughter.)   170 **bend one wrinkle on** (1) once frown at, or (2) cause one wrinkle on   172 **thy father . . . Wales** the Black Prince, eldest son of Edward III   173 **was . . . fierce** never was there a lion more fiercely enraged   177 **Accomplished . . . hours** i.e., when he was your age   179 **His noble hand** i.e., He, the Black Prince

Did win what he did spend, and spent not that 180
Which his triumphant father's hand had won. 181
His hands were guilty of no kindred blood, 182
But bloody with the enemies of his kin.
Oh, Richard! York is too far gone with grief,
Or else he never would compare between. 185

KING RICHARD
Why, uncle, what's the matter?

YORK                                              O my liege,
Pardon me, if you please; if not, I, pleased 187
Not to be pardoned, am content withal. 188
Seek you to seize and grip into your hands
The royalties and rights of banished Hereford? 190
Is not Gaunt dead? And doth not Hereford live?
Was not Gaunt just? And is not Harry true?
Did not the one deserve to have an heir?
Is not his heir a well-deserving son?
Take Hereford's rights away, and take from Time 195
His charters and his customary rights; 196
Let not tomorrow then ensue today; 197
Be not thyself; for how art thou a king
But by fair sequence and succession?
Now, afore God—God forbid I say true!—
If you do wrongfully seize Hereford's rights,
Call in the letters patents that he hath 202
By his attorneys general to sue 203
His livery, and deny his offered homage, 204
You pluck a thousand dangers on your head,
You lose a thousand well-disposèd hearts,
And prick my tender patience to those thoughts 207
Which honor and allegiance cannot think.

KING RICHARD
Think what you will, we seize into our hands
His plate, his goods, his money, and his lands.

YORK
I'll not be by the while. My liege, farewell. 211
What will ensue hereof there's none can tell;
But by bad courses may be understood 213
That their events can never fall out good.            *Exit.* 214

KING RICHARD
Go, Bushy, to the Earl of Wiltshire straight. 215
Bid him repair to us to Ely House 216
To see this business. Tomorrow next 217
We will for Ireland, and 'tis time, I trow. 218
And we create, in absence of ourself,
Our uncle York Lord Governor of England,
For he is just and always loved us well.—

Come on, our queen. Tomorrow must we part.
Be merry, for our time of stay is short. 223
    [*Flourish.*] *Exeunt King and Queen [with attendants].*
    *Manet Northumberland [with Willoughby and Ross].*

NORTHUMBERLAND
Well, lords, the Duke of Lancaster is dead.

ROSS
And living too, for now his son is duke.

WILLOUGHBY
Barely in title, not in revenues.

NORTHUMBERLAND
Richly in both, if justice had her right.

ROSS
My heart is great, but it must break with silence, 228
Ere't be disburdened with a liberal tongue. 229

NORTHUMBERLAND
Nay, speak thy mind; and let him ne'er speak more 230
That speaks thy words again to do thee harm! 231

WILLOUGHBY
Tends that thou wouldst speak to the Duke of
    Hereford? 232
If it be so, out with it boldly, man.
Quick is mine ear to hear of good towards him.

ROSS
No good at all that I can do for him,
Unless you call it good to pity him,
Bereft and gelded of his patrimony. 237

NORTHUMBERLAND
Now, afore God, 'tis shame such wrongs are borne
In him, a royal prince, and many more 239
Of noble blood in this declining land.
The King is not himself, but basely led
By flatterers; and what they will inform 242
Merely in hate 'gainst any of us all, 243
That will the King severely prosecute
'Gainst us, our lives, our children, and our heirs.

ROSS
The commons hath he pilled with grievous taxes, 246
And quite lost their hearts; the nobles hath he fined
For ancient quarrels, and quite lost their hearts.

WILLOUGHBY
And daily new exactions are devised,
As blanks, benevolences, and I wot not what. 250
But what i' God's name doth become of this? 251

NORTHUMBERLAND
Wars hath not wasted it, for warred he hath not,
But basely yielded upon compromise
That which his noble ancestors achieved with blows. 254
More hath he spent in peace than they in wars.

ROSS
The Earl of Wiltshire hath the realm in farm. 256

---

**180–1 Did . . . won** never allowed his expenditures to exceed what he took in, and never spent in excess of what Edward III had gained through his victories.   **182 kindred blood** of one's relatives   **185 compare between** draw comparisons.   **187 pleased** satisfied   **188 withal** with that, nonetheless.   **190 royalties** privileges granted through the King and belonging, in this case, to a member of the royal family   **195 Take . . . and take** i.e., If you take . . . you take   **196 His** Time's   **197 ensue** follow   **202–4 Call . . . livery** i.e., revoke the royal grant giving him the privilege to sue through his attorneys for possession of his inheritance   **204 deny** refuse.   **homage** avowal of allegiance (by which ceremony Bolingbroke would be able legally to secure his inheritance)   **207 prick** i.e., incite   **211 by the while** present while this is going on.   **213 But . . . understood** but with respect to bad proceedings it may be understood   **214 events** outcomes   **215 Earl of Wiltshire** (The King's Lord Treasurer and one of his notorious favorites.)   **216 repair** come   **217 see** see to.   **Tomorrow next** Tomorrow   **218 trow** believe.

**223.2 *Manet*** He remains on stage   **228 great** i.e., great with sorrow   **229 Ere't . . . tongue** rather than allowing itself to speak freely.   **230–1 and let . . . harm!** and let anyone not live to speak again who puts you in danger by repeating anything you say!   **232 Tends . . . to** Does what you wish to say concern   **237 gelded** i.e., deprived. (Literally, castrated.)   **239 In him** by him   **242 inform** charge, report as spies   **243 Merely in hate** out of pure hatred   **246 pilled** plundered   **250 blanks** blank charters.   **benevolences** forced loans to the crown (not actually employed until considerably later, in 1473).   **wot** know   **251 this** i.e., this unjustly collected revenue.   **254 with blows** through military might.   **256 in farm** on lease.

**WILLOUGHBY**

The King's grown bankrupt, like a broken man. 257

**NORTHUMBERLAND**

Reproach and dissolution hangeth over him.

**ROSS**

He hath not money for these Irish wars,
His burdenous taxations notwithstanding,
But by the robbing of the banished Duke.

**NORTHUMBERLAND**

His noble kinsman. Most degenerate king! 262
But, lords, we hear this fearful tempest sing,
Yet seek no shelter to avoid the storm;
We see the wind sit sore upon our sails, 265
And yet we strike not, but securely perish. 266

**ROSS**

We see the very wrack that we must suffer, 267
And unavoided is the danger now, 268
For suffering so the causes of our wrack. 269

**NORTHUMBERLAND**

Not so. Even through the hollow eyes of death 270
I spy life peering; but I dare not say
How near the tidings of our comfort is.

**WILLOUGHBY**

Nay, let us share thy thoughts, as thou dost ours.

**ROSS**

Be confident to speak, Northumberland.
We three are but thyself, and speaking so 275
Thy words are but as thoughts. Therefore be bold.

**NORTHUMBERLAND**

Then thus: I have from Port le Blanc,
A bay in Brittany, received intelligence
That Harry Duke of Hereford, Rainold Lord Cobham,
. . . . . . . . . . . . . 280
That late broke from the Duke of Exeter, 281
His brother, Archbishop late of Canterbury, 282
Sir Thomas Erpingham, Sir John Ramston,
Sir John Norbery, Sir Robert Waterton, and Francis
     Coint,
All these well furnished by the Duke of Brittany
With eight tall ships, three thousand men of war, 286
Are making hither with all due expedience 287
And shortly mean to touch our northern shore.
Perhaps they had ere this, but that they stay 289
The first departing of the King for Ireland. 290
If then we shall shake off our slavish yoke,

Imp out our drooping country's broken wing, 292
Redeem from broking pawn the blemished crown, 293
Wipe off the dust that hides our scepter's gilt, 294
And make high majesty look like itself,
Away with me in post to Ravenspurgh; 296
But if you faint, as fearing to do so, 297
Stay and be secret, and myself will go.

**ROSS**

To horse, to horse! Urge doubts to them that fear.

**WILLOUGHBY**

Hold out my horse, and I will first be there.     *Exeunt.* 300

❧

# [2.2]

*Enter the Queen, Bushy, [and] Bagot.*

**BUSHY**

Madam, Your Majesty is too much sad.
You promised, when you parted with the King, 2
To lay aside life-harming heaviness 3
And entertain a cheerful disposition. 4

**QUEEN**

To please the King I did; to please myself
I cannot do it. Yet I know no cause
Why I should welcome such a guest as grief,
Save bidding farewell to so sweet a guest 8
As my sweet Richard. Yet again methinks 9
Some unborn sorrow ripe in Fortune's womb
Is coming towards me, and my inward soul
With nothing trembles. At something it grieves
More than with parting from my lord the King.

**BUSHY**

Each substance of a grief hath twenty shadows, 14
Which shows like grief itself but is not so; 15
For sorrow's eyes, glazèd with blinding tears,
Divides one thing entire to many objects, 17
Like perspectives, which rightly gazed upon 18
Show nothing but confusion, eyed awry 19
Distinguish form. So your sweet Majesty, 20
Looking awry upon your lord's departure, 21
Find shapes of grief more than himself to wail, 22
Which, looked on as it is, is naught but shadows 23
Of what it is not. Then, thrice-gracious Queen,

257 **broken** financially ruined    262 **His noble kinsman** (Said bitterly: how could he do this to one of his own royal family!)    265 **sore** sorely, grievously    266 **strike** (1) furl the sails (2) strike blows.    **securely** heedlessly, overconfidently    267 **wrack** ruin    268 **unavoided** unavoidable    269 **For suffering** if we permit    270 **eyes** eye sockets    275 **are but thyself** share everything with you    280 . . . (A line is probably missing here, perhaps because of censorship. From information contained in Holinshed, it may have read something like "Thomas, son and heir to the Earl of Arundel" or "The son of Richard, Earl of Arundel.")    281 **late broke from** lately escaped from the custody of. (Holinshed records that "the Earl of Arundel's son, named Thomas, which was kept in the Duke of Exeter's house, escaped out of the realm . . . and went to his uncle Thomas Arundel, late Archbishop of Canterbury.")    282 **His** i.e., the Earl of Arundel's.    **late** until recently    286 **tall** stately.    **men of war** troops    287 **making** coming.    **expedience** expedition, speed    289–90 **stay . . . King** wait until the King departs

292 **Imp out** piece out. (A term from falconry, meaning to attach new feathers to a disabled wing of a bird.)    293 **from broking pawn** from being pledged to pawnbrokers    294 **gilt** gold (with pun on *guilt*)    296 **past** haste.    **Ravenspurgh** on the Yorkshire coast, at the mouth of the Humber River    297 **faint** are fainthearted    300 **Hold . . . and** If my horse holds out
**2.2. Location:** The court. According to Holinshed, the Queen remained at Windsor Castle when Richard left for Ireland.
2 **with** from    3 **heaviness** melancholy    4 **entertain** put on    8–9 **Save . . . Richard** (Only having to say farewell to so sweet a person as Richard, says the Queen, could justify my grieving.)    14 **Each . . . shadows** i.e., For every real grief there exist twenty imagined ones    15 **Which . . . itself** which looks like grief    17 **thing entire to** complete thing into    18 **perspectives** (In lines 16–17, Bushy seems to have in mind a glass with a multifaceted lens, multiplying images of the object being viewed; in lines 18–20, *perspectives* are pictures of figures made to appear distorted or confused, except when viewed obliquely, *eyed awry.*)    **rightly** directly, straight    19 **awry** obliquely    20 **Distinguish form** make the form distinct and normal.    21 **awry** i.e., mistakenly, distortedly    22 **himself** i.e., the grief itself.    **wail** bewail    23 **as it is** in a true perspective

More than your lord's departure weep not. More is not
    seen, 25
Or if it be, 'tis with false sorrow's eye,
Which for things true weeps things imaginary. 27

QUEEN
It may be so, but yet my inward soul
Persuades me it is otherwise. Howe'er it be,
I cannot but be sad—so heavy sad
As, though on thinking on no thought I think, 31
Makes me with heavy nothing faint and shrink. 32

BUSHY
'Tis nothing but conceit, my gracious lady. 33

QUEEN
'Tis nothing less. Conceit is still derived 34
From some forefather grief. Mine is not so, 35
For nothing hath begot my something grief, 36
Or something hath the nothing that I grieve. 37
'Tis in reversion that I do possess; 38
But what it is, that is not yet known what, 39
I cannot name. 'Tis nameless woe, I wot. 40

[Enter Green.]

GREEN
God save Your Majesty! And well met, gentlemen.
I hope the King is not yet shipped for Ireland.

QUEEN
Why hopest thou so? 'Tis better hope he is,
For his designs crave haste, his haste good hope. 44
Then wherefore dost thou hope he is not shipped?

GREEN
That he, our hope, might have retired his power, 46
And driven into despair an enemy's hope,
Who strongly hath set footing in this land.
The banished Bolingbroke repeals himself 49
And with uplifted arms is safe arrived 50
At Ravenspurgh.

QUEEN     Now God in heaven forbid!

GREEN
Ah, madam, 'tis too true; and that is worse, 52
The lord Northumberland, his son young Harry
    Percy,
The lords of Ross, Beaumont, and Willoughby,
With all their powerful friends, are fled to him.

BUSHY
Why have you not proclaimed Northumberland
And all the rest revolted faction traitors? 57

GREEN
We have, whereupon the Earl of Worcester
Hath broken his staff, resigned his stewardship, 59
And all the household servants fled with him
To Bolingbroke.

QUEEN
So, Green, thou art the midwife to my woe,
And Bolingbroke my sorrow's dismal heir. 63
Now hath my soul brought forth her prodigy, 64
And I, a gasping new-delivered mother,
Have woe to woe, sorrow to sorrow joined. 66

BUSHY
Despair not, madam.

QUEEN     Who shall hinder me?
I will despair, and be at enmity
With cozening hope. He is a flatterer, 69
A parasite, a keeper-back of death
Who gently would dissolve the bonds of life 71
Which false hope lingers in extremity. 72

[Enter York.]

GREEN     Here comes the Duke of York.

QUEEN
With signs of war about his agèd neck. 74
Oh, full of careful business are his looks! 75
Uncle, for God's sake, speak comfortable words. 76

YORK
Should I do so, I should belie my thoughts.
Comfort's in heaven, and we are on the earth,
Where nothing lives but crosses, cares, and grief. 79
Your husband, he is gone to save far off, 80
Whilst others come to make him lose at home.
Here am I left to underprop his land, 82
Who, weak with age, cannot support myself.
Now comes the sick hour that his surfeit made;
Now shall he try his friends that flattered him. 85

[Enter a Servingman.]

SERVINGMAN
My lord, your son was gone before I came. 86

YORK
He was? Why, so. Go all which way it will!
The nobles they are fled, the commons they are cold,
And will, I fear, revolt on Hereford's side.
Sirrah, get thee to Pleshey, to my sister Gloucester; 90
Bid her send me presently a thousand pound. 91
Hold, take my ring. 92

SERVINGMAN
My lord, I had forgot to tell Your Lordship:
Today, as I came by, I callèd there—
But I shall grieve you to report the rest.
YORK    What is't, knave?                                          96
SERVINGMAN
An hour before I came, the Duchess died.
YORK
God for his mercy, what a tide of woes
Comes rushing on this woeful land at once!
I know not what to do. I would to God,
So my untruth had not provoked him to it,             101
The King had cut off my head with my brother's.    102
What, are there no posts dispatched for Ireland?
How shall we do for money for these wars?
Come, sister—cousin, I would say—pray pardon
    me.—
Go, fellow, get thee home. Provide some carts
And bring away the armor that is there.
                                        [Exit Servingman.]
Gentlemen, will you go muster men?
If I know how or which way to order these affairs
Thus disorderly thrust into my hands,
Never believe me. Both are my kinsmen:
Th'one is my sovereign, whom both my oath
And duty bids defend; t'other again
Is my kinsman, whom the King hath wronged,
Whom conscience and my kindred bids to right.    115
Well, somewhat we must do.—Come, cousin,        116
I'll dispose of you.—Gentlemen,                              117
Go, muster up your men, and meet me presently
At Berkeley. I should to Pleshey too,                       119
But time will not permit. All is uneven,
And everything is left at six and seven.                   121
                            Exeunt Duke [of York], Queen.
                            Manent Bushy, [Bagot,] Green.
BUSHY
The wind sits fair for news to go to Ireland,
But none returns. For us to levy power
Proportionable to the enemy
Is all unpossible.
GREEN
Besides, our nearness to the King in love
Is near the hate of those love not the King.         127
BAGOT
And that is the wavering commons, for their love
Lies in their purses, and whoso empties them      129
By so much fills their hearts with deadly hate.
BUSHY
Wherein the King stands generally condemned.    131

BAGOT
If judgment lie in them, then so do we,                132
Because we ever have been near the King.         133
GREEN
Well, I will for refuge straight to Bristol Castle.
The Earl of Wiltshire is already there.
BUSHY
Thither will I with you, for little office              136
Will the hateful commons perform for us,        137
Except like curs to tear us all to pieces.
[To Bagot] Will you go along with us?
BAGOT
No, I will to Ireland to His Majesty.
Farewell. If heart's presages be not vain,          141
We three here part that ne'er shall meet again.
BUSHY
That's as York thrives to beat back Bolingbroke.   143
GREEN
Alas, poor duke! The task he undertakes
Is numbering sands and drinking oceans dry.
Where one on his side fights, thousands will fly.   146
Farewell at once, for once, for all, and ever.
BUSHY
Well, we may meet again.
BAGOT                            I fear me, never.
                                                    [Exeunt.]

❖

# [2.3]

*Enter [Bolingbroke, Duke of] Hereford, [and]*
*Northumberland [with forces].*

BOLINGBROKE
How far is it, my lord, to Berkeley now?
NORTHUMBERLAND    Believe me, noble lord,
I am a stranger here in Gloucestershire.
These high wild hills and rough uneven ways
Draws out our miles and makes them wearisome;
And yet your fair discourse hath been as sugar,
Making the hard way sweet and delectable.
But I bethink me what a weary way                    8
From Ravenspurgh to Cotswold will be found    9
In Ross and Willoughby, wanting your company,   10
Which, I protest, hath very much beguiled         11
The tediousness and process of my travel.           12
But theirs is sweetened with the hope to have
The present benefit which I possess;
And hope to joy is little less in joy                       15
Than hope enjoyed. By this the weary lords        16

---

96 **knave** i.e., fellow.    101 **So my untruth** provided that some act of disloyalty on my part    102 **brother's** i.e., the Duke of Gloucester's.
115 **my . . . right** my kinship to him bids that I right his wrong.
116 **somewhat** something.    **cousin** i.e., the Queen    117 **dispose of** make arrangements for    119 **Berkeley** a castle near Bristol.
121 **at six and seven** i.e., in confusion.    121.2 **Manent** They remain on stage    127 **Is . . . King** makes us enemies of those who oppose the King.    129 **whoso empties them** whoever spends money that might belong to citizens. (Bagot seems to have in mind the hated blank charters, used to tax citizens arbitrarily; see 2.1.250.)    131 **generally** by everyone

132 **If . . . we** i.e., If the power to pass judgment is given to the wavering commons, then we, too, stand condemned    133 **ever** always    136 **office** service    137 **hateful** full of hate, angry    141 **If . . . vain** If our hearts' predictions are not speaking in vain
143 **That's . . . thrives** i.e., That depends upon York's efforts and success    146 **fly** flee.
2.3. **Location:** In Gloucestershire, near Berkeley Castle.
8 **But . . . me** But I can't help thinking    9 **Cotswold** hilly district in Gloucestershire    10 **In** by.    **wanting** lacking    11 **protest** declare
12 **tediousness and process** tedious process    15–16 **And hope . . . enjoyed** and the hope of future happiness is only slightly less joyous than happiness already enjoyed.    16 **this** this expectation

Shall make their way seem short, as mine hath done
By sight of what I have: your noble company.

**BOLINGBROKE**
Of much less value is my company
Than your good words. But who comes here?

*Enter Harry Percy.*

**NORTHUMBERLAND**
It is my son, young Harry Percy,
Sent from my brother Worcester whencesoever.— 22
Harry, how fares your uncle? 23

**PERCY**
I had thought, my lord, to have learned his health of
you.

**NORTHUMBERLAND**    Why, is he not with the Queen?

**PERCY**
No, my good lord. He hath forsook the court, 26
Broken his staff of office, and dispersed
The household of the King.

**NORTHUMBERLAND**      What was his reason?
He was not so resolved when last we spake together.

**PERCY**
Because Your Lordship was proclaimèd traitor.
But he, my lord, is gone to Ravenspurgh
To offer service to the Duke of Hereford,
And sent me over by Berkeley to discover
What power the Duke of York had levied there, 34
Then with directions to repair to Ravenspurgh. 35

**NORTHUMBERLAND**
Have you forgot the Duke of Hereford, boy? 36

**PERCY**
No, my good lord, for that is not forgot
Which ne'er I did remember. To my knowledge
I never in my life did look on him.

**NORTHUMBERLAND**
Then learn to know him now. This is the Duke.

**PERCY**
My gracious lord, I tender you my service, 41
Such as it is, being tender, raw, and young,
Which elder days shall ripen and confirm 43
To more approvèd service and desert. 44

**BOLINGBROKE**
I thank thee, gentle Percy, and be sure
I count myself in nothing else so happy
As in a soul rememb'ring my good friends; 47
And as my fortune ripens with thy love, 48
It shall be still thy true love's recompense. 49
My heart this covenant makes, my hand thus seals it.
*[He offers Percy his hand.]*

**NORTHUMBERLAND**
How far is it to Berkeley? And what stir 51
Keeps good old York there with his men of war?

**PERCY**
There stands the castle by yon tuft of trees,
Manned with three hundred men, as I have heard,
And in it are the lords of York, Berkeley, and Seymour,
None else of name and noble estimate. 56

*[Enter Ross and Willoughby.]*

**NORTHUMBERLAND**
Here come the lords of Ross and Willoughby,
Bloody with spurring, fiery red with haste. 58

**BOLINGBROKE**
Welcome, my lords. I wot your love pursues 59
A banished traitor. All my treasury 60
Is yet but unfelt thanks, which, more enriched, 61
Shall be your love and labor's recompense.

**ROSS**
Your presence makes us rich, most noble lord.

**WILLOUGHBY**
And far surmounts our labor to attain it.

**BOLINGBROKE**
Evermore thank's the exchequer of the poor, 65
Which, till my infant fortune comes to years, 66
Stands for my bounty. But who comes here? 67

*[Enter Berkeley.]*

**NORTHUMBERLAND**
It is my lord of Berkeley, as I guess.

**BERKELEY**
My lord of Hereford, my message is to you.

**BOLINGBROKE**
My lord, my answer is—to "Lancaster"; 70
And I am come to seek that name in England,
And I must find that title in your tongue
Before I make reply to aught you say.

**BERKELEY**
Mistake me not, my lord, 'tis not my meaning
To raze one title of your honor out. 75
To you, my lord, I come, what lord you will, 76
From the most gracious regent of this land,
The Duke of York, to know what pricks you on 78
To take advantage of the absent time 79
And fright our native peace with self-borne arms. 80

*[Enter York.]*

---

**22 whencesoever** from wherever he is.   **23 your uncle** i.e., the Earl of Worcester.   **26 forsook** forsaken, abandoned   **34 power** troops   **35 directions** instructions.   **repair** go   **36 boy** (A rebuke for not respectfully greeting Bolingbroke, though historically Percy was two years Bolingbroke's senior.)   **41 tender** offer. (With a pun in the next line on the meaning "inexperienced.")   **my service** (Presumably Percy kneels to Bolingbroke, and so do Ross and Willoughby when they enter.)   **43 Which elder days** which the passage of time **44 approvèd** proven, demonstrated.   **desert** deserving.   **47 in a** in my   **48–9 And . . . recompense** and as my fortunes improve, assisted by your loyalty to me, I will be increasingly enabled to reward you for that loyalty.

**51 stir** action   **56 estimate** rank.   **58 spurring** i.e., hard riding   **59 wot** am aware that. (Bolingbroke graciously indicates his awareness of the risk they are taking in supporting him.)   **60 All my treasury** All the wealth I have at present   **61 unfelt** impalpable, expressed in words, not gifts.   **which** i.e., which treasury.   **more enriched** i.e., with still more thanks added, or, with substantial gifts at a later date   **65 Evermore . . . poor** "Thank you" is always the exchequer of the poor, i.e., the only means they have to repay favors   **66 comes to years** reaches maturity   **67 Stands for** serves in place of and stands as assurance for future reward   **70 "Lancaster"** (Bolingbroke will enter into no negotiations unless his proper title, taken away by Richard, is given him.)   **75 raze** scrape (or perhaps *rase,* "erase")   **76 what . . . will** whatever title you prefer to be addressed by. (Said sardonically.) **78 pricks** spurs   **79 the absent time** i.e., the time of the King's absence   **80 self-borne** borne in your own private cause, not the country's welfare. (Also suggesting *self-born,* "originating in the self.")

BOLINGBROKE
I shall not need transport my words by you;
Here comes His Grace in person.—My noble uncle!
                                                    [*He kneels.*]

YORK
Show me thy humble heart, and not thy knee,
Whose duty is deceivable and false.                               84

BOLINGBROKE   My gracious uncle—

YORK   Tut, tut!
Grace me no grace, nor uncle me no uncle.
I am no traitor's uncle; and that word "grace"
In an ungracious mouth is but profane.
Why have those banished and forbidden legs
Dared once to touch a dust of England's ground?                   91
But then more "why?" Why have they dared to march
So many miles upon her peaceful bosom,
Frighting her pale-faced villages with war
And ostentation of despisèd arms?                                 95
Com'st thou because the anointed King is hence?                   96
Why, foolish boy, the King is left behind,                        97
And in my loyal bosom lies his power.
Were I but now the lord of such hot youth                         99
As when brave Gaunt, thy father, and myself
Rescued the Black Prince, that young Mars of men,                101
From forth the ranks of many thousand French,
Oh, then how quickly should this arm of mine,
Now prisoner to the palsy, chastise thee
And minister correction to thy fault!                            105

BOLINGBROKE
My gracious uncle, let me know my fault.
On what condition stands it and wherein?                         107

YORK
Even in condition of the worst degree:
In gross rebellion and detested treason.
Thou art a banished man, and here art come
Before the expiration of thy time
In braving arms against thy sovereign.                           112

BOLINGBROKE [*standing*]
As I was banished, I was banished Hereford;
But as I come, I come for Lancaster.                             114
And, noble uncle, I beseech Your Grace
Look on my wrongs with an indifferent eye.
You are my father, for methinks in you
I see old Gaunt alive. Oh, then, my father,
Will you permit that I shall stand condemned
A wandering vagabond, my rights and royalties
Plucked from my arms perforce and given away
To upstart unthrifts? Wherefore was I born?                      122
If that my cousin king be King in England,
It must be granted I am Duke of Lancaster.
You have a son, Aumerle, my noble cousin;

Had you first died, and he been thus trod down,                  126
He should have found his uncle Gaunt a father
To rouse his wrongs and chase them to the bay.                   128
I am denied to sue my livery here,                               129
And yet my letters patents give me leave.                        130
My father's goods are all distrained and sold,                   131
And these, and all, are all amiss employed.
What would you have me do? I am a subject,
And I challenge law. Attorneys are denied me,                    134
And therefore personally I lay my claim
To my inheritance of free descent.                               136

NORTHUMBERLAND
The noble Duke hath been too much abused.

ROSS
It stands Your Grace upon to do him right.                       138

WILLOUGHBY
Base men by his endowments are made great.                       139

YORK
My lords of England, let me tell you this:
I have had feeling of my cousin's wrongs                         141
And labored all I could to do him right;
But in this kind to come, in braving arms,                       143
Be his own carver, and cut out his way                           144
To find out right with wrong—it may not be;                      145
And you that do abet him in this kind                            146
Cherish rebellion and are rebels all.

NORTHUMBERLAND
The noble Duke hath sworn his coming is
But for his own, and for the right of that                       149
We all have strongly sworn to give him aid;
And let him never see joy that breaks that oath!                 151

YORK
Well, well, I see the issue of these arms.                       152
I cannot mend it, I must needs confess,
Because my power is weak and all ill-left;                       154
But if I could, by Him that gave me life,
I would attach you all and make you stoop                        156
Unto the sovereign mercy of the King.
But since I cannot, be it known unto you
I do remain as neuter. So fare you well—
Unless you please to enter in the castle
And there repose you for this night.

BOLINGBROKE
An offer, uncle, that we will accept.
But we must win Your Grace to go with us
To Bristol Castle, which they say is held
By Bushy, Bagot, and their complices,

---

84 duty gesture of obeisance.   deceivable deceitful, deceptive
91 dust particle of dust   95 And . . . arms? and display of such an
unwelcome and despicable display of military might?
96 anointed i.e., sanctified by the holy oil and other tokens of divine
authority   97 the King i.e., the King's authority   99 Were . . . youth
i.e., Were I in the prime of my youth   101 the Black Prince i.e.,
Edward, the eldest son of Edward III and King Richard's father
105 minister administer   107 condition defect in me, or provision of
the law.   wherein in what does it consist.   112 braving either (1) as
an adjective, "defiant" or (2) as a verb, "brandishing." (Also at line 143.)
114 for Lancaster i.e., under the title of Lancaster and in order
to claim it.   122 unthrifts spendthrifts (such as the King's favorites).   Wherefore . . . born? i.e., Am I not the legal heir of my father?

126 first i.e., before Gaunt   128 rouse chase from cover, expose.   the
bay the extremity where the hunted animal turns on its pursuers.
129 I am . . . here I am denied the right to sue for possession of hereditary rights in England. (See 2.1.202–4 and note.)   130 letters patents
i.e., letters from the King indicating a subject's legal rights.   give me
leave provide me with legal authority to pursue my right to the title of
Duke of Lancaster.   131 distrained seized officially   134 challenge
law claim my legal rights.   136 of free descent by legal succession.
138 stands . . . upon is incumbent upon Your Grace   139 Base men
i.e., the King's favorites.   his endowments i.e., the properties that
rightly belong to Bolingbroke   141 cousin's nephew's   143 kind fashion.   in braving arms brandishing weapons   144 Be . . . carver i.e.,
act on his own authority, help himself   145 To find . . . wrong to
achieve one's rights by the illegal use of force   146 abet assist, encourage (illegally)   149 his own i.e., the Dukedom of Lancaster   151 joy
i.e., the joy of heaven   152 issue outcome   154 power army.   ill-left
left in dismay and with inadequate means   156 attach arrest

The caterpillars of the commonwealth,
Which I have sworn to weed and pluck away.

YORK
It may be I will go with you; but yet I'll pause,
For I am loath to break our country's laws.
Nor friends nor foes, to me welcome you are.          170
Things past redress are now with me past care.

*Exeunt.*

## [2.4]

*Enter Earl of Salisbury and a Welsh Captain.*

WELSH CAPTAIN
My lord of Salisbury, we have stayed ten days          1
And hardly kept our countrymen together,               2
And yet we hear no tidings from the King.              3
Therefore we will disperse ourselves. Farewell.

SALISBURY
Stay yet another day, thou trusty Welshman.
The King reposeth all his confidence in thee.

WELSH CAPTAIN
'Tis thought the King is dead. We will not stay.
The bay trees in our country are all withered,
And meteors fright the fixèd stars of heaven;
The pale-faced moon looks bloody on the earth,
And lean-looked prophets whisper fearful change;      11
Rich men look sad, and ruffians dance and leap,
The one in fear to lose what they enjoy,
The other to enjoy by rage and war.                   14
These signs forerun the death or fall of kings.       15
Farewell. Our countrymen are gone and fled,
As well assured Richard their king is dead.  *[Exit.]* 17

SALISBURY
Ah, Richard! With the eyes of heavy mind
I see thy glory like a shooting star
Fall to the base earth from the firmament.
Thy sun sets weeping in the lowly west,
Witnessing storms to come, woe, and unrest.           22
Thy friends are fled to wait upon thy foes,           23
And crossly to thy good all fortune goes.   *[Exit.]* 24

## [3.1]

*Enter [Bolingbroke,] Duke of Hereford, York,
Northumberland, [with] Bushy and Green,
prisoners.*

BOLINGBROKE   Bring forth these men.
Bushy and Green, I will not vex your souls—
Since presently your souls must part your bodies—     3
With too much urging your pernicious lives,           4

For 'twere no charity; yet, to wash your blood        5
From off my hands, here in the view of men
I will unfold some causes of your deaths.             7
You have misled a prince, a royal king,
A happy gentleman in blood and lineaments,            9
By you unhappied and disfigured clean.                10
You have in manner with your sinful hours             11
Made a divorce betwixt his queen and him,
Broke the possession of a royal bed,
And stained the beauty of a fair queen's cheeks
With tears drawn from her eyes by your foul wrongs.
Myself—a prince by fortune of my birth,
Near to the King in blood, and near in love
Till you did make him misinterpret me—
Have stooped my neck under your injuries
And sighed my English breath in foreign clouds,       20
Eating the bitter bread of banishment,
Whilst you have fed upon my seigniories,              22
Disparked my parks and felled my forest woods,        23
From my own windows torn my household coat,           24
Razed out my imprese, leaving me no sign,             25
Save men's opinions and my living blood,
To show the world I am a gentleman.
This and much more, much more than twice all this,
Condemns you to the death.—See them delivered
    over
To execution and the hand of death.

BUSHY
More welcome is the stroke of death to me
Than Bolingbroke to England. Lords, farewell.

GREEN
My comfort is that heaven will take our souls
And plague injustice with the pains of hell.

BOLINGBROKE
My lord Northumberland, see them dispatched.
*[Exeunt Northumberland with the prisoners, guarded.]*
Uncle, you say the Queen is at your house.
For God's sake, fairly let her be entreated.          37
Tell her I send to her my kind commends.              38
Take special care my greetings be delivered.

YORK
A gentleman of mine I have dispatched
With letters of your love to her at large.            41

BOLINGBROKE
Thanks, gentle uncle. Come, lords, away,              42
To fight with Glendower and his complices.            43
Awhile to work, and after holiday.        *Exeunt.*   44

170 **Nor** Neither as
**2.4. Location:** A camp in Wales.
**1 stayed** waited   **2 hardly** with difficulty   **3 yet** still   **11 lean-looked**
lean-looking   **14 to . . . rage** in hopes of possessing by violence
**15 forerun** anticipate   **17 As** as being   **22 Witnessing** betokening
**23 wait upon** attend, offer allegiance to   **24 crossly** adversely
**3.1. Location:** Bristol. The castle.
**3 presently** immediately   **4 urging** emphasizing as reasons (for your
executions)

**5 'twere no charity** it would be uncharitable   **7 unfold** reveal
**9 happy** fortunate.   **blood and lineaments** birth and natural characteristics   **10 By . . . clean** by you made wretched and wholly marred
in reputation.   **11 in manner** as it were   **20 foreign clouds** i.e., the
air of foreign lands (and adding to the clouds with sighs)   **22 seigniories** estates   **23 Disparked** thrown open to uses other than hunting and forestry   **24 household coat** coat of arms (frequently
emblazoned on stained or painted windows)   **25 Razed** scraped (or
perhaps *rased*, "erased").   **imprese** heraldic device, emblematic design
**37 entreated** treated.   **38 commends** regards, compliments.   **41 at
large** conveyed in full.   **42 gentle** noble   **43 Glendower** (Owen
Glendower was not, according to Holinshed's *Chronicles,* at this time
in arms against Bolingbroke. Possibly he is to be identified here with
the Welsh captain of the preceding scene.)   **44 after** afterwards

# [3.2]

*[Drums. Flourish and colors.] Enter the King,
Aumerle, [the Bishop of] Carlisle, etc. [with
soldiers].*

KING RICHARD
　Barkloughly Castle call they this at hand?　　　　　　1
AUMERLE
　Yea, my lord. How brooks Your Grace the air　　　　　2
　After your late tossing on the breaking seas?　　　　　3
KING RICHARD
　Needs must I like it well. I weep for joy　　　　　　　4
　To stand upon my kingdom once again.
　Dear earth, I do salute thee with my hand,
　　　　　*[He bends and touches the ground.]*
　Though rebels wound thee with their horses' hoofs.
　As a long-parted mother with her child　　　　　　　8
　Plays fondly with her tears and smiles in meeting,
　So, weeping, smiling, greet I thee, my earth,
　And do thee favors with my royal hands.
　Feed not thy sovereign's foe, my gentle earth,
　Nor with thy sweets comfort his ravenous sense,　　　13
　But let thy spiders, that suck up thy venom,　　　　　14
　And heavy-gaited toads lie in their way,　　　　　　　15
　Doing annoyance to the treacherous feet
　Which with usurping steps do trample thee.
　Yield stinging nettles to mine enemies;
　And when they from thy bosom pluck a flower,
　Guard it, I pray thee, with a lurking adder,　　　　　20
　Whose double tongue may with a mortal touch　　　　21
　Throw death upon thy sovereign's enemies.—
　Mock not my senseless conjuration, lords.　　　　　　23
　This earth shall have a feeling, and these stones
　Prove armèd soldiers, ere her native king　　　　　　25
　Shall falter under foul rebellion's arms.
CARLISLE
　Fear not, my lord. That Power that made you king
　Hath power to keep you king in spite of all.
　The means that heavens yield must be embraced
　And not neglected; else heaven would,　　　　　　　30
　And we will not. Heaven's offer we refuse,　　　　　31
　The proffered means of succor and redress.　　　　　32
AUMERLE
　He means, my lord, that we are too remiss,
　Whilst Bolingbroke through our security　　　　　　34
　Grows strong and great in substance and in power.
KING RICHARD
　Discomfortable cousin, know'st thou not　　　　　　36

　That when the searching eye of heaven is hid　　　　37
　Behind the globe that lights the lower world,　　　　38
　Then thieves and robbers range abroad unseen
　In murders and in outrage boldly here;
　But when from under this terrestrial ball　　　　　　41
　He fires the proud tops of the eastern pines　　　　　42
　And darts his light through every guilty hole,
　Then murders, treasons, and detested sins,
　The cloak of night being plucked from off their backs,
　Stand bare and naked, trembling at themselves?　　46
　So when this thief, this traitor, Bolingbroke,
　Who all this while hath reveled in the night
　Whilst we were wand'ring with the Antipodes,　　　49
　Shall see us rising in our throne, the east,
　His treasons will sit blushing in his face,
　Not able to endure the sight of day,
　But, self-affrighted, tremble at his sin.
　Not all the water in the rough rude sea
　Can wash the balm off from an anointed king;　　　55
　The breath of worldly men cannot depose　　　　　　56
　The deputy elected by the Lord.　　　　　　　　　57
　For every man that Bolingbroke hath pressed　　　　58
　To lift shrewd steel against our golden crown,　　　　59
　God for his Richard hath in heavenly pay
　A glorious angel. Then, if angels fight,
　Weak men must fall, for heaven still guards the right.　62

　　　　　*Enter Salisbury.*

　Welcome, my lord. How far off lies your power?
SALISBURY
　Nor near nor farther off, my gracious lord,　　　　　64
　Than this weak arm. Discomfort guides my tongue　65
　And bids me speak of nothing but despair.
　One day too late, I fear me, noble lord,
　Hath clouded all thy happy days on earth.
　Oh, call back yesterday, bid time return,
　And thou shalt have twelve thousand fighting men!
　Today, today, unhappy day too late,
　O'erthrows thy joys, friends, fortune, and thy state;　72
　For all the Welshmen, hearing thou wert dead,
　Are gone to Bolingbroke, dispersed, and fled.
AUMERLE
　Comfort, my liege. Why looks Your Grace so pale?
KING RICHARD
　But now the blood of twenty thousand men　　　　　76
　　Did triumph in my face, and they are fled;　　　　77
　And till so much blood thither come again,
　　Have I not reason to look pale and dead?　　　　　79

---

**3.2. Location: The coast of Wales, near Harlech Castle.**
**1 Barkloughly** i.e., Harlech　**2 brooks** enjoys　**3 late** recent
**4 Needs must** Necessarily　**8 a long-parted mother** with a mother
long parted from　**13 sweets** i.e., bounty.　**sense** appetite　**14 suck . . .
venom** (Alludes to the belief that spiders drew their poison from the
earth.)　**15 heavy-gaited** lumbering, clumsy　**20 Guard it** let it be
guarded　**21 double** forked.　**mortal** deadly　**23 senseless conjuration** solemn entreaty of senseless things; or, one that makes no sense
to you, being so fanciful　**25 native** entitled (to the crown) by birth,
rightful. (Richard was born at Bordeaux.)　**30–1 else . . . not** i.e.,
otherwise, we spurn heaven's will.　**32 succor and redress** help and
remedy.　**34 security** overconfidence　**36 Discomfortable** Disheart-
ening, discouraging

**37–8 when . . . world** i.e., when the sun is hid behind the earth, lighting its lower side　**41 this terrestrial ball** the earth　**42 He fires** the
sun lights up. (Literally, "sets on fire.")　**46 at themselves** i.e., at
being caught in their crimes.　**49 Antipodes** people on the other side
of the world; here, the Irish. (A geographical hyperbole.)　**55 balm**
consecrated oil used in anointing a king　**56 worldly** earthly
**57 elected** chosen　**58 pressed** impressed, forced into the ranks
**59 shrewd** keen, biting　**62 still** always　**64 Nor near** Neither
nearer　**65 Discomfort** Discouragement　**72 state** royal power
**76 But now** Even now.　**twenty** (A seeming discrepancy with *twelve*
in line 70; perhaps the result of Richard's hyperbole.)　**77 triumph**
i.e., shine forth　**79 pale and dead** deathly pale.

All souls that will be safe, fly from my side,
For time hath set a blot upon my pride.    81

AUMERLE
Comfort, my liege. Remember who you are.

KING RICHARD
I had forgot myself. Am I not king?
Awake, thou coward majesty, thou sleepest!
Is not the king's name twenty thousand names?
Arm, arm, my name! A puny subject strikes
At thy great glory. Look not to the ground,
Ye favorites of a king. Are we not high?
High be our thoughts. I know my uncle York
Hath power enough to serve our turn. But who comes
  here?

*Enter Scroop.*

SCROOP
More health and happiness betide my liege    91
Than can my care-tuned tongue deliver him!    92

KING RICHARD
Mine ear is open and my heart prepared.
The worst is worldly loss thou canst unfold.    94
Say, is my kingdom lost? Why, 'twas my care,    95
And what loss is it to be rid of care?
Strives Bolingbroke to be as great as we?
Greater he shall not be; if he serve God,
We'll serve Him too, and be his fellow so.    99
Revolt our subjects? That we cannot mend;
They break their faith to God as well as us.
Cry woe, destruction, ruin, and decay;
The worst is death, and death will have his day.

SCROOP
Glad am I that Your Highness is so armed    104
To bear the tidings of calamity.
Like an unseasonable stormy day,
Which makes the silver rivers drown their shores    107
As if the world were all dissolved to tears,
So high above his limits swells the rage    109
Of Bolingbroke, covering your fearful land    110
With hard bright steel and hearts harder than steel.
Whitebeards have armed their thin and hairless scalps   112
Against Thy Majesty; boys with women's voices
Strive to speak big, and clap their female joints    114
In stiff unwieldy arms against thy crown.    115
Thy very beadsmen learn to bend their bows    116
Of double-fatal yew against thy state;    117

Yea, distaff-women manage rusty bills    118
Against thy seat. Both young and old rebel,    119
And all goes worse than I have power to tell.

KING RICHARD
Too well, too well thou tell'st a tale so ill.
Where is the Earl of Wiltshire? Where is Bagot?    122
What is become of Bushy? Where is Green,
That they have let the dangerous enemy
Measure our confines with such peaceful steps?    125
If we prevail, their heads shall pay for it.
I warrant they have made peace with Bolingbroke.

SCROOP
Peace have they made with him indeed, my lord.

KING RICHARD
Oh, villains, vipers, damned without redemption!
Dogs easily won to fawn on any man!
Snakes in my heart-blood warmed, that sting my
  heart!
Three Judases, each one thrice worse than Judas!
Would they make peace? Terrible hell
Make war upon their spotted souls for this!    134

SCROOP
Sweet love, I see, changing his property,    135
Turns to the sourest and most deadly hate.
Again uncurse their souls. Their peace is made
With heads and not with hands. Those whom you
  curse    138
Have felt the worst of death's destroying wound
And lie full low, graved in the hollow ground.    140

AUMERLE
Is Bushy, Green, and the Earl of Wiltshire dead?

SCROOP
Ay, all of them at Bristol lost their heads.

AUMERLE
Where is the Duke my father with his power?

KING RICHARD
No matter where. Of comfort no man speak!
Let's talk of graves, of worms, and epitaphs,
Make dust our paper, and with rainy eyes    146
Write sorrow on the bosom of the earth.    147
Let's choose executors and talk of wills.    148
And yet not so, for what can we bequeath
Save our deposèd bodies to the ground?    150
Our lands, our lives, and all are Bolingbroke's,
And nothing can we call our own but death
And that small model of the barren earth    153
Which serves as paste and cover to our bones.    154
For God's sake, let us sit upon the ground

---

**81 blot** stain   **91 More . . . betide** May more health and happiness befall.   **my liege** the lord to whom I owe allegiance   **92 care-tuned** i.e., tuned by sorrow and to the key of sorrow.   **deliver** deliver to **94 unfold** reveal.   **95 care** trouble   **99 his fellow** his (Bolingbroke's) equal   **104 armed** prepared   **107 silver** shiny   **109 his limits** (1) its banks (2) the limits properly allowed to Bolingbroke's rage **110 fearful** full of fears   **112 Whitebeards** Old men.   **thin** sparsely haired   **114 Strive . . . joints** strive to speak with deep manlike voices, and thrust their adolescent limbs   **115 arms** armor   **116 beadsmen** old almsmen or pensioners whose duty it was to pray for a benefactor; here, for the King   **117 double-fatal** doubly fatal (since the wood of the yew was used for bows and since its foliage and berries are poisonous; yews were also commonly planted in graveyards)

**118–19 distaff-women . . . seat** spinning women wield unused and hence rusty pikes (long-handled ax-like weapons) against your throne.   **122 Bagot** (Although the King names Bagot here, he mentions only *three Judases* in line 132 and Aumerle does not ask about Bagot in line 141; in 3.4 we learn that Bagot is not executed along with the other three but reappears instead in 4.1.)   **125 Measure our confines** travel over my kingdom.   **peaceful** unopposed   **134 spotted** stained with treason   **135 his property** its distinctive quality **138 hands** (Used in swearing oaths, surrendering, etc.)   **140 graved** buried   **146–7 Make . . . earth** make the dusty earth a surface on which to inscribe our sorrows with our tears.   **148 executors** those responsible for administering last wills and testaments   **150 deposèd** (1) dethroned, as in 4.1 (2) deprived of those functions carried out by the body in this transitory life (3) deposited   **153 model** microcosm or mold, i.e., the body   **154 paste** pastry, pie crust

And tell sad stories of the death of kings—
How some have been deposed, some slain in war,
Some haunted by the ghosts they have deposed, 158
Some poisoned by their wives, some sleeping killed,
All murdered. For within the hollow crown
That rounds the mortal temples of a king 161
Keeps Death his court, and there the antic sits, 162
Scoffing his state and grinning at his pomp, 163
Allowing him a breath, a little scene, 164
To monarchize, be feared, and kill with looks, 165
Infusing him with self and vain conceit, 166
As if this flesh which walls about our life
Were brass impregnable; and humored thus, 168
Comes at the last and with a little pin
Bores through his castle wall, and—farewell, king!
Cover your heads, and mock not flesh and blood 171
With solemn reverence. Throw away respect,
Tradition, form, and ceremonious duty,
For you have but mistook me all this while.
I live with bread like you, feel want,
Taste grief, need friends. Subjected thus, 176
How can you say to me I am a king?

CARLISLE
My lord, wise men ne'er sit and wail their woes,
But presently prevent the ways to wail. 179
To fear the foe, since fear oppresseth strength, 180
Gives in your weakness strength unto your foe, 181
And so your follies fight against yourself.
Fear, and be slain. No worse can come to fight; 183
And fight and die is death destroying death, 184
Where fearing dying pays death servile breath. 185

AUMERLE
My father hath a power. Inquire of him, 186
And learn to make a body of a limb. 187

KING RICHARD
Thou chid'st me well. Proud Bolingbroke, I come
To change blows with thee for our day of doom. 189
This ague fit of fear is overblown; 190
An easy task it is to win our own. 191

Say, Scroop, where lies our uncle with his power? 192
Speak sweetly, man, although thy looks be sour.

SCROOP
Men judge by the complexion of the sky 194
  The state and inclination of the day.
So may you by my dull and heavy eye;
  My tongue hath but a heavier tale to say.
I play the torturer, by small and small 198
To lengthen out the worst that must be spoken:
Your uncle York is joined with Bolingbroke,
And all your northern castles yielded up,
And all your southern gentlemen in arms 202
Upon his party.

KING RICHARD    Thou hast said enough. 203
[To Aumerle] Beshrew thee, cousin, which didst lead
  me forth 204
Of that sweet way I was in to despair.
What say you now? What comfort have we now?
By heaven, I'll hate him everlastingly
That bids me be of comfort any more.
Go to Flint Castle. There I'll pine away; 209
A king, woe's slave, shall kingly woe obey.
That power I have, discharge, and let them go
To ear the land that hath some hope to grow, 212
For I have none. Let no man speak again
To alter this, for counsel is but vain.

AUMERLE
My liege, one word.

KING RICHARD      He does me double wrong 215
That wounds me with the flatteries of his tongue.
Discharge my followers. Let them hence away,
From Richard's night to Bolingbroke's fair day.
[Exeunt.]

❧

# [3.3]

*Enter [with drum and colors] Bolingbroke, York,*
*Northumberland, [attendants, and forces].*

BOLINGBROKE
So that by this intelligence we learn 1
The Welshmen are dispersed, and Salisbury
Is gone to meet the King, who lately landed
With some few private friends upon this coast.

NORTHUMBERLAND
The news is very fair and good, my lord:
Richard not far from hence hath hid his head.

YORK
It would beseem the Lord Northumberland 7
To say "King Richard." Alack the heavy day
When such a sacred king should hide his head!

---

**158 deposed** deprived of life   **161 rounds** encircles   **162 antic** grotesque figure, jester   **163 Scoffing his state** scoffing at the King's regality   **164 breath** breathing space, moment   **165 monarchize** play the monarch.   **kill with looks** i.e., order someone's death with a mere glance   **166 self and vain conceit** vain conceit of himself   **168 and humored thus** and Death, having amused himself at the King's expense, having led the King on in this humor   **171 Cover your heads** Replace your hats (which have been removed out of respect for the King)   **176 Subjected** Made subject to grief, want, etc. (With pun on "being treated like a subject.")   **179 But . . . wail** but promptly anticipate and thus prevent the courses that result in lamentation. **180–1 To fear . . . your foe** i.e., To be afraid of the foe is merely a weakness that, by oppressing your own resolve, gives advantage to the foe   **183 Fear . . . fight** i.e., If you fear, you are sure to be slain, and no worse fate can come to you if you fight   **184–5 fight . . . breath** to die fighting is to conquer death in the very act of dying, whereas to die fearfully pays to death the tribute of servility.   **186 power** army (as also in line 192).   **of** about, or from   **187 learn . . . limb** i.e., discover how to make a partial force serve for a complete one.   **189 change** exchange.   **for . . . doom** i.e., in order to settle our fates, which of us is to die now.   **190 This ague . . . overblown** This paroxysm of shivering in fear has blown over   **191 our own** i.e., my own kingdom.

**192 lies** is located.   **194 complexion** appearance   **198 by small and small** little by little   **202–3 And . . . party** and all your men of rank in southern England are also in arms on Bolingbroke's side. **204 Beshrew** Confound. (Literally, *curse.*)   **forth** out   **209 Flint Castle** (Near Chester.)   **212 ear** plow   **215 double wrong** i.e., in deceiving me and in leading me into false hope once again
**3.3. Location: Wales. Before Flint Castle.**
**1 intelligence** information   **7 beseem** be appropriate for, be seemly behavior in

NORTHUMBERLAND
Your Grace mistakes. Only to be brief
Left I his title out.
YORK                    The time hath been,
Would you have been so brief with him, he would                12
Have been so brief with you to shorten you,                    13
For taking so the head, your whole head's length.             14
BOLINGBROKE
Mistake not, uncle, further than you should.
YORK
Take not, good cousin, further than you should,
Lest you mistake the heavens are over our heads.              17
BOLINGBROKE
I know it, uncle, and oppose not myself
Against their will. But who comes here?

            *Enter Percy.*

Welcome, Harry. What, will not this castle yield?
PERCY
The castle royally is manned, my lord,
Against thy entrance.
BOLINGBROKE
Royally? Why, it contains no king?
PERCY    Yes, my good lord,
It doth contain a king. King Richard lies                      25
Within the limits of yon lime and stone,                       26
And with him are the Lord Aumerle, Lord Salisbury,
Sir Stephen Scroop, besides a clergyman
Of holy reverence—who, I cannot learn.
NORTHUMBERLAND
Oh, belike it is the Bishop of Carlisle.                        30
BOLINGBROKE [*to Northumberland*]    Noble lord,
Go to the rude ribs of that ancient castle;                   32
Through brazen trumpet send the breath of parley              33
Into his ruined ears, and thus deliver:                        34
Henry Bolingbroke
On both his knees doth kiss King Richard's hand
And sends allegiance and true faith of heart
To his most royal person, hither come
Even at his feet to lay my arms and power,
Provided that my banishment repealed                           40
And lands restored again be freely granted.                    41
If not, I'll use the advantage of my power,                    42
And lay the summer's dust with showers of blood               43
Rained from the wounds of slaughtered Englishmen—
The which how far off from the mind of Bolingbroke
It is such crimson tempest should bedrench                     46
The fresh green lap of fair King Richard's land,
My stooping duty tenderly shall show.                          48

Go, signify as much while here we march
Upon the grassy carpet of this plain.
    [*Northumberland and attendants advance to the castle.*]
Let's march without the noise of threat'ning drum,
That from this castle's tottered battlements                   52
Our fair appointments may be well perused.                     53
Methinks King Richard and myself should meet
With no less terror than the elements
Of fire and water, when their thund'ring shock                 56
At meeting tears the cloudy cheeks of heaven.
Be he the fire, I'll be the yielding water;
The rage be his, whilst on the earth I rain                    59
My waters—on the earth, and not on him.                        60
March on, and mark King Richard how he looks.                  61

    [*Bolingbroke's forces march about the stage.*] *The
    trumpets sound* [*a parley without and answer
    within, then a flourish. King*] *Richard appeareth
    on the walls* [*with the Bishop of Carlisle, Aumerle,
    Scroop, and Salisbury*].

See, see, King Richard doth himself appear,
As doth the blushing discontented sun                          63
From out the fiery portal of the east
When he perceives the envious clouds are bent                  65
To dim his glory and to stain the track
Of his bright passage to the occident.                         67
YORK
Yet looks he like a king. Behold, his eye,                     68
As bright as is the eagle's, lightens forth                    69
Controlling majesty. Alack, alack, for woe,
That any harm should stain so fair a show!
KING RICHARD [*to Northumberland*]
We are amazed; and thus long have we stood
To watch the fearful bending of thy knee,                      73
Because we thought ourself thy lawful king.
And if we be, how dare thy joints forget
To pay their awful duty to our presence?                       76
If we be not, show us the hand of God                          77
That hath dismissed us from our stewardship;
For well we know, no hand of blood and bone                    79
Can grip the sacred handle of our scepter,
Unless he do profane, steal, or usurp.                         81
And though you think that all, as you have done,
Have torn their souls by turning them from us,                 83
And we are barren and bereft of friends,                       84
Yet know, my master, God omnipotent,                           85
Is mustering in his clouds on our behalf

---

**12–14 he would.... length** the King would have dealt with you by summarily ordering your head to be chopped off, in requital for your presumptuously omitting his title as you have done.    **17 mistake** fail to perceive that. (Plays on Bolingbroke's use of *mistake*, just as York has punned on *brief* and *head*.)    **25 lies** resides    **26 Within ... stone** within the stone fortifications of yonder castle. (*Lime* was traditionally the main ingredient of mortar, now replaced generally by Portland cement.)    **30 belike** probably    **32 rude ribs** i.e., rugged walls    **33 brazen** (1) brass (2) bold.    **breath of parley** i.e., call for a conference    **34 his ruined ears** i.e., its (the castle's) ancient and battered loopholes    **40 my banishment repealed** the revocation of my banishment    **41 lands restored again** the restoration of my lands    **42 advantage of my power** superiority of my army    **43 lay** lay flat    **46 is** is that    **48 stooping duty** submissive kneeling

**52 tottered** in tottering condition, or dilapidated    **53 fair appointments** handsome show of military preparedness    **56 fire and water** i.e., lightning and rain    **59–60 whilst ... waters** while I moisten the earth with my tears    **61.2 *parley*** trumpet summons to a negotiation    **61.4 *on the walls*** i.e., in the gallery of the tiring-house, above, to the rear of the stage    **63 blushing** i.e., turning red with anger    **65 he** i.e., the sun.    **envious** hostile    **67 occident** west.    **68 Yet** Still, or nevertheless.    **he** i.e., King Richard    **69 lightens forth** flashes out, like lightning    **73 watch** wait for    **76 awful** reverential, full of awe    **77 hand** signature    **79 no ... bone** no human hand    **81 Unless he do profane** without committing sacrilege    **83 Have ... us** have turned away from me, their king, thereby imperiling their souls    **84 And** and that    **85 know** know that

Armies of pestilence; and they shall strike
Your children yet unborn and unbegot,
That lift your vassal hands against my head                          89
And threat the glory of my precious crown.                          90
Tell Bolingbroke—for yon methinks he stands—
That every stride he makes upon my land
Is dangerous treason. He is come to open                            93
The purple testament of bleeding war;                               94
But ere the crown he looks for live in peace,
Ten thousand bloody crowns of mothers' sons                         96
Shall ill become the flower of England's face,                      97
Change the complexion of her maid-pale peace                        98
To scarlet indignation, and bedew
Her pastures' grass with faithful English blood.

NORTHUMBERLAND
The King of heaven forbid our lord the King
Should so with civil and uncivil arms                              102
Be rushed upon! Thy thrice-noble cousin
Harry Bolingbroke doth humbly kiss thy hand;
And by the honorable tomb he swears
That stands upon your royal grandsire's bones,                     106
And by the royalties of both your bloods,
Currents that spring from one most gracious head,                  108
And by the buried hand of warlike Gaunt,                           109
And by the worth and honor of himself,
Comprising all that may be sworn or said,
His coming hither hath no further scope                            112
Than for his lineal royalties, and to beg                          113
Enfranchisement immediate on his knees;                            114
Which on thy royal party granted once,                             115
His glittering arms he will commend to rust,                       116
His barbèd steeds to stables, and his heart                        117
To faithful service of Your Majesty.
This swears he, as he is a prince and just,
And as I am a gentleman I credit him.

KING RICHARD
Northumberland, say thus the King returns:                         121
His noble cousin is right welcome hither,
And all the number of his fair demands
Shall be accomplished without contradiction.                       124
With all the gracious utterance thou hast
Speak to his gentle hearing kind commends.                         126
        [Northumberland and attendants retire to Bolingbroke
                                                    and York.]
[To Aumerle] We do debase ourself, cousin, do we not,
To look so poorly and to speak so fair?                            128
Shall we call back Northumberland, and send
Defiance to the traitor, and so die?

AUMERLE
No, good my lord. Let's fight with gentle words
Till time lend friends, and friends their helpful swords.

KING RICHARD
Oh, God, oh, God, that e'er this tongue of mine,
That laid the sentence of dread banishment
On yon proud man, should take it off again
With words of sooth! Oh, that I were as great          136
As is my grief, or lesser than my name!
Or that I could forget what I have been,
Or not remember what I must be now!
Swell'st thou, proud heart? I'll give thee scope to beat,  140
Since foes have scope to beat both thee and me.        141
        [Northumberland returns to the castle walls.]

AUMERLE
Northumberland comes back from Bolingbroke.

KING RICHARD
What must the King do now? Must he submit?
The King shall do it. Must he be deposed?
The King shall be contented. Must he lose
The name of king? I' God's name, let it go.
I'll give my jewels for a set of beads,                147
My gorgeous palace for a hermitage,
My gay apparel for an almsman's gown,                  149
My figured goblets for a dish of wood,                 150
My scepter for a palmer's walking-staff,               151
My subjects for a pair of carvèd saints,
And my large kingdom for a little grave,
A little, little grave, an obscure grave;
Or I'll be buried in the King's highway,
Some way of common trade, where subjects' feet        156
May hourly trample on their sovereign's head;
For on my heart they tread now whilst I live,
And, buried once, why not upon my head?               159
Aumerle, thou weep'st, my tenderhearted cousin.
We'll make foul weather with despisèd tears;
Our sighs and they shall lodge the summer corn        162
And make a dearth in this revolting land.             163
Or shall we play the wantons with our woes            164
And make some pretty match with shedding tears?       165
As thus, to drop them still upon one place,           166
Till they have fretted us a pair of graves            167
Within the earth; and, therein laid, there lies
Two kinsmen digged their graves with weeping eyes. 169
Would not this ill do well? Well, well, I see
I talk but idly, and you laugh at me.—
Most mighty prince, my lord Northumberland,
What says King Bolingbroke? Will His Majesty
Give Richard leave to live till Richard die?
You make a leg, and Bolingbroke says ay.              175

---

**89 That** of you that. **vassal** subject   **90 threat** threaten   **93–4 open . . . testament** initiate a bloodstained legacy. (Blood was often said to be purple.)   **96–7 Ten . . . face** the bloody heads of 10,000 young men (the flower of England) will disfigure the blossoming face of our country   **98 maid-pale** i.e., pale like the complexion of a young English maid   **102 civil** used in civil strife.   **uncivil** barbarous, violent   **106 your royal grandsire's** King Edward III's   **108 head** source (i.e., Edward III)   **109 hand** (with which Gaunt bravely fought)   **112 scope** purpose, aim   **113 lineal royalties** hereditary rights as one of royal blood   **114 Enfranchisement** freedom (from banishment)   **115 Which . . . once** which, once that has been granted by your royal self   **116 commend** give over   **117 barbèd** armored   **121 returns** answers   **124 accomplished** fulfilled   **126 commends** regards.   **128 poorly** abject.   **fair** courteously.

**136 sooth** cajolery, flattery.   **140 scope** freedom, space   **141 scope** capacity, opportunity   **147 set of beads** rosary   **149 almsman's gown** plain attire of one who lives on alms or charity   **150 figured** ornamented, embossed   **151 palmer's** pilgrim's   **156 trade** passage   **159 buried once** once I am buried   **162 Our . . . corn** our sighs and tears will beat down the summer grain fields   **163 revolting** rebelling   **164 play the wantons** sport, frolic   **165 match** game, contest   **166 still** continually   **167 fretted us** eaten away for us, worn. (With a play on "complained.")   **169 digged** who dug   **175 a leg** a curtsy, an obeisance

**NORTHUMBERLAND**
My lord, in the base court he doth attend                    176
To speak with you, may it please you to come down.    177

**KING RICHARD**
Down, down I come, like glistering Phaëthon,            178
Wanting the manage of unruly jades.                          179
In the base court? Base court, where kings grow base,
To come at traitors' calls and do them grace.              181
In the base court? Come down? Down, court! Down, king!
For night owls shriek where mounting larks should sing.                    [*Exeunt from above.*]

[*Northumberland rejoins Bolingbroke.*]

**BOLINGBROKE**
What says His Majesty?

**NORTHUMBERLAND**                    Sorrow and grief of heart
Makes him speak fondly, like a frantic man.              185
Yet he is come.

[*Enter King Richard and his attendants below.*]

**BOLINGBROKE**    Stand all apart,                            187
And show fair duty to His Majesty.        *He kneels down.*  188
My gracious lord!

**KING RICHARD**
Fair cousin, you debase your princely knee              190
To make the base earth proud with kissing it.           191
Me rather had my heart might feel your love             192
Than my unpleased eye see your courtesy.
Up, cousin, up. Your heart is up, I know,
Thus high at least [*touching his crown*], although your knee be low.

**BOLINGBROKE** [*rising*]
My gracious lord, I come but for mine own.

**KING RICHARD**
Your own is yours, and I am yours, and all.

**BOLINGBROKE**
So far be mine, my most redoubted lord,                 198
As my true service shall deserve your love.

**KING RICHARD**
Well you deserve. They well deserve to have
That know the strong'st and surest way to get.
[*To York, who weeps*] Uncle, give me your hands. Nay, dry your eyes;
Tears show their love, but want their remedies.        203
[*To Bolingbroke*] Cousin, I am too young to be your father,                    204

Though you are old enough to be my heir.
What you will have, I'll give, and willing too,
For do we must what force will have us do.
Set on towards London, cousin, is it so?

**BOLINGBROKE**
Yea, my good lord.

**KING RICHARD**                    Then I must not say no.
                                        [*Flourish. Exeunt.*]

# [3.4]

*Enter the Queen with [two Ladies,] her attendants.*

**QUEEN**
What sport shall we devise here in this garden,
To drive away the heavy thought of care?

**LADY**    Madam, we'll play at bowls.                    3

**QUEEN**
'Twill make me think the world is full of rubs,        4
And that my fortune runs against the bias.            5

**LADY**    Madam, we'll dance.

**QUEEN**
My legs can keep no measure in delight                7
When my poor heart no measure keeps in grief.    8
Therefore, no dancing, girl; some other sport.

**LADY**    Madam, we'll tell tales.

**QUEEN**
Of sorrow or of joy?

**LADY**                    Of either, madam.

**QUEEN**    Of neither, girl;
For if of joy, being altogether wanting,              13
It doth remember me the more of sorrow;             14
Or if of grief, being altogether had,                 15
It adds more sorrow to my want of joy.               16
For what I have I need not to repeat,
And what I want it boots not to complain.            18

**LADY**
Madam, I'll sing.

**QUEEN**                    'Tis well that thou hast cause,
But thou shouldst please me better wouldst thou weep.                    20

**LADY**
I could weep, madam, would it do you good.

**QUEEN**
And I could sing, would weeping do me good,       22
And never borrow any tear of thee.                   23

*Enter Gardeners [a Master and two Men].*

But stay, here come the gardeners.
Let's step into the shadow of these trees.

---

**176 base court** outer or lower court of a castle    **177 may it please you** if you please    **178 glistering** glistening, glittering.    **Phaëthon** son of the sun-god, whose chariot he attempted to steer across the sky; unable to control the horses of the sun, he was hurled from the chariot by Jupiter    **179 Wanting . . . jades** lacking the skill in horsemanship to control unruly nags.    **181 do them grace** (1) bow to them (2) treat them graciously.    **185 fondly** foolishly.    **frantic** mad    **187 apart** aside    **188 fair duty** respect    **190–1 debase . . . base** (Continues the wordplay on *base* in line 180.)    **192 Me rather had** I had rather    **198 mine** i.e., my loved lord (changing Richard's meaning of *yours* in the previous line).    **redoubted** dread    **203 want their remedies** lack remedies for what caused them.    **204 too young** (Historically, Richard and Bolingbroke were both thirty-three.)

**3.4. Location: The Duke of York's garden.**
**3 bowls** lawn bowling. (A common Elizabethan game.)    **4 rubs** impediments (in the game of bowls)    **5 against the bias** i.e., contrary, athwart. (Literally, not following the naturally curved path of a bowl, which was weighted on one side.)    **7 measure** a stately slow dance    **8 measure** moderation    **13 wanting** lacking    **14 remember** remind    **15 being** since I am    **16 want** lack    **18 boots** helps    **20 wouldst thou** if you would    **22 would . . . good** i.e., if weeping would make me any less unhappy    **23 never borrow** never need to borrow

My wretchedness unto a row of pins, 26
They will talk of state, for everyone doth so 27
Against a change; woe is forerun with woe. 28
                    [*The Queen and Ladies stand apart.*]
GARDENER [*to one Man*]
Go bind thou up young dangling apricots
Which, like unruly children, make their sire 30
Stoop with oppression of their prodigal weight. 31
Give some supportance to the bending twigs.
[*To the other*] Go thou, and like an executioner
Cut off the heads of too-fast-growing sprays
That look too lofty in our commonwealth.
All must be even in our government. 36
You thus employed, I will go root away
The noisome weeds which without profit suck 38
The soil's fertility from wholesome flowers.
MAN
Why should we in the compass of a pale 40
Keep law and form and due proportion,
Showing as in a model our firm estate, 42
When our sea-wallèd garden, the whole land,
Is full of weeds, her fairest flowers choked up,
Her fruit trees all unpruned, her hedges ruined,
Her knots disordered, and her wholesome herbs 46
Swarming with caterpillars?
GARDENER                    Hold thy peace. 47
He that hath suffered this disordered spring 48
Hath now himself met with the fall of leaf. 49
The weeds which his broad-spreading leaves did
    shelter,
That seemed in eating him to hold him up, 51
Are plucked up root and all by Bolingbroke:
I mean the Earl of Wiltshire, Bushy, Green.
MAN
What, are they dead?
GARDENER                    They are; and Bolingbroke
Hath seized the wasteful King. Oh, what pity is it
That he had not so trimmed and dressed his land 56
As we this garden! We at time of year 57
Do wound the bark, the skin of our fruit trees,
Lest being overproud in sap and blood 59
With too much riches it confound itself;
Had he done so to great and growing men, 61
They might have lived to bear and he to taste
Their fruits of duty. Superfluous branches
We lop away, that bearing boughs may live; 64
Had he done so, himself had borne the crown 65
Which waste of idle hours hath quite thrown down.
MAN
What, think you the King shall be deposed?

GARDENER
Depressed he is already, and deposed 68
'Tis doubt he will be. Letters came last night 69
To a dear friend of the good Duke of York's,
That tell black tidings.
QUEEN [*coming forward*]    Oh, I am pressed to death 71
Through want of speaking! Thou, old Adam's likeness, 72
Set to dress this garden, how dares 73
Thy harsh rude tongue sound this unpleasing news?
What Eve, what serpent, hath suggested thee 75
To make a second fall of cursèd man? 76
Why dost thou say King Richard is deposed?
Dar'st thou, thou little better thing than earth,
Divine his downfall? Say where, when, and how 79
Cam'st thou by this ill tidings? Speak, thou wretch.
GARDENER
Pardon me, madam. Little joy have I
To breathe this news, yet what I say is true.
King Richard, he is in the mighty hold 83
Of Bolingbroke. Their fortunes both are weighed:
In your lord's scale is nothing but himself
And some few vanities that make him light;
But in the balance of great Bolingbroke,
Besides himself, are all the English peers,
And with that odds he weighs King Richard down.
Post you to London and you will find it so; 90
I speak no more than everyone doth know.
QUEEN
Nimble mischance, that art so light of foot,
Doth not thy embassage belong to me, 93
And am I last that knows it? Oh, thou thinkest
To serve me last, that I may longest keep
Thy sorrow in my breast.—Come, ladies, go 96
To meet at London London's king in woe.
What, was I born to this, that my sad look
Should grace the triumph of great Bolingbroke? 99
Gard'ner, for telling me these news of woe,
Pray God the plants thou graft'st may never grow.
                    *Exit* [*with Ladies*].
GARDENER
Poor queen! So that thy state might be no worse, 102
I would my skill were subject to thy curse.
Here did she fall a tear; here in this place 104
I'll set a bank of rue, sour herb of grace. 105
Rue even for ruth here shortly shall be seen, 106
In the remembrance of a weeping queen.    *Exeunt.*

❖

26 My . . . pins i.e., I'd bet my immeasurable grief against the merest trifle   27 state statecraft, politics   28 Against . . . with woe when change is imminent; sad times are heralded by gloomy predictions.   30 their sire the tree   31 prodigal excessive   36 even equal   38 noisome harmful   40 pale enclosure, enclosed garden   42 firm stable   46 knots flower beds laid out in intricate designs   47 Hold thy peace Be quiet.   48 suffered allowed   49 fall of leaf i.e., autumn.   51 in eating him i.e., while they were really eating his sustenance   56 dressed put in order   57 at . . . year in the appropriate season   59 overproud in swollen with   61 growing ambitious   64 bearing fruit-bearing   65 crown (1) royal crown (2) crown of a tree

68 Depressed Brought low   69 'Tis doubt there is fear   71 pressed to death (Allusion to the *peine forte et dure*, inflicted by pressure of heavy weights upon the chests of indicted persons who refused to plead and remained silent.)   72 old Adam (In his role as the first gardener.)   73 dress cultivate   75 suggested tempted   76 a second fall (recalling the sinful fall of humankind through disobedience to God's command in the Garden of Eden; see Genesis, chapter 3)   79 Divine prophesy   83 hold (1) custody (2) prison   90 Post Hasten. (See the note at 1.1.56.)   93 embassage message.   belong to concern   96 Thy sorrow the sorrow that you (mischance) report   99 triumph triumphal procession.   Bolingbroke (The original spelling, "Bullingbrooke," indicates the rhyme with *look* in the previous line, pronounced something like "bruke" and "luke.")   102 So that Provided that   104 fall let fall   105 rue "herb of grace," a plant symbolical of repentance, ruth, or sorrow for another's misery   106 ruth pity

# [4.1]

*Enter Bolingbroke with the Lords [Aumerle,*
*Northumberland, Harry Percy, Fitzwater, Surrey,*
*the Bishop of Carlisle, the Abbot of Westminster,*
*and another Lord, Herald, officers] to Parliament.*
*[The throne is provided on stage.]*

BOLINGBROKE
Call forth Bagot.

*Enter [officers with] Bagot.*

Now, Bagot, freely speak thy mind,
What thou dost know of noble Gloucester's death,
Who wrought it with the King, and who performed          4
The bloody office of his timeless end.                    5

BAGOT
Then set before my face the Lord Aumerle.

BOLINGBROKE [*to Aumerle*]
Cousin, stand forth, and look upon that man.
                              [*Aumerle comes forward.*]

BAGOT
My lord Aumerle, I know your daring tongue
Scorns to unsay what once it hath delivered.              9
In that dead time when Gloucester's death was plotted,   10
I heard you say, "Is not my arm of length,               11
That reacheth from the restful English court             12
As far as Calais, to mine uncle's head?"
Amongst much other talk that very time                   14
I heard you say that you had rather refuse               15
The offer of an hundred thousand crowns                  16
Than Bolingbroke's return to England—                    17
Adding withal how blest this land would be               18
In this your cousin's death.

AUMERLE          Princes and noble lords,
What answer shall I make to this base man?
Shall I so much dishonor my fair stars                   22
On equal terms to give him chastisement?                 23
Either I must, or have mine honor soiled
With the attainder of his slanderous lips.               25
                        [*He throws down his gage.*]
There is my gage, the manual seal of death,              26
That marks thee out for hell. I say thou liest,
And will maintain what thou hast said is false
In thy heart-blood, though being all too base
To stain the temper of my knightly sword.

BOLINGBROKE
Bagot, forbear. Thou shalt not take it up.

AUMERLE
Excepting one, I would he were the best                  32
In all this presence that hath moved me so.

FITZWATER [*throwing down a gage*]
If that thy valor stand on sympathy,                     34
There is my gage, Aumerle, in gage to thine.             35
By that fair sun which shows me where thou stand'st,
I heard thee say, and vauntingly thou spak'st it,        37
That thou wert cause of noble Gloucester's death.
If thou deny'st it twenty times, thou liest,
And I will turn thy falsehood to thy heart,              40
Where it was forgèd, with my rapier's point.

AUMERLE [*taking up the gage*]
Thou dar'st not, coward, live to see that day.

FITZWATER
Now, by my soul, I would it were this hour.

AUMERLE
Fitzwater, thou art damned to hell for this.

PERCY
Aumerle, thou liest. His honor is as true
In this appeal as thou art all unjust;                   46
And that thou art so, there I throw my gage
                        [*throwing down a gage*]
To prove it on thee to the extremest point               48
Of mortal breathing. Seize it if thou dar'st.            49

AUMERLE [*taking up the gage*]
An if I do not, may my hands rot off                     50
And never brandish more revengeful steel                 51
Over the glittering helmet of my foe!

ANOTHER LORD [*throwing down a gage*]
I task the earth to the like, forsworn Aumerle,          53
And spur thee on with full as many lies                  54
As may be holloed in thy treacherous ear
From sun to sun. There is my honor's pawn;               56
Engage it to the trial, if thou darest.                  57

AUMERLE [*taking up the gage*]
Who sets me else? By heaven, I'll throw at all!          58
I have a thousand spirits in one breast
To answer twenty thousand such as you.

SURREY
My lord Fitzwater, I do remember well
The very time Aumerle and you did talk.

FITZWATER
'Tis very true. You were in presence then,               63
And you can witness with me this is true.

SURREY          As false, by heaven, as heaven itself is true.

FITZWATER
Surrey, thou liest.

SURREY                    Dishonorable boy!
That lie shall lie so heavy on my sword

---

**4.1. Location:** Westminster Hall.
**4 Who . . . King** who prevailed upon the King to have the murder performed    **5 office** function.    **timeless** untimely    **9 unsay** deny, take back.    **delivered** reported.    **10 dead** (1) deadly (2) dark, silent    **11 of length** long enough    **12 restful** i.e., untroubled by Gloucester    **14 that very time** (An inconsistency; Gloucester's death occurred before Bolingbroke left England.)    **15–17 I heard . . . England** (See 1.4.12–19.)    **17 Than . . . return** than have Bolingbroke return    **18 withal** in addition    **22 stars** i.e., fortune, rank    **23 On . . . chastisement** as to challenge him as my equal. (Traditionally, noblemen were under no obligation to answer a challenge from a person of lower social rank.)    **25 attainder** dishonoring accusation    **25.1 gage** usually a glove or a gauntlet (a mailed or armored glove), as at 1.1.69 ff.    **26 manual . . . death** death warrant sealed by my hand

**32 one** i.e., Bolingbroke.    **best** highest in rank    **34 stand on sympathy** i.e., insists on correspondence of rank in your opponent    **35 in gage** engaged    **37 vauntingly** boastfully    **40 turn** turn back    **46 appeal** accusation. (As also in line 80.)    **all unjust** totally false    **48–9 to . . . breathing** to the point of death.    **50 An if** If    **51 more** any more, ever again    **53 I . . . like** I burden the ground in the same way    **54 lies** accusations of lying    **56 sun to sun** sunrise to sunset.    **honor's pawn** pledge of honor. (Also in line 71.)    **57 Engage . . . trial** take it up as a pledge to combat    **58 Who . . . else?** Who else puts up stakes against me or challenges me to a contest?    **throw** (1) throw dice (2) throw down gages    **63 in presence** present

That it shall render vengeance and revenge,    68
Till thou the lie-giver and that lie do lie
In earth as quiet as thy father's skull.
In proof whereof, there is my honor's pawn.
    *[He throws down a gage.]*
Engage it to the trial if thou dar'st.

FITZWATER *[taking up the gage]*
How fondly dost thou spur a forward horse!    73
If I dare eat, or drink, or breathe, or live,
I dare meet Surrey in a wilderness    75
And spit upon him whilst I say he lies,
And lies, and lies. There is my bond of faith,
To tie thee to my strong correction.
    *[He throws down a gage.]*
As I intend to thrive in this new world,    79
Aumerle is guilty of my true appeal.    80
Besides, I heard the banished Norfolk say
That thou, Aumerle, didst send two of thy men
To execute the noble Duke at Calais.

AUMERLE
Some honest Christian trust me with a gage.
    *[He borrows a gage and throws it down.]*
That Norfolk lies, here do I throw down this,
If he may be repealed, to try his honor.    86

BOLINGBROKE
These differences shall all rest under gage    87
Till Norfolk be repealed. Repealed he shall be,
And, though mine enemy, restored again
To all his lands and seigniories. When he is returned,
Against Aumerle we will enforce his trial.

CARLISLE
That honorable day shall never be seen.
Many a time hath banished Norfolk fought
For Jesu Christ in glorious Christian field,
Streaming the ensign of the Christian cross    95
Against black pagans, Turks, and Saracens;
And, toiled with works of war, retired himself    97
To Italy, and there at Venice gave
His body to that pleasant country's earth
And his pure soul unto his captain, Christ,
Under whose colors he had fought so long.

BOLINGBROKE    Why, Bishop, is Norfolk dead?
CARLISLE    As surely as I live, my lord.
BOLINGBROKE
Sweet peace conduct his sweet soul to the bosom    104
Of good old Abraham! Lords appellants,    105
Your differences shall all rest under gage    106
Till we assign you to your days of trial.    107

    *Enter York.*

YORK
Great Duke of Lancaster, I come to thee
From plume-plucked Richard, who with willing soul
Adopts thee heir, and his high scepter yields
To the possession of thy royal hand.
Ascend his throne, descending now from him,
And long live Henry, fourth of that name!

BOLINGBROKE
In God's name, I'll ascend the regal throne.

CARLISLE    Marry, God forbid!
Worst in this royal presence may I speak,    116
Yet best beseeming me to speak the truth.    117
Would God that any in this noble presence
Were enough noble to be upright judge
Of noble Richard! Then true noblesse would    120
Learn him forbearance from so foul a wrong.    121
What subject can give sentence on his king?
And who sits here that is not Richard's subject?
Thieves are not judged but they are by to hear,    124
Although apparent guilt be seen in them;    125
And shall the figure of God's majesty,    126
His captain, steward, deputy elect,
Anointed, crownèd, planted many years,
Be judged by subject and inferior breath,
And he himself not present? Oh, forfend it God    130
That in a Christian climate souls refined    131
Should show so heinous, black, obscene a deed!    132
I speak to subjects, and a subject speaks,
Stirred up by God thus boldly for his king.
My lord of Hereford here, whom you call king,    135
Is a foul traitor to proud Hereford's king.
And if you crown him, let me prophesy:
The blood of English shall manure the ground
And future ages groan for this foul act;
Peace shall go sleep with Turks and infidels,
And in this seat of peace tumultuous wars
Shall kin with kin and kind with kind confound;    142
Disorder, horror, fear, and mutiny
Shall here inhabit, and this land be called
The field of Golgotha and dead men's skulls.    145
Oh, if you raise this house against this house,    146
It will the woefullest division prove
That ever fell upon this cursèd earth.
Prevent it, resist it, let it not be so,
Lest child, child's children, cry against you woe!

NORTHUMBERLAND
Well have you argued, sir, and for your pains
Of capital treason we arrest you here.—    152

---

**68 it** i.e., my sword   **73 fondly** foolishly, unnecessarily. **forward** willing   **75 in a wilderness** i.e., where fighting might go on uninterrupted to the death   **79 in . . . world** i.e., under the new king   **80 appeal** accusation.   **86 repealed** recalled from exile. **try** test   **87 under gage** as challenges   **95 Streaming** flying   **97 toiled** wearied   **104–5 bosom . . . Abraham** i.e., heaven. (See Luke 16:22.) **105 Lords appellants** Lords who appear as formal accusers **106 differences** quarrels   **107.1 Enter York** (Probably Richard's scepter, etc., are brought in at line 162, but York here invites Bolingbroke to ascend the throne with the surrendered scepter, and so perhaps the regalia are brought on here.)

**116 Worst** Least in rank   **117 best beseeming me** i.e., most befitting me as a clergyman   **120 noblesse** nobleness   **121 Learn him forbearance** teach him to forbear   **124 judged . . . by** condemned unless they are present   **125 apparent** manifest   **126 figure** image   **130 forfend** forbid   **131 souls refined** civilized people   **132 obscene** odious, repulsive   **135 My . . . Hereford** (Carlisle refuses to refer to Bolingbroke as king or even as Duke of Lancaster, since he lost the latter title at the time of his banishment.)   **142 Shall . . . confound** will destroy kinsmen by means of kinsmen and fellow countrymen by means of fellow countrymen   **145 Golgotha** Calvary, the hill outside of Jerusalem called "the place of dead men's skulls" (see Mark 15:22 and John 19:17) where Jesus was crucified   **146 this house . . . this house** i.e., Lancaster against York. (See Mark 3:25.)   **152 Of** on a charge of

My lord of Westminster, be it your charge
To keep him safely till his day of trial.
                    [*Carlisle is taken into custody.*]
May it please you, lords, to grant the commons' suit? 155

BOLINGBROKE
Fetch hither Richard, that in common view
He may surrender; so we shall proceed                  157
Without suspicion.

YORK                    I will be his conduct.     *Exit.* 158

BOLINGBROKE
Lords, you that here are under our arrest,
Procure your sureties for your days of answer.         160
Little are we beholding to your love,                  161
And little looked for at your helping hands.           162

        *Enter Richard and York [with Officers bearing*
        *the crown and regalia].*

KING RICHARD
Alack, why am I sent for to a king,
Before I have shook off the regal thoughts
Wherewith I reigned? I hardly yet have learned
To insinuate, flatter, bow, and bend my knee.
Give sorrow leave awhile to tutor me
To this submission. Yet I well remember
The favors of these men. Were they not mine?           169
Did they not sometime cry, "All hail!" to me?
So Judas did to Christ. But he, in twelve,
Found truth in all but one; I, in twelve thousand, none.
God save the King! Will no man say amen?
Am I both priest and clerk? Well then, amen.           174
God save the King, although I be not he;
And yet, amen, if heaven do think him me.
To do what service am I sent for hither?

YORK
To do that office of thine own good will
Which tired majesty did make thee offer:
The resignation of thy state and crown
To Henry Bolingbroke.

KING RICHARD
Give me the crown. [*He takes the crown.*] Here, cousin,
    seize the crown.
Here, cousin,
On this side my hand, and on that side thine.
Now is this golden crown like a deep well
That owes two buckets, filling one another,           186
The emptier ever dancing in the air,
The other down, unseen, and full of water.

That bucket down and full of tears am I,
Drinking my griefs, whilst you mount up on high.

BOLINGBROKE
I thought you had been willing to resign.

KING RICHARD
My crown I am, but still my griefs are mine.
You may my glories and my state depose,
But not my griefs; still am I king of those.

BOLINGBROKE
Part of your cares you give me with your crown.

KING RICHARD
Your cares set up do not pluck my cares down.          196
My care is loss of care, by old care done;            197
Your care is gain of care, by new care won.           198
The cares I give I have, though given away;            199
They 'tend the crown, yet still with me they stay.    200

BOLINGBROKE
Are you contented to resign the crown?

KING RICHARD
Ay, no; no, ay; for I must nothing be;                 202
Therefore no, no, for I resign to thee.                203
Now mark me how I will undo myself:                    204
                [*He yields his crown and scepter.*]
I give this heavy weight from off my head
And this unwieldy scepter from my hand,
The pride of kingly sway from out my heart;
With mine own tears I wash away my balm,               208
With mine own hands I give away my crown,
With mine own tongue deny my sacred state,
With mine own breath release all duteous oaths.        211
All pomp and majesty I do forswear;
My manors, rents, revenues I forgo;
My acts, decrees, and statutes I deny.
God pardon all oaths that are broke to me!
God keep all vows unbroke are made to thee!            216
Make me, that nothing have, with nothing grieved,     217
And thou with all pleased, that hast all achieved!
Long mayst thou live in Richard's seat to sit,
And soon lie Richard in an earthy pit!
God save King Henry, unkinged Richard says,
And send him many years of sunshine days!—
What more remains?

NORTHUMBERLAND [*presenting a paper*]
                        No more but that you read       223
These accusations and these grievous crimes
Committed by your person and your followers
Against the state and profit of this land;

**155 the commons' suit** request of the commons (i.e., that Richard be formally tried and the causes of his deposition made public. This line begins the abdication passage omitted in early quartos of the play.) **157 surrender** i.e., surrender the crown, abdicate **158 conduct** escort. **160 sureties** persons who will guarantee your appearance. **your days of answer** the time when you must appear to stand trial. **161 beholding** beholden, indebted **162 little . . . hands** i.e., I did not expect this from you, thinking you were on our side. **169 favors** (1) faces (2) support, good will **174 priest and clerk** (In religious services, the clerk or assistant would say "Amen" to the priest's prayers.) **186 owes** owns, has. **filling one another** (The raising of the full bucket lowers the other to be filled in turn.)

**196–200 Your . . . stay** i.e., Your assuming the cares of office does not assuage my griefs. My grief is loss of kingly responsibility, destroyed by a failure in diligence; your concern is gaining of kingly responsibility, won by zealous effort. The anxieties I transfer to you I also keep for myself, despite my giving them to you; they accompany the crown and yet still remain with me. **202 Ay** (1) Yes (2) I. (But, says Richard, I am nothing, and therefore "Ay" is "I" or "nothing," that is, "no.") **203 no, no . . . thee** (Richard plays on the logic that a double negative equals a positive; with an aural pun on *no/know*.) **204 undo** (1) divest (2) unmake **208 balm** sacred ointment with which a king was anointed in the coronation ceremony **211 release . . . oaths** release my subjects from their oaths of duty. **216 are** that are **217 Make** i.e., May God make. **with nothing grieved** (1) grieved at nothing (2) grieved at having nothing **223 read** i.e., read aloud

That, by confessing them, the souls of men
May deem that you are worthily deposed.
KING RICHARD
Must I do so? And must I ravel out                         229
My weaved-up follies? Gentle Northumberland,
If thy offenses were upon record,
Would it not shame thee in so fair a troop               232
To read a lecture of them? If thou wouldst,              233
There shouldst thou find one heinous article
Containing the deposing of a king
And cracking the strong warrant of an oath,
Marked with a blot, damned in the book of heaven.       237
Nay, all of you that stand and look upon me,
Whilst that my wretchedness doth bait myself,           239
Though some of you, with Pilate, wash your hands,       240
Showing an outward pity, yet you Pilates
Have here delivered me to my sour cross,                242
And water cannot wash away your sin.
NORTHUMBERLAND
My lord, dispatch. Read o'er these articles.            244
KING RICHARD
Mine eyes are full of tears; I cannot see.
And yet salt water blinds them not so much
But they can see a sort of traitors here.               247
Nay, if I turn mine eyes upon myself,
I find myself a traitor with the rest;
For I have given here my soul's consent
T'undeck the pompous body of a king,                    251
Made glory base and sovereignty a slave,
Proud majesty a subject, state a peasant.               253
NORTHUMBERLAND          My lord—
KING RICHARD
No lord of thine, thou haught insulting man,            255
Nor no man's lord. I have no name, no title,
No, not that name was given me at the font,
But 'tis usurped. Alack the heavy day,
That I have worn so many winters out
And know not now what name to call myself!
Oh, that I were a mockery king of snow,
Standing before the sun of Bolingbroke,
To melt myself away in water drops!
Good king, great king, and yet not greatly good,
An if my word be sterling yet in England,               265
Let it command a mirror hither straight,                266
That it may show me what a face I have,
Since it is bankrupt of his majesty.                    268
BOLINGBROKE
Go some of you and fetch a looking glass.               269
                              [Exit an Attendant.]
NORTHUMBERLAND
Read o'er this paper while the glass doth come.

KING RICHARD
Fiend, thou torments me ere I come to hell!
BOLINGBROKE
Urge it no more, my lord Northumberland.
NORTHUMBERLAND
The commons will not then be satisfied.
KING RICHARD
They shall be satisfied. I'll read enough
When I do see the very book indeed
Where all my sins are writ, and that's myself.          276

          Enter one with a glass.

Give me that glass, and therein will I read.
                          [He takes the mirror.]
No deeper wrinkles yet? Hath sorrow struck
So many blows upon this face of mine,
And made no deeper wounds? O flattering glass,
Like to my followers in prosperity,                     281
Thou dost beguile me! Was this face the face           282
That every day under his household roof
Did keep ten thousand men? Was this the face
That, like the sun, did make beholders wink?            285
Is this the face which faced so many follies,           286
That was at last outfaced by Bolingbroke?              287
A brittle glory shineth in this face—
As brittle as the glory is the face,
                          [He throws down the mirror.]
For there it is, cracked in an hundred shivers.
Mark, silent king, the moral of this sport:
How soon my sorrow hath destroyed my face.
BOLINGBROKE
The shadow of your sorrow hath destroyed             293
The shadow of your face.
KING RICHARD              Say that again.              294
The shadow of my sorrow? Ha! Let's see.
'Tis very true, my grief lies all within;
And these external manners of laments                 297
Are merely shadows to the unseen grief                298
That swells with silence in the tortured soul.
There lies the substance; and I thank thee, King,     300
For thy great bounty, that not only giv'st            301
Me cause to wail, but teachest me the way
How to lament the cause. I'll beg one boon,           303
And then be gone and trouble you no more.
Shall I obtain it?
BOLINGBROKE          Name it, fair cousin.
KING RICHARD
"Fair cousin"? I am greater than a king.
For when I was a king, my flatterers
Were then but subjects; being now a subject,

---

229 **ravel out** unravel   232 **troop** company   233 **read a lecture** give a
public reading (as a warning)   237 **Marked . . . damned** (Modifying
*article* in line 234)   239 **bait** torment, harass (as in bearbaiting)
240 **Pilate . . . hands** Although Pontius Pilate, prefect of the Roman
province of Judaea, washed his hands to signify his belief in the innocence of Christ (Matthew 27.24), he delivered Christ over to the Jews
to be crucified. (Richard persistently compares himself to Christ; see
also 3.2.132; 4.1.171.)   242 **sour** bitter   244 **dispatch** conclude, be done.
247 **sort** gang   251 **pompous** stately, splendid   253 **state** high rank,
stateliness   255 **haught** haughty   265 **An if** if.   **sterling** valid currency   266 **straight** immediately   268 **his** its   269 **some** i.e., someone

276.1 *glass* mirror.   281 **in prosperity** when I prospered   282 **Was
this face** (An echo of Christopher Marlowe's *Doctor Faustus*, 5.1, in
which the protagonist addresses Helen of Troy.)   285 **wink** close the
eyes, blink.   286 **faced** countenanced   287 **outfaced** stared down,
discountenanced   293 **shadow** outward show, or, overshadowing
nature   294 **shadow** reflection (in the mirror)   297 **manners** forms,
manifestations   298 **shadows to** shadowings forth or embodiments
of   300 **There** i.e., In my soul   301 **that** you who   303 **boon** favor

I have a king here to my flatterer.                          309
Being so great, I have no need to beg.
BOLINGBROKE   Yet ask.
KING RICHARD   And shall I have?
BOLINGBROKE   You shall.
KING RICHARD   Then give me leave to go.                     314
BOLINGBROKE   Whither?
KING RICHARD
Whither you will, so I were from your sights.
BOLINGBROKE
Go some of you, convey him to the Tower.                     317
KING RICHARD
Oh, good! "Convey"? Conveyers are you all,                   318
That rise thus nimbly by a true king's fall.
        [*Exeunt King Richard, some lords, and a guard.*]
BOLINGBROKE
On Wednesday next we solemnly set down
Our coronation. Lords, prepare yourselves.                   321
        *Exeunt. Manent* [*the Abbot of*] *Westminster,* [*the*
                *Bishop of*] *Carlisle, Aumerle.*
ABBOT
A woeful pageant have we here beheld.
CARLISLE
The woe's to come, the children yet unborn
Shall feel this day as sharp to them as thorn.               324
AUMERLE
You holy clergymen, is there no plot
To rid the realm of this pernicious blot?
ABBOT   My lord,
Before I freely speak my mind herein,
You shall not only take the Sacrament
To bury mine intents, but also to effect                     330
Whatever I shall happen to devise.
I see your brows are full of discontent,
Your hearts of sorrow, and your eyes of tears.
Come home with me to supper; I'll lay
A plot shall show us all a merry day.         *Exeunt.* 335

                        ❖

# [5.1]

        *Enter the Queen with* [*Ladies,*] *her attendants.*

QUEEN
This way the King will come. This is the way
To Julius Caesar's ill-erected tower,                        2
To whose flint bosom my condemnèd lord
Is doomed a prisoner by proud Bolingbroke.
Here let us rest, if this rebellious earth
Have any resting for her true king's queen.

        *Enter Richard* [*and guard*].

But soft, but see, or rather do not see                      7
My fair rose wither. Yet look up, behold,

That you in pity may dissolve to dew,
And wash him fresh again with true-love tears.—
Ah, thou, the model where old Troy did stand,               11
Thou map of honor, thou King Richard's tomb,                12
And not King Richard! Thou most beauteous inn,              13
Why should hard-favored grief be lodged in thee             14
When triumph is become an alehouse guest?                   15
KING RICHARD
Join not with grief, fair woman, do not so,
To make my end too sudden. Learn, good soul,                17
To think our former state a happy dream,
From which awaked, the truth of what we are
Shows us but this. I am sworn brother, sweet,
To grim Necessity, and he and I
Will keep a league till death. Hie thee to France,          22
And cloister thee in some religious house.                  23
Our holy lives must win a new world's crown,                24
Which our profane hours here have thrown down.
QUEEN
What, is my Richard both in shape and mind
Transformed and weakened? Hath Bolingbroke
Deposed thine intellect? Hath he been in thy heart?
The lion dying thrusteth forth his paw
And wounds the earth, if nothing else, with rage
To be o'erpowered; and wilt thou, pupil-like,               31
Take the correction, mildly kiss the rod,
And fawn on rage with base humility,
Which art a lion and the king of beasts?                    34
KING RICHARD
A king of beasts, indeed! If aught but beasts,              35
I had been still a happy king of men.
Good sometimes queen, prepare thee hence for France.  37
Think I am dead and that even here thou takest,
As from my deathbed, thy last living leave.
In winter's tedious nights sit by the fire
With good old folks, and let them tell thee tales
Of woeful ages long ago betid;                              42
And ere thou bid good night, to quit their griefs           43
Tell thou the lamentable tale of me
And send the hearers weeping to their beds;
Forwhy the senseless brands will sympathize                 46
The heavy accent of thy moving tongue,                      47
And in compassion weep the fire out;
And some will mourn in ashes, some coal-black,              49
For the deposing of a rightful king.

        *Enter Northumberland* [*attended*].

309 to as   314 leave permission   317 convey escort   318 Convey
Steal.   321.1 *Manent* They remain on stage   324 Shall who will
330 To . . . intents to conceal my plans   335 shall that shall
5.1. Location: London. A street leading to the Tower.
2 Julius . . . tower (The Tower of London, ascribed by tradition to
Julius Caesar, was built by William the Conqueror to hold the city in
subordination.)   ill-erected erected for evil ends or with evil
results   7 soft gently, wait a minute

11 thou . . . stand i.e., you ruined majesty, pattern of fallen greatness
like the desolate waste where Troy once stood   12 map of honor i.e.,
the mere outline of a once-glorious honor   13 inn residence, house
14 hard-favored unpleasant-looking   15 is . . . guest lodges in such a
vulgar tavern (i.e., in Bolingbroke).   17 To . . . sudden to kill me
quickly with grief.   22 Hie Hasten   23 religious house convent.
24 new world's heaven's   31 To be at being   34 Which art you who
are   35 king of beasts (1) lion (2) ruler over beastly men   37 sometimes former   42 Of . . . betid of woe that happened ages ago
43 quit their griefs requite their tales of woe   46–7 Forwhy . . .
tongue because even the inanimate and unfeeling firebrands will
respond to the doleful tone of your affecting tale   49 And . . .
coal-black and some of the brands will heap ashes on themselves
like grieving mourners and turn black with charring as though
dressing themselves in the black of mourning

NORTHUMBERLAND
My lord, the mind of Bolingbroke is changed;
You must to Pomfret, not unto the Tower.                            52
And, madam, there is order ta'en for you:                           53
With all swift speed you must away to France.

KING RICHARD
Northumberland, thou ladder wherewithal
The mounting Bolingbroke ascends my throne,
The time shall not be many hours of age
More than it is ere foul sin, gathering head,                       58
Shall break into corruption. Thou shalt think,                      59
Though he divide the realm and give thee half,
It is too little, helping him to all;                               61
He shall think that thou, which knowest the way
To plant unrightful kings, wilt know again,
Being ne'er so little urged another way,                            64
To pluck him headlong from the usurpèd throne.                      65
The love of wicked men converts to fear,                            66
That fear to hate, and hate turns one or both                       67
To worthy danger and deservèd death.                                68

NORTHUMBERLAND
My guilt be on my head, and there an end.                           69
Take leave and part, for you must part forthwith.                   70

KING RICHARD
Doubly divorced! Bad men, you violate
A twofold marriage, twixt my crown and me,
And then betwixt me and my married wife.
[To Queen] Let me unkiss the oath twixt thee and me;                74
And yet not so, for with a kiss 'twas made.—
Part us, Northumberland: I towards the north,
Where shivering cold and sickness pines the clime;                  77
My wife to France, from whence, set forth in pomp,
She came adornèd hither like sweet May,
Sent back like Hallowmas or short'st of day.                        80

QUEEN
And must we be divided? Must we part?

KING RICHARD
Ay, hand from hand, my love, and heart from heart.

QUEEN [to Northumberland]
Banish us both and send the King with me.

NORTHUMBERLAND
That were some love, but little policy.                             84

QUEEN
Then whither he goes, thither let me go.

KING RICHARD
So two, together weeping, make one woe.
Weep thou for me in France, I for thee here;
Better far off than, near, be ne'er the near.                       88

Go count thy way with sighs, I mine with groans.

QUEEN
So longest way shall have the longest moans.                        90

KING RICHARD
Twice for one step I'll groan, the way being short,
And piece the way out with a heavy heart.                           92
Come, come, in wooing sorrow let's be brief,
Since, wedding it, there is such length in grief.                   94
One kiss shall stop our mouths, and dumbly part;                    95
Thus give I mine, and thus take I thy heart.
                                            [They kiss.]

QUEEN
Give me mine own again. 'Twere no good part                         97
To take on me to keep and kill thy heart.    [They kiss.]           98
So, now I have mine own again, begone,
That I may strive to kill it with a groan.

KING RICHARD
We make woe wanton with this fond delay.                            101
Once more, adieu! The rest let sorrow say.
                        Exeunt [in two separate groups].

# [5.2]

*Enter Duke of York and the Duchess.*

DUCHESS
My lord, you told me you would tell the rest,
When weeping made you break the story off,
Of our two cousins coming into London.                              3

YORK
Where did I leave?

DUCHESS                          At that sad stop, my lord,          4
Where rude misgoverned hands from windows' tops                     5
Threw dust and rubbish on King Richard's head.

YORK
Then, as I said, the Duke, great Bolingbroke,
Mounted upon a hot and fiery steed
Which his aspiring rider seemed to know,                            9
With slow but stately pace kept on his course,
Whilst all tongues cried, "God save thee, Bolingbroke!"
You would have thought the very windows spake,
So many greedy looks of young and old
Through casements darted their desiring eyes
Upon his visage, and that all the walls
With painted imagery had said at once,                              16
"Jesu preserve thee! Welcome, Bolingbroke!"

---

52 **Pomfret** Pontefract Castle in Yorkshire   53 **order ta'en** arrangement made   58 **gathering head** gathering to a head   59 **corruption** putrid matter, pus.   61 **helping** since you helped   64 **Being . . . way** though scarcely urged at all   65 **To** how to   66 **converts** changes   67 **That fear** i.e., that fear changes.   **one or both** i.e., the new king or his partner, or both   68 **worthy** well-merited   69 **and . . . end** and let the topic be closed on that note.   70 **part . . . part** separate . . . depart   74 **unkiss** annul with a kiss (regarded as the seal of a ceremonial bond)   77 **pines the clime** afflicts the climate   80 **Hallowmas** All Saints' Day (November 1), regarded as the beginning of winter. **short'st of day** the winter solstice.   84 **policy** political practicality. 88 **Better . . . the near** i.e., better to be far apart than near and yet unable to meet. (The second *near* means "nearer.")

**90 So . . . moans** i.e., Then I will have to sigh and groan all the more, since my journey is longer.   **92 piece . . . out** make the journey seem longer   **94 Since . . . grief** i.e., since wedding ourselves to grief, we embark on a sadness that is only beginning. (A wry joke on the commonplace that a brief and romantic courtship is often the prelude to an interminable marriage.)   **95 and dumbly part** and then let us part in silence   **97–8 'Twere . . . me** It would not be wise of me to take it upon myself   **101 We . . . wanton** We sport with our grief.   **fond** (1) loving (2) pointless, foolish
**5.2. Location:** The Duke of York's house.
**3 cousins** kinsmen, i.e., nephews (Richard and Bolingbroke)   **4 leave** leave off.   **5 misgoverned** unruly.   **windows' tops** upper windows
**9 Which . . . know** which seemed to know its ambitious rider
**16 With painted imagery** i.e., showing crowds of people, as on a tapestry or painted cloth, depicting a procession.   **at once** all together

Whilst he, from the one side to the other turning,
Bareheaded, lower than his proud steed's neck,                          19
Bespake them thus: "I thank you, countrymen."                           20
And thus still doing, thus he passed along.                             21

DUCHESS
Alack, poor Richard! Where rode he the whilst?

YORK
As in a theater the eyes of men,
After a well-graced actor leaves the stage,
Are idly bent on him that enters next,                                  25
Thinking his prattle to be tedious,
Even so, or with much more contempt, men's eyes
Did scowl on gentle Richard. No man cried, "God
    save him!"
No joyful tongue gave him his welcome home,
But dust was thrown upon his sacred head—
Which with such gentle sorrow he shook off,
His face still combating with tears and smiles,
The badges of his grief and patience,                                   33
That had not God for some strong purpose steeled
The hearts of men, they must perforce have melted,                      35
And barbarism itself have pitied him.
But heaven hath a hand in these events,
To whose high will we bound our calm contents.                          38
To Bolingbroke are we sworn subjects now,
Whose state and honor I for aye allow.                                   40

        [Enter Aumerle.]

DUCHESS
Here comes my son Aumerle.

YORK                                        Aumerle that was;           41
But that is lost for being Richard's friend,
And, madam, you must call him Rutland now.
I am in Parliament pledge for his truth                                 44
And lasting fealty to the new-made king.

DUCHESS
Welcome, my son. Who are the violets now                                46
That strew the green lap of the new-come spring?                        47

AUMERLE
Madam, I know not, nor I greatly care not.
God knows I had as lief be none as one.                                 49

YORK
Well, bear you well in this new spring of time,                         50
Lest you be cropped before you come to prime.                           51
What news from Oxford? Do these jousts and triumphs
    hold?                                                               52

AUMERLE ·  For aught I know, my lord, they do.
YORK    You will be there, I know.
AUMERLE
If God prevent not, I purpose so.
YORK
    What seal is that, that hangs without thy bosom?                    56
    Yea, look'st thou pale? Let me see the writing.
AUMERLE
My lord, 'tis nothing.
YORK                              No matter, then, who see it.
    I will be satisfied. Let me see the writing.
AUMERLE
I do beseech Your Grace to pardon me.                                   60
It is a matter of small consequence,
Which for some reasons I would not have seen.                           62
YORK
Which for some reasons, sir, I mean to see.
I fear, I fear—
DUCHESS            What should you fear?
'Tis nothing but some bond that he is entered into
For gay apparel 'gainst the triumph day.                                66
YORK
Bound to himself? What doth he with a bond                              67
That he is bound to? Wife, thou art a fool.—                            68
Boy, let me see the writing.
AUMERLE
I do beseech you, pardon me. I may not show it.
YORK
I will be satisfied. Let me see it, I say.
            *He plucks it out of his bosom and reads it.*
Treason! Foul treason! Villain! Traitor! Slave!
DUCHESS    What is the matter, my lord?
YORK [*calling offstage*]    Ho! Who is within there?

        [*Enter a Servingman.*]

                                        Saddle my horse!—
God for his mercy, what treachery is here?                              75
DUCHESS    Why, what is it, my lord?
YORK [*to the Servingman*]
    Give me my boots, I say! Saddle my horse!—
                                    [*Exit Servingman.*]
Now, by mine honor, by my life, my troth,                               78
I will appeach the villain.
DUCHESS                            What is the matter?                   79
YORK
Peace, foolish woman.
DUCHESS
I will not peace. What is the matter, Aumerle?
AUMERLE
Good mother, be content. It is no more
Than my poor life must answer.
DUCHESS                              Thy life answer?

---

**19 lower** bowing lower   **20 Bespake** addressed   **21 still** continually
**25 idly** indifferently   **33 badges** insignia, outward signs   **35 perforce**
necessarily   **38 we . . . contents** i.e., we bind ourselves to be calmly
content.   **40 state** i.e., royal title.   **for aye allow** forever acknowledge.   **41 Aumerle that was** (Aumerle, as a member of Richard's
party, lost his dukedom, though he remained Earl of Rutland.)
**44 pledge** the guarantor.   **truth** loyalty   **46–7 Who . . . spring** i.e.,
Who are the favorites of the new king?   **49 I had . . . one** I'd be just
as glad to be left out as to be a favorite at court.   **50 bear you** bear
yourself   **51 cropped** plucked, i.e., beheaded   **52 Do . . . hold?** Are
those tourneys and pageants going forward? (According to Holinshed, these tourneys at Oxford were part of a conspiracy against
Bolingbroke by the Abbot of Westminster and others; the new king
was to be invited to attend and there be assassinated.)

**56 seal** i.e., seal attached to the border of a document.   **without**
outside of   **60 pardon me** i.e., excuse me if I don't comply.   **62 have
seen** wish to be seen.   **66 'gainst** in anticipation of   **67–8 What . . .
bound to?** i.e., Why should *he* have the bond instead of the creditor to
whom the debt is owed?   **75 God** i.e., I pray God   **78 troth** faith,
allegiance   **79 appeach** inform against, publicly accuse

YORK [*calling*]
    Bring me my boots! I will unto the King.

    *His [Serving]man enters with his boots.*

DUCHESS
    Strike him, Aumerle. Poor boy, thou art amazed.                85
    [*To the Servingman*] Hence, villain! Never more come
        in my sight.
YORK    Give me my boots, I say.
    [*The Servingman helps him on with his boots, and exit.*]
DUCHESS    Why, York, what wilt thou do?
    Wilt thou not hide the trespass of thine own?                89
    Have we more sons? Or are we like to have?                90
    Is not my teeming date drunk up with time?                91
    And wilt thou pluck my fair son from mine age
    And rob me of a happy mother's name?
    Is he not like thee? Is he not thine own?
YORK    Thou fond mad woman,                95
    Wilt thou conceal this dark conspiracy?
    A dozen of them here have ta'en the Sacrament,                97
    And interchangeably set down their hands,                98
    To kill the King at Oxford.
DUCHESS                He shall be none;                99
    We'll keep him here. Then what is that to him?                100
YORK
    Away, fond woman! Were he twenty times my son
    I would appeach him.
DUCHESS                Hadst thou groaned for him                102
    As I have done, thou wouldst be more pitiful.                103
    But now I know thy mind. Thou dost suspect
    That I have been disloyal to thy bed,
    And that he is a bastard, not thy son.
    Sweet York, sweet husband, be not of that mind!
    He is as like thee as a man may be,
    Not like to me, or any of my kin,
    And yet I love him.
YORK                Make way, unruly woman!    *Exit.*
DUCHESS
    After, Aumerle! Mount thee upon his horse,                111
    Spur post, and get before him to the King,                112
    And beg thy pardon ere he do accuse thee.
    I'll not be long behind. Though I be old,
    I doubt not but to ride as fast as York.
    And never will I rise up from the ground
    Till Bolingbroke have pardoned thee. Away, begone!
                [*Exeunt separately.*]

---

# [5.3]

    *Enter [Bolingbroke, now] King [Henry], with his
    nobles [Harry Percy and others].*

KING HENRY
    Can no man tell me of my unthrifty son?                1
    'Tis full three months since I did see him last.
    If any plague hang over us, 'tis he.
    I would to God, my lords, he might be found.
    Inquire at London, 'mongst the taverns there,
    For there, they say, he daily doth frequent
    With unrestrainèd loose companions,
    Even such, they say, as stand in narrow lanes
    And beat our watch, and rob our passengers—                9
    While he, young wanton and effeminate boy,                10
    Takes on the point of honor to support                11
    So dissolute a crew.
PERCY
    My lord, some two days since I saw the Prince,
    And told him of those triumphs held at Oxford.                14
KING HENRY    And what said the gallant?
PERCY
    His answer was, he would unto the stews,                16
    And from the common'st creature pluck a glove,                17
    And wear it as a favor, and with that                18
    He would unhorse the lustiest challenger.                19
KING HENRY
    As dissolute as desperate! Yet through both
    I see some sparks of better hope, which elder years
    May happily bring forth. But who comes here?                22

    *Enter Aumerle, amazed.*

AUMERLE    Where is the King?
KING HENRY
    What means our cousin, that he stares and looks
    So wildly?
AUMERLE
    God save Your Grace! I do beseech Your Majesty
    To have some conference with Your Grace alone.
KING HENRY [*to his nobles*]
    Withdraw yourselves, and leave us here alone.
                [*Exeunt Percy and lords.*]
    What is the matter with our cousin now?
AUMERLE [*kneeling*]
    Forever may my knees grow to the earth,
    My tongue cleave to the roof within my mouth,                31
    Unless a pardon ere I rise or speak.
KING HENRY
    Intended or committed was this fault?
    If on the first, how heinous e'er it be,                34

---

85 **Strike him** i.e., Strike the servant.    **amazed** confused, bewildered.    89 **thine own** your own son.    90 **Have we more sons?** (Historically, this Duchess of York was the Duke's second wife and was not Aumerle's mother; she was, however, the mother of another son, Richard, subsequently Earl of Cambridge.)    **like** likely    91 **teeming date** period of childbearing    95 **fond** foolish    97–9 **A dozen . . . Oxford** ("Hereupon was an indenture sextipartite made, sealed with their seals and signed with their hands, in the which each stood bound to other, to do their whole endeavor for the accomplishing of their purposed exploit." [Holinshed])    100 **that** i.e., the plot    102 **appeach** accuse.    **groaned for** i.e., given birth to. (But see note, line 90.)    103 **pitiful** pitying.    111 **After** Go after him.    **his horse** i.e., one of York's horses    112 **Spur post** ride as fast as possible

5.3. **Location:** The court (i.e., Windsor Castle).
1 **unthrifty** profligate    9 **watch** night watchmen.    **passengers** passers-by, wayfarers    10 **wanton** pampered youth.    **effeminate** self-indulgent    11 **Takes on** i.e., makes it a    14 **held** i.e., to be held    16 **stews** brothels    17 **common'st** most promiscuous    18 **with that** i.e., wearing that as a favor    19 **lustiest** most vigorous and brave    22 **happily** with good fortune    22.1 **amazed** distraught.    31 **My . . . mouth** (See Psalm 137:6: "If I do not remember thee, let my tongue cleave to the roof of my mouth.")    34 **If on the first** i.e., If intended only

To win thy after-love I pardon thee.                                        35

AUMERLE [*rising*]
Then give me leave that I may turn the key,                     36
That no man enter till my tale be done.

KING HENRY    Have thy desire.
                    [*Aumerle locks the door.*] *The Duke of York*
                                    *knocks at the door and crieth.*

YORK [*within*]
My liege, beware! Look to thyself.
Thou hast a traitor in thy presence there.

KING HENRY [*drawing*]    Villain, I'll make thee safe.    41

AUMERLE
Stay thy revengeful hand. Thou hast no cause to fear.

YORK [*within*]
Open the door, secure, foolhardy King!                          43
Shall I for love speak treason to thy face?                      44
Open the door, or I will break it open.
                            [*King Henry unlocks the door.*]

[*Enter York.*]

KING HENRY
What is the matter, uncle? Speak.
Recover breath; tell us how near is danger,
That we may arm us to encounter it.

YORK [*giving letter*]
Peruse this writing here, and thou shalt know
The treason that my haste forbids me show.              50

AUMERLE
Remember, as thou read'st, thy promise passed.
I do repent me. Read not my name there;
My heart is not confederate with my hand.                53

YORK
It was, villain, ere thy hand did set it down.
I tore it from the traitor's bosom, King;
Fear, and not love, begets his penitence.
Forget to pity him, lest thy pity prove                          57
A serpent that will sting thee to the heart.

KING HENRY
Oh, heinous, strong, and bold conspiracy!
O loyal father of a treacherous son,
Thou sheer, immaculate, and silver fountain,            61
From whence this stream through muddy passages    62
Hath held his current and defiled himself,                  63
Thy overflow of good converts to bad,                        64
And thy abundant goodness shall excuse                    65
This deadly blot in thy digressing son.                        66

YORK
So shall my virtue be his vice's bawd,
And he shall spend mine honor with his shame,
As thriftless sons their scraping fathers' gold.         69

Mine honor lives when his dishonor dies,
Or my shamed life in his dishonor lies.                     71
Thou kill'st me in his life; giving him breath,          72
The traitor lives, the true man's put to death.

DUCHESS [*within*]
What ho, my liege! For God's sake, let me in.

KING HENRY
What shrill-voiced suppliant makes this eager cry?

DUCHESS [*within*]
A woman, and thy aunt, great King. 'Tis I.
Speak with me, pity me, open the door!
A beggar begs that never begged before.

KING HENRY
Our scene is altered from a serious thing,
And now changed to "The Beggar and the King."    80
My dangerous cousin, let your mother in.
I know she is come to pray for your foul sin.

[*Aumerle opens the door. Enter the Duchess. She
kneels.*]

YORK
If thou do pardon whosoever pray,                            83
More sins for this forgiveness prosper may.            84
This festered joint cut off, the rest rest sound;      85
This let alone will all the rest confound.                  86

DUCHESS
O King, believe not this hardhearted man.
Love loving not itself, none other can.                     88

YORK
Thou frantic woman, what dost thou make here?   89
Shall thy old dugs once more a traitor rear?          90

DUCHESS
Sweet York, be patient.—Hear me, gentle liege.

KING HENRY
Rise up, good aunt.

DUCHESS                    Not yet, I thee beseech.
Forever will I walk upon my knees,
And never see day that the happy sees,                   94
Till thou give joy, until thou bid me joy,
By pardoning Rutland, my transgressing boy.

AUMERLE [*kneeling*]
Unto my mother's prayers I bend my knee.            97

YORK [*kneeling*]
Against them both my true joints bended be.
Ill mayst thou thrive, if thou grant any grace!

DUCHESS
Pleads he in earnest? Look upon his face.
His eyes do drop no tears, his prayers are in jest;
His words come from his mouth, ours from our breast.
He prays but faintly and would be denied;

---

**35 thy after-love** your loyalty to me in times to come    **36 leave** permission    **41 I'll . . . safe** I'll make you harmless (by running you through).    **43 secure** unsuspecting, heedless    **44 speak . . . face** i.e., speak so disrespectfully as to call you *secure* and *foolhardy*.    **50 haste . . . show** i.e., breathlessness prevents me from revealing.    **53 hand** signature.    **57 Forget** Forget your promise    **61 sheer** clear, pure    **62–4 From . . . to bad** i.e., from whence this pure and noble stream has been muddied, blocked, and defiled by Aumerle's attempted treason, thereby converting your superabundant virtue into evil    **65 And** i.e., but    **66 digressing** deviating from his proper course, transgressing    **69 scraping** parsimonious

**71 in . . . lies** will be hostage to his dishonorable conduct.    **72 in his life** if you permit him to live    **80 "The Beggar . . . King"** (Probably one of Shakespeare's many allusions to the ballad of King Cophetua and the Beggar Maid.)    **83 whosoever pray** anyone who presents a petition    **84 More . . . may** more and more sinfulness will prosper as a result of this unjustified leniency.    **85 This . . . sound** If this infected limb is cut off, the rest of the body will remain sound and healthy    **86 alone** untreated. **confound** ruin.    **88 Love . . . can** i.e., He who does not love himself in his own son can love no one else, not even the King.    **89 make** do    **90 once . . . rear** i.e., give life again to a traitor by now redeeming Aumerle from death.    **94 And . . . sees** and never enjoy the happiness that those who are happy experience    **97 Unto** In support of

We pray with heart and soul and all beside. 104
His weary joints would gladly rise, I know;
Our knees still kneel till to the ground they grow. 106
His prayers are full of false hypocrisy,
Ours of true zeal and deep integrity.
Our prayers do outpray his; then let them have
That mercy which true prayer ought to have.

KING HENRY
Good aunt, stand up.

DUCHESS                    Nay, do not say "stand up."
Say "pardon" first, and afterwards "stand up."
An if I were thy nurse, thy tongue to teach, 113
"Pardon" should be the first word of thy speech.
I never longed to hear a word till now;
Say "pardon," King; let pity teach thee how.
The word is short, but not so short as sweet;
No word like "pardon" for kings' mouths so meet.

YORK
Speak it in French, King: say "pardonne moy." 119

DUCHESS
Dost thou teach pardon pardon to destroy? 120
Ah, my sour husband, my hardhearted lord,
That sets the word itself against the word!
Speak "pardon" as 'tis current in our land;
The chopping French we do not understand. 124
Thine eye begins to speak; set thy tongue there,
Or in thy piteous heart plant thou thine ear,
That hearing how our plaints and prayers do pierce, 127
Pity may move thee "pardon" to rehearse. 128

KING HENRY
Good aunt, stand up.

DUCHESS                    I do not sue to stand. 129
Pardon is all the suit I have in hand.

KING HENRY
I pardon him, as God shall pardon me.

DUCHESS
Oh, happy vantage of a kneeling knee! 132
Yet am I sick for fear. Speak it again;
Twice saying "pardon" doth not pardon twain
But makes one pardon strong.

KING HENRY                    With all my heart
I pardon him.                    [All rise.]

DUCHESS          A god on earth thou art.

KING HENRY
But for our trusty brother-in-law and the Abbot, 137
With all the rest of that consorted crew, 138
Destruction straight shall dog them at the heels. 139
Good uncle, help to order several powers 140
To Oxford, or where'er these traitors are.
They shall not live within this world, I swear,
But I will have them, if I once know where. 143
Uncle, farewell, and, cousin, adieu.

Your mother well hath prayed; and prove you true. 145

DUCHESS
Come, my old son. I pray God make thee new. 146
                    Exeunt [in two groups].

❧

## [5.4]

Enter Sir Pierce [of] Exton [and his Men].

EXTON
Didst thou not mark the King, what words he spake,
"Have I no friend will rid me of this living fear?" 2
Was it not so?

MAN                    These were his very words.

EXTON
"Have I no friend?" quoth he. He spake it twice,
And urged it twice together, did he not?

MAN   He did.

EXTON
And speaking it, he wishtly looked on me, 7
As who should say, "I would thou wert the man 8
That would divorce this terror from my heart"—
Meaning the King at Pomfret. Come, let's go.
I am the King's friend, and will rid his foe. 11
                    [Exeunt.]

❧

## [5.5]

Enter Richard alone.

KING RICHARD
I have been studying how I may compare
This prison where I live unto the world;
And, for because the world is populous, 3
And here is not a creature but myself,
I cannot do it. Yet I'll hammer it out. 5
My brain I'll prove the female to my soul,
My soul the father, and these two beget
A generation of still-breeding thoughts; 8
And these same thoughts people this little world, 9
In humors like the people of this world, 10
For no thought is contented. The better sort,
As thoughts of things divine, are intermixed 12
With scruples and do set the word itself 13
Against the word, as thus, "Come, little ones," 14
And then again,
"It is as hard to come as for a camel
To thread the postern of a small needle's eye." 17

104 beside besides.   106 still continually   113 An if If   119 pardonne moy pardonnez-moi, excuse me. (An affectedly polite
refusal.)   120 pardon pardon to destroy pardon to destroy or undo
pardon   124 chopping logic chopping, changing the sense   127
plaints complaints, petitions   128 rehearse pronounce.   129 sue
seek permission   132 happy vantage fortunate gain   137 But for But
as for.   brother-in-law i.e., John Holland, Earl of Huntingdon and
Duke of Exeter, who had married Bolingbroke's sister (see 2.1.281
and note).   Abbot Abbot of Westminster; see 4.1.321–34
138 consorted conspiring, confederate   139 straight straightway,
at once   140 powers forces   143 have arrest

145 prove you true may you prove loyal.   146 old unregenerate
5.4. Location: The court. The opening stage direction in the quarto
reads Manet Sir Pierce Exton, etc.,   suggesting continuity of action
with the preceding scene.
2 will who will   7 wishtly intently   8 As . . . say as if to say   11 rid
rid him of
5.5. Location: Pomfret Castle. A dungeon.
3 for because because   5 hammer i.e., work, puzzle   8 still-breeding
constantly breeding   9 this little world myself and this prison as a
microcosm of the world   10 humors temperaments, peculiar fancies
12 As such as   13 scruples doubts   13–14 do set . . . word i.e.,
oppose one scriptural passage against its apparent opposite
14–17 Come . . . eye (See Matthew 19:14, 24.)   17 postern narrow gate

Thoughts tending to ambition, they do plot
Unlikely wonders—how these vain weak nails
May tear a passage through the flinty ribs
Of this hard world, my ragged prison walls, 21
And, for they cannot, die in their own pride. 22
Thoughts tending to content flatter themselves 23
That they are not the first of fortune's slaves,
Nor shall not be the last—like seely beggars 25
Who, sitting in the stocks, refuge their shame 26
That many have and others must sit there;
And in this thought they find a kind of ease,
Bearing their own misfortunes on the back
Of such as have before endured the like.
Thus play I in one person many people,
And none contented. Sometimes am I king;
Then treason makes me wish myself a beggar, 33
And so I am. Then crushing penury 34
Persuades me I was better when a king;
Then am I kinged again, and by and by
Think that I am unkinged by Bolingbroke,
And straight am nothing. But whate'er I be,
Nor I, nor any man that but man is, 39
With nothing shall be pleased till he be eased 40
With being nothing. (*The music plays.*) Music do
    I hear? 41
Ha, ha, keep time! How sour sweet music is
When time is broke and no proportion kept! 43
So is it in the music of men's lives.
And here have I the daintiness of ear
To check time broke in a disordered string, 46
But for the concord of my state and time
Had not an ear to hear my true time broke.
I wasted time, and now doth time waste me;
For now hath Time made me his numb'ring clock. 50
My thoughts are minutes, and with sighs they jar 51
Their watches on unto mine eyes, the outward watch 52
Whereto my finger, like a dial's point, 53
Is pointing still in cleansing them from tears.
Now sir, the sounds that tell what hour it is
Are clamorous groans that strike upon my heart,
Which is the bell. So sighs and tears and groans
Show minutes, hours, and times. But my time 58
Runs posting on in Bolingbroke's proud joy, 59
While I stand fooling here, his jack of the clock. 60
This music mads me. Let it sound no more, 61
For though it have holp madmen to their wits, 62

In me it seems it will make wise men mad.
                                    [*The music ceases.*]
Yet blessing on his heart that gives it me!
For 'tis a sign of love; and love to Richard
Is a strange brooch in this all-hating world. 66

    *Enter a Groom of the table.*

GROOM
    Hail, royal prince!
KING RICHARD          Thanks, noble peer.
    The cheapest of us is ten groats too dear. 68
    What art thou, and how comest thou hither,
    Where no man never comes but that sad dog
    That brings me food to make misfortune live?
GROOM
    I was a poor groom of thy stable, King,
    When thou wert king; who, traveling towards York,
    With much ado at length have gotten leave
    To look upon my sometimes royal master's face. 75
    Oh, how it earned my heart when I beheld 76
    In London streets, that coronation day,
    When Bolingbroke rode on roan Barbary,
    That horse that thou so often hast bestrid,
    That horse that I so carefully have dressed! 80
KING RICHARD
    Rode he on Barbary? Tell me, gentle friend,
    How went he under him?
GROOM
    So proudly as if he disdained the ground.
KING RICHARD
    So proud that Bolingbroke was on his back!
    That jade hath eat bread from my royal hand; 85
    This hand hath made him proud with clapping him. 86
    Would he not stumble? Would he not fall down,
    Since pride must have a fall, and break the neck
    Of that proud man that did usurp his back?
    Forgiveness, horse! Why do I rail on thee,
    Since thou, created to be awed by man, 91
    Wast born to bear? I was not made a horse,
    And yet I bear a burden like an ass,
    Spurred, galled, and tired by jauncing Bolingbroke. 94

    *Enter one [a Keeper] to Richard with meat.*

KEEPER [*to Groom*]
    Fellow, give place. Here is no longer stay.
KING RICHARD [*to Groom*]
    If thou love me, 'tis time thou wert away.
GROOM
    What my tongue dares not, that my heart shall say.
                                        *Exit Groom.*

---

**21 ragged** rugged   **22 for** because.   **pride** prime.   **23 content** contentment   **25 seely** simpleminded   **26 refuge their shame** i.e., seek refuge from their disgrace by reflecting   **33 treason** i.e., the thought of treason   **34 penury** poverty   **39–41 Nor . . . nothing** neither I nor any person alive can be fully satisfied with the things of this life until he or she is released by death.   **43 When . . . broke** when the metrical rhythm of music is disrupted   **46 check** rebuke.   **string** stringed instrument   **50 numb'ring clock** i.e., a clock that numbers hours and minutes (not an hourglass).   **51–2 My . . . watch** My sad thoughts, occurring every minute, are parts of an inner clock that, by means of the sighs they provoke, transfer their cares to my eyes, like the face of the clock   **53 dial's point** clock hand   **58 times** quarters and halves.   **59 posting** hastening   **60 jack of the clock** manikin that struck the bell on a clock.   **61 mads** maddens   **62 holp** helped

**66 strange brooch** rare jewel   **68 ten groats too dear** (There is a pun on *royal* and *noble* in the preceding lines. A royal (ten shillings) is worth ten groats (ten times four pence) more than a noble (six shillings, eight pence) is; hence, Richard is saying that he, "the cheapest of us" because he is a prisoner, is worth no more than the groom, whom he greets as his "noble peer.")   **75 sometimes** former   **76 earned** grieved   **80 dressed** tended, groomed.   **85 eat** eaten. (Pronounced "et.")   **86 clapping** patting, stroking   **91 awed** subdued, made submissive   **94 galled** made sore.   **jauncing** prancing, hard-riding   **94.1 meat** food.

KEEPER
My lord, will't please you to fall to?                                    98
KING RICHARD
Taste of it first, as thou art wont to do.                                99
KEEPER
My lord, I dare not. Sir Pierce of Exton, who
Lately came from the King, commands the contrary.
KING RICHARD
The devil take Henry of Lancaster and thee!                              102
Patience is stale, and I am weary of it.
                                    [*He beats the Keeper.*]
KEEPER    Help, help, help!

        *The murderers [Exton and his men] rush in.*

KING RICHARD
How now, what means death in this rude assault?
Villain, thy own hand yields thy death's instrument.
        [*He snatches a weapon from a man and kills him.*]
Go thou, and fill another room in hell.                                  107
        [*He kills another.*] *Here Exton strikes him down.*
That hand shall burn in never-quenching fire
That staggers thus my person. Exton, thy fierce hand        109
Hath with the King's blood stained the King's own
    land.
Mount, mount, my soul! Thy seat is up on high,
Whilst my gross flesh sinks downward, here to die.
                                                [*He dies.*]
EXTON
As full of valor as of royal blood.
Both have I spilled. Oh, would the deed were good!
For now the devil, that told me I did well,
Says that this deed is chronicled in hell.
This dead king to the living king I'll bear.
Take hence the rest, and give them burial here.
                            [*Exeunt, with the bodies.*]

## [5.6]

        [*Flourish.*] *Enter Bolingbroke [as King], with
        the Duke of York, [other lords, and attendants].*

KING HENRY
Kind uncle York, the latest news we hear
Is that the rebels have consumed with fire
Our town of Ci'cester in Gloucestershire,                                3
But whether they be ta'en or slain we hear not.

        *Enter Northumberland.*

Wecome, my lord. What is the news?
NORTHUMBERLAND
First, to thy sacred state wish I all happiness.
The next news is, I have to London sent

The heads of Salisbury, Spencer, Blunt, and Kent.
The manner of their taking may appear                                    9
At large discoursèd in this paper here.                                  10
                                    [*He gives a paper.*]
KING HENRY
We thank thee, gentle Percy, for thy pains,
And to thy worth will add right worthy gains.                            12

        *Enter Lord Fitzwater.*

FITZWATER
My lord, I have from Oxford sent to London
The heads of Brocas and Sir Bennet Seely,
Two of the dangerous consorted traitors                                  15
That sought at Oxford thy dire overthrow.
KING HENRY
Thy pains, Fitzwater, shall not be forgot;
Right noble is thy merit, well I wot.                                     18

        *Enter Henry Percy [with the Bishop of Carlisle,
        guarded].*

PERCY
The grand conspirator, Abbot of Westminster,                             19
With clog of conscience and sour melancholy                              20
Hath yielded up his body to the grave;
But here is Carlisle living, to abide                                     22
Thy kingly doom and sentence of his pride.                               23
KING HENRY    Carlisle, this is your doom:
Choose out some secret place, some reverent room,                        25
More than thou hast, and with it joy thy life.                           26
So as thou liv'st in peace, die free from strife;                        27
For though mine enemy thou hast ever been,
High sparks of honor in thee have I seen.

        *Enter Exton, with [attendants bearing] the coffin.*

EXTON
Great King, within this coffin I present
Thy buried fear. Herein all breathless lies
The mightiest of thy greatest enemies,
Richard of Bordeaux, by me hither brought.
KING HENRY
Exton, I thank thee not, for thou hast wrought
A deed of slander with thy fatal hand
Upon my head and all this famous land.                                   35
EXTON
From your own mouth, my lord, did I this deed.
KING HENRY
They love not poison that do poison need,
Nor do I thee. Though I did wish him dead,
I hate the murderer, love him murderèd.

---

**98 to fall to** to eat.   **99 Taste . . . first** i.e., to ensure that it isn't poisoned   **102 Henry of Lancaster** (Richard demotes the King by referring to him by his ducal title only.)   **107 room** place   **109 staggers** causes to stagger
**5.6. Location:** The court.
**3 Ci'cester** Cirencester

**9 taking** capture   **10 At large discoursèd** related in full   **12 worth** (1) deserving (2) present wealth   **15 consorted** conspiring   **18 wot** know.   **19 grand** chief   **20 clog** burden   **22 abide** await   **23 doom** judgment   **25 reverent room** place suitable for religious retirement   **26 More . . . hast** i.e., more spacious and suited for spiritual meditation than the cell you occupy now.   **joy** enjoy, have the benefit of   **27 So as** Provided that   **35 deed of slander** i.e., a deed sure to arouse slanderous talk about the new king

The guilt of conscience take thou for thy labor,
But neither my good word nor princely favor.
With Cain go wander through the shades of night,          43
And never show thy head by day nor light.
               *[Exeunt Exton and attendants.]*
Lords, I protest my soul is full of woe
That blood should sprinkle me to make me grow.

Come mourn with me for what I do lament,
And put on sullen black incontinent.                      48
I'll make a voyage to the Holy Land
To wash this blood off from my guilty hand.
March sadly after. Grace my mournings here               51
In weeping after this untimely bier.
        *[Exeunt in procession, following the coffin.]*

---

**43 Cain** murderer of his brother Abel; see 1.1.104        **48 incontinent** immediately.   **51 Grace** Dignify

# The First Part of King Henry the Fourth

The opening of *1 Henry IV* is taut and grave in tone. England is "shaken" and "wan with care." The troubles of *Richard II,* to which this play (c. 1596–1597) is a close sequel, have not been left behind. However much King Henry would prefer to unite his countrymen against a common foreign enemy in a crusade to the Holy Lands, he is prevented from doing so by continuing civil war. The impassioned rhetoric of his opening speech can only end in anticlimax, for the actual purpose of this meeting in council is to receive and assess reports of military action against the throne.

Henry's current troubles are in the far reaches of his kingdom: Scots in the north, Welsh in the west. Fighting for Henry on these two fronts are the nobles of the Percy family who helped him to power: Harry Percy ("Hotspur"), his father (Henry Percy) the Earl of Northumberland, his uncle the Earl of Worcester, and his brother-in-law Edmund Mortimer, the Earl of March. Apparently, they have fought bravely. Yet we soon sense that all is not well between the new King and those who rebelled with him against Richard II. A quarrel breaks out because Hotspur refuses to deliver to Henry some prisoners as required by feudal obedience. The matter of the ransom money is only a technicality; what is really at issue? In part, it is Henry's insistence on being obeyed on principle. Admiring Hotspur inordinately, the King feels he must discipline affectionately this fine young warrior as a father would discipline his son. Even more deeply, however, the issue of the prisoners galls Henry because of the proviso that he ransom Mortimer, captured by the Welsh. Henry does not forget that Mortimer is his chief rival for the English crown, being descended from the Duke of Clarence (elder brother to Henry's father, Gaunt) and having been proclaimed by Richard as heir to the throne. (Shakespeare accentuates the dynastic threat by combining two Edmund Mortimers from his historical sources: one who married Glendower's daughter and another who claimed the English throne; see 1.3.80–5 and

note.) Mortimer is the last person Henry would wish ransomed. Moreover, the King suspects Mortimer of having fought with something less than total zeal against the Welsh Glendower. Mortimer's marriage to Glendower's daughter confirms the King's worst fears. Henry knows Northumberland and Worcester to be expert in treasonous plotting, since they conspired with him to overthrow Richard. Now, Henry believes, these Percys are extending their alliance by a series of calculated marriages in order to seize power once again. This time their claimant is Mortimer.

Shakespeare's sympathies are many sided. The Percy clan is, in fact, organizing against Henry, but not without cause. As they see it, the man they helped to the throne has done little for them since. His manner of disciplining them sounds too much like hostility and ingratitude. Other counselors attend the King constantly while Worcester is banished from court. In such an atmosphere of distrust, suspicion breeds still more suspicion. The situation has deteriorated, surely more than either party originally intended.

Hotspur is the most attractive of the rebels—to us as well as to King Henry. He is outspoken, courageous, witty, and domineering in conversation. Above all, he is a disciple of manliness, loyalty, chivalry, bravery in battle—the attributes of an upstanding and somewhat old-fashioned sense of honor. Yet a fatal defect dwells even in these attractive qualities. Hotspur is impatient, proud, unwilling to tolerate a rival—be it Glendower or Prince Hal (Henry, Prince of Wales). In his first speech, purporting to explain his refusal to deliver the prisoners, he brilliantly satirizes an effete courtier who had come to him from King Henry in the midst of a battle. The satire betrays many harsh qualities in Hotspur: the self-indulgent wrath that returns fully to him even in recollection of the encounter, the pride in his own stoical indifference to suffering, and especially the obsessive nature (revealed in the repetitive pattern of the rhetoric) of his contempt for courtiers generally. Surely his scorn for stay-at-home politicians is directed in part at King Henry himself. To Hotspur, all courtiers are perfume-wearing, affected in mannerism and speech, and scarcely masculine. This preoccupation of Hotspur's makes him extraordinarily prone to one-sided judgments. Like most excessive devotees of chivalry, he divides humanity into two categories: those who are gentlemen, like himself, and those who are beneath contempt. The "vile politician" Bolingbroke and his son, the "sword-and-buckler Prince of Wales" (1.3.240, 229) fall into the latter category.

Prone as he is to such an overly simple view of political behavior, Hotspur can see no good in the King's cause and no evil in his own. He is a poor listener because of his obsession and yet an easy prey to his uncle and father, who require his leadership for their cause. They need only implant the suggestion that King Henry is acting from a political motive in his refusal to ransom Mortimer, and Hotspur is ready to leap incautiously to the defense of their cause. The great irony is that Hotspur fails to see political motives in the machinations of his own relatives. While he fights for bright honor, they maneuver cautiously for position and prove to be uncertain allies when the hour of battle approaches. Most crucially, they betray Hotspur in the prebattle negotiations, at which he is not present. As Worcester explains to Vernon during their return to rebel headquarters (5.2.3–25), they cannot let Hotspur know of the King's offer to settle matters by a general pardon. Although, as they realize, the King could pardon Hotspur's youth, there can be no turning back for themselves. Thus, the honor for which Hotspur fights is at bottom a lie, and the mutual esteem that might have grown between him and a much-reformed Prince of Wales is thwarted by the polarization of attitudes in the two camps. Hotspur's brand of honor is the victim of its own excess and lends some credence to Falstaff's wry conclusion that honor "is a mere scutcheon" (5.1.139–40).

The contrasting of Falstaff and Hotspur on the theme of honor suggests that they are dramatic foils for each other, representing extremes between which Hal must choose. Shakespeare uses this foil device structurally and consciously; for example, he has considerably reduced the age of the Hotspur he found in Raphael Holinshed's Chronicles (1578) in order to stress the similarity between Hotspur and Prince Hal. Conversely, to emphasize the contrast between Falstaff and Hotspur, Shakespeare envisages Falstaff as old (nearly sixty, by his own admission), fat, humorous, and without honor. Falstaff's vices are Hotspur's virtues, and the reverse. Whereas Hotspur offers to Hal a model of chivalric striving and attention to duty, Falstaff is a highwayman and a liar. On the other hand, Hotspur is a fanatic, unbending and self-absorbed even in the company of his sprightly wife, Kate, and irritated by music and poetry; Falstaff is the epitome of merriment and joie de vivre. We excuse much in him because he lusts after life with such an appetite and ingratiates himself to others by inviting them to laugh at his expense.

Despite the nearly irresistible attractiveness of Falstaff as a jolly companion and butt of humorous joking, he and Prince Hal are perennially caught up in witty debate as to the importance of Falstaff in Hal's life and whether the young man will have to get rid of Falstaff once Hal is king. The bantering raillery of their first scene (1.2) seems designed to provide diverting entertainment for the Prince and for us, and yet, beneath the word games and oneupmanship, we perceive that Hal and Falstaff are talking about the hanging of thieves and the question of whether or not Hal should give in to sinful temptation. Can the relationship of Hal and Falstaff continue unchanged into the reign of Henry V? Will there be gallows standing and justice for highwaymen? Will "Monsieur Remorse," as Poins calls Falstaff, ever sincerely repent? Will the Prince, for that matter? To allay our fears, Hal soliloquizes at scene's end, vowing his determination to use these scapegrace companions as mere foils for his triumphal reformation at the appropriate time. But this explanation raises an opposite danger in our sympathies: is he callously using his companions merely to create a self-serving myth of Prince Hal, the Politician with the Common Touch? Is Francis the drawer no more to Hal than a butt for his raillery? Since the rejection of Falstaff is, by Hal's own words, already determined, can we credit him with a serious friendship? Where do Shakespeare's sympathies lie—with the need for political order or with the hedonistic spirit of youth? One possible interpretation is that he recognizes the validity of both, and accordingly shows us a prince who is genuinely fond of Falstaff's exuberant company but who also knows that he is a king's son and must sooner or later accept the consequences of that unsought role. Falstaff's gift to him is youthful irresponsibility, which must be cherished (by all of us), even though it cannot last.

This compassionate interpretation is, to be sure, only one of many possibilities. Recent theater history has demonstrated how supple the play is, allowing directors and actors to choose among an array of possibilities. At one extreme, Hal can be played as a matter-of-fact and even cynical young man who knows from the very start exactly where he is going and what use he can make of Falstaff and company—as played, for example, by Richard Burton at Stratford-upon-Avon in 1951 (directed by Anthony Quayle and John Kidd). At the opposite extreme, Hal can be seen as a defiant rebel whose hatred for his unsympathetically cold father makes him reluctant to grow up and accept adult responsibility; this was the line taken, for example, by Gerard Murphy in Trevor Nunn's 1982 production for the Royal Shakespeare Company. Murphy's Hal was an unruly child for whom Falstaff was a nurturing substitute parent. Between these polarities, Hal can be variously seen as an alcoholic or a prudish snob or a playboy or simply a young man who wants to enjoy life. Correspondingly, the role of Falstaff offers widely varying possibilities as a kind of jolly scapegrace older friend, a calculating con artist and jokester who knows how to play for sympathy through self-effacing humor, or a dangerously irresponsible hedonist. King Henry as father can be seen as a sorely tested father burdened with heavy responsibilities and an ungrateful son, a guilt-ridden monarch who fears remorsefully that Hal's waywardness is heaven's punishment for the King's sins, or a hard-bitten politician engaged in a life-and-death struggle for power with aristocrats as Machiavellian as he. An important reason for the play's great success is its openness to interpretation.

In the Gad's Hill robbery, Falstaff reveals that his "cowardice" differs from the natural craven fear of Bardolph and Peto. He fights no longer than he sees "reason," that is, not against unfair odds such as two athletic young men in the dark (or later, at Shrewsbury, against the burly Scots giant, the Douglas). A man could get killed that way. Falstaff's cowardice, then, is philosophic, seen by himself in a humorous perspective. The same is true of his lying about the robbery. However much Hal exults in exposing Falstaff as a fraud, we cannot dismiss the possibility that Falstaff may see through the Prince's scheme, and may then feed Hal the expectedly outlandish lie (two men in buckram become eleven men) as a means of begging for affection. Falstaff's only way of pleading his cause is to tickle the Prince's fancy, in his role as a kind of court fool. What Falstaff most wants is to be loved and retained for what he is, and that, poignantly enough, is the one thing the mature Henry V cannot grant.

Throughout *1 Henry IV*, Shakespeare seems interested in the relationships between fathers and sons. These relationships help structure the comparisons and contrasts among foil characters. Falstaff is a foil, not only for Hotspur, but also for Henry IV; that is, despite all his insistence on youthful irresponsibility, Falstaff acts as a kind of parental figure to Hal. In the tavern scene (2.4), Falstaff and Hal take turns playing king and crown prince, and in both roles Falstaff wittily argues his case as companion and guide to the heir to the throne. Is it better to be old and merry, fat and loved, or to be hated like Pharaoh's lean kine? Falstaff argues against the gravity of council meetings with the same amused fervor that he later directs at the grinning honor of a dead hero. Hal, in his turn as king, questions the propriety of a "devil" haunting the crown prince "in the likeness of an old fat man," a "reverend Vice," a "gray Iniquity," a "father ruffian" (2.4.442–9). For all the good humor in this exchange, both men are asking whether Falstaff or King Henry serves Hal as the better model. Hal anticipates some of the very arguments his father will use against him next day at court, and, indeed, the insistent presence of that sober adult world makes itself felt even in the tavern.

When, under the pressure of that looming responsibility, Falstaff's merrymaking turns to something like urgent self-justification in his moving litany of appeals that Hal "banish not him thy Harry's company—banish plump Jack, and banish all the world," the Prince seems aware that he must face the consequences of his destiny. "I do, I will," he answers (lines 472–6), in a tone that can vary onstage (depending on the actor) from sober resolution to fond regret to awakening as from a dream.

Hotspur, too, is regarded as a son by more than one father. King Henry only half-jokingly wishes it could be proved that some night-tripping fairy had exchanged his Harry in the cradle for Harry Percy (1.1.85–9). Paradoxically, the King admires Hotspur all the more for standing up to him, just as another imperious father figure, Owen Glendower, bestows grudging but real admiration on Hotspur for his outspokenness (3.1.1–185). Hotspur's rebellious ways are cherished because they seem to promise manliness and fame; Hal's rebellious ways are feared and despised because they seem to reject the values of duty and leadership on which King Henry bases his self-respect. In these terms, the play must resolve Hal's coming of age, his acceptance of his role as true son of the King, and his proving his worth to the King. Hal must find his adult self—a self that differs greatly from that of King Henry—but must do so in a way that preserves the integrity of their relationship and the real debt he owes his father.

Prince Hal's uncertain journey toward maturity does not involve him in any significant relationships with women. His task is to fulfill what is expected of him as his father's son in a world of political and military conflict. Women stand on the periphery of affairs, as in *Richard II*, and yet the scenes in which they appear offer important perspectives on male competitiveness and ambition. Hotspur's wife, Kate, must put up with being condescended to and told little about men's doings; yet Hotspur's genuine fondness for her shows the best side of his personality, and her worries about his obsessive ways indicate that she understands him better than he understands himself. Mortimer's Welsh wife, too, introduces into this play an element of tenderness and anxious concern that is notably lacking in the earlier part of 3.1, when Hotspur cannot stop himself from quarreling pointlessly with his senior ally, Glendower. Hotspur's insensitivity to the Welsh lady's beautiful song is perhaps a key to his impending tragedy, for he is never a good listener. On a lower social scale, Mistress Quickly devotedly looks after Falstaff, only to be repaid with misogynistic insults that she does not appear to understand and with mooching that she recognizes all too well. Prince Hal, meantime, plays the role of intelligent observer of the battle of the sexes, even while he postpones his own engagement in that merry war. He must first sort out who he is in terms of male goals of career and success.

These conflicts surrounding Hal reach their climax and resolution at the field of Shrewsbury in Act 5. Hal's worth must be proven at Hotspur's expense. The rivalry between the two has been intense throughout the play, as seen for example in Hal's brilliant mimicking of Hotspur's devotion to bloodshed (2.4.101–8). Aware that his tarnished reputation puts him at a disadvantage, Hal speaks nobly of his rival and impresses even the adversarial camp with his regal bearing (5.1.83–100, 5.2.51–68). He rescues his father in the battle, thereby proving to King Henry that his son does not wish to supplant him, as he had feared. After the battle, Hal frees his Scottish adversary the Douglas in a display of princely magnificence, doing so with a more generous motive than Hotspur had displayed in his earlier release of the Douglas as his prisoner (1.3.259–62). Meantime, Hal has put considerable distance between himself and Falstaff, though sensitive still to the warmth of old memories. When he sees Hotspur and Falstaff on the ground together, both seemingly dead, Hal views as in a tableau the contrasting models between which he has shaped his own identity. Yet Falstaff is not dead. He rises to mutilate Hotspur's body and to claim the honor due Hal for Hotspur's death. For all Falstaff's witty commentary at the expense of honor, his own opposite course is unsuited to a time of war or to Hal's new public role. Falstaff's abuse of military conscription, his carrying a bottle of sack in place of a pistol, show him at his wittiest still, but in a world that may not tolerate such pranks. The merry games are out of place and childish. With characteristic generosity and imprudence, Hal gives the credit for Hotspur's death to Falstaff, who claims it so cravenly. Even so, the magic of their association has vanished. The time of adulthood is upon Hal.

# *The First Part of King Henry The Fourth*

[*Dramatis Personae*

KING HENRY THE FOURTH
PRINCE HENRY, *Prince of Wales,* ⎫
PRINCE JOHN OF LANCASTER, ⎬ *sons of the King*
EARL OF WESTMORLAND ⎭
SIR WALTER BLUNT

EARL OF NORTHUMBERLAND, *Henry Percy,* ⎫
HARRY PERCY (HOTSPUR), *his son,*
EARL OF WORCESTER, *Northumberland's*
   *younger brother,*
LORD MORTIMER, *Edmund Mortimer*
   *also referred to as the Earl of March,* ⎬ *rebels against the King*
OWEN GLENDOWER,
EARL OF DOUGLAS, *Archibald Douglas,*
SIR RICHARD VERNON,
ARCHBISHOP OF YORK, *Richard Scroop,*
SIR MICHAEL, *a member of the*
   *Archbishop's household,* ⎭

LADY PERCY, *Hotspur's wife and Mortimer's sister*
LADY MORTIMER, *Mortimer's wife and Glendower's*
   *daughter*

    SCENE: *England and Wales*]

SIR JOHN FALSTAFF
NED POINS
BARDOLPH
PETO
GADSHILL, *arranger of the highway robbery*
HOSTESS OF THE TAVERN, *Mistress Quickly*
FRANCIS, *a drawer, or tapster*
VINTNER, *or tavern keeper*

FIRST CARRIER
SECOND CARRIER
HOSTLER
CHAMBERLAIN
FIRST TRAVELER
SHERIFF
SERVANT *to Hotspur*
MESSENGER
SECOND MESSENGER

*Soldiers, Travelers, Lords, Attendants*

## [1.1]

*Enter the King, Lord John of Lancaster, [the] Earl of Westmorland, [Sir Walter Blunt,] with others.*

KING
So shaken as we are, so wan with care,
Find we a time for frighted peace to pant,                    2
And breathe short-winded accents of new broils               3
To be commenced in strands afar remote.                       4
No more the thirsty entrance of this soil                     5
Shall daub her lips with her own children's blood;           6
No more shall trenching war channel her fields               7
Nor bruise her flowerets with the armèd hoofs
Of hostile paces. Those opposèd eyes,                         9
Which, like the meteors of a troubled heaven,
All of one nature, of one substance bred,
Did lately meet in the intestine shock                       12
And furious close of civil butchery,                         13
Shall now in mutual well-beseeming ranks
March all one way and be no more opposed
Against acquaintance, kindred, and allies.
The edge of war, like an ill-sheathèd knife,
No more shall cut his master. Therefore, friends,            18
As far as to the sepulcher of Christ—
Whose soldier now, under whose blessèd cross
We are impressèd and engaged to fight—                       21
Forthwith a power of English shall we levy,                  22
Whose arms were molded in their mothers' womb                23
To chase these pagans in those holy fields
Over whose acres walked those blessèd feet
Which fourteen hundred years ago were nailed
For our advantage on the bitter cross.
But this our purpose now is twelve month old,
And bootless 'tis to tell you we will go.                    29
Therefore we meet not now. Then let me hear                  30
Of you, my gentle cousin Westmorland,                        31
What yesternight our council did decree
In forwarding this dear expedience.                          33

WESTMORLAND
My liege, this haste was hot in question,                    34
And many limits of the charge set down                       35
But yesternight, when all athwart there came                 36
A post from Wales loaden with heavy news,                    37
Whose worst was that the noble Mortimer,
Leading the men of Herefordshire to fight
Against the irregular and wild Glendower,                    40

Was by the rude hands of that Welshman taken,
A thousand of his people butcherèd—
Upon whose dead corpse there was such misuse,                43
Such beastly shameless transformation,                       44
By those Welshwomen done as may not be
Without much shame retold or spoken of.

KING
It seems then that the tidings of this broil
Brake off our business for the Holy Land.                    48

WESTMORLAND
This matched with other did, my gracious lord;               49
For more uneven and unwelcome news                           50
Came from the north, and thus it did import:
On Holy Rood Day, the gallant Hotspur there,                 52
Young Harry Percy, and brave Archibald,
That ever-valiant and approved Scot,                         54
At Holmedon met, where they did spend                        55
A sad and bloody hour,
As by discharge of their artillery                           57
And shape of likelihood the news was told;                   58
For he that brought them, in the very heat                   59
And pride of their contention did take horse,                60
Uncertain of the issue any way.

KING
Here is a dear, a true industrious friend,                   62
Sir Walter Blunt, new lighted from his horse,                63
Stained with the variation of each soil
Betwixt that Holmedon and this seat of ours;
And he hath brought us smooth and welcome news.              66
The Earl of Douglas is discomfited;                          67
Ten thousand bold Scots, two-and-twenty knights,
Balked in their own blood, did Sir Walter see                69
On Holmedon's plains. Of prisoners, Hotspur took
Mordake, Earl of Fife and eldest son                         71
To beaten Douglas, and the Earl of Atholl,
Of Murray, Angus, and Menteith.
And is not this an honorable spoil?
A gallant prize? Ha, cousin, is it not?

WESTMORLAND
In faith, it is a conquest for a prince to boast of.

KING
Yea, there thou mak'st me sad, and mak'st me sin
In envy that my lord Northumberland
Should be the father to so blest a son—
A son who is the theme of honor's tongue,
Amongst a grove the very straightest plant,                  81
Who is sweet Fortune's minion and her pride,                 82
Whilst I, by looking on the praise of him,
See riot and dishonor stain the brow                         84
Of my young Harry. Oh, that it could be proved

---

**1.1. Location: The royal court.**
**2 Find we** let us find.   **frighted** frightened   **3 breathe short-winded accents** speak, even though we are out of breath.   **accents** words. **broils** battles   **4 strands afar remote** far-off shores, i.e., of the Holy Land (to which, at the end of *Richard II*, Henry has pledged himself to a crusade).   **5 thirsty entrance** i.e., parched mouth   **6 daub** coat, smear   **7 trenching** cutting, plowing   **9 paces** horses' tread. **12 intestine** internal   **13 close** hand-to-hand encounter.   **civil** (as in "civil war")   **18 his** its   **21 impressèd** conscripted   **22 power** army   **23 their mothers'** i.e., their own mothers', but also suggesting England's   **29 bootless** useless   **30 Therefore ... now** That is not the reason for our present meeting.   **31 Of** from.   **gentle cousin** noble kinsman   **33 dear expedience** urgent expedition.   **34 hot in question** being hotly debated   **35 limits ... charge** particulars of military responsibility   **36 athwart** at cross purposes, contrarily **37 post** messenger.   **loaden** laden   **40 irregular** using guerilla tactics

**43 corpse** corpses   **44 transformation** mutilation   **48 Brake** broke   **49 other** other news   **50 uneven** disconcerting, distressing **52 Holy Rood Day** Holy Cross day, September 14   **54 approved** proved by experience   **55 Holmedon** Humbleton in Northumberland   **57 by** judging from   **58 shape of likelihood** likely outcome   **59 them** the news   **60 pride** height   **62–3 Here ... Blunt** (Whether Blunt enters at the start of the scene, or now, or possibly not at all, is not certain in the original text.)   **66 smooth** pleasant **67 discomfited** defeated   **69 Balked** heaped up in balks, or ridges, or thwarted   **71 Mordake** i.e., Murdoch, son of the Earl of Albany **81 plant** young tree   **82 minion** favorite   **84 riot** debauchery

That some night-tripping fairy had exchanged    86
In cradle clothes our children where they lay,
And called mine Percy, his Plantagenet!    88
Then would I have his Harry, and he mine.
But let him from my thoughts. What think you, coz,    90
Of this young Percy's pride? The prisoners
Which he in this adventure hath surprised    92
To his own use he keeps, and sends me word    93
I shall have none but Mordake, Earl of Fife.    94

WESTMORLAND
This is his uncle's teaching. This is Worcester,
Malevolent to you in all aspects,    96
Which makes him prune himself and bristle up    97
The crest of youth against your dignity.

KING
But I have sent for him to answer this;
And for this cause awhile we must neglect
Our holy purpose to Jerusalem.
Cousin, on Wednesday next our council we
Will hold at Windsor. So inform the lords.
But come yourself with speed to us again,
For more is to be said and to be done
Than out of anger can be utterèd.

WESTMORLAND    I will, my liege.          *Exeunt.*

# [1.2]

*Enter Prince of Wales and Sir John Falstaff.*

FALSTAFF
Now, Hal, what time of day is it, lad?

PRINCE    Thou art so fat-witted with drinking of old sack,    2
and unbuttoning thee after supper, and sleeping upon
benches after noon, that thou hast forgotten to de-    4
mand that truly which thou wouldst truly know. What    5
a devil hast thou to do with the time of the day? Unless    6
hours were cups of sack, and minutes capons, and
clocks the tongues of bawds, and dials the signs of    8
leaping houses, and the blessed sun himself a fair hot    9
wench in flame-colored taffeta, I see no reason why    10
thou shouldst be so superfluous to demand the time    11
of the day.

FALSTAFF    Indeed, you come near me now, Hal, for we    13
that take purses go by the moon and the seven stars,    14

and not by Phoebus, "he, that wandering knight so    15
fair." And I prithee, sweet wag, when thou art king,    16
as, God save Thy Grace—Majesty I should say, for    17
grace thou wilt have none—

PRINCE    What, none?

FALSTAFF    No, by my troth, not so much as will serve to    20
be prologue to an egg and butter.    21

PRINCE    Well, how then? Come, roundly, roundly.    22

FALSTAFF    Marry, then, sweet wag, when thou art king, let    23
not us that are squires of the night's body be    24
called thieves of the day's beauty. Let us be Diana's for-    25
esters, gentlemen of the shade, minions of the moon;    26
and let men say we be men of good government,    27
being governed, as the sea is, by our noble and chaste
mistress the moon, under whose countenance we steal.    29

PRINCE    Thou sayest well, and it holds well too, for the    30
fortune of us that are the moon's men doth ebb and
flow like the sea, being governed, as the sea is, by the
moon. As, for proof, now: a purse of gold most
resolutely snatched on Monday night and most disso-
lutely spent on Tuesday morning, got with swearing
"Lay by" and spent with crying "Bring in," now in as    36
low an ebb as the foot of the ladder and by and by in    37
as high a flow as the ridge of the gallows.    38

FALSTAFF    By the Lord, thou say'st true, lad. And is not
my hostess of the tavern a most sweet wench?

PRINCE    As the honey of Hybla, my old lad of the castle.    41
And is not a buff jerkin a most sweet robe of durance?    42

FALSTAFF    How now, how now, mad wag, what, in thy
quips and thy quiddities? What a plague have I to do    44
with a buff jerkin?

PRINCE    Why, what a pox have I to do with my hostess    46
of the tavern?

FALSTAFF    Well, thou hast called her to a reckoning many    48
a time and oft.

PRINCE    Did I ever call for thee to pay thy part?

FALSTAFF    No, I'll give thee thy due, thou hast paid all
there.

PRINCE    Yea, and elsewhere, so far as my coin would
stretch, and where it would not I have used my credit.

---

**86 night-tripping** i.e., moving nimbly in the night    **88 Plantagenet** (Family name of English royalty since Henry II, here applied to Henry IV and his son.)    **90 let him** let him go.    **coz** cousin, i.e., kinsman    **92 surprised** ambushed, captured    **93 To . . . use** i.e., to collect ransom for them    **94 none but Mordake** (Since Mordake was of royal blood, being grandson to Robert II of Scotland, Hotspur could not claim him as his prisoner according to the law of arms.)    **96 Malevolent . . . aspects** (1) implacably hostile to you (2) in astrological terms, a planet in a disobedient orbit, ominous as seen from every angle    **97 Which . . . himself** i.e., which teaching makes Hotspur preen himself (as a falcon preens its feathers) **1.2. Location: London, perhaps in an apartment of the Prince's.** **2 sack** a Spanish white wine    **4 forgotten** forgotten how    **4–5 demand** ask    **6 a devil** in the devil's name    **8 dials** clocks    **9 leaping houses** houses of prostitution    **10 taffeta** (Commonly worn by prostitutes.) **11 superfluous** (1) unnecessarily concerned (2) self-indulgent **13 you . . . now** i.e., you've scored a point on me    **14 go by** (1) travel by the light of (2) tell time by.    **the seven stars** the Pleiades

**15–16 Phoebus . . . fair** (Phoebus, god of the sun, is here equated with the wandering knight of a ballad or popular romance.)    **16 wag** wit **17 Grace** royal highness. (With pun on spiritual *grace* and also on the *grace* or blessing before a meal.)    **20 troth** faith    **21 prologue . . . butter** i.e., grace before a brief meal.    **22 roundly** i.e., out with it. **23 Marry** Indeed. (Literally, "by the Virgin Mary.")    **23–5 let . . . beauty** i.e., let not us who are attendants on the goddess of night, members of her household, be blamed for stealing daylight by sleeping in the daytime.    **25–6 Diana's foresters** (An elegant name for thieves by night; Diana is goddess of the moon and the hunt.) **26 minions** favorites    **27 government** (1) conduct (2) commonwealth **29 countenance** (1) face (2) patronage, approval.    **steal** (1) move stealthily (2) rob.    **30 it holds well** the comparison is apt    **36 Lay by** (A cry of highwaymen, like "Hands up!")    **Bring in** (An order given to a waiter in a tavern.)    **37 ladder** (1) pier ladder (2) gallows ladder **38 ridge** crossbar    **41 Hybla** (A town, famed for its honey, in Sicily near Syracuse.)    **old . . . castle** (1) a roisterer (2) the name, Sir John Oldcastle, borne by Falstaff in an earlier version of this play.    **42 buff jerkin** a leather jacket worn by officers of the law.    **durance** (1) imprisonment (2) durability, durable cloth.    **44 quiddities** subtleties of speech.    **46 pox** syphilis. (Here, *what a pox* is used as an expletive, like "what the devil.")    **48 reckoning** settlement of the bill. (With bawdy suggestion that is continued in *pay thy part* and *my coin would stretch*.)

**FALSTAFF**  Yea, and so used it that, were it not here apparent that thou art heir apparent—But I prithee, sweet wag, shall there be gallows standing in England when thou art king? And resolution thus fubbed as it 58 is with the rusty curb of old father Antic the law? Do 59 not thou, when thou art king, hang a thief.

**PRINCE**  No, thou shalt.

**FALSTAFF**  Shall I? Oh, rare! By the Lord, I'll be a brave 62 judge.

**PRINCE**  Thou judgest false already. I mean, thou shalt have the hanging of the thieves, and so become a rare 65 hangman.

**FALSTAFF**  Well, Hal, well; and in some sort it jumps 67 with my humor as well as waiting in the court, I can 68 tell you.

**PRINCE**  For obtaining of suits? 70

**FALSTAFF**  Yea, for obtaining of suits, whereof the hangman hath no lean wardrobe. 'Sblood, I am as 72 melancholy as a gib cat or a lugged bear. 73

**PRINCE**  Or an old lion, or a lover's lute.

**FALSTAFF**  Yea, or the drone of a Lincolnshire bagpipe.

**PRINCE**  What sayest thou to a hare, or the melancholy 76 of Moorditch? 77

**FALSTAFF**  Thou hast the most unsavory similes, and art indeed the most comparative, rascalliest, sweet young 79 prince. But Hal, I prithee, trouble me no more with vanity. I would to God thou and I knew where a com- 81 modity of good names were to be bought. An old lord 82 of the council rated me the other day in the street 83 about you, sir, but I marked him not; and yet he talked very wisely, but I regarded him not; and yet he talked wisely, and in the street too.

**PRINCE**  Thou didst well, for wisdom cries out in the 87 streets and no man regards it. 88

**FALSTAFF**  Oh, thou hast damnable iteration, and art 89 indeed able to corrupt a saint. Thou hast done much harm upon me, Hal, God forgive thee for it. Before I knew thee, Hal, I knew nothing; and now am I, if a 92 man should speak truly, little better than one of the wicked. I must give over this life, and I will give it over. By the Lord, an I do not I am a villain. I'll be 95 damned for never a king's son in Christendom.

**PRINCE**  Where shall we take a purse tomorrow, Jack?

**FALSTAFF**  Zounds, where thou wilt, lad, I'll make one. 98 An I do not, call me villain and baffle me. 99

**PRINCE**  I see a good amendment of life in thee—from praying to purse taking.

**FALSTAFF**  Why, Hal, 'tis my vocation, Hal. 'Tis no sin 102 for a man to labor in his vocation. 103

*Enter Poins.*

Poins! Now shall we know if Gadshill have set a 104 match. Oh, if men were to be saved by merit, what 105 hole in hell were hot enough for him? This is the most omnipotent villain that ever cried "Stand!" to a 107 true man. 108

**PRINCE**  Good morrow, Ned.

**POINS**  Good morrow, sweet Hal.—What says Monsieur Remorse? What says Sir John, Sack-and-Sugar Jack? How agrees the devil and thee about thy soul that thou soldest him on Good Friday last for a cup of Madeira and a cold capon's leg?

**PRINCE**  Sir John stands to his word; the devil shall have 115 his bargain, for he was never yet a breaker of proverbs. He will give the devil his due.

**POINS**  Then art thou damned for keeping thy word with the devil.

**PRINCE**  Else he had been damned for cozening the 120 devil.

**POINS**  But my lads, my lads, tomorrow morning, by four o'clock early, at Gad's Hill, there are pilgrims 123 going to Canterbury with rich offerings and traders riding to London with fat purses. I have vizards for 125 you all; you have horses for yourselves. Gadshill lies 126 tonight in Rochester. I have bespoke supper tomorrow 127 night in Eastcheap. We may do it as secure as sleep. If 128 you will go, I will stuff your purses full of crowns; if 129 you will not, tarry at home and be hanged.

**FALSTAFF**  Hear ye, Yedward, if I tarry at home and go 131 not, I'll hang you for going. 132

**POINS**  You will, chops? 133

**FALSTAFF**  Hal, wilt thou make one?

**PRINCE**  Who, I rob? I a thief? Not I, by my faith.

**FALSTAFF**  There's neither honesty, manhood, nor good fellowship in thee, nor thou cam'st not of the blood royal, if thou darest not stand for ten shillings. 138

---

**58 resolution** courage (of a highwayman).   **fubbed** cheated **59 Antic** buffoon   **62 rare** splendid.   **brave** excellent   **65 have . . . thieves** (1) be in charge of hanging thieves (or protecting them from hanging) (2) hang like other thieves.   **rare** (1) rarely used (2) excellent   **67–8 jumps . . . humor** suits my temperament   **68 waiting in the court** being in attendance at the royal court   **70 suits** petitions. (But Falstaff uses the word to mean suits of clothes; clothes belonging to an executed man were given to the executioner.)   **72 'Sblood** By his (Christ's) blood   **73 gib cat** tomcat.   **lugged bear** bear led by a chain and baited by dogs.   **76 hare** (A proverbially melancholy animal.)   **77 Moorditch** (A foul ditch draining Moorfields, outside London walls.)   **79 comparative** given to abusive comparisons **81 vanity** worldliness.   **81–2 commodity** supply   **82 names** reputations   **83 rated** chastised   **87–8 wisdom . . . regards it** (Hal paraphrases Proverbs 1:20–4, "Wisdom crieth without, and putteth forth her voice in the streets . . . and no man regarded," in jocose reply to Falstaff's mock sanctimoniousness.)   **89 iteration** repetition (of biblical texts, with a neat twist)   **92 nothing** i.e., no evil   **95 an** if

**98 Zounds** By his (Christ's) wounds.   **make one** be one of the party.   **99 baffle** publicly disgrace   **102, 103 vocation** (A favorite term of the reforming Protestant ministers to describe the function or station to which one is called by God. Falstaff comically misapplies it to justify highway robbing.)   **104 Gadshill** (The name of one of the highwaymen.)   **104–5 set a match** arranged a robbery.   **105 by merit** i.e., according to their deservings rather than by God's grace **107 omnipotent** unparalleled, utter.   **"Stand!"** "Stand and deliver!" i.e., Hand over your money.   **108 true man** honest citizen. **115 stands to** keeps   **120 Else** Otherwise.   **cozening** cheating **123 Gad's Hill** (Location near Rochester on the road from London to Canterbury; one of the highwaymen is called Gadshill.)   **125 vizards** masks   **126 lies** lodges   **127 bespoke** ordered   **128 Eastcheap** market district in London, with many taverns.   **129 crowns** gold coins   **131 Yedward** (Nickname for *Edward,* Poins's first name.)   **131–2 if I . . . going** i.e., there's no chance of my not going; sooner than that, I'd see you hanged instead for going in my place.   **133 chops** i.e., fat jaws or cheeks.   **138 stand . . . shillings** (1) stand up and fight for booty (2) be worth ten shillings, the value of the *royal,* the gold coin alluded to in *blood royal* (line 138).

PRINCE    Well then, once in my days I'll be a madcap.

FALSTAFF    Why, that's well said.

PRINCE    Well, come what will, I'll tarry at home.

FALSTAFF    By the Lord, I'll be a traitor then, when thou art king.

PRINCE    I care not.

POINS    Sir John, I prithee leave the Prince and me alone. I will lay him down such reasons for this adventure that he shall go.

FALSTAFF    Well, God give thee the spirit of persuasion and him the ears of profiting, that what thou speakest may move and what he hears may be believed, that the true prince may, for recreation sake, prove a false thief; for the poor abuses of the time want counte- 152
nance. Farewell. You shall find me in Eastcheap.      153

PRINCE    Farewell, thou latter spring! Farewell, All- 154
hallown summer!                  [*Exit Falstaff.*]   155

POINS    Now, my good sweet honey lord, ride with us tomorrow. I have a jest to execute that I cannot manage alone. Falstaff, Peto, Bardolph, and Gadshill shall rob those men that we have already waylaid—    159
yourself and I will not be there—and when they have the booty, if you and I do not rob them, cut this head off from my shoulders.

PRINCE    How shall we part with them in setting forth?

POINS    Why, we will set forth before or after them and appoint them a place of meeting, wherein it is at our pleasure to fail; and then will they adventure upon the    166
exploit themselves, which they shall have no sooner achieved but we'll set upon them.

PRINCE    Yea, but 'tis like that they will know us by our    169
horses, by our habits, and by every other appoint-     170
ment, to be ourselves.               171

POINS    Tut, our horses they shall not see—I'll tie them in the wood; our vizards we will change after we leave them; and, sirrah, I have cases of buckram for the    174
nonce, to immask our noted outward garments.     175

PRINCE    Yea, but I doubt they will be too hard for us.    176

POINS    Well, for two of them, I know them to be as true-bred cowards as ever turned back; and for the    178
third, if he fight longer than he sees reason, I'll for-swear arms. The virtue of this jest will be the incompre-    180
hensible lies that this same fat rogue will tell us when    181
we meet at supper—how thirty at least he fought with, what wards, what blows, what extremities he    183
endured; and in the reproof of this lives the jest.      184

PRINCE    Well, I'll go with thee. Provide us all things necessary and meet me tomorrow night in Eastcheap. There I'll sup. Farewell.

POINS    Farewell, my lord.          *Exit Poins.*

PRINCE

I know you all, and will awhile uphold
The unyoked humor of your idleness.            190
Yet herein will I imitate the sun,
Who doth permit the base contagious clouds         192
To smother up his beauty from the world,
That when he please again to be himself,          194
Being wanted he may be more wondered at,          195
By breaking through the foul and ugly mists
Of vapors that did seem to strangle him.
If all the year were playing holidays,
To sport would be as tedious as to work;
But when they seldom come, they wished-for come,
And nothing pleaseth but rare accidents.           201
So when this loose behavior I throw off
And pay the debt I never promisèd,
By how much better than my word I am,
By so much shall I falsify men's hopes;           205
And like bright metal on a sullen ground,          206
My reformation, glitt'ring o'er my fault,
Shall show more goodly and attract more eyes
Than that which hath no foil to set it off.         209
I'll so offend to make offense a skill,            210
Redeeming time when men think least I will.    *Exit.* 211

## [1.3]

*Enter the King, Northumberland, Worcester,*
*Hotspur, Sir Walter Blunt, with others.*

KING

My blood hath been too cold and temperate,
Unapt to stir at these indignities,
And you have found me, for accordingly           3
You tread upon my patience. But be sure
I will from henceforth rather be myself,           5
Mighty and to be feared, than my condition,        6
Which hath been smooth as oil, soft as young down,
And therefore lost that title of respect
Which the proud soul ne'er pays but to the proud.

WORCESTER

Our house, my sovereign liege, little deserves    10
The scourge of greatness to be used on it—
And that same greatness too which our own hands
Have holp to make so portly.            13

NORTHUMBERLAND  [*to the King*]    My lord—

KING

Worcester, get thee gone, for I do see

---

Danger and disobedience in thine eye.
Oh, sir, your presence is too bold and peremptory,
And majesty might never yet endure
The moody frontier of a servant brow.                                                    19
You have good leave to leave us. When we need                   20
Your use and counsel, we shall send for you.                      21

                          *Exit Worcester.*

[*To Northumberland*] You were about to speak.

NORTHUMBERLAND             Yea, my good lord.
Those prisoners in Your Highness' name demanded,
Which Harry Percy here at Holmedon took,
Were, as he says, not with such strength denied
As is delivered to Your Majesty.                                          26
Either envy, therefore, or misprision                                    27
Is guilty of this fault, and not my son.

HOTSPUR [*to the King*]
My liege, I did deny no prisoners,
But I remember when the fight was done,
When I was dry with rage and extreme toil,
Breathless and faint, leaning upon my sword,
Came there a certain lord, neat and trimly dressed,
Fresh as a bridegroom, and his chin new reaped                   34
Showed like a stubble land at harvest home.                        35
He was perfumèd like a milliner,                                         36
And twixt his finger and his thumb he held
A pouncet box, which ever and anon                                    38
He gave his nose and took't away again,
Who therewith angry, when it next came there,                    40
Took it in snuff; and still he smiled and talked,                    41
And as the soldiers bore dead bodies by
He called them untaught knaves, unmannerly,
To bring a slovenly unhandsome corpse
Betwixt the wind and his nobility.
With many holiday and lady terms                                        46
He questioned me, amongst the rest demanded
My prisoners in Your Majesty's behalf.
I then, all smarting with my wounds being cold,
To be so pestered with a popinjay,                                        50
Out of my grief and my impatience                                       51
Answered neglectingly I know not what,
He should, or he should not; for he made me mad
To see him shine so brisk, and smell so sweet,
And talk so like a waiting-gentlewoman
Of guns and drums and wounds—God save the
    mark!—                                                                    56
And telling me the sovereignest thing on earth                     57
Was parmacety for an inward bruise,                                    58

And that it was great pity, so it was,
This villainous saltpeter should be digged                            60
Out of the bowels of the harmless earth,
Which many a good tall fellow had destroyed                       62
So cowardly, and but for these vile guns
He would himself have been a soldier.
This bald unjointed chat of his, my lord,                              65
I answered indirectly, as I said,                                             66
And I beseech you, let not his report
Come current for an accusation                                             68
Betwixt my love and your high majesty.

BLUNT [*to the King*]
The circumstance considered, good my lord,
Whate'er Lord Harry Percy then had said
To such a person and in such a place,
At such a time, with all the rest retold,
May reasonably die, and never rise
To do him wrong or any way impeach                                   75
What then he said, so he unsay it now.                                  76

KING
Why, yet he doth deny his prisoners,                                     77
But with proviso and exception                                            78
That we at our own charge shall ransom straight                   79
His brother-in-law, the foolish Mortimer,                             80
Who, on my soul, hath willfully betrayed
The lives of those that he did lead to fight
Against that great magician, damned Glendower,
Whose daughter, as we hear, that Earl of March                   84
Hath lately married. Shall our coffers then
Be emptied to redeem a traitor home?
Shall we buy treason and indent with fears                           87
When they have lost and forfeited themselves?
No, on the barren mountains let him starve!
For I shall never hold that man my friend
Whose tongue shall ask me for one penny cost
To ransom home revolted Mortimer.                                     92

HOTSPUR     Revolted Mortimer?
He never did fall off, my sovereign liege,                              94
But by the chance of war. To prove that true
Needs no more but one tongue for all those wounds,
Those mouthèd wounds, which valiantly he took,               97
When on the gentle Severn's sedgy bank,                             98
In single opposition, hand to hand,

---

**60 saltpeter** potassium nitrate, used to make gunpowder and also
used medicinally   **62 tall** brave   **65 bald** trivial   **66 indirectly** inat-
tentively, offhandedly   **68 Come current** (1) be taken at face value (2)
come rushing in   **75 impeach** discredit   **76 so** provided that   **77 yet**
(emphatic) i.e., even now.  **deny** refuse to surrender   **78 proviso
and exception** (synonymous terms)   **79 straight** straightway, at
once   **80 Mortimer** (There were two Edmund Mortimers;
Shakespeare combines their stories. It was the uncle [1376–1409?]
who was captured by Glendower and married Glendower's daughter; it was the nephew [1391–1425], fifth Earl of March, who was proclaimed heir presumptive to King Richard II after the death of his
father, the fourth earl, whom Richard had named as his heir. The
uncle was brother to the fourth earl and to Hotspur's wife, Elizabeth,
called Kate in this play.)   **84 Earl of March** (The "Mortimer" of line
80; see note there.)   **87 indent with fears** i.e., make a bargain or come
to terms with traitors whom we have reason to fear   **92 revolted**
rebellious   **94 fall off** change his allegiance   **97 mouthèd** gaping
and eloquent   **98 Severn's** (The Severn River flows from northern
Wales and western England into the Bristol Channel.)  **sedgy**
bordered with reeds

---

**19 moody frontier** i.e., angry brow, frown. (*Frontier* literally means
"outwork" or "fortification.")   **20 good leave** full permission
**21 Your . . . counsel** to make use of you and your advice   **26 delivered**
reported   **27 envy** malice.  **misprision** misunderstanding   **34 chin
new reaped** i.e., with beard freshly barbered according to the latest
fashion, not like a soldier's beard   **35 Showed** looked.  **harvest
home** end of harvest, fields being cut back to stubble.   **36 milliner**
dealer in fancy articles, such as gloves and hats   **38 pouncet box** perfume box with perforated lid   **40 Who** i.e., his nose   **41 Took it in
snuff** (1) inhaled it (2) took offense.  **still** continually   **46 holiday
and lady** dainty and effeminate   **50 popinjay** parrot   **51 grief**
pain   **56 God . . . mark** (Probably originally a formula to avert evil
omen; here, an expression of impatience.)   **57 sovereignest** most
efficacious   **58 parmacety** spermaceti, a fatty substance taken from
the head of the sperm whale, used as a medicinal ointment

He did confound the best part of an hour                                100
In changing hardiment with great Glendower.                             101
Three times they breathed, and three times did they
    drink,                                                               102
Upon agreement, of swift Severn's flood,                                103
Who then, affrighted with their bloody looks,                           104
Ran fearfully among the trembling reeds
And hid his crisp head in the hollow bank,                              106
Bloodstainèd with these valiant combatants.
Never did bare and rotten policy                                        108
Color her working with such deadly wounds,                              109
Nor never could the noble Mortimer
Receive so many, and all willingly.
Then let not him be slandered with revolt.                              112

KING
Thou dost belie him, Percy, thou dost belie him.
He never did encounter with Glendower.
I tell thee,
He durst as well have met the devil alone
As Owen Glendower for an enemy.
Art thou not ashamed? But, sirrah, henceforth
Let me not hear you speak of Mortimer.
Send me your prisoners with the speediest means,
Or you shall hear in such a kind from me                                121
As will displease you.—My lord Northumberland,
We license your departure with your son.
Send us your prisoners, or you will hear of it.

*Exit King* [*with Blunt, and train*].

HOTSPUR
An if the devil come and roar for them                                  125
I will not send them. I will after straight                             126
And tell him so, for I will ease my heart,
Albeit I make a hazard of my head.                                      128

NORTHUMBERLAND
What, drunk with choler? Stay and pause awhile.                         129
Here comes your uncle.

*Enter Worcester.*

HOTSPUR                       Speak of Mortimer?
Zounds, I will speak of him, and let my soul                            131
Want mercy if I do not join with him!                                   132
Yea, on his part I'll empty all these veins,                            133
And shed my dear blood drop by drop in the dust,
But I will lift the downtrod Mortimer
As high in the air as this unthankful king,
As this ingrate and cankered Bolingbroke.                               137

NORTHUMBERLAND
Brother, the King hath made your nephew mad.

WORCESTER
Who struck this heat up after I was gone?

HOTSPUR
He will forsooth have all my prisoners;
And when I urged the ransom once again
Of my wife's brother, then his cheek looked pale,
And on my face he turned an eye of death,                               143
Trembling even at the name of Mortimer.

WORCESTER
I cannot blame him. Was not he proclaimed                               145
By Richard, that dead is, the next of blood?                            146

NORTHUMBERLAND
He was; I heard the proclamation.
And then it was when the unhappy king—                                  148
Whose wrongs in us God pardon!—did set forth                            149
Upon his Irish expedition;                                              150
From whence he, intercepted, did return                                 151
To be deposed and shortly murderèd.

WORCESTER
And for whose death we in the world's wide mouth
Live scandalized and foully spoken of.

HOTSPUR
But, soft, I pray you, did King Richard then                            155
Proclaim my brother Edmund Mortimer                                     156
Heir to the crown?

NORTHUMBERLAND     He did; myself did hear it.

HOTSPUR
Nay, then I cannot blame his cousin king,                               158
That wished him on the barren mountains starve.
But shall it be that you that set the crown
Upon the head of this forgetful man,
And for his sake wear the detested blot
Of murderous subornation—shall it be                                    163
That you a world of curses undergo,
Being the agents, or base second means,                                 165
The cords, the ladder, or the hangman rather?
Oh, pardon me that I descend so low
To show the line and the predicament                                    168
Wherein you range under this subtle king!                               169
Shall it for shame be spoken in these days,
Or fill up chronicles in time to come,
That men of your nobility and power
Did gage them both in an unjust behalf,                                 173
As both of you—God pardon it!—have done,
To put down Richard, that sweet lovely rose,
And plant this thorn, this canker, Bolingbroke?                         176
And shall it in more shame be further spoken
That you are fooled, discarded, and shook off
By him for whom these shames ye underwent?
No! Yet time serves wherein you may redeem                              180
Your banished honors and restore yourselves

---

**100 confound** consume   **101 changing hardiment** exchanging blows, matching valor   **102 breathed** paused for breath   **103 flood** river   **104 Who** i.e., the river   **106 crisp** curly, i.e., rippled.   **hollow** concave   **108 bare** paltry.   **policy** cunning   **109 Color** disguise   **112 revolt** i.e., the accusation of rebellion.   **121 kind** manner   **125 An if** If   **126 will after straight** will go after him immediately   **128 Albeit . . . head** even if I risk being beheaded.   **129 choler** anger.   **131 Zounds** By his (Christ's) wounds   **132 Want mercy** lack mercy, be damned   **133 on his part** i.e., fighting on Mortimer's side   **137 cankered** spoiled, malignant.   **Bolingbroke** i.e., King Henry IV. (Hotspur pointedly refuses to acknowledge his royalty.)

**143 an eye of death** a fearful look   **145 he** i.e., Mortimer   **146 next of blood** heir to the throne.   **148 unhappy** unfortunate   **149 in us** caused by our doings   **150 Irish expedition** (Richard II was putting down a rebellion in Ireland when Bolingbroke returned to England from exile.)   **151 intercepted** interrupted   **155 soft** i.e., wait a minute   **156 brother** brother-in-law   **158 cousin** (With a pun on cozen, "cheat.")   **163 murderous subornation** the suborning of, or inciting to, murder   **165 second means** agents   **168 To . . . predicament** to show the direction things are moving and the danger to you   **169 range** (1) are ranked (2) stray   **173 gage them** engage, pledge themselves   **176 canker** (1) canker rose or dog rose, wild and unfragrant (2) ulcer   **180 Yet** Still

Into the good thoughts of the world again;
Revenge the jeering and disdained contempt                 183
Of this proud king, who studies day and night             184
To answer all the debt he owes to you                      185
Even with the bloody payment of your deaths.
Therefore, I say—

WORCESTER            Peace, cousin, say no more.           187
And now I will unclasp a secret book,
And to your quick-conceiving discontents                   189
I'll read you matter deep and dangerous,
As full of peril and adventurous spirit
As to o'erwalk a current roaring loud
On the unsteadfast footing of a spear.                     193

HOTSPUR
If he fall in, good night, or sink or swim!                194
Send danger from the east unto the west,
So honor cross it from the north to south,                 196
And let them grapple. Oh, the blood more stirs
To rouse a lion than to start a hare!

NORTHUMBERLAND [to Worcester]
Imagination of some great exploit
Drives him beyond the bounds of patience.

HOTSPUR
By heaven, methinks it were an easy leap
To pluck bright honor from the pale-faced moon,
Or dive into the bottom of the deep,                       203
Where fathom line could never touch the ground,            204
And pluck up drownèd honor by the locks,
So he that doth redeem her thence might wear
Without corrival all her dignities;                        207
But out upon this half-faced fellowship!                   208

WORCESTER [to Northumberland]
He apprehends a world of figures here,                     209
But not the form of what he should attend.—                210
Good cousin, give me audience for a while.

HOTSPUR
I cry you mercy.

WORCESTER            Those same noble Scots                212
That are your prisoners—

HOTSPUR                  I'll keep them all.
By God, he shall not have a Scot of them,                  214
No, if a scot would save his soul, he shall not!           215
I'll keep them, by this hand.

WORCESTER                       You start away
And lend no ear unto my purposes.
Those prisoners you shall keep.

HOTSPUR                    Nay, I will, that's flat.   218

He said he would not ransom Mortimer,
Forbade my tongue to speak of Mortimer,
But I will find him when he lies asleep,
And in his ear I'll holler "Mortimer!"
Nay, I'll have a starling shall be taught to speak
Nothing but "Mortimer," and give it him
To keep his anger still in motion.                         225

WORCESTER    Hear you, cousin, a word.

HOTSPUR
All studies here I solemnly defy,                          227
Save how to gall and pinch this Bolingbroke,
And that same sword-and-buckler Prince of Wales.           229
But that I think his father loves him not                  230
And would be glad he met with some mischance,
I would have him poisoned with a pot of ale.

WORCESTER
Farewell, kinsman. I'll talk to you
When you are better tempered to attend.

NORTHUMBERLAND [to Hotspur]
Why, what a wasp-stung and impatient fool
Art thou to break into this woman's mood,                  236
Tying thine ear to no tongue but thine own!

HOTSPUR
Why, look you, I am whipped and scourged with rods,
Nettled and stung with pismires, when I hear               239
Of this vile politician, Bolingbroke.                      240
In Richard's time—what do you call the place?—
A plague upon it, it is in Gloucestershire;
'Twas where the madcap duke his uncle kept,                243
His uncle York; where I first bowed my knee
Unto this king of smiles, this Bolingbroke—
'Sblood, when you and he came back from
   Ravenspurgh.                                            246

NORTHUMBERLAND    At Berkeley Castle.                      247

HOTSPUR    You say true.
Why, what a candy deal of courtesy                         249
This fawning greyhound then did proffer me!
"Look when his infant fortune came to age,"                251
And "gentle Harry Percy," and "kind cousin"—
Oh, the devil take such cozeners!—God forgive me!         253
Good uncle, tell your tale; I have done.

WORCESTER
Nay, if you have not, to it again;
We will stay your leisure.

HOTSPUR            I have done, i'faith.                   256

WORCESTER
Then once more to your Scottish prisoners.
Deliver them up without their ransom straight,             258
And make the Douglas' son your only mean                   259

---

183 **Revenge** and wherein you may revenge yourself against.
**disdained** disdainful   184 **studies . . . night** plots incessantly
185 **answer** satisfy, discharge   187 **cousin** nephew   189 **quick-
conceiving** comprehending quickly   193 **spear** i.e., spear laid across
a stream as a narrow bridge.   194 **If . . . swim** i.e., Anyone daring
such a thing will face a life-or-death challenge. (Hotspur's imagination is fired by the thought of risking everything on such an attempt.)
**or sink** either sink   196 **So** provided that. (Also at line 206.)
203 **the deep** the ocean   204 **fathom line** a weighted line marked at
fathom intervals (six feet), used for measuring the depth of water
207 **corrival** rival, competitor   208 **out . . . fellowship!** down with
this paltry business of sharing glory with others!   209 **apprehends**
snatches at.   **figures** figures of the imagination, or figures of
speech   210 **form** essential nature.   **attend** give attention to.   212 **cry
you mercy** beg your pardon.   214–15 **Scot . . . scot** Scotsman . . . trifling
amount   218 **that's flat** that's for sure.

225 **still** continually   227 **studies** pursuits.   **defy** renounce
229 **sword-and-buckler** swashbuckling. (Gentlemen generally preferred
to wear the rapier and the dagger.)   230 **But that** Were it not that
236 **woman's** womanly. (A common defamatory view of women is
that that they were incapable of holding their tongues.)   239 **Nettled**
stung with nettles.   **pismires** ants. (From the urinous smell of an
anthill.)   240 **politician** deceitful schemer   243 **kept** dwelled
246 **'Sblood** By His (Christ's blood).   **Ravenspurgh** on the Yorkshire
coast, at the mouth of the Humber River, where Bolingbroke landed
on his return from exile (*Richard II*, 2.1.296).   247 **Berkeley Castle**
castle near Bristol.   249 **candy** sugared, flattering   251 **Look when**
When, as soon as   253 **cozeners** cheats. (With pun on *cousins*.)
256 **stay** await   258 **Deliver them up** Free them   259 **the Douglas'
son** i.e., Mordake. (See 1.1.71 and note.)   **mean** means, agent

For powers in Scotland, which, for divers reasons   260
Which I shall send you written, be assured
Will easily be granted. [*To Northumberland*] You, my
      lord,
Your son in Scotland being thus employed,
Shall secretly into the bosom creep   264
Of that same noble prelate well beloved,
The Archbishop.
HOTSPUR   Of York, is it not?
WORCESTER   True, who bears hard   268
His brother's death at Bristol, the Lord Scroop.
I speak not this in estimation,   270
As what I think might be, but what I know
Is ruminated, plotted, and set down,
And only stays but to behold the face
Of that occasion that shall bring it on.
HOTSPUR
I smell it. Upon my life, it will do well.
NORTHUMBERLAND
Before the game is afoot thou still let'st slip.   276
HOTSPUR
Why, it cannot choose but be a noble plot.   277
And then the power of Scotland and of York   278
To join with Mortimer, ha?
WORCESTER                              And so they shall.
HOTSPUR
In faith, it is exceedingly well aimed.   280
WORCESTER
And 'tis no little reason bids us speed,
To save our heads by raising of a head;   282
For, bear ourselves as even as we can,   283
The King will always think him in our debt,   284
And think we think ourselves unsatisfied
Till he hath found a time to pay us home.   286
And see already how he doth begin
To make us strangers to his looks of love.
HOTSPUR
He does, he does. We'll be revenged on him.
WORCESTER
Cousin, farewell. No further go in this
Than I by letters shall direct your course.
When time is ripe, which will be suddenly,   292
I'll steal to Glendower and Lord Mortimer,
Where you and Douglas and our powers at once,   294
As I will fashion it, shall happily meet   295
To bear our fortunes in our own strong arms,   296
Which now we hold at much uncertainty.
NORTHUMBERLAND
Farewell, good brother. We shall thrive, I trust.
HOTSPUR
Uncle, adieu. Oh, let the hours be short
Till fields and blows and groans applaud our sport!   300
                    *Exeunt* [*in separate groups*].

❧

260 **For powers** for raising an army   264 **secretly . . . creep** win the
confidence   268 **bears hard** resents   270 **estimation** guesswork
276 **still let'st slip** always let loose the dogs.   277 **cannot choose but
be** cannot help being   278 **power** army   280 **aimed** designed.
282 **head** army (with pun on *heads*)   283 **even** carefully   284 **him**
himself   286 **home** (1) fully (2) with a thrust to the heart.
292 **suddenly** soon   294 **at once** all together   295 **happily** fortunately
296 **arms** (1) limbs (2) military might   300 **fields** battlefields

## [2.1]

*Enter a Carrier with a lantern in his hand.*

FIRST CARRIER   Heigh-ho! An it be not four by the day,   1
   I'll be hanged. Charles's Wain is over the new   2
   chimney, and yet our horse not packed. What, hostler!   3
HOSTLER [*within*]   Anon, anon.   4
FIRST CARRIER   I prithee, Tom, beat Cut's saddle, put a   5
   few flocks in the point. Poor jade is wrung in the   6
   withers out of all cess.   7

*Enter another Carrier.*

SECOND CARRIER   Peas and beans are as dank here as a   8
   dog, and that is the next way to give poor jades the   9
   bots. This house is turned upside down since Robin   10
   Hostler died.
FIRST CARRIER   Poor fellow never joyed since the price
   of oats rose. It was the death of him.
SECOND CARRIER   I think this be the most villainous
   house in all London road for fleas. I am stung like a
   tench.   16
FIRST CARRIER   Like a tench? By the Mass, there is ne'er
   a king Christian could be better bit than I have been   18
   since the first cock.   19
SECOND CARRIER   Why, they will allow us ne'er a jordan,   20
   and then we leak in your chimney, and your chamber-   21
   lye breeds fleas like a loach.   22
FIRST CARRIER [*calling*]   What, Hostler! Come away and   23
   be hanged! Come away.   24
SECOND CARRIER   I have a gammon of bacon and two   25
   races of ginger, to be delivered as far as Charing Cross.   26
FIRST CARRIER   God's body, the turkeys in my pannier   27
   are quite starved. What, hostler! A plague on thee!
   Hast thou never an eye in thy head? Canst not hear?
   An 'twere not as good deed as drink to break the pate   30
   on thee, I am a very villain. Come, and be hanged!   31
   Hast no faith in thee?   32

*Enter Gadshill.*

**2.1. Location:** An innyard on the London-Canterbury road.
**0.1 *Carrier*** one whose trade was conveying goods, usually by pack-
horses   **1 An** If.   **by the day** in the morning   **2 Charles's Wain** i.e.,
Charlemagne's wagon; the constellation Ursa Major (the Big Dipper)
**3 horse** horses.   **hostler** groom.   **4 Anon** Right away, coming
**5 beat** soften.   **Cut's saddle** packsaddle of the horse named *Cut*,
meaning "bobtailed"   **6 flocks** tufts of wool.   **point** pommel of the
saddle.   **jade** nag   **6–7 wrung . . . withers** chafed (by his saddle) on
the ridge between his shoulder-blades   **7 cess** measure, estimate.
**8 Peas and beans** i.e., Horse fodder   **8–9 dank . . . dog** i.e., damp as
can be   **9 next** nearest, quickest   **10 bots** intestinal maggots.   **house**
inn   **16 tench** a spotted fish, whose spots may have been likened to
flea bites.   **18 king Christian** Christian king, accustomed to have the
best of everything   **19 first cock** i.e., midnight.   **20 jordan** chamber-
pot   **21 leak . . . chimney** urinate in the fireplace. (*Your* is used idiomatically; *your fireplace* means something like "you know the kind of
fireplace I'm talking about." *Your chamber-lye* in lines 21–2 has the
same idea.)   **22 loach** a small freshwater fish, thought to harbor parasites.   **23–4 Come . . . hanged** i.e., Come along, damn you. (Idiomatic.)   **25 gammon of bacon** ham   **26 races** roots.   **Charing Cross** a
market town lying between London and Westminster.   **27 pannier**
basket   **30 An** If   **30–1 An . . . hanged!** i.e., I'll be hanged if it
wouldn't be a good idea to smack you on the head. Come along,
damn you!   **32 faith** trustworthiness

GADSHILL   Good morrow, carriers. What's o'clock?

FIRST CARRIER   I think it be two o'clock. 34

GADSHILL   I prithee, lend me thy lantern to see my gelding in the stable. 36

FIRST CARRIER   Nay, by God, soft, I know a trick worth 37 two of that, i'faith.

GADSHILL [to the Second Carrier]   I pray thee, lend me thine.

SECOND CARRIER   Ay, when, canst tell? Lend me thy 40 lantern, quoth he! Marry, I'll see thee hanged first. 41

GADSHILL   Sirrah carrier, what time do you mean to come to London?

SECOND CARRIER   Time enough to go to bed with a 44 candle, I warrant thee.—Come, neighbor Mugs, we'll 45 call up the gentlemen. They will along with company, 46 for they have great charge.          Exeunt [Carriers]. 47

GADSHILL   What, ho! Chamberlain! 48

*Enter Chamberlain.*

CHAMBERLAIN   At hand, quoth pickpurse. 49

GADSHILL   That's even as fair as—at hand, quoth the 50 chamberlain; for thou variest no more from picking of 51 purses than giving direction doth from laboring; thou 52 layest the plot how. 53

CHAMBERLAIN   Good morrow, Master Gadshill. It holds 54 current that I told you yesternight: there's a franklin in 55 the Weald of Kent hath brought three hundred marks 56 with him in gold. I heard him tell it to one of his company last night at supper—a kind of auditor, one that hath abundance of charge too, God knows what. They 59 are up already, and call for eggs and butter. They will away presently. 61

GADSHILL   Sirrah, if they meet not with Saint Nicholas' 62 clerks, I'll give thee this neck. 63

CHAMBERLAIN   No, I'll none of it. I pray thee, keep that 64 for the hangman, for I know thou worshipest Saint Nicholas as truly as a man of falsehood may.

GADSHILL   What talkest thou to me of the hangman? If 67 I hang, I'll make a fat pair of gallows; for if I hang, old Sir John hangs with me, and thou knowest he is no starveling. Tut, there are other Trojans that thou 70 dream'st not of, the which for sport sake are content to do the profession some grace, that would, if matters 72

should be looked into, for their own credit sake 73 make all whole. I am joined with no foot-landrakers, 74 no long-staff sixpenny strikers, none of these mad 75 mustachio purple-hued malt-worms, but with nobility 76 and tranquillity, burgomasters and great oneyers, such 77 as can hold in, such as will strike sooner than speak, 78 and speak sooner than drink, and drink sooner than pray. And yet, zounds, I lie, for they pray continually to their saint, the commonwealth, or rather not pray to her but prey on her, for they ride up and down on her and make her their boots. 83

CHAMBERLAIN   What, the commonwealth their boots? Will she hold out water in foul way? 85

GADSHILL   She will, she will. Justice hath liquored her. 86 We steal as in a castle, cocksure. We have the receipt 87 of fern seed; we walk invisible. 88

CHAMBERLAIN   Nay, by my faith, I think you are more beholding to the night than to fern seed for your 90 walking invisible.

GADSHILL   Give me thy hand. Thou shalt have a share in our purchase, as I am a true man. 93

CHAMBERLAIN   Nay, rather let me have it as you are a false thief.

GADSHILL   Go to; *homo* is a common name to all men. 96 Bid the hostler bring my gelding out of the stable. Farewell, you muddy knave.          [*Exeunt separately.*] 98

❧

# [2.2]

*Enter Prince, Poins, Peto, and [Bardolph].*

POINS   Come, shelter, shelter! I have removed Falstaff's horse, and he frets like a gummed velvet. 2

PRINCE   Stand close.          [*They step aside.*] 3

*Enter Falstaff.*

FALSTAFF   Poins! Poins, and be hanged! Poins!

PRINCE [*coming forward*]   Peace, ye fat-kidneyed rascal! What a brawling dost thou keep! 6

FALSTAFF   Where's Poins, Hal?

---

34 **two o'clock** (An evasive answer; the First Carrier knows that it is at least four o'clock; see line 1.)   36 **gelding** castrated male horse   37 **soft** i.e., wait a minute   40 **Ay . . . tell?** i.e., You must be joking. 41 **quoth he** forsooth, indeed.   **Marry** i.e., Indeed   44–5 **Time . . . candle** i.e., Soon enough. (Another evasive answer.)   45 **I warrant thee** I assure you.   46–7 **They . . . charge** i.e., They wish to travel in company, because they have lots of valuable cargo.   48 **Chamberlain** (Male equivalent of a chambermaid. His entrance in the Quarto at line 47 may suggest that he is visible before Gadshill calls for him, giving point to his remark about being "At hand.")   49 **At . . . pickpurse** i.e., I am right beside you, as the pickpurse said to his victim. 50 **fair** good, apt   51–3 **thou variest . . . how** i.e., you don't actually do the stealing, but you give directions, like a master workman to his apprentices.   54–5 **holds current that** holds true what   55 **a franklin** a yeoman owning his own land   56 **Weald** wooded region.   **hath** who has.   **marks** coins of the value of thirteen shillings four pence 59 **charge** valued goods and money   61 **presently** immediately. 62–3 **Saint Nicholas' clerks** highwaymen. (Saint Nicholas was popularly supposed the patron of thieves.)   64 **I'll none** I want none 67 **What** Why   70 **Trojans** i.e., jolly fellows, roisterers   72 **profession** i.e., robbery.   **grace** credit, favor

73–4 **for . . . whole** for the sake of their own reputation will make sure that all goes well. (Gadshill hints that they may be joined by some persons of social importance, such as the Prince.)   74 **foot-landrakers** thieves who travel on foot   75 **long-staff sixpenny strikers** robbers with long staves who would knock down their victims for sixpence 76 **mustachio . . . malt-worms** purple-faced drunkards with huge mustaches   77 **tranquillity** those who lead easy lives.   **oneyers** ones, persons; or perhaps it should read *"oyez"-ers*, court officials whose duty it was to cry "Oyez, oyez!", i.e., "Hear ye, hear ye!" 78 **hold in** keep a secret; hold fast   83 **boots** booty. (With pun on *boots*, "shoes.")   85 **Will . . . way?** Will she let you go dry in muddy roads? i.e., Will she protect you in tight places?   86 **liquored** (1) made waterproof by oiling (2) bribed (3) made drunk   87 **as in a castle** i.e., in complete security.   **receipt** recipe, formula   88 **of fern seed** i.e., of becoming invisible (since fern seed, almost invisible itself, was popularly supposed to render its possessor invisible)   90 **beholding** beholden   93 **purchase** booty   96 **Go to** (An expression of impatience.)   *homo . . . men* the Latin name for man applies to all types; the phrase "true man" applies to me as well as the next man.   98 **muddy** stupid 2.2. **Location: The highway, near Gad's Hill.** 2 **frets** (1) is vexed (2) rubs and frays like *gummed velvet*, velvet made glossy with a stiffening gum   3 **close** concealed.   6 **keep** keep up.

PRINCE   He is walked up to the top of the hill. I'll go seek him.                    [*He steps aside.*]

FALSTAFF   I am accursed to rob in that thief's company. The rascal hath removed my horse and tied him I know not where. If I travel but four foot by the square 12 further afoot, I shall break my wind. Well, I doubt not but to die a fair death for all this, if I scape hanging for 14 killing that rogue. I have forsworn his company hourly any time this two-and-twenty years, and yet I am be-witched with the rogue's company. If the rascal have not given me medicines to make me love him, I'll be 18 hanged; it could not be else—I have drunk medicines. 19 Poins! Hal! A plague upon you both! Bardolph! Peto! I'll starve ere I'll rob a foot further. An 'twere not as 21 good a deed as drink to turn true man and to leave 22 these rogues, I am the veriest varlet that ever chewed 23 with a tooth. Eight yards of uneven ground is three- 24 score-and-ten miles afoot with me, and the stony- 25 hearted villains know it well enough. A plague upon it when thieves cannot be true one to another! (*They whistle.*) Whew! A plague upon you all! Give me my horse, you rogues, give me my horse, and be hanged! 28

PRINCE [*coming forward*]   Peace, ye fat-guts! Lie down. Lay thine ear close to the ground and list if thou 31 canst hear the tread of travelers.

FALSTAFF   Have you any levers to lift me up again, being down? 'Sblood, I'll not bear mine own flesh so far afoot again for all the coin in thy father's Exchequer. 35 What a plague mean ye to colt me thus? 36

PRINCE   Thou liest. Thou art not colted, thou art uncolted.

FALSTAFF   I prithee, good Prince Hal, help me to my 39 horse, good king's son. 40

PRINCE   Out, ye rogue! Shall I be your hostler?

FALSTAFF   Go hang thyself in thine own heir-apparent garters! If I be ta'en, I'll peach for this. An I have not 43 ballads made on you all and sung to filthy tunes, let a cup of sack be my poison. When a jest is so forward, 45 and afoot too! I hate it. 46

*Enter Gadshill.*

GADSHILL   Stand! 47

FALSTAFF   So I do, against my will.

POINS [*coming forward with Bardolph and Peto*]   Oh, 'tis our setter. I know his voice. 50

BARDOLPH   What news?

GADSHILL   Case ye, case ye, on with your vizards! 52

There's money of the King's coming down the hill; 'tis going to the King's Exchequer.

FALSTAFF   You lie, ye rogue, 'tis going to the King's Tavern.

GADSHILL   There's enough to make us all. 57

FALSTAFF   To be hanged.

PRINCE   Sirs, you four shall front them in the narrow 59 lane; Ned Poins and I will walk lower. If they scape 60 from your encounter, then they light on us.

PETO   How many be there of them?

GADSHILL   Some eight or ten.

FALSTAFF   Zounds, will they not rob us?

PRINCE   What, a coward, Sir John Paunch?

FALSTAFF   Indeed, I am not John of Gaunt, your 66 grandfather, but yet no coward, Hal.

PRINCE   Well, we leave that to the proof. 68

POINS   Sirrah Jack, thy horse stands behind the hedge. When thou need'st him, there thou shalt find him. Farewell, and stand fast. 71

FALSTAFF   Now cannot I strike him, if I should be 72 hanged. 73

PRINCE [*to Poins*]   Ned, where are our disguises?

POINS [*to Prince*]   Here, hard by. Stand close. 75
          [*Exeunt Prince and Poins.*]

FALSTAFF   Now, my masters, happy man be his dole, 76 say I. Every man to his business.   [*They stand aside.*]

*Enter the Travelers.*

FIRST TRAVELER   Come, neighbor. The boy shall lead our horses down the hill; we'll walk afoot awhile, and ease our legs.

THIEVES [*coming forward*]   Stand!

TRAVELERS   Jesus bless us!

FALSTAFF   Strike! Down with them! Cut the villains' throats! Ah, whoreson caterpillars, bacon-fed knaves! 84 They hate us youth. Down with them, fleece them!

TRAVELERS   Oh, we are undone, both we and ours for-ever!

FALSTAFF   Hang ye, gorbellied knaves, are ye undone? 88 No, ye fat chuffs; I would your store were here. On, 89 bacons, on! What, ye knaves, young men must live. 90 You are grandjurors, are ye? We'll jure ye, 'faith. 91
          *Here they rob them and bind them. Exeunt.*

*Enter the Prince and Poins [in buckram].*

PRINCE   The thieves have bound the true men. Now could thou and I rob the thieves and go merrily to London, it would be argument for a week, laughter 94 for a month, and a good jest forever.

---

12 **square** a measuring tool   14 **fair** exemplary.   **for all** despite all   18 **medicines** love potions   19 **it . . . else** it can't be anything else   21–4 **An . . . tooth** i.e., If I don't think it's a good idea to reform and turn informer, I'm the damnedest scoundrel that ever lived. (Cf. 2.1.30–1 and n.)   24–5 **three-score-and-ten** seventy   28 **Whew** (Perhaps Falstaff tries to answer the whistling he hears, or mocks it.) 31 **list** listen   35 **Exchequer** treasury   36 **colt** trick, cheat. (In lines 37–8, Prince Hal puns on the common meaning.)   39–40 **help . . . horse** help me to find my horse. (But in line 41, the Prince comically retorts as though having been asked to hold the stirrup while Falstaff mounted, as a hostler would do.)   43 **peach** inform on you   45 **so forward** so far advanced   46 **afoot** (1) in progress (2) on foot, i.e., not on horseback   47 **Stand!** Don't move! (But Falstaff answers in the sense of "stand on one's feet.")   50 **setter** arranger of the robbery. (See 1.2.104–5 and note.)   52 **Case ye** Put on your masks

57 **make us all** make our fortunes (or, as Falstaff sees it, make us be hanged).   59 **front** confront   60 **lower** further downhill.   66 **John of Gaunt** Henry IV's father, born at Ghent (and hence giving Falstaff a chance to pun on *gaunt* as the opposite of his fatness)   68 **proof** test.   71 **stand fast** i.e., do your part.   72–3 **Now . . . hanged** (Falstaff wishes he could hit Poins, who is too quick for him)   75 **Stand close** Keep out of sight.   76 **masters** good sirs.   **happy . . . dole** may happiness be every man's portion or lot.   84 **Ah . . . knaves!** i.e., Ah, you abominable parasites, you over-fed rascals!   88 **gorbellied** big-bellied   89 **chuffs** churls, rich but miserly.   **store** total wealth   90 **bacons** fat men   91 **grandjurors** i.e., men of wealth, able to serve on juries   94 **argument** a subject for conversation

POINS    Stand close. I hear them coming.

*[They stand aside.]*

*Enter the thieves again.*

FALSTAFF    Come, my masters, let us share, and then to    97
horse before day. An the Prince and Poins be not two
arrant cowards, there's no equity stirring. There's no    99
more valor in that Poins than in a wild duck.

*[The thieves begin to share the booty.]*

PRINCE    Your money!

POINS    Villains!

*As they are sharing, the Prince and Poins set upon
them. They all run away, and Falstaff, after a blow
or two, runs away too, leaving the booty behind
them.*

PRINCE

Got with much ease. Now merrily to horse.
The thieves are all scattered and possessed with fear
So strongly that they dare not meet each other;
Each takes his fellow for an officer.
Away, good Ned. Falstaff sweats to death
And lards the lean earth as he walks along.    108
Were't not for laughing, I should pity him.

POINS    How the fat rogue roared!    *Exeunt.*

❖

# [2.3]

*Enter Hotspur, solus, reading a letter.*

HOTSPUR    "But, for mine own part, my lord, I could be
well contented to be there, in respect of the love I bear
your house." He could be contented; why is he not,    3
then? In respect of the love he bears our house! He
shows in this he loves his own barn better than he
loves our house. Let me see some more. "The purpose
you undertake is dangerous"—why, that's certain.
'Tis dangerous to take a cold, to sleep, to drink; but I
tell you, my lord fool, out of this nettle, danger, we
pluck this flower, safety. "The purpose you undertake
is dangerous, the friends you have named uncertain,
the time itself unsorted, and your whole plot too light    12
for the counterpoise of so great an opposition." Say    13
you so, say you so? I say unto you again, you are a
shallow, cowardly hind, and you lie. What a lack-brain    15
is this! By the Lord, our plot is a good plot as ever
was laid, our friends true and constant; a good plot,
good friends, and full of expectation; an excellent plot,    18
very good friends. What a frosty-spirited rogue is
this! Why, my lord of York commends the plot and    20

the general course of the action. Zounds, an I were now    21
by this rascal, I could brain him with his lady's    22
fan. Is there not my father, my uncle, and myself? Lord    23
Edmund Mortimer, my lord of York, and Owen Glendower? Is there not besides the Douglas? Have I not all
their letters to meet me in arms by the ninth of the next
month, and are they not some of them set forward
already? What a pagan rascal is this, an infidel! Ha,    28
you shall see now in very sincerity of fear and
cold heart will he to the King and lay open all our
proceedings. Oh, I could divide myself and go to buf-    31
fets for moving such a dish of skim milk with so hon-    32
orable an action! Hang him, let him tell the King, we
are prepared. I will set forward tonight.

*Enter his Lady.*

How now, Kate? I must leave you within these two
hours.

LADY PERCY

Oh, my good lord, why are you thus alone?
For what offense have I this fortnight been
A banished woman from my Harry's bed?
Tell me, sweet lord, what is't that takes from thee
Thy stomach, pleasure, and thy golden sleep?    41
Why dost thou bend thine eyes upon the earth
And start so often when thou sit'st alone?
Why hast thou lost the fresh blood in thy cheeks
And given my treasures and my rights of thee    45
To thick-eyed musing and curst melancholy?    46
In thy faint slumbers I by thee have watched    47
And heard thee murmur tales of iron wars,    48
Speak terms of manage to thy bounding steed,    49
Cry, "Courage! To the field!" And thou hast talked
Of sallies and retires, of trenches, tents,    51
Of palisadoes, frontiers, parapets,    52
Of basilisks, of cannon, culverin,    53
Of prisoners' ransom, and of soldiers slain,
And all the currents of a heady fight.    55
Thy spirit within thee hath been so at war,
And thus hath so bestirred thee in thy sleep,
That beads of sweat have stood upon thy brow
Like bubbles in a late-disturbèd stream,    59
And in thy face strange motions have appeared,
Such as we see when men restrain their breath
On some great sudden hest. Oh, what portents are
    these?    62
Some heavy business hath my lord in hand,
And I must know it, else he loves me not.

---

97 **masters** good sirs    99 **arrant** notorious, unmitigated.    **equity**
judgment, discernment    108 **lards** drips fat on, bastes
**2.3. Location: Hotspur's estate (identified historically as Warkworth
Castle in Northumberland).**
0.1 *solus* alone    3 **house** family. (But Hotspur replies derisively in
lines 4–6 as though to the literal sense of a building that one might
compare to a barn.)    12 **unsorted** unsuitable    13 **for . . . of** to counterbalance    15 **hind** menial, peasant    18 **expectation** promise
20 **lord of York** i.e., Archbishop Scroop. (Also in line 24.)

21–2 **an . . . rascal** if I were face to face with this rascal, instead of
reading his letter    22–3 **his lady's fan** his wife's fan—a suitable light
weapon with which to chastise such a milktoast.    28 **pagan** unbelieving    31–2 **divide . . . buffets** i.e., fight with myself    32 **moving** urging
41 **stomach** appetite    45 **And . . . thee** and given the precious right I
have as wife to share your thoughts    46 **thick-eyed** dull-sighted,
vacant, abstracted.    **curst** ill-tempered    47 **faint** restless.    **watched**
lain awake    48 **iron** steely, unrelenting    49 **manage** horsemanship
51 **sallies** swift military sorties.    **retires** retreats    52–3 **Of . . .
culverin** of stakes set in the ground for defense, of ramparts,
protective walls, of large and smaller cannon    55 **heady** headlong
59 **late-disturbèd** recently stirred up    62 **hest** command; endeavor.

HOTSPUR [*calling*]
What, ho!

[*Enter a Servant.*]

Is Gilliams with the packet gone?                              65
SERVANT   He is, my lord, an hour ago.
HOTSPUR
Hath Butler brought those horses from the sheriff?            67
SERVANT
One horse, my lord, he brought even now.                      68
HOTSPUR
What horse? A roan, a crop-ear, is it not?                    69
SERVANT
It is, my lord.
HOTSPUR          That roan shall be my throne.
Well, I will back him straight. Oh, *Esperance!*              71
Bid Butler lead him forth into the park.

[*Exit Servant.*]

LADY PERCY   But hear you, my lord.
HOTSPUR   What say'st thou, my lady?
LADY PERCY   What is it carries you away?                     75
HOTSPUR   Why, my horse, my love, my horse.
LADY PERCY   Out, you mad-headed ape!                         77
A weasel hath not such a deal of spleen                       78
As you are tossed with. In faith,                             79
I'll know your business, Harry, that I will.
I fear my brother Mortimer doth stir
About his title, and hath sent for you                        82
To line his enterprise; but if you go—                        83
HOTSPUR
So far afoot, I shall be weary, love.
LADY PERCY
Come, come, you paraquito, answer me                          85
Directly unto this question that I ask.
In faith, I'll break thy little finger, Harry,
An if thou wilt not tell me all things true.                  88
HOTSPUR   Away,
Away, you trifler! Love? I love thee not;
I care not for thee, Kate. This is no world
To play with mammets and to tilt with lips.                   92
We must have bloody noses and cracked crowns,                 93
And pass them current too. Gods me, my horse!                 94
What say'st thou, Kate? What wouldst thou have with
me?
LADY PERCY
Do you not love me? Do you not, indeed?
Well, do not, then, for since you love me not

I will not love myself. Do you not love me?
Nay, tell me if you speak in jest or no.
HOTSPUR   Come, wilt thou see me ride?
And when I am a-horseback I will swear
I love thee infinitely. But hark you, Kate,
I must not have you henceforth question me
Whither I go, nor reason whereabout.                          104
Whither I must, I must; and, to conclude,
This evening must I leave you, gentle Kate.
I know you wise, but yet no farther wise
Than Harry Percy's wife; constant you are,
But yet a woman; and for secrecy,
No lady closer, for I well believe                            110
Thou wilt not utter what thou dost not know,
And so far will I trust thee, gentle Kate.
LADY PERCY   How, so far?
HOTSPUR
Not an inch further. But hark you, Kate:
Whither I go, thither shall you go too.
Today will I set forth, tomorrow you.
Will this content you, Kate?
LADY PERCY          It must, of force.   *Exeunt.*   117

# [2.4]

*Enter Prince and Poins.*

PRINCE   Ned, prithee, come out of that fat room, and         1
lend me thy hand to laugh a little.
POINS   Where hast been, Hal?
PRINCE   With three or four loggerheads amongst three         4
or four score hogsheads. I have sounded the very bass         5
string of humility. Sirrah, I am sworn brother to a leash     6
of drawers, and can call them all by their Christian          7
names, as Tom, Dick, and Francis. They take it already        8
upon their salvation that, though I be but Prince of          9
Wales, yet I am the king of courtesy, and tell me flatly
I am no proud Jack like Falstaff, but a Corinthian, a lad    11
of mettle, a good boy—by the Lord, so they call me!—
and when I am King of England I shall command all
the good lads in Eastcheap. They call drinking deep          14
"dyeing scarlet"; and when you breathe in your water-        15
ing they cry "hem!" and bid you "play it off." To con-       16
clude, I am so good a proficient in one quarter of an
hour that I can drink with any tinker in his own language during my life. I tell thee, Ned, thou hast lost
much honor that thou wert not with me in this action.

65 **the packet** a message that Hotspur is sending   67 **sheriff** i.e., bailiff.   68 **even** just   69 **roan** roan-colored, i.e., with white or grey
interspersed in the overall color of the coat   71 **back** mount.
*Esperance* Hope. (The motto of the Percy family.)   75 **carries you
away** carries you beyond the bounds of reason and judgment. (But
Hotspur puns on the literal meaning.)   77 **Out** (An expression of
impatience.)   78 **spleen** (The spleen was thought to be the source of
impulsive and irritable behavior.)   79 **tossed** tossed about, agitated
82 **title** claim to the throne   83 **line** strengthen   85 **paraquito** little
parrot. (A term of endearment, suggestive of loquaciousness.)
88 **An if** if   92 **mammets** dolls. (With a quibble on the Latin *mamma*
meaning "breast.")   93 **crowns** (1) heads (2) coins worth five
shillings. (Cracked coins would not "pass current," as Hotspur jokes
in the next line.)   94 **Gods me** God save me

104 **reason whereabout** ask about what.   110 **closer** more close-
mouthed   117 **of force** perforce, of necessity.
**2.4. Location: A tavern in Eastcheap, London, usually identified
as the Boar's Head. Some tavern furniture, including stools, is
provided onstage.**
1 **fat** stuffy, or, a vat room   4 **loggerheads** blockheads   5 **hogsheads**
wine barrels.   **bass** (With a pun on *base*.)   6 **sworn brother** i.e.,
bound by sacred oaths of loyalty   6–7 **leash of drawers** three waiters
8–9 **take . . . salvation** already maintain it as they hope to be
saved   11 **Jack** (1) Jack Falstaff (2) fellow.   **Corinthian** i.e., gay
blade, good sport. (Corinth was reputed to be licentious.)
14–15 **They . . . scarlet** (Either because excessive drinking causes a red
complexion or because urine, produced by *drinking deep*, was sometimes used for fixing dyes.)   15–16 **breathe . . . watering** pause for
breath in your drinking   16 **play it off** drink it up.

But, sweet Ned—to sweeten which name of Ned, I give thee this pennyworth of sugar, clapped even now 22 into my hand by an underskinker, one that never 23 spake other English in his life than "Eight shillings and sixpence," and "You are welcome," with this shrill addition, "Anon, anon, sir! Score a pint of bas- 26 tard in the Half-Moon," or so. But, Ned, to drive away 27 the time till Falstaff come, I prithee do thou stand in some by-room while I question my puny drawer to 29 what end he gave me the sugar; and do thou never leave calling "Francis," that his tale to me may be 31 nothing but "Anon." Step aside, and I'll show thee a precedent.                                              [Exit Poins.] 33

POINS [within]   Francis!
PRINCE   Thou art perfect.
POINS [within]   Francis!

*Enter [Francis, a] drawer.*

FRANCIS   Anon, anon, sir.—Look down into the Pom- 37
garnet, Ralph.                                                         38
PRINCE   Come hither, Francis.
FRANCIS   My lord?
PRINCE   How long hast thou to serve, Francis?      41
FRANCIS   Forsooth, five years, and as much as to—  42
POINS [within]   Francis!
FRANCIS [calling]   Anon, anon, sir.
PRINCE   Five year! By'r Lady, a long lease for the 45
clinking of pewter. But Francis, darest thou be so valiant as to play the coward with thy indenture and 47 show it a fair pair of heels and run from it?
FRANCIS   Oh, Lord, sir, I'll be sworn upon all the books 49 in England, I could find in my heart—
POINS [within]   Francis!
FRANCIS [calling]   Anon, sir.
PRINCE   How old art thou, Francis?
FRANCIS   Let me see, about Michaelmas next I shall 54 be—
POINS [within]   Francis!
FRANCIS [calling]   Anon, sir. Pray, stay a little, my lord.
PRINCE   Nay, but hark you, Francis: for the sugar thou 57 gavest me, 'twas a pennyworth, was 't not?
FRANCIS   Oh, Lord, I would it had been two!
PRINCE   I will give thee for it a thousand pound. Ask me when thou wilt, and thou shalt have it.
POINS [within]   Francis!
FRANCIS [calling]   Anon, anon.
PRINCE   Anon, Francis? No, Francis; but tomorrow, Francis, or, Francis, o'Thursday, or indeed, Francis, when thou wilt. But, Francis—
FRANCIS   My lord?

PRINCE   Wilt thou rob this leathern-jerkin, crystal- 69
button, not-pated, agate-ring, puke-stocking, caddis- 70
garter, smooth-tongue, Spanish-pouch—                      71
FRANCIS   Oh, Lord, sir, who do you mean?
PRINCE   Why, then, your brown bastard is your only 73
drink; for look you, Francis, your white canvas 74
doublet will sully. In Barbary, sir, it cannot come to so 75
much.                                                                          76
FRANCIS   What, sir?
POINS [within]   Francis!
PRINCE   Away, you rogue! Dost thou not hear them call? 79
*Here they both call him; the drawer stands
amazed, not knowing which way to go.*

*Enter Vintner.*

VINTNER   What stand'st thou still and hear'st such a 80
calling? Look to the guests within.      [Exit Francis.]
My lord, old Sir John, with half a dozen more, are at the
door. Shall I let them in?
PRINCE   Let them alone awhile, and then open the door. 84
[Exit Vintner.]

[Calling]   Poins!

*Enter Poins.*

POINS   Anon, anon, sir.
PRINCE   Sirrah, Falstaff and the rest of the thieves are at the door. Shall we be merry?
POINS   As merry as crickets, my lad. But hark ye, what cunning match have you made with this jest of the 90 drawer? Come, what's the issue?                          91
PRINCE   I am now of all humors that have showed 92
themselves humors since the old days of Goodman 93
Adam to the pupil age of this present twelve o'clock at 94
midnight.                                                                      95

[*Enter Francis, hurrying across the stage with
wine.*]

What's o'clock, Francis?
FRANCIS   Anon, anon, sir.                              [Exit.]
PRINCE   That ever this fellow should have fewer words than a parrot, and yet the son of a woman! His indus-
try is upstairs and downstairs, his eloquence the parcel 100 of a reckoning. I am not yet of Percy's mind, the Hot- 101 spur of the north, he that kills me some six or seven 102 dozen of Scots at a breakfast, washes his hands, and says to his wife, "Fie upon this quiet life! I want work." "Oh, my sweet Harry," says she, "how many

---

22 **sugar** (Used to sweeten wine.)   23 **underskinker** assistant to a waiter or bartender   26–7 **Anon . . . Half-Moon** Coming, sir!—Charge a pint of a sweet Spanish wine to the customers in the room of the inn called "the Half-Moon."   29 **by-room** side-room.   **puny drawer** inexperienced tapster or bartender   31 **leave** leave off 33 **precedent** example.   37–8 **Pomgarnet** Pomegranate. (Another room in the inn.)   41 **serve** i.e., serve out your apprenticeship 42 **Forsooth** Truly   45 **By'r Lady** By Our Lady   47 **indenture** contract of apprenticeship   49 **books** i.e., Bibles   54 **Michaelmas** September 29   57 **for** as for, concerning

69–71 **Wilt . . . Spanish-pouch** i.e., Will you rob your master of your services by running away, this man with his leather jacket, transparent buttons, cropped hair, a ring with small figures in an agate stone for a seal, dark woolen stockings, worsted garters, an ingratiating flattering manner of speech, wallet of Spanish leather 73–6 **Why . . . much** (The Prince talks seeming nonsense in order to bewilder Francis, but he also implies that Francis should stick to his trade, since he will not cut much of a figure in the world.)   75 **it** i.e., sugar   79.3 *Vintner* i.e., Innkeeper.   80 **What** Why   84 **Let them alone** Let them be   90 **match** game, contest   91 **issue** outcome, point.   92–5 **I . . . midnight** i.e., I'm now in a mood for anything that has happened in the whole history of the world.   93 **Goodman** (Title for a yeoman.)   94 **pupil** youthful   100–1 **parcel . . . reckoning** items of a bill.   102 **kills me** i.e., kills. (*Me* is used colloquially.)

hast thou killed today?" "Give my roan horse a drench," says he, and answers, " Some fourteen," an *hour* after, "a trifle, a trifle." I prithee, call in Falstaff. I'll play Percy, and that damned brawn shall play Dame Mortimer his wife. "Rivo!" says the drunkard. Call in ribs, call in tallow. [107] [109] [110] [111]

*Enter Falstaff, [Gadshill, Bardolph, and Peto; Francis following with wine].*

POINS    Welcome, Jack. Where hast thou been?

FALSTAFF    A plague of all cowards, I say, and a vengeance too! Marry and amen! Give me a cup of sack, boy. Ere I lead this life long, I'll sew netherstocks, and mend them and foot them too. A plague of all cowards! Give me a cup of sack, rogue. Is there no virtue extant?               *He drinketh.* [113] [115] [116]

PRINCE    Didst thou never see Titan kiss a dish of butter, pitiful-hearted Titan, that melted at the sweet tale of the sun's? If thou didst, then behold that compound. [119] [120] [121]

FALSTAFF    You rogue, here's lime in this sack too. There is nothing but roguery to be found in villainous man, yet a coward is worse than a cup of sack with lime in it. A villainous coward! Go thy ways, old Jack, die when thou wilt. If manhood, good manhood, be not forgot upon the face of the earth, then am I a shotten herring. There lives not three good men unhanged in England, and one of them is fat and grows old, God help the while! A bad world, I say. I would I were a weaver; I could sing psalms or anything. A plague of all cowards, I say still. [122] [127] [128] [130] [131]

PRINCE    How now, woolsack, what mutter you? [133]

FALSTAFF    A king's son! If I do not beat thee out of thy kingdom with a dagger of lath, and drive all thy subjects afore thee like a flock of wild geese, I'll never wear hair on my face more. You, Prince of Wales! [135] [136] [137]

PRINCE    Why, you whoreson round man, what's the matter?

FALSTAFF    Are not you a coward? Answer me to that. And Poins there?

POINS    Zounds, ye fat paunch, an ye call me coward, by the Lord, I'll stab thee.

FALSTAFF    I call thee coward? I'll see thee damned ere I call thee coward, but I would give a thousand pound I could run as fast as thou canst. You are straight enough in the shoulders; you care not who sees your back. Call you that backing of your friends? A plague upon such backing! Give me them that will face me.

Give me a cup of sack. I am a rogue if I drunk today.

PRINCE    Oh, villain, thy lips are scarce wiped since thou drunk'st last.

FALSTAFF    All is one for that. (*He drinketh.*) A plague of all cowards, still say I. [153]

PRINCE    What's the matter?

FALSTAFF    What's the matter? There be four of us here have ta'en a thousand pound this day morning. [157]

PRINCE    Where is it, Jack, where is it?

FALSTAFF    Where is it? Taken from us it is. A hundred upon poor four of us.

PRINCE    What, a hundred, man?

FALSTAFF    I am a rogue if I were not at half-sword with a dozen of them two hours together. I have scaped by miracle. I am eight times thrust through the doublet, four through the hose, my buckler cut through and through, my sword hacked like a handsaw—*ecce signum!* I never dealt better since I was a man. All would not do. A plague of all cowards! Let them speak. If they speak more or less than truth, they are villains and the sons of darkness. [162] [163] [164] [165] [166] [167] [168]

PRINCE    Speak, sirs, how was it?

GADSHILL    We four set upon some dozen—

FALSTAFF    Sixteen at least, my lord.

GADSHILL    And bound them.

PETO    No, no, they were not bound.

FALSTAFF    You rogue, they were bound, every man of them, or I am a Jew else, an Hebrew Jew.

GADSHILL    As we were sharing, some six or seven fresh men set upon us—

FALSTAFF    And unbound the rest, and then come in the other. [181]

PRINCE    What, fought you with them all?

FALSTAFF    All? I know not what you call all, but if I fought not with fifty of them, I am a bunch of radish. If there were not two- or three-and-fifty upon poor old Jack, then am I no two-legged creature.

PRINCE    Pray God you have not murdered some of them.

FALSTAFF    Nay, that's past praying for. I have peppered two of them. Two I am sure I have paid, two rogues in buckram suits. I tell thee what, Hal, if I tell thee a lie, spit in my face, call me horse. Thou knowest my old ward. Here I lay, and thus I bore my point. [*He demonstrates his stance.*] Four rogues in buckram let drive at me— [192]

PRINCE    What, four? Thou said'st but two even now. [195]

FALSTAFF    Four, Hal, I told thee four.

POINS    Ay, ay, he said four.

FALSTAFF    These four came all afront, and mainly thrust at me. I made me no more ado but took all their seven points in my target, thus. [198] [199] [200]

---

**107 drench** draft (sometimes of medicine).   **says he** i.e., he tells a servant   **109 brawn** fat boar   **110 Rivo** (An exclamation of uncertain meaning, but related to drinking.)   **111 ribs** rib roast.   **tallow** fat drippings.   **113 of** on   **115–16 netherstocks** stockings (the sewing or mending of which is a menial occupation)   **116 foot** make a new foot for   **119 Titan** i.e., the sun   **120 that** i.e., the butter   **121 compound** melting butter, i.e., Falstaff.   **122 lime in this sack** i.e., lime added to make the wine sparkle   **127–8 a shotten herring** a herring that has cast its roe and is consequently thin.   **130 the while** i.e., in these bad times.   **131 weaver** (Many psalm-singing Protestant immigrants from the Low Countries were weavers.)   **133 woolsack** bale of wool   **135 dagger of lath** (The Vice, a stock comic figure in morality plays, was so armed.)   **136–7 I'll . . . more** i.e., I'll forswear manhood, signified by my beard.

**153 All . . . that** No matter.   **157 have** who have.   **this day morning** this morning.   **162 at half-sword** i.e., fighting at close quarters   **163 scaped** escaped   **164 doublet** Elizabethan upper garment like a jacket   **165 hose** close-fitting breeches.   **buckler** shield   **166–7 ecce signum** behold the proof. (Familiar words from the Mass.)   **167–8 All . . . do** All that I did was of no avail.   **181 other** others.   **192 ward** defensive stance, parry.   **lay** stood   **195 even** just   **198 afront** abreast.   **mainly** powerfully   **199 made me** made. (*Me* is used colloquially.)   **200 target** shield

PRINCE   Seven? Why, there were but four even now.

FALSTAFF   In buckram?

POINS   Ay, four, in buckram suits.

FALSTAFF   Seven, by these hilts, or I am a villain else.   204

PRINCE [aside to Poins]   Prithee, let him alone. We shall have more anon.

FALSTAFF   Dost thou hear me, Hal?

PRINCE   Ay, and mark thee too, Jack.   208

FALSTAFF   Do so, for it is worth the listening to. These nine in buckram that I told thee of—

PRINCE   So, two more already.

FALSTAFF   Their points being broken—   212

POINS   Down fell their hose.

FALSTAFF   Began to give me ground; but I followed 214 me close, came in foot and hand; and with a thought 215 seven of the eleven I paid.

PRINCE   Oh, monstrous! Eleven buckram men grown out of two!

FALSTAFF   But, as the devil would have it, three mis- 219 begotten knaves in Kendal green came at my back 220 and let drive at me; for it was so dark, Hal, that thou couldst not see thy hand.

PRINCE   These lies are like their father that begets them, 223 gross as a mountain, open, palpable. Why, thou claybrained guts, thou knotty-pated fool, thou whore- 225 son, obscene, greasy tallow-keech—   226

FALSTAFF   What, art thou mad? Art thou mad? Is not the truth the truth?

PRINCE   Why, how couldst thou know these men in Kendal green when it was so dark thou couldst not see thy hand? Come, tell us your reason. What sayest thou to this?

POINS   Come, your reason, Jack, your reason.

FALSTAFF   What, upon compulsion? Zounds, an I were at the strappado, or all the racks in the world, I would 235 not tell you on compulsion. Give you a reason on com- pulsion? If reasons were as plentiful as blackberries, 237 I would give no man a reason upon compulsion, I.

PRINCE   I'll be no longer guilty of this sin. This sanguine 239 coward, this bed-presser, this horse-backbreaker, this huge hill of flesh—

FALSTAFF   'Sblood, you starveling, you eel-skin, you dried neat's tongue, you bull's pizzle, you stockfish! 243 Oh, for breath to utter what is like thee! You tailor's 244 yard, you sheath, you bowcase, you vile standing 245 tuck—   246

PRINCE   Well, breathe awhile, and then to it again, and when thou hast tired thyself in base comparisons, hear me speak but this.

POINS   Mark, Jack.

PRINCE   We two saw you four set on four and bound them, and were masters of their wealth. Mark now how a plain tale shall put you down. Then did we two set on you four, and, with a word, outfaced you from 254 your prize, and have it, yea, and can show it you here in the house. And, Falstaff, you carried your guts away as nimbly, with as quick dexterity, and roared for mercy, and still run and roared, as ever I heard bull calf. What a slave art thou, to hack thy sword as thou 259 hast done, and then say it was in fight! What trick, what device, what starting-hole canst thou now find 261 out to hide thee from this open and apparent shame?

POINS   Come, let's hear, Jack. What trick hast thou now?

FALSTAFF   By the Lord, I knew ye as well as he that made ye. Why, hear you, my masters, was it for me to kill the heir apparent? Should I turn upon the true prince? Why, thou knowest I am as valiant as Her- cules, but beware instinct. The lion will not touch the true prince. Instinct is a great matter; I was now a coward on instinct. I shall think the better of myself and thee during my life—I for a valiant lion, and thou for a true prince. But by the Lord, lads, I am glad you have the money. Hostess, clap to the doors! Watch 273 tonight, pray tomorrow. Gallants, lads, boys, hearts 274 of gold, all the titles of good fellowship come to you! What, shall we be merry? Shall we have a play extempore?

PRINCE   Content; and the argument shall be thy run- 278 ning away.

FALSTAFF   Ah, no more of that, Hal, an thou lovest me!

*Enter Hostess.*

HOSTESS   Oh, Jesu, my lord the Prince!

PRINCE   How now, my lady the hostess, what say'st thou to me?

HOSTESS   Marry, my lord, there is a nobleman of the court at door would speak with you. He says he comes from your father.

PRINCE   Give him as much as will make him a royal 287 man, and send him back again to my mother.   288

FALSTAFF   What manner of man is he?

HOSTESS   An old man.

FALSTAFF   What doth Gravity out of his bed at mid- 291 night? Shall I give him his answer?

PRINCE   Prithee, do, Jack.

FALSTAFF   Faith, and I'll send him packing.   *Exit.*

PRINCE   Now, sirs. By'r Lady, you fought fair; so did you, Peto; so did you, Bardolph. You are lions too, you ran away upon instinct, you will not touch the true prince; no, fie!

BARDOLPH   Faith, I ran when I saw others run.

204 **by these hilts** by my sword hilt   208 **mark** (1) pay heed (2) keep count   212 **points** sword points. (But Poins puns on the sense of laces, by which the hose were attached to the doublet.)   214–5 **followed me** followed   215 **foot and hand** i.e., advancing with weapon in hand. **with a thought** quick as a thought   219–20 **misbegotten** i.e., bastard, worthless   220 **Kendal** a town known for its textiles   223 **their father** (1) Falstaff (2) the devil, proverbially the father of lies   225 **knotty-pated** thickheaded   226 **tallow-keech** lump of tallow   235 **strappado** a kind of torture   237 **reasons . . . blackberries** (Falstaff puns on *raisins*, pro- nounced nearly like *reasons*.)   239 **sanguine** ruddy   243 **neat's** ox's. **pizzle** penis. **stockfish** dried cod.   244–6 **You tailor's . . . tuck** You tailor's yardstick, you empty weaponcase, you long and thin case for the bow to a stringed instrument, you worthless rapier. (Tailors were often laughed at for supposed effeminacy; "standing" plays on the idea of an erection.)

254 **with a word** (1) in a word (2) with a minimum of speech.   **out- faced** frightened   259 **slave** i.e., wretch   261 **starting-hole** place of shelter (like a rabbit's hole)   273 **clap to** shut.   **Watch** (1) Keep watchful vigil. (See Matthew 26:41.) (2) Carouse   274 **pray** (1) pray to God (2) prey   278 **argument** plot of the play   287–8 **Give . . . man** (Prince Hal puns on the value of coins: a *noble* was worth six shillings eight pence; a *royal* was worth ten shillings.)   291 **What doth** Why is

PRINCE  Faith, tell me now in earnest, how came Falstaff's sword so hacked?

PETO  Why, he hacked it with his dagger, and said he would swear truth out of England but he would make 303 you believe it was done in fight, and persuaded us to do the like.

BARDOLPH  Yea, and to tickle our noses with spear grass to make them bleed, and then to beslubber our gar- 307 ments with it and swear it was the blood of true men. I did that I did not this seven year before: I blushed to 309 hear his monstrous devices.

PRINCE  Oh, villain, thou stolest a cup of sack eighteen years ago and wert taken with the manner, and ever 312 since thou hast blushed extempore. Thou hadst fire 313 and sword on thy side, and yet thou ran'st away. What instinct hadst thou for it?

BARDOLPH  My lord, do you see these meteors? Do you 316 behold these exhalations?  [Pointing to his own face.] 317

PRINCE  I do.

BARDOLPH  What think you they portend? 319

PRINCE  Hot livers and cold purses. 320

BARDOLPH  Choler, my lord, if rightly taken. 321

PRINCE  No, if rightly taken, halter. 322

*Enter Falstaff.*

Here comes lean Jack, here comes bare-bone.—How 323 now, my sweet creature of bombast? How long is't 324 ago, Jack, since thou sawest thine own knee?

FALSTAFF  My own knee? When I was about thy years, Hal, I was not an eagle's talon in the waist; I could have crept into any alderman's thumb ring. A plague of sighing and grief! It blows a man up like a bladder. There's villainous news abroad. Here was Sir John Bracy from your father. You must to the court in the morning. That same mad fellow of the north, Percy, and he of Wales that gave Amamon the bastinado and 333 made Lucifer cuckold and swore the devil his true 334 liegeman upon the cross of a Welsh hook— what a 335 plague call you him? 336

POINS  Owen Glendower.

FALSTAFF  Owen, Owen, the same; and his son-in-law Mortimer, and old Northumberland, and that sprightly Scot of Scots, Douglas, that runs a-horseback up a hill perpendicular—

PRINCE  He that rides at high speed, and with his pistol kills a sparrow flying.

FALSTAFF  You have hit it. 344

PRINCE  So did he never the sparrow.

FALSTAFF  Well, that rascal hath good mettle in him; he will not run. 347

PRINCE  Why, what a rascal art thou then to praise him so for running!

FALSTAFF  A-horseback, ye cuckoo; but afoot he will not budge a foot.

PRINCE  Yes, Jack, upon instinct.

FALSTAFF  I grant ye, upon instinct. Well, he is there too, and one Mordake, and a thousand blue-caps more. 354 Worcester is stolen away tonight. Thy father's beard is turned white with the news. You may buy land now as cheap as stinking mackerel.

PRINCE  Why, then, it is like, if there come a hot June 358 and this civil buffeting hold, we shall buy maiden- 359 heads as they buy hobnails, by the hundreds.

FALSTAFF  By the mass, lad, thou sayest true; it is like we shall have good trading that way. But tell me, Hal, 362 art not thou horrible afeard? Thou being heir appar-ent, could the world pick thee out three such enemies again as that fiend Douglas, that spirit Percy, and that devil Glendower? Art thou not horribly afraid? Doth not thy blood thrill at it?

PRINCE  Not a whit, i'faith. I lack some of thy instinct.

FALSTAFF  Well, thou wilt be horribly chid tomorrow 369 when thou comest to thy father. If thou love me, practice an answer.

PRINCE  Do thou stand for my father, and examine me upon the particulars of my life.

FALSTAFF  Shall I? Content. This chair shall be my state, 374 this dagger my scepter, and this cushion my crown. [Falstaff establishes himself on his "throne."]

PRINCE  Thy state is taken for a joint stool, thy golden 376 scepter for a leaden dagger, and thy precious rich 377 crown for a pitiful bald crown.

FALSTAFF  Well, an the fire of grace be not quite out of thee, now shalt thou be moved. Give me a cup of sack to make my eyes look red, that it may be thought I have wept; for I must speak in passion, and I will do it in King Cambyses' vein. 383

PRINCE  Well, here is my leg.  [He bows.]

FALSTAFF  And here is my speech. Stand aside, nobil-ity.

HOSTESS  Oh, Jesu, this is excellent sport, i'faith!

FALSTAFF

Weep not, sweet queen, for trickling tears are vain.

HOSTESS  Oh, the Father, how he holds his countenance! 389

---

303 **swear . . . would** swear oaths until they go out of fashion if he did not  307 **beslubber** smear, cover  309 **that** something  312 **taken . . . manner** caught with the goods  313 **extempore** without needing any occasion. (Bardolph is red-faced whether he blushes or not.) **fire** i.e., a red nose and complexion caused by heavy drinking 316, 317 **meteors, exhalations** i.e., the red blotches on Bardolph's face. 319 **portend** signify. (Meteors, comets, and other meteorological phe-nomena were widely regarded as omens of disaster.)  320 **Hot . . . purses** i.e., Livers inflamed by drink and purses made empty by spending.  321 **Choler** A choleric or combative temperament. **taken** understood. (But the Prince, in his next speech, uses the word to mean "arrested.")  322 **halter** hangman's noose. (The Prince plays on Bardolph's *choler,* which he takes as *collar.*)  323 **Lean Jack, bare bone** (Ironic allusions to Falstaff's excessive girth.)  324 **bombast** (1) cotton padding (2) fustian speech.  333 **Amamon** (The name of a demon.) **bastinado** beating on the soles of the feet  334 **made . . . cuckold** i.e., gave Lucifer his horns, the sign of cuckoldry  334–5 **and swore . . . liegeman** and made the devil take an oath of allegiance as a true subject  335 **Welsh hook** curved-bladed pike lacking the cross shape of the sword on which such oaths were usually sworn 335–6 **what a plague** i.e., what the devil

344 **hit it** described it exactly. (But the Prince takes *hit* literally in the next line.)  347 **run** flee. (But the Prince answers punningly in the sense of "ride at high speed.")  354 **blue-caps** Scottish soldiers  358 **like** likely  359 **hold** continues  362 **trading** dealings  369 **chid** chided 374 **state** chair of state, throne  376 **joint stool** a stool made by a joiner or furniture maker  377 **leaden** of soft metal, hence inferior  383 **in . . . vein** i.e., in the ranting and (by Shakespeare's time) old-fashioned style of Thomas Preston's *Cambyses,* an early Elizabethan tragedy. 389 **the Father** i.e., in God's name.  **holds his countenance** keeps a straight face.

FALSTAFF
For God's sake, lords, convey my tristful queen,    390
For tears do stop the floodgates of her eyes.    391
HOSTESS    Oh, Jesu, he doth it as like one of these harlotry    392
players as ever I see!    393
FALSTAFF
Peace, good pint pot; peace, good tickle-brain.—    394
Harry, I do not only marvel where thou spendest thy
time, but also how thou art accompanied; for though    396
the camomile, the more it is trodden on the faster it    397
grows, yet youth, the more it is wasted the sooner it    398
wears. That thou art my son I have partly thy mother's    399
word, partly my own opinion, but chiefly a villainous
trick of thine eye and a foolish hanging of thy nether    401
lip that doth warrant me. If then thou be son to me,    402
here lies the point: why, being son to me, art thou so
pointed at? Shall the blessed sun of heaven prove a
micher and eat blackberries? A question not to be    405
asked. Shall the son of England prove a thief and take
purses? A question to be asked. There is a thing, Harry,
which thou hast often heard of, and it is known
to many in our land by the name of pitch. This pitch,    409
as ancient writers do report, doth defile; so doth the    410
company thou keepest. For, Harry, now I do not speak
to thee in drink but in tears, not in pleasure but in
passion, not in words only but in woes also. And yet    413
there is a virtuous man whom I have often noted in
thy company, but I know not his name.
PRINCE    What manner of man, an it like Your Majesty?    416
FALSTAFF    A goodly portly man, i'faith, and a corpulent;    417
of a cheerful look, a pleasing eye, and a most noble
carriage; and, as I think, his age some fifty, or, by'r
Lady, inclining to threescore; and now I remember me,    420
his name is Falstaff. If that man should be lewdly    421
given, he deceiveth me; for, Harry, I see virtue in his
looks. If then the tree may be known by the fruit, as the    423
fruit by the tree, then peremptorily I speak it, there is    424
virtue in that Falstaff. Him keep with, the rest banish.
And tell me now, thou naughty varlet, tell me, where
hast thou been this month?
PRINCE    Dost thou speak like a king? Do thou stand for
me, and I'll play my father.
FALSTAFF    Depose me? If thou dost it half so gravely, so
majestically, both in word and matter, hang me up by
the heels for a rabbit-sucker or a poulter's hare.    432
[Hal takes Falstaff's place on the "throne."]

PRINCE    Well, here I am set.    433
FALSTAFF    And here I stand. Judge, my masters.    434
PRINCE    Now, Harry, whence come you?
FALSTAFF    My noble lord, from Eastcheap.
PRINCE    The complaints I hear of thee are grievous.
FALSTAFF    'Sblood, my lord, they are false.— Nay, I'll    438
tickle ye for a young prince, i'faith.    439
PRINCE    Swearest thou, ungracious boy? Henceforth
ne'er look on me. Thou art violently carried away from
grace. There is a devil haunts thee in the likeness of an
old fat man; a tun of man is thy companion. Why dost    443
thou converse with that trunk of humors, that bolting-    444
hutch of beastliness, that swollen parcel of dropsies,    445
that huge bombard of sack, that stuffed cloak-bag of    446
guts, that roasted Manningtree ox with the pudding in    447
his belly, that reverend Vice, that gray Iniquity, that    448
father ruffian, that vanity in years? Wherein is he good    449
but to taste sack and drink it? Wherein neat and
cleanly but to carve a capon and eat it? Wherein    451
cunning but in craft? Wherein crafty but in villainy?    452
Wherein villainous but in all things? Wherein worthy
but in nothing?
FALSTAFF    I would Your Grace would take me with    455
you. Whom means Your Grace?    456
PRINCE    That villainous abominable misleader of youth,
Falstaff, that old white-bearded Satan.
FALSTAFF    My lord, the man I know.
PRINCE    I know thou dost.
FALSTAFF    But to say I know more harm in him than in
myself were to say more than I know. That he is old,
the more the pity, his white hairs do witness it; but
that he is, saving your reverence, a whoremaster, that    464
I utterly deny. If sack and sugar be a fault, God help
the wicked! If to be old and merry be a sin, then many
an old host that I know is damned. If to be fat be to be    467
hated, then Pharaoh's lean kine are to be loved. No,    468
my good lord, banish Peto, banish Bardolph, banish
Poins; but for sweet Jack Falstaff, kind Jack Falstaff,
true Jack Falstaff, valiant Jack Falstaff, and therefore
more valiant being as he is old Jack Falstaff, banish not
him thy Harry's company, banish not him thy Harry's
company—banish plump Jack, and banish all the
world.

---

390 **convey** escort away.  **tristful** sorrowing    391 **stop** fill
392 **harlotry** scurvy, vagabond    393 **players** actors    394 **tickle-brain**
(A slang term for strong liquor, here applied as a nickname for the
tavern hostess.)    396–9 **for though . . . wears** (Falstaff parodies the
style of John Lyly's *Euphues*, with its elaborate balanced antitheses,
alliterative effects, and illustrations drawn from fanciful natural
history. *Camomile* is an aromatic creeping herb whose flowers and
leaves are used medicinally.)    401 **trick** trait    402 **warrant** assure
405 **micher** truant    409–10 **This . . . defile** (An allusion to the familiar
proverb from Ecclesiasticus 13:1 about the defilement of touching
pitch.)    **pitch** a sticky, black residue from the distillation of tar, used
to seal wood from moisture    413 **passion** sorrow    416 **an it like** if it
please    417 **portly** (1) stately (2) corpulent    420 **threescore** sixty
421 **lewdly** wickedly    423 **If . . . by the fruit** (See Matthew 12:33.)
424 **peremptorily** decisively    432 **rabbit-sucker** unweaned rabbit.
**a poulter's hare** a hare for sale in a poultry shop.

433 **set** seated.    434 **my masters** my good sirs.    438 **'Sblood** i.e., By
Christ's blood    439 **tickle ye for** amuse you in the role of    443 **tun**
(1) large barrel (2) ton    444 **converse** associate.    **humors** body fluids,
diseases    444–5 **bolting-hutch** large bin    445 **dropsies** accumula-
tions of fluids causing swelling    446 **bombard** leathern drinking vessel.    **cloak-bag** portmanteau    447 **Manningtree ox** (Manningtree, a
town in Essex, had noted fairs where, no doubt, oxen were roasted
whole.)    **pudding** sausage-like entrails    448 **Vice, Iniquity** (Allegorical names for the chief comic character and tempter in morality
plays.)    449 **vanity in years** old person given to worldly desires
451 **cleanly** (1) pure (2) deft.    **a capon** a castrated rooster for the
table    452 **cunning** (1) skillful (2) crafty    455–6 **take me with you** let
me catch up with your meaning.    464 **saving your reverence** i.e.,
with my apology for using offensive language    467 **host** innkeeper    468 **Pharaoh's lean kine** (See Genesis 41, where Pharaoh's
dream of seven well-fattened cattle being devoured by seven lean
ones is interpreted by Joseph as a prophecy of seven years' famine
to come.)

PRINCE   I do, I will.                   [*A knocking.*
*Exeunt Hostess, Francis, and Bardolph.*]

*Enter Bardolph, running.*

BARDOLPH   Oh, my lord, my lord! The sheriff with a
most monstrous watch is at the door.         478
FALSTAFF   Out, ye rogue! Play out the play. I have
much to say in the behalf of that Falstaff.

*Enter the Hostess.*

HOSTESS   Oh, Jesu, my lord, my lord!
PRINCE   Heigh, heigh! The devil rides upon a fiddle- 482
stick. What's the matter?               483
HOSTESS   The sheriff and all the watch are at the door.
They are come to search the house. Shall I let them in?
FALSTAFF   Dost thou hear, Hal? Never call a true piece 486
of gold a counterfeit. Thou art essentially made 487
without seeming so.                  488
PRINCE   And thou a natural coward without instinct.
FALSTAFF   I deny your major. If you will deny the 490
sheriff, so; if not, let him enter. If I become not a cart 491
as well as another man, a plague on my bringing up! 492
I hope I shall as soon be strangled with a halter as
another.
PRINCE   Go hide thee behind the arras. The rest walk 495
up above. Now, my masters, for a true face and good 496
conscience.
FALSTAFF   Both which I have had, but their date is out, 498
and therefore I'll hide me.    [*He hides behind the arras.*]
PRINCE   Call in the sheriff.
          [*Exeunt all except the Prince and Peto.*]

*Enter Sheriff and the Carrier.*

Now, Master Sheriff, what is your will with me?
SHERIFF
   First, pardon me, my lord. A hue and cry       502
   Hath followed certain men unto this house.
PRINCE   What men?
SHERIFF
   One of them is well known, my gracious lord,
   A gross, fat man.
CARRIER            As fat as butter.
PRINCE
   The man, I do assure you, is not here,
   For I myself at this time have employed him.
   And, Sheriff, I will engage my word to thee       509
   That I will, by tomorrow dinnertime,          510
   Send him to answer thee, or any man,

   For anything he shall be charged withal;        512
   And so let me entreat you leave the house.
SHERIFF
   I will, my lord. There are two gentlemen
   Have in this robbery lost three hundred marks.
PRINCE
   It may be so. If he have robbed these men,
   He shall be answerable; and so farewell.
SHERIFF    Good night, my noble lord.
PRINCE
   I think it is good morrow, is it not?          519
SHERIFF
   Indeed, my lord, I think it be two o'clock.
                  *Exit* [*with Carrier*].
PRINCE   This oily rascal is known as well as Paul's. Go 521
call him forth.
PETO [*discovering Falstaff*]   Falstaff—Fast asleep behind
the arras, and snorting like a horse.
PRINCE   Hark, how hard he fetches breath. Search his
pockets. (*He searcheth his pockets, and findeth certain
papers.*) What hast thou found?
PETO   Nothing but papers, my lord.
PRINCE   Let's see what they be. Read them.
PETO [*reads*]
    Item, A capon, ............................................... 2s. 2d.
    Item, Sauce, ..................................................... 4d.
    Item, Sack, two gallons,                5s. 8d.
    Item, Anchovies and sack after
       supper, .......................................................2s. 6d.
    Item, Bread, ....................................................... ob. 534
PRINCE   Oh, monstrous! But one halfpennyworth of
bread to this intolerable deal of sack? What there is
else, keep close; we'll read it at more advantage. There 537
let him sleep till day. I'll to the court in the morning.
We must all to the wars, and thy place shall be
honorable. I'll procure this fat rogue a charge of foot, 540
and I know his death will be a march of twelve score. 541
The money shall be paid back again with advantage. 542
Be with me betimes in the morning; and so, good 543
morrow, Peto.
PETO   Good morrow, good my lord.            545
              *Exeunt* [*separately. Falstaff is concealed
once more behind the arras.*]

# [3.1]

*Enter Hotspur, Worcester, Lord Mortimer,
[and] Owen Glendower.*

---

478 **watch** posse of constables   482–3 **The . . . fiddlestick** i.e., Here's
much ado about nothing.   486–8 **Dost . . . seeming so** (In this difficult passage, Falstaff seems to suggest that he is true gold, not counterfeit, and so should not be betrayed to the watch by the Prince,
who, he hopes, is not merely playacting at the tavern but is truly one
of its madcap members.)   490 **deny your major** reject your major
premise.   **deny** refuse entrance to   491 **so** so be it.   **become** befit,
adorn.   **cart** i.e., hangman's cart   492 **bringing up** (1) upbringing
(2) being brought before the authorities to be hanged.   495 **arras** wall
hanging or tapestry.   496 **up above** upstairs.   498 **date is out** lease
has run out   502 **hue and cry** outcry calling for the pursuit of a
felon   509 **engage** pledge   510 **dinnertime** i.e., about noon

512 **withal** with   519 **morrow** morning   521 **Paul's** Saint Paul's
Cathedral.   534 **ob.** obolus, i.e., halfpenny.   537 **close** hidden.   **advantage** favorable opportunity.   540 **charge of foot** command of a company of infantry   541 **twelve score** i.e., two hundred
and forty yards.   542 **advantage** interest.   543 **betimes** early
545.1–2 *Exeunt . . . arras* (On stage, the arras is evidently arranged so
that Falstaff can exit behind it once the scene is over.)
**3.1. Location: Wales. Glendower's residence.** (Holinshed places a
meeting of the rebel deputies at Bangor in the Archdeacon's house,
but in this present "unhistorical" scene, as invented by Shakespeare,
Glendower is host throughout.) Seats are provided onstage.

MORTIMER
These promises are fair, the parties sure,                    1
And our induction full of prosperous hope.                    2
HOTSPUR
Lord Mortimer, and cousin Glendower,
Will you sit down? And uncle Worcester—
A plague upon it, I have forgot the map.
GLENDOWER [*producing a map*]
No, here it is. Sit, cousin Percy,
Sit, good cousin Hotspur—for by that name
As oft as Lancaster doth speak of you             8
His cheek looks pale, and with a rising sigh
He wisheth you in heaven.
HOTSPUR                          And you in hell,
As oft as he hears Owen Glendower spoke of.
GLENDOWER
I cannot blame him. At my nativity
The front of heaven was full of fiery shapes,     13
Of burning cressets, and at my birth              14
The frame and huge foundation of the earth
Shaked like a coward.
HOTSPUR                Why, so it would have done
At the same season, if your mother's cat
Had but kittened, though yourself had never been
    born.
GLENDOWER
I say the earth did shake when I was born.
HOTSPUR
And I say the earth was not of my mind,
If you suppose as fearing you it shook.
GLENDOWER
The heavens were all on fire; the earth did tremble.
HOTSPUR
Oh, then the earth shook to see the heavens on fire,
And not in fear of your nativity.
Diseasèd nature oftentimes breaks forth
In strange eruptions; oft the teeming earth
Is with a kind of colic pinched and vexed
By the imprisoning of unruly wind
Within her womb, which, for enlargement striving,  29
Shakes the old beldam earth and topples down       30
Steeples and moss-grown towers. At your birth
Our grandam earth, having this distemp'rature,     32
In passion shook.
GLENDOWER          Cousin, of many men             33
I do not bear these crossings. Give me leave       34
To tell you once again that at my birth
The front of heaven was full of fiery shapes,
The goats ran from the mountains, and the herds
Were strangely clamorous to the frighted fields.
These signs have marked me extraordinary,
And all the courses of my life do show
I am not in the roll of common men.

Where is he living, clipped in with the sea        42
That chides the banks of England, Scotland, Wales,  43
Which calls me pupil or hath read to me?           44
And bring him out that is but woman's son          45
Can trace me in the tedious ways of art            46
And hold me pace in deep experiments.              47
HOTSPUR
I think there's no man speaks better Welsh.        48
I'll to dinner.
MORTIMER
Peace, cousin Percy; you will make him mad.
GLENDOWER
I can call spirits from the vasty deep.            51
HOTSPUR
Why, so can I, or so can any man;
But will they come when you do call for them?
GLENDOWER
Why, I can teach you, cousin, to command the devil.
HOTSPUR
And I can teach thee, coz, to shame the devil
By telling truth. Tell truth and shame the devil.
If thou have power to raise him, bring him hither,
And I'll be sworn I have power to shame him hence.
Oh, while you live, tell truth and shame the devil!
MORTIMER
Come, come, no more of this unprofitable chat.
GLENDOWER
Three times hath Henry Bolingbroke made head      61
Against my power; thrice from the banks of Wye     62
And sandy-bottomed Severn have I sent him          63
Bootless home and weather-beaten back.            64
HOTSPUR
Home without boots, and in foul weather too!
How scapes he agues, in the devil's name?         66
GLENDOWER
Come, here is the map. Shall we divide our right
According to our threefold order ta'en?            68
MORTIMER
The Archdeacon hath divided it                     69
Into three limits very equally:                    70
England, from Trent and Severn hitherto,           71
By south and east is to my part assigned;
All westward, Wales beyond the Severn shore,
And all the fertile land within that bound,
To Owen Glendower; and, dear coz, to you           75
The remnant northward, lying off from Trent.

42–4 Where . . . to me? i.e., Where is there anyone in all of sea-walled Great Britain who can claim to have been my instructor?   45–7 And . . . experiments And I challenge you to produce a single human being who can follow my tracks in the arcane craft of magic or keep up with me in occult experiments.   48 speaks better Welsh (Hotspur hides an insult behind the literal meaning, since "to speak Welsh" meant colloquially both "to boast" and "to speak nonsense.")   51 call summon. (But Hotspur sardonically replies in the sense of "call out to," whether or not there is any response.)   vasty deep lower world.   61 made head raised a force   62 power army   62–3, 71 Wye, Severn, Trent rivers in Wales and northwest England   64 Bootless without advantage. (But Hotspur quibbles on the sense of "barefoot.")   66 agues fevers   68 order ta'en arrangements made.   69 Archdeacon i.e., the Archdeacon of Bangor, in whose house, according to Holinshed, a meeting took place between deputies of the rebel leaders   70 limits regions   71 hitherto to this point   75 coz cousin, i.e., brother-in-law

1 the parties sure our allies remain firm in their commitment   2 induction beginning.   prosperous hope hope of prospering.   8 Lancaster i.e., King Henry, here demoted to Duke of Lancaster   13 front brow, face. (As also at line 36.)   14 cressets lights burning in metal baskets suspended from the ends of long poles or ceilings; hence, meteors   29 enlargement release   30 beldam grandmother   32 distemp'rature disorder   33 passion suffering.   of from   34 crossings contradictions.

And our indentures tripartite are drawn,                    77
Which being sealèd interchangeably—
A business that this night may execute—                    79
Tomorrow, cousin Percy, you and I
And my good lord of Worcester will set forth
To meet your father and the Scottish power,
As is appointed us, at Shrewsbury.
My father Glendower is not ready yet,                    84
Nor shall we need his help these fourteen days.
[*To Glendower*] Within that space you may have drawn
     together                    86
Your tenants, friends, and neighboring gentlemen.

GLENDOWER
A shorter time shall send me to you, lords;
And in my conduct shall your ladies come,                    89
From whom you now must steal and take no leave,
For there will be a world of water shed
Upon the parting of your wives and you.

HOTSPUR [*consulting the map*]
Methinks my moiety, north from Burton here,                    93
In quantity equals not one of yours.
See how this river comes me cranking in                    95
And cuts me from the best of all my land
A huge half-moon, a monstrous cantle, out.                    97
I'll have the current in this place dammed up,
And here the smug and silver Trent shall run                    99
In a new channel, fair and evenly.
It shall not wind with such a deep indent
To rob me of so rich a bottom here.                    102

GLENDOWER
Not wind? It shall, it must. You see it doth.

MORTIMER
Yea, but mark how he bears his course and runs me up    104
With like advantage on the other side,
Gelding the opposèd continent as much                    106
As on the other side it takes from you.

WORCESTER
Yea, but a little charge will trench him here                    108
And on this north side win this cape of land;
And then he runs straight and even.

HOTSPUR
I'll have it so. A little charge will do it.

GLENDOWER    I'll not have it altered.

HOTSPUR    Will not you?

GLENDOWER    No, nor you shall not.

HOTSPUR    Who shall say me nay?

GLENDOWER    Why, that will I.

HOTSPUR
Let me not understand you, then; speak it in Welsh.

GLENDOWER
I can speak English, lord, as well as you;
For I was trained up in the English court,
Where, being but young, I framèd to the harp                    120
Many an English ditty lovely well,
And gave the tongue a helpful ornament—                    122
A virtue that was never seen in you.

HOTSPUR
Marry, and I am glad of it with all my heart!
I had rather be a kitten and cry "mew"
Than one of these same meter balladmongers.
I had rather hear a brazen can'stick turned                    127
Or a dry wheel grate on the axletree,                    128
And that would set my teeth nothing on edge,                    129
Nothing so much as mincing poetry.
'Tis like the forced gait of a shuffling nag.                    131

GLENDOWER    Come, you shall have Trent turned.

HOTSPUR
I do not care. I'll give thrice so much land
To any well-deserving friend;
But in the way of bargain, mark ye me,
I'll cavil on the ninth part of a hair.                    136
Are the indentures drawn? Shall we be gone?                    137

GLENDOWER
The moon shines fair; you may away by night.
I'll haste the writer and withal                    139
Break with your wives of your departure hence.                    140
I am afraid my daughter will run mad,
So much she doteth on her Mortimer.                    *Exit.*

MORTIMER
Fie, cousin Percy, how you cross my father!

HOTSPUR
I cannot choose. Sometimes he angers me
With telling me of the moldwarp and the ant,                    145
Of the dreamer Merlin and his prophecies,                    146
And of a dragon and a finless fish,
A clip-winged griffin and a moulten raven,                    148
A couching lion and a ramping cat,                    149
And such a deal of skimble-skamble stuff                    150
As puts me from my faith. I tell you what:                    151
He held me last night at least nine hours
In reckoning up the several devils' names                    153

77 **tripartite** i.e., drawn up in triplicate, each document *sealèd interchangeably* (line 78) with the seal of all signatories.    **drawn** drawn up    79 **this night may execute** may be carried out tonight    84 **father** father-in-law    86 **may** will be able to    89 **conduct** escort    93 **moiety** share    95 **comes me cranking in** comes bending in on my share. (The Trent, by turning northward to the North Sea instead of continuing eastward into the Wash, cuts Hotspur off from rich land in Lincolnshire and its vicinity.)    97 **cantle** piece    99 **smug** smooth    102 **bottom** valley    104 **runs me** runs. (*Me* is used colloquially.)    106 **Gelding . . . continent** cutting off from the land which it bounds on the opposite side. (The Trent's southerly loop from Stoke to Burton deprives Mortimer of a piece of land, just as its later northerly course deprives Hotspur.)    108 **charge** expenditure.    **trench** provide a new channel for

120 **framèd to the harp** set to harp accompaniment    122 **gave . . . ornament** i.e., added to the words a pleasing ornament of music; also, gave to the English tongue the ornament of music and poetry    127 **can'stick turned** candlestick turned on a lathe    128 **axletree** axle    129 **nothing** not at all    131 **shuffling** hobbled    136 **cavil . . . hair** i.e., argue about the most trivial detail.    137 **drawn** drawn up.    139 **writer** i.e., scrivener who would be drawing the indentures.    **withal** also    140 **Break with** inform    145 **moldwarp** mole. (Holinshed tells us that the division was arranged because of a prophecy that represented King Henry as the mole and the others as the dragon, the lion, and the wolf, who should divide the land among them.)    146 **Merlin** the bard, prophet, and magician of Arthurian story, Welsh in origin    148 **griffin** a fabulous beast, half lion, half eagle.    **moulten** having molted    149 **couching** couchant, crouching. (Heraldic term.)    **ramping** rampant, advancing on its hind legs. (Hotspur is ridiculing the heraldic emblems that Glendower holds so dear.)    150 **skimble-skamble** foolish, nonsensical    151 **puts . . . faith** drives me from my (Christian) faith.    153 **several** various

That were his lackeys. I cried "Hum," and "Well, go to," 154
But marked him not a word. Oh, he is as tedious
As a tirèd horse, a railing wife,
Worse than a smoky house. I had rather live
With cheese and garlic in a windmill, far,
Than feed on cates and have him talk to me     159
In any summer house in Christendom.

MORTIMER
In faith, he is a worthy gentleman,
Exceedingly well read, and profited     162
In strange concealments, valiant as a lion     163
And wondrous affable, and as bountiful
As mines of India. Shall I tell you, cousin?
He holds your temper in a high respect     166
And curbs himself even of his natural scope     167
When you come 'cross his humor. Faith, he does.     168
I warrant you that man is not alive
Might so have tempted him as you have done     170
Without the taste of danger and reproof.
But do not use it oft, let me entreat you.

WORCESTER [to Hotspur]
In faith, my lord, you are too willful-blame,     173
And since your coming hither have done enough
To put him quite besides his patience.     175
You must needs learn, lord, to amend this fault.
Though sometimes it show greatness, courage,
    blood—     177
And that's the dearest grace it renders you—     178
Yet oftentimes it doth present harsh rage,     179
Defect of manners, want of government,     180
Pride, haughtiness, opinion, and disdain,     181
The least of which haunting a nobleman
Loseth men's hearts and leaves behind a stain
Upon the beauty of all parts besides,     184
Beguiling them of commendation.     185

HOTSPUR
Well, I am schooled. Good manners be your speed!     186
Here come our wives, and let us take our leave.

*Enter Glendower with the ladies.*

MORTIMER
This is the deadly spite that angers me:     188
My wife can speak no English, I no Welsh.

GLENDOWER
My daughter weeps she'll not part with you;
She'll be a soldier too, she'll to the wars.

MORTIMER
Good father, tell her that she and my aunt Percy     192

Shall follow in your conduct speedily.     193
    *Glendower speaks to her in Welsh, and she answers
        him in the same.*

GLENDOWER
She is desperate here; a peevish self-willed harlotry,     194
One that no persuasion can do good upon.
    *The lady speaks in Welsh.*

MORTIMER [to her]
I understand thy looks. That pretty Welsh     196
Which thou pourest down from these swelling heavens     197
I am too perfect in; and, but for shame,     198
In such a parley should I answer thee.     199
    *The lady again in Welsh.*
I understand thy kisses and thou mine,
And that's a feeling disputation.     201
But I will never be a truant, love,
Till I have learned thy language; for thy tongue
Makes Welsh as sweet as ditties highly penned,     204
Sung by a fair queen in a summer's bower,
With ravishing division, to her lute.     206

GLENDOWER
Nay, if you melt, then will she run mad.     207
    *The lady speaks again in Welsh.*

MORTIMER
Oh, I am ignorance itself in this!

GLENDOWER
She bids you on the wanton rushes lay you down     209
And rest your gentle head upon her lap,
And she will sing the song that pleaseth you
And on your eyelids crown the god of sleep,     212
Charming your blood with pleasing heaviness,     213
Making such difference twixt wake and sleep     214
As is the difference betwixt day and night
The hour before the heavenly-harnessed team     216
Begins his golden progress in the east.

MORTIMER
With all my heart I'll sit and hear her sing.
By that time will our book, I think, be drawn.     219

GLENDOWER   Do so;
And those musicians that shall play to you
Hang in the air a thousand leagues from hence,
And straight they shall be here. Sit, and attend.     222
    *[Mortimer reclines with his head
        in his wife's lap.]*

HOTSPUR   Come, Kate, thou art perfect in lying down;
come, quick, quick, that I may lay my head in thy lap.

LADY PERCY   Go, ye giddy goose.
    *[Hotspur lies with his head
        in Kate's lap.] The music plays.*

---

154 **go to** i.e., you don't say   159 **cates** delicacies   162 **profited** proficient   163 **concealments** occult practices   166 **temper** temperament   167 **scope** freedom of speech   168 **come 'cross** contradict   170 **Might** who could   173 **too willful-blame** blameworthy for too much self-will   175 **besides** out of   177 **blood** spirit   178 **dearest grace** best (and costliest) credit   179 **present** represent   180 **want of government** lack of self-control   181 **opinion** vanity, arrogance   184 **all parts besides** all other abilities   185 **Beguiling** depriving   186 **Good . . . speed!** i.e., May these good manners you praise so bring you success! (Said wryly; Hotspur doubts that good manners count for much in a time of war.)   188 **spite** vexation   192 **aunt** (Percy's wife, here called Kate, was aunt of Edmund Mortimer, the fifth Earl of March, but was sister-in-law to the Sir Edward Mortimer who married Glendower's daughter.)

193 **conduct** safe-conduct, escort   194 **desperate here** adamant on this point (i.e., her decision to accompany Mortimer).   **peevish self-willed harlotry** childish, willful, silly wench   196 **That pretty Welsh** i.e., Your eloquent tears   197 **heavens** i.e., eyes   198 **perfect** proficient   199 **such a parley** i.e., the same language (of weeping)   201 **disputation** conversation, debate.   204 **highly penned** eloquently composed, in high style   206 **division** variation, passage in which rapid short notes vary a theme   207 **melt** i.e., weep   209 **wanton rushes** i.e., soft floor covering   212 **crown . . . sleep** make sleep supreme ruler   213 **heaviness** drowsiness   214 **difference** nearly indistinguishable difference   216 **the heavenly-harnessed team** i.e., the team of horses drawing the chariot of the sun   219 **book** document, indentures   222 **straight** at once

HOTSPUR
Now I perceive the devil understands Welsh;
And 'tis no marvel he is so humorous.     228
By'r Lady, he is a good musician.
LADY PERCY   Then should you be nothing but musical,
for you are altogether governed by humors. Lie still,
ye thief, and hear the lady sing in Welsh.     232
HOTSPUR   I had rather hear Lady, my brach, howl in  233
Irish.
LADY PERCY   Wouldst thou have thy head broken?   235
HOTSPUR   No.
LADY PERCY   Then be still.
HOTSPUR   Neither, 'tis a woman's fault.   238
LADY PERCY   Now God help thee!   239
HOTSPUR   To the Welsh lady's bed.
LADY PERCY   What's that?
HOTSPUR   Peace, she sings.

*Here the lady sings a Welsh song.*

HOTSPUR
Come, Kate, I'll have your song too.
LADY PERCY
Not mine, in good sooth.   244
HOTSPUR   Not yours, in good sooth! Heart, you swear  245
like a comfit maker's wife. "Not you, in good sooth,"  246
and "as true as I live," and "as God shall mend me,"
and "as sure as day,"
And givest such sarcenet surety for thy oaths   249
As if thou never walk'st further than Finsbury.   250
Swear me, Kate, like a lady as thou art,   251
A good mouth-filling oath, and leave "in sooth,"
And such protest of pepper-gingerbread,   253
To velvet-guards and Sunday citizens.   254
Come, sing.
LADY PERCY   I will not sing.
HOTSPUR   'Tis the next way to turn tailor, or be redbreast  257
teacher. An the indentures be drawn, I'll away within  258
these two hours; and so, come in when ye will.   *Exit.*
GLENDOWER
Come, come, Lord Mortimer. You are as slow
As hot Lord Percy is on fire to go.
By this our book is drawn; we'll but seal,   262
And then to horse immediately.
MORTIMER   With all my heart.     *Exeunt.*

♣

228 **humorous** whimsical, capricious.   232 **thief** i.e., rascal
233 **brach** bitch hound   235 **broken** i.e., struck so as to break the
skin.   238 **Neither . . . fault** i.e., I won't do that either; it's womanish
to be submissive.   239 **help** amend. (But Hotspur answers in the
sense of "assist with an amour.")   244 **sooth** truth.   245 **Heart** i.e.,
By Christ's heart   246 **comfit maker's** confectioner's   249 **sarcenet**
soft, flimsy. (From the soft silken material known as *sarcenet*.)
250 **Finsbury** a field just outside London frequented by the London
citizenry. (Hotspur jokes with Kate as though she were a citizen's
wife, using the pious and modest oaths of such people.)   251 **Swear
me** Swear. (*Me* is used colloquially.)   253 **protest . . . gingerbread**
i.e., mealy-mouthed protestations   254 **velvet-guards** i.e., wives who
wear velvet trimming   257–8 **'Tis . . . teacher** i.e., The only use one
might put singing to is to become a tailor (since tailors were noted for
effeminacy and singing at their work) or an instructor to caged song-
birds before they are sold. (Hotspur airily dismisses singing, as he
does poetry.)   257 **next** quickest   258 **An** If   262 **By this** By this
time.   **but** just

## [3.2]

*Enter the King, Prince of Wales, and others.*

KING
Lords, give us leave. The Prince of Wales and I
Must have some private conference; but be near at
hand,
For we shall presently have need of you.
                            *Exeunt Lords.*
I know not whether God will have it so
For some displeasing service I have done,
That in his secret doom out of my blood   6
He'll breed revengement and a scourge for me;
But thou dost in thy passages of life   8
Make me believe that thou art only marked   9
For the hot vengeance and the rod of heaven   10
To punish my mistreadings. Tell me else,   11
Could such inordinate and low desires,   12
Such poor, such bare, such lewd, such mean attempts,   13
Such barren pleasures, rude society,
As thou art matched withal and grafted to,   15
Accompany the greatness of thy blood
And hold their level with thy princely heart?   17
PRINCE
So please Your Majesty, I would I could
Quit all offenses with as clear excuse   19
As well as I am doubtless I can purge   20
Myself of many I am charged withal.
Yet such extenuation let me beg
As, in reproof of many tales devised,   23
Which oft the ear of greatness needs must hear
By smiling pickthanks and base newsmongers,   25
I may, for some things true, wherein my youth
Hath faulty wandered and irregular,
Find pardon on my true submission.
KING
God pardon thee! Yet let me wonder, Harry,
At thy affections, which do hold a wing   30
Quite from the flight of all thy ancestors.   31
Thy place in Council thou hast rudely lost,   32
Which by thy younger brother is supplied,
And art almost an alien to the hearts
Of all the court and princes of my blood.
The hope and expectation of thy time   36
Is ruined, and the soul of every man
Prophetically do forethink thy fall.   38

**3.2 Location: The royal court (historically, Westminster).**
6 **doom** judgment.   **blood** offspring   8 **passages** course, conduct
9–11 **thou . . . mistreadings** (1) you are marked as the means of heav-
en's vengeance against me, or (2) you are marked to suffer heaven's
vengeance because of my sins.   11 **else** how otherwise   12 **inordinate** (1) immoderate (2) unworthy of your rank   13 **lewd** low, base.
**attempts** undertakings   15 **withal** with   17 **hold their level** claim
equality   19 **Quit** acquit myself of   20 **doubtless** certain   23 **in
reproof** upon disproof   25 **By . . . newsmongers** from smiling flatterers and ignoble talebearers   30 **affections** inclinations   **hold a wing**
fly a course   31 **from** at variance with   32 **rudely** by violence.
(According to an apocryphal story, Prince Hal boxed the ears of the
Lord Chief Justice and was sent to prison for it; see *2 Henry IV*,
1.2.54–5, 192, and 5.2.70–1.)   36 **The hope . . . time** The hopes that
people had for you   38 **do forethink** does predict

Had I so lavish of my presence been,
So common-hackneyed in the eyes of men,                    40
So stale and cheap to vulgar company,
Opinion, that did help me to the crown,                    42
Had still kept loyal to possession                    43
And left me in reputeless banishment,                    44
A fellow of no mark nor likelihood.                    45
By being seldom seen, I could not stir
But like a comet I was wondered at,
That men would tell their children, "This is he!"
Others would say, "Where, which is Bolingbroke?"
And then I stole all courtesy from heaven,                    50
And dressed myself in such humility
That I did pluck allegiance from men's hearts,
Loud shouts and salutations from their mouths,
Even in the presence of the crownèd King.
Thus did I keep my person fresh and new,
My presence, like a robe pontifical,                    56
Ne'er seen but wondered at; and so my state,                    57
Seldom but sumptuous, showed like a feast                    58
And won by rareness such solemnity.                    59
The skipping King, he ambled up and down
With shallow jesters and rash bavin wits,                    61
Soon kindled and soon burnt; carded his state,                    62
Mingled his royalty with cap'ring fools,
Had his great name profanèd with their scorns,                    64
And gave his countenance, against his name,                    65
To laugh at gibing boys and stand the push                    66
Of every beardless vain comparative;                    67
Grew a companion to the common streets,
Enfeoffed himself to popularity,                    69
That, being daily swallowed by men's eyes,
They surfeited with honey and began
To loathe the taste of sweetness, whereof a little
More than a little is by much too much.
So when he had occasion to be seen,
He was but as the cuckoo is in June,
Heard, not regarded—seen, but with such eyes
As, sick and blunted with community,                    77
Afford no extraordinary gaze,
Such as is bent on sunlike majesty
When it shines seldom in admiring eyes;
But rather drowsed and hung their eyelids down,
Slept in his face, and rendered such aspect                    82
As cloudy men use to their adversaries,                    83

Being with his presence glutted, gorged, and full.
And in that very line, Harry, standest thou;                    85
For thou hast lost thy princely privilege
With vile participation. Not an eye                    87
But is aweary of thy common sight,
Save mine, which hath desired to see thee more—
Which now doth that I would not have it do,                    90
Make blind itself with foolish tenderness.                    91

PRINCE
I shall hereafter, my thrice gracious lord,
Be more myself.

KING                    For all the world                    93
As thou art to this hour was Richard then
When I from France set foot at Ravenspurgh,
And even as I was then is Percy now.
Now, by my scepter, and my soul to boot,                    97
He hath more worthy interest to the state                    98
Than thou the shadow of succession.                    99
For of no right, nor color like to right,                    100
He doth fill fields with harness in the realm,                    101
Turns head against the lion's armèd jaws,                    102
And, being no more in debt to years than thou,                    103
Leads ancient lords and reverend bishops on
To bloody battles and to bruising arms,
What never-dying honor hath he got
Against renownèd Douglas! Whose high deeds,                    107
Whose hot incursions and great name in arms
Holds from all soldiers chief majority                    109
And military title capital                    110
Through all the kingdoms that acknowledge Christ.
Thrice hath this Hotspur, Mars in swaddling clothes,
This infant warrior, in his enterprises
Discomfited great Douglas, ta'en him once,                    114
Enlargèd him and made a friend of him,                    115
To fill the mouth of deep defiance up                    116
And shake the peace and safety of our throne.
And what say you to this? Percy, Northumberland,
The Archbishop's Grace of York, Douglas, Mortimer,                    119
Capitulate against us and are up.                    120
But wherefore do I tell these news to thee?
Why, Harry, do I tell thee of my foes,
Which art my nearest and dearest enemy?                    123
Thou that art like enough, through vassal fear,                    124
Base inclination, and the start of spleen,                    125
To fight against me under Percy's pay,

---

**40 common-hackneyed** cheapened, vulgarized   **42 Opinion** public opinion   **43 to possession** i.e., to Richard II's sovereignty **44 reputeless** inglorious   **45 mark nor likelihood** importance or likeliness to succeed.   **50 I . . . heaven** i.e., I assumed a bearing of the utmost meekness   **56 pontifical** like that of a pope or archbishop **57–9 and so . . . solemnity** and so my magnificence on public occasions, infrequent but always sumptuous, looked festive and achieved by this rarity a suitable formal impressiveness.   **61 bavin** brushwood, soon burnt out   **62 carded his state** debased his royal dignity. (To *card* is to stir or mix, hence to adulterate.)   **64 with their scorns** by his favorites' scornful and contemptuous behavior   **65–7 And gave . . . comparative** and lent his authority, to the detriment of his royal dignity and reputation, to find amusement in young scoffers and submit himself to the insolence of every frivolous witcracker **69 Enfeoffed himself** gave himself up   **77 community** commonness   **82–3 Slept . . . adversaries** dozed off right before his eyes, and looked at the King in the way sullen men look at their adversaries

**85 line** degree, category   **87 vile participation** base association or companionship.   **90 that** that which   **91 tenderness** i.e., tears. **93 For all the world** In every way   **97 to boot** in addition **98–9 He . . . succession** i.e., this rebel Hotspur has a better claim to the throne than your merely hereditary claim unsupported by deeds. **100 of . . . to right** having no rightful claim or even the pretext of one **101 fields** battlefields.   **harness** armor, i.e., men in armor **102 Turns head** leads an armed insurrection.   **lion's** i.e., King's **103 being . . . thou** i.e., being no older than you. (Though historically Hotspur was twenty-three years older than the Prince.)   **107 Whose** i.e., Hotspur's   **109 majority** preeminence   **110 capital** chief, principal   **114 Discomfited** defeated   **115 Enlargèd** freed   **116 To . . . up** to swell the roar of deep defiance   **119 The Archbishop's Grace** His Grace the Archbishop   **120 Capitulate** form a league, draw up articles. **up** up in arms.   **123 dearest** (1) most precious (2) direst   **124 like** likely.   **vassal** slavish   **125 Base . . . spleen** inclination for baseness, and sudden bursts of capricious irascibility

To dog his heels and curtsy at his frowns,
To show how much thou art degenerate.

PRINCE
Do not think so. You shall not find it so.
And God forgive them that so much have swayed
Your Majesty's good thoughts away from me!
I will redeem all this on Percy's head
And in the closing of some glorious day
Be bold to tell you that I am your son,
When I will wear a garment all of blood
And stain my favors in a bloody mask,                        136
Which, washed away, shall scour my shame with it.
And that shall be the day, whene'er it lights,               138
That this same child of honor and renown,
This gallant Hotspur, this all-praisèd knight,
And your unthought-of Harry chance to meet.                  141
For every honor sitting on his helm,                         142
Would they were multitudes, and on my head
My shames redoubled! For the time will come
That I shall make this northern youth exchange
His glorious deeds for my indignities.
Percy is but my factor, good my lord,                        147
To engross up glorious deeds on my behalf;                   148
And I will call him to so strict account
That he shall render every glory up,
Yea, even the slightest worship of his time,                 151
Or I will tear the reckoning from his heart.
This in the name of God I promise here,
The which if He be pleased I shall perform,
I do beseech Your Majesty may salve                          155
The long-grown wounds of my intemperance.                    156
If not, the end of life cancels all bonds,
And I will die a hundred thousand deaths
Ere break the smallest parcel of this vow.

KING
A hundred thousand rebels die in this!
Thou shalt have charge and sovereign trust herein.          161

*Enter Blunt.*

How now, good Blunt? Thy looks are full of speed.
BLUNT
So hath the business that I come to speak of.
Lord Mortimer of Scotland hath sent word                     164
That Douglas and the English rebels met
The eleventh of this month at Shrewsbury.
A mighty and a fearful head they are,                        167
If pròmises be kept on every hand,                           168
As ever offered foul play in a state.
KING
The Earl of Westmorland set forth today,
With him my son, Lord John of Lancaster;
For this advertisement is five days old.                     172
On Wednesday next, Harry, you shall set forward;

On Thursday we ourselves will march. Our meeting     174
Is Bridgnorth. And, Harry, you shall march           175
Through Gloucestershire; by which account,
Our business valuèd, some twelve days hence          177
Our general forces at Bridgnorth shall meet.
Our hands are full of business. Let's away!
Advantage feeds him fat while men delay.     *Exeunt.* 180

# [3.3]

*Enter Falstaff and Bardolph.*

FALSTAFF    Bardolph, am I not fallen away vilely since    1
this last action? Do I not bate? Do I not dwindle? Why,    2
my skin hangs about me like an old lady's loose gown;
I am withered like an old applejohn. Well, I'll repent,    4
and that suddenly, while I am in some liking. I shall be   5
out of heart shortly, and then I shall have no strength    6
to repent. An I have not forgotten what the inside of a
church is made of, I am a peppercorn, a brewer's           8
horse. The inside of a church! Company, villainous         9
company, hath been the spoil of me.
BARDOLPH    Sir John, you are so fretful you cannot live   11
long.
FALSTAFF    Why, there is it. Come sing me a bawdy
song; make me merry. I was as virtuously given as a        14
gentleman need to be, virtuous enough: swore little,
diced not above seven times—a week, went to a
bawdy house not above once in a quarter—of an
hour, paid money that I borrowed—three or four
times, lived well and in good compass; and now I live      19
out of all order, out of all compass.
BARDOLPH    Why, you are so fat, Sir John, that you must
needs be out of all compass, out of all reasonable
compass, Sir John.
FALSTAFF    Do thou amend thy face, and I'll amend my
life. Thou art our admiral, thou bearest the lantern       25
in the poop, but 'tis in the nose of thee. Thou art the    26
Knight of the Burning Lamp.                                27
BARDOLPH    Why, Sir John, my face does you no harm.
FALSTAFF    No, I'll be sworn, I make as good use of it as
many a man doth of a death's-head or a *memento mori.*  30
I never see thy face but I think upon hellfire and

---

136 **favors** features   138 **lights** dawns   141 **unthought-of** lightly
valued, disregarded   142 **For** As for   147 **factor** agent   148 **engross**
**up** amass, buy up   151 **even . . . time** every smallest honor he has
ever won   155 **salve** soothe, heal   156 **intemperance** dissolute living.
161 **charge** command (of troops)   164 **Lord Mortimer of Scotland**
(A Scottish nobleman, unrelated to Glendower's son-in-law.)
167 **head** armed force   168 **If . . . hand** if all the rebels show up at the
field of battle (at Shrewsbury)   172 **advertisement** tidings, news

174 **meeting** place of rendezvous   175 **Bridgnorth** a town near
Shrewsbury.   177 **Our business valuèd** estimating how long our
business will take   180 **Advantage . . . fat** Opportunity (for rebellion)
prospers.   **him** himself, itself
**3.3. Location: A tavern in Eastcheap, as in 2.4.**
1 **fallen away** shrunk   2 **action** i.e., the robbery at Gad's Hill.   **bate**
lose weight.   4 **applejohn** a kind of apple still in good eating condition when shriveled.   5 **liking** (1) good bodily condition (2) inclination.   6 **out of heart** (1) disinclined, disheartened (2) out of condition
8 **peppercorn** unground dried pepper berry   8–9 **brewer's horse**
i.e., one that is old, withered, and decrepit.   11 **fretful** (1) anxious
(2) fretted, frayed   14 **given** inclined   19 **good compass** reasonable
limits; also, in Bardolph's speech, girth, circumference   25 **admiral**
flagship.   **lantern** i.e., a light for the rest of the fleet to follow;
here applied to Bardolph's inflamed nose, red from overdrinking
26 **poop** upper deck at a ship's stern   27 **Knight . . . Lamp** Falstaff
parodies the names of heroes in popular chivalric romances.
30 *memento mori* reminder of death, such as a death's head or a skull
engraved on a seal ring.

Dives that lived in purple; for there he is in his robes, 32
burning, burning. If thou wert any way given to
virtue, I would swear by thy face; my oath should be
"By this fire, that's God's angel." But thou art 35
altogether given over, and wert indeed, but for the 36
light in thy face, the son of utter darkness. When thou
ran'st up Gad's Hill in the night to catch my horse, if
I did not think thou hadst been an *ignis fatuus* or a ball 39
of wildfire, there's no purchase in money. Oh, thou art 40
a perpetual triumph, an everlasting bonfire light! 41
Thou hast saved me a thousand marks in links and 42
torches, walking with thee in the night betwixt tavern
and tavern; but the sack that thou hast drunk me 44
would have bought me lights as good cheap at the 45
dearest chandler's in Europe. I have maintained that 46
salamander of yours with fire any time this two-and- 47
thirty years. God reward me for it!

BARDOLPH    'Sblood, I would my face were in your belly! 49

FALSTAFF    God-a-mercy! So should I be sure to be
heartburned.

*Enter Hostess.*

How now, Dame Partlet the hen? Have you inquired 52
yet who picked my pocket?

HOSTESS    Why, Sir John, what do you think, Sir John?
Do you think I keep thieves in my house? I have
searched, I have inquired, so has my husband, man
by man, boy by boy, servant by servant. The tithe of a 57
hair was never lost in my house before.

FALSTAFF    Ye lie, hostess. Bardolph was shaved and 59
lost many a hair; and I'll be sworn my pocket was 60
picked. Go to, you are a woman, go.

HOSTESS    Who, I? No, I defy thee! God's light, I was 62
never called so in mine own house before.

FALSTAFF    Go to, I know you well enough.

HOSTESS    No, Sir John, you do not know me, Sir John.
I know you, Sir John. You owe me money, Sir John,
and now you pick a quarrel to beguile me of it. I
bought you a dozen of shirts to your back.

FALSTAFF    Dowlas, filthy dowlas. I have given them 69
away to bakers' wives; they have made bolters of 70
them.

HOSTESS    Now, as I am a true woman, holland of eight 72
shillings an ell. You owe money here besides, Sir 73
John, for your diet and by-drinkings, and money lent 74
you, four-and-twenty pound.

FALSTAFF    He had his part of it. Let him pay. 76
HOSTESS    He? Alas, he is poor, he hath nothing.
FALSTAFF    How, poor? Look upon his face. What call
you rich? Let them coin his nose, let them coin his
cheeks. I'll not pay a denier. What, will you make a 80
younker of me? Shall I not take mine ease in mine inn 81
but I shall have my pocket picked? I have lost a seal
ring of my grandfather's worth forty mark.
HOSTESS    Oh, Jesu, I have heard the Prince tell him, I
know not how oft, that that ring was copper.
FALSTAFF    How? The Prince is a Jack, a sneak-up. 86
'Sblood, an he were here, I would cudgel him like a
dog if he would say so. 88

*Enter the Prince [with Peto], marching, and*
*Falstaff meets him playing upon his truncheon like*
*a fife.*

How now, lad, is the wind in that door, i'faith? Must 89
we all march?
BARDOLPH    Yea, two and two, Newgate fashion. 91
HOSTESS    My lord, I pray you, hear me.
PRINCE    What say'st thou, Mistress Quickly? How doth
thy husband? I love him well; he is an honest man.
HOSTESS    Good my lord, hear me.
FALSTAFF    Prithee, let her alone and list to me.
PRINCE    What say'st thou, Jack?
FALSTAFF    The other night I fell asleep here behind the
arras and had my pocket picked. This house is turned 99
bawdy house; they pick pockets.
PRINCE    What didst thou lose, Jack?
FALSTAFF    Wilt thou believe me, Hal? Three or four
bonds of forty pound apiece and a seal ring of my
grandfather's.
PRINCE    A trifle, some eightpenny matter.
HOSTESS    So I told him, my lord, and I said I heard Your
Grace say so; and, my lord, he speaks most vilely of
you, like a foulmouthed man as he is, and said he
would cudgel you.
PRINCE    What, he did not!
HOSTESS    There's neither faith, truth, nor womanhood
in me else.
FALSTAFF    There's no more faith in thee than in a stewed 113
prune, nor no more truth in thee than in a drawn fox; 114
and for womanhood, Maid Marian may be the dep- 115
uty's wife of the ward to thee. Go, you thing, go. 116
HOSTESS    Say, what thing, what thing?
FALSTAFF    What thing? Why, a thing to thank God on. 118
HOSTESS    I am no thing to thank God on, I would thou 119
shouldst know it! I am an honest man's wife, and,

**32 Dives** the rich man who went to hell, referred to in Luke
16:19–31.    **in purple** wealthily    **35 "By ... angel"** (Psalms 104:4,
Hebrews 1:7, and Exodus 3:2 describe angels that appear in flames of
fire.)    **36 given over** abandoned to wickedness    **39 *ignis fatuus*** will-
o'-the-wisp    **40 wildfire** fireworks; lightning; will-o'-the-wisp
**41 triumph** procession led by torches    **42 links** torches, flares
**44 me** at my expense    **45 good cheap** cheap    **46 dearest chandler's**
most expensive candle maker's    **47 salamander** lizard reputed to be
able to live in fire    **49 I ... belly** (A colloquial way of objecting to an
insult. Falstaff responds in the literal sense: A face like yours would
give me massive indigestion.)    **52 Partlet** (Traditional name of a
hen.)    **57 tithe** tenth part    **59 was shaved** (1) had his beard cut
(2) was cheated and robbed    **60 lost many a hair** (1) was shaved
(2) was made bald by syphilis    **62 God's light** (A mild oath.)
**69 Dowlas** a coarse kind of linen    **70 bolters** cloths for sifting
flour    **72 holland** fine linen    **73 an ell** a measure of forty-five
inches.    **74 diet** meals.    **by-drinkings** drinks between meals

**76 He** Bardolph    **80 denier** one-twelfth of a French sou; type of very
small coin.    **81 younker** greenhorn    **86 Jack** knave, rascal.    **sneak-**
**up** sneak.    **88.2 *truncheon*** officer's staff    **89 is ... door** i.e., is that
the way the wind is blowing    **91 Newgate** a famous city prison
in London. (Prisoners marched two by two.)    **99 arras** curtain
**113–14 stewed prune** (Customarily associated with bawdy
houses.)    **114 drawn fox** fox driven from cover and wily in getting
back, or a dead fox dragged for the purpose of laying a false
trail.    **115 for** as for    **115–16 Maid ... thee** i.e., Maid Marian,
a disreputable woman in Robin Hood ballads, morris dances,
and the like, was a model of respectability compared with you.
**118–19 What thing ... no thing** (With sexual quibbles.)

setting thy knighthood aside, thou art a knave to call 121
me so.

FALSTAFF   Setting thy womanhood aside, thou art a
beast to say otherwise.

HOSTESS   Say, what beast, thou knave, thou?

FALSTAFF   What beast? Why, an otter.

PRINCE   An otter, Sir John! Why an otter?

FALSTAFF   Why? She's neither fish nor flesh; a man 128
knows not where to have her.                     129

HOSTESS   Thou art an unjust man in saying so. Thou or
any man knows where to have me, thou knave, thou.

PRINCE   Thou say'st true, hostess, and he slanders thee
most grossly.

HOSTESS   So he doth you, my lord, and said this other
day you owed him a thousand pound.

PRINCE   Sirrah, do I owe you a thousand pound?

FALSTAFF   A thousand pound, Hal? A million. Thy love
is worth a million; thou owest me thy love.

HOSTESS   Nay, my lord, he called you Jack and said he
would cudgel you.

FALSTAFF   Did I, Bardolph?

BARDOLPH   Indeed, Sir John, you said so.

FALSTAFF   Yea, if he said my ring was copper.

PRINCE   I say 'tis copper. Darest thou be as good as thy
word now?

FALSTAFF   Why, Hal, thou knowest, as thou art but
man, I dare; but as thou art prince, I fear thee as I fear
the roaring of the lion's whelp.                 148

PRINCE   And why not as the lion?

FALSTAFF   The King himself is to be feared as the lion.
Dost thou think I'll fear thee as I fear thy father? Nay,
an I do, I pray God my girdle break.

PRINCE   Oh, if it should, how would thy guts fall about
thy knees! But, sirrah, there's no room for faith, truth,
nor honesty in this bosom of thine; it is all filled up
with guts and midriff. Charge an honest woman with
picking thy pocket? Why, thou whoreson, impudent,
embossed rascal, if there were anything in thy pocket 158
but tavern reckonings, memorandums of bawdy
houses, and one poor pennyworth of sugar candy to
make thee long-winded, if thy pocket were enriched
with any other injuries but these, I am a villain. And 162
yet you will stand to it; you will not pocket up wrong! 163
Art thou not ashamed?

FALSTAFF   Dost thou hear, Hal? Thou knowest in the
state of innocency Adam fell; and what should poor
Jack Falstaff do in the days of villainy? Thou see'st I
have more flesh than another man, and therefore
more frailty. You confess then you picked my pocket.

PRINCE   It appears so by the story.

FALSTAFF   Hostess, I forgive thee. Go make ready breakfast. Love thy husband, look to thy servants, cherish
thy guests. Thou shalt find me tractable to any honest
reason; thou see'st I am pacified still. Nay, prithee, 174
begone.                              *Exit Hostess.*
Now, Hal, to the news at court: for the robbery, lad,
how is that answered?

PRINCE   Oh, my sweet beef, I must still be good angel to
thee. The money is paid back again.

FALSTAFF   Oh, I do not like that paying back. 'Tis a
double labor.                                    181

PRINCE   I am good friends with my father and may do
anything.

FALSTAFF   Rob me the exchequer the first thing thou
dost, and do it with unwashed hands too.          185

BARDOLPH   Do, my lord.

PRINCE   I have procured thee, Jack, a charge of foot.  187

FALSTAFF   I would it had been of horse. Where shall I
find one that can steal well? Oh, for a fine thief, of the 189
age of two-and-twenty or thereabouts! I am heinously
unprovided. Well, God be thanked for these rebels; 191
they offend none but the virtuous. I laud them, I 192
praise them.

PRINCE   Bardolph!

BARDOLPH   My lord?

PRINCE [*giving letters*]
Go bear this letter to Lord John of Lancaster,
To my brother John; this to my lord of Westmorland. 197
                                    [*Exit Bardolph.*]
Go, Peto, to horse, to horse, for thou and I
Have thirty miles to ride yet ere dinnertime.
                                         [*Exit Peto.*]
Jack, meet me tomorrow in the Temple Hall      200
At two o'clock in the afternoon.
There shalt thou know thy charge, and there receive 202
Money and order for their furniture.            203
The land is burning. Percy stands on high,
And either we or they must lower lie.       [*Exit.*]

FALSTAFF
Rare words! Brave world! Hostess, my breakfast, come! 206
Oh, I could wish this tavern were my drum!   [*Exit.*] 207

# [4.1]

[*Enter Hotspur, Worcester, and Douglas.*]

HOTSPUR
Well said, my noble Scot. If speaking truth

---

121 **setting . . . aside** (Mistress Quickly means, "without wishing to offend your rank of knighthood," but Falstaff replies in line 123 with the meaning, "setting aside your womanhood as of no value or perti-nence.")   128 **She's . . . flesh** (The otter was thought to have the fea-tures of both fish and land-dwelling animals.)   129 **have** understand. (With a sly suggestion of sexual possession—a meaning that eludes Mistress Quickly.)   148 **whelp** cub.   158 **embossed** (1) swollen with fat (2) foaming at the mouth and exhausted, like a hunted animal. **rascal** (1) scoundrel (2) immature and inferior deer   162 **injuries** i.e., those things you claim to have lost, thereby suffering harm
163 **stand to it** make a stand, insist on your supposed rights.   **pocket up** endure silently

174 **still** always.   181 **double labor** i.e., the taking and the returning.
185 **with unwashed hands** without further ado   187 **charge of foot** command of a company of infantry.   189 **one** i.e., a companion in thievery. (Falstaff sees war as the opportunity for stealing and con-ning.)   191 **unprovided** ill-equipped.   192 **they . . . virtuous** i.e., the rebels, by providing the occasion of war, give dishonest men a chance to profiteer and hence offend only those who are honest.   197 **my brother John** i.e., John, Duke of Lancaster, mentioned in the previous line   200 **Temple Hall** i.e., at the Inner Temple, one of the Inns of Court   202 **charge** responsibility, assignment   203 **furniture** equip-ment, furnishing.   206 **Rare** Excellent.   **Brave** Splendid   207 **drum** (Possibly Falstaff means that he wishes he could continue to enjoy this tavern instead of risking his life in battle. He may also be pun-ning on *tavern/taborn*, i.e., *taborin*, a kind of drum.)
**4.1. Location:** The rebel camp near Shrewsbury.

In this fine age were not thought flattery,
Such attribution should the Douglas have                    3
As not a soldier of this season's stamp                     4
Should go so general current through the world.             5
By God, I cannot flatter; I do defy                         6
The tongues of soothers! But a braver place                 7
In my heart's love hath no man than yourself.
Nay, task me to my word; approve me, lord.                  9
DOUGLAS    Thou art the king of honor.
No man so potent breathes upon the ground                  11
But I will beard him.

*Enter one [a Messenger] with letters.*

HOTSPUR                 Do so, and 'tis well.—             12
What letters hast thou there?—I can but thank you.         13
MESSENGER
These letters come from your father.
HOTSPUR
Letters from him? Why comes he not himself?
MESSENGER
He cannot come, my lord. He is grievous sick.
HOTSPUR
Zounds, how has he the leisure to be sick
In such a jostling time? Who leads his power?              18
Under whose government come they along?                   19
MESSENGER
His letters bears his mind, not I, my lord.
                          *[Hotspur reads the letter.]*
WORCESTER
I prithee, tell me, doth he keep his bed?                 21
MESSENGER
He did, my lord, four days ere I set forth,
And at the time of my departure thence
He was much feared by his physicians.                     24
WORCESTER
I would the state of time had first been whole            25
Ere he by sickness had been visited.
His health was never better worth than now.
HOTSPUR
Sick now? Droop now? This sickness doth infect
The very life-blood of our enterprise;
'Tis catching hither, even to our camp.
He writes me here that inward sickness—
And that his friends by deputation                        32
Could not so soon be drawn, nor did he think it meet      33
To lay so dangerous and dear a trust
On any soul removed but on his own.                       35
Yet doth he give us bold advertisement                    36

That with our small conjunction we should on,             37
To see how fortune is disposed to us;
For, as he writes, there is no quailing now,              39
Because the King is certainly possessed                   40
Of all our purposes. What say you to it?
WORCESTER
Your father's sickness is a maim to us.                   42
HOTSPUR
A perilous gash, a very limb lopped off.
And yet, in faith, it is not! His present want            44
Seems more than we shall find it. Were it good            45
To set the exact wealth of all our states                 46
All at one cast? To set so rich a main                    47
On the nice hazard of one doubtful hour?                  48
It were not good, for therein should we read              49
The very bottom and the soul of hope,                     50
The very list, the very utmost bound                      51
Of all our fortunes.
DOUGLAS                 Faith, and so we should;
Where now remains a sweet reversion,                      53
We may boldly spend upon the hope
Of what is to come in.
A comfort of retirement lives in this.                    56
HOTSPUR
A rendezvous, a home to fly unto,
If that the devil and mischance look big                  58
Upon the maidenhead of our affairs.                       59
WORCESTER
But yet I would your father had been here.
The quality and hair of our attempt                       61
Brooks no division. It will be thought                    62
By some that know not why he is away
That wisdom, loyalty, and mere dislike                    64
Of our proceedings kept the Earl from hence.
And think how such an apprehension                        66
May turn the tide of fearful faction                      67
And breed a kind of question in our cause.
For well you know we of the off'ring side                 69
Must keep aloof from strict arbitrament,                  70
And stop all sight-holes, every loop from whence          71
The eye of reason may pry in upon us.
This absence of your father's draws a curtain             73
That shows the ignorant a kind of fear
Before not dreamt of.
HOTSPUR                 You strain too far.               75
I rather of his absence make this use:

---

3 **attribution** praise, tribute   4–5 **As . . . world** that no one coined as a soldier in this current campaign should enjoy such a current reputation. (To **go . . . current** is to be put into circulation, continuing the image of coining in line 4.)   6 **defy** proclaim against   7 **soothers** flatterers.   **braver** better, dearer   9 **task . . . word** challenge me to make good my word.   **approve** test   11–12 **No . . . him** i.e., I am ready to defy anyone alive.   13 **I can . . . you** (Said to Douglas.)   18 **jostling** contending, clashing   19 **government** command   21 **keep** keep to   24 **feared** feared for   25 **time** the times   32–3 **And that . . . drawn** and that his allies could not so soon be assembled by anyone other than himself, any deputy   33 **meet** appropriate   35 **On . . . own** on anyone other than himself.   36 **advertisement** counsel, advice

37 **conjunction** joint force.   **on** go on   39 **quailing** losing heart   40 **possessed** informed   42 **maim** injury   44 **want** absence   45 **more** more serious   46 **To . . . states** to stake the absolute total of our resources   47 **cast** throw of the dice.   **main** stake in gambling; also, an army   48 **nice** precarious, delicate.   **hazard** (1) game at dice (2) venture   49–50 **should . . . hope** we should discover the utmost foundation and basis of our hopes, the most we could rely on   51 **list** limit   53 **Where . . . reversion** since as things stand we can expect reinforcements. (A *reversion* is literally part of an estate yet to be inherited.)   56 **retirement** something to fall back on   58 **big** threateningly   59 **maidenhead** i.e., commencement   61 **hair** kind, nature   62 **Brooks** tolerates   64 **loyalty** i.e., to the crown   66 **apprehension** (1) perception (2) apprehensiveness   67 **fearful faction** timid support   69 **off'ring side** side that attacks   70 **strict arbitrament** just inquiry or investigation   71 **sight-holes** peep-holes. (*Loop*, i.e., loophole, has the same meaning.)   73 **draws** draws aside, opens   75 **strain too far** exaggerate.

It lends a luster and more great opinion,                                77
A larger dare to our great enterprise,                                   78
Than if the Earl were here; for men must think,
If we without his help can make a head                                   80
To push against a kingdom, with his help
We shall o'erturn it topsy-turvy down.
Yet all goes well, yet all our joints are whole.                         83

DOUGLAS
As heart can think. There is not such a word
Spoke of in Scotland as this term of fear.

*Enter Sir Richard Vernon.*

HOTSPUR
My cousin Vernon, welcome, by my soul.

VERNON
Pray God my news be worth a welcome, lord.
The Earl of Westmorland, seven thousand strong,
Is marching hitherwards; with him Prince John.

HOTSPUR
No harm. What more?

VERNON                         And further I have learned
The King himself in person is set forth,
Or hitherwards intended speedily,                                        92
With strong and mighty preparation.

HOTSPUR
He shall be welcome too. Where is his son,
The nimble-footed madcap Prince of Wales,
And his comrades, that doffed the world aside                            96
And bid it pass?

VERNON                    All furnished, all in arms                     97
All plumed like estridges, that with the wind                            98
Bated like eagles having lately bathed,                                  99
Glittering in golden coats, like images,                                 100
As full of spirit as the month of May
And gorgeous as the sun at midsummer,
Wanton as youthful goats, wild as young bulls.                           103
I saw young Harry, with his beaver on,                                   104
His cuisses on his thighs, gallantly armed,                              105
Rise from the ground like feathered Mercury,
And vaulted with such ease into his seat                                 107
As if an angel dropped down from the clouds
To turn and wind a fiery Pegasus                                         109
And witch the world with noble horsemanship.                             110

HOTSPUR
No more, no more! Worse than the sun in March                            111
This praise doth nourish agues. Let them come.                           112
They come like sacrifices in their trim,                                 113

And to the fire-eyed maid of smoky war                                   114
All hot and bleeding will we offer them.
The mailèd Mars shall on his altar sit                                   116
Up to the ears in blood. I am on fire
To hear this rich reprisal is so nigh,                                   118
And yet not ours. Come, let me taste my horse,                           119
Who is to bear me like a thunderbolt
Against the bosom of the Prince of Wales.
Harry to Harry shall, hot horse to horse,
Meet and ne'er part till one drop down a corse.                          123
Oh, that Glendower were come!

VERNON                                  There is more news:
I learned in Worcester, as I rode along,
He cannot draw his power this fourteen days.                             126

DOUGLAS
That's the worst tidings that I hear of yet.

WORCESTER
Ay, by my faith, that bears a frosty sound.

HOTSPUR
What may the King's whole battle reach unto?                             129

VERNON
To thirty thousand.

HOTSPUR                         Forty let it be!
My father and Glendower being both away,
The powers of us may serve so great a day.                               132
Come, let us take a muster speedily.
Doomsday is near; die all, die merrily.

DOUGLAS
Talk not of dying. I am out of fear                                      135
Of death or death's hand for this one half year.                        136
                                                            *Exeunt.*

❧

# [4.2]

*Enter Falstaff, [and] Bardolph.*

FALSTAFF   Bardolph, get thee before to Coventry; fill
me a bottle of sack. Our soldiers shall march through;
we'll to Sutton Coldfield tonight.                                        3

BARDOLPH   Will you give me money, Captain?

FALSTAFF   Lay out, lay out.                                              5

BARDOLPH   This bottle makes an angel.                                    6

FALSTAFF   An if it do, take it for thy labor; an if it make
twenty, take them all; I'll answer the coinage. Bid my      8
lieutenant Peto meet me at town's end.

BARDOLPH   I will, Captain. Farewell.                        *Exit.*

FALSTAFF   If I be not ashamed of my soldiers, I am a
soused gurnet. I have misused the King's press dam-         12
nably. I have got, in exchange of a hundred and fifty

---

**77 opinion** renown   **78 dare** daring   **80 make a head** raise an armed force   **83 Yet** Still.   **joints** limbs   **92 intended** on the verge of departure   **96–7 that doffed . . . pass?** i.e., that thumbed their noses at responsibilities, telling the world to mind its own business?   **97 furnished** equipped   **98–9 All . . . bathed** i.e., all plumed with ostrich feathers, fluttering their wings in the wind like eagles having just bathed. (The text may be defective.)   **100 coats** (1) coats of mail (2) heraldic coats of arms.   **images** gilded statues   **103 Wanton** sportive, frolicsome   **104 beaver** visor; hence, helmet   **105 cuisses** armor for the thighs   **107 seat** saddle   **109 wind** wheel about.   **Pegasus** winged horse of Greek mythology   **110 witch** bewitch   **111–12 Worse . . . agues** (The spring sun was believed to give impetus to chills and fevers, by drawing up vapors. Vernon's speech, says Hotspur, gives one the shudders.)   **113 sacrifices** beasts for sacrifice.   **trim** fine apparel, trappings

**114 maid** i.e., Bellona, goddess of war   **116 mailèd** dressed in mail, armor   **118 reprisal** prize   **119 taste** try, feel under me   **123 corse** corpse.   **126 draw his power** muster his army   **129 battle** army   **132 The . . . us** our forces   **135 out of** free from   **136 for . . . year** i.e., for any time soon.
**4.2. Location:** A public road near Coventry.
**3 Sutton Coldfield** (In Warwickshire near Coventry.)   **5 Lay out** Pay for it yourself   **6 makes an angel** i.e., makes ten shillings I've spent for you. (But Falstaff answers as though *makes* means "produces," implying that Bardolph can profit from the transaction.)   **8 I'll . . . coinage** I'll take responsibility for any proceeds.   **12 soused gurnet** a kind of pickled fish.   **King's press** royal warrant for the impressment of troops

soldiers, three hundred and odd pounds. I press me   14
none but good householders, yeomen's sons, inquire   15
me out contracted bachelors, such as had been asked   16
twice on the banns—such a commodity of warm   17
slaves as had as lief hear the devil as a drum, such as   18
fear the report of a caliver worse than a struck fowl or   19
a hurt wild duck. I pressed me none but such toasts-   20
and-butter, with hearts in their bellies no bigger than   21
pins' heads, and they have bought out their services;   22
and now my whole charge consists of ancients, cor-   23
porals, lieutenants, gentlemen of companies— slaves   24
as ragged as Lazarus in the painted cloth, where the   25
glutton's dogs licked his sores, and such as indeed
were never soldiers, but discarded unjust servingmen,   27
younger sons to younger brothers, revolted tapsters,   28
and hostlers trade-fallen, the cankers of a calm world   29
and a long peace, ten times more dishonorable-ragged
than an old feazed ancient. And such have I, to fill up   31
the rooms of them as have bought out their services,   32
that you would think that I had a hundred and fifty tattered prodigals lately come from swine keeping, from   34
eating draff and husks. A mad fellow met me on the way   35
and told me I had unloaded all the gibbets and pressed   36
the dead bodies. No eye hath seen such scarecrows. I'll
not march through Coventry with them, that's flat.   38
Nay, and the villains march wide betwixt the legs as if
they had gyves on, for indeed I had the most of them   40
out of prison. There's not a shirt and a half in all my
company, and the half shirt is two napkins tacked together and thrown over the shoulders like a herald's
coat without sleeves; and the shirt, to say the truth,
stolen from my host at Saint Albans, or the red-nose   45
innkeeper of Daventry. But that's all one; they'll find   46
linen enough on every hedge.   47

*Enter the Prince [and the] Lord of Westmorland.*

PRINCE   How now, blown Jack? How now, quilt?   48
FALSTAFF   What, Hal? How now, mad wag? What a
devil dost thou in Warwickshire?—My good lord of

Westmorland, I cry you mercy. I thought Your Honor   51
had already been at Shrewsbury.
WESTMORLAND   Faith, Sir John, 'tis more than time that
I were there, and you too; but my powers are there   54
already. The King, I can tell you, looks for us all. We
must away all night.   56
FALSTAFF   Tut, never fear me. I am as vigilant as a cat to   57
steal cream.
PRINCE   I think, to steal cream indeed, for thy theft hath   59
already made thee butter. But tell me, Jack, whose   60
fellows are these that come after?
FALSTAFF   Mine, Hal, mine.
PRINCE   I did never see such pitiful rascals.
FALSTAFF   Tut, tut, good enough to toss; food for   64
powder, food for powder. They'll fill a pit as well as   65
better. Tush, man, mortal men, mortal men.
WESTMORLAND   Ay, but, Sir John, methinks they are
exceeding poor and bare, too beggarly.   68
FALSTAFF   Faith, for their poverty, I know not where   69
they had that, and for their bareness, I am sure they
never learned that of me.
PRINCE   No, I'll be sworn, unless you call three fingers   72
in the ribs bare. But, sirrah, make haste. Percy is   73
already in the field.                                          *Exit.*
FALSTAFF   What, is the King encamped?   75
WESTMORLAND   He is, Sir John. I fear we shall stay too
long.                                                      [*Exit.*]
FALSTAFF   Well,
To the latter end of a fray and the beginning of a feast   79
Fits a dull fighter and a keen guest.          *Exit.*   80

# [4.3]

*Enter Hotspur, Worcester, Douglas, [and]
Vernon.*

HOTSPUR
We'll fight with him tonight.
WORCESTER                                   It may not be.
DOUGLAS
You give him then advantage.
VERNON                                     Not a whit.   2
HOTSPUR
Why say you so? Looks he not for supply?   3
VERNON
So do we.
HOTSPUR   His is certain; ours is doubtful.

---

14 **press me** draft, conscript   15 **good** i.e., wealthy.   **yeomen's** small freeholders'   16 **contracted** engaged to be married   17 **banns** public announcements, declared on three Sundays in succession, of an intent to marry.   **warm** i.e., loving their comfort   18 **lief** willingly   19 **report** firing.   **caliver** musket.   **struck** wounded   20–1 **toasts-and-butter** weaklings   22 **bought . . . services** i.e., paid, bribed, to be released from military duty   23 **charge** company, troop.   **ancients** ensigns, standard-bearers. (By appointing a disproportionate number of junior officers, Falstaff has made it possible to collect for himself their more substantial pay.)   24 **gentlemen of companies** gentlemen without official military rank   25 **painted cloth** cheap hangings for a room. (For the story of Lazarus the beggar and Dives the rich man, see Luke 16:19–31.)   27 **discarded** dismissed.   **unjust** dishonest   28 **younger sons . . . brothers** (i.e., with no possibility of inheritance).   **revolted** runaway   29 **trade-fallen** whose business has fallen away.   **cankers** cankerworms that destroy leaves and buds. (Used figuratively.)   31 **feazed ancient** frayed flag.   32 **the rooms . . . services** the places of those who have paid bribes to be excused from military service   34 **prodigals** spendthrifts (see Luke 15:15–16) now down on their luck   35 **draff** hogwash.   **mad** madcap   36 **gibbets** gallows.   **pressed** recruited or shanghaied   38 **that's flat** that's for sure.   40 **gyves** fetters   45 **my host** the innkeeper   45, 46 **Saint Albans, Daventry** (Towns north and west of London, on the road to Coventry.)   46 **that's all one** no matter   47 **hedge** (where wet linen was spread out to dry and could be easily stolen).   48 **blown** swollen, inflated; also, short of wind.   **quilt** thickly padded.

51 **cry you mercy** beg your pardon.   54 **powers** soldiers   56 **must away** must march   57 **fear** worry about   59–60 **thy . . . butter** i.e., all the cream (rich things) you have stolen has been churned into butterfat in your barrel-like belly.   64 **toss** toss on a pike   64–5 **food for powder** cannon fodder   68 **poor and bare** inferior and threadbare. (But Falstaff puns on the sense of "financially strapped and lean.")   69 **for** as for   72–3 **three . . . ribs** i.e., Falstaff's fat-covered ribs. (A *finger* was a measure of three-fourths of an inch.)   75 **encamped** set up in camp at Shrewsbury; or, perhaps, having broken up camp to move to battle   79–80 **To . . . guest** i.e., Better to be late to a battle and early to a feast. (*Keen* means "with keen appetite.")   **4.3. Location: The rebel camp near Shrewsbury.**   2 **then** i.e., if you wait. (Addressed to Worcester, not Hotspur.)   3 **supply** reinforcements.

**WORCESTER**
Good cousin, be advised, stir not tonight.
**VERNON**
Do not, my lord.
**DOUGLAS**                You do not counsel well.
You speak it out of fear and cold heart.
**VERNON**
Do me no slander, Douglas. By my life,
And I dare well maintain it with my life,
If well-respected honor bid me on,                                    10
I hold as little counsel with weak fear                               11
As you, my lord, or any Scot that this day lives.
Let it be seen tomorrow in the battle
Which of us fears.
**DOUGLAS**        Yea, or tonight.
**VERNON**      Content.
**HOTSPUR**      Tonight, say I.
**VERNON**
Come, come, it may not be. I wonder much,                             18
Being men of such great leading as you are,                           19
That you foresee not what impediments
Drag back our expedition. Certain horse                               21
Of my cousin Vernon's are not yet come up.
Your uncle Worcester's horse came but today,
And now their pride and mettle is asleep,                             24
Their courage with hard labor tame and dull,
That not a horse is half the half of himself.
**HOTSPUR**
So are the horses of the enemy
In general journey-bated and brought low.                             28
The better part of ours are full of rest.
**WORCESTER**
The number of the King exceedeth our.
For God's sake, cousin, stay till all come in.                        31
                    *The trumpet sounds a parley.*

                    *Enter Sir Walter Blunt.*

**BLUNT**
I come with gracious offers from the King,
If you vouchsafe me hearing and respect.                              33
**HOTSPUR**
Welcome, Sir Walter Blunt; and would to God
You were of our determination!                                        35
Some of us love you well; and even those some           36
Envy your great deservings and good name
Because you are not of our quality                                    38
But stand against us like an enemy.
**BLUNT**
And God defend but still I should stand so,                           40
So long as out of limit and true rule                                 41
You stand against anointed majesty.
But to my charge. The King hath sent to know                          43

The nature of your griefs and whereupon                               44
You conjure from the breast of civil peace
Such bold hostility, teaching his duteous land
Audacious cruelty. If that the King                                   47
Have any way your good deserts forgot,
Which he confesseth to be manifold,
He bids you name your griefs, and with all speed
You shall have your desires with interest
And pardon absolute for yourself and these
Herein misled by your suggestion.                                     53
**HOTSPUR**
The King is kind; and well we know the King
Knows at what time to promise, when to pay.
My father and my uncle and myself
Did give him that same royalty he wears,
And when he was not six-and-twenty strong,
Sick in the world's regard, wretched and low,
A poor unminded outlaw sneaking home,                                 60
My father gave him welcome to the shore;
And when he heard him swear and vow to God
He came but to be Duke of Lancaster,
To sue his livery and beg his peace                                   64
With tears of innocency and terms of zeal,
My father, in kind heart and pity moved,
Swore him assistance, and performed it too.
Now when the lords and barons of the realm
Perceived Northumberland did lean to him,
The more and less came in with cap and knee,                          70
Met him in boroughs, cities, villages,
Attended him on bridges, stood in lanes,                              72
Laid gifts before him, proffered him their oaths,
Gave him their heirs as pages, followed him                           74
Even at the heels in golden multitudes.                               75
He presently, as greatness knows itself,                              76
Steps me a little higher than his vow                                 77
Made to my father while his blood was poor                            78
Upon the naked shore at Ravenspurgh,
And now, forsooth, takes on him to reform
Some certain edicts and some strait decrees                           81
That lie too heavy on the commonwealth,
Cries out upon abuses, seems to weep
Over his country's wrongs; and by this face,                          84
This seeming brow of justice, did he win
The hearts of all that he did angle for;
Proceeded further—cut me off the heads                                87
Of all the favorites that the absent King
In deputation left behind him here
When he was personal in the Irish war.                                90

**44 griefs** grievances   **47 If that** If   **53 suggestion** instigation.
**60 unminded** disregarded   **64 To sue . . . peace** to petition to take
possession of his rightful inheritance and be reconciled with King
Richard II   **70 The more . . . knee** persons of all ranks came to Bolingbroke with cap in hand and with bended knee   **72 Attended** waited
for.   **stood in lanes** stood row-deep along the roads   **74 Gave . . .**
**pages** i.e., brought him their heirs to serve as pages and also as hostages to the fathers' loyalty   **75 golden** (1) auspicious, celebrating (2)
majestically attired   **76 knows itself** perceives its own strength
**77 Steps me** i.e., steps. (*Me* is used colloquially.)   **vow** i.e., Bolingbroke's vow to seek no more than his inheritance   **78 while . . . poor**
i.e., while Bolingbroke's spirits were still humbled and his dynastic
claim in question   **81 strait** strict   **84 face** show, pretense   **87 cut**
**me** i.e., cut   **90 personal** in person

**10 well-respected** well weighed or considered   **11 I hold . . . counsel**
I have as little to do   **18 it may not be** i.e., enough of this quarreling.   **19 leading** leadership   **21 expedition** speedy progress.   **horse**
cavalry. (As also at line 23.)   **24 pride and mettle** spirit   **28 journey-**
**bated** tired from the journey   **31.1 *parley*** trumpet summons to a
conference.   **33 respect** respectful attention.   **35 determination**
persuasion (in the fight).   **36 even those some** those same persons   **38 Because** all the more so in that.   **quality** party   **40 defend**
forbid.   **still** always   **41 limit** bounds of allegiance   **43 charge**
commission.

BLUNT
Tut, I came not to hear this.
HOTSPUR                               Then to the point.
In short time after, he deposed the King,
Soon after that, deprived him of his life,
And in the neck of that tasked the whole state;     94
To make that worse, suffered his kinsman March—
Who is, if every owner were well placed,     96
Indeed his king—to be engaged in Wales,     97
There without ransom to lie forfeited;     98
Disgraced me in my happy victories,     99
Sought to entrap me by intelligence;     100
Rated mine uncle from the Council board;     101
In rage dismissed my father from the court;
Broke oath on oath, committed wrong on wrong,
And in conclusion drove us to seek out
This head of safety, and withal to pry     105
Into his title, the which we find
Too indirect for long continuance.
BLUNT
Shall I return this answer to the King?
HOTSPUR
Not so, Sir Walter. We'll withdraw awhile.
Go to the King; and let there be impawned     110
Some surety for a safe return again,
And in the morning early shall mine uncle
Bring him our purposes. And so farewell.     113
BLUNT
I would you would accept of grace and love.
HOTSPUR
And maybe so we shall.
BLUNT                           Pray God you do.   [*Exeunt.*]

❧

## [4.4]

*Enter [the] Archbishop of York, [and] Sir Michael.*

ARCHBISHOP [*giving letters*]
Hie, good Sir Michael, bear this sealèd brief     1
With wingèd haste to the Lord Marshal,     2
This to my cousin Scroop, and all the rest     3
To whom they are directed. If you knew
How much they do import, you would make haste.
SIR MICHAEL   My good lord, I guess their tenor.
ARCHBISHOP   Like enough you do.     7
Tomorrow, good Sir Michael, is a day

Wherein the fortune of ten thousand men
Must bide the touch; for, sir, at Shrewsbury,     10
As I am truly given to understand,
The King with mighty and quick-raisèd power
Meets with Lord Harry. And I fear, Sir Michael,
What with the sickness of Northumberland,
Whose power was in the first proportion,     15
And what with Owen Glendower's absence thence,
Who with them was a rated sinew too     17
And comes not in, o'erruled by prophecies,
I fear the power of Percy is too weak
To wage an instant trial with the King.     20
SIR MICHAEL
Why, my good lord, you need not fear;
There is Douglas and Lord Mortimer.
ARCHBISHOP   No, Mortimer is not there.
SIR MICHAEL
But there is Mordake, Vernon, Lord Harry Percy,
And there is my lord of Worcester, and a head     25
Of gallant warriors, noble gentlemen.
ARCHBISHOP
And so there is. But yet the King hath drawn
The special head of all the land together:     28
The Prince of Wales, Lord John of Lancaster,
The noble Westmorland, and warlike Blunt,
And many more corrivals and dear men     31
Of estimation and command in arms.     32
SIR MICHAEL
Doubt not, my lord, they shall be well opposed.     33
ARCHBISHOP
I hope no less, yet needful 'tis to fear;
And, to prevent the worst, Sir Michael, speed.
For if Lord Percy thrive not, ere the King
Dismiss his power he means to visit us,     37
For he hath heard of our confederacy,
And 'tis but wisdom to make strong against him.
Therefore make haste. I must go write again
To other friends; and so farewell, Sir Michael.
                              *Exeunt [separately].*

❧

## [5.1]

*Enter the King, Prince of Wales, Lord John of Lancaster, Sir Walter Blunt, [and] Falstaff.*

KING
How bloodily the sun begins to peer
Above yon bosky hill! The day looks pale     2
At his distemperature.
PRINCE                         The southern wind     3
Doth play the trumpet to his purposes,     4

94 in . . . that next, immediately after.   tasked laid taxes upon   96 if . . . placed if every claimant were given his proper place   97 engaged held as hostage   98 lie forfeited remain prisoner, unreclaimed   99 Disgraced me (by demanding the prisoners; see 1.3.23 ff.)   happy fortunate   100 intelligence secret information, i.e., from spies   101 Rated scolded   105 head of safety armed force for our protection.   withal also   110 impawned pledged   113 purposes proposals.
4.4. Location: York. The Archbishop's palace.
1 brief letter, dispatch   2 Lord Marshal i.e., Thomas Mowbray, son of the Duke of Norfolk who is exiled in *Richard II*, and a longtime enemy of the new King   3 Scroop i.e., perhaps Sir Stephen Scroop of *Richard II*, 3.2.91–218, or Lord Scroop of Masham of *Henry* V, 2.2   7 Like Likely

10 bide the touch be put to the test (like gold)   15 in . . . proportion of the largest size   17 rated sinew main strength or support reckoned upon   20 instant immediate   25 head troop   28 special head notable leaders   31 corrivals partners in the enterprise   32 estimation reputation, importance   33 they i.e., the rebels   37 he i.e., the King
5.1. Location: The King's camp near Shrewsbury.
2 bosky bushy   3 his distemperature i.e., the sun's unhealthy appearance.   4 trumpet trumpeter.   his its, the sun's

And by his hollow whistling in the leaves
Foretells a tempest and a blust'ring day.

KING

Then with the losers let it sympathize,                         7
For nothing can seem foul to those that win.
                        *The trumpet sounds.*

*Enter Worcester [and Vernon].*

How now, my lord of Worcester? 'Tis not well
That you and I should meet upon such terms
As now we meet. You have deceived our trust
And made us doff our easy robes of peace              12
To crush our old limbs in ungentle steel.
This is not well, my lord, this is not well.
What say you to it? Will you again unknit
This churlish knot of all-abhorrèd war
And move in that obedient orb again                       17
Where you did give a fair and natural light,
And be no more an exhaled meteor,                        19
A prodigy of fear, and a portent                              20
Of broachèd mischief to the unborn times?           21

WORCESTER    Hear me, my liege:
For mine own part, I could be well content
To entertain the lag end of my life
With quiet hours, for I protest                                24
I have not sought the day of this dislike.            26

KING

You have not sought it? How comes it, then?

FALSTAFF    Rebellion lay in his way, and he found it.

PRINCE    Peace, chewet, peace!                            29

WORCESTER

It pleased Your Majesty to turn your looks
Of favor from myself and all our house;
And yet I must remember you, my lord,
We were the first and dearest of your friends.    32
For you my staff of office did I break
In Richard's time, and posted day and night         35
To meet you on the way, and kiss your hand,
When yet you were in place and in account
Nothing so strong and fortunate as I.                   38
It was myself, my brother, and his son
That brought you home and boldly did outdare    40
The dangers of the time. You swore to us,
And you did swear that oath at Doncaster,
That you did nothing purpose 'gainst the state,
Nor claim no further than your new-fall'n right,  44
The seat of Gaunt, dukedom of Lancaster.
To this we swore our aid. But in short space
It rained down fortune show'ring on your head,
And such a flood of greatness fell on you—

What with our help, what with the absent King,
What with the injuries of a wanton time,             50
The seeming sufferances that you had borne,       51
And the contrarious winds that held the King
So long in his unlucky Irish wars
That all in England did repute him dead—
And from this swarm of fair advantages
You took occasion to be quickly wooed                56
To grip the general sway into your hand;             57
Forgot your oath to us at Doncaster;
And being fed by us, you used us so
As that ungentle gull, the cuckoo's bird,             60
Useth the sparrow; did oppress our nest,
Grew by our feeding to so great a bulk
That even our love durst not come near your sight 63
For fear of swallowing; but with nimble wing
We were enforced, for safety sake, to fly
Out of your sight and raise this present head,      66
Whereby we stand opposèd by such means           67
As you yourself have forged against yourself
By unkind usage, dangerous countenance,           69
And violation of all faith and troth
Sworn to us in your younger enterprise.

KING

These things indeed you have articulate,             72
Proclaimed at market crosses, read in churches,  73
To face the garment of rebellion                          74
With some fine color that may please the eye       75
Of fickle changelings and poor discontents,         76
Which gape and rub the elbow at the news          77
Of hurly-burly innovation.                                    78
And never yet did insurrection want                     79
Such water-colors to impaint his cause,               80
Nor moody beggars, starving for a time                81
Of pell-mell havoc and confusion.                        82

PRINCE

In both your armies there is many a soul              83
Shall pay full dearly for this encounter,
If once they join in trial. Tell your nephew
The Prince of Wales doth join with all the world
In praise of Henry Percy. By my hopes—              87
This present enterprise set off his head—            88
I do not think a braver gentleman,
More active-valiant or more valiant-young,
More daring or more bold, is now alive
To grace this latter age with noble deeds.             92

7 **sympathize** accord    12 **easy** comfortable    17 **orb** orbit, sphere of action. (The King's subjects, like planets and stars in the Ptolemaic cosmos, were supposed to revolve around the kingly center, comparable to the earth, in fixed courses.)    19 **exhaled meteor** (Meteors were believed to be vapors drawn up or *exhaled* by the sun and visible as streaks of light; they were regarded as ill omens.)    20 **prodigy of fear** fearful omen    21 **broachèd** set flowing, already begun.    **the unborn times** the future.    24 **entertain** occupy    26 **the . . . dislike** this time of discord.    29 **chewet** chough, jackdaw. (Here, a chatterer.)    32 **remember** remind    35 **posted** rode swiftly    38 **Nothing** not at all    40 **home** back to England from exile    44 **new-fall'n** recently inherited (by the death of John of Gaunt)

50 **injuries** abuses.    **wanton** ill-managed    51 **sufferances** suffering, distress    56 **occasion** the opportunity    57 **the general sway** the kingship    60 **ungentle . . . bird** rude nestling, the cuckoo's young offspring. (The cuckoo lays its eggs in other birds' nests.)    63 **our love** we who loved you    66 **head** armed force    67 **opposèd . . . means** goaded into opposition by such factors    69 **dangerous countenance** threatening behavior    72 **articulate** set forth, specified    73 **market crosses** (Christian crosses were often erected in the centers of marketplaces—a good place for public announcements.)    74 **face** trim, adorn    75 **color** (1) hue (2) specious appearance    76 **changelings** turncoats    77 **rub the elbow** i.e., hug themselves with delight    78 **innovation** rebellion.    79 **want** lack    80 **water-colors** i.e., thin excuses. (See *color*, line 75.)    **his** its    81 **moody** sullen, angry    82 **havoc** plundering    83 **both your** i.e., your and our    87 **hopes** i.e., hopes of salvation    88 **This . . . head** i.e., if this present rebellion is taken from his account, not held against him    92 **this latter age** this present time

For my part, I may speak it to my shame,
I have a truant been to chivalry;
And so I hear he doth account me too.
Yet this before my father's majesty:
I am content that he shall take the odds                    97
Of his great name and estimation,                          98
And will, to save the blood on either side,
Try fortune with him in a single fight.

KING
And, Prince of Wales, so dare we venture thee,             101
Albeit considerations infinite                             102
Do make against it.—No, good Worcester, no.
We love our people well; even those we love
That are misled upon your cousin's part;                   105
And, will they take the offer of our grace,                106
Both he and they and you, yea, every man
Shall be my friend again, and I'll be his.
So tell your cousin, and bring me word
What he will do. But if he will not yield,
Rebuke and dread correction wait on us,                    111
And they shall do their office. So, begone.
We will not now be troubled with reply.
We offer fair; take it advisedly.
                        *Exit Worcester [with Vernon].*

PRINCE
It will not be accepted, on my life.
The Douglas and the Hotspur both together
Are confident against the world in arms.

KING
Hence, therefore, every leader to his charge;
For on their answer will we set on them,
And God befriend us as our cause is just!                  120
                        *Exeunt. Manent Prince, Falstaff.*
FALSTAFF  Hal, if thou see me down in the battle and
bestride me, so; 'tis a point of friendship.               122
PRINCE  Nothing but a colossus can do thee that friend-    123
ship. Say thy prayers, and farewell.
FALSTAFF  I would 'twere bedtime, Hal, and all well.
PRINCE  Why, thou owest God a death.        [*Exit.*] 126
FALSTAFF  'Tis not due yet; I would be loath to pay him
before his day. What need I be so forward with him
that calls not on me? Well, 'tis no matter; honor pricks   129
me on. Yea, but how if honor prick me off when I           130
come on? How then? Can honor set to a leg? No. Or          131
an arm? No. Or take away the grief of a wound? No.         132
Honor hath no skill in surgery, then? No. What is
honor? A word. What is in that word "honor"? What is
that "honor"? Air. A trim reckoning! Who hath it? He
that died o' Wednesday. Doth he feel it? No. Doth he
hear it? No. 'Tis insensible, then? Yea, to the dead. But
will it not live with the living? No. Why? Detraction      138

will not suffer it. Therefore I'll none of it. Honor is a   139
mere scutcheon. And so ends my catechism.                  140
                                            *Exit.*

❖

# [5.2]

*Enter Worcester [and] Sir Richard Vernon.*

WORCESTER
Oh, no, my nephew must not know, Sir Richard,
The liberal and kind offer of the King.
VERNON
'Twere best he did.
WORCESTER     Then are we all undone.
It is not possible, it cannot be,
The King should keep his word in loving us;
He will suspect us still and find a time
To punish this offense in other faults.                    7
Suspicion all our lives shall be stuck full of eyes;       8
For treason is but trusted like the fox,
Who, never so tame, so cherished, and locked up,           10
Will have a wild trick of his ancestors.                   11
Look how we can, or sad or merrily,                        12
Interpretation will misquote our looks,
And we shall feed like oxen at a stall,
The better cherished still the nearer death.
My nephew's trespass may be well forgot;
It hath the excuse of youth and heat of blood,
And an adopted name of privilege—                          18
A harebrained Hotspur, governed by a spleen.               19
All his offenses live upon my head
And on his father's. We did train him on,                  21
And, his corruption being ta'en from us,                   22
We as the spring of all shall pay for all.                 23
Therefore, good cousin, let not Harry know
In any case the offer of the King.

*Enter Hotspur [and Douglas, with soldiers].*

VERNON
Deliver what you will; I'll say 'tis so.                   26
Here comes your cousin.
HOTSPUR                    My uncle is returned.
Deliver up my lord of Westmorland.                         28
Uncle, what news?
WORCESTER
The King will bid you battle presently.
DOUGLAS
Defy him by the lord of Westmorland.                       31

---

**139 suffer** allow    **140 scutcheon** heraldic emblem carried in funerals, displayed on coaches, etc.; it was the lowest form of symbol, having no pennon or other insignia.    **catechism** the principles of faith given in the form of question and answer.
**5.2. Location:** Near the rebel camp.
**7 To . . . faults** to find other faults in us to punish (as a way of getting back at us for defying him militarily).    **8 stuck . . . eyes** i.e., provided with many eyes, suspiciously inquisitive    **10 never so** be he never so    **11 trick** trait    **12 or sad** either sad    **18 an adopted . . . privilege** i.e., a nickname, "Hotspur," to justify his rashness    **19 spleen** intemperate impulse.    **21 train** incite, draw    **22 his . . . us** i.e., since his guilt originated in us    **23 spring** source    **26 Deliver** Report
**28 Deliver up** Release (as hostage; see 4.3.110–11)    **31 Defy him by** Send back your defiance with

---

**97 take the odds** have the advantage    **98 estimation** reputation
**101 venture** hazard, risk    **102 Albeit** although it be that. (The subjunctive has the force of "were it not that.")    **105 cousin's** kinsman's
**106 will they** if they will.    **grace** pardon    **111 wait on us** are awaiting my royal command    **120.1 Manent** They remain on stage
**122 bestride** stand over in order to defend.    **so** well and good
**123 colossus** (Referring to the Colossus of Rhodes, a massive statue of Apollo reported to have stood astride the entrance to the harbor there.)
**126 thou . . . death** (Proverbial, with a pun on *debt.*)    **129 pricks**
spurs    **130 prick me off** mark me off (as one dead)    **131 set to** rejoin
or set    **132 grief** pain    **138 Detraction** Slander

HOTSPUR

Lord Douglas, go you and tell him so.

DOUGLAS

Marry, and shall, and very willingly.     *Exit Douglas.* 33

WORCESTER

There is no seeming mercy in the King.

HOTSPUR

Did you beg any? God forbid!

WORCESTER

I told him gently of our grievances,
Of his oathbreaking, which he mended thus,
By now forswearing that he is forsworn.
He calls us rebels, traitors, and will scourge
With haughty arms this hateful name in us.

*Enter Douglas.*

DOUGLAS

Arm, gentlemen, to arms! For I have thrown
A brave defiance in King Henry's teeth,                      42
And Westmorland, that was engaged, did bear it;             43
Which cannot choose but bring him quickly on.

WORCESTER

The Prince of Wales stepped forth before the King,
And, nephew, challenged you to single fight.

HOTSPUR

Oh, would the quarrel lay upon our heads,
And that no man might draw short breath today
But I and Harry Monmouth! Tell me, tell me,                 49
How showed his tasking? Seemed it in contempt?             50

VERNON

No, by my soul. I never in my life
Did hear a challenge urged more modestly,                   52
Unless a brother should a brother dare
To gentle exercise and proof of arms.                       54
He gave you all the duties of a man,                        55
Trimmed up your praises with a princely tongue,            56
Spoke your deservings like a chronicle,
Making you ever better than his praise
By still dispraising praise valued with you;               59
And, which became him like a prince indeed,
He made a blushing cital of himself,                        61
And chid his truant youth with such a grace
As if he mastered there a double spirit
Of teaching and of learning instantly.                      64
There did he pause. But let me tell the world,
If he outlive the envy of this day,                         66
England did never owe so sweet a hope,                      67
So much misconstrued in his wantonness.                     68

HOTSPUR

Cousin, I think thou art enamorèd
On his follies. Never did I hear
Of any prince so wild a liberty.                            71

But be he as he will, yet once ere night
I will embrace him with a soldier's arm,
That he shall shrink under my courtesy.                     74
Arm, arm with speed! And, fellows, soldiers, friends,
Better consider what you have to do
Than I, that have not well the gift of tongue,
Can lift your blood up with persuasion.

*Enter a Messenger.*

FIRST MESSENGER     My lord, here are letters for you.

HOTSPUR     I cannot read them now.
Oh, gentlemen, the time of life is short!
To spend that shortness basely were too long               82
If life did ride upon a dial's point,                       83
Still ending at the arrival of an hour.                     84
An if we live, we live to tread on kings;
If die, brave death, when princes die with us!              86
Now, for our consciences, the arms are fair                87
When the intent of bearing them is just.

*Enter another [Messenger].*

SECOND MESSENGER

My lord, prepare. The King comes on apace.

HOTSPUR

I thank him that he cuts me from my tale,
For I profess not talking. Only this—                       91
Let each man do his best. And here draw I
A sword, whose temper I intend to stain
With the best blood that I can meet withal
In the adventure of this perilous day.
Now, *Esperance!* Percy! And set on.                        96
Sound all the lofty instruments of war,
And by that music let us all embrace;
For, heaven to earth, some of us never shall                99
A second time do such a courtesy.
     *Here they embrace. The trumpets sound.*  [*Exeunt.*]

❖

# [5.3]

*The King enters with his power [and passes over
the stage]. Alarum to the battle. Then enter
Douglas, and Sir Walter Blunt [dressed like King
Henry].*

BLUNT

What is thy name, that in the battle thus
Thou crossest me? What honor dost thou seek                 2
Upon my head?

DOUGLAS                    Know then my name is Douglas,
And I do haunt thee in the battle thus
Because some tell me that thou art a king.

---

33 **Marry, and shall** i.e., Indeed, I will   42 **brave** proud   43 **engaged**
held as hostage   49 **Monmouth** (A name for the Prince, taken from
the Welsh town where he was born.)   50 **showed his tasking**
appeared his giving the challenge.   52 **urged** put forward   54 **gentle**
befitting noble birth.   **proof of arms** test of martial skill.   55 **duties**
due merits   56 **Trimmed . . . praises** adorned his praise of you
59 **By . . . you** by consistently disparaging praise itself as not sufficient
to measure your true worth   61 **cital** account, recital   64 **instantly**
simultaneously.   66 **envy** hostility   67 **owe** own   68 **wantonness**
playful sportiveness.   71 **liberty** licentiousness.

74 **shrink under my courtesy** (1) be daunted by my greater courtesy
(2) fall back before my attack.   **82–4 To . . . hour** Life is too short to
spend it basely, even if life were to last only the time needed for the dial
(or sundial) to advance a single hour, ending when that hour is up.
86 **brave death** (1) such a death would be glorious (2) let us defy death
itself by our courage   87 **for** as for.   **fair** just   91 **I . . . talking** I have
no calling as an orator.   96 ***Esperance!*** Hope! (The motto of the Percy
family.)   99 **heaven to earth** i.e., I'll wager heaven against earth
**5.3. Location:** Shrewsbury field. The scene is virtually continuous.
**0.1** *power* army.   **0.2** *Alarum* Trumpet signal to advance   **2 Thou
crossest me** you confront and challenge me.

BLUNT    They tell thee true.

DOUGLAS
The lord of Stafford dear today hath bought          7
Thy likeness, for instead of thee, King Harry,          8
This sword hath ended him. So shall it thee,
Unless thou yield thee as my prisoner.

BLUNT
I was not born a yielder, thou proud Scot,
And thou shalt find a king that will revenge
Lord Stafford's death.     *They fight. Douglas kills Blunt.*

            *Then enter Hotspur.*

HOTSPUR
Oh, Douglas, hadst thou fought at Holmedon thus,
I never had triumphed upon a Scot.

DOUGLAS
All's done, all's won; here breathless lies the King.     16

HOTSPUR    Where?

DOUGLAS    Here.

HOTSPUR
This, Douglas? No. I know this face full well.
A gallant knight he was; his name was Blunt,
Semblably furnished like the King himself.          21

DOUGLAS
A fool go with thy soul, whither it goes!          22
A borrowed title hast thou bought too dear.
Why didst thou tell me that thou wert a king?

HOTSPUR
The King hath many marching in his coats.          25

DOUGLAS
Now, by my sword, I will kill all his coats!
I'll murder all his wardrobe, piece by piece,
Until I meet the King.

HOTSPUR                    Up, and away!
Our soldiers stand full fairly for the day.     [*Exeunt.*]     29

            *Alarum. Enter Falstaff, solus.*

FALSTAFF    Though I could scape shot-free at London, I     30
fear the shot here; here's no scoring but upon the pate.     31
Soft, who are you? Sir Walter Blunt. There's honor for
you. Here's no vanity! I am as hot as molten lead, and     33
as heavy too. God keep lead out of me! I need no more
weight than mine own bowels. I have led my ragamuffins where they are peppered. There's not three of
my hundred and fifty left alive, and they are for the
town's end, to beg during life. But who comes here?     38

            *Enter the Prince.*

PRINCE
What, stands thou idle here? Lend me thy sword.

Many a nobleman lies stark and stiff          40
Under the hoofs of vaunting enemies,
Whose deaths are yet unrevenged. I prithee,
Lend me thy sword.

FALSTAFF    Oh, Hal, I prithee, give me leave to breathe
awhile. Turk Gregory never did such deeds in arms as     45
I have done this day. I have paid Percy, I have made     46
him sure.          47

PRINCE
He is, indeed, and living to kill thee.
I prithee, lend me thy sword.

FALSTAFF    Nay, before God, Hal, if Percy be alive, thou
gets not my sword; but take my pistol, if thou wilt.

PRINCE
Give it me. What, is it in the case?

FALSTAFF    Ay, Hal, 'tis hot, 'tis hot. There's that will     53
sack a city.
            *The Prince draws it out and finds it to be a bottle
of sack.*

PRINCE
What, is it a time to jest and dally now?
            *He throws the bottle at him. Exit.*

FALSTAFF    Well, if Percy be alive, I'll pierce him. If he do     56
come in my way, so; if he do not, if I come in his     57
willingly, let him make a carbonado of me. I like not     58
such grinning honor as Sir Walter hath. Give me life,     59
which if I can save, so; if not, honor comes unlooked
for, and there's an end.          [*Exit.*]     61

## [5.4]

            *Alarum. Excursions. Enter the King, the Prince,
Lord John of Lancaster, [and the] Earl of
Westmorland.*

KING    I prithee,
Harry, withdraw thyself; thou bleedest too much.
Lord John of Lancaster, go you with him.

LANCASTER
Not I, my lord, unless I did bleed too.

PRINCE
I beseech Your Majesty, make up,          5
Lest your retirement do amaze your friends.          6

KING
I will do so. My lord of Westmorland,
Lead him to his tent.

**7 dear** dearly   **7–8 bought Thy likeness** paid for his resemblance to you   **16 breathless** i.e., dead   **21 Semblably furnished** similarly accoutered   **22 A . . . soul** i.e., May the stigma of "fool" accompany your soul (for having dressed as a decoy of King Henry)   **25 coats** vests worn over armor embroidered with a coat of arms   **29 stand . . . day** i.e., seem in an auspicious position, likely to win the victory.   **30 scape shot-free** escape   **31 scoring** (1) cutting (2) marking up of charges, by notches on a stick or on the inn door   **33 Here's no vanity!** i.e. (ironically), If this doesn't show what I was saying about honor, then nothing does!   **38 town's end** i.e., city gate, frequented by beggars

**40 stark and stiff** in rigor mortis, utterly rigid   **45 Turk Gregory** (*Turk* is an abusive term signifying a tyrant, and Gregory refers probably to Pope Gregory XIII, who was assumed to have encouraged the Massacre of Saint Bartholomew [1572], in which many French Protestants were slain, and to have encouraged plots against Elizabeth.)   **46–7 made him sure** made sure of him. (But Prince Hal takes *sure* in a different sense, meaning "safe.")   **53 hot** (Falstaff implies he has been firing at the enemy.)   **56 Percy . . . pierce** (Elizabethan pronunciation rendered the pun more obvious than it is now.)   **57 so** well and good. (Also in line 60.)   **58 carbonado** meat scored across for broiling   **59 grinning honor** the seemingly grinning expression of a human skull   **61 there's an end** (1) that concludes the subject of my catechism (see 5.1.129–40) (2) thus life ends.
**5.4. Location:** Scene continues at Shrewsbury field.
**0.1 *Excursions*** Sorties. (The fallen body of Blunt may be removed at some point or may be onstage still at 5.4.77 when Hal kills Hotspur.)
**5 make up** go forward   **6 retirement** retreat   **amaze** alarm

**WESTMORLAND**
Come, my lord, I'll lead you to your tent.

**PRINCE**
Lead me, my lord? I do not need your help.
And God forbid a shallow scratch should drive
The Prince of Wales from such a field as this,
Where stained nobility lies trodden on
And rebels' arms triumph in massacres!

**LANCASTER**
We breathe too long. Come, cousin Westmorland,                    15
Our duty this way lies. For God's sake, come.
                    [*Exeunt Prince John and Westmorland.*]

**PRINCE**
By God, thou hast deceived me, Lancaster!
I did not think thee lord of such a spirit.
Before, I loved thee as a brother, John,
But now I do respect thee as my soul.

**KING**
I saw him hold Lord Percy at the point                            21
With lustier maintenance than I did look for                      22
Of such an ungrown warrior.

**PRINCE**
Oh, this boy lends mettle to us all!                    *Exit.*

          [*Enter Douglas.*]

**DOUGLAS**
Another king? They grow like Hydra's heads.                       25
I am the Douglas, fatal to all those
That wear those colors on them. What art thou                     27
That counterfeit'st the person of a king?

**KING**
The King himself, who, Douglas, grieves at heart
So many of his shadows thou hast met                              30
And not the very King. I have two boys                            31
Seek Percy and thyself about the field;                           32
But, seeing thou fall'st on me so luckily,
I will assay thee; and defend thyself.                            34

**DOUGLAS**
I fear thou art another counterfeit;
And yet, in faith, thou bearest thee like a king.
But mine I am sure thou art, whoe'er thou be,
And thus I win thee.
          *They fight; the King being in danger,*
                    *enter Prince of Wales.*

**PRINCE**
Hold up thy head, vile Scot, or thou art like                     39
Never to hold it up again! The spirits
Of valiant Shirley, Stafford, Blunt, are in my arms.
It is the Prince of Wales that threatens thee,
Who never promiseth but he means to pay.                          43
                    *They fight. Douglas flieth.*
Cheerly, my lord. How fares Your Grace?                           44

Sir Nicholas Gawsey hath for succor sent,
And so hath Clifton. I'll to Clifton straight.

**KING**     Stay and breathe awhile.
Thou hast redeemed thy lost opinion,                              48
And showed thou mak'st some tender of my life                     49
In this fair rescue thou hast brought to me.

**PRINCE**
Oh, God, they did me too much injury
That ever said I hearkened for your death.                        52
If it were so, I might have let alone
The insulting hand of Douglas over you,                           54
Which would have been as speedy in your end
As all the poisonous potions in the world,
And saved the treacherous labor of your son.

**KING**
Make up to Clifton; I'll to Sir Nicholas Gawsey.                  58
                    *Exit King.*

          *Enter Hotspur.*

**HOTSPUR**
If I mistake not, thou art Harry Monmouth.

**PRINCE**
Thou speak'st as if I would deny my name.

**HOTSPUR**
My name is Harry Percy.

**PRINCE**                    Why then, I see
A very valiant rebel of the name.
I am the Prince of Wales; and think not, Percy,
To share with me in glory any more.
Two stars keep not their motion in one sphere,
Nor can one England brook a double reign                          66
Of Harry Percy and the Prince of Wales.

**HOTSPUR**
Nor shall it, Harry, for the hour is come
To end the one of us; and would to God
Thy name in arms were now as great as mine!

**PRINCE**
I'll make it greater ere I part from thee,
And all the budding honors on thy crest
I'll crop to make a garland for my head.                          73

**HOTSPUR**
I can no longer brook thy vanities.     *They fight.*    74

          *Enter Falstaff.*

**FALSTAFF**     Well said, Hal! To it, Hal! Nay, you shall find    75
no boy's play here, I can tell you.                               76

          *Enter Douglas. He fighteth with Falstaff, who falls*
          *down as if he were dead.          [Exit Douglas.]*
          *The Prince killeth Percy.*

**HOTSPUR**
Oh, Harry, thou hast robbed me of my youth!
I better brook the loss of brittle life
Than those proud titles thou hast won of me;

---

**15 breathe** rest, pause for breath (as also at line 47)   **21 at the point**
at sword's point   **22 lustier maintenance** more vigorous bearing
**25 Hydra's heads** (The heads of the Lernaean Hydra grew again as
fast as they were cut off. The slaying of the Lernaean Hydra was the
second of Hercules's twelve mighty labors.)   **27 colors** i.e., the colors of
King's insignia   **30 shadows** likenesses   **31 two boys** Prince Hal and
his younger brother John   **32 Seek** who seek   **34 assay thee** put
you to the test   **39 like** likely   **43 pay** (1) settle a debt (2) kill.
**44 Cheerly** (A cry of encouragement; literally, "Cheerfully.")

**48 opinion** reputation   **49 thou . . . of** you have some care for
**52 hearkened for** desired   **54 insulting** exulting   **58 Make up**
Advance   **66 brook** endure   **73 crop** pluck   **74 brook thy vanities**
tolerate your empty boasts.   **75 Well said** Well done   **76.3 killeth**
mortally wounds

They wound my thoughts worse than thy sword my
    flesh.
But thoughts, the slaves of life, and life, time's fool,            81
And time, that takes survey of all the world,
Must have a stop. Oh, I could prophesy,
But that the earthy and cold hand of death
Lies on my tongue. No, Percy, thou art dust,
And food for—                                            [*He dies.*]

PRINCE
For worms, brave Percy. Fare thee well, great heart.
Ill-weaved ambition, how much art thou shrunk!
When that this body did contain a spirit,                          89
A kingdom for it was too small a bound;
But now two paces of the vilest earth
Is room enough. This earth that bears thee dead
Bears not alive so stout a gentleman.                              93
If thou wert sensible of courtesy,                                 94
I should not make so dear a show of zeal;                          95
But let my favors hide thy mangled face,                           96
And, even in thy behalf, I'll thank myself
For doing these fair rites of tenderness.
        [*He covers Hotspur's face with a scarf
                          or other favor.*]
Adieu, and take thy praise with thee to heaven!
Thy ignominy sleep with thee in the grave,
But not remembered in thy epitaph!
                *He spieth Falstaff on the ground.*
What, old acquaintance, could not all this flesh
Keep in a little life? Poor Jack, farewell!
I could have better spared a better man.
Oh, I should have a heavy miss of thee                            105
If I were much in love with vanity.                               106
Death hath not struck so fat a deer today,
Though many dearer, in this bloody fray.
Emboweled will I see thee by and by.                              109
Till then in blood by noble Percy lie.            *Exit.*
                                *Falstaff riseth up.*
FALSTAFF   Emboweled? If thou embowel me today, I'll
give you leave to powder me and eat me too tomor-        112
row. 'Sblood, 'twas time to counterfeit, or that hot ter-    113
magant Scot had paid me, scot and lot too. Counterfeit?  114
I lie, I am no counterfeit. To die is to be a counterfeit,
for he is but the counterfeit of a man who hath not the
life of a man; but to counterfeit dying, when a man
thereby liveth, is to be no counterfeit but the true and
perfect image of life indeed. The better part of valor is  119
discretion, in the which better part I have saved my
life. Zounds, I am afraid of this gunpowder Percy,
though he be dead. How if he should counterfeit too
and rise? By my faith, I am afraid he would prove the

better counterfeit. Therefore I'll make him sure; yea,
and I'll swear I killed him. Why may not he rise as well
as I? Nothing confutes me but eyes, and nobody sees     126
me. Therefore, sirrah [*stabbing him*], with a new
wound in your thigh, come you along with me.
                *He takes up Hotspur on his back.*

        *Enter Prince [and] John of Lancaster.*

PRINCE
Come, brother John; full bravely hast thou fleshed       129
Thy maiden sword.
LANCASTER              But soft, whom have we here?
Did you not tell me this fat man was dead?
PRINCE   I did; I saw him dead,
Breathless and bleeding on the ground.—Art thou
    alive?
Or is it fantasy that plays upon our eyesight?
I prithee, speak. We will not trust our eyes
Without our ears. Thou art not what thou seem'st.
FALSTAFF   No, that's certain, I am not a double man; but   137
if I be not Jack Falstaff, then am I a Jack. There is Percy  138
[*throwing the body down*]. If your father will do me
any honor, so; if not, let him kill the next Percy himself. I look to be either earl or duke, I can assure you.
PRINCE
Why, Percy I killed myself and saw thee dead.
FALSTAFF   Didst thou? Lord, Lord, how this world is
given to lying! I grant you I was down and out of
breath, and so was he; but we rose both at an instant   145
and fought a long hour by Shrewsbury clock. If I may
be believed, so; if not, let them that should reward
valor bear the sin upon their own heads. I'll take it    148
upon my death I gave him this wound in the thigh.        149
If the man were alive and would deny it, zounds, I
would make him eat a piece of my sword.
LANCASTER
This is the strangest tale that ever I heard.
PRINCE
This is the strangest fellow, brother John.—
Come, bring your luggage nobly on your back.
For my part, if a lie may do thee grace,                  155
I'll gild it with the happiest terms I have.              156
                        *A retreat is sounded.*
The trumpet sounds retreat; the day is our.               157
Come, brother, let us to the highest of the field,        158
To see what friends are living, who are dead.
            *Exeunt [Prince of Wales and Lancaster].*
FALSTAFF   I'll follow, as they say, for reward. He that re-
wards me, God reward him! If I do grow great, I'll
grow less; for I'll purge, and leave sack, and live        162
cleanly as a nobleman should do.
                        *Exit [bearing off the body].*

---

**81 thoughts . . . fool** i.e., our mental consciousness, which is dependent on physical existence, and our life itself, which is subject to time
**89 When that** When   **93 stout** valiant   **94 sensible of courtesy** able
to hear my praise   **95 dear** handsome, heartfelt.   **zeal** admiration
**96 favors** plume, scarf, glove, or similar article   **105 heavy** (1) serious
(2) corpulent   **106 vanity** frivolity.   **109 Emboweled** Disemboweled,
i.e., for embalming and burial   **112 powder** salt   **113–14 termagant**
violent and blustering, like the heathen god of the Saracens in medieval and Renaissance lore   **114 paid** i.e., killed.   **scot and lot** i.e., in
full. (Originally the phrase was the term for a parish tax.)   **119 part**
constituent part, quality, role

**126 Nothing . . . eyes** i.e., Nothing can contradict me but an eyewitness   **129 fleshed** initiated (in battle)   **137 double man** (1) specter
(2) two men   **138 a Jack** a knave.   **145 at an instant** simultaneously
**148–9 take . . . death** i.e., swear with my eternal soul at risk
**155 a lie** i.e., this lie of yours.   **grace** credit   **156 happiest** most
felicitous   **157 our** ours.   **158 highest** highest vantage point
**162 purge** (1) reduce in weight, using laxatives (2) repent

# [5.5]

*The trumpets sound. Enter the King, Prince of Wales, Lord John of Lancaster, Earl of Westmorland, with Worcester and Vernon prisoners.*

KING
Thus ever did rebellion find rebuke.
Ill-spirited Worcester! Did not we send grace,
Pardon, and terms of love to all of you?
And wouldst thou turn our offers contrary?
Misuse the tenor of thy kinsman's trust?                        5
Three knights upon our party slain today,
A noble earl, and many a creature else
Had been alive this hour,
If like a Christian thou hadst truly borne
Betwixt our armies true intelligence.                          10

WORCESTER
What I have done my safety urged me to;
And I embrace this fortune patiently,
Since not to be avoided it falls on me.

KING
Bear Worcester to the death, and Vernon too.
Other offenders we will pause upon.
          [*Exeunt Worcester and Vernon, guarded.*]
How goes the field?

PRINCE
The noble Scot, Lord Douglas, when he saw
The fortune of the day quite turned from him,
The noble Percy slain, and all his men
Upon the foot of fear, fled with the rest;                     20
And falling from a hill, he was so bruised
That the pursuers took him. At my tent
The Douglas is; and I beseech Your Grace
I may dispose of him.

KING                        With all my heart.

PRINCE
Then, brother John of Lancaster,
To you this honorable bounty shall belong.                     26
Go to the Douglas, and deliver him
Up to his pleasure, ransomless and free.
His valors shown upon our crests today                         29
Have taught us how to cherish such high deeds
Even in the bosom of our adversaries.

LANCASTER
I thank Your Grace for this high courtesy,
Which I shall give away immediately.                           33

KING
Then this remains, that we divide our power.
You, son John, and my cousin Westmorland
Towards York shall bend you with your dearest speed   36
To meet Northumberland and the prelate Scroop,
Who, as we hear, are busily in arms.
Myself and you, son Harry, will towards Wales,
To fight with Glendower and the Earl of March.
Rebellion in this land shall lose his sway,                    41
Meeting the check of such another day;                         42
And since this business so fair is done,                       43
Let us not leave till all our own be won.      *Exeunt.*       44

---

5.5. Location: The battlefield.
5 Misuse . . . trust? i.e., Would you abuse Hotspur's confidence in you (by concealing the generosity of my offer, in your role as emissary)?   10 intelligence information, report.

20 Upon . . . fear fleeing in panic   26 this honorable bounty the honor of this bounteous act   29 crests i.e., helmets   33 give away pass along, confer on Douglas   36 bend you direct your course. dearest most urgent   41 his its   42 Meeting . . . day i.e., when the rebellion is entirely repulsed at one more battlefield   43 fair successfully   44 leave leave off

# The Life of King Henry the Fifth

*H*enry V (1599) is Shakespeare's culminating statement in the genre of the English history play. Unlike the late and atypical *Henry VIII* (1613), which is separated from the rest of Shakespeare's history plays by some fourteen years, *Henry V* sums up the historical themes with which Shakespeare had been fascinated for an entire decade. The play, first published in a memorially reconstructed and abridged quarto in 1600, must have been written not long after *2 Henry IV*, perhaps as an opening production for the Chamberlain's Men's new Bankside theater, the Globe, in 1599. To be sure, the play does not entirely fulfill the promise made in *2 Henry IV* to "continue the story, with Sir John in it, and make you merry with fair Katharine of France." Falstaff is missing. As before, Shakespeare apparently saw a grand design to his four-play sequence (which had started with *Richard II*) but improvised when he came to the writing of each part. Despite these minor adjustments in the overall plan, however, *Henry V* is clearly intended to bring to fulfillment the education of a politician-prince and to illustrate the arts of political kingship that Prince Hal had derived from his experiences in the earlier plays.

In a sense, too, *Henry V* sums up the achievement of the English history play, not only for Shakespeare, but also for other popular playwrights. The patriotic history play, born in the excitement of the Armada era immediately after 1588, had nearly run its course by 1599 and was soon to be supplanted by other dramatic genres, such as satire and revenge tragedy. Dark and complex political realities were already changing the buoyant mood in which the history play had been born: the aging Queen Elizabeth was near death and without a Protestant heir, while fear of another invasion threatened. In *Henry V*, we sense the approaching end of an era, for the play both celebrates the achievements of the English monarchy and examines its limits.

*Henry V* has become a controversial play, chiefly because our recent experiences with war have led us to be wary of political leaders who, in the name of patriotism, lay claim to and invade another country. George Bernard Shaw is prominent among those who have deplored Henry as a priggish and complacent warmonger and imperialist. Many historically minded critics, on the other hand, warn of the dangers of reading anachronistically from a modern perspective, and they argue that Henry is an admirable model of conduct according to Renaissance notions of statecraft and military leadership. What is Shakespeare's attitude toward his war hero? Does he sympathize with Henry's condescension toward the French and his order to every soldier to kill his French prisoners? Or is Shakespeare's admiration qualified by ironic reservations? As is usual in Shakespeare's work, the perspective is complex and balanced. The play pulls us in two directions. Although the Chorus, which interprets the play for us, approves of Henry's military posture, the grandiose rhetoric of war is consistently undercut by matter-of-fact revelations of people's self-interested motives. This contrast between rhetorical illusion and political reality extends from the justification of Henry's French campaign to his state marriage with Katharine of France. On the ethical issue of killing the French prisoners, for example, the play offers us contradictory and seemingly irreconcilable impressions. At the end of 4.6, Henry orders that "every soldier" is to "kill his prisoners," evidently because the English are under attack and cannot spare men to guard those who have been captured. In 4.7 (lines 1–10 and 54–5), however, we are told by Gower that the King gave the order in retaliation for the massacre by the cowardly French of the boys guarding the English luggage. Similarly, on the eve of the battle of Agincourt, we are left to draw our own conclusions about King Henry's conversation with his soldiers (4.1. 98–227). Is he evading the question of whether his cause is just by turning to a really very different matter of responsibility for someone else's sins, or is he simply testing his men with hard questions to prepare them for battle? Ironic puzzles such as these probably never amount to open disillusionment in this play, although some modern critics and directors would argue otherwise; the ironies are perhaps, instead, the acknowledgment of a special kind of morality pertaining to kingship.

Skill in rhetoric is a key to Henry's success—in defying the French Dauphin, in preparing troops for battle, or in wooing the French princess for his queen. As the Archbishop of Canterbury notes approvingly, King Henry's versatility as a rhetorician applies to all the vital disciplines of kingship: Henry can "reason in divinity," "debate of commonwealth affairs," "discourse of war," handle "any cause of policy," and in all such matters speak in "sweet and honeyed sentences" (1.1.39–51). Through the arts of language, Henry displays piety, learning, administrative sagacity, political cunning, and military intrepidity. Like the contemporary play *Julius Caesar* (1599), *Henry V* is concerned with techniques of persuasion. (The earlier *Richard III* is also a highly rhetorical play, though chiefly through the negative example of tyrannical behavior.) Yet, however much we may be swayed emotionally by the rhetoric, we realize that the public figure of Henry V is a mask behind which we can perceive little. Only rarely do we glimpse the affable young companion of the *Henry IV* plays. King Henry has accepted the responsibility of playing a political role. It denies him a private and separate identity, even—or especially—in choosing a wife. And it complicates our task of assessing the sincerity of his utterances. Is he genuinely pious, or has he merely learned the usefulness of pious utterance in swaying people's hearts? What especially are his motives for going to war against France?

Shakespeare could have begun this play with the stirring scene (1.2) in which Henry, urged on by his advisers, issues a defiant challenge to the French ambassadors. Instead, Shakespeare treats us to a prior glimpse beneath the patriotic surface. It seems that the Archbishop of Canterbury, threatened with a bill in Parliament designed to take away the better half of the Church's possessions, has resolved to parry with a counterproposal, whereby the Church will give Henry a very substantial sum for his French campaign, provided the offensive tax bill can be conveniently forgotten. The Archbishop has already been negotiating with Henry and surmises that the plan will work. This revelation is not shocking to us; it merely reveals the political process at work. The faint undercurrent of anticlericalism suggests that Henry is to be admired for putting pressure on his clergy with such success; they are rich and can afford to support the war. In any case, the dramatic effect is to show how men's practical motives affect their rhetoric. When, in the subsequent scene, the Archbishop delivers a public lecture on the English claim to France, we know that this learned prelate has a prior and self-interested commitment to the

war. His intricate dynastic argument, which he proclaims to be "as clear as is the summer's sun" (1.2.86), gives to the war a much-needed public justification. Henry's questions indicate not only his genuine concern about the legitimacy of his claim but also his political need for the Church's endorsement of his cause; he has already claimed certain French dukedoms and must have the Church's official approval of those claims before he can proceed. He similarly needs the backing of his nobles, who also have their own reasons for approving the campaign. Henry skillfully orchestrates the scene to produce the desired effect of unanimous and patriotic consent.

Although never directly stated, Henry's own motives for going to war must also combine sincere zeal with calculated self-interest. As king, he longs to recover the French territory that England governed in the great days of Poitiers and Crécy. As a man, he bristles at the contemptuous challenge of the Dauphin; Henry must still strive to overcome his reputation as a wastrel and must prove himself worthy of honorable comparison with his great ancestors. Politically (and this motive remains most hidden), Henry has absorbed his father's sage advice to "busy giddy minds / With foreign quarrels" (*2 Henry IV*, 4.5.213–14), to blunt political opposition at home by uniting English resentment against a foreign scapegoat.

The exigencies of war do indeed provide Henry with an opportunity for proceeding against his political enemies. He arrests the Earl of Cambridge, Lord Scroop, and Sir Thomas Grey at Southampton on charges of conspiring with France. The scene (2.2) is, for Shakespeare, uncharacteristically one-sided. We are never even told that Cambridge is the chief pretender to the English throne, son of the Duke of York, married to Anne Mortimer, and founder of the Yorkist claim in the York-Lancastrian wars—the sort of rival whom Shakespeare elsewhere portrays with understanding. Instead, the rhetoric of the Chorus to Act 2 blatantly warns us to expect "hell and treason" (line 29). These three conspirators, like Judases, says the Chorus, have bargained away their king for gold. (In fact, Cambridge insists that his motive was not financial, though he is not permitted to say what it was.) The playwright does not give them complex motives; they are sinners, so horrified by their own intents that they are actually grateful to be caught. The scene serves, by such rhetorical devices, to strengthen Henry's claim to the English throne as well as to the territories in France. Opposition to his rule during wartime is, in the view of the Chorus, simply treasonous; all persuasive evidences of dynastic rival claims are hidden from our view.

Comedy also contributes to the rhetorical image-making of the hero in *Henry V*. The tavern crew is on hand, though deprived of the now-deceased Falstaff's beguiling company and more distant from Henry than in the earlier history plays. Only briefly and in disguise, on the night before the battle, does the King encounter Pistol. The name of Bardolph comes to Henry as though in recollection of a distant past, when he hears that Bardolph is about to be executed for stealing from French churches. Henry confirms the sentence: "We would have all such offenders so cut off" (3.6.107). Whatever momentary pang Henry may feel, he remains constant to his banishment of Falstaff. And, although Shakespeare pleads for our sympathies in the seriocomic account of Falstaff's death, seen through the childlike naiveté of Mistress Quickly, there is no hope of reconciliation between Henry and his former mates. Pistol, despite his ornamental language, is little more than a boaster, coward, and thief. The tavern revelers are now the opportunists of war, troublemakers such as are found in every army, engaging rascals deserving to be cudgeled by more honorable men.

Pistol gets his comeuppance from Captain Fluellen, who replaces Falstaff as the chief comic figure, both in prominence (his role is second in length to that of Henry) and in proximity to the King. Fluellen is a Welshman, like King Henry, who was born at Monmouth in what was then Wales (hence the appropriateness of his former title as Prince of Wales). Fluellen is proud of this kinship. Because he is loyal and valiant, he is a person worthy to be seen in Henry's company. Yet there is none of the brilliant duel of wits previously linking Henry and Falstaff. Fluellen is a humorous character, identified at once by such comically exaggerated features as his Welsh accent and mannerisms of speech, his old-fashioned and somewhat fanatical sense of military propriety, and his devotion to the ancient rules of military discipline. Fluellen is a caricature, subject to mild satirical laughter, and there is a note of condescension in Henry's habit of playing practical jokes on the captain. We tend to laugh at, rather than with, him. (Henry makes practical jokes at others' expense as well, such as the soldier named Williams, with whom he exchanges gloves.) Unlike Falstaff, Fluellen lacks perspective on his own pomposity. He is a zealot for duty, and one feels Henry is taking unfair advantage when he picks on one who is such an easy mark for laughter. We suspect that Henry is using people again, bolstering his public image as the king with the common touch, borrowing a little Welsh color for mythmaking purposes. At the same time, Fluellen is steadfast, upright, and a credit to his countryman Henry. With his fellow captains from Scotland, Ireland, and England, he demonstrates that Britishers can fight together, even if they do antagonize one another with their proud regional customs. Those customs are to be cherished as part of the British character; because Pistol offers gratuitous insult to the Welsh tradition of wearing a leek in the cap on Saint Davy's Day, he must be thrashed.

As with the comic characters and Henry's political enemies, *Henry V* is rhetorically one-sided in its presentation of the French. Patriotism is a raw emotion, and Henry cannot appeal to it without awakening hostility toward the enemy. (Ironically enough, the great film version of *Henry V* by Laurence Olivier was created in 1944 during World War II to arouse national feelings against the Germans rather than against the French, and with complete success. Any enemy will do in such patriotic moods.) The French are portrayed as haughty, vastly superior in numbers, envious of one another, contemptuous of their own leadership (especially the Dauphin), treacherous (attacking the boys with the luggage), and craven. Even their joking is characterized by an unattractively bestial kind of bawdry (3.7.48–68). The British—"we few, we happy few" (4.3.60)—are tired and outnumbered but invincible and seemingly protected by God. Henry's order to kill the French prisoners and his description of the rapes and pillages his soldiers will commit if Harfleur fails to surrender (3.3.1–27) do, to be sure, raise serious questions about the morality of war under the best of kings; the play may be caustic toward the French nobility but does not necessarily exonerate the English. Even here, however, we are led to believe that, because the French are so execrably governed, France will suffer less under English rule. Henry takes care that his soldiers will not despoil the French countryside except under conditions of military "necessity." Only in Montjoy, the Duke of Burgundy, and Katharine of France does Shakespeare offer redeeming portraits of the French character, and in these instances the terms of hierarchical ascendancy seem clear: masculine English dominance, gentle French submissiveness. Katharine becomes "la belle France," depicted in Burgundy's eloquent peacemaking speech as being so much in need of competent management.

Women exist only on the margins of this war play, as in Shakespeare's other historical plays. Mistress Quickly's role is chiefly as a reminder to us that men fight with one another for the possession of women; the ludicrous quarrel of Pistol and Nym over Mistress Quickly anticipates the way in which Katharine of France will be one of the chief spoils of the war itself. Women also wait patiently at home while their men fight, and tend them when they are sick. Mistress Quickly's recollection of the death of Falstaff (2.3.9–25) is masterful in its evocation of tender solicitude, illiterate piety, and unwitting eroticism. Later, in France, Pistol pauses with momentary regret over news of the death of his wife from venereal disease (5.1.80–1). Katharine of France, though vastly better born, finds her role as a woman no less circumscribed. We first see her learning English from Alice, her lady in waiting (3.4). Why is she learning English? The obvious political reason, never explicitly stated, emerges with a kind of violence: the scene of the English lesson follows immediately after King Henry's ultimatum to the citizens of Harfleur to surrender or see their women raped and their children impaled by English weapons (3.3.27–41). Katharine accepts her lot with good grace, as though she had any other choice but to do so. We gather from her scene with Alice that she is a woman of spirit who can be imperious, vain, and curious about sex. Because she also is very French, the wooing scene in Act 5 can play comically on the differences of temperament between her and Henry, who is as English as she is French. These differences make Henry and Katharine potentially compatible through complementarity—male and female, soldier and lady, English and French—but the compact is patently a hierarchical one of conqueror and conquered. (Emma Thompson, in Kenneth Branagh's film version of 1989, brings to the role of Katharine a gracefully and persuasively feminist interpretation of an independent-minded woman who is decidedly skeptical about the courtship to which she is subjected, but even she discovers that she has no choice other than to capitulate to Henry's—i.e., Branagh's—charm and the imperatives of international diplomacy.) Historically, we know that the product of their sexual union, Henry VI, will bring to a dismal end the harmony of discords that presides uncertainly over the end of *Henry V*.

Henry woos Katharine with real flair, despite their unstated mutual recognition that their courtship is, above all, a matter of state, in which they must play predetermined roles. The individual within Henry V gives way to the public personality, but he never loses his style. He manages always to be true to himself, as a wooer or as a soldier. We see him in disguise, hobnobbing with common soldiers of his camp on the eve of battle, earnestly discussing with them the morality of war. We see him, with endearing human inconsistency, coveting all the glory of victory over the French and then adjuring his soldiers to give credit for that victory to God alone. Even if we are at times less attracted to this successful warrior and politician than to the carefree young man of *1 Henry IV*, we can still honor Henry's choice of responsible maturity and see that it is even compassionately self-denying. A king cannot be like other men, and Henry is willing to accept this price of leadership.

The Chorus presents *Henry V* to us as if it were an epic poem as well as a drama. Henry is an epic hero, defined in terms of mythic allusions and abstractions. He is compared to Mars, the god of war, with Famine, Sword, and Fire leashed at his heels, crouched and ready for employment. He is the "mirror of all Christian kings," and his followers are "English Mercurys" (2.0.6–7) with winged heels. Personified Expectation sits in the air, promising crowns and crownets to Henry and his followers. Henry's fleet of ships in the English Channel becomes "A city on th'inconstant billows dancing" (3.0.15). On the eve of battle, amidst his brothers, friends, and countrymen, Henry warms every heart with "cheerful semblance and sweet majesty" and with his "largess universal like the sun" (4.0.40–3). He forbids vainglorious pride and gives credit for his victory "Quite from himself to God" (5.0.22).

The action the Chorus describes is comparably epic, as it moves from England to France and back again, leaping over time, surveying all levels of society in the English nation, portraying famous military encounters seemingly more suited to epic narration (or to film, as both Laurence Olivier's 1944 film and Kenneth Branagh's more recent film version brilliantly demonstrate) than to the stage. The stage's limitation forms, indeed, a major burden of the Chorus's argument. He apologizes to the spectators for the "flat unraisèd spirits" that have dared to bring forth so vast an object "On this unworthy scaffold," in this "cockpit" or "wooden O" (Prologue). The play confines "mighty men" "In little room," "Mangling by starts the full course of their glory" (Epilogue).

This apology sounds like becoming modesty on Shakespeare's part, in conceding the truth of Ben Jonson's objection that a few hired actors with rusty swords can scarcely do justice to England's great wars of the past. *Henry V* is not a Jonsonian neoclassical play. Paradoxically, however, Shakespeare's acknowledgment of the limited means at his disposal to create mimetic spectacle amounts to a defense of his own theater of the imagination. Through the Chorus's repeated urgings that we use our "imaginary forces" to supply what the actors and the theater necessarily lack, Shakespeare invites us as spectators and partners into his world of art. The play becomes a journey of thought, of making "imaginary puissance." When Shakespeare and his acting company talk of horses, we are to "see them / Printing their proud hoofs i'th' receiving earth" (Prologue). This is not to minimize the importance of the theatrical experience but, indeed, quite the opposite, since we are instructed to liberate ourselves through that theatrical experience and to re-create by means of Shakespeare's script an epic vision. Shakespeare's stage, bare of scenery, relying on good actors and the words they speak, becomes through its very flexibility more versatile in creating that vision than the most ornate and mechanically sophisticated illusionistic theater.

Nothing illustrates better the controversial and timely nature of this play than the history of recent productions, on stage and in film and television. Once viewed as a stalwart defense of England's national greatness, so much so that Winston Churchill could invoke Henry's famous speech before the Battle of Agincourt ("We few, we happy few") in celebration of Britain's "finest hour" of defending England against Nazi Germany, *Henry V* was destined to become, in the years of disillusionment following World War II and especially during the Vietnam era, a vehicle for a satirical and dismaying view of war. Directors have sometimes chosen to have the Boy who accompanies Pistol, Bardolph, and Nym to France brutally killed in open view of the audience by French soldiers. (The script does not specify such action.) A production by the Royal Shakespeare

Company in 1964, directed by Peter Hall, showed the influence of Bertolt Brecht and Jan Kott (author of *Shakespeare Our Contemporary*) by staging the Battle of Agincourt in terrifying darkness, with reminiscences of the Guernica atrocity of the Spanish Civil War celebrated by Pablo Picasso's famous painting on the subject. In a number of productions, King Henry has been presented as a brazen devotee of imperialistic war, or a calculating politician for whom even the business of wooing is a matter of wearisome diplomatic necessity (as in Ian Holm's portrayal at Stratford-upon-Avon in 1964). Alternatively, Henry has sometimes been seen as a self-doubting hero, keenly attuned to the absurdity of what it is that destiny has thrust upon him. Some of these remarkable contrasts can be discerned in the differences between Olivier's World War II film production and that of Branagh in 1989, in the wake of Vietnam and the Falklands episode.

# The Life of King Henry the Fifth

[*Dramatis Personae*

CHORUS

KING HENRY THE FIFTH
HUMPHREY, DUKE OF GLOUCESTER,
JOHN, DUKE OF BEDFORD,
DUKE OF CLARENCE,
} *the King's brothers*

DUKE OF EXETER, *the King's uncle*
DUKE OF YORK, *the King's cousin*
EARL OF SALISBURY
EARL OF WESTMORLAND
EARL OF WARWICK
EARL OF HUNTINGDON

ARCHBISHOP OF CANTERBURY
BISHOP OF ELY

RICHARD, EARL OF CAMBRIDGE,
HENRY, LORD SCROOP OF MASHAM,
SIR THOMAS GREY,
} *conspirators against the King*

SIR THOMAS ERPINGHAM,
CAPTAIN GOWER,
CAPTAIN FLUELLEN,
CAPTAIN MACMORRIS,
CAPTAIN JAMY,
} *officers in the King's army*

JOHN BATES,
ALEXANDER COURT,
MICHAEL WILLIAMS,
} *soldiers in the King's army*

*An English* HERALD

PISTOL,
NYM,
BARDOLPH,
} *Falstaff's former tavern-mates*

BOY, *formerly Falstaff's page*
HOSTESS, *formerly Mistress Quickly, now married to Pistol*

DUKE OF BURGUNDY

FRENCH KING, *Charles the Sixth*
QUEEN ISABEL *of France*
DAUPHIN, *Lewis*
KATHARINE, *Princess of France*
ALICE, *a lady attending Katharine*
DUKE OF ORLEANS
DUKE OF BERRI
DUKE OF BOURBON
DUKE OF BRITTANY
CONSTABLE OF FRANCE
LORD RAMBURES
LORD GRANDPRÉ
GOVERNOR OF HARFLEUR
MONSIEUR LE FER, *a French soldier*
MONTJOY, *the French herald*
*French* AMBASSADORS *to England*

*Lords, Ladies, Officers, Soldiers, Citizens, Messengers, and Attendants*

SCENE: *England, afterwards France*]

# Prologue

*Enter [Chorus as] Prologue.*

CHORUS

Oh, for a Muse of fire, that would ascend          1
The brightest heaven of invention!          2
A kingdom for a stage, princes to act,
And monarchs to behold the swelling scene!          4
Then should the warlike Harry, like himself,          5
Assume the port of Mars; and at his heels,          6
Leashed in like hounds, should famine, sword, and
   fire
Crouch for employment. But pardon, gentles all,          8
The flat unraisèd spirits that hath dared          9
On this unworthy scaffold to bring forth          10
So great an object. Can this cockpit hold          11
The vasty fields of France? Or may we cram          12
Within this wooden O the very casques          13
That did affright the air at Agincourt?
Oh, pardon! Since a crooked figure may          15
Attest in little place a million;          16
And let us, ciphers to this great account,          17
On your imaginary forces work.          18
Suppose within the girdle of these walls
Are now confined two mighty monarchies,
Whose high uprearèd and abutting fronts          21
The perilous narrow ocean parts asunder.          22
Piece out our imperfections with your thoughts:
Into a thousand parts divide one man,
And make imaginary puissance.          25
Think, when we talk of horses, that you see them
Printing their proud hoofs i'th' receiving earth.
For 'tis your thoughts that now must deck our kings,          28
Carry them here and there, jumping o'er times,
Turning th'accomplishment of many years
Into an hourglass—for the which supply,          31
Admit me Chorus to this history,
Who, Prologue-like, your humble patience pray
Gently to hear, kindly to judge, our play.          *Exit.*

**Prologue.**
**1 Muse of fire** (Of the four elements—earth, air, fire, and water—fire is the most sublime and mounting.)   **2 invention** poetic imagination.   **4 swelling** splendid, magnificent   **5 like himself** i.e., presented in a fashion worthy of so great a king   **6 port** bearing   **8 gentles** gentlemen and gentlewomen   **9 flat unraisèd** uninspired, lifeless.   **spirits** i.e., actors and playwright.   **hath** (Elizabethan usage often pairs a plural subject with a singular verb.)   **10 scaffold** stage   **11 cockpit** (Elizabethan theaters were shaped rather like arenas for animal fighting.)   **12 vasty** vast, spacious   **13 O** (Refers to a round theater such as the Globe; the play may have been performed at the Curtain Theater.)   **casques** helmets   **15 crooked figure** cipher or zero (which, added to a number, will multiply its value tenfold)   **16 Attest** stand for   **17 account** (1) sum total (continuing the metaphor of *crooked figure*) (2) story   **18 imaginary forces** forces of imagination   **21 abutting** touching, bordering.   **fronts** (1) frontiers, i.e., the cliffs of Dover and Calais (2) foreheads   **22 perilous . . . ocean** i.e., English Channel   **25 puissance** armed might, army.   **28 deck** dress, adorn   **31 the which supply** which service

# [1.1]

*Enter the two bishops, [the Archbishop] of Canterbury and [the Bishop of] Ely.*

CANTERBURY

My lord, I'll tell you. That self bill is urged          1
Which in th'eleventh year of the last king's reign
Was like, and had indeed against us passed,          3
But that the scambling and unquiet time          4
Did push it out of farther question.          5

ELY

But how, my lord, shall we resist it now?

CANTERBURY

It must be thought on. If it pass against us,
We lose the better half of our possession.
For all the temporal lands which men devout          9
By testament have given to the Church
Would they strip from us, being valued thus:
As much as would maintain, to the King's honor,
Full fifteen earls and fifteen hundred knights,
Six thousand and two hundred good esquires,          14
And, to relief of lazars and weak age          15
Of indigent faint souls past corporal toil,          16
A hundred almshouses right well supplied;          17
And to the coffers of the King beside          18
A thousand pounds by th' year. Thus runs the bill.

ELY     This would drink deep.

CANTERBURY     'Twould drink the cup and all.

ELY     But what prevention?

CANTERBURY

The King is full of grace and fair regard.

ELY

And a true lover of the holy Church.

CANTERBURY

The courses of his youth promised it not.
The breath no sooner left his father's body
But that his wildness, mortified in him,          27
Seemed to die too; yea, at that very moment
Consideration like an angel came          29
And whipped th'offending Adam out of him,          30
Leaving his body as a paradise
T'envelop and contain celestial spirits.
Never was such a sudden scholar made;
Never came reformation in a flood
With such a heady currance, scouring faults;          35
Nor never Hydra-headed willfulness          36
So soon did lose his seat, and all at once,          37
As in this king.

ELY          We are blessed in the change.

CANTERBURY

Hear him but reason in divinity,

**1.1. Location: England. The royal court.**
**1 self** same   **3 like** likely (to have passed)   **4 scambling** unsettled   **5 question** consideration.   **9 temporal** used for secular purposes   **14 esquires** members of the gentry, ranking just below knights   **15 lazars** lepers   **16 corporal** physical   **17 almshouses** poor houses   **18 coffers** strong boxes i.e., treasury   **27 mortified** killed   **29 Consideration** meditation, reflection   **30 offending Adam** original sin   **35 heady currance** headlong current   **36 Hydra-headed** i.e., many-headed. (Alludes to the Lernaean Hydra, a monster of many heads overcome by Hercules.)   **37 his seat** its throne

And, all-admiring, with an inward wish
You would desire the King were made a prelate.
Hear him debate of commonwealth affairs,
You would say it hath been all in all his study.
List his discourse of war, and you shall hear          44
A fearful battle rendered you in music.               45
Turn him to any cause of policy,                      46
The Gordian knot of it he will unloose,              47
Familiar as his garter, that, when he speaks,        48
The air, a chartered libertine, is still,            49
And the mute wonder lurketh in men's ears            50
To steal his sweet and honeyed sentences;            51
So that the art and practic part of life             52
Must be the mistress to this theoric.                53
Which is a wonder how His Grace should glean it,
Since his addiction was to courses vain,             55
His companies unlettered, rude, and shallow,         56
His hours filled up with riots, banquets, sports,    57
And never noted in him any study,
Any retirement, any sequestration
From open haunts and popularity.                     60
ELY
The strawberry grows underneath the nettle,
And wholesome berries thrive and ripen best
Neighbored by fruit of baser quality;
And so the Prince obscured his contemplation
Under the veil of wildness, which, no doubt,
Grew like the summer grass, fastest by night,
Unseen, yet crescive in his faculty.                 67
CANTERBURY
It must be so, for miracles are ceased.             68
And therefore we must needs admit the means         69
How things are perfected.
ELY                         But, my good lord,
How now for mitigation of this bill
Urged by the Commons? Doth His Majesty
Incline to it, or no?
CANTERBURY          He seems indifferent,            73
Or rather swaying more upon our part
Than cherishing th'exhibiters against us;            75
For I have made an offer to His Majesty,
Upon our spiritual convocation                       77
And in regard of causes now in hand,                 78
Which I have opened to His Grace at large,           79

As touching France, to give a greater sum           80
Than ever at one time the clergy yet
Did to his predecessors part withal.                 82
ELY
How did this offer seem received, my lord?
CANTERBURY
With good acceptance of His Majesty,
Save that there was not time enough to hear,
As I perceived His Grace would fain have done,       86
The severals and unhidden passages                   87
Of his true titles to some certain dukedoms,
And generally to the crown and seat of France,       89
Derived from Edward, his great-grandfather.          90
ELY
What was th'impediment that broke this off?
CANTERBURY
The French ambassador upon that instant
Craved audience; and the hour I think is come
To give him hearing. Is it four o'clock?
ELY   It is.
CANTERBURY
Then go we in to know his embassy,                   96
Which I could with a ready guess declare
Before the Frenchman speak a word of it.
ELY
I'll wait upon you, and I long to hear it.   *Exeunt.* 99

❖

## [1.2]

*Enter the King, Humphrey [Duke of Gloucester],
Bedford, Clarence, Warwick, Westmorland, and
Exeter [with attendants].*

KING
Where is my gracious lord of Canterbury?
EXETER
Not here in presence.
KING                    Send for him, good uncle.
WESTMORLAND
Shall we call in th'ambassador, my liege?
KING
Not yet, my cousin. We would be resolved,            4
Before we hear him, of some things of weight
That task our thoughts, concerning us and France.    6

*Enter two bishops, [the Archbishop of Canter-
bury and the Bishop of Ely].*

CANTERBURY
God and his angels guard your sacred throne,
And make you long become it!
KING                          Sure we thank you.      8
My learnèd lord, we pray you to proceed,

44 **List** Listen to   45 **rendered . . . music** i.e., eloquently narrated.
46 **cause of policy** matter of statecraft   47 **Gordian knot** i.e., great
difficulty resolved forcefully. (It was foretold that whoever should
untie the Gordian knot would rule Asia. Alexander solved the problem by cutting the knot.)   48 **Familiar** as offhandedly or routinely.
**that** so that   49 **chartered libertine** free spirit, licensed to roam at
will   50–1 **the mute . . . sentences** i.e., wonder makes men silent,
eagerly listening to hear more of his sweetly profitable wise sayings
52–3 **So . . . theoric** so that experience in practical life must have been
the teacher by which he acquired his theoretical conception.
55 **addiction** inclination   56 **companies** companions.   **rude** coarse
57 **riots** reveling.   **sports** amusements   60 **open . . . popularity**
places of public resort and low company.   67 **crescive . . . faculty**
naturally inclined to grow.   68 **miracles are ceased** (Protestants generally believed that no miracles occurred after the revelation of
Christ.)   69 **means** i.e., natural causes   73 **indifferent** impartial
75 **exhibiters** those who introduce bills in Parliament   77 **Upon** on
behalf of.   **convocation** formal assembly of the clergy   78 **in hand**
under consideration   79 **opened** expounded.   **at large** in full

80 **As touching** as regards, concerning   82 **withal** with.   86 **fain** gladly
87 **severals** details.   **unhidden passages** clear lines of descent   89 **seat**
throne   90 **Edward** Edward III   96 **embassy** message
99 **wait upon** attend
**1.2. Location: England. The royal court.**
4 **cousin** (A form of address customarily used by royalty in addressing their nobles. In this case, Westmorland is in fact related to the
King by marriage.)   **be resolved** come to a decision   6 **task** engage,
occupy   8 **become** adorn, grace

And justly and religiously unfold
Why the law Salic that they have in France 11
Or should or should not bar us in our claim. 12
And God forbid, my dear and faithful lord,
That you should fashion, wrest, or bow your reading,
Or nicely charge your understanding soul 15
With opening titles miscreate, whose right 16
Suits not in native colors with the truth; 17
For God doth know how many now in health
Shall drop their blood in approbation 19
Of what your reverence shall incite us to. 20
Therefore take heed how you impawn our person, 21
How you awake our sleeping sword of war.
We charge you in the name of God take heed;
For never two such kingdoms did contend
Without much fall of blood, whose guiltless drops 25
Are every one a woe, a sore complaint 26
'Gainst him whose wrongs gives edge unto the
    swords 27
That makes such waste in brief mortality. 28
Under this conjuration speak, my lord; 29
For we will hear, note, and believe in heart
That what you speak is in your conscience washed
As pure as sin with baptism.

CANTERBURY
Then hear me, gracious sovereign, and you peers,
That owe yourselves, your lives, and services
To this imperial throne. There is no bar
To make against Your Highness' claim to France
But this, which they produce from Pharamond: 37
*"In terram Salicam mulieres ne succedant,"*
"No woman shall succeed in Salic land."
Which Salic land the French unjustly gloze 40
To be the realm of France, and Pharamond
The founder of this law and female bar. 42
Yet their own authors faithfully affirm
That the land Salic is in Germany,
Between the floods of Saale and of Elbe; 45
Where, Charles the Great having subdued the Saxons, 46
There left behind and settled certain French,
Who, holding in disdain the German women
For some dishonest manners of their life, 49
Established then this law: to wit, no female
Should be inheritrix in Salic land—
Which Salic, as I said, twixt Elbe and Saale,
Is at this day in Germany called Meissen.
Then doth it well appear the Salic law
Was not devisèd for the realm of France;
Nor did the French possess the Salic land

Until four hundred one-and-twenty years
After defunction of King Pharamond, 58
Idly supposed the founder of this law, 59
Who died within the year of our redemption
Four hundred twenty-six; and Charles the Great
Subdued the Saxons, and did seat the French
Beyond the River Saale, in the year
Eight hundred five. Besides, their writers say,
King Pepin, which deposèd Childeric, 65
Did, as heir general, being descended 66
Of Blithild, which was daughter to King Clothair,
Make claim and title to the crown of France.
Hugh Capet also, who usurped the crown
Of Charles the Duke of Lorraine, sole heir male
Of the true line and stock of Charles the Great,
To find his title with some shows of truth, 72
Though, in pure truth, it was corrupt and naught,
Conveyed himself as th'heir to th' Lady Lingard, 74
Daughter to Charlemagne, who was the son 75
To Lewis the Emperor, and Lewis the son
Of Charles the Great. Also King Lewis the Tenth, 77
Who was sole heir to the usurper Capet,
Could not keep quiet in his conscience,
Wearing the crown of France, till satisfied
That fair Queen Isabel, his grandmother,
Was lineal of the Lady Ermengard, 82
Daughter to Charles the foresaid Duke of Lorraine;
By the which marriage the line of Charles the Great
Was reunited to the crown of France.
So that, as clear as is the summer's sun,
King Pepin's title and Hugh Capet's claim,
King Lewis his satisfaction, all appear 88
To hold in right and title of the female;
So do the kings of France unto this day,
Howbeit they would hold up this Salic law 91
To bar Your Highness claiming from the female,
And rather choose to hide them in a net 93
Than amply to imbar their crooked titles 94
Usurped from you and your progenitors.

KING
May I with right and conscience make this claim?

CANTERBURY
The sin upon my head, dread sovereign!
For in the Book of Numbers is it writ,
When the man dies, let the inheritance 99
Descend unto the daughter. Gracious lord, 100
Stand for your own; unwind your bloody flag! 101
Look back into your mighty ancestors:

---

**11 Salic** (See explanation at lines 39–45.)   **12 Or** either   **15 nicely charge** subtly and foolishly burden   **16 opening titles miscreate** expounding spurious claims   **17 Suits . . . colors** i.e., does not naturally harmonize   **19 approbation** support, proof   **20 your reverence** (1) an honorific title for an archbishop, Your Reverence (2) your sacred authority   **21 impawn** put under an obligation   **25 fall** shedding   **26 woe** grievance.   **sore** severe, grievous   **27 wrongs** wrongdoings   **28 in brief mortality** i.e., among mortal, short-lived men.   **29 conjuration** solemn adjuration   **37 Pharamond** legendary Frankish king   **40 gloze** gloss   **42 female bar** barring of females from royal succession.   **45 floods** rivers   **46 Charles the Great** Charlemagne   **49 dishonest** unchaste

**58 defunction** death   **59 Idly** foolishly   **65 which** who. (As also in line 67.)   **66 heir general** heir through male or female line   **72 find provide**   **74 Conveyed himself** passed himself off   **75 Charlemagne** (Holinshed's and Hall's error, followed by Shakespeare, for Charles the Bald or Charles II, emperor of the West; Luitgard [Shakespeare's Lingard] became Charlemagne's wife after the death of Fastrada in 794.)   **77 Lewis the Tenth** (Actually, Louis IX; an error copied from Holinshed.)   **82 lineal of** descended from   **88 Lewis his satisfaction** Lewis's conviction   **91 Howbeit** notwithstanding   **93 hide . . . net** i.e., conceal the weakness of their case in a tangle of contradictions   **94 amply to imbar** frankly to bar claim to   **99–100 When . . . daughter** (This paraphrase leaves out an important phrase. Numbers 27:8 reads, "When a man dies leaving no son, his patrimony shall pass to his daughter.")   **101 unwind** unfurl

Go, my dread lord, to your great-grandsire's tomb,   103
From whom you claim! Invoke his warlike spirit,
And your great-uncle's, Edward the Black Prince,
Who on the French ground played a tragedy,   106
Making defeat on the full power of France,   107
Whiles his most mighty father on a hill
Stood smiling to behold his lion's whelp   109
Forage in blood of French nobility.
O noble English, that could entertain   111
With half their forces the full pride of France
And let another half stand laughing by,
All out of work and cold for action!   114

ELY
Awake remembrance of these valiant dead,
And with your puissant arm renew their feats!   116
You are their heir; you sit upon their throne;
The blood and courage that renownèd them   118
Runs in your veins; and my thrice-puissant liege
Is in the very May morn of his youth,
Ripe for exploits and mighty enterprises.

EXETER
Your brother kings and monarchs of the earth
Do all expect that you should rouse yourself
As did the former lions of your blood.

WESTMORLAND
They know Your Grace hath cause, and means, and might;
So hath Your Highness. Never king of England   126
Had nobles richer and more loyal subjects,
Whose hearts have left their bodies here in England
And lie pavilioned in the fields of France.   129

CANTERBURY
Oh, let their bodies follow, my dear liege,
With blood, and sword, and fire to win your right!
In aid whereof we of the spiritualty   132
Will raise Your Highness such a mighty sum
As never did the clergy at one time
Bring in to any of your ancestors.

KING
We must not only arm t'invade the French,
But lay down our proportions to defend   137
Against the Scot, who will make road upon us   138
With all advantages.   139

CANTERBURY
They of those marches, gracious sovereign,   140
Shall be a wall sufficient to defend
Our inland from the pilfering borderers.

KING
We do not mean the coursing snatchers only,   143

But fear the main intendment of the Scot,   144
Who hath been still a giddy neighbor to us.   145
For you shall read that my great-grandfather
Never went with his forces into France
But that the Scot on his unfurnished kingdom   148
Came pouring like the tide into a breach
With ample and brim fullness of his force,   150
Galling the gleanèd land with hot assays,   151
Girding with grievous siege castles and towns;   152
That England, being empty of defense,
Hath shook and trembled at th'ill neighborhood.   154

CANTERBURY
She hath been then more feared than harmed, my
  liege.   155
For hear her but exampled by herself:   156
When all her chivalry hath been in France   157
And she a mourning widow of her nobles,   158
She hath herself not only well defended
But taken and impounded as a stray   160
The King of Scots, whom she did send to France   161
To fill King Edward's fame with prisoner kings
And make her chronicle as rich with praise   163
As is the ooze and bottom of the sea
With sunken wrack and sumless treasuries.   165

A LORD
But there's a saying very old and true:
  "If that you will France win,
    Then with Scotland first begin."
For once the eagle England being in prey,   169
To her unguarded nest the weasel Scot
Comes sneaking, and so sucks her princely eggs,
Playing the mouse in absence of the cat,
To 'tame and havoc more than she can eat.   173

EXETER
It follows then the cat must stay at home;
Yet that is but a crushed necessity,   175
Since we have locks to safeguard necessaries
And pretty traps to catch the petty thieves.   177
While that the armèd hand doth fight abroad,   178
Th'advisèd head defends itself at home;   179
For government, though high, and low, and lower,   180
Put into parts, doth keep in one consent,   181

---

**103 great-grandsire's** i.e., Edward III's. His descent through his mother Isabella from the French King Philip IV is the basis of English claims to the French kingdom—a claim through female inheritance. Hence the importance of lines 39–55.   **106 tragedy** i.e., the Battle of Crécy, 1346, a major defeat for the French   **107 power** army   **109 his lion's whelp** i.e., Edward the Black Prince   **111 entertain** engage, encounter   **114 for action** for want of action.   **116 puissant** powerful   **118 renownèd** brought renown to   **126 So** so indeed   **129 pavilioned** tented, encamped   **132 spiritualty** clergy   **137 lay . . . proportions** allocate our forces   **138 road** inroad, raid   **139 With all advantages** whenever a good opportunity presents itself.   **140 They . . . marches** Our English forces in the territories bordering Scotland   **143 coursing snatchers** hit-and-run Scottish raiders on fast-galloping horses

**144 intendment** plan, hostile intent   **145 still** always.   **giddy** unstable, fickle   **148 unfurnished** unprovided with defense   **150 brim** absolute, complete   **151 Galling . . . assays** harassing the land stripped of defenders with hot attacks   **152 Girding** surrounding   **154 th'ill neighborhood** the unneighborliness.   **155 feared** frightened   **156 hear . . . herself** i.e., only listen how England can be instructed by an example from her own history   **157 chivalry** knights   **158 And she . . . nobles** and she, England, widowlike in being deprived of her nobility while they fight in France   **160–1 impounded . . . Scots** (King David II of Scotland was captured and imprisoned in 1346 while Edward III was in France.)   **161 to France** (Historically, David II was imprisoned in London, not sent to France.)   **163 her** England's   **165 wrack** wreckage.   **sumless** inestimable   **169 For . . . prey** For whenever the English king, like an eagle, is out hunting   **173 To 'tame and havoc** to attame (i.e., break into) and ravage   **175 crushed necessity** distorted conclusion   **177 pretty** ingenious   **178 While that** While   **179 advisèd** wise, prudent   **180 though . . . lower** i.e., though composed of three broad social ranks (corresponding also to three singing voices from treble to bass)   **181 Put into parts** separated into different functions (and into different parts in part-music).   **one consent** mutual harmony

Congreeing in a full and natural close,                    182
Like music.

CANTERBURY    Therefore doth heaven divide
The state of man in divers functions,
Setting endeavor in continual motion,
To which is fixèd, as an aim or butt,                       186
Obedience; for so work the honeybees,
Creatures that by a rule in nature teach
The act of order to a peopled kingdom.
They have a king, and officers of sorts,                    190
Where some, like magistrates, correct at home;             191
Others, like merchants, venture trade abroad;
Others, like soldiers, armèd in their stings,
Make boot upon the summer's velvet buds,                   194
Which pillage they with merry march bring home
To the tent royal of their emperor,
Who, busied in his majesty, surveys
The singing masons building roofs of gold,
The civil citizens kneading up the honey,
The poor mechanic porters crowding in                      200
Their heavy burdens at his narrow gate,
The sad-eyed justice with his surly hum                     202
Delivering o'er to executors pale                          203
The lazy yawning drone. I this infer,
That many things, having full reference                    205
To one consent, may work contrariously.                    206
As many arrows loosèd several ways                         207
Come to one mark, as many ways meet in one town,          208
As many fresh streams meet in one salt sea,
As many lines close in the dial's center,                  210
So may a thousand actions once afoot
End in one purpose, and be all well borne                  212
Without defeat. Therefore to France, my liege!
Divide your happy England into four,
Whereof take you one quarter into France,
And you withal shall make all Gallia shake.                216
If we with thrice such powers left at home
Cannot defend our own doors from the dog,
Let us be worried, and our nation lose                      219
The name of hardiness and policy.                          220

KING
Call in the messengers sent from the Dauphin.              221
                                    [Exeunt some.]

Now are we well resolved, and by God's help
And yours, the noble sinews of our power,
France being ours, we'll bend it to our awe,               224

Or break it all to pieces. Or there we'll sit,             225
Ruling in large and ample empery                           226
O'er France and all her almost kingly dukedoms,
Or lay these bones in an unworthy urn,
Tombless, with no remembrance over them.
Either our history shall with full mouth
Speak freely of our acts, or else our grave,
Like Turkish mute, shall have a tongueless mouth,          232
Not worshiped with a waxen epitaph.                        233

*Enter Ambassadors of France.*

Now are we well prepared to know the pleasure
Of our fair cousin Dauphin; for we hear                    235
Your greeting is from him, not from the King.

FIRST AMBASSADOR
May't please Your Majesty to give us leave
Freely to render what we have in charge,
Or shall we sparingly show you far off
The Dauphin's meaning and our embassy?

KING
We are no tyrant, but a Christian king,
Unto whose grace our passion is as subject                 242
As is our wretches fettered in our prisons.
Therefore with frank and with uncurbèd plainness
Tell us the Dauphin's mind.

FIRST AMBASSADOR            Thus, then, in few:             245
Your Highness, lately sending into France,
Did claim some certain dukedoms, in the right
Of your great predecessor, King Edward the Third.
In answer of which claim, the Prince our master
Says that you savor too much of your youth,
And bids you be advised there's naught in France
That can be with a nimble galliard won;                    252
You cannot revel into dukedoms there.
He therefore sends you, meeter for your spirit,            254
This tun of treasure, and in lieu of this                  255
Desires you let the dukedoms that you claim
Hear no more of you. This the Dauphin speaks.
                           [*A casket is presented;
                        Exeter examines its contents.*]

KING
What treasure, uncle?
EXETER                        Tennis balls, my liege.
KING
We are glad the Dauphin is so pleasant with us.            259
His present and your pains we thank you for.
When we have matched our rackets to these balls,          261
We will in France, by God's grace, play a set
Shall strike his father's crown into the hazard.           263

<hr>

**182 Congreeing** agreeing together. **close** musical cadence **186 aim or butt** target. (All endeavor is to direct itself toward obedience.) **190 They . . . king** (A common error of early natural history, derived from Aristotle. The simile of the bees appears in Virgil, Sir Thomas Elyot, John Lyly, and others.) **of sorts** various kinds **191 correct** administer justice **194 Make boot** prey **200 mechanic** engaged in manual labor **202 sad-eyed** grave-eyed **203 executors pale** executioners, pale in their terrible sternness **205–6 having . . . consent** united by a common understanding **207 As** Just as. **loosèd several ways** shot from different directions **208 ways** roads **210 close** come together. **dial's** sundial's **212 borne** carried out, sustained **216 withal** with this. **Gallia** France. (Latin name.) **219 worried** (1) torn apart or harried, as by dogs (2) made anxious **220 hardiness and policy** bravery and statesmanship. **221 Dauphin** heir apparent to the French throne. **224 ours** i.e., ours by right. **our awe** submission to us

**225 Or there** Either there **226 empery** dominion **232 Turkish mute** (Those attending on harems of the Turkish Sultans were reputedly castrated and obliged to remain completely silent.) **233 Not . . . epitaph** i.e., with not even so much as a wax (as opposed to bronze) epitaph; one easily effaced. **235 cousin** fellow prince (though Henry does also claim a line of descent in the French royal family) **242 Unto . . . passion is** unto whose graceful authority our emotions are **245 in few** briefly **252 galliard** a lively dance **254 meeter** more fitting **255 tun** cask **259 pleasant** jocular. (Also in line 281.) **261 rackets** (1) tennis rackets (2) noisy military assaults **263 crown** (1) royal crown (2) final point scored, or a coin (worth five shillings in English coinage) staked in the game. **hazard** (1) in "royal" tennis, an opening in one of the high walls enclosing the court; hitting the ball into such a "hazard" scored a winning point (2) jeopardy.

Tell him he hath made a match with such a wrangler   264
That all the courts of France will be disturbed   265
With chases. And we understand him well,   266
How he comes o'er us with our wilder days,   267
Not measuring what use we made of them.
We never valued this poor seat of England,   269
And therefore, living hence, did give ourself   270
To barbarous license—as 'tis ever common
That men are merriest when they are from home.   272
But tell the Dauphin I will keep my state,   273
Be like a king, and show my sail of greatness   274
When I do rouse me in my throne of France.
For that I have laid by my majesty   276
And plodded like a man for working days,   277
But I will rise there with so full a glory
That I will dazzle all the eyes of France,
Yea, strike the Dauphin blind to look on us.
And tell the pleasant Prince this mock of his
Hath turned his balls to gunstones, and his soul   282
Shall stand sore chargèd for the wasteful vengeance   283
That shall fly with them; for many a thousand
   widows
Shall this his mock mock out of their dear husbands,
Mock mothers from their sons, mock castles down,
And some are yet ungotten and unborn   287
That shall have cause to curse the Dauphin's scorn.
But this lies all within the will of God,
To whom I do appeal, and in whose name
Tell you the Dauphin I am coming on
To venge me as I may, and to put forth
My rightful hand in a well-hallowed cause.
So get you hence in peace; and tell the Dauphin
His jest will savor but of shallow wit
When thousands weep more than did laugh at it.—
Convey them with safe conduct.—Fare you well.   297
                              *Exeunt Ambassadors.*
EXETER   This was a merry message.
KING
We hope to make the sender blush at it.
Therefore, my lords, omit no happy hour   300
That may give furth'rance to our expedition;   301
For we have now no thought in us but France,
Save those to God, that run before our business.   303
Therefore let our proportions for these wars   304
Be soon collected, and all things thought upon
That may with reasonable swiftness add
More feathers to our wings; for, God before,   307

We'll chide this Dauphin at his father's door.
Therefore let every man now task his thought,   309
That this fair action may on foot be brought.
                              *Flourish. Exeunt.*

## [2.0]

*Enter Chorus.*

CHORUS
Now all the youth of England are on fire,
And silken dalliance in the wardrobe lies.   2
Now thrive the armorers, and honor's thought
Reigns solely in the breast of every man.
They sell the pasture now to buy the horse,
Following the mirror of all Christian kings,   6
With wingèd heels, as English Mercurys.   7
For now sits Expectation in the air
And hides a sword from hilts unto the point   9
With crowns imperial, crowns and coronets,   10
Promised to Harry and his followers.
The French, advised by good intelligence   12
Of this most dreadful preparation,
Shake in their fear, and with pale policy   14
Seek to divert the English purposes.
O England! Model to thy inward greatness,   16
Like little body with a mighty heart,
What mightst thou do, that honor would thee do,   18
Were all thy children kind and natural?
But see, thy fault France hath in thee found out,
A nest of hollow bosoms, which he fills   21
With treacherous crowns; and three corrupted men,   22
One, Richard Earl of Cambridge, and the second,
Henry Lord Scroop of Masham, and the third,
Sir Thomas Grey, knight, of Northumberland,
Have, for the gilt of France—oh, guilt indeed!—   26
Confirmed conspiracy with fearful France,   27
And by their hands this grace of kings must die,
If hell and treason hold their promises,
Ere he take ship for France, and in Southampton.
Linger your patience on, and we'll digest   31
Th'abuse of distance, force a play.   32
The sum is paid, the traitors are agreed,
The King is set from London, and the scene
Is now transported, gentles, to Southampton.   35
There is the playhouse now, there must you sit,
And thence to France shall we convey you safe,

---

And bring you back, charming the narrow seas
To give you gentle pass; for, if we may,                              39
We'll not offend one stomach with our play.                          40
But, when the King come forth, and not till then,                    41
Unto Southampton do we shift our scene.            *Exit.*           42

# [2.1]

*Enter Corporal Nym and Lieutenant Bardolph.*

BARDOLPH    Well met, Corporal Nym.
NYM    Good morrow, Lieutenant Bardolph.
BARDOLPH    What, are Ancient Pistol and you friends     3
yet?
NYM    For my part, I care not. I say little; but when time
shall serve, there shall be smiles—but that shall be as
it may. I dare not fight, but I will wink and hold out     7
mine iron. It is a simple one, but what though? It will    8
toast cheese, and it will endure cold as another man's     9
sword will—and there's an end.                            10
BARDOLPH    I will bestow a breakfast to make you
friends, and we'll be all three sworn brothers to     12
France. Let 't be so, good Corporal Nym.
NYM    Faith, I will live so long as I may, that's the certain    14
of it; and when I cannot live any longer, I will do as I
may. That is my rest; that is the rendezvous of it.     16
BARDOLPH    It is certain, Corporal, that he is married to
Nell Quickly, and certainly she did you wrong, for
you were trothplight to her.                             19
NYM    I cannot tell. Things must be as they may. Men
may sleep, and they may have their throats about
them at that time, and some say knives have edges. It
must be as it may. Though Patience be a tired mare,     23
yet she will plod. There must be conclusions. Well, I     24
cannot tell.

*Enter Pistol and [Hostess] Quickly.*

BARDOLPH    Here comes Ancient Pistol and his wife.
Good Corporal, be patient here.
NYM    How now, mine host Pistol?
PISTOL
Base tike, call'st thou me host?                         29
Now, by this hand, I swear, I scorn the term!
Nor shall my Nell keep lodgers.
HOSTESS    No, by my troth, not long; for we cannot lodge
and board a dozen or fourteen gentlewomen that live

honestly by the prick of their needles, but it will be     34
thought we keep a bawdy house straight. [*Nym and
Pistol draw.*] Oh, welladay, Lady! If he be not hewn     36
now, we shall see willful adultery and murder com-     37
itted.
BARDOLPH    Good Lieutenant! Good Corporal! Offer     39
nothing here.                                            40
NYM    Pish!
PISTOL
Pish for thee, Iceland dog!                              42
Thou prick-eared cur of Iceland!
HOSTESS    Good Corporal Nym, show thy valor, and     44
put up your sword.            [*They sheathe their swords.*]
NYM    Will you shog off? I would have you solus.     46
PISTOL
Solus, egregious dog? O viper vile!
The solus in thy most mervailous face!                   48
The solus in thy teeth, and in thy throat,               49
And in thy hateful lungs, yea, in thy maw, pardie,       50
And, which is worse, within thy nasty mouth!
I do retort the solus in thy bowels;
For I can take, and Pistol's cock is up,                 53
And flashing fire will follow.
NYM    I am not Barbason; you cannot conjure me. I have     55
an humor to knock you indifferently well. If you grow     56
foul with me, Pistol, I will scour you with my rapier, as     57
I may, in fair terms. If you would walk off, I would     58
prick your guts a little, in good terms, as I may, and
that's the humor of it.                                  60
PISTOL
O braggart vile and damnèd furious wight!                61
The grave doth gape, and doting death is near.           62
Therefore exhale!            [*They draw their swords.*]     63
BARDOLPH [*drawing his sword*]    Hear me, hear me what
I say. He that strikes the first stroke, I'll run him up to
the hilts, as I am a soldier.
PISTOL
An oath of mickle might, and fury shall abate.           67
            [*Pistol and Nym sheathe their swords.*]
[*To Nym*] Give me thy fist, thy forefoot to me give.
Thy spirits are most tall.                               69

---

39 **pass** passage   40 **offend one stomach** (1) offend anyone's taste by sudden shifts in scene (2) make anyone seasick   41–2 **But . . . scene** i.e., The scene will be shifted to Southampton after a scene in London. (These lines sound as though they were added as an afterthought, to accommodate the inclusion of the comic scene in 2.1.)
**2.1. Location:** London. A street.
3 **Ancient** Ensign, standard-bearer   7 **wink** shut the eyes   8 **iron** sword.   **though** of that.   9 **endure cold** i.e., doesn't mind being drawn from its sheath   10 **there's an end** that's all there is to it.
12 **sworn brothers** bound by a sacred oath of loyalty   14 **Faith** In good faith   16 **rest** last stake (in the gambling game of primero).
**rendezvous** last resort   19 **trothplight** betrothed   23–4 **Though . . . plod** i.e., Patient persistence will ultimately achieve its goal. (Nym hints, as he does elsewhere, at violence toward Pistol.)   24 **conclusions** an end to matters. (Nym hints darkly that the end must come soon.)
29 **tike** cur

34 **prick** (With a bawdy double meaning, probably unintended, as also in *Pistol's cock*, line 53.)   36 **welladay** wellaway, alas.   **Lady** i.e., by Our Lady. (An oath.)   **hewn** struck down   37 **adultery** (Blunder for "battery"?)   39–40 **Offer nothing** Attempt no violence   42 **Iceland dog** a small, shaggy dog often kept as a house pet. (Pistol's humor is to use extravagant epithets, like this one, tags from current plays, and scraps of foreign languages.)   44 **valor** (She means "calm," "forbearance.")   46 **shog off** move along.   **solus** alone. (Nym proposes a duel; see *walk off* in line 58.)   48 **mervailous** marvelous, astonishing   49–50 **The solus . . . lungs** (The most offensive insult possible, as in *Hamlet's* "the lie i'th' throat / As deep as to the lungs," 2.2.574–5.)   50 **maw** belly.   **pardie** *par Dieu,* by God   53 **take** catch fire.   **cock is up** trigger is cocked. (With bawdy pun.)   55 **Barbason** (The name of a fiend.)   **conjure** exorcise. (Nym mocks Pistol's hyperbolic rant as though it were a conjuration.)   55–6 **I have an humor** I'm in the mood. (*Humor* is a favorite word with Nym, as in lines 60, 71, 97, 116, 121, and 126.)   57 **foul** (1) foulmouthed (2) fouled from firing and in need of scouring   58 **in fair terms** i.e., make no mistake about it. (*In good terms* at line 59 means the same.)   **walk off** walk aside (to fight)   60 **that's . . . it** that's my mood.   61 **wight** person.   62 **doting** amorous, senescent (a word perhaps chosen for the alliteration in "doting death")   63 **exhale** draw (sword, much as the sun draws forth vapors).   67 **mickle** great   69 **tall** valiant.

NYM   I will cut thy throat, one time or other, in fair
    terms. That is the humor of it.
PISTOL *Couple a gorge!*                                          72
    That is the word. I thee defy again.
    O hound of Crete, think'st thou my spouse to get?            74
    No, to the spital go,                                        75
    And from the powdering tub of infamy                         76
    Fetch forth the lazar kite of Cressid's kind,                77
    Doll Tearsheet she by name, and her espouse.                 78
    I have, and I will hold, the quondam Quickly                 79
    For the only she; and—*pauca!* There's enough.               80
    Go to.

        *Enter the Boy.*

BOY   Mine host Pistol, you must come to my master,
    and you, hostess. He is very sick and would to bed.
    Good Bardolph, put thy face between his sheets, and          84
    do the office of a warming pan. Faith, he's very ill.
BARDOLPH   Away, you rogue!
HOSTESS   By my troth, he'll yield the crow a pudding            87
    one of these days. The King has killed his heart. Good       88
    husband, come home presently.         *Exit [with Boy].*     89
BARDOLPH   Come, shall I make you two friends? We
    must to France together. Why the devil should we
    keep knives to cut one another's throats?
PISTOL
    Let floods o'erswell, and fiends for food howl on!
NYM   You'll pay me the eight shillings I won of you at
    betting?
PISTOL   Base is the slave that pays.
NYM   That now I will have. That's the humor of it.
PISTOL   As manhood shall compound. Push home.                  98
                              *[They] draw.*
BARDOLPH [*drawing*]   By this sword, he that makes
    the first thrust, I'll kill him! By this sword, I will.
PISTOL
    Sword is an oath, and oaths must have their course.         101
                        *[He sheathes his sword.]*
BARDOLPH   Corporal Nym, an thou wilt be friends, be            102
    friends; an thou wilt not, why, then, be enemies with
    me too. Prithee, put up.                                     104
NYM   I shall have my eight shillings I won of you at
    betting?
PISTOL
    A noble shalt thou have, and present pay;                   107
    And liquor likewise will I give to thee,

And friendship shall combine, and brotherhood.
I'll live by Nym, and Nym shall live by me.                     110
Is not this just? For I shall sutler be                         111
Unto the camp, and profits will accrue.
Give me thy hand.
NYM   I shall have my noble?
PISTOL   In cash most justly paid.
NYM   Well, then, that's the humor of't.
            *[Nym and Bardolph sheathe their swords.]*

    *Enter Hostess.*

HOSTESS   As ever you come of women, come in quickly 117
    to Sir John. Ah, poor heart, he is so shaked of a burn-
    ing quotidian tertian that it is most lamentable to be-     119
    hold. Sweet men, come to him.          *[Exit.]*
NYM   The King hath run bad humors on the knight,               121
    that's the even of it.                                       122
PISTOL   Nym, thou hast spoke the right.
    His heart is fracted and corroborate.                        124
NYM   The King is a good king, but it must be as it may;
    he passes some humors and careers.                           126
PISTOL
    Let us condole the knight, for, lambkins, we will live. 127
                              *[Exeunt.]*

                          ❖

# [2.2]

    *Enter Exeter, Bedford, and Westmorland.*

BEDFORD
'Fore God, His Grace is bold to trust these traitors.
EXETER
They shall be apprehended by and by.
WESTMORLAND
How smooth and even they do bear themselves!                    3
As if allegiance in their bosoms sat,
Crownèd with faith and constant loyalty.
BEDFORD
The King hath note of all that they intend,
By interception which they dream not of.
EXETER
Nay, but the man that was his bedfellow,                         8
Whom he hath dulled and cloyed with gracious
    favors—                                                      9

72 *Couple a gorge!* Couper la gorge!, "Cut the throat!"   74 hound of
Crete (Parallel to *Iceland dog,* line 42.)   75 spital hospital   76 powder-
ing tub (Originally a tub used for salting beef; here, alluding to a
method of curing venereal disease by sweating.)   77 lazar . . . kind
i.e., diseased, leprous whore (a *kite* is a bird of prey) like Cressida,
the fallen woman, who, in Robert Henryson's *Testament of Cresseid,*
is shown as being rejected by Diomede and infected with leprosy
78 Doll Tearsheet (a character in *2 Henry IV*)   79 quondam former
80 only she i.e., only woman in the world.   *pauca* i.e., in brief   84 face
(Bardolph's face is fiery with drinking.)   87 he'll (Refers to the Boy or
Falstaff.)   yield . . . pudding i.e., be hanged on the gallows and eaten
by carrion birds   88 his i.e., Falstaff's   89 presently immediately.
98 As . . . compound As valor shall settle the matter (in fight).   101
Sword is an oath (Quibbling on *sword* as '*s word,* i.e., "God's word.")
102 an if   104 put up i.e., put up your sword.   107 A noble . . . pay
i.e., I'll settle for paying you six shillings eight pence ready money

110 Nym (Quibbles on *nim,* meaning "thief.")   111 sutler seller of
liquor and provisions to the soldiers   117 come of were born of
119 quotidian tertian (A *quotidian* fever was one that came daily; a
*tertian* fever, one that came on alternate days, though some authorities believed that different fevers might mix and intensify their
effects.)   121 run bad humors i.e., vented his displeasure   122 even
level truth   124 fracted broken.   corroborate (Blunder for "broken
to pieces" or "corrupted"? The word means "strengthened, confirmed.")   126 passes . . . careers lets pass (i.e., indulges in) some
idiosyncrasies and capers. (A *career* is a full gallop.)   127 condole
express our commiseration of or sympathy with.   lambkins (A term
of endearment.)
2.2. Location: Southampton, a seaport on England's southern coast.
3 smooth and even pleasant and calm   8 bedfellow i.e., constant
companion. (Refers to Scroop.)   9 Whom . . . favors i.e., to whom
the King has been extraordinarily generous, having *dulled and cloyed*
the appetite with gifts

That he should, for a foreign purse, so sell    10
His sovereign's life to death and treachery!

*Sound trumpets. Enter the King, Scroop, Cambridge, and Grey, [and attendants].*

KING
Now sits the wind fair, and we will aboard.    12
My lord of Cambridge, and my kind lord of Masham,    13
And you, my gentle knight, give me your thoughts.    14
Think you not that the pow'rs we bear with us    15
Will cut their passage through the force of France,
Doing the execution and the act
For which we have in head assembled them?    18

SCROOP
No doubt, my liege, if each man do his best.

KING
I doubt not that, since we are well persuaded
We carry not a heart with us from hence
That grows not in a fair consent with ours,    22
Nor leave not one behind that doth not wish
Success and conquest to attend on us.

CAMBRIDGE
Never was monarch better feared and loved
Than is Your Majesty. There's not, I think, a subject
That sits in heart-grief and uneasiness
Under the sweet shade of your government.

GREY
True. Those that were your father's enemies
Have steeped their galls in honey, and do serve you    30
With hearts create of duty and of zeal.    31

KING
We therefore have great cause of thankfulness,
And shall forget the office of our hand    33
Sooner than quittance of desert and merit    34
According to the weight and worthiness.

SCROOP
So service shall with steelèd sinews toil,    36
And labor shall refresh itself with hope,
To do Your Grace incessant services.

KING
We judge no less.—Uncle of Exeter,
Enlarge the man committed yesterday    40
That railed against our person. We consider
It was excess of wine that set him on,
And on his more advice we pardon him.    43

SCROOP
That's mercy, but too much security.    44
Let him be punished, sovereign, lest example
Breed, by his sufferance, more of such a kind.    46

KING    Oh, let us yet be merciful.

CAMBRIDGE
So may Your Highness, and yet punish too.

GREY
Sir, you show great mercy if you give him life    49
After the taste of much correction.    50

KING
Alas, your too much love and care of me
Are heavy orisons 'gainst this poor wretch!    52
If little faults proceeding on distemper    53
Shall not be winked at, how shall we stretch our eye    54
When capital crimes, chewed, swallowed, and
digested,    55
Appear before us? We'll yet enlarge that man,    56
Though Cambridge, Scroop, and Grey, in their dear
care
And tender preservation of our person,
Would have him punished. And now to our French
causes.
Who are the late commissioners?    60

CAMBRIDGE    I one, my lord.
Your Highness bade me ask for it today.    62

SCROOP    So did you me, my liege.

GREY    And I, my royal sovereign.

KING [*giving them papers*]
Then, Richard Earl of Cambridge, there is yours;
There yours, Lord Scroop of Masham; and sir knight,
Grey of Northumberland, this same is yours.
Read them, and know I know your worthiness.—
My lord of Westmorland, and uncle Exeter,
We will aboard tonight.—Why, how now, gentlemen?
What see you in those papers, that you lose
So much complexion?—Look ye how they change!    72
Their cheeks are paper.—Why, what read you there    73
That have so cowarded and chased your blood
Out of appearance?

CAMBRIDGE    I do confess my fault,    75
And do submit me to Your Highness' mercy.

GREY, SCROOP    To which we all appeal.

KING
The mercy that was quick in us but late    78
By your own counsel is suppressed and killed.
You must not dare, for shame, to talk of mercy,
For your own reasons turn into your bosoms,
As dogs upon their masters, worrying you.—    82
See you, my princes and my noble peers,
These English monsters! My lord of Cambridge here,
You know how apt our love was to accord    85
To furnish him with all appurtenants    86
Belonging to his honor; and this man
Hath for a few light crowns lightly conspired    88
And sworn unto the practices of France    89

---

**10 foreign** i.e., French (with whom Lord Scroop of Masham is accused of having arranged to betray King Henry in return for gold)    **12 sits . . . fair** the wind blows from a favorable quarter    **13 lord of Masham** Lord Scroop    **14 my gentle knight** Sir Thomas Grey    **15 pow'rs** armed forces    **18 in head** as an army    **22 grows . . . consent** does not act in harmony    **30 galls** i.e., resentment    **31 create** composed    **33 office** use, function    **34 quittance** requital    **36 So . . . toil** And so we will labor to perform the service we owe you with all our strength    **40 Enlarge** set free.    **committed** arrested    **43 his more advice** his more sober explanation and apology for what he had drunkenly said    **44 security** overconfidence.    **46 sufferance** being pardoned

**49 give him life** allow him to live    **50 correction** punishment.    **52 heavy orisons** weighty prayers, pleas    **53 proceeding on distemper** resulting from excessive drinking    **54 winked at** overlooked by shutting our eyes.    **how . . . eye** i.e., how can we gaze with open eye    **55 capital** punishable by death.    **chewed . . . digested** i.e., premeditated    **56 yet** in spite of what you say    **60 late** recently appointed (to serve while Henry is in France)    **62 it** i.e., my commission    **72 complexion** color.    **73 paper** i.e., white as a sheet.    **75 appearance** (1) sight (2) your faces. (Presumably the traitors kneel at this point.)    **78 quick** alive    **82 worrying you** tearing at your throat.    **85 accord** consent    **86 appurtenants** appurtenances    **88 light** insignificant.    **lightly** readily, casually    **89 practices** plots

To kill us here in Hampton. To the which
This knight, no less for bounty bound to us                91
Than Cambridge is, hath likewise sworn. But oh,
What shall I say to thee, Lord Scroop, thou cruel,
Ingrateful, savage, and inhuman creature?
Thou that didst bear the key of all my counsels,
That knew'st the very bottom of my soul,
That almost mightst have coined me into gold,
Wouldst thou have practiced on me for thy use?            98
May it be possible that foreign hire
Could out of thee extract one spark of evil
That might annoy my finger? 'Tis so strange              101
That though the truth of it stands off as gross          102
As black and white, my eye will scarcely see it.
Treason and murder ever kept together,
As two yoke-devils sworn to either's purpose,            105
Working so grossly in a natural cause                    106
That admiration did not whoop at them.                   107
But thou, 'gainst all proportion, didst bring in         108
Wonder to wait on treason and on murder;                 109
And whatsoever cunning fiend it was
That wrought upon thee so preposterously                 111
Hath got the voice in hell for excellence.               112
All other devils that suggest by treasons                113
Do botch and bungle up damnation                         114
With patches, colors, and with forms being fetched       115
From glist'ring semblances of piety;                     116
But he that tempered thee bade thee stand up,            117
Gave thee no instance why thou shouldst do treason,      118
Unless to dub thee with the name of traitor.             119
If that same demon that hath gulled thee thus
Should with his lion gait walk the whole world,          121
He might return to vasty Tartar back                     122
And tell the legions, "I can never win
A soul so easy as that Englishman's."
Oh, how hast thou with jealousy infected                 125
The sweetness of affiance! Show men dutiful?             126
Why, so didst thou. Seem they grave and learnèd?
Why, so didst thou. Come they of noble family?
Why, so didst thou. Seem they religious?
Why, so didst thou. Or are they spare in diet,
Free from gross passion or of mirth or anger,            131
Constant in spirit, not swerving with the blood,         132

Garnished and decked in modest complement,               133
Not working with the eye without the ear,                134
And but in purgèd judgment trusting neither?             135
Such and so finely bolted didst thou seem.               136
And thus thy fall hath left a kind of blot               137
To mark the full-fraught man and best endued             138
With some suspicion. I will weep for thee;               139
For this revolt of thine, methinks, is like
Another fall of man.—Their faults are open.              141
Arrest them to the answer of the law;                    142
And God acquit them of their practices!

EXETER  I arrest thee of high treason, by the name of
Richard Earl of Cambridge.
I arrest thee of high treason, by the name of Henry Lord
Scroop of Masham.
I arrest thee of high treason, by the name of Thomas
Grey, knight, of Northumberland.

SCROOP
Our purposes God justly hath discovered,                 150
And I repent my fault more than my death,
Which I beseech Your Highness to forgive,
Although my body pay the price of it.

CAMBRIDGE
For me, the gold of France did not seduce,
Although I did admit it as a motive                      155
The sooner to effect what I intended.                    156
But God be thankèd for prevention,
Which I in sufferance heartily will rejoice,             158
Beseeching God and you to pardon me.

GREY
Never did faithful subject more rejoice
At the discovery of most dangerous treason
Than I do at this hour joy o'er myself,
Prevented from a damnèd enterprise.
My fault, but not my body, pardon, sovereign.

KING
God quit you in his mercy! Hear your sentence.           165
You have conspired against our royal person,
Joined with an enemy proclaimed, and from his
  coffers
Received the golden earnest of our death,                168
Wherein you would have sold your king to slaughter,
His princes and his peers to servitude,
His subjects to oppression and contempt,
And his whole kingdom into desolation.
Touching our person seek we no revenge,                  173

---

**91 This knight** i.e., Grey  **98 practiced on** plotted against.  **use** profit. (With play on the meaning "interest derived from usury"; Scroop had served as Lord Treasurer.)  **101 annoy** injure  **102 stands . . . gross** appears as obvious  **105 yoke-devils** partners in a diabolical cause  **106–7 Working . . . them** working together so manifestly toward a purpose suited to their evil natures that they provoked no outcry of wonder.  **108 proportion** fitness of things  **109 Wonder** astonishment (that Scroop should be a murderer).  **wait on** attend, accompany  **111 wrought** worked.  **preposterously** unnaturally  **112 voice** vote  **113–16 All . . . piety** All other devils that tempt make at least some effort to dress damnation up in a plausible semblance of piety  **117–19 But . . . traitor** but the devil that tempted you to treason simply ordered you to stand up an unabashed rebel, and gave you no specious justification to do treason other than for the sheer sake of having the name of traitor.  **121 lion gait** (The devil, according to 1 Peter 5:8, strides about the world like a roaring lion, "seeking whom he may devour.")  **122 vasty** vast.  **Tartar** Tartarus, the hell of classical mythology  **125 jealousy** suspicion  **126 affiance** trust.  **Show** Appear  **131 or of** either of  **132 swerving with the blood** sinning through passion

**133 decked . . . complement** wearing the look of modesty  **134–5 Not . . . neither** trusting neither eye nor ear alone, and not trusting either one except when refined by wisdom and judgment.  **136 bolted** sifted  **137–9 And . . . suspicion** And thus your fall into sin has been such as to cast some suspicion on even those who seem fully and richly endowed with virtuous qualities.  **141 fall of man** humankind's original disobedience to God in the Garden of Eden.  **open** apparent, obvious.  **142 to the answer of** so that they will be answerable to  **150 discovered** revealed  **155 did . . . motive** i.e., accepted money from France as a means  **156 The . . . intended** (Cambridge's real motive, barely hinted at here, was to assist his brother-in-law Edmund Mortimer, fifth Earl of March, to the throne as the standard-bearer of the Yorkist claim against the Lancastrian Henry.)  **158 sufferance** my suffering and patient endurance  **165 quit** (1) pardon (2) requite, punish  **168 golden earnest of** advance payment for  **173 Touching our person** As regards my own personal safety

But we our kingdom's safety must so tender,                              174
Whose ruin you have sought, that to her laws
We do deliver you. Get you therefore hence,
Poor miserable wretches, to your death,
The taste whereof God of his mercy give
You patience to endure, and true repentance
Of all your dear offenses!—Bear them hence.                              180
     *Exeunt* [*Cambridge, Scroop, and Grey, guarded*].
Now, lords, for France, the enterprise whereof
Shall be to you, as us, like glorious.                                   182
We doubt not of a fair and lucky war,
Since God so graciously hath brought to light
This dangerous treason lurking in our way
To hinder our beginnings. We doubt not now
But every rub is smoothèd on our way.                                    187
Then forth, dear countrymen! Let us deliver
Our puissance into the hand of God,                                      189
Putting it straight in expedition.                                       190
Cheerly to sea! The signs of war advance!                                191
No king of England, if not king of France!
     *Flourish.* [*Exeunt.*]

# [2.3]

*Enter Pistol, Nym, Bardolph, Boy, and Hostess.*

HOSTESS Prithee, honey-sweet husband, let me bring
thee to Staines.                                                         2
PISTOL No, for my manly heart doth earn. Bardolph, be    3
blithe; Nym, rouse thy vaunting veins; Boy, bristle thy
courage up; for Falstaff he is dead, and we must earn
therefore.
BARDOLPH Would I were with him, wheresome'er he is,
either in heaven or in hell!
HOSTESS Nay, sure he's not in hell. He's in Arthur's      9
bosom, if ever man went to Arthur's bosom. 'A made    10
a finer end, and went away an it had been any         11
christom child. 'A parted ev'n just between twelve    12
and one, ev'n at the turning o'th' tide. For after I saw
him fumble with the sheets, and play with flowers,
and smile upon his finger's end, I knew there was but
one way; for his nose was as sharp as a pen, and 'a    16
babbled of green fields. "How now, Sir John?" quoth I.   17
"What, man? Be o' good cheer." So 'a cried out, "God,
God, God!" three or four times. Now I, to comfort him,
bid him 'a should not think of God; I hoped there was

no need to trouble himself with any such thoughts yet.
So 'a bade me lay more clothes on his feet. I put my
hand into the bed and felt them, and they were as cold
as any stone; then I felt to his knees, and so upward   24
and upward, and all was as cold as any stone.           25
NYM They say he cried out of sack.                     26
HOSTESS Ay, that 'a did.
BARDOLPH And of women.
HOSTESS Nay, that 'a did not.
BOY Yes, that 'a did, and said they were devils incar-
nate.
HOSTESS 'A could never abide carnation; 'twas a color
he never liked.
BOY 'A said once the devil would have him about
women.
HOSTESS 'A did in some sort, indeed, handle women;   36
but then he was rheumatic, and talked of the Whore of   37
Babylon.
BOY Do you not remember, 'a saw a flea stick upon
Bardolph's nose, and 'a said it was a black soul
burning in hell?
BARDOLPH Well, the fuel is gone that maintained that   42
fire. That's all the riches I got in his service.
NYM Shall we shog? The King will be gone from South-   44
ampton.
PISTOL
Come, let's away.—My love, give me thy lips.
     [*He kisses the Hostess.*]
Look to my chattels and my movables.                     47
Let senses rule. The word is "Pitch and pay."            48
Trust none,
For oaths are straws, men's faiths are wafer cakes,      50
And Holdfast is the only dog, my duck.                   51
Therefore, *caveto* be thy counselor.                    52
Go, clear thy crystals.—Yokefellows in arms,             53
Let us to France, like horseleeches, my boys,
To suck, to suck, the very blood to suck!
BOY And that's but unwholesome food, they say.
PISTOL Touch her soft mouth, and march.
BARDOLPH Farewell, hostess.   [*Kissing her.*]
NYM I cannot kiss, that is the humor of it; but adieu.
PISTOL
Let huswifery appear. Keep close, I thee command.        60
HOSTESS Farewell! Adieu!  *Exeunt* [*separately*].

174 **tender** regard, hold dear 180 **dear** grievous, dire 182 **like**
alike, equally 187 **But** but that. **rub** obstacle. (A bowling term.)
189 **puissance** armed might 190 **straight in expedition** immediately
in action. 191 **The signs . . . advance!** Lift high our banners!
**2.3. London. A street.**
2 **Staines** town on the road from London to Southampton. 3 **earn**
grieve. (But in line 5 there may also be a play on the sense of "find
other employment," since Pistol and the others are now on their
own.) 9–10 **Arthur's bosom** (Malapropism for "Abraham's bosom";
see Luke 16:22.) 10 **'A** He 11 **an** as if 12 **christom** (Mistress
Quickly means "new christened." A *chrisom* is a white robe put on a
child at baptism to betoken innocence. Christenings were performed
soon after birth because of the high rate of infant mortality.) 16–17 **'a
babbled of green fields** (This line contains Theobald's famous emendation. The Folio has "and a Table of greene fields." Mistress Quickly
seems unaware that Falstaff was reciting the Twenty-third Psalm.)

24–5 **upward . . . stone** (The Hostess seems unaware of the sexual
implications of her speech. *Stone* can mean "testicle.") 26 **of sack**
against sack (a Spanish wine). 36 **handle** discuss. (Though an unintended literal sense is also comically present.) 37 **rheumatic** feverish,
or perhaps an error for "lunatic." (Because "Rome" was pronounced
"room," *rheumatic* also prepares for the allusion to the Whore of Babylon, i.e., the Church of Rome. See also Revelation 17:4–5.) 42 **fuel** i.e.,
liquor, supplied by Falstaff, that has given Bardolph his red face
44 **shog** be off. 47 **chattels . . . movables** personal property. 48 **Let . . .
pay** i.e., Keep your eyes and ears open, and let your motto as hostess be
"cash down." 50 **wafer cakes** i.e., easily broken 51 **Holdfast . . . dog**
i.e., a large clamp or *holdfast* is best at holding things tight, like a tena-
cious dog. (Compare the proverb, "Brag is a good dog, but Holdfast is
better.") Mistress Quickly is bidden to keep a tight hold on things.
52 *caveto* beware. (The correct imperative plural of the Latin is *cavete*.)
53 **clear thy crystals** wipe your eyes. **Yokefellows** Companions
60 **Let . . . close** i.e., Be a thrifty housekeeper and stay at home

# [2.4]

*Flourish. Enter the French King, the Dauphin, the*
*Dukes of Berri and Brittany, [the Constable, and*
*others].*

FRENCH KING
Thus comes the English with full power upon us,
And more than carefully it us concerns
To answer royally in our defenses.
Therefore the Dukes of Berri and of Brittany,
Of Brabant and of Orleans, shall make forth,                                        5
And you, Prince Dauphin, with all swift dispatch,
To line and new-repair our towns of war                                              7
With men of courage and with means defendant;                                        8
For England his approaches makes as fierce                                           9
As waters to the sucking of a gulf.                                                  10
It fits us then to be as provident
As fear may teach us, out of late examples                                           12
Left by the fatal and neglected English                                              13
Upon our fields.

DAUPHIN                         My most redoubted father,                           14
It is most meet we arm us 'gainst the foe;                                           15
For peace itself should not so dull a kingdom,
Though war nor no known quarrel were in question,
But that defenses, musters, preparations,
Should be maintained, assembled, and collected
As were a war in expectation.                                                        20
Therefore, I say 'tis meet we all go forth
To view the sick and feeble parts of France.
And let us do it with no show of fear—
No, with no more than if we heard that England
Were busied with a Whitsun morris dance.                                             25
For, my good liege, she is so idly kinged,                                           26
Her scepter so fantastically borne
By a vain, giddy, shallow, humorous youth,                                           28
That fear attends her not.

CONSTABLE                         Oh, peace, Prince Dauphin!
You are too much mistaken in this king.
Question Your Grace the late ambassadors,
With what great state he heard their embassy,                                        32
How well supplied with noble counselors,
How modest in exception, and withal                                                  34
How terrible in constant resolution,                                                 35
And you shall find his vanities forespent                                            36
Were but the outside of the Roman Brutus,                                            37
Covering discretion with a coat of folly,
As gardeners do with ordure hide those roots                                         39

That shall first spring and be most delicate.
DAUPHIN
Well, 'tis not so, my Lord High Constable;
But though we think it so, it is no matter.
In cases of defense 'tis best to weigh
The enemy more mighty than he seems.
So the proportions of defense are filled,                                            45
Which of a weak and niggardly projection                                             46
Doth, like a miser, spoil his coat with scanting
A little cloth.
FRENCH KING        Think we King Harry strong;
And, princes, look you strongly arm to meet him.                                     49
The kindred of him hath been fleshed upon us;                                        50
And he is bred out of that bloody strain
That haunted us in our familiar paths.
Witness our too-much-memorable shame
When Crécy battle fatally was struck,                                                54
And all our princes captived by the hand
Of that black name, Edward, Black Prince of Wales;
Whiles that his mountain sire, on mountain standing,                                 57
Up in the air, crowned with the golden sun,
Saw his heroical seed and smiled to see him                                          59
Mangle the work of nature and deface                                                 60
The patterns that by God and by French fathers                                       61
Had twenty years been made. This is a stem                                          62
Of that victorious stock; and let us fear
The native mightiness and fate of him.                                               64

*Enter a Messenger.*

MESSENGER
Ambassadors from Harry King of England
Do crave admittance to Your Majesty.
FRENCH KING
We'll give them present audience. Go and bring them.
                                         *[Exit Messenger.]*
You see this chase is hotly followed, friends.
DAUPHIN
Turn head and stop pursuit; for coward dogs                                          69
Most spend their mouths when what they seem to
   threaten                                                                          70
Runs far before them. Good my sovereign,
Take up the English short, and let them know
Of what a monarchy you are the head.
Self-love, my liege, is not so vile a sin
As self-neglecting.

*Enter Exeter [and others].*

FRENCH KING              From our brother of England?                               75

---

2.4. Location: France. The royal court.
0.1 *Flourish* fanfare announcing the arrival of royalty or other dignitaries   **5 make forth** set forth   **7 line** reinforce   **8 defendant** defensive   **9 England** the King of England   **10 gulf** whirlpool.   **12 late** recent   **13 fatal and neglected** fatally underestimated   **14 redoubted** formidable   **15 meet** appropriate   **20 As were** as if there were   **25 Whitsun morris dance** folk dance often performed during Whitsuntide, in early summer, by persons in fancy costumes and decked with bells.   **26 idly** frivolously   **28 humorous** capricious   **32 state** dignity   **34 exception** making objections.   **withal** in addition   **35 terrible** awesome, terrifying   **36 vanities forespent** follies used up and now a thing of the past   **37 Brutus** i.e., the elder Brutus, Lucius Junius Brutus, who pretended to be stupid (*brutus*) as a ruse to allay the suspicions of the tyrant Tarquin until the time for overthrow was ripe   **39 ordure** manure, mulch

**45 So . . . filled** In that way an adequate and full defense is provided   **46 Which . . . projection** which defense, if designed on too small and miserly a scale   **49 look** be sure   **50 kindred** i.e., his great-grandfather Edward III and great-uncle Edward the Black Prince.   **fleshed** initiated in the shedding of blood, with foretaste of further success   **54 Crécy** French defeat in 1346.   **struck** waged   **57 mountain sire** i.e., Edward III, born in mountainous Wales, and of sturdy proportions   **59–62 Saw . . . made** beheld his heroical son (the Black Prince) and smiled to see him mangle Nature's handiwork in the shape of young Frenchmen, whom, some twenty or so years earlier, God and their French fathers had created and begotten.   **64 fate** what he is destined to do   **69 Turn . . . pursuit** Turn and face the pursuing hounds. (Hunting terms.)   **70 Most . . . mouths** bay the loudest   **75 brother** fellow monarch

EXETER
From him, and thus he greets Your Majesty:
He wills you, in the name of God Almighty,
That you divest yourself and lay apart                          78
The borrowed glories that by gift of heaven,
By law of nature and of nations, 'longs                         80
To him and to his heirs, namely, the crown
And all wide-strechèd honors that pertain                       82
By custom and the ordinance of times                            83
Unto the crown of France. That you may know
'Tis no sinister nor no awkward claim,                          85
Picked from the wormholes of long-vanished days,
Nor from the dust of old oblivion raked,
He sends you this most memorable line,                          88
                                    [giving a paper]
In every branch truly demonstrative,
Willing you overlook this pedigree.                             90
And when you find him evenly derived                            91
From his most famed of famous ancestors,
Edward the Third, he bids you then resign
Your crown and kingdom, indirectly held                         94
From him the native and true challenger.                        95
FRENCH KING    Or else what follows?
EXETER
Bloody constraint; for if you hide the crown                    97
Even in your hearts, there will he rake for it.
Therefore in fierce tempest is he coming,
In thunder and in earthquake, like a Jove,
That if requiring fail, he will compel;                         101
And bids you, in the bowels of the Lord,                        102
Deliver up the crown, and to take mercy
On the poor souls for whom this hungry war
Opens his vasty jaws, and on your head                          105
Turning the widows' tears, the orphans' cries,                  106
The dead men's blood, the privèd maidens' groans,              107
For husbands, fathers, and betrothèd lovers
That shall be swallowed in this controversy.
This is his claim, his threat'ning, and my message—
Unless the Dauphin be in presence here,
To whom expressly I bring greeting too.
FRENCH KING
For us, we will consider of this further.
Tomorrow shall you bear our full intent
Back to our brother of England.
DAUPHIN                          For the Dauphin,
I stand here for him. What to him from England?
EXETER
Scorn and defiance, slight regard, contempt,
And anything that may not misbecome                             118
The mighty sender, doth he prize you at.                        119

Thus says my king, and if your father's Highness
Do not, in grant of all demands at large,                       121
Sweeten the bitter mock you sent His Majesty,
He'll call you to so hot an answer of it                        123
That caves and womby vaultages of France                        124
Shall chide your trespass and return your mock
In second accent of his ordinance.                              126
DAUPHIN
Say if my father render fair return                             127
It is against my will, for I desire
Nothing but odds with England. To that end,                     129
As matching to his youth and vanity,
I did present him with the Paris balls.                         131
EXETER
He'll make your Paris Louvre shake for it,                      132
Were it the mistress court of mighty Europe.
And be assured, you'll find a diff'rence,
As we his subjects have in wonder found,
Between the promise of his greener days                         136
And these he masters now. Now he weighs time
Even to the utmost grain. That you shall read                   138
In your own losses, if he stay in France.
FRENCH KING
Tomorrow shall you know our mind at full.                       140
                                              Flourish.
EXETER
Dispatch us with all speed, lest that our king
Come here himself to question our delay;
For he is footed in this land already.
FRENCH KING
You shall be soon dispatched with fair conditions.
A night is but small breath and little pause
To answer matters of this consequence.
                                    Flourish. Exeunt.

                            ♣

# [3.0]

*Enter Chorus.*

CHORUS
Thus with imagined wing our swift scene flies                   1
In motion of no less celerity
Than that of thought. Suppose that you have seen
The well-appointed King at Dover pier                           4
Embark his royalty, and his brave fleet                         5
With silken streamers the young Phoebus fanning.                6
Play with your fancies, and in them behold

78 apart aside   80 'longs belongs   82 wide-strechèd stretching far
and wide   83 ordinance of times decrees of tradition   85 sinister illegitimate.   awkward oblique   88 line pedigree   90 Willing you overlook desiring that you look over   91 evenly directly   94 indirectly
wrongfully   95 native natural (by birthright).   challenger claimant.
97 constraint coercion, compulsion   101 requiring requesting   102 in
. . . Lord in the name of God's compassion. (See Philippians 1:8.)
105–6 and on . . . tears and who, poor souls, are pouring on your head
their widows' tears. (Perhaps the Quarto reading, "turnes he," is correct in
place of the Folio "Turning.")   107 privèd deprived (by loss of loved
ones)   118 misbecome be inappropriate for   119 prize value, appraise

121 in grant of in assenting to.   at large in full   123 of it for it
124 womby vaultages hollow recesses   126 In . . . ordinance in loud
echoing of the sound of King Henry's ordnance (cannon).   127 fair
return courteous reply   129 odds (1) strife (2) betting odds, as in tennis
131 Paris balls tennis balls.   132 Louvre the French royal palace
136 greener younger   138 grain grain of sand (in an hourglass).
That . . . read i.e., You will see this new seriousness manifested
140.1 Flourish (This trumpet call is sounded as the French King arises
from his throne, thereby dismissing the embassy, but Exeter boldly
insists on speaking further.)
3.0. Chorus.
1 imagined wing wings of imagination   4 well-appointed well-
equipped.   Dover (Seemingly an error for Hampton, i.e.,
Southampton.)   5 brave handsome   6 the . . . fanning i.e., fluttering
in the rising sun.

Upon the hempen tackle shipboys climbing;                               8
Hear the shrill whistle, which doth order give
To sounds confused; behold the threaden sails,                          10
Borne with th'invisible and creeping wind,
Draw the huge bottoms through the furrowed sea,                         12
Breasting the lofty surge. Oh, do but think                             13
You stand upon the rivage and behold                                    14
A city on th'inconstant billows dancing;
For so appears this fleet majestical,
Holding due course to Harfleur. Follow, follow!                         17
Grapple your minds to sternage of this navy,                            18
And leave your England as dead midnight still,
Guarded with grandsires, babies, and old women,
Either past or not arrived to pith and puissance;                       21
For who is he whose chin is but enriched
With one appearing hair that will not follow
These culled and choice-drawn cavaliers to France?                      24
Work, work your thoughts, and therein see a siege;
Behold the ordnance on their carriages,
With fatal mouths gaping on girded Harfleur.                            27
Suppose th'ambassador from the French comes back,
Tells Harry that the King doth offer him
Katharine his daughter, and with her, to dowry,
Some petty and unprofitable dukedoms.
The offer likes not; and the nimble gunner                              32
With linstock now the devilish cannon touches,                          33
                        *Alarum, and chambers go off.*
And down goes all before them. Still be kind,
And eke out our performance with your mind.
                                                    *Exit.*

✤

## [3.1]

*Enter the King, Exeter, Bedford, and Gloucester.*
*Alarum, [with soldiers carrying] scaling ladders at*
*Harfleur.*

KING
Once more unto the breach, dear friends, once more,                     1
Or close the wall up with our English dead!
In peace there's nothing so becomes a man
As modest stillness and humility.
But when the blast of war blows in our ears,
Then imitate the action of the tiger:
Stiffen the sinews, conjure up the blood,
Disguise fair nature with hard-favored rage.                            8
Then lend the eye a terrible aspect:                                    9
Let it pry through the portage of the head                             10
Like the brass cannon; let the brow o'erwhelm it                       11

As fearfully as doth a gallèd rock                                     12
O'erhang and jutty his confounded base,                                13
Swilled with the wild and wasteful ocean.                              14
Now set the teeth and stretch the nostril wide,
Hold hard the breath, and bend up every spirit
To his full height. On, on, you noblest English,
Whose blood is fet from fathers of war-proof,                          18
Fathers that, like so many Alexanders,                                 19
Have in these parts from morn till even fought,                        20
And sheathed their swords for lack of argument.                        21
Dishonor not your mothers; now attest
That those whom you called fathers did beget you.
Be copy now to men of grosser blood,                                   24
And teach them how to war. And you, good yeomen,
Whose limbs were made in England, show us here
The mettle of your pasture. Let us swear                               27
That you are worth your breeding, which I doubt not,
For there is none of you so mean and base                              29
That hath not noble luster in your eyes.
I see you stand like greyhounds in the slips,                          31
Straining upon the start. The game's afoot.                            32
Follow your spirit, and upon this charge                               33
Cry, "God for Harry! England and Saint George!"                        34
            *Alarum, and chambers go off. [Exeunt.]*

✤

## [3.2]

*Enter Nym, Bardolph, Pistol, and Boy.*

BARDOLPH   On, on, on, on, on! To the breach, to the
breach!
NYM   Pray thee, Corporal, stay. The knocks are too hot,
and for mine own part I have not a case of lives. The       4
humor of it is too hot, that is the very plainsong of it.   5
PISTOL
"The plainsong" is most just; for humors do abound.
Knocks go and come; God's vassals drop and die;            7
[*He sings*] "And sword and shield
            In bloody field
        Doth win immortal fame."
BOY   Would I were in an alehouse in London! I would
give all my fame for a pot of ale and safety.
PISTOL   And I:
[*He sings*] "If wishes would prevail with me,             14
My purpose should not fail with me,
        But thither would I hie."                           16

---

8 **hempen tackle** rope rigging   10 **threaden** woven of thread   12 **bottoms** hulls of ships   13 **surge** swell of the sea.   14 **rivage** shore   17 **Harfleur** at the mouth of the Seine   18 **Grapple** Attach, hook. **to sternage** to the sterns   21 **pith** strength   24 **culled and choice-drawn** carefully selected   27 **fatal** deadly.   **girded** besieged   32 **likes** pleases   33 **linstock** staff holding a gunner's match   33.1 *Alarum* Call to arms.   *chambers* small cannon (fired off backstage, or "within")
**3.1. Location: France. Before Harfleur.**
**0.2** *scaling ladders* (Presumably these are set up against the facade of the tiring-house, upstage, which is perceived to be the walls of Harfleur.)   1 **breach** gap in fortifications opened up by artillery
8 **hard-favored** unsightly, ugly   9 **terrible aspect** terrifying appearance   10 **portage** portholes, eyes   11 **o'erwhelm** project over

12 **fearfully** frighteningly.   **gallèd** washed away, eroded   13 **O'erhang ... base** hang and project over its worn-away base   14 **Swilled** washed.   **wasteful** destructive   18 **fet** fetched, derived.   **of war-proof** tested in war   19 **Alexanders** (Alexander grieved that there were no new worlds for him to conquer.)   20 **even** evening   21 **argument** opposition.   24 **copy** models   27 **mettle ... pasture** quality of your breeding. (Literally, *pasture* means "feeding.")   29 **mean and base** of low social station   31 **slips** leashes   32 **The game's afoot** The quarry is out of its lair and running.   33 **Follow your spirit** i.e., Obey the impulse of your vital powers   34 **Saint George** patron saint of England.
**3.2. Location: Before Harfleur, as in the previous scene; the action is essentially continuous.**
4 **case** set   5 **plainsong** simple melody, simple truth   7 **God's vassals** i.e., mortal men   14 **with me** in my case   16 **hie** hasten.

BOY [*sings*]
> "As duly, but not as truly,
> As bird doth sing on bough."

*Enter Fluellen.*

FLUELLEN   Up to the breach, you dogs! Avaunt, you cul-   19
lions!                                    [*Driving them forward.*]   20
PISTOL
Be merciful, great duke, to men of mold.   21
Abate thy rage, abate thy manly rage,
Abate thy rage, great duke!
Good bawcock, bate thy rage! Use lenity, sweet chuck!   24
NYM   These be good humors! Your Honor runs bad   25
humors.                              *Exit* [*with all but Boy*].   26
BOY   As young as I am, I have observed these three
swashers. I am boy to them all three, but all they three,   28
though they would serve me, could not be man to me;   29
for indeed three such antics do not amount to a man.   30
For Bardolph, he is white-livered and red-faced, by the   31
means whereof 'a faces it out but fights not. For Pistol,   32
he hath a killing tongue and a quiet sword, by the
means whereof 'a breaks words and keeps whole   34
weapons. For Nym, he hath heard that men of few
words are the best men, and therefore he scorns to say
his prayers, lest 'a should be thought a coward; but
his few bad words are matched with as few good
deeds, for 'a never broke any man's head but his own,
and that was against a post when he was drunk. They
will steal anything and call it purchase. Bardolph   41
stole a lute case, bore it twelve leagues, and sold it for   42
three halfpence. Nym and Bardolph are sworn brothers in filching, and in Calais they stole a fire shovel. I
knew by that piece of service the men would carry   45
coals. They would have me as familiar with men's   46
pockets as their gloves or their handkerchiefs, which
makes much against my manhood, if I should take   48
from another's pocket to put into mine, for it is plain
pocketing up of wrongs. I must leave them and seek   50
some better service. Their villainy goes against my   51
weak stomach, and therefore I must cast it up.   *Exit.*   52

*Enter Gower* [*and Fluellen, meeting*].

GOWER   Captain Fluellen, you must come presently to
the mines. The Duke of Gloucester would speak with   54
you.
FLUELLEN   To the mines? Tell you the Duke it is not so
good to come to the mines; for look you, the mines is
not according to the disciplines of the war. The   58
concavities of it is not sufficient. For look you, th'athver-   59
sary, you may discuss unto the Duke, look you,   60
is digt himself four yard under the countermines. By   61
Cheshu, I think 'a will plow up all, if there is not better   62
directions.
GOWER   The Duke of Gloucester, to whom the order of   64
the siege is given, is altogether directed by an Irish-
man, a very valiant gentleman, i'faith.
FLUELLEN   It is Captain Macmorris, is it not?
GOWER   I think it be.
FLUELLEN   By Cheshu, he is an ass, as in the world! I
will verify as much in his beard. He has no more di-   70
rections in the true disciplines of the wars, look you,
of the Roman disciplines, than is a puppy dog.

*Enter Macmorris and Captain Jamy.*

GOWER   Here 'a comes, and the Scots captain, Captain
Jamy, with him.
FLUELLEN   Captain Jamy is a marvelous falorous gen-   75
tleman, that is certain, and of great expedition and   76
knowledge in th'aunchient wars, upon my particular
knowledge of his directions. By Cheshu, he will
maintain his argument as well as any military man in
the world, in the disciplines of the pristine wars of the   80
Romans.
JAMY   I say gud day, Captain Fluellen.   82
FLUELLEN   Good e'en to Your Worship, good Captain   83
James.
GOWER   How now, Captain Macmorris, have you quit
the mines? Have the pioneers given o'er?   86
MACMORRIS   By Chrish, la, 'tish ill done! The work ish   87
give over, the trompet sound the retreat. By my hand
I swear, and my father's soul, the work ish ill done; it
ish give over. I would have blowed up the town, so
Chrish save me, la, in an hour. Oh, 'tish ill done, 'tish
ill done! By my hand, 'tish ill done!
FLUELLEN   Captain Macmorris, I beseech you now, will
you voutsafe me, look you, a few disputations with   94
you, as partly touching or concerning the disciplines
of the war, the Roman wars, in the way of argument,

---

**19 Avaunt** Be off   **19–20 cullions** rascals. (The original meaning was "testicles.")   **21 duke** leader, commander. (Latin *dux*.) A flattering title for a captain.   **men of mold** mere mortals.   **24 bawcock** fine fellow. (French *beau coq*.)   **lenity** leniency   **25–6 Your . . . humors** i.e., (1) You are behaving very idiosyncratically, Your Honor (2) Your fury is out of control. (Addressed to Fluellen, who is doubtless threatening or beating Nym, Bardolph, and Pistol to make them go forward.)   **28 swashers** swashbucklers.   **29 man** (1) servant (2) a manly, brave person   **30 antics** buffoons, zanies   **31 For** As for. (Also in lines 32 and 35.)   **white-livered** i.e., cowardly. (In extreme fear, the blood was thought to sink below the liver, leaving it bloodless.)   **32 'a faces it out** he has the martial-looking face for it, puts on a brave front   **34 breaks words** (1) misuses language and fails to keep his word (2) uses words as weapons   **41 purchase** (1) something paid for (2) thieves' cant for stolen goods.   **42 leagues** (about three miles each)   **45–6 carry coals** (1) do dirty, hard work, such as hauling coal (2) put up with insults.   **48 makes** goes   **50 pocketing . . . wrongs** (1) putting up with insults (2) receiving stolen goods.   **51–2 goes . . . stomach** (1) goes against my inclination (2) makes me sick   **52 cast it up** (1) cast it aside (2) vomit it.   **s.d. Exit** (A scene break may occur here, though it is not marked as such in most editions. Possibly Fluellen did not leave the stage at line 26.)

**54 mines** tunnels dug under the walls of the beseiged city to plant explosives.   **58 disciplines of the war** science of warfare (about which there were many books from Greek and Roman times down to the Renaissance; Fluellen's humor involves an obsession with this study and a preference for traditional methods).   **59 concavities** i.e., depth   **59–60 athversary** (Fluellen's pronunciation of *adversary*.)   **60 discuss** explain   **61 is digt . . . countermines** has dug himself countermines four yards beneath our mines.   **62 Cheshu** Jesu, Jesus.   **plow** blow. (In Fluellen's Welsh dialect, *p* is regularly substituted for *b* and *f* for *v*.)   **64 order** management   **70 in his beard** i.e., to his face.   **75 falorous** valorous   **76 expedition** readiness of argument, quickness of wit   **80 pristine** ancient   **82 gud** good. (In Jamie's Scots speech, *good* is pronounced "gud," *shall* "sall," *both* "bath," *Mass* "Mess," etc.; see lines 101–18.)   **83 Good e'en** Good afternoon or evening   **86 pioneers** sappers, diggers   **87 Chrish** (In Macmorris's Irish speech, *Christ*, *'tis*, and *is* are pronounced "Chrish," "'tish," and "ish," etc.)   **94 voutsafe** vouchsafe, permit

look you, and friendly communication—partly to satisfy my opinion, and partly for the satisfaction, look
you, of my mind, as touching the direction of the military discipline, that is the point.

JAMY  It sall be vary gud, gud feith, gud captens bath, 101
and I sall quite you with gud leve, as I may pick 102
occasion. That sall I, marry. 103

MACMORRIS  It is no time to discourse, so Chrish save
me! The day is hot, and the weather, and the wars,
and the King, and the dukes. It is no time to discourse.
The town is beseeched, and the trumpet call us to the 107
breach, and we talk, and, be Chrish, do nothing. 'Tis 108
shame for us all. So God sa' me, 'tis shame to stand
still, it is shame, by my hand! And there is throats to
be cut, and works to be done, and there ish nothing
done, so Chrish sa' me, la! 112

JAMY  By the Mess, ere theise eyes of mine take 113
themselves to slomber, ay'll de gud service, or I'll lig i'th' 114
grund for it, ay, or go to death! And I'll pay't as
valorously as I may, that sall I suerly do, that is the
breff and the long. Marry, I wad full fain heard some 117
question 'tween you twae. 118

FLUELLEN  Captain Macmorris, I think, look you, under
your correction, there is not many of your nation—

MACMORRIS  Of my nation? What ish my nation? Ish a 121
villain, and a bastard, and a knave, and a rascal? What 122
ish my nation? Who talks of my nation?

FLUELLEN  Look you, if you take the matter otherwise
than is meant, Captain Macmorris, peradventure I
shall think you do not use me with that affability as in
discretion you ought to use me, look you, being as
good a man as yourself, both in the disciplines of war
and in the derivation of my birth, and in other partic-
ularities.

MACMORRIS  I do not know you so good a man as myself. So Chrish save me, I will cut off your head!

GOWER  Gentlemen both, you will mistake each other. 133

JAMY  Ah, that's a foul fault!          *A parley* [*is sounded*]. 134

GOWER  The town sounds a parley.

FLUELLEN  Captain Macmorris, when there is more better opportunity to be required, look you, I will be so 137
bold as to tell you I know the disciplines of war; and
there is an end.          *Exit* [*with others*].

❧

---

## [3.3]

[*Enter the Governor and some citizens on the
walls.*] *Enter the King* [*Henry*] *and all his train
before the gates.*

KING
How yet resolves the Governor of the town?
This is the latest parle we will admit.                    2
Therefore to our best mercy give yourselves,
Or, like to men proud of destruction,                    4
Defy us to our worst; for as I am a soldier,
A name that in my thoughts becomes me best,
If I begin the batt'ry once again                         7
I will not leave the half-achievèd Harfleur
Till in her ashes she lie buried.
The gates of mercy shall be all shut up,
And the fleshed soldier, rough and hard of heart,       11
In liberty of bloody hand shall range                    12
With conscience wide as hell, mowing like grass          13
Your fresh fair virgins and your flow'ring infants.
What is it then to me if impious War,
Arrayed in flames like to the prince of fiends,          16
Do with his smirched complexion all fell feats           17
Enlinked to waste and desolation?
What is't to me, when you yourselves are cause,
If your pure maidens fall into the hand
Of hot and forcing violation?
What rein can hold licentious Wickedness
When down the hill he holds his fierce career?           23
We may as bootless spend our vain command               24
Upon th'enragèd soldiers in their spoil
As send precepts to the leviathan                        26
To come ashore. Therefore, you men of Harfleur,
Take pity of your town and of your people
Whiles yet my soldiers are in my command
Whiles yet the cool and temperate wind of grace         30
O'erblows the filthy and contagious clouds              31
Of heady murder, spoil, and villainy.                    32
If not, why, in a moment look to see                     33
The blind and bloody soldier with foul hand             34
Defile the locks of your shrill-shrieking daughters;
Your fathers taken by the silver beards,
And their most reverend heads dashed to the walls;
Your naked infants spitted upon pikes,

---

**3.3. Location: Before the gates of Harfleur, as in the previous scene.
The action is essentially continuous, as it is usually in battle
sequences; possibly some of the captains in 3.2 do not need to exit
here. The gates are represented by the tiring-house facade. Those
who appear *on the walls* are seen in the gallery backstage.
2 latest parle** last parley   **4 like ... destruction** i.e., like men elated
at the prospect of slaughter and glorying in destruction   **7 batt'ry**
attack   **11 fleshed** made fierce with the taste of blood   **12–13 In liberty
... as hell** will range with free license to shed blood and with a conscience wide and loose enough to sanction anything that hell itself
would justify   **16 like ... fiends** like the devil himself   **17 smirched**
blackened, covered with grime.   **fell** savage   **23 career** gallop.
**24 bootless** fruitlessly   **26 precepts** written summons.   **leviathan**
whale   **30 grace** mercy   **31 O'erblows** blows away. (Contagion was
thought to reside in clouds and mists.)   **32 heady** violent; headstrong   **33 look** expect   **34 blind** i.e., blinded with lust and rage

---

**101 bath** both   **102 quite** requite, answer.   **with gud leve** with good
leave, with your kind permission   **103 marry** indeed. (Originally,
"by the Virgin Mary.")   **107 beseeched** besieged   **108 be** by   **112
Chrish sa' me** Christ save me   **113 Mess** Mass   **114 ay'll de** I'll do.
**lig** lie   **117 breff** brief.   **wad full fain heard** would very willingly
have heard   **118 question** discussion.   **twae** two.   **121 What ish** i.e.,
What about   **121–2 Ish a villain** i.e., Is my nation a villain (etc.)?, or
Macmorris may be making a declarative statement, saying that anyone who says anything against my nation is a villain, etc.   **133 will
mistake** (Two possible meanings: [1] insist on misunderstanding
[2] are going to misunderstand.)   **134 s.d. *parley*** trumpet summons
to a negotiation   **137 required** found

Whiles the mad mothers with their howls confused
Do break the clouds, as did the wives of Jewry   40
At Herod's bloody-hunting slaughtermen.   41
What say you? Will you yield, and this avoid,
Or, guilty in defense, be thus destroyed?   43

GOVERNOR
Our expectation hath this day an end.
The Dauphin, whom of succors we entreated,   45
Returns us that his powers are yet not ready   46
To raise so great a siege. Therefore, great King,
We yield our town and lives to thy soft mercy.
Enter our gates, dispose of us and ours,
For we no longer are defensible.

KING
Open your gates.         [*Exit Governor.*]
         Come, uncle Exeter,
Go you and enter Harfleur; there remain,
And fortify it strongly 'gainst the French.
Use mercy to them all. For us, dear uncle,   54
The winter coming on and sickness growing
Upon our soldiers, we will retire to Calais.
Tonight in Harfleur will we be your guest;
Tomorrow for the march are we addressed.   58

         *Flourish, and enter the town.*

# [3.4]

*Enter Katharine and [Alice,] an old gentlewoman.*

KATHARINE   Alice, tu as été en Angleterre, et tu bien parles le langage.   1

ALICE   Un peu, madame.

KATHARINE   Je te prie, m'enseignez; il faut que j'apprenne à parler. Comment appelez-vous la main en anglais?

ALICE   La main? Elle est appelée de hand.

KATHARINE   De hand. Et les doigts?

ALICE   Les doigts? Ma foi, j'oublie les doigts; mais je me souviendrai. Les doigts? Je pense qu'ils sont appelés   10 de fingres; oui, de fingres.

KATHARINE   La main, de hand; les doigts, de fingres. Je pense que je suis le bon écolier; j'ai gagné deux mots d'anglais vîtement. Comment appelez-vous les ongles?

40 **Jewry** Judaea   41 **Herod's . . . slaughtermen** (For the account of Herod's slaughter of the innocent children in his attempt to murder the infant Jesus, see Matthew 2:16–18.)   43 **in defense** i.e., by not surrendering   45 **of succors** for help   46 **Returns** replies to   54 **For** As for   58 **addressed** prepared.
**3.4. Location: The French court at Rouen.**

**Translation:**
KATHARINE   Alice, you have been in England and speak the language well.
ALICE   A little, my lady.
KATHARINE   I pray you teach me; I have to learn to speak it. What do you call *la main* in English?
ALICE   *La main?* It is called de hand.
KATHARINE   De hand. And *les doigts?*
ALICE   *Les doigts?* Dear me, I forget *les doigts;* but I shall remember. I think that they are called de fingres; yes, de fingres.
KATHARINE   *La main,* de hand; *les doigts,* de fingres. I think that I am a clever scholar; I have learned two English words in no time. What do you call *les ongles?*

ALICE   Les ongles? Nous les appelons de nailes.

KATHARINE   De nailes. Écoutez, dites-moi si je parle bien: de hand, de fingres, et de nailes.

ALICE   C'est bien dit, madame; il est fort bon anglais.

KATHARINE   Dites-moi l'anglais pour le bras.   20

ALICE   De arm, madame.

KATHARINE   Et le coude?

ALICE   D' elbow.

KATHARINE   D' elbow. Je m'en fais la répétition de tous les mots que vous m'avez appris dès à présent.

ALICE   Il est trop difficile, madame, comme je pense.

KATHARINE   Excusez-moi, Alice; écoutez: d' hand, de fingre, de nailes, d' arma, de bilbow.

ALICE   D' elbow, madame.

KATHARINE   Oh, Seigneur Dieu, je m'en oublie! D' elbow.   30 Comment appelez-vous le col?

ALICE   De nick, madame.

KATHARINE   De nick. Et le menton?

ALICE   De chin.

KATHARINE   De sin. Le col, de nick; le menton, de sin.

ALICE   Oui. Sauf votre honneur, en vérité, vous prononcez les mots aussi droit que les natifs d'Angleterre.

KATHARINE   Je ne doute point d'apprendre, par la grâce de Dieu, et en peu de temps.

ALICE   N'avez-vous pas déjà oublié ce que je vous ai   40 enseigné?

KATHARINE   Non, je réciterai à vous promptement: d' hand, de fingre, de mailes—

ALICE   De nailes, madame.

KATHARINE   De nailes, de arm, de ilbow.

ALICE   Sauf votre honneur, d' elbow.

KATHARINE   Ainsi dis-je; d' elbow, de nick, et de sin. Comment appelez-vous le pied et la robe?

ALICE   *Les ongles?* We call them de nailes.
KATHARINE   De nailes. Listen; tell me whether or not I speak correctly: de hand, de fingres, and de nailes.
ALICE   That is correct, my lady; it is very good English.
KATHARINE   Tell me the English for *le bras.*
ALICE   De arm, my lady.
KATHARINE   And *le coude?*
ALICE   D' elbow.
KATHARINE   D' elbow. I am going to repeat all the words you have taught me so far.
ALICE   It is too hard, my lady, I fear.
KATHARINE   Pardon me, Alice; listen: d' hand, de fingre, de nailes, d' arma, de bilbow.
ALICE   D' elbow, my lady.
KATHARINE   Oh, Lord, I can't remember! D' elbow. What do you call *le col?*
ALICE   De nick, my lady.
KATHARINE   De nick. And *le menton?*
ALICE   De chin.
KATHARINE   De sin. *Le col,* de nick; *le menton,* de sin.
ALICE   Yes. If I may say so, really you pronounce the words just as correctly as native Englishmen.
KATHARINE   I have no doubt that I shall learn, with God's help, in a very short time.
ALICE   Haven't you already forgotten what I have taught you?
KATHARINE   No. I shall recite to you at once: d' hand, de fingre, de mailes—
ALICE   De nailes, my lady.
KATHARINE   De nailes, de arm, de ilbow.
ALICE   By your leave, d' elbow.
KATHARINE   That's what I said; d' elbow, de nick, and de sin. What do you call *le pied* and *la robe?*

ALICE   Le foot, madame, et le count.

KATHARINE   Le foot et le count! Oh, Seigneur Dieu! Ils 50
sont les mots de son mauvais, corruptible, gros, et
impudique, et non pour les dames d'honneur d'user.
Je ne voudrais prononcer ces mots devant les seig-
neurs de France pour tout le monde. Foh! Le foot et le
count! Néanmoins, je réciterai une autre fois ma leçon
ensemble: d' hand, de fingre, de nailes, de arm,
d' elbow, de nick, de sin, de foot, le count.

ALICE   Excellent, madame!

KATHARINE   C'est assez pour une fois. Allons-nous à
dîner.                                    Exit [with Alice].

❖

# [3.5]

*Enter the King of France, the Dauphin, [the Duke
of Brittany,] the Constable of France, and others.*

FRENCH KING
'Tis certain he hath passed the River Somme.

CONSTABLE
And if he be not fought withal, my lord,            2
Let us not live in France; let us quit all
And give our vineyards to a barbarous people.

DAUPHIN
*O Dieu vivant!* Shall a few sprays of us,          5
The emptying of our fathers' luxury,                6
Our scions, put in wild and savage stock,           7
Spurt up so suddenly into the clouds                8
And overlook their grafters?                        9

BRITTANY
Normans, but bastard Normans, Norman bastards!
*Mort de ma vie,* if they march along               11
Unfought withal, but I will sell my dukedom         12
To buy a slobbery and a dirty farm                  13
In that nook-shotten isle of Albion.                14

CONSTABLE
*Dieu de batailles,* where have they this mettle?   15
Is not their climate foggy, raw, and dull,

On whom as in despite the sun looks pale,           17
Killing their fruit with frowns? Can sodden water,  18
A drench for sur-reined jades, their barley broth,  19
Decoct their cold blood to such valiant heat?       20
And shall our quick blood, spirited with wine,      21
Seem frosty? Oh, for honor of our land,
Let us not hang like roping icicles                 23
Upon our houses' thatch, whiles a more frosty people
Sweat drops of gallant youth in our rich fields!
"Poor" may we call them in their native lords.      26

DAUPHIN   By faith and honor,
Our madams mock at us and plainly say               28
Our mettle is bred out, and they will give          29
Their bodies to the lust of English youth
To new-store France with bastard warriors.          31

BRITTANY
They bid us to the English dancing schools          32
And teach lavoltas, high and swift corantos,        33
Saying our grace is only in our heels               34
And that we are most lofty runaways.                35

FRENCH KING
Where is Montjoy the herald? Speed him hence.       36
Let him greet England with our sharp defiance.
Up, princes, and with spirit of honor edged         38
More sharper than your swords, hie to the field!    39
Charles Delabreth, High Constable of France,
You Dukes of Orleans, Bourbon, and of Berri,
Alençon, Brabant, Bar, and Burgundy,
Jaques Chatillion, Rambures, Vaudemont,
Beaumont, Grandpré, Roussi, and Faulconbridge,
Foix, Lestrelles, Boucicault, and Charolais,
High dukes, great princes, barons, lords, and knights,
For your great seats now quit you of great shames.   47
Bar Harry England, that sweeps through our land      48
With pennons painted in the blood of Harfleur.       49
Rush on his host, as doth the melted snow            50
Upon the valleys, whose low vassal seat
The Alps doth spit and void his rheum upon.          52
Go down upon him—you have power enough—
And in a captive chariot into Rouen
Bring him our prisoner.

CONSTABLE             This becomes the great.          55
Sorry am I his numbers are so few,
His soldiers sick and famished in their march,
For I am sure, when he shall see our army,

ALICE   Le foot, my lady, and le count. [As she pronounces them, *foot* sounds to Katharine like *foutre*, fornicate, and *count* (for *gown*) sounds like French for the female sexual organ, *cunt* in English.]

KATHARINE   Le foot and le count! Oh, Lord! Those are naughty words, wicked, coarse, and immodest, and are not fit to be used by ladies. I wouldn't say those words before French gentlemen for the whole world. Bah! Le foot and le count! Nevertheless, I shall recite my whole lesson once more: d' hand, de fingre, de nailes, de arm, d' elbow, de nick, de sin, de foot, le count.

ALICE   Excellent, my lady.

KATHARINE   That's enough for one time. Let's go to dinner.

**3.5. Location:** The French court at Rouen.
**2 withal** with. (As also in line 12.)   **5–9** *O . . .* **grafters?** O living God, shall a few sprigs derived from native French stock, from the pouring out of our forefathers' lust (during and after the Norman Conquest) being grafted onto the wild and savage stock (of English Saxons), sprout up suddenly to lofty heights and domineer over the plants or trees from which the grafts were taken, i.e., us native French?   **11** *Mort de ma vie* Death to my life   **12 but I will** i.e., if I do not   **13 slobbery** wet and slimy   **14 nook-shotten** full of nooks and angles. (Refers to the coastline.)   **isle of Albion** island of England, Scotland, and Wales.   **15** *Dieu de batailles* God of battles.   **where** from where

**17 as in despite** as if despising them, the English   **18 sodden water** boiled water   **19 A drench . . . jades** i.e., stuff no better than what they give their overridden horses to drink.   **barley broth** ale   **20 Decoct** warm up   **21 quick** lively   **23 roping** hanging down like a rope   **26 "Poor" . . . lords** i.e., Their fields, though rich in themselves, may be called poor in that they are owned by a spiritless aristocracy.   **28 madams** wives, ladies   **29 bred out** exhausted   **31 new-store** newly supply   **32 bid us** bid us go   **33 lavoltas, corantos** fashionable dances   **34 in our heels** (1) in dancing gracefully (2) in running away   **35 lofty** (1) noble (2) leaping.   **runaways** cowards. (But referring also to the movements of the dances.)   **36 Montjoy** title of the chief herald of France   **38 edged** given a sharp edge   **39 hie** hasten   **47 For** in the name of, in defense of.   **seats** positions.   **quit you** revenge yourselves   **48 Bar** Stop; bar the claim of   **49 pennons** banners, streamers   **50 host** army   **52 rheum** watery discharge, i.e., streams or avalanches   **55 becomes the great** befits greatness.

He'll drop his heart into the sink of fear    59
And for achievement offer us his ransom.    60

FRENCH KING

Therefore, Lord Constable, haste on Montjoy,
And let him say to England that we send
To know what willing ransom he will give.
Prince Dauphin, you shall stay with us in Rouen.

DAUPHIN

Not so, I do beseech Your Majesty.

FRENCH KING

Be patient, for you shall remain with us.
Now forth, Lord Constable and princes all,
And quickly bring us word of England's fall.    *Exeunt.*

❖

# [3.6]

*Enter Captains, English and Welsh: Gower and*
*Fluellen, [meeting].*

GOWER   How now, Captain Fluellen? Come you from
the bridge?    2

FLUELLEN   I assure you, there is very excellent services    3
committed at the bridge.

GOWER   Is the Duke of Exeter safe?

FLUELLEN   The Duke of Exeter is as magnanimous as
Agamemnon, and a man that I love and honor with    7
my soul, and my heart, and my duty, and my live,    8
and my living, and my uttermost power. He is not—
God be praised and blessed!—any hurt in the world,
but keeps the bridge most valiantly, with excellent discipline. There is an aunchient lieutenant there at the    12
pridge, I think in my very conscience he is as valiant
a man as Mark Antony, and he is a man of no esti-    14
mation in the world, but I did see him do as gallant    15
service.

GOWER   What do you call him?

FLUELLEN   He is called Aunchient Pistol.

GOWER   I know him not.

*Enter Pistol.*

FLUELLEN   Here is the man.

PISTOL

Captain, I thee beseech to do me favors.
The Duke of Exeter doth love thee well.

FLUELLEN   Ay, I praise God, and I have merited some
love at his hands.

PISTOL

Bardolph, a soldier, firm and sound of heart,
And of buxom valor, hath, by cruel fate    26
And giddy Fortune's furious fickle wheel,

That goddess blind
That stands upon the rolling restless stone—

FLUELLEN   By your patience, Aunchient Pistol. Fortune
is painted blind, with a muffler afore her eyes, to sig-    31
nify to you that Fortune is blind; and she is painted
also with a wheel, to signify to you, which is the moral
of it, that she is turning, and inconstant, and mutabil-
ity, and variation; and her foot, look you, is fixed upon
a spherical stone, which rolls, and rolls, and rolls. In
good truth, the poet is make a most excellent descrip-    37
tion of it. Fortune is an excellent moral.    38

PISTOL

Fortune is Bardolph's foe, and frowns on him;    39
For he hath stol'n a pax,    40
And hangèd must 'a be—a damnèd death!
Let gallows gape for dog; let man go free,
And let not hemp his windpipe suffocate.
But Exeter hath given the doom of death    44
For pax of little price.
Therefore, go speak—the Duke will hear thy voice—
And let not Bardolph's vital thread be cut
With edge of penny cord and vile reproach.    48
Speak, Captain, for his life, and I will thee requite.    49

FLUELLEN   Aunchient Pistol, I do partly understand
your meaning.

PISTOL   Why then rejoice therefor.

FLUELLEN   Certainly, Aunchient, it is not a thing to to rejoice at. For if, look you, he were my brother, I would
desire the Duke to use his good pleasure and put him
to execution; for discipline ought to be used.

PISTOL

Die and be damned! And *figo* for thy friendship!    57

FLUELLEN   It is well.

PISTOL   The fig of Spain!        *Exit.*

FLUELLEN   Very good.

GOWER   Why, this is an arrant counterfeit rascal! I
remember him now; a bawd, a cutpurse.

FLUELLEN   I'll assure you, 'a uttered as prave words at
the pridge as you shall see in a summer's day. But it is
very well. What he has spoke to me, that is well, I
warrant you, when time is serve.

GOWER   Why, 'tis a gull, a fool, a rogue, that now and    67
then goes to the wars, to grace himself at his return
into London under the form of a soldier. And such
fellows are perfect in the great commanders' names,    70
and they will learn you by rote where services were    71
done—at such and such a sconce, at such a breach, at    72
such a convoy; who came off bravely, who was shot,
who disgraced, what terms the enemy stood on—and    74
this they con perfectly in the phrase of war, which    75

---

**59 sink** pit    **60 for achievement** instead of achieving victory, as his sole accomplishment
**3.6. Location:** The English camp in northern France.
**2 bridge** (According to Holinshed, the French were beaten in their attempt to break down the bridge over the Ternoise. The audience is not told this, however, and might assume the river to be the Somme, mentioned in 3.5.1.)    **3 services** exploits. (As also in line 71.)
**7 Agamemnon** leader of the Greeks against Troy    **8 live** life
**12 aunchient lieutenant** (Pistol is elsewhere given the rank of ancient, or ensign.)    **14 Mark Antony** Roman politician and general
**14–15 estimation** fame    **26 buxom** vigorous

**31 muffler** blindfold    **37 is make** has made    **38 moral** emblem.
**39 Fortune . . . foe** (Probably alludes to the ballad "Fortune, my foe!")    **40 pax** metal disk with a crucifix stamped on it, kissed by the priest and communicants during Mass. (But Holinshed describes an incident in which the object stolen is a *pyx*, the vessel containing the consecrated host.)    **44 doom** judgment, sentence    **48 With . . . cord** with a hangman's noose, able to cut the windpipe as though with a sharp edge    **49 requite** pay.    **57 *figo*** gesture of contempt made by thrusting the thumb between the index and middle fingers    **67 gull** simpleton    **70 are perfect in** i.e., can recite perfectly    **71 learn** teach, recite    **72 sconce** fortification    **74 terms . . . stood on** conditions the enemy insisted on    **75 con** learn by heart

they trick up with new-tuned oaths. And what a  76
beard of the General's cut and a horrid suit of the  77
camp will do among foaming bottles and ale-washed  78
wits is wonderful to be thought on. But you must
learn to know such slanders of the age, or else you  80
may be marvelously mistook.  81

FLUELLEN    I tell you what, Captain Gower, I do perceive
he is not the man that he would gladly make show
to the world he is. If I find a hole in his coat, I will tell  84
him my mind. [*Drum heard.*] Hark you, the King is
coming, and I must speak with him from the pridge.  86

*Drum and colors. Enter the King and his poor
soldiers [and Gloucester].*

God pless Your Majesty!

KING    How now, Fluellen, cam'st thou from the bridge?

FLUELLEN    Ay, so please Your Majesty. The Duke of
Exeter has very gallantly maintained the pridge. The
French is gone off, look you, and there is gallant and
most prave passages. Marry, th'athversary was have  92
possession of the pridge, but he is enforced to retire,
and the Duke of Exeter is master of the pridge. I can
tell Your Majesty, the Duke is a prave man.

KING    What men have you lost, Fluellen?

FLUELLEN    The perdition of th'athversary hath been very  97
great, reasonable great. Marry, for my part, I think the
Duke hath lost never a man, but one that is like to be ex-  99
ecuted for robbing a church, one Bardolph, if Your Majesty know the man. His face is all bubukles, and whelks,  101
and knobs, and flames o' fire, and his lips blows at his
nose, and it is like a coal of fire, sometimes plue and
sometimes red; but his nose is executed, and his fire's
out.

KING    We would have all such offenders so cut off. And we
give express charge that, in our marches through the  107
country, there be nothing compelled from the villages,
nothing taken but paid for, none of the French up-
braided or abused in disdainful language; for when len-  110
ity and cruelty play for a kingdom, the gentler gamester  111
is the soonest winner.  112

*Tucket. Enter Montjoy.*

MONTJOY    You know me by my habit.  113

KING    Well then, I know thee. What shall I know of thee?

MONTJOY    My master's mind.

KING    Unfold it.

MONTJOY    Thus says my King: "Say thou to Harry of
England, though we seemed dead, we did but sleep.
Advantage is a better soldier than rashness. Tell him  119
we could have rebuked him at Harfleur, but that we

thought not good to bruise an injury till it were full  121
ripe. Now we speak upon our cue, and our voice is
imperial. England shall repent his folly, see his  123
weakness, and admire our sufferance. Bid him there-  124
fore consider of his ransom, which must proportion  125
the losses we have borne, the subjects we have lost,
the disgrace we have digested; which in weight to re-  127
answer, his pettiness would bow under. For our losses,  128
his exchequer is too poor; for th'effusion of our blood,  129
the muster of his kingdom too faint a number; and for  130
our disgrace, his own person kneeling at our feet but
a weak and worthless satisfaction. To this add defiance; and tell him, for conclusion, he hath betrayed his
followers, whose condemnation is pronounced." So far  134
my King and master; so much my office.

KING
What is thy name? I know thy quality.  136

MONTJOY    Montjoy.

KING
Thou dost thy office fairly. Turn thee back
And tell thy King I do not seek him now,
But could be willing to march on to Calais
Without impeachment. For, to say the sooth,  141
Though 'tis no wisdom to confess so much
Unto an enemy of craft and vantage,  143
My people are with sickness much enfeebled,
My numbers lessened, and those few I have
Almost no better than so many French,
Who when they were in health, I tell thee, herald,
I thought upon one pair of English legs  148
Did march three Frenchmen. Yet, forgive me, God,  149
That I do brag thus! This your air of France
Hath blown that vice in me. I must repent.  151
Go, therefore, tell thy master here I am;
My ransom is this frail and worthless trunk,  153
My army but a weak and sickly guard.
Yet, God before, tell him we will come on,
Though France himself and such another neighbor
Stand in our way. There's for thy labor, Montjoy.
*[He gives a purse.]*
Go bid thy master well advise himself.  158
If we may pass, we will; if we be hindered,
We shall your tawny ground with your red blood
Discolor. And so, Montjoy, fare you well.
The sum of all our answer is but this:
We would not seek a battle as we are,
Nor, as we are, we say we will not shun it.  164
So tell your master.

---

**76 trick** dress.    **new-tuned** i.e., of the latest fashion    **77–8 horrid . . .
camp** fierce battle outfit    **80 slanders of the age** persons who are a
disgrace to the times    **81 mistook** mistaken, deluded.    **84 a hole . . .
coat** i.e., a weak spot in him. (Proverbial.)    **86 from the pridge** with
news concerning the bridge.    **86.1 poor** bedraggled    **92 passages**
deeds of arms.    **was** did    **97 perdition** losses    **99 like** likely
**101 bubukles** carbuncles, abscesses.    **whelks** boils, pimples
**107 express charge** explicit orders    **110–11 lenity** leniency
**111 gamester** player    **112.1 Tucket** Trumpet signal, fanfare.
**113 habit** i.e., tabard, herald's coat.    **119 Advantage** Knowing how
to wait for favorable circumstance and position

**121 bruise an injury** squeeze a boil or pimple    **123 England** i.e.,
King Henry    **124 admire our sufferance** wonder at our patience.
**125 proportion** be proportional to    **127 digested** had to swallow
**127–8 which . . . under** i.e., to compensate for which his means are too
slender.    **129 exchequer** treasury    **130 muster** roll call    **134 condemnation** death sentence    **136 quality** rank and profession; ability.
**141 impeachment** impediment.    **sooth** truth    **143 vantage** superiority in resources    **148–9 upon . . . Frenchman** i.e., an English soldier is
worth three Frenchmen.    **151 blown** swelled; caused to blossom
**153 trunk** body    **158 advise himself** consider.    **164 as we are** being
who we are. (Playing on the meaning "in the condition we are" in the
previous line.)

MONTJOY
I shall deliver so. Thanks to Your Highness.          [*Exit.*]

GLOUCESTER
I hope they will not come upon us now.

KING
We are in God's hand, brother, not in theirs.
March to the bridge. It now draws toward night.
Beyond the river we'll encamp ourselves,
And on tomorrow bid them march away          *Exeunt.* 171

## [3.7]

*Enter the Constable of France, the Lord Rambures,*
*Orleans, Dauphin, with others.*

CONSTABLE          Tut, I have the best armor of the world.
Would it were day!

ORLEANS          You have an excellent armor; but let my
horse have his due.

CONSTABLE          It is the best horse of Europe.

ORLEANS          Will it never be morning?

DAUPHIN          My lord of Orleans and my Lord High
Constable, you talk of horse and armor?

ORLEANS          You are as well provided of both as any
prince in the world.

DAUPHIN          What a long night is this! I will not change
my horse with any that treads but on four pasterns. 12
Ça, ha! He bounds from the earth as if his entrails 13
were hairs; *le cheval volant,* the Pegasus, *qui a les narines* 14
*de feu!* When I bestride him, I soar, I am a hawk. He 15
trots the air. The earth sings when he touches it. The
basest horn of his hoof is more musical than the pipe 17
of Hermes. 18

ORLEANS          He's of the color of the nutmeg.

DAUPHIN          And of the heat of the ginger. It is a beast for
Perseus. He is pure air and fire; and the dull elements 21
of earth and water never appear in him, but only in 22
patient stillness while his rider mounts him. He is indeed a horse, and all other jades you may call beasts.

CONSTABLE          Indeed, my lord, it is a most absolute and 25
excellent horse.

DAUPHIN          It is the prince of palfreys. His neigh is like 27
the bidding of a monarch, and his countenance
enforces homage.

ORLEANS          No more, cousin.

DAUPHIN          Nay, the man hath no wit that cannot, from
the rising of the lark to the lodging of the lamb, vary 32

deserved praise on my palfrey. It is a theme as fluent
as the sea; turn the sands into eloquent tongues, and
my horse is argument for them all. 'Tis a subject for a 35
sovereign to reason on, and for a sovereign's sovereign 36
to ride on, and for the world, familiar to us and un- 37
known, to lay apart their particular functions and 38
wonder at him. I once writ a sonnet in his praise, and 39
began thus: "Wonder of nature—"

ORLEANS          I have heard a sonnet begin so to one's
mistress.

DAUPHIN          Then did they imitate that which I composed
to my courser, for my horse is my mistress. 44

ORLEANS          Your mistress bears well. 45

DAUPHIN          Me well, which is the prescript praise and 46
perfection of a good and particular mistress. 47

CONSTABLE          Nay, for methought yesterday your mistress shrewdly shook your back. 49

DAUPHIN          So perhaps did yours.

CONSTABLE          Mine was not bridled. 51

DAUPHIN          Oh, then belike she was old and gentle, and 52
you rode like a kern of Ireland, your French hose off, 53
and in your strait strossers. 54

CONSTABLE          You have good judgment in horsemanship.

DAUPHIN          Be warned by me, then: they that ride so,
and ride not warily, fall into foul bogs. I had rather
have my horse to my mistress. 58

CONSTABLE          I had as lief have my mistress a jade. 59

DAUPHIN          I tell thee, Constable, my mistress wears his 60
own hair. 61

CONSTABLE          I could make as true a boast as that, if I had
a sow to my mistress.

DAUPHIN          *"Le chien est retourné à son propre vomissement,* 64
*et la truie lavée au bourbier."* Thou mak'st use of 65
anything.

CONSTABLE          Yet do I not use my horse for my mistress,
or any such proverb so little kin to the purpose. 68

RAMBURES          My Lord Constable, the armor that I saw in
your tent tonight, are those stars or suns upon it?

CONSTABLE          Stars, my lord.

DAUPHIN          Some of them will fall tomorrow, I hope.

CONSTABLE          And yet my sky shall not want. 73

DAUPHIN          That may be, for you bear a many superflu- 74
ously, and 'twere more honor some were away. 75

---

**171 bid . . . away** bid our army march toward Calais.
**3.7. Location:** The French camp, near Agincourt.
**12 pasterns** i.e., hooves. (The *pastern* literally is the part of the horse's
leg just above the hoof.)          **13–14 as . . . hairs** i.e., as if he were a tennis
ball. (Tennis balls were stuffed with hair. Or perhaps *hairs* should
read *hares.*)          **14–15 le cheval . . . feu** the flying horse, Pegasus, with
nostrils breathing fire.          **17 basest horn** (1) lowest part (2) hoofbeat
**17–18 pipe of Hermes** (Hermes, messenger of the gods, charmed
Argus of the hundred eyes asleep with playing on his pipe.)
**21 Perseus** (According to some Greek legends and to Ovid, Perseus
rode Pegasus when he rescued Andromeda from the dragon.)
**21–2 air . . . water** (Of the four elements supposed to make up all
matter, water and earth are the heavier, while fire and air ascend.)
**25 absolute** perfect          **27 palfreys** saddle horses.          **32 lodging** lying
down.          **vary** produce variations of

**35 argument** subject          **36 reason** discourse          **37–9 for . . . him** for both
the known and unknown worlds to put aside their differences and
join in wondering at him.          **44 courser** swift and strong horse often
used in warfare.          **horse is my mistress** (Here begins a series of
bawdy double entendres involving human and animal sexuality:
*bears, shook your back, rode, foul bogs, doing,* etc.)          **45 bears well** carries
weight well (with sexual insinuation).          **46 prescript** prescribed
**47 particular** acknowledging only one master          **49 shrewdly**
viciously          **51 Mine . . . bridled** i.e., At least my mistress was not a
horse.          **52 belike** probably          **53 kern** Irish foot soldier. (Here it is
used to mean "rustic" or "boor.")          **French hose** wide breeches
**54 strait strossers** tights.          **58 to** as          **59 lief** happily.          **jade** (1) worn-
out horse (2) slut.          **60–1 wears . . . hair** i.e., is not artificially wigged,
like an elegant court lady, and perhaps bald from syphilis.
**64–5 "Le chien . . . bourbier"** The dog is returned to his own vomit,
and the washed sow to the mire. (See 2 Peter 2:22.)          **68 kin**
related          **73 sky** i.e., sky of honor.          **want** be lacking (in honor).
**74 a many** many. (Parallel to "a few.")          **75 'twere . . . away** i.e.,
it would be more honest and proper if some of your stars were done
away with.

CONSTABLE   Even as your horse bears your praises, who would trot as well, were some of your brags dismounted.

DAUPHIN   Would I were able to load him with his desert! Will it never be day? I will trot tomorrow a mile, and my way shall be paved with English faces. 79 80

CONSTABLE   I will not say so, for fear I should be faced out of my way. But I would it were morning, for I would fain be about the ears of the English. 82 83 84

RAMBURES   Who will go to hazard with me for twenty prisoners? 85

CONSTABLE   You must first go yourself to hazard, ere you have them.

DAUPHIN   'Tis midnight. I'll go arm myself.          *Exit.*

ORLEANS   The Dauphin longs for morning.

RAMBURES   He longs to eat the English.

CONSTABLE   I think he will eat all he kills.

ORLEANS   By the white hand of my lady, he's a gallant prince.

CONSTABLE   Swear by her foot, that she may tread out the oath. 95 96

ORLEANS   He is simply the most active gentleman of France.

CONSTABLE   Doing is activity, and he will still be doing. 99

ORLEANS   He never did harm, that I heard of. 100

CONSTABLE   Nor will do none tomorrow. He will keep that good name still.

ORLEANS   I know him to be valiant.

CONSTABLE   I was told that by one that knows him better than you.

ORLEANS   What's he?

CONSTABLE   Marry, he told me so himself, and he said he cared not who knew it.

ORLEANS   He needs not; it is no hidden virtue in him. 109

CONSTABLE   By my faith, sir, but it is. Never anybody saw it but his lackey. 'Tis a hooded valor, and when it appears it will bate. 110 111 112

ORLEANS   Ill will never said well.

CONSTABLE   I will cap that proverb with "There is flattery in friendship."

ORLEANS   And I will take up that with "Give the devil his due." 116 117

CONSTABLE   Well placed. There stands your friend for the devil. Have at the very eye of that proverb with "A pox of the devil." 118 119

ORLEANS   You are the better at proverbs by how much "A fool's bolt is soon shot." 122

CONSTABLE   You have shot over. 123

ORLEANS   'Tis not the first time you were overshot. 124

*Enter a Messenger.*

MESSENGER   My Lord High Constable, the English lie within fifteen hundred paces of your tents.

CONSTABLE   Who hath measured the ground?

MESSENGER   The Lord Grandpré.

CONSTABLE   A valiant and most expert gentleman.
                              [*Exit Messenger.*]
Would it were day! Alas, poor Harry of England! He longs not for the dawning as we do.

ORLEANS   What a wretched and peevish fellow is this King of England, to mope with his fat-brained followers so far out of his knowledge! 133

CONSTABLE   If the English had any apprehension, they would run away. 135

ORLEANS   That they lack; for if their heads had any intellectual armor, they could never wear such heavy headpieces.

RAMBURES   That island of England breeds very valiant creatures; their mastiffs are of unmatchable courage.

ORLEANS   Foolish curs, that run winking into the mouth of a Russian bear and have their heads crushed like rotten apples. You may as well say "That's a valiant flea that dare eat his breakfast on the lip of a lion." 142

CONSTABLE   Just, just! And the men do sympathize with the mastiffs in robustious and rough coming on, leaving their wits with their wives; and then give them great meals of beef and iron and steel, they will eat like wolves and fight like devils. 146 147

ORLEANS   Ay, but these English are shrewdly out of beef. 151

CONSTABLE   Then shall we find tomorrow they have only stomachs to eat and none to fight. Now is it time to arm. Come, shall we about it? 154

ORLEANS
It is now two o'clock; but let me see, by ten
We shall have each a hundred Englishmen.   *Exeunt.*

❧

# [4.0]

[*Enter*] *Chorus.*

CHORUS
Now entertain conjecture of a time          1
When creeping murmur and the poring dark    2
Fills the wide vessel of the universe.
From camp to camp, through the foul womb of night,
The hum of either army stilly sounds,        5

**79–80 Would . . . desert!** I wish I could find words to equal his deserving! **82–3 faced . . . way** braved out of my way, put to shame.   **84 fain** gladly.   **about the ears** buffeting the heads   **85 go to hazard** bet, play at dice. (But the Constable replies in the sense of "encounter danger.") **95–6 tread . . . oath** (1) fulfill the oath by dancing (2) stamp on, spurn the oath.   **99 Doing** (1) Acting, pretending (2) Copulating.   **still** continually   **100 did harm** i.e., offended. (But the Constable uses it to mean "hurt any enemy.")   **109 He needs not** i.e., There is no need for him to proclaim it himself.   **it** i.e., valor   **110–11 Never . . . lackey** i.e., He shows "valor" only in beating his servant.   **111 hooded valor** (The hawk was kept hooded to prevent it from beating its wings, or "bating.") **112 bate** (1) beat its wings (2) abate, be downcast.   **116–17 Give . . . due** Give even the devil his due; everyone deserves some praise. (But the Constable turns this proverb against the Dauphin by likening him to the devil.)   **118–19 There . . . devil** i.e., You just called the Dauphin the devil.   **119 Have . . . eye** Shoot straight at the bull's-eye. (A sporting term appropriate to this verbal contest of "capping proverbs.")

**122 bolt** short, blunt arrow   **123 shot over** i.e., shot over the mark. **124 overshot** i.e., outshot, defeated.   **133 mope** (1) wander about (2) be downcast   **135 apprehension** (1) sense (2) sense of danger **142 winking** shutting their eyes   **146 Just** Exactly.   **sympathize with** resemble   **147 robustious** violent, boisterous   **151 shrewdly out of** devilishly short of   **154 stomachs** appetites **4.0. Chorus.** **1 entertain conjecture of** imagine   **2 poring** in which one must strain the eyes to see   **5 stilly** softly

That the fixed sentinels almost receive
The secret whispers of each other's watch.
Fire answers fire, and through their paly flames    8
Each battle sees the other's umbered face.    9
Steed threatens steed, in high and boastful neighs
Piercing the night's dull ear; and from the tents
The armorers, accomplishing the knights,    12
With busy hammers closing rivets up,
Give dreadful note of preparation.
The country cocks do crow, the clocks do toll,
And the third hour of drowsy morning name.
Proud of their numbers and secure in soul,    17
The confident and overlusty French    18
Do the low-rated English play at dice,    19
And chide the cripple tardy-gaited night,    20
Who like a foul and ugly witch doth limp
So tediously away. The poor condemnèd English,
Like sacrifices, by their watchful fires
Sit patiently and inly ruminate    24
The morning's danger; and their gesture sad,    25
Investing lank-lean cheeks and war-worn coats,    26
Presenteth them unto the gazing moon
So many horrid ghosts. Oh, now, who will behold
The royal captain of this ruined band
Walking from watch to watch, from tent to tent,
Let him cry, "Praise and glory on his head!"
For forth he goes and visits all his host,    32
Bids them good morrow with a modest smile,
And calls them brothers, friends, and countrymen.
Upon his royal face there is no note
How dread an army hath enrounded him.    36
Nor doth he dedicate one jot of color    37
Unto the weary and all-watchèd night,    38
But freshly looks and overbears attaint    39
With cheerful semblance and sweet majesty;
That every wretch, pining and pale before,
Beholding him, plucks comfort from his looks.
A largess universal like the sun
His liberal eye doth give to everyone,
Thawing cold fear, that mean and gentle all    45
Behold, as may unworthiness define,    46
A little touch of Harry in the night.
And so our scene must to the battle fly;
Where—oh, for pity!—we shall much disgrace
With four or five most vile and ragged foils,    50
Right ill-disposed in brawl ridiculous,
The name of Agincourt. Yet sit and see,
Minding true things by what their mockeries be.    53

*Exit.*

❖

8 **paly** pale   9 **battle** army.   **umbered** shadowed   12 **accomplishing** equipping   17 **secure** overconfident   18 **overlusty** overly merry   19 **play** gamble for   20 **tardy-gaited** slow-paced   24 **inly** inwardly   25 **gesture sad** serious bearing   26 **Investing** clothing   32 **host** army   36 **enrounded** surrounded   37 **dedicate** yield up.   **color** i.e., bright color of complexion   38 **all-watchèd** spent entirely in wakefulness and waiting   39 **overbears attaint** overcomes the effects of weariness and depression   45 **mean and gentle** those of low and of high birth   46 **unworthiness** I, who am unworthy of praising so great an object   50 **foils** blunted fencing swords   53 **Minding** bearing in mind.   **mockeries** inadequate imitations

# [4.1]

*Enter the King, Bedford, and Gloucester.*

KING
Gloucester, 'tis true that we are in great danger;
The greater therefore should our courage be.
Good morrow, brother Bedford. God Almighty!
There is some soul of goodness in things evil,
Would men observingly distill it out;    5
For our bad neighbor makes us early stirrers,
Which is both healthful and good husbandry.    7
Besides, they are our outward consciences,
And preachers to us all, admonishing
That we should dress us fairly for our end.    10
Thus may we gather honey from the weed
And make a moral of the devil himself.

*Enter Erpingham.*

Good morrow, old Sir Thomas Erpingham.
A good soft pillow for that good white head
Were better than a churlish turf of France.    15

ERPINGHAM
Not so, my liege. This lodging likes me better,    16
Since I may say, "Now lie I like a king."

KING
'Tis good for men to love their present pains
Upon example; so the spirit is eased.    19
And when the mind is quickened, out of doubt
The organs, though defunct and dead before,
Break up their drowsy grave and newly move    22
With casted slough and fresh legerity.    23
Lend me thy cloak, Sir Thomas. [*The King puts on
Erpingham's cloak.*] Brothers both,    24
Commend me to the princes in our camp;    25
Do my good morrow to them, and anon    26
Desire them all to my pavilion.

GLOUCESTER   We shall, my liege.
ERPINGHAM   Shall I attend Your Grace?
KING   No, my good knight,
Go with my brothers to my lords of England.
I and my bosom must debate awhile,
And then I would no other company.

ERPINGHAM
The Lord in heaven bless thee, noble Harry!
*Exeunt [all but the King].*

KING
God-a-mercy, old heart! Thou speak'st cheerfully.    35

*Enter Pistol.*

PISTOL   *Che vous là?*    36

4.1. Location: The English camp at Agincourt.
5 **Would men** if one could   7 **husbandry** economy, thrift.   10 **dress us fairly** prepare ourselves well   15 **churlish** rough, hard   16 **likes** pleases   19 **Upon example** i.e., following or considering the example of persons such as King Henry and Erpingham   22–3 **Break . . . legerity** break out of their lethargy and move nimbly, like a snake having cast off its old skin.   24 **Brothers both** i.e., Bedford and Gloucester   25 **Commend me** convey my greetings   26 **Do . . . morrow** deliver my morning's greetings   35 **God-a-mercy** i.e., Thanks   36 **Che vous là?** i.e., *Qui va là?* ("Who goes there?") or *Qui vous là?* ("Who are you there?"). (Pistol's imperfect French.)

KING   A friend.

PISTOL
>     Discuss unto me: art thou officer,                                      38
>     Or art thou base, common, and popular?                                  39

KING   I am a gentleman of a company.                                         40

PISTOL   Trail'st thou the puissant pike?                                     41

KING   Even so. What are you?

PISTOL
>     As good a gentleman as the Emperor.

KING   Then you are a better than the King.

PISTOL
>     The King's a bawcock and a heart of gold,                               45
>     A lad of life, an imp of fame,                                          46
>     Of parents good, of fist most valiant.
>     I kiss his dirty shoe, and from heartstring
>     I love the lovely bully. What is thy name?                              49

KING   Harry le Roy.                                                          50

PISTOL
>     Le Roy? A Cornish name. Art thou of Cornish crew?

KING   No, I am a Welshman.                                                   52

PISTOL   Know'st thou Fluellen?

KING   Yes.

PISTOL
>     Tell him I'll knock his leek about his pate                             55
>     Upon Saint Davy's Day.                                                  56

KING   Do not you wear your dagger in your cap that
day, lest he knock that about yours.

PISTOL   Art thou his friend?

KING   And his kinsman too.

PISTOL   The *figo* for thee, then!                                          61

KING   I thank you. God be with you!

PISTOL   My name is Pistol called.                              *Exit.*

KING   It sorts well with your fierceness.                                   64

*Manet King [standing apart].*

*Enter Fluellen and Gower [meeting].*

GOWER   Captain Fluellen!

FLUELLEN   So, in the name of Jesu Christ, speak fewer.                      66
It is the greatest admiration in the universal world,                        67
when the true and aunchient prerogatifes and laws of
the wars is not kept. If you would take the pains but
to examine the wars of Pompey the Great, you shall                           70
find, I warrant you, that there is no tiddle-taddle nor                      71
pibble-pabble in Pompey's camp. I warrant you, you                           72
shall find the ceremonies of the wars, and the cares of
it, and the forms of it, and the sobriety of it, and the                     74
modesty of it, to be otherwise.                                              75

GOWER   Why, the enemy is loud; you hear him all
night.

FLUELLEN   If the enemy is an ass and a fool and a prating                   78
coxcomb, is it meet, think you, that we should also,                         79
look you, be an ass and a fool and a prating coxcomb?
In your own conscience, now?

GOWER   I will speak lower.

FLUELLEN   I pray you and beseech you that you will.
*Exit [with Gower].*

KING
>     Though it appear a little out of fashion,
>     There is much care and valor in this Welshman.

*Enter three soldiers, John Bates, Alexander Court,
and Michael Williams.*

COURT   Brother John Bates, is not that the morning
which breaks yonder?

BATES   I think it be. But we have no great cause to
desire the approach of day.

WILLIAMS   We see yonder the beginning of the day, but
I think we shall never see the end of it.—Who goes
there?

KING   A friend.

WILLIAMS   Under what captain serve you?

KING   Under Sir Thomas Erpingham.

WILLIAMS   A good old commander and a most kind
gentleman. I pray you, what thinks he of our estate?             97

KING   Even as men wrecked upon a sand, that look to                         98
be washed off the next tide.

BATES   He hath not told his thought to the King?

KING   No, nor it is not meet he should. For, though I
speak it to you, I think the King is but a man, as I am.
The violet smells to him as it doth to me; the element          103
shows to him as it doth to me; all his senses have but         104
human conditions. His ceremonies laid by, in his               105
nakedness he appears but a man; and though his
affections are higher mounted than ours, yet when              107
they stoop, they stoop with the like wing. Therefore
when he sees reason of fears, as we do, his fears, out
of doubt, be of the same relish as ours are. Yet, in           110
reason, no man should possess him with any appear-             111
ance of fear, lest he, by showing it, should dishearten
his army.

BATES   He may show what outward courage he will; but
I believe, as cold a night as 'tis, he could wish himself
in Thames up to the neck; and so I would he were,
and I by him, at all adventures, so we were quit here.          117

KING   By my troth, I will speak my conscience of the
King: I think he would not wish himself anywhere but
where he is.

---

**38 Discuss** Declare   **39 popular** of low birth.   **40 gentleman of a company** gentleman serving as a volunteer.   **41 Trail'st . . . pike?** i.e., Are you in the infantry?   **45 bawcock** fine fellow. (From the French *beau coq*.)   **46 imp of fame** child or scion of renown   **49 bully** (A term of endearment meaning "fine fellow.")   **50 le Roy** the King (French)   **52 Welshman** (Henry was born at Monmouth, then considered part of Wales.)   **55–6 leek . . . Day** (On Saint David's Day, March 1, the leek was worn in memory of a Welsh victory over the Saxons in 540 A.D., since Saint David, the Welsh leader, had commanded his followers to wear leeks in their caps on that occasion.)   **61 figo** (A provoking gesture of contempt; see the note for 3.6.57.)   **64 sorts** fits, agrees   **64.1 Manet King** The King remains.   **66 fewer** i.e., calmly, more quietly.   **67 admiration** wonder   **70 Pompey the Great** Roman general defeated by Julius Caesar   **71–2 tiddle-taddle nor pibble-pabble** tittle-tattle nor bibble-babble   **74 sobriety** orderliness, decorum   **75 modesty** propriety

**78–9 prating coxcomb** chattering fool   **79 meet** fitting. (Also in line 101.)   **97 estate** situation.   **98 wrecked** shipwrecked   **103–4 element shows** sky appears   **105 ceremonies** symbols of royalty   **107 affections . . . mounted** desires soar higher. (A falconry metaphor continued in *stoop*, "descend," "swoop down," and *with the like wing*, "similarly.")   **110 relish** taste   **111 possess him with** induce in him   **117 at all adventures** at all events (since the Thames would be less risky under any circumstances than the impending battle).   **quit here** out of this situation.

BATES  Then I would he were here alone. So should he be sure to be ransomed, and a many poor men's lives saved.

KING  I dare say you love him not so ill to wish him here alone, howsoever you speak this to feel other men's 125 minds. Methinks I could not die anywhere so contented as in the King's company, his cause being just and his quarrel honorable.

WILLIAMS  That's more than we know.

BATES  Ay, or more than we should seek after; for we know enough if we know we are the King's subjects. If his cause be wrong, our obedience to the King wipes the crime of it out of us.

WILLIAMS  But if the cause be not good, the King himself hath a heavy reckoning to make, when all those legs and arms and heads, chopped off in a battle, shall join together at the Latter Day and cry all, 137 "We died at such a place"—some swearing, some crying for a surgeon, some upon their wives left poor behind them, some upon the debts they owe, some upon their children rawly left. I am afeard there are 141 few die well that die in a battle; for how can they charitably dispose of anything, when blood is their argument? Now, if these men do not die well, it will be a black matter for the King that led them to it; who 145 to disobey were against all proportion of subjection. 146

KING  So, if a son that is by his father sent about merchandise do sinfully miscarry upon the sea, the 148 imputation of his wickedness, by your rule, should be 149 imposed upon his father that sent him; or if a servant, under his master's command transporting a sum of money, be assailed by robbers and die in many 152 irreconciled iniquities, you may call the business of the 153 master the author of the servant's damnation. But this is not so. The King is not bound to answer the particular endings of his soldiers, the father of his son, nor 157 the master of his servant; for they purpose not their deaths when they propose their services. Besides, there is no king, be his cause never so spotless, if it 159 come to the arbitrament of swords, can try it out with 160 all unspotted soldiers. Some, peradventure, have on 161 them the guilt of premeditated and contrived murder; some, of beguiling virgins with the broken seals of 163 perjury; some, making the wars their bulwark, that 164 have before gored the gentle bosom of peace with pillage and robbery. Now, if these men have defeated 166 the law and outrun native punishment, though they 167 can outstrip men, they have no wings to fly from God. War is his beadle, war is his vengeance; so that here 169

men are punished for before-breach of the King's laws 170 in now the King's quarrel. Where they feared the 171 death, they have borne life away; and where they 172 would be safe, they perish. Then if they die unpro- 173 vided, no more is the King guilty of their damnation 174 than he was before guilty of those impieties for the which they are now visited. Every subject's duty is the 176 King's; but every subject's soul is his own. Therefore should every soldier in the wars do as every sick man in his bed, wash every mote out of his conscience; and 179 dying so, death is to him advantage, or not dying, the time was blessedly lost wherein such preparation was gained. And in him that escapes, it were not sin to think that, making God so free an offer, He let him outlive that day to see His greatness and to teach others how they should prepare.

WILLIAMS  'Tis certain, every man that dies ill, the ill 186 upon his own head, the King is not to answer it.

BATES  I do not desire he should answer for me, and yet I determine to fight lustily for him.

KING  I myself heard the King say he would not be ransomed.

WILLIAMS  Ay, he said so, to make us fight cheerfully; but when our throats are cut, he may be ransomed and we ne'er the wiser.

KING  If I live to see it, I will never trust his word after.

WILLIAMS  You pay him then! That's a perilous shot out 196 of an elder-gun, that a poor and a private displeasure 197 can do against a monarch. You may as well go about to turn the sun to ice with fanning in his face with a peacock's feather. You'll never trust his word after! Come, 'tis a foolish saying.

KING  Your reproof is something too round. I should be 202 angry with you, if the time were convenient.

WILLIAMS  Let it be a quarrel between us, if you live.

KING  I embrace it.

WILLIAMS  How shall I know thee again?

KING  Give me any gage of thine, and I will wear it in 207 my bonnet. Then if ever thou dar'st acknowledge it, I will make it my quarrel.

WILLIAMS  Here's my glove. Give me another of thine.

KING  There.                          [*They exchange gloves.*]

WILLIAMS  This will I also wear in my cap. If ever thou come to me and say, after tomorrow, "This is my glove," by this hand, I will take thee a box on the ear. 214

KING  If ever I live to see it, I will challenge it.

WILLIAMS  Thou dar'st as well be hanged.

KING  Well, I will do it, though I take thee in the King's company.

WILLIAMS  Keep thy word. Fare thee well.

125 **feel** feel out   137 **Latter Day** last day, Christian Day of Judgment   141 **rawly** without provision   145 **who** whom   146 **proportion of subjection** proper duty of a subject.   148 **sinfully miscarry** die in his sins   149 **imputation . . . wickedness** wickedness imputed to him   152–3 **in . . . iniquities** with his wicked deeds unabsolved   155 **answer** answer for   157 **purpose** intend   159–60 **if . . . swords** if a dispute can be settled only by swords   161 **unspotted** innocent   163 **broken seals** (1) broken promises (2) violated maidenheads   164 **bulwark** refuge from punishment (for offenses committed)   166 **defeated** broken   167 **native** at home   169 **beadle** parish officer responsible for punishing petty offenders

170 **before-breach** prior violation   171–3 **Where . . . perish** i.e., Whereas before they feared execution but escaped punishment, here where they look for safety they die in battle.   173–4 **unprovided** spiritually unprepared   176 **visited** i.e., by punishment.   179 **mote** small impurity   186 **dies ill** dies in sin   196 **You pay him then!** i.e., That will really pay him back for his perfidy, won't it? (Said sarcastically.)   197 **elder-gun** popgun made from a branch of elder with the pith hollowed out   202 **round** direct, brusque.   207 **gage** pledge   214 **take** give, strike

BATES   Be friends, you English fools, be friends. We
have French quarrels enough, if you could tell how to 221
reckon.
KING   Indeed, the French may lay twenty French crowns 223
to one they will beat us, for they bear them on their
shoulders; but it is no English treason to cut French 225
crowns, and tomorrow the King himself will be a
clipper.                                    *Exeunt soldiers.*
Upon the King! Let us our lives, our souls,
Our debts, our careful wives,                         229
Our children, and our sins lay on the King!
We must bear all. Oh, hard condition,
Twin-born with greatness, subject to the breath       232
Of every fool, whose sense no more can feel           233
But his own wringing! What infinite heartsease        234
Must kings neglect that private men enjoy!
And what have kings that privates have not too,       236
Save ceremony, save general ceremony?
And what art thou, thou idol ceremony?
What kind of god art thou, that suffer'st more        239
Of mortal griefs than do thy worshipers?              240
What are thy rents? What are thy comings-in?          241
O ceremony, show me but thy worth!
What is thy soul of adoration?                        243
Art thou aught else but place, degree, and form,      244
Creating awe and fear in other men?
Wherein thou art less happy, being feared,
Than they in fearing.
What drink'st thou oft, instead of homage sweet,
But poisoned flattery? Oh, be sick, great greatness,  249
And bid thy ceremony give thee cure!                  250
Think'st thou the fiery fever will go out             251
With titles blown from adulation?                     252
Will it give place to flexure and low bending?        253
Canst thou, when thou command'st the beggar's
     knee,
Command the health of it? No, thou proud dream,
That play'st so subtly with a king's repose.
I am a king that find thee, and I know               257
'Tis not the balm, the scepter, and the ball,        258
The sword, the mace, the crown imperial,             259

The intertissued robe of gold and pearl,             260
The farcèd title running 'fore the king,             261
The throne he sits on, nor the tide of pomp          262
That beats upon the high shore of this world—        263
No, not all these, thrice-gorgeous ceremony,
Not all these, laid in bed majestical,
Can sleep so soundly as the wretched slave
Who, with a body filled and vacant mind,             267
Gets him to rest, crammed with distressful bread;    268
Never sees horrid night, the child of hell,
But like a lackey from the rise to set               270
Sweats in the eye of Phoebus, and all night          271
Sleeps in Elysium; next day after dawn               272
Doth rise and help Hyperion to his horse,            273
And follows so the ever-running year
With profitable labor to his grave.
And but for ceremony, such a wretch,
Winding up days with toil and nights with sleep,
Had the forehand and vantage of a king.              278
The slave, a member of the country's peace,          279
Enjoys it, but in gross brain little wots            280
What watch the King keeps to maintain the peace,     281
Whose hours the peasant best advantages.             282

*Enter Erpingham.*

ERPINGHAM
My lord, your nobles, jealous of your absence,       283
Seek through your camp to find you.
KING                                Good old knight,
Collect them all together at my tent.
I'll be before thee.
ERPINGHAM           I shall do't, my lord.    *Exit.* 286
KING
O God of battles, steel my soldiers' hearts;
Possess them not with fear! Take from them now
The sense of reck'ning, ere th'opposèd numbers       289
Pluck their hearts from them. Not today, O Lord,
Oh, not today, think not upon the fault              291
My father made in compassing the crown!              292
I Richard's body have interrèd new,                  293
And on it have bestowed more contrite tears
Than from it issued forcèd drops of blood.
Five hundred poor I have in yearly pay
Who twice a day their withered hands hold up
Toward heaven, to pardon blood; and I have built
Two chantries, where the sad and solemn priests      299
Sing still for Richard's soul. More will I do;       300

**221 could tell** knew   **223 lay** bet. (But also anticipating the meaning "lay down or lose in battle.")   **crowns** (1) coins (2) heads   **225 English treason** (It was a treasonable offense to clip or "cut" English coins; it obviously is no offense to slash French heads, and even King Henry will be such a "clipper.")   **229 careful** full of cares   **232–4 Twin-born . . . wringing** i.e., inseparable from the condition of being born of royal rank, a condition that makes a king the subject of the idle gossip of every fool, even those whose sensibilities pay attention to nothing other than the rumbling of their own stomachs.   **236 privates** private persons   **239–40 What kind . . . worshipers?** i.e., What sort of idol is a king, who, despite all the ceremony he enjoys, suffers more from bearing the heavy burdens of his office than do those citizens who worship him and the ceremony he embodies?   **241 rents, comings-in** income, revenues   **243 thy soul of adoration** the essential quality that makes you so much admired.   **244 place** rank   **249–50 Oh . . . cure!** Learn to cure yourself by being sick, by treating poisoned flattery and ceremoniousness as a medicine that will purge you of being in love with your own great greatness.   **251–2 Think'st . . . adulation?** Do you really think that the fever of vain pride will be extinguished by speeches breathed by flatterers? (*Blown* also suggests "inflated.")   **253 Will . . . bending?** i.e., Will the sickness be cured by bowing and scraping?   **257 find thee** i.e., experience greatness and am able to appraise its worth and limitations   **258 balm** consecrating oil used to anoint a king in his coronation.   **ball** orb of sovereignty   **259 mace** ceremonial staff

**260 intertissued** interwoven   **261 farcèd** stuffed (with pompous phrases)   **262–3 the tide . . . world** the flood of pomp and ceremony that assails all human life, most of all at the very height of the social hierarchy   **267 vacant mind** mind free of cares   **268 distressful** earned by hard work   **270 lackey** (1) footman running alongside the chariot of the sun (2) peasant.   **rise to set** sunrise to sunset   **271 Phoebus** the sun god   **272 Elysium** in Greek mythology, the abode of the blessed   **273 Hyperion** the father of the sun, or the sun itself. (The peasant is up before the sun.)   **278 Had** would have.   **forehand** upper hand   **279 member** sharer   **280 it** i.e., peace.   **wots** knows   **281 watch** wakeful guard   **282 Whose . . . advantages** whose hours of watchful care most benefit the peasant.   **283 jealous of** apprehensive because of   **286 be** be there   **289 sense of reck'ning** ability to reckon up the odds   **291 the fault** i.e., the deposition and murder of Richard II   **292 compassing** obtaining   **293 new** anew   **299 chantries** chapels in which masses for the dead were celebrated.   **sad** grave   **300 still** continually

Though all that I can do is nothing worth,
Since that my penitence comes after all,                    302
Imploring pardon.

*Enter Gloucester.*

GLOUCESTER  My liege!
KING  My brother Gloucester's voice? Ay;
I know thy errand. I will go with thee.
The day, my friends, and all things stay for me.
*Exeunt.*

# [4.2]

*Enter the Dauphin, Orleans, Rambures, and
Beaumont.*

ORLEANS
The sun doth gild our armor. Up, my lords!
DAUPHIN  *Monte* à *cheval!* My horse! *Varlet! Lacquais!* Ha!  2
ORLEANS  Oh, brave spirit!
DAUPHIN  *Via, les eaux et terre!*                            4
ORLEANS  *Rien puis? L'air et feu?*                           5
DAUPHIN  *Cieux,* cousin Orleans.                             6

*Enter Constable.*

Now, my Lord Constable?

CONSTABLE
Hark, how our steeds for present service neigh!              8
DAUPHIN
Mount them, and make incision in their hides,               9
That their hot blood may spin in English eyes              10
And dout them with superfluous courage. Ha!                11
RAMBURES
What, will you have them weep our horses' blood?
How shall we then behold their natural tears?

*Enter Messenger.*

MESSENGER
The English are embattled, you French peers.               14
CONSTABLE
To horse, you gallant princes, straight to horse!
Do but behold yond poor and starvèd band,
And your fair show shall suck away their souls,            17
Leaving them but the shales and husks of men.              18
There is not work enough for all our hands,
Scarce blood enough in all their sickly veins
To give each naked curtal ax a stain                       21

That our French gallants shall today draw out
And sheathe for lack of sport. Let us but blow on
    them,
The vapor of our valor will o'erturn them.
'Tis positive against all exceptions, lords,               25
That our superfluous lackeys and our peasants,
Who in unnecessary action swarm
About our squares of battle, were enough                   28
To purge this field of such a hilding foe,                 29
Though we upon this mountain's basis by                    30
Took stand for idle speculation—                           31
But that our honors must not. What's to say?               32
A very little little let us do
And all is done. Then let the trumpets sound
The tucket sonance and the note to mount;                  35
For our approach shall so much dare the field              36
That England shall couch down in fear and yield.

*Enter Grandpré.*

GRANDPRÉ
Why do you stay so long, my lords of France?
Yond island carrions, desperate of their bones,           39
Ill-favoredly become the morning field.                   40
Their ragged curtains poorly are let loose,               41
And our air shakes them passing scornfully.               42
Big Mars seems bankrupt in their beggared host            43
And faintly through a rusty beaver peeps.                  44
The horsemen sit like fixèd candlesticks,
With torch staves in their hand, and their poor jades      46
Lob down their heads, drooping the hides and hips,         47
The gum down-roping from their pale-dead eyes,             48
And in their pale dull mouths the gimmaled bit             49
Lies foul with chewed grass, still and motionless;
And their executors, the knavish crows,                    51
Fly o'er them all impatient for their hour.
Description cannot suit itself in words
To demonstrate the life of such a battle                   54
In life so lifeless as it shows itself.
CONSTABLE
They have said their prayers, and they stay for death.  56
DAUPHIN
Shall we go send them dinners and fresh suits,
And give their fasting horses provender,                   58
And after fight with them?
CONSTABLE
I stay but for my guard. On to the field!                  60
I will the banner from a trumpet take,                     61

---

302 **Since that** necessitating that
**4.2. Location:** The French camp.
**0.2** *Beaumont* (The Folio text mentions Lord Beaumont but does not
give him a speaking part.)  **2** *Monte* à *cheval!* To horse!  *Varlet!*
*Lacquais!* liveried servant, valet  **4** *Via . . . terre!* Begone, waters and
earth! (The Dauphin imagines himself riding through and over rivers
and solid ground.)  **5** *Rien . . . feu?* Nothing more? What about air
and fire? (i.e., Why not soar above all four elements, not just water
and earth?)  **6** *Cieux* The heavens. (The Dauphin carries the metaphor
one step further to its ultimate height.)  **8 present service** immediate
action  **9 incision** i.e., with spurs  **10 spin** gush, spatter
**11 And . . . courage** i.e., and put out the English eyes with the horses'
superfluous blood, the proof of their excessive courage.  **dout** put out
**14 embattled** arranged in battle order  **17 fair show** impressive
appearance  **18 shales** shells  **21 curtal ax** cutlass, short sword

25 **exceptions** objections  **28 squares of battle** four-sided military
formations.  **were** would be  **29 hilding** worthless, base  **30 basis**
foot.  **by** nearby  **31 Took . . . speculation** stood still and idly looked
on  **32 But that** except for the fact that  **35 tucket sonance** trumpet
call.  **mount** mount our horses  **36 dare** (1) defy (2) stupify with fear
**39 carrions** cadavers for the scavenger birds.  **desperate of** without
hope of saving  **40 Ill-favoredly become** i.e., are an eyesore to
**41 curtains** colors, banners  **42 passing** exceedingly  **43 Mars** the
god of war  **44 beaver** visor  **46 torch staves** i.e., tapers in place of
lances. (The horsemen themselves look like carved candleholders.)
**47 Lob down** hang down.  **drooping** letting droop  **48 gum** watery
discharge.  **down-roping** hanging down ropelike  **49 gimmaled**
jointed  **51 their executors** the disposers of their remains  **54 battle**
army  **56 stay for** await  **58 provender** fodder  **60 guard** (Including
a standard-bearer.)  **61 trumpet** trumpeter

And use it for my haste. Come, come, away!
The sun is high, and we outwear the day.          *Exeunt.*  63

❖

# [4.3]

*Enter Gloucester, Bedford, Exeter, Erpingham,*
*with all his host, Salisbury, and Westmorland.*

GLOUCESTER   Where is the King?
BEDFORD
The King himself is rode to view their battle.          2
WESTMORLAND
Of fighting men they have full threescore thousand.
EXETER
There's five to one. Besides, they all are fresh.
SALISBURY
God's arm strike with us! 'Tis a fearful odds.
God b'wi' you, princes all; I'll to my charge.
If we no more meet till we meet in heaven,
Then, joyfully, my noble lord of Bedford,
My dear lord Gloucester, and my good lord Exeter,
And my kind kinsman, warriors all, adieu!          10
BEDFORD
Farewell, good Salisbury, and good luck go with thee!
EXETER
Farewell, kind lord. Fight valiantly today!
And yet I do thee wrong to mind thee of it,          13
For thou art framed of the firm truth of valor.          14
                              [*Exit Salisbury.*]
BEDFORD
He is as full of valor as of kindness,
Princely in both.
                    *Enter the King.*
WESTMORLAND   Oh, that we now had here
But one ten thousand of those men in England
That do no work today!
KING                          What's he that wishes so?          18
My cousin Westmorland? No, my fair cousin.
If we are marked to die, we are enough          20
To do our country loss; and if to live,          21
The fewer men, the greater share of honor.
God's will, I pray thee, wish not one man more.
By Jove, I am not covetous for gold,
Nor care I who doth feed upon my cost;          25
It yearns me not if men my garments wear;          26
Such outward things dwell not in my desires.
But if it be a sin to covet honor
I am the most offending soul alive.
No, faith, my coz, wish not a man from England.          30
God's peace, I would not lose so great an honor          31
As one man more, methinks, would share from me          32
For the best hope I have. Oh, do not wish one more!          33

Rather proclaim it, Westmorland, through my host          34
That he which hath no stomach to this fight,          35
Let him depart; his passport shall be made
And crowns for convoy put into his purse.          37
We would not die in that man's company
That fears his fellowship to die with us.          39
This day is called the Feast of Crispian.          40
He that outlives this day and comes safe home
Will stand a-tiptoe when this day is named
And rouse him at the name of Crispian.
He that shall see this day and live old age          44
Will yearly on the vigil feast his neighbors          45
And say, "Tomorrow is Saint Crispian."
Then will he strip his sleeve and show his scars,
And say, "These wounds I had on Crispin's Day."
Old men forget; yet all shall be forgot,          49
But he'll remember with advantages          50
What feats he did that day. Then shall our names,
Familiar in his mouth as household words—
Harry the King, Bedford and Exeter,
Warwick and Talbot, Salisbury and Gloucester—
Be in their flowing cups freshly remembered.
This story shall the good man teach his son;
And Crispin Crispian shall ne'er go by,
From this day to the ending of the world,
But we in it shall be rememberèd—
We few, we happy few, we band of brothers.
For he today that sheds his blood with me
Shall be my brother; be he ne'er so vile,          62
This day shall gentle his condition.          63
And gentlemen in England now abed
Shall think themselves accurst they were not here,
And hold their manhoods cheap whiles any speaks
That fought with us upon Saint Crispin's Day.

                    *Enter Salisbury.*

SALISBURY
My sovereign lord, bestow yourself with speed.          68
The French are bravely in their battles set,          69
And will with all expedience charge on us.          70
KING
All things are ready, if our minds be so.
WESTMORLAND
Perish the man whose mind is backward now!          72
KING
Thou dost not wish more help from England, coz?
WESTMORLAND
God's will, my liege, would you and I alone,
Without more help, could fight this royal battle!

---

63 **outwear** waste
4.3. **Location:** The English camp.
2 **battle** army.   6 **charge** post, command.   10 **kinsman** i.e., Westmorland, whose son had married Salisbury's daughter   13 **mind** remind   14 **framed** made, built   18 **What's** Who is   20–1 **enough . . . loss** enough loss for our country to suffer   25–6 **Nor . . . wear** (Henry professes not to crave liveried dependents, swelling his greatness.)   25 **upon my cost** at my expense   26 **yearns** grieves   30 **coz** cousin, kinsman   31 **God's peace** (A mild oath.)   32 **share from me** take from me as his share   33 **For . . . have** i.e., in exchange for my hope of eternal life.

34 **host** army   35 **stomach to** appetite for   37 **crowns for convoy** travel money   39 **That . . . us** who is afraid to risk his life in my company.   40 **Feast of Crispian** Saint Crispin's Day, October 25. (Crispinus and Crispianus were martyrs who fled from Rome in the third century; according to legend, they disguised themselves as shoemakers and afterward became the patron saints of that craft.)   44 **live** live to see   45 **vigil** evening before a feast day   49 **yet** in time   50 **advantages** additions of his own   62 **vile** lowly   63 **gentle his condition** i.e., raise his social status to the equivalent of gentleman in that he is my "brother."   68 **bestow yourself** take up your battle position   69 **bravely . . . set** finely arrayed in their battalions   70 **expedience** speed   72 **backward** reluctant

KING
Why, now thou hast unwished five thousand men,
Which likes me better than to wish us one.—    77
You know your places. God be with you all!

     *Tucket. Enter Montjoy.*

MONTJOY
Once more I come to know of thee, King Harry,
If for thy ransom thou wilt now compound    80
Before thy most assurèd overthrow;
For certainly thou art so near the gulf    82
Thou needs must be englutted. Besides, in mercy    83
The Constable desires thee thou wilt mind    84
Thy followers of repentance, that their souls
May make a peaceful and a sweet retire    86
From off these fields where, wretches, their poor
     bodies
Must lie and fester.
KING            Who hath sent thee now?
MONTJOY    The Constable of France.
KING
I pray thee, bear my former answer back:
Bid them achieve me, and then sell my bones.    91
Good God, why should they mock poor fellows thus?
The man that once did sell the lion's skin
While the beast lived was killed with hunting him.
A many of our bodies shall no doubt    95
Find native graves, upon the which, I trust,    96
Shall witness live in brass of this day's work.
And those that leave their valiant bones in France,
Dying like men, though buried in your dunghills,
They shall be famed; for there the sun shall greet them
And draw their honors reeking up to heaven,    101
Leaving their earthly parts to choke your clime,
The smell whereof shall breed a plague in France.
Mark then abounding valor in our English,    104
That, being dead, like to the bullets crazing    105
Break out into a second course of mischief,
Killing in relapse of mortality.    107
Let me speak proudly. Tell the Constable
We are but warriors for the working day.    109
Our gayness and our gilt are all besmirched
With rainy marching in the painful field.
There's not a piece of feather in our host—    112
Good argument, I hope, we will not fly—    113
And time hath worn us into slovenry.    114
But, by the Mass, our hearts are in the trim!    115
And my poor soldiers tell me, yet ere night

They'll be in fresher robes, or they will pluck    117
The gay new coats o'er the French soldiers' heads    118
And turn them out of service. If they do this—    119
As, if God please, they shall—my ransom then
Will soon be levied. Herald, save thou thy labor.    121
Come thou no more for ransom, gentle herald.    122
They shall have none, I swear, but these my joints,
Which if they have as I will leave 'em them,
Shall yield them little, tell the Constable.
MONTJOY
I shall, King Harry. And so fare thee well.
Thou never shalt hear herald any more.      *Exit.*
KING
I fear thou wilt once more come again for a ransom.

     *Enter York [and kneels].*

YORK
My lord, most humbly on my knee I beg
The leading of the vaward.    130
KING
Take it, brave York. Now, soldiers, march away.
And how thou pleasest, God, dispose the day!
                         *Exeunt.*

           ❖

## [4.4]

     *Alarum. Excursions. Enter Pistol, French Soldier,*
     *[and] Boy.*

PISTOL    Yield, cur!
FRENCH SOLDIER    *Je pense que vous êtes le gentilhomme de*    2
   *bonne qualité.*    3
PISTOL
   *Qualtitie calmie custure me!*    4
   Art thou a gentleman? What is thy name? Discuss.    5
FRENCH SOLDIER    *O Seigneur Dieu!*    6
PISTOL
   Oh, Signieur Dew should be a gentleman.    7
   Perpend my words, O Signieur Dew, and mark:    8
   O Signieur Dew, thou diest on point of fox,    9
   Except, O signieur, thou do give to me    10
   Egregious ransom.      *[He threatens him with his sword.]*    11
FRENCH SOLDIER    *Oh, prenez miséricorde! Ayez pitié de*    12
   *moi!*    13
PISTOL
   "Moy" shall not serve. I will have forty moys,    14
   Or I will fetch thy rim out at thy throat    15

---

77 **likes** pleases   80 **compound** make terms   82 **gulf** whirlpool
83 **englutted** swallowed up.   84 **mind** remind   86 **retire** retreat
91 **achieve** capture   95 **A many** Many   96 **native** in our own land
(i.e., England)   101 **reeking** (1) breathing (2) smelling   104 **abound-ing** overflowing, abundant   105 **crazing** shattering, with a suggestion
also of *grazing*, "ricocheting"   107 **Killing . . . mortality** killing (their
foes) as they (the English) fall back (decompose) into their elements;
also, like the bullet, with a deadly ricochet.   109 **for the working day**
to do serious work, not take a holiday.   112 **feather** decorative
plume   113 **fly** flee   114 **slovenry** slovenliness, untidiness.
115 **in the trim** fully rigged, ready for action.

117–19 **They'll . . . service** they will be more freshly dressed by nightfall, if no other way than by defrocking the French soldiers like incapable servants being dismissed and stripped of their livery. (Soldiers
got to keep such spoils of war from their victims.)
121 **levied** collected.   122 **gentle** noble   130 **vaward** vanguard.
**4.4. Location:** The field of battle.
0.1 *Excursions* Sorties.   2–3 *Je . . . qualité* I think that you are a gentleman
of high rank.   4 *calmie custure me* (These words are perhaps derived
from the refrain of a popular song, supposed to be Irish, "Calen o custure
me.")   5 **Discuss** Speak.   6 *O Seigneur Dieu!* O Lord God!   7 **should**
must   8 **Perpend** Attend to, consider   9 **fox** sword   10 **Except** unless
11 **Egregious** huge   12–13 *Oh . . . moi!* Oh, have mercy! Take pity on me!
14 **Moy** (Pistol, not understanding, takes *moi* for the name of a coin or a
sum of money, a moiety or half.)   15 **rim** midriff, diaphragm

In drops of crimson blood.

FRENCH SOLDIER    *Est-il impossible d'échapper la force de ton* 17
*bras?* 18

PISTOL    Brass, cur?
Thou damnèd and luxurious mountain goat, 20
Offer'st me brass?

FRENCH SOLDIER    *Oh, pardonnez-moi!*

PISTOL
Say'st thou me so? Is that a ton of moys?— 23
Come hither, boy. Ask me this slave in French 24
What is his name.

BOY    *Écoutez: comment êtes-vous appelé?* 26

FRENCH SOLDIER    *Monsieur Le Fer.*

BOY    He says his name is Master Fer.

PISTOL    Master Fer? I'll fer him, and firk him, and ferret 29
him. Discuss the same in French unto him.

BOY    I do not know the French for fer, and ferret, and
firk.

PISTOL
Bid him prepare, for I will cut his throat.

FRENCH SOLDIER    *Que dit-il, monsieur?* 34

BOY    *Il me commande à vous dire que vous faites vous* 35
*prêt; car ce soldat ici est disposé tout à cette heure de* 36
*couper votre gorge.* 37

PISTOL
*Owy, cuppele gorge, permafoy,* 38
Peasant, unless thou give me crowns, brave crowns, 39
Or mangled shalt thou be by this my sword.

FRENCH SOLDIER    *Oh, je vous supplie, pour l'amour de* 41
*Dieu, me pardonner! Je suis le gentilhomme de bonne* 42
*maison. Gardez ma vie, et je vous donnerai deux cents* 43
*écus.* 44

PISTOL    What are his words?

BOY    He prays you to save his life. He is a gentleman of
a good house, and for his ransom he will give you two 47
hundred crowns.

PISTOL
Tell him my fury shall abate, and I
The crowns will take.

FRENCH SOLDIER    *Petit monsieur, que dit-il?* 51

BOY    *Encore qu'il est contre son jurement de pardonner* 52
*aucun prisonnier, néanmoins, pour les écus que vous* 53
*l'avez promis, il est content à vous donner la liberté,* 54
*le franchisement.* 55

FRENCH SOLDIER [*kneeling*]    *Sur mes genoux je vous* 56
*donne mille remercîments; et je m'estime heureux que* 57
*j'ai tombé entre les mains d'un chevalier, je pense,* 58
*le plus brave, vaillant, et très-distingué seigneur* 59
*d'Angleterre.* 60

PISTOL    Expound unto me, boy.

BOY    He gives you, upon his knees, a thousand thanks,
and he esteems himself happy that he hath fallen into
the hands of one, as he thinks, the most brave, valorous, and thrice-worthy signieur of England.

PISTOL
As I suck blood, I will some mercy show.
Follow me!

BOY    *Suivez-vous le grand capitaine.* 68

       [*Exeunt Pistol and French Soldier.*]
I did never know so full a voice issue
from so empty a heart! But the saying is true, "The
empty vessel makes the greatest sound." Bardolph and
Nym had ten times more valor than this roaring devil 72
i'th'old play, that everyone may pare his nails with 73
a wooden dagger, and they are both hanged; and so 74
would this be, if he durst steal anything adventur-
ously. I must stay with the lackeys, with the luggage
of our camp. The French might have a good prey of 77
us, if he knew of it, for there is none to guard it but
boys.           *Exit.*

❖

## [4.5]

*Enter Constable, Orleans, Bourbon, Dauphin,*
*and Rambures.*

CONSTABLE    *Oh, diable!* 1

ORLEANS    *Oh, Seigneur! Le jour est perdu, tout est perdu!* 2

DAUPHIN
*Mort de ma vie!* All is confounded, all. 3
Reproach and everlasting shame
Sits mocking in our plumes.      *A short alarum.*
*Oh, méchante fortune!* Do not run away.

CONSTABLE    Why, all our ranks are broke. 6

DAUPHIN
Oh, perdurable shame! Let's stab ourselves. 8
Be these the wretches that we played at dice for?

ORLEANS
Is this the king we sent to for his ransom?

BOURBON
Shame and eternal shame, nothing but shame!
Let us die! In once more! Back again!

---

17–18 *Est-il . . . bras?* Is it impossible to escape the strength of your arm? (But Pistol takes *bras*, "arm," for *brass*.)   **20 luxurious** lecherous   **23 a ton of moys** (This is what Pistol phonetically makes out of *pardonnez-moi*, pardon me.)   **24 slave** wretch   **26 *Écoutez . . . appelé?*** Listen: what is your name?   **29 firk** trounce.   **ferret** worry (like a ferret)   **34–7 *Que . . . gorge*** What does he say, sir? BOY He bids me tell you that you must prepare yourself, because this soldier intends to cut your throat immediately.   **38 *Owy*** *Oui,* "yes." **permafoy** *per ma foi,* by my faith   **39 brave** fine, splendid   **41–4 *Oh . . . écus*** Oh, I pray you, for the love of God, to pardon me! I am a gentleman of a good house; preserve my life, and I shall give you two hundred crowns.   **47 house** family   **51–5 *Petit . . . franchisement*** What does he say, little sir? BOY Although it is against his oath to pardon any prisoner, nevertheless, in return for the crowns you have promised, he is willing to give you your liberty, your freedom.

**56–60 *Sur . . . d'Angleterre*** On my knees, I give you a thousand thanks, and I consider myself happy that I have fallen into the hands of a knight, as I think, the bravest, most valiant, and very distinguished gentleman in England.   **68 *Suivez-vous . . . capitaine*** Follow the great captain.   **72–4 this roaring . . . dagger** Shakespeare refers several times to the devil in the morality play with his dagger of lath; see *2H6*, 4.2.2 and *Twelfth Night*, 4.2.126. The paring of the devil's nails was a proverbial act of bravado.   **77 a good prey** i.e., easy pickings
**4.5. Location: The field of battle still.**
**1 *Oh, diable!*** Oh, the devil!   **2 *Oh . . . perdu!*** Oh, Lord, the day is lost, all is lost!   **3 *Mort . . . vie!*** Death of my life!   **confounded** lost   **6 *Oh, méchante fortune!*** Oh, malicious fortune!   **8 perdurable** everlasting

And he that will not follow Bourbon now,
Let him go hence, and with his cap in hand,
Like a base pander, hold the chamber door
Whilst by a slave, no gentler than my dog,
His fairest daughter is contaminated.                            16

CONSTABLE
Disorder, that hath spoiled us, friend us now!                   18
Let us on heaps go offer up our lives.                           19

ORLEANS
We are enough yet living in the field
To smother up the English in our throngs,
If any order might be thought upon.

BOURBON
The devil take order now! I'll to the throng.
Let life be short, else shame will be too long.
                                              *Exeunt.*

# [4.6]

*Alarum. Enter the King and his train, [Exeter,
and others,] with prisoners.*

KING
Well have we done, thrice valiant countrymen!
But all's not done; yet keep the French the field.               2

EXETER
The Duke of York commends him to Your Majesty.

KING
Lives he, good uncle? Thrice within this hour
I saw him down, thrice up again and fighting.
From helmet to the spur all blood he was.

EXETER
In which array, brave soldier, doth he lie,
Larding the plain; and by his bloody side,                       8
Yokefellow to his honor-owing wounds,                            9
The noble Earl of Suffolk also lies.
Suffolk first died; and York, all haggled over,                  11
Comes to him, where in gore he lay insteeped,                    12
And takes him by the beard, kisses the gashes
That bloodily did yawn upon his face.                            14
He cries aloud, "Tarry, my cousin Suffolk!
My soul shall thine keep company to heaven;
Tarry, sweet soul, for mine, then fly abreast,
As in this glorious and well-foughten field
We kept together in our chivalry!"
Upon these words I came and cheered him up.
He smiled me in the face, raught me his hand,                    21
And with a feeble grip says, "Dear my lord,
Commend my service to my sovereign."
So did he turn, and over Suffolk's neck
He threw his wounded arm, and kissed his lips,
And so, espoused to death, with blood he sealed

A testament of noble-ending love.
The pretty and sweet manner of it forced
Those waters from me which I would have stopped;                 29
But I had not so much of man in me,
And all my mother came into mine eyes                            31
And gave me up to tears.

KING                              I blame you not;
For, hearing this, I must perforce compound                      33
With mistful eyes, or they will issue too.        *Alarum.*  34
But, hark, what new alarum is this same?
The French have reinforced their scattered men.
Then every soldier kill his prisoners!                           37
Give the word through.                            *Exeunt.*

# [4.7]

*Enter Fluellen and Gower.*

FLUELLEN   Kill the poys and the luggage? 'Tis expressly      1
against the law of arms. 'Tis as arrant a piece of
knavery, mark you now, as can be offert; in your
conscience, now, is it not?

GOWER   'Tis certain there's not a boy left alive; and the
cowardly rascals that ran from the battle ha' done this
slaughter. Besides, they have burned and carried
away all that was in the King's tent, wherefore the
King most worthily hath caused every soldier to cut
his prisoner's throat. Oh, 'tis a gallant king!

FLUELLEN   Ay, he was porn at Monmouth, Captain   11
Gower. What call you the town's name where Alexander the Pig was born?

GOWER   Alexander the Great.

FLUELLEN   Why, I pray you, is not "pig" great? The pig,
or the great, or the mighty, or the huge, or the
magnanimous, are all one reckonings, save the phrase   17
is a little variations.

GOWER   I think Alexander the Great was born in
Macedon. His father was called Philip of Macedon, as
I take it.

FLUELLEN   I think it is e'en Macedon where Alexander is
porn. I tell you, Captain, if you look in the maps of the
'orld, I warrant you sall find, in the comparisons between Macedon and Monmouth, that the situations,
look you, is both alike. There is a river in Macedon,
and there is also moreover a river at Monmouth. It is
called Wye at Monmouth, but it is out of my prains
what is the name of the other river; but 'tis all one, 'tis
alike as my fingers is to my fingers, and there is sal-
mons in both. If you mark Alexander's life well, Harry
of Monmouth's life is come after it indifferent well, for   32
there is figures in all things. Alexander, God knows,   33

---

**16 gentler** (1) more nobly born (2) tenderer   **18 friend** befriend
**19 on** in
**4.6. Location: The field of battle still.**
**2 yet . . . field** the French are in the field of battle still.   **8 Larding**
fattening, enriching (with his blood)   **9 honor-owing** honor-owning,
honorable   **11 haggled over** mangled, hacked   **12 insteeped**
steeped, soaked   **14 yawn** gape   **21 me in the** in my.   **raught**
reached

**29 waters** i.e., tears   **31 my mother** i.e., the tenderer part of me
**33 perforce** necessarily.   **compound** come to terms   **34 issue** issue
forth tears   **37 kill his prisoners** (This follows Holinshed, who says
that Henry, alarmed by the outcry of the lackeys and boys of the
camp, feared a new attack and ordered the prisoners killed as a precaution. Gower, 4.7.7–10, attributes the King's action to revenge.)
**4.7. Location: The field of battle still.**
**1 luggage** i.e., lackeys guarding the luggage.   **11 Monmouth** (i.e.,
in Wales)   **17 are . . . reckonings** come to the same thing   **32 is . . .
well** resembles it fairly well   **33 figures** comparisons, similes

and you know, in his rages, and his furies, and his
wraths, and his cholers, and his moods, and his dis-
pleasures, and his indignations, and also being a little
intoxicates in his prains, did, in his ales and his angers,    37
look you, kill his best friend, Cleitus.    38

GOWER    Our King is not like him in that. He never killed
any of his friends.

FLUELLEN    It is not well done, mark you now, to take
the tales out of my mouth ere it is made and finished.
I speak but in the figures and comparisons of it. As
Alexander killed his friend Cleitus, being in his ales
and his cups, so also Harry Monmouth, being in his
right wits and his good judgments, turned away the
fat knight with the great-belly doublet. He was full of    47
jests, and gipes, and knaveries, and mocks. I have    48
forgot his name.

GOWER    Sir John Falstaff.

FLUELLEN    That is he. I'll tell you there is good men
porn at Monmouth.

GOWER    Here comes His Majesty.

*Alarum. Enter King Harry, [Warwick, Gloucester,
Exeter, and others,] and Bourbon, with [other]
prisoners. Flourish.*

KING

I was not angry since I came to France
Until this instant. Take a trumpet, herald;    55
Ride thou unto the horsemen on yond hill.
If they will fight with us, bid them come down,
Or void the field. They do offend our sight.    58
If they'll do neither, we will come to them,
And make them skirr away as swift as stones    60
Enforcèd from the old Assyrian slings.    61
Besides, we'll cut the throats of those we have,
And not a man of them that we shall take
Shall taste our mercy. Go and tell them so.

*Enter Montjoy.*

EXETER

Here comes the herald of the French, my liege.

GLOUCESTER

His eyes are humbler than they used to be.

KING

How now, what means this, herald? Know'st thou
not
That I have fined these bones of mine for ransom?    68
Com'st thou again for ransom?

MONTJOY                    No, great King.
I come to thee for charitable license,
That we may wander o'er this bloody field
To book our dead and then to bury them,    72
To sort our nobles from our common men.

For many of our princes—woe the while!—
Lie drowned and soaked in mercenary blood;    75
So do our vulgar drench their peasant limbs    76
In blood of princes; and the wounded steeds
Fret fetlock-deep in gore and with wild rage    78
Yerk out their armèd heels at their dead masters,    79
Killing them twice. Oh, give us leave, great King,
To view the field in safety, and dispose
Of their dead bodies!

KING                    I tell thee truly, herald,
I know not if the day be ours or no,
For yet a many of your horsemen peer    84
And gallop o'er the field.

MONTJOY                    The day is yours.

KING

Praisèd be God, and not our strength, for it!
What is this castle called that stands hard by?

MONTJOY    They call it Agincourt.

KING

Then call we this the field of Agincourt,
Fought on the day of Crispin Crispianus.

FLUELLEN    Your grandfather of famous memory, an't    91
please Your Majesty, and your great-uncle Edward the
Plack Prince of Wales, as I have read in the chronicles,
fought a most prave pattle here in France.

KING    They did, Fluellen.

FLUELLEN    Your Majesty says very true. If Your Majesties is remembered of it, the Welshmen did good
service in a garden where leeks did grow, wearing
leeks in their Monmouth caps, which, Your Majesty    99
know, to this hour is an honorable badge of the
service; and I do believe Your Majesty takes no scorn
to wear the leek upon Saint Tavy's Day.    102

KING

I wear it for a memorable honor,
For I am Welsh, you know, good countryman.

FLUELLEN    All the water in Wye cannot wash Your
Majesty's Welsh plood out of your pody, I can tell you
that. God pless it and preserve it, as long as it pleases
His Grace, and His Majesty too!

KING    Thanks, good my countryman.

FLUELLEN    By Jeshu, I am Your Majesty's countryman.
I care not who know it. I will confess it to all the 'orld.
I need not to be ashamed of Your Majesty, praised be
God, so long as Your Majesty is an honest man.

KING

God keep me so!

*Enter Williams [with a glove in his cap].*

Our heralds go with him.
Bring me just notice of the numbers dead    115

---

37 **in his ales** i.e., under the influence of ale    38 **Cleitus** a general and close associate of Alexander, whom Alexander killed in a drinking bout. 47 **great-belly doublet** a man's close-fitting jacket, in which the lower part was stuffed out with bombast or padding.    48 **gipes** gibes, jokes 55 **trumpet** trumpeter    58 **void** leave    60 **skirr** scurry    61 **Enforcèd** discharged. (The Assyrians were famous for their deadly use of stones projected by slings.)    68 **fined . . . ransom** i.e., agreed to pay as a fine or ransom only these bones of mine and no more.    72 **book** record

75 **mercenary** i.e., of common soldiers, who fought for pay    76 **So** that way.    **vulgar** commoners    78 **fetlock-deep** (The *fetlock* is above the hoof, at the back of the leg.)    79 **Yerk** kick    84 **peer** (1) look about anxiously (2) appear    91 **grandfather** i.e., great-grandfather, Edward III.    **an't** if it    99 **Monmouth caps** round and rimless caps with a tapering crown, commonly worn by the Welsh    102 **Saint Tavy's Day** the festival of Saint David, patron saint of Wales, March 1—an occasion for the celebration of Welsh traditions, though the wearing of leeks to commemorate the great victory in 540 against the Saxons did not begin until well after the setting of this play.    115 **just** exact

On both our parts.
                    [*Exeunt Heralds and Gower with Montjoy.*]
                    Call yonder fellow hither.
EXETER [*to Williams*]   Soldier, you must come to the King.
KING   Soldier, why wear'st thou that glove in thy cap?
WILLIAMS   An't please Your Majesty, 'tis the gage of  119
one that I should fight withal, if he be alive.  120
KING   An Englishman?
WILLIAMS   An't please Your Majesty, a rascal that swag-
gered with me last night, who, if 'a live and ever dare
to challenge this glove, I have sworn to take him a box  124
o'th'ear; or if I can see my glove in his cap, which he
swore, as he was a soldier, he would wear if 'a lived, I
will strike it out soundly.
KING   What think you, Captain Fluellen, is it fit this
soldier keep his oath?
FLUELLEN   He is a craven and a villain else, an't please  130
Your Majesty, in my conscience.
KING   It may be his enemy is a gentleman of great sort,  132
quite from the answer of his degree.  133
FLUELLEN   Though he be as good a gentleman as the
devil is, as Lucifer and Beelzebub himself, it is
necessary, look Your Grace, that he keep his vow and
his oath. If he be perjured, see you now, his reputation
is as arrant a villain and a Jack-sauce as ever his  138
black shoe trod upon God's ground and His earth, in
my conscience, la!
KING [*to Williams*]   Then keep thy vow, sirrah, when
thou meet'st the fellow.
WILLIAMS   So I will, my liege, as I live.
KING   Who serv'st thou under?
WILLIAMS   Under Captain Gower, my liege.
FLUELLEN   Gower is a good captain, and is good
knowledge and literatured in the wars.  147
KING   Call him hither to me, soldier.
WILLIAMS   I will, my liege.                              *Exit.*
KING   Here, Fluellen, wear thou this favor for me and
stick it in thy cap. [*He gives Fluellen Williams's glove.*]
When Alençon and myself were down together, I  152
plucked this glove from his helm. If any man challenge  153
this, he is a friend to Alençon and an enemy to our
person. If thou encounter any such, apprehend him,
an thou dost me love.  156
FLUELLEN [*putting the glove in his cap*]   Your Grace doo's  157
me as great honors as can be desired in the hearts of
his subjects. I would fain see the man that  159
has but two legs that shall find himself aggriefed at  160
this glove, that is all. But I would fain see it once, an't  161
please God of his grace that I might see.
KING   Know'st thou Gower?
FLUELLEN   He is my dear friend, an't please you.
KING   Pray thee, go seek him and bring him to my tent.
FLUELLEN   I will fetch him.                             *Exit.*

119 An't If it. (Also in line 130.)   120 should am engaged to
124 take give   130 craven coward   132 sort rank   133 quite . . .
degree i.e., too high in rank to answer the challenge of one so
low.   138 Jack-sauce saucy knave   147 literatured well read
152 Alençon a french duke, not appearing in this play, but a familiar
name to the English. (Also in line 154 and 4.8.18.)   153 helm helmet.   156 an if   157 doo's does   159 fain willingly   159–60 the
man . . . legs i.e., any man   161 an't if it. (Also in line 164.)

KING
My lord of Warwick, and my brother Gloucester,
Follow Fluellen closely at the heels.
The glove which I have given him for a favor
May haply purchase him a box o'th'ear.  170
It is the soldier's; I by bargain should
Wear it myself. Follow, good cousin Warwick.
If that the soldier strike him, as I judge  173
By his blunt bearing he will keep his word,
Some sudden mischief may arise of it;
For I do know Fluellen valiant
And touched with choler, hot as gunpowder,  177
And quickly will return an injury.  178
Follow, and see there be no harm between them.
Go you with me, uncle of Exeter.    *Exeunt* [*separately*].

# [4.8]

*Enter Gower and Williams.*

WILLIAMS   I warrant it is to knight you, Captain.  1

*Enter Fluellen.*

FLUELLEN   God's will and his pleasure, Captain, I
beseech you now, come apace to the King. There is
more good toward you, peradventure, than is in your
knowledge to dream of.
WILLIAMS   Sir, know you this glove?
FLUELLEN   Know the glove? I know the glove is a glove.
WILLIAMS   I know this, and thus I challenge it.
                                               *Strikes him.*
FLUELLEN   'Sblood, an arrant traitor as any 's in the  9
universal world, or in France, or in England!
GOWER [*to Williams*]   How now, sir? You villain!
WILLIAMS   Do you think I'll be forsworn?
FLUELLEN   Stand away, Captain Gower. I will give
treason his payment into plows, I warrant you.  14
WILLIAMS   I am no traitor.
FLUELLEN   That's a lie in thy throat.—I charge you in His  16
Majesty's name, apprehend him. He's a friend of the
Duke Alençon's.

*Enter Warwick and Gloucester.*

WARWICK   How now, how now, what's the matter?
FLUELLEN   My lord of Warwick, here is—praised be
God for it!—a most contagious treason come to light,  21
look you, as you shall desire in a summer's day.—
Here is His Majesty.

*Enter King* [*Henry*] *and Exeter.*

KING   How now, what's the matter?
FLUELLEN   My liege, here is a villain and a traitor that,
look Your Grace, has struck the glove which Your
Majesty is take out of the helmet of Alençon.

170 haply perhaps   173 If that If   177 touched with choler
hot-tempered   178 return an injury repay an insult.
4.8. Location: The English camp.
1 warrant guarantee   9 'Sblood By His (Christ's) blood   14 his its.
into plows in blows   16 lie in thy throat i.e., inexcusable lie.
21 contagious noxious; or Fluellen may mean "notorious"

WILLIAMS   My liege, this was my glove; here is the fellow of it. [*Showing his other glove.*] And he that I gave it
to in change promised to wear it in his cap. I promised   30
to strike him, if he did. I met this man with my glove
in his cap, and I have been as good as my word.

FLUELLEN   Your Majesty hear now, saving Your Majesty's manhood, what an arrant, rascally, beggarly,
lousy knave it is. I hope Your Majesty is pear me   35
testimony and witness, and will avouchment, that this   36
is the glove of Alençon that Your Majesty is give me,
in your conscience, now.

KING   Give me thy glove, soldier. Look, here is the
fellow of it.                          [*He shows his other glove.*]
'Twas I indeed thou promisèd'st to strike,
And thou hast given me most bitter terms.   42

FLUELLEN   An't please Your Majesty, let his neck
answer for it, if there is any martial law in the world.

KING
How canst thou make me satisfaction?

WILLIAMS   All offenses, my lord, come from the heart.
Never came any from mine that might offend Your
Majesty.

KING   It was ourself thou didst abuse.

WILLIAMS   Your Majesty came not like yourself. You
appeared to me but as a common man—witness the
night, your garments, your lowliness. And what Your   52
Highness suffered under that shape, I beseech you take
it for your own fault and not mine; for had you been
as I took you for, I made no offense. Therefore I be-   55
seech Your Highness pardon me.

KING
Here, uncle Exeter, fill this glove with crowns,
And give it to this fellow.—Keep it, fellow,
And wear it for an honor in thy cap
Till I do challenge it.—Give him the crowns.
              [*Exeter gives the glove and gold to Williams.*]
And Captain, you must needs be friends with him.

FLUELLEN   By this day and this light, the fellow has
mettle enough in his belly.—Hold, there is twelve-
pence for you. [*He offers Williams a coin.*] And I pray you
to serve God, and keep you out of prawls, and
prabbles, and quarrels, and dissensions, and I warrant   66
you it is the better for you.

WILLIAMS   I will none of your money.

FLUELLEN   It is with a good will. I can tell you, it will
serve you to mend your shoes. Come, wherefore
should you be so pashful? Your shoes is not so good.
'Tis a good silling, I warrant you, or I will change it.

              *Enter [an English] Herald.*

KING   Now, herald, are the dead numbered?

HERALD [*giving a paper*]
Here is the number of the slaughtered French.

KING
What prisoners of good sort are taken, uncle?   75

EXETER [*reading*]
Charles Duke of Orleans, nephew to the King;   76
John Duke of Bourbon, and Lord Boucicault;
Of other lords and barons, knights and squires,
Full fifteen hundred, besides common men.

KING
This note doth tell me of ten thousand French
That in the field lie slain. Of princes, in this number,
And nobles bearing banners, there lie dead   82
One hundred twenty-six; added to these,
Of knights, esquires, and gallant gentlemen,
Eight thousand and four hundred, of the which
Five hundred were but yesterday dubbed knights.
So that in these ten thousand they have lost
There are but sixteen hundred mercenaries;
The rest are princes, barons, lords, knights, squires,
And gentlemen of blood and quality.
The names of those their nobles that lie dead:
Charles Delabreth, High Constable of France;
Jaques of Chatillion, Admiral of France;
The Master of the Crossbows, Lord Rambures;
Great-Master of France, the brave Sir Guichard
   Dauphin   95
John, Duke of Alençon; Anthony, Duke of Brabant,
The brother to the Duke of Burgundy;
And Edward, Duke of Bar; of lusty earls,   98
Grandpré and Roussi, Faulconbridge and Foix,
Beaumont and Marle, Vaudemont and Lestrelles.
Here was a royal fellowship of death!
Where is the number of our English dead?
              [*He is given another paper.*]
Edward the Duke of York, the Earl of Suffolk,
Sir Richard Keighley, Davy Gam, esquire;
None else of name, and of all other men   105
But five-and-twenty. O God, thy arm was here!   106
And not to us, but to thy arm alone,
Ascribe we all. When, without stratagem,
But in plain shock and even play of battle,   109
Was ever known so great and little loss
On one part and on th'other? Take it, God,
For it is none but thine.

EXETER                              'Tis wonderful.

KING
Come, go we in procession to the village.
And be it death proclaimèd through our host
To boast of this or take that praise from God
Which is his only.

FLUELLEN   Is it not lawful, an't please Your Majesty, to
tell how many is killed?

KING
Yes, Captain, but with this acknowledgment,
That God fought for us.

---

30 **change** exchange   35 **is pear** will bear   36 **avouchment** avouch
42 **terms** words.   52 **lowliness** humble mien.   55 **made** would have
made   66 **prabbles** i.e., brabbles, scuffles   75 **good sort** high rank

76–106 **Charles . . . here** (The catalogue of the captured and slain is
from Holinshed.)   82 **bearing banners** i.e., with coats of arms
95 **Great-Master** grandmaster, i.e., the chief officer of the royal household   98 **lusty** vigorous   105 **name** rank, social importance
109 **even** equal

FLUELLEN   Yes, in my conscience, he did us great good.
KING   Do we all holy rites.
    Let there be sung *Non nobis* and *Te Deum*,    123
    The dead with charity enclosed in clay;
    And then to Calais, and to England then,
    Where ne'er from France arrived more happy men.    126
                             *Exeunt.*

❖

## [5.0]

*Enter Chorus.*

CHORUS
    Vouchsafe to those that have not read the story    1
    That I may prompt them; and of such as have,
    I humbly pray them to admit th'excuse    3
    Of time, of numbers, and due course of things,    4
    Which cannot in their huge and proper life    5
    Be here presented. Now we bear the King
    Toward Calais. Grant him there. There seen,
    Heave him away upon your wingèd thoughts
    Athwart the sea. Behold, the English beach    9
    Pales-in the flood with men, wives, and boys,    10
    Whose shouts and claps outvoice the deep-mouthed
        sea,    11
    Which like a mighty whiffler 'fore the King    12
    Seems to prepare his way. So let him land,
    And solemnly see him set on to London.    14
    So swift a pace hath thought that even now
    You may imagine him upon Blackheath,    16
    Where that his lords desire him to have borne    17
    His bruisèd helmet and his bended sword
    Before him through the city. He forbids it,
    Being free from vainness and self-glorious pride,
    Giving full trophy, signal, and ostent    21
    Quite from himself to God. But now behold,
    In the quick forge and working-house of thought,
    How London doth pour out her citizens!
    The Mayor and all his brethren, in best sort,    25
    Like to the senators of th'antique Rome
    With the plebeians swarming at their heels,
    Go forth and fetch their conquering Caesar in;

    As by a lower but loving likelihood,    29
    Were now the General of our gracious Empress,    30
    As in good time he may, from Ireland coming,
    Bringing rebellion broachèd on his sword,    32
    How many would the peaceful city quit    33
    To welcome him! Much more, and much more cause,    34
    Did they this Harry. Now in London place him;
    As yet the lamentation of the French    36
    Invites the King of England's stay at home;    37
    The Emperor's coming in behalf of France,    38
    To order peace between them . . . and omit    39
    All the occurrences, whatever chanced,
    Till Harry's back-return again to France.    41
    There must we bring him; and myself have played
    The interim by rememb'ring you 'tis past.    43
    Then brook abridgment, and your eyes advance,    44
    After your thoughts, straight back again to France.
                             *Exit.*

❖

## [5.1]

*Enter Fluellen [with a leek in his cap, and a
cudgel], and Gower.*

GOWER   Nay, that's right. But why wear you your leek
   today? Saint Davy's Day is past.
FLUELLEN   There is occasions and causes why and
   wherefore in all things. I will tell you asse my friend,    4
   Captain Gower. The rascally, scald, beggarly, lousy,    5
   pragging knave, Pistol, which you and yourself and all
   the world know to be no petter than a fellow, look you
   now, of no merits, he is come to me and prings me
   pread and salt yesterday, look you, and bid me eat my
   leek. It was in a place where I could not breed no contention with him; but I will be so bold as to wear it in
   my cap till I see him once again, and then I will tell
   him a little piece of my desires.

    *Enter Pistol.*

GOWER   Why, here he comes, swelling like a turkey-
   cock.
FLUELLEN   'Tis no matter for his swellings nor his
   turkey-cocks.—God pless you, Aunchient Pistol! You
   scurvy, lousy knave, God pless you!
PISTOL
   Ha, art thou bedlam? Dost thou thirst, base Trojan,    19

---

**123 *Non nobis*** i.e., Psalm 115, beginning, "Not unto us, O Lord,
not unto us, but unto thy name give glory." **   *Te Deum*** a hymn of
thanksgiving, beginning, "We praise thee O God" **   126 happy**
fortunate
**5.0. (Between Acts 4 and 5, there is historically an interval of about
five years during which Henry made a second campaign in France
that brought the French to terms in the Treaty of Troyes, with
which the play ends.)**
**1 Vouchsafe** Permit it    **3 admit th'excuse** excuse our handling
**4 Of time . . . things** (Shakespeare may glance here at the ancient critical tradition of the so-called "classical unities" of time, place, and
action, based on Aristotle's *Poetics*, limiting a play's staging representation to twenty-four hours, to a single locale, and to a single plot.)
**5 proper** true    **9 Athwart** across    **10 Pales-in the flood** surrounds and
fences in the sea    **11 outvoice . . . sea** drown out even the sound of the
thundering sea    **12 whiffler** an usher heading the procession to clear
the way    **14 solemnly** ceremoniously    **16 Blackheath** open area just
outside London, to the southeast    **17 Where that** where    **21 Giving . . .
ostent** giving every memorial, token, and display of victory
**25 brethren** fellow officers of the city.    **sort** array

**29–34 As . . . him** (Seemingly, an allusion to the Earl of Essex, who left
London on his Irish expedition on March 27, 1599, in an attempt to put
down Tyrone's rebellion; he returned unsuccessful and under a cloud on
September 28 of the same year. These lines, therefore, were probably
written between the dates mentioned.)    **29 a . . . likelihood** a less exalted
comparison but one that shows much love    **30 Empress** i.e., Elizabeth
**32 broachèd** transfixed, spitted    **33 quit** leave (by going to the city gate
to greet Henry)    **36–7 As . . . home** i.e., the French are so dejected that
Henry can stay in England without fear of loss in France    **38 Emperor's
coming** (The Holy Roman Emperor, Sigismund, came to England on
behalf of France in May 1416.)    **39 them . . . and omit** (Something
appears to be left out here. Possibly it should read, "them, and the death /
O' the Dauphin, leap we over, and omit . . .")    **41 Harry's back-return**
i.e., Henry's second campaign, commencing in 1417    **43 rememb'ring**
reminding    **44 brook** tolerate, excuse
**5.1. Location: France. The English camp.**
**4 asse** as    **5 scald** scurvy    **19 bedlam** crazy.    **Trojan** i.e., rascal

To have me fold up Parca's fatal web?                    20
Hence, I am qualmish at the smell of leek.               21
FLUELLEN    I peseech you heartily, scurvy, lousy knave,
at my desires, and my requests, and my petitions, to
eat, look you, this leek. [*He offers the leek.*] Because,
look you, you do not love it, nor your affections and
your appetites and your disgestions doo's not agree
with it, I would desire you to eat it.
PISTOL
Not for Cadwallader and all his goats.                   28
FLUELLEN    There is one goat for you. (*Strikes him.*) Will
you be so good, scald knave, as eat it?
PISTOL    Base Trojan, thou shalt die.
FLUELLEN    You say very true, scald knave, when God's
will is. I will desire you to live in the meantime and
eat your victuals. Come, there is sauce for it. [*He strikes
him.*] You called me yesterday mountain squire, but I    35
will make you today a squire of low degree. I pray       36
you, fall to. If you can mock a leek, you can eat a leek. 37
GOWER    Enough, Captain, you have astonished him.        38
FLUELLEN    By Jesu, I will make him eat some part of my
leek, or I will peat his pate four days. Bite, I pray you; 40
it is good for your green wound and your ploody          41
coxcomb.                                                  42
PISTOL    Must I bite?
FLUELLEN    Yes, certainly, and out of doubt and out of
question too, and ambiguities.
PISTOL
By this leek, I will most horribly revenge—
                    [*Fluellen threatens him.*]
I eat and eat—I swear—
FLUELLEN    Eat, I pray you. Will you have some more
sauce to your leek? There is not enough leek to
swear by.
PISTOL
Quiet thy cudgel; thou dost see I eat.
FLUELLEN    Much good do you, scald knave, heartily.      52
Nay, pray you, throw none away; the skin is good for
your broken coxcomb. When you take occasions to see      54
leeks hereafter, I pray you, mock at 'em, that is all.
PISTOL    Good.
FLUELLEN    Ay, leeks is good. Hold you, there is a groat  57
to heal your pate.                    [*He offers a coin.*]
PISTOL    Me, a groat?
FLUELLEN    Yes, verily, and in truth you shall take it, or
I have another leek in my pocket which you shall eat.
PISTOL
I take thy groat in earnest of revenge.                  62

FLUELLEN    If I owe you anything, I will pay you in
cudgels. You shall be a woodmonger and buy nothing
of me but cudgels. God b'wi'you, and keep you, and
heal your pate.                                  *Exit.*
PISTOL    All hell shall stir for this.
GOWER    Go, go, you are a counterfeit cowardly knave.
Will you mock at an ancient tradition, begun upon an
honorable respect and worn as a memorable trophy of      70
predeceased valor, and dare not avouch in your deeds     71
any of your words? I have seen you gleeking and          72
galling at this gentleman twice or thrice. You thought    73
because he could not speak English in the native garb
he could not therefore handle an English cudgel. You
find it otherwise; and henceforth let a Welsh cor-
rection teach you a good English condition. Fare
ye well.                                         *Exit.*
PISTOL
Doth Fortune play the huswife with me now?               79
News have I that my Doll is dead                         80
I'th' spital of a malady of France,                     81
And there my rendezvous is quite cut off.
Old I do wax, and from my weary limbs                    83
Honor is cudgeled. Well, bawd I'll turn,
And something lean to cutpurse of quick hand.            85
To England will I steal, and there I'll steal;
And patches will I get unto these cudgeled scars,
And swear I got them in the Gallia wars.        *Exit.*  88

❖

## [5.2]

*Enter, at one door, King Henry, Exeter, Bedford,
[Gloucester, Clarence,] Warwick, [Westmorland,]
and other lords; at another, Queen Isabel, the
[French] King, the Duke of Burgundy, [the
Princess Katharine, Alice,] and other French.*

KING HENRY
Peace to this meeting, wherefor we are met!
Unto our brother France and to our sister,               2
Health and fair time of day; joy and good wishes
To our most fair and princely cousin Katharine;          4
And, as a branch and member of this royalty,             5
By whom this great assembly is contrived,
We do salute you, Duke of Burgundy;
And princes French, and peers, health to you all!
FRENCH KING
Right joyous are we to behold your face,
Most worthy brother England. Fairly met!
So are you, princes English, every one.

---

**20 Parca's** (The Parcae, or Fates, spun, drew out, and cut the thread of destiny.)  **21 qualmish** squeamish, nauseated  **28 Cadwallader** seventh-century Welsh warrior king.  **goats** (Pistol makes the customary taunt that the Welsh were goatherds.)  **35 mountain squire** i.e., a squire owning mountainous, poor land  **36 squire of low degree** (Allusion to a popular medieval romance, *The Squire of Low Degree*. Fluellen threatens to make Pistol into a lowly, contemptible figure, towered over by a mountain squire.)  **37 fall** to eat.  **38 astonished** dazed, terrified  **40 pate** head  **41 green** raw  **42 coxcomb** fool's cap; here, the scalp.  **52 Much . . . you** Much good may it do you  **54 broken** bleeding (not "fractured")  **57 groat** fourpenny coin  **62 in earnest of** as a down payment for

**70 respect** consideration  **71 predeceased valor** valor of those now dead  **72–3 gleeking and galling** mocking and scoffing  **79 huswife** hussy, fickle jade  **80 Doll** (At 2.1.17–18 we learn that Pistol was married to Nell Quickly. The similarity of *Doll* and *Nell* could suggest a textual error here, or authorial forgetfulness, or a change in the characters' fortunes.)  **81 spital** hospital.  **malady of France** venereal disease  **83 wax** grow  **85 something lean to** I'll incline somewhat to  **88 Gallia** French
**5.2. Location: The French court.**
**2 brother, sister** i.e., fellow monarch and his queen  **4 cousin** kinswoman (i.e., allied in royal lineage)  **5 royalty** royal family

QUEEN ISABEL
So happy be the issue, brother England,    12
Of this good day and of this gracious meeting,
As we are now glad to behold your eyes—
Your eyes, which hitherto have borne in them
Against the French that met them in their bent   16
The fatal balls of murdering basilisks.   17
The venom of such looks, we fairly hope,
Have lost their quality, and that this day   19
Shall change all griefs and quarrels into love.   20

KING HENRY
To cry amen to that, thus we appear.

QUEEN ISABEL
You English princes all, I do salute you.

BURGUNDY
My duty to you both, on equal love,
Great Kings of France and England! That I have
  labored
With all my wits, my pains, and strong endeavors
To bring your most imperial Majesties
Unto this bar and royal interview,   27
Your mightiness on both parts best can witness.
Since, then, my office hath so far prevailed
That, face to face and royal eye to eye,
You have congreeted, let it not disgrace me   31
If I demand, before this royal view,   32
What rub or what impediment there is   33
Why that the naked, poor, and mangled Peace,   34
Dear nurse of arts, plenties, and joyful births,
Should not in this best garden of the world,
Our fertile France, put up her lovely visage?   37
Alas, she hath from France too long been chased,
And all her husbandry doth lie on heaps,   39
Corrupting in it own fertility.   40
Her vine, the merry cheerer of the heart,   41
Unprunèd dies; her hedges even-pleached,   42
Like prisoners wildly overgrown with hair,
Put forth disordered twigs; her fallow leas   44
The darnel, hemlock, and rank fumitory   45
Doth root upon, while that the coulter rusts   46
That should deracinate such savagery.   47
The even mead, that erst brought sweetly forth   48
The freckled cowslip, burnet, and green clover,   49
Wanting the scythe, all uncorrected, rank,   50
Conceives by idleness, and nothing teems   51
But hateful docks, rough thistles, kecksies, burrs,   52
Losing both beauty and utility.
And all our vineyards, fallows, meads, and hedges,   54

Defective in their natures, grow to wildness;   55
Even so our houses and ourselves and children   56
Have lost, or do not learn for want of time,
The sciences that should become our country,   58
But grow like savages—as soldiers will
That nothing do but meditate on blood—
To swearing and stern looks, diffused attire,   61
And everything that seems unnatural.
Which to reduce into our former favor   63
You are assembled, and my speech entreats
That I may know the let why gentle Peace   65
Should not expel these inconveniences
And bless us with her former qualities.

KING HENRY
If, Duke of Burgundy, you would the peace,   68
Whose want gives growth to th'imperfections   69
Which you have cited, you must buy that peace
With full accord to all our just demands,
Whose tenors and particular effects   72
You have enscheduled briefly in your hands.   73

BURGUNDY
The King hath heard them, to the which as yet
There is no answer made.

KING HENRY                Well then, the peace,
Which you before so urged, lies in his answer.

FRENCH KING
I have but with a cursitory eye   77
O'erglanced the articles. Pleaseth Your Grace   78
To appoint some of your council presently
To sit with us once more, with better heed
To re-survey them, we will suddenly   81
Pass our accept and peremptory answer.   82

KING HENRY
Brother, we shall.—Go, uncle Exeter,
And brother Clarence, and you, brother Gloucester,
Warwick, and Huntingdon, go with the King,
And take with you free power to ratify,
Augment, or alter, as your wisdoms best
Shall see advantageable for our dignity,   88
Anything in or out of our demands,
And we'll consign thereto.—Will you, fair sister,   90
Go with the princes, or stay here with us?

QUEEN ISABEL
Our gracious brother, I will go with them.
Haply a woman's voice may do some good   93
When articles too nicely urged be stood on.   94

KING HENRY
Yet leave our cousin Katharine here with us.
She is our capital demand, comprised   96
Within the fore-rank of our articles.   97

---

12 issue outcome   16 in their bent (1) as they were directed (2) in their glance   17 fatal balls (1) cannonballs (2) eyeballs.   basilisks (1) large cannon (2) monsters supposed to kill with their gaze.   19 quality characteristic deadliness   20 griefs grievances   27 bar tribunal   31 congreeted greeted each other   32 demand ask   33 rub obstacle. (A term from bowls.)   34 Why that why   37 put up show, lift up   39 husbandry harvest, foison   40 it its   41 Her vine i.e., Her wine grapes   42 even-pleached smoothly intertwined   44 fallow leas uncultivated open fields   45 darnel . . . fumitory i.e., weeds that grow in cultivated land   46 while that while. coulter plow blade   47 deracinate root out   48 even mead level meadow. erst formerly   49 burnet a herb   50 Wanting lacking   51 Conceives gives birth (to weeds).   teems flourishes   52 kecksies dry stalks   54 fallows land plowed and left lying

55 Defective . . . natures naturally inclined to wildness   56 houses households   58 sciences skills   61 diffused disordered   63 reduce . . . favor return to our former good appearance and good graces   65 let hindrance   68 would wish   69 want lack   72 tenors . . . effects general purport and specific details   73 enscheduled drawn up in writing   77 cursitory cursory, hasty   78 Pleaseth May it please   81 suddenly speedily   82 Pass . . . answer deliver our agreed-to and final answer.   88 advantageable advantageous   90 consign agree, subscribe   93 Haply Perhaps   94 nicely punctiliously, with insistence on detail.   stood on insisted on.   96 capital chief   97 fore-rank first row

QUEEN ISABEL
She hath good leave.

*Exeunt omnes. Manent King [Henry]*
*and Katharine [with Alice].*

KING HENRY     Fair Katharine, and most fair,     98
Will you vouchsafe to teach a soldier terms
Such as will enter at a lady's ear
And plead his love suit to her gentle heart?

KATHARINE     Your Majesty shall mock at me. I cannot
speak your England.

KING HENRY     O fair Katharine, if you will love me
soundly with your French heart, I will be glad to hear
you confess it brokenly with your English tongue. Do
you like me, Kate?

KATHARINE     *Pardonnez-moi,* I cannot tell wat is "like
me."

KING HENRY     An angel is like you, Kate, and you are
like an angel.

KATHARINE     [*to Alice*]     *Que dit-il? Que je suis semblable à*     112
*les anges?*     113

ALICE     *Oui, vraiment, sauf Votre Grâce, ainsi dit-il.*     114

KING HENRY     I said so, dear Katharine, and I must not
blush to affirm it.

KATHARINE     *Oh, bon Dieu! Les langues des hommes sont*
*pleines de tromperies.*

KING HENRY     What says she, fair one? That the tongues
of men are full of deceits?

ALICE     *Oui,* dat de tongues of de mans is be full of
deceits. Dat is de Princess.

KING HENRY     The Princess is the better Englishwoman.     123
I'faith, Kate, my wooing is fit for thy understanding.
I am glad thou canst speak no better English, for if
thou couldst, thou wouldst find me such a plain king
that thou wouldst think I had sold my farm to buy my
crown. I know no ways to mince it in love, but directly     128
to say, "I love you." Then if you urge me farther than
to say, "Do you, in faith?" I wear out my suit. Give me     130
your answer, i'faith, do, and so clap hands and a     131
bargain. How say you, lady?

KATHARINE     *Sauf votre honneur,* me understand well.

KING HENRY     Marry, if you would put me to verses or
to dance for your sake, Kate, why, you undid me. For
the one I have neither words nor measure, and for the     136
other I have no strength in measure, yet a reasonable     137
measure in strength. If I could win a lady at leapfrog,     138
or by vaulting into my saddle with my armor on my
back, under the correction of bragging be it spoken, I
should quickly leap into a wife. Or if I might buffet for     141
my love, or bound my horse for her favors, I could lay     142
on like a butcher and sit like a jackanapes, never off.     143
But before God, Kate, I cannot look greenly, nor gasp     144
out my eloquence, nor I have no cunning in protesta-

tion—only downright oaths, which I never use till     146
urged, nor never break for urging. If thou canst love a     147
fellow of this temper, Kate, whose face is not worth     148
sunburning, that never looks in his glass for love of     149
anything he sees there, let thine eye be thy cook. I     150
speak to thee plain soldier. If thou canst love me for
this, take me. If not, to say to thee that I shall die is
true; but for thy love, by the Lord, no. Yet I love thee
too. And while thou liv'st, dear Kate, take a fellow of
plain and uncoined constancy, for he perforce must     155
do thee right, because he hath not the gift to woo in
other places. For these fellows of infinite tongue that
can rhyme themselves into ladies' favors, they do
always reason themselves out again. What? A speaker
is but a prater, a rhyme is but a ballad. A good leg will
fall, a straight back will stoop, a black beard will turn     161
white, a curled pate will grow bald, a fair face will
wither, a full eye will wax hollow; but a good heart,
Kate, is the sun and the moon—or rather the sun and
not the moon, for it shines bright and never changes,
but keeps his course truly. If thou would have such a
one, take me. And take me, take a soldier; take a
soldier, take a king. And what say'st thou then to my
love? Speak, my fair, and fairly, I pray thee.

KATHARINE     Is it possible dat I sould love de *ennemi* of
France?

KING HENRY     No, it is not possible you should love the
enemy of France, Kate; but in loving me you should
love the friend of France, for I love France so well that
I will not part with a village of it. I will have it all mine.
And, Kate, when France is mine and I am yours, then
yours is France and you are mine.

KATHARINE     I cannot tell wat is dat.

KING HENRY     No, Kate? I will tell thee in French, which
I am sure will hang upon my tongue like a new-
married wife about her husband's neck, hardly to be
shook off. *Je quand sur le possession de France, et quand*     182
*vous avez le possession de moi*—let me see, what?     183
Saint Denis be my speed!—*donc vôtre est France et vous*     184
*êtes mienne.* It is as easy for me, Kate, to conquer the     185
kingdom as to speak so much more French. I shall
never move thee in French, unless it be to laugh at
me.

KATHARINE     *Sauf votre honneur, le français que vous parlez,*     189
*il est meilleur que l' anglais lequel je parle.*     190

KING HENRY     No, faith, is't not, Kate. But thy speaking
of my tongue, and I thine, most truly-falsely, must     192
needs be granted to be much at one. But, Kate, dost     193
thou understand thus much English: Canst thou
love me?

KATHARINE   I cannot tell.

KING HENRY   Can any of your neighbors tell, Kate? I'll ask them. Come, I know thou lovest me. And at night, when you come into your closet, you'll question 199 this gentlewoman about me; and I know, Kate, you will to her dispraise those parts in me that you love with your heart. But, good Kate, mock me mercifully, the rather, gentle Princess, because I love thee cruelly. If ever thou be'st mine, Kate, as I have a saving faith within me tells me thou shalt, I get thee with scambling, and thou must therefore needs prove a 206 good soldier-breeder. Shall not thou and I, between Saint Denis and Saint George, compound a boy, half French, half English, that shall go to Constantinople and take the Turk by the beard? Shall we not? What say'st thou, my fair flower-de-luce? 211

KATHARINE   I do not know dat.

KING HENRY   No; 'tis hereafter to know, but now to promise. Do but now promise, Kate, you will endeavor for your French part of such a boy, and for my English moiety take the word of a king and a bachelor. 216 How answer you, *la plus belle Katharine du monde, mon* 217 *très cher et devin déesse?* 218

KATHARINE   Your Majestee 'ave *fausse* French enough 219 to deceive de most *sage demoiselle* dat is *en France.*

KING HENRY   Now, fie upon my false French! By mine honor, in true English, I love thee, Kate; by which honor I dare not swear thou lovest me, yet my blood begins to flatter me that thou dost, notwithstanding the poor and untempering effect of my visage. Now 215 beshrew my father's ambition! He was thinking of civil 226 wars when he got me; therefore was I created with a stubborn outside, with an aspect of iron, that when I 228 come to woo ladies I fright them. But in faith, Kate, the elder I wax the better I shall appear. My comfort is that old age, that ill layer-up of beauty, can do no more spoil upon my face. Thou hast me, if thou hast me, at the worst; and thou shalt wear me, if thou wear me, better and better. And therefore tell me, most fair Katharine, will you have me? Put off your maiden blushes; avouch the thoughts of your heart with the 236 looks of an empress; take me by the hand, and say, "Harry of England, I am thine." Which word thou shalt no sooner bless mine ear withal, but I will tell thee aloud, "England is thine, Ireland is thine, France is thine, and Henry Plantagenet is thine"—who, though I speak it before his face, if he be not fellow with the best king, thou shalt find the best king 243 of good fellows. Come, your answer in broken music! 244 For thy voice is music, and thy English broken. Therefore, queen of all, Katharine, break thy mind to 246 me in broken English. Wilt thou have me?

KATHARINE   Dat is as it shall please de *roi mon père.* 248

KING HENRY   Nay, it will please him well, Kate. It shall please him, Kate.

KATHARINE   Den it sall also content me.

KING HENRY   Upon that I kiss your hand, and I call you my queen.          [*He attempts to kiss her hand.*]

KATHARINE   *Laissez, mon seigneur, laissez, laissez! Ma* 254 *foi, je ne veux point que vous abaissiez votre grandeur* 255 *en baisant la main d'une—Notre Seigneur!—indigne* 256 *serviteur. Excusez-moi, je vous supplie, mon très-puissant* 257 *seigneur.* 258

KING HENRY   Then I will kiss your lips, Kate.

KATHARINE   *Les dames et demoiselles pour être baisées* 260 *devant leur noces, il n'est pas la coutume de France.* 261

KING HENRY   [*to Alice*]   Madam my interpreter, what says she?

ALICE   Dat it is not be de fashion *pour les* ladies of France—I cannot tell wat is *baiser* en Anglish.

KING HENRY   To kiss.

ALICE   Your Majestee *entend* bettre *que moi.* 267

KING HENRY   It is not a fashion for the maids in France to kiss before they are married, would she say?

ALICE   *Oui, vraiment.* 270

KING HENRY   Oh, Kate, nice customs curtsy to great kings. 271 Dear Kate, you and I cannot be confined within the weak list of a country's fashion. We are the makers of 273 manners, Kate; and the liberty that follows our places 274 stops the mouth of all find-faults, as I will do yours, for upholding the nice fashion of your country in denying me a kiss. Therefore, patiently and yielding. [*He kisses her.*] You have witchcraft in your lips, Kate. There is more eloquence in a sugar touch of them than in the tongues of the French council, and they should 280 sooner persuade Harry of England than a general petition of monarchs.—Here comes your father.

*Enter the French power and the English lords.*

BURGUNDY   God save Your Majesty! My royal cousin, teach you our princess English?

KING HENRY   I would have her learn, my fair cousin, how perfectly I love her, and that is good English.

BURGUNDY   Is she not apt?

KING HENRY   Our tongue is rough, coz, and my condi- 288 tion is not smooth; so that, having neither the voice 289 nor the heart of flattery about me, I cannot so conjure up the spirit of love in her that he will appear in his 291 true likeness.

---

**199 closet** private chamber   **206 scambling** the scuffles of war
**211 flower-de-luce** fleur-de-lis, the emblem of France.   **216 moiety** half   **217–18 la plus . . . déesse** the most beautiful Katharine in the world, my very dear and divine goddess.   **219 fausse** i.e., false (both "incorrect" and "deceptive")   **225 untempering** unsettling, unsoftening   **226 beshrew** curses on   **228 aspect** appearance **236 avouch** vouch for, confirm   **243 fellow with** on equal terms with   **244 broken music** (Henry quibbles on the term for music composed in parts for different instruments.)   **246 break** open

**248 de *roi mon père*** the King my father.   **254–8 *Laissez . . . seigneur*** Don't, my lord, don't, don't! By my faith, I do not wish you to lower your greatness by kissing the hand of an—our dear Lord!—unworthy servant; excuse me, I beg you, my most powerful lord. (*Serviteur* is masculine and not appropriately applied to a lady, but the error may be Shakespeare's.)   **260–1 *Les dames . . . France*** It is not customary in France for ladies and young girls to be kissed before their marriage.   **267 *entend . . . moi*** understands better than I. **270 *Oui, vraiment*** Yes, truly.   **271 nice** fastidious   **273 list** limit, barrier   **274 follows our places** attends our (high) rank   **280 they** your lips **288 Our tongue** (1) Our English language (2) My soldierly speech   **288–9 condition** soldierly manner   **291 his** its

BURGUNDY  Pardon the frankness of my mirth, if I
answer you for that. If you would conjure in her, you 294
must make a circle; if conjure up love in her in his true
likeness, he must appear naked and blind. Can you 296
blame her then, being a maid yet rosed over with the 297
virgin crimson of modesty, if she deny the appearance 298
of a naked blind boy in her naked seeing self? It were, 299
my lord, a hard condition for a maid to consign to.  300
KING HENRY  Yet they do wink and yield, as love is 301
blind and enforces.  302
BURGUNDY  They are then excused, my lord, when they
see not what they do.
KING HENRY  Then, good my lord, teach your cousin to
consent winking.
BURGUNDY  I will wink on her to consent, my lord, if 307
you will teach her to know my meaning; for maids,
well summered and warm kept, are like flies at Bar- 309
tholomew-tide: blind, though they have their eyes, 310
and then they will endure handling, which before 311
would not abide looking on.
KING HENRY  This moral ties me over to time and a hot 313
summer; and so I shall catch the fly, your cousin, in 314
the latter end, and she must be blind too.
BURGUNDY  As love is, my lord, before it loves.  316
KING HENRY  It is so; and you may, some of you, thank
love for my blindness, who cannot see many a fair 318
French city for one fair French maid that stands in 319
my way.  320
FRENCH KING  Yes, my lord, you see them perspectively, 321
the cities turned into a maid; for they are all girdled
with maiden walls that war hath never entered.  323
KING HENRY  Shall Kate be my wife?
FRENCH KING  So please you.
KING HENRY  I am content, so the maiden cities you talk 326
of may wait on her. So the maid that stood in the way 327
for my wish shall show me the way to my will.  328
FRENCH KING
We have consented to all terms of reason.
KING HENRY  Is't so, my lords of England?

WESTMORLAND
The King hath granted every article:
His daughter first, and then in sequel all
According to their firm proposèd natures.  333
EXETER
Only he hath not yet subscribèd this:  334
Where Your Majesty demands that the King of France,
having any occasion to write for matter of grant, shall 336
name Your Highness in this form and with this ad- 337
dition, in French, *Notre très cher fils Henri, Roi* 338
*d'Angleterre, Héritier de France*; and thus in Latin, 339
*Praeclarissimus filius noster Henricus, Rex Angliae et* 340
*Haeres Franciae.*
FRENCH KING
Nor this I have not, brother, so denied  342
But your request shall make me let it pass.  343
KING HENRY
I pray you then, in love and dear alliance,
Let that one article rank with the rest,
And thereupon give me your daughter.
FRENCH KING
Take her, fair son, and from her blood raise up
Issue to me, that the contending kingdoms
Of France and England, whose very shores look pale
With envy of each other's happiness,
May cease their hatred, and this dear conjunction
Plant neighborhood and Christian-like accord
In their sweet bosoms, that never war advance
His bleeding sword twixt England and fair France.
LORDS  Amen!
KING HENRY
Now, welcome, Kate; and bear me witness all,
That here I kiss her as my sovereign queen.
                    [*He kisses her.*] *Flourish.*
QUEEN ISABEL
God, the best maker of all marriages,
Combine your hearts in one, your realms in one!
As man and wife, being two, are one in love,
So be there twixt your kingdoms such a spousal  361
That never may ill office, or fell jealousy,  362
Which troubles oft the bed of blessèd marriage,
Thrust in between the paction of these kingdoms  364
To make divorce of their incorporate league;
That English may as French, French Englishmen,
Receive each other. God speak this "Amen"!
ALL  Amen!
KING HENRY
Prepare we for our marriage, on which day,
My lord of Burgundy, we'll take your oath,
And all the peers', for surety of our leagues.  371
Then shall I swear to Kate, and you to me;

---

**294 conjure in her** (with bawdy double meaning of raising up something within her *circle*, line 295)  **296 naked and blind** (as Cupid is
conventionally portrayed)  **297 yet rosed over** still blushing
**298–9 if . . . self** if she refuses to admit the entry of a naked boy in her
sight, or herself being naked?  **300 a hard condition** (Suggesting
erection.)  **consign** agree  **301–2 Yet . . . enforces** Yet young maidens do close their eyes and say yes, prompted to do so by their own
bashfulness and male importunity.  **307 wink on her** give her an
encouraging wink  **309 summered** nurtured  **309–10 Bartholomew-
tide** August 24 (when flies, bees, etc., are sluggish)  **311 handling**
(1) handling of the beehive (2) sexual handling  **313–14 This moral
. . . summer** The lesson of your fable would oblige me to wait for the
heat of summer  **316 As . . . loves** (Love is blind before it loves,
because it cannot yet see the beloved and because love has not yet
opened the lover's eyes.)  **318–20 who . . . my way** i.e., since I am so
preoccupied with Katharine that I have forgotten for the moment
about all those French towns I want. (He is joking; he gets the French
towns, along with her.)  **321 perspectively** i.e., as in an optical
device that presents different images when viewed from different
angles  **323 maiden** unbreached. (With a sexual metaphor, continued
in *entered*.)  **326 so** provided that  **327 wait on her** attend her, go
along with her (as part of her dowry).  **328 will** (1) intention of ruling France (2) sexual desire.

**333 According . . . natures** exactly as specified in the proposals.
**334 subscribèd** agreed to, signed to  **336 for . . . grant** in official
deeds, granting title to land and the like  **337–8 addition** title
**338–9 Notre . . . France** i.e., Our very dear son Henry, King of England, Heir of France  **340 Praeclarissimus** most famous. (Presumably
an error for "Praecharissimus" or "Praecarissimus," "most dear." Shakespeare is following Holinshed, who took the error from Hall.)  **342 so**
so firmly  **343 But** but that  **361 spousal** marriage  **362 ill office**
unfriendly dealings.  **fell** cruel  **364 paction** alliance, compact
**371 surety . . . leagues** guarantees of our negotiated agreement.

And may our oaths well kept and prosperous be!
                              *Sennet.*        *Exeunt.*

# [Epilogue]

*Enter Chorus.*

CHORUS
    Thus far, with rough and all-unable pen,
        Our bending author hath pursued the story,                    2
    In little room confining mighty men,
        Mangling by starts the full course of their glory.            4

Small time, but in that small most greatly lived                      5
    This star of England. Fortune made his sword,
By which the world's best garden he achieved,                         7
    And of it left his son imperial lord.
Henry the Sixth, in infant bands crowned King                         9
    Of France and England, did this king succeed;
Whose state so many had the managing
    That they lost France and made his England bleed,
Which oft our stage hath shown; and, for their sake,                  13
In your fair minds let this acceptance take.         [*Exit.*]        14

---

**Epilogue.**
**2 bending** i.e., under the weight of his task   **4 by starts** in fits and
starts, in fragments

**5 Small time** (Henry V ruled for only nine years, dying at the age of
thirty-five.)   **7 best garden** i.e., France   **9 infant bands** swaddling
clothes   **13 Which . . . shown** (Refers to the three parts of *King Henry
VI.*)   **their** i.e., the actors and the author, the presenters on *our stage*
(line 13)   **14 let . . . take** let this play meet with your approval.

# The Tragedies

Romeo and Juliet

Julius Caesar

Hamlet, Prince of Denmark

Othello, The Moor of Venice

King Lear

Macbeth

Antony and Cleopatra

# Romeo and Juliet

Though a tragedy, *Romeo and Juliet* is, in some ways, more closely comparable to Shakespeare's romantic comedies and early writings than to his later tragedies. Stylistically belonging to the years 1594–1596, it is in the lyric vein of *A Midsummer Night's Dream, The Merchant of Venice,* and *Richard II,* all of which are from the mid 1590s. Like them, it uses a variety of rhyme schemes (couplets, quatrains, octets, and even sonnets) and revels in punning, metaphor, and wit combat. It is separated in tone and in time from the earliest of the great tragedies, *Julius Caesar* and *Hamlet,* by almost half a decade, and, except for the experimental *Titus Andronicus,* it is the only tragedy (that is not also a history) that Shakespeare wrote in the first decade of his career—a period devoted otherwise to romantic comedy and English history.

Like many comedies, *Romeo and Juliet* is a love story, celebrating the exquisite, brief joy of youthful passion. Even its tragic ending stresses the poignancy of that brief beauty, not the bitter futility of love, as in *Troilus and Cressida* or *Othello.* The tragic ending of *Romeo and Juliet* underscores the observation made by a vexed lover in *A Midsummer Night's Dream* that "The course of true love never did run smooth" (1.1.134). True love in *Romeo and Juliet,* as in *A Midsummer Night's Dream,* is destined to be crossed by differences in blood or family background, differences in age, arbitrary choices of family or friends, or uncontrollable catastrophes, such as war, death, and sickness. Love is thus, as in *A Midsummer Night's Dream,* "momentary as a sound, / Swift as a shadow, short as any dream," swallowed up by darkness; "So quick bright things come to confusion" (1.1.143–9). A dominant pattern of imagery in *Romeo and Juliet* evokes a corresponding sense of suddenness and violence: fire, gunpowder, hot blood, lightning, the inconstant wind, the storm-tossed or shipwrecked vessel. The beauty of a love that is so threatened and so fragile is intensified by the brevity of the experience. A tragic outcome therefore affirms the uniqueness and pristine quality of youthful ecstasy. The flowering and fading of a joy "too rich for use, for earth too dear" (1.5.48), does not so much condemn the unfeeling world as welcome the martyrdom of literally dying for love.

As protagonists, Romeo and Juliet lack tragic stature by any classical definition or in terms of the medieval convention of the Fall of Princes. The lovers are not extraordinary except in their passionate attachment to one another. They belong to prominent merchant families rather than to the nobility. They (especially Juliet) are very young, more so than any other of Shakespeare's tragic protagonists, and are indeed younger than most couples marrying in England at the time the play was written; Juliet is not yet fourteen (1.2.9, 1.3.13). Romeo and Juliet's dilemma of parental opposition is of the domestic sort often found in comedy. In fact, several characters in the play partly resemble the conventional character types of the Latin comic playwright Plautus or of Italian neoclassical comedy: the domineering father who insists that his daughter marry according to his choice, the unwelcome rival wooer, the garrulous and bawdy nurse, and, of course, the lovers. The Italian *novella,* to which Shakespeare often turned for his plots, made use of these same types and paid little attention to the classical precept that protagonists in a tragic story ought to be persons of high rank who are humbled through some inner flaw, or hamartia.

The story of Romeo and Juliet goes back ultimately to the fifth-century A.D. Greek romance of *Ephesiaca,* in which we find the motif of the sleeping potion as a means of escaping an unwelcome marriage. Masuccio of Salerno, in his *Il Novellino,* in 1476, combined the narrative of the heroine's deathlike trance and seeming burial alive with that of the hero's tragic failure to receive news from the friar that she is still alive. Luigi da Porto, in his *novella* (c. 1530), set the scene at Verona, provided the names of Romeo and Giulietta for the hero and heroine, added the account of their feuding families, the Montecchi and Cappelletti, introduced the killing of Tybalt (Theobaldo), and provided other important details. Luigi's version was followed by Matteo Bandello's famous *Novelle* of 1554, which was translated into French by Pierre Boaistuau (1559). The French version became the source for Arthur Brooke's long narrative poem in English, *The Tragical History of Romeus and Juliet* (1562). Brooke mentions having seen a play on the subject, but it is doubtful that Shakespeare knew this old play or, if he did know it, made use of it. Brooke's poem was his chief and probably only source. Shakespeare has condensed Brooke's action from nine months to less than a week, has greatly expanded the role of Mercutio, and has given to the Nurse a warmth and humorous richness not found in the usual Italian duenna, or *balia*. He has also tidied up the Friar's immorality and deleted the anti-papal tone. Inheriting from Brooke a cautionary narrative against unruly yielding to sexual passion, in the homiletic vein of Puritan preachers, Shakespeare instead sympathizes with the perils of young lovers whose desires are unappreciated by an unfeeling world. Throughout all these changes, Shakespeare retains Brooke's romantic (rather than classically tragic) conception of love overwhelmed by external obstacles.

Like the romantic comedies, *Romeo and Juliet* is often funny and bawdy. Samson and Gregory in the first scene are slapstick cowards, hiding behind the law and daring to quarrel only when reinforcements arrive. The Nurse delights us with her earthy recollections of the day she weaned Juliet: the child tasting "the wormwood on the nipple / Of my dug" (1.3.31–2), the warm Italian sun, an earthquake, the Nurse's husband telling his lame but often-repeated bawdy joke about women falling on their backs. Mercutio employs his inventive and sardonic humor to twit Romeo for lovesickness and the Nurse for her pomposity. She, in turn, scolds Peter and plagues Juliet (who is breathlessly awaiting news from Romeo) with a history of her back ailments. Mercutio and the Nurse are among Shakespeare's bawdiest characters. Their wry and salacious view of love contrasts with the nobly innocent and yet physically passionate love of Romeo and Juliet. Mercutio and the Nurse cannot take part in the play's denouement; one dies, misinterpreting Romeo's appeasement of Tybalt, and the other proves insensitive to Juliet's depth of feeling. Yet the disappearance of these engaging companions takes from the play some of its vitality and most of its funniness. The death of Tybalt turns the play from comedy to tragedy.

The lovers, too, are at first well suited to Shakespearean romantic comedy. When we meet Romeo, he is not in love with Juliet at all, despite the play's title, but is mooning over a "hardhearted wench" (in Mercutio's words) named Rosaline. This "goddess" appropriately never appears in the play; she is almost a disembodied idea in Romeo's mind, a scornful beauty like Phoebe in *As You Like It*. Romeo's love for her is tedious and self-pitying, like that of the conventional wooer in a sonnet sequence by Francesco Petrarch or one of his imitators. Juliet, although not yet fourteen, must change all this by teaching Romeo the nature of true love. She will have none of his shopworn clichés learned in the service of Rosaline, his flowery protestations and swearing by the moon, lest they prove to be love's perjuries. With her innocent candor, she insists (like many heroines of the romantic comedies) on dispelling the mask of pretense that lovers too often show one another. "Capulet" and "Montague" are mere labels, not the inner self. Although Juliet would have been more coy, she confesses, had she known that Romeo was overhearing her, she will now "prove more true / Than those that have more cunning to be strange" (2.2.100–1). She is more practical than he in assessing danger and making plans. Later she also proves herself remarkably able to bear misfortune.

The comedy of the play's first half is, to be sure, over-shadowed by the certainty of disaster. The opening chorus plainly warns us that the lovers will die. They are "star-crossed," and they speak of themselves as such. Romeo fears "Some consequence yet hanging in the stars" when he reluctantly goes to the Capulets' feast (1.4.107); after he has slain Tybalt, he cries, "Oh, I am fortune's fool!" (3.1.135); and, at the news of Juliet's supposed death, he proclaims, "Then I defy you, stars!" (5.1.24). Yet in what sense are Romeo and Juliet "star-crossed"? The concept is deliberately broad in this play, encompassing many factors, such as hatred, bumbling, bad luck, and simple lack of awareness.

The first scene presents feuding as a major cause in the tragedy. The quarrel between the two families is so ancient that the original motives are no longer even discussed. Inspired by the "fiery" Tybalt, factionalism pursues its mindless course, despite the efforts of the Prince to end it. Although the elders of both families talk of peace, they call for their swords quickly enough when a fray begins. Still, this senseless hatred does not lead to tragedy until its effects are fatally complicated through misunderstanding. With poignant irony, good intentions are repeatedly undermined by lack of knowledge. We can see why Juliet does not tell her family of her secret marriage with a presumably hated Montague, but, in fact, Capulet has accepted Romeo as a guest in his house under the terms of chivalric hospitality, praising him as a "virtuous and well governed youth" (1.5.69). For all his dictatorial ways, and the manifest advantages he may see in marrying his daughter to an aristocrat like Paris, Capulet would, of course, never propose the match if he knew his daughter to be married already. Not knowing of Juliet's marriage, he and his wife can only interpret her refusal to marry Paris as caprice. Count Paris himself is victim of this tragedy of unawareness. He is an eminently suitable wooer for Juliet, rich and nobly born, considerate, peace-loving, and deeply fond of Juliet (as he shows by his private and sincere grief at her tomb). Certainly, he would never intentionally woo a married woman. Not knowing, he plays the unattractive role of the rival wooer and dies for it. Similarly, Mercutio cannot understand Romeo's seemingly craven behavior toward Tybalt and so begins the duel that leads to Romeo's banishment. The final scene, with Friar Laurence's retelling of the story, allows us to see the survivors confronted with what they have all unknowingly done.

Chance, or accident, plays a role of importance equal to that of hatred and unawareness. An outbreak of the plague prevents Friar John from conveying Friar Laurence's letter to Romeo at Mantua. Friar Laurence, going hurriedly to the Capulets' tomb, arrives in time for Juliet's awakening but some minutes after Romeo has killed Paris and taken poison. Juliet awakens only moments later. The Watch comes just too late to prevent her suicide. Friar Laurence expresses well the sense of frustration at plans gone awry by such narrow margins: "what an unkind hour / Is guilty of this lamentable chance!" (5.3.145–6). Earlier, Capulet's decision to move the wedding date up one day has crucially affected the timing. Human miscalculation contributes also to the catastrophe: Mercutio is killed under Romeo's arm, and Friar Laurence wonders unhappily if any of his complicated plans "Miscarried by my fault" (5.3.267). Character and human decision play a part in this tragedy, for Romeo should not have dueled with Tybalt, no matter what the provocation. In choosing to kill Tybalt, he has deliberately cast aside as "effeminate" the gentle and forgiving qualities he has learned from his love of Juliet (3.1.113) and thus is guilty of a rash and self-destructive action. To ascribe the cause of the tragedy in Aristotelian fashion to his and Juliet's impulsiveness is, however, to ignore much of the rest of the play.

Instead, the ending of the play brings a pattern out of the seeming welter of mistakes and animosities. "A greater power than we can contradict / Hath thwarted our intents," says Friar Laurence, suggesting that the seeming bad luck of the delayed letter was, in fact, the intent of a mysterious higher intelligence (5.3.153–4). Prince Escalus, too, finds a necessary meaning in the tragic event. "See what a scourge is laid upon your hate," he admonishes the Montagues and Capulets, "That heaven finds means to kill your joys with love." Romeo and Juliet are "Poor sacrifices of our enmity" (lines 292–304). As the Prologue had foretold, their deaths will "bury their parents' strife"; the families' feud is a stubborn evil force "Which, but their children's end, naught could remove." Order is preciously restored; the price is great, but the sacrifice nonetheless confirms a sense of a larger intention in what had appeared to be simply hatred and misfortune. Throughout the play, love and

hate are interrelated opposites, yoked through the rhetorical device of oxymoron, or inherent contradiction. Romeo apostrophizes, "O brawling love, O loving hate" (1.1.176), and Juliet later echoes his words: "My only love sprung from my only hate" (1.5.139). This paradox expresses a conflict in humankind, as in the universe itself. "Two such opposèd kings encamp them still / In man as well as herbs," says Friar Laurence, "grace and rude will" (2.3.27–8). Hatred is a condition of our corrupted wills, of our fall from grace, and it attempts to destroy what is gracious in human beings. In this cosmic strife, love must pay the sacrifice, as Romeo and Juliet do with their lives, but, because their deaths are finally perceived as the cost of so much hatred, the two families come to terms with their collective guilt and resolve henceforth to be worthy of the sacrifice.

Structurally, *Romeo and Juliet* gives considerable prominence to the feuding of the two families. Public scenes occur at key points—at beginning, middle, and end (1.1, 3.1, and 5.3)—and each such scene concerns violence and its consequences. The play begins with a brawl. Tybalt is a baleful presence in 1.1 and 3.1, implacably bent on vengeance. The three public scenes are alike, too, in that they bring into confrontation the entire families of Capulets and Montagues, who call for swords and demand reprisal from the state for what they themselves have set in motion. Prince Escalus dominates these three public scenes. He must offer judgment in each, giving the families fair warning, then exiling Romeo for Tybalt's death, and finally counseling the families on the meaning of their collective tragedy. He is a spokesman for public order and security ("Mercy but murders, pardoning those that kill," 3.1.196), even though he is also unable to prevent the tragedy. He stands above the conflict and yet is affected by it; his own kinsman, Mercutio, is one of the casualties. For all his dignity and impartiality, Escalus's official function is somehow tangential to the central emotional experience of the play. The law does not provide a remedy. Still, it can preside and arbitrate. To Escalus is given the final speech promising both punishment and pardon, and it is he who sums up the paradoxical interdependence of love and hate. Although the morning after the catastrophe brings with it sorrow, it also brings peace, however "glooming." Escalus is master of ceremonies for a restored order through which the families and we are reconciled to what has occurred.

In good part, the public scenes of the play serve to frame the love plot and the increasing isolation of the separated lovers, but these public scenes have a function of their own to the extent that the tragedy has touched and altered everyone. The final tableau is not the kiss of the dying lovers but the handclasp of the reconciled fathers. The long, last public ceremonial is important because, although the private catastrophe of the lovers is unalterably complete, recognition occurs only when the Friar recounts at great length to all the community the story we already know. As we watch the bereaved families responding with shock to the story of Romeo and Juliet's tragedy, we understand the reason for its length: only when it is too late do the families begin to comprehend their own complicity in the disaster that has occurred. This recognition is not that of the protagonists, as in the Aristotelian conception of recognition, nor does it accompany a reversal in the love tragedy; that reversal already has taken place in Romeo's banishment and the lovers' deaths. This lack of correspondence with an Aristotelian definition of tragedy is not, however, a structural flaw; rather, it is a manifestation of the dual focus of the tragedy on the lovers and on all Verona. The city itself is a kind of protagonist, suffering through its own violence and coming at last to the sad comfort that wisdom brings.

The timeless nature of a tragic story about young lovers has resulted in its being an irresistible vehicle for modern updatings in the theater and in film, many of them highly successful in bringing the play into the lives of modern and young audiences. Productions in this vein have raised important questions about the protagonists' attitudes toward love and the nature of the social environment in which their tragedy occurs. The play's vivid bawdry embraces an atmosphere of hedonism that can be understood, implicitly at least, in terms of the sexual revolution of the 1960s and afterwards. The boy actor who originally played Juliet on Shakespeare's stage has been replaced by Olivia Hussey, for example, in Franco Zeffirelli's popular film of 1968; Hussey is so gorgeously appealing in her first long night-time conversation with Romeo that his insistent "Oh, wilt thou leave me so unsatisfied?" takes on new urgency. Subsequently, the film briefly shows the lovers in bed, unclothed. Mercutio is sometimes portrayed as homosexual: mutedly so in the Zeffirelli film, aggressively so in Terry Hands's 1973 production at Stratford-upon-Avon, and flamboyantly so in Baz Luhrmann's immensely successful film, *Romeo + Juliet*, of 1996. In this last version, Mercutio is an African American drag queen, while Friar Laurence is a New Age priest. Juliet's mother in this same film is hilarious as a pill-popping, chain-smoking, and hard-drinking society dame slithering her ectomorphically slim body into a Cleopatra outfit for the huge masked ball that she and her nouveau riche husband are putting on in their tastelessly expensive block-long mansion—just the sort of parents whom one can count on not to understand their daughter. Luhrmann's Nurse is an Hispanic woman bellowing "Huliet! Huliet!" to remind us that the film is set in a southern United States city like Los Angeles or Miami. (Parts were actually filmed in Mexico City.) The street violence is also Hispanic, with rival gangs setting fire to gas stations and shooting automatic weapons during high-speed car chases. This updating of the violence with which the play begins owes some of its inspiration, presumably, to Leonard Bernstein's *West Side Story* (1957), set in Spanish Harlem.

Such innovations are at their best when they point to the play's insistent dramatization of violence and love in conflict. What responsibility does society bear for youthful tragedy when the models for behavior available to young people are what they are in today's world? How can a young man like Romeo escape the peer pressures of gang loyalties and macho stereotypes? Romeo struggles against these pressures in his crucial moment of decision; knowing that Juliet has taught him a better way, he yet succumbs to the mores of his tribe and to his own need to revenge on Tybalt the death of Mercutio. In these modern productions, as in the play itself, the violent response is too believable. As Friar Laurence says, "grace and rude will" do battle within the human psyche, too often with tragic outcome, and young love must pay the price.

# Romeo and Juliet

[Dramatis Personae

CHORUS

ESCALUS, *Prince of Verona*
MERCUTIO, *the Prince's kinsman and Romeo's friend*
PARIS, *a young count and kinsman of the Prince*
PAGE *to Count Paris*

MONTAGUE
MONTAGUE'S WIFE
ROMEO, *son of the Montagues*
BENVOLIO, *Montague's nephew and Romeo's friend*
ABRAHAM, *a servant of the Montague household*
BALTHASAR, *a servant of the Montague household attending Romeo*

CAPULET
CAPULET'S WIFE
JULIET, *daughter of the Capulets*
NURSE
TYBALT, *nephew of Capulet's Wife*

SCENE: *Verona; Mantua*]

PETRUCHIO, *Capulet's kinsman*
SECOND CAPULET, *an old man, Capulet's kinsman*
PETER, *a servant of the Capulet household attending the Nurse*
SAMSON,
GREGORY,
ANTHONY,
POTPAN,
CLOWN *or* SERVANT,
*Other* SERVANTS,
} *servants of the Capulet household*

FRIAR LAURENCE,
FRIAR JOHN,
} *Franciscan friars*

APOTHECARY
*Three* MUSICIANS (*Simon Catling, Hugh Rebeck, and James Soundpost*)
*Three* WATCHMEN

*Citizens, Maskers, Torchbearers, Guards, Servants, and Attendants*

## The Prologue

[*Enter Chorus.*]

CHORUS
Two households, both alike in dignity,                                    1
　In fair Verona, where we lay our scene,
From ancient grudge break to new mutiny,                                 3
　Where civil blood makes civil hands unclean.                          4
From forth the fatal loins of these two foes
　A pair of star-crossed lovers take their life;                         6
Whose misadventured piteous overthrows                                   7

Doth with their death bury their parents' strife.
The fearful passage of their death-marked love,                          9
　And the continuance of their parents' rage,
Which, but their children's end, naught could remove,
　Is now the two hours' traffic of our stage;                          12
The which if you with patient ears attend,
What here shall miss, our toil shall strive to mend.                    14
                                                        [*Exit.*]

❖

**Prologue.**
**1–14** (The Prologue is in the form of a sonnet.)
**1 dignity** rank, status   **3 mutiny** strife, discord   **4 Where . . . unclean** where citizens' hands uncivilly are stained in civil strife with their fellow citizens' blood.   **6 star-crossed** thwarted by destiny, by adverse stars   **7 misadventured** unlucky

**9 passage** progress   **12 two hours' traffic** A conventional way of referring to the length of stage performances in the early modern period, not to be taken too literally, but indicative of a brisk pace   **14 What . . . mend** what is defective or inadequate in the short summary I have given you here, the actors' efforts in the following two hours will strive amply and fully to make clear.

464

# [1.1]

*Enter Samson and Gregory, with swords*
*and bucklers, of the house of Capulet.*

SAMSON   Gregory, on my word, we'll not carry coals.    1

GREGORY   No, for then we should be colliers.    2

SAMSON   I mean, an we be in choler, we'll draw.    3

GREGORY   Ay, while you live, draw your neck out of    4
collar.    5

SAMSON   I strike quickly, being moved.    6

GREGORY   But thou art not quickly moved to strike.

SAMSON   A dog of the house of Montague moves me.    8

GREGORY   To move is to stir, and to be valiant is to
stand. Therefore, if thou art moved, thou run'st away.    10

SAMSON   A dog of that house shall move me to stand. I
will take the wall of any man or maid of Montague's.    12

GREGORY   That shows thee a weak slave, for the    13
weakest goes to the wall.    14

SAMSON   'Tis true, and therefore women, being the
weaker vessels, are ever thrust to the wall. Therefore I    16
will push Montague's men from the wall and thrust
his maids to the wall.

GREGORY   The quarrel is between our masters and us    19
their men.    20

SAMSON   'Tis all one. I will show myself a tyrant: when    21
I have fought with the men, I will be civil with the
maids—I will cut off their heads.

GREGORY   The heads of the maids?

SAMSON   Ay, the heads of the maids, or their maidenheads. Take it in what sense thou wilt.    26

GREGORY   They must take it in sense that feel it.    27

SAMSON   Me they shall feel while I am able to stand,    28
and 'tis known I am a pretty piece of flesh.    29

GREGORY   'Tis well thou art not fish; if thou hadst, thou    30
hadst been Poor John. Draw thy tool. Here comes of    31
the house of Montagues.

*Enter two other Servingmen*
*[Abraham and another].*

SAMSON   My naked weapon is out. Quarrel, I will back
thee.

GREGORY   How, turn thy back and run?

SAMSON   Fear me not.    36

GREGORY   No, marry. I fear thee!    37

SAMSON   Let us take the law of our side. Let them    38
begin.

GREGORY   I will frown as I pass by, and let them take it
as they list.    41

SAMSON   Nay, as they dare. I will bite my thumb at    42
them, which is disgrace to them if they bear it.
                    *[Samson makes taunting gestures.]*

ABRAHAM   Do you bite your thumb at us, sir?

SAMSON   I do bite my thumb, sir.

ABRAHAM   Do you bite your thumb at us, sir?

SAMSON   *[aside to Gregory]*   Is the law of our side if I
say ay?

GREGORY   *[aside to Samson]*   No.

SAMSON   *[to Abraham]*   No, sir, I do not bite my thumb
at you, sir, but I bite my thumb, sir.

GREGORY   Do you quarrel, sir?

ABRAHAM   Quarrel, sir? No, sir.

SAMSON   But if you do, sir, I am for you. I serve as good
a man as you.

ABRAHAM   No better.

SAMSON   Well, sir.

*Enter Benvolio.*

GREGORY   *[to Samson]*   Say "better." Here comes one of    58
my master's kinsmen.    59

SAMSON   *[to Abraham]*   Yes, better, sir.

ABRAHAM   You lie.

SAMSON   Draw, if you be men. Gregory, remember thy
washing blow.    *They fight.*    63

BENVOLIO   Part, fools!
Put up your swords. You know not what you do.

*Enter Tybalt [with sword drawn].*

TYBALT
What, art thou drawn among these heartless hinds?    66
Turn thee, Benvolio. Look upon thy death.

BENVOLIO
I do but keep the peace. Put up thy sword,
Or manage it to part these men with me.    69

TYBALT
What, drawn and talk of peace? I hate the word
As I hate hell, all Montagues, and thee.
Have at thee, coward!    *[They fight.]*    72

*Enter three or four Citizens with clubs*
*or partisans.*

---

**1.1. Location: Verona. A public place.**
**0.2 *bucklers*** small shields   **1 carry coals** i.e., endure insults.   **2 colliers**
(Coal carriers were regarded as dirty and of evil repute.)   **3 an** if.
**choler** anger (produced by one of the four humors).   **draw** draw
swords.   **5 collar** i.e., hangman's noose. (With pun on *colliers* and
*choler*.)   **6 moved** i.e., to anger. (With pun in next line.)   **8 moves**
incites   **10 stand** i.e., stand one's ground.   **12 take the wall** take the
cleaner side of the walk nearest the wall, thus forcing others out into
the gutter   **13–14 the weakest . . . wall** (A proverb expressing the
idea that the weakest are always forced to give way.)   **16 weaker
vessels** (Saint Paul bids husbands give honor to their wives "as unto
the weaker vessel," 1 Peter 3:7.)   **thrust to the wall** (With suggestion
of amorous assault.)   **19–20 between . . . men** i.e., between the males
of one household and the males of the other household; we have
no quarrel with the women.   **21 'Tis all one** It comes to the same
thing.   **26 what sense** whatever meaning   **27 They . . . feel it** i.e., It
is the maids who must receive by way of physical sensation (*sense*)
what I have to offer, because they are the ones who can feel it.
**28 stand** (With suggestion of "have an erection," continued in
the next few lines in *draw thy tool* and *my naked weapon is out.*)
**29–30 flesh . . . fish** (Refers to the proverbial phrase, "neither fish nor
flesh.")   **31 Poor John** hake salted and dried—a poor Lenten kind
of food. (Probably with a bawdy suggestion of sexual insufficiency.)
**comes of** i.e., come members of

**36 Fear** Mistrust. (But Gregory deliberately misunderstands in the
next line, saying, in effect, "No indeed, do you think I'd be afraid of
you?")   **37 marry** i.e., indeed. (Originally an oath, "by the Virgin
Mary.")   **38 take the law of** have the law on   **41 list** please.   **42 bite
my thumb** i.e., make an insulting and probably obscene gesture
**58–9 one . . . kinsmen** i.e., Tybalt, who is approaching. (Not Benvolio,
who has just entered unobserved by the servingmen.)   **63 washing**
slashing with great force   **66 heartless hinds** cowardly menials.
**69 manage** use   **72 Have at thee** i.e., On guard, here I come
**72.2 *partisans*** long-handled spears.

CITIZENS
Clubs, bills, and partisans! Strike! Beat them down!    73
Down with the Capulets! Down with the Montagues!    74

*Enter old Capulet in his gown, and his Wife.*

CAPULET
What noise is this? Give me my long sword, ho!    75
CAPULET'S WIFE
A crutch, a crutch! Why call you for a sword?
CAPULET
My sword, I say! Old Montague is come
And flourishes his blade in spite of me.    78

*Enter old Montague and his Wife.*

MONTAGUE
Thou villain Capulet!—Hold me not; let me go.
MONTAGUE'S WIFE
Thou shalt not stir one foot to seek a foe.    80

*Enter Prince Escalus, with his train.*

PRINCE
Rebellious subjects, enemies to peace,
Profaners of this neighbor-stainèd steel—    82
Will they not hear? What, ho! You men, you beasts,
That quench the fire of your pernicious rage
With purple fountains issuing from your veins,    85
On pain of torture, from those bloody hands
Throw your mistempered weapons to the ground    87
And hear the sentence of your movèd prince.    88
Three civil brawls, bred of an airy word,    89
By thee, old Capulet, and Montague,
Have thrice disturbed the quiet of our streets
And made Verona's ancient citizens
Cast by their grave-beseeming ornaments    93
To wield old partisans in hands as old,
Cankered with peace, to part your cankered hate.    95
If ever you disturb our streets again
Your lives shall pay the forfeit of the peace.    97
For this time all the rest depart away.
You, Capulet, shall go along with me,
And Montague, come you this afternoon,
To know our farther pleasure in this case,
To old Freetown, our common judgment-place.    102
Once more, on pain of death, all men depart.
*Exeunt [all but Montague, Montague's Wife,*
*and Benvolio].*

MONTAGUE
Who set this ancient quarrel new abroach?    104
Speak, nephew, were you by when it began?    105
BENVOLIO
Here were the servants of your adversary,
And yours, close fighting ere I did approach.
I drew to part them. In the instant came
The fiery Tybalt with his sword prepared,    109
Which, as he breathed defiance to my ears,
He swung about his head and cut the winds
Who, nothing hurt withal, hissed him in scorn.    112
While we were interchanging thrusts and blows,
Came more and more, and fought on part and part    114
Till the Prince came, who parted either part.    115
MONTAGUE'S WIFE
Oh, where is Romeo? Saw you him today?
Right glad I am he was not at this fray.
BENVOLIO
Madam, an hour before the worshiped sun
Peered forth the golden window of the east,    119
A troubled mind drave me to walk abroad,    120
Where, underneath the grove of sycamore
That westward rooteth from this city side,    122
So early walking did I see your son.
Towards him I made, but he was ware of me    124
And stole into the covert of the wood.    125
I, measuring his affections by my own,    126
Which then most sought where most might not be
found,    127
Being one too many by my weary self,
Pursued my humor, not pursuing his,    129
And gladly shunned who gladly fled from me.    130
MONTAGUE
Many a morning hath he there been seen,
With tears augmenting the fresh morning's dew,
Adding to clouds more clouds with his deep sighs;
But all so soon as the all-cheering sun
Should in the farthest east begin to draw
The shady curtains from Aurora's bed,    136
Away from light steals home my heavy son    137
And private in his chamber pens himself,
Shuts up his windows, locks fair daylight out,
And makes himself an artificial night.
Black and portentous must this humor prove
Unless good counsel may the cause remove.
BENVOLIO
My noble uncle, do you know the cause?
MONTAGUE
I neither know it nor can learn of him.

---

**73 Clubs** Rallying cry, summoning apprentices with their clubs.   **bills** long-handled spears with hooked blades   **74.1** *gown* nightgown, dressing gown   **75 long sword** heavy, old-fashioned sword   **78 spite** defiance, despite   **80.1** *train* retinue.   **82 Profaners . . . steel** you who profane your weapons by staining them with neighbors' blood   **85 purple** bloody, dark red   **87 mistempered** (1) having been tempered, or hardened, in hot blood rather than cold water (2) malignant, ill-tempered   **88 movèd** angry   **89 airy** flippant, saucy   **93 grave-beseeming ornaments** i.e., staffs and other appurtenances suited to wise old age   **95 Cankered . . . cankered** corroded (from disuse) . . . malignant   **97 Your . . . peace** death will be the penalty for breaking the peace.   **102 Freetown** (Brooke's translation, in his poem *Romeus and Juliet*, of *Villa Franca*, as found in the Italian story.)   **common** public

**104 set . . . abroach** reopened this old quarrel, set it flowing.   **105 by** near   **109 prepared** drawn, ready   **112 Who . . . withal** which winds, not at all injured thereby   **114 on part and part** on one side and the other   **115 either part** the two parties.   **119 forth** from forth   **120 drave . . . abroad** drove me to take a walk   **122 That . . . side** that grows on the west side of this city   **124 made** moved.   **ware** wary, aware   **125 covert** cover, hiding place   **126 affections** wishes, inclination   **127 Which . . . found** which then chiefly desired a place where I might be alone   **129 humor** mood   **130 who** him who   **136 Aurora** goddess of dawn   **137 heavy** (1) sad (2) the opposite of *light*.   **son** (punning on *sun*, line 134)

**BENVOLIO**
  Have you importuned him by any means?                145
**MONTAGUE**
  Both by myself and many other friends.
  But he, his own affections' counselor,
  Is to himself—I will not say how true,              148
  But to himself so secret and so close,              149
  So far from sounding and discovery,                 150
  As is the bud bit with an envious worm              151
  Ere he can spread his sweet leaves to the air
  Or dedicate his beauty to the sun.
  Could we but learn from whence his sorrows grow,
  We would as willingly give cure as know.

            *Enter Romeo.*

**BENVOLIO**
  See where he comes. So please you, step aside.      156
  I'll know his grievance or be much denied.
**MONTAGUE**
  I would thou wert so happy by thy stay              158
  To hear true shrift.—Come, madam, let's away.       159
            *Exeunt [Montague and his Wife].*
**BENVOLIO**
  Good morrow, cousin.
**ROMEO**                      Is the day so young?    160
**BENVOLIO**
  But new struck nine.
**ROMEO**                      Ay me! Sad hours seem long.
  Was that my father that went hence so fast?
**BENVOLIO**
  It was. What sadness lengthens Romeo's hours?
**ROMEO**
  Not having that which, having, makes them short.
**BENVOLIO**   In love?
**ROMEO**   Out—
**BENVOLIO**   Of love?
**ROMEO**
  Out of her favor where I am in love.
**BENVOLIO**
  Alas, that Love, so gentle in his view,             169
  Should be so tyrannous and rough in proof!          170
**ROMEO**
  Alas, that Love, whose view is muffled still,       171
  Should without eyes see pathways to his will!       172
  Where shall we dine?—Oh, me! What fray was here?
  Yet tell me not, for I have heard it all.
  Here's much to do with hate, but more with love.
  Why, then, O brawling love, O loving hate,
  O anything of nothing first create,                 177
  O heavy lightness, serious vanity,
  Misshapen chaos of well-seeming forms,
  Feather of lead, bright smoke, cold fire, sick health,

  Still-waking sleep, that is not what it is!         181
  This love feel I, that feel no love in this.
  Dost thou not laugh?
**BENVOLIO**          No, coz, I rather weep.           183
**ROMEO**
  Good heart, at what?
**BENVOLIO**              At thy good heart's oppression.
**ROMEO**
  Why, such is love's transgression.
  Griefs of mine own lie heavy in my breast,
  Which thou wilt propagate, to have it pressed       187
  With more of thine. This love that thou hast shown  188
  Doth add more grief to too much of mine own.
  Love is a smoke made with the fume of sighs;
  Being purged, a fire sparkling in lovers' eyes;     191
  Being vexed, a sea nourished with lovers' tears.
  What is it else? A madness most discreet,           193
  A choking gall, and a preserving sweet.
  Farewell, my coz.
**BENVOLIO**          Soft! I will go along.            195
  An if you leave me so, you do me wrong.             196
**ROMEO**
  Tut, I have lost myself. I am not here.
  This is not Romeo; he's some other where.
**BENVOLIO**
  Tell me in sadness, who is that you love?           199
**ROMEO**   What, shall I groan and tell thee?
**BENVOLIO**
  Groan? Why, no, but sadly tell me who.              201
**ROMEO**
  Bid a sick man in sadness make his will—
  A word ill urged to one that is so ill!             203
  In sadness, cousin, I do love a woman.
**BENVOLIO**
  I aimed so near when I supposed you loved.
**ROMEO**
  A right good markman! And she's fair I love.        206
**BENVOLIO**
  A right fair mark, fair coz, is soonest hit.        207
**ROMEO**
  Well, in that hit you miss. She'll not be hit
  With Cupid's arrow. She hath Dian's wit,            209
  And, in strong proof of chastity well armed,        210
  From Love's weak childish bow she lives unharmed.
  She will not stay the siege of loving terms,        212
  Nor bide th'encounter of assailing eyes,            213
  Nor ope her lap to saint-seducing gold.
  Oh, she is rich in beauty, only poor
  That when she dies, with beauty dies her store.     216

**181 Still-waking** continually awake   **183 coz** cousin, kinsman   **187–8 propagate . . . thine** increase by having it, i.e., my own grief, oppressed or made still heavier with your grief on my account. (The image of propagating and pressing is appropriately sexual.)   **191 purged** cleansed, purified   **193 discreet** judicious, prudent   **195 Soft!** i.e., Wait a moment!   **196 An if** If   **199 sadness** seriousness.   **is that** is it that   **201 sadly** seriously. (But Romeo plays on the word, and on *in sadness*, in the sense of "sorrowfully.")   **203 A word** i.e., *sadly* or *in sadness*—too sad a word, says Romeo, for a melancholy lover   **206 fair** beautiful   **207 fair mark** clear, distinct target   **209 Dian's** Diana was huntress and goddess of chastity   **210 proof** armor   **212 stay** submit to   **213 bide** abide, endure   **216 store** wealth. (She will die without children, and therefore her beauty will die with her.)

**145 any means** every means possible.   **148 true** i.e., wise in counseling himself   **149 close** secretive   **150 sounding** being fathomed (to discover deep or inner secrets)   **151 envious worm** malicious grub or larva   **156 So please you** If you please   **158 happy** fortunate, successful   **159 To** as to.   **shrift** confession.   **160 cousin** kinsman.   **169 Love** Cupid.   **view** appearance   **170 in proof** in reality, in experience.   **171 view . . . still** sight is blindfolded always. (Love is blind.)   **172 to his will** to what he wants.   **177 create** created

**BENVOLIO**

Then she hath sworn that she will still live chaste?   217

**ROMEO**

She hath, and in that sparing makes huge waste,   218
For beauty starved with her severity   219
Cuts beauty off from all posterity.
She is too fair, too wise, wisely too fair,
To merit bliss by making me despair.   222
She hath forsworn to love, and in that vow   223
Do I live dead, that live to tell it now.

**BENVOLIO**

Be ruled by me. Forget to think of her.

**ROMEO**

Oh, teach me how I should forget to think!

**BENVOLIO**

By giving liberty unto thine eyes:
Examine other beauties.

**ROMEO**                              'Tis the way
To call hers, exquisite, in question more.   229
These happy masks that kiss fair ladies' brows,
Being black, puts us in mind they hide the fair.
He that is strucken blind cannot forget
The precious treasure of his eyesight lost.
Show me a mistress that is passing fair:   234
What doth her beauty serve but as a note
Where I may read who passed that passing fair?   236
Farewell. Thou canst not teach me to forget.

**BENVOLIO**

I'll pay that doctrine, or else die in debt.   *Exeunt.* 238

❧

## [1.2]

*Enter Capulet, County Paris, and the Clown
[a Servingman].*

**CAPULET**

But Montague is bound as well as I,   1
In penalty alike, and 'tis not hard, I think,
For men so old as we to keep the peace.

**PARIS**

Of honorable reckoning are you both,   4
And pity 'tis you lived at odds so long.
But now, my lord, what say you to my suit?

**CAPULET**

But saying o'er what I have said before:   7
My child is yet a stranger in the world;
She hath not seen the change of fourteen years.
Let two more summers wither in their pride
Ere we may think her ripe to be a bride.

**PARIS**

Younger than she are happy mothers made.

**CAPULET**

And too soon marred are those so early made.
The earth hath swallowed all my hopes but she;
She is the hopeful lady of my earth.   15
But woo her, gentle Paris, get her heart;
My will to her consent is but a part;
And, she agreed, within her scope of choice   18
Lies my consent and fair-according voice.   19
This night I hold an old accustomed feast,   20
Whereto I have invited many a guest
Such as I love; and you among the store,   22
One more, most welcome, makes my number more.
At my poor house look to behold this night
Earth-treading stars that make dark heaven light.   25
Such comfort as do lusty young men feel   26
When well-appareled April on the heel   27
Of limping winter treads, even such delight
Among fresh fennel buds shall you this night   29
Inherit at my house. Hear all, all see,   30
And like her most whose merit most shall be;
Which on more view of many, mine, being one,   32
May stand in number, though in reck'ning none.   33
Come, go with me. [*To the Servingman, giving a paper*]
Go, sirrah, trudge about   34
Through fair Verona; find those persons out
Whose names are written there, and to them say,
My house and welcome on their pleasure stay.   37
*Exit [with Paris].*

**SERVINGMAN**   Find them out whose names are written
here! It is written that the shoemaker should meddle   39
with his yard and the tailor with his last, the fisher   40
with his pencil, and the painter with his nets; but I am   41
sent to find those persons whose names are here writ,   42
and can never find what names the writing person   43
hath here writ. I must to the learned.—In good time!   44

*Enter Benvolio and Romeo.*

**217 still** always   **218 sparing** miserliness   **219 starved with** killed by
**222 To . . . despair** to achieve her own salvation through chaste living
while driving me to the spiritually dangerous state of despair.
**223 forsworn to** renounced, repudiated   **229 in question more** even
more keenly to mind, into consideration.   **234 mistress** i.e., eligible
young woman.   **passing** surpassingly   **236 passed** surpassed
**238 I'll . . . debt** i.e., I'll fulfill my obligation to do that, or feel I have
failed as a friend.
**1.2. Location:** Verona.
**0.1** *County* Count   **1 bound** legally obligated (to keep the peace)
**4 reckoning** estimation, repute   **7 o'er** again

**15 the hopeful . . . earth** i.e., my heir and hope for posterity. (*Earth*
includes property and lands.)   **18–19 And . . . voice** and, if she agrees,
my consent will happily confirm her choice.   **19 according** agreeing
**20 old accustomed** traditional   **22 store** group   **25 Earth-treading
. . . light** i.e., earthly beauty and splendor that will outshine the heavens themselves   **26 lusty** lively   **27 well-appareled** newly clothed
in green   **29 fennel** flowering herb thought to have the power of
awakening passion. (Or perhaps "fennel" should read "female.")
**30 Inherit** possess   **32–3 Which . . . none** i.e., when you have looked
over many ladies, my daughter, being one of them, may be numeri-
cally counted among the lot, but you may not think her worth your
notice. (Capulet refers to the proverbial saying, "one is no number.")
**34 sirrah** (Customary form of address to servants.)   **37 on . . . stay**
wait to serve their pleasure.   **39–41 It is . . . nets** i.e., If a shoemaker
cannot be expected to have any skill with a *yard* (a tailor's yardstick)
and conversely a tailor with a *last* (a shoemaker's form), and similarly
with a painter's *pencil* (a paintbrush) in a fisherman's hands or a net
in a painter's hands, why should I, an illiterate servant, be expected
to be able to read a written note of invitation? (*Meddle, yard*, and *pencil* are often slang expressions for sexual activity and the male sexual
organ, but since *last* and *nets* don't seem to convey sexual meaning
here, the humor is more directed at comic inappropriateness.)
**42 find** locate   **43 find** figure out   **44 In good time** i.e., Here
comes help.

BENVOLIO
Tut, man, one fire burns out another's burning,
One pain is lessened by another's anguish; 46
Turn giddy, and be holp by backward turning; 47
One desperate grief cures with another's languish. 48
Take thou some new infection to thy eye,
And the rank poison of the old will die. 50

ROMEO
Your plaintain leaf is excellent for that. 51

BENVOLIO
For what, I pray thee?

ROMEO           For your broken shin.

BENVOLIO   Why, Romeo, art thou mad?

ROMEO
Not mad, but bound more than a madman is; 54
Shut up in prison, kept without my food,
Whipped and tormented and—Good e'en, good
fellow. 56

SERVINGMAN   God gi' good e'en. I pray, sir, can you read? 57

ROMEO
Ay, mine own fortune in my misery.

SERVINGMAN   Perhaps you have learned it without 59
book. But, I pray, can you read anything you see? 60

ROMEO
Ay, if I know the letters and the language.

SERVINGMAN   Ye say honestly. Rest you merry! 62
                         [*Going.*]

ROMEO    Stay, fellow, I can read.     *He reads the letter.*
"Signor Martino and his wife and daughters,
County Anselme and his beauteous sisters,
The lady widow of Vitruvio,
Signor Placentio and his lovely nieces,
Mercutio and his brother Valentine,
Mine uncle Capulet, his wife, and daughters,
My fair niece Rosaline, and Livia,
Signor Valentio and his cousin Tybalt,
Lucio and the lively Helena."
A fair assembly. Whither should they come?

SERVINGMAN   Up.

ROMEO   Whither? To supper?

SERVINGMAN   To our house.

ROMEO   Whose house?

SERVINGMAN   My master's.

ROMEO
Indeed, I should have asked thee that before.

SERVINGMAN   Now I'll tell you without asking. My
master is the great rich Capulet; and if you be not of
the house of Montagues, I pray, come and crush a cup 82
of wine. Rest you merry!              [*Exit.*]

BENVOLIO
At this same ancient feast of Capulet's 84
Sups the fair Rosaline whom thou so loves,
With all the admirèd beauties of Verona.
Go thither, and with unattainted eye 87
Compare her face with some that I shall show,
And I will make thee think thy swan a crow.

ROMEO
When the devout religion of mine eye 90
Maintains such falsehood, then turn tears to fires; 91
And these who, often drowned, could never die, 92
Transparent heretics, be burnt for liars! 93
One fairer than my love? The all-seeing sun
Ne'er saw her match since first the world begun.

BENVOLIO
Tut, you saw her fair, none else being by,
Herself poised with herself in either eye; 97
But in that crystal scales let there be weighed 98
Your lady's love against some other maid
That I will show you shining at this feast,
And she shall scant show well that now seems best. 101

ROMEO
I'll go along, no such sight to be shown,
But to rejoice in splendor of mine own.    [*Exeunt.*] 103

❖

# [1.3]

*Enter Capulet's Wife and Nurse.*

WIFE
Nurse, where's my daughter? Call her forth to me.

NURSE
Now, by my maidenhead at twelve year old, 2
I bade her come. What, lamb! What, ladybird! 3
God forbid, where's this girl? What, Juliet! 4

*Enter Juliet.*

JULIET   How now? Who calls?
NURSE   Your mother.
JULIET
Madam, I am here. What is your will?

WIFE
This is the matter.—Nurse, give leave awhile, 8
We must talk in secret.—Nurse, come back again;
I have remembered me, thou's hear our counsel. 10
Thou knowest my daughter's of a pretty age.

---

46 **another's anguish** the anguish of another pain   47 **holp . . . turning** helped by turning in the reverse direction   48 **cures . . . languish** is cured by the suffering of a second *grief* or pain.   50 **rank** foul
51 **Your . . . that** i.e., (sardonically) Your proverbial nostrums are about as useful in curing my real grief as is a folk remedy for minor abrasions such as a *broken shin* (line 52) or surface wound on the leg—that is, no use at all.   54 **bound** (The usual treatment for madness.)
56 **Good e'en** Good evening. (Used after noon.)   57 **gi'** give you
59–60 **Perhaps . . . book** (1) Perhaps that's some sort of book that you've committed to memory (2) Misery is something one can learn without knowing how to read.   62 **Rest you merry** i.e., Farewell. (The servingman can see he is getting nowhere.)   82 **crush** i.e., drink

84 **ancient** customary   87 **unattainted** unbiased   90–3 **When . . . liars!** (Romeo, recalling that persons suspected of witchcraft were sometimes thrown into water to see if they would drown or float, and that those who did not drown were declared witches and burned at the stake, protests that whenever he is a heretic in love by looking at some woman other than Rosaline he should be similarly burned by having his own tears turn into flames, since he will have shown that his flood of tears could not drown him, i.e., was insufficient. *Transparent* means "manifest," "clear.")   97 **poised** weighed, balanced   98 **crystal scales** i.e., Romeo's eyes   101 **scant** scarcely
103 **mine own** i.e., the sight of my own Rosaline.
**1.3. Location: Verona. Capulet's house.**
2 **by . . . old** I swear by the virginity I still had when I was twelve
3 **ladybird** (A term of affection.)   4 **God forbid** (A mild oath.)
8 **give leave** leave us   10 **thou's** thou shalt

NURSE
Faith, I can tell her age unto an hour.

WIFE
She's not fourteen.

NURSE                                    I'll lay fourteen of my teeth—
And yet, to my teen be it spoken, I have but four—        14
She's not fourteen. How long is it now
To Lammastide?

WIFE                          A fortnight and odd days.                16

NURSE
Even or odd, of all days in the year,
Come Lammas Eve at night shall she be fourteen.
Susan and she—God rest all Christian souls!—             19
Were of an age. Well, Susan is with God;
She was too good for me. But, as I said,
On Lammas Eve at night shall she be fourteen,
That shall she, marry, I remember it well.               23
'Tis since the earthquake now eleven years,
And she was weaned—I never shall forget it—
Of all the days of the year, upon that day;
For I had then laid wormwood to my dug,                  27
Sitting in the sun under the dovehouse wall.
My lord and you were then at Mantua—
Nay, I do bear a brain! But, as I said,                  30
When it did taste the wormwood on the nipple
Of my dug and felt it bitter, pretty fool,               32
To see it tetchy and fall out wi'th' dug!                33
"Shake" quoth the dovehouse. 'Twas no need, I trow,      34
To bid me trudge!                                        35
And since that time it is eleven years,
For then she could stand high-lone; nay, by the rood,    37
She could have run and waddled all about.
For even the day before, she broke her brow,             39
And then my husband—God be with his soul!
'A was a merry man—took up the child.                    41
"Yea," quoth he, "dost thou fall upon thy face?
Thou wilt fall backward when thou hast more wit,         43
Wilt thou not, Jule?" and, by my halidom,                44
The pretty wretch left crying and said "Ay."
To see now how a jest shall come about!                  46
I warrant, an I should live a thousand years,
I never should forget it. "Wilt thou not, Jule?" quoth
    he,
And, pretty fool, it stinted and said "Ay."              49

WIFE
Enough of this. I pray thee, hold thy peace.

NURSE
Yes, madam. Yet I cannot choose but laugh
To think it should leave crying and say "Ay."
And yet, I warrant, it had upon it brow                  53
A bump as big as a young cockerel's stone—               54
A perilous knock—and it cried bitterly.
"Yea," quoth my husband, "fall'st upon thy face?
Thou wilt fall backward when thou comest to age,
Wilt thou not, Jule?" It stinted and said "Ay."

JULIET
And stint thou too, I pray thee, Nurse, say I.           59

NURSE
Peace, I have done. God mark thee to his grace!          60
Thou wast the prettiest babe that e'er I nursed.
An I might live to see thee married once,                62
I have my wish.

WIFE
Marry, that "marry" is the very theme
I came to talk of. Tell me, daughter Juliet,
How stands your disposition to be married?               66

JULIET
It is an honor that I dream not of.

NURSE
An honor? Were not I thine only nurse,
I would say thou hadst sucked wisdom from thy teat.      69

WIFE
Well, think of marriage now. Younger than you
Here in Verona, ladies of esteem,
Are made already mothers. By my count
I was your mother much upon these years                  73
That you are now a maid. Thus then in brief:
The valiant Paris seeks you for his love.

NURSE
A man, young lady! Lady, such a man
As all the world—why, he's a man of wax.                 77

WIFE
Verona's summer hath not such a flower.

NURSE
Nay, he's a flower, in faith, a very flower.             79

WIFE
What say you? Can you love the gentleman?
This night you shall behold him at our feast.
Read o'er the volume of young Paris' face,
And find delight writ there with beauty's pen;
Examine every married lineament,                         84
And see how one another lends content;                   85
And what obscured in this fair volume lies               86
Find written in the margent of his eyes.                 87
This precious book of love, this unbound lover,          88

---

14 teen sorrow. (Playing on *teen* and *four* in *fourteen.*)  16 Lammastide the days near August 1.  19 Susan the Nurse's own child, who
has evidently died  23 marry i.e., by the Virgin Mary. (A mild oath.)
27 wormwood (A bitter-tasting plant used to wean the child from the
*dug* or "teat.")  30 bear a brain maintain a keen memory.  32 fool
(A term of endearment here.)  33 tetchy peevish, irritable  34 "Shake"
. . . dovehouse i.e., The dovehouse shook.  trow believe, assure you
35 trudge be off quickly.  37 high-lone on her feet, without help.
rood cross  39 broke her brow bruised her forehead (by falling)
41 'A He  43 wit understanding  44 by my halidom (A mild oath:
"by all things holy," but popularly confused with "by my Holy
Dame.")  46 come about come true.  49 it stinted the child ceased
crying. (The use of "it" for an infant was common in Elizabethan
England, as in the German *"das kind."*)

53 it brow its brow  54 cockerel's stone young rooster's testicle
59 say I (With a pun on *said "Ay"* of previous line.)  60 mark
choose  62 An If.  once someday  66 disposition inclination
69 thy teat the teat that nourished you.  73 much . . . years at much
the same age  77 a man of wax as handsome as a figure modeled in
wax.  79 Nay Indeed  84 married lineament harmonized feature
85 And . . . content and see how his handsome features enhance one
another  86–7 And what . . . eyes and whatever you don't fully
grasp by seeing his handsome features, find explained in his eyes, as
though they were a kind of marginal gloss or commentary found in
books.  88 unbound i.e., because not bound in marriage. (With a
double meaning in the continuing metaphor of an unbound book.)

To beautify him, only lacks a cover.                                    89
The fish lives in the sea, and 'tis much pride                          90
For fair without the fair within to hide.                               91
That book in many's eyes doth share the glory,                          92
That in gold clasps locks in the golden story;                          93
So shall you share all that he doth possess
By having him, making yourself no less.

NURSE
No less? Nay, bigger. Women grow by men.                                96

WIFE
Speak briefly, can you like of Paris' love?                             97

JULIET
I'll look to like, if looking liking move;                              98
But no more deep will I endart mine eye
Than your consent gives strength to make it fly.

*Enter Servingman.*

SERVINGMAN    Madam, the guests are come, supper
served up, you called, my young lady asked for, the
Nurse cursed in the pantry, and everything in extremity. I must hence to wait. I beseech you, follow straight. 104
WIFE    We follow thee.                          [*Exit Servingman.*]
                            Juliet, the County stays.             105

NURSE
Go, girl, seek happy nights to happy days.        *Exeunt.*

# [1.4]

*Enter Romeo, Mercutio, Benvolio, with five or
six other masquers; torchbearers.*

ROMEO
What, shall this speech be spoke for our excuse?                         1
Or shall we on without apology?                                          2

BENVOLIO
The date is out of such prolixity.                                       3
We'll have no Cupid hoodwinked with a scarf,                             4
Bearing a Tartar's painted bow of lath,                                  5
Scaring the ladies like a crowkeeper,                                    6
Nor no without-book prologue, faintly spoke                              7
After the prompter, for our entrance;
But let them measure us by what they will,                               9
We'll measure them a measure, and be gone.                              10

ROMEO
Give me a torch. I am not for this ambling.
Being but heavy, I will bear the light.                                 12
MERCUTIO
Nay, gentle Romeo, we must have you dance.
ROMEO
Not I, believe me. You have dancing shoes
With nimble soles; I have a soul of lead                                15
So stakes me to the ground I cannot move.
MERCUTIO
You are a lover; borrow Cupid's wings,
And soar with them above a common bound.                               18
ROMEO
I am too sore enpiercèd with his shaft                                  19
To soar with his light feathers, and so bound
I cannot bound a pitch above dull woe.                                  21
Under love's heavy burden do I sink.
MERCUTIO
And, to sink in it, should you burden love—                            23
Too great oppression for a tender thing.
ROMEO
Is love a tender thing? It is too rough,
Too rude, too boisterous, and it pricks like thorn.
MERCUTIO
If love be rough with you, be rough with love;
Prick love for pricking, and you beat love down.                       28
Give me a case to put my visage in.                                    29
                              [*He puts on a mask.*]
A visor for a visor! What care I                                       30
What curious eye doth quote deformities?                               31
Here are the beetle brows shall blush for me.
BENVOLIO
Come, knock and enter, and no sooner in
But every man betake him to his legs.                                  34
ROMEO
A torch for me. Let wantons light of heart
Tickle the senseless rushes with their heels,                          36
For I am proverbed with a grandsire phrase:                            37
I'll be a candle-holder and look on.                                   38
The game was ne'er so fair, and I am done.                             39

---

**89 a cover** i.e., marriage, an embracing wife.   **90–1 The fish . . . hide** i.e., The fish has its own suitable environment, and similarly in mar- riage the fair Juliet (here imagined as a beautiful book-cover "binding" Paris) would suitably enhance Paris's worth.   **92–3 That book . . . story** i.e., In many persons' eyes, a good story is all the more admira- ble for being handsomely bound. (*Clasps* means [1] book fastenings [2] embraces.)   **96 bigger** i.e., by pregnancy.   **97 like of** be pleased with   **98 liking move** may provoke affection   **104 straight** at once.   **105 County stays** Count (Paris) waits for you.
**1.4. Location: Verona. A street.**
**1 speech** (Masquers were customarily preceded by a messenger or "presenter" with a set speech of compliment.)   **2 on** go on, approach   **3 The date . . . prolixity** Such windy rhetoric is out of fashion.   **4 Cupid** i.e., messenger or "presenter," probably a boy, disguised as Cupid.   **hoodwinked** blindfolded   **5 Tartar's . . . bow** (Tartars' bows, shorter and more curved than the English longbow, were thought to have resembled the old Roman bow with which Cupid was pictured.)   **lath** flimsy wood   **6 crowkeeper** scarecrow   **7 without-book** memorized   **9 measure** judge   **10 measure . . . measure** tread a dance for them

**12 heavy** (1) sad (2) the opposite of *light* (as at 1.1.137)   **15 soul** (Pun- ning on *sole*.)   **18 common bound** (1) ordinary limit (2) normal dance leap.   **19 sore** sorely. (With pun on *soar.*)   **21 bound** leap. (With wordplay on *bound*, "confined," in the previous line.)   **pitch** height. (A term from falconry for the highest point of a hawk's flight.)
**23 And . . . love** i.e., You wouldn't just sink *under* love's heavy bur- den, you'd sink *into* it and burden it. (Suggesting sexual penetration.)
**28 Prick . . . down** i.e., If love gets rough, fight back. (But with bawdy suggestion of *pricking* as a way to satisfy desire and end in detumes- cence.)   **29 case** mask   **30 A visor . . . visor** i.e., A mask for an ugly masklike face.   **31 quote** take notice of   **34 to his legs** to danc- ing.   **36 senseless rushes** reeds used as floor covering, or insensate green rushes   **37 proverbed . . . phrase** furnished with an old prov- erb   **38 candle-holder** i.e., bystander. (Referring to the proverbial idea that one who lacks ability himself can hold the candle and thus provide light for one who is able to act.)   **39 The game . . . done** (Another proverbial truism, that it is best to quit when one is ahead.)

MERCUTIO
Tut, dun's the mouse, the constable's own word.    40
If thou art dun, we'll draw thee from the mire    41
Of—save your reverence—love, wherein thou stickest    42
Up to the ears. Come, we burn daylight, ho!    43
ROMEO
Nay, that's not so.
MERCUTIO    I mean, sir, in delay
We waste our lights in vain, like lamps by day.
Take our good meaning, for our judgment sits    46
Five times in that ere once in our five wits.    47
ROMEO
And we mean well in going to this masque,
But 'tis no wit to go.
MERCUTIO    Why, may one ask?    49
ROMEO
I dreamt a dream tonight.
MERCUTIO    And so did I.    50
ROMEO
Well, what was yours?
MERCUTIO    That dreamers often lie.    51
ROMEO
In bed asleep, while they do dream things true.
MERCUTIO
Oh, then, I see Queen Mab hath been with you.    53
She is the fairies' midwife, and she comes
In shape no bigger than an agate stone    55
On the forefinger of an alderman,    56
Drawn with a team of little atomi    57
Over men's noses as they lie asleep.
Her chariot is an empty hazelnut,
Made by the joiner squirrel or old grub,    60
Time out o' mind the fairies' coachmakers.
Her wagon spokes made of long spinners' legs,    62
The cover of the wings of grasshoppers,
Her traces of the smallest spider web,    64
Her collars of the moonshine's wat'ry beams,    65
Her whip of cricket's bone, the lash of film,    66
Her wagoner a small gray-coated gnat,    67

Not half so big as a round little worm    68
Pricked from the lazy finger of a maid.    69
And in this state she gallops night by night
Through lovers' brains, and then they dream of love;
O'er courtiers' knees, that dream on curtsies straight;    72
O'er lawyers' fingers, who straight dream on fees;
O'er ladies' lips, who straight on kisses dream,
Which oft the angry Mab with blisters plagues
Because their breaths with sweetmeats tainted are.    76
Sometime she gallops o'er a courtier's nose,
And then dreams he of smelling out a suit.    78
And sometime comes she with a tithe-pig's tail    79
Tickling a parson's nose as 'a lies asleep;
Then dreams he of another benefice.    81
Sometime she driveth o'er a soldier's neck,
And then dreams he of cutting foreign throats,
Of breaches, ambuscadoes, Spanish blades,    84
Of healths five fathom deep, and then anon    85
Drums in his ear, at which he starts and wakes,
And being thus frighted swears a prayer or two
And sleeps again. This is that very Mab
That plats the manes of horses in the night,    89
And bakes the elflocks in foul sluttish hairs,    90
Which once untangled much misfortune bodes.    91
This is the hag, when maids lie on their backs,
That presses them and learns them first to bear,    93
Making them women of good carriage.    94
This is she—
ROMEO    Peace, peace, Mercutio, peace!
Thou talk'st of nothing.
MERCUTIO    True, I talk of dreams,
Which are the children of an idle brain,
Begot of nothing but vain fantasy,    98
Which is as thin of substance as the air,
And more inconstant than the wind, who woos
Even now the frozen bosom of the north,
And being angered, puffs away from thence,
Turning his side to the dew-dropping south.
BENVOLIO
This wind you talk of blows us from ourselves.    104
Supper is done, and we shall come too late.
ROMEO
I fear, too early; for my mind misgives    106
Some consequence yet hanging in the stars

**40 dun's . . . word** i.e., "keep still"—just the sort of thing a constable might say. (Matching proverb with proverb, Mercutio answers Romeo's "I am done" by twitting him for being mousy. Constables were much laughed at for inappropriately pompous speech.)
**41–3 If . . . ears** (To Mercutio, Romeo's love melancholy recalls the Christmas game called "Dun is in the mire," in which a heavy log, representing a horse named Dun, was hauled out of an imaginary mire by the players. *Save your reverence* is Mercutio's mock apology for speaking of so improper an expression as being mired up to the ears in love.)
**43 burn daylight** i.e., waste time. (But Romeo quibbles, protesting that it is not literally daytime.)
**46–7 Take . . . wits** Try to understand what I am trying to say (rather than quibbling with phrases like "burn daylight"), for wise judgment is five times more pleased with good meaning than with the ingenious wit of our frail senses.
**49 wit** wisdom (playing on *wits* in line 47; *mean* in line 48 plays on *meaning* in line 46)
**50 tonight** last night.
**51 lie** tell falsehoods. (But Mercutio answers in the sense of "lie down in bed.")
**53 Queen Mab** (Possibly a name of Celtic origin for the Fairy Queen.)
**55 agate stone** (Precious stone often carved with diminutive figures and set in a ring.)
**56 alderman** member of the municipal council
**57 atomi** tiny creatures (atoms)
**60 joiner** furniture maker.   **grub** insect larva (which bores holes in nuts)
**62 spinners'** spiders'
**64 traces** harness for the team of tiny creatures, the *atomi* (line 57), that pull Queen Mab's carriage
**65 collars** part of the harness for the team, fitted over their shoulders, to take the strain when they pull the carriage
**66 film** gossamer thread
**67 wagoner** chariot driver

**68–9 a round . . . maid** (Worms proverbially breed in the fingers of the idle.)
**72 curtsies** bows, obeisances.   **straight** immediately
**76 sweetmeats** candies or candied preserves
**78 smelling . . . suit** i.e., finding a petitioner who will pay for the use of his influence at court.
**79 tithe-pig** pig given to the parson in lieu of money as the parishioner's tithing, or granting of a tenth
**81 benefice** ecclesiastical living.
**84 Of breaches . . . blades** of opening up gaps in fortifications, of ambushes, of swords from Toledo in Spain, where the best swords were made
**85 Of healths . . . deep** of toasts drunk deep
**89 That plats . . . night** (According to popular superstition, the tangles that persistently turn up in the manes of horses were "witches' stirrups," i.e., footholds for witches as they rode.)
**90–1 And bakes . . . bodes** (*Elflocks* or clumps of matted hair were so named because they were imagined to be the work of elves, who would torment anyone so presumptuous as to untangle the elflocks.)
**93 learns** teaches
**94 good carriage** (1) commendable deportment (2) skill in bearing the weight of men in sexual intercourse (3) able subsequently to carry a child.
**98 vain fantasy** delusive imagination
**104 from ourselves** from our plans.
**106 misgives** fears

Shall bitterly begin his fearful date 108
With this night's revels, and expire the term 109
Of a despisèd life closed in my breast
By some vile forfeit of untimely death.
But He that hath the steerage of my course
Direct my suit! On, lusty gentlemen. 113
BENVOLIO Strike, drum. *They march about the stage,* 114
*and* [*retire to one side*].

# [1.5]

*Servingmen come forth with napkins.*

FIRST SERVINGMAN Where's Potpan, that he helps not
to take away? He shift a trencher? He scrape a trencher? 2
SECOND SERVINGMAN When good manners shall lie all
in one or two men's hands, and they unwashed too, 4
'tis a foul thing. 5
FIRST SERVINGMAN Away with the joint stools, remove 6
the court cupboard, look to the plate. Good thou, save 7
me a piece of marchpane, and, as thou loves me, let 8
the porter let in Susan Grindstone and Nell. 9
                        [*Exit Second Servingman.*]
Anthony and Potpan!

[*Enter two more Servingmen.*]

THIRD SERVINGMAN Ay, boy, ready.
FIRST SERVINGMAN You are looked for and called for,
asked for and sought for, in the great chamber.
FOURTH SERVINGMAN We cannot be here and there
too. Cheerly, boys! Be brisk awhile, and the longest 15
liver take all.                  *Exeunt.* 16

*Enter* [*Capulet and family and*] *all the guests
and gentlewomen to the masquers.*

CAPULET [*to the masquers*]
Welcome, gentlemen! Ladies that have their toes
Unplagued with corns will walk a bout with you. 18
Ah, my mistresses, which of you all 19
Will now deny to dance? She that makes dainty, 20
She, I'll swear, hath corns. Am I come near ye now? 21
Welcome, gentlemen! I have seen the day
That I have worn a visor and could tell
A whispering tale in a fair lady's ear
Such as would please. 'Tis gone, 'tis gone, 'tis gone.
You are welcome, gentlemen! Come, musicians, play.
                 *Music plays, and they dance.*

A hall, a hall! Give room! And foot it, girls. 27
[*To Servingmen*] More light, you knaves, and turn the
tables up, 28
And quench the fire; the room is grown too hot.
[*To his cousin*] Ah, sirrah, this unlooked-for sport
comes well. 30
Nay, sit, nay, sit, good cousin Capulet, 31
For you and I are past our dancing days.
How long is't now since last yourself and I
Were in a mask?
SECOND CAPULET By'r Lady, thirty years.
CAPULET
What, man? 'Tis not so much, 'tis not so much;
'Tis since the nuptial of Lucentio,
Come Pentecost as quickly as it will, 37
Some five-and-twenty years, and then we masked.
SECOND CAPULET
'Tis more, 'tis more. His son is elder, sir;
His son is thirty.
CAPULET           Will you tell me that?
His son was but a ward two years ago. 41
ROMEO [*to a Servingman*]
What lady's that which doth enrich the hand
Of yonder knight?
SERVINGMAN I know not, sir.
ROMEO
Oh, she doth teach the torches to burn bright!
It seems she hangs upon the cheek of night
As a rich jewel in an Ethiop's ear—
Beauty too rich for use, for earth too dear! 48
So shows a snowy dove trooping with crows 49
As yonder lady o'er her fellows shows.
The measure done, I'll watch her place of stand, 51
And, touching hers, make blessèd my rude hand. 52
Did my heart love till now? Forswear it, sight! 53
For I ne'er saw true beauty till this night.
TYBALT
This, by his voice, should be a Montague.
Fetch me my rapier, boy. What dares the slave 56
Come hither, covered with an antic face, 57
To fleer and scorn at our solemnity? 58
Now, by the stock and honor of my kin,
To strike him dead I hold it not a sin.
CAPULET
Why, how now, kinsman? Wherefore storm you so?

---

**108 date** appointed time   **109 expire** bring to an end   **113 lusty**
lively   **114 drum** drummer.
**1.5. Location: The action, continuous from the previous scene, is
now imaginatively transferred to a hall in Capulet's house.**
**2 take away** clear the table.   **trencher** wooden dish or plate.
**4 unwashed** (1) dirty (2) belonging to an ignorant or underprivileged
class   **5 foul** (1) dirty (2) bad   **6 joint stools** stools of which the parts
are fitted by a joiner or furniture maker   **7 court cupboard** sideboard.   **plate** silverware.   **Good thou** i.e., You there   **8 marchpane**
cake made from sugar and almonds, marzipan   **9 Susan and Nell**
(Presumably, kitchenmaids that the First Servingman would like to
see admitted to the festivities.)   **15 the longest . . . all** (A proverb
in defense of merriment.)   **18 walk a bout** dance a turn   **19 mis-**
**tresses** ladies   **20 makes dainty** seems coyly reluctant (to dance)
**21 Am . . . now?** Have I hit a sensitive point, struck home?

**27 A hall** i.e., Clear the hall for dancing.   **foot it** dance   **28 turn . . .**
**up** move the tables out of the way for the dancing (by taking up
the boards and then removing the supporting trestles)   **30 sirrah**
(Normally used in addressing social inferiors. Perhaps Capulet uses
a jesting tone toward his kinsman or possibly addresses himself.)
**unlooked-for sport** i.e., arrival of the masquers, providing more
men for the dancing   **31 cousin** (*Cousin* often means "kinsman";
at 1.2.69, "Mine uncle Capulet" is named on the invitation list.)
**37 Pentecost** seventh Sunday after Easter (and never as late as mid-
July, two weeks before Lammas or August 1, when according to 1.3.16,
the play takes place; a seeming inconsistency).   **41 a ward** a minor
under guardianship   **48 dear** precious.   **49 shows** appears   **51 The**
**measure done** When this dance is over.   **her place of stand** where
she stands   **52 hers** her hand.   **rude** rough   **53 Forswear it** Deny
any previous oath   **56 What** How.   **slave** wretch   **57 antic face** grotesque mask   **58 fleer** jeer.   **solemnity** time-honored festivity.

TYBALT
Uncle, this is a Montague, our foe,
A villain that is hither come in spite                                            63
To scorn at our solemnity this night.

CAPULET
Young Romeo is it?

TYBALT                                    'Tis he, that villain Romeo.

CAPULET
Content thee, gentle coz, let him alone.
'A bears him like a portly gentleman,                                            67
And, to say truth, Verona brags of him
To be a virtuous and well governed youth.
I would not for the wealth of all this town
Here in my house do him disparagement.
Therefore be patient; take no note of him.
It is my will, the which if thou respect,
Show a fair presence and put off these frowns,                       74
An ill-beseeming semblance for a feast.                                 75

TYBALT
It fits when such a villain is a guest.
I'll not endure him.

CAPULET                        He shall be endured.
What, goodman boy? I say he shall. Go to!                            78
Am I the master here, or you? Go to.
You'll not endure him! God shall mend my soul,
You'll make a mutiny among my guests!                                81
You will set cock-a-hoop! You'll be the man!                         82

TYBALT
Why, uncle, 'tis a shame.

CAPULET                                    Go to, go to,
You are a saucy boy. Is't so, indeed?
This trick may chance to scathe you. I know what,               85
You must contrary me. Marry, 'tis time.—                             86
Well said, my hearts!—You are a princox, go.                       87
Be quiet, or—More light, more light!—For shame!
I'll make you quiet.—What, cheerly, my hearts!

TYBALT
Patience perforce with willful choler meeting                         90
Makes my flesh tremble in their different greeting.                91
I will withdraw. But this intrusion shall,
Now seeming sweet, convert to bitt'rest gall.          *Exit.*

ROMEO [*to Juliet*]
If I profane with my unworthiest hand                                    94
     This holy shrine, the gentle sin is this:                              95
My lips, two blushing pilgrims, ready stand
     To smooth that rough touch with a tender kiss.

JULIET
Good pilgrim, you do wrong your hand too much,

Which mannerly devotion shows in this;
For saints have hands that pilgrims' hands do touch,   100
     And palm to palm is holy palmers' kiss.                          101

ROMEO
Have not saints lips, and holy palmers too?

JULIET
Ay, pilgrim, lips that they must use in prayer.

ROMEO
Oh, then, dear saint, let lips do what hands do.           104
     They pray; grant thou, lest faith turn to despair.

JULIET
Saints do not move, though grant for prayers' sake.   106

ROMEO
Then move not, while my prayer's effect I take.          107
                                                   [*He kisses her.*]
Thus from my lips, by thine, my sin is purged.

JULIET
Then have my lips the sin that they have took.

ROMEO
Sin from my lips? Oh, trespass sweetly urged!
     Give me my sin again.                  [*He kisses her.*]

JULIET                                    You kiss by th' book.        111

NURSE [*approaching*]
Madam, your mother craves a word with you.
                                                   [*Juliet retires.*]

ROMEO
What is her mother?

NURSE                                    Marry, bachelor,              113
Her mother is the lady of the house,
And a good lady, and a wise and virtuous.
I nursed her daughter that you talked withal.              116
I tell you, he that can lay hold of her
Shall have the chinks.

ROMEO [*aside*]                        Is she a Capulet?             118
Oh, dear account! My life is my foe's debt.                  119

BENVOLIO [*approaching*]
Away, begone! The sport is at the best.                        120

ROMEO
Ay, so I fear; the more is my unrest.
                                   [*The masquers prepare to leave.*]

CAPULET
Nay, gentlemen, prepare not to be gone.
We have a trifling foolish banquet towards.                  123
                                   [*One whispers in his ear.*]
Is it e'en so? Why, then, I thank you all.
I thank you, honest gentlemen. Good night.             125

---

63 **spite** malice   67 **'A** He.   **portly** of good deportment   74 **presence** demeanor   75 **semblance** facial expression   78 **goodman boy** (A belittling term for Tybalt; *goodman* applied to one below the rank of gentleman but still of some substance, like a wealthy farmer.)   **Go to** (An expression of irritation.)   81 **mutiny** disturbance   82 **You ...man!** i.e., You'll set mischief abroach (literally, turn the tap and let the liquor flow)! You'll be the big shot!   85 **scathe** harm   86 **contrary** oppose, thwart.   **'tis time** i.e., it's time you were taught a lesson.   87 **Well said** Well done. (Said to the dancers.)   **princox** saucy boy   90-1 **Patience ... greeting** The attempt to be patient under duress when I am so angry causes me to tremble at the contrary meeting of these two opposite impulses.   94-107 (These lines are in the form of a Shakespearean sonnet; they are followed by a quatrain.)   95 **shrine** i.e., Juliet's hand

100 **saints** i.e., images of saints that are venerated by pilgrims   101 **palmers** pilgrims who have been to the Holy Land and have brought back a palm. (With a pun on the palm of the hand.)   104 **let ... do** let lips touch, just as hands touch.   106 **Saints ... sake** Venerated images and statues of saints remain motionless but nonetheless intercede on behalf of praying pilgrims.   107 **move** (Romeo quibbles on Juliet's metaphorical use of the word *move* to urge that she remain motionless while he kisses her.)   111 **by th' book** by the rules, like an expert.   113 **What** Who   116 **withal** with.   118 **the chinks** plenty of coins, money. (A slang expression.)   119 **dear account** heavy reckoning.   **my foe's debt** due to my foe, at his mercy.   120 **The sport ... best** i.e., It is time to leave. (Refers to the proverb, "When play is at the best, it is time to leave"; compare at 1.4.39.)   123 **foolish banquet towards** insignificant light refreshment just ready.   125 **honest** honorable

More torches here! Come on then, let's to bed.                                         126
[*To his cousin*] Ah, sirrah, by my fay, it waxes late.                                127
I'll to my rest.
                    [*All proceed to leave but Juliet and the Nurse.*]

JULIET
Come hither, Nurse. What is yond gentleman?

NURSE
The son and heir of old Tiberio.

JULIET
What's he that now is going out of door?

NURSE
Marry, that, I think, be young Petruchio.

JULIET
What's he that follows here, that would not dance?

NURSE    I know not.

JULIET
Go ask his name. [*The Nurse goes.*] If he be marrièd,
My grave is like to be my wedding bed.                                                 136

NURSE [*returning*]
His name is Romeo, and a Montague,
The only son of your great enemy.

JULIET
My only love sprung from my only hate!
Too early seen unknown, and known too late!
Prodigious birth of love it is to me                                                   141
That I must love a loathèd enemy.

NURSE
What's tis? What's tis?

JULIET                          A rhyme I learned even now                             143
Of one I danced withal.        *One calls within* "Juliet."

NURSE                             Anon, anon!                                           144
Come, let's away. The strangers all are gone.   *Exeunt.*

❖

# [2.0]

          [*Enter*] Chorus.

CHORUS
Now old desire doth in his deathbed lie,                                               1
    And young affection gapes to be his heir;                                          2
That fair for which love groaned for and would die,                                    3
    With tender Juliet matched, is now not fair.                                       4
Now Romeo is beloved and loves again,
    Alike bewitchèd by the charm of looks;                                             6
But to his foe supposed he must complain,                                              7
    And she steal love's sweet bait from fearful hooks.                                8
Being held a foe, he may not have access
    To breathe such vows as lovers use to swear;                                       10
And she as much in love, her means much less
    To meet her new-belovèd anywhere.

126 **torches** i.e., to light the guests as they leave   127 **fay** faith
136 **like** likely   141 **Prodigious** Ominous   143 **tis** this. (Dialect
pronunciation.)   144 **withal** with.   **Anon** i.e., We're coming
**2.0. Chorus.**
**1–14** (This chorus is a sonnet.)   **2 gapes** waits open-mouthed
**3 fair** beauty, i.e., Rosaline   **4 matched** compared   **6 Alike** i.e.,
equally with Juliet   **7 foe supposed** i.e., Juliet, a Capulet; also, his
opposite number in the war of love.   **complain** offer his love
plaint   **8 And she . . . hooks** and she must steal moments of happy
love from frightening circumstances designed to catch her
unawares.   **10 use** are accustomed

But passion lends them power, time means, to meet,                                     13
Temp'ring extremities with extreme sweet.        [*Exit.*]                             14

❖

# [2.1]

          *Enter Romeo alone.*

ROMEO
Can I go forward when my heart is here?                                                 1
Turn back, dull earth, and find thy center out.                                        2
                                    [*Romeo retires.*]

          *Enter Benvolio with Mercutio.*

BENVOLIO
Romeo! My cousin Romeo! Romeo!

MERCUTIO    He is wise
And, on my life, hath stol'n him home to bed.

BENVOLIO
He ran this way and leapt this orchard wall.
Call, good Mercutio.

MERCUTIO                          Nay, I'll conjure too.                               7
Romeo! Humors! Madman! Passion! Lover!                                                 8
Appear thou in the likeness of a sigh.
Speak but one rhyme, and I am satisfied;
Cry but "Ay me!" Pronounce but "love" and "dove."
Speak to my gossip Venus one fair word,                                                12
One nickname for her purblind son and heir,                                            13
Young Abraham Cupid, he that shot so trim                                              14
When King Cophetua loved the beggar maid.—                                             15
He heareth not, he stirreth not, he moveth not;
The ape is dead, and I must conjure him.—                                              17
I conjure thee by Rosaline's bright eyes,
By her high forehead and her scarlet lip,
By her fine foot, straight leg, and quivering thigh,
And the demesnes that there adjacent lie,                                              21
That in thy likeness thou appear to us.

BENVOLIO
An if he hear thee, thou wilt anger him.                                               23

MERCUTIO
This cannot anger him. 'Twould anger him
To raise a spirit in his mistress' circle                                              25
Of some strange nature, letting it there stand                                         26

13 **time means** time lends them means   14 **Temp'ring extremities**
mitigating the hardships.   **sweet** sweetness, pleasure.
**2.1. Location: Verona. Outside of Capulet's walled orchard.**
**1 forward** i.e., away   **2 Turn . . . out** (Romeo bids his own earthbound body find out its *center*, its soul or heart [i.e., Juliet], much as in
the Ptolemaic system all earthly things seek out their center, the earth,
standing at the center of the universe. His body is *dull* in that, like
earth, it is the lowest and heaviest of the four elements, associated
with melancholy.)   **7 conjure** raise him with magical incantation
**8 Humors** Moods.   **12 gossip** crony   **13 purblind** dim-sighted
**14 Young Abraham** i.e., one who is young and yet, like the biblical
Abraham, old; Cupid was paradoxically the youngest and the oldest
of the gods   **15 King Cophetua** (In an old ballad, the King falls in
love with a beggar maid and makes her his queen.)   **17 ape** (Used as
a term of endearment.)   **21 demesnes** regions. (With bawdy suggestion as to what is adjacent to the thighs; bawdy puns on terms of conjuration continue in *raise, spirit,* i.e., "phallus" or "semen," *circle, stand,
laid it, raise up.*)   **23 An if** If   **25 circle** (1) conjuring circle (2) vagina
**26 strange** belonging to another person. (With suggestion of a rival
possessing Rosaline sexually.)   **stand** (suggesting an erection)

Till she had laid it and conjured it down; 　　27
That were some spite. My invocation 　　28
Is fair and honest; in his mistress' name
I conjure only but to raise up him.

BENVOLIO

Come, he hath hid himself among these trees
To be consorted with the humorous night. 　　32
Blind is his love, and best befits the dark.

MERCUTIO

If love be blind, love cannot hit the mark.
Now will he sit under a medlar tree 　　35
And wish his mistress were that kind of fruit
As maids call medlars when they laugh alone. 　　37
Oh, Romeo, that she were, oh, that she were
An open-arse, and thou a pop'ring pear! 　　39
Romeo, good night. I'll to my truckle bed; 　　40
This field bed is too cold for me to sleep. 　　41
Come, shall we go?

BENVOLIO　　　　　　　　　Go, then, for 'tis in vain
To seek him here that means not to be found.
　　　　　　　　　　　　　　　　*Exit [with Mercutio].*

❖

## [2.2]

ROMEO　　*[coming forward]*
He jests at scars that never felt a wound. 　　1
　　　　　　　*[A light appears above, as at Juliet's window.]*
But soft, what light through yonder window breaks? 　　2
It is the east, and Juliet is the sun.
Arise, fair sun, and kill the envious moon,
Who is already sick and pale with grief
That thou her maid art far more fair than she. 　　6
Be not her maid, since she is envious; 　　7
Her vestal livery is but sick and green 　　8
And none but fools do wear it. Cast it off.
　　　　　　　*[Juliet appears aloft as at her window.]*
It is my lady, oh, it is my love.
Oh, that she knew she were!
She speaks, yet she says nothing. What of that?

**27 laid it** (1) laid the spirit to rest (2) provided sexual satisfaction leading to detumescence　**28 were some spite** would be vexing. **32 consorted** associated.　**humorous** (1) moist, damp (2) well suited to the *humor* of melancholy　**35 medlar** a fruit that was edible only when partly decayed, used as a slang term for women's sexual organs **37 alone** i.e., with no male company.　**39 open-arse** (Another name for the *medlar*, making explicit the sexual metaphor.)　**pop'ring pear** poppering pear (named after Poperinghe in Flanders). A fruit with phallic associations because of its shape and its suggestive name ("pop 'er in").　**40 truckle bed** a bed on casters to be rolled under a standing bed when not in use　**41 field bed** i.e., the ground **2.2. Location:** The action, continuous from the previous scene, is now imaginatively transferred to inside Capulet's orchard. A rhymed couplet links the two scenes. Romeo has been hiding from his friends as though concealed by the orchard wall. He speaks at once and then turns to observe Juliet's window, which is probably in the gallery above, rear stage.
**1.1** *A light appears* (Some editors assume that Juliet is visible at line 1.) **2 soft** gently, wait a minute　**6 maid** i.e., votary of Diana, goddess of the moon and patroness of virgins　**7 her** the moon's, Diana's, as the goddess of chastity. (Addressed to Juliet as the sun; Romeo hopes that she will not be a devotee of chastity.)　**8 Her vestal livery** the uniform of Diana's chaste votaries.　**sick and green** (Suggesting the pallor of moonlight, as well as anemia or *greensickness* [see 3.5.156], to which teenage girls were susceptible.)

Her eye discourses. I will answer it.
I am too bold. 'Tis not to me she speaks.
Two of the fairest stars in all the heaven,
Having some business, do entreat her eyes
To twinkle in their spheres till they return. 　　17
What if her eyes were there, they in her head? 　　18
The brightness of her cheek would shame those stars
As daylight doth a lamp; her eyes in heaven
Would through the airy region stream so bright 　　21
That birds would sing and think it were not night.
See how she leans her cheek upon her hand!
Oh, that I were a glove upon that hand,
That I might touch that cheek!

JULIET　　　　　　　　　　　Ay me!

ROMEO *[aside]*　　　　　　　　　　　She speaks.
Oh, speak again, bright angel, for thou art
As glorious to this night, being o'er my head,
As is a wingèd messenger of heaven
Unto the white-upturnèd wond'ring eyes 　　29
Of mortals that fall back to gaze on him
When he bestrides the lazy puffing clouds
And sails upon the bosom of the air.

JULIET *[to herself]*
O Romeo, Romeo, wherefore art thou Romeo? 　　33
Deny thy father and refuse thy name!
Or, if thou wilt not, be but sworn my love,
And I'll no longer be a Capulet.

ROMEO *[aside]*
Shall I hear more, or shall I speak at this?

JULIET
'Tis but thy name that is my enemy;
Thou art thyself, though not a Montague. 　　39
What's Montague? It is nor hand, nor foot, 　　40
Nor arm, nor face, nor any other part
Belonging to a man. Oh, be some other name!
What's in a name? That which we call a rose
By any other word would smell as sweet;
So Romeo would, were he not Romeo called,
Retain that dear perfection which he owes 　　46
Without that title. Romeo, doff thy name, 　　47
And for thy name, which is no part of thee, 　　48
Take all myself.

ROMEO　　　　　I take thee at thy word!
Call me but love, and I'll be new baptized;
Henceforth I never will be Romeo.

JULIET
What man art thou that, thus bescreened in night, 　　52
So stumblest on my counsel?

ROMEO　　　　　　　　　　By a name 　　53
I know not how to tell thee who I am.
My name, dear saint, is hateful to myself,
Because it is an enemy to thee;
Had I it written, I would tear the word.

**17 spheres** transparent concentric shells supposed to carry the heavenly bodies with them in their revolution around the earth　**18 there** i.e., in the spheres　**21 stream** shine　**29 white-upturnèd** looking upward so that the whites of the eyes are visible　**33 wherefore** why **39 though not** (1) even if you were not (2) though not in anything essential　**40 nor hand** neither hand　**46 owes** owns　**47 doff** cast off　**48 for** in exchange for　**52 bescreened** concealed　**53 counsel** secret thoughts.

JULIET
My ears have yet not drunk a hundred words
Of thy tongue's uttering, yet I know the sound:
Art thou not Romeo and a Montague?
ROMEO
Neither, fair maid, if either thee dislike.                         61
JULIET
How camest thou hither, tell me, and wherefore?
The orchard walls are high and hard to climb,
And the place death, considering who thou art,
If any of my kinsmen find thee here.
ROMEO
With love's light wings did I o'erperch these walls,       66
For stony limits cannot hold love out,
And what love can do, that dares love attempt;
Therefore thy kinsmen are no stop to me.
JULIET
If they do see thee, they will murder thee.
ROMEO
Alack, there lies more peril in thine eye
Than twenty of their swords. Look thou but sweet,
And I am proof against their enmity.                               73
JULIET
I would not for the world they saw thee here.
ROMEO
I have night's cloak to hide me from their eyes;
And but thou love me, let them find me here.               76
My life were better ended by their hate
Than death proroguèd, wanting of thy love.               78
JULIET
By whose direction found'st thou out this place?
ROMEO
By Love, that first did prompt me to inquire.
He lent me counsel, and I lent him eyes.
I am no pilot; yet, wert thou as far
As that vast shore washed with the farthest sea,
I should adventure for such merchandise.
JULIET
Thou knowest the mask of night is on my face,
Else would a maiden blush bepaint my cheek
For that which thou hast heard me speak tonight.
Fain would I dwell on form—fain, fain deny               88
What I have spoke; but farewell compliment!               89
Dost thou love me? I know thou wilt say "Ay,"
And I will take thy word. Yet if thou swear'st
Thou mayst prove false. At lovers' perjuries,
They say, Jove laughs. O gentle Romeo,
If thou dost love, pronounce it faithfully.
Or if thou thinkest I am too quickly won,
I'll frown and be perverse and say thee nay,
So thou wilt woo, but else not for the world.               97
In truth, fair Montague, I am too fond,                          98
And therefore thou mayst think my havior light.          99
But trust me, gentleman, I'll prove more true
Than those that have more cunning to be strange.      101

I should have been more strange, I must confess,
But that thou overheard'st, ere I was ware,                   103
My true-love passion. Therefore pardon me,
And not impute this yielding to light love,
Which the dark night hath so discoverèd.                    106
ROMEO
Lady, by yonder blessèd moon I vow,
That tips with silver all these fruit-tree tops—
JULIET
Oh, swear not by the moon, th'inconstant moon,
That monthly changes in her circled orb,                     110
Lest that thy love prove likewise variable.
ROMEO
What shall I swear by?
JULIET                                       Do not swear at all;
Or, if thou wilt, swear by thy gracious self,
Which is the god of my idolatry,
And I'll believe thee.
ROMEO                              If my heart's dear love—
JULIET
Well, do not swear. Although I joy in thee,
I have no joy of this contract tonight.                           117
It is too rash, too unadvised, too sudden,                      118
Too like the lightning, which doth cease to be
Ere one can say it lightens. Sweet, good night!
This bud of love, by summer's ripening breath,
May prove a beauteous flower when next we meet.
Good night, good night! As sweet repose and rest       123
Come to thy heart as that within my breast!
ROMEO
Oh, wilt thou leave me so unsatisfied?
JULIET
What satisfaction canst thou have tonight?
ROMEO
Th'exchange of thy love's faithful vow for mine.
JULIET
I gave thee mine before thou didst request it;
And yet I would it were to give again.
ROMEO
Wouldst thou withdraw it? For what purpose, love?
JULIET
But to be frank and give it thee again.                          131
And yet I wish but for the thing I have.
My bounty is as boundless as the sea,
My love as deep; the more I give to thee,
The more I have, for both are infinite.
                                    [*The Nurse calls within.*]
I hear some noise within. Dear love, adieu!—
Anon, good Nurse!—Sweet Montague, be true.
Stay but a little; I will come again.          [*Exit, above.*]
ROMEO
Oh, blessèd, blessèd night! I am afeard,
Being in night, all this is but a dream,
Too flattering-sweet to be substantial.

        [*Enter Juliet, above.*]

**61 thee dislike** displeases you.  **66 o'erperch** fly over  **73 proof** protected  **76 but** unless  **78 prorogued** postponed.  **wanting of** lacking  **88 Fain** Gladly.  **dwell on form** preserve the proper formalities  **89 compliment** etiquette, convention.  **97 So** provided that  **98 fond** infatuated  **99 havior light** behavior frivolous.  **101 strange** reserved, aloof, modest.

**103 ware** aware  **106 Which** i.e., which yielding.  **discoverèd** revealed.  **110 orb** orbit, sphere  **117 contract** exchanging of vows  **118 unadvised** unconsidered  **123 As** May just as  **131 frank** liberal, bounteous

JULIET
Three words, dear Romeo, and good night indeed.
If that thy bent of love be honorable,                              143
Thy purpose marriage, send me word tomorrow,
By one that I'll procure to come to thee,
Where and what time thou wilt perform the rite,
And all my fortunes at thy foot I'll lay
And follow thee my lord throughout the world.

NURSE [*within*]   Madam!

JULIET
I come, anon.—But if thou meanest not well,
I do beseech thee—

NURSE [*within*]            Madam!

JULIET                          By and by, I come—            151
To cease thy strife and leave me to my grief.                      152
Tomorrow will I send.

ROMEO    So thrive my soul—

JULIET    A thousand times good night!        [*Exit, above.*]

ROMEO
A thousand times the worse, to want thy light.
Love goes toward love as schoolboys from their
   books,
But love from love, toward school with heavy looks.
                                      [*He starts to leave.*]

*Enter Juliet [above] again.*

JULIET
Hist! Romeo, hist! Oh, for a falconer's voice,
To lure this tassel-gentle back again!                             160
Bondage is hoarse and may not speak aloud,                         161
Else would I tear the cave where Echo lies                         162
And make her airy tongue more hoarse than mine
With repetition of "My Romeo!"

ROMEO
It is my soul that calls upon my name.
How silver-sweet sound lovers' tongues by night,
Like softest music to attending ears!

JULIET
Romeo!

ROMEO    My nyas?

JULIET                    What o'clock tomorrow            168
Shall I send to thee?

ROMEO                          By the hour of nine.

JULIET
I will not fail. 'Tis twenty year till then.—
I have forgot why I did call thee back.

ROMEO
Let me stand here till thou remember it.

JULIET
I shall forget, to have thee still stand there,                    173
Remembering how I love thy company.

ROMEO
And I'll still stay, to have thee still forget,
Forgetting any other home but this.

JULIET
'Tis almost morning. I would have thee gone—
And yet no farther than a wanton's bird,                           178
That lets it hop a little from his hand,
Like a poor prisoner in his twisted gyves,                         180
And with a silken thread plucks it back again,
So loving-jealous of his liberty.                                  182

ROMEO
I would I were thy bird.

JULIET                      Sweet, so would I.
Yet I should kill thee with much cherishing.
Good night, good night! Parting is such sweet sorrow
That I shall say good night till it be morrow.
                                      [*Exit, above.*]

ROMEO
Sleep dwell upon thine eyes, peace in thy breast!
Would I were sleep and peace, so sweet to rest!
Hence will I to my ghostly friar's close cell,                     189
His help to crave, and my dear hap to tell.      *Exit.* 190

❖

# [2.3]

*Enter Friar [Laurence] alone, with a basket.*

FRIAR LAURENCE
The gray-eyed morn smiles on the frowning night,
Check'ring the eastern clouds with streaks of light,
And fleckled darkness like a drunkard reels                        3
From forth day's path and Titan's fiery wheels.                    4
Now, ere the sun advance his burning eye,                          5
The day to cheer and night's dank dew to dry,
I must up-fill this osier cage of ours                             7
With baleful weeds and precious-juicèd flowers.                    8
The earth that's nature's mother is her tomb;
What is her burying grave, that is her womb;
And from her womb children of divers kind
We sucking on her natural bosom find,
Many for many virtues excellent,
None but for some, and yet all different.                          14
Oh, mickle is the powerful grace that lies                         15
In plants, herbs, stones, and their true qualities.                16
For naught so vile that on the earth doth live                     17
But to the earth some special good doth give;
Nor aught so good but, strained from that fair use,                19
Revolts from true birth, stumbling on abuse.
Virtue itself turns vice, being misapplied,
And vice sometime by action dignified.

*Enter Romeo.*

---

143 **bent** purpose, inclination   151 **By and by** Immediately
152 **strife** striving   160 **tassel-gentle** tercel gentle, the male of the
goshawk   161 **Bondage is hoarse** i.e., In confinement one can speak
only in a loud whisper   162 **tear** pierce (with noise).   **Echo** (In Book
3 of Ovid's *Metamorphoses*, Echo, rejected by Narcissus, pines away in
lonely caves until only her voice is left.)   168 **nyas** eyas, fledgling
hawk. (Here a term of endearment.)   173 **still** always

178 **wanton's** spoiled child's   180 **gyves** fetters   182 **his** its
189 **ghostly** spiritual.   **close** narrow   190 **dear hap** good fortune
2.3. **Location: Verona. Friar Laurence's monastery garden.**
3 **fleckled** dappled   4 **From forth** out of the way of.   **Titan's** (Helios,
the sun god, was a descendant of the race of Titans.)   5 **advance** raise
7 **osier cage** willow basket   8 **baleful** harmful   14 **None but for some**
there are none that are not useful for something   15 **mickle** great.
**grace** beneficent virtue   16 **true** proper, inherent   17 **For naught so
vile** For there is nothing so vile   19 **strained** forced, perverted

Within the infant rind of this weak flower
Poison hath residence and medicine power:
For this, being smelt, with that part cheers each part;     25
Being tasted, slays all senses with the heart.             26
Two such opposèd kings encamp them still                   27
In man as well as herbs—grace and rude will;
And where the worser is predominant,
Full soon the canker death eats up that plant.             30

ROMEO
Good morrow, Father.

FRIAR LAURENCE          Benedicite!                          31
What early tongue so sweet saluteth me?
Young son, it argues a distempered head                     33
So soon to bid good morrow to thy bed.
Care keeps his watch in every old man's eye,
And where care lodges sleep will never lie;
But where unbruisèd youth with unstuffed brain              37
Doth couch his limbs, there golden sleep doth reign.
Therefore thy earliness doth me assure
Thou art uproused with some distemp'rature;
Or if not so, then here I hit it right:
Our Romeo hath not been in bed tonight.

ROMEO
That last is true. The sweeter rest was mine.

FRIAR LAURENCE
God pardon sin! Wast thou with Rosaline?

ROMEO
With Rosaline, my ghostly father? No.
I have forgot that name, and that name's woe.

FRIAR LAURENCE
That's my good son. But where hast thou been, then?

ROMEO
I'll tell thee ere thou ask it me again.
I have been feasting with mine enemy,
Where on a sudden one hath wounded me
That's by me wounded. Both our remedies                     51
Within thy help and holy physic lies.                       52
I bear no hatred, blessèd man, for, lo,
My intercession likewise steads my foe.                     54

FRIAR LAURENCE
Be plain, good son, and homely in thy drift.                55
Riddling confession finds but riddling shrift.              56

ROMEO
Then plainly know my heart's dear love is set
On the fair daughter of rich Capulet.
As mine on hers, so hers is set on mine,
And all combined, save what thou must combine
By holy marriage. When and where and how
We met, we wooed, and made exchange of vow
I'll tell thee as we pass; but this I pray,
That thou consent to marry us today.

FRIAR LAURENCE
Holy Saint Francis, what a change is here!
Is Rosaline, that thou didst love so dear,

So soon forsaken? Young men's love then lies
Not truly in their hearts, but in their eyes.
Jesu Maria, what a deal of brine
Hath washed thy sallow cheeks for Rosaline!
How much salt water thrown away in waste
To season love, that of it doth not taste!                  72
The sun not yet thy sighs from heaven clears,
Thy old groans yet ringing in mine ancient ears.
Lo, here upon thy cheek the stain doth sit
Of an old tear that is not washed off yet.
If e'er thou wast thyself and these woes thine,             77
Thou and these woes were all for Rosaline.
And art thou changed? Pronounce this sentence then:        79
Women may fall, when there's no strength in men.

ROMEO
Thou chid'st me oft for loving Rosaline.

FRIAR LAURENCE
For doting, not for loving, pupil mine.

ROMEO
And bad'st me bury love.

FRIAR LAURENCE          Not in a grave
To lay one in, another out to have.

ROMEO
I pray thee, chide not. She whom I love now
Doth grace for grace and love for love allow.               86
The other did not so.

FRIAR LAURENCE          Oh, she knew well
Thy love did read by rote, that could not spell.            88
But come, young waverer, come, go with me,
In one respect I'll thy assistant be;                       90
For this alliance may so happy prove
To turn your households' rancor to pure love.               92

ROMEO
Oh, let us hence! I stand on sudden haste.                  93

FRIAR LAURENCE
Wisely and slow. They stumble that run fast.
                                              *Exeunt.*

❧

# [2.4]

*Enter Benvolio and Mercutio.*

MERCUTIO
Where the devil should this Romeo be?                        1
Came he not home tonight?                                     2

BENVOLIO
Not to his father's. I spoke with his man.

MERCUTIO
Why, that same pale hardhearted wench, that
  Rosaline,
Torments him so that he will sure run mad.

BENVOLIO
Tybalt, the kinsman to old Capulet,
Hath sent a letter to his father's house.

25 **with . . . each part** i.e., with the odor enlivens each bodily part
26 **with** together with   27 **them still** themselves always   30 **canker**
cankerworm   31 **Benedicite!** A blessing on you!   33 **argues** demonstrates, provides evidence of.   **distempered** disturbed, disordered
37 **unstuffed** not overcharged, carefree   51 **Both our remedies** The
remedy for both of us   52 **physic** medicine, healing property
54 **intercession** petition.   **steads my foe** i.e., benefits Juliet.
55 **homely** simple   56 **shrift** absolution.

72 **season** flavor   77 **If . . . thine** If ever you had any proper sense of
self and understanding of your love sorrows   79 **sentence** maxim
86 **grace** favor   88 **did read . . . spell** i.e., was like a schoolboy's exercise, repeating words without understanding.   90 **In one respect** for
one reason (at least)   92 **To** as to   93 **stand on** am in need of, insist on
**2.4. Location:** Verona. A street.
1 **should** can   2 **tonight** last night.

MERCUTIO    A challenge, on my life.

BENVOLIO    Romeo will answer it.       9

MERCUTIO    Any man that can write may answer a letter.

BENVOLIO    Nay, he will answer the letter's master, how he dares, being dared.

MERCUTIO    Alas poor Romeo! He is already dead, stabbed with a white wench's black eye, run through the ear with a love song, the very pin of his heart cleft 15 with the blind bow-boy's butt shaft. And is he a man 16 to encounter Tybalt?

BENVOLIO    Why, what is Tybalt?

MERCUTIO    More than prince of cats. Oh, he's the cou- 19 rageous captain of compliments. He fights as you 20 sing pricksong, keeps time, distance, and proportion; 21 he rests his minim rests, one, two, and the third in 22 your bosom. The very butcher of a silk button, a 23 duellist, a duellist, a gentleman of the very first house, 24 of the first and second cause. Ah, the immortal 25 *passado!* The *punto reverso!* The *hay!* 26

BENVOLIO    The what?

MERCUTIO    The pox of such antic, lisping, affecting phan- 28 tasimes, these new tuners of accent! "By Jesu, a very 29 good blade! A very tall man! A very good whore!" 30 Why, is not this a lamentable thing, grandsire, that we 31 should be thus afflicted with these strange flies, these 32 fashionmongers, these pardon-me's, who stand so 33 much on the new form that they cannot sit at ease on 34 the old bench? Oh, their bones, their bones! 35

*Enter Romeo.*

BENVOLIO    Here comes Romeo, here comes Romeo.

MERCUTIO    Without his roe, like a dried herring. Oh, 37 flesh, flesh, how art thou fishified! Now is he for the numbers that Petrarch flowed in. Laura to his lady 39 was but a kitchen wench—marry, she had a better

love to berhyme her—Dido a dowdy, Cleopatra a 41 gypsy, Helen and Hero hildings and harlots, Thisbe a 42 gray eye or so, but not to the purpose. Signor Romeo, 43 *bonjour!* There's a French salutation to your French 44 slop. You gave us the counterfeit fairly last night. 45

ROMEO    Good morrow to you both. What counterfeit did I give you?

MERCUTIO    The slip, sir, the slip. Can you not conceive? 48

ROMEO    Pardon, good Mercutio. My business was great, and in such a case as mine a man may strain courtesy.

MERCUTIO    That's as much as to say, such a case as yours 51 constrains a man to bow in the hams. 52

ROMEO    Meaning, to curtsy. 53

MERCUTIO    Thou hast most kindly hit it. 54

ROMEO    A most courteous exposition.

MERCUTIO    Nay, I am the very pink of courtesy. 56

ROMEO    Pink for flower.

MERCUTIO    Right.

ROMEO    Why then is my pump well flowered. 59

MERCUTIO    Sure wit, follow me this jest now till thou hast worn out thy pump, that when the single sole of it is worn, the jest may remain, after the wearing, solely singular. 63

ROMEO    Oh, single-soled jest, solely singular for the 64 singleness! 65

MERCUTIO    Come between us, good Benvolio. My wits faints.

ROMEO    Switch and spurs, switch and spurs! Or I'll cry 68 a match. 69

MERCUTIO    Nay, if our wits run the wild-goose chase, I 70 am done, for thou hast more of the wild goose in one of thy wits than, I am sure, I have in my whole five. Was I with you there for the goose? 73

ROMEO    Thou wast never with me for anything when thou wast not there for the goose. 75

MERCUTIO    I will bite thee by the ear for that jest. 76

ROMEO    Nay, good goose, bite not.

MERCUTIO    Thy wit is a very bitter sweeting; it is a most 78 sharp sauce. 79

ROMEO    And is it not, then, well served in to a sweet goose?

---

**9 answer it** accept the challenge. (But Mercutio replies in the sense of "write in reply.")   **15 pin** peg in the center of a target   **16 butt shaft** unbarbed arrow, allotted to children and thus to Cupid.   **19 prince of cats** (The name of the king of cats in *Reynard the Fox* was Tybalt or Tybert.)   **20 captain of compliments** master of ceremony and dueling etiquette.   **21 pricksong** music written out.   **proportion** rhythm   **22 minim rests** short rests in musical notation   **23 butcher . . . button** i.e., one able to strike a specific button on his adversary's person   **24 first house** best school of fencing   **25 first and second cause** causes according to the code of dueling that would oblige one to seek the satisfaction of one's honor.   **26 passado** forward thrust.   **punto reverso** backhanded stroke.   **hay** thrust through. (From the Italian *hai,* meaning "you have [it].")   **28 The pox of** Plague take.   **antic** grotesque   **28–9 phantasimes** coxcombs, fantastically dressed or mannered   **29 new tuners of accent** those who introduce new foreign words and slang phrases into their speech.   **30 tall** valiant   **31 grandsire** i.e., one who disapproves of the new fashion and prefers old custom   **32 flies** parasites   **33 pardon-me's** i.e., those who affect overly polite manners.   **stand** (1) insist (2) the opposite of *sit,* line 34   **34–5 form . . . bench** (*Form* means both "fashion" or "code of manners" and "bench.")   **35 bones** French *bon,* "good" (with play on English *bone*)   **37 Without his roe** i.e., Looking thin and emaciated, sexually spent. (With a pun on the first syllable of Romeo's name; the remaining syllables, *me-oh,* sound like the expression of a melancholy lover. *Roe* also suggests a female deer or "dear.")   **39 numbers** verses.   **Laura** the lady to whom the Italian Renaissance poet Petrarch addressed his love poems. (Other romantic heroines are named in the following passage: Dido, Queen of Carthage; Cleopatra; Helen of Troy; Hero, beloved of Leander; and Thisbe, beloved of Pyramus.)   **to** in comparison with

**41 dowdy** homely woman   **42 gypsy** Egyptian; whore. **hildings** good-for-nothings   **43 not** i.e., that is not   **44 to** to match   **44–5 French slop** loose trousers of French fashion.   **45 fairly** handsomely, effectively   **48 slip** (Counterfeit coins were called "slips.") **conceive** i.e., get the joke.   **51 case** (1) situation (2) physical condition. (Mercutio also bawdily suggests that Romeo has been in a *case,* i.e., the female genitalia.)   **52 bow in the hams** (1) make a low bow (2) show the effects of venereal disease.   **53 curtsy** bow, make obeisance.   **54 kindly** graciously. (But also suggesting natural and physical explanations.)   **56 pink** embodied perfection. (But suggesting also the flower called *pink,* the color, and *pinking* of a shoe; see next note.)   **59 pump well flowered** shoe expertly pinked or perforated in ornamental figures suggesting flowers.   **63 solely singular** unique.   **64 single-soled** i.e., thin, contemptible   **65 singleness** feebleness.   **68 Switch and spurs** i.e., Keep up the rapid pace of the hunt (in the game of wits)   **68–9 cry a match** claim victory.   **70 wildgoose chase** a horse race in which the leading rider dares his competitors to follow him wherever he goes   **73 Was . . . goose?** Did I score a point in calling you a goose?   **75 for the goose** (1) behaving like a goose (2) looking for a prostitute.   **76 bite . . . ear** i.e., give you an affectionate nibble on the ear. (Said ironically, however, and Romeo parries.)   **78 sweeting** sweet-flavored variety of apple   **79 sharp sauce** (1) "biting" retort (2) tart sauce, of the sort that should be served with cooked goose (as Romeo points out).

MERCUTIO   Oh, here's a wit of cheveril, that stretches 82
from an inch narrow to an ell broad!                       83

ROMEO   I stretch it out for that word "broad," which,
added to the goose, proves thee far and wide a broad 85
goose.

MERCUTIO   Why, is not this better now than groaning
for love? Now art thou sociable, now art thou Romeo;
now art thou what thou art, by art as well as by nature.
For this driveling love is like a great natural that runs 90
lolling up and down to hide his bauble in a hole.      91

BENVOLIO   Stop there, stop there.

MERCUTIO   Thou desirest me to stop in my tale against 93
the hair.                                                            94

BENVOLIO   Thou wouldst else have made thy tale large.

MERCUTIO   Oh, thou art deceived; I would have made it
short, for I was come to the whole depth of my tale
and meant indeed to occupy the argument no longer.

ROMEO   Here's goodly gear!                              99

*Enter Nurse and her man [Peter].*

A sail, a sail!                                               100

MERCUTIO   Two, two: a shirt and a smock.            101

NURSE   Peter!

PETER   Anon!

NURSE   My fan, Peter.

MERCUTIO   Good Peter, to hide her face, for her fan's
the fairer face.

NURSE   God gi' good morrow, gentlemen.

MERCUTIO   God gi' good e'en, fair gentlewoman.

NURSE   Is it good e'en?                                    109

MERCUTIO   'Tis no less, I tell ye, for the bawdy hand of
the dial is now upon the prick of noon.                111

NURSE   Out upon you! What a man are you?        112

ROMEO   One, gentlewoman, that God hath made for
himself to mar.                                             114

NURSE   By my troth, it is well said. "For himself to mar," 115
quoth 'a? Gentlemen, can any of you tell me where I 116
may find the young Romeo?

ROMEO   I can tell you; but young Romeo will be older
when you have found him than he was when you
sought him. I am the youngest of that name, for fault 120
of a worse.

NURSE   You say well.

MERCUTIO   Yea, is the worst well? Very well took, i'faith, 123
wisely, wisely.

NURSE   If you be he, sir, I desire some confidence with 125
you.

BENVOLIO   She will indite him to some supper.     127

MERCUTIO   A bawd, a bawd, a bawd! So ho!        128

ROMEO   What hast thou found?

MERCUTIO   No hare, sir, unless a hare, sir, in a lenten 130
pie, that is something stale and hoar ere it be spent.  131
                                                        *[He sings.]*

> An old hare hoar,
> And an old hare hoar,
> Is very good meat in Lent.
> But a hare that is hoar
> Is too much for a score,                          136
> When it hoars ere it be spent.

Romeo, will you come to your father's? We'll to dinner thither.

ROMEO   I will follow you.

MERCUTIO   Farewell, ancient lady. Farewell,   *[singing]*
"Lady, lady, lady."   *Exeunt [Mercutio and Benvolio].* 142

NURSE   I pray you, sir, what saucy merchant was this 143
that was so full of his ropery?                           144

ROMEO   A gentleman, Nurse, that loves to hear himself
talk, and will speak more in a minute than he will
stand to in a month.                                       147

NURSE   An 'a speak anything against me, I'll take him 148
down, an 'a were lustier than he is, and twenty such 149
Jacks; and if I cannot, I'll find those that shall. Scurvy 150
knave! I am none of his flirt-gills. I am none of his 151
skains-mates. *[To Peter]* And thou must stand by, too, 152
and suffer every knave to use me at his pleasure!

PETER   I saw no man use you at his pleasure. If I had,
my weapon should quickly have been out; I warrant 155
you, I dare draw as soon as another man, if I see
occasion in a good quarrel, and the law on my side.

NURSE   Now, afore God, I am so vexed that every part 158
about me quivers. Scurvy knave! Pray you, sir, a 159
word; and as I told you, my young lady bid me
inquire you out. What she bid me say, I will keep to
myself. But first let me tell ye, if ye should lead her
in a fool's paradise, as they say, it were a very gross
kind of behavior, as they say. For the gentlewoman
is young; and therefore if you should deal double

---

**82 cheveril** kid leather, easily stretched   **83 ell** (forty-five inches)
**85 broad** large, complete; perhaps also wanton   **90 natural** idiot
**91 lolling** with his tongue (or bauble) hanging out.   **bauble** (1) jester's
wand (2) phallus   **93 stop in my tale** (1) stop short in my story
(2) stuff in my penis   **93–4 against the hair** against the grain, against
my wish. (With bawdy suggestion of pubic hair. The sexual punning
continues in *large* [erect], *short* [detumescent], *come to the depth of my
tale, occupy*, etc.)   **99 goodly gear** matter for mockery. (With suggestion of "ample sexual apparatus.")   **100 A sail** (To Romeo, the Nurse
is an imposing galleon in full sail.)   **101 a shirt and a smock** i.e., a
man and a woman.   **109 Is it good e'en?** Is it afternoon already?
**111 prick** point on the dial of a clock. (With bawdy suggestion.)
**112 Out upon you** (Expression of indignation.)   **What** What kind
of   **114 mar** i.e., disfigure morally through sin. (Humankind, made
in God's image, mars that image sinfully.)   **115 troth** faith
**116 quoth 'a** said he. (A sarcastic interjection, meaning "forsooth"
or "indeed.")   **120 fault** lack

**123 took** understood   **125 confidence** (The Nurse's mistake for
"conference.")   **127 indite** (Benvolio's deliberate malapropism for
"invite.")   **128 So ho** (Cry of hunter sighting game.)   **130 hare**
(Slang word for "prostitute"; similarly, with *stale* and *meat* in the following lines.)   **130–1 a lenten pie** a pie that should contain no meat,
in observance of Lent   **131 hoar** moldy. (With pun on "whore"; *stale*
also can mean "whore.")   **spent** consumed.   **136 for a score** for a
reckoning, to pay good money for   **142 "Lady, lady, lady"** (Refrain
from the ballad *Chaste Susanna*.)   **143 merchant** i.e., fellow   **144 ropery** vulgar humor, knavery.   **147 stand to** carry out, stand in support
of   **148 An 'a** If he   **148–9 take him down** cut him down to size.
(With unintended bawdy suggestion.)   **149 lustier** stronger (with a
suggestion, perhaps unintended, of "more horny")   **150 Jacks**
knaves   **151 flirt-gills** loose women.   **152 skains-mates** (Perhaps
daggermates, outlaws, or gangster molls.)   **155 weapon** (With
bawdy suggestion, perhaps unrecognized by the speaker, as also in
*at his pleasure*.)   **warrant** assure   **158–9 every part ... quivers** (More
bawdy suggestion, unrecognized by the Nurse.)

with her, truly it were an ill thing to be offered to any
gentlewoman, and very weak dealing.                              167

ROMEO    Nurse, commend me to thy lady and mistress.
I protest unto thee—                                            169

NURSE    Good heart, and i'faith I will tell her as much.      170
Lord, Lord, she will be a joyful woman.

ROMEO    What wilt thou tell her, Nurse? Thou dost not
mark me.                                                        173

NURSE    I will tell her, sir, that you do protest, which, as
I take it, is a gentlemanlike offer.

ROMEO    Bid her devise
Some means to come to shrift this afternoon,                    177
And there she shall at Friar Laurence' cell
Be shrived and married. Here is for thy pains.                  179
                              [He offers money.]

NURSE    No, truly, sir, not a penny.

ROMEO    Go to, I say you shall.

NURSE
This afternoon, sir? Well, she shall be there.

ROMEO
And stay, good Nurse, behind the abbey wall.
Within this hour my man shall be with thee
And bring thee cords made like a tackled stair,                185
Which to the high topgallant of my joy                         186
Must be my convoy in the secret night.                         187
Farewell. Be trusty, and I'll quit thy pains.                  188
Farewell. Commend me to thy mistress.
                         [Romeo starts to leave.]

NURSE
Now God in heaven bless thee! Hark you, sir.

ROMEO    What say'st thou, my dear Nurse?

NURSE
Is your man secret? Did you ne'er hear say,                    192
"Two may keep counsel, putting one away"?                      193

ROMEO
'Warrant thee, my man's as true as steel.                      194

NURSE    Well, sir, my mistress is the sweetest lady—
Lord, Lord! When 'twas a little prating thing—Oh,
there is a nobleman in town, one Paris, that would
fain lay knife aboard; but she, good soul, had as lief         198
see a toad, a very toad, as see him. I anger her
sometimes and tell her that Paris is the properer man,         200
but I'll warrant you, when I say so, she looks as pale
as any clout in the versal world. Doth not rosemary            202
and Romeo begin both with a letter?                            203

ROMEO    Ay, Nurse, what of that? Both with an R.

NURSE    Ah, mocker! That's the dog's name; R is for          205
the—No; I know it begins with some other letter; and           206
she hath the prettiest sententious of it, of you and           207
rosemary, that it would do you good to hear it.

ROMEO    Commend me to thy lady.

NURSE    Ay, a thousand times.            [Exit Romeo.]
Peter!

PETER    Anon!

NURSE    Before, and apace.                    Exeunt. 212

❧

# [2.5]

*Enter Juliet.*

JULIET
The clock struck nine when I did send the Nurse;
In half an hour she promised to return.
Perchance she cannot meet him. That's not so.
Oh, she is lame! Love's heralds should be thoughts,
Which ten times faster glides than the sun's beams
Driving back shadows over louring hills.                        6
Therefore do nimble-pinioned doves draw Love,                   7
And therefore hath the wind-swift Cupid wings.
Now is the sun upon the highmost hill
Of this day's journey, and from nine till twelve
Is three long hours, yet she is not come.
Had she affections and warm youthful blood,                     12
She would be as swift in motion as a ball;
My words would bandy her to my sweet love,                      14
And his to me.
But old folks, many feign as they were dead—                    16
Unwieldy, slow, heavy, and pale as lead.

*Enter Nurse [and Peter].*

Oh, God, she comes!—O honey Nurse, what news?
Hast thou met with him? Send thy man away.

NURSE    Peter, stay at the gate.            [Exit Peter.]

JULIET
Now, good sweet Nurse—Oh, Lord, why lookest thou
sad?
Though news be sad, yet tell them merrily;
If good, thou shamest the music of sweet news
By playing it to me with so sour a face.

NURSE
I am aweary. Give me leave awhile.                              25
Fie, how my bones ache! What a jaunce have I had!              26

JULIET
I would thou hadst my bones and I thy news.
Nay, come, I pray thee, speak. Good, good Nurse,
speak.

---

167 **weak** contemptible    169 **protest** vow. (Romeo may intend only to protest his good intentions, but the Nurse seemingly takes the word to mean "propose," as if Romeo is making a *gentlemanlike offer* [line 175] of marriage that would ensure against Juliet's being led into a *fool's paradise* [line 163]—i.e., being seduced.)    170 **Good heart** (A mild oath.)    173 **mark me** pay attention to what I say.    177 **shrift** confession and absolution    179 **shrived** absolved    185 **tackled stair** rope ladder    186 **topgallant** highest mast and sail of a ship, the summit    187 **convoy** conveyance, means of passage    188 **quit** reward, requite    192 **secret** trustworthy.    193 **keep counsel** keep a secret    194 **'Warrant** I assure    198 **fain lay knife aboard** like to assert his claim (just as a guest at an inn did by bringing his knife to the dinner table; with sexual suggestion also).    **lief** willingly    200 **properer** handsomer    202 **clout** faded rag.    **versal** universal.    **rosemary** (Associated with weddings and funerals.)    203 **a letter** one and the same letter.

205 **the dog's name** (The letter *R* was thought to resemble the dog's growl.)    205–6 **R is for . . . letter** (Perhaps the Nurse is about to say "arse," but has a notion that it begins with some other letter. In any case, she decides against saying such an indelicate word.)    207 **sententious** (The Nurse probably means "sentences," maxims.)    212 **Before, and apace** Go before me quickly.    **2.5. Location:** Verona. Outside Capulet's house, perhaps in the orchard or garden.    6 **louring** dark, threatening    7 **Love** i.e., Venus, whose chariot was drawn by swift-winged doves    12 **affections** desires    14 **bandy** toss to and fro, as in tennis.    16 **feign as** act as though    25 **Give me leave** Let me alone    26 **jaunce** jouncing, jolting

NURSE
    Jesu, what haste! Can you not stay awhile?                          29
    Do you not see that I am out of breath?
JULIET
    How art thou out of breath, when thou hast breath
    To say to me that thou art out of breath?
    The excuse that thou dost make in this delay
    Is longer than the tale thou dost excuse.                          34
    Is thy news good or bad? Answer to that;
    Say either, and I'll stay the circumstance.                        36
    Let me be satisfied: is't good or bad?
NURSE    Well, you have made a simple choice. You know    38
    not how to choose a man. Romeo? No, not he. Though
    his face be better than any man's, yet his leg excels all
    men's; and for a hand, and a foot, and a body, though
    they be not to be talked on, yet they are past compare.    42
    He is not the flower of courtesy, but, I'll warrant him,
    as gentle as a lamb. Go thy ways, wench. Serve God.
    What, have you dined at home?
JULIET
    No, no; but all this did I know before.
    What says he of our marriage? What of that?
NURSE
    Lord, how my head aches! What a head have I!
    It beats as it would fall in twenty pieces.
    My back o' t'other side—ah, my back, my back!        50
    Beshrew your heart for sending me about                      51
    To catch my death with jauncing up and down!
JULIET
    I'faith, I am sorry that thou art not well.
    Sweet, sweet, sweet Nurse, tell me, what says my
        love?
NURSE
    Your love says, like an honest gentleman,
    And a courteous, and a kind, and a handsome,
    And, I warrant, a virtuous—Where is your mother?
JULIET
    Where is my mother? Why, she is within,
    Where should she be? How oddly thou repliest!
    "Your love says, like an honest gentleman,               60
    'Where is your mother?'"
NURSE                                    O God's Lady dear!
    Are you so hot? Marry, come up, I trow.                      62
    Is this the poultice for my aching bones?
    Henceforward do your messages yourself.
JULIET
    Here's such a coil! Come, what says Romeo?            65
NURSE
    Have you got leave to go to shrift today?
JULIET    I have.
NURSE
    Then hie you hence to Friar Laurence' cell;            68
    There stays a husband to make you a wife.

    Now comes the wanton blood up in your cheeks;
    They'll be in scarlet straight at any news.                  71
    Hie you to church. I must another way,
    To fetch a ladder, by the which your love
    Must climb a bird's nest soon when it is dark.        74
    I am the drudge, and toil in your delight,
    But you shall bear the burden soon at night.
    Go. I'll to dinner. Hie you to the cell.                        77
JULIET
    Hie to high fortune! Honest Nurse, farewell.
                                        Exeunt [separately].

# [2.6]

*Enter Friar [Laurence] and Romeo.*

FRIAR LAURENCE
    So smile the heavens upon this holy act                      1
    That after-hours with sorrow chide us not!
ROMEO
    Amen, amen! But come what sorrow can,
    It cannot countervail the exchange of joy                    4
    That one short minute gives me in her sight.
    Do thou but close our hands with holy words,         6
    Then love-devouring death do what he dare;
    It is enough I may but call her mine.
FRIAR LAURENCE
    These violent delights have violent ends
    And in their triumph die, like fire and powder,        10
    Which as they kiss consume. The sweetest honey
    Is loathsome in his own deliciousness,                        12
    And in the taste confounds the appetite.                    13
    Therefore love moderately. Long love doth so;
    Too swift arrives as tardy as too slow.

*Enter Juliet.*

    Here comes the lady. Oh, so light a foot
    Will ne'er wear out the everlasting flint.
    A lover may bestride the gossamers                             18
    That idles in the wanton summer air,                          19
    And yet not fall, so light is vanity.                             20
JULIET
    Good even to my ghostly confessor.                            21
FRIAR LAURENCE
    Romeo shall thank thee, daughter, for us both.     22
JULIET
    As much to him, else is his thanks too much.         23

---

71 **in scarlet straight** i.e., blushing immediately    74 **bird's nest**
i.e., Juliet's room. (Continues the association of Juliet as a bird, as
at 1.3.3, 2.2.168–82, with erotic suggestion. The bawdry is continued
in *bear the burden* two lines later.)    77 **Hie you** Hurry. (With a pun
on *high* in line 78.)
**2.6. Location:** Verona. Friar Laurence's cell.
1 **So . . . heavens** May the heavens so smile    4 **countervail** outweigh,
counterbalance    6 **close** join    10 **powder** gunpowder    12 **his** its
13 **confounds** destroys    18 **gossamers** filmy cobwebs    19 **wanton**
playful    20 **vanity** transitory human joy.    21 **Good even** Good afternoon. (See 2.4.177.)    **ghostly** spiritual    22 **thank thee** i.e., give a kiss
in thanks for your greeting    23 **As . . . too much** either (1) Then I
must repay him with a kiss, lest I be overpaid, or (2) My greeting is to
Romeo as much as to you; otherwise, his greeting would exceed mine.

---

29 **stay** wait    34 **excuse** excuse yourself from telling.    36 **stay the
circumstance** wait patiently for the details.    38 **simple** foolish
42 **be not to be talked on** are beneath mention (especially in refined
ladylike company)    50 **o' t'other** on the other    51 **Beshrew** A curse
on. (Used as a mild oath.)    60 **honest** honorable    62 **hot** impatient.
**Marry, come up** (An expression of impatient reproof.)    **I trow**
Literally, I think, I believe.    65 **coil** turmoil, fuss.    68 **hie** hasten

ROMEO
    Ah, Juliet, if the measure of thy joy
    Be heaped like mine, and that thy skill be more    25
    To blazon it, then sweeten with thy breath    26
    This neighbor air, and let rich music's tongue
    Unfold the imagined happiness that both    28
    Receive in either by this dear encounter.    29
JULIET
    Conceit, more rich in matter than in words,    30
    Brags of his substance, not of ornament.    31
    They are but beggars that can count their worth.
    But my true love is grown to such excess
    I cannot sum up sum of half my wealth.    34
FRIAR LAURENCE
    Come, come with me, and we will make short work;
    For, by your leaves, you shall not stay alone
    Till Holy Church incorporate two in one.    *[Exeunt.]*

# [3.1]

*Enter Mercutio, Benvolio, and men.*

BENVOLIO
    I pray thee, good Mercutio, let's retire.
    The day is hot, the Capels are abroad,    2
    And if we meet we shall not scape a brawl,
    For now, these hot days, is the mad blood stirring.
MERCUTIO    Thou art like one of these fellows that when
    he enters the confines of a tavern, claps me his sword    6
    upon the table and says, "God send me no need of
    thee!" and by the operation of the second cup draws    8
    him on the drawer, when indeed there is no need.    9
BENVOLIO    Am I like such a fellow?
MERCUTIO    Come, come, thou art as hot a Jack in thy    11
    mood as any in Italy, and as soon moved to be moody,    12
    and as soon moody to be moved.    13
BENVOLIO    And what to?
MERCUTIO    Nay, an there were two such, we should    15
    have none shortly, for one would kill the other. Thou!
    Why, thou wilt quarrel with a man that hath a hair
    more or a hair less in his beard than thou hast. Thou
    wilt quarrel with a man for cracking nuts, having no
    other reason but because thou hast hazel eyes. What
    eye but such an eye would spy out such a quarrel? Thy
    head is as full of quarrels as an egg is full of meat, and    22
    yet thy head hath been beaten as addle as an egg for    23
    quarreling. Thou hast quarreled with a man for cough-
    ing in the street, because he hath wakened thy dog that

    hath lain asleep in the sun. Didst thou not fall out
    with a tailor for wearing his new doublet before    27
    Easter? With another, for tying his new shoes with old    28
    ribbon? And yet thou wilt tutor me from quarreling!
BENVOLIO    An I were so apt to quarrel as thou art, any
    man should buy the fee simple of my life for an hour    31
    and a quarter.    32
MERCUTIO    The fee simple! Oh, simple!    33

*Enter Tybalt, Petruchio, and others.*

BENVOLIO    By my head, here comes the Capulets.
MERCUTIO    By my heel, I care not.
TYBALT    *[to his companions]*
    Follow me close, for I will speak to them.—
    Gentlemen, good e'en. A word with one of you.
MERCUTIO    And but one word with one of us? Couple it
    with something: make it a word and a blow.
TYBALT    You shall find me apt enough to that, sir, an
    you will give me occasion.
MERCUTIO    Could you not take some occasion without
    giving?
TYBALT    Mercutio, thou consortest with Romeo.    44
MERCUTIO    "Consort"? What, dost thou make us min-
    strels? An thou make minstrels of us, look to hear
    nothing but discords. Here's my fiddlestick; here's    47
    that shall make you dance. Zounds, "consort"!    48
BENVOLIO
    We talk here in the public haunt of men.
    Either withdraw unto some private place,
    Or reason coldly of your grievances,    51
    Or else depart; here all eyes gaze on us.    52
MERCUTIO
    Men's eyes were made to look, and let them gaze.
    I will not budge for no man's pleasure, I.

*Enter Romeo.*

TYBALT
    Well, peace be with you, sir. Here comes my man.
MERCUTIO
    But I'll be hanged, sir, if he wear your livery.    56
    Marry, go before to field, he'll be your follower;    57
    Your Worship in that sense may call him "man."    58
TYBALT
    Romeo, the love I bear thee can afford
    No better term than this: thou art a villain.    60
ROMEO
    Tybalt, the reason that I have to love thee
    Doth much excuse the appertaining rage    62
    To such a greeting. Villain am I none.

---

**25 that** if  **26 blazon** describe, set forth. (A heraldic term.)
**28 Unfold** make known.  **imagined** i.e., unexpressed  **29 in either** from each other  **30–1 Conceit . . . ornament** True understanding, more enriched by the actual reality (of love) than by mere words, finds more worth in the substance of that reality than in outward show.  **34 sum up sum** add up the total
**3.1. Location: Verona. A public place.**
**2 Capels** Capulets  **6 claps me** claps. (*Me* is a now-archaic dative of reference, used colloquially.)  **8–9 draws . . . drawer** draws his sword against the tapster or waiter  **9 there is no need** i.e., of his sword.
**11 as hot a Jack** as hot-tempered a fellow  **12 moody** angry  **13 to be moved** at being provoked.  **15 an** if  **22 meat** i.e., edible matter
**23 addle** addled, confused

**27 doublet** man's jacket  **27–8 before Easter** (A new outfit should be saved for Easter, not worn during the penitential days of Lent.)
**31 fee simple** outright possession  **31–2 an hour . . . quarter** i.e., my life would last no longer in such circumstances.  **33 Oh, simple!** Oh, how stupid!  **44 consortest** keep company with. (But Mercutio quibbles on its musical sense of "accompany" or "play together.")
**47 fiddlestick** (Mercutio means his sword.)  **48 that** that which.
**Zounds** By God's (Christ's) wounds  **51 coldly** calmly  **52 depart** go away separately  **56 livery** servant's uniform. (Mercutio deliberately mistakes Tybalt's phrase *my man* to mean "my servant.")  **57 field** field where a duel might occur  **58 Your Worship** (A title of honor used here with mock politeness.)  **60 villain** lowly wretch, rogue.
**62 the appertaining rage** the rage that would ordinarily be appropriate

Therefore, farewell. I see thou knowest me not.

TYBALT
Boy, this shall not excuse the injuries    65
That thou hast done me. Therefore turn and draw.

ROMEO
I do protest I never injured thee,    67
But love thee better than thou canst devise    68
Till thou shalt know the reason of my love.
And so, good Capulet—which name I tender    70
As dearly as mine own—be satisfied.

MERCUTIO
Oh, calm, dishonorable, vile submission!
*Alla stoccata* carries it away.     [*He draws.*]   73
Tybalt, you ratcatcher, will you walk?    74

TYBALT    What wouldst thou have with me?

MERCUTIO    Good king of cats, nothing but one of your
nine lives, that I mean to make bold withal, and, as   77
you shall use me hereafter, dry-beat the rest of the   78
eight. Will you pluck your sword out of his pilcher by   79
the ears? Make haste, lest mine be about your ears ere   80
it be out.

TYBALT    I am for you.         [*He draws.*]

ROMEO
Gentle Mercutio, put thy rapier up.

MERCUTIO    Come, sir, your *passado*.     [*They fight.*]   84

ROMEO
Draw, Benvolio, beat down their weapons.
Gentlemen, for shame, forbear this outrage!    86
Tybalt, Mercutio, the Prince expressly hath
Forbid this bandying in Verona streets.    88
Hold, Tybalt! Good Mercutio!
     [*Tybalt under Romeo's arm stabs Mercutio.*] *Away*
                   *Tybalt* [*with his followers*].

MERCUTIO                 I am hurt.    89
A plague o' both your houses! I am sped.    90
Is he gone, and hath nothing?

BENVOLIO           What, art thou hurt?    91

MERCUTIO
Ay, ay, a scratch, a scratch; marry, 'tis enough.
Where is my page? Go, villain, fetch a surgeon.
                     [*Exit Page.*]

ROMEO
Courage, man, the hurt cannot be much.

MERCUTIO    No, 'tis not so deep as a well, nor so wide as
a church door, but 'tis enough, 'twill serve. Ask for me
tomorrow, and you shall find me a grave man. I am   97
peppered, I warrant, for this world. A plague o' both   98
your houses! Zounds, a dog, a rat, a mouse, a cat, to
scratch a man to death! A braggart, a rogue, a villain,
that fights by the book of arithmetic! Why the devil   101
came you between us? I was hurt under your arm.

ROMEO    I thought all for the best.

MERCUTIO
Help me into some house, Benvolio,
Or I shall faint. A plague o' both your houses!
They have made worm's meat of me. I have it,
And soundly too. Your houses!
            *Exit* [*supported by Benvolio*].

ROMEO
This gentleman, the Prince's near ally,    108
My very friend, hath got this mortal hurt    109
In my behalf; my reputation stained
With Tybalt's slander—Tybalt, that an hour
Hath been my cousin! O sweet Juliet,    112
Thy beauty hath made me effeminate,    113
And in my temper softened valor's steel.    114

      *Enter Benvolio.*

BENVOLIO
O Romeo, Romeo, brave Mercutio is dead!
That gallant spirit hath aspired the clouds,    116
Which too untimely here did scorn the earth.    117

ROMEO
This day's black fate on more days doth depend;    118
This but begins the woe others must end.    119

      [*Enter Tybalt.*]

BENVOLIO
Here comes the furious Tybalt back again.

ROMEO
Alive in triumph, and Mercutio slain!
Away to heaven, respective lenity,    122
And fire-eyed fury be my conduct now!    123
Now, Tybalt, take the "villain" back again
That late thou gavest me, for Mercutio's soul
Is but a little way above our heads,
Staying for thine to keep him company.
Either thou or I, or both, must go with him.

TYBALT
Thou, wretched boy, that didst consort him here,
Shalt with him hence.

ROMEO            This shall determine that.
             *They fight. Tybalt falls.*

BENVOLIO    Romeo, away, begone!
The citizens are up, and Tybalt slain.

---

**65 Boy** (A deliberate and grave insult when addressed to a grown man. Tybalt's use of *thee* and *thou* in lines 59–60 and following is similarly insulting; Romeo's use of this personal form in lines 61–4 and 67–9, on the other hand, is appropriate to a close family tie that he privately acknowledges but is of course misunderstood by Tybalt and the bystanders.) **67 protest** insist **68 devise** imagine **70 tender** value **73 *Alla stoccata* . . . away** i.e. (scornfully), This elegant Italian way of fencing, and the fancy terminology to go with it, will win the day, I suppose. (*Alla stoccata* means "at the thrust.") **74 ratcatcher** (An allusion to Tybalt as king of cats; see 2.4.19.) **77 make bold withal** make free with **78 dry-beat** beat soundly (without drawing blood) **79–80 out . . . ears** out of its scabbard by the handle or hilt. **84 *passado*** forward thrust. (Another fancy Italian fencing term of the sort Mercutio despises.) **86 outrage** disgraceful quarreling. **88 bandying** exchange of blows **89 s.d. *Away Tybalt*** (Because the phrase is unusual for an exit stage direction, some editors plausibly assign this as a speech to Petruchio, who enters at line 33.1 and is otherwise silent.) **90 sped** done for. **91 and hath nothing** and has received no hurt in payment for his blows.

**97 grave** (Mercutio thus puns with his last breath.) **98 peppered** finished, done for **101 by . . . arithmetic** by the numbers, as in a textbook on fencing (as at 2.4.20–3). **108 ally** kinsman **109 very** true **112 cousin** kinsman. **113 effeminate** weak **114 temper** disposition. (But with a play on the tempering of a steel sword.) **116 aspired** ascended to **117 Which . . . earth** whose spirit, before his untimely death, scorned anything he found unworthy. **118 This day's . . . depend** This day hangs threateningly over the time to come **119 others** other days to come **122 respective lenity** considerate gentleness **123 conduct** guide

Stand not amazed. The Prince will doom thee death    133
If thou art taken. Hence, begone, away!

ROMEO
Oh, I am fortune's fool!

BENVOLIO                    Why dost thou stay?    135

*Exit Romeo.*

*Enter Citizens.*

FIRST CITIZEN
Which way ran he that killed Mercutio?
Tybalt, that murderer, which way ran he?

BENVOLIO
There lies that Tybalt.

FIRST CITIZEN                    Up, sir, go with me.
I charge thee in the Prince's name, obey.

*Enter Prince [attended], old Montague,
Capulet, their Wives, and all.*

PRINCE
Where are the vile beginners of this fray?

BENVOLIO
O noble Prince, I can discover all    141
The unlucky manage of this fatal brawl.    142
There lies the man, slain by young Romeo,
That slew thy kinsman, brave Mercutio.

CAPULET'S WIFE
Tybalt, my cousin! O my brother's child!
O Prince! O cousin! Husband! Oh, the blood is spilled
Of my dear kinsman! Prince, as thou art true,
For blood of ours shed blood of Montague.
O cousin, cousin!

PRINCE
Benvolio, who began this bloody fray?

BENVOLIO
Tybalt, here slain, whom Romeo's hand did slay.
Romeo, that spoke him fair, bid him bethink    152
How nice the quarrel was, and urged withal    153
Your high displeasure. All this—utterèd
With gentle breath, calm look, knees humbly bowed—
Could not take truce with the unruly spleen    156
Of Tybalt deaf to peace, but that he tilts
With piercing steel at bold Mercutio's breast,
Who, all as hot, turns deadly point to point,
And, with a martial scorn, with one hand beats
Cold death aside and with the other sends
It back to Tybalt, whose dexterity
Retorts it. Romeo, he cries aloud,    163
"Hold, friends! Friends, part!" and swifter than his
      tongue
His agile arm beats down their fatal points,
And twixt them rushes; underneath whose arm
An envious thrust from Tybalt hit the life    167
Of stout Mercutio, and then Tybalt fled;    168
But by and by comes back to Romeo,
Who had but newly entertained revenge,    170

And to't they go like lightning, for, ere I
Could draw to part them was stout Tybalt slain,
And, as he fell, did Romeo turn and fly.
This is the truth, or let Benvolio die.

CAPULET'S WIFE
He is a kinsman to the Montague.
Affection makes him false; he speaks not true.    176
Some twenty of them fought in this black strife,
And all those twenty could but kill one life.
I beg for justice, which thou, Prince, must give.
Romeo slew Tybalt; Romeo must not live.

PRINCE
Romeo slew him, he slew Mercutio.
Who now the price of his dear blood doth owe?

MONTAGUE
Not Romeo, Prince, he was Mercutio's friend;
His fault concludes but what the law should end,    184
The life of Tybalt.

PRINCE                    And for that offense
Immediately we do exile him hence.
I have an interest in your hate's proceeding;
My blood for your rude brawls doth lie a-bleeding;    188
But I'll amerce you with so strong a fine    189
That you shall all repent the loss of mine.
I will be deaf to pleading and excuses;
Nor tears nor prayers shall purchase out abuses.    192
Therefore use none. Let Romeo hence in haste,    193
Else, when he is found, that hour is his last.    194
Bear hence this body and attend our will.    195
Mercy but murders, pardoning those that kill.    196

*Exeunt, [some carrying Tybalt's body].*

❧

# [3.2]

*Enter Juliet alone.*

JULIET
Gallop apace, you fiery-footed steeds,    1
Towards Phoebus' lodging! Such a wagoner    2
As Phaëthon would whip you to the west    3
And bring in cloudy night immediately.    4
Spread thy close curtain, love-performing night,    5

133 **amazed** dazed.   **doom thee death** sentence you to death
135 **fool** dupe.   141 **discover** reveal   142 **manage** conduct   152 **fair**
civilly.   **bethink** consider   153 **nice** trivial.   **withal** besides   156 **take**
**truce** make peace   163 **Retorts** returns   167 **envious** malicious
168 **stout** brave   170 **entertained** harbored thoughts of

176 **Affection** Partiality   184 **concludes but** only finishes   188 **My**
**blood** i.e., blood of my kinsman. (Here we learn that Mercutio was
kin to the Prince.)   189 **amerce** penalize   192 **Nor** neither.   **purchase**
**out abuses** redeem misdeeds.   193 **hence** depart   194 **Else** otherwise
195 **attend our will** be on hand to hear further judgment.   196 **but**
**murders** merely encourages murder by excessive leniency
**3.2. Location: Verona. Capulet's house.**
1 **apace** quickly.   **steeds** i.e., the horses of the sun god's chariot
2 **Phoebus** (Often equated with Helios, the sun god.)   **lodging** i.e., in
the west, below the horizon.   2–4 **Such . . . immediately** i.e., One
who is impetuously young, as we are, would understand the need to
make the day as short as possible and would quickly bring it to an
end. (The mythical allusion is sadly ironic, for Phaëthon drove the
chariot of the sun so badly that he had to be destroyed by Zeus.)
5 **close** enclosing

That runaways' eyes may wink, and Romeo                  6
Leap to these arms, untalked of and unseen.              7
Lovers can see to do their amorous rites
By their own beauties; or, if love be blind,
It best agrees with night. Come, civil night,           10
Thou sober-suited matron all in black,
And learn me how to lose a winning match                 12
Played for a pair of stainless maidenhoods.
Hood my unmanned blood, bating in my cheeks,             14
With thy black mantle till strange love grown bold       15
Think true love acted simple modesty.
Come, night. Come, Romeo. Come, thou day in night;
For thou wilt lie upon the wings of night
Whiter than new snow upon a raven's back.
Come, gentle night, come, loving, black-browed night,
Give me my Romeo, and when I shall die                   21
Take him and cut him out in little stars,
And he will make the face of heaven so fine
That all the world will be in love with night
And pay no worship to the garish sun.                    25
Oh, I have bought the mansion of a love
But not possessed it, and though I am sold,
Not yet enjoyed. So tedious is this day
As is the night before some festival
To an impatient child that hath new robes
And may not wear them. Oh, here comes my nurse,          31

       *Enter Nurse, with cords.*

And she brings news, and every tongue that speaks
But Romeo's name speaks heavenly eloquence.
Now, Nurse, what news? What hast thou there? The
   cords
That Romeo bid thee fetch?

NURSE               Ay, ay, the cords.
                           [*She throws them down.*]

JULIET
Ay me, what news? Why dost thou wring thy hands?

NURSE
Ah, weraday! He's dead, he's dead, he's dead!           37
We are undone, lady, we are undone!
Alack the day, he's gone, he's killed, he's dead!

JULIET
Can heaven be so envious?

NURSE               Romeo can,         40
Though heaven cannot. Oh, Romeo, Romeo!
Who ever would have thought it? Romeo!

---

JULIET
What devil art thou that dost torment me thus?
This torture should be roared in dismal hell.
Hath Romeo slain himself? Say thou but "Ay,"
And that bare vowel "I" shall poison more               46
Than the death-darting eye of cockatrice.               47
I am not I, if there be such an "Ay,"
Or those eyes shut, that makes thee answer "Ay."        49
If he be slain, say "Ay," or if not, "No."
Brief sounds determine of my weal or woe.               51

NURSE
I saw the wound. I saw it with mine eyes—
God save the mark!—here on his manly breast.            53
A piteous corpse, a bloody piteous corpse;
Pale, pale as ashes, all bedaubed in blood,
All in gore-blood. I swoonèd at the sight.              56

JULIET
Oh, break, my heart! Poor bankrupt, break at once!
To prison, eyes; ne'er look on liberty!
Vile earth, to earth resign; end motion here,           59
And thou and Romeo press one heavy bier!                60

NURSE
O Tybalt, Tybalt, the best friend I had!
O courteous Tybalt! Honest gentleman!                   62
That ever I should live to see thee dead!

JULIET
What storm is this that blows so contrary?
Is Romeo slaughtered, and is Tybalt dead?
My dearest cousin, and my dearer lord?
Then, dreadful trumpet, sound the general doom!         67
For who is living, if those two are gone?

NURSE
Tybalt is gone, and Romeo banishèd;
Romeo that killed him, he is banishèd.

JULIET
Oh, God! Did Romeo's hand shed Tybalt's blood?

NURSE
It did, it did. Alas the day it did!

JULIET
O serpent heart, hid with a flow'ring face!             73
Did ever dragon keep so fair a cave?                    74
Beautiful tyrant! Fiend angelical!
Dove-feathered raven! Wolvish-ravening lamb!
Despisèd substance of divinest show!                    77
Just opposite to what thou justly seem'st,
A damnèd saint, an honorable villain!
O nature, what hadst thou to do in hell
When thou didst bower the spirit of a fiend             81
In mortal paradise of such sweet flesh?
Was ever book containing such vile matter

---

**6–7 That runaways' . . . unseen** (Perhaps Juliet is thinking of the elopement that will surely be necessary once she and Romeo secretly marry; they will embrace in the dark of *love-performing night*, untalked of and unseen by others and by each other. A difficult passage that is sometimes interpreted, uncertainly, as referring to the sun's horses as the *runaways*. *Wink* means "close, be shut.")   **10 civil** circumspect, somberly attired   **12 learn** teach.   **to lose . . . match** to lose my virginity in order to gain a happy marriage   **14 Hood** Cover. (A term in falconry; the hawk's eyes were covered so that it would not *bate* or beat its wings.)   **unmanned** untamed (in falconry; with a pun on "not yet sexually possessed")   **15 strange** diffident   **21 I** (Often emended to *he*, following the fourth quarto, but Juliet may mean that when she is dead she will share Romeo's beauty with the world. Dying may also hint at sexual climax.)   **25 garish** dazzling   **31.1 cords** ropes (for the ladder).   **37 weraday!** welladay, alas!   **40 envious** malicious.

**46 "I"** (Pronounced identically with "Ay.")   **47 cockatrice** basilisk, a mythical serpent that could kill by its look.   **49 those eyes shut** if Romeo's eyes are shut (in death)   **51 weal** welfare, happiness   **53 God . . . mark** (An oath registering shock and horror.)   **56 gore-blood** clotted blood.   **59 Vile . . . here** May my vile body resign itself to burial, ending life itself   **60 press** weigh down.   **bier** litter for carrying corpses.   **62 Honest** Honorable   **67 trumpet** i.e., the last trumpet.   **general doom** Day of Judgment.   **73 hid . . . face** concealed beneath a beautiful face.   **74 keep** occupy, guard.   **cave** i.e., one with treasure in it.   **77 show** appearance.   **81 bower** give lodging to

So fairly bound? Oh, that deceit should dwell
In such a gorgeous palace!
NURSE                                    There's no trust,
No faith, no honesty in men; all perjured,
All forsworn, all naught, all dissemblers.                  87
Ah, where's my man? Give me some aqua vitae.               88
These griefs, these woes, these sorrows make me old.
Shame come to Romeo!
JULIET                        Blistered be thy tongue
For such a wish! He was not born to shame.
Upon his brow shame is ashamed to sit,
For 'tis a throne where honor may be crowned
Sole monarch of the universal earth.
Oh, what a beast was I to chide at him!
NURSE
Will you speak well of him that killed your cousin?
JULIET
Shall I speak ill of him that is my husband?
Ah, poor my lord, what tongue shall smooth thy name   98
When I, thy three-hours wife, have mangled it?
But wherefore, villain, didst thou kill my cousin?
That villain cousin would have killed my husband.
Back, foolish tears, back to your native spring!
Your tributary drops belong to woe,                       103
Which you, mistaking, offer up to joy.
My husband lives, that Tybalt would have slain,          105
And Tybalt's dead, that would have slain my
     husband.
All this is comfort. Wherefore weep I then?
Some word there was, worser than Tybalt's death,
That murdered me. I would forget it fain,                 109
But oh, it presses to my memory
Like damnèd guilty deeds to sinners' minds!
"Tybalt is dead, and Romeo—banishèd."
That "banishèd," that one word "banishèd"
Hath slain ten thousand Tybalts. Tybalt's death
Was woe enough, if it had ended there;
Or, if sour woe delights in fellowship
And needly will be ranked with other griefs,             117
Why followed not, when she said "Tybalt's dead,"
"Thy father," or "thy mother," nay, or both,
Which modern lamentation might have moved?               120
But with a rearward following Tybalt's death,            121
"Romeo is banishèd"—to speak that word
Is father, mother, Tybalt, Romeo, Juliet,
All slain, all dead. "Romeo is banishèd!"
There is no end, no limit, measure, bound,
In that word's death; no words can that woe sound.        126
Where is my father and my mother, Nurse?
NURSE
Weeping and wailing over Tybalt's corpse.
Will you go to them? I will bring you thither.

JULIET
Wash they his wounds with tears? Mine shall be spent,
When theirs are dry, for Romeo's banishment.
Take up those cords.—Poor ropes, you are beguiled,
Both you and I, for Romeo is exiled.
He made you for a highway to my bed,
But I, a maid, die maiden-widowèd.
Come, cords, come, Nurse. I'll to my wedding bed,
And death, not Romeo, take my maidenhead.
NURSE [*taking up the cords*]
Hie to your chamber. I'll find Romeo
To comfort you. I wot well where he is.                   139
Hark ye, your Romeo will be here at night.
I'll to him. He is hid at Laurence' cell.
JULIET [*giving a ring*]
Oh, find him! Give this ring to my true knight,
And bid him come to take his last farewell.
                        *Exeunt* [*separately*].

# [3.3]

*Enter Friar* [*Laurence*].

FRIAR LAURENCE
Romeo, come forth; come forth, thou fearful man.          1
Affliction is enamored of thy parts,                       2
And thou art wedded to calamity.

     [*Enter*] *Romeo.*

ROMEO
Father, what news? What is the Prince's doom?              4
What sorrow craves acquaintance at my hand
That I yet know not?
FRIAR LAURENCE           Too familiar
Is my dear son with such sour company.
I bring thee tidings of the Prince's doom.
ROMEO
What less than doomsday is the Prince's doom?             9
FRIAR LAURENCE
A gentler judgment vanished from his lips:               10
Not body's death, but body's banishment.
ROMEO
Ha, banishment? Be merciful, say "death";
For exile hath more terror in his look,
Much more than death. Do not say "banishment."
FRIAR LAURENCE
Here from Verona art thou banishèd.
Be patient, for the world is broad and wide.
ROMEO
There is no world without Verona walls                   17
But purgatory, torture, hell itself.
Hence "banishèd" is banished from the world,
And world's exile is death. Then "banishèd"             20
Is death mistermed. Calling death "banishèd,"

87 **naught** worthless, evil   88 **man** servant.  **aqua vitae** alcoholic
spirits.   98 **poor my lord** my poor lord.  **smooth thy name** speak
your name kindly   103 **Your . . . woe** You should be shed, offered as
a tribute, on some occasion of real woe   105 **that** whom   109 **fain**
gladly   117 **needly** of necessity.  **ranked with** accompanied by
120 **Which . . . moved** which might have prompted a normal grief-
stricken response.   121 **rearward** rearguard, following afterward
126 **can . . . sound** can fathom and adequately express that woe.

139 **wot** know
3.3. Location: Verona. Friar Laurence's cell.
1 **fearful** full of fear   2 **parts** qualities   4 **doom** judgment.
9 **doomsday** the Day of Judgment, i.e., end of the world
10 **vanished** issued, escaped   17 **without** outside of   20 **world's**
**exile** exile from the world

Thou cut'st my head off with a golden ax
And smilest upon the stroke that murders me.

FRIAR LAURENCE
Oh, deadly sin! Oh, rude unthankfulness!
Thy fault our law calls death, but the kind Prince,    25
Taking thy part, hath rushed aside the law    26
And turned that black word "death" to "banishment."
This is dear mercy, and thou see'st it not.

ROMEO
'Tis torture, and not mercy. Heaven is here
Where Juliet lives, and every cat and dog
And little mouse, every unworthy thing,
Live here in heaven and may look on her,
But Romeo may not. More validity,    33
More honorable state, more courtship lives    34
In carrion flies than Romeo. They may seize
On the white wonder of dear Juliet's hand
And steal immortal blessing from her lips,
Who even in pure and vestal modesty    38
Still blush, as thinking their own kisses sin;    39
But Romeo may not, he is banishèd.
Flies may do this, but I from this must fly.
They are free men, but I am banishèd.
And sayest thou yet that exile is not death?
Hadst thou no poison mixed, no sharp-ground knife,
No sudden mean of death, though ne'er so mean,    45
But "banishèd" to kill me? "Banishèd"?
Oh, Friar, the damnèd use that word in hell;
Howling attends it. How hast thou the heart,
Being a divine, a ghostly confessor,    49
A sin absolver, and my friend professed,    50
To mangle me with that word "banishèd"?

FRIAR LAURENCE
Thou fond mad man, hear me a little speak.    52

ROMEO
Oh, thou wilt speak again of banishment.

FRIAR LAURENCE
I'll give thee armor to keep off that word,
Adversity's sweet milk, philosophy,
To comfort thee, though thou art banishèd.

ROMEO
Yet "banishèd"? Hang up philosophy!    57
Unless philosophy can make a Juliet,
Displant a town, reverse a prince's doom,    59
It helps not, it prevails not. Talk no more.

FRIAR LAURENCE
Oh, then I see that madmen have no ears.

ROMEO
How should they, when that wise men have no eyes?

FRIAR LAURENCE
Let me dispute with thee of thy estate.    63

ROMEO
Thou canst not speak of that thou dost not feel.    64
Wert thou as young as I, Juliet thy love,
An hour but married, Tybalt murderèd,
Doting like me, and like me banishèd,
Then mightst thou speak, then mightst thou tear thy
   hair,
And fall upon the ground, as I do now,
Taking the measure of an unmade grave.
            [He falls upon the ground.] Knock [within].

FRIAR LAURENCE
Arise. One knocks. Good Romeo, hide thyself.

ROMEO
Not I, unless the breath of heartsick groans,
Mistlike, infold me from the search of eyes.    Knock.

FRIAR LAURENCE
Hark, how they knock!—Who's there?—Romeo, arise.
Thou wilt be taken.—Stay awhile!—Stand up.
                                    Knock.
Run to my study.—By and by!—God's will,
What simpleness is this?—I come, I come!    Knock.   77
Who knocks so hard? Whence come you? What's your
   will?                        [Going to the door.]

NURSE [within]
Let me come in, and you shall know my errand.
I come from Lady Juliet.

FRIAR LAURENCE            Welcome, then.
                        [He opens the door.]

        Enter Nurse.

NURSE
O holy Friar, oh, tell me, holy Friar,
Where's my lady's lord, where's Romeo?

FRIAR LAURENCE
There on the ground, with his own tears made drunk.

NURSE
Oh, he is even in my mistress' case,    84
Just in her case! Oh, woeful sympathy!    85
Piteous predicament! Even so lies she,
Blubb'ring and weeping, weeping and blubb'ring.—
Stand up, stand up! Stand, an you be a man.
For Juliet's sake, for her sake, rise and stand!
Why should you fall into so deep an O?    90

ROMEO   Nurse!                        [He rises.]

NURSE
Ah, sir, ah, sir! Death's the end of all.

ROMEO
Spakest thou of Juliet? How is it with her?
Doth not she think me an old murderer,    94
Now I have stained the childhood of our joy
With blood removed but little from her own?
Where is she? And how doth she? And what says
My concealed lady to our canceled love?    98

---

**25 Thy fault . . . death** For your crime, the law demands a death sentence   **26 rushed** thrust   **33 validity** true worth   **34 courtship** (1) courtliness (2) occasion for wooing   **38 vestal** maidenly   **39 Still . . . sin** continually look red, as though blushing to think that their touching each other is sin   **45 mean . . . mean** means . . . base   **49 ghostly** spiritual   **50 A sin absolver** (One of the priest's most sacred duties was to hear confession and prescribe penance leading to absolution for the sin or sins committed.)   **52 fond** foolish, frantic   **57 Yet** Still   **59 Displant** uproot (by moving Romeo's place of banishment, wherever that is to be [Mantua, as it turns out], near to Verona and Juliet)   **63 dispute** reason.   **estate** situation.

**64 that** that which   **77 simpleness** foolishness   **84 even** exactly.   **case** situation   **85 woeful sympathy** mutuality of grief.   **90 an O** a fit of groaning. (A sexual meaning, unrecognized by the speaker, is suggested by *rise and stand* in the previous line and *case* in lines 84–5.)   **94 old** hardened   **98 concealed** secret.   **canceled** nullified (by the impending exile)

NURSE
    Oh, she says nothing, sir, but weeps and weeps,
    And now falls on her bed, and then starts up,
    And "Tybalt" calls, and then on Romeo cries,
    And then down falls again.
ROMEO               As if that name,
    Shot from the deadly level of a gun,        103
    Did murder her, as that name's cursèd hand
    Murdered her kinsman. Oh, tell me, Friar, tell me,
    In what vile part of this anatomy
    Doth my name lodge? Tell me, that I may sack    107
    The hateful mansion.
           [*He draws a weapon, but is restrained.*]
FRIAR LAURENCE      Hold thy desperate hand!
    Art thou a man? Thy form cries out thou art;
    Thy tears are womanish, thy wild acts denote
    The unreasonable fury of a beast.
    Unseemly woman in a seeming man,
    And ill-beseeming beast in seeming both!
    Thou hast amazed me. By my holy order,
    I thought thy disposition better tempered.    115
    Hast thou slain Tybalt? Wilt thou slay thyself,
    And slay thy lady, that in thy life lives,
    By doing damnèd hate upon thyself?
    Why railest thou on thy birth, the heaven, and earth,
    Since birth, and heaven, and earth, all three do meet  120
    In thee at once, which thou at once wouldst lose?
    Fie, fie, thou shamest thy shape, thy love, thy wit,  122
    Which, like a usurer, abound'st in all,    123
    And usest none in that true use indeed    124
    Which should bedeck thy shape, thy love, thy wit.  125
    Thy noble shape is but a form of wax,    126
    Digressing from the valor of a man;
    Thy dear love sworn but hollow perjury,
    Killing that love which thou hast vowed to cherish;
    Thy wit, that ornament to shape and love,
    Misshapen in the conduct of them both,    131
    Like powder in a skilless soldier's flask    132
    Is set afire by thine own ignorance,
    And thou dismembered with thine own defense.  134
    What, rouse thee, man! Thy Juliet is alive,
    For whose dear sake thou wast but lately dead;  136
    There art thou happy. Tybalt would kill thee,  137
    But thou slewest Tybalt; there art thou happy.
    The law that threatened death becomes thy friend
    And turns it to exile; there art thou happy.
    A pack of blessings light upon thy back,
    Happiness courts thee in her best array,
    But like a mishavèd and sullen wench    143
    Thou pout'st upon thy fortune and thy love.

    Take heed, take heed, for such die miserable.
    Go, get thee to thy love, as was decreed.    146
    Ascend her chamber; hence and comfort her.
    But look thou stay not till the watch be set,  148
    For then thou canst not pass to Mantua,
    Where thou shalt live till we can find a time
    To blaze your marriage, reconcile your friends,  151
    Beg pardon of the Prince, and call thee back
    With twenty hundred thousand times more joy
    Than thou went'st forth in lamentation.
    Go before, Nurse. Commend me to thy lady,
    And bid her hasten all the house to bed,
    Which heavy sorrow makes them apt unto.
    Romeo is coming.
NURSE
    Oh, Lord, I could have stayed here all the night
    To hear good counsel. Oh, what learning is!—
    My lord, I'll tell my lady you will come.
ROMEO
    Do so, and bid my sweet prepare to chide.
NURSE [*giving a ring*]
    Here, sir, a ring she bid me give you, sir.
    Hie you, make haste, for it grows very late.    [*Exit.*]
ROMEO
    How well my comfort is revived by this!
FRIAR LAURENCE
    Go hence. Good night. And here stands all your state: 166
    Either be gone before the watch be set,
    Or by the break of day disguised from hence.
    Sojourn in Mantua. I'll find out your man,
    And he shall signify from time to time
    Every good hap to you that chances here.    171
    Give me thy hand. 'Tis late. Farewell, good night.
ROMEO
    But that a joy past joy calls out on me,
    It were a grief so brief to part with thee.    174
    Farewell.              *Exeunt* [*separately*].

❖

# [3.4]

*Enter old Capulet, his Wife, and Paris.*

CAPULET
    Things have fall'n out, sir, so unluckily,    1
    That we have had no time to move our daughter.  2
    Look you, she loved her kinsman Tybalt dearly,
    And so did I. Well, we were born to die.
    'Tis very late. She'll not come down tonight.
    I promise you, but for your company    6
    I would have been abed an hour ago.
PARIS
    These times of woe afford no times to woo.
    Madam, good night. Commend me to your daughter.

---

103 **level** aim   107 **sack** destroy   115 **tempered** harmonized, balanced.   120 **birth . . . earth** life, soul, and body   122–5 **thou shamest . . . wit** you shame your physical form, love, and mind (corresponding to life, soul, and body), all of which you have in abundance but which you misuse as a usurer misuses wealth, using improperly the treasure that you should put to proper use.   126 **form of wax** waxwork, mere outer form   131 **conduct** guidance   132 **powder** gunpowder.  **flask** powder horn   134 **dismembered . . . defense** blown to pieces by that which should defend you, i.e., your *wit*, or intellect.   136 **wast . . . dead** i.e., only recently were wishing yourself dead. (See line 70.)   137 **happy** fortunate.   143 **mishavèd** misbehaved

146 **decreed** (1) arranged earlier (2) decreed by heaven for those who have married.   148 **look** see to it that.  **the watch be set** guards are posted (at the city gates)   151 **blaze** publish, divulge.  **friends** relations   166 **here . . . state** your fortune depends on what follows   171 **good hap** fortunate event   174 **brief** quickly   **3.4. Location:** Verona. Capulet's house.   1 **fall'n out** happened   2 **move** persuade   6 **promise** assure

**WIFE**
I will, and know her mind early tomorrow.
Tonight she's mewed up to her heaviness.     11

**CAPULET**
Sir Paris, I will make a desperate tender     12
Of my child's love. I think she will be ruled
In all respects by me; nay, more, I doubt it not.
Wife, go you to her ere you go to bed.
Acquaint her here of my son Paris' love,
And bid her, mark you me, on Wednesday next—     17
But soft, what day is this?

**PARIS**                           Monday, my lord.     18

**CAPULET**
Monday! Ha, ha! Well, Wednesday is too soon;
O' Thursday let it be. O'Thursday, tell her,
She shall be married to this noble earl.
Will you be ready? Do you like this haste?
We'll keep no great ado—a friend or two;
For hark you, Tybalt being slain so late,     24
It may be thought we held him carelessly,     25
Being our kinsman, if we revel much.
Therefore we'll have some half a dozen friends,
And there an end. But what say you to Thursday?

**PARIS**
My lord, I would that Thursday were tomorrow.

**CAPULET**
Well, get you gone. O' Thursday be it, then.
[*To his Wife*] Go you to Juliet ere you go to bed;
Prepare her, wife, against this wedding day.—     32
Farewell, my lord.—Light to my chamber, ho!—
Afore me, it is so very late     34
That we may call it early by and by.
Good night.                           *Exeunt.*

❧

## [3.5]

*Enter Romeo and Juliet aloft [at the window].*

**JULIET**
Wilt thou be gone? It is not yet near day.
It was the nightingale, and not the lark,
That pierced the fearful hollow of thine ear;     3
Nightly she sings on yond pomegranate tree.
Believe me, love, it was the nightingale.

**ROMEO**
It was the lark, the herald of the morn,
No nightingale. Look, love, what envious streaks
Do lace the severing clouds in yonder east.     8
Night's candles are burnt out, and jocund day     9
Stands tiptoe on the misty mountain tops.
I must be gone and live, or stay and die.

**JULIET**
Yond light is not daylight, I know it, I.
It is some meteor that the sun exhaled     13
To be to thee this night a torchbearer
And light thee on thy way to Mantua.
Therefore stay yet. Thou need'st not to be gone.

**ROMEO**
Let me be ta'en; let me be put to death.
I am content, so thou wilt have it so.     18
I'll say yon gray is not the morning's eye;
'Tis but the pale reflex of Cynthia's brow.     20
Nor that is not the lark whose notes do beat
The vaulty heaven so high above our heads.
I have more care to stay than will to go.     23
Come, death, and welcome! Juliet wills it so.
How is't, my soul? Let's talk. It is not day.

**JULIET**
It is, it is. Hie hence, begone, away!     26
It is the lark that sings so out of tune,
Straining harsh discords and unpleasing sharps.     28
Some say the lark makes sweet division;     29
This doth not so, for she divideth us.
Some say the lark and loathèd toad changed eyes;     31
Oh, now I would they had changed voices too,
Since arm from arm that voice doth us affray,     33
Hunting thee hence with hunt's-up to the day.     34
Oh, now begone! More light and light it grows.

**ROMEO**
More light and light, more dark and dark our woes!

*Enter Nurse [hastily].*

**NURSE**  Madam!
**JULIET**  Nurse?
**NURSE**
Your lady mother is coming to your chamber.
The day is broke; be wary, look about.     [*Exit.*]

**JULIET**
Then window, let day in, and let life out.

**ROMEO**
Farewell, farewell! One kiss, and I'll descend.
          [*They kiss. He climbs down from the window.*]

**JULIET**
Art thou gone so? Love, lord, ay, husband, friend!     43
I must hear from thee every day in the hour,
For in a minute there are many days.
Oh, by this count I shall be much in years     46
Ere I again behold my Romeo!

**ROMEO** [*from below her window*]     Farewell!

---

**11 mewed up to** cooped up with. (A term from falconry, reminiscent of 2.2.159–68.)  **heaviness** sorrow.  **12 desperate tender** bold offer  **17 mark you me** listen to this  **18 soft** wait a minute  **24 late** recently  **25 held him carelessly** did not regard him highly  **32 against** in anticipation of  **34 Afore me** i.e., By my life. (A mild oath.)
**3.5. Location:** Verona. Capulet's orchard with Juliet's chamber window above, and, at lines 68 ff., the interior of Juliet's chamber.
**3 fearful** apprehensive, anxious  **8 severing** separating  **9 jocund** cheerful

**13 exhaled** i.e., has drawn out of the ground. (Meteors were thought to be vapors of luminous gas drawn up by the sun.)  **18 so** as long as, since  **20 reflex** reflection.  **Cynthia's** the moon's  **23 care** desire, concern  **26 Hie hence** Hasten away  **28 Straining . . . sharps** compressing together notes in harsh discord and that are pitched too high to be pleasingly harmonious.  **29 division** variations on a melody, made by dividing each note into notes of briefer duration  **31 changed** exchanged. (A popular saying, to account for the observation that the lark has very ordinary eyes and the toad remarkable ones.)  **33 arm from arm** from one another's arms.  **affray** frighten  **34 hunt's-up** a song or tune originally designed to awaken huntsmen; later, used also to serenade a newly married couple  **43 friend** lover  **46 much in years** much older

I will omit no opportunity
That may convey my greetings, love, to thee.
JULIET
Oh, think'st thou we shall ever meet again?
ROMEO
I doubt it not, and all these woes shall serve
For sweet discourses in our times to come.
JULIET
Oh, God, I have an ill-divining soul!                                     54
Methinks I see thee, now thou art so low,
As one dead in the bottom of a tomb.
Either my eyesight fails or thou lookest pale.
ROMEO
And trust me, love, in my eye so do you.
Dry sorrow drinks our blood. Adieu, adieu!         *Exit.*  59
JULIET
O Fortune, Fortune! All men call thee fickle.
If thou art fickle, what dost thou with him
That is renowned for faith? Be fickle, Fortune.
For then, I hope, thou wilt not keep him long,
But send him back.

*Enter Mother [Capulet's Wife].*

WIFE                       Ho, daughter, are you up?
JULIET
Who is't that calls? It is my lady mother.
Is she not down so late, or up so early?                                  66
What unaccustomed cause procures her hither?                              67
                  *[She goeth down from the window.]*
WIFE
Why, how now, Juliet?
JULIET                        Madam, I am not well.
WIFE
Evermore weeping for your cousin's death?
What, wilt thou wash him from his grave with tears?
An if thou couldst, thou couldst not make him live;
Therefore, have done. Some grief shows much of love,                      72
But much of grief shows still some want of wit.                           73
JULIET
Yet let me weep for such a feeling loss.                                  74
WIFE
So shall you feel the loss, but not the friend                            75
Which you weep for.
JULIET                        Feeling so the loss,
I cannot choose but ever weep the friend.                                 77
WIFE
Well, girl, thou weep'st not so much for his death
As that the villain lives which slaughtered him.

JULIET
What villain, madam?
WIFE                          That same villain, Romeo.
JULIET *[aside]*
Villain and he be many miles asunder.—
God pardon him! I do, with all my heart;
And yet no man like he doth grieve my heart.                              83
WIFE
That is because the traitor murderer lives.
JULIET
Ay, madam, from the reach of these my hands.
Would none but I might venge my cousin's death!
WIFE
We will have vengeance for it, fear thou not.
Then weep no more. I'll send to one in Mantua,
Where that same banished runagate doth live,                              89
Shall give him such an unaccustomed dram                                  90
That he shall soon keep Tybalt company.
And then, I hope, thou wilt be satisfied.
JULIET
Indeed, I never shall be satisfied
With Romeo till I behold him—dead—
Is my poor heart so for a kinsman vexed.
Madam, if you could find out but a man
To bear a poison, I would temper it,                                      97
That Romeo should, upon receipt thereof,
Soon sleep in quiet. Oh, how my heart abhors
To hear him named, and cannot come to him
To wreak the love I bore my cousin                                        101
Upon his body that hath slaughtered him!                                  102
WIFE
Find thou the means, and I'll find such a man.
But now I'll tell thee joyful tidings, girl.
JULIET
And joy comes well in such a needy time.
What are they, beseech Your Ladyship?
WIFE
Well, well, thou hast a careful father, child,                            107
One who, to put thee from thy heaviness,                                  108
Hath sorted out a sudden day of joy                                       109
That thou expects not, nor I looked not for.
JULIET
Madam, in happy time, what day is that?
WIFE
Marry, my child, early next Thursday morn,                                112
The gallant, young, and noble gentleman,
The County Paris, at Saint Peter's Church
Shall happily make thee there a joyful bride.
JULIET
Now, by Saint Peter's Church, and Peter too,
He shall not make me there a joyful bride!

**54 ill-divining** prophesying of misfortune   **59 Dry sorrow** (The heat of the body in sorrow and despair was thought to descend into the bowels and dry up the blood.)   **66 down** in bed   **67 procures her** induces her to come   **67.1** (As indicated by the bracketed stage direction, which is from the first quarto, Juliet, who has appeared until now at her "window" above the stage, evidently descends quickly to the main stage and joins her mother for the remainder of the scene. The stage, which before was to have been imagined as Capulet's orchard, is now Juliet's chamber. Juliet's mother has entered onto the main stage four lines earlier.)   **72 have done** cease.   **73 want of wit** lack of intelligence.   **74 feeling** deeply felt   **75 feel** experience.   **the friend** the kinsman   **77 the friend** (Juliet secretly means "my lover," as at line 43, but, of course, her mother hears it as "Tybalt.")

**83 no man like he** no man so much as he.   **grieve** (1) anger (2) grieve with longing. (Juliet speaks to her mother throughout in intentional ambiguities, at lines 85, 86, 99, 100–2, etc.)   **89 runagate** renegade, fugitive   **90 Shall** who will.   **dram** dose. (Literally, one-eighth of a fluid ounce.)   **97 temper** (1) mix, concoct (2) alloy, dilute. (In her intended double meanings about Romeo dead, poisoned, and sleeping in quiet, Juliet is, of course, unaware of an ironic anticipation of how these things will be fulfilled.)   **101 wreak** (1) avenge (2) bestow   **102 his body that** the body of him who   **107 careful** full of care (for you)   **108 heaviness** sorrow   **109 sorted** chosen   **112 Marry** i.e., By the Virgin Mary

I wonder at this haste, that I must wed
Ere he that should be husband comes to woo.
I pray you, tell my lord and father, madam,
I will not marry yet, and when I do I swear
It shall be Romeo, whom you know I hate,
Rather than Paris. These are news indeed!

WIFE
Here comes your father. Tell him so yourself,
And see how he will take it at your hands.

*Enter Capulet and Nurse.*

CAPULET
When the sun sets, the earth doth drizzle dew,
But for the sunset of my brother's son                                        127
It rains downright.—
How now, a conduit, girl? What, still in tears?                          129
Evermore show'ring? In one little body
Thou counterfeits a bark, a sea, a wind;                                    131
For still thy eyes, which I may call the sea,                               132
Do ebb and flow with tears; the bark thy body is,                       133
Sailing in this salt flood; the winds, thy sighs,                           134
Who, raging with thy tears, and they with them,                        135
Without a sudden calm, will overset                                           136
Thy tempest-tossèd body.—How now, wife?
Have you delivered to her our decree?

WIFE
Ay, sir, but she will none, she gives you thanks.                        139
I would the fool were married to her grave!

CAPULET
Soft, take me with you, take me with you, wife.                       141
How? Will she none? Doth she not give us thanks?
Is she not proud? Doth she not count her blest,                        143
Unworthy as she is, that we have wrought                                 144
So worthy a gentleman to be her bride?                                     145

JULIET
Not proud you have, but thankful that you have.
Proud can I never be of what I hate,
But thankful even for hate that is meant love.                          148

CAPULET
How, how, how, how, chopped logic? What is this?
"Proud," and "I thank you," and "I thank you not,"
And yet "not proud"? Mistress minion, you,                            151
Thank me no thankings, nor proud me no prouds,
But fettle your fine joints 'gainst Thursday next                       153
To go with Paris to Saint Peter's Church,
Or I will drag thee on a hurdle thither.                                       155
Out, you greensickness carrion! Out, you baggage!               156
You tallow-face!

WIFE [*to Capulet*]   Fie, fie! What, are you mad?                 157

JULIET [*kneeling*]
Good father, I beseech you on my knees,
Hear me with patience but to speak a word.

CAPULET
Hang thee, young baggage, disobedient wretch!
I tell thee what: get thee to church o' Thursday
Or never after look me in the face.
Speak not, reply not, do not answer me!
My fingers itch. Wife, we scarce thought us blest
That God had lent us but this only child;
But now I see this one is one too much,
And that we have a curse in having her.
Out on her, hilding!

NURSE                          God in heaven bless her!            168
You are to blame, my lord, to rate her so.                              169

CAPULET
And why, my Lady Wisdom? Hold your tongue,
Good Prudence. Smatter with your gossips, go.                     171

NURSE
I speak no treason.

CAPULET                     Oh, God-i'-good-e'en!                   172

NURSE
May not one speak?

CAPULET                     Peace, you mumbling fool!
Utter your gravity o'er a gossip's bowl,                                   174
For here we need it not.

WIFE                            You are too hot.

CAPULET   God's bread, it makes me mad!                         176
Day, night, hour, tide, time, work, play,                              177
Alone, in company, still my care hath been                          178
To have her matched. And having now provided
A gentleman of noble parentage,
Of fair demesnes, youthful, and nobly liened,                     181
Stuffed, as they say, with honorable parts,                          182
Proportioned as one's thought would wish a man—
And then to have a wretched puling fool,                            184
A whining mammet, in her fortune's tender,                       185
To answer, "I'll not wed, I cannot love,
I am too young; I pray you, pardon me."
But, an you will not wed, I'll pardon you.                          188
Graze where you will, you shall not house with me.
Look to't, think on't. I do not use to jest.                          190
Thursday is near. Lay hand on heart; advise.                    191
An you be mine, I'll give you to my friend;
An you be not, hang, beg, starve, die in the streets,
For, by my soul, I'll ne'er acknowledge thee,
Nor what is mine shall never do thee good.
Trust to't, bethink you. I'll not be forsworn.     *Exit.*   196

JULIET
Is there no pity sitting in the clouds
That sees into the bottom of my grief?

---

**127 the sunset . . . son** the death of my nephew Tybalt   **129 conduit** water pipe, fountain   **131 bark** sailing vessel   **132 still** continually **133 bark** sailing vessel   **134 flood** sea   **135 Who . . . them** which windy sighs, at war with thy tears. (Juliet's storm of grief is one in which her tears and sighs, like the two contending elements of water and wind, are imagined to be in conflict with each other.)   **136 Without** unless there is **139 will . . . thanks** says "no thank you," she'll have no part of it. **141 take . . . you** let me understand you   **143 count her** consider herself **144 wrought** arranged for   **145 bride** bridegroom.   **148 hate . . . love** that which is hateful but which was meant lovingly.   **151 minion** spoiled darling, minx   **153 fettle** make ready.   **'gainst** in anticipation of   **155 a hurdle** a conveyance on which criminals were dragged to execution **156 greensickness** (An anemic ailment of young unmarried women; it suggests Juliet's paleness.)   **baggage** hussy.   **157 tallow-face** paleface.

**168 hilding** jade, baggage.   **169 rate** berate, scold   **171 Smatter** Chatter.   **gossips** gossiping women friends   **172 God-i'-good-e'en** i.e., For God's sake. (Literally, God give you good evening.) **174 gravity** wisdom. (Said contemptuously.)   **176 God's bread** i.e., By God's (Christ's) Sacrament   **177 tide** season   **178 still** incessantly   **181 demesnes** estates.   **liened** descended   **182 parts** qualities   **184 puling** whining   **185 mammet** doll.   **in . . . tender** when an offer of good fortune is made to her   **188 pardon you** i.e., allow you to depart. (Said caustically.)   **190 do not use** am not accustomed   **191 advise** consider carefully.   **196 be forsworn** i.e., go back on my word.

O sweet my mother, cast me not away!
Delay this marriage for a month, a week;
Or if you do not, make the bridal bed
In that dim monument where Tybalt lies.

WIFE
Talk not to me, for I'll not speak a word.
Do as thou wilt, for I have done with thee.        *Exit.*

JULIET [*rising*]
Oh, God!—O Nurse, how shall this be prevented?
My husband is on earth, my faith in heaven.        206
How shall that faith return again to earth,        207
Unless that husband send it me from heaven         208
By leaving earth? Comfort me, counsel me.          209
Alack, alack, that heaven should practice stratagems
Upon so soft a subject as myself!
What say'st thou? Hast thou not a word of joy?
Some comfort, Nurse.

NURSE                        Faith, here it is.
Romeo is banished, and all the world to nothing    214
That he dares ne'er come back to challenge you,    215
Or if he do, it needs must be by stealth.
Then, since the case so stands as now it doth,
I think it best you married with the County.
Oh, he's a lovely gentleman!
Romeo's a dishclout to him. An eagle, madam,       220
Hath not so green, so quick, so fair an eye
As Paris hath. Beshrew my very heart,              222
I think you are happy in this second match,
For it excels your first; or if it did not,
Your first is dead—or 'twere as good he were,
As living here and you no use of him.

JULIET   Speak'st thou from thy heart?

NURSE
And from my soul too. Else beshrew them both.

JULIET   Amen!                                     229

NURSE   What?

JULIET
Well, thou hast comforted me marvelous much.
Go in, and tell my lady I am gone,
Having displeased my father, to Laurence' cell
To make confession and to be absolved.

NURSE
Marry, I will; and this is wisely done.        [*Exit.*]

JULIET
Ancient damnation! Oh, most wicked fiend!          236
Is it more sin to wish me thus forsworn,           237
Or to dispraise my lord with that same tongue
Which she hath praised him with above compare
So many thousand times? Go, counselor,
Thou and my bosom henceforth shall be twain.       241

---

I'll to the Friar to know his remedy.
If all else fail, myself have power to die.        *Exit.*

# [4.1]

*Enter Friar [Laurence] and County Paris.*

FRIAR LAURENCE
On Thursday, sir? The time is very short.

PARIS
My father Capulet will have it so,
And I am nothing slow to slack his haste.          3

FRIAR LAURENCE
You say you do not know the lady's mind?
Uneven is the course. I like it not.

PARIS
Immoderately she weeps for Tybalt's death,
And therefore have I little talked of love,
For Venus smiles not in a house of tears.          8
Now, sir, her father counts it dangerous
That she do give her sorrow so much sway,
And in his wisdom hastes our marriage
To stop the inundation of her tears,
Which, too much minded by herself alone,           13
May be put from her by society.                    14
Now do you know the reason of this haste.

FRIAR LAURENCE [*aside*]
I would I knew not why it should be slowed.—
Look, sir, here comes the lady toward my cell.

*Enter Juliet.*

PARIS
Happily met, my lady and my wife!

JULIET
That may be, sir, when I may be a wife.

PARIS
That "may be" must be, love, on Thursday next.

JULIET
What must be shall be.

FRIAR LAURENCE            That's a certain text.

PARIS
Come you to make confession to this father?

JULIET
To answer that, I should confess to you.

PARIS
Do not deny to him that you love me.

JULIET
I will confess to you that I love him.

PARIS
So will ye, I am sure, that you love me.

JULIET
If I do so, it will be of more price,              27
Being spoke behind your back, than to your face.

---

206 **my faith in heaven** i.e., I am married to Romeo in the sight of
heaven.   **207–9 How . . . leaving earth?** i.e., How can I remarry while
Romeo is still alive?   **214 all . . . nothing** the odds are overwhelming
**215 challenge** lay claim to   **220 dishclout** dishrag   **222 Beshrew**
(A mild oath. Also in line 228.)   **229 Amen** (Juliet says "Amen" as
though to answer the Nurse's prayer that her heart and soul be
cursed. The Nurse does not get the point.)   **236 Ancient damnation!**
Damnable old woman!   **237 forsworn** i.e., false to my marriage
vows   **241 bosom** secret thoughts.   **twain** separated.

**4.1. Location:** Verona. Friar Laurence's cell.
**3 nothing . . . haste** not at all reluctant to lessen his haste, i.e., willing
to speed matters along.   **8 Venus . . . tears** (1) amorousness is not
appropriate in a house of mourning (2) the planet Venus does not exert
a favorable influence when it is in an inauspicious *house* or constellation of the zodiac.   **13 too . . . alone** too mind-consuming when she is
alone   **14 society** companionship.   **27 more price** greater worth

**PARIS**
Poor soul, thy face is much abused with tears.

**JULIET**
The tears have got small victory by that,
For it was bad enough before their spite.    31

**PARIS**
Thou wrong'st it more than tears with that report.    32

**JULIET**
That is no slander, sir, which is a truth;
And what I spake, I spake it to my face.    34

**PARIS**
Thy face is mine, and thou hast slandered it.

**JULIET**
It may be so, for it is not mine own.—    36
Are you at leisure, holy Father, now,
Or shall I come to you at evening Mass?

**FRIAR LAURENCE**
My leisure serves me, pensive daughter, now.—    39
My lord, we must entreat the time alone.    40

**PARIS**
God shield I should disturb devotion!    41
Juliet, on Thursday early will I rouse ye.
Till then, adieu, and keep this holy kiss.    *Exit.*

**JULIET**
Oh, shut the door! And when thou hast done so,
Come weep with me—past hope, past cure, past help!

**FRIAR LAURENCE**
Ah, Juliet, I already know thy grief;
It strains me past the compass of my wits.    47
I hear thou must, and nothing may prorogue it,    48
On Thursday next be married to this county.

**JULIET**
Tell me not, Friar, that thou hearest of this,
Unless thou tell me how I may prevent it.
If in thy wisdom thou canst give no help,
Do thou but call my resolution wise
And with this knife I'll help it presently.    54
    *[She shows a knife.]*
God joined my heart and Romeo's, thou our hands;
And ere this hand, by thee to Romeo sealed,
Shall be the label to another deed,    57
Or my true heart with treacherous revolt
Turn to another, this shall slay them both.    59
Therefore, out of thy long-experienced time,    60
Give me some present counsel, or, behold,
Twixt my extremes and me this bloody knife    62
Shall play the umpire, arbitrating that
Which the commission of thy years and art    64
Could to no issue of true honor bring.
Be not so long to speak; I long to die    66
If what thou speak'st speak not of remedy.

**FRIAR LAURENCE**
Hold, daughter. I do spy a kind of hope,
Which craves as desperate an execution
As that is desperate which we would prevent.
If, rather than to marry County Paris,
Thou hast the strength of will to slay thyself,
Then is it likely thou wilt undertake
A thing like death to chide away this shame,
That cop'st with Death himself to scape from it;    75
And if thou darest, I'll give thee remedy.

**JULIET**
Oh, bid me leap, rather than marry Paris,
From off the battlements of any tower,
Or walk in thievish ways, or bid me lurk    79
Where serpents are; chain me with roaring bears,
Or hide me nightly in a charnel house,    81
O'ercovered quite with dead men's rattling bones,
With reeky shanks and yellow chopless skulls;    83
Or bid me go into a new-made grave
And hide me with a dead man in his tomb—
Things that, to hear them told, have made me
    tremble—
And I will do it without fear or doubt,
To live an unstained wife to my sweet love.

**FRIAR LAURENCE**
Hold, then. Go home, be merry, give consent
To marry Paris. Wednesday is tomorrow.
Tomorrow night look that thou lie alone;
Let not the Nurse lie with thee in thy chamber.
Take thou this vial, being then in bed,
    *[showing her a vial]*
And this distilling liquor drink thou off,    94
When presently through all thy veins shall run
A cold and drowsy humor; for no pulse    96
Shall keep his native progress, but surcease;    97
No warmth, no breath shall testify thou livest;
The roses in thy lips and cheeks shall fade
To wanny ashes, thy eyes' windows fall    100
Like death when he shuts up the day of life;
Each part, deprived of supple government,    102
Shall, stiff and stark and cold, appear like death.    103
And in this borrowed likeness of shrunk death
Thou shalt continue two-and-forty hours,
And then awake as from a pleasant sleep.
Now, when the bridegroom in the morning comes
To rouse thee from thy bed, there art thou dead.
Then, as the manner of our country is,
In thy best robes uncovered on the bier
Thou shalt be borne to that same ancient vault
Where all the kindred of the Capulets lie.
In the meantime, against thou shalt awake,    113
Shall Romeo by my letters know our drift,    114

31 **spite** malice.   32 **Thou . . . report** Your apology for your face slanders it more than your tears do.   34 **to my face** (1) openly (2) about my face.   36 **is not mine own** (1) is beyond my control, does not reveal me truly (2) belongs to Romeo.   39 **pensive** sorrowful   40 **entreat . . . alone** ask you to leave us alone.   41 **God shield** God forbid   47 **compass** bounds   48 **prorogue** delay   54 **presently** at once.   57 **label** strip attached to a deed to carry the seal; hence, confirmation, seal   59 **both** i.e., hand and heart.   60 **time** age   62 **extremes** extreme difficulties   64 **commission** authority.   **art** skill   66 **so long** so slow. (With wordplay on *long*, "yearn," later in this same line.)

75 **That . . . himself** either (1) you who are willing to encounter Death by killing yourself, or (2) that simulates Death itself.   **it** this shame   79 **thievish ways** roads frequented by thieves   81 **charnel house** vault for human bones   83 **reeky** reeking, malodorous.   **chopless** without the lower jaw   94 **distilling** infusing the body, or distilled   96 **humor** fluid   97 **his native** its natural.   **surcease** cease   100 **wanny** wan, pale.   **eyes' windows** eyelids   102 **part** bodily part.   **supple government** control of motion   103 **stark** rigid in death   113 **against** anticipating when   114 **drift** plan

And hither shall he come; and he and I
Will watch thy waking, and that very night          116
Shall Romeo bear thee hence to Mantua.
And this shall free thee from this present shame,
If no inconstant toy nor womanish fear            119
Abate thy valor in the acting it.

JULIET [*taking the vial*]
Give me, give me! Oh, tell not me of fear!

FRIAR LAURENCE
Hold, get you gone. Be strong and prosperous      122
In this resolve. I'll send a friar with speed
To Mantua, with my letters to thy lord.

JULIET
Love give me strength, and strength shall help afford.  125
Farewell, dear Father!              *Exeunt [separately].*

❧

## [4.2]

*Enter Father Capulet, Mother [Capulet's Wife],*
*Nurse, and Servingmen, two or three.*

CAPULET
So many guests invite as here are writ.
                    [*Exit one or two Servingmen.*]
Sirrah, go hire me twenty cunning cooks.            2

SERVINGMAN   You shall have none ill, sir, for I'll try if  3
they can lick their fingers.

CAPULET   How canst thou try them so?

SERVINGMAN   Marry, sir, 'tis an ill cook that cannot lick
his own fingers; therefore he that cannot lick his
fingers goes not with me.

CAPULET   Go, begone.              [*Exit Servingman.*]
We shall be much unfurnished for this time.         10
What, is my daughter gone to Friar Laurence?

NURSE   Ay, forsooth.

CAPULET
Well, he may chance to do some good on her.
A peevish self-willed harlotry it is.               14

        *Enter Juliet.*

NURSE
See where she comes from shrift with merry look.

CAPULET
How now, my headstrong, where have you been
    gadding?

JULIET
Where I have learned me to repent the sin
Of disobedient opposition
To you and your behests, and am enjoined           19
By holy Laurence to fall prostrate here,    [*kneeling*]
To beg your pardon. Pardon, I beseech you!
Henceforward I am ever ruled by you.

CAPULET
Send for the County! Go tell him of this.
I'll have this knot knit up tomorrow morning.

JULIET
I met the youthful lord at Laurence' cell
And gave him what becomèd love I might,            26
Not stepping o'er the bounds of modesty.

CAPULET
Why, I am glad on't. This is well. Stand up.
                    [*Juliet rises.*]
This is as 't should be. Let me see the County;
Ay, marry, go, I say, and fetch him hither.
Now, afore God, this reverend holy friar,
All our whole city is much bound to him.           32

JULIET
Nurse, will you go with me into my closet           33
To help me sort such needful ornaments             34
As you think fit to furnish me tomorrow?

WIFE
No, not till Thursday. There is time enough.

CAPULET
Go, Nurse, go with her. We'll to church tomorrow.
                    *Exeunt [Juliet and Nurse].*

WIFE
We shall be short in our provision.
'Tis now near night.

CAPULET              Tush, I will stir about,
And all things shall be well, I warrant thee, wife.
Go thou to Juliet, help to deck up her.
I'll not to bed tonight. Let me alone.             42
I'll play the huswife for this once.—What, ho!—    43
They are all forth. Well, I will walk myself
To County Paris, to prepare up him
Against tomorrow. My heart is wondrous light,      46
Since this same wayward girl is so reclaimed.
                    *Exeunt.*

❧

## [4.3]

*Enter Juliet and Nurse.*

JULIET
Ay, those attires are best. But, gentle Nurse,
I pray thee, leave me to myself tonight;
For I have need of many orisons                     3
To move the heavens to smile upon my state,        4
Which, well thou knowest, is cross and full of sin.  5

        *Enter Mother [Capulet's Wife].*

WIFE
What, are you busy, ho? Need you my help?

JULIET
No, madam, we have culled such necessaries         7
As are behooveful for our state tomorrow.          8
So please you, let me now be left alone,
And let the Nurse this night sit up with you,

---

**116 watch** keep a watch over, be on hand for   **119 toy** idle fancy
**122 prosperous** successful   **125 help afford** provide help.
**4.2. Location:** Verona. Capulet's house.
**2 cunning** skilled   **3 none ill** no bad ones.   **try** test   **4 unfurnished**
unprovided   **14 A peevish . . . is** i.e., She's a silly good-for-nothing.
**19 behests** commands

**26 becomèd** befitting   **32 bound** indebted   **33 closet** private chamber
**34 sort** choose   **42 Let me alone** Leave things to me.   **43 huswife**
housewife   **46 Against** in anticipation of
**4.3. Location:** Verona. Capulet's house; Juliet's bed, enclosed by
bedcurtains, is set up in the discovery space.
**3 orisons** prayers   **4 state** spiritual condition   **5 cross** perverse
**7 culled** picked out   **8 behooveful** needful.   **state** ceremony

For I am sure you have your hands full all
In this so sudden business.
WIFE                              Good night.
Get thee to bed and rest, for thou hast need.
                              *Exeunt [Capulet's Wife and Nurse].*

JULIET
Farewell! God knows when we shall meet again.
I have a faint cold fear thrills through my veins        15
That almost freezes up the heat of life.
I'll call them back again to comfort me.—
Nurse!—What should she do here?
My dismal scene I needs must act alone.
Come, vial.                        *[She takes out the vial.]*
What if this mixture do not work at all?
Shall I be married then tomorrow morning?
No, no, this shall forbid it. Lie thou there.
                        *[She lays down a dagger.]*
What if it be a poison, which the Friar
Subtly hath ministered to have me dead,
Lest in this marriage he should be dishonored
Because he married me before to Romeo?
I fear it is; and yet methinks it should not,
For he hath still been tried a holy man.                29
How if, when I am laid into the tomb,
I wake before the time that Romeo
Come to redeem me? There's a fearful point!
Shall I not then be stifled in the vault,
To whose foul mouth no healthsome air breathes in,
And there die strangled ere my Romeo comes?
Or, if I live, is it not very like                      36
The horrible conceit of death and night,                37
Together with the terror of the place—
As in a vault, an ancient receptacle,                   39
Where for this many hundred years the bones
Of all my buried ancestors are packed;
Where bloody Tybalt, yet but green in earth,            42
Lies fest'ring in his shroud; where, as they say,
At some hours in the night spirits resort—
Alack, alack, is it not like that I,
So early waking, what with loathsome smells,
And shrieks like mandrakes torn out of the earth,       47
That living mortals, hearing them, run mad—             48
Oh, if I wake, shall I not be distraught,
Environèd with all these hideous fears,                 50
And madly play with my forefathers' joints,
And pluck the mangled Tybalt from his shroud,
And in this rage, with some great kinsman's bone        53
As with a club dash out my desp'rate brains?
Oh, look! Methinks I see my cousin's ghost
Seeking out Romeo, that did spit his body               56

Upon a rapier's point. Stay, Tybalt, stay!              57
Romeo, Romeo, Romeo! Here's drink—I drink to thee.
                  *[She drinks and falls upon her bed,*
                              *within the curtains.]*

## [4.4]

*Enter Lady of the House [Capulet's Wife]*
*and Nurse.*

WIFE
Hold, take these keys, and fetch more spices, Nurse.
NURSE
They call for dates and quinces in the pastry.         2

        *Enter old Capulet.*

CAPULET
Come, stir, stir, stir! The second cock hath crowed.
The curfew bell hath rung; 'tis three o'clock.         4
Look to the baked meats, good Angelica.                5
Spare not for cost.
NURSE                    Go, you cotquean, go,          6
Get you to bed. Faith, you'll be sick tomorrow         7
For this night's watching.                             8
CAPULET
No, not a whit. What, I have watched ere now
All night for lesser cause, and ne'er been sick.
WIFE
Ay, you have been a mouse-hunt in your time,           11
But I will watch you from such watching now.           12
                        *Exeunt Lady and Nurse.*
CAPULET    A jealous hood, a jealous hood!             13

        *Enter three or four [Servingmen] with spits and*
        *logs, and baskets.*

Now, fellow, what is there?
FIRST SERVINGMAN
Things for the cook, sir, but I know not what.
CAPULET    Make haste, make haste. *[Exit First Servingman.]*
[*To Second Servingman*]         Sirrah, fetch drier logs.
Call Peter. He will show thee where they are.
SECOND SERVINGMAN
I have a head, sir, that will find out logs            18
And never trouble Peter for the matter.
CAPULET
Mass, and well said. A merry whoreson, ha!            20

**15 faint** producing faintness.    **thrills** that pierces, shivers    **29 still been tried** always been tried and proven to be    **36 like** likely. (Also at line 45.)    **37 conceit** idea    **39 As** namely    **42 green** new, freshly    **47 mandrakes** (The root of the mandragora or mandrake resembled the human form; the plant was fabled to utter a shriek when torn from the ground.)    **48 That** so that    **50 fears** objects of fear    **53 rage** madness.    **great** i.e., of an earlier generation, as in *great*-grandfather    **56 spit** impale

**57 Stay** Stop, wait
**4.4. Location: Scene continues. Juliet's bed remains visible.**
**2 pastry** room in which pastry was made.    **4 curfew bell** a bell rung at evening, but also in the morning; here, after the "second cock," line 3, the second crowing of the cock or rooster, who greeted the day early    **5 baked meats** pies, pastry    **6 cotquean** i.e., a man who acts the housewife. (Literally, a cottage housewife.)    **7 Faith** In good faith. (A mild oath.)    **8 watching** being awake.    **11 mouse-hunt** i.e., hunter of women. (Literally, a weasel.)    **12 watch . . . watching** i.e., keep an eye on you to prevent such nighttime activity. (Playing on *watching* in line 8.)    **13 A jealous hood** i.e., You wear the cap of jealousy    **18 I . . . logs** i.e., (1) I have a good head for finding things (2) My wooden head knows all about logs    **20 Mass** By the Mass. **whoreson** i.e., fellow. (An abusive term used familiarly.)

Thou shalt be loggerhead.            [*Exit Servingman.*]
            Good faith, 'tis day.                      21
The County will be here with music straight,          22
For so he said he would.         *Play music* [*within*].
            I hear him near.
Nurse! Wife! What, ho! What, Nurse, I say!

            *Enter Nurse.*

Go waken Juliet, go and trim her up.
I'll go and chat with Paris. Hie, make haste,
Make haste. The bridegroom he is come already.
Make haste, I say.                      [*Exit Capulet.*]

# [4.5]

            [*The Nurse goes to the bed.*]

NURSE
Mistress! What, mistress! Juliet!—Fast, I warrant her,
    she.                                          1
Why, lamb, why, lady! Fie, you slugabed!
Why, love, I say! Madam! Sweetheart! Why, bride!
What, not a word? You take your pennyworths now.   4
Sleep for a week; for the next night, I warrant,
The County Paris hath set up his rest              6
That you shall rest but little. God forgive me,    7
Marry, and amen! How sound is she asleep!          8
I needs must wake her.—Madam, madam, madam!
Ay, let the County take you in your bed;           10
He'll fright you up, i'faith.—Will it not be?
                    [*She opens the bedcurtains.*]
What, dressed, and in your clothes, and down again?
I must needs wake you. Lady, lady, lady!
Alas, alas! Help, help! My lady's dead!
Oh, weraday, that ever I was born!                 15
Some aqua vitae, ho! My lord! My lady!             16

            [*Enter Capulet's Wife.*]

WIFE
What noise is here?
NURSE                Oh, lamentable day!
WIFE
What is the matter?
NURSE                Look, look! Oh, heavy day!    18
WIFE
Oh, me, oh, me! My child, my only life!
Revive, look up, or I will die with thee!
Help, help! Call help.

            *Enter Father* [*Capulet*].

CAPULET
For shame, bring Juliet forth. Her lord is come.

NURSE
She's dead, deceased. She's dead, alack the day!
WIFE
Alack the day, she's dead, she's dead, she's dead!
CAPULET
Ha! Let me see her. Out, alas! She's cold.
Her blood is settled, and her joints are stiff;         26
Life and these lips have long been separated.
Death lies on her like an untimely frost
Upon the sweetest flower of all the field.
NURSE
Oh, lamentable day!
WIFE                Oh, woeful time!
CAPULET
Death, that hath ta'en her hence to make me wail,
Ties up my tongue and will not let me speak.

            *Enter Friar* [*Laurence*] *and the County* [*Paris,
            with Musicians*].

FRIAR LAURENCE
Come, is the bride ready to go to church?
CAPULET
Ready to go, but never to return.
Oh, son, the night before thy wedding day
Hath Death lain with thy wife. There she lies,
Flower as she was, deflowered by him.
Death is my son-in-law, Death is my heir;
My daughter he hath wedded. I will die,
And leave him all; life, living, all is Death's.        40
PARIS
Have I thought long to see this morning's face,        41
And doth it give me such a sight as this?
WIFE
Accurst, unhappy, wretched, hateful day!
Most miserable hour that e'er time saw
In lasting labor of his pilgrimage!                    45
But one, poor one, one poor and loving child,
But one thing to rejoice and solace in,
And cruel Death hath catched it from my sight!
NURSE
O woe! O woeful, woeful, woeful day!
Most lamentable day, most woeful day
That ever, ever I did yet behold!
O day, O day, O day! O hateful day!
Never was seen so black a day as this.
O woeful day, O woeful day!
PARIS
Beguiled, divorcèd, wrongèd, spited, slain!
Most detestable Death, by thee beguiled,
By cruel, cruel thee quite overthrown!
O love! O life! Not life, but love in death!
CAPULET
Despised, distressèd, hated, martyred, killed!
Uncomfortable time, why cam'st thou now              60

---

21 **loggerhead** (1) put in charge of getting logs (2) a blockhead.
22 **straight** straightway, immediately
**4.5. Location: Scene continues. Juliet's bed remains visible.**
1 **Fast** Fast asleep   4 **pennyworths** small portions (of sleep)   6 **set
. . . rest** staked his all, resolved to play all out. (From the card game of
primero, here with obviously bawdy meaning.)   7–8 **God . . . amen!**
(The Nurse apologizes amiably for her bawdy talk.)   10 **take . . . bed**
(1) find you still abed (2) possess you sexually   15 **weraday** wellaway,
alas   16 **aqua vitae** strong alcoholic spirits   18 **heavy** sorrowful

26 **settled** congealed   40 **living** means of living, property
41–64 **Have . . . burièd** (A stage direction in the first quarto, "*All at once
cry out and wring their hands,*" may suggest that the four mourners are
to speak simultaneously, a possibility since all have six lines of text;
Paris's six lines are divided at 41–2 and 65–8)   45 **lasting** unceasing
60 **Uncomfortable** Comfortless

To murder, murder our solemnity?                               61
O child! O child! My soul, and not my child!
Dead art thou! Alack, my child is dead,
And with my child my joys are buried.

FRIAR LAURENCE
Peace, ho, for shame! Confusion's cure lives not    65
In these confusions. Heaven and yourself
Had part in this fair maid; now heaven hath all,
And all the better is it for the maid.
Your part in her you could not keep from death,    69
But heaven keeps his part in eternal life.
The most you sought was her promotion,             71
For 'twas your heaven she should be advanced;      72
And weep ye now, seeing she is advanced
Above the clouds, as high as heaven itself?
Oh, in this love you love your child so ill
That you run mad, seeing that she is well.
She's not well married that lives married long,
But she's best married that dies married young.
Dry up your tears, and stick your rosemary         79
On this fair corpse, and, as the custom is,
And in her best array, bear her to church;
For though fond nature bids us all lament,         82
Yet nature's tears are reason's merriment.         83

CAPULET
All things that we ordainèd festival               84
Turn from their office to black funeral:           85
Our instruments to melancholy bells,
Our wedding cheer to a sad burial feast,
Our solemn hymns to sullen dirges change,          88
Our bridal flowers serve for a buried corpse,
And all things change them to the contrary.        90

FRIAR LAURENCE
Sir, go you in, and, madam, go with him,
And go, Sir Paris. Everyone prepare
To follow this fair corpse unto her grave.
The heavens do lour upon you for some ill;         94
Move them no more by crossing their high will.     95

*Exeunt. Manet [Nurse with Musicians].*

FIRST MUSICIAN
Faith, we may put up our pipes and be gone.

NURSE
Honest good fellows, ah, put up, put up!
For well you know this is a pitiful case.          [*Exit.*]

FIRST MUSICIAN
Ay, by my troth, the case may be amended.          99

*Enter Peter.*

PETER    Musicians, oh, musicians, "Heart's ease," 100
"Heart's ease." Oh, an you will have me live, play 101
"Heart's ease."

FIRST MUSICIAN    Why "Heart's ease"?

PETER    Oh, musicians, because my heart itself plays "My
heart is full." Oh, play me some merry dump to     105
comfort me.

FIRST MUSICIAN    Not a dump we! 'Tis no time to play
now.

PETER    You will not, then?

FIRST MUSICIAN    No.

PETER    I will then give it you soundly.

FIRST MUSICIAN    What will you give us?

PETER    No money, on my faith, but the gleek; I will give 113
you the minstrel.                                  114

FIRST MUSICIAN    Then will I give you the serving- 115
creature.                                          116

PETER    Then will I lay the serving-creature's dagger on 117
your pate. I will carry no crotchets. I'll re you, I'll fa 118
you. Do you note me?                               119

FIRST MUSICIAN    An you re us and fa us, you note us. 120

SECOND MUSICIAN    Pray you, put up your dagger and 121
put out your wit.                                  122

PETER    Then have at you with my wit! I will dry-beat 123
you with an iron wit, and put up my iron dagger.   124
Answer me like men:
  "When griping griefs the heart doth wound,       126
     And doleful dumps the mind oppress,           127
  Then music with her silver sound—"               128
Why "silver sound"? Why "music with her silver
sound"? What say you, Simon Catling?               130

FIRST MUSICIAN    Marry, sir, because silver hath a sweet
sound.

PETER    Pretty! What say you, Hugh Rebeck?        133

SECOND MUSICIAN    I say "silver sound" because musicians sound for silver.                            135

PETER    Pretty too! What say you, James Soundpost? 136

THIRD MUSICIAN    Faith, I know not what to say.   137

---

**PETER** Oh, I cry you mercy, you are the singer. I will say 138
for you. It is "music with her silver sound" because
musicians have no gold for sounding: 140
    "Then music with her silver sound
        With speedy help doth lend redress." *Exit.*
**FIRST MUSICIAN** What a pestilent knave is this same!
**SECOND MUSICIAN** Hang him, Jack! Come, we'll in here,
tarry for the mourners, and stay dinner. *Exeunt.* 145

❖

## [5.1]

*Enter Romeo.*

**ROMEO**
If I may trust the flattering truth of sleep, 1
My dreams presage some joyful news at hand.
My bosom's lord sits lightly in his throne, 3
And all this day an unaccustomed spirit
Lifts me above the ground with cheerful thoughts.
I dreamt my lady came and found me dead—
Strange dream, that gives a dead man leave to
    think!—
And breathed such life with kisses in my lips
That I revived and was an emperor.
Ah me, how sweet is love itself possessed 10
When but love's shadows are so rich in joy! 11

*Enter Romeo's man [Balthasar, booted].*

News from Verona! How now, Balthasar,
Dost thou not bring me letters from the Friar?
How doth my lady? Is my father well?
How fares my Juliet? That I ask again,
For nothing can be ill if she be well.
**BALTHASAR**
Then she is well, and nothing can be ill.
Her body sleeps in Capels' monument,
And her immortal part with angels lives.
I saw her laid low in her kindred's vault,
And presently took post to tell it you. 21
Oh, pardon me for bringing these ill news,
Since you did leave it for my office, sir. 23
**ROMEO**
Is it e'en so? Then I defy you, stars!—
Thou knowest my lodging. Get me ink and paper,
And hire post-horses. I will hence tonight.
**BALTHASAR**
I do beseech you, sir, have patience.
Your looks are pale and wild, and do import 28
Some misadventure.
**ROMEO**                    Tush, thou art deceived.
Leave me, and do the thing I bid thee do.
Hast thou no letters to me from the Friar?

**BALTHASAR**
No, my good lord.
**ROMEO**                    No matter. Get thee gone,
And hire those horses. I'll be with thee straight.
                                *Exit [Balthasar].*
Well, Juliet, I will lie with thee tonight.
Let's see for means. O mischief, thou art swift 35
To enter in the thoughts of desperate men!
I do remember an apothecary— 37
And hereabouts 'a dwells—which late I noted 38
In tattered weeds, with overwhelming brows, 39
Culling of simples. Meager were his looks; 40
Sharp misery had worn him to the bones;
And in his needy shop a tortoise hung,
An alligator stuffed, and other skins
Of ill-shaped fishes; and about his shelves
A beggarly account of empty boxes, 45
Green earthen pots, bladders, and musty seeds,
Remnants of packthread, and old cakes of roses 47
Were thinly scattered to make up a show.
Noting this penury, to myself I said,
"An if a man did need a poison now, 50
Whose sale is present death in Mantua, 51
Here lives a caitiff wretch would sell it him." 52
Oh, this same thought did but forerun my need,
And this same needy man must sell it me.
As I remember, this should be the house.
Being holiday, the beggar's shop is shut.—
What, ho! Apothecary!

*[Enter Apothecary.]*

**APOTHECARY**                    Who calls so loud?
**ROMEO**
Come hither, man. I see that thou art poor.
Hold, there is forty ducats. [*He shows gold.*] Let me
    have 59
A dram of poison, such soon-speeding gear 60
As will disperse itself through all the veins,
That the life-weary taker may fall dead,
And that the trunk may be discharged of breath 63
As violently as hasty powder fired 64
Doth hurry from the fatal cannon's womb. 65
**APOTHECARY**
Such mortal drugs I have, but Mantua's law 66
Is death to any he that utters them. 67
**ROMEO**
Art thou so bare and full of wretchedness,
And fearest to die? Famine is in thy cheeks,

---

**138 cry you mercy** beg your pardon   **140 have . . . sounding** i.e.,
(1) are paid only silver for playing (2) have no gold to jingle in their
pockets   **145 stay** await
**5.1. Location:** Mantua. A street.
**1 flattering** i.e., telling me what I want to believe   **3 bosom's lord**
i.e., heart   **10 itself possessed** actually enjoyed   **11 love's shadows**
dreams of love   **11.1 booted** wearing riding boots—a conventional
stage sign of traveling.   **21 presently took post** at once started off
with post-horses   **23 for my office** as my duty   **28 import** denote

**35 for means** by what means.   **37 apothecary** druggist   **38 which . . .
noted** whom lately I noticed   **39 weeds** garments.   **overwhelming
brows** forehead and eyebrows jutting out over his eyes   **40 simples**
medicinal herbs.   **Meager** Impoverished   **45 beggarly account** poor
array   **47 cakes of roses** petals pressed into cakes to be used as perfume   **50 An if** If   **51 present** immediate   **52 caitiff** miserable.
**would** who would   **59 ducats** gold coins.   **60 soon-speeding gear**
quickly effective stuff   **63 trunk** body.   **discharged** unloaded
**64 hasty powder fired** volatile gunpowder ignited   **65 fatal cannon's
womb** deadly cannon's mouth.   **66 mortal** deadly   **67 any he**
anyone.   **utters** issues, sells

Need and oppression starveth in thy eyes,　70
Contempt and beggary hangs upon thy back.
The world is not thy friend, nor the world's law;
The world affords no law to make thee rich.
Then be not poor, but break it, and take this.　74

APOTHECARY
My poverty but not my will consents.

ROMEO
I pay thy poverty and not thy will.

APOTHECARY [*giving poison*]
Put this in any liquid thing you will
And drink it off, and if you had the strength
Of twenty men it would dispatch you straight.　79

ROMEO [*giving gold*]
There is thy gold—worse poison to men's souls,
Doing more murder in this loathsome world
Than these poor compounds that thou mayst not sell.
I sell thee poison; thou hast sold me none.
Farewell. Buy food, and get thyself in flesh.　84
　　　　　　　　　　　　[*Exit Apothecary.*]
Come, cordial and not poison, go with me　85
To Juliet's grave, for there must I use thee.　*Exit.*

❖

# [5.2]

*Enter Friar John to Friar Laurence.*

FRIAR JOHN
Holy Franciscan friar! Brother, ho!

*Enter [Friar] Laurence.*

FRIAR LAURENCE
This same should be the voice of Friar John.
Welcome from Mantua! What says Romeo?
Or if his mind be writ, give me his letter.

FRIAR JOHN
Going to find a barefoot brother out—
One of our order—to associate me　6
Here in this city visiting the sick,
And finding him, the searchers of the town,　8
Suspecting that we both were in a house
Where the infectious pestilence did reign,
Sealed up the doors and would not let us forth,
So that my speed to Mantua there was stayed.　12

FRIAR LAURENCE
Who bare my letter, then, to Romeo?　13

FRIAR JOHN
I could not send it—here it is again—
Nor get a messenger to bring it thee,
So fearful were they of infection.　[*He gives a letter.*]

FRIAR LAURENCE
Unhappy fortune! By my brotherhood,　17
The letter was not nice but full of charge,　18
Of dear import, and the neglecting it　19
May do much danger. Friar John, go hence.
Get me an iron crow and bring it straight　21
Unto my cell.

FRIAR JOHN　Brother, I'll go and bring it thee.　*Exit.*

FRIAR LAURENCE
Now must I to the monument alone.
Within this three hours will fair Juliet wake.
She will beshrew me much that Romeo　26
Hath had no notice of these accidents;　27
But I will write again to Mantua,
And keep her at my cell till Romeo come—
Poor living corpse, closed in a dead man's tomb!
　　　　　　　　　　　　　　　*Exit.*

❖

# [5.3]

*Enter Paris, and his Page [bearing flowers, perfumed water, and a torch. Juliet, lying in seeming death atop her bier and perhaps concealed at first from the audience's view, is understood to be in the Capulets' burial vault, with Tybalt's body also there.]*

PARIS
Give me thy torch, boy. Hence, and stand aloof.　1
Yet put it out, for I would not be seen.
Under yond yew trees lay thee all along,　3
Holding thy ear close to the hollow ground.
So shall no foot upon the churchyard tread,
Being loose, unfirm, with digging up of graves,　6
But thou shalt hear it. Whistle then to me
As signal that thou hearest something approach.
Give me those flowers. Do as I bid thee. Go.

PAGE [*aside*]
I am almost afraid to stand alone　10
Here in the churchyard, yet I will adventure.
　　　　　　　　　　　　　　[*He retires.*]

PARIS [*strewing flowers and perfumed water*]
Sweet flower, with flowers thy bridal bed I strew—　12
　Oh, woe! Thy canopy is dust and stones—　13
Which with sweet water nightly I will dew,　14
　Or wanting that, with tears distilled by moans.　15
The obsequies that I for thee will keep　16
Nightly shall be to strew thy grave and weep.
　　　　　　　　　　　　*Whistle Boy.*
The boy gives warning something doth approach.
What cursèd foot wanders this way tonight

---

70 **starveth** are revealed by the starving look　74 **poor** (1) impoverished (2) spiritless, timid　79 **straight** immediately.　84 **get . . . flesh** grow fat and prosperous.　85 **cordial** restorative for the heart
5.2. Location: Verona. Friar Laurence's cell.
6 **order** fraternal and monastic society.　**associate** accompany
8 **searchers of the town** town officials charged with public health (and especially concerned about the *pestilence* or plague)　12 **speed** successful journey, progress.　**stayed** stopped.　13 **bare** bore, carried

17 **brotherhood** monastic order　18 **nice** trivial.　**charge** importance
19 **dear** precious, urgent　21 **crow** crowbar　26 **beshrew** i.e., reprove
27 **accidents** events
5.3. Location: Verona. A churchyard and the vault or tomb belonging to the Capulets. Juliet's bier may be thrust onstage from the "discovery" space or may be concealed until the tomb is "opened" by Romeo at 83.1, perhaps by the drawing back of curtains.
1 **aloof** to one side, at a distance.　3 **all along** stretched out　6 **Being** i.e., the soil being　10 **stand** stay　12 **Sweet flower** i.e., Juliet
13 **canopy** covering　14 **sweet** perfumed.　**dew** moisten　15 **wanting** lacking　16 **obsequies** ceremonies in memory of the dead

To cross my obsequies and true love's rite?                              20
What, with a torch? Muffle me, night, awhile.                            21
                                        [*He retires.*]

    *Enter Romeo and Balthasar, [with a torch, a*
    *mattock, and a crowbar].*

ROMEO
Give me that mattock and the wrenching iron.                             22
                                        [*He takes the tools.*]
Hold, take this letter. Early in the morning
See thou deliver it to my lord and father.
                        [*He gives a letter and takes a torch.*]
Give me the light. Upon thy life I charge thee,
Whate'er thou hearest or see'st, stand all aloof
And do not interrupt me in my course                                     27
Why I descend into this bed of death
Is partly to behold my lady's face,
But chiefly to take thence from her dead finger
A precious ring—a ring that I must use
In dear employment. Therefore hence, begone.                             32
But if thou, jealous, dost return to pry                                 33
In what I farther shall intend to do,
By heaven, I will tear thee joint by joint
And strew this hungry churchyard with thy limbs.                         36
The time and my intents are savage-wild,
More fierce and more inexorable far
Than empty tigers or the roaring sea.                                    39

BALTHASAR
I will be gone, sir, and not trouble ye.

ROMEO
So shalt thou show me friendship. Take thou that.
                                        [*He gives him money.*]
Live, and be prosperous; and farewell, good fellow.

BALTHASAR [*aside*]
For all this same, I'll hide me hereabout.                               43
His looks I fear, and his intents I doubt.   [*He retires.*]             44

ROMEO
Thou detestable maw, thou womb of death,                                 45
Gorged with the dearest morsel of the earth,
Thus I enforce thy rotten jaws to open,
And in despite I'll cram thee with more food.                            48
                            [*He begins to open the tomb.*]

PARIS
This is that banished haughty Montague
That murdered my love's cousin, with which grief
It is supposèd the fair creature died,
And here is come to do some villainous shame
To the dead bodies. I will apprehend him.
                                        [*He comes forward.*]
Stop thy unhallowed toil, vile Montague!
Can vengeance be pursued further than death?

Condemnèd villain, I do apprehend thee.
Obey and go with me, for thou must die.

ROMEO
I must indeed, and therefore came I hither.
Good gentle youth, tempt not a desperate man.
Fly hence and leave me. Think upon these gone;                           60
Let them affright thee. I beseech thee, youth,
Put not another sin upon my head
By urging me to fury. Oh, begone!
By heaven, I love thee better than myself,
For I come hither armed against myself.
Stay not, begone. Live, and hereafter say
A madman's mercy bid thee run away.

PARIS
I do defy thy conjuration,                                               68
And apprehend thee for a felon here.

ROMEO
Wilt thou provoke me? Then have at thee, boy!
                                        [*They fight.*]

PAGE
Oh, Lord, they fight! I will go call the watch.   [*Exit.*]

PARIS
Oh, I am slain! [*He falls.*] If thou be merciful,
Open the tomb, lay me with Juliet.           [*He dies.*]

ROMEO
In faith, I will. Let me peruse this face.
Mercutio's kinsman, noble County Paris!
What said my man when my betossèd soul                                   76
Did not attend him as we rode? I think
He told me Paris should have married Juliet.                             78
Said he not so? Or did I dream it so?
Or am I mad, hearing him talk of Juliet,
To think it was so? Oh, give me thy hand,
One writ with me in sour misfortune's book.
I'll bury thee in a triumphant grave.
                                        [*He opens the tomb.*]
A grave? Oh, no! A lantern, slaughtered youth,                           84
For here lies Juliet, and her beauty makes
This vault a feasting presence full of light.                            86
Death, lie thou there, by a dead man interred.
                                    [*He lays Paris in the tomb.*]
How oft when men are at the point of death
Have they been merry, which their keepers call                          89
A lightening before death! Oh, how may I                                 90
Call this a lightening? O my love, my wife!
Death, that hath sucked the honey of thy breath,
Hath had no power yet upon thy beauty.
Thou art not conquered; beauty's ensign yet                              94
Is crimson in thy lips and in thy cheeks,
And death's pale flag is not advancèd there.                             96
Tybalt, liest thou there in thy bloody sheet?                            97
Oh, what more favor can I do to thee
Than with that hand that cut thy youth in twain
To sunder his that was thine enemy?                                      100

---

**20 cross** interrupt   **21 Muffle** Conceal   **22 wrenching iron** crowbar.   **27 course** intended action   **32 dear employment** important business.   **33 jealous** suspicious   **36 hungry** hungry for corpses   **39 empty** hungry   **43 For all this same** All the same   **44 fear** distrust. **doubt** suspect.   **45 womb** belly   **48 in despite** defiantly   **48.1 He . . . tomb** Whether the tomb is represented by a bier thrust onstage or by a curtained recess (see indication of scene location above at the start of 5.3), Romeo may mime the action here and at line 83.1 of using tools to open it.

**60 gone** dead   **68 conjuration** solemn entreaty   **76 betossèd** storm-tossed   **78 should have** was to have   **84 lantern** turret room full of windows, lighthouse   **86 feasting presence** reception chamber for feasting   **89 keepers** attendants, jailers   **90 lightening** exhilaration (supposed to occur just before death)   **94 ensign** banner   **96 advancèd** raised   **97 sheet** shroud.   **100 his** i.e., my (Romeo's) own

Forgive me, cousin!—Ah, dear Juliet,
Why art thou yet so fair? Shall I believe
That unsubstantial Death is amorous,                              103
And that the lean abhorrèd monster keeps
Thee here in dark to be his paramour?
For fear of that I still will stay with thee                      106
And never from this palace of dim night
Depart again. Here, here will I remain
With worms that are thy chambermaids. Oh, here
Will I set up my everlasting rest                                 110
And shake the yoke of inauspicious stars
From this world-wearied flesh. Eyes, look your last!
Arms, take your last embrace! And lips, O you
The doors of breath, seal with a righteous kiss
A dateless bargain to engrossing death!                          115
                                    [*He kisses Juliet.*]
Come, bitter conduct, come, unsavory guide,                       116
Thou desperate pilot, now at once run on                          117
The dashing rocks thy seasick weary bark!
Here's to my love. [*He drinks.*] O true apothecary!
Thy drugs are quick. Thus with a kiss I die. [*He dies.*]

               *Enter Friar* [*Laurence*] *with lantern, crow,*
               *and spade.*

FRIAR LAURENCE
Saint Francis be my speed! How oft tonight                        121
Have my old feet stumbled at graves! Who's there?
BALTHASAR
Here's one, a friend, and one that knows you well.
FRIAR LAURENCE
Bliss be upon you. Tell me, good my friend,
What torch is yond that vainly lends his light                    125
To grubs and eyeless skulls? As I discern,                        126
It burneth in the Capels' monument.
BALTHASAR
It doth so, holy sir, and there's my master,
One that you love.
FRIAR LAURENCE    Who is it?
BALTHASAR                      Romeo.
FRIAR LAURENCE
How long hath he been there?
BALTHASAR                      Full half an hour.
FRIAR LAURENCE
Go with me to the vault.
BALTHASAR                  I dare not, sir.
My master knows not but I am gone hence,
And fearfully did menace me with death
If I did stay to look on his intents.
FRIAR LAURENCE
Stay, then, I'll go alone. Fear comes upon me.
Oh, much I fear some ill unthrifty thing.                         136

BALTHASAR
As I did sleep under this yew tree here
I dreamt my master and another fought,
And that my master slew him.
FRIAR LAURENCE [*advancing to the tomb*]    Romeo!
Alack, alack, what blood is this which stains
The stony entrance of this sepulcher?
What mean these masterless and gory swords
To lie discolored by this place of peace?                         143
                            [*He looks in the tomb.*]
Romeo! Oh, pale! Who else? What, Paris too?
And steeped in blood? Ah, what an unkind hour                     145
Is guilty of this lamentable chance!
The lady stirs.                    [*Juliet wakes.*]
JULIET
O comfortable Friar, where is my lord?                            148
I do remember well where I should be,
And there I am. Where is my Romeo?
                            [*A noise within.*]
FRIAR LAURENCE
I hear some noise. Lady, come from that nest
Of death, contagion, and unnatural sleep.
A greater power than we can contradict
Hath thwarted our intents. Come, come away.
Thy husband in thy bosom there lies dead,
And Paris, too. Come, I'll dispose of thee
Among a sisterhood of holy nuns.
Stay not to question, for the watch is coming.
Come, go, good Juliet. [*A noise again.*] I dare no longer
    stay.                    *Exit* [*Friar Laurence*].
JULIET
Go, get thee hence, for I will not away.
What's here? A cup, closed in my true love's hand?
Poison, I see, hath been his timeless end.                        162
O churl, drunk all, and left no friendly drop                     163
To help me after? I will kiss thy lips;
Haply some poison yet doth hang on them,                          165
To make me die with a restorative.    [*She kisses him.*]
Thy lips are warm.

               *Enter* [*Paris's*] *Boy and Watch.*

FIRST WATCH                  Lead, boy. Which way?
JULIET
Yea, noise? Then I'll be brief. O happy dagger!                   169
                            [*She takes Romeo's dagger.*]
This is thy sheath. There rust, and let me die.
                            [*She stabs herself and dies.*]
PAGE
This is the place, there where the torch doth burn.
FIRST WATCH
The ground is bloody. Search about the churchyard.
Go, some of you, whoe'er you find attach.                         173
                            [*Exeunt some.*]
Pitiful sight! Here lies the County slain,

---

103 **unsubstantial** lacking material existence   106 **still** always
110 **set . . . rest** (See 4.5.6. The meaning is, "make my final determination," with allusion to the idea of repose.)   115 **dateless bargain**
everlasting contract.   **engrossing** monopolizing, taking all; also,
drawing up the contract   116 **conduct** guide (i.e., the poison)
117 **desperate** reckless, despairing   121 **be my speed** prosper me
and let me arrive in time.   125 **vainly** uselessly.   **his** its   126 **grubs**
insect larvae   136 **unthrifty** unfortunate

143.1 *He looks . . . tomb* Whether the Friar is to enter the tomb depends
on staging arrangements.   145 **unkind** unnatural   148 **comfortable**
comforting   162 **timeless** (1) untimely (2) everlasting   163 **churl**
miser   165 **Haply** perhaps   169 **happy** opportune   173 **attach**
arrest, detain.

And Juliet bleeding, warm, and newly dead,
Who here hath lain these two days burièd.
Go tell the Prince. Run to the Capulets.
Raise up the Montagues. Some others search.
                              [*Exeunt others.*]
We see the ground whereon these woes do lie,
But the true ground of all these piteous woes      180
We cannot without circumstance descry.             181

       Enter [*some of the Watch, with*] *Romeo's*
       man [*Balthasar*].

SECOND WATCH
Here's Romeo's man. We found him in the
   churchyard.
FIRST WATCH
Hold him in safety till the Prince come hither.    183

       Enter Friar [*Laurence*], *and another Watchman*
       [*with tools*].

THIRD WATCH
Here is a friar, that trembles, sighs, and weeps.
We took this mattock and this spade from him
As he was coming from this churchyard's side.
FIRST WATCH
A great suspicion. Stay the Friar, too.            187

       Enter the Prince [*and attendants*].

PRINCE
What misadventure is so early up
That calls our person from our morning rest?        189

       Enter Capels [*Capulet and his Wife*].

CAPULET
What should it be that is so shrieked abroad?
CAPULET'S WIFE
Oh, the people in the street cry "Romeo,"
Some "Juliet," and some "Paris," and all run
With open outcry toward our monument.
PRINCE
What fear is this which startles in our ears?      194
FIRST WATCH
Sovereign, here lies the County Paris slain,
And Romeo dead, and Juliet, dead before,
Warm and new killed.
PRINCE
Search, seek, and know how this foul murder comes. 198
FIRST WATCH
Here is a friar, and slaughtered Romeo's man,
With instruments upon them fit to open             200
These dead men's tombs.
CAPULET
O heavens! O wife, look how our daughter bleeds!
This dagger hath mista'en, for lo, his house       203
Is empty on the back of Montague,
And it mis-sheathèd in my daughter's bosom!

---

180 **ground** basis. (Playing on the meaning "earth" in line 179.)
181 **circumstance** details   183 **in safety** under guard   187 **Stay** Detain
189 **our person** (The royal "we.")   194 **startles** cries alarmingly
198 **know** learn.  **comes** came about.   200 **instruments** tools
203 **his house** its scabbard

CAPULET'S WIFE
Oh, me! This sight of death is as a bell
That warns my old age to a sepulcher.              207

       Enter Montague.

PRINCE
Come, Montague, for thou art early up
To see thy son and heir more early down.
MONTAGUE
Alas, my liege, my wife is dead tonight;
Grief of my son's exile hath stopped her breath.
What further woe conspires against mine age?
PRINCE   Look, and thou shalt see.
MONTAGUE [*seeing Romeo's body*]
O thou untaught! What manners is in this,          214
To press before thy father to a grave?             215
PRINCE
Seal up the mouth of outrage for a while,          216
Till we can clear these ambiguities
And know their spring, their head, their true descent; 218
And then will I be general of your woes            219
And lead you even to death. Meantime, forbear,     220
And let mischance be slave to patience.            221
Bring forth the parties of suspicion.              222
FRIAR LAURENCE
I am the greatest, able to do least,
Yet most suspected, as the time and place
Doth make against me, of this direful murder;      225
And here I stand, both to impeach and purge        226
Myself condemnèd and myself excused.               227
PRINCE
Then say at once what thou dost know in this.
FRIAR LAURENCE
I will be brief, for my short date of breath       229
Is not so long as is a tedious tale.
Romeo, there dead, was husband to that Juliet,
And she, there dead, that Romeo's faithful wife.
I married them, and their stol'n marriage day
Was Tybalt's doomsday, whose untimely death
Banished the new-made bridegroom from this city,
For whom, and not for Tybalt, Juliet pined.
You, to remove that siege of grief from her,
Betrothed and would have married her perforce      238
To County Paris. Then comes she to me,
And with wild looks bid me devise some means
To rid her from this second marriage,
Or in my cell there would she kill herself.
Then gave I her—so tutored by my art—
A sleeping potion, which so took effect
As I intended, for it wrought on her               245
The form of death. Meantime I writ to Romeo        246

---

207 **warns . . . age** summons me in my old age   214 **untaught** ill-mannered youth. (Said with affectionate irony.)   215 **press** hasten, go
216 **mouth of outrage** (1) popular outcry (2) entrance to the tomb
218 **spring, head** (Both words mean "source.")   219 **be . . . woes** be leader in lamentation   220 **even to death** in lamentation for the dead.
221 **let . . . patience** i.e., let us bear our misfortune patiently.   222 **of** under   225 **make** conspire, tell   226–7 **to . . . excused** to accuse myself of what is to be condemned in me and to exonerate myself where I ought to be excused.   229 **date of breath** time left to live   238 **perforce** by compulsion   245 **wrought** fashioned   246 **form** appearance

That he should hither come as this dire night 247
To help to take her from her borrowed grave,
Being the time the potion's force should cease.
But he which bore my letter, Friar John,
Was stayed by accident, and yesternight 251
Returned my letter back. Then all alone
At the prefixèd hour of her waking
Came I to take her from her kindred's vault,
Meaning to keep her closely at my cell 255
Till I conveniently could send to Romeo.
But when I came, some minute ere the time
Of her awakening, here untimely lay
The noble Paris and true Romeo dead.
She wakes, and I entreated her come forth
And bear this work of heaven with patience.
But then a noise did scare me from the tomb,
And she, too desperate, would not go with me,
But, as it seems, did violence on herself.
All this I know, and to the marriage
Her nurse is privy; and if aught in this 266
Miscarried by my fault, let my old life
Be sacrificed some hour before his time 268
Unto the rigor of severest law.

PRINCE
We still have known thee for a holy man. 270
Where's Romeo's man? What can he say to this?

BALTHASAR
I brought my master news of Juliet's death,
And then in post he came from Mantua 273
To this same place, to this same monument.
This letter he early bid me give his father, 275
[*showing a letter*]
And threatened me with death, going in the vault,
If I departed not and left him there.

PRINCE [*taking the letter*]
Give me the letter. I will look on it.
Where is the County's page, that raised the watch?
Sirrah, what made your master in this place? 280

PAGE
He came with flowers to strew his lady's grave,
And bid me stand aloof, and so I did.
Anon comes one with light to ope the tomb,
And by and by my master drew on him,
And then I ran away to call the watch.

PRINCE
This letter doth make good the Friar's words,
Their course of love, the tidings of her death;
And here he writes that he did buy a poison
Of a poor 'pothecary, and therewithal 289
Came to this vault to die, and lie with Juliet.
Where be these enemies? Capulet, Montague,
See what a scourge is laid upon your hate,
That heaven finds means to kill your joys with love. 293
And I, for winking at your discords, too 294
Have lost a brace of kinsmen. All are punished. 295

CAPULET
O brother Montague, give me thy hand.
This is my daughter's jointure, for no more 297
Can I demand.

MONTAGUE        But I can give thee more,
For I will raise her statue in pure gold, 299
That whiles Verona by that name is known
There shall no figure at such rate be set 301
As that of true and faithful Juliet.

CAPULET
As rich shall Romeo's by his lady's lie;
Poor sacrifices of our enmity!

PRINCE
A glooming peace this morning with it brings;
    The sun, for sorrow, will not show his head.
Go hence to have more talk of these sad things.
    Some shall be pardoned, and some punishèd;
For never was a story of more woe
Than this of Juliet and her Romeo.        [*Exeunt.*]

---

**247 as this** this very  **251 stayed** stopped  **255 closely** secretly  **266 privy** in on the secret  **268 his** its  **270 still** always  **273 post** haste  **275 This . . . father** He bade me give this letter to his father early in the morning (5.3.23–4)  **280 made** did

**289 therewithal** with the poison  **293 kill your joys** (1) destroy your happiness (2) kill your children.  **with** by means of  **294 winking at** shutting my eyes to  **295 a brace of** two  **297 jointure** marriage settlement  **299 raise** (The second quarto reading, "raie," is defended by some editors in the sense of "array," make ready.)  **301 rate** value

# Julius Caesar

*Julius Caesar* stands midway in Shakespeare's dramatic career, at a critical juncture. In some ways, it is an epilogue to his English history plays of the 1590s; in other ways, it introduces the period of the great tragedies. The play evidently was first performed at the new Globe playhouse in the fall of 1599, shortly after *Henry V* (the last of Shakespeare's history plays about medieval England) and around the time of *As You Like It* (one of the last of Shakespeare's happy romantic comedies). It shortly preceded *Hamlet*. It is placed among the tragedies in the Folio of 1623, where it was first published, and is entitled *The Tragedy of Julius Caesar*, but in the table of contents it is listed as *The Life and Death of Julius Caesar* as though it were a history.

*Julius Caesar* shares with Shakespeare's history plays an absorption in the problems of civil war and popular unrest. Rome, like England, suffers an internal division that is reflected in the perturbed state of the heavens themselves. The commoners, or plebeians, are easily swayed by demagogues. Opportunists prosper in this atmosphere of crisis, although fittingly even they are sometimes undone by their own scheming. Politics seems to require a morality quite apart from that of personal life, posing a tragic dilemma for Brutus, as it did for Richard II or Henry VI. The blending of history and tragedy in *Julius Caesar*, then, is not unlike that found in several English history plays. Rome was a natural subject to which Shakespeare might turn in his continuing depiction of political behavior. Roman culture had recently been elevated to new importance by the classical orientation of the Renaissance. As a model of political organization, it loomed larger in Elizabethan consciousness than it does in ours, because so few other models were available and because Greek culture was less accessible in language and tradition. According to a widely accepted mythology, Elizabethans considered themselves descended from the Romans through another Brutus, the great-grandson of Aeneas.

Yet the differences between Roman and English history are as important as the similarities. Rome's choice during her civil wars lay between a senatorial republican form of government and a strong single ruler. Although the monarchical English might be inclined to be suspicious of republicanism, they had no experience to compare with it—certainly not their various peasants' revolts, such as Jack Cade's rebellion (in *2 Henry VI*). On the other hand, Roman one-man rule as it flourished under Octavius Caesar lacked the English sanctions of divine right. Rome was, after all, a pagan culture, and Shakespeare carefully preserves this non-Christian frame of reference. The gods are frequently invoked and appear to respond with prophetic dreams and auguries, but their ultimate intentions are baffling. Human beings strive blindly; the will of the gods is inscrutable. The outcome of *Julius Caesar* is far different from the restoration of providentially ordained order at the end of *Richard III*. Calm is restored and political authority reestablished, but we are by no means sure that a divine morality has been served. Roman history for Shakespeare is history divested of its divine imperatives and located in a distant political setting, making dispassionate appraisal less difficult.

In Plutarch's *Lives of the Noble Grecians and Romans*, as translated by Sir Thomas North, Shakespeare discovered a rich opportunity for pursuing the ironies of political life to which he had been increasingly attracted in the English histories. In fact, he was drawn throughout his career to Plutarch: to the portrait of Portia in "The Life of Marcus Brutus," not only for Portia in *Julius Caesar*, but also for Lucrece in *The Rape of Lucrece*, Kate in *1 Henry IV,* and Portia in *The Merchant of Venice*; to "The Life of Theseus" for the Duke of *A Midsummer Night's Dream*; and to various lives for *Julius Caesar, Coriolanus, Antony and Cleopatra,* and *Timon of Athens*. Freed from the orthodoxies of the Elizabethan world view, Shakespeare turned in the Roman or classical plays toward irony or outright satire (as in *Troilus and Cressida*) and toward the personal tragedy of political dilemma (as in *Coriolanus* and *Julius Caesar*). These are to be the dominant motifs of the Roman or classical plays, as distinguished from both the English histories and the great tragedies of evil, in which politics plays a lesser part (*Hamlet, Othello, King Lear, Macbeth*).

*Julius Caesar* is an ambivalent study of civil conflict. As in *Richard II*, the play is structured around two protagonists rather than one. Caesar and Brutus, men of extraordinary abilities and debilitating weaknesses, are more like one another than either would care to admit. This antithetical balance reflects a dual tradition: the medieval view of Dante and of Geoffrey Chaucer condemning Brutus and Cassius as conspirators, and the Renaissance view of Sir Philip Sidney and Ben Jonson condemning Caesar as a tyrant. These opposing views still live on in various twentieth-century productions that seek to enlist the play on the side of conservatism or liberalism. In one famous production by Orson Welles for the Mercury Theatre in 1937, Caesar was made out to resemble Benito Mussolini, Italy's fascist dictator, with reference also to Franco's fascists in Spain when that civil war was at its peak. Welles's subtitle for his production, "Death of a Dictator," left no doubt as to the intended statement. The film version of 1953 by John Houseman and Joseph Maniewicz dyed its khaki military uniforms green to suggest the German Wehrmacht; the music adopted for the production deliberately aped the music that accompanied Nazi marching columns in newsreels in the 1930s. Trevor Nunn, at Stratford-upon-Avon in 1972, similarly drew overt parallels to German fascism. At Stratford, Connecticut, in 1979, director Gerald Freedman presented Caesar as a Latin American dictator; at Ashland, Oregon, in 1982, Jerry Turner likened Caesar to Che Guevara. Such interpretations reflect what the conspirators themselves believe, as they cry "Liberty! Freedom! Tyranny is dead!" but the play itself invites widely varying interpretations. Caesar has sometimes appeared as a great leader and a man of great natural authority despite his manifest weaknesses, involved in a struggle to the death with conspirators whose motives and personalities are as complex as his. Anthony Quayle and Michael Langham sought such a balance in their 1950 production at Stratford-upon-Avon; so did Glen Byam Shaw in 1957. The film version of 1953 by John Houseman and Joseph Mankiewicz achieved a kind of balance, despite its antifascist leanings, by evenly distributing its major roles among various well-known actors and actresses—John Gielgud as Cassius, Marlon Brando as Antony, James Mason as Brutus, Louis Calhern as Caesar, Greer Garson as Calpurnia, Deborah Kerr as Portia—instead of allowing one actor to dominate the play. Most recent criticism similarly has abandoned the fruitless debate as to whether Brutus or Caesar is the tragic protagonist, and whether one or the other of them is to be seen as morally superior, in favor of a multiple perspective.

Caesar is a study in paradox. He is unquestionably a great general, astute in politics, decisive in his judgments, and sharp in his evaluation of men, as, for example, in his distrust of Cassius with his "lean and hungry look" (1.2.194). Yet this mightiest of men, who in Cassius's phrase bestrides the narrow world "like a Colossus" (line 136), is also deaf in one ear, prone to fevers and epilepsy, unable to compete with Cassius by swimming the Tiber fully armed, and afflicted with a sterile marriage. Physical limitations of this sort are common enough, but in Caesar they are constantly juxtaposed with his aspirations to be above mortal weakness. He dies boasting that he is like the "northern star," constant, unique, "Unshaked of motion" (3.1.61–71). He professes to fear nothing and yet is notoriously superstitious. He calmly reflects that "death, a necessary end, / Will come when it will come," and then arrogantly boasts in the next moment that "Danger knows full well / That Caesar is more dangerous than he" (2.2.36–45). As his wife puts it, Caesar's "wisdom is consumed in confidence" (line 49). He willfully betrays his own best instincts and ignores plain warnings through self-deception. He stops a procession to hear a soothsayer and then dismisses the man as "a dreamer" (1.2.24). He commissions his augurers to determine whether he should stay at home on the ides of March and then persuades himself that acting on their advice would be a sign of weakness. Most fatally, he thinks himself above flattery and so is especially vulnerable to it. So wise and powerful a man as this cannot stop the process of his own fate, because his fate and character are interwoven: he is the victim of his own hubris. His insatiable desire for the crown overbalances his judgment; no warnings of the gods can save him. Even his virtues conspire against him, for he regards himself as one who puts public interest ahead of personal affairs, and so he brushes aside the letter of Artemidorus that would have told him of the conspiracy.

Brutus, for all his opposition to Caesar, is also a paradoxical figure. His strengths are quite unlike those of Caesar, but his weaknesses are surprisingly similar. Brutus is a noble Roman from an ancient family whose glory it has been to defend the personal liberties of Rome, the republican tradition. Brutus's virtues are personal virtues. He enjoys an admirable rapport with his courageous and intelligent wife, and is genuinely kind to his servants. In friendship he is trustworthy. He deplores oaths in the conspiracy because his word is his bond. He finds Caesar's ambition for power distasteful and vulgar; his opposition to Caesar is both idealistic and patrician. Brutus's hubris is a pride of family, and on this score he is vulnerable to flattery. As Cassius reminds him, alluding to Brutus's ancestor Lucius Junius Brutus, who founded the Roman Republic in 509 B.C.: "There was a Brutus once that would have brooked / Th'eternal devil to keep his state in Rome / As easily as a king"

(1.2.159–61). Should not Marcus Brutus be the savior of his country from a return to tyranny? Is not he a more fit leader for Rome than Caesar? " 'Brutus' and 'Caesar.' What should be in that 'Caesar'? / Why should that name be sounded more than yours?" (lines 142–3). Cassius's strategy is to present to Brutus numerous testimonials "all tending to the great opinion / That Rome holds of his name" (lines 318–19). Cassius plays the role of tempter here, but the notion he suggests is not new to Brutus.

The parallelism of Brutus's pride and Caesar's ambition is strongly underscored by the way in which these great figures appear to us in two adjoining scenes: 2.1 and 2.2. In these two scenes, the protagonists enter alone during the troubled night, call for a servant, receive the conspirators, and dispute the wise caution of their wives. Both men are predisposed to the temptations that are placed before them. Brutus has often thought of himself as the indispensable man for the preservation of Rome's liberties. Despite his good breeding and coolly rational manner, he is as dominating a personality as Caesar and as hard to move once his mind is made up. Indeed, the conspiracy founders on Brutus's repeated insistence on having his own way. He allows no oaths among the conspirators and will not kill Antony along with Caesar. He permits Antony to speak after him at Caesar's funeral. He vetoes Cicero as a fellow conspirator. In each instance, the other conspirators are unanimously opposed to Brutus's choice but yield to him. Brutus cuts off Cassius's objections before hearing them fully, being accustomed to having his way without dispute. His motives are in part noble and idealistic: Brutus wishes to have the conspirators behave generously and openly, as heroes rather than as henchmen. Yet there is something loftily patrician in his desire to have the fruits of conspiracy without any of the dirty work. His willingness to have Antony speak after him betrays a vain confidence in his own oratory and an unjustified faith in the plebeian mob. Moreover, when Brutus overrides Cassius once more in the decision to fight at Philippi and is proved wrong by the event, no idealistic motive can excuse Brutus's insistence on being obeyed; Cassius is the more experienced soldier. Still, Brutus's fatal limitations as leader of a coup d'état are inseparable from his virtues as a private man. The truth is that such a noble man is, by his very nature, unsuited for the stern exigencies of assassination and civil war. Brutus is strong-minded about his ideals, but he cannot be ruthless. The means and the end of revolution drift further and further apart. He cannot supply his troops at Philippi because he will not forage among the peasants of the countryside and will not countenance among his allies the routine corruptions of an army in time of war, though at the same time that he upbraids Cassius for not sending him gold he does not stop to ask where the gold would come from. Even suicide is distasteful for Brutus, obliging him to embarrass his friends

by asking their help. Brutus is too high-minded and genteel a man for the troubled times in which he lives.

The times indeed seem to demand ruthless action of the sort Antony and Octavius are all too ready to provide. The greatest irony of Brutus's fall is that the coup he undertakes for Roman liberty yields only further diminutions of that liberty. The plebeians are not ready for the commonwealth Brutus envisages. From the first, they are portrayed as amiable but "saucy" (even in the opinion of their tribunes, Flavius and Marullus). They adulate Caesar at the expense of their previous idol, Pompey. When Brutus successfully appeals for a moment to their changeable loyalties, they cry "Let him be Caesar," and "Caesar's better parts / Shall be crowned in Brutus" (3.2.51–2). If Brutus were not swayed by this hero-worship, he would have good cause to be disillusioned. To his credit, he is not the demagogue the plebeians take him for and so cannot continue to bend them to his will. Cassius, too, for all his villainlike role as tempter to Brutus, his envious motive, and his Epicurean skepticism, reveals a finer nature as the play progresses. Inspired perhaps by Brutus's philosophic idealism, Cassius turns philosopher also and accepts defeat in a noble but ineffectual cause. Yet even his death is futile; Cassius is misinformed about the fate of his friend Titinius and so stabs himself just when the battle is going well for the conspirators.

The ultimate victors are Antony and Octavius. Antony, whatever finer nature he may possess, becomes under the stress of circumstance a cunning bargainer with the conspirators and a masterful rhetorician who characterizes himself to the plebeians as a "plain blunt man" (3.2.219). In sardonic soliloquy at the end of his funeral oration, he observes, "Now let it work. Mischief, thou art afoot. / Take thou what course thou wilt" (lines 261–2). He is, to be sure, stirred by loyalty to Caesar's memory, but to the end of avenging Caesar's death he is prepared to unleash violence at whatever risk to the state. He regards Lepidus contemptuously as a mere creature under his command. Antony is older than Octavius and teaches the younger man about political realities, but an Elizabethan audience would probably savor the irony that Octavius will subsequently beat Antony at his own game. At Philippi, Octavius's refusal to accept Antony's directions in the battle (5.1.16–20) gives us a glimpse of the peremptory manner for which he is to become famous, like his predecessor. Antony and Octavius together are, in any case, a fearsome pair, matter-of-factly noting down the names of those who must die, including their own kinsmen. They cut off the bequests left to the populace in Caesar's will, by which Antony had won the hearts of the plebeians (3.2, 4.1–2). Many innocent persons are sacrificed in the new reign of terror, including Cicero and the poet unluckily named Cinna. In such deaths, art and civilization yield to expediency. Rationality gives way to frenzied rhetoric and to a struggle for power in which Rome's republican tradition is buried forever. Such is the achievement of Brutus's noble revolution.

Appropriately for such a depiction of ambivalent political strife, *Julius Caesar* is written chiefly in the oratorical mode. It resembles its near contemporary, *Henry V*, in devoting so much attention to speeches of public persuasion. The famous orations following Caesar's assassination—one by Brutus in the so-called Laconic style (that is, concise and sententious) and one by Antony in the Asiatic style (that is, more florid, anecdotal, and literary)—are only the most prominent of many public utterances. In the first scene, Marullus rebukes the plebeians for their disloyalty to Pompey and for the moment dissuades them from idolizing Caesar. Decius Brutus changes Caesar's presumably unalterable mind about staying home on the ides of March (2.2). Caesar lectures the Senate on the virtues of constancy. Before Philippi, the contending armies clash with verbal taunts. Antony and Octavius end the play with tributes to the dead Brutus. In less public scenes as well, oratory serves to win Brutus over to the conspirators, to urge unavailingly that Brutus confide in his wife, or to warn the unheeding Caesar of his danger. The decline of the conspirators' cause shows in their descent from rational discourse to private bickering (4.3). The play gives us a range of rhetorical styles, from the deliberative (having to do with careful consideration of choices) to the forensic (analogous to pleading at law, maintaining one side or the other of a given question), to the epideictic (for display, as in set orations). The imagery, suitably public and rhetorical in its function, is of a fixed star in the firmament, a Colossus bestriding the petty world of humans, a tide of fortune in the affairs of humankind, a statue spouting fountains of blood. The city of Rome is a vivid presence in the play, conveyed at times through Elizabethan anachronisms, such as striking clocks, sweaty nightcaps, "towers and windows, yea, . . . chimney tops" (1.1.39), but in an eclectic fusion of native and classical traditions wherein anachronisms become functionally purposeful. Style affords us one more way of considering *Julius Caesar* as a Janus play, looking back to Shakespeare's history plays and forward to his tragedies.

Women are marginalized in *Julius Caesar*, much as in Shakespeare's English history plays. Portia and Calpurnia are alike, not only in their concern for their husbands' welfare, but also in their inability to do anything to ensure their husbands' safety and prosperity. Fittingly in such an unremittingly patriarchal play, Portia and Calpurnia are noble Roman matrons of the type we also see earlier in *The Rape of Lucrece* or *Titus Andronicus* and later in Octavia (*Antony and Cleopatra*) and Valeria (*Coriolanus*): unassailably virtuous, descended from patrician stock, and submissive to the essentially male values of unflinching duty and stoical reserve. Portia, daughter of the great Cato of

Utica who committed suicide rather than submit to Caesar's tyranny, emulates her father's example by taking her own life rather than outlive her husband's shame in defeat. Calpurnia expounds her prophetic dream of Caesar's bleeding statue (2.2.76–9) only to be rebuked for womanly cowardice. These women do what they can to offer their men an alternative perspective on political ambition—one in which caution and attentiveness to family values stand in opposition to the competitive mores of the male-dominated world—but the women are doomed, like Cassandra and Andromache (in *Troilus and Cressida*), to see their quiet wisdom ignored or misinterpreted. Most touching of all is the scene of marital mutuality between Portia and Brutus (2.1.234–310), in which we realize that Portia's concern and sympathy for her husband cannot save Brutus from himself.

A structural pattern to be found in *Julius Caesar*, as noted by John Velz (see bibliography), is the replicating action of rise and fall by which the great men of ancient Rome succeed one another. The process antedates the play itself, for Pompey's faded glory mentioned in Act 1 is a reminder—or should be a reminder—that good fortune lasts but a day. We behold Caesar at the point of his greatest triumph and his imminent decline to death. "O mighty Caesar! Dost thou lie so low?" asks Antony when he sees the prostrate body of the once most powerful man alive. "Are all thy conquests, glories, triumphs, spoils, / Shrunk to this little measure?" (3.1.150–2). Brutus and Cassius step forward into prominence only to be supplanted by Antony and Octavius. Antony is unaware, though presumably the audience is aware, that Antony is to fall at the hands of Octavius. The process of incessant change, reinforced by such metaphors as the tide in the affairs of humans (already noted), offering its mocking comment on Caesar's self-comparison to the fixed northern star, is not simply a meaningless descent on the grand staircase of history, for Octavius's *Pax Romana* lies at the end of the cycle from republic to empire. Still, that resting place is beyond the conclusion of this open-ended play. What we see here again and again is a human blindness to history, through which a succession of protagonists repeat one another's errors without intending to do so. Cassius, like Caesar, goes to his death in the face of unpropitious omens that he now partly believes to be true. The eagles that accompanied Cassius and his army to Philippi desert him as the moment of battle approaches. These omens suggest a balance between character and fate, for, though the leaders of Rome have one by one fallen through their own acts and choices, they have also, it seems, fulfilled a prearranged destiny. Brutus, confronted by the Ghost of Caesar and assured that he will see this spirit of Caesar at Philippi, answers resolutely, "Why, I will see thee at Philippi, then" (4.3.288). Defeated in battle, as he sensed he would be, Brutus takes his own life. Cassius dies on his birthday. *Sic transit gloria mundi.*

# Julius Caesar

[*Dramatis Personae*

JULIUS CAESAR
CALPURNIA, *Caesar's wife*
MARK ANTONY,
OCTAVIUS CAESAR, } *triumvirs after Caesar's death*
LEPIDUS,

MARCUS BRUTUS
PORTIA, *Brutus's wife*
CAIUS CASSIUS,
CASCA,
DECIUS BRUTUS,
CINNA, } *conspirators with Brutus*
METELLUS CIMBER,
TREBONIUS,
CAIUS LIGARIUS,

CICERO,
PUBLIUS, } *senators*
POPILIUS LENA,
FLAVIUS, } *tribunes of the people*
MARULLUS,

SOOTHSAYER
ARTEMIDORUS, *a teacher of rhetoric*
CINNA, *a poet*
*Another* POET

LUCILIUS,
TITINIUS,
MESSALA,
YOUNG CATO,
VOLUMNIUS,
VARRO, } *officers and soldiers in the army*
CLAUDIUS, *of Brutus and Cassius*
CLITUS,
DARDANIUS,
LABEO,
FLAVIUS,

PINDARUS, *Cassius's servant*
LUCIUS, } *Brutus's servants*
STRATO,
*Caesar's* SERVANT
*Antony's* SERVANT
*Octavius's* SERVANT

CARPENTER
COBBLER
*Five* PLEBEIANS
*Three* SOLDIERS *in Brutus' army*
*Two* SOLDIERS *in Antony's army*
MESSENGER

GHOST *of Caesar*

*Senators, Plebeians, Officers, Soldiers, and Attendants*

SCENE: *Rome; the neighborhood of Sardis; the neighborhood of Philippi*]

## 1.1

*Enter Flavius, Marullus, and certain commoners over the stage.*

FLAVIUS
Hence! Home, you idle creatures, get you home!

Is this a holiday? What, know you not,
Being mechanical, you ought not walk           3
Upon a laboring day without the sign           4
Of your profession?—Speak, what trade art thou?
CARPENTER   Why, sir, a carpenter.
MARULLUS
Where is thy leather apron and thy rule?        7

1.1. Location: Rome. A street.

3 **mechanical** practicioner of a trade   4 **sign** garb and implements
7 **rule** carpenter's ruler

510

What dost thou with thy best apparel on?—
You, sir, what trade are you?
COBBLER   Truly, sir, in respect of a fine workman, I am    10
but, as you would say, a cobbler.    11
MARULLUS
But what trade art thou? Answer me directly.
COBBLER   A trade, sir, that I hope I may use with a safe
conscience, which is indeed, sir, a mender of bad soles.    14
FLAVIUS
What trade, thou knave? Thou naughty knave, what
trade?    15
COBBLER   Nay, I beseech you, sir, be not out with me.    16
Yet if you be out, sir, I can mend you.    17
FLAVIUS
What mean'st thou by that? Mend me, thou saucy
fellow?
COBBLER   Why, sir, cobble you.    19
FLAVIUS   Thou art a cobbler, art thou?
COBBLER   Truly, sir, all that I live by is with the awl. I    21
meddle with no tradesman's matters nor women's    22
matters, but withal I am indeed, sir, a surgeon to old    23
shoes. When they are in great danger, I recover them.    24
As proper men as ever trod upon neat's leather have    25
gone upon my handiwork.
FLAVIUS
But wherefore art not in thy shop today?
Why dost thou lead these men about the streets?
COBBLER   Truly, sir, to wear out their shoes, to get myself
into more work. But indeed, sir, we make holiday
to see Caesar and to rejoice in his triumph.    31
MARULLUS
Wherefore rejoice? What conquest brings he home?
What tributaries follow him to Rome    33
To grace in captive bonds his chariot wheels?
You blocks, you stones, you worse than senseless
things!    35
O you hard hearts, you cruel men of Rome,
Knew you not Pompey? Many a time and oft    37
Have you climbed up to walls and battlements,    38
To towers and windows, yea, to chimney tops,    39
Your infants in your arms, and there have sat
The livelong day, with patient expectation,

To see great Pompey pass the streets of Rome.    42
And when you saw his chariot but appear,
Have you not made an universal shout,
That Tiber trembled underneath her banks    45
To hear the replication of your sounds    46
Made in her concave shores?    47
And do you now put on your best attire?
And do you now cull out a holiday?    49
And do you now strew flowers in his way
That comes in triumph over Pompey's blood?    51
Begone!
Run to your houses, fall upon your knees,
Pray to the gods to intermit the plague    54
That needs must light on this ingratitude.    55
FLAVIUS
Go, go, good countrymen, and for this fault
Assemble all the poor men of your sort;    57
Draw them to Tiber banks, and weep your tears
Into the channel, till the lowest stream    59
Do kiss the most exalted shores of all.    60
*Exeunt all the commoners.*
See whe'er their basest mettle be not moved.    61
They vanish tongue-tied in their guiltiness.
Go you down that way towards the Capitol;
This way will I. Disrobe the images    64
If you do find them decked with ceremonies.    65
MARULLUS   May we do so?
You know it is the Feast of Lupercal.    67
FLAVIUS
It is no matter. Let no images
Be hung with Caesar's trophies. I'll about    69
And drive away the vulgar from the streets;    70
So do you too, where you perceive them thick.    71
These growing feathers plucked from Caesar's wing
Will make him fly an ordinary pitch,    73
Who else would soar above the view of men    74
And keep us all in servile fearfulness.    *Exeunt.*

**10 in . . . workman** (1) as far as skilled work is concerned (2) compared with a skilled worker   **11 cobbler** (1) one who works with shoes (2) bungler.   **14 soles** (With pun on "souls.")   **15 naughty** good-for-nothing   **16 out** out of temper   **17 out** having worn-out shoes. **mend you** (1) cure your bad temper (2) repair your shoes.   **19 cobble you** mend your shoes. (The meaning "to pelt with stones" also suggests itself here, though perhaps it was not in general use until later in the seventeenth century.)   **21 awl** a shoemaker's pointed spike. (Punning on *all.*)   **22 meddle with** (1) have to do with (2) have sexual intercourse with   **23 withal** indeed, yet. (With pun on *with awl.*) **24 recover** (1) resole (2) cure   **25 proper** fine, handsome.   **as . . . leather** (Proverbial. *Neat's leather* is cowhide.)   **31 triumph** triumphal procession. (Caesar had overthrown the sons of Pompey the Great in Spain at the Battle of Munda, March 17, 45 B.C. The triumph was held that October.)   **33 tributaries** captives who will pay ransom (tribute)   **35 senseless** insensible like stone (hence, unfeeling) **37 Pompey** (Caesar had overthrown the great soldier and onetime triumvir at the Battle of Pharsalus in 48 B.C. Pompey fled to Egypt, where he was murdered.)   **38–9 battlements . . . chimney tops** (The details are appropriate to an Elizabethan cityscape.)

**42 great** (Alludes to Pompey's epithet, *Magnus*, "great.")   **pass** pass through   **45 Tiber** the Tiber River   **46 replication** echo   **47 concave** hollow, overhanging   **49 cull** pick   **51 Pompey's blood** (1) Pompey's offspring (2) the blood of the Pompeys.   **54 intermit** suspend, discontinue   **55 needs must** must necessarily   **57 sort** rank, social class   **59–60 till . . . all** until even at its lowest reach the river is filled to the brim.   **61 See . . . moved** See how even their ignoble natures can be moved to pity and feelings of guilt. (*Mettle* and *metal* are interchangeable, meaning both "temperament" and the natural substance. A base *metal* is one that is easily changed or *moved*, unlike gold; compare 1.2.308–10.)   **64 images** statues (of Caesar in royal regalia, set up by his followers)   **65 ceremonies** ceremonial trappings.   **67 Feast of Lupercal** a feast of purification (*Februa*, whence *February*) in honor of Pan, celebrated from ancient times in Rome on February 15 of each year. (Historically, this celebration came some months after Caesar's triumph in October of 45 B.C. The celebrants, called *Luperci*, raced around the Palatine Hill and the Circus carrying thongs of goatskin, with which they lightly struck those who came in their way. Women so touched were suppposed to be cured of barrenness; hence Caesar's wish that Antony would strike Calpurnia, 1.2.6–9.)   **69 trophies** spoils of war hung up as memorials of victory.   **about** go around the other way   **70 vulgar** commoners, plebeians   **71 thick** thronged.   **73 pitch** highest point in flight. (A term from falconry.) **74 else** otherwise

# [1.2]

*Enter Caesar, Antony for the course, Calpurnia,*
*Portia, Decius, Cicero, Brutus, Cassius, Casca, a*
*Soothsayer; after them, Marullus and Flavius;*
*[citizens following].*

CAESAR
Calpurnia!

CASCA            Peace, ho! Caesar speaks.

CAESAR                                    Calpurnia!

CALPURNIA    Here, my lord.

CAESAR
Stand you directly in Antonio's way                      3
When he doth run his course. Antonio!

ANTONY    Caesar, my lord?

CAESAR
Forget not, in your speed, Antonio,
To touch Calpurnia; for our elders say
The barren, touchèd in this holy chase,
Shake off their sterile curse.

ANTONY                      I shall remember.            9
When Caesar says "Do this," it is performed.

CAESAR
Set on, and leave no ceremony out.        [*Flourish.*]   11

SOOTHSAYER    Caesar!

CAESAR    Ha? Who calls?

CASCA
Bid every noise be still. Peace yet again!
                                    [*The music ceases.*]

CAESAR
Who is it in the press that calls on me?                 15
I hear a tongue shriller than all the music
Cry "Caesar!" Speak. Caesar is turned to hear.

SOOTHSAYER
Beware the ides of March.

CAESAR                      What man is that?             18

BRUTUS
A soothsayer bids you beware the ides of March.

CAESAR
Set him before me. Let me see his face.

CASSIUS
Fellow, come from the throng. [*The Soothsayer comes*
   *forward.*] Look upon Caesar.

CAESAR
What say'st thou to me now? Speak once again.

SOOTHSAYER    Beware the ides of March.

CAESAR
He is a dreamer. Let us leave him. Pass.                 24
          *Sennet. Exeunt. Manent Brutus and Cassius.*

CASSIUS
Will you go see the order of the course?                 25

BRUTUS    Not I.

CASSIUS    I pray you, do.

BRUTUS
I am not gamesome. I do lack some part                   28
Of that quick spirit that is in Antony.
Let me not hinder, Cassius, your desires;
I'll leave you.

CASSIUS
Brutus, I do observe you now of late.
I have not from your eyes that gentleness
And show of love as I was wont to have.                  34
You bear too stubborn and too strange a hand             35
Over your friend that loves you.

BRUTUS                      Cassius,
Be not deceived. If I have veiled my look,               37
I turn the trouble of my countenance
Merely upon myself. Vexèd I am                           39
Of late with passions of some difference,                40
Conceptions only proper to myself,                       41
Which give some soil, perhaps, to my behaviors.          42
But let not therefore my good friends be grieved—
Among which number, Cassius, be you one—
Nor construe any further my neglect
Than that poor Brutus, with himself at war,
Forgets the shows of love to other men.

CASSIUS
Then, Brutus, I have much mistook your passion,
By means whereof this breast of mine hath buried         49
Thoughts of great value, worthy cogitations.             50
Tell me, good Brutus, can you see your face?

BRUTUS
No, Cassius, for the eye sees not itself
But by reflection, by some other things.

CASSIUS    'Tis just.                                    54
And it is very much lamented, Brutus,
That you have no such mirrors as will turn
Your hidden worthiness into your eye,
That you might see your shadow. I have heard             58
Where many of the best respect in Rome,                  59
Except immortal Caesar, speaking of Brutus
And groaning underneath this age's yoke,
Have wished that noble Brutus had his eyes.              62

BRUTUS
Into what dangers would you lead me, Cassius,
That you would have me seek into myself
For that which is not in me?

CASSIUS
Therefore, good Brutus, be prepared to hear;
And since you know you cannot see yourself

---

1.2. **Location:** A public place or street, perhaps as in the previous
scene.
**0.1** *for the course* i.e., stripped for the race, carrying a goatskin
thong   **3** *Antonio's* (Here and occasionally elsewhere Shakespeare
employs Italian forms of Latin proper names, perhaps for metrical
reasons.)   **9 sterile curse** curse of barrenness.   **11 Set on** Proceed
**15 press** throng   **18 ides of March** March 15.   **24.1** *Sennet* Trumpet
call signaling the arrival or departure of a dignitary.   *Manent* They
remain on stage   **25 order of the course** ritual and progress of the race.

**28 gamesome** fond of sports, merry.   **34 wont** accustomed   **35 You
. . . hand** You behave too stubbornly and in too unfriendly a manner.
(The metaphor is from horsemanship.)   **37 veiled my look** hidden
my inner feelings   **39 Merely** entirely   **40 passions of some difference** conflicting emotions   **41 only proper to** relating only to
**42 soil** blemish   **49–50 By . . . value** because of which misunderstanding (my assuming you were displeased with me) I have kept to
myself important thoughts   **54 just** true.   **58 shadow** image, reflection.   **59 best respect** highest repute and station   **62 had his eyes**
(1) could see things from the perspective of Caesar's critics, or
(2) could see better with his own eyes.

So well as by reflection, I, your glass, 68
Will modestly discover to yourself 69
That of yourself which you yet know not of.
And be not jealous on me, gentle Brutus. 71
Were I a common laughter, or did use 72
To stale with ordinary oaths my love 73
To every new protester; if you know 74
That I do fawn on men and hug them hard
And after scandal them, or if you know 76
That I profess myself in banqueting 77
To all the rout, then hold me dangerous. 78

*Flourish, and shout.*

BRUTUS
What means this shouting? I do fear the people
Choose Caesar for their king.

CASSIUS                         Ay, do you fear it?
Then must I think you would not have it so.

BRUTUS
I would not, Cassius, yet I love him well.
But wherefore do you hold me here so long?
What is it that you would impart to me?
If it be aught toward the general good,
Set honor in one eye and death i'th'other
And I will look on both indifferently; 87
For let the gods so speed me as I love 88
The name of honor more than I fear death.

CASSIUS
I know that virtue to be in you, Brutus,
As well as I do know your outward favor. 91
Well, honor is the subject of my story.
I cannot tell what you and other men
Think of this life; but, for my single self,
I had as lief not be as live to be 95
In awe of such a thing as I myself. 96
I was born free as Caesar, so were you;
We both have fed as well, and we can both
Endure the winter's cold as well as he.
For once, upon a raw and gusty day,
The troubled Tiber chafing with her shores,
Caesar said to me, "Dar'st thou, Cassius, now
Leap in with me into this angry flood
And swim to yonder point?" Upon the word,
Accoutred as I was, I plungèd in 105
And bade him follow; so indeed he did.
The torrent roared, and we did buffet it
With lusty sinews, throwing it aside 108
And stemming it with hearts of controversy. 109

But ere we could arrive the point proposed,
Caesar cried, "Help me, Cassius, or I sink!"
Ay, as Aeneas, our great ancestor, 112
Did from the flames of Troy upon his shoulder
The old Anchises bear, so from the waves of Tiber
Did I the tirèd Caesar. And this man
Is now become a god, and Cassius is
A wretched creature and must bend his body 117
If Caesar carelessly but nod on him.
He had a fever when he was in Spain,
And when the fit was on him I did mark
How he did shake. 'Tis true, this god did shake.
His coward lips did from their color fly, 122
And that same eye whose bend doth awe the world 123
Did lose his luster. I did hear him groan. 124
Ay, and that tongue of his that bade the Romans
Mark him and write his speeches in their books,
Alas, it cried, "Give me some drink, Titinius,"
As a sick girl. Ye gods, it doth amaze me
A man of such a feeble temper should 129
So get the start of the majestic world 130
And bear the palm alone.    *Shout. Flourish.* 131

BRUTUS    Another general shout!
I do believe that these applauses are
For some new honors that are heaped on Caesar.

CASSIUS
Why, man, he doth bestride the narrow world
Like a Colossus, and we petty men 136
Walk under his huge legs and peep about
To find ourselves dishonorable graves.
Men at some time are masters of their fates.
The fault, dear Brutus, is not in our stars,
But in ourselves, that we are underlings.
"Brutus" and "Caesar." What should be in that
   "Caesar"?
Why should that name be sounded more than yours? 143
Write them together, yours is as fair a name;
Sound them, it doth become the mouth as well;
Weigh them, it is as heavy; conjure with 'em,
"Brutus" will start a spirit as soon as "Caesar." 147
Now, in the names of all the gods at once,
Upon what meat doth this our Caesar feed
That he is grown so great? Age, thou art shamed!
Rome, thou hast lost the breed of noble bloods! 151
When went there by an age since the great flood 152

68 **glass** mirror   69 **modestly discover** reveal without exaggeration   71 **jealous on** suspicious of.   **gentle** noble   72 **laughter** laughingstock, as at 4.3.114; or perhaps *laugher*, a shallow fellow who laughs at every jest.   **did use** were accustomed   73 **stale** cheapen, make common.   **ordinary** (1) commonplace (2) customary (3) tavern   74 **protester** one who protests or declares friendship   76 **after scandal** afterwards slander   77 **profess myself** make declarations of friendship   78 **rout** mob   78.1 *Flourish* Fanfare for a dignitary   87 **indifferently** impartially   88 **speed me** make me prosper   91 **favor** appearance.   95 **as lief not be** just as soon not exist   96 **such ... myself** i.e., a fellow mortal.   105 **Accoutred** fully dressed in armor   108 **lusty sinews** vigorous might. (Literally, tendons.)   109 **stemming** making headway against.   **hearts of controversy** hearts fired up by rivalry.

112 **Aeneas** hero of Virgil's *Aeneid*, the legendary founder of Rome (hence *our great ancestor*), who bore his aged father Anchises out of burning Troy as it was falling to the Greeks   117 **bend his body** bow   122 **color** (1) i.e., normal healthy hue (2) military colors, flag. (The lips are personified as deserters.)   123 **bend** glance, gaze   124 **his** its   129 **temper** constitution   130 **get ... of** gain ascendancy over   131 **palm** victor's prize   136 **Colossus** (A 100-foot-high bronze statue of Helios, the sun god, one of the seven wonders of the ancient world, was commonly supposed to have stood astride the entrance to the harbor of Rhodes.)   143 **be sounded** (1) be spoken and celebrated (2) resound   147 **start** raise. (Perhaps the crowd is heard to shout a third time at this point, or somewhere else in this conversation. At line 226 below, we are told that "They shouted thrice.")   151 **the breed ... bloods** the bloodline of men of noble stock and valiant spirit.   152 **flood** i.e., the classical analogue of Noah's flood, in which all humanity was destroyed except for Deucalion and his wife Pyrrha

But it was famed with more than with one man?                    153
When could they say, till now, that talked of Rome,
That her wide walks encompassed but one man?
Now is it Rome indeed, and room enough,                          156
When there is in it but one only man.
Oh, you and I have heard our fathers say
There was a Brutus once that would have brooked                  159
Th'eternal devil to keep his state in Rome                       160
As easily as a king.                                             161

BRUTUS
That you do love me, I am nothing jealous.                       162
What you would work me to, I have some aim.                      163
How I have thought of this and of these times
I shall recount hereafter. For this present,
I would not, so with love I might entreat you,                   166
Be any further moved. What you have said                         167
I will consider; what you have to say
I will with patience hear and find a time
Both meet to hear and answer such high things.                   170
Till then, my noble friend, chew upon this:
Brutus had rather be a villager
Than to repute himself a son of Rome
Under these hard conditions as this time
Is like to lay upon us.                                          175

CASSIUS   I am glad that my weak words
Have struck but thus much show of fire from Brutus.   177

*Enter Caesar and his train.* [*Brutus and
Cassius continue to confer privately.*]

BRUTUS
The games are done, and Caesar is returning.

CASSIUS
As they pass by, pluck Casca by the sleeve,
And he will, after his sour fashion, tell you
What hath proceeded worthy note today.

BRUTUS
I will do so. But look you, Cassius,
The angry spot doth glow on Caesar's brow,
And all the rest look like a chidden train.                      184
Calpurnia's cheek is pale, and Cicero
Looks with such ferret and such fiery eyes                       186
As we have seen him in the Capitol,
Being crossed in conference by some senators.                    188

CASSIUS
Casca will tell us what the matter is.

CAESAR   Antonio!

ANTONY   Caesar?

CAESAR
Let me have men about me that are fat,

Sleek-headed men, and such as sleep o' nights.
Yond Cassius has a lean and hungry look.
He thinks too much. Such men are dangerous.

ANTONY
Fear him not, Caesar, he's not dangerous.
He is a noble Roman, and well given.                             197

CAESAR
Would he were fatter! But I fear him not.
Yet if my name were liable to fear,
I do not know the man I should avoid
So soon as that spare Cassius. He reads much,
He is a great observer, and he looks
Quite through the deeds of men. He loves no plays,   203
As thou dost, Antony; he hears no music.             204
Seldom he smiles, and smiles in such a sort          205
As if he mocked himself and scorned his spirit
That could be moved to smile at anything.
Such men as he be never at heart's ease
Whiles they behold a greater than themselves,
And therefore are they very dangerous.
I rather tell thee what is to be feared
Than what I fear, for always I am Caesar.
Come on my right hand, for this ear is deaf,
And tell me truly what thou think'st of him.
*Sennet. Exeunt Caesar and his train.* [*Casca remains
with Brutus and Cassius.*]

CASCA   You pulled me by the cloak. Would you speak   215
with me?

BRUTUS
Ay, Casca. Tell us what hath chanced today,          217
That Caesar looks so sad.                            218

CASCA   Why, you were with him, were you not?

BRUTUS
I should not then ask Casca what had chanced.

CASCA   Why, there was a crown offered him; and, being
offered him, he put it by with the back of his hand,
thus, and then the people fell a-shouting.

BRUTUS   What was the second noise for?

CASCA   Why, for that too.

CASSIUS
They shouted thrice. What was the last cry for?      226

CASCA   Why, for that too.

BRUTUS   Was the crown offered him thrice?

CASCA   Ay, marry, was't, and he put it by thrice, every   229
time gentler than other, and at every putting-by mine
honest neighbors shouted.                                     231

CASSIUS   Who offered him the crown?

CASCA   Why, Antony.

BRUTUS
Tell us the manner of it, gentle Casca.              234

CASCA   I can as well be hanged as tell the manner of it.
It was mere foolery; I did not mark it. I saw Mark An-

---

**153 famed with** famous for   **156 Rome, room** (Pronounced alike.)
**159 Brutus** i.e., Lucius Junius Brutus, who expelled the Tarquins
and founded the Roman republic (c. 509 B.C.).   **brooked** tolerated
**160 keep his state** set himself up in majesty   **161 As . . . king** as
readily as he would tolerate a king.   **162 nothing jealous** not at all
doubtful.   **163 work** persuade.   **aim** inkling.   **166 so . . . you** if I
might entreat you in the name of friendship   **167 moved** urged.
**170 meet** fitting   **175 like** likely   **177.1 train** retinue. (See 1.2.0.1–4
for the names of those in the procession.)   **184 a chidden train**
scolded followers.   **186 ferret** ferretlike, i.e., small and red
**188 crossed in conference** opposed in debate

**197 given** disposed.   **203 through** i.e., into the motives of   **204 hears
no music** (Regarded as a sign of a morose and treacherous character.)
**205 sort** manner   **215 cloak** (Elizabethan costume; see also *sleeve*, line
179, and *doublet*, line 265. The Roman toga was sleeveless.)   **217 chanced**
happened   **218 sad** serious.   **226 thrice** (See note at 1.2.147.)   **229 marry**
i.e., indeed. (Originally, "by the Virgin Mary.")   **231 honest** worthy.
(Said contemptuously.)   **234 gentle** noble

tony offer him a crown—yet 'twas not a crown neither, 'twas one of these coronets—and, as I told you, 238 he put it by once; but for all that, to my thinking, he would fain have had it. Then he offered it to him again; 240 then he put it by again; but to my thinking he was very loath to lay his fingers off it. And then he offered it the third time. He put it the third time by, and still 243 as he refused it the rabblement hooted and clapped 244 their chapped hands, and threw up their sweaty night- 245 caps, and uttered such a deal of stinking breath be- 246 cause Caesar refused the crown that it had almost choked Caesar, for he swooned and fell down at it. And for mine own part I durst not laugh for fear of opening my lips and receiving the bad air.

CASSIUS
But soft, I pray you. What, did Caesar swoon?            251

CASCA   He fell down in the marketplace, and foamed at mouth, and was speechless.

BRUTUS
'Tis very like. He hath the falling sickness.            254

CASSIUS
No, Caesar hath it not, but you and I,
And honest Casca, we have the falling sickness.

CASCA   I know not what you mean by that, but I am sure Caesar fell down. If the tag-rag people did not 258 clap him and hiss him, according as he pleased and displeased them, as they use to do the players in the 260 theater, I am no true man.                               261

BRUTUS
What said he when he came unto himself?

CASCA   Marry, before he fell down, when he perceived the common herd was glad he refused the crown, he plucked me ope his doublet and offered them his throat 265 to cut. An I had been a man of any occupation, if I 266 would not have taken him at a word, I would I might go to hell among the rogues. And so he fell. When he came to himself again, he said if he had done or said anything amiss, he desired Their Worships to think it 270 was his infirmity. Three or four wenches where I stood cried, "Alas, good soul!" and forgave him with all their hearts. But there's no heed to be taken of them; if Caesar had stabbed their mothers they would have done no less.

BRUTUS
And after that, he came thus sad away?                   276

CASCA   Ay.

CASSIUS   Did Cicero say anything?

CASCA   Ay, he spoke Greek.

CASSIUS   To what effect?

CASCA   Nay, an I tell you that, I'll ne'er look you i'th' face again. But those that understood him smiled at one another and shook their heads; but, for mine own part, it was Greek to me. I could tell you more news too. Marullus and Flavius, for pulling scarves off 285 Caesar's images, are put to silence. Fare you well. 286 There was more foolery yet, if I could remember it.

CASSIUS   Will you sup with me tonight, Casca?

CASCA   No, I am promised forth.                         289

CASSIUS   Will you dine with me tomorrow?

CASCA   Ay, if I be alive, and your mind hold, and your dinner worth the eating.

CASSIUS   Good. I will expect you.

CASCA   Do so. Farewell both.                    *Exit.*

BRUTUS
What a blunt fellow is this grown to be!
He was quick mettle when he went to school.             296

CASSIUS
So is he now in execution
Of any bold or noble enterprise,
However he puts on this tardy form.                      299
This rudeness is a sauce to his good wit,                300
Which gives men stomach to digest his words             301
With better appetite.

BRUTUS
And so it is. For this time I will leave you.
Tomorrow, if you please to speak with me,
I will come home to you; or, if you will,
Come home to me, and I will wait for you.

CASSIUS
I will do so. Till then, think of the world.            307
                                        *Exit Brutus.*

Well, Brutus, thou art noble. Yet I see
Thy honorable mettle may be wrought                      309
From that it is disposed. Therefore it is meet          310
That noble minds keep ever with their likes;
For who so firm that cannot be seduced?
Caesar doth bear me hard, but he loves Brutus.          313
If I were Brutus now, and he were Cassius,
He should not humor me. I will this night                315
In several hands in at his windows throw,                316
As if they came from several citizens,
Writings, all tending to the great opinion

---

**285 scarves** decorations, festoons   **286 put to silence** dismissed from office. (So reported in Plutarch. Shakespeare's wording ominously suggests that they were executed.)   **289 promised forth** engaged to dine out.   **296 quick mettle** of a lively temperament   **299 However** however much.   **tardy form** air of ennui and disengagement. **300 rudeness** rough manner.   **wit** intellect   **301 stomach** appetite, inclination   **307 the world** i.e., the state of the world.   **309 mettle** (As often, the word combines the senses of *mettle*, "temperament," and *metal*, "substance." The latter meaning continues here in the chemical metaphor of metal that is *wrought* or transmuted. As *honorable mettle* [or noble metal], gold cannot be transmuted into base substances, and yet Cassius proposes to do just that with Brutus. Compare this with 1.1.61.)   **309–10 wrought . . . disposed** turned away from its natural disposition.   **310 meet** fitting   **313 doth . . . hard** bears me a grudge and keeps me on a short rein   **315 He . . . humor me** i.e., I wouldn't put up with being cajoled or humored. (*He* could refer to Caesar or Brutus.)   **316 several hands** different handwritings

---

**238 coronets** chaplets, garlands   **240 fain** gladly   **243–4 still as** whenever   **245–6 nightcaps** (Scornful allusion to the *pilleus*, a felt cap worn by the plebeians on festival days.)   **251 soft** i.e., wait a minute **254 like** likely.   **falling sickness** epilepsy. (But Cassius takes it to mean "falling into servitude.")   **258 tag-rag** ragtag, riffraff   **260 use** are accustomed.   **players** actors   **261 true** honest   **265 plucked me ope** pulled open. (*Me* is used colloquially.)   **doublet** Elizabethan upper garment, like a jacket   **266 An** If.   **man . . . occupation** (1) working man (2) man of action   **270 Their Worships** (Said mockingly; in Casca's view, the commoners certainly do not deserve respectful titles like "Your Honor.")   **276 sad** somberly

That Rome holds of his name, wherein obscurely
Caesar's ambition shall be glancèd at.                    320
And after this let Caesar seat him sure,                  321
For we will shake him, or worse days endure.      *Exit.*

## [1.3]

*Thunder and lightning. Enter, [meeting,] Casca
[with his sword drawn] and Cicero.*

CICERO
Good even, Casca. Brought you Caesar home?            1
Why are you breathless? And why stare you so?

CASCA
Are not you moved, when all the sway of earth         3
Shakes like a thing unfirm? Oh, Cicero,
I have seen tempests when the scolding winds
Have rived the knotty oaks, and I have seen           6
Th'ambitious ocean swell and rage and foam
To be exalted with the threat'ning clouds;            8
But never till tonight, never till now,
Did I go through a tempest dropping fire.
Either there is a civil strife in heaven,
Or else the world, too saucy with the gods,          12
Incenses them to send destruction.

CICERO
Why, saw you anything more wonderful?               14

CASCA
A common slave—you know him well by sight—
Held up his left hand, which did flame and burn
Like twenty torches joined, and yet his hand,
Not sensible of fire, remained unscorched.           18
Besides—I ha' not since put up my sword—            19
Against the Capitol I met a lion,                    20
Who glazed upon me and went surly by                 21
Without annoying me. And there were drawn            22
Upon a heap a hundred ghastly women,                 23
Transformèd with their fear, who swore they saw
Men all in fire walk up and down the streets.
And yesterday the bird of night did sit             26
Even at noonday upon the marketplace,
Hooting and shrieking. When these prodigies          28
Do so conjointly meet, let not men say,              29
"These are their reasons, they are natural,"
For I believe they are portentous things
Unto the climate that they point upon.               32

CICERO
Indeed, it is a strange-disposèd time.
But men may construe things after their fashion,     34

Clean from the purpose of the things themselves.     35
Comes Caesar to the Capitol tomorrow?

CASCA
He doth; for he did bid Antonio
Send word to you he would be there tomorrow.

CICERO
Good night then, Casca. This disturbèd sky
Is not to walk in.

CASCA                      Farewell, Cicero.        *Exit Cicero.*

*Enter Cassius.*

CASSIUS
Who's there?

CASCA               A Roman.

CASSIUS                            Casca, by your voice.

CASCA
Your ear is good. Cassius, what night is this!       42

CASSIUS
A very pleasing night to honest men.

CASCA
Who ever knew the heavens menace so?

CASSIUS
Those that have known the earth so full of faults.
For my part, I have walked about the streets,
Submitting me unto the perilous night,
And thus unbracèd, Casca, as you see,                48
Have bared my bosom to the thunder-stone;            49
And when the cross blue lightning seemed to open     50
The breast of heaven, I did present myself
Even in the aim and very flash of it.

CASCA
But wherefore did you so much tempt the heavens?
It is the part of men to fear and tremble            54
When the most mighty gods by tokens send             55
Such dreadful heralds to astonish us.                56

CASSIUS
You are dull, Casca, and those sparks of life
That should be in a Roman you do want,               58
Or else you use not. You look pale, and gaze,
And put on fear, and cast yourself in wonder,        60
To see the strange impatience of the heavens.
But if you would consider the true cause
Why all these fires, why all these gliding ghosts,
Why birds and beasts from quality and kind,          64
Why old men, fools, and children calculate,          65
Why all these things change from their ordinance,    66
Their natures, and preformèd faculties,              67
To monstrous quality—why, you shall find             68
That heaven hath infused them with these spirits
To make them instruments of fear and warning
Unto some monstrous state.                           71

---

320 **glancèd** hinted   321 **seat him sure** seat himself securely in
power (i.e., watch out)
**1.3. Location: A street.**
1 **even** evening.   **Brought you** Did you escort   3 **sway** established
order   6 **rived** split   8 **exalted with** raised to the level of   12 **saucy**
insolent   14 **more wonderful** else that was wondrous.   18 **Not sensible of** not feeling   19 **put up** sheathed   20 **Against** in front of, opposite
21 **glazed** stared glassily   22 **annoying** harming   22–3 **drawn . . . heap**
huddled together   23 **ghastly** pallid   26 **bird of night** owl, a bird of
evil omen   28 **prodigies** abnormalities, wonders   29 **conjointly**
**meet** coincide   32 **climate** region   34 **construe** interpret.   **after their**
**fashion** in their own way

35 **Clean . . . purpose** contrary to the actual import or meaning
42 **what night** what a night   48 **unbracèd** with doublet unfastened
49 **thunder-stone** thunderbolt   50 **cross** forked, jagged   54 **part**
appropriate role   55 **tokens** signs   56 **astonish** stun, terrify   58 **want**
lack   60 **put on** adopt, show signs of.   **in wonder** into a state of
wonder   64 **from . . . kind** (behaving) contrary to their true nature
65 **calculate** reckon, prophesy   66 **ordinance** established nature
67 **preformèd** innate, congenital   68 **monstrous** unnatural
71 **Unto . . . state** pointing to some disorder in the commonwealth or
state of affairs.

Now could I, Casca, name to thee a man
Most like this dreadful night,
That thunders, lightens, opens graves, and roars
As doth the lion in the Capitol—
A man no mightier than thyself or me
In personal action, yet prodigious grown                          77
And fearful, as these strange eruptions are.                      78

CASCA
'Tis Caesar that you mean, is it not, Cassius?

CASSIUS
Let it be who it is. For Romans now
Have thews and limbs like to their ancestors';                    81
But, woe the while, our fathers' minds are dead,                  82
And we are governed with our mothers' spirits.
Our yoke and sufferance show us womanish.                         84

CASCA
Indeed, they say the senators tomorrow
Mean to establish Caesar as a king,
And he shall wear his crown by sea and land
In every place save here in Italy.                                88

CASSIUS
I know where I will wear this dagger then;
Cassius from bondage will deliver Cassius.
Therein, ye gods, you make the weak most strong;                  91
Therein, ye gods, you tyrants do defeat.
Nor stony tower, nor walls of beaten brass,                       93
Nor airless dungeon, nor strong links of iron,
Can be retentive to the strength of spirit;                       95
But life, being weary of these worldly bars,                      96
Never lacks power to dismiss itself.
If I know this, know all the world besides,                       98
That part of tyranny that I do bear
I can shake off at pleasure.              *Thunder still.*

CASCA                        So can I.                             100
So every bondman in his own hand bears
The power to cancel his captivity.

CASSIUS
And why should Caesar be a tyrant then?
Poor man, I know he would not be a wolf
But that he sees the Romans are but sheep;
He were no lion, were not Romans hinds.                           106
Those that with haste will make a mighty fire
Begin it with weak straws. What trash is Rome,
What rubbish and what offal, when it serves                       109
For the base matter to illuminate                                 110
So vile a thing as Caesar! But, O grief,
Where hast thou led me? I perhaps speak this
Before a willing bondman; then I know
My answer must be made. But I am armed,                           114
And dangers are to me indifferent.                                115

CASCA
You speak to Casca, and to such a man
That is no fleering telltale. Hold. My hand.                      117
Be factious for redress of all these griefs,                      118
And I will set this foot of mine as far
As who goes farthest.              [*They shake hands.*]

CASSIUS              There's a bargain made.                       120
Now know you, Casca, I have moved already                         121
Some certain of the noblest-minded Romans
To undergo with me an enterprise
Of honorable dangerous consequence;
And I do know by this they stay for me                            125
In Pompey's porch. For now, this fearful night,                   126
There is no stir or walking in the streets,
And the complexion of the element                                 128
In favor 's like the work we have in hand,                        129
Most bloody, fiery, and most terrible.

*Enter Cinna.*

CASCA
Stand close awhile, for here comes one in haste.                  131

CASSIUS
'Tis Cinna; I do know him by his gait.
He is a friend.—Cinna, where haste you so?

CINNA
To find out you. Who's that? Metellus Cimber?

CASSIUS
No, it is Casca, one incorporate                                  135
To our attempts. Am I not stayed for, Cinna?                      136

CINNA
I am glad on't. What a fearful night is this!                     137
There's two or three of us have seen strange sights.

CASSIUS     Am I not stayed for? Tell me.

CINNA
Yes, you are. Oh, Cassius, if you could
But win the noble Brutus to our party—

CASSIUS
Be you content. Good Cinna, take this paper,                      142
                              [*giving papers*]
And look you lay it in the praetor's chair,                       143
Where Brutus may but find it. And throw this                      144
In at his window. Set this up with wax                            145
Upon old Brutus' statue. All this done,                           146
Repair to Pompey's porch, where you shall find us.                147
Is Decius Brutus and Trebonius there?

CINNA
All but Metellus Cimber, and he's gone

---

77 **prodigious** ominous   78 **fearful** inspiring fear   81 **thews** sinews, muscles   82 **woe the while** alas for the age.   **are dead** no longer live in us   84 **yoke and sufferance** patience under the yoke   88 **save** except   91 **Therein** i.e., In the ability to commit suicide   93 **Nor** Neither   95 **Can . . . spirit** can confine a resolute spirit   96 **bars** (1) prison bars (2) burdens (such as tyranny)   98 **know . . . besides** let the rest of the world know   100 **s.d.** *Thunder still* Continuous thunder.   106 **were no lion** would not be a lion.   **hinds** (1) female of the red deer (2) servants, menials.   109 **offal** refuse, wood shavings   110 **matter** i.e., fuel   114 **My answer . . . made** I will have to answer (to Caesar) for what I have said.   **armed** (1) provided with weapons (2) morally fortified   115 **indifferent** unimportant.

117 **fleering** fawning; scornful.   **Hold. My hand** Enough; here is my hand.   118 **factious** active as a partisan.   **griefs** grievances   120 **who** whoever   121 **moved** urged   125 **by this** by this time.   **stay** wait   126 **Pompey's porch** the colonnade of Pompey's great open theater, dedicated in 55 B.C. (Caesar was assassinated there, though Shakespeare has the assassination take place in the Capitol [i.e., the Senate chamber].)   128 **element** sky   129 **favor 's** appearance is   131 **close** concealed, still   135 **incorporate** admitted as a member   136 **stayed for** waited for.   137 **on't** of it.   142 **Be you content** Set your mind at rest.   143 **praetor's chair** official seat of a praetor, Roman magistrate ranking next below the consul. (Brutus was praetor, one of sixteen.)   144 **Where . . . it** where Brutus cannot help finding it.   144–5 **this . . . this** (Cassius hands several letters to Cinna to be placed in various strategic places.)   146 **old Brutus' statue** the statue of Lucius Junius Brutus, famous ancestor of the Brutus in this play.   147 **Repair** proceed. (Also in line 152.)   **Pompey's porch** (See line 126 and note above.)

To seek you at your house. Well, I will hie,                                150
And so bestow these papers as you bade me.

CASSIUS
That done, repair to Pompey's theater.      *Exit Cinna.*
Come, Casca, you and I will yet ere day
See Brutus at his house. Three parts of him                                154
Is ours already, and the man entire
Upon the next encounter yields him ours.

CASCA
Oh, he sits high in all the people's hearts;
And that which would appear offense in us,                                 158
His countenance, like richest alchemy,                                     159
Will change to virtue and to worthiness.                                   160

CASSIUS
Him and his worth, and our great need of him,
You have right well conceited. Let us go,                                  162
For it is after midnight, and ere day
We will awake him and be sure of him.       *Exeunt.*

❖

## 2.1

*Enter Brutus in his orchard.*

BRUTUS   What, Lucius, ho!—
I cannot by the progress of the stars
Give guess how near to day.—Lucius, I say!—
I would it were my fault to sleep so soundly.—
When, Lucius, when? Awake, I say! What, Lucius!          5

*Enter Lucius.*

LUCIUS   Called you, my lord?
BRUTUS
Get me a taper in my study, Lucius.                                         7
When it is lighted, come and call me here.
LUCIUS   I will, my lord.                              *Exit.*
BRUTUS
It must be by his death. And for my part
I know no personal cause to spurn at him,                                  11
But for the general. He would be crowned.                                  12
How that might change his nature, there's the
    question.
It is the bright day that brings forth the adder,
And that craves wary walking. Crown him—that—    15
And then I grant we put a sting in him
That at his will he may do danger with.
Th'abuse of greatness is when it disjoins
Remorse from power. And to speak truth of Caesar,     19

I have not known when his affections swayed             20
More than his reason. But 'tis a common proof          21
That lowliness is young ambition's ladder,             22
Whereto the climber-upward turns his face;
But when he once attains the upmost round              24
He then unto the ladder turns his back,
Looks in the clouds, scorning the base degrees         26
By which he did ascend. So Caesar may.
Then, lest he may, prevent. And since the quarrel
Will bear no color for the thing he is,                29
Fashion it thus: that what he is, augmented,           30
Would run to these and these extremities;
And therefore think him as a serpent's egg
Which, hatched, would, as his kind, grow
    mischievous;                                       33
And kill him in the shell.

*Enter Lucius.*

LUCIUS
The taper burneth in your closet, sir.                 35
Searching the window for a flint, I found
This paper, thus sealed up, and I am sure
It did not lie there when I went to bed.
                              *Gives him the letter.*
BRUTUS
Get you to bed again. It is not day.
Is not tomorrow, boy, the ides of March?               40
LUCIUS   I know not, sir.
BRUTUS
Look in the calendar and bring me word.
LUCIUS   I will, sir.                              *Exit.*
BRUTUS
The exhalations whizzing in the air                    44
Give so much light that I may read by them.
                              *Opens the letter and reads.*
"Brutus, thou sleep'st. Awake, and see thyself!
Shall Rome, etc. Speak, strike, redress!"
"Brutus, thou sleep'st. Awake!"
Such instigations have been often dropped
Where I have took them up.
"Shall Rome, etc." Thus must I piece it out:
Shall Rome stand under one man's awe? What, Rome?
My ancestors did from the streets of Rome
The Tarquin drive, when he was called a king.
"Speak, strike, redress!" Am I entreated
To speak and strike? O Rome, I make thee promise,
If the redress will follow, thou receivest           57
Thy full petition at the hand of Brutus.             58

*Enter Lucius.*

LUCIUS   Sir, March is wasted fifteen days.
                              *Knock within.*

---

**150 hie** go quickly   **154 parts** i.e., quarters   **158–60 that which . . .
worthiness** his endorsement and honorable name will convert into
virtue and worthiness those things in our conspiracy that would otherwise seem offensive, just as alchemy is supposed to transform base
metals into richest gold.   **162 conceited** (1) conceived, grasped (2)
expressed in a figure of speech.
**2.1. Location: Rome. Brutus' orchard, or garden.**
**5 When** (An exclamation of impatience.)   **7 Get . . . taper** Put a candle for me   **11 spurn** kick   **12 general** general cause, common good.
**15 craves** requires.   **that** that is the issue   **19 Remorse** scruple,
compassion

**20 affections swayed** passions ruled   **21 proof** experience   **22 lowliness** pretended humbleness   **24 round** rung   **26 base degrees**
(1) lower rungs (2) persons of lower social station   **29 Will . . . is** can
carry no appearance of justice so far as his conduct to date is concerned
**30 Fashion it** put the matter   **33 as his kind** according to its nature.
**mischievous** harmful   **35 closet** private chamber, study   **40 ides**
fifteenth day   **44 exhalations** meteors   **57 If . . . follow** i.e., if striking
Caesar will lead to the reform of grievances   **57–8 thou . . . Brutus**
you will be granted all you ask for from me, Brutus.

**BRUTUS**
'Tis good. Go to the gate; somebody knocks.
[*Exit Lucius.*]
Since Cassius first did whet me against Caesar,
I have not slept.
Between the acting of a dreadful thing
And the first motion, all the interim is                                    64
Like a phantasma or a hideous dream.                                        65
The genius and the mortal instruments                                       66
Are then in council; and the state of man,                                  67
Like to a little kingdom, suffers then
The nature of an insurrection.                                              69

*Enter Lucius.*

**LUCIUS**
Sir, 'tis your brother Cassius at the door,                                 70
Who doth desire to see you.

**BRUTUS**                              Is he alone?

**LUCIUS**
No, sir. There are more with him.

**BRUTUS**                              Do you know them?

**LUCIUS**
No, sir. Their hats are plucked about their ears,
And half their faces buried in their cloaks,
That by no means I may discover them                                        75
By any mark of favor.

**BRUTUS**                  Let 'em enter.        [*Exit Lucius.*]   76
They are the faction. O conspiracy,
Sham'st thou to show thy dangerous brow by night,
When evils are most free? Oh, then, by day                                  79
Where wilt thou find a cavern dark enough
To mask thy monstrous visage? Seek none,
    conspiracy!
Hide it in smiles and affability;
For if thou put thy native semblance on,                                    83
Not Erebus itself were dim enough                                           84
To hide thee from prevention.                                               85

*Enter the conspirators, Cassius, Casca, Decius,
Cinna, Metellus [Cimber], and Trebonius.*

**CASSIUS**
I think we are too bold upon your rest.                                     86
Good morrow, Brutus. Do we trouble you?

**BRUTUS**
I have been up this hour, awake all night.
Know I these men that come along with you?

**CASSIUS**
Yes, every man of them, and no man here
But honors you; and every one doth wish
You had but that opinion of yourself

Which every noble Roman bears of you.
This is Trebonius.

**BRUTUS**                              He is welcome hither.

**CASSIUS**
This, Decius Brutus.

**BRUTUS**                              He is welcome too.

**CASSIUS**
This, Casca; this, Cinna; and this, Metellus Cimber.

**BRUTUS**    They are all welcome.
What watchful cares do interpose themselves                                 98
Betwixt your eyes and night?

**CASSIUS**    Shall I entreat a word?
*They [Brutus and Cassius] whisper.*

**DECIUS**
Here lies the east. Doth not the day break here?                          101

**CASCA**    No.

**CINNA**
Oh, pardon, sir, it doth; and yon gray lines
That fret the clouds are messengers of day.                               104

**CASCA**
You shall confess that you are both deceived.                             105
Here, as I point my sword, the sun arises,
Which is a great way growing on the south,                                 107
Weighing the youthful season of the year.                                 108
Some two months hence, up higher toward the north  109
He first presents his fire; and the high east                             110
Stands, as the Capitol, directly here.

**BRUTUS** [*coming forward*]
Give me your hands all over, one by one.                                  112

**CASSIUS**
And let us swear our resolution.

**BRUTUS**
No, not an oath. If not the face of men,                                  114
The sufferance of our souls, the time's abuse—                            115
If these be motives weak, break off betimes,                              116
And every man hence to his idle bed;                                      117
So let high-sighted tyranny range on                                      118
Till each man drop by lottery. But if these,                              119
As I am sure they do, bear fire enough
To kindle cowards and to steel with valor                                 121
The melting spirits of women, then, countrymen,
What need we any spur but our own cause
To prick us to redress? What other bond                                   124
Than secret Romans that have spoke the word                               125
And will not palter? And what other oath                                  126
Than honesty to honesty engaged                                           127
That this shall be or we will fall for it?                                128

---

64 **motion** proposal or impulse   65 **phantasma** hallucination
66–7 **The genius . . . council** The tutelary god or attendant spirit allotted
to every person at birth is then intensely at debate with the person's
physical faculties and passionate nature   69 **The nature of an** a kind of
70 **brother** i.e., brother-in-law. (Cassius had married a sister of Brutus.)
75 **discover** identify   76 **favor** appearance.   79 **free** free to roam at
will.   83 **native** natural, true   84 **Erebus** primeval Darkness (sprung,
according to Hesiod, from Chaos and his sister Night)   85 **prevention**
detection and being forestalled.   86 **upon** in intruding upon

98 **watchful cares** sleep-preventing worries   101 **Here** (Decius points
eastward.)   104 **fret** mark with interlacing lines   105 **deceived** mistaken.   107 **growing** encroaching   108 **Weighing** considering, in consequence of   109 **two months hence** i.e., in May, when the sun rises
in the northeast; before spring, it rises southeast   110 **high** due
112 **all over** one and all   114–16 **If . . . betimes** If the gravely serious
faces of Romans, the suffering we feel, and the corruptions of the
present day are insufficient to move us, we should break off at once
117 **idle** (1) unused (2) in which men are idle   118 **high-sighted**
upward-gazing, ambitious; or haughtily (compare with 2.1.26); or
looking down from on high   119 **by lottery** i.e., as the capricious tyrant
chances to pick on him.   **these** i.e., these injustices just cited
121 **cowards** even cowards.   **steel** harden   124 **prick** spur
125 **Than . . . word** than the word of Romans who, having given their
word of honor, will remain secret   126 **palter** shift position evasively.
127 **honesty** personal honor   128 **shall be** shall be accomplished

Swear priests and cowards and men cautelous,    129
Old feeble carrions, and such suffering souls    130
That welcome wrongs; unto bad causes swear    131
Such creatures as men doubt. But do not stain    132
The even virtue of our enterprise,    133
Nor th'insuppressive mettle of our spirits,    134
To think that or our cause or our performance    135
Did need an oath, when every drop of blood
That every Roman bears—and nobly bears—
Is guilty of a several bastardy    138
If he do break the smallest particle
Of any promise that hath passed from him.

CASSIUS
But what of Cicero? Shall we sound him?    141
I think he will stand very strong with us.    142

CASCA
Let us not leave him out.

CINNA                   No, by no means.

METELLUS
Oh, let us have him, for his silver hairs
Will purchase us a good opinion    145
And buy men's voices to commend our deeds.
It shall be said his judgment ruled our hands;
Our youths and wildness shall no whit appear,
But all be buried in his gravity.

BRUTUS
Oh, name him not. Let us not break with him,    150
For he will never follow anything
That other men begin.

CASSIUS     Then leave him out.

CASCA     Indeed he is not fit.

DECIUS
Shall no man else be touched but only Caesar?

CASSIUS
Decius, well urged. I think it is not meet    156
Mark Antony, so well beloved of Caesar,
Should outlive Caesar. We shall find of him    158
A shrewd contriver; and you know his means,    159
If he improve them, may well stretch so far    160
As to annoy us all. Which to prevent,    161
Let Antony and Caesar fall together.

BRUTUS
Our course will seem too bloody, Caius Cassius,
To cut the head off and then hack the limbs,
Like wrath in death and envy afterwards;    165
For Antony is but a limb of Caesar.
Let's be sacrificers, but not butchers, Caius.
We all stand up against the spirit of Caesar,
And in the spirit of men there is no blood.

Oh, that we then could come by Caesar's spirit
And not dismember Caesar! But, alas,
Caesar must bleed for it. And, gentle friends,    172
Let's kill him boldly, but not wrathfully;
Let's carve him as a dish fit for the gods,
Not hew him as a carcass fit for hounds.
And let our hearts, as subtle masters do,
Stir up their servants to an act of rage    177
And after seem to chide 'em. This shall make    178
Our purpose necessary, and not envious;    179
Which so appearing to the common eyes,
We shall be called purgers, not murderers.    181
And for Mark Antony, think not of him;    182
For he can do no more than Caesar's arm
When Caesar's head is off.

CASSIUS           Yet I fear him,
For in the engrafted love he bears to Caesar—    185

BRUTUS
Alas, good Cassius, do not think of him.
If he love Caesar, all that he can do
Is to himself—take thought and die for Caesar.    188
And that were much he should, for he is given    189
To sports, to wildness, and much company.

TREBONIUS
There is no fear in him. Let him not die,    191
For he will live, and laugh at this hereafter.    192

*Clock strikes.*

BRUTUS
Peace! Count the clock.

CASSIUS         The clock hath stricken three.

TREBONIUS
'Tis time to part.

CASSIUS         But it is doubtful yet
Whether Caesar will come forth today or no;
For he is superstitious grown of late,
Quite from the main opinion he held once
Of fantasy, of dreams, and ceremonies.    198
It may be these apparent prodigies,    199
The unaccustomed terror of this night,
And the persuasion of his augurers    201
May hold him from the Capitol today.

DECIUS
Never fear that. If he be so resolved,
I can o'ersway him; for he loves to hear
That unicorns may be betrayed with trees,    205
And bears with glasses, elephants with holes,    206
Lions with toils, and men with flatterers;    207

---

**129–32 Swear . . . doubt** Let priests and cowards and crafty old men tottering on the brink of the grave swear oaths, and long-suffering souls that submit supinely to wrongs; it is contemptible, untrustworthy persons like these who swear oaths to bad causes. **133 even** steadfast, consistent   **134 insuppressive** indomitable   **135 or . . . or** either . . . or   **138 a several bastardy** an individual act unworthy of his parentage   **141 sound him** sound him out.   **142 stand . . . us** add great credence to our enterprise.   **145 purchase** procure. (Playing on the financial sense of *silver*, line 144.)   **150 break with** confide in   **156 meet** fitting   **158 of** in   **159 shrewd** malicious; artful   **160 improve** exploit, make good use of   **161 annoy** injure   **165 envy** malice

**172 gentle** noble   **177 their servants** i.e., our hands   **178 And after . . . 'em** and then blame our hands as though they had acted without our hearts' consent.   **179 envious** malicious   **181 purgers** those who heal by bleeding the patient   **182 for** as for   **185 engrafted** firmly implanted   **188 take thought** give way to melancholy **189 were much he should** would be an eminently suitable thing for him to do   **191 no fear** nothing to fear   **192.1 Clock strikes** (An anachronism much commented upon; the mechanical clock was not invented until c. 1300.)   **198 fantasy** imaginings.   **ceremonies** omens drawn from the performance of some rite.   **199 apparent** manifest, both visible and obvious   **201 augurers** augurs, official interpreters of omens   **205 may . . . trees** can be tricked by luring the unicorns to drive their single horns into trees   **206 with glasses** by dazzling them with mirrors.   **holes** pitfalls   **207 toils** nets, snares

But when I tell him he hates flatterers,
He says he does, being then most flattered.
Let me work;
For I can give his humor the true bent, 211
And I will bring him to the Capitol.

CASSIUS

Nay, we will all of us be there to fetch him.

BRUTUS

By the eighth hour. Is that the uttermost? 214

CINNA

Be that the uttermost, and fail not then.

METELLUS

Caius Ligarius doth bear Caesar hard, 216
Who rated him for speaking well of Pompey. 217
I wonder none of you have thought of him.

BRUTUS

Now, good Metellus, go along by him. 219
He loves me well, and I have given him reasons;
Send him but hither, and I'll fashion him. 221

CASSIUS

The morning comes upon 's. We'll leave you, Brutus.
And, friends, disperse yourselves; but all remember
What you have said, and show yourselves true
　　　Romans.

BRUTUS

Good gentlemen, look fresh and merrily;
Let not our looks put on our purposes, 226
But bear it as our Roman actors do,
With untired spirits and formal constancy. 228
And so good morrow to you every one. 229
　　　　　　　　　　　　*Exeunt. Manet Brutus.*
Boy! Lucius!—Fast asleep? It is no matter. 230
Enjoy the honey-heavy dew of slumber.
Thou hast no figures nor no fantasies 232
Which busy care draws in the brains of men; 233
Therefore thou sleep'st so sound.

　　*Enter Portia.*

PORTIA　　　　　　　　　　　　　Brutus, my lord!

BRUTUS

Portia, what mean you? Wherefore rise you now?
It is not for your health thus to commit
Your weak condition to the raw cold morning.

PORTIA

Nor for yours neither. You've ungently, Brutus, 238
Stole from my bed. And yesternight, at supper,
You suddenly arose, and walked about
Musing and sighing, with your arms across, 241

And when I asked you what the matter was,
You stared upon me with ungentle looks.
I urged you further; then you scratched your head
And too impatiently stamped with your foot.
Yet I insisted, yet you answered not, 246
But with an angry wafture of your hand 247
Gave sign for me to leave you. So I did,
Fearing to strengthen that impatience
Which seemed too much enkindled, and withal 250
Hoping it was but an effect of humor, 251
Which sometime hath his hour with every man. 252
It will not let you eat, nor talk, nor sleep,
And could it work so much upon your shape
As it hath much prevailed on your condition, 255
I should not know you Brutus. Dear my lord, 256
Make me acquainted with your cause of grief.

BRUTUS

I am not well in health, and that is all.

PORTIA

Brutus is wise, and were he not in health
He would embrace the means to come by it.

BRUTUS

Why, so I do. Good Portia, go to bed. 261

PORTIA

Is Brutus sick? And is it physical 262
To walk unbracèd and suck up the humors 263
Of the dank morning? What, is Brutus sick,
And will he steal out of his wholesome bed
To dare the vile contagion of the night,
And tempt the rheumy and unpurgèd air 267
To add unto his sickness? No, my Brutus,
You have some sick offense within your mind,
Which by the right and virtue of my place
I ought to know of. [*She kneels.*] And upon my knees
I charm you, by my once-commended beauty, 272
By all your vows of love, and that great vow
Which did incorporate and make us one,
That you unfold to me, your self, your half,
Why you are heavy, and what men tonight 276
Have had resort to you; for here have been
Some six or seven, who did hide their faces
Even from darkness.

BRUTUS　　　　　　　Kneel not, gentle Portia. 279
　　　　　　　　　　　　　　　　　　[*He raises her.*]

PORTIA

I should not need if you were gentle Brutus. 280
Within the bond of marriage, tell me, Brutus,
Is it excepted I should know no secrets 282
That appertain to you? Am I your self
But as it were in sort or limitation, 284

---

**211 humor** disposition　**214 the eighth hour** i.e., 8 A.M. (The Elizabethan way of reckoning time. By Roman reckoning, the day began at 6 A.M., so that *the eighth hour* would be 2 P.M.)　**uttermost** latest.　**216 doth bear Caesar hard** bears a grudge toward Caesar. (See 1.2.313n.)　**217 rated** rebuked　**219 by him** by way of his house.　**221 fashion** shape (to our purposes)　**226 put on** expose to open view　**228 formal constancy** steadfast appearance, decorum.　**229.1 Manet** He remains on stage　**230 Lucius** (Brutus calls to his servant, who is evidently within, asleep, after having admitted the conspirators at line 85; later, at line 310, he is still within when Brutus calls to him.)　**232 figures** imaginings　**233 care** anxiety　**238 ungently** discourteously, unkindly　**241 across** folded. (A sign of melancholy.)

**246 Yet . . . yet** Still . . . still　**247 wafture** waving　**250 withal** moreover　**251 humor** imbalance of temperament　**252 his** its　**255 condition** inner state of mind　**256 know you** recognize you as　**261 so I do** (Said with a double meaning not perceived by Portia: I seek through Caesar's death the means to better the health of the state.)　**262 physical** healthful　**263 unbracèd** with loosened clothing.　**humors** damps, mists　**267 rheumy and unpurgèd** conducive to illness and not cleansed of its impurities (which night air was thought to contain)　**272 charm** conjure, entreat　**276 heavy** sad　**279, 280 gentle** noble; gracious, kind　**282 excepted** made an exception that　**284 in . . . limitation** only up to a point. (A legal phrase.)

To keep with you at meals, comfort your bed,                285
And talk to you sometimes? Dwell I but in the suburbs  286
Of your good pleasure? If it be no more,
Portia is Brutus' harlot, not his wife.

BRUTUS
You are my true and honorable wife,
As dear to me as are the ruddy drops
That visit my sad heart.

PORTIA
If this were true, then should I know this secret.
I grant I am a woman, but withal                            293
A woman that Lord Brutus took to wife.
I grant I am a woman, but withal
A woman well reputed, Cato's daughter.                      296
Think you I am no stronger than my sex,
Being so fathered and so husbanded?
Tell me your counsels, I will not disclose 'em.            299
I have made strong proof of my constancy,
Giving myself a voluntary wound
Here, in the thigh. Can I bear that with patience,
And not my husband's secrets?

BRUTUS                                        O ye gods,
Render me worthy of this noble wife!
                                        Knock [within].
Hark, hark, one knocks. Portia, go in awhile,
And by and by thy bosom shall partake
The secrets of my heart.
All my engagements I will construe to thee,                308
All the charactery of my sad brows.                        309
Leave me with haste.                        Exit Portia.
    [Calling]            Lucius, who's that knocks?

        Enter Lucius and [Caius] Ligarius [wearing a
        kerchief].

LUCIUS
Here is a sick man that would speak with you.              311

BRUTUS
Caius Ligarius, that Metellus spake of.
Boy, stand aside.                           [Exit Lucius.]
                    Caius Ligarius, how?                   313

LIGARIUS
Vouchsafe good morrow from a feeble tongue.                314

BRUTUS
Oh, what a time have you chose out, brave Caius,           315
To wear a kerchief! Would you were not sick!               316

LIGARIUS
I am not sick, if Brutus have in hand
Any exploit worthy the name of honor.

BRUTUS
Such an exploit have I in hand, Ligarius,

Had you a healthful ear to hear of it.

LIGARIUS
By all the gods that Romans bow before,
I here discard my sickness!  [He throws off his kerchief.]
                            Soul of Rome!
Brave son, derived from honorable loins!
Thou like an exorcist hast conjured up
My mortifièd spirit. Now bid me run,                       325
And I will strive with things impossible,
Yea, get the better of them. What's to do?

BRUTUS
A piece of work that will make sick men whole.             328

LIGARIUS
But are not some whole that we must make sick?

BRUTUS
That must we also. What it is, my Caius,
I shall unfold to thee as we are going
To whom it must be done.

LIGARIUS                        Set on your foot,           332
And with a heart new-fired I follow you
To do I know not what; but it sufficeth
That Brutus leads me on.                    Thunder.

BRUTUS                        Follow me, then.    Exeunt.

                            ❧

# [2.2]

        Thunder and lightning. Enter Julius Caesar, in his
        nightgown.

CAESAR
Nor heaven nor earth have been at peace tonight.            1
Thrice hath Calpurnia in her sleep cried out,
"Help, ho, they murder Caesar!"—Who's within?

        Enter a Servant.

SERVANT    My lord?

CAESAR
Go bid the priests do present sacrifice                     5
And bring me their opinions of success.                     6

SERVANT    I will, my lord.                        Exit.

        Enter Calpurnia.

CALPURNIA
What mean you, Caesar? Think you to walk forth?
You shall not stir out of your house today.

CAESAR
Caesar shall forth. The things that threatened me
Ne'er looked but on my back. When they shall see
The face of Caesar, they are vanishèd.

CALPURNIA
Caesar, I never stood on ceremonies,                       13

---

285 keep stay, be   286 suburbs periphery. (In Elizabethan London, prostitutes frequented the suburbs.)   293 withal in addition   296 Cato's daughter (Cato the Younger of Utica was famous for his integrity; he sided with Pompey against Caesar in 48 B.C. and later killed himself rather than submit to Caesar's tyranny. He was Brutus's uncle as well as his father-in-law.)   299 Tell me (1) If you tell me (2) Do tell me.   counsels secrets   308 construe explain fully   309 charactery handwriting, i.e., what is figured there   311 sick man (In Elizabethan medicine, a poultice was often applied to the forehead of a patient and wrapped in a handkerchief; hence the kerchief in line 316.)   313 how? i.e., how are you?   314 Vouchsafe Deign (to accept)   315 brave noble; courageous   316 Would If only

325 mortifièd deadened   328 whole healthy, i.e., free of the disease of tyranny.   332 To whom i.e., to him to whom
2.2. Location: Caesar's house.
0.2 nightgown housecoat.   1 Nor Neither   5 present sacrifice immediate examination of the entrails of sacrificed animals for omens   6 success the result, what will follow.   13 stood on ceremonies attached importance to omens

Yet now they fright me. There is one within,
Besides the things that we have heard and seen,
Recounts most horrid sights seen by the watch.                16
A lioness hath whelpèd in the streets,                        17
And graves have yawned and yielded up their dead.            18
Fierce fiery warriors fight upon the clouds
In ranks and squadrons and right form of war,                20
Which drizzled blood upon the Capitol.
The noise of battle hurtled in the air;                       22
Horses did neigh, and dying men did groan,
And ghosts did shriek and squeal about the streets.
Oh, Caesar, these things are beyond all use,                  25
And I do fear them.
CAESAR                    What can be avoided
Whose end is purposed by the mighty gods?
Yet Caesar shall go forth; for these predictions
Are to the world in general as to Caesar.
CALPURNIA
When beggars die there are no comets seen;
The heavens themselves blaze forth the death of
    princes.                                                  31
CAESAR
Cowards die many times before their deaths;
The valiant never taste of death but once.
Of all the wonders that I yet have heard,
It seems to me most strange that men should fear,
Seeing that death, a necessary end,
Will come when it will come.

*Enter a Servant.*

                            What say the augurers?
SERVANT
They would not have you to stir forth today.
Plucking the entrails of an offering forth,
They could not find a heart within the beast.
CAESAR
The gods do this in shame of cowardice.
Caesar should be a beast without a heart
If he should stay at home today for fear.
No, Caesar shall not. Danger knows full well
That Caesar is more dangerous than he.
We are two lions littered in one day,                         46
And I the elder and more terrible;
And Caesar shall go forth.
CALPURNIA              Alas, my lord,
Your wisdom is consumed in confidence.                        49
Do not go forth today! Call it my fear
That keeps you in the house, and not your own.
We'll send Mark Antony to the Senate House,
And he shall say you are not well today.
Let me, upon my knee, prevail in this.        [*She kneels.*]
CAESAR
Mark Antony shall say I am not well,

And for thy humor I will stay at home.                        56
                            [*He raises her.*]

    *Enter Decius.*

Here's Decius Brutus. He shall tell them so.
DECIUS
Caesar, all hail! Good morrow, worthy Caesar.
I come to fetch you to the Senate House.
CAESAR
And you are come in very happy time                           60
To bear my greeting to the senators
And tell them that I will not come today.
Cannot is false, and that I dare not, falser;
I will not come today. Tell them so, Decius.
CALPURNIA
Say he is sick.
CAESAR             Shall Caesar send a lie?
Have I in conquest stretched mine arm so far
To be afeard to tell graybeards the truth?
Decius, go tell them Caesar will not come.
DECIUS
Most mighty Caesar, let me know some cause,
Lest I be laughed at when I tell them so.
CAESAR
The cause is in my will: I will not come.
That is enough to satisfy the Senate.
But for your private satisfaction,
Because I love you, I will let you know.
Calpurnia here, my wife, stays me at home.                    75
She dreamt tonight she saw my statue,                         76
Which like a fountain with an hundred spouts
Did run pure blood; and many lusty Romans                     78
Came smiling and did bathe their hands in it.
And these does she apply for warnings and portents           80
Of evils imminent, and on her knee
Hath begged that I will stay at home today.
DECIUS
This dream is all amiss interpreted;
It was a vision fair and fortunate.
Your statue spouting blood in many pipes,
In which so many smiling Romans bathed,
Signifies that from you great Rome shall suck
Reviving blood, and that great men shall press              88
For tinctures, stains, relics, and cognizance.              89
This by Calpurnia's dream is signified.
CAESAR
And this way have you well expounded it.
DECIUS
I have, when you have heard what I can say;
And know it now. The Senate have concluded
To give this day a crown to mighty Caesar.
If you shall send them word you will not come,

---

16 **watch** (An anachronism, since there was no *watch,* or "body of
night watchmen," in Caesar's Rome.)  17 **whelpèd** given birth
18 **yawned** gaped  20 **right form** regular formation  22 **hurtled**
clashed  25 **use** normal experience  31 **blaze forth** proclaim (in a
blaze of light)  46 **littered** born (as in a litter of cats)  49 **consumed
in confidence** eaten up by your overconfidence.

56 **humor** whim  60 **happy** opportune  75 **stays** detains  76 **tonight**
last night  78 **lusty** lively, merry  80 **apply for** interpret as
88 **press** crowd around  89 **tinctures** handkerchiefs dipped in the
blood of martyrs, with healing powers; or colors in a coat of arms.
(*Tinctures, stains,* and *relics* are all venerated properties, as though
Caesar were a saint.)  **cognizance** heraldic emblems worn by a
nobleman's followers.

Their minds may change. Besides, it were a mock 96
Apt to be rendered for someone to say 97
"Break up the Senate till another time
When Caesar's wife shall meet with better dreams."
If Caesar hide himself, shall they not whisper
"Lo, Caesar is afraid"?
Pardon me, Caesar, for my dear dear love
To your proceeding bids me tell you this, 103
And reason to my love is liable. 104

CAESAR
How foolish do your fears seem now, Calpurnia!
I am ashamèd I did yield to them.
Give me my robe, for I will go.

*Enter Brutus, Ligarius, Metellus, Casca,*
*Trebonius, Cinna, and Publius.*

And look where Publius is come to fetch me.

PUBLIUS
Good morrow, Caesar.

CAESAR                    Welcome, Publius.
What, Brutus, are you stirred so early too?
Good morrow, Casca. Caius Ligarius,
Caesar was ne'er so much your enemy
As that same ague which hath made you lean. 113
What is't o'clock?

BRUTUS                    Caesar, 'tis strucken eight. 114

CAESAR
I thank you for your pains and courtesy.

*Enter Antony.*

See, Antony, that revels long o' nights,
Is notwithstanding up. Good morrow, Antony.

ANTONY    So to most noble Caesar.

CAESAR [*to a Servant*]    Bid them prepare within. 119
                    [*Exit Servant.*]
I am to blame to be thus waited for.
Now, Cinna. Now, Metellus. What, Trebonius,
I have an hour's talk in store for you;
Remember that you call on me today.
Be near me, that I may remember you.

TREBONIUS
Caesar, I will. [*Aside*] And so near will I be
That your best friends shall wish I had been further.

CAESAR
Good friends, go in and taste some wine with me,
And we, like friends, will straightway go together.

BRUTUS [*aside*]
That every like is not the same, O Caesar, 129
The heart of Brutus earns to think upon!    *Exeunt.* 130

♣

## [2.3]

*Enter Artemidorus [reading a paper].*

ARTEMIDORUS    "Caesar, beware of Brutus; take heed of
Cassius; come not near Casca; have an eye to Cinna;
trust not Trebonius; mark well Metellus Cimber; De-
cius Brutus loves thee not; thou hast wronged Caius
Ligarius. There is but one mind in all these men, and
it is bent against Caesar. If thou be'st not immortal,
look about you. Security gives way to conspiracy. The 7
mighty gods defend thee! Thy lover, 8
                    Artemidorus."
Here will I stand till Caesar pass along,
And as a suitor will I give him this.
My heart laments that virtue cannot live
Out of the teeth of emulation. 13
If thou read this, O Caesar, thou mayest live;
If not, the Fates with traitors do contrive.    *Exit.* 15

♣

## [2.4]

*Enter Portia and Lucius.*

PORTIA
I prithee, boy, run to the Senate House.
Stay not to answer me, but get thee gone.—
Why dost thou stay?

LUCIUS                    To know my errand, madam.

PORTIA
I would have had thee there and here again
Ere I can tell thee what thou shouldst do there.
[*Aside*] O constancy, be strong upon my side; 6
Set a huge mountain 'tween my heart and tongue! 7
I have a man's mind, but a woman's might.
How hard it is for women to keep counsel!— 9
Art thou here yet?

LUCIUS                    Madam, what should I do?
Run to the Capitol, and nothing else?
And so return to you, and nothing else?

PORTIA
Yes, bring me word, boy, if thy lord look well,
For he went sickly forth; and take good note
What Caesar doth, what suitors press to him.
Hark, boy, what noise is that?

LUCIUS    I hear none, madam.

PORTIA    Prithee, listen well.
I heard a bustling rumor, like a fray, 19
And the wind brings it from the Capitol.

LUCIUS    Sooth, madam, I hear nothing. 21

*Enter the Soothsayer.*

---

96–7 a mock . . . rendered a sarcastic remark likely to be made
103 proceeding advancement    104 reason . . . liable my reasoning
is swayed by my affection.    113 ague fever    114 eight 8 A.M.
(See 2.1.214n on Roman time.)    119 prepare within i.e., set out wine
in the other room and prepare to leave. (Perhaps addressed to the
servant who entered at line 37, or to Calpurnia.) The ritual drinking
of wine is a pledge of friendship that should preclude violence; see
lines 127–8.    129 That . . . same i.e., That not all those who behave "like
friends" (line 128) are actually so. (Proverbial).    130 earns grieves

2.3. Location: A street near the Capitol.
7 Security gives way Overconfidence opens a path    8 lover
friend    13 Out . . . emulation beyond the bite of grudging envy.
15 contrive conspire.
2.4. Location: Before the house of Brutus.
6 constancy resolution    7 Set . . . tongue i.e., let my brave resolution keep
my tongue from blabbing what my heart fears.    9 counsel a secret.
19 bustling rumor confused sound.    fray fight    21 Sooth Truly

PORTIA
Come hither, fellow. Which way hast thou been?
SOOTHSAYER    At mine own house, good lady.
PORTIA
What is't o'clock?
SOOTHSAYER          About the ninth hour, lady.          24
PORTIA
Is Caesar yet gone to the Capitol?
SOOTHSAYER
Madam, not yet. I go to take my stand,
To see him pass on to the Capitol.
PORTIA
Thou hast some suit to Caesar, hast thou not?
SOOTHSAYER
That I have, lady, if it will please Caesar
To be so good to Caesar as to hear me:
I shall beseech him to befriend himself.
PORTIA
Why, know'st thou any harm 's intended towards him?
SOOTHSAYER
None that I know will be, much that I fear may chance.
Good morrow to you. Here the street is narrow.
The throng that follows Caesar at the heels,
Of senators, of praetors, common suitors,          36
Will crowd a feeble man almost to death.
I'll get me to a place more void, and there          38
Speak to great Caesar as he comes along.          *Exit.*
PORTIA
I must go in. Ay me, how weak a thing
The heart of woman is! O Brutus,
The heavens speed thee in thine enterprise!—
Sure, the boy heard me.—Brutus hath a suit
That Caesar will not grant.—Oh, I grow faint.—
Run, Lucius, and commend me to my lord;          45
Say I am merry. Come to me again          46
And bring me word what he doth say to thee.
                                   *Exeunt [separately].*

❖

# 3.1

*Flourish. Enter Caesar, Brutus, Cassius, Casca,*
*Decius, Metellus [Cimber], Trebonius, Cinna,*
*Antony, Lepidus, Artemidorus, Publius, [Popilius*
*Lena], and the Soothsayer; [others following].*

CAESAR [*to the Soothsayer*]    The ides of March are come.
SOOTHSAYER    Ay, Caesar, but not gone.
ARTEMIDORUS    Hail, Caesar! Read this schedule.          3
DECIUS
Trebonius doth desire you to o'erread,

At your best leisure, this his humble suit.
ARTEMIDORUS
O Caesar, read mine first, for mine's a suit
That touches Caesar nearer. Read it, great Caesar.
CAESAR
What touches us ourself shall be last served.
ARTEMIDORUS
Delay not, Caesar, read it instantly.
CAESAR
What, is the fellow mad?
PUBLIUS                      Sirrah, give place.          10
CASSIUS
What, urge you your petitions in the street?
Come to the Capitol.

          [*Caesar goes to the Capitol and takes his place, the*
          *rest following.*]

POPILIUS [*to Cassius*]
I wish your enterprise today may thrive.
CASSIUS    What enterprise, Popilius?
POPILIUS [*to Cassius*]    Fare you well.
                              [*He advances to Caesar.*]
BRUTUS    What said Popilius Lena?
CASSIUS
He wished today our enterprise might thrive.
I fear our purpose is discoverèd.
BRUTUS
Look how he makes to Caesar. Mark him.          19
                    [*Popilius speaks apart to Caesar.*]
CASSIUS
Casca, be sudden, for we fear prevention.
Brutus, what shall be done? If this be known,
Cassius or Caesar never shall turn back,          22
For I will slay myself.
BRUTUS                      Cassius, be constant.          23
Popilius Lena speaks not of our purposes;
For look, he smiles, and Caesar doth not change.          25
CASSIUS
Trebonius knows his time, for look you, Brutus,
He draws Mark Antony out of the way.
                         [*Exit Trebonius with Antony.*]
DECIUS
Where is Metellus Cimber? Let him go
And presently prefer his suit to Caesar.          29
BRUTUS
He is addressed. Press near and second him.          30
CINNA
Casca, you are the first that rears your hand.
                              [*They press near Caesar.*]
CAESAR
Are we all ready? What is now amiss
That Caesar and his Senate must redress?

24 **the ninth hour** i.e., 9 A.M. (In Roman reckoning, the ninth hour
would be 3 P.M.)    36 **praetors** judges    38 **void** empty, uncrowded
45 **commend me** bear my greetings    46 **merry** cheerful. (Not "mirthful.")
3.1 Location: Before the Capitol, and, following line 12, within the
Capitol.
0.4 *others following* (Citizens may be present, though not certainly
so; see lines 83 and 93–4.)    3 **schedule** document.

10 **Sirrah** Fellow. (A form of address to a social inferior.)    **place**
way.    19 **makes to** advances toward    22–3 **Cassius . . . myself** Either
Cassius or Caesar will never return from the Capitol alive, for I will
commit suicide if this attempt fails.    23 **be constant** hold steady.
25 **change** change expression.    29 **presently prefer** immediately urge
30 **addressed** ready.

METELLUS [*kneeling*]
Most high, most mighty, and most puissant Caesar, 34
Metellus Cimber throws before thy seat
An humble heart—
CAESAR                    I must prevent thee, Cimber. 36
These couchings and these lowly courtesies 37
Might fire the blood of ordinary men, 38
And turn preordinance and first decree 39
Into the law of children. Be not fond 40
To think that Caesar bears such rebel blood 41
That will be thawed from the true quality 42
With that which melteth fools—I mean, sweet words,
Low-crookèd curtsies, and base spaniel fawning. 44
Thy brother by decree is banishèd.
If thou dost bend and pray and fawn for him, 46
I spurn thee like a cur out of my way. 47
Know, Caesar doth not wrong, nor without cause
Will he be satisfied.
METELLUS
Is there no voice more worthy than my own
To sound more sweetly in great Caesar's ear
For the repealing of my banished brother? 52
BRUTUS [*kneeling*]
I kiss thy hand, but not in flattery, Caesar,
Desiring thee that Publius Cimber may
Have an immediate freedom of repeal. 55
CAESAR
What, Brutus?
CASSIUS [*kneeling*]    Pardon, Caesar! Caesar, pardon!
As low as to thy foot doth Cassius fall,
To beg enfranchisement for Publius Cimber. 58
CAESAR
I could be well moved, if I were as you;
If I could pray to move, prayers would move me. 60
But I am constant as the northern star, 61
Of whose true-fixed and resting quality 62
There is no fellow in the firmament. 63
The skies are painted with unnumbered sparks;
They are all fire and every one doth shine;
But there's but one in all doth hold his place.
So in the world: 'tis furnished well with men,
And men are flesh and blood, and apprehensive; 68
Yet in the number I do know but one
That unassailable holds on his rank, 70
Unshaked of motion. And that I am he, 71
Let me a little show it even in this:

That I was constant Cimber should be banished,
And constant do remain to keep him so.
CINNA [*kneeling*]
O Caesar—
CAESAR          Hence! Wilt thou lift up Olympus? 75
DECIUS [*kneeling*]
Great Caesar—
CAESAR             Doth not Brutus bootless kneel? 76
CASCA    Speak hands for me!
            *They stab Caesar, [Casca first, Brutus last].*
CAESAR    *Et tu, Brutè?* Then fall, Caesar!    *Dies.* 78
CINNA
Liberty! Freedom! Tyranny is dead!
Run hence, proclaim, cry it about the streets.
CASSIUS
Some to the common pulpits, and cry out 81
"Liberty, freedom, and enfranchisement!" 82
BRUTUS
People and senators, be not affrighted.
Fly not; stand still. Ambition's debt is paid. 84
CASCA
Go to the pulpit, Brutus.
DECIUS              And Cassius too.
BRUTUS    Where's Publius? 86
CINNA
Here, quite confounded with this mutiny. 87
METELLUS
Stand fast together, lest some friend of Caesar's
Should chance—
BRUTUS
Talk not of standing. Publius, good cheer. 90
There is no harm intended to your person,
Nor to no Roman else. So tell them, Publius.
CASSIUS
And leave us, Publius, lest that the people,
Rushing on us, should do your age some mischief.
BRUTUS
Do so, and let no man abide this deed 95
But we the doers.    [*Exeunt all but the conspirators.*]

            *Enter Trebonius.*

CASSIUS
Where is Antony?
TREBONIUS          Fled to his house amazed. 97
Men, wives, and children stare, cry out, and run
As it were doomsday.
BRUTUS              Fates, we will know your pleasures. 99
That we shall die, we know; 'tis but the time, 100
And drawing days out, that men stand upon. 101

34 **puissant** powerful  36 **prevent** forestall  37 **couchings . . . courtesies** kneelings and submissive bows  38 **fire the blood of** inflame the passions of  39–40 **And turn . . . children** and turn preordained law into the kinds of childish and flexible rules that children use in their games.  40 **fond** so foolish as  41 **rebel** rebellious against reason  42 **true quality** proper firmness and stability. (The metaphor is from alchemy.)  44 **Low-crookèd curtsies** obsequious bows  46 **bend** bow  47 **spurn** kick  52 **repealing** recall  55 **freedom of repeal** permission to return.  58 **enfranchisement** i.e., restoration of citizenship  60 **pray to move** make petition (as you do)  61 **northern star** polestar  62 **resting** remaining stationary  63 **fellow** equal  68 **apprehensive** capable of perception  70 **rank** place, position  71 **Unshaked of motion** (1) unswayed by petitions (2) with perfect steadiness.

75 **Olympus** mountain dwelling of the Greek gods  76 **bootless** in vain  78 *Et tu, Brutè?* You too, Brutus? (Literally, "Even thou.")  81 **common pulpits** public platforms or rostra  82 **enfranchisement** restoration of civil rights (as in line 58 above)  84 **Ambition's debt** What Caesar's ambition deserved  86 **Publius** (An old senator, too confused to flee.)  87 **mutiny** uprising, discord.  90 **standing** making a stand.  95 **abide** (1) suffer the consequences of (2) remain here with  97 **amazed** stupified.  99 **As** as if.  **doomsday** the day of final judgment.  100–1 **'tis . . . upon** i.e., it is only the time of our deaths, and how long we have to live, that we are uncertain about, make a question of.

CASCA

Why, he that cuts off twenty years of life
Cuts off so many years of fearing death.

BRUTUS

Grant that, and then is death a benefit.
So are we Caesar's friends, that have abridged
His time of fearing death. Stoop, Romans, stoop,
And let us bathe our hands in Caesar's blood
Up to the elbows and besmear our swords.
Then walk we forth even to the marketplace,                    109
And, waving our red weapons o'er our heads,
Let's all cry "Peace, freedom, and liberty!"

CASSIUS

Stoop, then, and wash. [*They bathe their hands and
         weapons.*] How many ages hence
Shall this our lofty scene be acted over
In states unborn and accents yet unknown!                      114

BRUTUS

How many times shall Caesar bleed in sport,                    115
That now on Pompey's basis lies along                          116
No worthier than the dust!

CASSIUS   So oft as that shall be,
So often shall the knot of us be called                        119
The men that gave their country liberty.

DECIUS

What, shall we forth?

CASSIUS                    Ay, every man away.
Brutus shall lead, and we will grace his heels                 122
With the most boldest and best hearts of Rome.

*Enter a Servant.*

BRUTUS

Soft, who comes here? A friend of Antony's.

SERVANT [*kneeling*]

Thus, Brutus, did my master bid me kneel;
Thus did Mark Antony bid me fall down,
And, being prostrate, thus he bade me say:
"Brutus is noble, wise, valiant, and honest;                   128
Caesar was mighty, bold, royal, and loving.
Say I love Brutus and I honor him;
Say I feared Caesar, honored him, and loved him.
If Brutus will vouchsafe that Antony                           132
May safely come to him and be resolved                         133
How Caesar hath deserved to lie in death,
Mark Antony shall not love Caesar dead
So well as Brutus living, but will follow
The fortunes and affairs of noble Brutus
Thorough the hazards of this untrod state                      138
With all true faith." So says my master Antony.

BRUTUS

Thy master is a wise and valiant Roman;
I never thought him worse.

Tell him, so please him come unto this place,                  142
He shall be satisfied and, by my honor,
Depart untouched.

SERVANT         I'll fetch him presently.                      144

                                    *Exit Servant.*

BRUTUS

I know that we shall have him well to friend.                  145

CASSIUS

I wish we may. But yet have I a mind
That fears him much, and my misgiving still                    147
Falls shrewdly to the purpose.                                 148

*Enter Antony.*

BRUTUS

But here comes Antony.—Welcome, Mark Antony.

ANTONY

O mighty Caesar! Dost thou lie so low?
Are all thy conquests, glories, triumphs, spoils,              151
Shrunk to this little measure? Fare thee well.—
I know not, gentlemen, what you intend,
Who else must be let blood, who else is rank;                  154
If I myself, there is no hour so fit
As Caesar's death's hour, nor no instrument
Of half that worth as those your swords, made rich
With the most noble blood of all this world.
I do beseech ye, if you bear me hard,                          159
Now, whilst your purpled hands do reek and smoke,              160
Fulfill your pleasure. Live a thousand years,                  161
I shall not find myself so apt to die;                         162
No place will please me so, no mean of death,
As here by Caesar, and by you cut off,
The choice and master spirits of this age.

BRUTUS

Oh, Antony, beg not your death of us.
Though now we must appear bloody and cruel,
As by our hands and this our present act
You see we do, yet see you but our hands
And this the bleeding business they have done.
Our hearts you see not. They are pitiful;                      171
And pity to the general wrong of Rome—
As fire drives out fire, so pity pity—                         173
Hath done this deed on Caesar. For your part,
To you our swords have leaden points, Mark Antony.             175
Our arms in strength of malice, and our hearts                 176
Of brothers' temper, do receive you in                         177
With all kind love, good thoughts, and reverence.

CASSIUS

Your voice shall be as strong as any man's                     179
In the disposing of new dignities.                             180

---

109 **the marketplace** i.e., the Forum   114 **accents** languages   115 **in sport** for entertainment   116 **on Pompey's ... along** lies prostrate on the pedestal of Pompey's statue   119 **knot** group   122 **grace his heels** follow him close at heels (in a triumphal procession; cf. 1.1.34)   128 **honest** honorable   132 **vouchsafe** grant   133 **be resolved** receive an explanation   138 **Thorough** through.   **untrod state** still unexplored state of affairs

142 **so** if it should   144 **presently** immediately.   145 **to friend** for a friend.   147 **fears** distrusts   148 **Falls ... purpose** is intensely to the point.   151 **spoils** valuables seized from the enemy   154 **let blood** bled (a medical term), i.e., killed.   **rank** steamy; ripe   159 **bear me hard** bear ill will to me   160 **purpled** bloody   161 **Live** If I should live   162 **apt** ready   171 **pitiful** full of pity   173 **pity pity** i.e., pity for the general wrong of Rome has driven out pity for Caesar   175 **leaden** i.e., blunt   176–7 **Our ... temper** i.e., Both our arms, though seeming strong in enmity, and our hearts, full of brotherly feeling   179 **voice** vote, authority   180 **dignities** offices of state.

**BRUTUS**
Only be patient till we have appeased
The multitude, beside themselves with fear,
And then we will deliver you the cause                            183
Why I, that did love Caesar when I struck him,
Have thus proceeded.

**ANTONY**                         I doubt not of your wisdom.
Let each man render me his bloody hand.
[*He shakes hands with the conspirators.*]
First, Marcus Brutus, will I shake with you;
Next, Caius Cassius, do I take your hand;
Now, Decius Brutus, yours; now yours, Metellus;
Yours, Cinna; and, my valiant Casca, yours;
Though last, not least in love, yours, good Trebonius.
Gentlemen all—alas, what shall I say?
My credit now stands on such slippery ground            193
That one of two bad ways you must conceit me,            194
Either a coward or a flatterer.
That I did love thee, Caesar, oh, 'tis true!
If then thy spirit look upon us now,
Shall it not grieve thee dearer than thy death            198
To see thy Antony making his peace,
Shaking the bloody fingers of thy foes—
Most noble—in the presence of thy corpse?
Had I as many eyes as thou hast wounds,
Weeping as fast as they stream forth thy blood,
It would become me better than to close                    204
In terms of friendship with thine enemies.
Pardon me, Julius! Here wast thou bayed, brave hart, 206
Here didst thou fall, and here thy hunters stand,
Signed in thy spoil and crimsoned in thy lethe.          208
O world, thou wast the forest to this hart,
And this indeed, O world, the heart of thee!
How like a deer, strucken by many princes,
Dost thou here lie!

**CASSIUS**
Mark Antony—

**ANTONY**                         Pardon me, Caius Cassius.
The enemies of Caesar shall say this;                        214
Then in a friend it is cold modesty.                          215

**CASSIUS**
I blame you not for praising Caesar so,
But what compact mean you to have with us?
Will you be pricked in number of our friends,            218
Or shall we on and not depend on you?

**ANTONY**
Therefore I took your hands, but was indeed
Swayed from the point by looking down on Caesar.
Friends am I with you all, and love you all,

Upon this hope, that you shall give me reasons
Why and wherein Caesar was dangerous.

**BRUTUS**
Or else were this a savage spectacle.                        225
Our reasons are so full of good regard                      226
That were you, Antony, the son of Caesar,
You should be satisfied.

**ANTONY**                         That's all I seek,
And am moreover suitor that I may
Produce his body to the marketplace,                        230
And in the pulpit, as becomes a friend,                    231
Speak in the order of his funeral.                            232

**BRUTUS**
You shall, Mark Antony.

**CASSIUS**                         Brutus, a word with you.
[*Aside to Brutus*] You know not what you do. Do not
consent
That Antony speak in his funeral.
Know you how much the people may be moved
By that which he will utter?

**BRUTUS** [*aside to Cassius*]          By your pardon:
I will myself into the pulpit first
And show the reason of our Caesar's death.
What Antony shall speak, I will protest                      240
He speaks by leave and by permission,
And that we are contented Caesar shall
Have all true rites and lawful ceremonies.
It shall advantage more than do us wrong.

**CASSIUS** [*aside to Brutus*]
I know not what may fall. I like it not.                      245

**BRUTUS**
Mark Antony, here, take you Caesar's body.
You shall not in your funeral speech blame us,
But speak all good you can devise of Caesar,
And say you do't by our permission.
Else shall you not have any hand at all
About his funeral. And you shall speak
In the same pulpit whereto I am going,
After my speech is ended.

**ANTONY**                         Be it so.
I do desire no more.

**BRUTUS**
Prepare the body then, and follow us.                        255
*Exeunt. Manet Antony.*

**ANTONY**
Oh, pardon me, thou bleeding piece of earth,
That I am meek and gentle with these butchers!
Thou art the ruins of the noblest man
That ever livèd in the tide of times.                        259
Woe to the hand that shed this costly blood!              260
Over thy wounds now do I prophesy—
Which, like dumb mouths, do ope their ruby lips          262

---

**183 deliver** report to   **193 credit** credibility   **194 conceit** think,
judge   **198 dearer** more deeply   **204 become** suit.   **close** come to an
agreement   **206 bayed** brought to bay.   **hart** stag. (With pun on
*heart*.)   **208 Signed . . . spoil** marked with the tokens of your slaughter. (The *spoil* in hunting is the cutting up of the quarry and distribution of reward to the hounds.)   **lethe** river of oblivion in the
underworld, here associated with death and blood. (Perhaps fused
with Cocytus, river of blood in the underworld.)   **214 The enemies**
Even the enemies   **215 cold modesty** sober moderation.
**218 pricked** marked down

**225 Or else were this** Otherwise this would be   **226 regard** account,
consideration   **230 Produce** bring forth.   **marketplace** Forum   **231
pulpit** public platform   **232 order** ceremony   **240 protest** announce,
insist   **245 fall** befall, happen.   **255.1 Manet** He remains on stage
**259 tide of times** course of all history.   **260 costly** (1) valuable
(2) fraught with dire consequences   **262 ruby** (1) red (2) bloody

To beg the voice and utterance of my tongue—
A curse shall light upon the limbs of men;
Domestic fury and fierce civil strife
Shall cumber all the parts of Italy;                    266
Blood and destruction shall be so in use
And dreadful objects so familiar                    268
That mothers shall but smile when they behold
Their infants quartered with the hands of war,    270
All pity choked with custom of fell deeds;    271
And Caesar's spirit, ranging for revenge,    272
With Ate by his side come hot from hell,    273
Shall in these confines with a monarch's voice    274
Cry havoc and let slip the dogs of war,    275
That this foul deed shall smell above the earth
With carrion men, groaning for burial.

*Enter Octavius's Servant.*

You serve Octavius Caesar, do you not?
SERVANT    I do, Mark Antony.
ANTONY
Caesar did write for him to come to Rome.
SERVANT
He did receive his letters, and is coming,    281
And bid me say to you by word of mouth—
O Caesar!—    *[Seeing the body.]*
ANTONY
Thy heart is big. Get thee apart and weep.
Passion, I see, is catching, for mine eyes,    285
Seeing those beads of sorrow stand in thine,
Began to water. Is thy master coming?
SERVANT
He lies tonight within seven leagues of Rome.    288
ANTONY
Post back with speed and tell him what hath chanced. 289
Here is a mourning Rome, a dangerous Rome,
No Rome of safety for Octavius yet;    291
Hie hence and tell him so. Yet stay awhile;
Thou shalt not back till I have borne this corpse
Into the marketplace. There shall I try,    294
In my oration, how the people take
The cruel issue of these bloody men,    296
According to the which thou shalt discourse    297
To young Octavius of the state of things.    298
Lend me your hand.    *Exeunt [with Caesar's body].*

---

**[3.2]**

*Enter Brutus and [presently] goes into the pulpit,
and Cassius, with the Plebeians.*

PLEBEIANS
We will be satisfied! Let us be satisfied!    1
BRUTUS
Then follow me, and give me audience, friends.—
Cassius, go you into the other street
And part the numbers.    4
Those that will hear me speak, let 'em stay here;
Those that will follow Cassius, go with him;
And public reasons shall be renderèd
Of Caesar's death.
FIRST PLEBEIAN    I will hear Brutus speak.
SECOND PLEBEIAN
I will hear Cassius, and compare their reasons
When severally we hear them renderèd.    10
    *[Exit Cassius, with some of the Plebeians.]*
THIRD PLEBEIAN
The noble Brutus is ascended. Silence!
BRUTUS    Be patient till the last.
Romans, countrymen, and lovers, hear me for my    13
cause, and be silent that you may hear. Believe me for
mine honor, and have respect to mine honor, that you
may believe. Censure me in your wisdom, and awake    16
your senses, that you may the better judge. If there be    17
any in this assembly, any dear friend of Caesar's, to
him I say that Brutus' love to Caesar was no less than
his. If then that friend demand why Brutus rose
against Caesar, this is my answer: not that I loved Caesar less, but that I loved Rome more. Had you rather
Caesar were living and die all slaves, than that Caesar
were dead, to live all free men? As Caesar loved me, I
weep for him; as he was fortunate, I rejoice at it; as he
was valiant, I honor him; but, as he was ambitious, I
slew him. There is tears for his love; joy for his fortune;
honor for his valor; and death for his ambition.
Who is here so base that would be a bondman? If any,
speak, for him have I offended. Who is here so rude    30
that would not be a Roman? If any, speak, for him
have I offended. Who is here so vile that will not love
his country? If any, speak, for him have I offended. I
pause for a reply.
ALL    None, Brutus, none!
BRUTUS    Then none have I offended. I have done no
more to Caesar than you shall do to Brutus. The ques-    37
tion of his death is enrolled in the Capitol, his glory    38
not extenuated wherein he was worthy, nor his    39

---

**266 cumber** overwhelm; entangle, burden    **268 objects** sights
**270 quartered** cut to pieces    **271 custom . . . deeds** the familiarity
of cruel deeds    **272 ranging** roaming up and down in search of
prey    **273 Ate** goddess of discord and moral chaos    **274 confines**
regions.    **monarch's** i.e., authoritative    **275 Cry havoc** give the
signal for sack, pillage, and slaughter, taking no prisoners.    **let slip**
unleash    **281 letters** (Not necessarily plural. The Latin word for
letter, *litterae*, has a plural form.)    **285 Passion** Sorrow    **288 lies**
lodges.    **seven leagues** about twenty miles    **289 Post** Ride.
**chanced** happened.    **291 Rome** (With pun on "room," as at 1.2.156.)
**294 try** test    **296 issue** outcome, deed    **297 the which** the outcome
of which    **298 young Octavius** (He was eighteen in March of
44 B.C.)

**3.2. Location: The Forum.**
**1 be satisfied** have an explanation.    **4 part** divide    **10 severally** separately    **13 lovers** friends. (This speech by Brutus is in what Plutarch
calls the Lacedemonian or Spartan style, brief and sententious. Its
content is original with Shakespeare.)    **16 Censure** Judge    **17 senses**
intellectual powers    **30 rude** barbarous    **37 than . . . Brutus** (In lines
45–7 below, Brutus offers to die for Rome if his country should
ask.)    **37–8 The question . . . enrolled** The considerations that neces-
sitated his death are recorded    **39 extenuated** minimized

offenses enforced for which he suffered death.                                    40

   *Enter Mark Antony [and others] with Caesar's body.*

Here comes his body, mourned by Mark Antony, who, though he had no hand in his death, shall receive the benefit of his dying, a place in the commonwealth, as which of you shall not? With this I depart, that, as I slew my best lover for the good of Rome, I have the   45
same dagger for myself when it shall please my country to need my death.

ALL   Live, Brutus, live, live!          *[Brutus comes down.]*

FIRST PLEBEIAN
Bring him with triumph home unto his house.

SECOND PLEBEIAN
Give him a statue with his ancestors.                                   50

THIRD PLEBEIAN
Let him be Caesar.

FOURTH PLEBEIAN   Caesar's better parts
Shall be crowned in Brutus.

FIRST PLEBEIAN
We'll bring him to his house with shouts and clamors.

BRUTUS
My countrymen—

SECOND PLEBEIAN   Peace, silence! Brutus speaks.

FIRST PLEBEIAN   Peace, ho!

BRUTUS
Good countrymen, let me depart alone,
And, for my sake, stay here with Antony.
Do grace to Caesar's corpse, and grace his speech   58
Tending to Caesar's glories, which Mark Antony,   59
By our permission, is allowed to make.
I do entreat you, not a man depart,
Save I alone, till Antony have spoke.          *Exit.*

FIRST PLEBEIAN
Stay, ho, and let us hear Mark Antony.

THIRD PLEBEIAN
Let him go up into the public chair.
We'll hear him. Noble Antony, go up.

ANTONY
For Brutus' sake I am beholding to you.              66
   *[He goes into the pulpit.]*

FOURTH PLEBEIAN   What does he say of Brutus?

THIRD PLEBEIAN   He says, for Brutus' sake
He finds himself beholding to us all.

FOURTH PLEBEIAN
'Twere best he speak no harm of Brutus here.

FIRST PLEBEIAN
This Caesar was a tyrant.

THIRD PLEBEIAN          Nay, that's certain.
We are blest that Rome is rid of him.

SECOND PLEBEIAN
Peace! Let us hear what Antony can say.

ANTONY
You gentle Romans—

ALL                 Peace, ho! Let us hear him.

ANTONY
Friends, Romans, countrymen, lend me your ears.   75
I come to bury Caesar, not to praise him.
The evil that men do lives after them;
The good is oft interrèd with their bones.
So let it be with Caesar. The noble Brutus
Hath told you Caesar was ambitious.
If it were so, it was a grievous fault,
And grievously hath Caesar answered it.          82
Here, under leave of Brutus and the rest—        83
For Brutus is an honorable man,
So are they all, all honorable men—
Come I to speak in Caesar's funeral.
He was my friend, faithful and just to me;
But Brutus says he was ambitious,
And Brutus is an honorable man.
He hath brought many captives home to Rome,
Whose ransoms did the general coffers fill.
Did this in Caesar seem ambitious?
When that the poor have cried, Caesar hath wept;   93
Ambition should be made of sterner stuff.
Yet Brutus says he was ambitious,
And Brutus is an honorable man.
You all did see that on the Lupercal             97
I thrice presented him a kingly crown,
Which he did thrice refuse. Was this ambition?
Yet Brutus says he was ambitious,
And sure he is an honorable man.
I speak not to disprove what Brutus spoke,
But here I am to speak what I do know.
You all did love him once, not without cause.
What cause withholds you then to mourn for him?
O judgment! Thou art fled to brutish beasts,
And men have lost their reason. Bear with me;
My heart is in the coffin there with Caesar,
And I must pause till it come back to me.

FIRST PLEBEIAN
Methinks there is much reason in his sayings.

SECOND PLEBEIAN
If thou consider rightly of the matter,
Caesar has had great wrong.

THIRD PLEBEIAN          Has he, masters?   112
I fear there will a worse come in his place.

FOURTH PLEBEIAN
Marked ye his words? He would not take the crown,
Therefore 'tis certain he was not ambitious.

FIRST PLEBEIAN
If it be found so, some will dear abide it.       116

**40 enforced** exaggerated, insisted upon   **45 lover** friend   **50** SECOND PLEBEIAN (Not the same person who exited at line 10; the numbering here refers to those who stay to hear Brutus.)   **58 Do grace** Show respect.   **grace his speech** listen courteously to Antony's speech   **59 Tending to** relating to, dealing with   **66 beholding** beholden

**75 Friends** (This speech by Antony is thought to illustrate the Asiatic or "florid" style of speaking. In it Shakespeare gathers various hints from Plutarch ("Marcus Antonius" and "Dion") and Appian, but the speech is Shakespeare's invention.)   **82 answered** paid the penalty for   **83 under leave** by permission   **93 When that** When   **97 Lupercal** (See 1.1.67 and note.)   **112 masters** good sirs.   **116 dear abide it** pay a heavy penalty for it.

SECOND PLEBEIAN
    Poor soul, his eyes are red as fire with weeping.
THIRD PLEBEIAN
    There's not a nobler man in Rome than Antony.
FOURTH PLEBEIAN
    Now mark him. He begins again to speak.
ANTONY
    But yesterday the word of Caesar might
    Have stood against the world. Now lies he there,
    And none so poor to do him reverence.    122
    Oh, masters, if I were disposed to stir    123
    Your hearts and minds to mutiny and rage,    124
    I should do Brutus wrong, and Cassius wrong,
    Who, you all know, are honorable men.
    I will not do them wrong; I rather choose
    To wrong the dead, to wrong myself and you,
    Than I will wrong such honorable men.
    But here's a parchment with the seal of Caesar.
    I found it in his closet; 'tis his will.    131
                    [He shows the will.]
    Let but the commons hear this testament—    132
    Which, pardon me, I do not mean to read—
    And they would go and kiss dead Caesar's wounds
    And dip their napkins in his sacred blood,    135
    Yea, beg a hair of him for memory,
    And dying, mention it within their wills,
    Bequeathing it as a rich legacy
    Unto their issue.    139
FOURTH PLEBEIAN
    We'll hear the will! Read it, Mark Antony.
ALL
    The will, the will! We will hear Caesar's will.
ANTONY
    Have patience, gentle friends: I must not read it.
    It is not meet you know how Caesar loved you.    143
    You are not wood, you are not stones, but men;
    And being men, hearing the will of Caesar,
    It will inflame you, it will make you mad.
    'Tis good you know not that you are his heirs,
    For if you should, oh, what would come of it?
FOURTH PLEBEIAN
    Read the will! We'll hear it, Antony.
    You shall read us the will, Caesar's will.
ANTONY
    Will you be patient? Will you stay awhile?
    I have o'ershot myself to tell you of it.    152
    I fear I wrong the honorable men
    Whose daggers have stabbed Caesar; I do fear it.
FOURTH PLEBEIAN
    They were traitors. "Honorable men"!
ALL    The will! The testament!
SECOND PLEBEIAN
    They were villains, murderers. The will! Read the will!

ANTONY
    You will compel me then to read the will?
    Then make a ring about the corpse of Caesar
    And let me show you him that made the will.
    Shall I descend? And will you give me leave?
ALL    Come down.
SECOND PLEBEIAN    Descend.
THIRD PLEBEIAN    You shall have leave.
            [Antony comes down. They gather around Caesar.]
FOURTH PLEBEIAN    A ring; stand round.
FIRST PLEBEIAN
    Stand from the hearse. Stand from the body.    166
SECOND PLEBEIAN
    Room for Antony, most noble Antony!
ANTONY
    Nay, press not so upon me. Stand farre off.    168
ALL    Stand back! Room! Bear back!
ANTONY
    If you have tears, prepare to shed them now.
    You all do know this mantle. I remember    171
    The first time ever Caesar put it on;
    'Twas on a summer's evening in his tent,
    That day he overcame the Nervii.    174
    Look, in this place ran Cassius' dagger through.
    See what a rent the envious Casca made.    176
    Through this the well-belovèd Brutus stabbed,
    And as he plucked his cursèd steel away,
    Mark how the blood of Caesar followed it,
    As rushing out of doors to be resolved    180
    If Brutus so unkindly knocked or no;    181
    For Brutus, as you know, was Caesar's angel.    182
    Judge, O you gods, how dearly Caesar loved him!
    This was the most unkindest cut of all;    184
    For when the noble Caesar saw him stab,
    Ingratitude, more strong than traitors' arms,
    Quite vanquished him. Then burst his mighty heart,
    And in his mantle muffling up his face,
    Even at the base of Pompey's statue,
    Which all the while ran blood, great Caesar fell.
    Oh, what a fall was there, my countrymen!
    Then I, and you, and all of us fell down,
    Whilst bloody treason flourished over us.    193
    Oh, now you weep, and I perceive you feel
    The dint of pity. These are gracious drops.    195
    Kind souls, what, weep you when you but behold
    Our Caesar's vesture wounded? Look you here,    197
    Here is himself, marred as you see with traitors.
                    [He lifts Caesar's mantle.]
FIRST PLEBEIAN    Oh, piteous spectacle!
SECOND PLEBEIAN    O noble Caesar!

---

122 And none . . . reverence i.e., and yet no one is below him in fortune now, no one of even the lowest social station to look up to and
revere him.    123 masters good sirs    124 mutiny riot, tumult
131 closet private chamber, study    132 commons common people
135 napkins handkerchiefs    139 issue descendants, heirs.    143 meet
fitting that    152 o'ershot myself gone further than I should

166 hearse bier.    168 farre farther    171 mantle cloak, toga.    174 the
Nervii the Belgian tribe whose defeat in 57 B.C. is described in Caesar's
*Gallic Wars*, 2.15–28    176 rent tear, hole.    envious malicious, spiteful
180 As as if.    be resolved learn for certain    181 unkindly cruelly and
unnaturally    182 angel (1) daimon or genius, guardian angel (2) best
beloved.    184 most unkindest (1) most cruel (2) most unnatural. (The
double superlative was grammatically acceptable in Shakespeare's day.)
193 flourished (1) triumphed insolently (2) brandished its sword    195
dint impression    197 vesture clothing

**THIRD PLEBEIAN**  Oh, woeful day!

**FOURTH PLEBEIAN**  Oh, traitors, villains!

**FIRST PLEBEIAN**  Oh, most bloody sight!

**SECOND PLEBEIAN**  We will be revenged.

**ALL**  Revenge! About! Seek! Burn! Fire! Kill! Slay! Let     205
not a traitor live!

**ANTONY**  Stay, countrymen.

**FIRST PLEBEIAN**  Peace there! Hear the noble Antony.

**SECOND PLEBEIAN**  We'll hear him, we'll follow him,
we'll die with him!

**ANTONY**
Good friends, sweet friends, let me not stir you up
To such a sudden flood of mutiny.
They that have done this deed are honorable.
What private griefs they have, alas, I know not,     214
That made them do it. They are wise and honorable,
And will no doubt with reasons answer you.
I come not, friends, to steal away your hearts.
I am no orator, as Brutus is,
But, as you know me all, a plain blunt man
That love my friend, and that they know full well
That gave me public leave to speak of him.     221
For I have neither wit, nor words, nor worth,     222
Action, nor utterance, nor the power of speech     223
To stir men's blood. I only speak right on.
I tell you that which you yourselves do know,
Show you sweet Caesar's wounds, poor poor dumb
     mouths,
And bid them speak for me. But were I Brutus,
And Brutus Antony, there were an Antony
Would ruffle up your spirits and put a tongue     229
In every wound of Caesar that should move
The stones of Rome to rise and mutiny.

**ALL**
We'll mutiny!

**FIRST PLEBEIAN**  We'll burn the house of Brutus!

**THIRD PLEBEIAN**
Away, then! Come, seek the conspirators.

**ANTONY**
Yet hear me, countrymen. Yet hear me speak.

**ALL**
Peace, ho! Hear Antony, most noble Antony!

**ANTONY**
Why, friends, you go to do you know not what.
Wherein hath Caesar thus deserved your loves?
Alas, you know not. I must tell you then:
You have forgot the will I told you of.

**ALL**
Most true. The will! Let's stay and hear the will.

**ANTONY**
Here is the will, and under Caesar's seal.
To every Roman citizen he gives,
To every several man, seventy-five drachmas.     243

**SECOND PLEBEIAN**
Most noble Caesar! We'll revenge his death.

**THIRD PLEBEIAN**  O royal Caesar!

**ANTONY**  Hear me with patience.

**ALL**  Peace, ho!

**ANTONY**
Moreover, he hath left you all his walks,
His private arbors, and new-planted orchards,
On this side Tiber; he hath left them you,
And to your heirs forever—common pleasures,     251
To walk abroad and recreate yourselves.
Here was a Caesar! When comes such another?

**FIRST PLEBEIAN**
Never, never! Come, away, away!
We'll burn his body in the holy place
And with the brands fire the traitors' houses.
Take up the body.

**SECOND PLEBEIAN**  Go fetch fire!

**THIRD PLEBEIAN**  Pluck down benches!

**FOURTH PLEBEIAN**  Pluck down forms, windows, any-     259
thing!                     *Exeunt Plebeians [with the body].*

**ANTONY**
Now let it work. Mischief, thou art afoot.
Take thou what course thou wilt.

           *Enter [Octavius's] Servant.*

                              How now, fellow?

**SERVANT**
Sir, Octavius is already come to Rome.

**ANTONY**  Where is he?

**SERVANT**
He and Lepidus are at Caesar's house.

**ANTONY**
And thither will I straight to visit him.     266
He comes upon a wish. Fortune is merry,     267
And in this mood will give us anything.

**SERVANT**
I heard him say Brutus and Cassius
Are rid like madmen through the gates of Rome.     270

**ANTONY**
Belike they had some notice of the people,     271
How I had moved them. Bring me to Octavius.
                                   *Exeunt.*

                      ❧

## [3.3]

*Enter Cinna the poet, and after him the Ple-
beians.*

**CINNA**
I dreamt tonight that I did feast with Caesar,     1

---

**205 About!** To work!  **214 griefs** grievances  **221 public leave** permission to speak publicly  **222–3 neither . . . speech** neither intelligence, vocabulary, moral authority, gesture, rhetorical skill, nor
polished delivery  **229 ruffle up** stir to anger  **243 several** individual.  **drachmas** coins. (This is a substantial bequest.)

**251 common pleasures** public pleasure gardens (in which)
**259 forms, windows** benches, window frames and shutters
**266 straight** straightway, at once  **267 upon a wish** just when
wanted.  **merry** favorably disposed  **270 Are rid** have ridden
**271 Belike** Likely enough.  **of** about; or, from
**3.3. Location:** A street.
**1 tonight** last night

And things unluckily charge my fantasy.                                    2
I have no will to wander forth of doors,
Yet something leads me forth.

FIRST PLEBEIAN    What is your name?

SECOND PLEBEIAN    Whither are you going?

THIRD PLEBEIAN    Where do you dwell?

FOURTH PLEBEIAN    Are you a married man or a
bachelor?

SECOND PLEBEIAN    Answer every man directly.

FIRST PLEBEIAN    Ay, and briefly.

FOURTH PLEBEIAN    Ay, and wisely.

THIRD PLEBEIAN    Ay, and truly, you were best.          13

CINNA    What is my name? Whither am I going? Where
do I dwell? Am I a married man or a bachelor? Then
to answer every man directly and briefly, wisely and
truly: wisely I say, I am a bachelor.

SECOND PLEBEIAN    That's as much as to say they are
fools that marry. You'll bear me a bang for that, I fear.   19
Proceed directly.                                          20

CINNA    Directly, I am going to Caesar's funeral.         21

FIRST PLEBEIAN    As a friend or an enemy?

CINNA    As a friend.

SECOND PLEBEIAN    That matter is answered directly.

FOURTH PLEBEIAN    For your dwelling—briefly.

CINNA    Briefly, I dwell by the Capitol.

THIRD PLEBEIAN    Your name, sir, truly.

CINNA    Truly, my name is Cinna.

FIRST PLEBEIAN    Tear him to pieces! He's a conspirator!

CINNA    I am Cinna the poet, I am Cinna the poet!

FOURTH PLEBEIAN    Tear him for his bad verses, tear him
for his bad verses!

CINNA    I am not Cinna the conspirator.

FOURTH PLEBEIAN    It is no matter, his name's Cinna.
Pluck but his name out of his heart, and turn him         35
going.                                                    36

THIRD PLEBEIAN    Tear him, tear him! Come, brands, ho,
firebrands! To Brutus', to Cassius'; burn all! Some to
Decius' house, and some to Casca's; some to Ligarius'.
Away, go!

*Exeunt all the Plebeians, [dragging off Cinna].*

❖

# 4.1

*Enter Antony [with a list], Octavius, and Lepidus.*

ANTONY
These many, then, shall die. Their names are pricked.      1

OCTAVIUS
Your brother too must die. Consent you, Lepidus?

LEPIDUS
I do consent—

OCTAVIUS                    Prick him down, Antony.

LEPIDUS
Upon condition Publius shall not live,
Who is your sister's son, Mark Antony.

ANTONY
He shall not live. Look, with a spot I damn him.            6
But Lepidus, go you to Caesar's house.
Fetch the will hither, and we shall determine                8
How to cut off some charge in legacies.                      9

LEPIDUS    What, shall I find you here?

OCTAVIUS    Or here or at the Capitol.          *Exit Lepidus.*  11

ANTONY
This is a slight, unmeritable man,                           12
Meet to be sent on errands. Is it fit,
The threefold world divided, he should stand                14
One of the three to share it?

OCTAVIUS                    So you thought him,
And took his voice who should be pricked to die             16
In our black sentence and proscription.                     17

ANTONY
Octavius, I have seen more days than you;
And though we lay these honors on this man
To ease ourselves of divers sland'rous loads,               20
He shall but bear them as the ass bears gold,
To groan and sweat under the business,
Either led or driven as we point the way;
And having brought our treasure where we will,
Then take we down his load, and turn him off,
Like to the empty ass, to shake his ears                    26
And graze in commons.

OCTAVIUS                    You may do your will;           27
But he's a tried and valiant soldier.

ANTONY
So is my horse, Octavius, and for that
I do appoint him store of provender.                        30
It is a creature that I teach to fight,
To wind, to stop, to run directly on,                       32
His corporal motion governed by my spirit.                  33
And in some taste is Lepidus but so.                        34
He must be taught, and trained, and bid go forth—
A barren-spirited fellow, one that feeds
On objects, arts, and imitations,                           37
Which, out of use and staled by other men,                  38
Begin his fashion. Do not talk of him                       39
But as a property. And now, Octavius,                       40

---

2 **unluckily . . . fantasy** oppress my imagination with foreboding.
13 **you were best** you'd better.   19 **bear . . . bang** get a beating from
me   20 **directly** without evasion.   21 **Directly** (1) Straight there
(2) At once   35–6 **turn him going** send him packing.
**4.1. Location:** Rome. A table is perhaps set out.
1 **pricked** marked down on a list (with a stylus making an impression
on a wax tablet, or piercing a sheet of paper).

6 **spot** mark (on the list).   **damn** condemn   8–9 **determine . . . legacies** find a way to reduce the outlay of Caesar's estate, by altering the
will.   11 **Or** Either   12 **slight, unmeritable** insignificant and undeserving   14 **threefold world** The Roman world was governed after the
assassination of Julius Caesar (44 B.C.) by the so-called Second Triumvirate, consisting of Mark Antony, Octavius Caesar, and Lepidus. After
40 B.C., Antony's power lay mainly in the Middle East, Lepidus's in
Africa, and Octavius's in Spain, Gaul, and northern Italy.   16 **took his
voice** acceded to his opinion (i.e., about Publius)   17 **black sentence**
death sentence.   **proscription** (Proscription branded a man as an outlaw,
confiscated his property, offered a reward for his murder, and prohibited
his sons and grandsons from holding public office.)   20 **sland'rous** burdensome   26 **empty** unloaded   27 **commons** public pasture.
30 **appoint** assign, provide.   **provender** fodder.   32 **wind** turn.
(Horse trainer's term.)   **directly on** straight ahead   33 **corporal** bodily
34 **taste** degree, sense   37 **On . . . imitations** on curiosities, artificial
things, and the following of fashion—copied things merely, taken up
secondhand   38 **staled** made common or cheap   39 **Begin his fashion**
are for him the ultimate in fashion.   40 **property** tool.

Listen great things. Brutus and Cassius               41
Are levying powers. We must straight make head.       42
Therefore let our alliance be combined,               43
Our best friends made, our means stretched;           44
And let us presently go sit in council
How covert matters may be best disclosed              46
And open perils surest answerèd.                      47

OCTAVIUS
Let us do so, for we are at the stake                 48
And bayed about with many enemies;                    49
And some that smile have in their hearts, I fear,
Millions of mischiefs.                    *Exeunt.*    51

❖

# [4.2]

*Drum. Enter Brutus, Lucilius, [Lucius,] and the*
*army. Titinius and Pindarus meet them.*

BRUTUS   Stand, ho!                                    1
LUCILIUS   Give the word, ho, and stand!               2
BRUTUS
What now, Lucilius, is Cassius near?
LUCILIUS
He is at hand, and Pindarus is come
To do you salutation from his master.
BRUTUS
He greets me well. Your master, Pindarus,             6
In his own change, or by ill officers,                7
Hath given me some worthy cause to wish               8
Things done, undone; but if he be at hand
I shall be satisfied.
PINDARUS            I do not doubt                     10
But that my noble master will appear
Such as he is, full of regard and honor.              12
BRUTUS
He is not doubted.—A word, Lucilius.
        *[Brutus and Lucilius speak apart.]*
How he received you let me be resolved.               14
LUCILIUS
With courtesy and with respect enough,
But not with such familiar instances                  16
Nor with such free and friendly conference            17
As he hath used of old.
BRUTUS                 Thou hast described

A hot friend cooling. Ever note, Lucilius:
When love begins to sicken and decay
It useth an enforcèd ceremony.                         21
There are no tricks in plain and simple faith.
But hollow men, like horses hot at hand,              23
Make gallant show and promise of their mettle;        24
                              *Low march within.*
But when they should endure the bloody spur,          25
They fall their crests and like deceitful jades       26
Sink in the trial. Comes his army on?                 27
LUCILIUS
They mean this night in Sardis to be quartered.       28
The greater part, the horse in general,               29
Are come with Cassius.

        *Enter Cassius and his powers.*

BRUTUS                    Hark, he is arrived.
March gently on to meet him.                           31
CASSIUS   Stand, ho!
BRUTUS   Stand, ho! Speak the word along.
FIRST SOLDIER   Stand!
SECOND SOLDIER   Stand!
THIRD SOLDIER   Stand!
CASSIUS
Most noble brother, you have done me wrong.
BRUTUS
Judge me, you gods! Wrong I mine enemies?
And if not so, how should I wrong a brother?
CASSIUS
Brutus, this sober form of yours hides wrongs;        40
And when you do them—
BRUTUS                 Cassius, be content;            41
Speak your griefs softly. I do know you well.         42
Before the eyes of both our armies here,
Which should perceive nothing but love from us,
Let us not wrangle. Bid them move away.
Then in my tent, Cassius, enlarge your griefs,        46
And I will give you audience.
CASSIUS                      Pindarus,                 47
Bid our commanders lead their charges off             48
A little from this ground.
BRUTUS
Lucius, do you the like, and let no man
Come to our tent till we have done our conference.
Let Lucilius and Titinius guard our door.             52
            *Exeunt. Manent Brutus and Cassius.*
        *[Lucilius and Titinius stand guard at the door.]*

❖

41 **Listen** hear   42 **powers** armies.   **straight make head** immediately raise an army.   43 **let . . . combined** let us work as one   44 **made** mustered, made certain.   **stretched** used to fullest advantage, extended to the utmost   46 **How . . . disclosed** (to determine) how hidden dangers may best be discovered   47 **surest answerèd** most safely dealt with.   48 **at the stake** i.e., like a bear in the sport of bearbaiting   49 **bayed about** surrounded as by baying dogs   51 **mischiefs** harms, evils.
**4.2. Location:** Camp near Sardis, in Asia Minor. Before Brutus's tent.   1–2 **Stand . . . stand!** Halt! Pass the word!   6 **He . . . well** His greetings are welcome.   **Your master** Cassius   7 **In . . . officers** whether from an alteration in his feelings toward me or through the acts of unworthy subordinates   8 **worthy** justifiable   10 **shall be satisfied** will insist on having things explained.   12 **full . . . honor** deserving all respect and honor.   14 **resolved** informed, put out of doubt.   16 **familiar instances** proofs of intimate friendship   17 **conference** conversation

21 **enforcèd** constrained   23 **hollow** insincere.   **hot at hand** restless and full of spirit when held in, at the start   24 **mettle** spirit   25 **But . . . spur** but when the spur digs into their flanks   26 **fall their crests** lower their necks (literally, the ridge or mane of the neck), hang their heads.   **jades** worthless horses   27 **Sink** give way, fail   28 **Sardis** (The capital city of Lydia in Asia Minor.)   **quartered** lodged, stationed.   29 **the horse in general** all the cavalry   31 **gently** mildly, not hostilely   40 **sober form** dignified manner, appearance   41 **be content** keep calm   42 **griefs** grievances.   **I . . . well** i.e., We've known one another long and can proceed calmly.   46 **enlarge** speak freely   47 **give you audience** hear what you have to say.   48 **charges** troops   52 **Lucilius** (The Folio reads *Lucius* here and *Lucillius* in line 50, but, when Shakespeare interpolated a passage in the next scene at lines 124–66, he evidently intended to have Lucilius guarding the door.)

# [4.3]

**CASSIUS**
That you have wronged me doth appear in this:
You have condemned and noted Lucius Pella  2
For taking bribes here of the Sardians,
Wherein my letters, praying on his side,  4
Because I knew the man, was slighted off.  5
**BRUTUS**
You wronged yourself to write in such a case.
**CASSIUS**
In such a time as this it is not meet  7
That every nice offense should bear his comment.  8
**BRUTUS**
Let me tell you, Cassius, you yourself
Are much condemned to have an itching palm,  10
To sell and mart your offices for gold  11
To undeservers.
**CASSIUS**    I an itching palm?
You know that you are Brutus that speaks this,
Or, by the gods, this speech were else your last.  14
**BRUTUS**
The name of Cassius honors this corruption,  15
And chastisement doth therefore hide his head.  16
**CASSIUS**    Chastisement?
**BRUTUS**
Remember March, the ides of March remember.
Did not great Julius bleed for justice' sake?
What villain touched his body that did stab  20
And not for justice? What, shall one of us,  21
That struck the foremost man of all this world
But for supporting robbers, shall we now  23
Contaminate our fingers with base bribes,
And sell the mighty space of our large honors  25
For so much trash as may be graspèd thus?  26
I had rather be a dog and bay the moon  27
Than such a Roman.
**CASSIUS**    Brutus, bait not me.  28
I'll not endure it. You forget yourself
To hedge me in. I am a soldier, I,  30
Older in practice, abler than yourself
To make conditions.  32
**BRUTUS**    Go to! You are not, Cassius.

**CASSIUS**    I am.
**BRUTUS**    I say you are not.
**CASSIUS**
Urge me no more; I shall forget myself.  36
Have mind upon your health. Tempt me no farther.  37
**BRUTUS**    Away, slight man!  38
**CASSIUS**
Is't possible?
**BRUTUS**    Hear me, for I will speak.
Must I give way and room to your rash choler?  40
Shall I be frighted when a madman stares?  41
**CASSIUS**
O ye gods, ye gods! Must I endure all this?
**BRUTUS**
All this? Ay, more. Fret till your proud heart break.
Go show your slaves how choleric you are,
And make your bondmen tremble. Must I budge?  45
Must I observe you? Must I stand and crouch  46
Under your testy humor? By the gods,  47
You shall digest the venom of your spleen  48
Though it do split you; for, from this day forth,
I'll use you for my mirth, yea, for my laughter,
When you are waspish.
**CASSIUS**    Is it come to this?  51
**BRUTUS**
You say you are a better soldier.
Let it appear so; make your vaunting true,  53
And it shall please me well. For mine own part,
I shall be glad to learn of noble men.  55
**CASSIUS**
You wrong me every way! You wrong me, Brutus.
I said an elder soldier, not a better.
Did I say "better"?
**BRUTUS**    If you did, I care not.
**CASSIUS**
When Caesar lived he durst not thus have moved me.  59
**BRUTUS**
Peace, peace! You durst not so have tempted him.  60
**CASSIUS**    I durst not?
**BRUTUS**    No.
**CASSIUS**
What, durst not tempt him?
**BRUTUS**    For your life you durst not.
**CASSIUS**
Do not presume too much upon my love.
I may do that I shall be sorry for.
**BRUTUS**
You have done that you should be sorry for.
There is no terror, Cassius, in your threats,
For I am armed so strong in honesty
That they pass by me as the idle wind,

**4.3. Location:** The scene is continuous. Brutus and Cassius remain on stage, which now represents the interior of Brutus's tent. **2 noted** publicly disgraced. **Lucius Pella** a Roman praetor in Sardis **4 letters** i.e., letter. (See 3.1.281n.) **praying** entreating **5 slighted off** slightingly dismissed. **7 meet** fitting **8 nice** trivial. **bear his comment** be taken note of. (*His* means "its.") **10 condemned to have** accused of having **11 mart** traffic in **14 else** otherwise **15 honors** lends the appearance of honor to, countenances **16 And . . . head** and for that reason those who might rebuke such corruption are reluctant to speak out. **20–1 What . . . justice?** Which of us was villain enough to stab for any cause other than justice? **23 But** only. **robbers** (According to Plutarch, Caesar "was a favorer and suborner of all of them that did rob and spoil by his countenance and authority.") **25 the mighty . . . honors** the greatness of our honorable reputations and the high offices we have power to confer **26 trash** i.e., money (despised in Brutus's stoic philosophy) **27 bay** howl at **28 bait** provoke **30 hedge me in** crowd me, limit my authority. **32 make conditions** i.e., manage affairs, make decisions about Lucius Pella and other officers.

**36 Urge** Provoke **37 Tempt** Provoke **38 slight** insignificant **40 way and room** free course and scope. **choler** wrathful temperament. **41 stares** looks wildly at me. **45 bondmen** (Probably not distinguished from "slaves" in line 44.) **budge** flinch. **46 observe** defer to. **crouch** cringe **47 humor** temperament. **48 digest** swallow. **spleen** i.e., irascibility **51 waspish** hotheaded. **53 vaunting** boasting **55 I shall . . . men** (Said sarcastically: "Wouldn't it be a nice surprise to learn that some men can be noble after all?", or, "I am glad to be corrected by such a noble person as yourself.") **59 moved** angered **60 tempted** provoked

Which I respect not. I did send to you
For certain sums of gold, which you denied me;
For I can raise no money by vile means.                                72
By heaven, I had rather coin my heart                                  73
And drop my blood for drachmas than to wring                           74
From the hard hands of peasants their vile trash                       75
By any indirection. I did send                                         76
To you for gold to pay my legions,
Which you denied me. Was that done like Cassius?
Should I have answered Caius Cassius so?
When Marcus Brutus grows so covetous
To lock such rascal counters from his friends,                         81
Be ready, gods, with all your thunderbolts,
Dash him to pieces!
CASSIUS                    I denied you not.
BRUTUS
    You did.
CASSIUS    I did not. He was but a fool
    That brought my answer back. Brutus hath rived my
        heart.                                                         85
    A friend should bear his friend's infirmities,
    But Brutus makes mine greater than they are.
BRUTUS
    I do not, till you practice them on me.
CASSIUS
    You love me not.
BRUTUS              I do not like your faults.
CASSIUS
    A friendly eye could never see such faults.
BRUTUS
    A flatterer's would not, though they do appear
    As huge as high Olympus.
CASSIUS
    Come, Antony, and young Octavius, come,
    Revenge yourselves alone on Cassius;
    For Cassius is aweary of the world,
    Hated by one he loves, braved by his brother,                      96
    Checked like a bondman, all his faults observed,                   97
    Set in a notebook, learned and conned by rote                      98
    To cast into my teeth. Oh, I could weep
    My spirit from mine eyes! There is my dagger,
            [offering his unsheathed dagger]
    And here my naked breast; within, a heart
    Dearer than Pluto's mine, richer than gold.                        102
    If that thou be'st a Roman, take it forth.
    I, that denied thee gold, will give my heart.
    Strike, as thou didst at Caesar; for I know,
    When thou didst hate him worst, thou loved'st him
        better
    Than ever thou loved'st Cassius.
BRUTUS                        Sheathe your dagger.
    Be angry when you will, it shall have scope;

Do what you will, dishonor shall be humor.                             109
Oh, Cassius, you are yokèd with a lamb                                 110
That carries anger as the flint bears fire,
Who, much enforcèd, shows a hasty spark                                112
And straight is cold again.
CASSIUS                Hath Cassius lived                              113
To be but mirth and laughter to his Brutus
When grief and blood ill-tempered vexeth him?                          115
BRUTUS
When I spoke that, I was ill-tempered too.
CASSIUS
Do you confess so much? Give me your hand.
BRUTUS
And my heart too.            [They embrace.]
CASSIUS            Oh, Brutus!
BRUTUS                    What's the matter?
CASSIUS
Have not you love enough to bear with me,
When that rash humor which my mother gave me           120
Makes me forgetful?
BRUTUS          Yes, Cassius, and from henceforth,
When you are overearnest with your Brutus,
He'll think your mother chides, and leave you so.      123

    Enter a Poet [followed by Lucilius and Titinius,
    who have been standing guard at the door].

POET
Let me go in to see the generals!
There is some grudge between 'em; 'tis not meet
They be alone.
LUCILIUS            You shall not come to them.
POET    Nothing but death shall stay me.
CASSIUS    How now? What's the matter?
POET
For shame, you generals! What do you mean?
Love and be friends, as two such men should be;
For I have seen more years, I'm sure, than ye.
CASSIUS
Ha, ha, how vilely doth this cynic rhyme!               132
BRUTUS
Get you hence, sirrah. Saucy fellow, hence!             133
CASSIUS
Bear with him, Brutus. 'Tis his fashion.
BRUTUS
I'll know his humor when he knows his time.             135
What should the wars do with these jigging fools?      136
Companion, hence!
CASSIUS          Away, away, begone!    Exit Poet. 137
BRUTUS
Lucilius and Titinius, bid the commanders

72 I . . . means i.e., I refuse to raise money by unethical or illegal means.
73 coin my heart turn my very heart into coinage  74 drachmas silver
coins  75 their vile trash the pitifully small amounts of money they earn
76 indirection devious or unjust means.  81 lock . . . counters withhold
such paltry sums. (Counters were uncurrent coins or disks used by shop-
keepers as tokens in making reckonings.)  85 rived cleft, split  96 braved
defied.  brother i.e., follow general  97 Checked rebuked.  bondman
slave  98 conned by rote memorized  102 Dearer . . . mine richer than
the opulent wealth of the underworld, presided over by Pluto (here conflated with Plutus, god of riches)

109 dishonor . . . humor i.e., I'll regard your dishonorable conduct
and self-righteous anger as the effects of temperament, something to
be humored.  110 yokèd with allied with  112 enforcèd provoked,
struck upon  113 straight at once  115 blood ill-tempered disposition imbalanced by the humors of the body  120 that rash humor
i.e., choler, anger  123 leave you so let it go at that.  132 cynic i.e.,
rude fellow; also one claiming to be a Cynic philosopher, hence outspoken  133 sirrah (A term of address for a boy or a man of inferior
social status.)  135 I'll . . . time I'll indulge his eccentric behavior
when he knows the proper time for it.  136 jigging rhyming in jerky
doggerel  137 Companion Fellow

Prepare to lodge their companies tonight.

CASSIUS
And come yourselves, and bring Messala with you
Immediately to us.      [*Exeunt Lucilius and Titinius.*]

BRUTUS [*to Lucius within*]     Lucius, a bowl of wine.

CASSIUS
I did not think you could have been so angry.

BRUTUS
Oh, Cassius, I am sick of many griefs.

CASSIUS
Of your philosophy you make no use
If you give place to accidental evils.       145

BRUTUS
No man bears sorrow better. Portia is dead.

CASSIUS    Ha? Portia?

BRUTUS    She is dead.

CASSIUS
How scaped I killing when I crossed you so?    149
Oh, insupportable and touching loss!
Upon what sickness?

BRUTUS            Impatient of my absence,
And grief that young Octavius with Mark Antony
Have made themselves so strong—for with her death 153
That tidings came—with this she fell distract
And, her attendants absent, swallowed fire.     155

CASSIUS
And died so?

BRUTUS      Even so.

CASSIUS          O ye immortal gods!

*Enter Boy [Lucius] with wine and tapers.*

BRUTUS
Speak no more of her.—Give me a bowl of wine.—
In this I bury all unkindness, Cassius.        *Drinks.*

CASSIUS
My heart is thirsty for that noble pledge.
Fill, Lucius, till the wine o'erswell the cup;
I cannot drink too much of Brutus' love.      161
             [*He drinks. Exit Lucius.*]

*Enter Titinius and Messala.*

BRUTUS
Come in, Titinius. Welcome, good Messala.
Now sit we close about this taper here
And call in question our necessities.     [*They sit.*] 164

CASSIUS
Portia, art thou gone?

BRUTUS         No more, I pray you.
Messala, I have here receivèd letters        166

That young Octavius and Mark Antony
Come down upon us with a mighty power,    168
Bending their expedition toward Philippi.    169
             [*He shows a letter.*]

MESSALA
Myself have letters of the selfsame tenor.

BRUTUS    With what addition?

MESSALA
That by proscription and bills of outlawry    172
Octavius, Antony, and Lepidus
Have put to death an hundred senators.

BRUTUS
Therein our letters do not well agree;
Mine speak of seventy senators that died
By their proscriptions, Cicero being one.

CASSIUS
Cicero one?

MESSALA      Cicero is dead,
And by that order of proscription.
Had you your letters from your wife, my lord?    180

BRUTUS    No, Messala.

MESSALA
Nor nothing in your letters writ of her?       182

BRUTUS
Nothing, Messala.

MESSALA         That, methinks, is strange.

BRUTUS
Why ask you? Hear you aught of her in yours?

MESSALA    No, my lord.

BRUTUS
Now, as you are a Roman, tell me true.

MESSALA
Then like a Roman bear the truth I tell,
For certain she is dead, and by strange manner.

BRUTUS
Why, farewell, Portia. We must die, Messala.
With meditating that she must die once,      190
I have the patience to endure it now.

MESSALA
Even so great men great losses should endure.   192

CASSIUS
I have as much of this in art as you,        193
But yet my nature could not bear it so.      194

BRUTUS
Well, to our work alive. What do you think    195
Of marching to Philippi presently?

---

**145 place** way. **accidental evils** misfortunes caused by chance (which should be a matter of indifference to a Stoic philosopher like Brutus). **149 scaped I killing** did I escape being killed **153 her death** i.e., news of her death **155 swallowed fire** (According to Plutarch, as translated by Thomas North, Portia "took hot burning coals and cast them in her mouth, and kept her mouth so close that she choked herself.") **161.2 *Titinius*** (Lucilius does not return with Titinius, as he was ordered to do at lines 140–1, probably because he was not in Shakespeare's original version of this scene.) **164 call in question** consider, discuss **166 letters** (Probably a single letter. See 3.1.281n and 4.3.4n.)

**168 power** army   **169 Bending** directing.   **expedition** rapid march; warlike enterprise   **172 proscription** (See the note at 4.1.17.) **180–94 Had . . . so** (This passage is sometimes regarded as contradictory to lines 142–65 and redundant. Perhaps it is the original account of Portia's death, and lines 142–65 are part of a later interpolation, but it is also possible that both are intended, the first being Brutus's intimate revelation of the news to his friend and the second being Brutus's recovery of his stoic reserve now on display for Messala and Titinius.)   **182 nothing . . . her** nothing written about her in the letter or letters you've received.   **190 once** at some time   **192 Even so** In just such a way   **193 art** i.e., the acquired theoretical wisdom of stoical fortitude (as contrasted with the gifts of *nature* in line 194)   **195 alive** concerning us who are alive and dealing with present and future realities.

CASSIUS
I do not think it good.
BRUTUS                    Your reason?
CASSIUS                              This it is:
'Tis better that the enemy seek us.
So shall he waste his means, weary his soldiers,
Doing himself offense, whilst we, lying still,            200
Are full of rest, defense, and nimbleness.
BRUTUS
Good reasons must of force give place to better.          202
The people twixt Philippi and this ground
Do stand but in a forced affection,
For they have grudged us contribution.
The enemy, marching along by them,
By them shall make a fuller number up,
Come on refreshed, new-added, and encouraged;
From which advantage shall we cut him off
If at Philippi we do face him there,
These people at our back.
CASSIUS                     Hear me, good brother—         211
BRUTUS
Under your pardon. You must note beside                   212
That we have tried the utmost of our friends;
Our legions are brim full, our cause is ripe.
The enemy increaseth every day;
We, at the height, are ready to decline.
There is a tide in the affairs of men
Which, taken at the flood, leads on to fortune;
Omitted, all the voyage of their life
Is bound in shallows and in miseries.                     220
On such a full sea are we now afloat,
And we must take the current when it serves
Or lose our ventures.
CASSIUS               Then, with your will, go on.         223
We'll along ourselves and meet them at Philippi.
BRUTUS
The deep of night is crept upon our talk,
And nature must obey necessity,
Which we will niggard with a little rest.                 227
There is no more to say.
CASSIUS                  No more. Good night.
Early tomorrow will we rise and hence.                    229
BRUTUS
Lucius!

   *Enter Lucius.*

      My gown.                    [*Exit Lucius.*]
               Farewell, good Messala.                    230
Good night, Titinius. Noble, noble Cassius,
Good night and good repose.
CASSIUS                    Oh, my dear brother!

This was an ill beginning of the night.
Never come such division 'tween our souls!
Let it not, Brutus.

   *Enter Lucius with the gown.*

BRUTUS   Everything is well.
CASSIUS   Good night, my lord.
BRUTUS   Good night, good brother.
TITINIUS, MESSALA   Good night, Lord Brutus.
BRUTUS   Farewell, everyone.
               *Exeunt [all but Brutus and Lucius].*
Give me the gown. Where is thy instrument?               241
LUCIUS
Here in the tent.
BRUTUS               What, thou speak'st drowsily!
Poor knave, I blame thee not; thou art o'erwatched.      243
Call Claudius and some other of my men;
I'll have them sleep on cushions in my tent.
LUCIUS [*calling*]   Varro and Claudius!

   *Enter Varro and Claudius.*

VARRO   Calls my lord?
BRUTUS
I pray you, sirs, lie in my tent and sleep.
It may be I shall raise you by and by                    249
On business to my brother Cassius.
VARRO
So please you, we will stand and watch your pleasure.    251
BRUTUS
I will not have it so. Lie down, good sirs.
It may be I shall otherwise bethink me.                  253
               [*Varro and Claudius lie down.*]
Look, Lucius, here's the book I sought for so;
I put it in the pocket of my gown.
LUCIUS
I was sure Your Lordship did not give it me.
BRUTUS
Bear with me, good boy, I am much forgetful.
Canst thou hold up thy heavy eyes awhile
And touch thy instrument a strain or two?                259
LUCIUS
Ay, my lord, an't please you.
BRUTUS                        It does, my boy.            260
I trouble thee too much, but thou art willing.
LUCIUS   It is my duty, sir.
BRUTUS
I should not urge thy duty past thy might;
I know young bloods look for a time of rest.             264
LUCIUS   I have slept, my lord, already.
BRUTUS
It was well done, and thou shalt sleep again;
I will not hold thee long. If I do live,

---

**200 offense** harm   **202 of force** necessarily   **211 These ... back** i.e., with the people our enemy would otherwise recruit being instead in territory we control.   **212 Under your pardon** i.e., Excuse me, let me continue.   **220 bound in** confined to   **223 ventures** investments (of enterprise at sea).   **with your will** as you wish   **227 niggard** stint (by sleeping only briefly)   **229 hence** depart.   **230 gown** housecoat, dressing gown

**241 instrument** i.e., perhaps a lute or cittern.   **243 knave** boy. **o'erwatched** tired from lack of sleep.   **249 raise** rouse   **251 watch your pleasure** wakefully await your commands.   **253 otherwise bethink me** think of something else.   **259 touch** i.e., play on.   **strain** tune, musical phrase   **260 an't** if it   **264 young bloods** youthful constitutions

I will be good to thee.
                    *Music, and a song. [Lucius falls asleep.]*
This is a sleepy tune. O murd'rous slumber,                269
Layest thou thy leaden mace upon my boy,                   270
That plays thee music? Gentle knave, good night;
I will not do thee so much wrong to wake thee.
If thou dost nod, thou break'st thy instrument;
I'll take it from thee. And, good boy, good night.
                    *[He removes Lucius's instrument,*
                    *and begins to read.]*
Let me see, let me see; is not the leaf turned down
Where I left reading? Here it is, I think.

      *Enter the Ghost of Caesar.*

How ill this taper burns! Ha! Who comes here?             277
I think it is the weakness of mine eyes
That shapes this monstrous apparition.
It comes upon me.—Art thou any thing?                     280
Art thou some god, some angel, or some devil,
That mak'st my blood cold and my hair to stare?           282
Speak to me what thou art.

GHOST
Thy evil spirit, Brutus.

BRUTUS                    Why com'st thou?

GHOST
To tell thee thou shalt see me at Philippi.

BRUTUS    Well; then I shall see thee again?

GHOST    Ay, at Philippi.

BRUTUS
Why, I will see thee at Philippi, then.    *[Exit Ghost.]*
Now I have taken heart, thou vanishest.
Ill spirit, I would hold more talk with thee.—
Boy, Lucius! Varro! Claudius! Sirs, awake!
Claudius!

LUCIUS        The strings, my lord, are false.            292

BRUTUS
He thinks he still is at his instrument.—
Lucius, awake!

LUCIUS    My lord?

BRUTUS
Didst thou dream, Lucius, that thou so cried'st out?

LUCIUS
My lord, I do not know that I did cry.

BRUTUS
Yes, that thou didst. Didst thou see anything?

LUCIUS    Nothing, my lord.

BRUTUS
Sleep again, Lucius. Sirrah Claudius!
*[To Varro]* Fellow thou, awake!

VARRO                    My lord?

CLAUDIUS                        My lord?
                    *[They get up.]*

BRUTUS
Why did you so cry out, sirs, in your sleep?

VARRO, CLAUDIUS
Did we, my lord?

BRUTUS                Ay. Saw you anything?

VARRO
No, my lord, I saw nothing.

CLAUDIUS                        Nor I, my lord.

BRUTUS
Go and commend me to my brother Cassius.                 305
Bid him set on his powers betimes before,                306
And we will follow.

VARRO, CLAUDIUS        It shall be done, my lord.
                    *Exeunt.*

❖

## 5.1

    *Enter Octavius, Antony, and their army.*

OCTAVIUS
Now, Antony, our hopes are answerèd.
You said the enemy would not come down,
But keep the hills and upper regions.                     3
It proves not so. Their battles are at hand;              4
They mean to warn us at Philippi here,                    5
Answering before we do demand of them.

ANTONY
Tut, I am in their bosoms, and I know                     7
Wherefore they do it. They could be content
To visit other places, and come down                      9
With fearful bravery, thinking by this face               10
To fasten in our thoughts that they have courage;
But 'tis not so.

    *Enter a Messenger.*

MESSENGER        Prepare you, generals.                   12
The enemy comes on in gallant show.
Their bloody sign of battle is hung out,                  14
And something to be done immediately.                     15

ANTONY
Octavius, lead your battle softly on                      16
Upon the left hand of the even field.

OCTAVIUS
Upon the right hand, I. Keep thou the left.

ANTONY
Why do you cross me in this exigent?                      19

269 **murd'rous** producing the likeness of death    270 **leaden mace**
heavy staff of office (used by a sheriff to touch the shoulder of one
being placed under arrest)    277 **How . . . burns!** (Ghostly apparitions
were thought to be accompanied by such effects as lights burning low
and blue.)    280 **upon** toward    282 **stare** stand on end.    292 **false** out
of tune.

305 **commend me** deliver my greetings    306 **set . . . before** march
away with his troops early in the morning, before me
**5.1. Location:** The plains of Philippi, in Macedonia.
3 **keep** remain in    4 **battles** armies    5 **warn** challenge    7 **bosoms**
secret councils    9 **visit other places** i.e., be elsewhere    10 **fearful
bravery** (1) awesome ostentation (2) a show of bravery to conceal
their fear.    **face** pretense (of courage)    12 **'tis not so** (1) their plan
cannot deceive us (2) they have no courage.    14 **bloody sign** red flag
or crimson coat of arms as battle signal    15 **to be** is to be    16 **softly**
warily, with restraint    19 **cross** contradict.    **exigent** critical
moment.

**OCTAVIUS**
I do not cross you, but I will do so.        *March.*    20

*Drum. Enter Brutus, Cassius, and their army;*
*[Lucilius, Titinius, Messala, and others].*

**BRUTUS**    They stand and would have parley.    21
**CASSIUS**
Stand fast, Titinius. We must out and talk.    22
**OCTAVIUS**
Mark Antony, shall we give sign of battle?
**ANTONY**
No, Caesar, we will answer on their charge.    24
Make forth. The generals would have some words.    25
**OCTAVIUS** [*to his officers*]    Stir not until the signal.
[*The two sides advance toward one another.*]
**BRUTUS**
Words before blows. Is it so, countrymen?
**OCTAVIUS**
Not that we love words better, as you do.
**BRUTUS**
Good words are better than bad strokes, Octavius.
**ANTONY**
In your bad strokes, Brutus, you give good words.    30
Witness the hole you made in Caesar's heart,
Crying "Long live! Hail, Caesar!"
**CASSIUS**                                Antony,
The posture of your blows are yet unknown;    33
But for your words, they rob the Hybla bees,    34
And leave them honeyless.
**ANTONY**    Not stingless too?
**BRUTUS**    Oh, yes, and soundless too.
For you have stol'n their buzzing, Antony,
And very wisely threat before you sting.    39
**ANTONY**
Villains! You did not so when your vile daggers    40
Hacked one another in the sides of Caesar.
You showed your teeth like apes, and fawned like
  hounds,    42
And bowed like bondmen, kissing Caesar's feet,
Whilst damnèd Casca, like a cur, behind,
Struck Caesar on the neck. Oh, you flatterers!
**CASSIUS**
Flatterers? Now, Brutus, thank yourself!
This tongue had not offended so today
If Cassius might have ruled.    48
**OCTAVIUS**
Come, come, the cause. If arguing make us sweat,    49
The proof of it will turn to redder drops.    50
Look,                                    [*He draws.*]

I draw a sword against conspirators.
When think you that the sword goes up again?    53
Never, till Caesar's three-and-thirty wounds    54
Be well avenged, or till another Caesar    55
Have added slaughter to the sword of traitors.    56
**BRUTUS**
Caesar, thou canst not die by traitors' hands,    57
Unless thou bring'st them with thee.
**OCTAVIUS**                            So I hope.    58
I was not born to die on Brutus' sword.    59
**BRUTUS**
Oh, if thou wert the noblest of thy strain,    60
Young man, thou couldst not die more honorable.    61
**CASSIUS**
A peevish schoolboy, worthless of such honor,    62
Joined with a masker and a reveler!    63
**ANTONY**
Old Cassius still.
**OCTAVIUS**            Come, Antony, away!—    64
Defiance, traitors, hurl we in your teeth.
If you dare fight today, come to the field;
If not, when you have stomachs.    67
                *Exeunt Octavius, Antony, and army.*
**CASSIUS**
Why, now, blow wind, swell billow, and swim bark!    68
The storm is up, and all is on the hazard.    69
**BRUTUS**
Ho, Lucilius! Hark, a word with you.
**LUCILIUS** (*stands forth*)    My lord?
                [*Brutus and Lucilius converse apart.*]
**CASSIUS**    Messala!
**MESSALA** (*stands forth*)    What says my general?
**CASSIUS**    Messala,
This is my birthday, as this very day    75
Was Cassius born. Give me thy hand, Messala.
Be thou my witness that against my will,
As Pompey was, am I compelled to set    78
Upon one battle all our liberties.
You know that I held Epicurus strong    80
And his opinion. Now I change my mind
And partly credit things that do presage.    82
Coming from Sardis, on our former ensign    83

---

**20 cross you** contradict you perversely.    **do so** do as I said.    **21 parley** conference between the opposing sides.    **22 out** go out to meet them    **24 answer on their charge** respond when they attack.    **25 Make forth** March forward.    **30 In . . . words** i.e., As you deliver cruel blows, Brutus, you use deceiving flattery.    **33 The posture . . . unknown** i.e., your might as a warrior is as yet untested    **34 for** as for.    **Hybla** a mountain and a town in ancient Sicily, famous for honey    **39 very wisely** (Said ironically; Brutus suggests that Antony is all bluster and no action.)    **threat** threaten    **40 so** i.e., give warning    **42 showed your teeth** i.e., in smiles    **48 ruled** prevailed (in urging that Antony be killed).    **49 the cause** to our business.    **50 proof** trial

**53 up** in its sheath    **54 three-and-thirty** (Plutarch reports it as three-and-twenty.)    **55 another Caesar** i.e., myself, Octavius Caesar    **56 Have . . . to** has also been slaughtered by    **57–8 thou . . . thee** i.e., the only traitors here are in your own army.    **58–9 So . . . sword** i.e. (sardonically), I'm glad to hear you say that, since you are the traitor I mean, and, since you are not in my army, I cannot, according to your assertion, die at your hands.    **60 if** even if.    **strain** lineage    **61 honorable** honorably.    **62 peevish** silly, childish.    **schoolboy** (Octavius was eighteen at the time of Caesar's assassination.)    **worthless** unworthy    **63 a masker . . . reveler** i.e., Antony, noted for his dissipation.    **64 Old . . . still** i.e., Listen to Cassius, as envious and ill-willed as ever. (Said sardonically.)    **67 stomachs** appetites (for fighting), courage.    **68 Why . . . bark** i.e., Well, then, let the storm of battle blow so fiercely that the mountainous waves will force the ship of state to swim for its life.    **69 on the hazard** at stake.    **75 as** inasmuch as    **78 Pompey** (The reference is to the battle of Pharsalus, 48 B.C., where Pompey was persuaded to fight Julius Caesar against his own judgment.)    **set** stake    **80 Epicurus** Greek philosopher (341–270 B.C.) who, because he held the gods to be indifferent to human affairs, spurned belief in omens or superstitions    **82 presage** foretell events.    **83 former ensign** foremost standard, the legion's *aquila*, a tall standard surmounted by the image of an eagle

Two mighty eagles fell, and there they perched,                  84
Gorging and feeding from our soldiers' hands,
Who to Philippi here consorted us.                               86
This morning are they fled away and gone,
And in their steads do ravens, crows, and kites                  88
Fly o'er our heads and downward look on us
As we were sickly prey. Their shadows seem                       90
A canopy most fatal, under which                                 91
Our army lies, ready to give up the ghost.

MESSALA
Believe not so.

CASSIUS              I but believe it partly,                    93
For I am fresh of spirit and resolved
To meet all perils very constantly.                              95

BRUTUS
Even so, Lucilius.                    [*He rejoins Cassius.*]

CASSIUS              Now, most noble Brutus,                     96
The gods today stand friendly, that we may,                      97
Lovers in peace, lead on our days to age!                        98
But since the affairs of men rest still incertain,               99
Let's reason with the worst that may befall.                     100
If we do lose this battle, then is this
The very last time we shall speak together.
What are you then determinèd to do?

BRUTUS
Even by the rule of that philosophy
By which I did blame Cato for the death                          105
Which he did give himself—I know not how,
But I do find it cowardly and vile,
For fear of what might fall, so to prevent                       108
The time of life—arming myself with patience                     109
To stay the providence of some high powers                       110
That govern us below.

CASSIUS              Then, if we lose this battle,
You are contented to be led in triumph
Thorough the streets of Rome?                                    113

BRUTUS
No, Cassius, no. Think not, thou noble Roman,
That ever Brutus will go bound to Rome;
He bears too great a mind. But this same day
Must end that work the ides of March begun.
And whether we shall meet again I know not;
Therefore our everlasting farewell take.
Forever and forever farewell, Cassius!
If we do meet again, why, we shall smile;
If not, why then this parting was well made.

CASSIUS
Forever and forever farewell, Brutus!
If we do meet again, we'll smile indeed;
If not, 'tis true this parting was well made.

BRUTUS
Why, then, lead on. Oh, that a man might know
The end of this day's business ere it come!                      127
But it sufficeth that the day will end,
And then the end is known.—Come, ho, away!
                                        *Exeunt.*

❧

## [5.2]

*Alarum. Enter Brutus and Messala.*

BRUTUS
Ride, ride, Messala, ride, and give these bills                  1
Unto the legions on the other side.                              2
                    [*He hands him written orders.*]
                                *Loud alarum.*
Let them set on at once; for I perceive                          3
But cold demeanor in Octavio's wing,                             4
And sudden push gives them the overthrow.
Ride, ride, Messala! Let them all come down.                     6
                            *Exeunt* [*separately*].

❧

## [5.3]

*Alarums. Enter Cassius* [*carrying a standard*], *and
Titinius.*

CASSIUS
Oh, look, Titinius, look, the villains fly!                      1
Myself have to mine own turned enemy.                            2
This ensign here of mine was turning back;                       3
I slew the coward and did take it from him.                      4

TITINIUS
Oh, Cassius, Brutus gave the word too early,
Who, having some advantage on Octavius,
Took it too eagerly. His soldiers fell to spoil,                 7
Whilst we by Antony are all enclosed.                            8

*Enter Pindarus.*

---

84 **fell** swooped down   86 **Who** which (the eagles).   **consorted** accompanied   88 **kites** scavenger birds (also raptors)   90 **As** as if   91 **fatal** presaging death   93 **but** only   95 **constantly** resolutely.   96 **Even so, Lucilius** (This phrase marks the end of Brutus's private conversation apart with Lucilius.)   97 **The gods** May the gods   98 **Lovers** friends.   **age** old age.   99 **still** always   100 **reason** reckon   105 **Cato** i.e., Marcus Porcius Cato, Brutus' father-in-law, who killed himself to avoid submission to Caesar in 46 B.C. (See 2.1.296 and note.) Brutus's condemnation of Cato's suicide out of fear of failure can perhaps be reconciled with lines 114–17 below and with Brutus's own later suicide (5.5.50), since on that occasion Brutus is responding to certain defeat and disgrace. The seeming contradiction may also be owing to an ambiguity in North's Plutarch.   108 **fall** befall.   **prevent** anticipate the end, cut short   109 **time** term, extent   110 **stay** await   113 **Thorough** through

127 **ere** before
**5.2. Location:** The plains of Philippi. The field of battle.
**0.1** *Alarum* (This is seemingly an anticipatory stage direction; the battle actually begins with the *Loud alarum* at line 2. An *alarum* off stage sounds, signifying a battle.)   1 **bills** orders   2 **side** wing (i.e., Cassius's wing).   3 **set on** attack   4 **cold demeanor** faintheartedness
6 **come down** i.e., from the hills, where the Republican army has been awaiting the signal to attack. (See 5.1.2–3.)
**5.3. Location:** The field of battle still.
1 **the villains** i.e., my own troops   2 **mine own** my own men
3 **ensign** bearer of the standard. (A legion's *aquila*, or "eagle standard," had great significance and needed to be guarded.)   4 **it** i.e., the standard   7 **spoil** looting   8 **enclosed** surrounded.

PINDARUS
    Fly further off, my lord, fly further off!
    Mark Antony is in your tents, my lord.
    Fly therefore, noble Cassius, fly far off.
CASSIUS
    This hill is far enough. Look, look, Titinius:
    Are those my tents where I perceive the fire?
TITINIUS
    They are, my lord.
CASSIUS                 Titinius, if thou lovest me,
    Mount thou my horse, and hide thy spurs in him
    Till he have brought thee up to yonder troops
    And here again, that I may rest assured
    Whether yond troops are friend or enemy.
TITINIUS
    I will be here again even with a thought.          Exit.  19
CASSIUS
    Go, Pindarus, get higher on that hill.
    My sight was ever thick. Regard Titinius,          21
    And tell me what thou not'st about the field.      22
                              [Pindarus goes up.]
    This day I breathèd first. Time is come round,      23
    And where I did begin, there shall I end.
    My life is run his compass.—Sirrah, what news?     25
PINDARUS (above)   Oh, my lord!
CASSIUS   What news?
PINDARUS [above]
    Titinius is enclosèd round about
    With horsemen, that make to him on the spur,       29
    Yet he spurs on. Now they are almost on him.
    Now, Titinius! Now some light. Oh, he             31
    Lights too. He's ta'en. (Shout.) And hark! They shout
       for joy.
CASSIUS   Come down, behold no more.
    Oh, coward that I am, to live so long
    To see my best friend ta'en before my face!        35

              Enter Pindarus [from above].

    Come hither, sirrah.
    In Parthia did I take thee prisoner,               37
    And then I swore thee, saving of thy life,         38
    That whatsoever I did bid thee do
    Thou shouldst attempt it. Come now, keep thine oath;
    Now be a freeman, and with this good sword,
    That ran through Caesar's bowels, search this bosom. 42
    Stand not to answer. Here, take thou the hilts,    43
    And when my face is covered, as 'tis now,
    Guide thou the sword. [Pindarus does so.] Caesar, thou
       art revenged,
    Even with the sword that killed thee.      [He dies.]

PINDARUS
    So, I am free, yet would not so have been,         47
    Durst I have done my will. Oh, Cassius!            48
    Far from this country Pindarus shall run,
    Where never Roman shall take note of him.    [Exit.]

          Enter Titinius [wearing a garland of laurel] and
          Messala.

MESSALA
    It is but change, Titinius; for Octavius           51
    Is overthrown by noble Brutus' power,
    As Cassius' legions are by Antony.
TITINIUS
    These tidings will well comfort Cassius.
MESSALA
    Where did you leave him?
TITINIUS                 All disconsolate,
    With Pindarus his bondman, on this hill.
MESSALA
    Is not that he that lies upon the ground?
TITINIUS
    He lies not like the living.—Oh, my heart!
MESSALA
    Is not that he?
TITINIUS        No, this was he, Messala,
    But Cassius is no more. O setting sun,
    As in thy red rays thou dost sink to night,
    So in his red blood Cassius' day is set.
    The sun of Rome is set. Our day is gone;          63
    Clouds, dews, and dangers come; our deeds are done.
    Mistrust of my success hath done this deed.        65
MESSALA
    Mistrust of good success hath done this deed.
    O hateful Error, Melancholy's child,               67
    Why dost thou show to the apt thoughts of men      68
    The things that are not? O Error, soon conceived,
    Thou never com'st unto a happy birth,              70
    But kill'st the mother that engendered thee.       71
TITINIUS
    What, Pindarus! Where art thou, Pindarus?
MESSALA
    Seek him, Titinius, whilst I go to meet
    The noble Brutus, thrusting this report
    Into his ears. I may say "thrusting" it,
    For piercing steel and darts envenomèd
    Shall be as welcome to the ears of Brutus
    As tidings of this sight.
TITINIUS                 Hie you, Messala,
    And I will seek for Pindarus the while.           79
                              [Exit Messala.]
    Why didst thou send me forth, brave Cassius?
    Did I not meet thy friends? And did not they
    Put on my brows this wreath of victory

19 even . . . thought as quick as thought.  21 thick imperfect, dim.  Regard Observe  22.1 Pindarus goes up (Pindarus may climb to the gallery, or may exit and ascend behind the scenes; see line 35.1 and note.)  23 I breathèd first I first breathed the air as a newborn infant. (Compare 5.1.75–6.)  25 his compass its circuit, circle (as drawn by a geometer's compass).  29 make . . . spur approach him, spurring their horses to great speed  31 some light some horsemen dismount.  35.1 Enter (Pindarus may descend in full view of the audience; see note at 22.1.)  37 Parthia (What is now northeastern Iran.)  38 swore . . . of made you swear, when I spared  42 search probe, penetrate  43 Stand Delay.  hilts sword hilt

47 so in this manner  48 Durst . . . will if I had dared do what I wished: disobey Cassius's command  51 change exchange of advantage, quid pro quo  63 sun (With pun on son.)  65 Mistrust . . . deed i.e., Cassius's mistaken impression that Titinius has been captured in battle (see 14–32 above) has prompted him to commit suicide. (Messala then rephrases in line 66 what Titinius has just said: Cassius's doubt that the Republican army can hope for good success has prompted the suicide.)  67 Melancholy's child i.e., bred of pessimism  68 apt impressionable  70–1 Thou . . . thee You perish like an abortive fetus, killing the person whose melancholic predilection to expect the worst has given rise to fatal error.  79 the while meanwhile.

And bid me give it thee? Didst thou not hear their
   shouts?
Alas, thou hast misconstrued everything.
But, hold thee, take this garland on thy brow.       85
          [*He places the garland on Cassius's brow.*]
Thy Brutus bid me give it thee, and I
Will do his bidding. Brutus, come apace              87
And see how I regarded Caius Cassius.
By your leave, gods! This is a Roman's part.
Come, Cassius' sword, and find Titinius' heart.
          [*He stabs himself and*] *dies.*

   *Alarum. Enter Brutus, Messala, young Cato,*
   *Strato, Volumnius, and Lucilius,* [*Labeo, and*
   *Flavius*].

BRUTUS
   Where, where, Messala, doth his body lie?
MESSALA
   Lo, yonder, and Titinius mourning it.
BRUTUS
   Titinius' face is upward.
CATO                          He is slain.
BRUTUS
   O Julius Caesar, thou art mighty yet!
   Thy spirit walks abroad and turns our swords
   In our own proper entrails.        *Low alarums.*
CATO                    Brave Titinius!               96
   Look whe'er he have not crowned dead Cassius.     97
BRUTUS
   Are yet two Romans living such as these?
   The last of all the Romans, fare thee well!
   It is impossible that ever Rome
   Should breed thy fellow. Friends, I owe more tears
   To this dead man than you shall see me pay.—
   I shall find time, Cassius, I shall find time.—
   Come, therefore, and to Thasos send his body.     104
   His funerals shall not be in our camp,             105
   Lest it discomfort us. Lucilius, come,             106
   And come, young Cato, let us to the field.
   Labeo and Flavius, set our battles on.             108
   'Tis three o'clock, and, Romans, yet ere night    109
   We shall try fortune in a second fight.
          *Exeunt* [*with the bodies*].

❖

# [5.4]

   *Alarum. Enter Brutus, Messala,* [*young*] *Cato,*
   *Lucilius, and Flavius.*

BRUTUS
   Yet, countrymen, oh, yet hold up your heads!
          [*Exit, followed by Messala and Flavius.*]
CATO
   What bastard doth not? Who will go with me?        2
   I will proclaim my name about the field:
   I am the son of Marcus Cato, ho!                   4
   A foe to tyrants, and my country's friend.
   I am the son of Marcus Cato, ho!

          *Enter soldiers, and fight.*

LUCILIUS
   And I am Brutus, Marcus Brutus I!
   Brutus, my country's friend! Know me for Brutus!
          [*Young Cato is slain by Antony's men.*]
   O young and noble Cato, art thou down?
   Why, now thou diest as bravely as Titinius,
   And mayst be honored, being Cato's son.
FIRST SOLDIER [*capturing Lucilius*]
   Yield, or thou diest.
LUCILIUS [*offering money*]   Only I yield to die.     12
   There is so much that thou wilt kill me straight;  13
   Kill Brutus, and be honored in his death.
FIRST SOLDIER
   We must not. A noble prisoner!
SECOND SOLDIER
   Room, ho! Tell Antony, Brutus is ta'en.

          *Enter Antony.*

FIRST SOLDIER
   I'll tell the news. Here comes the General.—
   Brutus is ta'en, Brutus is ta'en, my lord.
ANTONY   Where is he?
LUCILIUS
   Safe, Antony, Brutus is safe enough.
   I dare assure thee that no enemy
   Shall ever take alive the noble Brutus.
   The gods defend him from so great a shame!
   When you do find him, or alive or dead,            24
   He will be found like Brutus, like himself.        25
ANTONY [*to First Soldier*]
   This is not Brutus, friend, but, I assure you,
   A prize no less in worth. Keep this man safe;
   Give him all kindness. I had rather have
   Such men my friends than enemies.—Go on,
   And see whe'er Brutus be alive or dead;            30
   And bring us word unto Octavius' tent
   How everything is chanced.                         32
          *Exeunt* [*separately, some bearing Cato's body*].

❖

**85 hold thee** wait   **87 apace** quickly   **96 own proper** very own
**96 s.d.** *Low alarums* Offstage sound effects suggesting the activity
of distant battle.   **97 whe'er** whether   **104 Thasos** an island off the
coast of Thrace, near Philippi   **105 funerals** funeral obsequies
**106 discomfort us** discourage our troops.   **108 battles** armies
**109 yet ere night** (The historical battles fought at Philippi were
actually weeks apart.)
**5.4. Location:** Scene continues at the field of battle.

**2 What . . . not?** Who is so base that he would not do so?   **4 Marcus
Cato** Cato the Younger, a noted Republican and man of great moral
integrity, who committed a bungled suicide in 46 B.C. as a protest
against the encroachments of Julius Caesar on Rome's senatorial tradition.   **12 Only . . . die** I surrender only on condition that I die at
your hands.   **13 There . . . straight** Here is money if you will kill me
at once   **24 or alive** either alive   **25 like Brutus** true to his noblest
self   **30 whe'er** whether   **32 is chanced** has fallen out.

## [5.5]

*Enter Brutus, Dardanius, Clitus, Strato, and*
*Volumnius.*

**BRUTUS**
Come, poor remains of friends, rest on this rock.
                                              [*He sits.*]
**CLITUS**
Statilius showed the torchlight, but, my lord,          2
He came not back. He is or ta'en or slain.              3
**BRUTUS**
Sit thee down, Clitus. Slaying is the word.
It is a deed in fashion. Hark thee, Clitus.
                                           [*He whispers.*]
**CLITUS**
What, I, my lord? No, not for all the world.
**BRUTUS**
Peace then. No words.
**CLITUS**                    I'll rather kill myself.
**BRUTUS**
Hark thee, Dardanius.              [*He whispers.*]
**DARDANIUS**          Shall I do such a deed?
      [*Dardanius and Clitus move away from Brutus.*]
**CLITUS**   Oh, Dardanius!
**DARDANIUS**   Oh, Clitus!
**CLITUS**
What ill request did Brutus make to thee?
**DARDANIUS**
To kill him, Clitus. Look, he meditates.
**CLITUS**
Now is that noble vessel full of grief,
That it runs over even at his eyes.
**BRUTUS**
Come hither, good Volumnius. List a word.             15
**VOLUMNIUS**
What says my lord?
**BRUTUS**                    Why, this, Volumnius:
The ghost of Caesar hath appeared to me
Two several times by night—at Sardis once,            18
And this last night here in Philippi fields.
I know my hour is come.
**VOLUMNIUS**                    Not so, my lord.
**BRUTUS**
Nay, I am sure it is, Volumnius.
Thou see'st the world, Volumnius, how it goes;
Our enemies have beat us to the pit.   *Low alarums.*  23
It is more worthy to leap in ourselves
Than tarry till they push us. Good Volumnius,
Thou know'st that we two went to school together.
Even for that our love of old, I prithee,             27

Hold thou my sword hilts whilst I run on it.          28
**VOLUMNIUS**
That's not an office for a friend, my lord.
                                        *Alarum still.*
**CLITUS**
Fly, fly, my lord! There is no tarrying here.
**BRUTUS**
Farewell to you, and you, and you, Volumnius.
Strato, thou hast been all this while asleep;
Farewell to thee too, Strato. Countrymen,
My heart doth joy that yet in all my life
I found no man but he was true to me.
I shall have glory by this losing day
More than Octavius and Mark Antony
By this vile conquest shall attain unto.
So fare you well at once, for Brutus' tongue          39
Hath almost ended his life's history.
Night hangs upon mine eyes; my bones would rest,
That have but labored to attain this hour.            42
           *Alarum. Cry within, "Fly, fly, fly!"*
**CLITUS**
Fly, my lord, fly!
**BRUTUS**          Hence, I will follow.
        [*Exeunt Clitus, Dardanius, and Volumnius.*]
I prithee, Strato, stay thou by thy lord.
Thou art a fellow of a good respect;                  45
Thy life hath had some smatch of honor in it.         46
Hold then my sword, and turn away thy face,
While I do run upon it. Wilt thou, Strato?
**STRATO**
Give me your hand first. Fare you well, my lord.
**BRUTUS**
Farewell, good Strato. [*He runs on his sword.*] Caesar,
   now be still.
I killed not thee with half so good a will. *Dies.* 51

        *Alarum. Retreat. Enter Antony, Octavius;*
        *Messala, Lucilius [as prisoners]; and the army.*

**OCTAVIUS**   What man is that?
**MESSALA**
My master's man. Strato, where is thy master?
**STRATO**
Free from the bondage you are in, Messala.
The conquerors can but make a fire of him,
For Brutus only overcame himself,                     56
And no man else hath honor by his death.
**LUCILIUS**
So Brutus should be found. I thank thee, Brutus,
That thou hast proved Lucilius' saying true.          59
**OCTAVIUS**
All that served Brutus, I will entertain them.        60

---

**5.5. Location: The field of battle still.**
**2–3 Statilius . . . slain** (According to Plutarch, a scout named Statilius
has gone through the enemy lines to reconnoitre and to hold up a
torch if all is well at Cassius's camp; he signals back but is then
captured and slain.)   **3 or ta'en** either taken   **15 List** Listen to
**18 several** separate   **23 beat** driven.   **pit** trap for wild animals; also,
a grave.   **27 that our love** that friendship of ours

**28 hilts** hilt   **39 at once** all together, or without further ado
**42 That . . . hour** that have striven all life long only to achieve this
moment of death.   **45 respect** reputation   **46 some smatch** some
flavor, a touch   **51.1 *Retreat*** Signal to retire.   **56 Brutus . . . himself**
only Brutus conquered Brutus   **59 saying** (See 5.4.21–5.)   **60 entertain**
take into service

Fellow, wilt thou bestow thy time with me?

STRATO
Ay, if Messala will prefer me to you.                                    62

OCTAVIUS    Do so, good Messala.

MESSALA    How died my master, Strato?

STRATO
I held the sword, and he did run on it.

MESSALA
Octavius, then take him to follow thee,                                   66
That did the latest service to my master.                                67

ANTONY
This was the noblest Roman of them all.
All the conspirators save only he
Did that they did in envy of great Caesar;
He only in a general honest thought                                       71
And common good to all made one of them.

His life was gentle, and the elements                                     73
So mixed in him that Nature might stand up
And say to all the world, "This was a man!"

OCTAVIUS
According to his virtue let us use him,
With all respect and rites of burial.
Within my tent his bones tonight shall lie,
Most like a soldier, ordered honorably.                                   79
So call the field to rest, and let's away                                 80
To part the glories of this happy day.                                    81

*Exeunt omnes [with Brutus's body].*

---

**62 prefer** recommend   **66 follow** serve   **67 latest** last   **71 general** i.e., selfless. (Cf. 2.1.2 n.)

**73 gentle** noble.   **elements** (Humankind as a microcosm is made up of earth, air, fire, and water, formed into the four humors of phlegm, blood, yellow bile [or choler], and black bile [or melancholy], whose qualities were mingled in Brutus in due proportions.)   **79 ordered** treated, arranged for; accorded solemn rites. (Cf. 1.2.25 n.)   **80 field** army in the field   **81 part** share.   **happy** fortunate   **81.1 *omnes*** all

# Hamlet, Prince of Denmark

A recurring motif in *Hamlet* is of a seemingly healthy exterior concealing an interior sickness. Mere pretense of virtue, as Hamlet warns his mother, "will but skin and film the ulcerous place, / Whiles rank corruption, mining all within, / Infects unseen" (3.4.154–6). Polonius confesses, when he is about to use his daughter as a decoy for Hamlet, that "with devotion's visage / And pious action we do sugar o'er / The devil himself"; and his observation elicits a more anguished mea culpa from Claudius in an aside: "How smart a lash that speech doth give my conscience! / The harlot's cheek, beautied with plast'ring art, / Is not more ugly to the thing that helps it / Than is my deed to my most painted word" (3.1.47–54).

This motif of concealed evil and disease continually reminds us that, in both a specific and a broader sense, "Something is rotten in the state of Denmark" (1.4.90). The specific source of contamination is a poison: the poison with which Claudius has killed Hamlet's father, the poison in the players' enactment of "The Murder of Gonzago," and the two poisons (envenomed sword and poisoned drink) with which Claudius and Laertes plot to rid themselves of young Hamlet. More generally, the poison is an evil nature seeking to destroy humanity's better self, as in the archetypal murder of Abel by Cain. "Oh, my offense is rank! It smells to heaven," laments Claudius, "It hath the primal eldest curse upon't, / A brother's murder" (3.3.36–8). To Hamlet, his father and Claudius typify what is best and worst in humanity; one is the sun-god Hyperion and the other, a satyr. Claudius is a "serpent" and a "mildewed ear, / Blasting his wholesome brother" (1.5.40; 3.4.65–6). Many a person, in Hamlet's view, is tragically destined to behold his or her better qualities corrupted by "some vicious mole of nature" over which the individual seems to have no control. "His virtues else, be they as pure as grace, / As infinite as man may undergo, / Shall in the general censure take corruption / From that particular fault." The "dram of evil" pollutes "all the noble substance" (1.4.24–37). Thus, poison spreads outward to infect the whole individual, just as bad individuals can infect an entire court or nation.

Hamlet, his mind attuned to philosophical matters, is keenly and poetically aware of humanity's fallen condition. He is, moreover, a shrewd observer of the Danish court, familiar with its ways and at the same time newly returned from abroad, looking at Denmark with a stranger's eyes. What particularly darkens his view of humanity, however, is not the general fact of corrupted human nature but rather Hamlet's knowledge of a dreadful secret. Even before he learns of his father's murder, Hamlet senses that there is something more deeply amiss than his mother's overhasty marriage to her deceased husband's brother. This is serious enough, to be sure, for it violates a taboo (parallel to the marriage of a widower to his deceased wife's sister, long regarded as incestuous by the English) and is thus understandably referred to as "incest" by Hamlet and his father's ghost. The appalling spectacle of Gertrude's "wicked speed, to post / With such dexterity to incestuous sheets" (1.2.156–7) overwhelms Hamlet with revulsion at carnal appetite and intensifies the emotional crisis any son would go through when forced to contemplate his father's death and his mother's remarriage. Still, the Ghost's revelation is of something far worse, something Hamlet has subconsciously feared and suspected. "Oh, my prophetic soul! My uncle!" (1.5.42). Now Hamlet believes he has confirming evidence for his intuition that the world itself is "an unweeded garden / That grows to seed. Things rank and gross in nature / Possess it merely" (1.2.135–7).

Something is indeed rotten in the state of Denmark. The monarch on whom the health and safety of the kingdom depend is a murderer. Yet few persons know his secret: Hamlet, Horatio only belatedly, Claudius himself, and ourselves as audience. Many ironies and misunderstandings within the play cannot be understood without a proper awareness of this gap between Hamlet's knowledge and most others' ignorance of the murder. For, according to their own lights, Polonius and the rest behave as courtiers normally behave, obeying and flattering a king who has been chosen by a constitutional process of "election" and can therefore claim to be their legitimate ruler. They do not know that he is a murderer. Hamlet, for his part, is so obsessed with the secret murder that he overreacts to those around him, rejecting overtures of friendship and becoming embittered, callous, brutal, and even violent. His antisocial behavior gives the others good reason to fear him as a menace to the state. Nevertheless, we share with Hamlet a knowledge of the truth and know that he is right, whereas the others are at best unhappily deceived by their own blind complicity in evil.

Rosencrantz and Guildenstern, for instance, are boyhood friends of Hamlet but are now dependent on the favor of King Claudius. Despite their seeming concern for their one-time comrade and Hamlet's initial pleasure in receiving them, they are faceless courtiers whose very names, like their personalities, are virtually interchangeable. "Thanks, Rosencrantz and gentle Guildenstern," says the King, and "Thanks, Guildenstern and gentle Rosencrantz," echoes the Queen (2.2.33–4). They cannot understand why Hamlet increasingly mocks their overtures of friendship, whereas Hamlet cannot stomach their subservience to the King. The secret murder divides Hamlet from them, since only he knows of it. As the confrontation between Hamlet and Claudius grows more deadly, Rosencrantz and Guildenstern, not knowing the true cause, can only interpret Hamlet's behavior as dangerous madness. The wild display he puts on during the performance of "The Murder of Gonzago" and then the killing of Polonius are evidence of a treasonous threat to the crown, eliciting from them staunch assertions of the divine right of kings. "Most holy and religious fear it is / To keep those many many bodies safe / That live and feed upon Your Majesty," professes Guildenstern, and Rosencrantz reiterates the theme: "The cease of majesty / Dies not alone, but like a gulf doth draw / What's near it with it" (3.3.8–17). These sentiments of Elizabethan orthodoxy, similar to ones frequently heard in Shakespeare's history plays, are here undercut by a devastating irony, since they are spoken unwittingly in defense of a murderer. This irony pursues Rosencrantz and Guildenstern to their graves, for they are killed performing what they see as their duty to convey Hamlet safely to England. They are as ignorant of Claudius's secret orders for the murder of Hamlet in England as they are of Claudius's real reason for wishing to be rid of his stepson. That Hamlet should ingeniously remove the secret commission from Rosencrantz and Guildenstern's packet and substitute an order for their execution is ironically fitting, even though they are guiltless of having plotted Hamlet's death. "Why, man, they did make love to this employment," says Hamlet to Horatio. "They are not near my

conscience. Their defeat / Does by their own insinuation grow" (5.2.57–9). They have condemned themselves, in Hamlet's eyes, by interceding officiously in deadly affairs of which they had no comprehension. Hamlet's judgment of them is harsh, and he himself appears hardened and pitiless in his role as agent in their deaths, but he is right that they have courted their own destiny.

Polonius, too, dies for meddling. It seems an unfair fate, since he wishes no physical harm to Hamlet and is only trying to ingratiate himself with Claudius. Yet Polonius's complicity in jaded court politics is deeper than his fatuous parental sententiousness might lead one to suppose. His famous advice to his son, often quoted out of context as though it were wise counsel, is, in fact, a worldly gospel of self-interest and concern for appearances. Like his son, Laertes, he cynically presumes that Hamlet's affection for Ophelia cannot be serious, since princes are not free to marry ladies of the court; accordingly, Polonius obliges his daughter to return the love letters she so cherishes. Polonius's spies are everywhere, seeking to entrap Polonius's own son in fleshly sin or to discover symptoms of Hamlet's presumed lovesickness. Polonius may cut a ridiculous figure as a prattling busybody, but he is wily and even menacing in his intent. He has actually helped Claudius to the throne and is an essential instrument of royal policy. His ineffectuality and ignorance of the murder do not really excuse his guilty involvement.

Ophelia is more innocent than her father and brother, and more truly affectionate toward Hamlet. She earns our sympathy because she is caught between the conflicting wills of the men who are supremely important to her—her wooer, her father, and her brother. Obedient by instinct and training to patriarchal instruction, she is unprepared to cope with divided authority and so takes refuge in passivity. Nevertheless, her pitiable story suggests that weak-willed acquiescence is poisoned by the evil to which it surrenders. However passively, Ophelia becomes an instrument through which Claudius attempts to spy on Hamlet. She is much like Gertrude, for the Queen has yielded to Claudius's importunity without ever knowing fully what awful price Claudius has paid for her and for the throne. The resemblance between Ophelia and Gertrude confirms Hamlet's tendency to generalize about feminine weakness—"frailty, thy name is woman" (1.2.146)—and prompts his misogynistic outburst against Ophelia when he concludes she, too, is spying on him. His rejection of love and friendship (except for Horatio's) seems paranoid in character and yet is at least partially justified by the fact that so many of the court are in fact conspiring to learn what he is up to.

Their oversimplification of his dilemma and their facile analyses vex Hamlet as much as their meddling. When they presume to diagnose his malady, the courtiers actually reveal more about themselves than about Hamlet— something we as readers and viewers might well bear in mind. Rosencrantz and Guildenstern think in political terms, reflecting their own ambitious natures, and Hamlet takes mordant delight in leading them on. "Sir, I lack advancement," he mockingly answers Rosencrantz's questioning as to the cause of his distemper. Rosencrantz is immediately taken in: "How can that be, when you have the voice of the King himself for your succession in Denmark?" (3.2.338–41). Actually, Hamlet does hold a grudge against Claudius for having "Popped in between th'election and my hopes" (5.2.65), using the Danish custom of "election" by the chief lords of the realm to deprive young Hamlet of the succession that would normally have been his. Nevertheless, it is a gross oversimplification to suppose that political frustration is the key to Hamlet's sorrow, and to speculate thus is presumptuous. "Why, look you now, how unworthy a thing you make of me!" Hamlet protests to Rosencrantz and Guildenstern. "You would play upon me, you would seem to know my stops, you would pluck out the heart of my mystery" (3.2.362–5). An even worse offender in the distortion of complex truth is Polonius, whose facile diagnosis of lovesickness appears to have been inspired by recollections of Polonius's own far-off youth. ("Truly in my youth I suffered much extremity for love, very near this," 2.2.189–91). Polonius's fatuous complacency in his own powers of analysis—"If circumstances lead me, I will find / Where truth is hid, though it were hid indeed / Within the center" (2.2.157–9)—reads like a parody of Hamlet's struggle to discover what is true and what is not.

Thus, although Hamlet may seem to react with excessive bitterness toward those who are set to watch over him, the corruption he decries in Denmark is both real and universal. "The time is out of joint," he laments. "Oh, cursèd spite / That ever I was born to set it right!" (1.5.197–8). How is he to proceed in setting things right? Ever since the nineteenth century, it has been fashionable to discover reasons for Hamlet's delaying his revenge. The basic Romantic approach is to find a defect, or tragic flaw, in Hamlet himself. In Coleridge's words, Hamlet suffers from "an overbalance in the contemplative faculty" and is "one who vacillates from sensibility and procrastinates from thought, and loses the power of action in the energy of resolve." More recent psychological critics, such as Freud and his disciple Ernest Jones, still seek answers to the Romantics' question by explaining Hamlet's failure of will. In this interpretation, Hamlet is the victim of an Oedipal trauma: he has longed unconsciously to possess his mother and for that very reason cannot bring himself to punish the hated uncle who has supplanted him in his incestuous and forbidden desire. Such interpretations suggest, among other things, that Hamlet continues to serve as a mirror in which analysts who would pluck out the heart of his mystery see an image of their own concerns—just as Rosencrantz and Guildenstern read politics, and Polonius reads lovesickness, into Hamlet's distress.

We can ask, however, not only whether the explanations for Hamlet's supposed delay are valid but also whether the question they seek to answer is itself valid. Is the delay unnecessary or excessive? The question did not even arise until the nineteenth century. Earlier audiences were evidently satisfied that Hamlet must test the Ghost's credibility, since apparitions can tell half-truths to deceive people, and that, once Hamlet has confirmed the Ghost's word, he proceeds as resolutely as his canny adversary allows. More recent criticism, perhaps reflecting a modern absorption in existentialist philosophy, has proposed that Hamlet's dilemma is a matter, not of personal failure, but of the absurdity of action itself in a corrupt world. Does what Hamlet is asked to do make any sense, given the bestial nature of humanity and the impossibility of knowing what is right? In part, it is a matter of style: Claudius's Denmark is crassly vulgar, and to combat this vulgarity on its own terms seems to require the sort of bad histrionics Hamlet derides in actors who mouth their lines or tear a passion to tatters. Hamlet's dilemma of action can best be studied in the play by comparing him with various characters who are obliged to act in situations similar to his own and who respond in meaningfully different ways.

Three young men—Hamlet, Laertes, and Fortinbras—are called upon to avenge their fathers' violent deaths. Ophelia, too, has lost a father by violent means, and her madness and death are another kind of reaction to such a loss. The responses of Laertes and Fortinbras offer rich parallels to Hamlet, in both cases implying the futility of positive and forceful action. Laertes thinks he has received an unambiguous mandate to take revenge, since Hamlet has undoubtedly slain Polonius and helped to deprive Ophelia of her sanity. Accordingly, Laertes comes back to Denmark in a fury, stirring the rabble with his demagoguery and spouting Senecan rant about dismissing conscience "to the profoundest pit" in his quest for vengeance (4.5.135). When Claudius asks what Laertes would do to Hamlet "To show yourself in deed your father's son / More than in words," Laertes fires back: "To cut his throat i'th' church" (4.7.126–7). This resolution is understandable. The pity is, however, that Laertes has only superficially identified the murderer in the case. He is too easily deceived by Claudius, because he has jumped to easy and fallacious conclusions, and so is doomed to become a pawn in Claudius's sly maneuverings. Too late he sees his error and must die for it, begging and receiving Hamlet's forgiveness. Before we accuse Hamlet of thinking too deliberately before acting, we must consider that Laertes does not think enough.

Fortinbras of Norway, as his name implies ("strong in arms"), is one who believes in decisive action. At the beginning of the play, we learn that his father has been slain in battle by old Hamlet and that Fortinbras has collected an army to win back by force the territory fairly won by the Danes in that encounter. Like Hamlet, young

Fortinbras does not succeed his father to the throne but must now contend with an uncle-king. When this uncle, at Claudius's instigation, forbids Fortinbras to march against the Danes and rewards him for his restraint with a huge annual income and a commission to fight the Poles instead, Fortinbras sagaciously welcomes the new opportunity. He pockets the money, marches against Poland, and waits for occasion to deliver Denmark as well into his hands. Clearly this is more of a success story than that of Laertes, and Hamlet does, after all, give his blessing to the "election" of Fortinbras to the Danish throne. Fortinbras is the man of the hour, the representative of a restored political stability. Yet Hamlet's admiration for this man on horseback is qualified by a profound reservation. Hamlet's dying prophecy that the election will light on Fortinbras (5.2.357–8) is suffused with ironies, so much so that the incongruity is sometimes made conscious and deliberate in performance. Earlier in the play, the spectacle of Fortinbras marching against Poland "to gain a little patch of ground / That hath in it no profit but the name" prompts Hamlet to berate himself for inaction, but he cannot ignore the absurdity of the effort. "Two thousand souls and twenty thousand ducats / Will not debate the question of this straw." The soldiers will risk their very lives "Even for an eggshell" (4.4.19–54). It is only one step from this view of the vanity of ambitious striving to the speculation that great Caesar or Alexander, dead and turned to dust, may one day produce the loam or clay with which to stop the bunghole of a beer barrel. Fortinbras epitomizes the ongoing political order after Hamlet's death, but is that order of any consequence to us after we have imagined with Hamlet the futility of most human endeavor?

To ask such a question is to seek passive or self-abnegating answers to the riddle of life, and Hamlet is attuned to such inquiries. Even before he learns of his father's murder, he contemplates suicide, wishing "that the Everlasting had not fixed / His canon 'gainst self-slaughter" (1.2.131–2). As with the alternative of action, other characters serve as foils to Hamlet, revealing both the attractions and perils of withdrawal. Ophelia is destroyed by meekly acquiescing in others' desires. Whether she commits suicide is uncertain, but the very possibility reminds us that Hamlet has twice considered and reluctantly rejected this despairing path as forbidden by Christian teaching—the second such occasion being his "To be, or not to be" soliloquy in 3.1. He has also play-acted at the madness to which Ophelia succumbs. Gertrude identifies herself with Ophelia and like her has surrendered her will to male aggressiveness. We suspect she knows little of the actual murder (see 3.4.31) but dares not think how deeply she may be implicated. Although her death is evidently not a suicide (see 5.2.291–7), it is passive and expiatory.

A more attractive alternative to decisive action for Hamlet is acting in the theater, and he is full of exuberant advice to the visiting players. The play they perform before Claudius at Hamlet's request and with some lines added by him—a play consciously archaic in style—offers to the Danish court a kind of heightened reflection of itself, a homiletic artifact, rendering in conventional terms the taut anxieties and terrors of murder for the sake of noble passion. Structurally, the play within the play becomes not an escape for Hamlet into inaction but rather the point on which the whole drama pivots and the scene in which contemplation of past events is largely replaced with stirrings toward action. When Lucianus in the Mousetrap play turns out to be nephew rather than brother to the dead king, the audience finds itself face to face, not with history, but with prophecy. We are not surprised when, in his conversations with the players, Hamlet openly professes his admiration for the way in which art holds "the mirror up to nature, to show virtue her feature, scorn her own image, and the very age and body of the time his form and pressure" (3.2.22–4). Hamlet admires the dramatist's ability to transmute raw human feeling into tragic art, depicting and ordering reality as Shakespeare's play of *Hamlet* does for us. Yet play-acting can also be, Hamlet recognizes, a self-indulgent escape for him, a way of unpacking his heart with words and of verbalizing his situation without doing something to remedy it. Acting and talking remind him too much of Polonius, who was an actor in his youth and who continues to be, like Hamlet, an inveterate punster.

Of the passive responses in the play, the stoicism of Horatio is by far the most attractive to Hamlet. "More an antique Roman than a Dane" (5.2.343), Horatio is, as Hamlet praises him, immune to flattering or to opportunities for cheap self-advancement. He is "As one, in suffering all, that suffers nothing, / A man that Fortune's buffets and rewards / Hast ta'en with equal thanks" (3.2.65–7). Such a person has a sure defense against the worst that life can offer. Hamlet can trust and love Horatio as he can no one else. Yet even here there are limits, for Horatio's skeptical and Roman philosophy cuts him off from a Christian and metaphysical overview. "There are more things in heaven and earth, Horatio, / Than are dreamt of in your philosophy" (1.5.175–6). After they have beheld together the skulls of Yorick's graveyard, Horatio seemingly does not share with Hamlet the exulting Christian perception that, although human life is indeed vain, Providence will reveal a pattern transcending human sorrow.

Hamlet's path must lie somewhere between the rash suddenness of Laertes or the canny resoluteness of Fortinbras on the one hand, and the passivity of Ophelia or Gertrude and the stoic resignation of Horatio on the other. At first he alternates between action and inaction, finding neither satisfactory. The Ghost has commanded Hamlet to revenge but has not explained how this is to be done; indeed, Gertrude is to be left passively to heaven and her conscience. If this method will suffice for her (and Christian wisdom taught that such a purgation was as thorough as it was sure), why not for Claudius? If Claudius must be killed, should it be while he is at his sin rather than at his prayers? The play is full of questions, stemming chiefly from the enigmatic queries put to the Ghost. "Say, why is this? Wherefore? What should we do?" (1.4.57). Hamlet is not incapable of action. He shows unusual strength and cunning on the pirate ship, in his duel with Laertes ("I shall win at the odds"; 5.2.209), and especially in his slaying of Polonius—an action hardly characterized by "thinking too precisely on th'event" (4.4.42). Here is forthright action of the sort Laertes espouses. Yet, when the corpse behind his mother's arras turns out to be Polonius rather than Claudius, Hamlet concludes from the mistake that he has offended heaven. Even if Polonius deserves what he got, Hamlet believes he has made himself into a cruel "scourge" of Providence who must himself suffer retribution as well as deal it out. Swift action has not accomplished what the Ghost commanded.

The Ghost does not appear to speak for Providence in any case. His message is of revenge, a pagan concept deeply embedded in most societies but at odds with Christian teaching. His wish that Claudius be sent to hell and that Gertrude be more gently treated might, in fact, be the judgment of an impartial deity but here comes wrapped in the passionate involvement of a murdered man's restless spirit. This is not to say that Hamlet is being tempted to perform a damnable act, as he fears is possible, but that the Ghost's command cannot readily be reconciled with a complex and balanced view of justice. If Hamlet were to spring on Claudius in the fullness of his vice and cut his throat, we would pronounce Hamlet a murderer. What Hamlet believes he has learned instead is that he must become the instrument of Providence according to *its* plans, not his own. After his return from England, he senses triumphantly that all will be for the best if he allows an unseen power to decide the time and place for his final act. Under these conditions, rash action will be right. "Rashly, / And praised be rashness for it—let us know / Our indiscretion sometime serves us well / When our deep plots do pall, and that should learn us / There's a divinity that shapes our ends, / Rough-hew them how we will" (5.2.6–11). Passivity, too, is now a proper course, for Hamlet puts himself wholly at the disposal of Providence. What had seemed so impossible when Hamlet tried to formulate his own design proves elementary once he trusts to a divine justice in which he now firmly believes. Rashness and passivity are perfectly fused. Hamlet is revenged without having to commit premeditated murder and is relieved of his painful existence without having to commit suicide.

The circumstances of *Hamlet'*s catastrophe do indeed seem to accomplish all that Hamlet desires, by a route so circuitous that no one could ever have foreseen or devised it. Polonius's death, as it turns out, was instrumental after all, for it led to Laertes's angry return to Denmark and the challenge to a duel. Every seemingly unrelated event has its place; "There's a special providence in the fall of a sparrow" (5.2.217–18). Repeatedly, the characters stress the role of seeming accident leading to just retribution. Even Horatio, for whom the events of the play suggest a pattern of randomness and violence, of "accidental judgments" and "casual slaughters," can see at last, "in this upshot, purposes mistook / Fall'n on th'inventors' heads" (5.2.384–7). In a similar vein, Laertes confesses himself "a woodcock to mine own springe" (line 309). As Hamlet had said earlier, of Rosencrantz and Guildenstern, "'tis the sport to have the engineer / Hoised with his own petard" (3.4.213–14). Thus, too, Claudius's poisoned cup, intended for Hamlet, kills the Queen for whom Claudius had done such evil in order to acquire her and the throne. The destiny of evil in this play is to overreach itself.

In its final resolution, *Hamlet* incorporates a broader conception of justice than its revenge formula seemed at first to make possible. Yet, in its origins, *Hamlet* is a revenge story, and these traditions have left some residual savagery in the play. In the *Historia Danica* of Saxo Grammaticus, 1180–1208, and in the rather free translation of Saxo into French by François de Belleforest, *Histoires Tragiques* (1576), Hamlet is cunning and bloodily resolute throughout. He kills an eavesdropper without a qualm during the interview with his mother and exchanges letters on his way to England with characteristic shrewdness. Ultimately, he returns to Denmark, sets fire to his uncle's hall, slays its courtly inhabitants, and claims his rightful throne from a grateful people. The Ghost, absent in this account, may well have been derived from Thomas Kyd's *The Spanish Tragedy* (c. 1587) and perhaps a lost *Hamlet* play in existence by 1589. *The Spanish Tragedy* bears many resemblances to our *Hamlet* and suggests what the lost *Hamlet* may well have contained: a sensational murder, a Senecan Ghost demanding revenge, the avenger hampered by court intrigue, his resort to a feigned madness, and his difficulty in authenticating the ghostly vision. A German version of *Hamlet*, called *Der bestrafte Brudermord* (1710), based seemingly on the older *Hamlet*, includes such details as the play within the play, the sparing of the King at his prayers in order to damn his soul, Ophelia's madness, the fencing match with poisoned swords and poisoned drink, and the final catastrophe of vengeance and death. Similarly, the early unauthorized first quarto of *Hamlet* (1603) offers some passages seemingly based on the older play by Kyd.

Although this evidence suggests that Shakespeare received most of the material for the plot intact, his transformation of that material was nonetheless immeasurable. To be sure, Kyd's *The Spanish Tragedy* contains many rhetorical passages on the inadequacy of human justice, but the overall effect is still sensational and the outcome is a triumph for the pagan spirit of revenge. So, too, with the many revenge plays of the 1590s and 1600s that Kyd's dramatic genius had inspired, including Shakespeare's own *Titus Andronicus* (c. 1589–1592). *Hamlet,* written in about 1599–1601 (it is not mentioned by Frances Meres in his *Palladis Tamia: Wit's Treasury,* in 1598, and was entered in the Stationers' Register, the official record book of the London Company of Stationers [booksellers and printers], in 1602), is unparalleled in its philosophical richness. Its ending is truly cathartic, for Hamlet dies, not as a bloodied avenger, but as one who has affirmed the tragic dignity of the human race. His courage and faith, maintained in the face of great odds, atone for the dismal corruption in which Denmark has festered. His resolutely honest inquiries have taken him beyond the revulsion and doubt that express so eloquently, among other matters, the fearful response of Shakespeare's own generation to a seeming breakdown of established political, theological, and cosmological beliefs. Hamlet finally perceives that "if it be not now, yet it will come," and that "The readiness is all" (5.2.219–20). This discovery, this revelation of necessity and meaning in Hamlet's great reversal of fortune, enables him to confront the tragic circumstance of his life with understanding and heroism and to demonstrate the triumph of the human spirit even in the moment of his catastrophe.

Such an assertion of the individual will does not lessen the tragic waste with which *Hamlet* ends. Hamlet is dead, and the great promise of his life is forever lost. Few others have survived. Justice has seemingly been fulfilled in the deaths of Claudius, Gertrude, Rosencrantz and Guildenstern, Polonius, Laertes, and perhaps even Ophelia, but in a wild and extravagant way, as though Justice herself, more vengeful than providential, were unceasingly hungry for victims. Hamlet, the minister of that justice, has likewise grown hardened to the spilling of blood, even if he submits himself at last to the will of a force he recognizes as providential. Denmark faces the kind of political uncertainty with which the play began. However much Hamlet may admire Fortinbras's resolution, the prince of Norway seems an alien choice for Denmark—even an ironic one. Horatio sees so little point in outliving the catastrophe of this play that he would choose death, were it not that he must draw his breath in pain to ensure that Hamlet's story is truly told. Still, that truth has been rescued from oblivion. Amid the ruin of the final scene, we share the artist's vision, through which we struggle to interpret and give order to the tragedy that proves inseparable from human existence.

The performance history of *Hamlet* is extraordinarily rich. It also attests to a variety of interpetations that is equally textured. Eighteenth-century versions by David Garrick and others often took out or severely reduced the Fortinbras plot; indeed, the play is so long that it almost certainly was not acted in its entirety even in Shakespeare's day. Garrick also deleted the Gravediggers' scene and much besides in Act 5. Pictorial scenery in the nineteenth century tended to favor opulent renditions of the play-within-the-play and Ophelia's mad scenes. Hamlet was portrayed in 1864, at the Lyceum Theater, as a Viking in a primitive medieval decor. Henry Irving, undertaking the role of Hamlet from 1864 to 1885, chose a decor of the fifth or sixth century, with castle battlements set among massive rocks glimmering under the soft light of the moon in the first act. John Gielgud became famous as a leading Hamlet of his day, beginning in 1930 at the Old Vic, emphasizing the pale, introspective, sonorous-voiced Hamlet that Coleridge had imagined. More recently, *Hamlet* has been seen from an existential vantage (by Tyrone Guthrie, 1938, at the Old Vic) in the modern-dress context of a Europe precariously trapped between the first World War and a second about to begin. Laurence Olivier, in his film version of 1948, explored the Freudian dimensions of "a man who could not make up his mind"; influenced by Ernest Jones's *Hamlet and Oedipus,* Olivier allowed the camera eye to linger on the Queen's bedchamber and its bed, where Hamlet encountered his mother in a scene (3.4) heavy with incestuous overtones.

Recent productions on stage, in film, and on television amply demonstrate how Shakespeare's best-known play can lend itself to other kinds of relevance to our modern world. Political interpretations sometimes focus on Claudius as a Machiavel in the school of modern spin-doctoring. At the Wisdom Bridge Theater's Chicago production in the 1970s, for example, directed by Robert Falls with Aidan Quinn as Hamlet, Claudius was the Great Communicator in the style of Ronald Reagan. His first scene (1.2) featured the new king on an array of television sets, blandly explaining to the Danish public the reasons for his rapid assumption of power and marriage with the widow of his dead brother. Claudius and Gertrude never appeared onstage in this scene; the audience saw the king on television, while the stage itself was given over to his zealous public relations team, nattily dressed, preparing a reception for the press representatives, making sure the event went smoothly. Fading posters of the dead king offered contrasting reminders of the regime which Claudius had so astutely supplanted.

More recently, in Michael Almereyda's low-budget film of 2000, the setting throughout is the New York world of privilege and high finance. Claudius (Kyle MacLachlan) is a chief executive officer of a superconglomerate financial empire. Gertrude (Diane Venora) is a suburban wife utterly seduced by the expensive privileges she now enjoys, of stretch limousines, private bathing pools in their high-rise empire, and the surroundings of obsequious flattery that immense wealth can command. Hamlet (Ethan Hawke), conversely, is a rebel with a cause, ostentatiously out of step in his moth-eaten ski cap, his scruffy clothes, his mania for the latest film and computer technology, and his disdain for corrupting privilege. The ghost of Hamlet's father (Sam Shepard) eerily appears on the swank penthouse battlements of New York's concrete skyscrapers, berattling the television monitors of up-to-date security systems. The overall effect is indeed strikingly modern and plausible. Another popular film version is that of Franco Zeffirelli (1990), with Mel Gibson as a matinee idol Hamlet, Alan Bates as a believably sexy Claudius, Glenn Close as a Gertrude who is erotically infatuated with her new husband, and some compellingly handsome scenery. Grigori Kozintsev's Russian film version of 1964, based on a script by Boris Pasternak, is visually eloquent in its recurring images of stone, iron, fire, sea, and earth. Kenneth Branagh's four-hour *Hamlet* (1996) is notable for its intrepedity in offering an essentially uncut version and for some superb performances, especially that of Derek Jacobi as Claudius. Jacobi had starred earlier as Hamlet onstage (Old Vic, 1979) and in the BBC television series of all the plays beginning in 1979. Richard Burton's memorable stage performance (1964, at New York's Lunt-Fontanne Theater) is available on video. This play is especially fortunate in a rich archive of filmed or televised versions that make possible a comparative study in production by some of the greatest Shakespearean actors of the twentieth and twenty-first centuries. These varied interpretations abundantly show how *Hamlet* and its fascinating protagonist can be satirical, rebellious, mordant, funny, disillusioned, melancholic, introspective, and much more. The play that puzzles and fascinates readers is also immensely disturbing in performance.

# *Hamlet, Prince of Denmark*

[*Dramatis Personae*

GHOST *of Hamlet, the former King of Denmark*
CLAUDIUS, *King of Denmark, the former King's brother*
GERTRUDE, *Queen of Denmark, widow of the former King and now wife of Claudius*
HAMLET, *Prince of Denmark, son of the late King and of Gertrude*

POLONIUS, *councillor to the King*
LAERTES, *his son*
OPHELIA, *his daughter*
REYNALDO, *his servant*

HORATIO, *Hamlet's friend and fellow student*

VOLTEMAND,
CORNELIUS,
ROSENCRANTZ,
GUILDENSTERN,  } *members of the Danish court*
OSRIC,
A GENTLEMAN,
A LORD,

BERNARDO,
FRANCISCO,  } *officers and soldiers on watch*
MARCELLUS,

FORTINBRAS, *Prince of Norway*
CAPTAIN *in his army*

*Three or Four* PLAYERS, *taking the roles of* PROLOGUE, PLAYER KING, PLAYER QUEEN, *and* LUCIANUS
*Two* MESSENGERS
FIRST SAILOR
*Two* CLOWNS, *a gravedigger and his companion*
PRIEST
FIRST AMBASSADOR *from England*

*Lords, Soldiers, Attendants, Guards, other Players, Followers of Laertes, other Sailors, another Ambassador or Ambassadors from England*

SCENE: *Denmark*]

## [1.1]

*Enter Bernardo and Francisco, two sentinels,*
*[meeting].*

BERNARDO    Who's there?

FRANCISCO
Nay, answer me. Stand and unfold yourself.    2

BERNARDO    Long live the King!

FRANCISCO    Bernardo?

BERNARDO    He.

FRANCISCO
You come most carefully upon your hour.

BERNARDO
'Tis now struck twelve. Get thee to bed, Francisco.

FRANCISCO
For this relief much thanks. 'Tis bitter cold,
And I am sick at heart.

BERNARDO    Have you had quiet guard?

FRANCISCO    Not a mouse stirring.

BERNARDO    Well, good night.
If you do meet Horatio and Marcellus,
The rivals of my watch, bid them make haste.    14

*Enter Horatio and Marcellus.*

FRANCISCO
I think I hear them.—Stand, ho! Who is there?

HORATIO    Friends to this ground.    16

MARCELLUS    And liegemen to the Dane.    17

FRANCISCO    Give you good night.    18

MARCELLUS
Oh, farewell, honest soldier. Who hath relieved you?

FRANCISCO
Bernardo hath my place. Give you good night.
                              *Exit Francisco.*

MARCELLUS    Holla! Bernardo!

BERNARDO    Say, what, is Horatio there?

HORATIO    A piece of him.

BERNARDO
Welcome, Horatio. Welcome, good Marcellus.

HORATIO
What, has this thing appeared again tonight?

BERNARDO    I have seen nothing.

MARCELLUS
Horatio says 'tis but our fantasy,    27
And will not let belief take hold of him
Touching this dreaded sight twice seen of us.
Therefore I have entreated him along    30
With us to watch the minutes of this night,    31
That if again this apparition come
He may approve our eyes and speak to it.    33

HORATIO
Tush, tush, 'twill not appear.

BERNARDO                Sit down awhile

And let us once again assail your ears,
That are so fortified against our story,
What we two nights have seen.

HORATIO                Well, sit we down,
And let us hear Bernardo speak of this.

BERNARDO    Last night of all,    39
When yond same star that's westward from the pole    40
Had made his course t'illume that part of heaven    41
Where now it burns, Marcellus and myself,
The bell then beating one—

*Enter the Ghost.*

MARCELLUS
Peace, break thee off! Look where it comes again!

BERNARDO
In the same figure like the King that's dead.

MARCELLUS
Thou art a scholar. Speak to it, Horatio.    46

BERNARDO
Looks it not like the King? Mark it, Horatio.

HORATIO
Most like. It harrows me with fear and wonder.

BERNARDO
It would be spoke to.

MARCELLUS                Question it, Horatio.    49

HORATIO
What art thou that usurp'st this time of night,    50
Together with that fair and warlike form
In which the majesty of buried Denmark    52
Did sometimes march? By heaven, I charge thee, speak!    53

MARCELLUS
It is offended.

BERNARDO                See, it stalks away.

HORATIO
Stay! Speak, speak! I charge thee, speak!    *Exit the Ghost.*

MARCELLUS    'Tis gone and will not answer.

BERNARDO
How now, Horatio? You tremble and look pale.
Is not this something more than fantasy?
What think you on't?    59

HORATIO
Before my God, I might not this believe
Without the sensible and true avouch    61
Of mine own eyes.

MARCELLUS                Is it not like the King?

HORATIO    As thou art to thyself.
Such was the very armor he had on
When he the ambitious Norway combated.    65
So frowned he once when, in an angry parle,    66
He smote the sledded Polacks on the ice.    67
'Tis strange.

---

**1.1. Location:** Elsinore castle. A guard platform.
**2 me** (Francisco emphasizes that *he* is the sentry currently on watch.)
**unfold yourself** reveal your identity.    **14 rivals** partners    **16 ground**
country, land.    **17 liegemen to the Dane** men sworn to serve the
Danish king.    **18 Give** May God give    **27 fantasy** imagination
**30 along** to come along    **31 watch** keep watch during    **33 approve**
corroborate

**39 Last . . . all** i.e., This *very* last night. (Emphatic.)    **40 pole** polestar,
north star    **41 his** its.    **t'illume** to illuminate    **46 scholar** one
learned enough to know how to question a ghost properly.    **49 It . . .
to** (It was commonly believed that a ghost could not speak until
spoken to.)    **50 usurp'st** wrongfully takes over    **52 buried Denmark**
the buried King of Denmark    **53 sometimes** formerly    **59 on't** of it.
**61 sensible** confirmed by the senses.    **avouch** warrant, evidence
**65 Norway** King of Norway    **66 parle** parley    **67 sledded** traveling
on sleds.    **Polacks** Poles

MARCELLUS

Thus twice before, and jump at this dead hour,    69
With martial stalk hath he gone by our watch.    70

HORATIO

In what particular thought to work I know not,    71
But in the gross and scope of mine opinion    72
This bodes some strange eruption to our state.

MARCELLUS

Good now, sit down, and tell me, he that knows,    74
Why this same strict and most observant watch
So nightly toils the subject of the land,    76
And why such daily cast of brazen cannon    77
And foreign mart for implements of war,    78
Why such impress of shipwrights, whose sore task    79
Does not divide the Sunday from the week.
What might be toward, that this sweaty haste    81
Doth make the night joint-laborer with the day?
Who is't that can inform me?

HORATIO                          That can I;
At least, the whisper goes so. Our last king,
Whose image even but now appeared to us,
Was, as you know, by Fortinbras of Norway,
Thereto pricked on by a most emulate pride,    87
Dared to the combat; in which our valiant Hamlet—
For so this side of our known world esteemed him—    89
Did slay this Fortinbras; who by a sealed compact    90
Well ratified by law and heraldry    91
Did forfeit, with his life, all those his lands
Which he stood seized of, to the conqueror;    93
Against the which a moiety competent    94
Was gagèd by our king, which had returned    95
To the inheritance of Fortinbras    96
Had he been vanquisher, as, by the same cov'nant    97
And carriage of the article designed,    98
His fell to Hamlet. Now, sir, young Fortinbras,
Of unimprovèd mettle hot and full,    100
Hath in the skirts of Norway here and there    101
Sharked up a list of landless resolutes    102
For food and diet to some enterprise    103
That hath a stomach in't, which is no other—    104
As it doth well appear unto our state—
But to recover of us, by strong hand    106
And terms compulsative, those foresaid lands    107
So by his father lost. And this, I take it,
Is the main motive of our preparations,

The source of this our watch, and the chief head    110
Of this post-haste and rummage in the land.    111

BERNARDO

I think it be no other but e'en so.
Well may it sort that this portentous figure    113
Comes armèd through our watch so like the King
That was and is the question of these wars.    115

HORATIO

A mote it is to trouble the mind's eye.    116
In the most high and palmy state of Rome,    117
A little ere the mightiest Julius fell,    118
The graves stood tenantless, and the sheeted dead    119
Did squeak and gibber in the Roman streets;
As stars with trains of fire and dews of blood,    121
Disasters in the sun; and the moist star    122
Upon whose influence Neptune's empire stands    123
Was sick almost to doomsday with eclipse.    124
And even the like precurse of feared events,    125
As harbingers preceding still the fates    126
And prologue to the omen coming on,    127
Have heaven and earth together demonstrated
Unto our climatures and countrymen.    129

*Enter Ghost again.*

But soft, behold! Lo, where it comes again!    130
I'll cross it, though it blast me. (*It spreads his arms.*) Stay,
    illusion!    131
If thou hast any sound or use of voice,
Speak to me!
If there be any good thing to be done
That may to thee do ease and grace to me,
Speak to me!
If thou art privy to thy country's fate,    137
Which, happily, foreknowing may avoid,    138
Oh, speak!
Or if thou hast uphoarded in thy life
Extorted treasure in the womb of earth,
For which, they say, you spirits oft walk in death,
Speak of it! (*The cock crows.*) Stay and speak!—Stop it,
    Marcellus.

MARCELLUS

Shall I strike at it with my partisan?    144

HORATIO    Do, if it will not stand.    [*They strike at it.*]

BERNARDO    'Tis here!    146

HORATIO    'Tis here!                        *Exit Ghost.*  147

---

**69 jump** exactly    **70 stalk** stride    **71 to work** i.e., to collect my thoughts and try to understand this    **72 gross and scope** general drift    **74 Good now** (An expression denoting entreaty or expostulation.)    **76 toils** causes to toil.    **subject** subjects    **77 cast** casting    **78 mart** shopping    **79 impress** impressment, conscription    **81 toward** in preparation    **87 Thereto . . . pride** (Refers to old Fortinbras, not the Danish King.)    **pricked on** incited.    **emulate** emulous, ambitious    **89 this . . . world** i.e., all Europe, the Western world    **90 sealed** certified, confirmed    **91 heraldry** chivalry    **93 seized** possessed    **94 Against the** in return for.    **moiety competent** corresponding portion    **95 gagèd** engaged, pledged.    **had returned** would have passed    **96 inheritance** possession    **97 cov'nant** i.e., the *sealed compact* of line 90    **98 carriage . . . designed** purport of the article referred to    **100 unimprovèd mettle** untried, undisciplined spirits    **101 skirts** outlying regions, outskirts    **102–4 Sharked . . . in't** rounded up (as a shark scoops up fish) a troop of restlessly ambitious younger sons lacking landed title to feed and supply an enterprise of considerable daring    **106 of us** from us    **107 compulsative** compulsatory

**110 head** source    **111 post-haste and rummage** frenetic activity and bustle    **113 Well . . . sort** That would explain why    **115 question** focus of contention    **116 mote** speck of dust    **117 palmy** flourishing    **118 Julius** Julius Caesar    **119 sheeted** shrouded    **121 As** (This abrupt transition suggests that matter is possibly omitted between lines 120 and 121.)    **stars** comets.    **trains** trails    **122 Disasters** unfavorable signs or aspects.    **moist star** i.e., moon, governing tides    **123 Neptune's . . . stands** the sea depends    **124 Was . . . eclipse** was eclipsed nearly to the cosmic darkness predicted for the second coming of Christ and the ending of the world. (See Matthew 24:29 and Revelation 6:12.)    **125 precurse** heralding, foreshadowing    **126 harbingers** forerunners.    **still** always    **127 omen** calamitous event    **129 climatures** climes, regions    **130 soft** i.e., enough, break off    **131 cross** stand in its path, confront.    **blast** wither, strike with a curse.    **131 s.d. his** its    **137 privy to** in on the secret of    **138 happily** haply, perchance    **144 partisan** long-handled spear.    **146–7 'Tis Here! / 'Tis here!** (Perhaps they attempt to strike at the Ghost, but are baffled by its seeming ability to be here and there and nowhere.)

MARCELLUS    'Tis gone.
We do it wrong, being so majestical,
To offer it the show of violence,
For it is as the air invulnerable,
And our vain blows malicious mockery.

BERNARDO
It was about to speak when the cock crew.

HORATIO
And then it started like a guilty thing
Upon a fearful summons. I have heard
The cock, that is the trumpet to the morn,    156
Doth with his lofty and shrill-sounding throat
Awake the god of day, and at his warning,
Whether in sea or fire, in earth or air,
Th'extravagant and erring spirit hies    160
To his confine; and of the truth herein
This present object made probation.    162

MARCELLUS
It faded on the crowing of the cock.
Some say that ever 'gainst that season comes    164
Wherein our Savior's birth is celebrated,
The bird of dawning singeth all night long,
And then, they say, no spirit can walk abroad;
The nights are wholesome, then no planets strike,    168
No fairy takes, nor witch hath power to charm,    169
So hallowed and so gracious is that time.    170

HORATIO
So have I heard and do in part believe it.
But, look, the morn in russet mantle clad    172
Walks o'er the dew of yon high eastward hill.
Break we our watch up, and by my advice
Let us impart what we have seen tonight
Unto young Hamlet; for upon my life,
This spirit, dumb to us, will speak to him.
Do you consent we shall acquaint him with it,
As needful in our loves, fitting our duty?

MARCELLUS
Let's do't, I pray, and I this morning know
Where we shall find him most conveniently.
                               *Exeunt.*

# [1.2]

*Flourish. Enter Claudius, King of Denmark,*
*Gertrude the Queen, [the] Council, as Polonius*
*and his son Laertes, Hamlet, cum aliis [including*
*Voltemand and Cornelius].*

KING
Though yet of Hamlet our dear brother's death    1
The memory be green, and that it us befitted
To bear our hearts in grief and our whole kingdom

To be contracted in one brow of woe,
Yet so far hath discretion fought with nature
That we with wisest sorrow think on him
Together with remembrance of ourselves.
Therefore our sometime sister, now our queen,    8
Th'imperial jointress to this warlike state,    9
Have we, as 'twere with a defeated joy—
With an auspicious an one dropping eye,    11
With mirth in funeral and with dirge in marriage,
In equal scale weighing delight and dole—    13
Taken to wife. Nor have we herein barred
Your better wisdoms, which have freely gone
With this affair along. For all, our thanks.
Now follows that you know young Fortinbras,    17
Holding a weak supposal of our worth,    18
Or thinking by our late dear brother's death
Our state to be disjoint and out of frame,    20
Co-leaguèd with this dream of his advantage,    21
He hath not failed to pester us with message
Importing the surrender of those lands    23
Lost by his father, with all bonds of law,    24
To our most valiant brother. So much for him.
Now for ourself and for this time of meeting.
Thus much the business is: we have here writ
To Norway, uncle of young Fortinbras—
Who, impotent and bed-rid, scarcely hears    29
Of this his nephew's purpose—to suppress
His further gait herein, in that the levies,    31
The lists, and full proportions are all made    32
Out of his subject; and we here dispatch    33
You, good Cornelius, and you, Voltemand,
For bearers of this greeting to old Norway,
Giving to you no further personal power
To business with the King more than the scope
Of these dilated articles allow.     *[He gives a paper.]*   38
Farewell, and let your haste commend your duty.    39

CORNELIUS, VOLTEMAND
In that, and all things, will we show our duty.

KING
We doubt it nothing. Heartily farewell.    41
                *Exeunt Voltemand and Cornelius.*
And now, Laertes, what's the news with you?
You told us of some suit; what is't, Laertes?
You cannot speak of reason to the Dane    44
And lose your voice. What wouldst thou beg, Laertes,    45
That shall not be my offer, not thy asking?
The head is not more native to the heart,    47

---

**156 trumpet** trumpeter    **160 extravagant and erring** wandering beyond bounds. (The words have similar meaning.)    **hies** hastens
**162 probation** proof.    **164 'gainst** just before    **168 strike** destroy by evil influence    **169 takes** bewitches.    **charm** cast a spell, control by enchantment    **170 gracious** full of grace    **172 russet** reddish brown
**1.2. Location: The castle.**
**0.1** *Flourish* Trumpet fanfare announcing the arrival of royalty, etc.
**0.2** *as* i.e., such as, including.    **0.3** *cum aliis* with others    **1 our** my. (The royal "we"; also in the following lines.)

**8 sometime** former    **9 jointress** woman possessing property with her husband    **11 With . . . eye** with one eye smiling and the other weeping    **13 dole** grief    **17 Now . . . know** Next, you need to be informed that    **18 weak supposal** low estimate    **20 disjoint . . . frame** in a state of total disorder    **21 Co-leaguèd . . . advantage** joined to his illusory sense of having the advantage over us and to his vision of future success    **23 Importing** having for its substance    **24 with . . . law** (See 1.1.91, "Well ratified by law and heraldry.")    **29 impotent** helpless    **31 His** i.e., Fortinbras'.    **gait** proceeding    **31–3 in that . . . subject** since the levying of troops and supplies is drawn entirely from the King of Norway's own subjects    **38 dilated** set out at length    **39 let . . . duty** let your swift obeying of orders, rather than mere words, express your dutifulness.    **41 nothing** not at all. **44 the Dane** the Danish king    **45 lose your voice** waste your speech. **47 native** closely connected, related

The hand more instrumental to the mouth,                                48
Than is the throne of Denmark to thy father.
What wouldst thou have, Laertes?

LAERTES                                           Dread my lord,        50
Your leave and favor to return to France,                               51
From whence though willingly I came to Denmark
To show my duty in your coronation,
Yet now I must confess, that duty done,
My thoughts and wishes bend again toward France
And bow them to your gracious leave and pardon.                         56

KING
Have you your father's leave? What says Polonius?

POLONIUS
H'ath, my lord, wrung from me my slow leave                             58
By laborsome petition, and at last
Upon his will I sealed my hard consent.                                 60
I do beseech you, give him leave to go.

KING
Take thy fair hour, Laertes. Time be thine,                             62
And thy best graces spend it at thy will.                               63
But now, my cousin Hamlet, and my son—                                  64

HAMLET
A little more than kin, and less than kind.                             65

KING
How is it that the clouds still hang on you?

HAMLET
Not so, my lord. I am too much i' th' sun.                              67

QUEEN
Good Hamlet, cast thy nighted color off,                                68
And let thine eye look like a friend on Denmark.                        69
Do not forever with thy vailèd lids                                     70
Seek for thy noble father in the dust.
Thou know'st 'tis common, all that lives must die,                      72
Passing through nature to eternity.

HAMLET
Ay, madam, it is common.

QUEEN                                             If it be,
Why seems it so particular with thee?                                   75

HAMLET
Seems, madam? Nay, it is. I know not "seems."
'Tis not alone my inky cloak, good mother,
Nor customary suits of solemn black,                                    78
Nor windy suspiration of forced breath,                                 79

No, nor the fruitful river in the eye,                                  80
Nor the dejected havior of the visage,                                  81
Together with all forms, moods, shapes of grief,                        82
That can denote me truly. These indeed seem,
For they are actions that a man might play.
But I have that within which passeth show;
These but the trappings and the suits of woe.

KING
'Tis sweet and commendable in your nature, Hamlet,
To give these mourning duties to your father.
But you must know your father lost a father,
That father lost, lost his, and the survivor bound
In filial obligation for some term
To do obsequious sorrow. But to persever                                92
In obstinate condolement is a course                                    93
Of impious stubbornness. 'Tis unmanly grief.
It shows a will most incorrect to heaven,
A heart unfortified, a mind impatient,                                  96
An understanding simple and unschooled.                                 97
For what we know must be and is as common
As any the most vulgar thing to sense,                                  99
Why should we in our peevish opposition
Take it to heart? Fie, 'tis a fault to heaven,
A fault against the dead, a fault to nature,
To reason most absurd, whose common theme
Is death of fathers, and who still hath cried,                          104
From the first corpse till he that died today,                          105
"This must be so." We pray you, throw to earth
This unprevailing woe and think of us                                   107
As of a father; for let the world take note,
You are the most immediate to our throne,                               109
And with no less nobility of love
Than that which dearest father bears his son
Do I impart toward you. For your intent                                 112
In going back to school in Wittenberg,                                  113
It is most retrograde to our desire,                                    114
And we beseech you bend you to remain                                   115
Here in the cheer and comfort of our eye,
Our chiefest courtier, cousin, and our son.

QUEEN
Let not thy mother lose her prayers, Hamlet.
I pray thee, stay with us, go not to Wittenberg.

HAMLET
I shall in all my best obey you, madam.                                 120

KING
Why, 'tis a loving and a fair reply.
Be as ourself in Denmark.—Madam, come.
This gentle and unforced accord of Hamlet
Sits smiling to my heart, in grace whereof                              124
No jocund health that Denmark drinks today                              125

---

**48 instrumental** serviceable    **50 Dread my lord** My revered lord
**51 leave and favor** kind permission    **56 bow . . . pardon** entreatingly
make a deep bow, asking your permission to depart.    **58 H'ath** He
has    **60 sealed** (as if sealing a legal document).    **hard** reluctant
**62 Take thy fair hour** Enjoy your time of youth    **63 And . . . will** and
may your time be spent in exercising your best qualities.    **64 cousin**
any kin not of the immediate family    **65 A little . . . kind** Too close a
blood relation, and yet we are less than kinsmen in that our relationship
lacks affection and is indeed unnatural. (Hamlet plays on *kind* as [1]
kindly [2] belonging to nature, suggesting that Claudius is not the same
kind of being as the rest of humanity. The line is often delivered as an
aside, though it need not be.)    **67 th' sun** i.e., the sunshine of the King's
royal favor. (With pun on *son*.)    **68 nighted color** (1) mourning garments
of black (2) dark melancholy    **69 Denmark** the King of Denmark.
**70 vailèd lids** lowered eyes    **72 common** of universal occurrence. (But
Hamlet plays on the sense of "vulgar" in line 74.)    **75 particular** personal    **78 customary** customary to mourning    **79 suspiration** sighing

**80 fruitful** abundant    **81 havior** expression    **82 moods** outward
expression of feeling    **92 obsequious** suited to obsequies or funerals
**93 condolement** sorrowing    **96 unfortified** i.e., against adversity
**97 simple** ignorant    **99 As . . . sense** as the most ordinary experience
**104 still** always    **105 the first corpse** (Abel's)    **107 unprevailing**
unavailing, useless    **109 most immediate** next in succession
**112 impart toward** liberally bestow on.    **For** As for    **113 to school** i.e.,
to your studies.    **Wittenberg** famous German university where Luther
posted his 95 theses in 1517    **114 retrograde** contrary    **115 bend you** to
incline yourself    **120 in all my best** to the best of my ability    **124 to** i.e.,
at.    **grace** thanksgiving    **125 jocund** merry

But the great cannon to the clouds shall tell,                     126
And the King's rouse the heavens shall bruit again,               127
Respeaking earthly thunder. Come, away.                           128
                    *Flourish. Exeunt all but Hamlet.*

HAMLET
Oh, that this too too solid flesh would melt,                     129
Thaw, and resolve itself into a dew!                              130
Or that the Everlasting had not fixed
His canon 'gainst self-slaughter! Oh, God, God,                   132
How weary, stale, flat, and unprofitable
Seem to me all the uses of this world!                            134
Fie on't, ah, fie! 'Tis an unweeded garden
That grows to seed. Things rank and gross in nature
Possess it merely. That it should come to this!                  137
But two months dead—nay, not so much, not two.
So excellent a king, that was to this                             139
Hyperion to a satyr, so loving to my mother                      140
That he might not beteem the winds of heaven                     141
Visit her face too roughly. Heaven and earth,
Must I remember? Why, she would hang on him
As if increase of appetite had grown
By what it fed on, and yet within a month—
Let me not think on't; frailty, thy name is woman!—
A little month, or ere those shoes were old                      147
With which she followed my poor father's body,
Like Niobe, all tears, why she, even she—                        149
Oh, God, a beast, that wants discourse of reason,               150
Would have mourned longer!—married with my
   uncle,
My father's brother, but no more like my father
Than I to Hercules. Within a month,
Ere yet the salt of most unrighteous tears
Had left the flushing in her gallèd eyes,                        155
She married. Oh, most wicked speed, to post                      156
With such dexterity to incestuous sheets!                        157
It is not, nor it cannot come to good.
But break, my heart, for I must hold my tongue.

*Enter Horatio, Marcellus, and Bernardo.*

HORATIO
Hail to Your Lordship!
HAMLET                          I am glad to see you well.
   Horatio!—or I do forget myself.
HORATIO
The same, my lord, and your poor servant ever.

HAMLET
Sir, my good friend; I'll change that name with you.    163
And what make you from Wittenberg, Horatio?—            164
   Marcellus.
MARCELLUS   My good lord.
HAMLET
I am very glad to see you. [*To Bernardo*] Good even,
   sir.—
But what in faith make you from Wittenberg?
HORATIO
A truant disposition, good my lord.
HAMLET
I would not have your enemy say so,
Nor shall you do my ear that violence                   171
To make it truster of your own report                   172
Against yourself. I know you are no truant.             173
But what is your affair in Elsinore?
We'll teach you to drink deep ere you depart.           175
HORATIO
My lord, I came to see your father's funeral.
HAMLET
I prithee, do not mock me, fellow student;
I think it was to see my mother's wedding.
HORATIO
Indeed, my lord, it followed hard upon.                 179
HAMLET
Thrift, thrift, Horatio! The funeral baked meats        180
Did coldly furnish forth the marriage tables.           181
Would I had met my dearest foe in heaven                182
Ere I had ever seen that day, Horatio!
My father!—Methinks I see my father.
HORATIO
Oh, where, my lord?
HAMLET                          In my mind's eye, Horatio.
HORATIO
I saw him once. 'A was a goodly king.                   186
HAMLET
'A was a man. Take him for all in all,
I shall not look upon his like again.
HORATIO
My lord, I think I saw him yesternight.
HAMLET   Saw? Who?
HORATIO   My lord, the King your father.
HAMLET   The King my father?
HORATIO
Season your admiration for a while                      193
With an attent ear till I may deliver,                  194
Upon the witness of these gentlemen,
This marvel to you.
HAMLET                          For God's love, let me hear!
HORATIO
Two nights together had these gentlemen,

126 **tell** sound, announce   127 **rouse** drinking of a draft of liquor.
**bruit again** loudly echo   128 **Respeaking earthly thunder** echoing
our salvos of trumpet and kettledrum, sounded when the King drinks;
see 1.4.8–12.   129 **solid** (The early quartos read "sallied"; the Folio,
"solid.")   130 **resolve** dissolve   132 **canon** law   134 **uses** customs,
doings   137 **merely** completely   139 **to this** in comparison with
Claudius   140 **Hyperion** Titan sun-god, father of Helios.   **satyr** a
lecherous creature of classical mythology, half-human but with a
goat's legs, tail, ears, and horns   141 **beteem** allow   147 **or ere** even
before   149 **Niobe** Tantalus's daughter, Queen of Thebes, who
boasted that she had more sons and daughters than Leto; for this,
Apollo and Artemis, children of Leto, slew her fourteen children. She
was turned by Zeus into a stone that continually dropped tears.
150 **wants . . . reason** lacks the faculty of reason   155 **gallèd** irritated,
inflamed   156 **post** hasten   157 **incestuous** (In Shakespeare's day, the
marriage of a man like Claudius to his deceased brother's wife was
considered incestuous.)

163 **change that name** i.e., give and receive reciprocally the name of
"friend" rather than talk of "servant." Or Hamlet may be saying, "No,
I am *your* servant."   164 **make you from** are you doing away from
171–3 **Nor . . . yourself** nor will I trust my own ears if they were to tell
me that you call yourself a *truant* or delinquent.   175 **to drink deep**
i.e., to accept our hospitality   179 **hard upon** in rapid succession.
180 **baked meats** meat pies   181 **coldly** i.e., as cold leftovers
182 **dearest** closest (and therefore deadliest)   186 **'A** He   193 **Season
your admiration** Moderate your astonishment   194 **attent** attentive

Marcellus and Bernardo, on their watch,
In the dead waste and middle of the night,                               199
Been thus encountered. A figure like your father,
Armed at all points, exactly, cap-à-pie,                                 201
Appears before them, and with solemn march
Goes slow and stately by them. Thrice he walked
By their oppressed and fear-surprisèd eyes
Within his truncheon's length, whilst they, distilled                    205
Almost to jelly with the act of fear,                                    206
Stand dumb and speak not to him. This to me
In dreadful secrecy impart they did,                                     208
And I with them the third night kept the watch,
Where, as they had delivered, both in time,
Form of the thing, each word made true and good,
The apparition comes. I knew your father;
These hands are not more like.

HAMLET                                  But where was this?        213

MARCELLUS
My lord, upon the platform where we watched.

HAMLET
Did you not speak to it?

HORATIO                        My lord, I did,
But answer made it none. Yet once methought
It lifted up it head and did address                                     217
Itself to motion, like as it would speak;                                218
But even then the morning cock crew loud,                                219
And at the sound it shrunk in haste away
And vanished from our sight.

HAMLET                                   'Tis very strange.

HORATIO
As I do live, my honored lord, 'tis true,
And we did think it writ down in our duty
To let you know of it.

HAMLET
Indeed, indeed, sirs. But this troubles me.
Hold you the watch tonight?

ALL                              We do, my lord.

HAMLET   Armed, say you?

ALL   Armed, my lord.

HAMLET   From top to toe?

ALL   My lord, from head to foot.

HAMLET   Then saw you not his face?

HORATIO
Oh, yes, my lord, he wore his beaver up.                                 232

HAMLET   What looked he, frowningly?                                     233

HORATIO
A countenance more in sorrow than in anger.

HAMLET   Pale or red?

HORATIO   Nay, very pale.

HAMLET   And fixed his eyes upon you?

HORATIO   Most constantly.

HAMLET   I would I had been there.

HORATIO   It would have much amazed you.

HAMLET   Very like, very like. Stayed it long?                          241

HORATIO
While one with moderate haste might tell a hundred.   242

MARCELLUS, BERNARDO   Longer, longer.

HORATIO   Not when I saw't.

HAMLET   His beard was grizzled—no?

HORATIO
It was, as I have seen it in his life,
A sable silvered.

HAMLET                       I will watch tonight.
Perchance 'twill walk again.

HORATIO                          I warr'nt it will.

HAMLET
If it assume my noble father's person,
I'll speak to it though hell itself should gape
And bid me hold my peace. I pray you all,
If you have hitherto concealed this sight,
Let it be tenable in your silence still,                    253
And whatsomever else shall hap tonight,
Give it an understanding but no tongue.
I will requite your loves. So, fare you well.
Upon the platform twixt eleven and twelve
I'll visit you.

ALL                Our duty to Your Honor.

HAMLET
Your loves, as mine to you. Farewell.                      259
                    Exeunt [all but Hamlet].
My father's spirit in arms! All is not well.
I doubt some foul play. Would the night were come!   261
Till then sit still, my soul. Foul deeds will rise,
Though all the earth o'erwhelm them, to men's eyes.
                                          Exit.

## [1.3]

*Enter Laertes and Ophelia, his sister.*

LAERTES   My necessaries are embarked. Farewell.          1
And, sister, as the winds give benefit
And convoy is assistant, do not sleep                      3
But let me hear from you.

OPHELIA                       Do you doubt that?           4

LAERTES
For Hamlet, and the trifling of his favor,                 5
Hold it a fashion and a toy in blood,                      6
A violet in the youth of primy nature,                     7
Forward, not permanent, sweet, not lasting,               8
The perfume and suppliance of a minute—                   9
No more.

OPHELIA   No more but so?

LAERTES                       Think it no more.

242 **tell** count   253 **tenable** held   259 **Your loves** i.e., Say "Your loves" to me, not just your "duty."   261 **doubt** suspect
**1.3. Location:** Polonius's chambers.
1 **embarked** loaded on board.   3 **convoy is assistant** means of conveyance are available   4 **But let** without letting   5 **For** As for   6 **toy in blood** passing amorous fancy   7 **primy** in its prime, springtime
8 **Forward** precocious   9 **suppliance** pastime, something to fill the time

For nature crescent does not grow alone 11
In thews and bulk, but as this temple waxes 12
The inward service of the mind and soul 13
Grows wide withal. Perhaps he loves you now, 14
And now no soil nor cautel doth besmirch 15
The virtue of his will; but you must fear, 16
His greatness weighed, his will is not his own. 17
For he himself is subject to his birth.
He may not, as unvalued persons do,
Carve for himself, for on his choice depends 20
The safety and health of this whole state,
And therefore must his choice be circumscribed
Unto the voice and yielding of that body 23
Whereof he is the head. Then if he says he loves you,
It fits your wisdom so far to believe it
As he in his particular act and place 26
May give his saying deed, which is no further
Than the main voice of Denmark goes withal. 28
Then weigh what loss your honor may sustain
If with too credent ear you list his songs, 30
Or lose your heart, or your chaste treasure open
To his unmastered importunity. 32
Fear it, Ophelia, fear it, my dear sister,
And keep you in the rear of your affection, 34
Out of the shot and danger of desire.
The chariest maid is prodigal enough 36
If she unmask her beauty to the moon. 37
Virtue itself scapes not calumnious strokes.
The canker galls the infants of the spring 39
Too oft before their buttons be disclosed, 40
And in the morn and liquid dew of youth 41
Contagious blastments are most imminent. 42
Be wary then; best safety lies in fear.
Youth to itself rebels, though none else near. 44

OPHELIA
I shall the effect of this good lesson keep
As watchman to my heart. But, good my brother,
Do not, as some ungracious pastors do, 47
Show me the steep and thorny way to heaven,
Whilst like a puffed and reckless libertine 49
Himself the primrose path of dalliance treads,
And recks not his own rede.

*Enter Polonius.*

LAERTES                    Oh, fear me not. 51

11–14 For nature . . . withal For nature, as it ripens, does not grow only in physical strength, but as the body matures the inner qualities of mind and soul grow along with it. (Laertes warns Ophelia that Hamlet's mind and soul may change as his body ages.)  15 soil nor cautel blemish nor deceit  16 The . . . will the purity of his desire  17 His greatness weighed taking into account his high fortune  20 Carve i.e., choose  23 voice and yielding assent, approval  26 in . . . place in his particular restricted circumstances  28 main voice general assent.  withal along with.  30 credent credulous.  list listen to  32 unmastered uncontrolled  34 keep . . . affection don't advance as far as your affection might lead you. (A military metaphor.)  36 chariest most scrupulously modest  37 If she unmask if she does no more than show her beauty.  moon (Symbol of chastity.)  39 canker galls cankerworm destroys  40 buttons be disclosed buds be opened  41 liquid dew i.e., time when dew is fresh and bright  42 blastments blights  44 Youth . . . rebels Youth yields to the rebellion of the flesh  47 ungracious ungodly  49 puffed bloated, or swollen with pride  51 recks heeds.  rede counsel.  fear me not don't worry on my account.

I stay too long. But here my father comes.
A double blessing is a double grace; 53
Occasion smiles upon a second leave. 54
POLONIUS
Yet here, Laertes? Aboard, aboard, for shame!
The wind sits in the shoulder of your sail, 56
And you are stayed for. There—my blessing with thee!
And these few precepts in thy memory
Look thou character. Give thy thoughts no tongue, 59
Nor any unproportioned thought his act. 60
Be thou familiar, but by no means vulgar. 61
Those friends thou hast, and their adoption tried, 62
Grapple them to thy soul with hoops of steel,
But do not dull thy palm with entertainment 64
Of each new-hatched, unfledged comrade. Beware 65
Of entrance to a quarrel, but being in,
Bear't that th'opposèd may beware of thee. 67
Give every man thy ear, but few thy voice;
Take each man's censure, but reserve thy judgment. 69
Costly thy habit as thy purse can buy, 70
But not expressed in fancy; rich, not gaudy, 71
For the apparel oft proclaims the man,
And they in France of the best rank and station
Are of all most select and generous chief in that. 74
Neither a borrower nor a lender be,
For loan oft loses both itself and friend,
And borrowing dulleth edge of husbandry. 77
This above all: to thine own self be true,
And it must follow, as the night the day,
Thou canst not then be false to any man.
Farewell. My blessing season this in thee! 81
LAERTES
Most humbly do I take my leave, my lord.
POLONIUS
The time invites you. Go, your servants tend. 83
LAERTES
Farewell, Ophelia, and remember well
What I have said to you.
OPHELIA   'Tis in my memory locked,
And you yourself shall keep the key of it.
LAERTES   Farewell.                    *Exit Laertes.*
POLONIUS
What is't, Ophelia, he hath said to you?
OPHELIA
So please you, something touching the Lord Hamlet. 90
POLONIUS   Marry, well bethought. 91
'Tis told me he hath very oft of late
Given private time to you, and you yourself

53–4 A double . . . leave The goddess Occasion or Opportunity smiles on the happy circumstance of being able to say good-bye twice and thus receive a second blessing.  56 The wind . . . sail i.e., You have a favorable wind  59 Look thou character see to it that you inscribe.  60 unproportioned badly calculated, intemperate.  his its  61 familiar sociable.  vulgar common.  62 and . . . tried and their suitability to be your friends having been put to the test  64 dull thy palm i.e., shake hands so often as to make the gesture meaningless  67 Bear't that manage it so that  69 censure opinion, judgment  70 habit clothing  71 fancy excessive ornament, decadent fashion  74 Are . . . that are of a most refined and well-bred preeminence in choosing what to wear.  77 husbandry thrift.  81 season mature  83 tend attend, wait.  90 So please you If you please.  touching concerning  91 Marry i.e., By the Virgin Mary. (A mild oath.)

Have of your audience been most free and bounteous.
If it be so—as so 'tis put on me, 95
And that in way of caution—I must tell you
You do not understand yourself so clearly
As it behooves my daughter and your honor. 98
What is between you? Give me up the truth.

OPHELIA
He hath, my lord, of late made many tenders 100
Of his affection to me.

POLONIUS
Affection? Pooh! You speak like a green girl,
Unsifted in such perilous circumstance. 103
Do you believe his tenders, as you call them?

OPHELIA
I do not know, my lord, what I should think.

POLONIUS
Marry, I'll teach you. Think yourself a baby
That you have ta'en these tenders for true pay
Which are not sterling. Tender yourself more dearly, 108
Or—not to crack the wind of the poor phrase, 109
Running it thus—you'll tender me a fool. 110

OPHELIA
My lord, he hath importuned me with love
In honorable fashion.

POLONIUS
Ay, fashion you may call it. Go to, go to. 113

OPHELIA
And hath given countenance to his speech, my lord, 114
With almost all the holy vows of heaven.

POLONIUS
Ay, springes to catch woodcocks. I do know, 116
When the blood burns, how prodigal the soul 117
Lends the tongue vows. These blazes, daughter,
Giving more light than heat, extinct in both 119
Even in their promise as it is a-making, 120
You must not take for fire. From this time, daughter,
Be something scanter of your maiden presence. 122
Set your entreatments at a higher rate 123
Than a command to parley. For Lord Hamlet, 124
Believe so much in him that he is young, 125
And with a larger tether may he walk
Than may be given you. In few, Ophelia, 127
Do not believe his vows, for they are brokers, 128
Not of that dye which their investments show, 129
But mere implorators of unholy suits, 130

Breathing like sanctified and pious bawds, 131
The better to beguile. This is for all: 132
I would not, in plain terms, from this time forth
Have you so slander any moment leisure 134
As to give words or talk with the Lord Hamlet.
Look to 't, I charge you. Come your ways. 136

OPHELIA    I shall obey, my lord.        *Exeunt.*

❖

## [1.4]

*Enter Hamlet, Horatio, and Marcellus.*

HAMLET    The air bites shrewdly; it is very cold. 1

HORATIO
It is a nipping and an eager air. 2

HAMLET
What hour now?

HORATIO                I think it lacks of twelve. 3

MARCELLUS
No, it is struck.

HORATIO    Indeed? I heard it not.
It then draws near the season 5
Wherein the spirit held his wont to walk. 6
        *A flourish of trumpets, and two pieces goes off*
                                    [*within*].
What does this mean, my lord?

HAMLET
The King doth wake tonight and takes his rouse, 8
Keeps wassail, and the swagg'ring upspring reels; 9
And as he drains his drafts of Rhenish down, 10
The kettledrum and trumpet thus bray out
The triumph of his pledge.

HORATIO                Is it a custom? 12

HAMLET    Ay, marry, is 't,
But to my mind, though I am native here
And to the manner born, it is a custom 15
More honored in the breach than the observance. 16
This heavy-headed revel east and west 17
Makes us traduced and taxed of other nations. 18
They clepe us drunkards, and with swinish phrase 19
Soil our addition; and indeed it takes 20
From our achievements, though performed at height, 21
The pith and marrow of our attribute. 22

---

95 **put on** impressed on, told to    98 **behooves** befits    100 **tenders** offers    103 **Unsifted** i.e., untried    108 **sterling** legal currency.    **Tender . . . dearly** (1) Bargain for your favors at a higher rate—i.e., hold out for marriage (2) Show greater care of yourself    109 **crack the wind** i.e., run it until it is broken-winded    110 **tender . . . fool** (1) make a fool of me (2) present me with a *fool* or baby.    113 **fashion** mere form, pretense.    **Go to** (An expression of impatience.)    114 **countenance** credit, confirmation    116 **springes** snares.    **woodcocks** birds easily caught; here used to connote gullibility.    117 **prodigal** prodigally    119–20 **extinct . . . a-making** i.e., lacking any true warmth of affection even from the very moment when these vows were uttered    122 **something** somewhat    123–4 **Set . . . parley** i.e., As defender of your chastity, negotiate for something better than a surrender simply because the besieger requests an interview.    124 **For** As for    125 **so . . . him** this much concerning him    127 **In few** Briefly    128 **brokers** go-betweens, procurers    129 **dye** color or sort.    **investments** clothes. (The vows are not what they seem.)    130 **mere implorators** out-and-out solicitors

131 **Breathing** speaking    132 **for all** once for all, in sum    134 **slander** abuse, misuse.    **moment** moment's    136 **Come your ways** Come along.
**1.4. Location: The guard platform.**
1 **shrewdly** keenly, sharply    2 **eager** biting    3 **lacks of** is just short of    5 **season** time    6 **held his wont** was accustomed    6.1 *pieces* i.e., of ordnance, cannon    8 **wake** stay awake and hold revel.    **takes his rouse** carouses    9 **Keeps . . . reels** carouses, and riotously dances a German dance called the upspring    10 **Rhenish** Rhine wine    12 **The triumph . . . pledge** the celebration of his offering a toast.    15 **manner** custom (of drinking)    16 **More . . . observance** better neglected than followed.    17 **east and west** i.e., everywhere    18 **taxed of** censured by    19 **clepe** call.    **with swinish phrase** i.e., by calling us swine    20 **addition** reputation    21 **at height** outstandingly    22 **The pith . . . attribute** the most essential part of the esteem that should be attributed to us.

So, oft it chances in particular men,
That for some vicious mole of nature in them,                    24
As in their birth—wherein they are not guilty,
Since nature cannot choose his origin—                           26
By the o'ergrowth of some complexion,                            27
Oft breaking down the pales and forts of reason,                 28
Or by some habit that too much o'erleavens                       29
The form of plausive manners, that these men,                    30
Carrying, I say, the stamp of one defect,
Being nature's livery or fortune's star,                         32
His virtues else, be they as pure as grace,                      33
As infinite as man may undergo,                                  34
Shall in the general censure take corruption                     35
From that particular fault. The dram of evil                     36
Doth all the noble substance often dout                          37
To his own scandal.

       *Enter Ghost.*

HORATIO           Look, my lord, it comes!    38
HAMLET
Angels and ministers of grace defend us!                         39
Be thou a spirit of health or goblin damned,                     40
Bring with thee airs from heaven or blasts from hell,            41
Be thy intents wicked or charitable,                             42
Thou com'st in such a questionable shape                         43
That I will speak to thee. I'll call thee Hamlet,
King, father, royal Dane. Oh, answer me!
Let me not burst in ignorance, but tell
Why thy canonized bones, hearsèd in death,                       47
Have burst their cerements; why the sepulcher                    48
Wherein we saw thee quietly inurned                              49
Hath oped his ponderous and marble jaws
To cast thee up again. What may this mean,
That thou, dead corpse, again in complete steel,                 52
Revisits thus the glimpses of the moon,                          53
Making night hideous, and we fools of nature                     54
So horridly to shake our disposition                             55
With thoughts beyond the reaches of our souls?
Say, why is this? Wherefore? What should we do?
        *[The] Ghost beckons Hamlet.*

HORATIO
It beckons you to go away with it,
As if it some impartment did desire                              59
To you alone.
MARCELLUS     Look with what courteous action
It wafts you to a more removèd ground.
But do not go with it.
HORATIO           No, by no means.
HAMLET
It will not speak. Then I will follow it.
HORATIO
Do not, my lord!
HAMLET        Why, what should be the fear?
I do not set my life at a pin's fee,                             65
And for my soul, what can it do to that,                         66
Being a thing immortal as itself?
It waves me forth again. I'll follow it.
HORATIO
What if it tempt you toward the flood, my lord,                  69
Or to the dreadful summit of the cliff
That beetles o'er his base into the sea,                         71
And there assume some other horrible form
Which might deprive your sovereignty of reason                   73
And draw you into madness? Think of it.
The very place puts toys of desperation,                         75
Without more motive, into every brain
That looks so many fathoms to the sea
And hears it roar beneath.
HAMLET
It wafts me still.—Go on, I'll follow thee.
MARCELLUS
You shall not go, my lord.    *[They try to stop him.]*
HAMLET             Hold off your hands!
HORATIO
Be ruled. You shall not go.
HAMLET              My fate cries out,    81
And makes each petty artery in this body                         82
As hardy as the Nemean lion's nerve.                             83
Still am I called. Unhand me, gentlemen.
By heaven, I'll make a ghost of him that lets me!                85
I say, away!—Go on, I'll follow thee.
        *Exeunt Ghost and Hamlet.*
HORATIO
He waxes desperate with imagination.
MARCELLUS
Let's follow. 'Tis not fit thus to obey him.
HORATIO
Have after. To what issue will this come?                        89
MARCELLUS
Something is rotten in the state of Denmark.

---

**24 for . . . mole** on account of some natural defect in their constitutions   **26 his** its   **27 the o'ergrowth . . . complexion** the excessive growth in individuals of some natural trait   **28 pales** palings, fences (as of a fortification)   **29–30 o'erleavens . . . manners** i.e., infects the way we should behave (much as bad yeast spoils the dough). *Plausive* means "pleasing."   **32 Being . . . star** (that stamp of defect) being a sign identifying one as wearing the livery of, and hence being the servant to, nature (unfortunate inherited qualities) or fortune (mischance)   **33 His virtues else** i.e., the other qualities of *these men* (line 30)   **34 may undergo** can sustain   **35 in . . . censure** in overall appraisal, in people's opinion generally   **36–8 The dram . . . scandal** i.e., The small drop of evil blots out or works against the noble substance of the whole and brings it into disrepute. (To *dout* is to blot out. A famous crux.)   **39 ministers of grace** messengers of God   **40 Be . . . health** Whether you are a good angel   **41 Bring** whether you bring   **42 Be thy intents** whether your intentions are   **43 questionable** inviting question   **47 canonized** buried according to the canons of the church.   **hearsèd** coffined   **48 cerements** grave clothes   **49 inurned** entombed   **52 complete steel** full armor   **53 the glimpses . . . moon** i.e., the sublunary world, all that is beneath the moon   **54 fools of nature** mere mortals, limited to natural knowledge and subject to nature   **55 So . . . disposition** to distress our mental composure so violently

**59 impartment** communication   **65 fee** value   **66 for** as for   **69 flood** sea   **71 beetles o'er** overhangs threateningly (like bushy eyebrows).   **his** its   **73 deprive . . . reason** take away the rule of reason over your mind   **75 toys of desperation** fancies of desperate acts, i.e., suicide   **81 My fate cries out** My destiny summons me   **82 petty** weak.   **artery** blood vessel system through which the vital spirits were thought to have been conveyed   **83 As . . . nerve** as a sinew of the huge lion slain by Hercules as the first of his twelve labors.   **85 lets** hinders   **89 Have after** Let's go after him.   **issue** outcome

**HORATIO**
Heaven will direct it.
**MARCELLUS** Nay, let's follow him. *Exeunt.* 91

❖

# [1.5]

*Enter Ghost and Hamlet.*

**HAMLET**
Whither wilt thou lead me? Speak. I'll go no further.
**GHOST**
Mark me.
**HAMLET** I will.
**GHOST** My hour is almost come,
When I to sulf'rous and tormenting flames
Must render up myself.
**HAMLET** Alas, poor ghost!
**GHOST**
Pity me not, but lend thy serious hearing
To what I shall unfold.
**HAMLET** Speak. I am bound to hear. 7
**GHOST**
So art thou to revenge, when thou shalt hear.
**HAMLET** What?
**GHOST** I am thy father's spirit,
Doomed for a certain term to walk the night,
And for the day confined to fast in fires, 12
Till the foul crimes done in my days of nature 13
Are burnt and purged away. But that I am forbid 14
To tell the secrets of my prison house,
I could a tale unfold whose lightest word
Would harrow up thy soul, freeze thy young blood, 17
Make thy two eyes like stars start from their spheres, 18
Thy knotted and combinèd locks to part, 19
And each particular hair to stand on end
Like quills upon the fretful porcupine.
But this eternal blazon must not be 22
To ears of flesh and blood. List, Hamlet, oh, list!
If thou didst ever thy dear father love—
**HAMLET** O God!
**GHOST**
Revenge his foul and most unnatural murder.
**HAMLET** Murder?
**GHOST**
Murder most foul, as in the best it is, 28
But this most foul, strange, and unnatural.
**HAMLET**
Haste me to know't, that I, with wings as swift
As meditation or the thoughts of love,
May sweep to my revenge.
**GHOST** I find thee apt;

And duller shouldst thou be than the fat weed 33
That rots itself in ease on Lethe wharf, 34
Wouldst thou not stir in this. Now, Hamlet, hear.
'Tis given out that, sleeping in my orchard, 36
A serpent stung me. So the whole ear of Denmark
Is by a forgèd process of my death 38
Rankly abused. But know, thou noble youth, 39
The serpent that did sting thy father's life
Now wears his crown.
**HAMLET** Oh, my prophetic soul! My uncle!
**GHOST**
Ay, that incestuous, that adulterate beast, 43
With witchcraft of his wit, with traitorous gifts— 44
Oh, wicked wit and gifts, that have the power
So to seduce!—won to his shameful lust
The will of my most seeming-virtuous queen.
Oh, Hamlet, what a falling off was there!
From me, whose love was of that dignity
That it went hand in hand even with the vow 50
I made to her in marriage, and to decline
Upon a wretch whose natural gifts were poor
To those of mine! 53
But virtue, as it never will be moved, 54
Though lewdness court it in a shape of heaven, 55
So lust, though to a radiant angel linked,
Will sate itself in a celestial bed 57
And prey on garbage.
But soft, methinks I scent the morning's air. 59
Brief let me be. Sleeping within my orchard,
My custom always of the afternoon,
Upon my secure hour thy uncle stole, 62
With juice of cursèd hebona in a vial, 63
And in the porches of my ears did pour 64
The leperous distillment, whose effect 65
Holds such an enmity with blood of man
That swift as quicksilver it courses through 67
The natural gates and alleys of the body, 68
And with a sudden vigor it doth posset 69
And curd, like eager droppings into milk, 70
The thin and wholesome blood. So did it mine,
And a most instant tetter barked about, 72
Most lazar-like, with vile and loathsome crust, 73
All my smooth body.
Thus was I, sleeping, by a brother's hand
Of life, of crown, of queen at once dispatched, 76

---

**91 it** i.e., the outcome.
**1.5. Location: The battlements of the castle.**
**7 bound** (1) ready (2) obligated by duty and fate. (The Ghost, in line 8, answers in the second sense.)   **12 fast** do penance by fasting
**13 crimes** sins.   **of nature** as a mortal   **14 But that** Were it not that
**17 harrow up** lacerate, tear   **18 spheres** i.e., eye-sockets, here compared to the orbits or transparent revolving spheres in which, according to Ptolemaic astronomy, the heavenly bodies were fixed
**19 knotted . . . locks** hair neatly arranged and confined   **22 eternal blazon** revelation of the secrets of eternity   **28 in the best** even at best

**33 shouldst thou be** you would have to be.   **fat** torpid, lethargic
**34 Lethe** the river of forgetfulness in Hades   **36 'Tis given out** The official story goes.   **orchard** garden   **38 forgèd process** falsified account   **39 abused** deceived.   **43 adulterate** adulterous   **44 gifts** (1) talents (2) presents   **50 even with the vow** with the very vow   **53 To** compared with   **54 virtue, as it** just as virtue   **55 shape of heaven** heavenly form   **57 sate . . . bed** gratify its lustful appetite to the point of revulsion or ennui, even in a virtuously lawful marriage   **59 soft** wait a minute, hold on   **62 secure hour** time of being free from worries and threats   **63 hebona** a poison. (The word seems to be a form of *ebony*, though it is thought perhaps to be related to *henbane*, a poison, or to *ebenus*, "yew.")   **64 porches** gateways   **65 leperous distillment** distillation causing leprosylike disfigurement   **67 quicksilver** mercury   **68 gates** entry ways   **69–70 posset . . . curd** coagulate and curdle   **70 eager** sour, acid   **72 tetter** eruption of scabs.   **barked** covered with a rough covering, like bark on a tree   **73 lazar-like** leperlike
**76 dispatched** suddenly deprived

Cut off even in the blossoms of my sin,    77
Unhouseled, disappointed, unaneled,    78
No reck'ning made, but sent to my account    79
With all my imperfections on my head.
Oh, horrible! Oh, horrible, most horrible!
If thou hast nature in thee, bear it not.    82
Let not the royal bed of Denmark be
A couch for luxury and damnèd incest.    84
But, howsomever thou pursues this act,
Taint not thy mind nor let thy soul contrive
Against thy mother aught. Leave her to heaven
And to those thorns that in her bosom lodge,
To prick and sting her. Fare thee well at once.
The glowworm shows the matin to be near,    90
And 'gins to pale his uneffectual fire.    91
Adieu, adieu, Hamlet! Remember me.    [*Exit.*]
HAMLET
O all you host of heaven! O earth! What else?
And shall I couple hell? Oh, fie! Hold, hold, my heart,    94
And you, my sinews, grow not instant old,    95
But bear me stiffly up. Remember thee?
Ay, thou poor ghost, whiles memory holds a seat
In this distracted globe. Remember thee?    98
Yea, from the table of my memory    99
I'll wipe away all trivial fond records,    100
All saws of books, all forms, all pressures past    101
That youth and observation copied there,
And thy commandment all alone shall live
Within the book and volume of my brain,
Unmixed with baser matter. Yes, yes, by heaven!
Oh, most pernicious woman!
Oh, villain, villain, smiling, damnèd villain!
My tables, my tables—meet it is I set it down    108
That one may smile, and smile, and be a villain.
At least I am sure it may be so in Denmark.
So, uncle, there you are. Now to my word:    111
It is "Adieu, adieu! Remember me."
I have sworn't.

*Enter Horatio and Marcellus.*

HORATIO    My lord, my lord!
MARCELLUS    Lord Hamlet!
HORATIO    Heavens secure him!    116
HAMLET    So be it.
MARCELLUS    Illo, ho, ho, my lord!
HAMLET    Hillo, ho, ho, boy! Come, bird, come.    119
MARCELLUS    How is't, my noble lord?

HORATIO    What news, my lord?
HAMLET    Oh, wonderful!
HORATIO    Good my lord, tell it.
HAMLET    No, you'll reveal it.
HORATIO    Not I, my lord, by heaven.
MARCELLUS    Nor I, my lord.
HAMLET
How say you, then, would heart of man once think it?    127
But you'll be secret?
HORATIO, MARCELLUS    Ay, by heaven, my lord.
HAMLET
There's ne'er a villain dwelling in all Denmark
But he's an arrant knave.    130
HORATIO
There needs no ghost, my lord, come from the grave
To tell us this.
HAMLET    Why, right, you are i' th' right.
And so, without more circumstance at all,    133
I hold it fit that we shake hands and part,
You as your business and desires shall point you—
For every man hath business and desire,
Such as it is—and for my own poor part,
Look you, I'll go pray.
HORATIO
These are but wild and whirling words, my lord.
HAMLET
I am sorry they offend you, heartily;
Yes, faith, heartily.
HORATIO    There's no offense, my lord.
HAMLET
Yes, by Saint Patrick, but there is, Horatio,    142
And much offense too. Touching this vision here,    143
It is an honest ghost, that let me tell you.    144
For your desire to know what is between us,    145
O'ermaster't as you may. And now, good friends,
As you are friends, scholars, and soldiers,
Give me one poor request.
HORATIO    What is't, my lord? We will.
HAMLET
Never make known what you have seen tonight.
HORATIO, MARCELLUS    My lord, we will not.
HAMLET    Nay, but swear't.
HORATIO    In faith, my lord, not I.    153
MARCELLUS    Nor I, my lord, in faith.
HAMLET    Upon my sword.    [*He holds out his sword.*]    155
MARCELLUS    We have sworn, my lord, already.    156
HAMLET    Indeed, upon my sword, indeed.
GHOST    (*cries under the stage*) Swear.
HAMLET
Ha, ha, boy, say'st thou so? Art thou there, truepenny?    159

**77 blossoms** full flowering    **78 Unhouseled . . . unaneled** without having received the Sacrament or other last rites including confession, absolution, and the holy oil of extreme unction    **79 reck'ning** settling of accounts    **82 nature** i.e., the promptings of a son    **84 luxury** lechery    **90 matin** morning    **91 his** its    **94 couple** add.    **Hold** Hold together    **95 sinews** tendons, muscles.    **instant** instantly    **98 globe** (1) head (2) world (3) Globe Theater.    **99 table** tablet, slate    **100 fond** foolish    **101 All . . . past** all wise sayings, all shapes or images imprinted on the tablets of my memory, all past impressions    **108 My tables . . . down** (Editors often specify that Hamlet makes a note in his writing tablet, but he may simply mean that he is making a mental observation of lasting impression.)    **111 there you are** i.e., there, I've noted that against you.    **116 secure him** keep him safe.    **119 Hillo . . . come** (A falconer's call to a hawk in air. Hamlet mocks the hallooing as though it were a part of hawking.)

**127 once** ever    **130 But . . . knave** (Hamlet jokingly gives a self-evident answer: every villain is a thoroughgoing knave.)    **133 circumstance** ceremony, elaboration    **142 Saint Patrick** the keeper of Purgatory    **143 offense** (Hamlet deliberately changes Horatio's "no offense taken" to "an offense against all decency.")    **Touching** Concerning, with regard to    **144 honest** genuine    **145 For** As for, regarding    **153 In faith . . . I** i.e., I swear not to tell what I have seen. (Horatio is not refusing to swear.)    **155 sword** i.e., the hilt in the form of a cross.    **156 We . . . already** i.e., We swore *in faith*.    **159 truepenny** honest old fellow.

Come on, you hear this fellow in the cellarage.
Consent to swear.
HORATIO                    Propose the oath, my lord.
HAMLET
Never to speak of this that you have seen,
Swear by my sword.
GHOST [*beneath*]    Swear.                    [*They swear.*] 164
HAMLET
*Hic et ubique?* Then we'll shift our ground.          165
                        [*He moves to another spot.*]
Come hither, gentlemen,
And lay your hands again upon my sword.
Never to speak of this that you have heard,
Swear by my sword.
GHOST [*beneath*]    Swear by his sword.        [*They swear.*]
HAMLET
Well said, old mole. Canst work i'th'earth so fast?
A worthy pioneer!—Once more remove, good friends. 172
                        [*They move again.*]
HORATIO
Oh, day and night, but this is wondrous strange!
HAMLET
And therefore as a stranger give it welcome.          174
There are more things in heaven and earth, Horatio,
Than are dreamt of in your philosophy.                176
But come;
Here, as before, never, so help you mercy,            178
How strange or odd some'er I bear myself—
As I perchance hereafter shall think meet
To put an antic disposition on—                       181
That you, at such times seeing me, never shall,
With arms encumbered thus, or this headshake,         183
Or by pronouncing of some doubtful phrase
As "Well, we know," or "We could, an if we would,"    185
Or "If we list to speak," or "There be, an if they
   might,"                                            186
Or such ambiguous giving out, to note               187
That you know aught of me—this not to do,           188
So grace and mercy at your most need help you, swear.
GHOST [*beneath*]    Swear.               [*They swear.*]
HAMLET
Rest, rest, perturbèd spirit!—So, gentlemen,
With all my love I do commend me to you;              192
And what so poor a man as Hamlet is
May do t'express his love and friending to you,       194
God willing, shall not lack. Let us go in together,   195
And still your fingers on your lips, I pray.          196

The time is out of joint. Oh, cursèd spite            197
That ever I was born to set it right!
                        [*They wait for him to leave first.*]
Nay, come, let's go together.              *Exeunt.* 199

                        ❖

## [2.1]

*Enter old Polonius with his man [Reynaldo].*

POLONIUS
Give him this money and these notes, Reynaldo.
                        [*He gives money and papers.*]
REYNALDO    I will, my lord.
POLONIUS
You shall do marv'lous wisely, good Reynaldo,          3
Before you visit him, to make inquire                  4
Of his behavior.
REYNALDO            My lord, I did intend it.
POLONIUS
Marry, well said, very well said. Look you, sir,       6
Inquire me first what Danskers are in Paris,           7
And how, and who, what means, and where they
   keep,                                               8
What company, at what expense; and finding
By this encompassment and drift of question           10
That they do know my son, come you more nearer        11
Than your particular demands will touch it.           12
Take you, as 'twere, some distant knowledge of him,   13
As thus, "I know his father and his friends,
And in part him." Do you mark this, Reynaldo?
REYNALDO    Ay, very well, my lord.
POLONIUS
"And in part him, but," you may say, "not well.
But if't be he I mean, he's very wild,
Addicted so and so," and there put on him             19
What forgeries you please—marry, none so rank         20
As may dishonor him, take heed of that,
But, sir, such wanton, wild, and usual slips          22
As are companions noted and most known
To youth and liberty.
REYNALDO    As gaming, my lord.                        25
POLONIUS    Ay, or drinking, fencing, swearing, Quarrel-
ing, drabbing—you may go so far.                       27
REYNALDO    My lord, that would dishonor him.
POLONIUS
Faith, no, as you may season it in the charge.        29
You must not put another scandal on him
That he is open to incontinency;                      31

---

**164 s.d. *They swear*** (Seemingly they swear here, and at lines 170 and
190, as they lay their hands on Hamlet's sword. Triple oaths would
have particular force; these three oaths deal with what they have
seen, what they have heard, and what they promise about Hamlet's
*antic disposition.*)    **165 *Hic et ubique?*** Here and everywhere? (Latin.)
**172 pioneer** foot soldier assigned to dig tunnels and excavations.
**174 as a stranger** i.e., needing your hospitality    **176 your philosophy**
this subject that is called "natural philosophy" or "science." (*Your* is
not personal.)    **178 so help you mercy** as you hope for God's mercy
when you are judged    **181 antic** grotesque, strange    **183 encumbered** folded    **185 an if** if    **186 list** wished.    **There . . . might** There
are those who could talk if they were at liberty to do so    **187 giving
out** utterance.    **note** indicate    **188 aught** anything    **192 commend . . .
you** give you my best wishes    **194 friending** friendliness    **195 lack**
be lacking.    **196 still** always

**197 out of joint** in utter disorder.    **199 let's go together** (Probably
they wait for him to leave first, but he refuses this ceremoniousness.)
**2.1. Location: Polonius's chambers.**
**3 marv'lous** marvelously    **4 inquire** inquiry    **6 Marry** i.e., By the Virgin Mary. (A mild oath.)    **7 Inquire me** Inquire on my behalf. (The
"me" is colloquial.)    **Danskers** Danes    **8 how** how they live.    **what
means** what wealth (they have).    **keep** dwell    **10 encompassment . . .
question** roundabout way of questioning    **11–12 come . . . it** you will
find out more this way than by asking pointed questions (*particular
demands*).    **13 Take you** Assume, pretend    **19 put on** impute to
**20 forgeries** invented tales.    **rank** gross    **22 wanton** sportive, unrestrained    **25 gaming** gambling    **27 drabbing** whoring    **29 season**
temper, soften    **31 incontinency** habitual sexual excess

That's not my meaning. But breathe his faults so
    quaintly                                         32
That they may seem the taints of liberty,    33
The flash and outbreak of a fiery mind,
A savageness in unreclaimèd blood,    35
Of general assault.    36
REYNALDO    But, my good lord—
POLONIUS    Wherefore should you do this?
REYNALDO    Ay, my lord, I would know that.
POLONIUS    Marry, sir, here's my drift,    41
And I believe it is a fetch of warrant.    42
You laying these slight sullies on my son,    43
As 'twere a thing a little soiled i' th' working,
Mark you,
Your party in converse, him you would sound,    45
Having ever seen in the prenominate crimes    46
The youth you breathe of guilty, be assured    47
He closes with you in this consequence:    48
"Good sir," or so, or "friend," or "gentleman,"
According to the phrase or the addition    50
Of man and country.
REYNALDO            Very good, my lord.
POLONIUS    And then, sir, does 'a this—'a does—what
was I about to say? By the Mass, I was about to say
something. Where did I leave?    54
REYNALDO    At "closes in the consequence."
POLONIUS
At "closes in the consequence," ay, marry.
He closes thus: "I know the gentleman,
I saw him yesterday," or "th'other day,"
Or then, or then, with such or such, "and as you say,
There was 'a gaming," "there o'ertook in 's rouse,"    60
"There falling out at tennis," or perchance    61
"I saw him enter such a house of sale,"    62
Videlicet a brothel, or so forth. See you now,    63
Your bait of falsehood takes this carp of truth;    64
And thus do we of wisdom and of reach,    65
With windlasses and with assays of bias,    66
By indirections find directions out.    67
So by my former lecture and advice    68
Shall you my son. You have me, have you not?    69
REYNALDO
My lord, I have.
POLONIUS           God b'wi'ye; fare ye well.
REYNALDO    Good my lord.

POLONIUS
    Observe his inclination in yourself.    72
REYNALDO    I shall, my lord.
POLONIUS    And let him ply his music.
REYNALDO    Well, my lord.
POLONIUS
    Farewell.                      *Exit Reynaldo.*

        *Enter Ophelia.*

            How now, Ophelia, what's the matter?
OPHELIA
    Alas, my lord, I have been so affrighted!
POLONIUS    With what, i'th' name of God?
OPHELIA
    My lord, as I was sewing in my chamber,
    Lord Hamlet, with his doublet all unbraced,    80
    No hat upon his head, his stockings fouled,    81
    Ungartered, and down-gyvèd to his ankle,    82
    Pale as his shirt, his knees knocking each other,
    And with a look so piteous in purport    84
    As if he had been loosèd out of hell
    To speak of horrors—he comes before me.
POLONIUS
    Mad for thy love?
OPHELIA            My lord, I do not know,
    But truly I do fear it.
POLONIUS            What said he?
OPHELIA
    He took me by the wrist and held me hard.
    Then goes he to the length of all his arm,
    And, with his other hand thus o'er his brow
    He falls to such perusal of my face
    As 'a would draw it. Long stayed he so.    93
    At last, a little shaking of mine arm
    And thrice his head thus waving up and down,
    He raised a sigh so piteous and profound
    That it did seem to shatter all his bulk    97
    And end his being. That done, he lets me go,
    And with his head over his shoulder turned
    He seemed to find his way without his eyes,
    For out o' doors he went without their help,
    And to the last bended their light on me.    102
POLONIUS
    Come, go with me. I will go seek the King.
    This is the very ecstasy of love,    104
    Whose violent property fordoes itself    105
    And leads the will to desperate undertakings
    As oft as any passion under heaven
    That does afflict our natures. I am sorry.
    What, have you given him any hard words of late?
OPHELIA
    No, my good lord, but as you did command
    I did repel his letters and denied

---

**32 breathe** name, utter.  **quaintly** artfully, subtly  **33 taints of liberty** faults resulting from free living  **35–6 A savageness . . . assault** a wildness in untamed youth that assails all indiscriminately.  **41 fetch of warrant** legitimate trick.  **42 sullies** stains, blemish  **43 i' th' working** in the process of being made, i.e., in everyday experience  **45 Your . . . converse** the person you are conversing with.  **sound** sound out  **46 Having ever** if he has ever.  **prenominate crimes** aforenamed offenses  **47 breathe** speak  **48 closes . . . consequence** takes you into his confidence as follows  **50 addition** title  **54 leave** leave off.  **60 o'ertook in 's rouse** overcome by drink  **61 falling out** quarreling  **62 house of sale** whorehouse  **63 Videlicet** namely  **64 carp** a fish  **65 reach** capacity, ability  **66 windlasses** i.e., circuitous paths. (Literally, circuits made to head off the game in hunting.)  **assays of bias** attempts through indirection (like the curving path of the bowling ball, which is biased or weighted to one side)  **67 directions** i.e., the way things really are  **68 former lecture** just-ended set of instructions  **69 have** understand

**72 in yourself** in your own person (as well as by asking questions of others).  **80 doublet** close-fitting jacket.  **unbraced** unfastened  **81 No . . . head** (Hats were customarily worn indoors in the England of Shakespeare's day.)  **fouled** untidy, dirty  **82 down-gyvèd** fallen to the ankles (like gyves or fetters)  **84 in purport** in what it expressed  **93 As 'a** as if he  **97 bulk** body  **102 bended . . . on me** (The eyes were thought to emit rays, enabling them to see by bringing back images to the eyes.)  **104 ecstasy** madness  **105 property fordoes** nature destroys

His access to me.
POLONIUS          That hath made him mad.
I am sorry that with better heed and judgment
I had not quoted him. I feared he did but trifle      114
And meant to wrack thee. But beshrew my jealousy!   115
By heaven, it is as proper to our age                116
To cast beyond ourselves in our opinions             117
As it is common for the younger sort
To lack discretion. Come, go we to the King.
This must be known, which, being kept close, might
    move                                              120
More grief to hide than hate to utter love.          121
Come.                                        *Exeunt.*

❖

## [2.2]

*Flourish. Enter King and Queen, Rosencrantz,
and Guildenstern, cum aliis.*

KING
Welcome, dear Rosencrantz and Guildenstern.
Moreover that we much did long to see you,            2
The need we have to use you did provoke
Our hasty sending. Something have you heard
Of Hamlet's transformation—so I call it,
Since not th'exterior nor the inward man
Resembles that it was. What it should be,             7
More than his father's death, that thus hath put him
So much from th'understanding of himself,
I cannot dream of. I entreat you both
That, being of so young days brought up with him,    11
And since so neighbored to his youth and humor,      12
That you vouchsafe your rest here in our court       13
Some little time, so by your companies
To draw him on to pleasures, and to gather
So much as from occasions you may glean,             16
Whether aught to us unknown afflicts him thus
That, opened, lies within our remedy.                18
QUEEN
Good gentlemen, he hath much talked of you,
And sure I am two men there is not living
To whom he more adheres. If it will please you
To show us so much gentry and good will              22
As to expend your time with us awhile
For the supply and profit of our hope,               24

Your visitation shall receive such thanks
As fits a kings's remembrance.
ROSENCRANTZ                 Both Your Majesties       26
Might, by the sovereign power you have of us,         27
Put your dread pleasures more into command           28
Than to entreaty.
GUILDENSTERN    But we both obey,
And here give up ourselves in the full bent          30
To lay our service freely at your feet,
To be commanded.
KING
Thanks, Rosencrantz and gentle Guildenstern.
QUEEN
Thanks, Guildenstern and gentle Rosencrantz.
And I beseech you instantly to visit
My too much changèd son.—Go, some of you,
And bring these gentlemen where Hamlet is.
GUILDENSTERN
Heavens make our presence and our practices          38
Pleasant and helpful to him!
QUEEN                  Ay, amen!
      *Exeunt Rosencrantz and Guildenstern [with some
                                     attendants].*

*Enter Polonius.*

POLONIUS
Th'ambassadors from Norway, my good lord,
Are joyfully returned.
KING
Thou still hast been the father of good news.        42
POLONIUS
Have I, my lord? Assure you, my good liege,
I hold my duty, as I hold my soul,
Both to my God and to my gracious king;
And I do think, or else this brain of mine
Hunts not the trail of policy so sure                47
As it hath used to do, that I have found             48
The very cause of Hamlet's lunacy.
KING
Oh, speak of that! That do I long to hear.
POLONIUS
Give first admittance to th'ambassadors.
My news shall be the fruit to that great feast.      52
KING
Thyself do grace to them and bring them in.          53
                               *[Exit Polonius.]*
He tells me, my sweet queen, that he hath found
The head and source of all your son's distemper.
QUEEN
I doubt it is no other but the main,                 56
His father's death and our o'erhasty marriage.

*Enter Polonius, Voltemand, and Cornelius.*

---

114 **quoted** observed   115 **wrack** ruin, seduce.   **beshrew my jealousy!** a plague upon my suspicious nature!   116 **proper . . . age** characteristic of us (old) men   117 **cast beyond** overshoot, miscalculate. (A metaphor from hunting.)   120 **known** made known (to the King). **close** secret   120–1 **might . . . love** i.e., might cause more grief (because of what Hamlet might do) by hiding the knowledge of Hamlet's strange behavior to Ophelia than unpleasantness by telling it.
**2.2. Location: The castle.**
0.2 *cum aliis* with others.   2 **Moreover that** Besides the fact that   7 **that** what   11–12 **That . . . humor** that, seeing as you were brought up with him from early youth (see 3.4.209, where Hamlet refers to Rosencrantz and Guildenstern as "my two schoolfellows"), and since you have been intimately acquainted with his youthful ways   13 **vouchsafe your rest** consent to stay   16 **occasions** opportunity   18 **opened** being revealed   22 **gentry** courtesy   24 **supply . . . hope** aid and furtherance of what we hope for

26 **As fits . . . remembrance** as would be a fitting gift of a king who rewards true service.   27 **of** over   28 **dread** inspiring awe   30 **in . . . bent** to the utmost degree of our capacity. (An archery metaphor.)   38 **practices** doings   42 **still** always   47 **policy** statecraft   48 **hath used to do** has customarily done   52 **fruit** dessert   53 **grace** honor. (Punning on *grace* said before a *feast*, line 52.)   56 **doubt** fear, suspect

KING
Well, we shall sift him.—Welcome, my good friends!     58
Say, Voltemand, what from our brother Norway?     59
VOLTEMAND
Most fair return of greetings and desires.     60
Upon our first, he sent out to suppress     61
His nephew's levies, which to him appeared     62
To be a preparation 'gainst the Polack,
But, better looked into, he truly found
It was against Your Highness. Whereat grieved
That so his sickness, age, and impotence     66
Was falsely borne in hand, sends out arrests     67
On Fortinbras, which he, in brief, obeys,
Receives rebuke from Norway, and in fine     69
Makes vow before his uncle never more
To give th'assay of arms against Your Majesty.     71
Whereon old Norway, overcome with joy,
Gives him three thousand crowns in annual fee
And his commission to employ those soldiers,
So levied as before, against the Polack,
With an entreaty, herein further shown,
                                            [giving a paper]
That it might please you to give quiet pass
Through your dominions for his enterprise
On such regards of safety and allowance     79
As therein are set down.
KING                          It likes us well,     80
And at our more considered time we'll read,     81
Answer, and think upon this business.
Meantime we thank you for your well-took labor.
Go to your rest; at night we'll feast together.
Most welcome home!               Exeunt Ambassadors.
POLONIUS                 This business is well ended.
My liege, and madam, to expostulate     86
What majesty should be, what duty is,
Why day is day, night night, and time is time,
Were nothing but to waste night, day, and time.
Therefore, since brevity is the soul of wit,     90
And tediousness the limbs and outward flourishes,
I will be brief. Your noble son is mad.
Mad call I it, for, to define true madness,
What is't but to be nothing else but mad?
But let that go.
QUEEN               More matter, with less art.
POLONIUS
Madam, I swear I use no art at all.
That he is mad, 'tis true; 'tis true 'tis pity,
And pity 'tis 'tis true—a foolish figure,     98
But farewell it, for I will use no art.
Mad let us grant him, then, and now remains
That we find out the cause of this effect,

Or rather say, the cause of this defect,
For this effect defective comes by cause.     103
Thus it remains, and the remainder thus.
Perpend.     105
I have a daughter—have whilst she is mine—     106
Who, in her duty and obedience, mark,
Hath given me this. Now gather and surmise.     108
[He reads] the letter. "To the celestial and my soul's
idol, the most beautified Ophelia"—
That's an ill phrase, a vile phrase; "beautified" is a
vile phrase. But you shall hear.          [He reads.]
"These in her excellent white bosom, these, etc."     113
QUEEN     Came this from Hamlet to her?
POLONIUS
Good madam, stay awhile, I will be faithful.     115
                                            [He reads.]
        "Doubt thou the stars are fire,
            Doubt that the sun doth move,
        Doubt truth to be a liar,     118
            But never doubt I love.
O dear Ophelia, I am ill at these numbers. I have not     120
art to reckon my groans. But that I love thee best, O     121
most best, believe it. Adieu.
                Thine evermore, most dear lady, whilst this
                        machine is to him, Hamlet."  124
This in obedience hath my daughter shown me,
And, more above, hath his solicitings,     126
As they fell out by time, by means, and place,     127
All given to mine ear.
KING                         But how hath she     128
Received his love?
POLONIUS                 What do you think of me?
KING
As of a man faithful and honorable.
POLONIUS
I would fain prove so. But what might you think,     131
When I had seen this hot love on the wing—
As I perceived it, I must tell you that,
Before my daughter told me—what might you,
Or my dear Majesty your queen here, think,
If I had played the desk or table book,     136
Or given my heart a winking, mute and dumb,     137
Or looked upon this love with idle sight?     138
What might you think? No, I went round to work,     139
And my young mistress thus I did bespeak:     140
"Lord Hamlet is a prince out of thy star;     141
This must not be." And then I precepts gave her,     142

---

58 **sift him** question Polonius (or Hamlet) closely.   59 **brother** fellow king   60 **desires** good wishes.   61 **Upon our first** At our first words on the business   62 **His nephew's levies** young Fortinbras's raising of troops   66 **impotence** weakness   67 **borne in hand** deluded, taken advantage of.   **arrests** orders to desist   69 **in fine** in conclusion   71 **give th'assay** make trial of strength, challenge   79 **On . . . allowance** i.e., with such considerations for the safety of Denmark and permission for Fortinbras   80 **likes** pleases   81 **considered** suitable for deliberation   86 **expostulate** expound, inquire into   90 **wit** sense or judgment   98 **figure** figure of speech

103 **For . . . cause** i.e., for this defective behavior, this madness, must have a cause.   105 **Perpend** Consider.   106 **whilst . . . mine** i.e., until she marries   108 **gather and surmise** draw your own conclusions.   113 **"In . . . etc."** (The letter is poetically addressed to her heart, where a letter would be kept by a young lady.)   115 **stay . . . faithful** i.e., hold on, I will do as I said I would.   118 **Doubt** suspect   120 **ill . . . numbers** unskilled at writing verses.   121 **reckon** (1) count (2) number metrically, scan   124 **machine** i.e., body   126–8 **And . . . ear** and moreover she has told me when, how, and where his solicitings of her occurred.   131 **fain** gladly   136–7 **If . . . dumb** if I had acted as go-between, passing love notes, or if I had refused to let my heart acknowledge what my eyes could see   138 **with idle sight** complacently or incomprehendingly.   139 **round** roundly, plainly   140 **bespeak** address   141 **out of thy star** above your sphere, position   142 **precepts** orders

That she should lock herself from his resort,                    143
Admit no messengers, receive no tokens.
Which done, she took the fruits of my advice;
And he, repulsèd—a short tale to make—
Fell into a sadness, then into a fast,
Thence to a watch, thence into a weakness,          148
Thence to a lightness, and by this declension       149
Into the madness wherein now he raves,
And all we mourn for.

KING [*to the Queen*]          Do you think 'tis this?
QUEEN   It may be, very like.                         152
POLONIUS
Hath there been such a time—I would fain know
   that—                                             153
That I have positively said "'Tis so,"
When it proved otherwise?
KING                         Not that I know.
POLONIUS
Take this from this, if this be otherwise.           156
If circumstances lead me, I will find
Where truth is hid, though it were hid indeed
Within the center.
KING              How may we try it further?          159
POLONIUS
You know sometimes he walks four hours together
Here in the lobby.
QUEEN              So he does indeed.
POLONIUS
At such a time I'll loose my daughter to him.        162
Be you and I behind an arras then.                   163
Mark the encounter. If he love her not
And be not from his reason fall'n thereon,           165
Let me be no assistant for a state,
But keep a farm and carters.
KING                         We will try it.          167

*Enter Hamlet reading on a book.*

QUEEN
But look where sadly the poor wretch comes reading.
POLONIUS
Away, I do beseech you both, away.
I'll board him presently. Oh, give me leave.         170
              *Exit King and Queen [with attendants].*
How does my good Lord Hamlet?
HAMLET   Well, God-a-mercy.                           172
POLONIUS   Do you know me, my lord?
HAMLET   Excellent, excellent well. You're a fishmonger.  174
POLONIUS   Not I, my lord.
HAMLET   Then I would you were so honest a man.

POLONIUS   Honest, my lord?
HAMLET   Ay, sir. To be honest, as this world goes, is to
   be one man picked out of ten thousand.
POLONIUS   That's very true, my lord.
HAMLET   For if the sun breed maggots in a dead dog,
   being a good kissing carrion—Have you a daughter?  182
POLONIUS   I have, my lord.
HAMLET   Let her not walk i'th' sun. Conception is a   184
   blessing, but as your daughter may conceive, friend,
   look to't.                                          186
POLONIUS [*aside*]   How say you by that? Still harping
   on my daughter. Yet he knew me not at first; 'a said
   I was a fishmonger. 'A is far gone. And truly in my
   youth I suffered much extremity for love, very near
   this. I'll speak to him again.—What do you read,
   my lord?
HAMLET   Words, words, words.
POLONIUS   What is the matter, my lord?               194
HAMLET   Between who?
POLONIUS   I mean, the matter that you read, my lord.
HAMLET   Slanders, sir; for the satirical rogue says here
   that old men have gray beards, that their faces are wrinkled, their eyes purging thick amber and plum-tree  199
   gum, and that they have a plentiful lack of wit, together  200
   with most weak hams. All which, sir, though I most
   powerfully and potently believe, yet I hold it not hon-  202
   esty to have it thus set down, for you yourself, sir, shall  203
   grow old as I am, if like a crab you could go backward.  204
POLONIUS [*aside*]   Though this be madness, yet there is
   method in't.—Will you walk out of the air, my lord?  206
HAMLET   Into my grave.
POLONIUS   Indeed, that's out of the air. [*Aside*] How
   pregnant sometimes his replies are! A happiness that  209
   often madness hits on, which reason and sanity could
   not so prosperously be delivered of. I will leave him  211
   and suddenly contrive the means of meeting between  212
   him and my daughter.—My honorable lord, I will
   most humbly take my leave of you.
HAMLET   You cannot, sir, take from me anything that I
   will more willingly part withal—except my life, except  216
   my life, except my life.

*Enter Guildenstern and Rosencrantz.*

POLONIUS   Fare you well, my lord.
HAMLET   These tedious old fools!
POLONIUS   You go to seek the Lord Hamlet. There he is.
ROSENCRANTZ [*to Polonius*]   God save you, sir!
                                    [*Exit Polonius.*]
GUILDENSTERN   My honored lord!

---

**143 resort** visits   **148 watch** state of sleeplessness   **149 lightness**
lightheadedness.   **declension** decline, deterioration. (With a pun on
the grammatical sense.)   **152 like** likely.   **153 fain** gladly   **156 Take
this from this** (The actor probably gestures, indicating that he means
his head from his shoulders, or his staff of office or chain from his
hands or neck, or something similar.)   **159 center** center of the earth,
traditionally an extraordinarily inaccessible place.   **try** test   **162
loose** (As if she were a caged animal about to be mated.)   **163 arras**
hanging, tapestry   **165 thereon** on that account   **167 carters** wagon
drivers.   **170 I'll . . . leave** I'll accost him at once. Please leave us
alone; leave him to me.   **172 God-a-mercy** God have mercy, i.e.,
thank you.   **174 fishmonger** fish merchant.

**182 a good kissing carrion** i.e., a good piece of flesh for kissing, or for
the sun to kiss   **184 i'th' sun** in public. (With additional implication
of the sunshine of princely favors.)   **Conception** (1) Understanding
(2) Pregnancy   **186 look to't** watch out.   **194 matter** substance. (But
Hamlet plays on the sense of "basis for a dispute.")   **199 purging**
discharging.   **amber** i.e., resin, like the resinous *plum-tree gum*
**200 wit** understanding   **202–3 honesty** decency, decorum   **204 old**
as old   **206 out of the air** (The open air was considered dangerous
for sick people.)   **209 pregnant** quick-witted, full of meaning.
**happiness** felicity of expression   **211 prosperously** successfully
**212 suddenly** immediately   **216 withal** with

ROSENCRANTZ   My most dear lord!

HAMLET   My excellent good friends! How dost thou, Guildenstern? Ah, Rosencrantz! Good lads, how do ye both?

ROSENCRANTZ
As the indifferent children of the earth.                                227

GUILDENSTERN
Happy in that we are not over-happy.
On Fortune's cap we are not the very button.

HAMLET   Nor the soles of her shoe?

ROSENCRANTZ   Neither, my lord.

HAMLET   Then you live about her waist, or in the mid-   232
dle of her favors?                                             233

GUILDENSTERN   Faith, her privates we.            234

HAMLET   In the secret parts of Fortune? Oh, most true, she is a strumpet. What news?                     236

ROSENCRANTZ   None, my lord, but that the world's grown honest.

HAMLET   Then is doomsday near. But your news is not true. Let me question more in particular. What have you, my good friends, deserved at the hands of Fortune that she sends you to prison hither?

GUILDENSTERN   Prison, my lord?

HAMLET   Denmark's a prison.

ROSENCRANTZ   Then is the world one.

HAMLET   A goodly one, in which there are many confines, wards, and dungeons, Denmark being one   247
o'th' worst.

ROSENCRANTZ   We think not so, my lord.

HAMLET   Why then 'tis none to you, for there is nothing either good or bad but thinking makes it so. To me it is a prison.

ROSENCRANTZ   Why then, your ambition makes it one. 'Tis too narrow for your mind.

HAMLET   Oh, God, I could be bounded in a nutshell and count myself a king of infinite space, were it not that I have bad dreams.

GUILDENSTERN   Which dreams indeed are ambition, for the very substance of the ambitious is merely the   259
shadow of a dream.                                           260

HAMLET   A dream itself is but a shadow.

ROSENCRANTZ   Truly, and I hold ambition of so airy and light a quality that it is but a shadow's shadow.

HAMLET   Then are our beggars bodies, and our mon-   264
archs and outstretched heroes the beggars' shadows.   265
Shall we to th' court? For, by my fay, I cannot reason.   266

ROSENCRANTZ, GUILDENSTERN   We'll wait upon you.   267

HAMLET   No such matter. I will not sort you with the   268
rest of my servants, for, to speak to you like an honest man, I am most dreadfully attended. But, in the   270
beaten way of friendship, what make you at Elsinore?   271

ROSENCRANTZ   To visit you, my lord, no other occasion.

HAMLET   Beggar that I am, I am even poor in thanks; but I thank you; and sure, dear friends, my thanks are too dear a halfpenny. Were you not sent for? Is it your   275
own inclining? Is it a free visitation? Come, deal   276
justly with me. Come, come. Nay, speak.

GUILDENSTERN   What should we say, my lord?

HAMLET   Why, anything but to th' purpose. You were sent   279
for, and there is a kind of confession in your looks which your modesties have not craft enough to color.   281
I know the good King and Queen have sent for you.

ROSENCRANTZ   To what end, my lord?

HAMLET   That you must teach me. But let me conjure   284
you, by the rights of our fellowship, by the consonancy   285
of our youth, by the obligation of our ever-preserved   286
love, and by what more dear a better proposer   287
could charge you withal, be even and direct with me   288
whether you were sent for or no.

ROSENCRANTZ   [aside to Guildenstern]   What say you?

HAMLET   [aside]   Nay, then, I have an eye of you.—If   291
you love me, hold not off.                                    292

GUILDENSTERN   My lord, we were sent for.

HAMLET   I will tell you why; so shall my anticipation   294
prevent your discovery, and your secrecy to the King   295
and Queen molt no feather. I have of late—but   296
wherefore I know not—lost all my mirth, forgone all custom of exercise; and indeed it goes so heavily with my disposition that this goodly frame, the earth, seems to me a sterile promontory; this most excellent canopy, the air, look you, this brave o'erhanging   301
firmament, this majestical roof fretted with golden   302
fire, why, it appears no other thing to me than a foul and pestilent congregation of vapors. What a piece of work   304
is a man! How noble in reason, how infinite in faculties, in form and moving how express and admirable, in   306
action how like an angel, in apprehension how like a   307
god! The beauty of the world, the paragon of animals! And yet, to me, what is this quintessence of dust?   309
Man delights not me—no, nor woman neither, though by your smiling you seem to say so.

---

227 **indifferent** ordinary, at neither extreme of fortune or misfortune
**232–3 the middle . . . favors** i.e., her genitals.   234 **her privates we** (1) we dwell in her privates, her genitals, in the middle of her favors (2) we are her ordinary footsoldiers.   236 **strumpet** (Fortune was proverbially thought of as fickle.)   247 **confines** places of confinement   259–60 **the very . . . a dream** i.e, the goal of ambition is without sustance, being nothing more than unreal image of something that is itself mere illusion. (Rosencrantz rephrases this idea in lines 262–3.)   264–5 **Then . . . shadows** (Hamlet pursues their argument about ambition to its absurd extreme: if ambition is only a shadow of a shadow, then beggars, who are presumably without ambition, must be real, whereas monarchs and heroes are only their shadows—*outstretched* like elongated shadows, made to look bigger than they are.)   266 **fay** faith   267 **wait upon** accompany, attend. (But Hamlet uses the phrase in the sense of providing menial service.)

268 **sort** class, categorize   270 **dreadfully attended** waited upon in slovenly fashion.   271 **beaten way** familiar path, tried-and-true course.   **make** do   275 **too dear a halfpenny** (1) too expensive at even a halfpenny, i.e., of little worth (2) too expensive by a halfpenny in return for worthless kindness.   276 **free** voluntary   279 **Why . . . but to th' purpose** Anything except a straightforward answer. (Said ironically.)   281 **color** disguise.   284 **conjure** adjure, entreat   285–6 **the consonancy of our youth** our closeness in our younger days   287 **better** more skillful   288 **charge** urge.   **even** straight, honest   291 **of** on   292 **hold not off** don't hold back.   294–5 **so . . . discovery** in that way my saying it first will spare you from having to reveal the truth   296 **molt no feather** i.e., not diminish in the least.   301 **brave** splendid   302 **fretted** adorned (with fretwork, as in a vaulted ceiling)   304 **congregation** mass.   **piece of work** masterpiece   306 **express** well-framed, exact, expressive   307 **apprehension** power of comprehending   309 **quintessence** very essence. (Literally, the fifth essence beyond earth, water, air, and fire, supposed to be extractable from them.)

ROSENCRANTZ   My lord, there was no such stuff in my
thoughts.

HAMLET   Why did you laugh, then, when I said man
delights not me?

ROSENCRANTZ   To think, my lord, if you delight not in
man, what lenten entertainment the players shall 317
receive from you. We coted them on the way, and 318
hither are they coming to offer you service.

HAMLET   He that plays the king shall be welcome; His
Majesty shall have tribute of me. The adventurous 321
knight shall use his foil and target, the lover shall not 322
sigh gratis, the humorous man shall end his part in 323
peace, the clown shall make those laugh whose lungs 324
are tickle o'th' sear, and the lady shall say her mind 325
freely, or the blank verse shall halt for't. What players 326
are they?

ROSENCRANTZ   Even those you were wont to take such 328
delight in, the tragedians of the city.                        329

HAMLET   How chances it they travel? Their residence, 330
both in reputation and profit, was better both ways.

ROSENCRANTZ   I think their inhibition comes by the 332
means of the late innovation.                               333

HAMLET   Do they hold the same estimation they did
when I was in the city? Are they so followed?

ROSENCRANTZ   No, indeed they are not.

HAMLET   How comes it? Do they grow rusty?           337

ROSENCRANTZ   Nay, their endeavor keeps in the wonted 338
pace. But there is, sir, an eyrie of children, little eyases, 339
that cry out on the top of question and are most tyran- 340
nically clapped for't. These are now the fashion, and 341
so berattle the common stages—so they call them— 342
that many wearing rapiers are afraid of goose quills 343
and dare scarce come thither.

HAMLET   What, are they children? Who maintains 'em?
How are they escotted? Will they pursue the quality no 346
longer than they can sing? Will they not say after- 347

wards, if they should grow themselves to common 348
players—as it is most like, if their means are not 349
better—their writers do them wrong to make them 350
exclaim against their own succession?                      351

ROSENCRANTZ   Faith, there has been much to-do on 352
both sides, and the nation holds it no sin to tarre them to 353
controversy. There was for a while no money bid for 354
argument unless the poet and the player went to cuffs 355
in the question.                                          356

HAMLET   Is't possible?

GUILDENSTERN   Oh, there has been much throwing
about of brains.

HAMLET   Do the boys carry it away?                      360

ROSENCRANTZ   Ay, that they do, my lord—Hercules 361
and his load too.                                         362

HAMLET   It is not very strange; for my uncle is King of
Denmark, and those that would make mows at him 364
while my father lived give twenty, forty, fifty, a
hundred ducats apiece for his picture in little. 'Sblood, 366
there is something in this more than natural, if philosophy could find it out.

        [A] *flourish for the players* [*within*].

GUILDENSTERN   There are the players.

HAMLET   Gentlemen, you are welcome to Elsinore. Your
hands, come. Th'appurtenance of welcome is 371
fashion and ceremony. Let me comply with you in this 372
garb, lest my extent to the players, which, I tell you, 373
must show fairly outward, should more appear like 374
entertainment than yours. You are welcome. But my 375
uncle-father and aunt-mother are deceived.

GUILDENSTERN   In what, my dear lord?

HAMLET   I am but mad north-north-west. When the 378
wind is southerly I know a hawk from a handsaw.     379

        *Enter Polonius.*

POLONIUS   Well be with you, gentlemen!

HAMLET   Hark you, Guildenstern, and you too; at each
ear a hearer. That great baby you see there is not yet
out of his swaddling clouts.                              383

ROSENCRANTZ   Haply he is the second time come to 384
them, for they say an old man is twice a child.

---

317 **lenten entertainment** meager reception (appropriate to
Lent)   318 **coted** overtook and passed by   321 **tribute** (1) applause
(2) homage paid in money.   **of** from   322 **foil and target** sword and
shield   323 **gratis** for nothing.   **humorous man** eccentric character,
dominated by one trait or "humor"   323–4 **in peace** i.e., with full
license   325 **tickle o'th' sear** hair trigger, ready to laugh easily. (A
*sear* is part of a gun-lock.)   326 **halt** limp   328 **wont** accustomed   329 **tragedians** actors   330 **residence** remaining in their
usual place, i.e., in the city   332 **inhibition** formal prohibition (from
acting plays in the city)   333 **late innovation** i.e., recent new fashion
in satirical plays performed by boy actors in the "private" theaters; or
the Earl of Essex's abortive rebellion in 1601 against Elizabeth's government. (A much debated passage of seemingly topical reference.)
337 **How . . . rusty?** Have they lost their polish, gone out of fashion?
(This passage, through line 362, alludes to the rivalry between the
children's companies and the adult actors, given strong impetus by
the reopening of the Children of the Chapel at the Blackfriars Theater
in late 1600.)   338 **keeps . . . wonted** continues in the usual   339
**eyrie** nest.   **eyases** young hawks   340 **cry . . . question** speak shrilly,
dominating the controversy (in decrying the public theaters)
340–1 **tyrannically** vehemently   342 **berattle . . . stages** clamor against
the public theaters   343 **many wearing rapiers** i.e., many men of fashion, afraid to patronize the common players for fear of being satirized
by the poets writing for the boy actors.   **goose quills** i.e., pens of sati-
rists   346 **escotted** maintained.   **quality** (acting) profession
346–7 **no longer . . . sing** i.e., only until their voices change.

348 **common** regular, adult   349 **like** likely   349–50 **if . . . better** if
they find no better way to support themselves   351 **succession** i.e.,
future careers.   352 **to-do** ado   353 **tarre** incite (as in inciting dogs to
attack a chained bear)   354–6 **There . . . question** i.e., For a while, no
money was offered by the acting companies to playwrights for the
plot to a play unless the satirical poets who wrote for the boys and
the adult actors came to blows in the play itself.   360 **carry it away**
i.e., win the day.   361–2 **Hercules . . . load** (Thought to be an allusion
to the sign of the Globe Theatre, which allegedly was Hercules bearing the world on his shoulders.)   364 **mows** faces   366 **ducats** gold
coins.   **in little** in miniature.   **'Sblood** By God's (Christ's) blood
371 **Th'appurtenance** The proper accompaniment   372 **comply**
observe the formalities of courtesy   373 **garb** i.e., manner.   **my
extent** that which I extend, i.e., my polite behavior   374 **show fairly
outward** show every evidence of cordiality   375 **entertainment** a
(warm) reception   378 **north-north-west** just off true north, only
partly.   379 **I . . . handsaw** (Speaking in his mad guise, Hamlet perhaps suggests that he can tell true from false. A *handsaw* may be a
*hernshaw* or heron. Still, a supposedly mad disposition might compare hawks and handsaws.)   383 **swaddling clouts** cloths in which
to wrap a newborn baby.   384 **Haply** Perhaps

HAMLET   I will prophesy he comes to tell me of the players. Mark it.—You say right, sir, o' Monday morning, 'twas then indeed. 387 388

POLONIUS   My lord, I have news to tell you.

HAMLET   My lord, I have news to tell you. When Roscius was an actor in Rome— 390

POLONIUS   The actors are come hither, my lord.

HAMLET   Buzz, buzz! 393

POLONIUS   Upon my honor—

HAMLET   Then came each actor on his ass.

POLONIUS   The best actors in the world, either for tragedy, comedy, history, pastoral, pastoral-comical, historical-pastoral, tragical-historical, tragical-comical-historical-pastoral, scene individable, or poem unlimited. Seneca cannot be too heavy, nor Plautus too light. For the law of writ and the liberty, these are the only men. 399 400 401

HAMLET   O Jephthah, judge of Israel, what a treasure hadst thou! 403

POLONIUS   What a treasure had he, my lord?

HAMLET   Why,
        "One fair daughter, and no more,
        The which he lovèd passing well." 408

POLONIUS   [aside]   Still on my daughter.

HAMLET   Am I not i'th' right, old Jephthah?

POLONIUS   If you call me Jephthah, my lord, I have a daughter that I love passing well.

HAMLET   Nay, that follows not. 413

POLONIUS   What follows then, my lord? 414

HAMLET   Why,
        "As by lot, God wot," 416
and then, you know,
        "It came to pass, as most like it was"— 418
the first row of the pious chanson will show you more, 419
for look where my abridgment comes. 420

        *Enter four or five Players.*

You are welcome, masters; welcome, all. I am glad to 421
see thee well. Welcome, good friends. Oh, my old friend!
Thy face is valanced since I saw thee last. Com'st 423
thou to beard me in Denmark? What, my young lady 424

and mistress! By'r Lady, Your Ladyship is nearer 425
heaven than when I saw you last, by the altitude of a 426
chopine. Pray God your voice, like a piece of uncur- 427
rent gold, be not cracked within the ring. Masters, you 428
are all welcome. We'll e'en to't like French falconers, 429
fly at anything we see. We'll have a speech straight. 430
Come, give us a taste of your quality. Come, a 431
passionate speech.

FIRST PLAYER   What speech, my good lord?

HAMLET   I heard thee speak me a speech once, but it
was never acted, or if it was, not above once, for the
play, I remember, pleased not the million; 'twas cav- 436
iare to the general. But it was—as I received it, and 437
others, whose judgments in such matters cried in the 438
top of mine—an excellent play, well digested in the 439
scenes, set down with as much modesty as cunning. I 440
remember one said there were no sallets in the lines to 441
make the matter savory, nor no matter in the phrase
that might indict the author of affectation, but called it 443
an honest method, as wholesome as sweet, and by very
much more handsome than fine. One speech in't I 445
chiefly loved: 'twas Aeneas' tale to Dido, and there- 446
about of it especially where he speaks of Priam's 447
slaughter. If it live in your memory, begin at this line: 448
let me see, let me see—
"The rugged Pyrrhus, like the Hyrcanian beast"— 450
'Tis not so. It begins with Pyrrhus:
"The rugged Pyrrhus, he whose sable arms, 452
Black as his purpose, did the night resemble
When he lay couchèd in the ominous horse, 454
Hath now this dread and black complexion
    smeared
With heraldry more dismal. Head to foot 456
Now is he total gules, horridly tricked 457
With blood of fathers, mothers, daughters, sons,
Baked and impasted with the parching streets, 459
That lend a tyrannous and damnèd light 460

387–8 You say . . . then indeed (Said to impress upon Polonius the idea that Hamlet is in serious conversation with his friends.)   390 Roscius a famous Roman actor who died in 62 B.C.   393 Buzz (An interjection used to denote stale news.)   399–400 scene . . . unlimited plays that are unclassifiable and all-inclusive. (An absurdly catchall conclusion to Polonius's pompous list of categories.)   400 Seneca writer of Latin tragedies (c. 3 B.C.–65 A.D.).   Plautus writer of Latin comedies (c. 254–184 B.C.).   401 law . . . liberty dramatic composition both according to the rules and disregarding the rules.   these i.e., the actors 403 Jephthah . . . Israel (Jephthah had to sacrifice his daughter; see Judges 11. Hamlet goes on to quote from a fragment of a ballad on the theme.)   408 passing surpassingly   413 that follows not i.e., just because you resemble Jephthah in having a daughter does not logically prove that you love her.   414 What . . . lord? What does follow logically? (But Hamlet, pretending madness, answers with a fragment of a ballad, as if Polonius had asked, "What comes next?" See 419n.)   416 lot chance.   wot knows   418 like likely, probable   419 the first . . . more the first stanza of this biblically based ballad will satisfy your stated desire to know *what follows* (line 414)   420 my abridgment something that cuts short my conversation; also, a diversion   421 masters good sirs 423 valanced fringed (with a beard)   424 beard confront, challenge. (With obvious pun.)   young lady i.e., boy playing women's parts

425 By'r Lady By Our Lady   425–6 nearer heaven i.e., taller 427 chopine thick-soled shoe of Italian fashion.   427–8 uncurrent not passable as lawful coinage   428 cracked . . . ring i.e., changed from adolescent to male voice, no longer suitable for women's roles. (Coins featured rings enclosing the sovereign's head; if the coin was sufficiently clipped to invade within this ring, it was unfit for currency.)   429 e'en to't go at it   430 straight at once.   431 quality professional skill. 436–7 caviare to the general i.e., an expensive delicacy not generally palatable to uneducated tastes.   438–9 cried in the top of i.e., spoke with greater authority than   439 digested arranged, ordered 440 modesty moderation, restraint.   cunning skill.   441 sallets i.e., something savory, spicy improprieties   443 indict convict   445 handsome well-proportioned.   fine elaborately ornamented, showy. 446 Aeneas' . . . Dido Aeneas' visit to Dido, Queen of Carthage, in Book I of Virgil' *Aeneid*   447–8 Priam's slaughter the slaying of the ruler of Troy, when the Greeks finally took the city.   450 Pyrrhus a Greek hero in the Trojan War, also known as Neoptolemus, son of Achilles—another avenging son.   the Hyrcanian beast i.e., the tiger. (On the death of Priam, see Virgil, *Aeneid*, 2.506 ff.; compare the whole speech with Marlowe's *Dido Queen of Carthage*, 2.1.214 ff. On the *Hyrcanian* tiger, see *Aeneid*, 4.366–7. Hyrcania is on the Caspian Sea.)   452 rugged shaggy, savage.   sable black (for reasons of camouflage during the episode of the Trojan horse)   454 couchèd concealed.   ominous horse fateful Trojan horse, by which the Greeks gained access to Troy   456 dismal calamitous.   457 total gules entirely red. (A heraldic term.)   tricked spotted and smeared. (Heraldic.)   459 Baked . . . streets roasted and encrusted, like a thick paste, by the parching heat of the streets (because of the fires everywhere)   460 tyrannous cruel

To their vile murders. Roasted in wrath and fire,
And thus o'ersizèd with coagulate gore,                              462
With eyes like carbuncles, the hellish Pyrrhus                       463
Old grandsire Priam seeks."
So proceed you.

POLONIUS   'Fore God, my lord, well spoken, with good
accent and good discretion.

FIRST PLAYER   "Anon he finds him
Striking too short at Greeks. His antique sword,                     469
Rebellious to his arm, lies where it falls,
Repugnant to command. Unequal matched,                              471
Pyrrhus at Priam drives, in rage strikes wide,
But with the whiff and wind of his fell sword                        473
Th'unnervèd father falls. Then senseless Ilium,                      474
Seeming to feel this blow, with flaming top
Stoops to his base, and with a hideous crash                         476
Takes prisoner Pyrrhus' ear. For, lo! His sword,
Which was declining on the milky head                                478
Of reverend Priam, seemed i'th'air to stick.
So as a painted tyrant Pyrrhus stood,                                480
And, like a neutral to his will and matter,                          481
Did nothing.
But as we often see against some storm                               483
A silence in the heavens, the rack stand still,                      484
The bold winds speechless, and the orb below                         485
As hush as death, anon the dreadful thunder
Doth rend the region, so, after Pyrrhus' pause,                      487
A rousèd vengeance sets him new a-work,
And never did the Cyclops' hammers fall                              489
On Mars his armor forged for proof eterne                            490
With less remorse than Pyrrhus' bleeding sword                       491
Now falls on Priam.
Out, out, thou strumpet Fortune! All you gods                        493
In general synod take away her power!                                494
Break all the spokes and fellies from her wheel,                     495
And bowl the round nave down the hill of heaven                      496
As low as to the fiends!"

POLONIUS   This is too long.

HAMLET   It shall to the barber's with your beard.—Pri-
thee, say on. He's for a jig or a tale of bawdry, or he               500
sleeps. Say on; come to Hecuba.                                       501

FIRST PLAYER
"But who, oh, who, had seen the moblèd queen"—                       502

HAMLET   "The moblèd queen"?

POLONIUS   That's good. "Moblèd queen" is good.

FIRST PLAYER
"Run barefoot up and down, threat'ning the flames                    505
With bisson rheum, a clout upon that head                            506
Where late the diadem stood, and, for a robe,                        507
About her lank and all o'erteemèd loins                              508
A blanket, in th' alarm of fear caught up—
Who this had seen, with tongue in venom steeped,
'Gainst Fortune's state would treason have
      pronounced.                                                     511
But if the gods themselves did see her then                          512
When she saw Pyrrhus make malicious sport
In mincing with his sword her husband's limbs,
The instant burst of clamor that she made,
Unless things mortal move them not at all,
Would have made milch the burning eyes of heaven,    517
And passion in the gods."                                            518

POLONIUS   Look whe'er he has not turned his color and    519
has tears in 's eyes. Prithee, no more.

HAMLET   'Tis well; I'll have thee speak out the rest of
this soon.—Good my lord, will you see the players well
bestowed? Do ye hear, let them be well used, for they    523
are the abstracts and brief chronicles of the time. After    524
your death you were better have a bad epitaph than
their ill report while you live.

POLONIUS   My lord, I will use them according to their
desert.

HAMLET   God's bodikins, man, much better. Use every    529
man after his desert, and who should scape whipping?
Use them after your own honor and dignity. The less    531
they deserve, the more merit is in your bounty. Take
them in.

POLONIUS   Come, sirs.                              *Exit Polonius.*

HAMLET   Follow him, friends. We'll hear a play tomor-
row. [*As they start to leave, Hamlet detains the First
Player.*] Dost thou hear me, old friend? Can you play
*The Murder of Gonzago?*

FIRST PLAYER   Ay, my lord.

HAMLET   We'll ha 't tomorrow night. You could, for a    540
need, study a speech of some dozen or sixteen lines    541
which I would set down and insert in 't, could you not?

FIRST PLAYER   Ay, my lord.

HAMLET   Very well. Follow that lord, and look you mock
him not.                                          *Exeunt players.*
My good friends, I'll leave you till night. You are welcome to Elsinore.

ROSENCRANTZ   Good my lord!
                    *Exeunt [Rosencrantz and Guildenstern].*

HAMLET
Ay, so, God b' wi' ye.—Now I am alone.
Oh, what a rogue and peasant slave am I!

---

**462 o'ersizèd** covered as with size or glue.   **coagulate** congealed
**463 carbuncles** large fiery-red precious stones thought to emit their own
light   **469 antique** ancient, long-used   **471 Repugnant** disobedient,
resistant.   **Unequal matched** They being unequally matched   **473 fell**
cruel   **474 Th'unnervèd** the strengthless.   **senseless Ilium** the citadel of
Troy, inanimate and unable to defend itself   **476 his** its   **478 declining**
descending.   **milky** white-haired   **480 painted** motionless, as in a painting   **481 like . . . matter** i.e., as though suspended between his intention
and its fulfillment   **483 against** just before   **484 rack** mass of clouds
**485 orb** globe, earth   **487 region** sky   **489 Cyclops'.** The Cyclopes were
giant armor makers in the smithy of Vulcan.   **490 Mars his** Mars's.
**proof** proven or tested resistance to assault   **491 remorse** pity   **493 Out**
(An expression of outrage, fury, etc.)   **494 synod** assembly   **495 fellies**
pieces of wood forming the rim of a wheel   **496 nave** hub.   **hill of
heaven** Mount Olympus   **500 jig** comic song and dance often given at
the end of a play   **501 Hecuba** wife of Priam.   **502 moblèd** muffled.

**505 threat'ning the flames** i.e., weeping hard enough to dampen the
flames   **506 bisson rheum** blinding tears.   **clout** cloth   **507 late**
lately.   **diadem** crown   **508 all o'erteemèd** utterly worn out with
bearing children   **511 state** rule, managing.   **pronounced** proclaimed.
**512 But if** But even if   **517 milch** milky, moist with tears.   **burning
eyes of heaven** i.e., stars, heavenly bodies   **518 passion** overpowering
emotion   **519 whe'er** whether   **523 bestowed** lodged.   **524 abstracts**
summary accounts   **529 God's bodikins** By God's (Christ's) little body,
*bodikin.* (Not to be confused with *bodkin,* "dagger.")   **531 after** according to   **540 ha 't** have it performed   **541 study** memorize

Is it not monstrous that this player here,
But in a fiction, in a dream of passion,    552
Could force his soul so to his whole conceit    553
That from her working all his visage wanned,    554
Tears in his eyes, distraction in's aspect,    555
A broken voice, and his whole function suiting    556
With forms to his conceit? And all for nothing!    557
For Hecuba!
What's Hecuba to him, or he to Hecuba,
That he should weep for her? What would he do
Had he the motive and the cue for passion
That I have? He would drown the stage with tears
And cleave the general ear with horrid speech,    563
Make mad the guilty and appal the free,    564
Confound the ignorant, and amaze indeed    565
The very faculties of eyes and ears. Yet I,
A dull and muddy-mettled rascal, peak    567
Like John-a-dreams, unpregnant of my cause,    568
And can say nothing—no, not for a king
Upon whose property and most dear life    570
A damned defeat was made. Am I a coward?    571
Who calls me villain? Breaks my pate across?    572
Plucks off my beard and blows it in my face?
Tweaks me by th' nose? Gives me the lie i'th' throat    574
As deep as to the lungs? Who does me this?
Ha, 'swounds, I should take it; for it cannot be    576
But I am pigeon-livered and lack gall    577
To make oppression bitter, or ere this    578
I should ha' fatted all the region kites    579
With this slave's offal. Bloody, bawdy villain!    580
Remorseless, treacherous, lecherous, kindless villain!    581
Oh, vengeance!
Why, what an ass am I! This is most brave,    583
That I, the son of a dear father murdered,
Prompted to my revenge by heaven and hell,
Must like a whore unpack my heart with words
And fall a-cursing, like a very drab,    587
A scullion! Fie upon't, foh! About, my brains!    588
Hum, I have heard
That guilty creatures sitting at a play
Have by the very cunning of the scene    591
Been struck so to the soul that presently    592

They have proclaimed their malefactions;
For murder, though it have no tongue, will speak
With most miraculous organ. I'll have these players
Play something like the murder of my father
Before mine uncle. I'll observe his looks;
I'll tent him to the quick. If 'a but blench,    598
I know my course. The spirit that I have seen
May be the devil, and the devil hath power
T'assume a pleasing shape; yea, and perhaps,
Out of my weakness and my melancholy,
As he is very potent with such spirits,    603
Abuses me to damn me. I'll have grounds    604
More relative than this. The play's the thing    605
Wherein I'll catch the conscience of the King.    *Exit.*

## [3.1]

*Enter King, Queen, Polonius, Ophelia,*
*Rosencrantz, Guildenstern, and lords.*

KING
And can you by no drift of circumstance    1
Get from him why he puts on this confusion,
Grating so harshly all his days of quiet
With turbulent and dangerous lunacy?
ROSENCRANTZ
He does confess he feels himself distracted,
But from what cause 'a will by no means speak.
GUILDENSTERN
Nor do we find him forward to be sounded,    7
But with a crafty madness keeps aloof
When we would bring him on to some confession
Of his true state.
QUEEN                    Did he receive you well?
ROSENCRANTZ    Most like a gentleman.
GUILDENSTERN
But with much forcing of his disposition.    12
ROSENCRANTZ
Niggard of question, but of our demands    13
Most free in his reply.
QUEEN                    Did you assay him    14
To any pastime?
ROSENCRANTZ
Madam, it so fell out that certain players
We o'erraught on the way. Of these we told him,    17
And there did seem in him a kind of joy
To hear of it. They are about the court,
And, as I think, they have already order
This night to play before him.
POLONIUS                    'Tis most true,
And he beseeched me to entreat Your Majesties
To hear and see the matter.

552 But merely   553 force . . . conceit bring his innermost being so entirely into accord with his conception (of the role)   554 from her working as a result of, or in response to, his soul's activity.   wanned grew pale   555 aspect look, glance   556–7 his whole . . . conceit all his bodily powers responding with actions to suit his thought.
563 the general ear everyone's ear.   horrid horrible   564 appal (Literally, make pale.)   free innocent   565 Confound the ignorant i.e., dumbfound those who know nothing of the crime that has been committed.   amaze stun   567 muddy-mettled dull-spirited
567–8 peak . . . cause mope, like a dreaming idler, not quickened by my cause   570 property person and function   571 damned defeat damnable act of destruction   572 pate head   574 Gives . . . throat Calls me an out-and-out liar   576 'swounds by his (Christ's) wounds   577 pigeon-livered (The pigeon or dove was popularly supposed to be mild because it secreted no gall.)   578 To . . . bitter to make things bitter for oppressors   579 region kites kites (birds of prey) of the air   580 offal entrails.   581 Remorseless Pitiless.   kindless unnatural   583 brave fine, admirable. (Said ironically.)
587 drab whore   588 scullion menial kitchen servant. (Apt to be foul-mouthed.)   About About it, to work   591 cunning art, skill.   scene dramatic presentation   592 presently at once

598 tent probe.   the quick the tender part of a wound, the core.   blench quail, flinch   603 spirits humors (of melancholy)   604 Abuses deludes   605 relative cogent, pertinent
3.1. Location: The castle.
1 drift of circumstance tactful inquiry   7 forward willing.   sounded questioned   12 disposition inclination.   13 Niggard of question Laconic.   demands questions   14 assay try to win   17 o'erraught overtook

KING
    With all my heart, and it doth much content me
    To hear him so inclined.
    Good gentlemen, give him a further edge      26
    And drive his purpose on to these delights.

ROSENCRANTZ
    We shall, my lord.
                *Exeunt Rosencrantz and Guildenstern.*

KING             Sweet Gertrude, leave us too,
    For we have closely sent for Hamlet hither,      29
    That he, as 'twere by accident, may here
    Affront Ophelia.      31
    Her father and myself, lawful espials,      32
    Will so bestow ourselves that seeing, unseen,
    We may of their encounter frankly judge,
    And gather by him, as he is behaved,
    If't be th'affliction of his love or no
    That thus he suffers for.

QUEEN             I shall obey you.
    And for your part, Ophelia, I do wish
    That your good beauties be the happy cause
    Of Hamlet's wildness. So shall I hope your virtues
    Will bring him to his wonted way again,      41
    To both your honors.

OPHELIA        Madam, I wish it may.
                     *[Exit Queen.]*

POLONIUS
    Ophelia, walk you here.—Gracious, so please you,      43
    We will bestow ourselves. *[To Ophelia]* Read on this
        book,            *[giving her a book]*      44
    That show of such an exercise may color      45
    Your loneliness. We are oft to blame in this—      46
    'Tis too much proved—that with devotion's visage      47
    And pious action we do sugar o'er
    The devil himself.

KING *[aside]*      Oh, 'tis too true!
    How smart a lash that speech doth give my
        conscience!
    The harlot's cheek, beautied with plast'ring art,
    Is not more ugly to the thing that helps it      53
    Than is my deed to my most painted word.      54
    Oh, heavy burden!

POLONIUS
    I hear him coming. Let's withdraw, my lord.      56
            *[The King and Polonius withdraw.]*

    *Enter Hamlet. [Ophelia pretends to read a book.]*

HAMLET
    To be, or not to be, that is the question:
    Whether 'tis nobler in the mind to suffer
    The slings and arrows of outrageous fortune,

    Or to take arms against a sea of troubles
    And by opposing end them. To die, to sleep—
    No more—and by a sleep to say we end
    The heartache and the thousand natural shocks
    That flesh is heir to. 'Tis a consummation
    Devoutly to be wished. To die, to sleep;
    To sleep, perchance to dream. Ay, there's the rub,      66
    For in that sleep of death what dreams may come,
    When we have shuffled off this mortal coil,      68
    Must give us pause. There's the respect      69
    That makes calamity of so long life.      70
    For who would bear the whips and scorns of time,
    Th'oppressor's wrong, the proud man's contumely,      72
    The pangs of disprized love, the law's delay,      73
    The insolence of office, and the spurns      74
    That patient merit of th'unworthy takes,      75
    When he himself might his quietus make      76
    With a bare bodkin? Who would these fardels bear,      77
    To grunt and sweat under a weary life,
    But that the dread of something after death,
    The undiscovered country from whose bourn      80
    No traveler returns, puzzles the will,
    And makes us rather bear those ills we have
    Than fly to others that we know not of?
    Thus conscience does make cowards of us all;      84
    And thus the native hue of resolution      85
    Is sicklied o'er with the pale cast of thought,      86
    And enterprises of great pith and moment      87
    With this regard their currents turn awry      88
    And lose the name of action.—Soft you now,      89
    The fair Ophelia.—Nymph, in thy orisons      90
    Be all my sins remembered.

OPHELIA              Good my lord,      91
    How does Your Honor for this many a day?

HAMLET
    I humbly thank you; well, well, well.

OPHELIA
    My lord, I have remembrances of yours,
    That I have longèd long to redeliver.
    I pray you, now receive them.      *[She offers tokens.]*

HAMLET
    No, not I. I never gave you aught.

OPHELIA
    My honored lord, you know right well you did,
    And with them words of so sweet breath composed
    As made the things more rich. Their perfume lost,
    Take these again, for to the noble mind

---

**26 edge** incitement    **29 closely** privately    **31 Affront** confront, meet    **32 espials** spies    **41 wonted** customary    **43 Gracious** Your Grace (i.e., the King)    **44 bestow** conceal    **45 exercise** religious exercise. (The book she reads is one of devotion.)    **color** give a plausible appearance to    **46 loneliness** being alone.    **47 too much proved** too often shown to be true, too often practiced    **53 to . . . helps it** in comparison with the cosmetic that fashions the cheek's false beauty    **54 painted word** deceptive utterances.    **56.1 *withdraw*** (The King and Polonius may retire behind an arras. The stage directions specify that they "enter" again near the end of the scene.)

**66 rub** (Literally, an obstacle in the game of bowls.)    **68 shuffled** sloughed, cast.    **coil** turmoil    **69 respect** consideration    **70 of . . . life** so long-lived, something we willingly endure for so long. (Also suggesting that long life is itself a calamity.)    **72 contumely** insolent abuse    **73 disprized** unvalued    **74 office** officialdom.    **spurns** insults    **75 of . . . takes** receives from unworthy persons    **76 quietus** acquittance; here, death    **77 a bare bodkin** a mere dagger, unsheathed.    **fardels** burdens    **80 bourn** frontier, boundary    **84 conscience** (1) introspection (2) moral promptings    **85 native hue** natural color, complexion    **86 cast** tinge, shade of color    **87 pith** profundity.    **moment** importance    **88 regard** respect, consideration.    **currents** courses    **89 Soft you** i.e., Wait a minute, gently    **90–1 in . . . remembered** i.e., pray for me, sinner that I am.

Rich gifts wax poor when givers prove unkind.
There, my lord.                              [*She gives tokens.*]

HAMLET   Ha, ha! Are you honest?                                    104

OPHELIA   My lord?

HAMLET   Are you fair?                                              106

OPHELIA   What means Your Lordship?

HAMLET   That if you be honest and fair, your honesty               108
should admit no discourse to your beauty.                           109

OPHELIA   Could beauty, my lord, have better commerce               110
than with honesty?

HAMLET   Ay, truly, for the power of beauty will sooner
transform honesty from what it is to a bawd than the
force of honesty can translate beauty into his likeness.            114
This was sometime a paradox, but now the time gives                 115
it proof. I did love you once.                                      116

OPHELIA   Indeed, my lord, you made me believe so.

HAMLET   You should not have believed me, for virtue                118
cannot so inoculate our old stock but we shall relish of            119
it. I loved you not.                                                120

OPHELIA   I was the more deceived.

HAMLET   Get thee to a nunnery. Why wouldst thou be a               122
breeder of sinners? I am myself indifferent honest, but             123
yet I could accuse me of such things that it were better
my mother had not borne me: I am very proud,
revengeful, ambitious, with more offenses at my beck                126
than I have thoughts to put them in, imagination to
give them shape, or time to act them in. What should
such fellows as I do crawling between heaven and
earth? We are arrant knaves all; believe none of us.
Go thy ways to a nunnery. Where's your father?

OPHELIA   At home, my lord.

HAMLET   Let the doors be shut upon him, that he may
play the fool nowhere but in 's own house. Farewell.

OPHELIA   Oh, help him, you sweet heavens!

HAMLET   If thou dost marry, I'll give thee this plague for
thy dowry: be thou as chaste as ice, as pure as snow,
thou shalt not escape calumny. Get thee to a nunnery,
go, farewell. Or, if thou wilt needs marry, marry a fool, for
wise men know well enough what monsters you                         140
make of them. To a nunnery, go, and quickly too.
Farewell.

OPHELIA   O heavenly powers, restore him!

HAMLET   I have heard of your paintings too, well                   144
enough. God hath given you one face, and you make
yourselves another. You jig, you amble, and you                     146
lisp, you nickname God's creatures, and make your                   147
wantonness your ignorance. Go to, I'll no more on't;                148

it hath made me mad. I say we will have no more
marriages. Those that are married already—all but
one—shall live. The rest shall keep as they are. To a
nunnery, go.                                          *Exit.*

OPHELIA
Oh, what a noble mind is here o'erthrown!
The courtier's, soldier's, scholar's, eye, tongue, sword,
Th'expectancy and rose of the fair state,                           155
The glass of fashion and the mold of form,                          156
Th'observed of all observers, quite, quite down!                    157
And I, of ladies most deject and wretched,
That sucked the honey of his music vows,                            159
Now see that noble and most sovereign reason
Like sweet bells jangled out of tune and harsh,
That unmatched form and feature of blown youth                      162
Blasted with ecstasy. Oh, woe is me,                                163
T'have seen what I have seen, see what I see!

*Enter King and Polonius.*

KING
Love? His affections do not that way tend;                          165
Nor what he spake, though it lacked form a little,
Was not like madness. There's something in his soul
O'er which his melancholy sits on brood,                            168
And I do doubt the hatch and the disclose                           169
Will be some danger; which to prevent,
I have in quick determination
Thus set it down: he shall with speed to England                    172
For the demand of our neglected tribute.
Haply the seas and countries different                              174
With variable objects shall expel                                   175
This something-settled matter in his heart,                         176
Whereon his brains still beating puts him thus                      177
From fashion of himself. What think you on't?                       178

POLONIUS
It shall do well. But yet do I believe
The origin and commencement of his grief
Sprung from neglected love.—How now, Ophelia?
You need not tell us what Lord Hamlet said;
We heard it all.—My lord, do as you please,
But, if you hold it fit, after the play
Let his queen-mother all alone entreat him
To show his grief. Let her be round with him;                       186
And I'll be placed, so please you, in the ear
Of all their conference. If she find him not,                       188
To England send him, or confine him where

---

**104 honest** (1) truthful (2) chaste.   **106 fair** (1) beautiful (2) just, honorable.   **108 your honesty** your chastity   **109 discourse to** familiar dealings with   **110 commerce** dealings, intercourse   **114 his** its   **115–16 This . . . proof** This was formerly a seeming absurdity, but now the present age confirms how true it is.   **118–20 virtue . . . of it** virtue cannot be grafted onto our sinful condition without our retaining some taste of the old stock.   **122 nunnery** convent. (With an awareness that the word was also used derisively to denote a brothel.)   **123 indifferent honest** reasonably virtuous   **126 beck** command   **140 monsters** (An allusion to the horns of a cuckold.)   **you** i.e., you women   **144 paintings** use of cosmetics   **146–8 You jig . . . ignorance** i.e., You prance about frivolously and speak with affected coyness, you put new labels on God's creatures (by your use of cosmetics), and you excuse your affectations on the grounds of pretended ignorance.   **148 Go to** (Expressing anger.)   **on't** of it

**155 Th'expectancy and rose** the hope and ornament   **156 The glass . . . form** the mirror of true self-fashioning and the pattern of courtly behavior   **157 Th'observed . . . observers** i.e., the center of attention and honor in the court   **159 music** musical, sweetly uttered   **162 blown** blossoming   **163 Blasted with ecstasy** blighted with madness.   **165 affections** emotions, feelings   **168 sits on brood** sits like a bird on a nest, about to *hatch* mischief (line 169)   **169 doubt** suspect, fear.   **disclose** disclosure, hatching   **172 set it down** resolved   **174 Haply** Perhaps   **175 variable objects** various sights and surroundings to divert him   **176 This something . . . heart** the strange matter settled in his heart   **177 still** continually   **178 From . . . himself** out of his natural manner.   **186 round** blunt   **188 find him not** fails to discover what is troubling him

Your wisdom best shall think.

KING                                    It shall be so.

Madness in great ones must not unwatched go.

*Exeunt.*

❖

## [3.2]

*Enter Hamlet and two or three of the Players.*

HAMLET    Speak the speech, I pray you, as I pronounced
it to you, trippingly on the tongue. But if you mouth    2
it, as many of your players do, I had as lief the town crier    3
spoke my lines. Nor do not saw the air too much with
your hand, thus, but use all gently; for in the very
torrent, tempest, and, as I may say, whirlwind of your
passion, you must acquire and beget a temperance
that may give it smoothness. Oh, it offends me to the
soul to hear a robustious periwig-pated fellow tear a    9
passion to tatters, to very rags, to split the ears of the
groundlings, who for the most part are capable of    11
nothing but inexplicable dumb shows and noise. I    12
would have such a fellow whipped for o'erdoing Ter-    13
magant. It out-Herods Herod. Pray you, avoid it.    14

FIRST PLAYER    I warrant Your Honor.    15

HAMLET    Be not too tame neither, but let your own
discretion be your tutor. Suit the action to the word,
the word to the action, with this special observance,
that you o'erstep not the modesty of nature. For    19
anything so o'erdone is from the purpose of playing,    20
whose end, both at the first and now, was and is to
hold as 'twere the mirror up to nature, to show virtue
her feature, scorn her own image, and the very age    23
and body of the time his form and pressure. Now this    24
overdone or come tardy off, though it makes the    25
unskillful laugh, cannot but make the judicious grieve,    26
the censure of the which one must in your allowance    27
o'erweigh a whole theater of others. Oh, there be players that I have seen play, and heard others praise, and
that highly, not to speak it profanely, that, neither    30
having th'accent of Christians nor the gait of Chris-    31
tian, pagan, nor no man, have so strutted and bellowed    32
that I have thought some of nature's journeymen had    33

made men and not made them well, they imitated
humanity so abominably.    35

FIRST PLAYER    I hope we have reformed that indifferently    36
with us, sir.

HAMLET    Oh, reform it altogether. And let those that play
your clowns speak no more than is set down for them;
for there be of them that will themselves laugh, to set    40
on some quantity of barren spectators to laugh too,    41
though in the meantime some necessary question of
the play be then to be considered. That's villainous,
and shows a most pitiful ambition in the fool that uses
it. Go make you ready.                    [*Exeunt Players.*]

*Enter Polonius, Guildenstern, and Rosencrantz.*

How now, my lord, will the King hear this piece of
work?

POLONIUS    And the Queen too, and that presently.    48

HAMLET    Bid the players make haste.    [*Exit Polonius.*]
Will you two help to hasten them?

ROSENCRANTZ
Ay, my lord.                              *Exeunt they two.*

HAMLET              What ho, Horatio!

*Enter Horatio.*

HORATIO    Here, sweet lord, at your service.

HAMLET
Horatio, thou art e'en as just a man
As e'er my conversation coped withal.    54

HORATIO
Oh, my dear lord—

HAMLET                    Nay, do not think I flatter,
For what advancement may I hope from thee
That no revenue hast but thy good spirits
To feed and clothe thee? Why should the poor be
    flattered?
No, let the candied tongue lick absurd pomp,    59
And crook the pregnant hinges of the knee    60
Where thrift may follow fawning. Dost thou hear?    61
Since my dear soul was mistress of her choice
And could of men distinguish her election,    63
Sh' hath sealed thee for herself, for thou hast been    64
As one, in suffering all, that suffers nothing,
A man that Fortune's buffets and rewards
Hast ta'en with equal thanks; and blest are those
Whose blood and judgment are so well commingled    68
That they are not a pipe for Fortune's finger
To sound what stop she please. Give me that man    70
That is not passion's slave, and I will wear him
In my heart's core, ay, in my heart of heart,
As I do thee.—Something too much of this.—
There is a play tonight before the King.
One scene of it comes near the circumstance
Which I have told thee of my father's death.

**3.2. Location: The castle.**
**2–3 mouth it** declaim, speak exaggeratedly    **3 your players** actors nowadays.    **I had as lief** I would just as soon    **town crier** minor official making public announcements    **9 robustious** bombastic.    **periwig-pated**
wig-wearing    **11 groundlings** spectators who paid least and stood in the
yard of the theater.    **capable of** able to understand    **12 dumb shows
and noise** noisy spectacle (rather than thoughtful drama).    **13–14 Termagant** a supposed deity of the Mohammedans, not found in any English medieval play but elsewhere portrayed as violent and blustering.
**14 Herod** King of Judea who order the massacre of all male children in
an attempt to kill Jesus (Mathew 2:2). He appears in many medieval cycle
plays as a blustering tyrant.    **15 warrant** assure.    **19 modesty** restraint,
moderation    **20 from** contrary to    **23 scorn** i.e., something foolish and
deserving of scorn    **23–4 and the . . . pressure** and the present state of
affairs its likeness as seen in an impression, such as wax.    **25 come tardy
off** done lamely    **25–6 the unskillful** those lacking in judgment    **27 the
censure . . . one** the judgment of even one of whom.    **your allowance**
your scale of values    **30 not . . . profanely** (Hamlet anticipates his idea in
lines 33–4 that some men were not made by God at all.)    **31 Christians**
i.e., ordinary decent folk    **32 nor no man** i.e., nor any human being at
all    **33 journeymen** common workmen

**35 abominably** (Shakespeare's usual spelling, "abhominably," suggests a literal though etymologically incorrect meaning, "removed
from human nature.")    **36 indifferently** tolerably    **40 of them** some
among them    **41 barren** i.e., of wit    **48 presently** at once.    **54 my . . .
withal** my dealings encountered.    **59 candied** sugared, flattering    **60 pregnant** compliant    **61 thrift** profit    **63 could . . . election**
could make distinguishing choices among persons    **64 sealed thee**
(Literally, as one would seal a legal document to mark possession.)    **68 blood** passion    **70 stop** hole in a wind instrument for
controlling the sound

I prithee, when thou see'st that act afoot,
Even with the very comment of thy soul    78
Observe my uncle. If his occulted guilt    79
Do not itself unkennel in one speech,    80
It is a damnèd ghost that we have seen,
And my imaginations are as foul
As Vulcan's stithy. Give him heedful note,    83
For I mine eyes will rivet to his face,
And after we will both our judgments join
In censure of his seeming.
HORATIO                    Well, my lord.    86
If 'a steal aught the whilst this play is playing    87
And scape detecting, I will pay the theft.    88

*Enter King, Queen, Polonius, Ophelia, Rosen-*
*crantz, Guildenstern, and other lords attendant,*
*with his guard carrying torches. Danish march.*
*Sound a flourish.*

HAMLET    They are coming to the play. I must be idle.    89
Get you a place.    [*The King, Queen, and courtiers sit.*]
KING    How fares our cousin Hamlet?    91
HAMLET    Excellent, i'faith, of the chameleon's dish: I eat    92
the air, promise-crammed. You cannot feed capons so.    93
KING    I have nothing with this answer, Hamlet. These    94
words are not mine.    95
HAMLET    No, nor mine now. [*To Polonius*] My lord, you    96
played once i'th'university, you say?
POLONIUS    That I did, my lord, and was accounted a
good actor.
HAMLET    And what did you enact?
POLONIUS    I did enact Julius Caesar. I was killed i'th'    101
Capitol; Brutus killed me.    102
HAMLET    It was a brute part of him to kill so capital a    103
calf there.—Be the players ready?    104
ROSENCRANTZ    Ay, my lord. They stay upon your    105
patience.
QUEEN    Come hither, my dear Hamlet, sit by me.
HAMLET    No, good mother, here's mettle more attractive.    108
POLONIUS [*to the King*]    Oho, do you mark that?
HAMLET    Lady, shall I lie in your lap?    110
[*Lying down at Ophelia's feet.*]

OPHELIA    No, my lord.
HAMLET    I mean, my head upon your lap?
OPHELIA    Ay, my lord.
HAMLET    Do you think I meant country matters?    114
OPHELIA    I think nothing, my lord.
HAMLET    That's a fair thought to lie between maids'
legs.
OPHELIA    What is, my lord?
HAMLET    Nothing.    119
OPHELIA    You are merry, my lord.
HAMLET    Who, I?
OPHELIA    Ay, my lord.
HAMLET    Oh, God, your only jig maker. What should a    123
man do but be merry? For look you how cheerfully my
mother looks, and my father died within 's two hours.    125
OPHELIA    Nay, 'tis twice two months, my lord.
HAMLET    So long? Nay then, let the devil wear black, for    127
I'll have a suit of sables. O heavens! Die two months    128
ago, and not forgotten yet? Then there's hope a great
man's memory may outlive his life half a year. But, by'r    130
Lady, 'a must build churches, then, or else shall 'a    131
suffer not thinking on, with the hobbyhorse, whose    132
epitaph is "For oh, for oh, the hobbyhorse is forgot."    133

*Hautboys play. The dumb show enters.*

*Enter a King and Queen, very lovingly, the*
*Queen embracing him. She kneels,*
*and makes show of protestation unto him. He*
*takes her up, and declines his head upon her neck.*
*[He] lays him down upon a bank of flowers. She,*
*seeing him asleep, leaves him. Anon comes in*
*a fellow, takes off his crown, kisses it, and pours*
*poison in the King's ears, and exits. The*
*Queen returns, finds the King dead, and makes*
*passionate action. The Poisoner, with some two or*
*three mutes, comes in again, seeming to lament with her.*
*The dead body is carried away. The Poisoner wooes the*
*Queen with gifts; she seems loath and unwilling*
*awhile, but in the end accepts his love.*
*Exeunt [players].*

OPHELIA    What means this, my lord?
HAMLET    Marry, this is miching mallico; it means mis-    135
chief.

---

**78 the very . . . soul** your most penetrating observation and consideration    **79 occulted** hidden    **80 unkennel** (As one would say of a fox driven from its lair.)    **83 Vulcan's stithy** the smithy, the place of stiths (anvils) of the Roman god of fire and metalworking.    **86 censure of his seeming** judgment of his appearance or behavior.    **87 If 'a steal aught** If he gets away with anything    **88.2 *lords attendant*** lords in attendance    **89 idle** (1) unoccupied (2) mad.    **91 cousin** i.e., close relative    **92 chameleon's dish** (Chameleons were supposed to feed on air. Hamlet deliberately misinterprets the King's *fares* as "feeds." By his phrase *eat the air* he also plays on the idea of feeding himself with the promise of succession, of being the *heir*.)    **93 capons** roosters castrated and *crammed* with feed to make them succulent    **94 have . . . with** make nothing of, or gain nothing from    **95 are not mine** do not respond to what I asked.    **96 nor mine now** (Once spoken, words are proverbially no longer the speaker's own—and hence should be uttered warily.)    **101–2 i'th' Capitol** (where Caesar was assassinated, according to *Julius Caesar*, 3.1, but see 1.3.126n in that play)    **103 brute** (Hamlet puns on Latin, *brutus*, "stupid," referring to the mad guise adopted by Lucius Junius Brutus in order to confuse his enemies, the tyrannical Tarquins, whose overthrow ushered in the Roman republic, c. 509 B.C.)    **part** (1) deed (2) role    **104 calf** fool    **105 stay upon** await    **108 mettle** disposition; also suggesting "metal," with attractive magnetic properties    **110 Lady . . . lap?** On stage, Hamlet often lies at Ophelia's feet, but he could instead offer to do this and continue to stand.

**114 country matters** i.e., sexual intercourse. (With a bawdy pun on the first syllable of *country*.)    **119 Nothing** The figure zero or naught, suggesting the female sexual anatomy. (*Thing* not infrequently has a bawdy connotation of male or female anatomy, and the reference here could be male.)    **123 only jig maker** very best composer of jigs, i.e., pointless merriment. (Hamlet replies sardonically to Ophelia's observation that he is merry by saying, "If you're looking for someone who is really merry, you've come to the right person.")    **125 within 's** within this (i.e., these)    **127–8 let . . . sables** i.e., if mourning for a dead father can last only two months, then let the devil mourn in black for all I care, while I'll wear sable robes, suitably black in appearance but actually quite luxurious and soft.    **130–1 by'r Lady** i.e., by Mary, mother of God. (A common oath.)    **132 suffer . . . on** undergo oblivion    **133 "For . . . forgot"** (Verse of a song occurring also in *Love's Labor's Lost*, 3.1.27–8. The hobbyhorse was a character made up to resemble a horse and rider, appearing in the morris dance and such May-game sports. This song laments the disappearance of such customs under pressure from the Puritans.)    **133.12 *mutes*** i.e., nonspeaking actors    **135 this is miching mallico** this is sneaking mischief

OPHELIA    Belike this show imports the argument of the 137
play.

*Enter Prologue.*

HAMLET    We shall know by this fellow. The players can-
not keep counsel; they'll tell all.                          140
OPHELIA    Will 'a tell us what this show meant?
HAMLET    Ay, or any show that you will show him. Be 142
not you ashamed to show, he'll not shame to tell you 143
what it means.
OPHELIA    You are naught, you are naught. I'll mark the 145
play.
PROLOGUE
    For us, and for our tragedy,
    Here stooping to your clemency,                          148
    We beg your hearing patiently.            [*Exit.*]
HAMLET    Is this a prologue, or the posy of a ring?       150
OPHELIA    'Tis brief, my lord.
HAMLET    As woman's love.

*Enter [two Players as] King and his Queen.*

PLAYER KING
    Full thirty times hath Phoebus' cart gone round        153
    Neptune's salt wash and Tellus' orbèd ground,          154
    And thirty dozen moons with borrowed sheen             155
    About the world have times twelve thirties been,
    Since love our hearts and Hymen did our hands          157
    Unite commutual in most sacred bands.                  158
PLAYER QUEEN
    So many journeys may the sun and moon
    Make us again count o'er ere love be done!
    But, woe is me, you are so sick of late,
    So far from cheer and from your former state,
    That I distrust you. Yet, though I distrust,           163
    Discomfort you, my lord, it nothing must.              164
    For women's fear and love holds quantity;              165
    In neither aught, or in extremity.                     166
    Now, what my love is, proof hath made you know,        167
    And as my love is sized, my fear is so.
    Where love is great, the littlest doubts are fear;     169
    Where little fears grow great, great love grows there.
PLAYER KING
    Faith, I must leave thee, love, and shortly too;
    My operant powers their functions leave to do.         172
    And thou shalt live in this fair world behind,         173
    Honored, beloved; and haply one as kind
    For husband shalt thou—
PLAYER QUEEN                      Oh, confound the rest!

Such love must needs be treason in my breast.
In second husband let me be accurst!
None wed the second but who killed the first.               178
HAMLET    Wormwood, wormwood.                                179
PLAYER QUEEN
    The instances that second marriage move                 180
    Are base respects of thrift, but none of love.          181
    A second time I kill my husband dead
    When second husband kisses me in bed.
PLAYER KING
    I do believe you think what now you speak,
    But what we do determine oft we break.
    Purpose is but the slave to memory,                     186
    Of violent birth, but poor validity,                    187
    Which now, like fruit unripe, sticks on the tree,       188
    But fall unshaken when they mellow be.
    Most necessary 'tis that we forget                      190
    To pay ourselves what to ourselves is debt.             191
    What to ourselves in passion we propose,
    The passion ending, doth the purpose lose.
    The violence of either grief or joy
    Their own enactures with themselves destroy.            195
    Where joy most revels, grief doth most lament;          196
    Grief joys, joy grieves, on slender accident.           197
    This world is not for aye, nor 'tis not strange         198
    That even our loves should with our fortunes change;
    For 'tis a question left us yet to prove,
    Whether love lead fortune, or else fortune love.
    The great man down, you mark his favorite flies;        202
    The poor advanced makes friends of enemies.             203
    And hitherto doth love on fortune tend;                 204
    For who not needs shall never lack a friend,            205
    And who in want a hollow friend doth try                206
    Directly seasons him his enemy.                         207
    But, orderly to end where I begun,
    Our wills and fates do so contrary run                  209
    That our devices still are overthrown;                  210
    Our thoughts are ours, their ends none of our own.      211
    So think thou wilt no second husband wed,
    But die thy thoughts when thy first lord is dead.
PLAYER QUEEN
    Nor earth to me give food, nor heaven light,            214
    Sport and repose lock from me day and night,            215

---

137 **Belike** Probably.   **argument** plot   140 **counsel** secret   142–3 **Be not you** Provided you are not   145 **naught** indecent. (Ophelia is reacting to Hamlet's pointed remarks about not being ashamed to show all.)   148 **stooping** bowing   150 **posy . . . ring** brief motto in verse inscribed in a ring.   153 **Phoebus' cart** the sun-god's chariot, making its yearly cycle   154 **salt wash** the sea.   **Tellus'** Tellus was goddess of the earth, of the *orbèd ground*   155 **borrowed** i.e., reflected   157 **Hymen** god of matrimony   158 **commutual** mutually.   **bands** bonds.   163 **distrust** am anxious about   164 **Discomfort . . . must** it must not distress you at all.   165 **hold quantity** keep proportion with one another   166 **In . . . extremity** women experience fear and love either minimally or extremely.   167 **proof** experience   169 **the littlest** even the littlest   172 **My . . . to do** my vital functions are shutting down.   173 **behind** after I have gone

178 **None** (1) Let no woman; or (2) No woman does.   **but who** except the one who   179 **Wormwood** i.e., How bitter. (Literally, a bitter-tasting plant.)   180 **instances** motives.   **move** motivate   181 **base . . . thrift** ignoble considerations of material prosperity   186 **Purpose . . . memory** Our good intentions are subject to forgetfulness   187 **validity** strength, durability   188 **Which** i.e., purpose   190–1 **Most . . . debt** It's inevitable that in time we forget the obligations we have imposed on ourselves.   195 **enactures** fulfillments   196–7 **Where . . . accident** The capacity for extreme joy and grief go together, and often one extreme is instantly changed into its opposite on the slightest provocation.   198 **aye** ever   202 **down** fallen in fortune   203 **The poor . . . enemies** when one of humble station is promoted, you see his enemies suddenly becoming his friends.   204 **hitherto** up to this point in the argument, or, to this extent.   **tend** attend   205 **who not needs** he who is not in need (of wealth)   206 **who in want** he who, being in need.   **try** test (his generosity)   207 **seasons him** ripens him into   209 **Our . . . run** what we want and what we get go contrarily   210 **devices** intentions.   **still** continually   211 **ends** results   214 **Nor** Let neither   215 **Sport . . . night** may day deny me its pastimes and night its repose

To desperation turn my trust and hope,
An anchor's cheer in prison be my scope!                217
Each opposite that blanks the face of joy               218
Meet what I would have well and it destroy!             219
Both here and hence pursue me lasting strife            220
If, once a widow, ever I be wife!

HAMLET   If she should break it now!

PLAYER KING

'Tis deeply sworn. Sweet, leave me here awhile;
My spirits grow dull, and fain I would beguile         224
The tedious day with sleep.

PLAYER QUEEN                        Sleep rock thy brain,
And never come mischance between us twain!

                    [He sleeps.] Exit [Player Queen].

HAMLET   Madam, how like you this play?

QUEEN   The lady doth protest too much, methinks.      228

HAMLET   Oh, but she'll keep her word.

KING   Have you heard the argument? Is there no of-    230
fense in't?

HAMLET   No, no, they do but jest, poison in jest. No  232
offense i'th' world.                                   233

KING   What do you call the play?

HAMLET   The Mousetrap. Marry, how? Tropically.       235
This play is the image of a murder done in Vienna.
Gonzago is the Duke's name, his wife, Baptista. You   237
shall see anon. 'Tis a knavish piece of work, but what
of that? Your Majesty, and we that have free souls, it 239
touches us not. Let the galled jade wince, our withers 240
are unwrung.                                           241

            Enter Lucianus.

This is one Lucianus, nephew to the King.

OPHELIA   You are as good as a chorus, my lord.       243

HAMLET   I could interpret between you and your love,  244
if I could see the puppets dallying.                  245

OPHELIA   You are keen, my lord, you are keen.        246

HAMLET   It would cost you a groaning to take off mine
edge.

OPHELIA   Still better, and worse.                    249

HAMLET   So you mis-take your husbands.—Begin, mur-   250
derer. Pox, leave thy damnable faces and begin. Come,
the croaking raven doth bellow for revenge.

LUCIANUS

Thoughts black, hands apt, drugs fit, and time
   agreeing,
Confederate season, else no creature seeing,          254
Thou mixture rank, of midnight weeds collected,       255
With Hecate's ban thrice blasted, thrice infected,    256
Thy natural magic and dire property                   257
On wholesome life usurp immediately.

   [He] pours the poison in his [the Player King's] ears.

HAMLET   'A poisons him i'th' garden for his estate. His 259
name's Gonzago. The story is extant, and written in
very choice Italian. You shall see anon how the
murderer gets the love of Gonzago's wife.

                              [Claudius rises.]

OPHELIA   The King rises.

HAMLET   What, frighted with false fire?              264

QUEEN   How fares my lord?

POLONIUS   Give o'er the play.

KING   Give me some light. Away!

COURTIERS   Lights, lights, lights!

            Exeunt all but Hamlet and Horatio.

HAMLET

"Why, let the strucken deer go weep,                  269
   The hart ungallèd play.                            270
For some must watch, while some must sleep;           271
   Thus runs the world away."                         272
Would not this, sir, and a forest of feathers—if the  273
rest of my fortunes turn Turk with me—with two        274
Provincial roses on my razed shoes, get me a fellow-  275
ship in a cry of players?                              276

HORATIO   Half a share.

HAMLET   A whole one, I.
"For thou dost know, O Damon dear,                    279
   This realm dismantled was                          280
Of Jove himself, and now reigns here                  281
   A very, very—pajock."                              282

217 anchor's cheer anchorite's or hermit's fare.  my scope the extent of my happiness.  218–19 Each . . . destroy! May every adverse thing that causes the face of joy to turn pale meet and destroy everything that I desire to see prosper!  220 hence in the life hereafter  224 spirits vital spirits  228 doth . . . much makes too many promises and protestations  230 argument plot.  232 jest make believe.  232–3 offense crime, injury. (Hamlet playfully alters the King's use of the word in line 231 to mean "cause for objection.")  235 Tropically Figuratively. (The first quarto reading, "trapically," suggests a pun on trap in Mousetrap.)  237 Duke's i.e., King's. (An inconsistency that may be due to Shakespeare's possible acquaintance with a historical incident, the alleged murder of the Duke of Urbino by Luigi Gonzaga in 1538.)  239 free guiltless  240 galled jade horse whose hide is rubbed by saddle or harness.  withers the part between the horse's shoulder blades  241 unwrung not rubbed sore.  243 chorus (In many Elizabethan plays, the forthcoming action was explained by an actor known as the "chorus"; at a puppet show, the actor who spoke the dialogue was known as an "interpreter," as indicated by the lines following.)  244 interpret (1) ventriloquize the dialogue, as in a puppet show (2) act as pander  245 puppets dallying (With suggestion of sexual play, continued in keen, "sexually aroused," groaning, "moaning in pregnancy," and edge, "sexual desire" or "impetuosity.")  246 keen sharp, bitter  249 Still . . . worse More keen, always bettering what other people say with witty wordplay, but at the same time more offensive.

250 So Even thus (in marriage).  mis-take take falseheartedly and cheat on. (The marriage vows say "for better, for worse.")  254 Confederate . . . seeing the time and occasion conspiring (to assist me), and also no one seeing me  255 rank foul, offensive  256 Hecate's ban the curse of Hecate, the goddess of witchcraft  257 dire property baleful quality  259 estate i.e., the kingship.  His i.e., the King's  264 false fire the blank discharge of a gun loaded with powder but no shot.  269–72 Why . . . away (Perhaps from an old ballad, with allusion to the popular belief that a wounded deer retires to weep and die; compare with As You Like It, 2.1.33–66.)  270 ungallèd unafflicted  271 watch remain awake  272 Thus . . . away Thus the world goes.  273 this i.e., this success with the play I have just presented.  feathers (Allusion to the plumes that Elizabethan actors were fond of wearing.)  274 turn Turk with turn renegade against, go back on  275 Provincial roses rosettes of ribbon, named for roses grown in a part of France.  razed with ornamental slashing  275–6 fellowship . . . players partnership in a theatrical company.  276 cry pack (of hounds, etc.)  279 Damon the friend of Pythias, as Horatio is friend of Hamlet; or, a traditional pastoral name  280–2 This realm . . . pajock i.e., Jove, representing divine authority and justice, has abandoned this realm to its own devices, leaving in his stead only a peacock or vain pretender to virtue (though the rhyme-word expected in place of pajock or "peacock" suggests that the realm is now ruled over by an "ass").  280 dismantled stripped, divested

HORATIO   You might have rhymed.

HAMLET   Oh, good Horatio, I'll take the ghost's word for a thousand pound. Didst perceive?

HORATIO   Very well, my lord.

HAMLET   Upon the talk of the poisoning?

HORATIO   I did very well note him.

*Enter Rosencrantz and Guildenstern.*

HAMLET   Aha! Come, some music! Come, the recorders.
    "For if the King like not the comedy,
      Why then, belike, he likes it not, perdy."   292
Come, some music.

GUILDENSTERN   Good my lord, vouchsafe me a word with you.

HAMLET   Sir, a whole history.

GUILDENSTERN   The King, sir—

HAMLET   Ay, sir, what of him?

GUILDENSTERN   Is in his retirement marvelous dis-  299
tempered.                                300

HAMLET   With drink, sir?

GUILDENSTERN   No, my lord, with choler.   302

HAMLET   Your wisdom should show itself more richer to signify this to his doctor, for for me to put him to his purgation would perhaps plunge him into far more  305
choler.

GUILDENSTERN   Good my lord, put your discourse into some frame and start not so wildly from my affair.   308

HAMLET   I am tame, sir. Pronounce.

GUILDENSTERN   The Queen, your mother, in most great affliction of spirit, hath sent me to you.

HAMLET   You are welcome.

GUILDENSTERN   Nay, good my lord, this courtesy is not of the right breed. If it shall please you to make me a  314
wholesome answer, I will do your mother's command-
ment; if not, your pardon and my return shall be the  316
end of my business.

HAMLET   Sir, I cannot.

GUILDENSTERN   What, my lord?

HAMLET   Make you a wholesome answer; my wit's dis-
eased. But, sir, such answer as I can make, you shall command, or rather, as you say, my mother. Therefore no more, but to the matter. My mother, you say—

ROSENCRANTZ   Then thus she says: your behavior hath struck her into amazement and admiration.   325

HAMLET   Oh, wonderful son, that can so 'stonish a mother! But is there no sequel at the heels of this mother's admiration? Impart.   328

ROSENCRANTZ   She desires to speak with you in her closet ere you go to bed.   330

HAMLET   We shall obey, were she ten times our mother. Have you any further trade with us?

ROSENCRANTZ   My lord, you once did love me.

HAMLET   So I do still, by these pickers and stealers.   334

ROSENCRANTZ   Good my lord, what is your cause of distemper? You do surely bar the door upon your own liberty if you deny your griefs to your friend.   337

HAMLET   Sir, I lack advancement.

ROSENCRANTZ   How can that be, when you have the voice of the King himself for your succession in Denmark?

HAMLET   Ay, sir, but "While the grass grows"—the  342
proverb is something musty.   343

*Enter the Players with recorders.*

Oh, the recorders. Let me see one. [*He takes a recorder.*]
To withdraw with you: why do you go about to recover  345
the wind of me, as if you would drive me into a toil?  346

GUILDENSTERN   Oh, my lord, if my duty be too bold, my  347
love is too unmannerly.   348

HAMLET   I do not well understand that. Will you play  349
upon this pipe?

GUILDENSTERN   My lord, I cannot.

HAMLET   I pray you.

GUILDENSTERN   Believe me, I cannot.

HAMLET   I do beseech you.

GUILDENSTERN   I know no touch of it, my lord.

HAMLET   It is as easy as lying. Govern these ventages  356
with your fingers and thumb, give it breath with your mouth, and it will discourse most eloquent music. Look you, these are the stops.

GUILDENSTERN   But these cannot I command to any utterance of harmony. I have not the skill.

HAMLET   Why, look you now, how unworthy a thing you make of me! You would play upon me, you would seem to know my stops, you would pluck out the heart of my mystery, you would sound me from my lowest  365
note to the top of my compass, and there is much  366
music, excellent voice, in this little organ, yet cannot  367
you make it speak. 'Sblood, do you think I am easier to be played on than a pipe? Call me what instrument you will, though you can fret me, you cannot play  370
upon me.

*Enter Polonius.*

God bless you, sir!

<hr/>

292 **belike** perhaps.   **perdy** (A corruption of the French *par dieu*, "by God.")   299 **retirement** withdrawal to his chambers   299–300 **distem-pered** out of humor. (But Hamlet deliberately plays on the wider appli-cation to any illness of mind or body, as in lines 335–6, especially to drunkenness.)   302 **choler** anger. (But Hamlet takes the word in its more basic humoral sense of "bilious disorder.")   305 **purgation** (Ham-let hints at something going beyond medical treatment to bloodletting and the extraction of confession.)   308 **frame** order.   **start** shy or jump away (like a horse; the opposite of *tame* in line 309)   314 **breed** (1) kind (2) breeding, manners.   316 **pardon** permission to depart   325 **admira-tion** bewilderment.   328 **Impart** Speak.   330 **closet** private chamber

334 **pickers and stealers** i.e., hands. (So called from the catechism, "to keep my hands from picking and stealing.")   337 **liberty** i.e., being freed from *distemper*, line 336; but perhaps with a veiled threat as well.   **deny** refuse to share   342 **"While . . . grows"** (The rest of the proverb is "the silly horse starves"; Hamlet implies that his hopes of succession are distant in time at best.)   343 **something** somewhat 343.1 *Players* actors   345 **withdraw** speak privately   345–6 **recover the wind** get to the windward side (thus allowing the game to scent the hunter and thereby be driven in the opposite direction into the *toil* or net) 346 **toil** snare.   347–8 **if . . . unmannerly** if I am using an unmannerly boldness, it is my love that occasions it.   349 **I . . . that** i.e., I don't understand how genuine love can be unmannerly.   356 **ventages** finger-holes or *stops* (line 359) of the recorder   365 **sound** (1) fathom (2) produce sound in   366 **compass** range (of voice)   367 **organ** musical instrument   370 **fret** irritate. (With a quibble on the *frets* or ridges on the fingerboard of some stringed instruments to regulate the fingering.)

POLONIUS    My lord, the Queen would speak with you,
and presently.                                                                    374
HAMLET    Do you see yonder cloud that's almost in
shape of a camel?
POLONIUS    By th' Mass, and 'tis, like a camel indeed.
HAMLET    Methinks it is like a weasel.
POLONIUS    It is backed like a weasel.
HAMLET    Or like a whale.
POLONIUS    Very like a whale.
HAMLET    Then I will come to my mother by and by.
[*Aside*] They fool me to the top of my bent.—I will   383
come by and by.
POLONIUS    I will say so.                                          *Exit.*
HAMLET    "By and by" is easily said. Leave me, friends.
                    [*Exeunt Rosencrantz and Guildenstern.*]
'Tis now the very witching time of night,                     387
When churchyards yawn and hell itself breathes out
Contagion to this world. Now could I drink hot
    blood
And do such bitter business as the day
Would quake to look on. Soft, now to my mother.
O heart, lose not thy nature! Let not ever                    392
The soul of Nero enter this firm bosom.                       393
Let me be cruel, not unnatural;
I will speak daggers to her, but use none.
My tongue and soul in this be hypocrites:
How in my words somever she be shent,                         397
To give them seals never my soul consent!          *Exit.* 398

❖

# [3.3]

*Enter King, Rosencrantz, and Guildenstern.*

KING
I like him not, nor stands it safe with us                    1
To let his madness range. Therefore prepare you.
I your commission will forthwith dispatch,                    3
And he to England shall along with you.
The terms of our estate may not endure                        5
Hazard so dangerous as doth hourly grow
Out of his lunacies.
GUILDENSTERN            We will ourselves provide.              7
Most holy and religious fear it is                            8
To keep those many many bodies safe
That live and feed upon Your Majesty.
ROSENCRANTZ
The single and peculiar life is bound                         11

With all the strength and armor of the mind
To keep itself from noyance, but much more                    13
That spirit upon whose weal depends and rests                 14
The lives of many. The cease of majesty                       15
Dies not alone, but like a gulf doth draw                     16
What's near it with it. It is a massy wheel                   17
Fixed on the summit of the highest mount,
To whose huge spokes ten thousand lesser things
Are mortised and adjoined, which, when it falls,              20
Each small annexment, petty consequence,                      21
Attends the boist'rous ruin. Never alone                      22
Did the King sigh, but with a general groan.
KING
Arm you, I pray you, to this speedy voyage,                   24
For we will fetters put upon this fear,
Which now goes too free-footed.
ROSENCRANTZ AND GUILDENSTERN       We will haste us.
        *Exeunt gentlemen [Rosencrantz and Guildenstern].*

        *Enter Polonius.*

POLONIUS
My lord, he's going to his mother's closet.                   27
Behind the arras I'll convey myself                           28
To hear the process. I'll warrant she'll tax him home,        29
And, as you said—and wisely was it said—
'Tis meet that some more audience than a mother,              31
Since nature makes them partial, should o'erhear
The speech of vantage. Fare you well, my liege.               33
I'll call upon you ere you go to bed
And tell you what I know.
KING                            Thanks, dear my lord.
                                        *Exit [Polonius].*
Oh, my offense is rank! It smells to heaven.
It hath the primal eldest curse upon't,                       37
A brother's murder. Pray can I not,
Though inclination be as sharp as will;                       39
My stronger guilt defeats my strong intent,
And like a man to double business bound                       41
I stand in pause where I shall first begin,
And both neglect. What if this cursèd hand
Were thicker than itself with brother's blood,
Is there not rain enough in the sweet heavens
To wash it white as snow? Whereto serves mercy               46
But to confront the visage of offense?                        47
And what's in prayer but this twofold force,

---

**13 noyance** harm    **14 That spirit** the King.    **weal** well-being
**15 cease** decease, cessation    **16 gulf** whirlpool    **17 massy** massive
**20 mortised** fastened (as with a fitted joint).    **when it falls** i.e., when
it descends, like the wheel of Fortune, bringing a king down with it
**21 Each . . . consequence** i.e., every hanger-on and unimportant person or thing connected with the King    **22 Attends** participates in
**24 Arm** Provide, prepare    **27 closet** private chamber    **28 arras**
screen of tapestry placed around the walls of household apartments.
(On the Elizabethan stage, the arras was presumably over a door or
aperture in the tiring-house facade.)    **29 process** proceedings.
**tax him home** reprove him severely    **31 meet** fitting    **33 of vantage**
from an advantageous place, or, in addition.    **37 the primal eldest
curse** the curse of Cain, the first murderer; he killed his brother Abel
**39 Though . . . will** though my desire is as strong as my determination
**41 bound** (1) destined (2) obliged. (The King wants to repent and still
enjoy what he has gained.)    **46–7 Whereto . . . offense?** What function does mercy serve other than to confront sin face to face?

---

**374 presently** at once.    **383 They fool . . . bent** They humor my odd
behavior to the limit of my ability or endurance. (Literally, the extent
to which a bow may be bent.)    **387 witching time** time when spells
are cast and evil is abroad    **392 nature** natural feeling.    **393 Nero**
(This infamous Roman emperor, 37–68 A.D., put to death his mother,
Agrippina, who had murdered her husband, Claudius.)    **397–8
How . . . consent!** however much she is to be rebuked by my words, may
my soul never consent to ratify those words with deeds of violence!
**3.3. Location: The castle.**
**1 him** i.e., Hamlet's behavior    **3 dispatch** prepare, cause to be drawn
up    **5 terms of our estate** circumstances of my royal position
**7 We . . . provide** We'll put ourselves in readiness.    **8 religious fear**
sacred concern    **11 single and peculiar** individual and private

To be forestallèd ere we come to fall,                              49
Or pardoned being down? Then I'll look up.
My fault is past. But oh, what form of prayer
Can serve my turn? "Forgive me my foul murder"?
That cannot be, since I am still possessed
Of those effects for which I did the murder:
My crown, mine own ambition, and my queen.
May one be pardoned and retain th'offense?                          56
In the corrupted currents of this world                             57
Offense's gilded hand may shove by justice,                         58
And oft 'tis seen the wicked prize itself                           59
Buys out the law. But 'tis not so above.
There is no shuffling, there the action lies                        61
In his true nature, and we ourselves compelled,                     62
Even to the teeth and forehead of our faults,                       63
To give in evidence. What then? What rests?                         64
Try what repentance can. What can it not?
Yet what can it, when one cannot repent?
O wretched state, O bosom black as death,
O limèd soul that, struggling to be free,                           68
Art more engaged! Help, angels! Make assay.                         69
Bow, stubborn knees, and heart with strings of steel,
Be soft as sinews of the newborn babe!
All may be well.                               [He kneels.]

*Enter Hamlet.*

HAMLET
Now might I do it pat, now 'a is a-praying;                         73
And now I'll do't. [He draws his sword.] And so 'a goes
    to heaven,
And so am I revenged. That would be scanned:                        75
A villain kills my father, and for that,
I, his sole son, do this same villain send
To heaven.
Why, this is hire and salary, not revenge.
'A took my father grossly, full of bread,                           80
With all his crimes broad blown, as flush as May;                   81
And how his audit stands who knows save heaven?                     82
But in our circumstance and course of thought                       83
'Tis heavy with him. And am I then revenged,
To take him in the purging of his soul,
When he is fit and seasoned for his passage?                        86
No!
Up, sword, and know thou a more horrid hent.                        88
                              [He puts up his sword.]

---

When he is drunk asleep, or in his rage,                            89
Or in th'incestuous pleasure of his bed,
At gaming, swearing, or about some act                              91
That has no relish of salvation in't—                               92
Then trip him, that his heels may kick at heaven,
And that his soul may be as damned and black
As hell, whereto it goes. My mother stays.                          95
This physic but prolongs thy sickly days.      *Exit.*              96
KING
My words fly up, my thoughts remain below.
Words without thoughts never to heaven go.     *Exit.*

❖

## [3.4]

*Enter Queen [Gertrude] and Polonius.*

POLONIUS
'A will come straight. Look you lay home to him.                    1
Tell him his pranks have been too broad to bear with,               2
And that Your Grace hath screened and stood
    between
Much heat and him. I'll silence me even here.                       4
Pray you, be round with him.                                        5
HAMLET (*within*)   Mother, mother, mother!
QUEEN   I'll warrant you, fear me not.                              7
Withdraw, I hear him coming.
                     [*Polonius hides behind the arras.*]

*Enter Hamlet.*

HAMLET   Now, mother, what's the matter?
QUEEN
Hamlet, thou hast thy father much offended.                         10
HAMLET
Mother, you have my father much offended.
QUEEN
Come, come, you answer with an idle tongue.                         12
HAMLET
Go, go, you question with a wicked tongue.
QUEEN
Why, how now, Hamlet?
HAMLET                         What's the matter now?
QUEEN
Have you forgot me?
HAMLET                         No, by the rood, not so:             15
You are the Queen, your husband's brother's wife,
And—would it were not so!—you are my mother.
QUEEN
Nay, then, I'll set those to you that can speak.                    18

---

49 **forestallèd** prevented (from sinning)   56 **th'offense** the thing for which one offended.   57 **currents** courses of events   58 **gilded hand** hand offering gold as a bribe.   **shove by** thrust aside   59 **wicked prize** prize won by wickedness   61 **There . . . lies** There in heaven can be no evasion, there the deed lies exposed to view   62 **his** its   63 **to the teeth and forehead** face to face, concealing nothing   64 **give in** provide.   **rests** remains.   68 **limèd** caught as with bird-lime, a sticky substance used to ensnare birds   69 **engaged** entangled.   **assay** trial. (Said to himself, or to the angels to try him.)   73 **pat** opportunely   75 **would be scanned** needs to be looked into, or, could be interpreted as follows   80 **grossly, full of bread** i.e., enjoying his worldly pleasures rather than fasting. (See Ezekiel 16:49.)   81 **crimes broad blown** sins in full bloom.   **flush** vigorous   82 **audit** account.   **save** except for   83 **in . . . thought** as we see it from our mortal perspective   86 **seasoned** matured, readied   88 **know . . . hent** await to be grasped by me on a more horrid occasion. (*Hent* means "act of seizing.")

89 **drunk . . . rage** dead drunk, or in a fit of sexual passion   91 **gaming** gambling   92 **relish** trace, savor   95 **stays** awaits (me).   96 **physic** purging (by prayer), or, Hamlet's postponement of the killing   **3.4. Location:** The Queen's private chamber.   1 **lay . . . him** reprove him soundly.   2 **broad** unrestrained   4 **Much heat** i.e., the King's anger.   **I'll silence me** I'll quietly conceal myself. (Ironic, since it is his crying out at line 24 that leads to his death. Some editors emend *silence* to "sconce." The first quarto's reading, "shroud," is attractive.)   5 **round** blunt   7 **I'll . . . not** I assure you, you needn't worry about me.   10 **thy father** i.e., your stepfather, Claudius   12 **idle** foolish   15 **forgot me** i.e., forgotten that I am your mother.   **rood** cross of Christ   18 **speak** i.e., talk sense into you.

HAMLET
Come, come, and sit you down; you shall not budge.
You go not till I set you up a glass
Where you may see the inmost part of you.

QUEEN
What wilt thou do? Thou wilt not murder me?
Help, help, ho!

POLONIUS [*behind the arras*]  What ho! Help, help, help!

HAMLET [*drawing*]
How now? A rat? Dead for a ducat, dead!          25
                    [*He thrusts his rapier through the arras.*]

POLONIUS [*behind the arras*]
Oh, I am slain!                    [*He falls and dies.*]

QUEEN          Oh, me, what hast thou done?

HAMLET  Nay, I know not. Is it the King?

QUEEN
Oh, what a rash and bloody deed is this!

HAMLET
A bloody deed—almost as bad, good mother,
As kill a king, and marry with his brother.

QUEEN
As kill a king!

HAMLET          Ay, lady, it was my word.
                    [*He parts the arras and discovers Polonius.*]
Thou wretched, rash, intruding fool, farewell!
I took thee for thy better. Take thy fortune.          33
Thou find'st to be too busy is some danger.—          34
Leave wringing of your hands. Peace, sit you down,
And let me wring your heart, for so I shall,
If it be made of penetrable stuff,
If damnèd custom have not brazed it so          38
That it is proof and bulwark against sense.          39

QUEEN
What have I done, that thou dar'st wag thy tongue
In noise so rude against me?

HAMLET                    Such an act
That blurs the grace and blush of modesty,
Calls virtue hypocrite, takes off the rose
From the fair forehead of an innocent love
And sets a blister there, makes marriage vows          45
As false as dicers' oaths. Oh, such a deed
As from the body of contraction plucks          47
The very soul, and sweet religion makes          48
A rhapsody of words. Heaven's face does glow          49
O'er this solidity and compound mass          50
With tristful visage, as against the doom,          51
Is thought-sick at the act.

QUEEN                    Ay me, what act,          52
That roars so loud and thunders in the index?          53

HAMLET [*showing her two likenesses*]
Look here upon this picture, and on this,

The counterfeit presentment of two brothers.          55
See what a grace was seated on this brow:          56
Hyperion's curls, the front of Jove himself,          57
An eye like Mars to threaten and command,          58
A station like the herald Mercury          59
New-lighted on a heaven-kissing hill—          60
A combination and a form indeed
Where every god did seem to set his seal          62
To give the world assurance of a man.
This was your husband. Look you now what follows:
Here is your husband, like a mildewed ear,          65
Blasting his wholesome brother. Have you eyes?          66
Could you on this fair mountain leave to feed          67
And batten on this moor? Ha, have you eyes?          68
You cannot call it love, for at your age
The heyday in the blood is tame, it's humble,          70
And waits upon the judgment, and what judgment          71
Would step from this to this? Sense, sure, you have,          72
Else could you not have motion, but sure that sense
Is apoplexed, for madness would not err,          74
Nor sense to ecstasy was ne'er so thralled,          75
But it reserved some quantity of choice          76
To serve in such a difference. What devil was't          77
That thus hath cozened you at hoodman-blind?          78
Eyes without feeling, feeling without sight,
Ears without hands or eyes, smelling sans all,          80
Or but a sickly part of one true sense
Could not so mope. O shame, where is thy blush?          82
Rebellious hell,
If thou canst mutine in a matron's bones,          84
To flaming youth let virtue be as wax          85
And melt in her own fire. Proclaim no shame          86
When the compulsive ardor gives the charge,          87
Since frost itself as actively doth burn,          88
And reason panders will.          89

QUEEN  Oh, Hamlet, speak no more!
Thou turn'st mine eyes into my very soul,
And there I see such black and grainèd spots          92

**25 Dead for a ducat** i.e., I bet a ducat he's dead; or, a ducat is his life's fee.  **33 thy better** the King.  **34 busy** nosey  **38 damnèd custom** habitual wickedness.  **brazed** brazened, hardened  **39 proof** impenetrable, like *proof* or tested armor.  **sense** feeling.  **45 sets a blister** i.e., brands as a harlot  **47 contraction** the marriage contract  **48 sweet religion makes** i.e., makes marriage vows  **49 rhapsody** senseless string  **49–52 Heaven's . . . act** Heaven's face blushes at this solid world compounded of the various elements, with sorrowful face as though the day of doom were near, and is sick with horror at the deed (i.e., Gertrude's second marriage).  **53 index** table of contents, prelude or preface.

**55 counterfeit presentment** representation in portraiture  **56 this brow** King Hamlet's brow  **57 Hyperion's** the sun-god's.  **front** brow  **58 Mars** god of war  **59 station** stance.  **Mercury** winged messenger of the gods  **60 New-lighted** newly alighted.  **heaven-kissing** reaching to the sky  **62 set his seal** i.e., affix his approval  **65 ear** i.e., of grain.  **66 Blasting** blighting  **67 leave** cease  **68 batten** gorge.  **moor** barren or marshy ground. (Suggesting also "dark-skinned.")  **70 The heyday . . . blood** (The blood was thought to be the source of sexual desire.)  **71 waits upon** is subservient to  **72 Sense** Perception through the five senses (the functions of the middle or sensible soul)  **74 apoplexed** paralyzed.  **err** so err  **75–7 Nor . . . difference** nor could your physical senses ever have been so enthralled to *ecstasy* or lunacy that they could not distinguish to some degree between Hamlet Senior and Claudius.  **78 cozened** cheated.  **hoodman-blind** blindman's buff. (In this game, says Hamlet, the devil must have pushed Claudius toward Gertrude while she was blindfolded.)  **80 sans** without  **82 mope** be dazed, act aimlessly.  **84 mutine** mutiny  **85–6 To . . . fire** when it comes to sexually passionate youth, let virtue melt like a candle or stick of sealing wax held over a candle flame. (There's no point in hoping for self-restraint among young people when matronly women set such a bad example.)  **86–9 Proclaim . . . will** Call it no shameful business when the compelling ardor of youth delivers the attack, i.e., commits lechery, since the *frost* of advanced age burns with as active a fire of lust and reason perverts itself by fomenting lust rather than restraining it.  **92 grainèd** ingrained, indelible

As will not leave their tinct.

HAMLET                    Nay, but to live    93
In the rank sweat of an enseamèd bed,    94
Stewed in corruption, honeying and making love    95
Over the nasty sty!    96

QUEEN    Oh, speak to me no more!
These words like daggers enter in my ears.
No more, sweet Hamlet!

HAMLET                    A murderer and a villain,
A slave that is not twentieth part the tithe    100
Of your precedent lord, a vice of kings,    101
A cutpurse of the empire and the rule,    102
That from a shelf the precious diadem stole    103
And put it in his pocket!

QUEEN    No more!    105

*Enter Ghost [in his nightgown].*

HAMLET    A king of shreds and patches—    106
Save me, and hover o'er me with your wings,
You heavenly guards! What would you, gracious
    figure?

QUEEN    Alas, he's mad!

HAMLET
Do you not come your tardy son to chide,
That, lapsed in time and passion, lets go by    111
Th'important acting of your dread command?    112
Oh, say!

GHOST
Do not forget. This visitation
Is but to whet thy almost blunted purpose.    115
But look, amazement on thy mother sits.    116
Oh, step between her and her fighting soul!
Conceit in weakest bodies strongest works.    118
Speak to her, Hamlet.

HAMLET                    How is it with you, lady?

QUEEN    Alas, how is't with you,
That you do bend your eye on vacancy,    121
And with th'incorporal air do hold discourse?    122
Forth at your eyes your spirits wildly peep,
And, as the sleeping soldiers in th'alarm,    124
Your bedded hair, like life in excrements,    125
Start up and stand on end. O gentle son,
Upon the heat and flame of thy distemper    127
Sprinkle cool patience. Whereon do you look?

HAMLET
On him, on him! Look you how pale he glares!
His form and cause conjoined, preaching to stones,    130
Would make them capable.—Do not look upon me,    131
Lest with this piteous action you convert    132
My stern effects. Then what I have to do    133
Will want true color—tears perchance for blood.    134

QUEEN    To whom do you speak this?

HAMLET    Do you see nothing there?

QUEEN
Nothing at all, yet all that is I see.

HAMLET    Nor did you nothing hear?

QUEEN    No, nothing but ourselves.

HAMLET
Why, look you there, look how it steals away!
My father, in his habit as he lived!    141
Look where he goes even now out at the portal!    142

                                    *Exit Ghost.*

QUEEN
This is the very coinage of your brain.    143
This bodiless creation ecstasy    144
Is very cunning in.    145

HAMLET    Ecstasy?
My pulse as yours doth temperately keep time,
And makes as healthful music. It is not madness
That I have uttered. Bring me to the test,
And I the matter will reword, which madness    150
Would gambol from. Mother, for love of grace,    151
Lay not that flattering unction to your soul    152
That not your trespass but my madness speaks.
It will but skin and film the ulcerous place,    154
Whiles rank corruption, mining all within,    155
Infects unseen. Confess yourself to heaven,
Repent what's past, avoid what is to come,
And do not spread the compost on the weeds    158
To make them ranker. Forgive me this my virtue;    159
For in the fatness of these pursy times    160
Virtue itself of vice must pardon beg,
Yea, curb and woo for leave to do him good.    162

QUEEN
Oh, Hamlet, thou hast cleft my heart in twain.

HAMLET
Oh, throw away the worser part of it,
And live the purer with the other half.
Good night. But go not to my uncle's bed;
Assume a virtue, if you have it not.
That monster, custom, who all sense doth eat,    168
Of habits devil, is angel yet in this,    169

---

**93 leave their tinct** surrender their dark stain.    **94 enseamèd** saturated in the grease and filth of passionate lovemaking    **95 Stewed** soaked, bathed. (With a suggestion of "stew," brothel.)    **96 Over ... sty** (Like barnyard animals.)    **100 tithe** tenth part    **101 precedent lord** former husband. **vice** (From the morality plays, a model of iniquity and buffoonery.) **102 cutpurse** pickpocket.    **the rule** the kingdom    **103 diadem** crown **105 .1 nightgown** a robe for indoor wear.    **106 A king ... patches** i.e., a king whose splendor is all sham; a clown or fool dressed in motley    **111 lapsed ... passion** having let time and passionate commitment slip away **112 Th'important** the importunate, urgent    **115 whet** sharpen **116 amazement** distraction    **118 Conceit** Imagination    **121 bend** direct, focus    **122 th'incorporal** the immaterial    **124 as ... th'alarm** like soldiers called out of sleep by an alarum    **125 bedded** laid flat.    **like life in excrements** i.e., as though hair, an outgrowth of the body, had a life of its own. (Hair was thought to be lifeless because it lacks sensation, and so its standing on end would be unnatural and ominous.)    **127 distemper** disorder

**130 His ... conjoined** His appearance joined to his cause for appearing and speaking.    **to stones** even to stones    **131 capable** capable of feeling, receptive.    **132–3 convert ... effects** divert me from my stern duty. **134 want ... blood** lack plausibility so that (with a play on the normal sense of *color*) I shall shed colorless tears instead of blood.    **141 habit** clothes. **as** as when    **142 portal** doorway    **143 very** mere    **144–5 This ... in** Madness is skillful in creating this kind of hallucination.    **150 reword** repeat word for word    **151 gambol** skip away    **152 unction** ointment **154 skin** grow a skin over    **155 mining** working under the surface **158 compost** manure    **159 this my virtue** my virtuous talk in reproving you    **160 fatness** grossness.    **pursy** flabby, out of shape    **162 curb** bow, bend the knee.    **leave** permission    **168 who ... eat** which consumes and overwhelms the physical senses    **169 Of habits devil** devil-like in prompting evil habits

That to the use of actions fair and good
He likewise gives a frock or livery                                171
That aptly is put on. Refrain tonight,                             172
And that shall lend a kind of easiness
To the next abstinence; the next more easy;
For use almost can change the stamp of nature,                     175
And either [in] the devil, or throw him out                        176
With wondrous potency. Once more, good night;
And when you are desirous to be blest,                             178
I'll blessing beg of you. For this same lord,                      179
                              [*pointing to Polonius*]
I do repent; but heaven hath pleased it so
To punish me with this, and this with me,                          181
That I must be their scourge and minister.                         182
I will bestow him, and will answer well                            183
The death I gave him. So, again, good night.
I must be cruel only to be kind.
Thus bad begins, and worse remains behind.                         186
One word more, good lady.
QUEEN                              What shall I do?
HAMLET
Not this by no means that I bid you do:
Let the bloat king tempt you again to bed,                         189
Pinch wanton on your cheek, call you his mouse,                    190
And let him, for a pair of reechy kisses,                          191
Or paddling in your neck with his damned fingers,                  192
Make you to ravel all this matter out                              193
That I essentially am not in madness,
But mad in craft. 'Twere good you let him know,                    195
For who that's but a queen, fair, sober, wise,
Would from a paddock, from a bat, a gib,                           197
Such dear concernings hide? Who would do so?                       198
No, in despite of sense and secrecy,                               199
Unpeg the basket on the house's top,                               200
Let the birds fly, and like the famous ape,                        201
To try conclusions, in the basket creep                            202
And break your own neck down.                                      203
QUEEN
Be thou assured, if words be made of breath,
And breath of life, I have no life to breathe
What thou hast said to me.

HAMLET
I must to England. You know that?
QUEEN                                          Alack,
I had forgot. 'Tis so concluded on.
HAMLET
There's letters sealed, and my two schoolfellows,
Whom I will trust as I will adders fanged,
They bear the mandate; they must sweep my way                      211
And marshal me to knavery. Let it work.                            212
For 'tis the sport to have the engineer                            213
Hoised with his own petard, and 't shall go hard                   214
But I will delve one yard below their mines                        215
And blow them at the moon. Oh, 'tis most sweet
When in one line two crafts directly meet.                         217
This man shall set me packing.                                      218
I'll lug the guts into the neighbor room.
Mother, good night indeed. This counselor
Is now most still, most secret, and most grave,
Who was in life a foolish prating knave.—
Come, sir, to draw toward an end with you.—                        223
Good night, mother.
                         *Exit Hamlet, tagging in Polonius.*

## [4.1]

*Enter King [and Queen], with Rosencrantz and Guildenstern.*

KING
There's matter in these sighs, these profound heaves.          1
You must translate; 'tis fit we understand them.
Where is your son?
QUEEN
Bestow this place on us a little while.
                  [*Exeunt Rosencrantz and Guildenstern.*]
Ah, my good lord, what have I seen tonight!

---

**171 livery** an outer appearance, a customary garb (and hence a pre-disposition easily assumed in time of stress)   **172 aptly** readily   **175 use** habit.   **the stamp of nature** our inborn traits   **176 [in]** let in. (Other suggested emendations for this defective passage include "master," "shame," "lodge," "curb," or "house.")   **178–9 when . . . you** i.e., when you are ready to be penitent and seek God's blessing, I will ask your blessing as a dutiful son should.   **179 For** As for   **181 To punish . . . with me** i.e., to seek retribution from me for killing Polonius, and from him for meddling   **182 their scourge and minister** i.e., agent of heavenly retribution.   **183 bestow** stow, dispose of.   **answer** account or pay for   **186 behind** either (1) having now been left behind, or (2) still to come.   **189 bloat** bloated   **190 Pinch wanton** i.e., leave his love pinches on your cheeks, branding you as wanton   **191 reechy** dirty, filthy   **192 paddling** fingering amorously   **193 ravel . . . out** unravel, disclose   **195 in craft** by cunning.   **'Twere good** (Said sarcastically; also the following eight lines.)   **197 paddock** toad.   **gib** tomcat   **198 dear concernings** important affairs   **199 sense and secrecy** secrecy that common sense requires   **200 Unpeg the basket** open the cage, i.e., let out the secret   **201 famous ape** (In a story now lost.)   **202 try conclusions** test the outcome (in which the ape apparently enters a cage from which birds have been released and then tries to fly out of the cage as they have done, falling to its death)   **203 down** in the fall.

**211–12 sweep . . . knavery** sweep a path before me and conduct me to some *knavery* or treachery prepared for me.   **212 work** proceed.   **213 'tis the sport** it's a fine ironic joke.   **engineer** maker of *engines* of war   **214 Hoised with** blown up by.   **petard** an explosive used to blow in a door or make a breach   **214–15 't shall . . . will** unless luck is against me, I will   **215 mines** tunnels used in warfare to undermine the enemy's emplacements; Hamlet will countermine by going under their mines   **217 in one line** i.e., mines and countermines on a collision course, or the countermines directly below the mines.   **crafts** acts of guile, plots   **218 set me packing** set me to making schemes, and set me to lugging (him), and, also, send me off in a hurry.   **223 draw . . . end** finish up. (With a pun on *draw*, "pull.")
**4.1. Location:** The castle.
**0.1 Enter King [and Queen]** (In the Folio text, Gertrude evidently does not exit at the end of 3.4; the scene is continuous here. The Folio ends 3.4 with "*Exit Hamlet tugging in Polonius*," not naming Gertrude, and opens 4.1 with "*Enter King.*" Yet the second quarto concludes 3.4 with a simple "*Exit*," which often stands ambiguously for a single exit or an exeunt in early modern texts, and then starts 4.1 with "*Enter King, and Queene, with Rosencraus and Guyldensterne.*" The King's opening lines in 4.1 suggest that he has had time, during a brief intervening pause, to become aware of Gertrude's highly wrought emotional state. In line 35, the King refers to Gertrude's *closet* as though it were elsewhere. The differences between the second quarto and the Folio offer an alternative staging. In either case, 4.1 follows swiftly upon 3.4.)   **1 matter** significance.   **heaves** heavy sighs.

KING
    What, Gertrude? How does Hamlet?
QUEEN
    Mad as the sea and wind when both contend
    Which is the mightier. In his lawless fit,
    Behind the arras hearing something stir,
    Whips out his rapier, cries, "A rat, a rat!"
    And in this brainish apprehension kills                11
    The unseen good old man.
KING                           Oh, heavy deed!             12
    It had been so with us, had we been there.             13
    His liberty is full of threats to all—
    To you yourself, to us, to everyone.
    Alas, how shall this bloody deed be answered?          16
    It will be laid to us, whose providence                17
    Should have kept short, restrained, and out of haunt   18
    This mad young man. But so much was our love,
    We would not understand what was most fit,
    But, like the owner of a foul disease,                 21
    To keep it from divulging, let it feed                 22
    Even on the pith of life. Where is he gone?
QUEEN
    To draw apart the body he hath killed,
    O'er whom his very madness, like some ore              25
    Among a mineral of metals base,                        26
    Shows itself pure: 'a weeps for what is done.
KING    Oh, Gertrude, come away!
    The sun no sooner shall the mountains touch
    But we will ship him hence, and this vile deed
    We must with all our majesty and skill
    Both countenance and excuse.—Ho, Guildenstern!        32

        *Enter Rosencrantz and Guildenstern.*

    Friends both, go join you with some further aid.
    Hamlet in madness hath Polonius slain,
    And from his mother's closet hath he dragged him.
    Go seek him out, speak fair, and bring the body
    Into the chapel. I pray you, haste in this.            36
        *Exit gentleman [Rosencrantz and Guildenstern].*
    Come, Gertrude, we'll call up our wisest friends
    And let them know both what we mean to do
    And what's untimely done [So envious slander,]        40
    Whose whisper o'er the world's diameter,               41
    As level as the cannon to his blank,                   42
    Transports his poisoned shot, may miss our name
    And hit the woundless air. Oh, come away!              44
    My soul is full of discord and dismay.    *Exeunt.*

11 **brainish apprehension** frenzied misapprehension   12 **heavy** grievous   13 **us** i.e., me. (The royal "we"; also in line 15.) 16 **answered** explained.   17 **laid to** blamed on.   **providence** foresight   18 **short** i.e., on a short tether.   **out of haunt** secluded 21 **owner** victim   22 **from divulging** from becoming publicly known   25 **ore** vein of gold   26 **mineral** mine   32 **countenance** put the best face on   36 **fair** gently, courteously   40 [**So envious slander,**] (These words, or others like them, are missing from the early texts.)   41 **diameter** extent from side to side   42 **As level** with as direct aim.   **his blank** its target at point-blank range 44 **woundless** invulnerable

## [4.2]

        *Enter Hamlet.*

HAMLET    Safely stowed.
ROSENCRANTZ, GUILDENSTERN (*within*)    Hamlet! Lord
    Hamlet!
HAMLET    But soft, what noise? Who calls on Hamlet? Oh,    4
    here they come.

        *Enter Rosencrantz and Guildenstern.*

ROSENCRANTZ
    What have you done, my lord, with the dead body?
HAMLET
    Compounded it with dust, whereto 'tis kin.
ROSENCRANTZ
    Tell us where 'tis, that we may take it thence
    And bear it to the chapel.
HAMLET    Do not believe it.
ROSENCRANTZ    Believe what?
HAMLET    That I can keep your counsel and not mine        12
    own. Besides, to be demanded of a sponge, what rep-   13
    lication should be made by the son of a king?          14
ROSENCRANTZ    Take you me for a sponge, my lord?
HAMLET    Ay, sir, that soaks up the King's countenance,   16
    his rewards, his authorities. But such officers do the  17
    King best service in the end. He keeps them, like an
    ape, an apple, in the corner of his jaw, first mouthed
    to be last swallowed. When he needs what you have
    gleaned, it is but squeezing you, and, sponge, you
    shall be dry again.
ROSENCRANTZ    I understand you not, my lord.
HAMLET    I am glad of it. A knavish speech sleeps in a    24
    foolish ear.
ROSENCRANTZ    My lord, you must tell us where the
    body is and go with us to the King.
HAMLET    The body is with the King, but the King is not   28
    with the body. The King is a thing—                    29
GUILDENSTERN    A thing, my lord?
HAMLET    Of nothing. Bring me to him. Hide fox, and all   31
    after!                     *Exeunt [running, with Rosencrantz and*
                                *Guildenstern in pursuit].*    32

                    *

## [4.3]

        *Enter King, and two or three.*

**4.2. Location: The castle.**
**4 soft** wait a minute.   **12–13 That . . . own** i.e., Don't expect me to do as you bid me and not follow my own counsel.   **13 demanded of** questioned by   **13–14 replication** reply   **16 countenance** favor **17 authorities** delegated power, influence.   **24 sleeps in** has no meaning to   **28–9 The . . . body** (Perhaps alludes to the legal commonplace of "the king's two bodies," which drew a distinction between the sacred office of kingship and the particular mortal who possessed it at any given time. Hence, although Claudius's body is necessarily a part of him, true kingship is not contained in it. Similarly, Claudius will have Polonius's body when it is found, but there is no kingship in this business either.)   **31 Of nothing** (1) Of no account (2) Lacking the essence of kingship, as in lines 28–9 and note. **31–2 Hide . . . after** (An old signal cry in the game of hide-and-seek, suggesting that Hamlet now runs away from them.)
**4.3. Location: The castle.**

KING
I have sent to seek him, and to find the body.
How dangerous is it that this man goes loose!
Yet must not we put the strong law on him.
He's loved of the distracted multitude,                                4
Who like not in their judgment, but their eyes,                         5
And where 'tis so, th'offender's scourge is weighed,                    6
But never the offense. To bear all smooth and even,                     7
This sudden sending him away must seem
Deliberate pause. Diseases desperate grown                              9
By desperate appliance are relieved,                                    10
Or not at all.

*Enter Rosencrantz.*

How now, what hath befall'n?
ROSENCRANTZ
Where the dead body is bestowed, my lord,
We cannot get from him.
KING                                    But where is he?
ROSENCRANTZ
Without, my lord; guarded, to know your pleasure.                       14
KING
Bring him before us.
ROSENCRANTZ [*calling*]    Ho, Guildenstern! Bring in the lord.

*Enter Hamlet and Guildenstern [with Guards].*

KING    Now, Hamlet, where's Polonius?
HAMLET    At supper.
KING    At supper? Where?
HAMLET    Not where he eats, but where 'a is eaten. A
certain convocation of politic worms are e'en at him.                   20
Your worm is your only emperor for diet. We fat all                     21
creatures else to fat us, and we fat ourselves for mag-
gots. Your fat king and your lean beggar is but
variable service—two dishes, but to one table. That's                   24
the end.
KING    Alas, alas!
HAMLET    A man may fish with the worm that hath eat                    27
of a king, and eat of the fish that hath fed of that
worm.
KING    What dost thou mean by this?
HAMLET    Nothing but to show you how a king may go
a progress through the guts of a beggar.                                32
KING    Where is Polonius?
HAMLET    In heaven. Send thither to see. If your messenger find him not there, seek him i'th'other place yourself. But if indeed you find him not within this month,

you shall nose him as you go up the stairs into the                     37
lobby.
KING [*to some attendants*]    Go seek him there.
HAMLET    'A will stay till you come. [*Exeunt attendants.*]
KING
Hamlet, this deed of thine, for thine especial safety—
Which we do tender, as we dearly grieve                                 42
For that which thou hast done—must send thee hence
With fiery quickness. Therefore prepare thyself.
The bark is ready, and the wind at help,                                45
Th'associates tend, and everything is bent                              46
For England.
HAMLET    For England!
KING    Ay, Hamlet.
HAMLET    Good.
KING
So is it, if thou knew'st our purposes.
HAMLET    I see a cherub that sees them. But come, for                  52
England! Farewell, dear mother.
KING    Thy loving father, Hamlet.
HAMLET    My mother. Father and mother is man and
wife, man and wife is one flesh, and so, my mother.
Come, for England!                                          *Exit.*
KING
Follow him at foot; tempt him with speed aboard.                        58
Delay it not. I'll have him hence tonight.
Away! For everything is sealed and done
That else leans on th'affair. Pray you, make haste.                     61
                            [*Exeunt all but the King.*]
And, England, if my love thou hold'st at aught—                         62
As my great power thereof may give thee sense,                          63
Since yet thy cicatrice looks raw and red                               64
After the Danish sword, and thy free awe                                65
Pays homage to us—thou mayst not coldly set                             66
Our sovereign process, which imports at full,                           67
By letters conguring to that effect,                                    68
The present death of Hamlet. Do it, England,                            69
For like the hectic in my blood he rages,                               70
And thou must cure me. Till I know 'tis done,
Howe'er my haps, my joys were ne'er begun.          *Exit.*    72

❖

# [4.4]

*Enter Fortinbras with his army over the stage.*

FORTINBRAS
Go, Captain, from me greet the Danish king.

---

**4 of** by.    **distracted** fickle, unstable    **5 Who . . . eyes** who choose not by judgment but by appearance    **6–7 th'offender's . . . offense** i.e., the populace often takes umbrage at the severity of a punishment without taking into account the gravity of the crime.    **7 To . . . even** To manage the business in an unprovocative way    **9 Deliberate pause** carefully considered action.    **10 appliance** remedies    **14 Without** Outside    **20 convocation** assembly.    **politic worms** crafty worms (suited to a master spy like Polonius).    **e'en** even now    **21 Your worm** Your average worm. (Compare *your fat king and your lean beggar* in line 23.)    **diet** food, eating. (With a punning reference to the Diet of Worms, a famous *convocation* held in 1521.)    **24 service** food served at table. (Worms feed on kings and beggars alike.)    **27 eat** eaten. (Pronounced *et.*)    **32 progress** royal journey of state

**37 nose** smell    **42 tender** value, hold dear.    **dearly** intensely    **45 bark** sailing vessel    **46 tend** wait.    **bent** in readiness    **52 cherub** (Cherubim are angels of knowledge. Hamlet hints that both he and heaven are onto Claudius's tricks.)    **58 at foot** close behind, at his heels.    **tempt** persuade    **61 leans on** bears upon, is related to    **62 England** i.e., King of England.    **at aught** at any value    **63 As . . . sense** for so my great power may give you a just appreciation of the importance of valuing my love    **64 cicatrice** scar    **65 free awe** unconstrained show of respect    **66 coldly set** regard with indifference    **67 process** command.    **imports at full** conveys specific directions for    **68 conguring** agreeing    **69 present** immediate    **70 hectic** persistent fever    **72 Howe'er . . . begun** whatever else happens, I cannot begin to be happy.    **4.4. Location: The coast of Denmark.**

Tell him that by his license Fortinbras 2
Craves the conveyance of a promised march 3
Over his kingdom. You know the rendezvous.
If that His Majesty would aught with us, 5
We shall express our duty in his eye; 6
And let him know so.
CAPTAIN   I will do't, my lord.
FORTINBRAS   Go softly on.   [*Exeunt all but the Captain.*] 9

*Enter Hamlet, Rosencrantz, [Guildenstern,] etc.*

HAMLET   Good sir, whose powers are these? 10
CAPTAIN   They are of Norway, sir.
HAMLET   How purposed, sir, I pray you?
CAPTAIN   Against some part of Poland.
HAMLET   Who commands them, sir?
CAPTAIN
The nephew to old Norway, Fortinbras.
HAMLET
Goes it against the main of Poland, sir, 16
Or for some frontier?
CAPTAIN
Truly to speak, and with no addition, 18
We go to gain a little patch of ground
That hath in it no profit but the name.
To pay five ducats, five, I would not farm it; 21
Nor will it yield to Norway or the Pole
A ranker rate, should it be sold in fee. 23
HAMLET
Why, then the Polack never will defend it.
CAPTAIN
Yes, it is already garrisoned.
HAMLET
Two thousand souls and twenty thousand ducats
Will not debate the question of this straw. 27
This is th'impostume of much wealth and peace, 28
That inward breaks, and shows no cause without 29
Why the man dies. I humbly thank you, sir.
CAPTAIN
God b'wi'you, sir.   [*Exit.*]
ROSENCRANTZ   Will't please you go, my lord?
HAMLET
I'll be with you straight. Go a little before.
[*Exeunt all except Hamlet.*]
How all occasions do inform against me 33
And spur my dull revenge! What is a man,
If his chief good and market of his time 35
Be but to sleep and feed? A beast, no more.
Sure he that made us with such large discourse, 37
Looking before and after, gave us not 38
That capability and godlike reason

To fust in us unused. Now, whether it be 40
Bestial oblivion, or some craven scruple 41
Of thinking too precisely on th'event— 42
A thought which, quartered, hath but one part
wisdom
And ever three parts coward—I do not know
Why yet I live to say "This thing's to do,"
Sith I have cause, and will, and strength, and means 46
To do't. Examples gross as earth exhort me: 47
Witness this army of such mass and charge, 48
Led by a delicate and tender prince, 49
Whose spirit with divine ambition puffed
Makes mouths at the invisible event, 51
Exposing what is mortal and unsure
To all that fortune, death, and danger dare, 53
Even for an eggshell. Rightly to be great 54
Is not to stir without great argument, 55
But greatly to find quarrel in a straw 56
When honor's at the stake. How stand I, then, 57
That have a father killed, a mother stained,
Excitements of my reason and my blood, 59
And let all sleep, while to my shame I see
The imminent death of twenty thousand men
That for a fantasy and trick of fame 62
Go to their graves like beds, fight for a plot 63
Whereon the numbers cannot try the cause, 64
Which is not tomb enough and continent 65
To hide the slain? Oh, from this time forth
My thoughts be bloody or be nothing worth!   *Exit.*

❖

## [4.5]

*Enter Queen and Horatio.*

QUEEN
I will not speak with her.
HORATIO                       She is importunate,
Indeed distract. Her mood will needs be pitied. 2
QUEEN   What would she have?
HORATIO
She speaks much of her father, says she hears
There's tricks i'th' world, and hems, and beats her
heart, 5
Spurns enviously at straws, speaks things in doubt 6

2 **license** permission   3 **conveyance** unhindered passage
5 **would . . . us** wishes to confer with me for any reason   6 **We . . . eye** I will come pay my respects in person   9 **softly** slowly, circumspectly   10 **powers** armed forces   16 **main** main part   18 **addition** exaggeration   21 **To pay** i.e., For a yearly rental of.   **farm it** take a lease of it   23 **ranker** higher.   **in fee** fee simple, outright.   27 **debate . . . straw** argue about this trifling matter.
28 **th'impostume** the abscess   29 **inward breaks** festers within.   **without** externally   33 **inform against** denounce; take shape against   35 **market of** profit of   37 **discourse** power of reasoning   38 **Looking before and after** able to review past events and anticipate the future

40 **fust** grow moldy   41 **oblivion** forgetfulness.   **craven** cowardly   42 **precisely** scrupulously.   **th'event** the outcome   46 **Sith** since   47 **gross** obvious   48 **charge** expense   49 **delicate and tender** of fine and youthful qualities   51 **Makes mouths** makes scornful faces.   **invisible event** unforeseeable outcome   53 **dare** could do (to him)   54–7 **Rightly . . . stake** True greatness is not a matter of being moved to action solely by a great cause; rather, it is to respond greatly to an apparently trivial cause when honor is at the stake.
59 **blood** (The supposed seat of the passions.)   62 **fantasy** fanciful caprice, illusion.   **trick** trifle, deceit   63 **plot** plot of ground
64 **Whereon . . . cause** on which there is insufficient room for the soldiers needed to fight for it   65 **continent** receptacle, container
**4.5. Location: The castle.**
2 **distract** out of her mind.   5 **tricks** deceptions.   **hems** clears her throat, makes "hmm" sounds.   **heart** i.e., breast   6 **Spurns . . . straws** kicks spitefully, takes offense at trifles.   **in doubt** of obscure meaning

That carry but half sense. Her speech is nothing,  
Yet the unshapèd use of it doth move     8  
The hearers to collection; they yawn at it,     9  
And botch the words up fit to their own thoughts,     10  
Which, as her winks and nods and gestures yield  
    them,     11  
Indeed would make one think there might be thought,     12  
Though nothing sure, yet much unhappily.     13  

QUEEN  
'Twere good she were spoken with, for she may strew  
Dangerous conjectures in ill-breeding minds.     15  
Let her come in.       [*Horatio withdraws to admit Ophelia.*]  
[*Aside*] To my sick soul, as sin's true nature is,  
Each toy seems prologue to some great amiss.     18  
So full of artless jealousy is guilt,     19  
It spills itself in fearing to be spilt.     20  

*Enter Ophelia distracted, playing on a lute, and*  
*her hair down, singing* [*escorted by Horatio*].  

OPHELIA  
Where is the beauteous majesty of Denmark?  
QUEEN   How now, Ophelia?  
OPHELIA   (*she sings*)  
    "How should I your true love know  
       From another one?  
    By his cockle hat and staff,     25  
       And his sandal shoon."     26  
QUEEN   Alas, sweet lady, what imports this song?  
OPHELIA   Say you? Nay, pray you, mark.  
    "He is dead and gone, lady,       (*Song.*)  
       He is dead and gone;  
    At his head a grass-green turf,  
       At his heels a stone."  
   Oho!     33  
QUEEN   Nay, but Ophelia—  
OPHELIA   Pray you, mark.  
[*Sings*] "White his shroud as the mountain snow"—  

*Enter King.*  

QUEEN   Alas, look here, my lord.  
OPHELIA  
    "Larded with sweet flowers;       (*Song.*)   38  
    Which bewept to the grave did not go  
       With true-love showers."     40  
KING   How do you, pretty lady?  
OPHELIA   Well, God 'ield you! They say the owl was a    42  

baker's daughter. Lord, we know what we are, but  
know not what we may be. God be at your table!  
KING   Conceit upon her father.     45  
OPHELIA   Pray you, let's have no words of this; but when  
they ask you what it means, say you this:  
    "Tomorrow is Saint Valentine's day,     (*Song.*)  
       All in the morning betime,     49  
    And I a maid at your window,  
       To be your Valentine.  
    Then up he rose, and donned his clothes,  
       And dupped the chamber door,     53  
    Let in the maid, that out a maid     54  
       Never departed more."     55  
KING   Pretty Ophelia—  
OPHELIA   Indeed, la, without an oath, I'll make an end  
on't:     58  
   [*Sings*] "By Gis and by Saint Charity,     59  
       Alack, and fie for shame!  
    Young men will do't, if they come to't;  
       By Cock, they are to blame.     62  
    Quoth she, 'Before you tumbled me,  
       You promised me to wed.'"  
   He answers:  
    "'So would I ha' done, by yonder sun,  
       An thou hadst not come to my bed.'"     67  
KING   How long hath she been thus?  
OPHELIA   I hope all will be well. We must be patient,  
but I cannot choose but weep to think they would lay  
him i'th' cold ground. My brother shall know of it.  
And so I thank you for your good counsel. Come, my  
coach! Good night, ladies, good night, sweet ladies,  
good night, good night.        [*Exit.*]  
KING   [*to Horatio*]  
Follow her close. Give her good watch, I pray you.  
          [*Exit Horatio.*]  
Oh, this is the poison of deep grief; it springs  
All from her father's death—and now behold!  
Oh, Gertrude, Gertrude,  
When sorrows come, they come not single spies,     79  
But in battalions. First, her father slain;  
Next, your son gone, and he most violent author  
Of his own just remove; the people muddied,     82  
Thick and unwholesome in their thoughts and  
    whispers     83  
For good Polonius' death—and we have done but  
    greenly,     84  
In hugger-mugger to inter him; poor Ophelia     85  
Divided from herself and her fair judgment,  
Without the which we are pictures or mere beasts;  
Last, and as much containing as all these,     88  
Her brother is in secret come from France,  

---

**8 unshapèd use** incoherent manner   **9 collection** inference, a guess at some sort of meaning.   **yawn** gape, wonder; grasp. (The Folio reading, "aim," is possible.)   **10 botch** patch   **11 Which** which words.   **yield** deliver, represent   **12–13 there might . . . unhappily** that a great deal could be guessed at of a most unfortunate nature, even if one couldn't be at all sure.   **15 ill-breeding** prone to suspect the worst and to make mischief   **18 toy** trifle.   **amiss** calamity. **19–20 So . . . spilt** Guilt is so burdened with conscience and guileless fear of detection that it reveals itself through apprehension of disaster.   **20.1 Enter Ophelia** (In the first quarto, Ophelia enters "*playing on a lute, and her hair down, singing.*")   **25 cockle hat** hat with cockleshell stuck in it as a sign that the wearer had been a pilgrim to the shrine of Saint James of Compostella in Spain   **26 shoon** shoes.   **33 Oho!** (Perhaps a sigh.)   **38 Larded** strewn, bedecked   **40 showers** i.e., tears.   **42 God 'ield** God yield or reward.   **owl** (Refers to a legend about a baker's daughter who was turned into an owl for being ungenerous when Jesus begged a loaf of bread.)

**45 Conceit** Fancy, brooding   **49 betime** early   **53 dupped** did up, opened   **54–5 that out . . . more** who, when she departed, was no longer a virgin.   **58 on't** of it   **59 Gis** Jesus   **62 Cock** (A perversion of "God" in oaths; here also with a quibble on the slang word for penis.) **67 An** if   **79 spies** scouts sent in advance of the main force   **82 just remove** justly deserved removal (to England).   **muddied** stirred up, confused   **83 Thick** bewildered, muddled   **84 greenly** foolishly **85 hugger-mugger** secret haste   **88 as much containing** as full of serious matter

Feeds on this wonder, keeps himself in clouds,                                   90
And wants not buzzers to infect his ear                                          91
With pestilent speeches of his father's death,
Wherein necessity, of matter beggared,                                           93
Will nothing stick our person to arraign                                         94
In ear and ear. Oh, my dear Gertrude, this,                                      95
Like to a murd'ring piece, in many places                                        96
Gives me superfluous death.                    *A noise within.*                 97
QUEEN    Alack, what noise is this?
KING    Attend!                                                                  99
    Where is my Switzers? Let them guard the door.                               100

        *Enter a Messenger.*

    What is the matter?
MESSENGER                    Save yourself, my lord!
    The ocean, overpeering of his list,                                          102
    Eats not the flats with more impetuous haste                                 103
    Than young Laertes, in a riotous head,                                       104
    O'erbears your officers. The rabble call him lord,
    And, as the world were now but to begin,                                     106
    Antiquity forgot, custom not known,                                          107
    The ratifiers and props of every word,                                      108
    They cry, "Choose we! Laertes shall be king!"
    Caps, hands, and tongues applaud it to the clouds,                           110
    "Laertes shall be king, Laertes king!"
QUEEN
    How cheerfully on the false trail they cry!
                                            *A noise within.*
    Oh, this is counter, you false Danish dogs!                                  113

        *Enter Laertes with others.*

KING    The doors are broke.
LAERTES
    Where is this King?—Sirs, stand you all without.
ALL    No, let's come in.
LAERTES    I pray you, give me leave.
ALL    We will, we will.
LAERTES    I thank you. Keep the door. [*Exeunt followers.*]
                                    Oh, thou vile king,
    Give me my father!
QUEEN [*restraining him*]    Calmly, good Laertes.
LAERTES
    That drop of blood that's calm proclaims me bastard,

Cries cuckold to my father, brands the harlot                                    122
Even here between the chaste unsmirchèd brow                                     123
Of my true mother.
KING                        What is the cause, Laertes,                          124
    That thy rebellion looks so giantlike?                                       125
    Let him go, Gertrude. Do not fear our person.                                126
    There's such divinity doth hedge a king                                      127
    That treason can but peep to what it would,                                  128
    Acts little of his will. Tell me, Laertes,                                   129
    Why thou art thus incensed. Let him go, Gertrude.
    Speak, man.
LAERTES            Where is my father?
KING                            Dead.
QUEEN
    But not by him.
KING                    Let him demand his fill.
LAERTES
    How came he dead? I'll not be juggled with.                                  133
    To hell, allegiance! Vows, to the blackest devil!
    Conscience and grace, to the profoundest pit!
    I dare damnation. To this point I stand,                                     136
    That both the worlds I give to negligence,                                   137
    Let come what comes, only I'll be revenged
    Most throughly for my father.                                                139
KING    Who shall stay you?
LAERTES    My will, not all the world's.                                         141
    And for my means, I'll husband them so well                                  142
    They shall go far with little.
KING                            Good Laertes,
    If you desire to know the certainty
    Of your dear father, is't writ in your revenge
    That, swoopstake, you will draw both friend and foe,   146
    Winner and loser?
LAERTES    None but his enemies.
KING    Will you know them, then?
LAERTES
    To his good friends thus wide I'll ope my arms,
    And like the kind life-rendering pelican                                     151
    Repast them with my blood.
KING                        Why, now you speak                                   152
    Like a good child and a true gentleman.
    That I am guiltless of your father's death,
    And am most sensibly in grief for it,                                        155
    It shall as level to your judgment 'pear                                     156
    As day does to your eye.            *A noise within.*

---

90 **Feeds . . . clouds** feeds his resentment on this whole shocking turn of events, keeps himself aloof and mysterious    91 **wants** lacks.    **buzzers** gossipers, informers    93 **necessity** i.e., the need to invent some plausible explanation.    **of matter beggared** unprovided with facts    94–5 **Will . . . ear** will not hesitate to accuse my (royal) person in everybody's ears.    96 **murd'ring piece** cannon loaded so as to scatter its shot    97 **Gives . . . death** kills me over and over. 99 **Attend!** Guard me!    100 **Switzers** Swiss guards, mercenaries. 102 **overpeering of his list** overflowing its shore, boundary 103 **flats** i.e., flatlands near shore.    **impetuous** violent (perhaps also with the meaning of *impiteous* ["impitious," Q2], "pitiless")    104 **riotous head** insurrectionary advance    106–8 **And . . . word** and, as if the world were to be started all over afresh, utterly setting aside all ancient traditional customs that should confirm and underprop our every word and promise    110 **Caps** (The caps are thrown in the air.) 113 **counter** (A hunting term, meaning to follow the trail in a direction opposite to that which the game has taken.)

122–4 **brands . . . mother** i.e, seems to proclaim my chaste mother a whore, as though a brand were printed on her pure forehead, much like the horns of cuckoldry that are imagined to sprout on the heads of husbands whose wives have cheated on them.    123 **between** amidst 125 **giantlike** (Recalling the rising of the giants of Greek mythology against Olympus.)    126 **fear our person** fear for my personal safety. 127 **hedge** protect, as with a surrounding barrier    128 **can . . . would** can only peep furtively, as through a barrier, at what it would intend 129 **Acts . . . will** (but) performs little of what it intends.    133 **juggled with** cheated, deceived.    136 **To . . . stand** I am resolved in this 137 **both . . . negligence** i.e., both this world and the next are of no consequence to me    139 **throughly** thoroughly    141 **My will . . . world's** I'll stop (*stay*) when my will is accomplished, not for anyone else's.    142 **for** as for    146 **swoopstake** i.e., indiscriminately. (Literally, taking all stakes on the gambling table at once. *Draw* is also a gambling term, meaning "take from.")    151 **pelican** (Refers to the belief that the female pelican fed its young with its own blood.)    152 **Repast** feed    155 **sensibly** feelingly    156 **level** plain

VOICES WITHIN           Let her come in!

LAERTES

How now, what noise is that?

*Enter Ophelia [as before].*

O heat, dry up my brains! Tears seven times salt
Burn out the sense and virtue of mine eye!    160
By heaven, thy madness shall be paid with weight    161
Till our scale turns the beam. O rose of May!    162
Dear maid, kind sister, sweet Ophelia!
O heavens, is't possible a young maid's wits
Should be as mortal as an old man's life?
Nature is fine in love, and where 'tis fine    166
It sends some precious instance of itself    167
After the thing it loves.    168

OPHELIA

"They bore him barefaced on the bier,      (*Song.*)
     Hey non nonny, nonny, hey nonny,
     And on his grave rained many a tear—"
Fare you well, my dove!

LAERTES

Hadst thou thy wits and didst persuade revenge,
It could not move thus.

OPHELIA    You must sing "A-down a-down," and you  175
"call him a-down-a." Oh, how the wheel becomes it! It  176
is the false steward that stole his master's daughter.  177

LAERTES    This nothing's more than matter.  178

OPHELIA    There's rosemary, that's for remembrance;  179
pray you, love, remember. And there is pansies; that's  180
for thoughts.

LAERTES    A document in madness, thoughts and re-  182
membrance fitted.

OPHELIA    There's fennel for you, and columbines.  184
There's rue for you, and here's some for me; we may  185
call it herb of grace o' Sundays. Oh, you must wear your
rue with a difference. There's a daisy. I would give  187
you some violets, but they withered all when my  188
father died. They say 'a made a good end—

---

[Sings] "For bonny sweet Robin is all my joy."

LAERTES

Thought and affliction, passion, hell itself,    191
She turns to favor and to prettiness.    192

OPHELIA

"And will 'a not come again?       (*Song.*)
And will 'a not come again?
     No, no, he is dead.
     Go to thy deathbed,
He never will come again.

"His beard was as white as snow,
All flaxen was his poll.    199
     He is gone, he is gone,
     And we cast away moan.
God ha' mercy on his soul!"
And of all Christian souls, I pray God. God b'wi'you.
     *Exeunt Ophelia [and the Queen, following her].*

LAERTES    Do you see this, O God?

KING

Laertes, I must commune with your grief,
Or you deny me right. Go but apart,    206
Make choice of whom your wisest friends you will,    207
And they shall hear and judge twixt you and me.
If by direct or by collateral hand    209
They find us touched, we will our kingdom give,    210
Our crown, our life, and all that we call ours
To you in satisfaction; but if not,
Be you content to lend your patience to us,
And we shall jointly labor with your soul
To give it due content.

LAERTES         Let this be so.
His means of death, his obscure burial—
No trophy, sword, nor hatchment o'er his bones,    217
No noble rite, nor formal ostentation—    218
Cry to be heard, as 'twere from heaven to earth,
That I must call't in question.

KING             So you shall,    220
And where th'offense is, let the great ax fall.
I pray you, go with me.          *Exeunt.*

❧

# [4.6]

*Enter Horatio, with an Attendant [i.e., Servingman].*

HORATIO    What are they that would speak with me?

SERVINGMAN    Sailors, sir. They say they have
letters for you.

HORATIO    Let them come in.      [*Exit Servingman.*]    3
I do not know from what part of the world

---

160 **virtue** faculty, power   161 **paid with weight** repaid, avenged equally or more   162 **beam** crossbar of a balance.   **166–8 Nature . . . loves** Human nature is exquisitely sensitive in matters of love, and in cases of sudden loss it sends some precious part of itself after the lost object of that love. (In this case, Ophelia's sanity deserts her out of sorrow for her lost father and perhaps too out of her love for Hamlet.)   **175–6 You . . . a-down-a** (Ophelia assigns the singing of refrains, like her own "Hey non nonny," to others present.)   **176 wheel** spinning wheel as accompaniment to the song, or refrain   **177 false steward** (The story is unknown.)   **178 This . . . matter** This seeming nonsense is more eloquent than sane utterance.   **179 rosemary** (Used as a symbol of remembrance both at weddings and at funerals.)   **180 pansies** (Emblems of love and courtship; perhaps from French *pensèes,* "thoughts.")   **182 document** instruction, lesson   **184 There's fennel . . . columbines** (*Fennel* betokens flattery; *columbines,* unchastity or ingratitude. Throughout, Ophelia addresses her various listeners, giving one flower to one and another to another, perhaps with particular symbolic significance in each case.)   **185 rue** (Emblem of repentance—a signification that is evident in its popular name, *herb of grace.*)   **187 with a difference** (A device used in heraldry to distinguish one family from another on the coat of arms, here suggesting that Ophelia and the others have different causes of sorrow and repentance; perhaps with a play on *rue* in the sense of "ruth," "pity.")   **daisy** (Emblem of love's victims and of faithlessness.)   **188 violets** (Emblems of faithfulness.)

191 **Thought** Melancholy.   **passion** suffering   192 **favor** grace, beauty   199 **poll** head.   206 **Go but apart** i.e., Go with me where we can talk privately   207 **whom** whichever of   209 **collateral hand** indirect agency   210 **us touched** me implicated   217 **trophy** memorial.   **hatchment** tablet displaying the armorial bearings of a deceased person   218 **ostentation** ceremony   220 **That** so that.   **call't in question** demand an explanation.   **4.6. Location:** The castle.   3 **letters** a letter

I should be greeted, if not from Lord Hamlet.

*Enter Sailors.*

[A] SAILOR    God bless you, sir.

HORATIO    Let him bless thee too.

[A] SAILOR    'A shall, sir, an't please him. There's a    9
letter for you, sir—it comes from th'ambassador that    10
was bound for England—if your name be Horatio, as
I am let to know it is.                [*He gives a letter.*]    12

HORATIO (*reads the letter*)    "Horatio, when thou shalt have over-    13
looked this, give these fellows some means to the King;    14
they have letters for him. Ere we were two days old at    15
sea, a pirate of very warlike appointment gave us    16
chase. Finding ourselves too slow of sail, we put on a
compelled valor, and in the grapple I boarded them.    18
On the instant they got clear of our ship, so I alone
became their prisoner. They have dealt with me like
thieves of mercy, but they knew what they did: I am to    21
do a good turn for them. Let the King have the letters
I have sent, and repair thou to me with as much haste    23
as thou wouldest fly death. I have words to speak in
thine ear will make thee dumb, yet are they much too
light for the bore of the matter. These good fellows will    26
bring thee where I am. Rosencrantz and Guildenstern
hold their course for England. Of them I have much to
tell thee. Farewell.

He that thou knowest thine, Hamlet."

Come, I will give you way for these your letters,    31
And do't the speedier that you may direct me
To him from whom you brought them.        *Exeunt.*

❧

# [4.7]

*Enter King and Laertes.*

KING
Now must your conscience my acquittance seal,    1
And you must put me in your heart for friend,
Sith you have heard, and with a knowing ear,    3
That he which hath your noble father slain
Pursued my life.

LAERTES                It well appears. But tell me
Why you proceeded not against these feats    6
So crimeful and so capital in nature,    7
As by your safety, greatness, wisdom, all things else,
You mainly were stirred up.    9

KING        Oh, for two special reasons,
Which may to you perhaps seem much unsinewed,    11
But yet to me they're strong. The Queen his mother
Lives almost by his looks, and for myself—
My virtue or my plague, be it either which—

She's so conjunctive to my life and soul    15
That, as the star moves not but in his sphere,    16
I could not but by her. The other motive
Why to a public count I might not go    18
Is the great love the general gender bear him,    19
Who, dipping all his faults in their affection,
Would, like the spring that turneth wood to stone,    21
Convert his gyves to graces, so that my arrows,    22
Too slightly timbered for so loud a wind,    23
Would have reverted to my bow again
But not where I had aimed them.

LAERTES
And so have I a noble father lost,
A sister driven into desp'rate terms,    27
Whose worth, if praises may go back again,    28
Stood challenger on mount of all the age    29
For her perfections. But my revenge will come.

KING
Break not your sleeps for that. You must not think
That we are made of stuff so flat and dull
That we can let our beard be shook with danger
And think it pastime. You shortly shall hear more.
I loved your father, and we love ourself;
And that, I hope, will teach you to imagine—

*Enter a Messenger with letters.*

How now? What news?

MESSENGER                Letters, my lord, from Hamlet:
This to Your Majesty, this to the Queen.
                            [*He gives letters.*]

KING    From Hamlet? Who brought them?

MESSENGER
Sailors, my lord, they say. I saw them not.
They were given me by Claudio. He received them
Of him that brought them.

KING                Laertes, you shall hear them.—
Leave us.                    *Exit Messenger.*
[*He reads.*] "High and mighty, you shall know I am set
naked on your kingdom. Tomorrow shall I beg leave    45
to see your kingly eyes, when I shall, first asking your
pardon, thereunto recount the occasion of my sudden    47
and more strange return.            Hamlet."
What should this mean? Are all the rest come back?
Or is it some abuse, and no such thing?    50

LAERTES
Know you the hand?

KING                'Tis Hamlet's character. "Naked!"    51
And in a postscript here he says "alone."

---

**9 an't** if it    **10 th'ambassador** (Hamlet's ostensible role; see 3.1.172–3.)
**12 am let to know** am given to understand    **13–14 overlooked** looked
over    **14 means** means of access    **15–16 were . . . sea** had been at sea
two days    **16 pirate** pirate ship    **18 grapple** hand-to-hand fight when
the attacking vessel has fastened itself to its victim by means of grappling hooks    **21 thieves of mercy** merciful thieves    **23 repair** come
**26 bore** caliber, i.e., importance    **31 way** means of access
**4.7. Location: The castle.**
**1 my acquittance seal** confirm or acknowledge my innocence
**3 Sith** since    **6 feats** acts    **7 capital** punishable by death    **9 mainly**
greatly    **11 unsinewed** weak

**15 conjunctive** closely united. (An astronomical metaphor.)    **16 his**
its.    **sphere** one of the hollow spheres in which, according to Ptolemaic astronomy, the planets were supposed to move    **18 count**
account, reckoning, indictment    **19 general gender** common people
**21 spring** i.e., a spring with such a concentration of time that it coats
a piece of wood with timestone, in effect gilding and petrifying it
**22 gyves** fetters (which, gilded by the people's praise, would look like
badges of honor)    **23 Too . . . wind** with too light a shaft for so powerful a gust (of popular sentiment)    **27 terms** state, condition    **28 go
back** recall what she was    **29 on mount** set up on high    **45 naked**
destitute, unarmed, without followers    **47 pardon** (for returning
without authorization)    **50 abuse** deceit.    **no such thing** not what
the letter says.    **51 character** handwriting.

Can you advise me?

**LAERTES**
I am lost in it, my lord. But let him come.
It warms the very sickness in my heart
That I shall live and tell him to his teeth,
"Thus diddest thou."

**KING**                    If it be so, Laertes—                57
As how should it be so? How otherwise?—        58
Will you be ruled by me?

**LAERTES**                    Ay, my lord,
If so you'll not o'errule me to a peace.        60

**KING**
To thine own peace. If he be now returned,
As checking at his voyage, and that he means    62
No more to undertake it, I will work him
To an exploit, now ripe in my device,           64
Under the which he shall not choose but fall;
And for his death no wind of blame shall breathe,
But even his mother shall uncharge the practice  67
And call it accident.

**LAERTES**                    My lord, I will be ruled,
The rather if you could devise it so
That I might be the organ.

**KING**                    It falls right.        70
You have been talked of since your travel much,
And that in Hamlet's hearing, for a quality
Wherein they say you shine. Your sum of parts    73
Did not together pluck such envy from him
As did that one, and that, in my regard,
Of the unworthiest siege.                        76

**LAERTES**   What part is that, my lord?

**KING**
A very ribbon in the cap of youth,
Yet needful too, for youth no less becomes       79
The light and careless livery that it wears
Than settled age his sables and his weeds        81
Importing health and graveness. Two months since 82
Here was a gentleman of Normandy.
I have seen myself, and served against, the French,
And they can well on horseback, but this gallant 85
Had witchcraft in't; he grew into his seat,
And to such wondrous doing brought his horse
As had he been incorpsed and deminatured        88
With the brave beast. So far he passed my thought 89
That I in forgery of shapes and tricks           90
Come short of what he did.

**LAERTES**                    A Norman was't?

**KING**   A Norman.                              92

**LAERTES**
Upon my life, Lamord.

**KING**                    The very same.

**LAERTES**
I know him well. He is the brooch indeed          94
And gem of all the nation.

**KING**   He made confession of you,              96
And gave you such a masterly report
For art and exercise in your defense,            98
And for your rapier most especially,
That he cried out 'twould be a sight indeed
If one could match you. Th'escrimers of their nation, 101
He swore, had neither motion, guard, nor eye     102
If you opposed them. Sir, this report of his
Did Hamlet so envenom with his envy
That he could nothing do but wish and beg
Your sudden coming o'er, to play with him.       106
Now, out of this—

**LAERTES**          What out of this, my lord?

**KING**
Laertes, was your father dear to you?
Or are you like the painting of a sorrow,
A face without a heart?

**LAERTES**                    Why ask you this?

**KING**
Not that I think you did not love your father,
But that I know love is begun by time,           112
And that I see, in passages of proof,            113
Time qualifies the spark and fire of it.         114
There lives within the very flame of love
A kind of wick or snuff that will abate it,      116
And nothing is at a like goodness still,         117
For goodness, growing to a pleurisy,             118
Dies in his own too much. That we would do,      119
We should do when we would; for this "would"
changes
And hath abatements and delays as many           121
As there are tongues, are hands, are accidents,  122
And then this "should" is like a spendthrift's sigh, 123
That hurts by easing. But, to the quick of th'ulcer: 124
Hamlet comes back. What would you undertake
To show yourself in deed your father's son
More than in words?

**LAERTES**                    To cut his throat i'th' church.

---

**57 Thus diddest thou** i.e., Here's for what you did to my father.   **58 As . . . otherwise?** how can this (Hamlet's return) be true? Yet how otherwise than true (since we have the evidence of his letter)?   **60 If you'll** so long as you will   **62 checking at** i.e., turning aside from (like a falcon leaving the quarry to fly at a chance bird).   **that** if   **64 device** devising, invention   **67 uncharge the practice** acquit the stratagem of being a plot   **70 organ** agent, instrument.   **73 Your . . . parts** All your other virtues   **76 unworthiest siege** least important rank.   **79 no less becomes** is no less adorned by   **81–2 his sables . . . graveness** its rich robes furred with sable and its garments denoting dignified well-being and seriousness.   **85 can well** are skilled   **88–9 As . . . beast** as if, centaurlike, he had been made into one body with the horse, possessing half its nature.   **89 passed my thought** surpassed my expectation   **90 in . . . tricks** in my imagining what feats of horsemanship might be possible

**92 A Norman** One who hails from Normandy.   **94 brooch** ornament   **96 confession** testimonial, admission of superiority   **98 For . . . defense** with respect to your skill and practice with your weapon   **101 Th'escrimers** The fencers   **102 had . . . eye** would have neither movement, defensive strategy, or visual sharpness   **106 sudden** immediate.   **play** fence   **112 begun by time** i.e., created by the right circumstance and hence subject to change   **113 passages of proof** actual well-attested instances   **114 qualifies** weakens, moderates   **116 wick or snuff** the charred part of a candlewick   **117 nothing . . . still** nothing remains at a constant level of perfection   **118 pleurisy** excess, plethora. (Literally, a chest inflammation.)   **119 in . . . much** of its own excess.   **That** That which   **121 abatements** diminutions   **122 As . . . accidents** as there are tongues to dissuade, hands to prevent, and chance events to intervene   **123 spendthrift's sigh** (An allusion to the belief that sighs draw blood from the heart.)   **124 hurts by easing** i.e., costs the heart blood and wastes precious opportunity even while it affords emotional relief.   **quick of th'ulcer** i.e., heart of the matter

KING
　　No place, indeed, should murder sanctuarize;　　128
　　Revenge should have no bounds. But good Laertes,
　　Will you do this, keep close within your chamber.　130
　　Hamlet returned shall know you are come home.
　　We'll put on those shall praise your excellence　132
　　And set a double varnish on the fame　133
　　The Frenchman gave you, bring you in fine together,　134
　　And wager on your heads. He, being remiss,　135
　　Most generous, and free from all contriving,　136
　　Will not peruse the foils, so that with ease,　137
　　Or with a little shuffling, you may choose
　　A sword unbated, and in a pass of practice　139
　　Requite him for your father.
LAERTES　　　　　　　　　I will do't,
　　And for that purpose I'll anoint my sword.
　　I bought an unction of a mountebank　142
　　So mortal that, but dip a knife in it,
　　Where it draws blood no cataplasm so rare,　144
　　Collected from all simples that have virtue　145
　　Under the moon, can save the thing from death　146
　　That is but scratched withal. I'll touch my point
　　With this contagion, that if I gall him slightly,　148
　　It may be death.
KING　　　　　　Let's further think of this,
　　Weigh what convenience both of time and means
　　May fit us to our shape. If this should fail,　151
　　And that our drift look through our bad performance,　152
　　'Twere better not essayed. Therefore this project
　　Should have a back or second, that might hold
　　If this should blast in proof. Soft, let me see.　155
　　We'll make a solemn wager on your cunnings—　156
　　I ha 't!
　　When in your motion you are hot and dry—
　　As make your bouts more violent to that end—　159
　　And that he calls for drink, I'll have prepared him
　　A chalice for the nonce, whereon but sipping,　161
　　If he by chance escape your venomed stuck,　162
　　Our purpose may hold there.

　　　　　　　*Enter Queen.*

　　　　　　　　　　How [now], sweet queen?
QUEEN
　　One woe doth tread upon another's heel,
　　So fast they follow. Your sister's drowned, Laertes.
LAERTES　　Drowned! Oh, where?

QUEEN
　　There is a willow grows aslant a brook　167
　　That shows his hoar leaves in the glassy stream;　168
　　Therewith fantastic garlands did she make
　　Of crowflowers, nettles, daisies, and long purples,　170
　　That liberal shepherds give a grosser name,　171
　　But our cold maids do dead men's fingers call them.　172
　　There on the pendent boughs her crownet weeds　173
　　Clamb'ring to hang, an envious sliver broke,　174
　　When down her weedy trophies and herself　175
　　Fell in the weeping brook. Her clothes spread wide,
　　And mermaidlike awhile they bore her up,
　　Which time she chanted snatches of old lauds,　178
　　As one incapable of her own distress,　179
　　Or like a creature native and endued　180
　　Unto that element. But long it could not be
　　Till that her garments, heavy with their drink,　182
　　Pulled the poor wretch from her melodious lay　183
　　To muddy death.
LAERTES　　　　　　Alas, then she is drowned?
QUEEN　　Drowned, drowned.
LAERTES
　　Too much of water hast thou, poor Ophelia,
　　And therefore I forbid my tears. But yet
　　It is our trick; nature her custom holds,　188
　　Let shame say what it will. [*He weeps.*] When these
　　　are gone,　189
　　The woman will be out. Adieu, my lord.　190
　　I have a speech of fire that fain would blaze,　191
　　But that this folly douts it.　　　　　*Exit.*
KING　　　　　　　　Let's follow, Gertrude.　192
　　How much I had to do to calm his rage!
　　Now fear I this will give it start again;
　　Therefore let's follow.　　　　　*Exeunt.*

　　　　　　　　　　❖

# [5.1]

　　　*Enter two Clowns [with spades and mattocks].*

FIRST CLOWN　　Is she to be buried in Christian burial,
　　that willfully seeks her own salvation?　　2

128 **sanctuarize** protect from punishment. (Alludes to the right of sanctuary with which certain religious places were invested.)　**130 Will you do this** if you will do this　**132 put on those shall** arrange for some to **133 And . . . fame** and enhance the lustrous reputation　**134 in fine** finally **135 remiss** negligently unsuspicious　**136 generous** noble-minded **137 foils** fencing weapons　**139 unbated** not blunted, having no button. **pass of practice** treacherous thrust in an arranged bout　**142 unction** ointment.　**mountebank** quack doctor　**144 cataplasm** plaster or poultice.　**rare** excellent　**145 simples** herbs.　**virtue** potency　**146 Under the moon** i.e., anywhere (with reference perhaps to the belief that herbs gathered at night had a special power)　**148 gall** graze, wound　**151 shape** part we propose to act.　**152 drift . . . performance** intention should be betrayed by our bungling　**155 blast in proof** come to grief when put to the test. **156 cunnings** respective skills　**159 As** i.e., and you should　**161 nonce** occasion　**162 stuck** thrust. (From *stoccado*, a fencing term.)

167 **aslant a** obliquely across the　168 **hoar leaves** white or gray undersides of the leaves　170 **crowflowers** wild buttercups.　**long purples** early purple orchids　171 **liberal** free-speaking.　**a grosser name** (The testicle-resembling tubers of the orchid, which also in some cases resemble *dead men's fingers*, have earned various slang names like "dogstones" and "cullions.")　172 **cold** chaste　173–4 **There . . . hang** As she clambered up to hang on the overhanging boughs her coronet-like garland of wild flowers　174 **envious sliver** malicious branch　175 **weedy** i.e., of plants　178 **lauds** hymns　179 **incapable of** lacking capacity to apprehend　180 **endued** adapted by nature　182 **Till** that until　183 **lay** ballad, song　188 **It is our trick** i.e., weeping is our natural way (when sad)　189–90 **When . . . out** When my tears are all shed, the woman in me will have run its course.　191 **fain** willingly　192 **douts** extinguishes. (The second quarto reads "drownes.")
**5.1. Location:** A churchyard.
0.1 *Clowns* rustics　2 **salvation** (A blunder for "damnation," or perhaps a suggestion that Ophelia was taking her own shortcut to heaven.)

SECOND CLOWN    I tell thee she is; therefore make her
grave straight. The crowner hath sat on her, and finds    4
it Christian burial.                                       5

FIRST CLOWN    How can that be, unless she drowned
herself in her own defense?

SECOND CLOWN    Why, 'tis found so.                        8

FIRST CLOWN    It must be *se offendendo*, it cannot be else.    9
For here lies the point: if I drown myself wittingly, it
argues an act, and an act hath three branches—it is
to act, to do, and to perform. Argal, she drowned her-    12
self wittingly.

SECOND CLOWN    Nay, but hear you, Goodman Delver—         14

FIRST CLOWN    Give me leave. Here lies the water; good.
Here stands the man; good. If the man go to this
water and drown himself, it is, will he, nill he, he       17
goes, mark you that. But if the water come to him and
drown him, he drowns not himself. Argal, he that is
not guilty of his own death shortens not his own life.

SECOND CLOWN    But is this law?

FIRST CLOWN    Ay, marry, is't—crowner's quest law.        22

SECOND CLOWN    Will you ha' the truth on't? If this had
not been a gentlewoman, she should have been
buried out o' Christian burial.

FIRST CLOWN    Why, there thou say'st. And the more        26
pity that great folk should have countenance in this      27
world to drown or hang themselves, more than their
even-Christian. Come, my spade. There is no ancient       29
gentlemen but gardeners, ditchers, and grave makers.
They hold up Adam's profession.                            31

SECOND CLOWN    Was he a gentleman?

FIRST CLOWN    'A was the first that ever bore arms.       33

SECOND CLOWN    Why, he had none.

FIRST CLOWN    What, art a heathen? How dost thou
understand the Scripture? The Scripture says Adam
digged. Could he dig without arms? I'll put another       37
question to thee. If thou answerest me not to the
purpose, confess thyself—                                  39

SECOND CLOWN    Go to.                                     40

FIRST CLOWN    What is he that builds stronger than
either the mason, the shipwright, or the carpenter?       42

SECOND CLOWN    The gallows maker, for that frame         43
outlives a thousand tenants.

FIRST CLOWN    I like thy wit well, in good faith. The
gallows does well. But how does it well? It does well to   46
those that do ill. Now thou dost ill to say the gallows

is built stronger than the church. Argal, the gallows
may do well to thee. To't again, come.

SECOND CLOWN    "Who builds stronger than a mason, a
shipwright, or a carpenter?"

FIRST CLOWN    Ay, tell me that, and unyoke.              52

SECOND CLOWN    Marry, now I can tell.

FIRST CLOWN    To't.

SECOND CLOWN    Mass, I cannot tell.                      55

*Enter Hamlet and Horatio [at a distance afar off].*

FIRST CLOWN    Cudgel thy brains no more about it, for
your dull ass will not mend his pace with beating; and    57
when you are asked this question next, say "a grave-
maker." The houses that he makes lasts till doomsday.
Go get thee to Johan. Fetch me a stoup of liquor.        60

*[Exit Second Clown. First Clown digs.]*
*Song.*

"In youth, when I did love, did love,                    61
    Methought it was very sweet,
To contract—oh—the time for—a—my behove,                 63
    Oh, methought there—a—was nothing—a—
        meet."                                            64

HAMLET    Has this fellow no feeling of his business, that 'a    65
sings at grave-making?

HORATIO    Custom hath made it in him a property of       67
easiness.                                                  68

HAMLET    'Tis e'en so. The hand of little employment      69
hath the daintier sense.                                   70

FIRST CLOWN                                        *Song.*
"But age with his stealing steps
    Hath clawed me in his clutch,
And hath shipped me intil the land,                       73
    As if I had never been such."                        74

*[He throws up a skull.]*

HAMLET    That skull had a tongue in it and could sing
once. How the knave jowls it to the ground, as if        76
'twere Cain's jawbone, that did the first murder! This    77
might be the pate of a politician, which this ass now     78
o'er-offices, one that would circumvent God, might        79
it not?

HORATIO    It might, my lord.

HAMLET    Or of a courtier, which could say, "Good
morrow, sweet lord! How dost thou, good lord?"
This might be my Lord Such-a-one, that praised my
Lord Such-a-one's horse when 'a meant to beg it,
might it not?

HORATIO    Ay, my lord.

---

4 **straight** straightway, immediately. (But with a pun on *strait*, "narrow.")   **crowner** coroner.   **sat on her** conducted an inquest on her
case   4–5 **finds it** gives his official verdict that her means of death was
consistent with   8 **found so** determined so in the coroner's verdict.
9 *se offendendo* (A comic mistake for *se defendendo*, a term used in ver-
dicts of self-defense.)   12 **Argal** (Corruption of *ergo*, "therefore.")
14 **Goodman** (An honorific title often used with the name of a profession or craft.)   17 **will he, nill he** whether he will or no, willy-nilly
22 **quest** inquest   26 **there thou say'st** i.e., that's right.   27 **countenance**
privilege   29 **even-Christian** fellow Christians.   **ancient** going back to
ancient times   31 **hold up** maintain   33 **bore arms** (To be entitled to
bear a coat of arms would make Adam a gentleman, but as one who
bore a spade, our common ancestor was an ordinary delver in the
earth.)   37 **arms** i.e., the arms of the body.   39 **confess thyself** (The
saying continues, "and be hanged.")   40 **Go to** (An expression of impatience.)   42 **mason** stonemason   43 **frame** (1) gallows (2) structure
46 **does well** (1) is an apt answer (2) does a good turn.

52 **unyoke** i.e., after this great effort, you may unharness the team of
your wits.   55 **Mass** By the Mass   57 **your . . . beating** your ordinary
plodding beast of burden won't move quickly without a beating
60 **stoup** flagon, tankard   61 **In . . . love** (This and the two following
stanzas, with nonsensical variations, are from a poem attributed to Lord
Vaux and printed in *Tottel's Miscellany*, 1557. The *oh* and *a* [for "ah"] seemingly are the grunts of the digger.)   63 **To contract . . . behove** i.e., to
shorten the time for my own advantage. (Perhaps he means to *prolong* it.)
64 **meet** suitable, i.e., more suitable.   65 **that 'a** that he   67–8 **property
of easiness** something he can do easily, without distress.   69 **'Tis e'en
so** Exactly.   70 **daintier sense** more delicate sense of feeling.   73 **intil
the land** into the earth. (But note the lack of rhyme in *steps, land*.)
74 **such** i.e., alive and in love.   76 **jowls** dashes. (With a pun on *jowl*,
"jawbone.")   77 **first murder** Cain's murder of his brother Abel (Genesis
4:8).   78 **politician** schemer, plotter   79 **o'er-offices** gets the better of

HAMLET    Why, e'en so, and now my Lady Worm's, chapless, and knocked about the mazard with a sexton's spade. Here's fine revolution, an we had the trick to see't. Did these bones cost no more the breeding but to play at loggets with them? Mine ache to think on't. 89 90 91 92

FIRST CLOWN                                        *Song.*
    "A pickax and a spade, a spade,
        For and a shrouding sheet;                              95
    Oh, a pit of clay for to be made
        For such a guest is meet."
                        [*He throws up another skull.*]

HAMLET    There's another. Why might not that be the skull of a lawyer? Where be his quiddities now, his quillets, his cases, his tenures, and his tricks? Why does he suffer this rude knave now to knock him about the sconce with a dirty shovel, and will not tell him of his action of battery? H'm, this fellow might be in 's time a great buyer of land, with his statutes, his recognizances, his fines, his double vouchers, his recoveries. Is this the fine of his fines and the recovery of his recoveries, to have his fine pate full of fine dirt? Will his vouchers vouch him no more of his purchases, and double ones too, than the length and breadth of a pair of indentures? The very conveyances of his lands will hardly lie in this box, and must th'inheritor himself have no more, ha? 99 100 101 102 103 104 105 106 107 108 109 110 111

HORATIO    Not a jot more, my lord.

HAMLET    Is not parchment made of sheepskins?

HORATIO    Ay, my lord, and of calves' skins too.

HAMLET    They are sheep and calves which seek out assurance in that. I will speak to this fellow.—Whose grave's this, sirrah? 116 117 118

FIRST CLOWN    Mine, sir.
    [*Sings*]    "Oh, pit of clay for to be made
                For such a guest is meet."

HAMLET    I think it be thine, indeed, for thou liest in't.

FIRST CLOWN    You lie out on't, sir, and therefore 'tis not yours. For my part, I do not lie in't, yet it is mine.

HAMLET    Thou dost lie in't, to be in't and say it is thine. 'Tis for the dead, not for the quick; therefore thou liest. 126

FIRST CLOWN    'Tis a quick lie, sir; 'twill away again from me to you.

HAMLET    What man dost thou dig it for?

FIRST CLOWN    For no man, sir.

HAMLET    What woman, then?

FIRST CLOWN    For none, neither.

HAMLET    Who is to be buried in't?

FIRST CLOWN    One that was a woman, sir, but, rest her soul, she's dead.

HAMLET    How absolute the knave is! We must speak by the card, or equivocation will undo us. By the Lord, Horatio, these three years I have taken note of it: the age is grown so picked that the toe of the peasant comes so near the heel of the courtier he galls his kibe.—How long hast thou been grave-maker? 137 138 139 140 141

FIRST CLOWN    Of all the days i'th' year, I came to't that day that our last king Hamlet overcame Fortinbras.

HAMLET    How long is that since?

FIRST CLOWN    Cannot you tell that? Every fool can tell that. It was the very day that young Hamlet was born—he that is mad and sent into England.

HAMLET    Ay, marry, why was he sent into England?

FIRST CLOWN    Why, because 'a was mad. 'A shall recover his wits there, or if 'a do not, 'tis no great matter there.

HAMLET    Why?

FIRST CLOWN    'Twill not be seen in him there. There the men are as mad as he.

HAMLET    How came he mad?

FIRST CLOWN    Very strangely, they say.

HAMLET    How strangely?

FIRST CLOWN    Faith, e'en with losing his wits.

HAMLET    Upon what ground?                                        160

FIRST CLOWN    Why, here in Denmark. I have been sexton here, man and boy, thirty years.                         162

HAMLET    How long will a man lie i'th'earth ere he rot?

FIRST CLOWN    I'faith, if 'a be not rotten before 'a die—as we have many pocky corpses nowadays, that will scarce hold the laying in—'a will last you some eight year or nine year. A tanner will last you nine year. 165 166

HAMLET    Why he more than another?

FIRST CLOWN    Why, sir, his hide is so tanned with his trade that 'a will keep out water a great while, and

---

89 **chapless** having no lower jaw.    **mazard** i.e., head. (Literally, a drinking vessel.)    90 **revolution** turn of Fortune's wheel, change.    **trick** knack    91–2 **cost . . . but** involve so little expense and care in upbringing that we may    92 **loggets** a game in which pieces of hard wood shaped like Indian clubs or bowling pins are thrown to lie as near as possible to a stake    95 **For and** and moreover    99–100 **his quiddities . . . quillets** his subtleties, his legal niceties    100 **tenures** the holding of a piece of property or office, or the conditions or period of such holding    101 **rude** foolish    102 **sconce** head    103 **action of battery** lawsuit about physical assault.    104 **his statutes** his legal documents acknowledging obligation of a debt    104–5 **recognizances** bonds undertaking to repay debts    105 **fines** procedures for converting entailed estates into "fee simple" or freehold.    **double vouchers** vouchers signed by two signatories guaranteeing the legality of real estate titles.    **recoveries** suits to obtain the authority of a court judgment for the holding of land.    106–7 **Is this . . . dirt?** Is this the end of his legal maneuvers and profitable land deals, to have the skull of his elegant head filled full of minutely sifted dirt? (With multiple wordplay on *fine* and *fines*.)    107–10 **Will . . . indentures?** Will his vouchers, even double ones, guarantee him no more land than is needed to bury him in, being no bigger than the deed of conveyance? (An *indenture* is literally a legal document drawn up in duplicate on a single sheet and then cut apart on a zigzag line so that each pair was uniquely matched.)    111 **box** (1) deed box (2) coffin.    **th'inheritor** the acquirer, owner    116–17 **assurance in that** safety in legal parchments.    118 **sirrah** (A term of address to inferiors.)

126 **quick** living    137 **absolute** strict, precise    137–8 **by the card** i.e., with precision. (Literally, by the mariner's compass-card, on which the points of the compass were marked.)    138 **equivocation** ambiguity in the use of terms    139–41 **the age . . . kibe** i.e., the age has grown so finical and mannered that the lower classes ape their social betters, chafing at their heels. (*Kibes* are chilblains on the heels.)    160 **ground** cause. (But, in the next line, the gravedigger takes the word in the sense of "land," "country.")    162 **sexton** a minor functionary who tends to church property, digging graves, etc.    165 **pocky** rotten, diseased. (Literally, with the pox, or syphilis.)    166 **hold the laying in** hold together long enough to be interred.    **last you** last. (*You* is used colloquially here and in the following lines.)

your water is a sore decayer of your whoreson dead 171
body. [*He picks up a skull.*] Here's a skull now: this skull
hath lain you i'th'earth three-and-twenty years.          173

HAMLET   Whose was it?

FIRST CLOWN   A whoreson mad fellow's it was. Whose
do you think it was?

HAMLET   Nay, I know not.

FIRST CLOWN   A pestilence on him for a mad rogue! 'A
poured a flagon of Rhenish on my head once. This 179
same skull, sir, was Yorick's skull, the King's jester.

HAMLET   This?

FIRST CLOWN   E'en that.

HAMLET   Let me see. [*He takes the skull.*] Alas, poor
Yorick! I knew him, Horatio, a fellow of infinite jest,
of most excellent fancy. He hath borne me on his
back a thousand times, and now how abhorred in my 185
imagination it is! My gorge rises at it. Here hung those 187
lips that I have kissed I know not how oft. Where be
your gibes now? Your gambols, your songs, your 189
flashes of merriment that were wont to set the table on
a roar? Not one now, to mock your own grinning?
Quite chopfallen? Now get you to my lady's chamber 192
and tell her, let her paint an inch thick, to this favor 193
she must come. Make her laugh at that. Prithee,
Horatio, tell me one thing.

HORATIO   What's that, my lord?

HAMLET   Dost thou think Alexander looked o' this 197
fashion i'th'earth?

HORATIO   E'en so.

HAMLET   And smelt so? Pah! [*He throws down the skull.*]

HORATIO   E'en so, my lord.

HAMLET   To what base uses we may return, Horatio!
Why may not imagination trace the noble dust of
Alexander till 'a find it stopping a bunghole?       204

HORATIO   'Twere to consider too curiously to consider 205
so.

HAMLET   No, faith, not a jot, but to follow him thither
with modesty enough, and likelihood to lead it. As 208
thus: Alexander died, Alexander was buried, Alexander returneth into dust, the dust is earth, of earth we
make loam, and why of that loam whereto he was 211
converted might they not stop a beer barrel?
Imperious Caesar, dead and turned to clay,          213
Might stop a hole to keep the wind away.
Oh, that that earth which kept the world in awe      215
Should patch a wall t'expel the winter's flaw!       216

*Enter King, Queen, Laertes, and a coffin*
[*containing the corpse of Ophelia*], *with*
[*a Priest and*] *lords attendant.*

But soft, but soft, aside! Here comes the King,      217

The Queen, the courtiers. Who is that they follow?
And with such maimèd rites? This doth betoken        219
The corpse they follow did with desperate hand
Fordo it own life. 'Twas of some estate.             221
Couch we awhile and mark.                            222

        [*He and Horatio conceal themselves.*
        *Ophelia's body is taken to the grave.*]

LAERTES   What ceremony else?

HAMLET   [*to Horatio*]
That is Laertes, a very noble youth. Mark.

LAERTES   What ceremony else?

PRIEST
Her obsequies have been as far enlarged
As we have warrantise. Her death was doubtful,       227
And but that great command o'ersways the order      228
She should in ground unsanctified been lodged        229
Till the last trumpet. For charitable prayers,       230
Shards, flints, and pebbles should be thrown on her. 231
Yet here she is allowed her virgin crants,           232
Her maiden strewments, and the bringing home         233
Of bell and burial.                                  234

LAERTES
Must there no more be done?

PRIEST                          No more be done.
We should profane the service of the dead
To sing sage requiem and such rest to her            237
As to peace-parted souls.

LAERTES                    Lay her i'th'earth,        238
And from her fair and unpolluted flesh
May violets spring! I tell thee, churlish priest,    240
A ministering angel shall my sister be
When thou liest howling.

HAMLET   [*to Horatio*]       What, the fair Ophelia!  242

QUEEN   [*scattering flowers*]   Sweets to the sweet! Farewell.
I hoped thou shouldst have been my Hamlet's wife.
I thought thy bride-bed to have decked, sweet maid,
And not t' have strewed thy grave.

LAERTES                        Oh, treble woe
Fall ten times treble on that cursèd head
Whose wicked deed thy most ingenious sense           248
Deprived thee of! Hold off the earth awhile,
Till I have caught her once more in mine arms.
        [*He*] *leaps in the grave* [*and embraces Ophelia*].
Now pile your dust upon the quick and dead,          251
Till of this flat a mountain you have made
T' o'ertop old Pelion or the skyish head             253
Of blue Olympus.

171 **sore** keen, veritable.   **whoreson** (An expression of contemptuous familiarity.)   173 **lain you** lain. (See the note at line 166.)   179 **Rhenish** Rhine wine   187 **My gorge rises** i.e., I feel nauseated   189 **gibes** taunts   192 **chopfallen** (1) lacking the lower jaw (2) dejected.   193 **favor** aspect, appearance   197 **Alexander** Alexander the Great   204 **bunghole** hole for filling or emptying a cask.   205 **curiously** minutely   208 **with . . . lead it** with moderation and plausibility.   211 **loam** a mixture of clay, straw, sand, etc. used to mold bricks, or, in this case, bungs for a beer barrel   213 **Imperious** Imperial   215 **that earth** Caesar's body   216 **flaw** gust of wind.   216.3 *attendant* in attendance.   217 **soft** i.e., wait, be careful

219 **maimèd** mutilated, incomplete   221 **Fordo it** destroy its.   **estate** rank.   222 **Couch we** Let's hide, lie low   227 **warrantise** i.e., ecclesiastical authority.   228 **order** (1) prescribed practice (2) religious order of clerics   229 **She should . . . lodged** she should have been buried in unsanctified ground   230 **For** In place of   231 **Shards** broken bits of pottery   232 **crants** garlands betokening maidenhood   233 **strewments** flowers strewn on a coffin   233–4 **bringing . . . burial** laying the body to rest, to the sound of the bell.   237 **sage requiem** a solemn mass for the dead.   **such rest** i.e., to pray for such rest   238 **peace-parted souls** those who have died at peace with God.   240 **violets** (See 4.5.188 and note.)   242 **howling** i.e., in hell.   248 **ingenious sense** a mind that is quick, alert, of fine qualities   251 **quick** living   253 **Pelion** a mountain in northern Thessaly; compare *Olympus* and *Ossa* in lines 254 and 286. (In their rebellion against the Olympian gods, the giants attempted to heap Ossa on Pelion in order to scale Olympus.)

HAMLET [*coming forward*]    What is he whose grief
Bears such an emphasis, whose phrase of sorrow    255
Conjures the wandering stars and makes them stand    256
Like wonder-wounded hearers? This is I,    257
Hamlet the Dane.    258

LAERTES [*grappling with him*]    The devil take thy soul!    259

HAMLET    Thou pray'st not well.
I prithee, take thy fingers from my throat,
For though I am not splenitive and rash,    262
Yet have I something in me dangerous,
Which let thy wiseness fear. Away thy hand!

KING    Pluck them asunder.

QUEEN    Hamlet, Hamlet!

ALL    Gentlemen!

HORATIO    Good my lord, be quiet.
[*Hamlet and Laertes are parted.*]

HAMLET
Why, I will fight with him upon this theme
Until my eyelids will no longer wag.    270

QUEEN    Oh, my son, what theme?

HAMLET
I loved Ophelia. Forty thousand brothers
Could not with all their quantity of love
Make up my sum. What wilt thou do for her?

KING    Oh, he is mad, Laertes.

QUEEN    For love of God, forbear him.    276

HAMLET
'Swounds, show me what thou'lt do.    277
Woo't weep? Woo't fight? Woo't fast? Woo't tear
thyself?    278
Woo't drink up eisel? Eat a crocodile?    279
I'll do't. Dost thou come here to whine?
To outface me with leaping in her grave?
Be buried quick with her, and so will I.    282
And if thou prate of mountains, let them throw
Millions of acres on us, till our ground,
Singeing his pate against the burning zone,    285
Make Ossa like a wart! Nay, an thou'lt mouth,    286
I'll rant as well as thou.

QUEEN                        This is mere madness,    287
And thus awhile the fit will work on him;
Anon, as patient as the female dove

When that her golden couplets are disclosed,    290
His silence will sit drooping.

HAMLET                        Hear you, sir.
What is the reason that you use me thus?
I loved you ever. But it is no matter.
Let Hercules himself do what he may,    294
The cat will mew, and dog will have his day.    295
*Exit Hamlet.*

KING
I pray you, good Horatio, wait upon him.
[*Exit*] *Horatio.*
[*To Laertes*] Strengthen your patience in our last
night's speech;    297
We'll put the matter to the present push.—    298
Good Gertrude, set some watch over your son.—
This grave shall have a living monument.    300
An hour of quiet shortly shall we see;    301
Till then, in patience our proceeding be.    *Exeunt.*

♣

# [5.2]

*Enter Hamlet and Horatio.*

HAMLET
So much for this, sir; now let me see, the other.    1
You do remember all the circumstance?

HORATIO    Remember it, my lord!

HAMLET
Sir, in my heart there was a kind of fighting
That would not let me sleep. Methought I lay
Worse than the mutines in the bilboes. Rashly,    6
And praised be rashness for it—let us know    7
Our indiscretion sometime serves us well    8
When our deep plots do pall, and that should learn us    9
There's a divinity that shapes our ends,
Rough-hew them how we will—

HORATIO                        That is most certain.    11

HAMLET    Up from my cabin,
My sea-gown scarfed about me, in the dark    13
Groped I to find out them, had my desire,    14
Fingered their packet, and in fine withdrew    15
To mine own room again, making so bold,
My fears forgetting manners, to unseal
Their grand commission; where I found, Horatio—
Oh, royal knavery!—an exact command,

---

255 **emphasis** i.e., rhetorical and florid emphasis. (*Phrase* has a similar rhetorical connotation.)    256 **wandering stars** planets    257 **wonder-wounded** struck with amazement    258 **the Dane** (This title normally signifies the King; see 1.1.17 and note.)    259 **s.d.** *grappling with him* The testimony of the first quarto that *"Hamlet leaps in after Laertes"* and of the ballad "Elegy on Burbage," published in *Gentleman's Magazine* in 1825 ("Oft have I seen him leap into a grave") seem to indicate one way in which this fight was staged; however, the difficulty of fitting two contenders and Ophelia's body into a confined space (probably the trapdoor) suggests to many editors the alternative, that Laertes jumps out of the grave to attack Hamlet.)    262 **splenitive** hot-tempered    270 **wag** move. (A fluttering eyelid is a conventional sign that life has not yet gone.)    276 **forbear him** leave him alone.    277 **'Swounds** By His (Christ's) wounds    278 **Woo't** Wilt thou    279 **Woo't . . . eisel?** Will you drink up a whole draft of vinegar? (An extremely self-punishing task as a way of expressing grief.) **crocodile** (Crocodiles were tough and dangerous, and were supposed to shed crocodile tears.)    282 **quick** alive    285 **his pate** its head, i.e., top.    **burning zone** zone in the celestial sphere containing the sun's orbit, between the tropics of Cancer and Capricorn    286 **Ossa** (See 253n.)    **an thou'lt mouth** if you want to rant    287 **mere** utter

290 **golden couplets** two baby pigeons, covered with yellow down.    **disclosed** hatched    **294–5 Let . . . day** i.e., (1) Even Hercules couldn't stop Laertes's theatrical rant (2) I, too, will have my turn; i.e., despite any blustering attempts at interference, every person will sooner or later do what he or she must do.    297 **in** i.e., by recalling    298 **present push** immediate test.    300 **living** lasting. (For Laertes's private understanding, Claudius also hints that Hamlet's death will serve as such a monument.)    301 **hour of quiet** time free of conflict
**5.2. Location: The castle.**
1 **the other** the other matter. (See 4.6.24–6.)    6 **mutines** mutineers.    **bilboes** shackles.    **Rashly** On impulse. (This adverb goes with lines 12 ff.)    7 **know** acknowledge    8 **indiscretion** lack of foresight and judgment (not an indiscreet act)    9 **pall** fail, falter, go stale.    **learn** teach    11 **Rough-hew** shape roughly    13 **sea-gown** seaman's coat.    **scarfed** loosely wrapped    14 **them** i.e., Rosencrantz and Guildenstern    15 **Fingered** pilfered, pinched.    **in fine** finally, in conclusion

Larded with many several sorts of reasons   20
Importing Denmark's health and England's too,   21
With, ho! such bugs and goblins in my life,   22
That on the supervise, no leisure bated,   23
No, not to stay the grinding of the ax,   24
My head should be struck off.

**HORATIO**             Is't possible?

**HAMLET** [*giving a document*]
Here's the commission. Read it at more leisure.
But wilt thou hear me how I did proceed?

**HORATIO**    I beseech you.

**HAMLET**
Being thus benetted round with villainies—
Ere I could make a prologue to my brains,   30
They had begun the play—I sat me down,   31
Devised a new commission, wrote it fair.   32
I once did hold it, as our statists do,   33
A baseness to write fair, and labored much   34
How to forget that learning, but, sir, now
It did me yeoman's service. Wilt thou know
Th'effect of what I wrote?

**HORATIO**          Ay, good my lord.

**HAMLET**
An earnest conjuration from the King,   38
As England was his faithful tributary,
As love between them like the palm might flourish,   40
As peace should still her wheaten garland wear   41
And stand a comma 'tween their amities,   42
And many suchlike "as"es of great charge,   43
That on the view and knowing of these contents,
Without debatement further more or less,
He should the bearers put to sudden death,
Not shriving time allowed.

**HORATIO**         How was this sealed?   47

**HAMLET**
Why, even in that was heaven ordinant.   48
I had my father's signet in my purse,   49
Which was the model of that Danish seal;   50
Folded the writ up in the form of th'other,   51
Subscribed it, gave't th'impression, placed it safely,   52
The changeling never known. Now, the next day   53
Was our sea fight, and what to this was sequent   54
Thou knowest already.

**HORATIO**
So Guildenstern and Rosencrantz go to't.

**HAMLET**
Why, man, they did make love to this employment.
They are not near my conscience. Their defeat   58
Does by their own insinuation grow.   59
'Tis dangerous when the baser nature comes   60
Between the pass and fell incensèd points   61
Of mighty opposites.

**HORATIO**        Why, what a king is this!   62

**HAMLET**
Does it not, think'st thee, stand me now upon—   63
He that hath killed my king and whored my mother,
Popped in between th'election and my hopes,   65
Thrown out his angle for my proper life,   66
And with such coz'nage—is't not perfect conscience   67
To quit him with this arm? And is't not to be damned   68
To let this canker of our nature come   69
In further evil?   70

**HORATIO**
It must be shortly known to him from England
What is the issue of the business there.

**HAMLET**
It will be short. The interim's mine,
And a man's life's no more than to say "one."   74
But I am very sorry, good Horatio,
That to Laertes I forgot myself,
For by the image of my cause I see
The portraiture of his. I'll court his favors.   78
But, sure, the bravery of his grief did put me   79
Into a tow'ring passion.

**HORATIO**          Peace, who comes here?

*Enter young Osric, [a courtier].*

**OSRIC**   Your Lordship is right welcome back to Denmark.

**HAMLET**   I humbly thank you, sir. [*To Horatio*] Dost
know this water-fly?

**HORATIO**   No, my good lord.

**HAMLET**   Thy state is the more gracious, for 'tis a vice to
know him. He hath much land, and fertile. Let a beast   86
be lord of beasts, and his crib shall stand at the King's   87
mess. 'Tis a chuff, but, as I say, spacious in the   88
possession of dirt.

**OSRIC**   Sweet lord, if Your Lordship were at leisure, I
should impart a thing to you from His Majesty.

**HAMLET**   I will receive it, sir, with all diligence of spirit.
Put your bonnet to his right use; 'tis for the head.   93

---

**20 Larded** garnished.   **several** different   **21 Importing** relating to   **22 With . . . life** i.e., with all sorts of warnings of imaginary dangers if I were allowed to continue living. (*Bugs* are bugbears, hobgoblins.)   **23 That . . . bated** that on the reading of this commission, no delay being allowed   **24 stay** await   **30–1 Ere . . . play** before I could consciously turn my brain to the matter, it had started working on a plan   **32 fair** in a clear hand.   **33 statists** politicians, men of public affairs   **34 A baseness** beneath my dignity   **38 conjuration** entreaty   **40 palm** (An image of flourishing; see Psalm 92:12.)   **41 still** always.   **wheaten garland** (Symbolic of fruitful agriculture, of peace and plenty.)   **42 comma** (Indicating continuity, link.)   **43 "as"es** (1) the "whereases" of a formal document (2) asses.   **charge** (1) import (2) burden (appropriate to asses)   **47 shriving time** time for confession and absolution   **48 ordinant** directing.   **49 signet** small seal   **50 model** replica   **51 writ** writing   **52 Subscribed** signed (with forged signature).   **impression** i.e., with a wax seal   **53 changeling** i.e., substituted letter. (Literally, a fairy child substituted for a human one.)   **54 was sequent** followed

**58 defeat** destruction   **59 insinuation** intrusive intervention, sticking their noses in my business   **60 baser** of lower social station   **61 pass** thrust.   **fell** fierce   **62 opposites** antagonists.   **63 stand me now upon** become incumbent on me now   **65 th'election** (The Danish monarch was "elected" by a small number of high-ranking electors.)   **66 angle** fishhook.   **proper** very   **67 coz'nage** trickery   **68 quit** requite, pay back   **69 canker** ulcer   **69–70 come In** grow into   **74 a man's . . . "one"** one's whole life occupies such a short time, only as long as it takes to count to 1.   **78 court his favors** ingratiate myself with Laertes.   **79 bravery** bravado   **86–8 Let . . . mess** i.e., If a man, no matter how beastlike, is as rich in livestock and possessions as Osric, he may eat at the King's table.   **87 crib** manger   **88 chuff** boor, churl. (The second quarto spelling, "chough," is a variant spelling that also suggests the meaning here of "chattering jackdaw.")   **93 bonnet** any kind of cap or hat.   **his** its

OSRIC   I thank Your Lordship, it is very hot.

HAMLET   No, believe me, 'tis very cold. The wind is northerly.

OSRIC   It is indifferent cold, my lord, indeed.    97

HAMLET   But yet methinks it is very sultry and hot for my complexion.    99

OSRIC   Exceedingly, my lord. It is very sultry, as 'twere—I cannot tell how. But, my lord, His Majesty bade me signify to you that 'a has laid a great wager on your head. Sir, this is the matter—

HAMLET   I beseech you, remember.

*[Hamlet moves him to put on his hat.]*

OSRIC   Nay, good my lord; for my ease, in good faith.   105 Sir, here is newly come to court Laertes—believe me, an absolute gentleman, full of most excellent differ-   107 ences of very soft society and great showing. Indeed,   108 to speak feelingly of him, he is the card or calendar of   109 gentry, for you shall find in him the continent of what   110 part a gentleman would see.    111

HAMLET   Sir, his definement suffers no perdition in   112 you, though I know to divide him inventorially would   113 dazzle th'arithmetic of memory, and yet but yaw   114 neither in respect of his quick sail. But, in the verity of   115 extolment, I take him to be a soul of great article, and   116 his infusion of such dearth and rareness as, to make   117 true diction of him, his semblable is his mirror and   118 who else would trace him his umbrage, nothing   119 more.    120

OSRIC   Your Lordship speaks most infallibly of him.

HAMLET   The concernancy, sir? Why do we wrap the   122 gentleman in our more rawer breath?    123

OSRIC   Sir?

HORATIO   Is't not possible to understand in another   125 tongue? You will do't, sir, really.    126

HAMLET   What imports the nomination of this gentle-   127 man?

OSRIC   Of Laertes?

HORATIO   *[to Hamlet]*   His purse is empty already; all 's golden words are spent.

HAMLET   Of him, sir.

OSRIC   I know you are not ignorant—

HAMLET   I would you did, sir. Yet in faith if you did, it   134 would not much approve me. Well, sir?    135

OSRIC   You are not ignorant of what excellence Laertes is—

HAMLET   I dare not confess that, lest I should compare   138 with him in excellence. But to know a man well were   139 to know himself.    140

OSRIC   I mean, sir, for his weapon; but in the imputation   141 laid on him by them, in his meed he's unfellowed.    142

HAMLET   What's his weapon?

OSRIC   Rapier and dagger.

HAMLET   That's two of his weapons—but well.    145

OSRIC   The King, sir, hath wagered with him six Barbary   146 horses, against the which he has impawned, as I take   147 it, six French rapiers and poniards, with their assigns,   148 as girdle, hangers, or so. Three of the carriages, in   149 faith, are very dear to fancy, very responsive to the   150 hilts, most delicate carriages, and of very liberal con-   151 ceit.    152

HAMLET   What call you the carriages?    153

HORATIO   *[to Hamlet]*   I knew you must be edified by the margin ere you had done.    155

OSRIC   The carriages, sir, are the hangers.

HAMLET   The phrase would be more germane to the matter if we could carry cannon by our sides; I would it might be hangers till then. But, on: six Barbary horses against six French swords, their assigns, and three lib-eral-conceited carriages; that's the French bet against the Danish. Why is this impawned, as you call it?

OSRIC   The King, sir, hath laid, sir, that in a dozen   163 passes between yourself and him, he shall not exceed   164 you three hits. He hath laid on't twelve for nine, and it would come to immediate trial, if Your Lordship would vouchsafe the answer.    167

HAMLET   How if I answer no?

---

**97 indifferent** somewhat   **99 complexion** constitution.   **105 for my ease** (A conventional reply declining the invitation to put the hat back on.)   **107 absolute** perfect   **107–8 differences** special qualities   **108 soft society** agreeable manners.   **great showing** distinguished appearance.   **109 feelingly** with just perception   **109–10 the card ... gentry** the model or paradigm (literally, a chart or directory) of good breeding   **110–11 the continent ... see** one who contains in himself all the qualities a gentleman would like to see. (A *continent* is that which contains.)   **112–15 his definement ... sail** the task of defining Laertes's excellences suffers no diminution in your description of him, though I know that to enumerate all his graces would stupify one's powers of memory, and even so could do no more than veer unsteadily off course in a vain attempt to keep up with his rapid forward motion. (Hamlet mocks Osric by parodying his jargon-filled speeches.)   **115–20 But ... more** But, in true praise of him, I take him to be a person of remarkable substance, and his essence of such rarity and excellence as, to speak truly of him, none can compare with him other than his own mirror; anyone following in his footsteps can only hope to be the shadow to his substance, nothing more.   **122 concernancy** import, relevance   **123 rawer breath** unrefined speech that can only come short in praising him.   **125–6 Is't ... tongue?** i.e., Is it not possible for you, Osric, to understand and communicate in any other tongue than the overblown rhetoric you have used? (Alternatively, Horatio could be asking Hamlet to speak more plainly.)   **126 You will do't** i.e., You can if you try, or, you may well have to try (to speak plainly).   **127 nomination** naming

**134–5 I would ... approve me** (Responding to Osric's incompleted sentence as though it were a complete statement, Hamlet says, with mock politeness, "I wish you did know me to be not ignorant [i.e., to be knowledgeable] about matters," and then turns this into an insult: "But if you did, your recommendation of me would be of little value in any case.")   **138–40 I dare ... himself** I dare not boast of knowing Laertes's excellence lest I seem to imply a comparable excellence in myself. Certainly, to know another person well, one must know oneself.   **141–2 I mean ... unfellowed** I mean his excellence with his rapier, not his general excellence; in the reputation he enjoys for use of his weapons, his merit is unequaled.   **145 but well** but never mind.   **146 Barbary** i.e., from the Barbary region of northern Africa   **147 he** i.e., Laertes.   **impawned** staked, wagered   **148 poniards** daggers.   **assigns** appurtenances   **149 hangers** straps on the sword belt (*girdle*), from which the sword hung.   **or so** and so on.   **149–52 Three ... conceit** Three of the hangers, truly, are very pleasing to the fancy, decoratively matched with the hilts, delicate in workmanship, and made with elaborate ingenuity.   **153 What call you** What do you refer to when you say   **155 margin** margin of a book, place for explanatory notes   **163 laid** wagered   **164 passes** bouts. (The odds of the betting are hard to explain. Possibly the King bets that Hamlet will win at least five out of twelve, at which point Laertes raises the odds against himself by betting he will win nine.)   **167 vouchsafe the answer** be so good as to accept the challenge. (Hamlet deliberately takes the phrase in its literal sense of replying.)

OSRIC    I mean, my lord, the opposition of your person in trial.

HAMLET    Sir, I will walk here in the hall. If it please His Majesty, it is the breathing time of day with me. Let 172 the foils be brought, the gentleman willing, and the King hold his purpose, I will win for him an I can; if not, I will gain nothing but my shame and the odd hits.

OSRIC    Shall I re-deliver you e'en so?    177

HAMLET    To this effect, sir—after what flourish your nature will.

OSRIC    I commend my duty to Your Lordship.    180

HAMLET    Yours, yours.    [Exit Osric.] 'A does well to commend it himself; there are no tongues else for 's turn.    183

HORATIO    This lapwing runs away with the shell on his 184 head.

HAMLET    'A did comply with his dug before 'a sucked 186 it. Thus has he—and many more of the same bevy 187 that I know the drossy age dotes on—only got the 188 tune of the time, and, out of an habit of encounter, a 189 kind of yeasty collection, which carries them through 190 and through the most fanned and winnowed opin- 191 ions; and do but blow them to their trial, the bubbles 192 are out.    193

*Enter a Lord.*

LORD    My lord, His Majesty commended him to you by young Osric, who brings back to him that you attend him in the hall. He sends to know if your pleasure hold to play with Laertes, or that you will take longer 197 time.

HAMLET    I am constant to my purposes; they follow the King's pleasure. If his fitness speaks, mine is ready; 200 now or whensoever, provided I be so able as now.

LORD    The King and Queen and all are coming down.

HAMLET    In happy time.    203

LORD    The Queen desires you to use some gentle enter- 204 tainment to Laertes before you fall to play.    205

HAMLET    She well instructs me.    [Exit Lord.]

HORATIO    You will lose this wager, my lord.

HAMLET    I do not think so. Since he went into France, I have been in continual practice; I shall win at the odds.

172 **breathing time** exercise period.   **Let** i.e., If   177 **re-deliver you** report what you say   180 **commend** commit to your favor. (A conventional salutation, but Hamlet wryly uses a more literal meaning, "recommend," "praise," in line 182.)   183 **for 's turn** for his purposes, i.e., to do it for him.   184 **lapwing** (A proverbial type of youthful forwardness. Also, a bird that draws intruders away from its nest and was thought to run about with its head in the shell when newly hatched; a seeming reference to Osric's hat.)   186 **comply . . . dug** observe ceremonious formality toward his nurse's or mother's teat   187–93 **Thus . . . are out** Thus has he—and many like him of the sort our frivolous age dotes on—acquired the trendy manner of speech of the time, and, out of habitual conversation with courtiers of their own kind, have collected together a kind of frothy medley of current phrases, which enables such gallants to hold their own among persons of the most select and well-sifted views; and yet do but test them by merely blowing on them, and their bubbles burst.   197 **play** fence.   **that** if   200 **If . . . ready** If he declares his readiness, my convenience waits on his   203 **In happy time** (A phrase of courtesy indicating that the time is convenient.)   204–5 **entertainment** greeting

But thou wouldst not think how ill all's here about my heart; but it is no matter.

HORATIO    Nay, good my lord—

HAMLET    It is but foolery, but it is such a kind of gain- 213 giving as would perhaps trouble a woman.    214

HORATIO    If your mind dislike anything, obey it. I will forestall their repair hither and say you are not fit.    216

HAMLET    Not a whit, we defy augury. There's a special 217 providence in the fall of a sparrow. If it be now, 'tis not to come; if it be not to come, it will be now; if it be not now, yet it will come. The readiness is all. Since 220 no man has aught of what he leaves, what is't to leave 221 betimes? Let be.    222

*Trumpets, drums, and officers with cushions. Enter King, Queen, and Lords [including Laertes and Osric, and all the state], with other Attendants, with foils and gauntlets, a table, and flagons of wine on it.*

KING
Come, Hamlet, come and take this hand from me.
    [The King puts Laertes's hand into Hamlet's.]

HAMLET [to Laertes]
Give me your pardon, sir. I have done you wrong,
But pardon't as you are a gentleman.
This presence knows,    226
And you must needs have heard, how I am punished 227
With a sore distraction. What I have done
That might your nature, honor, and exception    229
Roughly awake, I here proclaim was madness.
Was't Hamlet wronged Laertes? Never Hamlet.
If Hamlet from himself be ta'en away,
And when he's not himself does wrong Laertes,
Then Hamlet does it not, Hamlet denies it.
Who does it, then? His madness. If't be so,
Hamlet is of the faction that is wronged;    236
His madness is poor Hamlet's enemy.
Sir, in this audience
Let my disclaiming from a purposed evil
Free me so far in your most generous thoughts
That I have shot my arrow o'er the house
And hurt my brother.

LAERTES                        I am satisfied in nature,    242
Whose motive in this case should stir me most    243
To my revenge. But in my terms of honor
I stand aloof, and will no reconcilement    245
Till by some elder masters of known honor    246
I have a voice and precedent of peace    247
To keep my name ungored. But till that time    248
I do receive your offered love like love,

213–14 **gaingiving** misgiving   216 **repair** coming   217 **augury** the attempt to read signs of future events in order to avoid predicted trouble. 220–2 **Since . . . Let be** Since no one has knowledge of what he is leaving behind, what does an early death matter after all? Enough; forbear. 222.1 *Trumpets, drums* Trumpeters, drummers   222.3 *all the state* the entire court   226 **presence** royal assembly   227 **punished** afflicted 229 **exception** disapproval   236 **faction** party   242 **in nature** i.e., as to my personal feelings   243 **Whose motive** the prompting of which 245 **will** desire, will allow   246–8 **Till . . . ungored** until by the official judgment of those gentlemen of the court who preside over the duel I can obtain an authoritative pronouncement and previous instance of a similar reconciliation to clear my reputation of any injury.

And will not wrong it.

HAMLET                     I do embrace it freely,
And will this brothers' wager frankly play.—          251
Give us the foils. Come on.

LAERTES                     Come, one for me.

HAMLET
I'll be your foil, Laertes. In mine ignorance          253
Your skill shall, like a star i'th' darkest night,
Stick fiery off indeed.

LAERTES                     You mock me, sir.          255

HAMLET     No, by this hand.

KING
Give them the foils, young Osric. Cousin Hamlet,
You know the wager?

HAMLET                     Very well, my lord.
Your Grace has laid the odds o'th' weaker side.        259

KING
I do not fear it; I have seen you both.
But since he is bettered, we have therefore odds.      261

LAERTES
This is too heavy. Let me see another.
          [He exchanges his foil for another.]

HAMLET
This likes me well. These foils have all a length?     263
          [They] prepare to play.

OSRIC     Ay, my good lord.

KING
Set me the stoups of wine upon that table.             265
If Hamlet give the first or second hit,
Or quit in answer of the third exchange,               267
Let all the battlements their ordnance fire.
The King shall drink to Hamlet's better breath,        269
And in the cup an union shall he throw                  270
Richer than that which four successive kings
In Denmark's crown have worn. Give me the cups,
And let the kettle to the trumpet speak,               273
The trumpet to the cannoneer without,
The cannons to the heavens, the heaven to earth,
"Now the King drinks to Hamlet." Come, begin.
          Trumpets the while.
And you, the judges, bear a wary eye.

HAMLET     Come on, sir.

LAERTES     Come, my lord. They play. [Hamlet scores a hit.]

HAMLET     One.

LAERTES     No.

HAMLET     Judgment.

OSRIC     A hit, a very palpable hit.

LAERTES     Well, again.

KING
Stay, give me drink. Hamlet, this pearl is thine.
          [He drinks, and throws a pearl in Hamlet's cup.]
Here's to thy health. Give him the cup.
          Trumpets sound, and shot goes off.

HAMLET
I'll play this bout first. Set it by awhile.
Come. [They fence.] Another hit; what say you?

LAERTES     A touch, a touch, I do confess.

KING
Our son shall win.

QUEEN                     He's fat and scant of breath.     289
Here, Hamlet, take my napkin, rub thy brows.               290
The Queen carouses to thy fortune, Hamlet.                 291

HAMLET     Good madam!

KING     Gertrude, do not drink.

QUEEN
I will, my lord, I pray you pardon me.     [She drinks.]

KING [aside]
It is the poisoned cup. It is too late.

HAMLET
I dare not drink yet, madam; by and by.

QUEEN     Come, let me wipe thy face.

LAERTES [aside to the King]
My lord, I'll hit him now.

KING                     I do not think't.

LAERTES [aside]
And yet it is almost against my conscience.

HAMLET
Come, for the third, Laertes. You do but dally.
I pray you, pass with your best violence;              301
I am afeard you make a wanton of me.                   302

LAERTES     Say you so? Come on.          [They] play.

OSRIC
Nothing neither way.

LAERTES
Have at you now!                                       305
          [Laertes wounds Hamlet; then,] in scuffling,
          they change rapiers, [and Hamlet wounds Laertes].

KING     Part them! They are incensed.

HAMLET
Nay, come, again.          [The Queen falls.]

OSRIC                     Look to the Queen there, ho!

HORATIO
They bleed on both sides. How is it, my lord?

OSRIC     How is't, Laertes?

LAERTES
Why, as a woodcock to mine own springe, Osric;        309
I am justly killed with mine own treachery.

HAMLET
How does the Queen?

KING     She swoons to see them bleed.

251 frankly without ill feeling or the burden of rancor   253 foil thin
metal background which sets a jewel off. (With pun on the blunted
rapier for fencing.)   255 Stick fiery off stand out brilliantly   259 laid . . .
side backed the weaker side.   261 is bettered is the odds-on favorite.
(Laertes's handicap is the "three hits" specified in line 165.)
263 likes pleases   263.1 play fence.   265 stoups flagons   267 Or . . .
exchange or draws even with Laertes by winning the third exchange
269 better breath improved vigor   270 union pearl. (So called, according to Pliny's Natural History, 9, because pearls are unique, never identical.)   273 kettle kettledrum

289 fat not physically fit, out of training   290 napkin handkerchief   291 carouses drinks a toast   301 pass thrust   302 make . . .
me i.e., treat me like a spoiled child, trifle with me.   305.1–2 in scuffling, they change rapiers (This stage direction occurs in the Folio.
According to a widespread stage tradition, Hamlet receives a scratch,
realizes that Laertes's sword is unbated, and accordingly forces an
exchange.)   309 woodcock a bird, a type of stupidity or as a
decoy.   springe trap, snare

QUEEN
No, no, the drink, the drink—Oh, my dear Hamlet—
The drink, the drink! I am poisoned.          [*She dies.*]

HAMLET
Oh, villainy! Ho, let the door be locked!
Treachery! Seek it out.          [*Laertes falls. Exit Osric.*]

LAERTES
It is here, Hamlet. Hamlet, thou art slain.
No med'cine in the world can do thee good;
In thee there is not half an hour of life.
The treacherous instrument is in thy hand,
Unbated and envenomed. The foul practice          320
Hath turned itself on me. Lo, here I lie,
Never to rise again. Thy mother's poisoned.
I can no more. The King, the King's to blame.

HAMLET
The point envenomed too? Then, venom, to thy work.
          [*He*] hurts the King.

ALL   Treason! Treason!

KING
Oh, yet defend me, friends! I am but hurt.

HAMLET [*forcing the King to drink*]
Here, thou incestuous, murd'rous, damnèd Dane,
Drink off this potion. Is thy union here?          328
Follow my mother.          [*The*] King dies.

LAERTES                    He is justly served.
It is a poison tempered by himself.          330
Exchange forgiveness with me, noble Hamlet.
Mine and my father's death come not upon thee,
Nor thine on me!          [*He*] dies.

HAMLET
Heaven make thee free of it! I follow thee.
I am dead, Horatio. Wretched Queen, adieu!
You that look pale and tremble at this chance,          336
That are but mutes or audience to this act,          337
Had I but time—as this fell sergeant, Death,          338
Is strict in his arrest—oh, I could tell you—          339
But let it be. Horatio, I am dead;
Thou liv'st. Report me and my cause aright
To the unsatisfied.

HORATIO                    Never believe it.
I am more an antique Roman than a Dane.          343
Here's yet some liquor left.
          [*He attempts to drink from the poisoned cup.*
          *Hamlet prevents him.*]

HAMLET                    As thou'rt a man,
Give me the cup! Let go! By heaven, I'll ha 't.
Oh, God, Horatio, what a wounded name,
Things standing thus unknown, shall live behind
          me!
If thou didst ever hold me in thy heart,
Absent thee from felicity awhile,

And in this harsh world draw thy breath in pain
To tell my story. *A march afar off* [*and a volley within*].
     What warlike noise is this?

          *Enter Osric.*

OSRIC
Young Fortinbras, with conquest come from Poland,
To th'ambassadors of England gives
This warlike volley.

HAMLET                    Oh, I die, Horatio!
The potent poison quite o'ercrows my spirit.          355
I cannot live to hear the news from England,
But I do prophesy th'election lights
On Fortinbras. He has my dying voice.          358
So tell him, with th'occurrents more and less          359
Which have solicited. The rest is silence.          360
Oh, oh, oh, oh!          [*He*] dies.

HORATIO
Now cracks a noble heart. Good night, sweet prince,
And flights of angels sing thee to thy rest!
          [*March within.*]
Why does the drum come hither?

          *Enter Fortinbras and English Ambassadors,*
          *with drum, colors, and Attendants.*

FORTINBRAS
Where is this sight?

HORATIO                    What is it you would see?
If aught of woe or wonder, cease your search.

FORTINBRAS
This quarry cries on havoc. O proud Death,          367
What feast is toward in thine eternal cell,          368
That thou so many princes at a shot
So bloodily hast struck?

FIRST AMBASSADOR                    The sight is dismal,
And our affairs from England come too late.
The ears are senseless that should give us hearing,
To tell him his commandment is fulfilled,
That Rosencrantz and Guildenstern are dead.
Where should we have our thanks?

HORATIO                    Not from his mouth,   375
Had it th'ability of life to thank you.
He never gave commandment for their death.
But since, so jump upon this bloody question,          378
You from the Polack wars and you from England
Are here arrived, give order that these bodies
High on a stage be placèd to the view,          381
And let me speak to th' yet unknowing world
How these things came about. So shall you hear
Of carnal, bloody, and unnatural acts,
Of accidental judgments, casual slaughters,          385

---

**320 Unbated** not blunted with a button.   **practice** plot   **328 union** pearl. (See line 270; with grim puns on the word's other meanings: marriage, shared death.)   **330 tempered** mixed   **336 chance** mischance   **337 mutes** silent witnesses. (Literally, actors with nonspeaking parts.)   **338 fell sergeant** remorseless arresting officer   **339 strict** (1) severely just (2) unavoidable.   **arrest** (1) taking into custody (2) stopping my speech   **343 Roman** (Suicide was an honorable choice for many Romans as an alternative to a dishonorable life.)

**355 o'ercrows** triumphs over (like the winner in a cockfight)   **358 voice** vote.   **359 th'occurrents** the events, incidents   **360 solicited** moved, urged. (Hamlet doesn't finish saying what the events have prompted—presumably, his acts of vengeance, or his reporting of those events to Fortinbras.)   **367 This . . . havoc** This heap of dead bodies loudly proclaims a general slaughter.   **368 feast** i.e., Death feasting on those who have fallen.   **toward** in preparation   **375 his** Claudius's   **378 so jump . . . question** so hard on the heels of this bloody business   **381 stage** platform   **385 judgments** retributions.   **casual** occurring by chance

Of deaths put on by cunning and forced cause,                         386
And, in this upshot, purposes mistook
Fall'n on th'inventors' heads. All this can I
Truly deliver.
FORTINBRAS        Let us haste to hear it,
And call the noblest to the audience.
For me, with sorrow I embrace my fortune.
I have some rights of memory in this kingdom,                          392
Which now to claim my vantage doth invite me.                         393
HORATIO
Of that I shall have also cause to speak,
And from his mouth whose voice will draw on more.                     395
But let this same be presently performed,                             396

Even while men's minds are wild, lest more
    mischance
On plots and errors happen.
FORTINBRAS                            Let four captains                398
Bear Hamlet, like a soldier, to the stage,
For he was likely, had he been put on,                                400
To have proved most royal; and for his passage,                       401
The soldiers' music and the rite of war
Speak loudly for him.                                                 403
Take up the body. Such a sight as this
Becomes the field, but here shows much amiss.                         405
Go bid the soldiers shoot.

*Exeunt marching, [bearing off the dead body,]
after the which a peal of ordnance are shot off.*

---

**386 put on** instigated.   **forced cause** contrivance   **392 of memory**
traditional, remembered, unforgotten   **393 vantage** favorable
opportunity   **395 voice . . . more** vote will influence still others.
**396 presently** immediately

**398 On** on top of   **400 put on** i.e., invested in royal office and so put
to the test   **401 for his passage** to mark his passing   **403 Speak** (let
them) speak   **405 Becomes the field** suits the field of battle

# Othello, the Moor of Venice

*O*thello differs in several respects from the other three major Shakespearean tragedies with which it is usually ranked. Written seemingly about the time of its performance at court by the King's Men (Shakespeare's acting company) on November 1, 1604, after *Hamlet* (c. 1599–1601) and before *King Lear* (1605–1606) and *Macbeth* (c. 1606–1607), *Othello* shares with these other plays a fascination with evil in its most virulent and universal aspect. These plays study the devastating effects of ambitious pride, ingratitude, wrath, jealousy, and vengeful hate—the deadly sins of the spirit—with only a passing interest in the political strife to which Shakespeare's Roman or classical tragedies are generally devoted. Of the four, *Othello* is the most concentrated upon one particular evil. The action concerns sexual jealousy, and, although human sinfulness is such that jealousy ceaselessly touches on other forms of depravity, the center of interest always returns in *Othello* to the destruction of a love through jealousy. *Othello* is a tragic portrait of a marriage. The protagonist is not a king or a prince, as in the tragedies already mentioned, but a general recently married. There are no supernatural visitations, as in *Hamlet* and *Macbeth*. Ideas of divine justice, while essential to *Othello*'s portrayal of a battle between good and evil for the allegiance of the protagonist, do not encompass the wide sweep of *King Lear*, nor do we find here the same broad indictment of humanity. Social order is not seriously shaken by Othello's tragedy. The fair-minded Duke of Venice remains firmly in control, and his deputy Lodovico oversees a just conclusion on Cyprus.

By the same token, *Othello* does not offer the remorseless questioning about humanity's relationship to the cosmos that we find in *King Lear, Hamlet,* and *Macbeth.* The battle of good and evil is, of course, cosmic, but in *Othello* that battle is realized through a taut narrative of jealousy and murder. Its poetic images are accordingly focused to a large extent on the natural world. One cluster of images is domestic and animal, having to do with goats, monkeys, wolves, baboons, guinea hens, wildcats, spiders, flies, asses, dogs, copulating horses and sheep, serpents, and toads; other images, more wide-ranging in scope, include green-eyed monsters, devils, poisons, money purses, tarnished jewels, music untuned, and light extinguished. The story is immediate and direct, retaining the sensational atmosphere of its Italian prose source by Giovanni Baptista Giraldi Cinthio, in his *Hecatommithi* of 1565 (translated into French in 1584). Events move even more swiftly than in Cinthio's work, for Shakespeare has compressed the story into two or three nights and days (albeit with an intervening sea journey and with an elastic use of stage time to allow for the maturing of long-term plans, as when we learn that Iago has begged Emilia "a hundred times" to steal Desdemona's handkerchief, 3.3.308, or that Iago has accused Cassio of making love to Desdemona "A thousand times," 5.2.219). *Othello* does not have a fully developed double plot, as in *King Lear,* or a comparatively large group of characters serving as foils to the protagonist, as in *Hamlet. Othello*'s cast is small, and the plot is concentrated to an unusual degree on Othello, Desdemona, and Iago. What *Othello* may lose in breadth it gains in dramatic intensity.

Daringly, Shakespeare opens this tragedy of love, not with a direct and sympathetic portrayal of the lovers themselves, but with a scene of vicious insinuation about their marriage. The images employed by Iago to describe the coupling of Othello and Desdemona are revoltingly animalistic, sodomistic. "Even now, now, very now, an old black ram / Is tupping your white ewe," he taunts Desdemona's father, Brabantio. (Tupping is a word used specifically for the copulating of sheep.) "You'll have your daughter covered with a Barbary horse; you'll have your nephews neigh to you"; "your daughter and the Moor are now making the beast with two backs"; "the devil will make a grandsire of you" (1.1.90–3, 113–20). This degraded view reduces the marriage to one of utter carnality, with repeated emphasis on the word "gross": Desdemona has yielded "to the gross clasps of a lascivious Moor" and has made "a gross revolt" against her family and society (lines 129, 137). Iago's second theme, one that is habitual with him, is money. "What ho, Brabantio! Thieves, thieves, thieves! / Look to your house, your daughter, and your bags" (lines 81–2). The implication is of a sinister bond between thievery in sex and thievery in gold. Sex and money are both commodities to be protected by watchful fathers against libidinous and opportunistic children.

We as audience make plentiful allowance for Iago's bias in all this, since he has admitted to Roderigo his knavery and resentment of Othello. Even so, the carnal vision of love we confront is calculatedly disturbing, because it seems so equated with a pejorative image of blackness. Othello is unquestionably a black man, referred to disparagingly by his detractors as the "thick-lips," with a "sooty bosom" (1.1.68; 1.2.71); Elizabethan usage applied the term "Moor" without attempting to distinguish between Arabian and African peoples. From the ugly start of the play, Othello and Desdemona have to prove the worth of their love in the face of preset attitudes against miscegenation. Brabantio takes refuge in the thought that Othello must have bewitched Desdemona. His basic assumption—one to be echoed later by Iago and when Othello's confidence is undermined by Othello himself—is that miscegenation is unnatural by definition. In confronting and accusing Othello, he repeatedly appeals "to all things of sense" (that is, to common sense) and asks if it is not "gross in sense" (self-evident) that Othello has practiced magic on her, since nothing else could prompt human nature so to leave its natural path. "For nature so preposterously to err, / Being not deficient, blind, or lame of sense, / Sans witchcraft could not" (1.2.65, 73; 1.3.64–6). We as audience can perceive the racial bias in Brabantio's view and can recognize also in him the type of imperious father who conventionally opposes romantic love. It is sadly ironic that he should now prefer Roderigo as a son-in-law, evidently concluding that any white Venetian would be preferable to the prince of blacks. Still, Brabantio has been hospitable to the Moor and trusting of his daughter. He is a sorrowful rather than ridiculous figure, and the charge he levels at the married pair, however much it is based on a priori assumptions of what is "natural" in human behavior, remains to be answered.

After all, we find ourselves wondering, what did attract Othello and Desdemona to one another? Even though he certainly did not use witchcraft, may Othello not have employed a subtler kind of enchantment in the exotic character of his travels among "the Cannibals that each other eat, / The Anthropophagi, and men whose heads / Do grow beneath their shoulders" (1.3.145–7)? These "passing strange" events fascinate Desdemona as they do everyone, including the Duke of Venice ("I think this tale would win my daughter too"). Othello has not practiced unfairly on her—"This only is the witchcraft I have used" (lines 162, 171–3). Yet may he not represent for Desdemona a radical novelty, being a man at once less devious and more interesting than the dissolute Venetian swaggerers, such as Roderigo and the "wealthy curlèd darlings of our nation" (1.2.69), who follow her about? Was her deceiving of her father by means of the elopement a protest, an escape from conventionality? Why has she been attracted to a man older than herself? For his part, Othello gives the impression of being inexperienced with women, at least of Desdemona's rank and complexion, and is both intrigued and flattered by her attentions. "She loved me for the dangers I had passed, / And I loved her that she did pity them" (1.3.169–70). Desdemona fulfills a place in Othello's view of himself. Does she also represent status for him in Venetian society, where he has been employed as a military commander but treated nonetheless as something of an alien?

These subtle but impertinent ways of doubting the motivations of Othello and Desdemona, adding to the difficulties that are inherent in an attempt to understand the mysteries of attraction in any relationship, are thrust upon us by the play's opening and are later crucial to Iago's strategy of breeding mistrust. Just as importantly, however, these insinuations are refuted by Othello and especially by Desdemona. Whatever others may think, she never gives the slightest indication of regarding her husband as different because he is black and old. In fact, the images of blackness and age are significantly reversed during the play's early scenes. Othello has already embraced the Christian faith, whereas Iago, a white Italian in a Christian culture, emerges as innately evil from the very start of the play. Othello's first appearance onstage, when he confronts a party of torch-bearing men coming to arrest him and bids his followers sheathe their swords (1.2.60), is perhaps reminiscent of Christ's arrest in the Garden of Gethsemane; if so, it suggests a fleeting comparison between Othello and the Christian God whose charity and forbearance he seeks to emulate. Othello's blackness may be used in part as an emblem of fallen humanity, but so are we all fallen. His age similarly strengthens our impression of his wisdom, restraint, and leadership. Any suggestions of comic sexual infidelity in the marriage of an older man and an attractive young bride are confuted by what we see in Desdemona's chaste yet sensual regard for the good man she has chosen.

Desdemona is devoted to Othello, admiring, and faithful. We believe her when she says that she does not even know what it means to be unfaithful; the word *whore* is not in her vocabulary. She is defenseless against the charges brought against her because she does not even comprehend them and cannot believe that anyone would imagine such things. Her love, both erotic and chaste, is of that transcendent wholesomeness common to several late Shakespearean heroines, such as Cordelia in *King Lear* and Hermione in *The Winter's Tale*. Her "pre-ferring" Othello to her father, like Cordelia's placing her duty to a husband before that to a father, is not ungrate-ful but natural and proper. And Othello, however much he may regard Desdemona in terms of his own identity (he calls her "my fair warrior"), does cherish Desdemona as she deserves. "I cannot speak enough of this content," he exclaims when he rejoins her on Cyprus. "It stops me here; it is too much of joy" (2.1.182, 196–7). The passion-ate intensity of his love prepares the way for his tragedy; he speaks more truly than he knows in saying, "when I love thee not, / Chaos is come again" (3.3.99–100). Iago speaks truly also when he observes that Othello "Is of a constant, loving, noble nature" (2.1.290). Othello's trag-edy is not that he is easily duped, but that his strong faith can be destroyed at such terrible cost. Othello never for-gets how much he is losing. The threat to his love is not an initial lack of his being happily married, but rather the insidious assumption that Desdemona cannot love him because such a love might be unnatural. The fear of being unlovable exists in Othello's mind, but the human instru-ment of this vicious gospel is Iago.

Iago belongs to a select group of villains in Shakespeare who, while plausibly motivated in human terms, also take delight in evil for its own sake: Aaron the Moor in *Titus Andronicus*, Richard III, Don John in *Much Ado About Nothing*, and Edmund in *King Lear*. They are not, like Macbeth or like Claudius in *Hamlet*, men driven by ambi-tion to commit crimes they clearly recognize to be wrong. Although Edmund does belatedly try to make amends, these villains are essentially conscienceless, sinister, and amused by their own cunning. They are related to one another by a stage metaphor of personified evil derived from the Vice of the morality play, whose typical role is to win the Mankind figure away from virtue and to cor-rupt him with worldly enticements. Like that engaging tempter, Shakespeare's villains in these plays take the audience into their confidence, boast in soliloquy of their cleverness, exult in the triumph of evil, and improvise plans with daring and resourcefulness. They are all superb actors, deceiving virtually every character onstage until late in the action with their protean and hypocritical display. They take pleasure in this "sport" and amaze us by their virtuosity. The role is paradoxically comic in its use of ingenious and resourceful deception— the grim and ironic comedy of vice. We know that we are to con-demn morally even while we applaud the skill.

This theatrical tradition of the Vice may best explain a puzzling feature of Iago, noted long ago and memorably phrased by Samuel Taylor Coleridge as "the motive hunting of a motiveless malignity." To be sure, Iago does offer plausible motives for what he does. Despite his resemblance to the morality Vice, he is no allegorized abstraction but an ensign in the army, a junior field offi-cer who hates being out-ranked by a theoretician or staff officer. As an old-school professional, he also resents that he has not been promoted on the basis of seniority, the "old gradation" (1.1.38). Even his efforts at using influ-ence with Othello have come to naught, and Iago can scarcely be blamed for supposing that Cassio's friend-ship with Othello has won him special favor. Thus, Iago has reason to plot against Cassio as well as Othello. Nevertheless a further dimension is needed to explain Iago's gloating, his utter lack of moral reflection, his con-centration on destroying Desdemona (who has not wronged Iago), his absorption in ingenious methods of plotting, his finesse and style. Hatred precedes any plau-sible motive in Iago and ultimately does not depend on psychological causality. Probably the tradition of the stage Machiavel (another type of gloating villain based on stereotyped attitudes toward the heretical political ideas of Niccolò Machiavelli), as in Marlowe's *The Jew of Malta*, contributes to the portraiture; this tradition was readily assimilated with that of the Vice.

Iago's machinations yield him both "sport" and "profit" (1.3.387); that is, he enjoys his evildoing, although he is also driven by a motive. This Vice-like behavior in human garb creates a restless sense of a destructive meta-physical reality lying behind his visible exterior. Even his stated motives do not always make sense. When in an outburst of hatred he soliloquizes that "I hate the Moor; / And it is thought abroad that twixt my sheets / He's done my office," Iago goes on to concede the unlikeli-hood of this charge. "I know not if't be true; / But I, for mere suspicion in that kind, / Will do as if for surety" (lines 387–91). The charge is so absurd, in fact, that we have to look into Iago himself for the origin of this jealous paranoia. The answer may be partly emblematic: as the embodiment and genius of sexual jealousy, Iago suffers with ironic appropriateness from the evil he preaches, and without external cause. Emilia understands that jeal-ousy is not a rational affliction but a self-induced disease of the mind. Jealous persons, she tells Desdemona, "are not ever jealous for the cause, / But jealous for they're jealous. It is a monster / Begot upon itself, born on itself" (3.4.161–3). Iago's own testimonial bears this out, for his jealousy is at once wholly irrational and agonizingly self-destructive. "I do suspect the lusty Moor / Hath leaped into my seat, the thought whereof / Doth, like a poison-ous mineral, gnaw my innards" (2.1.296–8). In light of this nightmare, we can see that even his seemingly plau-sible resentment of Cassio's promotion is jealous envy. The "daily beauty" in Cassio's life makes Iago feel "ugly" by comparison (5.1.19–20), engendering in Iago a pro-found sense of lack of worth from which he can tempo-rarily find relief only by reducing Othello and others to his own miserable condition. He is adept at provoking self-hatred in others because he suffers from it himself. His declaration to Othello that "I am your own forever" (3.3.495) is, of course, cynical, but it also signals the extent to which Iago has succeeded in wooing Othello away from Desdemona and Cassio into a murderous union between two women-hating men. The Iago who thus dedicates himself as partner in the fulfillment of Othello's homicidal fantasies is, we learn, capable of fantasizing a bizarre amorous encounter between himself and Cassio (lines 429–41).

Othello comes at last to regard Iago as a "demi-devil" who has tempted Othello to damn himself "beneath all depth in hell"; Lodovico speaks of Iago in the closing lines of the play as a "hellish villain" (5.2.142, 309, 379); and Iago himself boasts that "When devils will the blackest sins put on, / They do suggest at first with heavenly shows, / As I do now" (2.3.345–7). Iago thus bears some affinity to both the Vice and the devil, suggesting his relationship both to Othello's inner temptation and to a preexistent evil force in the universe itself. Conversely, Desdemona is in Emilia's words an "angel," purely chaste; "So come my soul to bliss as I speak true" (5.2.134, 259). When Desdemona lands on Cyprus, she is greeted in words that echo the *Ave Maria:* "Hail to thee, lady! And the grace of heaven . . . Enwheel thee round" (2.1.87–9). These images introduce metaphorically a conflict of good and evil in which Othello, typical of fallen humanity, has chosen evil and destroyed the good at the prompting of a diabolical counselor. Again we see the heritage of the morality play, especially of the later morality play in which the Mankind figure was sometimes damned rather than saved. Even so, to allegorize *Othello* is to obscure and misread its clash of human passion. In fact, we see that the impulse to reduce human complexity to simplistic moral absolutes is a fatal weakness in Othello; by insisting on viewing Desdemona as a type or abstraction, he loses sight of her wonderful humanity. The theological issue of salvation or damnation is not relevant in dramatic terms; the play is not a homily on the dangers of jealousy. The metaphysical dimensions of a homiletic tradition are transmuted into human drama. Acknowledging these limitations, we can notwithstanding see a spiritual analogy in Iago's devil-like method of undoing his victims.

His trick resembles that of the similarly mischief-making Don John in *Much Ado About Nothing:* an optical illusion by which the blameless heroine is impugned as an adulteress. The concealed Othello must watch Cassio boasting of sexual triumphs and believe he is talking about Desdemona. Like the devil, Iago is given power over people's frail senses, especially the eyes. He can create illusions to induce Othello to see what Iago wants him to see, as Don John does with Claudio, but Othello's acceptance of the lie must be his own responsibility, a failure of his corrupted will. Iago practices on Othello with an a priori logic used before on Brabantio and Roderigo, urging the proneness of all mortals to sin and the alleged unnaturalness of a black-white marriage. All women have appetites; Desdemona is a woman; hence, Desdemona has appetites. "The wine she drinks is made of grapes," he scoffs to Roderigo. "If she had been blessed, she would never have loved the Moor" (2.1.253–5). She is a Venetian, and "In Venice they do let God see the pranks / They dare not show their husbands" (3.3.216–17). Therefore, she, too, is a hypocrite; "She did deceive her father" (line 220). Most of all, it stands to reason that she must long for a man of her own race. Iago succeeds in getting Othello to concur: "And yet, how nature erring from itself—" (line 243). This proposition that Nature teaches all persons, including Desdemona, to seek a harmonious matching of "clime, complexion, and degree" strikes a responsive chord in Othello, since he knows that even though he has authority as a general serving his adopted city he is also black and in some senses a foreigner, an alien. "Haply, for I am black / And have not those soft parts of conversation / That chamberers have." Then, too, he is sensitive that he is older than she, "declined / Into the vale of years" (lines 246, 279–82), "the young affects / In me defunct" (1.3.266–7). And so, if one must conclude from the preceding that Desdemona will seek a lover, the only question is who. "This granted—as it is a most pregnant and unforced position—who stands so eminent in the degree of this fortune as Cassio does?" (2.1.236–9). Once Othello has accepted this syllogistic sequence of proofs, specious not through any lapse in logic but because the axiomatic assumptions about human nature are degraded and do not apply to Desdemona, Othello has arrived at an unshakable conclusion to which all subsequent evidence must be applied. "Villain, be sure thou prove my love a whore," he commissions Iago (3.3.375). Desdemona's innocent pleading for Cassio only makes things look worse. Cassio's reputed muttering while asleep, like the handkerchief seen in his possession or his giddy talk about his mistress Bianca, "speaks against her [Desdemona] with the other proofs" (line 456).

How has Othello fallen so far? His bliss with Desdemona as they are rejoined on Cyprus knows no limit. These two persons represent married love at its very best, erotic and spiritual, she enhancing his manliness, he cherishing her beauty and virtue. His blackness and age are positive images in him, despite earlier insinuations to the contrary. Indeed, we have no reason to suppose that Othello is what we would call "old," despite his worries about being "declined / Into the vale of years" and having lost the "young effects" of sexual desire; he appears to be middle-aged and vigorous, so much so that Desdemona is attracted to him sexually as well as in other ways. He is a man of public worthiness, of command, of self-assurance. Desdemona is the most domestic of Shakespeare's tragic heroines, even while she is also representative of so much that is transcendent. Husband and wife are bound happily in one of Shakespeare's few detailed portraits of serious commitment in marriage. Othello initially has the wisdom to know that Desdemona's feminine attractiveness ought not to be threatening to him: he need not be jealous because she is beautiful, "free of speech," and loves dancing and music, since "Where virtue is, these are more virtuous." Nor does he see any reason at first to fear her "revolt" simply because he is black and older than his wife; "she had eyes, and chose me" (3.3.197–203). Othello's self-assurance through the love he perceives in Desdemona is the strongest sign of his happiness in marriage.

What then gives way? We look at Iago for one important insight, but ultimately the cause must be in Othello himself. Arthur Kirsch has argued persuasively (in *Shakespeare and the Experience of Love,* 1981) that Othello's most grave failing is an insufficient regard for himself. It is in part an inability to counter the effects on him of a culture that regards him as an outsider; he is at last persuaded to see himself with the eyes of Venice, not just of Iago, but of Brabantio (who gladly entertains Othello until he has the presumption to elope with Brabantio's white daughter) and others. The resulting destruction of self-regard is devastating. Othello's jealousy stems from a profound suspicion that others cannot love him because he does not deem himself lovable.

Othello has loved Desdemona as an extention of himself, and, in his moments of greatest contentedness, his marriage is sustained by an idealized vision of himself serving as the object of his exalted romantic passion. When he destroys Desdemona, as he realizes with a terrible clarity, Othello destroys himself; the act is a prelude to his actual suicide. Iago's means of temptation, then, is to persuade Othello to regard himself with the eyes of Venice, to accept the view that Othello is himself alien and that any woman who loves him does so perversely. In Othello's tainted state of mind, Desdemona's very sexuality becomes an unbearable threat to him, her warmth and devotion a "proof" of disloyalty. Othello's most tortured speeches (3.4.57–77, 4.2.49–66) reveal the extent to which he equates the seemingly betraying woman, whom he has so depended on for happiness, with his own mother, who was given a handkerchief by an Egyptian sorceress and was warned that, if she should lose it, she would lose her husband's affection. Othello has briefly learned and then forgotten the precious art of harmonizing erotic passion and spiritual love, and, as these two great aims of love are driven apart in him, he comes to loathe and fear the sexuality that puts him so much in mind of his physical frailty and dependence on woman. The horror and pity of *Othello* rests, above all, in the spectacle of a love that was once so whole and noble made filthy by self-hatred. The tragic flaw thus lies in Othello's maleness, in his fear of betrayal by the innocent woman he loves, and in his apparent need to degrade her for the very thing he finds desirable in her— a tendency so common among men that

Freud, in the early twentieth century, could declare it to be "the most prevalent form of degradation in erotic life" (in Freud's *Sammlung,* volume 4).

The increasing surrender of Othello's judgment to passion can be measured in three successive trial scenes in the play: the entirely fair trial of Othello himself by the Venetian Senate concerning the elopement, Othello's trial of Cassio for drinking and rioting (when, ominously, Othello's "blood begins my safer guides to rule," 2.3.199), and finally the prejudged sentencing of Desdemona without providing her any opportunity to defend herself. In a corollary decline, Othello falls from the Christian compassion of the opening scenes (he customarily confesses to heaven "the vices of my blood," 1.3.125) to the pagan savagery of his vengeful and ritualistic execution of his wife. "My heart is turned to stone" (4.1.184–5), he vows, and at the play's end he grievingly characterizes himself as a "base Indian" who "threw a pearl away / Richer than all his tribe" (5.2.357–8). Iago knows that he must persuade Othello to sentence and to execute Desdemona himself, for only by active commitment to evil will Othello damn himself. In nothing does Iago so resemble the devil as in his wish to see Othello destroy the innocence and goodness on which his happiness depends.

The fate of some of the lesser characters echoes that of Othello, for Iago's evil intent is to "enmesh them all" (2.3.356). Cassio, in particular, is, like Othello, an attractive man with a single, vulnerable weakness—in his case, a fleshly appetite for wine and women. For him, alternately idolizing and depreciating women as he does, the gap between spiritual and sensual love remains vast, but he is essentially good-natured and trustworthy. His seemingly genial flaws lead to disaster, because they put him at the mercy of a remorseless enemy. Iago is, with fitting irony, the apostle of absolute self-control: "Our bodies are our gardens, to the which our wills are gardeners" (1.3.323–4). Thus, Cassio's tragedy is anything but a straightforward homily on the virtues of temperance. Similarly, Bianca is undone, not through any simple cause-and-effect punishment of her sexual conduct—she is, after all, fond of Cassio and loyal to him, even if he will not marry her— but because Iago is able to turn appearances against her. With his usual appeal to a priori logic, he builds a case that she and Cassio are in cahoots: "I do suspect this trash / To be a party in this injury . . . This is the fruits of whoring" (5.1.86–7, 118). Roderigo is another of Iago's victims, a contemptible one, led by the nose because he, too, has surrendered reason to passion. Emilia cannot escape Iago's evil influence and steals the handkerchief for him, despite knowing its value for Desdemona. Flaws are magnified into disasters by a remorseless evil intelligence. Men and women both must be ceaselessly circumspect; a good reputation is sooner lost than recovered. Emilia is a conventionally decent enough woman—she jests to Desdemona that she would be faithless in marriage only for a very high price—and yet her one small compromise with her conscience contributes to the murder of her mistress. Like Othello, she offers atonement too late, by denouncing her husband in a gesture of defiance toward male authority that says much about the tragic consequences of male mistrust of women. Desdemona is the only person in the play too good to be struck down through some inner flaw, which may explain why Iago is so intent on destroying her along with Othello and Cassio.

As a tragic hero, Othello obtains self-knowledge at a terrible price. He knows finally that what he has destroyed was ineffably good. The discovery is too late for him to make amends, and he dies by his own hand as atonement. The deaths of Othello and Desdemona are, in their separate ways, equally devastating: he is in part the victim of racism, though he nobly refuses to deny his own culpability, and she is the victim of sexism, lapsing sadly into the stereotypical role of passive and silent sufferer that the Venetian world expects of women. Despite the loss, however, Othello's reaffirmation of faith in Desdemona's goodness undoes what the devil-like Iago had most hoped to achieve: the separation of Othello from his loving trust in one who is good. In this important sense, Othello's self-knowledge is cathartic and a compensation for the terrible price he has paid. The very existence of a person as good as Desdemona gives the lie to Iago's creed that everyone has his or her price. She is the sacrificial victim who must die for Othello's loss of faith and, by dying, rekindle that faith. ("My life upon her faith!" Othello prophetically affirms, in response to her father's warning that she may deceive [1.3.297].) She cannot restore him to himself, for self-hatred has done its ugly work, but she is the means by which he understands at last the chimerical and wantonly destructive nature of his jealousy. His greatness appears in his acknowledgment of this truth and in the heroic struggle with which he has confronted an inner darkness we all share.

Onstage and in film and television, *Othello* proves itself to be jarringly relevant to modern concerns about racial conflict and about men's mistreatment of women. Janet Suzman chose to produce the play onstage and subsequently for educational television in Johannesburg, South Africa, at a time when apartheid was soon to be dismantled, even though that surprising if inevitable event was not yet discernible. A racially mixed audience came to see a racially mixed cast, with John Kani, a well-known South African black actor, as Othello, and a very fair-haired South African actress as Desdemona. Iago unmistakably represented the mindset of a state police officer obsessed with preserving the purity of the white race and therefore venemous in his racial hatred of Othello for his miscegenated marriage with a white woman. The explosively powerful emotions of that production carry over into a memorable film version. Orson Welles's 1951 film version, recently remastered, featured Othello in blackface as the protagonist; so did Laurence Olivier's film of 1965, based on a National Theatre stage production of 1964 with Frank Finlay as Iago and Maggie Smith as Desdemona. Indeed, most Othellos onstage over the centuries have been white actors (including Edmund Kean, John Philip Kemble, Edwin Booth, Charles Macready, Edwin Forrest, Henry Irving, Tommaso Salvini, and Paul Scofield, many of whom also played Iago), with notable exceptions that include Ira Aldridge, Earle Hyman, and Paul Robeson. Robeson's galvanizing performances at the Savoy Theatre in 1930 with Peggy Ashcroft as Desdemona, and then in Margaret Webster's New York production of 1943–1945 with Uta Hagen as Desdemona and José Ferrer as Iago, helped establish the role of Othello as one that great black actors could perform. Today racially mixed casting allows for all sorts of permutations, though Kenneth Branagh's recent film chooses the more recognizable pattern with Branagh himself as Iago and Laurence Fishburne as Othello. Iqbal Khan, in his much-admired modern-dress production of *Othello* for the Royal Shakespeare Company at Stratford-upon-Avon in 2015, cast two black actors, Hugh Quarshie and Lucian Msamati, as Othello and Iago. In another recent development, Emilia has stood out in several productions as the raisonneur and heroic figure in the play, speaking as she does on behalf of maltreated women, urging Desdemona to stand up for her rights. One recent Chicago production went so far as to rewrite the ending: Othello and Iago both survive unpunished for what they have done, while Desdemona and Emilia lie dead as their innocent victims. This deliberate and provocative overstatement might seem extreme to some viewers, but unquestionably did signal the direction of recent performance history of this profoundly disturbing play.

# Othello, the Moor of Venice

## The Names of the Actors

OTHELLO, *the Moor*
BRABANTIO, *[a senator,] father to Desdemona*
CASSIO, *an honorable lieutenant [to Othello]*
IAGO, *[Othello's ancient,] a villain*
RODERIGO, *a gulled gentleman*
DUKE OF VENICE
SENATORS *[of Venice]*
MONTANO, *Governor of Cyprus*
GENTLEMEN *of Cyprus*
LODOVICO *and* GRATIANO, *[kinsmen to Brabantio,] two noble Venetians*
SAILORS
CLOWN

DESDEMONA, *[daughter to Brabantio and] wife to Othello*
EMILIA, *wife to Iago*
BIANCA, *a courtesan [and mistress to Cassio]*

[A MESSENGER
A HERALD
A MUSICIAN

*Servants, Attendants, Officers, Senators, Musicians, Gentlemen*

SCENE: *Venice; a seaport in Cyprus]*

## 1.1

*Enter Roderigo and Iago.*

RODERIGO
  Tush, never tell me! I take it much unkindly          1
  That thou, Iago, who hast had my purse
  As if the strings were thine, shouldst know of this.   3
IAGO  'Sblood, but you'll not hear me.                   4
  If ever I did dream of such a matter,
  Abhor me.
RODERIGO
  Thou told'st me thou didst hold him in thy hate.       7
IAGO  Despise me
  If I do not. Three great ones of the city,             9
  In personal suit to make me his lieutenant,
  Off-capped to him; and by the faith of man,
  I know my price, I am worth no worse a place.
  But he, as loving his own pride and purposes,
  Evades them with a bombast circumstance               14

  Horribly stuffed with epithets of war,                15
  And, in conclusion,
  Nonsuits my mediators. For, "Certes," says he,        17
  "I have already chose my officer."
  And what was he?
  Forsooth, a great arithmetician,                      20
  One Michael Cassio, a Florentine,
  A fellow almost damned in a fair wife,                22
  That never set a squadron in the field
  Nor the division of a battle knows                    24
  More than a spinster—unless the bookish theoric,     25
  Wherein the togaed consuls can propose                26
  As masterly as he. Mere prattle without practice
  Is all his soldiership. But he, sir, had th'election;
  And I, of whom his eyes had seen the proof            29
  At Rhodes, at Cyprus, and on other grounds            30

---

1.1. **Location: Venice. A street.**
**1 never tell me** (An expression of incredulity, like "tell me another one.")
**3 this** i.e., Desdemona's elopement.   **4 'Sblood** By His (Christ's) blood
**7 him** Othello   **9 great ones** members of the ruling elite   **14 bombast circumstance** wordy evasion. (*Bombast* is cotton padding.)

**15 epithets of war** military expressions   **17 Nonsuits** rejects the petition of.   **Certes** Certainly   **20 arithmetician** i.e., a man whose military knowledge is merely theoretical, based on books of tactics
**22 A . . . wife** (Cassio does not seem to be married, but his counterpart in Shakespeare's source "had a woman in the house who made the most marvelous embroidery on fine linen." See also 4.1.131.)   **24 division of a battle** disposition of a military unit   **25 a spinster** i.e., a housewife, one whose regular occupation is spinning.   **theoric** theory
**26 togaed consuls** toga-wearing counselors or senators.   **propose** discuss   **29 his** Othello's   **30 grounds** arenas of military conflict

Christened and heathen, must be beleed and calmed 31
By debitor and creditor. This countercaster, 32
He, in good time, must his lieutenant be, 33
And I—God bless the mark!—His Moorship's ancient. 34
RODERIGO
By heaven, I rather would have been his hangman. 35
IAGO
Why, there's no remedy. 'Tis the curse of service;
Preferment goes by letter and affection, 37
And not by old gradation, where each second 38
Stood heir to th' first. Now, sir, be judge yourself 39
Whether I in any just term am affined 40
To love the Moor.
RODERIGO    I would not follow him then.
IAGO    Oh, sir, content you. 43
I follow him to serve my turn upon him.
We cannot all be masters, nor all masters
Cannot be truly followed. You shall mark 46
Many a duteous and knee-crooking knave
That, doting on his own obsequious bondage,
Wears out his time, much like his master's ass,
For naught but provender, and when he's old,
    cashiered. 50
Whip me such honest knaves. Others there are 51
Who, trimmed in forms and visages of duty, 52
Keep yet their hearts attending on themselves,
And, throwing but shows of service on their lords,
Do well thrive by them, and when they have lined
    their coats, 55
Do themselves homage. These fellows have some
    soul, 56
And such a one do I profess myself. For, sir,
It is as sure as you are Roderigo,
Were I the Moor I would not be Iago. 59
In following him, I follow but myself—
Heaven is my judge, not I for love and duty,
But seeming so for my peculiar end. 62
For when my outward action doth demonstrate
The native act and figure of my heart 64
In compliment extern, 'tis not long after 65

But I will wear my heart upon my sleeve
For daws to peck at. I am not what I am. 67
RODERIGO
What a full fortune does the thick-lips owe 68
If he can carry't thus!
IAGO                         Call up her father. 69
Rouse him, make after him, poison his delight,
Proclaim him in the streets; incense her kinsmen, 71
And, though he in a fertile climate dwell, 72
Plague him with flies. Though that his joy be joy, 73
Yet throw such changes of vexation on't 74
As it may lose some color. 75
RODERIGO
Here is her father's house. I'll call aloud.
IAGO
Do, with like timorous accent and dire yell 77
As when, by night and negligence, the fire 78
Is spied in populous cities.
RODERIGO

What ho, Brabantio! Signor Brabantio, ho!

IAGO

Awake! What ho, Brabantio! Thieves, thieves, thieves!
Look to your house, your daughter, and your bags!
Thieves, thieves! 83

*Brabantio [enters] above [at a window].*

BRABANTIO
What is the reason of this terrible summons?
What is the matter there?
RODERIGO
Signor, is all your family within?
IAGO
Are your doors locked?
BRABANTIO                         Why, wherefore ask you this?
IAGO
Zounds, sir, you're robbed. For shame, put on your
    gown! 88
Your heart is burst; you have lost half your soul.
Even now, now, very now, an old black ram
Is tupping your white ewe. Arise, arise! 91
Awake the snorting citizens with the bell, 92
Or else the devil will make a grandsire of you. 93
Arise, I say!
BRABANTIO    What, have you lost your wits?
RODERIGO
Most reverend signor, do you know my voice?

31 **Christened and heathen** Christian and pagan.    **beleed and calmed** left to leeward without wind, becalmed. (A sailing metaphor.)    32 **debitor and creditor** (A name for a system of bookkeeping, here used as a contemptuous nickname for Cassio.)    **countercaster** i.e., bookkeeper, one who tallies with *counters*, or "metal disks." (Said contemptuously.)    33 **in good time** opportunely, i.e., forsooth    34 **God bless the mark** (Perhaps originally a formula to ward off evil; here an expression of impatience.)    **ancient** standard-bearer, ensign (whose rank is below that of lieutenant, line 33).    35 **his hangman** the executioner of him.    37 **Preferment** promotion.    **letter and affection** personal influence and favoritism    38 **old gradation** step-by-step seniority, the traditional way    39 **Stood heir to** ranked below    40 **term** respect.    **affined** bound    43 **content you** don't you worry about that.    46 **truly** faithfully    50 **cashiered** dismissed from service.    51 **Whip me** Whip, as far as I'm concerned    52 **trimmed . . . duty** dressed up in the mere form and show of dutifulness    55 **lined their coats** i.e., stuffed their purses    56 **Do themselves homage** i.e., attend to self-interest solely.    59 **Were . . . Iago** i.e., if I were able to assume command, I certainly would not choose to remain a subordinate, or, I would keep a suspicious eye on a flattering subordinate.    62 **peculiar** particular, personal    64 **native** innate.    **figure** shape, intent    65 **compliment extern** outward show (conforming in this case to the inner workings and intention of the heart)

67 **daws** small crowlike birds, proverbially stupid and avaricious.    **I am not what I am** i.e., I am not one who wears his heart on his sleeve.    68 **full** swelling.    **thick-lips** (Elizabethans often applied the term "Moor" to Negroes.)    **owe** own    69 **carry't** carry out the elopement    71 **him** Othello    72–3 **though . . . flies** though he seems prosperous and happy now, vex him with misery.    73 **Though . . . be joy** Although he seems fortunate and happy. (Repeats the idea of line 72.)    74 **changes of vexation** vexing changes    75 **As . . . color** that may cause it to lose some of its original gloss.    77 **timorous** frightening    78 **As . . . fire** as when a fire, having gained hold by negligence at night    83.1 **at a window** (This stage direction, from the quarto, probably calls for an appearance on the gallery above and rearstage.)    88 **Zounds** By His (Christ's) wounds    91 **tupping** covering, copulating with. (Said of sheep.)    92 **snorting** snoring    93 **Or . . . of you** or else you will discover that the devil is the father of your grandchildren.

BRABANTIO    Not I. What are you?
RODERIGO    My name is Roderigo.
BRABANTIO    The worser welcome.
I have charged thee not to haunt about my doors.
In honest plainness thou hast heard me say
My daughter is not for thee; and now, in madness,
Being full of supper and distemp'ring drafts,                              102
Upon malicious bravery dost thou come                                      103
To start my quiet.                                                         104
RODERIGO
Sir, sir, sir—
BRABANTIO    But thou must needs be sure
My spirits and my place have in their power                                106
To make this bitter to thee.
RODERIGO                               Patience, good sir.
BRABANTIO
What tell'st thou me of robbing? This is Venice;
My house is not a grange.
RODERIGO                               Most grave Brabantio,               109
In simple and pure soul I come to you.                                     110
IAGO    Zounds, sir, you are one of those that will not
serve God if the devil bid you. Because we come to do
you service and you think we are ruffians, you'll have
your daughter covered with a Barbary horse; you'll   114
have your nephews neigh to you; you'll have coursers   115
for cousins and jennets for germans.                                       116
BRABANTIO    What profane wretch art thou?
IAGO    I am one, sir, that comes to tell you your daughter
and the Moor are now making the beast with two
backs.
BRABANTIO
Thou art a villain.
IAGO                               You are—a senator.                      121
BRABANTIO
This thou shalt answer. I know thee, Roderigo.                             122
RODERIGO
Sir, I will answer anything. But I beseech you,
If't be your pleasure and most wise consent—                               124
As partly I find it is—that your fair daughter,
At this odd-even and dull watch o'th' night,                               126
Transported with no worse nor better guard                                 127
But with a knave of common hire, a gondolier,                              128
To the gross clasps of a lascivious Moor—
If this be known to you and your allowance                                 130
We then have done you bold and saucy wrongs.                               131
But if you know not this, my manners tell me
We have your wrong rebuke. Do not believe

That, from the sense of all civility,                                      134
I thus would play and trifle with your reverence.                          135
Your daughter, if you have not given her leave,
I say again, hath made a gross revolt,
Tying her duty, beauty, wit, and fortunes                                  138
In an extravagant and wheeling stranger                                    139
Of here and everywhere. Straight satisfy yourself.                         140
If she be in her chamber or your house,
Let loose on me the justice of the state
For thus deluding you.
BRABANTIO  [calling]    Strike on the tinder, ho!                          144
Give me a taper! Call up all my people!
This accident is not unlike my dream.                                      146
Belief of it oppresses me already.
Light, I say, light!                               Exit [above].
IAGO                               Farewell, for I must leave you.
It seems not meet nor wholesome to my place                                149
To be produced—as, if I stay, I shall—                                     150
Against the Moor. For I do know the state,
However this may gall him with some check,                                 152
Cannot with safety cast him, for he's embarked                             153
With such loud reason to the Cyprus wars,                                  154
Which even now stands in act, that, for their souls,                       155
Another of his fathom they have none                                       156
To lead their business; in which regard,                                   157
Though I do hate him as I do hell pains,
Yet for necessity of present life                                          159
I must show out a flag and sign of love,
Which is indeed but sign. That you shall surely find
him,
Lead to the Sagittary the raisèd search,                                   162
And there will I be with him. So farewell.        Exit. 163

*Enter [below] Brabantio [in his nightgown] with
servants and torches.*

BRABANTIO
It is too true an evil. Gone she is;
And what's to come of my despisèd time                                     165
Is naught but bitterness. Now, Roderigo,
Where didst thou see her?—Oh, unhappy girl!—
With the Moor, say'st thou?—Who would be a father!—
How didst thou know 'twas she?—Oh, she deceives
me
Past thought!—What said she to you?—Get more
tapers.
Raise all my kindred.—Are they married, think you?

---

**102 distemp'ring** intoxicating   **103 Upon malicious bravery** with hostile intent to defy me   **104 start** startle, disrupt   **106 My . . . power** my temperament and my authority of office have it in their power   **109 grange** isolated country house.   **grave** reverend   **110 simple** sincere   **114 covered with** mounted sexually by.   **Barbary** from northern Africa (and hence associated with Othello)   **115 nephews** i.e., grandsons   **115–16 you'll . . . germans** you'll consent to have powerful horses for kinfolks and small Spanish horses for near relatives.   **121 a senator** (Said with mock politeness, as though the word itself were an insult.)   **122 answer** be held accountable for.   **124 wise** well-informed   **126 At . . . night** at this hour that is between day and night, neither the one nor the other   **127 with** by   **128 But with a knave** than by a low fellow, a servant   **130 and your allowance** and has your permission   **131 saucy** insolent

**134 from** contrary to.   **civility** good manners, decency   **135 your reverence** (1) the respect due to you (2) Your Reverence.   **138 wit** intelligence   **139–40 In . . . everywhere** to a wandering and vagabond foreigner of uncertain origins.   **140 Straight** Straightaway   **144 tinder** charred linen ignited by a spark from flint and steel, used to light torches or *tapers* (lines 145, 170)   **146 accident** occurrence, event   **149 meet** fitting.   **place** position (as ensign)   **150 produced** produced (as a witness)   **152 gall** rub; oppress.   **check** rebuke   **153 cast** dismiss.   **embarked** engaged   **154 loud** urgent   **155 stands in act** have started.   **for their souls** to save their souls   **156 fathom** i.e., ability, depth of experience   **157 in which regard** out of regard for which   **159 life** livelihood   **162 Sagittary** (An inn or house where Othello and Desdemona are staying, named for its sign of Sagittarius, or Centaur.)   **raisèd search** search party called to duty   **163.1 nightgown** dressing gown. (This costuming is specified in the quarto text.)   **165 time** i.e., remainder of life

**RODERIGO**  Truly, I think they are.

**BRABANTIO**
Oh, heaven! How got she out? Oh, treason of the
    blood!                                                   173
Fathers, from hence trust not your daughters' minds   174
By what you see them act. Is there not charms          175
By which the property of youth and maidhood            176
May be abused? Have you not read, Roderigo,            177
Of some such thing?

**RODERIGO**                    Yes, sir, I have indeed.

**BRABANTIO**
Call up my brother.—Oh, would you had had her!—
Some one way, some another.—Do you know
Where we may apprehend her and the Moor?

**RODERIGO**
I think I can discover him, if you please             182
To get good guard and go along with me.

**BRABANTIO**
Pray you, lead on. At every house I'll call;
I may command at most.—Get weapons, ho!              185
And raise some special officers of night.—
On, good Roderigo. I will deserve your pains.        187

                              *Exeunt.*

❖

## 1.2

*Enter Othello, Iago, attendants with torches.*

**IAGO**
Though in the trade of war I have slain men,
Yet do I hold it very stuff o'th' conscience           2
To do no contrived murder. I lack iniquity             3
Sometime to do me service. Nine or ten times
I had thought t'have yerked him here under the ribs.   5

**OTHELLO**
'Tis better as it is.

**IAGO**                    Nay, but he prated,
And spoke such scurvy and provoking terms
Against your honor
That, with the little godliness I have,
I did full hard forbear him. But, I pray you, sir,    10
Are you fast married? Be assured of this,
That the magnifico is much beloved,                   12
And hath in his effect a voice potential              13
As double as the Duke's. He will divorce you,
Or put upon you what restraint or grievance
The law, with all his might to enforce it on,
Will give him cable.

**OTHELLO**          Let him do his spite.            17
My services which I have done the seigniory           18

Shall out-tongue his complaints. 'Tis yet to know—    19
Which, when I know that boasting is an honor,          20
I shall promulgate—I fetch my life and being          21
From men of royal siege, and my demerits              22
May speak unbonneted to as proud a fortune            23
As this that I have reached. For know, Iago,          24
But that I love the gentle Desdemona,
I would not my unhousèd free condition                26
Put into circumscription and confine                  27
For the seas' worth. But look, what lights come yond? 28

*Enter Cassio [and officers] with torches.*

**IAGO**
Those are the raisèd father and his friends.
You were best go in.

**OTHELLO**             Not I. I must be found.
My parts, my title, and my perfect soul               31
Shall manifest me rightly. Is it they?

**IAGO**  By Janus, I think no.                        33

**OTHELLO**
The servants of the Duke? And my lieutenant?
The goodness of the night upon you, friends!
What is the news?

**CASSIO**             The Duke does greet you, General,
And he requires your haste-post-haste appearance
Even on the instant.

**OTHELLO**            What is the matter, think you?

**CASSIO**
Something from Cyprus, as I may divine.               39
It is a business of some heat. The galleys            40
Have sent a dozen sequent messengers                  41
This very night at one another's heels,
And many of the consuls, raised and met,             43
Are at the Duke's already. You have been hotly called
    for,
When, being not at your lodging to be found,
The Senate hath sent about three several quests      46
To search you out.

**OTHELLO**           'Tis well I am found by you.
I will but spend a word here in the house
And go with you.                      [*Exit.*]

**CASSIO**             Ancient, what makes he here?    49

**IAGO**
Faith, he tonight hath boarded a land carrack.        50
If it prove lawful prize, he's made forever.          51

---

**173 treason of the blood** disobedience prompted by sexual passion. **174–5 trust . . . act** don't assume that your daughters' intents can be judged by the way they appear to behave. **175 charms** spells **176 property** special quality, nature **177 abused** deceived. **182 discover** reveal, uncover **185 command** demand assistance **187 deserve** show gratitude for
**1.2. Location:** Venice. Another street, before Othello's lodgings. **2 very stuff** essence, basic material. (Continuing the metaphor of *trade* from line 1.) **3 contrived** premeditated **5 yerked** stabbed. **him** i.e., Roderigo. **10 I . . . him** I restrained myself with great difficulty from assaulting him. **12 magnifico** Venetian grandee, i.e., Brabantio. **13 in his effect** at his command. **potential** powerful **17 cable** i.e., scope. **18 seigniory** Venetian government

**19 yet to know** not yet widely known **20–1 Which . . . promulgate** i.e., which I will never proclaim, since boasting is dishonorable **22 siege** i.e., rank. (Literally, a seat used by a person of distinction.) **22–4 my demerits . . . reached** my deservings may be proudly proclaimed as worthy of the greatness I have attained in my career. (*Unbonneted* means "with hat modestly removed in deference.") **26 unhousèd** unconfined, undomesticated **27 circumscription and confine** restriction and confinement **28 the seas' worth** all the riches at the bottom of the sea. **28.1 officers** (The quarto text specifies, "*Enter* Cassio *with lights, Officers, and torches.*") **31 My . . . soul** My natural gifts, my position or reputation, and my unflawed conscience **33 Janus** Roman two-faced god of beginnings **39 divine** guess. **40 heat** urgency. **41 sequent** successive **43 consuls** senators **46 about** all over the city. **several** separate **49 Ancient** Ensign. **makes** does **50 boarded** gone aboard and seized as an act of piracy. (With sexual suggestion.) **carrack** large merchant ship. **51 prize** booty

CASSIO
I do not understand.
IAGO                                 He's married.
CASSIO                                           To who?

[*Enter Othello.*]

IAGO
Marry, to—Come, Captain, will you go?                              53
OTHELLO   Have with you.                                           54
CASSIO
Here comes another troop to seek for you.                         55

*Enter Brabantio, Roderigo, with officers and
torches.*

IAGO
It is Brabantio. General, be advised.                             56
He comes to bad intent.
OTHELLO                            Holla! Stand there!
RODERIGO
Signor, it is the Moor.
BRABANTIO                          Down with him, thief!
                                   [*They draw on both sides.*]
IAGO
You, Roderigo! Come, sir, I am for you.
OTHELLO
Keep up your bright swords, for the dew will rust
    them.                                                         60
Good signor, you shall more command with years                   61
Than with your weapons.
BRABANTIO
O thou foul thief, where hast thou stowed my
    daughter?
Damned as thou art, thou hast enchanted her!
For I'll refer me to all things of sense,                         65
If she in chains of magic were not bound
Whether a maid so tender, fair, and happy,
So opposite to marriage that she shunned
The wealthy curlèd darlings of our nation,
Would ever have, t'incur a general mock,
Run from her guardage to the sooty bosom                          71
Of such a thing as thou—to fear, not to delight.
Judge me the world if 'tis not gross in sense                     73
That thou hast practiced on her with foul charms,
Abused her delicate youth with drugs or minerals                  75
That weakens motion. I'll have't disputed on;                     76
'Tis probable and palpable to thinking.
I therefore apprehend and do attach thee                          78
For an abuser of the world, a practicer                           79
Of arts inhibited and out of warrant.—                            80
Lay hold upon him! If he do resist,

Subdue him at his peril.
OTHELLO                            Hold your hands,
Both you of my inclining and the rest.                            83
Were it my cue to fight, I should have known it
Without a prompter.—Whither will you that I go
To answer this your charge?
BRABANTIO      To prison, till fit time
Of law and course of direct session                              88
Call thee to answer.
OTHELLO                            What if I do obey?
How may the Duke be therewith satisfied,
Whose messengers are here about my side
Upon some present business of the state
To bring me to him?
OFFICER                    'Tis true, most worthy signor.
The Duke's in council, and your noble self,
I am sure, is sent for.
BRABANTIO             How? The Duke in council?
In this time of the night? Bring him away.                        96
Mine's not an idle cause. The Duke himself,                       97
Or any of my brothers of the state,                               98
Cannot but feel this wrong as 'twere their own;
For if such actions may have passage free,                       100
Bondslaves and pagans shall our statesmen be.
                                             *Exeunt.*

❖

# 1.3

*Enter Duke [and] Senators [and sit at a table, with
lights], and Officers. [The Duke and Senators
are reading dispatches.]*

DUKE
There is no composition in these news                             1
That gives them credit.
FIRST SENATOR      Indeed, they are disproportioned.              3
My letters say a hundred and seven galleys.
DUKE
And mine, a hundred forty.
SECOND SENATOR                     And mine, two hundred.
But though they jump not on a just account—                       6
As in these cases, where the aim reports                          7
'Tis oft with difference—yet do they all confirm                  8
A Turkish fleet, and bearing up to Cyprus.
DUKE
Nay, it is possible enough to judgment.
I do not so secure me in the error                               11
But the main article I do approve                                12
In fearful sense.

53 **Marry** (An oath, originally "by the Virgin Mary"; here used with wordplay on *married.*)   54 **Have with you** i.e., Let's go.   **55.1–2 *officers and torches*** (The quarto text calls for "*others with lights and weapons.*")   56 **be advised** be on your guard.   60 **Keep up** Keep in the sheath   61 **years** the authority of old age   65 **For . . . sense** For I appeal to common sense   71 **guardage** guardianship   73 **gross in sense** obvious   75 **minerals** i.e., poisons   76 **weakens motion** impair the vital faculties.   **disputed on** argued in court by professional counsel, debated by experts   78 **attach** arrest   79 **abuser** deceiver   80 **arts inhibited** prohibited arts, black magic.   **out of warrant** illegal.

83 **inclining** following, party   88 **course of direct session** regular or specially convened legal proceedings   96 **away** right along.   97 **idle** trifling   98 **brothers** fellow senators   100 **may . . . free** are allowed to go unchecked
**1.3. Location:** Venice. A council chamber.
**0.1–2 *Enter . . . Officers*** (The quarto text calls for the Duke and senators to "*set at a Table with lights and Attendants.*")   1 **composition** consistency   3 **disproportioned** inconsistent.   6 **jump** agree. **just** exact   7–8 **where . . . difference** when the reports are estimates, they often differ in what they say   11–12 **I do not . . . approve** I do not take such (false) comfort in the discrepancies that I fail to perceive the main point, i.e., that the Turkish fleet is threatening

SAILOR (*within*)   What ho, what ho, what ho!

*Enter Sailor.*

OFFICER   A messenger from the galleys.

DUKE   Now, what's the business?

SAILOR

The Turkish preparation makes for Rhodes.   16
So was I bid report here to the state
By Signor Angelo.

DUKE

How say you by this change?

FIRST SENATOR                This cannot be   19
By no assay of reason. 'Tis a pageant   20
To keep us in false gaze. When we consider   21
Th'importancy of Cyprus to the Turk,
And let ourselves again but understand
That, as it more concerns the Turk than Rhodes,   24
So may he with more facile question bear it,   25
For that it stands not in such warlike brace,   26
But altogether lacks th'abilities   27
That Rhodes is dressed in—if we make thought of this,   28
We must not think the Turk is so unskillful   29
To leave that latest which concerns him first,   30
Neglecting an attempt of ease and gain
To wake and wage a danger profitless.   32

DUKE

Nay, in all confidence, he's not for Rhodes.

OFFICER   Here is more news.

*Enter a Messenger.*

MESSENGER

The Ottomites, reverend and gracious,   35
Steering with due course toward the isle of Rhodes,
Have there injointed them with an after fleet.   37

FIRST SENATOR

Ay, so I thought. How many, as you guess?

MESSENGER

Of thirty sail; and now they do restem   39
Their backward course, bearing with frank
     appearance   40
Their purposes toward Cyprus. Signor Montano,
Your trusty and most valiant servitor,   42
With his free duty recommends you thus,   43
And prays you to believe him.

DUKE   'Tis certain then for Cyprus.
Marcus Luccicos, is not he in town?

FIRST SENATOR   He's now in Florence.

DUKE

Write from us to him, post-post-haste. Dispatch.

FIRST SENATOR

Here comes Brabantio and the valiant Moor.

*Enter Brabantio, Othello, Cassio, Iago,
Roderigo, and officers.*

DUKE

Valiant Othello, we must straight employ you   50
Against the general enemy Ottoman.   51
[*To Brabantio*] I did not see you; welcome, gentle
     signor.   52
We lacked your counsel and your help tonight.

BRABANTIO

So did I yours. Good Your Grace, pardon me;
Neither my place nor aught I heard of business   55
Hath raised me from my bed, nor doth the general
     care
Take hold on me, for my particular grief   57
Is of so floodgate and o'erbearing nature   58
That it engluts and swallows other sorrows   59
And it is still itself.

DUKE                Why, what's the matter?   60

BRABANTIO

My daughter! Oh, my daughter!

DUKE AND SENATORS                Dead?

BRABANTIO                                Ay, to me.
She is abused, stol'n from me, and corrupted   62
By spells and medicines bought of mountebanks;
For nature so preposterously to err,
Being not deficient, blind, or lame of sense,   65
Sans witchcraft could not.   66

DUKE

Whoe'er he be that in this foul proceeding
Hath thus beguiled your daughter of herself,
And you of her, the bloody book of law
You shall yourself read in the bitter letter
After your own sense—yea, though our proper son   71
Stood in your action.

BRABANTIO                Humbly I thank Your Grace.   72
Here is the man, this Moor, whom now it seems
Your special mandate for the state affairs
Hath hither brought.

ALL                We are very sorry for't.

DUKE [*to Othello*]

What, in your own part, can you say to this?

BRABANTIO   Nothing, but this is so.

OTHELLO

Most potent, grave, and reverend signors,
My very noble and approved good masters:   79
That I have ta'en away this old man's daughter,
It is most true; true, I have married her.
The very head and front of my offending   82

---

**16 preparation** fleet prepared for battle   **19 by** about   **20 assay** test.   **pageant** mere show   **21 in false gaze** looking the wrong way.   **24 as it more concerns** i.e., since Cyprus is more valuable to   **25 So may . . . it** so also he (the Turk) can more easily capture it (Cyprus)   **26–8 For that . . . is dressed in** since Cyprus is not as well defended militarily as is Rhodes   **29 unskillful** deficient in judgment   **30 latest** last   **32 wake and wage** stir up and risk   **35 Ottomites** Turks   **37 injointed them** joined themselves.   **after** second, reinforcing following   **39–40 restem . . . course** retrace their original course   **40 frank appearance** undisguised intent   **42 servitor** officer under your command   **43 free duty** freely given and loyal service.   **recommends** commends himself and reports to

**50 straight** straightaway   **51 general enemy** universal enemy to all Christendom   **52 gentle** noble   **55 place** official position   **57 particular** personal   **58 floodgate** i.e., overwhelming (as when floodgates are opened)   **59 engluts** engulfs   **60 is still itself** remains undiminished.   **62 abused** deceived   **65 deficient** defective.   **lame of sense** deficient in sensory perception   **66 Sans** without   **71 After . . . sense** according to your own interpretation.   **our proper** my own   **72 Stood . . . action** were under your accusation.   **79 approved** proved, esteemed   **82 head and front** height and breadth, entire extent

Hath this extent, no more. Rude am I in my speech, 83
And little blessed with the soft phrase of peace;
For since these arms of mine had seven years' pith, 85
Till now some nine moons wasted, they have used 86
Their dearest action in the tented field; 87
And little of this great world can I speak
More than pertains to feats of broils and battle,
And therefore little shall I grace my cause
In speaking for myself. Yet, by your gracious patience,
I will a round unvarnished tale deliver 92
Of my whole course of love—what drugs, what charms,
What conjuration, and what mighty magic,
For such proceeding I am charged withal, 95
I won his daughter.

BRABANTIO　　　　　A maiden never bold;
Of spirit so still and quiet that her motion 97
Blushed at herself; and she, in spite of nature, 98
Of years, of country, credit, everything, 99
To fall in love with what she feared to look on!
It is a judgment maimed and most imperfect
That will confess perfection so could err 102
Against all rules of nature, and must be driven
To find out practices of cunning hell 104
Why this should be. I therefore vouch again 105
That with some mixtures powerful o'er the blood, 106
Or with some dram conjured to this effect, 107
He wrought upon her.

DUKE　　　　　　To vouch this is no proof,
Without more wider and more overt test 109
Than these thin habits and poor likelihoods 110
Of modern seeming do prefer against him. 111

FIRST SENATOR　　But Othello, speak.
Did you by indirect and forcèd courses 113
Subdue and poison this young maid's affections?
Or came it by request and such fair question 115
As soul to soul affordeth?

OTHELLO　　　　　　I do beseech you,
Send for the lady to the Sagittary
And let her speak of me before her father.
If you do find me foul in her report,
The trust, the office I do hold of you
Not only take away, but let your sentence
Even fall upon my life.

DUKE　　　　　　Fetch Desdemona hither.

OTHELLO [to Iago]
Ancient, conduct them. You best know the place.
　　　　　　　　　　　[Exeunt Iago and attendants.]

And, till she come, as truly as to heaven
I do confess the vices of my blood, 125
So justly to your grave ears I'll present 126
How I did thrive in this fair lady's love,
And she in mine.

DUKE　Say it, Othello.

OTHELLO
Her father loved me, oft invited me,
Still questioned me the story of my life 131
From year to year—the battles, sieges, fortunes
That I have passed.
I ran it through, even from my boyish days
To th' very moment that he bade me tell it,
Wherein I spoke of most disastrous chances,
Of moving accidents by flood and field, 137
Of hairbreadth scapes i'th'imminent deadly breach, 138
Of being taken by the insolent foe
And sold to slavery, of my redemption thence,
And portance in my travels' history, 141
Wherein of antres vast and deserts idle, 142
Rough quarries, rocks, and hills whose heads touch
　　heaven, 143
It was my hint to speak—such was my process— 144
And of the Cannibals that each other eat,
The Anthropophagi, and men whose heads 146
Do grow beneath their shoulders. These things to hear
Would Desdemona seriously incline;
But still the house affairs would draw her thence,
Which ever as she could with haste dispatch
She'd come again, and with a greedy ear
Devour up my discourse. Which I, observing,
Took once a pliant hour, and found good means 153
To draw from her a prayer of earnest heart
That I would all my pilgrimage dilate, 155
Whereof by parcels she had something heard, 156
But not intentively. I did consent, 157
And often did beguile her of her tears,
When I did speak of some distressful stroke
That my youth suffered. My story being done,
She gave me for my pains a world of sighs.
She swore, in faith, 'twas strange, 'twas passing
　　strange, 162
'Twas pitiful, 'twas wondrous pitiful.
She wished she had not heard it, yet she wished
That heaven had made her such a man. She thanked
　　me, 165
And bade me, if I had a friend that loved her,
I should but teach him how to tell my story,
And that would woo her. Upon this hint I spake. 168
She loved me for the dangers I had passed,

---

**83 Rude** Unpolished　**85 since . . . pith** i.e., since I was seven. (*Pith* means "strength, vigor.")　**86 Till . . . wasted** until some nine months ago (since when Othello has evidently not been on active duty, but in Venice)　**87 dearest** most valuable　**92 round** plain　**95 withal** with　**97–8 that . . . herself** that she was blushingly hesitant to assert herself　**99 years** i.e., difference in age.　**credit** virtuous reputation　**102 confess** concede (that)　**104 practices** plots　**105 vouch** assert　**106 blood** passions　**107 dram . . . effect** dose made by magical spells to have this effect　**109 more wider** fuller.　**test** testimony　**110 habits** garments, i.e., appearances.　**poor likelihoods** weak inferences　**111 modern seeming** popular conjecture.　**prefer** bring forth　**113 forcèd courses** means used against her will　**115 question** conversation

**125 blood** passions, human nature　**126 justly** truthfully, accurately　**131 Still** continually　**137 moving accidents** stirring happenings　**138 i'th'imminent . . . breach** in death-threatening gaps made in a fortification　**141 portance** conduct　**142 antres** caverns.　**idle** barren, desolate　**143 Rough quarries** rugged rock formations　**144 hint** occasion, opportunity　**146 Anthropophagi** man-eaters. (A term from Pliny's *Natural History*.)　**153 pliant** well-suiting　**155 dilate** relate in detail　**156 by parcels** piecemeal　**157 intentively** with full attention, continuously.　**162 passing** exceedingly　**165 made her** (1) created her to be (2) made for her　**168 hint** (1) opportunity (2) hint (in the modern sense)

And I loved her that she did pity them.
This only is the witchcraft I have used.
Here comes the lady. Let her witness it.

*Enter Desdemona, Iago, [and] attendants.*

DUKE
I think this tale would win my daughter too.
Good Brabantio,
Take up this mangled matter at the best.                    175
Men do their broken weapons rather use
Than their bare hands.
BRABANTIO                    I pray you, hear her speak.
If she confess that she was half the wooer,
Destruction on my head if my bad blame
Light on the man!—Come hither, gentle mistress.
Do you perceive in all this noble company
Where most you owe obedience?
DESDEMONA                        My noble father,
I do perceive here a divided duty.
To you I am bound for life and education;            184
My life and education both do learn me            185
How to respect you. You are the lord of duty;            186
I am hitherto your daughter. But here's my husband,
And so much duty as my mother showed
To you, preferring you before her father,
So much I challenge that I may profess            190
Due to the Moor my lord.
BRABANTIO    God be with you! I have done.
Please it Your Grace, on to the state affairs.
I had rather to adopt a child than get it.            194
Come hither, Moor.        [*He joins the hands of Othello
and Desdemona.*]
I here do give thee that with all my heart            196
Which, but thou hast already, with all my heart            197
I would keep from thee.—For your sake, jewel,            198
I am glad at soul I have no other child,
For thy escape would teach me tyranny,            200
To hang clogs on them.—I have done, my lord.            201
DUKE
Let me speak like yourself, and lay a sentence            202
Which, as a grece or step, may help these lovers            203
Into your favor.
When remedies are past, the griefs are ended            205
By seeing the worst, which late on hopes depended.            206
To mourn a mischief that is past and gone            207
Is the next way to draw new mischief on.            208
What cannot be preserved when fortune takes,            209
Patience her injury a mock'ry makes.            210

The robbed that smiles steals something from the thief;
He robs himself that spends a bootless grief.            212
BRABANTIO
So let the Turk of Cyprus us beguile,
We lose it not, so long as we can smile.
He bears the sentence well that nothing bears            215
But the free comfort which from thence he hears,            216
But he bears both the sentence and the sorrow            217
That, to pay grief, must of poor patience borrow.            218
These sentences, to sugar or to gall,            219
Being strong on both sides, are equivocal.            220
But words are words. I never yet did hear
That the bruisèd heart was piercèd through the ear.            222
I humbly beseech you, proceed to th'affairs of state.
DUKE    The Turk with a most mighty preparation makes
for Cyprus. Othello, the fortitude of the place is best            225
known to you; and though we have there a substitute            226
of most allowed sufficiency, yet opinion, a sovereign            227
mistress of effects, throws a more safer voice on you.            228
You must therefore be content to slubber the gloss of            229
your new fortunes with this more stubborn and            230
boisterous expedition.            231
OTHELLO
The tyrant custom, most grave senators,
Hath made the flinty and steel couch of war
My thrice-driven bed of down. I do agnize            234
A natural and prompt alacrity
I find in hardness, and do undertake            236
These present wars against the Ottomites.
Most humbly therefore bending to your state,            238
I crave fit disposition for my wife,
Due reference of place and exhibition,            240
With such accommodation and besort            241
As levels with her breeding.            242
DUKE
Why, at her father's.
BRABANTIO                        I will not have it so.
OTHELLO
Nor I.
DESDEMONA    Nor I. I would not there reside,
To put my father in impatient thoughts
By being in his eye. Most gracious Duke,
To my unfolding lend your prosperous ear,            247

---

175 Take . . . best make the best of a bad bargain.    184 education upbringing    185 learn teach    186 of duty to whom duty is due    190 challenge claim    194 get beget    196 with all my heart wherein my whole affection has been engaged    197 with all my heart willingly, gladly    198 For your sake Because of you    200 escape elopement    201 clogs (Literally, blocks of wood fastened to the legs of criminals or animals to inhibit escape.)    202 like yourself i.e., as you would, in your proper temper.    lay a sentence apply a maxim    203 grece step    205–6 When . . . depended When all hope of remedy is past, our sorrows are ended by realizing that the worst has already happened which lately we hoped would not happen.    207 mischief misfortune, injury    208 next nearest    209–10 What . . . makes When fortune takes away what cannot be saved, patience makes a mockery of fortune's wrongdoing.

212 spends a bootless grief indulges in unavailing grief.    215–18 He bears . . . borrow A person can easily be comforted by your maxim that enjoys its platitudinous comfort without having to experience the misfortune that occasions sorrow, but anyone whose grief bankrupts his poor patience is left with your saying and his sorrow, too. (*Bears the sentence* also plays on the meaning, "receives judicial sentence.")    219–20 These . . . equivocal These fine maxims are equivocal, being equally appropriate to happiness or bitterness.    222 piercèd . . . ear relieved by mere words reaching it through the ear.    225 fortitude strength    226 substitute deputy    227 allowed acknowledged    227–8 opinion . . . on you general opinion, an important determiner of affairs, chooses you as the best man.    229 slubber soil, sully    230–1 stubborn . . . expedition rough and violent expedition, for which haste is needed.    234 thrice-driven thrice sifted, winnowed.    agnize know in myself, acknowledge    236 hardness hardship    238 bending . . . state bowing or kneeling to your authority    240–2 Due . . . breeding proper respect for her place (as my wife) and maintenance, with such suitable provision and attendance as befits her upbringing.    247 my unfolding what I shall unfold or say.    prosperous favorable

And let me find a charter in your voice,                                    248
T'assist my simpleness.
DUKE   What would you, Desdemona?
DESDEMONA
That I did love the Moor to live with him,
My downright violence and storm of fortunes                                252
May trumpet to the world. My heart's subdued
Even to the very quality of my lord.                                       254
I saw Othello's visage in his mind,
And to his honors and his valiant parts                                    256
Did I my soul and fortunes consecrate.
So that, dear lords, if I be left behind
A moth of peace, and he go to the war,                                     259
The rites for why I love him are bereft me,                                260
And I a heavy interim shall support                                        261
By his dear absence. Let me go with him.                                   262
OTHELLO   Let her have your voice.                                         263
Vouch with me, heaven, I therefor beg it not
To please the palate of my appetite,
Nor to comply with heat—the young affects                                 266
In me defunct—and proper satisfaction,                                    267
But to be free and bounteous to her mind.                                 268
And heaven defend your good souls that you think                          269
I will your serious and great business scant
When she is with me. No, when light-winged toys
Of feathered Cupid seel with wanton dullness                              272
My speculative and officed instruments,                                   273
That my disports corrupt and taint my business,                          274
Let huswives make a skillet of my helm,
And all indign and base adversities                                       276
Make head against my estimation!                                          277
DUKE
Be it as you shall privately determine,
Either for her stay or going. Th'affair cries haste,
And speed must answer it.
A SENATOR                      You must away tonight.
DESDEMONA
Tonight, my lord?
DUKE                      This night.
OTHELLO                      With all my heart.
DUKE
At nine i'th' morning here we'll meet again.
Othello, leave some officer behind,
And he shall our commission bring to you,
With such things else of quality and respect                              285
As doth import you.
OTHELLO                      So please Your Grace, my ancient;   286

A man he is of honesty and trust.
To his conveyance I assign my wife,
With what else needful Your Good Grace shall think
To be sent after me.
DUKE                      Let it be so.
Good night to everyone. [*To Brabantio*] And, noble
  signor,
If virtue no delighted beauty lack,                                       292
Your son-in-law is far more fair than black.
FIRST SENATOR
Adieu, brave Moor. Use Desdemona well.
BRABANTIO
Look to her, Moor, if thou hast eyes to see.
She has deceived her father, and may thee.
        *Exeunt* [*Duke, Brabantio, Cassio, Senators, and
                                          officers*].
OTHELLO
My life upon her faith!—Honest Iago,
My Desdemona must I leave to thee.
I prithee, let thy wife attend on her,
And bring them after in the best advantage.                               300
Come, Desdemona. I have but an hour
Of love, of worldly matters and direction,                                302
To spend with thee. We must obey the time.                                303
        *Exit* [*with Desdemona*].
RODERIGO   Iago—
IAGO   What say'st thou, noble heart?
RODERIGO   What will I do, think'st thou?
IAGO   Why, go to bed and sleep.
RODERIGO   I will incontinently drown myself.                             308
IAGO   If thou dost, I shall never love thee after. Why,
  thou silly gentleman?
RODERIGO   It is silliness to live when to live is torment;
  and then have we a prescription to die when death is   312
  our physician.                                                          313
IAGO   Oh, villainous! I have looked upon the world for   314
  four times seven years, and since I could distinguish    315
  betwixt a benefit and an injury I never found man that
  knew how to love himself. Ere I would say I would
  drown myself for the love of a guinea hen, I would       318
  change my humanity with a baboon.                                       319
RODERIGO   What should I do? I confess it is my shame
  to be so fond, but it is not in my virtue to amend it.    321
IAGO   Virtue? A fig! 'Tis in ourselves that we are thus or   322
  thus. Our bodies are our gardens, to the which our
  wills are gardeners; so that if we will plant nettles or   324
  sow lettuce, set hyssop and weed up thyme, supply it     325
  with one gender of herbs or distract it with many,        326
  either to have it sterile with idleness or manured with   327

---

**248 charter** privilege, authorization   **252 My . . . fortunes** my plain and total breach of social custom   **254 quality** moral and spiritual identity   **256 parts** qualities   **259 moth** i.e., one who consumes merely   **260 rites** rites of love. (With a suggestion, too, of "rights," sharing.)   **261 heavy** burdensome   **262 dear** grievous   **263 voice** consent.   **266 heat** sexual passion.   **young affects** passions of youth, adolescent desires   **267 defunct** done with, at an end.   **proper** personal   **268 free** generous   **269 defend** forbid.   **think** should think   **272 seel** i.e., make blind (as in falconry, by sewing up the eyes of the hawk during training)   **273 My . . . instruments** my eyes, whose function is to see   **274 That . . . business** in such a way that my sexual pastimes interfere with my official duties   **276 indign** unworthy, shameful   **277 Make head** raise an army.   **estimation** reputation.   **285 of quality and respect** of importance and relevance   **286 import** concern

**292 delighted** capable of delighting   **300 in . . . advantage** at the most favorable opportunity.   **302 direction** instructions   **303 the time** the urgency of the present crisis.   **308 incontinently** immediately, without self-restraint   **312 prescription** (1) right based on long-established custom (2) doctor's prescription   **312–13 when . . . physician** i.e., when death is the only way of ending our torments.   **314 villainous** i.e., what perfect nonsense.   **315 since** ever since   **318 guinea hen** (A slang term for a prostitute.)   **319 change** exchange   **321 fond** infatuated.   **virtue** strength, nature   **322 fig** (To give a fig is to thrust the thumb between the first and second fingers in a vulgar and insulting gesture.)   **324 nettles** stinging weeds   **325 hyssop** a herb of the mint family   **326 gender** kind.   **distract it with** make wasteful use of   **327 idleness** want of cultivation

industry—why, the power and corrigible authority of 328
this lies in our wills. If the beam of our lives had not 329
one scale of reason to poise another of sensuality, the 330
blood and baseness of our natures would conduct us 331
to most preposterous conclusions. But we have reason
to cool our raging motions, our carnal stings, our 333
unbitted lusts, whereof I take this that you call love to 334
be a sect or scion.                                          335

RODERIGO   It cannot be.

IAGO   It is merely a lust of the blood and a permission
of the will. Come, be a man. Drown thyself? Drown
cats and blind puppies. I have professed me thy friend, 339
and I confess me knit to thy deserving with cables of
perdurable toughness. I could never better stead thee 341
than now. Put money in thy purse. Follow thou the
wars; defeat thy favor with an usurped beard. I say, 343
put money in thy purse. It cannot be long that Desdemona should continue her love to the Moor—put
money in thy purse—nor he his to her. It was a violent commencement in her, and thou shalt see an an- 347
swerable sequestration—put but money in thy purse. 348
These Moors are changeable in their wills—fill thy 349
purse with money. The food that to him now is as
luscious as locusts shall be to him shortly as bitter as 351
coloquintida. She must change for youth; when she is 352
sated with his body, she will find the error of her
choice. She must have change, she must. Therefore
put money in thy purse. If thou wilt needs damn thyself, do it a more delicate way than drowning. Make
all the money thou canst. If sanctimony and a frail vow 357
betwixt an erring barbarian and a supersubtle Vene- 358
tian be not too hard for my wits and all the tribe of
hell, thou shalt enjoy her. Therefore make money. A
pox of drowning thyself! It is clean out of the way. 361
Seek thou rather to be hanged in compassing thy joy 362
than to be drowned and go without her.

RODERIGO   Wilt thou be fast to my hopes if I depend on 364
   the issue?                                                365

IAGO   Thou art sure of me. Go, make money. I have
told thee often, and I retell thee again and again, I hate
the Moor. My cause is hearted; thine hath no less rea- 368
son. Let us be conjunctive in our revenge against him. 369
If thou canst cuckold him, thou dost thyself a pleasure,
me a sport. There are many events in the womb of
time which will be delivered. Traverse, go, provide thy 372
money. We will have more of this tomorrow. Adieu.

RODERIGO   Where shall we meet i'th' morning?
IAGO   At my lodging.
RODERIGO   I'll be with thee betimes. [*He starts to leave.*] 376
IAGO   Go to, farewell.—Do you hear, Roderigo?          377
RODERIGO   What say you?
IAGO   No more of drowning, do you hear?
RODERIGO   I am changed.
IAGO   Go to, farewell. Put money enough in your
   purse.
RODERIGO   I'll sell all my land.                    *Exit.*
IAGO
Thus do I ever make my fool my purse;
For I mine own gained knowledge should profane
If I would time expend with such a snipe           386
But for my sport and profit. I hate the Moor;
And it is thought abroad that twixt my sheets       388
He's done my office. I know not if't be true;       389
But I, for mere suspicion in that kind,
Will do as if for surety. He holds me well;          391
The better shall my purpose work on him.
Cassio's a proper man. Let me see now:              393
To get his place and to plume up my will            394
In double knavery—How, how?—Let's see:
After some time, to abuse Othello's ear             396
That he is too familiar with his wife.               397
He hath a person and a smooth dispose               398
To be suspected, framed to make women false.        399
The Moor is of a free and open nature,              400
That thinks men honest that but seem to be so,
And will as tenderly be led by the nose             402
As asses are.
I have't. It is engendered. Hell and night
Must bring this monstrous birth to the world's light.
                                                [*Exit.*]

❖

# 2.1

*Enter Montano and two Gentlemen.*

MONTANO
What from the cape can you discern at sea?
FIRST GENTLEMAN
Nothing at all. It is a high-wrought flood.          2
I cannot, twixt the heaven and the main,             3
Descry a sail.
MONTANO
Methinks the wind hath spoke aloud at land;
A fuller blast ne'er shook our battlements.
If it hath ruffianed so upon the sea,                7

---

**328 corrigible authority** power to correct   **329 beam** balance
**330 poise** counterbalance   **331 blood** natural passions   **333 motions**
appetites   **334 unbitted** unbridled, uncontrolled   **335 sect or scion**
cutting or offshoot.   **339 blind** i.e., newborn and helpless   **341 perdurable** very durable.   **stead** assist   **343 defeat thy favor** disguise
your face.   **usurped** (The suggestion is that Roderigo is not man
enough to have a beard of his own.)   **347–8 an answerable sequestration** a corresponding cutting off or estrangement   **349 wills** carnal
appetites   **351 locusts** fruit of the carob tree (see Matthew 3:4), or
perhaps honeysuckle   **352 coloquintida** colocynth or bitter apple,
a purgative.   **357 sanctimony** (1) an aura of goodness (2) love-
worship   **358 erring** wandering, vagabond, unsteady   **361 clean . . .
way** entirely unsuitable as a course of action.   **362 compassing**
encompassing, embracing   **364 fast** true   **365 issue** (successful) outcome.   **368 hearted** fixed in the heart, heartfelt   **369 conjunctive**
united   **372 Traverse** (A military marching term.)

**376 betimes** early.   **377 Go to** (An expression of impatience or jolly-
ing along others.)   **386 snipe** woodcock, i.e., fool   **388 it is thought
abroad** it is rumored   **389 my office** i.e., my sexual function as husband.   **391 do . . . surety** act as if on certain knowledge.   **holds me
well** regards me favorably   **393 proper** handsome   **394 plume up**
put a feather in the cap of, i.e., glorify, gratify   **396 abuse** deceive
**397 he** Cassio.   **his** Othello's   **398 dispose** disposition   **399 framed**
formed, made   **400 free and open** frank and unsuspecting
**402 tenderly** readily
**2.1. Location: A seaport in Cyprus. An open place near the quay.**
**2 high-wrought flood** very agitated sea.   **3 main** ocean. (Also at line
41.)   **7 ruffianed** raged

What ribs of oak, when mountains melt on them,   8
Can hold the mortise? What shall we hear of this?   9

SECOND GENTLEMAN
A segregation of the Turkish fleet.   10
For do but stand upon the foaming shore,
The chidden billow seems to pelt the clouds;   12
The wind-shaked surge, with high and monstrous
    mane,   13
Seems to cast water on the burning Bear   14
And quench the guards of th'ever-fixèd pole.
I never did like molestation view   16
On the enchafèd flood.   17

MONTANO   If that the Turkish fleet   18
Be not ensheltered and embayed, they are drowned;   19
It is impossible to bear it out.   20

     *Enter a [Third] Gentleman.*

THIRD GENTLEMAN   News, lads! Our wars are done.
The desperate tempest hath so banged the Turks
That their designment halts. A noble ship of Venice   23
Hath seen a grievous wreck and sufferance   24
On most part of their fleet.

MONTANO   How? Is this true?

THIRD GENTLEMAN   The ship is here put in,
A Veronesa; Michael Cassio,   28
Lieutenant to the warlike Moor Othello,
Is come on shore; the Moor himself at sea,
And is in full commission here for Cyprus.

MONTANO
I am glad on't. 'Tis a worthy governor.

THIRD GENTLEMAN
But this same Cassio, though he speak of comfort
Touching the Turkish loss, yet he looks sadly   34
And prays the Moor be safe, for they were parted
With foul and violent tempest.

MONTANO               Pray heaven he be,
For I have served him, and the man commands
Like a full soldier. Let's to the seaside, ho!   38
As well to see the vessel that's come in
As to throw out our eyes for brave Othello,   40
Even till we make the main and th'aerial blue   41
An indistinct regard.

THIRD GENTLEMAN   Come, let's do so,   42
For every minute is expectancy   43

Of more arrivance.   44

     *Enter Cassio.*

CASSIO
Thanks, you the valiant of this warlike isle,
That so approve the Moor! Oh, let the heavens   46
Give him defense against the elements,
For I have lost him on a dangerous sea.

MONTANO   Is he well shipped?

CASSIO
His bark is stoutly timbered, and his pilot   50
Of very expert and approved allowance;   51
Therefore my hopes, not surfeited to death,   52
Stand in bold cure.
           [*A cry*] *within:* "A sail, a sail, a sail!"   53

CASSIO   What noise?

A GENTLEMAN
The town is empty. On the brow o'th' sea   55
Stand ranks of people, and they cry "A sail!"

CASSIO
My hopes do shape him for the governor.   57
                  [*A shot within.*]

SECOND GENTLEMAN
They do discharge their shot of courtesy;   58
Our friends at least.

CASSIO            I pray you, sir, go forth,
And give us truth who 'tis that is arrived.

SECOND GENTLEMAN   I shall.           *Exit.*

MONTANO
But, good Lieutenant, is your general wived?

CASSIO
Most fortunately. He hath achieved a maid
That paragons description and wild fame,   64
One that excels the quirks of blazoning pens,   65
And in th'essential vesture of creation   66
Does tire the engineer.

     *Enter [Second] Gentleman.*

                           How now? Who has put in?   67

SECOND GENTLEMAN
'Tis one Iago, ancient to the General.

CASSIO
He's had most favorable and happy speed.
Tempests themselves, high seas, and howling winds,
The guttered rocks and congregated sands—   71
Traitors ensteeped to clog the guiltless keel—   72
As having sense of beauty, do omit   73
Their mortal natures, letting go safely by   74

---

**8 mountains** i.e., of water   **9 hold the mortise** hold their joints together. (A *mortise* is the socket hollowed out in fitting timbers.)   **shall we hear** can we expect   **10 segregation** dispersal **12 chidden** i.e., rebuked, repelled (by the shore), and thus shot into the air   **13 monstrous mane** (The surf is like the mane of a wild beast.)   **14 the burning Bear** i.e., the constellation Ursa Minor or the Little Bear, which includes the polestar (and hence regarded as the *guards of th'ever-fixèd pole* in the next line; sometimes the term *guards* is applied to the two "pointers" of the Big Bear or Dipper, which may be intended here.)   **16 like molestation** comparable disturbance **17 enchafèd** angry   **18 If that** If   **19 embayed** sheltered by a bay **20 bear it out** survive, weather the storm.   **23 designment halts** enterprise is crippled. (Literally, "is lame.")   **24 wreck** shipwreck. **sufferance** damage, disaster   **28 Veronesa** from Verona (and perhaps in service with Venice)   **34 Touching** regarding.   **sadly** gravely   **38 full** perfect   **40 throw . . . eyes** keep on eyes peeled **41 the main . . . blue** the sea and the sky   **42 An indistinct regard** indistinguishable in our view.   **43 is expectancy** gives expectation

---

**44 arrivance** arrival.   **46 approve** admire, honor   **50 stoutly** strongly   **51 approved allowance** tested reputation   **52–3 not . . . cure** not exhausted through repeated application or delayed fulfillment, strongly persist.   **55 brow o'th' sea** cliff-edge   **57 My . . . governor** I hope and imagine this ship to be Othello's.   **58 discharge . . . courtesy** fire a salute in token of respect and courtesy   **64 paragons** surpasses.   **wild fame** extravagant report   **65 quirks** witty conceits.   **blazoning** setting forth as though in heraldic language   **66–7 And in . . . engineer** and in her real, God-given, beauty, (she) defeats any attempt to praise her. (An *engineer* is one who devises, here a poet.)   **67 put in** i.e., to harbor.   **71 guttered** jagged,   **72 ensteeped** lying under water.   **guiltless** unsuspecting **73 As** as if.   **omit** forbear to exercise   **74 mortal** deadly

The divine Desdemona.

MONTANO                          What is she?

CASSIO
She that I spake of, our great captain's captain,
Left in the conduct of the bold Iago,                                      77
Whose footing here anticipates our thoughts                                78
A sennight's speed. Great Jove, Othello guard,                             79
And swell his sail with thine own powerful breath,
That he may bless this bay with his tall ship,                             81
Make love's quick pants in Desdemona's arms,
Give renewed fire to our extincted spirits,
And bring all Cyprus comfort!

*Enter Desdemona, Iago, Roderigo, and Emilia.*

                              Oh, behold,
The riches of the ship is come on shore!
You men of Cyprus, let her have your knees.
        [*The gentlemen make curtsy to Desdemona.*]
Hail to thee, lady! And the grace of heaven
Before, behind thee, and on every hand
Enwheel thee round!

DESDEMONA             I thank you, valiant Cassio.
What tidings can you tell me of my lord?

CASSIO
He is not yet arrived, nor know I aught
But that he's well and will be shortly here.

DESDEMONA
Oh, but I fear—How lost you company?

CASSIO
The great contention of the sea and skies
Parted our fellowship.
                    (*Within*) "A sail, a sail!" [*A shot.*]
                    But hark. A sail!

SECOND GENTLEMAN
They give their greeting to the citadel.
This likewise is a friend.

CASSIO                          See for the news.               97
                    [*Exit Second Gentleman.*]
Good ancient, you are welcome. [*Kissing Emilia.*]
    Welcome, mistress.
Let it not gall your patience, good Iago,
That I extend my manners; 'tis my breeding                     100
That gives me this bold show of courtesy.

IAGO
Sir, would she give you so much of her lips
As of her tongue she oft bestows on me,
You would have enough.

DESDEMONA    Alas, she has no speech!                          105

IAGO    In faith, too much.
I find it still, when I have list to sleep.                    107
Marry, before Your Ladyship, I grant,
She puts her tongue a little in her heart
And chides with thinking.

EMILIA                    You have little cause to say so.     110

IAGO
Come on, come on. You are pictures out of doors,              111
Bells in your parlors, wildcats in your kitchens,            112
Saints in your injuries, devils being offended,             113
Players in your huswifery, and huswives in your beds. 114

DESDEMONA    Oh, fie upon thee, slanderer!

IAGO
Nay, it is true, or else I am a Turk.                        116
You rise to play, and go to bed to work.

EMILIA
You shall not write my praise.

IAGO                              No, let me not.

DESDEMONA
What wouldst write of me, if thou shouldst praise me?

IAGO
Oh, gentle lady, do not put me to't,
For I am nothing if not critical.                            121

DESDEMONA
Come on, essay.—There's one gone to the harbor?             122

IAGO    Ay, madam.

DESDEMONA
I am not merry, but I do beguile
The thing I am by seeming otherwise.                         125
Come, how wouldst thou praise me?

IAGO
I am about it, but indeed my invention
Comes from my pate as birdlime does from frieze—            128
It plucks out brains and all. But my Muse labors,           129
And thus she is delivered:
If she be fair and wise, fairness and wit,                   131
The one's for use, the other useth it.                       132

DESDEMONA
Well praised! How if she be black and witty?                133

IAGO
If she be black, and thereto have a wit,
She'll find a white that shall her blackness fit.           135

DESDEMONA
Worse and worse.

EMILIA                    How if fair and foolish?

IAGO
She never yet was foolish that was fair,                     137
For even her folly helped her to an heir.                    138

DESDEMONA    These are old fond paradoxes to make fools 139

77 in the conduct of to be escorted by    78–9 Whose . . . speed whose
arrival here has happened a week sooner than we expected.    81 tall
tall-masted    97 See for the news i.e., Go look and determine if this is
true.    100 extend give scope to.    breeding training in the niceties of
etiquette    105 she has no speech i.e., she's not a chatterbox, as you
allege.    107 still always.    list desire    110 with thinking i.e., in her
thoughts only.

111 pictures out of doors i.e., as pretty as pictures, and silently well-
behaved in public    112 Bells i.e., jangling, noisy, and brazen.    in your
kitchens i.e., in domestic affairs. (Ladies would not do the cooking.)
113 Saints . . . injuries i.e., putting on airs of sanctity and innocence when
wronged by others    114 Players . . . beds play-actors at domesticity and
truly energetic only as lovers in bed.    116 a Turk an infidel, not to be
believed.    121 critical censorious.    122 essay try.    125 The thing I am
i.e., my anxious self    128 birdlime sticky substance used to catch small
birds.    frieze coarse woolen cloth    129 labors (1) exerts herself (2) prepares to deliver a child. (With a following pun on *delivered* in line 130.)
131 she some woman    132 The one's . . . it i.e., her cleverness will make use
of her beauty.    133 black dark-complexioned, brunette    135 She'll . . .
fit she will find a fair-complexioned mate suited to her dark complexion.
(Punning on *wight*, person, and contrasting *white* and *black*, with suggestion of sexual coupling.)    137–8 She . . . heir i.e., No beautiful woman
can really be called foolish, since with her enticing beauty she will seduce
her lover and that way beget a child.    139 fond foolish

laugh i'th'alehouse. What miserable praise hast thou for her that's foul and foolish? 141

IAGO
There's none so foul and foolish thereunto, 142
But does foul pranks which fair and wise ones do. 143

DESDEMONA   Oh, heavy ignorance! Thou praisest the worst best. But what praise couldst thou bestow on a deserving woman indeed, one that, in the authority of her merit, did justly put on the vouch of very malice itself? 147

IAGO
She that was ever fair, and never proud,
Had tongue at will, and yet was never loud, 149
Never lacked gold and yet went never gay, 150
Fled from her wish, and yet said, "Now I may," 151
She that being angered, her revenge being nigh,
Bade her wrong stay and her displeasure fly, 153
She that in wisdom never was so frail
To change the cod's head for the salmon's tail, 155
She that could think and ne'er disclose her mind,
See suitors following and not look behind,
She was a wight, if ever such wight were—

DESDEMONA   To do what?

IAGO
To suckle fools and chronicle small beer. 160

DESDEMONA   Oh, most lame and impotent conclusion! Do not learn of him, Emilia, though he be thy husband. How say you, Cassio? Is he not a most profane and 163 liberal counselor? 164

CASSIO   He speaks home, madam. You may relish him 165 more in the soldier than in the scholar. 166

   [Cassio and Desdemona stand together, conversing intimately.]

IAGO [aside]   He takes her by the palm. Ay, well said, 167 whisper. With as little a web as this will I ensnare as great a fly as Cassio. Ay, smile upon her, do; I will gyve thee in thine own courtship. You say true; 'tis so, 170 indeed. If such tricks as these strip you out of your lieutenantry, it had been better you had not kissed your three fingers so oft, which now again you are most apt to play the sir in. Very good; well kissed! An 174 excellent courtesy! 'Tis so, indeed. Yet again your fingers to your lips? Would they were clyster pipes for 176 your sake! [Trumpet within.] The Moor! I know his trumpet.

CASSIO   'Tis truly so.

DESDEMONA            Let's meet him and receive him.

CASSIO   Lo, where he comes!

   Enter Othello and attendants.

OTHELLO
Oh, my fair warrior!

DESDEMONA            My dear Othello!

OTHELLO
It gives me wonder great as my content
To see you here before me. O my soul's joy,
If after every tempest come such calms,
May the winds blow till they have wakened death,
And let the laboring bark climb hills of seas 187
Olympus-high, and duck again as low 188
As hell's from heaven! If it were now to die, 189
'Twere now to be most happy, for I fear
My soul hath her content so absolute
That not another comfort like to this
Succeeds in unknown fate.

DESDEMONA            The heavens forbid 193
But that our loves and comforts should increase
Even as our days do grow!

OTHELLO   Amen to that, sweet powers! 196
I cannot speak enough of this content.
It stops me here; it is too much of joy.
And this, and this, the greatest discords be 199
            [They kiss.]
That e'er our hearts shall make!

IAGO [aside]   Oh, you are well tuned now!
But I'll set down the pegs that make this music, 202
As honest as I am. 203

OTHELLO   Come, let us to the castle.
News, friends! Our wars are done, the Turks are drowned.
How does my old acquaintance of this isle?— 206
Honey, you shall be well desired in Cyprus; 207
I have found great love amongst them. Oh, my sweet,
I prattle out of fashion, and I dote 209
In mine own comforts.—I prithee, good Iago,
Go to the bay and disembark my coffers. 211
Bring thou the master to the citadel; 212
He is a good one, and his worthiness
Does challenge much respect.—Come, Desdemona.— 214
Once more, well met at Cyprus!
            Exeunt Othello and Desdemona [and all but Iago and Roderigo].

IAGO [to a departing attendant]   Do thou meet me presently at 216 the harbor. [To Roderigo] Come hither. If thou be'st valiant—as, they say, base men being in love have 218 then a nobility in their natures more than is native to them—list me. The Lieutenant tonight watches on 220 the court of guard. First, I must tell thee this: 221 Desdemona is directly in love with him.

141 foul ugly   142 thereunto in addition   143 foul sluttish   147 put . . . vouch compel the approval   149 Had . . . will was never at a loss for words   150 gay extravagantly clothed   151 Fled . . . may avoided temptation where the choice was hers   153 Bade . . . fly i.e., resolved to put up with her injury and bade her anger to cease   155 To . . . tail i.e., to make an unworthy exchange that is selfishly demanding and ambitious. (The fish's lower body, below the rib cage, has fewest bones and is generally the succulent portion. With implication of sexual infidelity as well: cod's head can be slang for "penis" and tail for "vulva.")   160 To . . . beer i.e., To breastfeed babies and keep track of petty household accounts—the routine responsibilities of a very ordinary wife.   163–4 profane and liberal irreverent and licentious   165 home right to the target. (A term from fencing.)   relish appreciate   166 in in the character of   167 well said well done   170 gyve fetter, shackle.   courtship courtliness.   174 the sir i.e., the fine gentleman   176 clyster pipes enema tubes

187 bark boat   188 Olympus-high as high as the fabled home of the ancient gods   189 hell's hell is   193 Succeeds . . . fate i.e., can hope to follow after death.   196 powers gods.   199.1 They kiss (The direction is from the quarto.)   202 set down loosen (and hence untune the instrument)   203 As . . . I am for all my supposed honesty.   206 my old acquaintance presumably Montana, governor of Cyprus   207 desired sought after   209 out of fashion indecorously, incoherently   211 coffers chests, baggage.   212 master ship's captain   214 challenge lay claim to, deserve   216 presently right away   218 base men even ignoble men   220 list listen to   220–1 The Lieutenant . . . guard Cassio is in charge tonight at the guardhouse.

RODERIGO    With him? Why, 'tis not possible.

IAGO    Lay thy finger thus, and let thy soul be instructed.  224
Mark me with what violence she first loved the Moor,
but for bragging and telling her fantastical lies. To love  226
him still for prating? Let not thy discreet heart think it.
Her eye must be fed; and what delight shall she have
to look on the devil? When the blood is made dull with
the act of sport, there should be, again to inflame it  230
and to give satiety a fresh appetite, loveliness in favor,  231
sympathy in years, manners, and beauties—all which  232
the Moor is defective in. Now, for want of these
required conveniences, her delicate tenderness will  234
find itself abused, begin to heave the gorge, disrelish  235
and abhor the Moor. Very nature will instruct her in it  236
and compel her to some second choice. Now, sir,
this granted—as it is a most pregnant and unforced  238
position—who stands so eminent in the degree of this  239
fortune as Cassio does? A knave very voluble, no fur-  240
ther conscionable than in putting on the mere form  241
of civil and humane seeming for the better compass-  242
ing of his salt and most hidden loose affection. Why,  243
none, why, none. A slipper and subtle knave, a finder  244
out of occasions, that has an eye can stamp and  245
counterfeit advantages, though true advantage never  246
present itself; a devilish knave. Besides, the knave is
handsome, young, and hath all those requisites in him
that folly and green minds look after. A pestilent  249
complete knave, and the woman hath found him  250
already.

RODERIGO    I cannot believe that in her. She's full of
most blessed condition.  253

IAGO    Blessed fig's end! The wine she drinks is made of  254
grapes. If she had been blessed, she would never have
loved the Moor. Blessed pudding! Didst thou not see  256
her paddle with the palm of his hand? Didst not mark
that?

RODERIGO    Yes, that I did; but that was but courtesy.

IAGO    Lechery, by this hand. An index and obscure pro-  260
logue to the history of lust and foul thoughts. They
met so near with their lips that their breaths embraced
together. Villainous thoughts, Roderigo! When these  263
mutualities so marshal the way, hard at hand comes  264
the master and main exercise, th'incorporate conclu-  265
sion. Pish! But, sir, be you ruled by me. I have brought  266
you from Venice. Watch you tonight; for the com-  267
mand, I'll lay't upon you. Cassio knows you not. I'll  268
not be far from you. Do you find some occasion to
anger Cassio, either by speaking too loud, or tainting  270
his discipline, or from what other course you please,  271
which the time shall more favorably minister.  272

RODERIGO    Well.

IAGO    Sir, he's rash and very sudden in choler, and haply  274
may strike at you. Provoke him that he may, for
even out of that will I cause these of Cyprus to mutiny,  276
whose qualification shall come into no true taste again  277
but by the displanting of Cassio. So shall you have a
shorter journey to your desires by the means I shall
then have to prefer them, and the impediment most  280
profitably removed, without the which there were no  281
expectation of our prosperity.

RODERIGO    I will do this, if you can bring it to any
opportunity.

IAGO    I warrant thee. Meet me by and by at the citadel.  285
I must fetch his necessaries ashore. Farewell.  286

RODERIGO    Adieu.                                    *Exit.*

IAGO
That Cassio loves her, I do well believe't;
That she loves him, 'tis apt and of great credit.  289
The Moor, howbeit that I endure him not,
Is of a constant, loving, noble nature,
And I dare think he'll prove to Desdemona
A most dear husband. Now, I do love her too,  293
Not out of absolute lust—though peradventure
I stand accountant for as great a sin—  295
But partly led to diet my revenge  296
For that I do suspect the lusty Moor
Hath leaped into my seat, the thought whereof  298
Doth, like a poisonous mineral, gnaw my inwards;  299
And nothing can or shall content my soul
Till I am evened with him, wife for wife,
Or failing so, yet that I put the Moor
At least into a jealousy so strong
That judgment cannot cure. Which thing to do,
If this poor trash of Venice, whom I trace  305
For his quick hunting, stand the putting on,  306
I'll have our Michael Cassio on the hip,  307
Abuse him to the Moor in the rank garb—  308
For I fear Cassio with my nightcap too—  309
Make the Moor thank me, love me, and reward me
For making him egregiously an ass
And practicing upon his peace and quiet  312

---

**224 thus** i.e., on your lips    **226 but** only    **230 the act of sport** sex
**231 favor** appearance    **232 sympathy** correspondence, similarity
**234 required conveniences** things conducive to sexual compatibil-
ity    **235 abused** cheated, revolted.    **heave the gorge** experience
nausea    **236 Very nature** Her very instincts    **238 pregnant** evident,
cogent    **239 in . . . of** as next in line for    **240 voluble** facile, glib    **241
conscionable** conscientious, conscience-bound    **242 humane** polite,
courteous    **243 salt** licentiousness.    **244 slipper**
slippery    **245 an eye can stamp** an eye that can coin, create    **246
advantages** favorable opportunities    **249 folly** wantonness.    **green**
immature.    **pestilent** i.e., wretched, nefarious    **250 found him** sized
him up, perceived his intent    **253 condition** disposition.    **254 fig's
end** (See 1.3.322 for the vulgar gesture of the fig.)    **256 pudding** sausage. (Here used as a kind of swear word.)    **260 index** table of contents.    **obscure** veiled, hidden    **263–6 When . . . conclusion** When
these intimate exchanges have led the way, like the official at the
head of some procession, the main event closely follows, concluding
in carnal embrace.

**267 Watch you** Stand watch    **267–8 for . . . you** I'll arrange for you to be
appointed, given orders; or, I'll put you in charge.    **270–1 tainting his
discipline** disparaging his authority    **272 minister** provide.    **274 choler**
wrath.    **haply** perhaps    **276 mutiny** riot    **277 whose . . . again** who will
not be satisfied and pacified    **280 prefer** advance    **281 were** would
be    **285 warrant** assure.    **by and by** immediately    **286 his necessaries**
Othello's possessions    **289 apt** probable.    **credit** credibility.    **293 dear**
(1) loving (2) costly    **295 accountant . . . sin** i.e., accountable for the sin of
desiring revenge by whatever means    **296 diet** feed    **298 Hath . . . seat** has
taken possession of my marriage bed    **299 inwards** innards    **305–6 If . . .
putting on** if this miserable wretch Roderigo, whom I use as my hunting
dog, responds as he should to my whetting him on. (*Trace* is difficult. It
could mean "pursue," or "keep hungry," or "train," or "slow down by
putting weights on the dog.")    **307 on the hip** at my mercy, where I can
throw him. (A wrestling term.)    **308 Abuse** slander.    **rank garb** coarse
manner, gross fashion    **309 with my nightcap** i.e., as a rival in my bed, as
one who gives me cuckold's horns    **312 practicing upon** plotting against

Even to madness. 'Tis here, but yet confused.
Knavery's plain face is never seen till used.     *Exit.*

## 2.2

*Enter Othello's Herald with a proclamation.*

HERALD   It is Othello's pleasure, our noble and valiant
general, that, upon certain tidings now arrived, importing the mere perdition of the Turkish fleet, every   3
man put himself into triumph: some to dance, some to   4
make bonfires, each man to what sport and revels his
addiction leads him. For, besides these beneficial   6
news, it is the celebration of his nuptial. So much was
his pleasure should be proclaimed. All offices are open,   8
and there is full liberty of feasting from this present
hour of five till the bell have told eleven. Heaven bless
the isle of Cyprus and our noble general Othello!
                                     *Exit.*

## [2.3]

*Enter Othello, Desdemona, Cassio, and
attendants.*

OTHELLO
Good Michael, look you to the guard tonight.
Let's teach ourselves that honorable stop   2
Not to outsport discretion.   3
CASSIO
Iago hath direction what to do,
But notwithstanding, with my personal eye
Will I look to't.
OTHELLO       Iago is most honest.
Michael, good night. Tomorrow with your earliest   7
Let me have speech with you. [*To Desdemona*] Come,
    my dear love,
The purchase made, the fruits are to ensue;   9
That profit's yet to come 'tween me and you.—   10
Good night.
        *Exit* [*Othello, with Desdemona and attendants*].

      *Enter Iago.*

CASSIO   Welcome, Iago. We must to the watch.
IAGO   Not this hour, Lieutenant; 'tis not yet ten o'th'   13
clock. Our general cast us thus early for the love of his   14
Desdemona; who let us not therefore blame. He hath   15
not yet made wanton the night with her, and she is
sport for Jove.
CASSIO   She's a most exquisite lady.
IAGO   And, I'll warrant her, full of game.

CASSIO   Indeed, she's a most fresh and delicate creature.
IAGO   What an eye she has! Methinks it sounds a parley   21
to provocation.
CASSIO   An inviting eye, and yet methinks right modest.
IAGO   And when she speaks, is it not an alarum to love?   24
CASSIO   She is indeed perfection.
IAGO   Well, happiness to their sheets! Come, Lieutenant,
I have a stoup of wine, and here without are a brace of   27
Cyprus gallants that would fain have a measure to the   28
health of black Othello.
CASSIO   Not tonight, good Iago. I have very poor and
unhappy brains for drinking. I could well wish cour-
tesy would invent some other custom of entertain-
ment.
IAGO   Oh, they are our friends. But one cup! I'll drink for   34
you.   35
CASSIO   I have drunk but one cup tonight, and that was
craftily qualified too, and behold what innovation it   37
makes here. I am unfortunate in the infirmity and   38
dare not task my weakness with any more.
IAGO   What, man? 'Tis a night of revels. The gallants
desire it.
CASSIO   Where are they?
IAGO   Here at the door. I pray you, call them in.
CASSIO   I'll do't, but it dislikes me.          *Exit.*   44
IAGO
If I can fasten but one cup upon him,
With that which he hath drunk tonight already,
He'll be as full of quarrel and offense   47
As my young mistress' dog. Now, my sick fool
    Roderigo,
Whom love hath turned almost the wrong side out,
To Desdemona hath tonight caroused   50
Potations pottle-deep; and he's to watch.   51
Three lads of Cyprus—noble swelling spirits,   52
That hold their honors in a wary distance,   53
The very elements of this warlike isle—   54
Have I tonight flustered with flowing cups,
And they watch too. Now, 'mongst this flock of
    drunkards   56
Am I to put our Cassio in some action
That may offend the isle.—But here they come.

    *Enter Cassio, Montano, and gentlemen;* [*servants
following with wine*].

If consequence do but approve my dream,   59
My boat sails freely both with wind and stream.   60
CASSIO   'Fore God, they have given me a rouse already.   61

---

**2.2. Location: Cyprus.**
**3 mere perdition** complete destruction   **4 triumph** public celebration
**6 addiction** inclination   **8 offices** rooms where food and drink are kept
**2.3. Location: Cyprus. The citadel.**
**2 stop** restraint   **3 outsport** celebrate beyond the bounds of   **7 with
your earliest** at your earliest convenience   **9–10 The purchase . . . you**
i.e., though married, we haven't yet consummated our love. (Possibly,
too, Othello is referring to pregnancy. At all events, his desire for sexual union is manifest.)   **13 Not this hour** Not for an hour yet   **14 cast**
dismissed   **15 who** i.e., Othello

**21 sounds a parley** calls for a conference, issues an invitation
**24 alarum** signal calling men to arms. (Continuing the military
metaphor of *parley,* line 21.)   **27 stoup** measure of liquor, two quarts.
**without** outside.   **brace** pair   **28 fain have a measure** gladly drink a
toast   **34–5 for you** in your place. (Iago will do the steady drinking
to keep the gallants company while Cassio has only one cup.)
**37 qualified** diluted.   **innovation** disturbance, insurrection   **38 here**
i.e., in my head.   **44 it dislikes me** i.e., I'm reluctant.   **47 offense**
readiness to give or take offense   **50 caroused** drunk off   **51 pottle-
deep** to the bottom of the tankard.   **watch** stand watch.   **52 swelling** proud   **53 hold . . . distance** i.e., are extremely sensitive of their
honor   **54 elements** lifeblood   **56 watch** are members of the
guard   **59 If . . . dream** If subsequent events will only confirm my
dreams and hopes   **60 stream** current.   **61 rouse** full draft of liquor

MONTANO    Good faith, a little one; not past a pint, as I
am a soldier.

IAGO    Some wine, ho!

[*He sings.*]    "And let me the cannikin clink, clink,    65
        And let me the cannikin clink.
            A soldier's a man,
            Oh, man's life's but a span;    68
            Why, then, let a soldier drink."

Some wine, boys!

CASSIO    'Fore God, an excellent song.

IAGO    I learned it in England, where indeed they are
most potent in potting. Your Dane, your German, and    73
your swag-bellied Hollander—drink, ho!—are noth-    74
ing to your English.

CASSIO    Is your Englishman so exquisite in his drinking?

IAGO    Why, he drinks you, with facility, your Dane    77
dead drunk; he sweats not to overthrow your Almain;    78
he gives your Hollander a vomit ere the next pottle can
be filled.

CASSIO    To the health of our general!

MONTANO    I am for it, Lieutenant, and I'll do you justice.    82

IAGO    O sweet England! [*He sings.*]

"King Stephen was and-a worthy peer,
    His breeches cost him but a crown;
He held them sixpence all too dear,
    With that he called the tailor lown.    87

He was a wight of high renown,    88
    And thou art but of low degree.
'Tis pride that pulls the country down;    90
    Then take thy auld cloak about thee."    91

Some wine, ho!

CASSIO    'Fore God, this is a more exquisite song than
the other.

IAGO    Will you hear't again?

CASSIO    No, for I hold him to be unworthy of his place
that does those things. Well, God's above all; and
there be souls must be saved, and there be souls must    98
not be saved.    99

IAGO    It's true, good Lieutenant.

CASSIO    For mine own part—no offense to the General,
nor any man of quality—I hope to be saved.    102

IAGO    And so do I too, Lieutenant.

CASSIO    Ay, but, by your leave, not before me; the lieutenant is to be saved before the ancient. Let's have no
more of this; let's to our affairs.—God forgive us our
sins!—Gentlemen, let's look to our business. Do not
think, gentlemen, I am drunk. This is my ancient; this
is my right hand, and this is my left. I am not drunk
now. I can stand well enough, and speak well enough.

GENTLEMEN    Excellent well.

CASSIO    Why, very well then. You must not think then
that I am drunk.    *Exit.*

MONTANO
To th' platform, masters. Come, let's set the watch.    114
            [*Exeunt Gentlemen.*]

IAGO
You see this fellow that is gone before.
He's a soldier fit to stand by Caesar
And give direction; and do but see his vice.
'Tis to his virtue a just equinox,    118
The one as long as th'other. 'Tis pity of him.
I fear the trust Othello puts him in,
On some odd time of his infirmity,
Will shake this island.

MONTANO                But is he often thus?

IAGO
'Tis evermore the prologue to his sleep.
He'll watch the horologe a double set,    124
If drink rock not his cradle.

MONTANO                It were well
The General were put in mind of it.
Perhaps he sees it not, or his good nature
Prizes the virtue that appears in Cassio
And looks not on his evils. Is not this true?

*Enter Roderigo.*

IAGO [*aside to him*]    How now, Roderigo?
I pray you, after the Lieutenant; go.    [*Exit Roderigo.*]

MONTANO
And 'tis great pity that the noble Moor
Should hazard such a place as his own second    133
With one of an engraffed infirmity.    134
It were an honest action to say so
To the Moor.

IAGO                Not I, for this fair island.
I do love Cassio well and would do much
To cure him of this evil.    [*Cry within:* "Help! Help!"]
            But, hark! What noise?    138

*Enter Cassio, pursuing Roderigo.*

CASSIO    Zounds, you rogue! You rascal!

MONTANO    What's the matter, Lieutenant?

CASSIO    A knave teach me my duty? I'll beat the knave
into a twiggen bottle.    142

RODERIGO    Beat me?

CASSIO    Dost thou prate, rogue?    [*He strikes Roderigo.*]

MONTANO    Nay, good Lieutenant.    [*Restraining him.*] I
pray you, sir, hold your hand.

CASSIO    Let me go, sir, or I'll knock you o'er the
mazard.    148

---

**65 cannikin** small drinking vessel    **68 span** brief span of time. (Compare Psalm 39:5 as rendered in the Book of Common Prayer: "Thou hast made my days as it were a span long.")    **73 potent in potting** adept at drinking.    **Your Dane** Your typical Dane. (Similarly with the colloquial "your" in lines 74–8.)    **74 swag-bellied Hollander** fat and sagging-bellied Dutchman    **77 drinks you** drinks.    **your Dane** your typical Dane.    **78 sweats not** i.e., need not exert himself.    **Almain** German    **82 I'll . . . justice** i.e., I'll match you drink for drink.    **87 lown** lout, rascal.    **88 wight** person    **90 pride** i.e., extravagance in dress    **91 auld** old    **98–9 there be . . . not be saved** According to Calvinist theology, some mortals are destined from the beginning of time to be saved, while others are predeterminately damned.    **102 quality** rank

**114 masters** good sirs.    **set the watch** mount the guard.    **118 just equinox** exact counterpart. (*Equinox* is an equal length of days and nights.)    **124 watch . . . set** stay awake twice around the clock or *horologe*    **133–4 hazard . . . With** risk giving such an important position as his second in command to    **134 engraffed** engrafted, inveterate    **138.1 *pursuing*** (The quarto text reads, "*driuing in.*")    **142 twiggen** wicker-encased. (Cassio vows to assail Roderigo until his skin resembles wickerwork or until he has driven Roderigo through the holes in a wickerwork.)    **148 mazard** i.e., head. (Literally, a drinking vessel.)

MONTANO　Come, come, you're drunk.

CASSIO　Drunk?　　　　　　　　　　　　　　　　[*They fight.*]

IAGO [*aside to Roderigo*]

Away, I say. Go out and cry a mutiny.　　　　　　151

　　　　　　　　　　　　　　　　　　　[*Exit Roderigo.*]

Nay, good Lieutenant—God's will, gentlemen—

Help, ho!—Lieutenant—sir—Montano—sir—

Help, masters!—Here's a goodly watch indeed!　154

　　　　　　　　　　　　　　　　　　　[*A bell rings.*]

Who's that which rings the bell?—Diablo, ho!　155

The town will rise. God's will, Lieutenant, hold!　156

You'll be ashamed forever.

*Enter Othello and attendants* [*with weapons*].

OTHELLO

What is the matter here?

MONTANO　　　　　　　　　Zounds, I bleed still.

I am hurt to th' death. He dies!　[*He thrusts at Cassio.*]

OTHELLO　　　　　　　　　　　Hold, for your lives!

IAGO

Hold, ho! Lieutenant—sir—Montano—gentlemen—

Have you forgot all sense of place and duty?

Hold! The General speaks to you. Hold, for shame!

OTHELLO

Why, how now, ho! From whence ariseth this?

Are we turned Turks, and to ourselves do that　164

Which heaven hath forbid the Ottomites?　165

For Christian shame, put by this barbarous brawl!

He that stirs next to carve for his own rage　167

Holds his soul light; he dies upon his motion.　168

Silence that dreadful bell. It frights the isle

From her propriety. What is the matter, masters?　170

Honest Iago, that looks dead with grieving,

Speak. Who began this? On thy love, I charge thee.　172

IAGO

I do not know. Friends all but now, even now,

In quarter and in terms like bride and groom　174

Devesting them for bed; and then, but now—　175

As if some planet had unwitted men—　176

Swords out, and tilting one at others' breasts　177

In opposition bloody. I cannot speak　178

Any beginning to this peevish odds;　179

And would in action glorious I had lost　180

Those legs that brought me to a part of it!　181

OTHELLO

How comes it, Michael, you are thus forgot?　182

CASSIO

I pray you, pardon me. I cannot speak.

OTHELLO

Worthy Montano, you were wont be civil;　184

The gravity and stillness of your youth　185

The world hath noted, and your name is great

In mouths of wisest censure. What's the matter　187

That you unlace your reputation thus　188

And spend your rich opinion for the name　189

Of a night-brawler? Give me answer to it.

MONTANO

Worthy Othello, I am hurt to danger.

Your officer, Iago, can inform you—

While I spare speech, which something now offends

　me—　　　　　　　　　　　　　　　193

Of all that I do know; nor know I aught

By me that's said or done amiss this night,

Unless self-charity be sometimes a vice,　196

And to defend ourselves it be a sin

When violence assails us.

OTHELLO　　　　　　　　　Now, by heaven,

My blood begins my safer guides to rule,　199

And passion, having my best judgment collied,　200

Essays to lead the way. Zounds, if I stir,　201

Or do but lift this arm, the best of you

Shall sink in my rebuke. Give me to know

How this foul rout began, who set it on;　204

And he that is approved in this offense,　205

Though he had twinned with me, both at a birth,

Shall lose me. What? In a town of war　207

Yet wild, the people's hearts brim full of fear,　208

To manage private and domestic quarrel?　209

In night, and on the court and guard of safety?　210

'Tis monstrous. Iago, who began't?

MONTANO [*to Iago*]

If partially affined, or leagued in office,　212

Thou dost deliver more or less than truth,

Thou art no soldier.

IAGO　　　　　　　　　Touch me not so near.

I had rather have this tongue cut from my mouth

Than it should do offense to Michael Cassio;

Yet, I persuade myself, to speak the truth

Shall nothing wrong him. Thus it is, General:

Montano and myself being in speech,

There comes a fellow crying out for help,

And Cassio following him with determined sword

To execute upon him. Sir, this gentleman　222

　　　　　　　　　　　　　[*indicating Montano*]

Steps in to Cassio and entreats his pause.　223

Myself the crying fellow did pursue,

Lest by his clamor—as it so fell out—

The town might fall in fright. He, swift of foot,　226

---

**151 cry a mutiny** proclaim a riot.　**154 masters** sirs.　**154.1 *A bell rings*** (This direction is from the quarto, as are *Exit Roderigo* at line 131, *They fight* at line 150, and *with weapons* at line 157.1.)　**155 Diablo** The devil　**156 rise** grow riotous.　**164–5 to ourselves . . . Ottomites** inflict on ourselves the harm that heaven has prevented the Turks from doing (by destroying their fleet).　**167 to carve . . . rage** to satisfy his rage by carving with his weapon　**168 Holds . . . light** i.e., places little value on his life.　**upon his motion** if he moves.　**170 propriety** proper state or condition.　**172 On thy love** On the love and duty you owe me　**174 In quarter . . . terms** in conduct and speech　**175 Devesting them** undressing themselves　**176 some planet** some malign influence emanating from heavenly bodies　**177 tilting** tilting at　**178 speak** explain　**179 peevish odds** childish quarrel　**180–1 And would . . . of it** and I would rather have lost my legs in military action than find myself caught up in this sordid quarrel.　**182 are thus forgot** have forgotten yourself thus.

**184 wont be** accustomed to be　**185 stillness** sobriety　**187 censure** judgment.　**188 unlace** undo, lay open (as one might loose the strings of a purse containing reputation)　**189 opinion** reputation　**193 something** somewhat.　**offends** pains　**196 self-charity** defending oneself　**199 blood** passion (of anger).　**guides** i.e., reason　**200 collied** darkened　**201 Essays** undertakes　**204 rout** riot　**205 approved in** found guilty of　**207 town of** town garrisoned for　**208 Yet** still　**209 manage** undertake　**210 on . . . safety** at the main guardhouse or headquarters and on watch.　**212 If . . . office** If made partial by personal relationships with any fellow officers (especially Cassio)　**222 execute upon him** (1) proceed violently against him (2) execute him.　**223 his pause** him to stop.　**226 fall in** fall into a state of

Outran my purpose, and I returned, the rather          227
For that I heard the clink and fall of swords          228
And Cassio high in oath, which till tonight
I ne'er might say before. When I came back—
For this was brief—I found them close together
At blow and thrust, even as again they were
When you yourself did part them.
More of this matter cannot I report.
But men are men; the best sometimes forget.           235
Though Cassio did some little wrong to him,
As men in rage strike those that wish them best,      237
Yet surely Cassio, I believe, received
From him that fled some strange indignity,
Which patience could not pass.

OTHELLO                                I know, Iago,   240
Thy honesty and love doth mince this matter,          241
Making it light to Cassio.—Cassio, I love thee,
But nevermore be officer of mine.

*Enter Desdemona, attended.*

Look if my gentle love be not raised up.
I'll make thee an example.

DESDEMONA
What is the matter, dear?

OTHELLO                          All's well now, sweeting;
Come away to bed. [*To Montano*] Sir, for your hurts,
Myself will be your surgeon.—Lead him off.           248
                              [*Montano is led off.*]
Iago, look with care about the town
And silence those whom this vile brawl distracted.
Come, Desdemona. 'Tis the soldiers' life
To have their balmy slumbers waked with strife.
                    *Exit [with all but Iago and Cassio].*

IAGO    What, are you hurt, Lieutenant?

CASSIO    Ay, past all surgery.

IAGO    Marry, God forbid!

CASSIO    Reputation, reputation, reputation! Oh, I have
lost my reputation! I have lost the immortal part of
myself, and what remains is bestial. My reputation,
Iago, my reputation!

IAGO    As I am an honest man, I thought you had
received some bodily wound; there is more sense in
that than in reputation. Reputation is an idle and most
false imposition, oft got without merit and lost with-   263
out deserving. You have lost no reputation at all,
unless you repute yourself such a loser. What, man,   265
there are more ways to recover the General again. You  266
are but now cast in his mood—a punishment more in     267
policy than in malice, even so as one would beat his  268
offenseless dog to affright an imperious lion. Sue to  269
him again and he's yours.

CASSIO    I will rather sue to be despised than to deceive
so good a commander with so slight, so drunken, and   272
so indiscreet an officer. Drunk? And speak parrot?   273
And squabble? Swagger? Swear? And discourse fustian with one's own shadow? O thou invisible spirit
of wine, if thou hast no name to be known by, let us
call thee devil!

IAGO    What was he that you followed with your sword?
What had he done to you?

CASSIO    I know not.

IAGO    Is't possible?

CASSIO    I remember a mass of things, but nothing
distinctly; a quarrel, but nothing wherefore. Oh, God,  283
that men should put an enemy in their mouths to steal   284
away their brains! That we should, with joy, pleas-
ance, revel, and applause transform ourselves into    286
beasts!

IAGO    Why, but you are now well enough. How came
you thus recovered?

CASSIO    It hath pleased the devil drunkenness to give
place to the devil wrath. One unperfectness shows me
another, to make me frankly despise myself.

IAGO    Come, you are too severe a moraler. As the time,   293
the place, and the condition of this country stands, I
could heartily wish this had not befallen; but since it is
as it is, mend it for your own good.

CASSIO    I will ask him for my place again; he shall tell
me I am a drunkard. Had I as many mouths as Hydra,    298
such an answer would stop them all. To be now a
sensible man, by and by a fool, and presently a beast!
Oh, strange! Every inordinate cup is unblessed, and the  301
ingredient is a devil.

IAGO    Come, come, good wine is a good familiar
creature, if it be well used. Exclaim no more against it.
And, good Lieutenant, I think you think I love you.

CASSIO    I have well approved it, sir. I drunk!          306

IAGO    You or any man living may be drunk at a time,   307
man. I'll tell you what you shall do. Our general's wife
is now the general—I may say so in this respect, for   309
that he hath devoted and given up himself to the      310
contemplation, mark, and denotement of her parts     311
and graces. Confess yourself freely to her; importune
her help to put you in your place again. She is of so
free, so kind, so apt, so blessed a disposition, she   314
holds it a vice in her goodness not to do more than she
is requested. This broken joint between you and her
husband entreat her to splinter; and, my fortunes     317
against any lay worth naming, this crack of your love  318
shall grow stronger than it was before.

CASSIO    You advise me well.

---

227 **rather** sooner    228 **For that** because    235 **forget** forget themselves.    237 **those . . . best** i.e., even those who are well disposed
toward them    240 **pass** let pass.    241 **mince** minimize    248 **be your
surgeon** i.e., make sure you receive medical attention.    263 **false
imposition** thing artificially imposed and of no real value    265
**unless . . . loser** unless you give yourself the name of one who has
lost his good reputation.    266 **recover** regain favor with    267 **cast in
his mood** dismissed in a moment of anger    267–8 **in policy** done for
expediency's sake and as a public gesture    268–9 **would . . . lion** i.e.,
would make an example of a minor offender in order to deter more
important and dangerous offenders.    269 **Sue to** Petition

272 **slight** worthless    273 **speak parrot** talk nonsense, rant. (*Discourse
fustian*, lines 274–5, has much the same meaning.)    283 **wherefore**
why.    284 **an enemy** i.e., alcohol    286 **applause** desire for
applause    293 **moraler** moralizer.    298 **Hydra** the Lernaean Hydra,
a monster with many heads and the ability to grow two heads when
one was cut off, slain by Hercules as the second of his twelve
labors    301 **inordinate** immoderate    306 **approved** proved by
experience    307 **at a time** at one time or another    309–10 **for that**
that    311 **mark, and denotement** (Both words mean "observation.")
**parts** qualities    314 **free** generous    317 **splinter** bind with splints
318 **lay** stake, wager

IAGO    I protest, in the sincerity of love and honest 321
kindness.

CASSIO    I think it freely; and betimes in the morning I 323
will beseech the virtuous Desdemona to undertake for
me. I am desperate of my fortunes if they check me 325
here.

IAGO    You are in the right. Good night, Lieutenant. I
must to the watch.

CASSIO    Good night, honest Iago.          *Exit Cassio.*

IAGO
And what's he then that says I play the villain,
When this advice is free I give, and honest,           331
Probal to thinking, and indeed the course               332
To win the Moor again? For 'tis most easy
Th'inclining Desdemona to subdue                        334
In any honest suit; she's framed as fruitful            335
As the free elements. And then for her                  336
To win the Moor—were't to renounce his baptism,
All seals and symbols of redeemèd sin—                  338
His soul is so enfettered to her love
That she may make, unmake, do what she list,            340
Even as her appetite shall play the god                 341
With his weak function. How am I then a villain,        342
To counsel Cassio to this parallel course               343
Directly to his good? Divinity of hell!                 344
When devils will the blackest sins put on,              345
They do suggest at first with heavenly shows,           346
As I do now. For whiles this honest fool
Plies Desdemona to repair his fortune,
And she for him pleads strongly to the Moor,
I'll pour this pestilence into his ear,
That she repeals him for her body's lust;               351
And by how much she strives to do him good,
She shall undo her credit with the Moor.
So will I turn her virtue into pitch,                   354
And out of her own goodness make the net
That shall enmesh them all.

                 *Enter Roderigo.*

                            How now, Roderigo?

RODERIGO    I do follow here in the chase, not like a
hound that hunts, but one that fills up the cry. My 358
money is almost spent; I have been tonight exceedingly well cudgeled; and I think the issue will be I shall 360
have so much experience for my pains, and so, 361
with no money at all and a little more wit, return again
to Venice.

IAGO
How poor are they that have not patience!
What wound did ever heal but by degrees?
Thou know'st we work by wit, and not by witchcraft,
And wit depends on dilatory time.                       367
Does't not go well? Cassio hath beaten thee,
And thou, by that small hurt, hast cashiered Cassio. 369
Though other things grow fair against the sun,          370
Yet fruits that blossom first will first be ripe.       371
Content thyself awhile. By the Mass, 'tis morning!      372
Pleasure and action make the hours seem short.
Retire thee; go where thou art billeted.                374
Away, I say! Thou shalt know more hereafter.
Nay, get thee gone.          *Exit Roderigo.*
              Two things are to be done.
My wife must move for Cassio to her mistress;           377
I'll set her on;
Myself the while to draw the Moor apart
And bring him jump when he may Cassio find              380
Soliciting his wife. Ay, that's the way.
Dull not device by coldness and delay.         *Exit.* 382

# 3.1

*Enter Cassio [and] Musicians.*

CASSIO
Masters, play here—I will content your pains—          1
Something that's brief, and bid "Good morrow,
General."                       [*They play.*]

              [*Enter*] *Clown.*

CLOWN    Why, masters, have your instruments been in
Naples, that they speak i'th' nose thus?                4
A MUSICIAN    How, sir, how?
CLOWN    Are these, I pray you, wind instruments?
A MUSICIAN    Ay, marry, are they, sir.
CLOWN    Oh, thereby hangs a tail.
A MUSICIAN    Whereby hangs a tale, sir?
CLOWN    Marry, sir, by many a wind instrument that I 10
know. But, masters, here's money for you. [*He gives
money.*] And the General so likes your music that he
desires you, for love's sake, to make no more noise
with it.
A MUSICIAN    Well, sir, we will not.
CLOWN    If you have any music that may not be heard, 16
to't again; but, as they say, to hear music the General
does not greatly care.
A MUSICIAN    We have none such, sir.

---

**321 I protest** i.e., I insist that I am advising you well    **323 freely** unre-
servedly.    **betimes** early    **325 check** repulse, stop    **331 free** (1) free
from guile (2) freely given    **332 Probal** probable, reasonable    **334
Th'inclining** the favorably disposed.    **subdue** persuade    **335 framed
as fruitful** created as generous    **336 free elements** i.e., earth, air, fire,
and water, unrestrained and spontaneous.    **338 seals** tokens.
**redeemèd sin** redemption from sin    **340 list** choose    **341–2 Even . . .
function** just as her wishes mold his weak ways to her will.    **343–4
to . . . good** i.e., to this course of action that seems in his best interests
(but is actually threatening).    **344 Divinity of hell!** Inverted theology
of hell (which seduces the soul to its damnation)!    **345 put on** further,
instigate    **346 suggest** tempt    **351 repeals him** attempts to get him
restored    **354 pitch** i.e., (1) foul blackness (2) a snaring substance
**358 fills up the cry** merely takes part as one of the pack.    **360 issue**
outcome    **361 so much** just so much and no more

**367 dilatory** drawn-out    **369 cashiered** dismissed from service
**370–1 Though . . . ripe** i.e., Plans that are well prepared and set expeditiously in motion will soonest ripen into success.    **372 By the Mass**
(A oath.)    **374 billeted** assigned to quarters.    **377 move** plead
**380 jump** precisely    **382 device** plot.    **coldness** lack of zeal
**3.1. Location: Before the chamber of Othello and Desdemona.**
**1 Masters** Good sirs.    **content your pains** reward your efforts
**4 speak i'th' nose** (1) sound nasal (2) sound like one whose nose has
been attacked by syphilis. (Naples was popularly supposed to have a
high incidence of venereal disease.)    **10 wind instrument** (With a
joke on flatulence. The *tail*, line 8, that hangs nearby the *wind instrument* suggests the penis.)    **16 may not** cannot

CLOWN    Then put up your pipes in your bag, for I'll away. Go, vanish into air, away!    *Exeunt Musicians.*

CASSIO    Dost thou hear, mine honest friend?

CLOWN    No, I hear not your honest friend; I hear you.

CASSIO    Prithee, keep up thy quillets. There's a poor 24
piece of gold for thee. [*He gives money.*] If the gentlewoman that attends the General's wife be stirring, tell
her there's one Cassio entreats her a little favor of 27
speech. Wilt thou do this? 28

CLOWN    She is stirring, sir. If she will stir hither, I shall 29
seem to notify unto her. 30

CASSIO
Do, good my friend.                    *Exit Clown.*

*Enter Iago.*

In happy time, Iago. 31

IAGO    You have not been abed, then?

CASSIO    Why, no. The day had broke
Before we parted. I have made bold, Iago,
To send in to your wife. My suit to her
Is that she will to virtuous Desdemona
Procure me some access.

IAGO    I'll send her to you presently;
And I'll devise a mean to draw the Moor 39
Out of the way, that your converse and business
May be more free.

CASSIO
I humbly thank you for't.                    *Exit [Iago].*
I never knew
A Florentine more kind and honest. 43

*Enter Emilia.*

EMILIA
Good morrow, good Lieutenant. I am sorry
For your displeasure; but all will sure be well. 45
The General and his wife are talking of it,
And she speaks for you stoutly. The Moor replies 47
That he you hurt is of great fame in Cyprus 48
And great affinity, and that in wholesome wisdom 49
He might not but refuse you; but he protests he loves
you 50
And needs no other suitor but his likings
To take the safest occasion by the front 52
To bring you in again.

CASSIO                    Yet I beseech you,
If you think fit, or that it may be done,
Give me advantage of some brief discourse
With Desdemon alone.

EMILIA                    Pray you, come in.
I will bestow you where you shall have time
To speak your bosom freely. 58

CASSIO    I am much bound to you.            [*Exeunt.*]

❖

## 3.2

*Enter Othello, Iago, and Gentlemen.*

OTHELLO [*giving letters*]
These letters give, Iago, to the pilot,
And by him do my duties to the Senate. 2
That done, I will be walking on the works; 3
Repair there to me.

IAGO                    Well, my good lord, I'll do't. 4

OTHELLO
This fortification, gentlemen, shall we see't?

GENTLEMEN    We'll wait upon Your Lordship.    *Exeunt.* 6

❖

## 3.3

*Enter Desdemona, Cassio, and Emilia.*

DESDEMONA
Be thou assured, good Cassio, I will do
All my abilities in thy behalf.

EMILIA
Good madam, do. I warrant it grieves my husband
As if the cause were his.

DESDEMONA
Oh, that's an honest fellow. Do not doubt, Cassio,
But I will have my lord and you again
As friendly as you were.

CASSIO                    Bounteous madam,
Whatever shall become of Michael Cassio,
He's never anything but your true servant.

DESDEMONA
I know't. I thank you. You do love my lord;
You have known him long, and be you well assured
He shall in strangeness stand no farther off 12
Than in a politic distance.

CASSIO                    Ay, but, lady, 13
That policy may either last so long,
Or feed upon such nice and waterish diet, 15
Or breed itself so out of circumstance, 16
That, I being absent and my place supplied, 17
My general will forget my love and service.

DESDEMONA
Do not doubt that. Before Emilia here 19
I give thee warrant of thy place. Assure thee, 20
If I do vow a friendship I'll perform it
To the last article. My lord shall never rest.
I'll watch him tame and talk him out of patience; 23

---

24 **keep . . . quillets** refrain from quibbling.    27–8 **entreats . . . speech**
who begs the favor of a brief talk.    29 **stir** bestir herself. (With a play
on *stirring*, "rousing herself from rest.")    30 **seem** deem it good,
think fit    31 **In happy time** i.e., Well met    39 **mean** means    43 **Florentine** i.e., even a fellow Florentine. (Iago is a Venetian; Cassio is a
Florentine.)    45 **displeasure** fall from favor    47 **stoutly** spiritedly.    48 **fame** reputation, importance    49 **affinity** kindred, family
connection    50 **He . . . refuse you** he had no alternative but to dismiss you.    **protests** insists    52 **occasion . . . front** opportunity by the
forelock    58 **bosom** inmost thoughts

**3.2. Location: The citadel.**
2 **do my duties** convey my respects    3 **works** breastworks, fortifications
4 **Repair** return, come    6 **wait upon** attend
**3.3. Location: The citadel.**
12 **strangeness** aloofness    13 **politic** required by wise policy
15 **Or . . . diet** or sustain itself at length upon such trivial and meager
technicalities    16 **breed . . . circumstance** continually renew itself so
out of chance events, or yield so few chances for my being pardoned
17 **supplied** filled by another person    19 **doubt** fear    20 **warrant**
guarantee    23 **watch him tame** tame him by keeping him from sleeping. (A term from falconry.)    **out of patience** past his endurance

His bed shall seem a school, his board a shrift;   24
I'll intermingle everything he does
With Cassio's suit. Therefore be merry, Cassio,
For thy solicitor shall rather die   27
Than give thy cause away.   28

*Enter Othello and Iago [at a distance].*

EMILIA   Madam, here comes my lord.
CASSIO   Madam, I'll take my leave.
DESDEMONA   Why, stay, and hear me speak.
CASSIO
Madam, not now. I am very ill at ease,
Unfit for mine own purposes.
DESDEMONA   Well, do your discretion.   *Exit Cassio.*   34
IAGO   Ha? I like not that.
OTHELLO   What dost thou say?
IAGO
Nothing, my lord; or if—I know not what.
OTHELLO
Was not that Cassio parted from my wife?
IAGO
Cassio, my lord? No, sure, I cannot think it,
That he would steal away so guilty-like,
Seeing you coming.
OTHELLO   I do believe 'twas he.
DESDEMONA [*joining them*]   How now, my lord?
I have been talking with a suitor here,
A man that languishes in your displeasure.
OTHELLO   Who is't you mean?
DESDEMONA
Why, your lieutenant, Cassio. Good my lord,
If I have any grace or power to move you,
His present reconciliation take;   49
For if he be not one that truly loves you,
That errs in ignorance and not in cunning,   51
I have no judgment in an honest face.
I prithee, call him back.
OTHELLO   Went he hence now?
DESDEMONA   Yes, faith, so humbled
That he hath left part of his grief with me
To suffer with him. Good love, call him back.
OTHELLO
Not now, sweet Desdemon. Some other time.
DESDEMONA   But shall't be shortly?
OTHELLO   The sooner, sweet, for you.
DESDEMONA   Shall't be tonight at supper?
OTHELLO   No, not tonight.
DESDEMONA   Tomorrow dinner, then?   63
OTHELLO   I shall not dine at home.
I meet the captains at the citadel.
DESDEMONA
Why, then, tomorrow night, or Tuesday morn,
On Tuesday noon, or night, on Wednesday morn.
I prithee, name the time, but let it not
Exceed three days. In faith, he's penitent;

And yet his trespass, in our common reason—   70
Save that, they say, the wars must make example   71
Out of her best—is not almost a fault   72
T'incur a private check. When shall he come?   73
Tell me, Othello. I wonder in my soul
What you would ask me that I should deny,
Or stand so mamm'ring on. What? Michael Cassio,   76
That came a-wooing with you, and so many a time,
When I have spoke of you dispraisingly,
Hath ta'en your part—to have so much to do
To bring him in! By'r Lady, I could do much—   80
OTHELLO
Prithee, no more. Let him come when he will;
I will deny thee nothing.
DESDEMONA   Why, this is not a boon.
'Tis as I should entreat you wear your gloves,
Or feed on nourishing dishes, or keep you warm,
Or sue to you to do a peculiar profit   86
To your own person. Nay, when I have a suit
Wherein I mean to touch your love indeed,   88
It shall be full of poise and difficult weight,   89
And fearful to be granted.
OTHELLO   I will deny thee nothing.
Whereon, I do beseech thee, grant me this,   92
To leave me but a little to myself.
DESDEMONA
Shall I deny you? No. Farewell, my lord.
OTHELLO
Farewell, my Desdemona. I'll come to thee straight.   95
DESDEMONA
Emilia, come.—Be as your fancies teach you;   96
Whate'er you be, I am obedient.   *Exit [with Emilia].*
OTHELLO
Excellent wretch! Perdition catch my soul   98
But I do love thee! And when I love thee not,   99
Chaos is come again.   100
IAGO   My noble lord—
OTHELLO   What dost thou say, Iago?
IAGO
Did Michael Cassio, when you wooed my lady,
Know of your love?
OTHELLO
He did, from first to last. Why dost thou ask?
IAGO
But for a satisfaction of my thought;
No further harm.
OTHELLO   Why of thy thought, Iago?

---

**24 board** dining table.   **shrift** confessional   **27 solicitor** advocate
**28 away** up.   **34 do your discretion** do as you think fit.   **49 His . . .
take** let him be reconciled to you right away   **51 in cunning**
wittingly   **63 dinner** (The midday meal.)

**70 common reason** everyday judgments   **71–2 Save . . . best** were it
not that, as the saying goes, military discipline requires making an
example of the very best men. (*Her* refers to wars as a singular concept.)   **72 not almost** scarcely   **73 a private check** even a private
reprimand.   **76 mamm'ring on** wavering or muttering about.   **80
bring him in** restore him to favor.   **86 peculiar** particular, personal   **88 touch** test   **89 poise . . . weight** delicacy and weightiness   **92 Whereon** In return for which   **95 straight**
straightaway.   **96 fancies** inclinations   **98 wretch** (A term of affectionate endearment.)   **99–100 And . . . again** i.e., My love for you will
last forever, until the end of time when chaos will return. (But with
an unconscious, ironic suggestion that, if anything should induce
Othello to cease loving Desdemona, the result would be chaos.)

IAGO
  I did not think he had been acquainted with her.
OTHELLO
  Oh, yes, and went between us very oft.
IAGO  Indeed?
OTHELLO
  Indeed? Ay, indeed. Discern'st thou aught in that?
  Is he not honest?
IAGO  Honest, my lord?
OTHELLO  Honest. Ay, honest.
IAGO  My lord, for aught I know.
OTHELLO  What dost thou think?
IAGO  Think, my lord?
OTHELLO
  "Think, my lord?" By heaven, thou echo'st me,
  As if there were some monster in thy thought
  Too hideous to be shown. Thou dost mean something.
  I heard thee say even now, thou lik'st not that,
  When Cassio left my wife. What didst not like?
  And when I told thee he was of my counsel      123
  In my whole course of wooing, thou cried'st "Indeed?"
  And didst contract and purse thy brow together   125
  As if thou then hadst shut up in thy brain
  Some horrible conceit. If thou dost love me,    127
  Show me thy thought.
IAGO  My lord, you know I love you.
OTHELLO  I think thou dost;
  And, for I know thou'rt full of love and honesty,  131
  And weigh'st thy words before thou giv'st them
    breath,
  Therefore these stops of thine fright me the more;  133
  For such things in a false disloyal knave
  Are tricks of custom, but in a man that's just   135
  They're close dilations, working from the heart   136
  That passion cannot rule.
IAGO                    For Michael Cassio,   137
  I dare be sworn I think that he is honest.
OTHELLO
  I think so too.
IAGO          Men should be what they seem;
  Or those that be not, would they might seem none!  140
OTHELLO
  Certain, men should be what they seem.
IAGO
  Why, then, I think Cassio's an honest man.
OTHELLO  Nay, yet there's more in this.
  I prithee, speak to me as to thy thinkings,
  As thou dost ruminate, and give thy worst of thoughts
  The worst of words.
IAGO            Good my lord, pardon me.
  Though I am bound to every act of duty,
  I am not bound to that all slaves are free to.   148
  Utter my thoughts? Why, say they are vile and false,
  As where's that palace whereinto foul things

Sometimes intrude not? Who has that breast so pure
But some uncleanly apprehensions
Keep leets and law days, and in sessions sit     153
With meditations lawful?               154
OTHELLO
  Thou dost conspire against thy friend, Iago,   155
  If thou but think'st him wronged and mak'st his ear
  A stranger to thy thoughts.
IAGO                I do beseech you,
  Though I perchance am vicious in my guess—     158
  As I confess it is my nature's plague
  To spy into abuses, and oft my jealousy       160
  Shapes faults that are not—that your wisdom then,
  From one that so imperfectly conceits,        162
  Would take no notice, nor build yourself a trouble  163
  Out of his scattering and unsure observance.    164
  It were not for your quiet nor your good,      165
  Nor for my manhood, honesty, and wisdom,
  To let you know my thoughts.
OTHELLO              What dost thou mean?
IAGO
  Good name in man and woman, dear my lord,
  Is the immediate jewel of their souls.        169
  Who steals my purse steals trash; 'tis something,
    nothing;                     170
  'Twas mine, 'tis his, and has been slave to thousands;
  But he that filches from me my good name
  Robs me of that which not enriches him
  And makes me poor indeed.
OTHELLO  By heaven, I'll know thy thoughts.
IAGO
  You cannot, if my heart were in your hand,     176
  Nor shall not, whilst 'tis in my custody.
OTHELLO  Ha?
IAGO  Oh, beware, my lord, of jealousy.
  It is the green-eyed monster, which doth mock   179
  The meat it feeds on. That cuckold lives in bliss  180
  Who, certain of his fate, loves not his wronger;  181
  But oh, what damnèd minutes tells he o'er      182
  Who dotes, yet doubts, suspects, yet fondly loves!  183
OTHELLO  Oh, misery!
IAGO
  Poor and content is rich, and rich enough,     185
  But riches fineless is as poor as winter       186
  To him that ever fears he shall be poor.

123 of my counsel in my confidence  125 purse knit  127 conceit fancy, thought.  131 for because  133 stops pauses  135 of custom customary  136–7 They're . . . rule they are secret or involuntary expressions of feeling that are too strong to be kept back.  137 For As for  140 those . . . none I wish that those who are not honest might at least not pretend to be.  148 that that which.  free to free with respect to.

153 Keep leets and law days i.e., hold court, set up their authority in one's heart. (Leets are a kind of manor court; law days are the days when courts sit in session, or those sessions.)  153–4 and in sessions . . . lawful i.e., and debate in that court with virtuous thoughts just as though the uncleanly thoughts were of equal legitimacy.  155 thy friend i.e., Othello  158 vicious wrong  160 jealousy suspicious nature  162 one i.e., myself, Iago.  conceits judges, conjectures  163 Would I beseech you that, in your wisdom, you would  164 scattering random, incoherent  165 were not would not be  169 immediate essential, most precious  170 Who He who  176 if even if  179–80 which . . . feeds on (Jealousy mocks both itself and the sufferer of jealousy; it is self-devouring and is its own punishment.)  180–1 That . . . wronger A cuckolded husband who knows his wife to be unfaithful can at least take comfort in knowing the truth, so that he will not continue to love her or to befriend her lover. (Othello echoes this sentiment in lines 204–6, when he vows that he would end uncertainty and cease to love an unfaithful wife.)  182 tells counts  183 fondly (1) adoringly (2) foolishly  185 Poor . . . enough To be content with what little one has is the greatest wealth of all. (Proverbial.)  186 fineless boundless

Good God, the souls of all my tribe defend
From jealousy!
OTHELLO    Why, why is this?
Think'st thou I'd make a life of jealousy,
To follow still the changes of the moon     192
With fresh suspicions? No! To be once in doubt    193
Is once to be resolved. Exchange me for a goat    194
When I shall turn the business of my soul
To such exsufflicate and blowed surmises    196
Matching thy inference. 'Tis not to make me jealous   197
To say my wife is fair, feeds well, loves company,
Is free of speech, sings, plays, and dances well;
Where virtue is, these are more virtuous.
Nor from mine own weak merits will I draw
The smallest fear or doubt of her revolt,    202
For she had eyes, and chose me. No, Iago,
I'll see before I doubt; when I doubt, prove;
And on the proof, there is no more but this—
Away at once with love or jealousy.
IAGO
I am glad of this, for now I shall have reason
To show the love and duty that I bear you
With franker spirit. Therefore, as I am bound,    209
Receive it from me. I speak not yet of proof.
Look to your wife; observe her well with Cassio.
Wear your eyes thus, not jealous nor secure.    212
I would not have your free and noble nature,
Out of self-bounty, be abused. Look to't.    214
I know our country disposition well;
In Venice they do let God see the pranks
They dare not show their husbands; their best
    conscience
Is not to leave't undone, but keep't unknown.
OTHELLO    Dost thou say so?
IAGO
She did deceive her father, marrying you;
And when she seemed to shake and fear your looks,
She loved them most.
OTHELLO         And so she did.
IAGO                Why, go to, then! 222
She that, so young, could give out such a seeming,    223
To seel her father's eyes up close as oak,    224
He thought 'twas witchcraft! But I am much to blame.
I humbly do beseech you of your pardon
For too much loving you.
OTHELLO    I am bound to thee forever.    228
IAGO
I see this hath a little dashed your spirits.

OTHELLO
Not a jot, not a jot.
IAGO          I'faith, I fear it has.
I hope you will consider what is spoke
Comes from my love. But I do see you're moved.
I am to pray you not to strain my speech
To grosser issues nor to larger reach    234
Than to suspicion.
OTHELLO    I will not.
IAGO    Should you do so, my lord,
My speech should fall into such vile success    238
Which my thoughts aimed not. Cassio's my worthy
    friend.
My lord, I see you're moved.
OTHELLO         No, not much moved.
I do not think but Desdemona's honest.    241
IAGO
Long live she so! And long live you to think so!
OTHELLO
And yet, how nature erring from itself—
IAGO
Ay, there's the point! As—to be bold with you—
Not to affect many proposèd matches    245
Of her own clime, complexion, and degree,    246
Whereto we see in all things nature tends—
Foh! One may smell in such a will most rank,    248
Foul disproportion, thoughts unnatural.    249
But pardon me. I do not in position    250
Distinctly speak of her, though I may fear
Her will, recoiling to her better judgment,    252
May fall to match you with her country forms    253
And happily repent.
OTHELLO         Farewell, farewell!    254
If more thou dost perceive, let me know more.
Set on thy wife to observe. Leave me, Iago.
IAGO [*going*]    My lord, I take my leave.
OTHELLO
Why did I marry? This honest creature doubtless
Sees and knows more, much more, than he unfolds.
IAGO [*returning*]
My lord, I would I might entreat Your Honor
To scan this thing no farther. Leave it to time.    261
Although 'tis fit that Cassio have his place—
For, sure, he fills it up with great ability—
Yet, if you please to hold him off awhile,
You shall by that perceive him and his means.    265
Note if your lady strain his entertainment    266
With any strong or vehement importunity;
Much will be seen in that. In the meantime,
Let me be thought too busy in my fears—    269

---

**192–3 To follow . . . suspicions?** to be plagued by jealous uncertainties, changing incessantly like the moon?   **194 once** once and for all.   **resolved** free of doubt, having settled the matter.   **196 exsufflicate and blowed** inflated and blown up or flyblown, hence, loathsome, disgusting   **197 inference** description or allegation.   **202 doubt . . . revolt** fear of her unfaithfulness   **209 bound** dutybound   **212 not . . . secure** neither jealous nor free from uncertainty.   **214 self-bounty** inherent or natural goodness and generosity.   **abused** deceived.   **222 go to** (An expression of impatience.)   **223 seeming** false appearance   **224 seel** blind. (A term from falconry.)   **oak** (A close-grained wood.)   **228 bound** indebted. (But perhaps with ironic sense of "tied.")

**234 grosser issues** greater significances.   **reach** meaning, scope   **238 success** effect, result   **241 honest** chaste.   **245 affect** prefer, desire   **246 clime . . . degree** country, temperament or skin color, and social position   **248 will** sensuality, appetite   **249 disproportion** abnormality   **250 in position** in making this argument or proposition   **252 recoiling** reverting.   **better** i.e., more natural and reconsidered   **253 fall . . . forms** undertake to compare you with Venetian norms of handsomeness   **254 happily repent** perhaps repent her marriage.   **261 scan** scrutinize   **265 his means** the method he uses (to regain his post).   **266 strain his entertainment** urge Cassio's reinstatement   **269 busy** officious

As worthy cause I have to fear I am—
And hold her free, I do beseech Your Honor.                       271
OTHELLO   Fear not my government.                                  272
IAGO   I once more take my leave.                    *Exit.*
OTHELLO
This fellow's of exceeding honesty,
And knows all qualities, with a learnèd spirit,                   275
Of human dealings. If I do prove her haggard,                     276
Though that her jesses were my dear heartstrings,                 277
I'd whistle her off and let her down the wind                     278
To prey at fortune. Haply, for I am black                         279
And have not those soft parts of conversation                     280
That chamberers have, or for I am declined                        281
Into the vale of years—yet that's not much—
She's gone. I am abused, and my relief                            283
Must be to loathe her. Oh, curse of marriage,
That we can call these delicate creatures ours
And not their appetites! I had rather be a toad
And live upon the vapor of a dungeon
Than keep a corner in the thing I love
For others' uses. Yet, 'tis the plague of great ones;
Prerogatived are they less than the base.                         290
'Tis destiny unshunnable, like death.
Even then this forkèd plague is fated to us                       292
When we do quicken. Look where she comes.                         293

            *Enter Desdemona and Emilia.*

If she be false, oh, then heaven mocks itself!
I'll not believe't.
DESDEMONA       How now, my dear Othello?
Your dinner, and the generous islanders                           296
By you invited do attend your presence.                           297
OTHELLO
I am to blame.
DESDEMONA       Why do you speak so faintly?
Are you not well?
OTHELLO
I have a pain upon my forehead here.
DESDEMONA
Faith, that's with watching. 'Twill away again.                   301
                    *[She offers her handkerchief.]*
Let me but bind it hard, within this hour
It will be well.
OTHELLO       Your napkin is too little.                           303
Let it alone. Come, I'll go in with you.                          304
        *[He puts the handkerchief from him, and it drops.]*

DESDEMONA
I am very sorry that you are not well.
                        *Exit [with Othello].*
EMILIA [*picking up the handkerchief*]
I am glad I have found this napkin.
This was her first remembrance from the Moor.
My wayward husband hath a hundred times               308
Wooed me to steal it, but she so loves the token—
For he conjured her she should ever keep it—
That she reserves it evermore about her
To kiss and talk to. I'll have the work ta'en out,    312
And give't Iago. What he will do with it
Heaven knows, not I;
I nothing but to please his fantasy.                  315

            *Enter Iago.*

IAGO
How now? What do you here alone?
EMILIA
Do not you chide. I have a thing for you.
IAGO
You have a thing for me? It is a common thing—        318
EMILIA   Ha?
IAGO   To have a foolish wife.
EMILIA
Oh, is that all? What will you give me now
For that same handkerchief?
IAGO   What handkerchief?
EMILIA   What handkerchief?
Why, that the Moor first gave to Desdemona;           325
That which so often you did bid me steal.
IAGO   Hast stol'n it from her?
EMILIA
No, faith. She let it drop by negligence,
And to th'advantage I, being here, took't up.         329
Look, here 'tis.
IAGO           A good wench! Give it me.
EMILIA
What will you do with't, that you have been so earnest
To have me filch it?
IAGO [*snatching it*]   Why, what is that to you?
EMILIA
If it be not for some purpose of import,
Give't me again. Poor lady, she'll run mad
When she shall lack it.
IAGO               Be not acknown on't.      335
I have use for it. Go, leave me.          *Exit Emilia.*
I will in Cassio's lodging lose this napkin            337
And let him find it. Trifles light as air
Are to the jealous confirmations strong
As proofs of Holy Writ. This may do something.
The Moor already changes with my poison.

---

271 **hold her free** regard her as innocent   272 **government** self-control, conduct.   275 **qualities** natures, types   276 **haggard** wild (like a wild female hawk)   277 **Though that** though.   **jesses** straps fastened around the legs of a trained hawk   278 **I'd . . . wind** i.e., I'd let her go forever. (To release a hawk downwind was to turn it loose.)   279 **prey at fortune** fend for herself in the wild.   **Haply, for** Perhaps because   280 **soft . . . conversation** pleasing social graces   281 **chamberers** drawing-room gallants.   **for** because   283 **abused** deceived   290 **Prerogatived** privileged (to have honest wives).   **the base** ordinary citizens. (Socially prominent men are especially prone to the common destiny of being cuckolded and to the public shame that goes with it.)   292 **forkèd** (An allusion to the horns of the cuckold.)   293 **quicken** receive life. (*Quicken* may also mean to swarm with maggots as the body festers, as in 4.2.69, in which case lines 292–3 suggest that *even then*, in death, we are cuckolded by *forkèd* worms.)   296 **generous** noble   297 **attend** await   301 **watching** too little sleep.   303 **napkin** handkerchief   304 **Let it alone** i.e., Never mind.

308 **wayward** capricious   312 **work ta'en out** design of the embroidery copied   315 **fantasy** whim.   318 **common thing** (With bawdy suggestion; *common* suggests coarseness and availability to all comers, and *thing* is a slang term for the vagina.)   325 **that** that which   329 **to th'advantage** taking the opportunity   335 **lack** miss.   **Be . . . on't** Do not confess knowledge of it; keep out of this.   337 **lose** (The Folio spelling, "loose," is a normal spelling for "lose," but it may also contain the idea of "let go," "release.")

Dangerous conceits are in their natures poisons, 342
Which at the first are scarce found to distaste, 343
But with a little act upon the blood 344
Burn like the mines of sulfur.

*Enter Othello.*

         I did say so.
Look where he comes! Not poppy nor mandragora 346
Nor all the drowsy syrups of the world
Shall ever medicine thee to that sweet sleep
Which thou owed'st yesterday.

**OTHELLO**        Ha, ha, false to me? 349

**IAGO**
 Why, how now, General? No more of that.

**OTHELLO**
 Avaunt! Begone! Thou hast set me on the rack.
 I swear 'tis better to be much abused
 Than but to know't a little.

**IAGO**       How now, my lord?

**OTHELLO**
 What sense had I of her stol'n hours of lust?
 I saw't not, thought it not, it harmed not me.
 I slept the next night well, fed well, was free and
  merry; 356
 I found not Cassio's kisses on her lips.
 He that is robbed, not wanting what is stolen, 358
 Let him not know't and he's not robbed at all.

**IAGO**  I am sorry to hear this.

**OTHELLO**
 I had been happy if the general camp,
 Pioneers and all, had tasted her sweet body, 362
 So I had nothing known. Oh, now, forever 363
 Farewell the tranquil mind! Farewell content!
 Farewell the plumèd troops and the big wars 365
 That makes ambition virtue! Oh, farewell!
 Farewell the neighing steed and the shrill trump,
 The spirit-stirring drum, th'ear-piercing fife,
 The royal banner, and all quality, 369
 Pride, pomp, and circumstance of glorious war! 370
 And O you mortal engines, whose rude throats 371
 Th'immortal Jove's dread clamors counterfeit, 372
 Farewell! Othello's occupation's gone.

**IAGO**  Is't possible, my lord?

**OTHELLO**
 Villain, be sure thou prove my love a whore!
 Be sure of it. Give me the ocular proof,
 Or, by the worth of mine eternal soul,
 Thou hadst been better have been born a dog
 Than answer my waked wrath!

**IAGO**       Is't come to this?

**OTHELLO**
 Make me to see't, or at the least so prove it

That the probation bear no hinge nor loop 381
To hang a doubt on, or woe upon thy life!

**IAGO**  My noble lord—

**OTHELLO**
 If thou dost slander her and torture me,
 Never pray more; abandon all remorse; 385
 On horror's head horrors accumulate; 386
 Do deeds to make heaven weep, all earth amazed; 387
 For nothing canst thou to damnation add
 Greater than that.

**IAGO**     O grace! O heaven forgive me!
 Are you a man? Have you a soul or sense?
 God b'wi'you; take mine office. O wretched fool, 391
 That lov'st to make thine honesty a vice! 392
 O monstrous world! Take note, take note, O world,
 To be direct and honest is not safe.
 I thank you for this profit, and from hence 395
 I'll love no friend, sith love breeds such offense. 396

**OTHELLO**  Nay, stay. Thou shouldst be honest. 397

**IAGO**
 I should be wise, for honesty's a fool
 And loses that it works for.

**OTHELLO**      By the world, 399
 I think my wife be honest and think she is not;
 I think that thou art just and think thou art not.
 I'll have some proof. My name, that was as fresh
 As Dian's visage, is now begrimed and black 403
 As mine own face. If there be cords, or knives,
 Poison, or fire, or suffocating streams,
 I'll not endure it. Would I were satisfied!

**IAGO**
 I see, sir, you are eaten up with passion.
 I do repent me that I put it to you.
 You would be satisfied?

**OTHELLO**      Would? Nay, and I will.

**IAGO**
 And may; but how? How satisfied, my lord?
 Would you, the supervisor, grossly gape on? 411
 Behold her topped?

**OTHELLO**     Death and damnation! Oh!

**IAGO**
 It were a tedious difficulty, I think,
 To bring them to that prospect. Damn them then, 414
 If ever mortal eyes do see them bolster 415
 More than their own. What then? How then? 416
 What shall I say? Where's satisfaction?
 It is impossible you should see this,
 Were they as prime as goats, as hot as monkeys, 419

---

**381 probation** proof  **385 remorse** pity, penitent hope for salvation  **386 horrors accumulate** add still more horrors  **387 amazed** confounded with horror  **391 take mine office** I offer my resignation.  **O wretched fool** (Iago addresses himself as a fool for having carried honesty too far.)  **392 vice** failing, something overdone.  **395 profit** profitable instruction.  **from hence** henceforth  **396 sith** since.  **offense** i.e., harm to the one who offers help and friendship.  **397 Thou shouldst be** It appears that you are. (But Iago replies in the sense of "ought to be.")  **399 that** what  **403 Dian** Diana, goddess of the moon and of chastity  **411 supervisor** onlooker  **414 Damn them then** i.e., They would have to be really incorrigible  **415 bolster** go to bed together, share a pillow  **416 More** other.  **own** own eyes.  **419 prime** lustful

---

**342 conceits** fancies, ideas.  **in their natures** inherently  **343 distaste** be distasteful  **344 act** action, working  **346 mandragora** a narcotic made of the mandrake root  **349 thou owed'st** you did own  **356 free** carefree  **358 wanting** missing  **362 Pioneers** diggers of mines, the lowest grade of soldiers  **363 So** provided  **365 plumèd** with plume-decked headgear.  **big** mighty  **369 quality** character, essential nature  **370 Pride** rich display.  **circumstance** pageantry  **371 mortal engines** deadly cannon  **372 Jove's dread clamors** i.e., thunder

As salt as wolves in pride, and fools as gross                    420
As ignorance made drunk. But yet I say,                    421
If imputation and strong circumstances                    422
Which lead directly to the door of truth
Will give you satisfaction, you might have't.

OTHELLO
Give me a living reason she's disloyal.

IAGO   I do not like the office.
But sith I am entered in this cause so far,                    427
Pricked to't by foolish honesty and love,                    428
I will go on. I lay with Cassio lately,                    429
And being troubled with a raging tooth
I could not sleep. There are a kind of men
So loose of soul that in their sleeps will mutter
Their affairs. One of this kind is Cassio.
In sleep I heard him say, "Sweet Desdemona,
Let us be wary, let us hide our loves!"
And then, sir, would he grip and wring my hand,
Cry "O sweet creature!", then kiss me hard,
As if he plucked up kisses by the roots
That grew upon my lips; then laid his leg
Over my thigh, and sighed, and kissed, and then
Cried, "Cursèd fate that gave thee to the Moor!"

OTHELLO
Oh, monstrous! Monstrous!

IAGO                    Nay, this was but his dream.

OTHELLO
But this denoted a foregone conclusion.                    443
'Tis a shrewd doubt, though it be but a dream.                    444

IAGO
And this may help to thicken other proofs
That do demonstrate thinly.

OTHELLO                    I'll tear her all to pieces.

IAGO
Nay, but be wise. Yet we see nothing done;
She may be honest yet. Tell me but this:
Have you not sometimes seen a handkerchief
Spotted with strawberries in your wife's hand?                    450

OTHELLO
I gave her such a one. 'Twas my first gift.

IAGO
I know not that; but such a handkerchief—
I am sure it was your wife's—did I today
See Cassio wipe his beard with.

OTHELLO                    If it be that—

IAGO
If it be that, or any that was hers,
It speaks against her with the other proofs.

OTHELLO
Oh, that the slave had forty thousand lives!                    457
One is too poor, too weak for my revenge.
Now do I see 'tis true. Look here, Iago,
All my fond love thus do I blow to heaven.                    460

'Tis gone.
Arise, black vengeance, from the hollow hell!
Yield up, O love, thy crown and hearted throne                    463
To tyrannous hate! Swell, bosom, with thy freight,                    464
For 'tis of aspics' tongues!                    465

IAGO   Yet be content.                    466

OTHELLO   Oh, blood, blood, blood!

IAGO
Patience, I say. Your mind perhaps may change.

OTHELLO
Never, Iago. Like to the Pontic Sea,                    469
Whose icy current and compulsive course
Ne'er knows retiring ebb, but keeps due on
To the Propontic and the Hellespont,                    472
Even so my bloody thoughts with violent pace
Shall ne'er look back, ne'er ebb to humble love,
Till that a capable and wide revenge                    475
Swallow them up. Now, by yond marble heaven,                    476
[Kneeling] In the due reverence of a sacred vow
I here engage my words.

IAGO                    Do not rise yet.
[He kneels.] Witness, you ever-burning lights above,                    479
You elements that clip us round about,                    480
Witness that here Iago doth give up
The execution of his wit, hands, heart,                    482
To wronged Othello's service. Let him command,
And to obey shall be in me remorse,                    484
What bloody business ever.                    [They rise.]

OTHELLO                    I greet thy love,                    485
Not with vain thanks, but with acceptance bounteous,
And will upon the instant put thee to't.                    487
Within these three days let me hear thee say
That Cassio's not alive.

IAGO                    My friend is dead;
'Tis done at your request. But let her live.

OTHELLO
Damn her, lewd minx! Oh, damn her, damn her!                    491
Come, go with me apart. I will withdraw
To furnish me with some swift means of death
For the fair devil. Now art thou my lieutenant.

IAGO   I am your own forever.                    Exeunt.

❦

# 3.4

*Enter Desdemona, Emilia, and Clown.*

DESDEMONA   Do you know, sirrah, where Lieutenant                    1
Cassio lies?                    2

---

420 **salt** wanton, lustful.   **pride** heat   421 **As . . . drunk** as ignorant drunken persons.   422 **imputation . . . circumstances** strong circumstantial evidence   427 **sith** since   428 **Pricked** spurred   429 **lay with** (A common arrangement in times of military engagement.)   443 **foregone conclusion** previous experience or action.   444 **shrewd doubt** suspicious circumstance   450 **Spotted with strawberries** embroidered with a strawberry pattern   457 **the slave** i.e., Cassio   460 **fond** foolish. (But also suggesting "affectionate.")

463 **hearted** fixed in the heart   464 **freight** burden   465 **aspics'** venomous serpents'   466 **content** calm.   469 **Pontic Sea** Black Sea   472 **Propontic** Sea of Marmora, between the Black Sea and the Aegean.   **Hellespont** Dardanelles, straits where the Sea of Marmora joins with the Aegean   475 **capable** ample, capacious   476 **marble** i.e., gleaming, polished, and indifferent to human suffering   479 **s.d.** *He kneels* (In the quarto text, Iago kneels here after Othello has knelt at line 477.)   **lights** stars and planets   480 **clip** encompass, embrace   482 **execution** exercise, action.   **wit** mind   484 **remorse** pity (for Othello's wrongs)   485 **ever** soever.   487 **to't** to the proof.   491 **minx** wanton.   
**3.4. Location: Before the citadel.**   
1 **sirrah** (A form of address to an inferior.)   2 **lies** lodges. (But the Clown makes the obvious pun.)

CLOWN   I dare not say he lies anywhere.

DESDEMONA   Why, man?

CLOWN   He's a soldier, and for me to say a soldier lies, 'tis stabbing.

DESDEMONA   Go to. Where lodges he?

CLOWN   To tell you where he lodges is to tell you where I lie.

DESDEMONA   Can anything be made of this?

CLOWN   I know not where he lodges, and for me to devise a lodging and say he lies here, or he lies there, were to lie in mine own throat.   13

DESDEMONA   Can you inquire him out, and be edified   14 by report?   15

CLOWN   I will catechize the world for him; that is, make questions, and by them answer.

DESDEMONA   Seek him, bid him come hither. Tell him I have moved my lord on his behalf and hope all will be   19 well.

CLOWN   To do this is within the compass of man's wit,   21 and therefore I will attempt the doing it.   *Exit Clown.*

DESDEMONA
Where should I lose that handkerchief, Emilia?   23

EMILIA   I know not, madam.

DESDEMONA
Believe me, I had rather have lost my purse
Full of crusadoes; and but my noble Moor   26
Is true of mind and made of no such baseness
As jealous creatures are, it were enough
To put him to ill thinking.

EMILIA             Is he not jealous?

DESDEMONA
Who, he? I think the sun where he was born
Drew all such humors from him.

EMILIA           Look where he comes.   31

*Enter Othello.*

DESDEMONA
I will not leave him now till Cassio
Be called to him.—How is 't with you, my lord?

OTHELLO
Well, my good lady. [*Aside*] Oh, hardness to dissemble!—
How do you, Desdemona?

DESDEMONA        Well, my good lord.

OTHELLO
Give me your hand. [*She gives her hand.*] This hand is moist, my lady.

DESDEMONA
It yet hath felt no age nor known no sorrow.

OTHELLO
This argues fruitfulness and liberal heart.   38
Hot, hot, and moist. This hand of yours requires
A sequester from liberty, fasting and prayer,   40

Much castigation, exercise devout;   41
For here's a young and sweating devil here
That commonly rebels. 'Tis a good hand,
A frank one.

DESDEMONA   You may indeed say so,   44
For 'twas that hand that gave away my heart.

OTHELLO
A liberal hand. The hearts of old gave hands,   46
But our new heraldry is hands, not hearts.   47

DESDEMONA
I cannot speak of this. Come now, your promise.

OTHELLO   What promise, chuck?   49

DESDEMONA
I have sent to bid Cassio come speak with you.

OTHELLO
I have a salt and sorry rheum offends me;   51
Lend me thy handkerchief.

DESDEMONA   Here, my lord. [*She offers a handkerchief.*]

OTHELLO
That which I gave you.

DESDEMONA        I have it not about me.

OTHELLO   Not?

DESDEMONA   No, faith, my lord.

OTHELLO
That's a fault. That handkerchief
Did an Egyptian to my mother give.
She was a charmer, and could almost read   59
The thoughts of people. She told her, while she kept it
'Twould make her amiable and subdue my father   61
Entirely to her love, but if she lost it
Or made a gift of it, my father's eye
Should hold her loathèd and his spirits should hunt   64
After new fancies. She, dying, gave it me,   65
And bid me, when my fate would have me wived,
To give it her. I did so; and take heed on 't;   67
Make it a darling like your precious eye.   68
To lose 't or give 't away were such perdition   69
As nothing else could match.

DESDEMONA        Is 't possible?

OTHELLO
'Tis true. There's magic in the web of it.   71
A sibyl, that had numbered in the world   72
The sun to course two hundred compasses,   73
In her prophetic fury sewed the work;   74
The worms were hallowed that did breed the silk,
And it was dyed in mummy which the skillful   76
Conserved of maidens' hearts.

DESDEMONA       I' faith! Is 't true?   77

---

13 **lie . . . throat** lie egregiously and deliberately.   14–15 **be edified by report** learn the truth from what you hear.   19 **moved my lord** petitioned Othello   21 **compass** scope   23 **should I lose** could I have lost   26 **crusadoes** Portuguese gold coins.   **but** were it not that   31 **humors** whimsical ideas. (Refers to the four bodily fluids thought to determine temperament.)   38 **argues** gives evidence of.   **fruitfulness** generosity, amorousness, and fecundity.   **liberal** generous and sexually free   40 **sequester** sequestration

41 **castigation** corrective discipline.   **exercise devout** i.e., prayer, religious meditation, etc.   44 **frank** generous, open. (With sexual suggestion.)   46–7 **The hearts . . . hearts** i.e., In former times, people would give their hearts when they gave their hands to something, but in our dedacent present age the joining of hands no longer has that spiritual sense.   49 **chuck** (A term of endearment.)   51 **salt . . . rheum** distressful head cold or watering of the eyes   59 **charmer** sorceress   61 **amiable** desirable   64 **hold her** regard her as   65 **fancies** loves.   67 **her** i.e., to my wife.   68 **like . . . eye** as precious as eyesight.   69 **perdition** loss, damnation   71 **web** fabric, weaving   72–3 **A sibyl . . . compasses** a prophetess, who was two hundred years old.. (*Compasses* means "annual circlings.")   74 **prophetic fury** frenzy of prophetic inspiration.   **work** embroidered pattern   76 **mummy** medicinal or magical preparation drained from mummified bodies   77 **Conserved of** prepared or preserved out of

**OTHELLO**
Most veritable. Therefore look to't well.
**DESDEMONA**
Then would to God that I had never seen't!
**OTHELLO** Ha? Wherefore?
**DESDEMONA**
Why do you speak so startingly and rash? 81
**OTHELLO**
Is't lost? Is't gone? Speak, is't out o'th' way? 82
**DESDEMONA** Heaven bless us!
**OTHELLO** Say you?
**DESDEMONA**
It is not lost; but what an if it were? 85
**OTHELLO** How?
**DESDEMONA**
I say it is not lost.
**OTHELLO** Fetch't, let me see't.
**DESDEMONA**
Why, so I can, sir, but I will not now.
This is a trick to put me from my suit.
Pray you, let Cassio be received again.
**OTHELLO**
Fetch me the handkerchief! My mind misgives.
**DESDEMONA** Come, come,
You'll never meet a more sufficient man. 93
**OTHELLO**
The handkerchief!
**DESDEMONA** I pray, talk me of Cassio. 94
**OTHELLO**
The handkerchief!
**DESDEMONA** A man that all his time 95
Hath founded his good fortunes on your love, 96
Shared dangers with you—
**OTHELLO** The handkerchief!
**DESDEMONA** I'faith, you are to blame.
**OTHELLO** Zounds! *Exit Othello.*
**EMILIA** Is not this man jealous?
**DESDEMONA** I ne'er saw this before.
Sure, there's some wonder in this handkerchief.
I am most unhappy in the loss of it. 104
**EMILIA**
'Tis not a year or two shows us a man. 105
They are all but stomachs, and we all but food; 106
They eat us hungerly, and when they are full 107
They belch us.

*Enter Iago and Cassio.*

Look you, Cassio and my husband.
**IAGO** [*to Cassio*]
There is no other way; 'tis she must do't.
And, lo, the happiness! Go and importune her. 110

**DESDEMONA**
How now, good Cassio? What's the news with you?
**CASSIO**
Madam, my former suit. I do beseech you
That by your virtuous means I may again 113
Exist and be a member of his love
Whom I, with all the office of my heart, 115
Entirely honor. I would not be delayed.
If my offense be of such mortal kind 117
That nor my service past, nor present sorrows, 118
Nor purposed merit in futurity
Can ransom me into his love again,
But to know so must be my benefit; 121
So shall I clothe me in a forced content,
And shut myself up in some other course, 123
To fortune's alms.
**DESDEMONA** Alas, thrice-gentle Cassio, 124
My advocation is not now in tune. 125
My lord is not my lord; nor should I know him,
Were he in favor as in humor altered. 127
So help me every spirit sanctified 128
As I have spoken for you all my best
And stood within the blank of his displeasure 130
For my free speech! You must awhile be patient. 131
What I can do I will, and more I will
Than for myself I dare. Let that suffice you.
**IAGO**
Is my lord angry?
**EMILIA** He went hence but now,
And certainly in strange unquietness.
**IAGO**
Can he be angry? I have seen the cannon
When it hath blown his ranks into the air, 137
And like the devil from his very arm 138
Puffed his own brother—and is he angry? 139
Something of moment then. I will go meet him. 140
There's matter in't indeed, if he be angry.
**DESDEMONA**
I prithee, do so. *Exit* [*Iago*].
Something, sure, of state, 142
Either from Venice, or some unhatched practice 143
Made demonstrable here in Cyprus to him, 144
Hath puddled his clear spirit; and in such cases 145
Men's natures wrangle with inferior things,
Though great ones are their object. 'Tis even so;
For let our finger ache, and it indues 148
Our other, healthful members even to a sense
Of pain. Nay, we must think men are not gods, 150

**113 virtuous** (1) efficacious (2) morally good **115 office** loyal service **117 mortal** fatal **118 nor...nor** neither...nor **121 But...benefit** simply to know that my case is hopeless will have to content me (and will be better than uncertainty) **123 shut...in** commit myself to **124 To fortune's alms** throwing myself on the mercy of fortune. **125 advocation** advocacy **127 favor** appearance. **humor** mood **128 So...sanctified** So help me all the heavenly host **130 within the blank** within point-blank range. (The *blank* is the center of the target.) **131 free** frank **137 ranks** ranks of soldiers **138–9 And...brother** i.e., and I have seen the devilish cannon blow up his right-hand man standing at his side, a solider as dear to Othello as his own brother **140 of moment** momentous **142 of state** concerning state affairs **143 unhatched practice** as yet unexecuted or undiscovered plot **144 Made demonstrable** revealed, uncovered **145 puddled** muddied **148 indues** induces, brings to the same condition **150 think** consider that

**81 startingly and rash** disjointedly and impetuously, excitedly. **82 out o'th' way** lost, misplaced. **85 an if** if **93 sufficient** able, complete **94 talk** talk to **95–6 A man...love** A man who throughout his career has relied on your favor for his advancement **104 unhappy** (1) unfortunate (2) sad **105 'Tis...man** A year or two is not enough time for us women to know what men really are. **106 but** nothing but **107 hungerly** hungrily **110 the happiness** in happy time, fortunately met.

Nor of them look for such observancy                          151
As fits the bridal. Beshrew me much, Emilia,                  152
I was, unhandsome warrior as I am,                            153
Arraigning his unkindness with my soul;                       154
But now I find I had suborned the witness,                    155
And he's indicted falsely.

EMILIA                               Pray heaven it be
State matters, as you think, and no conception
Nor no jealous toy concerning you.                            158

DESDEMONA
Alas the day! I never gave him cause.

EMILIA
But jealous souls will not be answered so;
They are not ever jealous for the cause,
But jealous for they're jealous. It is a monster             162
Begot upon itself, born on itself.                            163

DESDEMONA
Heaven keep that monster from Othello's mind!

EMILIA    Lady, amen.

DESDEMONA
I will go seek him. Cassio, walk hereabout.
If I do find him fit, I'll move your suit
And seek to effect it to my uttermost.

CASSIO
I humbly thank Your Ladyship.
*Exit [Desdemona with Emilia].*

*Enter Bianca.*

BIANCA
Save you, friend Cassio!

CASSIO                               What make you from home?   170
How is't with you, my most fair Bianca?
I' faith, sweet love, I was coming to your house.

BIANCA
And I was going to your lodging, Cassio.
What, keep a week away? Seven days and nights?
Eightscore-eight hours? And lovers' absent hours             175
More tedious than the dial eightscore times?                 176
Oh, weary reck'ning!

CASSIO                               Pardon me, Bianca.
I have this while with leaden thoughts been pressed;
But I shall, in a more continuate time,                       179
Strike off this score of absence. Sweet Bianca,              180
                [*giving her Desdemona's handkerchief*]
Take me this work out.

BIANCA                               Oh, Cassio, whence came this?  181
This is some token from a newer friend.                       182
To the felt absence now I feel a cause.                       183
Is't come to this? Well, well.

CASSIO                               Go to, woman!
Throw your vile guesses in the devil's teeth,

From whence you have them. You are jealous now
That this is from some mistress, some remembrance.
No, by my faith, Bianca.

BIANCA                               Why, whose is it?

CASSIO
I know not, neither. I found it in my chamber.
I like the work well. Ere it be demanded—                     190
As like enough it will—I would have it copied.                191
Take it and do't, and leave me for this time.

BIANCA    Leave you? Wherefore?

CASSIO
I do attend here on the General,
And think it no addition, nor my wish,                        195
To have him see me womaned.

BIANCA    Why, I pray you?

CASSIO    Not that I love you not.

BIANCA    But that you do not love me.
I pray you, bring me on the way a little,                     200
And say if I shall see you soon at night.

CASSIO
'Tis but a little way that I can bring you,
For I attend here; but I'll see you soon.

BIANCA
'Tis very good. I must be circumstanced.                      204
                                *Exeunt omnes.*

❖

# 4.1

*Enter Othello and Iago.*

IAGO
Will you think so?

OTHELLO                               Think so, Iago?

IAGO                                                    What,
To kiss in private?

OTHELLO                               An unauthorized kiss!

IAGO
Or to be naked with her friend in bed
An hour or more, not meaning any harm?

OTHELLO
Naked in bed, Iago, and not mean harm?
It is hypocrisy against the devil.                            6
They that mean virtuously and yet do so,                      7
The devil their virtue tempts, and they tempt heaven.         8

IAGO
If they do nothing, 'tis a venial slip.                       9
But if I give my wife a handkerchief—

OTHELLO    What then?

IAGO
Why then, 'tis hers, my lord, and being hers,
She may, I think, bestow't on any man.

OTHELLO
She is protectress of her honor too.
May she give that?

---

**151–2 Nor . . . bridal** nor must we expect of most people the courteous attentiveness that one hopes to find among newly-weds.    **152 Beshrew me** (A mild curse.)    **153 unhandsome** insufficient, unskillful    **154 with** before the bar of    **155 suborned the witness** induced the witness to give false testimony    **158 toy** fancy    **162 for** because    **163 Begot upon itself** generated solely from itself    **170 Save** God save.    **make do**    **175 Eight-score-eight** one hundred sixty-eight, the number of hours in a week    **176 the dial** a complete revolution of the clock    **179 continuate** uninterrupted    **180 Strike . . . score** settle this account    **181 Take . . . out** copy this embroidery for me.    **182 friend** mistress.    **183 To . . . cause** Now I understand why you've been away so long.

**190 demanded** inquired for    **191 like** likely    **195 addition** i.e., addition to my reputation    **200 bring** accompany    **204 be circumstanced** be governed by circumstance, yield to your conditions.
**4.1. Location: Before the citadel.**
**6 It is . . . devil** That would be hypocrisy enough to daunt the devil himself.    **7–8 They . . . heaven** Those who are virtuously inclined and yet recklessly disregard the importance of *appearing* virtuous are laying themselves open to the devil's insinuations and are even tempting heaven itself to behave as if appearances didn't matter.    **9 venial** pardonable

IAGO
    Her honor is an essence that's not seen;
    They have it very oft that have it not.                                      17
    But, for the handkerchief—
OTHELLO
    By heaven, I would most gladly have forgot it.
    Thou said'st—Oh, it comes o'er my memory
    As doth the raven o'er the infectious house,                                 21
    Boding to all—he had my handkerchief.
IAGO
    Ay, what of that?
OTHELLO                        That's not so good now.
IAGO                                              What
    If I had said I had seen him do you wrong?
    Or heard him say—as knaves be such abroad,                                   25
    Who having, by their own importunate suit,                                   26
    Or voluntary dotage of some mistress,                                        27
    Convincèd or supplied them, cannot choose                                    28
    But they must blab—
OTHELLO                        Hath he said anything?                            29
IAGO
    He hath, my lord; but, be you well assured,
    No more than he'll unswear.
OTHELLO                        What hath he said?
IAGO
    Faith, that he did—I know not what he did.
OTHELLO    What? What?
IAGO
    Lie—
OTHELLO    With her?
IAGO                        With her, on her; what you will.
OTHELLO    Lie with her? Lie on her? We say "lie on her"
    when they belie her. Lie with her? Zounds, that's ful-             36
    some.—Handkerchief—confessions—handkerchief!                       37
    —To confess and be hanged for his labor—first to be               38
    hanged and then to confess.—I tremble at it. Nature               39
    would not invest herself in such shadowing passion                40
    without some instruction. It is not words that shakes             41
    me thus. Pish! Noses, ears, and lips.—Is't possible?
    —Confess—handkerchief!—O devil!
                                        *Falls in a trance.*
IAGO    Work on,
    My medicine, work! Thus credulous fools are caught,
    And many worthy and chaste dames even thus,
    All guiltless, meet reproach.—What, ho! My lord!
    My lord, I say! Othello!

                        *Enter Cassio.*

                        How now, Cassio?

CASSIO    What's the matter?
IAGO
    My lord is fall'n into an epilepsy.
    This is his second fit. He had one yesterday.
CASSIO
    Rub him about the temples.
IAGO                                        No, forbear.
    The lethargy must have his quiet course.                                     53
    If not, he foams at mouth, and by and by
    Breaks out to savage madness. Look, he stirs.
    Do you withdraw yourself a little while.
    He will recover straight. When he is gone,                                   57
    I would on great occasion speak with you.                                    58
                                        [*Exit Cassio.*]
    How is it, General? Have you not hurt your head?
OTHELLO
    Dost thou mock me?
IAGO                        I mock you not, by heaven.                            60
    Would you would bear your fortune like a man!
OTHELLO
    A hornèd man's a monster and a beast.
IAGO
    There's many a beast then in a populous city,                                63
    And many a civil monster.                                                    64
OTHELLO    Did he confess it?
IAGO    Good sir, be a man.
    Think every bearded fellow that's but yoked                                  67
    May draw with you. There's millions now alive                                68
    That nightly lie in those unproper beds                                      69
    Which they dare swear peculiar. Your case is better.                         70
    Oh, 'tis the spite of hell, the fiend's arch-mock,                           71
    To lip a wanton in a secure couch                                            72
    And to suppose her chaste! No, let me know,
    And knowing what I am, I know what she shall be.                             74
OTHELLO    Oh, thou art wise. 'Tis certain.
IAGO    Stand you awhile apart;
    Confine yourself but in a patient list.                                      77
    Whilst you were here o'erwhelmèd with your grief—
    A passion most unsuiting such a man—
    Cassio came hither. I shifted him away,                                      80
    And laid good 'scuse upon your ecstasy,                                      81
    Bade him anon return and here speak with me,
    The which he promised. Do but encave yourself                                83
    And mark the fleers, the gibes, and notable scorns                           84
    That dwell in every region of his face;
    For I will make him tell the tale anew,
    Where, how, how oft, how long ago, and when
    He hath and is again to cope your wife.                                      88

---

**17 They have it** i.e., They enjoy a reputation for it    **21 raven ... house** (Allusion to the belief that the raven hovered over a house of sickness or infection, such as one visited by the plague.)    **25–9 as ... blab—** since there are rascals enough who, having seduced a woman either through their own importunity or through the woman's willing infatuation, cannot keep quiet about it—    **36 belie** slander    **36–7 fulsome** foul.    **38–9 first ... to confess** (Othello reverses the proverbial *confess and be hanged*; Cassio is to be given no time to confess before he dies.)    **39–41 Nature ... instruction** i.e., Without some foundation in fact, nature would not have dressed herself in such an overwhelming passion that comes over me now and fills my mind with images, or in such a lifelike fantasy as Cassio had in his dream of lying with Desdemona.    **41 words** mere words

**53 lethargy** trance.    **his** its    **57 straight** immediately.    **58 on great occasion** on a matter of great importance    **60 mock me** (Othello takes Iago's question about hurting his head to be a mocking reference to the cuckold's horns.)    **63 There's ... city** i.e., One finds cuckolds wherever people dwell    **64 civil** i.e., dwelling in a city    **67 yoked** (1) married (2) put into the yoke of infamy and cuckoldry    **68 draw with you** pull as you do, like oxen who are yoked, i.e., share your fate as cuckold.    **69 unproper** not exclusively their own    **70 Which ... peculiar** which they are fatuous enough to insist are exclusively theirs in marriage.    **better** i.e., because you know the truth.    **71 arch-mock** supreme mockery of married men    **72 lip** kiss.    **secure** free from suspicion    **74 And ... shall be** and, knowing myself to be a cuckold, I'll know for certain that she's a whore.    **77 in ... list** within the bounds of patience.    **80–1 I shifted ... ecstasy** I got him out of the way, using your fit as my excuse for doing so    **83 encave** conceal    **84 fleers** sneers    **88 cope** encounter with, have sex with

I say, but mark his gesture. Marry, patience!    89
Or I shall say you're all-in-all in spleen,    90
And nothing of a man.

OTHELLO                    Dost thou hear, Iago?
I will be found most cunning in my patience;
But—dost thou hear?—most bloody.

IAGO                              That's not amiss;
But yet keep time in all. Will you withdraw?    94
                    [*Othello stands apart.*]
Now will I question Cassio of Bianca,
A huswife that by selling her desires    96
Buys herself bread and clothes. It is a creature
That dotes on Cassio—as 'tis the strumpet's plague
To beguile many and be beguiled by one.
He, when he hears of her, cannot restrain    100
From the excess of laughter. Here he comes.

*Enter Cassio.*

As he shall smile, Othello shall go mad;
And his unbookish jealousy must conster    103
Poor Cassio's smiles, gestures, and light behaviors
Quite in the wrong.—How do you now, Lieutenant?

CASSIO
The worser that you give me the addition    106
Whose want even kills me.    107

IAGO
Ply Desdemona well and you are sure on't.
[*Speaking lower*] Now, if this suit lay in Bianca's power,
How quickly should you speed!

CASSIO [*laughing*]    Alas, poor caitiff!    111

OTHELLO [*aside*]    Look how he laughs already!

IAGO
I never knew a woman love man so.

CASSIO
Alas, poor rogue! I think, i'faith, she loves me.

OTHELLO [*aside*]
Now he denies it faintly, and laughs it out.

IAGO
Do you hear, Cassio?

OTHELLO [*aside*]        Now he importunes him
To tell it o'er. Go to! Well said, well said.    117

IAGO
She gives it out that you shall marry her.    118
Do you intend it?

CASSIO    Ha, ha, ha!

OTHELLO [*aside*]
Do you triumph, Roman? Do you triumph?    121

CASSIO    I marry her? What? A customer? Prithee, bear    122
some charity to my wit; do not think it so unwhole-    123
some. Ha, ha, ha!

OTHELLO [*aside*]    So, so, so, so! They laugh that win.    125

IAGO    Faith, the cry goes that you shall marry her.    126

CASSIO    Prithee, say true.

IAGO    I am a very villain else.    128

OTHELLO [*aside*]    Have you scored me? Well.    129

CASSIO    This is the monkey's own giving out. She is    130
persuaded I will marry her out of her own love and
flattery, not out of my promise.    132

OTHELLO [*aside*]    Iago beckons me. Now he begins the    133
story.

CASSIO    She was here even now; she haunts me in every
place. I was the other day talking on the seabank with    136
certain Venetians, and thither comes the bauble, and,    137
by this hand, she falls me thus about my neck—    138
                    [*He embraces Iago.*]

OTHELLO [*aside*]    Crying, "Oh, dear Cassio!" as it were; his
gesture imports it.

CASSIO    So hangs and lolls and weeps upon me, so
shakes and pulls me. Ha, ha, ha!

OTHELLO [*aside*]    Now he tells how she plucked him to my
chamber. Oh, I see that nose of yours, but not that dog    144
I shall throw it to.    145

CASSIO    Well, I must leave her company.

IAGO    Before me, look where she comes.    147

*Enter Bianca [with Desdemona's handkerchief].*

CASSIO    'Tis such another fitchew! Marry, a perfumed    148
one.—What do you mean by this haunting of me?

BIANCA    Let the devil and his dam haunt you! What did    150
you mean by that same handkerchief you gave me
even now? I was a fine fool to take it. I must take out    152
the work? A likely piece of work, that you should find    153
it in your chamber and know not who left it there!
This is some minx's token, and I must take out the
work? There; give it your hobby-horse. [*She gives him    156
the handkerchief.*] Wheresoever you had it, I'll take out
no work on't.

CASSIO    How now, my sweet Bianca? How now? How
now?

OTHELLO [*aside*]    By heaven, that should be my hand-    161
kerchief!

BIANCA    If you'll come to supper tonight, you may; if
you will not, come when you are next prepared for.    164
                            *Exit.*

IAGO    After her, after her.

CASSIO    Faith, I must. She'll rail in the streets else.

IAGO    Will you sup there?

CASSIO    Faith, I intend so.

IAGO    Well, I may chance to see you, for I would very
fain speak with you.    170

---

**89 but** only    **90 all-in-all in spleen** utterly governed by passionate
impulses    **94 keep time** keep yourself steady (as in music)    **96 huswife** hussy    **100 restrain** refrain    **103 his unbookish** Othello's unin-
structed.    **conster** construe    **106 addition** title    **107 Whose want** the
lack of which    **111 caitiff** wretch.    **117 Go to** (An expression of
remonstrance.)    **Well said** Well done. (Sarcastic.)    **118 gives it out**
spreads the word    **121 Roman** (The Romans were noted for their *triumphs* or triumphal processions.)    **122 A customer?** Who, I, the
whore's customer? (Or, *customer* could mean "prostitute.")    **122–3
bear . . . wit** be more charitable to my judgment

**125 They . . . win** i.e., They that laugh last laugh best.
**126 cry** rumor    **128 I . . . else** Call me a complete rogue if I'm not telling the truth.    **129 scored me** scored off me sexually, branded
me.    **130 giving out** telling.    **132 flattery** self-flattery, self-deception    **133 beckons** signals to    **136 seabank** seashore    **137 bauble**
plaything    **138 by this hand** I make my vow    **144–5 not . . . to**
(Othello imagines himself cutting off Cassio's nose and throwing it to
a dog.)    **147 Before me** i.e., On my soul    **148 'Tis . . . fitchew!** What
a whore she is! Just like all the others. (*Fitchew* or "polecat" was a
common term of contempt for a courtesan or prostitute.)    **150 dam**
mother    **152 take out** copy    **153 A likely . . . work** A fine story
**156 hobby-horse** harlot.    **161 should be** must be    **164 when . . . for**
when I'm ready for you (i.e., never).    **170 fain** gladly

CASSIO   Prithee, come. Will you?

IAGO   Go to. Say no more.                    [*Exit Cassio.*] 172

OTHELLO [*advancing*]   How shall I murder him, Iago?

IAGO   Did you perceive how he laughed at his vice?

OTHELLO   Oh, Iago!

IAGO   And did you see the handkerchief?

OTHELLO   Was that mine?

IAGO   Yours, by this hand. And to see how he prizes the foolish woman your wife! She gave it him, and he hath given it his whore.

OTHELLO   I would have him nine years a-killing. A fine woman! A fair woman! A sweet woman!

IAGO   Nay, you must forget that.

OTHELLO   Ay, let her rot and perish, and be damned tonight, for she shall not live. No, my heart is turned to stone; I strike it, and it hurts my hand. Oh, the world hath not a sweeter creature! She might lie by an emperor's side and command him tasks.

IAGO   Nay, that's not your way.                        189

OTHELLO   Hang her! I do but say what she is. So delicate with her needle! An admirable musician! Oh, she will sing the savageness out of a bear. Of so high and plenteous wit and invention!                        193

IAGO   She's the worse for all this.

OTHELLO   Oh, a thousand, a thousand times! And then, of so gentle a condition!                        196

IAGO   Ay, too gentle.                        197

OTHELLO   Nay, that's certain. But yet the pity of it, Iago! Oh, Iago, the pity of it, Iago!

IAGO   If you are so fond over her iniquity, give her patent 200 to offend, for if it touch not you it comes near nobody.

OTHELLO   I will chop her into messes. Cuckold me?    202

IAGO   Oh, 'tis foul in her.

OTHELLO   With mine officer?

IAGO   That's fouler.

OTHELLO   Get me some poison, Iago, this night. I'll not expostulate with her, lest her body and beauty unpro-   207 vide my mind again. This night, Iago.                        208

IAGO   Do it not with poison. Strangle her in her bed, even the bed she hath contaminated.

OTHELLO   Good, good! The justice of it pleases. Very good.

IAGO   And for Cassio, let me be his undertaker. You 212 shall hear more by midnight.

OTHELLO   Excellent good. [*A trumpet within.*] What trumpet is that same?

IAGO   I warrant, something from Venice.

*Enter Lodovico, Desdemona, and attendants.*

'Tis Lodovico. This comes from the Duke.
See, your wife's with him.

LODOVICO   God save you, worthy General!

OTHELLO                                   With all my heart, sir. 218

LODOVICO [*giving him a letter*]   The Duke and the senators of Venice greet you.

OTHELLO   I kiss the instrument of their pleasures.
                        [*He opens the letter, and reads.*]

DESDEMONA   And what's the news, good cousin Lodovico?

IAGO   I am very glad to see you, signor.
Welcome to Cyprus.

LODOVICO   I thank you. How does Lieutenant Cassio?

IAGO   Lives, sir.

DESDEMONA   Cousin, there's fall'n between him and my lord An unkind breach; but you shall make all well.    227

OTHELLO   Are you sure of that?

DESDEMONA   My lord?

OTHELLO [*reads*]   "This fail you not to do, as you will—"

LODOVICO   He did not call; he's busy in the paper.
Is there division twixt my lord and Cassio?

DESDEMONA   A most unhappy one. I would do much T'atone them, for the love I bear to Cassio.    234

OTHELLO   Fire and brimstone!

DESDEMONA   My lord?

OTHELLO   Are you wise?

DESDEMONA   What, is he angry?

LODOVICO                         Maybe the letter moved him; For, as I think, they do command him home, Deputing Cassio in his government.    240

DESDEMONA   By my troth, I am glad on't.    241

OTHELLO   Indeed?

DESDEMONA   My lord?

OTHELLO   I am glad to see you mad.    244

DESDEMONA   Why, sweet Othello—

OTHELLO [*striking her*]   Devil!

DESDEMONA   I have not deserved this.

LODOVICO   My lord, this would not be believed in Venice, Though I should swear I saw't. 'Tis very much.    249 Make her amends; she weeps.

OTHELLO                         Oh, devil, devil!
If that the earth could teem with woman's tears,    251 Each drop she falls would prove a crocodile.    252 Out of my sight!

DESDEMONA                         I will not stay to offend you. [*Going.*]

**LODOVICO**  Truly, an obedient lady.
I do beseech Your Lordship, call her back.

**OTHELLO** [*calling*]  Mistress!

**DESDEMONA** [*returning*]  My lord?

**OTHELLO**  What would you with her, sir?  258

**LODOVICO**  Who, I, my lord?

**OTHELLO**
Ay, you did wish that I would make her turn.  260
Sir, she can turn, and turn, and yet go on  261
And turn again; and she can weep, sir, weep;
And she's obedient, as you say, obedient,  263
Very obedient.—Proceed you in your tears.—
Concerning this, sir—Oh, well-painted passion!—  265
I am commanded home.—Get you away;
I'll send for you anon.—Sir, I obey the mandate
And will return to Venice.—Hence, avaunt!
                              [*Exit Desdemona.*]
Cassio shall have my place. And, sir, tonight
I do entreat that we may sup together.
You are welcome, sir, to Cyprus.—Goats and
    monkeys!                              *Exit.* 271

**LODOVICO**
Is this the noble Moor whom our full Senate
Call all in all sufficient? Is this the nature
Whom passion could not shake? Whose solid virtue
The shot of accident nor dart of chance
Could neither graze nor pierce?

**IAGO**                              He is much changed.

**LODOVICO**
Are his wits safe? Is he not light of brain?

**IAGO**
He's that he is. I may not breathe my censure  278
What he might be. If what he might he is not,  279
I would to heaven he were!

**LODOVICO**                    What, strike his wife?  280

**IAGO**
Faith, that was not so well; yet would I knew  281
That stroke would prove the worst!

**LODOVICO**                              Is it his use?  282
Or did the letters work upon his blood  283
And new-create his fault?

**IAGO**                    Alas, alas!
It is not honesty in me to speak
What I have seen and known. You shall observe him,
And his own courses will denote him so  287
That I may save my speech. Do but go after,
And mark how he continues.

**LODOVICO**
I am sorry that I am deceived in him.          *Exeunt.*

❧

258 **What would you** What do you wish. (Othello implies that Desdemona is pliant and will do a *turn* sexually with any man.)  260 **turn** return  261 **turn** do a sexual turn  263 **obedient** (With much the same sexual connotation as *turn* in lines 260–2.)  265 **passion** i.e., grief.  271 **Goats and monkeys** (Symbols of animalistic lust. See 3.3.419.)  278–80 **I may . . . were!** i.e., I dare not venture an opinion as to whether he's of unsound mind, as you suggest, but, if he isn't, then it might be better to wish he were in fact insane, since only that could excuse his wild behavior!  281 **would I knew** I wish I could be sure  282 **use** custom.  283 **blood** passions  287 **courses will denote** actions will reveal

# 4.2

*Enter Othello and Emilia.*

**OTHELLO**  You have seen nothing, then?

**EMILIA**
Nor ever heard, nor ever did suspect.

**OTHELLO**
Yes, you have seen Cassio and she together.

**EMILIA**
But then I saw no harm, and then I heard
Each syllable that breath made up between them.  5

**OTHELLO**  What, did they never whisper?

**EMILIA**  Never, my lord.

**OTHELLO**  Nor send you out o'th' way?

**EMILIA**  Never.

**OTHELLO**
To fetch her fan, her gloves, her mask, nor nothing?

**EMILIA**  Never, my lord.

**OTHELLO**  That's strange.

**EMILIA**
I durst, my lord, to wager she is honest,
Lay down my soul at stake. If you think other,  14
Remove your thought; it doth abuse your bosom.  15
If any wretch have put this in your head,
Let heaven requite it with the serpent's curse!  17
For if she be not honest, chaste, and true,
There's no man happy; the purest of their wives
Is foul as slander.

**OTHELLO**          Bid her come hither. Go.
                              *Exit Emilia.*
She says enough; yet she's a simple bawd  21
That cannot say as much. This is a subtle whore,  22
A closet lock and key of villainous secrets.  23
And yet she'll kneel and pray; I have seen her do't.

*Enter Desdemona and Emilia.*

**DESDEMONA**  My lord, what is your will?

**OTHELLO**  Pray you, chuck, come hither.  26

**DESDEMONA**
What is your pleasure?

**OTHELLO**          Let me see your eyes.
Look in my face.

**DESDEMONA**          What horrible fancy's this?

**OTHELLO** [*to Emilia*]  Some of your function, mistress.  29
Leave procreants alone and shut the door;  30
Cough or cry "hem" if anybody come.
Your mystery, your mystery! Nay, dispatch.  32
                              *Exit Emilia.*

**DESDEMONA** [*kneeling*]
Upon my knees, what doth your speech import?

4.2. **Location: The citadel.**
5 **Each . . . them** every syllable they uttered.  14 **at stake** as the wager.  15 **abuse your bosom** deceive your breast, your heart.  17 **the serpent's curse** the curse pronounced by God on the serpent for deceiving Eve, just as some man has done to Othello and Desdemona. (See Genesis 3:14.)  21–2 **she's . . . much** i.e., any procuress or go-between who couldn't make up as plausible a story as Emilia's would have to be pretty stupid.  22 **This** i.e., Desdemona  23 **closet lock and key** i.e., concealer  26 **chuck** (A term of endearment.)  29 **Some . . . function** i.e., Practice your chosen profession, that of bawd (by guarding the door)  30 **procreants** mating couples  32 **mystery** trade, occupation

     I understand a fury in your words,
     But not the words.

OTHELLO
     Why, what art thou?

DESDEMONA           Your wife, my lord, your true
     And loyal wife.

OTHELLO          Come, swear it, damn thyself,
     Lest, being like one of heaven, the devils themselves    38
     Should fear to seize thee. Therefore be double
         damned:
     Swear thou art honest.

DESDEMONA          Heaven doth truly know it.

OTHELLO
     Heaven truly knows that thou art false as hell.

DESDEMONA
     To whom, my lord? With whom? How am I false?

OTHELLO [weeping]
     Ah, Desdemon! Away, away, away!

DESDEMONA
     Alas the heavy day! Why do you weep?
     Am I the motive of these tears, my lord?    45
     If haply you my father do suspect    46
     An instrument of this your calling back,
     Lay not your blame on me. If you have lost him,
     I have lost him too.

OTHELLO          Had it pleased God
     To try me with affliction, had He rained
     All kinds of sores and shames on my bare head,
     Steeped me in poverty to the very lips,
     Given to captivity me and my utmost hopes,
     I should have found in some place of my soul
     A drop of patience. But, alas, to make me
     A fixèd figure for the time of scorn    56
     To point his slow and moving finger at!    57
     Yet could I bear that too, well, very well.
     But there where I have garnered up my heart,    59
     Where either I must live or bear no life,    60
     The fountain from the which my current runs    61
     Or else dries up—to be discarded thence!
     Or keep it as a cistern for foul toads    63
     To knot and gender in! Turn thy complexion there,    64
     Patience, thou young and rose-lipped cherubin—    65
     Ay, there look grim as hell!    66

DESDEMONA
     I hope my noble lord esteems me honest.    67

OTHELLO
     Oh, ay, as summer flies are in the shambles,    68
     That quicken even with blowing. O thou weed,    69
     Who art so lovely fair and smell'st so sweet
     That the sense aches at thee, would thou hadst ne'er
     been born!

DESDEMONA
     Alas, what ignorant sin have I committed?    72

OTHELLO
     Was this fair paper, this most goodly book,    73
     Made to write "whore" upon? What committed?
     Committed? Oh, thou public commoner!    75
     I should make very forges of my cheeks,
     That would to cinders burn up modesty,
     Did I but speak thy deeds. What committed?
     Heaven stops the nose at it and the moon winks;    79
     The bawdy wind, that kisses all it meets,    80
     Is hushed within the hollow mine of earth    81
     And will not hear't. What committed?
     Impudent strumpet!

DESDEMONA          By heaven, you do me wrong.

OTHELLO
     Are not you a strumpet?

DESDEMONA    No, as I am a Christian.
     If to preserve this vessel for my lord    86
     From any other foul unlawful touch
     Be not to be a strumpet, I am none.

OTHELLO    What, not a whore?

DESDEMONA    No, as I shall be saved.

OTHELLO    Is't possible?

DESDEMONA
     Oh, heaven forgive us!

OTHELLO          I cry you mercy, then.    92
     I took you for that cunning whore of Venice
     That married with Othello. [Calling out] You, mistress,
     That have the office opposite to Saint Peter    95
     And keep the gate of hell!

         Enter Emilia.

              You, you, ay, you!
     We have done our course. There's money for your
         pains.              [He gives money.]    97
     I pray you, turn the key and keep our counsel.    Exit.

EMILIA
     Alas, what does this gentleman conceive?    99
     How do you, madam? How do you, my good lady?

DESDEMONA    Faith, half asleep.    101

EMILIA
     Good madam, what's the matter with my lord?

DESDEMONA    With who?

EMILIA    Why, with my lord, madam.

DESDEMONA
     Who is thy lord?

EMILIA          He that is yours, sweet lady.

DESDEMONA
     I have none. Do not talk to me, Emilia.
     I cannot weep, nor answers have I none
     But what should go by water. Prithee, tonight    108

---

**38 being . . . heaven** looking like an angel    **45 motive** cause    **46 haply** perhaps    **56–7 A fixèd . . . finger at** a figure of ridicule to be pointed at scornfully for all of eternity by the slowly moving finger of Time. **59 garnered** stored    **60 bear no life** die    **61 fountain** spring    **63 cistern** cesspool    **64 To . . . gender in** to couple sexually and conceive in. **64–6 Turn . . . hell!** Direct your gaze there, Patience, and your youthful and rosy cherubic countenance will turn grim and pale at this hellish spectacle!    **67 honest** chaste.    **68 shambles** slaughterhouse **69 That . . . blowing** that come to life with the puffing up of the rotten meat on which the flies and their maggots are breeding.

**72 ignorant sin** sin in ignorance    **73 this fair . . . book** i.e., Desdemona's beautiful countenance    **75 commoner** prostitute. **79 winks** closes her eyes. (The moon symbolizes chastity.)    **80 bawdy** kissing one and all    **81 mine** cave (where the winds were thought to dwell)    **86 vessel** body    **92 cry you mercy** beg your pardon. (Sarcastic.)    **95 Saint Peter** (who keeps the gate of heaven)    **97 course** business. (With an indecent suggestion of "trick," turn at sex.)    **99 conceive** suppose, think.    **101 half asleep** i.e., dazed.    **108 go by water** be conveyed by tears.

Lay on my bed my wedding sheets, remember;
And call thy husband hither.
EMILIA   Here's a change indeed!                                    *Exit.*
DESDEMONA
'Tis meet I should be used so, very meet.                           112
How have I been behaved, that he might stick                        113
The small'st opinion on my least misuse?                            114

　　　　*Enter Iago and Emilia.*

IAGO
What is your pleasure, madam? How is't with you?
DESDEMONA
I cannot tell. Those that do teach young babes
Do it with gentle means and easy tasks.
He might have chid me so, for, in good faith,
I am a child to chiding.
IAGO   What is the matter, lady?
EMILIA
Alas, Iago, my lord hath so bewhored her,                           121
Thrown such despite and heavy terms upon her,
That true hearts cannot bear it.
DESDEMONA   Am I that name, Iago?
IAGO   What name, fair lady?
DESDEMONA
Such as she said my lord did say I was.
EMILIA
He called her whore. A beggar in his drink
Could not have laid such terms upon his callet.                     128
IAGO   Why did he so?
DESDEMONA [*weeping*]
I do not know. I am sure I am none such.
IAGO   Do not weep, do not weep. Alas the day!
EMILIA
Hath she forsook so many noble matches,
Her father and her country and her friends,
To be called whore? Would it not make one weep?
DESDEMONA
It is my wretched fortune.
IAGO                         Beshrew him for't!                      135
How comes this trick upon him?
DESDEMONA                    Nay, heaven doth know.  136
EMILIA
I will be hanged if some eternal villain,                           137
Some busy and insinuating rogue,                                    138
Some cogging, cozening slave, to get some office,                   139
Have not devised this slander. I will be hanged else.               140
IAGO
Fie, there is no such man. It is impossible.
DESDEMONA
If any such there be, heaven pardon him!
EMILIA
A halter pardon him! And hell gnaw his bones!                       143

Why should he call her whore? Who keeps her
　　company?
What place? What time? What form? What
　　likelihood?                                                      145
The Moor's abused by some most villainous knave,
Some base notorious knave, some scurvy fellow.
Oh, heaven, that such companions thou'dst unfold,                   148
And put in every honest hand a whip
To lash the rascals naked through the world
Even from the east to th' west!
IAGO                         Speak within door.                     151
EMILIA
Oh, fie upon them! Some such squire he was                          152
That turned your wit the seamy side without                         153
And made you to suspect me with the Moor.
IAGO
You are a fool. Go to.
DESDEMONA               Oh, God, Iago,                               155
What shall I do to win my lord again?
Good friend, go to him; for, by this light of heaven,
I know not how I lost him. Here I kneel.   [*She kneels.*]
If e'er my will did trespass 'gainst his love,
Either in discourse of thought or actual deed,                      160
Or that mine eyes, mine ears, or any sense                          161
Delighted them in any other form;                                   162
Or that I do not yet, and ever did,                                 163
And ever will—though he do shake me off
To beggarly divorcement—love him dearly,
Comfort forswear me! Unkindness may do much,                        166
And his unkindness may defeat my life,                              167
But never taint my love. I cannot say "whore."
It does abhor me now I speak the word;                              169
To do the act that might the addition earn                          170
Not the world's mass of vanity could make me.                       171
　　　　　　　　　　　　　　　　　　　　　　　[*She rises.*]
IAGO
I pray you, be content. 'Tis but his humor.                         172
The business of the state does him offense,
And he does chide with you.
DESDEMONA   If 'twere no other—
IAGO   It is but so, I warrant.    [*Trumpets within.*]
Hark, how these instruments summon you to supper!
The messengers of Venice stays the meat.                            178
Go in, and weep not. All things shall be well.
　　　　　　　　　　*Exeunt Desdemona and Emilia.*

　　　　*Enter Roderigo.*

How now, Roderigo?
RODERIGO   I do not find that thou deal'st justly with me.
IAGO   What in the contrary?

---

**112 'Tis . . . very meet** i.e., It must be I somehow have deserved this.   **113–14 How . . . misuse?** What have I done that prompts Othello to attach even the slightest censure to whatever little fault I may have committed?   **121 bewhored her** called her whore **128 callet** whore.   **135 Beshrew** May evil befall. (An oath.)   **136 trick** strange behavior, delusion   **137 eternal** inveterate   **138 insinuating** ingratiating, fawning, wheedling   **139 cogging, cozening** cheating, defrauding   **140 else** otherwise.   **143 halter** hangman's noose

**145 form** manner, circumstance.   **148 that . . . unfold** would that you would expose such fellows   **151 within door** i.e., not so loud.   **152 squire** fellow   **153 seamy side without** wrong side out   **155 Go to** i.e., That's enough.   **160 discourse of thought** process of thinking   **161 that** if. (Also in line 163.)   **162 Delighted . . . form** took delight in anyone other then Othello   **163 yet** still   **166 Comfort forswear** may heavenly comfort forsake   **167 defeat** destroy **169 abhor** (1) fill me with abhorrence (2) make me whorelike **170 addition** title   **171 vanity** showy splendor   **172 humor** mood. **178 stays the meat** are waiting to dine.

RODERIGO    Every day thou daff'st me with some device, 183
Iago, and rather, as it seems to me now, keep'st
from me all conveniency than suppliest me with the 185
least advantage of hope. I will indeed no longer 186
endure it, nor am I yet persuaded to put up in peace 187
what already I have foolishly suffered.

IAGO    Will you hear me, Roderigo?

RODERIGO    Faith, I have heard too much, for your words
and performances are no kin together.

IAGO    You charge me most unjustly.

RODERIGO    With naught but truth. I have wasted myself
out of my means. The jewels you have had from me to
deliver Desdemona would half have corrupted a vo- 195
tarist. You have told me she hath received them and 196
returned me expectations and comforts of sudden re- 197
spect and acquaintance, but I find none. 198

IAGO    Well, go to, very well.

RODERIGO    "Very well"! "Go to"! I cannot go to, man, 200
nor 'tis not very well. By this hand, I think it is scurvy,
and begin to find myself fopped in it. 202

IAGO    Very well.

RODERIGO    I tell you 'tis not very well. I will make myself 204
known to Desdemona. If she will return me my jewels,
I will give over my suit and repent my unlawful solicitation; if not, assure yourself I will seek satisfaction 207
of you.

IAGO    You have said now? 209

RODERIGO    Ay, and said nothing but what I protest 210
intendment of doing. 211

IAGO    Why, now I see there's mettle in thee, and even
from this instant do build on thee a better opinion
than ever before. Give me thy hand, Roderigo. Thou 214
hast taken against me a most just exception; but yet I 215
protest I have dealt most directly in thy affair.

RODERIGO    It hath not appeared.

IAGO    I grant indeed it hath not appeared, and your
suspicion is not without wit and judgment. But,
Roderigo, if thou hast that in thee indeed which I have
greater reason to believe now than ever—I mean
purpose, courage, and valor—this night show it. If
thou the next night following enjoy not Desdemona,
take me from this world with treachery and devise
engines for my life. 225

RODERIGO    Well, what is it? Is it within reason and
compass?

IAGO    Sir, there is especial commission come from
Venice to depute Cassio in Othello's place.

RODERIGO    Is that true? Why, then Othello and Desdemona return again to Venice.

IAGO    Oh, no; he goes into Mauritania and takes away
with him the fair Desdemona, unless his abode be 233
lingered here by some accident; wherein none can be
so determinate as the removing of Cassio. 235

RODERIGO    How do you mean, removing of him?

IAGO    Why, by making him uncapable of Othello's
place—knocking out his brains.

RODERIGO    And that you would have me to do?

IAGO    Ay, if you dare do yourself a profit and a right.
He sups tonight with a harlotry, and thither will I go to 241
him. He knows not yet of his honorable fortune. If
you will watch his going thence, which I will fashion
to fall out between twelve and one, you may take him 244
at your pleasure. I will be near to second your attempt,
and he shall fall between us. Come, stand not amazed 246
at it, but go along with me. I will show you such a
necessity in his death that you shall think yourself
bound to put it on him. It is now high suppertime, 249
and the night grows to waste. About it. 250

RODERIGO    I will hear further reason for this.

IAGO    And you shall be satisfied.          *Exeunt.*

## 4.3

*Enter Othello, Lodovico, Desdemona, Emilia, and
attendants.*

LODOVICO
I do beseech you, sir, trouble yourself no further.

OTHELLO
Oh, pardon me; 'twill do me good to walk.

LODOVICO
Madam, good night. I humbly thank Your Ladyship.

DESDEMONA
Your Honor is most welcome.

OTHELLO                          Will you walk, sir?
Oh, Desdemona!

DESDEMONA    My lord?

OTHELLO    Get you to bed on th'instant. I will be returned forthwith. Dismiss your attendant there. Look't
be done.

DESDEMONA    I will, my lord.
                    *Exit [Othello, with Lodovico and attendants].*

EMILIA    How goes it now? He looks gentler than he did.

DESDEMONA
He says he will return incontinent,                     12
And hath commanded me to go to bed,
And bid me to dismiss you.

EMILIA    Dismiss me?

DESDEMONA
It was his bidding. Therefore, good Emilia,
Give me my nightly wearing, and adieu.
We must not now displease him.

EMILIA    I would you had never seen him!

183 **thou daff'st me** you put me off.   **device** excuse, trick
185 **conveniency** advantage, opportunity   186 **advantage** increase
187 **put up** submit to, tolerate   195 **deliver** deliver to   195–6 **votarist**
nun.   197–8 **sudden respect** immediate consideration   200 **I cannot
go to** (Roderigo changes Iago's *go to*, an expression urging patience,
to *I cannot go to*, "I have no opportunity for success in wooing.")
202 **fopped** fooled, duped   204 **not very well** (Roderigo changes Iago's
*Very well*, "All right, then," to *not very well*, "not at all good.")
207 **satisfaction** repayment. (The term normally means settling of
accounts in a duel.)   209 **You . . . now?** Have you finished?   210–11
**protest intendment** avow my intention   214–15 **Thou . . . exception**
you have accused me most unjustly   225 **engines** plots, snares

233 **his abode** his dwelling here   235 **determinate** instrumental
241 **harlotry** slut   244 **fall out** occur   246 **between us** at the hands
of one or the other of us.   249 **high** fully   250 **grows to waste** wastes
away.
4.3. Location: The citadel.
12 **incontinent** immediately

DESDEMONA
So would not I. My love doth so approve him
That even his stubbornness, his checks, his frowns—   21
Prithee, unpin me—have grace and favor in them.
                    [*Emilia prepares Desdemona for bed.*]
EMILIA   I have laid those sheets you bade me on the
bed.
DESDEMONA
All's one. Good faith, how foolish are our minds!   25
If I do die before thee, prithee shroud me
In one of these same sheets.
EMILIA                             Come, come, you talk.   27
DESDEMONA
My mother had a maid called Barbary.
She was in love, and he she loved proved mad   29
And did forsake her. She had a song of "Willow."
An old thing 'twas, but it expressed her fortune,
And she died singing it. That song tonight
Will not go from my mind; I have much to do   33
But to go hang my head all at one side   34
And sing it like poor Barbary. Prithee, dispatch.   35
EMILIA   Shall I go fetch your nightgown?   36
DESDEMONA   No, unpin me here.
This Lodovico is a proper man.   38
EMILIA   A very handsome man.
DESDEMONA   He speaks well.
EMILIA   I know a lady in Venice would have walked
barefoot to Palestine for a touch of his nether lip.
DESDEMONA [*singing*]
      "The poor soul sat sighing by a sycamore tree,
          Sing all a green willow;   44
      Her hand on her bosom, her head on her knee,
          Sing willow, willow, willow.
      The fresh streams ran by her and murmured her
              moans;
          Sing willow, willow, willow;
      Her salt tears fell from her, and softened the
              stones—"
Lay by these.
[*Singing*] "Sing willow, willow, willow—"
Prithee, hie thee. He'll come anon.   52
[*Singing*] "Sing all a green willow must be my garland.
      Let nobody blame him; his scorn I approve—"
Nay, that's not next.—Hark! Who is't that knocks?
EMILIA   It's the wind.
DESDEMONA [*singing*]
      "I called my love false love; but what said he
          then?
          Sing willow, willow, willow;
      If I court more women, you'll couch with more
              men."   59
So, get thee gone. Good night. Mine eyes do itch;
Doth that bode weeping?
EMILIA                             'Tis neither here nor there.

DESDEMONA
I have heard it said so. Oh, these men, these men!
Dost thou in conscience think—tell me, Emilia—
That there be women do abuse their husbands   64
In such gross kind?
EMILIA                     There be some such, no question.   65
DESDEMONA
Wouldst thou do such a deed for all the world?
EMILIA
Why, would not you?
DESDEMONA                     No, by this heavenly light!
EMILIA
Nor I neither by this heavenly light;
I might do't as well i'th' dark.
DESDEMONA
Wouldst thou do a deed for all the world?
EMILIA
The world's a huge thing. It is a great price
For a small vice.
DESDEMONA
Good troth, I think thou wouldst not.
EMILIA   By my troth, I think I should, and undo't when   74
I had done. Marry, I would not do such a thing for a
joint ring, nor for measures of lawn, nor for gowns,   76
petticoats, nor caps, nor any petty exhibition. But for   77
all the whole world! Uds pity, who would not make   78
her husband a cuckold to make him a monarch? I
should venture Purgatory for't.
DESDEMONA
Beshrew me if I would do such a wrong
For the whole world.
EMILIA   Why, the wrong is but a wrong i'th' world, and
having the world for your labor, 'tis a wrong in your
own world, and you might quickly make it right.
DESDEMONA
I do not think there is any such woman.
EMILIA   Yes, a dozen, and as many   87
To th' vantage as would store the world they played
    for.   88
But I do think it is their husbands' faults
If wives do fall. Say that they slack their duties   90
And pour our treasures into foreign laps,   91
Or else break out in peevish jealousies,
Throwing restraint upon us? Or say they strike us,   93
Or scant our former having in despite?   94
Why, we have galls, and though we have some grace,   95
Yet have we some revenge. Let husbands know
Their wives have sense like them. They see, and smell,   97
And have their palates both for sweet and sour,
As husbands have. What is it that they do   99

**64 do abuse** who do deceive   **65 kind** fashion.   **74 undo't** i.e., pretend I hadn't   **76 joint ring** a ring made in separate halves.   **lawn** fine linen   **77 exhibition** gift.   **78 Uds** God's   **87–8 and . . . played for** and as many as would populate the world they won with their sexual sporting.   **90 Say . . . duties** Suppose that our husbands neglect their marital duties   **91 pour . . . laps** i.e., are unfaithful, give what is rightfully ours (their semen) to other women   **93 Throwing . . . us** jealously restricting our freedom.   **94 Or . . . despite** or spitefully take away from us whatever we enjoyed before.   **95 have galls** i.e., are capable of resenting injury and insult.   **grace** inclination to be merciful   **97 sense** sensory perception and appetite   **99 they** husbands

**21 stubbornness** roughness.   **checks** rebukes   **25 All's one** All right. It doesn't really matter.   **27 talk** i.e., prattle.   **29 mad** wild, lunatic   **33–4 I . . . hang** I can scarcely keep myself from hanging   **35 dispatch** finish up.   **36 nightgown** dressing gown.   **38 proper** handsome   **44 willow** (A conventional emblem of disappointed love.)   **52 hie thee** hurry.   **anon** right away.   **59 couch** lie, sleep

When they change us for others? Is it sport? 100
I think it is. And doth affection breed it? 101
I think it doth. Is't frailty that thus errs?
It is so, too. And have not we affections,
Desires for sport, and frailty, as men have?
Then let them use us well; else let them know,
The ills we do, their ills instruct us so. 106

DESDEMONA
Good night, good night. God me such uses send 107
Not to pick bad from bad, but by bad mend! 108
                                        *Exeunt.*

❖

# 5.1

*Enter Iago and Roderigo.*

IAGO
Here stand behind this bulk. Straight will he come. 1
Wear thy good rapier bare, and put it home. 2
Quick, quick! Fear nothing. I'll be at thy elbow.
It makes us or it mars us. Think on that,
And fix most firm thy resolution.

RODERIGO
Be near at hand. I may miscarry in't. 6

IAGO
Here, at thy hand. Be bold, and take thy stand.
          [*Iago stands aside, Roderigo conceals himself.*]

RODERIGO
I have no great devotion to the deed;
And yet he hath given me satisfying reasons.
'Tis but a man gone. Forth, my sword! He dies.
                                        [*He draws.*]

IAGO
I have rubbed this young quat almost to the sense, 11
And he grows angry. Now, whether he kill Cassio
Or Cassio him, or each do kill the other,
Every way makes my gain. Live Roderigo, 14
He calls me to a restitution large
Of gold and jewels that I bobbed from him 16
As gifts to Desdemona.
It must not be. If Cassio do remain,
He hath a daily beauty in his life
That makes me ugly; and besides, the Moor
May unfold me to him; there stand I in much peril. 21
No, he must die. Be't so. I hear him coming.

*Enter Cassio.*

RODERIGO [*coming forth*]
I know his gait, 'tis he.—Villain, thou diest!
                              [*He attacks Cassio.*]

CASSIO
That thrust had been mine enemy indeed,
But that my coat is better than thou know'st. 25
I will make proof of thine.
          [*He draws, and wounds Roderigo.*]

RODERIGO          Oh, I am slain!   [*He falls.* 26
                    *Iago, from behind, wounds Cassio
                          in the leg, and exit.*]

CASSIO
I am maimed forever. Help, ho! Murder! Murder!

*Enter Othello.*

OTHELLO   The voice of Cassio! Iago keeps his word.
RODERIGO   Oh, villain that I am!
OTHELLO   It is even so.
CASSIO   Oh, help, ho! Light! A surgeon!
OTHELLO
'Tis he. O brave Iago, honest and just,
That hast such noble sense of thy friend's wrong! 33
Thou teachest me.—Minion, your dear lies dead, 34
And your unblest fate hies. Strumpet, I come. 35
Forth of my heart those charms, thine eyes, are blotted; 36
Thy bed, lust-stained, shall with lust's blood be
      spotted.                          *Exit Othello.*

*Enter Lodovico and Gratiano.*

CASSIO
What ho! No watch? No passage? Murder! Murder! 38
GRATIANO
'Tis some mischance. The voice is very direful.
CASSIO   Oh, help!
LODOVICO   Hark!
RODERIGO   Oh, wretched villain!
LODOVICO
Two or three groan. 'Tis heavy night; 43
These may be counterfeits. Let's think't unsafe
To come in to the cry without more help. 45
                    [*They remain near the entrance.*]
RODERIGO
Nobody come? Then shall I bleed to death.

*Enter Iago [in his shirtsleeves, with a light].*

LODOVICO   Hark!
GRATIANO
Here's one comes in his shirt, with light and weapons.
IAGO
Who's there? Whose noise is this that cries on murder? 49
LODOVICO
We do not know.
IAGO                Did not you hear a cry?
CASSIO
Here, here! For heaven's sake, help me!
IAGO                      What's the matter?
                          [*He moves toward Cassio.*]

---

**100 change** exchange.   **sport** sexual pastime.   **101 affection** passion
**106 The ills . . . so** their ill behavior teaches us the way to do ill.
**107 uses** habit, practice   **108 Not . . . mend** i.e., not to learn bad conduct from others' badness (as Emilia has suggested women learn
from men), but to mend my ways by perceiving what badness is,
making spiritual benefit out of evil and adversity.
**5.1. Location: A street in Cyprus.**
**1 bulk** framework projecting from the front of a shop.   **Straight** Immediately.   **he** Cassio   **2 bare** unsheathed.   **home** all the way into the target.
**6 I . . . in't** I may not succeed.   **11 quat** pimple, pustule.   **to the sense** to
the quick   **14 Live Roderigo** If Roderigo lives   **16 bobbed** swindled
**21 unfold** expose, reveal

**25 coat** (Possibly a garment of mail under the outer clothing, or simply
a tougher coat than Roderigo expected.)   **26 proof** a test   **33 thy
friend's** Othello's   **34 Minion** Hussy (i.e., Desdemona)   **35 hies**
hastens on.   **36 Forth of** From out   **38 passage** people passing by.
**43 heavy** thick, dark   **45 come in to** approach   **49 cries** cries out

GRATIANO [*to Lodovico*]
  This is Othello's ancient, as I take it.
LODOVICO [*to Gratiano*]
  The same indeed, a very valiant fellow.
IAGO [*to Cassio*]
  What are you here that cry so grievously?     54
CASSIO
  Iago? Oh, I am spoiled, undone by villains!     55
  Give me some help.
IAGO
  Oh, me, Lieutenant! What villains have done this?
CASSIO
  I think that one of them is hereabout,
  And cannot make away.
IAGO            Oh, treacherous villains!     59
  [*To Lodovico and Gratiano*] What are you there? Come
    in, and give some help.           [*They advance.*]
RODERIGO    Oh, help me there!
CASSIO
  That's one of them.
IAGO             Oh, murderous slave! Oh, villain!
                          [*He stabs Roderigo.*]
RODERIGO
  Oh, damned Iago! Oh, inhuman dog!
IAGO
  Kill men i'th' dark?—Where be these bloody thieves?—
  How silent is this town!—Ho! Murder, murder!—
  [*To Lodovico and Gratiano*] What may you be? Are you
    of good or evil?
LODOVICO    As you shall prove us, praise us.     67
IAGO    Signor Lodovico?
LODOVICO    He, sir.
IAGO
  I cry you mercy. Here's Cassio hurt by villains.     70
GRATIANO    Cassio?
IAGO    How is't, brother?
CASSIO    My leg is cut in two.
IAGO    Marry, heaven forbid!
  Light, gentlemen! I'll bind it with my shirt.
           [*He hands them the light, and tends to Cassio's
                               wound.*]

         *Enter Bianca.*

BIANCA
  What is the matter, ho? Who is't that cried?
IAGO    Who is't that cried?
BIANCA             Oh, my dear Cassio!
  My sweet Cassio! Oh, Cassio, Cassio, Cassio!
IAGO
  Oh, notable strumpet! Cassio, may you suspect
  Who they should be that have thus mangled you?
CASSIO    No.
GRATIANO
  I am sorry to find you thus. I have been to seek you.

IAGO
  Lend me a garter. [*He applies a tourniquet.*] So.—Oh, for
    a chair,     83
  To bear him easily hence!
BIANCA
  Alas, he faints! Oh, Cassio, Cassio, Cassio!
IAGO
  Gentlemen all, I do suspect this trash
  To be a party in this injury.—
  Patience awhile, good Cassio.—Come, come;
  Lend me a light. [*He shines the light on Roderigo.*] Know
    we this face or no?
  Alas, my friend and my dear countryman
  Roderigo! No.—Yes, sure.—Oh, heaven! Roderigo!
GRATIANO    What, of Venice?
IAGO    Even he, sir. Did you know him?
GRATIANO    Know him? Ay.
IAGO
  Signor Gratiano? I cry your gentle pardon.     95
  These bloody accidents must excuse my manners     96
  That so neglected you.
GRATIANO            I am glad to see you.
IAGO
  How do you, Cassio?—Oh, a chair, a chair!
GRATIANO    Roderigo!
IAGO
  He, he, 'tis he. [*A litter is brought in.*] Oh, that's well
    said; the chair.     100
  Some good man bear him carefully from hence;
  I'll fetch the General's surgeon. [*To Bianca*] For you,
    mistress,     102
  Save you your labor.—He that lies slain here, Cassio,     103
  Was my dear friend. What malice was between you?     104
CASSIO
  None in the world, nor do I know the man.
IAGO [*to Bianca*]
  What, look you pale?—Oh, bear him out o'th'air.     106
                [*Cassio and Roderigo are borne off.*]
  Stay you, good gentlemen.—Look you pale,
    mistress?—     107
  Do you perceive the gastness of her eye?—     108
  Nay, if you stare, we shall hear more anon.—     109
  Behold her well; I pray you, look upon her.
  Do you see, gentlemen? Nay, guiltiness
  Will speak, though tongues were out of use.

     [*Enter Emilia.*]

EMILIA
  'Las, what's the matter? What's the matter, husand?
IAGO
  Cassio hath here been set on in the dark
  By Roderigo and fellows that are scaped.
  He's almost slain, and Roderigo dead.     116

---

**83 chair** litter  **95 gentle** noble  **96 accidents** sudden events
**100 well said** well done  **102 For** As for  **103 Save ... labor** i.e., never
you mind tending Cassio.  **He** Roderigo  **104 malice** enmity
**106 bear ... air** (Fresh air was thought to be dangerous for a wound.)
**107 Stay you** (Lodovico and Gratiano are evidently about to leave.)
**108 gastness** terror  **109 stare** (Iago pretends to interpret Bianca's
wild looks as an involuntary confession of guilt.)  **116 He's** Cassio is

---

**54 What** Who. (Also at lines 60 and 66.)  **55 spoiled** ruined, done
for  **59 make** get  **67 prove us** prove us to be.  **praise** appraise
**70 I cry you mercy** I beg your pardon.

**EMILIA**
Alas, good gentleman! Alas, good Cassio!
**IAGO**
This is the fruits of whoring. Prithee, Emilia,
Go know of Cassio where he supped tonight.   119
[*To Bianca*] What, do you shake at that?
**BIANCA**
He supped at my house, but I therefore shake not.
**IAGO**
Oh, did he so? I charge you go with me.
**EMILIA**    Oh, fie upon thee, strumpet!
**BIANCA**
I am no strumpet, but of life as honest   124
As you that thus abuse me.
**EMILIA**    As I? Faugh! Fie upon thee!
**IAGO**
Kind gentlemen, let's go see poor Cassio dressed.—   127
Come, mistress, you must tell 's another tale.—   128
Emilia, run you to the citadel
And tell my lord and lady what hath happed.—
Will you go on afore? [*Aside*] This is the night
That either makes me or fordoes me quite.   *Exeunt.* 132

❖

## 5.2

*Enter Othello [with a light], and Desdemona in her bed.*

**OTHELLO**
It is the cause, it is the cause, my soul.   1
Let me not name it to you, you chaste stars!
It is the cause. Yet I'll not shed her blood,
Nor scar that whiter skin of hers than snow,
And smooth as monumental alabaster.   5
Yet she must die, else she'll betray more men.
Put out the light, and then put out the light.   7
If I quench thee, thou flaming minister,   8
I can again thy former light restore,
Should I repent me; but once put out thy light,   10
Thou cunning'st pattern of excelling nature,   11
I know not where is that Promethean heat   12
That can thy light relume. When I have plucked thy
rose,   13
I cannot give it vital growth again;
It needs must wither. I'll smell thee on the tree.   15
[*He kisses her.*]
Oh, balmy breath, that dost almost persuade
Justice to break her sword! One more, one more.

119 **know** learn   124 **honest** chaste   127 **Cassio dressed** Cassio's wounds dressed.   128 **tell's . . . tale** i.e., tell us the truth for a change.   132 **fordoes** undoes, ruins
**5.2. Location:** A bedchamber in the citadel.
0.1–2 *in her bed* (Either the curtains are drawn back to reveal the bed in a recessed area backstage, or the bed is "thrust out" onstage as the scene begins.)   1 **cause** i.e., cause of justice, the offense itself, which must be corrected in the name of justice   5 **monumental alabaster** stone used in making tombs and funeral monuments.   7 **the light . . . light** the torch or lamp . . . Desdemona's life.   8 **minister** servant   10 **repent me** change my mind   11 **Thou . . . pattern** you skillfully wrought perfect example   12 **Promethean heat** (Alludes to two myths: that of Prometheus stealing fire from heaven for humanity, and that of his animating humankind from clay.)   13 **relume** rekindle.   15 **needs** necessarily

Be thus when thou art dead, and I will kill thee,
And love thee after. One more, and that's the last.
[*He kisses her.*]
So sweet was ne'er so fatal. I must weep,   20
But they are cruel tears. This sorrow's heavenly;   21
It strikes where it doth love. She wakes.   22
**DESDEMONA**    Who's there? Othello?
**OTHELLO**    Ay, Desdemona.
**DESDEMONA**    Will you come to bed, my lord?
**OTHELLO**    Have you prayed tonight, Desdemon?
**DESDEMONA**    Ay, my lord.
**OTHELLO**
If you bethink yourself of any crime   28
Unreconciled as yet to heaven and grace,
Solicit for it straight.   30
**DESDEMONA**
Alack, my lord, what may you mean by that?
**OTHELLO**
Well, do it, and be brief. I will walk by.
I would not kill thy unprepared spirit.
No, heaven forfend! I would not kill thy soul.   34
**DESDEMONA**
Talk you of killing?
**OTHELLO**    Ay, I do.
**DESDEMONA**    Then heaven
Have mercy on me!
**OTHELLO**    Amen, with all my heart!
**DESDEMONA**
If you say so, I hope you will not kill me.
**OTHELLO**    Humh!
**DESDEMONA**
And yet I fear you; for you're fatal then
When your eyes roll so. Why I should fear I know not,
Since guiltiness I know not; but yet I feel I fear.
**OTHELLO**
Think on thy sins.
**DESDEMONA**    They are loves I bear to you.   42
**OTHELLO**    Ay, and for that thou diest.
**DESDEMONA**
That death's unnatural that kills for loving.
Alas, why gnaw you so your nether lip?
Some bloody passion shakes your very frame.
These are portents; but yet I hope, I hope,
They do not point on me.
**OTHELLO**    Peace, and be still!
**DESDEMONA**    I will so. What's the matter?
**OTHELLO**
That handkerchief which I so loved and gave thee
Thou gav'st to Cassio.
**DESDEMONA**    No, by my life and soul!
Send for the man and ask him.
**OTHELLO**
Sweet soul, take heed, take heed of perjury.
Thou art on thy deathbed.

20 **So sweet . . . fatal** So sweet a kiss was never before associated with sin and death.   21 **they are cruel tears** these tears betoken a sorrowful cruelty, regrettable but just.   22 **It . . . love** (Compare Hebrews 12:6: "For whom the Lord loveth he chasteneth.")   28 **crime** sin   30 **Solicit** petition, ask forgiveness.   **straight** immediately.   34 **forfend** forbid.   42 **They . . . you** i.e., My only sins are my idolatry of loving you.

DESDEMONA
  Ay, but not yet to die.
OTHELLO                              Yes, presently.          56
  Therefore confess thee freely of thy sin;
  For to deny each article with oath
  Cannot remove nor choke the strong conception   59
  That I do groan withal. Thou art to die.        60
DESDEMONA
  Then Lord have mercy on me!
OTHELLO                              I say, amen.
DESDEMONA
  And have you mercy too! I never did
  Offend you in my life; never loved Cassio
  But with such general warranty of heaven        64
  As I might love. I never gave him token.
OTHELLO
  By heaven, I saw my handkerchief in 's hand.
  Oh, perjured woman! Thou dost stone my heart,   67
  And makes me call what I intend to do
  A murder, which I thought a sacrifice.
  I saw the handkerchief.
DESDEMONA                  He found it, then.
  I never gave it him. Send for him hither;
  Let him confess a truth.
OTHELLO                    He hath confessed.
DESDEMONA   What, my lord?
OTHELLO
  That he hath used thee.
DESDEMONA                  How? Unlawfully?
OTHELLO                                       Ay.
DESDEMONA
  He will not say so.
OTHELLO               No, his mouth is stopped;
  Honest Iago hath ta'en order for't.             76
DESDEMONA
  Oh, my fear interprets. What, is he dead?
OTHELLO
  Had all his hairs been lives, my great revenge
  Had stomach for them all.
DESDEMONA
  Alas, he is betrayed and I undone!       [She weeps.]
OTHELLO
  Out, strumpet! Weep'st thou for him to my face?
DESDEMONA
  Oh, banish me, my lord, but kill me not!
OTHELLO   Down, strumpet!
DESDEMONA
  Kill me tomorrow; let me live tonight!
OTHELLO   Nay, if you strive—
DESDEMONA
  But half an hour!
OTHELLO              Being done, there is no pause.  86

DESDEMONA
  But while I say one prayer!
OTHELLO                          It is too late.         56
                                 Smothers her.
EMILIA (at the door)
  My lord, my lord! What, ho! My lord, my lord!
OTHELLO
  What noise is this? Not dead? Not yet quite dead?
  I that am cruel am yet merciful;
  I would not have thee linger in thy pain.
                             [He dispatches her.]
  So, so.
EMILIA (within)   What, ho! My lord, my lord!
OTHELLO                                 Who's there?
EMILIA [within]
  Oh, good my lord, I would speak a word with you!
OTHELLO
  Yes, 'tis Emilia.—By and by.—She's dead.
  'Tis like she comes to speak of Cassio's death.—    95
  The noise was high. Ha! No more moving?             96
  Still as the grave. Shall she come in? Were't good?—
  I think she stirs again. No. What's best to do?
  If she come in, she'll sure speak to my wife.
  My wife! My wife! What wife? I have no wife.
  Oh, insupportable! Oh, heavy hour!
  Methinks it should be now a huge eclipse
  Of sun and moon, and that th'affrighted globe
  Should yawn at alteration.
EMILIA [within]                I do beseech you       104
  That I may speak with you, O good my lord!
OTHELLO
  I had forgot thee. Oh, come in, Emilia.—
  Soft, by and by. Let me the curtains draw.—        107
         [He closes the bedcurtains and opens the door.]
  Where art thou?

         Enter Emilia.

                   What's the matter with thee now?
EMILIA
  Oh, my good lord, yonder's foul murders done!
OTHELLO   What, now?
EMILIA   But now, my lord.                            111
OTHELLO
  It is the very error of the moon;                  112
  She comes more nearer earth than she was wont,     113
  And makes men mad.                                 114
EMILIA
  Cassio, my lord, hath killed a young Venetian
  Called Roderigo.
OTHELLO              Roderigo killed?

56 presently immediately.   59 conception (1) belief in your guilt
(2) plan in my mind   60 groan withal (1) groan at in sorrow
(2) groan as in giving birth.   64 warranty sanction   67 stone turn
to stone, harden   76 ta'en order taken measures   86 Being done
i.e., Since justice has begun its relentless course

95 like likely that   96 The noise was high i.e., She must have heard
about it.   104 Should . . . alteration should gape wide in an earthquake, as if expressing amazement at an eclipse. (According to Pliny,
earthquakes often happen during eclipses. The cataclismic event here
is especially terrifying if it imagines the impossible concurrence of a
solar and lunar eclipse—an apocalyptic scenario befitting the horror
of Desdemona's death. If Othello means a solar eclipse, with the
moon blocking out the sun, that rare event would be terrible enough.)
107 Soft Wait a minute   111 But Just   112 error aberration, irregularity
113 She Luna, the moon goddess   114 mad i.e., "lunatic."

And Cassio killed?

EMILIA                    No, Cassio is not killed.

OTHELLO
Not Cassio killed? Then murder's out of tune,
And sweet revenge grows harsh.

DESDEMONA    Oh, falsely, falsely murdered!

EMILIA    Oh, Lord, what cry is that?

OTHELLO    That? What?

EMILIA
Out and alas, that was my lady's voice.                    123
                    [*She opens the bedcurtains.*]
Help, help, ho, help! O lady, speak again!
Sweet Desdemona! O sweet mistress, speak!

DESDEMONA    A guiltless death I die.

EMILIA    Oh, who hath done this deed?

DESDEMONA    Nobody; I myself. Farewell.
Commend me to my kind lord. Oh, farewell! [*She dies.*]

OTHELLO
Why, how should she be murdered?

EMILIA                    Alas, who knows?

OTHELLO
You heard her say herself it was not I.

EMILIA
She said so. I must needs report the truth.                    132

OTHELLO
She's like a liar gone to burning hell!
'Twas I that killed her.

EMILIA                    Oh, the more angel she,
And you the blacker devil!

OTHELLO
She turned to folly, and she was a whore.                    136

EMILIA
Thou dost belie her, and thou art a devil.                    137

OTHELLO    She was false as water.

EMILIA    Thou art rash as fire to say
That she was false. Oh, she was heavenly true!

OTHELLO
Cassio did top her. Ask thy husband else.                    141
Oh, I were damned beneath all depth in hell
But that I did proceed upon just grounds
To this extremity. Thy husband knew it all.

EMILIA    My husband?

OTHELLO    Thy husband.

EMILIA    That she was false to wedlock?

OTHELLO
Ay, with Cassio. Nay, had she been true,
If heaven would make me such another world
Of one entire and perfect chrysolite,                    150
I'd not have sold her for it.

EMILIA    My husband?

OTHELLO
Ay, 'twas he that told me on her first.
An honest man he is, and hates the slime
That sticks on filthy deeds.

EMILIA    My husband?

OTHELLO
What needs this iterance, woman? I say thy husband.    157

EMILIA
Oh, mistress, villainy hath made mocks with love!    158
My husband say she was false?

OTHELLO                    He, woman;
I say thy husband. Dost understand the word?
My friend, thy husband, honest, honest Iago.

EMILIA
If he say so, may his pernicious soul
Rot half a grain a day! He lies to th' heart.
She was too fond of her most filthy bargain.

OTHELLO    Ha?                    [*He draws.*]

EMILIA    Do thy worst!
This deed of thine is no more worthy heaven
Than thou wast worthy her.

OTHELLO                    Peace, you were best.    168

EMILIA
Thou hast not half that power to do me harm
As I have to be hurt. O gull! O dolt!                    170
As ignorant as dirt! Thou hast done a deed—
I care not for thy sword; I'll make thee known,
Though I lost twenty lives.—Help! Help, ho, help!
The Moor hath killed my mistress! Murder, murder!

*Enter Montano, Gratiano, and Iago.*

MONTANO
What is the matter? How now, General?

EMILIA
Oh, are you come, Iago? You have done well,
That men must lay their murders on your neck.    177

GRATIANO    What is the matter?

EMILIA [*to Iago*]
Disprove this villain, if thou be'st a man.
He says thou told'st him that his wife was false.
I know thou didst not; thou'rt not such a villain.    181
Speak, for my heart is full.

IAGO
I told him what I thought, and told no more
Than what he found himself was apt and true.    184

EMILIA
But did you ever tell him she was false?

IAGO    I did.

EMILIA
You told a lie, an odious, damnèd lie!
Upon my soul, a lie, a wicked lie.
She false with Cassio? Did you say with Cassio?

IAGO
With Cassio, mistress. Go to, charm your tongue.    190

EMILIA
I will not charm my tongue; I am bound to speak.
My mistress here lies murdered in her bed—

ALL    Oh, heavens forfend!

EMILIA
And your reports have set the murder on.

**123 Out** (A cry of dismay, intensifying *alas*.)   **132 must needs**
must   **136 folly** i.e., wantonness, fleshly sin   **137 belie** slander
**141 else** i.e., if you don't believe me.   **150 chrysolite** precious topaz

**157 iterance** iteration, repetition   **158 made mocks with** cruelly
mocked   **168 Peace . . . best** You'd better be quiet.   **170 to be hurt**
i.e., to endure hurt.   **gull** dupe.   **177 on your neck** to your charge.
**181 such a villain** such a villain as all that.   **184 apt** plausible
**190 charm** control

OTHELLO
Nay, stare not, masters. It is true indeed.

GRATIANO 'Tis a strange truth.

MONTANO
Oh, monstrous act!

EMILIA                    Villainy, villainy, villainy!
I think upon't—I think I smell't! Oh, villainy!
I thought so then—I'll kill myself for grief—          199
Oh, villainy, villainy!

IAGO
What, are you mad? I charge you, get you home.

EMILIA
Good gentlemen, let me have leave to speak.
'Tis proper I obey him, but not now.
Perchance, Iago, I will ne'er go home.

OTHELLO
Oh! Oh! Oh!                    [Othello falls on the bed.]

EMILIA          Nay, lay thee down and roar,              205
For thou hast killed the sweetest innocent
That e'er did lift up eye.

OTHELLO [rising]          Oh, she was foul!              207
I scarce did know you, uncle. There lies your niece,
Whose breath indeed these hands have newly
      stopped.
I know this act shows horrible and grim.                210

GRATIANO
Poor Desdemon! I am glad thy father's dead.
Thy match was mortal to him, and pure grief
Shore his old thread in twain. Did he live now,        213
This sight would make him do a desperate turn,         214
Yea, curse his better angel from his side,
And fall to reprobance.                                216

OTHELLO
'Tis pitiful. But yet Iago knows
That she with Cassio hath the act of shame
A thousand times committed. Cassio confessed it;
And she did gratify his amorous works                  220
With that recognizance and pledge of love             221
Which I first gave her. I saw it in his hand;
It was a handkerchief, an antique token
My father gave my mother.

EMILIA    O God! O heavenly God!

IAGO
Zounds, hold your peace.

EMILIA                    'Twill out, 'twill out! I peace?
No, I will speak as liberal as the north.             227
Let heaven and men and devils, let them all,
All, all, cry shame against me, yet I'll speak.

IAGO
Be wise, and get you home.

EMILIA                    I will not.
                    [Iago threatens Emilia.]

GRATIANO                              Fie,

Your sword upon a woman?

EMILIA
Oh, thou dull Moor! That handkerchief thou speak'st of
I found by fortune and did give my husband;
For often, with a solemn earnestness,
More than indeed belonged to such a trifle,           235
He begged of me to steal't.

IAGO                    Villainous whore!

EMILIA
She give it Cassio? No, alas! I found it,
And I did give't my husband.

IAGO                    Filth, thou liest!

EMILIA
By heaven, I do not, I do not, gentlemen.
Oh, murderous coxcomb! What should such a fool        240
Do with so good a wife?

OTHELLO    Are there no stones in heaven              242
But what serves for the thunder?—Precious villain!    243
          [He runs at Iago; Montano disarms Othello. Iago,
                              from behind, stabs Emilia.]

GRATIANO
The woman falls! Sure he hath killed his wife.

EMILIA
Ay, ay. Oh, lay me by my mistress' side.
                                        [Exit Iago.]

GRATIANO    He's gone, but his wife's killed.

MONTANO
'Tis a notorious villain. Take you this weapon,
Which I have here recovered from the Moor.
Come, guard the door without. Let him not pass,
But kill him rather. I'll after that same villain,
For 'tis a damnèd slave.
                    Exit [with all but Othello and Emilia,
                        who has been laid by Desdemona's side].

OTHELLO    I am not valiant neither,
But every puny whipster gets my sword.                253
But why should honor outlive honesty?                 254
Let it go all.

EMILIA          What did thy song bode, lady?
Hark, canst thou hear me? I will play the swan,       256
And die in music. [She sings] "Willow, willow, willow."
Moor, she was chaste. She loved thee, cruel Moor.
So come my soul to bliss as I speak true.
So speaking as I think, alas, I die.          [She dies.]

OTHELLO
I have another weapon in this chamber;
It was a sword of Spain, the ice-brook's temper—      262
Oh, here it is. [He finds a sword.] Uncle, I must come
      forth.

GRATIANO [within]
If thou attempt it, it will cost thee dear.

199 then (Perhaps at 3.3.331–2 and 4.2.137–54.)    205 s.d. Othello . . .
bed (This direction is from the quarto, as also He kisses her at line 19
and She dies at line 129.)    207 lift up eye i.e., lift her eyes to heaven.
210 shows looks    213 Shore . . . thread sheared the thread of his old
age (as Atropos, one of the three Fates, was thought to do)    214 turn
deed    216 reprobance the unforgivable sin of despair and suicide.
220 gratify reward    221 recognizance token    227 liberal as the
north freely as the north wind (blows).

235 belonged was appropriate    240 coxcomb fool. (Addressed to
Othello.)    242 stones bolts, such as those used for thunderbolts
243 Precious i.e., Arrant, utter    243.1–2 He . . . Emilia (The quarto
text reads, "The Moore runnes at Iago. Iago kils his wife." The quarto also
specifies the exit of Iago at line 245 and the death of Emilia at line 260.)
253 every . . . sword every whipper-snapper can get the better of
me and my sword.    254 why . . . honesty? why should a soldier's
reputation for bravery outlive true integrity?    256 play the swan
(The swan was fabled to sing only at its death.)    262 the ice-brook's
temper tempered in ice-cold water

Thou hast no weapon, and perforce must suffer.

OTHELLO
Look in upon me then and speak with me,
Or, naked as I am, I will assault thee.    267

    *[Enter Gratiano.]*

GRATIANO
What is the matter?

OTHELLO        Behold, I have a weapon;
A better never did itself sustain
Upon a soldier's thigh. I have seen the day
That, with this little arm and this good sword,
I have made my way through more impediments
Than twenty times your stop. But oh, vain boast!    273
Who can control his fate? 'Tis not so now.
Be not afraid, though you do see me weaponed;
Here is my journey's end, here is my butt    276
And very seamark of my utmost sail.    277
             *[Gratiano steps back.]*
Do you go back dismayed? 'Tis a lost fear;    278
Man but a rush against Othello's breast    279
And he retires. Where should Othello go?
             *[He turns to Desdemona.]*
Now, how dost thou look now? Oh, ill-starred wench!
Pale as thy smock! When we shall meet at compt,    282
This look of thine will hurl my soul from heaven,
And fiends will snatch at it. Cold, cold, my girl?
Even like thy chastity. Oh, cursèd, cursèd slave!    285
Whip me, ye devils,
From the possession of this heavenly sight!
Blow me about in winds! Roast me in sulfur!
Wash me in steep-down gulfs of liquid fire!
Oh, Desdemon! Dead, Desdemon! Dead! Oh! Oh!    290

    *Enter Lodovico, Cassio [carried in a litter],
Montano, and Iago [prisoner], with officers.*

LODOVICO
Where is this rash and most unfortunate man?

OTHELLO
That's he that was Othello. Here I am.

LODOVICO
Where is that viper? Bring the villain forth.
             *[Iago is led forward.]*

OTHELLO
I look down towards his feet; but that's a fable.    294
If that thou be'st a devil, I cannot kill thee.
             *[He wounds Iago.]*

LODOVICO
Wrench his sword from him.      *[Othello is disarmed.]*

IAGO              I bleed, sir, but not killed.

OTHELLO
I am not sorry neither. I'd have thee live,

---

For in my sense 'tis happiness to die.    298

LODOVICO
O thou Othello, that was once so good,
Fall'n in the practice of a cursèd slave,    300
What shall be said to thee?

OTHELLO          Why, anything.
An honorable murderer, if you will,
For naught I did in hate, but all in honor.

LODOVICO
This wretch hath part confessed his villainy.
Did you and he consent in Cassio's death?    305

OTHELLO    Ay.

CASSIO
Dear General, I never gave you cause.

OTHELLO
I do believe it, and I ask your pardon.
Will you, I pray, demand that demi-devil
Why he hath thus ensnared my soul and body?

IAGO
Demand me nothing. What you know, you know.
From this time forth I never will speak word.

LODOVICO    What, not to pray?

GRATIANO    Torments will ope your lips.    314

OTHELLO    Well, thou dost best.    315

LODOVICO
Sir, you shall understand what hath befall'n,
Which, as I think, you know not. Here is a letter
Found in the pocket of the slain Roderigo;
And here another. *[He produces letters.]* The one of them
   imports
The death of Cassio, to be undertook
By Roderigo.

OTHELLO
Oh, villain!

CASSIO        Most heathenish and most gross!    322

LODOVICO *[showing another paper]*
Now here's another discontented paper    323
Found in his pocket too. And this, it seems,
Roderigo meant t'have sent this damnèd villain;
But that belike Iago in the interim    326
Came in and satisfied him.    327

OTHELLO *[to Iago]*    Oh, thou pernicious caitiff!—    328
How came you, Cassio, by that handkerchief
That was my wife's?

CASSIO          I found it in my chamber;
And he himself confessed but even now    331
That there he dropped it for a special purpose
Which wrought to his desire.

OTHELLO          Oh, fool, fool, fool!    333

CASSIO
There is besides in Roderigo's letter
How he upbraids Iago, that he made him

---

267 **naked** unarmed    273 **your stop** the obstruction you present.
276 **butt** goal, limit. (An archery term.)    277 **seamark** beacon (marking
his destination or limit)    278 **lost** groundless    279 **Man . . . rush**
wield no more than a reed    282 **compt** account, judgment day
285 **slave** i.e., Othello himself.    290.1 **in a litter** (The quarto specifies
that Cassio is *"in a Chaire."*)    294 **towards his feet** i.e., to see if they
are cloven, as the devil's are fabled to be

298 **in my sense** to one who feels as I do    300 **in the practice** through
the plotting, into the snare.    **slave** villain    305 **consent** agree
314 **Torments** Torture    315 **thou dost best** you (Iago) do best not
to talk.    322 **gross** monstrous.    323 **discontented** full of discontent
326 **belike** most likely    327 **Came . . . him** interposed and gave him
satisfactory explanation.    328 **caitiff** wretch    331 **he** Iago    333
**wrought . . . desire** worked out as he wished, fitted in with his plan.

Brave me upon the watch, whereon it came                    336
That I was cast; and even but now he spake,                  337
After long seeming dead, Iago hurt him,                      338
Iago set him on.                                             339

LODOVICO [*to Othello*]
You must forsake this room and go with us.
Your power and your command is taken off,                    341
And Cassio rules in Cyprus. For this slave,                  342
If there be any cunning cruelty
That can torment him much and hold him long,                 344
It shall be his. You shall close prisoner rest               345
Till that the nature of your fault be known                  346
To the Venetian state.—Come, bring away.

OTHELLO
Soft you; a word or two before you go.                       348
I have done the state some service, and they know't.
No more of that. I pray you, in your letters,
When you shall these unlucky deeds relate,                   351
Speak of me as I am; nothing extenuate,
Nor set down aught in malice. Then must you speak
Of one that loved not wisely but too well;
Of one not easily jealous but, being wrought,               355
Perplexed in the extreme; of one whose hand,                356
Like the base Indian, threw a pearl away                     357
Richer than all his tribe; of one whose subdued eyes,        358

Albeit unusèd to the melting mood,                           359
Drops tears as fast as the Arabian trees
Their medicinable gum. Set you down this;                    361
And say besides that in Aleppo once,                         362
Where a malignant and a turbaned Turk
Beat a Venetian and traduced the state,
I took by th' throat the circumcisèd dog
And smote him, thus.                    [*He stabs himself.*] 366

LODOVICO    Oh, bloody period!                               367
GRATIANO    All that is spoke is marred.
OTHELLO
I kissed thee ere I killed thee. No way but this,
Killing myself, to die upon a kiss.
                    [*He kisses Desdemona and*] *dies.*

CASSIO
This did I fear, but thought he had no weapon;
For he was great of heart.
LODOVICO [*to Iago*]            O Spartan dog,                372
More fell than anguish, hunger, or the sea!                  373
Look on the tragic loading of this bed.
This is thy work. The object poisons sight;
Let it be hid. Gratiano, keep the house,                     376
                    [*The bedcurtains are drawn.*]
And seize upon the fortunes of the Moor,                     377
For they succeed on you. [*To Cassio*] To you, Lord
    Governor,                                                378
Remains the censure of this hellish villain,                379
The time, the place, the torture. Oh, enforce it!
Myself will straight aboard, and to the state
This heavy act with heavy heart relate.          *Exeunt.*

---

**336 Brave** defy.   **whereon it came** whereof it came about   **337 cast** dismissed   **337–9 even . . . him on** i.e., and a short time ago, after having apparently died, Roderigo revived enough to tell how Iago had egged him on to kill Cassio and then had mortally wounded Roderigo.   **341 taken off** taken away   **342 For** As for   **344 hold him long** keep him alive a long time (during his torture)
**345 You . . . rest** You will remain a closely-guarded prisoner
**346 Till that** until   **348 Soft you** One moment   **351 unlucky** unfortunate   **355 wrought** worked upon, worked into a frenzy
**356 Perplexed** distraught   **357 Indian** (This reading from the quarto pictures an ignorant savage who cannot recognize the value of a precious jewel. The Folio reading, "Iudean," i.e., infidel or disbeliever, may refer to Herod, who slew Miriamne in a fit of jealousy, or to Judas Iscariot, the betrayer of Christ.)   **358 subdued** i.e., overcome by grief

**359 Albeit . . . mood** although not accustomed to weeping
**361 gum** i.e., myrrh.   **362 Aleppo** (in modern-day Syria)
**366 s.d.** *He stabs himself* (This direction is in the quarto text.)
**367 period** termination, conclusion.   **372 Spartan dog** (Spartan dogs were noted for their savagery and silence.)   **373 fell** cruel
**376 Let it be hid** i.e., draw the bedcurtains. (No stage direction specifies that the dead are to be carried offstage at the end of the play.)
**keep** guard   **377 seize upon** take legal possession of   **378 succeed on** pass as though by inheritance to   **379 censure** sentencing

# King Lear

In *King Lear*, Shakespeare pushes to its limit the hypothesis of a malign or at least indifferent universe in which human life is meaningless and brutal. Few plays other than *Hamlet* and *Macbeth* approach *King Lear* in evoking the wretchedness of human existence, and even they cannot match the devastating spectacle of the Earl of Gloucester blinded or Cordelia dead in Lear's arms. The responses of the chief characters are correspondingly searing. "Is man no more than this?" rages Lear. "Unaccommodated man is no more but such a poor, bare, forked animal as thou art" (3.4.101–7). Life he calls a "great stage of fools," an endless torment: "the first time that we smell the air / We wawl and cry" (4.6.179–83). Gloucester's despair takes the form of accusing the gods of gleeful malice toward humanity: "As flies to wanton boys are we to th' gods; / They kill us for their sport" (4.1.36–7). Gloucester's ministering son Edgar can offer him no greater consolation than stoic resolve: "Men must endure / Their going hence, even as their coming hither; / Ripeness is all" (5.2.9–11). These statements need not be read as choric expressions of meaning for the play as a whole, but they do attest to the depth of suffering. In no other Shakespearean play does injustice appear to triumph so ferociously, for so long, and with such impunity. Will the heavens countenance this reign of injustice on earth? Retribution is late in coming and is not certainly the work of the heavens themselves. For, at the last, we must confront the wanton death of the innocent Cordelia—a death no longer willed even by the villain who arranged her execution. "Is this the promised end?" (5.3.268) asks the Earl of Kent, stressing the unparalleled horror of the catastrophe.

Throughout its earlier history, the ancient story of King Lear had always ended happily. In the popular folktale of Cinderella, to which the legend of Lear's daughters bears a significant resemblance, the youngest and virtuous daughter triumphs over her two older wicked sisters and is married to her princely wooer. Geoffrey of Monmouth's *Historia Regum Britanniae* (c. 1136), the earliest known version of the Lear story, records that, after Lear is overthrown by his sons-in-law (more than by his daughters), he is restored to his throne by the intervention of the French King and is allowed to enjoy his kingdom and Cordelia's love until his natural death. (Cordelia, as his successor, is later dethroned and murdered by her wicked nephews, but that is another story.) Sixteenth-century Tudor versions of the Lear story with which Shakespeare was familiar—John Higgins's account in *The First Part of the Mirror for Magistrates* (1574), Raphael Holinshed's *Chronicles* (1587), Edmund Spenser's *The Faerie Queene*, 2.10.27–32, and a play called *The True Chronicle History of King Leir* (by 1594, published 1605)—all retain the happy ending. The tragic pattern may have been suggested instead by Shakespeare's probable source for the Gloucester-Edgar-Edmund plot, Sir Philip Sidney's *Arcadia*, 2.10, in which the Paphlagonian King is the victim of filial ingratitude and deceit.

Yet even Shakespeare's authority was not sufficient to put down the craving for a happy resolution. Nahum Tate's adaptation (1681), which banished the Fool as indecorous for a tragedy and united Edgar and Cordelia in marriage, placing Lear once again on his throne, held the English stage for about 150 years. David Garrick restored some of Shakespeare's lines, and Edmund Kean restored the tragic ending, but it was not until 1838 that *King Lear* was again performed more or less as the dramatist wrote it. One of Shakespeare's editors, Dr. Samuel Johnson, evidently spoke for most eighteenth-century audiences when he confessed that he could hardly bring himself to read Shakespeare's text. Cordelia's slaughter violated that age's longing for "poetic justice." Her death implied a wanton universe and so counseled philosophic despair. Today, Shakespeare's relentless honesty and refusal to accept easy answers convince us that he was right to defy the conventions of his source, though no doubt we, too, distort the play to conform with our supposed toughness of vision.

Shakespeare evidently wrote *King Lear* some time before it was performed at court in December of 1606, probably in 1605 and certainly no earlier than 1603–1604; Edgar's speeches as Tom o' Bedlam contain references to Samuel Harsnett's *Declaration of Egregious Popish Impostures,* which was registered for publication in March of 1603. Thus, *King Lear* was probably written between *Othello* (c. 1603–1604) and *Macbeth* (c. 1606–1607), when Shakespeare was at the height of his literary power in the writing of tragedies.

When we look at the play in formal terms, we are apt to be struck first by its complex double plot. Nowhere else in Shakespearean tragedy do we find anything approaching the rich orchestration of the double plotting in *King Lear*. The links and parallels between the two plots are established on a narrative level early in the play and continue to the end. King Lear misjudges his children and disinherits his loving daughter Cordelia in favor of her duplicitous sisters, whereas Gloucester falls prey to Edmund's deceptions and disinherits his loyal son Edgar; Lear is turned out into the storm by his false daughters, while Gloucester is branded as a traitor by Edmund and deprived of his eyesight; Lear in his madness realizes his fault against Cordelia, while the blind Gloucester "sees" at last the truth about Edgar; and both fathers are cared for by their loving children and are belatedly reconciled to them, but then die brokenhearted. As recent criticism has noted, these narrative parallels are not especially significant in themselves; we are moved, not by the mere repetition of events, but by the enlargement of tragic vision that results from the counterpointing of two such actions. When we see juxtaposed to each other two scenes of trial, Lear's mad arraignment of the absent Goneril and Regan and then the cruel imposition of the mere "form of justice" on the pinioned Gloucester (3.6 and 3.7), we begin to measure the extent to which justice and injustice are inverted by cruelty. When at last the two old men come together, during the storm scenes and especially at Dover, the sad comfort they derive from sharing the wreckage of their lives calls forth piercing eloquence against the stench of mortality. The sight is "most pitiful in the meanest wretch, / Past speaking of in a king" (4.6.204–5).

The play's double structure suggests another duality central to *King Lear:* an opposition of parable and realism, in which "divided and distinguished worlds" are bound together for instructive contrast. (These terms are Maynard Mack's, in his *King Lear in Our Time,* 1965.) To a remarkable degree, this play derives its story from folklore and legend, with many of the wondrous and implausible circumstances of popular romance. A prose rendition might almost begin, "Once upon a time there was a king who had three daughters. . . ." Yet Shakespeare arouses romantic expectation only to crush it by aborting the conventional happy ending, setting up a dramatic tension between an idealized world of make-believe and the actual world of disappointed hopes. We are aware of artifice and convention, and yet are deeply moved by the "truth" of suffering, love, and hatred. The characters pull us two ways at once; we regard them as types with universalized characteristics—a king and father, his cruel daughters, his loving daughter, and the like—and yet we scrutinize them for psychological motivation because they seem so real and individual.

This duality appears in both the central and the secondary characters. The King of France is in part a hero out of romance, who makes selfless choices and rescues the heroine Cordelia from her distress; yet his motive must also be appraised in the context of a bitter struggle for power. Why does he leave the English court "in choler," and why does he return to England with an army? Is it only to aid his wife and her beleaguered father, or is he negotiating for military advantage? Certainly, a French invasion of England on behalf of Lear complicates the issues of loyalty for the well-meaning Duke of Albany (and perhaps as well for an English Renaissance audience, with its habitual mistrust of the French). The dual focus of the play invites conflicting interpretation. Similarly, Edgar is presented to us on the one hand as the traduced victim in a starkly pessimistic story, dominated by his rationalistic brother, Edmund, who scoffs at religion and undertakes to manipulate those around him for personal gain; on the other hand, Edgar's story grows increasingly improbable as he undertakes a series of disguises and emerges finally as an anonymous champion of chivalry, challenging his brother in the lists like a knight-errant out of Arthurian romance. Edgar's motives are hard to follow. Is he the hero of a fabulous story whose disguises and contriving of illusions for his father are simply part of that storytelling tradition, or is he, in more realistic terms, a man whose disguises are a defensive mask and whose elaborate contrivances defeat themselves? Edmund, his brother, is no less complex. Onstage today he is usually interpreted as smooth and plausible, well-motivated by his father's condescending attitude and by the arbitrariness of the law that has excluded him from legitimacy and inheritance. Yet parable elevates Edmund into something monstrous. He becomes an embodiment of gleeful villainy, like Iago in *Othello,* malignantly evil simply because the evil that is in the universe must find a human form through which to express itself. Edmund's belated attempt to do some good adds to our difficulties in appraising his character, but the restless power of the dual conception supplies a vitality not to be found in pure fable or in realistic literature.

What we see then in Edmund and in others is the union of the universal and the particular, making *King Lear* at once parable and compellingly real. The parable or folktale element is prominent at the beginning of the play and focuses attention on the archetypal situations with which the story is concerned: rivalry between siblings, fear of parental rejection, and, at the same time, parental fear of children's callousness. The "unrealistic" contrast between Cordelia and her wicked sisters, or between Edgar and Edmund, is something we accept as a convention of storytelling, because it expresses vividly the psychic truth of rivalry between brothers and sisters. We identify with Cordelia and Edgar as virtuous children whose worth is misjudged, and who are losing to wicked siblings the contest for parental approval. (In folklore, the rejecting parent is usually a stepparent, which signifies our conviction that he or she is not a true parent at all.) Similarly, we accept as a meaningful convention of storytelling the equally "unrealistic" device by which Lear tests the love of his daughters. Like any parent, he wishes to be loved and appreciated in response to the kindnesses he has performed. The tension between fathers and their marriageable daughters is a recurrent pattern in Shakespeare's late plays, as in *Othello* (in which Brabantio accuses Desdemona of deceiving and deserting him), in *Pericles, Cymbeline,* and *The Winter's Tale,* and in *The Tempest,* in which the pattern is best resolved. In *King Lear,* Shakespeare explores the inherently explosive situation of an imperious father who, having provided for his children and having grown old, assumes he has a right to expect that those children will express their love and gratitude by looking after him.

The difficulty is that the parable of Lear and his children presents two contrasting viewpoints—that of the unappreciated child and that of the unwanted aging parent. Tragic misunderstanding is inevitable, and it outweighs the question of assessing blame. From Lear's point of view, Cordelia's silence is a truculent scanting of obedience. What he has devised is, after all, only a prearranged formality, with Cordelia to receive the richest third of England. Cannot such a ceremony be answered with the conventional hyperbole of courtly language, to which the King's ear is attuned? Don't parents have a right to be verbally reassured of their children's love? How can children be so laconic about such a precious matter? For her part, however, Cordelia senses that Lear is demanding love as payment for his parental kindliness, quid pro quo. Genuine love ought rather to be selfless, as the King of France tells the Duke of Burgundy: "Love's not love / When it is mingled with regards that stands / Aloof from th'entire point" (1.1.242–4). Is Cordelia being asked to prefer Lear before her own husband-to-be? Is this the price she must pay for her upbringing? Lear's ego seems fully capable of demanding this sacrifice from his daughters, especially from his favorite, Cordelia; he has given them his whole kingdom, now let them care for him as befits his royal rank and patriarchal role. The "second childishness" of his old age brings with it a self-centered longing to monopolize the lives of his children and to be a child again. Besides, as king, Lear has long grown accustomed to flattery and absolute obedience. Goneril and Regan are content to flatter and promise obedience, knowing they will turn him out once he has relinquished his authority. Cordelia refuses to lie in this fashion, but she also will not yield to Lear's implicit request for her undivided affection. Part of her must be loyal to her own husband and her children, in the natural cycle of the generations. "When I shall wed, / That lord whose hand must take my plight shall carry / Half my love with him, half my care and duty" (1.1.100–2). Marriage will not prevent her from obeying, loving, and honoring her father as is fit but will establish for her a new priority. To Lear, as to other fathers contemplating a daughter's marriage in late Shakespearean plays, this savors of desertion.

Lear is sadly deficient in self-knowledge. As Regan dryly observes, "he hath ever but slenderly known himself" (1.1.296–7) and has grown ever more changeable and imperious with age. By dividing his kingdom in three, ostensibly so that "future strife / May be prevented now" (lines 44–5), he instead sets in motion a civil war and French invasion. His intention of putting aside his regal authority while still retaining "The name and all th'additions to a king" (line 136) perhaps betrays a lack of comprehension of the realities of power, although Lear may also have plausible political reasons for what he does, in view of the restive ambitions of the Dukes of Cornwall, Albany, and Burgundy. In any case, he welcomes poisoned flattery but interprets well-intended criticism, whether from Cordelia or Kent, as treason. These failures in no sense justify what Lear's ungrateful children do to him; as he later says, just before going mad, "I am a man / More sinned against than sinning" (3.2.59–60). His failures are, however, tokens of his worldly insolence, for which he must fall. The process is a painful one, but, since it brings self-discovery, it is not without its compensations. Indeed, a central paradox of the play is that by no other way could Lear have learned what human suffering and need are all about.

Lear's Fool is instrumental in elucidating this paradox. The Fool offers Lear advice in palatable form as mere foolery or entertainment and thus obtains a hearing when Kent and Cordelia have been angrily dismissed. Beneath his seemingly innocent jibes, however, are plain warnings of the looming disaster Lear blindly refuses to acknowledge. The Fool knows, as indeed any fool could tell, that Goneril and Regan are remorseless and unnatural. The real fool, therefore, is Lear himself, for having placed himself in their power. In a paradox familiar to Renaissance audiences—as in Erasmus's *In Praise of Folly,* Cervantes's *Don Quixote,* and Shakespeare's own earlier *As You Like It* and *Twelfth Night*—folly and wisdom exchange places. By a similar inversion of logic, the Fool offers his coxcomb to the Earl of Kent for siding with Lear in his exile, "for taking one's part that's out of favor" (1.4.97). Worldly wisdom suggests that we serve those whose fortunes are on the rise, as the obsequious and servile Oswald does.

Indeed, the sinister progress of the first half of the play seems to confirm the Fool's contention that kindness and love are a sure way to exile and poverty. "Let go thy hold when a great wheel runs down a hill lest it break thy neck with following; but the great one that goes upward, let him draw thee after" (2.4.70–3). Yet the Fool resolves to ignore his own sardonic advice; "I would have none but knaves follow it, since a fool gives it" (lines 74–5). Beneath his mocking, the Fool expresses the deeper truth that it is better to be a "fool" and suffer than to win on the cynical world's terms. The greatest fools truly are those who prosper through cruelty and become hardened in sin. As the Fool puts it, deriving a seemingly contrary lesson from Lear's rejection of Cordelia: "Why, this fellow has banished two on 's daughters and did the third a blessing against his will" (1.4.99–101).

These inversions find a parallel in Christian teaching, although the play is nominally pagan in setting. (The lack of explicit Christian reference may be in part the result of a parliamentary order in 1606 banning references to "God" onstage as blasphemous.) Christianity does not hold a monopoly on the idea that one must lose the world in order to win a better world, but its expressions of that idea were plentifully available to Shakespeare: "Blessed are the meek, for they shall inherit the earth" (the Sermon on the Mount); "Go and sell that thou hast, and give to the poor, and thou shalt have treasure in heaven" (Matthew 19:21); "He hath put down the mighty from their seats, and exalted them of low degree" (Luke 1:52). Cordelia's vision of genuine love is of this exalted spiritual order. She is, as the King of France extols her, "most rich being poor, / Most choice, forsaken, and most loved, despised" (1.1.254–5). This is the sense in which Lear has bestowed on her an unintended blessing, by exiling her from a worldly prosperity that is inherently pernicious. Now, with poetic fitness, Lear must learn the same lesson himself. He does so, paradoxically, at the very moment he goes mad, parting ways with the conventional truths of the corrupted world. "My wits begin to turn," he says (3.2.67), and then speaks his first kind words to the Fool, who is his companion in the storm. Lear senses companionship with a fellow mortal who is cold and outcast as he is. In his madness, he perceives both the worth of this insight and the need for suffering to attain it: "The art of our necessities is strange, / And can make vile things precious" (lines 70–1). Misery teaches Lear things he never could know as king about other "Poor naked wretches" who "bide the pelting of this pitiless storm." How are such poor persons to be fed and clothed? "Oh, I have ta'en / Too little care of this! Take physic, pomp; / Expose thyself to feel what wretches feel, / That thou mayst shake the superflux to them / And show the heavens more just" (3.4.28–36). This vision of perfect justice is visionary and utopian, utterly mad, in fact, but it is also spiritual wisdom dearly bought.

Gloucester learns a similar truth and expresses it in much the same way. Like Lear, he has driven into exile a virtuous child and has placed himself in the power of the wicked. Enlightenment comes only through suffering. Just as Lear achieves spiritual wisdom when he goes mad, Gloucester achieves spiritual vision when he is physically blinded. His eyes having been ground out by the heel of Cornwall's boot, Gloucester asks for Edmund only to learn that Edmund has betrayed him in return for siding with Lear in the approaching civil war. Gloucester's response, however, is not to accuse Edmund of treachery but to beg forgiveness of the wronged Edgar. No longer does Gloucester need eyes to see this truth: "I stumbled when I saw." Although the discovery is shattering, Gloucester perceives, as does Lear, that adversity is paradoxically of some benefit, since prosperity had previously caused him to be so spiritually blind. "Full oft 'tis seen / Our means secure us, and our mere defects / Prove our commodities" (4.1.19–21). And this realization leads him, as it does Lear, to express a longing for utopian social justice in which arrogant men will be humbled and the poor raised up by redistributed wealth. "Heavens, deal so still! / Let the superfluous and lust-dieted man, / That slaves your ordinance, that will not see / Because he does not feel, feel your pow'r quickly! / So distribution should undo excess / And each man have enough" (lines 65–70).

To say that Lear and Gloucester learn something precious is not, however, to deny that they are also devastated and broken by their savage humiliation. Indeed, Gloucester is driven to a despairing attempt at suicide, and Lear remains obsessed with the rotten stench of his own mortality, "bound / Upon a wheel of fire" (4.7.47–8). Every decent value that we like to associate with civilization is grotesquely inverted during the storm scenes. Justice, for example, is portrayed in two sharply contrasting scenes: the mere "form of justice" by which Cornwall condemns Gloucester for treason (3.7.26) and the earnestly playacted trial by which the mad Lear arraigns Goneril and Regan of filial ingratitude (3.6). The appearance and the reality of justice have exchanged places, as have folly and wisdom or blindness and seeing. The trial of Gloucester is outwardly correct, for Cornwall possesses the legal authority to try his subjects and at least goes through the motions of interrogating his prisoner. The outcome is, however, cruelly predetermined. In the playacting trial concurrently taking place in a wretched hovel, the outward appearance of justice is pathetically absurd. Here, justice on earth is personified by a madman (Lear), Edgar disguised as another madman (Tom o' Bedlam), and a Fool, of whom the latter two are addressed by Lear as "Thou robèd man of justice" and "thou, his yokefellow of equity" (lines 36–7). They are caught up in a pastime of illusion, using a footstool to represent Lear's ungrateful daughters. Yet true justice is here and not inside the manor house.

Similar contrasts invert the values of loyalty, obedience, and family bonds. Edmund becomes, in the language of the villains, the "loyal" son whose loyalty is demonstrated by turning on his own "traitorous" father. Cornwall becomes a new father to Edmund ("thou shalt find a dearer father in my love," 3.5.25–6). Conversely, a servant who tries to restrain Cornwall from blinding Gloucester is, in Regan's eyes, monstrously insubordinate. "A peasant stand up thus?" (3.7.83). Personal and sexual relationships betray signs of the universal malaise. The explicitly sexual ties in the play, notably those of Goneril, Regan, and Edmund, are grossly carnal and lead to jealousy and murder, while in Cordelia's wifely role the sensual is underplayed. The relationships we are invited to cherish—those of Cordelia, Kent, the Fool, and Gloucester to King Lear, and Edgar to Gloucester—are filial or are characterized by loyal service, both of which are pointedly nonsexual. Nowhere do we find an embodiment of love that is both sensual and spiritual, as in Desdemona in *Othello* or Hermione in *The Winter's Tale*. The Fool's and Tom o' Bedlam's (i.e., Edgar's) gibes about codpieces and plackets (3.2.27–40, 3.4.96) anticipate Lear's towering indictment of carnality, in which his fear of woman's insatiable appetite and his revulsion at her body "Down from the waist" ("there is the sulfurous pit, burning, scalding, stench, consumption. Fie, fie, fie! Pah, pah!") combine with a destructive self-hatred (4.6.124–30).

All these inversions and polarizations are subsumed in the inversion of the word "natural." Edmund is the "natural" son of Gloucester, meaning literally that he is illegitimate. Figuratively, he therefore represents a violation of traditional moral order. In appearance he is smooth and plausible, but in reality he is an archdeceiver like the Vice in a morality play, a superb actor who boasts to the audience in soliloquy of his protean villainy. "Nature" is Edmund's goddess, and by this he means something like a naturalistic universe in which the race goes to the swiftest and in which conscience, morality, and religion are empty myths. Whereas Lear invokes Nature as a goddess who will punish ungrateful daughters and defend rejected fathers (1.4.274–88) and whereas Gloucester believes in a cosmic correspondence between eclipses of the moon or sun and mutinous discords among people (1.2.106–17), Edmund scoffs at all such metaphysical speculations. He spurns, in other words, the Boethian conception of a divine harmony uniting the cosmos and humankind, with humankind at the center of the universe. As a rationalist, Edmund echoes Jacobean disruptions of the older world order in politics and religion as well as in science. He is Machiavellian, an atheist, and Epicurean—everything inimical to traditional Elizabethan ideals of order. To him, "natural" means precisely what Lear and Gloucester call "unnatural."

His creed provides the play with its supreme test. Which definition of "natural" is true? Does heaven exist, and will it let Edmund and the other villainous persons get away with their evil? The question is frequently asked, but the answers are ambiguous. "If you do love old men," Lear implores the gods, "if your sweet sway / Allow obedience, if you yourselves are old, / Make it your cause" (2.4.191–3). His exhortations mount into frenzied rant, until finally the heavens do send down a terrible storm—on Lear himself. Witnesses agree that the absence of divine order in the universe would have the gravest consequences. "If that the heavens do not their visible spirits / Send quickly down to tame these vile offenses," says Albany of Lear's ordeal, "It will come, / Humanity must perforce prey on itself, / Like monsters of the deep" (4.2.47–51). And Cornwall's servants (in a passage missing from the Folio text) have perceived earlier the dire implications of their masters' evil deeds. "I'll never care what wickedness I do, / If this man come to good," says one, and his fellow agrees: "If she [Regan] live long, / And in the end meet the old course of death, / Women will all turn monsters" (3.7.102–5). Yet these servants do, in fact, obey their own best instincts, turning on Cornwall and ministering to Gloucester despite danger to themselves. Similarly, Albany abandons his mild attempts to conciliate his domineering wife and instead uses his power for good. Cordelia's ability to forgive and cherish her father, and Edgar's comparable ministering to Gloucester, give the lie to Edmund's "natural" or amoral view of humanity; a few people, at least, are capable of charity, even when it does not serve their own material self-interest. Conversely, the play suggests that villainy will at last destroy itself, and not simply because the gods are just; Albany's hopeful insistence that "This shows you are above, / You justicers" (4.2.79–80) may be a little more than wishful thinking, to be undercut by some fresh disaster, but at least the insatiable ambitions of Edmund, Goneril, Regan, Cornwall, and Oswald do lead to their violent deaths. Edmund's belated attempt to save the life of Cordelia, though unsuccessful, suggests that this intelligent villain has at last begun to understand the great flaw in his naturalistic creed and to see that, like Goneril and Regan, he has been consumed by his own lust.

Even with such reassurances that villainy will eventually undo itself, the devastation at the end of *King Lear* is so appalling that our questions about justice remain finally unanswered. To ask the question "Who must pay for Lear's self-knowledge?" is to remind ourselves that women must often die in Shakespeare's tragedies so that men may learn, and to perceive even further that, in the absurdist world of *Lear*, the Cartesian logic of cause and effect and poetic justice simply will not account for all that we long to understand. As Roland Barthes well expresses the matter in an essay on Racine, "tragedy is only a means of reclaiming human unhappiness, of subsuming it, thus justifying it under the form of necessity, or wisdom, or purification." Tragedy cannot explain away the death of Cordelia and the heartbreak of her father. The last tableau is a vision of doomsday, with Cordelia strangled, Lear broken and dying, and the "gored state" in such disarray that we cannot be sure what restoration can occur. The very question of political order is dwarfed by the enormity of the personal disaster of Lear and Cordelia. No one wishes longer life for the King: "He hates him / That would upon the rack of this tough world / Stretch him out longer." He is dead; "The wonder is he hath endured so long" (5.3.319–26). Lear's view of life's terrible corruption, pronounced in his madness, seems confirmed in his end. Perhaps the only way in which this tragedy can redeem so much unhappiness is to suggest that, given the incurable badness of the world, we can at least choose whether to attempt to be like Cordelia and Edgar (knowing what the price may be for such courage) or to settle for being our worst selves, like Edmund, Goneril, and Regan. Overwhelmed as we are by the testimonial before us of humankind's vicious capacity for self-destruction, we are stirred nonetheless by the ability of some men and women to confront their fearful destiny with probity and stoic renunciation, adhering to what they believe to be good and expecting Fortune to give them absolutely nothing. The power of love, though learned too late to avert catastrophe, is at last discovered in its very defeat.

*King Lear* has become a fable for our times, on stage, in film and television, and in fictional adaptations in novel form. The role of Lear has been a compelling one for so many great Shakespearean actors, including Philip Kemble, Henry Irving, Edwin Forrest, John Gielgud, Donald Wolfit, Donald Sinden, Brian Cox, Michael Gambon, Robert Stephens, Greg Hicks, Ian McKellen, Colm Feore, and John Wood. Peter Brook's film version of 1970, based on a stage production of 1962, with Paul Scofield as Lear, did much to equate the play's bleak vision with that of our modern existential world. Stimulated by Jan Kott's *Shakespeare Our Contemporary* (translated 1964), a post–World War II apocalyptic interpretation of Shakespeare from the perspective of an ideologically embattled eastern Europe, Brook unfolds a narrative of unrelieved disillusionment. The medium of film enables him to show what it would be like, for example, to have a hundred knights and all their followers descend on Albany's castle at the same time, demanding to be fed and quarreling with the servants of Goneril and Albany; the din and confusion are overwhelming, to such an extent that one can see Goneril's point in wanting to cut back on the King's retinue. A barren, wintry landscape adds visual reinforcement to the savage energies of family and dynastic conflict. Grigori Kozintsev's film of 1971, the work of a great Soviet director, sees the larger movements of the play in Marxist terms as the dialectical imperatives of political and social history; again, the medium of film makes it possible for Kozintsev to do

what the stage cannot do, deploy huge casts of anonymous soldiers and workers as both victims and movers of social change. Laurence Olivier's performance of Lear for Granada Television (directed by Michael Elliott, 1983, Granada Video, 1984) came at the very end of Olivier's life, as his climactic and final role; his interpretation is deeply enhanced by one's perception that the actor is literally dying of cancer. Olivier, weakened but determined, had to be helped through the rigors of the screening, with the result that his Lear is tender, vulnerable, frail, though capable of the outbursts of rage that often come with advanced age. His *King Lear* is about the approach of death. Akira Kurosawa, in his epic *Ran* (1985), chose a more radical adaptation, that of telling a story of a Japanese warlord and his three sons, one of them (like Cordelia) dear but misunderstood, the others treacherous. One of their wives (the Lady Kaede) turns out to be another Edmund, Goneril, Regan, and Lady Macbeth all combined in one, fiercely and murderously determined that her husband succeed by whatever means possible. Kurosawa's vision of evil in the human heart is meant to be terrifying, and it is. The Royal National Theatre production of *King Lear* won several awards for Best Actor (Ian Holm as Lear) and Best Director (Richard Eyre), and is available on video from the BBC and Mobil Masterpiece Theatre (1998). In fiction, Jane Smiley's *A Thousand Acres* (1991) features a similar transposition, in this case to a midwestern American farm run by an aging farmer who transfers his land to his daughters and then sinks into alcoholism and insanity as two daughters squabble over their inheritance and end up losing everything, including their husbands, while their sister Caroline (Cordelia), unwilling to take part in the dividing of the farm, tries unsuccessfully as a lawyer to have the property restored to her father. Edward Bond's stage play called *Lear* (1971) accentuated *King Lear*'s already formidable bleakness by adding to its cruelty and violence; in it, war became a never-ending cycle of repression and escalating oppression. In these varied reworkings, we see the remarkable malleability of *King Lear* as an endlessly fascinating subject for new historicist, cultural materialist, deconstructive, and feminist readings that open up topics of misogyny and patriarchy, political ideologies, and philosophical pessimism.

*King Lear* exists in two early texts, the quarto of 1608 and the considerably changed Folio version of 1623. Similar disparities appear in *Hamlet*, *Othello*, *Troilus and Cressida*, *Henry IV Part II*, and a number of other plays, but the problem is especially acute in *King Lear*. Shakespeare must have had a hand in the revisions that led to the Folio text. It contains new material. At the same time, the quarto text contains passages not found in the Folio. The revisions may have resulted from a number of circumstances: cutting for performance (the play as it stands in either version is probably too long to have been produced in its entirety on the Jacobean stage), censorship, errors in transcription, and still more. The Folio version does alter some matters especially having to do with the French invasion; characters like Albany appear in a different light. The very ending is changed as to which characters speak the concluding lines.

Given these factors, many editions today present two or even three texts for the reader, or mark the text with brackets and other indicators of textual variation. This present edition does not do so, though the textual notes do indicate the differences that occur. The reasons for choosing to present here the more traditional composite or eclectic text are these: *King Lear's* textual variations between quarto and Folio are more extensive than in some other plays, but are not always different in kind, so that it is a distortion to treat this play alone as a multiple-text play. To choose either quarto or Folio is to lose important material that is unquestionably Shakespeare's. To print two or even three versions is to add pages to an already weighty collection. And the presentation of multiple texts, or of a single text that is flagged with bracketed markers, also imposes on the reader a task of sorting out a complex and uncertain textual history that, however important ultimately in studying Shakespeare as a writer and as a reviser, is perhaps best left to subsequent investigation in a full-scale critical edition after one has absorbed the greatness of this play as a piece of writing for the theater. The present composite *King Lear*, based chiefly on the Folio text but including the 300 or so lines found only in the first quarto along with some quarto readings where the Folio version seems less textually reliable, is in a sense a compromise, but it is one that seems well suited to the purposes of this present edition.

# *King Lear*

[*Dramatis Personae*

KING LEAR
GONERIL,
REGAN,        } *Lear's daughters*
CORDELIA,
DUKE OF ALBANY, *Goneril's husband*
DUKE OF CORNWALL, *Regan's husband*
KING OF FRANCE, *Cordelia's suitor and husband*
DUKE OF BURGUNDY, *suitor to Cordelia*

EARL OF KENT, *later disguised as Caius*
EARL OF GLOUCESTER
EDGAR, *Gloucester's son and heir, later disguised as poor Tom*
EDMUND, *Gloucester's bastard son*

OSWALD, *Goneril's steward*
A KNIGHT *serving King Lear*
*Lear's* FOOL
CURAN, *in Gloucester's household*
GENTLEMEN
*Three* SERVANTS
OLD MAN, *a tenant of Gloucester*
*Three* MESSENGERS
A GENTLEMAN *attending Cordelia as a Doctor*
*Two* CAPTAINS
HERALD

*Knights, Gentlemen, Attendants, Servants, Officers, Soldiers, Trumpeters*

SCENE: *Britain*]

# 1.1

*Enter Kent, Gloucester, and Edmund.*

KENT     I thought the King had more affected the Duke of     1
Albany than Cornwall.     2

GLOUCESTER     It did always seem so to us; but now in
the division of the kingdom it appears not which of     4
the dukes he values most, for equalities are so weighed     5
that curiosity in neither can make choice of either's     6
moiety.     7

KENT     Is not this your son, my lord?

GLOUCESTER     His breeding, sir, hath been at my charge.     9
I have so often blushed to acknowledge him that now
I am brazed to't.     11

KENT     I cannot conceive you.     12

GLOUCESTER     Sir, this young fellow's mother could;
whereupon she grew round-wombed and had indeed,
sir, a son for her cradle ere she had a husband
for her bed. Do you smell a fault?     16

KENT     I cannot wish the fault undone, the issue of it     17
being so proper.     18

GLOUCESTER     But I have a son, sir, by order of law, some     19
year elder than this, who yet is no dearer in my ac-     20
count. Though this knave came something saucily to     21
the world before he was sent for, yet was his mother
fair, there was good sport at his making, and the     23
whoreson must be acknowledged.—Do you know this     24
noble gentleman, Edmund?

EDMUND     No, my lord.

GLOUCESTER     My lord of Kent. Remember him hereafter
as my honorable friend.

EDMUND     My services to Your Lordship.     29

KENT     I must love you, and sue to know you better.     30

EDMUND     Sir, I shall study deserving.     31

GLOUCESTER     He hath been out nine years, and away     32
he shall again. The King is coming.     33

*Sennet. Enter [one bearing a coronet, then] King
Lear, Cornwall, Albany, Goneril, Regan, Cordelia,
and attendants.*

LEAR
Attend the lords of France and Burgundy, Gloucester.     34

GLOUCESTER     I shall, my liege.     *Exit.*     35

LEAR
Meantime we shall express our darker purpose.     36
Give me the map there. [*He takes a map.*] Know that we
have divided
In three our kingdom; and 'tis our fast intent     38
To shake all cares and business from our age,
Conferring them on younger strengths while we
Unburdened crawl toward death. Our son of
Cornwall,     41
And you, our no less loving son of Albany,     42
We have this hour a constant will to publish     43
Our daughters' several dowers, that future strife     44
May be prevented now. The princes, France and
Burgundy,
Great rivals in our youngest daughter's love,
Long in our court have made their amorous sojourn
And here are to be answered. Tell me, my
daughters—
Since now we will divest us both of rule,
Interest of territory, cares of state—     50
Which of you shall we say doth love us most?
That we our largest bounty may extend     52
Where nature doth with merit challenge. Goneril,     53
Our eldest born, speak first.

GONERIL
Sir, I love you more than words can wield the matter,
Dearer than eyesight, space, and liberty,     56
Beyond what can be valued, rich or rare,
No less than life, with grace, health, beauty, honor;
As much as child e'er loved, or father found;     59
A love that makes breath poor and speech unable.     60
Beyond all manner of so much I love you.

CORDELIA [*aside*]
What shall Cordelia speak? Love and be silent.

LEAR [*indicating on map*]
Of all these bounds, even from this line to this,
With shadowy forests and with champains riched,     64
With plenteous rivers and wide-skirted meads,     65
We make thee lady. To thine and Albany's issue
Be this perpetual.—What says our second daughter,
Our dearest Regan, wife of Cornwall? Speak.

REGAN
Sir, I am made of that self mettle as my sister,     69
And prize me at her worth. In my true heart     70
I find she names my very deed of love;     71
Only she comes too short, that I profess     72
Myself an enemy to all other joys
Which the most precious square of sense possesses,     74

---

**1.1. Location: King Lear's palace.**
**1 affected** favored     **2 Albany** i.e., Scotland     **4 it appears not** it is not clear
**5–7 equalities . . . moiety** the shares balance so equally that close scrutiny
cannot find advantage in either's portion.     **9 breeding** raising, care.
**charge** expense.     **11 brazed** hardened     **12 conceive** understand. (But
Gloucester puns in the sense of "become pregnant.")     **16 fault** (1) sin (2) loss
of scent by the hounds.     **17 issue** (1) result (2) offspring     **18 proper**
(1) excellent (2) handsome.     **19 by order of law** legitimate     **19–20 some
year** about a year     **20–1 account** estimation.     **21 knave** young fellow,
scamp.     **something** somewhat     **23 fair** beautiful     **24 whoreson** low
fellow; suggesting bastardy, but (like *knave* above) used with affectionate
condescension     **29 services** duty     **30 sue** petition, beg     **31 study
deserving** strive to be worthy (of your esteem).     **32 out** i.e., abroad,
absent     **33.1** *Sennet* trumpet signal heralding a procession.     *one . . . then*
(This direction is from the quarto. The *coronet* is perhaps intended for
Cordelia or her betrothed. A coronet signifies nobility below the rank of
king.)     **34 Attend** Wait upon, usher ceremoniously     **35 liege** lord to
whom I owe feudal obedience.

---

**36 we, our** (The royal plural; also in lines 37–44, etc.)     **darker purpose**
undeclared intention.     **38 fast** firm     **41, 42 son** son-in-law
**43 constant . . . publish** firm resolve to proclaim     **44 several dowers**
individual dowries     **50 Interest of** right or title to, possession of
**52 That** So that     **53 Where . . . challenge** where both natural affection and
merit claim our bounty as their due.     **56 space, and liberty** possession of
land, and freedom of action     **59 found** i.e., found himself to be loved
**60 breath . . . unable** utterance impoverished and speech inadequate.
**64 shadowy** shady.     **champains riched** fertile plains     **65 plenteous . . .
meads** abundant rivers bordered with wide meadows     **69 that self
mettle** that same spirited temperament     **70 prize . . . worth** value myself
as her equal (in love for you). (*Prize* suggests "price.")     **71 names . . .
love** describes my love in action     **72 that** in that     **74 Which . . .
possesses** which the most delicately sensitive part of my nature can enjoy

And find I am alone felicitate 75
In your dear Highness' love.

CORDELIA [*aside*]        Then poor Cordelia!
And yet not so, since I am sure my love's
More ponderous than my tongue. 78

LEAR
To thee and thine hereditary ever
Remain this ample third of our fair kingdom,
No less in space, validity, and pleasure 81
Than that conferred on Goneril.—Now, our joy,
Although our last and least, to whose young love 83
The vines of France and milk of Burgundy 84
Strive to be interessed, what can you say to draw 85
A third more opulent than your sisters'? Speak.

CORDELIA   Nothing, my lord.

LEAR   Nothing?

CORDELIA   Nothing.

LEAR
Nothing will come of nothing. Speak again.

CORDELIA
Unhappy that I am, I cannot heave
My heart into my mouth. I love Your Majesty
According to my bond, no more nor less. 93

LEAR
How, how, Cordelia? Mend your speech a little,
Lest you may mar your fortunes.

CORDELIA        Good my lord,
You have begot me, bred me, loved me. I
Return those duties back as are right fit, 97
Obey you, love you, and most honor you.
Why have my sisters husbands if they say
They love you all? Haply, when I shall wed, 100
That lord whose hand must take my plight shall carry 101
Half my love with him, half my care and duty.
Sure I shall never marry like my sisters,
To love my father all.

LEAR
But goes thy heart with this?

CORDELIA        Ay, my good lord.

LEAR   So young, and so untender?

CORDELIA   So young, my lord, and true.

LEAR
Let it be so! Thy truth then be thy dower!
For, by the sacred radiance of the sun,
The mysteries of Hecate and the night, 110
By all the operation of the orbs 111
From whom we do exist and cease to be, 112
Here I disclaim all my paternal care,
Propinquity, and property of blood, 114
And as a stranger to my heart and me

Hold thee from this forever. The barbarous Scythian, 116
Or he that makes his generation messes 117
To gorge his appetite, shall to my bosom
Be as well neighbored, pitied, and relieved 119
As thou my sometime daughter.

KENT        Good my liege— 120

LEAR   Peace, Kent!
Come not between the dragon and his wrath.
I loved her most, and thought to set my rest 123
On her kind nursery. [*To Cordelia*] Hence, and avoid
   my sight!— 124
So be my grave my peace, as here I give 125
Her father's heart from her. Call France. Who stirs? 126
Call Burgundy.        [*Exit one.*]
        Cornwall and Albany,
With my two daughters' dowers digest the third. 128
Let pride, which she calls plainness, marry her. 129
I do invest you jointly with my power,
Preeminence, and all the large effects 131
That troop with majesty. Ourself by monthly course, 132
With reservation of an hundred knights 133
By you to be sustained, shall our abode
Make with you by due turns. Only we shall retain
The name and all th'additions to a king. 136
The sway, revenue, execution of the rest, 137
Belovèd sons, be yours, which to confirm,
This coronet part between you.

KENT        Royal Lear, 139
Whom I have ever honored as my king,
Loved as my father, as my master followed,
As my great patron thought on in my prayers—

LEAR
The bow is bent and drawn. Make from the shaft. 143

KENT
Let it fall rather, though the fork invade 144
The region of my heart. Be Kent unmannerly
When Lear is mad. What wouldst thou do, old man?
Think'st thou that duty shall have dread to speak
When power to flattery bows?
To plainness honor's bound 149
When majesty falls to folly. Reserve thy state, 150
And in thy best consideration check 151
This hideous rashness. Answer my life my judgment, 152

---

**116 this** this time forth.   **Scythian** (Scythians were famous in antiquity for savagery.)   **117 makes . . . messes** makes meals of his children or parents   **119 neighbored** helped in a neighborly way
**120 sometime** former   **123 set my rest** rely wholly. (A phrase from a
game of cards, meaning "to stake all.")   **124 nursery** nursing, care.
**avoid** get out of   **125 So . . . peace, as** As I hope to rest peacefully in
my grave   **126 Who stirs?** i.e., Jump to it; don't just stand there.
**128 digest** assimilate, incorporate   **129 Let . . . her** Let pride, which
she calls plain speaking, be her dowry and get her a husband.
**131 effects** outward shows   **132 troop with** accompany, serve.
**Ourself** (The royal "we.")   **133 With reservation of** reserving to myself
the right to be attended by   **136 th'additions** the honors and prerogatives   **137 sway** sovereign authority   **139 coronet** (Perhaps Lear
gestures toward this coronet that was to have symbolized Cordelia's
dowry and marriage, hands it to his sons-in-law, or actually attempts
to divide it.)   **143 Make from** Get out of the way of   **144 fall** strike.
**fork** barbed head of an arrow   **149 To . . . bound** Loyalty demands
frankness   **150 Reserve thy state** Retain your royal authority
**151 And . . . check** and with wise deliberation restrain   **152 Answer . . .
judgment** I wager my life on my judgment that

**75 I am alone felicitate** I am only made happy   **78 ponderous** weighty
**81 validity** value.   **pleasure** pleasing features   **83 least** youngest
**84 vines** vineyards.   **milk** pastures (?)   **85 be interessed** be affiliated,
establish a claim, be admitted as to a privilege.   **draw** win   **93 bond**
filial obligation   **97 right fit** proper and fitting   **100 all** exclusively,
and with all of themselves.   **Haply** Perhaps, with luck   **101 plight**
pledge in marriage   **110 mysteries** secret rites.   **Hecate** goddess of
witchcraft and the moon   **111 operation** influence.   **orbs** planets and
stars   **112 From whom** under whose influence   **114 Propinquity . . .
blood** close kinship, and rights and duties entailed in blood ties

Thy youngest daughter does not love thee least,
Nor are those emptyhearted whose low sounds
Reverb no hollowness.

LEAR                          Kent, on thy life, no more.       155

KENT
My life I never held but as a pawn                             156
To wage against thine enemies, nor fear to lose it,            157
Thy safety being motive.

LEAR                          Out of my sight!                 158

KENT
See better, Lear, and let me still remain
The true blank of thine eye.                                   160

LEAR    Now, by Apollo—

KENT    Now, by Apollo, King,
Thou swear'st thy gods in vain.                                163

LEAR    Oh, vassal! Miscreant!                                 164

            [*Laying his hand on his sword.*]

ALBANY, CORNWALL    Dear sir, forbear.

KENT
Do, kill thy physician, and the fee bestow
Upon the foul disease. Revoke thy gift,
Or whilst I can vent clamor from my throat
I'll tell thee thou dost evil.

LEAR
Hear me, recreant, on thine allegiance hear me!               170
Since thou hast sought to make us break our vows,
Which we durst never yet, and with strained pride             172
To come betwixt our sentence and our power,                   173
Which nor our nature nor our place can bear,                   174
Our potency made good, take thy reward.                       175
Five days we do allot thee for provision
To shield thee from disasters of the world,
And on the sixth to turn thy hated back
Upon our kingdom. If on the tenth day following
Thy banished trunk be found in our dominions,                 180
The moment is thy death. Away! By Jupiter,
This shall not be revoked.

KENT
Fare thee well, King. Sith thus thou wilt appear,             183
Freedom lives hence and banishment is here.
[*To Cordelia*] The gods to their dear shelter take thee,
    maid,
That justly think'st and hast most rightly said!
[*To Regan and Goneril*] And your large speeches may
    your deeds approve,                                        187
That good effects may spring from words of love.
Thus Kent, O princes, bids you all adieu.

He'll shape his old course in a country new.       *Exit.* 190

    *Flourish. Enter Gloucester, with France and*
    *Burgundy; attendants.*

GLOUCESTER
Here's France and Burgundy, my noble lord.

LEAR    My lord of Burgundy,
We first address toward you, who with this king               193
Hath rivaled for our daughter. What in the least              194
Will you require in present dower with her
Or cease your quest of love?

BURGUNDY                      Most royal Majesty,
I crave no more than hath Your Highness offered,
Nor will you tender less.

LEAR                          Right noble Burgundy,            198
When she was dear to us we did hold her so,                   199
But now her price is fallen. Sir, there she stands.
If aught within that little-seeming substance,                201
Or all of it, with our displeasure pieced,                    202
And nothing more, may fitly like Your Grace,                  203
She's there, and she is yours.

BURGUNDY                      I know no answer.

LEAR
Will you, with those infirmities she owes,                    205
Unfriended, new-adopted to our hate,
Dowered with our curse and strangered with our
    oath,                                                      207
Take her, or leave her?

BURGUNDY                  Pardon me, royal sir.
Election makes not up in such conditions.                     209

LEAR
Then leave her, sir, for by the power that made me,
I tell you all her wealth. [*To France*] For you, great King, 211
I would not from your love make such a stray                  212
To match you where I hate; therefore beseech you             213
T'avert your liking a more worthier way                       214
Than on a wretch whom Nature is ashamed
Almost t'acknowledge hers.

FRANCE                        This is most strange,
That she whom even but now was your best object,
The argument of your praise, balm of your age,                218
Most best, most dearest, should in this trice of time         219
Commit a thing so monstrous to dismantle                      220
So many folds of favor. Sure her offense
Must be of such unnatural degree
That monsters it, or your fore-vouched affection              223
Fall into taint, which to believe of her                      224

---

**155 Reverb no hollowness** do not reverberate like a hollow drum, insincerely.    **156–7 My . . . wage** I never regarded my life other than as a pledge to hazard in battle. (A *pawn* suggests also a chess piece or a stake here wagered on behalf of the King.)    **158 motive** that which prompts me to act.    **160 The true . . . eye** i.e., the means to enable you to see better. (*Blank* means "the white center of the target," or, "the true direct aim," as in "point-blank," traveling in a straight line.)    **163 Thou . . . in vain** i.e., you invoke Apollo and other gods in vain when you ask them to aid you in disowning Cordelia.    **164 vassal** i.e., wretch.    **Miscreant** (Literally, infidel, heretic; hence, villain, rascal.)    **170 recreant** traitor    **172 strained** excessive    **173 To . . . power** i.e., to block my power to command and judge    **174 Which . . . place** which neither my temperament nor my office as king    **175 Our . . . good** my power enacted, demonstrated    **180 trunk** body    **183 Sith** Since    **187 your . . . approve** may your deeds confirm your speeches with their vast claims

**190 shape . . . course** follow his traditional plainspoken ways    **190.1 Flourish** trumpet fanfare used for the entrance or exit of important persons    **193 address** address myself    **194 rivaled** competed. **in the least** at the lowest    **198 tender** offer    **199 so** i.e., *dear*, beloved and valued at a high price    **201 little-seeming substance** one who seems substantial but whose substance is, in fact, little, or, one who refuses to flatter    **202 pieced** added, joined    **203 like** please    **205 owes** owns    **207 strangered** disowned    **209 Election . . . conditions** No choice is possible under such conditions.    **211 tell you** (1) inform you of (2) enumerate for you.    **For** As for    **212 make such a stray** stray so far    **213 To** as to. **beseech** I beseech    **214 T'avert your liking** to turn your affections    **218 argument** theme    **219 trice** moment    **220 to** as to    **223 monsters it** makes it monstrous    **223–4 or . . . taint** or else the affection for her you have hitherto affirmed must fall into suspicion

Must be a faith that reason without miracle
Should never plant in me.

CORDELIA     I yet beseech Your Majesty—
If for I want that glib and oily art      228
To speak and purpose not, since what I well intend      229
I'll do't before I speak—that you make known
It is no vicious blot, murder, or foulness,      231
No unchaste action or dishonored step
That hath deprived me of your grace and favor,
But even for want of that for which I am richer:      234
A still-soliciting eye and such a tongue      235
That I am glad I have not, though not to have it
Hath lost me in your liking.

LEAR                  Better thou
Hadst not been born than not t'have pleased me better.

FRANCE
Is it but this? A tardiness in nature
Which often leaves the history unspoke      240
That it intends to do?—My lord of Burgundy,
What say you to the lady? Love's not love
When it is mingled with regards that stands      243
Aloof from th'entire point. Will you have her?      244
She is herself a dowry.

BURGUNDY [to Lear]     Royal King,
Give but that portion which yourself proposed,
And here I take Cordelia by the hand,
Duchess of Burgundy.

LEAR
Nothing. I have sworn. I am firm.

BURGUNDY [to Cordelia]
I am sorry, then, you have so lost a father
That you must lose a husband.

CORDELIA            Peace be with Burgundy!
Since that respects of fortune are his love,      252
I shall not be his wife.

FRANCE
Fairest Cordelia, that art most rich being poor,
Most choice, forsaken, and most loved, despised,
Thee and thy virtues here I seize upon,
Be it lawful I take up what's cast away.      257
                    [He takes her hand.]
Gods, gods! 'Tis strange that from their cold'st neglect  258
My love should kindle to inflamed respect.—      259
Thy dowerless daughter, King, thrown to my chance,   260
Is queen of us, of ours, and our fair France.
Not all the dukes of wat'rish Burgundy      262
Can buy this unprized precious maid of me.—     263
Bid them farewell, Cordelia, though unkind.      264
Thou losest here, a better where to find.      265

LEAR
Thou hast her, France. Let her be thine, for we
Have no such daughter, nor shall ever see
That face of hers again. Therefore begone
Without our grace, our love, our benison.      269
Come, noble Burgundy.
          Flourish. Exeunt [all but France, Goneril, Regan,
                          and Cordelia].

FRANCE     Bid farewell to your sisters.

CORDELIA
Ye jewels of our father, with washed eyes      272
Cordelia leaves you. I know you what you are,
And like a sister am most loath to call      274
Your faults as they are named. Love well our father.  275
To your professèd bosoms I commit him.      276
But yet, alas, stood I within his grace,
I would prefer him to a better place.      278
So, farewell to you both.

REGAN
Prescribe not us our duty.

GONERIL            Let your study
Be to content your lord, who hath received you
At Fortune's alms. You have obedience scanted,     282
And well are worth the want that you have wanted.   283

CORDELIA
Time shall unfold what plighted cunning hides;     284
Who covers faults, at last shame them derides.     285
Well may you prosper!

FRANCE            Come, my fair Cordelia.
               Exeunt France and Cordelia.

GONERIL     Sister, it is not little I have to say of what most
nearly appertains to us both. I think our father will
hence tonight.

REGAN     That's most certain, and with you; next month
with us.

GONERIL     You see how full of changes his age is; the   292
observation we have made of it hath not been little.   293
He always loved our sister most, and with what poor
judgment he hath now cast her off appears too grossly.  295

REGAN     'Tis the infirmity of his age. Yet he hath ever
but slenderly known himself.

GONERIL     The best and soundest of his time hath been  298
but rash. Then must we look from his age to receive  299
not alone the imperfections of long-engraffed condi-  300
tion, but therewithal the unruly waywardness that in-  301
firm and choleric years bring with them.

REGAN     Such unconstant starts are we like to have from  303
him as this of Kent's banishment.

228 for I want because I lack   229 purpose not not intend to do what
I say   231 foulness immorality   234 for which for lack of which
235 still-soliciting ever begging   240 history tale, narrative   243–4
regards . . . point irrelevant considerations.   252 Since . . . fortune
Since concern for wealth and position   257 Be it lawful if it be lawful
that   258–9 'Tis . . . respect It's strange that my love for one whom the
gods seem to regard with cold neglect should kindle to such an ardent
degree.   260 chance lot   262 wat'rish (1) well-watered with rivers
(2) feeble, watery   263 unprized not appreciated. (With perhaps a sense
also of "priceless.")   264 though unkind though they have behaved
unnaturally.   265 here this place.   where place elsewhere

269 benison blessing.   272 washed tear-washed   274 like a sister
i.e., because I am your sister   275 as . . . named by their true names.
276 professèd bosoms publicly avowed love   278 prefer advance, recommend   282 At . . . alms as a pittance or dole from Fortune.   283 And
well . . . wanted i.e., and well deserve to be without the dowry and the
parental affection that you have both lacked and flouted.   284–5 Time . . .
derides Time will bring to light what cunning attempts to conceal as if
in the folds of a cloak; those who hide their faults may do so for a while,
but in time they will be shamed and derided.   292–3 the observation . . .
little we have had ample opportunity to observe this changeability
in our father.   295 grossly obviously.   298–9 The best . . . rash Even in
the prime of his life, he was stormy and unpredictable.   300–1 long-
engraffed condition long-implanted habit   301 therewithal added
thereto   303 unconstant starts impulsive outbursts.   like likely

GONERIL  There is further compliment of leave-taking 305
  between France and him. Pray you, let us hit together. 306
  If our father carry authority with such disposition as 307
  he bears, this last surrender of his will but offend us. 308
REGAN  We shall further think of it.
GONERIL  We must do something, and i'th' heat. 310

Exeunt.

❖

## 1.2

Enter Bastard [Edmund, with a letter].

EDMUND
  Thou, Nature, art my goddess; to thy law 1
  My services are bound. Wherefore should I
  Stand in the plague of custom and permit 3
  The curiosity of nations to deprive me, 4
  For that I am some twelve or fourteen moonshines 5
  Lag of a brother? Why bastard? Wherefore base? 6
  When my dimensions are as well compact, 7
  My mind as generous, and my shape as true, 8
  As honest madam's issue? Why brand they us 9
  With base? With baseness? Bastardy? Base, base?
  Who in the lusty stealth of nature take 11
  More composition and fierce quality 12
  Than doth within a dull, stale, tirèd bed
  Go to th' creating a whole tribe of fops 14
  Got 'tween asleep and wake? Well, then, 15
  Legitimate Edgar, I must have your land.
  Our father's love is to the bastard Edmund 17
  As to th' legitimate. Fine word, "legitimate"!
  Well, my legitimate, if this letter speed 19
  And my invention thrive, Edmund the base 20
  Shall top the legitimate. I grow, I prosper.
  Now, gods, stand up for bastards!

Enter Gloucester.

GLOUCESTER
  Kent banished thus? And France in choler parted? 23
  And the King gone tonight? Prescribed his power, 24
  Confined to exhibition? All this done 25
  Upon the gad? Edmund, how now? What news? 26
EDMUND  So please Your Lordship, none.

[Putting up the letter.]

GLOUCESTER  Why so earnestly seek you to put up that
  letter?
EDMUND  I know no news, my lord.
GLOUCESTER  What paper were you reading?
EDMUND  Nothing, my lord.
GLOUCESTER  No? What needed then that terrible dis- 33
  patch of it into your pocket? The quality of nothing 34
  hath not such need to hide itself. Let's see. Come, if it
  be nothing I shall not need spectacles.
EDMUND  I beseech you, sir, pardon me. It is a letter
  from my brother, that I have not all o'erread; and for 38
  so much as I have perused, I find it not fit for your
  o'erlooking. 40
GLOUCESTER  Give me the letter, sir.
EDMUND  I shall offend either to detain or give it. The
  contents, as in part I understand them, are to blame. 43
GLOUCESTER  Let's see, let's see.

[Edmund gives the letter.]

EDMUND  I hope for my brother's justification he wrote
  this but as an essay or taste of my virtue. 46
GLOUCESTER (reads)  "This policy and reverence of age 47
  makes the world bitter to the best of our times, keeps 48
  our fortunes from us till our oldness cannot relish
  them. I begin to find an idle and fond bondage in the 50
  oppression of aged tyranny, who sways not as it hath 51
  power but as it is suffered. Come to me, that of this I 52
  may speak more. If our father would sleep till I waked
  him, you should enjoy half his revenue forever and live
  the beloved of your brother,                  Edgar."
  Hum! Conspiracy! "Sleep till I waked him, you should
  enjoy half his revenue." My son Edgar! Had he
  a hand to write this? A heart and brain to breed it
  in? When came this to you? Who brought it?
EDMUND  It was not brought me, my lord; there's the
  cunning of it. I found it thrown in at the casement of 61
  my closet. 62
GLOUCESTER  You know the character to be your 63
  brother's?
EDMUND  If the matter were good, my lord, I durst 65
  swear it were his; but in respect of that I would fain 66
  think it were not.
GLOUCESTER  It is his.
EDMUND  It is his hand, my lord, but I hope his heart is
  not in the contents.
GLOUCESTER  Has he never before sounded you in this 71
  business?
EDMUND  Never, my lord. But I have heard him oft
  maintain it to be fit that, sons at perfect age and fathers 74
  declined, the father should be as ward to the son, and 75
  the son manage his revenue.

---

**305 compliment** ceremony  **306 hit** agree  **307–8 If . . . offend us** If our father continues to boss us around with his accustomed imperiousness, this most recent display of willfullness will do us nothing but harm.  **310 i'th' heat** i.e., while the iron is hot.
**1.2. Location:** The Earl of Gloucester's house.
**1 Nature** i.e., the sanction that governs the material world through mechanistic amoral forces  **3 Stand . . . custom** submit to the vexatious injustice of inheritance law  **4 The curiosity of nations** arbitrary social gradations  **5 For that** because.  **moonshines** months  **6 Lag of** lagging behind, younger than  **7 dimensions** proportions.  **compact** knit together, fitted  **8 generous** noble, refined  **9 honest** chaste  **11–12 Who . . . quality** Whose begetting in the sexual act both requires and engenders a fuller mixture and more energetic force  **14 fops** fools  **15 Got** begotten  **17 to** as much to  **19 speed** succeed, prosper  **20 invention thrive** scheme prosper  **23 in choler parted** having left angrily.  **24 tonight** last night.  **Prescribed** Limited  **25 exhibition** an allowance, pension.  **26 Upon the gad** suddenly, as if pricked by a gad or spur.

**33–4 terrible dispatch** fearful quick disposal  **38 for** as for  **40 o'erlooking** perusal.  **43 to blame** (The Folio reading, "too blame," "too blameworthy to be shown," may be correct.)  **46 essay or taste** assay, test  **47 policy and reverence of** policy of reverencing  **48 the best . . . times** the best years of our lives, i.e., our youth  **50 idle and fond** useless and foolish  **51 who sways** which rules  **52 suffered** permitted.  **61 casement** window  **62 closet** private room.  **63 character** handwriting  **65 matter** contents  **66 in . . . that** considering what the contents are.  **fain** gladly  **71 sounded you** sounded you out  **74 fit** fitting, appropriate.  **perfect age** full maturity  **75 declined** having become feeble

GLOUCESTER     Oh, villain, villain! His very opinion in the 77
letter! Abhorred villain! Unnatural, detested, brutish 78
villain! Worse than brutish! Go, sirrah, seek him. I'll 79
apprehend him. Abominable villain! Where is he?

EDMUND     I do not well know, my lord. If it shall please
you to suspend your indignation against my brother
till you can derive from him better testimony of his
intent, you should run a certain course; where, if you 84
violently proceed against him, mistaking his purpose,
it would make a great gap in your own honor and
shake in pieces the heart of his obedience. I dare pawn 87
down my life for him that he hath writ this to feel my 88
affection to Your Honor, and to no other pretense of 89
danger. 90

GLOUCESTER     Think you so?

EDMUND     If Your Honor judge it meet, I will place you 92
where you shall hear us confer of this, and by an 93
auricular assurance have your satisfaction, and that 94
without any further delay than this very evening.

GLOUCESTER     He cannot be such a monster—

EDMUND     Nor is not, sure.

GLOUCESTER     To his father, that so tenderly and entirely loves him. Heaven and earth! Edmund, seek
him out; wind me into him, I pray you. Frame the 100
business after your own wisdom. I would unstate 101
myself to be in a due resolution. 102

EDMUND     I will seek him, sir, presently, convey the 103
business as I shall find means, and acquaint you
withal. 105

GLOUCESTER     These late eclipses in the sun and moon 106
portend no good to us. Though the wisdom of nature 107
can reason it thus and thus, yet nature finds itself
scourged by the sequent effects. Love cools, friend- 109
ship falls off, brothers divide; in cities, mutinies; in
countries, discord; in palaces, treason; and the bond
cracked twixt son and father. This villain of mine
comes under the prediction; there's son against father.
The King falls from bias of nature; there's father 114
against child. We have seen the best of our time.
Machinations, hollowness, treachery, and all ruinous 116
disorders follow us disquietly to our graves. Find out
this villain, Edmund; it shall lose thee nothing. Do it 118
carefully. And the noble and truehearted Kent banished! His offense, honesty! 'Tis strange.     *Exit.*

EDMUND     This is the excellent foppery of the world, that 121

when we are sick in fortune—often the surfeit of our 122
own behavior—we make guilty of our disasters the 123
sun, the moon, and the stars, as if we were villains by
necessity, fools by heavenly compulsion, knaves,
thieves, and treachers by spherical predominance, 126
drunkards, liars, and adulterers by an enforced obedience of planetary influence, and all that we are evil
in, by a divine thrusting on. An admirable evasion of 129
whoremaster man, to lay his goatish disposition to 130
the charge of a star! My father compounded with my 131
mother under the Dragon's tail and my nativity was 132
under Ursa Major, so that it follows I am rough and 133
lecherous. Fut, I should have been that I am, had the 134
maidenliest star in the firmament twinkled on my
bastardizing. Edgar—

*Enter Edgar.*

and pat he comes like the catastrophe of the old 137
comedy. My cue is villainous melancholy, with a sigh
like Tom o' Bedlam.—Oh, these eclipses do portend 139
these divisions! Fa, sol, la, mi. 140

EDGAR     How now, brother Edmund, what serious
contemplation are you in?

EDMUND     I am thinking, brother, of a prediction I read
this other day, what should follow these eclipses. 144

EDGAR     Do you busy yourself with that?

EDMUND     I promise you, the effects he writes of succeed 146
unhappily, as of unnaturalness between the child and 147
the parent, death, dearth, dissolutions of ancient amities, divisions in state, menaces and maledictions
against king and nobles, needless diffidences, banish- 150
ment of friends, dissipation of cohorts, nuptial 151
breaches, and I know not what.

EDGAR     How long have you been a sectary astronom- 153
ical? 154

EDMUND     Come, come, when saw you my father last?

EDGAR     The night gone by.

EDMUND     Spake you with him?

EDGAR     Ay, two hours together.

EDMUND     Parted you in good terms? Found you no
displeasure in him by word nor countenance? 160

EDGAR     None at all.

**77 villain** vile wretch, diabolical schemer   **78 Abhorred** Abhorrent. **detested** hated and hateful   **79 sirrah** (Form of address used to inferiors or children.)   **84 run a certain course** proceed with safety and certainty.   **where** whereas   **87–8 pawn down** stake   **88 feel** feel out   **89–90 pretense of danger** dangerous purpose.   **92 meet** fitting, proper   **93–4 by an . . . satisfaction** satisfy yourself as to the truth by what you hear   **100 wind me into him** insinuate yourself into his confidence. (*Me* is used colloquially.)   **Frame** Arrange   **101 after your own wisdom** as you think best.   **101–2 I would . . . resolution** I would give up my wealth and rank to know the truth, have my doubts resolved.   **103 presently** immediately.   **convey** manage   **105 withal** therewith.   **106 late** recent   **107 the wisdom of nature** natural science   **109 sequent effects** i.e., devastating consequences.   **114 bias of nature** natural inclination   **116 hollowness** insincerity   **118 lose thee nothing** i.e., earn you a reward.   **121 foppery** foolishness

**122–3 surfeit . . . behavior** consequences of our own overindulgence   **126 treachers** traitors.   **spherical predominance** astrological determinism, because a certain planet was ascendant at the hour of our birth   **129 divine** supernatural   **130–1 to the charge** to the responsibility   **131–2 compounded . . . Dragon's tail** had sex with my mother under the constellation Draco (not one of the regular signs of the zodiac), or under the descending point at which the moon's orbit intersects with the ecliptic or apparent orbit of the sun (when an eclipse might occur)   **133 Ursa Major** the Big Bear or Dipper—not one of the regular signs of the zodiac   **134 Fut** i.e., 'Sfoot, by Christ's foot.   **that** what   **137 pat** on cue.   **catastrophe** conclusion, resolution (of a play)   **139 Tom o' Bedlam** a lunatic patient of Bethlehem Hospital in London turned out to beg for his bread.   **140 divisions** social and family conflicts. (But with a musical sense also of florid variations on a theme, thus prompting Edmund's singing.)   **144 this other day** the other day   **146 promise** assure   **146–7 succeed unhappily** follow unluckily   **150 needless diffidences** groundless distrust of others   **151 dissipation of cohorts** breaking up of military companies, large-scale desertions   **153–4 sectary astronomical** believer in astrology.   **160 countenance** demeanor.

EDMUND   Bethink yourself wherein you may have offended him, and at my entreaty forbear his presence 163
until some little time hath qualified the heat of his 164
displeasure, which at this instant so rageth in him that
with the mischief of your person it would scarcely 166
allay.                                                    167

EDGAR   Some villain hath done me wrong.

EDMUND   That's my fear. I pray you, have a continent 169
forbearance till the speed of his rage goes slower; and, 170
as I say, retire with me to my lodging, from whence I
will fitly bring you to hear my lord speak. Pray ye, go! 172
There's my key. [*He gives a key.*] If you do stir abroad,
go armed.

EDGAR   Armed, brother?

EDMUND   Brother, I advise you to the best. I am no honest man if there be any good meaning toward you. I 177
have told you what I have seen and heard, but faintly, 178
nothing like the image and horror of it. Pray you, 179
away.

EDGAR   Shall I hear from you anon?

EDMUND
I do serve you in this business.            *Exit* [*Edgar*].
A credulous father and a brother noble,
Whose nature is so far from doing harms
That he suspects none; on whose foolish honesty
My practices ride easy. I see the business.          186
Let me, if not by birth, have lands by wit.          187
All with me's meet that I can fashion fit.      *Exit.* 188

## 1.3

*Enter Goneril, and [Oswald, her] steward.*

GONERIL   Did my father strike my gentleman for chiding of his fool?

OSWALD   Ay, madam.

GONERIL   By day and night he wrongs me! Every hour
He flashes into one gross crime or other                5
That sets us all at odds. I'll not endure it.
His knights grow riotous, and himself upbraids us
On every trifle. When he returns from hunting
I will not speak with him. Say I am sick.
If you come slack of former services                   10
You shall do well; the fault of it I'll answer.        11
                                        [*Horns within.*]

OSWALD   He's coming, madam. I hear him.

GONERIL
Put on what weary negligence you please,
You and your fellows. I'd have it come to question.    14
If he distaste it, let him to my sister,               15

---

163 **forbear his presence** avoid meeting him    164 **qualified** moderated    166 **with . . . person** with the harmful effect of your presence;
or, even if there were injury done to you    167 **allay** be allayed.
169–70 **have . . . forbearance** keep a wary distance    172 **fitly** at a fit
time.    **my lord** our father    177 **meaning** intention    178 **but faintly**
only with a faint impression    179 **image and horror** horrid reality
186 **practices** plots.    **the business** i.e., how my plots should proceed.
187 **wit** cleverness.    188 **meet** justifiable.    **fit** to my purpose.
**1.3. Location:** The Duke of Albany's palace.
5 **crime** offense    10 **If . . . services** If you serve him with less alacrity
than you did before    11 **answer** be answerable for.    14 **come to
question** be made an issue.    15 **distaste** dislike

---

Whose mind and mine, I know, in that are one,
Not to be overruled. Idle old man,                     17
That still would manage those authorities              18
That he hath given away! Now, by my life,
Old fools are babes again, and must be used
With checks as flatteries, when they are seen abused.  21
Remember what I have said.

OSWALD   Well, madam.

GONERIL
And let his knights have colder looks among you.
What grows of it, no matter. Advise your fellows so.
I would breed from hence occasions, and I shall,       26
That I may speak. I'll write straight to my sister     27
To hold my very course. Prepare for dinner.   *Exeunt.*

## 1.4

*Enter Kent [disguised].*

KENT
If but as well I other accents borrow                   1
That can my speech diffuse, my good intent              2
May carry through itself to that full issue             3
For which I razed my likeness. Now, banished Kent,      4
If thou canst serve where thou dost stand condemned,    5
So may it come thy master, whom thou lov'st,            6
Shall find thee full of labors.                         7

   *Horns within. Enter Lear, [Knights,] and
   attendants.*

LEAR   Let me not stay a jot for dinner. Go get it ready.  8
                            [*Exit an Attendant.*]
[*To Kent*] How now, what art thou?

KENT   A man, sir.

LEAR   What dost thou profess? What wouldst thou with  11
us?

KENT   I do profess to be no less than I seem: to serve
him truly that will put me in trust, to love him that is
honest, to converse with him that is wise and says     15
little, to fear judgment, to fight when I cannot choose, 16
and to eat no fish.                                    17

LEAR   What art thou?

KENT   A very honest-hearted fellow, and as poor as the
King.

---

17 **Idle** Foolish    18 **manage those authorities** exercise those prerogatives
21 **With . . . abused** with rebukes in place of flattering attentiveness, when
such flattery is seen to be taken advantage of.    26 **occasions** opportunities for taking offense    27 **speak** speak bluntly.    **straight** immediately
**1.4. Location:** The Duke of Albany's palace still. The sense of time
is virtually continuous.
1 **as well** i.e., as well as I have disguised myself by means of costume
2 **diffuse** render confused or indistinct    3–4 **May . . . likeness** may
achieve the desired result for which I scraped off my beard and
erased my outward appearance.    5 **If . . . condemned** i.e., if you
can obtain service under the very king who has banished you
6 **come** come to pass that    7.1 *within* offstage.    8 **stay** wait
8.1 *Attendant* (This attendant may be a knight; certainly the one who
speaks at line 50 is a knight.)    11 **What . . . profess?** What is your
special calling? (But Kent puns in his answer on *profess* meaning to
"claim.")    15 **honest** honorable.    **converse** associate    16 **judgment**
i.e., God's judgment.    **choose** i.e., choose but to fight    17 **eat no fish**
i.e., eat a manly diet (?), be a good Protestant (?).

**LEAR**    If thou be'st as poor for a subject as he's for a king, thou'rt poor enough. What wouldst thou?

**KENT**    Service.

**LEAR**    Who wouldst thou serve?

**KENT**    You.

**LEAR**    Dost thou know me, fellow?

**KENT**    No, sir, but you have that in your countenance 27 which I would fain call master. 28

**LEAR**    What's that?

**KENT**    Authority.

**LEAR**    What services canst thou do?

**KENT**    I can keep honest counsel, ride, run, mar a curi- 32 ous tale in telling it, and deliver a plain message 33 bluntly. That which ordinary men are fit for I am qualified in, and the best of me is diligence.

**LEAR**    How old art thou?

**KENT**    Not so young, sir, to love a woman for singing, 37 nor so old to dote on her for anything. I have years on my back forty-eight.

**LEAR**    Follow me; thou shalt serve me. If I like thee no worse after dinner, I will not part from thee yet.— Dinner, ho, dinner! Where's my knave, my fool? Go you and call my fool hither.      [*Exit one.*]

      *Enter steward* [*Oswald*].

You! You, sirrah, where's my daughter?

**OSWALD**    So please you—                    *Exit.*

**LEAR**    What says the fellow there? Call the clodpoll 46 back.                            [*Exit a knight.*] Where's my fool, ho? I think the world's asleep.

      [*Enter Knight.*]

How now? Where's that mongrel?

**KNIGHT**    He says, my lord, your daughter is not well.

**LEAR**    Why came not the slave back to me when I called 51 him?

**KNIGHT**    Sir, he answered me in the roundest manner, 53 he would not.

**LEAR**    He would not?

**KNIGHT**    My lord, I know not what the matter is, but to my judgment Your Highness is not entertained with 57 that ceremonious affection as you were wont. There's 58 a great abatement of kindness appears as well in the 59 general dependents as in the Duke himself also and 60 your daughter.

**LEAR**    Ha? Say'st thou so?

**KNIGHT**    I beseech you, pardon me, my lord, if I be mistaken, for my duty cannot be silent when I think Your Highness wronged.

**LEAR**    Thou but rememberest me of mine own concep- 66 tion. I have perceived a most faint neglect of late, 67 which I have rather blamed as mine own jealous 68

curiosity than as a very pretense and purpose of 69 unkindness. I will look further into't. But where's my fool? I have not seen him this two days. 71

**KNIGHT**    Since my young lady's going into France, sir, the Fool hath much pined away.

**LEAR**    No more of that. I have noted it well. Go you and tell my daughter I would speak with her.    [*Exit one.*] Go you call hither my fool.           [*Exit one.*]

      *Enter steward* [*Oswald*].

Oh, you, sir, you, come you hither, sir. Who am I, sir?

**OSWALD**    My lady's father.

**LEAR**    "My lady's father"? My lord's knave! You whore-son dog, you slave, you cur!

**OSWALD**    I am none of these, my lord, I beseech your pardon.

**LEAR**    Do you bandy looks with me, you rascal? 83                             [*He strikes Oswald.*]

**OSWALD**    I'll not be strucken, my lord. 84

**KENT**    Nor tripped neither, you base football player. 85                     [*He trips up Oswald's heels.*]

**LEAR**    I thank thee, fellow. Thou serv'st me, and I'll love thee.

**KENT**    Come, sir, arise, away! I'll teach you differences. 88 Away, away! If you will measure your lubber's length 89 again, tarry; but away! Go to. Have you wisdom? So. 90                      [*He pushes Oswald out.*]

**LEAR**    Now, my friendly knave, I thank thee. There's earnest of thy service.    [*He gives Kent money.*] 92

      *Enter Fool.*

**FOOL**    Let me hire him too. Here's my coxcomb. 93                      [*Offering Kent his cap.*]

**LEAR**    How now, my pretty knave, how dost thou?

**FOOL**    [*to Kent*]    Sirrah, you were best take my coxcomb. 95

**KENT**    Why, Fool?

**FOOL**    Why? For taking one's part that's out of favor. Nay, an thou canst not smile as the wind sits, thou'lt 98 catch cold shortly. There, take my coxcomb. Why, this 99 fellow has banished two on 's daughters and did the 100 third a blessing against his will. If thou follow him, thou 101 must needs wear my coxcomb.—How now, nuncle? 102 Would I had two coxcombs and two daughters.

**LEAR**    Why, my boy?

---

**27 countenance** face and bearing   **28 fain** willingly   **32 keep honest counsel** respect confidences   **32–3 curious** ornate, elaborate   **37 to love** as to love   **46 clodpoll** blockhead   **51 slave** wretch   **53 roundest** bluntest   **57 entertained** treated   **58 wont** accustomed to.   **59 appears** that appears   **60 general dependents** servants generally   **66 rememberest** remind   **66–7 conception** idea, thought.   **67 faint** halfhearted   **68–9 jealous curiosity** overscrupulous regard for matters of etiquette

**69 very pretense** true intention   **71 this** these   **83 bandy looks** exchange glances (in such a way as to imply that Oswald and Lear are social equals)   **84 strucken** struck   **85 football** (A raucous street game played by the lower classes.)   **88 differences** distinctions in rank.   **89–90 If . . . again** i.e., If you want to be laid out flat again, you clumsy ox   **90 Go to** (An expression of impatience or anger.) **Have you wisdom?** i.e., Wise up.   **92 earnest of** a first payment for **93 coxcomb** fool's cap, crested with a red comb.   **95 you were best** you had better   **98–9 an . . . shortly** i.e., if you can't play along with those in power, you'll find yourself out in the cold.   **100 banished** (Paradoxically, by giving Goneril and Regan his kingdom, Lear has lost them, given them power over him.)   **on 's** of his   **101 blessing** i.e., bestowing Cordelia on France and saving her from the curse of insolent prosperity   **102 nuncle** (Contraction of "mine uncle," the Fool's way of addressing Lear.)

FOOL   If I gave them all my living, I'd keep my coxcombs myself. There's mine; beg another of thy daughters. 105 106 107

LEAR   Take heed, sirrah—the whip.

FOOL   Truth's a dog must to kennel. He must be whipped out, when Lady the Brach may stand by th' fire and stink. 109 110

LEAR   A pestilent gall to me! 112

FOOL   Sirrah, I'll teach thee a speech.

LEAR   Do.

FOOL   Mark it, nuncle:

Have more than thou showest, 116
Speak less than thou knowest,
Lend less than thou owest, 118
Ride more than thou goest, 119
Learn more than thou trowest, 120
Set less than thou throwest; 121
Leave thy drink and thy whore,
And keep in-a-door, 123
And thou shalt have more 124
Than two tens to a score. 125

KENT   This is nothing, Fool.

FOOL   Then 'tis like the breath of an unfee'd lawyer; you gave me nothing for't. Can you make no use of nothing, nuncle? 127 128

LEAR   Why, no, boy. Nothing can be made out of nothing.

FOOL   [to Kent]   Prithee, tell him; so much the rent of his land comes to. He will not believe a fool. 132 133

LEAR   A bitter fool! 134

FOOL   Dost know the difference, my boy, between a bitter fool and a sweet one?

LEAR   No, lad. Teach me.

FOOL

That lord that counseled thee
To give away thy land,
Come place him here by me;
Do thou for him stand. 141
The sweet and bitter fool
Will presently appear: 143
The one in motley here, 144
The other found out there. 145

LEAR   Dost thou call me fool, boy?

FOOL   All thy other titles thou hast given away; that thou wast born with.

KENT   This is not altogether fool, my lord.

FOOL   No, faith, lords and great men will not let me; if I had a monopoly out, they would have part on't. And ladies too, they will not let me have all the fool to myself; they'll be snatching. Nuncle, give me an egg and I'll give thee two crowns. 150 151 153

LEAR   What two crowns shall they be?

FOOL   Why, after I have cut the egg i'th' middle and eat up the meat, the two crowns of the egg. When thou clovest thy crown i'th' middle and gav'st away both parts, thou bor'st thine ass on thy back o'er the dirt. Thou hadst little wit in thy bald crown when thou gav'st thy golden one away. If I speak like myself in this, let him be whipped that first finds it so. 156 157 158 159 160 161 162

[Sings.]   "Fools had ne'er less grace in a year, 163
For wise men are grown foppish 164
And know not how their wits to wear, 165
Their manners are so apish." 166

LEAR   When were you wont to be so full of songs, sirrah? 167

FOOL   I have used it, nuncle, e'er since thou mad'st thy daughters thy mother; for when thou gav'st them the rod and putt'st down thine own breeches, 169

[Sings]   "Then they for sudden joy did weep,
And I for sorrow sung,
That such a king should play bo-peep 174
And go the fools among."

Prithee, nuncle, keep a schoolmaster that can teach thy fool to lie. I would fain learn to lie.

LEAR   An you lie, sirrah, we'll have you whipped. 178

FOOL   I marvel what kin thou and thy daughters are. They'll have me whipped for speaking true, thou'lt have me whipped for lying, and sometimes I am whipped for holding my peace. I had rather be any kind o' thing than a fool. And yet I would not be thee, nuncle. Thou hast pared thy wit o' both sides and left nothing i'th' middle. Here comes one o' th' parings. 182

*Enter Goneril.*

LEAR

How now, daughter? What makes that frontlet on? You are too much of late i'th' frown. 186

105 **living** property   105–6 **keep my coxcombs** (as proof of my folly)   106–7 **beg . . . daughters** i.e., beg for the coxcomb that you deserve for dealing with your daughters as you did.   109 **must to** that must go to   110 **Brach** bitch hound (here likened to Goneril and Regan, who have been given favored places despite their reeking of dishonest flattery)   112 **gall** irritation, bitterness—literally, a painful swelling, or bile. (Lear is stung by the Fool's gibe because it is so true.)   116 **Have . . . showest** Don't display your wealth ostentatiously   118 **owest** own   119 **goest** i.e., on foot. (Travel on horseback, not afoot; more practical advice.)   120 **Learn** i.e., listen to.   **trowest** believe   121 **Set . . . throwest** don't stake everything on a single throw of the dice   123 **in-a-door** indoors, at home   124–5 **And . . . score** and you will do better than break even (since a *score* equals two tens, or twenty).   127–8 **'tis . . . for't** i.e., it's like adivce given you by an unpaid lawyer, presumably worth just about what you paid for it.   132–3 **so . . . to** (Because Lear has given away his land, he can collect no rent.)   134 **bitter** satirical   141 **Do . . . stand** take his place.   143 **presently** immediately   144 **motley** the parti-colored dress of the professional fool. (The Fool identifies himself as the sweet fool, Lear as the bitter fool who counseled himself to give away his kingdom.)   145 **found out there** discovered there. (The Fool points at Lear.)

150 **No . . . let me** i.e., Great persons at court will not let me monopolize folly; I am not *altogether fool* in the sense of being "all the fool there is"   151 **a monopoly out** a corner on the market. (The granting of monopolies was a common abuse under King James and Queen Elizabeth.)   **on't** of it.   153 **snatching** seizing their share (including sexual pleasure).   156–7 **and eat . . . meat** and have eaten the edible part   157 **the two crowns of the egg** i.e., the two halves of the eggshell.   158 **clovest** cleaved   159 **bor'st . . . dirt** i.e., bore the ass instead of letting the ass bear you.   160 **wit** sense   161–2 **If . . . so** If I speak like a fool in saying this, let the first person to discover the truth of this be whipped (since in this corrupt world those who speak truth are punished for doing so).   163–6 **"Fools . . . apish"** "Fools have never been so out of favor, for wise men foppishly trade places with the fools and no longer know how to show off their wit to advantage, they have grown so foolish in their manners."   167 **wont** accustomed   169 **used** practiced   174 **bo-peep** (A child's game).   178 **An** If   182 **holding my peace** holding my tongue.   186 **What . . . on?** What is that frown doing on your forehead? (A *frontlet* is a band worn on the forehead.)

FOOL    Thou wast a pretty fellow when thou hadst no
need to care for her frowning; now thou art an O with- 189
out a figure. I am better than thou art now; I am a fool, 190
thou art nothing. [*To Goneril*] Yes, forsooth, I will
hold my tongue; so your face bids me, though you say
nothing.
        Mum, mum,
        He that keeps nor crust nor crumb,                    195
        Weary of all, shall want some.                        196
    [*Pointing to Lear*] That's a shelled peascod.            197

GONERIL
    Not only, sir, this your all-licensed fool,               198
    But other of your insolent retinue
    Do hourly carp and quarrel, breaking forth                200
    In rank and not-to-be-endurèd riots. Sir,                 201
    I had thought by making this well known unto you
    To have found a safe redress, but now grow fearful,       203
    By what yourself too late have spoke and done,            204
    That you protect this course and put it on                205
    By your allowance; which if you should, the fault         206
    Would not scape censure, nor the redresses sleep          207
    Which in the tender of a wholesome weal                   208
    Might in their working do you that offense,               209
    Which else were shame, that then necessity                210
    Will call discreet proceeding.                            211

FOOL    For you know, nuncle,
        "The hedge sparrow fed the cuckoo so long             213
        That it had it head bit off by it young."             214
    So, out went the candle, and we were left darkling.       215

LEAR [*to Goneril*]    Are you our daughter?

GONERIL                                          Come, sir,
    I would you would make use of your good wisdom,
    Whereof I know you are fraught, and put away              218
    These dispositions which of late transport you            219
    From what you rightly are.

FOOL    May not an ass know when the cart draws the           221
    horse? Whoop, Jug! I love thee.                           222

LEAR
    Doth any here know me? This is not Lear.
    Doth Lear walk thus, speak thus? Where are his eyes?
    Either his notion weakens, or his discernings             225
    Are lethargied—Ha! Waking? 'Tis not so.                   226
    Who is it that can tell me who I am?

FOOL    Lear's shadow.

LEAR
    I would learn that; for, by the marks of sovereignty,     229
    Knowledge, and reason, I should be false persuaded        230
    I had daughters.                                          231

FOOL    Which they will make an obedient father.              232

LEAR    Your name, fair gentlewoman?

GONERIL
    This admiration, sir, is much o'th' savor                 234
    Of other your new pranks. I do beseech you                235
    To understand my purposes aright.
    As you are old and reverend, should be wise.              237
    Here do you keep a hundred knights and squires,
    Men so disordered, so debauched and bold                  239
    That this our court, infected with their manners,
    Shows like a riotous inn. Epicurism and lust              241
    Make it more like a tavern or a brothel
    Than a graced palace. The shame itself doth speak         243
    For instant remedy. Be then desired,                      244
    By her that else will take the thing she begs,
    A little to disquantity your train,                       246
    And the remainders that shall still depend                247
    To be such men as may besort your age,                    248
    Which know themselves and you.

LEAR                                   Darkness and devils! 249
    Saddle my horses! Call my train together!   [*Exit one.*] 250
    Degenerate bastard, I'll not trouble thee.
    Yet have I left a daughter.

GONERIL
    You strike my people, and your disordered rabble
    Make servants of their betters.                           254

        *Enter Albany.*

LEAR
    Woe, that too late repents!—Oh, sir, are you come?        255
    Is it your will? Speak, sir.—Prepare my horses.
                                              [*Exit one.*]
    Ingratitude, thou marble-hearted fiend,
    More hideous when thou show'st thee in a child
    Than the sea monster!

ALBANY    Pray, sir, be patient.

LEAR [*to Goneril*]    Detested kite, thou liest!             261
    My train are men of choice and rarest parts,              262
    That all particulars of duty know
    And in the most exact regard support                      264
    The worships of their name. Oh, most small fault,         265

189–90 O without a figure zero, cipher of no value unless preceded
by a digit.   195–6 He . . . some i.e., That person who, having grown
weary of his possessions, gives all away, will find himself in need of
part of what is gone.   196 want lack   197 shelled peascod shelled
pea pod, empty of its contents.   198 all-licensed allowed to speak or
act as he pleases   200 carp find fault   201 rank gross, excessive
203 safe certain   204 too late all too recently   205 put it on encourage it   206 allowance approval   207–11 nor . . . proceeding nor
would the punishments lie dormant which, out of care for the common welfare, might prove unpleasant to you—proceedings that the
stern necessity of the times will regard as prudent even if under normal circumstances they might seem shameful.   213 cuckoo a bird
that lays its eggs in other birds' nests   214 it head its head.   it young
i.e., the young cuckoo. (A cautionary fable about ungrateful children.)
215 darkling in the dark.   218 fraught freighted, provided   219 dispositions inclinations, moods   221–2 May . . . horse? i.e., May not
even a fool see that matters are backwards when a daughter lectures
her father?   222 Jug i.e., Joan. (A nickname for a whore.)   225 notion
intellectual power   225–6 or his . . . lethargied or his faculties are
asleep   226 Waking? i.e., Am I really awake?

229 I would learn that I would like to learn who I am.   marks of
sovereignty outward and visible evidence of being king   230–1 I
should . . . daughters i.e., all these outward signs of sanity and status
would seem to suggest (falsely) that I am the king who had obedient
daughters.   232 Which Whom   234 admiration (guise of) wonderment   235 other other of   237 should i.e., you should   239 Men . . .
bold men so disorderly, so depraved and impudent   241 Shows
appears.   Epicurism Gluttony, hedonism   243 graced dignified
244 desired requested   246 disquantity your train diminish the
number of your attendants   247 the remainders . . . depend those
who remain to attend you   248 besort befit   249 Which . . . you servants who have proper self-knowledge and an awareness of how they
should serve you.   250 train retinue   254 Make . . . betters treat their
masters like servants.   255 Woe, that Woe to the person who
261 kite bird of prey   262 parts qualities   264–5 And . . . name and
with utter scrupulousness uphold the honor of their reputation.

How ugly didst thou in Cordelia show!
Which, like an engine, wrenched my frame of nature 267
From the fixed place, drew from my heart all love, 268
And added to the gall. Oh, Lear, Lear, Lear! 269
Beat at this gate [*striking his head*] that let thy folly in
And thy dear judgment out!—Go, go, my people. 271

                          [*Exeunt some.*]

ALBANY
My lord, I am guiltless as I am ignorant
Of what hath moved you.

LEAR                 It may be so, my lord.—
Hear, Nature, hear! Dear goddess, hear!
Suspend thy purpose if thou didst intend
To make this creature fruitful!
Into her womb convey sterility;
Dry up in her the organs of increase,
And from her derogate body never spring 279
A babe to honor her! If she must teem, 280
Create her child of spleen, that it may live 281
And be a thwart disnatured torment to her! 282
Let it stamp wrinkles in her brow of youth,
With cadent tears fret channels in her cheeks, 284
Turn all her mother's pains and benefits 285
To laughter and contempt, that she may feel
How sharper than a serpent's tooth it is
To have a thankless child! Away, away!

       *Exit* [*with Kent and the rest of Lear's followers*].

ALBANY
Now, gods that we adore, whereof comes this?

GONERIL
Never afflict yourself to know more of it, 290
But let his disposition have that scope 291
As dotage gives it. 292

         *Enter Lear.*

LEAR
What, fifty of my followers at a clap?
Within a fortnight?

ALBANY            What's the matter, sir?

LEAR
I'll tell thee. [*To Goneril*] Life and death! I am ashamed
That thou hast power to shake my manhood thus,
That these hot tears, which break from me perforce, 296
Should make thee worth them. Blasts and fogs upon
      thee! 298
Th'untented woundings of a father's curse 299
Pierce every sense about thee! Old fond eyes, 300
Beweep this cause again, I'll pluck ye out 301
And cast you, with the waters that you loose, 302

To temper clay. Yea, is't come to this? 303
Let it be so. Yet have I left a daughter,
Who, I am sure, is kind and comfortable. 305
When she shall hear this of thee, with her nails
She'll flay thy wolvish visage. Thou shalt find
That I'll resume the shape which thou dost think 308
I have cast off forever.               *Exit.*

GONERIL [*to Albany*]    Do you mark that? 309

ALBANY
I cannot be so partial, Goneril,
To the great love I bear you— 311

GONERIL
Pray you, content.—What, Oswald, ho! 312
[*To the Fool*] You, sir, more knave than fool, after your
      master.

FOOL    Nuncle Lear, nuncle Lear! Tarry, take the Fool 314
     with thee. 315
         A fox, when one has caught her,
         And such a daughter
         Should sure to the slaughter, 318
         If my cap would buy a halter. 319
         So the Fool follows after.         *Exit.*

GONERIL
This man hath had good counsel. A hundred knights? 321
'Tis politic and safe to let him keep 322
At point a hundred knights—yes, that on every
      dream, 323
Each buzz, each fancy, each complaint, dislike, 324
He may enguard his dotage with their powers 325
And hold our lives in mercy.—Oswald, I say! 326

ALBANY    Well, you may fear too far. 327

GONERIL    Safer than trust too far.
Let me still take away the harms I fear, 329
Not fear still to be taken. I know his heart. 330
What he hath uttered I have writ my sister.
If she sustain him and his hundred knights
When I have showed th'unfitness—

       *Enter steward* [*Oswald*].

                      How now, Oswald?
What, have you writ that letter to my sister?

OSWALD    Ay, madam.

GONERIL
Take you some company and away to horse.
Inform her full of my particular fear,
And thereto add such reasons of your own
As may compact it more. Get you gone, 339

---

**267–8 Which . . . place** which, like a powerful mechanical contrivance, wrenched my natural affection away from where it belonged  **269 gall** bitterness.  **271 dear** precious  **279 derogate** debased  **280 teem** produce offspring  **281 spleen** violent ill nature  **282 thwart disnatured** obstinate, perverse, and unnatural  **284 cadent** cascading.  **fret** wear away  **285 benefits** pleasures of motherhood  **290 Never . . . know** Don't distress yourself by seeking to know  **291 disposition** humor, mood  **292 As** that  **296 perforce** against my will  **298 Should . . . them** should seem to suggest that you are worth a king's tears.  **Blasts and fogs** Infectious blights and disease-bearing fogs  **299 untented woundings** wounds that have not been probed and cleansed  **300 fond** foolish  **301 Beweep** if you weep for  **302 loose** let loose (in tears)

**303 To temper clay** to mix with earth. (Lear threatens to cast both his eyes and their tears to the ground.)  **305 comfortable** comforting. **308 the shape** i.e., the kingship  **309 Do . . . that?** i.e., Did you hear his threat to resume royal power?  **311 To** because of  **312 content** be quiet.  **314–15 take . . . thee** (1) take me with you (2) take the name "fool" with you. (A stock phrase of taunting farewell.)  **318 Should sure** should certainly be sent  **319 halter** (1) rope for leading an animal (2) hangman's noose.  **321 This . . . counsel** (Said sarcastically.) **322 politic** prudent. (Said ironically.)  **323 At point** armed and ready. **dream** i.e., imagined wrong  **324 buzz** idle rumor  **325 enguard** protect  **326 in mercy** at his mercy.  **327 fear too far** overestimate the danger.  **329 still take away** always remove  **330 Not . . . taken** rather than dwell continually in the fear of being taken prisoner by such harms.  **339 compact** confirm, compound

And hasten your return.                     [*Exit Oswald.*]
                        No, no, my lord,
This milky gentleness and course of yours                    341
Though I condemn not, yet, under pardon,                     342
You are much more attaxed for want of wisdom                 343
Than praised for harmful mildness.                           344

ALBANY
How far your eyes may pierce I cannot tell.                  345
Striving to better, oft we mar what's well.

GONERIL    Nay, then—

ALBANY    Well, well, th'event.                [*Exeunt.*] 348

❧

# 1.5

*Enter Lear, Kent [disguised as Caius], and Fool.*

LEAR [*giving a letter to Kent*]    Go you before to Gloucester   1
with these letters. Acquaint my daughter no further          2
with anything you know than comes from her demand            3
out of the letter. If your diligence be not speedy, I shall  4
be there afore you.

KENT    I will not sleep, my lord, till I have delivered your
letter.                                              *Exit.*

FOOL    If a man's brains were in 's heels, were't not in    8
danger of kibes?                                             9

LEAR    Ay, boy.

FOOL    Then, I prithee, be merry. Thy wit shall ne'er go   11
slipshod.                                                   12

LEAR    Ha, ha, ha!

FOOL    Shalt see thy other daughter will use thee kindly,  14
for though she's as like this as a crab's like an apple,    15
yet I can tell what I can tell.

LEAR    What canst tell, boy?

FOOL    She will taste as like this as a crab does to a crab.
Thou canst tell why one's nose stands i'th' middle
on 's face?                                                 20

LEAR    No.

FOOL    Why, to keep one's eyes of either side 's nose,     22
that what a man cannot smell out he may spy into.

LEAR    I did her wrong.                                    24

FOOL    Canst tell how an oyster makes his shell?

LEAR    No.

FOOL    Nor I neither. But I can tell why a snail has a
house.

LEAR    Why?

FOOL    Why, to put 's head in, not to give it away to his  30
daughters and leave his horns without a case.               31

LEAR    I will forget my nature. So kind a father!—Be my    32
horses ready?

FOOL    Thy asses are gone about 'em. The reason why        34
the seven stars are no more than seven is a pretty          35
reason.

LEAR    Because they are not eight.

FOOL    Yes, indeed. Thou wouldst make a good fool.

LEAR    To take't again perforce! Monster ingratitude!      39

FOOL    If thou wert my fool, nuncle, I'd have thee beaten
for being old before thy time.

LEAR    How's that?

FOOL    Thou shouldst not have been old till thou hadst
been wise.

LEAR
Oh, let me not be mad, not mad, sweet heaven!
Keep me in temper; I would not be mad!                      46

[*Enter Gentleman.*]

How now, are the horses ready?

GENTLEMAN    Ready, my lord.

LEAR    Come, boy.              [*Exeunt Lear and Gentleman.*]

FOOL
She that's a maid now, and laughs at my departure,
Shall not be a maid long, unless things be cut
    shorter.                                        *Exit.* 51

❧

# 2.1

*Enter Bastard [Edmund] and Curan, severally.*

EDMUND    Save thee, Curan.                                  1

CURAN    And you, sir. I have been with your father and
given him notice that the Duke of Cornwall and Regan
his duchess will be here with him this night.

EDMUND    How comes that?

CURAN    Nay, I know not. You have heard of the news
abroad—I mean the whispered ones, for they are yet          7
but ear-bussing arguments?                                  8

EDMUND    Not I. Pray you, what are they?

CURAN    Have you heard of no likely wars toward twixt     10
the Dukes of Cornwall and Albany?

EDMUND    Not a word.

CURAN    You may do, then, in time. Fare you well, sir.
                                                    *Exit.*

---

**341 milky . . . course** effeminate and gentle way    **342 under pardon**
if you'll excuse my saying so    **343 attaxed** taken to task for, blamed
**344 harmful mildness** mildness that causes harm.    **345 pierce**
i.e., see into matters    **348 th'event** i.e., time will tell.
**1.5. Location: Before Albany's palace.**
**1 before** on ahead.    **Gloucester** i.e., the place in Gloucestershire
**2 these letters** this letter.    **3 demand** inquiry    **4 out of** prompted by
**8–9 were't . . . kibes?** wouldn't his brains be in danger of that common
affliction of the heel called chilblains?    **11–12 Thy wit . . . slipshod**
i.e., Your brains would have no need for slippers to avoid chafing the
chilblains, since you have no brains. (Anyone who journeys to Regan
in hopes of kind treatment is utterly brainless.)    **14 Shalt** Thou
shalt.    **kindly** (1) with filial kindness (2) according to her own
nature    **15 crab** crab apple    **20 on 's** of one's    **22 of either side 's**
on either side of his    **24 her** i.e., Cordelia

**30–1 Why, to . . . case** i.e., The snail's head and horns are unendan-
gered with its *case* or shell; Lear, conversely, has given away his
crown to his daughters, leaving his brows unadorned and vulnerable.
(With a suggestion too of the cuckold's horned head, as though Lear's
victimization had a sexual dimension.)    **32 nature** natural affection.
(Compare line 14 and note.)    **34 Thy . . . 'em** i.e., Your servants (who
labor like asses in your service) have gone about readying the horses.
**35 seven stars** Pleiades    **39 To take't . . . perforce!** i.e., To think that
Goneril would forcibly take back again the privileges guaranteed to
me! (Or perhaps Lear is meditating an armed restoration of his monarchy.)    **46 temper** mental equilibrium    **51 things** i.e., penises.
**cut shorter** (A bawdy joke addressed to the audience.)
**2.1. Location: The Earl of Gloucester's house.**
**0.1 severally** separately.    **1 Save** God save    **7 abroad** going the
rounds.    **ones** i.e., the news, regarded as plural    **8 ear-bussing**
**arguments** lightly whispered topics.    **10 toward** impending

EDMUND
The Duke be here tonight? The better! Best!                14
This weaves itself perforce into my business.
My father hath set guard to take my brother,
And I have one thing, of a queasy question,                17
Which I must act. Briefness and fortune, work!—           18
Brother, a word. Descend. Brother, I say!

        *Enter Edgar.*

My father watches. Oh, sir, fly this place!
Intelligence is given where you are hid.
You have now the good advantage of the night.
Have you not spoken 'gainst the Duke of Cornwall?
He's coming hither, now, i'th' night, i'th' haste,         24
And Regan with him. Have you nothing said
Upon his party 'gainst the Duke of Albany?                 26
Advise yourself.
EDGAR                I am sure on't, not a word.            27
EDMUND
I hear my father coming. Pardon me;
In cunning I must draw my sword upon you.
Draw. Seem to defend yourself. Now, quit you well.—  30
                        [*They draw.*]
Yield! Come before my father!—Light, ho, here!—           31
Fly, brother.—Torches, torches!—So, farewell.             32
                                *Exit Edgar.*
Some blood drawn on me would beget opinion                 33
Of my more fierce endeavor. I have seen drunkards          34
Do more than this in sport. [*He wounds himself in the
    arm.*] Father, father!
Stop, stop! No help?

        *Enter Gloucester, and servants with torches.*

GLOUCESTER        Now, Edmund, where's the villain?
EDMUND
Here stood he in the dark, his sharp sword out,
Mumbling of wicked charms, conjuring the moon
To stand 's auspicious mistress.
GLOUCESTER                But where is he?                  39
EDMUND
Look, sir, I bleed.
GLOUCESTER        Where is the villain, Edmund?
EDMUND
Fled this way, sir. When by no means he could—
GLOUCESTER    Pursue him, ho! Go after.
                        [*Exeunt some servants.*]
                        By no means what?

EDMUND
Persuade me to the murder of Your Lordship,
But that I told him the revenging gods                     44

14 **The better! Best!** So much the better; in fact, the best that could
happen!   17 **queasy question** matter not for queasy stomachs
18 **Briefness and fortune** Expeditious dispatch and good luck
24 **i'th' haste** in great haste   26 **Upon his party** i.e., recklessly on
Cornwall's behalf (? It would be dangerous to speak on either side.)
27 **Advise yourself** Consider your situation.   **on't** of it   30 **quit you**
defend, acquit yourself   31–2 **Yield . . . farewell** (Edmund speaks
loudly as though trying to arrest Edgar, calls for others to help, and
privately bids Edgar to flee.)   33–4 **beget . . . endeavor** create an
impression of my having fought fiercely.   39 **stand 's** stand his, act
as his   44 **that** when

'Gainst parricides did all the thunder bend,               45
Spoke with how manifold and strong a bond
The child was bound to th' father; sir, in fine,           47
Seeing how loathly opposite I stood                        48
To his unnatural purpose, in fell motion                   49
With his preparèd sword he charges home                    50
My unprovided body, latched mine arm;                      51
And when he saw my best alarumed spirits,                  52
Bold in the quarrel's right, roused to th'encounter,       53
Or whether ghasted by the noise I made,                    54
Full suddenly he fled.
GLOUCESTER            Let him fly far.                      55
Not in this land shall he remain uncaught;
And found—dispatch. The noble Duke my master,             57
My worthy arch and patron, comes tonight.                  58
By his authority I will proclaim it
That he which finds him shall deserve our thanks,
Bringing the murderous caitiff to the stake;               61
He that conceals him, death.
EDMUND
When I dissuaded him from his intent
And found him pight to do it, with curst speech            64
I threatened to discover him. He replied,                  65
"Thou unpossessing bastard, dost thou think,              66
If I would stand against thee, would the reposal           67
Of any trust, virtue, or worth in thee
Make thy words faithed? No. What I should deny—           69
As this I would, ay, though thou didst produce
My very character—I'd turn it all                          71
To thy suggestion, plot, and damnÈd practice;              72
And thou must make a dullard of the world                  73
If they not thought the profits of my death                74
Were very pregnant and potential spirits                   75
To make thee seek it."
GLOUCESTER            Oh, strong and fastened villain!  76
Would he deny his letter, said he?
I never got him.                        *Tucket within.*  78
Hark, the Duke's trumpets! I know not why he comes.
All ports I'll bar; the villain shall not scape.           80
The Duke must grant me that. Besides, his picture          81
I will send far and near, that all the kingdom
May have due note of him; and of my land,

45 **bend** aim   47 **in fine** in conclusion   48 **loathly opposite**
loathingly opposed   49 **fell motion** deadly thrust   50 **preparèd**
unsheathed and ready.   **home** to the very heart   51 **unprovided**
unprotected.   **latched** nicked, lanced   52 **best alarumed** thoroughly
aroused to action, as by a trumpet   53 **quarrel's right** justice of the
cause   54 **ghasted** frightened   55 **Let him fly far** i.e., Any fleeing, no
matter how far, will be in vain.   57 **dispatch** i.e., that will be the end
for him.   58 **arch and patron** chief patron   61 **caitiff** wretch   **to
the stake** i.e., to reckoning   64 **pight** determined.   **curst** angry
65 **discover** expose   66 **unpossessing** unable to inherit, beggarly
67 **reposal** placing   69 **faithed** believed.   **What** That which, whatever   71 **character** written testimony, handwriting.   **turn** attribute
72 **suggestion** instigation.   **practice** scheming   73–6 **And . . . seek it**
and you must think everyone slow-witted indeed not to suppose that
they would see how the profits to be gained by my death would be
fertile and potent tempters to make you seek my death.   76 **strong
and fastened** flagrant and hardened   78 **got** begot.   **s.d.** *Tucket*
series of notes on the trumpet, here indicating Cornwall's arrival
80 **ports** seaports, or gateways   81 **picture** description and image

Loyal and natural boy, I'll work the means                                84
To make thee capable.                                                      85

*Enter Cornwall, Regan, and attendants.*

CORNWALL
How now, my noble friend? Since I came hither,
Which I can call but now, I have heard strange news.
REGAN
If it be true, all vengeance comes too short
Which can pursue th'offender. How dost, my lord?
GLOUCESTER
Oh madam, my old heart is cracked, it's cracked!
REGAN
What, did my father's godson seek your life?
He whom my father named? Your Edgar?
GLOUCESTER
Oh, lady, lady, shame would have it hid!
REGAN
Was he not companion with the riotous knights
That tend upon my father?
GLOUCESTER
I know not, madam. 'Tis too bad, too bad.
EDMUND
Yes, madam, he was of that consort.                                        97
REGAN
No marvel, then, though he were ill affected.                              98
'Tis they have put him on the old man's death,                             99
To have th'expense and spoil of his revenues.                              100
I have this present evening from my sister
Been well informed of them, and with such cautions
That if they come to sojourn at my house
I'll not be there.
CORNWALL                         Nor I, assure thee, Regan.
Edmund, I hear that you have shown your father
A childlike office.
EDMUND                          'Twas my duty, sir.                        106
GLOUCESTER [*to Cornwall*]
He did bewray his practice, and received                                   107
This hurt you see striving to apprehend him.                               108
CORNWALL    Is he pursued?
GLOUCESTER    Ay, my good lord.
CORNWALL
If he be taken, he shall never more
Be feared of doing harm. Make your own purpose,                            112
How in my strength you please. For you, Edmund,                            113
Whose virtue and obedience doth this instant
So much commend itself, you shall be ours.
Natures of such deep trust we shall much need;
You we first seize on.
EDMUND                          I shall serve you, sir,
Truly, however else.                                                       118
GLOUCESTER    For him I thank Your Grace.

CORNWALL
You know not why we came to visit you—
REGAN
—Thus out of season, threading dark-eyed night:
Occasions, noble Gloucester, of some poise,                                122
Wherein we must have use of your advice.
Our father he hath writ, so hath our sister,
Of differences, which I least thought it fit                               125
To answer from our home. The several messengers                            126
From hence attend dispatch. Our good old friend,                           127
Lay comforts to your bosom, and bestow
Your needful counsel to our businesses,
Which craves the instant use.
GLOUCESTER                         I serve you, madam.                     130
Your Graces are right welcome.        *Flourish. Exeunt.*

❧

## 2.2

*Enter Kent [disguised as Caius] and steward
[Oswald], severally.*

OSWALD    Good dawning to thee, friend. Art of this          1
house?
KENT    Ay.
OSWALD    Where may we set our horses?
KENT    I'th' mire.
OSWALD    Prithee, if thou lov'st me, tell me.               6
KENT    I love thee not.
OSWALD    Why then, I care not for thee.
KENT    If I had thee in Lipsbury pinfold, I would make     9
thee care for me.                                           10
OSWALD    Why dost thou use me thus? I know thee not.
KENT    Fellow, I know thee.                                 12
OSWALD    What dost thou know me for?
KENT    A knave, a rascal, an eater of broken meats;        14
a base, proud, shallow, beggarly, three-suited,            15
hundred-pound, filthy worsted-stocking knave; a            16
lily-livered, action-taking, whoreson, glass-gazing,       17
superserviceable, finical rogue; one-trunk-inheriting      18
slave; one that wouldst be a bawd in way of good ser-      19
vice, and art nothing but the composition of a knave,      20
beggar, coward, pander, and the son and heir of a

**122 poise** weight   **125 differences** quarrels.   **which** which letters
**126 from our home** while still at our palace in Cornwall.   **several**
various   **127 attend dispatch** wait to be dispatched.   **130 the instant
use** immediate attention.
**2.2. Location: Before Gloucester's house.**
**0.2 *severally*** at separate doors.   **1 dawning** (It is not yet day.)   **6 if
thou lov'st me** i.e., if you bear good will toward me. (But Kent deliberately takes the phrase in its literal, not courtly, sense.)   **9 in Lipsbury pinfold** i.e., within the pinfold of the lips, between my teeth.
(A *pinfold* is a pound for stray animals.)   **10 care for** i.e., be wary of.
(Playing on *care not for*, "do not like," in line 8.)   **12 I know thee**
i.e., I know you for what you are. (Playing on *know thee not*, "am
unacquainted with you," in line 11.)   **14 broken meats** scraps of food
(such as were passed out to the most lowly)   **15–16 three-suited . . .
knave** i.e., a steward of a household, with an allowance of three suits
a year and a comfortable income of one hundred pounds, dressed in
dirty wool stockings appropriate to the servant class   **16–19 a lily-
livered . . . slave** a cowardly, litigious, insufferable, self-infatuated,
officious, foppish rogue, whose personal property all fits into one
trunk   **19–20 bawd . . . service** i.e., pimp or pander as a way of
providing whatever is wanted   **20 composition** compound

**84 natural** (1) prompted by natural feelings of loyalty and affection
(2) bastard   **85 capable** legally able to become the inheritor.   **97 consort** crew.   **98 though** if.   **ill affected** ill-disposed, disloyal.   **99 put
him on** incited him to seek   **100 th'expense and spoil** the squandering
**106 childlike** filial   **107 bewray his practice** expose his (Edgar's)
plot   **108 apprehend** arrest   **112–13 Make . . . please** Go about
achieving your purpose, making free use of my authority and
resources.   **113 For** As for   **118 however else** above all else.

mongrel bitch; one whom I will beat into clamorous whining if thou deniest the least syllable of thy addi-  23
tion.  24

OSWALD   Why, what a monstrous fellow art thou thus to rail on one that is neither known of thee nor knows thee!

KENT   What a brazen-faced varlet art thou to deny thou  28
knowest me! Is it two days since I tripped up thy heels and beat thee before the King? Draw, you rogue, for though it be night, yet the moon shines. I'll make a sop o'th' moonshine of you, you whoreson, cullionly  32
barbermonger. Draw!          [*He brandishes his sword.*]  33

OSWALD   Away! I have nothing to do with thee.

KENT   Draw, you rascal! You come with letters against the King, and take Vanity the puppet's part against  36
the royalty of her father. Draw, you rogue, or I'll so carbonado your shanks—draw, you rascal! Come  38
your ways.  39

OSWALD   Help, ho! Murder! Help!

KENT   Strike, you slave! Stand, rogue, stand, you neat  41
slave, strike!                    [*He beats him.*]

OSWALD   Help, ho! Murder! Murder!

*Enter Bastard [Edmund, with his rapier
drawn], Cornwall, Regan, Gloucester, servants.*

EDMUND   How now, what's the matter? Part!  44

KENT   With you, goodman boy, an you please! Come,  45
I'll flesh ye. Come on, young master.  46

GLOUCESTER   Weapons? Arms? What's the matter here?

CORNWALL   Keep peace, upon your lives! [*Kent and
Oswald are parted.*] He dies that strikes again. What is the matter?

REGAN   The messengers from our sister and the King.

CORNWALL   What's your difference? Speak.  52

OSWALD   I am scarce in breath, my lord.

KENT   No marvel, you have so bestirred your valor. You cowardly rascal, nature disclaims in thee. A tailor  55
made thee.

CORNWALL   Thou art a strange fellow. A tailor make a man?

KENT   Ay, a tailor, sir. A stonecutter or a painter could not have made him so ill, though he had been but two  60
years at the trade.

CORNWALL   Speak yet, how grew your quarrel?

OSWALD   This ancient ruffian, sir, whose life I have spared at suit of his gray beard—  64

KENT   Thou whoreson zed! Thou unnecessary letter!—  65
My lord, if you'll give me leave, I will tread this un-  66
bolted villain into mortar and daub the wall of a jakes  67
with him.—Spare my gray beard, you wagtail?  68

CORNWALL   Peace, sirrah!
You beastly knave, know you no reverence?  70

KENT
Yes, sir, but anger hath a privilege.

CORNWALL   Why art thou angry?

KENT
That such a slave as this should wear a sword,
Who wears no honesty. Such smiling rogues as these,
Like rats, oft bite the holy cords atwain  75
Which are too intrinse t'unloose; smooth every
    passion  76
That in the natures of their lords rebel,  77
Bring oil to fire, snow to their colder moods,  78
Renege, affirm, and turn their halcyon beaks  79
With every gale and vary of their masters,  80
Knowing naught, like dogs, but following.—  81
A plague upon your epileptic visage!  82
Smile you my speeches, as I were a fool?  83
Goose, an I had you upon Sarum plain,  84
I'd drive ye cackling home to Camelot.  85

CORNWALL   What, art thou mad, old fellow?

GLOUCESTER   How fell you out? Say that.

KENT
No contraries hold more antipathy
Than I and such a knave.

CORNWALL
Why dost thou call him knave? What is his fault?

KENT   His countenance likes me not.  91

CORNWALL
No more, perchance, does mine, nor his, nor hers.

KENT
Sir, 'tis my occupation to be plain:
I have seen better faces in my time
Than stands on any shoulder that I see
Before me at this instant.

CORNWALL                    This is some fellow
Who, having been praised for bluntness, doth affect  97

---

**23–4 thy addition** the titles I've given you.   **28 varlet** rogue   **32 sop o'th' moonshine** something so perforated that it will soak up moonshine as a sop (floating piece of toast) soaks up liquor   **32–3 cullionly barbermonger** base frequenter of barber shops, fop. (*Cullion* originally meant "testicle.")   **36 Vanity . . . part** i.e., the part of Goneril (here personified as a character in a morality play)   **38 carbonado** cut crosswise, like meat for broiling   **38–9 Come your ways** Come on.   **41 neat** (1) foppish (2) calflike. (*Neat* means "horned cattle.")   **44 matter** i.e., trouble. (But Kent takes the meaning "cause for quarrel.")   **45 With you** I'll fight with you; my quarrel is with you.   **goodman boy** (A contemptuous epithet, a title of mock respect, addressed seemingly to Edmund.)   **an if**   **46 flesh** initiate into combat   **52 difference** quarrel.   **55 disclaims in** disowns   **60 ill** badly   **64 at suit of** on account of

**65 zed** the letter z (regarded as unnecessary and often not included in dictionaries of the time).   **66–7 unbolted** unsifted; hence, coarse   **67 daub** plaster.   **jakes** privy   **68 wagtail** i.e., bird wagging its tail feathers in pert obsequiousness.   **70 reverence** respect.   **75 holy cords** sacred bonds of loyalty and order   **76 intrinse** intricate, tightly knotted.   **smooth** flatter, humor   **77 rebel** rebel against reason   **78 Bring . . . moods** flatteringly fuel the flame of their masters' angry passions, while similarly exacerbating their downward mood swings   **79 Renege, affirm** nay-say one moment (when their lords are in a denying mood) and serve as yes-men the next.   **halcyon beaks** (The halcyon or kingfisher, if hung up, would supposedly turn its beak into the wind.)   **80 gale and vary** shifting wind   **81 following** fawning and flattery.   **82 epileptic** i.e., trembling and pale with fright and distorted with a grin   **83 Smile you** Do you smile at.   **as** as if   **84–5 Goose . . . Camelot** (The reference is obscure, but the general sense is that Kent, if given space and opportunity, would send Oswald packing like a cackling goose. Camelot, the legendary seat of King Arthur and his Knights of the Round Table, was thought to have been in the general vicinity of Salisbury, Sarum, and Gloucester.)   **91 likes** pleases   **97 affect** adopt the style of

A saucy roughness, and constrains the garb          98
Quite from his nature. He cannot flatter, he;          99
An honest mind and plain, he must speak truth!
An they will take't, so; if not, he's plain.          101
These kind of knaves I know, which in this plainness
Harbor more craft and more corrupter ends
Than twenty silly-ducking observants          104
That stretch their duties nicely.          105

KENT
Sir, in good faith, in sincere verity,          106
Under th'allowance of your great aspect,          107
Whose influence, like the wreath of radiant fire          108
On flickering Phoebus' front—

CORNWALL                         What mean'st by this?   109

KENT    To go out of my dialect, which you discommend   110
so much. I know, sir, I am no flatterer. He that be-   111
guiled you in a plain accent was a plain knave, which   112
for my part I will not be, though I should win your   113
displeasure to entreat me to't.          114

CORNWALL [to Oswald]  What was th'offense you gave him?

OSWALD    I never gave him any.
It pleased the King his master very late          117
To strike at me, upon his misconstruction;          118
When he, conjunct, and flattering his displeasure,          119
Tripped me behind; being down, insulted, railed,          120
And put upon him such a deal of man          121
That worthied him, got praises of the King          122
For him attempting who was self-subdued;          123
And, in the fleshment of this dread exploit,          124
Drew on me here again.

KENT    None of these rogues and cowards          126
But Ajax is their fool.

CORNWALL                         Fetch forth the stocks!   127

You stubborn, ancient knave, you reverend braggart,   128
We'll teach you.

KENT                    Sir, I am too old to learn.
Call not your stocks for me. I serve the King,
On whose employment I was sent to you.
You shall do small respect, show too bold malice
Against the grace and person of my master,          133
Stocking his messenger.

CORNWALL
Fetch forth the stocks! As I have life and honor,
There shall he sit till noon.

REGAN
Till noon? Till night, my lord, and all night too.

KENT
Why, madam, if I were your father's dog
You should not use me so.          139

REGAN    Sir, being his knave, I will.          140

CORNWALL
This is a fellow of the selfsame color          141
Our sister speaks of.—Come, bring away the stocks!   142
                              Stocks brought out.

GLOUCESTER
Let me beseech Your Grace not to do so.
His fault is much, and the good King his master
Will check him for't. Your purposed low correction   145
Is such as basest and contemned'st wretches          146
For pilferings and most common trespasses
Are punished with. The King must take it ill
That he, so slightly valued in his messenger,
Should have him thus restrained.

CORNWALL                         I'll answer that.   150

REGAN
My sister may receive it much more worse
To have her gentleman abused, assaulted,          152
For following her affairs. Put in his legs.          153
                    [Kent is put in the stocks.]
Come, my good lord, away.
                    Exeunt [all but Gloucester and Kent].

GLOUCESTER
I am sorry for thee, friend. 'Tis the Duke's pleasure,
Whose disposition, all the world well knows,
Will not be rubbed nor stopped. I'll entreat for thee.   157

KENT
Pray, do not, sir. I have watched and traveled hard.   158
Some time I shall sleep out; the rest I'll whistle.
A good man's fortune may grow out at heels.          160
Give you good morrow!          161

GLOUCESTER
The Duke's to blame in this. 'Twill be ill taken.   *Exit.*

---

**98–9 constrains . . . nature** i.e., distorts plainness quite from its true purpose so that it becomes instead a way of deceiving the listener. **99 He . . . he** He professes to be one who abhors the use of flattering speech. (Said sardonically.)   **101 An . . . plain** If people will take his rudeness, fine; if not, his excuse is that he speaks plain truth. **104–5 Than . . . nicely** than twenty foolishly bowing, obsequious courtiers who outdo themselves in the punctilious performance of their courtly duties.   **106 Sir, in good faith** (Kent assumes the wordy mannerisms of courtly flattery.)   **107 th'allowance** the approval. **aspect** (1) countenance (2) astrological position   **108 influence** astrological power   **109 Phoebus' front** i.e., the sun's forehead **110 dialect** usual mode of speech   **111–14 He . . . to't** The man who used plain speech to you craftily (see lines 102–5) and thereby taught you to suspect plain speakers of being deceitful was in fact a plain rascal, which part I will not play, much as it would please me to incur your displeasure if speaking thus would have that effect. (Kent would prefer to displease Cornwall, since Cornwall is pleased only by flatterers, and Kent has assumed until now that plain speech was the best way to offend, but he now argues mockingly that he can no longer speak plainly, since his honest utterance would be interpreted as duplicity.)   **117 late** recently   **118 upon his misconstruction** as a result of the King's misunderstanding (me)   **119 When . . . displeasure** whereupon Kent, in cahoots with the King and his party, and wishing to gratify the King's anger at me   **120 being down, insulted** when I was down, he exulted over me   **121–2 And put . . . him** and acted with a bravado that earned him an accolade of being a worthy fellow   **123 For . . . self-subdued** for assailing one (i.e., myself) who chose not to resist   **124 And . . . exploit** and, in the excitement of his first success in this fearless deed. (Said ironically.)   **126–7 None . . . fool** i.e., You never find any rogues and cowards of this sort who do not outdo the blustering Ajax in their boasting.

**128 reverend** (because old)   **133 grace** sovereignty, royal grace **139 should** would   **140 being** since you are   **141 color** complexion, character   **142 sister** sister-in-law.   **away** along   **145 check** rebuke, correct.   **purposed** i.e., insultingly intended   **146 contemned'st** most despised   **150 answer** be answerable for   **152 her gentleman** Oswald   **153 following** carrying out   **157 rubbed** hindered, obstructed. (A term from bowls.)   **158 watched** gone sleepless **160 A . . . heels** i.e., Even good men suffer decline in fortune at times. (To be out at heels is literally to be threadbare, coming through one's stockings.)   **161 Give you** i.e., God give you

KENT

Good King, that must approve the common saw,    163
Thou out of heaven's benediction com'st
To the warm sun!                    [*He takes out a letter.*]
Approach, thou beacon to this under globe,    166
That by thy comfortable beams I may    167
Peruse this letter. Nothing almost sees miracles    168
But misery. I know 'tis from Cordelia,    169
Who hath most fortunately been informed
Of my obscurèd course, "and shall find time    171
From this enormous state, seeking to give    172
Losses their remedies." All weary and o'erwatched,    173
Take vantage, heavy eyes, not to behold    174
This shameful lodging.    175
Fortune, good night. Smile once more; turn thy wheel!    176
                                    [*He sleeps.*]

❖

## [2.3]

*Enter Edgar.*

EDGAR    I heard myself proclaimed,
And by the happy hollow of a tree    2
Escaped the hunt. No port is free, no place    3
That guard and most unusual vigilance    4
Does not attend my taking. Whiles I may scape    5
I will preserve myself, and am bethought    6
To take the basest and most poorest shape
That ever penury, in contempt of man,    8
Brought near to beast. My face I'll grime with filth,
Blanket my loins, elf all my hairs in knots,    10
And with presented nakedness outface    11
The winds and persecutions of the sky.
The country gives me proof and precedent    13
Of Bedlam beggars who with roaring voices    14
Strike in their numbed and mortified bare arms    15
Pins, wooden pricks, nails, sprigs of rosemary;    16
And with this horrible object, from low farms,    17

Poor pelting villages, sheepcotes, and mills,    18
Sometime with lunatic bans, sometime with prayers,    19
Enforce their charity. Poor Turlygod! Poor Tom!    20
That's something yet. Edgar I nothing am.    *Exit.*    21

❖

## [2.4]

*Enter Lear, Fool, and Gentleman.*

LEAR

'Tis strange that they should so depart from home    1
And not send back my messenger.
GENTLEMAN                    As I learned,
The night before there was no purpose in them
Of this remove.
KENT                    Hail to thee, noble master!    4
LEAR    Ha?
Mak'st thou this shame thy pastime?
KENT                    No, my lord.
FOOL    Ha, ha, he wears cruel garters. Horses are tied by    7
the heads, dogs and bears by th' neck, monkeys by
th' loins, and men by th' legs. When a man's over-    9
lusty at legs, then he wears wooden netherstocks.    10
LEAR

What's he that hath so much thy place mistook    11
To set thee here?
KENT                    It is both he and she:    12
Your son and daughter.    13
LEAR    No.
KENT    Yes.
LEAR    No, I say.
KENT    I say yea.
LEAR    No, no, they would not.
KENT    Yes, they have.
LEAR    By Jupiter, I swear no.
KENT

By Juno, I swear ay.
LEAR                    They durst not do't!
They could not, would not do't. 'Tis worse than
    murder
To do upon respect such violent outrage.    23
Resolve me with all modest haste which way    24
Thou mightst deserve, or they impose, this usage,
Coming from us.

---

163 **approve** prove true.  **saw** proverb (i.e., "To run out of God's blessing into the warm sun," meaning "to go from better to worse," from a state of bliss into the pitiless world. Kent sees Lear as heading for trouble.)  166 **beacon . . . globe** i.e., the sun. (Daylight is coming soon to this *under globe*, the earth.)  167 **comfortable** comforting  168–9 **Nothing . . . misery** Scarcely anything can make one appreciate miracles like being in a state of misery; to the miserable, any relief seems miraculous.  171 **obscurèd** disguised  171–3 **"and shall . . . remedies"** i.e., "and who, in the fullness of time, will bring relief to the monstrous state of affairs under which we suffer, seeking to remedy what has been destroyed." (The passage may be corrupt. Kent seems to be reading from his letter.)  173 **o'erwatched** exhausted with staying awake  174 **vantage** advantage (of sleep)  175 **lodging** i.e., the stocks.  176 **wheel** (Since Kent is at the bottom of Fortune's wheel, any turning should improve his situation.)  **2.3. Location: Scene continues. Kent is dozing in the stocks.**  2 **happy** luckily found  3 **port** (See 2.1.80 and note.)  4 **That** in which  5 **attend my taking** lie in wait to capture me.  6 **bethought** resolved  8 **in . . . man** in order to show how contemptible humankind is  10 **elf** tangle into elflocks  11 **presented** exposed to view, displayed  13 **proof** example  14 **Bedlam** (See the note to 1.2.139.)  15 **Strike** stick.  **mortified** deadened  16 **wooden pricks** skewers  17 **object** spectacle.  **low** lowly

18 **pelting** paltry  19 **bans** curses  20 **Enforce their charity** manage to beg something.  **Poor . . . Tom** (Edgar practices the begging role he is about to adopt. Beggars were known as "poor Toms.")  **Turlygod** (A name of unknown origin.)  21 **That's . . . am** There's some kind of existence for me as poor Tom. I am Edgar no longer.
**2.4. Location: Scene continues before Gloucester's house. Kent still dozing in the stocks.**
1 **they** Cornwall and Regan  4 **remove** change of residence.  7 **cruel** (1) unkind (2) crewel (compare the quarto spelling, "crewell"), a thin yarn of which hose were made: The Fool is referring to the stocks that bind Kent's feet like garters.  9–10 **overlusty at legs** given to running away, or overly active sexually  10 **netherstocks** stockings.
11 **What's** Who is.  **place** i.e., role as messenger from the King
12 **To** as to  13 **son** son-in-law  23 **upon respect** i.e., against my officers (who deserve respect)  24 **Resolve** Enlighten.  **modest** moderate

KENT         My lord, when at their home 26
I did commend Your Highness' letters to them, 27
Ere I was risen from the place that showed 28
My duty kneeling, came there a reeking post, 29
Stewed in his haste, half breathless, panting forth 30
From Goneril his mistress salutations;
Delivered letters, spite of intermission, 32
Which presently they read; on whose contents 33
They summoned up their meiny, straight took horse, 34
Commanded me to follow and attend
The leisure of their answer, gave me cold looks;
And meeting here the other messenger,
Whose welcome, I perceived, had poisoned mine—
Being the very fellow which of late
Displayed so saucily against Your Highness— 40
Having more man than wit about me, drew. 41
He raised the house with loud and coward cries.
Your son and daughter found this trespass worth
The shame which here it suffers.

FOOL    Winter's not gone yet if the wild geese fly that 45
way. 46
    Fathers that wear rags
        Do make their children blind, 48
    But fathers that bear bags 49
        Shall see their children kind.
    Fortune, that arrant whore, 51
    Ne'er turns the key to th' poor. 52
But, for all this, thou shalt have as many dolors for thy 53
daughters as thou canst tell in a year. 54

LEAR
Oh, how this mother swells up toward my heart! 55
*Hysterica passio*, down, thou climbing sorrow! 56
Thy element's below.—Where is this daughter? 57

KENT    With the Earl, sir, here within.

LEAR    Follow me not. Stay here.                    *Exit.*

GENTLEMAN
Made you no more offense but what you speak of?

KENT    None. How chance the King comes with so small 61
a number?

FOOL    An thou hadst been set i'th' stocks for that ques- 63
tion, thou'dst well deserved it.

KENT    Why, Fool?

FOOL    We'll set thee to school to an ant to teach thee 66
there's no laboring i'th' winter. All that follow their 67
noses are led by their eyes but blind men, and there's 68
not a nose among twenty but can smell him that's 69
stinking. Let go thy hold when a great wheel runs 70
down a hill lest it break thy neck with following; but
the great one that goes upward, let him draw thee after. When a wise man gives thee better counsel, give
me mine again. I would have none but knaves follow
it, since a fool gives it.
    That sir which serves and seeks for gain,
        And follows but for form,
    Will pack when it begins to rain 78
        And leave thee in the storm.
    But I will tarry; the fool will stay,
        And let the wise man fly.
    The knave turns fool that runs away; 82
        The fool no knave, pardie. 83

*Enter Lear and Gloucester.*

KENT    Where learned you this, Fool?

FOOL    Not i'th' stocks, fool.

LEAR
Deny to speak with me? They are sick? They are
    weary?
They have traveled all the night? Mere fetches, 87
The images of revolt and flying off. 88
Fetch me a better answer.

GLOUCESTER                My dear lord,
You know the fiery quality of the Duke,
How unremovable and fixed he is
In his own course.

LEAR
Vengeance! Plague! Death! Confusion! 93
Fiery? What quality? Why, Gloucester, Gloucester,
I'd speak with the Duke of Cornwall and his wife.

GLOUCESTER
Well, my good lord, I have informed them so.

LEAR
Informed them? Dost thou understand me, man?

GLOUCESTER    Ay, my good lord.

LEAR
The King would speak with Cornwall. The dear father
Would with his daughter speak, commands, tends
    service. 100
Are they informed of this? My breath and blood! 101
Fiery? The fiery Duke? Tell the hot Duke that—
No, but not yet. Maybe he is not well.
Infirmity doth still neglect all office 104
Whereto our health is bound; we are not ourselves 105

26 **their home** (Kent and Oswald went first to Cornwall's palace after leaving Albany's palace.)   27 **commend** deliver   28–9 **from . . . kneeling** from the kneeling posture that showed my duty   29 **reeking** steaming (with heat of travel)   30 **Stewed** i.e., thoroughly heated, soaked   32 **spite of intermission** in disregard of interrupting me, or, in spite of the interruptions caused by his being out of breath   33 **presently** instantly.   **on** on the basis of   34 **meiny** retinue of servants, household   40 **Displayed so saucily** behaved so insolently   41 **more man than wit** more courage than good sense   45–6 **Winter's . . . way** i.e., The signs still point to continued and worsening fortune; the wild geese are still flying south.   48 **blind** i.e., indifferent to their father's needs   49 **bags** i.e., of gold   51 **arrant** outright, egregious   52 **turns the key** opens the door   53 **dolors** griefs. (With pun on "dollars," English word for an Austrian or Spanish coin.)   **for** (1) on account of (2) in exchange for   54 **tell** (1) relate (2) count   55, 56 **mother, Hysterica passio** i.e., hysteria, giving the sensation of choking or suffocating   57 **element's** proper place is. (Hysteria, from the Greek *hystera*, womb, was thought to be produced by vapors ascending from the uterus or abdomen.)   61 **chance** chances it   63 **An** If

66–7 **We'll . . . winter** i.e., Just as the ant knows not to labor in the winter, the wise man knows not to labor for one whose fortunes are fallen.   67–70 **All . . . stinking** i.e., One who is out of favor can be easily detected (he smells of misfortune) and so is easily avoided by timeservers.   78 **pack** be off   82 **The knave . . . away** i.e., Deserting one's master is the greatest folly   83 **pardie** *par Dieu* (French), "by God."   87 **fetches** pretexts, dodges   88 **images** signs. **flying off** desertion.   93 **Confusion!** Destruction!   100 **tends** attends, waits for   101 **My . . . blood!** i.e., By my very life. (An oath.)   104–5 **Infirmity . . . bound** Sickness always prompts us to neglect all duties which in good health we are bound to perform

When nature, being oppressed, commands the mind
To suffer with the body. I'll forbear,
And am fallen out with my more headier will,                                108
To take the indisposed and sickly fit                                       109
For the sound man. [*Looking at Kent*] Death on my
    state! Wherefore                                                        110
Should he sit here? This act persuades me
That this remotion of the Duke and her                                      112
Is practice only. Give me my servant forth.                                 113
Go tell the Duke and 's wife I'd speak with them,
Now, presently. Bid them come forth and hear me,                            115
Or at their chamber door I'll beat the drum
Till it cry sleep to death.                                                 117

GLOUCESTER   I would have all well betwixt you.   *Exit.*

LEAR
Oh, me, my heart, my rising heart! But down!

FOOL   Cry to it, nuncle, as the cockney did to the eels  120
when she put 'em i'th' paste alive. She knapped 'em  121
o'th' coxcombs with a stick and cried, "Down, wan-  122
tons, down!" 'Twas her brother that, in pure kindness  123
to his horse, buttered his hay.                                            124

*Enter Cornwall, Regan, Gloucester, [and]
servants.*

LEAR   Good morrow to you both.
CORNWALL   Hail to Your Grace!

                                    *Kent here set at liberty.*

REGAN   I am glad to see Your Highness.
LEAR
Regan, I think you are. I know what reason
I have to think so. If thou shouldst not be glad,
I would divorce me from thy mother's tomb,                                  130
Sepulch'ring an adultress. [*To Kent*] Oh, are you free?  131
Some other time for that.—Belovèd Regan,
Thy sister's naught. Oh, Regan, she hath tied                               133
Sharp-toothed unkindness, like a vulture, here.
                          [*He lays his hand on his heart.*]
I can scarce speak to thee. Thou'lt not believe
With how depraved a quality—Oh, Regan!                                      136

REGAN
I pray you, sir, take patience. I have hope                                 137
You less know how to value her desert                                       138
Than she to scant her duty.
LEAR                         Say? How is that?                              139
REGAN
I cannot think my sister in the least
Would fail her obligation. If, sir, perchance
She have restrained the riots of your followers,
'Tis on such ground and to such wholesome end
As clears her from all blame.
LEAR   My curses on her!
REGAN   Oh, sir, you are old;
Nature in you stands on the very verge                                      147
Of his confine. You should be ruled and led                                148
By some discretion that discerns your state                                 149
Better than you yourself. Therefore, I pray you,
That to our sister you do make return.
Say you have wronged her.
LEAR                       Ask her forgiveness?
Do you but mark how this becomes the house:                                 153
[*Kneeling*] "Dear daughter, I confess that I am old;
Age is unnecessary. On my knees I beg
That you'll vouchsafe me raiment, bed, and food."                          156
REGAN
Good sir, no more. These are unsightly tricks.
Return you to my sister.
LEAR [*rising*]              Never, Regan.
She hath abated me of half my train,                                        159
Looked black upon me, struck me with her tongue
Most serpentlike upon the very heart.
All the stored vengeances of heaven fall                                    162
On her ingrateful top! Strike her young bones,                              163
You taking airs, with lameness!
CORNWALL                         Fie, sir, fie!                             164
LEAR
You nimble lightnings, dart your blinding flames
Into her scornful eyes! Infect her beauty,
You fen-sucked fogs drawn by the powerful sun                               167
To fall and blister!                                                        168
REGAN
O the blest gods! So will you wish on me
When the rash mood is on.
LEAR
No, Regan, thou shalt never have my curse.
Thy tender-hafted nature shall not give                                     172
Thee o'er to harshness. Her eyes are fierce, but thine
Do comfort and not burn. 'Tis not in thee
To grudge my pleasures, to cut off my train,

---

**108–10 And . . . man** and now disapprove of my more impetuous will
in having rashly supposed that those who are indisposed and sickly
were in sound health.   **110 Death . . . state!** (A common oath, here
ironically appropriate to a king whose royal authority is dying.)
**112 remotion** removal, inaccessibility   **113 practice** deception.
**forth** out of the stocks.   **115 presently** at once.   **117 cry sleep to
death** i.e., puts an end to sleep by the noise.   **120 cockney** i.e., a
Londoner, ignorant of ways of cooking eels   **121 paste** pastry pie.
**knapped** rapped   **122 coxcombs** heads   **122–3 wantons** playful
creatures, sexy rogues. (A term of affectionate abuse. The cockney
wife is trying to coax and wheedle the eels into laying down their
lives for the making of the pastry pie—a plea that is about as ineffectual as Lear's imploring his rising heart to subside.)   **123–4 'Twas . . .
hay** (Another city ignorance; the act is well intended, but horses do
not like greasy hay. As with Lear, good intentions are not enough.
The *brother* is related to the cockney wife in that they are both misguidedly tenderhearted.)   **130–1 I would . . . adultress** i.e., I would
cease to honor your dead mother's tomb, since it would surely
contain the dead body of an adultress. (Only such a fantasy of
illegitimacy could explain to Lear filial ingratitude of the monstrous
sort that now confronts him.)   **133 naught** wicked.   **136 quality**
disposition

**137–9 I have . . . duty** I trust this is more a matter of your undervaluing
her merit than of her falling slack in her duty to you.   **139 Say?** Come
again?   **147–8 Nature . . . confine** i.e., Your life has almost completed its
allotted scope.   **149 By . . . state** by some discreet person who understands your situation and condition   **153 becomes the house** suits
domestic decorum and the royal family line. (Said with bitter irony.)
**156 vouchsafe me raiment** do me the great favor of granting me clothing   **159 abated** deprived   **162 All** Let all   **163 ingrateful top** ungrateful head.   **164 taking** infectious   **167 fen-sucked** (It was supposed that
the sun sucked up poisonous vapors from fens or marshes.)   **168 To
fall and blister** to fall upon her and blister her beauty.   **172 tender-
hafted** gentle. (Literally, set in a tender *haft*, i.e., handle or frame.)

To bandy hasty words, to scant my sizes, 176
And, in conclusion, to oppose the bolt 177
Against my coming in. Thou better know'st
The offices of nature, bond of childhood, 179
Effects of courtesy, dues of gratitude. 180
Thy half o'th' kingdom hast thou not forgot,
Wherein I thee endowed.
REGAN                              Good sir, to th' purpose. 182
LEAR
Who put my man i'th' stocks?          *Tucket within.*
CORNWALL                           What trumpet's that?
REGAN
I know't—my sister's. This approves her letter, 184
That she would soon be here.

          *Enter steward [Oswald].*

                              Is your lady come?
LEAR
This is a slave, whose easy-borrowed pride 186
Dwells in the fickle grace of her he follows.— 187
Out, varlet, from my sight!
CORNWALL                        What means Your Grace? 188
LEAR
Who stocked my servant? Regan, I have good hope
Thou didst not know on't.

          *Enter Goneril.*

                         Who comes here? O heavens,
If you do love old men, if your sweet sway
Allow obedience, if you yourselves are old, 192
Make it your cause; send down, and take my part!
[*To Goneril*] Art not ashamed to look upon this beard? 194
          [*Goneril and Regan join hands.*]
Oh, Regan, will you take her by the hand?
GONERIL
Why not by th' hand, sir? How have I offended?
All's not offense that indiscretion finds 197
And dotage terms so.
LEAR                    O sides, you are too tough! 198
Will you yet hold?—How came my man i'th' stocks?
CORNWALL
I set him there, sir; but his own disorders
Deserved much less advancement.
LEAR                              You? Did you? 201
REGAN
I pray you, father, being weak, seem so. 202
If till the expiration of your month
You will return and sojourn with my sister,
Dismissing half your train, come then to me.

I am now from home, and out of that provision 206
Which shall be needful for your entertainment. 207
LEAR
Return to her? And fifty men dismissed?
No! Rather I abjure all roofs, and choose
To wage against the enmity o'th'air, 210
To be a comrade with the wolf and owl—
Necessity's sharp pinch. Return with her?
Why, the hot-blooded France, that dowerless took 213
Our youngest born—I could as well be brought
To knee his throne and, squirelike, pension beg 215
To keep base life afoot. Return with her?
Persuade me rather to be slave and sumpter 217
To this detested groom.          [*He points to Oswald.*]
GONERIL                         At your choice, sir.
LEAR
I prithee, daughter, do not make me mad.
I will not trouble thee, my child. Farewell.
We'll no more meet, no more see one another.
But yet thou art my flesh, my blood, my daughter—
Or rather a disease that's in my flesh,
Which I must needs call mine. Thou art a boil,
A plague-sore, or embossèd carbuncle 225
In my corrupted blood. But I'll not chide thee;
Let shame come when it will, I do not call it. 227
I do not bid the thunder-bearer shoot, 228
Nor tell tales of thee to high-judging Jove. 229
Mend when thou canst; be better at thy leisure.
I can be patient. I can stay with Regan,
I and my hundred knights.
REGAN    Not altogether so.
I looked not for you yet, nor am provided 234
For your fit welcome. Give ear, sir, to my sister;
For those that mingle reason with your passion 236
Must be content to think you old, and so— 237
But she knows what she does.
LEAR                    Is this well spoken?
REGAN
I dare avouch it, sir. What, fifty followers? 239
Is it not well? What should you need of more?
Yea, or so many, sith that both charge and danger 241
Speak 'gainst so great a number? How in one house
Should many people under two commands
Hold amity? 'Tis hard, almost impossible.
GONERIL
Why might not you, my lord, receive attendance
From those that she calls servants, or from mine?
REGAN
Why not, my lord? If then they chanced to slack ye, 247
We could control them. If you will come to me— 248
For now I spy a danger—I entreat you

---

176 **bandy** volley, exchange.    **scant my sizes** diminish my allow-
ances    177 **oppose the bolt** lock the door    179 **The offices . . .
childhood** the natural duties and filial obligations due to parents
180 **Effects** actions, manifestations    182 **to th' purpose** get to the
point.    184 **approves** confirms    186 **easy-borrowed** easily put
on    187 **grace** favor.    **her** Goneril    188 **varlet** worthless fellow
192 **Allow** approve, sanction    194 **beard** (A sign of age and presumed
entitlement to respect.)    197–8 **All's . . . so** Not everything that the
poor judgment and dotage of old age deem offensive is actually so.
198 **sides** i.e., sides of the chest (stretched by the swelling heart)
201 **much less advancement** far less honor, i.e., far worse treatment.
202 **seem so** i.e., don't act as if you were strong.

206 **from** away from    207 **entertainment** proper reception.
210 **wage** wage war    213 **hot-blooded** spirited, youthful; choleric
215 **knee** fall on my knees before    217 **sumpter** packhorse; hence,
drudge    225 **embossèd** swollen, tumid    227 **call** summon    228 **the
thunder-bearer** i.e., Jove    229 **high-judging** judging from on high
234 **looked not for** did not expect    236–7 **For . . . old** for those who
dispassionately consider your intemperate outbursts must conclude
that you are old    239 **avouch** vouch for    241 **sith that** since.    **charge**
expense.    **danger** i.e., the danger of rivalry and disaffection in such a
large household    247 **slack** neglect    248 **control** correct

To bring but five-and-twenty. To no more
Will I give place or notice.                                    251

LEAR
I gave you all—

REGAN                         And in good time you gave it.

LEAR
Made you my guardians, my depositaries,          253
But kept a reservation to be followed               254
With such a number. What, must I come to you
With five-and-twenty? Regan, said you so?

REGAN
And speak't again, my lord. No more with me.

LEAR
Those wicked creatures yet do look well-favored   258
When others are more wicked; not being the worst
Stands in some rank of praise. [*To Goneril*] I'll go with
  thee.                                                        260
Thy fifty yet doth double five-and-twenty,
And thou art twice her love.

GONERIL                       Hear me, my lord:
What need you five-and-twenty, ten, or five,
To follow in a house where twice so many        264
Have a command to tend you?

REGAN                         What need one?       265

LEAR
Oh, reason not the need! Our basest beggars         266
Are in the poorest thing superfluous.               267
Allow not nature more than nature needs,            268
Man's life is cheap as beast's. Thou art a lady;
If only to go warm were gorgeous,                   270
Why, nature needs not what thou gorgeous wear'st,  271
Which scarcely keeps thee warm. But, for true need—  272
You heavens, give me that patience, patience I need!
You see me here, you gods, a poor old man,
As full of grief as age, wretched in both.
If it be you that stirs these daughters' hearts
Against their father, fool me not so much           277
To bear it tamely; touch me with noble anger,       278
And let not women's weapons, water drops,
Stain my man's cheeks. No, you unnatural hags,
I will have such revenges on you both
That all the world shall—I will do such things—
What they are yet I know not, but they shall be
The terrors of the earth. You think I'll weep;
No, I'll not weep.                 *Storm and tempest.*
I have full cause of weeping; but this heart
Shall break into a hundred thousand flaws           287

Or ere I'll weep. Oh, Fool, I shall go mad!         288
          *Exeunt [Lear, Gloucester, Kent, Gentleman,*
                                    *and Fool].*

CORNWALL
Let us withdraw. 'Twill be a storm.

REGAN
This house is little. The old man and 's people
Cannot be well bestowed.                            291

GONERIL
'Tis his own blame hath put himself from rest,      292
And must needs taste his folly.                     293

REGAN
For his particular, I'll receive him gladly,        294
But not one follower.

GONERIL
So am I purposed. Where is my lord of Gloucester?

CORNWALL
Followed the old man forth.

          *Enter Gloucester.*

                         He is returned.

GLOUCESTER
The King is in high rage.

CORNWALL               Whither is he going?

GLOUCESTER
He calls to horse, but will I know not whither.

CORNWALL
'Tis best to give him way. He leads himself.        300

GONERIL [*to Gloucester*]
My lord, entreat him by no means to stay.           301

GLOUCESTER
Alack, the night comes on, and the bleak winds
Do sorely ruffle. For many miles about              303
There's scarce a bush.

REGAN              Oh, sir, to willful men
The injuries that they themselves procure
Must be their schoolmasters. Shut up your doors.
He is attended with a desperate train,              307
And what they may incense him to, being apt         308
To have his ear abused, wisdom bids fear.           309

CORNWALL
Shut up your doors, my lord; 'tis a wild night.
My Regan counsels well. Come out o'th' storm.
                                          *Exeunt.*

                         ❖

# 3.1

*Storm still. Enter Kent [disguised as Caius]*
*and a Gentleman, severally.*

KENT   Who's there, besides foul weather?

GENTLEMAN
One minded like the weather, most unquietly.
KENT    I know you. Where's the King?
GENTLEMAN
Contending with the fretful elements;
Bids the wind blow the earth into the sea
Or swell the curlèd waters 'bove the main,                     6
That things might change or cease; tears his white hair,       7
Which the impetuous blasts with eyeless rage
Catch in their fury and make nothing of;                       9
Strives in his little world of man to outstorm                 10
The to-and-fro-conflicting wind and rain.
This night, wherein the cub-drawn bear would couch,            12
The lion and the belly-pinchèd wolf
Keep their fur dry, unbonneted he runs
And bids what will take all.
KENT                             But who is with him?          15
GENTLEMAN
None but the Fool, who labors to outjest                       16
His heart-struck injuries.
KENT                             Sir, I do know you,           17
And dare upon the warrant of my note                           18
Commend a dear thing to you. There is division,               19
Although as yet the face of it is covered
With mutual cunning, twixt Albany and Cornwall;
Who have—as who have not, that their great stars              22
Throned and set high?—servants, who seem no less,            23
Which are to France the spies and speculations               24
Intelligent of our state. What hath been seen,               25
Either in snuffs and packings of the dukes,                  26
Or the hard rein which both of them hath borne               27
Against the old kind King, or something deeper,              28
Whereof perchance these are but furnishings—                 29
But true it is, from France there comes a power              30
Into this scattered kingdom, who already,                    31
Wise in our negligence, have secret feet                     32
In some of our best ports and are at point                   33
To show their open banner. Now to you:
If on my credit you dare build so far                        35
To make your speed to Dover, you shall find
Some that will thank you, making just report                 37
Of how unnatural and bemadding sorrow
The King hath cause to plain.                                39
I am a gentleman of blood and breeding,                      40

And from some knowledge and assurance offer                  41
This office to you.                                          42
GENTLEMAN
I will talk further with you.
KENT                             No, do not.
For confirmation that I am much more
Than my outwall, open this purse and take                    45
What it contains. [*He gives a purse and a ring.*] If you
shall see Cordelia—
As fear not but you shall—show her this ring,                47
And she will tell you who that fellow is                     48
That yet you do not know. Fie on this storm!
I will go seek the King.
GENTLEMAN
Give me your hand. Have you no more to say?
KENT
Few words, but, to effect, more than all yet:                52
That when we have found the King—in which your
  pain                                                       53
That way, I'll this—he that first lights on him              54
Holla the other.                          *Exeunt* [*separately*].

❖

## 3.2

*Storm still. Enter Lear and Fool.*

LEAR
Blow, winds, and crack your cheeks! Rage, blow!
You cataracts and hurricanoes, spout                         2
Till you have drenched our steeples, drowned the
  cocks!                                                     3
You sulfurous and thought-executing fires,                   4
Vaunt-couriers of oak-cleaving thunderbolts,                 5
Singe my white head! And thou, all-shaking thunder,
Strike flat the thick rotundity o'th' world!
Crack nature's molds, all germens spill at once              8
That make ingrateful man!
FOOL    Oh, nuncle, court holy water in a dry house is bet-  10
ter than this rainwater out o'door. Good nuncle, in,
ask thy daughters' blessing. Here's a night pities          12
neither wise men nor fools.
LEAR
Rumble thy bellyful! Spit, fire! Spout, rain!
Nor rain, wind, thunder, fire are my daughters.             15
I tax not you, you elements, with unkindness;               16
I never gave you kingdom, called you children.
You owe me no subscription. Then let fall                   18

---

**6 curlèd** with mighty billows.   **main** mainland    **7 things** all things
**9 make nothing of** blow about contemptuously   **10 little world of
man** i.e., microcosm, which is an epitome of the macrocosm or universe
**12 cub-drawn** famished, with udders sucked dry (and hence ravenous).
**couch** lie close in its den    **15 bids . . . all** (A cry of desperate defiance;
"take all" is the cry of a gambler in staking his last.)   **16 outjest** exorcise or relieve by jesting    **17 heart-struck injuries** injuries that strike to
the very heart.    **18–19 And . . . to you** and dare, on the strength of what
I know about you, entrust a precious undertaking to you.   **22–3 as . . .
high** as who does not, among those whom a mighty destiny has
enthroned on high   **23 no less** i.e., no other than servants   **24 speculations** scouts, spies   **25 Intelligent of** supplying intelligence pertinent to
**26 snuffs and packings** resentments and intrigues   **27–8 Or . . . King** or
the harsh reining in they both have inflicted on King Lear   **29 furnishings**
outward shows    **30 power** army   **31 scattered** divided   **32 Wise in**
aware of.   **feet** footholds   **33 at point** ready   **35 credit** trustworthiness.
**so far** so far as    **37 making just report** for making an accurate report
**39 plain** complain.   **40 blood and breeding** good family and education

**41 assurance** confidence, certainty   **42 office** assignment   **45 outwall** exterior appearance   **47 fear not but** be assured that   **48 fellow**
i.e., Kent   **52 to effect** in their consequences   **53–4 in which . . . this**
in which task, you search in that direction while I go this way
**3.2. Location: An open place, as before.**
**2 hurricanoes** waterspouts   **3 drenched** drowned.   **cocks** weather-
vanes.   **4 thought-executing fires** lightning that acts with the quickness of thought   **5 Vaunt-couriers** forerunners   **8 Crack . . . at once**
Crack the molds in which nature makes all life; destroy all seeds at
once   **10 court holy water** flattery   **12 ask . . . blessing** (For Lear to
do so would be to acknowledge their authority.)   **15 Nor** Neither
**16 tax** accuse.   **with** of   **18 subscription** allegiance.

Your horrible pleasure. Here I stand your slave,
A poor, infirm, weak, and despised old man.
But yet I call you servile ministers,                             21
That will with two pernicious daughters join
Your high-engendered battles 'gainst a head                       23
So old and white as this. Oho! 'Tis foul.

FOOL   He that has a house to put 's head in has a good
headpiece.                                                       26
     The codpiece that will house          27
       Before the head has any,   28
     The head and he shall louse;          29
       So beggars marry many.     30
     The man that makes his toe            31
       What he his heart should make   32
     Shall of a corn cry woe,              33
       And turn his sleep to wake.   34
For there was never yet fair woman but she made                   35
mouths in a glass.                                                36

LEAR
No, I will be the pattern of all patience;
I will say nothing.

     *Enter Kent, [disguised as Caius].*

KENT   Who's there?
FOOL   Marry, here's grace and a codpiece; that's a wise   40
man and a fool.

KENT
Alas, sir, are you here? Things that love night
Love not such nights as these. The wrathful skies
Gallow the very wanderers of the dark                             44
And make them keep their caves. Since I was man,                  45
Such sheets of fire, such bursts of horrid thunder,
Such groans of roaring wind and rain I never
Remember to have heard. Man's nature cannot carry                 48
Th'affliction nor the fear.

LEAR                            Let the great gods,               49
That keep this dreadful pother o'er our heads,                    50
Find out their enemies now. Tremble, thou wretch,
That hast within thee undivulgèd crimes
Unwhipped of justice! Hide thee, thou bloody hand,                53
Thou perjured, and thou simular of virtue                         54
That art incestuous! Caitiff, to pieces shake,                    55
That under covert and convenient seeming                          56

Has practiced on man's life! Close pent-up guilts,                57
Rive your concealing continents and cry                           58
These dreadful summoners grace! I am a man                        59
More sinned against than sinning.

KENT                            Alack, bareheaded?
Gracious my lord, hard by here is a hovel;
Some friendship will it lend you 'gainst the tempest.
Repose you there while I to this hard house—
More harder than the stones whereof 'tis raised,
Which even but now, demanding after you,                          65
Denied me to come in—return and force
Their scanted courtesy.

LEAR                            My wits begin to turn.            67
Come on, my boy. How dost, my boy? Art cold?
I am cold myself.—Where is this straw, my fellow?
The art of our necessities is strange,
And can make vile things precious. Come, your
   hovel.—
Poor fool and knave, I have one part in my heart
That's sorry yet for thee.

FOOL [*sings*]
     "He that has and a little tiny wit,        74
       With heigh-ho, the wind and the rain,
     Must make content with his fortunes fit,
       Though the rain it raineth every day."    77

LEAR
True, boy.—Come, bring us to this hovel.
           *Exit [with Kent].*

FOOL   This is a brave night to cool a courtesan. I'll speak   79
a prophecy ere I go:

     When priests are more in word than matter;    81
     When brewers mar their malt with water;        82
     When nobles are their tailors' tutors,         83
     No heretics burned but wenches' suitors,       84
     Then shall the realm of Albion                 85
     Come to great confusion.                       86

     When every case in law is right,               87
     No squire in debt, nor no poor knight;
     When slanders do not live in tongues,          89
     Nor cutpurses come not to throngs;

---

**21 ministers** agents   **23 high-engendered battles** battalions engendered in the heavens   **26 headpiece** (1) helmetlike covering for the head (2) head for common sense.   **27–30 The codpiece . . . many** i.e., A man who houses his genitals in a sexual embrace before he has a roof over his head can expect the lice-infested penury of a penniless marriage. (The *codpiece* is a covering for the genitals worn by men with their close-fitting hose; here representing the genitals themselves.) **31–4 The man . . . wake** i.e., Anyone who unwisely places his affection on base things will be afflicted with sorrow and sleeplessness. (The *corn* is a bunion on the toe.)   **35–6 made . . . glass** practiced making attractive faces in a mirror.   **40 Marry** (An oath, originally "by the Virgin Mary.")   **grace** royal grace.   **codpiece** (Often prominent in the Fool's costume.)   **44 Gallow . . . dark** frighten the very wild beasts of the night   **45 keep** occupy, remain inside   **48 carry** endure **49 Th'affliction** the physical affliction   **50 pother** hubbub, turmoil **53 Unwhipped of** unpunished by   **54 simular** pretender   **55 Caitiff** Wretch   **56 convenient seeming** deception fitted to the purpose

**57 practiced on** plotted against   **57–9 Close . . . grace!** O you secret and buried consciousnesses of guilt, burst open the hiding places that conceal you, and pray to the gods for mercy! (*Summoners* are the officers who cited offenders to appear before ecclesiastical courts.)   **65 Which** i.e., the occupants of which.   **demanding** I inquiring   **67 scanted** stinted **74–7 "He . . . day"** (Derived from the popular song that Feste sings in *Twelfth Night*, 5.1.389 ff.)   **79 This . . . courtesan** i.e., This night is stormy enough to cool even the lust of a courtesan. (*Brave* means "fine, excellent.") **81 When priests . . . matter** i.e., When priests do not practice what they preach. (This and the next three lines satirize the present state of affairs.)   **82 mar** adulterate   **83 are . . . tutors** can instruct their own tailors about fashion   **84 No heretics . . . suitors** i.e., when the prevailing heresy is lechery (a heresy, in other words, against love rather than against true religion), punished by burning not at the stake but by means of venereal infection   **85 realm of Albion** kingdom of England. (The Fool is parodying a pseudo-Chaucerian prophetic verse.)   **85–6 Then . . . confusion** (In F, these lines follow line 92; Q omits lines 79–96.) **87 right** just. (This and the next five lines offer a utopian vision of justice and charity that will never be realized in this corrupted world.) **89 When slanders . . . tongues** when no tongues speak slanders

When usurers tell their gold i'th' field,    91
And bawds and whores do churches build,
Then comes the time, who lives to see't,    93
That going shall be used with feet.    94

This prophecy Merlin shall make, for I live before his    95
time.           *Exit.*

❖

## 3.3

*Enter Gloucester and Edmund [with lights].*

GLOUCESTER   Alack, alack, Edmund, I like not this unnatural dealing. When I desired their leave that I might
pity him, they took from me the use of mine own    3
house, charged me on pain of perpetual displeasure
neither to speak of him, entreat for him, or any way
sustain him.

EDMUND   Most savage and unnatural!

GLOUCESTER   Go to; say you nothing. There is division    8
between the dukes, and a worse matter than that. I
have received a letter this night; 'tis dangerous to be
spoken; I have locked the letter in my closet. These in-    11
juries the King now bears will be revenged home;    12
there is part of a power already footed. We must in-    13
cline to the King. I will look him and privily relieve    14
him. Go you and maintain talk with the Duke, that
my charity be not of him perceived. If he ask for me,    16
I am ill and gone to bed. If I die for't, as no less is
threatened me, the King my old master must be relieved. There is strange things toward, Edmund. Pray    19
you, be careful.           *Exit.*

EDMUND
This courtesy forbid thee shall the Duke    21
Instantly know, and of that letter too.
This seems a fair deserving, and must draw me    23
That which my father loses—no less than all.    24
The younger rises when the old doth fall.      *Exit.*

❖

## 3.4

*Enter Lear, Kent [disguised as Caius], and Fool.*

KENT
Here is the place, my lord. Good my lord, enter.

---

91 **tell** count.  **i'th' field** i.e., openly, without fear  **93 who** whoever
**94 That . . . feet** that walking will be done on foot. (A comical anticlimax: Nothing will have been changed; don't expect these utopian
dreams to have materialized.)  **95 Merlin** (A great wizard of the
court of King Arthur, who came after Lear. The Fool's comical inversion ends his song on a note of paradox and impossibility.)
**3.3. Location: Gloucester's house.**
**3 pity** be merciful to, relieve  **8 Go to** i.e., No more of that
**11 closet** private chamber.  **12 home** thoroughly  **13 power** armed
force.  **footed** landed.  **13–14 incline to** side with  **14 look** look for.
**privily** secretly  **16 of** by  **19 toward** impending  **21 courtesy
forbid thee** kindess (to Lear) which you were forbidden to show
**23–4 This . . . all** i.e., This betraying by me of my father is something
he has brought on himself, and will surely confer upon me the earldom of Gloucester and all his wealth.
**3.4. Location: An open place. Before a hovel.**

---

The tyranny of the open night's too rough
For nature to endure.           *Storm still.*

LEAR            Let me alone.    3

KENT
Good my lord, enter here.

LEAR            Wilt break my heart?    4

KENT
I had rather break mine own. Good my lord, enter.

LEAR
Thou think'st 'tis much that this contentious storm
Invades us to the skin. So 'tis to thee,
But where the greater malady is fixed    8
The lesser is scarce felt. Thou'dst shun a bear,
But if thy flight lay toward the roaring sea
Thou'dst meet the bear i'th' mouth. When the
mind's free,    11
The body's delicate. This tempest in my mind    12
Doth from my senses take all feeling else
Save what beats there. Filial ingratitude!    14
Is it not as this mouth should tear this hand    15
For lifting food to't? But I will punish home.    16
No, I will weep no more. In such a night
To shut me out? Pour on; I will endure.
In such a night as this? Oh, Regan, Goneril,
Your old kind father, whose frank heart gave all—    20
Oh, that way madness lies; let me shun that!
No more of that.

KENT           Good my lord, enter here.

LEAR
Prithee, go in thyself; seek thine own ease.
This tempest will not give me leave to ponder    24
On things would hurt me more. But I'll go in.    25
[*To the Fool*] In, boy; go first. You houseless poverty—
Nay, get thee in. I'll pray, and then I'll sleep.
           *Exit [Fool into the hovel].*
Poor naked wretches, wheresoe'er you are,
That bide the pelting of this pitiless storm,    29
How shall your houseless heads and unfed sides,    30
Your looped and windowed raggedness, defend you    31
From seasons such as these? Oh, I have ta'en
Too little care of this! Take physic, pomp;    33
Expose thyself to feel what wretches feel,
That thou mayst shake the superflux to them    35
And show the heavens more just.

EDGAR [*within*]   Fathom and half, fathom and half!    37
Poor Tom!

*Enter Fool [from the hovel].*

---

3 **nature** human nature  4 **Wilt . . . heart?** i.e., Do you want to relieve
my physical wants and thereby force me to remember my daughters'
ingratitude?  8 **fixed** lodged, implanted  11 **i'th' mouth** i.e., head-on.
**free** free of anxiety  12 **delicate** sensitive, aware to its surroundings.
14 **Save** except  15–16 **Is it . . . to't** i.e., The ingratitude of daughters is
as if the mouth of our body should ungratefully attack the hand, forgetting that the mouth owes everything to the hand for providing it with food.
15 **as** as if  16 **home** fully.  20 **frank** liberal  24 **will . . . leave** i.e., keeps
me too preoccupied  25 **things would** things (such as filial ingratitude)
that would  29 **bide** endure  30 **unfed sides** i.e., lean ribs  31 **looped
and windowed** full of openings like windows and loopholes  33 **Take
physic, pomp** Cure yourself, O distempered great ones  35 **superflux**
superfluity. (With suggestion of *flux*, "bodily discharge," introduced by
*physic*, "purgative," in line 33.)  37 **Fathom and half** (A sailor's cry
while taking soundings, hence appropriate to a deluge.)

**FOOL**   Come not in here, nuncle; here's a spirit. Help
me, help me!

**KENT**   Give me thy hand. Who's there?

**FOOL**   A spirit, a spirit! He says his name's poor Tom.

**KENT**
What art thou that dost grumble there i'th' straw?   43
Come forth.

*Enter Edgar [disguised as a madman].*

**EDGAR**   Away! The foul fiend follows me! Through the   45
sharp hawthorn blows the cold wind. Humh! Go to thy   46
bed and warm thee.

**LEAR**   Didst thou give all to thy daughters? And art
thou come to this?

**EDGAR**   Who gives anything to poor Tom? Whom the
foul fiend hath led through fire and through flame,
through ford and whirlpool, o'er bog and quagmire;
that hath laid knives under his pillow and halters in   53
his pew, set ratsbane by his porridge, made him   54
proud of heart to ride on a bay trotting horse over   55
four-inched bridges to course his own shadow for a   56
traitor. Bless thy five wits! Tom's a-cold. Oh, do de,   57
do de, do de. Bless thee from whirlwinds, star-blast-   58
ing, and taking! Do poor Tom some charity, whom the   59
foul fiend vexes. There could I have him now—and   60
there—and there again—and there.       *Storm still.*

**LEAR**
Has his daughters brought him to this pass?—   62
Couldst thou save nothing? Wouldst thou give 'em
all?

**FOOL**   Nay, he reserved a blanket, else we had been all   64
shamed.

**LEAR**
Now, all the plagues that in the pendulous air   66
Hang fated o'er men's faults light on thy daughters!   67

**KENT**   He hath no daughters, sir.

**LEAR**
Death, traitor! Nothing could have subdued nature
To such a lowness but his unkind daughters.
Is it the fashion that discarded fathers
Should have thus little mercy on their flesh?   72
Judicious punishment! 'Twas this flesh begot   73
Those pelican daughters.   74

**EDGAR**   Pillicock sat on Pillicock Hill. Alow, alow, loo,   75
loo!

**FOOL**   This cold night will turn us all to fools and madmen.

**EDGAR**   Take heed o'th' foul fiend. Obey thy parents;
keep thy word's justice; swear not; commit not with   80
man's sworn spouse; set not thy sweet heart on proud
array. Tom's a-cold.

**LEAR**   What hast thou been?

**EDGAR**   A servingman, proud in heart and mind, that   84
curled my hair, wore gloves in my cap, served the lust   85
of my mistress' heart, and did the act of darkness with
her; swore as many oaths as I spake words, and broke
them in the sweet face of heaven. One that slept in the
contriving of lust and waked to do it. Wine loved I
deeply, dice dearly, and in woman out-paramoured   90
the Turk. False of heart, light of ear, bloody of hand;   91
hog in sloth, fox in stealth, wolf in greediness, dog in
madness, lion in prey. Let not the creaking of shoes   93
nor the rustling of silks betray thy poor heart to   94
woman. Keep thy foot out of brothels, thy hand out of
plackets, thy pen from lenders' books, and defy the   96
foul fiend. Still through the hawthorn blows the cold
wind; says suum, mun, nonny. Dolphin my boy, boy,   98
sessa! Let him trot by.       *Storm still.*   99

**LEAR**   Thou wert better in a grave than to answer with
thy uncovered body this extremity of the skies. Is man
no more than this? Consider him well. Thou ow'st the   102
worm no silk, the beast no hide, the sheep no wool,   103
the cat no perfume. Ha! Here's three on 's are sophis-   104
ticated; thou art the thing itself. Unaccommodated   105
man is no more but such a poor, bare, forked animal   106
as thou art. Off, off, you lendings! Come, unbutton
here.       *[Tearing off his clothes.]*

**FOOL**   Prithee, nuncle, be contented; 'tis a naughty night   109
to swim in. Now a little fire in a wild field were like   110
an old lecher's heart—a small spark, all the rest on 's   111
body cold.

*Enter Gloucester, with a torch.*

Look, here comes a walking fire.

43 **grumble** mutter, mumble   45 **Away!** Keep away!   45–6 **Through . . .
wind** (Possibly a line from a ballad.)   53–4 **that hath . . . porridge**
(The fiend has laid in poor Tom's way tempting means to despairing
suicide, the most damnable of sins: knives under his pillow when he
is asleep, nooses in his church pew when he should be at prayer, and
rat poison set beside his soup when he should eat.)   54–7 **made him . . .
traitor** (The next temptation is an act of suicidal bravado that would be
impossible without the devil's aid: riding a horse over bridges only
four inches wide in pursuit of one's own shadow.)   57 **five wits**
(Either the five physical senses—sight, hearing, etc.—or the five faculties of the mind: common wit, imagination, fantasy, estimation, and
memory.)   58–9 **star-blasting** being blighted by influence of the stars
59 **taking** infection, evil influence, enchantment.   60 **There** (Perhaps
he slaps at lice and other vermin as if they were devils.)   62 **pass** miserable plight.   64 **reserved a blanket** kept a wrap (for his nakedness)
66 **pendulous** suspended, overhanging   67 **fated** having the power of
fate   72 **have . . . flesh** i.e., punish themselves, as Edgar has done (probably with pins and thorns stuck in his flesh.)   73 **Judicious** Appropriate
to the crime   74 **pelican** greedy. (Young pelicans supposedly smote
their parents and fed on the blood of their mothers' breasts.)

75 **Pillicock** (From an old rhyme, suggested by the sound of *pelican*.
*Pillicock* in nursery rhyme seems to have been a euphemism for penis;
*Pillicock Hill*, for the Mount of Venus.)   80 **justice** integrity.   **commit
not** i.e., do not commit adultery. (Edgar's mad homily contains fragments of the Ten Commandments.)   84 **servingman** either a "servant"
in the language of courtly love or an ambitious servant in a household   85 **gloves** i.e., my mistress's favors   90–1 **out-paramoured the
Turk** outdid the Sultan in keeping mistresses.   91 **light of ear** i.e., listening intently for information that can be used criminally   93 **prey**
preying.   93–4 **creaking . . . silks** (Telltale noises of lovers in a secret
assignation.)   96 **plackets** slits in skirts or petticoats.   **thy pen . . .
books** i.e., do not sign a contract for a loan   98 **suum . . . nonny**
(Imitative of the wind?)   **Dolphin my boy** (A slang phrase or bit of
song?)   99 **sessa** i.e., away, cease (?).   102–4 **Thou . . . perfume**
Stripped of your finery, you are not indebted to the silkworm for silk,
cattle for hide, the sheep for wool, or the civet cat for the perfume
derived from its anal pouch.   104–5 **Here's . . . itself** The three of us
here (Kent, the Fool, and Lear) are decked out in the sophistication of
supposedly civilized society; you (Edgar) are the unadorned, natural
essence, the natural man.   105 **Unaccommodated** Unfurnished with
the trappings of civilization, such as clothing   106 **forked** two-legged
109 **naughty** bad, nasty   110 **wild** barren, uncultivated   111 **on 's** of his

EDGAR   This is the foul fiend Flibbertigibbet! He begins 114
at curfew and walks till the first cock; he gives the web 115
and the pin, squinnies the eye and makes the harelip, 116
mildews the white wheat, and hurts the poor creature 117
of earth.
        Swithold footed thrice the 'old; 119
        He met the nightmare and her ninefold; 120
          Bid her alight,
          And her troth plight, 122
        And aroint thee, witch, aroint thee! 123
KENT   How fares Your Grace?
LEAR   What's he?
KENT   Who's there? What is't you seek?
GLOUCESTER   What are you there? Your names?
EDGAR   Poor Tom, that eats the swimming frog, the
toad, the tadpole, the wall newt and the water; that in 129
the fury of his heart, when the foul fiend rages, eats
cow dung for salads, swallows the old rat and the
ditch-dog, drinks the green mantle of the standing 132
pool; who is whipped from tithing to tithing and 133
stock-punished and imprisoned; who hath had three 134
suits to his back, six shirts to his body, 135
        Horse to ride, and weapon to wear;
        But mice and rats and such small deer 137
        Have been Tom's food for seven long year.
Beware my follower. Peace, Smulkin! Peace, thou fiend! 139
GLOUCESTER
What, hath Your Grace no better company?
EDGAR   The Prince of Darkness is a gentleman. Modo 141
he's called, and Mahu.
GLOUCESTER [to Lear]
Our flesh and blood, my lord, is grown so vile 143
That it doth hate what gets it. 144
EDGAR   Poor Tom's a-cold.
GLOUCESTER
Go in with me. My duty cannot suffer 146
To obey in all your daughters' hard commands. 147
Though their injunction be to bar my doors
And let this tyrannous night take hold upon you,

Yet have I ventured to come seek you out
And bring you where both fire and food is ready.
LEAR
First let me talk with this philosopher.
[To Edgar] What is the cause of thunder?
KENT                                          Good my lord,
Take his offer. Go into th' house.
LEAR
I'll talk a word with this same learnéd Theban. 155
[To Edgar] What is your study? 156
EDGAR   How to prevent the fiend, and to kill vermin. 157
LEAR   Let me ask you one word in private.
             [Lear and Edgar talk apart.]
KENT [to Gloucester]
Importune him once more to go, my lord.
His wits begin to unsettle.
GLOUCESTER                    Canst thou blame him?
                   Storm still.
His daughters seek his death. Ah, that good Kent!
He said it would be thus, poor banished man.
Thou say'st the King grows mad; I'll tell thee, friend,
I am almost mad myself. I had a son,
Now outlawed from my blood; he sought my life 165
But lately, very late. I loved him, friend, 166
No father his son dearer. True to tell thee,
The grief hath crazed my wits. What a night's this!—
I do beseech Your Grace—
LEAR   Oh, cry you mercy, sir. 170
[To Edgar] Noble philosopher, your company.
EDGAR   Tom's a-cold.
GLOUCESTER [to Edgar]
In, fellow, there, in th' hovel. Keep thee warm.
LEAR [starting toward the hovel]
Come, let's in all.
KENT                    This way, my lord.
LEAR                                          With him!
I will keep still with my philosopher.
KENT [to Gloucester]
Good my lord, soothe him. Let him take the fellow. 176
GLOUCESTER [to Kent]   Take you him on. 177
KENT [to Edgar]
Sirrah, come on. Go along with us.
LEAR   Come, good Athenian. 179
GLOUCESTER   No words, no words! Hush.
EDGAR
Child Rowland to the dark tower came; 181
His word was still, "Fie, foh, and fum, 182
I smell the blood of a British man." Exeunt. 183

114 Flibbertigibbet (A devil from Elizabethan folklore whose name appears in Samuel Harsnett's *Declaration of Egregious Popish Impostures*, 1603, and elsewhere.)   114–15 He . . . cock He walks from nightfall till dawn   115–16 web and the pin cataract of the eye   116 squinnies squints   117 white ripening, ready for harvest   119 Swithold Saint Withold, an Anglo-Saxon exorcist, who here provides defense against the *nightmare*, or demon thought to afflict sleepers, by commanding the nightmare to *alight*, i.e., stop riding over the sleeper, and *plight* her *troth*, i.e., vow true faith, promise to do no harm. (Or, an error for *Swithin*.)   footed . . . 'old thrice traversed the wold (tract of hilly upland)   120 ninefold nine offspring. (With possible pun on *fold, foal*.)   122 And . . . plight and gave her pledge   123 aroint thee begone   129 water water newt   132 ditch-dog dead dog in a ditch. mantle scum.   standing stagnant   133 from . . . to tithing from one ward or parish to another   134 stock-punished placed in the stocks   134–5 three suits (Like the menial servant at 2.2.15.)   137 deer animals   139 follower familiar, attendant devil.   Smulkin a devil's name (in Samuel Harsnet's *Declaration*, as are *Modo* and *Mahu* in lines 141–2).   141 The Prince of Darkness The devil   143–4 Our . . . gets it (1) Children have become so hardened in sin that they hate their parents (2) Life is so intolerable that humans cry out at having been born.   146 suffer permit me   147 in all in all matters

155 Theban i.e., a Greek wise man, one deeply versed in "philosophy" or natural science.   156 study special competence.   157 prevent thwart   165 outlawed . . . blood disowned, disinherited, and legally outlawed   166 late recently.   170 cry you mercy I beg your pardon   176 soothe humor   177 Take . . . on i.e., Go on ahead with Edgar.   179 Athenian i.e., philosopher.   181 Child Rowland, etc. (Probably a fragment of a ballad about the hero of the Charlemagne legends. A *child* is a candidate for knighthood.)   182 word watchword.   still incessantly   182–3 "Fie . . . man" (This is essentially what the Giant says in "Jack, the Giant Killer.")

## 3.5

*Enter Cornwall and Edmund [with a letter].*

**CORNWALL**    I will have my revenge ere I depart his house.

**EDMUND**    How, my lord, I may be censured, that nature 3
thus gives way to loyalty, something fears me to 4
think of.

**CORNWALL**    I now perceive it was not altogether your
brother's evil disposition made him seek his death, 7
but a provoking merit set awork by a reprovable 8
badness in himself. 9

**EDMUND**    How malicious is my fortune, that I must 10
repent to be just! This is the letter he spoke of, which 11
approves him an intelligent party to the advantages 12
of France. Oh, heavens! That this treason were not, or 13
not I the detector!

**CORNWALL**    Go with me to the Duchess.

**EDMUND**    If the matter of this paper be certain, you have
mighty business in hand.

**CORNWALL**    True or false, it hath made thee Earl of
Gloucester. Seek out where thy father is, that he may
be ready for our apprehension. 20

**EDMUND** [*aside*]    If I find him comforting the King, it 21
will stuff his suspicion more fully.—I will persevere 22
in my course of loyalty, though the conflict be sore
between that and my blood. 24

**CORNWALL**    I will lay trust upon thee, and thou shalt
find a dearer father in my love.    *Exeunt.*

## 3.6

*Enter Kent [disguised as Caius] and
Gloucester.*

**GLOUCESTER**    Here is better than the open air; take it
thankfully. I will piece out the comfort with what 2
addition I can. I will not be long from you.

**KENT**    All the power of his wits have given way to his
impatience. The gods reward your kindness! 5
*Exit [Gloucester].*

*Enter Lear, Edgar [as poor Tom], and Fool.*

**EDGAR**    Fraterretto calls me, and tells me Nero is an 6
angler in the lake of darkness. Pray, innocent, and 7
beware the foul fiend.

**FOOL**    Prithee, nuncle, tell me whether a madman be a
gentleman or a yeoman? 10

**LEAR**    A king, a king!

**FOOL**    No, he's a yeoman that has a gentleman to his
son; for he's a mad yeoman that sees his son a
gentleman before him.

**LEAR**
To have a thousand with red burning spits
Come hizzing in upon 'em— 16

**EDGAR**    The foul fiend bites my back. 17

**FOOL**    He's mad that trusts in the tameness of a wolf, a 18
horse's health, a boy's love, or a whore's oath. 19

**LEAR**
It shall be done; I will arraign them straight. 20
[*To Edgar*] Come, sit thou here, most learnèd justicer. 21
[*To the Fool*] Thou, sapient sir, sit here. Now, you she-
foxes! 22

**EDGAR**    Look where he stands and glares! Want'st thou 23
eyes at trial, madam? 24
[*Sings.*] "Come o'er the burn, Bessy, to me—" 25

**FOOL** [*sings*]
Her boat hath a leak,
And she must not speak
Why she dares not come over to thee.

**EDGAR**    The foul fiend haunts poor Tom in the voice of a
nightingale. Hoppedance cries in Tom's belly for two 30
white herring. Croak not, black angel; I have no food 31
for thee.

**KENT** [*to Lear*]
How do you, sir? Stand you not so amazed. 33
Will you lie down and rest upon the cushions?

**LEAR**
I'll see their trial first. Bring in their evidence. 35
[*To Edgar*] Thou robèd man of justice, take thy place; 36
[*To the Fool*] And thou, his yokefellow of equity, 37

**3.5. Location: Gloucester's house.**
**3** censured judged.    **nature** attachment to family    **4 something fears**
somewhat frightens    **7 his** his father's    **8–9 but . . . himself** but
a wickedness in Gloucester deserving punishment that was given
further stimulus by Edgar's own reprehensibly evil nature.
**10–11 How . . . just!** i.e., How cruel of fate to oblige me to be upright
and loyal by betraying my own father!    **11–13 which . . . France**
which proves him to be a spy on behalf of the French.    **20 for our**
**apprehension** for our arresting of him.    **21 If . . . comforting** If I find
Gloucester giving aid and comfort to    **22 his suspicion** Cornwall's
suspicion of Gloucester    **24 blood** family loyalty, filial instincts.
**3.6. Location: Within a building on Gloucester's estate, near or**
**adjoining his house, or part of the house itself. See 3.4.146–54.**
**Cushions are provided, and stools.**
**2 piece** eke    **5 impatience** rage, inability to endure more.    **The gods**
May the gods

**6 Fraterretto** (Another of the fiends from Harsnett.)    **6–7 Nero . . .**
**darkness** (Chaucer's "Monk's Tale," lines 2474–5, tells how Nero
fished in the Tiber with nets of gold thread; in Rabelais, 2.30, Nero is
described as a hurdy-gurdy player and Trajan an angler for frogs in the
underworld.)    **7 innocent** simpleton, fool (i.e., the Fool)    **10 yeoman**
property owner below the rank of gentleman. (The Fool's bitter jest in
lines 12–14 is that such a man might go mad to see his son advanced
over him.)    **16 hizzing** hissing. (Lear imagines his wicked daughters
suffering torments in hell or being attacked by enemies.)
**17 bites** (i.e., in the shape of a louse)    **18–19 tameness . . . health**
(Wolves are untamable, and horses are prone to disease.)    **20 arraign**
**them** (Lear now imagines the trial of his cruel daughters.)    **straight** at
once.    **21 justicer** judge, justice.    **22 sapient** wise    **23 he** (Probably
one of Edgar's devils, or, Lear.)    **23–4 Want'st . . . trial** Do you lack
spectators at your trial? or, Can't you see who's looking at you?
**25 "Come . . . me"** (First line of a ballad by William Birche, 1558. A
*burn* is a brook. The Fool makes a ribald reply, in which the *leaky boat*
suggests the woman's easy virtue or perhaps her menstrual period.)
**30 nightingale** (Edgar pretends to take the Fool's singing for that of a
fiend disguised as a nightingale.)    **Hoppedance** (Harsnett mentions
"Hoberdidance.")    **31 white** unsmoked (contrasted with *black angel*,
a demon).    **Croak** (Refers to the rumbling in Edgar's stomach, denoting hunger.)    **33 amazed** bewildered.    **35 their evidence** the witnesses against them.    **36 robèd man** i.e., Edgar, with his blanket
**37 yokefellow of equity** partner in the law

Bench by his side. [*To Kent*] You are o'th' commission;  38
Sit you, too.                                    [*They sit.*]
EDGAR   Let us deal justly.                    [*He sings.*]
      Sleepest or wakest thou, jolly shepherd?
            Thy sheep be in the corn;            42
      And for one blast of thy minikin mouth,    43
            Thy sheep shall take no harm.        44
      Purr the cat is gray.                       45
LEAR   Arraign her first; 'tis Goneril, I here take my oath
before this honorable assembly, kicked the poor King  47
her father.
FOOL   Come hither, mistress. Is your name Goneril?
LEAR   She cannot deny it.
FOOL   Cry you mercy, I took you for a joint stool.  51
LEAR
      And here's another, whose warped looks proclaim  52
      What store her heart is made on. Stop her there!  53
      Arms, arms, sword, fire! Corruption in the place!  54
      False justicer, why hast thou let her scape?
EDGAR   Bless thy five wits!
KENT
      Oh, pity! Sir, where is the patience now
      That you so oft have boasted to retain?
EDGAR [*aside*]
      My tears begin to take his part so much
      They mar my counterfeiting.
LEAR   The little dogs and all
      Tray, Blanch, and Sweetheart, see, they bark at me.
EDGAR   Tom will throw his head at them.—Avaunt, you  63
      curs!
            Be thy mouth or black or white,        65
            Tooth that poisons if it bite,
            Mastiff, greyhound, mongrel grim,
            Hound or spaniel, brach or lym,        68
            Bobtail tike or trundle-tail,          69
            Tom will make him weep and wail;
            For, with throwing thus my head,
            Dogs leap the hatch, and all are fled.  72
      Do de, de, de. Sessa! Come, march to wakes and fairs  73
      and market towns. Poor Tom, thy horn is dry.  74
LEAR   Then let them anatomize Regan; see what breeds  75
      about her heart. Is there any cause in nature that makes
      these hard hearts? [*To Edgar*] You, sir, I entertain  77

for one of my hundred; only I do not like the fashion of
your garments. You will say they are Persian; but let  79
them be changed.
KENT
      Now, good my lord, lie here and rest awhile.
LEAR [*lying on cushions*]   Make no noise, make no
      noise. Draw the curtains. So, so, so. We'll go to supper  83
      i'th' morning.                      [*He sleeps.*]
FOOL   And I'll go to bed at noon.

      *Enter Gloucester.*

GLOUCESTER [*to Kent*]
      Come hither, friend. Where is the King my master?
KENT
      Here, sir, but trouble him not; his wits are gone.
GLOUCESTER
      Good friend, I prithee, take him in thy arms.
      I have o'erheard a plot of death upon him.    89
      There is a litter ready; lay him in't
      And drive toward Dover, friend, where thou shalt
            meet
      Both welcome and protection. Take up thy master.
      If thou shouldst dally half an hour, his life,
      With thine and all that offer to defend him,
      Stand in assurèd loss. Take up, take up,       95
      And follow me, that will to some provision     96
      Give thee quick conduct.
KENT                           Oppressèd nature sleeps.  97
      This rest might yet have balmed thy broken sinews,  98
      Which, if convenience will not allow,          99
      Stand in hard cure. [*To the Fool*] Come, help to bear thy
            master.                                  100
      Thou must not stay behind.    [*They pick up Lear.*]
GLOUCESTER                      Come, come, away!
                              *Exeunt [all but Edgar].*
EDGAR
      When we our betters see bearing our woes,      102
      We scarcely think our miseries our foes.       103
      Who alone suffers suffers most i'th' mind,     104
      Leaving free things and happy shows behind;    105
      But then the mind much sufferance doth o'erskip  106
      When grief hath mates, and bearing fellowship.  107
      How light and portable my pain seems now,      108
      When that which makes me bend makes the King
            bow—
      He childed as I fathered. Tom, away!           110

**38 Bench** take your place on the bench.   **o'th' commission** one commissioned to be a justice   **42 corn** grainfield   **43–4 And . . . harm** i.e., one shout from your dainty (*minikin*) mouth can recall the sheep from the grainfield and thus save them from dangerous overeating.   **45 Purr the cat** (A devil or familiar from Harsnett; see the note for 3.4.114. *Purr* may be the sound the familiar makes.)   **47 kicked** who kicked   **51 Cry you mercy** I beg your pardon.   **joint stool** low stool made by a joiner, or maker of furniture with joined parts. (Proverbially, the phrase "I took . . . stool" meant "I beg your pardon for failing to notice you." The reference is also presumably to a real stool on stage.)   **52 another** i.e., Regan   **53 store** abundance, material.   **on** of.   **54 Corruption in the place!** i.e., There is iniquity or bribery in this court!   **63 throw his head at** i.e., threaten.   **Avaunt!** Begone!   **65 or black** either black   **68 brach or lym** bitch-hound or bloodhound   **69 Bobtail . . . trundle-tail** mongrel dog with a docked or bobbed tail, or one that is curly-tailed   **72 hatch** lower half of a divided door   **73 Sessa** i.e., Away, cease.   **wakes** parish festivals   **74 horn** horn-bottle, used by beggars to drink from and to beg for alms   **75 anatomize** dissect   **77 entertain** take into my service

**79 Persian** (Lear madly asks if Edgar's wretched blanket is a rich Persian fabric.)   **83 curtains** bedcurtains. (They presumably exist only in Lear's mad imagination.)   **89 upon** against   **95 Stand . . . loss** will assuredly be lost.   **96 provision** supplies, or, means of providing for safety   **97 conduct** guidance.   **98 balmed** soothed, healed.   **sinews** nerves   **99 convenience** circumstances   **100 Stand . . . cure** will be hard to cure.   **102 our woes** woes like ours   **103 We . . . foes** we almost forget our own miseries (since we see how human suffering afflicts even the great).   **104–7 Who . . . fellowship** Anyone who has no companionship in suffering undergoes the mental anguish of forgetting entirely the carefree ways and happy scenes that were once enjoyed, whereas fellowship in grief enables the mind to rise above such suffering. (I.e., Misery loves company.)   **108 portable** bearable, endurable   **110 He . . . fathered** i.e., he suffering cruelty from his children as I from my father.

Mark the high noises, and thyself bewray 111
When false opinion, whose wrong thoughts defile
    thee, 112
In thy just proof repeals and reconciles thee. 113
What will hap more tonight, safe scape the King! 114
Lurk, lurk. [*Exit.*] 115

❖

## 3.7

*Enter Cornwall, Regan, Goneril, Bastard*
[*Edmund*], *and Servants.*

CORNWALL [*to Goneril*]    Post speedily to my lord your hus- 1
band; show him this letter. [*He gives a letter.*] The army
of France is landed.—Seek out the traitor Gloucester.
[*Exeunt some Servants.*]
REGAN    Hang him instantly.
GONERIL    Pluck out his eyes.
CORNWALL    Leave him to my displeasure. Edmund,
keep you our sister company. The revenges we are 7
bound to take upon your traitorous father are not fit 8
for your beholding. Advise the Duke, where you are 9
going, to a most festinate preparation; we are bound 10
to the like. Our posts shall be swift and intelligent 11
betwixt us. Farewell, dear sister; farewell, my lord of 12
Gloucester. 13

*Enter steward* [*Oswald*].

How now? Where's the King?
OSWALD
My lord of Gloucester hath conveyed him hence. 15
Some five- or six-and-thirty of his knights, 16
Hot questrists after him, met him at gate, 17
Who, with some other of the lord's dependents, 18
Are gone with him toward Dover, where they boast
To have well-armèd friends.
CORNWALL    Get horses for your mistress. [*Exit Oswald.*]
GONERIL    Farewell, sweet lord, and sister.
CORNWALL
Edmund, farewell.    *Exeunt* [*Goneril and Edmund*].
Go seek the traitor Gloucester. 24
Pinion him like a thief; bring him before us.
[*Exeunt Servants.*]
Though well we may not pass upon his life 25
Without the form of justice, yet our power 26

111–13 Mark . . . thee Observe what is being said about those in high
places or about great events, and reveal your identity only when the
general opinion that now slanders you, at length establishing your
innocence, recalls you from banishment and restores you to favor.
114 What . . . King! Whatever else happens tonight, may the King
escape safely!    115 Lurk Keep out of sight
3.7. Location: Gloucester's house.
1 Post Ride    7 sister sister-in-law, Goneril    8 bound intending;
obliged    9–11 Advise . . . the like Tell the Duke of Albany, when you get
there, to prepare quickly; we intend and are committed to do the same.
11 posts messengers.    intelligent well informed    12 sister sister-in-law,
Goneril    12–13 my . . . Gloucester i.e., Edmund, the recipient now of his
father's forfeited estate and title. (Two lines later, Oswald uses the same
title to refer to Edmund's father.)    15 hence i.e., toward Dover (but
Gloucester is quickly arrested).    16 his Lear's    17 questrists after him
searchers for Lear    18 the lord's i.e., Gloucester's    24 Pinion him Bind
his arms    25 pass upon his life pass the death sentence upon him
26 form of justice formal legal proceedings

Shall do a court'sy to our wrath, which men 27
May blame but not control.

*Enter Gloucester, and Servants* [*leading him*].

Who's there? The traitor?
REGAN    Ingrateful fox! 'Tis he.
CORNWALL    Bind fast his corky arms. 30
GLOUCESTER
What means Your Graces? Good my friends, consider
You are my guests. Do me no foul play, friends.
CORNWALL
Bind him, I say. [*Servants bind him.*]
REGAN    Hard, hard. Oh, filthy traitor!
GLOUCESTER
Unmerciful lady as you are, I'm none.
CORNWALL
To this chair bind him.—Villain, thou shalt find—
[*Regan plucks Gloucester's beard.*]
GLOUCESTER
By the kind gods, 'tis most ignobly done
To pluck me by the beard.
REGAN
So white, and such a traitor?
GLOUCESTER    Naughty lady, 38
These hairs which thou dost ravish from my chin
Will quicken and accuse thee. I am your host. 40
With robbers' hands my hospitable favors 41
You should not ruffle thus. What will you do? 42
CORNWALL
Come, sir, what letters had you late from France? 43
REGAN
Be simple-answered, for we know the truth. 44
CORNWALL
And what confederacy have you with the traitors
Late footed in the kingdom?
REGAN    To whose hands 46
You have sent the lunatic King. Speak.
GLOUCESTER
I have a letter guessingly set down, 48
Which came from one that's of a neutral heart,
And not from one opposed.
CORNWALL    Cunning.
REGAN    And false.
CORNWALL    Where hast thou sent the King?
GLOUCESTER    To Dover.
REGAN
Wherefore to Dover? Wast thou not charged at peril— 55
CORNWALL
Wherefore to Dover? Let him answer that.
GLOUCESTER
I am tied to th' stake, and I must stand the course. 57

27 do a court'sy i.e., bow before, yield precedence    30 corky withered with age    38 white white-haired, venerable.    Naughty
Wicked    40 quicken come to life    41–2 With . . . thus You should
not roughly handle my welcoming features with your hands as
though you were robbers.    43 late lately    44 simple-answered
straightforward in your answers    46 Late footed recently landed
48 guessingly set down conjecturally written    55 Wherefore Why.
charged at peril commanded on peril of your life    57 tied to th'
stake i.e., like a bear to be baited with dogs.    the course the dogs'
attack.

REGAN   Wherefore to Dover?

GLOUCESTER
Because I would not see thy cruel nails
Pluck out his poor old eyes, nor thy fierce sister
In his anointed flesh stick boarish fangs.              61
The sea, with such a storm as his bare head
In hell-black night endured, would have buoyed up       63
And quenched the stellèd fires;                          64
Yet, poor old heart, he holp the heavens to rain.       65
If wolves had at thy gate howled that dern time,        66
Thou shouldst have said, "Good porter, turn the key."   67
All cruels else subscribe. But I shall see              68
The wingèd Vengeance overtake such children.            69

CORNWALL
See't shalt thou never.—Fellows, hold the chair.
Upon these eyes of thine I'll set my foot.

GLOUCESTER
He that will think to live till he be old,              72
Give me some help!
              [Servants hold the chair as Cornwall grinds
              out one of Gloucester's eyes with his boot.]
              Oh, cruel! O you gods!

REGAN
One side will mock another. Th'other too.

CORNWALL [to Gloucester]
If you see Vengeance—

FIRST SERVANT            Hold your hand, my lord!
I have served you ever since I was a child;
But better service have I never done you
Than now to bid you hold.

REGAN                    How now, you dog?

FIRST SERVANT [to Regan]
If you did wear a beard upon your chin,
I'd shake it on this quarrel.—What do you mean?        80

CORNWALL   My villain?        [He draws his sword.]    81

FIRST SERVANT [drawing]
Nay, then, come on, and take the chance of anger.       82
              [They fight. Cornwall is wounded.]

REGAN [to another Servant]
Give me thy sword. A peasant stand up thus?             83
     [She takes a sword and] kills him [the First Servant].

FIRST SERVANT
Oh, I am slain! My lord, you have one eye left          84
To see some mischief on him. Oh!     [He dies.]        85

CORNWALL
Lest it see more, prevent it. Out, vile jelly!
              [He puts out Gloucester's other eye.]

Where is thy luster now?

GLOUCESTER
All dark and comfortless. Where's my son Edmund?
Edmund, enkindle all the sparks of nature               89
To quit this horrid act.

REGAN                    Out, treacherous villain!      90
Thou call'st on him that hates thee. It was he
That made the overture of thy treasons to us,           92
Who is too good to pity thee.

GLOUCESTER
Oh, my follies! Then Edgar was abused.                  94
Kind gods, forgive me that, and prosper him!

REGAN [to a Servant]
Go thrust him out at gates and let him smell
His way to Dover.        Exit [a Servant] with Gloucester.
              How is't, my lord? How look you?  97

CORNWALL
I have received a hurt. Follow me, lady.—
Turn out that eyeless villain. Throw this slave
Upon the dunghill.—Regan, I bleed apace.
Untimely comes this hurt. Give me your arm.
              Exeunt [Cornwall, supported by Regan].

SECOND SERVANT
I'll never care what wickedness I do,
If this man come to good.

THIRD SERVANT            If she live long,              103
And in the end meet the old course of death,            104
Women will all turn monsters.

SECOND SERVANT
Let's follow the old Earl, and get the Bedlam           106
To lead him where he would. His roguish madness         107
Allows itself to anything.                              108

THIRD SERVANT
Go thou. I'll fetch some flax and whites of eggs
To apply to his bleeding face. Now, heaven help him! 110
              Exeunt [with the body].

❧

# 4.1

*Enter Edgar [as poor Tom].*

EDGAR
Yet better thus, and known to be contemned,             1
Than still contemned and flattered. To be worst,        2
The lowest and most dejected thing of fortune,          3
Stands still in esperance, lives not in fear.           4

---

**61 anointed** consecrated with holy oil   **63–4 would . . . fires** would have swelled high enough, like a wave-lifted buoy, to quench the stars. (*Stellèd* means "starry" or "fixed.")   **65 holp** helped.   **rain** i.e., by his weeping. (Q reads "rage.")   **66 dern** dire, dreadful   **67 turn the key** i.e., let them in.   **68 All . . . subscribe** All other cruel creatures would show forgiveness except you; this cruelty is unparalleled.   **69 The wingèd Vengeance** the swift vengeance of the avenging angel of divine wrath   **72 will think** hopes   **80 I'd . . . quarrel** i.e., I'd pull your beard in vehement defiance in this cause.   **What do you mean?** i.e., What are you thinking of, what do you think you're doing? (Said perhaps to Cornwall.)   **81 villain** servant, bondman. (Cornwall's question implies, "How dare you do such a thing?")   **82 the chance of anger** the risks of an angry encounter.   **83.1 She . . . kills him** (The Quarto stage direction reads "Shee takes a sword and runs at him behind." The Folio reads "Killes him.")   **84 My Lord** Gloucester   **85 mischief** injury

**89 nature** i.e., filial love   **90 quit** requite.   **Out** (An exclamation of anger or impatience.)   **92 overture** disclosure   **94 abused** wronged. **97 How look you?** How is it with you?   **103 this man** Cornwall. (Lines 102–10 are found in Q only.) If Cornwall goes unpunished, says the Servant, I may as well commit any crime I please.   **104 old** customary, natural   **106 Bedlam** i.e., lunatic discharged from the insane asylum and licensed to beg   **107–8 His . . . anything** His being a madman and derelict allows him to do anything we ask. **110.1 Exeunt** (At some point after lines 99–100, the body of the slain First Servant must be removed.)
**4.1. Location: An open place.**
**1–2 Yet . . . flattered** It is better to be openly despised as a beggar than continually despised behind one's back and flattered to one's face. **3 dejected** cast down   **4 Stands . . . fear** gives one some cause for hope, having nothing to fear (since everything is already lost).

The lamentable change is from the best;                      5
The worst returns to laughter. Welcome, then,                6
Thou unsubstantial air that I embrace!
The wretch that thou hast blown unto the worst
Owes nothing to thy blasts.

*Enter Gloucester, and an Old Man [leading him].*

But who comes here?                      9
My father, parti-eyed? World, world, O world!              10
But that thy strange mutations make us hate thee,          11
Life would not yield to age.                                12

OLD MAN
Oh, my good lord, I have been your tenant
And your father's tenant these fourscore years.

GLOUCESTER
Away, get thee away! Good friend, begone.
Thy comforts can do me no good at all;
Thee they may hurt.

OLD MAN                      You cannot see your way.

GLOUCESTER
I have no way and therefore want no eyes;
I stumbled when I saw. Full oft 'tis seen
Our means secure us, and our mere defects              20
Prove our commodities. O dear son Edgar,              21
The food of thy abusèd father's wrath!              22
Might I but live to see thee in my touch,              23
I'd say I had eyes again!

OLD MAN                      How now? Who's there?

EDGAR [*aside*]
O gods! Who is't can say, "I am at the worst"?
I am worse than e'er I was.

OLD MAN                      'Tis poor mad Tom.

EDGAR [*aside*]
And worse I may be yet. The worst is not              27
So long as we can say, "This is the worst."              28

OLD MAN [*to Edgar*]
Fellow, where goest?

GLOUCESTER                      Is it a beggar-man?

OLD MAN    Madman and beggar too.

GLOUCESTER
He has some reason, else he could not beg.              31
I'th' last night's storm I such a fellow saw,
Which made me think a man a worm. My son
Came then into my mind, and yet my mind
Was then scarce friends with him. I have heard more
  since.
As flies to wanton boys are we to th' gods;              36

They kill us for their sport.

EDGAR [*aside*]                      How should this be?      37
Bad is the trade that must play fool to sorrow,          38
Ang'ring itself and others.—Bless thee, master!          39

GLOUCESTER
Is that the naked fellow?

OLD MAN                      Ay, my lord.

GLOUCESTER
Then, prithee, get thee gone. If for my sake
Thou wilt o'ertake us hence a mile or twain              42
I'th' way toward Dover, do it for ancient love,          43
And bring some covering for this naked soul,
Who I'll entreat to lead me.

OLD MAN                      Alack, sir, he is mad.

GLOUCESTER
'Tis the time's plague, when madmen lead the blind.    46
Do as I bid thee, or rather do thy pleasure;
Above the rest, begone.                                48

OLD MAN
I'll bring him the best 'parel that I have,
Come on't what will.                      *Exit.*

GLOUCESTER                      Sirrah, naked fellow—          50

EDGAR
Poor Tom's a-cold. [*Aside*] I cannot daub it further.    51

GLOUCESTER    Come hither, fellow.

EDGAR [*aside*]
And yet I must.—Bless thy sweet eyes, they bleed.

GLOUCESTER    Know'st thou the way to Dover?

EDGAR    Both stile and gate, horseway and footpath.
Poor Tom hath been scared out of his good wits. Bless
thee, good man's son, from the foul fiend! Five fiends
have been in poor Tom at once: of lust, as Obidicut;    58
Hobbididance, prince of dumbness; Mahu, of stealing;    59
Modo, of murder; Flibbertigibbet, of mopping          60
and mowing, who since possesses chambermaids and      61
waiting women. So, bless thee, master!

GLOUCESTER [*giving a purse*]
Here, take this purse, thou whom the heavens'
  plagues
Have humbled to all strokes. That I am wretched        64
Makes thee the happier. Heavens, deal so still!
Let the superfluous and lust-dieted man,                66

---

**5–6 The lamentable . . . laughter** Any change from the best is grievous, whereas any change from the worst is bound to be for the better. **9 Owes nothing** can pay no more, is free of obligation  **10 parti-eyed** i.e., with eyes red with blood and bandaged in white, thus multicolored like a fool's costume.  **11–12 But . . . age** If it were not for your hateful inconstancy, we would never be reconciled to old age and death. **20–1 Our . . . commodities** Our prosperity makes us proudly overconfident, whereas the sheer afflictions we suffer prove beneficial (by teaching us humility).  **22 The . . . wrath** on whom thy deceived father's wrath fed, the object of his anger.  **23 in** by means of  **27–8 The worst . . . worst** So long as we can speak and act and delude ourselves with false hopes, our fortunes can, in fact, grow worse.  **31 reason** sanity **36 wanton** childishly cruel

**37 How . . . be?** i.e., How can he have suffered so much, changed so much?  **38–9 Bad . . . others** It's a bad business to have to play the fool to my sorrowing father, vexing myself and others (with this delay in revealing my true identity).  **42 o'ertake us** catch up to us (after you have found clothing for Tom o' Bedlam)  **43 ancient love** i.e., the mutually trusting relationship of master and tenant that you and I have long enjoyed  **46 'Tis the time's plague** It well expresses the spreading sickness of our present state  **48 the rest** all  **50 Come . . . will** whatever comes of this as regards myself.  **51 I . . . further** i.e., I cannot keep up this pretense any longer. (Literally, "I cannot plaster up the wall.")  **58–60 Obidicut . . . Flibbertigibbet** (Fiends borrowed, as before in 3.4.114 and 139–42, from Harsnett.) **60–1 mopping and mowing** making grimaces and mouths  **61 since** ever since then  **64 Have . . . strokes** have brought so low as to bear every blow of Fortune.  **66 superfluous and lust-dieted** immoderately gluttonous and luxuriously fed

That slaves your ordinance, that will not see        67
Because he does not feel, feel your pow'r quickly!    68
So distribution should undo excess                    69
And each man have enough. Dost thou know Dover?

EDGAR   Ay, master.

GLOUCESTER
There is a cliff, whose high and bending head         72
Looks fearfully in the confinèd deep.                 73
Bring me but to the very brim of it
And I'll repair the misery thou dost bear
With something rich about me. From that place         76
I shall no leading need.

EDGAR                          Give me thy arm.
Poor Tom shall lead thee.                    *Exeunt.*

❖

# 4.2

*Enter Goneril [and] Bastard [Edmund].*

GONERIL
Welcome, my lord. I marvel our mild husband          1
Not met us on the way.

          *[Enter] steward [Oswald].*

                          Now, where's your master?   2
OSWALD
Madam, within, but never man so changed.
I told him of the army that was landed;
He smiled at it. I told him you were coming;
His answer was "The worse." Of Gloucester's
    treachery
And of the loyal service of his son
When I informed him, then he called me sot           8
And told me I had turned the wrong side out.
What most he should dislike seems pleasant to him;
What like, offensive.

GONERIL *[to Edmund]*   Then shall you go no further.
It is the cowish terror of his spirit,               12
That dares not undertake. He'll not feel wrongs      13
Which tie him to an answer. Our wishes on the way    14
May prove effects. Back, Edmund, to my brother;      15
Hasten his musters and conduct his powers.           16
I must change arms at home and give the distaff      17

Into my husband's hands. This trusty servant
Shall pass between us. Ere long you are like to hear,   19
If you dare venture in your own behalf,
A mistress's command. Wear this; spare speech.       21
                    *[She gives him a favor.]*
Decline your head. [*She kisses him.*] This kiss, if it durst
    speak,
Would stretch thy spirits up into the air.
Conceive, and fare thee well.                        24

EDMUND
Yours in the ranks of death.                *Exit.*
GONERIL                    My most dear Gloucester!  25
Oh, the difference of man and man!
To thee a woman's services are due;
My fool usurps my body.                              28

OSWALD   Madam, here comes my lord.       *[Exit.]*  29

          *Enter Albany.*

GONERIL
I have been worth the whistling.

ALBANY                              Oh, Goneril,     30
You are not worth the dust which the rude wind
Blows in your face. I fear your disposition;         32
That nature which contemns it origin                 33
Cannot be bordered certain in itself.                34
She that herself will sliver and disbranch           35
From her material sap perforce must wither           36
And come to deadly use.                              37

GONERIL   No more. The text is foolish.             38

ALBANY
Wisdom and goodness to the vile seem vile;
Filths savor but themselves. What have you done?     40
Tigers, not daughters, what have you performed?
A father, and a gracious agèd man,
Whose reverence even the head-lugged bear would
    lick,                                            43
Most barbarous, most degenerate, have you madded.   44
Could my good brother suffer you to do it?           45
A man, a prince, by him so benefited?
If that the heavens do not their visible spirits     47
Send quickly down to tame these vile offenses,
It will come,
Humanity must perforce prey on itself,
Like monsters of the deep.

GONERIL                          Milk-livered man,   51

---

**67 That . . . ordinance** who enslaves your divine ordinances to his own corrupt will   **67–8 that . . . feel** who is resistant to spiritual insight because, not having suffered himself, he lacks the sympathy of fellow feeling   **69 So . . . excess** In that way, radical redistribution of wealth would remedy the evil of the rich having too much wealth for their own good   **72 bending** overhanging   **73 in . . . deep** i.e., into the sea below, which is confined by its shores.   **76 about me** on my person.
**4.2. Location: Before the Duke of Albany's palace.**
**1 Welcome** (Goneril, who has just arrived home from Gloucestershire escorted by Edmund, bids him brief welcome before he must return.)
**2 Not met** has not met   **8 sot** fool   **12 cowish** cowardly   **13 undertake** venture.   **13–14 He'll . . . answer** He will ignore insults that, if he took notice, would oblige him to respond, to fight.   **14–15 Our . . . effects** The hopes we discussed on our journey here (presumably concerning the supplanting of Albany by Edmund) may come to pass.   **15 brother** brother-in-law, Cornwall   **16 musters** assembling of troops.   **powers** armed forces.   **17 change arms** i.e., exchange the woman's distaff for the soldier's sword.   **distaff** spinning staff, symbolizing the wife's role

**19 like** likely   **21 mistress's** (With sexual double meaning.)
**24 Conceive** Understand, take my meaning. (With sexual double entendre, continuing from *stretch thy spirits* in the previous line and continued in *death*, line 25, and *a woman's services*, line 27.)   **25 in** even in
**28 My fool . . . body** i.e., my husband claims possession of me but is unfit to do so.   **29 s.d. Exit** (Oswald could exit later with Goneril, at line 88.)   **30 worth the whistling** i.e., worth the attentions of men. (Alludes to the proverb, "it is a poor dog that is not worth the whistling.")   **32 fear your disposition** mistrust your nature   **33 contemns it** spurns its   **34 bordered certain** safely restrained, kept within bounds   **35 sliver and disbranch** tear off and split   **36 material sap** nourishing substance, the stock from which she grew   **37 to deadly use** to a bad end, to a destructive purpose.   **38 The text** i.e., on which you have been preaching   **40 savor but themselves** hunger only for that which is filthy.   **43 head-lugged** dragged by the head (or by the ring in its nose) and infuriated   **44 madded** driven mad.   **45 brother** brother-in-law (Cornwall).   **suffer** allow   **47 If that** If.   **visible** manifested   **51 Milk-livered** White-livered, cowardly

That bear'st a cheek for blows, a head for wrongs,    52
Who hast not in thy brows an eye discerning    53
Thine honor from thy suffering, that not know'st    54
Fools do those villains pity who are punished    55
Ere they have done their mischief. Where's thy drum?    56
France spreads his banners in our noiseless land,    57
With plumèd helm thy state begins to threat,    58
Whilst thou, a moral fool, sits still and cries,    59
"Alack, why does he so?"

ALBANY                    See thyself, devil!    60
Proper deformity shows not in the fiend    61
So horrid as in woman.

GONERIL                    Oh, vain fool!    62

ALBANY
Thou changèd and self-covered thing, for shame,    63
Bemonster not thy feature. Were't my fitness    64
To let these hands obey my blood,    65
They are apt enough to dislocate and tear    66
Thy flesh and bones. Howe'er thou art a fiend,    67
A woman's shape doth shield thee.    68

GONERIL    Marry, your manhood! Mew!    69

*Enter a Messenger.*

ALBANY    What news?

MESSENGER
Oh, my good lord, the Duke of Cornwall's dead,
Slain by his servant, going to put out
The other eye of Gloucester.

ALBANY                    Gloucester's eyes!

MESSENGER
A servant that he bred, thrilled with remorse,    74
Opposed against the act, bending his sword    75
To his great master, who, threat enraged,    76
Flew on him and amongst them felled him dead,    77
But not without that harmful stroke which since
Hath plucked him after.

ALBANY                    This shows you are above,    79

You justicers, that these our nether crimes    80
So speedily can venge! But, oh, poor Gloucester!
Lost he his other eye?

MESSENGER                    Both, both, my lord.—
This letter, madam, craves a speedy answer;
'Tis from your sister.    [*He gives her a letter.*]

GONERIL [*aside*]    One way I like this well;    84
But being widow, and my Gloucester with her,    85
May all the building in my fancy pluck    86
Upon my hateful life. Another way    87
The news is not so tart.—I'll read, and answer.    88
                    [*Exit.*]

ALBANY
Where was his son when they did take his eyes?    89

MESSENGER
Come with my lady hither.

ALBANY                    He is not here.    90

MESSENGER
No, my good lord. I met him back again.    91

ALBANY    Knows he the wickedness?

MESSENGER
Ay, my good lord. 'Twas he informed against him,    93
And quit the house on purpose that their punishment
Might have the freer course.

ALBANY                    Gloucester, I live    95
To thank thee for the love thou show'dst the King
And to revenge thine eyes.—Come hither, friend.
Tell me what more thou know'st.    *Exeunt.*

❖

# 4.[3]

*Enter Kent [disguised] and a Gentleman.*

KENT    Why the King of France is so suddenly gone back
know you no reason?    2

GENTLEMAN    Something he left imperfect in the state,    3
which since his coming forth is thought of, which im-    4
ports to the kingdom so much fear and danger that his    5
personal return was most required and necessary.

KENT
Who hath he left behind him general?

GENTLEMAN
The Marshal of France, Monsieur la Far.

KENT    Did your letters pierce the Queen to any demonstration of grief?

GENTLEMAN
Ay, sir. She took them, read them in my presence,
And now and then an ample tear trilled down    12
Her delicate cheek. It seemed she was a queen

---

**52 That . . . wrongs** you whose cheek is fit for receiving blows and whose head deserves cuckold's horns    **53–4 discerning . . . suffering** able to tell the difference between an insult to your honor and something you should tolerate    **54–6 that not . . . mischief** you who fail to understand that only fools like yourself are so tenderhearted as to pity villains (like Gloucester, Lear, and Cordelia) who are apprehended and punished before they have committed a crime.    **56 Where's thy drum?** Where is your military preparedness?    **57 noiseless** peaceful, unprepared for war    **58 With . . . threat** the French soldiers, with their plumed helmets, begin to threaten your kingdom    **59 moral** moralizing    **60 "Alack . . . so?"** (An utterly ineffectual response to invasion.)    **See thyself, devil!** i.e., Take a good look at yourself, see what a monster you have become.    **61–2 Proper . . . woman** The deformity that is appropriate in a fiend's features is even uglier in a woman's (since it is so at variance with her nominally feminine appearance).    **62 vain** useless, ridiculous    **63–4 Thou . . . feature** You creature whose transformation into a fiend now overwhelms your womanliness, do not, however evil you are, take on the outward form of a monster or fiend.    **64 Were't my fitness** If it were suitable for me    **65 blood** passion    **66 apt** ready    **67 Howe'er . . . fiend** However much you may be a fiend in reality    **68 shield** (Since I, as a gentleman, cannot lay violent hands on a lady.)    **69 Mew** (An exclamation of disgust, a derisive catcall: You speak of manhood in shielding me as a woman. Some manhood!)    **74 bred** kept in his household.    **thrilled with remorse** deeply moved with pity    **75 Opposed** opposed himself    **75–6 bending . . . To** directing his sword against    **77 amongst them** together with the others (?) in their midst (?) out of their number (?) during the fighting (?)    **79 after** along (to death).

**80 justicers** (heavenly) judges.    **nether** i.e., (1) committed here below, on earth (2) hellish    **84 One way** (i.e., because Edmund is now Duke of Gloucester, and Cornwall, a dangerous rival for the throne, is dead)    **85–7 But . . . life** but she being now a widow, and Edmund in her company, may pull down my imagined happiness (of having the entire kingdom with Edmund), leaving my hopes in ruins.    **88 tart** bitter, sour. (See line 84 and note.)    **89 his son** Edmund.    **his** Gloucester's.    **90 my lady** Goneril    **91 back again** on the way back (from Albany's palace).    **93 him** Gloucester    **95 Gloucester** The old Earl of Gloucester    **4.3. Location: The French camp near Dover. This scene is omitted in F.**    **2 no reason** the reason.    **3 imperfect in the state** unsettled in state affairs    **4 is thought of** came into his memory    **4–5 imports** portends    **12 trilled** trickled

Over her passion, who, most rebel-like,                                    14
Sought to be king o'er her.

KENT                                        Oh, then it moved her?

GENTLEMAN
Not to a rage. Patience and sorrow strove
Who should express her goodliest. You have seen           17
Sunshine and rain at once. Her smiles and tears
Were like a better way; those happy smilets               19
That played on her ripe lip seemed not to know            20
What guests were in her eyes, which parted thence         21
As pearls from diamonds dropped. In brief,
Sorrow would be a rarity most beloved                     23
If all could so become it.                                24

KENT    Made she no verbal question?                      25

GENTLEMAN
Faith, once or twice she heaved the name of "father"      26
Pantingly forth, as if it pressed her heart;
Cried, "Sisters, sisters! Shame of ladies, sisters!
Kent! Father! Sisters! What, i'th' storm, i'th' night?
Let pity not be believed!" There she shook                30
The holy water from her heavenly eyes,
And, clamor-moistened, then away she started              32
To deal with grief alone.

KENT                              It is the stars,
The stars above us, govern our conditions,                34
Else one self mate and make could not beget               35
Such different issues. You spoke not with her since?      36

GENTLEMAN    No.

KENT
Was this before the King returned?

GENTLEMAN                                  No, since.      38

KENT
Well, sir, the poor distressèd Lear's i'th' town,
Who sometime in his better tune remembers                 40
What we are come about, and by no means
Will yield to see his daughter.

GENTLEMAN                            Why, good sir?        42

KENT
A sovereign shame so elbows him—his own
    unkindness                                            43
That stripped her from his benediction, turned her        44
To foreign casualties, gave her dear rights               45
To his dog-hearted daughters—these things sting
His mind so venomously that burning shame
Detains him from Cordelia.                                48

GENTLEMAN    Alack, poor gentleman!

KENT
Of Albany's and Cornwall's powers you heard not?          50

GENTLEMAN    'Tis so. They are afoot.                     51

KENT
Well, sir, I'll bring you to our master Lear
And leave you to attend him. Some dear cause              53
Will in concealment wrap me up awhile.
When I am known aright, you shall not grieve              55
Lending me this acquaintance. I pray you, go             56
Along with me.                              *Exeunt.*

# 4.[4]

*Enter, with drum and colors, Cordelia,*
*Doctor, and soldiers.*

CORDELIA
Alack, 'tis he! Why, he was met even now
As mad as the vexed sea, singing aloud,
Crowned with rank fumiter and furrow weeds,               3
With hardocks, hemlock, nettles, cuckooflowers,           4
Darnel, and all the idle weeds that grow                  5
In our sustaining corn. A century send forth!             6
Search every acre in the high-grown field
And bring him to our eye.    [*Exit a soldier or soldiers.*]
                              What can man's wisdom        8
In the restoring his bereavèd sense,
He that helps him take all my outward worth.              10

DOCTOR    There is means, madam.
Our foster nurse of nature is repose,
The which he lacks. That to provoke in him                13
Are many simples operative, whose power                   14
Will close the eye of anguish.

CORDELIA                            All blest secrets,
All you unpublished virtues of the earth,                 16
Spring with my tears! Be aidant and remediate            17
In the good man's distress! Seek, seek for him,
Lest his ungoverned rage dissolve the life                19
That wants the means to lead it.

*Enter Messenger.*

MESSENGER                            News, madam.          20
The British powers are marching hitherward.               21

**14 who** which    **17 Who . . . goodliest** which of the two could portray her best.    **19 like a better way** better than that, though similar    **20–1 seemed . . . eyes** seemed oblivious of her tears    **23 a rarity** i.e., a precious thing, like a jewel    **24 If . . . it** i.e., if all persons were as attractive in sorrow as she.    **25 verbal** i.e., as distinguished from her tears and looks    **26 heaved** breathed out with difficulty    **30 Let . . . believed!** i.e., Let no show of pity be trusted (since they are proved to be so false)!    **32 clamor-moistened** i.e., her outcry of grief assuaged by tears.    **started** i.e., went    **34 conditions** characters    **35 Else . . . make** otherwise, one couple (husband and wife)    **36 issues** offspring.    **38 before . . . returned** before the King of France returned to his kingdom.    **40 better tune** more composed state of mind    **42 yield** consent    **43 sovereign** overruling.    **elbows him** i.e., prods his memory, jostles him, thrusts him back    **44 turned her** turned her out    **45 foreign casualties** chances of fortune abroad    **48 Detains him from** holds him back from seeing

**50 powers** troops, armies    **51 afoot** on the march.    **53 dear cause** important purpose    **55–6 grieve . . . acquaintance** regret having made my acquaintance.
**4.4. Location: The French camp.**
**0.2** *Doctor* (The Folio reads "Gentleman" here and at line 11.)
**3 fumiter** fumitory, a weed or herb.    **furrow weeds** weeds growing in plowed furrows    **4 hardocks** probably burdock, a coarse weedy plant.    **cuckooflowers** flowers of late spring, when the cuckoo is heard    **5 Darnel** weed of the grass kind.    **idle** worthless    **6 sustaining corn** sustenance-giving grain.    **A century** (Literally, a troop of one hundred men.)    **8 What . . . wisdom** i.e., What medical knowledge can accomplish    **10 outward** material    **13 That to provoke** To induce that    **14 Are . . . operative** many herbal remedies are efficacious; or, there are many effective remedies. (*Simples* are prepared from a single herb.)    **16 unpublished virtues** little-known benign herbs    **17 Spring** grow.    **aidant and remediate** helpful and remedial    **19 rage** frenzy    **20 That . . . lead it** that lacks the means to live sanely.    **21 powers** armies

CORDELIA
'Tis known before. Our preparation stands
In expectation of them. O dear father,
It is thy business that I go about;
Therefore great France
My mourning and importuned tears hath pitied.              26
No blown ambition doth our arms incite,                   27
But love, dear love, and our aged father's right.
Soon may I hear and see him!                    *Exeunt.*

❦

## 4.[5]

*Enter Regan and steward [Oswald].*

REGAN    But are my brother's powers set forth?            1
OSWALD    Ay, madam.
REGAN    Himself in person there?
OSWALD    Madam, with much ado.                            4
    Your sister is the better soldier.
REGAN
    Lord Edmund spake not with your lord at home?        6
OSWALD    No, madam.
REGAN
    What might import my sister's letter to him?         8
OSWALD    I know not, lady.
REGAN
    Faith, he is posted hence on serious matter.         10
    It was great ignorance, Gloucester's eyes being out,  11
    To let him live. Where he arrives he moves
    All hearts against us. Edmund, I think, is gone,
    In pity of his misery, to dispatch                   14
    His nighted life; moreover to descry                 15
    The strength o'th'enemy.
OSWALD
    I must needs after him, madam, with my letter.
REGAN
    Our troops set forth tomorrow. Stay with us;
    The ways are dangerous.
OSWALD                        I may not, madam.
    My lady charged my duty in this business.            20
REGAN
    Why should she write to Edmund? Might not you
    Transport her purposes by word? Belike               22
    Something—I know not what. I'll love thee much;
    Let me unseal the letter.
OSWALD                        Madam, I had rather—
REGAN
    I know your lady does not love her husband,
    I am sure of that; and at her late being here        26
    She gave strange oeillades and most speaking looks    27
    To noble Edmund. I know you are of her bosom.        28
OSWALD    I, madam?

REGAN
    I speak in understanding; y'are, I know't.           30
    Therefore I do advise you, take this note:           31
    My lord is dead; Edmund and I have talked,           32
    And more convenient is he for my hand                33
    Than for your lady's. You may gather more.           34
    If you do find him, pray you, give him this;         35
    And when your mistress hears thus much from you,     36
    I pray, desire her call her wisdom to her.           37
    So, fare you well.
    If you do chance to hear of that blind traitor,
    Preferment falls on him that cuts him off.           40
OSWALD
    Would I could meet him, madam! I should show
    What party I do follow.
REGAN                        Fare thee well.
                                *Exeunt [separately].*

❦

## 4.[6]

*Enter Gloucester, and Edgar [in peasant's clothes,
leading his father].*

GLOUCESTER
    When shall I come to th' top of that same hill?      1
EDGAR
    You do climb up it now. Look how we labor.
GLOUCESTER
    Methinks the ground is even.
EDGAR                        Horrible steep.
    Hark, do you hear the sea?
GLOUCESTER                    No, truly.
EDGAR
    Why, then, your other senses grow imperfect
    By your eyes' anguish.
GLOUCESTER                So may it be, indeed.
    Methinks thy voice is altered, and thou speak'st
    In better phrase and matter than thou didst.
EDGAR
    You're much deceived. In nothing am I changed
    But in my garments.
GLOUCESTER            Methinks you're better spoken.
EDGAR
    Come on, sir, here's the place. Stand still. How fearful
    And dizzy 'tis to cast one's eyes so low!
    The crows and choughs that wing the midway air       13
    Show scarce so gross as beetles. Halfway down        14
    Hangs one that gathers samphire—dreadful trade!      15
    Methinks he seems no bigger than his head.
    The fishermen that walk upon the beach

26 **importuned** importunate    27 **blown** swollen
**4.5. Location: Gloucester's house.**
1 **my brother's powers** Albany's forces    4 **with much ado** after
much fuss and persuasion.    6 **your lord** Albany    8 **What . . . to him?**
What might Goneril have communicated to him in her letter?
10 **is posted** has hurried    11 **ignorance** error, folly    14 **his** Gloucester's    15 **nighted** benighted, blinded.    **descry** spy out    20 **charged**
**my duty** laid great stress on my obedience    22 **Belike** It may be
26 **late** recently    27 **oeillades** amorous glances    28 **of her bosom** in
her confidence.

30 **in understanding** with certain knowledge.    **y'are** you are in Regan's
confidence    31 **take this note** take note of this    32 **have talked** have
come to an understanding    33 **convenient** fitting    34 **gather more** infer
what I am trying to suggest.    35 **this** i.e., this information, or a love
token, or possibly a letter (though only one letter, Goneril's, is found on
his dead body at 4.6.262)    36 **thus much** what I have told you    37 **call . . .**
**to her** to recall herself to her senses.    40 **Preferment** advancement
**4.6. Location: Open place near Dover.**
1 **that same hill** i.e., the cliff we talked about (4.1.72–4).    13 **choughs**
jackdaws.    **midway** halfway down    14 **Show** appear.    **gross**
large    15 **samphire** (A herb used in pickling.)

Appear like mice, and yond tall anchoring bark   18
Diminished to her cock; her cock, a buoy   19
Almost too small for sight. The murmuring surge,
That on th'unnumbered idle pebble chafes,   21
Cannot be heard so high. I'll look no more,
Lest my brain turn, and the deficient sight   23
Topple down headlong.

GLOUCESTER                   Set me where you stand.   24

EDGAR
Give me your hand. You are now within a foot
Of th'extreme verge. For all beneath the moon   26
Would I not leap upright.

GLOUCESTER                 Let go my hand.   27
Here, friend, 's another purse; in it a jewel
Well worth a poor man's taking.     [*He gives a purse.*]
   Fairies and gods   29
Prosper it with thee! Go thou further off.   30
Bid me farewell, and let me hear thee going.

EDGAR [*moving away*]
Now fare you well, good sir.

GLOUCESTER               With all my heart.

EDGAR [*aside*]
Why I do trifle thus with his despair
Is done to cure it.

GLOUCESTER [*kneeling*]   O you mighty gods!
This world I do renounce, and in your sights
Shake patiently my great affliction off.
If I could bear it longer and not fall
To quarrel with your great opposeless wills,   38
My snuff and loathèd part of nature should   39
Burn itself out. If Edgar live, oh, bless him!   40
Now, fellow, fare thee well.     [*He falls forward.*]

EDGAR               Gone, sir. Farewell.—
And yet I know not how conceit may rob   42
The treasury of life, when life itself
Yields to the theft. Had he been where he thought,   44
By this had thought been past. Alive or dead?—   45
Ho, you, sir! Friend! Hear you, sir! Speak!—
Thus might he pass indeed; yet he revives.—   47
What are you, sir?

GLOUCESTER         Away, and let me die.   48

EDGAR
Hadst thou been aught but gossamer, feathers, air,   49
So many fathom down precipitating,   50
Thou'dst shivered like an egg; but thou dost breathe,   51
Hast heavy substance, bleed'st not, speak'st, art
   sound.   52

Ten masts at each make not the altitude   53
Which thou hast perpendicularly fell.   54
Thy life's a miracle. Speak yet again.

GLOUCESTER   But have I fall'n or no?

EDGAR
From the dread summit of this chalky bourn.   57
Look up a-height; the shrill-gorged lark so far   58
Cannot be seen or heard. Do but look up.

GLOUCESTER   Alack, I have no eyes.
Is wretchedness deprived that benefit   61
To end itself by death? 'Twas yet some comfort
When misery could beguile the tyrant's rage   63
And frustrate his proud will.

EDGAR               Give me your arm.
               [*He lifts him up.*]
Up—so. How is't? Feel you your legs? You stand.

GLOUCESTER
Too well, too well.

EDGAR         This is above all strangeness.
Upon the crown o'th' cliff what thing was that
Which parted from you?

GLOUCESTER        A poor unfortunate beggar.

EDGAR
As I stood here below, methought his eyes
Were two full moons; he had a thousand noses,
Horns whelked and waved like the enridgèd sea.   71
It was some fiend. Therefore, thou happy father,   72
Think that the clearest gods, who make them honors   73
Of men's impossibilities, have preserved thee.   74

GLOUCESTER
I do remember now. Henceforth I'll bear
Affliction till it do cry out itself   76
"Enough, enough," and die. That thing you speak of,   77
I took it for a man; often 'twould say
"The fiend, the fiend." He led me to that place.

EDGAR
Bear free and patient thoughts.

   *Enter Lear* [*mad, fantastically dressed with wild
   flowers*].

                           But who comes here?   80
The safer sense will ne'er accommodate   81
His master thus.   82

LEAR   No, they cannot touch me for coining. I am the   83
King himself.   84

EDGAR   Oh, thou side-piercing sight!   85

---

18 **bark** small sailing vessel   19 **Diminished . . . cock** apparently reduced to the size of her cockboat, small ship's boat   21 **th'unnumbered idle pebble** innumerable, randomly shifting, pebbles   23–4 **Lest . . . headlong** lest I become dizzy, and my failing sight topple me headlong. 26 **For . . . moon** i.e., For the whole world   27 **upright** i.e., up and down, much less forward.   29–30 **Fairies . . . thee**! May the fairies and gods cause this to multiply in your possession!   38 **To quarrel with** into rebellion against.   **opposeless** irresistible   39–40 **My . . . out** i.e., rather than commit suicide, I would wait until the useless residue of my loathed life, like the smoking wick of a candle, should burn itself out.   42 **conceit** imagination   44 **Yields** consents   45 **By this** by this time   47 **pass** die 48 **What** Who. (Edgar now speaks in a new voice, differing from that of "poor Tom" and also from the "altered" voice he used at the start of this scene; see lines 7–10.)   49 **aught** anything   50 **precipitating** plunging 51 **shivered** shattered   52 **heavy substance** the substance of the flesh

53 **at each** end to end   54 **fell** fallen.   57 **bourn** limit, boundary (i.e., the edge of the sea).   58 **a-height** on high.   **shrill-gorged** shrill-throated   61 **deprived** deprived of   63 **beguile** outwit   71 **whelked** twisted, convoluted.   **enridgèd** furrowed (by the wind)   72 **happy father** lucky old man   73 **clearest** purest, most righteous   73–4 **who . . . impossibilities** who win our awe and reverence by doing things impossible to men   76–7 **till . . . die** i.e., until affliction itself has had enough, or until I die.   80 **free** i.e., free from despair   81–2 **The safer . . . thus** i.e., A person in his right senses would never dress himself in such a fashion. (*His master* is the owner of the *safer sense* or sane mind. *His* means "its.")   83–4 **they . . . himself** they cannot prosecute me for minting coins. As king, I enjoy the exclusive royal prerogative for doing so. (Lear madly goes on to discuss his need for money to pay his imaginary soldiers.)   85 **side-piercing** heartrending. (With a suggestion of Christ's suffering on the cross.)

LEAR　Nature's above art in that respect. There's your 86
press money. That fellow handles his bow like a crow- 87
keeper. Draw me a clothier's yard. Look, look, a 88
mouse! Peace, peace; this piece of toasted cheese will
do't. There's my gauntlet; I'll prove it on a giant. Bring 90
up the brown bills. Oh, well flown, bird! I'th' clout, 91
i'th' clout—hewgh! Give the word. 92

EDGAR　Sweet marjoram. 93

LEAR　Pass.

GLOUCESTER　I know that voice.

LEAR　Ha! Goneril with a white beard? They flattered
me like a dog and told me I had white hairs in my 97
beard ere the black ones were there. To say ay and 98
no to everything that I said ay and no to was 99
no good divinity. When the rain came to wet me 100
once and the wind to make me chatter, when the 101
thunder would not peace at my bidding, there I found 102
'em, there I smelt 'em out. Go to, they are not men o' 103
their words. They told me I was everything. 'Tis a
lie. I am not ague-proof. 105

GLOUCESTER
The trick of that voice I do well remember. 106
Is't not the King?

LEAR　　　　　　　　Ay, every inch a king.
When I do stare, see how the subject quakes.
I pardon that man's life. What was thy cause? 109
Adultery?
Thou shalt not die. Die for adultery? No.
The wren goes to't, and the small gilded fly
Does lecher in my sight.
Let copulation thrive; for Gloucester's bastard son
Was kinder to his father than my daughters
Got 'tween the lawful sheets.
To't, luxury, pell-mell, for I lack soldiers. 117
Behold yond simpering dame,
Whose face between her forks presages snow, 119
That minces virtue and does shake the head 120
To hear of pleasure's name; 121
The fitchew nor the soilèd horse goes to't 122

With a more riotous appetite.
Down from the waist they are Centaurs, 124
Though women all above.
But to the girdle do the gods inherit; 126
Beneath is all the fiends'.
There's hell, there's darkness, there is the sulfurous pit, 128
burning, scalding, stench, consumption. Fie, fie, fie!
Pah, pah! Give me an ounce of civet, good apothecary, 130
to sweeten my imagination. There's money for thee.

GLOUCESTER　Oh, let me kiss that hand!

LEAR　Let me wipe it first; it smells of mortality.

GLOUCESTER
Oh, ruined piece of nature! This great world 134
Shall so wear out to naught. Dost thou know me? 135

LEAR　I remember thine eyes well enough. Dost thou
squinny at me? No, do thy worst, blind Cupid; I'll not 137
love. Read thou this challenge. Mark but the penning 138
of it.

GLOUCESTER
Were all thy letters suns, I could not see.

EDGAR　[aside]
I would not take this from report. It is, 141
And my heart breaks at it.

LEAR　Read.

GLOUCESTER　What, with the case of eyes? 144

LEAR　Oho, are you there with me? No eyes in your 145
head, nor no money in your purse? Your eyes are in a
heavy case, your purse in a light, yet you see how this 147
world goes.

GLOUCESTER　I see it feelingly. 149

LEAR　What, art mad? A man may see how this world
goes with no eyes. Look with thine ears. See how
yond justice rails upon yond simple thief. Hark in 152
thine ear: change places and, handy-dandy, which is 153
the justice, which is the thief? Thou hast seen a
farmer's dog bark at a beggar?

GLOUCESTER　Ay, sir.

LEAR　And the creature run from the cur? There thou 157
mightst behold the great image of authority: a dog's 158
obeyed in office. 159
Thou rascal beadle, hold thy bloody hand! 160
Why dost thou lash that whore? Strip thine own back;
Thou hotly lusts to use her in that kind 162
For which thou whipp'st her. The usurer hangs the
cozener. 163

---

**86 Nature's . . . respect** Real life can offer more heart-piercing examples than art. **87 press money** enlistment bonus. **87–8 crowkeeper** laborer hired to scare away the crows. **88 Draw . . . yard** i.e., Draw your bow to the full length of the arrow, a cloth-yard long. **90 do't** i.e., capture the mouse, an imagined enemy. **gauntlet** armored glove thrown down as a challenge. **prove it on** maintain it against **91 brown bills** soldiers carrying pikes (painted brown), or the pikes themselves. **well flown, bird** (Lear uses the language of hawking to describe the flight of an arrow.) **clout** target, bull's-eye **92 hewgh** (The arrow's noise.) **word** password. **93 Sweet marjoram** (A herb used to cure madness.) **97 like a dog** fawningly **97–8 told . . . there** i.e., told me I had the white-haired wisdom of old age before I had even attained the manliness of a beard. **98–100 To . . . divinity** i.e., To agree flatteringly with everything I said was not good theology, since the Bible teaches us to "let your yea be yea and your nay, nay" (James 5:12; see also Matthew 5:37 and 2 Cor. 1:18). **100–3 When . . . out** i.e., Suffering wet, cold, and storm have taught me about the frailty of the human condition. **103 Go to** (An expression of impatience.) **105 ague-proof** immune against illness (literally, fever). **106 trick** peculiar characteristic **109 cause** offense. **117 luxury** lechery **119 Whose . . . snow** whose frosty countenance seems to suggest frigidity between her legs **120 minces** affects, mimics **121 of pleasure's name** the very name of pleasure **122 The fitchew . . . to't** neither the polecat nor the well-pastured horse indulges in sexual pleasure

**124 Centaurs** fabulous creatures with the head, trunk, and arms of a man joined to the body and legs of a horse **126 But** Only. **girdle** waist. **inherit** have possession **128 hell** (Often equated in Renaissance writing with the female sexual anatomy.) **130 civet** musk perfume **134 piece** (1) fragment (2) masterpiece **134–5 This . . . naught** Even so will the whole universe come to an apocalyptic end. **137 squinny** squint **138 challenge** (Lear madly imagines writing a challenge to a rival over a woman.) **141 take** believe, credit. **It is** It is taking place, incredibly enough **144 case** mere sockets **145 are . . . me?** is that your meaning, the point you are making? **147 heavy case** sad plight. (With pun on *case* in line 144.) **149 feelingly** (1) by touch (2) keenly, painfully. **152 simple** of humble station **153 handy-dandy** take your choice of hands (as in a well-known child's game) **157 creature** poor fellow **158–9 a dog's . . . office** i.e., even currish power commands submission. **160 beadle** parish officer, responsible for giving whippings **162 kind** way **163 The usurer . . . cozener** The moneylender (who can buy out justice) hangs the con man.

Through tattered clothes small vices do appear; 164
Robes and furred gowns hide all. Plate sin with gold, 165
And the strong lance of justice hurtless breaks; 166
Arm it in rags, a pygmy's straw does pierce it.
None does offend, none, I say, none. I'll able 'em. 168
Take that of me, my friend, who have the power 169
To seal th'accuser's lips. Get thee glass eyes, 170
And like a scurvy politician seem 171
To see the things thou dost not. Now, now, now, now! 172
Pull off my boots. Harder, harder! So.

EDGAR [*aside*]
Oh, matter and impertinency mixed, 174
Reason in madness!

LEAR
If thou wilt weep my fortunes, take my eyes.
I know thee well enough; thy name is Gloucester.
Thou must be patient. We came crying hither.
Thou know'st the first time that we smell the air
We wawl and cry. I will preach to thee. Mark.

GLOUCESTER   Alack, alack the day!

LEAR
When we are born, we cry that we are come
To this great stage of fools.—This' a good block. 183
It were a delicate stratagem to shoe 184
A troop of horse with felt. I'll put 't in proof, 185
And when I have stol'n upon these son-in-laws,
Then, kill, kill, kill, kill, kill, kill!

*Enter a Gentleman [with attendants].*

GENTLEMAN
Oh, here he is. Lay hand upon him.—Sir,
Your most dear daughter—

LEAR
No rescue? What, a prisoner? I am even
The natural fool of fortune. Use me well; 191
You shall have ransom. Let me have surgeons;
I am cut to th' brains.

GENTLEMAN                You shall have anything. 193

LEAR   No seconds? All myself? 194
Why, this would make a man a man of salt 195
To use his eyes for garden waterpots,
Ay, and laying autumn's dust.

GENTLEMAN                Good sir— 197

LEAR   I will die bravely, like a smug bridegroom. What? 198

I will be jovial. Come, come, I am a king, 199
Masters, know you that? 200

GENTLEMAN
You are a royal one, and we obey you.

LEAR   Then there's life in't. Nay, an you get it, you 202
shall get it by running. Sa, sa, sa, sa. 203

*Exit [running, followed by attendants].*

GENTLEMAN
A sight most pitiful in the meanest wretch, 204
Past speaking of in a king! Thou hast one daughter
Who redeems nature from the general curse 206
Which twain have brought her to. 207

EDGAR   Hail, gentle sir. 208

GENTLEMAN   Sir, speed you. What's your will? 209

EDGAR
Do you hear aught, sir, of a battle toward? 210

GENTLEMAN
Most sure and vulgar. Everyone hears that 211
Which can distinguish sound.

EDGAR                But, by your favor, 212
How near's the other army?

GENTLEMAN
Near and on speedy foot. The main descry 214
Stands on the hourly thought. 215

EDGAR   I thank you, sir; that's all.

GENTLEMAN
Though that the Queen on special cause is here, 217
Her army is moved on.

EDGAR                I thank you, sir.

*Exit [Gentleman].*

GLOUCESTER
You ever-gentle gods, take my breath from me;
Let not my worser spirit tempt me again 220
To die before you please!

EDGAR   Well pray you, father. 222

GLOUCESTER   Now, good sir, what are you? 223

EDGAR
A most poor man, made tame to fortune's blows, 224
Who, by the art of known and feeling sorrows, 225
Am pregnant to good pity. Give me your hand. 226
I'll lead you to some biding.   [*He offers his arm.*]

GLOUCESTER                Hearty thanks. 227

**164–5 Through . . . all** i.e., Beggars' small vices are apparent for all to see; rich folk, in expensive clothes, succeed in hiding a great deal.   **165 Plate** Arm in plate armor   **166 hurtless breaks** splinters harmlessly   **168–72 None . . . dost not** Lear's mad fantasy is one of imagining what it would be like to have the corrupt power to dismiss charges against persons he wishes to shield from the law: Absolutely no one is guilty. I'll empower and give warrant to such offenders. Learn this from me, my friend, and take the protection I offer, I who have power to silence your accusers. Fit yourself out with artificial eyes, so that, like a hypocritical politician, you can pretend to see the true state of affairs when in fact you are insensitively blind to the way things are.   **174 matter and impertinency** sense and nonsense   **183 This'** This is.   **block** mold for a felt hat. (Lear may refer to the weeds strewn in his hair, which he removes as though doffing a hat before preaching a sermon.)   **184 delicate** subtle   **185 felt** i.e., padding to deaden the sound of the horses' footfall.   **in proof** to the test   **191 natural fool** born plaything.   **Use** Treat   **193 cut** wounded   **194 seconds** supporters.   **195 of salt** of salt tears   **197 laying** sprinkling and settling   **198 bravely** (1) courageously (2) splendidly attired.   **smug** trimly dressed. (*Bridegroom* continues the punning sexual suggestion of *die bravely,* "have sex successfully.")

**199 jovial** (1) Jovelike, majestic (2) jolly.   **200 Masters** good sirs   **202 life** i.e., hope still.   **an** if   **203 Sa . . . sa** (A hunting cry.)   **204 meanest** lowliest   **206 general curse** fallen condition of the human race   **207 twain** (1) Goneril and Regan (2) Adam and Eve   **208 gentle** noble   **209 speed you** Godspeed, may God prosper you.   **210 toward** imminent.   **211 vulgar** in everyone's mouth, generally known.   **212 Which . . . sound** i.e., who can understand speech.   **by your favor** if you please, if I may ask   **214–15 The main . . . thought** The full view of the main body is expected any hour now.   **217 Though that** Although.   **on special cause** for a special reason, i.e., to minister to Lear   **220 worser spirit** bad angel, or ill thoughts   **222 father** (A term of respect to older men, as also in lines 72, 259, and 290, though with ironic double meaning throughout the scene.)   **223 what** who. (Again, Edgar alters his voice to personate a new stranger assisting Gloucester. See line 48, above, and note.)   **224 tame** submissive   **225 known and feeling** personally experienced and heartfelt   **226 pregnant** prone   **227 biding** abode, resting place.

The bounty and the benison of heaven 228
To boot, and boot!

*Enter steward [Oswald].*

OSWALD     A proclaimed prize! Most happy! 229
*[He draws his sword.]*
That eyeless head of thine was first framed flesh 230
To raise my fortunes. Thou old unhappy traitor,
Briefly thyself remember. The sword is out 232
That must destroy thee.
GLOUCESTER     Now let thy friendly hand 233
Put strength enough to't.     *[Edgar intervenes.]*
OSWALD     Wherefore, bold peasant,
Dar'st thou support a published traitor? Hence, 235
Lest that th'infection of his fortune take 236
Like hold on thee. Let go his arm. 237
EDGAR   'Chill not let go, zir, without vurther 'cagion. 238
OSWALD   Let go, slave, or thou diest!
EDGAR   Good gentleman, go your gait, and let poor volk 240
pass. An 'chud ha' bin zwaggered out of my life, 241
'twould not ha' bin zo long as 'tis by a vortnight. Nay, 242
come not near th' old man; keep out, 'che vor ye, or 243
Ise try whether your costard or my ballow be the 244
harder. 'Chill be plain with you.
OSWALD   Out, dunghill!
EDGAR   'Chill pick your teeth, zir. Come, no matter vor
your foins.   *[They fight. Edgar fells him with his cudgel.]* 248
OSWALD
Slave, thou hast slain me. Villain, take my purse. 249
If ever thou wilt thrive, bury my body 250
And give the letters which thou find'st about me 251
To Edmund, Earl of Gloucester. Seek him out
Upon the English party. Oh, untimely death! 253
Death!     *[He dies.]*
EDGAR
I know thee well: a serviceable villain, 255
As duteous to the vices of thy mistress
As badness would desire.
GLOUCESTER   What, is he dead?
EDGAR   Sit you down, father. Rest you. *[Gloucester sits.]*
Let's see these pockets; the letters that he speaks of
May be my friends. He's dead; I am only sorry
He had no other deathsman. Let us see. 262
*[He finds a letter and opens it.]*
Leave, gentle wax, and, manners, blame us not. 263

To know our enemies' minds we rip their hearts;
Their papers is more lawful.     *(Reads the letter.)*
"Let our reciprocal vows be remembered. You have
many opportunities to cut him off; if your will want 267
not, time and place will be fruitfully offered. There is 268
nothing done if he return the conqueror. Then am I 269
the prisoner, and his bed my jail, from the loathed
warmth whereof deliver me and supply the place for 271
your labor. 272
Your—wife, so I would say—affectionate servant,
and for you her own for venture, Goneril." 274
Oh, indistinguished space of woman's will! 275
A plot upon her virtuous husband's life,
And the exchange my brother! Here in the sands
Thee I'll rake up, the post unsanctified 278
Of murderous lechers; and in the mature time 279
With this ungracious paper strike the sight 280
Of the death-practiced Duke. For him 'tis well 281
That of thy death and business I can tell.
*[Exit with the body.]*
GLOUCESTER
The King is mad. How stiff is my vile sense, 283
That I stand up and have ingenious feeling 284
Of my huge sorrows! Better I were distract; 285
So should my thoughts be severed from my griefs,
And woes by wrong imaginations lose 287
The knowledge of themselves.     *Drum afar off.*

*[Enter Edgar.]*
EDGAR     Give me your hand.
Far off, methinks, I hear the beaten drum.
Come, father, I'll bestow you with a friend. 290
*Exeunt, [Edgar leading his father].*

❖

## 4.7

*Enter Cordelia, Kent [dressed still in his disguise
costume, Doctor], and Gentleman.*

CORDELIA
O thou good Kent, how shall I live and work
To match thy goodness? My life will be too short,
And every measure fail me. 3

228–9 **The bounty . . . and boot!** In addition to my thanks, I wish you the bounty and blessings of heaven.   229 **proclaimed prize** one with a price on his head.   **happy** fortunate.   230 **framed flesh** born   232 **thyself remember** i.e., say your prayers.   233 **friendly** i.e., welcome, since I desire death   235 **published** proclaimed   236 **Lest that** lest   237 **Like** similar   238 **'Chill** I will. (Literally, a contraction of *Ich will*. Edgar adopts Somerset dialect, a stage convention regularly used for peasants.)   **vurther 'cagion** further occasion.   240 **go your gait** go your own way   241 **An 'chud** If I could.   **zwaggered** swaggered, bullied   242 **'twould . . . vortnight** it (my life) wouldn't have lasted as long as it has.   243 **'che vor ye** I warrant you   244 **Ise** I shall.   **costard** head. (Literally, an apple.)   **ballow** cudgel   248 **foins** thrusts.   249 **Villain** Serf   250 **If . . . thrive** If you hope to live and prosper   251 **letters** letter. (See 4.5.35 and note.)   **about me** upon my person   253 **Upon** on, within.   **party** side.   255 **serviceable** officious   262 **deathsman** executioner.   263 **Leave** By your leave.   **wax** wax seal on the letter

267 **him** Albany   267–8 **want not** is not lacking   268 **fruitfully** plentifully and with results   268–9 **There is nothing done** i.e., We will have accomplished nothing   271 **supply** fill   271–2 **for your labor** (1) as recompense for your efforts (2) as a place for your amorous labors.   274 **and for . . . venture** and one ready to venture her own fortunes for your sake   275 **indistinguished . . . will** limitless and incalculable expanse of woman's appetite.   278 **rake up** cover up. **post unsanctified** unholy messenger   279 **in . . . time** when the time is ripe   280 **ungracious** wicked.   **strike** blast   281 **Of . . . well** of Albany, whose death is plotted. It's a good thing for him   283 **How . . . sense** How obstinate is my deplorable sanity and power of sensation   284 **ingenious** conscious. (Gloucester laments that he remains sane and hence fully conscious of his troubles, unlike Lear.)   285 **distract** distracted, crazy   287 **wrong imaginations** delusions   290 **bestow** lodge. (At the scene's end, Edgar leads off Gloucester; presumably, at line 282 or else here, he must also dispose of Oswald's body in the trapdoor or by lugging it offstage.)
**4.7. Location: The French camp.**
**0.2** *Doctor* ("*Gentleman*" in F.)   **3 every . . . me** every attempt (to match your goodness) will fall short.

KENT
To be acknowledged, madam, is o'erpaid. 4
All my reports go with the modest truth, 5
Nor more nor clipped, but so.

CORDELIA                    Be better suited. 6
These weeds are memories of those worser hours; 7
I prithee, put them off.

KENT                Pardon, dear madam;
Yet to be known shortens my made intent. 9
My boon I make it that you know me not 10
Till time and I think meet. 11

CORDELIA
Then be't so, my good lord. [*To the Doctor*] How
   does the King? 12

DOCTOR    Madam, sleeps still.

CORDELIA    O you kind gods,
Cure this great breach in his abusèd nature!
Th'untuned and jarring senses, oh, wind up 16
Of this child-changèd father! 17

DOCTOR    So please Your Majesty
That we may wake the King? He hath slept long.

CORDELIA
Be governed by your knowledge, and proceed
I'th' sway of your own will.—Is he arrayed? 21

*Enter Lear in a chair carried by servants.*

DOCTOR
Ay, madam. In the heaviness of sleep
We put fresh garments on him.
Be by, good madam, when we do awake him.
I doubt not of his temperance.

CORDELIA              Very well.    [*Music.*] 25

DOCTOR
Please you, draw near.—Louder the music there!

CORDELIA [*kissing him*]
O my dear father! Restoration hang
Thy medicine on my lips, and let this kiss
Repair those violent harms that my two sisters
Have in thy reverence made!

KENT            Kind and dear princess! 30

CORDELIA
Had you not been their father, these white flakes 31
Had challenged pity of them. Was this a face 32
To be opposed against the warring winds?
To stand against the deep dread-bolted thunder 34
In the most terrible and nimble stroke

Of quick cross lightning? To watch—poor perdu!— 36
With this thin helm? Mine enemy's dog, 37
Though he had bit me, should have stood that night
Against my fire; and wast thou fain, poor father, 39
To hovel thee with swine and rogues forlorn 40
In short and musty straw? Alack, alack! 41
'Tis wonder that thy life and wits at once
Had not concluded all.—He wakes! Speak to him. 43

DOCTOR    Madam, do you; 'tis fittest.

CORDELIA
How does my royal lord? How fares Your Majesty?

LEAR
You do me wrong to take me out o'th' grave.
Thou art a soul in bliss; but I am bound
Upon a wheel of fire, that mine own tears 48
Do scald like molten lead.

CORDELIA           Sir, do you know me?

LEAR
You are a spirit, I know. Where did you die?

CORDELIA    Still, still, far wide! 51

DOCTOR
He's scarce awake. Let him alone awhile.

LEAR
Where have I been? Where am I? Fair daylight?
I am mightily abused. I should ev'n die with pity 54
To see another thus. I know not what to say. 55
I will not swear these are my hands. Let's see;
I feel this pinprick. Would I were assured
Of my condition!

CORDELIA [*kneeling*]    Oh, look upon me, sir,
And hold your hands in benediction o'er me.
                  [*He attempts to kneel.*]
No, sir, you must not kneel.

LEAR               Pray, do not mock me.
I am a very foolish fond old man, 61
Fourscore and upward, not an hour more nor less;
And, to deal plainly,
I fear I am not in my perfect mind.
Methinks I should know you, and know this man,
Yet I am doubtful; for I am mainly ignorant 66
What place this is, and all the skill I have
Remembers not these garments, nor I know not
Where I did lodge last night. Do not laugh at me,
For, as I am a man, I think this lady
To be my child Cordelia.

CORDELIA [*weeping*]    And so I am, I am.

LEAR
Be your tears wet? Yes, faith. I pray, weep not.
If you have poison for me I will drink it.
I know you do not love me, for your sisters
Have, as I do remember, done me wrong.
You have some cause, they have not.

---

**4 o'erpaid** more than enough.  **5 All the reports go** i.e., May all my reports of service as Caius to Lear conform  **6 Nor . . . clipped** i.e., neither more nor less.  **so** exactly accurate.  **suited** dressed.  **7 weeds** garments. **memories** remembrances  **9 Yet . . . intent** to reveal my true identity now would alter my carefully made plan.  **10 My . . . it** The favor I seek is. **know** acknowledge  **11 meet** appropriate.  **12 s.d.** *Doctor* Named *"Doctor"* in Q here and *"Gentleman"* in F and throughout this scene to line 86. Compare 4.4, where the same difference between Q and F occurs. The role seems medical; at line 20, Cordelia appeals to the Doctor's professional knowledge.  **16 wind up** tune (as by tightening the tension on the string of an instrument)  **17 child-changèd** changed by childrens' cruelty, and changed into a child  **21 I'th' sway** under the direction.  **arrayed** clothed. **25 temperance** self-control, calm behavior.  **30 reverence** venerable condition  **31 Had you** Even if you had.  **flakes** locks of hair  **32 Had challenged** would have demanded  **34 deep** bass-voiced.  **dread-bolted** furnished with the dreadful thunderbolt

**36 cross** zigzag.  **watch** stay awake (like a sentry on duty).  **perdu** lost one; a sentinel placed in a position of peculiar danger  **37 helm** helmet, i.e., scanty hair.  **39 Against** before, in front of.  **fain** constrained  **40 rogues forlorn** abandoned vagabonds  **41 short** broken up and hence uncomfortable  **43 concluded all** come to an end altogether.  **48 wheel of fire** (A hellish torment for the eternally damned.) **that** so that  **51 wide** wide of the mark, wandering.  **54 abused** confused, deluded.  **55 thus** i.e., thus confused, bewildered.  **61 fond** in my dotage  **66 mainly** entirely

CORDELIA  No cause, no cause.

LEAR  Am I in France?

KENT  In your own kingdom, sir.

LEAR  Do not abuse me.   81

DOCTOR
Be comforted, good madam. The great rage,  82
You see, is killed in him, and yet it is danger
To make him even o'er the time he has lost.  84
Desire him to go in. Trouble him no more
Till further settling.  86

CORDELIA  Will't please Your Highness walk?  87

LEAR  You must bear with me.
Pray you now, forget and forgive.
I am old and foolish.
        *Exeunt [all but Kent and Gentleman].*

GENTLEMAN  Holds it true, sir, that the Duke of Corn-  91
wall was so slain?

KENT  Most certain, sir.

GENTLEMAN  Who is conductor of his people?  94

KENT  As 'tis said, the bastard son of Gloucester.

GENTLEMAN  They say Edgar, his banished son, is with
the Earl of Kent in Germany.

KENT  Report is changeable. 'Tis time to look about; the  98
powers of the kingdom approach apace.  99

GENTLEMAN  The arbitrament is like to be bloody. Fare  100
you well, sir.    *[Exit.]*

KENT
My point and period will be throughly wrought,  102
Or well or ill, as this day's battle's fought.  *Exit.*  103

❖

# 5.1

*Enter, with drum and colors, Edmund, Regan,
Gentlemen, and soldiers.*

EDMUND  *[to a Gentleman]*
Know of the Duke if his last purpose hold,  1
Or whether since he is advised by aught  2
To change the course. He's full of alteration  3
And self-reproving. Bring his constant pleasure.  4
        *[Exit Gentleman.]*

REGAN
Our sister's man is certainly miscarried.  5

EDMUND
'Tis to be doubted, madam.

REGAN        Now, sweet lord,  6
You know the goodness I intend upon you.  7
Tell me, but truly—but then speak the truth—
Do you not love my sister?

EDMUND        In honored love.  9

REGAN
But have you never found my brother's way
To the forfended place?  11

EDMUND  That thought abuses you.  12

REGAN
I am doubtful that you have been conjunct  13
And bosomed with her, as far as we call hers.  14

EDMUND  No, by mine honor, madam.

REGAN
I never shall endure her. Dear my lord,
Be not familiar with her.  17

EDMUND
Fear me not.—She and the Duke her husband!  18

*Enter, with drum and colors, Albany, Goneril,
[and] soldiers.*

GONERIL  *[aside]*
I had rather lose the battle than that sister
Should loosen him and me.  20

ALBANY  *[to Regan]*
Our very loving sister, well bemet.  21
*[To Edmund]* Sir, this I hear: the King is come to his
  daughter,
With others whom the rigor of our state  23
Forced to cry out. Where I could not be honest,  24
I never yet was valiant. For this business,  25
It touches us as France invades our land,  26
Not bolds the King, with others whom, I fear,  27
Most just and heavy causes make oppose.  28

EDMUND  Sir, you speak nobly.

REGAN  Why is this reasoned?  30

GONERIL
Combine together 'gainst the enemy;
For these domestic and particular broils  32
Are not the question here.

ALBANY        Let's then determine
With th'ancient of war on our proceeding.  34

EDMUND
I shall attend you presently at your tent.  35

REGAN  Sister, you'll go with us?  36

GONERIL  No.

---

81 **abuse** deceive. (Or perhaps Lear feels hurt by the reminder of his having divided the kingdom.)  82 **rage** frenzy  84 **even o'er** fill in, go over in his mind  86 **settling** composing of his mind.  87 **walk** withdraw.  91 **Holds it true** Is it still held to be true  94 **conductor** commander, general  98 **Report** Rumor.  **look about** take stock of the situation, prepare defenses  99 **powers of the kingdom** British armies (marching against the French invaders)  100 **arbitrament** decision by arms, decisive encounter  102 **My . . . wrought** i.e., The conclusion of my destiny (literally, the full stop at the end of my life's sentence) will be thoroughly shaped  103 **Or** either.  **as** according as
**5.1. Location: The British camp near Dover.**
1 **Know** Inquire.  **the Duke** Albany.  **last purpose hold** most recent intention (to fight) remains firm  2 **since** since then.  **advised by aught** persuaded by any consideration  3 **alteration** vacillation  4 **constant pleasure** settled decision.  5 **man** i.e., Oswald.  **miscarried** lost, perished.

6 **doubted** feared  7 **intend** intend to confer  9 **honored** honorable
11 **forfended** forbidden (by the commandment against adultery)
12 **abuses** degrades, wrongs  13–14 **I . . . hers** I fear that you have been sexually intimate with her to the fullest extent possible.  17 **familiar** intimate  18 **Fear me not** Don't worry about me on that score.  20 **loosen** separate  21 **bemet** met.  23 **rigor of our state** harshness of our rule  24 **cry out** rebel.  **Where** In a case where.  **honest** honorable  25 **For** As for  26 **touches us as** concerns us insofar as  27–8 **Not . . . oppose** not because the matter emboldens the King and others who, I fear, are driven into opposition by just and weighty grievances.  30 **Why . . . reasoned?** i.e., Why are we arguing about reasons for fighting, instead of fighting?  32 **particular broils** private quarrels  34 **th'ancient of war** the veteran officers  35 **presently** shortly  36 **with us** i.e., rather than stay with Edmund

REGAN
'Tis most convenient. Pray, go with us.                    38
GONERIL [*aside*]
Oho, I know the riddle.—I will go.                         39

[*As they are going out,*] enter Edgar [*disguised*].

EDGAR [*to Albany*]
If e'er Your Grace had speech with man so poor,
Hear me one word.
ALBANY [*to the others*]     I'll overtake you.
                              *Exeunt both the armies.*
                                        Speak.

EDGAR [*giving a letter*]
Before you fight the battle, ope this letter.              42
If you have victory, let the trumpet sound                 43
For him that brought it. Wretched though I seem,           44
I can produce a champion that will prove                   45
What is avouchèd there. If you miscarry,                   46
Your business of the world hath so an end,
And machination ceases. Fortune love you!                  48
ALBANY     Stay till I have read the letter.
EDGAR     I was forbid it.
When time shall serve, let but the herald cry
And I'll appear again.               *Exit* [*Edgar*].
ALBANY
Why, fare thee well. I will o'erlook thy paper.            53

*Enter Edmund.*

EDMUND
The enemy's in view. Draw up your powers.                  54
                    [*He offers Albany a paper.*]
Here is the guess of their true strength and forces        55
By diligent discovery; but your haste                      56
Is now urged on you.
ALBANY               We will greet the time.   *Exit.*  57
EDMUND
To both these sisters have I sworn my love,
Each jealous of the other as the stung                     59
Are of the adder. Which of them shall I take?
Both? One? Or neither? Neither can be enjoyed
If both remain alive. To take the widow
Exasperates, makes mad her sister Goneril,
And hardly shall I carry out my side,                      64
Her husband being alive. Now then, we'll use
His countenance for the battle, which being done,          66
Let her who would be rid of him devise
His speedy taking off. As for the mercy                    68
Which he intends to Lear and to Cordelia,
The battle done and they within our power,

Shall never see his pardon, for my state                   71
Stands on me to defend, not to debate.                     72
                                        *Exit.*

❖

## 5.2

*Alarum within. Enter, with drum and colors, Lear,
Cordelia, and soldiers, over the stage; and exeunt.*

*Enter Edgar and Gloucester.*

EDGAR
Here, father, take the shadow of this tree                 1
For your good host. Pray that the right may thrive.        2
If ever I return to you again,
I'll bring you comfort.
GLOUCESTER               Grace go with you, sir!            4
                              *Exit* [*Edgar*].

*Alarum and retreat within. Enter Edgar.*

EDGAR
Away, old man! Give me thy hand. Away!
King Lear hath lost, he and his daughter ta'en.
Give me thy hand. Come on.
GLOUCESTER
No further, sir. A man may rot even here.                  8
EDGAR
What, in ill thoughts again? Men must endure
Their going hence, even as their coming hither;
Ripeness is all. Come on.
GLOUCESTER               And that's true too.              11
                                        *Exeunt.*

❖

## 5.3

*Enter, in conquest, with drum and colors, Edmund;
Lear and Cordelia, as prisoners; soldiers, Captain.*

EDMUND
Some officers take them away. Good guard                   1
Until their greater pleasures first be known               2
That are to censure them.
CORDELIA [*to Lear*]          We are not the first         3
Who with best meaning have incurred the worst.             4
For thee, oppressèd King, I am cast down;                  5
Myself could else outfrown false Fortune's frown.
Shall we not see these daughters and these sisters?        7

---

**38 convenient** proper, fitting.    **39 I know the riddle** i.e., I understand the reason for Regan's enigmatic demand that I accompany her, which is that she wants to keep me away from Edmund.    **42 this letter** i.e., Goneril's letter to Edmund found on Oswald's body.    **43 sound** sound a summons **44 For him** for myself (Edgar)    **45 prove** i.e., in trial by combat **46 avouchèd** affirmed.    **miscarry** lose the battle and die    **48 machination** plotting    **53 o'erlook** peruse    **54 powers** troops.    **55 guess** estimate **56 discovery** reconnoitering    **57 We . . . time** We will be ready for whatever happens.    **59 jealous** suspicious.    **the stung** those who have been stung    **64 carry . . . side** carry out my end of the bargain in our *reciprocal vows* (4.6.266)    **66 countenance** backing, authority of his name **68 taking off** killing.

**71 Shall** they shall    **71–2 my state . . . debate** my position depends upon maintenance by forceful action, not by talk.
**5.2. Location: The battlefield.**
**0.1 Alarum** trumpet call to arms    **1 father** (1) reverend old man (2) biological father    **2 host** shelterer.    **4.2 retreat** trumpet signal for withdrawal    **8 even here** right here.    **11 Ripeness** (Humans shouldn't die before their time, just as fruit doesn't fall until it's ripe.)
**5.3. Location: The British camp.**
**1 Good guard** Guard them well    **2 their greater pleasures** the wishes of those in command    **3 censure** judge    **4 meaning** intentions **5 cast down** saddened    **7 Shall . . . sisters?** i.e., Aren't we even allowed to speak to Goneril and Regan before they order to prison their own father and sister?

LEAR
No, no, no, no! Come, let's away to prison.
We two alone will sing like birds i'th' cage.
When thou dost ask me blessing, I'll kneel down
And ask of thee forgiveness. So we'll live,
And pray, and sing, and tell old tales, and laugh
At gilded butterflies, and hear poor rogues       13
Talk of court news; and we'll talk with them too—
Who loses and who wins; who's in, who's out—
And take upon 's the mystery of things,           16
As if we were God's spies; and we'll wear out,    17
In a walled prison, packs and sects of great ones, 18
That ebb and flow by th' moon.
EDMUND                              Take them away.  19
LEAR
Upon such sacrifices, my Cordelia,
The gods themselves throw incense. Have I caught
    thee?                                          21
He that parts us shall bring a brand from heaven   22
And fire us hence like foxes. Wipe thine eyes;     23
The good years shall devour them, flesh and fell,  24
Ere they shall make us weep. We'll see 'em starved
    first.                                         25
Come.                     *Exit [with Cordelia, guarded].*
EDMUND   Come hither, Captain. Hark.
Take thou this note. [*He gives a paper.*] Go follow them
    to prison.
One step I have advanced thee; if thou dost        29
As this instructs thee, thou dost make thy way
To noble fortunes. Know thou this: that men
Are as the time is. To be tender-minded            32
Does not become a sword. Thy great employment      33
Will not bear question; either say thou'lt do't    34
Or thrive by other means.
CAPTAIN                         I'll do't, my lord.
EDMUND   About it, and write "happy" when th' hast done. 36
Mark, I say, instantly, and carry it so            37
As I have set it down.
CAPTAIN
I cannot draw a cart, nor eat dried oats;          39
If it be man's work, I'll do't.        *Exit Captain.*

*Flourish. Enter Albany, Goneril, Regan, [another
Captain, and] soldiers.*

ALBANY
Sir, you have showed today your valiant strain,
And fortune led you well. You have the captives
Who were the opposites of this day's strife;       43
I do require them of you, so to use them           44
As we shall find their merits and our safety
May equally determine.
EDMUND                          Sir, I thought it fit
To send the old and miserable King
To some retention and appointed guard,             49
Whose age had charms in it, whose title more,      50
To pluck the common bosom on his side              51
And turn our impressed lances in our eyes          52
Which do command them. With him I sent the Queen,  53
My reason all the same; and they are ready
Tomorrow, or at further space, t'appear            55
Where you shall hold your session. At this time    56
We sweat and bleed; the friend hath lost his friend,
And the best quarrels in the heat are cursed       58
By those that feel their sharpness.                59
The question of Cordelia and her father
Requires a fitter place.
ALBANY                      Sir, by your patience,   61
I hold you but a subject of this war,              62
Not as a brother.
REGAN                   That's as we list to grace him.  63
Methinks our pleasure might have been demanded     64
Ere you had spoke so far. He led our powers,       65
Bore the commission of my place and person,
The which immediacy may well stand up              67
And call itself your brother.
GONERIL                          Not so hot!
In his own grace he doth exalt himself             69
More than in your addition.
REGAN                          In my rights,         70
By me invested, he compeers the best.              71
GONERIL
That were the most if he should husband you.       72
REGAN
Jesters do oft prove prophets.
GONERIL                          Holla, holla!       73
That eye that told you so looked but asquint.      74
REGAN
Lady, I am not well, else I should answer
From a full-flowing stomach. [*To Edmund*] General, 76

---

**13 gilded butterflies** i.e., gaily dressed courtiers and other ephemeral types, or perhaps actual butterflies   **16 take upon 's** assume the burden of, or profess to understand   **17 God's spies** i.e., detached observers surveying the deeds of humanity from an eternal vantage point.   **wear out** outlast   **18–19 packs . . . moon** i.e., followers and cliques attached to persons of high station, whose fortunes change erratically and constantly.   **21 The gods . . . incense** (The gods make offerings to Cordelia instead of receiving them.)   **22–3 He . . . foxes** i.e., Nothing short of a firebrand from heaven will ever part us again. (Firebrands were used to smoke foxes from their lairs; compare also Samson's use of firebrands tied to the tails of foxes in order to punish the Philistines for denying him his wife, in Judges 15:4–5.)   **24–5 The good . . . weep** i.e., the years will be good to us and will utterly foil our enemies' attempts to make us sorrowful as long as we are together (?) (*Flesh and fell* means "meat and skin," i.e., utterly.)   **29 advanced** promoted   **32 Are . . . is** i.e., must adapt themselves to stern exigencies.   **33 become a sword** i.e., suit a warrior.   **34 bear question** admit of discussion   **36 write "happy"** call yourself fortunate.   **th'** thou   **37 Mark** Be attentive.   **carry it** carry it out   **39 draw . . . dried oats** (as a horse would do)

**43 opposites** enemies   **44 require** request.   **use** treat   **49 retention** confinement   **50–3 Whose . . . them** whose advanced age had magic in it, and whose title as king had even more, to win the sympathy of the commoners and turn against us the weapons of those very troops whom we impressed into service. (*In our eyes* may suggest retaliation for the blinding of Gloucester.)   **55 at further space** at some future time   **56 session** court session.   **58–9 And . . . sharpness** and even the best of causes, at this moment when the passions of battle have not cooled, are viewed with hatred by those who have suffered the painful consequences. (Edmund pretends to worry that sentencing right now would be swayed by emotional desires for vengeance.)   **61 by your patience** if you please   **62 subject of** subordinate in   **63 list** please   **64 pleasure** wish.   **demanded** asked about   **65 powers** armed forces   **67 immediacy** nearness of connection   **69 grace** merit   **70 your addition** the titles you confer.   **71 compeers** is equal with   **72 That . . . most** That investiture would be most complete   **73 prove** turn out to be   **74 asquint** (Jealousy proverbially makes the eye look *asquint*, "furtively, suspiciously.")   **76 full-flowing stomach** full tide of angry rejoinder.

Take thou my soldiers, prisoners, patrimony;    77
Dispose of them, of me; the walls is thine.    78
Witness the world that I create thee here
My lord and master.
GONERIL                    Mean you to enjoy him?
ALBANY
The let-alone lies not in your good will.    81
EDMUND
Nor in thine, lord.
ALBANY                    Half-blooded fellow, yes.    82
REGAN [to Edmund]
Let the drum strike and prove my title thine.
ALBANY
Stay yet; hear reason. Edmund, I arrest thee
On capital treason; and, in thy attaint    85
This gilded serpent. [Pointing to Goneril] For your
    claim, fair sister,    86
I bar it in the interest of my wife;
'Tis she is subcontracted to this lord,
And I, her husband, contradict your banns.    89
If you will marry, make your loves to me;    90
My lady is bespoke.
GONERIL                    An interlude!    91
ALBANY
Thou art armed, Gloucester. Let the trumpet sound.    92
If none appear to prove upon thy person
Thy heinous, manifest, and many treasons,
There is my pledge. [He throws down a glove.] I'll make
    it on thy heart,    95
Ere I taste bread, thou art in nothing less    96
Than I have here proclaimed thee.
REGAN    Sick, oh, sick!
GONERIL [aside]    If not, I'll ne'er trust medicine.    99
EDMUND [throwing down a glove]
There's my exchange. What in the world he is    100
That names me traitor, villain-like he lies.
Call by the trumpet. He that dares approach,
On him, on you—who not?—I will maintain
My truth and honor firmly.
ALBANY
A herald, ho!
EDMUND        A herald, ho, a herald!

        Enter a Herald.

ALBANY [to Edmund]
Trust to thy single virtue; for thy soldiers,    106
All levied in my name, have in my name
Took their discharge.
REGAN                    My sickness grows upon me.

ALBANY [to Soldiers]
She is not well. Convey her to my tent.
                    [Exit Regan, supported.]
Come hither, herald. Let the trumpet sound,
And read out this.            [He gives a paper.]
CAPTAIN    Sound, trumpet!        A trumpet sounds.
HERALD (reads)    "If any man of quality or degree within    113
the lists of the army will maintain upon Edmund, sup-    114
posed Earl of Gloucester, that he is a manifold traitor,
let him appear by the third sound of the trumpet. He    116
is bold in his defense."
EDMUND    Sound!                First trumpet.
HERALD    Again!                Second trumpet.
HERALD    Again!                Third trumpet.
                    Trumpet answers within.

        Enter Edgar, armed, [with a trumpeter before
        him].

ALBANY
Ask him his purposes, why he appears
Upon this call o'th' trumpet.
HERALD                    What are you?    122
Your name, your quality, and why you answer    123
This present summons?
EDGAR                    Know my name is lost,
By treason's tooth bare-gnawn and canker-bit.    125
Yet am I noble as the adversary
I come to cope.
ALBANY            Which is that adversary?    127
EDGAR
What's he that speaks for Edmund, Earl of
    Gloucester?
EDMUND
Himself. What say'st thou to him?
EDGAR                    Draw thy sword,
That, if my speech offend a noble heart,    130
Thy arm may do thee justice. Here is mine.    131
                    [He draws his sword.]
Behold, it is the privilege of mine honors,    132
My oath, and my profession. I protest,    133
Maugre thy strength, place, youth, and eminence,    134
Despite thy victor sword and fire-new fortune,    135
Thy valor, and thy heart, thou art a traitor—    136
False to thy gods, thy brother, and thy father,
Conspirant 'gainst this high-illustrious prince,    138
And from th'extremest upward of thy head    139
To the descent and dust below thy foot    140
A most toad-spotted traitor. Say thou no,    141
This sword, this arm, and my best spirits are bent    142
To prove upon thy heart, whereto I speak,
Thou liest.

77 patrimony inheritance   78 the walls is thine i.e., the citadel of my heart and body surrenders completely to you.   81 let-alone preventing, denying   82 Half-blooded Only partly of noble blood, bastard   85–6 and, in thy . . . serpent i.e., and I also arrest this superficially attractive monster (Goneril) as partner in your corruption and as one who has (unwittingly) provided the attaint or accusation against you. 86 For As for.   sister sister-in-law   89 banns public announcement of a proposed marriage.   90 make . . . me i.e., sue to me for permission   91 An interlude! A play; i.e., you are being melodramatic, or, what a farce this is!   92 Gloucester Edmund.   95 make prove (the Q reading)   96 in nothing less in no respect less guilty   99 medicine i.e., the poison used to kill Regan.   100 What Whoever   106 single virtue unaided prowess

113 quality or degree noble birth or rank. (Also in line 123.)   114 lists roster   116 He i.e., The challenger   122 What Who   123 quality rank 125 canker-bit worm-eaten.   127 cope encounter.   130–1 That . . . justice so that if what I have to say insults one who is truly noble (i.e., not illegitimate), you may prove the nobility you claim by vanquishing with your sword.   132 of mine honors i.e., of my knighthood   133 profession i.e., knighthood.   134 Maugre in spite of   135 victor victorious. fire-new newly minted   136 heart courage   138 this . . . prince Albany 139 upward top   140 descent lowest extreme   141 toad-spotted venomous, and spotted with infamy.   Say thou If you say   142 bent prepared

EDMUND    In wisdom I should ask thy name.                                   144
   But since thy outside looks so fair and warlike,
   And that thy tongue some say of breeding breathes,      146
   What safe and nicely I might well delay                       147
   By rule of knighthood, I disdain and spurn.                   148
   Back do I toss those treasons to thy head,                    149
   With the hell-hated lie o'erwhelm thy heart,                  150
   Which—for they yet glance by and scarcely bruise—   151
   This sword of mine shall give them instant way,              152
   Where they shall rest forever.—Trumpets, speak!          153
             *[He draws.] Alarums. Fight. [Edmund falls.]*
ALBANY [*to Edgar*]
   Save him, save him!
GONERIL                              This is practice, Gloucester.           154
   By th' law of arms thou wast not bound to answer
   An unknown opposite. Thou art not vanquished,
   But cozened and beguiled.
ALBANY                              Shut your mouth, dame,                   157
   Or with this paper shall I stopple it.—Hold, sir—            158
   Thou worse than any name, read thine own evil.
             *[He shows the letter.]*
   [*To Goneril*] No tearing, lady; I perceive you know it.
GONERIL
   Say if I do, the laws are mine, not thine.
   Who can arraign me for't?
ALBANY                              Most monstrous! Oh!
   Know'st thou this paper?
GONERIL                              Ask me not what I know.
                         *Exit.*
ALBANY
   Go after her. She's desperate; govern her.                     164
            *[Exit a soldier.]*
EDMUND
   What you have charged me with, that have I done,
   And more, much more. The time will bring it out.
   'Tis past, and so am I. But what art thou
   That hast this fortune on me? If thou'rt noble,                 168
   I do forgive thee.
EDGAR                              Let's exchange charity.                  169
   I am no less in blood than thou art, Edmund;
   If more, the more ignobly thou hast wronged me.
   My name is Edgar, and thy father's son.
   The gods are just, and of our pleasant vices                  173
   Make instruments to plague us.
   The dark and vicious place where thee he got                  175

   Cost him his eyes.
EDMUND                              Th' hast spoken right. 'Tis true.
   The wheel is come full circle; I am here.                      177
ALBANY [*to Edgar*]
   Methought thy very gait did prophesy
   A royal nobleness. I must embrace thee.
                *[They embrace.]*
   Let sorrow split my heart if ever I
   Did hate thee or thy father!
EDGAR    Worthy prince, I know't.
ALBANY    Where have you hid yourself?
   How have you known the miseries of your father?
EDGAR
   By nursing them, my lord. List a brief tale,                   185
   And when 'tis told, oh, that my heart would burst!
   The bloody proclamation to escape                              187
   That followed me so near—oh, our lives' sweetness,          188
   That we the pain of death would hourly die                    189
   Rather than die at once!—taught me to shift                  190
   Into a madman's rags, t'assume a semblance
   That very dogs disdained; and in this habit                   192
   Met I my father with his bleeding rings,                       193
   Their precious stones new lost; became his guide,            194
   Led him, begged for him, saved him from despair;
   Never—oh, fault!—revealed myself unto him
   Until some half hour past, when I was armed.
   Not sure, though hoping, of this good success,                198
   I asked his blessing, and from first to last
   Told him our pilgrimage. But his flawed heart—              200
   Alack, too weak the conflict to support—
   Twixt two extremes of passion, joy and grief,
   Burst smilingly.
EDMUND                              This speech of yours hath moved me,
   And shall perchance do good. But speak you on;
   You look as you had something more to say.
ALBANY
   If there be more, more woeful, hold it in,
   For I am almost ready to dissolve,                             207
   Hearing of this.
EDGAR                              This would have seemed a period         208
   To such as love not sorrow; but another,                      209
   To amplify too much, would make much more                    210
   And top extremity. Whilst I                                    211
   Was big in clamor, came there in a man                        212
   Who, having seen me in my worst estate,
   Shunned my abhorred society; but then, finding
   Who 'twas that so endured, with his strong arms
   He fastened on my neck and bellowed out

---

**144 wisdom** prudence   **146 that** since.   **say** smack, taste, indication   **147 safe and nicely** prudently and punctiliously   **148 I . . . spurn** i.e., I disdain to insist on my right to refuse combat with one of lower rank.   **149 treasons . . . head** i.e., accusations of treason in your teeth   **150 hell-hated** hated as hell is hated   **151 Which . . . bruise** i.e., which charges of treason—since as yet they merely glance off my armor and do no harm   **152 give . . . way** provide them an immediate pathway (to your heart)   **153 Where . . . forever** i.e., my victory in trial by combat will prove forever that the charges of treason apply to you.   **154 Save** Spare. (Albany wishes to spare Edmund's life so that he may confess and be found guilty.)   **practice** trickery, or (said sardonically) astute management.   **Gloucester** Edmund.   **157 cozened** tricked   **158 stopple** stop up.   **Hold, sir** (Addressed to Edgar or, more probably, Edmund.)   **164 govern** restrain   **168 fortune on** victory over   **169 charity** forgiveness (for Edmund's wickedness toward Edgar and Edgar's having slain Edmund).   **173 pleasant** pleasurable   **175 got** begot

**177 The wheel . . . here** (Alludes both to the wheel of fortune and to the idea of a completed circle whereby crime meets its appropriate punishment. Edmund sees that everything has at last come around to where it began.)   **185 List** Listen to   **187 The . . . escape** In order to escape the death-threatening proclamation   **188–90 oh . . . at once!** oh, the perversity of our attachment to our lives' sweetness, that we prefer to suffer continually the fear of death rather than die at once and be done with it!   **192 habit** garb   **193 rings** sockets   **194 stones** i.e., eyeballs   **198 success** outcome   **200 flawed** cracked   **207 dissolve** i.e., in tears   **208 a period** the limit   **209–11 but . . . extremity** i.e., but another sorrowful circumstance, adding to what is already too much, would increase it and exceed the limit.   **212 big in clamor** loud in my lamenting

As he'd burst heaven, threw him on my father,                217
Told the most piteous tale of Lear and him                    218
That ever ear received, which in recounting
His grief grew puissant, and the strings of life              220
Began to crack. Twice then the trumpets sounded,
And there I left him tranced.

ALBANY                                    But who was this?    222

EDGAR
Kent, sir, the banished Kent, who in disguise
Followed his enemy king and did him service                   224
Improper for a slave.                                          225

*Enter a Gentleman [with a bloody knife].*

GENTLEMAN
Help, help, oh, help!

EDGAR                        What kind of help?

ALBANY                                         Speak, man.

EDGAR
What means this bloody knife?

GENTLEMAN                         'Tis hot, it smokes.        227
It came even from the heart of—Oh, she's dead!

ALBANY    Who dead? Speak, man.

GENTLEMAN
Your lady, sir, your lady! And her sister                     230
By her is poisoned; she confesses it.

EDMUND
I was contracted to them both. All three
Now marry in an instant.

EDGAR                         Here comes Kent.

*Enter Kent.*

ALBANY
Produce the bodies, be they alive or dead.
                              *[Exit Gentleman.]*
This judgment of the heavens, that makes us tremble,
Touches us not with pity.—Oh, is this he?
*[To Kent]* The time will not allow the compliment            237
Which very manners urges.

KENT                          I am come                       238
To bid my king and master aye good night.                    239
Is he not here?

ALBANY                Great thing of us forgot!
Speak, Edmund, where's the King? And where's
    Cordelia?
               *Goneril and Regan's bodies [are] brought out.*
See'st thou this object, Kent?                                242

KENT    Alack, why thus?

EDMUND    Yet Edmund was beloved.                             244
The one the other poisoned for my sake                        245
And after slew herself.

ALBANY    Even so. Cover their faces.

217 **As** as if.  **threw . . . father** threw himself on my father's body
218 **him** himself    220 **His** i.e., Kent's.  **puissant** powerful.  **strings of
life** heartstrings    222 **tranced** entranced, senseless.    224 **his enemy
king** i.e., the king who had rejected and banished him    225 **Improper . . .
slave** inappropriate even for a slave.    227 **smokes** steams.    230 **Your
lady** Goneril    237 **compliment** ceremony    238 **Which . . . urges** which
common courtesy requires.    239 **aye good night** farewell forever. (Kent
believes he himself is near death, his heartstrings having begun to
crack.)    242 **object** sight    244 **Yet** Despite all    245 **The one** Goneril

EDMUND
I pant for life. Some good I mean to do,
Despite of mine own nature. Quickly send—
Be brief in it—to th' castle, for my writ
Is on the life of Lear and on Cordelia.
Nay, send in time.

ALBANY                    Run, run, oh, run!

EDGAR
To who, my lord? Who has the office? *[To Edmund]*
    Send                                                      253
Thy token of reprieve.

EDMUND    Well thought on. Take my sword. The captain!
Give it the Captain.

EDGAR                    Haste thee, for thy life.
                    *[Exit one with Edmund's sword.]*

EDMUND
He hath commission from thy wife and me
To hang Cordelia in the prison and
To lay the blame upon her own despair,
That she fordid herself.                                      260

ALBANY
The gods defend her! Bear him hence awhile.
                              *[Edmund is borne off.]*

*Enter Lear, with Cordelia in his arms; [Captain].*

LEAR
Howl, howl, howl! Oh, you are men of stones!
Had I your tongues and eyes, I'd use them so
That heaven's vault should crack. She's gone forever.
I know when one is dead and when one lives;
She's dead as earth. Lend me a looking glass;
If that her breath will mist or stain the stone,             267
Why, then she lives.

KENT                    Is this the promised end?            268

EDGAR
Or image of that horror?

ALBANY                    Fall and cease!                    269

LEAR
This feather stirs; she lives! If it be so,
It is a chance which does redeem all sorrows
That ever I have felt.

KENT *[kneeling]*          O my good master!

LEAR
Prithee, away.

EDGAR              'Tis noble Kent, your friend.

LEAR
A plague upon you, murderers, traitors all!
I might have saved her; now she's gone forever!
Cordelia, Cordelia! Stay a little. Ha?
What is't thou say'st? Her voice was ever soft,
Gentle, and low, an excellent thing in woman.
I killed the slave that was a-hanging thee.

CAPTAIN
'Tis true, my lords, he did.

LEAR                          Did I not, fellow?

253 **office** commission.    260 **fordid** destroyed    267 **If that** if.  **stone**
crystal or polished stone of which the mirror is made    268 **Is . . .
end?** (Kent may mean "Is this what all our hopes have come to?"
Edgar replies by invoking the Last Judgment.)    269 **image** representation.  **Fall and cease!** i.e., Let all things cease to be!

I have seen the day, with my good biting falchion    281
I would have made them skip. I am old now,
And these same crosses spoil me.—Who are you?    283
Mine eyes are not o'th' best; I'll tell you straight.    284

KENT
If Fortune brag of two she loved and hated,    285
One of them we behold.    286

LEAR
This is a dull sight. Are you not Kent?

KENT                                            The same,    287
Your servant Kent. Where is your servant Caius?    288

LEAR
He's a good fellow, I can tell you that;
He'll strike, and quickly too. He's dead and rotten.

KENT
No, my good lord, I am the very man—

LEAR    I'll see that straight.    292

KENT
That from your first of difference and decay    293
Have followed your sad steps—

LEAR                                You are welcome hither.

KENT
Nor no man else. All's cheerless, dark, and deadly.
Your eldest daughters have fordone themselves,    296
And desperately are dead.

LEAR                        Ay, so I think.    297

ALBANY
He knows not what he says, and vain it is
That we present us to him.

EDGAR                        Very bootless.    299

*Enter a Captain.*

CAPTAIN    Edmund is dead, my lord.

ALBANY    That's but a trifle here.
You lords and noble friends, know our intent:
What comfort to this great decay may come    303

Shall be applied. For us, we will resign,    304
During the life of this old majesty,
To him our absolute power; [*to Edgar and Kent*] you, to
    your rights,
With boot and such addition as your honors    307
Have more than merited. All friends shall taste
The wages of their virtue, and all foes
The cup of their deservings.—Oh, see, see!

LEAR
And my poor fool is hanged! No, no, no life?    311
Why should a dog, a horse, a rat have life,
And thou no breath at all? Thou'lt come no more,
Never, never, never, never, never!
Pray you, undo this button. Thank you, sir.
Do you see this? Look on her, look, her lips,
Look there, look there!                    *He dies.*

EDGAR                        He faints.—My lord, my lord!

KENT
Break, heart, I prithee, break!

EDGAR                        Look up, my lord.

KENT
Vex not his ghost. Oh, let him pass! He hates him    319
That would upon the rack of this tough world    320
Stretch him out longer.

EDGAR                        He is gone indeed.

KENT
The wonder is he hath endured so long.
He but usurped his life.

ALBANY
Bear them from hence. Our present business
Is general woe. [*To Kent and Edgar*] Friends of my soul,
    you twain
Rule in this realm, and the gored state sustain.

KENT
I have a journey, sir, shortly to go.    327
My master calls me; I must not say no.

EDGAR
The weight of this sad time we must obey;    329
Speak what we feel, not what we ought to say.
The oldest hath borne most; we that are young
Shall never see so much nor live so long.    332

                        *Exeunt, with a dead march.*

---

281 **falchion** light sword    283 **crosses spoil me** adversities take away my strength.    284 **I'll . . . straight** I'll recognize you in a moment.
285–6 **If . . . behold** If Fortune were to brag of two persons whom she has subjected to the greatest fall from her favor into her hatred, Lear would have to be one of them.    287 **This . . . sight** i.e., My vision is clouding, or, this is a dismal spectacle.    288 **Caius** (Kent's disguise name.)    292 **see that straight** attend to that in a moment.    293 **That from . . . decay** who from the beginning of your quarrel (with Cordelia) to your decline of fortune    295 **Nor . . . else** No, not I nor anyone else, or, I am the *very man* (line 291), him and no one else.    296 **fordone** destroyed    297 **desperately** in despair    299 **bootless** in vain.
299.1 s.d. **Captain** (Identified as *Messenger* in F.)    303 **What . . . come** i.e., whatever means of comforting this ruined king and state of affairs may present themselves

304 **For** As for    307 **With . . . honors** with reward and such further distinctions as your honorable conduct in this war    311 **poor fool** i.e., Cordelia. (*Fool* is here a term of endearment.)    319 **ghost** departing spirit.    320 **rack** torture rack. (The F/Q spelling, "wracke," also suggests shipwreck, disaster.)    327 **journey** i.e., to another world, to death    329–32 **The weight . . . so long** (This final speech is assigned in Q to Albany, in F to Edgar.)    332.1 *Exeunt* (Presumably the dead bodies are borne out in procession.)

# Macbeth

*Macbeth* is seemingly the last of four great Shakespearean tragedies—*Hamlet* (c. 1599–1601), *Othello* (c. 1603–1604), *King Lear* (1605–1606), and *Macbeth* (c. 1606–1607)—that examine the dimensions of spiritual evil, as distinguished from the political strife of Roman tragedies such as *Julius Caesar, Antony* and *Cleopatra,* and *Coriolanus.* Whether or not Shakespeare intended *Macbeth* as a culmination of a series of tragedies on evil, the play does offer a particularly terse and gloomy view of humanity's encounter with the powers of darkness. Macbeth, more consciously than any other of Shakespeare's major tragic protagonists, has to face the temptation of committing what he knows to be a monstrous crime. Like Doctor Faustus in Christopher Marlowe's play, *The Tragedy of Doctor Faustus* (c. 1588), and to a lesser extent like Adam in John Milton's *Paradise Lost* (1667), Macbeth understands the reasons for resisting evil and yet goes ahead with his disastrous plan. His awareness and sensitivity to moral issues, together with his conscious choice of evil, produce an unnerving account of human failure, all the more distressing because Macbeth is so representatively human. He seems to possess freedom of will and accepts personal responsibility for his fate, and yet his tragic doom seems unavoidable. Nor is there eventual salvation to be hoped for, as there is in *Paradise Lost*, since Macbeth's crime is too heinous and his heart too hardened. He is more like Doctor Faustus—damned and in despair.

To an extent not found in the other tragedies, the issue is stated in terms of salvation versus damnation. Macbeth knows before he acts that King Duncan's virtues "Will plead like angels, trumpet-tongued, against / The deep damnation of his taking-off" (1.7.19–20). After the murder, he is equally aware that he has "Put rancors in the vessel of my peace . . . and mine eternal jewel / Given to the common enemy of man" (3.1.68–70). His enemies later describe him as a devil and a "hellhound" (5.8.3). He, like Marlowe's Doctor Faustus before him, has knowingly sold his soul for gain. And, although as a mortal he still has time to repent his crimes, horrible as they are, Macbeth cannot find the words to be penitent. "Wherefore could not I pronounce 'Amen'?" he implores his wife after they have committed the murder. "I had most need of blessing, and 'Amen' / Stuck in my throat" (2.2.35–7). Macbeth's own answer seems to be that he has committed himself so inexorably to evil that he cannot turn back. Sentence has been pronounced: "Glamis hath murdered sleep, and therefore Cawdor / Shall sleep no more; Macbeth shall sleep no more" (lines 46–7).

*Macbeth* is not a conventional morality play (even less so than *Doctor Faustus*) and is not concerned primarily with preaching against sinfulness or demonstrating that Macbeth is finally damned for what he does. A tradition of moral and religious drama has been transformed into an intensely human study of the psychological effects of evil on a particular man and, to a lesser extent, on his wife. That moral tradition nevertheless provides as its legacy a perspective on the operation of evil in human affairs. A perverse ambition seemingly inborn in Macbeth himself is abetted by dark forces dwelling in the universe, waiting to catch him off guard. Among Shakespeare's tragedies, indeed, *Macbeth* is remarkable for its focus on evil in the protagonist and on his relationship to the sinister forces tempting him. In no other Shakespearean play is the audience asked to identify to such an extent with the evildoer himself. *Richard III* also focuses on an evil protagonist, but in that play the spectators are distanced by the character's gloating and are not partakers to the same extent in the introspective soliloquies of a man confronting his own ambition. Macbeth is more representatively human. If he betrays an inclination toward brutality, he also humanely attempts to resist that urge. We witness and struggle to understand his downfall through two phases: the spiritual struggle before he actually commits the crime, and then the despairing aftermath, with its vain quest for security through continued violence. Evil is thus presented in two aspects: first as an insidious suggestion leading Macbeth on toward an illusory promise of gain and then as a frenzied addiction to the hated thing by which he is possessed.

In the first phase, before the commission of the crime, we wonder to what extent the powers of darkness are a determining factor in what Macbeth does. Can he avoid the fate the witches proclaim? Evidently, he and Lady Macbeth have previously considered murdering Duncan; the witches appear after the thought, not before. Lady Macbeth reminds her wavering husband that he was the first to "break this enterprise" to her, on some previous occasion when "Nor time nor place / Did then adhere, and yet you would make both" (1.7.49–53). Elizabethans would probably understand that evil spirits such as witches appear when summoned, whether by our conscious or unconscious minds. Macbeth is ripe for their insinuations: a mind free of taint would see no sinister invitation in their prophecy of greatness to come. And, in a saner moment, Macbeth knows that his restless desire to interfere with destiny is arrogant and useless. "If chance will have me king, why, chance may crown me / Without my stir" (1.3.145–6). Banquo, his companion, serves as his dramatic opposite by consistently displaying a more stoical attitude toward the witches. "Speak then to me," he addresses them, "who neither beg nor fear / Your favors nor your hate" (lines 60–1). Like Horatio in *Hamlet*, Banquo strongly resists the blandishments of fortune as well as its buffets, though not without an agonizing night of moral struggle. Indeed, promises of success are often more ruinous than setbacks—as in the seemingly paradoxical instance of the farmer, cited by Macbeth's porter, who "hanged himself on th'expectation of plenty" (2.3.4–5). It is by showing Macbeth that he is two-thirds of his way to the throne that the witches tempt him to seize the last third at whatever cost. "Glamis, and Thane of Cawdor! / The greatest is behind" (1.3.116–17).

Banquo comprehends the nature of temptation. "To win us to our harm," he observes, "The instruments of darkness tell us truths, / Win us with honest trifles, to betray's / In deepest consequence" (1.3.123–6). The devil can speak true, and his strategy is to invite us into a trap we help prepare. Without our active consent in evil (as Othello also learns), we cannot fall. Yet in what sense are the witches trifling with Macbeth or prevaricating? When they address him as one "that shalt be king hereafter" (line 50), they are stating a certainty, for they can "look into the seeds of time / And say which grain will grow and which will not," as Banquo says (lines 58–9). They know that Banquo will be "Lesser than Macbeth, and greater. / Not so happy, yet much happier" (lines 65–6), since Banquo will beget a race of kings and Macbeth will not. How then do they know that Macbeth will be king? If we consider the hypothetical question, what if Macbeth does *not* murder Duncan, we can gain some understanding of the relationship between character and fate; for the only valid answer is that the question remains hypothetical—Macbeth *does* kill Duncan, the witches are right in their prediction. It is idle to speculate that Providence would

have found another way to make Macbeth king, for the witches' prophecy is self-fulfilling in the very way they foresee. Character is fate; they know Macbeth's fatal weakness and know they can "enkindle" him to seize the crown by laying irresistible temptations before him. This does not mean that they determine his choice but, rather, that Macbeth's choice is predictable and therefore unvoidable, even though not preordained. He has free choice, but that choice will, in fact, go only one way—as with Adam and Eve in Milton's *Paradise Lost* and in the medieval tradition from which this poem was derived.

Although the powers of evil cannot determine Macbeth's choice, they can influence the external conditions affecting that choice. By a series of apparently circumstantial events, well timed in their effect, they can repeatedly assail him just when he is about to rally to the call of conscience. The witches, armed with supernatural knowledge, inform Macbeth of his new title shortly before the King's ambassadors confirm that he is to be the Thane of Cawdor. Duncan chooses this night to lodge under Macbeth's roof. And, just when Macbeth resolves to abandon even this unparalleled opportunity, his wife intervenes on the side of the witches. Macbeth commits the murder in part to keep his word to her and to prove he is no coward (like Donwald, the slayer of King Duff in one of Shakespeare's chief sources, Raphael Holinshed's *Chronicles*). Not only the opportunities presented to Macbeth, but also the obstacles put in his way are cannily timed to overwhelm his conscience. When King Duncan announces that his son Malcolm is now Prince of Cumberland and official heir to the throne (1.4.36–42), the unintended threat deflects Macbeth's mood from one of gratitude and acceptance to one of hostility. These are mitigating circumstances that affect our judgment of Macbeth, and, even though they cannot excuse him, they certainly increase our sympathetic identification.

We are moved, too, by the poetic intensity of Macbeth's moral vision. His soliloquies are memorable as poetry, not merely because Shakespeare wrote them, but because Macbeth is sensitive and aware. The horror, indeed, of his crime is that his cultivated self is revolted by what he cannot prevent himself from doing. He understands with a terrible clarity, not only the moral wrong of what he is about to do, but also the inescapably destructive consequences for himself. He is as reluctant as we to see the crime committed, and yet he goes to it with a sad and rational deliberateness rather than in a self-blinding fury. For Macbeth, there is no seeming loss of perspective, and yet there is total alienation of the act from his moral consciousness. The arguments for and against murdering Duncan, as Macbeth pictures them in his acutely visual imagination, when weighed, are overwhelmingly opposed to the deed. Duncan is his king and his guest, deserving Macbeth's duty and hospitality. The King is virtuous and able. He has shown every favor to

Macbeth, thereby removing any sane motive for striving after further promotion. All human history shows that murders of this sort "return / To plague th'inventor" (1.7.9–10), that is, provide only guilt and punishment rather than satisfaction. Finally, judgment in "the life to come" includes the prospect of eternal torment. On the other side of the argument is nothing but Macbeth's "Vaulting ambition, which o'erleaps itself" (line 27)—a perverse refusal to be content with his present good fortune because there is more that beckons. Who could weigh the issues so dispassionately and still choose the wrong? Yet the failure is, in fact, predictable; Macbeth is presented to us as typically human, both in his understanding and in his perverse ambition.

Macbeth's clarity of moral imagination is contrasted with his wife's imperceptiveness. He is always seeing visions or hearing voices—a dagger in the air, the ghost of Banquo, a voice crying "Sleep no more!"—and she is always denying them. "The sleeping and the dead / Are but as pictures," she insists. He knows that "all great Neptune's ocean" cannot wash the blood from his hands; "No, this my hand will rather / The multitudinous seas incarnadine, / Making the green one red." To Lady Macbeth, contrastingly, "A little water clears us of this deed. / How easy is it, then!" (2.2.57–72). Macbeth knows that the murder of Duncan is but the beginning: "We have scorched the snake, not killed it." Lady Macbeth would prefer to believe that "What's done is done" (3.2.14–15). Ironically, it is she, finally, who must endure visions of the most agonizing sort, sleepwalking in her distress and trying to rub away the "damned spot" that before seemed so easy to remove. "All the perfumes of Arabia will not sweeten this little hand," she laments (5.1.33–52). This relationship between Macbeth and Lady Macbeth owes much to traditional contrasts between male and female principles. As in the pairing of Adam and Eve, the man is putatively the more rational of the two but knowingly shares his wife's sin through fondness for her. She has failed to foresee the long-range consequences of sinful ambition and so becomes a temptress to her husband. The fall of man and woman into the bondage of sin takes place in an incongruous atmosphere of domestic intimacy and mutual concern; Lady Macbeth is motivated by ambition for her husband in much the same way that he sins to win her approbation.

The fatal disharmony flawing this domestic accord is conveyed through images of sexual inversion. Lady Macbeth prepares for her ordeal with the incantation, "Come, you spirits / That tend on mortal thoughts, unsex me here . . . Come to my woman's breasts / And take my milk for gall" (1.5.40–8). When she accuses her husband of unmanly cowardice and vows she would dash out the brains of her own infant for such effeminacy as he has displayed, he extols her with "Bring forth men-children only! / For thy undaunted mettle should compose / Nothing but males" (1.7.73–5). She takes the initiative,

devising and then carrying out the plan to drug Duncan's chamber-guards with wine. This assumption of the dominant male role by the woman might well remind Elizabethan spectators of numerous biblical, medieval, and classical parallels deploring the ascendancy of passion over reason: Eve choosing for Adam, Noah's wife taking command of the ark, Samson succumbing to the temptations of Delilah, the Wife of Bath dominating her husbands, Venus emasculating Mars, and others.

In *Macbeth*, sexual inversion also allies Lady Macbeth with the witches or weird sisters, the bearded women. Their unnaturalness betokens disorder in nature, for they can sail in a sieve and "look not like th'inhabitants o'th'earth / And yet are on't" (1.3.41–2). Characteristically, they speak in paradoxes: "When the battle's lost and won," "Fair is foul, and foul is fair" (1.1.4,11). Shakespeare probably drew on numerous sources to depict the witches: Holinshed's *Chronicles* (from which he conflated two accounts, one of Duncan and Macbeth, and the other of King Duff slain by Donwald with the help of his wife), King James's writings on witchcraft, Samuel Harsnett's *Declaration of Egregious Popish Impostures* (used also for *King Lear*), and the accounts of the Scottish witch trials published around 1590. In the last, particularly, Shakespeare could have found mention of witches raising storms and sailing in sieves to endanger vessels at sea, performing threefold rituals blaspheming the Trinity, and brewing witches' broth. Holinshed's *Chronicles* refer to the Weird Sisters as "goddesses of destiny," associating them with the three fates, Clotho, Lachesis, and Atropos, who hold the spinning distaff, draw off the thread of life, and cut it. In *Macbeth*, the Weird Sisters' power to control fortune is curtailed, and they are portrayed as witches according to popular contemporary understanding, rather than as goddesses of destiny; nonetheless, witches were thought to be servants of the devil (Banquo wonders if the devil can speak true in their utterances, 1.3.107), and through them Macbeth has made an ominous pact with evil itself. His visit to their seething cauldron in 4.1 brings him to the witches' masters, those unknown powers that know his very thought and who tempt him with those equivocations of which Banquo has warned Macbeth. The popularity of witchlore tempted Shakespeare's acting company to expand the witches' scenes with spectacles of song and dance; even the Folio text we have evidently contains interpolations derived in part from Thomas Middleton's *The Witch* (see especially 3.5 and part of 4.1, containing mention of Middleton's songs "Come away" and "Black spirits"). Nevertheless, Shakespeare's original theme of a disharmony in nature remains clearly visible.

The disharmonies of gender relations in *Macbeth* suggest another disturbing dimension of this tragedy. The play is filled with what Janet Adelman (in *Cannibals, Witches, and Divorce*, edited by Marjorie Garber, 1985) aptly calls fantasies of maternal power. Macbeth, like many males, attempts to cope with his imaginings of a destructive maternal power and his fantasies of escape into a world fashioned and controlled solely by himself. Initially, he submits to his wife's idea of manliness and commits murder in order to win her approval, destroying in the process a fatherly figure whose manhood is nonetheless ambivalently presented to us: Duncan is to be sure a nurturing father-king, but he is also too soft and trusting for his own good. Macbeth chooses to side with his masculinized wife against the gentler side of human nature, lauding her as a woman who should "Bring forth men-children only," since her "undaunted mettle should compose / Nothing but males" (1.7.73–5), but, in the longer term, Macbeth finds himself desiccated by his own vulnerability to this masculinized mother. He turns unsuccessfully to the witches for the power he needs to make him author of himself; in the process of attempting to make himself wholly "masculine," he manages instead to strip away from himself "honor, love, obedience, troops of friends," and all the graces that should "accompany old age" (5.3.24–5). His nemesis is appropriately one who was not, in the normal sense, "of woman born," since Macduff "was from his mother's womb / Untimely ripped" (5.8.13–16). Macduff represents, in other words, the self-creating and invulnerable masculinity that Macbeth cannot fashion for himself. The ending of the play is distressingly absolute in its consolidation of male power—a reestablishment of control that seems necessary in view of the virulence of the maternal power the play has dared to unleash.

Patterns of imagery throughout the play point similarly to disorders in nature and in human relationships. The murder of Duncan, like that of Caesar in *Julius Caesar*, is accompanied by signs of the heavens' anger. Various observers report that chimneys blow down during the unruly night, that owls clamor and attack falcons, that the earth shakes, and that Duncan's horses devour each other. (Some of these portents are from Holinshed.) Banquo's ghost returns from the dead to haunt his murderer, prompting Macbeth to speak in metaphors of charnel houses and graves that send back their dead and of birds of prey that devour the corpses. The drunken porter who opens the gate to Macduff and Lennox after the murder (2.3) invokes images of judgment and everlasting bonfire, through which the scene takes on the semblance of hell gate and the Harrowing of Hell. Owls appear repeatedly in the imagery, along with other creatures associated with nighttime and horror: wolves, serpents, scorpions, bats, toads, beetles, crows, rooks. Darkness itself assumes tangible and menacing shapes of hidden stars or extinguished candles, a thick blanket shrouded "in the dunnest smoke of hell" (1.5.51), an entombment of the earth in place of "living light" (2.4.10), a scarf to hoodwink the eye of "pitiful day" (3.2.50), and a "bloody and invisible hand" to tear to pieces the lives of the virtuous (3.2.51–2). Sleep is transformed from "great nature's second course" and a "nourisher" of life that "knits up the raveled sleeve of

care" (2.2.41–4) into "death's counterfeit" (2.3.77) and a living hell for Lady Macbeth. Life becomes sterile for Macbeth, a denial of harvest, the lees or dregs of the wine and "the sere, the yellow leaf" (5.3.23). In a theatrical metaphor, life becomes for him unreal, "a walking shadow, a poor player / That struts and frets his hour upon the stage / And then is heard no more" (5.5.24–6). This theme of empty illusion carries over into the recurring image of borrowed or ill-fitting garments that belie the wearer. Macbeth is an actor, a hypocrite, whose "False face must hide what the false heart doth know" (1.7.83) and who must "Look like th'innocent flower, / But be the serpent under't" (1.5.65–6). Even the show of grief is an assumed mask whereby evildoers deceive the virtuous, so much so that Malcolm, Donalbain, and Macduff learn to conceal their true feelings rather than be thought to "show an unfelt sorrow" (2.3.138).

Blood is not only a literal sign of disorder but an emblem of Macbeth's remorseless butchery, a "damned spot" on the conscience, and a promise of divine vengeance: "It will have blood, they say; blood will have blood" (3.4.123). The emphasis on corrupted blood also suggests disease, in which Macbeth's tyranny is a sickness to his country as well as to himself. Scotland bleeds (4.3.32), needing a physician; Macduff and his allies call themselves "the med'cine of the sickly weal" (5.2.27). Lady Macbeth's disease is incurable, something spiritually corrupt wherein "the patient / Must minister to himself" (5.3.47–8). Conversely, the English King Edward is renowned for his divine gift of curing what was called the king's evil, or scrofula (4.3.147–8). These images are generally paternalistic in their invocation of kings and fathers who heal and unite.

Throughout, the defenders of righteousness are associated with positive images of natural order and with patriarchal control. Duncan rewards his subjects by saying, "I have begun to plant thee, and will labor / To make thee full of growing" (1.4.28–9). His arrival at Inverness Castle is heralded by signs of summer, sweet air, and "the temple-haunting martlet" (1.6.4). He is a fatherly figure, so much so that even Lady Macbeth balks at an act so like patricide. Macduff, too, is a father and husband whose family is butchered. The forest of Birnam marching to confront Macbeth, although rationally explainable as a device of camouflage for Macduff's army, is emblematic of the natural order itself rising up against the monstrosity of Macbeth's crimes. Banquo is, above all, a patriarchal figure, ancestor of the royal line governing Scotland and England at the time the play was written. These harmonies are to an extent restorative. Even the witches' riddling prophecies, "th'equivocation of the fiend" (5.5.43), luring Macbeth into further atrocities with the vain promise of security, anticipate a just retribution.

Nonetheless, the play's vision of evil shakes us deeply. Scotland's peace has been violated, so much so that "to do harm / Is often laudable, to do good sometime /

Accounted dangerous folly" (4.2.76–8). Macduff has been forced to deny his proper manly role of protecting his wife and family; Lady Macduff and her son, along with young Siward, have had to pay with their innocent lives the terrible price of Scotland's tyranny. In his frenzied attempt to prevent the fulfillment of the prophecy about Banquo's lineage inheriting the kingdom, Macbeth has, like King Herod, slaughtered much of the younger generation on whom the future depends. We can only hope that the stability to which Scotland returns after his death will be lasting. Banquo's line is to rule eventually and to produce a line of kings reaching down to the royal occupant to whom Shakespeare will present his play, but, when *Macbeth* ends, it is Malcolm who is king. The killing of a traitor (Macbeth) and the placing of his head on a pole replicate the play's beginning in the treason and beheading of the Thane of Cawdor—a gentleman on whom Duncan built "An absolute trust" (1.4.14). Most troublingly, the humanly representative nature of Macbeth's crime leaves us with little assurance that we could resist his temptation. The most that can be said is that wise and good persons such as Banquo and Macduff have learned to know the evil in themselves and to resist it as nobly as they can.

Along with its timeless interest in murder and the human conscience, *Macbeth* is an intensely political play. It surely was viewed as such when it was first produced in 1606–1607. The drunken porter in 2.3 seemingly refers to the infamous attempt to blow up the houses of Parliament known as the Gunpowder Plot of 1605, and to the subsequent trial of the Jesuit Henry Garnet, the notorious "equivocator," for his part in the conspiracy (2.3.8). Banquo fulfills a historical role as progenitor of the dynastic line that would lead eventually to James VI of Scotland, who had become James I of England in 1603. The pageant of *"eight Kings and Banquo last"* that Macbeth must witness on the occasion of his final visit to the Weird Sisters (4.1.111.1) ends with a *glass* or magic mirror showing many more kings bearing the appurtenances of royal office, including the "twofold balls and treble scepters" (4.1.121) that seemingly refer to James's double coronation in 1603 as King of England and Scotland. James was keenly interested in witchcraft. Scotland was a constant worry on England's northern border, aligning itself with France, marauding across the English border, tearing itself apart through clan violence, and, from an English point of view, manifesting the kind of tyranny that the English especially feared. The Scotland of this play thus helps to define, largely by contrast, what is thought to be truly English. The English King who is described as doing "A most miraculous work" in curing "the evil," or scrofula, by his touch (4.3.147–8) suggests a flattering reference to James, who claimed this power of curing. This unnamed English king lends his support to the military attack against Macbeth through which the tyrant is finally overthrown. The play simultaneously incorporates an uneasy attitude of hostility toward Scotland along with a vision of union between the two countries that is brought about by the subjugation of Scotland to her southern neighbor. A rough kind of harmony is achieved out of disharmony. Macbeth's act of murderous regicide is answered by another regicide in the name of English law. The quandaries of such a resolution may point to the ambivalence that many English people felt about their odd ruler from the north, the man who came to be known as "the wisest fool in Christendom."

*Macbeth* is a difficult play to present on stage, at least according to stage tradition: ever since the early twentieth century, actors have referred to it superstitiously as "the Scottish play" as a way of avoiding bad luck that otherwise can hover menacingly over the acting company. Presumably this is a theatrical response to the play's dark probing of irrational magic, fatal determinism, and human frailty. Not coincidentally, perhaps, some of the greatest successes in performance have been on film. Akira Kurosawa's *Throne of Blood* (1957) retells the story of Macbeth, in black and white, as a devastating exploration of ambitious strife among Japanese warlords. Although the dialogue and characters' names of Shakespeare's play are altered throughout, this version captures magnificently the mysterious and malign intent of the prophetic figure that Washizu (the Macbeth figure) encounters in a forest, tempting him to evil by the ambiguous promises of future greatness. The forest itself is a striking presence in this film, invested as it is with supernatural terror in the midst of a thunderstorm. The Lady Asaji, wife to Washizu, is horrifyingly obsessed with ambition for her husband; her seeming role as an obedient and decorously aristocratic Japanese wife accentuates the contrast between the surfaces of civilized behavior and the dark inner promptings of competitive self-assertion. A film version with Ian McKellen and Judi Dench as Macbeth and his wife, based on a stage version directed by Trevor Nunn (1976–1978) at Stratford-upon-Avon, London, and Newcastle-upon-Tyne, emphasizes the demonic in such a way as to give the Weird Sisters a real power that is both psychologically plausible and frighteningly irrational. Roman Polanski's film version (1971), though faulted for its sponsorship by Playboy Productions and its consequent flaunting of some grotesque nakedness, does successfully portray Macbeth and Lady Macbeth as a vitally young couple for whom sexuality is integral to their ambition. And of course there have been great stage productions, despite the shibboleth of the bad-luck legend, notably Glen Byam Shaw's production at Stratford-upon-Avon in 1955 starring Laurence Olivier and Vivien Leigh that invited admiration for husband and wife as magnificent, courageous, loyal, and of genuinely tragic stature even if fatally flawed by their hearkening to the voice of evil.

# Macbeth

[*Dramatis Personae*

DUNCAN, *King of Scotland*
MALCOLM, } *his sons*
DONALBAIN

MACBETH, *Thane of Glamis, later of Cawdor, later King of Scotland*
LADY MACBETH

BANQUO, *a thane of Scotland*
FLEANCE, *his son*
MACDUFF, *Thane of Fife*
LADY MACDUFF
SON *of Macduff and Lady Macduff*

LENNOX,
ROSS,
MENTEITH, } *thanes and noblemen of Scotland*
ANGUS,
CAITHNESS,

SIWARD, *Earl of Northumberland*
YOUNG SIWARD, *his son*

SEYTON, *an officer attending Macbeth*
*Another* LORD
ENGLISH DOCTOR
SCOTTISH DOCTOR
GENTLEWOMAN *attending Lady Macbeth*
CAPTAIN *serving Duncan*
PORTER
OLD MAN
*Three* MURDERERS *of Banquo*
FIRST MURDERER *at Macduff's castle*
MESSENGER *to Lady Macbeth*
MESSENGER *to Lady Macduff*
SERVANT *to Macbeth*
SERVANT *to Lady Macbeth*
*Three* WITCHES *or* WEIRD SISTERS
HECATE
*Three* APPARITIONS

*Lords, Gentlemen, Officers, Soldiers, Murderers, and Attendants*

SCENE: *Scotland; England*]

## 1.1

*Thunder and lightning. Enter three Witches.*

FIRST WITCH
When shall we three meet again?
In thunder, lightning, or in rain?
SECOND WITCH
When the hurlyburly's done,
When the battle's lost and won.
THIRD WITCH
That will be ere the set of sun.                    3

FIRST WITCH
Where the place?
SECOND WITCH          Upon the heath.
THIRD WITCH
There to meet with Macbeth.
FIRST WITCH    I come, Grimalkin!                    8
SECOND WITCH    Paddock calls.                       9
THIRD WITCH    Anon.                                 10

---

1.1. Location: An open place.
3 hurlyburly's tumult's

8 Grimalkin i.e., gray cat, name of the witch's familiar—a demon or evil spirit supposed to answer a witch's call and to allow him or her to perform black magic.   9 Paddock toad; also a familiar   10 Anon At once, right away.

ALL
Fair is foul, and foul is fair.
Hover through the fog and filthy air.          *Exeunt.*

❖

## 1.2

*Alarum within. Enter King [Duncan], Malcolm,*
*Donalbain, Lennox, with attendants, meeting a*
*bleeding Captain.*

DUNCAN
What bloody man is that? He can report,
As seemeth by his plight, of the revolt
The newest state.
MALCOLM                This is the sergeant          3
Who like a good and hardy soldier fought
'Gainst my captivity.—Hail, brave friend!
Say to the King the knowledge of the broil          6
As thou didst leave it.
CAPTAIN                Doubtful it stood,
As two spent swimmers that do cling together          8
And choke their art. The merciless Macdonwald—          9
Worthy to be a rebel, for to that          10
The multiplying villainies of nature          11
Do swarm upon him—from the Western Isles          12
Of kerns and gallowglasses is supplied;          13
And Fortune, on his damnèd quarrel smiling,          14
Showed like a rebel's whore. But all's too weak;          15
For brave Macbeth—well he deserves that name—          16
Disdaining Fortune, with his brandished steel,
Which smoked with bloody execution,          18
Like valor's minion carved out his passage          19
Till he faced the slave,          20
Which ne'er shook hands nor bade farewell to him          21
Till he unseamed him from the nave to th' chops,          22
And fixed his head upon our battlements.
DUNCAN
Oh, valiant cousin, worthy gentleman!          24

CAPTAIN
As whence the sun 'gins his reflection          25
Shipwrecking storms and direful thunders break,          26
So from that spring whence comfort seemed to come          27
Discomfort swells. Mark, King of Scotland, mark.          28
No sooner justice had, with valor armed,
Compelled these skipping kerns to trust their heels          30
But the Norweyan lord, surveying vantage,          31
With furbished arms and new supplies of men,          32
Began a fresh assault.
DUNCAN
Dismayed not this our captains, Macbeth and
    Banquo?
CAPTAIN
Yes, as sparrows eagles, or the hare the lion.          35
If I say sooth, I must report they were          36
As cannons overcharged with double cracks,          37
So they doubly redoubled strokes upon the foe.          38
Except they meant to bathe in reeking wounds          39
Or memorize another Golgotha,          40
I cannot tell.
But I am faint. My gashes cry for help.
DUNCAN
So well thy words become thee as thy wounds;
They smack of honor both.—Go get him surgeons.
                    [*Exit Captain, attended.*]

*Enter Ross and Angus.*

Who comes here?
MALCOLM                The worthy Thane of Ross.          45
LENNOX    What a haste looks through his eyes!
So should he look that seems to speak things strange.          47
ROSS    God save the King!
DUNCAN    Whence cam'st thou, worthy thane?
ROSS    From Fife, great King,
Where the Norweyan banners flout the sky          51
And fan our people cold.          52
Norway himself, with terrible numbers,          53
Assisted by that most disloyal traitor,
The Thane of Cawdor, began a dismal conflict,          55
Till that Bellona's bridegroom, lapped in proof,          56
Confronted him with self-comparisons,          57

---

**1.2. Location: A camp near Forres.**
**0.1** *Alarum* trumpet call to arms    **3 newest state** latest news.
**sergeant** i.e., staff officer. (There may be no inconsistency with his
rank of "captain" in the stage direction and speech prefixes in the
Folio.)    **6 broil** battle    **8 spent** tired out    **9 choke their art** render
their skill in swimming useless.    **9–13 The merciless . . . supplied**
The merciless Macdonwald—worthy of the hated name of rebel, for
in the cause of rebellion an ever-increasing number of villainous persons and unnatural qualities swarm about him like vermin—is joined
by light-armed Irish footsoldiers and ax-armed horsemen from the
western islands of Scotland (the Hebrides and perhaps Ireland)
**14–15 And Fortune . . . whore** i.e., Fortune, proverbially a false
strumpet, smiles at first on Macdonwald's damned rebellion but deserts him in his hour of need.    **16 well . . . name** well he deserves a
name that is synonymous with "brave"    **18 Which . . . execution** from
which smoke and steam arose as if caused by its bloody business
**19 minion** darling. (Macbeth is Valor's darling, not Fortune's.)
**20 the slave** i.e., Macdonwald    **21 Which . . . to him** i.e., Macbeth
paused for no ceremonious greeting or farewell to Macdonwald
**22 nave** navel.    **chops** jaws    **24 cousin** kinsman

**25–8 As . . . swells** Just as terrible storms at sea arise out of the east,
from the place where the sun first begins its return from winter
and shows itself in the seeming comfort of the dawn, even thus did
a new military threat come on the heels of the seeming good news
of Macdonwald's execution.    **30 skipping** (1) lightly armed, quick
at maneuvering (2) skittish.    **trust their heels** take to their heels
**31 surveying vantage** seeing an opportunity    **32 furbished** polished,
newly renovated    **35 Yes . . . eagles** Yes, about as much as sparrows
terrify eagles. (Said ironically.)    **36 say sooth** tell the truth    **37 cracks**
charges of explosive    **38 So . . . strokes** so vigorously did they redou-
ble their blows    **39 Except** Unless    **40 memorize** make memorable
or famous.    **Golgotha** "place of a skull," where Christ was crucified.
(Mark 15:22.)    **45 Thane** Scottish title of honor, roughly equivalent to
"Earl"    **47 seems to** seems about to    **51 flout** mock, insult    **52 fan . . .
cold** fan cold fear into our troops.    **53 Norway** The King of Norway.
**terrible numbers** terrifying numbers of troops    **55 dismal** ominous
**56 Till . . . proof** i.e., until Macbeth, clad in well-tested armor.
(Bellona was the Roman goddess of war.)    **57 him** i.e., the King
of Norway.    **self-comparisons** i.e., matching counterthrusts

Point against point, rebellious arm 'gainst arm,    58
Curbing his lavish spirit; and to conclude,
The victory fell on us.

DUNCAN                    Great happiness!

ROSS    That now
Sweno, the Norways' king, craves composition;    62
Nor would we deign him burial of his men
Till he disbursèd at Saint Colme's Inch    64
Ten thousand dollars to our general use.    65

DUNCAN
No more that Thane of Cawdor shall deceive
Our bosom interest. Go pronounce his present death,    67
And with his former title greet Macbeth.

ROSS    I'll see it done.

DUNCAN
What he hath lost noble Macbeth hath won.
                                    *Exeunt.*

❖

# 1.3

*Thunder. Enter the three Witches.*

FIRST WITCH    Where hast thou been, sister?

SECOND WITCH    Killing swine.

THIRD WITCH    Sister, where thou?

FIRST WITCH
A sailor's wife had chestnuts in her lap,
And munched, and munched, and munched. "Give
    me," quoth I.
"Aroint thee, witch!" the rump-fed runnion cries.    6
Her husband's to Aleppo gone, master o'th' *Tiger*;    7
But in a sieve I'll thither sail,
And like a rat without a tail    9
I'll do, I'll do, and I'll do.    10

SECOND WITCH
I'll give thee a wind.

FIRST WITCH
Thou'rt kind.

THIRD WITCH
And I another.

FIRST WITCH
I myself have all the other,    14
And the very ports they blow,    15
All the quarters that they know    16
I'th' shipman's card.    17
I'll drain him dry as hay.    18

Sleep shall neither night nor day
Hang upon his penthouse lid.    20
He shall live a man forbid.    21
Weary sev'nnights nine times nine    22
Shall he dwindle, peak, and pine.    23
Though his bark cannot be lost,    24
Yet it shall be tempest-tossed.
Look what I have.

SECOND WITCH    Show me, show me.

FIRST WITCH
Here I have a pilot's thumb,
Wrecked as homeward he did come.    *Drum within.*

THIRD WITCH
A drum, a drum!
Macbeth doth come.

ALL  [*dancing in a circle*]
The Weird Sisters, hand in hand,    32
Posters of the sea and land,    33
Thus do go about, about,
Thrice to thine, and thrice to mine,
And thrice again, to make up nine.
Peace! The charm's wound up.

*Enter Macbeth and Banquo.*

MACBETH
So foul and fair a day I have not seen.

BANQUO
How far is't called to Forres?—What are these,    39
So withered and so wild in their attire,
That look not like th'inhabitants o'th'earth
And yet are on't?—Live you? Or are you aught
That man may question? You seem to understand me
By each at once her choppy finger laying    44
Upon her skinny lips. You should be women,
And yet your beards forbid me to interpret
That you are so.

MACBETH                    Speak, if you can. What are you?

FIRST WITCH
All hail, Macbeth! Hail to thee, Thane of Glamis!

SECOND WITCH
All hail, Macbeth! Hail to thee, Thane of Cawdor!

THIRD WITCH
All hail, Macbeth, that shalt be king hereafter!

BANQUO
Good sir, why do you start and seem to fear
Things that do sound so fair?—I'th' name of truth,
Are ye fantastical or that indeed    53
Which outwardly ye show? My noble partner    54
You greet with present grace and great prediction    55
Of noble having and of royal hope,
That he seems rapt withal. To me you speak not.    57
If you can look into the seeds of time

---

**58 point** sword point  **62 Norways'** Norwegians'.  **composition** agreement, treaty of peace  **64 Saint Colme's Inch** Inchcolm, the Isle of St. Columba in the Firth of Forth  **65 dollars** Spanish or Dutch coins  **67 Our** (The royal "we.")  **bosom** close and intimate.  **present** immediate

**1.3. Location: A heath near Forres.**

**6 Aroint thee** Begone.  **rump-fed runnion** fat-rumped baggage
**7 Aleppo** (in modern-day Syria).  *Tiger* (A ship's name.)  **9–10 like . . . do** (Suggestive of the witches' deformity and sexual insatiability. Witches were thought to seduce men sexually. *Do* means [1] act [2] perform sexually.)  **14–17 I . . . card** I can summon all other winds, wherever they blow and from whatever *quarter* in the shipman's compass card.  **18 I'll . . . hay** (With a suggestion of sexually draining the seaman's semen.)

**20 penthouse lid** i.e., eyelid (which projects out over the eye like a *penthouse* or slope-roofed structure).  **21 forbid** accursed.  **22 sev'n-nights** weeks  **23 peak** grow peaked or thin  **24 bark** small sailing vessel  **32 Weird Sisters** women connected with fate or destiny; also women having a mysterious or unearthly, uncanny appearance. Old English "wyrd" means "fate." F reads "weyward."  **33 Posters of** swift travelers over  **39 is't called** is it said to be  **44 choppy** chapped  **53 fantastical** creatures of fantasy or imagination  **54 show** appear.  **55 grace** honor, title  **57 rapt withal** entranced.

And say which grain will grow and which will not,
Speak then to me, who neither beg nor fear                          60
Your favors nor your hate.                                          61
FIRST WITCH    Hail!
SECOND WITCH    Hail!
THIRD WITCH    Hail!
FIRST WITCH
Lesser than Macbeth, and greater.
SECOND WITCH
Not so happy, yet much happier.                                    66
THIRD WITCH
Thou shalt get kings, though thou be none.                         67
So all hail, Macbeth and Banquo!
FIRST WITCH
Banquo and Macbeth, all hail!
MACBETH
Stay, you imperfect speakers, tell me more!                        70
By Sinel's death I know I am Thane of Glamis,                      71
But how of Cawdor? The Thane of Cawdor lives
A prosperous gentleman; and to be king
Stands not within the prospect of belief,
No more than to be Cawdor. Say from whence                         75
You owe this strange intelligence, or why                          76
Upon this blasted heath you stop our way                           77
With such prophetic greeting? Speak, I charge you.
                                        *Witches vanish.*
BANQUO
The earth hath bubbles, as the water has,
And these are of them. Whither are they vanished?
MACBETH
Into the air; and what seemed corporal melted,                     81
As breath into the wind. Would they had stayed!
BANQUO
Were such things here as we do speak about?
Or have we eaten on the insane root                                84
That takes the reason prisoner?
MACBETH
Your children shall be kings.
BANQUO                                    You shall be king.
MACBETH
And Thane of Cawdor too. Went it not so?
BANQUO
To th' selfsame tune and words.—Who's here?

                    *Enter Ross and Angus.*

ROSS
The King hath happily received, Macbeth,
The news of thy success; and when he reads                         90
Thy personal venture in the rebels' fight,                         91
His wonders and his praises do contend                             92
Which should be thine or his. Silenced with that,                  93
In viewing o'er the rest o'th' selfsame day

He finds thee in the stout Norweyan ranks,                         95
Nothing afeard of what thyself didst make,                         96
Strange images of death. As thick as tale                          97
Came post with post, and every one did bear                        98
Thy praises in his kingdom's great defense,
And poured them down before him.
ANGUS                                    We are sent
To give thee from our royal master thanks,
Only to herald thee into his sight,
Not pay thee.
ROSS
And, for an earnest of a greater honor,                           104
He bade me, from him, call thee Thane of Cawdor;
In which addition, hail, most worthy thane,                       106
For it is thine.
BANQUO              What, can the devil speak true?
MACBETH
The Thane of Cawdor lives. Why do you dress me
In borrowed robes?
ANGUS                      Who was the thane lives yet,            109
But under heavy judgment bears that life
Which he deserves to lose. Whether he was combined 111
With those of Norway, or did line the rebel               112
With hidden help and vantage, or that with both
He labored in his country's wrack, I know not;            114
But treasons capital, confessed and proved,               115
Have overthrown him.
MACBETH *[aside]*            Glamis, and Thane of Cawdor!
The greatest is behind. *[To Ross and Angus]* Thanks for
    your pains.                                                   117
*[Aside to Banquo]* Do you not hope your children shall
    be kings
When those that gave the Thane of Cawdor to me
Promised no less to them?
BANQUO *[to Macbeth]*            That, trusted home,              120
Might yet enkindle you unto the crown,
Besides the Thane of Cawdor. But 'tis strange;
And oftentimes to win us to our harm
The instruments of darkness tell us truths,
Win us with honest trifles, to betray 's
In deepest consequence.—                                          126
Cousins, a word, I pray you.                                      127
                *[He converses apart with Ross and Angus.]*
MACBETH *[aside]*    Two truths are told,
As happy prologues to the swelling act                            129
Of the imperial theme.—I thank you, gentlemen.
*[Aside]* This supernatural soliciting                            131
Cannot be ill, cannot be good. If ill,
Why hath it given me earnest of success

---

60–1 **beg . . . hate** beg your favors nor fear your hate.    **66 happy**
fortunate    **67 get** beget    **70 imperfect** cryptic    **71 Sinel's** (Sinel was
Macbeth's father.)    **75–6 Say . . . intelligence** Say from what source
you have this disturbing information    **77 blasted** blighted    **81 corporal**
corporeal    **84 on** of.    **insane root** root causing insanity; variously
identified    **90–3 and when . . . his** and when he reads or hears of
your extraordinary valor in fighting the rebels, he concludes that
your wondrous deeds outdo any praise he could offer.

**95 stout** haughty, determined, valiant    **96 Nothing** not at all
**97–8 As . . . with post** As fast as could be told, i.e., counted, came
messenger after messenger. (Unless the text should be amended to
"As thick as hail.")    **104 earnest** token payment    **106 addition** title
**109 Who** He who    **111 combined** confederate    **112 line the rebel** reinforce Macdonwald    **114 in . . . wrack** to bring about his country's ruin
**115 capital** deserving death    **117 The greatest is behind** either
(1) Two of the three prophecies (and thus the greatest number of them)
have already been fulfilled, or (2) The greatest one, the kingship, is
still to come.    **120 home** all the way    **126 In deepest consequence**
in the profoundly important sequel.    **127 Cousins** i.e., Fellow lords
**129 swelling act** stately drama    **131 soliciting** tempting

Commencing in a truth? I am Thane of Cawdor.
If good, why do I yield to that suggestion
Whose horrid image doth unfix my hair                                    136
And make my seated heart knock at my ribs,
Against the use of nature? Present fears                                 138
Are less than horrible imaginings.
My thought, whose murder yet is but fantastical,                        140
Shakes so my single state of man                                        141
That function is smothered in surmise,                                  142
And nothing is but what is not.                                         143

BANQUO    Look how our partner's rapt.

MACBETH [aside]
If chance will have me king, why, chance may crown
    me
Without my stir.

BANQUO                    New honors come upon him,                     146
Like our strange garments, cleave not to their mold                     147
But with the aid of use.

MACBETH [aside]                    Come what come may,                  148
Time and the hour runs through the roughest day.                        149

BANQUO
Worthy Macbeth, we stay upon your leisure.                              150

MACBETH
Give me your favor. My dull brain was wrought                           151
With things forgotten. Kind gentlemen, your pains
Are registered where every day I turn                                   153
The leaf to read them. Let us toward the King.
[Aside to Banquo]    Think upon what hath chanced,
    and at more time,                                                   155
The interim having weighed it, let us speak                             156
Our free hearts each to other.                                          157

BANQUO [to Macbeth]    Very gladly.

MACBETH [to Banquo]    Till then, enough.—Come, friends.
                                                        Exeunt.

❧

# 1.4

*Flourish. Enter King [Duncan], Lennox, Malcolm,*
*Donalbain, and attendants.*

DUNCAN
Is execution done on Cawdor? Are not
Those in commission yet returned?

MALCOLM                    My liege,                                     2
They are not yet come back. But I have spoke

With one that saw him die, who did report
That very frankly he confessed his treasons,
Implored Your Highness' pardon, and set forth
A deep repentance. Nothing in his life
Became him like the leaving it. He died                                 8
As one that had been studied in his death                               9
To throw away the dearest thing he owed                                 10
As 'twere a careless trifle.

DUNCAN                    There's no art                                11
To find the mind's construction in the face.
He was a gentleman on whom I built
An absolute trust.

*Enter Macbeth, Banquo, Ross, and Angus.*

                    O worthiest cousin!
The sin of my ingratitude even now
Was heavy on me. Thou art so far before                                 16
That swiftest wing of recompense is slow
To overtake thee. Would thou hadst less deserved,
That the proportion both of thanks and payment                         19
Might have been mine! Only I have left to say,                          20
More is thy due than more than all can pay.

MACBETH
The service and the loyalty I owe,
In doing it, pays itself. Your Highness' part
Is to receive our duties; and our duties
Are to your throne and state children and servants,                    25
Which do but what they should by doing everything
Safe toward your love and honor.

DUNCAN                    Welcome hither!                               27
I have begun to plant thee, and will labor
To make thee full of growing. Noble Banquo,
That hast no less deserved, nor must be known
No less to have done so, let me infold thee
And hold thee to my heart.

BANQUO                    There if I grow,
The harvest is your own.

DUNCAN                    My plenteous joys,
Wanton in fullness, seek to hide themselves                            34
In drops of sorrow.—Sons, kinsmen, thanes,
And you whose places are the nearest, know
We will establish our estate upon                                      37
Our eldest, Malcolm, whom we name hereafter
The Prince of Cumberland; which honor must                             39
Not unaccompanied invest him only,                                     40
But signs of nobleness, like stars, shall shine
On all deservers.—From hence to Inverness,                             42
And bind us further to you.                                            43

---

**136 unfix my hair** make my hair stand on end    **138 use** custom.
**fears** things feared    **140 whose . . . fantastical** in which the conception
of murder is merely imaginary at this point    **141 single . . . man** weak
human condition    **142 function** normal power of action.    **surmise**
speculation, imaginings    **143 And . . . not** and everything seems
unreal.    **146 stir** bestirring (myself).    **come** i.e., which have come
**147–8 cleave . . . use** do not take the shape of the wearer until often
worn. (Macbeth is often connected in the text with clothes that don't
really fit him.)    **149 Time . . . day** time moves relentlessly on, no matter what else happens.    **150 stay** wait    **151 favor** pardon.    **wrought**
shaped, preoccupied    **153 registered** recorded (in my memory)
**155 at more time** at a time of greater leisure    **156 weighed it** given
opportunity for reflection on its meaning    **157 Our free hearts** our
hearts freely
**1.4. Location: Forres. The palace.**
**2 in commission** having warrant (to see to the execution of Cawdor)

**8 Became** graced, befitted    **9 been studied** made it his study
**10 owed** owned    **11 careless** uncared for    **16 before** ahead (in
deserving)    **19–20 That . . . mine** that I might have thanked and
rewarded you in ample proportion to your worth.    **25 Are . . .
servants** are like children and servants in relation to your throne
and dignity, existing only to serve you    **27 Safe . . . honor** to safeguard you whom we love and honor.    **34 Wanton** unrestrained
**37 We** (The royal "we.")    **establish our estate** fix the succession of
the kingdom    **39 Prince of Cumberland** title of the heir apparent
to the Scottish throne    **40 Not . . . only** not be bestowed on Malcolm
alone; other deserving nobles are to share honors    **42 Inverness** the
seat or location of Macbeth's castle, Dunsinane    **43 bind . . . you** put
me further in your (Macbeth's) obligation by your hospitality.

MACBETH

The rest is labor which is not used for you. 44
I'll be myself the harbinger and make joyful 45
The hearing of my wife with your approach;
So humbly take my leave.

DUNCAN            My worthy Cawdor!

MACBETH [*aside*]

The Prince of Cumberland! That is a step
On which I must fall down or else o'erleap,
For in my way it lies. Stars, hide your fires; 50
Let not light see my black and deep desires.
The eye wink at the hand; yet let that be 52
Which the eye fears, when it is done, to see.   *Exit.* 53

DUNCAN

True, worthy Banquo. He is full so valiant, 54
And in his commendations I am fed; 55
It is a banquet to me. Let's after him,
Whose care is gone before to bid us welcome.
It is a peerless kinsman.      *Flourish. Exeunt.*

❖

# 1.5

*Enter Macbeth's Wife, alone, with a letter.*

LADY MACBETH [*reads*]   "They met me in the day of success; and I have learned by the perfect'st report they 2
have more in them than mortal knowledge. When I
burnt in desire to question them further, they made
themselves air, into which they vanished. Whiles I
stood rapt in the wonder of it came missives from the 6
King, who all-hailed me 'Thane of Cawdor,' by which
title, before, these Weird Sisters saluted me, and referred me to the coming on of time with 'Hail, king
that shalt be!' This have I thought good to deliver thee, 10
my dearest partner of greatness, that thou mightst not
lose the dues of rejoicing by being ignorant of what
greatness is promised thee. Lay it to thy heart, and
farewell."
Glamis thou art, and Cawdor, and shalt be
What thou art promised. Yet do I fear thy nature; 16
It is too full o'th' milk of human kindness
To catch the nearest way. Thou wouldst be great,
Art not without ambition, but without
The illness should attend it. What thou wouldst
   highly, 20
That wouldst thou holily; wouldst not play false,

And yet wouldst wrongly win. Thou'dst have, great
   Glamis,
That which cries "Thus thou must do," if thou have it, 23
And that which rather thou dost fear to do 24
Than wishest should be undone. Hie thee hither, 25
That I may pour my spirits in thine ear
And chastise with the valor of my tongue
All that impedes thee from the golden round 28
Which fate and metaphysical aid doth seem 29
To have thee crowned withal.

*Enter [a servant as] Messenger.*

                  What is your tidings? 30

MESSENGER

The King comes here tonight.

LADY MACBETH           Thou'rt mad to say it!
Is not thy master with him, who, were't so,
Would have informed for preparation? 33

MESSENGER

So please you, it is true. Our thane is coming.
One of my fellows had the speed of him, 35
Who, almost dead for breath, had scarcely more
Than would make up his message.

LADY MACBETH          Give him tending; 37
He brings great news.       *Exit Messenger.*
           The raven himself is hoarse
That croaks the fatal entrance of Duncan
Under my battlements. Come, you spirits
That tend on mortal thoughts, unsex me here 41
And fill me from the crown to the toe top-full
Of direst cruelty! Make thick my blood;
Stop up th'access and passage to remorse, 44
That no compunctious visitings of nature 45
Shake my fell purpose, nor keep peace between 46
Th'effect and it! Come to my woman's breasts 47
And take my milk for gall, you murd'ring ministers, 48
Wherever in your sightless substances 49
You wait on nature's mischief! Come, thick night, 50
And pall thee in the dunnest smoke of hell, 51
That my keen knife see not the wound it makes,
Nor heaven peep through the blanket of the dark
To cry "Hold, hold!"

*Enter Macbeth.*

         Great Glamis! Worthy Cawdor! 54
Greater than both by the all-hail hereafter!
Thy letters have transported me beyond 56

---

**44 The rest . . . you** All activity not devoted to serving you is mere tediousness and hard work.   **45 harbinger** forerunner, messenger   **50 in my way it lies** (The monarchy was not hereditary, and Macbeth had a right to believe that he himself might be chosen as Duncan's successor; he here questions whether he will interfere with the course of events.)   **52–3 The eye . . . see** Let the eye shut itself and not see the hand's deed; yet when the deed is done, let it be fearful to behold.   **54 full so valiant** fully as valiant as you say. (Apparently, Duncan and Banquo have been conversing privately on this subject during Macbeth's soliloquy.)   **55 in . . . fed** it nourishes me to hear him praised
**1.5. Location:** Inverness. Macbeth's castle.
**2 perfect'st** most accurate   **6 missives** messengers   **10 deliver thee** inform you of   **16 do I fear** I mistrust   **20 illness** evil (that). **highly** greatly

**23 have** are to have, want to have   **24–5 And that . . . undone** i.e., and the thing you ambitiously crave frightens you more in terms of the means needed to achieve it than in the idea of having it; if you could have it without those means, you certainly wouldn't wish it undone.   **25 Hie** Hasten   **28 round** crown   **29 metaphysical** super-natural   **30 withal** with.   **33 informed for preparation** i.e., sent me word so that I might get things ready.   **35 had . . . of** outstripped **37 Give him tending** Tend to his needs   **41 tend . . . thoughts** attend on, act as the instruments of, deadly or murderous thoughts **44 remorse** pity   **45 nature** natural feelings   **46 fell** fierce, cruel **46–7 nor . . . and it** nor intervene between my *fell purpose* and its accomplishment.   **48 for gall** in exchange for gall, or perhaps *as* gall. **ministers** agents   **49 sightless** invisible   **50 You . . . mischief** you aid and abet the wickedness of human nature.   **51 pall** envelop. **dunnest** darkest   **54 Hold** Stop   **56 letters have** i.e., letter has

This ignorant present, and I feel now 57
The future in the instant.

MACBETH                    My dearest love, 58
Duncan comes here tonight.

LADY MACBETH                    And when goes hence?

MACBETH
Tomorrow, as he purposes.

LADY MACBETH                    Oh, never
Shall sun that morrow see!
Your face, my thane, is as a book where men
May read strange matters. To beguile the time, 63
Look like the time; bear welcome in your eye, 64
Your hand, your tongue. Look like th'innocent flower,
But be the serpent under't. He that's coming
Must be provided for; and you shall put
This night's great business into my dispatch, 68
Which shall to all our nights and days to come
Give solely sovereign sway and masterdom.

MACBETH
We will speak further.

LADY MACBETH                    Only look up clear. 71
To alter favor ever is to fear. 72
Leave all the rest to me.                    *Exeunt.*

❖

# 1.6

*Hautboys and torches. Enter King [Duncan],
Malcolm, Donalbain, Banquo, Lennox, Macduff,
Ross, Angus, and attendants.*

DUNCAN
This castle hath a pleasant seat. The air 1
Nimbly and sweetly recommends itself
Unto our gentle senses.

BANQUO                    This guest of summer, 3
The temple-haunting martlet, does approve 4
By his loved mansionry that the heaven's breath 5
Smells wooingly here. No jutty, frieze, 6
Buttress, nor coign of vantage but this bird 7
Hath made his pendent bed and procreant cradle. 8
Where they most breed and haunt, I have observed
The air is delicate.

*Enter Lady [Macbeth].*

DUNCAN                    See, see, our honored hostess!
The love that follows us sometime is our trouble, 11
Which still we thank as love. Herein I teach you 12

---

How you shall bid God 'ild us for your pains, 13
And thank us for your trouble.

LADY MACBETH                    All our service
In every point twice done, and then done double,
Were poor and single business to contend 16
Against those honors deep and broad wherewith 17
Your Majesty loads our house. For those of old, 18
And the late dignities heaped up to them, 19
We rest your hermits.

DUNCAN                    Where's the Thane of Cawdor? 20
We coursed him at the heels, and had a purpose 21
To be his purveyor; but he rides well, 22
And his great love, sharp as his spur, hath holp him 23
To his home before us. Fair and noble hostess,
We are your guest tonight.

LADY MACBETH                    Your servants ever 25
Have theirs, themselves, and what is theirs in compt 26
To make their audit at Your Highness' pleasure, 27
Still to return your own.

DUNCAN                    Give me your hand. 28
Conduct me to mine host. We love him highly,
And shall continue our graces towards him.
By your leave, hostess.                    *Exeunt.*

❖

# 1.7

*Hautboys. Torches. Enter a sewer, and divers
servants with dishes and service, [and pass] over
the stage. Then enter Macbeth.*

MACBETH
If it were done when 'tis done, then 'twere well
It were done quickly. If th'assassination 2
Could trammel up the consequence, and catch 3
With his surcease success—that but this blow 4
Might be the be-all and the end-all!—here, 5
But here, upon this bank and shoal of time,
We'd jump the life to come. But in these cases 7

---

**57–8 I feel . . . instant** I sense a glorious future almost as though it were with us right now.   **63–4 To beguile . . . time** To deceive everyone, look the way people expect you to look   **68 dispatch** management   **71–2 Only . . . fear** Whatever else you do, keep an innocent countenance. To alter one's countenance is to betray a guilty conscience.
**1.6. Location: Before Macbeth's castle.**
**0.1** *Hautboys* oboelike instruments   **1 seat** site.   **3 gentle** (1) noble (2) refined (by the delicate air)   **4–5 The . . . mansionry** The house martin, that loves to nest in churches, proves by his devoted nest building   **6 jutty** projection of wall or building   **7 coign of vantage** convenient corner, i.e., for nesting   **8 pendent** hanging, suspended. **procreant** for breeding   **11–12 The love . . . love** The love that sometimes forces itself inconveniently upon us we still appreciate, since it is meant as love. (Duncan is graciously suggesting that his visit is a bother, but, he hopes, a welcome one.)

**13 bid . . . pains** ask God to reward me for the trouble I'm giving you. (This is said in the same gently jocose spirit as lines 11–12.)   **'ild** yield, repay   **16–17 Were . . . Against** would be poor and small when compared with   **18–20 For . . . hermits** In gratitude for the dignities heaped upon us in former days and still others more recently added to them, we are your thankful worshipers who pray for you like hermits or beadsmen.   **21 coursed** followed (as in a hunt)   **22 purveyor** an officer sent ahead to provide for entertainment; here, forerunner   **23 holp** helped   **25 We** (the royal "we," also in lines 13–14 and 29)
**25–8 Your . . . own** Those who serve you hold their own servants, themselves, and all their possessions in trust from you, and can render an account whenever you wish, ready always to render back to you what is yours. (A feudal concept of obligation.)
**1.7. Location: Macbeth's castle; an inner courtyard.**
**0.1** *sewer* chief waiter, butler   **2–4 If . . . success** i.e., If only the assassination of Duncan could proceed without further consequences and end the matter with the completion of the deed itself. (To *trammel* is to bind up or entangle in a net; *surcease* means "cessation"; *success* means "what succeeds or follows.")   **4 that but** so that only   **5 here** in this world   **7 jump** risk. (But imaging the physical act is characteristic of Macbeth; compare this with line 27.)

We still have judgment here, that we but teach 8
Bloody instructions, which, being taught, return 9
To plague th'inventor. This evenhanded justice 10
Commends th'ingredience of our poisoned chalice 11
To our own lips. He's here in double trust:
First, as I am his kinsman and his subject,
Strong both against the deed; then, as his host,
Who should against his murderer shut the door,
Not bear the knife myself. Besides, this Duncan
Hath borne his faculties so meek, hath been 17
So clear in his great office, that his virtues 18
Will plead like angels, trumpet-tongued, against
The deep damnation of his taking-off; 20
And Pity, like a naked newborn babe
Striding the blast, or heaven's cherubin, horsed 22
Upon the sightless couriers of the air, 23
Shall blow the horrid deed in every eye,
That tears shall drown the wind. I have no spur 25
To prick the sides of my intent, but only
Vaulting ambition, which o'erleaps itself
And falls on th'other— 28

*Enter Lady [Macbeth].*

How now, what news?

LADY MACBETH
He has almost supped. Why have you left the
chamber?

MACBETH
Hath he asked for me?

LADY MACBETH                    Know you not he has?

MACBETH
We will proceed no further in this business.
He hath honored me of late, and I have bought 33
Golden opinions from all sorts of people,
Which would be worn now in their newest gloss, 35
Not cast aside so soon.

LADY MACBETH                    Was the hope drunk
Wherein you dressed yourself? Hath it slept since? 37
And wakes it now, to look so green and pale 38
At what it did so freely? From this time 39
Such I account thy love. Art thou afeard
To be the same in thine own act and valor 41
As thou art in desire? Wouldst thou have that 42
Which thou esteem'st the ornament of life, 43
And live a coward in thine own esteem,
Letting "I dare not" wait upon "I would," 45

Like the poor cat i'th' adage?

MACBETH                    Prithee, peace! 46
I dare do all that may become a man;
Who dares do more is none.

LADY MACBETH                    What beast was't, then,
That made you break this enterprise to me? 49
When you durst do it, then you were a man;
And, to be more than what you were, you would 51
Be so much more the man. Nor time nor place 52
Did then adhere, and yet you would make both. 53
They have made themselves, and that their fitness
now 54
Does unmake you. I have given suck, and know
How tender 'tis to love the babe that milks me;
I would, while it was smiling in my face,
Have plucked my nipple from his boneless gums
And dashed the brains out, had I so sworn as you
Have done to this.

MACBETH                    If we should fail?

LADY MACBETH                    We fail?
But screw your courage to the sticking place 61
And we'll not fail. When Duncan is asleep—
Whereto the rather shall his day's hard journey
Soundly invite him—his two chamberlains 64
Will I with wine and wassail so convince 65
That memory, the warder of the brain, 66
Shall be a fume, and the receipt of reason 67
A limbeck only. When in swinish sleep 68
Their drenchèd natures lies as in a death, 69
What cannot you and I perform upon
Th'unguarded Duncan? What not put upon
His spongy officers, who shall bear the guilt 72
Of our great quell?

MACBETH                    Bring forth men-children only! 73
For thy undaunted mettle should compose 74
Nothing but males. Will it not be received, 75
When we have marked with blood those sleepy two
Of his own chamber and used their very daggers,
That they have done't?

LADY MACBETH                    Who dares receive it other, 78
As we shall make our griefs and clamor roar 79
Upon his death?

MACBETH                    I am settled, and bend up 80
Each corporal agent to this terrible feat. 81

---

**8–10 We . . . th'inventor** i.e., we still have punishment for crime in this world, whereby our bloody acts establish guilty precedents and thereby invite the just reciprocity of punishing blood with blood.   **11 Commends** presents.   **th'ingredience** the contents of a mixture   **17 faculties** authority   **18 clear** free of taint   **20 taking-off** murder   **22 Striding the blast** bestriding the tempest. (Putti and cherubs are often portrayed this way in Renaissance graphic arts.)   **23 sightless couriers** invisible steeds or runners, i.e., the winds   **25 tears . . . wind** (Showers of rain were popularly supposed to still the wind.)   **28 th'other** the other side. (The image is of a horseman vaulting into his saddle and ignominiously falling on the opposite side.)   **33 bought** acquired (by bravery in battle)
**35 would** ought to, should   **37 dressed yourself?** i.e., put on the "newest gloss" (line 35) that you have won by your bravery?   **38 green** sickly   **39 At . . . freely** i.e., at what it dared to hope for by killing Duncan.
**41–2 To . . . desire?** i.e., to undertake valiantly what you desire?   **43 the ornament of life** i.e., the crown   **45 wait upon** accompany, always follow

**46 adage** (i.e., "The cat would eat fish but she will not wet her feet.")
**49 break** broach   **51–2 to be . . . the man** for you to seize the opportunity of becoming far greater than before would surely be a manifestation of true manhood.   **52 Nor** Neither   **53 adhere** agree, suit.
**would** wanted to   **54 that their fitness** that very suitability of time and place   **61 But** Only.   **the sticking place** the notch into which is fitted the string of a crossbow cranked taut for shooting   **64 chamberlains** attendants on the bedchamber   **65 wassail** carousal, drink.   **convince** overpower   **66–8 warder . . . only** (The brain was thought to be divided into three ventricles: imagination in front, memory at the back, and between them the seat of reason. The fumes of wine, arising from the stomach, would deaden memory and judgment.)   **67 receipt** receptacle, ventricle   **68 limbeck** device for distilling liquids   **69 drenchèd** drowned (in wine)   **72 spongy** soaked, drunken   **73 quell** murder.
**74 mettle** (the same word as *metal*): substance, temperament
**75 received** i.e., as truth   **78 other** otherwise   **79 As** inasmuch as
**80–1 bend up . . . agent** harness and direct every part of me

Away, and mock the time with fairest show.    82
False face must hide what the false heart doth know.
             *Exeunt.*

❖

# 2.1

*Enter Banquo, and Fleance, with a torch before him.*

BANQUO   How goes the night, boy?

FLEANCE
The moon is down. I have not heard the clock.

BANQUO
And she goes down at twelve.

FLEANCE            I take't, 'tis later, sir.    3

BANQUO
Hold, take my sword. [*He gives him his sword.*] There's
   husbandry in heaven;    4
Their candles are all out. Take thee that too.
           [*He gives him his belt and dagger.*]
A heavy summons lies like lead upon me,    6
And yet I would not sleep. Merciful powers,    7
Restrain in me the cursèd thoughts that nature
Gives way to in repose!

*Enter Macbeth, and a Servant with a torch.*

Give me my sword. Who's there? [*He takes his sword.*]

MACBETH   A friend.

BANQUO
What, sir, not yet at rest? The King's abed.
He hath been in unusual pleasure,
And sent forth great largess to your offices.    14
This diamond he greets your wife withal,
By the name of most kind hostess, and shut up    16
In measureless content.     [*He gives a diamond.*]

MACBETH         Being unprepared,    17
Our will became the servant to defect,    18
Which else should free have wrought.    19

BANQUO   All's well.
I dreamt last night of the three Weird Sisters.
To you they have showed some truth.

MACBETH            I think not of them.
Yet, when we can entreat an hour to serve,
We would spend it in some words upon that business,
If you would grant the time.

BANQUO           At your kind'st leisure.

MACBETH
If you shall cleave to my consent when 'tis,    26
It shall make honor for you.

BANQUO           So I lose none    27
In seeking to augment it, but still keep
My bosom franchised and allegiance clear,    29
I shall be counseled.

MACBETH           Good repose the while!    30

BANQUO   Thanks, sir. The like to you.
          *Exit Banquo [with Fleance].*

MACBETH [*to Servant*]
Go bid thy mistress, when my drink is ready,    32
She strike upon the bell. Get thee to bed.
          *Exit [Servant].*
Is this a dagger which I see before me,
The handle toward my hand? Come, let me clutch
   thee.
I have thee not, and yet I see thee still.
Art thou not, fatal vision, sensible    37
To feeling as to sight? Or art thou but
A dagger of the mind, a false creation,
Proceeding from the heat-oppressèd brain?    40
I see thee yet, in form as palpable
As this which now I draw.     [*He draws a dagger.*]
Thou marshall'st me the way that I was going,    43
And such an instrument I was to use.
Mine eyes are made the fools o'th'other senses,
Or else worth all the rest. I see thee still,
And on thy blade and dudgeon gouts of blood,    47
Which was not so before. There's no such thing.
It is the bloody business which informs    49
Thus to mine eyes. Now o'er the one half world
Nature seems dead, and wicked dreams abuse    51
The curtained sleep. Witchcraft celebrates    52
Pale Hecate's offerings, and withered Murder,    53
Alarumed by his sentinel, the wolf,    54
Whose howl's his watch, thus with his stealthy pace,    55
With Tarquin's ravishing strides, towards his design    56
Moves like a ghost. Thou sure and firm-set earth,
Hear not my steps which way they walk, for fear
Thy very stones prate of my whereabout
And take the present horror from the time    60
Which now suits with it. Whiles I threat, he lives;    61

---

**26 cleave . . . 'tis** give me your support, adhere to my view, when the time comes   **27 So** Provided that   **29 franchised** free (from guilt). **clear** unstained   **30 counseled** receptive to suggestion.   **32 drink** i.e., posset or bedtime drink of hot spiced milk curdled with ale or wine, as also in 2.2.6   **37 fatal** ominous.   **sensible** perceivable by the senses   **40 heat-oppressèd** fevered   **43 Thou . . . going** You seem to guide me toward the destiny I intended, toward Duncan's chambers   **47 dudgeon** hilt of a dagger.   **gouts** drops   **49 informs** creates images   **51 abuse** deceive   **52 curtained** curtained by night (and by bedcurtains)   **53 Pale Hecate's offerings** sacrificial offerings to Hecate, the goddess of night and witchcraft. (She is *pale* because she is identified with the pale moon.)   **withered** (Murder is pictured as in images of Death, shrunken and wasted.)   **54 Alarumed** given the signal to action   **55 watch** watchword or cry   **56 Tarquin's** (Tarquin was a Roman tyrant who ravished Lucrece.)   **60–1 And take . . . with it** and thus echo and augment the horror which is so suited to this evil hour, or, usurp the present horror by breaking the silence. **61 Whiles I threat** i.e., While I merely threaten to kill Duncan

---

**82 mock** deceive
**2.1. Location:** Inner courtyard of Macbeth's castle. Time is virtually continuous from the previous scene.
**0.1 torch** (This may mean "torchbearer," although it does not at line 9.1.)
**3 she** the moon   **4 husbandry** thrift (careful management of resources in the domestic economy)   **6 summons** i.e., to sleep   **7 would not** am reluctant to (owing to my uneasy fears).   **powers** order of angels deputed by God to resist demons   **14 largess** gifts, gratuities. **offices** quarters used for the household work.   **16–17 and shut . . . content** and went to bed professing himself endlessly pleased.
**18–19 Our . . . wrought** our good will (to entertain the King) was limited by our meager resources (on such short notice), which otherwise would have poured forth hospitality without restraint.

Words to the heat of deeds too cold breath gives.              62
                                        *A bell rings.*

I go, and it is done. The bell invites me.
Hear it not, Duncan, for it is a knell
That summons thee to heaven or to hell.              *Exit.*

❧

## 2.2

*Enter Lady [Macbeth].*

LADY MACBETH
That which hath made them drunk hath made me
    bold;
What hath quenched them hath given me fire. Hark!
    Peace!
It was the owl that shrieked, the fatal bellman,              3
Which gives the stern'st good-night. He is about it.              4
The doors are open; and the surfeited grooms              5
Do mock their charge with snores. I have drugged
    their possets,              6
That death and nature do contend about them              7
Whether they live or die.
MACBETH [*within*]              Who's there? What, ho!              8
LADY MACBETH
Alack, I am afraid they have awaked,
And 'tis not done. Th'attempt and not the deed
Confounds us. Hark! I laid their daggers ready;              11
He could not miss 'em. Had he not resembled              12
My father as he slept, I had done't.

*Enter Macbeth, [bearing bloody daggers].*

My husband!
MACBETH
I have done the deed. Didst thou not hear a noise?
LADY MACBETH
I heard the owl scream and the crickets cry.              16
Did not you speak?
MACBETH   When?
LADY MACBETH   Now.
MACBETH   As I descended?
LADY MACBETH   Ay.
MACBETH   Hark! Who lies i'th' second chamber?
LADY MACBETH   Donalbain.
MACBETH [*looking at his hands*]   This is a sorry sight.
LADY MACBETH
A foolish thought, to say a sorry sight.
MACBETH
There's one did laugh in 's sleep, and one cried
    "Murder!"
That they did wake each other. I stood and heard
    them.

But they did say their prayers, and addressed them              28
Again to sleep.
LADY MACBETH   There are two lodged together.
MACBETH
One cried "God bless us!" and "Amen!" the other,
As they had seen me with these hangman's hands.              31
List'ning their fear, I could not say "Amen"
When they did say "God bless us!"
LADY MACBETH   Consider it not so deeply.
MACBETH
But wherefore could not I pronounce "Amen"?
I had most need of blessing, and "Amen"
Stuck in my throat.
LADY MACBETH         These deeds must not be thought              37
After these ways; so, it will make us mad.              38
MACBETH
Methought I heard a voice cry "Sleep no more!
Macbeth does murder sleep," the innocent sleep,
Sleep that knits up the raveled sleave of care,              41
The death of each day's life, sore labor's bath,              42
Balm of hurt minds, great nature's second course,              43
Chief nourisher in life's feast—
LADY MACBETH                         What do you mean?
MACBETH
Still it cried "Sleep no more!" to all the house;
"Glamis hath murdered sleep, and therefore Cawdor
Shall sleep no more; Macbeth shall sleep no more."
LADY MACBETH
Who was it that thus cried? Why, worthy thane,
You do unbend your noble strength to think              49
So brainsickly of things. Go get some water
And wash this filthy witness from your hand.              51
Why did you bring these daggers from the place?
They must lie there. Go, carry them and smear
The sleepy grooms with blood.
MACBETH                         I'll go no more.
I am afraid to think what I have done;
Look on't again I dare not.
LADY MACBETH                    Infirm of purpose!
Give me the daggers. The sleeping and the dead
Are but as pictures. 'Tis the eye of childhood
That fears a painted devil. If he do bleed,
I'll gild the faces of the grooms withal,              60
For it must seem their guilt.
        [*She takes the daggers, and] exit. Knock within.*
MACBETH                         Whence is that knocking?
How is't with me, when every noise appalls me?
What hands are here? Ha! They pluck out mine eyes.
Will all great Neptune's ocean wash this blood
Clean from my hand? No, this my hand will rather
The multitudinous seas incarnadine,              66

62 **Words . . . gives** Words give only lifeless expression to live deeds, are no substitute for deeds.
**2.2. Location: Scene continues.**
3 **bellman** one who rings a bell to announce a death or to mark the hours of the night   4 **Which . . . good-night** i.e., that announces the last good-night, death.   5 **grooms** servants   6 **mock their charge** make a mockery of their guard duty.   **possets** hot bedtime drinks (as in 2.1.32)   7–8 **That . . . die** that they almost seem more dead than alive.   11 **Confounds** ruins   12 **He** Macbeth.   **he** Duncan   16 **owl, crickets** (The sounds of both could be ominous and prophetic of death.)

28 **addressed them** settled themselves   31 **As** as if.   **hangman's hands** bloody hands of the executioner.   37 **thought** thought about   38 **so** if we do so   41 **raveled sleave** tangled skein   42 **bath** i.e., to relieve the soreness   43 **second course** (Ordinary feasts had two courses, of which the second was the *chief nourisher;* here, sleep is seen as following eating in a restorative process.)   49 **unbend** slacken (as one would a bow; contrast with "bend up" in 1.7.80)   51 **witness** evidence   60 **gild** smear, coat, as if with a thin layer of gold. (Gold was ordinarily spoken of as red.)   66 **multitudinous** vast and teeming.   **incarnadine** stain red

Making the green one red.                                    67

*Enter Lady [Macbeth].*

LADY MACBETH
My hands are of your color, but I shame
To wear a heart so white. (*Knock.*) I hear a knocking
At the south entry. Retire we to our chamber.
A little water clears us of this deed.
How easy is it, then! Your constancy                          72
Hath left you unattended. (*Knock.*) Hark! More
    knocking.                                                 73
Get on your nightgown, lest occasion call us                  74
And show us to be watchers. Be not lost                       75
So poorly in your thoughts.

MACBETH
To know my deed, 'twere best not know myself.                 77
                                                    *Knock.*

Wake Duncan with thy knocking! I would thou
    couldst!                                        *Exeunt.*

## 2.3

*Knocking within. Enter a Porter.*

PORTER   Here's a knocking indeed! If a man were porter
of hell gate, he should have old turning the key.              2
(*Knock.*) Knock, knock, knock! Who's there, i'th'
name of Beelzebub? Here's a farmer that hanged                 4
himself on th'expectation of plenty. Come in time!             5
Have napkins enough about you; here you'll sweat for't.        6
(*Knock.*) Knock, knock! Who's there, in th'other
devil's name? Faith, here's an equivocator, that could         8
swear in both the scales against either scale, who
committed treason enough for God's sake, yet could
not equivocate to heaven. Oh, come in, equivocator.
(*Knock.*) Knock, knock, knock! Who's there? Faith,
here's an English tailor come hither for stealing out of      13
a French hose. Come in, tailor. Here you may roast            14
your goose. (*Knock.*) Knock, knock! Never at quiet!          15

---

**67 one red** one all-pervading red.   **72–3 Your . . . unattended** Your preoccupation with yourself has left you inattentive to other matters.
**74 nightgown** dressing gown   **75 to be watchers** to have been awake and
not abed.   **77 To know . . . myself** To come to terms with what I have
done, I would do best to shut out the horror entirely and deny who I am.
**2.3. Location: Scene continues. The knocking at the door has
already been heard in 2.2. It is not necessary to assume literally,
however, that Macbeth and Lady Macbeth have been talking near
the** *south entry* **(2.2.70) where the knocking is heard.**
**2 old** plenty of   **4 Beelzebub** a devil.   **4–5 Here's . . . plenty** i.e.,
Here's a farmer who has hoarded in anticipation of a scarcity and will
be justly punished by a crop surplus and low prices.   **5 Come in
time!** i.e., You have come in good time!   **6 napkins** handkerchiefs or
towels (to mop up the sweat)   **8 equivocator** (This is regarded by
many editors as an allusion to the trial of the Jesuit Henry Garnet for
treason in the spring of 1606 and to the doctrine of equivocation said
to have been presented in his defense; according to this doctrine, a lie
was not a lie if the utterer had in his mind a different meaning in
which the utterance was true.)   **13–14 for stealing . . . hose** (French
fashions, much in demand by style-conscious courtiers, no doubt provided opportunities for tailors to skimp in the making of garments
while charging customers the full amount.)   **14–15 roast your goose**
heat your tailor's smoothing iron—something easily done in the
flames of hell. (With a pun on the sense, "cook your goose." A *goose*
could also be a long-handled iron, or a prostitute.)

What are you? But this place is too cold for hell. I'll
devil-porter it no further. I had thought to have let in
some of all professions that go the primrose way to
th'everlasting bonfire. (*Knock.*) Anon, anon! [*He opens the
gate.*] I pray you, remember the porter.

*Enter Macduff and Lennox.*

MACDUFF
Was it so late, friend, ere you went to bed,
That you do lie so late?

PORTER   Faith, sir, we were carousing till the second      23
cock; and drink, sir, is a great provoker of three things.   24

MACDUFF   What three things does drink especially
provoke?

PORTER   Marry, sir, nose-painting, sleep, and urine.       27
Lechery, sir, it provokes and unprovokes: it provokes
the desire but it takes away the performance. Therefore much drink may be said to be an equivocator
with lechery: it makes him and it mars him; it sets him
on and it takes him off; it persuades him and dis-
heartens him, makes him stand to and not stand to;         33
in conclusion, equivocates him in a sleep and, giving      34
him the lie, leaves him.                                    35

MACDUFF   I believe drink gave thee the lie last night.    36

PORTER   That it did, sir, i'the very throat on me. But I   37
requited him for his lie, and, I think, being too strong
for him, though he took up my legs sometimes, yet I         39
made a shift to cast him.                                   40

MACDUFF   Is thy master stirring?

*Enter Macbeth.*

Our knocking has awaked him. Here he comes.
                                            [*Exit Porter.*]
LENNOX
Good morrow, noble sir.

MACBETH                             Good morrow, both.

MACDUFF
Is the King stirring, worthy thane?

MACBETH                                        Not yet.

MACDUFF
He did command me to call timely on him.                    45
I have almost slipped the hour.

MACBETH                             I'll bring you to him.   46

MACDUFF
I know this is a joyful trouble to you,
But yet 'tis one.

---

**23–4 second cock** second crowing of the cock before dawn; 3:00 a.m.
**27 Marry** (Originally, an oath, "by the Virgin Mary.")   **nose-painting**
i.e., reddening of the nose through drink   **33 makes . . . not stand to**
arouses him sexually but then takes away the ability to perform sexually. (Repeating the idea of the previous phrases about how it *makes
him and mars him*, etc.)   **34 equivocates . . . sleep** (1) lulls him asleep
(2) gives him an erotic experience in dream only   **34–5 giving him
the lie** (1) deceiving him (2) laying him out flat   **35 leaves him**
(1) dissipates as intoxication (2) is passed off as urine.   **36 gave thee
the lie** (1) called you a liar (2) made you unable to stand and put you
to sleep   **37 i'the . . . me** (1) giving me the deepest insult imaginable
(2) literally, going down my throat. (*On* means "of.")   **39 took . . .
legs** made me unable to stand and threw me to the ground as a
wrestler might do   **40 made a shift** managed.   **cast** (1) throw, as in
wrestling (2) vomit   **45 timely** betimes, early   **46 slipped** let slip

MACBETH
The labor we delight in physics pain.                                    49
This is the door.
MACDUFF          I'll make so bold to call,
For 'tis my limited service.                    *Exit Macduff.*    51
LENNOX    Goes the King hence today?
MACBETH    He does; he did appoint so.
LENNOX
The night has been unruly. Where we lay,
Our chimneys were blown down, and, as they say,
Lamentings heard i'th'air, strange screams of death,
And prophesying with accents terrible                          57
Of dire combustion and confused events                         58
New hatched to th' woeful time. The obscure bird               59
Clamored the livelong night. Some say the earth
Was feverous and did shake.
MACBETH                              'Twas a rough night.
LENNOX
My young remembrance cannot parallel
A fellow to it.

          *Enter Macduff.*

MACDUFF          Oh, horror, horror, horror!
Tongue nor heart cannot conceive nor name thee!
MACBETH AND LENNOX    What's the matter?
MACDUFF
Confusion now hath made his masterpiece!                       66
Most sacrilegious murder hath broke ope
The Lord's anointed temple and stole thence                    68
The life o'th' building!
MACBETH    What is't you say? The life?
LENNOX    Mean you His Majesty?
MACDUFF
Approach the chamber and destroy your sight
With a new Gorgon. Do not bid me speak;                        73
See, and then speak yourselves.
                    *Exeunt Macbeth and Lennox.*
                    Awake, awake!
Ring the alarum bell. Murder and treason!
Banquo and Donalbain, Malcolm, awake!
Shake off this downy sleep, death's counterfeit,               77
And look on death itself! Up, up, and see
The great doom's image! Malcolm, Banquo,                       79
As from your graves rise up and walk like sprites              80
To countenance this horror! Ring the bell.    *Bell rings.*    81

          *Enter Lady [Macbeth].*

LADY MACBETH    What's the business,
That such a hideous trumpet calls to parley                    83

The sleepers of the house? Speak, speak!
MACDUFF    Oh, gentle lady,                                     85
'Tis not for you to hear what I can speak.
The repetition in a woman's ear                                87
Would murder as it fell.

          *Enter Banquo.*

                              Oh, Banquo, Banquo,
Our royal master's murdered!
LADY MACBETH                              Woe, alas!
What, in our house?
BANQUO                    Too cruel anywhere.
Dear Duff, I prithee, contradict thyself
And say it is not so.

          *Enter Macbeth, Lennox, and Ross.*

MACBETH
Had I but died an hour before this chance                      93
I had lived a blessèd time; for from this instant
There's nothing serious in mortality.                          95
All is but toys. Renown and grace is dead;                     96
The wine of life is drawn, and the mere lees                   97
Is left this vault to brag of.                                 98

          *Enter Malcolm and Donalbain.*

DONALBAIN
What is amiss?
MACBETH          You are, and do not know't.
The spring, the head, the fountain of your blood
Is stopped, the very source of it is stopped.
MACDUFF
Your royal father's murdered.
MALCOLM                              Oh, by whom?
LENNOX
Those of his chamber, as it seemed, had done't.
Their hands and faces were all badged with blood;             104
So were their daggers, which unwiped we found
Upon their pillows. They stared and were distracted;
No man's life was to be trusted with them.
MACBETH
Oh, yet I do repent me of my fury,
That I did kill them.
MACDUFF                    Wherefore did you so?             109
MACBETH
Who can be wise, amazed, temp'rate and furious,             110
Loyal and neutral, in a moment? No man.
Th'expedition of my violent love                             112
Outran the pauser, reason. Here lay Duncan,
His silver skin laced with his golden blood,                 114
And his gashed stabs looked like a breach in nature          115
For ruin's wasteful entrance; there the murderers,           116
Steeped in the colors of their trade, their daggers

Unmannerly breeched with gore. Who could refrain 118
That had a heart to love, and in that heart
Courage to make 's love known?
LADY MACBETH [*fainting*]        Help me hence, ho! 120
MACDUFF
Look to the lady.
MALCOLM [*aside to Donalbain*]
        Why do we hold our tongues,
That most may claim this argument for ours? 122
DONALBAIN [*aside to Malcolm*]
What should be spoken here, where our fate,
Hid in an auger hole, may rush and seize us? 124
Let's away. Our tears are not yet brewed. 125
MALCOLM [*aside to Donalbain*]
Nor our strong sorrow upon the foot of motion. 126
BANQUO    Look to the lady.

             [*Lady Macbeth is helped out.*]
And when we have our naked frailties hid, 128
That suffer in exposure, let us meet
And question this most bloody piece of work 130
To know it further. Fears and scruples shake us. 131
In the great hand of God I stand, and thence 132
Against the undivulged pretense I fight 133
Of treasonous malice.
MACDUFF      And so do I.
ALL           So all. 134
MACBETH
Let's briefly put on manly readiness 135
And meet i'th' hall together.
ALL           Well contented.
    *Exeunt [all but Malcolm and Donalbain].*
MALCOLM
What will you do? Let's not consort with them. 137
To show an unfelt sorrow is an office
Which the false man does easy. I'll to England. 139
DONALBAIN
To Ireland, I. Our separated fortune
Shall keep us both the safer. Where we are,
There's daggers in men's smiles; the nea'er in blood, 142
The nearer bloody.
MALCOLM    This murderous shaft that's shot 143
Hath not yet lighted, and our safest way 144
Is to avoid the aim. Therefore to horse,
And let us not be dainty of leave-taking, 146
But shift away. There's warrant in that theft 147

Which steals itself when there's no mercy left. 148
                    *Exeunt.*

# 2.4

*Enter Ross with an Old Man.*

OLD MAN
Threescore and ten I can remember well,
Within the volume of which time I have seen
Hours dreadful and things strange, but this sore night 3
Hath trifled former knowings.
ROSS           Ha, good father, 4
Thou see'st the heavens, as troubled with man's act, 5
Threatens his bloody stage. By th' clock 'tis day, 6
And yet dark night strangles the traveling lamp. 7
Is't night's predominance or the day's shame
That darkness does the face of earth entomb
When living light should kiss it?
OLD MAN         'Tis unnatural,
Even like the deed that's done. On Tuesday last
A falcon, tow'ring in her pride of place, 12
Was by a mousing owl hawked at and killed. 13
ROSS
And Duncan's horses—a thing most strange and
    certain—
Beauteous and swift, the minions of their race, 15
Turned wild in nature, broke their stalls, flung out,
Contending 'gainst obedience, as they would 17
Make war with mankind.
OLD MAN     'Tis said they eat each other. 18
ROSS
They did so, to th'amazement of mine eyes
That looked upon't.

    *Enter Macduff.*

              Here comes the good Macduff.—
How goes the world, sir, now?
MACDUFF         Why, see you not?
ROSS
Is't known who did this more than bloody deed?
MACDUFF
Those that Macbeth hath slain.
ROSS           Alas the day,
What good could they pretend?
MACDUFF        They were suborned. 24
Malcolm and Donalbain, the King's two sons,
Are stol'n away and fled, which puts upon them
Suspicion of the deed.
ROSS          'Gainst nature still!

---

**118 breeched with gore** covered (as with breeches) to the hilts with gore. **120 make 's love known** make manifest his love. **122 That . . . ours** we to whom this business matters most. **124 in an auger hole** i.e., in some hiding place, in ambush. (An *auger* is a hole-drilling tool.) **125 Our . . . brewed** i.e., Our real sorrow has not yet ripened. **126 upon . . . motion** yet prepared to express itself fully. **128 our naked frailties hid** clothed our poor, shivering bodies (which remind us of our human frailty) **130 question** discuss **131 scruples** doubts, suspicions **132–4 thence . . . malice** with God's help, I will fight against the as-yet-unknown purpose that prompted this treason. **133 pretense** design **134 malice** enmity. **135 briefly** quickly. **manly readiness** men's clothing and resolute purpose **137 consort** keep company, associate **139 easy** easily. **142–3 the nea'er . . . bloody** the closer the relationship, the greater the danger to be feared of bloody intent. **144 lighted** alighted, fallen **146 dainty of** tediously ceremonious in **147 shift away** disappear by stealth. **warrant** justification

**148 Which steals itself** i.e., which slips away to avoid danger. **2.4. Location:** Outside Macbeth's castle of Inverness. **3 sore** dreadful, grievous **4 trifled former knowings** made trivial all former experiences. **father** old man **5–6 the heavens . . . stage** the heavens threateningly show their disapproval of this murder by staging a solar eclipse. (With a theatrical metaphor in *heavens* [the decorated roof over the stage], *act*, and *stage*.) **7 the traveling lamp** i.e., the sun. **12 tow'ring** circling higher and higher. (A term in falconry.) **place** pitch, highest point in the falcon's flight **13 mousing** ordinarily preying on mice **15 minions** darlings **17 as** as if **18 eat** ate. (Pronounced "et.") **24 What . . . pretend?** i.e., what could they hope to gain by it? **suborned** bribed, hired.

Thriftless ambition, that will ravin up                    28
Thine own life's means! Then 'tis most like              29
The sovereignty will fall upon Macbeth.
MACDUFF
He is already named and gone to Scone              31
To be invested.
ROSS                    Where is Duncan's body?
MACDUFF    Carried to Colmekill,                        33
The sacred storehouse of his predecessors
And guardian of their bones.
ROSS                          Will you to Scone?
MACDUFF
No, cousin, I'll to Fife.
ROSS                      Well, I will thither.          36
MACDUFF
Well, may you see things well done there. Adieu,
Lest our old robes sit easier than our new!
ROSS    Farewell, father.
OLD MAN
God's benison go with you, and with those        40
That would make good of bad, and friends of foes!  41
                                    *Exeunt omnes.*

❧

# 3.1

*Enter Banquo.*

BANQUO
Thou hast it now—King, Cawdor, Glamis, all
As the weird women promised, and I fear
Thou played'st most foully for't. Yet it was said
It should not stand in thy posterity,
But that myself should be the root and father        4
Of many kings. If there come truth from them—
As upon thee, Macbeth, their speeches shine—
Why, by the verities on thee made good,              7
May they not be my oracles as well
And set me up in hope? But hush, no more.         10

    *Sennet sounded. Enter Macbeth as King, Lady*
    *[Macbeth], Lennox, Ross, lords, and attendants.*

MACBETH
Here's our chief guest.
LADY MACBETH          If he had been forgotten,
It had been as a gap in our great feast
And all-thing unbecoming.                            13
MACBETH
Tonight we hold a solemn supper, sir,                14
And I'll request your presence.
BANQUO                Let Your Highness
Command upon me, to the which my duties           16

Are with a most indissoluble tie
Forever knit.
MACBETH    Ride you this afternoon?
BANQUO    Ay, my good lord.
MACBETH
We should have else desired your good advice,
Which still hath been both grave and prosperous,    22
In this day's council; but we'll take tomorrow.
Is't far you ride?
BANQUO
As far, my lord, as will fill up the time
Twixt this and supper. Go not my horse the better,  26
I must become a borrower of the night
For a dark hour or twain.
MACBETH    Fail not our feast.
BANQUO    My lord, I will not.
MACBETH
We hear our bloody cousins are bestowed           31
In England and in Ireland, not confessing
Their cruel parricide, filling their hearers
With strange invention. But of that tomorrow,      34
When therewithal we shall have cause of state       35
Craving us jointly. Hie you to horse. Adieu,        36
Till you return at night. Goes Fleance with you?
BANQUO
Ay, my good lord. Our time does call upon 's.
MACBETH
I wish your horses swift and sure of foot,
And so I do commend you to their backs.           40
Farewell.                          *Exit Banquo.*
Let every man be master of his time
Till seven at night. To make society
The sweeter welcome, we will keep ourself           44
Till suppertime alone. While then, God be with you!  45
    *Exeunt Lords [and all but Macbeth and a Servant].*
Sirrah, a word with you. Attend those men           46
Our pleasure?
SERVANT
They are, my lord, without the palace gate.         48
MACBETH
Bring them before us.                *Exit Servant.*
                        To be thus is nothing,        49
But to be safely thus.—Our fears in Banquo        50
Stick deep, and in his royalty of nature            51
Reigns that which would be feared. 'Tis much he
   dares;                                            52
And to that dauntless temper of his mind           53
He hath a wisdom that doth guide his valor
To act in safety. There is none but he
Whose being I do fear; and under him
My genius is rebuked, as it is said                 57

---

**28 Thriftless** Spendthrift.   **ravin up** devour ravenously   **29 like**
likely   **31 named** chosen. (See the note for 1.4.50.)   **Scone** ancient
royal city of Scotland near Perth   **33 Colmekill** Icolmkill, i.e., Cell of
St. Columba, the barren islet of Iona in the Western Islands, a sacred
spot where the kings were buried; here, called a *storehouse*   **36 Fife**
(Of which Macduff is Thane.)   **40 bension** blessing   **41.1 omnes** all.
**3.1. Location: Forres. The palace.**
**4 stand** stay, remain   **7 shine** beam favorably   **10.1 Sennet** trumpet call
**13 all-thing** in every way   **14 solemn** ceremonious   **16 Command**
lay your command

**22 still** always.   **grave and prosperous** weighty and profitable
**26 this** this present moment.   **Go ... better** Unless my horse makes better time than I expect   **31 bestowed** lodged   **34 invention** falsehood.
**35 therewithal** besides that   **35–6 cause ... jointly** questions of state
occupying our joint attention.   **40 commend** commit, entrust
**44 we ... ourself** I will keep to myself   **45 While** Till   **46 Sirrah**
(A form of address to a social inferior.)   **48 without** outside   **49 thus**
i.e., king   **50 But** unless.   **in** concerning   **51 royalty of nature** natural
kingly bearing   **52 would be** deserves to be   **53 to** added to   **57 My**
**genius is rebuked** my guardian spirit is daunted or abashed

Mark Antony's was by Caesar. He chid the sisters                    58
When first they put the name of king upon me,
And bade them speak to him. Then, prophetlike,
They hailed him father to a line of kings.
Upon my head they placed a fruitless crown
And put a barren scepter in my grip,
Thence to be wrenched with an unlineal hand,              64
No son of mine succeeding. If't be so,
For Banquo's issue have I filed my mind;                        66
For them the gracious Duncan have I murdered,
Put rancors in the vessel of my peace                              68
Only for them, and mine eternal jewel                            69
Given to the common enemy of man                              70
To make them kings, the seeds of Banquo kings.
Rather than so, come fate into the list,                             72
And champion me to th'utterance!—Who's there?        73

*Enter Servant and two Murderers.*

Now go to the door, and stay there till we call.
                                                            *Exit Servant.*
Was it not yesterday we spoke together?
MURDERERS
  It was, so please Your Highness.
MACBETH                                              Well then, now
  Have you considered of my speeches? Know
  That it was he in the times past which held you         78
  So under fortune, which you thought had been         79
  Our innocent self. This I made good to you
  In our last conference, passed in probation with you  81
  How you were borne in hand, how crossed, the
    instruments,                                                           82
  Who wrought with them, and all things else that
    might                                                                     83
  To half a soul and to a notion crazed                          84
  Say, "Thus did Banquo."
FIRST MURDERER                   You made it known to us.
MACBETH
  I did so, and went further, which is now
  Our point of second meeting. Do you find
  Your patience so predominant in your nature
  That you can let this go? Are you so gospeled           89
  To pray for this good man and for his issue,
  Whose heavy hand hath bowed you to the grave
  And beggared yours forever?
FIRST MURDERER                   We are men, my liege.      92
MACBETH
  Ay, in the catalogue ye go for men,                           93
  As hounds and greyhounds, mongrels, spaniels, curs,

Shoughs, water-rugs, and demi-wolves are clept          95
All by the name of dogs. The valued file                        96
Distinguishes the swift, the slow, the subtle,
The housekeeper, the hunter, every one                        98
According to the gift which bounteous nature
Hath in him closed, whereby he does receive             100
Particular addition from the bill                                    101
That writes them all alike; and so of men.                   102
Now, if you have a station in the file,                          103
Not i'th' worst rank of manhood, say't,                       104
And I will put that business in your bosoms
Whose execution takes your enemy off,                      106
Grapples you to the heart and love of us,
Who wear our health but sickly in his life,                 108
Which in his death were perfect.
SECOND MURDERER                   I am one, my liege,
  Whom the vile blows and buffets of the world
  Hath so incensed that I am reckless what
  I do to spite the world.
FIRST MURDERER                   And I another,
  So weary with disasters, tugged with fortune,         113
  That I would set my life on any chance                    114
  To mend it or be rid on't.
MACBETH                                    Both of you         115
  Know Banquo was your enemy.
BOTH MURDERERS                         True, my lord.
MACBETH
  So is he mine, and in such bloody distance               117
  That every minute of his being thrusts                       118
  Against my near'st of life. And though I could          119
  With barefaced power sweep him from my sight       120
  And bid my will avouch it, yet I must not,                121
  For certain friends that are both his and mine,         122
  Whose loves I may not drop, but wail his fall          123
  Who I myself struck down. And thence it is             124
  That I to your assistance do make love,                     125
  Masking the business from the common eye
  For sundry weighty reasons.
SECOND MURDERER                   We shall, my lord,
  Perform what you command us.
FIRST MURDERER                         Though our lives—
MACBETH
  Your spirits shine through you. Within this hour at
    most                                                                       129
  I will advise you where to plant yourselves,

**58 Caesar** Octavius Caesar.   **64 with** by.   **unlineal** not of lineal descent from me   **66 issue** descendants.   **filed** defiled   **68 rancors** malignant enemies (here visualized as a poison added to a vessel full of wholesome drink)   **69 eternal jewel** i.e., soul   **70 common . . . man** i.e., devil   **72 list** lists, place of combat   **73 champion me** fight with me in single combat.   **to th'utterance** to the last extremity (French, *à l'outrance*).   **78 he** Banquo   **79 under fortune** down in your fortunes   **81–3 passed . . . with them** went over the proof with you how you were deceived by false promises, how you were thwarted, who the agents were, who directed their activities   **84 To . . . crazed** even to a half-wit of unsound mind   **89 gospeled** imbued with the gospel spirit   **92 yours** your family   **93 go for** pass for, are entered for

**95 Shoughs . . . clept** shaggy lap-dogs, long-haired water dogs, and dogs that have been crossbred with wolves are called   **96 valued file** list classified according to value   **98 housekeeper** watchdog   **100 in him closed** enclosed in him   **101–2 Particular . . . alike** particular qualification apart from the catalog that lists them all indiscriminately   **103–4 if . . . manhood** if you occupy not the worst of places in the *rank and file* of men   **106 Whose execution** the doing of which   **108 in his life** while he lives   **113 tugged with** pulled about by (as in wrestling)   **114 set** risk, stake   **115 on't** of it.   **117 distance** (1) hostility, enmity (2) interval of distance between fencers   **118–19 thrusts . . . life** stabs me to the heart.   **120 With barefaced power** by open use of my supreme royal authority   **121 And . . . avouch it** and use my mere wish as my justification   **122 For** because of, for the sake of   **123–4 wail . . . Who** I must bewail the death of him whom   **125 That . . . love** that I woo your aid   **129 Your . . . you** i.e., Enough; I can see your determination in your faces.

Acquaint you with the perfect spy o'th' time,                131
The moment on't, for 't must be done tonight,               132
And something from the palace; always thought               133
That I require a clearness. And with him—                    134
To leave no rubs nor botches in the work—                   135
Fleance his son, that keeps him company,
Whose absence is no less material to me
Than is his father's, must embrace the fate
Of that dark hour. Resolve yourselves apart;                139
I'll come to you anon.
BOTH MURDERERS    We are resolved, my lord.
MACBETH
I'll call upon you straight. Abide within.                  141
                            *Exeunt [Murderers]*.
It is concluded. Banquo, thy soul's flight,
If it find heaven, must find it out tonight.    [*Exit.*]

❧

## 3.2

*Enter Macbeth's Lady and a Servant.*

LADY MACBETH    Is Banquo gone from court?
SERVANT
Ay, madam, but returns again tonight.
LADY MACBETH
Say to the King I would attend his leisure
For a few words.
SERVANT    Madam, I will.                            *Exit.*
LADY MACBETH    Naught's had, all's spent,
Where our desire is got without content.                     7
'Tis safer to be that which we destroy
Than by destruction dwell in doubtful joy.                   9

*Enter Macbeth.*

How now, my lord? Why do you keep alone,
Of sorriest fancies your companions making,                  11
Using those thoughts which should indeed have died           12
With them they think on? Things without all remedy
Should be without regard. What's done is done.               14
MACBETH
We have scorched the snake, not killed it.                   15
She'll close and be herself, whilst our poor malice          16
Remains in danger of her former tooth.                       17
But let the frame of things disjoint, both the worlds
    suffer,                                                  18
Ere we will eat our meal in fear and sleep
In the affliction of these terrible dreams

That shake us nightly. Better be with the dead,
Whom we, to gain our peace, have sent to peace,              22
Than on the torture of the mind to lie                       23
In restless ecstasy. Duncan is in his grave;                24
After life's fitful fever he sleeps well.
Treason has done his worst; nor steel, nor poison,          26
Malice domestic, foreign levy, nothing                       27
Can touch him further.
LADY MACBETH                Come on,
Gentle my lord, sleek o'er your rugged looks.               30
Be bright and jovial among your guests tonight.
MACBETH
So shall I, love, and so, I pray, be you.
Let your remembrance apply to Banquo;                       33
Present him eminence, both with eye and tongue—             34
Unsafe the while, that we                                    35
Must lave our honors in these flattering streams             36
And make our faces vizards to our hearts,                    37
Disguising what they are.
LADY MACBETH                You must leave this.
MACBETH
Oh, full of scorpions is my mind, dear wife!
Thou know'st that Banquo and his Fleance lives.
LADY MACBETH
But in them nature's copy's not eterne.                      41
MACBETH
There's comfort yet; they are assailable.
Then be thou jocund. Ere the bat hath flown
His cloistered flight, ere to black Hecate's summons         44
The shard-borne beetle with his drowsy hums                  45
Hath rung night's yawning peal, there shall be done          46
A deed of dreadful note.
LADY MACBETH                What's to be done?
MACBETH
Be innocent of the knowledge, dearest chuck,                48
Till thou applaud the deed. Come, seeling night,             49
Scarf up the tender eye of pitiful day,                      50
And with thy bloody and invisible hand
Cancel and tear to pieces that great bond                    52
Which keeps me pale! Light thickens,                         53
And the crow makes wing to th' rooky wood;                   54
Good things of day begin to droop and drowse,

---

131–2 with . . . on't with full and precise instructions as to when it is to be done. (*Spy* means "espial, observation.")   133 something from some distance removed from.   thought being borne in mind   134 clearness freedom from suspicion.   135 rubs defects, rough spots   139 Resolve yourselves apart Make up your minds in private conference   141 straight shortly, soon.   Abide Wait
3.2. Location: The palace.
7 content contentedness.   9 Than . . . joy than by destroying achieve only an apprehensive joy.   11 sorriest most despicable or wretched   12 Using keeping company with, entertaining   14 without regard not pondered upon.   15 scorched slashed, cut   16 close heal, close up again.   poor malice feeble hostility   17 her former tooth her fang, just as before.   18 let . . . suffer let the universe itself fall apart, both heaven and earth perish

22 to gain . . . to peace to gain contentedness through satisfied ambition, have sent to eternal rest   23 torture rack   24 ecstasy frenzy.   26 nor steel neither steel   27 Malice domestic civil war.   foreign levy the levying of troops abroad (against Scotland)   30 Gentle . . . looks my noble lord, smooth over your rough looks.   33 Let . . . apply Remember to pay special attention   34 eminence favor   35–6 Unsafe . . . streams we, being unsafe at present, must put on a show of flattering cordiality to make clean our honor. (To *lave* is to wash.)   37 vizards masks   41 nature's . . . eterne nature's lease on life will not continue forever.   44 cloistered secluded, restricted.   Hecate goddess of night and witchcraft, as in 2.1.53   45 shard-borne borne on shards, or horny wing cases, or, *shard-born*, bred in cow-droppings (shards)   46 yawning drowsy   48 chuck (A term of endearment.)   49 seeling eye-closing. (Night is pictured here as a falconer sewing up the eyes of day lest it should struggle against the deed that is to be done.)   50 Scarf up blindfold.   pitiful compassionate   52 that great bond i.e., the bond of natural and moral law (here associated with the full light of day); Banquo's lease on life   53 pale sickly, pallid (like moonlight, contrasted with the full light of day); also, pallid from fear.   Light thickens Darkness is coming on   54 crow rook.   rooky full of rooks

Whiles night's black agents to their preys do rouse. 56
Thou marvel'st at my words, but hold thee still.
Things bad begun make strong themselves by ill.
So, prithee, go with me.                    *Exeunt.*

❖

## 3.3

*Enter three Murderers.*

FIRST MURDERER  [*to the Third Murderer*]
But who did bid thee join with us?
THIRD MURDERER                    Macbeth.
SECOND MURDERER  [*to the First Murderer*]
He needs not our mistrust, since he delivers     2
Our offices and what we have to do               3
To the direction just.
FIRST MURDERER     Then stand with us.          4
The west yet glimmers with some streaks of day.
Now spurs the lated traveler apace             6
To gain the timely inn, and near approaches    7
The subject of our watch.
THIRD MURDERER     Hark, I hear horses.
BANQUO (*within*)  Give us a light there, ho!
SECOND MURDERER    Then 'tis he. The rest
That are within the note of expectation       12
Already are i'th' court.
FIRST MURDERER     His horses go about.       14
THIRD MURDERER
Almost a mile; but he does usually—
So all men do—from hence to th' palace gate
Make it their walk.

*Enter Banquo and Fleance, with a torch.*

SECOND MURDERER   A light, a light!
THIRD MURDERER    'Tis he.
FIRST MURDERER    Stand to't.
BANQUO    It will be rain tonight.
FIRST MURDERER    Let it come down!
                    [*They attack Banquo.*]
BANQUO
Oh, treachery! Fly, good Fleance, fly, fly, fly!
Thou mayst revenge.—Oh, slave!
                [*He dies. Fleance escapes.*]
THIRD MURDERER
Who did strike out the light?
FIRST MURDERER          Was't not the way?   25
THIRD MURDERER
There's but one down; the son is fled.
SECOND MURDERER
We have lost best half of our affair.

FIRST MURDERER
Well, let's away and say how much is done.     28
                    *Exeunt.*

❖

## 3.4

*Banquet prepared. Enter Macbeth, Lady
[Macbeth], Ross, Lennox, Lords, and attendants.*

MACBETH
You know your own degrees; sit down. At first   1
And last, the hearty welcome.        [*They sit.*]
LORDS                    Thanks to Your Majesty.  2
MACBETH
Ourself will mingle with society               3
And play the humble host.
Our hostess keeps her state, but in best time  5
We will require her welcome.                   6
LADY MACBETH
Pronounce it for me, sir, to all our friends,
For my heart speaks they are welcome.

*Enter First Murderer [to the door].*

MACBETH
See, they encounter thee with their hearts' thanks.  9
Both sides are even. Here I'll sit i'th' midst.     10
Be large in mirth; anon we'll drink a measure      11
The table round. [*He goes to the Murderer.*] There's
    blood upon thy face.
MURDERER    'Tis Banquo's, then.
MACBETH
'Tis better thee without than he within.        14
Is he dispatched?
MURDERER
My lord, his throat is cut. That I did for him.
MACBETH    Thou art the best o'th' cutthroats.
Yet he's good that did the like for Fleance;
If thou didst it, thou art the nonpareil.       19
MURDERER    Most royal sir, Fleance is scaped.
MACBETH
Then comes my fit again. I had else been perfect,
Whole as the marble, founded as the rock,       22
As broad and general as the casing air.         23
But now I am cabined, cribbed, confined, bound in 24
To saucy doubts and fears. But Banquo's safe?   25

---

56 to . . . rouse bestir themselves to hunt their prey.
3.3. Location: A park near the palace.
2–4 He . . . just We need not mistrust this man, since the instructions he brings from Macbeth are so precise and so like what Macbeth said to us.   6 lated belated   7 timely arrived at in good time   12 within . . . expectation in the list of those expected   14 go about i.e., can be heard as servants take the horses to the stables (while Banquo and Fleance, provided with a torch, walk from the palace gate to the castle).
25 way i.e., thing to do.

28.1 *Exeunt* (Presumably, the murderers drag the body of Banquo offstage as they go.)
3.4. Location: A room of state in the palace.
1 degrees ranks (as a determinant of seating)   1–2 At . . . last Once for all   3 mingle with society i.e., leave the chair of state and circulate among the guests   5 keeps her state remains in her chair of state. in best time when it is most appropriate   6 require her welcome call upon her to give the welcome.   9 encounter respond to   10 even full, with equal numbers on both sides.   11 large liberal, free.   measure i.e., cup filled to the brim for a toast   14 'Tis . . . within It is better to have his blood on you than he to have it within him.   19 the nonpareil without equal.   22 founded firmly established   23 broad and general unconfined.   casing encasing, enveloping   24 cribbed shut in   25 saucy sharp, impudent, importunate

MURDERER
Ay, my good lord. Safe in a ditch he bides,
With twenty trenchèd gashes on his head,
The least a death to nature.

MACBETH                                  Thanks for that.
There the grown serpent lies; the worm that's fled     29
Hath nature that in time will venom breed,
No teeth for th' present. Get thee gone. Tomorrow
We'll hear ourselves again.                 *Exit Murderer.*

LADY MACBETH                        My royal lord,     32
You do not give the cheer. The feast is sold           33
That is not often vouched, while 'tis a-making,        34
'Tis given with welcome. To feed were best at home;    35
From thence, the sauce to meat is ceremony;            36
Meeting were bare without it.

> *Enter the Ghost of Banquo, and sits in Macbeth's place.*

MACBETH                          Sweet remembrancer!     37
Now, good digestion wait on appetite,                    38
And health on both!

LENNOX                May't please Your Highness sit?     39

MACBETH
Here had we now our country's honor roofed              40
Were the gracèd person of our Banquo present,
Who may I rather challenge for unkindness              42
Than pity for mischance.

ROSS                              His absence, sir,
Lays blame upon his promise. Please't Your Highness
To grace us with your royal company?

MACBETH [*seeing his place occupied*]
The table's full.

LENNOX             Here is a place reserved, sir.

MACBETH    Where?

LENNOX
Here, my good lord. What is't that moves Your
    Highness?

MACBETH
Which of you have done this?

LORDS                        What, my good lord?

MACBETH [*to the Ghost*]
Thou canst not say I did it. Never shake
Thy gory locks at me.

ROSS
Gentlemen, rise. His Highness is not well.
                              [*They start to rise.*]

LADY MACBETH
Sit, worthy friends. My lord is often thus,
And hath been from his youth. Pray you, keep seat.
The fit is momentary; upon a thought                   55
He will again be well. If much you note him

You shall offend him and extend his passion.           57
Feed, and regard him not.—[*She confers apart with
    Macbeth.*] Are you a man?

MACBETH
Ay, and a bold one, that dare look on that
Which might appall the devil.

LADY MACBETH                    Oh, proper stuff!     60
This is the very painting of your fear.
This is the air-drawn dagger which, you said,          62
Led you to Duncan. Oh, these flaws and starts,         63
Impostors to true fear, would well become              64
A woman's story at a winter's fire,
Authorized by her grandam. Shame itself!               66
Why do you make such faces? When all's done,
You look but on a stool.

MACBETH                      Prithee, see there!
Behold, look! Lo, how say you?—
Why, what care I? If thou canst nod, speak too.        70
If charnel houses and our graves must send             71
Those that we bury back, our monuments                 72
Shall be the maws of kites.        [*Exit Ghost.*]     73

LADY MACBETH   What, quite unmanned in folly?

MACBETH
If I stand here, I saw him.

LADY MACBETH            Fie, for shame!

MACBETH
Blood hath been shed ere now, i'th'olden time,
Ere humane statute purged the gentle weal;             77
Ay, and since too, murders have been performed         78
Too terrible for the ear. The time has been
That, when the brains were out, the man would die,
And there an end; but now they rise again
With twenty mortal murders on their crowns,            82
And push us from our stools. This is more strange
Than such a murder is.

LADY MACBETH            My worthy lord,
Your noble friends do lack you.

MACBETH                        I do forget.
Do not muse at me, my most worthy friends;
I have a strange infirmity, which is nothing
To those that know me. Come, love and health to all!
Then I'll sit down. Give me some wine. Fill full.
                              [*He is given wine.*]

> *Enter Ghost.*

I drink to th' general joy o'th' whole table,
And to our dear friend Banquo, whom we miss.
Would he were here! To all, and him, we thirst,        92

---

29 **worm** young serpent    32 **hear ourselves** personally confer    33 **give the cheer** welcome your guests.    33–5 **The feast . . . welcome** A feast seems grudgingly and mercenarily given unless it is repeatedly graced with assurances of welcome.    35–7 **To feed . . . without it** Plain eating is best done in one's own domestic setting; on more social occasions, the spice to a feast is ceremony; gatherings are too unadorned without it.    37 **Sweet remembrancer!** A gracious reminder!    38 **wait on** attend    39 **And . . . both!** and may good health accompany both good appetite and good digestion!    40 **had we** we would have.    **roofed** under one roof    42 **Who . . . unkindness** whom I hope I may sooner reprove for negligence    55 **upon a thought** in a moment

57 **offend him** make him worse    60 **Oh, proper stuff!** Oh, stuff and nonsense!    62 **air-drawn** made of thin air, or floating disembodied in space    63 **flaws** gusts, outbursts    64 **Imposters to** mimickers of. **become** befit    66 **Authorized by** told on the authority of.    **grandam** grandmother    70 **thou** Banquo    71 **charnel houses** depositories for bones or bodies    72–3 **our . . . kites** i.e., we will have to leave the unburied bodies to scavenging birds of prey.    77 **Ere . . . weal** before the institution of law cleansed the commonwealth of violence and made it civilized. (*Humane*, interchangeable with *human*, means both "appertaining to humankind" and "benevolent, civilizing.")    78 **since** i.e., ever since the "olden time" (line 76)    82 **mortal murders** deadly wounds.    **crowns** heads    92 **thirst** desire to drink

And all to all.
LORDS                    Our duties and the pledge.                              93
                                        [*They drink.*]
MACBETH [*seeing the Ghost*]
    Avaunt, and quit my sight! Let the earth hide thee!
    Thy bones are marrowless, thy blood is cold;
    Thou hast no speculation in those eyes                                      96
    Which thou dost glare with!
LADY MACBETH                      Think of this, good peers,
    But as a thing of custom. 'Tis no other;
    Only it spoils the pleasure of the time.
MACBETH    What man dare, I dare.
    Approach thou like the rugged Russian bear,
    The armed rhinoceros, or th' Hyrcan tiger;                                  102
    Take any shape but that, and my firm nerves                                 103
    Shall never tremble. Or be alive again
    And dare me to the desert with thy sword.                                   105
    If trembling I inhabit then, protest me                                     106
    The baby of a girl. Hence, horrible shadow!                                 107
    Unreal mock'ry, hence!        [*Exit Ghost.*]
                        Why, so; being gone,
    I am a man again. Pray you, sit still.
LADY MACBETH
    You have displaced the mirth, broke the good meeting
    With most admired disorder.
MACBETH                          Can such things be,                            111
    And overcome us like a summer's cloud,                                      112
    Without our special wonder? You make me strange                            113
    Even to the disposition that I owe,                                         114
    When now I think you can behold such sights
    And keep the natural ruby of your cheeks
    When mine is blanched with fear.
ROSS                            What sights, my lord?
LADY MACBETH
    I pray you, speak not. He grows worse and worse;
    Question enrages him. At once, good night.                                  119
    Stand not upon the order of your going,                                     120
    But go at once.
LENNOX          Good night, and better health
    Attend His Majesty!
LADY MACBETH        A kind good night to all!
                    *Exeunt Lords* [*and attendants*].
MACBETH
    It will have blood, they say; blood will have blood.
    Stones have been known to move, and trees to speak;  124
    Augurs and understood relations have                                       125
    By maggot-pies and choughs and rooks brought forth  126
    The secret'st man of blood. What is the night?                             127

LADY MACBETH
    Almost at odds with morning, which is which.
MACBETH
    How say'st thou, that Macduff denies his person                            129
    At our great bidding?
LADY MACBETH            Did you send to him, sir?
MACBETH
    I hear it by the way; but I will send.                                      131
    There's not a one of them but in his house                                 132
    I keep a servant fee'd. I will tomorrow—                                    133
    And betimes I will—to the Weird Sisters.                                    134
    More shall they speak, for now I am bent to know                           135
    By the worst means the worst. For mine own good
    All causes shall give way. I am in blood                                   137
    Stepped in so far that, should I wade no more,                             138
    Returning were as tedious as go o'er.                                      139
    Strange things I have in head, that will to hand,                          140
    Which must be acted ere they may be scanned.                               141
LADY MACBETH
    You lack the season of all natures, sleep.                                 142
MACBETH
    Come, we'll to sleep. My strange and self-abuse                            143
    Is the initiate fear that wants hard use.                                  144
    We are yet but young in deed.            *Exeunt.*

❖

## 3.5

*Thunder. Enter the three Witches, meeting Hecate.*

FIRST WITCH
    Why, how now, Hecate? You look angerly.                                     1
HECATE
    Have I not reason, beldams as you are?                                      2
    Saucy and overbold, how did you dare
    To trade and traffic with Macbeth
    In riddles and affairs of death,
    And I, the mistress of your charms,
    The close contriver of all harms,                                          7
    Was never called to bear my part
    Or show the glory of our art?
    And, which is worse, all you have done
    Hath been but for a wayward son,
    Spiteful and wrathful, who, as others do,
    Loves for his own ends, not for you.
    But make amends now. Get you gone,
    And at the pit of Acheron                                                  15

93 **all to all** all good wishes to all, or, let all drink to everyone else.
**Our ... pledge** We dutifully drink this toast.    96 **speculation** power
of sight    102 **armed** armor-plated.    **Hyrcan** of Hyrcania, in ancient
times a region near the Caspian Sea    103 **nerves** sinews    105 **the
desert** some solitary place    106–7 **If ... girl** If then I tremble, proclaim me a baby girl, or a girl's doll.    111 **admired disorder** wondered-
at lack of self-control.    112 **overcome** come over    113–14 **You make ...
owe** You cause me to feel I do not know my own nature (which I had
supposed brave)    119 **At once** To you all; now    120 **Stand ... going**
Do not take the time to leave in ceremonious order of rank, as you
entered    124 **Stones ... speak** i.e., Even inanimate nature speaks in
such a way as to reveal the unnatural act of murder    125–7 **Augurs ...
blood** Prophets versed in the interpretation of occult mysteries have,
by reading the signs of magpies and jackdaws, revealed secret
murderers.    127 **the night** i.e., the time of night.

129 **How say'st thou** What do you say to the fact    131 **by the way**
indirectly    132 **them** my Scottish nobles    133 **fee'd** i.e., paid to spy.
134 **betimes** (1) early (2) while there is still time    135 **bent** determined
137 **All causes** all other considerations    138 **should ... more** even if
I were to wade no farther    139 **were** would be.    **go o'er** to proceed.
140 **that ... hand** that must be performed    141 **acted ... scanned**
put into performance even before there is time to scrutinize them.
142 **season** preservative    143–4 **My ... use** My strange self-punishing
fear is that felt by a novice who lacks toughening experience.
**3.5. Location:** A heath. (This scene is probably by another author.)
1 **angerly** angrily, angry.    2 **beldams** hags    7 **close** secret
15 **Acheron** the river of sorrows in Hades; here, hell itself

Meet me i'th' morning. Thither he
Will come to know his destiny.
Your vessels and your spells provide,
Your charms and everything beside.
I am for th'air. This night I'll spend
Unto a dismal and a fatal end.                                          21
Great business must be wrought ere noon.
Upon the corner of the moon
There hangs a vap'rous drop profound;                                   24
I'll catch it ere it come to ground,
And that, distilled by magic sleights,
Shall raise such artificial sprites                                     27
As by the strength of their illusion
Shall draw him on to his confusion.                                     29
He shall spurn fate, scorn death, and bear
His hopes 'bove wisdom, grace, and fear.
And you all know, security                                              32
Is mortals' chiefest enemy.            *Music and a song.*
Hark! I am called. My little spirit, see,
Sits in a foggy cloud and stays for me.            [*Exit.*] 35
                *Sing within,* "Come away, come away," *etc.*
FIRST WITCH
Come, let's make haste. She'll soon be back again.
                                                        *Exeunt.*

❖

## 3.6

*Enter Lennox and another Lord.*

LENNOX
My former speeches have but hit your thoughts,                          1
Which can interpret farther. Only I say                                 2
Things have been strangely borne. The gracious
    Duncan                                                              3
Was pitied of Macbeth; marry, he was dead.                              4
And the right valiant Banquo walked too late,
Whom you may say, if't please you, Fleance killed,
For Fleance fled. Men must not walk too late.
Who cannot want the thought how monstrous                               8
It was for Malcolm and for Donalbain
To kill their gracious father? Damnèd fact!                             10
How it did grieve Macbeth! Did he not straight                          11
In pious rage the two delinquents tear
That were the slaves of drink and thralls of sleep?                     13
Was not that nobly done? Ay, and wisely too;
For 'twould have angered any heart alive
To hear the men deny't. So that I say

He has borne all things well; and I do think                            17
That had he Duncan's sons under his key—
As, an't please heaven, he shall not—they should find                   19
What 'twere to kill a father. So should Fleance.
But peace! For from broad words, and 'cause he failed                   21
His presence at the tyrant's feast, I hear                              22
Macduff lives in disgrace. Sir, can you tell
Where he bestows himself?
LORD                              The son of Duncan,                     24
From whom this tyrant holds the due of birth,                           25
Lives in the English court, and is received
Of the most pious Edward with such grace                                27
That the malevolence of fortune nothing
Takes from his high respect. Thither Macduff                            29
Is gone to pray the holy king, upon his aid,                            30
To wake Northumberland and warlike Siward,                              31
That by the help of these—with Him above
To ratify the work—we may again
Give to our tables meat, sleep to our nights,                           34
Free from our feasts and banquets bloody knives,                        35
Do faithful homage, and receive free honors—                            36
All which we pine for now. And this report
Hath so exasperate the King that he                                     38
Prepares for some attempt of war.
LENNOX   Sent he to Macduff?
LORD
He did; and with an absolute "Sir, not I,"                              41
The cloudy messenger turns me his back                                  42
And hums, as who should say, "You'll rue the time                       43
That clogs me with this answer."
LENNOX                              And that well might                  44
Advise him to a caution, t' hold what distance                          45
His wisdom can provide. Some holy angel                                 46
Fly to the court of England and unfold
His message ere he come, that a swift blessing                          48
May soon return to this our suffering country                           49
Under a hand accursed!                                                  50
LORD   I'll send my prayers with him.            *Exeunt.*

❖

21 **Unto** working toward.   **dismal** disastrous, ill-omened   24 **profound** i.e., heavily pendent, ready to drop off   27 **artificial sprites** spirits produced by magical arts   29 **confusion** ruin.   32 **security** overconfidence   35.1 **"Come away,"** *etc.* (The song occurs in Thomas Middleton's *The Witch.*)
**3.6. Location: Somewhere in Scotland.**
1–2 **My . . . farther** What I've just said has coincided with your own thought. I needn't say more; you can surmise the rest.   3 **borne** carried on.   3–4 **The gracious . . . dead** (Lennox ironically implies that Macbeth's show of sorrow for the dead Duncan was hypocritical.)
8 **cannot . . . thought** can help thinking   10 **fact** deed, crime.
11 **straight** straightaway, at once   13 **thralls** slaves

17 **borne all things well** managed everything cleverly   19 **an't** if it.   **should** would be sure to   21 **from broad words** on account of plain speech   22 **His presence** i.e., to be present   24 **bestows himself** is quartered, has taken refuge.   **The son of Duncan** Malcolm   25 **holds . . . birth** withholds the birthright (i.e., the Scottish crown)   27 **Of** by.   **Edward** Edward the Confessor, King of England   29 **his high respect** the high respect paid to him. (Being out of fortune has not lessened the dignity with which Malcolm is received in England.)   30 **to pray . . . aid** to petition King Edward, in aid of Malcolm   31 **wake Northumberland** rouse the people of Northumberland   34 **meat** food   35 **Free . . . banquets** free our feasts and banquets from   36 **free** freely bestowed, or, pertaining to freemen   38 **exasperate the King** exasperated Macbeth   41 **with . . . I** i.e., when Macduff answered the messenger curtly with a refusal   42 **cloudy** louring, scowling.   **turns me** i.e., turns. (*Me* is used colloquially for emphasis.)   43 **hums . . . say** says "umph!" as if to say   44 **clogs** encumbers, loads   45–6 **Advise . . . provide** warn him (Macduff) to keep what safe distance he can (from Macbeth).   48 **His message** i.e., the request for aid against Scotland that Macduff is going to present to King Edward (see lines 29 ff.)
49–50 **suffering country Under** country suffering under

# 4.1

*[A cauldron.] Thunder. Enter the three Witches.*

**FIRST WITCH**
Thrice the brinded cat hath mewed.    1

**SECOND WITCH**
Thrice, and once the hedgepig whined.    2

**THIRD WITCH**
Harpier cries, 'Tis time, 'tis time!    3

**FIRST WITCH**
Round about the cauldron go;
In the poisoned entrails throw.
Toad, that under cold stone
Days and nights has thirty-one    7
Sweltered venom sleeping got,    8
Boil thou first i'th' charmèd pot.

**ALL** *[as they dance round the cauldron]*
Double, double, toil and trouble;
Fire burn, and cauldron bubble.

**SECOND WITCH**
Fillet of a fenny snake,    12
In the cauldron boil and bake;
Eye of newt and toe of frog,
Wool of bat and tongue of dog,
Adder's fork and blindworm's sting,    16
Lizard's leg and owlet's wing,
For a charm of powerful trouble,
Like a hell-broth boil and bubble.

**ALL**
Double, double, toil and trouble;
Fire burn, and cauldron bubble.

**THIRD WITCH**
Scale of dragon, tooth of wolf,
Witches' mummy, maw and gulf    23
Of the ravined salt-sea shark,    24
Root of hemlock digged i'th' dark,
Liver of blaspheming Jew,
Gall of goat, and slips of yew    27
Slivered in the moon's eclipse,    28
Nose of Turk and Tartar's lips,
Finger of birth-strangled babe
Ditch-delivered by a drab,    31
Make the gruel thick and slab.    32
Add thereto a tiger's chaudron    33
For th'ingredient of our cauldron.    34

**ALL**
Double, double, toil and trouble;
Fire burn, and cauldron bubble.

**SECOND WITCH**
Cool it with a baboon's blood,
Then the charm is firm and good.    38

*Enter Hecate to the other three Witches.*

**HECATE**
Oh, well done! I commend your pains,    39
And everyone shall share i'th' gains.
And now about the cauldron sing
Like elves and fairies in a ring,
Enchanting all that you put in.    43
*Music and a song:* "Black spirits," *etc.*
*[Exit Hecate.]*

**SECOND WITCH**
By the pricking of my thumbs,
Something wicked this way comes.
Open, locks,
Whoever knocks!

*Enter Macbeth.*

**MACBETH**
How now, you secret, black, and midnight hags?    48
What is't you do?

**ALL**                    A deed without a name.

**MACBETH**
I conjure you, by that which you profess,
Howe'er you come to know it, answer me.
Though you untie the winds and let them fight
Against the churches, though the yeasty waves    53
Confound and swallow navigation up,    54
Though bladed corn be lodged and trees blown down,    55
Though castles topple on their warders' heads,    56
Though palaces and pyramids do slope    57
Their heads to their foundations, though the treasure
Of nature's germens tumble all together    59
Even till destruction sicken, answer me    60
To what I ask you.

**FIRST WITCH**          Speak.

**SECOND WITCH**              Demand.

**THIRD WITCH**                  We'll answer.

**FIRST WITCH**
Say if thou'dst rather hear it from our mouths
Or from our masters?

**MACBETH**              Call 'em. Let me see 'em.

**FIRST WITCH**
Pour in sow's blood, that hath eaten
Her nine farrow; grease that's sweaten    65

**4.1. Location:** A cavern (see 3.5.15). In the middle, a boiling cauldron (provided presumably by means of the trapdoor; see 4.1.106. The trapdoor must also be used in this scene for the apparitions.) **1 brinded** marked by streaks (as by fire), brindled   **2 hedgepig** hedgehog   **3 Harpier** (The name of a familiar spirit; probably derived from *harpy*.)   **cries** i.e., gives the signal to begin   **7–8 Days . . . got** has for thirty-one days and nights exuded venom formed during sleep   **12 Fillet** Slice.   **fenny** inhabiting fens or swamps   **16 fork** forked tongue.   **blindworm's** A blindworm is a slowworm, a harmless burrowing lizard.   **23 mummy** mummified flesh made into a magical potion.   **maw and gulf** gullet and stomach   **24 ravined** ravenous, or glutted with prey (?)   **27 Gall** gall bladder.   **slips** cuttings for grafting or planting.   **yew** (A tree often planted in churchyards and associated with mourning.)   **28 Slivered** broken off (as a branch)   **31 Ditch . . . drab** born in a ditch of a harlot   **32 slab** viscous.   **33 chaudron** entrails   **34 th'ingredient** the ingredients

**38.1 other** (Said because Hecate is a witch, too, not because more witches enter.)   **39–43 Oh . . . in** (These lines are universally regarded as non-Shakespearean.)   **43.1 "Black spirits,"** *etc.* (This song is found in Middleton's *The Witch*.)   **48 black** i.e., dealing in black magic   **53 yeasty** foamy   **54 Confound** destroy   **55 Though . . . lodged** though unripe grain be laid flat   **56 warders'** guardsmen's   **57 slope** bend   **59 nature's germens** seed or elements from which all nature operates   **60 sicken** be surfeited with its own excess   **65 nine farrow** litter of nine.   **sweaten** sweated

From the murderer's gibbet throw                                       66
Into the flame.
ALL                    Come high or low,                              67
Thyself and office deftly show!                                       68

*Thunder. First Apparition, an armed Head.*

MACBETH
Tell me, thou unknown power—
FIRST WITCH                        He knows thy thought.
Hear his speech, but say thou naught.
FIRST APPARITION
Macbeth! Macbeth! Macbeth! Beware Macduff,
Beware the Thane of Fife. Dismiss me. Enough.          72
                            *He descends.*
MACBETH
Whate'er thou art, for thy good caution, thanks;
Thou hast harped my fear aright. But one word
more—                                                                  74
FIRST WITCH
He will not be commanded. Here's another,
More potent than the first.                                            76

*Thunder. Second Apparition, a bloody Child.*

SECOND APPARITION    Macbeth! Macbeth! Macbeth!
MACBETH    Had I three ears, I'd hear thee.
SECOND APPARITION
Be bloody, bold, and resolute; laugh to scorn
The power of man, for none of woman born
Shall harm Macbeth.                        *Descends.*
MACBETH
Then live, Macduff; what need I fear of thee?
But yet I'll make assurance double sure,
And take a bond of fate. Thou shalt not live,           84
That I may tell pale-hearted fear it lies,
And sleep in spite of thunder.                          86

*Thunder. Third Apparition, a Child crowned, with
a tree in his hand.*

                          What is this
That rises like the issue of a king                     87
And wears upon his baby brow the round                  88
And top of sovereignty?
ALL                    Listen, but speak not to't.      89
THIRD APPARITION
Be lion-mettled, proud, and take no care                90
Who chafes, who frets, or where conspirers are.
Macbeth shall never vanquished be until

Great Birnam Wood to high Dunsinane Hill
Shall come against him.                    *Descends.*
MACBETH                    That will never be.
Who can impress the forest, bid the tree                95
Unfix his earthbound root? Sweet bodements, good!       96
Rebellious dead, rise never till the wood               97
Of Birnam rise, and our high-placed Macbeth             98
Shall live the lease of nature, pay his breath          99
To time and mortal custom. Yet my heart                 100
Throbs to know one thing. Tell me, if your art
Can tell so much: shall Banquo's issue ever
Reign in this kingdom?
ALL                        Seek to know no more.
MACBETH
I will be satisfied. Deny me this,
And an eternal curse fall on you! Let me know.          105
          [*The cauldron descends.*] *Hautboys.*
Why sinks that cauldron? And what noise is this?        106
FIRST WITCH    Show!
SECOND WITCH    Show!
THIRD WITCH    Show!
ALL
Show his eyes, and grieve his heart;
Come like shadows, so depart!                           111

*A show of eight kings and Banquo last; [the eighth
King] with a glass in his hand.*

MACBETH
Thou art too like the spirit of Banquo. Down!
Thy crown does sear mine eyeballs. And thy hair,
Thou other gold-bound brow, is like the first.         114
A third is like the former. Filthy hags,
Why do you show me this? A fourth? Start, eyes!        116
What, will the line stretch out to th' crack of doom?   117
Another yet? A seventh? I'll see no more.
And yet the eighth appears, who bears a glass
Which shows me many more; and some I see
That twofold balls and treble scepters carry.          121
Horrible sight! Now I see 'tis true,
For the blood-boltered Banquo smiles upon me           123
And points at them for his. [*The apparitions vanish.*]
    What, is this so?                                   124

66 **gibbet** gallows   67 **high or low** of the upper or lower air, from under the earth or in hell; or, one and all   68 **office** function   68.1 *armed Head* (Perhaps symbolizes the head of Macbeth cut off by Macduff and presented by him to Malcolm, or else the head of Macduff, armed in rebellion against Macbeth.)   72.1 *He descends* (i.e., by means of the trapdoor).   74 **harped** hit, touched (as in touching a harp to make it sound)   76.1 *bloody Child* (Symbolizes Macduff untimely ripped from his mother's womb; see 5.8.15–16.)   84 **take a bond of** get a guarantee from (i.e., by killing Macduff, to make doubly sure he can do no harm)   86.1–2 *Child . . . hand* (Symbolizes Malcolm, the royal child; the tree anticipates the cutting of boughs in Birnam Wood, 5.4.)   87 **like** in the likeness of   88–9 **round And top** crown   90 **lion-mettled** as bold as a lion

95 **impress** press into service, like soldiers   96 **bodements** prophecies   97–8 **Rebellious . . . rise** i.e., May the souls of those I have murdered (Banquo, Duncan) never rise again, since trees themselves cannot rise; the souls of Banquo and Duncan are rebellious in presuming to do so, defying death itself. (An image of the Day of Judgment, when bodies are prophesied to rise again; see *Henry V*, 4.1.135–8.)   98 **high-placed** placed on the throne as king   99–100 **Shall . . . custom** will live out his full life span until it is time for him to expire (*pay his breath*) in the way of all mortals.   105.1 *Hautboys* oboelike instruments.   106 **noise** music   111.1 *eight kings* (Banquo was the supposed ancestor of the Stuart dynasty, leading forward to King James VI of Scotland and James I of England, the *eighth King* here.)   111.2 *glass* (magic) mirror (also in line 119)   114 **other** i.e., second   116 **Start** Bulge from their sockets   117 **th' crack of doom** the Day of judgment.   121 **twofold balls** (A probable reference to the double coronation of James at Scone and Westminster, as King of England and Scotland.)   **treble scepters** (Probably refers to James' assumed title as King of Great Britain, France, and Ireland.)   123 **blood-boltered** having his hair matted with blood   124 **for his** as his descendants.

FIRST WITCH

Ay, sir, all this is so. But why                                  125
Stands Macbeth thus amazedly?                                     126
Come, sisters, cheer we up his sprites                            127
And show the best of our delights.
I'll charm the air to give a sound,
While you perform your antic round,                               130
That this great king may kindly say
Our duties did his welcome pay.                                   132

*Music. The Witches dance, and vanish.*

MACBETH

Where are they? Gone? Let this pernicious hour
Stand aye accursèd in the calendar!
Come in, without there!

*Enter Lennox.*

LENNOX                          What's Your Grace's will?

MACBETH

Saw you the Weird Sisters?

LENNOX                          No, my lord.

MACBETH

Came they not by you?

LENNOX                          No, indeed, my lord.

MACBETH

Infected be the air whereon they ride,
And damned all those that trust them! I did hear
The galloping of horse. Who was't came by?                        140

LENNOX

'Tis two or three, my lord, that bring you word
Macduff is fled to England.

MACBETH                          Fled to England!

LENNOX

Ay, my good lord.

MACBETH [*aside*]

Time, thou anticipat'st my dread exploits.                        144
The flighty purpose never is o'ertook                             145
Unless the deed go with it. From this moment                      146
The very firstlings of my heart shall be                          147
The firstlings of my hand. And even now,                          148
To crown my thoughts with acts, be it thought and
    done:
The castle of Macduff I will surprise,                            150
Seize upon Fife, give to th'edge o'th' sword
His wife, his babes, and all unfortunate souls
That trace him in his line. No boasting like a fool;              153
This deed I'll do before this purpose cool.
But no more sights!—Where are these gentlemen?
Come, bring me where they are.                          *Exeunt.*

❖

**125–32 Ay . . . pay** (These lines are assumed to have been written by someone other than Shakespeare.)   **126 amazedly** stunned.   **127 sprites** spirits   **130 antic round** grotesque dance in a circle   **132 Our . . . pay** the entertainment we provided has repaid the welcome he provided for us.   **140 horse** horses.   **144 thou anticipat'st** you forestall. Macduff has moved so quickly that he has stayed ahead of my murderous plan.
**145–6 The flighty . . . go with it** Whatever we fleetingly propose is never realized unless we do the deed the moment it is thought of.   **147–8 The very . . . hand** the firstborn promptings of my heart will become my first of deeds.   **150 surprise** attack without warning   **153 trace . . . line** follow him in the line of inheritance.

## 4.2

*Enter Macduff's Wife, her Son, and Ross.*

LADY MACDUFF

What had he done to make him fly the land?

ROSS

You must have patience, madam.

LADY MACDUFF                          He had none.

His flight was madness. When our actions do not,               3
Our fears do make us traitors.

ROSS                          You know not                         4

Whether it was his wisdom or his fear.

LADY MACDUFF

Wisdom? To leave his wife, to leave his babes,
His mansion, and his titles in a place                          7
From whence himself does fly? He loves us not,
He wants the natural touch; for the poor wren,                  9
The most diminutive of birds, will fight,
Her young ones in her nest, against the owl.                    11
All is the fear and nothing is the love,
As little is the wisdom, where the flight
So runs against all reason.

ROSS                          My dearest coz,                     14

I pray you, school yourself. But, for your husband,             15
He is noble, wise, judicious, and best knows
The fits o'th' season. I dare not speak much further,           17
But cruel are the times when we are traitors                    18
And do not know ourselves, when we hold rumor                   19
From what we fear, yet know not what we fear,                   20
But float upon a wild and violent sea
Each way and none. I take my leave of you;                      22
Shall not be long but I'll be here again.                       23
Things at the worst will cease, or else climb upward
To what they were before.—My pretty cousin,
Blessing upon you!

LADY MACDUFF

Fathered he is, and yet he's fatherless.

ROSS

I am so much a fool, should I stay longer
It would be my disgrace and your discomfort.                    29
I take my leave at once.                          *Exit Ross.*

LADY MACDUFF    Sirrah, your father's dead;                       31
And what will you do now? How will you live?

SON

As birds do, mother.

LADY MACDUFF                          What, with worms and flies?

SON

With what I get, I mean; and so do they.

**4.2. Location: Fife. Macduff's castle.**
**3–4 When . . . traitors** Even when we have committed no treasonous act, our fearful responses make us look guilty.   **7 titles** possessions to which he has title   **9 wants . . . touch** lacks the natural instinct to protect his family   **11 Her . . . nest** when her young ones are in the nest   **14 coz** kinswoman   **15 school** control.   **for** as for   **17 fits o'th' season** violent convulsions of the time.   **18–19 are traitors . . . ourselves** are alienated from one another by a climate of fear and suspected treason   **19–20 when . . . not what we fear** when our fearful worries teach us to believe every rumor without our really knowing what there is for us to fear   **22 Each . . . none** this way and that.   **23 Shall** it shall.   **but** before   **29 It . . . discomfort** I should disgrace my manhood by weeping and cause you distress.   **31 Sirrah** (Here, an affectionate form of address to a child.)

LADY MACDUFF    Poor bird! Thou'dst never fear                    35
The net nor lime, the pitfall nor the gin.                        36
SON
Why should I, mother? Poor birds they are not set for.            37
My father is not dead, for all your saying.
LADY MACDUFF
Yes, he is dead. How wilt thou do for a father?
SON    Nay, how will you do for a husband?
LADY MACDUFF    Why, I can buy me twenty at any
market.
SON    Then you'll buy 'em to sell again.
LADY MACDUFF
Thou speak'st with all thy wit,
And yet, i'faith, with wit enough for thee.
SON    Was my father a traitor, mother?
LADY MACDUFF    Ay, that he was.
SON    What is a traitor?
LADY MACDUFF    Why, one that swears and lies.         48
SON    And be all traitors that do so?
LADY MACDUFF
Every one that does so is a traitor,
And must be hanged.
SON
And must they all be hanged that swear and lie?
LADY MACDUFF    Every one.
SON    Who must hang them?
LADY MACDUFF    Why, the honest men.
SON    Then the liars and swearers are fools, for there are
liars and swearers enough to beat the honest men and
hang up them.
LADY MACDUFF    Now, God help thee, poor monkey!
But how wilt thou do for a father?
SON    If he were dead, you'd weep for him; if you would
not, it were a good sign that I should quickly have a
new father.
LADY MACDUFF    Poor prattler, how thou talk'st!

*Enter a Messenger.*

MESSENGER
Bless you, fair dame! I am not to you known,
Though in your state of honor I am perfect.               67
I doubt some danger does approach you nearly.            68
If you will take a homely man's advice,                  69
Be not found here. Hence with your little ones!
To fright you thus, methinks, I am too savage;
To do worse to you were fell cruelty,                    72
Which is too nigh your person. Heaven preserve you!      73
I dare abide no longer.                  *Exit Messenger.*
LADY MACDUFF                  Whither should I fly?
I have done no harm. But I remember now
I am in this earthly world, where to do harm
Is often laudable, to do good sometime
Accounted dangerous folly. Why then, alas,

Do I put up that womanly defense
To say I have done no harm?

*Enter Murderers.*

What are these faces?
FIRST MURDERER    Where is your husband?
LADY MACDUFF
I hope in no place so unsanctified
Where such as thou mayst find him.
FIRST MURDERER                  He's a traitor.
SON
Thou liest, thou shag-haired villain!
FIRST MURDERER                  What, you egg?
                                 [*He stabs him.*]
Young fry of treachery!
SON                  He has killed me, mother.      85
Run away, I pray you!              [*He dies.*]
      *Exit* [*Lady Macduff*] *crying "Murder!"*
      [*followed by the Murderers with the Son's body*].

♣

## 4.3

*Enter Malcolm and Macduff.*

MALCOLM
Let us seek out some desolate shade, and there
Weep our sad bosoms empty.
MACDUFF                  Let us rather
Hold fast the mortal sword, and like good men       3
Bestride our downfall'n birthdom. Each new morn     4
New widows howl, new orphans cry, new sorrows
Strike heaven on the face, that it resounds         6
As if it felt with Scotland and yelled out          7
Like syllable of dolor.
MALCOLM                  What I believe, I'll wail;   8
What know, believe; and what I can redress,          9
As I shall find the time to friend, I will.         10
What you have spoke it may be so, perchance.
This tyrant, whose sole name blisters our tongues,  12
Was once thought honest. You have loved him well;
He hath not touched you yet. I am young; but
    something                                       14
You may deserve of him through me, and wisdom       15
To offer up a weak, poor, innocent lamb
T'appease an angry god.
MACDUFF    I am not treacherous.
MALCOLM    But Macbeth is.

85 **fry** spawn, progeny
**4.3. Location:** England. Before King Edward the Confessor's palace.
**3 mortal** deadly   **4 Bestride . . . birthdom** stand in defense over our
downtrodden native land. (F reads "downfall.")   **6 that it resounds** so
that it echoes   **7–8 As . . . dolor** as if heaven, feeling itself the blow
delivered to Scotland, cried out with a similar cry of pain.   **8–9 What . . .
believe** i.e., What I believe to be amiss in Scotland I will grieve for,
and anything I am certain to be true I will believe. (But one must
be cautious in these duplicitous times.)   **10 to friend** opportune,
congenial   **12 sole** mere   **14 He . . . yet** i.e., the fact that Macbeth
hasn't hurt you yet makes me suspicious of your loyalties.   **young**
i.e., inexperienced   **14–15 something . . . me** i.e., you may win favor
with Macbeth by betraying me to him. (F reads "discerne" in place of
"deserve.")   **15 wisdom** i.e., it would be worldly-wise

35 **Thou'dst never fear** You are too innocent to be prudently wary of
36 **lime** birdlime (a sticky substance put on branches to snare birds).   **gin**
snare.   **37 Poor . . . for** i.e., Traps are not set for *poor* birds, as you call me.
48 **swears and lies** swears an oath and then breaks it.   **67 Though . . . per-**
**fect** though I am perfectly acquainted with your honorable state and rank.
68 **doubt** fear   **69 homely** plain   **72–3 To . . . person** to frighten you still
further would be savage cruelty, which is already too near at hand.

A good and virtuous nature may recoil                                      20
In an imperial charge. But I shall crave your pardon.                      21
That which you are my thoughts cannot transpose;                           22
Angels are bright still, though the brightest fell.                        23
Though all things foul would wear the brows of grace,                      24
Yet grace must still look so.
MACDUFF                              I have lost my hopes.                  25
MALCOLM
Perchance even there where I did find my doubts.                           26
Why in that rawness left you wife and child,                               27
Those precious motives, those strong knots of love,                        28
Without leave-taking? I pray you,
Let not my jealousies be your dishonors,                                   30
But mine own safeties. You may be rightly just,                            31
Whatever I shall think.
MACDUFF                        Bleed, bleed, poor country!
Great tyranny, lay thou thy basis sure,                                    33
For goodness dare not check thee; wear thou thy
   wrongs,                                                                 34
The title is affeered! Fare thee well, lord.                               35
I would not be the villain that thou think'st                              36
For the whole space that's in the tyrant's grasp,
And the rich East to boot.
MALCOLM                          Be not offended.                         38
I speak not as in absolute fear of you.                                    39
I think our country sinks beneath the yoke;
It weeps, it bleeds, and each new day a gash
Is added to her wounds. I think withal                                     42
There would be hands uplifted in my right;                                 43
And here from gracious England have I offer                                44
Of goodly thousands. But, for all this,
When I shall tread upon the tyrant's head,
Or wear it on my sword, yet my poor country
Shall have more vices than it had before,
More suffer, and more sundry ways than ever,                               49
By him that shall succeed.
MACDUFF                          What should he be?                        50
MALCOLM
It is myself I mean, in whom I know

All the particulars of vice so grafted                                     52
That, when they shall be opened, black Macbeth                             53
Will seem as pure as snow, and the poor state
Esteem him as a lamb, being compared
With my confineless harms.
MACDUFF                              Not in the legions                    56
Of horrid hell can come a devil more damned
In evils to top Macbeth.
MALCOLM                          I grant him bloody,                       58
Luxurious, avaricious, false, deceitful,                                   59
Sudden, malicious, smacking of every sin                                   60
That has a name. But there's no bottom, none,
In my voluptuousness. Your wives, your daughters,
Your matrons, and your maids could not fill up
The cistern of my lust, and my desire
All continent impediments would o'erbear                                   65
That did oppose my will. Better Macbeth                                    66
Than such an one to reign.
MACDUFF                          Boundless intemperance
In nature is a tyranny; it hath been                                       68
Th'untimely emptying of the happy throne
And fall of many kings. But fear not yet                                   70
To take upon you what is yours. You may
Convey your pleasures in a spacious plenty,                                72
And yet seem cold; the time you may so hoodwink.                           73
We have willing dames enough. There cannot be
That vulture in you to devour so many
As will to greatness dedicate themselves,
Finding it so inclined.
MALCOLM                          With this there grows                     77
In my most ill-composed affection such                                     78
A stanchless avarice that, were I king,                                    79
I should cut off the nobles for their lands,
Desire his jewels and this other's house,                                  81
And my more-having would be as a sauce
To make me hunger more, that I should forge                                83
Quarrels unjust against the good and loyal,
Destroying them for wealth.
MACDUFF                          This avarice
Sticks deeper, grows with more pernicious root
Than summer-seeming lust, and it hath been                                 87
The sword of our slain kings. Yet do not fear;                             88
Scotland hath foisons to fill up your will                                 89
Of your mere own. All these are portable,                                  90
With other graces weighed.                                                 91
MALCOLM
But I have none. The king-becoming graces,
As justice, verity, temp'rance, stableness,

---

**20–1 A good . . . charge** i.e., Even as good a virtuous nature as you have, Macduff, may give way to the insinuations of a royal command from Macbeth. (With wordplay on the *recoil* of a firearm that is *charged* with power and shot.)   **22 That . . . transpose** My suspicious thoughts cannot change you from what you are, cannot make you evil   **23 the brightest** i.e., Lucifer   **24–5 Though . . . so** Even though evil puts on the appearance of good so often as to cast that appearance into deep suspicion, yet goodness must go on looking and acting like itself.   **25 hopes** i.e., hopes of persuading Malcolm to lead the cause against Macbeth.   **26 Perchance even there** i.e., Perhaps in that same mistrustful frame of mind.   **doubts** i.e., fears such as that Macduff may covertly be on Macbeth's side.   **27 rawness** unprotected condition. (Malcolm suggests that Macduff's leaving his family unprotected could be construed as more evidence of his not having anything to fear from Macbeth.)   **28 motives** i.e., inducements to be protective of them   **30–1 Let . . . safeties** may it be true that my suspicions of your lack of honor are founded only in my own wariness.   **33 basis** foundation   **34 check** rebuke, call to account.   **wear . . . wrongs** continue to enjoy your wrongfully gained powers   **35 affeered** confirmed, certified.   **36 that thou think'st** that you think me   **38 to boot** in addition.   **39 absolute fear** complete mistrust   **42 withal** even so   **43 right** cause   **44 England** the King of England   **49 More . . . ways** suffer more grievously and in more varied ways   **50 What . . . be?** Whom could you possibly mean?

---

**52 grafted** (1) engrafted, indissolubly mixed (2) grafted like a plant that will then *open* or unfold   **53 opened** unfolded (like a bud)   **56 confineless** limitless   **58 top** surpass   **59 Luxurious** lecherous   **60 Sudden** violent, impetuous   **65 continent** (1) chaste (2) restraining, containing   **66 will** lust. (Also in line 89.)   **68 nature** human nature   **70 yet** nevertheless   **72 Convey** manage with secrecy   **73 cold** comparatively chaste. **the time . . . hoodwink** you may thus deceive the age.   **77 With this** Along with this lustfulness   **78 ill-composed affection** evil disposition   **79 stanchless** insatiable   **81 his** one man's.   **this other's** another's   **83 that** so that   **87 summer-seeming** appropriate to youth (and lessening in later years)   **88 sword** i.e., means of overthrow   **89 foisons** resources, plenty   **90 Of . . . own** out of your own royal estates alone. **portable** bearable   **91 weighed** counterbalanced.

Bounty, perseverance, mercy, lowliness,                         94
Devotion, patience, courage, fortitude,
I have no relish of them, but abound                            96
In the division of each several crime,                          97
Acting it many ways. Nay, had I power, I should
Pour the sweet milk of concord into hell,
Uproar the universal peace, confound                            100
All unity on earth.
MACDUFF                    O Scotland, Scotland!
MALCOLM
If such a one be fit to govern, speak.
I am as I have spoken.
MACDUFF                    Fit to govern?
No, not to live. O nation miserable,
With an untitled tyrant bloody-sceptered,                       105
When shalt thou see thy wholesome days again,
Since that the truest issue of thy throne                       107
By his own interdiction stands accurst                          108
And does blaspheme his breed? Thy royal father                  109
Was a most sainted king; the queen that bore thee,
Oft'ner upon her knees than on her feet,
Died every day she lived. Fare thee well.                       112
These evils thou repeat'st upon thyself                         113
Hath banished me from Scotland. O my breast,                    114
Thy hope ends here!
MALCOLM                    Macduff, this noble passion,
Child of integrity, hath from my soul                           116
Wiped the black scruples, reconciled my thoughts
To thy good truth and honor. Devilish Macbeth
By many of these trains hath sought to win me                   119
Into his power, and modest wisdom plucks me                     120
From overcredulous haste. But God above
Deal between thee and me! For even now
I put myself to thy direction and
Unspeak mine own detraction, here abjure                        124
The taints and blames I laid upon myself
For strangers to my nature. I am yet                            126
Unknown to woman, never was forsworn,                           127
Scarcely have coveted what was mine own,
At no time broke my faith, would not betray
The devil to his fellow, and delight                            130
No less in truth than life. My first false speaking
Was this upon myself. What I am truly                           132
Is thine and my poor country's to command—
Whither indeed, before thy here-approach,
Old Siward with ten thousand warlike men,
Already at a point, was setting forth.                          136

Now we'll together; and the chance of goodness                  137
Be like our warranted quarrel!—Why are you silent?              138
MACDUFF
Such welcome and unwelcome things at once
'Tis hard to reconcile.

                    *Enter a Doctor.*

MALCOLM
Well, more anon.—Comes the King forth, I pray you?              141
DOCTOR
Ay, sir. There are a crew of wretched souls
That stay his cure. Their malady convinces                      143
The great essay of art; but at his touch—                       144
Such sanctity hath heaven given his hand—
They presently amend.
MALCOLM                    I thank you, Doctor.                 146
                              *Exit [Doctor].*
MACDUFF
What's the disease he means?
MALCOLM                              'Tis called the evil.      147
A most miraculous work in this good king,
Which often, since my here-remain in England,                  149
I have seen him do. How he solicits heaven                      150
Himself best knows; but strangely-visited people,              151
All swoll'n and ulcerous, pitiful to the eye,
The mere despair of surgery, he cures,                          153
Hanging a golden stamp about their necks                        154
Put on with holy prayers; and 'tis spoken,                      155
To the succeeding royalty he leaves                             156
The healing benediction. With this strange virtue              157
He hath a heavenly gift of prophecy,
And sundry blessings hang about his throne
That speak him full of grace.

                    *Enter Ross.*

MACDUFF                              See who comes here.
MALCOLM
My countryman, but yet I know him not.                          161
MACDUFF
My ever-gentle cousin, welcome hither.                          162
MALCOLM
I know him now. Good God betimes remove                         163
The means that makes us strangers!
ROSS                                        Sir, amen.
MACDUFF
Stands Scotland where it did?
ROSS                              Alas, poor country,
Almost afraid to know itself. It cannot

---

94 **lowliness** humility    96 **relish** flavor or trace    97 **division** subdivisions, various possible forms.    **several** separate    100 **Uproar** throw into an uproar    105 **untitled** lacking rightful title, usurping    107 **Since that** since.    **issue** descendant, heir    108 **interdiction** debarring of self    109 **does blaspheme his breed** defames his breeding, i.e., is a disgrace to his royal lineage.    112 **Died . . . lived** lived a life of daily mortification.    113 **thou repeat'st** that you recite or declare    114 **breast** heart    116 **Child of integrity** a product of your integrity of spirit; or, you person of perfect integrity    119 **trains** plots, stratagems    120 **modest . . . me** wise prudence holds me back    124 **Unspeak . . . detraction** take back all I said in detraction of myself    126 **For** as    127 **Unknown to woman** a virgin    130 **The devil** even the devil    132 **upon** against    136 **at a point** prepared

137–8 **the chance . . . quarrel** may our chance of success be proportionate to the justice of our cause.    141 **the King** King Edward the Confessor    143 **stay** wait for.    **convinces** defeats    144 **essay of art** efforts of medical skill    146 **presently** immediately    147 **the evil** "the King's evil," scrofula, supposedly cured by the royal touch; James I claimed this power.    149 **here-remain** stay    150 **solicits** prevails by prayer with    151 **strangely-visited** afflicted by strange diseases    153 **mere** utter    154 **stamp** minted coin    155–7 **and 'tis . . . benediction** it is said that he bequeaths this healing blessedness to his royal progeny.    157 **virtue** healing power    161 **My countryman** (So identified by his dress.)    **know** recognize    162 **gentle** noble.    **cousin** kinsman.    163 **betimes** speedily

Be called our mother, but our grave, where nothing    167
But who knows nothing is once seen to smile;    168
Where sighs and groans and shrieks that rend the air
Are made, not marked; where violent sorrow seems    170
A modern ecstasy. The dead man's knell    171
Is there scarce asked for who, and good men's lives    172
Expire before the flowers in their caps,    173
Dying or ere they sicken.

MACDUFF    Oh, relation    174
Too nice, and yet too true!

MALCOLM    What's the newest grief?    175

ROSS
That of an hour's age doth hiss the speaker;    176
Each minute teems a new one.

MACDUFF    How does my wife?    177

ROSS
Why, well.    178

MACDUFF    And all my children?

ROSS    Well too.

MACDUFF
The tyrant has not battered at their peace?

ROSS
No, they were well at peace when I did leave 'em.

MACDUFF
Be not a niggard of your speech. How goes't?

ROSS
When I came hither to transport the tidings
Which I have heavily borne, there ran a rumor    183
Of many worthy fellows that were out,    184
Which was to my belief witnessed the rather    185
For that I saw the tyrant's power afoot.    186
Now is the time of help. [To Malcolm] Your eye in
    Scotland    187
Would create soldiers, make our women fight,    188
To doff their dire distresses.

MALCOLM    Be't their comfort    189
We are coming thither. Gracious England hath    190
Lent us good Siward and ten thousand men;
An older and a better soldier none    192
That Christendom gives out.

ROSS    Would I could answer    193
This comfort with the like! But I have words
That would be howled out in the desert air,    195
Where hearing should not latch them.

MACDUFF    What concern they?    196

The general cause? Or is it a fee-grief    197
Due to some single breast?

ROSS    No mind that's honest    198
But in it shares some woe, though the main part
Pertains to you alone.

MACDUFF    If it be mine,
Keep it not from me; quickly let me have it.

ROSS
Let not your ears despise my tongue forever,
Which shall possess them with the heaviest sound    203
That ever yet they heard.

MACDUFF    Hum! I guess at it.

ROSS
Your castle is surprised, your wife and babes
Savagely slaughtered. To relate the manner
Were, on the quarry of these murdered deer,    207
To add the death of you.

MALCOLM    Merciful heaven!
What, man, ne'er pull your hat upon your brows;    209
Give sorrow words. The grief that does not speak
Whispers the o'erfraught heart and bids it break.    211

MACDUFF
My children too?

ROSS    Wife, children, servants, all
That could be found.

MACDUFF    And I must be from thence!    213
My wife killed too?

ROSS    I have said.

MALCOLM    Be comforted.
Let's make us med'cines of our great revenge
To cure this deadly grief.

MACDUFF
He has no children. All my pretty ones?    217
Did you say all? O hell-kite! All?    218
What, all my pretty chickens and their dam
At one fell swoop?    220

MALCOLM    Dispute it like a man.    221

MACDUFF    I shall do so;
But I must also feel it as a man.
I cannot but remember such things were,
That were most precious to me. Did heaven look on
And would not take their part? Sinful Macduff,
They were all struck for thee! Naught that I am,    227
Not for their own demerits, but for mine,
Fell slaughter on their souls. Heaven rest them now!

MALCOLM
Be this the whetstone of your sword. Let grief
Convert to anger; blunt not the heart, enrage it.

---

167–8 nothing But who nobody except a person who    168 once ever
170 marked noticed (because they are so common)    171 modern
ecstasy commonplace emotion.    171–2 The dead . . . who Scarcely anyone ever asks for whom the bell tolls    173 flowers (Often worn in
Elizabethan caps.)    174 or ere they sicken before they have had time
to fall ill.    relation report    175 nice minutely accurate, elaborately
phrased    176 That . . . speaker The speaker of news that is scarcely an
hour old is hissed at for reporting stale news    177 teems teems with,
yields    178 well (Ross quibbles, in his reluctance to tell the bad news.
"The dead are well" means they are at rest.)    183 heavily sadly
184–6 Of . . . afoot about many worthy Scots driven into exile and
armed rebellion, which rumor was strengthened all the more when
I saw Macbeth's army on the move (in anticipation of being attacked).
187 time of help time when help is sorely needed.    188 our women
even our women    189 doff put off, get rid of    190 Gracious England
i.e., Edward the Confessor    192 none there is none    193 gives out tells
of, proclaims.    195 would should    196 latch catch (the sound of)

197 fee-grief a grief with an individual owner, having absolute ownership    198 Due to i.e., owned by    203 possess them with put them
in possession of    207 quarry heap of slaughtered deer at a hunt.
(With a pun on dear, deer.)    209 pull your hat (A conventional gesture
of silent grief.)    211 Whispers whispers to.    o'erfraught overburdened    213 must had to    217 He has no children (Referring either to
Macbeth, who must not be a father if he can do such a thing, or, to
Malcolm, who speaks comfortingly without knowing what such a
loss feels like to a father.)    218 hell-kite (The kite is a rapacious bird
of prey; a term of disdain and dislike.)    220 fell cruel    221 Dispute
Strive against, debate    227 for thee i.e., as divine punishment for
your sins.    Naught Wicked

MACDUFF
Oh, I could play the woman with mine eyes
And braggart with my tongue! But, gentle heavens,
Cut short all intermission. Front to front                         234
Bring thou this fiend of Scotland and myself;
Within my sword's length set him. If he scape,                     236
Heaven forgive him too!

MALCOLM                                This tune goes manly.         237
Come, go we to the King. Our power is ready;                       238
Our lack is nothing but our leave. Macbeth                         239
Is ripe for shaking, and the powers above
Put on their instruments. Receive what cheer you may.              241
The night is long that never finds the day.        *Exeunt.*

❖

## 5.1

*Enter a Doctor of Physic and a Waiting-*
*Gentlewoman.*

DOCTOR    I have two nights watched with you, but can-
perceive no truth in your report. When was it she last
walked?

GENTLEWOMAN    Since His Majesty went into the field, I
have seen her rise from her bed, throw her nightgown
upon her, unlock her closet, take forth paper, fold it,            6
write upon't, read it, afterwards seal it, and again
return to bed, yet all this while in a most fast sleep.

DOCTOR    A great perturbation in nature, to receive at
once the benefit of sleep and do the effects of                    10
watching! In this slumbery agitation, besides her                  11
walking and other actual performances, what, at any
time, have you heard her say?

GENTLEWOMAN    That, sir, which I will not report after her.

DOCTOR    You may to me, and 'tis most meet you should.            16

GENTLEWOMAN    Neither to you nor anyone, having no
witness to confirm my speech.

*Enter Lady [Macbeth], with a taper.*

Lo you, here she comes! This is her very guise, and,
upon my life, fast asleep. Observe her. Stand close.               20
                          [*They stand aside.*]

DOCTOR    How came she by that light?

GENTLEWOMAN    Why, it stood by her. She has light by
her continually. 'Tis her command.

DOCTOR    You see her eyes are open.

GENTLEWOMAN    Ay, but their sense are shut.

DOCTOR    What is it she does now? Look how she rubs
her hands.

GENTLEWOMAN    It is an accustomed action with her to
seem thus washing her hands. I have known her
continue in this a quarter of an hour.

LADY MACBETH    Yet here's a spot.

DOCTOR    Hark, she speaks. I will set down what comes
from her, to satisfy my remembrance the more          33
strongly.

LADY MACBETH    Out, damned spot! Out, I say! One—
two—why then, 'tis time to do't. Hell is murky.—
Fie, my lord, fie, a soldier, and afeard? What need we
fear who knows it, when none can call our power to
account? Yet who would have thought the old man to
have had so much blood in him?

DOCTOR    Do you mark that?

LADY MACBETH    The Thane of Fife had a wife. Where is
she now?—What, will these hands ne'er be
clean?—No more o'that, my lord, no more o' that;
you mar all with this starting.                        45

DOCTOR    Go to, go to. You have known what you         46
should not.

GENTLEWOMAN    She has spoke what she should not, I
am sure of that. Heaven knows what she has known!

LADY MACBETH    Here's the smell of the blood still. All
the perfumes of Arabia will not sweeten this little
hand. Oh, oh, oh!

DOCTOR    What a sigh is there! The heart is sorely      53
charged.                                                54

GENTLEWOMAN    I would not have such a heart in my
bosom for the dignity of the whole body.               56

DOCTOR    Well, well, well.

GENTLEWOMAN    Pray God it be, sir.                     58

DOCTOR    This disease is beyond my practice. Yet I have
known those which have walked in their sleep who
have died holily in their beds.

LADY MACBETH    Wash your hands, put on your nightgown; look not so pale! I tell you yet again, Banquo's
buried. He cannot come out on 's grave.                 64

DOCTOR    Even so?

LADY MACBETH    To bed, to bed! There's knocking at the
gate. Come, come, come, come, give me your hand.
What's done cannot be undone. To bed, to bed,
to bed!                                         *Exit Lady.*

DOCTOR    Will she go now to bed?

GENTLEWOMAN    Directly.

DOCTOR
Foul whisperings are abroad. Unnatural deeds
Do breed unnatural troubles. Infected minds
To their deaf pillows will discharge their secrets.
More needs she the divine than the physician.          75
God, God forgive us all! Look after her;
Remove from her the means of all annoyance,            77
And still keep eyes upon her. So, good night.          78
My mind she has mated, and amazed my sight.            79
I think, but dare not speak.

GENTLEWOMAN                       Good night, good Doctor.
                                            *Exeunt.*

❖

234 **intermission** delay, interval.   **Front to front** Face to face
**236–7 If . . . too!** If I let him escape, may he find forgiveness not only
from me but from heaven itself! (This is a condition that Macduff will
not allow to happen.)   **238 power** army   **239 Our . . . leave** we need
only to take our leave (of the English King).   **241 Put . . . instruments**
set us on as their agents, or, arm themselves.
**5.1. Location: Dunsinane. Macbeth's castle.**
**0.1** *Physic* medicine   **6 closet** chest or cabinet   **10–11 do . . . watch-**
**ing** act as though awake.   **16 meet** suitable   **20 close** concealed.

**33 satisfy** confirm, support   **45 this starting** these startled movements.
**46 Go to** (An exclamation of reproof, directed at Lady Macbeth.)
**53–4 sorely charged** heavily burdened.   **56 dignity** worth, value
**58 Pray . . . sir** Pray God it will turn out well, as you say, sir. (Playing
on the Doctor's *"Well, well,"* i.e., "Dear, dear.")   **64 on 's** of his
**75 divine** priest   **77 annoyance** i.e., harming herself   **78 still**
constantly   **79 mated** bewildered, stupefied

# 5.2

*Drum and colors. Enter Menteith, Caithness,*
*Angus, Lennox, [and] soldiers.*

MENTEITH
  The English power is near, led on by Malcolm,
  His uncle Siward, and the good Macduff.
  Revenges burn in them, for their dear causes   3
  Would to the bleeding and the grim alarm   4
  Excite the mortified man.
ANGUS             Near Birnam Wood   5
  Shall we well meet them; that way are they coming.   6
CAITHNESS
  Who knows if Donalbain be with his brother?
LENNOX
  For certain, sir, he is not. I have a file   8
  Of all the gentry. There is Siward's son,
  And many unrough youths that even now   10
  Protest their first of manhood.
MENTEITH         What does the tyrant?   11
CAITHNESS
  Great Dunsinane he strongly fortifies.
  Some say he's mad, others that lesser hate him
  Do call it valiant fury; but for certain
  He cannot buckle his distempered cause   15
  Within the belt of rule.
ANGUS          Now does he feel   16
  His secret murders sticking on his hands;
  Now minutely revolts upbraid his faith-breach.   18
  Those he commands move only in command,   19
  Nothing in love. Now does he feel his title
  Hang loose about him, like a giant's robe
  Upon a dwarfish thief.
MENTEITH        Who then shall blame
  His pestered senses to recoil and start,   23
  When all that is within him does condemn
  Itself for being there?
CAITHNESS       Well, march we on
  To give obedience where 'tis truly owed.
  Meet we the med'cine of the sickly weal,   27
  And with him pour we in our country's purge   28
  Each drop of us.
LENNOX        Or so much as it needs   29
  To dew the sovereign flower and drown the weeds.   30
  Make we our march towards Birnam.
                         *Exeunt, marching.*

# 5.3

*Enter Macbeth, Doctor, and attendants.*

MACBETH
  Bring me no more reports. Let them fly all!   1
  Till Birnam Wood remove to Dunsinane,
  I cannot taint with fear. What's the boy Malcolm?   3
  Was he not born of woman? The spirits that know
  All mortal consequences have pronounced me thus:   5
  "Fear not, Macbeth. No man that's born of woman
  Shall e'er have power upon thee." Then fly, false
    thanes,
  And mingle with the English epicures!   8
  The mind I sway by and the heart I bear   9
  Shall never sag with doubt nor shake with fear.

      *Enter Servant.*

  The devil damn thee black, thou cream-faced loon!   11
  Where got'st thou that goose look?
SERVANT
  There is ten thousand—
MACBETH           Geese, villain?
SERVANT              Soldiers, sir.
MACBETH
  Go prick thy face and over-red thy fear,   14
  Thou lily-livered boy. What soldiers, patch?   15
  Death of thy soul! Those linen cheeks of thine   16
  Are counselors to fear. What soldiers, whey-face?   17
SERVANT   The English force, so please you.
MACBETH   Take thy face hence.      *[Exit Servant.]*
        *[Calling]* Seyton!—I am sick at heart
  When I behold—Seyton, I say!—This push   20
  Will cheer me ever, or disseat me now.   21
  I have lived long enough. My way of life   22
  Is fall'n into the sere, the yellow leaf,   23
  And that which should accompany old age,
  As honor, love, obedience, troops of friends,   25
  I must not look to have, but in their stead
  Curses, not loud but deep, mouth-honor, breath   27
  Which the poor heart would fain deny and dare not.   28
  Seyton!

      *Enter Seyton.*

SEYTON
  What's your gracious pleasure?
MACBETH              What news more?

---

**5.2. Location: The country near Dunsinane.**
**3–5 their . . . man** their grievous wrongs would awaken even the dead
to answer the bloody and grim call to battle.  **6 well** conveniently;
doubtless  **8 file** list, roster  **10 unrough** beardless  **11 Protest**
assert publicly  **15 distempered** disease-swollen, dropsical  **16 rule**
restraint, self-control.  **18 Now . . . faith-breach** every minute now,
revolts upbraid him for his violation of all trust and sacred vows.
**19 in command** under orders  **23 pestered** troubled, tormented
**27 Meet we . . . weal** i.e., Let us join forces with Malcolm, the physician
of our sick land  **28–9 pour . . . of us** i.e., let us shed all our blood
as a bloodletting or *purge* for our country.  **30 dew** bedew, water.
**sovereign** (1) royal (2) medically efficacious

**5.3. Location: Dunsinane. Macbeth's castle.**
**1 Let . . . all!** Let all the thanes desert!  **3 taint with** become imbued or
infected with, weakened by  **5 All . . . consequences** all that happens in
this mortal life  **8 English epicures** luxury-loving Englishmen.  **9 sway**
rule myself  **11 loon** stupid fellow.  **14 Go . . . fear** i.e., Go prick or
pinch your pale cheeks to bring some color into them. (Current medical
theory held that fear caused a retreat of the blood to the abdominal
organs, leaving the countenance pale or *lily-livered*, line 15.)  **15 patch**
domestic fool.  **16 Death . . . soul!** May your soul die an eternal death!
(An oath.)  **linen** i.e., pale, white  **17 Are . . . fear** (The fear is contagious to the rest of the body and to other observers.)  **whey-face** paleface. (Whey, the watery serum in milk separated from the curd in the
making of cheese, is whitish.)  **20 behold** (Macbeth does not finish this
thought.)  **push** effort, crisis  **21 cheer** (With a suggestion of "chair.")
**disseat** dethrone  **22 way** course  **23 sere** dry and withered  **25 As**
such as  **27 mouth-honor** lip service  **28 fain** willingly

SEYTON
　All is confirmed, my lord, which was reported.
MACBETH
　I'll fight till from my bones my flesh be hacked.
　Give me my armor.
SEYTON　　　　　'Tis not needed yet.
MACBETH　　I'll put it on.
　Send out more horses. Skirr the country round.　　　36
　Hang those that talk of fear. Give me mine armor.
　How does your patient, Doctor?
DOCTOR　　Not so sick, my lord,
　As she is troubled with thick-coming fancies
　That keep her from her rest.
MACBETH　　　　　　　　Cure her of that.
　Canst thou not minister to a mind diseased,
　Pluck from the memory a rooted sorrow,
　Raze out the written troubles of the brain,　　　　44
　And with some sweet oblivious antidote　　　　　　45
　Cleanse the stuffed bosom of that perilous stuff　　46
　Which weighs upon the heart?
DOCTOR　　　　　　　　　Therein the patient
　Must minister to himself.
MACBETH
　Throw physic to the dogs! I'll none of it.　　　　　49
　Come, put mine armor on. Give me my staff.　　　50
　　　　　　　　　　　　　[Attendants arm him.]
　Seyton, send out. Doctor, the thanes fly from me.—
　Come, sir, dispatch.—If thou couldst, Doctor, cast　52
　The water of my land, find her disease,　　　　　53
　And purge it to a sound and pristine health,
　I would applaud thee to the very echo,
　That should applaud again.—Pull't off, I say.—　56
　What rhubarb, senna, or what purgative drug　　57
　Would scour these English hence? Hear'st thou of
　　　them?　　　　　　　　　　　　　　　　58
DOCTOR
　Ay, my good lord. Your royal preparation
　Makes us hear something.
MACBETH　　　　　　　　Bring it after me.—　　60
　I will not be afraid of death and bane　　　　　　61
　Till Birnam Forest come to Dunsinane.
　　　　　　　　　　　　Exeunt [all but the Doctor].
DOCTOR
　Were I from Dunsinane away and clear,
　Profit again should hardly draw me here.　　[Exit.]　64

❧

# 5.4

*Drum and colors. Enter Malcolm, Siward,*
*Macduff, Siward's Son, Menteith, Caithness,*
*Angus, [Lennox, Ross,] and soldiers, marching.*

36 Skirr Scour　44 Raze scrape; erase.　written troubles of troubles
recorded in　45 oblivious causing forgetfulness　46 stuffed overfilled
49 physic medicine　50 staff lance or baton of office.　52 dispatch
hurry.　52–3 cast The water diagnose disease by the inspection of urine
56 That . . . again (The sound of applause would be heard to echo.)
Pull't off (Refers to some part of the armor not properly put on.)
57 senna a purgative drug. (F reads "Cyme.")　58 scour purge, cleanse,
rid　60 it i.e., the armor not yet put on　61 bane ruin　64 Profit . . . here
No hope of profit could lure me back again.
5.4. Location: Country near Birnam Wood.

MALCOLM
　Cousins, I hope the days are near at hand　　　　1
　That chambers will be safe.
MENTEITH　　　　　　　　We doubt it nothing.　　2
SIWARD
　What wood is this before us?
MENTEITH　　　　　　　　The wood of Birnam.
MALCOLM
　Let every soldier hew him down a bough
　And bear't before him. Thereby shall we shadow　　5
　The numbers of our host and make discovery　　　6
　Err in report of us.
SOLDIERS　　　　　　　It shall be done.
SIWARD
　We learn no other but the confident tyrant　　　　8
　Keeps still in Dunsinane and will endure　　　　　9
　Our setting down before't.
MALCOLM　　　　　　　'Tis his main hope;　　　10
　For where there is advantage to be given,　　　　11
　Both more and less have given him the revolt,　　12
　And none serve with him but constrainèd things
　Whose hearts are absent too.
MACDUFF　　　　　　　　Let our just censures　14
　Attend the true event, and put we on　　　　　　15
　Industrious soldiership.
SIWARD　　　　　　　　The time approaches
　That will with due decision make us know
　What we shall say we have and what we owe.　　18
　Thoughts speculative their unsure hopes relate,　19
　But certain issue strokes must arbitrate—　　　　20
　Towards which advance the war.　Exeunt, marching.　21

❧

# 5.5

*Enter Macbeth, Seyton, and soldiers, with drum*
*and colors.*

MACBETH
　Hang out our banners on the outward walls.
　The cry is still, "They come!" Our castle's strength
　Will laugh a siege to scorn. Here let them lie　　　3
　Till famine and the ague eat them up.　　　　　4
　Were they not forced with those that should be ours,　5
　We might have met them dareful, beard to beard,　6

1 Cousins Kinsmen, peers　2 chambers . . . safe i.e., we may sleep
safely in our bedchambers.　nothing not at all.　5 shadow disguise,
conceal　6 discovery scouting reports　8 no other but no other news
but that　9 Keeps remains.　endure allow, not attempt to prevent
10 setting down before't laying siege to it.　11 advantage opportunity (i.e., in military operations outside Macbeth's castle in which it is
possible for would-be deserters to slip away; in a siege, his forces will
be more confined to the castle and under his watchful eye)　12 more
and less high and low　14–15 Let . . . event Let us postpone judgment about these uncertain matters until we've achieved our goal
18 What . . . owe what we only claim to have, as distinguished from
what we actually have. (Owe can mean "own.")　19–20 Thoughts . . .
arbitrate Speculating can only convey our sense of hope; blows must
decide the actual outcome　21 war army.
5.5. Location: Dunsinane. Macbeth's castle.
3 laugh . . . scorn laugh scornfully at the siege.　4 the ague fever,
disease　5 forced reinforced.　should be ours are our Scottish
countrymen　6 dareful boldly, in open battle

And beat them backward home.
*A cry within of women.*
What is that noise?

SEYTON
It is the cry of women, my good lord.
[*He goes to the door.*]

MACBETH
I have almost forgot the taste of fears.
The time has been my senses would have cooled          10
To hear a night-shriek, and my fell of hair            11
Would at a dismal treatise rouse and stir              12
As life were in't. I have supped full with horrors;    13
Direness, familiar to my slaughterous thoughts,
Cannot once start me.

[*Seyton returns.*]

Wherefore was that cry?          15
SEYTON    The Queen, my lord, is dead.
MACBETH    She should have died hereafter;          17
There would have been a time for such a word.
Tomorrow, and tomorrow, and tomorrow                   19
Creeps in this petty pace from day to day              20
To the last syllable of recorded time,
And all our yesterdays have lighted fools              22
The way to dusty death. Out, out, brief candle!        23
Life's but a walking shadow, a poor player
That struts and frets his hour upon the stage
And then is heard no more. It is a tale
Told by an idiot, full of sound and fury,
Signifying nothing.          28

*Enter a Messenger.*

Thou com'st to use thy tongue; thy story quickly.
MESSENGER    Gracious my lord,
I should report that which I say I saw,
But know not how to do't.
MACBETH                    Well, say, sir.
MESSENGER
As I did stand my watch upon the hill,
I looked toward Birnam, and anon, methought,
The wood began to move.
MACBETH                    Liar and slave!          35
MESSENGER
Let me endure your wrath if't be not so.
Within this three mile may you see it coming;
I say, a moving grove.
MACBETH                    If thou speak'st false,
Upon the next tree shalt thou hang alive
Till famine cling thee. If thy speech be sooth,        40
I care not if thou dost for me as much.                41

I pull in resolution, and begin                        42
To doubt th'equivocation of the fiend
That lies like truth. "Fear not, till Birnam Wood
Do come to Dunsinane," and now a wood
Comes toward Dunsinane. Arm, arm, and out!
If this which he avouches does appear,
There is nor flying hence nor tarrying here.
I 'gin to be aweary of the sun,
And wish th'estate o'th' world were now undone.        50
Ring the alarum bell! Blow wind, come wrack,           51
At least we'll die with harness on our back.   *Exeunt.*   52

## 5.6

*Drum and colors. Enter Malcolm, Siward,*
*Macduff, and their army, with boughs.*

MALCOLM
Now near enough. Your leafy screens throw down,
And show like those you are. You, worthy uncle,        2
Shall with my cousin, your right noble son,
Lead our first battle. Worthy Macduff and we           4
Shall take upon 's what else remains to do,
According to our order.
SIWARD                    Fare you well.          6
Do we but find the tyrant's power tonight,             7
Let us be beaten, if we cannot fight.
MACDUFF
Make all our trumpets speak! Give them all breath,
Those clamorous harbingers of blood and death!        10
*Exeunt. Alarums continued.*

## 5.7

*Enter Macbeth.*

MACBETH
They have tied me to a stake. I cannot fly,
But bearlike I must fight the course. What's he        2
That was not born of woman? Such a one
Am I to fear, or none.

*Enter young Siward.*

YOUNG SIWARD    What is thy name?
MACBETH    Thou'lt be afraid to hear it.
YOUNG SIWARD
No, though thou call'st thyself a hotter name
Than any is in hell.
MACBETH                    My name's Macbeth.

---

10 **cooled** felt the chill of terror   11 **my fell of hair** the hair of my scalp and skin   12 **dismal treatise** sad story   13 **As** as if   15 **start me** make me start.   **Wherefore** Why   17 **She … hereafter** She would have died someday, or, she should have died at some more appropriate time, freed from the relentless pressures of the moment   19–28 **Tomorrow … nothing** (For biblical echoes in this speech, see Psalms 18:28, 22:15, 90:9; Job 8:9, 14:1–2, 18:6.)   20 **in this** in at this   22 **lighted** (The metaphor is of a candle used to light one to bed, just as life is a brief transit for wretched mortals to their deathbeds.)   23 **dusty** (Since life, made out of dust, returns to dust.)   35 **slave** wretch.   40 **cling** cause to shrivel.   **sooth** truth   41 **as much** the same thing.

42 **pull in resolution** can no longer give free rein to my self-confident determination   50 **th'estate** the settled order   51 **wrack** ruin   52 **harness** armor
**5.6. Location:** Dunsinane. Before Macbeth's castle.
2 **show** appear.   **uncle** i.e., Siward   4 **battle** battalion.   6 **order** plan of battle.   7 **Do we** If we do.   **power** army   10 **harbingers** forerunners
**5.7. Location:** Before Macbeth's castle; the battle action is continuous here.
2 **course** bout or round of bearbaiting, in which the bear was tied to a stake and dogs were set upon him.

**YOUNG SIWARD**
The devil himself could not pronounce a title
More hateful to mine ear.
**MACBETH**                              No, nor more fearful.
**YOUNG SIWARD**
Thou liest, abhorrèd tyrant! With my sword
I'll prove the lie thou speak'st.
                    *Fight, and young Siward slain.*
**MACBETH**                    Thou wast born of woman.    12
But swords I smile at, weapons laugh to scorn,
Brandished by man that's of a woman born.    *Exit.*

        *Alarums. Enter Macduff.*

**MACDUFF**
That way the noise is. Tyrant, show thy face!
If thou be'st slain, and with no stroke of mine,    16
My wife and children's ghosts will haunt me still.    17
I cannot strike at wretched kerns, whose arms    18
Are hired to bear their staves. Either thou, Macbeth,    19
Or else my sword with an unbattered edge
I sheathe again undeeded. There thou shouldst be;    21
By this great clatter one of greatest note
Seems bruited. Let me find him, Fortune,    23
And more I beg not.              *Exit. Alarums.*

        *Enter Malcolm and Siward.*

**SIWARD**
This way, my lord. The castle's gently rendered:    25
The tyrant's people on both sides do fight,    26
The noble thanes do bravely in the war,
The day almost itself professes yours,    28
And little is to do.
**MALCOLM**              We have met with foes
That strike beside us.
**SIWARD**              Enter, sir, the castle.    30
                    *Exeunt. Alarum.*

# [5.8]

        *Enter Macbeth.*

**MACBETH**
Why should I play the Roman fool and die    1
On mine own sword? Whiles I see lives, the gashes    2

---

Do better upon them.

        *Enter Macduff.*

**MACDUFF**              Turn, hellhound, turn!
**MACBETH**
Of all men else I have avoided thee.
But get thee back! My soul is too much charged
With blood of thine already.
**MACDUFF**              I have no words;
My voice is in my sword, thou bloodier villain
Than terms can give thee out!    *Fight. Alarum.*
**MACBETH**              Thou losest labor.    8
As easy mayst thou the intrenchant air    9
With thy keen sword impress as make me bleed.    10
Let fall thy blade on vulnerable crests;
I bear a charmèd life, which must not yield
To one of woman born.
**MACDUFF**              Despair thy charm,    13
And let the angel whom thou still hast served    14
Tell thee, Macduff was from his mother's womb
Untimely ripped.    16
**MACBETH**
Accursèd be that tongue that tells me so,
For it hath cowed my better part of man!    18
And be these juggling fiends no more believed    19
That palter with us in a double sense,    20
That keep the word of promise to our ear    21
And break it to our hope. I'll not fight with thee.    22
**MACDUFF**    Then yield thee, coward,
And live to be the show and gaze o'th' time!    24
We'll have thee, as our rarer monsters are,
Painted upon a pole, and underwrit,    26
"Here may you see the tyrant."
**MACBETH**              I will not yield
To kiss the ground before young Malcolm's feet
And to be baited with the rabble's curse.    29
Though Birnam Wood be come to Dunsinane,
And thou opposed, being of no woman born,
Yet I will try the last. Before my body    32
I throw my warlike shield. Lay on, Macduff,
And damned be him that first cries, "Hold, enough!"    34
                *Exeunt, fighting. Alarums.*

        *Enter fighting, and Macbeth slain. [Exit Macduff*
        *with Macbeth's body.] Retreat, and flourish. Enter,*
        *with drum and colors, Malcolm, Siward, Ross,*
        *thanes, and soldiers.*

---

**12 s.d. young Siward slain** (In some unspecified way, young Siward's body must be removed from the stage; his own father enters at line 24.1 and perceives nothing amiss, and in 5.8.38 young Siward is reported *missing* in action. Perhaps Macbeth drags off the body, or perhaps it is removed by soldiers during the alarums.)   **16 with** by   **17 still** forever.   **18 kerns** (Properly, Irish foot soldiers; here, applied contemptuously to the rank and file.)   **19 staves** spears.   **Either thou** i.e., Either I find you and sheathe my sword in you   **21 undeeded** having seen no action.   **shouldst be** ought to be (judging by the noise)   **23 bruited** announced.   **25 gently rendered** surrendered with little fighting   **26 The tyrant's ... fight** i.e., some of Macbeth's Scottish countrymen have deserted to our side   **28 professes** declares itself   **30 strike beside us** fight on our side, or miss us deliberately.
**5.8. Location:** Before Macbeth's castle, as the battle continues; after line 34, within the castle.
**1 Roman fool** i.e., suicide, like Brutus, Mark Antony, and others.   **die** i.e., fall   **2–3 Whiles ... them** As long as I see enemy forces still living, the gashes that my sword can offer are more fitly bestowed upon the enemy (than on myself).

**8 give thee out** name you, describe you.   **9 intrenchant** that cannot be cut, indivisible   **10 impress** make an impression on   **13 Despair** Despair of   **14 angel** evil angel, Macbeth's genius.   **still** always   **16 Untimely** prematurely, i.e., by Caesarian delivery   **18 better ... man** i.e., courage.   **19 juggling** deceiving   **20 palter ... sense** equivocate with us   **21–2 That ... hope** that make promises we hear (and think we understand) but then break promise with what we hoped and expected.   **24 gaze o'th' time** spectacle or sideshow of the age.   **26 Painted ... pole** i.e., painted on a board or cloth and suspended on a pole   **29 baited** harassed   **32 the last** i.e., my last resort: my own strength and resolution.   **34.3 Retreat** a trumpet call ordering an end to the fighting.   **34.3–4 Enter, with drum and colors, etc.** (The remainder of the play is perhaps imagined as taking place in Macbeth's castle and could be marked as a separate scene. In Shakespeare's theater, however, the shift is so nonrepresentational and without scenic alteration that the action is virtually continuous.)

**MALCOLM**

I would the friends we miss were safe arrived.                    35

**SIWARD**

Some must go off; and yet, by these I see                         36
So great a day as this is cheaply bought.

**MALCOLM**

Macduff is missing, and your noble son.

**ROSS** [*to Siward*]

Your son, my lord, has paid a soldier's debt.
He only lived but till he was a man,
The which no sooner had his prowess confirmed
In the unshrinking station where he fought,            42
But like a man he died.

**SIWARD**                    Then he is dead?

**ROSS**

Ay, and brought off the field. Your cause of sorrow
Must not be measured by his worth, for then
It hath no end.

**SIWARD**          Had he his hurts before?

**ROSS**

Ay, on the front.

**SIWARD**          Why then, God's soldier be he!
Had I as many sons as I have hairs
I would not wish them to a fairer death.
And so, his knell is knolled.

**MALCOLM**                    He's worth more sorrow,
And that I'll spend for him.

**SIWARD**                    He's worth no more.
They say he parted well and paid his score,            52
And so, God be with him! Here comes newer comfort.

*Enter Macduff, with Macbeth's head.*

**MACDUFF** [*to Malcolm*]

Hail, King! For so thou art. Behold where stands      54
Th'usurper's cursèd head. The time is free.           55
I see thee compassed with thy kingdom's pearl,        56
That speak my salutation in their minds,
Whose voices I desire aloud with mine:
Hail, King of Scotland!

**ALL**    Hail, King of Scotland!              *Flourish.*

**MALCOLM**

We shall not spend a large expense of time
Before we reckon with your several loves              62
And make us even with you. My thanes and kinsmen,     63
Henceforth be earls, the first that ever Scotland
In such an honor named. What's more to do
Which would be planted newly with the time,           66
As calling home our exiled friends abroad
That fled the snares of watchful tyranny,
Producing forth the cruel ministers                   69
Of this dead butcher and his fiendlike queen—
Who, as 'tis thought, by self and violent hands       71
Took off her life—this, and what needful else
That calls upon us, by the grace of Grace
We will perform in measure, time, and place.          74
So, thanks to all at once and to each one,
Whom we invite to see us crowned at Scone.            76

*Flourish. Exeunt omnes.*

**54 stands** i.e., on a pole   **55 free** released from tyranny.
**56 compassed . . . pearl** surrounded by the nobles of your kingdom
(literally, the pearls encircling a crown)   **62 reckon** come to a reckoning.
**several** individual   **63 make . . . you** repay your worthiness.
**66 would . . . time** should be established at the commencement of this
new era   **69 Producing forth** bringing forward to trial.   **ministers**
agents   **71 self and violent** her own violent   **74 in measure . . . place**
in proper order and at fit time and place.   **76.1 *omnes*** all.

**35 would** wish   **36 go off** die.   **by these** to judge by these (assembled)   **42 unshrinking station** post from which he did not shrink   **52 parted** departed, died.   **score** reckoning

# Antony and Cleopatra

Shakespeare probably wrote *Antony and Cleopatra* in 1606 or 1607; it was registered for publication on May 20, 1608, and apparently influenced a revision of Samuel Daniel's *Cleopatra* that was published "newly altered" in 1607. *Antony and Cleopatra* was thus roughly contemporary with *King Lear* and *Macbeth*. Yet the contrast between those two tragedies and *Antony and Cleopatra* is immense. Unlike *Macbeth*, with its taut focus on a murderer and his wife, *Antony and Cleopatra* moves back and forth across the Mediterranean in its epic survey of characters and events, bringing together the fates of Pompey, Octavius Caesar, Octavia, and Lepidus with those of the protagonists. *King Lear* gives proper names to fourteen characters, *Macbeth* to eighteen, *Antony and Cleopatra* to thirty-one. The Roman play requires no fewer than forty-two separate scenes, of which most occur in what modern editors label Acts 3 and 4, although no play is less suited to the classical rigors of five-act structure, and these divisions are not found in the reliable Folio text of 1623. Indeed, it is as though Shakespeare resolved at the height of his career to show that he could dispense entirely with the classical "rules," which had never taken serious hold of the English popular stage in any case. The flouting of the unities is so extreme that John Dryden, in his *All for Love, or The World Well Lost* (1678), undertook not so much to revise Shakespeare as to start afresh on the same subject. Dryden's play is restricted to the last few hours of the protagonists' lives, at Cleopatra's tomb in Alexandria, with a severely limited cast of characters and much of the narrative revealed through recollection. Although a substantial achievement in its own right, *All for Love* surely demonstrates that Shakespeare knew what he was doing, for Dryden has excised a good deal of the panorama, the excitement, and the "infinite variety" (2.2.246).

Shakespeare departs also from the somber tone of his tragedies of evil. He creates, instead, a world that bears affinities to the ambiguous conflicts of the other Roman plays, to the varying humorous perspectives of the comedies, and to the imaginative reconstructions of the late romances. As protagonists, Antony and Cleopatra lack tragic stature, or so it first appears: she is a tawny gypsy temptress and he a "strumpet's fool," a once-great general now bound in "strong Egyptian fetters" and lost in "dotage" (1.1.13; 1.2.122–3). Several scenes, especially those set in Egypt, are comic and delightfully bawdy: Charmian learning her fortune from the soothsayer, Cleopatra practicing her charms in vain to keep Antony from leaving Egypt or raunchily daydreaming of being Antony's horse "to bear the weight of Antony" (1.5.22), Cleopatra flying into a magnificent rage at the news of Antony's marriage to Octavia and then consoling herself with catty reflections on Octavia's reported low voice and shortness of stature ("I think so, Charmian. Dull of tongue, and dwarfish," 3.3.17). In its comic texture, the play somewhat resembles *Romeo and Juliet*, an earlier play about a younger pair of lovers, although there the bawdry is used chiefly to characterize the lovers' companions and confidants, whereas in *Antony and Cleopatra* it is central to our vision of Cleopatra especially. In any case, the later play is a tragedy about lovers who, despite their quarrels and uncertainties and betrayals of self, are reconciled in a vision of the greatness of their love. In its depiction of two contrasting worlds, also, *Antony and Cleopatra* recalls the movement of several earlier comedies from the realistic world of political conniving to a dreamworld of the romantic and the unexpected. We can endorse neither world fully in *Antony and Cleopatra*, and, accordingly, the vision of life presented is often ambivalent and ironic as much as it is tragic. The contrast of values separating Egypt and Rome underscores the paradox of humanity's quest for seemingly irreconcilable goals. The ending is neither a triumph nor a defeat for the lovers but something of both. If Antony and Cleopatra seem in one way too small to be tragic protagonists, in another way they seem too large, creating imaginative visions of themselves and their union that escape the realm of tragedy altogether. Our attention is focused less on the way in which the protagonists come to understand some meaningful relationship between their character and the fate required of them by a tragic universe than on the almost comic way in which the absurdities of Roman worldly striving and Egyptian dissipation are transfigured in the world of the imagination.

The Roman point of view opens the play and never entirely loses its force. At first, it may seem superior to that of Egypt. Demetrius and Philo, who invite us to view the play's first encounter between Antony and Cleopatra (1.1) from the perspective of the professional Roman soldier, lament the decline of Antony into Circean enslavement. Their tragic concept is of the Fall of Princes, all the more soberly edifying because of the height from which Antony has toppled. "You shall see in him / The triple pillar of the world transformed / Into a strumpet's fool" (1.1.11–13). Egypt is enchanting but clearly enervating— a bizarre assemblage of soothsayers, eunuchs, and waiting-gentlewomen who wish to be "married to three kings in a forenoon and widow them all" (1.2.28–9). Their mirth is all bawdry, tinged with practices, such as transvestitism, that Roman custom views as licentious. The prevailing images are of procreation in various shapes, sleep (mandragora, Lethe), the oriental opulence of Cleopatra's barge (a golden poop, purple sails, silver oars, divers-colored fans), Epicurean feasting, and drinking. As Enobarbus says, "Mine, and most of our fortunes tonight, shall be—drunk to bed" (1.2.47–8).

Antony, for all his reckless defiance of Rome, agrees in his more reflective moments with what Demetrius and Philo have said. "A Roman thought hath struck him," Cleopatra observantly remarks, and Antony has indeed determined that "I must from this enchanting queen break off" (1.2.88, 135). His later return to Cleopatra is at least in part a surrender, a betrayal of his marriage vows to Octavia and his political assurances to Caesar. In the ensuing battles, Antony submits himself recklessly to Cleopatra's governance, and this inversion of dominance in sexual roles, as conventionally understood by the Roman patriarchal world, is emblematic of a deeper disorder within Antony. As Enobarbus concludes bitterly, Antony "would make his will / Lord of his reason" and so has subverted his "judgment" (3.13.3–4, 37) to passion.

From the beginning, Cleopatra has sought dominance over Antony in the war of the sexes. When Antony first came to her on the River Cydnus, we learn, he was so overcome in all his senses that he was "barbered ten times o'er" (2.2.234). Cleopatra boasts that she "angled" for Antony on many occasions, catching him the way fishermen "betray" fish, and that, when she had "drunk him to his bed," she "put my tires and mantles on him, whilst / I wore his sword Philippan" (2.5.10–23). Caesar, affronted by such transvestite debauchery, charges that Antony "is not more manlike / Than Cleopatra, nor the queen of Ptolemy / More womanly than he" (1.4.5–7).

During the battle scenes, Antony's followers complain that "Photinus, an eunuch" (probably Mardian), and Cleopatra's maids manage the war: "So our leader's led, / And we are women's men" (3.7.14–15, 70–1). Antony confesses too late that they were right. He becomes a "doting mallard," one whose heart is "tied by th' strings" to Cleopatra's rudder when her ships retreat in the naval engagement at Actium (3.10.20, 3.11.56). In the mythic images used to raise their relationship to heroic proportions, Antony is like Mars to Cleopatra's Venus (1.5.19), in both a positive and a negative sense. The image has positive connotations of the way in which, as Milton puts it, the "two great sexes animate the world," the masterful soldier and his attractive consort complementing one another in a right relationship of martial prowess and beauty, bravery and love, reason and will; however, to the Renaissance, the myth of Mars and Venus could also be read in a destructive sense, as an adulterous relationship in which reason is subverted to appetite. In another mythic comparison, Antony is like Hercules, not in his prime, but with the shirt of Nessus on his back—a poisoned shirt given to Hercules by his wife in a mistaken hope of thereby assuring his love for her (4.12.43). Antony's soldiers understandably believe that the god Hercules has deserted his reputed descendant and onetime champion (4.3.21–2).

Despite Antony's shameful violation of manhood, honor, attention to duty, self-knowledge, and all that Rome stands for, however, the end of his story is anything but a one-sided endorsement for the Roman point of view. The actual Rome, disfigured by political conniving, falls far short of the ideal. Antony has a point when he protests that "Kingdoms are clay" (1.1.37). Alliances are unstable and are governed by mere political expediency. At first, Antony's wife Fulvia and his brother Lucius have fought one another until forced to unite against the greater threat of Octavius Caesar. Similarly, Antony and Caesar come together only because Pompey has become dangerously powerful at sea and has won the favor of the fickle mob, "Our slippery people" (1.2.192). This detente is not meant to last. As Enobarbus bluntly puts it, "if you borrow one another's love for the instant, you may, when you hear no more words of Pompey, return it again" (2.2.109–11). Enobarbus is rebuked for his unstatesmanlike tone, but no one denies the validity of what he says. In this cynical negotiation, Octavia is a pawn between husband and brother, shabbily treated by both. Caesar coldly bargains away the happiness of the one person of whom he protests that "no brother / Did ever love so dearly" (2.2.159–60). Antony, although hating false promises and resolving to be loyal to Octavia, knows within himself that it won't work. To make matters worse for the fair-minded Antony, he has received great favors from Pompey that he must now uncharitably repudiate in the interests of politics. Pompey does not miss the opportunity to remind Antony of his ingratitude, but the prevailing mood is not so much of bitterness as of ironic futility. Old friendships must be sacrificed; no one seems wholly to blame, and no one can stop the game. Pompey is as much in the wrong as anyone and as powerless. Despite his idealistic hope of restoring republican government to Rome, he has had to ally himself with pirates who offer him sinister temptations. He could be "lord of all the world" (2.7.62) if he would only murder on occasion, but Pompey is destined to be trapped between lofty ends and ignoble means. Lepidus is still another dismaying victim of political callousness, used condescendingly by Caesar and permitted to drink himself into oblivion, until he is cashiered on a trumped-up charge and imprisoned for life.

Octavius Caesar embodies most of all the ironic limits of political ambition. He has avoided enslavement to passion at the very real cost of enslaving himself to his public career as general, triumvir, and future emperor. His ideal warrior is one who, driven by military necessity, would "drink / The stale [urine] of horses and the gilded puddle / Which beasts would cough at" (1.4.62–4). As a general, he is Antony's opposite in every way. He attacks only when he has the advantage and places those who have deserted Antony in his own front lines so "That Antony may seem to spend his fury / Upon himself" (4.6.10–11). He controls his supplies cannily, believing it a "waste" to feast his army (4.1.17). He, of course, declines Antony's offers of single combat. Antony meantime recklessly accepts Caesar's challenge to fight at sea, feasts debauchingly in one "gaudy night" after another (3.13.186), and generously refuses to blame or penalize those who leave him. His sending Enobarbus's belongings after him into Caesar's camp convinces that honest soldier he has made a fatal error, for, however imprudent Antony's chivalry may be, it is unquestionably noble and great-hearted. Caesar is a superb general and political genius, but he is also a military automaton, a logistical reckoner, a Machiavellian pragmatist. In his personal life, he is no less austere and puritanical. He deplores loosening his tongue with alcohol. About women, he is deeply cynical, believing that "want will perjure / The ne'er-touched vestal" (3.12.30–1). Between him and Cleopatra, there is a profound antipathy, based in part on his revulsion at her earlier affair with his namesake and adoptive father, Julius Caesar (3.6.6). Cleopatra may entertain briefly the notion of trying to seduce this new Caesar (3.13.46 ff.), for like Charmian she loves long life "better than figs"(1.2.34), but, if so, she soon discovers that she and Caesar are not compatible. All that he represents she must instead grandly repudiate, choosing death and the fantasy of an eternity with Antony as her way to "call great Caesar ass / Unpolicied" (5.2.307–8).

Cleopatra is a "lass unparalleled" (5.2.316), whose greatness is elusive and all the more enthralling because it is so mysterious. She rises above her counterpart in Shakespeare's source, Plutarch's Lives of the Noble Grecians and Romans, in which she is an impressive queenly woman but still essentially a temptress causing the lamentable fall of the hero. Shakespeare's Cleopatra is that but is also something indefinable that can be gotten at only through paradox. Her very character is the essence of contradiction: she knows how "to chide, to laugh, / To weep" (1.1.51–2), to be sullen or violent, like a skillful actor keeping Antony continually off guard. Dispassionately examined, she is a woman no longer young who abuses messengers like an oriental despot, who sends Antony a false report of her death out of fear for her own safety, who will not risk leaving her monument even when Antony lies outside mortally wounded, and who lies about her wealth when captured by Caesar (what is she planning to do with that wealth, anyway?). We cannot be sure that she would not have "packed cards with Caesar" (4.14.19) if she had found him susceptible to her charms. Yet we are not invited to see her dispassionately. Her charm is eternal, and so are the myths surrounding that charm. Observers evoking her splendor do not describe her person directly but, rather, her effects and surroundings: Enobarbus says simply that "For her own person, / It beggared all description" and goes on to catalogue her cloth-of-gold pavilion and her mermaid-like attendants. Most of all, she is a paradox: she makes defect perfection, age cannot wither her, and "vilest things / Become themselves in her, that the holy priests / Bless her when she is riggish" (2.2.207–50). She is both a whore and the Lucretian Venus; both sluttish and holy.

Inspired by Cleopatra, Antony shows himself ready to break down conventional barriers between the sexes and to explore new emotional territory by giving up part of his self-protective masculinity. Antony's embracing of an attractive but sexually dangerous woman is all the more remarkable in a play that follows the harrowing depictions of sexual conflict in Hamlet, Othello, and King Lear and the degrading portrait of erotic enslavement in the "Dark Lady" sonnets, for here the relationship of the lovers, though doomed, is also triumphant. Shakespeare takes a look at something like midlife crisis, conceding freely how ridiculous the male appears to himself and to others in his compulsive tendency to polarize women into saints and whores. Yet Shakespeare also explores ways in which the man and the woman attempt to become increasingly like each other, enabling the man to participate in a vision of union with the feminine principle of generative, erotic, fertile, life-giving vitality, and enabling the woman to join her "husband" in the noble resolve of a Roman suicide.

In Cleopatra, "fancy" exceeds "nature"; the fertility of her Egypt overflows the measure, exceeding the sterility of Rome as her own imaginative fertility exceeds reality itself. When she protests that she will not go to Rome to behold herself in a wretched play and thus see "Some squeaking Cleopatra boy my greatness / I'th' posture of a whore" (5.2.220–1), we realize that Shakespeare is calling attention to his own art as well, pointing out how Elizabethan boy actors on a bare stage can transform reality into a dream that we believe. Cleopatra's mystery is like that of poetry itself. The "real" world pales into insignificance of a "little O, the earth," something "No better than a sty," full of illusory shadows that "mock our eyes with air" (5.2.80, 4.15.64, 4.14.7); and Caesar's triumph vanishes with it. In its place, Antony and Cleopatra raise up a vision of themselves as lovers who, through art, have indeed become eternal. Together they will overpicture Venus and Mars, and will be so renowned that "Dido and her Aeneas shall want troops, / And all the haunt be ours" (4.14.53–4). They are virtually husband and wife—"Husband, I come!" exclaims Cleopatra just before she dies (5.2.287)—united at last in a re-creative vision almost appropriate to comedy; and in their marriage they find a kind of redemption for the defeat that history can inflict. Antony is no longer dying Hercules but the god of Cleopatra's dream whose "legs bestrid the ocean; his reared arm / Crested the world; his voice was propertied / As all the tunèd spheres" (lines 81–3). Through Cleopatra's vision, we realize how all the characteristics that made Antony at once so noble and so sure to fall before Caesar—his generosity amounting to imprudence, his spontaneity, his impatience with the ordinary, his staking his all on love when he hears of Cleopatra's supposed death—have not deserted him. His death serves to reaffirm the magnificence of the very qualities that have brought him down. His essential nobility is confirmed, even if it must be defined in non-Roman ways. He and Cleopatra share the "immortal longings" for which she goes willingly to her death, dressed in her "best attires" like a queen (lines 281, 228), for neither lover will accept anything less than greatness.

*Antony and Cleopatra* is a daunting play to stage, because the main characters take on a mythic character that seems larger than life, larger than art itself. Michael Goldman imagines what it would be like for an actor to audition for the part of Antony only to be instructed by the casting director, "Now, stand there and be a triple pillar of the world." How can an actor convey the charisma of a man whose very name is legendary? The problem in acting Cleopatra is even more acute. The great actresses who have taken on the assignment have all been praised for many things but also faulted for lacking other dimensions of this amazing character. Vivien Leigh, playing opposite Laurence Olivier's Antony at the St. James Theatre, London, in 1951, was applauded by the critics for her coquettish sexiness and magnetism but perhaps deficient in animal heat and duskiness. Peggy Ashcroft, in Glen Byam Shaw's production at Stratford-upon-Avon in 1953, was lauded as impressively intelligent and capable of huge emotional variation, but was seen as physically small and not as sexually glamorous as Leigh. Margaret Whiting, at the Old Vic in 1957, was regarded by most viewers as simply too young for the part. Vanessa Redgrave, at the Bankside Globe Playhouse in 1973, threw cola bottles at her servants in her fits of temper, and somehow lacked dignity for the final scenes. Glenda Jackson, playing Cleopatra in Peter Brook's de-romanticized version at Stratford-upon-Avon in 1978, was brilliant for her iciness of tone and angularity in wit combat, but at the expense of tenderness and erotic feeling. The role has attracted the greatest of talent, from Janet Suzman to Helen Mirren to Judi Dench, with similar praise and qualifications. These limits are a tribute to the play itself but a thorny problem for those who are producing the play. Film versions have tended to succumb to the temptations of visual splendor, in the style of Cecil B. DeMille, thus missing the point of the play's verbal and theatrical invocation of the ineffable. One singularly successful production is that on audiotape with Michael Redgrave as Antony and Peggy Ashcroft as Cleopatra; here the listener can imagine the lovers to be as toweringly great as the play's language suggests, magnificently assisted by the voices of two great actors. This is not to say that *Antony and Cleopatra* is unplayable; to the contrary, it shows Shakespeare at the very height of his powers as a professional writer for the theater. At the same time, few plays have ever posed a greater challenge for an acting ensemble.

# Antony and Cleopatra

[*Dramatis Personae*

MARK ANTONY,
OCTAVIUS CAESAR, } *triumvirs*
LEPIDUS,

CLEOPATRA,
CHARMIAN,
IRAS,
ALEXAS,
MARDIAN, *a eunuch,* } *Cleopatra's attendants*
DIOMEDES,
SELEUCUS, *Cleopatra's treasurer,*

OCTAVIA, *sister of Octavius Caesar and wife of Antony*

DEMETRIUS,
PHILO,
DOMITIUS ENOBARBUS,
VENTIDIUS,
SILIUS, } *Antony's friends and followers*
EROS,
CANIDIUS,
SCARUS,
DERCETUS,
A SCHOOLMASTER, *Antony's* AMBASSADOR *to Caesar*

MAECENAS,
AGRIPPA,
TAURUS,
THIDIAS, } *Octavius Caesar's friends and followers*
DOLABELLA,
GALLUS,
PROCULEIUS,

SEXTUS POMPEIUS *or* POMPEY
MENAS,
MENECRATES, } *Pompey's friends*
VARRIUS,

MESSENGERS *to Antony, Octavius, Caesar, and Cleopatra*
A SOOTHSAYER
*Two* SERVANTS *of Pompey*
SERVANTS *of Antony and Cleopatra*
A BOY
SOLDIERS, SENTRIES, GUARDSMEN *of Antony and Octavius Caesar*
A CAPTAIN *in Antony's army*
*An* EGYPTIAN
A CLOWN *with figs*

*Ladies attending Cleopatra, Eunuchs, Servants, Soldiers, Captains, Officers, silent named characters (Rannius, Lucillius, Lamprius)*

SCENE: *In several parts of the Roman Empire*]

## [1.1]

*Enter Demetrius and Philo.*

PHILO
  Nay, but this dotage of our general's          1
  O'erflows the measure. Those his goodly eyes,   2

  That o'er the files and musters of the war      3
  Have glowed like plated Mars, now bend, now turn  4
  The office and devotion of their view           5
  Upon a tawny front. His captain's heart,        6
  Which in the scuffles of great fights hath burst  7
  The buckles on his breast, reneges all temper   8

---

1.1. **Location:** Alexandria. Cleopatra's palace.
1 **dotage** foolish affection, sometimes associated with old age
2 **O'erflows the measure** exceeds moderation, exceeds the means of measuring it.

3 **files and musters** orderly formations   4 **plated** clothed in armor
5 **office** function   6 **tawny front** dark face. (Literally, forehead.)
8 **reneges all temper** renounces all moderation

And is become the bellows and the fan
To cool a gypsy's lust.

*Flourish. Enter Antony, Cleopatra, her ladies, the*
*train, with eunuchs fanning her.*

Look, where they come.                                 10
Take but good note, and you shall see in him
The triple pillar of the world transformed            12
Into a strumpet's fool. Behold and see.               13

CLEOPATRA
If it be love indeed, tell me how much.

ANTONY
There's beggary in the love that can be reckoned.     15

CLEOPATRA
I'll set a bourn how far to be beloved.               16

ANTONY
Then must thou needs find out new heaven, new
    earth.                                            17

*Enter a Messenger.*

MESSENGER    News, my good lord, from Rome.
ANTONY    Grates me! The sum.                          19
CLEOPATRA    Nay, hear them, Antony.                   20
Fulvia perchance is angry, or who knows               21
If the scarce-bearded Caesar have not sent            22
His powerful mandate to you, "Do this, or this;
Take in that kingdom, and enfranchise that;           24
Perform't, or else we damn thee."                     25
ANTONY    How, my love?                                26
CLEOPATRA    Perchance? Nay, and most like.           27
You must not stay here longer; your dismission        28
Is come from Caesar. Therefore hear it, Antony.
Where's Fulvia's process? Caesar's, I would say. Both? 30
Call in the messengers. As I am Egypt's queen,
Thou blushest, Antony, and that blood of thine
Is Caesar's homager; else so thy cheek pays shame     33
When shrill-tongued Fulvia scolds. The messengers!

ANTONY
Let Rome in Tiber melt and the wide arch
Of the ranged empire fall! Here is my space.          36
Kingdoms are clay; our dungy earth alike
Feeds beast as man. The nobleness of life

Is to do thus; when such a mutual pair                39
And such a twain can do't, in which I bind,           40
On pain of punishment, the world to weet              41
We stand up peerless.
CLEOPATRA                    Excellent falsehood!      42
Why did he marry Fulvia, and not love her?            43
I'll seem the fool I am not. Antony                    44
Will be himself.
ANTONY                    But stirred by Cleopatra.    45
Now, for the love of Love and her soft hours,
Let's not confound the time with conference harsh.    47
There's not a minute of our lives should stretch      48
Without some pleasure now. What sport tonight?        49

CLEOPATRA
Hear the ambassadors.
ANTONY                    Fie, wrangling queen!
Whom everything becomes—to chide, to laugh,
To weep; whose every passion fully strives
To make itself, in thee, fair and admired!
No messenger but thine; and all alone                 54
Tonight we'll wander through the streets and note
The qualities of people. Come, my queen,
Last night you did desire it.—Speak not to us.
*Exeunt [Antony and Cleopatra] with the train.*

DEMETRIUS
Is Caesar with Antonius prized so slight?             58
PHILO
Sir, sometimes when he is not Antony
He comes too short of that great property             60
Which still should go with Antony.
DEMETRIUS                    I am full sorry           61
That he approves the common liar, who                 62
Thus speaks of him at Rome; but I will hope
Of better deeds tomorrow. Rest you happy!    *Exeunt.*  64

## [1.2]

*Enter Enobarbus, Lamprius, a Soothsayer, Ran-*
*nius, Lucillius, Charmian, Iras, Mardian the*
*eunuch, and Alexas.*

CHARMIAN    Lord Alexas, sweet Alexas, most anything
    Alexas, almost most absolute Alexas, where's the   2
    soothsayer that you praised so to th' Queen? Oh, that

I knew this husband, which, you say, must charge his
horns with garlands!                                                    5

ALEXAS   Soothsayer!

SOOTHSAYER   Your will?

CHARMIAN
Is this the man?—Is't you, sir, that know things?

SOOTHSAYER
In nature's infinite book of secrecy
A little I can read.

ALEXAS [to Charmian]   Show him your hand.

ENOBARBUS [to servants within]
Bring in the banquet quickly; wine enough           12
Cleopatra's health to drink.

CHARMIAN [giving her hand to the Soothsayer]   Good sir,
give me good fortune.

SOOTHSAYER   I make not, but foresee.

CHARMIAN   Pray, then, foresee me one.

SOOTHSAYER
You shall be yet far fairer than you are.

CHARMIAN   He means in flesh.                              19

IRAS   No, you shall paint when you are old.             20

CHARMIAN   Wrinkles forbid!

ALEXAS   Vex not his prescience. Be attentive.

CHARMIAN   Hush!

SOOTHSAYER
You shall be more beloving than beloved.

CHARMIAN   I had rather heat my liver with drinking.    25

ALEXAS   Nay, hear him.

CHARMIAN   Good now, some excellent fortune! Let me   27
be married to three kings in a forenoon and widow
them all. Let me have a child at fifty, to whom Herod   29
of Jewry may do homage. Find me to marry me with     30
Octavius Caesar, and companion me with my mis-        31
tress.                                                                      32

SOOTHSAYER
You shall outlive the lady whom you serve.

CHARMIAN   Oh, excellent! I love long life better than figs.   34

SOOTHSAYER
You have seen and proved a fairer former fortune      35
Than that which is to approach.

CHARMIAN   Then belike my children shall have no      37
names. Prithee, how many boys and wenches must I    38
have?                                                                      39

SOOTHSAYER
If every of your wishes had a womb,
And fertile every wish, a million.

CHARMIAN   Out, fool! I forgive thee for a witch.        42

ALEXAS   You think none but your sheets are privy to   43
your wishes.

CHARMIAN   Nay, come, tell Iras hers.

ALEXAS   We'll know all our fortunes.

ENOBARBUS   Mine, and most of our fortunes tonight,
shall be—drunk to bed.

IRAS [giving her hand to the Soothsayer]   There's a palm
presages chastity, if nothing else.

CHARMIAN   E'en as the o'erflowing Nilus presageth   51
famine.                                                                    52

IRAS   Go, you wild bedfellow, you cannot soothsay.   53

CHARMIAN   Nay, if an oily palm be not a fruitful prog-   54
nostication, I cannot scratch mine ear. Prithee, tell her   55
but a workaday fortune.                                          56

SOOTHSAYER   Your fortunes are alike.

IRAS   But how, but how? Give me particulars.

SOOTHSAYER   I have said.                                     59

IRAS   Am I not an inch of fortune better than she?

CHARMIAN   Well, if you were but an inch of fortune better than I, where would you choose it?

IRAS   Not in my husband's nose.                            63

CHARMIAN   Our worser thoughts heavens mend! Al-   64
exas—come, his fortune, his fortune! Oh, let him marry
a woman that cannot go, sweet Isis, I beseech thee,    66
and let her die too, and give him a worse, and let
worse follow worse till the worst of all follow him
laughing to his grave, fiftyfold a cuckold! Good Isis,
hear me this prayer, though thou deny me a matter of   70
more weight; good Isis, I beseech thee!

IRAS   Amen, dear goddess, hear that prayer of the people! For, as it is a heart-breaking to see a handsome
man loose-wived, so it is a deadly sorrow to behold a   74
foul knave uncuckolded. Therefore, dear Isis, keep de-   75
corum, and fortune him accordingly!                       76

CHARMIAN   Amen.

ALEXAS   Lo now, if it lay in their hands to make me a
cuckold, they would make themselves whores but     79
they'd do't.                                                           80

*Enter Cleopatra.*

ENOBARBUS
Hush! Here comes Antony.

CHARMIAN   Not he. The Queen.

CLEOPATRA [to Enobarbus]   Saw you my lord?

---

**4 this husband** (Evidently Alexas has told Charmian that the Sooth-sayer will prophesy a husband for her.)   **4–5 must . . . garlands** i.e., must decorate his cuckold's horns with a garland of flowers, like a sacrificial beast. (Cuckolded men were derisively thought of as grow-ing horns, as a badge of their infamy.)   **12 banquet** light repast, des-sert   **19 in flesh** i.e., by putting on weight.   **20 paint** i.e., use makeup   **25 heat . . . drinking** i.e., heat my liver with wine rather than with unrequited love. (The liver was believed to be the seat of sexual desire.)   **27 Good now** Come on, now   **29–30 Herod of Jewry** i.e., even the blustering tyrant who massacred the children of Judea   **30 Find me** i.e., Find in my palm   **31–2 companion . . . mistress** give me equal fortune with Cleopatra; or, perhaps, let Cleopatra become my "companion" or attendant.   **34 better than figs** (Proba-bly a proverbial expression; with genital suggestion.)   **35 proved** experienced   **37 belike** probably   **37–8 have no names** be illegitimate.   **38 wenches** girls   **38–9 must I have** am I to have.

**42 Out . . . witch** (Charmian jokingly says that, since soothsayers, like fools, are allowed to speak freely without penalty, she will forgive him for slander.)   **43 privy to** in on the secret of   **51–2 E'en . . . fam-ine** (Charmian speaks ironically; the overflowing Nile presages abun-dance. See 2.7.17–23.)   **53 wild** wanton   **54 oily palm** sweaty or moist palm (indicating a sensual disposition)   **54–5 fruitful prognos-tication** omen of fertility   **56 workaday** ordinary   **59 I have said** I have no more to say.   **63 Not . . . nose** (Iras bawdily hints at some place other than in the nose where she would prefer to see her hus-band well endowed.)   **64 Our . . . mend!** (Charmian pretends to be shocked: May heaven improve our dirty minds!)   **66 cannot go** (1) is lame (2) cannot make love satisfactorily or cannot bear children. **Isis** Egyptian goddess usually identified with fertility and the moon   **70 hear me** hear (on my behalf)   **74 loose-wived** with an unfaithful wife   **75 foul** ugly   **75–6 keep decorum** deal suitably with the case   **76 fortune him** grant him fortune   **79–80 they . . . do't** i.e., they would stop at nothing, even becoming whores, to cuckold me.

ENOBARBUS    No, lady.
CLEOPATRA  [to Charmian]    Was he not here?
CHARMIAN    No, madam.
CLEOPATRA
He was disposed to mirth, but on the sudden
A Roman thought hath struck him. Enobarbus!
ENOBARBUS    Madam?
CLEOPATRA
Seek him and bring him hither. Where's Alexas?
ALEXAS
Here at your service.—My lord approaches.

*Enter Antony with a Messenger.*

CLEOPATRA
We will not look upon him. Go with us.
                    *Exeunt [all but Antony and the Messenger].*
FIRST MESSENGER
Fulvia thy wife first came into the field.                         93
ANTONY    Against my brother Lucius?
FIRST MESSENGER    Ay.
But soon that war had end, and the time's state          96
Made friends of them, jointing their force 'gainst
    Caesar,                                                               97
Whose better issue in the war from Italy                        98
Upon the first encounter drave them.                            99
ANTONY    Well, what worst?
FIRST MESSENGER
The nature of bad news infects the teller.                     101
ANTONY
When it concerns the fool or coward. On.
Things that are past are done with me. 'Tis thus:
Who tells me true, though in his tale lie death,          104
I hear him as he flattered.
FIRST MESSENGER                    Labienus—                105
This is stiff news—hath with his Parthian force
Extended Asia; from Euphrates                                 107
His conquering banner shook, from Syria
To Lydia and to Ionia,
Whilst—
ANTONY    Antony, thou wouldst say.
FIRST MESSENGER                        Oh, my lord!
ANTONY
Speak to me home; mince not the general tongue.     111
Name Cleopatra as she is called in Rome;
Rail thou in Fulvia's phrase, and taunt my faults     113
With such full license as both truth and malice
Have power to utter. Oh, then we bring forth weeds
When our quick minds lie still, and our ills told us     116
Is as our earing. Fare thee well awhile.                     117

FIRST MESSENGER    At your noble pleasure.
                                *Exit [First] Messenger.*

*Enter another Messenger.*

ANTONY
From Sicyon, ho, the news! Speak there.
SECOND MESSENGER
The man from Sicyon—is there such an one?          120
THIRD MESSENGER  [at the door]
He stays upon your will.
ANTONY                        Let him appear.—          121
            [*Exeunt Second and Third Messengers.*]
These strong Egyptian fetters I must break,
Or lose myself in dotage.

*Enter another Messenger, with a letter.*

                        What are you?
FOURTH MESSENGER    Fulvia thy wife is dead.
ANTONY    Where died she?
FOURTH MESSENGER    In Sicyon.
Her length of sickness, with what else more serious
Importeth thee to know, this bears.   [*He gives a letter.*]
ANTONY                        Forbear me.          128
                        [*Exit Fourth Messenger.*]
There's a great spirit gone! Thus did I desire it.
What our contempts doth often hurl from us
We wish it ours again. The present pleasure,
By revolution lowering, does become                       132
The opposite of itself. She's good, being gone;         133
The hand could pluck her back that shoved her on.     134
I must from this enchanting queen break off.
Ten thousand harms more than the ills I know
My idleness doth hatch.—How now, Enobarbus!

*Enter Enobarbus.*

ENOBARBUS    What's your pleasure, sir?
ANTONY    I must with haste from hence.
ENOBARBUS    Why, then, we kill all our women. We see
how mortal an unkindness is to them; if they suffer
our departure, death's the word.
ANTONY    I must be gone.
ENOBARBUS    Under a compelling occasion, let women
die. It were pity to cast them away for nothing, though
between them and a great cause they should be esteemed nothing. Cleopatra, catching but the least noise    147
of this, dies instantly; I have seen her die twenty times    148
upon far poorer moment. I do think there is mettle in    149

---

**93 field** battlefield.    **96 time's state** circumstances prevailing at the moment    **97 jointing** uniting    **98–9 Whose . . . them** whose better military success drove them from Italy upon the very first encounter.    **101 infects the teller** i.e., makes the teller seem unwelcome.    **104 Who** he who    **105 as** as if.    **Labienus** (Brutus and Cassius [see *Julius Caesar*] had sent Quintus Labienus to Orodes, King of Parthia, to seek aid against Antony and Octavius Caesar; with a force thus obtained, he is now overrunning the Roman provinces in the Middle East.)    **107 Extended** seized upon. (A legal phrase.)    **111 Speak . . . tongue** Speak bluntly; don't minimize the common report.    **113 Rail . . . phrase** Scold me as Fulvia would    **116 quick** alive, inventive    **116–17 our ills . . . earing** hearing our faults told to us improves us, as plowing (*earing*) improves land by rooting out the weeds.

**120 The man from Sicyon** (The messenger who has just entered, not being from Sicyon, realizes in some confusion that Antony wants to hear the news from Sicyon. This second messenger therefore calls out to ask if the messenger from Sicyon is to be found. Another messenger at the door replies that such a man is indeed waiting, and in a moment that messenger from Sicyon enters with his report. Some editors change the second and third messengers into attendants.) *Sicyon* is an ancient city in Greece, where Antony left Fulvia.    **121 stays upon** awaits    **128 Importeth** concerns.    **Forbear** Leave    **132 By revolution lowering** sinking in our estimation in the course of time and Fortune's turning wheel    **133 The opposite of itself** the opposite of pleasure: unhappiness and dishonor.    **134 could** would be willing to    **147 noise** hint, rumor    **148 die** (Playing on a common second meaning of "achieve sexual orgasm.")    **149 poorer moment** lesser cause.    **mettle** i.e., sexual vigor

death, which commits some loving act upon her, she
hath such a celerity in dying.

ANTONY    She is cunning past man's thought.

ENOBARBUS    Alack, sir, no, her passions are made of
nothing but the finest part of pure love. We cannot call
her winds and waters sighs and tears; they are greater 155
storms and tempests than almanacs can report. This
cannot be cunning in her; if it be, she makes a shower
of rain as well as Jove.

ANTONY    Would I had never seen her!

ENOBARBUS    Oh, sir, you had then left unseen a wonderful piece of work, which not to have been blessed
withal would have discredited your travel.

ANTONY    Fulvia is dead.

ENOBARBUS    Sir?

ANTONY    Fulvia is dead.

ENOBARBUS    Fulvia?

ANTONY    Dead.

ENOBARBUS    Why, sir, give the gods a thankful sacrifice.
When it pleaseth their deities to take the wife of a man
from him, it shows to man the tailors of the earth; 170
comforting therein, that when old robes are worn out,
there are members to make new. If there were no more 172
women but Fulvia, then had you indeed a cut, and the
case to be lamented. This grief is crowned with consolation; your old smock brings forth a new petticoat, 175
and indeed the tears live in an onion that should water 176
this sorrow. 177

ANTONY
The business she hath broachèd in the state 178
Cannot endure my absence.

ENOBARBUS    And the business you have broached here
cannot be without you, especially that of Cleopatra's,
which wholly depends on your abode. 182

ANTONY
No more light answers. Let our officers 183
Have notice what we purpose. I shall break 184
The cause of our expedience to the Queen 185
And get her leave to part. For not alone 186
The death of Fulvia, with more urgent touches, 187
Do strongly speak to us, but the letters too
Of many our contriving friends in Rome 189
Petition us at home. Sextus Pompeius 190
Hath given the dare to Caesar and commands
The empire of the sea. Our slippery people, 192

Whose love is never linked to the deserver
Till his deserts are past, begin to throw 194
Pompey the Great and all his dignities 195
Upon his son, who—high in name and power,
Higher than both in blood and life—stands up 197
For the main soldier; whose quality, going on, 198
The sides o'th' world may danger. Much is breeding, 199
Which, like the courser's hair, hath yet but life, 200
And not a serpent's poison. Say our pleasure, 201
To such whose place is under us, requires 202
Our quick remove from hence. 203

ENOBARBUS    I shall do't.                [*Exeunt separately.*]

## [1.3]

*Enter Cleopatra, Charmian, Alexas, and Iras.*

CLEOPATRA
Where is he?

CHARMIAN    I did not see him since. 1

CLEOPATRA [*to Alexas*]
See where he is, who's with him, what he does.
I did not send you. If you find him sad, 3
Say I am dancing; if in mirth, report
That I am sudden sick. Quick, and return. 5
                                    [*Exit Alexas.*]

CHARMIAN
Madam, methinks, if you did love him dearly,
You do not hold the method to enforce 7
The like from him.

CLEOPATRA                What should I do I do not? 8

CHARMIAN
In each thing give him way. Cross him in nothing.

CLEOPATRA
Thou teachest like a fool: the way to lose him.

CHARMIAN
Tempt him not so too far. I wish, forbear; 11
In time we hate that which we often fear.

*Enter Antony.*

But here comes Antony.

CLEOPATRA                I am sick and sullen. 13

ANTONY
I am sorry to give breathing to my purpose— 14

---

155 **sighs** i.e., mere sighs    170 **tailors** (The gods can fashion a new
wife for a man, much as a tailor can mend or replace a worn-out garment.)    172 **members** (The word has a bawdy suggestion, pursued
in lines 173–4 and 180 in *cut, case, business,* and *broached; cut* and *case*
suggest the female sexual organs; *broached* suggests something that is
stabbed, pricked, opened.)    175 **smock** undergarment. (Also used
defamatorily of women.)    176–7 **the tears . . . sorrow** i.e., only an
onion could produce tears on this occasion of Fulvia's death.
178 **broachèd** opened up. (But see the note for line 172.)    182 **abode**
staying.    183 **light** frivolous, indelicate    184 **break** i.e., break the
news of    185 **expedience** haste    186 **leave** consent    187 **urgent
touches** pressing matters    189 **Of . . . friends** from many friends
working in our interest    190 **at home** to come home.    **Sextus
Pompeius** son of Pompey the Great, who, though outlawed, has been
able to exploit the division between Antony and Octavius and
thereby gain command of Sicily and the sea; he appears in Act 2
192 **slippery** fickle

194 **throw** bestow    195 **Pompey the Great** i.e., the title and honored
status of "Pompey the Great"    197 **blood and life** mettle and vitality
197–8 **stands . . . soldier** lays claim to being the greatest soldier
198–9 **whose . . . danger** whose aspiring character and situation, if
allowed to continue unchecked, may endanger the frame of the
Roman world.    200 **like . . . hair** (Allusion to the popular belief that a
horsehair put into water would turn to a snake.)    200–1 **hath . . .
poison** is alive at this point but not yet a poisonous full-grown serpent.    201–3 **Say . . . hence** Inform those who serve me that my wish
is to depart quickly.
**1.3. Location: Alexandria. Cleopatra's palace.**
1 **since** lately.    3 **I did . . . you** i.e., Do not let him know I sent you.
**sad** serious    5 **sudden** suddenly taken    7 **hold the method** follow
the right course    8 **I do not** that I am not doing.    11 **Tempt** Try.
**I wish** I wish you would    13 **sullen** depressed, melancholy.
14 **breathing** utterance

CLEOPATRA
　Help me away, dear Charmian! I shall fall.
　It cannot be thus long; the sides of nature　　　16
　Will not sustain it.
ANTONY　　　　　　　Now, my dearest queen—
CLEOPATRA
　Pray you, stand farther from me.
ANTONY　　　　　　　　　　　What's the matter?　18
CLEOPATRA
　I know by that same eye there's some good news.
　What says the married woman, you may go?　20
　Would she had never given you leave to come!
　Let her not say 'tis I that keep you here.
　I have no power upon you; hers you are.
ANTONY
　The gods best know—
CLEOPATRA　　　　　　　Oh, never was there queen
　So mightily betrayed! Yet at the first
　I saw the treasons planted.
ANTONY　　　　　　Cleopatra—
CLEOPATRA
　Why should I think you can be mine, and true—
　Though you in swearing shake the thronèd gods—
　Who have been false to Fulvia? Riotous madness,　29
　To be entangled with those mouth-made vows　30
　Which break themselves in swearing!
ANTONY　　　　　　　　　　Most sweet queen—　31
CLEOPATRA
　Nay, pray you, seek no color for your going,　32
　But bid farewell and go. When you sued staying,　33
　Then was the time for words. No going then.
　Eternity was in our lips and eyes,　　　　35
　Bliss in our brows' bent; none our parts so poor　36
　But was a race of heaven. They are so still,　37
　Or thou, the greatest soldier of the world,
　Art turned the greatest liar.
ANTONY　　　　　　　How now, lady?
CLEOPATRA
　I would I had thy inches. Thou shouldst know　40
　There were a heart in Egypt.
ANTONY　　　　　　Hear me, Queen:　41
　The strong necessity of time commands
　Our services awhile, but my full heart
　Remains in use with you. Our Italy　　　44
　Shines o'er with civil swords; Sextus Pompeius　45
　Makes his approaches to the port of Rome;

　Equality of two domestic powers　　　　47
　Breed scrupulous faction; the hated, grown to
　　strength,　　　　　　　　　　　　48
　Are newly grown to love; the condemned Pompey,　49
　Rich in his father's honor, creeps apace　50
　Into the hearts of such as have not thrived
　Upon the present state, whose numbers threaten;　52
　And quietness, grown sick of rest, would purge　53
　By any desperate change. My more particular,　54
　And that which most with you should safe my going,　55
　Is Fulvia's death.
CLEOPATRA
　Though age from folly could not give me freedom,
　It does from childishness. Can Fulvia die?
ANTONY　　She's dead, my queen.　　　[*He offers letters.*]
　Look here, and at thy sovereign leisure read
　The garboils she awaked; at the last, best,　61
　See when and where she died.
CLEOPATRA　　　　　Oh, most false love!
　Where be the sacred vials thou shouldst fill　63
　With sorrowful water? Now I see, I see,
　In Fulvia's death how mine received shall be.
ANTONY
　Quarrel no more, but be prepared to know
　The purposes I bear, which are or cease　67
　As you shall give th'advice. By the fire　68
　That quickens Nilus' slime, I go from hence　69
　Thy soldier, servant, making peace or war
　As thou affects.
CLEOPATRA　　　Cut my lace, Charmian, come!　71
　But let it be; I am quickly ill, and well,
　So Antony loves.
ANTONY　　　　　My precious queen, forbear,　73
　And give true evidence to his love which stands　74
　An honorable trial.
CLEOPATRA　　　　So Fulvia told me.　75
　I prithee, turn aside and weep for her;
　Then bid adieu to me, and say the tears
　Belong to Egypt. Good now, play one scene　78

16 **It . . . long** I can't last long at this rate.　**sides of nature** human body, frame　18 **stand farther from me** give me air.　20 **the married woman** Fulvia　29 **Who** you who.　**Riotous madness** What folly on my part　30 **mouth-made** insincerely spoken　31 **in swearing** even while they are being sworn.　32 **color** pretext　33 **sued staying** begged to stay　35 **our** i.e., my. (The royal plural.)　36 **bent** arch, curve. **none . . . poor** none of my features, however poor　37 **race of heaven** of heavenly origin, or, possibly, of the flavor of heaven.　40 **inches** (1) height (2) manly strength. (With perhaps a bawdy suggestion of phallic size.)　41 **There . . . Egypt** i.e., that the Egyptian queen has the courage to stand up to such graceless behavior.　44 **in use with you** for your use, in trust.　45 **Shines . . . swords** glitters everywhere with weapons of civil war

**47–8 Equality . . . faction** the equal splitting of domestic power between two (Antony and Caesar) breeds petty bickering　**48–9 the hated . . . love** those (like Pompey) who were out of favor, being now strong, have recently come back into popular favor　**49–50 Pompey . . . apace** i.e., Sextus Pompeius, richly inheriting the honor once accorded Pompey the Great, quickly insinuates himself　**52 state** government (of the triumvirate).　**whose numbers** the large numbers of which disaffected persons　**53–4 And quietness . . . change** and peace, bored with its own long continuance, longs to purge itself by the violence of war (medically speaking, by vomiting, bowel evacuation, or bloodletting). **54 particular** personal concern　**55 safe** make safe　**61 garboils** disturbances, commotions.　**best** i.e., best of all　**63 sacred vials** (Alludes to the supposed Roman custom of putting bottles filled with tears in the tombs of the departed.)　**67 which are** which will proceed　**68 fire** i.e., sun　**69 quickens . . . slime** brings to life the mud left by the overflow of the Nile　**71 thou affects** you desire.　**lace** cord or laces fastening the bodice. (Cleopatra pretends she is fainting.)　**73 So** provided that, or, possibly, "in the same way, as suddenly and violently as my own" **74–5 And . . . trial** and bear true witness to the love of one who withstands any honorable test.　**75 So . . . me** i.e., So Fulvia would have said, no doubt. (Said as a taunt.)　**78 Belong to Egypt** are shed for the Queen of Egypt.　**Good now** (An expression of entreaty.)

Of excellent dissembling, and let it look
Like perfect honor.

ANTONY     You'll heat my blood. No more.    80

CLEOPATRA
You can do better yet; but this is meetly.    81

ANTONY
Now, by my sword—

CLEOPATRA     And target. Still he mends.    82
But this is not the best. Look, prithee, Charmian,
How this Herculean Roman does become    84
The carriage of his chafe.    85

ANTONY    I'll leave you, lady.

CLEOPATRA    Courteous lord, one word.
Sir, you and I must part, but that's not it;
Sir, you and I have loved, but there's not it;
That you know well. Something it is I would—    90
Oh, my oblivion is a very Antony,    91
And I am all forgotten.

ANTONY     But that your royalty    92
Holds idleness your subject, I should take you    93
For idleness itself.

CLEOPATRA     'Tis sweating labor    94
To bear such idleness so near the heart    95
As Cleopatra this. But sir, forgive me,    96
Since my becomings kill me when they do not    97
Eye well to you. Your honor calls you hence;    98
Therefore be deaf to my unpitied folly,
And all the gods go with you! Upon your sword    100
Sit laurel victory, and smooth success    101
Be strewed before your feet!

ANTONY     Let us go. Come;
Our separation so abides and flies    103
That thou, residing here, goes yet with me,
And I, hence fleeting, here remain with thee.
Away!      *Exeunt.*

❧

# [1.4]

*Enter Octavius [Caesar], reading a letter, Lepidus,
and their train.*

CAESAR
You may see, Lepidus, and henceforth know,
It is not Caesar's natural vice to hate

Our great competitor. From Alexandria    3
This is the news: he fishes, drinks, and wastes
The lamps of night in revel; is not more manlike
Than Cleopatra, nor the queen of Ptolemy    6
More womanly than he; hardly gave audience, or    7
Vouchsafed to think he had partners. You shall find
    there
A man who is the abstract of all faults    9
That all men follow.

LEPIDUS     I must not think there are
Evils enough to darken all his goodness.
His faults in him seem as the spots of heaven,    12
More fiery by night's blackness, hereditary    13
Rather than purchased, what he cannot change    14
Than what he chooses.    15

CAESAR
You are too indulgent. Let's grant it is not    16
Amiss to tumble on the bed of Ptolemy,
To give a kingdom for a mirth, to sit    18
And keep the turn of tippling with a slave,    19
To reel the streets at noon, and stand the buffet    20
With knaves that smells of sweat. Say this becomes
    him—    21
As his composure must be rare indeed    22
Whom these things cannot blemish—yet must Antony
No way excuse his foils when we do bear    24
So great weight in his lightness. If he filled    25
His vacancy with his voluptuousness,    26
Full surfeits and the dryness of his bones    27
Call on him for't. But to confound such time    28
That drums him from his sport and speaks as loud    29
As his own state and ours, 'tis to be chid    30
As we rate boys who, being mature in knowledge,    31
Pawn their experience to their present pleasure    32
And so rebel to judgment.

*Enter a Messenger.*

LEPIDUS     Here's more news.    33

FIRST MESSENGER
Thy biddings have been done, and every hour,
Most noble Caesar, shalt thou have report
How 'tis abroad. Pompey is strong at sea,

---

**80 heat my blood** i.e., anger me.   **81 meetly** i.e., fairly well acted. (Said mockingly.)   **82 target** shield.   **mends** improves (in his "scene / Of excellent dissembling").   **84–5 How . . . chafe** i.e., how Antony, who claims descent from Hercules, plays the role of his enraged ancestor well. (Hercules had become a stock figure of the enraged hero or tyrant.)   **chafe** rage.   **90 would** wished to say   **91 my . . . Antony** my forgetful memory is like Antony (who is now leaving and thus forgetting me)   **92 I . . . forgotten** (1) I have forgotten what I was going to say (2) I am entirely forgotten (by Antony).   **92–4 But . . . itself** Since you are a queen, your frivolousness must be your subject (i.e., ruled by you); otherwise, I'd think you were frivolousness itself.   **94–6 'Tis . . . this** i.e., I am not being frivolous; this is hard for me to bear. (*Sweating, labor,* and *bear* are all associated with pregnancy.)   **97 my becomings** (1) those qualities that become me (2) the various roles that I adopt   **98 Eye** appear   **100–1 Upon . . . victory** May your military exploits be crowned with the laurel wreath betokening victory   **103 so abides and flies** mingles remaining and going in such a paradoxical fashion   **1.4. Location: Rome.**

**3 competitor** partner. (With a suggestion also of "rival.")   **6 Ptolemy** (Cleopatra's royal half-brother, to whom she had been married according to Egyptian custom and at the behest of Julius Caesar.)   **7 gave audience** i.e., received messengers (from Octavius)   **9 abstract** epitome   **12–13 His . . . blackness** His faults and virtues stand out in contrast to one another, just as the stars in the sky stand out from night's darkness   **14 purchased** acquired   **15 Than** rather than   **16 Let's grant** Even if we were to grant   **18 mirth** jest, diversion   **19 keep . . . of** take turns   **20 stand the buffet** exchange blows   **21 Say** Supposing   **22 As his composure** and a man's composition or temperament   **24 foils** blemishes   **24–5 when . . . lightness** when we have to carry the heavy burden imposed by his levity.   **26 His vacancy** his leisure time   **27–8 Full . . . for't** the physical disabilities resulting from such voluptuousness (such as venereal disease) would call him to account and would be adequate punishment.   **28 confound** waste   **29 drums** summons (as by a military drum).   **sport** amorous pastime   **29–30 speaks . . . ours** summons him urgently in view of his political position and ours as well   **30 chid** chided, reprimanded   **31 rate** berate.   **mature in knowledge** old enough to know better   **32 Pawn . . . pleasure** risk for the sake of immediate gratification what experience tells them will be ultimately painful   **33 to judgment** against better judgment.

And it appears he is beloved of those                                37
That only have feared Caesar. To the ports                           38
The discontents repair, and men's reports                            39
Give him much wronged.                              [*Exit.*]

CAESAR                        I should have known no less.   40
It hath been taught us from the primal state                         41
That he which is was wished until he were;                           42
And the ebbed man, ne'er loved till ne'er worth love,                43
Comes deared by being lacked. This common body,                      44
Like to a vagabond flag upon the stream,                             45
Goes to and back, lackeying the varying tide                         46
To rot itself with motion.

*[Enter a Second Messenger.]*

SECOND MESSENGER   Caesar, I bring thee word
Menecrates and Menas, famous pirates,                                49
Makes the sea serve them, which they ear and wound    50
With keels of every kind. Many hot inroads
They make in Italy. The borders maritime                             52
Lack blood to think on't, and flush youth revolt.                    53
No vessel can peep forth but 'tis as soon
Taken as seen; for Pompey's name strikes more     55
Than could his war resisted.                          [*Exit.*]

CAESAR                                    Antony,     56
Leave thy lascivious wassails. When thou once       57
Was beaten from Modena, where thou slew'st
Hirtius and Pansa, consuls, at thy heel
Did famine follow, whom thou fought'st against,                      60
Though daintily brought up, with patience more
Than savages could suffer. Thou didst drink                          62
The stale of horses and the gilded puddle                            63
Which beasts would cough at. Thy palate then did
    deign                                                            64
The roughest berry on the rudest hedge.
Yea, like the stag, when snow the pasture sheets,                    66
The barks of trees thou browsèd. On the Alps                         67
It is reported thou didst eat strange flesh,
Which some did die to look on. And all this—
It wounds thine honor that I speak it now—
Was borne so like a soldier that thy cheek
So much as lanked not.                                               72
LEPIDUS   'Tis pity of him.                                          73
CAESAR   Let his shames quickly
Drive him to Rome. 'Tis time we twain
Did show ourselves i'th' field, and to that end

Assemble we immediate council. Pompey
Thrives in our idleness.
LEPIDUS                         Tomorrow, Caesar,
I shall be furnished to inform you rightly
Both what by sea and land I can be able             80
To front this present time.
CAESAR                         Till which encounter   81
It is my business too. Farewell.
LEPIDUS
Farewell, my lord. What you shall know meantime
Of stirs abroad, I shall beseech you, sir,           84
To let me be partaker.
CAESAR
Doubt not, sir, I knew it for my bond.               86
                                *Exeunt [separately].*

❧

# [1.5]

*Enter Cleopatra, Charmian, Iras, and Mardian.*

CLEOPATRA   Charmian!
CHARMIAN   Madam?
CLEOPATRA
Ha, ha! Give me to drink mandragora.                 3
CHARMIAN   Why, madam?
CLEOPATRA
That I might sleep out this great gap of time
My Antony is away.
CHARMIAN   You think of him too much.
CLEOPATRA
Oh, 'tis treason!
CHARMIAN             Madam, I trust not so.
CLEOPATRA
Thou, eunuch Mardian!
MARDIAN                    What's Your Highness' pleasure?
CLEOPATRA
Not now to hear thee sing. I take no pleasure
In aught an eunuch has. 'Tis well for thee           11
That, being unseminared, thy freer thoughts          12
May not fly forth of Egypt. Hast thou affections?    13
MARDIAN   Yes, gracious madam.
CLEOPATRA   Indeed?
MARDIAN
Not in deed, madam, for I can do nothing             16
But what indeed is honest to be done.                17
Yet have I fierce affections, and think
What Venus did with Mars.
CLEOPATRA                    Oh, Charmian,
Where think'st thou he is now? Stands he or sits he?
Or does he walk? Or is he on his horse?
Oh, happy horse, to bear the weight of Antony!

---

**37 of** by   **38 That . . . Caesar** that have obeyed Caesar only out of fear.   **39 discontents** discontented. (See 1.3.48–52.)   **40 Give him** represent him as   **41–4 It . . . lacked** It is an ironic lesson of history from the earliest times that the man currently in the public eye is avidly sought after only until he becomes ruler, whereas the public figure whose fortunes have decayed, sought after only when he is no longer worthy of love, becomes loved once he is gone.   **44 common body** populace   **45 vagabond flag** shifting and drifting weeds   **46 lackeying** following in servile fashion, like a lackey   **49 famous** notorious   **50 ear** plow   **52 borders maritime** coastal territories   **53 Lack blood** turn pale.   **flush** vigorous; flushed, ruddy (contrasted with those who *Lack blood*)   **55–6 strikes . . . resisted** inflicts more damage than his forces could against our resistance.   **57 wassails** carousals.   **60 whom** i.e., famine   **62 suffer** show in suffering.   **63 stale** urine.   **gilded** covered with iridescent slime   **64 deign** not disdain   **66 sheets** covers   **67 browsèd** fed upon.   **72 So . . . lanked not** did not even grow thin.   **73 of** about

**80 be able** be capable of mustering   **81 front** confront, deal with   **84 stirs** commotions   **86 knew** already knew.   **bond** duty, obligation.
**1.5. Location: Egypt. Cleopatra's palace.**
**3 mandragora** juice of the mandrake (a narcotic).   **11 aught** (With bawdy suggestion.)   **12 unseminared** castrated   **13 of** from.   **affections** passions.   **16 Not in deed** (Mardian punningly takes the *deed* of *Indeed* in line 15 to mean "physical act.")   **do** (With suggestion of sexual intercourse.)   **17 honest** chaste

Do bravely, horse, for wot'st thou whom thou mov'st?   23
The demi-Atlas of this earth, the arm   24
And burgonet of men. He's speaking now,   25
Or murmuring, "Where's my serpent of old Nile?"
For so he calls me. Now I feed myself
With most delicious poison. Think on me,   28
That am with Phoebus' amorous pinches black   29
And wrinkled deep in time. Broad-fronted Caesar,   30
When thou wast here above the ground, I was
A morsel for a monarch. And great Pompey   32
Would stand and make his eyes grow in my brow;   33
There would he anchor his aspect, and die   34
With looking on his life.   35

*Enter Alexas.*

ALEXAS   Sovereign of Egypt, hail!
CLEOPATRA
How much unlike art thou Mark Antony!
Yet, coming from him, that great med'cine hath   38
With his tinct gilded thee.   39
How goes it with my brave Mark Antony?   40
ALEXAS   Last thing he did, dear Queen,
He kissed—the last of many doubled kisses—
This orient pearl. [*He gives a pearl.*] His speech sticks in
   my heart.   43
CLEOPATRA
Mine ear must pluck it thence.
ALEXAS                               "Good friend," quoth he,
"Say the firm Roman to great Egypt sends   45
This treasure of an oyster; at whose foot,
To mend the petty present, I will piece   47
Her opulent throne with kingdoms. All the East,
Say thou, shall call her mistress." So he nodded,
And soberly did mount an arm-gaunt steed,   50
Who neighed so high that what I would have spoke
Was beastly dumbed by him.   52
CLEOPATRA   What, was he sad, or merry?
ALEXAS
Like to the time o'th' year between the extremes
Of hot and cold, he was nor sad nor merry.   55

CLEOPATRA
Oh, well-divided disposition! Note him,   56
Note him, good Charmian, 'tis the man; but note him.   57
He was not sad, for he would shine on those   58
That make their looks by his; he was not merry,   59
Which seemed to tell them his remembrance lay
In Egypt with his joy; but between both.
Oh, heavenly mingle! Be'st thou sad or merry,
The violence of either thee becomes,   63
So does it no man else.—Met'st thou my posts?   64
ALEXAS
Ay, madam, twenty several messengers.   65
Why do you send so thick?
CLEOPATRA                               Who's born that day   66
When I forget to send to Antony
Shall die a beggar. Ink and paper, Charmian.   68
Welcome, my good Alexas. Did I, Charmian,
Ever love Caesar so?
CHARMIAN                 Oh, that brave Caesar!
CLEOPATRA
Be choked with such another emphasis!   71
Say, "the brave Antony."
CHARMIAN                             The valiant Caesar!
CLEOPATRA
By Isis, I will give thee bloody teeth
If thou with Caesar paragon again   74
My man of men.
CHARMIAN             By your most gracious pardon,
I sing but after you.
CLEOPATRA             My salad days,
When I was green in judgment, cold in blood,   77
To say as I said then. But, come, away,
Get me ink and paper.
He shall have every day a several greeting,
Or I'll unpeople Egypt.                    *Exeunt.*   81

❖

# [2.1]

*Enter Pompey, Menecrates, and Menas, in war-
like manner.*

POMPEY
If the great gods be just, they shall assist
The deeds of justest men.
MENAS                             Know, worthy Pompey,   2
That what they do delay they not deny.   3

23 **Do** (With sexual suggestion, as in line 16.)   **wot'st thou** do you know   24 **demi-Atlas** one who (together with Caesar) supports the weight of the whole world, as Atlas did. (Cleopatra disregards Lepidus as a triumvir.)   **arm** strong right arm or weapon   25 **burgonet** light helmet or steel cap, i.e., protector   28–30 **Think . . . time** (Cleopatra reflects on her ability to attract Antony, given the fact that she is dark-skinned [as from the amorous pinches of her lover, the sun] and increasingly wrinkled with age.)   29 **Phoebus'** the sun's   30 **Broad-fronted Caesar** Broad-foreheaded Julius Caesar   32 **great Pompey** Gnaeus Pompey, oldest son of Pompey the Great and brother of the Sextus Pompey of this play. (Shakespeare may here conflate Gnaeus Pompey with Pompey the Great.)   33 **die . . . brow** i.e., rivet his eyes on my face   34 **aspect** look, gaze.   **die** i.e., suffer the extremity of love. (And with suggestion of orgasm, as at 1.2.148.)   35 **his life** that which he lived for.   38 **great med'cine** i.e., Antony, here equated with the elixir of life, the so-called philosopher's stone, the supposed substance by which alchemists hoped to turn all baser metals into gold   39 **his tinct** its alchemical potency; also, its color   40 **brave** splendid   43 **orient** shining, bright. (The best pearls were from the East or Orient.)   45 **firm** constant, true.   **Egypt** the Queen of Egypt   47 **mend** improve.   **piece** augment   50 **arm-gaunt** made trim and hard by warlike service, or hungry for battle   52 **dumbed** drowned out, made inaudible   55 **nor sad** neither sad

56 **well-divided disposition** well-balanced temperament.   57 **the man** i.e., perfectly characteristic of him.   **but** do but, only   58 **would** wished to   59 **make . . . his** model their demeanor on his look   63 **thee becomes** is becoming to you   64 **So does it** as it does to.   **posts** messengers.   65 **several** separate, distinct. (Also in line 80.)   66 **Who's** Anyone who is   68 **Shall . . . beggar** (since that day, sure never to come, would be ill-omened).   71 **emphasis** emphatic expression.   74 **paragon** match or compare   77 **green** immature.   **blood** passion, feeling   81 **Or . . . Egypt** Or I will send so many messengers that Egypt will be unpeopled. (Perhaps too with a darker threat of violence.)
**2.1. Location:** Pompey's camp, probably at Messina, Sicily.
2 MENAS (The Folio assigns the speeches in this scene to "*Mene.*"; some could be for Menecrates, but Pompey ignores him entirely at lines 33–53, and Menecrates never reappears in the play.)   3 **not deny** i.e., do not necessarily deny.

POMPEY
Whiles we are suitors to their throne, decays                    4
The thing we sue for.
MENAS                                    We, ignorant of ourselves,    5
Beg often our own harms, which the wise powers
Deny us for our good; so find we profit
By losing of our prayers.
POMPEY                                    I shall do well.
The people love me, and the sea is mine;
My powers are crescent, and my auguring hope        10
Says it will come to th' full. Mark Antony                11
In Egypt sits at dinner, and will make
No wars without doors. Caesar gets money where        13
He loses hearts. Lepidus flatters both,
Of both is flattered; but he neither loves,                15
Nor either cares for him.
MENAS                                    Caesar and Lepidus
Are in the field. A mighty strength they carry.        17
POMPEY
Where have you this? 'Tis false.
MENAS                                    From Silvius, sir.
POMPEY
He dreams. I know they are in Rome together
Looking for Antony. But all the charms of love,        20
Salt Cleopatra, soften thy waned lip!                21
Let witchcraft joined with beauty, lust with both,
Tie up the libertine in a field of feasts,                23
Keep his brain fuming. Epicurean cooks                24
Sharpen with cloyless sauce his appetite,                25
That sleep and feeding may prorogue his honor        26
Even till a Lethe'd dullness—

*Enter Varrius.*

                                        How now, Varrius?    27
VARRIUS
This is most certain that I shall deliver:                28
Mark Antony is every hour in Rome
Expected. Since he went from Egypt 'tis
A space for further travel.                        31
POMPEY    I could have given less matter                32
A better ear. Menas, I did not think
This amorous surfeiter would have donned his helm    34
For such a petty war. His soldiership
Is twice the other twain. But let us rear                36
The higher our opinion, that our stirring                37
Can from the lap of Egypt's widow pluck                38

The ne'er-lust-wearied Antony.
MENAS                                    I cannot hope        39
Caesar and Antony shall well greet together.        40
His wife that's dead did trespasses to Caesar;        41
His brother warred upon him, although, I think,        42
Not moved by Antony.
POMPEY                                    I know not, Menas,    43
How lesser enmities may give way to greater.
Were't not that we stand up against them all,
'Twere pregnant they should square between
    themselves,                                    46
For they have entertainèd cause enough                47
To draw their swords. But how the fear of us
May cement their divisions and bind up
The petty difference, we yet not know.
Be't as our gods will have't! It only stands        51
Our lives upon to use our strongest hands.            52
Come, Menas.                            *Exeunt.*

❖

# [2.2]

*Enter Enobarbus and Lepidus.*

LEPIDUS
Good Enobarbus, 'tis a worthy deed,
And shall become you well, to entreat your captain
To soft and gentle speech.
ENOBARBUS                        I shall entreat him
To answer like himself. If Caesar move him,            4
Let Antony look over Caesar's head                5
And speak as loud as Mars. By Jupiter,
Were I the wearer of Antonio's beard,
I would not shave't today.                        8
LEPIDUS
'Tis not a time for private stomaching.
ENOBARBUS                                    Every time    9
Serves for the matter that is then born in't.
LEPIDUS
But small to greater matters must give way.
ENOBARBUS
Not if the small come first.
LEPIDUS                                    Your speech is passion;
But pray you stir no embers up. Here comes
The noble Antony.

*Enter Antony and Ventidius [in conversation].*

ENOBARBUS                        And yonder, Caesar.

*Enter Caesar, Maecenas, and Agrippa, [also in
conversation, by another door].*

4–5 Whiles . . . for While we are praying, that for which we pray is being destroyed.    10 My . . . crescent My armed forces are on the increase.    auguring prophesying    11 it i.e., my powers or fortune (seen as a crescent moon, becoming full)    13 without doors outdoors, i.e., in the battlefield, rather than in the bedroom.    15 Of by.    neither loves loves neither    17 A . . . carry They command a mighty army.    20 Looking for awaiting.    charms spells    21 Salt lustful.    waned faded, withered    23 Tie . . . feasts i.e., tether him like an animal in a rich pasture    24 Epicurean Let epicurean    25 cloyless i.e., which will not satiate    26 prorogue defer the operation of    27 Lethe'd oblivious. (From the river of the underworld whose waters cause forgetfulness in those who drink.)    28 deliver report    31 space . . . travel time enough for an even longer journey and labor (travail).    32 less important    34 helm helmet    36 rear raise    37 opinion i.e., of ourselves    38 Egypt's widow i.e., Cleopatra, widow of the young King Ptolemy XIV

39 hope expect    40 well greet greet one another kindly    41 did trespasses to wronged    42 brother i.e., Lucius Antonius. (See 1.2.94 ff.)    43 moved provoked, incited    46 pregnant clear, obvious.    square quarrel    47 entertainèd maintained    51–2 It . . . hands Our very lives depend upon our using our greatest strength.
**2.2. Location:** Rome. Furniture is put out on which Antony and Caesar are to sit.
4 like himself i.e., in a way befitting his greatness.    move him i.e., to anger    5 look . . . head i.e., condescend to Caesar as a smaller man    8 I . . . shave't i.e., I would continue to wear it and thereby dare Caesar to pluck it (in a symbolic gesture for starting a fight)    9 private stomaching personal resentment.

ANTONY
If we compose well here, to Parthia.                          15
Hark, Ventidius.                    [*They confer apart.*]

CAESAR
I do not know, Maecenas, ask Agrippa.

LEPIDUS   Noble friends,
That which combined us was most great, and let not
A leaner action rend us. What's amiss,                        20
May it be gently heard. When we debate
Our trivial difference loud, we do commit
Murder in healing wounds. Then, noble partners,              23
The rather for I earnestly beseech,                          24
Touch you the sourest points with sweetest terms,
Nor curstness grow to th' matter.

ANTONY                          'Tis spoken well.            26
Were we before our armies, and to fight,                     27
I should do thus.                         *Flourish.*        28

CAESAR   Welcome to Rome.

ANTONY    Thank you.

CAESAR   Sit.

ANTONY    Sit, sir.

CAESAR   Nay, then.                       [*They sit.*]

ANTONY
I learn you take things ill which are not so,
Or being, concern you not.

CAESAR                      I must be laughed at             35
If, or for nothing or a little, I                            36
Should say myself offended, and with you
Chiefly i'th' world; more laughed at that I should          38
Once name you derogately, when to sound your name           39
It not concerned me.                                         40

ANTONY
My being in Egypt, Caesar, what was't to you?

CAESAR
No more than my residing here at Rome
Might be to you in Egypt. Yet if you there
Did practice on my state, your being in Egypt               44
Might be my question.

ANTONY                      How intend you "practiced"?      45

CAESAR
You may be pleased to catch at mine intent                  46
By what did here befall me. Your wife and brother
Made wars upon me, and their contestation
Was theme for you. You were the word of war.                49

ANTONY
You do mistake your business. My brother never
Did urge me in his act. I did inquire it,                    51
And have my learning from some true reports                 52

That drew their swords with you. Did he not rather          53
Discredit my authority with yours,                          54
And make the wars alike against my stomach,                 55
Having alike your cause? Of this my letters                 56
Before did satisfy you. If you'll patch a quarrel,          57
As matter whole you have to make it with,                   58
It must not be with this.

CAESAR                      You praise yourself              59
By laying defects of judgment to me, but
You patched up your excuses.

ANTONY                          Not so, not so.
I know you could not lack—I am certain on't—                62
Very necessity of this thought, that I,                     63
Your partner in the cause 'gainst which he fought,          64
Could not with graceful eyes attend those wars              65
Which fronted mine own peace. As for my wife,               66
I would you had her spirit in such another.                 67
The third o'th' world is yours, which with a snaffle        68
You may pace easy, but not such a wife.                     69

ENOBARBUS   Would we had all such wives, that the men
might go to wars with the women!

ANTONY
So much uncurbable, her garboils, Caesar,                   72
Made out of her impatience—which not wanted               73
Shrewdness of policy too—I grieving grant                   74
Did you too much disquiet. For that you must                75
But say I could not help it.

CAESAR                      I wrote to you                   76
When rioting in Alexandria; you                             77
Did pocket up my letters and with taunts
Did gibe my missive out of audience.

ANTONY                          Sir,                         79
He fell upon me ere admitted, then.                         80
Three kings I had newly feasted, and did want               81
Of what I was i'th' morning. But next day                   82
I told him of myself, which was as much                     83
As to have asked him pardon. Let this fellow
Be nothing of our strife; if we contend,                    85
Out of our question wipe him.

CAESAR                      You have broken                  86
The article of your oath, which you shall never             87
Have tongue to charge me with.

LEPIDUS   Soft, Caesar!                                      89

ANTONY   No, Lepidus, let him speak.

---

15 **compose** come to an agreement   20 **leaner** lesser, more trivial.
**rend** divide.   **What's** Whatever is   23 **healing** i.e., attempting to heal
24 **The rather for** all the more because   26 **Nor . . . grow** nor let ill humor
be added   27 **to** about to   28 **thus** i.e., embrace (? as they may do here) or,
speak calmly, as Lepidus urges.   35 **being** being so, i.e., even if they are
amiss   36 **or . . . or** either . . . or   38 **i'th' world** of all people   39 **Once**
under any circumstances.   **derogately** disparagingly   39–40 **when . . .**
**concerned me** i.e., if, as you say, it were none of my business.   44 **practice**
**on my state** plot against my position   45 **question** business.   **How**
**intend you** What do you mean   46 **catch at** infer, grasp   49 **Was . . . war**
had you for its theme. They made war in your name. (*Word* here means
"watchword.")   51 **urge . . . act** claim that he was fighting in my behalf.
**inquire** inquire into   52 **my learning** what I have learned.   **true reports**
reliable sources

53 **That . . . you** that fought in your army.   54 **Discredit** injure.
**with** along with   55 **stomach** desire   56 **Having . . . cause** i.e., I having just as much reason as you to deplore Lucius's action.   57–9 **If . . .**
**this** If you insist on manufacturing a quarrel out of shreds and patches,
as if you had substantial material to make it with, you've chosen a
weak matter to use.   62–3 **I know . . . thought** I'm certain you must
have realized   64 **he** i.e., Lucius   65 **with . . . attend** regard favorably   66 **fronted** confronted, opposed   67 **I would . . . another** I wish
one could find another as full of spirit.   68 **snaffle** bridle bit   69 **pace**
put through its paces, manage   72–5 **So . . . disquiet** I unhappily concede that Fulvia's unmanageable commotions, caused by her impatience (at my being in Egypt) but not lacking in keenness of stratagem,
did much to disquiet you, Caesar.   76 **But say** concede that   77 **When**
while you were   79 **Did . . . audience** taunted my messenger out of
your presence.   80 **fell** burst in   81–2 **did want . . . morning** was not
at my best as I had been earlier in the day.   83 **of myself** i.e., of my
having had a lot to drink   85 **Be . . . of** have no part in   86 **question**
contention   87 **article** terms   89 **Soft** Gently, go easy

The honor is sacred which he talks on now,
Supposing that I lacked it. But, on, Caesar:　92
The article of my oath—

CAESAR
To lend me arms and aid when I required them,　94
The which you both denied.

ANTONY　　　　　　　　　　　Neglected, rather;
And then when poisoned hours had bound me up
From mine own knowledge. As nearly as I may　97
I'll play the penitent to you, but mine honesty　98
Shall not make poor my greatness, nor my power　99
Work without it. Truth is that Fulvia,　100
To have me out of Egypt, made wars here,
For which myself, the ignorant motive, do　102
So far ask pardon as befits mine honor
To stoop in such a case.

LEPIDUS　　　　　　　　　　'Tis noble spoken.　104

MAECENAS
If it might please you to enforce no further
The griefs between ye; to forget them quite　106
Were to remember that the present need
Speaks to atone you.

LEPIDUS　　　　　　　　Worthily spoken, Maecenas.　108

ENOBARBUS　Or, if you borrow one another's love for the
instant, you may, when you hear no more words of
Pompey, return it again. You shall have time to wrangle in when you have nothing else to do.

ANTONY
Thou art a soldier only. Speak no more.

ENOBARBUS　That truth should be silent I had almost
forgot.

ANTONY
You wrong this presence. Therefore speak no more.　116

ENOBARBUS　Go to, then; your considerate stone.　117

CAESAR
I do not much dislike the matter, but
The manner of his speech; for 't cannot be
We shall remain in friendship, our conditions　120
So diff'ring in their acts. Yet, if I knew
What hoop should hold us staunch, from edge to edge　122
O'th' world I would pursue it.

AGRIPPA　Give me leave, Caesar.

CAESAR　Speak, Agrippa.

AGRIPPA
Thou hast a sister by the mother's side,
Admired Octavia. Great Mark Antony
Is now a widower.

CAESAR　　　　　　　Say not so, Agrippa.
If Cleopatra heard you, your reproof　129
Were well deserved of rashness.　130

ANTONY
I am not married, Caesar. Let me hear
Agrippa further speak.

AGRIPPA
To hold you in perpetual amity,
To make you brothers, and to knit your hearts
With an unslipping knot, take Antony　135
Octavia to his wife, whose beauty claims　136
No worse a husband than the best of men,
Whose virtue and whose general graces speak　138
That which none else can utter. By this marriage　139
All little jealousies, which now seem great,　140
And all great fears, which now import their dangers,　141
Would then be nothing. Truths would be tales,　142
Where now half tales be truths. Her love to both　143
Would each to other and all loves to both
Draw after her. Pardon what I have spoke,
For 'tis a studied, not a present thought,　146
By duty ruminated.

ANTONY　　　　　　　　Will Caesar speak?

CAESAR
Not till he hears how Antony is touched　148
With what is spoke already.　149

ANTONY　What power is in Agrippa
If I would say, "Agrippa, be it so,"
To make this good?

CAESAR　　　　　　　The power of Caesar and
His power unto Octavia.

ANTONY　　　　　　　　May I never　153
To this good purpose, that so fairly shows,　154
Dream of impediment! Let me have thy hand
Further this act of grace, and from this hour　156
The heart of brothers govern in our loves
And sway our great designs!

CAESAR　　　　　　　　There's my hand.
　　　　　　　　　　　　　[They clasp hands.]
A sister I bequeath you whom no brother
Did ever love so dearly. Let her live
To join our kingdoms and our hearts; and never　161
Fly off our loves again!

LEPIDUS　　　　　　　Happily, amen!　162

ANTONY
I did not think to draw my sword 'gainst Pompey,
For he hath laid strange courtesies and great　164
Of late upon me. I must thank him only,　165
Lest my remembrance suffer ill report;　166
At heel of that, defy him.

LEPIDUS　　　　　　　Time calls upon 's.　167
Of us must Pompey presently be sought,　168
Or else he seeks out us.

---

92 **Supposing** implying, or, even if we were to suppose　94 **required**
requested　97 **From . . . knowledge** from realizing what I was
doing.　98–100 **mine . . . it** my honesty (in admitting my overindulgence) will not go so far as to dishonor my greatness, nor, conversely,
will my authority be used in a dishonorable way.　102 **motive** moving or inciting cause　104 **noble** nobly　106 **griefs** grievances
108 **atone** reconcile　116 **presence** company.　117 **Go . . . stone** i.e.,
All right, all right. I'll keep my thoughts to myself.　120 **conditions**
temperaments, dispositions　122 **hoop** barrel hoop.　**staunch** firm,
watertight　129–30 **your . . . rashness** the rebuke you would get for
such rash speech would be richly deserved.

135 **take Antony** let Antony take　136 **to** to be, for　138–9 **Whose . . .
utter** whose virtues declare themselves better than any words about
them could do.　140 **jealousies** misunderstandings, suspicions
141 **import** imply; carry with them　142–3 **Truths . . . truths** True
reports (no matter how distressing) would then be discounted as
mere rumors, whereas at present half-true reports are taken for the
whole truth.　146 **present** spur-of-the-moment　148–9 **touched With**
affected by　153 **unto** over　154 **so fairly shows** looks so promising
156 **Further** in furtherance of　161–2 **never . . . again** may our amity
never desert us again.　164 **strange** remarkable　165 **only** at
least　166 **Lest . . . report** lest I be accused of ingratitude　167 **At
heel of** immediately after　168 **Of** By.　**presently** at once

ANTONY    Where lies he?

CAESAR
About the mount Misena.

ANTONY                                    What is his strength    171
By land?

CAESAR    Great and increasing; but by sea
He is an absolute master.

ANTONY                                    So is the fame.    173
Would we had spoke together! Haste we for it.    174
Yet, ere we put ourselves in arms, dispatch we
The business we have talked of.

CAESAR                                    With most gladness,    176
And do invite you to my sister's view,    177
Whither straight I'll lead you.    178

ANTONY
Let us, Lepidus, not lack your company.

LEPIDUS
Noble Antony, not sickness should detain me.    180
        *Flourish. Exeunt. Manent Enobarbus, Agrippa,*
                                            *Maecenas.*

MAECENAS [*to Enobarbus*]    Welcome from Egypt, sir.

ENOBARBUS    Half the heart of Caesar, worthy Maecenas!    182
My honorable friend, Agrippa!

AGRIPPA    Good Enobarbus!

MAECENAS    We have cause to be glad that matters are so
well digested. You stayed well by't in Egypt.    186

ENOBARBUS    Ay, sir, we did sleep day out of counte-    187
nance and made the night light with drinking.    188

MAECENAS    Eight wild boars roasted whole at a breakfast, and but twelve persons there; is this true?

ENOBARBUS    This was but as a fly by an eagle. We had    191
much more monstrous matter of feast, which worthily
deserved noting.

MAECENAS    She's a most triumphant lady, if report be    194
square to her.    195

ENOBARBUS    When she first met Mark Antony, she
pursed up his heart upon the river of Cydnus.    197

AGRIPPA    There she appeared indeed, or my reporter de-    198
vised well for her.    199

ENOBARBUS    I will tell you.
The barge she sat in, like a burnished throne    201
Burnt on the water. The poop was beaten gold;    202
Purple the sails, and so perfumèd that
The winds were lovesick with them. The oars were
        silver,
Which to the tune of flutes kept stroke, and made
The water which they beat to follow faster,

As amorous of their strokes. For her own person,    207
It beggared all description: she did lie
In her pavilion—cloth-of-gold of tissue—    209
O'erpicturing that Venus where we see    210
The fancy outwork nature. On each side her    211
Stood pretty dimpled boys, like smiling Cupids,
With divers-colored fans, whose wind did seem    213
To glow the delicate cheeks which they did cool,    214
And what they undid did.

AGRIPPA                                    Oh, rare for Antony!    215

ENOBARBUS
Her gentlewomen, like the Nereides,    216
So many mermaids, tended her i'th'eyes    217
And made their bends adornings. At the helm    218
A seeming mermaid steers. The silken tackle    219
Swell with the touches of those flower-soft hands,
That yarely frame the office. From the barge    221
A strange invisible perfume hits the sense
Of the adjacent wharfs. The city cast    223
Her people out upon her; and Antony,
Enthroned i'th' marketplace, did sit alone,
Whistling to th'air, which, but for vacancy,    226
Had gone to gaze on Cleopatra too,
And made a gap in nature.

AGRIPPA                                    Rare Egyptian!

ENOBARBUS
Upon her landing, Antony sent to her,
Invited her to supper. She replied
It should be better he became her guest,
Which she entreated. Our courteous Antony,
Whom ne'er the word of "No" woman heard speak,
Being barbered ten times o'er, goes to the feast,
And for his ordinary pays his heart    235
For what his eyes eat only.

AGRIPPA                                    Royal wench!    236
She made great Caesar lay his sword to bed;    237
He plowed her, and she cropped.

ENOBARBUS                                    I saw her once    238
Hop forty paces through the public street,
And having lost her breath, she spoke and panted,
That she did make defect perfection,    241
And, breathless, pour breath forth.

MAECENAS
Now Antony must leave her utterly.

ENOBARBUS    Never. He will not.
Age cannot wither her, nor custom stale    245
Her infinite variety. Other women cloy
The appetites they feed, but she makes hungry

**171 Misena** i.e., Misenum, in southern Italy. (Not in Sicily, where 2.1 perhaps takes place.)    **173 So is the fame** So it is reported.    **174 Would . . . together!** Would that we had had a chance to parley before battle!    **176 most** the greatest    **177 to my sister's view** to see my sister    **178 straight** straightway    **180.1 Manent** They remain on stage    **182 Half . . . Caesar** You who are very close to Caesar, one of his closest advisers    **186 digested** disposed.    **stayed well by't** kept at it    **187–8 we . . . countenance** we disconcerted day by sleeping right through it    **188 light** (1) brightly lit (2) debauched and giddy    **191 This . . . eagle** i.e., This was nothing compared with greater feasting.    **194 triumphant** magnificent    **195 square** just    **197 pursed up** pocketed up, put in her purse.    **river of Cydnus** (in modern-day southeastern Turkey)    **198–9 devised** invented    **201 burnished** lustrous, shiny    **202 poop** a short deck built over the main deck at the stern of the vessel

**207 As** as if.    **For** As for    **209 cloth-of-gold of tissue** cloth interwoven with gold thread    **210 that Venus** a painting of Venus    **211 fancy** imagination    **213 divers-colored** multicolored    **214 glow** cause to glow    **215 rare** excellent    **216 Nereides** sea nymphs    **217 So . . . i'th'eyes** as if they were so many mermaids, attended to her every glance or nod    **218 made . . . adornings** made their graceful bowings beautiful.    **219 tackle** sails and sailing apparatus    **221 yarely . . . office** nimbly perform their function.    **223 wharfs** banks.    **226 but for vacancy** except that it would have created a vacuum    **235 ordinary** meal, supper (such as one might obtain at a public table in a tavern)    **236 eat** ate. (Pronounced *et*.)    **237 Caesar** i.e., Julius Caesar, by whom Cleopatra had a son named Caesarion    **238 cropped** bore fruit (a son).    **241 That** so that    **245 custom stale** repeated experience make stale

Where most she satisfies; for vilest things
Become themselves in her, that the holy priests    249
Bless her when she is riggish.    250

MAECENAS
If beauty, wisdom, modesty can settle
The heart of Antony, Octavia is
A blessèd lottery to him.

AGRIPPA                              Let us go.    253
Good Enobarbus, make yourself my guest
Whilst you abide here.

ENOBARBUS                    Humbly, sir, I thank you.
                                                    *Exeunt.*

❧

## [2.3]

*Enter Antony, Caesar, Octavia between them.*

ANTONY
The world and my great office will sometimes
Divide me from your bosom.

OCTAVIA                              All which time
Before the gods my knee shall bow my prayers    3
To them for you.

ANTONY                    Good night, sir. My Octavia,
Read not my blemishes in the world's report.    5
I have not kept my square, but that to come    6
Shall all be done by th' rule. Good night, dear lady.
Good night, sir.

CAESAR    Good night.    *Exit [with Octavia].*

*Enter Soothsayer.*

ANTONY
Now, sirrah: you do wish yourself in Egypt?    10

SOOTHSAYER    Would I had never come from thence,
nor you thither!    12

ANTONY    If you can, your reason?

SOOTHSAYER    I see it in my motion, have it not in my    14
tongue; but yet hie you to Egypt again.    15

ANTONY
Say to me, whose fortunes shall rise higher,
Caesar's or mine?

SOOTHSAYER    Caesar's.
Therefore, O Antony, stay not by his side.
Thy daemon—that thy spirit which keeps thee—is    20
Noble, courageous, high unmatchable,    21
Where Caesar's is not; but near him thy angel    22
Becomes afeard, as being o'erpowered. Therefore    23
Make space enough between you.

ANTONY                              Speak this no more.

SOOTHSAYER
To none but thee; no more but when to thee.    25
If thou dost play with him at any game,
Thou art sure to lose; and of that natural luck    27
He beats thee 'gainst the odds. Thy luster thickens    28
When he shines by. I say again, thy spirit    29
Is all afraid to govern thee near him;
But, he away, 'tis noble.

ANTONY                              Get thee gone.
Say to Ventidius I would speak with him.
                                        *Exit [Soothsayer].*
He shall to Parthia.—Be it art or hap,    33
He hath spoken true. The very dice obey him,    34
And in our sports my better cunning faints    35
Under his chance. If we draw lots, he speeds;    36
His cocks do win the battle still of mine    37
When it is all to naught, and his quails ever    38
Beat mine, inhooped, at odds. I will to Egypt;    39
And though I make this marriage for my peace,
I'th'East my pleasure lies.

*Enter Ventidius.*

                              Oh, come, Ventidius.
You must to Parthia. Your commission's ready;
Follow me, and receive't.    *Exeunt.*

❧

## [2.4]

*Enter Lepidus, Maecenas, and Agrippa.*

LEPIDUS
Trouble yourselves no further. Pray you, hasten
Your generals after.

AGRIPPA                    Sir, Mark Antony    2
Will e'en but kiss Octavia, and we'll follow.    3

LEPIDUS
Till I shall see you in your soldier's dress,    4
Which will become you both, farewell.

MAECENAS                              We shall,    5
As I conceive the journey, be at th' Mount    6
Before you, Lepidus.

LEPIDUS                    Your way is shorter;
My purposes do draw me much about.    8
You'll win two days upon me.

MAECENAS, AGRIPPA                    Sir, good success!

LEPIDUS    Farewell.    *Exeunt.*

❧

---

249 **Become themselves** are becoming, attractive.    **that** so that
250 **riggish** lustful.    253 **lottery** prize, gift of fortune
**2.3. Location: Rome.**
3 **my knee . . . prayers** my knee will bend in prayer    5 **Read** interpret.
**in** according to    6 **kept my square** kept to a straight course
(as guided by a carpenter's square; with pun on *rule*, "ruler" in next
line).    **that** that which is    10 **sirrah** (A form of address to a social
inferior.)    12 **thither** to that place.    14 **in my motion** intuitively, by
inward prompting    15 **hie** hasten    20 **Thy . . . thee** Your guardian
spirit, the spirit that protects you    21 **high unmatchable** unmatchable
in the extreme    22 **Where . . . not** wherever Caesar's spirit is not
present (to daunt yours)    23 **as** as if

25 **no more but when** only when    27 **of** by    28 **thickens** grows dim
29 **by** nearby.    33 **art or hap** skill or luck    34 **He** the soothsayer.
**him** Octavius    35 **cunning** skill    36 **chance** luck.    **speeds** wins
37 **still of** always from    38 **When . . . naught** when the odds are
everything to nothing (in my favor)    39 **inhooped** (The birds were
enclosed in hoops to make them fight.)    **at odds** against the odds.
**2.4. Location: Rome.**
2 **Your generals after** after your generals.    3 **e'en but** only, just
4 **dress** garb, apparel    5 **become** suit    6 **conceive** understand.
**th' Mount** i.e., Mount Misenum    8 **about** roundabout.

# [2.5]

*Enter Cleopatra, Charmian, Iras, and Alexas.*

CLEOPATRA
Give me some music; music, moody food
Of us that trade in love.

ALL                                         The music, ho!

*Enter Mardian the eunuch.*

CLEOPATRA
Let it alone. Let's to billiards. Come, Charmian.

CHARMIAN
My arm is sore. Best play with Mardian.

CLEOPATRA
As well a woman with an eunuch played
As with a woman. Come, you'll play with me, sir?

MARDIAN    As well as I can, madam.

CLEOPATRA
And when good will is showed, though't come too
    short,                                                            8
The actor may plead pardon. I'll none now.                            9
Give me mine angle; we'll to th' river. There,                       10
My music playing far off, I will betray
Tawny-finned fishes. My bended hook shall pierce
Their slimy jaws, and as I draw them up
I'll think them every one an Antony,
And say, "Aha! You're caught."

CHARMIAN                             'Twas merry when
You wagered on your angling, when your diver
Did hang a salt fish on his hook, which he                           17
With fervency drew up.

CLEOPATRA                   That time—oh, times!—
I laughed him out of patience; and that night
I laughed him into patience. And next morn,
Ere the ninth hour, I drunk him to his bed,                          21
Then put my tires and mantles on him, whilst                         22
I wore his sword Philippan.

*Enter a Messenger.*

                                    Oh, from Italy!                   23
Ram thou thy fruitful tidings in mine ears,
That long time have been barren.

MESSENGER                         Madam, madam—

CLEOPATRA
Antonio's dead! If thou say so, villain,
Thou kill'st thy mistress; but well and free,
If thou so yield him, there is gold, and here                        28
My bluest veins to kiss—a hand that kings
Have lipped, and trembled kissing.
                *[She offers him gold, and her hand to kiss.]*

MESSENGER    First, madam, he is well.

CLEOPATRA
Why, there's more gold. But, sirrah, mark, we use
To say the dead are well. Bring it to that,                          33
The gold I give thee will I melt and pour
Down thy ill-uttering throat.

MESSENGER    Good madam, hear me.

CLEOPATRA    Well, go to, I will.                                     37
But there's no goodness in thy face, if Antony
Be free and healthful—so tart a favor                                39
To trumpet such good tidings! If not well,
Thou shouldst come like a Fury crowned with snakes,                  41
Not like a formal man.

MESSENGER                Will't please you hear me?                   42

CLEOPATRA
I have a mind to strike thee ere thou speak'st.
Yet, if thou say Antony lives, is well,
Or friends with Caesar, or not captive to him,
I'll set thee in a shower of gold and hail
Rich pearls upon thee.

MESSENGER                Madam, he's well.

CLEOPATRA                                    Well said.

MESSENGER
And friends with Caesar.

CLEOPATRA                  Thou'rt an honest man.                     48

MESSENGER
Caesar and he are greater friends than ever.

CLEOPATRA
Make thee a fortune from me.

MESSENGER                      But yet, madam—

CLEOPATRA
I do not like "But yet"; it does allay                               51
The good precedence. Fie upon "But yet"!                             52
"But yet" is as a jailer to bring forth
Some monstrous malefactor. Prithee, friend,
Pour out the pack of matter to mine ear,                             55
The good and bad together. He's friends with Caesar,
In state of health, thou say'st, and, thou say'st, free.

MESSENGER
Free, madam? No, I made no such report.
He's bound unto Octavia.

CLEOPATRA                  For what good turn?                        59

MESSENGER
For the best turn i'th' bed.

CLEOPATRA          I am pale, Charmian.

MESSENGER
Madam, he's married to Octavia.

CLEOPATRA
The most infectious pestilence upon thee!
                                    *Strikes him down.*

MESSENGER
Good madam, patience.

CLEOPATRA          What say you?    *Strikes him.*
                                    Hence,

---

**2.5. Location:** Alexandria. Cleopatra's palace.
**8 too short** (A bawdy joke on Mardian's being castrated; *will* suggests
"sexual desire"; *come* suggests "reach orgasm.")   **9 I'll none now** i.e., I won't
play billiards after all.   **10 angle** rod and line   **17 salt** dried, preserved in
salt. (This practical joke, as reported in Plutarch, was Cleopatra's way of
poking fun at Antony's boasting about his prowess as a fisher.)
**21 ninth hour** i.e., 9 A.M.   **drunk** drank   **22 tires** headdresses, or perhaps
attire.   **mantles** robes, garments   **23 Philippan** (Named for Antony's victory over Brutus and Cassius at Philippi.)   **28 yield** (1) grant (2) report

**33 well** i.e., well out of it, in heaven.   **Bring it to that** If that is your
meaning   **37 go to** i.e., all right, then. (Said remonstratingly.)
**39 tart a favor** sour a face   **41 Fury** avenging goddess of classical
mythology   **42 like . . . man** in ordinary human form.   **48 honest**
worthy   **51–2 allay . . . precedence** annul the good news that preceded it.   **55 pack of matter** entire contents (as of a peddler's pack)
**59 turn** deed, favor, purpose. (But the Messenger replies in the sense
of "feat, bout," with sexual suggestion.)

Horrible villain, or I'll spurn thine eyes                          64
Like balls before me! I'll unhair thy head!                        65
                          *She hales him up and down.*
Thou shalt be whipped with wire and stewed in brine,
Smarting in ling'ring pickle!
MESSENGER                              Gracious madam,              67
I that do bring the news made not the match.
CLEOPATRA
Say 'tis not so, a province I will give thee
And make thy fortunes proud. The blow thou hadst
Shall make thy peace for moving me to rage,                        71
And I will boot thee with what gift beside                         72
Thy modesty can beg.
MESSENGER                    He's married, madam.                  73
CLEOPATRA
Rogue, thou hast lived too long!          *Draw a knife.*
MESSENGER                          Nay then, I'll run.
What mean you, madam? I have made no fault.        *Exit.*
CHARMIAN
Good madam, keep yourself within yourself.                         76
The man is innocent.
CLEOPATRA
Some innocents scape not the thunderbolt.
Melt Egypt into Nile, and kindly creatures                         79
Turn all to serpents! Call the slave again.
Though I am mad, I will not bite him. Call!                        81
CHARMIAN
He is afeard to come.
CLEOPATRA                    I will not hurt him.
                          [*The Messenger is sent for.*]
These hands do lack nobility, that they strike
A meaner than myself, since I myself                               84
Have given myself the cause.

          *Enter the Messenger again.*

                              Come hither, sir.                    85
Though it be honest, it is never good
To bring bad news. Give to a gracious message
An host of tongues, but let ill tidings tell                       88
Themselves when they be felt.                                      89
MESSENGER    I have done my duty.
CLEOPATRA    Is he married?
I cannot hate thee worser than I do
If thou again say "Yes."
MESSENGER                    He's married, madam.
CLEOPATRA
The gods confound thee! Dost thou hold there still?                94
MESSENGER
Should I lie, madam?
CLEOPATRA                    Oh, I would thou didst,

So half my Egypt were submerged and made                          96
A cistern for scaled snakes! Go, get thee hence.                   97
Hadst thou Narcissus in thy face, to me                            98
Thou wouldst appear most ugly. He is married?
MESSENGER
I crave Your Highness' pardon.
CLEOPATRA                    He is married?
MESSENGER
Take no offense that I would not offend you.                       101
To punish me for what you make me do
Seems much unequal. He's married to Octavia.                       103
CLEOPATRA
Oh, that his fault should make a knave of thee,                    104
That art not what thou'rt sure of! Get thee hence.                 105
The merchandise which thou hast brought from
     Rome
Are all too dear for me. Lie they upon thy hand,                   107
And be undone by 'em!                [*Exit Messenger.*]
CHARMIAN              Good Your Highness, patience.  108
CLEOPATRA
In praising Antony, I have dispraised Caesar.
CHARMIAN    Many times, madam.
CLEOPATRA
I am paid for't now. Lead me from hence;                           111
I faint. Oh, Iras, Charmian! 'Tis no matter.
Go to the fellow, good Alexas. Bid him
Report the feature of Octavia: her years,
Her inclination. Let him not leave out                             115
The color of her hair. Bring me word quickly.
                              [*Exit Alexas.*]
Let him forever go!—Let him not, Charmian.                         117
Though he be painted one way like a Gorgon,                        118
The other way's a Mars. [*To Mardian*] Bid you Alexas  119
Bring me word how tall she is.—Pity me, Charmian,
But do not speak to me. Lead me to my chamber.
                                        *Exeunt.*

❖

# [2.6]

*Flourish. Enter Pompey [and] Menas at one
door, with drum and trumpet; at another, Caesar, Lepidus, Antony, Enobarbus, Maecenas,
Agrippa, with soldiers marching.*

---

**64 spurn** kick   **65.1 hales** drags   **67 pickle** pickling solution.
**71 make thy peace** compensate, mollify me   **72 boot thee with** give
you into the bargain, or, make amends with.   **what** whatever
**73 Thy modesty** one of your modest expectations   **76 keep . . .
yourself** i.e., control yourself.   **79 kindly** endowed with innately
good qualities   **81 mad** (1) angry (2) insane, and so apt to bite
**84 A meaner** one of lower social station   **84–5 since . . . cause** since I
am the one I ought to blame.   **85 the cause** i.e., by loving Antony.
**88 host** multitude   **89 when . . . felt** i.e., by being felt rather than
spoken aloud. Let bad tidings announce themselves.   **94 confound**
destroy.   **hold there still** stick to your story.

**96 So** even if   **97 cistern** tank.   **scaled** scaly   **98 Narcissus** beautiful
youth of Greek mythology who fell in love with his own reflected
image   **101 Take . . . offend you** Don't be offended that I hesitate to
offend you (by telling bad news), or, don't interpret as offense what is not
meant to offend.   **103 much unequal** most unjust.   **104–5 Oh, that . . .
sure of!** How regrettable that Antony's fault puts you in the wrong, you
who are not yourself hateful even if you have had to report hateful news
as a certain fact!   **107 dear** (1) expensive (2) emotionally precious
**107–8 Lie . . . by 'em** May they remain in your possession unsold, and may
you be bankrupt, financially ruined! (i.e., May you never profit from your
bad tidings!)   **111 I am . . . now** (in that Octavius Caesar has arranged for
Antony to marry Octavius's sister).   **115 inclination** disposition.
**117 him** Antony   **118–19 Though . . . Mars** (Alludes to a type of picture
known as a perspective, which shows different images when looked at
from different angles of vision. A *Gorgon* is a female monster with serpents
in her hair, capable of turning to stone anything that meets her gaze.)
**2.6. Location:** Near Misenum, in southern Italy near modern
Naples. (But 2.1 perhaps took place in Messina, Sicily.)

POMPEY
　Your hostages I have, so have you mine,　　　　　　1
　And we shall talk before we fight.
CAESAR　　　　　　　　　　　　　　Most meet　　　2
　That first we come to words; and therefore have we
　Our written purposes before us sent,　　　　　　　4
　Which if thou hast considered, let us know
　If 'twill tie up thy discontented sword　　　　　　6
　And carry back to Sicily much tall youth　　　　　7
　That else must perish here.
POMPEY　　　　　　　　　　　　To you all three,
　The senators alone of this great world,　　　　　　9
　Chief factors for the gods: I do not know　　　　　10
　Wherefore my father should revengers want,　　　11
　Having a son and friends, since Julius Caesar,　　12
　Who at Philippi the good Brutus ghosted,　　　　13
　There saw you laboring for him. What was't　　　14
　That moved pale Cassius to conspire? And what
　Made th'all-honored, honest Roman Brutus,　　　16
　With the armed rest, courtiers of beauteous freedom,　17
　To drench the Capitol, but that they would　　　　18
　Have one man but a man? And that is it　　　　　19
　Hath made me rig my navy, at whose burden
　The angered ocean foams, with which I meant
　To scourge th'ingratitude that despiteful Rome
　Cast on my noble father.
CAESAR　　　　　　　　　　Take your time.
ANTONY
　Thou canst not fear us, Pompey, with thy sails;　　24
　We'll speak with thee at sea. At land thou know'st　25
　How much we do o'ercount thee.
POMPEY　　　　　　　　　　　At land indeed　　　26
　Thou dost o'ercount me of my father's house;
　But since the cuckoo builds not for himself,　　　28
　Remain in't as thou mayst.
LEPIDUS　　　　　　　　　Be pleased to tell us—　　29
　For this is from the present—how you take　　　　30
　The offers we have sent you.
CAESAR　　　　　　　　　　　There's the point.

ANTONY
　Which do not be entreated to, but weigh　　　　　32
　What it is worth embraced.
CAESAR　　　　　　　　　　And what may follow,　33
　To try a larger fortune.
POMPEY　　　　　　　　　You have made me offer　34
　Of Sicily, Sardinia; and I must
　Rid all the sea of pirates; then, to send　　　　　36
　Measures of wheat to Rome. This 'greed upon,
　To part with unhacked edges and bear back　　　38
　Our targes undinted.
CAESAR, ANTONY, LEPIDUS　That's our offer.
POMPEY　　　　　　　　　　　　　　Know then　39
　I came before you here a man prepared
　To take this offer, but Mark Antony
　Put me to some impatience. Though I lose　　　　42
　The praise of it by telling, you must know,　　　43
　When Caesar and your brother were at blows,
　Your mother came to Sicily and did find
　Her welcome friendly.
ANTONY　　　　　　　　I have heard it, Pompey,
　And am well studied for a liberal thanks　　　　47
　Which I do owe you.
POMPEY　　　　　　　Let me have your hand.
　　　　　　　　　　　　　[They shake hands.]
　I did not think, sir, to have met you here.
ANTONY
　The beds i'th'East are soft; and thanks to you,
　That called me timelier than my purpose hither,　51
　For I have gained by't.
CAESAR [to Pompey]　　　Since I saw you last
　There's a change upon you.
POMPEY　　　　　　　　　　Well, I know not
　What counts harsh Fortune casts upon my face,　54
　But in my bosom shall she never come
　To make my heart her vassal.
LEPIDUS　　　　　　　　　　Well met here.
POMPEY
　I hope so, Lepidus. Thus we are agreed.
　I crave our composition may be written　　　　58
　And sealed between us.
CAESAR　　　　　　　　That's the next to do.　　59
POMPEY
　We'll feast each other ere we part, and let's
　Draw lots who shall begin.
ANTONY　　　　　　　　　That will I, Pompey.　61
POMPEY
　No, Antony, take the lot. But, first or last,　　　62

---

**1 hostages** persons held on both sides as security during negotiations prior to fighting　**2 meet** fitting　**4 purposes** propositions　**6 tie . . . sword** i.e., satisfy your concerns and allow you to forgo a fight　**7 tall** brave　**9 senators alone** i.e., sole rulers of the state (who have thus supplanted the Senate)　**10 factors** agents　**10–14 I do . . . for him** (Julius Caesar defeated Pompey's father, Pompey the Great, and was subsequently assassinated by Brutus and Cassius, among others. Caesar's ghost appeared to Brutus at Philippi, where the combined forces of Antony, Octavius, and Lepidus defeated Brutus and Cassius. [See *Julius Caesar*.] Since Antony, Octavius, and Lepidus thus defeated the avengers of Pompey the Great's death, Pompey the Great's sons and friends should become his avengers by continuing to war on Antony, Octavius, and Lepidus.)　**11 want** lack　**13 ghosted** haunted　**16 honest** honorable　**17 the armed rest** i.e., the rest of those who were armed.　**courtiers . . . freedom** those who seek and serve freedom only　**18 drench** bathe in blood　**19 Have . . . a man** (The republican conspirators acted to keep Julius Caesar from accepting the crown.)　**24 fear** frighten　**25 speak with** confront　**26 o'ercount** outnumber. (But Pompey's use of the word in the next line implies that Antony has cheated him. Plutarch informs us that Antony bought the elder Pompey's house at auction and later refused to pay for it.)　**28 cuckoo** a bird that builds no nest for itself but lays its eggs in other birds' nests　**29 as thou mayst** as long as you can, or, since you can.　**30 from the present** digressing from the business at hand

**32 do . . . to** i.e., do not accept merely because we ask　**33 embraced** if accepted by you.　**34 To . . . fortune** i.e., if you decide to risk war with the triumvirs, or, if you join with us to share a greater fortune.　**36 to send** I am to send　**38 To part** we are to part company.　**edges** swords　**39 targes** shields　**42–3 Though . . . telling** i.e., Though I forfeit praise from others by praising myself　**47 well studied for** well prepared to deliver　**51 timelier** earlier　**54 counts** tally marks. (From the practice of casting accounts or reckonings by means of marks or notches on tallies.)　**casts** calculates　**58 composition** agreement　**59 sealed between us** stamped with the official seal of each co-signer.　**61 That will I** I will begin (to serve first as host)　**62 take the lot** draw lots with the rest of us, accept the results of the lottery.　**first or last** whether you win the lottery to go first or last

Your fine Egyptian cookery shall have
The fame. I have heard that Julius Caesar
Grew fat with feasting there.
ANTONY    You have heard much.
POMPEY    I have fair meanings, sir.                          67
ANTONY    And fair words to them.                            68
POMPEY    Then so much have I heard.                         69
    And I have heard Apollodorus carried—                    70
ENOBARBUS
    No more of that. He did so.
POMPEY                          What, I pray you?             71
ENOBARBUS
    A certain queen to Caesar in a mattress.                 72
POMPEY
    I know thee now. How far'st thou, soldier?
ENOBARBUS                                      Well,
    And well am like to do, for I perceive                   74
    Four feasts are toward.
POMPEY                   Let me shake thy hand.              75
                          [*They shake hands.*]
    I never hated thee. I have seen thee fight
    When I have envied thy behavior.
ENOBARBUS                              Sir,
    I never loved you much, but I ha' praised ye
    When you have well deserved ten times as much
    As I have said you did.
POMPEY                  Enjoy thy plainness;                 80
    It nothing ill becomes thee.                             81
    Aboard my galley I invite you all.
    Will you lead, lords?
CAESAR, ANTONY, LEPIDUS    Show 's the way, sir.
POMPEY                                      Come.  83
                *Exeunt. Manent Enobarbus and Menas.*
MENAS [*aside*]    Thy father, Pompey, would ne'er have
    made this treaty.—You and I have known, sir.            85
ENOBARBUS    At sea, I think.
MENAS    We have, sir.
ENOBARBUS    You have done well by water.
MENAS    And you by land.
ENOBARBUS    I will praise any man that will praise me,
    though it cannot be denied what I have done by land.
MENAS    Nor what I have done by water.
ENOBARBUS    Yes, something you can deny for your own
    safety: you have been a great thief by sea.
MENAS    And you by land.
ENOBARBUS    There I deny my land service. But give me  96
    your hand, Menas. [*They shake hands.*] If our eyes had
    authority, here they might take two thieves kissing.  98

MENAS    All men's faces are true, whatsome'er their hands
    are.
ENOBARBUS    But there is never a fair woman has a true  101
    face.
MENAS    No slander; they steal hearts.                     103
ENOBARBUS    We came hither to fight with you.
MENAS    For my part, I am sorry it is turned to a drinking.  105
    Pompey doth this day laugh away his fortune.
ENOBARBUS    If he do, sure he cannot weep't back
    again.
MENAS    You've said, sir. We looked not for Mark  109
    Antony here. Pray you, is he married to Cleopatra?
ENOBARBUS    Caesar's sister is called Octavia.
MENAS    True, sir. She was the wife of Caius Marcellus.
ENOBARBUS    But she is now the wife of Marcus Anto-
    nius.
MENAS    Pray ye, sir?                                       115
ENOBARBUS    'Tis true.
MENAS    Then is Caesar and he forever knit together.
ENOBARBUS    If I were bound to divine of this unity, I  118
    would not prophesy so.
MENAS    I think the policy of that purpose made more in  120
    the marriage than the love of the parties.
ENOBARBUS    I think so too. But you shall find the band
    that seems to tie their friendship together will be
    the very strangler of their amity. Octavia is of a holy, cold,
    and still conversation.                                  125
MENAS    Who would not have his wife so?
ENOBARBUS    Not he that himself is not so, which is
    Mark Antony. He will to his Egyptian dish again.
    Then shall the sighs of Octavia blow the fire up in
    Caesar, and, as I said before, that which is the strength
    of their amity shall prove the immediate author of  131
    their variance. Antony will use his affection where it  132
    is; he married but his occasion here.                    133
MENAS    And thus it may be. Come, sir, will you
    aboard? I have a health for you.                         135
ENOBARBUS    I shall take it, sir. We have used our
    throats in Egypt.
MENAS    Come, let's away.                          *Exeunt.*

❖

# [2.7]

*Music plays. Enter two or three Servants with a
banquet.*

FIRST SERVANT    Here they'll be, man. Some o' their
    plants are ill-rooted already; the least wind i'th' world  2
    will blow them down.

67 **fair** i.e., friendly  68 **fair** i.e., well-chosen  69 **Then . . . heard** i.e., I am not implying more about Antony in Egypt than my words honestly mean.  70–2 **Apollodorus . . . mattress** (Alludes to a tale told by Plutarch according to which Cleopatra had herself rolled up in a mattress and carried secretly by Apollodorus to meet Julius Caesar.)  74 **like** likely  75 **toward** coming up.  80 **Enjoy thy plainness** Give free rein to your bluntness  81 **nothing . . . thee** suits you not at all badly.  83.1 *Manent* They remain on stage  85 **known** known each other  96 **There** In respect of that  98 **authority** i.e., to make arrests, like a constable.  **take** arrest.  **two thieves kissing** (1) our two thieving hands shaking (2) two thieves greeting each other.

101 **true** honest (because women use cosmetic art to conceal defects)  103 **No . . . hearts** i.e., You speak true, since women in their own way are thieves, stealing men's affections.  105 **a drinking** an occasion for drinking.  109 **You've said** You've spoken truly  115 **Pray ye, sir?** Are you in earnest?  118 **divine of** prophesy about  120 **made more** played more of a role  125 **conversation** demeanor.  131–2 **author . . . variance** cause of their falling out.  132–3 **use . . . it is** i.e., satisfy his passion in Egypt  133 **his occasion** what his interests demanded  135 **health** toast  **2.7. Location:** On board Pompey's galley, off Misenum in southern Italy. A table and stools are brought on.  **0.2 banquet** a course of the feast, probably dessert  **2 plants** (1) planted trees (2) soles of the feet.  **are ill-rooted** i.e., are unsteady (owing to drinking heavily)

SECOND SERVANT   Lepidus is high-colored.   4

FIRST SERVANT   They have made him drink alms-drink.   5

SECOND SERVANT   As they pinch one another by the   6
disposition, he cries out, "No more," reconciles them   7
to his entreaty, and himself to th' drink.   8

FIRST SERVANT   But it raises the greater war between
him and his discretion.

SECOND SERVANT   Why, this it is to have a name in   11
great men's fellowship. I had as lief have a reed that   12
will do me no service as a partisan I could not heave.   13

FIRST SERVANT   To be called into a huge sphere,   14
and not to be seen to move in't, are the holes where   15
eyes should be, which pitifully disaster the cheeks.   16

*A sennet sounded. Enter Caesar, Antony,*
*Pompey, Lepidus, Agrippa, Maecenas, Enobarbus,*
*Menas, with other captains [and a Boy].*

ANTONY
Thus do they, sir: they take the flow o'th' Nile   17
By certain scales i'th' pyramid. They know   18
By th' height, the lowness, or the mean if dearth   19
Or foison follow. The higher Nilus swells   20
The more it promises; as it ebbs, the seedsman
Upon the slime and ooze scatters his grain,
And shortly comes to harvest.

LEPIDUS   You've strange serpents there?

ANTONY   Ay, Lepidus.

LEPIDUS   Your serpent of Egypt is bred now of your   26
mud by the operation of your sun; so is your crocodile.

ANTONY   They are so.

POMPEY   Sit—and some wine. A health to Lepidus!   29
*[They sit and drink.]*

LEPIDUS   I am not so well as I should be, but I'll   30
ne'er out.   31

ENOBARBUS   Not till you have slept; I fear me you'll be
in till then.   33

LEPIDUS   Nay, certainly, I have heard the Ptolemies'
pyramises are very goodly things; without contradic-   35
tion I have heard that.

MENAS *[aside to Pompey]*   Pompey, a word.

POMPEY *[to Menas]*   Say in mine ear. What is't?

MENAS *(whispers in 's ear)*
Forsake thy seat, I do beseech thee, captain,
And hear me speak a word.

POMPEY *[to Menas]*
Forbear me till anon.—This wine for Lepidus!   41

LEPIDUS   What manner o' thing is your crocodile?

ANTONY   It is shaped, sir, like itself, and it is as broad as
it hath breadth. It is just so high as it is, and moves
with it own organs. It lives by that which nourisheth   45
it, and, the elements once out of it, it transmigrates.   46

LEPIDUS   What color is it of?

ANTONY   Of it own color too.

LEPIDUS   'Tis a strange serpent.

ANTONY   'Tis so. And the tears of it are wet.   50

CAESAR   Will this description satisfy him?

ANTONY   With the health that Pompey gives him, else
he is a very epicure.   *[Menas whispers again.]*   53

POMPEY *[aside to Menas]*
Go hang, sir, hang! Tell me of that? Away!
Do as I bid you.—Where's this cup I called for?

MENAS *[aside to Pompey]*
If for the sake of merit thou wilt hear me,   56
Rise from thy stool.

POMPEY *[rising]*   I think thou'rt mad. The matter?
*[They walk aside.]*

MENAS
I have ever held my cap off to thy fortunes.   58

POMPEY
Thou hast served me with much faith. What's else to
say?—   59
Be jolly, lords.

ANTONY   These quicksands, Lepidus,
Keep off them, for you sink.
*[Menas and Pompey speak aside.]*

MENAS
Wilt thou be lord of all the world?

POMPEY                          What say'st thou?

MENAS
Wilt thou be lord of the whole world? That's twice.

POMPEY
How should that be?

MENAS                    But entertain it,   64
And, though thou think me poor, I am the man
Will give thee all the world.

POMPEY                    Hast thou drunk well?

MENAS
No, Pompey, I have kept me from the cup.
Thou art, if thou dar'st be, the earthly Jove.

---

**4 high-colored** flushed.   **5 alms-drink** i.e., drink charitably consumed in the furtherance of reconciliation. (See next speech and note.)   **6–8 As . . . drink** As they chafe one another, prompted by their various temperaments, Lepidus entreats them to stop quarreling, and reconciles himself to the peacemaking business of downing one drink after another in response to their toasts.   **11 a name** a name only   **12 had as lief** would just as soon   **13 partisan** long-bladed spear. (Here, metaphorically, too large a weapon for Lepidus to wield.)   **14–16 To . . . cheeks** To be summoned by fortune to greatness and yet not be able to fulfill the role greatly is like having eye sockets with no eyes in them, a defect that will disfigure (*disaster*) the cheeks. (The underlying image is of a heavenly body that cannot move properly in its sphere, causing *disaster*, meaning both disfigurement and the evil effects of unfavorable aspect of a planet.)
**16.1 sennet** trumpet call signaling the approach of a procession
**17 sir** (Usually thought to refer to Caesar, but the matter is uncertain.)
**take** measure   **18 scales** graduated markings   **19 mean** middle
**20 foison** plenty   **26 Your serpent** i.e., This serpent that people talk about. (The colloquial indefinite *your*.)   **29 health** toast. (Lepidus is obliged to drink up every time a toast is proposed to him.)   **30–1 I'll ne'er out** i.e., I'll never refuse a toast, never quit.   **33 in** in drink, in your cups. (With a play of antitheses between *in* and *out* in line 31.)
**35 pyramises** (Lepidus's drunken error for *pyramides*, plural of *pyramis* or *pyramid*.)

**41 Forbear . . . anon** Excuse me for a moment.   **45 it own** its own. (Also in line 48.)   **46 elements** vital elements   **50 tears** (Alludes to the ancient belief that the crocodile wept insincere "crocodile tears" over its victim before devouring it.)   **53 epicure** (1) glutton (2) atheist. (The Epicureans did not believe in an afterlife. Antony's jesting point is that only an atheist or epicure would be skeptical of such a satisfying description as Antony has just given of the crocodile.)
**56 merit** i.e., my merits as a loyal follower, or, the merit of my ideas
**58 held . . . off** i.e., been a respectful and faithful servant   **59 faith** faithfulness.   **64 But entertain it** Only accept the possibility

Whate'er the ocean pales or sky inclips                                                69
Is thine, if thou wilt ha 't.
POMPEY                                    Show me which way.
MENAS
These three world-sharers, these competitors,                                          71
Are in thy vessel. Let me cut the cable,
And, when we are put off, fall to their throats.                                       73
All there is thine.
POMPEY                             Ah, this thou shouldst have done
And not have spoke on't! In me 'tis villainy;                                          75
In thee 't had been good service. Thou must know,                                      76
'Tis not my profit that does lead mine honor;
Mine honor, it. Repent that e'er thy tongue                                            78
Hath so betrayed thine act. Being done unknown,                                        79
I should have found it afterwards well done,
But must condemn it now. Desist, and drink.
                                   *[He returns to the feast.]*
MENAS *[aside]*    For this,
I'll never follow thy palled fortunes more.                                            83
Who seeks and will not take when once 'tis offered                                     84
Shall never find it more.
POMPEY                              This health to Lepidus!
ANTONY
Bear him ashore. I'll pledge it for him, Pompey.                                       86
ENOBARBUS
Here's to thee, Menas!                          *[They drink.]*
MENAS                            Enobarbus, welcome!
POMPEY   Fill till the cup be hid.                                                     88
ENOBARBUS   There's a strong fellow, Menas.
                  *[Pointing to one who carries off Lepidus.]*
MENAS   Why?
ENOBARBUS   'A bears the third part of the world, man;                                 91
see'st not?
MENAS
The third part, then, is drunk. Would it were all,
That it might go on wheels!                                                            94
ENOBARBUS   Drink thou; increase the reels.                                            95
MENAS   Come.
POMPEY
This is not yet an Alexandrian feast.
ANTONY
It ripens towards it. Strike the vessels, ho!                                          98
Here's to Caesar!
CAESAR                       I could well forbear't.
It's monstrous labor when I wash my brain
And it grows fouler.
ANTONY                       Be a child o'th' time.
CAESAR   Possess it, I'll make answer.                                                 102
But I had rather fast from all four days                                               103

Than drink so much in one.
ENOBARBUS *[to Antony]*          Ha, my brave emperor!                                 104
Shall we dance now the Egyptian Bacchanals                                             105
And celebrate our drink?                                                               106
POMPEY   Let's ha 't, good soldier.
ANTONY   Come, let's all take hands
Till that the conquering wine hath steeped our sense                                   109
In soft and delicate Lethe.
ENOBARBUS                          All take hands.                                      110
Make battery to our ears with the loud music,                                          111
The while I'll place you; then the boy shall sing.                                     112
The holding every man shall bear as loud                                               113
As his strong sides can volley.                                                        114
          *Music plays. Enobarbus places them hand in hand.*

                        *The Song.*

BOY *[sings]*
              Come, thou monarch of the vine,
              Plumpy Bacchus with pink eyne!                                           116
              In thy fats our cares be drowned,                                        117
              With thy grapes our hairs be crowned.
ALL       Cup us till the world go round,                                              119
              Cup us till the world go round!
CAESAR
What would you more? Pompey, good night.—Good
  brother,
Let me request you off. Our graver business                                           122
Frowns at this levity. Gentle lords, let's part;
You see we have burnt our cheeks. Strong Enobarb                                       124
Is weaker than the wine, and mine own tongue
Splits what it speaks. The wild disguise hath almost                                   126
Anticked us all. What needs more words? Good night.                                    127
Good Antony, your hand.
POMPEY                            I'll try you on the shore.                           128
ANTONY
And shall, sir. Give 's your hand.
POMPEY                              Oh, Antony,
You have my father's house. But what? We are
  friends.
Come down into the boat.
ENOBARBUS                       Take heed you fall not.                                131
             *[Exeunt all but Enobarbus and Menas.]*
Menas, I'll not on shore.
MENAS                           No, to my cabin.
These drums, these trumpets, flutes! What!
Let Neptune hear we bid a loud farewell
To these great fellows. Sound and be hanged, sound
  out!                              *Sound a flourish, with drums.*

---

69 **pales** impales, fences in.   **inclips** embraces   71 **competitors** partners. (With secondary sense of "rivals.")   73 **are put off** have put to sea   75 **on't** of it.   76 **Thou must know** I must inform you that   78 **Mine honor, it** i.e., my honor comes before my personal profit. 78–9 **Repent . . . act** Regret that your speaking of this has disabled your opportunity to act.   79 **unknown** i.e., without my knowledge 83 **palled** decayed, darkened   84 **Who** He who   86 **pledge it** i.e., drink the toast (since Lepidus is too far gone to drink)   88 **be hid** is so full that one cannot see the inside of the cup itself.   91 **'A** He   94 **go on wheels** go fast or easily. (Proverbial.)   95 **reels** (1) revels (2) reeling and whirling of drunkenness.   98 **Strike the vessels** Broach or tap more casks   102 **Possess . . . answer** My answer is, be master of the time; or, possibly, Drink it off, I'll drink in return.   103 **all** all nourishment

---

104 **brave** splendid   105 **Bacchanals** drunken dance to Bacchus, god of wine   106 **celebrate** consecrate with observances   109 **Till that** until 110 **Lethe** i.e., forgetfulness. (Literally, the river of oblivion in Hades.) 111 **Make battery to** Assault   112 **The while** while   113 **holding** refrain.   **bear** carry, sing   114 **volley** sing in return, answering the stanza with the refrain; or, fire off.   116 **pink eyne** i.e., eyes half-shut and red from drinking.   117 **fats** vats, vessels   119 **Cup** Intoxicate 122 **off** to disembark.   124 **we . . . cheeks** our complexions are flushed with drinking.   126 **disguise** (1) masque (2) transforming drunkenness 127 **Anticked us** (1) made dancers of us in a masque (2) made buffoons or fools of us   128 **try you** i.e., take you on in a drinking contest 131 **boat** small boat for taking the party ashore.

ENOBARBUS   Hoo! says 'a. There's my cap.
                                      [*He flings it in the air.*]
MENAS   Hoo! Noble captain, come.                    *Exeunt.*

❧

## [3.1]

*Enter Ventidius as it were in triumph [with Silius,
and other Romans, officers, and soldiers], the dead
body of Pacorus [son of Orodes] borne before him.*

VENTIDIUS
    Now, darting Parthia, art thou struck, and now      1
    Pleased fortune does of Marcus Crassus' death       2
    Make me revenger. Bear the King's son's body
    Before our army. Thy Pacorus, Orodes,               4
    Pays this for Marcus Crassus.
SILIUS                    Noble Ventidius,
    Whilst yet with Parthian blood thy sword is warm,
    The fugitive Parthians follow. Spur through Media,  7
    Mesopotamia, and the shelters whither
    The routed fly. So thy grand captain, Antony,
    Shall set thee on triumphant chariots and          10
    Put garlands on thy head.
VENTIDIUS                    Oh, Silius, Silius,
    I have done enough. A lower place, note well,      12
    May make too great an act. For learn this, Silius:
    Better to leave undone than by our deed
    Acquire too high a fame when him we serve's away.
    Caesar and Antony have ever won
    More in their officer than person. Sossius,        17
    One of my place in Syria, his lieutenant,          18
    For quick accumulation of renown,
    Which he achieved by th' minute, lost his favor.   20
    Who does i'th' wars more than his captain can      21
    Becomes his captain's captain; and ambition,
    The soldier's virtue, rather makes choice of loss  23
    Than gain which darkens him.                       24
    I could do more to do Antonius good,
    But 'twould offend him, and in his offense         26
    Should my performance perish.
SILIUS   Thou hast, Ventidius, that                    28
    Without the which a soldier and his sword          29
    Grants scarce distinction. Thou wilt write to Antony?  30
VENTIDIUS
    I'll humbly signify what in his name,

That magical word of war, we have effected:           32
How with his banners and his well-paid ranks          33
The ne'er-yet-beaten horse of Parthia                 34
We have jaded out o'th' field.
SILIUS                    Where is he now?             35
VENTIDIUS
    He purposeth to Athens, whither, with what haste
    The weight we must convey with 's will permit,     37
    We shall appear before him.—On, there. Pass along!
                                              *Exeunt.*

❧

## [3.2]

*Enter Agrippa at one door, Enobarbus at another.*

AGRIPPA   What, are the brothers parted?               1
ENOBARBUS
    They have dispatched with Pompey; he is gone.      2
    The other three are sealing. Octavia weeps         3
    To part from Rome; Caesar is sad; and Lepidus,     4
    Since Pompey's feast, as Menas says, is troubled
    With the greensickness.
AGRIPPA                    'Tis a noble Lepidus.       6
ENOBARBUS
    A very fine one. Oh, how he loves Caesar!          7
AGRIPPA
    Nay, but how dearly he adores Mark Antony!
ENOBARBUS
    Caesar? Why, he's the Jupiter of men.
AGRIPPA
    What's Antony? The god of Jupiter.
ENOBARBUS
    Spake you of Caesar? How, the nonpareil!           11
AGRIPPA
    O Antony, O thou Arabian bird!                     12
ENOBARBUS
    Would you praise Caesar, say "Caesar"; go no further.
AGRIPPA
    Indeed, he plied them both with excellent praises.
ENOBARBUS
    But he loves Caesar best; yet he loves Antony.
    Hoo! Hearts, tongues, figures, scribes, bards, poets,
        cannot                                         16
    Think, speak, cast, write, sing, number, hoo!     17
    His love to Antony. But as for Caesar,
    Kneel down, kneel down, and wonder.
AGRIPPA                    Both he loves.

---

3.1. Location: The Middle East.
**1 darting** (The Parthians were famous for archery and for the Parthian dart which they discharged as they fled.)   **Parthia** i.e., Orodes,
King of Parthia   **2 Crassus' death** (Crassus, member of the first triumvirate with Pompey the Great and Julius Caesar, was overthrown
and treacherously murdered by Orodes in 53 B.C.)   **4 Pacorus,
Orodes** (Pacorus was the son of Orodes.)   **7 The ... follow** follow
the fleeing Parthians.   **10 triumphant** triumphal   **12 A lower place**
One of lower rank   **17 More ... person** more through the actions of
their lieutenants than by their own efforts.   **18 of my place** of the
same rank as I.   **his lieutenant** i.e., the commanding officer acting
for Antony   **20 by th' minute** minute by minute, continually
**21 Who** He who   **23–4 rather ... him** prefers to lose rather than gain
in such a way as to darken his reputation.   **26 offense** taking offense
**28–30 that ... distinction** i.e., discretion, without which a soldier can
scarcely be distinguished from the sword he uses.

**32 word** watchword.   **effected** achieved   **33 with** despite   **34 horse**
cavalry   **35 jaded** driven exhausted like jades, inferior horses
**37 weight** heavy equipment.   **with 's** with us.
3.2. Location: Rome.
**1 are ... parted?** have the brothers-in-law departed?   **2 dispatched**
concluded the business   **3 The other three** The triumvirs, Octavius,
Antony, and Lepidus.   **sealing** affixing seals for their agreements, settling matters.   **4 sad** somber   **6 greensickness** a kind of anemia supposed to affect young women, especially those afflicted with love-longing.
(Used ironically here to refer to Lepidus's hangover and to his love for
Antony and Caesar.)   **7 fine** (*Lepidus* in Latin means "fine," "elegant.")
**11 How** Hoo   **12 Arabian bird** i.e., the fabled phoenix. (Only one
existed at a time; it re-created itself by arising from its ashes.)
**16 figures** figures of speech   **17 cast** calculate.   **number** write verses

ENOBARBUS
They are his shards, and he their beetle. [*Trumpets
   within.*] So;                                                20
This is to horse. Adieu, noble Agrippa.              21
AGRIPPA
Good fortune, worthy soldier, and farewell.

*Enter Caesar, Antony, Lepidus, and Octavia.*

ANTONY   No further, sir.                            23
CAESAR
You take from me a great part of myself;
Use me well in't.—Sister, prove such a wife
As my thoughts make thee, and as my farthest bond   26
Shall pass on thy approof.—Most noble Antony,        27
Let not the piece of virtue which is set             28
Betwixt us as the cement of our love
To keep it builded be the ram to batter
The fortress of it; for better might we
Have loved without this mean, if on both parts       32
This be not cherished.
ANTONY                    Make me not offended
In your distrust.
CAESAR            I have said.
ANTONY                      You shall not find,        34
Though you be therein curious, the least cause        35
For what you seem to fear. So the gods keep you,      36
And make the hearts of Romans serve your ends!
We will here part.
CAESAR
Farewell, my dearest sister, fare thee well.
The elements be kind to thee, and make               40
Thy spirits all of comfort! Fare thee well.
OCTAVIA [*weeping*]   My noble brother!
ANTONY
The April's in her eyes; it is love's spring,         43
And these the showers to bring it on.—Be cheerful.
OCTAVIA [*to Caesar*]
Sir, look well to my husband's house; and—            45
CAESAR
What, Octavia?
OCTAVIA          I'll tell you in your ear.
                   [*She whisper to Caesar.*]
ANTONY
Her tongue will not obey her heart, nor can           47
Her heart inform her tongue—the swan's down
   feather,                                           48
That stands upon the swell at full of tide,           49
And neither way inclines.                             50

ENOBARBUS [*aside to Agrippa*]   Will Caesar weep?
AGRIPPA [*aside to Enobarbus*]   He has a cloud in 's face.
ENOBARBUS [*aside to Agrippa*]
He were the worse for that, were he a horse;          53
So is he, being a man.
AGRIPPA [*aside to Enobarbus*]   Why, Enobarbus,      54
When Antony found Julius Caesar dead,
He cried almost to roaring; and he wept
When at Philippi he found Brutus slain.
ENOBARBUS [*aside to Agrippa*]
That year indeed he was troubled with a rheum.        58
What willingly he did confound he wailed,             59
Believe't, till I wept too.
CAESAR                 No, sweet Octavia,
You shall hear from me still. The time shall not      61
Outgo my thinking on you.
ANTONY                   Come, sir, come,              62
I'll wrestle with you in my strength of love.
Look, here I have you [*embracing him*]; thus I let you
   go,
And give you to the gods.
CAESAR                 Adieu. Be happy!
LEPIDUS
Let all the number of the stars give light
To thy fair way!
CAESAR        Farewell, farewell!   *Kisses Octavia.*
ANTONY                       Farewell!
      *Trumpets sound. Exeunt [in separate groups].*

❖

## [3.3]

*Enter Cleopatra, Charmian, Iras, and Alexas.*

CLEOPATRA
Where is the fellow?
ALEXAS             Half afeard to come.
CLEOPATRA
Go to, go to.

*Enter the Messenger as before.*

            Come hither, sir.
ALEXAS              Good Majesty,                      2
Herod of Jewry dare not look upon you                 3
But when you are well pleased.
CLEOPATRA              That Herod's head               4
I'll have; but how, when Antony is gone,              5
Through whom I might command it?—Come thou
   near.
MESSENGER   Most gracious Majesty!
CLEOPATRA   Didst thou behold Octavia?

20 **shards** patches of dung, or, perhaps, wings or wing-cases, i.e., pro-
tectors, patrons   21 **This is to horse** i.e., The trumpet call gives the
signal to depart.   23 **No further** i.e., You need not go on urging your
point, or, you need accompany me no further   26–7 **as . . . approof**
such that my most solemn commitment shall be justified in certifying
what you will prove to be.   28 **piece** masterpiece   32 **mean** intermediary, or means   34 **In** by.   **I have said** i.e., I stand by what I've said.
35 **curious** overly inquisitive or touchy   36 **keep** protect   40 **The
elements** May the heavens   43 **The April's . . . eyes** She weeps
45 **husband's house** i.e., Antony's house, as at 2.7.130, though Octavia
is also a widow; see 3.3.29   47–50 **Her . . . inclines** i.e., Her conflicting
emotions make her unable to speak aloud, like a swan's down feather
floating at full tide, moving neither up nor down stream.

53 **He . . . horse** (Alludes to the belief that a horse with a dark spot or
star on its face was apt to be bad-tempered.)   54 **So . . . man** (Such
weeping is here viewed as unmanly.)   58 **rheum** i.e., running at the
eyes. (Said of any discharge of secretion from the head.)   59 **What . . .
wailed** He wept for what he intentionally destroyed   61 **still** regularly.
61–2 **The time . . . you** Time itself will not outlast my thinking of you.
3.3. **Location: Alexandria. Cleopatra's palace.**
2 **Go to** (An expression of impatience.)   3 **Herod of Jewry** i.e., Even the
famous tyrant who slaughtered the children. (See 1.2.29–30.)   4–5 **That . . .
have** (Cleopatra perhaps unwittingly alludes to the story of Salome, who,
to please her mother Herodias, demanded the head of John the Baptist as
the reward for her dancing before her father, Herod II (Mark 6:14–28).)

MESSENGER
    Ay, dread Queen.
CLEOPATRA                         Where?
MESSENGER                                 Madam, in Rome.
    I looked her in the face, and saw her led
    Between her brother and Mark Antony.
CLEOPATRA
    Is she as tall as me?
MESSENGER                     She is not, madam.
CLEOPATRA
    Didst hear her speak? Is she shrill-tongued or low?
MESSENGER
    Madam, I heard her speak. She is low-voiced.
CLEOPATRA
    That's not so good. He cannot like her long.            15
CHARMIAN
    Like her! Oh, Isis, 'tis impossible.
CLEOPATRA
    I think so, Charmian. Dull of tongue, and dwarfish.—
    What majesty is in her gait? Remember,
    If e'er thou looked'st on majesty.
MESSENGER                           She creeps:
    Her motion and her station are as one.                  20
    She shows a body rather than a life,                    21
    A statue than a breather.
CLEOPATRA                     Is this certain?              22
MESSENGER
  · Or I have no observance.
CHARMIAN                      Three in Egypt               23
    Cannot make better note.
CLEOPATRA                     He's very knowing,           24
    I do perceive't. There's nothing in her yet.
    The fellow has good judgment.
CHARMIAN                           Excellent.
CLEOPATRA   Guess at her years, I prithee.
MESSENGER   Madam,
    She was a widow—
CLEOPATRA               Widow? Charmian, hark.
MESSENGER   And I do think she's thirty.                    30
CLEOPATRA
    Bear'st thou her face in mind? Is't long or round?
MESSENGER   Round, even to faultiness.
CLEOPATRA
    For the most part, too, they are foolish that are so.—
    Her hair, what color?
MESSENGER   Brown, madam; and her forehead
    As low as she would wish it.
CLEOPATRA [giving money]      There's gold for thee.        36
    Thou must not take my former sharpness ill.
    I will employ thee back again; I find thee              39
    Most fit for business. Go make thee ready;

    Our letters are prepared.            [Exit Messenger.]
CHARMIAN                      A proper man.                 41
CLEOPATRA
    Indeed, he is so. I repent me much
    That so I harried him. Why, methinks, by him,           43
    This creature's no such thing.
CHARMIAN                          Nothing, madam.          44
CLEOPATRA
    The man hath seen some majesty, and should know.
CHARMIAN
    Hath he seen majesty? Isis else defend,                 46
    And serving you so long!                                47
CLEOPATRA
    I have one thing more to ask him yet, good
        Charmian—
    But 'tis no matter; thou shalt bring him to me
    Where I will write. All may be well enough
CHARMIAN   I warrant you, madam.            Exeunt.   51

❖

# [3.4]

*Enter Antony and Octavia.*

ANTONY
    Nay, nay, Octavia, not only that—
    That were excusable, that and thousands more
    Of semblable import—but he hath waged              3
    New wars 'gainst Pompey; made his will, and read it  4
    To public ear;
    Spoke scantly of me; when perforce he could not      6
    But pay me terms of honor, cold and sickly
    He vented them, most narrow measure lent me;          8
    When the best hint was given him, he not took't,      9
    Or did it from his teeth.
OCTAVIA                       Oh, my good lord,            10
    Believe not all, or, if you must believe,
    Stomach not all. A more unhappy lady,                 12
    If this division chance, ne'er stood between,         13
    Praying for both parts.
    The good gods will mock me presently                  15
    When I shall pray, "Oh, bless my lord and husband!"
    Undo that prayer by crying out as loud,               17
    "Oh, bless my brother!" Husband win, win brother,
    Prays and destroys the prayer; no midway
    Twixt these extremes at all.
ANTONY                          Gentle Octavia,
    Let your best love draw to that point which seeks     21
    Best to preserve it. If I lose mine honor,            22

---

15 **not so good** i.e., not so good for her.   20 **Her . . . one** i.e., she moves with so little animation that it's all the same whether she's moving or standing.   21 **shows** appears as   22 **than a breather** rather than a living being.   23 **observance** power of observation.   23–4 **Three . . . note** There are not three people in all Egypt who are better observers.   30 **thirty** (i.e., considerably younger than Cleopatra, who, historically, was 38 at this time).   36 **As . . . it** i.e., such that she wouldn't wish it to be any lower. (A colloquial way of suggesting she is ugly; high foreheads were thought more beautiful.)   39 **employ . . . again** send you back with a message

41 **proper** good   43 **harried** maltreated.   **by** according to   44 **no such thing** nothing much.   46 **else defend** forbid that it be otherwise. (An interjection.)   47 **serving** i.e., he having served   51 **warrant** assure
**3.4. Location: Athens.**
3 **semblable** similar   4 **read it** (in order to win the populace by showing them what benefits they might expect from him)   6 **scantly** slightingly   8 **vented** gave vent to, expressed.   **narrow measure lent me** gave me minimal praise   9 **hint** occasion (to praise Antony)   10 **from his teeth** i.e., between clenched teeth, not from the heart.   12 **Stomach** resent   13 **chance** occurs   15 **presently** right away   17 **Undo** i.e., and then undo, or, I shall undo   21–2 **Let . . . it** let your warmest love be given to that one of us who seeks to preserve it (your love) best.

I lose myself; better I were not yours
Than yours so branchless. But, as you requested, 24
Yourself shall go between 's. The meantime, lady, 25
I'll raise the preparation of a war 26
Shall stain your brother. Make your soonest haste; 27
So your desires are yours.

OCTAVIA                                    Thanks to my lord. 28
The Jove of power make me, most weak, most weak, 29
Your reconciler! Wars twixt you twain would be
As if the world should cleave, and that slain men 31
Should solder up the rift. 32

ANTONY
When it appears to you where this begins, 33
Turn your displeasure that way, for our faults 34
Can never be so equal that your love 35
Can equally move with them. Provide your going; 36
Choose your own company and command what cost
Your heart has mind to.                    *Exeunt.*

❖

## [3.5]

*Enter Enobarbus and Eros, [meeting].*

ENOBARBUS   How now, friend Eros?
EROS   There's strange news come, sir.
ENOBARBUS   What, man?
EROS   Caesar and Lepidus have made wars upon Pompey.
ENOBARBUS   This is old. What is the success? 6
EROS   Caesar, having made use of him in the wars 7
'gainst Pompey, presently denied him rivality, would 8
not let him partake in the glory of the action; and, not
resting here, accuses him of letters he had formerly 10
wrote to Pompey; upon his own appeal seizes him. 11
So the poor third is up, till death enlarge his confine. 12

ENOBARBUS
Then, world, thou hast a pair of chops, no more; 13
And throw between them all the food thou hast, 14
They'll grind the one the other. Where's Antony? 15

EROS
He's walking in the garden—thus, and spurns 16
The rush that lies before him; cries, "Fool Lepidus!" 17

And threats the throat of that his officer 18
That murdered Pompey.
ENOBARBUS                    Our great navy's rigged. 19

EROS
For Italy and Caesar. More, Domitius: 20
My lord desires you presently. My news 21
I might have told hereafter.
ENOBARBUS                    'Twill be naught, 22
But let it be. Bring me to Antony.
EROS                                    Come, sir.   *Exeunt.*

❖

## [3.6]

*Enter Agrippa, Maecenas, and Caesar.*

CAESAR
Contemning Rome, he has done all this and more 1
In Alexandria. Here's the manner of 't:
I'th' marketplace, on a tribunal silvered, 3
Cleopatra and himself in chairs of gold
Were publicly enthroned. At the feet sat
Caesarion, whom they call my father's son, 6
And all the unlawful issue that their lust
Since then hath made between them. Unto her
He gave the stablishment of Egypt, made her 9
Of lower Syria, Cyprus, Lydia,
Absolute queen.
MAECENAS                    This in the public eye?
CAESAR
I'th' common showplace, where they exercise. 12
His sons he there proclaimed the kings of kings:
Great Media, Parthia, and Armenia
He gave to Alexander; to Ptolemy he assigned
Syria, Cilicia, and Phoenicia. She
In th' habiliments of the goddess Isis 17
That day appeared, and oft before gave audience,
As 'tis reported, so. 19
MAECENAS   Let Rome be thus informed.
AGRIPPA   Who, queasy with his insolence already, 21
Will their good thoughts call from him. 22
CAESAR
The people knows it, and have now received
His accusations.
AGRIPPA                    Who does he accuse?
CAESAR
Caesar, and that, having in Sicily
Sextus Pompeius spoiled, we had not rated him 26
His part o'th'isle. Then does he say he lent me 27

---

24 **branchless** pruned (of honor).   25 **The meantime** In the meantime
26–7 **I'll . . . brother** I'll raise an army that will deprive your brother of
his luster.   28 **So . . . yours** i.e., thus you have obtained your desire (to
go). (Or, *so* may mean "as long as.")   29 **most weak** I who am utterly
powerless   31 **cleave** split   32 **Should solder** would be needed to fill
and close   33 **where this begins** who started this quarrel   34 **our** i.e.,
Caesar's and my   34–6 **our faults . . . them** i.e., you will have to judge
between our faults and choose.   36 **Provide** Make arrangements for
**3.5. Location: Athens.**
6 **success** outcome, result.   7 **him** i.e., Lepidus   8 **presently** immediately.   **rivality** rights of a partner. (Caesar and Lepidus have newly
gone to war against Pompey and have defeated him.)   10 **resting
here** stopping with this insult   11 **wrote** written.   **his own appeal**
Caesar's own accusation   12 **third** triumvir.   **up** shut up (in
prison).   **enlarge his confine** set him free.   13 **a pair . . . more** a single pair of jaws, with no third partner   14 **throw** if you were to
throw   15 **They'll . . . other** the jaws would still grind against each
other, grind each other down.   16 **thus** (Eros imitates Antony's
angry walk.)   **spurns** kicks   17 **rush** strewn rushes

18 **And . . . officer** and threatens the life of the officer of his
19 **Pompey** (After his defeat by Caesar and Lepidus, Pompey was
murdered—perhaps, according to history, on Antony's orders, but
here Antony blames his officer.)   20 **More** I have more to say
21 **presently** immediately.   22 **be naught** come to nothing
**3.6. Location: Rome.**
1 **Contemning** Disdaining   3 **tribunal** seat of state, dais   6 **my
father's** i.e., Julius Caesar's. (Julius Caesar had adopted his grand-
nephew Octavius as his son.)   9 **stablishment** settled possession
12 **exercise** put on entertainments and sports.   17 **habiliments** attire
19 **so** in this attire.   21 **queasy** nauseated, "fed up." (Refers to the
Roman people's attitude.)   22 **call** withdraw   26 **spoiled** despoiled,
plundered.   **rated him** allotted to Antony   27 **th'isle** i.e., Sicily.

Some shipping, unrestored. Lastly, he frets   28
That Lepidus of the triumvirate   29
Should be deposed, and, being, that we detain   30
All his revenue.

AGRIPPA          Sir, this should be answered.

CAESAR
'Tis done already, and the messenger gone.
I have told him Lepidus was grown too cruel,
That he his high authority abused
And did deserve his change. For what I have
    conquered,   35
I grant him part; but then in his Armenia,   36
And other of his conquered kingdoms, I
Demand the like.

MAECENAS          He'll never yield to that.

CAESAR
Nor must not then be yielded to in this.

*Enter Octavia with her train.*

OCTAVIA
Hail, Caesar, and my lord! Hail, most dear Caesar!

CAESAR
That ever I should call thee castaway!

OCTAVIA
You have not called me so, nor have you cause.

CAESAR
Why have you stol'n upon us thus? You come not
Like Caesar's sister. The wife of Antony
Should have an army for an usher and
The neighs of horse to tell of her approach   46
Long ere she did appear. The trees by th' way   47
Should have borne men, and expectation fainted,
Longing for what it had not. Nay, the dust
Should have ascended to the roof of heaven,
Raised by your populous troops. But you are come
A market maid to Rome, and have prevented   52
The ostentation of our love, which, left unshown,   53
Is often left unloved. We should have met you   54
By sea and land, supplying every stage   55
With an augmented greeting.

OCTAVIA          Good my lord,
To come thus was I not constrained, but did it
On my free will. My lord, Mark Antony,
Hearing that you prepared for war, acquainted
My grievèd ear withal, whereon I begged
His pardon for return.

CAESAR          Which soon he granted,   61
Being an obstruct 'tween his lust and him.   62

OCTAVIA
Do not say so, my lord.

CAESAR          I have eyes upon him,
And his affairs come to me on the wind.
Where is he now?

OCTAVIA      My lord, in Athens.   28

CAESAR   29
No, my most wrongèd sister. Cleopatra
Hath nodded him to her. He hath given his empire
Up to a whore; who now are levying   69
The kings o'th'earth for war. He hath assembled
Bocchus, the King of Libya; Archelaus,
Of Cappadocia; Philadelphos, King
Of Paphlagonia; the Thracian king, Adallas;
King Manchus of Arabia; King of Pont;
Herod of Jewry; Mithridates, King
Of Comagene; Polemon and Amyntas,
The Kings of Mede and Lycaonia,
With a more larger list of scepters.   78

OCTAVIA      Ay me, most wretched,
That have my heart parted betwixt two friends
That does afflict each other!

CAESAR          Welcome hither.
Your letters did withhold our breaking forth   82
Till we perceived both how you were wrong led   83
And we in negligent danger. Cheer your heart.   84
Be you not troubled with the time, which drives   85
O'er your content these strong necessities,   86
But let determined things to destiny   87
Hold unbewailed their way. Welcome to Rome,   88
Nothing more dear to me. You are abused   89
Beyond the mark of thought, and the high gods,   90
To do you justice, makes his ministers   91
Of us and those that love you. Best of comfort,   92
And ever welcome to us.

AGRIPPA      Welcome, lady.

MAECENAS      Welcome, dear madam.
Each heart in Rome does love and pity you.
Only th'adulterous Antony, most large   97
In his abominations, turns you off   98
And gives his potent regiment to a trull   99
That noises it against us.

OCTAVIA      Is it so, sir?   100

CAESAR
Most certain. Sister, welcome. Pray you
Be ever known to patience. My dear'st sister! *Exeunt.*   102

❖

# [3.7]

*Enter Cleopatra and Enobarbus.*

28 **unrestored** that I did not return to him.   29 **of** from   30 **being** having been deposed   35 **For** As for   36 **him** Antony   46 **horse** horses   47 **by** along   52 **prevented** forestalled (by your unannounced arrival)   53 **ostentation** ceremonial display   53–4 **which . . . unloved** which, if not made manifest through ceremonious display, often remains unappreciated or ceases to exist.   55 **stage** stage of your journey   61 **pardon for** permission to   62 **Being . . . him** i.e., since your return to Rome removed the obstacle between him and the gratification of his desires.

69 **who** i.e., and they   78 **a more larger** an even longer   82 **withhold . . . forth** restrain my advancing to battle   83 **wrong led** wronged, abused   84 **negligent danger** danger through neglect of taking necessary action.   85 **the time** the present state of affairs   85–6 **which . . . necessities** i.e., which tramples your happiness underfoot like a team of animals pulling a wagon   87–8 **let . . . way** allow inevitable events to go unbewailed to their destined conclusion.   89 **Nothing . . . me** i.e., you who are more dear to me than anything.   90 **mark** reach   90–2 **the high . . . you** i.e., the high gods (here treated as a singular subject of the verb "makes," and referred to as "his" in line 91) make us and those that love you their ministers of justice in your cause.   97 **large** unrestrained   98 **turns you off** rejects you   99 **regiment** government, rule.   **trull** prostitute   100 **noises it** is clamorous   102 **Be . . . patience** be patient.
3.7. **Location: Near Actium, on the northwestern coast of Greece. Antony's camp.**

CLEOPATRA
I will be even with thee, doubt it not.
ENOBARBUS    But why, why, why?
CLEOPATRA
Thou hast forspoke my being in these wars,                    3
And say'st it is not fit.
ENOBARBUS                    Well, is it, is it?                4
CLEOPATRA
If not denounced against us, why should not we                5
Be there in person?
ENOBARBUS [aside]    Well, I could reply.
If we should serve with horse and mares together,            7
The horse were merely lost; the mares would bear            8
A soldier and his horse.
CLEOPATRA                    What is't you say?               9
ENOBARBUS
Your presence needs must puzzle Antony,                      10
Take from his heart, take from his brain, from's time
What should not then be spared. He is already
Traduced for levity, and 'tis said in Rome                    13
That Photinus, an eunuch, and your maids                      14
Manage this war.
CLEOPATRA              Sink Rome, and their tongues rot
That speak against us! A charge we bear i'th' war,           16
And as the president of my kingdom will                       17
Appear there for a man. Speak not against it.                 18
I will not stay behind.

*Enter Antony and Canidius.*

ENOBARBUS              Nay, I have done.
Here comes the Emperor.
ANTONY                    Is it not strange, Canidius,
That from Tarentum and Brundusium
He could so quickly cut the Ionian sea                        22
And take in Toryne?—You have heard on't, sweet?             23
CLEOPATRA
Celerity is never more admired                                24
Than by the negligent.
ANTONY                    A good rebuke,
Which might have well becomed the best of men,               26
To taunt at slackness. Canidius, we
Will fight with him by sea.
CLEOPATRA                    By sea, what else?
CANIDIUS    Why will my lord do so?
ANTONY    For that he dares us to't.                          30
ENOBARBUS
So hath my lord dared him to single fight.

CANIDIUS
Ay, and to wage this battle at Pharsalia,
Where Caesar fought with Pompey. But these offers,
Which serve not for his vantage, he shakes off,
And so should you.
ENOBARBUS              Your ships are not well manned;
Your mariners are muleteers, reapers, people                 36
Engrossed by swift impress. In Caesar's fleet                37
Are those that often have 'gainst Pompey fought;
Their ships are yare, yours heavy. No disgrace               39
Shall fall you for refusing him at sea,                       40
Being prepared for land.
ANTONY                    By sea, by sea.
ENOBARBUS
Most worthy sir, you therein throw away
The absolute soldiership you have by land,
Distract your army, which doth most consist                  44
Of war-marked footmen, leave unexecuted                      45
Your own renownèd knowledge, quite forgo
The way which promises assurance, and
Give up yourself merely to chance and hazard                 48
From firm security.
ANTONY              I'll fight at sea.
CLEOPATRA
I have sixty sails, Caesar none better.
ANTONY
Our overplus of shipping will we burn,
And with the rest full-manned, from th' head of
Actium                                                        52
Beat th'approaching Caesar. But if we fail,
We then can do't at land.

*Enter a Messenger.*

                         Thy business?
MESSENGER
The news is true, my lord; he is descried.                    55
Caesar has taken Toryne.
ANTONY
Can he be there in person? 'Tis impossible;
Strange that his power should be. Canidius,                   58
Our nineteen legions thou shalt hold by land,
And our twelve thousand horse. We'll to our ship.
Away, my Thetis!

*Enter a Soldier.*

                    How now, worthy soldier?                  61
SOLDIER
O noble Emperor, do not fight by sea;
Trust not to rotten planks. Do you misdoubt
This sword and these my wounds? Let th'Egyptians
And the Phoenicians go a-ducking; we                          65

---

**3 forspoke** spoken against   **4 fit** appropriate.   **5 If . . . us** i.e., Even if
the war were not declared against me (which it is)   **7 horse** stallions
**8 merely** utterly   **8–9 bear . . . horse** be mounted by a rider and a stallion.   **10 puzzle** bewilder   **13 Traduced** criticized, censured   **14 an
eunuch** (Probably Mardian. In North's Plutarch, Caesar complains
that "Mardian the eunuch, Photinus, and Iras . . . and Charmian . . .
ruled the affairs of Antonius' empire." But Photinus [or Pothinus] was
a eunuch, too.)   **16 charge** responsibility, cost   **17 president** ruler
**18 for** in the capacity of   **22 Ionian** (Often applied to the Aegean, but
here the Adriatic. Tarentum and Brundusium or Brundisium are in the
"heel" of Italy, across the Adriatic from Actium and Toryne.)   **23 take
in** conquer.   **on't** of it   **24 Celerity** Swiftness.   **admired** wondered
at   **26 becomed** become, suited   **30 For that** Because

**36 muleteers** mule-drivers, peasants   **37 Engrossed** collected wholesale.   **impress** impressment, conscription.   **39 yare** quick, maneu-
verable   **40 fall** befall   **44 Distract** divide, divert.   **most** for the
most part   **45 footmen** foot soldiers.   **unexecuted** unused, untapped
**48 merely** entirely   **52 head** promontory   **55 he is descried** he has
been sighted.   **58 his power** i.e., his army, let alone himself   **61 Thetis** sea goddess, the mother of Achilles.   **65 go a-ducking** (1) go to
sea (2) get drenched (3) cringe

Have used to conquer standing on the earth                          66
And fighting foot to foot.
ANTONY                      Well, well, away!
       *Exeunt Antony, Cleopatra, and Enobarbus.*
SOLDIER
By Hercules, I think I am i'th' right.
CANIDIUS
Soldier, thou art; but his whole action grows                       69
Not in the power on't. So our leader's led,                         70
And we are women's men.
SOLDIER                     You keep by land                         71
The legions and the horse whole, do you not?                        72
CANIDIUS
Marcus Octavius, Marcus Justeius,
Publicola, and Caelius are for sea;
But we keep whole by land. This speed of Caesar's                   75
Carries beyond belief.                                              76
SOLDIER    While he was yet in Rome
His power went out in such distractions as                          78
Beguiled all spies.
CANIDIUS               Who's his lieutenant, hear you?
SOLDIER
They say, one Taurus.
CANIDIUS               Well I know the man.

    *Enter a Messenger.*

MESSENGER    The Emperor calls Canidius.
CANIDIUS
With news the time's in labor, and throws forth                     82
Each minute some.                    *Exeunt.*   83

❖

# [3.8]

    *Enter Caesar [and Taurus] with his army,
marching.*

CAESAR    Taurus!
TAURUS    My lord?
CAESAR
Strike not by land; keep whole. Provoke not battle                  3
Till we have done at sea. Do not exceed
The prescript of this scroll. [*He gives a scroll.*] Our
   fortune lies                                          5
Upon this jump.                      *Exeunt.*   6

❖

# [3.9]

    *Enter Antony and Enobarbus.*

ANTONY
Set we our squadrons on yond side o'th' hill,
In eye of Caesar's battle, from which place                         2
We may the number of the ships behold
And so proceed accordingly.              *Exeunt.*

❖

# [3.10]

    *Canidius marcheth with his land army one way
over the stage, and Taurus, the lieutenant of
Caesar, the other way. After their going in is heard
the noise of a sea fight.*

    *Alarum. Enter Enobarbus.*

ENOBARBUS
Naught, naught, all naught! I can behold no longer.                 1
Th'*Antoniad*, the Egyptian admiral,                                2
With all their sixty, fly and turn the rudder.
To see't mine eyes are blasted.

    *Enter Scarus.*

SCARUS                       Gods and goddesses,
All the whole synod of them!
ENOBARBUS                    What's thy passion?                     5
SCARUS
The greater cantle of the world is lost                             6
With very ignorance; we have kissed away                            7
Kingdoms and provinces.
ENOBARBUS              How appears the fight?
SCARUS
On our side like the tokened pestilence,                            9
Where death is sure. Yon ribaudred nag of Egypt—                    10
Whom leprosy o'ertake!—i'th' midst o'th' fight,
When vantage like a pair of twins appeared                          12
Both as the same, or rather ours the elder,                         13
The breeze upon her, like a cow in June,                            14
Hoists sails and flies.
ENOBARBUS                That I beheld.
Mine eyes did sicken at the sight, and could not
Endure a further view.
SCARUS                   She once being loofed,                      18
The noble ruin of her magic, Antony,                                19
Claps on his sea wing and, like a doting mallard,                   20
Leaving the fight in height, flies after her.                       21
I never saw an action of such shame.
Experience, manhood, honor, ne'er before

**66 Have used** are accustomed.    **standing on the earth** (1) fighting on
land (2) standing upright, not *ducking,* or "cringing"    **69–70 his . . .
on't** his whole strategy has been developed without regard to where
his power really lies.    **71 men** servingmen.    **72 horse** cavalry.
**whole** undivided, held in reserve    **75 keep whole** stay as a single unit
**76 Carries** surpasses (like an arrow in archery)    **78 distractions**
detachments, divisions    **82–3 With . . . some** More news is born each
minute. (*Throws forth* means "gives birth.")
**3.8. Location: A field near Actium, as before.**
**3 keep whole** stay in reserve.    **5 prescript** orders    **6 jump** chance,
hazard, strategy.
**3.9. Location: A field near Actium, as before.**

**2 eye** sight.    **battle** battle line
**3.10. Location: A field near Actium, as before.**
**1 Naught** All has come to naught    **2 admiral** flagship    **5 synod**
assembly    **6 cantle** corner; hence, piece or part    **7 With very ignorance** through utter stupidity    **9 tokened pestilence** (Certain red
spots appeared on the bodies of the plague-smitten, called tokens.)
**10 ribaudred** foul, obscene    **12–13 When . . . same** i.e., when the
advantage was equal on either side    **13 elder** i.e., more advanced,
more likely to inherit    **14 breeze** (1) gadfly (2) light wind    **18 loofed**
luffed, with ship's head brought close to the wind. (With a pun on
*aloofed,* "becoming distant.")    **19 ruin of** object ruined by    **20 Claps . . .
sea wing** i.e., hoists sail, preparing for flight like a water bird.    **mallard**
drake    **21 in** at its

Did violate so itself.

ENOBARBUS                    Alack, alack!

*Enter Canidius.*

CANIDIUS
Our fortune on the sea is out of breath,
And sinks most lamentably. Had our general
Been what he knew himself, it had gone well.  27
Oh, he has given example for our flight
Most grossly by his own!

ENOBARBUS
Ay, are you thereabouts? Why then, good night
indeed.  30

CANIDIUS
Toward Peloponnesus are they fled.  31

SCARUS
'Tis easy to't, and there I will attend  32
What further comes.

CANIDIUS                    To Caesar will I render  33
My legions and my horse. Six kings already  34
Show me the way of yielding.

ENOBARBUS                    I'll yet follow
The wounded chance of Antony, though my reason  36
Sits in the wind against me.        *[Exeunt separately.]*  37

❖

# [3.11]

*Enter Antony with attendants.*

ANTONY
Hark! The land bids me tread no more upon't;
It is ashamed to bear me. Friends, come hither.
I am so lated in the world that I  3
Have lost my way forever. I have a ship
Laden with gold. Take that, divide it; fly,  5
And make your peace with Caesar.

ALL                              Fly? Not we.

ANTONY
I have fled myself, and have instructed cowards
To run and show their shoulders. Friends, begone.  8
I have myself resolved upon a course
Which has no need of you. Begone.
My treasure's in the harbor. Take it. Oh,
I followed that I blush to look upon!  12
My very hairs do mutiny, for the white  13
Reprove the brown for rashness, and they them  14

For fear and doting. Friends, begone. You shall
Have letters from me to some friends that will
Sweep your way for you. Pray you, look not sad,  17
Nor make replies of loathness. Take the hint  18
Which my despair proclaims. Let that be left  19
Which leaves itself. To the seaside straightway!  20
I will possess you of that ship and treasure.
Leave me, I pray, a little. Pray you now,  22
Nay, do so, for indeed I have lost command.  23
Therefore I pray you. I'll see you by and by.  24
*[Exeunt attendants. Antony] sits down.*

*Enter Cleopatra led by Charmian, [Iras,] and Eros.*

EROS
Nay, gentle madam, to him, comfort him.

IRAS    Do, most dear Queen.

CHARMIAN    Do; why, what else?

CLEOPATRA    Let me sit down. O Juno!

ANTONY    No, no, no, no, no.

EROS    See you here, sir?

ANTONY    Oh, fie, fie, fie!

CHARMIAN    Madam!

IRAS    Madam, O good Empress!

EROS    Sir, sir!

ANTONY
Yes, my lord, yes. He at Philippi kept  35
His sword e'en like a dancer, while I struck  36
The lean and wrinkled Cassius, and 'twas I
That the mad Brutus ended. He alone  38
Dealt on lieutenantry, and no practice had  39
In the brave squares of war; yet now—no matter.  40

CLEOPATRA
Ah, stand by.

EROS                    The Queen, my lord, the Queen.  41

IRAS
Go to him, madam, speak to him.
He's unqualitied with very shame.  43

CLEOPATRA    Well then, sustain me. Oh!

EROS
Most noble sir, arise. The Queen approaches.
Her head's declined, and death will seize her but  46
Your comfort makes the rescue.

ANTONY
I have offended reputation,
A most unnoble swerving.

EROS                    Sir, the Queen.  49

---

27 **himself** himself to be   30 **thereabouts** i.e., of that mind, thinking of desertion.   **good night indeed** i.e., it's all over.   31 **Peloponnesus** southern Greece (from which Antony then crosses the Mediterranean to Egypt)   32 **to't** to get to it.   **attend** await   33 **render** surrender   34 **horse** cavalry.   36 **wounded chance** broken fortunes   37 **Sits . . . me** i.e., is on my windward side, tracking me and hunting me down.   **3.11. Location:** Historically, events such as dispatching the Schoolmaster to Caesar took place in Egypt; however, the dramatic impression of this scene is that it occurs soon after the battle.   3 **lated** belated, like a traveler still journeying when night falls   5 **fly** flee   8 **shoulders** i.e., backs.   12 **that** that which   13 **mutiny** contend among themselves   14 **they them** i.e., the brown hairs reprove the white

17 **Sweep your way** clear your way (to Caesar)   18 **loathness** unwillingness.   **hint** opportunity   19 **that** i.e., Antony and his cause   20 **leaves** is untrue to, deserts   22 **a little** for a little while.   23 **lost command** i.e., of myself and of my authority.   24 **pray** entreat (as opposed to "command")   35 **Yes . . . yes** (Antony is absorbed in his own bitter thoughts, as also in lines 29 and 31.)   **He** i.e., Octavius.   **kept** kept in its sheath   36 **e'en . . . dancer** i.e., as though for ornament only, in a dance   38 **ended** i.e., defeated. (Not *killed*; Brutus and Cassius committed suicide.)   **He alone** Caesar merely   39 **Dealt on lieutenantry** let his subordinates do the fighting   40 **brave squares** splendid squadrons, bodies of troops drawn up in square formation   41 **stand by** (Cleopatra indicates she is about to faint and needs assistance.)   43 **unqualitied** dispossessed of his own nature, i.e., not himself   46 **but** unless   49 **swerving** lapse, transgression.

ANTONY
    Oh, whither hast thou led me, Egypt? See       50
    How I convey my shame out of thine eyes     51
    By looking back what I have left behind     52
    'Stroyed in dishonor.
CLEOPATRA        Oh, my lord, my lord,   53
    Forgive my fearful sails! I little thought    54
    You would have followed.
ANTONY          Egypt, thou knew'st too well
    My heart was to thy rudder tied by th' strings,  56
    And thou shouldst tow me after. O'er my spirit
    Thy full supremacy thou knew'st, and that
    Thy beck might from the bidding of the gods   59
    Command me.
CLEOPATRA    Oh, my pardon!
ANTONY    ·       Now I must   60
    To the young man send humble treaties, dodge  61
    And palter in the shifts of lowness, who    62
    With half the bulk o'th' world played as I pleased,
    Making and marring fortunes. You did know
    How much you were my conqueror, and that
    My sword, made weak by my affection, would  66
    Obey it on all cause.
CLEOPATRA      Pardon, pardon!   67
ANTONY
    Fall not a tear, I say; one of them rates    68
    All that is won and lost. Give me a kiss.     [*They kiss.*]
    Even this repays me.—We sent our schoolmaster;  70
    Is 'a come back?—Love, I am full of lead.—
    Some wine, within there, and our viands! Fortune
      knows   72
    We scorn her most when most she offers blows.
                      *Exeunt.*

❖

# [3.12]

*Enter Caesar, Agrippa, [Thidias,] and Dolabella,*
*with others.*

CAESAR
    Let him appear that's come from Antony.
    Know you him?
DOLABELLA     Caesar, 'tis his schoolmaster—
    An argument that he is plucked, when hither   3
    He sends so poor a pinion of his wing,     4
    Which had superfluous kings for messengers  5

    Not many moons gone by.

        *Enter Ambassador from Antony.*

CAESAR                Approach and speak.
AMBASSADOR
    Such as I am, I come from Antony.
    I was of late as petty to his ends     8
    As is the morn-dew on the myrtle leaf
    To his grand sea.
CAESAR       Be't so. Declare thine office.  10
AMBASSADOR
    Lord of his fortunes he salutes thee, and
    Requires to live in Egypt; which not granted,  12
    He lessens his requests, and to thee sues   13
    To let him breathe between the heavens and earth  14
    A private man in Athens. This for him.
    Next, Cleopatra does confess thy greatness,
    Submits her to thy might, and of thee craves
    The circle of the Ptolemies for her heirs,  18
    Now hazarded to thy grace.
CAESAR           For Antony,  19
    I have no ears to his request. The Queen
    Of audience nor desire shall fail, so she   21
    From Egypt drive her all-disgracèd friend
    Or take his life there. This if she perform
    She shall not sue unheard. So to them both.
AMBASSADOR
    Fortune pursue thee!
CAESAR       Bring him through the bands.  25
            [*Exit Ambassador, attended.*]
    [*To Thidias*] To try thy eloquence now 'tis time.
      Dispatch.
    From Antony win Cleopatra. Promise,
    And in our name, what she requires; add more,  28
    From thine invention, offers. Women are not  29
    In their best fortunes strong, but want will perjure  30
    The ne'er-touched vestal. Try thy cunning, Thidias.  31
    Make thine own edict for thy pains, which we  32
    Will answer as a law.
THIDIAS        Caesar, I go.  33
CAESAR
    Observe how Antony becomes his flaw,   34
    And what thou think'st his very action speaks  35
    In every power that moves.
THIDIAS        Caesar, I shall.    *Exeunt.*  36

❖

---

**50–3 See . . . dishonor** i.e., See how ashamed I am to have you see me like this, looking back on what I have left behind dishonorably destroyed.  **54 fearful** timorous  **56 th' strings** (1) the heartstrings (2) towing cable  **59–60 Thy . . . Command me** your mere beckoning would command me away from doing the bidding of the gods themselves.  **61 treaties** entreaties, propositions for settlement.  **dodge** shuffle, cringe  **62 palter** use trickery, prevaricate, equivocate. **shifts of lowness** pitiful evasions used by those lacking power  **66 affection** passion  **67 on all cause** whatever the reason.  **68 Fall** Let fall.  **rates** equals  **70 Even this** This by itself.  **schoolmaster** (Identified in Plutarch as Euphronius, tutor to Antony's children by Cleopatra.)  **72 viands** food.
**3.12. Location:** Egypt. Caesar's camp.
**3 An argument** an indication  **4 pinion** i.e., pinion-feather, outer feather  **5 Which** who

**8 petty to** insignificant in terms of  **10 To . . . sea** compared to its, the dewdrop's, great source, the sea.  **thine office** your official business.  **12 Requires** asks.  **which not granted** and if that request is not granted  **13 sues** petitions  **14 breathe** i.e., live  **18 circle** crown  **19 hazarded . . . grace** dependent on your favor.  **For** As for  **21 Of . . . fail** will not fail to be granted a hearing with Caesar, nor will she fail to be granted what she desires.  **so** provided that  **25 Bring** Escort.  **bands** troops on guard, military lines.  **28 requires** asks  **28–9 add . . . offers** add ideas of your own.  **29–31 Women . . . vestal** Women are not strong even at the height of their good fortune, but need will cause even an untouched vestal virgin to break her vows.  **31 cunning** skill  **32 Make . . . edict** Decree your own reward  **33 answer as a law** confirm as if it were a law. **34 becomes his flaw** bears his misfortune and disgrace  **35–6 And . . . moves** and what you think his gestures reveal in every move he makes.

# [3.13]

*Enter Cleopatra, Enobarbus, Charmian, and Iras.*

CLEOPATRA
What shall we do, Enobarbus?

ENOBARBUS                          Think, and die.                1

CLEOPATRA
Is Antony or we in fault for this?                                2

ENOBARBUS
Antony only, that would make his will                             3
Lord of his reason. What though you fled
From that great face of war, whose several ranges                5
Frighted each other? Why should he follow?
The itch of his affection should not then                         7
Have nicked his captainship, at such a point,                     8
When half to half the world opposed, he being                    9
The meerèd question. 'Twas a shame no less                        10
Than was his loss, to course your flying flags                    11
And leave his navy gazing.

CLEOPATRA                          Prithee, peace.

*Enter the Ambassador with Antony.*

ANTONY   Is that his answer?

AMBASSADOR   Ay, my lord.

ANTONY
The Queen shall then have courtesy, so she                        15
Will yield us up.

AMBASSADOR         He says so.

ANTONY                             Let her know't.—                16
To the boy Caesar send this grizzled head,
And he will fill thy wishes to the brim
With principalities.

CLEOPATRA           That head, my lord?

ANTONY [*to the Ambassador*]
To him again. Tell him he wears the rose
Of youth upon him, from which the world should
     note
Something particular. His coin, ships, legions,                  22
May be a coward's, whose ministers would prevail                 23
Under the service of a child as soon
As i'th' command of Caesar. I dare him therefore
To lay his gay caparisons apart                                   26
And answer me declined, sword against sword,                     27
Ourselves alone. I'll write it. Follow me.
                    [*Exeunt Antony and Ambassador.*]

ENOBARBUS [*aside*]
Yes, like enough, high-battled Caesar will                       29

Unstate his happiness and be staged to th' show                  30
Against a sworder! I see men's judgments are                     31
A parcel of their fortunes, and things outward                   32
Do draw the inward quality after them                            33
To suffer all alike. That he should dream,                       34
Knowing all measures, the full Caesar will                       35
Answer his emptiness! Caesar, thou hast subdued                  36
His judgment too.

*Enter a Servant.*

SERVANT             A messenger from Caesar.

CLEOPATRA
What, no more ceremony? See, my women,
Against the blown rose may they stop their nose                  39
That kneeled unto the buds.—Admit him, sir.                      40
                              [*Exit Servant.*]

ENOBARBUS [*aside*]
Mine honesty and I begin to square.                              41
The loyalty well held to fools does make                         42
Our faith mere folly; yet he that can endure                     43
To follow with allegiance a fall'n lord
Does conquer him that did his master conquer                     45
And earns a place i'th' story.

*Enter Thidias.*

CLEOPATRA                   Caesar's will?

THIDIAS
Hear it apart.

CLEOPATRA         None but friends. Say boldly.                  47

THIDIAS
So haply are they friends to Antony.                             48

ENOBARBUS
He needs as many, sir, as Caesar has,
Or needs not us. If Caesar please, our master                    50
Will leap to be his friend. For us, you know                     51
Whose he is we are, and that is Caesar's.

THIDIAS                                  So.                      52
Thus then, thou most renowned: Caesar entreats
Not to consider in what case thou stand'st                       54
Further than he is Caesar.

CLEOPATRA                   Go on: right royal.                  55

---

**30–1 Unstate . . . sworder** set aside his advantageous fortune and be
exhibited publicly in a sword-fight contest with a mere gladiator.
**31–4 I see . . . alike** I see that men's judgments are inextricably linked
to their fortunes, whereby outward circumstances draw after them
inward qualities of character in such a way that both suffer at the
same time.   **35 Knowing all measures** i.e., having experienced every
degree of fortune.   **full** at full fortune   **36 Answer** (1) meet man to
man with (2) correspond with (3) reply to   **39 blown** overblown,
starting to decay   **40 That** who formerly   **41 honesty** (With meaning
also of "honor.")   **square** quarrel.   **42–3 The . . . folly** A stubborn
loyalty bestowed on fools is folly itself   **45 Does . . . conquer** i.e.,
achieves a moral victory over the very fortune that subdued his own
master   **47 apart** in private.   **48 haply** perhaps   **50 Or . . . us** i.e., or
else he doesn't need even us, his case being hopeless.
**51 For** As for   **52 Whose . . . Caesar's** i.e., we are Antony's friends,
and he is Caesar's, so that we, too, are Caesar's.   **54–5 Not . . . Caesar**
i.e., not to worry about your situation other than to consider that you
are dealing with Caesar, the embodiment of magnanimity.   **55 right
royal** i.e., that is very magnanimous.

---

**3.13. Location:** Alexandria. Cleopatra's palace.
**1 Think, and die** Think despondently, and die of melancholy or by suicide.   **2 we** I   **3 will** desire (especially sexual)   **5 ranges** ranks, lines
(of ships)   **7 affection** sexual passion   **8 nicked** cut short or maimed,
or got the better of.   **point** crisis   **9–10 When . . . question** when the
two halves of the world found themselves in conflict, Antony being the
sole ground of the quarrel.   **11 course** pursue (as in hunting)   **15 so**
provided that   **16 us** me   **22 Something particular** some exceptional
exploit.   **23 May be** could as well be.   **ministers** agents, subordinates   **26 gay caparisons** resplendent trappings   **27 answer me
declined** meet me as I am, lowered in fortune and advanced in
years   **29 like** likely.   **high-battled** provided with a mighty army

THIDIAS
He knows that you embrace not Antony
As you did love, but as you feared him.

CLEOPATRA                           Oh!

THIDIAS
The scars upon your honor therefore he
Does pity as constrainèd blemishes,
Not as deserved.

CLEOPATRA           He is a god and knows
What is most right. Mine honor was not yielded,          61
But conquered merely.

ENOBARBUS [aside]           To be sure of that,          62
I will ask Antony. Sir, sir, thou art so leaky
That we must leave thee to thy sinking, for
Thy dearest quit thee.           Exit Enobarbus.

THIDIAS           Shall I say to Caesar
What you require of him? For he partly begs          66
To be desired to give. It much would please him
That of his fortunes you should make a staff
To lean upon; but it would warm his spirits
To hear from me you had left Antony
And put yourself under his shroud,          71
The universal landlord.

CLEOPATRA           What's your name?

THIDIAS
My name is Thidias.

CLEOPATRA           Most kind messenger,
Say to great Caesar this in deputation:          74
I kiss his conquering hand. Tell him I am prompt          75
To lay my crown at 's feet, and there to kneel
Till from his all-obeying breath I hear          77
The doom of Egypt.

THIDIAS           'Tis your noblest course.          78
Wisdom and fortune combating together,          79
If that the former dare but what it can,          80
No chance may shake it. Give me grace to lay          81
My duty on your hand.           [He kisses her hand.]

CLEOPATRA   Your Caesar's father oft,          83
When he hath mused of taking kingdoms in,          84
Bestowed his lips on that unworthy place,
As it rained kisses.

Enter Antony and Enobarbus.

ANTONY           Favors? By Jove that thunders!          86
What art thou, fellow?

THIDIAS           One that but performs
The bidding of the fullest man, and worthiest          88
To have command obeyed.

ENOBARBUS [aside]           You will be whipped.

ANTONY [calling for Servants]
Approach, there!—Ah, you kite!—Now, gods and
   devils!          90
Authority melts from me of late. When I cried "Ho!",
Like boys unto a muss kings would start forth          92
And cry, "Your will?"—Have you no ears? I am
Antony yet.

Enter a Servant [followed by others].

           Take hence this jack and whip him.          94

ENOBARBUS [aside]
'Tis better playing with a lion's whelp          95
Than with an old one dying.

ANTONY           Moon and stars!
Whip him. Were't twenty of the greatest tributaries          97
That do acknowledge Caesar, should I find them
So saucy with the hand of she here—what's her name
Since she was Cleopatra? Whip him, fellows,
Till like a boy you see him cringe his face          101
And whine aloud for mercy. Take him hence.

THIDIAS
Mark Antony—

ANTONY           Tug him away! Being whipped,
Bring him again. This jack of Caesar's shall
Bear us an errand to him.

           Exeunt [Servants] with Thidias.
[To Cleopatra] You were half blasted ere I knew you.
   Ha?          106
Have I my pillow left unpressed in Rome,
Forborne the getting of a lawful race,          108
And by a gem of women, to be abused          109
By one that looks on feeders?          110

CLEOPATRA   Good my lord—

ANTONY   You have been a boggler ever.          112
But when we in our viciousness grow hard—
Oh, misery on't!—the wise gods seel our eyes,          114
In our own filth drop our clear judgments, make us
Adore our errors, laugh at 's while we strut
To our confusion.

CLEOPATRA           Oh, is't come to this?          117

ANTONY
I found you as a morsel cold upon
Dead Caesar's trencher; nay, you were a fragment          119
Of Gnaeus Pompey's, besides what hotter hours,          120
Unregistered in vulgar fame, you have          121
Luxuriously picked out. For I am sure,          122
Though you can guess what temperance should be,

---

61 right true.   62 merely utterly.   66 require ask.   partly i.e., as commensurate with his dignity   71 shroud shelter. (With suggestion too of a burial cloth.)   74 in deputation by you as deputy   75 prompt ready   77 all-obeying obeyed by all   78 The doom of Egypt i.e., my and my country's fate.   79–81 Wisdom . . . shake it i.e., When offered a choice between wise counsel and fortune's blandishments, the wise person who dares to ask only for what is possible cannot be disappointed by misfortune.   83 Your Caesar's father i.e., Julius Caesar, actually Octavius' great-uncle. (See note at 3.6.6.)   84 mused . . . in thought about conquering kingdoms   86 As as if   88 fullest most fortunate, best

90 kite a rapacious bird of prey that feeds on ignoble objects, and a slang word for "whore." (Said of Cleopatra.)   92 muss game in which small objects are thrown down to be scrambled for   94 jack fellow. (Contemptuous.)   95 whelp cub   97 tributaries rulers paying tribute   101 cringe contract in pain   106 blasted withered, blighted   108 getting begetting.   lawful legitimate   109 abused deceived, betrayed   110 By . . . feeders? i.e., by a woman (Cleopatra) who is so depraved as to let her hand be kissed by a mere creature of Caesar's, one who clings to him for sustenance?   112 boggler waverer, shifty person. (Often used of shying horses.)   114 seel blind. (A term in falconry for sewing shut the eyes of wild hawks in order to tame them.)   117 confusion destruction.   119 trencher wooden plate.   fragment leftover   120 Gnaeus Pompey's (See 1.5.32 and note.)   121 vulgar fame common gossip   122 Luxuriously lustfully

You know not what it is.

CLEOPATRA                          Wherefore is this?                    124

ANTONY
To let a fellow that will take rewards
And say "God quit you!" be familiar with          126
My playfellow, your hand, this kingly seal
And plighter of high hearts! Oh, that I were      128
Upon the hill of Basan, to outroar                129
The hornèd herd! For I have savage cause,         130
And to proclaim it civilly were like
A haltered neck which does the hangman thank      132
For being yare about him.

*Enter a Servant with Thidias.*

                          Is he whipped?           133

SERVANT   Soundly, my lord.

ANTONY   Cried he? And begged 'a pardon?

SERVANT   He did ask favor.

ANTONY [*to Thidias*]
If that thy father live, let him repent            137
Thou wast not made his daughter; and be thou sorry
To follow Caesar in his triumph, since
Thou hast been whipped for following him.
    Henceforth
The white hand of a lady fever thee;              141
Shake thou to look on't. Get thee back to Caesar.
Tell him thy entertainment. Look thou say         143
He makes me angry with him; for he seems
Proud and disdainful, harping on what I am,
Not what he knew I was. He makes me angry,
And at this time most easy 'tis to do't,
When my good stars, that were my former guides,
Have empty left their orbs and shot their fires   149
Into th'abysm of hell. If he mislike               150
My speech and what is done, tell him he has
Hipparchus, my enfranchèd bondman, whom            152
He may at pleasure whip, or hang, or torture,
As he shall like, to quit me. Urge it thou.—       154
Hence with thy stripes, begone!
                    *Exit* [*Servant with*] *Thidias.*

CLEOPATRA                          Have you done yet?

ANTONY
Alack, our terrene moon is now eclipsed,           156
And it portends alone the fall of Antony.

CLEOPATRA   I must stay his time.                   158

ANTONY
To flatter Caesar, would you mingle eyes

With one that ties his points?

CLEOPATRA                          Not know me yet?   160

ANTONY
Coldhearted toward me?

CLEOPATRA                          Ah, dear, if I be so,
From my cold heart let heaven engender hail,
And poison it in the source, and the first stone
Drop in my neck; as it determines, so              164
Dissolve my life! The next Caesarion smite,
Till by degrees the memory of my womb,             166
Together with my brave Egyptians all,              167
By the discandying of this pelleted storm          168
Lie graveless till the flies and gnats of Nile
Have buried them for prey!

ANTONY                          I am satisfied.        170
Caesar sits down in Alexandria, where              171
I will oppose his fate. Our force by land          172
Hath nobly held; our severed navy too
Have knit again, and fleet, threat'ning most sealike.   174
Where hast thou been, my heart? Dost thou hear,
    lady?                                          175
If from the field I shall return once more
To kiss these lips, I will appear in blood;        177
I and my sword will earn our chronicle.            178
There's hope in't yet.

CLEOPATRA   That's my brave lord!

ANTONY
I will be treble-sinewed, hearted, breathed,       181
And fight maliciously. For when mine hours         182
Were nice and lucky, men did ransom lives          183
Of me for jests; but now I'll set my teeth         184
And send to darkness all that stop me. Come,       185
Let's have one other gaudy night. Call to me       186
All my sad captains. Fill our bowls once more;
Let's mock the midnight bell.

CLEOPATRA                          It is my birthday.
I had thought t'have held it poor; but since my lord   189
Is Antony again, I will be Cleopatra.

ANTONY   We will yet do well.

CLEOPATRA [*to attendants*]
Call all his noble captains to my lord.

ANTONY
Do so. We'll speak to them, and tonight I'll force
The wine peep through their scars. Come on, my
    queen,
There's sap in't yet. The next time I do fight     195

---

124 **Wherefore is this**? i.e., What brought this on?   126 **quit** reward. (*God quit you* is said obsequiously to acknowledge a tip.)   128 **plighter** pledger   129–30 **hill of Basan . . . The hornèd herd** (Allusion to the strong bulls of Bashan, Psalms 22:12 and 68:15. Antony imagines himself as the greatest horned beast, i.e., cuckold, of that herd.)   132–3 **A haltered . . . him** a person about to be hanged by a *halter* or noose who asks the hangman to kill him quickly.   133 **yare** deft, quick   137 **If that** If   141 **fever thee** make you shiver   143 **entertainment** reception.   **Look** Be sure that   149 **orbs** spheres   150 **th'abysm** the abyss   152 **Hipparchus** (According to Plutarch, the man was a deserter to Caesar's side.)   **enfranchèd** enfranchised, emancipated   154 **quit** requite, pay back   156 **our . . . eclipsed** i.e., (1) the moon in eclipse portends disaster (2) the waning of the love of Cleopatra (equated with Isis, the moon goddess) spells the end for me   158 **stay his time** i.e., be patient until his fury has subsided.

160 **ties his points** i.e., helps Caesar as a valet with the metal-tipped laces used to fasten articles of clothing.   164 **neck** throat or head.   **determines** comes to an end, dissolves. (See line 168.)   166 **memory of my womb** i.e., my offspring   167 **brave** splendid. (Also in line 180.)   168 **discandying** melting.   **pelleted** falling in pellets   170 **for prey** i.e., by eating them.   171 **sits down in** lays siege to   172 **oppose his fate** confront his (seemingly irresistible) fortune.   174 **fleet** float   175 **heart** courage.   177 **in blood** (1) bloody from battle (2) full-spirited   178 **chronicle** place in history.   181 **treble-sinewed . . . breathed** thrice myself in strength, courage, and endurance   182 **maliciously** furiously, fiercely.   183 **nice** delicate, refined   183–4 **men . . . jests** I allowed enemies to be ransomed for trifles or as a magnanimous gesture   185 **to darkness** i.e., to death, the underworld   186 **gaudy** festive   189 **held it poor** celebrated it simply   195 **sap in't** i.e., life in our enterprise

I'll make Death love me, for I will contend       196
Even with his pestilent scythe.                    197

*Exeunt [all but Enobarbus].*

ENOBARBUS
Now he'll outstare the lightning. To be furious    198
Is to be frighted out of fear, and in that mood
The dove will peck the estridge; and I see still   200
A diminution in our captain's brain
Restores his heart. When valor preys on reason,    202
It eats the sword it fights with. I will seek      203
Some way to leave him.                   *Exit.*

❧

# [4.1]

*Enter Caesar, Agrippa, and Maecenas, with his army, Caesar reading a letter.*

CAESAR
He calls me boy, and chides as he had power        1
To beat me out of Egypt. My messenger
He hath whipped with rods, dares me to personal
   combat,
Caesar to Antony. Let the old ruffian know
I have many other ways to die, meantime
Laugh at his challenge.
MAECENAS          Caesar must think,
When one so great begins to rage, he's hunted      8
Even to falling. Give him no breath, but now       9
Make boot of his distraction. Never anger          10
Made good guard for itself.
CAESAR                      Let our best heads      11
Know that tomorrow the last of many battles
We mean to fight. Within our files there are,      13
Of those that served Mark Antony but late,         14
Enough to fetch him in. See it done,               15
And feast the army; we have store to do't,         16
And they have earned the waste. Poor Antony!       17

*Exeunt.*

❧

# [4.2]

*Enter Antony, Cleopatra, Enobarbus, Charmian, Iras, Alexas, with others.*

ANTONY
He will not fight with me, Domitius?

ENOBARBUS   No.
ANTONY   Why should he not?
ENOBARBUS
He thinks, being twenty times of better fortune,
He is twenty men to one.
ANTONY                   Tomorrow, soldier,
By sea and land I'll fight. Or I will live         6
Or bathe my dying honor in the blood
Shall make it live again. Woo't thou fight well?   8
ENOBARBUS
I'll strike, and cry, "Take all."
ANTONY                     Well said. Come on!     9
Call forth my household servants. Let's tonight    10

*Enter three or four servitors.*

Be bounteous at our meal.—Give me thy hand.
Thou hast been rightly honest—so hast thou—        12
Thou—and thou—and thou. You have served me
   well,
And kings have been your fellows.
CLEOPATRA *[aside to Enobarbus]*     What means this?   14
ENOBARBUS *[aside to Cleopatra]*
'Tis one of those odd tricks which sorrow shoots
Out of the mind.
ANTONY               And thou art honest too.
I wish I could be made so many men,                17
And all of you clapped up together in             18
An Antony, that I might do you service
So good as you have done.
ALL                      The gods forbid!
ANTONY
Well, my good fellows, wait on me tonight:
Scant not my cups, and make as much of me          22
As when mine empire was your fellow too,           23
And suffered my command.
CLEOPATRA *[aside to Enobarbus]*     What does he mean?  24
ENOBARBUS *[aside to Cleopatra]*
To make his followers weep.
ANTONY                     Tend me tonight;
May be it is the period of your duty.              26
Haply you shall not see me more, or if,            27
A mangled shadow. Perchance tomorrow              28
You'll serve another master. I look on you
As one that takes his leave. Mine honest friends,
I turn you not away, but, like a master
Married to your good service, stay till death.
Tend me tonight two hours, I ask no more,
And the gods yield you for't!
ENOBARBUS                   What mean you, sir,    34
To give them this discomfort? Look, they weep,

---

196–7 **I will . . . scythe** i.e., I will outdo even Death himself and his plague-dealing scythe.   **198 outstare** stare down.   **furious** frenzied   **200 estridge** ostrich, or, a kind of hawk.   **still** constantly 202–3 **When . . . with** When valor turns to unreasonable fury, it destroys the very quality of reasonableness that valor depends on in battle.
**4.1. Location: Before Alexandria. Caesar's camp.**
**1 as** as if   **8 rage** rave   **9 breath** breathing space   **10 Make boot** take advantage.   **distraction** frenzy.   **10–11 Never anger Made** Never did anger make   **11 best heads** commanding officers   **13 files** (As in "rank and file.")   **14 late** lately   **15 fetch him in** surround, capture him.   **16 store** provisions   **17 waste** lavish expenditure.
**4.2. Location: Alexandria. Cleopatra's palace.**

---

**6 Or** Either   **8 Shall** that will.   **Woo't** Wilt   **9 strike . . . Take all** (1) fight to the finish, crying, "Winner take all" (2) strike sail and surrender.   **10.1 servitors** attendants.   **12 honest** true, loyal   **14 fellows** i.e., fellow servants of me.   **17 made . . . men** divided into as many men as you are   **18 clapped up** combined   **22 Scant not my cups** i.e., Provide generously   **23 fellow** i.e., fellow servant   **24 suffered** acknowledged, submitted to   **26 period** end   **27 Haply** Perhaps.   **if** if you do   **28 shadow** ghost.   **34 yield** reward

And I, an ass, am onion-eyed. For shame,                                    36
Transform us not to women.
ANTONY                                        Ho, ho, ho!
Now the witch take me if I meant it thus!                                    38
Grace grow where those drops fall! My hearty friends,                        39
You take me in too dolorous a sense,
For I spake to you for your comfort, did desire you
To burn this night with torches. Know, my hearts,                            42
I hope well of tomorrow, and will lead you
Where rather I'll expect victorious life
Than death and honor. Let's to supper, come,
And drown consideration.                              *Exeunt.*    46

❧

## [4.3]

*Enter a company of Soldiers.*

FIRST SOLDIER
Brother, good night. Tomorrow is the day.
SECOND SOLDIER
It will determine one way. Fare you well.                                    2
Heard you of nothing strange about the streets?                              3
FIRST SOLDIER   Nothing. What news?
SECOND SOLDIER
Belike 'tis but a rumor. Good night to you.                                  5
FIRST SOLDIER   Well, sir, good night.

*They meet other Soldiers.*

SECOND SOLDIER   Soldiers, have careful watch.
THIRD SOLDIER   And you. Good night, good night.
        *They place themselves in every corner of the stage.*
SECOND SOLDIER   Here we. And if tomorrow                                     9
Our navy thrive, I have an absolute hope
Our landmen will stand up.                                                   11
FIRST SOLDIER   'Tis a brave army, and full of purpose.                      12
        *Music of the hautboys is under the stage.*
SECOND SOLDIER   Peace! What noise?
FIRST SOLDIER   List, list!                                                  14
SECOND SOLDIER   Hark!
FIRST SOLDIER   Music i'th'air.
THIRD SOLDIER   Under the earth.
FOURTH SOLDIER   It signs well, does it not?                                 18
THIRD SOLDIER   No.
FIRST SOLDIER   Peace, I say! What should this mean?
SECOND SOLDIER
'Tis the god Hercules, whom Antony loved,
Now leaves him.
FIRST SOLDIER   Walk; let's see if other watchmen
Do hear what we do.
        [*They advance toward their fellow watchmen.*]
SECOND SOLDIER   How now, masters?                                           24

ALL (*speak together*)   How now? How now? Do you
hear this?
FIRST SOLDIER   Ay. Is't not strange?
THIRD SOLDIER   Do you hear, masters? Do you hear?
FIRST SOLDIER
Follow the noise so far as we have quarter;                                  29
Let's see how it will give off.                                              30
ALL   Content. 'Tis strange.                              *Exeunt.*

❧

## [4.4]

*Enter Antony and Cleopatra, with [Charmian and]
others [attending].*

ANTONY
Eros! Mine armor, Eros!
CLEOPATRA                                Sleep a little.
ANTONY
No, my chuck.—Eros, come, mine armor, Eros!                                  2

*Enter Eros [with armor].*

Come, good fellow, put thine iron on.                                        3
If fortune be not ours today, it is
Because we brave her. Come.
CLEOPATRA                        Nay, I'll help too.                          5
What's this for?              [*She helps to arm him.*]
ANTONY              Ah, let be, let be! Thou art
The armorer of my heart. False, false; this, this.                           7
CLEOPATRA
Sooth, la, I'll help. Thus it must be.
ANTONY                                Well, well,                            8
We shall thrive now. See'st thou, my good fellow?
Go, put on thy defenses.
EROS                            Briefly, sir.                                10
CLEOPATRA
Is not this buckled well?
ANTONY                      Rarely, rarely.                                  11
He that unbuckles this, till we do please                                    12
To doff't for our repose, shall hear a storm.                                13
Thou fumblest, Eros, and my queen's a squire                                 14
More tight at this than thou. Dispatch. O love,                              15
That thou couldst see my wars today, and knew'st                             16
The royal occupation! Thou shouldst see                                      17
A workman in't.

*Enter an armed Soldier.*

                        Good morrow to thee. Welcome.                        18
Thou look'st like him that knows a warlike charge.                           19

---

29 **as we have quarter** as our watch post extends   30 **give off** cease.
**4.4. Location:** Alexandria. The palace.
2 **chuck** (A term of endearment.)   3 **thine iron** i.e., my armor that
you have there. (Or perhaps he is telling Eros to arm.)   5 **brave** defy
7 **False** You're putting it on wrong   8 **Sooth** In truth   10 **defenses**
armor.   **Briefly** In a moment   11 **Rarely** Excellently   12–13 **He . . .
storm** i.e., Anyone who attempts to burst my armor in the fight,
before I choose myself to unarm and rest, will be greeted by a storm
of blows.   14 **squire** armor-bearer of a knight   15 **tight** deft, skillful.
**Dispatch** Finish up.   16–17 **knew'st . . . occupation** (would that) you
could appreciate how excellently I carry out the royal art of warfare.
18 **workman** craftsman, professional   19 **him** one.   **charge** duty,
responsibility.

36 **onion-eyed** weepy.   38 **the witch take me** may I be bewitched
39 **Grace grow** (1) May rue or herb of grace grow (2) May gracious fortune
flourish.   **hearty** loving   42 **burn . . . torches** i.e., revel through the night.
46 **drown consideration** drown brooding thought in our wine cups.
**4.3. Location:** Alexandria. Before the palace.
2 **determine one way** be decided, come to an end one way or the
other.   3 **about** in   5 **Belike** Probably   9 **Here we** Here's our station.   11 **stand up** make a stand.   12 **brave** splendid, gallant
12.1 *hautboys* oboelike instruments   14 **List** Listen   18 **signs well** is
a good sign   24 **masters** good sirs. (Also in line 28.)

To business that we love we rise betime                         20
And go to't with delight.
SOLDIER                         A thousand, sir,
Early though 't be, have on their riveted trim                  22
And at the port expect you.   *Shout. Trumpets flourish.*       23

          *Enter Captains and soldiers.*

CAPTAIN
The morn is fair. Good morrow, General.
ALL
Good morrow, General.
ANTONY                         'Tis well blown, lads.           25
This morning, like the spirit of a youth
That means to be of note, begins betimes.
So, so. Come, give me that. This way. Well said.                28
Fare thee well, dame. Whate'er becomes of me,
This is a soldier's kiss. [*He kisses her.*] Rebukable,
And worthy shameful check it were, to stand                     31
On more mechanic compliment. I'll leave thee                    32
Now like a man of steel.—You that will fight,
Follow me close. I'll bring you to't. Adieu.
          *Exeunt* [*Antony, Eros, Captains, and soldiers*].
CHARMIAN
Please you, retire to your chamber?
CLEOPATRA                         Lead me.
He goes forth gallantly. That he and Caesar might
Determine this great war in single fight!
Then Antony—but now—Well, on.          *Exeunt.*

                          ❧

# [4.5]

          *Trumpets sound. Enter Antony and Eros; [a
          Soldier meeting them].*

SOLDIER
The gods make this a happy day to Antony!                        1
ANTONY
Would thou and those thy scars had once prevailed               2
To make me fight at land!
SOLDIER                         Hadst thou done so,
The kings that have revolted, and the soldier                    4
That has this morning left thee, would have still
Followed thy heels.
ANTONY                   Who's gone this morning?
SOLDIER                                        Who?
One ever near thee. Call for Enobarbus,
He shall not hear thee, or from Caesar's camp
Say, "I am none of thine."
ANTONY                   What sayest thou?
SOLDIER                                        Sir,
He is with Caesar.
EROS                   Sir, his chests and treasure

He has not with him.
ANTONY               Is he gone?
SOLDIER                         Most certain.
ANTONY
Go, Eros, send his treasure after. Do it.
Detain no jot, I charge thee. Write to him—
I will subscribe—gentle adieus and greetings.                   14
Say that I wish he never find more cause
To change a master. Oh, my fortunes have
Corrupted honest men! Dispatch.—Enobarbus!                      17
                              *Exeunt.*

                          ❧

# [4.6]

          *Flourish. Enter Agrippa, Caesar, with Enobarbus,
          and Dolabella.*

CAESAR
Go forth, Agrippa, and begin the fight.
Our will is Antony be took alive;
Make it so known.
AGRIPPA   Caesar, I shall.          [*Exit.*]
CAESAR
The time of universal peace is near.                             5
Prove this a prosp'rous day, the three-nooked world             6
Shall bear the olive freely.

          *Enter a Messenger.*

MESSENGER               Antony                                   7
Is come into the field.
CAESAR               Go charge Agrippa                           8
Plant those that have revolted in the van,                       9
That Antony may seem to spend his fury
Upon himself.          *Exeunt* [*all but Enobarbus*].
ENOBARBUS
Alexas did revolt and went to Jewry on                          12
Affairs of Antony, there did dissuade                           13
Great Herod to incline himself to Caesar
And leave his master Antony. For this pains,
Caesar hath hanged him. Canidius and the rest
That fell away have entertainment but                           17
No honorable trust. I have done ill,
Of which I do accuse myself so sorely                           19
That I will joy no more.

          *Enter a Soldier of Caesar's.*

SOLDIER               Enobarbus, Antony
Hath after thee sent all thy treasure, with
His bounty overplus. The messenger                              22

**20 betime** betimes, early   **22 riveted trim** i.e., armor riveted into place   **23 port** gate   **25 'Tis well blown** i.e., The morning begins well. (Or, refers to trumpets in line 23 s.d.)   **28 Well said** Well done.   **31 check** reproof   **31–2 stand . . . compliment** insist on vulgar and routine ceremonies of leavetaking.
**4.5. Location: Before Alexandria. Antony's camp.**
**1 happy** fortunate   **2 once** earlier   **4 revolted** deserted

**14 subscribe** sign   **17 Dispatch** Make haste, get on with it.
**4.6. Location: Before Alexandria. Caesar's camp.**
**5 The . . . near** (The Renaissance identified Octavius Caesar, or the Emperor Augustus as he was subsequently titled, with this *Pax Romana,* peace under the Roman Empire.)   **6 Prove this** If this proves to be.   **three-nooked** three-cornered. (Refers to Asia, Europe, and Africa.)   **7 bear** (1) bring forth (2) wear as a triumphal garland. **olive** symbol of peace   **8 charge Agrippa** order Agrippa to   **9 van** vanguard, front lines   **12 Jewry** Judaea   **13 dissuade** i.e., from following Antony   **17 entertainment** employment, maintenance **19 sorely** heavily   **22 overplus** in addition.

Came on my guard, and at thy tent is now    23
Unloading of his mules.

ENOBARBUS    I give it you.

SOLDIER    Mock not, Enobarbus,
I tell you true. Best you safed the bringer    27
Out of the host. I must attend mine office,    28
Or would have done't myself. Your emperor
Continues still a Jove.    *Exit.*

ENOBARBUS
I am alone the villain of the earth,    31
And feel I am so most. O Antony,    32
Thou mine of bounty, how wouldst thou have paid    33
My better service, when my turpitude
Thou dost so crown with gold! This blows my heart.    35
If swift thought break it not, a swifter mean    36
Shall outstrike thought; but thought will do't, I feel.    37
I fight against thee? No, I will go seek
Some ditch wherein to die. The foul'st best fits
My latter part of life.    *Exit.*

❧

# [4.7]

*Alarum. Drums and trumpets. Enter Agrippa
[and others].*

AGRIPPA
Retire! We have engaged ourselves too far.
Caesar himself has work, and our oppression    2
Exceeds what we expected.    *Exeunt.*    3

*Alarums. Enter Antony, and Scarus wounded.*

SCARUS
O my brave Emperor, this is fought indeed!
Had we done so at first, we had droven them home    5
With clouts about their heads.

ANTONY    Thou bleed'st apace.    6

SCARUS
I had a wound here that was like a T,
But now 'tis made an H.    *[Sound retreat] far off.*

ANTONY    They do retire.    8

SCARUS
We'll beat 'em into bench holes. I have yet    9
Room for six scotches more.    10

*Enter Eros.*

EROS
They are beaten, sir, and our advantage serves    11
For a fair victory.

SCARUS    Let us score their backs    12
And snatch 'em up, as we take hares, behind!
'Tis sport to maul a runner.

ANTONY    I will reward thee    14
Once for thy spritely comfort and tenfold
For thy good valor. Come thee on.

SCARUS    I'll halt after.    *Exeunt.*    17

❧

# [4.8]

*Alarum. Enter Antony again in a march; Scarus,
with others.*

ANTONY
We have beat him to his camp. Run one before    1
And let the Queen know of our gests.  *[Exit a Soldier.]*
Tomorrow,    2
Before the sun shall see 's, we'll spill the blood    3
That has today escaped. I thank you all,    4
For doughty-handed are you, and have fought    5
Not as you served the cause, but as 't had been    6
Each man's like mine; you have shown all Hectors.    7
Enter the city, clip your wives, your friends,    8
Tell them your feats, whilst they with joyful tears
Wash the congealment from your wounds and kiss
The honored gashes whole.

*Enter Cleopatra [attended].*

[*To Scarus*] Give me thy hand;
To this great fairy I'll commend thy acts,
Make her thanks bless thee. [*To Cleopatra*] O thou day    12
o'th' world,    13
Chain mine armed neck; leap thou, attire and all,    14
Through proof of harness to my heart, and there    15
Ride on the pants triumphing!    *[They embrace.]*

CLEOPATRA    Lord of lords,    16
O infinite virtue, com'st thou smiling from    17
The world's great snare uncaught?

ANTONY    My nightingale,
We have beat them to their beds. What, girl, though
gray
Do something mingle with our younger brown, yet
ha' we    20
A brain that nourishes our nerves and can    21

---

23 **on my guard** while I was standing guard    27 **Best you safed** You
would do well to provide safe-conduct for    28 **host** army.    **attend
mine office** see to my duties    31 **alone the** the only, the greatest
32 **And . . . most** and am the one who feels it most.    33 **mine** abundant store    35 **blows** causes to swell to the bursting point    36 **mean**
i.e., suicide    37 **thought** melancholy.    **do't** i.e., break my heart
**4.7. Location:** Field of battle between the camps.
2 **has work** is hard pressed.    **our oppression** the heavy attacks
against us    3 **s.d.** *Exeunt* (The cleared stage technically marks a new
scene, although the alarums provide a sense of continuous action.)
5 **droven** driven    6 **clouts** (1) bandages (2) blows and knocks
8 **H** i.e., the bottom of the T has been cut across to make an H lying on
its side. (There is a pun on *ache,* pronounced *aitch.*)    9 **bench holes** the
holes of latrines, i.e., any desperate place to hide.    10 **scotches** cuts

11–12 **our . . . victory** i.e., we are in such a favorable position that a
complete victory seems in prospect.    12 **score** mark by cuts from a
whip    14 **a runner** one in retreat.    17 **halt** limp
**4.8. Location:** Before Alexandria. The action is virtually continuous.
1 **beat** driven.    **Run one** Let someone run    2 **gests** deeds.    3–4 **spill . . .
escaped** slaughter those enemy soldiers who managed to survive yes-
terday's battle.    5 **doughty-handed** valiant    6–7 **Not . . . mine** not as if
you were merely serving the general cause, but as if it were your cause
personally    7 **shown** shown yourselves    8 **clip** embrace    12 **fairy**
enchantress, dispenser of good fortune    13 **day** light    14 **Chain . . .
neck** hang around my neck in an embrace like a medal on a chain
15 **proof of harness** proof-armor, tested armor    16 **pants** heartbeats
17 **virtue** valor    20 **something** somewhat    21 **nerves** sinews, tendons

Get goal for goal of youth. Behold this man;                    22
Commend unto his lips thy favoring hand.—                    23
Kiss it, my warrior. [*Scarus kisses Cleopatra's hand.*] He
   hath fought today
As if a god, in hate of mankind, had
Destroyed in such a shape.

CLEOPATRA                              I'll give thee, friend,
An armor all of gold; it was a king's.

ANTONY

He has deserved it, were it carbuncled                    28
Like holy Phoebus' car. Give me thy hand.                    29
Through Alexandria make a jolly march;
Bear our hacked targets like the men that owe them.    31
Had our great palace the capacity
To camp this host, we all would sup together              33
And drink carouses to the next day's fate,                    34
Which promises royal peril. Trumpeters,                    35
With brazen din blast you the city's ear;
Make mingle with our rattling taborins,                    37
That heaven and earth may strike their sounds
   together,                                                             38
Applauding our approach. [*Trumpets sound.*] *Exeunt.*

❧

## [4.9]

*Enter a Sentry and his company. Enobarbus
follows.*

SENTRY

If we be not relieved within this hour,
We must return to th' court of guard. The night     2
Is shiny, and they say we shall embattle                    3
By th' second hour i'th' morn.

FIRST WATCH     This last day was a shrewd one to 's.  5

ENOBARBUS     Oh, bear me witness, night—

SECOND WATCH

What man is this?

FIRST WATCH     Stand close, and list him.                    8
                        [*They stand aside.*]

ENOBARBUS

Be witness to me, O thou blessèd moon,
When men revolted shall upon record                    10
Bear hateful memory: poor Enobarbus did
Before thy face repent.

SENTRY     Enobarbus?

SECOND WATCH     Peace! Hark further.

ENOBARBUS

O sovereign mistress of true melancholy,              15
The poisonous damp of night disponge upon me,    16
That life, a very rebel to my will,
May hang no longer on me. Throw my heart
Against the flint and hardness of my fault,
Which, being dried with grief, will break to powder  20
And finish all foul thoughts. O Antony,
Nobler than my revolt is infamous,
Forgive me in thine own particular,                    23
But let the world rank me in register                    24
A master-leaver and a fugitive.                              25
O Antony! O Antony!                              [*He dies.*]

FIRST WATCH     Let's speak to him.

SENTRY

Let's hear him, for the things he speaks
May concern Caesar.

SECOND WATCH                    Let's do so. But he sleeps.

SENTRY

Swoons rather, for so bad a prayer as his
Was never yet for sleep.

FIRST WATCH                    Go we to him.                    31
                [*They approach Enobarbus.*]

SECOND WATCH     Awake, sir, awake. Speak to us.

FIRST WATCH     Hear you, sir?

SENTRY     The hand of death hath raught him.              34
                         *Drums afar off.*

Hark, the drums demurely wake the sleepers.          35
Let us bear him to th' court of guard;
He is of note. Our hour is fully out.                    37

SECOND WATCH

Come on, then. He may recover yet.
                  *Exeunt* [*with the body*].

❧

## [4.10]

*Enter Antony and Scarus, with their army.*

ANTONY

Their preparation is today by sea;
We please them not by land.

SCARUS                              For both, my lord.

ANTONY

I would they'd fight i'th' fire or i'th' air;              3
We'd fight there too. But this it is: our foot            4
Upon the hills adjoining to the city
Shall stay with us. Order for sea is given;              6

---

22 **Get . . . of** i.e., stay competitively equal with.   **this man** i.e., Scarus
23 **Commend** entrust, commit   28 **carbuncled** set with jewels
29 **Phoebus' car** the chariot of the sun.   31 **Bear . . . them** bear our
hacked shields, well suited to the warriors who, like their shields, have
sustained blows. (*Owe* means "own.")   33 **camp this host** accommodate this army   34 **carouses** toasts   35 **royal peril** i.e., war, the sport of
monarchs.   37 **taborins** drums   38 **That . . . together** i.e., that the heavens may echo and augment the loud noise of the drums and trumpets
**4.9. Location:** Caesar's camp.
2 **court of guard** guardroom.   3 **shiny** bright, moonlit.   **embattle**
assemble for the combat   5 **shrewd** unlucky   8 **close** concealed.
**list** listen to   10 **revolted** who have broken their allegiance.   **upon
record** in the record of history

15 **mistress . . . melancholy** i.e., the moon, so addressed because of
her supposed influence in causing lunacy   16 **disponge** pour down
(as from a squeezed sponge)   20 **Which** i.e., the heart.   **dried with
grief** (Cold and melancholy blood was thought to strangle and dry
up the heart.)   23 **in . . . particular** in your own person   24 **rank me
in register** put me down in its records   25 **master-leaver** (1) one who
deserts his master (2) nonpareil of deserters.   **fugitive** deserter.
31 **for** a prelude to   34 **raught** reached, taken   35 **demurely** with
solemn sound   37 **of note** of rank.   **out** expired.
**4.10. Location:** The field of battle.
3 **fire . . . air** (Along with earth and water, where Antony is already
prepared, fire and air make up the traditional four elements of all
matter.)   4 **foot** foot soldiers   6 **for sea** to fight at sea

They have put forth the haven—                                          7
Where their appointment we may best discover          8
And look on their endeavor.                    *Exeunt.*

❖

# [4.11]

*Enter Caesar and his army.*

CAESAR
But being charged, we will be still by land,          1
Which, as I take't, we shall; for his best force      2
Is forth to man his galleys. To the vales,            3
And hold our best advantage.            *Exeunt.*      4

❖

# [4.12]

*Enter Antony and Scarus.*

ANTONY
Yet they are not joined. Where yond pine does stand,    1
I shall discover all. I'll bring thee word
Straight how 'tis like to go.                    *Exit.*
                    *Alarum afar off, as at a sea fight.*
SCARUS                              Swallows have built    3
In Cleopatra's sails their nests. The augurers          4
Say they know not, they cannot tell, look grimly,
And dare not speak their knowledge. Antony
Is valiant, and dejected, and by starts
His fretted fortunes give him hope and fear             8
Of what he has and has not.

*Enter Antony.*

ANTONY                              All is lost!
This foul Egyptian hath betrayèd me.
My fleet hath yielded to the foe, and yonder
They cast their caps up and carouse together
Like friends long lost. Triple-turned whore! 'Tis thou    13
Hast sold me to this novice, and my heart
Makes only wars on thee. Bid them all fly;
For when I am revenged upon my charm,                    16
I have done all. Bid them all fly. Begone!
                                        *[Exit Scarus.]*
O sun, thy uprise shall I see no more.
Fortune and Antony part here; even here
Do we shake hands. All come to this? The hearts          20
That spanieled me at heels, to whom I gave              21
Their wishes, do discandy, melt their sweets            22

On blossoming Caesar; and this pine is barked          23
That overtopped them all. Betrayed I am.
Oh, this false soul of Egypt! This grave charm,        25
Whose eye becked forth my wars and called them
    home,                                              26
Whose bosom was my crownet, my chief end,              27
Like a right gypsy hath at fast and loose              28
Beguiled me to the very heart of loss.                 29
*[Calling]* What, Eros, Eros!

*Enter Cleopatra.*

                    Ah, thou spell! Avaunt!             30
CLEOPATRA
Why is my lord enraged against his love?
ANTONY
Vanish, or I shall give thee thy deserving
And blemish Caesar's triumph. Let him take thee        33
And hoist thee up to the shouting plebeians!
Follow his chariot, like the greatest spot             35
Of all thy sex; most monsterlike be shown              36
For poor'st diminutives, for dolts, and let            37
Patient Octavia plow thy visage up
With her preparèd nails!            *Exit Cleopatra.*
                    'Tis well thou'rt gone,
If it be well to live; but better 'twere
Thou fell'st into my fury, for one death               41
Might have prevented many.—Eros, ho!—                  42
The shirt of Nessus is upon me. Teach me,              43
Alcides, thou mine ancestor, thy rage.                 44
Let me lodge Lichas on the horns o'th' moon,           45
And with those hands, that grasped the heaviest club,
Subdue my worthiest self. The witch shall die.
To the young Roman boy she hath sold me, and I fall
Under this plot. She dies for't.—Eros, ho!    *Exit.*

❖

# [4.13]

*Enter Cleopatra, Charmian, Iras, [and] Mardian.*

CLEOPATRA
Help me, my women! Oh, he's more mad

---

**7 forth** forth from   **8 appointment** disposition of forces, equipment.
**discover** descry
**4.11. Location: The field of battle.**
**1 But being** Unless we are.   **still** inactive   **2 we shall** i.e., we will be
left undisturbed   **3 Is forth** has gone forth.   **vales** valleys   **4 hold . . .
advantage** take the most advantageous position.
**4.12. Location: The field of battle at first, though by scene's end the
action appears to be located in Alexandria.**
**1 joined** joined in battle.   **3 Straight** immediately.   **like** likely
**4 augurers** augurs, soothsayers   **8 fretted** worn away, vexed, checkered
**13 Triple-turned** Three times faithless (to Julius Caesar, Gnaeus
Pompey, and now Antony)   **16 charm** practicer of charms or spells
**20 shake hands** i.e., in parting.   **hearts** good fellows   **21 spanieled**
fawned upon like a spaniel   **22 Their wishes** whatever they wished.
**discandy** melt, dissolve

**23 this pine** i.e., Antony.   **barked** stripped of its bark and thus killed
**25 This grave charm** i.e., This sorceress who casts fatal spells
**26 Whose . . . home** whose seductive glance tempted me into making
wars on her behalf, bestowing the fruits of victories on her   **27 Whose . . .
end** whose embraces were the crown of my achievement and my goal
**28 right** veritable.   **fast and loose** a cheating game in which the victim
bets that he can make fast a knot in an ingeniously coiled rope, whereupon the knot is pulled loose   **29 Beguiled** cheated.   **loss** ruin.
**30 spell** enchantment.   **Avaunt!** Begone!   **33 blemish Caesar's triumph**
i.e., kill you and thereby frustrate Caesar's plan to display you in his
triumphal procession into Rome.   **35 spot** blemish, disgrace
**36 shown** exhibited   **37 diminutives** underlings, i.e., the populace
**41 Thou fell'st into** you had fallen a victim to   **42 many** i.e., many other
deaths resulting from my rage.   **43–5 Nessus . . . Lichas** (When Hercules or *Alcides* had fatally wounded the centaur *Nessus* for trying to rape
Hercules's wife Deianira, Nessus vengefully gave his blood-soaked shirt
to Deianira as a supposed love charm for her husband. The poison gave
Hercules such agony that he cast his page *Lichas* into the air.)
**4.13. Location: Alexandria. This scene appears to follow scene 12
closely. The sense of location is very fluid, and it is not clear where
the end of scene 12 takes place.**

Than Telamon for his shield; the boar of Thessaly      2
Was never so embossed.
CHARMIAN                    To th' monument!              3
There lock yourself and send him word you are dead.
The soul and body rive not more in parting              5
Than greatness going off.
CLEOPATRA                   To th' monument!              6
Mardian, go tell him I have slain myself.
Say that the last I spoke was "Antony,"
And word it, prithee, piteously. Hence, Mardian,
And bring me how he takes my death. To th'
   monument!                                   *Exeunt.*

❧

# [4.14]

*Enter Antony and Eros.*

ANTONY
Eros, thou yet behold'st me?
EROS                          Ay, noble lord.
ANTONY
Sometime we see a cloud that's dragonish,               2
A vapor sometime like a bear or lion,
A towered citadel, a pendant rock,                       4
A forkèd mountain, or blue promontory
With trees upon't that nod unto the world
And mock our eyes with air. Thou hast seen these
   signs;
They are black vesper's pageants.
EROS                            Ay, my lord.              8
ANTONY
That which is now a horse, even with a thought
The rack dislimns and makes it indistinct               10
As water is in water.
EROS                 It does, my lord.
ANTONY
My good knave Eros, now thy captain is                  12
Even such a body. Here I am Antony,
Yet cannot hold this visible shape, my knave.
I made these wars for Egypt, and the Queen,
Whose heart I thought I had, for she had mine—
Which whilst it was mine had annexed unto't
A million more, now lost—she, Eros, has
Packed cards with Caesar and false-played my glory      19
Unto an enemy's triumph.                                20

Nay, weep not, gentle Eros. There is left us
Ourselves to end ourselves.

*Enter Mardian.*

                              Oh, thy vile lady!
She has robbed me of my sword.
MARDIAN                        No, Antony,               23
My mistress loved thee, and her fortunes mingled
With thine entirely.
ANTONY             Hence, saucy eunuch, peace!
She hath betrayed me and shall die the death.           26
MARDIAN
Death of one person can be paid but once,
And that she has discharged. What thou wouldst do       28
Is done unto thy hand. The last she spake               29
Was, "Antony, most noble Antony!"
Then in the midst a tearing groan did break
The name of Antony; it was divided                      32
Between her heart and lips. She rendered life           33
Thy name so buried in her.
ANTONY              Dead, then?
MARDIAN                      Dead.                       34
ANTONY
Unarm, Eros. The long day's task is done,
And we must sleep. [*To Mardian*] That thou depart'st
   hence safe
Does pay thy labor richly; go.      *Exit Mardian.*
             Off, pluck off! [*Eros unarms him.*]
The sevenfold shield of Ajax cannot keep               38
The battery from my heart. Oh, cleave, my sides!       39
Heart, once be stronger than thy continent;            40
Crack thy frail case! Apace, Eros, apace.              41
No more a soldier. Bruisèd pieces, go;                 42
You have been nobly borne.—From me awhile.             43
                                   *Exit Eros.*
I will o'ertake thee, Cleopatra, and
Weep for my pardon. So it must be, for now
All length is torture; since the torch is out,        46
Lie down, and stray no farther. Now all labor
Mars what it does; yea, very force entangles           48
Itself with strength. Seal then, and all is done.      49
Eros!—I come, my queen.—Eros!—Stay for me.            50
Where souls do couch on flowers, we'll hand in hand,   51
And with our sprightly port make the ghosts gaze.      52

2 **Telamon** Ajax Telamon, who after the capture of Troy went mad and slew himself when he was not awarded the shield and armor of Achilles.  **the boar of Thessaly** the boar sent by Diana or Artemis to ravage the fields of Calydon, slain by Meleager  3 **embossed** foaming at the mouth from rage and exhaustion.  **monument** tomb presumably built to house Cleopatra's royal remains after her death, like the pyramids.  5 **rive** split, sever  6 **going off** i.e., bidding farewell to its glory.
**4.14. Location: Alexandria. (See location of scene 13; again, the sense of time is immediate and the place is fluid.)**
2 **dragonish** shaped like a dragon  4 **pendant** overhanging  8 **black . . . pageants** i.e., illusory visions heralding the approach of night.  10 **The rack dislimns** the mass of cloud changes its shape  12 **knave** lad  19 **Packed cards** i.e., stacked the deck.  **false-played** falsely played away  20 **triumph** (1) victory (2) trump card.

23 **sword** i.e., prowess as a soldier, masculinity.  26 **die the death** be put to death.  28 **discharged** paid.  29 **unto thy hand** for you, without your having to lift a finger.  32–3 **it . . . lips** i.e., she groaned out half of Antony's name and then died with the unspoken part in her heart only.  33–4 **She . . . in her** She gave back to Nature that part of your name thus buried in her heart.  38 **sevenfold** with seven thicknesses. (The shield of Ajax was of brass reinforced with seven thicknesses of oxhide.)  39 **battery** battering  40–1 **Heart . . . case** My breaking heart, for once show greater strength than that of the body which contains it; take my frail body along with you into death.  41 **Apace** Quickly  42 **pieces** pieces of armor  43 **From** Go from  46 **length** prolongation of life.  **the torch** i.e., the life of Cleopatra  48–9 **very force . . . strength** any resolute action undoes itself by its own exertions.  49 **Seal** Finish the business (as in sealing a letter)  50 **Eros** (The meaning of Eros's name, erotic love, is especially apt here.)  51 **couch** lie (among the blessed dead in the Elysian fields, as pictured for example in Virgil's *Aeneid*)  52 **sprightly** (1) high-spirited (2) spiritlike, ghostly.  **port** bearing

Dido and her Aeneas shall want troops,    53
And all the haunt be ours.—Come, Eros, Eros!    54

*Enter Eros.*

EROS
What would my lord?
ANTONY           Since Cleopatra died
I have lived in such dishonor that the gods
Detest my baseness. I, that with my sword
Quartered the world, and o'er green Neptune's back    58
With ships made cities, condemn myself to lack    59
The courage of a woman—less noble mind
Than she which by her death our Caesar tells    61
"I am conqueror of myself." Thou art sworn, Eros,
That when the exigent should come which now    63
Is come indeed, when I should see behind me    64
Th'inevitable prosecution of    65
Disgrace and horror, that on my command
Thou then wouldst kill me. Do't. The time is come.
Thou strik'st not me, 'tis Caesar thou defeat'st.
Put color in thy cheek.
EROS           The gods withhold me!    69
Shall I do that which all the Parthian darts,
Though enemy, lost aim and could not?
ANTONY           Eros,
Wouldst thou be windowed in great Rome and see    72
Thy master thus with pleached arms, bending down    73
His corrigible neck, his face subdued    74
To penetrative shame, whilst the wheeled seat    75
Of fortunate Caesar, drawn before him, branded    76
His baseness that ensued?
EROS           I would not see't.    77
ANTONY
Come, then, for with a wound I must be cured.
Draw that thy honest sword, which thou hast worn    79
Most useful for thy country.
EROS           Oh, sir, pardon me!    80
ANTONY
When I did make thee free, swor'st thou not then
To do this when I bade thee? Do it at once,
Or thy precedent services are all    83
But accidents unpurposed. Draw, and come.    84
EROS
Turn from me then that noble countenance

Wherein the worship of the whole world lies.    86
ANTONY   Lo thee!          *[He turns away.]*
EROS *[drawing his sword]*
My sword is drawn.
ANTONY        Then let it do at once
That thing why thou hast drawn it.
EROS          My dear master,
My captain, and my emperor, let me say,
Before I strike this bloody stroke, farewell.
ANTONY   'Tis said, man, and farewell.
EROS
Farewell, great chief. Shall I strike now?
ANTONY          Now, Eros.
EROS *(kills himself)*
Why, there then! Thus I do escape the sorrow
Of Antony's death.        *[He dies.]*
ANTONY        Thrice nobler than myself!
Thou teachest me, O valiant Eros, what
I should, and thou couldst not. My queen and Eros    97
Have by their brave instruction got upon me    98
A nobleness in record. But I will be    99
A bridegroom in my death, and run into't
As to a lover's bed. Come, then, and Eros,
Thy master dies thy scholar. To do thus
I learned of thee.     *[He falls on his sword.]*
       How, not dead? Not dead?
The guard, ho! Oh, dispatch me!    104

*Enter [Dercetus and others of] a Guard.*

FIRST GUARD   What's the noise?
ANTONY   I have done my work ill, friends.
Oh, make an end of what I have begun!
SECOND GUARD   The star is fallen.
FIRST GUARD   And time is at his period.    109
ALL   Alas, and woe!
ANTONY   Let him that loves me strike me dead.
FIRST GUARD   Not I.
SECOND GUARD   Nor I.
THIRD GUARD   Nor anyone.      *Exeunt [Guard].*
DERCETUS
Thy death and fortunes bid thy followers fly.
This sword but shown to Caesar, with this tidings,
Shall enter me with him. [*He takes up Antony's sword.*]   117

*Enter Diomedes.*

DIOMEDES   Where's Antony?
DERCETUS   There, Diomed, there.
DIOMEDES
Lives he? Wilt thou not answer, man? [*Exit Dercetus.*]
ANTONY
Art thou there, Diomed? Draw thy sword and give me
Sufficing strokes for death.
DIOMEDES        Most absolute lord,
My mistress Cleopatra sent me to thee.

---

**53 Dido . . . troops** We will be the most distinguished lovers in the Elysian fields, outshining even the Queen of Carthage and her famous lover. (In the *Aeneid*, Aeneas deserts Dido in order to found Rome, putting public good ahead of private passion as Antony does not. Dido scorns Aeneas when they meet in the underworld; Antony here imagines himself and Cleopatra in the Elysian fields.) **want troops** lack followers   **54 And . . . ours** i.e., and we will be the envy of all the spirits in that place.   **58–9 Quartered . . . cities** divided and conquered the world, and at sea assembled flotillas as dense and populous as cities   **59 to lack** for lacking   **61 our Caesar tells** tells Octavius Caesar that   **63 exigent** exigency, time of compelling need   **64 behind me** coming at my back   **65 prosecution** pursuit, consequence   **69 The gods withhold me!** i.e., God forbid!   **72 windowed** placed as in a window   **73 pleached** bound   **74 corrigible** submissive   **75 penetrative** penetrating. **wheeled seat** chariot   **76–7 branded . . . ensued** stigmatized, as by a brand, the shame of him that followed.   **79 honest** honorable   **80 pardon me!** excuse me from doing this!   **83 precedent** former   **84 accidents unpurposed** events leading to no purpose.

**86 worship** honor, worth   **97 I should . . . not** I should have done for myself and you couldn't bring yourself to do for me.   **98–9 got . . . record** won a noble place in history before I have.   **104 dispatch** finish   **109 his period** its end.   **117 enter . . . him** admit me to his service, put me in his good graces.

**ANTONY**
When did she send thee?

**DIOMEDES**            Now, my lord.

**ANTONY**                    Where is she?

**DIOMEDES**
Locked in her monument. She had a prophesying fear
Of what hath come to pass. For when she saw—
Which never shall be found—you did suspect    127
She had disposed with Caesar, and that your rage    128
Would not be purged, she sent you word she was
     dead;
But, fearing since how it might work, hath sent
Me to proclaim the truth, and I am come,
I dread, too late.

**ANTONY**
Too late, good Diomed. Call my guard, I prithee.

**DIOMEDES** [*calling*]
What ho, the Emperor's guard! The guard, what ho!
Come, your lord calls.

     *Enter four or five of the Guard of Antony.*

**ANTONY**
Bear me, good friends, where Cleopatra bides.    136
'Tis the last service that I shall command you.

**FIRST GUARD**
Woe, woe are we, sir, you may not live to wear    138
All your true followers out.

**ALL**                 Most heavy day!    139

**ANTONY**
Nay, good my fellows, do not please sharp fate
To grace it with your sorrows. Bid that welcome    141
Which comes to punish us, and we punish it,
Seeming to bear it lightly. Take me up.
I have led you oft; carry me now, good friends,
And have my thanks for all.

     *Exeunt, bearing Antony [and Eros].*

## [4.15]

     *Enter Cleopatra and her maids aloft, with*
     *Charmian and Iras.*

**CLEOPATRA**
Oh, Charmian, I will never go from hence.

**CHARMIAN**
Be comforted, dear madam.

**CLEOPATRA**             No, I will not.
All strange and terrible events are welcome,
But comforts we despise. Our size of sorrow,
Proportioned to our cause, must be as great
As that which makes it.

     *Enter [below] Diomedes.*

                 How now? Is he dead?

**DIOMEDES**
His death's upon him, but not dead.
Look out o'th'other side your monument;
His guard have brought him thither.

     *Enter [below] Antony, and the Guard*
     [*bearing him*].

**CLEOPATRA**    O sun,
Burn the great sphere thou mov'st in; darkling stand    11
The varying shore o'th' world! O Antony,
Antony, Antony! Help, Charmian, help, Iras, help!
Help, friends below! Let's draw him hither.

**ANTONY**                 Peace!
Not Caesar's valor hath o'erthrown Antony,
But Antony's hath triumphed on itself.

**CLEOPATRA**
So it should be, that none but Antony
Should conquer Antony; but woe 'tis so!

**ANTONY**
I am dying, Egypt, dying. Only
I here importune death awhile, until    20
Of many thousand kisses the poor last
I lay upon thy lips.

**CLEOPATRA**          I dare not, dear—    22
Dear my lord, pardon—I dare not,
Lest I be taken. Not th'imperious show    24
Of the full-fortuned Caesar ever shall
Be brooched with me. If knife, drugs, serpents, have    26
Edge, sting, or operation, I am safe.    27
Your wife Octavia, with her modest eyes
And still conclusion, shall acquire no honor    29
Demuring upon me. But come, come, Antony—    30
Help me, my women—we must draw thee up.
Assist, good friends.

**ANTONY**           Oh, quick, or I am gone.
                     [*They begin lifting.*]

**CLEOPATRA**
Here's sport indeed! How heavy weighs my lord!
Our strength is all gone into heaviness,    34
That makes the weight. Had I great Juno's power,
The strong-winged Mercury should fetch thee up
And set thee by Jove's side. Yet come a little;
Wishers were ever fools. Oh, come, come, come!    38
         *They heave Antony aloft to Cleopatra.*
And welcome, welcome! Die when thou hast lived;    39
Quicken with kissing. Had my lips that power,    40
Thus would I wear them out.      [*She kisses him.*]

**ALL**    A heavy sight!    42

**ANTONY**    I am dying, Egypt, dying.
Give me some wine, and let me speak a little.

---

**127 found** found to be true    **128 disposed with** come to terms with    **136 bides** abides, dwells.    **138–9 live . . . out** outlive all those that serve you.    **141 To grace** by gracing or honoring
**4.15. Location: Alexandria. Cleopatra's monument.**
**0.1 *aloft*** in the gallery above the main stage

**11 sphere** concentric sphere in which, according to Ptolemaic astronomy, the sun moved about the earth, as did the planets and stars. **darkling** in darkness    **20 importune** i.e., beg a delay of    **22 I dare not** i.e., I dare not come down    **24 th'imperious show** the imperial triumphal procession    **26 Be . . . me** be decorated with me as a brooch-like adornment.    **27 operation** power, efficacy    **29 still conclusion** silent judgment    **30 Demuring** looking demurely    **34 heaviness** (1) sadness (2) weight    **38 Wishers . . . fools** Those who constantly wish for things are foolish.    **39 Die . . . lived** i.e., Die after living intensely. (With a pun on *die* suggesting sexual consummation; hence *Quicken* in line 40.)    **40 Quicken** revive    **42 heavy** doleful

ANTONY AND CLEOPATRA: 5.1

CLEOPATRA
No, let me speak, and let me rail so high
That the false huswife Fortune break her wheel, 46
Provoked by my offense.
ANTONY                    One word, sweet Queen: 47
Of Caesar seek your honor, with your safety. Oh! 48
CLEOPATRA
They do not go together.
ANTONY                    Gentle, hear me.
None about Caesar trust but Proculeius.
CLEOPATRA
My resolution and my hands I'll trust,
None about Caesar.
ANTONY
The miserable change now at my end 53
Lament nor sorrow at, but please your thoughts 54
In feeding them with those my former fortunes, 55
Wherein I lived the greatest prince o'th' world,
The noblest; and do now not basely die,
Not cowardly put off my helmet to
My countryman—a Roman by a Roman
Valiantly vanquished. Now my spirit is going;
I can no more.
CLEOPATRA          Noblest of men, woo't die? 61
Hast thou no care of me? Shall I abide
In this dull world, which in thy absence is
No better than a sty? [*Antony dies.*] Oh, see, my
    women,
The crown o'th'earth doth melt. My lord!
Oh, withered is the garland of the war;
The soldier's pole is fall'n! Young boys and girls 67
Are level now with men. The odds is gone, 68
And there is nothing left remarkable
Beneath the visiting moon.          [*She faints.*]
CHARMIAN    Oh, quietness, lady!
IRAS    She's dead too, our sovereign.
CHARMIAN    Lady!
IRAS    Madam!
CHARMIAN    Oh, madam, madam, madam!
IRAS    Royal Egypt, Empress!          [*Cleopatra stirs.*]
CHARMIAN    Peace, peace, Iras.
CLEOPATRA
No more but e'en a woman, and commanded
By such poor passion as the maid that milks
And does the meanest chares. It were for me 80
To throw my scepter at the injurious gods,
To tell them that this world did equal theirs
Till they had stol'n our jewel. All's but naught;
Patience is sottish, and impatience does 84
Become a dog that's mad. Then is it sin 85
To rush into the secret house of death
Ere death dare come to us? How do you, women?

What, what, good cheer! Why, how now, Charmian?
My noble girls! Ah, women, women! Look,
Our lamp is spent, it's out. Good sirs, take heart. 90
We'll bury him; and then, what's brave, what's noble, 91
Let's do't after the high Roman fashion
And make death proud to take us. Come, away.
This case of that huge spirit now is cold.
Ah, women, women! Come. We have no friend
But resolution, and the briefest end. 96
          *Exeunt, [those above] bearing off Antony's body.*

## [5.1]

*Enter Caesar, Agrippa, Dolabella, Maecenas,*
*[Gallus, Proculeius,] with his council of war.*

CAESAR
Go to him, Dolabella, bid him yield;
Being so frustrate, tell him, he mocks 2
The pauses that he makes.
DOLABELLA          Caesar, I shall.          [*Exit.*] 3

*Enter Dercetus, with the sword of Antony.*

CAESAR
Wherefore is that? And what art thou that dar'st
Appear thus to us?
DERCETUS          I am called Dercetus. 5
Mark Antony I served, who best was worthy 6
Best to be served. Whilst he stood up and spoke
He was my master, and I wore my life
To spend upon his haters. If thou please 9
To take me to thee, as I was to him
I'll be to Caesar; if thou pleasest not,
I yield thee up my life.
CAESAR          What is't thou say'st?
DERCETUS
I say, O Caesar, Antony is dead.
CAESAR
The breaking of so great a thing should make 14
A greater crack. The round world 15
Should have shook lions into civil streets 16
And citizens to their dens. The death of Antony 17
Is not a single doom; in the name lay 18
A moiety of the world.
DERCETUS          He is dead, Caesar, 19
Not by a public minister of justice,
Nor by a hirèd knife; but that self hand 21
Which writ his honor in the acts it did
Hath, with the courage which the heart did lend it,

46 **false huswife** treacherous hussy    47 **offense** offensive speech.    48 **Of** from    53–5 **The miserable ... fortunes** Neither lament or sorrow at my sad decline of fortune now that I am dying, but feed your thoughts with pleasing recollections of what I was like in my best days    61 **woo't** wilt thou    67 **pole** polestar or battle standard. (Probably with a suggestion of a sexual potency now withered and fallen through death.)    68 **The odds is gone** The distinction between great and small has disappeared    80 **chares** chores, drudgery.    **were** would be fitting    84–5 **Patience ... mad** i.e., Patience is for fools, and impatience is for the mad; both are useless here.

90 **Good sirs** (Addressed to the women.)    91 **brave** fine
96 **briefest** swiftest
**5.1. Location:** Alexandria. Caesar's camp.
2 **frustrate** helpless, baffled    2–3 **mocks ... makes** makes himself ridiculous by his delays (in yielding).    5 **thus** i.e., with a drawn sword. (An illegal act in the presence of royalty.)    6 **who best** who at his best    9 **spend** expend    14 **breaking** (1) destruction (2) disclosure    15 **crack** (1) cracking apart (2) loud report.    16 **civil** city    17 **their** i.e., the lions', or else, the citizens scurry to safety indoors, in their own "dens." (In either case, nature is inverted in a kind of disorder that earlier accompanied the death of Julius Caesar.)    18 **Is ... doom** i.e., signifies the death and destruction of much more than a single man    19 **moiety** half    21 **self** same

Splitted the heart. This is his sword.
                              [*He offers the sword.*]
I robbed his wound of it. Behold it stained
With his most noble blood.

CAESAR                    Look you sad, friends?
The gods rebuke me, but it is tidings                    27
To wash the eyes of kings.

AGRIPPA                   And strange it is
That nature must compel us to lament
Our most persisted deeds.

MAECENAS                  His taints and honors          30
Waged equal with him.

AGRIPPA                   A rarer spirit never           31
Did steer humanity; but you gods will give us           32
Some faults to make us men. Caesar is touched.

MAECENAS
When such a spacious mirror's set before him,           34
He needs must see himself.

CAESAR                    O Antony,                      35
I have followed thee to this; but we do launch          36
Diseases in our bodies. I must perforce                 37
Have shown to thee such a declining day,                38
Or look on thine; we could not stall together           39
In the whole world. But yet let me lament
With tears as sovereign as the blood of hearts          41
That thou, my brother, my competitor                    42
In top of all design, my mate in empire,                43
Friend and companion in the front of war,               44
The arm of mine own body, and the heart                 45
Where mine his thoughts did kindle—that our stars,      46
Unreconcilable, should divide                           47
Our equalness to this. Hear me, good friends—           48

              *Enter an Egyptian.*

But I will tell you at some meeter season.              49
The business of this man looks out of him;              50
We'll hear him what he says.—Whence are you?            51

EGYPTIAN
A poor Egyptian yet, the Queen my mistress,             52
Confined in all she has, her monument,
Of thy intents desires instruction,
That she preparedly may frame herself                   55
To th' way she's forced to.

CAESAR                    Bid her have good heart.
She soon shall know of us, by some of ours,             57

How honorable and how kindly we
Determine for her; for Caesar cannot live               59
To be ungentle.

EGYPTIAN        So the gods preserve thee!     *Exit.*  60

CAESAR
Come hither, Proculeius. Go and say
We purpose her no shame. Give her what comforts         62
The quality of her passion shall require,               63
Lest, in her greatness, by some mortal stroke           64
She do defeat us; for her life in Rome                  65
Would be eternal in our triumph. Go,                    66
And with your speediest bring us what she says          67
And how you find of her.

PROCULEIUS               Caesar, I shall.               68
                         *Exit Proculeius.*

CAESAR   Gallus, go you along.      [*Exit Gallus.*]
                         Where's Dolabella,
To second Proculeius?

ALL                      Dolabella!

CAESAR
Let him alone, for I remember now                       71
How he's employed. He shall in time be ready.
Go with me to my tent, where you shall see
How hardly I was drawn into this war,                   74
How calm and gentle I proceeded still                   75
In all my writings. Go with me and see                  76
What I can show in this.           *Exeunt.*

                    ❖

# [5.2]

*Enter Cleopatra, Charmian, Iras, and Mardian.*

CLEOPATRA
My desolation does begin to make
A better life. 'Tis paltry to be Caesar;                2
Not being Fortune, he's but Fortune's knave,            3
A minister of her will. And it is great
To do that thing that ends all other deeds,             5
Which shackles accidents and bolts up change,           6
Which sleeps and never palates more the dung,           7
The beggar's nurse and Caesar's.                        8
          *Enter [to the gates of the monument] Proculeius.*

PROCULEIUS
Caesar sends greeting to the Queen of Egypt,
And bids thee study on what fair demands                10
Thou mean'st to have him grant thee.

CLEOPATRA                     What's thy name?

27 but it is if it is not   30 persisted persistently desired or pursued
31 Waged equal with battled equally in.   rarer more extraordinary
32 steer humanity govern any individual.   will give insist on giving
34–5 When . . . himself Such an image of mixed virtues and vices in a
great man is bound to prompt Caesar (or anyone) to think about his own
weaknesses and strengths.   36 followed pursued   36–7 but . . . bodies
i.e., I have hurt you to cure a malaise in the state and in ourselves, as men
lance diseases in their own bodies.   37 perforce necessarily   38 shown to
thee i.e., suffered myself at your hands   39 stall dwell   41 as sovereign . . .
hearts as precious or efficacious as heart's blood   42 competitor associate,
partner (and rival)   43 In . . . design at the head of every grand enterprise
44 front forehead, face   45–6 the heart . . . kindle the brave heart where
my heart kindled its (*his*) thoughts of courage   47–8 should . . . this
should divide our equal partnership to this extreme.   49 meeter season
more suitable time.   50 looks . . . him reveals itself in his appearance and
expression   51 Whence are you? Where do you come from?   52 A . . .
yet i.e., Egyptian Cleopatra, still reduced in circumstance (and awaiting
your will), or, I am a poor Egyptian still, though subject to Rome's authority
55 frame herself shape her course of action   57 ours my people

59–60 Caesar . . . ungentle i.e., lack of graciousness is entirely foreign to
Caesar's nature.   62 purpose intend   63 quality strength.   passion
grief   64 greatness greatness of spirit   65 life in Rome presence in
Rome alive   66 eternal in our triumph an eternal glory in my triumphal procession.   67 with your speediest as quickly as you can   68 of
concerning   71 Let him alone Don't bother about him now   74 hardly
reluctantly   75 still always   76 writings i.e., letters to Antony.
5.2. Location: Alexandria. Cleopatra's monument.
2 better i.e., rising above the vicissitudes of fortune   3 knave servant
5–8 To do . . . Caesar's i.e., to commit suicide, a sleep that arrests accident and change, and in which the sleeper relishes no more the
dungy earth that sustains all living creatures, both Caesar and the
beggar.   10 study on consider carefully

PROCULEIUS
My name is Proculeius.
CLEOPATRA                     Antony
Did tell me of you, bade me trust you; but
I do not greatly care to be deceived,                    14
That have no use for trusting. If your master            15
Would have a queen his beggar, you must tell him
That majesty, to keep decorum, must
No less beg than a kingdom. If he please
To give me conquered Egypt for my son,
He gives me so much of mine own as I                     20
Will kneel to him with thanks.
PROCULEIUS                    Be of good cheer;
You're fall'n into a princely hand. Fear nothing.
Make your full reference freely to my lord,              23
Who is so full of grace that it flows over
On all that need. Let me report to him
Your sweet dependency, and you shall find               26
A conqueror that will pray in aid for kindness          27
Where he for grace is kneeled to.
CLEOPATRA                     Pray you, tell him
I am his fortune's vassal, and I send him               29
The greatness he has got. I hourly learn                30
A doctrine of obedience, and would gladly
Look him i'th' face.
PROCULEIUS            This I'll report, dear lady.
Have comfort, for I know your plight is pitied
Of him that caused it.                                  34
                    [Roman soldiers enter from
            behind Cleopatra and take her prisoner.]
You see how easily she may be surprised.
[To the soldiers] Guard her till Caesar come.
IRAS                          Royal Queen!
CHARMIAN
Oh, Cleopatra! Thou art taken, Queen.
CLEOPATRA [drawing a dagger]
Quick, quick, good hands.
PROCULEIUS            Hold, worthy lady, hold!
                              [He disarms her.]
Do not yourself such wrong, who are in this
Relieved, but not betrayed.
CLEOPATRA                     What, of death too,      40
That rids our dogs of languish?
PROCULEIUS                     Cleopatra,              41
Do not abuse my master's bounty by
Th'undoing of yourself. Let the world see
His nobleness well acted, which your death             44
Will never let come forth.
CLEOPATRA                     Where art thou, Death?   45
Come hither, come! Come, come, and take a queen

Worth many babes and beggars!
PROCULEIUS              Oh, temperance, lady!          47
CLEOPATRA
Sir, I will eat no meat, I'll not drink, sir;          48
If idle talk will once be necessary,                   49
I'll not sleep, neither. This mortal house I'll ruin,
Do Caesar what he can. Know, sir, that I
Will not wait pinioned at your master's court,         52
Nor once be chastised with the sober eye
Of dull Octavia. Shall they hoist me up
And show me to the shouting varletry                   55
Of censuring Rome? Rather a ditch in Egypt
Be gentle grave unto me! Rather on Nilus' mud
Lay me stark nak'd and let the waterflies
Blow me into abhorring! Rather make                    59
My country's high pyramides my gibbet                  60
And hang me up in chains!
PROCULEIUS             You do extend
These thoughts of horror further than you shall
Find cause in Caesar.

            Enter Dolabella.

DOLABELLA             Proculeius,
What thou hast done thy master Caesar knows,
And he hath sent for thee. For the Queen,              65
I'll take her to my guard.
PROCULEIUS             So, Dolabella,
It shall content me best. Be gentle to her.
[To Cleopatra] To Caesar I will speak what you shall
    please,                                            68
If you'll employ me to him.
CLEOPATRA             Say I would die.
                    Exit Proculeius [with soldiers].
DOLABELLA
Most noble Empress, you have heard of me?
CLEOPATRA
I cannot tell.
DOLABELLA    Assuredly you know me.
CLEOPATRA
No matter, sir, what I have heard or known.
You laugh when boys or women tell their dreams;
Is't not your trick?
DOLABELLA             I understand not, madam.         74
CLEOPATRA
I dreamt there was an emperor Antony.
Oh, such another sleep, that I might see
But such another man!
DOLABELLA             If it might please ye—
CLEOPATRA
His face was as the heav'ns, and therein stuck         78
A sun and moon, which kept their course and lighted

14 do . . . to be am wary of being  15 That since I  20 as that
23 Make . . . reference Refer your case  26 dependency submissiveness  27 pray . . . kindness beg your assistance to ensure that he may
omit no kindness  29–30 I send . . . got i.e., I acknowledge his superiority over all he has won, including myself.  34 Of by.  34.1 Roman
soldiers (Perhaps led by Gallus; see 5.1.69. Possibly some speech for
him has been omitted.)  40 Relieved rescued.  of death too i.e., (1) am I
relieved or deprived even of death (2) am I betrayed even of the right to die
41 our dogs of languish even our dogs of lingering disease.  44 acted
accomplished  45 let come forth allow to be displayed.

47 babes and beggars i.e., those whom death takes easily and
often.  48 meat food  49 If . . . necessary even if on occasion I must
resort to idle talk (to keep myself awake)  52 wait pinioned wait
shackled in attendance, like a bird with clipped wings, unable to
fly  55 varletry rabble  59 Blow . . . abhorring cause me to swell
abhorrently with maggots, or, deposit their eggs on me until I become
abhorrent.  60 gibbet gallows  65 For As for  68 what whatever
74 trick manner, way.  78 stuck were set

The little O, the earth.

DOLABELLA                     Most sovereign creature—

CLEOPATRA   His legs bestrid the ocean; his reared arm   81
Crested the world; his voice was propertied   82
As all the tunèd spheres, and that to friends;   83
But when he meant to quail and shake the orb,   84
He was as rattling thunder. For his bounty,   85
There was no winter in't; an autumn 'twas
That grew the more by reaping. His delights   87
Were dolphin-like; they showed his back above   88
The element they lived in. In his livery   89
Walked crowns and crownets; realms and islands
were   90
As plates dropped from his pocket.

DOLABELLA                     Cleopatra—   91

CLEOPATRA
Think you there was or might be such a man
As this I dreamt of?

DOLABELLA                     Gentle madam, no.

CLEOPATRA
You lie, up to the hearing of the gods.
But if there be nor ever were one such,   95
It's past the size of dreaming. Nature wants stuff   96
To vie strange forms with fancy; yet t'imagine   97
An Antony were nature's piece 'gainst fancy,   98
Condemning shadows quite.

DOLABELLA                     Hear me, good madam:   99
Your loss is as yourself, great; and you bear it
As answering to the weight. Would I might never   101
O'ertake pursued success but I do feel,   102
By the rebound of yours, a grief that smites   103
My very heart at root.

CLEOPATRA                     I thank you, sir.
Know you what Caesar means to do with me?

DOLABELLA
I am loath to tell you what I would you knew.   106

CLEOPATRA
Nay, pray you, sir.

DOLABELLA            Though he be honorable—

CLEOPATRA   He'll lead me, then, in triumph.

DOLABELLA   Madam, he will, I know't.        Flourish.

*Enter Proculeius, Caesar, Gallus, Maecenas,
and others of his train.*

ALL   Make way there! Caesar!

CAESAR   Which is the Queen of Egypt?

DOLABELLA   It is the Emperor, madam.

*Cleopatra kneels.*

CAESAR   Arise, you shall not kneel. I pray you, rise.
Rise, Egypt.

CLEOPATRA [*rising*]   Sir, the gods will have it thus;   114
My master and my lord I must obey.

CAESAR   Take to you no hard thoughts.   116
The record of what injuries you did us,
Though written in our flesh, we shall remember   118
As things but done by chance.

CLEOPATRA                     Sole sir o'th' world,   119
I cannot project mine own cause so well   120
To make it clear, but do confess I have   121
Been laden with like frailties which before   122
Have often shamed our sex.

CAESAR                     Cleopatra, know
We will extenuate rather than enforce.   124
If you apply yourself to our intents,   125
Which towards you are most gentle, you shall find
A benefit in this change; but if you seek
To lay on me a cruelty by taking   128
Antony's course, you shall bereave yourself   129
Of my good purposes and put your children
To that destruction which I'll guard them from
If thereon you rely. I'll take my leave.

CLEOPATRA
And may, through all the world! 'Tis yours, and we,   133
Your scutcheons and your signs of conquest, shall   134
Hang in what place you please. Here, my good lord.   135

*[She gives him a scroll.]*

CAESAR
You shall advise me in all for Cleopatra.   136

CLEOPATRA
This is the brief of money, plate, and jewels   137
I am possessed of. 'Tis exactly valued,
Not petty things admitted. Where's Seleucus?   139

*[Enter Seleucus.]*

SELEUCUS   Here, madam.

CLEOPATRA
This is my treasurer. Let him speak, my lord,
Upon his peril, that I have reserved
To myself nothing.—Speak the truth, Seleucus.

SELEUCUS
Madam, I had rather seal my lips
Than to my peril speak that which is not.

CLEOPATRA   What have I kept back?

SELEUCUS
Enough to purchase what you have made known.

---

81 **bestrid** straddled (like the Colossus of Rhodes)   82 **Crested** surmounted as with a heraldic crest   82–3 **propertied . . . friends** endowed with qualities which, when he spoke to friends, recalled the harmony of the heavenly bodies in their spheres   84 **quail** make quail, overawe. **orb** globe   85 **For** As for   87–9 **His . . . in** i.e., Like the dolphin sportfully rising up out of the sea, his pleasures arose out of the element in which he lived, both glorying in and transcending that element. 89–90 **In . . . crownets** i.e., Among his retainers (those who would wear his livery) were kings and princes   91 **plates** coins   95 **nor ever were** or if there never existed   96 **It's . . . dreaming** no dream can come up to it, my image of him.   96–9 **Nature . . . quite** Nature lacks material to equal the remarkable forms produced by fancy or imagination; yet an Antony such as I have pictured forth would himself be a work of nature, in fact would be Nature's masterpiece in competition with the imagination.   101 **As . . . weight** commensurate with the weightiness of the loss.   101–2 **Would . . . feel** May I never succeed at what I desire if I do not feel   103 **rebound** reflection   106 **would** wish

114 **thus** i.e., that I kneel and obey you   116 **Take . . . thoughts** Don't torment yourself with reproaches or regrets.   118 **in our flesh** i.e. in the wounds and losses we have suffered in battle   119 **sir** master   120 **project** set forth   121 **To** as to.   **clear** free of blame   122 **before** since the beginning of time   124 **enforce** press home.   125 **If . . . intents** If you comply with my plans   128 **lay . . . cruelty** force me to be cruel   129 **bereave** rob   133 **And may** i.e., (1) You may leave when you choose (2) You may have your will in anything   134 **scutcheons** shields showing armorial bearings; hence, shields hung up as monuments of victory   135 **Hang** be hung up in display as your trophies. (But with a hidden suggestion of "be hanged as your captives.")   136 **in all for Cleopatra** i.e., in all matters pertaining to yourself.   137 **brief** list, summary   139 **Not . . . admitted** petty things omitted.

CAESAR
    Nay, blush not, Cleopatra. I approve
    Your wisdom in the deed.
CLEOPATRA                    See, Caesar! Oh, behold
    How pomp is followed! Mine will now be yours,        150
    And, should we shift estates, yours would be mine.   151
    The ingratitude of this Seleucus does
    Even make me wild.—Oh, slave, of no more trust
    Than love that's hired! [*Seleucus retreats from her.*]
        What, goest thou back? Thou shalt             154
    Go back, I warrant thee! But I'll catch thine eyes,
    Though they had wings. Slave, soulless villain, dog!
    Oh, rarely base!
CAESAR                  Good Queen, let us entreat you.   157
CLEOPATRA
    Oh, Caesar, what a wounding shame is this,
    That thou vouchsafing here to visit me,
    Doing the honor of thy lordliness                   160
    To one so meek, that mine own servant should        161
    Parcel the sum of my disgraces by                   162
    Addition of his envy! Say, good Caesar,             163
    That I some lady trifles have reserved,             164
    Immoment toys, things of such dignity               165
    As we greet modern friends withal, and say          166
    Some nobler token I have kept apart
    For Livia and Octavia, to induce                    168
    Their mediation; must I be unfolded                 169
    With one that I have bred? The gods! It smites me   170
    Beneath the fall I have. [*To Seleucus*] Prithee, go hence,  171
    Or I shall show the cinders of my spirits           172
    Through th'ashes of my chance. Wert thou a man,     173
    Thou wouldst have mercy on me.                      174
CAESAR    Forbear, Seleucus.          [*Exit Seleucus.*]
CLEOPATRA
    Be it known that we, the greatest, are misthought   176
    For things that others do; and when we fall
    We answer others' merits in our name,               178
    Are therefore to be pitied.
CAESAR                    Cleopatra,
    Not what you have reserved nor what acknowledged
    Put we i'th' roll of conquest. Still be't yours;
    Bestow it at your pleasure, and believe
    Caesar's no merchant, to make prize with you        183
    Of things that merchants sold. Therefore be cheered.
    Make not your thoughts your prisons. No, dear
        Queen,                                          185
    For we intend so to dispose you as                  186

150 **How . . . followed!** how greatness is served!   **Mine** All the pomp and
followers that attend me   151 **shift estates** reverse fortunes   154 **hired**
paid for.   157 **rarely** exceptionally.   **entreat you** i.e., entreat you to let
this matter go.   160–1 **Doing . . . meek** stooping in your lordly greatness
to honor such a meek and submissive person as myself   161–3 **should . . .
envy** itemize and add to my discomfiture in such a spiteful way.   163 **Say**
Suppose for a moment   164 **lady** ladylike, feminine   165 **Immoment
toys** trifles of no importance   166 **modern** ordinary.   **withal** with
168 **Livia** Octavius Caesar's wife   168–9 **to . . . mediation** in hopes that
they might intercede on my behalf   169–70 **unfolded . . . bred** exposed
by one of my household.   171 **Beneath . . . have** even more woundingly
than my own disgrace.   172 **cinders** smoldering hot coals   173 **chance**
(fallen) fortune.   173–4 **Wert . . . on me** i.e., If you were a real man instead
of a eunuch, you wouldn't behave in such an unmanly fashion.   176 **mis-
thought** misjudged   178 **We . . . name** we are held accountable for the
deeds of others done in our name   183 **make prize** haggle   185 **Make . . .
prisons** i.e., Don't imprison yourself in your thoughts by misconceiving of
your situation.   186 **dispose** dispose of

    Yourself shall give us counsel. Feed and sleep.
    Our care and pity is so much upon you
    That we remain your friend; and so adieu.
CLEOPATRA
    My master, and my lord!
CAESAR                    Not so. Adieu.
            *Flourish. Exeunt Caesar and his train.*
CLEOPATRA
    He words me, girls, he words me, that I should not   191
    Be noble to myself. But hark thee, Charmian.         192
            [*She whispers to Charmian.*]
IRAS
    Finish, good lady. The bright day is done,
    And we are for the dark.
CLEOPATRA [*to Charmian*]    Hie thee again.             194
    I have spoke already, and it is provided;            195
    Go put it to the haste.
CHARMIAN                Madam, I will.

        *Enter Dolabella.*

DOLABELLA
    Where's the Queen?
CHARMIAN              Behold, sir.           [*Exit.*]
CLEOPATRA                    Dolabella!
DOLABELLA
    Madam, as thereto sworn by your command,
    Which my love makes religion to obey,
    I tell you this: Caesar through Syria
    Intends his journey, and within three days
    You with your children will he send before.
    Make your best use of this. I have performed
    Your pleasure and my promise.
CLEOPATRA                    Dolabella,
    I shall remain your debtor.
DOLABELLA                I your servant.
    Adieu, good Queen. I must attend on Caesar.
CLEOPATRA
    Farewell, and thanks.            *Exit [Dolabella].*
            Now, Iras, what think'st thou?
    Thou an Egyptian puppet shall be shown
    In Rome as well as I. Mechanic slaves               209
    With greasy aprons, rules, and hammers shall        210
    Uplift us to the view. In their thick breaths,
    Rank of gross diet, shall we be enclouded           212
    And forced to drink their vapor.
IRAS                    The gods forbid!                213
CLEOPATRA
    Nay, 'tis most certain, Iras. Saucy lictors         214
    Will catch at us like strumpets, and scald rhymers  215
    Ballad us out o' tune. The quick comedians          216
    Extemporally will stage us and present              217

191–2 **he words . . . myself** he tries to deceive me with mere words
to keep me from suicide.   194 **Hie thee again** Return quickly.
195 **spoke** given orders (for the means of suicide)   209 **Mechanic
slaves** Common laborers   210 **rules** straight-edged measuring sticks
212 **Rank . . . diet** reeking of coarse food   213 **drink** drink in, breathe
deeply   214 **lictors** minor officials in attendance on Roman magistrates   215 **scald** scurvy   216 **Ballad us** sing ballads about us.
**quick** quick-witted   217 **Extemporally** in improvised performance

Our Alexandrian revels; Antony
Shall be brought drunken forth, and I shall see
Some squeaking Cleopatra boy my greatness     220
I'th' posture of a whore.

IRAS                O the good gods!

CLEOPATRA   Nay, that's certain.

IRAS
I'll never see't! For I am sure my nails
Are stronger than mine eyes.

CLEOPATRA            Why, that's the way
To fool their preparation and to conquer
Their most absurd intents.

*Enter Charmian.*

                Now, Charmian!
Show me, my women, like a queen. Go fetch    227
My best attires. I am again for Cydnus,        228
To meet Mark Antony. Sirrah Iras, go—        229
Now, noble Charmian, we'll dispatch indeed—   230
And when thou hast done this chare I'll give thee
   leave                                   231
To play till doomsday. Bring our crown and all.   232
         *[Exit Iras.] A noise within.*
Wherefore's this noise?

*Enter a Guardsman.*

GUARDSMAN           Here is a rural fellow
That will not be denied Your Highness' presence.
He brings you figs.

CLEOPATRA
Let him come in.                 *Exit Guardsman.*
             What poor an instrument    236
May do a noble deed! He brings me liberty.
My resolution's placed, and I have nothing     238
Of woman in me. Now from head to foot
I am marble-constant; now the fleeting moon    240
No planet is of mine.

*Enter Guardsman, and Clown [bringing in a
basket].*

GUARDSMAN          This is the man.      241

CLEOPATRA   Avoid, and leave him.    *Exit Guardsman.* 242
Hast thou the pretty worm of Nilus there,      243
That kills and pains not?

CLOWN    Truly, I have him, but I would not be the party
that should desire you to touch him, for his biting is
immortal. Those that do die of it do seldom or never 247
recover.

CLEOPATRA   Remember'st thou any that have died on't? 249

CLOWN    Very many, men and women too. I heard of 250
one of them no longer than yesterday—a very honest
woman, but something given to lie, as a woman 252
should not do but in the way of honesty—how she
died of the biting of it, what pain she felt. Truly, she
makes a very good report o'th' worm. But he that will
believe all that they say shall never be saved by half 256
that they do. But this is most falliable, the worm's an 257
odd worm.

CLEOPATRA   Get thee hence, farewell.

CLOWN    I wish you all joy of the worm.
               *[He sets down his basket.]*

CLEOPATRA   Farewell.

CLOWN    You must think this, look you, that the worm
will do his kind.                             263

CLEOPATRA   Ay, ay; farewell.

CLOWN    Look you, the worm is not to be trusted but in
the keeping of wise people, for indeed there is no
goodness in the worm.

CLEOPATRA   Take thou no care; it shall be heeded.     268

CLOWN    Very good. Give it nothing, I pray you, for it is
not worth the feeding.

CLEOPATRA   Will it eat me?

CLOWN    You must not think I am so simple but I know
the devil himself will not eat a woman. I know that a
woman is a dish for the gods, if the devil dress her 274
not. But truly, these same whoreson devils do the 275
gods great harm in their women, for in every ten that
they make, the devils mar five.

CLEOPATRA   Well, get thee gone. Farewell.

CLOWN    Yes, forsooth. I wish you joy o'th' worm.
                               *Exit.*

*[Enter Iras with royal attire.]*

CLEOPATRA
Give me my robe. Put on my crown. I have
Immortal longings in me. Now no more         281
The juice of Egypt's grape shall moist this lip.
             *[The women dress her.]*
Yare, yare, good Iras; quick. Methinks I hear     283
Antony call; I see him rouse himself
To praise my noble act. I hear him mock
The luck of Caesar, which the gods give men     286
To excuse their after wrath. Husband, I come!    287
Now to that name my courage prove my title!     288
I am fire and air; my other elements             289

---

**220 boy** (Allusion to the practice of having women's parts acted by boys on the Elizabethan stage.)   **227 Show** Display   **228–9 I . . . Antony** (See 2.2.196 ff.)   **229 Sirrah** (Compare *sirs*, addressed to the women, in 4.15.90.)   **230 dispatch** (1) finish (2) hasten   **231 chare** task, chore   **232.1 *Exit Iras*** (It is possible that Charmian leaves, too.)   **236 What** How   **238 placed** fixed   **240 fleeting** inconstant, changing   **241 planet** (The Greek word *planetes* means "wanderer," a heavenly body that moves among the fixed stars.)   **s.d. *Clown*** rustic   **242 Avoid** Withdraw   **243 worm** snake, serpent. (But elsewhere in this scene with the added connotations of "the male sexual organ" and "earthworm.")   **247 immortal** (Blunder for "mortal.")   **249 on't** of it.

**250 heard of** heard from   **252 to lie** (With sexual second meaning hinted at also in *honest*, i.e., "chaste," *die*, i.e., "reach orgasm," and *worm*.)   **256 all . . . half** (The Clown comically reverses the sensible order of these two words.)   **257 falliable** (Blunder for "infallible.")   **263 his kind** its natural function.   **268 Take thou no care** Don't worry   **274 dress** prepare, as in cooking. (With a suggestion also of dressing in alluring clothes.)   **275 whoreson** i.e., rascally, abominable. (A slang expression.)   **281 Immortal longings** longings for immortality   **283 Yare** Quickly   **286–7 which . . . wrath** the luck that the gods give men when they intend to mock and punish them subsequently for their hubris.   **288 to . . . title!** may my courage prove my right to call myself Antony's wife!   **289 other elements** i.e., earth and water, the heavier elements

I give to baser life. So, have you done?
Come then, and take the last warmth of my lips.
Farewell, kind Charmian. Iras, long farewell.
                              [*She kisses them. Iras falls and dies.*]
Have I the aspic in my lips? Dost fall?                           293
If thou and nature can so gently part,
The stroke of death is as a lover's pinch,
Which hurts, and is desired. Dost thou lie still?
If thus thou vanishest, thou tell'st the world
It is not worth leave-taking.                                     298

CHARMIAN
Dissolve, thick cloud, and rain, that I may say
The gods themselves do weep!
CLEOPATRA                           This proves me base.          300
If she first meet the curlèd Antony,                              301
He'll make demand of her, and spend that kiss                     302
Which is my heaven to have. [*To an asp*] Come, thou
   mortal wretch,                                                 303
With thy sharp teeth this knot intrinsicate                       304
Of life at once untie. Poor venomous fool,
Be angry, and dispatch. Oh, couldst thou speak,
That I might hear thee call great Caesar ass
Unpolicied!
CHARMIAN      O eastern star!
CLEOPATRA                           Peace, peace!                 308
Dost thou not see my baby at my breast,
That sucks the nurse asleep?
CHARMIAN                  Oh, break! Oh, break!
CLEOPATRA
As sweet as balm, as soft as air, as gentle—
O Antony!—Nay, I will take thee too.
                        [*Applying another asp to her arm.*]
What should I stay—                         *Dies.* 313
CHARMIAN
In this wild world? So, fare thee well.                           314
Now boast thee, Death, in thy possession lies
A lass unparalleled. Downy windows, close;                        316
And golden Phoebus never be beheld                                317
Of eyes again so royal! Your crown's awry;                        318
I'll mend it, and then play—                                      319

*Enter the Guard, rustling in.*

FIRST GUARD
Where's the Queen?
CHARMIAN                Speak softly. Wake her not.
FIRST GUARD
Caesar hath sent—
CHARMIAN                Too slow a messenger.
                        [*She applies an asp to herself.*]

Oh, come apace, dispatch! I partly feel thee.
FIRST GUARD
Approach, ho! All's not well. Caesar's beguiled.                  323
SECOND GUARD
There's Dolabella sent from Caesar. Call him.
                                        [*Exit a guard.*]
FIRST GUARD
What work is here, Charmian? Is this well done?
CHARMIAN
It is well done, and fitting for a princess
Descended of so many royal kings.
Ah, soldier!                             *Charmian dies.*

*Enter Dolabella.*

DOLABELLA
How goes it here?
SECOND GUARD          All dead.
DOLABELLA                      Caesar, thy thoughts
Touch their effects in this. Thyself art coming          330
To see performed the dreaded act which thou
So sought'st to hinder.

*Enter Caesar and all his train, marching.*

ALL    A way there, a way for Caesar!                    333
DOLABELLA
Oh, sir, you are too sure an augurer;
That you did fear is done.
CAESAR                      Bravest at the last,          335
She leveled at our purposes and, being royal,            336
Took her own way. The manner of their deaths?
I do not see them bleed.
DOLABELLA                  Who was last with them?
FIRST GUARD
A simple countryman, that brought her figs.              339
This was his basket.
CAESAR               Poisoned, then.
FIRST GUARD                          Oh, Caesar,
This Charmian lived but now; she stood and spake.
I found her trimming up the diadem
On her dead mistress; tremblingly she stood,
And on the sudden dropped.
CAESAR                     Oh, noble weakness!
If they had swallowed poison, 'twould appear
By external swelling; but she looks like sleep,          346
As she would catch another Antony                        347
In her strong toil of grace.
DOLABELLA                    Here on her breast           348
There is a vent of blood and something blown;            349
The like is on her arm.

---

293 **aspic** asp   298 **is . . . leave-taking** does not deserve a ceremonious farewell.   **300 base** ignoble.   **301 curlèd** with curled hair
**302 make demand** (1) ask questions (2) ask pleasure.   **spend that
kiss** expend his desire on her   **303 mortal** deadly.   **wretch** (An
affectionate term of abuse, like *fool* in line 305.)   **304 intrinsicate**
intricate   **308 Unpolicied** outwitted.   **eastern star** i.e., Venus,
the morning star, here applied to Cleopatra.   **313 What** Why
**314 wild** savage. (Sometimes taken to be a variant of *vild*, "vile.")
**316 Downy windows** i.e., Soft eyelids   **317 golden Phoebus** the
sun   **318 Of** by   **319 mend** fix, straighten

323 **beguiled** cheated, tricked.   **330 Touch their effects** meet with
realization   **333 A way** Make a path   **335 That** that which   **336 leveled at** aimed at, guessed   **339 simple** humbly born   **346 like sleep**
as if asleep   **347 As** as if   **348 toil** net   **349 vent** discharge.   **blown**
deposited, or, swollen

**FIRST GUARD**
This is an aspic's trail, and these fig leaves
Have slime upon them, such as th'aspic leaves
Upon the caves of Nile.
**CAESAR**                    Most probable
That so she died; for her physician tells me
She hath pursued conclusions infinite                        355
Of easy ways to die. Take up her bed,
And bear her women from the monument.
She shall be buried by her Antony.
No grave upon the earth shall clip in it                     359

**355 conclusions** experimental results   **359 clip** embrace, clasp

A pair so famous. High events as these
Strike those that make them; and their story is             361
No less in pity than his glory which                         362
Brought them to be lamented. Our army shall                 363
In solemn show attend this funeral,
And then to Rome. Come, Dolabella, see
High order in this great solemnity.                          366
              *Exeunt omnes, [bearing the dead bodies].*

**361 Strike . . . them** touch with sorrow those who brought about these deeds   **361–3 their story . . . lamented** the story of these famous lovers is no less pitiable than the fame of him (Octavius Caesar) who brought them low is glorious.   **366.1 *omnes*** all

# The Romances

*The Winter's Tale*     *The Tempest*

# The Winter's Tale

*T*he *Winter's Tale* (c. 1609–1611), with its almost symmetrical division into two halves of bleak tragedy and comic romance, illustrates perhaps more clearly than any other Shakespearean play the genre of tragicomedy. To be sure, all the late romances feature journeys of separation, apparent deaths, and tearful reconciliations. Marina and Thaisa in *Pericles*, Imogen in *Cymbeline*, and Ferdinand in *The Tempest*, all supposed irrecoverably lost, are brought back to life by apparently miraculous devices. Of the four late romances, however, *The Winter's Tale* uses the most formal structure to evoke the antithesis of tragedy and romance. It is sharply divided into contrasting halves by a gap of sixteen years. The tragic first half takes place almost entirely in Sicilia, whereas the action of the second half is limited for the most part to Bohemia. At the court of Sicilia, we see tyrannical jealousy producing a spiritual climate of "winter / In storm perpetual"; in Bohemia, we witness a pastoral landscape and a sheep-shearing evoking "the sweet o'th' year," "When daffodils begin to peer" (3.2.212–13; 4.3.1–3). Paradoxically, the contrast between the two halves is intensified by parallels between the two: both begin with Camillo onstage and proceed to scenes of confrontation and jealousy in which, ironically, the innocent cause of jealousy in the first half, Polixenes, becomes the jealous tyrant of the second half. The mirroring reminds us of the cyclical nature of time and the hope it brings of renewal as we move from tragedy to romantic comedy.

Although this motif of a renewing journey from jaded court to idealized countryside reminds us of *As You Like It* and other early comedies, we sense in the late romances and especially in *The Winter's Tale* a new preoccupation with humanity's tragic folly. The vision of human depravity is world-weary and pessimistic, as though infected by the gloomy spirit of the great tragedies. And because humanity is so bent on destroying itself, the restoration is at once more urgently needed and more

miraculous than in the "festive" world of early comedy. Renewal is mythically associated with the seasonal cycle from winter to summer.

King Leontes's tragedy seems at first irreversible and terrifying, like that of Shakespeare's greatest tragic protagonists. He suffers from irrational jealousy, as does Othello, and attempts to destroy the person on whom all his happiness depends. As with Othello, his jealousy stems from a characteristically male fear of inadequacy and rejection. Unlike Othello, however, Leontes needs no diabolical tempter such as Iago to poison his mind against Queen Hermione. Leontes is undone by his own fantasies. No differences in race or age can explain Leontes's fears of estrangement from Hermione. She is not imprudent in her conduct, like her counterpart in Robert Greene's *Pandosto* (1588), the prose romance from which Shakespeare drew his narrative. Although Hermione is graciously fond of Leontes's dear friend Polixenes and urges him to stay longer in Sicilia, she does so only with a hospitable warmth demanded by the occasion and encouraged by her husband. In every way, then, Shakespeare strips away from Leontes the motive and the occasion for plausible doubting of his wife. All observers in the Sicilian court are incredulous and shocked at the King's accusations. Even so, Leontes is neither an unsympathetic nor an unbelievable character. Like Othello, Leontes cherishes his wife and perceives with a horrifying intensity what a fearful cost they both must pay for his suspicions. Not only his marriage, but also his lifelong friendship with Polixenes, his sense of pride in his children, and his enjoyment of his subjects' warm regard, all must be sacrificed to a single overwhelming compulsion.

Whatever may be the psychological cause of this obsession, it manifests itself as a revulsion against all sexual behavior. Like mad Lear, Leontes imagines lechery to be the unavoidable fact of the cosmos and of the human condition, the lowest common denominator to which all persons (including Hermione) must stoop. He is persuaded that "It is a bawdy planet," in which cuckolded man has "his pond fished by his next neighbor, by / Sir Smile, his neighbor" (1.2.195–201). Leontes's tortured soliloquies are laden with sexual images, of unattended "gates" letting in and out the enemy "With bag and baggage," and of a "dagger" that must be "muzzled / Lest it should bite its master" (lines 197, 206, 156–7). As in *King Lear*, order is inverted to disorder, sanity to madness, legitimacy to illegitimacy. Sexual misconduct is emblematic of a universal malaise: "Why, then the world and all that's in't is nothing, / The covering sky is nothing, Bohemia nothing, / My wife is nothing" (lines 292–4). Other characters, too, see the trial of Hermione as a testing of humanity's worth: if Hermione proves false, Antigonus promises, he will treat his own wife as a stable horse and will "geld" his three daughters (2.1.148). Prevailing images are of spiders, venom, infection, sterility, and the "dungy earth" (line 158).

Cosmic order is never really challenged, however, even though the human suffering is very real and the injustice to women especially apparent. Leontes's fantasies of universal disorder are chimerical. His wife is, in fact, chaste, Polixenes true, and the King's courtiers loyal. Camillo refuses to carry out Leontes's order to murder Polixenes, not only because he knows murder to be wrong, but also because history offers not one example of a man "that had struck anointed kings / And flourished after" (1.2.357–8). The cosmos of this play is one in which crimes are invariably and swiftly punished. The Delphic oracle vindicates Hermione and gives Leontes stern warning. When Leontes persists in his madness, his son Mamillius's death follows as an immediate consequence. As Leontes at once perceives, "Apollo's angry, and the heavens themselves / Do strike at my injustice" (3.2.146–7). Leontes paradoxically welcomes the lengthy contrition he must undergo, for it confirms a pattern in the universe of just cause and effect. Although as tragic protagonist he has discovered the truth about Hermione moments too late and so must pay richly for his error, Leontes has at least recovered faith in Hermione's transcendent goodness. His nightmare now over, he accepts and embraces suffering as a necessary atonement.

The transition to romance is therefore anticipated to an extent by the play's first half, even though the tone of the last two acts is strikingly different. The old Shepherd signals a momentous change when he speaks to his son of a cataclysmic storm and a ravenous bear set in opposition to the miraculous discovery of a child: "Now bless thyself. Thou met'st with things dying, I with things newborn" (3.3.110–11). Time comes onstage as Chorus, like Gower in *Pericles*, to remind us of the conscious artifice of the dramatist. He can "o'erthrow law" and carry us over sixteen years as if we had merely dreamed out the interim (4.1). Shakespeare flaunts the improbability

of his story by giving Bohemia a seacoast (much to the dismay of Ben Jonson) and by bringing onstage either a live bear or an actor costumed as one ("*Exit, pursued by a bear,*" 3.3.57 s.d.). The narrative uses many typical devices of romance: a babe abandoned to the elements, a princess brought up by shepherds, a prince disguised as a swain, a sea voyage, and a recognition scene. Love is threatened, not by the internal psychic obstacle of jealousy, but by the external obstacles of parental opposition and a seeming disparity of social rank between the lovers. Comedy easily finds solutions for such difficulties by the unraveling of illusion. This comic world also properly includes clownish shepherds, coy shepherdesses, and Autolycus, the roguish peddler, whose machinations contribute in an unforeseen manner to the working out of the love plot. Autolycus is in many ways the presiding genius of the play's second half, as dominant a character as Leontes in the first half and one whose delightful function is to do good "against my will" (5.2.125). In this paradox of knavery converted surprisingly to benign ends, we see how the comic providence of Shakespeare's tragicomic world makes use of the most implausible and outrageous happenings in pursuit of its own inscrutable design.

The conventional romantic ending is infused, however, with a sadness and a mystery that take the play well beyond what is usual in comedy. Mamillius and Antigonus are really dead, and that irredeemable fact is not forgotten in the play's final happy moments. Hermione, although vindicated by the gods, has suffered public shame, the death of one child, separation from her other child, and prolonged isolation from her husband; like Imogen in *Cymbeline*, she has had to endure the consequences of male frailty and thereby redeem her husband through her suffering. Her husband, having thrown her aside, must, like Pericles, rediscover and learn to cherish the woman he once chose who now has aged; he must reconfirm his marriage to her, even as he learns to accept the marriage of his daughter to a younger man. All of these crucial turnings hinge upon Shakespeare's most notable departure from his source, Greene's *Pandosto*: Hermione is brought back to life. All observers regard this event, and the rediscovery of Perdita, as grossly implausible, "so like an old tale that the verity of it is in strong suspicion" (5.2.29–30). The play's very title, *The Winter's Tale*, reinforces this sense of naive improbability. Why does Shakespeare stress this riddling paradox of an unbelievable reality, and why does he deliberately mislead his audience into believing that Hermione has, in fact, died (3.3.15–45), using a kind of theatrical trickery found in no other Shakespearean play? The answer may well be that, in Paulina's words, we must awake our faith, accepting a narrative of death and return to life that cannot ultimately be comprehended by reason. On the rational level, we are told that Hermione has been kept in hiding for sixteen years, in order to fulfill the condition of the oracle that Leontes is to live without an heir (and hence without a wife) until Perdita is found. Such an explanation seems psychologically incomprehensible, however, for it demands that Hermione live in extended isolation and that Paulina serve as the King's conscience for such a long period of time without any way for the participants to know when their suffering will end. Instead, we are drawn toward an emblematic interpretation, bearing in mind that it is more an evocative hint than a complete truth. Throughout the play, Hermione has been repeatedly associated with "Grace" and with the goddess Proserpina, whose return from the underworld, after "Three crabbèd months had soured themselves to death" (1.2.102), signals the coming of spring. Perdita, also associated with Proserpina (4.4.116), is welcomed by her father "As is the spring to th' earth" (5.1.152). The emphasis on the bond of father and daughter, so characteristic of Shakespeare's late plays and especially his romances, goes importantly beyond the patriarchalism of Shakespeare's earlier history plays in its exploration of family relationships. Paulina has a similarly emblematic role, that of Conscience, patiently guiding the King to a divinely appointed renewal of his joy. Paulina speaks of herself as an artist figure, like Prospero in *The Tempest*, performing wonders of illusion, though she rejects the assistance of wicked powers. These emblematic hints do not rob the story of its human drama, but they do lend a transcendent significance to Leontes's bittersweet story of sinful error, affliction, and an unexpected second happiness.

On stage in recent decades, the play has shown its remarkable dramaturgic effectiveness, especially in the restoration of Hermione to her husband as a living and breathing statue. Peter Brook, at the Phoenix Theatre in London, 1951, chose a permanent set to underscore the play's malleable swift action and its need for the audience to participate imaginatively in the fashioning of theatrical illusion. Trevor Nunn's set at Stratford-upon-Avon in 1969 was a three-sided white box in which nothing was realistically represented. Nunn and John Barton, at Stratford-upon-Avon in 1976, visualized bears everywhere: in motifs of wall hangings and carpets, in a bearskin draped on a couch. The violent irrationality of Ian McKellen's Leontes seemed plausible in such a symbolic and mythic landscape. In Terry Hands's 1986 production also at Stratford-upon-Avon, a huge bear rug on the cool marble floor of Leontes's Regency palace during the play's first half became, in Bohemia, the live bear that tore into the shoulder of Antigonus. Above all, the apparent bringing back to life of Hermione's statue in the final scene has proven again and again to be a masterly *coup de théâtre*. What we see in the theater is of course an illusion, but at what level? Are we to understand that a statue comes to life? Much depends on the actress's skill in appearing motionless and then warm to her husband's touch. The moment is indeed one calculated to awaken our faith in the miracle of renewal and in the power of art to confound illusion and reality. We are led to ponder deeply the mysteries of our own uncertain existence.

# The Winter's Tale

## The Names of the Actors

LEONTES, *King of Sicilia*
MAMILLIUS, *young prince of Sicilia*
CAMILLO,
ANTIGONUS,  } *four Lords of Sicilia*
CLEOMENES,
DION,

HERMIONE, *Queen to Leontes*
PERDITA, *daughter to Leontes and Hermione*
PAULINA, *wife to Antigonus*
EMILIA, *a lady [attending on Hermione]*

POLIXENES, *King of Bohemia*
FLORIZEL, *Prince of Bohemia*
ARCHIDAMUS, *a lord of Bohemia*
Old SHEPHERD, *reputed father of Perdita*
CLOWN, *his son*
AUTOLYCUS, *a rogue*

[SCENE: *Sicilia, and Bohemia*]

[MOPSA,  } *Shepherdesses*
[DORCAS,

[A MARINER
A JAILER
*Two* LADIES *attending Hermione*
*Two* SERVANTS *attending Leontes*
*One or more* LORDS *attending Leontes*
*An* OFFICER *of the court*
A GENTLEMAN *attending Leontes*
*Three* GENTLEMEN *of the court of Sicilia*
A SERVANT *of the Old Shepherd*

TIME, *as Chorus*]

*Other Lords and Gentlemen, [Ladies, Officers,] and*
*Servants; Shepherds and Shepherdesses; [Twelve*
*Countrymen disguised as Satyrs]*

## 1.1

*Enter Camillo and Archidamus.*

ARCHIDAMUS  If you shall chance, Camillo, to visit Bohemia on the like occasion whereon my services are  2
now on foot, you shall see, as I have said, great  3
difference betwixt our Bohemia and your Sicilia.
CAMILLO  I think this coming summer the King of Sicilia
means to pay Bohemia the visitation which he justly  6
owes him.
ARCHIDAMUS  Wherein our entertainment shall shame  8
us, we will be justified in our loves; for indeed—  9
CAMILLO  Beseech you—

ARCHIDAMUS  Verily, I speak it in the freedom of my  11
knowledge. We cannot with such magnificence—in  12
so rare—I know not what to say. We will give you
sleepy drinks, that your senses, unintelligent of our  14
insufficience, may, though they cannot praise us, as
little accuse us.
CAMILLO  You pay a great deal too dear for what's
given freely.
ARCHIDAMUS  Believe me, I speak as my understanding
instructs me and as mine honesty puts it to utterance.
CAMILLO  Sicilia cannot show himself overkind to Bo-  21
hemia. They were trained together in their childhoods,
and there rooted betwixt them then such an affection
which cannot choose but branch now. Since their  24
more mature dignities and royal necessities made
separation of their society, their encounters, though  26

---

1.1. Location: Sicilia. The court of Leontes.
**2–3 on the . . . foot** on an occasion like this one that I am engaged in
(attending on King Polixenes)  **6 Bohemia** the King of Bohemia.
(Also at lines 21–2.)  **8–9 Wherein . . . loves** In whatever way our
attempts to entertain you will shame us by falling short, we will
make up for by our affection

**11–12 in . . . knowledge** as my knowledge entitles me to speak.
**14 sleepy** sleep-inducing.  **unintelligent** unaware  **21 Sicilia**
The King of Sicilia  **24 branch** put forth new growth, flourish.
(Also perhaps with opposite and unconscious suggestion of "divide.")
**26 their society** their being together

not personal, hath been royally attorneyed with 27
interchange of gifts, letters, loving embassies, that 28
they have seemed to be together though absent,
shook hands as over a vast, and embraced as it were 30
from the ends of opposed winds. The heavens con- 31
tinue their loves!

ARCHIDAMUS   I think there is not in the world either
malice or matter to alter it. You have an unspeakable 34
comfort of your young prince Mamillius. It is a 35
gentleman of the greatest promise that ever came into
my note. 37

CAMILLO   I very well agree with you in the hopes of
him. It is a gallant child, one that indeed physics the 39
subject, makes old hearts fresh. They that went on 40
crutches ere he was born desire yet their life to see him 41
a man.

ARCHIDAMUS   Would they else be content to die? 43

CAMILLO   Yes, if there were no other excuse why they 44
should desire to live.

ARCHIDAMUS   If the King had no son, they would desire 46
to live on crutches till he had one.           *Exeunt.* 47

## 1.2

*Enter Leontes, Hermione, Mamillius, Polixenes,
Camillo.*

POLIXENES
Nine changes of the wat'ry star hath been 1
The shepherd's note since we have left our throne 2
Without a burden. Time as long again 3
Would be filled up, my brother, with our thanks,
And yet we should for perpetuity 5
Go hence in debt. And therefore, like a cipher, 6
Yet standing in rich place, I multiply 7
With one "We thank you" many thousands more
That go before it.

LEONTES             Stay your thanks awhile 9
And pay them when you part.

POLIXENES                     Sir, that's tomorrow.
I am questioned by my fears of what may chance 11
Or breed upon our absence, that may blow 12
No sneaping winds at home to make us say, 13
"This is put forth too truly." Besides, I have stayed 14

To tire your royalty.
LEONTES               We are tougher, brother,
Than you can put us to't.
POLIXENES               No longer stay. 16
LEONTES
One sev'nnight longer.
POLIXENES               Very sooth, tomorrow. 17
LEONTES
We'll part the time between 's, then, and in that 18
I'll no gainsaying.
POLIXENES           Press me not, beseech you, so. 19
There is no tongue that moves, none, none i' th' world
So soon as yours could win me. So it should now,
Were there necessity in your request, although 22
'Twere needful I denied it. My affairs
Do even drag me homeward, which to hinder
Were in your love a whip to me, my stay 25
To you a charge and trouble. To save both, 26
Farewell, our brother.
LEONTES             Tongue-tied, our Queen? Speak you.
HERMIONE
I had thought, sir, to have held my peace until 28
You had drawn oaths from him not to stay. You, sir, 29
Charge him too coldly. Tell him you are sure
All in Bohemia's well; this satisfaction 31
The bygone day proclaimed. Say this to him, 32
He's beat from his best ward.
LEONTES               Well said, Hermione. 33
HERMIONE
To tell he longs to see his son were strong. 34
But let him say so then, and let him go.
But let him swear so and he shall not stay; 36
We'll thwack him hence with distaffs. 37
[*To Polixenes*] Yet of your royal presence I'll adventure 38
The borrow of a week. When at Bohemia 39
You take my lord, I'll give him my commission 40
To let him there a month behind the gest 41
Prefixed for 's parting.—Yet, good deed, Leontes, 42
I love thee not a jar o' th' clock behind 43
What lady she her lord.—You'll stay?
POLIXENES                     No, madam. 44
HERMIONE
Nay, but you will?
POLIXENES           I may not, verily.
HERMIONE   Verily?

---

**27 personal** in person.   **attorneyed** carried out by deputy   **28 that** so that   **30 vast** boundless space   **31 ends . . . winds** i.e., opposite ends of the earth.   **The heavens** May the heavens   **34 unspeakable** inexpressible   **35 of** in the person of.   **It** He (Also in line 39.)   **37 note** observation.   **39–40 physics the subject** brings health to the subjects of this kingdom   **40–1 went on crutches** i.e., were old and infirm   **41 their life** to continue living   **43 else** otherwise   **44 excuse** reason   **46–7 If . . . one** Even if there were no living heir to the throne, these old people would still wish to go on living in hopes of one.
**1.2. Location: The same.**
**1 wat'ry star** moon. (The moon is governor of tides.)   **2 note** observation. (Shepherds and other simple folk mark the passage of months by the moon.)   **we** I. (The royal "we.")   **3 burden** occupant.   **5–6 And . . . debt** and yet I still would depart forever unable to repay the debt I owe for your hospitality.   **5 for perpetuity** forever   **6–7 like . . . place** like a zero at the end of a number, increasing its value by powers of ten, though of itself without value   **9 Stay** Postpone   **11–14 I am . . . truly** I am anxious about what may happen in my absence, especially a stirring up of envy and backbiting that would cause me to say my fears were all too plausible.

**16 Than . . . to't** than anything you can do to try me.   **No longer** I can no longer   **17 sev'nnight** week.   **Very sooth** Truly   **18 part the time** split the difference, i.e., divide a week in two   **19 I'll no gainsaying** I won't take "no" for an answer.   **beseech** I beseech   **22 although** even if   **25 Were . . . to me** would be a punishment to me, though done lovingly   **26 charge** expense, burden   **28–9 I . . . to stay** i.e., I almost thought that you were going to get him to swear he *won't* stay, before I got a chance to say anything.   **31–2 this . . . proclaimed** yesterday brought news to satisfy on that score.   **32 Say** If you say   **33 ward** defensive posture. (A fencing term.)   **34 tell** tell us that.   **were strong** would be a strong argument.   **36 he shall not stay** i.e., we wouldn't let him stay even if he wanted to   **37 distaffs** sticks used in spinning, here employed as a domestic kind of weapon.   **38 adventure** risk   **39 borrow** borrowing   **40 commission** permission   **41–2 To . . . parting** to let him stay there a month longer than the originally agreed-upon time (the "gest") for his departure.   **42 good deed** indeed   **43–4 I love . . . lord** I love you not even a tiny bit (literally, a tick of the clock) less than any noble lady loves her husband.

You put me off with limber vows; but I,                                47
Though you would seek t'unsphere the stars with
    oaths,
Should yet say, "Sir, no going." Verily,
You shall not go. A lady's "verily" is
As potent as a lord's. Will you go yet?
Force me to keep you as a prisoner,
Not like a guest: so you shall pay your fees                           53
When you depart, and save your thanks. How say
    you?
My prisoner or my guest? By your dread "verily,"
One of them you shall be.

POLIXENES              Your guest, then, madam.
To be your prisoner should import offending,                           57
Which is for me less easy to commit
Than you to punish.

HERMIONE         Not your jailer, then,
But your kind hostess. Come, I'll question you
Of my lord's tricks and yours when you were boys.
You were pretty lordings then?

POLIXENES           We were, fair Queen,        62
Two lads that thought there was no more behind             63
But such a day tomorrow as today,
And to be boy eternal.

HERMIONE        Was not my lord
The verier wag o'th' two?                                              66

POLIXENES
We were as twinned lambs that did frisk i'th' sun
And bleat the one at th'other. What we changed             68
Was innocence for innocence; we knew not
The doctrine of ill-doing, nor dreamed
That any did. Had we pursued that life,
And our weak spirits ne'er been higher reared
With stronger blood, we should have answered
    heaven                                                                73
Boldly "Not guilty," the imposition cleared               74
Hereditary ours.

HERMIONE      By this we gather                        75
You have tripped since.

POLIXENES        Oh, my most sacred lady,
Temptations have since then been born to 's, for
In those unfledged days was my wife a girl;               78
Your precious self had then not crossed the eyes
Of my young playfellow.

HERMIONE        Grace to boot!                          80
Of this make no conclusion, lest you say                   81
Your queen and I are devils. Yet go on.
Th'offenses we have made you do we'll answer,             83
If you first sinned with us, and that with us
You did continue fault, and that you slipped not

With any but with us.

LEONTES          Is he won yet?                       86

HERMIONE
He'll stay, my lord.

LEONTES         At my request he would not.
Hermione, my dearest, thou never spok'st
To better purpose.

HERMIONE      Never?

LEONTES          Never but once.

HERMIONE
What? Have I twice said well? When was 't before?
I prithee, tell me. Cram 's with praise and make 's        91
As fat as tame things. One good deed dying
    tongueless                                                           92
Slaughters a thousand waiting upon that.                   93
Our praises are our wages. You may ride 's
With one soft kiss a thousand furlongs ere
With spur we heat an acre. But to th' goal:                96
My last good deed was to entreat his stay.
What was my first? It has an elder sister,
Or I mistake you. Oh, would her name were Grace!
But once before I spoke to the purpose. When?
Nay, let me have't; I long.

LEONTES        Why, that was when
Three crabbèd months had soured themselves to
    death
Ere I could make thee open thy white hand
And clap thyself my love. Then didst thou utter,          104
"I am yours forever."

HERMIONE      'Tis grace indeed.
Why, lo you now, I have spoke to th' purpose twice:
The one forever earned a royal husband,
Th'other for some while a friend.
             [She gives her hand to Polixenes.]

LEONTES [aside]        Too hot, too hot!
To mingle friendship far is mingling bloods.              109
I have tremor cordis on me. My heart dances,              110
But not for joy, not joy. This entertainment              111
May a free face put on, derive a liberty                  112
From heartiness, from bounty, fertile bosom,              113
And well become the agent. 'T may, I grant.               114
But to be paddling palms and pinching fingers,
As now they are, and making practiced smiles
As in a looking glass, and then to sigh, as 'twere
The mort o'th' deer; oh, that is entertainment            118
My bosom likes not, nor my brows.—Mamillius,             119
Art thou my boy?

MAMILLIUS      Ay, my good lord.

LEONTES                 I'fecks,          120

---

**47 limber** limp  **53 fees** payments demanded by jailers of prisoners at the time of their release  **57 import offending** imply my having offended  **62 lordings** young lords  **63 behind** still to come  **66 The verier wag** truly the more mischievous  **68 changed** exchanged **73 stronger blood** mature sexual passions  **74–5 the imposition . . . ours** i.e., being freed from original sin itself (if we had continued in that state); or, excepting of course the original sin that is the common condition of all mortals.  **78 unfledged** not yet feathered, i.e., immature  **80 Grace to boot!** Heaven help me!  **81 Of . . . conclusion** Don't follow your implied line of reasoning to its logical conclusion **83 answer** answer for

**86 Is he won yet?** (Leontes has been out of hearing for much of their conversation.)  **91 Cram's** Cram us.  **make's** make us  **92 tongueless** unpraised, unsung  **93 Slaughters . . . that** i.e., will inhibit many other good deeds that would have been inspired by that praise. **96 heat** traverse as in a race.  **to th' goal** to come to the point **104 clap** clasp hands, pledge  **109 mingling bloods** (Sexual intercourse was thought to produce a mingling of bloods.)  **110 tremor cordis** fluttering of the heart  **111 entertainment** i.e., of Polixenes by Hermione  **112 free face** innocent appearance  **113 fertile bosom** i.e., generous affection  **114 well . . . agent** do credit to the doer. **118 mort** note sounded on a horn at the death of the hunted deer **119 brows** (Alludes to cuckolds' horns, the supposed badge of men whose wives are unfaithful.)  **120 I'fecks** In faith

Why, that's my bawcock. What, hast smutched thy
   nose?                                                                      121
They say it is a copy out of mine. Come, captain,
We must be neat; not neat, but cleanly, captain.                               123
And yet the steer, the heifer, and the calf
Are all called neat.—Still virginaling                                         125
Upon his palm?—How now, you wanton calf?                                       126
Art thou my calf?

MAMILLIUS              Yes, if you will, my lord.

LEONTES
Thou want'st a rough pash and the shoots that I have   128
To be full like me. Yet they say we are                                        129
Almost as like as eggs. Women say so,
That will say anything. But were they false
As o'erdyed blacks, as wind, as waters, false                                  132
As dice are to be wished by one that fixes                                     133
No bourn twixt his and mine, yet were it true                                  134
To say this boy were like me. Come, sir page,
Look on me with your welkin eye. Sweet villain!                                136
Most dear'st! My collop! Can thy dam?—may't be?—   137
Affection, thy intention stabs the center.                                     138
Thou dost make possible things not so held,                                    139
Communicat'st with dreams—how can this be?—                                    140
With what's unreal thou coactive art,                                          141
And fellow'st nothing. Then 'tis very credent                                  142
Thou mayst cojoin with something; and thou dost,                               143
And that beyond commission, and I find it,                                     144
And that to the infection of my brains
And hard'ning of my brows.

POLIXENES           What means Sicilia?                      146

HERMIONE
He something seems unsettled.

POLIXENES           How, my lord?                          147
What cheer? How is't with you, best brother?

HERMIONE                You look
As if you held a brow of much distraction.
Are you moved, my lord?

LEONTES           No, in good earnest.                       150
How sometimes nature will betray its folly,                                    151
Its tenderness, and make itself a pastime                                      152
To harder bosoms! Looking on the lines                                         153

---

Of my boy's face, methoughts I did recoil                                      154
Twenty-three years, and saw myself unbreeched,                                 155
In my green velvet coat, my dagger muzzled                                     156
Lest it should bite its master and so prove,
As ornaments oft do, too dangerous.
How like, methought, I then was to this kernel,
This squash, this gentleman.—Mine honest friend,     160
Will you take eggs for money?                                                  161

MAMILLIUS    No, my lord, I'll fight.

LEONTES
You will? Why, happy man be 's dole!—My brother,  163
Are you so fond of your young prince as we
Do seem to be of ours?

POLIXENES          If at home, sir,
He's all my exercise, my mirth, my matter,                                     166
Now my sworn friend and then mine enemy,
My parasite, my soldier, statesman, all.
He makes a July's day short as December,
And with his varying childness cures in me                                     170
Thoughts that would thick my blood.

LEONTES              So stands this squire   171
Officed with me. We two will walk, my lord,                                    172
And leave you to your graver steps. Hermione,
How thou lov'st us, show in our brother's welcome.    174
Let what is dear in Sicily be cheap.                                           175
Next to thyself and my young rover, he's
Apparent to my heart.

HERMIONE          If you would seek us,                         177
We are yours i'th' garden. Shall 's attend you there?   178

LEONTES
To your own bents dispose you. You'll be found,       179
Be you beneath the sky. [*Aside*] I am angling now,
Though you perceive me not how I give line.           181
Go to, go to!                                                                  182
How she holds up the neb, the bill to him,            183
And arms her with the boldness of a wife              184
To her allowing husband!
         [*Exeunt Polixenes and Hermione.*]
            Gone already!                                    185
Inch thick, knee-deep, o'er head and ears a forked
   one!—                                                                    186
Go play, boy, play. Thy mother plays, and I           187
Play too, but so disgraced a part, whose issue        188

---

121 **bawcock** i.e., fine fellow. (French *beau coq*.)   123 **not . . . cleanly**
(Leontes changes the word because *neat* also means "cattle" and
hence reminds him of cuckolds' horns.)   125 **virginaling** touching
hands, as in playing on the virginals, a keyboard instrument   126
**wanton** frisky   128 **Thou . . . have** You lack a shaggy head and the
horns that I have. (Again alluding to cuckolds' horns.)   129 **full**
fully   132 **o'erdyed blacks** black garments, or ones that have been
weakened by too much dye or that have been dyed over another
color (thereby betraying a falseness in the mourner)   132–4 **false . . .
mine** as false as dice are wished false by one who intends to cheat
me, and who respects no boundary between what is his and
mine   136 **welkin** sky-blue   137 **collop** small piece of meat; i.e., of
my own flesh.   **dam** mother   138–43 **Affection . . . something**
Strong passion, your intense power pierces to the very center, the
soul. You make possible things normally considered fantastic, partak-
ing as you do of the nature of dreams. How can this be? You collabo-
rate with unreality and imagined fantasies. It's all the likelier, then,
that such imaginings may also fasten on a real object   144 **commission** what is lawful   146 **What means Sicilia?** Why is the King of
Sicilia looking so distracted?   147 **something** somewhat   150 **moved**
angry   151 **nature** i.e., affectionate feeling between parent and
child   152 **pastime** occasion for amusement   153 **To harder bosoms**
for persons who are less tender-hearted.

154 **methoughts** it seemed to me.   **recoil** i.e., go back in memory
155 **unbreeched** not yet wearing breeches   156 **muzzled** i.e., sheathed.
(With phallic suggestion.)   160 **squash** unripe peascod or pea pod.
**honest** worthy   161 **take eggs for money** i.e., be imposed upon, taken
advantage of, cheated. (Proverbial.)   163 **happy . . . dole** may good
fortune be his lot. (Proverbial.)   166 **matter** concern   170 **childness**
childlike ways   171 **thick my blood** (Melancholy thoughts were supposed to thicken the blood.)   171–2 **So . . . with me** Mamillius does the
same for me.   174–5 **How . . . cheap** (A hidden second meaning in these
lines may be intentional: show just how much you love me by the way
you encourage Polixenes's attentions and thereby cheapen the most
precious thing in Sicily.)   177 **Apparent** heir apparent (perhaps with a
suggestion too of "evident, revealed")   178 **Shall 's** Shall we   179 **To . . .
dispose you** Act according to your inclinations. (With more bitter
double meaning, continued in *You'll be found*, i.e., found out.)   181 **give
line** pay out line (to let the fish hook itself well).   182 **Go to** (An
expression of remonstrance.)   183 **the neb, the bill** her face and mouth.
("Neb" means "beak.")   184 **arms her with** assumes   185 **allowing**
approving   186 **forked** horned   187 **play** play games.   **plays** i.e., in
a sexual liaison   188 **Play** play a role.   **issue** outcome. (With a pun
on the sense of "offspring" and "theatrical exit.")

Will hiss me to my grave. Contempt and clamor
Will be my knell. Go play, boy, play. There have been,
Or I am much deceived, cuckolds ere now;
And many a man there is, even at this present,
Now while I speak this, holds his wife by th' arm,
That little thinks she has been sluiced in 's absence    194
And his pond fished by his next neighbor, by
Sir Smile, his neighbor. Nay, there's comfort in't
Whiles other men have gates and those gates opened,    197
As mine, against their will. Should all despair
That have revolted wives, the tenth of mankind    199
Would hang themselves. Physic for't there's none.    200
It is a bawdy planet, that will strike    201
Where 'tis predominant; and 'tis powerful, think it,    202
From east, west, north, and south. Be it concluded,
No barricado for a belly. Know't,    204
It will let in and out the enemy
With bag and baggage. Many thousand on 's    206
Have the disease and feel't not.—How now, boy?

MAMILLIUS
I am like you, they say.

LEONTES                     Why, that's some comfort.
What, Camillo there?

CAMILLO [coming forward]  Ay, my good lord.

LEONTES
Go play, Mamillius; thou'rt an honest man.
                         [Exit Mamillius.]
Camillo, this great sir will yet stay longer.

CAMILLO
You had much ado to make his anchor hold.
When you cast out, it still came home.

LEONTES                     Didst note it?    213

CAMILLO
He would not stay at your petitions, made
His business more material.

LEONTES                     Didst perceive it?    215
[Aside] They're here with me already, whisp'ring,
     rounding,    216
"Sicilia is a so-forth." 'Tis far gone    217
When I shall gust it last.—How came't, Camillo,    218
That he did stay?

CAMILLO          At the good Queen's entreaty.

LEONTES
"At the Queen's" be't. "Good" should be pertinent,    220
But so it is, it is not. Was this taken    221
By any understanding pate but thine?    222

For thy conceit is soaking, will draw in    223
More than the common blocks. Not noted, is't,    224
But of the finer natures? By some severals    225
Of headpiece extraordinary? Lower messes    226
Perchance are to this business purblind? Say.    227

CAMILLO
Business, my lord? I think most understand
Bohemia stays here longer.

LEONTES
Ha?

CAMILLO     Stays here longer.

LEONTES                     Ay, but why?

CAMILLO
To satisfy Your Highness and the entreaties
Of our most gracious mistress.

LEONTES                     Satisfy?    232
Th'entreaties of your mistress? Satisfy?
Let that suffice. I have trusted thee, Camillo,
With all the nearest things to my heart, as well    235
My chamber councils, wherein, priestlike, thou    236
Hast cleansed my bosom. I from thee departed    237
Thy penitent reformed. But we have been    238
Deceived in thy integrity, deceived
In that which seems so.

CAMILLO          Be it forbid, my lord!    240

LEONTES
To bide upon't, thou art not honest; or,    241
If thou inclin'st that way, thou art a coward,    242
Which hoxes honesty behind, restraining    243
From course required; or else thou must be counted    244
A servant grafted in my serious trust    245
And therein negligent; or else a fool
That see'st a game played home, the rich stake drawn,    247
And tak'st it all for jest.

CAMILLO          My gracious lord,
I may be negligent, foolish, and fearful;
In every one of these no man is free
But that his negligence, his folly, fear,
Among the infinite doings of the world
Sometime puts forth. In your affairs, my lord,    253
If ever I were willful-negligent,
It was my folly; if industriously    255
I played the fool, it was my negligence,
Not weighing well the end; if ever fearful
To do a thing where I the issue doubted,    258

194 **sluiced** drawn off, as by a sluice. (The water in his pond, so to speak, has been drawn off by a cheating neighbor.)    197 **gates** sluice gates, suggestive of the wife's chastity that has been opened and robbed    199 **revolted** unfaithful    200 **Physic** Medicine    201 **It . . . planet** i.e., This unchastity is like the planet Venus.    **strike** blast, destroy by a malign influence    202 **predominant** in the ascendant. (Said of a planet.)    **think it** be assured of this    204 **barricado** barricade.    **Know 't** Be certain of this    206 **bag and baggage** (With sexual suggestion, as earlier in *dagger* [line 156], *sluiced, gates, let in and out,* etc.)    **on 's** of us    213 **still came home** always came back to the ship, failed to hold.    215 **material** important.    216 **They're . . . already** People are already onto my situation.    **rounding** whispering, gossiping    217 **a so-forth** a so-and-so, a you-know-what.    218 **gust** taste, i.e., hear of    220 **pertinent** i.e., appropriate    221 **so it is** as things stand.    **taken** perceived    222 **pate** head

223 **conceit is soaking** understanding is receptive    224 **blocks** blockheads.    225 **But . . . natures** except by those of rarefied intellect.    **severals** individuals    226 **headpiece** i.e., intellect.    **Lower messes** Those who sit lower at table, i.e., inferior persons    227 **purblind** totally blind.    232 **Satisfy?** (Leontes takes the word in a sexual sense.)    235–6 **as well . . . councils** as well as with my private affairs    237–8 **I . . . reformed** I left your company as from a priest to whom I had penitently confessed my sins and received absolution.    240 **Be it forbid** i.e., God forbid I should do such a thing    241–4 **To bide . . . required** If you hold back from saying what you think, you are not being honest; or, if you would like to speak but remain silent, you are a coward, allowing frankness to be hamstrung or shackled from carrying out the duty it should perform    245 **grafted . . . trust** taken into my complete confidence. (*Grafted* means "deeply embedded," like a graft.)    247 **home** i.e., for keeps, in earnest. (With perhaps a sexual double meaning, continued in *rich stake drawn*.)    **drawn** won    253 **Sometime puts forth** sometimes shows itself.    255 **industriously** deliberately    258 **the issue doubted** feared the outcome

Whereof the execution did cry out                                                259
Against the nonperformance, 'twas a fear                                         260
Which oft infects the wisest. These, my lord,
Are such allowed infirmities that honesty                                        262
Is never free of. But, beseech Your Grace,
Be plainer with me. Let me know my trespass
By its own visage. If I then deny it,                                            265
'Tis none of mine.

LEONTES                        Ha' not you seen, Camillo—
But that's past doubt; you have, or your eyeglass                                267
Is thicker than a cuckold's horn—or heard—                                       268
For to a vision so apparent, rumor                                               269
Cannot be mute—or thought—for cogitation
Resides not in that man that does not think—                                     271
My wife is slippery? If thou wilt confess,
Or else be impudently negative                                                   273
To have nor eyes nor ears nor thought, then say                                  274
My wife's a hobbyhorse, deserves a name                                          275
As rank as any flax-wench that puts to                                           276
Before her trothplight. Say't and justify't.                                     277

CAMILLO
I would not be a stander-by to hear
My sovereign mistress clouded so without
My present vengeance taken. 'Shrew my heart,                                     280
You never spoke what did become you less
Than this, which to reiterate were sin                                           282
As deep as that, though true.

LEONTES                          Is whispering nothing?                          283
Is leaning cheek to cheek? Is meeting noses?
Kissing with inside lip? Stopping the career                                     285
Of laughter with a sigh—a note infallible                                        286
Of breaking honesty? Horsing foot on foot?                                       287
Skulking in corners? Wishing clocks more swift,
Hours minutes, noon midnight? And all eyes                                       289
Blind with the pin and web but theirs, theirs only,                              290
That would unseen be wicked? Is this nothing?
Why, then the world and all that's in't is nothing,
The covering sky is nothing, Bohemia nothing,
My wife is nothing, nor nothing have these nothings,
If this be nothing.

CAMILLO                 Good my lord, be cured
Of this diseased opinion, and betimes,                                           296
For 'tis most dangerous.

LEONTES                          Say it be, 'tis true.                           297

CAMILLO
No, no, my lord.

LEONTES                        It is. You lie, you lie!
I say thou liest, Camillo, and I hate thee,
Pronounce thee a gross lout, a mindless slave,
Or else a hovering temporizer, that                                              301
Canst with thine eyes at once see good and evil,
Inclining to them both. Were my wife's liver                                     303
Infected as her life, she would not live                                         304
The running of one glass.

CAMILLO                          Who does infect her?                            305

LEONTES
Why, he that wears her like her medal, hanging                                   306
About his neck, Bohemia—who, if I
Had servants true about me, that bare eyes                                       308
To see alike mine honor as their profits,                                        309
Their own particular thrifts, they would do that                                 310
Which should undo more doing. Ay, and thou,                                      311
His cupbearer—whom I from meaner form                                            312
Have benched and reared to worship, who mayst see   313
Plainly as heaven sees earth and earth sees heaven
How I am galled—mightst bespice a cup                                            315
To give mine enemy a lasting wink,                                               316
Which draft to me were cordial.

CAMILLO                                    Sir, my lord,                          317
I could do this, and that with no rash potion,                                   318
But with a ling'ring dram that should not work
Maliciously like poison. But I cannot                                            320
Believe this crack to be in my dread mistress,                                   321
So sovereignly being honorable.                                                  322
I have loved thee—

LEONTES                     Make that thy question, and go rot!   323
Dost think I am so muddy, so unsettled,                                          324
To appoint myself in this vexation, sully                                        325
The purity and whiteness of my sheets—
Which to preserve is sleep, which being spotted
Is goads, thorns, nettles, tails of wasps—
Give scandal to the blood o' th' prince my son,
Who I do think is mine and love as mine,
Without ripe moving to't? Would I do this?                                       331
Could man so blench?

CAMILLO                          I must believe you, sir.                        332
I do, and will fetch off Bohemia for't;                                          333
Provided that, when he's removed, Your Highness
Will take again your queen as yours at first,

---

**259–60 Whereof . . . nonperformance** in which the completion of the task showed how wrong I was in being reluctant to undertake it **262 allowed** acknowledged. **that** as **265 visage** face, i.e., plain appearance. **267 eyeglass** lens of the eye **268 cuckold's horn** (A thin sheet of horn can be seen through like a lens, though a cuckold's horn is another matter.) **269 to a vision so apparent** about something so plainly visible **271 think** i.e., think so **273–4 Or . . . eyes** or, as the only possible alternative, insist impudently that you have neither eyes **275 hobbyhorse** wanton woman **276 flax-wench** common slut. **puts to** engages in sex **277 justify't** affirm it. **280 present** immediate. **'Shrew** Beshrew, curse **282–3 which . . . true** i.e., to repeat which accusation would be to sin as deeply as her supposed adultery, even if it were true (which it isn't). **285 career** full gallop **286 note** sign **287 honesty** chastity. **Horsing foot on foot** Placing one's foot on that of another person and then moving the feet up and down together. **289 Hours minutes** wishing hours were minutes **290 pin and web** cataract of the eye. (The lovers wish to think themselves unobserved.) **296 betimes** quickly **297 Say it be** Even if it is dangerous

**301 hovering** wavering **303 Inclining . . . both** being tolerant of evil along with the good. **304 Infected as her life** as full of disease as is her moral conduct **305 glass** hourglass. **306 like her medal** like a miniature portrait of her, worn in a locket **308–9 that . . . profits** who have eyes as attentive to matters affecting my honor as to their own personal concerns **310 thrifts** gains **311 undo more doing** i.e., prevent more deceitful sexual carryings-on. **312 cupbearer** servant who, along with his other responsibilities, serves wine to his aristocratic master **312–13 whom . . . worship** whom I have elevated from his humble station to one of dignity and honor, with a worthy bench or place at table **315 galled** rubbed, chafed. **bespice** i.e., lace with poison **316–17 To . . . cordial** to serve Polixenes a drink that would close his eyes in death forever, which at the same time would be a medical restorative to me. **318 rash** quick-acting (and therefore easily detected) **320 Maliciously** virulently **321 crack** flaw. **dread** worthy of awe **322 sovereignly** supremely **323 Make . . . rot!** i.e., If you're going to question my accusations, may you rot in hell! **324 muddy** muddle-headed **325 To . . . vexation** to give myself this vexation **331 ripe moving** ample persuasion **332 blench** swerve (from sensible conduct). **333 fetch off** do away with; or, with deliberate ambiguity, rescue. (As also in *removed* in the next line.)

Even for your son's sake, and thereby for sealing      336
The injury of tongues in courts and kingdoms
Known and allied to yours.

LEONTES                              Thou dost advise me
Even so as I mine own course have set down.
I'll give no blemish to her honor, none.

CAMILLO   My lord,
Go then, and with a countenance as clear
As friendship wears at feasts, keep with Bohemia      343
And with your queen. I am his cupbearer.
If from me he have wholesome beverage,
Account me not your servant.

LEONTES                              This is all.
Do't and thou hast the one half of my heart;
Do't not, thou splitt'st thine own.

CAMILLO                              I'll do't, my lord.

LEONTES
I will seem friendly, as thou hast advised me.      *Exit.*

CAMILLO
Oh, miserable lady! But, for me,
What case stand I in? I must be the poisoner
Of good Polixenes, and my ground to do't
Is the obedience to a master, one
Who in rebellion with himself will have
All that are his so too. To do this deed,      355
Promotion follows. If I could find example
Of thousands that had struck anointed kings
And flourished after, I'd not do't; but since      358
Nor brass, nor stone, nor parchment bears not one,      359
Let villainy itself forswear't. I must      360
Forsake the court. To do't or no is certain      361
To me a breakneck. Happy star reign now!      362
Here comes Bohemia.

*Enter Polixenes.*

POLIXENES [*to himself*]   This is strange. Methinks
My favor here begins to warp. Not speak?—      364
Good day, Camillo.

CAMILLO                              Hail, most royal sir!

POLIXENES
What is the news i'th' court?

CAMILLO                              None rare, my lord.      366

POLIXENES
The King hath on him such a countenance
As he had lost some province and a region      368
Loved as he loves himself. Even now I met him
With customary compliment, when he,
Wafting his eyes to th' contrary and falling      371
A lip of much contempt, speeds from me, and

So leaves me to consider what is breeding      373
That changeth thus his manners.

CAMILLO   I dare not know, my lord.

POLIXENES
How, dare not? Do not? Do you know, and dare not?   376
Be intelligent to me. 'Tis thereabouts,      377
For to yourself what you do know you must,      378
And cannot say you dare not. Good Camillo,      379
Your changed complexions are to me a mirror
Which shows me mine changed too; for I must be      381
A party in this alteration, finding      382
Myself thus altered with't.

CAMILLO                              There is a sickness
Which puts some of us in distemper, but
I cannot name the disease; and it is caught
Of you that yet are well.

POLIXENES                       How? Caught of me?      386
Make me not sighted like the basilisk.      387
I have looked on thousands who have sped the better   388
By my regard, but killed none so. Camillo,      389
As you are certainly a gentleman, thereto      390
Clerklike experienced, which no less adorns      391
Our gentry than our parents' noble names,      392
In whose success we are gentle, I beseech you,      393
If you know aught which does behoove my
      knowledge      394
Thereof to be informed, imprison't not      395
In ignorant concealment.

CAMILLO                              I may not answer.      396

POLIXENES
A sickness caught of me, and yet I well?
I must be answered. Dost thou hear, Camillo?
I conjure thee, by all the parts of man      399
Which honor does acknowledge, whereof the least      400
Is not this suit of mine, that thou declare      401
What incidency thou dost guess of harm      402
Is creeping toward me; how far off, how near;
Which way to be prevented, if to be;      404
If not, how best to bear it.

CAMILLO                       Sir, I will tell you,
Since I am charged in honor and by him      406
That I think honorable. Therefore mark my counsel,
Which must be ev'n as swiftly followed as
I mean to utter it, or both yourself and me

---

336 **for sealing** for the sake of silencing. (Some editors prefer *forsealing*, sealing up tight.)   343 **keep** remain in company   355 **All . . . too** i.e., all his followers like him in rebelling against the best in themselves and in obeying his worst self.   **To do** If I do   358 **after** afterwards   358–9 **but . . . one** but since neither brass monuments nor stone markers nor written documents can show a single instance of persons who have killed a king and prospered afterwards   360 **forswear't** swear not to do it.   361 **To do 't or no** i.e., Either to kill Polixenes or not to kill him   362 **breakneck** destruction, ruin. **Happy star** May a propitious star or constellation   364 **favor** welcome. **warp** change, shrivel, grow askew (as wood warps).   **Not speak?** (Leontes has just passed by Polixenes without speaking.)   366 **rare** noteworthy   368 **As** as if   371 **Wafting . . . contrary** averting his eyes.   **falling** letting fall

373 **breeding** hatching   376 **Do not?** i.e., Or do you mean you don't know?   377 **intelligent** intelligible.   **'Tis thereabouts** It must be something of this sort, i.e., that you know and dare not tell   378–9 **For . . . dare not** i.e., for in your heart, whatever it is you know, you must in fact know, and can't claim it's a matter of not daring to know.   381–2 **for . . . alteration** for my appearance must have changed too along with the alteration in Leontes's behavior   386 **Of** from   387 **sighted** provided with a gaze.   **basilisk** a fabled serpent whose gaze was fatal.   388 **sped** prospered   389 **regard** look   390–3 **thereto . . . gentle** in addition to which you are a cultivated and educated person—something that graces our gentlemanlike condition no less than the worthy name of our ancestors, by succession from whom we are made noble   394–5 **which . . . informed** which it behooves me to know   396 **ignorant concealment** concealment that would keep me ignorant or that would proceed from pretended ignorance on your part.   399 **parts** obligations   400–1 **whereof . . . not** not the least of which is (to answer)   402 **incidency** likely incident   404 **if to be** if it can be (prevented)   406 **by him** i.e., by you yourself

Cry lost, and so good night!

POLIXENES                    On, good Camillo.                    410

CAMILLO

I am appointed him to murder you.                    411

POLIXENES

By whom, Camillo?

CAMILLO                    By the King.

POLIXENES                    For what?

CAMILLO

He thinks, nay, with all confidence he swears,
As he had seen't or been an instrument                    414
To vice you to't, that you have touched his queen                    415
Forbiddenly.

POLIXENES          Oh, then my best blood turn                    416
To an infected jelly, and my name
Be yoked with his that did betray the Best!                    418
Turn then my freshest reputation to
A savor that may strike the dullest nostril                    420
Where I arrive, and my approach be shunned,                    421
Nay, hated too, worse than the great'st infection
That e'er was heard or read!

CAMILLO                    Swear his thought over                    423
By each particular star in heaven and
By all their influences, you may as well                    425
Forbid the sea for to obey the moon                    426
As or by oath remove or counsel shake                    427
The fabric of his folly, whose foundation                    428
Is piled upon his faith and will continue                    429
The standing of his body.

POLIXENES                    How should this grow?                    430

CAMILLO

I know not. But I am sure 'tis safer to
Avoid what's grown than question how 'tis born.
If therefore you dare trust my honesty,
That lies enclosèd in this trunk which you                    434
Shall bear along impawned, away tonight!                    435
Your followers I will whisper to the business,                    436
And will by twos and threes at several posterns                    437
Clear them o'th' city. For myself, I'll put                    438
My fortunes to your service, which are here
By this discovery lost. Be not uncertain,                    440
For, by the honor of my parents, I
Have uttered truth, which if you seek to prove,                    442
I dare not stand by; nor shall you be safer                    443
Than one condemned by the King's own mouth,
     thereon                    444
His execution sworn.

POLIXENES                    I do believe thee;                    445

410 good night i.e., this is the end.    411 him by him (Leontes), or, the one    414 As as if    415 vice force, as with a carpenter's tool, or, impel, tempt. (The *Vice* was a tempter in the morality play.)    416 then my if that were so, may my    418 his . . . Best the name of him (Judas) who betrayed Christ.    420 savor stench    421 Where wherever    423 read read about.    Swear . . . over i.e., Even if you should deny his suspicion with oaths    425 influences astrological emanations thought to influence human destiny    426 for to to    427 or . . . or either . . . or    428 fabric substance    428–30 whose . . . body the foundation of which is built upon an unshaken conviction and which will last as long as he lives.    430 How . . . grow? How could this suspicion have arisen?    434 trunk body. (With a suggestion too of a traveling trunk.)    435 impawned i.e., as a pledge of good faith    436 whisper to secretly inform of and urge    437 posterns rear gates    438 For As for    440 discovery revelation, disclosure    442 prove test    443 stand by affirm publicly; stay    444–5 thereon . . . sworn thereby certain to be executed by order of King Leontes.

I saw his heart in 's face. Give me thy hand.
Be pilot to me, and thy places shall                    447
Still neighbor mine. My ships are ready, and                    448
My people did expect my hence departure
Two days ago. This jealousy
Is for a precious creature. As she's rare,                    451
Must it be great; and as his person's mighty,
Must it be violent; and as he does conceive
He is dishonored by a man which ever
Professed to him, why, his revenges must                    455
In that be made more bitter. Fear o'ershades me.                    456
Good expedition be my friend, and comfort                    457
The gracious Queen, part of his theme, but nothing                    458
Of his ill-ta'en suspicion! Come, Camillo,                    459
I will respect thee as a father if
Thou bear'st my life off. Hence! Let us avoid.                    461

CAMILLO

It is in mine authority to command
The keys of all the posterns. Please Your Highness
To take the urgent hour. Come, sir, away.          *Exeunt.*          464

❖

## 2.1

*Enter Hermione, Mamillius, [and] Ladies.*

HERMIONE

Take the boy to you. He so troubles me,
'Tis past enduring.

FIRST LADY [*taking Mamillius from the Queen*]
                    Come, my gracious lord,
Shall I be your playfellow?

MAMILLIUS

No, I'll none of you.

FIRST LADY                    Why, my sweet lord?                    4

MAMILLIUS

You'll kiss me hard and speak to me as if
I were a baby still.—I love you better.

SECOND LADY

And why so, my lord?

MAMILLIUS                    Not for because                    7
Your brows are blacker; yet black brows, they say,                    8
Become some women best, so that there be not                    9
Too much hair there, but in a semicircle,
Or a half-moon made with a pen.

SECOND LADY                    Who taught' this?                    11

MAMILLIUS

I learned it out of women's faces. Pray now,
What color are your eyebrows?

FIRST LADY                    Blue, my lord.

MAMILLIUS

Nay, that's a mock. I have seen a lady's nose

447–8 thy . . . mine officially you will always be near to me.    451 rare a nonpareil    455 Professed openly professed friendship    456 In that for that reason    457–9 Good . . . suspicion! May good speed befriend me, and may my quick departure ease the predicament of the gracious Queen, who is the object of the King's suspicions but who is guiltless of them!    461 bear'st my life off can get me out of this alive.    avoid depart.    464 take . . . hour seize the opportune moment.

2.1. Location: Sicilia. The royal court.
4 none of you have nothing to do with you.    7 for because because    8 brows eyebrows    9 so provided    11 taught' taught you

That has been blue, but not her eyebrows.

FIRST LADY                                      Hark ye,                15
The Queen your mother rounds apace. We shall                16
Present our services to a fine new prince
One of these days, and then you'd wanton with us,           18
If we would have you.

SECOND LADY                      She is spread of late
Into a goodly bulk. Good time encounter her!                20

HERMIONE [*calling to her women*]
What wisdom stirs amongst you?—Come, sir, now
I am for you again. Pray you, sit by us                       22
And tell 's a tale.

MAMILLIUS                      Merry or sad shall 't be?

HERMIONE    As merry as you will.

MAMILLIUS
A sad tale's best for winter. I have one
Of sprites and goblins.

HERMIONE                      Let's have that, good sir.
Come on, sit down. Come on, and do your best
To fright me with your sprites. You're powerful at it.

MAMILLIUS
There was a man—

HERMIONE                      Nay, come sit down, then on.
                                      [*Mamillius sits.*]

MAMILLIUS
Dwelt by a churchyard. I will tell it softly;
Yond crickets shall not hear it.                              31

HERMIONE
Come on, then, and give't me in mine ear.
                                      [*They converse privately.*]

[*Enter*] *Leontes, Antigonus, Lords,* [*and others*].

LEONTES
Was he met there? His train? Camillo with him?              33

A LORD
Behind the tuft of pines I met them. Never
Saw I men scour so on their way. I eyed them               35
Even to their ships.

LEONTES                      How blest am I
In my just censure, in my true opinion!                     37
Alack, for lesser knowledge! How accurst                    38
In being so blest! There may be in the cup                  39
A spider steeped, and one may drink, depart,                40
And yet partake no venom, for his knowledge
Is not infected; but if one present
Th'abhorred ingredient to his eye, make known
How he hath drunk, he cracks his gorge, his sides,          44
With violent hefts. I have drunk, and seen the spider.      45
Camillo was his help in this, his pander.
There is a plot against my life, my crown.
All's true that is mistrusted. That false villain           48

Whom I employed was pre-employed by him.
He has discovered my design, and I                          50
Remain a pinched thing, yea, a very trick                   51
For them to play at will. How came the posterns             52
So easily open?

A LORD                      By his great authority,
Which often hath no less prevailed than so
On your command.

LEONTES    I know't too well.
[*To Hermione*] Give me the boy. I am glad you did not
   nurse him.
Though he does bear some signs of me, yet you
Have too much blood in him.

HERMIONE                      What is this? Sport?          59

LEONTES [*to a Lord*]
Bear the boy hence; he shall not come about her.
Away with him! And let her sport herself
With that she's big with, [*to Hermione*] for 'tis Polixenes
Has made thee swell thus.          [*Mamillius is led out.*]

HERMIONE                      But I'd say he had not,       63
And I'll be sworn you would believe my saying,
Howe'er you lean to th' nayward.

LEONTES                      You, my lords,                 65
Look on her, mark her well. Be but about
To say "She is a goodly lady," and                          67
The justice of your hearts will thereto add
"'Tis pity she's not honest, honorable."                    69
Praise her but for this her without-door form,             70
Which on my faith deserves high speech, and straight       71
The shrug, the hum or ha, these petty brands               72
That calumny doth use—oh, I am out,                        73
That mercy does, for calumny will sear                      74
Virtue itself—these shrugs, these hums and ha's,           75
When you have said she's goodly, come between              76
Ere you can say she's honest. But be't known,              77
From him that has most cause to grieve it should be,
She's an adulteress.

HERMIONE                      Should a villain say so,
The most replenished villain in the world,                 80
He were as much more villain. You, my lord,                81
Do but mistake.

LEONTES                      You have mistook, my lady,     82
Polixenes for Leontes. Oh, thou thing!
Which I'll not call a creature of thy place,               84
Lest barbarism, making me the precedent,
Should a like language use to all degrees                  86
And mannerly distinguishment leave out                     87

**50 discovered** disclosed   **51 pinched** tortured, ridiculous.   **trick** plaything   **52 play** play with.   **posterns** gates   **59 Sport?** A joke?   **63 I'd** I need only   **65 th' nayward** the contrary.   **67 goodly** attractive   **69 honest** chaste   **70 without-door** outward, external   **71 straight** straightaway, at once   **72 brands** i.e., signs, stigmas   **73 calumny** slander.   **out** wrong, in error   **74–7 That . . . honest** i.e., we can't call it slander attacking virtue in this case, since Hermione has only the appearance of virtue. I should have said that mercy itself will speak in suggestive hums and ha's about Hermione, interrupting you when you are about to say she's chaste.   **80 replenished** complete   **81 He . . . villain** his saying so would double his villainy.   **82 mistook** taken wrongfully. (Playing bitterly on *mistake*, "misapprehend.")   **84 Which . . . place** whose exalted rank I will not desecrate by calling you what you really are   **86 like** similar.   **degrees** social ranks   **87 And . . . out** and leave out proper distinctions

**15 blue** blue with cold   **16 rounds apace** grows round-wombed quickly.   **18 wanton** sport, play   **20 Good . . . her!** May she have a happy issue!   **22 for you** ready for you   **31 crickets** i.e., the court ladies, tittering and laughing   **33 train** retinue.   **35 scour** scurry   **37 censure** judgment   **38 Alack . . . knowledge!** Would that there were less for me to know!   **39 blest** i.e., with knowledge (that causes unhappiness).   **40 A spider** (The superstition referred to here is that the drinker is not poisoned by the spider in the cup unless the spider is known to be there.)   **44 gorge** throat   **45 hefts** heavings, retchings.   **48 mistrusted** suspected.

Betwixt the prince and beggar. I have said
She's an adultress; I have said with whom.
More, she's a traitor, and Camillo is
A fedarary with her, and one that knows                          91
What she should shame to know herself                            92
But with her most vile principal, that she's                     93
A bed-swerver, even as bad as those                              94
That vulgars give bold'st titles, ay, and privy                  95
To this their late escape.

HERMIONE                        No, by my life,                  96
Privy to none of this. How will this grieve you,
When you shall come to clearer knowledge, that
You thus have published me! Gentle my lord,                      99
You scarce can right me throughly than to say                    100
You did mistake.

LEONTES                  No. If I mistake
In those foundations which I build upon,
The center is not big enough to bear                             103
A schoolboy's top.—Away with her to prison!
He who shall speak for her is afar off guilty                    105
But that he speaks.

HERMIONE                  There's some ill planet reigns.        106
I must be patient till the heavens look
With an aspect more favorable. Good my lords,                    108
I am not prone to weeping, as our sex
Commonly are, the want of which vain dew                         110
Perchance shall dry your pities; but I have
That honorable grief lodged here which burns
Worse than tears drown. Beseech you all, my lords,
With thoughts so qualified as your charities                     114
Shall best instruct you, measure me; and so                      115
The King's will be performed!

LEONTES                        Shall I be heard?                 116

HERMIONE
Who is't that goes with me? Beseech Your Highness
My women may be with me, for you see
My plight requires it.—Do not weep, good fools;                 119
There is no cause. When you shall know your mistress
Has deserved prison, then abound in tears
As I come out. This action I now go on                          122
Is for my better grace.—Adieu, my lord.                         123
I never wished to see you sorry; now
I trust I shall. My women, come, you have leave.                125

LEONTES    Go, do our bidding. Hence!
                    [*Exit Queen, guarded, with Ladies.*]

A LORD
Beseech Your Highness, call the Queen again.

ANTIGONUS
Be certain what you do, sir, lest your justice

Prove violence, in the which three great ones suffer:
Yourself, your queen, your son.

A LORD                          For her, my lord,
I dare my life lay down and will do't, sir,
Please you t'accept it, that the Queen is spotless
I'th'eyes of heaven and to you—I mean
In this which you accuse her.

ANTIGONUS                        If it prove
She's otherwise, I'll keep my stables where                     135
I lodge my wife. I'll go in couples with her;                   136
Than when I feel and see her no farther trust her.              137
For every inch of woman in the world,
Ay, every dram of woman's flesh is false,                       139
If she be.

LEONTES    Hold your peaces.

A LORD                          Good my lord—                   140

ANTIGONUS
It is for you we speak, not for ourselves.
You are abused, and by some putter-on                           142
That will be damned for't. Would I knew the villain;
I would land-damn him. Be she honor-flawed,                     144
I have three daughters—the eldest is eleven,
The second and the third, nine and some five—                   146
If this prove true, they'll pay for't. By mine honor,
I'll geld 'em all! Fourteen they shall not see                  148
To bring false generations. They are co-heirs,                  149
And I had rather glib myself than they                          150
Should not produce fair issue.

LEONTES                        Cease, no more!                  151
You smell this business with a sense as cold
As is a dead man's nose; but I do see't and feel't
As you feel doing thus, and see withal                          154
The instruments that feel.

ANTIGONUS                  If it be so,                          155
We need no grave to bury honesty;
There's not a grain of it the face to sweeten                   157
Of the whole dungy earth.

LEONTES                        What? Lack I credit?             158

A LORD
I had rather you did lack than I, my lord,
Upon this ground; and more it would content me                 160
To have her honor true than your suspicion,
Be blamed for't how you might.

LEONTES                        Why, what need we                162
Commune with you of this, but rather follow                     163

---

**91 fedarary** confederate   **92–3 to know ... principal** to acknowledge
privately even with her contemptible partner   **94 bed-swerver** adulteress   **95 That ... titles** that common people call by the rudest
names.   **privy** in on the secret   **96 late** recent   **99 published** proclaimed.   **Gentle my** My noble   **100 You ... say** you can scarcely
find a better way to right the wrong you have done me than by
admitting   **103 center** earth   **105 afar off** indirectly   **106 But ...
speaks** merely by speaking.   **108 aspect** astrological influence.
**Good my** My good   **110 want** lack   **114 qualified** tempered
**115 measure** judge   **116 heard** i.e., obeyed.   **119 fools** (Here, a term
of endearment for Hermione's attendant women.)   **122 come out** am
released from prison.   **122–3 The action ... grace** What I now must
undergo will ultimately make me seem more gracious in others' eyes
and ennoble me by suffering.   **125 leave** permission (to attend me).

**135–6 I'll ... wife** (If Hermione is an adulteress, says Antigonus,
then all women are no better than animals, to be penned up and
guarded suspiciously.)   **136 in couples** i.e., like two hounds leashed
together and hence inseparable   **137 Than ... trust her** trust her no
further than I can feel her next to me and actually see her.   **139 dram**
smallest part   **140 she** i.e., Hermione   **142 abused** deceived.
**putter-on** instigator   **144 land-damn** i.e., ruin utterly (?)
**146 some** about   **148 geld** sterilize, de-sex.   **Fourteen ... see** i.e., If
necessary I will sterilize them before they reach fourteen   **149 bring
false generations** have illegitimate children.   **They are co-heirs**
i.e., They will share my inheritance (since I have no son to inherit all)
**150 glib** castrate, geld   **151 fair issue** legitimate offspring.   **154 thus**
(Leontes presumably grasps Antigonus by the arm or pinches him or
tweaks his nose.)   **154–5 and see ... feel** i.e., just as you and I see
these fingers that pinch, I see in my mind's eye the amorous touching
of Hermione and Polixenes. (*Withal* means "in addition.")   **157–8 the
face ... earth** that could sweeten the face of the entire dung-laden
earth.   **158 credit** credibility.   **160 Upon this ground** in this matter
**162 we** I. (The royal "we.")   **163 Commune** converse

Our forceful instigation? Our prerogative    164
Calls not your counsels, but our natural goodness    165
Imparts this; which if you—or stupefied    166
Or seeming so in skill—cannot or will not    167
Relish a truth like us, inform yourselves    168
We need no more of your advice. The matter,
The loss, the gain, the ordering on't, is all    170
Properly ours.

ANTIGONUS          And I wish, my liege,
You had only in your silent judgment tried it,
Without more overture.

LEONTES                    How could that be?    173
Either thou art most ignorant by age,    174
Or thou wert born a fool. Camillo's flight,
Added to their familiarity—
Which was as gross as ever touched conjecture,    177
That lacked sight only, naught for approbation    178
But only seeing, all other circumstances
Made up to th' deed—doth push on this proceeding.    180
Yet, for a greater confirmation—
For in an act of this importance 'twere    182
Most piteous to be wild—I have dispatched in post    183
To sacred Delphos, to Apollo's temple,    184
Cleomenes and Dion, whom you know
Of stuffed sufficiency. Now from the oracle    186
They will bring all, whose spiritual counsel had    187
Shall stop or spur me. Have I done well?

A LORD    Well done, my lord.

LEONTES
Though I am satisfied, and need no more
Than what I know, yet shall the oracle
Give rest to th' minds of others, such as he    192
Whose ignorant credulity will not
Come up to th' truth. So have we thought it good    194
From our free person she should be confined,    195
Lest that the treachery of the two fled hence
Be left her to perform. Come, follow us.
We are to speak in public, for this business
Will raise us all.

ANTIGONUS [aside]    To laughter, as I take it,    199
If the good truth were known.          Exeunt.

❧

## 2.2

*Enter Paulina, a Gentleman, [and attendants].*

PAULINA
The keeper of the prison, call to him.
Let him have knowledge who I am.
                    [*The Gentleman goes to the door.*]
                              Good lady,    2
No court in Europe is too good for thee;
What dost thou then in prison?

          [*Enter*] *Jailer.*

                              Now, good sir,
You know me, do you not?

JAILER                    For a worthy lady
And one who much I honor.

PAULINA                    Pray you then,
Conduct me to the Queen.

JAILER                    I may not, madam.
To the contrary I have express commandment.

PAULINA
Here's ado, to lock up honesty and honor from
Th'access of gentle visitors! Is't lawful, pray you,    10
To see her women? Any of them? Emilia?

JAILER    So please you, madam,
To put apart these your attendants, I    13
Shall bring Emilia forth.

PAULINA                    I pray now, call her.—
Withdraw yourselves.
                    [*Gentleman and attendants withdraw.*]

JAILER    And, madam,
I must be present at your conference.

PAULINA    Well, be't so, prithee.          [*Exit Jailer.*]
Here's such ado, to make no stain a stain    19
As passes coloring.

          [*Enter Jailer, with*] *Emilia.*

                    Dear gentlewoman,    20
How fares our gracious lady?

EMILIA
As well as one so great and so forlorn
May hold together. On her frights and griefs—    23
Which never tender lady hath borne greater—    24
She is something before her time delivered.    25

PAULINA
A boy?

EMILIA    A daughter, and a goodly babe,
Lusty and like to live. The Queen receives    27
Much comfort in't, says, "My poor prisoner,
I am innocent as you."

PAULINA                    I dare be sworn.
These dangerous unsafe lunes i'th' King, beshrew
them!    30
He must be told on't, and he shall. The office    31
Becomes a woman best; I'll take't upon me.    32

164 Our . . . instigation my own strong inclination.    164–6 Our
prerogative . . . this My royal prerogative is under no obligation to
consult you, but rather out of natural generosity I inform you of the
matter    166 or either    167 Or . . . skill or pretending to be stupefied
out of cunning    168 Relish savor, appreciate    170 on't of it
173 overture public disclosure.    174 by age through the folly of old
age    177 as gross . . . conjecture as palpably evident as any matter
ever conjectured about    178 naught for approbation lacking nothing
for proof    180 Made up to confirming.    push on urge onward
182 'twere it would be    183 wild rash.    post haste    184 Delphos
(See note at 3.1.2.)    186 Of stuffed sufficiency abundantly qualified
and trustworthy.    187 all the whole truth.    had having been obtained
192 he any person (such as Antigonus)    194 Come up to face
195 From away from.    free accessible    199 raise rouse
2.2. Location: Sicilia. A prison.

2 Good lady (Addressed to the absent Hermione.)    10 gentle noble;
kind, gracious    13 put apart dismiss    19–20 to make . . . coloring to
make out of no stain at all a besmirching of honor that surpasses any
justification. (Expressed in a metaphor of dyeing and painting.)
23 On In consequence of    24 Which than which    25 something
somewhat. (Also in line 55.)    27 Lusty vigorous.    like likely
30 lunes fits of lunacy    31 on't of it    32 Becomes suits

If I prove honey-mouthed, let my tongue blister 33
And never to my red-looked anger be 34
The trumpet any more. Pray you, Emilia, 35
Commend my best obedience to the Queen. 36
If she dares trust me with her little babe,
I'll show't the King and undertake to be
Her advocate to th' loud'st. We do not know 39
How he may soften at the sight o'th' child.
The silence often of pure innocence
Persuades when speaking fails.

EMILIA                    Most worthy madam,
Your honor and your goodness is so evident
That your free undertaking cannot miss 44
A thriving issue. There is no lady living 45
So meet for this great errand. Please Your Ladyship 46
To visit the next room, I'll presently 47
Acquaint the Queen of your most noble offer,
Who but today hammered of this design, 49
But durst not tempt a minister of honor 50
Lest she should be denied.

PAULINA                    Tell her, Emilia,
I'll use that tongue I have. If wit flow from't 52
As boldness from my bosom, let 't not be doubted
I shall do good.

EMILIA            Now be you blest for it!
I'll to the Queen.—Please you, come something nearer. 55

JAILER
Madam, if't please the Queen to send the babe,
I know not what I shall incur to pass it, 57
Having no warrant.

PAULINA            You need not fear it, sir.
This child was prisoner to the womb and is
By law and process of great Nature thence
Freed and enfranchised, not a party to
The anger of the King, nor guilty of—
If any be—the trespass of the Queen.

JAILER     I do believe it.

PAULINA
Do not you fear. Upon mine honor, I
Will stand betwixt you and danger.          *Exeunt.*

❖

## 2.3

*Enter Leontes.*

LEONTES
Nor night nor day, no rest! It is but weakness 1
To bear the matter thus, mere weakness. If 2
The cause were not in being—part o'th' cause, 3
She th'adulteress, for the harlot King 4

Is quite beyond mine arm, out of the blank 5
And level of my brain, plot-proof, but she 6
I can hook to me—say that she were gone, 7
Given to the fire, a moiety of my rest 8
Might come to me again.—Who's there?

*[Enter a] Servant.*

SERVANT                    My lord?
LEONTES     How does the boy?
SERVANT
He took good rest tonight; 'tis hoped 11
His sickness is discharged.
LEONTES            To see his nobleness!
Conceiving the dishonor of his mother, 13
He straight declined, drooped, took it deeply, 14
Fastened and fixed the shame on't in himself, 15
Threw off his spirit, his appetite, his sleep, 16
And downright languished.—Leave me solely. Go, 17
See how he fares.          [*Exit Servant.*] 18
              Fie, fie! No thought of him.
The very thought of my revenges that way
Recoil upon me—in himself too mighty,
And in his parties, his alliance. Let him be, 21
Until a time may serve. For present vengeance,
Take it on her. Camillo and Polixenes
Laugh at me, make their pastime at my sorrow.
They should not laugh if I could reach them, nor
Shall she, within my power.

*Enter Paulina [with a baby]; Antigonus and Lords [trying to hold her back].*

A LORD                    You must not enter.
PAULINA
Nay, rather, good my lords, be second to me. 27
Fear you his tryannous passion more, alas,
Than the Queen's life? A gracious innocent soul,
More free than he is jealous.
ANTIGONUS            That's enough. 30
SERVANT
Madam, he hath not slept tonight, commanded
None should come at him.
PAULINA            Not so hot, good sir.
I come to bring him sleep. 'Tis such as you,
That creep like shadows by him and do sigh
At each his needless heavings, such as you 35
Nourish the cause of his awaking. I 36
Do come with words as medicinal as true,
Honest as either, to purge him of that humor 38
That presses him from sleep.
LEONTES            What noise there, ho?

33 **honey-mouthed** i.e., flattering and obsequious, rather than telling the harsh truth.  **blister** (It was popularly supposed that lying blistered the tongue.)  34 **red-looked** red-faced  35 **trumpet** i.e., herald, speaker  36 **Commend** deliver  39 **to th' loud'st** as loudly as I can.  44 **free** generous  45 **thriving issue** successful outcome (punning also on *issue*, offspring).  46 **meet** well suited.  **Please** If it please  47 **presently** at once  49 **hammered of** mused upon  50 **But . . . honor** but did not dare to solicit a high-ranking person of the court  52 **wit** wisdom  55 **come . . . nearer** i.e., come into the next room (as in lines 46–7).  57 **to pass it** if I let it pass  **2.3. Location:** Sicilia. The royal court.
1 **Nor** Neither  2–3 **If . . . in being** If the person responsible for this disgrace were not alive  4 **harlot** lewd. (Originally applied to either sex.)

5–6 **out . . . level** beyond the range. (Archery terms: *blank* is the center of the target or the close range needed for a direct shot at it, as in "point-blank"; *level* is the action of aiming.)  6 **plot-proof** beyond the reach of my plotting to capture him  7 **hook** (As with grappling hooks.)  **say . . . gone** suppose she were dead  8 **Given to the fire** burned at the stake (as a traitor conspiring against the King).  **moiety** portion  11 **tonight** last night  13 **Conceiving** Grasping the enormity of  14 **straight** immediately  15 **on't** of it  16 **spirit** liveliness  17 **solely** alone.  18 **him** i.e., Polixenes.  21 **his parties . . . alliance** his supporters and allies.  27 **be second to** aid, second  30 **free** innocent  35 **heavings** sighs or groans  36 **awaking** inability to sleep.  38 **humor** distemper

PAULINA
No noise, my lord, but needful conference
About some gossips for Your Highness.

LEONTES                 How?    41
Away with that audacious lady! Antigonus,
I charged thee that she should not come about me.
I knew she would.

ANTIGONUS        I told her so, my lord,
On your displeasure's peril and on mine,
She should not visit you.

LEONTES          What, canst not rule her?

PAULINA
From all dishonesty he can. In this,
Unless he take the course that you have done—
Commit me for committing honor—trust it,    49
He shall not rule me.

ANTIGONUS       La you now, you hear!    50
When she will take the rein I let her run,
But she'll not stumble.

PAULINA          Good my liege, I come—
And, I beseech you hear me, who professes
Myself your loyal servant, your physician,
Your most obedient counselor, yet that dares
Less appear so in comforting your evils    56
Than such as most seem yours—I say, I come    57
From your good queen.

LEONTES    Good queen?

PAULINA
Good queen, my lord, good queen, I say good queen,
And would by combat make her good, so were I    61
A man, the worst about you.

LEONTES [to Lords]         Force her hence.    62

PAULINA
Let him that makes but trifles of his eyes
First hand me. On mine own accord I'll off,
But first I'll do my errand. The good Queen,
For she is good, hath brought you forth a daughter—
Here 'tis—commends it to your blessing.
                 [She lays down the baby.]

LEONTES                  Out!
A mankind witch! Hence with her, out o' door!    68
A most intelligencing bawd!

PAULINA          Not so.    69
I am as ignorant in that as you
In so entitling me, and no less honest
Than you are mad; which is enough, I'll warrant,
As this world goes, to pass for honest.

LEONTES [to Lords]           Traitors!
Will you not push her out? [To Antigonus] Give her the
   bastard.
Thou dotard, thou art woman-tired, unroosted    75

By thy Dame Partlet here. Take up the bastard!    76
Take't up, I say. Give't to thy crone.

PAULINA [to Antigonus]       Forever    77
Unvenerable be thy hands if thou    78
Tak'st up the Princess by that forcèd baseness    79
Which he has put upon't!

LEONTES        He dreads his wife.

PAULINA
So I would you did. Then 'twere past all doubt
You'd call your children yours.

LEONTES        A nest of traitors!

ANTIGONUS
I am none, by this good light.

PAULINA          Nor I, nor any    83
But one that's here, and that's himself; for he
The sacred honor of himself, his queen's,
His hopeful son's, his babe's, betrays to slander,
Whose sting is sharper than the sword's; and will
   not—
For, as the case now stands, it is a curse    88
He cannot be compelled to't—once remove    89
The root of his opinion, which is rotten    90
As ever oak or stone was sound.

LEONTES           A callet    91
Of boundless tongue, who late hath beat her husband    92
And now baits me! This brat is none of mine;    93
It is the issue of Polixenes.    94
Hence with it, and together with the dam    95
Commit them to the fire!

PAULINA          It is yours;
And, might we lay th'old proverb to your charge,
So like you, 'tis the worse. Behold, my lords,    98
Although the print be little, the whole matter    99
And copy of the father—eye, nose, lip,
The trick of 's frown, his forehead, nay, the valley,    101
The pretty dimples of his chin and cheek, his smiles,
The very mold and frame of hand, nail, finger.
And thou, good goddess Nature, which hast made it
So like to him that got it, if thou hast    105
The ordering of the mind too, 'mongst all colors
No yellow in't, lest she suspect, as he does,    107
Her children not her husband's!

LEONTES        A gross hag!
And, lozel, thou art worthy to be hanged,    109
That wilt not stay her tongue.

ANTIGONUS       Hang all the husbands    110
That cannot do that feat, you'll leave yourself

---

76 **Partlet** or Pertilote, a common name for a hen (as in *Reynard the Fox* and in Chaucer's "Nun's Priest's Tale")   77 **crone** old woman.   78 **Unvenerable** unworthy of respect   79 **by that forcèd baseness** under that wrongfully imposed name of bastard   83 **by this good light** by the light of day. (A common oath.)   88–90 **as . . . opinion** i.e., since he is King, he regrettably can't be compelled to change his deeply rooted opinion   91 **callet** scold   92 **late** recently   93 **baits** (With a pun on *beat* in the previous line, pronounced "bate.")   94 **issue** child   95 **dam** mother   98 **So . . . worse** she's so like you that she fares the worse for it.   99 **print** copy   101 **trick** characteristic expression.   **valley** cleft above the upper lip or on the chin   105 **got** begot   107 **No yellow** let there be no yellow, i.e., the color of jealousy. (A chaste woman could hardly expect that her own children are illegitimate, but Paulina may be hyperbolically ridiculing Leontes's suspicions.)   109 **lozel** worthless person, scoundrel. (Addressed to Antigonus.)   110 **stay** restrain

---

41 **gossips** godparents for the baby at its baptism   49 **Commit** i.e., to prison   50 **La . . . hear!** i.e., There now, you hear how she will go on talking!   56–7 **in comforting . . . yours** when it comes to encouraging your evil courses than those flatterers who seem to be your most loyal servants   61 **by combat** by trial by combat.   **make** prove.   **so were I** if I were   62 **worst** least manly, or, lowest in rank   68 **mankind** masculine, behaving like a man   69 **intelligencing bawd** acting as go-between and spy (for the Queen and Polixenes).   75 **woman-tired** henpecked. (From *tire* in falconry, meaning "tear with the beak.")   **unroosted** driven from your perch

Hardly one subject.

**LEONTES**                    Once more, take her hence.

**PAULINA**
A most unworthy and unnatural lord
Can do no more.

**LEONTES**                    I'll ha' thee burnt.

**PAULINA**                         I care not.
It is an heretic that makes the fire,                        115
Not she which burns in't. I'll not call you tyrant;          116
But this most cruel usage of your queen,
Not able to produce more accusation                          118
Than your own weak-hinged fancy, something savors
Of tyranny and will ignoble make you,
Yea, scandalous to the world.

**LEONTES** [*to Antigonus*]        On your allegiance,
Out of the chamber with her! Were I a tyrant,
Where were her life? She durst not call me so               123
If she did know me one. Away with her!

**PAULINA**
I pray you, do not push me; I'll be gone.
Look to your babe, my lord; 'tis yours. Jove send her
A better guiding spirit!—What needs these hands?           127
You that are thus so tender o'er his follies                128
Will never do him good, not one of you.
So, so. Farewell, we are gone.                    *Exit.*

**LEONTES** [*to Antigonus*]
Thou, traitor, hast set on thy wife to this.
My child? Away with't! Even thou, that hast
A heart so tender o'er it, take it hence
And see it instantly consumed with fire;
Even thou and none but thou. Take it up straight.
Within this hour bring me word 'tis done,
And by good testimony, or I'll seize thy life,
With what thou else call'st thine. If thou refuse
And wilt encounter with my wrath, say so;
The bastard brains with these my proper hands              140
Shall I dash out. Go, take it to the fire,
For thou set'st on thy wife.

**ANTIGONUS**                    I did not, sir.
These lords, my noble fellows, if they please,
Can clear me in't.

**LORDS**                    We can. My royal liege,
He is not guilty of her coming hither.

**LEONTES**  You're liars all.

**A LORD**
Beseech Your Highness, give us better credit.             147
We have always truly served you, and beseech'             148
So to esteem of us; and on our knees we beg,
As recompense of our dear services                        150
Past and to come, that you do change this purpose,
Which being so horrible, so bloody, must
Lead on to some foul issue. We all kneel.

**LEONTES**
I am a feather for each wind that blows.
Shall I live on to see this bastard kneel
And call me father? Better burn it now
Than curse it then. But be it; let it live.
It shall not neither. [*To Antigonus*] You, sir, come you
    hither,
You that have been so tenderly officious
With Lady Margery, your midwife there,                     160
To save this bastard's life—for 'tis a bastard,
So sure as this beard's gray. What will you adventure     162
To save this brat's life?

**ANTIGONUS**                    Anything, my lord,
That my ability may undergo
And nobleness impose. At least thus much:
I'll pawn the little blood which I have left
To save the innocent—anything possible.

**LEONTES** [*holding his sword*]
It shall be possible. Swear by this sword
Thou wilt perform my bidding.

**ANTIGONUS** [*his hand on the hilt*]    I will, my lord.

**LEONTES**
Mark and perform it, see'st thou; for the fail            170
Of any point in't shall not only be
Death to thyself but to thy lewd-tongued wife,
Whom for this time we pardon. We enjoin thee,
As thou art liegeman to us, that thou carry               174
This female bastard hence, and that thou bear it
To some remote and desert place quite out
Of our dominions, and that there thou leave it,
Without more mercy, to it own protection                  178
And favor of the climate. As by strange fortune
It came to us, I do in justice charge thee,
On thy soul's peril and thy body's torture,
That thou commend it strangely to some place              182
Where chance may nurse or end it. Take it up.

**ANTIGONUS** [*taking up the baby*]
I swear to do this, though a present death
Had been more merciful.—Come on, poor babe.
Some powerful spirit instruct the kites and ravens        186
To be thy nurses! Wolves and bears, they say,
Casting their savageness aside, have done
Like offices of pity.—Sir, be prosperous                  189
In more than this deed does require!—And blessing         190
Against this cruelty fight on thy side,                    191
Poor thing, condemned to loss!    *Exit* [*with the baby*].

**LEONTES**                    No, I'll not rear             192
Another's issue.

        *Enter a Servant.*

**SERVANT**            Please Your Highness, posts          193
From those you sent to th'oracle are come
An hour since. Cleomenes and Dion,                         195

---

**115–16 It is . . . in 't** i.e., In burning me, you who would be making or building the fire are the heretic, not me (since loss of faith in innocence is a kind of heresy), or, you can burn a woman if you like, but it's a heretic's fire only if she is, in fact, a heretic.   **118 Not able** you not being able   **123 Where . . . life?** how could she escape execution at my command?   **127 What . . . hands?** What need is there to push me?   **128 tender o'er** gentle with   **140 proper** own   **147 credit** belief.   **148 beseech'** we beseech you   **150 dear** loyal, heartfelt

**160 Margery** (A derisive term, evidently equivalent to *Partlet* in line 76.)   **162 this beard's** (Probably Antigonus's.)   **adventure** risk   **170 see'st thou** i.e., do you hear.   **fail** failure   **174 liegeman** loyal subject   **178 it** its   **182 commend . . . place** commit it to some foreign place   **186 kites** preying and scavenging hawks   **189 Like** similar   **190 more** i.e., more ways, more extent.   **require** deserve.   **191 Against** to counteract   **192 loss** destruction.   **193 posts** messengers   **195 since** ago.

Being well arrived from Delphos, are both landed,
Hasting to th' court.

A LORD                     So please you, sir, their speed
Hath been beyond account.

LEONTES                     Twenty-three days    198
They have been absent. 'Tis good speed, foretells
The great Apollo suddenly will have    200
The truth of this appear. Prepare you, lords.
Summon a session, that we may arraign    202
Our most disloyal lady; for, as she hath
Been publicly accused, so shall she have
A just and open trial. While she lives
My heart will be a burden to me. Leave me,
And think upon my bidding.        *Exeunt [separately].*

❧

## 3.1

*Enter Cleomenes and Dion.*

CLEOMENES
The climate's delicate, the air most sweet,
Fertile the isle, the temple much surpassing    2
The common praise it bears.

DION                     I shall report,
For most it caught me, the celestial habits—    4
Methinks I so should term them—and the reverence
Of the grave wearers. Oh, the sacrifice!
How ceremonious, solemn, and unearthly
It was i'th'offering!

CLEOMENES           But of all, the burst
And the ear-deaf'ning voice o'th'oracle,
Kin to Jove's thunder, so surprised my sense    10
That I was nothing.

DION                     If th'event o'th' journey    11
Prove as successful to the Queen—Oh, be't so!—
As it hath been to us rare, pleasant, speedy,    13
The time is worth the use on't.

CLEOMENES                     Great Apollo    14
Turn all to th' best! These proclamations,
So forcing faults upon Hermione,
I little like.

DION           The violent carriage of it    17
Will clear or end the business. When the oracle,
Thus by Apollo's great divine sealed up,    19
Shall the contents discover, something rare    20
Even then will rush to knowledge. Go. Fresh horses!
And gracious be the issue!           *Exeunt.*

❧

---

198 **beyond account** unprecedented, or, beyond explanation.
200 **suddenly** at once   202 **session** trial
**3.1. Location: Sicilia. On the way to Leontes's court.**
2 **isle** (Shakespeare follows Greene's *Pandosto* in fictitiously placing
Delphi on an island. Delphi, sometimes known as Delphos [see
2.1.184, 2.3.196, and 3.2.126], was often confused with Delos, the
island birthplace of Apollo and location also of an oracle.)
4 **caught me** caught my attention.   **habits** vestments   10 **surprised**
overwhelmed   11 **th'event** the outcome   13 **rare** outstanding
14 **is worth . . . on't** will have been well employed.   17 **carriage**
execution, management   19 **great divine** chief priest
20 **discover** reveal

## 3.2

*Enter Leontes, Lords, [and] Officers.*

LEONTES
This sessions, to our great grief we pronounce,
Even pushes 'gainst our heart: the party tried
The daughter of a king, our wife, and one
Of us too much beloved. Let us be cleared    4
Of being tyrannous, since we so openly
Proceed in justice, which shall have due course
Even to the guilt or the purgation.    7
Produce the prisoner.

OFFICER
It is His Highness' pleasure that the Queen
Appear in person here in court. Silence!

*[Enter] Hermione, as to her trial, [Paulina, and]
Ladies.*

LEONTES   Read the indictment.
OFFICER *[reads]*   "Hermione, Queen to the worthy
Leontes, King of Sicilia, thou art here accused and ar-
raigned of high treason, in committing adultery with
Polixenes, King of Bohemia, and conspiring with
Camillo to take away the life of our sovereign lord the
King, thy royal husband; the pretense whereof being    17
by circumstances partly laid open, thou, Hermione,
contrary to the faith and allegiance of a true subject,
didst counsel and aid them, for their better safety, to
fly away by night."

HERMIONE
Since what I am to say must be but that
Which contradicts my accusation, and
The testimony on my part no other
But what comes from myself, it shall scarce boot me    25
To say "not guilty." Mine integrity,
Being counted falsehood, shall, as I express it,
Be so received. But thus: if powers divine
Behold our human actions, as they do,
I doubt not then but innocence shall make
False accusation blush and tyranny
Tremble at patience. You, my lord, best know,
Who least will seem to do so, my past life
Hath been as continent, as chaste, as true    34
As I am now unhappy; which is more
Than history can pattern, though devised    36
And played to take spectators. For behold me—    37
A fellow of the royal bed, which owe    38
A moiety of the throne, a great king's daughter,    39
The mother to a hopeful prince—here standing    40
To prate and talk for life and honor 'fore

---

**3.2. Location: Sicilia. A place of justice, probably at court.**
4 **Of us** by me   7 **purgation** acquittal.   17 **pretense** purpose, design
25 **boot** avail   34 **continent** self-restrained from desire   36 **history**
story, drama.   **pattern** show a similar example for   37 **take** please,
charm   38 **which owe** who owns   39 **moiety** share   40 **a hopeful**
**prince** a prince of whom much is hoped and expected

Who please to come and hear. For life, I prize it        42
As I weigh grief, which I would spare. For honor,        43
'Tis a derivative from me to mine,                       44
And only that I stand for. I appeal                      45
To your own conscience, sir, before Polixenes            46
Came to your court, how I was in your grace,
How merited to be so; since he came,
With what encounter so uncurrent I                       49
Have strained t'appear thus; if one jot beyond           50
The bound of honor, or in act or will                    51
That way inclining, hardened be the hearts               52
Of all that hear me, and my near'st of kin
Cry "Fie" upon my grave!

LEONTES                         I ne'er heard yet
That any of these bolder vices wanted                    55
Less impudence to gainsay what they did                  56
Than to perform it first.

HERMIONE                         That's true enough,     57
Though 'tis a saying, sir, not due to me.                58

LEONTES
You will not own it.

HERMIONE                         More than mistress of    59
Which comes to me in name of fault, I must not           60
At all acknowledge. For Polixenes,                       61
With whom I am accused, I do confess
I loved him as in honor he required;                     63
With such a kind of love as might become
A lady like me; with a love even such,
So, and no other, as yourself commanded;
Which not to have done I think had been in me            67
Both disobedience and ingratitude
To you and toward your friend, whose love had
     spoke,                                              69
Even since it could speak, from an infant, freely        70
That it was yours. Now, for conspiracy,                  71
I know not how it tastes, though it be dished            72
For me to try how. All I know of it
Is that Camillo was an honest man;
And why he left your court, the gods themselves,
Wotting no more than I, are ignorant.                    76

LEONTES
You knew of his departure, as you know
What you have underta'en to do in 's absence.

HERMIONE    Sir,
You speak a language that I understand not.
My life stands in the level of your dreams,              81

Which I'll lay down.

LEONTES                         Your actions are my dreams.  82
You had a bastard by Polixenes,
And I but dreamed it. As you were past all shame—        84
Those of your fact are so—so past all truth,             85
Which to deny concerns more than avails; for as          86
Thy brat hath been cast out, like to itself,             87
No father owning it—which is indeed                      88
More criminal in thee than it—so thou                    89
Shalt feel our justice, in whose easiest passage         90
Look for no less than death.

HERMIONE                         Sir, spare your threats.  91
The bug which you would fright me with I seek.           92
To me can life be no commodity.                          93
The crown and comfort of my life, your favor,
I do give lost, for I do feel it gone,                   95
But know not how it went. My second joy                  96
And firstfruits of my body, from his presence
I am barred, like one infectious. My third comfort,
Starred most unluckily, is from my breast,               99
The innocent milk in it most innocent mouth,             100
Haled out to murder; myself on every post                101
Proclaimed a strumpet; with immodest hatred              102
The childbed privilege denied, which longs               103
To women of all fashion; lastly, hurried                 104
Here to this place, i'th'open air, before                105
I have got strength of limit. Now, my liege,             106
Tell me what blessings I have here alive
That I should fear to die? Therefore proceed.
But yet hear this; mistake me not. No life,              109
I prize it not a straw. But for mine honor,
Which I would free, if I shall be condemned              111
Upon surmises, all proofs sleeping else                  112
But what your jealousies awake, I tell you               113
'Tis rigor and not law. Your Honors all,                 114
I do refer me to the oracle.                             115
Apollo be my judge!

A LORD                         This your request
Is altogether just. Therefore bring forth,
And in Apollo's name, his oracle.

                         [*Exeunt certain Officers.*]

HERMIONE
The Emperor of Russia was my father.
Oh, that he were alive and here beholding
His daughter's trial! That he did but see

---

**42 Who please** whoever chooses    **42–5 For . . . stand for** As for life, I value it as I value grief, and would as willingly do without; as for honor, it is to be transmitted from me to my descendants, and that only I make a stand for.    **46 conscience** consideration, inward knowledge **49–50 With . . . thus** (I ask) by what behavior so unacceptable I have transgressed so that I appear thus (in disgrace and on trial)    **51 or in act or will** either in act or intent    **52 hardened . . . hearts** may the hearts be hardened against me    **55–6 wanted Less** were more lacking in    **56 gainsay** deny    **57 first** in the first place.    **58 due** applicable **59 own** admit    **59–61 More . . . acknowledge** I must not acknowledge or answer for more faults than I actually have.    **61 For** As for **63 required** deserved    **67 had been** would have been    **69–71 your friend . . . yours** i.e., Polixenes, who professed love for you from earliest childhood (as you for him).    **71 for** as for    **72 though . . . dished** even if it were to be served up    **76 Wotting** supposing they know **81 in . . . dreams** as a target in the aim and range of your delusions

**82 Which** i.e., my life.    **Your . . . dreams** i.e., You have performed what I have fantasized, and what you have done preys on my mind. **84 but** merely    **85 Those of your fact** All those who do what you did **86 Which . . . avails** your denial of which is understandable, but it won't do you any good    **87 like to itself** as an outcast, fatherless brat ought to be    **88 owning** acknowledging    **89 More . . . it** more a criminal act on your part than on your child's    **90–1 in whose . . . death** i.e., which will impose the death sentence at least, perhaps torture also. **92 bug** bugbear, bogey, imaginary object of terror    **93 commodity** asset.    **95 give** reckon as, or give up for    **96 My second joy** i.e., Mamillius    **99 Starred most unluckily** born under a most unlucky star    **100 it** its    **101 Haled** dragged.    **post** posting place for public notices    **102 immodest** immoderate    **103 The childbed . . . longs** denied the privilege of bedrest after giving birth, something that is the right    **104 all fashion** every rank    **105 open air** (considered unhealthy, especially here to women weakened by childbirth)    **106 got . . . limit** regained my strength after having borne a child.    **109 No life** i.e., I do not ask for life    **111 free** vindicate    **112–13 else But** other than what **114 rigor** tyranny    **115 refer me** appeal my case

The flatness of my misery, yet with eyes                    122
Of pity, not revenge!

[*Enter Officers, with*] Cleomenes [*and*] Dion.

OFFICER [*holding a sword*]
You here shall swear upon this sword of justice
That you, Cleomenes and Dion, have
Been both at Delphos, and from thence have brought
This sealed-up oracle, by the hand delivered
Of great Apollo's priest, and that since then
You have not dared to break the holy seal
Nor read the secrets in't.
CLEOMENES, DION          All this we swear.
LEONTES
Break up the seals and read.                                131
OFFICER [*reads*]    "Hermione is chaste, Polixenes blame-
less, Camillo a true subject, Leontes a jealous tyrant,
his innocent babe truly begotten, and the King shall
live without an heir if that which is lost be not
found."
LORDS
Now blessèd be the great Apollo!
HERMIONE                          Praised!
LEONTES
Hast thou read truth?
OFFICER                     Ay, my lord, even so
As it is here set down.
LEONTES
There is no truth at all i'th'oracle.
The sessions shall proceed. This is mere falsehood.

[*Enter a Servant.*]

SERVANT
My lord the King, the King!
LEONTES                     What is the business?
SERVANT
Oh, sir, I shall be hated to report it!                     143
The Prince your son, with mere conceit and fear            144
Of the Queen's speed, is gone.
LEONTES                        How? Gone?
SERVANT                              Is dead.              145
LEONTES
Apollo's angry, and the heavens themselves
Do strike at my injustice. [*Hermione swoons.*] How now
    there?
PAULINA
This news is mortal to the Queen. Look down
And see what death is doing.
LEONTES                        Take her hence.
Her heart is but o'ercharged; she will recover.
I have too much believed mine own suspicion.
Beseech you, tenderly apply to her
Some remedies for life.
            [*Exeunt Paulina and Ladies, with Hermione.*]
                        Apollo, pardon
My great profaneness 'gainst thine oracle!
I'll reconcile me to Polixenes,

New woo my queen, recall the good Camillo,
Whom I proclaim a man of truth, of mercy;
For, being transported by my jealousies
To bloody thoughts and to revenge, I chose
Camillo for the minister to poison
My friend Polixenes; which had been done,
But that the good mind of Camillo tardied             162
My swift command, though I with death and with
Reward did threaten and encourage him,
Not doing it and being done. He, most humane       165
And filled with honor, to my kingly guest
Unclasped my practice, quit his fortunes here,      167
Which you knew great, and to the hazard
Of all incertainties himself commended,             169
No richer than his honor. How he glisters           170
Through my rust! And how his piety                  171
Does my deeds make the blacker!

[*Enter Paulina.*]

PAULINA                            Woe the while!
Oh, cut my lace, lest my heart, cracking it,        173
Break too!
A LORD          What fit is this, good lady?
PAULINA
What studied torments, tyrant, hast for me?         175
What wheels, racks, fires? What flaying, boiling    176
In leads or oils? What old or newer torture
Must I receive, whose every word deserves           178
To taste of thy most worst? Thy tyranny,            179
Together working with thy jealousies—
Fancies too weak for boys, too green and idle       181
For girls of nine—oh, think what they have done,
And then run mad indeed, stark mad! For all
Thy bygone fooleries were but spices of it.         184
That thou betrayed'st Polixenes, 'twas nothing;
That did but show thee, of a fool, inconstant       186
And damnable ingrateful. Nor was 't much
Thou wouldst have poisoned good Camillo's honor,
To have him kill a king—poor trespasses,           189
More monstrous standing by; whereof I reckon        190
The casting forth to crows thy baby daughter        191
To be or none or little, though a devil             192
Would have shed water out of fire ere done't.       193
Nor is't directly laid to thee, the death
Of the young Prince, whose honorable thoughts,
Thoughts high for one so tender, cleft the heart    196
That could conceive a gross and foolish sire        197

162 **tardied** delayed   165 **Not . . . done** i.e., death if he did not do it
and reward if he did.   167 **Unclasped my practice** disclosed my
plot   169 **himself commended** entrusted himself   170 **No richer than**
with no riches except   170–1 **How . . . rust!** How he shines in contrast
with my fault!   173 **my lace** the lace of my stays   175 **studied** ingeniously devised   176 **wheels . . . flaying** (Various methods of torture:
being stretched on a wheel or rack until the bones are broken or pulled
apart at the joints, being burned or skinned alive.)   178–9 **whose . . .
worst?** i.e., since all I can say must accuse you of tyranny and thus
earn your most heinous punishments?   181 **too weak for boys** too
flimsy even for boys to have come up with.   **green and idle** immature and foolish   184 **spices** foretastes, samples   186 **of** for   189 **To
have** by having.   **poor** slight   190 **More . . . by** when more monstrous sins are at hand for comparison   191 **crows** carrion birds
192 **or none** either none   193 **shed . . . fire** wept from his fiery eyes or
while surrounded by hellfire   196 **tender** young   197 **conceive**
apprehend that

122 **flatness** boundlessness   131 **up** open   143 **to report** for reporting
144 **conceit and fear** i.e., anxious concern   145 **speed** fate, fortune

Blemished his gracious dam. This is not, no,    198
Laid to thy answer. But the last—Oh, lords,    199
When I have said, cry woe! The Queen, the Queen,    200
The sweet'st, dear'st creature's dead, and vengeance for't
Not dropped down yet.
A LORD                                The higher powers forbid!
PAULINA
I say she's dead. I'll swear't. If word nor oath
Prevail not, go and see. If you can bring
Tincture or luster in her lip, her eye,    205
Heat outwardly or breath within, I'll serve you
As I would do the gods. But, O thou tyrant!
Do not repent these things, for they are heavier
Than all thy woes can stir. Therefore betake thee    209
To nothing but despair. A thousand knees
Ten thousand years together, naked, fasting,
Upon a barren mountain, and still winter    212
In storm perpetual, could not move the gods
To look that way thou wert.
LEONTES                                Go on, go on.    214
Thou canst not speak too much. I have deserved
All tongues to talk their bitt'rest.
A LORD [to Paulina]                    Say no more.
Howe'er the business goes, you have made fault
I'th' boldness of your speech.
PAULINA                                I am sorry for't.
All faults I make, when I shall come to know them,    219
I do repent. Alas, I have showed too much
The rashness of a woman. He is touched
To th' noble heart. What's gone and what's past help
Should be past grief.—Do not receive affliction    223
At my petition. I beseech you, rather    224
Let me be punished, that have minded you    225
Of what you should forget. Now, good my liege,
Sir, royal sir, forgive a foolish woman.
The love I bore your queen—lo, fool again!
I'll speak of her no more, nor of your children;
I'll not remember you of my own lord,    230
Who is lost too. Take your patience to you,    231
And I'll say nothing.
LEONTES                        Thou didst speak but well
When most the truth, which I receive much better
Than to be pitied of thee. Prithee, bring me
To the dead bodies of my queen and son.
One grave shall be for both. Upon them shall
The causes of their death appear, unto
Our shame perpetual. Once a day I'll visit
The chapel where they lie, and tears shed there
Shall be my recreation. So long as nature    240
Will bear up with this exercise, so long

I daily vow to use it. Come and lead me
To these sorrows.                                Exeunt.

## 3.3

*Enter Antigonus [and] a Mariner, [with a] babe.*

ANTIGONUS
Thou art perfect then, our ship hath touched upon    1
The deserts of Bohemia?
MARINER                                Ay, my lord, and fear    2
We have landed in ill time. The skies look grimly
And threaten present blusters. In my conscience,    4
The heavens with that we have in hand are angry
And frown upon 's.
ANTIGONUS    Their sacred wills be done! Go, get aboard;
Look to thy bark. I'll not be long before    8
I call upon thee.
MARINER                    Make your best haste, and go not
Too far i'th' land. 'Tis like to be loud weather.    10
Besides, this place is famous for the creatures
Of prey that keep upon't.
ANTIGONUS                        Go thou away.    12
I'll follow instantly.
MARINER                    I am glad at heart
To be so rid o'th' business.                    Exit.
ANTIGONUS                        Come, poor babe.
I have heard, but not believed, the spirits o'th' dead
May walk again. If such thing be, thy mother
Appeared to me last night, for ne'er was dream
So like a waking. To me comes a creature,
Sometimes her head on one side, some another;    19
I never saw a vessel of like sorrow,
So filled and so becoming. In pure white robes,    21
Like very sanctity, she did approach
My cabin where I lay, thrice bowed before me,
And, gasping to begin some speech, her eyes
Became two spouts. The fury spent, anon
Did this break from her: "Good Antigonus,
Since fate, against thy better disposition,
Hath made thy person for the thrower-out
Of my poor babe, according to thine oath,
Places remote enough are in Bohemia;
There weep and leave it crying. And, for the babe    31
Is counted lost forever, Perdita,    32
I prithee, call't. For this ungentle business    33
Put on thee by my lord, thou ne'er shalt see
Thy wife Paulina more." And so, with shrieks,
She melted into air. Affrighted much,
I did in time collect myself and thought    37
This was so and no slumber. Dreams are toys;    38

---

198 **dam** mother.    199 **Laid . . . answer** presented as a charge that you must answer.    200 **said** finished speaking    205 **Tincture** color    209 **woes can stir** penance can remove.    212 **still** always    214 **To look . . . wert** to regard you.    219 **I make** that I make    223–4 **Do . . . petition** Do not afflict yourself with remorse at my urging.    225 **minded you** put you in mind    230 **remember** remind    231 **Take . . . you** Arm yourself with patience    240 **my recreation** (1) my sole diversion (2) my spiritual regeneration.    **nature** my physical being

3.3. **Location: Bohemia. The seacoast.**
1 **perfect** certain    2 **deserts of Bohemia** i.e., deserted region on the coast. (Shakespeare follows Greene's *Pandosto* in giving Bohemia a seacoast.)    4 **present** immediate.    **conscience** opinion    8 **bark** ship.    10 **like** likely.    **loud** stormy    12 **keep upon't** inhabit it.    19 **some another** sometimes the other    21 **So . . . becoming** i.e., so filled with sorrow and able to bear it so gracefully.    31 **for** because    32 **Perdita** i.e., the lost one    33 **ungentle** ignoble    37 **collect myself** compose myself    38 **toys** trifles

Yet for this once, yea, superstitiously,
I will be squared by this. I do believe                                  40
Hermione hath suffered death, and that
Apollo would, this being indeed the issue                                42
Of King Polixenes, it should here be laid,
Either for life or death, upon the earth
Of its right father. Blossom, speed thee well!
                             *[He lays down the baby.]*
There lie, and there thy character; there these,                         46
        *[He places a box and a fardel beside the baby.]*
Which may, if fortune please, both breed thee, pretty,                   47
And still rest thine. [*Thunder.*] The storm begins. Poor
    wretch,                                                           48
That for thy mother's fault art thus exposed
To loss and what may follow! Weep I cannot,                              50
But my heart bleeds; and most accurst am I
To be by oath enjoined to this. Farewell!
The day frowns more and more. Thou'rt like to have                      53
A lullaby too rough. I never saw
The heavens so dim by day. A savage clamor!
Well may I get aboard! This is the chase.
I am gone forever!            *Exit, pursued by a bear.*

      *[Enter a] Shepherd.*

SHEPHERD   I would there were no age between ten and
three-and-twenty, or that youth would sleep out the
rest, for there is nothing in the between but getting
wenches with child, wronging the ancientry, stealing,    61
fighting—Hark you now, would any but these boiled        62
brains of nineteen and two-and-twenty hunt this          63
weather? They have scared away two of my best sheep,
which I fear the wolf will sooner find than the master.
If anywhere I have them, 'tis by the seaside, browsing
of ivy. Good luck, an't be thy will! [*Seeing the child.*]  67
What have we here? Mercy on 's, a bairn, a very pretty    68
bairn! A boy or a child, I wonder? A pretty one, a very  69
pretty one. Sure some scape. Though I am not bookish,    70
yet I can read waiting-gentlewoman in the scape.
This has been some stair-work, some trunk-work,          72
some behind-door-work. They were warmer that got        73
this than the poor thing is here. I'll take it up for pity.
Yet I'll tarry till my son come; he hallooed but even
now.—Whoa, ho, hoa!                                       76

     *Enter Clown.*

CLOWN   Hilloa, loa!

SHEPHERD   What, art so near? If thou'lt see a thing to
talk on when thou art dead and rotten, come hither.
What ail'st thou, man?
CLOWN   I have seen two such sights, by sea and by
land! But I am not to say it is a sea, for it is now the sky;
betwixt the firmament and it you cannot thrust a
bodkin's point.                                                          84
SHEPHERD   Why, boy, how is it?
CLOWN   I would you did but see how it chafes, how it
rages, how it takes up the shore! But that's not to the   87
point. Oh, the most piteous cry of the poor souls! Some–
times to see 'em, and not to see 'em; now the ship
boring the moon with her mainmast, and anon swallowed with yeast and froth, as you'd thrust a cork into   91
a hogshead. And then for the land service, to see how    92
the bear tore out his shoulder bone; how he cried to
me for help and said his name was Antigonus, a nobleman. But to make an end of the ship: to see how
the sea flapdragoned it! But first, how the poor souls    96
roared and the sea mocked them, and how the poor
gentleman roared and the bear mocked him, both
roaring louder than the sea or weather.
SHEPHERD   Name of mercy, when was this, boy?       100
CLOWN   Now, now. I have not winked since I saw these   101
sights. The men are not yet cold under water, nor the
bear half dined on the gentleman. He's at it now.
SHEPHERD   Would I had been by, to have helped the
old man!
CLOWN   I would you had been by the ship side, to have
helped her. There your charity would have lacked
footing.                                                                 108
SHEPHERD   Heavy matters, heavy matters! But look thee
here, boy. Now bless thyself. Thou met'st with things
dying, I with things newborn. Here's a sight for thee;
look thee, a bearing cloth for a squire's child! Look      112
thee here; take up, take up, boy. Open't. So, let's see.
It was told me I should be rich by the fairies. This is
some changeling. Open't. What's within, boy?            115
                         *[The Clown opens the box.]*
CLOWN   You're a made old man. If the sins of your
youth are forgiven you, you're well to live. Gold, all     117
gold!
SHEPHERD   This is fairy gold, boy, and 'twill prove so.
Up with't, keep it close. Home, home, the next way.      120
We are lucky, boy, and to be so still requires nothing    121
but secrecy. Let my sheep go. Come, good boy, the       122
next way home.

---

**40 squared** directed in my course  **42 issue** child  **46 thy character**
the written account of your history and parentage (i.e., the one that
subsequently will serve to identify Perdita).  **these** i.e., the gold
and jewels found by the Shepherd, also later used to identify her.
**46.1 box, fardel** (The box, containing gold and jewels, is later produced
by the old Shepherd and the Clown; see 4.4.758–9. They also have a
*fardel*, or "bundle," consisting evidently of the bearing cloth [3.3.112]
and/or mantle [5.2.34] in which the babe was found.)  **47 breed thee**
keep you, pay for your support.  **pretty** pretty one  **48 And still rest**
**thine** i.e., and still provide a heritage with what is unspent.  **50 Weep**
**I cannot** i.e., I cannot weep as the Queen instructed me (line 31)
**53 like** likely  **61 ancientry** old people  **62–3 boiled brains** addlepa-
ted youths  **67 of** on.  **Good . . . will!** i.e., May God grant me good
luck in finding my sheep!  **68 bairn** child  **69 child** i.e., female infant
**70 scape** sexual escapade.  **72–3 stair-work . . . behind-door-work**
i.e., sexual liaisons under or behind the stairs or using a room or a
trunk for concealment.  **73 got** begot  **76.1 Clown** country fellow,
rustic.

**84 bodkin's** needle's. (A *bodkin* can also be a dagger, awl, etc.)
**87 takes up** (1) contends with, rebukes (2) swallows  **91 yeast** foam
**92 hogshead** large barrel. (The image is of a cork swimming in a turbulent expanse of frothing liquid.)  **land service** (1) dish of food
served on land (2) military service on land (as distinguished from
naval service); here, the doings on land  **96 flapdragoned** swallowed
as one would a flapdragon, i.e., a raisin or the like swallowed out
of flaming brandy in the game of snapdragon  **100 Name of mercy**
In the name of mercy  **101 winked** blinked an eye  **108 footing**
(1) foothold (2) establishment of a charitable foundation, one that would
provide *charity* (line 107).  **112 bearing cloth** rich cloth or mantle in
which a child was carried to its baptism.  **for . . . child** i.e., for a child
born into the gentry.  **115 changeling** child secretly substituted for a
mortal child by the fairies.  **117 well to live** well-to-do.  **120 close**
secret.  **next** nearest  **121–2 to be . . . secrecy** (To talk about fairy
gifts would be to insure bad luck.)  **121 still** on a continuing basis

CLOWN    Go you the next way with your findings. I'll go
see if the bear be gone from the gentleman, and how
much he hath eaten. They are never curst but when  126
they are hungry. If there be any of him left, I'll bury it.

SHEPHERD    That's a good deed. If thou mayest discern
by that which is left of him what he is, fetch me to th'  129
sight of him.

CLOWN    Marry, will I; and you shall help to put him i'th'  131
ground.

SHEPHERD    'Tis a lucky day, boy, and we'll do good
deeds on't.                                                   *Exeunt.*

❧

## 4.1

*Enter Time, the Chorus.*

TIME
I, that please some, try all, both joy and terror            1
Of good and bad, that makes and unfolds error,              2
Now take upon me, in the name of Time,
To use my wings. Impute it not a crime
To me or my swift passage that I slide
O'er sixteen years and leave the growth untried             6
Of that wide gap, since it is in my power
To o'erthrow law and in one self-born hour                  8
To plant and o'erwhelm custom. Let me pass                  9
The same I am ere ancient'st order was                      10
Or what is now received. I witness to                       11
The times that brought them in; so shall I do               12
To th' freshest things now reigning, and make stale
The glistering of this present as my tale                   14
Now seems to it. Your patience this allowing,               15
I turn my glass and give my scene such growing              16
As you had slept between. Leontes leaving                   17
Th'effects of his fond jealousies, so grieving              18
That he shuts up himself, imagine me,
Gentle spectators, that I now may be
In fair Bohemia. And remember well
I mentioned a son o'th' King's, which Florizel
I now name to you; and with speed so pace                   23
To speak of Perdita, now grown in grace                     24
Equal with wond'ring. What of her ensues                    25
I list not prophesy; but let Time's news                    26
Be known when 'tis brought forth. A shepherd's
daughter,

---

126 **curst** mean, fierce    129 **what he is** what is his identity or rank
131 **Marry** i.e., Indeed. (Originally an oath, "by the Virgin Mary.")
**4.1.**
**1 try** test    **2 that . . . error** i.e., I who make error, thus bringing joy to
the bad and terror to the good, and then at last unfold or disclose
error, thus bringing joy to the good and terror to the bad    **6 growth
untried** developments unexplored    **8 law** any established order
(including the rule of the unity of time in a dramatic performance,
conventionally limiting the action to twenty-four hours).    **self-born**
selfsame, or born of myself (since hours are the creations of Time)
**9 To . . . o'erwhelm** to establish and then subvert    **9–11 Let . . .
received** Let me continue as I have been from before the beginning
of time to the present.    **12 them** i.e., law and custom    **14 glistering**
glittering shine    **14–15 as my . . . to it** in the same way that my hoary
tale now seems old-fashioned when compared with the shiny fashion
of today.    **16 glass** hourglass    **17 As** as if    **18 fond** foolish
**23 pace** proceed    **24–5 now . . . wond'ring** now grown so gracious
(and graceful) as to inspire wonderment.    **26 list not** prefer not to

---

And what to her adheres, which follows after,              28
Is th'argument of Time. Of this allow,                     29
If ever you have spent time worse ere now;
If never, yet that Time himself doth say                   31
He wishes earnestly you never may.          *Exit.*

❧

## 4.2

*Enter Polixenes and Camillo.*

POLIXENES    I pray thee, good Camillo, be no more
importunate. 'Tis a sickness denying thee anything, a
death to grant this.

CAMILLO    It is fifteen years since I saw my country.   4
Though I have for the most part been aired abroad, I     5
desire to lay my bones there. Besides, the penitent
King, my master, hath sent for me, to whose feeling      7
sorrows I might be some allay—or I o'erween to think     8
so—which is another spur to my departure.

POLIXENES    As thou lov'st me, Camillo, wipe not out the
rest of thy services by leaving me now. The need I
have of thee thine own goodness hath made. Better
not to have had thee than thus to want thee. Thou,       13
having made me businesses which none without thee        14
can sufficiently manage, must either stay to execute     15
them thyself or take away with thee the very services    16
thou hast done; which if I have not enough
considered—as too much I cannot—to be more thank-       18
ful to thee shall be my study, and my profit therein the
heaping friendships. Of that fatal country, Sicilia,    20
prithee, speak no more, whose very naming punishes
me with the remembrance of that penitent, as thou
call'st him, and reconciled King, my brother, whose
loss of his most precious queen and children are even
now to be afresh lamented. Say to me, when saw'st
thou the Prince Florizel, my son? Kings are no less
unhappy, their issue not being gracious, than they are   27
in losing them when they have approved their virtues.    28

CAMILLO    Sir, it is three days since I saw the Prince.
What his happier affairs may be are to me unknown;
but I have missingly noted he is of late much retired    31
from court and is less frequent to his princely exercises 32
than formerly he hath appeared.                          33

POLIXENES    I have considered so much, Camillo, and     34
with some care, so far that I have eyes under my ser-    35
vice which look upon his removedness; from whom I        36
have this intelligence, that he is seldom from the       37
house of a most homely shepherd—a man, they say,        38

---

28 **to her adheres** concerns her    29 **th'argument** the subject matter
31 **yet that** i.e., yet allow that
**4.2. Location: Bohemia. The court of Polixenes.**
4 **fifteen** (Compare "sixteen" at 4.1.6.)    5 **been aired abroad** lived
abroad    7 **feeling** heartfelt    8 **allay** means of abatement.    **o'erween**
am presumptuous enough    13 **want** lack    14 **made me businesses**
done things for me    15–16 **execute them** carry them out    18 **considered** rewarded    20 **heaping friendships** accumulation of your kind
services and our mutual affection.    27 **their . . . gracious** if their children behave ungraciously    28 **approved** proved (as young Mamillius
had done before he so unhappily died)    31 **missingly noted** sur-
mised by his absences (that)    32 **frequent to** devoted to.    **princely
exercises** (which might include fencing and horseback riding)
33 **appeared** seemed to be.    34 **so much** as much    35–6 **eyes . . .
removedness** spies who keep an eye on him in his absence from the
court    37 **intelligence** news.    **from** away from    38 **homely** simple

that from very nothing, and beyond the imagination of his neighbors, is grown into an unspeakable estate. 40

CAMILLO   I have heard, sir, of such a man, who hath a daughter of most rare note. The report of her is 42 extended more than can be thought to begin from 43 such a cottage.

POLIXENES   That's likewise part of my intelligence; but, I fear, the angle that plucks our son thither. Thou shalt 46 accompany us to the place, where we will, not appearing what we are, have some question with the shep- 48 herd; from whose simplicity I think it not uneasy to 49 get the cause of my son's resort thither. Prithee, be my present partner in this business, and lay aside the thoughts of Sicilia.

CAMILLO   I willingly obey your command.

POLIXENES   My best Camillo! We must disguise ourselves.                                 *Exit [with Camillo].*

## 4.3

*Enter Autolycus, singing.*

AUTOLYCUS
When daffodils begin to peer,                    1
    With heigh, the doxy over the dale!           2
Why, then comes in the sweet o'the year,
    For the red blood reigns in the winter's pale. 4

The white sheet bleaching on the hedge,          5
    With heigh, the sweet birds, oh, how they
        sing!
Doth set my pugging tooth on edge,               7
    For a quart of ale is a dish for a king.      8

The lark, that tirralirra chants,
    With heigh, with heigh, the thrush and the jay!
Are summer songs for me and my aunts,            11
    While we lie tumbling in the hay.

I have served Prince Florizel and in my time wore three-pile, but now I am out of service.         14

But shall I go mourn for that, my dear?          15
    The pale moon shines by night,
And when I wander here and there,                17
    I then do most go right.                      18

If tinkers may have leave to live,               19
    And bear the sow-skin budget,                 20

Then my account I well may give,                 21
    And in the stocks avouch it.                  22

My traffic is sheets; when the kite builds, look to lesser 23 linen. My father named me Autolycus, who, being, as 24 I am, littered under Mercury, was likewise a snap- 25 per-up of unconsidered trifles. With die and drab I 26 purchased this caparison, and my revenue is the silly 27 cheat. Gallows and knock are too powerful on the 28 highway; beating and hanging are terrors to me. For 29 the life to come, I sleep out the thought of it. A prize, 30 a prize!

*Enter Clown.*

CLOWN   Let me see: every 'leven wether tods; every tod 32 yields pound and odd shilling; fifteen hundred shorn, what comes the wool to?

AUTOLYCUS [*aside*]   If the springe hold, the cock's mine. 35

CLOWN   I cannot do't without counters. Let me see; 36 what am I to buy for our sheepshearing feast? Three pound of sugar, five pound of currants, rice—what will this sister of mine do with rice? But my father hath made her mistress of the feast, and she lays it on. She hath made me four-and-twenty nosegays for the shear- 41 ers—three-man-song men all, and very good ones; 42 but they are most of them means and basses, but one 43 Puritan amongst them, and he sings psalms to horn- 44 pipes. I must have saffron to color the warden pies; 45 mace; dates?—none, that's out of my note; nutmegs, 46 seven; a race or two of ginger, but that I may beg; four 47 pound of prunes, and as many of raisins o'th' sun. 48

AUTOLYCUS   Oh, that ever I was born! [*He grovels on the ground.*]

CLOWN   I'th' name of me!                         50

AUTOLYCUS   Oh, help me, help me! Pluck but off these rags, and then death, death!

---

**21 my account** an account of myself   **22 in . . . avouch it** i.e., affirm that I am a tinker if I find myself sitting in the stocks, where vagabonds often end up. (Autolycus passes himself off as a tinker to mask his real calling of thief.)   **23–4 when . . . linen** (The kite, a bird of prey, was thought to carry off small pieces of linen with which to construct its nest, whereas Autolycus makes off with larger linen or sheets hung out to dry.)   **24 Autolycus** (Like his namesake, Ulysses's grandfather, the son of Mercury, this Autolycus is an expert thief.) **who** (Refers ambiguously to Autolycus and "My father"; see next note.)   **25 littered under Mercury** (1) sired by Mercury, the god of thieves (2) born when the planet Mercury was in the ascendant **26 unconsidered** left unattended, not worth thinking about **26–8 With . . . cheat** Gambling and whoring have brought me to the wearing of these tattered rags, and my source of income is petty trickery used to cheat simpletons.   **28–9 Gallows . . . to me** i.e., Hanging and being beaten, the ordinary hazards of being a highwayman, are too much for me; I'll stick to being a petty thief.   **29 For** As for **30 sleep . . . it** i.e., don't give a thought to punishment in the next world.   **prize** booty   **32 every . . . tods** every eleven sheep yield a *tod*, i.e., a bulk of wool weighing twenty-eight pounds   **35 springe** snare.   **cock** woodcock. (A proverbially stupid bird.)   **36 counters** metal disks used in reckoning.   **41 made me** made. (*Me* is used colloquially.)   **nosegays** bouquets   **42 three-man-song men** singers of songs for three male voices: bass, tenor, and treble   **43 means** tenors   **43–5 but . . . hornpipes** (Puritans were often laughed at for their pious singing; this Puritan is imagined as singing hymns even to the sounds of raucous merriment at a fair.)   **45 warden** made of the warden pear   **46 out of my note** not on my list   **47 race** root   **48 o'th' sun** dried in the sun.   **50 I'th' name of me!** (An unusual and perhaps comic oath.)

---

**40 unspeakable** beyond description   **42 note** distinction.   **43 begin** emanate, originate   **46 angle** baited fishhook.   **our** (The royal plural; also in *us*, line 47.)   **48 question** talk   **49 uneasy** difficult

**4.3. Location: Bohemia. A road near the Shepherd's cottage.**
**1 peer** peep out, appear   **2 doxy** beggar's wench   **4 pale** (1) paleness (2) domain, region of authority. (The image is of red blood restoring vitality to a pale complexion.)   **5 bleaching** drying   **7 set . . . on edge** i.e., whets the appetite of my thieving tooth, my taste for thieving. (To *pug* is to "pull, tug.")   **8 quart of ale** (To be paid for perhaps with profits from theft of sheets.)   **11 aunts** i.e., whores   **14 three-pile** velvet having very rich pile or nap   **15 for that** i.e., for being out of service   **17 wander** i.e., as a thief)   **18 most go right** i.e., live the life that is meant for me.   **19 leave to live** permission to practice their trade of mending metal pots (and thieving)   **20 budget** tool bag

CLOWN  Alack, poor soul! Thou hast need of more rags 53
to lay on thee, rather than have these off. 54

AUTOLYCUS  Oh, sir, the loathsomeness of them offend
me more than the stripes I have received, which are
mighty ones and millions.

CLOWN  Alas, poor man! A million of beating may come
to a great matter.

AUTOLYCUS  I am robbed, sir, and beaten; my money
and apparel ta'en from me, and these detestable things
put upon me.

CLOWN  What, by a horseman or a footman? 63

AUTOLYCUS  A footman, sweet sir, a footman.

CLOWN  Indeed, he should be a footman by the garments he has left with thee. If this be a horseman's
coat, it hath seen very hot service. Lend me thy hand;
I'll help thee. Come, lend me thy hand. [*He helps him
up.*]

AUTOLYCUS  Oh, good sir, tenderly. Oh!

CLOWN  Alas, poor soul!

AUTOLYCUS  Oh, good sir, softly, good sir! I fear, sir, my
shoulder blade is out.

CLOWN  How now? Canst stand?

AUTOLYCUS  [*picking his pocket*]  Softly, dear sir; good
sir, softly. You ha' done me a charitable office. 75

CLOWN  [*reaching for his purse*]  Dost lack any money? I 76
have a little money for thee. 77

AUTOLYCUS  No, good sweet sir; no, I beseech you, sir.
I have a kinsman not past three quarters of a mile
hence, unto whom I was going; I shall there have
money or anything I want. Offer me no money, I pray
you. That kills my heart.

CLOWN  What manner of fellow was he that robbed
you?

AUTOLYCUS  A fellow, sir, that I have known to go about
with troll-my-dames. I knew him once a servant of the 85
Prince. I cannot tell, good sir, for which of his virtues
it was, but he was certainly whipped out of the court.

CLOWN  His vices, you would say. There's no virtue
whipped out of the court. They cherish it to make it
stay there; and yet it will no more but abide. 90

AUTOLYCUS  Vices, I would say, sir. I know this man
well. He hath been since an ape bearer, then a process 92
server, a bailiff. Then he compassed a motion of 93
the Prodigal Son and married a tinker's wife within a 94
mile where my land and living lies, and, having flown 95
over many knavish professions, he settled only in
rogue. Some call him Autolycus.

CLOWN  Out upon him! Prig, for my life, prig! He 98
haunts wakes, fairs, and bearbaitings. 99

AUTOLYCUS  Very true, sir. He, sir, he. That's the rogue
that put me into this apparel.

CLOWN  Not a more cowardly rogue in all Bohemia. If
you had but looked big and spit at him, he'd have
run.

AUTOLYCUS  I must confess to you, sir, I am no fighter.
I am false of heart that way, and that he knew, I 106
warrant him.

CLOWN  How do you now?

AUTOLYCUS  Sweet sir, much better than I was. I can
stand and walk. I will even take my leave of you and
pace softly towards my kinsman's. 111

CLOWN  Shall I bring thee on the way? 112

AUTOLYCUS  No, good-faced sir, no, sweet sir.

CLOWN  Then fare thee well. I must go buy spices for
our sheep-shearing. *Exit.*

AUTOLYCUS  Prosper you, sweet sir! Your purse is not 116
hot enough to purchase your spice. I'll be with you at 117
your sheep-shearing too. If I make not this cheat bring 118
out another, and the shearers prove sheep, let me be 119
unrolled and my name put in the book of virtue! 120

*Song.*

Jog on, jog on, the footpath way,
　　And merrily hent the stile-a; 122
A merry heart goes all the day,
　　Your sad tires in a mile-a. *Exit.*

❧

## 4.4

*Enter Florizel [in shepherd's garb, and] Perdita [in
holiday attire].*

FLORIZEL
These your unusual weeds to each part of you 1
Does give a life; no shepherdess, but Flora 2
Peering in April's front. This your sheepshearing 3
Is as a meeting of the petty gods, 4
And you the queen on't.

PERDITA　　　　　　　Sir, my gracious lord, 5
To chide at your extremes it not becomes me. 6
Oh, pardon that I name them! Your high self,
The gracious mark o'th' land, you have obscured 8
With a swain's wearing, and me, poor lowly maid, 9

53–4 **Thou . . . off** i.e., For modesty's sake, you need more clothing,
not less, to cover your nakedness.　63 **horseman** highwayman.
**footman** footpad. (As the Clown observes in line 65, a common robber on foot would have poorer clothes than a mounted highwayman.)　75 **office** service.　76–7 **I have . . . thee** (The Clown reaches
for his money and might have discovered the robbery if Autolycus
had not quickly begged him not to bother.)　85 **troll-my-dames** or
troll-madams (from the French *trou-madame*), a game in which the
object was to *troll* balls through arches set on a board. (Autolycus
uses the word to suggest women who *troll* or saunter about.)　90 **no
more but abide** make only a temporary or unwilling stay.　92 **ape
bearer** one who carries a trained monkey about for exhibition
92–3 **process server** sheriff's officer who serves processes or summonses
93 **compassed a motion** devised a puppet show　94 **the Prodigal Son**
the son who, in one of Jesus's parables, returns to his father and is forgiven for his spendthrift ways (Luke 15:11-24).　95 **living** property

98 **Prig** Thief　99 **wakes** village festivals　106 **false** cowardly
111 **softly** slowly　112 **bring . . . way** go part of the way with you.
116 **Prosper . . . sir!** (Said to the departing Clown.)　116–17 **Your . . .
spice** i.e., You'll find but a cold purse to pay for your hot spices; an
empty purse is a cold one. (Said after the Clown's departure.)
118–19 **cheat bring out** swindle lead to　120 **unrolled** taken off the
roll (of thieves and vagabonds)　122 **hent** take hold of (as a means
of climbing over a *stile*, a structure providing steps over a fence or wall).
**4.4. Location: Bohemia. The Shepherd's cottage.** (See lines 181–2,
187, etc.)
1 **unusual weeds** special, holiday attire　2 **Flora** goddess of flowers
3 **Peering . . . front** peeping forth in early April, or, in April's countenance or garb.　4 **petty** minor　5 **on't** of it.　6 **extremes** extravagant
statements　8 **mark o'th' land** one who is noted and used as a model
by everyone　9 **swain's wearing** shepherd's garb

Most goddesslike pranked up. But that our feasts          10
In every mess have folly, and the feeders                 11
Digest it with a custom, I should blush                   12
To see you so attired, swoon, I think,
To show myself a glass.
FLORIZEL                        I bless the time            14
When my good falcon made her flight across
Thy father's ground.
PERDITA                  Now Jove afford you cause!         16
To me the difference forges dread; your greatness          17
Hath not been used to fear. Even now I tremble
To think your father by some accident
Should pass this way as you did. Oh, the Fates!
How would he look to see his work, so noble,              21
Vilely bound up? What would he say? Or how                22
Should I, in these my borrowed flaunts, behold            23
The sternness of his presence?
FLORIZEL                            Apprehend
Nothing but jollity. The gods themselves,
Humbling their deities to love, have taken
The shapes of beasts upon them. Jupiter                   27
Became a bull, and bellowed; the green Neptune            28
A ram, and bleated; and the fire-robed god,               29
Golden Apollo, a poor humble swain,                       30
As I seem now. Their transformations
Were never for a piece of beauty rarer,
Nor in a way so chaste, since my desires                  33
Run not before mine honor, nor my lusts
Burn hotter than my faith.
PERDITA                    Oh, but sir,
Your resolution cannot hold when 'tis
Opposed, as it must be, by th' power of the King.
One of these two must be necessities,
Which then will speak: that you must change this
    purpose
Or I my life.
FLORIZEL          Thou dearest Perdita,                    40
With these forced thoughts, I prithee, darken not          41
The mirth o'th' feast. Or I'll be thine, my fair,          42
Or not my father's. For I cannot be
Mine own, nor anything to any, if
I be not thine. To this I am most constant,
Though destiny say no. Be merry, gentle!                  46
Strangle such thoughts as these with anything            47
That you behold the while. Your guests are coming.       48

Lift up your countenance as it were the day              49
Of celebration of that nuptial which
We two have sworn shall come.
PERDITA                        O Lady Fortune,
Stand you auspicious!
FLORIZEL               See, your guests approach.
Address yourself to entertain them sprightly,            53
And let's be red with mirth.

    [*Enter*] *Shepherd, Clown; Polixenes, Camillo*
    [*disguised*]; *Mopsa, Dorcas; servants.*

SHEPHERD
Fie, daughter! When my old wife lived, upon
This day she was both pantler, butler, cook,             56
Both dame and servant; welcomed all, served all;        57
Would sing her song and dance her turn; now here,
At upper end o'th' table, now i'th' middle;
On his shoulder, and his; her face afire                 60
With labor, and the thing she took to quench it          61
She would to each one sip. You are retired,              62
As if you were a feasted one and not
The hostess of the meeting. Pray you, bid
These unknown friends to 's welcome, for it is           65
A way to make us better friends, more known.             66
Come, quench your blushes and present yourself
That which you are, mistress o'th' feast. Come on,
And bid us welcome to your sheepshearing,
As your good flock shall prosper.
PERDITA [*to Polixenes*]              Sir, welcome.
It is my father's will I should take on me
The hostess-ship o'th' day. [*To Camillo*] You're
    welcome, sir.—
Give me those flowers there, Dorcas.—Reverend sirs,
For you there's rosemary and rue; these keep             74
Seeming and savor all the winter long.                   75
Grace and remembrance be to you both,                    76
And welcome to our shearing!  [*Giving them flowers.*]
POLIXENES                        Shepherdess—
A fair one are you—well you fit our ages
With flowers of winter.
PERDITA                   Sir, the year growing ancient,   79
Not yet on summer's death nor on the birth
Of trembling winter, the fairest flow'rs o'th' season
Are our carnations and streaked gillyvors,               82
Which some call nature's bastards. Of that kind          83
Our rustic garden's barren, and I care not
To get slips of them.
POLIXENES             Wherefore, gentle maiden,            85
Do you neglect them?
PERDITA              For I have heard it said             86

**10 pranked up** bedecked.   **10–12 But . . . custom** Were it not that
whenever folks gather for merry feasting one encounters some folly,
which the guests take in their stride so as to be expected   **14 To show . . .
glass** if I were to see myself in a mirror.   **16 Jove . . . cause!** May Jove
grant that you have good reason to be thankful!   **17 To me . . . dread**
To me, the difference in our social rank is a source of dread   **21–2 How
. . . bound up?** What would he think to see the nobly-born son he created so vilely outfitted? (The *work*, Florizel, is metaphorically a piece
of writing, and his garments are the binding of the book.)   **23 flaunts**
finery   **27–30 Jupiter . . . swain** (Jupiter disguised himself as a bull to
woo Europa, Neptune took the shape of a ram in order to seduce Bisalter
or Theophane [Ovid, *Metamorphoses*, 6.117], and Apollo took on the
role of "a poor humble swain" (line 30) to enable his master Admetus
to woo Alcestis.)   **33 in a way** i.e., pursuing a purpose   **40 Or I my
life** i.e., or I will be threatened with loss of life (as Polixenes indeed
threatens at lines 436–43).   **41 forced** farfetched, unnatural   **42 Or**
Either   **46 gentle** i.e., my gentle love.   **47–8 Strangle . . . while** i.e.,
Put down such thoughts by attending to matters at hand.

**49 as** as if   **53 Address** Prepare   **56 pantler** pantry servant   **57 dame**
mistress of the household   **60 On his . . . his** at one person's . . .
another's   **61–2 and . . . sip** and she would toast each one with the
drink she took to quench the fire of her labor.   **65 to 's** each one to his
**66 more known** better acquainted.   **74 keep** retain   **75 Seeming**
outward appearance, color   **76 Grace and remembrance** Divine
grace and remembrance after death. (Equated respectively with rue
and rosemary.)   **79 the year . . . ancient** i.e., when autumn arrives
**82 gillyvors** gillyflowers, a kind of carnation   **83 nature's bastards**
i.e., the result of artificial breeding. (See lines 86–8.)   **85 slips** cuttings
**86 For** Because

There is an art which in their piedness shares    87
With great creating nature.
POLIXENES                          Say there be;    88
Yet nature is made better by no mean    89
But nature makes that mean. So, over that art    90
Which you say adds to nature is an art
That nature makes. You see, sweet maid, we marry
A gentler scion to the wildest stock,    93
And make conceive a bark of baser kind    94
By bud of nobler race. This is an art    95
Which does mend nature—change it, rather—but
The art itself is nature.
PERDITA                          So it is.
POLIXENES
Then make your garden rich in gillyvors,
And do not call them bastards.
PERDITA                          I'll not put
The dibble in earth to set one slip of them,    100
No more than, were I painted, I would wish    101
This youth should say 'twere well, and only therefore
Desire to breed by me. Here's flowers for you:
                    [giving them flowers]
Hot lavender, mints, savory, marjoram,    104
The marigold, that goes to bed wi'th' sun
And with him rises weeping. These are flowers    106
Of middle summer, and I think they are given    107
To men of middle age. You're very welcome.
CAMILLO
I should leave grazing, were I of your flock,
And only live by gazing.
PERDITA                          Out, alas!    110
You'd be so lean that blasts of January
Would blow you through and through. [To Florizel]
    Now, my fair'st friend,
I would I had some flow'rs o'th' spring that might
Become your time of day; [to the Shepherdesses] and
    yours, and yours,    114
That wear upon your virgin branches yet    115
Your maidenheads growing. O Proserpina,    116
For the flow'rs now that, frighted, thou let'st fall
From Dis's wagon! Daffodils,
That come before the swallow dares, and take    119
The winds of March with beauty; violets dim,    120
But sweeter than the lids of Juno's eyes
Or Cytherea's breath; pale primroses,    122
That die unmarried ere they can behold

Bright Phoebus in his strength—a malady    124
Most incident to maids; bold oxlips and    125
The crown imperial; lilies of all kinds,    126
The flower-de-luce being one. Oh, these I lack    127
To make you garlands of, and my sweet friend,    128
To strew him o'er and o'er!
FLORIZEL                          What, like a corpse?
PERDITA
No, like a bank for Love to lie and play on,    130
Not like a corpse; or if, not to be buried,    131
But quick and in mine arms. Come, take your flowers.    132
                    [Giving flowers.]
Methinks I play as I have seen them do
In Whitsun pastorals. Sure this robe of mine    134
Does change my disposition.
FLORIZEL                          What you do    135
Still betters what is done. When you speak, sweet,    136
I'd have you do it ever. When you sing,
I'd have you buy and sell so, so give alms,
Pray so; and, for the ord'ring your affairs,
To sing them too. When you do dance, I wish you
A wave o'th' sea, that you might ever do
Nothing but that—move still, still so,
And own no other function. Each your doing,    143
So singular in each particular,    144
Crowns what you are doing in the present deeds,    145
That all your acts are queens.
PERDITA                          Oh, Doricles,    146
Your praises are too large. But that your youth    147
And the true blood which peeps fairly through 't
Do plainly give you out an unstained shepherd,    149
With wisdom I might fear, my Doricles,
You wooed me the false way.
FLORIZEL                          I think you have
As little skill to fear as I have purpose    152
To put you to't. But come, our dance, I pray.    153
Your hand, my Perdita. So turtles pair,    154
That never mean to part.
PERDITA                          I'll swear for 'em.    155
                    [They speak apart.]
POLIXENES [to Camillo]
This is the prettiest lowborn lass that ever

87 **art** i.e., of crossbreeding.    **piedness** particolored appearance. (Perdita disclaims the art of crossbreeding, since it infringes on what nature itself does as well.)    88 **Say** Suppose    89 **mean** means    90 **But** unless. (Polixenes's point is that the art of improving on nature is itself natural.)    93 **gentler** nobler, more cultivated.    **scion** (1) descendant, child (2) cutting of a plant joined to a stock in grafting    94–5 **And . . . race** and thereby bring forth, out of the inferior stock, a flower of superior breed.    100 **dibble** trowel.    **set** plant    101 **painted** made artificially beautiful by cosmetics    104 **Hot** eager, ardent, aromatic (?) (Spices were classified as hot or cold.)    106 **weeping** i.e., dew-drenched.    107 **middle summer** (Having no autumn flowers in any case [lines 79–82], since it is too early in the season, Perdita flatters her older guests by giving them flowers appropriate to *middle age*.)    110 **Out** (An exclamation of dismay.)    114 **Become** suit    115–16 **That . . . growing** you who are still virgins.    116 **Proserpina** daughter of Ceres, stolen away by Pluto (*Dis*) and taken to Hades when, according to Ovid, she was gathering flowers    119 **dares** i.e., returns from seasonal migration.    **take** charm    120 **dim** with hanging heads    122 **Cytherea's** Venus's

124 **Phoebus** the sun-god    124–5 **a malady . . . maids** (Young maids, suffering from greensickness, a kind of anemia, are pale like the primrose.)    126 **crown imperial** flower from the Levant, cultivated in English gardens    127 **flower-de-luce** fleur-de-lis.    **I lack** (Because the season is too late for them.)    128 **To . . . friend** to make garlands of them for you (Polixenes and Camillo) and for my sweet friend (Florizel)    130 **like . . . play on** as if one were strewing a bank where Cupid himself might lie in amorous play    131 **or if** or if not like a corpse, that is, like a living body    132 **quick** alive    134 **Whitsun pastorals** plays (including Robin Hood plays) and English morris dances often performed at Whitsuntide, seven Sundays after Easter.    134–5 **Sure . . . disposition** (Perdita wonders if the wearing of festive garments is inviting her to play a role quite unlike her usual one.)    136 **Still . . . done** gets better and better.    143 **own** have.    **Each your doing** Each thing you do and how you do it    144 **singular** unique and peerless    145 **Crowns . . . deeds** makes whatever you are doing at the moment seem supremely wonderful    146 **Doricles** (Florizel's disguise name.)    147 **large** lavish.    **But that** Were it not that    149 **give you out** proclaim you to be    152 **skill** reason    153 **To . . . to't** i.e., to woo you "the false way," with intent to seduce you.    154 **turtles** turtledoves, as symbols of faithful love    155 **I'll swear for 'em** i.e., I'll be sworn they do.

Ran on the greensward. Nothing she does or seems     157
But smacks of something greater than herself,
Too noble for this place.

CAMILLO                          He tells her something
That makes her blood look out. Good sooth, she is     160
The queen of curds and cream.

CLOWN                                  Come on, strike up!

DORCAS
Mopsa must be your mistress. Marry, garlic,     162
To mend her kissing with!

MOPSA                              Now, in good time!     163

CLOWN
Not a word, a word. We stand upon our manners.     164
Come, strike up!     165

[Music.] *Here a dance of shepherds and*
*shepherdesses.*

POLIXENES
Pray, good shepherd, what fair swain is this
Which dances with your daughter?

SHEPHERD
They call him Doricles, and boasts himself     168
To have a worthy feeding; but I have it     169
Upon his own report and I believe it.
He looks like sooth. He says he loves my daughter.     171
I think so too, for never gazed the moon
Upon the water as he'll stand and read,
As 'twere, my daughter's eyes; and, to be plain,
I think there is not half a kiss to choose
Who loves another best.

POLIXENES                          She dances featly.     176

SHEPHERD
So she does anything—though I report it
That should be silent. If young Doricles
Do light upon her, she shall bring him that     179
Which he not dreams of.

*Enter Servant.*

SERVANT   Oh, master, if you did but hear the peddler at
the door, you would never dance again after a tabor     182
and pipe; no, the bagpipe could not move you. He
sings several tunes faster than you'll tell money. He     184
utters them as he had eaten ballads and all men's ears     185
grew to his tunes.     186

CLOWN   He could never come better. He shall come in.     187
I love a ballad but even too well, if it be doleful matter     188
merrily set down, or a very pleasant thing indeed and     189
sung lamentably.     190

SERVANT   He hath songs for man or woman, of all sizes.     191
No milliner can so fit his customers with gloves. He     192

has the prettiest love songs for maids, so without
bawdry, which is strange, with such delicate burdens     194
of dildos and fadings, "Jump her and thump her"; and     195
where some stretchmouthed rascal would, as it were,     196
mean mischief and break a foul gap into the matter,     197
he makes the maid to answer, "Whoop, do me no
harm, good man"; puts him off, slights him, with
"Whoop, do me no harm, good man."

POLIXENES   This is a brave fellow.     201

CLOWN   Believe me, thou talkest of an admirable con-     202
ceited fellow. Has he any unbraided wares?     203

SERVANT   He hath ribbons of all the colors i'th'
rainbow; points more than all the lawyers in Bohemia     205
can learnedly handle, though they come to him by th'     206
gross; inkles, caddisses, cambrics, lawns. Why, he     207
sings 'em over as they were gods or goddesses; you     208
would think a smock were a she-angel, he so chants to     209
the sleevehand and the work about the square on't.     210

CLOWN   Prithee, bring him in, and let him approach
singing.

PERDITA   Forewarn him that he use no scurrilous words
in 's tunes.                          [*The Servant goes to the door.*]

CLOWN   You have of these peddlers that have more in     215
them than you'd think, sister.

PERDITA   Ay, good brother, or go about to think.     217

*Enter Autolycus, singing.*

AUTOLYCUS
Lawn as white as driven snow,     218
Cypress black as e'er was crow,     219
Gloves as sweet as damask roses,     220
Masks for faces and for noses,
Bugle bracelet, necklace amber,     222
Perfume for a lady's chamber,
Golden coifs and stomachers,     224
For my lads to give their dears,
Pins and poking-sticks of steel,     226
What maids lack from head to heel,     227
Come buy of me, come. Come buy, come buy.
Buy, lads, or else your lasses cry.
Come buy!

CLOWN   If I were not in love with Mopsa, thou shouldst

---

**157 greensward** grassy turf.   **160 makes . . . out** makes her blush.
**162 mistress** i.e., partner in the dance.   **163 kissing** i.e., bad breath.
(Dorcas jests that even garlic would improve Mopsa's breath.)   **in
good time** (An expression of indignation.)   **164 stand upon** set store
by   **165.1 dance** (Probably a morris dance.)   **168 and** i.e., and they
say he   **169 feeding** pasturage, lands   **171 He . . . sooth** He appears to
be honest.   **176 another** the other.   **featly** gracefully.   **179 light upon**
choose   **182 after a tabor** to the tune of a small drum   **184 several**
various.   **tell** count   **185 as . . . ballads** as if he had grown up on
ballads   **186 grew to** listened intently to   **187 better** at a better
time.   **188 but even too well** all too well   **189 pleasant** merry
**190 lamentably** mournfully.   **191 sizes** sorts.   **192 milliner** vendor
of fancy ware and apparel, including gloves, ribbons, and bonnets

**194 burdens** refrains   **195 dildos and fadings** words in the ballad
refrains (with bawdy double meanings, "artificial penises" and
"orgasms," of which the servant is evidently unaware, as is true also
of *jump her, thump her, do me no harm,* etc.)   **196 stretchmouthed**
widemouthed, foulmouthed   **197 break . . . matter** insert some gross
obscenity into the song, or, act in a suggestive way   **201 brave** excellent   **202–3 admirable conceited** wonderfully witty and clever
**203 unbraided** not shopworn, new   **205 points** (1) laces for fastening
clothes (2) headings in an argument   **206–7 by th' gross** in huge
quantities   **207 inkles . . . lawns** linen tapes, worsted tape used for
garters, fine heavy linen fabrics, fine sheer linens.   **208 sings 'em
over as** touts his wares as if   **209 smock** petticoat   **210 sleevehand**
wristband.   **square on't** embroidered bosom or yoke of the garment.
**215 You . . . peddlers** You'll find peddlers   **217 go about** intend,
wish   **217.1 Enter Autolycus** (Apparently he is wearing a false beard;
later in this scene, he removes it to impersonate a courtier to the
Clown and Shepherd.)   **218 Lawn** Fine linen   **219 Cypress** crepe
imported from Cyprus, used for mourning   **220 sweet** i.e., perfumed.
(Also in line 249.)   **222 Bugle bracelet** bracelet of black glossy beads
**224 coifs** close-fitting caps.   **stomachers** embroidered fronts for ladies'
dresses   **226 poking-sticks** rods used for ironing and stiffening the
plaits of ruffs. (With bawdy suggestion.)   **227 What** whatever

take no money of me, but being enthralled as I am, it ²³²
will also be the bondage of certain ribbons and gloves. ²³³

MOPSA   I was promised them against the feast, but they ²³⁴
come not too late now.

DORCAS   He hath promised you more than that, or ²³⁶
there be liars.   ²³⁷

MOPSA   He hath paid you all he promised you. Maybe
he has paid you more, which will shame you to give ²³⁹
him again.   ²⁴⁰

CLOWN   Is there no manners left among maids? Will ²⁴¹
they wear their plackets where they should bear their ²⁴²
faces? Is there not milking time, when you are going to ²⁴³
bed, or kilnhole, to whistle of these secrets, but you ²⁴⁴
must be tittle-tattling before all our guests? 'Tis well
they are whisp'ring. Clamor your tongues, and not a ²⁴⁶
word more.

MOPSA   I have done. Come, you promised me a tawdry ²⁴⁸
lace and a pair of sweet gloves.   ²⁴⁹

CLOWN   Have I not told thee how I was cozened by the ²⁵⁰
way and lost all my money?

AUTOLYCUS   And indeed, sir, there are cozeners abroad;
therefore it behooves men to be wary.

CLOWN   Fear not thou, man, thou shalt lose nothing
here.

AUTOLYCUS   I hope so, sir, for I have about me many ²⁵⁶
parcels of charge.   ²⁵⁷

CLOWN   What hast here? Ballads?

MOPSA   Pray now, buy some. I love a ballad in print,
alife, for then we are sure they are true.   ²⁶⁰

AUTOLYCUS   Here's one to a very doleful tune, how a
usurer's wife was brought to bed of twenty moneybags at a burden, and how she longed to eat adders' ²⁶³
heads and toads carbonadoed.   ²⁶⁴

MOPSA   Is it true, think you?

AUTOLYCUS   Very true, and but a month old.

DORCAS   Bless me from marrying a usurer!   ²⁶⁷

AUTOLYCUS   Here's the midwife's name to't, one
Mistress Taleporter, and five or six honest wives that ²⁶⁹
were present. Why should I carry lies abroad?

MOPSA   Pray you now, buy it.

CLOWN   Come on, lay it by, and let's first see more
ballads. We'll buy the other things anon.

AUTOLYCUS   Here's another ballad, of a fish that appeared upon the coast on Wednesday the fourscore of ²⁷⁵
April, forty thousand fathom above water, and sung ²⁷⁶
this ballad against the hard hearts of maids. It was

thought she was a woman and was turned into a cold
fish for she would not exchange flesh with one that ²⁷⁹
loved her. The ballad is very pitiful, and as true.

DORCAS   Is it true too, think you?

AUTOLYCUS   Five justices' hands at it, and witnesses ²⁸²
more than my pack will hold.

CLOWN   Lay it by too. Another.

AUTOLYCUS   This is a merry ballad, but a very pretty
one.

MOPSA   Let's have some merry ones.

AUTOLYCUS   Why, this is a passing merry one and goes ²⁸⁸
to the tune of "Two Maids Wooing a Man." There's
scarce a maid westward but she sings it. 'Tis in ²⁹⁰
request, I can tell you.

MOPSA   We can both sing it. If thou'lt bear a part, thou ²⁹²
shalt hear; 'tis in three parts.

DORCAS   We had the tune on't a month ago.   ²⁹⁴

AUTOLYCUS   I can bear my part; you must know 'tis my
occupation. Have at it with you.   ²⁹⁶

*Song.*

AUTOLYCUS
     Get you hence, for I must go
     Where it fits not you to know.
DORCAS
          Whither?
MOPSA               Oh, whither?
DORCAS                          Whither?
MOPSA
     It becomes thy oath full well,
     Thou to me thy secrets tell.
DORCAS
          Me too. Let me go thither.
MOPSA
     Or thou goest to th' grange or mill.   ³⁰³
DORCAS
     If to either, thou dost ill.
AUTOLYCUS
          Neither.
DORCAS          What, neither?
AUTOLYCUS                      Neither.
DORCAS
     Thou hast sworn my love to be.
MOPSA
     Thou hast sworn it more to me.
          Then whither goest? Say, whither?

CLOWN   We'll have this song out anon by ourselves. ³⁰⁹
My father and the gentlemen are in sad talk, and we'll ³¹⁰
not trouble them. Come, bring away thy pack after
me. Wenches, I'll buy for you both. Peddler, let's have
the first choice. Follow me, girls.
          [*Exit with Dorcas and Mopsa.*]
AUTOLYCUS   And you shall pay well for 'em.
          [*He follows singing.*]

---

232–3 **it will . . . bondage** it will also mean the taking into custody
(by means of purchase and tying up into a parcel)   234 **against** in
anticipation of, in time for   236–7 **He . . . liars** i.e., He promised to
marry you, too, or else rumor is a liar.   239 **paid you more** i.e., made
you pregnant   239–40 **which . . . again** i.e., which will shame you by
giving birth to his child.   241–3 **Will . . . faces?** i.e., Will they always
be talking and revealing personal secrets?   **plackets** slits in petticoats. (With bawdy suggestion of the pudendum, as in line 613.)
244 **kilnhole** fire hole of a baking oven (where maids might gossip).
**whistle** whisper   246 **Clamor** i.e., Silence   248–9 **tawdry lace** cheap
and showy lace, or, neckerchief. (So called from St. Audrey's Fair.)
249 **sweet** perfumed   250 **cozened** cheated   256 **about me** on my
person   257 **parcels of charge** valuable items.   260 **alife** on my
life   263 **at a burden** in one childbirth   264 **carbonadoed** scored
across and grilled.   267 **Bless** God protect, keep   269 **Taleporter** i.e.,
talebearer, gossip   275 **fourscore** eightieth (!)   276 **forty . . . water**
i.e., 240,000 feet, or about 7.5 miles, in the sky

279 **for** because.   **exchange flesh** have sex   282 **hands at it** signatures on it   288 **passing** surpassingly   290 **westward** in the West
Country   292 **bear a part** sing one of the voices in the part-song
294 **on't** of it   296 **Have at it** Here goes   303 **Or** Either.   **grange**
farm   309 **have this song out** finish this song   310 **sad** serious

*Song.*

Will you buy any tape,
Or lace for your cape,
My dainty duck, my dear-a?
Any silk, any thread,
And toys for your head,                                    319
Of the new'st and fin'st, fin'st wear-a?
Come to the peddler;
Money's a meddler,                                         322
That doth utter all men's ware-a.          *Exit.* 323

[*Enter a Servant.*]

SERVANT   Master, there is three carters, three shep-  324
herds, three neatherds, three swineherds, that have  325
made themselves all men of hair. They call themselves  326
saultiers, and they have a dance which the wenches say  327
is a gallimaufry of gambols, because they are not in't;  328
but they themselves are o'th' mind, if it be not too  329
rough for some that know little but bowling, it will  330
please plentifully.

SHEPHERD   Away! We'll none on't. Here has been too
much homely foolery already.—I know, sir, we  333
weary you.

POLIXENES   You weary those that refresh us. Pray, let's
see these four threes of herdsmen.                        336

SERVANT   One three of them, by their own report, sir,  337
hath danced before the King, and not the worst of the
three but jumps twelve foot and a half by th' square.  339

SHEPHERD   Leave your prating. Since these good men  340
are pleased, let them come in; but quickly now.

SERVANT   Why, they stay at door, sir.
                                        [*He goes to the door.*]

*Here a dance of twelve Satyrs.*

POLIXENES [*to the Shepherd*]
Oh, father, you'll know more of that hereafter.  343
[*To Camillo*] Is it not too far gone? 'Tis time to part
them.
He's simple and tells much. [*To Florizel*] How now, fair
shepherd?                                                 345
Your heart is full of something that does take
Your mind from feasting. Sooth, when I was young  347
And handed love as you do, I was wont                     348
To load my she with knacks. I would have ransacked  349
The peddler's silken treasury and have poured it
To her acceptance; you have let him go,                   351
And nothing marted with him. If your lass                 352

Interpretation should abuse and call this               353
Your lack of love or bounty, you were straited          354
For a reply, at least if you make a care
Of happy holding her.
FLORIZEL                    Old sir, I know                356
She prizes not such trifles as these are.
The gifts she looks from me are packed and locked       358
Up in my heart, which I have given already,
But not delivered. [*To Perdita*] Oh, hear me breathe my
    life                                                  360
Before this ancient sir, who, it should seem,            361
Hath sometime loved! I take thy hand, this hand,
As soft as dove's down and as white as it,
Or Ethiopian's tooth, or the fanned snow that's bolted 364
By th' northern blasts twice o'er.   [*He takes her hand.*]
POLIXENES                    What follows this?
How prettily the young swain seems to wash
The hand was fair before! I have put you out.            367
But to your protestation; let me hear                    368
What you profess.
FLORIZEL          Do, and be witness to't.
POLIXENES
And this my neighbor too?
FLORIZEL                    And he, and more
Than he, and men—the earth, the heavens, and all:
That, were I crowned the most imperial monarch,
Thereof most worthy, were I the fairest youth            373
That ever made eye swerve, had force and knowledge 374
More than was ever man's, I would not prize them
Without her love; for her employ them all,
Commend them and condemn them to her service          377
Or to their own perdition.
POLIXENES                    Fairly offered.               378
CAMILLO
This shows a sound affection.
SHEPHERD                    But, my daughter,
Say you the like to him?
PERDITA                    I cannot speak
So well, nothing so well; no, nor mean better.
By th' pattern of mine own thoughts I cut out            382
The purity of his.
SHEPHERD          Take hands, a bargain!                   383
And, friends unknown, you shall bear witness to't:
I give my daughter to him and will make
Her portion equal his.
FLORIZEL                    Oh, that must be                386
I'th' virtue of your daughter. One being dead,           387

---

**319 toys** trifles   **322 meddler** i.e., go-between in commercial transactions
**323 utter** put on the market   **324 carters** cart drivers   **325 neatherds**
cowherds   **326 of hair** dressed in skins.   **327 saultiers** leapers or
vaulters. (With perhaps a play on *Saltiers* as a blunder for "satyrs.")
**327–8 the wenches . . . in't** the young women, envious because they
are not dancing it themselves, criticize the saultiers' dance as a confused
mess   **329 they themselves** the satyr dancers   **330 bowling** (A more
sedate sport than the vigorous satyr dancing.)   **333 homely** unpolished
**336 threes** trios   **337 three** threesome   **339 by th' square** precisely.
**340 Leave** Leave off   **343 Oh, . . . hereafter** (Polixenes completes the
conversation he has been having with the old Shepherd during the
dance. *Father* is a respectful term of address for older men.)   **345 He's
simple** The old Shepherd is guileless   **347 Sooth** In truth   **348 handed**
handled, dealt in.   **wont** accustomed   **349 she** lass.   **knacks** trifling
gifts.   **351 To her acceptance** for her to choose   **352 nothing marted
with** have done no business with

**353 Interpretation should abuse** should interpret wrongly
**354 were straited** would be hard-pressed   **356 happy holding her**
keeping her happy.   **358 looks** looks for   **360 But not delivered**
i.e., but I have not confirmed it by a solemn vow before witnesses,
making binding the contract.   **breathe my life** i.e., pronounce eternal
vows   **361 this ancient sir** Polixenes   **364 fanned** blown.   **bolted**
sifted   **367 was** that was.   **put you out** interrupted what you were
saying.   **368 to your protestation** on with your public affirmation
**373 Thereof most worthy** and fully worthy of that great office
**374 swerve** turn in my direction (out of awe and respect).   **force**
strength   **377–8 Commend . . . perdition** either commend them to her
service, or, failing that, condemn them to deserved destruction.
**382–3 By . . . of his** By the purity of my own thoughts I can define the
purity of his. (A metaphor of clothes-making; Perdita has formed her
own thoughts on the model of his.)   **386 portion** dowry   **387 One
being dead** When a certain person dies

I shall have more than you can dream of yet;
Enough then for your wonder. But come on:        389
Contract us 'fore these witnesses.

**SHEPHERD**                              Come, your hand;
And, daughter, yours.

**POLIXENES**               Soft, swain, awhile, beseech you.   391
Have you a father?

**FLORIZEL**    I have, but what of him?

**POLIXENES**    Knows he of this?

**FLORIZEL**    He neither does nor shall.

**POLIXENES**    Methinks a father
Is at the nuptial of his son a guest
That best becomes the table. Pray you, once more,    398
Is not your father grown incapable
Of reasonable affairs? Is he not stupid             400
With age and altering rheums? Can he speak? Hear?   401
Know man from man? Dispute his own estate?          402
Lies he not bed-rid, and again does nothing
But what he did being childish?

**FLORIZEL**                     No, good sir,      404
He has his health and ampler strength indeed
Than most have of his age.

**POLIXENES**                   By my white beard,
You offer him, if this be so, a wrong
Something unfilial. Reason my son                   408
Should choose himself a wife, but as good reason
The father, all whose joy is nothing else
But fair posterity, should hold some counsel        411
In such a business.

**FLORIZEL**             I yield all this;           412
But for some other reasons, my grave sir,
Which 'tis not fit you know, I not acquaint
My father of this business.

**POLIXENES**                  Let him know't.

**FLORIZEL**
He shall not.

**POLIXENES**    Prithee, let him.

**FLORIZEL**                       No, he must not.

**SHEPHERD**
Let him, my son. He shall not need to grieve
At knowing of thy choice.

**FLORIZEL**                  Come, come, he must not.
Mark our contract.

**POLIXENES** [*discovering himself*]    Mark your divorce,
young sir,
Whom son I dare not call. Thou art too base
To be acknowledged. Thou a scepter's heir,
That thus affects a sheephook?—Thou old traitor,   422
I am sorry that by hanging thee I can
But shorten thy life one week.—And thou, fresh piece

Of excellent witchcraft, who of force must know     425
The royal fool thou cop'st with—

**SHEPHERD**                       Oh, my heart!      426

**POLIXENES**
I'll have thy beauty scratched with briers and made
More homely than thy state.—For thee, fond boy,     428
If I may ever know thou dost but sigh
That thou no more shalt see this knack—as never     430
I mean thou shalt—we'll bar thee from succession,
Not hold thee of our blood, no, not our kin,
Farre than Deucalion off. Mark thou my words.       433
Follow us to the court.—Thou churl, for this time,  434
Though full of our displeasure, yet we free thee
From the dead blow of it.—And you, enchantment,     436
Worthy enough a herdsman—yea, him too,              437
That makes himself, but for our honor therein,      438
Unworthy thee—if ever henceforth thou               439
These rural latches to his entrance open,
Or hoop his body more with thy embraces,
I will devise a death as cruel for thee
As thou art tender to't.                      *Exit.*

**PERDITA**                Even here undone!
I was not much afeard; for once or twice
I was about to speak and tell him plainly
The selfsame sun that shines upon his court
Hides not his visage from our cottage, but
Looks on alike. Will't please you, sir, be gone?    448
I told you what would come of this. Beseech you,
Of your own state take care. This dream of mine—
Being now awake, I'll queen it no inch farther,
But milk my ewes and weep.

**CAMILLO**                   Why, how now, father?
Speak ere thou diest.

**SHEPHERD**              I cannot speak, nor think,   453
Nor dare to know that which I know. [*To Florizel*] Oh,
sir,
You have undone a man of fourscore three,           455
That thought to fill his grave in quiet, yea,
To die upon the bed my father died,                 457
To lie close by his honest bones; but now
Some hangman must put on my shroud and lay me
Where no priest shovels in dust. [*To Perdita*] Oh,
cursed wretch,
That knew'st this was the Prince, and wouldst adven-
ture
To mingle faith with him! Undone, undone!           462
If I might die within this hour, I have lived
To die when I desire.                         *Exit.*

**FLORIZEL** [*to Perdita*]    Why look you so upon me?

389 **Enough . . . wonder** there will be enough then for you to wonder
at.    391 **Soft** Wait a minute    398 **becomes** befits    400 **reasonable
affairs** matters requiring the use of reason.    401 **altering rheums**
weakening catarrhs or other diseases.    402 **Dispute** Discuss.    **estate**
affairs, condition.    404 **being childish** when he was a child.
408 **Something** somewhat.    **Reason my son** It is reasonable that my
son. (The disguised Polixenes purports to be speaking hypothetically,
using himself as an example, but of course the application to Florizel
is direct.)    411 **hold some counsel** be consulted    412 **yield** concede
422 **affects** desires, shows inclination for

425 **of force** of necessity    426 **thou cop'st** you deal    428 **homely**
(1) unattractive (2) humble.    **state** social status.    **fond** foolish
430 **knack** trifle, schemer    433 **Farre . . . off** farther in kinship than
Deucalion (the Noah of classical legend and hence the primal, distant
ancestor of the whole human race).    434 **churl** i.e., the Shepherd
436 **dead** deadly.    **enchantment** i.e., Perdita    437–9 **him too . . . thee**
worthy indeed of him (Florizel) whose behavior renders him unwor-
thy even of you, if we were to set aside for the moment the question
of the dignity of our royal house    448 **alike** both alike.    453 **ere thou
diest** before you die of grief (?). (Although Polixenes has relented of
his threat to hang the Shepherd, the Shepherd is gloomily sure it will
come to a hanging, lines 459–60.)    455 **fourscore three** 83    457 **died**
died on    462 **mingle faith** exchange pledges

I am but sorry, not afeard; delayed,
But nothing altered. What I was, I am,
More straining on for plucking back, not following 468
My leash unwillingly.

CAMILLO　　　　Gracious my lord,
You know your father's temper. At this time
He will allow no speech, which I do guess
You do not purpose to him; and as hardly 472
Will he endure your sight as yet, I fear.
Then, till the fury of His Highness settle,
Come not before him.

FLORIZEL　　　　I not purpose it.
I think Camillo?

CAMILLO　　　　Even he, my lord.

PERDITA
How often have I told you 'twould be thus?
How often said my dignity would last 478
But till 'twere known?

FLORIZEL　　　　It cannot fail but by 479
The violation of my faith; and then 480
Let nature crush the sides o'th'earth together
And mar the seeds within! Lift up thy looks. 482
From my succession wipe me, father; I 483
Am heir to my affection.

CAMILLO　　　　Be advised. 484

FLORIZEL
I am, and by my fancy. If my reason 485
Will thereto be obedient, I have reason; 486
If not, my senses, better pleased with madness,
Do bid it welcome.

CAMILLO　　　　This is desperate, sir.

FLORIZEL
So call it, but it does fulfill my vow;
I needs must think it honesty. Camillo,
Not for Bohemia nor the pomp that may
Be thereat gleaned, for all the sun sees or
The close earth wombs or the profound seas hides 493
In unknown fathoms, will I break my oath
To this my fair beloved. Therefore, I pray, you,
As you have ever been my father's honored friend,
When he shall miss me—as, in faith, I mean not
To see him any more—cast your good counsels
Upon his passion. Let myself and fortune 499
Tug for the time to come. This you may know 500
And so deliver: I am put to sea 501
With her who here I cannot hold on shore; 502
And most opportune to our need I have
A vessel rides fast by, but not prepared 504

For this design. What course I mean to hold
Shall nothing benefit your knowledge nor 506
Concern me the reporting.

CAMILLO　　　　Oh, my lord, 507
I would your spirit were easier for advice, 508
Or stronger for your need.

FLORIZEL　　　　Hark, Perdita.
[To Camillo] I'll hear you by and by.
[He draws Perdita aside.]

CAMILLO [aside]　　　　He's irremovable, 510
Resolved for flight. Now were I happy if
His going I could frame to serve my turn, 512
Save him from danger, do him love and honor,
Purchase the sight again of dear Sicilia
And that unhappy king, my master, whom
I so much thirst to see.

FLORIZEL　　　　Now, good Camillo,
I am so fraught with curious business that 517
I leave out ceremony.

CAMILLO　　　　Sir, I think 518
You have heard of my poor services i'th' love
That I have borne your father?

FLORIZEL　　　　Very nobly
Have you deserved. It is my father's music
To speak your deeds, not little of his care
To have them recompensed as thought on.

CAMILLO　　　　Well, my lord, 523
If you may please to think I love the King
And through him what's nearest to him, which is
Your gracious self, embrace but my direction, 526
If your more ponderous and settled project 527
May suffer alteration. On mine honor, 528
I'll point you where you shall have such receiving
As shall become Your Highness, where you may 530
Enjoy your mistress—from the whom I see
There's no disjunction to be made but by,
As heavens forfend, your ruin—marry her, 533
And, with my best endeavors in your absence 534
Your discontenting father strive to qualify 535
And bring him up to liking.

FLORIZEL　　　　How, Camillo, 536
May this, almost a miracle, be done,
That I may call thee something more than man,
And after that trust to thee?

CAMILLO　　　　Have you thought on 539
A place whereto you'll go?

FLORIZEL　　　　Not any yet.
But as th'unthought-on accident is guilty 541
To what we wildly do, so we profess 542

---

**468 More . . . back** i.e., like a hound on the leash, all the more eager to go forward for being restrained　**472 purpose** intend　**478 my dignity** i.e., the new status this marriage would have offered　**479 But** only　**480 then** when that happens　**482 mar the seeds within** i.e., destroy the very sources of life on earth (since all material life was thought to be derived from *seeds*).　**483 From . . . father** (Florizel apostrophizes the absent Polixenes.)　**483–4 I . . . affection** i.e., I will be content with my passionate love for Perdita in place of my inheritance.　**484 Be advised** Think carefully, be receptive to wise advice.　**485 fancy** love.　**486 have reason** (1) will be reasonable (2) will be sane　**493 close** secret.　**wombs** encloses, conceals　**499 passion** anger.　**500 Tug** contend　**501 deliver** report　**502 who** whom　**504 rides fast by** that rides at anchor nearby　**but** though

**506–7 Shall . . . reporting** would not behoove you to know nor me to report.　**508 easier for** more open to　**510 irremovable** immovable　**512 frame** shape　**517 curious** demanding care　**518 I . . . ceremony** (Florizel apologizes for failing to observe proper ceremony toward Camillo under the pressures of the present crisis.)　**523 as thought on** as deservingly as they merit.　**526 embrace . . . direction** simply follow my advice　**527 ponderous** weighty　**528 suffer** permit　**530 become Your Highness** suit your royal rank, suit Your Highness　**533 forfend** forbid　**534 with** together with　**535 discontenting** discontented, displeased.　**qualify** appease, pacify　**536 bring . . . liking** get him to the point of approval.　**539 after** ever after　**541–2 as . . . wildly do** just as the unexpected happening (e.g., of our being discovered by the King) is responsible for what we rashly do at this point

Ourselves to be the slaves of chance and flies                                     543
Of every wind that blows.

CAMILLO                              Then list to me.
This follows, if you will not change your purpose
But undergo this flight: make for Sicilia,
And there present yourself and your fair princess—
For so I see she must be—'fore Leontes.
She shall be habited as it becomes                                                 549
The partner of your bed. Methinks I see
Leontes opening his free arms and weeping                                          551
His welcomes forth; asks thee there "Son,
    forgiveness!"
As 'twere i'th' father's person; kisses the hands
Of your fresh princess; o'er and o'er divides him                                  554
Twixt his unkindness and his kindness. Th'one                                      555
He chides to hell, and bids the other grow
Faster than thought or time.

FLORIZEL                             Worthy Camillo,                               557
What color for my visitation shall I                                               558
Hold up before him?

CAMILLO                     Sent by the King your father                          559
To greet him and to give him comforts. Sir,
The manner of your bearing towards him, with
What you, as from your father, shall deliver—                                      562
Things known betwixt us three—I'll write you down,
The which shall point you forth at every sitting                                   564
What you must say, that he shall not perceive
But that you have your father's bosom there                                        566
And speak his very heart.

FLORIZEL                             I am bound to you.
There is some sap in this.

CAMILLO                     A course more promising                               568
Than a wild dedication of yourselves
To unpathed waters, undreamed shores, most certain
To miseries enough; no hope to help you,
But as you shake off one, to take another;                                         572
Nothing so certain as your anchors, who                                            573
Do their best office if they can but stay you                                      574
Where you'll be loath to be. Besides, you know                                     575
Prosperity's the very bond of love,                                                576
Whose fresh complexion and whose heart together                                    577
Affliction alters.

PERDITA                        One of these is true:                               578
I think affliction may subdue the cheek,                                           579
But not take in the mind.

CAMILLO                              Yea, say you so?                              580

There shall not at your father's house these seven
    years                                                                          581
Be born another such.

FLORIZEL                     My good Camillo,
She's as forward of her breeding as she is                                         583
I'th' rear 'our birth.

CAMILLO                     I cannot say 'tis pity                                 584
She lacks instructions, for she seems a mistress                                   585
To most that teach.

PERDITA                     Your pardon, sir; for this
I'll blush you thanks.

FLORIZEL                     My prettiest Perdita!
But oh, the thorns we stand upon! Camillo,
Preserver of my father, now of me,
The medicine of our house, how shall we do?
We are not furnished like Bohemia's son,
Nor shall appear so in Sicilia.

CAMILLO  My lord,
Fear none of this. I think you know my fortunes
Do all lie there. It shall be so my care
To have you royally appointed as if                                                595
The scene you play were mine. For instance, sir,
That you may know you shall not want, one word.

                                                    [*They talk aside.*]

*Enter Autolycus.*

AUTOLYCUS  Ha, ha, what a fool Honesty is! And Trust,
his sworn brother, a very simple gentleman! I have
sold all my trumpery; not a counterfeit stone, not a
ribbon, glass, pomander, brooch, table book, ballad,        601
knife, tape, glove, shoe tie, bracelet, horn ring, to
keep my pack from fasting. They throng who should        603
buy first, as if my trinkets had been hallowed and          604
brought a benediction to the buyer; by which means
I saw whose purse was best in picture, and what I            606
saw, to my good use I remembered. My clown, who
wants but something to be a reasonable man, grew so       608
in love with the wenches' song that he would not stir
his pettitoes till he had both tune and words, which        610
so drew the rest of the herd to me that all their other
senses stuck in ears. You might have pinched a             612
placket, it was senseless. 'Twas nothing to geld a cod-   613
piece of a purse. I could have filed keys off that hung    614
in chains. No hearing, no feeling, but my sir's song,      615
and admiring the nothing of it. So that in this time of    616
lethargy I picked and cut most of their festival purses;
and had not the old man come in with a hubbub

---

543 **flies** i.e., insignificant insects, blown about by the winds of
chance   549 **habited** (richly) dressed   551 **free** generous, noble
554 **fresh** young and beautiful   554–5 **divides . . . kindness** divides
his speech between his former unkindness (which he condemns) and
his present intention of kindness.   557 **Faster** firmer; also, more swiftly
558 **color** excuse, pretext   559 **Hold up before** present to.   **Sent**
i.e., Say you are sent   562 **deliver** say   564 **point you forth** indicate
to you.   **sitting** conference   566 **bosom** inmost thoughts   568 **sap** life
572 **one** one misery, one misfortune.   **take** encounter   573 **Nothing**
not at all.   573–5 **who . . . to be** which are doing as well as can be
hoped if they simply hold you in some undesirable place (rather
than allowing you to proceed on toward even greater disaster).
576–8 **Prosperity's . . . alters** i.e., young love flourishes while things
are going well but loses its fresh complexion and strength of feeling
under the test of adversity.   579 **subdue the cheek** make the complexion look pale and wasted   580 **take in** overcome

581 **your father's** (Said to Perdita, but applicable to Florizel as well.)
**these seven years** i.e., for a long time to come. (Camillo's point is that
she is a nonpareil.)   583 **forward . . . breeding** far in advance of her
lowly upbringing   584 **I'th' rear 'our** below me in   585 **instructions**
formal schooling.   **a mistress** a teacher   595 **appointed** equipped,
outfitted   601 **pomander** scent-ball.   **table book** notebook   603 **from
fasting** i.e., from going empty.   604 **hallowed** made sacred, like
relics   606 **best in picture** best to look at, most promising
608 **wants but something** lacks one thing only (i.e., intelligence)
610 **pettitoes** pig's toes; here, toes   612 **stuck in ears** were occupied
with hearing.   613 **placket** (Literally, slit in a petticoat; with bawdy
suggestion.)   **senseless** insensible.   613–14 **geld . . . purse** cut a
purse loose from the pouch worn at the front of a man's breeches.
615 **my sir's** i.e., the Clown's   616 **nothing** (1) vacuity (2) noting, tune.
(*Nothing* and *noting* were sounded alike in Elizabethan English.)

against his daughter and the King's son and scared my
choughs from the chaff, I had not left a purse alive in    620
the whole army.

[*Camillo, Florizel, and Perdita come forward.*]

CAMILLO
Nay, but my letters by this means being there
So soon as you arrive shall clear that doubt.

FLORIZEL
And those that you'll procure from King Leontes—

CAMILLO
Shall satisfy your father.

PERDITA                                    Happy be you!
All that you speak shows fair.

CAMILLO [*seeing Autolycus*]          Who have we here?
We'll make an instrument of this, omit
Nothing may give us aid.                                    628

AUTOLYCUS [*aside*]    If they have overheard me now,
why, hanging.

CAMILLO    How now, good fellow? Why shak'st thou so?
Fear not, man, here's no harm intended to thee.

AUTOLYCUS    I am a poor fellow, sir.

CAMILLO    Why, be so still. Here's nobody will steal that
from thee. Yet for the outside of thy poverty we must    635
make an exchange. Therefore discase thee instantly—    636
thou must think there's a necessity in't—and change    637
garments with this gentleman. Though the penny-    638
worth on his side be the worst, yet hold thee, there's    639
some boot.                              [*He gives money.*]    640

AUTOLYCUS    I am a poor fellow, sir. [*Aside*] I know ye    641
well enough.                                    642

CAMILLO    Nay, prithee, dispatch. The gentleman is half    643
flayed already.                                    644

AUTOLYCUS    Are you in earnest, sir? [*Aside*] I smell the
trick on't.

FLORIZEL    Dispatch, I prithee.

AUTOLYCUS    Indeed, I have had earnest, but I cannot    648
with conscience take it.

CAMILLO    Unbuckle, unbuckle.

[*Florizel and Autolycus exchange garments.*]

Fortunate mistress—let my prophecy                    651
Come home to ye!—you must retire yourself            652
Into some covert. Take your sweetheart's hat            653
And pluck it o'er your brows, muffle your face,
Dismantle you, and, as you can, disliken                655
The truth of your own seeming, that you may—        656
For I do fear eyes—over to shipboard                    657
Get undescried.

PERDITA                        I see the play so lies
That I must bear a part.

CAMILLO                            No remedy.—

Have you done there?

FLORIZEL                        Should I now meet my father,
He would not call me son.

CAMILLO    Nay, you shall have no hat.
                            [*He gives it to Perdita.*]
Come, lady, come. Farewell, my friend.

AUTOLYCUS                                    Adieu, sir.

FLORIZEL
Oh, Perdita, what have we twain forgot?
Pray you, a word.                    [*They speak aside.*]

CAMILLO [*aside*]
What I do next shall be to tell the King
Of this escape and whither they are bound;
Wherein my hope is I shall so prevail
To force him after, in whose company
I shall re-view Sicilia, for whose sight            670
I have a woman's longing.

FLORIZEL                        Fortune speed us!    671
Thus we set on, Camillo, to th' seaside.

CAMILLO    The swifter speed the better.

                    *Exit* [*with Florizel and Perdita*].

AUTOLYCUS    I understand the business; I hear it. To
have an open ear, a quick eye, and a nimble hand is
necessary for a cutpurse; a good nose is requisite also,
to smell out work for th'other senses. I see this is the
time that the unjust man doth thrive. What an
exchange had this been without boot! What a boot is    679
here with this exchange! Sure the gods do this year
connive at us, and we may do anything extempore.    681
The Prince himself is about a piece of iniquity, stealing    682
away from his father with his clog at his heels. If I    683
thought it were a piece of honesty to acquaint the King
withal, I would not do't. I hold it the more knavery to    685
conceal it; and therein am I constant to my profession.

*Enter Clown and Shepherd* [*carrying a bundle and
a box*]

Aside, aside! Here is more matter for a hot brain.
Every lane's end, every shop, church, session, hang-    688
ing, yields a careful man work.        [*He stands aside.*]

CLOWN    See, see, what a man you are now! There is no
other way but to tell the King she's a changeling and    691
none of your flesh and blood.

SHEPHERD    Nay, but hear me.

CLOWN    Nay, but hear me.

SHEPHERD    Go to, then.                                    695

CLOWN    She being none of your flesh and blood, your
flesh and blood has not offended the King, and so
your flesh and blood is not to be punished by him.
Show those things you found about her, those secret
things, all but what she has with her. This being done,
let the law go whistle, I warrant you.

SHEPHERD    I will tell the King all, every word, yea, and
his son's pranks too; who, I may say, is no honest

---

620 **choughs** jackdaws    628 **Nothing** nothing that    635 **the outside . . .
poverty** i.e., your ragged clothing    636 **discase** undress    637 **think**
understand    638–9 **pennyworth** i.e., value of the bargain    640 **some
boot** something in addition.    641–2 **I know . . . enough** i.e., I bet you
are up to some trick. (See lines 645–6.)    643 **dispatch** hurry. (Also in
line 647.)    644 **flayed** skinned, i.e., undressed    648 **earnest** advance
payment. (Playing on *in earnest* in line 645.)    651–2 **let . . . to ye!** i.e.,
let my prophecy that you, Perdita, will be fortunate be fulfilled for
you!    653 **covert** hiding place.    655–6 **as you . . . seeming** as much as
you can, disguise your outward appearance    657 **eyes** spying eyes

670 **re-view** see again    671 **a woman's longing** i.e., a highly emotional desire.    679 **without boot** i.e., even without added payment.
**What a boot** What a profit    681 **connive at** look indulgently at
682 **about** engaged in    683 **clog** encumbrance (i.e., Perdita)
685 **withal** with it    688 **session** court session    691 **changeling**
child left by the fairies    695 **Go to** Go ahead. (Or, an expression
of impatience.)

man, neither to his father nor to me, to go about to 704
make me the King's brother-in-law.

CLOWN   Indeed, brother-in-law was the farthest off you
could have been to him, and then your blood had
been the dearer by I know not how much an ounce.

AUTOLYCUS [aside]   Very wisely, puppies!

SHEPHERD   Well, let us to the King. There is that in this
fardel will make him scratch his beard.                      711

AUTOLYCUS [aside]   I know not what impediment this
complaint may be to the flight of my master.                713

CLOWN   Pray heartily he be at' palace.                     714

AUTOLYCUS [aside]   Though I am not naturally honest,
I am so sometimes by chance. Let me pocket up my
peddler's excrement. [He takes off his false beard.] How 717
now, rustics, whither are you bound?

SHEPHERD   To the palace, an it like Your Worship.          719

AUTOLYCUS   Your affairs there, what, with whom, the
condition of that fardel, the place of your dwelling, 721
your names, your ages, of what having, breeding, and 722
anything that is fitting to be known, discover.             723

CLOWN   We are but plain fellows, sir.                      724

AUTOLYCUS   A lie; you are rough and hairy. Let me have
no lying. It becomes none but tradesmen, and they 726
often give us soldiers the lie, but we pay them for it 727
with stamped coin, not stabbing steel; therefore they
do not give us the lie.                                     729

CLOWN   Your Worship had like to have given us one, if 730
you had not taken yourself with the manner.                 731

SHEPHERD   Are you a courtier, an't like you, sir?

AUTOLYCUS   Whether it like me or no, I am a courtier.
See'st thou not the air of the court in these enfoldings? 734
Hath not my gait in it the measure of the court? Re- 735
ceives not thy nose court odor from me? Reflect I not 736
on thy baseness court contempt? Think'st thou, for 737
that I insinuate to toze from thee thy business, I am 738
therefore no courtier? I am courtier cap-à-pie, and one 739
that will either push on or pluck back thy business
there. Whereupon I command thee to open thy affair. 741

SHEPHERD   My business, sir, is to the King.

AUTOLYCUS   What advocate hast thou to him?

SHEPHERD   I know not, an't like you.

CLOWN [aside to Shepherd]   "Advocate" 's the court
word for a pheasant. Say you have none.                     746

SHEPHERD   None, sir. I have no pheasant, cock nor hen.

AUTOLYCUS [aside]
How blessed are we that are not simple men!
Yet nature might have made me as these are;
Therefore I will not disdain.

CLOWN [to Shepherd]   This cannot be but a great cour- 751
tier.

SHEPHERD   His garments are rich, but he wears them
not handsomely.

CLOWN   He seems to be the more noble in being fantas- 755
tical. A great man, I'll warrant. I know by the picking 756
on's teeth.                                                 757

AUTOLYCUS   The fardel there? What's i'th' fardel?
Wherefore that box?

SHEPHERD   Sir, there lies such secrets in this fardel and
box which none must know but the King, and which
he shall know within this hour if I may come to th'
speech of him.

AUTOLYCUS   Age, thou hast lost thy labor.                  764

SHEPHERD   Why, sir?

AUTOLYCUS   The King is not at the palace. He is gone
aboard a new ship to purge melancholy and air 767
himself; for, if thou be'st capable of things serious, 768
thou must know the King is full of grief.

SHEPHERD   So 'tis said, sir; about his son, that should 770
have married a shepherd's daughter.                         771

AUTOLYCUS   If that shepherd be not in handfast, let him 772
fly. The curses he shall have, the tortures he shall feel,
will break the back of man, the heart of monster.

CLOWN   Think you so, sir?

AUTOLYCUS   Not he alone shall suffer what wit can make 776
heavy and vengeance bitter, but those that are ger- 777
mane to him, though removed fifty times, shall all 778
come under the hangman—which, though it be great 779
pity, yet it is necessary. An old sheep-whistling rogue, 780
a ram tender, to offer to have his daughter come into 781
grace? Some say he shall be stoned; but that death is 782
too soft for him, say I. Draw our throne into a sheep- 783
cote? All deaths are too few, the sharpest too easy. 784

CLOWN   Has the old man e'er a son, sir, do you hear,
an't like you, sir?

AUTOLYCUS   He has a son, who shall be flayed alive; then,
'nointed over with honey, set on the head of a wasp's
nest; then stand till he be three-quarters and a dram 789
dead; then recovered again with aqua vitae or some 790
other hot infusion; then, raw as he is, and in the hot-
test day prognostication proclaims, shall he be set 792
against a brick wall, the sun looking with a southward
eye upon him, where he is to behold him with flies 794
blown to death. But what talk we of these traitorly ras- 795
cals, whose miseries are to be smiled at, their offenses

---

704 go about make it his object   711 fardel bundle   713 my master
i.e., Florizel. (See 4.3.13.)   714 at' at the   717 excrement outgrowth of
hair, beard.   719 an it like if it please. (Also in lines 732, 744, and 786.)
721 condition nature   722 having property   723 discover reveal.
724 plain simple. (But Autolycus plays on the meaning "smooth.")
726 becomes suits   727 give . . . lie i.e., cheat us. (But giving the lie also
means to accuse a person to his face of lying, an affront which a soldier
would repay with stabbing steel.)   729 give (Autolycus punningly
observes that, since soldiers pay tradesmen for their wares, the tradesmen cannot be said to have given the lie, and so a duel is avoided.)
730 had like was about   731 taken . . . manner i.e., caught yourself in
the act, stopped short. (The Clown observes that Autolycus has once
again avoided the "giving of the lie" and its consequences in a duel by
his clever equivocation. Compare with Touchstone in As You Like It, 5.4.)
734 enfoldings clothes.   735 measure stately tread   736–7 Reflect . . .
contempt? Do I not cast contempt on your ignobility of spirit and
social station?   737–8 for that . . . business because I undertake to toze
or pry out of you what your business may be   739 cap-à-pie from
head to foot   741 open reveal   746 pheasant (The rustics suppose that
Autolycus has asked them what gift they propose to present as a bribe,
as one might do to a judge in a court of law.)

751 be but be anyone but   755–6 fantastical eccentric.   756–7 picking on's teeth (A stylish affectation in Shakespeare's time.)   764 Age
Old man   767 purge rid himself of   768 be'st capable of know anything about   770–1 should have was to have   772 handfast custody.
(With a play on "betrothal.")   776 wit ingenuity (in devising tortures)   777–8 germane related   779 under the hangman into the
hands of the executioner   780 sheep-whistling tending sheep by
whistling after them   781 offer dare   782 grace favor.   783 Draw
Drag   783–4 sheepcote pen for sheep.   789 a dram i.e., a small
amount, a fraction   790 aqua vitae brandy   792 prognostication fore-
casting (in the almanac)   794 he i.e., the sun   795 blown swollen.
what i.e., why

being so capital? Tell me, for you seem to be honest plain men, what you have to the King. Being some- 798 thing gently considered, I'll bring you where he is 799 aboard, tender your persons to his presence, whisper 800 him in your behalfs; and if it be in man besides the King to effect your suits, here is man shall do it.

CLOWN [*to Shepherd*]   He seems to be of great authority. Close with him, give him gold; and though authority 804 be a stubborn bear, yet he is oft led by the nose with gold. Show the inside of your purse to the out- 806 side of his hand, and no more ado. Remember— 807 "stoned," and "flayed alive."

SHEPHERD   An't please you, sir, to undertake the business for us, here is that gold I have. [*He offers* 810 *money.*] I'll make it as much more, and leave this young man in pawn till I bring it you.   812

AUTOLYCUS   After I have done what I promised?

SHEPHERD   Ay, sir.

AUTOLYCUS [*taking the money*]   Well, give me the moiety. 815 [*To the Clown*] Are you a party in this business?

CLOWN   In some sort, sir. But, though my case be a piti- 817 ful one, I hope I shall not be flayed out of it.

AUTOLYCUS   Oh, that's the case of the shepherd's son. Hang him, he'll be made an example.

CLOWN [*to Shepherd*]   Comfort, good comfort! We must to the King and show our strange sights. He must know 'tis none of your daughter nor my sister; we are gone else.—Sir, I will give you as much as this old 824 man does when the business is performed, and remain, as he says, your pawn till it be brought you.

AUTOLYCUS   I will trust you. Walk before toward the 827 seaside; go on the right hand. I will but look upon the 828 hedge and follow you.   829

CLOWN [*to Shepherd*]   We are blessed in this man, as I may say, even blessed.

SHEPHERD   Let's before, as he bids us. He was provided to do us good.   *Exeunt* [*Shepherd and Clown*].

AUTOLYCUS   If I had a mind to be honest, I see Fortune would not suffer me; she drops booties in my mouth. 835 I am courted now with a double occasion: gold, and a 836 means to do the Prince my master good, which who knows how that may turn back to my advancement? I 838 will bring these two moles, these blind ones, aboard 839 him. If he think it fit to shore them again and that the 840 complaint they have to the King concerns him noth- 841 ing, let him call me rogue for being so far officious, for 842 I am proof against that title and what shame else 843 belongs to't. To him will I present them. There may be 844 matter in it.   [*Exit.*]

798 **what you have to** what business you have with   **798–9 Being . . . considered** i.e., (1) Being a gentleman of some influence (2) If I receive a gentlemanly consideration, a bribe   **800 tender your persons** introduce you   **804 Close with him** Accept his offer   **806–7 outside** i.e., palm   **810 that** what   **812 in pawn** as security   **815 moiety** half. **817 case** (1) cause (2) skin   **824 gone else** undone otherwise. **827 before** ahead of me   **828–9 look . . . hedge** i.e., relieve myself **835 suffer** allow.   **booties** prizes   **836 occasion** opportunity **838 turn back** redound   **839–40 aboard him** i.e., to him (Prince Florizel) aboard his ship.   **840 shore** put ashore   **841–2 nothing** not at all   **843 proof against** invulnerable to   **844 him** the King

# 5.1

*Enter Leontes, Cleomenes, Dion, Paulina, [and] servants.*

CLEOMENES
Sir, you have done enough, and have performed
A saintlike sorrow. No fault could you make
Which you have not redeemed—indeed, paid down
More penitence than done trespass. At the last,
Do as the heavens have done: forget your evil.
With them, forgive yourself.

LEONTES                                 Whilst I remember
Her and her virtues, I cannot forget
My blemishes in them, and so still think of          8
The wrong I did myself, which was so much
That heirless it hath made my kingdom and
Destroyed the sweet'st companion that e'er man
Bred his hopes out of. True?

PAULINA                              Too true, my lord.       12
If one by one you wedded all the world,
Or from the all that are took something good          14
To make a perfect woman, she you killed
Would be unparalleled.

LEONTES                           I think so. Killed?
She I killed? I did so, but thou strik'st me
Sorely to say I did. It is as bitter
Upon thy tongue as in my thought. Now, good now,   19
Say so but seldom.

CLEOMENES                 Not at all, good lady.        20
You might have spoken a thousand things that would  21
Have done the time more benefit and graced           22
Your kindness better.

PAULINA                        You are one of those        23
Would have him wed again.

DION                               If you would not so,      24
You pity not the state nor the remembrance            25
Of his most sovereign name, consider little            26
What dangers by His Highness' fail of issue            27
May drop upon his kingdom and devour
Incertain lookers-on. What were more holy             29
Than to rejoice the former queen is well?              30
What holier than, for royalty's repair,
For present comfort and for future good,
To bless the bed of majesty again
With a sweet fellow to't?

PAULINA                          There is none worthy,
Respecting her that's gone. Besides, the gods          35
Will have fulfilled their secret purposes;             36
For has not the divine Apollo said,
Is't not the tenor of his oracle,                      38
That King Leontes shall not have an heir

**5.1. Location:** Sicilia. The royal court.
**8 in them** in relation to them   **12 his hope** his hopes of an heir
**14 the all that are** all the women that there are   **19 good now** i.e., if you please   **20 Not at all** Never say these things   **21–3 that . . . better** that would have helped with matters today and would have bettered your reputation for gracious kindness.   **24 Would** who would   **25–6 You . . . name** you do not pity the kingdom nor do you bear in mind the need of an heir to the throne   **26 consider little** and you consider too little **27 fail of issue** failure to produce an heir   **29 Incertain** bewildered (about the royal succession).   **were** would be   **30 rejoice** rejoice that.   **is well** i.e., is in heaven.   **35 Respecting** in comparison with   **36 Will . . . purposes** are determined to have their secret purposes fulfilled   **38 tenor** purport

Till his lost child be found? Which that it shall
Is all as monstrous to our human reason          41
As my Antigonus to break his grave                42
And come again to me, who, on my life,
Did perish with the infant. 'Tis your counsel     44
My lord should to the heavens be contrary,
Oppose against their wills. [*To Leontes*] Care not for     46
   issue.
The crown will find an heir. Great Alexander
Left his to th' worthiest; so his successor        48
Was like to be the best.

LEONTES                         Good Paulina,      49
Who hast the memory of Hermione,
I know, in honor, oh, that ever I
Had squared me to thy counsel! Then even now     52
I might have looked upon my queen's full eyes,
Have taken treasure from her lips—

PAULINA                         And left them
More rich for what they yielded.

LEONTES                         Thou speak'st truth.    55
No more such wives, therefore no wife. One worse,     56
And better used, would make her sainted spirit     57
Again possess her corpse, and on this stage,       58
Where we're offenders now, appear soul-vexed,
And begin, "Why to me?"

PAULINA                         Had she such power,     60
She had just cause.

LEONTES                         She had, and would incense me     61
To murder her I married.

PAULINA                         I should so.          62
Were I the ghost that walked, I'd bid you mark
Her eye and tell me for what dull part in't
You chose her. Then I'd shriek, that even your ears
Should rift to hear me, and the words that followed     66
Should be, "Remember mine."

LEONTES                         Stars, stars,        67
And all eyes else dead coals! Fear thou no wife;     68
I'll have no wife, Paulina.

PAULINA                         Will you swear
Never to marry but by my free leave?

LEONTES
Never, Paulina, so be blest my spirit!

PAULINA
Then, good my lords, bear witness to his oath.

CLEOMENES
You tempt him overmuch.

PAULINA                         Unless another,       73
As like Hermione as is her picture,

Affront his eye.

CLEOMENES          Good madam—                       41

PAULINA                         I have done.        75
Yet if my lord will marry—if you will, sir,
No remedy but you will—give me the office
To choose you a queen. She shall not be so young
As was your former, but she shall be such
As, walked your first queen's ghost, it should take joy     80
To see her in your arms.

LEONTES                         My true Paulina,
We shall not marry till thou bidd'st us.

PAULINA                         That
Shall be when your first queen's again in breath;
Never till then.                                    84

*Enter a Gentleman.*

GENTLEMAN
One that gives out himself Prince Florizel,        85
Son of Polixenes, with his princess—she
The fairest I have yet beheld—desires access
To your high presence.

LEONTES                         What with him? He comes not     88
Like to his father's greatness. His approach,      89
So out of circumstance and sudden, tells us        90
'Tis not a visitation framed, but forced           91
By need and accident. What train?

GENTLEMAN                         But few,          92
And those but mean.

LEONTES                         His princess, say you, with him?     93

GENTLEMAN
Ay, the most peerless piece of earth, I think,
That e'er the sun shone bright on.

PAULINA                         Oh, Hermione,
As every present time doth boast itself            96
Above a better gone, so must thy grave             97
Give way to what's seen now! [*To the Gentleman*] Sir,
   you yourself                                     98
Have said and writ so, but your writing now
Is colder than that theme. She had not been        100
Nor was not to be equaled—thus your verse          101
Flowed with her beauty once. 'Tis shrewdly ebbed   102
To say you have seen a better.

GENTLEMAN                         Pardon, madam.
The one I have almost forgot—your pardon!          104
The other, when she has obtained your eye,
Will have your tongue too. This is a creature,     106
Would she begin a sect, might quench the zeal
Of all professors else, make proselytes            108

---

**41 monstrous** incredible   **42 As** as for   **44 'Tis your counsel** It's your advice that   **46 Oppose** oppose himself.   **Care not for** Do not be anxious about   **48 Left . . . worthiest** (When Alexander the Great died in 323 B.C., his son Alexander was yet unborn, necessitating the choice of an heir.)   **49 like** likely   **52 squared me** adjusted or regulated myself   **55 for . . . yielded** for the assurance they showed of her love for her husband.   **56–7 One . . . used** i.e., If I took a new, less excellent wife and treated her better   **57 her** Hermione's   **58 possess her corpse** return to earth (*this stage*) in Hermione's human shape   **60 Why to me?** Why this offense to me?   **61 had** would have.   **incense** stir up, incite   **62 should so** would similarly incite you.   **66 rift** rive, split   **67 mine** my eyes.   **Stars** i.e., Her eyes were stars   **68 all eyes else** all other eyes   **73 tempt** bear down on

**75 Affront** confront   **80 walked . . . ghost** if your first queen's ghost were to appear.   **take joy** be overjoyed   **84.1 Enter a Gentleman** (He is called a "Servant" in the Folio text, but his writing poetry in lines 100–4 is more consistent with his being a courtier. Any such person at court is a servant of the king.)   **85 gives out himself** reports himself to be   **88 What** What retinue   **89 Like to** in a manner consistent with   **90 out of circumstance** without ceremony   **91 framed** planned   **92 train** retinue.   **93 mean** lowly.   **96–8 As . . . now!** As every present age boasts its superiority to past times that were in point of fact better, so you, long dead, must give way to present fashion!   **100 that theme** i.e., Hermione, the subject of your verses.   **100–1 She . . . equaled** (Presumably, the poet wrote "She has not been or is not to be equaled.")   **102 'Tis shrewdly ebbed** i.e., You've egregiously gone back on your word   **104 The one** Hermione   **106 tongue** i.e., approval   **108 professors else** believers in other sects or deities

Of who she but bid follow.

PAULINA                              How? Not women!     109

GENTLEMAN
Women will love her that she is a woman
More worth than any man; men, that she is
The rarest of all women.

LEONTES                              Go, Cleomenes.
Yourself, assisted with your honored friends,
Bring them to our embracement.

                    *Exit [Cleomenes with others].*
                              Still, 'tis strange
He thus should steal upon us.

PAULINA                              Had our prince,
Jewel of children, seen this hour, he had paired
Well with this lord. There was not full a month
Between their births.

LEONTES     Prithee, no more, cease. Thou know'st
He dies to me again when talked of. Sure,
When I shall see this gentleman, thy speeches
Will bring me to consider that which may
Unfurnish me of reason. They are come.     123

*Enter Florizel, Perdita, Cleomenes, and others.*

Your mother was most true to wedlock, Prince,
For she did print your royal father off,     125
Conceiving you. Were I but twenty-one,
Your father's image is so hit in you,     127
His very air, that I should call you brother,
As I did him, and speak of something wildly
By us performed before. Most dearly welcome!
And your fair princess—goddess! Oh! Alas,
I lost a couple that twixt heaven and earth
Might thus have stood begetting wonder as
You, gracious couple, do. And then I lost—
All mine own folly—the society,
Amity too, of your brave father, whom,     136
Though bearing misery, I desire my life     137
Once more to look on him.

FLORIZEL                              By his command     138
Have I here touched Sicilia, and from him
Give you all greetings that a king, at friend,     140
Can send his brother; and but infirmity,     141
Which waits upon worn times, hath something seized     142
His wished ability, he had himself     143
The lands and waters twixt your throne and his
Measured to look upon you, whom he loves—     145
He bade me say so—more than all the scepters
And those that bear them living.

LEONTES                              O my brother!     147
Good gentleman, the wrongs I have done thee stir
Afresh within me, and these thy offices,     149

So rarely kind, are as interpreters     150
Of my behindhand slackness. Welcome hither,     151
As is the spring to th'earth. And hath he too
Exposed this paragon to th' fearful usage—
At least ungentle—of the dreadful Neptune,     154
To greet a man not worth her pains, much less
Th'adventure of her person?

FLORIZEL                              Good my lord,     156
She came from Libya.

LEONTES                              Where the warlike Smalus,
That noble honored lord, is feared and loved?

FLORIZEL
Most royal sir, from thence, from him, whose daughter     159
His tears proclaimed his, parting with her. Thence,     160
A prosperous south wind friendly, we have crossed,
To execute the charge my father gave me     162
For visiting Your Highness. My best train
I have from your Sicilian shores dismissed,
Who for Bohemia bend, to signify     165
Not only my success in Libya, sir,
But my arrival and my wife's in safety
Here where we are.

LEONTES                              The blessèd gods
Purge all infection from our air whilst you
Do climate here! You have a holy father,     170
A graceful gentleman, against whose person,     171
So sacred as it is, I have done sin,
For which the heavens, taking angry note,
Have left me issueless; and your father's blest,
As he from heaven merits it, with you,
Worthy his goodness. What might I have been,
Might I a son and daughter now have looked on,
Such goodly things as you?

                    *Enter a Lord.*

LORD                              Most noble sir,
That which I shall report will bear no credit
Were not the proof so nigh. Please you, great sir,
Bohemia greets you from himself by me;
Desires you to attach his son, who has—     182
His dignity and duty both cast off—     183
Fled from his father, from his hopes, and with
A shepherd's daughter.

LEONTES                              Where's Bohemia? Speak.     185

LORD
Here in your city. I now came from him.
I speak amazedly, and it becomes     187
My marvel and my message. To your court     188
Whiles he was hast'ning—in the chase, it seems,
Of this fair couple—meets he on the way
The father of this seeming lady and

---

**109 Of . . . follow** of all those whom she merely invited to follow her.
**How? Not women!** What do you mean? Surely women wouldn't become converts!     **123 Unfurnish** deprive, divest     **125 print . . . off** make you an exact copy of Polixenes, as if in printing     **127 hit** exactly reproduced     **136 brave** noble     **137 my life** i.e., to live long enough     **138 him** (Redundant in modern syntax.)     **140 at friend** in friendship     **141 but** were it not that     **142 waits . . . times** attends old age     **142–3 something . . . ability** to some extent taken away his ability (to travel) as he wishes     **145 Measured** traversed     **147 those . . . living** those living kings who bear scepters.     **149 offices** messages of good will, courteous attentions

**150 rarely** exceptionally     **150–1 are . . . slackness** are like commentators on my slowness in greeting you.     **154 Neptune** god of the sea     **156 Th'adventure** the hazard     **159–60 whose . . . her** whose tears, as he parted with her, proclaimed her to be his daughter.     **162 execute the charge** carry out the mission     **165 bend** direct their course     **170 climate** dwell, reside (in this clime)     **171 graceful** full of grace, gracious     **182 attach** arrest     **183 dignity and duty** princely dignity and filial duty     **185 Bohemia** Polixenes, King of Bohemia.
**187–8 I . . . message** i.e., I speak perplexedly as befits my perplexity and my astonishing news.

Her brother, having both their country quitted
With this young prince.

FLORIZEL                    Camillo has betrayed me,
Whose honor and whose honesty till now
Endured all weathers.

LORD                          Lay't so to his charge.          195
He's with the King your father.

LEONTES                      Who? Camillo?

LORD
Camillo, sir. I spake with him, who now
Has these poor men in question. Never saw I          198
Wretches so quake. They kneel, they kiss the earth,
Forswear themselves as often as they speak.          200
Bohemia stops his ears and threatens them
With divers deaths in death.

PERDITA                      Oh, my poor father!          202
The heaven sets spies upon us, will not have
Our contract celebrated.

LEONTES                      You are married?

FLORIZEL
We are not, sir, nor are we like to be.          205
The stars, I see, will kiss the valleys first;
The odds for high and low's alike.

LEONTES                      My lord,          207
Is this the daughter of a king?

FLORIZEL                      She is,
When once she is my wife.

LEONTES
That "once," I see, by your good father's speed
Will come on very slowly. I am sorry,
Most sorry, you have broken from his liking
Where you were tied in duty, and as sorry
Your choice is not so rich in worth as beauty,          214
That you might well enjoy her.

FLORIZEL [to Perdita]          Dear, look up.
Though Fortune, visible an enemy,          216
Should chase us with my father, power no jot          217
Hath she to change our loves.—Beseech you, sir,          218
Remember since you owed no more to time          219
Than I do now. With thought of such affections,          220
Step forth mine advocate. At your request
My father will grant precious things as trifles.

LEONTES
Would he do so, I'd beg your precious mistress,
Which he counts but a trifle.

PAULINA                      Sir, my liege,
Your eye hath too much youth in't. Not a month
'Fore your queen died, she was more worth such
     gazes
Than what you look on now.

LEONTES                      I thought of her
Even in these looks I made. [To Florizel] But your
     petition

Is yet unanswered. I will to your father.
Your honor not o'erthrown by your desires,          230
I am friend to them and you. Upon which errand
I now go toward him. Therefore follow me,
And mark what way I make. Come, good my lord.          233
                                        Exeunt.

❖

## 5.2

*Enter Autolycus and a Gentleman.*

AUTOLYCUS    Beseech you, sir, were you present at this          1
relation?          2

FIRST GENTLEMAN    I was by at the opening of the fardel,
heard the old shepherd deliver the manner how he          4
found it; whereupon, after a little amazedness, we
were all commanded out of the chamber. Only this,
methought, I heard the shepherd say he found the
child.

AUTOLYCUS    I would most gladly know the issue of it.          9

FIRST GENTLEMAN    I make a broken delivery of the busi-          10
ness, but the changes I perceived in the King and Camillo were very notes of admiration. They seemed al-          12
most, with staring on one another, to tear the cases of          13
their eyes. There was speech in their dumbness, lan-          14
guage in their very gesture. They looked as they had          15
heard of a world ransomed, or one destroyed. A notable
passion of wonder appeared in them, but the wisest
beholder, that knew no more but seeing, could not say          18
if th'importance were joy or sorrow; but in the ex-          19
tremity of the one it must needs be.          20

*Enter another Gentleman.*

Here comes a gentleman that happily knows more.—          21
The news, Rogero?          22

SECOND GENTLEMAN    Nothing but bonfires. The oracle
is fulfilled; the King's daughter is found. Such a deal of          24
wonder is broken out within this hour that ballad
makers cannot be able to express it.

*Enter another Gentleman.*

Here comes the Lady Paulina's steward. He can deliver
you more.—How goes it now, sir? This news which is
called true is so like an old tale that the verity of it is in
strong suspicion. Has the King found his heir?

THIRD GENTLEMAN    Most true, if ever truth were preg-          31
nant by circumstance. That which you hear you'll          32
swear you see, there is such unity in the proofs. The
mantle of Queen Hermione's, her jewel about the neck

---

195 **Lay't . . . charge** Confront him with it directly.   **198 in question**
under interrogation.   **200 Forswear** perjure   **202 divers deaths** various tortures   **205 like** likely   **207 The odds . . . alike** Fortune treats
high and low alike.   **214 worth** rank   **216–18 Though . . . loves** Even
though the goddess Fortune herself, taking visible form as our
enemy, has apparently joined forces with King Polixenes to chase us
down, she has no power to alter our love for each other.   **219–20
since . . . now** when you were no older than I am now.   **220 With . . .
affections** Recalling what it was to be in love at that age

230 **Your . . . desires** If your chaste honor has not been overcome by
sexual desire, and, if what you want in this match is compatible with
your royal honor   **233 way** progress
**5.2. Location: Sicilia. At court.**
**1–2 at this relation?** when this was told?   **4 deliver** report   **9 issue**
outcome   **10 broken** disjointed, fragmented   **12 very notes of admiration** veritable marks of wonderment.   **13–14 to tear . . . eyes** to
burst their eyesockets.   **14 dumbness** silence   **15 as** as if   **18 no . . .
seeing** nothing except what he could see   **19 th'importance** the import,
meaning   **20 of the one** of one or the other   **21 happily** haply,
perhaps   **22 Rogero** Ruggiero.   **24 deal** huge quantity   **31–2 pregnant
by circumstance** made apparent by circumstantial evidence.

of it, the letters of Antigonus found with it which they
know to be his character, the majesty of the creature in 36
resemblance of the mother, the affection of nobleness 37
which nature shows above her breeding, and many 38
other evidences proclaim her with all certainty to be
the King's daughter. Did you see the meeting of the
two kings?

SECOND GENTLEMAN No.

THIRD GENTLEMAN Then have you lost a sight which
was to be seen, cannot be spoken of. There might you
have beheld one joy crown another, so and in such
manner that it seemed Sorrow wept to take leave of
them, for their joy waded in tears. There was casting
up of eyes, holding up of hands, with countenance of 48
such distraction that they were to be known by
garment, not by favor. Our king, being ready to leap 50
out of himself for joy of his found daughter, as if that
joy were now become a loss, cries, "Oh, thy mother,
thy mother!" then asks Bohemia forgiveness; then
embraces his son-in-law; then again worries he his 54
daughter with clipping her; now he thanks the old 55
shepherd, which stands by like a weather-bitten con- 56
duit of many kings' reigns. I never heard of such 57
another encounter, which lames report to follow it and 58
undoes description to do it. 59

SECOND GENTLEMAN What, pray you, became of Antigonus, that carried hence the child?

THIRD GENTLEMAN Like an old tale still, which will have
matter to rehearse though credit be asleep and not an 63
ear open. He was torn to pieces with a bear. This 64
avouches the shepherd's son, who has not only his 65
innocence, which seems much, to justify him, but a 66
handkerchief and rings of his that Paulina knows. 67

FIRST GENTLEMAN What became of his bark and his 68
followers?

THIRD GENTLEMAN Wrecked the same instant of their
master's death and in the view of the shepherd; so that
all the instruments which aided to expose the child
were even then lost when it was found. But oh, the
noble combat that twixt joy and sorrow was fought in
Paulina! She had one eye declined for the loss of her 75
husband, another elevated that the oracle was fulfilled. 76
She lifted the Princess from the earth, and so locks her
in embracing as if she would pin her to her heart, that
she might no more be in danger of losing. 79

FIRST GENTLEMAN The dignity of this act was worth
the audience of kings and princes, for by such was it
acted.

THIRD GENTLEMAN One of the prettiest touches of all,
and that which angled for mine eyes—caught the

water, though not the fish—was when, at the relation
of the Queen's death, with the manner how she came
to't bravely confessed and lamented by the King,
how attentiveness wounded his daughter; till, from 88
one sign of dolor to another, she did, with an "Alas!" I 89
would fain say, bleed tears, for I am sure my heart
wept blood. Who was most marble there changed 91
color; some swooned, all sorrowed. If all the world
could have seen't, the woe had been universal.

FIRST GENTLEMAN Are they returned to the court?

THIRD GENTLEMAN No. The Princess hearing of her
mother's statue, which is in the keeping of Paulina—a
piece many years in doing and now newly performed 97
by that rare Italian master, Julio Romano, who, had he 98
himself eternity and could put breath into his work,
would beguile Nature of her custom, so perfectly he is 100
her ape; he so near to Hermione hath done Hermione 101
that they say one would speak to her and stand in
hope of answer—thither with all greediness of affec- 103
tion are they gone, and there they intend to sup. 104

SECOND GENTLEMAN I thought she had some great matter there in hand, for she hath privately twice or thrice
a day, ever since the death of Hermione, visited that
removed house. Shall we thither and with our com- 108
pany piece the rejoicing? 109

FIRST GENTLEMAN Who would be thence that has the
benefit of access? Every wink of an eye some new
grace will be born. Our absence makes us unthrifty to 112
our knowledge. Let's along. *Exeunt [Gentlemen].*

AUTOLYCUS Now, had I not the dash of my former life 114
in me, would preferment drop on my head. I brought 115
the old man and his son aboard the Prince, told him I 116
heard them talk of a fardel and I know not what. But
he at that time overfond of the shepherd's daughter—so he then took her to be—who began to be 119
much seasick, and himself little better, extremity of
weather continuing, this mystery remained undiscovered. But 'tis all one to me, for had I been the finder 122
out of this secret, it would not have relished among 123
my other discredits.

*Enter Shepherd and Clown, [dressed in finery].*

Here come those I have done good to against my will,
and already appearing in the blossoms of their fortune.

SHEPHERD Come, boy. I am past more children, but
thy sons and daughters will be all gentlemen born.

CLOWN [to Autolycus] You are well met, sir. You denied to fight
with me this other day because I was no gentleman 131

36 **character** handwriting    37 **affection of** natural disposition to
38 **breeding** upbringing    48 **countenance** bearing, demeanor
50 **favor** features.    54 **worries he** he pesters    55 **clipping** embracing
56–7 **which . . . reigns** who stands by weeping like a weather-beaten
fountain that has stood there over the course of many kings' reigns.
58–9 **which . . . do it** which makes any account of it seem inadequate
and beggars the powers of description in an attempt to do justice to it.
63 **rehearse** relate.    **credit** belief    64 **with** by    65 **avouches** confirms,
corroborates    66 **innocence** simplemindedness (such that he would
seem unable to invent such a story)    67 **his** Antigonus's    68 **bark**
ship    75–6 **She . . . fulfilled** i.e., She wept and laughed at the same
time.    79 **losing** being lost.

88 **attentiveness** listening to it    89 **dolor** grief    91 **Who . . . marble**
Even the most hardhearted    97 **performed** completed    98 **Julio
Romano** Italian painter and sculptor of the sixteenth century, better
known as a painter (and an anachronism in this play)    100 **beguile**
deprive, cheat.    **custom** trade    101 **ape** imitator    103–4 **greediness
of affection** eagerness born of love    104 **sup** i.e., feed their hungry
eyes (?) or, perhaps, have a commemorative banquet (?).    108 **removed**
sequestered    109 **piece** add to, augment    112 **unthrifty to** passing
up an opportunity to increase    114–15 **had I . . . head** if it weren't for
the lingering aura of petty thievery that hangs about me, royal favor
would be sure to fall to my lot.    116 **the Prince** the Prince's ship
119 **who** Perdita    122 **'tis all one** it's all the same    123 **relished**
tasted well, suited    131 **this other** the other

born. See you these clothes? Say you see them not and think me still no gentleman born. You were best say these robes are not gentlemen born. Give me the lie, 134 do, and try whether I am not now a gentleman born.

AUTOLYCUS  I know you are now, sir, a gentleman born.

CLOWN  Ay, and have been so any time these four hours.

SHEPHERD  And so have I, boy.

CLOWN  So you have. But I was a gentleman born before my father; for the King's son took me by the hand and called me brother; and then the two kings called my father brother; and then the Prince my brother and the Princess my sister called my father father; and so we wept, and there was the first gentlemanlike tears that ever we shed.

SHEPHERD  We may live, son, to shed many more.

CLOWN  Ay, or else 'twere hard luck, being in so pre- 148 posterous estate as we are. 149

AUTOLYCUS  I humbly beseech you, sir, to pardon me all the faults I have committed to Your Worship, and to give me your good report to the Prince my master. 152

SHEPHERD  Prithee, son, do; for we must be gentle, now 153 we are gentlemen.

CLOWN [to Autolycus]  Thou wilt amend thy life?

AUTOLYCUS  Ay, an it like Your good Worship. 156

CLOWN  Give me thy hand. I will swear to the Prince thou art as honest a true fellow as any is in Bohemia. 158

SHEPHERD  You may say it, but not swear it.

CLOWN  Not swear it, now I am a gentleman? Let boors 160 and franklins say it; I'll swear it. 161

SHEPHERD  How if it be false, son?

CLOWN  If it be ne'er so false, a true gentleman may 163 swear it in the behalf of his friend.—And I'll swear to the Prince thou art a tall fellow of thy hands and that 165 thou wilt not be drunk; but I know thou art no tall fellow of thy hands and that thou wilt be drunk. But I'll swear it, and I would thou wouldst be a tall fellow of thy hands.

AUTOLYCUS  I will prove so, sir, to my power. 170

CLOWN  Ay, by any means prove a tall fellow. If I do not wonder how thou dar'st venture to be drunk, not being a tall fellow, trust me not. Hark, the kings and the princes, our kindred, are going to see the Queen's picture. Come, follow us. We'll be thy good masters. 175

*Exeunt.*

❖

# 5.3

*Enter Leontes, Polixenes, Florizel, Perdita,*

*Camillo, Paulina, lords, etc.*

LEONTES
O grave and good Paulina, the great comfort
That I have had of thee!

PAULINA               What, sovereign sir, 2
I did not well, I meant well. All my services
You have paid home. But that you have vouchsafed, 4
With your crowned brother and these your contracted
Heirs of your kingdoms, my poor house to visit,
It is a surplus of your grace which never 7
My life may last to answer.

LEONTES             O Paulina, 8
We honor you with trouble. But we came 9
To see the statue of our queen. Your gallery
Have we passed through, not without much content
In many singularities; but we saw not 12
That which my daughter came to look upon,
The statue of her mother.

PAULINA           As she lived peerless,
So her dead likeness, I do well believe,
Excels whatever yet you looked upon
Or hand of man hath done. Therefore I keep it
Lonely, apart. But here it is. Prepare 18
To see the life as lively mocked as ever 19
Still sleep mocked death. Behold, and say 'tis well. 20
[*Paulina draws a curtain, and discovers*]
*Hermione [standing] like a statue.*
I like your silence; it the more shows off
Your wonder. But yet speak; first, you, my liege.
Comes it not something near?

LEONTES             Her natural posture! 23
Chide me, dear stone, that I may say indeed
Thou art Hermione; or rather, thou art she
In thy not chiding, for she was as tender
As infancy and grace. But yet, Paulina,
Hermione was not as much wrinkled, nothing 28
So agèd as this seems.

POLIXENES          Oh, not by much.

PAULINA
So much the more our carver's excellence,
Which lets go by some sixteen years and makes her
As she lived now.

LEONTES        As now she might have done, 32
So much to my good comfort as it is
Now piercing to my soul. Oh, thus she stood,
Even with such life of majesty—warm life,
As now it coldly stands—when first I wooed her!
I am ashamed. Does not the stone rebuke me
For being more stone than it? O royal piece! 38
There's magic in thy majesty, which has
My evils conjured to remembrance and
From thy admiring daughter took the spirits, 41

---

134 **Give me the lie** Accuse me to my face of lying (an insult that requires a challenge to a duel)  148–9 **preposterous** (Blunder for "prosperous.")  152 **me** on my behalf  153 **gentle** nobly generous
156 **an it like** if it please  158 **honest a true** worthy an honest
160 **boors** peasants  161 **franklins** farmers owning their own small farms  163 **If . . . false** No matter how false the oath may be
165 **tall . . . hands** brave fellow  170 **my power** the best of my ability. (Autolycus slyly promises to use his hands well—in picking pockets.)
175 **picture** i.e., likeness, painted statue.

**5.3. Location:** Sicilia. Paulina's house.
2 **What** Whatever  4 **home** fully.  7–8 **which . . . answer** which I can never live long enough to be able to repay.  9 **We . . . trouble** i.e., we trouble you with the demands of hospitality, though you are kind enough to call it an honor.  12 **singularities** rarities, curiosities
18 **Lonely** isolated  19 **as lively mocked** as realistically counterfeited
20 **Still** motionless, quiet  23 **something** somewhat  28 **nothing** not at all  32 **As she** as if she  38 **stone** hard-hearted.  **piece** work of art.  41 **admiring** filled with wonder.  **spirits** vital spirits

Standing like stone with thee.
PERDITA                              And give me leave,
And do not say 'tis superstition, that
I kneel and then implore her blessing.—Lady,
                                        [kneeling]
Dear Queen, that ended when I but began,          45
Give me that hand of yours to kiss.
PAULINA                              Oh, patience!
The statue is but newly fixed; the color's          47
Not dry.
CAMILLO
My lord, your sorrow was too sore laid on,          49
Which sixteen winters cannot blow away,
So many summers dry. Scarce any joy                51
Did ever so long live; no sorrow
But killed itself much sooner.
POLIXENES                        Dear my brother,    53
Let him that was the cause of this have power        54
To take off so much grief from you as he
Will piece up in himself.
PAULINA                        Indeed, my lord,       56
If I had thought the sight of my poor image
Would thus have wrought you—for the stone is
    mine—                                           58
I'd not have showed it.
LEONTES                      Do not draw the curtain.
PAULINA
No longer shall you gaze on't, lest your fancy
May think anon it moves.
LEONTES                      Let be, let be.
Would I were dead but that methinks already—
What was he that did make it? See, my lord,
Would you not deem it breathed? And that those veins
Did verily bear blood?
POLIXENES                Masterly done.
The very life seems warm upon her lip.
LEONTES
The fixture of her eye has motion in't,              67
As we are mocked with art.
PAULINA                        I'll draw the curtain.  68
My lord's almost so far transported that
He'll think anon it lives.
LEONTES                      Oh, sweet Paulina,
Make me to think so twenty years together!
No settled senses of the world can match           72
The pleasure of that madness. Let't alone.
PAULINA
I am sorry, sir, I have thus far stirred you; but
I could afflict you farther.
LEONTES                      Do, Paulina;
For this affliction has a taste as sweet

As any cordial comfort. Still methinks                77
There is an air comes from her. What fine chisel
Could ever yet cut breath? Let no man mock me,
For I will kiss her.
PAULINA            Good my lord, forbear.
The ruddiness upon her lip is wet;
You'll mar it if you kiss it, stain your own
With oily painting. Shall I draw the curtain?         83
LEONTES
No, not these twenty years.
PERDITA                    So long could I
Stand by, a looker on.
PAULINA              Either forbear,
Quit presently the chapel, or resolve you             86
For more amazement. If you can behold it,
I'll make the statue move indeed, descend
And take you by the hand. But then you'll think—
Which I protest against—I am assisted
By wicked powers.
LEONTES            What you can make her do
I am content to look on, what to speak
I am content to hear; for 'tis as easy
To make her speak as move.
PAULINA                It is required
You do awake your faith. Then all stand still.
On; those that think it is unlawful business          96
I am about, let them depart.
LEONTES                    Proceed.
No foot shall stir.
PAULINA          Music, awake her; strike!  [Music.]  98
'Tis time. Descend. Be stone no more. Approach.
Strike all that look upon with marvel. Come,          100
I'll fill your grave up. Stir, nay, come away,
Bequeath to death your numbness, for from him         102
Dear life redeems you.—You perceive she stirs.
                            [Hermione comes down.]
Start not. Her actions shall be holy as
You hear my spell is lawful. Do not shun her          105
Until you see her die again, for then                 106
You kill her double. Nay, present your hand.          107
When she was young you wooed her. Now in age
Is she become the suitor?      [Leontes touches her.]
LEONTES                    Oh, she's warm!
If this be magic, let it be an art
Lawful as eating.
POLIXENES        She embraces him.
CAMILLO        She hangs about his neck.
If she pertain to life, let her speak too.            114
POLIXENES
Ay, and make it manifest where she has lived,
Or how stol'n from the dead.
PAULINA                  That she is living,
Were it but told you, should be hooted at
Like an old tale; but it appears she lives,
Though yet she speak not. Mark a little while.

45 ended died.  began was born  47 fixed made fast in its color
49 sore heavily  51 So . . . dry i.e., and sixteen summers cannot dry
up. (Camillo tells the King that he has imposed too heavy a sorrow
on himself if even sixteen years' time cannot end it.)  53 But killed
itself that did not end  54 him i.e., myself (as an innocent cause,
but still a cause)  56 piece up in himself add to his own burden.
58 wrought affected  67 The fixture . . . in't i.e., Her eye, though
motionless, gives the appearance of motion  68 As . . . art in such a
way that we are fooled by artistic illusion.  72 No settled . . . world
No calm mind in the world

77 cordial restorative, heartwarming  83 painting paint.  86 presently
immediately  96 On; those (Often emended to Or those.)  98 strike
strike up.  100 upon on  102 him i.e., death  105–7 Do . . . double
i.e., If you ever shun her during the rest of her life, you will kill her
again.  114 pertain to life is truly alive

[*To Perdita*] Please you to interpose, fair madam. Kneel, 120
And pray your mother's blessing.—Turn, good lady;
Our Perdita is found.

HERMIONE                     You gods, look down
And from your sacred vials pour your graces
Upon my daughter's head!—Tell me, mine own,
Where hast thou been preserved? Where lived? How
  found
Thy father's court? For thou shalt hear that I,
Knowing by Paulina that the oracle
Gave hope thou wast in being, have preserved        128
Myself to see the issue.                            129

PAULINA     There's time enough for that,
Lest they desire upon this push to trouble          131
Your joys with like relation. Go together,          132
You precious winners all; your exultation
Partake to everyone. I, an old turtle,              134
Will wing me to some withered bough and there
My mate, that's never to be found again,            136
Lament till I am lost.

LEONTES                 Oh, peace, Paulina!          137

**120 madam** (Addressed to Perdita as Princess and affianced to be
married.)    **128 in being** alive    **129 the issue** (1) the outcome (2) my
child.    **131–2 Lest . . . relation** lest they (bystanders) insist, at this
critical juncture, on interrupting this moment of joy with your relating of your story or with their telling what has happened to them.
**134 Partake to** share with, communicate to.    **turtle** turtledove
**136–7 My mate . . . lost** grieve for my lost mate until I die.

Thou shouldst a husband take by my consent,
As I by thine a wife. This is a match,
And made between 's by vows. Thou hast found
  mine,
But how is to be questioned, for I saw her,
As I thought, dead, and have in vain said many
A prayer upon her grave. I'll not seek far—
For him, I partly know his mind—to find thee        144
An honorable husband. Come, Camillo,
And take her by the hand, whose worth and honesty  146
Is richly noted and here justified                  147
By us, a pair of kings. Let's from this place.
[*To Hermione*] What? Look upon my brother. Both your
  pardons,
That e'er I put between your holy looks
My ill suspicion. This' your son-in-law             151
And son unto the King, whom, heavens directing,
Is trothplight to your daughter. Good Paulina,      153
Lead us from hence, where we may leisurely
Each one demand and answer to his part              155
Performed in this wide gap of time since first
We were dissevered. Hastily lead away.     *Exeunt.*

**144 For** as for    **146 whose** i.e., Camillo's    **147 richly noted** abundantly acknowledged.    **justified** avouched    **151 This'** This is
**153 trothplight** betrothed    **155 demand** ask

# The Tempest

Shakespeare creates in *The Tempest* a world of the imagination, a place of conflict and ultimately of magical rejuvenation, like the forests of *A Midsummer Night's Dream* and *As You Like It*. The journey to Shakespeare's island is to a realm of art where everything is controlled by the artist-figure. Yet the journey is no escape from reality, for the island shows people what they are, as well as what they ought to be. Even its location juxtaposes the "real" world with an idealized landscape: like Plato's New Atlantis or Thomas More's Utopia, Shakespeare's island is to be found both somewhere and nowhere. On the narrative level, it is located in the Mediterranean Sea. Yet there are overtones of the New World, the Western Hemisphere, where Thomas More had situated his island of Utopia. Ariel fetches dew at Prospero's command from the "Bermudas" (1.2.230). Caliban when prostrate reminds Trinculo of a "dead Indian" (2.2.33) who might be displayed before gullible crowds eager to see such a prodigious creature from across the seas, and Caliban's god, Setebos, was, according to Richard Eden's account of Magellan's circumnavigation of the globe (in *History of Travel*, 1577), worshiped by South American natives. An inspiration for Shakespeare's story (for which no direct literary source is known) may well have been various accounts of the shipwreck in the Bermudas in 1609 of the *Sea Venture*, which was carrying settlers to the new Virginian colony. Shakespeare borrowed details from Sylvester Jourdain's *A Discovery of the Bermudas, Otherwise Called the Isle of Devils*, published in 1610, and from William Strachey's *A True Reportory of the Wreck and Redemption . . . from the Islands of the Bermudas*, which Shakespeare must have seen in manuscript since it was not published until after his death. He wrote the play shortly after reading these works, for *The Tempest* was acted at court in 1611. He may also have known or heard of various accounts of Magellan's circumnavigation of the world in 1519–1522 (including Richard Eden's shortened English version, as part of his *History of Travel*, of an Italian

narrative by Antonio Pigafetta), Francis Fletcher's journal of Sir Francis Drake's circumnavigation in 1577–1580, Richard Rich's *News from Virginia* (1610), and still other potential sources of information. Shakespeare's fascination with the Western Hemisphere gave him, not the actual location of his story, which remains Mediterranean, but a state of mind associated with newness and the unfamiliar. From this strange and unknown place, we gain a radical perspective on the old world of European culture. Miranda sees on the island a "new world" in which humankind appears "brave" (5.1.185), and, although her wonder must be tempered by Prospero's rejoinder that "'Tis new to thee" (line 186) and by Aldous Huxley's still more ironic use of her phrase in the title of his satirical novel *Brave New World*, the island endures as a restorative vision. Even though we experience it fleetingly, as in a dream, this nonexistent realm assumes a permanence enjoyed by all great works of art.

Prospero rules autocratically as artist-king and patriarch over this imaginary world, conjuring up trials and visions to test people's intentions and awaken their consciences. To the island come an assortment of persons who, because they require varied ordeals, are separated by Prospero and Ariel into three groups: King Alonso and those accompanying him; Alonso's son, Ferdinand; and Stephano and Trinculo. Prospero's authority over them, though strong, has limits. As Duke of Milan, he was bookishly inattentive to political matters and thus vulnerable to the Machiavellian conniving of his younger brother, Antonio. Only in a world apart, the artist's world, do his powers derived from learning find their proper sphere. Because he cannot control the world beyond his isle, he must wait for "strange, bountiful Fortune, / Now my dear lady" (1.2.179–80) to bring his enemies near his shore. He eschews, moreover, the black arts of diabolism. His is a white magic, devoted ultimately to what he considers moral ends: rescuing Ariel from the spell of the witch Sycorax, curbing the appetite of Caliban, spying on Antonio and Sebastian in the role of Conscience. He thus comes to see Fortune's gift of delivering his enemies into his hands as an opportunity for him to forgive and restore them, not be revenged.

Such an assumption of godlike power is close to arrogance, even blasphemy, for Prospero is no god. His chief power, learned from books and exercised through Ariel, is to control the elements so as to create illusion—of separation, of death, of the gods' blessing. Yet, since he is human, even this power is an immense burden and temptation. Prospero has much to learn, like those whom he controls. He must subdue his anger, his self-pity, his readiness to blame others, and his domineering over Miranda. He must overcome the vengeful impulse he experiences toward those who have wronged him, and he must conquer the longing many a father feels to hold on to his daughter when she is desired by another man. He struggles with these problems through his art, devising games and shows in which his angry self-pity and jealousy are transmuted into playacting scenes of divine warning and forgiveness toward his enemies and watchful parental austerity toward Miranda and Ferdinand. Prospero's responsibilities cause him to behave magisterially and to be resented by the spirits of the isle. His authority is problematic to us because he seems so patriarchal, colonialist, even sexist and racist in his arrogating to himself the right and responsibility to control others in the name of values they may not share. Ariel longs to be free of this authority. Perhaps our sympathy for Prospero is greatest when we perceive that he, too, with mixed feelings of genuine relief and melancholy, is ready to lay aside his demanding and self-important role as creative moral intelligence.

Alonso and his court party variously illustrate the unregenerate world left behind in Naples and Milan. We first see them on shipboard, panicky and desperate, their titles and finery mocked by roaring waves. Futile ambition seems destined for a watery demise. Yet death by water in this play is a transfiguration rather than an end, a mystical rebirth, as in the regenerative cycle of the seasons from winter to summer. Ariel suggests as much in his song about a drowned father: "Those are pearls that were his eyes. / Nothing of him that doth fade / But doth suffer a sea change / Into something rich and strange" (1.2.402–5). Still, this miracle is not apparent at first to those who are caught in the illusion of death. As in T. S. Eliot's *The Waste Land*, which repeatedly alludes to *The Tempest*, self-blinded human beings fear a disaster that is ironically the prelude to reawakening.

The illusions created on the island serve to test these imperfect men and to make them reveal their true selves. Only Gonzalo, who long ago aided Prospero and Miranda when they were banished from Milan, responds affirmatively to illusion. In his eyes, their having been saved from drowning is a miracle: they breathe fresh air, the grass is green on the island, and their very garments appear not to have been stained by the salt water. His ideal commonwealth (2.1.150–71), which Shakespeare drew in part from an essay by Montaigne, postulates a natural goodness in humanity and makes no allowance for the darker propensities of human behavior, but at least Gonzalo's cheerfulness is in refreshing contrast to the jaded sneers of some of his companions. Sebastian and Antonio react to the magic isle, as to Gonzalo's commonwealth, by cynically refusing to believe in miracles. They scoff at Gonzalo for insistently looking on the bright side; if he were to examine his supposedly unstained clothes more carefully, they jest, he would discover that his pockets are filled with mud. Confident that they are unobserved, they seize the opportunity afforded by Alonso's being asleep to plot a murder and political coup. This attempt is not only despicable but also madly ludicrous, for they are all shipwrecked and no longer have kingdoms over which to quarrel. Even more ironically, Sebastian and Antonio, despite their insolent belief in their self-sufficiency, are being observed. The villains must be taught that an unseen power keeps track of their misdeeds. However presumptuous Prospero may be to assume through Ariel's means the role of godlike observer, he does awaken conscience and prevent murder. The villains may revert to type when returned to their usual habitat, but even they are at least briefly moved to an awareness of the unseen (3.3.21–7). Alonso, more worthy than they, though burdened, too, with sin, responds to his situation with guilt and despair, for he assumes that his son Ferdinand's death is the just punishment of the gods for Alonso's part in the earlier overthrow of Prospero. Alonso must be led, by means of curative illusions, through the purgative experience of contrition to the reward he thinks impossible and undeserved: reunion with his lost son.

Alonso is thus, like Posthumus in *Cymbeline* or Leontes in *The Winter's Tale*, a tragicomic figure—sinful, contrite, ultimately forgiven. Alonso's son Ferdinand must also undergo ordeals and visions devised by Prospero to test his worth, but more on the level of romantic comedy. Ferdinand is young, innocent, and hopeful, well matched to Miranda. From the start, Prospero obviously approves of his prospective son-in-law. Yet even Prospero, needing to prepare himself for a life in which Miranda will no longer be solely his, is not ready to lay aside at least the comic fiction of parental opposition. He invents difficulties, imposes tasks of logbearing (like those assigned Caliban), and issues stern warnings against premarital sex. In the comic mode, parents are expected to cross their children in matters of the heart. Prospero is so convincing in his role of overbearing parent, insisting on absolute unthinking obedience from his daughter, that we remain unsure whether he is truly like that or whether we are meant to sense in his performance a grappling with his own deepest feelings of possessiveness and autocratic authority, tempered finally by his awareness of the arbitrariness of such a role and his readiness to let Miranda decide for herself. As a teacher of youth, moreover, Prospero is convinced by long experience that prizes too easily won are too lightly esteemed. Manifold are the temptations urging Ferdinand to surrender to the natural rhythms of the isle as Caliban would. In place of ceremonies conducted in civilized societies by the church, Prospero must create the illusion of ceremony by his art. The betrothal of Ferdinand and Miranda accordingly unites the best of both worlds: the natural innocence of the island, which teaches them to avoid the corruptions of civilization at its worst, and the higher law of nature achieved through moral wisdom at its best. To this marriage, the goddesses Iris, Ceres, and Juno, the embodiments of Prospero's artistic imagination, bring promises of bounteous harvest, "refreshing showers," celestial harmony, and a springtime brought back to the earth by Proserpina's return from Hades (4.1.76–117). In Ferdinand and Miranda, "nurture" is wedded to "nature." This bond unites spirit and flesh, legitimizing erotic pleasure by incorporating it within Prospero's vision of a cosmic moral order.

At the lowest level of this traditional cosmic and moral framework, in Prospero's view, are Stephano and Trinculo. Their comic scenes juxtapose them with Caliban, for he represents untutored Nature, whereas they represent the unnatural depths to which human beings brought up in civilized society can fall. In this they resemble Sebastian and Antonio, who have learned in supposedly civilized Italy arts of intrigue and political murder. The antics of Stephano and Trinculo burlesque the conduct of their presumed betters, thereby exposing to ridicule the self-deceptions of ambitious men. The clowns desire to exploit the natural wonders of the isle by taking Caliban back to civilization to be shown in carnivals or by plying him with strong drink and whetting his resentment against authority. These plottings are in vain, however, for, like Sebastian and Antonio, the clowns are being watched. The clowns teach Caliban to cry out for "freedom" (2.2.184), by which they mean license to do as one pleases, but are foiled by Ariel as comic nemesis. Because they are degenerate buffoons, Prospero as satirist devises for them an exposure that is appropriately humiliating and satirical.

In contrast with them, Caliban is in many ways a sympathetic character. His sensitivity to natural beauty, as in his descriptions of the "nimble marmoset" or the dreaming music he so often hears (2.2.168; 3.2.137–45), is entirely appropriate to this child of nature. He is, to be sure, the child of a witch and is called many harsh names by Miranda and Prospero, such as "Abhorrèd slave" and "a born devil, on whose nature / Nurture can never stick" (1.2.354; 4.1.188–9). Yet he protests with some justification that the island was his in the first place and that Prospero and Miranda are interlopers. His very existence calls radically into question the value of civilization, which has shown itself capable of limitless depravity. What profit has

Caliban derived from learning Prospero's language other than, as he puts it, to "know how to curse" (1.2.367)? With instinctive cunning, he senses that books are his chief enemy and plots to destroy them first in his attempt at rebellion. The unspoiled natural world does indeed offer civilization a unique perspective on itself. In this it resembles Gonzalo's Montaigne-inspired ideal commonwealth, which, no matter how laughably implausible from the cynic's point of view, does at least question some assumptions—economic, political, and social—common in western societies.

Radical perspectives of this kind invite consideration of many unsettling questions about exploration, colonialist empire building, and sexual imperialism. The fleeting comparison of Caliban to an indigenous native (2.2.33), although ignored in stage productions of the play until the late nineteenth century, suggests a discourse on colonialism in *The Tempest* that anticipates to a remarkable degree a doleful history of exploitation, of providing rum and guns to the natives, and of taking away land through violent expropriation in the name of bringing civilization and God to the New World. Stephano and Trinculo, pouring wine down Caliban's throat and thus reducing him to a worshiping slave, show exploitation at its worst, but surely the play allows us to wonder also if Prospero's enslavement of Caliban, however high-minded in its claims of preventing disorder and rape, is not tainted by the same imperatives of possession and control. The issue is wonderfully complex. Caliban is a projection of both the naturally depraved savage described in many explorers' accounts and the nobly innocent savage described by Montaigne. By dramatizing the conflict without taking sides, Shakespeare leaves open a debate about the worth of Prospero's endeavor to contain Caliban's otherness and produces an ambivalent result in which the apparent victory of colonialism and censorship does not entirely conceal the contradictory struggle through which those values are imposed. The play's many open-ended questions apply not only to the New World but also, nearer at hand, to Ireland—an island on the margins of Britain that was regarded as both savage and threatening.

The play's discourse also raises issues of class and political justice. The battle between Prospero and Caliban is one of "master" and "man" (2.2.183); even if Caliban's cry of "freedom" leads him only into further enslavement by Stephano and Trinculo (who are themselves masterless men), the play does not resolve the conflict by simply reimposing social hierarchy. Caliban, Stephano, and Trinculo are all taught a lesson and are satirically punished for their rebellious behavior, but Caliban at least is pardoned and is left behind on the island at the play's end where presumably he will no longer be a slave. In political terms, Prospero resolves the long-standing hostilities between Milan and Naples by his astute arranging of the betrothal of Miranda to Ferdinand. However much it is idealized as a romantic match presided over harmoniously by the gods, it is also a political union aimed at bringing together the ruling families of those two city-states. Prospero's masque, his ultimate vision of the triumph of civilization, transforms the myth of the rape of a daughter (Proserpina) in such a way as to preserve the daughter's chaste honor in a union that will repair the political and social damage done by the ouster of Prospero from his dukedom of Milan. For these reasons, the betrothal of Ferdinand and Miranda must have seemed politically relevant to Shakespeare's audience when *The Tempest* was performed before King James at Whitehall in November of 1611 and then again at court in 1613 in celebration of the marriage of James's daughter Elizabeth to Frederick, the Elector Palatine.

The play's ending is far from perfectly stable. Antonio never repents, and we cannot be sure what the island will be like once Prospero has disappeared from the scene. Since Prospero's occupation of the island replicates in a sense the process by which he himself was overthrown, we cannot know when the cycle of revolution will ever cease. We cannot even be sure of the extent to which Shakespeare is master of his own colonial debate in *The Tempest* or, conversely, the extent to which today we should feel ourselves free to relativize, ironize, or in other ways criticize this play for apparent or probable prejudices. Not even a great author like Shakespeare can escape the limits of his own time, any more than we can escape the limits of our own. Perhaps we can nonetheless project ourselves, as spectators and readers, into Shakespeare's attempt to celebrate humanity's highest achievement in the union of the island with the civilized world. Miranda and Ferdinand have bright hopes for the future, even if those hopes must be qualified by Prospero's melancholic observation that the "brave new world" with "such people in't" is only "new to thee," to those who are young and not yet experienced in the world's vexations. Even Caliban may be at last reconciled to Prospero's insistent idea of a harmony between will and reason, no matter how perilously and delicately achieved. Prospero speaks of Caliban as a "thing of darkness I / Acknowledge mine," and Caliban vows to "be wise hereafter / And seek for grace" (5.1.278–9, 298–9). Prospero's view is that the natural self-aggrandizing ego within is more contented, better understood, and more truly free when harmonized with reason.

Caliban is a part of humanity; Ariel is not. Ariel can comprehend what compassion and forgiveness would be like, "were I human" (5.1.20), and can take good-natured part in Prospero's designs to castigate or reform his fellow mortals, but Ariel longs to be free in quite another sense from that meant by Caliban. Ariel takes no part in the final integration of human society. This spirit belongs to a magic world of song, music, and illusion that the artist borrows for his use but that exists eternally outside of him. Like the elements of air, earth, fire, and water in which it mysteriously dwells, this spirit is morally neutral but incredibly vital. From it the artist achieves powers of imagination, enabling him to bedim the noontide sun or call forth the dead from their graves. These visions are illusory in the profound sense that all life is illusory, an "insubstantial pageant" melted into thin air (4.1.150–5). Prospero the artist cherishes his own humanity, as a promise of surcease from his labors. Yet the artifact created by the artist endures, existing apart from time and place, as does Ariel: "Then to the elements / Be free, and fare thou well!" (5.1.321–2). No doubt it is a romantic fiction to associate the dramatist Shakespeare with Prospero's farewell to his art, but it is an almost irresistible idea, because we are so moved by the sense of completion and yet humility, the exultation and yet the calm contained in this leave-taking.

As though to demonstrate the summation of his artistry as magician-poet in what he may indeed have designed as his farewell to the stage, Shakespeare puts on a dazzling display of the verbal artistry for which he had already become famous. His command of blank verse is, by this time, more flexible and protean than ever before, with a marked increase in run-on lines, caesuras in mid line, the sharing of blank verse lines between two or more speakers, feminine endings, and other features of the late Shakespearean style. The play is notable for its bravura passages, such as those that begin "Our revels now are ended" (4.1.148–58) and "Ye elves of hills" (5.1.33–57). With its opening storm scene and its solemn shows and masques—the "*several strange shapes*" bringing in a banquet and the appearance of Ariel "*like a harpy*" in 3.3, the masque of Iris, Ceres, and Juno in 4.1, and Prospero's confining the Neapolitans to a charmed circle in 5.1—*The Tempest* presents itself as a tour de force of spectacle and grandeur in which all of these dazzling events are also astutely interrupted by the resurgence of human appetite and by satiric correction. At every turn the drama manifests a deft compression of time and event. The tone is masterfully assured, in prose as in verse. Images of a dreamlike world come together in a remarkable amalgam whereby the characters participate in a fluid world that moves through them even as they move through it, becoming one with the tempest of time.

In performance, *The Tempest* reveals an extraordinary range of interpretive possibilities. Caliban, in late-nineteenth-century stage versions, was apt to be a grotesque specimen of Darwinian evolution, outfitted with gills, fishy scales, and long fingernails for prying shellfish out of rocks (the long fingernails are in fact mentioned, at 2.2.166). Herbert Beerbohm Tree, in 1904, saw Caliban as hairy from head to foot, with unkempt beard, pointed ears, sinister eyes, and long fingernails. To Frank Benson, at Stratford-upon-Avon in 1891, Caliban (played by Benson himself) was the missing link in an evolutionary chain of monkeys, baboons, and other presumably human ancestors; the Caliban of this production climbed a tree on stage, hung upside down, and gibbered. More recently, in accord with critical interest in the play as a potential critique of colonialism, Caliban has often been seen as a Caribbean native, physically imposing and even handsome, restive under his slavery, a man of immense human dignity. An example is that of David Suchet in Clifford Williams's 1987 production for the Royal Shakespeare Company; Suchet's Caliban, a sympathetic victim of imperialism, evoked unmistakable echoes of third-world exploited populations from the West Indies and sub-Saharan Africa. Prospero has undergone no less of a sea change, from the benign authorial stand-in of traditional nineteenth-century productions to a man who can be tyrannical, arbitrary, menacing, close to violence, deeply angry, as in Derek Jarman's 1980 film. Interpretations of Ariel have varied from saccharine sweetness to the punk-haired and drug-inebriated, as in Mark Rylance's Ariel in Ron Daniels's 1982 RSC production. Underlying sexual tensions are evident on all sides in recent productions. Some of the most remarkable versions of the play have abandoned Shakespeare's script to varying degrees, as in Peter Brook's Round House production of 1968 featuring an enormous Sycorax giving birth to Caliban, a takeover of the island and capture of Prospero by Caliban, and a wild orgy. Derek Jarman's film version of 1980 saw the play as dominantly gay, with Caliban as an aging "queen." Giorgio Strehler's *La Tempesta*, Milan, 1977, pictured Ariel as a *commedia dell'arte* Pierrot attached to a wire, soaring through the air and landing as though on Prospero's raised finger. Peter Greenaway's 1991 film called *Prospero's Books* presented the entire play through Prospero's eyes; John Gielgud, as Prospero, spoke virtually all the lines. The extraordinary range of theatrical innovations that has been brought to this play testifies to the script's own remarkable theatrical self-consciousness and its delight in magic and illusion.

# The Tempest

## Names of the Actors

ALONSO, *King of Naples*
SEBASTIAN, *his brother*
PROSPERO, *the right Duke of Milan*
ANTONIO, *his brother, the usurping Duke of Milan*
FERDINAND, *son to the King of Naples*
GONZALO, *an honest old counselor*
ADRIAN *and* ⎱
FRANCISCO, ⎰ *lords*
CALIBAN, *a savage and deformed slave*
TRINCULO, *a jester*
STEPHANO, *a drunken butler*
MASTER *of a ship*

BOATSWAIN
MARINERS

MIRANDA, *daughter to Prospero*

ARIEL, *an airy spirit*
IRIS,
CERES,
JUNO,       *[presented by] spirits*
NYMPHS,
REAPERS,

[*Other Spirits attending on Prospero*]

THE SCENE: *An uninhabited island*

# 1.1

*A tempestuous noise of thunder and lightning heard. Enter a Shipmaster and a Boatswain.*

MASTER   Boatswain!

BOATSWAIN   Here, Master. What cheer?

MASTER   Good, speak to th' mariners. Fall to't yarely, or we run ourselves aground. Bestir, bestir!    *Exit.*    3

*Enter Mariners.*

BOATSWAIN   Heigh, my hearts! Cheerly, cheerly, my hearts! Yare, yare! Take in the topsail. Tend to th' Master's whistle.—Blow till thou burst thy wind, if room enough!    6 7 8

*Enter Alonso, Sebastian, Antonio, Ferdinand, Gonzalo, and others.*

ALONSO   Good Boatswain, have care. Where's the Master? Play the men.    10

BOATSWAIN   I pray now, keep below.

ANTONIO   Where is the Master, Boatswain?

BOATSWAIN   Do you not hear him? You mar our labor. Keep your cabins! You do assist the storm.    14

GONZALO   Nay, good, be patient.    15

BOATSWAIN   When the sea is. Hence! What cares these roarers for the name of king? To cabin! Silence! Trouble us not.    17

GONZALO   Good, yet remember whom thou hast aboard.

BOATSWAIN   None that I more love than myself. You are a councillor; if you can command these elements to silence and work the peace of the present, we will not hand a rope more. Use your authority. If you cannot, give thanks you have lived so long and make yourself ready in your cabin for the mischance of the hour, if it so hap.—Cheerly, good hearts!—Out of our way, I say.    *Exit.*    23 24 27

GONZALO   I have great comfort from this fellow. Methinks he hath no drowning mark upon him; his complexion is perfect gallows. Stand fast, good Fate, to his hanging! Make the rope of his destiny our cable, for our own doth little advantage. If he be not born to be    30 31 32 33

hanged, our case is miserable.    *Exeunt [courtiers].*    34

*Enter Boatswain.*

BOATSWAIN   Down with the topmast! Yare! Lower, lower! Bring her to try wi'th' main course. (*A cry within.*) A plague upon this howling! They are louder than the weather or our office.    36 38

*Enter Sebastian, Antonio, and Gonzalo.*

Yet again? What do you here? Shall we give o'er and drown? Have you a mind to sink?    39

SEBASTIAN   A pox o'your throat, you bawling, blasphemous, incharitable dog!

BOATSWAIN   Work you, then.

ANTONIO   Hang, cur! Hang, you whoreson, insolent noisemaker! We are less afraid to be drowned than thou art.

GONZALO   I'll warrant him for drowning, though the ship were no stronger than a nutshell and as leaky as an unstanched wench.    47 49

BOATSWAIN   Lay her ahold, ahold! Set her two courses. Off to sea again! Lay her off!    50

*Enter Mariners, wet.*

MARINERS   All lost! To prayers, to prayers! All lost! [*The Mariners run about in confusion, exiting at random.*]

BOATSWAIN   What, must our mouths be cold?    53

GONZALO
The King and Prince at prayers! Let's assist them,
For our case is as theirs.

SEBASTIAN              I am out of patience.

ANTONIO
We are merely cheated of our lives by drunkards.    56
This wide-chapped rascal! Would thou mightst lie drowning    57
The washing of ten tides!

GONZALO            He'll be hanged yet,    58
Though every drop of water swear against it
And gape at wid'st to glut him.
(*A confused noise within:*)      "Mercy on us!"—    60
"We split, we split!"—"Farewell my wife and
children!"—    61
"Farewell, brother!"—"We split, we split, we split!"
                   [*Exit Boatswain.*]

ANTONIO   Let's all sink wi'th' King.

SEBASTIAN   Let's take leave of him.
                      *Exit [with Antonio].*

GONZALO   Now would I give a thousand furlongs of sea    65

---

**Names of the Actors** This list appears at the end of the play in the First Folio, in this order, with Miranda's name below that of the men, as was conventional in lists of the period.   PROSPERO, *the right* the rightful   CALIBAN . . . *slave* The Folio reads "*saluage*," a common alternative spelling of *savage* but perhaps also with a resonance of being salvaged from shipwreck. *Slave* has a range of meanings: wretch, rascal, servile creature, one who is owned by another person, one who is divested of freedom and personal rights.
**1.1. Location: On board ship, off the island's coast.**
**3 Good** i.e., It's good you've come, or, my good fellow.   **yarely** nimbly
**6 Tend** Attend   **7 Blow** (Addressed to the wind.)   **7–8 if room enough** as long as we have sea room enough.   **10 Play the men** Act like men, with spirit.   **14 Keep** Remain in   **15 good** good fellow   **17 roarers** waves or winds, or both; spoken to as though they were "bullies" or "blusterers"   **23 work . . . present** bring calm to our present circumstances
**24 hand** handle   **27 hap** happens.   **30–1 complexion . . . gallows** appearance shows he was born to be hanged (and therefore, according to the proverb, in no danger of drowning)   **32 our cable** our means of security   **33 our . . . advantage** our own cable is of little benefit.

**34 case is miserable** circumstances are desperate.   **36 Bring . . . course** Sail her close to the wind by means of the mainsail.   **38 our office** i.e., the noise we make at our work.   **39 give o'er** give up **47 warrant him for drowning** guarantee that he will never be drowned **49 unstanched** insatiable, loose, unrestrained. (Suggesting also "incontinent" and "menstrual.")   **50 ahold** ahull, close to the wind. **courses** sails, i.e., foresail as well as mainsail, set in an attempt to get the ship back out into open water.   **53 must . . . cold?** i.e., must we drown in the cold sea?   **56 merely** utterly   **57 wide-chapped** big-mouthed **57–8 Would . . . tides!** (Pirates were hanged on the shore and left until three tides had come in.)   **60 at wid'st** wide open.   **glut** swallow **61 split** break apart.   **65 furlongs** (A furlong is 220 yards.)

for an acre of barren ground: long heath, brown furze, 66
anything. The wills above be done! But I would fain 67
die a dry death.                                    *Exit.*

❖

## 1.2

*Enter Prospero [in his magic cloak] and Miranda.*

MIRANDA
If by your art, my dearest father, you have               1
Put the wild waters in this roar, allay them.             2
The sky, it seems, would pour down stinking pitch,
But that the sea, mounting to th' welkin's cheek,         4
Dashes the fire out. Oh, I have suffered
With those that I saw suffer! A brave vessel,             6
Who had, no doubt, some noble creature in her,
Dashed all to pieces. Oh, the cry did knock
Against my very heart! Poor souls, they perished.
Had I been any god of power, I would
Have sunk the sea within the earth or ere                11
It should the good ship so have swallowed and
The freighting souls within her.
PROSPERO                          Be collected.            13
No more amazement. Tell your piteous heart               14
There's no harm done.
MIRANDA                    Oh, woe the day!
PROSPERO                             No harm.
I have done nothing but in care of thee,                 16
Of thee, my dear one, thee, my daughter, who
Art ignorant of what thou art, naught knowing
Of whence I am, nor that I am more better                19
Than Prospero, master of a full poor cell,               20
And thy no greater father.
MIRANDA                      More to know                 21
Did never meddle with my thoughts.
PROSPERO                              'Tis time           22
I should inform thee farther. Lend thy hand
And pluck my magic garment from me. So,
            [*laying down his magic cloak and staff*]
Lie there, my art.—Wipe thou thine eyes. Have
   comfort.
The direful spectacle of the wreck, which touched        26
The very virtue of compassion in thee,                   27
I have with such provision in mine art
So safely ordered that there is no soul—
No, not so much perdition as an hair                     30
Betid to any creature in the vessel                      31
Which thou heard'st cry, which thou saw'st sink. Sit
   down,                                                 32

For thou must now know farther.
MIRANDA [*sitting*]                  You have often
Begun to tell me what I am, but stopped
And left me to a bootless inquisition,                   35
Concluding, "Stay, not yet."
PROSPERO                    The hour's now come;
The very minute bids thee ope thine ear.
Obey, and be attentive. Canst thou remember
A time before we came unto this cell?
I do not think thou canst, for then thou wast not
Out three years old.
MIRANDA              Certainly, sir, I can.               41
PROSPERO
By what? By any other house or person?
Of anything the image, tell me, that
Hath kept with thy remembrance.
MIRANDA                      'Tis far off,
And rather like a dream than an assurance                45
That my remembrance warrants. Had I not                  46
Four or five women once that tended me?
PROSPERO
Thou hadst, and more, Miranda. But how is it
That this lives in thy mind? What see'st thou else
In the dark backward and abysm of time?                  50
If thou rememb'rest aught ere thou cam'st here,          51
How thou cam'st here thou mayst.
MIRANDA                      But that I do not.
PROSPERO
Twelve year since, Miranda, twelve year since,
Thy father was the Duke of Milan and
A prince of power.
MIRANDA            Sir, are not you my father?
PROSPERO
Thy mother was a piece of virtue, and                    56
She said thou wast my daughter; and thy father
Was Duke of Milan, and his only heir
And princess no worse issued.
MIRANDA                  Oh, the heavens!                 59
What foul play had we, that we came from thence?
Or blessèd was't we did?
PROSPERO            Both, both, my girl.
By foul play, as thou say'st, were we heaved thence,
But blessedly holp hither.
MIRANDA              Oh, my heart bleeds                  63
To think o'th' teen that I have turned you to,           64
Which is from my remembrance! Please you, farther.       65
PROSPERO
My brother and thy uncle, called Antonio—
I pray thee mark me—that a brother should
Be so perfidious!—he whom next thyself                   68
Of all the world I loved, and to him put
The manage of my state, as at that time                  70
Through all the seigniories it was the first,            71

66 **heath** heather.   **furze** gorse, a weed that grows on wasteland
67 **fain** rather
**1.2. Location: The island, near Prospero's cell. On the Elizabethan
stage, this cell is implicitly at hand throughout the play, although
in some scenes the convention of flexible distance allows us to
imagine characters in other parts of the island.**
1 **art** magic   2 **allay** pacify   4 **welkin's cheek** sky's face   6 **brave**
gallant, splendid   11 **or ere** before   13 **freighting souls** cargo of
souls.   **collected** calm, composed.   14 **amazement** consternation.
**piteous** pitying   16 **but** except   19 **more better** of higher rank
20 **full** very   21 **no greater** i.e., master of nothing greater than a very
poor cell   22 **meddle** mingle   26 **wreck** shipwreck   27 **virtue**
essence   30 **perdition** loss   31 **Betid** happened   32 **Which** whom

35 **bootless inquisition** profitless inquiry   41 **Out** fully   45–6 **assurance . . . warrants** certainty that my memory guarantees.   50 **backward
. . . time** abyss of the past.   51 **aught** anything.   56 **piece** masterpiece,
exemplar   59 **no worse issued** no less nobly born, descended.   63 **holp**
helped   64 **teen . . . to** trouble I've caused you to remember, or put you
to   65 **from** out of   68 **next** next to   70 **manage** management, admin-
istration   71 **seigniories** i.e., city-states of northern Italy

And Prospero the prime duke, being so reputed 72
In dignity, and for the liberal arts
Without a parallel; those being all my study,
The government I cast upon my brother
And to my state grew stranger, being transported 76
And rapt in secret studies. Thy false uncle—
Dost thou attend me?

MIRANDA      Sir, most heedfully.

PROSPERO
Being once perfected how to grant suits, 79
How to deny them, who t'advance and who
To trash for overtopping, new created 81
The creatures that were mine, I say, or changed 'em, 82
Or else new formed 'em; having both the key 83
Of officer and office, set all hearts i'th' state 84
To what tune pleased his ear, that now he was 85
The ivy which had hid my princely trunk
And sucked my verdure out on't. Thou attend'st not. 87

MIRANDA
Oh, good sir, I do.

PROSPERO      I pray thee, mark me.
I, thus neglecting worldly ends, all dedicated
To closeness and the bettering of my mind 90
With that which, but by being so retired, 91
O'erprized all popular rate, in my false brother 92
Awaked an evil nature; and my trust,
Like a good parent, did beget of him 94
A falsehood in its contrary as great
As my trust was, which had indeed no limit,
A confidence sans bound. He being thus lorded 97
Not only with what my revenue yielded
But what my power might else exact, like one 99
Who, having into truth by telling of it, 100
Made such a sinner of his memory 101
To credit his own lie, he did believe 102
He was indeed the Duke, out o'th' substitution 103
And executing th'outward face of royalty 104
With all prerogative. Hence his ambition growing— 105
Dost thou hear?

MIRANDA      Your tale, sir, would cure deafness.

PROSPERO
To have no screen between this part he played 107
And him he played it for, he needs will be 108
Absolute Milan. Me, poor man, my library 109
Was dukedom large enough. Of temporal royalties 110
He thinks me now incapable; confederates— 111
So dry he was for sway—wi'th' King of Naples 112
To give him annual tribute, do him homage, 113
Subject his coronet to his crown, and bend 114
The dukedom yet unbowed—alas, poor Milan!— 115
To most ignoble stooping.

MIRANDA      O the heavens!

PROSPERO
Mark his condition and th'event, then tell me 117
If this might be a brother.

MIRANDA      I should sin
To think but nobly of my grandmother. 119
Good wombs have borne bad sons.

PROSPERO      Now the condition.
This King of Naples, being an enemy
To me inveterate, hearkens my brother's suit, 122
Which was that he, in lieu o'th' premises 123
Of homage and I know not how much tribute,
Should presently extirpate me and mine 125
Out of the dukedom and confer fair Milan,
With all the honors, on my brother. Whereon,
A treacherous army levied, one midnight
Fated to th' purpose did Antonio open
The gates of Milan, and, i'th' dead of darkness,
The ministers for th' purpose hurried thence 131
Me and thy crying self.

MIRANDA      Alack, for pity!
I, not rememb'ring how I cried out then,
Will cry it o'er again. It is a hint 134
That wrings mine eyes to 't.

PROSPERO      Hear a little further, 135
And then I'll bring thee to the present business
Which now 's upon 's, without the which this story
Were most impertinent.

MIRANDA      Wherefore did they not 138
That hour destroy us?

PROSPERO      Well demanded, wench. 139
My tale provokes that question. Dear, they durst not,
So dear the love my people bore me, nor set 141
A mark so bloody on the business, but 142

---

72 **prime** first in rank and importance    76 **to . . . stranger** i.e., withdrew from my responsibilities as duke.   **transported** carried away   79 **perfected** grown skillful   81 **trash** check a hound by tying a cord or weight to its neck.   **overtopping** running too far ahead of the pack; surmounting, exceeding one's authority   81–3 **new . . . formed 'em** won the loyalty of my officers by appointing them to new posts, or replaced them with others who would be loyal to Antonio, or else redefined the positions and their occupants   83–5 **having . . . ear** having now under his control both the officers and the positions, he set a tone for his rule according to his own inclination. (*Key* is also a metaphor for tuning stringed instruments.)   85 **that** so that   87 **verdure** vitality. **on't** of it.   90 **closeness** retirement, seclusion   91–2 **but . . . rate** i.e., were it not that its private nature caused me to neglect my public responsibilities, had a value far beyond what public opinion could appreciate, or, simply because it was done in such seclusion, had a value not appreciated by popular opinion   94 **good parent** (Alludes to the proverb that good parents often bear bad children; see also line 120.)   **of** in   97 **sans** without.   **lorded** raised to lordship, with power and wealth   99 **else** otherwise, additionally   100–2 **Who . . . lie** i.e., who, by repeatedly telling the lie (that he was indeed Duke of Milan), made his memory such a confirmed sinner against truth that he began to believe his own lie   103–5 **out . . . prerogative** as a result of his making himself my substitute and carrying out all the visible functions of royalty with all its rights and privileges.

107–9 **To have . . . Milan** In order to eliminate all separation between his role and himself, he insisted on becoming the Duke of Milan in name as well as in fact.   109 **Me** As for me   110 **temporal royalties** practical prerogatives and responsibilities of a sovereign   111 **confederates** conspires, allies himself   112 **dry** thirsty.   **sway** power   113 **him** i.e., the King of Naples   114 **his . . . his** Antonio's . . . the King of Naples's. **bend** make bow down   115 **yet** hitherto   117 **condition** pact.   **th'event** the outcome   119 **but** other than   122 **hearkens** listens to   123 **he** the King of Naples.   **in . . . premises** in return for the stipulation   125 **presently extirpate** at once remove   131 **ministers . . . purpose** agents employed to do this.   **thence** from there   134 **hint** prompting   135 **wrings** (1) constrains (2) wrings tears from   138 **impertinent** irrelevant.   **Wherefore** Why   139 **demanded** asked.   **wench** (Here a term of endearment.)   141–2 **set . . . bloody** i.e., make obvious their murderous intent. (From the practice of marking with the blood of the prey those who have participated in a successful hunt.)

With colors fairer painted their foul ends. 143
In few, they hurried us aboard a bark, 144
Bore us some leagues to sea, where they prepared 145
A rotten carcass of a butt, not rigged, 146
Nor tackle, sail, nor mast; the very rats 147
Instinctively have quit it. There they hoist us, 148
To cry to th' sea that roared to us, to sigh
To th' winds, whose pity, sighing back again,
Did us but loving wrong.

MIRANDA                         Alack, what trouble 151
Was I then to you!

PROSPERO             Oh, a cherubin
Thou wast that did preserve me. Thou didst smile,
Infusèd with a fortitude from heaven, 154
When I have decked the sea with drops full salt, 155
Under my burden groaned, which raised in me 156
An undergoing stomach, to bear up 157
Against what should ensue.

MIRANDA    How came we ashore?

PROSPERO    By Providence divine.
Some food we had, and some fresh water, that
A noble Neapolitan, Gonzalo,
Out of his charity, who being then appointed
Master of this design, did give us, with
Rich garments, linens, stuffs, and necessaries, 165
Which since have steaded much. So, of his
    gentleness, 166
Knowing I loved my books, he furnished me
From mine own library with volumes that
I prize above my dukedom.

MIRANDA                         Would I might 169
But ever see that man!

PROSPERO             Now I arise. 170
            [*He puts on his magic cloak.*]
Sit still, and hear the last of our sea sorrow. 171
Here in this island we arrived; and here
Have I, thy schoolmaster, made thee more profit 173
Than other princes can, that have more time 174
For vainer hours and tutors not so careful. 175

MIRANDA
Heavens thank you for't! And now, I pray you, sir—
For still 'tis beating in my mind—your reason
For raising this sea storm?

PROSPERO             Know thus far forth:
By accident most strange, bountiful Fortune,
Now my dear lady, hath mine enemies 180
Brought to this shore; and by my prescience
I find my zenith doth depend upon 182

A most auspicious star, whose influence 183
If now I court not, but omit, my fortunes 184
Will ever after droop. Here cease more questions.
Thou art inclined to sleep. 'Tis a good dullness, 186
And give it way. I know thou canst not choose. 187
            [*Miranda sleeps.*]
Come away, servant, come! I am ready now. 188
Approach, my Ariel, come.

        *Enter Ariel.*

ARIEL
All hail, great master, grave sir, hail! I come
To answer thy best pleasure; be't to fly,
To swim, to dive into the fire, to ride
On the curled clouds, to thy strong bidding task 193
Ariel and all his quality.

PROSPERO                         Hast thou, spirit, 194
Performed to point the tempest that I bade thee? 195

ARIEL    To every article.
I boarded the King's ship. Now on the beak, 197
Now in the waist, the deck, in every cabin, 198
I flamed amazement. Sometime I'd divide 199
And burn in many places; on the topmast,
The yards, and bowsprit would I flame distinctly, 201
Then meet and join. Jove's lightning, the precursors 202
O'th' dreadful thunderclaps, more momentary 203
And sight-outrunning were not. The fire and cracks 204
Of sulfurous roaring the most mighty Neptune 205
Seem to besiege and make his bold waves tremble,
Yea, his dread trident shake.

PROSPERO                         My brave spirit! 207
Who was so firm, so constant, that this coil 208
Would not infect his reason?

ARIEL                         Not a soul
But felt a fever of the mad and played 210
Some tricks of desperation. All but mariners
Plunged in the foaming brine and quit the vessel,
Then all afire with me. The King's son, Ferdinand,
With hair up-staring—then like reeds, not hair— 214
Was the first man that leapt; cried, "Hell is empty,
And all the devils are here!"

PROSPERO                         Why, that's my spirit!
But was not this nigh shore?

ARIEL                         Close by, my master.

PROSPERO
But are they, Ariel, safe?

ARIEL                         Not a hair perished.
On their sustaining garments not a blemish, 219
But fresher than before; and, as thou bad'st me, 220

---

143 **fairer** apparently more attractive   144 **In few** In short.   **bark** ship
145 **leagues** anywhere from two to five nautical miles   146 **butt** cask, tub
147 **Nor tackle** neither rigging   148 **quit** abandoned   151 **Did . . .
wrong** i.e., pitied us even as they drove us on.   154 **Infusèd** filled, suffused   155 **decked** covered (with salt tears); adorned   156 **which** i.e.,
the smile   157 **undergoing stomach** courage to go on   165 **stuffs**
supplies   166 **steaded much** been of much use.   **So, of** Similarly, out of
169 **Would** I wish   170 **But ever** i.e., someday   171 **sea sorrow**
sorrowful adventure at sea.   173–4 **made . . . can** provided a more
valuable education than other royal children (of either sex) can enjoy
175 **vainer** more foolishly spent.   **careful** caring.   180 **my dear lady**
(Refers to Fortune, not Miranda.)   182 **zenith** height of fortune.
(Astrological term.)

183 **influence** astrological power   184 **but omit** but ignore instead
186 **dullness** drowsiness   187 **give it way** let it happen (i.e., don't fight it).
188 **Come away** Come   193 **task** make demands upon   194 **quality**
(1) fellow spirits (2) abilities.   195 **to point** to the smallest detail   197 **beak**
prow   198 **waist** midships.   **deck** poop deck at the stern   199 **flamed
amazement** struck terror in the guise of fire, i.e., Saint Elmo's fire.
201 **yards** spars supporting the sails.   **bowsprit** large spar aft.   **distinctly**
in different places   202–4 **Jove's . . . were not** Even lightning, which is
visible before the sound of thunder, could not have been swifter than the
flames that I caused to appear on the ship's rigging.   205 **Neptune** Roman
god of the sea   207 **trident** three-pronged weapon   208 **coil** tumult
210 **of the mad** such as madmen feel   214 **up-staring** standing on end
219 **sustaining** protecting   220 **bad'st** ordered

In troops I have dispersed them 'bout the isle.    221
The King's son have I landed by himself,
Whom I left cooling of the air with sighs    223
In an odd angle of the isle, and sitting,    224
His arms in this sad knot.            [*He folds his arms.*]

PROSPERO                    Of the King's ship,    225
The mariners, say how thou hast disposed,
And all the rest o'th' fleet.

ARIEL                        Safely in harbor
Is the King's ship; in the deep nook where once    228
Thou called'st me up at midnight to fetch dew    229
From the still-vexed Bermudas, there she's hid;    230
The mariners all under hatches stowed,
Who, with a charm joined to their suffered labor,    232
I have left asleep. And for the rest o'th' fleet,
Which I dispersed, they all have met again
And are upon the Mediterranean float    235
Bound sadly home for Naples,
Supposing that they saw the King's ship wrecked
And his great person perish.

PROSPERO                        Ariel, thy charge
Exactly is performed. But there's more work.
What is the time o'th' day?

ARIEL                    Past the mid season.    240

PROSPERO
At least two glasses. The time twixt six and now    241
Must by us both be spent most preciously.

ARIEL
Is there more toil? Since thou dost give me pains,    243
Let me remember thee what thou hast promised,    244
Which is not yet performed me.

PROSPERO                    How now? Moody?
What is't thou canst demand?

ARIEL                    My liberty.

PROSPERO
Before the time be out? No more!

ARIEL                    I prithee,
Remember I have done thee worthy service,
Told thee no lies, made thee no mistakings, served
Without or grudge or grumblings. Thou did promise    250
To bate me a full year.

PROSPERO            Dost thou forget    251
From what a torment I did free thee?

ARIEL                    No.

PROSPERO
Thou dost, and think'st it much to tread the ooze
Of the salt deep,
To run upon the sharp wind of the north,
To do me business in the veins o'th' earth    256

When it is baked with frost.

ARIEL                    I do not, sir.    257

PROSPERO
Thou liest, malignant thing! Hast thou forgot
The foul witch Sycorax, who with age and envy    259
Was grown into a hoop? Hast thou forgot her?    260

ARIEL    No, sir.

PROSPERO
Thou hast. Where was she born? Speak. Tell me.

ARIEL
Sir, in Argier.

PROSPERO        Oh, was she so? I must    263
Once in a month recount what thou hast been,
Which thou forget'st. This damned witch Sycorax,
For mischiefs manifold and sorceries terrible    266
To enter human hearing, from Argier,
Thou know'st, was banished. For one thing she did    268
They would not take her life. Is not this true?

ARIEL    Ay, sir.

PROSPERO
This blue-eyed hag was hither brought with child    271
And here was left by th' sailors. Thou, my slave,
As thou report'st thyself, was then her servant;
And, for thou wast a spirit too delicate    274
To act her earthy and abhorred commands,
Refusing her grand hests, she did confine thee,    276
By help of her more potent ministers
And in her most unmitigable rage,
Into a cloven pine, within which rift
Imprisoned thou didst painfully remain
A dozen years; within which space she died    281
And left thee there, where thou didst vent thy
    groans
As fast as mill wheels strike. Then was this island—    283
Save for the son that she did litter here,    284
A freckled whelp, hag-born—not honored with    285
A human shape.

ARIEL            Yes, Caliban her son.    286

PROSPERO
Dull thing, I say so: he, that Caliban    287
Whom now I keep in service. Thou best know'st
What torment I did find thee in. Thy groans
Did make wolves howl, and penetrate the breasts
Of ever-angry bears. It was a torment
To lay upon the damned, which Sycorax
Could not again undo. It was mine art,
When I arrived and heard thee, that made gape    294
The pine and let thee out.

ARIEL                    I thank thee, master.

**221 troops** groups   **223 cooling of** cooling   **224 angle** corner   **225 sad knot** (Folded arms are indicative of melancholy.)   **228 nook** bay   **229 dew** (Collected at midnight for magical purposes; compare with line 324.)   **230 still-vexed Bermudas** ever stormy Bermudas. (Perhaps refers to the then recent Bermuda shipwreck; see play Introduction. The Folio text reads "*Bermoothes.*")   **232 with . . . labor** by means of a spell added to all the labor they have undergone   **235 float** sea   **240 mid season** noon.   **241 glasses** hourglasses.   **243 pains** labors   **244 remember** remind   **250 or grudge** either complaining   **251 bate** remit, deduct   **256 do me** do for me.   **veins** veins of minerals, or, underground streams, thought to be analogous to the veins of the human body

**257 baked** hardened   **259 envy** malice   **260 grown into a hoop** i.e., so bent over with age as to resemble a hoop.   **263 Argier** Algiers.   **266 terrible** too terrible   **268 one . . . did** (Perhaps a reference to her pregnancy, for which her life would be spared.)   **271 blue-eyed** with dark circles under the eyes or with blue eyelids, implying pregnancy.   **with child** pregnant   **274 for** because   **276 hests** commands   **281 space** space of time   **283 as mill wheels strike** as the blades of a mill wheel strike the water.   **284 Save** except.   **litter** give birth to   **285 whelp** offspring. (Used of animals.)   **hag-born** born of a female demon   **286 Yes . . . son** (Ariel is probably concurring with Prospero's comment about a "freckled whelp," not contradicting the point about "A human shape.")   **287 Dull . . . so** i.e., Exactly, that's what I said, you dullard   **294 gape** open wide

PROSPERO
 If thou more murmur'st, I will rend an oak
 And peg thee in his knotty entrails till     297
 Thou hast howled away twelve winters.
ARIEL            Pardon, master.
 I will be correspondent to command     299
 And do my spriting gently.         300
PROSPERO Do so, and after two days
 I will discharge thee.
ARIEL       That's my noble master!
 What shall I do? Say what? What shall I do?
PROSPERO
 Go make thyself like a nymph o'th' sea. Be subject
 To no sight but thine and mine, invisible
 To every eyeball else. Go take this shape
 And hither come in't. Go, hence with diligence!
            *Exit [Ariel].*
 [*To Miranda*] Awake, dear heart, awake! Thou hast
  slept well.
 Awake!
MIRANDA  The strangeness of your story put
 Heaviness in me.
PROSPERO    Shake it off. Come on,   310
 We'll visit Caliban, my slave, who never
 Yields us kind answer.
MIRANDA      'Tis a villain, sir,
 I do not love to look on.
PROSPERO     But, as 'tis,
 We cannot miss him. He does make our fire,  314
 Fetch in our wood, and serves in offices   315
 That profit us.—What ho! Slave! Caliban!
 Thou earth, thou! Speak.
CALIBAN (*within*)   There's wood enough within.
PROSPERO
 Come forth, I say! There's other business for thee.
 Come, thou tortoise! When?       319

    *Enter Ariel like a water nymph.*

 Fine apparition! My quaint Ariel,     320
 Hark in thine ear.      [*He whispers.*]
ARIEL    My lord, it shall be done.  *Exit.*
PROSPERO
 Thou poisonous slave, got by the devil himself 322
 Upon thy wicked dam, come forth!    323

    *Enter Caliban.*

CALIBAN
 As wicked dew as e'er my mother brushed  324
 With raven's feather from unwholesome fen  325
 Drop on you both! A southwest blow on ye  326
 And blister you all o'er!
PROSPERO
 For this, be sure, tonight thou shalt have cramps,

Side-stitches that shall pen thy breath up. Urchins 329
Shall forth at vast of night that they may work  330
All exercise on thee. Thou shalt be pinched  331
As thick as honeycomb, each pinch more stinging 332
Than bees that made 'em.
CALIBAN      I must eat my dinner. 333
 This island's mine, by Sycorax my mother,
 Which thou tak'st from me. When thou cam'st first,
 Thou strok'st me and made much of me, wouldst give
  me
 Water with berries in't, and teach me how
 To name the bigger light, and how the less,  338
 That burn by day and night. And then I loved thee
 And showed thee all the qualities o'th'isle,
 The fresh springs, brine pits, barren place and fertile.
 Cursed be I that did so! All the charms   342
 Of Sycorax, toads, beetles, bats, light on you!
 For I am all the subjects that you have,
 Which first was mine own king; and here you sty me 345
 In this hard rock, whiles you do keep from me
 The rest o'th'island.
PROSPERO     Thou most lying slave,
 Whom stripes may move, not kindness! I have used
  thee,               348
 Filth as thou art, with humane care, and lodged thee 349
 In mine own cell, till thou didst seek to violate
 The honor of my child.
CALIBAN
 Oho, oho! Would't had been done!
 Thou didst prevent me; I had peopled else  353
 This isle with Calibans.
MIRANDA     Abhorrèd slave,  354
 Which any print of goodness wilt not take,  355
 Being capable of all ill! I pitied thee,
 Took pains to make thee speak, taught thee each hour
 One thing or other. When thou didst not, savage,
 Know thine own meaning, but wouldst gabble like
 A thing most brutish, I endowed thy purposes 360
 With words that made them known. But thy vile race, 361
 Though thou didst learn, had that in't which good
  natures
 Could not abide to be with; therefore wast thou
 Deservedly confined into this rock,
 Who hadst deserved more than a prison.   365
CALIBAN
 You taught me language, and my profit on't
 Is I know how to curse. The red plague rid you 367

---

297 **his** its 299 **correspondent** responsive, submissive 300 **spriting gently** duties as a spirit willingly. 310 **Heaviness** drowsiness 314 **miss** do without 315 **offices** functions, duties 319 **When** (An exclamation of impatience.) 320 **quaint** ingenious 322 **got** begotten, sired 323 **dam** mother. (Used of animals.) 324 **wicked** mischievous, harmful. **brushed** collected by brushing 325 **fen** marsh, bog 326 **southwest** i.e., wind thought to bring disease

329 **Urchins** Hedgehogs; here, suggesting goblins in the guise of hedgehogs 330 **vast** lengthy, desolate time. (Malignant spirits were thought to be restricted to the hours of darkness.) 330–1 **work All exercise** effect their spells 332 **as honeycomb** i.e., as a honeycomb full of bees 333 **'em** i.e., the honeycomb. 338 **the bigger . . . less** i.e., the sun and the moon. (See Genesis 1:16: "God then made two great lights: the greater light to rule the day, and the less light to rule the night.") 342 **charms** spells 345 **Which** who. **sty** confine as in a sty 348 **stripes** lashes. **used** treated 349 **humane** (Not distinguished as a word from *human*.) 353 **peopled else** otherwise populated 354–65 **Abhorrèd . . . prison** (Sometimes assigned by editors to Prospero.) 355 **print** imprint, impression 360 **purposes** meanings, desires 361 **race** natural disposition; species, nature 367 **red plague** plague characterized by red sores and evacuation of blood. **rid** destroy

For learning me your language!

PROSPERO          Hagseed, hence!   368
Fetch us in fuel, and be quick, thou'rt best,   369
To answer other business. Shrugg'st thou, malice?   370
If thou neglect'st or dost unwillingly
What I command, I'll rack thee with old cramps,   372
Fill all thy bones with aches, make thee roar   373
That beasts shall tremble at thy din.

CALIBAN          No, pray thee.
[*Aside*] I must obey. His art is of such power
It would control my dam's god, Setebos,   376
And make a vassal of him.

PROSPERO          So, slave, hence!   377
         *Exit Caliban.*

*Enter Ferdinand; and Ariel, invisible, playing and singing. [Ferdinand does not see Prospero and Miranda.]*

*Ariel's Song.*

ARIEL
Come unto these yellow sands,
And then take hands;
Curtsied when you have, and kissed   380
The wild waves whist;   381
Foot it featly here and there,   382
And, sweet sprites, bear   383
The burden. Hark, hark!   384
*Burden, dispersedly [within].* Bow-wow. 385
The watchdogs bark.
[*Burden, dispersedly within.*] Bow-wow.
Hark, hark! I hear
The strain of strutting chanticleer   389
Cry Cock-a-diddle-dow.

FERDINAND
Where should this music be? I'th'air or th'earth?   391
It sounds no more; and sure it waits upon   392
Some god o'th'island. Sitting on a bank,   393
Weeping again the King my father's wreck,
This music crept by me upon the waters,
Allaying both their fury and my passion   396
With its sweet air. Thence I have followed it,   397
Or it hath drawn me rather. But 'tis gone.
No, it begins again.

*Ariel's Song.*

ARIEL
Full fathom five thy father lies.
Of his bones are coral made.

Those are pearls that were his eyes.
Nothing of him that doth fade
But doth suffer a sea change
Into something rich and strange.
Sea nymphs hourly ring his knell.   406
*Burden [within].* Ding dong.
Hark, now I hear them, ding dong bell.   408

FERDINAND
The ditty does remember my drowned father.   409
This is no mortal business, nor no sound
That the earth owes. I hear it now above me.   411

PROSPERO [*to Miranda*]
The fringèd curtains of thine eye advance   412
And say what thou see'st yond.

MIRANDA        What is't? A spirit?   413
Lord, how it looks about! Believe me, sir,   414
It carries a brave form. But 'tis a spirit.   415

PROSPERO
No, wench, it eats and sleeps and hath such senses
As we have, such. This gallant which thou see'st   417
Was in the wreck; and, but he's something stained   418
With grief, that's beauty's canker, thou mightst
call him   419
A goodly person. He hath lost his fellows
And strays about to find 'em.

MIRANDA      I might call him
A thing divine, for nothing natural
I ever saw so noble.

PROSPERO [*aside*]    It goes on, I see,
As my soul prompts it.—Spirit, fine spirit, I'll free thee 424
Within two days for this.

FERDINAND [*seeing Miranda*]   Most sure, the goddess
On whom these airs attend!—Vouchsafe my prayer   426
May know if you remain upon this island,   427
And that you will some good instruction give
How I may bear me here. My prime request,   429
Which I do last pronounce, is—O you wonder!—   430
If you be maid or no?

MIRANDA       No wonder, sir,   431
But certainly a maid.

FERDINAND      My language? Heavens!
I am the best of them that speak this speech,   433
Were I but where 'tis spoken.

PROSPERO [*coming forward*]    How? The best?
What wert thou if the King of Naples heard thee?

FERDINAND
A single thing, as I am now, that wonders   436
To hear thee speak of Naples. He does hear me,   437

**368 learning** teaching. **Hagseed** Offspring of a female demon **369 thou'rt best** you'd be well advised **370 answer other business** perform other tasks. **372 old** such as old people suffer, long-accustomed and plentiful **373 aches** (Pronounced "aitches.") **376 dam's** mother's. **Setebos** (A god of the Patagonians, named in Richard Eden's *History of Travel*, 1577.) **377.2 Ariel, invisible** (Ariel wears a garment that by convention indicates he is invisible to Ferdinand and Miranda.) **380 Curtsied...have** when you have curtsied **380–1 kissed...whist** kissed the waves into silence, or, kissed while the waves are being hushed **382 Foot it featly** dance nimbly **383 sprites** spirits. **bear** carry, sing **384 burden** refrain, undersong. **385 s.d. dispersedly** i.e., from all directions, not in unison **389 chanticleer** a rooster **391 should** can **392 waits upon** serves, attends **393 bank** sandbank **396 passion** grief **397 air** melody. **Thence** i.e., From the bank on which I sat

**406 knell** announcement of a death by the tolling of a bell. **408 ding...bell** (Perhaps sung as part of the song's *burden* or refrain, as in the previous line.) **409 remember** commemorate **411 owes** owns. **412 The fringèd... advance** Open your eyes **413 yond** yon, yonder. **414 about** around. **415 brave** excellent **417 gallant** fine gentleman **418 but...stained** were it not that his luster is somewhat darkened **419 canker** cankerworm (feeding on buds and leaves) **424 Spirit** Ariel **426 airs** songs. **Vouchsafe** Grant **427 remain** dwell **429 bear me** conduct myself. **prime** chief **430 wonder** (Miranda's name means "to be wondered at.") **431 maid** (1) a human maiden as opposed to a goddess (2) unmarried (3) a virgin **433 best** i.e., in birth **436 A single...now** (1) A single figure who combines into one person both self and King of Naples (since Ferdinand believes he has inherited the kingship) (2) A lonely shipwrecked figure **437 Naples** the King of Naples. **He...me** I who hear my own words am the King of Naples

And that he does I weep. Myself am Naples,    438
Who with mine eyes, never since at ebb, beheld    439
The King my father wrecked.

MIRANDA                               Alack, for mercy!

FERDINAND
Yes, faith, and all his lords, the Duke of Milan
And his brave son being twain.

PROSPERO [aside]                  The Duke of Milan    442
And his more braver daughter could control thee,    443
If now 'twere fit to do't. At the first sight
They have changed eyes.—Delicate Ariel,    445
I'll set thee free for this. [To Ferdinand] A word, good
    sir.
I fear you have done yourself some wrong. A word!    447

MIRANDA [aside]
Why speaks my father so ungently? This
Is the third man that e'er I saw, the first
That e'er I sighed for. Pity move my father    450
To be inclined my way!

FERDINAND [to Miranda]   Oh, if a virgin,
And your affection not gone forth, I'll make you    452
The Queen of Naples.

PROSPERO                   Soft, sir! One word more.    453
[Aside] They are both in either's powers; but this swift
    business    454
I must uneasy make, lest too light winning    455
Make the prize light. [To Ferdinand] One word more: I
    charge thee    456
That thou attend me. Thou dost here usurp    457
The name thou ow'st not, and hast put thyself    458
Upon this island as a spy, to win it
From me, the lord on't.

FERDINAND                  No, as I am a man.    460

MIRANDA
There's nothing ill can dwell in such a temple.
If the ill spirit have so fair a house,
Good things will strive to dwell with't.

PROSPERO                              Follow me.—    463
Speak not you for him; he's a traitor.—Come,
I'll manacle thy neck and feet together.
Seawater shalt thou drink; thy food shall be
The fresh-brook mussels, withered roots, and husks
Wherein the acorn cradled. Follow.

FERDINAND                              No!    
I will resist such entertainment till    469
Mine enemy has more pow'r.
                    He draws, and is charmed from moving.

MIRANDA                          O dear father,    470
Make not too rash a trial of him, for    471

He's gentle, and not fearful.

PROSPERO                          What, I say,    472
My foot my tutor?—Put thy sword up, traitor,    473
Who mak'st a show but dar'st not strike, thy
    conscience
Is so possessed with guilt. Come from thy ward,    475
For I can here disarm thee with this stick    476
And make thy weapon drop.    [He brandishes his staff.]

MIRANDA [trying to hinder him]   Beseech you, father!

PROSPERO
Hence! Hang not on my garments.

MIRANDA                          Sir, have pity!
I'll be his surety.

PROSPERO          Silence! One word more    479
Shall make me chide thee, if not hate thee. What,
An advocate for an impostor? Hush!
Thou think'st there is no more such shapes as he,
Having seen but him and Caliban. Foolish wench,
To th' most of men this is a Caliban,    484
And they to him are angels.

MIRANDA                    My affections
Are then most humble; I have no ambition
To see a goodlier man.

PROSPERO [to Ferdinand]   Come on, obey.
Thy nerves are in their infancy again    488
And have no vigor in them.

FERDINAND                    So they are.
My spirits, as in a dream, are all bound up.    490
My father's loss, the weakness which I feel,
The wreck of all my friends, nor this man's threats
To whom I am subdued, are but light to me,    493
Might I but through my prison once a day
Behold this maid. All corners else o'th'earth    495
Let liberty make use of; space enough
Have I in such a prison.

PROSPERO [aside]   It works. [To Ferdinand] Come on.—
Thou hast done well, fine Ariel! [To Ferdinand] Follow
    me.
[To Ariel] Hark what thou else shalt do me.

MIRANDA [to Ferdinand]                   Be of comfort. 499
My father's of a better nature, sir,
Than he appears by speech. This is unwonted    501
Which now came from him.

PROSPERO [to Ariel]              Thou shalt be as free
As mountain winds; but then exactly do    503
All points of my command.

ARIEL                        To th' syllable.

PROSPERO [to Ferdinand]
Come, follow. [To Miranda] Speak not for him.
                                        Exeunt.

❖

438 And ... weep i.e., and I weep at this reminder that my father is seemingly dead, leaving me heir. 439 never ... ebb never dry, continually
weeping 442 son (The only reference in the play to a son of Antonio.) The Duke of Milan (Prospero insists that he is the proper Duke of
Milan, not Antonio or Ferdinand; see lines 436–41.) 443 more braver
more splendid. control refute and control 445 changed eyes
exchanged amorous glances. 447 done ... wrong i.e., spoken falsely.
450 Pity May pity 452 not gone forth not given to someone else
453 Soft Gently, wait a moment 454 both in either's each in the other's
455 uneasy difficult 456 light cheap. (Playing on light, "easy," in 455.)
457 attend follow, obey 458 ow'st ownest 460 on't of it. 463 strive ...
with't i.e., expel the evil and occupy the temple, the body. 469 entertainment treatment 470 s.d. charmed magically prevented 471 rash harsh

472 gentle (1) wellborn (2) easily managed. fearful frightening,
dangerous; or, cowardly. 473 My ... tutor? i.e., Do you, as my
daughter and thus bound to me by obedience, dare presume to teach
me what to do? 475 ward defensive posture (in fencing) 476 stick
magician's staff or wand 479 surety guarantee. 484 To compared
with 488 nerves sinews 490 spirits vital powers 493 light unimportant 495 corners else other corners, regions 499 me for me.
501 unwonted unusual 503 then until then

## 2.1

*Enter Alonso, Sebastian, Antonio, Gonzalo,*
*Adrian, Francisco, and others.*

GONZALO [*to Alonso*]
Beseech you, sir, be merry. You have cause,
So have we all, of joy, for our escape
Is much beyond our loss. Our hint of woe    3
Is common; every day some sailor's wife,
The masters of some merchant, and the merchant,    5
Have just our theme of woe. But for the miracle,    6
I mean our preservation, few in millions
Can speak like us. Then wisely, good sir, weigh    8
Our sorrow with our comfort.

ALONSO                Prithee, peace.    9

SEBASTIAN [*aside to Antonio*]    He receives comfort like
cold porridge.    11

ANTONIO [*aside to Sebastian*]    The visitor will not give    12
him o'er so.    13

SEBASTIAN    Look, he's winding up the watch of his wit;
by and by it will strike.

GONZALO [*to Alonso*]    Sir—

SEBASTIAN [*aside to Antonio*]    One. Tell.    17

GONZALO    When every grief is entertained    18
That's offered, comes to th'entertainer—    19

SEBASTIAN    A dollar.    20

GONZALO    Dolor comes to him, indeed. You have spoken truer than you purposed.

SEBASTIAN    You have taken it wiselier than I meant you
should.

GONZALO [*to Alonso*]    Therefore, my lord—

ANTONIO    Fie, what a spendthrift is he of his tongue!

ALONSO [*to Gonzalo*]    I prithee, spare.    27

GONZALO    Well, I have done. But yet—

SEBASTIAN [*aside to Antonio*]    He will be talking.

ANTONIO [*aside to Sebastian*]    Which, of he or Adrian,    30
for a good wager, first begins to crow?    31

SEBASTIAN    The old cock.    32

ANTONIO    The cockerel.    33

SEBASTIAN    Done. The wager?

ANTONIO    A laughter.    35

SEBASTIAN    A match!    36

ADRIAN    Though this island seem to be desert—    37

ANTONIO    Ha, ha, ha!

SEBASTIAN    So, you're paid.    39

ADRIAN    Uninhabitable and almost inaccessible—

SEBASTIAN    Yet—

ADRIAN    Yet—

ANTONIO    He could not miss't.    43

ADRIAN    It must needs be of subtle, tender, and delicate    44
temperance.    45

ANTONIO    Temperance was a delicate wench.    46

SEBASTIAN    Ay, and a subtle, as he most learnedly    47
delivered.    48

ADRIAN    The air breathes upon us here most sweetly.

SEBASTIAN    As if it had lungs, and rotten ones.

ANTONIO    Or as 'twere perfumed by a fen.    51

GONZALO    Here is everything advantageous to life.

ANTONIO    True, save means to live.    53

SEBASTIAN    Of that there's none, or little.

GONZALO    How lush and lusty the grass looks! How    55
green!

ANTONIO    The ground indeed is tawny.    57

SEBASTIAN    With an eye of green in't.    58

ANTONIO    He misses not much.

SEBASTIAN    No. He doth but mistake the truth totally.    60

GONZALO    But the rarity of it is—which is indeed
almost beyond credit—

SEBASTIAN    As many vouched rarities are.    63

GONZALO    That our garments, being, as they were,
drenched in the sea, hold notwithstanding their fresh-
ness and glosses, being rather new-dyed than stained
with salt water.

ANTONIO    If but one of his pockets could speak, would    68
it not say he lies?    69

SEBASTIAN    Ay, or very falsely pocket up his report.    70

GONZALO    Methinks our garments are now as fresh as
when we put them on first in Afric, at the marriage of
the King's fair daughter Claribel to the King of Tunis.

SEBASTIAN    'Twas a sweet marriage, and we prosper
well in our return.

ADRIAN    Tunis was never graced before with such a
paragon to their queen.    77

---

**2.1. Location: Another part of the island.**
**3 hint** occasion    **5 The masters . . . the merchant** the officers or owners of some merchant vessel and the merchant who owns the cargo
**6 for** as for    **8–9 weigh . . . comfort** balance our sorrow against our
comfort.    **11 porridge** (Punningly suggested by *peace*, i.e., "peas" or
"pease," a common ingredient of porridge.)    **12 visitor** one bringing
nourishment and comfort to the sick, as Gonzalo is doing    **12–13 give
him o'er** abandon him. Gonzalo is persistent.    **17 Tell** Keep count.
**18–19 When . . . entertainer** When every sorrow that presents itself is
accepted without resistance, there comes to the recipient    **20 dollar**
widely circulated coin, the German thaler and the Spanish piece of
eight. (Sebastian puns on *entertainer* in the sense of paid performer or
innkeeper; to Gonzalo, *dollar* suggests "dolor," grief.)    **27 spare** forbear, cease.    **30–1 Which . . . crow?** Which of the two, Gonzalo or
Adrian, do you bet will speak (crow) first?    **32 The old cock** Gonzalo.
**33 The cockerel** Adrian.    **35 laughter** (1) burst of laughter (2) sitting
of eggs. (When Adrian, the *cockerel*, begins to speak two lines later,
Sebastian loses the bet. The Folio speech prefixes in lines 38–9 are here
reversed so that Antonio enjoys his laugh as the prize for winning, as
in the proverb "He who laughs last laughs best" or "He laughs that
wins." The Folio assignment can work in the theater, however, if
Sebastian pays for losing with a sardonic laugh of concession.)

**36 A match!** A bargain; agreed!    **37 desert** uninhabited    **39 you're
paid** i.e., you've had your laugh; that's your prize.    **43 miss't**
(1) avoid saying "Yet" (2) miss the island.    **44 must needs be** has to be
**45 temperance** mildness of climate.    **46 Temperance** a girl's name.
**delicate** (Here it means "given to pleasure, voluptuous"; in line 44,
"pleasant." Antonio is evidently suggesting that *tender, and delicate temperance* sounds like a Puritan phrase, which Antonio then mocks by
applying the words to a woman rather than an island. He began this
bawdy comparison with a double entendre on *inaccessible*, line 40.)
**47 subtle** (Here it means "tricky, sexually crafty"; in line 44, "delicate.")
**48 delivered** uttered. (Sebastian joins Antonio in baiting the Puritans
with his use of the pious cant phrase *learnedly delivered*.)    **51 fen** evil-
smelling marshland.    **53 save** except    **55 lusty** healthy    **57 tawny**
dull brown, yellowish.    **58 eye** tinge, or spot. (Sebastian is mocking
Gonzalo's optimism by saying there's precious little green to be anywhere. Antonio echoes him in line 59 with similar sarcasm.)    **60 He . . .
totally** i.e., He's only a tiny 100% wrong. (Sarcastic.)    **63 As . . . are**
(More sarcasm: Just as many alleged strange sights are doubtful,
including this one.)    **68–70 If . . . report** (More wisecracking: Gonzalo's mud-filled pockets would surely give the lie to his talk of clean
fresh garments, thereby *pocketing up* or tabling the *report*.)    **77 to** for

GONZALO   Not since widow Dido's time.    78

ANTONIO [*aside to Sebastian*]   Widow? A pox o' that!
How came that "widow" in? Widow Dido!

SEBASTIAN   What if he had said "widower Aeneas"
too? Good Lord, how you take it!    82

ADRIAN [*to Gonzalo*]   "Widow Dido" said you? You make
me study of that. She was of Carthage, not of Tunis.    84

GONZALO   This Tunis, sir, was Carthage.

ADRIAN   Carthage?

GONZALO   I assure you, Carthage.

ANTONIO   His word is more than the miraculous harp.    88

SEBASTIAN   He hath raised the wall, and houses too.

ANTONIO   What impossible matter will he make easy
next?

SEBASTIAN   I think he will carry this island home in his
pocket and give it his son for an apple.    93

ANTONIO   And, sowing the kernels of it in the sea,    94
bring forth more islands.

GONZALO   Ay.    96

ANTONIO   Why, in good time.    97

GONZALO [*to Alonso*]   Sir, we were talking that our garments seem now as fresh as when we were at Tunis
at the marriage of your daughter, who is now queen.

ANTONIO   And the rarest that e'er came there.    101

SEBASTIAN   Bate, I beseech you, widow Dido.    102

ANTONIO   Oh, widow Dido? Ay, widow Dido.

GONZALO   Is not, sir, my doublet as fresh as the first    104
day I wore it? I mean, in a sort.    105

ANTONIO   That "sort" was well fished for.    106

GONZALO   When I wore it at your daughter's marriage.

ALONSO
You cram these words into mine ears against
The stomach of my sense. Would I had never    109
Married my daughter there! For, coming thence,    110
My son is lost and, in my rate, she too,    111
Who is so far from Italy removed
I ne'er again shall see her. O thou mine heir
Of Naples and of Milan, what strange fish
Hath made his meal on thee?

FRANCISCO               Sir, he may live.
I saw him beat the surges under him    116
And ride upon their backs. He trod the water,

Whose enmity he flung aside, and breasted
The surge most swoll'n that met him. His bold head
'Bove the contentious waves he kept, and oared    120
Himself with his good arms in lusty stroke    121
To th' shore, that o'er his wave-worn basis bowed,    122
As stooping to relieve him. I not doubt    123
He came alive to land.

ALONSO            No, no, he's gone.

SEBASTIAN [*to Alonso*]
Sir, you may thank yourself for this great loss,
That would not bless our Europe with your daughter,    126
But rather loose her to an African,    127
Where she at least is banished from your eye,    128
Who hath cause to wet the grief on't.

ALONSO            Prithee, peace.    129

SEBASTIAN
You were kneeled to and importuned otherwise    130
By all of us, and the fair soul herself    131
Weighed between loathness and obedience at    132
Which end o'th' beam should bow. We have lost your
son,    133
I fear, forever. Milan and Naples have
More widows in them of this business' making    135
Than we bring men to comfort them.
The fault's your own.

ALONSO   So is the dear'st o'th' loss.    138

GONZALO   My lord Sebastian,
The truth you speak doth lack some gentleness
And time to speak it in. You rub the sore    141
When you should bring the plaster.

SEBASTIAN           Very well.    142

ANTONIO   And most chirurgeonly.    143

GONZALO [*to Alonso*]
It is foul weather in us all, good sir,
When you are cloudy.

SEBASTIAN [*to Antonio*]   Fowl weather?

ANTONIO [*to Sebastian*]        Very foul.    145

GONZALO
Had I plantation of this isle, my lord—    146

ANTONIO [*to Sebastian*]
He'd sow 't with nettle seed.

SEBASTIAN        Or docks, or mallows.    147

GONZALO
And were the king on't, what would I do?

---

**78 widow Dido's** Queen of Carthage, deserted by Aeneas. (She was, in fact, a widow when Aeneas, a widower, met her, but Antonio may be amused at Gonzalo's prudish use of the term "widow" to describe a woman deserted by her lover.)   **82 take** understand, respond to, interpret   **84 study of** think about   **88 miraculous harp** (Alludes to Amphion's harp, with which he raised the walls of Thebes; Gonzalo has exceeded that deed by recreating ancient Carthage—*wall and houses*—mistakenly on the site of modern-day Tunis. Some Renaissance commentators believed, like Gonzalo, that the two sites were near each other.)   **93 for an apple** as one might give an apple.   **94 kernels** seeds   **96 Ay** (Gonzalo may be reasserting his point about Carthage, or he may be responding ironically to Antonio, who, in turn, answers sarcastically.)   **97 in good time** (An expression of ironical acquiescence or amazement, i.e., "sure, right away.")   **101 rarest** most remarkable, beautiful   **102 Bate** Abate, except, leave out. (Sebastian says sardonically, surely you should allow widow Dido to be an exception.)   **104 doublet** close-fitting jacket   **105 in a sort** in a way.   **106 sort** (Antonio plays on the idea of drawing lots and on "fishing" for something to say.)   **109 The stomach . . . sense** my appetite for hearing them.   **110 Married** given in marriage   **111 rate** estimation, opinion   **116 surges** waves

**120 oared** propelled as by an oar   **121 lusty** vigorous   **122 that . . . bowed** that projected out over its (*his*) surf-eroded base, bending down toward the sea   **123 As** as if   **126 That** you who   **127 But . . . her** but would rather turn her loose (or, "lose her")   **128–9 Where . . . on't** where at least she is not a constant reproach in your eye, which has good reason to weep sorrowfully for this unhappy development.   **130 importuned** urged, implored   **131–3 the fair . . . bow** Claribel herself was poised uncertainly, as in a balancing scale, between being unwilling to marry and yet wishing to obey her father.   **135 of . . . making** on account of this marriage and subsequent shipwreck   **138 dear'st** heaviest, most costly   **141 time** appropriate time   **142 plaster** (A medical application.)   **143 chirurgeonly** like a skilled surgeon. (Antonio mocks Gonzalo's medical analogy of a *plaster* applied curatively to a wound.)   **145 Fowl** (With a pun on *foul*, returning to the imagery of lines 30–5.)   **146 plantation** colonial settlement. (With subsequent wordplay on the literal meaning, "planting.")   **147 docks . . . mallows** (Weeds; the first was used as an antidote for nettle stings.)

SEBASTIAN   Scape being drunk for want of wine.  149

GONZALO
I'th' commonwealth I would by contraries  150
Execute all things; for no kind of traffic  151
Would I admit; no name of magistrate;
Letters should not be known; riches, poverty,  153
And use of service, none; contract, succession,  154
Bourn, bound of land, tilth, vineyard, none;  155
No use of metal, corn, or wine, or oil;  156
No occupation; all men idle, all,
And women too, but innocent and pure;
No sovereignty—

SEBASTIAN          Yet he would be king on't.

ANTONIO   The latter end of his commonwealth forgets
the beginning.

GONZALO
All things in common nature should produce
Without sweat or endeavor. Treason, felony,
Sword, pike, knife, gun, or need of any engine  164
Would I not have; but nature should bring forth,
Of it own kind, all foison, all abundance,  166
To feed my innocent people.

SEBASTIAN   No marrying 'mong his subjects?

ANTONIO   None, man, all idle—whores and knaves.

GONZALO
I would with such perfection govern, sir,
T'excel the Golden Age.

SEBASTIAN          'Save His Majesty!  171

ANTONIO
Long live Gonzalo!

GONZALO          And—do you mark me, sir?

ALONSO
Prithee, no more. Thou dost talk nothing to me.

GONZALO   I do well believe Your Highness, and did it
to minister occasion to these gentlemen, who are of  175
such sensible and nimble lungs that they always use  176
to laugh at nothing.

ANTONIO   'Twas you we laughed at.

GONZALO   Who in this kind of merry fooling am nothing
to you; so you may continue, and laugh at nothing still.

ANTONIO   What a blow was there given!

SEBASTIAN   An it had not fallen flat-long.  182

GONZALO   You are gentlemen of brave mettle; you  183
would lift the moon out of her sphere if she would  184

continue in it five weeks without changing.

*Enter Ariel [invisible] playing solemn music.*

SEBASTIAN   We would so, and then go a-batfowling.  186
ANTONIO   Nay, good my lord, be not angry.
GONZALO   No, I warrant you, I will not adventure my  188
discretion so weakly. Will you laugh me asleep? For I  189
am very heavy.  190
ANTONIO   Go sleep, and hear us.  191
       *[All sleep except Alonso, Sebastian, and Antonio.]*
ALONSO
What, all so soon asleep? I wish mine eyes
Would, with themselves, shut up my thoughts. I find  193
They are inclined to do so.
SEBASTIAN          Please you, sir,
Do not omit the heavy offer of it.  195
It seldom visits sorrow; when it doth,
It is a comforter.
ANTONIO          We two, my lord,
Will guard your person while you take your rest,
And watch your safety.
ALONSO          Thank you. Wondrous heavy.
       *[Alonso sleeps. Exit Ariel.]*
SEBASTIAN
What a strange drowsiness possesses them!
ANTONIO
It is the quality o'th' climate.
SEBASTIAN          Why
Doth it not then our eyelids sink? I find not
Myself disposed to sleep.
ANTONIO          Nor I. My spirits are nimble.
They fell together all, as by consent;  204
They dropped, as by a thunderstroke. What might,
Worthy Sebastian, oh, what might—? No more.
And yet methinks I see it in thy face
What thou shouldst be. Th'occasion speaks thee, and  208
My strong imagination sees a crown
Dropping upon thy head.
SEBASTIAN          What, art thou waking?  210
ANTONIO
Do you not hear me speak?
SEBASTIAN          I do, and surely
It is a sleepy language, and thou speak'st  212
Out of thy sleep. What is it thou didst say?
This is a strange repose, to be asleep
With eyes wide open—standing, speaking, moving—
And yet so fast asleep.
ANTONIO          Noble Sebastian,
Thou let'st thy fortune sleep—die, rather; wink'st  217

**149 Scape** Escape.   **want** lack. (Sebastian jokes sarcastically that this hypothetical ruler would be saved from dissipation only by the barrenness of the island.)   **150 by contraries** by what is directly opposite to usual custom. (Lines 150-67 are based on John Florio's translation of Montaigne's essay "Of the Cannibals.")   **151 traffic** trade   **153 Letters** learning   **154 use of service** custom of employing servants.   **succession** holding of property by right of inheritance   **155 Bourn . . . tilth** boundaries, property limits, tillage of soil   **156 corn** grain   **164 pike** lance.   **engine** instrument of warfare   **166 it** its.   **foison** plenty   **171 the Golden Age** an age of prelapsarian abundance and peace; the first of four "ages" of human history, followed by silver, bronze, and lead.   **'Save** God save   **175 minister occasion** furnish opportunity (for laughter)   **176 sensible** sensitive.   **use** are accustomed   **182 An** If.   **flat-long** with the flat of the sword, i.e., ineffectually.   **183 mettle** temperament, courage. (The sense of *metal*, indistinguishable as a form from *mettle*, continues the metaphor of the sword. F reads "mettall.")   **184 sphere** orbit. (Literally, one of the concentric zones occupied by planets in Ptolemaic astronomy.)

**186 a-batfowling** hunting birds at night with lantern and *bat*, or "stick"; also, gulling a simpleton. (Gonzalo is the simpleton, or fowl, and Sebastian will use the moon as his lantern.)   **188–9 adventure . . . weakly** risk my reputation for discretion for so trivial a cause (by getting angry).   **190 heavy** sleepy.   **191 Go . . . us** i.e., Get ready for sleep, and we'll do our part by laughing.   **193 Would . . . thoughts** would shut off my melancholy brooding when they (my eyes) close themselves in sleep.   **195 Do . . . it** do not decline the invitation to drowsiness.   **204 They . . . consent** The others all fell asleep simultaneously, as if by common agreement   **208 Th'occasion . . . thee** The opportunity of the moment calls upon you   **210 waking** awake.   **212 sleepy** dreamlike, fantastic   **217 wink'st** (you) shut your eyes

Whiles thou art waking.

SEBASTIAN                    Thou dost snore distinctly;    218
There's meaning in thy snores.

ANTONIO
I am more serious than my custom. You
Must be so too if heed me, which to do    221
Trebles thee o'er.

SEBASTIAN          Well, I am standing water.    222

ANTONIO
I'll teach you how to flow.

SEBASTIAN                    Do so. To ebb    223
Hereditary sloth instructs me.

ANTONIO                            Oh,    224
If you but knew how you the purpose cherish    225
Whiles thus you mock it! How, in stripping it,    226
You more invest it! Ebbing men, indeed,    227
Most often do so near the bottom run    228
By their own fear or sloth.

SEBASTIAN                    Prithee, say on.
The setting of thine eye and cheek proclaim    230
A matter from thee, and a birth indeed    231
Which throes thee much to yield.

ANTONIO                        Thus, sir:    232
Although this lord of weak remembrance, this    233
Who shall be of as little memory    234
When he is earthed, hath here almost persuaded—    235
For he's a spirit of persuasion, only    236
Professes to persuade—the King his son's alive,    237
'Tis as impossible that he's undrowned
As he that sleeps here swims.

SEBASTIAN                    I have no hope
That he's undrowned.

ANTONIO          Oh, out of that "no hope"
What great hope have you! No hope that way is    241
Another way so high a hope that even    242
Ambition cannot pierce a wink beyond,    243
But doubt discovery there. Will you grant with me    244
That Ferdinand is drowned?

SEBASTIAN                    He's gone.

ANTONIO                        Then tell me,
Who's the next heir of Naples?

SEBASTIAN                        Claribel.

ANTONIO
She that is Queen of Tunis; she that dwells
Ten leagues beyond man's life; she that from Naples    248
Can have no note, unless the sun were post—    249
The Man i'th' Moon's too slow—till newborn chins
Be rough and razorable; she that from whom    251
We all were sea-swallowed, though some cast again,    252
And by that destiny to perform an act
Whereof what's past is prologue, what to come    254
In yours and my discharge.    255

SEBASTIAN    What stuff is this? How say you?
'Tis true my brother's daughter's Queen of Tunis;    257
So is she heir of Naples; twixt which regions
There is some space.

ANTONIO                    A space whose ev'ry cubit    259
Seems to cry out, "How shall that Claribel
Measure us back to Naples? Keep in Tunis,    261
And let Sebastian wake." Say this were death    262
That now hath seized them, why, they were no worse
Than now they are. There be that can rule Naples    264
As well as he that sleeps, lords that can prate    265
As amply and unnecessarily
As this Gonzalo. I myself could make    267
A chough of as deep chat. Oh, that you bore    268
The mind that I do! What a sleep were this
For your advancement! Do you understand me?

SEBASTIAN
Methinks I do.

ANTONIO          And how does your content    271
Tender your own good fortune?

SEBASTIAN                    I remember    272
You did supplant your brother Prospero.

ANTONIO                            True.
And look how well my garments sit upon me,
Much feater than before. My brother's servants    275
Were then my fellows. Now they are my men.

SEBASTIAN    But, for your conscience?    277

ANTONIO
Ay, sir, where lies that? If 'twere a kibe,    278
'Twould put me to my slipper; but I feel not    279
This deity in my bosom. Twenty consciences    280
That stand twixt me and Milan, candied be they    281
And melt ere they molest! Here lies your brother,    282
No better than the earth he lies upon,
If he were that which now he's like—that's dead,
Whom I, with this obedient steel, three inches of it,

218 **distinctly** articulately    221 **if heed** if you heed    222 **Trebles thee o'er** makes you three times as great and rich.    **standing water** water that neither ebbs nor flows, at a standstill.    223 **ebb** recede, decline    224 **Hereditary sloth** i.e., natural laziness and the position of younger brother, one who cannot inherit    225–6 **If . . . mock it!** If you only knew how much you secretly cherish ambition even while your words mock it!    226–7 **How . . . invest it!** How the more you speak flippantly of ambition, the more you, in effect, affirm it, clothing what you have stripped!    227 **Ebbing men** People whose fortunes are on the decline    228 **the bottom** i.e., on which unadventurous men may go aground and miss the tide of fortune    230 **setting** set expression (of earnestness)    231 **matter** matter of importance    232 **throes** causes pain, as in giving birth.    **yield** give forth, speak about.    233–7 **Although . . . alive** although this owner of weak memory, Gonzalo, he who will be only weakly remembered when he is dead, has nearly persuaded—since he's a mind or soul devoted solely to persuade—King Alonso that Ferdinand lives    241 **that way** i.e., in regard to Ferdinand's being saved    242–4 **that . . . there** that even ambition for high status cannot capture a glimpse of anything higher, and even there it doubts the reality of what it sees (because the place dreamed of is so supremely high). (What then follows is Antonio's analysis of why nevertheless they can proceed without fear.)

248 **Ten . . . life** i.e., further than the journey of a lifetime    249 **note** news, intimation.    **post** messenger    251 **razorable** ready for shaving.    **from** on our voyage from    252 **cast again** were disgorged, cast ashore. (With a pun on *casting* of parts for a play.)    254–5 **Whereof . . . discharge** i.e, of which our overthrow of Prospero for the Dukedom of Milan was only the start of a play that is now about to continue with your and my performances.    257 **daughter's** daughter is    259 **cubit** ancient measure of length of about twenty inches    261 **Measure . . . Naples?** i.e., know anything of our whereabouts on our trip back to Naples?    **Keep** You, Claribel, stay    262 **wake** i.e., to his good fortune.    264 **There be** There are those    265 **prate** speak foolishly    267–8 **I . . . chat** I could teach a jackdaw to talk as wisely, or, be such a garrulous talker myself.    271–2 **And . . . fortune?** And how does your contentment with what I've just said further your good fortune?    275 **feater** more becomingly, fittingly    277 **for** as for    278 **kibe** chilblain, here a sore on the heel    279 **put me to** oblige me to wear    280–2 **Twenty . . . molest!** Even if there were twenty consciences between me and the dukedom of Milan, may they be lumped together or crystallized like candy and then melted down before I'd let them interfere!

Can lay to bed forever; whiles you, doing thus,          286
To the perpetual wink for aye might put                  287
This ancient morsel, this Sir Prudence, who
Should not upbraid our course. For all the rest,         289
They'll take suggestion as a cat laps milk;              290
They'll tell the clock to any business that              291
We say befits the hour.

SEBASTIAN                    Thy case, dear friend,
Shall be my precedent. As thou got'st Milan,
I'll come by Naples. Draw thy sword. One stroke
Shall free thee from the tribute which thou payest,      295
And I the king shall love thee.

ANTONIO                      Draw together;
And when I rear my hand, do you the like
To fall it on Gonzalo.                    [*They draw.*]

SEBASTIAN             Oh, but one word.              298
                                      [*They talk apart.*]

*Enter Ariel [invisible], with music and song.*

ARIEL [*to Gonzalo*]
My master through his art foresees the danger
That you, his friend, are in, and sends me forth—
For else his project dies—to keep them living.          301
                           *Sings in Gonzalo's ear.*
    While you here do snoring lie,
    Open-eyed conspiracy
        His time doth take.                              304
    If of life you keep a care,
    Shake off slumber, and beware.
        Awake, awake!

ANTONIO   Then let us both be sudden.

GONZALO [*waking*]   Now, good angels preserve the King!
                                   [*The others wake.*]

ALONSO
Why, how now, ho, awake? Why are you drawn?
Wherefore this ghastly looking?

GONZALO                       What's the matter?

SEBASTIAN
Whiles we stood here securing your repose,               312
Even now, we heard a hollow burst of bellowing
Like bulls, or rather lions. Did 't not wake you?
It struck mine ear most terribly.

ALONSO                       I heard nothing.

ANTONIO
Oh, 'twas a din to fright a monster's ear,
To make an earthquake! Sure it was the roar
Of a whole herd of lions.

ALONSO                    Heard you this, Gonzalo?

GONZALO
Upon mine honor, sir, I heard a humming,
And that a strange one too, which did awake me.
I shaked you, sir, and cried. As mine eyes opened,       321
I saw their weapons drawn. There was a noise,

That's verily. 'Tis best we stand upon our guard,        323
Or that we quit this place. Let's draw our weapons.

ALONSO
Lead off this ground, and let's make further search
For my poor son.

GONZALO         Heavens keep him from these beasts!
For he is, sure, i'th'island.

ALONSO                        Lead away.

ARIEL [*aside*]
Prospero my lord shall know what I have done.
So, King, go safely on to seek thy son.
                           *Exeunt [separately].*

❧

# 2.2

*Enter Caliban with a burden of wood. A noise of
thunder heard.*

CALIBAN
All the infections that the sun sucks up
From bogs, fens, flats, on Prosper fall, and make him    2
By inchmeal a disease! His spirits hear me,              3
And yet I needs must curse. But they'll nor pinch,       4
Fright me with urchin shows, pitch me i'th' mire,        5
Nor lead me, like a firebrand, in the dark               6
Out of my way, unless he bid 'em. But
For every trifle are they set upon me,
Sometimes like apes, that mow and chatter at me,         9
And after bite me; then like hedgehogs, which
Lie tumbling in my barefoot way and mount
Their pricks at my footfall. Sometime am I
All wound with adders, who with cloven tongues           13
Do hiss me into madness.

        *Enter Trinculo.*

            Lo, now, lo!
Here comes a spirit of his, and to torment me
For bringing wood in slowly. I'll fall flat.
Perchance he will not mind me.        [*He lies down.*]  17

TRINCULO   Here's neither bush nor shrub to bear off     18
any weather at all. And another storm brewing; I hear
it sing i'th' wind. Yond same black cloud, yond huge
one, looks like a foul bombard that would shed his       21
liquor. If it should thunder as it did before, I know not
where to hide my head. Yond same cloud cannot            23
choose but fall by pailfuls. [*Seeing Caliban*] What have 24
we here, a man or a fish? Dead or alive? A fish, he
smells like a fish; a very ancient and fishlike smell; a
kind of not-of-the-newest Poor John. A strange fish!     27
Were I in England now, as once I was, and had but
this fish painted, not a holiday fool there but would    29

---

286 **thus** similarly. (The actor makes a stabbing gesture.)   287 **wink**
sleep, closing of eyes.   **aye** ever   289 **Should not upbraid** must not
be allowed to find fault with.   **For** As for   290 **take suggestion**
respond to prompting   291 **tell the clock** i.e., agree, answer appropriately, chime   295 **tribute** (See 1.2.113–24.)   298 **fall it** let it fall
301 **else** otherwise.   **them** Alonso and the rest   304 **time** opportunity   312 **securing** standing guard over   321 **cried** called out.

323 **verily** true.
**2.2. Location:** Another part of the island.
2 **flats** swamps   3 **By inchmeal** inch by inch   4 **needs must** have to.
**nor** neither   5 **urchin shows** elvish apparitions shaped like hedgehogs
6 **like a firebrand** they in the guise of a will-o'-the-wisp   9 **mow** make
faces   13 **wound with** entwined by   17 **mind** notice   18 **bear off** keep
off   21 **foul bombard** dirty leather jug.   **his** its   23–4 **cannot choose but**
must inevitably   27 **Poor John** salted fish, type of poor fare.   29 **painted**
i.e., painted on a sign set up outside a booth or tent at a fair

give a piece of silver. There would this monster make 30
a man. Any strange beast there makes a man. When 31
they will not give a doit to relieve a lame beggar, they 32
will lay out ten to see a dead Indian. Legged like a 33
man, and his fins like arms! Warm, o' my troth! I do 34
now let loose my opinion, hold it no longer: this is no 35
fish, but an islander, that hath lately suffered by a
thunderbolt. [*Thunder.*] Alas, the storm is come again!
My best way is to creep under his gaberdine. There is 38
no other shelter hereabout. Misery acquaints a man
with strange bedfellows. I will here shroud till the 40
dregs of the storm be past. 41
                    [*He creeps under Caliban's garment.*]

*Enter Stephano, singing, [a bottle in his hand].*

STEPHANO
        I shall no more to sea, to sea,
            Here shall I die ashore—
This is a very scurvy tune to sing at a man's funeral.
Well, here's my comfort.                    *Drinks.*
(*Sings.*)
        The master, the swabber, the boatswain, and I, 46
            The gunner and his mate,
        Loved Mall, Meg, and Marian, and Margery,
            But none of us cared for Kate.
        For she had a tongue with a tang, 50
        Would cry to a sailor, 'Go hang!'
        She loved not the savor of tar nor of pitch,
        Yet a tailor might scratch her where'er she did itch. 53
            Then to sea, boys, and let her go hang!
This is a scurvy tune too. But here's my comfort.
                                            *Drinks.*

CALIBAN    Do not torment me! Oh! 56
STEPHANO    What's the matter? Have we devils here? Do 57
    you put tricks upon 's with savages and men of Ind, 58
    ha? I have not scaped drowning to be afeard now of
    your four legs. For it hath been said, "As proper a man 60
    as ever went on four legs cannot make him give 61
    ground"; and it shall be said so again while Stephano 62
    breathes at' nostrils. 63
CALIBAN    This spirit torments me! Oh!
STEPHANO    This is some monster of the isle with four
    legs, who hath got, as I take it, an ague. Where the 66
    devil should he learn our language? I will give him 67
    some relief, if it be but for that. If I can recover him 68
    and keep him tame and get to Naples with him, he's

a present for any emperor that ever trod on neat's 70
leather. 71
CALIBAN    Do not torment me, prithee. I'll bring my
    wood home faster.
STEPHANO    He's in his fit now and does not talk after 74
    the wisest. He shall taste of my bottle. If he have never 75
    drunk wine afore, it will go near to remove his fit. If I 76
    can recover him and keep him tame, I will not take too 77
    much for him. He shall pay for him that hath him, and 78
    that soundly.
CALIBAN    Thou dost me yet but little hurt; thou wilt
    anon, I know it by thy trembling. Now Prosper works
    upon thee.
STEPHANO    Come on your ways. Open your mouth. Here 83
    is that which will give language to you, cat. Open your 84
    mouth. This will shake your shaking, I can tell you, 85
    and that soundly. [*Giving Caliban a drink.*] You cannot 86
    tell who's your friend. Open your chaps again. 87
TRINCULO    I should know that voice. It should be—but
    he is drowned, and these are devils. Oh, defend me!
STEPHANO    Four legs and two voices—a most delicate 90
    monster! His forward voice now is to speak well of his
    friend; his backward voice is to utter foul speeches and 92
    to detract. If all the wine in my bottle will recover him, 93
    I will help his ague. Come. [*Giving a drink.*] Amen! I
    will pour some in thy other mouth.
TRINCULO    Stephano!
STEPHANO    Doth thy other mouth call me? Mercy,
    mercy! This is a devil, and no monster. I will leave
    him. I have no long spoon. 99
TRINCULO    Stephano! If thou be'st Stephano, touch me
    and speak to me, for I am Trinculo—be not afeard—
    thy good friend Trinculo.
STEPHANO    If thou be'st Trinculo, come forth. I'll pull
    thee by the lesser legs. If any be Trinculo's legs, these
    are they. [*Pulling him out.*] Thou art very Trinculo
    indeed! How cam'st thou to be the siege of this 106
    mooncalf? Can he vent Trinculos? 107
TRINCULO    I took him to be killed with a thunderstroke.
    But art thou not drowned, Stephano? I hope now thou
    art not drowned. Is the storm overblown? I hid me 110
    under the dead mooncalf's gaberdine for fear of the
    storm. And art thou living, Stephano? Oh, Stephano,
    two Neapolitans scaped!    [*He capers with Stephano.*]

30–1 **make a man** (1) make a man's fortune (2) pass for a human being.
32 **doit** small coin    33 **Indian** (as Native Americans were exhibited in
England).    34 **o' my troth** by my faith.    35 **hold it** hold it in    38 **gaberdine** cloak, loose upper garment.    40 **shroud** take shelter    41 **dregs** i.e.,
last remains (as in a *bombard* or jug, line 21)    46 **swabber** crew member
whose job is to wash the decks    50 **tang** sting    53 **tailor ... itch** (A dig
at tailors for their supposed effeminacy and a bawdy suggestion of satisfying a sexual craving.)    56 **Do ... me!** (Caliban assumes that one of
Prospero's spirits has come to punish him.)    57 **What's the matter?**
What's going on here?    58 **put tricks upon 's** trick us with conjuring
shows.    **Ind** India    60 **proper** handsome    61 **four legs** (The conventional phrase would supply *two legs*, but the creature Stephano thinks he
sees has four.)    61–2 **cannot ... ground** cannot daunt a brave man and
make him yield. (Stephano vows to be brave like that.)    63 **at'** at the
66 **ague** fever. (Probably both Caliban and Trinculo are quaking; see
lines 56 and 81.)    67 **should he learn** could he have learned    68 **for
that** i.e., for knowing our language.    **recover** revive. (Also in line 77.)

70–1 **that ... leather** i.e., that ever walked. (*Neat's leather* is cowhide.)
74–5 **after the wisest** in the wisest fashion.    76 **afore** before.    **go near**
to be in a fair way to    77 **recover** restore    77–8 **I will ... much** i.e.,
no sum can be too much    78 **He shall ... hath him** Anyone who
wants him will have to pay dearly for him    83 **Come ... ways** Come
on.    84–5 **cat ... mouth** (Allusion to the proverb "Good liquor will
make a cat speak.")    85 **shake** shake off    86–7 **You ... friend** i.e.,
You can't tell who's your friend until someone like me provides you
with a drink.    87 **chaps** jaws    90 **delicate** ingenious    92 **backward
voice** (Trinculo and Caliban are facing in opposite directions. Stephano supposes the monster to have a rear end that can emit *foul
speeches* or foul-smelling wind at the monster's *other mouth*, line 95.)
93 **If ... him** Even if it takes all the wine in my bottle to cure him
99 **long spoon** (Allusion to the proverb "He that sups with the devil
has need of a long spoon.")    106 **siege** excrement    107 **mooncalf**
monstrous or misshapen creature (whose deformity is caused by the
malignant influence of the moon).    **vent** excrete, defecate
110 **overblown** blown over.

STEPHANO   Prithee, do not turn me about. My stomach
is not constant.                                                          115

CALIBAN
These be fine things, an if they be not spirits.                           116
That's a brave god, and bears celestial liquor.                            117
I will kneel to him.

STEPHANO   How didst thou scape? How cam'st thou
hither? Swear by this bottle how thou cam'st hither. I
escaped upon a butt of sack which the sailors heaved                       121
o'erboard—by this bottle, which I made of the bark of                      122
a tree with mine own hands since I was cast ashore.

CALIBAN [*kneeling*]   I'll swear upon that bottle to be
thy true subject, for the liquor is not earthly.

STEPHANO   Here. Swear then how thou escaped'st.

TRINCULO   Swum ashore, man, like a duck. I can swim
like a duck, I'll be sworn.

STEPHANO   Here, kiss the book. Though thou canst                          129
swim like a duck, thou art made like a goose.
                                        [*Giving him a drink.*]

TRINCULO   Oh, Stephano, hast any more of this?

STEPHANO   The whole butt, man. My cellar is in a rock
by th' seaside, where my wine is hid.—How now,
mooncalf? How does thine ague?

CALIBAN   Hast thou not dropped from heaven?

STEPHANO   Out o'th' moon, I do assure thee. I was the
man i'th' moon when time was.                                              137

CALIBAN
I have seen thee in her, and I do adore thee.
My mistress showed me thee, and thy dog, and thy
bush.                                                                      139

STEPHANO   Come, swear to that. Kiss the book. I will
furnish it anon with new contents. Swear.                                  141
                                        [*Giving him a drink.*]

TRINCULO   By this good light, this is a very shallow                      142
monster! I afeard of him? A very weak monster! The
man i'th' moon? A most poor credulous monster!
Well drawn, monster, in good sooth!                                        145

CALIBAN [*to Stephano*]
I'll show thee every fertile inch o'th'island,
And I will kiss thy foot. I prithee, be my god.

TRINCULO   By this light, a most perfidious and drunken
monster! When 's god's asleep, he'll rob his bottle.                       149

CALIBAN
I'll kiss thy foot. I'll swear myself thy subject.

STEPHANO   Come on then. Down, and swear.
                                        [*Caliban kneels.*]

TRINCULO   I shall laugh myself to death at this puppy-
headed monster. A most scurvy monster! I could find
in my heart to beat him—

STEPHANO   Come, kiss.

TRINCULO   But that the poor monster's in drink. An          156
abominable monster!

CALIBAN
I'll show thee the best springs. I'll pluck thee berries.
I'll fish for thee and get thee wood enough.
A plague upon the tyrant that I serve!
I'll bear him no more sticks, but follow thee,
Thou wondrous man.

TRINCULO   A most ridiculous monster, to make a
wonder of a poor drunkard!

CALIBAN
I prithee, let me bring thee where crabs grow,               165
And I with my long nails will dig thee pignuts,              166
Show thee a jay's nest, and instruct thee how
To snare the nimble marmoset. I'll bring thee                168
To clust'ring filberts, and sometimes I'll get thee
Young scamels from the rock. Wilt thou go with me?           170

STEPHANO   I prithee now, lead the way without any
more talking.—Trinculo, the King and all our com-           172
pany else being drowned, we will inherit here.—             173
Here, bear my bottle.—Fellow Trinculo, we'll fill him       174
by and by again.

CALIBAN (*sings drunkenly*)
Farewell, master, farewell, farewell!

TRINCULO   A howling monster; a drunken monster!

CALIBAN
No more dams I'll make for fish,                             178
  Nor fetch in firing                                        179
    At requiring,
  Nor scrape trenchering, nor wash dish.                     181
    'Ban, 'Ban, Ca–Caliban
      Has a new master. Get a new man!                       183
Freedom, high-day! High-day, freedom! Freedom,              184
high-day, freedom!

STEPHANO   O brave monster! Lead the way.      *Exeunt.*

❧

# 3.1

*Enter Ferdinand, bearing a log.*

FERDINAND
There be some sports are painful, and their labor            1
Delight in them sets off. Some kinds of baseness             2
Are nobly undergone, and most poor matters                   3
Point to rich ends. This my mean task                        4
Would be as heavy to me as odious, but                       5

115 constant steady.   116 an if if   117 brave fine, magnificent
121 butt of sack barrel of Canary wine   122 by this bottle i.e., I swear
by this bottle   129 book i.e., bottle. (But with ironic reference to the
practice of kissing the Bible in swearing an oath; see *I'll be sworn* in line
128.)   137 when time was once upon a time.   139 My mistress
Miranda.   dog . . . bush (The man in the moon was popularly imagined to have with him a dog and a bush of thorn.)   141 furnish . . .
contents fill it with wine.   142 By . . . light By God's light, by this good
light from the sun   145 Well . . . sooth! Well pulled on the bottle, truly!
149 When . . . bottle i.e., Caliban wouldn't even stop at robbing his god
(i.e., Stephano) of his bottle if he could catch him asleep.

156 But that Were it not that.   in drink drunk.   165 crabs crab
apples, or crabs   166 pignuts earthnuts, edible tuberous roots
168 marmoset small monkey.   170 scamels (Possibly *seamews*,
seagulls, mentioned in Strachey's letter, or shellfish, or perhaps from
*squamelle*, "furnished with little scales." Contemporary French and
Italian travel accounts report that the natives of Patagonia in South
America ate small fish described as *fort scameux* and *squame*.)
172–3 all . . . else all the rest of our shipboard companions   173 inherit
take possession   174 him it, the bottle   178 for fish to catch fish
179 firing firewood   181 trenchering trenchers, wooden plates
183 Get a new man (Addressed to Prospero.)   184 high-day holiday.
3.1. Location: Before Prospero's cell.
1–2 There . . . sets off Some pastimes are laborious, but the pleasure
we get from them compensates for the effort. (Pleasure is *set off* by
labor as a jewel is set off by its foil.)   2 baseness menial activity
3 undergone undertaken.   most poor poorest   4 mean lowly
5 but were it not that

The mistress which I serve quickens what's dead                    6
And makes my labors pleasures. Oh, she is
Ten times more gentle than her father's crabbed,
And he's composed of harshness. I must remove
Some thousands of these logs and pile them up,
Upon a sore injunction. My sweet mistress                          11
Weeps when she sees me work and says such baseness
Had never like executor. I forget;                                 13
But these sweet thoughts do even refresh my labors,
Most busy lest when I do it.

*Enter Miranda; and Prospero [at a distance,
unseen].*

MIRANDA                              Alas now, pray you,            15
Work not so hard. I would the lightning had
Burnt up those logs that you are enjoined to pile!                 17
Pray, set it down and rest you. When this burns,                   18
'Twill weep for having wearied you. My father                      19
Is hard at study. Pray now, rest yourself.
He's safe for these three hours.
FERDINAND                            O most dear mistress,          21
The sun will set before I shall discharge                          22
What I must strive to do.
MIRANDA                              If you'll sit down,
I'll bear your logs the while. Pray, give me that.
I'll carry it to the pile.
FERDINAND                            No, precious creature,
I had rather crack my sinews, break my back,
Than you should such dishonor undergo
While I sit lazy by.
MIRANDA                              It would become me
As well as it does you; and I should do it
With much more ease, for my good will is to it,
And yours it is against.
PROSPERO *[aside]*           Poor worm, thou art infected!
This visitation shows it.                                          32
MIRANDA                              You look wearily.
FERDINAND
No, noble mistress, 'tis fresh morning with me
When you are by at night. I do beseech you—                        34
Chiefly that I might set it in my prayers—
What is your name?
MIRANDA                              Miranda.—O my father,
I have broke your hest to say so.
FERDINAND                            Admired Miranda!               37
Indeed the top of admiration, worth
What's dearest to the world! Full many a lady                      39
I have eyed with best regard, and many a time                      40
The harmony of their tongues hath into bondage

Brought my too diligent ear. For several virtues                   42
Have I liked several women, never any
With so full soul but some defect in her
Did quarrel with the noblest grace she owed                        45
And put it to the foil. But you, O you,                            46
So perfect and so peerless, are created
Of every creature's best!
MIRANDA                   I do not know                            48
One of my sex; no woman's face remember,
Save, from my glass, mine own. Nor have I seen                     50
More that I may call men than you, good friend,
And my dear father. How features are abroad                        52
I am skilless of; but, by my modesty,                              53
The jewel in my dower, I would not wish                            54
Any companion in the world but you;
Nor can imagination form a shape,
Besides yourself, to like of. But I prattle                        57
Something too wildly, and my father's precepts                     58
I therein do forget.
FERDINAND                 I am in my condition                     59
A prince, Miranda; I do think, a king—
I would, not so!—and would no more endure                          61
This wooden slavery than to suffer                                 62
The flesh-fly blow my mouth. Hear my soul speak:                   63
The very instant that I saw you did
My heart fly to your service, there resides
To make me slave to it, and for your sake
Am I this patient log-man.
MIRANDA                              Do you love me?
FERDINAND
O heaven, O earth, bear witness to this sound,
And crown what I profess with kind event                           69
If I speak true! If hollowly, invert                               70
What best is boded me to mischief! I                               71
Beyond all limit of what else i'th' world                          72
Do love, prize, honor you.
MIRANDA *[weeping]*            I am a fool
To weep at what I am glad of.
PROSPERO *[aside]*             Fair encounter
Of two most rare affections! Heavens rain grace
On that which breeds between 'em!
FERDINAND                              Wherefore weep you?
MIRANDA
At mine unworthiness, that dare not offer
What I desire to give, and much less take
What I shall die to want. But this is trifling,                    79
And all the more it seeks to hide itself
The bigger bulk it shows. Hence, bashful cunning,                  81

---

**6 quickens** gives life to   **11 sore injunction** severe command.
**13 Had . . . executor** was never before undertaken by so noble a
being.   **I forget** i.e., I forget that I'm supposed to be working
**15 Most . . . do it** (Ferdinand seems to say that the busier he is, the
less likely he is to forget the sweet thoughts that make his labors
pleasant. The line may be in need of emendation.)   **17 enjoined** commanded   **18 this** i.e., the log   **19 weep** i.e., exude resin   **21 these** the
next   **22 discharge** complete   **32 visitation** (1) Miranda's visit to
Ferdinand (2) visitation of the plague, i.e., infection of love   **34 by**
nearby   **37 hest** command.   **Admired Miranda** (Her name means
"to be admired or wondered at.")   **39 dearest** most treasured
**40 best regard** thoughtful and approving attention

**42 diligent** attentive.   **several** various. (Also in line 43.)   **45 owed**
owned   **46 put . . . foil** (1) overthrew it (as in fencing or wrestling)
(2) served as a *foil*, or "contrast," to set it off.   **48 Of** out of   **50 glass**
mirror   **52 How . . . abroad** What people look like in other places
**53 skilless** ignorant.   **modesty** virginity   **54 dower** dowry   **57 like**
**of** be pleased with, be fond of.   **58 Something** somewhat   **59 condi-**
**tion** rank   **61 I would** I wish it were   **62 wooden slavery** being compelled to carry wood   **62–3 than . . . mouth** than I would allow flying
insects to deposit their eggs in my mouth as if in decaying flesh.
**69 kind event** favorable outcome   **70 hollowly** insincerely, falsely.
**invert** turn   **71 boded** in store for.   **mischief** harm.   **72 what** whatever   **79 die** (Probably with an unconscious sexual meaning that
underlies all of lines 77–81.)   **to want** through lacking.   **81 bashful**
**cunning** coyness

And prompt me, plain and holy innocence!
I am your wife, if you will marry me;
If not, I'll die your maid. To be your fellow 84
You may deny me, but I'll be your servant
Whether you will or no.

FERDINAND                    My mistress, dearest, 86
And I thus humble ever.

MIRANDA    My husband, then?

FERDINAND    Ay, with a heart as willing 89
As bondage e'er of freedom. Here's my hand.

MIRANDA [*clasping his hand*]
And mine, with my heart in't. And now farewell
Till half an hour hence.

FERDINAND                    A thousand thousand! 92

*Exeunt [Ferdinand and Miranda, separately].*

PROSPERO
So glad of this as they I cannot be,
Who are surprised with all; but my rejoicing 94
At nothing can be more. I'll to my book,
For yet ere suppertime must I perform
Much business appertaining.                    *Exit.* 97

❖

## 3.2

*Enter Caliban, Stephano, and Trinculo.*

STEPHANO    Tell not me. When the butt is out, we will 1
drink water, not a drop before. Therefore bear up and 2
board 'em. Servant monster, drink to me. 3

TRINCULO    Servant monster? The folly of this island! 4
They say there's but five upon this isle. We are three
of them; if th'other two be brained like us, the state 6
totters.

STEPHANO    Drink, servant monster, when I bid thee.
Thy eyes are almost set in thy head.    [*Giving a drink.*] 9

TRINCULO    Where should they be set else? He were a 10
brave monster indeed if they were set in his tail. 11

STEPHANO    My man-monster hath drowned his tongue
in sack. For my part, the sea cannot drown me. I 13
swam, ere I could recover the shore, five and thirty 14
leagues off and on. By this light, thou shalt be my 15
lieutenant, monster, or my standard. 16

TRINCULO    Your lieutenant, if you list; he's no standard. 17

STEPHANO    We'll not run, Monsieur Monster. 18

TRINCULO    Nor go neither, but you'll lie like dogs and 19
yet say nothing neither.

STEPHANO    Mooncalf, speak once in thy life, if thou
be'st a good mooncalf.

CALIBAN
How does Thy Honor? Let me lick thy shoe.
I'll not serve him. He is not valiant.

TRINCULO    Thou liest, most ignorant monster, I am in 25
case to jostle a constable. Why, thou deboshed fish, 26
thou, was there ever man a coward that hath drunk so 27
much sack as I today? Wilt thou tell a monstrous lie,
being but half a fish and half a monster?

CALIBAN
Lo, how he mocks me! Wilt thou let him, my lord?

TRINCULO    "Lord," quoth he? That a monster should be
such a natural! 32

CALIBAN
Lo, lo, again! Bite him to death, I prithee.

STEPHANO    Trinculo, keep a good tongue in your head.
If you prove a mutineer—the next tree! The poor mon- 35
ster's my subject, and he shall not suffer indignity.

CALIBAN
I thank my noble lord. Wilt thou be pleased
To hearken once again to the suit I made to thee?

STEPHANO    Marry, will I. Kneel and repeat it. I will 39
stand, and so shall Trinculo.    [*Caliban kneels.*] 40

*Enter Ariel, invisible.*

CALIBAN
As I told thee before, I am subject to a tyrant,
A sorcerer, that by his cunning hath
Cheated me of the island.

ARIEL [*mimicking Trinculo*]
Thou liest.

CALIBAN                    Thou liest, thou jesting monkey, thou!
I would my valiant master would destroy thee.
I do not lie.

STEPHANO    Trinculo, if you trouble him any more in 's
tale, by this hand, I will supplant some of your teeth. 48

TRINCULO    Why, I said nothing.

STEPHANO    Mum, then, and no more.—Proceed.

CALIBAN
I say by sorcery he got this isle;
From me he got it. If Thy Greatness will 52
Revenge it on him—for I know thou dar'st,
But this thing dare not— 54

STEPHANO    That's most certain.

CALIBAN
Thou shalt be lord of it, and I'll serve thee.

---

**84 maid** handmaiden, servant.  **fellow** mate    **86 will** desire it.
**My mistress** i.e., The woman I adore and serve (not an illicit sexual
partner)    **89 willing** desirous    **92 A thousand thousand!** A thousand thousand farewells!    **94 with all** by everything that has happened, or, *withal*, "by it"    **97 appertaining** related to this.
**3.2. Location: Another part of the island.**
**1 out** empty    **2–3 bear . . . 'em** (Stephano uses the terminology of
maneuvering at sea and boarding a vessel under attack as a way of
urging an assault on the liquor supply.)    **4 folly of** i.e., stupidity
found on    **6 be brained** are endowed with intelligence    **9 set . . .
head** fixed in a drunken stare. (But Trinculo answers in a literal sense.)
**10 set** placed.    **were** would be    **11 brave** fine, splendid    **13 sack** a
Spanish white wine. (Also in line 28.)    **14 recover** gain, reach
**14–15 five . . . on** i.e., something over a hundred miles, give or take, or,
off and on, intermittently. (A drunken hyperbole.)    **15 By this light**
(An oath: By the light of the sun.)    **16 standard** standard-bearer,
ensign. (But Trinculo answers in the literal sense: Caliban is *no standard*, not able to stand up because he's so drunk.)    **17 list** prefer

**18 run** run away, retreat (as a standard-bearer should not do)
**19 Nor . . . dogs** i.e., You won't even walk, much less run; you'll lie
down in the field like the proverbial cowardly dog. (With a play on
*lie*, tell falsehoods.)    **25–6 in case** ready, valiant enough
**26 deboshed** debauched, drunken    **27 ever . . . coward** ever a coward. (Trinculo appeals to his gargantuan drinking as refutation of the
charge that he is *not valiant*, line 24.)    **32 natural** fool, idiot.    **35 the
next tree** i.e., you'll hang.    **39 Marry** i.e., Indeed. (Originally an oath,
"by the Virgin Mary.")    **40.1 invisible** i.e., wearing a garment to connote invisibility, as at 1.2.377.2.    **48 supplant** uproot, displace    **52 he**
Prospero    **54 this thing** i.e., Trinculo

STEPHANO   How now shall this be compassed? Canst 57
thou bring me to the party? 58

CALIBAN
Yea, yea, my lord. I'll yield him thee asleep, 59
Where thou mayst knock a nail into his head.

ARIEL [*mimicking Trinculo*]   Thou liest; thou canst not.

CALIBAN
What a pied ninny's this! Thou scurvy patch!— 62
I do beseech Thy Greatness, give him blows
And take his bottle from him. When that's gone
He shall drink naught but brine, for I'll not show
him
Where the quick freshes are. 66

STEPHANO   Trinculo, run into no further danger. Interrupt the monster one word further and, by this hand,
I'll turn my mercy out o' doors and make a stockfish of 69
thee.

TRINCULO   Why, what did I? I did nothing. I'll go farther
off.

STEPHANO   Didst thou not say he lied?

ARIEL [*mimicking Trinculo*]   Thou liest.

STEPHANO   Do I so? Take thou that. [*He beats Trinculo.*]
As you like this, give me the lie another time. 76

TRINCULO   I did not give the lie. Out o' your wits and
hearing too? A pox o' your bottle! This can sack and 78
drinking do. A murrain on your monster, and the 79
devil take your fingers! 80

CALIBAN   Ha, ha, ha!

STEPHANO   Now, forward with your tale.
[*To Trinculo*] Prithee, stand further off.

CALIBAN
Beat him enough. After a little time
I'll beat him too.

STEPHANO   Stand farther.—Come, proceed.

CALIBAN
Why, as I told thee, 'tis a custom with him
I'th' afternoon to sleep. There thou mayst brain him,
Having first seized his books; or with a log
Batter his skull, or paunch him with a stake, 90
Or cut his weasand with thy knife. Remember 91
First to possess his books, for without them
He's but a sot, as I am, nor hath not 93
One spirit to command. They all do hate him
As rootedly as I. Burn but his books.
He has brave utensils—for so he calls them— 96
Which, when he has a house, he'll deck withal. 97
And that most deeply to consider is
The beauty of his daughter. He himself
Calls her a nonpareil. I never saw a woman 100
But only Sycorax my dam and she; 101
But she as far surpasseth Sycorax
As great'st does least.

STEPHANO                           Is it so brave a lass? 103

CALIBAN
Ay, lord. She will become thy bed, I warrant, 104
And bring thee forth brave brood.

STEPHANO   Monster, I will kill this man. His daughter
and I will be king and queen—save Our Graces!—and 107
Trinculo and thyself shall be viceroys. Dost thou like
the plot, Trinculo?

TRINCULO   Excellent.

STEPHANO   Give me thy hand. I am sorry I beat thee;
but, while thou liv'st, keep a good tongue in thy head.

CALIBAN
Within this half hour will he be asleep. 113
Wilt thou destroy him then?

STEPHANO   Ay, on mine honor.

ARIEL [*aside*]   This will I tell my master.

CALIBAN
Thou mak'st me merry; I am full of pleasure.
Let us be jocund. Will you troll the catch 118
You taught me but whilere? 119

STEPHANO   At thy request, monster, I will do reason, 120
any reason.—Come on, Trinculo, let us sing.     *Sings.* 121
    Flout 'em and scout 'em 122
    And scout 'em and flout 'em!
        Thought is free.

CALIBAN   That's not the tune. 125
            *Ariel plays the tune on a tabor and pipe.*

STEPHANO   What is this same?

TRINCULO   This is the tune of our catch, played by the
picture of Nobody. 128

STEPHANO   If thou be'st a man, show thyself in thy
likeness. If thou be'st a devil, take't as thou list. 130

TRINCULO   Oh, forgive me my sins!

STEPHANO   He that dies pays all debts. I defy thee. 132
Mercy upon us!

CALIBAN   Art thou afeard?

STEPHANO   No, monster, not I.

CALIBAN
Be not afeard. The isle is full of noises,
Sounds, and sweet airs, that give delight and hurt not. 137
Sometimes a thousand twangling instruments
Will hum about mine ears, and sometimes voices
That, if I then had waked after long sleep,
Will make me sleep again; and then, in dreaming,
The clouds methought would open and show riches
Ready to drop upon me, that when I waked
I cried to dream again. 144

STEPHANO   This will prove a brave kingdom to me,
where I shall have my music for nothing.

CALIBAN   When Prospero is destroyed.

---

**57 compassed** achieved.   **58 the party** i.e., Prospero, the subject of Caliban's plot.   **59 yield him thee** arrange matters so that you can steal upon him. (See lines 87–8 below.)   **62 pied ninny** fool in motley.   **patch** fool.   **66 quick freshes** running springs   **69 turn ... o' doors** banish all merciful feelings.   **stockfish** dried cod beaten before cooking   **76 give me the lie** call me a liar to my face   **78 A pox** i.e., A plague. (A curse.)   **79 murrain** plague. (Literally, a cattle disease.)   **80 fingers** i.e., the hand you used to beat me.   **90 paunch** stab in the belly   **91 weasand** windpipe   **93 sot** fool   **96 brave utensils** fine furnishings   **97 deck withal** furnish it with.   **100 nonpareil** one without equal.   **101 dam** mother

**103 brave** splendid, attractive   **104 become** suit (sexually)   **107 save God** save   **113 he** Prospero   **118 jocund** jovial, merry.   **troll the catch** sing the round   **119 but whilere** only a short time ago.   **120–1 reason, any reason** anything reasonable.   **122 Flout** Scoff at.   **scout** deride   **125.1 tabor** small drum   **128 picture of Nobody** (Refers to a familiar figure with head, arms, and legs but no trunk. Trinculo's point is that the musician appears to be invisible. Ariel on stage is indeed "invisible" [line 40.1] to the clowns.)   **130 take't ... list** (A proverbial formula of bravado and defiance, as in *Romeo and Juliet*, 1.1.40–1.)   **132 He ... debts** (Another proverbial swagger: Death settles all scores, I'm not afraid to fight. Stephano's swagger then collapses in the next line; perhaps Ariel has done something to scare him.)   **137 airs** melodies   **144 to dream** desirous of dreaming

STEPHANO    That shall be by and by. I remember the 148
story.

TRINCULO    The sound is going away. Let's follow it,
and after do our work.

STEPHANO    Lead, monster; we'll follow. I would I could
see this taborer! He lays it on.                              153

TRINCULO    Wilt come? I'll follow, Stephano.

*Exeunt [following Ariel's music].*

❖

## 3.3

*Enter Alonso, Sebastian, Antonio, Gonzalo,
Adrian, Francisco, etc.*

GONZALO
By'r lakin, I can go no further, sir.                          1
My old bones aches. Here's a maze trod indeed
Through forthrights and meanders! By your patience,           3
I needs must rest me.

ALONSO                        Old lord, I cannot blame thee,
Who am myself attached with weariness,                        5
To th' dulling of my spirits. Sit down and rest.              6
Even here I will put off my hope, and keep it
No longer for my flatterer. He is drowned                     8
Whom thus we stray to find, and the sea mocks
Our frustrate search on land. Well, let him go.               10
                              *[Alonso and Gonzalo sit.]*

ANTONIO *[aside to Sebastian]*
I am right glad that he's so out of hope.
Do not, for one repulse, forgo the purpose                    12
That you resolved t'effect.

SEBASTIAN *[to Antonio]*         The next advantage
Will we take throughly.

ANTONIO *[to Sebastian]*    Let it be tonight,                 14
For, now they are oppressed with travel, they                 15
Will not, nor cannot, use such vigilance                      16
As when they are fresh.

SEBASTIAN *[to Antonio]*    I say tonight. No more.            17

*Solemn and strange music; and Prospero on
the top, invisible.*

ALONSO
What harmony is this? My good friends, hark!

GONZALO    Marvelous sweet music!

*Enter several strange shapes, bringing in a ban-
quet, and dance about it with gentle actions of
salutations; and, inviting the King, etc., to eat,
they depart.*

ALONSO
Give us kind keepers, heavens! What were these?              20

SEBASTIAN
A living drollery. Now I will believe                         21
That there are unicorns; that in Arabia
There is one tree, the phoenix' throne, one phoenix          23
At this hour reigning there.

ANTONIO                              I'll believe both;
And what does else want credit, come to me                    25
And I'll be sworn 'tis true. Travelers ne'er did lie,
Though fools at home condemn 'em.

GONZALO                              If in Naples
I should report this now, would they believe me
If I should say I saw such islanders?
For, certes, these are people of the island,                  30
Who, though they are of monstrous shape, yet note,
Their manners are more gentle, kind, than of
Our human generation you shall find
Many, nay, almost any.

PROSPERO *[aside]*         Honest lord,
Thou hast said well, for some of you there present
Are worse than devils.

ALONSO                    I cannot too much muse               36
Such shapes, such gesture, and such sound,
expressing—
Although they want the use of tongue—a kind                   38
Of excellent dumb discourse.

PROSPERO *[aside]*         Praise in departing.                39

FRANCISCO
They vanished strangely.

SEBASTIAN                    No matter, since
They have left their viands behind, for we have
stomachs.                                                     41
Will 't please you taste of what is here?

ALONSO                              Not I.

GONZALO
Faith, sir, you need not fear. When we were boys,
Who would believe that there were mountaineers                44
Dewlapped like bulls, whose throats had hanging at
'em                                                           45
Wallets of flesh? Or that there were such men                 46
Whose heads stood in their breasts? Which now we
find                                                          47
Each putter-out of five for one will bring us                 48
Good warrant of.

ALONSO                    I will stand to and feed,            49

---

148 by and by very soon.    153 lays it on i.e., plays the drum
vigorously.
3.3. Location: Another part of the island.
1 By'r lakin By our Ladykin, by our Lady    3 forthrights and meanders
paths straight and crooked.    5 attached with seized by    6 To . . . spirits
to the point of being dull-spirited.    8 for my flatterer as an attendant
saying what I want to hear, telling me sweet lies.    10 frustrate frustrated
12 for because of    14 throughly thoroughly.    15 now now that.    travel
(Spelled "trauaile" in the Folio and carrying the sense of labor as well as
traveling.)    16 use such vigilance be as vigilant    17.1–2 *on the top* at
some high point of the tiring-house or the theater, on a third level above
the gallery

20 kind keepers guardian angels    21 living drollery comic entertainment, caricature, or puppet show put on by live actors.
23 phoenix' The phoenix was a mythical bird consumed to ashes
every five hundred to six hundred years, only to be renewed into
another cycle.    25 want credit lack credibility    30 certes certainly
36 muse wonder at    38 want lack    39 Praise in departing i.e.,
Save your praise until the end of the performance. (Proverbial.)
41 viands provisions.    stomachs appetites.    44 mountaineers
mountain dwellers    45 Dewlapped having a dewlap, or fold of skin
hanging from the neck, like cattle    46 Wallets pendent folds of skin,
wattles    47 in their breasts (i.e., like the Anthropophagi described in
*Othello*, 1.3.146.)    48 putter-out . . . one one who invests money or
gambles on the risks of travel on the condition that the traveler who
returns safely is to receive five times the amount deposited; hence,
any traveler    49 Good warrant assurance.    stand to come forward,
fall to. (Also in line 52.)

Although my last—no matter, since I feel                50
The best is past. Brother, my lord the Duke,             51
Stand to, and do as we.          [*They approach the table.*]   52

*Thunder and lightning. Enter Ariel, like a harpy,*
*claps his wings upon the table, and with a quaint*
*device the banquet vanishes.*

ARIEL

You are three men of sin, whom Destiny—                 53
That hath to instrument this lower world                 54
And what is in't—the never-surfeited sea                 55
Hath caused to belch up you, and on this island          56
Where man doth not inhabit, you 'mongst men
Being most unfit to live. I have made you mad;
And even with suchlike valor men hang and drown          59
Their proper selves.      [*Alonso, Sebastian, and Antonio*
                                        *draw their swords.*]
                              You fools! I and my fellows   60
Are ministers of Fate. The elements
Of whom your swords are tempered may as well            62
Wound the loud winds, or with bemocked-at stabs         63
Kill the still-closing waters, as diminish               64
One dowl that's in my plume. My fellow ministers         65
Are like invulnerable. If you could hurt,                66
Your swords are now too massy for your strengths         67
And will not be uplifted. But remember—
For that's my business to you—that you three
From Milan did supplant good Prospero;
Exposed unto the sea, which hath requit it,              71
Him and his innocent child; for which foul deed
The powers, delaying, not forgetting, have
Incensed the seas and shores, yea, all the creatures,
Against your peace. Thee of thy son, Alonso,
They have bereft; and do pronounce by me
Ling'ring perdition, worse than any death                77
Can be at once, shall step by step attend
You and your ways; whose wraths to guard you
    from—                                                79
Which here, in this most desolate isle, else falls       80
Upon your heads—is nothing but heart's sorrow           81
And a clear life ensuing.                                82

*He vanishes in thunder; then, to soft music,*
*enter the shapes again, and dance, with mocks*
*and mows, and carrying out the table.*

PROSPERO

Bravely the figure of this harpy hast thou               83
Performed, my Ariel; a grace it had devouring.           84
Of my instruction hast thou nothing bated                85
In what thou hadst to say. So, with good life            86
And observation strange, my meaner ministers            87
Their several kinds have done. My high charms work,     88
And these mine enemies are all knit up
In their distractions. They now are in my power;        90
And in these fits I leave them, while I visit
Young Ferdinand, whom they suppose is drowned,
And his and mine loved darling.          [*Exit above.*]

GONZALO

I'th' name of something holy, sir, why stand you        94
In this strange stare?

ALONSO                          Oh, it is monstrous, monstrous!  95
Methought the billows spoke and told me of it;           96
The winds did sing it to me, and the thunder,
That deep and dreadful organ pipe, pronounced
The name of Prosper; it did bass my trespass.           99
Therefor my son i'th'ooze is bedded; and
I'll seek him deeper than e'er plummet sounded,         101
And with him there lie mudded.                *Exit.*

SEBASTIAN        But one fiend at a time,               103
I'll fight their legions o'er.

ANTONIO                    I'll be thy second.          104
                *Exeunt* [*Sebastian and Antonio*].

GONZALO

All three of them are desperate. Their great guilt,     105
Like poison given to work a great time after,           106
Now 'gins to bite the spirits. I do beseech you,        107
That are of suppler joints, follow them swiftly          108
And hinder them from what this ecstasy                   109
May now provoke them to.

ADRIAN                        Follow, I pray you.
                                   *Exeunt omnes.*

❖

# 4.1

*Enter Prospero, Ferdinand, and Miranda.*

PROSPERO

If I have too austerely punished you,
Your compensation makes amends, for I

**50 Although my last** even if this were to be my last meal   **51 best** best part of life   **52.1 harpy** a fabulous monster with a woman's face and breasts and a vulture's body, supposed to be a minister of divine vengeance   **52.2–3 *with . . . vanishes*** by means of some ingenious stage contrivance, the food vanishes. (The table remains until line 82.)   **53–6 whom . . . up you** you whom Destiny, acting through this sublunary world as its instrument, has caused the ever-hungry sea to belch up   **54 to** as its   **59 suchlike valor** i.e., the reckless valor derived from madness   **60 Their . . . selves** themselves.   **62 whom** which.   **tempered** made hard   **63 bemocked-at** scorned   **64 still-closing** always closing again when parted   **65 dowl** soft, fine feather   **66 like** likewise, similarly.   **If** Even if   **67 massy** heavy   **71 requit** requited, avenged   **77 perdition** ruin, destruction   **79 whose . . . from** to guard you from which heavenly wrath   **80 else** otherwise   **81 is nothing** there is no way   **82 clear** unspotted, innocent   **82.2–3 *mocks and mows*** mocking gestures and grimaces

**83 Bravely** Finely, dashingly   **84 a grace . . . devouring** your impersonation displayed a ravishing grace. (With a punning suggestion of having caused the banquet to disappear as if by consuming it.)   **85 bated** abated, omitted   **86–8 So . . . done** Similarly, my lesser spirits assisting you have done their various tasks with observant care and attention to detail.   **90 distractions** trancelike state.   **94–5 why . . . stare?** (Gonzalo was not addressed in Ariel's speech to the *three men of sin*, line 53, and is not, as they are, in a maddened state; see lines 105–7.)   **95 it** i.e., my sin. (Also in line 96.)   **96 billows** waves   **99 bass my trespass** proclaim my trespass like a bass note in the music.   **101 than . . . sounded** than ever a lead weight attached to a line tested the depth   **103–4 But . . . o'er** If the demons come at me one at a time, I'll fight them all.   **105 desperate** despairing and reckless.   **106 Like . . . after** like poison, starting to work long after it has been administered   **107 bite the spirits** sap their vital powers through anguish.   **107–8 you . . . joints** Adrian, Francisco, and others not under Ariel's numbing spell   **109 ecstasy** mad frenzy
**4.1. Location: Before Prospero's cell.**

Have given you here a third of mine own life,                    3
Or that for which I live; who once again
I tender to thy hand. All thy vexations                          5
Were but my trials of thy love, and thou
Hast strangely stood the test. Here, afore heaven,              7
I ratify this my rich gift. O Ferdinand,
Do not smile at me that I boast her off,                         9
For thou shalt find she will outstrip all praise
And make it halt behind her.

**FERDINAND**                          I do believe it            11
Against an oracle.                                              12

**PROSPERO**
Then, as my gift and thine own acquisition
Worthily purchased, take my daughter. But
If thou dost break her virgin-knot before
All sanctimonious ceremonies may                                16
With full and holy rite be ministered,
No sweet aspersion shall the heavens let fall                   18
To make this contract grow; but barren hate,
Sour-eyed disdain, and discord shall bestrew
The union of your bed with weeds so loathly                     21
That you shall hate it both. Therefore take heed,
As Hymen's lamps shall light you.

**FERDINAND**                          As I hope                 23
For quiet days, fair issue, and long life,                      24
With such love as 'tis now, the murkiest den,
The most opportune place, the strong'st suggestion              26
Our worser genius can, shall never melt                         27
Mine honor into lust, to take away                              28
The edge of that day's celebration                              29
When I shall think or Phoebus' steeds are foundered             30
Or Night kept chained below.

**PROSPERO**                          Fairly spoke.
Sit then and talk with her. She is thine own.
       [*Ferdinand and Miranda sit and talk together.*]
What, Ariel! My industrious servant, Ariel!                     33

       *Enter Ariel.*

**ARIEL**
What would my potent master? Here I am.

**PROSPERO**
Thou and thy meaner fellows your last service                   35
Did worthily perform, and I must use you
In such another trick. Go bring the rabble,                     37

O'er whom I give thee power, here to this place.
Incite them to quick motion, for I must
Bestow upon the eyes of this young couple
Some vanity of mine art. It is my promise,                      41
And they expect it from me.

**ARIEL**                          Presently?                    42
**PROSPERO**     Ay, with a twink.                               43
**ARIEL**
       Before you can say "Come" and "Go,"
       And breathe twice, and cry "So, so,"
       Each one, tripping on his toe,
       Will be here with mop and mow.                            47
       Do you love me, master? No?

**PROSPERO**
Dearly, my delicate Ariel. Do not approach
Till thou dost hear me call.

**ARIEL**                          Well; I conceive.    *Exit.*  50
**PROSPERO** [*to Ferdinand*]
Look thou be true; do not give dalliance                        51
Too much the rein. The strongest oaths are straw                52
To th' fire i'th' blood. Be more abstemious,
Or else good night your vow!

**FERDINAND**                          I warrant you, sir,       54
The white cold virgin snow upon my heart                        55
Abates the ardor of my liver.

**PROSPERO**                          Well.                      56
Now come, my Ariel! Bring a corollary,                          57
Rather than want a spirit. Appear, and pertly!—                 58
No tongue! All eyes! Be silent.         *Soft music.*           59

       *Enter Iris.*

**IRIS**
Ceres, most bounteous lady, thy rich leas                       60
Of wheat, rye, barley, vetches, oats, and peas;                61
Thy turfy mountains, where live nibbling sheep,
And flat meads thatched with stover, them to keep;             63
Thy banks with pionèd and twillèd brims,                       64
Which spongy April at thy hest betrims                          65
To make cold nymphs chaste crowns; and thy
    broom groves,                                               66
Whose shadow the dismissèd bachelor loves,                     67
Being lass-lorn; thy pole-clipped vineyard;                    68
And thy sea marge, sterile and rocky hard,                     69
Where thou thyself dost air: the queen o'th' sky,              70

---

**3 a third** i.e., Miranda, into whose education I have put a third of my life, or (less precisely) who represents a large part of what I have cared about, along with my dukedom and my magical art   **5 tender** offer   **7 strangely** exceptionally   **9 boast her off** i.e., praise her so, or, perhaps an error for "boast of her"; the Folio reads "boast her of"   **11 halt** limp   **12 Against an oracle** even if an oracle should declare otherwise.   **16 sanctimonious** sacred   **18 aspersion** dew, shower   **21 weeds** (In place of the flowers customarily strewn on the marriage bed.)   **23 As . . . you** i.e., as you long for happiness and concord in your marriage. (Hymen was the Greek and Roman god of marriage; his symbolic torches, the wedding torches, were supposed to burn brightly for a happy marriage and smokily for a troubled one.)   **24 issue** offspring   **26–7 the strong'st . . . can** the strongest temptation that the evil spirit within us can propose   **28 to** so as to   **29 edge** keen enjoyment, sexual ardor   **30 or . . . foundered** either that the horses of the sun's chariot have gone lame (thus delaying the night for which I will be so eager)   **33 What** Now then   **35 meaner fellows** subordinates   **37 trick** device. **rabble** band, i.e., the *meaner fellows* of line 35

**41 vanity** (1) illusion (2) trifle (3) desire for admiration, conceit   **42 Presently?** Immediately?   **43 with a twink** in the twinkling of an eye.   **47 mop and mow** grimaces.   **50 conceive** understand.   **51 true** true to your promise   **52 Too . . . rein** too great a freedom.   **54 good night** i.e., say good-bye to. **warrant** guarantee   **55 The white . . . heart** i.e., the chaste ideal to which my heart is devoted   **56 liver** (The presumed seat of the passions).   **57 corollary** surplus, extra supply   **58 want** lack. **pertly** briskly.   **59 No tongue!** Quiet, everyone!   **59.1 Iris** goddess of the rainbow and Juno's messenger.   **60 Ceres** goddess of the generative power of nature.   **leas** meadows   **61 vetches** plants for forage, fodder   **63 meads** meadows. **stover** winter fodder for cattle.   **them to keep** to feed the sheep   **64 Thy . . . brims** your riverbanks protected from erosion by interwoven roots and branches   **65 spongy** wet.   **hest** command   **66 cold** chaste.   **broom groves** clumps of broom, gorse, yellow-flowered shrub   **67 dismissèd bachelor** rejected suitor   **68 pole-clipped vineyard** vines entwining poles or hedged in by them   **69 sea marge** shore   **70 thou . . . air** you take the air, go for walks.   **queen o'th' sky** i.e., Juno

Whose wat'ry arch and messenger am I,    71
Bids thee leave these, and with her sovereign grace,    72

*Juno descends [slowly in her car].*

Here on this grass plot, in this very place,
To come and sport. Her peacocks fly amain.    74
Approach, rich Ceres, her to entertain.    75

*Enter Ceres.*

**CERES**
Hail, many-colored messenger, that ne'er
Dost disobey the wife of Jupiter,
Who with thy saffron wings upon my flowers    78
Diffusest honeydrops, refreshing showers,
And with each end of thy blue bow dost crown    80
My bosky acres and my unshrubbed down,    81
Rich scarf to my proud earth. Why hath thy queen    82
Summoned me hither to this short-grassed green?

**IRIS**
A contract of true love to celebrate,
And some donation freely to estate    85
On the blest lovers.

**CERES**        Tell me, heavenly bow,
If Venus or her son, as thou dost know,    87
Do now attend the Queen? Since they did plot    88
The means that dusky Dis my daughter got,    89
Her and her blind boy's scandaled company    90
I have forsworn.

**IRIS**        Of her society    91
Be not afraid. I met Her Deity    92
Cutting the clouds towards Paphos, and her son    93
Dove-drawn with her. Here thought they to have
     done    94
Some wanton charm upon this man and maid,    95
Whose vows are that no bed-right shall be paid    96
Till Hymen's torch be lighted; but in vain.    97
Mars's hot minion is returned again;    98
Her waspish-headed son has broke his arrows,    99
Swears he will shoot no more, but play with
     sparrows    100
And be a boy right out.

*[Juno alights.]*

**CERES**        Highest Queen of state,    101
Great Juno, comes; I know her by her gait.    102

**JUNO**
How does my bounteous sister? Go with me    103
To bless this twain, that they may prosperous be,
And honored in their issue.      *They sing:* 105

**JUNO**
Honor, riches, marriage blessing,
Long continuance and increasing,
Hourly joys be still upon you!    108
Juno sings her blessings on you.

**CERES**
Earth's increase, foison plenty,    110
Barns and garners never empty,    111
Vines with clust'ring bunches growing,
Plants with goodly burden bowing;

Spring come to you at the farthest
In the very end of harvest!    115
Scarcity and want shall shun you;
Ceres' blessing so is on you.

**FERDINAND**
This is a most majestic vision, and
Harmonious charmingly. May I be bold    119
To think these spirits?

**PROSPERO**        Spirits, which by mine art
I have from their confines called to enact
My present fancies.

**FERDINAND**        Let me live here ever!
So rare a wondered father and a wise    123
Makes this place Paradise.

*Juno and Ceres whisper, and send*
*Iris on employment.*

**PROSPERO**        Sweet now, silence!
Juno and Ceres whisper seriously;
There's something else to do. Hush and be mute,
Or else our spell is marred.

**IRIS** *[calling offstage]*
You nymphs, called naiads, of the wind'ring brooks,    128
With your sedged crowns and ever-harmless looks,    129
Leave your crisp channels, and on this green land    130
Answer your summons; Juno does command.
Come, temperate nymphs, and help to celebrate    132
A contract of true love. Be not too late.

*Enter certain nymphs.*

You sunburned sicklemen, of August weary,    134
Come hither from the furrow and be merry.    135

---

**71 wat'ry arch** rainbow   **72.1 *Juno descends*** i.e., starts her descent from the "heavens" above the stage   **74 peacocks** birds sacred to Juno and used to pull her chariot.   **amain** with full speed.   **75 entertain** receive.   **78 saffron** yellow   **80 bow** rainbow   **81 bosky** wooded. **unshrubbed down** open upland   **82 scarf** (The rainbow is like a colored silk band adorning the earth.)   **85 estate** bestow   **87 son** i.e., Cupid. **as** as far as   **88–91 Since . . . forsworn** Since Venus and her blind son Cupid plotted the means by which Dis (Pluto) carried off my daughter Proserpina to be his bride in Hades, I have forsworn their scandalous company.   **92 Her Deity** i.e., Her Highness   **93 Paphos** place on the island of Cyprus, sacred to Venus   **94 Dove-drawn** (Venus's chariot was drawn by doves.)   **94–5 done . . . charm** inflicted some lustful spell **96–7 that . . . lighted** that their union will not be sexually consummated until the wedding ceremony has taken place   **98 Mars's hot minion** i.e., Venus, the beloved of Mars.   **returned** i.e., returned to Paphos **99 waspish-headed** hotheaded, peevish   **100 sparrows** (Supposed lustful, and sacred to Venus.)   **101 right out** outright.   **Highest . . . state** Most majestic Queen   **102 gait** i.e., majestic bearing.

**103 sister** i.e., fellow goddess.   **105 issue** offspring.   **108 still** always **110 foison plenty** plentiful harvest   **111 garners** granaries   **115 In . . . harvest** i.e., with no winter in between.   **119 charmingly** enchantingly. **bold** so bold as   **123 wondered** wonder-performing, wondrous.   **wise** (The Folio appears to read "wise" here, but with a tall "s" that resembles an "f," leading to much dispute over this reading. In some copies of the Folio the "s" looks like an "f," perhaps damaged, but evidently as the result of an inkblot, so that the true reading is "s." Even so, an error in transmission would be easy, so that the author's intention is uncertain. The matter bears importantly on whether or not Ferdinand includes Miranda in his vision of paradise.)   **128 naiads** nymphs of springs, rivers, or lakes.   **wind'ring** wandering, winding (?)   **129 sedged crowns** garlands made of reeds. **ever-harmless** perennially innocent   **130 crisp channels** rippled streams **132 temperate** chaste   **134 sicklemen** harvesters, field workers who cut down grain and grass.   **of August weary** i.e., weary of the hard work of the harvest   **135 furrow** i.e., plowed fields

Make holiday; your rye-straw hats put on,
And these fresh nymphs encounter every one          137
In country footing.                                 138

> *Enter certain reapers, properly habited. They join*
> *with the nymphs in a graceful dance, towards the*
> *end whereof Prospero starts suddenly, and speaks;*
> *after which, to a strange, hollow, and confused*
> *noise, they heavily vanish.*

PROSPERO [*aside*]
I had forgot that foul conspiracy
Of the beast Caliban and his confederates
Against my life. The minute of their plot
Is almost come. [*To the Spirits*] Well done! Avoid; no
   more!                                            142
FERDINAND [*to Miranda*]
This is strange. Your father's in some passion
That works him strongly.
MIRANDA                        Never till this day   144
Saw I him touched with anger so distempered.
PROSPERO
You do look, my son, in a moved sort,              146
As if you were dismayed. Be cheerful, sir.
Our revels now are ended. These our actors,        148
As I foretold you, were all spirits and
Are melted into air, into thin air;
And, like the baseless fabric of this vision,      151
The cloud-capped towers, the gorgeous palaces,
The solemn temples, the great globe itself,        153
Yea, all which it inherit, shall dissolve,         154
And, like this insubstantial pageant faded,
Leave not a rack behind. We are such stuff         156
As dreams are made on, and our little life         157
Is rounded with a sleep. Sir, I am vexed.          158
Bear with my weakness. My old brain is troubled.
Be not disturbed with my infirmity.                160
If you be pleased, retire into my cell             161
And there repose. A turn or two I'll walk
To still my beating mind.
FERDINAND, MIRANDA       We wish your peace.         163
                *Exeunt [Ferdinand and Miranda].*
PROSPERO
Come with a thought! I thank thee, Ariel. Come.    164

> *Enter Ariel.*

ARIEL
Thy thoughts I cleave to. What's thy pleasure?
PROSPERO                              Spirit,       165
We must prepare to meet with Caliban.

ARIEL
Ay, my commander. When I presented Ceres,          167
I thought to have told thee of it, but I feared
Lest I might anger thee.
PROSPERO
Say again, where didst thou leave these varlets?
ARIEL
I told you, sir, they were red-hot with drinking;
So full of valor that they smote the air
For breathing in their faces, beat the ground
For kissing of their feet; yet always bending      174
Towards their project. Then I beat my tabor,
At which, like unbacked colts, they pricked their ears, 176
Advanced their eyelids, lifted up their noses      177
As they smelt music. So I charmed their ears       178
That calflike they my lowing followed through      179
Toothed briers, sharp furzes, pricking gorse, and
   thorns,                                          180
Which entered their frail shins. At last I left them
I'th' filthy-mantled pool beyond your cell,        182
There dancing up to th' chins, that the foul lake  183
O'erstunk their feet.
PROSPERO            This was well done, my bird.    184
Thy shape invisible retain thou still.
The trumpery in my house, go bring it hither,      186
For stale to catch these thieves.
ARIEL                            I go, I go.   *Exit.* 187
PROSPERO
A devil, a born devil, on whose nature
Nurture can never stick; on whom my pains,
Humanely taken, all, all lost, quite lost!
And as with age his body uglier grows,
So his mind cankers. I will plague them all,       192
Even to roaring.

> *Enter Ariel, loaden with glistering apparel, etc.*

                    Come, hang them on this line.   193

> [*Ariel hangs up the showy finery; Prospero and*
> *Ariel remain, invisible.*] *Enter Caliban, Stephano,*
> *and Trinculo, all wet.*

CALIBAN
Pray you, tread softly, that the blind mole may
Not hear a foot fall. We now are near his cell.
STEPHANO   Monster, your fairy, which you say is a
harmless fairy, has done little better than played the
jack with us.                                       198

---

**137 encounter** join   **138 country footing** country dancing.
**138.1** *properly habited* suitably costumed.   **138.5** *heavily* slowly,
dejectedly   **142 Avoid** Withdraw   **144 works** affects, agitates
**146 moved sort** troubled state, condition   **148 revels** entertainment,
pageant   **151 baseless fabric** unsubstantial theatrical edifice or
contrivance   **153 great globe** (With a glance at the Globe Theatre.)
**154 which it inherit** who subsequently occupy it   **156 rack** wisp of
cloud   **157 on** of   **158 rounded** surrounded (before birth and after
death), or crowned, rounded off   **160 with** by   **161 retire** withdraw,
go   **163 beating** agitated   **164 with a thought** i.e., on the instant,
or, summoned by my thought, no sooner thought of than here.
**165 cleave** cling, adhere

**167 presented** acted the part of, or, introduced   **174 bending** aiming   **176 unbacked** unbroken, unridden   **177 Advanced** lifted up
**178 As** as if   **179 lowing** mooing   **180 furzes . . . gorse** prickly
shrubs   **182 filthy-mantled** covered with a slimy scum   **183 that** so
that   **184 O'erstunk** smelled worse than, or, caused to stink terribly
**186 trumpery** cheap goods, the *glistering apparel* mentioned in the following stage direction   **187 stale** (1) decoy (2) out-of-fashion garments. (With possible further suggestions of "horse piss," as in line
199, and "steal," pronounced like *stale. For stale* could also mean "fit
for a prostitute.")   **192 cankers** festers, grows malignant.   **193 line**
lime tree or linden.   **193.1–2** *Prospero and Ariel remain* (The staging
is uncertain. They may instead exit here and return with the spirits
at line 256.)   **198 jack** (1) knave (2) will-o'-the-wisp

TRINCULO   Monster, I do smell all horse piss, at which my nose is in great indignation.

STEPHANO   So is mine. Do you hear, monster? If I should take a displeasure against you, look you—

TRINCULO   Thou wert but a lost monster.

CALIBAN
Good my lord, give me thy favor still.
Be patient, for the prize I'll bring thee to
Shall hoodwink this mischance. Therefore speak
    softly.                                                    206
All's hushed as midnight yet.

TRINCULO   Ay, but to lose our bottles in the pool—

STEPHANO   There is not only disgrace and dishonor in that, monster, but an infinite loss.

TRINCULO   That's more to me than my wetting. Yet this is your harmless fairy, monster!

STEPHANO   I will fetch off my bottle, though I be o'er     213
ears for my labor.                                           214

CALIBAN
Prithee, my king, be quiet. See'st thou here,
This is the mouth o'th' cell. No noise, and enter.
Do that good mischief which may make this island
Thine own forever, and I thy Caliban
For aye thy footlicker.                                       219

STEPHANO   Give me thy hand. I do begin to have bloody thoughts.

TRINCULO [seeing the finery] O King Stephano! O peer!        222
O worthy Stephano! Look what a wardrobe here is for thee!

CALIBAN
Let it alone, thou fool, it is but trash.

TRINCULO   Oho, monster! We know what belongs to a frippery. O King Stephano!        [He puts on a gown.]  227

STEPHANO   Put off that gown, Trinculo. By this hand, I'll have that gown.

TRINCULO   Thy Grace shall have it.

CALIBAN
The dropsy drown this fool! What do you mean           231
To dote thus on such luggage? Let 't alone           232
And do the murder first. If he awake,
From toe to crown he'll fill our skins with pinches,   234
Make us strange stuff.

STEPHANO   Be you quiet, monster.—Mistress line, is      236
not this my jerkin? [He takes it down.] Now is the jerkin   237
under the line. Now, jerkin, you are like to lose your   238
hair and prove a bald jerkin.                               239

TRINCULO   Do, do! We steal by line and level, an't like   240
Your Grace.

STEPHANO   I thank thee for that jest. Here's a garment for't. [He gives a garment.] Wit shall not go unrewarded while I am king of this country. "Steal by line and level" is an excellent pass of pate. There's another   245
garment for't.

TRINCULO   Monster, come, put some lime upon your   247
fingers, and away with the rest.                           248

CALIBAN
I will have none on't. We shall lose our time,         249
And all be turned to barnacles, or to apes             250
With foreheads villainous low.                             251

STEPHANO   Monster, lay to your fingers. Help to bear   252
this away where my hogshead of wine is, or I'll turn   253
you out of my kingdom. Go to, carry this.             254

TRINCULO   And this.

STEPHANO   Ay, and this.
    [They load Caliban with more and more garments.]

    A noise of hunters heard. Enter divers spirits, in
    shape of dogs and hounds, hunting them about,
    Prospero and Ariel setting them on.

PROSPERO   Hey, Mountain, hey!                              257

ARIEL   Silver! There it goes, Silver!

PROSPERO   Fury, Fury! There, Tyrant, there! Hark! Hark!
    [Caliban, Stephano, and Trinculo are driven out.]
Go, charge my goblins that they grind their joints
With dry convulsions, shorten up their sinews        261
With agèd cramps, and more pinch-spotted make
    them                                                   262
Than pard or cat o' mountain.

ARIEL                          Hark, they roar!            263

PROSPERO
Let them be hunted soundly. At this hour              264
Lies at my mercy all mine enemies.
Shortly shall all my labors end, and thou
Shalt have the air at freedom. For a little          267
Follow, and do me service.               Exeunt.

                        ❖

# 5.1

    Enter Prospero in his magic robes, [with his
    staff,] and Ariel.

240 **Do, do!** i.e., Bravo! (Said in response to the jesting or to the taking of the jerkin, or both.)   **steal . . . level** i.e., steal by means of plumb line and carpenter's level, methodically. (With pun on *line*, "lime tree," line 238, and *steal*, pronounced like *stale*, i.e., prostitute, continuing Stephano's bawdy quibble.)   **an't like** if it please   245 **pass of pate** sally of wit. (The metaphor is from fencing.)   247 **lime** birdlime, sticky substance used to trap birds, here given to Caliban to provide him with the sticky fingers that are handy for thieves   248 **away . . . rest** let's get away with the rest of the trumpery.   249 **on't** of it.   250 **barnacles** barnacle geese, formerly supposed to be hatched from barnacles attached to trees or to rotting timber; here, evidently used, like *apes*, as types of simpletons   251 **villainous** vilely   252 **lay to** start using   253 **this** i.e., the *glistering apparel*.   **hogshead** large cask   254 **Go to** (An expression of exhortation or remonstrance.)   257 **Mountain** (One of the dogs, along with Silver, Fury, and Tyrant.)   261 **dry convulsions** racking cramps   262 **agèd** characteristic of old age   263 **pard** panther or leopard.   **cat o' mountain** wildcat.   264 **soundly** severely.   267 **little** little while longer   **5.1. Location: Before Prospero's cell.**

206 **hoodwink this mischance** cover up (literally, blindfold) this mistake.   213–14 **o'er ears** over my ears in the filthy horse pond (line 182)   219 **For aye** forever   222 **King . . . peer** (Alludes to the old ballad beginning, "King Stephen was a worthy peer.")   227 **frippery** second-hand-clothing shop. (Trinculo knows that what they have just found is much finer.)   231 **The dropsy drown** (An oath. *Dropsy* is a disease characterized by the accumulation of fluid in the connective tissue of the body.)   232 **luggage** cumbersome trash.   234 **crown** head   236 **Mistress line** (Addressed to the linden or lime tree upon which, at line 193, Ariel hung the *glistering apparel*.)   237 **jerkin** jacket made of leather   238 **under the line** under the lime tree. (With punning sense of being south of the equinoctial line or equator; sailors on long voyages to the southern regions were popularly supposed to lose their hair from scurvy or other diseases. Stephano also quibbles bawdily on losing hair through syphilis, and puns in *Mistress* and *jerkin*.)   **like** likely   239 **bald** (1) hairless, napless (2) meager

PROSPERO
Now does my project gather to a head.
My charms crack not, my spirits obey, and Time    2
Goes upright with his carriage. How's the day?    3

ARIEL
On the sixth hour, at which time, my lord,    4
You said our work should cease.

PROSPERO                                    I did say so,
When first I raised the tempest. Say, my spirit,
How fares the King and 's followers?

ARIEL                                    Confined together
In the same fashion as you gave in charge,
Just as you left them; all prisoners, sir,
In the line grove which weather-fends your cell.    10
They cannot budge till your release. The King,    11
His brother, and yours abide all three distracted,    12
And the remainder mourning over them,
Brim full of sorrow and dismay; but chiefly
Him that you termed, sir, the good old lord,
    Gonzalo.
His tears run down his beard like winter's drops
From eaves of reeds. Your charm so strongly works
    'em    17
That if you now beheld them your affections    18
Would become tender.

PROSPERO                    Dost thou think so, spirit?

ARIEL
Mine would, sir, were I human.

PROSPERO                                    And mine shall.
Hast thou, which art but air, a touch, a feeling    21
Of their afflictions, and shall not myself,
One of their kind, that relish all as sharply    23
Passion as they, be kindlier moved than thou art?    24
Though with their high wrongs I am struck to th'
    quick,    25
Yet with my nobler reason 'gainst my fury
Do I take part. The rarer action is    27
In virtue than in vengeance. They being penitent,
The sole drift of my purpose doth extend
Not a frown further. Go release them, Ariel.
My charms I'll break, their senses I'll restore,
And they shall be themselves.

ARIEL                                    I'll fetch them, sir.
                                                *Exit.*
    [*Prospero traces a charmed circle with his staff.*]

PROSPERO
Ye elves of hills, brooks, standing lakes, and groves,    33
And ye that on the sands with printless foot
Do chase the ebbing Neptune, and do fly him    35

When he comes back; you demi-puppets that    36
By moonshine do the green sour ringlets make,    37
Whereof the ewe not bites; and you whose pastime
Is to make midnight mushrooms, that rejoice    39
To hear the solemn curfew; by whose aid,    40
Weak masters though ye be, I have bedimmed    41
The noontide sun, called forth the mutinous winds,
And twixt the green sea and the azured vault    43
Set roaring war; to the dread rattling thunder    44
Have I given fire, and rifted Jove's stout oak    45
With his own bolt; the strong-based promontory    46
Have I made shake, and by the spurs plucked up    47
The pine and cedar; graves at my command
Have waked their sleepers, oped, and let 'em forth
By my so potent art. But this rough magic    50
I here abjure, and when I have required    51
Some heavenly music—which even now I do—
To work mine end upon their senses that    53
This airy charm is for, I'll break my staff,
Bury it certain fathoms in the earth,    55
And deeper than did ever plummet sound
I'll drown my book.                    *Solemn music.*

    *Here enters Ariel before; then Alonso, with a*
    *frantic gesture, attended by Gonzalo; Sebastian and*
    *Antonio in like manner, attended by Adrian and*
    *Francisco. They all enter the circle which Prospero*
    *had made, and there stand charmed; which*
    *Prospero observing, speaks:*

[*To Alonso*] A solemn air, and the best comforter    58
To an unsettled fancy, cure thy brains,    59
Now useless, boiled within thy skull! [*To Sebastian*
    *and Antonio*] There stand,
For you are spell-stopped.—    60
Holy Gonzalo, honorable man,
Mine eyes, e'en sociable to the show of thine,    63
Fall fellowly drops. [*Aside*] The charm dissolves
    apace,    64
And as the morning steals upon the night,
Melting the darkness, so their rising senses
Begin to chase the ignorant fumes that mantle    67
Their clearer reason.—O good Gonzalo,    68
My true preserver, and a loyal sir
To him thou follow'st! I will pay thy graces    70
Home both in word and deed.—Most cruelly    71
Didst thou, Alonso, use me and my daughter.
Thy brother was a furtherer in the act.—    73

---

2 **crack** collapse, fail. (The metaphor is probably alchemical, as in *project* and *gather to a head*, line 1.)    3 **his carriage** its burden. (Time is no longer heavily burdened and so can go *upright*, standing straight and unimpeded.)    4 **On** Approaching    10 **line grove** grove of lime trees. **weather-fends** protects from the weather    11 **your release** you release them.    12 **distracted** out of their wits    17 **eaves of reeds** thatched roofs. 18 **affections** disposition, feelings    21 **touch** sense, apprehension 23–4 **that . . . they** I who experience human emotions as acutely as they 24 **kindlier** (1) more sympathetically (2) more naturally, humanly 25 **high** heinous    27 **rarer** nobler    33 **Ye . . . groves** (This passage, down through line 50, is an embellished paraphrase of Golding's translation of Ovid's *Metamorphoses*, 7.197–219.)    35 **the ebbing Neptune** the sea, as it retreats along the sand, back to the ocean

36 **When . . . back** when the next wave surges up the sand beach. **demi-puppets** puppets of half size, i.e., elves and fairies    37 **green sour ringlets** fairy rings, circles in grass (actually produced by mushrooms)    39 **midnight mushrooms** mushrooms appearing overnight 40 **curfew** evening bell, usually rung at nine o'clock, ushering in the time when spirits are abroad    41 **Weak masters** i.e., subordinate spirits, as in 4.1.35    43 **the azured vault** i.e., the sky    44–5 **to . . . fire** I have discharged the dread rattling thunderbolt    45 **rifted** riven, split. **oak** a tree that was sacred to Jove    46 **bolt** thunderbolt    47 **spurs** roots    50 **rough** violent    51 **required** summoned    53 **their senses that** the senses of those whom    55 **certain** several    58 **air** song.    **and** i.e., which is 59 **fancy** imagination    60 **boiled** i.e., extremely agitated    63 **sociable** sympathetic.    **show** appearance    64 **Fall** let fall    67 **ignorant fumes** fumes that render them incapable of comprehension.    **mantle** envelop    68 **clearer** growing clearer    70 **pay thy graces** requite your favors and virtues    71 **Home** fully    73 **furtherer** accomplice

Thou art pinched for't now, Sebastian. [*To Antonio*]
    Flesh and blood,                                               74
You, brother mine, that entertained ambition,
Expelled remorse and nature, whom, with Sebastian,      76
Whose inward pinches therefore are most strong,
Would here have killed your king, I do forgive thee,
Unnatural though thou art.—Their understanding
Begins to swell, and the approaching tide
Will shortly fill the reasonable shore                          81
That now lies foul and muddy. Not one of them
That yet looks on me, or would know me.—Ariel,
Fetch me the hat and rapier in my cell.
          [*Ariel goes to the cell and returns immediately.*]
I will discase me and myself present                            85
As I was sometime Milan. Quickly, spirit!                       86
Thou shalt ere long be free.
                       *Ariel sings and helps to attire him.*

ARIEL
        Where the bee sucks, there suck I.
        In a cowslip's bell I lie;
        There I couch when owls do cry.                          90
        On the bat's back I do fly
        After summer merrily.                                    92
    Merrily, merrily shall I live now
    Under the blossom that hangs on the bough.

PROSPERO
    Why, that's my dainty Ariel! I shall miss thee,
    But yet thou shalt have freedom. So, so, so.                 96
    To the King's ship, invisible as thou art!
    There shalt thou find the mariners asleep
    Under the hatches. The Master and the Boatswain
    Being awake, enforce them to this place,
    And presently, I prithee.                                    101

ARIEL
    I drink the air before me, and return
    Or ere your pulse twice beat.              *Exit.* 103

GONZALO
    All torment, trouble, wonder, and amazement
    Inhabits here. Some heavenly power guide us
    Out of this fearful country!

PROSPERO                        Behold, sir King,        106
    The wrongèd Duke of Milan, Prospero.
    For more assurance that a living prince
    Does now speak to thee, I embrace thy body;
    And to thee and thy company I bid
    A hearty welcome.              [*Embracing him.*]

ALONSO                    Whe'er thou be'st he or no,      111
    Or some enchanted trifle to abuse me,                  112
    As late I have been, I not know. Thy pulse             113
    Beats as of flesh and blood; and, since I saw thee,
    Th'affliction of my mind amends, with which

I fear a madness held me. This must crave—               116
An if this be at all—a most strange story.               117
Thy dukedom I resign, and do entreat                     118
Thou pardon me my wrongs. But how should
    Prospero                                             119
Be living, and be here?
PROSPERO [*to Gonzalo*]        First, noble friend,
    Let me embrace thine age, whose honor cannot         121
    Be measured or confined.         [*Embracing him.*]
GONZALO                    Whether this be               122
    Or be not, I'll not swear.
PROSPERO                        You do yet taste
    Some subtleties o'th'isle, that will not let you     124
    Believe things certain. Welcome, my friends all!
    [*Aside to Sebastian and Antonio*] But you, my brace of
        lords, were I so minded,                         126
    I here could pluck His Highness' frown upon you
    And justify you traitors. At this time               128
    I will tell no tales.
SEBASTIAN                    The devil speaks in him.
PROSPERO                                No.               129
    [*To Antonio*] For you, most wicked sir, whom to call
        brother
    Would even infect my mouth, I do forgive
    Thy rankest fault—all of them; and require
    My dukedom of thee, which perforce I know            133
    Thou must restore.
ALONSO                    If thou be'st Prospero,
    Give us particulars of thy preservation,
    How thou hast met us here, whom three hours since    136
    Were wrecked upon this shore; where I have lost—
    How sharp the point of this remembrance is!—
    My dear son Ferdinand.
PROSPERO                    I am woe for't, sir.         139
ALONSO
    Irreparable is the loss, and Patience
    Says it is past her cure.
PROSPERO                    I rather think
    You have not sought her help, of whose soft grace    142
    For the like loss I have her sovereign aid           143
    And rest myself content.
ALONSO                    You the like loss?
PROSPERO
    As great to me as late, and supportable              145
    To make the dear loss, have I means much weaker      146
    Than you may call to comfort you; for I              147
    Have lost my daughter.
ALONSO    A daughter?
    O heavens, that they were living both in Naples,

---

74 **pinched** punished, afflicted   76 **remorse and nature** pity and natural feeling.   **whom** you who   81 **reasonable shore** shores of reason, i.e., minds. (Their reason returns, like the incoming tide.)   85 **discase** disrobe   86 **As . . . Milan** in my former appearance as Duke of Milan.   90 **couch** lie   92 **After summer** following summer as it moves to various parts of the world   96 **So, so, so** (Expresses approval of Ariel's help as valet.)   101 **presently** immediately   103 **Or ere** before   106 **fearful** frightening   111 **Whe'er** Whether   112 **trifle** trick of magic.   **abuse** deceive   113 **late** lately

116 **crave** require   117 **An . . . all** if this is actually happening.   **story** i.e., explanation.   118 **Thy . . . resign** (Alonso made arrangement with Antonio at the time of Prospero's banishment for Milan to pay tribute to Naples; see 1.2.113–27.)   119 **wrongs** wrongdoings.   121 **thine age** your venerable self   122 **this be** this is actually happening   124 **subtleties** illusions, magical powers. (Playing on the idea of "pastries, concoctions.")   126 **brace** pair   128 **justify you** prove you to be   129 **No** i.e., No, my knowledge of your evil deeds and intents is not black magic.   133 **perforce** of necessity   136 **whom** we who   139 **woe** sorry   142 **of** by.   **grace** mercy   143 **sovereign** efficacious   145 **late** recent   145–7 **and supportable . . . you** and I have much weaker means to make my loss supportable than you can call upon to comfort you

The king and queen there! That they were, I wish 151
Myself were mudded in that oozy bed 152
Where my son lies. When did you lose your daughter? 153

PROSPERO
In this last tempest. I perceive these lords
At this encounter do so much admire 155
That they devour their reason and scarce think 156
Their eyes do offices of truth, their words 157
Are natural breath. But, howsoev'r you have 158
Been jostled from your senses, know for certain
That I am Prospero and that very duke
Which was thrust forth of Milan, who most strangely 161
Upon this shore, where you were wrecked, was
    landed
To be the lord on't. No more yet of this,
For 'tis a chronicle of day by day, 164
Not a relation for a breakfast nor
Befitting this first meeting. Welcome, sir.
This cell's my court. Here have I few attendants,
And subjects none abroad. Pray you, look in. 168
My dukedom since you have given me again,
I will requite you with as good a thing, 170
At least bring forth a wonder to content ye
As much as me my dukedom. 172

*Here Prospero discovers Ferdinand and Miranda,*
*playing at chess.*

MIRANDA    Sweet lord, you play me false. 173
FERDINAND    No, my dearest love,
I would not for the world.
MIRANDA
Yes, for a score of kingdoms you should wrangle, 176
And I would call it fair play.
ALONSO                If this prove 177
A vision of the island, one dear son 178
Shall I twice lose.
SEBASTIAN         A most high miracle!
FERDINAND *[approaching his father]*
Though the seas threaten, they are merciful;
I have cursed them without cause.       *[He kneels.]*
ALONSO            Now all the blessings
Of a glad father compass thee about! 182
Arise, and say how thou cam'st here.
                    *[Ferdinand rises.]*
MIRANDA              Oh, wonder!
How many goodly creatures are there here!
How beauteous mankind is! Oh, brave new world 185

That has such people in't!
PROSPERO              'Tis new to thee.
ALONSO
What is this maid with whom thou wast at play?
Your eld'st acquaintance cannot be three hours. 188
Is she the goddess that hath severed us,
And brought us thus together?
FERDINAND          Sir, she is mortal;
But by immortal Providence she's mine.
I chose her when I could not ask my father
For his advice, nor thought I had one. She
Is daughter to this famous Duke of Milan,
Of whom so often I have heard renown,
But never saw before; of whom I have
Received a second life; and second father
This lady makes him to me.
ALONSO            I am hers. 198
But oh, how oddly will it sound that I
Must ask my child forgiveness!
PROSPERO           There, sir, stop.
Let us not burden our remembrances with
A heaviness that's gone.
GONZALO          I have inly wept, 202
Or should have spoke ere this. Look down, you gods,
And on this couple drop a blessèd crown!
For it is you that have chalked forth the way 205
Which brought us hither.
ALONSO          I say amen, Gonzalo!
GONZALO
Was Milan thrust from Milan, that his issue 207
Should become kings of Naples? Oh, rejoice
Beyond a common joy, and set it down
With gold on lasting pillars: in one voyage 210
Did Claribel her husband find at Tunis,
And Ferdinand, her brother, found a wife
Where he himself was lost; Prospero his dukedom
In a poor isle; and all of us ourselves 214
When no man was his own.
ALONSO *[to Ferdinand and Miranda]*    Give me your hands. 215
Let grief and sorrow still embrace his heart 216
That doth not wish you joy!
GONZALO          Be it so! Amen!

*Enter Ariel, with the Master and Boatswain*
*amazedly following.*

Oh, look, sir, look, sir! Here is more of us.
I prophesied, if a gallows were on land,
This fellow could not drown.—Now, blasphemy, 220
That swear'st grace o'erboard, not an oath on shore? 221
Hast thou no mouth by land? What is the news?
BOATSWAIN
The best news is that we have safely found

---

151–3 **That . . . lies** I would wish myself buried in that muddy bed where my son's body lies drowned if that would somehow make them alive and reigning in Naples.   155 **admire** wonder
156 **devour their reason** i.e., are openmouthed, dumbfounded
156–8 **and scarce . . . breath** and scarcely can believe their eyes or their own words.   161 **of** from   164 **of day by day** requiring days to tell, or covering a long span of time   168 **abroad** anywhere else.
170 **requite** repay   172.1 *discovers* i.e., by opening a curtain, presumably rearstage   173 **play me false** cheat me.   176–7 **Yes . . . play** i.e., Yes, even if we were playing for twenty kingdoms, something less than the whole world, you would still press your advantage against me, and I would lovingly let you do it as though it were fair play.
178 **vision** illusion   182 **compass** encompass, embrace   185 **brave** splendid, gorgeously appareled, handsome

188 **eld'st** longest   198 **I am hers** i.e., I am now a second father to her, by marriage (to which I heartily consent).   202 **heaviness** sadness. **inly** inwardly   205 **chalked . . . way** marked as with a piece of chalk the pathway   207 **Was Milan** Was the Duke of Milan. **issue** offspring
210 **on lasting pillars** i.e., on some commemorative monument
214–15 **all . . . own** all of us have found ourselves and our sanity when we all had lost our senses.   216 **still** always. **his** that person's
220 **blasphemy** i.e., blasphemer   221 **That swear'st grace o'erboard** i.e., you who expel heavenly grace from the ship by your blasphemies.
**not an oath** aren't you going to swear an oath

Our King and company; the next, our ship—
Which, but three glasses since, we gave out split—   225
Is tight and yare and bravely rigged as when   226
We first put out to sea.

ARIEL [*aside to Prospero*]   Sir, all this service
Have I done since I went.

PROSPERO [*aside to Ariel*]      My tricksy spirit!   228

ALONSO
These are not natural events; they strengthen   229
From strange to stranger. Say, how came you hither?

BOATSWAIN
If I did think, sir, I were well awake,
I'd strive to tell you. We were dead of sleep,   232
And—how we know not—all clapped under hatches,
Where but even now, with strange and several noises   234
Of roaring, shrieking, howling, jingling chains,
And more diversity of sounds, all horrible,
We were awaked; straightway at liberty;
Where we, in all her trim, freshly beheld
Our royal, good, and gallant ship, our Master
Cap'ring to eye her. On a trice, so please you,   240
Even in a dream, were we divided from them   241
And were brought moping hither.

ARIEL [*aside to Prospero*]            Was't well done?   242

PROSPERO [*aside to Ariel*]
Bravely, my diligence. Thou shalt be free.

ALONSO
This is as strange a maze as e'er men trod,   244
And there is in this business more than nature
Was ever conduct of. Some oracle   246
Must rectify our knowledge.

PROSPERO                     Sir, my liege,
Do not infest your mind with beating on   248
The strangeness of this business. At picked leisure,   249
Which shall be shortly, single I'll resolve you,   250
Which to you shall seem probable, of every   251
These happened accidents; till when, be cheerful   252
And think of each thing well. [*Aside to Ariel*] Come
hither, spirit.   253
Set Caliban and his companions free.
Untie the spell.                         [*Exit Ariel.*]
[*To Alonso*]   How fares my gracious sir?
There are yet missing of your company
Some few odd lads that you remember not.   257

*Enter Ariel, driving in Caliban, Stephano, and*
*Trinculo, in their stolen apparel.*

STEPHANO   Every man shift for all the rest, and let no   258
man take care for himself; for all is but fortune. *Corag-*   259

---

*gio*, bully monster, *coraggio!*   260

TRINCULO   If these be true spies which I wear in my   261
head, here's a goodly sight.

CALIBAN
O Setebos, these be brave spirits indeed!   263
How fine my master is! I am afraid   264
He will chastise me.

SEBASTIAN   Ha, ha!
What things are these, my lord Antonio?
Will money buy 'em?

ANTONIO                     Very like. One of them   268
Is a plain fish, and no doubt marketable.

PROSPERO
Mark but the badges of these men, my lords,   270
Then say if they be true. This misshapen knave,   271
His mother was a witch, and one so strong
That could control the moon, make flows and ebbs,
And deal in her command without her power.   274
These three have robbed me, and this demidevil—
For he's a bastard one—had plotted with them   276
To take my life. Two of these fellows you
Must know and own. This thing of darkness I   278
Acknowledge mine.

CALIBAN               I shall be pinched to death.

ALONSO
Is not this Stephano, my drunken butler?

SEBASTIAN   He is drunk now. Where had he wine?

ALONSO
And Trinculo is reeling ripe. Where should they   282
Find this grand liquor that hath gilded 'em?   283
[*To Trinculo*] How cam'st thou in this pickle?   284

TRINCULO   I have been in such a pickle since I saw you
last that, I fear me, will never out of my bones. I shall
not fear flyblowing.   287

SEBASTIAN   Why, how now, Stephano?

STEPHANO   Oh, touch me not! I am not Stephano, but a   289
cramp.   290

PROSPERO   You'd be king o'the isle, sirrah?   291

STEPHANO   I should have been a sore one, then.   292

ALONSO [*pointing to Caliban*]
This is a strange thing as e'er I looked on.

PROSPERO
He is as disproportioned in his manners
As in his shape.—Go, sirrah, to my cell.
Take with you your companions. As you look
To have my pardon, trim it handsomely.   297

---

259–60 **Coraggio . . . monster** Have courage, gallant monster   261 **true**
**spies** accurate observers (i.e., sharp eyes)   263 **brave** handsome
264 **fine** splendidly attired   268 **like** likely.   270 **badges** emblems worn
by servants to indicate whom they serve (perhaps in this case the stolen
apparel)   271 **say . . . true** say if they are worthy and loyal servants.
274 **And . . . power** and usurp the moon's command (over tides) without her authority. (Sycorax could control the moon and hence the
tides.)   276 **bastard** counterfeit   278 **own** acknowledge.   282 **reeling**
**ripe** staggeringly drunk.   **should they** were they able to   283 **gilded**
**'em** flushed their complexion (from the drink), giving them a ruddy or
gilded appearance.   284 **pickle** (1) fix, predicament (2) pickling brine
(in this case, horse urine).   287 **flyblowing** i.e., being fouled by fly eggs
(from which he is saved by being pickled).   289–90 **I . . . cramp** i.e., I am
all cramps, from head to toe.   291 **sirrah** (Standard form of address to
an inferior, here expressing reprimand.)   292 **sore** (1) tyrannical (2)
sorry, inept (3) wracked by pain   297 **trim** prepare, decorate

225 **glasses** hourglasses.   **gave out split** declared shipwrecked, gave
up for lost   226 **yare** ready.   **bravely** splendidly   228 **tricksy** ingenious, sportive   229 **strengthen** increase   232 **dead of sleep** deep in
sleep   234 **several** diverse   240 **Cap'ring to eye** dancing for joy to
see.   **On a trice** In an instant   241 **them** i.e., the other crew members
242 **moping** in a daze   244 **trod** i.e., attempted to find the way out of
246 **conduct** director   248 **infest** harass, disturb.   **beating on** worrying about   249 **picked** chosen, convenient   250 **single** privately.
**resolve** satisfy, explain to   251 **probable** plausible   251–2 **of every**
**These** about every one of these   252 **accidents** occurrences
253 **well** favorably.   257 **odd** unaccounted for   258–9 **Every . . . him-**
**self** (Stephano drunkenly inverts the saying "Every man for himself.")

CALIBAN

  Ay, that I will; and I'll be wise hereafter
  And seek for grace. What a thrice-double ass     299
  Was I to take this drunkard for a god
  And worship this dull fool!

PROSPERO           Go to. Away!

ALONSO

  Hence, and bestow your luggage where you found it.

SEBASTIAN    Or stole it, rather.

        [Exeunt Caliban, Stephano, and Trinculo.]

PROSPERO

  Sir, I invite Your Highness and your train
  To my poor cell, where you shall take your rest
  For this one night; which, part of it, I'll waste     306
  With such discourse as, I not doubt, shall make it
  Go quick away: the story of my life,
  And the particular accidents gone by     309
  Since I came to this isle. And in the morn
  I'll bring you to your ship, and so to Naples,
  Where I have hope to see the nuptial
  Of these our dear-belovèd solemnized;
  And thence retire me to my Milan, where
  Every third thought shall be my grave.

ALONSO                I long

  To hear the story of your life, which must
  Take the ear strangely.

PROSPERO         I'll deliver all;     317
  And promise you calm seas, auspicious gales,
  And sail so expeditious that shall catch     319
  Your royal fleet far off. [Aside to Ariel] My Ariel, chick,   320

---

That is thy charge. Then to the elements
Be free, and fare thou well!
        [To the others] Please you, draw near.  322
          Exeunt omnes [except Prospero].

# Epilogue    *Spoken by* PROSPERO.

Now my charms are all o'erthrown,
And what strength I have 's mine own,
Which is most faint. Now, 'tis true,
I must be here confined by you
Or sent to Naples. Let me not,
Since I have my dukedom got
And pardoned the deceiver, dwell
In this bare island by your spell,
But release me from my bands     9
With the help of your good hands.     10
Gentle breath of yours my sails     11
Must fill, or else my project fails,
Which was to please. Now I want     13
Spirits to enforce, art to enchant,
And my ending is despair,
Unless I be relieved by prayer,     16
Which pierces so that it assaults     17
Mercy itself, and frees all faults.     18
As you from crimes would pardoned be,     19
Let your indulgence set me free.    *Exit.*   20

---

**322 draw near** i.e., enter my cell.
**Epilogue.**
**9 bands** bonds, fetters   **10 hands** i.e., applause (the noise of which could break a charm).   **11 Gentle breath** Favorable breeze (produced by hands clapping or favorable comment)   **13 want** lack   **16 prayer** i.e., Prospero's petition to the audience   **17 assaults** penetrates the heart of   **18 frees** obtains forgiveness for   **19 crimes** sins   **20 indulgence** (1) humoring, lenient approval (2) remission of punishment for sin

---

**299 grace** pardon, favor.   **306 waste** spend   **309 accidents** occurrences   **317 Take** take effect upon, enchant.   **deliver** declare, relate **319–20 catch . . . far off** enable you to catch up with the main part of your royal fleet, now afar off en route to Naples. (See 1.2.235–6.)

# The Poems

*Sonnets*

# Sonnets

Shakespeare seems to have cared more about his reputation as a lyric poet than as a dramatist. He contributed to the major nondramatic genres of his day: to amatory Ovidian narrative in *Venus and Adonis*, to the Complaint in *The Rape of Lucrece*, to philosophical poetry in "The Phoenix and Turtle." He cooperated in the publication of his first two important poems, dedicating them to the young Earl of Southampton with a plea to him for sponsorship. To write poetry in this vein was more fashionable than to write plays, which one did mainly for money.

A poet with ambitions of this sort simply had to write a sonnet sequence. Sonneteering was the rage in England in the early and mid 1590s. Based on the sonneteering tradition of Francesco Petrarch, Sir Thomas Wyatt, and others, and gaining new momentum in 1591 with the publication of Sir Philip Sidney's *Astrophel and Stella*, the vogue ended almost as suddenly as it began, in 1596 or 1597. The sonnet sequences of this brief period bear the names of most well-known and minor poets of the day: *Amoretti* by Edmund Spenser (1595), *Delia* by Samuel Daniel (1591 and 1592), *Caelica* by Fulke Greville (not published until 1633), *Idea's Mirror* by Michael Drayton (1594), *Diana* by Henry Constable (1592), *Phyllis* by Thomas Lodge (1593), and the more imitative sequences of Barnabe Barnes, Giles Fletcher, William Percy, Bartholomew Griffin, William Smith, and Robert Tofte.

Shakespeare wrote sonnets during the heyday of the genre, for in 1598 Francis Meres, in his *Palladis Tamia: Wit's Treasury*, praised Shakespeare's "sugared sonnets among his private friends." Even though they were not printed at the time, we know from Meres's remark that they were circulated in manuscript among the cognoscenti and commanded respect. Shakespeare may actually have preferred to delay the publication of his sonnets, not through indifference to their literary worth, but through a desire not to seem too professional. The "courtly makers" of the English Renaissance, those gentlemen whose chivalric accomplishments were supposed to include versifying, looked on the writing of poetry as an avocation designed to amuse one's peers or to court a lady. Publication was not quite genteel, and many such authors affected dismay when their verses were pirated into print. The young wits about London of the 1590s, whether aristocratic or not, sometimes imitated this fashion. Like young John Donne, they sought the favorable verdict of their fellow wits at the Inns of Court (where young men studied law) and professed not to care about wider recognition. Whether Shakespeare was motivated in this way we do not know, but, in any event, his much-sought-after sonnet sequence was not published until 1609, long after the vogue had passed. The publisher, Thomas Thorpe, seems not to have obtained Shakespeare's authorization. Two sonnets, numbers 138 and 144, had been pirated ten years earlier by William Jaggard in *The Passionate Pilgrim*, 1599, a little anthology with some poems by Shakespeare and some wrongly attributed to him. The sonnets were not reprinted until 1640, either because the sonnet vogue had passed or because Thorpe's edition had been suppressed.

The unexplained circumstances of publication have given rise to a host of vexing and apparently unanswerable questions. Probably no puzzle in all English literature has provoked so much speculation and produced so little agreement. To whom are the sonnets addressed? Do they tell a consistent story, and, if so, do they tell us anything about Shakespeare's life? The basic difficulty is that we cannot be sure that the order in which Thorpe published the sonnets represents Shakespeare's intention, nor can we assume that Thorpe spoke for Shakespeare when he dedicated the sonnets to "Mr. W. H." As they stand, most of the first 126 sonnets appear to be addressed in warm friendship to a handsome young aristocrat, whereas sonnets 127–52 mostly speak of the poet's dark-haired mistress. Yet the last two sonnets, 153–4, seem unrelated to anything previous and cast some doubt on the reliability of the ordering. Within each large grouping of the sonnets, moreover, we find evident inconsistencies: jealousies disappear and suddenly reappear, the poet bewails his absolute rejection by the friend and then speaks a few sonnets later of harmonious affection as though nothing had happened, and so on. Some sonnets are closely linked to their predecessors; some are apparently disconnected (although even here we must allow for the real possibility that Shakespeare intends juxtaposition and contrast). We cannot be sure if the friend of sonnets 1–126 is really one person or several. We can only speculate that the unhappy love triangle described in sonnets 40–2, in which the friend has usurped the poet's mistress, can be identified with the love triangle of the "Dark Lady" sonnets, 127–52. Most readers sense a narrative continuity of the whole yet find blocks of sonnets stubbornly out of place. The temptation to rearrange the order has proved irresistible, but no alternative order has ever won acceptance. The consensus is that Thorpe's order is at times suspect but may have more rationale than at first appears. It is, in any case, the only authoritative order we have.

No less frustrating is Thorpe's dedication "To the Only Begetter of These Ensuing Sonnets, Mr. W. H." Given the late and unauthorized publication, we cannot assume that Thorpe speaks for Shakespeare. Quite possibly he is only thanking the person who obtained the sonnets for him, making publication possible. Mundanely enough, Mr. W. H. could be William Hall, an associate of Thorpe's in the publishing business. Yet Elizabethan usage affords few instances of "begetter" in this sense of "obtainer." Donald Foster has offered new and persuasive arguments for the idea that "Mr. W. H." is only a typographical error of a common sort and that Thorpe meant to say "Mr. W. S.," Master William Shakespeare. In this case, "begetter" would mean simply "creator." This solution has a wonderful neatness about it, but other readers have wondered if it answers the seeming contradiction when Thorpe speaks of "Mr. W. H." and "our ever-living poet" in the dedication as though they are two people. Thorpe offers to Mr. W. H. "that eternity promised by our ever-living poet," as though Mr. W. H. were the very subject of those sonnets whom Shakespeare vows to immortalize.

This interpretation of "begetter" as "inspirer" has prompted many enthusiasts to search for a Mr. W. H. in Shakespeare's life, a nobleman who befriended him. The chief candidates are two. First is the young Earl of Southampton, to whom Shakespeare had dedicated *Venus and Adonis* and *The Rape of Lucrece*. The dedication to the second of these poems bespeaks a warmth and gratitude that had been less evident in the first. The Earl's name, Henry Wriothesley, yields initials that are the reverse of W. H. If this correspondence seems unconvincing, W. H. could stand for Sir William Harvey, third husband of Mary, Lady Southampton, the young Earl's mother. Some

researchers would have us believe that Shakespeare wrote the sonnets for Lady Southampton, especially those urging a young man (her son) to marry and procreate. This entire case is speculative, however, and we have no evidence that Shakespeare had any dealings with Southampton after *The Rape of Lucrece*. The plain ascription "Mr. W. H." seems an oddly uncivil way for Thorpe to have addressed an earl. If meant for Southampton, the sonnets must have been written fairly early in the 1590s, for they give no hint of Southampton's later career: his courtship of Elizabeth Vernon, her pregnancy and their secret marriage in 1598, and his later involvement in Essex's Irish campaign and abortive uprising against Queen Elizabeth. Those literary sleuths who stress similarities to the Southampton relationship are too willing to overlook dissimilarities.

The next chief candidate for Mr. W. H. is William Herbert, third Earl of Pembroke, to whom, along with his brother, Shakespeare's colleagues dedicated the First Folio of 1623. In 1595, Pembroke's parents were attempting to arrange his marriage with Lady Elizabeth Carey, granddaughter of the first Lord Hunsdon, who was Lord Chamberlain and patron of Shakespeare's company. In 1597, another alliance was attempted with Bridget Vere, granddaughter of Lord Burghley. In both negotiations, young Pembroke objected to the girl in question. This hypothesis requires, however, an uncomfortably late date for the sonnets and postulates a gap in age between Shakespeare and Pembroke that would have afforded little opportunity for genuine friendship. Pembroke was only fifteen in 1595; Shakespeare was thirty-one. Besides, no evidence supports the claim other than historical coincidence. The common initials W. H. can be made to produce other candidates as well, such as the Lincolnshire lawyer named William Hatcliffe proposed (to no one's satisfaction) by Leslie Hotson. Hotson wants to date most of the sonnets before 1589, since Hatcliffe came to London in 1587–1588. When such speculations are constructed on the single enigmatic testimonial of the dedication by Thomas Thorpe, who may well have had no connection with Shakespeare, we are left with a case that would not be worth describing had it not captured the imagination of so many researchers.

Biographical identifications have also been proposed for the various personages in the sonnet sequence, predictably with no better success. The rival poet, with "the proud full sail of his great verse" (sonnet 86), has been linked to Christopher Marlowe (who died in 1593), George Chapman, and others. The sequence gives us little to go on, other than that the rival poet possesses a considerable enough talent to intimidate the author of the sonnets and to ingratiate himself with the author's aristocratic friend. No biographical circumstances resembling this rivalry have come to light. Various candidates have also been found for the "Dark Lady." One is Mary

Fitton, a lady-in-waiting at court who bore a child by Pembroke in 1601. Again, we have no evidence that Shakespeare knew her, nor is he likely to have carried on an affair with one of such high rank. A. L. Rowse has proposed Emilia Lanier, wife of Alfonso Lanier and daughter of a court musician named Bassano, a woman of suitably dark complexion perhaps but whose presumed connection with Shakespeare rests only on the reported rumor that she was a mistress of Lord Hunsdon. We are left finally without knowing who any of these people were, or whether indeed Shakespeare was attempting to be biographical at all.

The same irresolution afflicts the dating of the sonnets. Do they give hints of a personal chronicle extending over some years, following Thorpe's arrangement of the sonnets or some alternative order? Sonnet 104 speaks of three years having elapsed since the poet met his friend. Are there other signposts that relate to contemporary events? A line in sonnet 107 ("The mortal moon hath her eclipse endured") is usually linked to the death of Queen Elizabeth (known as Diana or Cynthia) in 1603, though Leslie Hotson prefers to see in it an allusion to the Spanish Armada, shaped for sea battle in a moonlike crescent when it met defeat in 1588. The newly built pyramids in sonnet 123 remind Hotson of the obelisks built by Pope Sixtus V in Rome, 1586–1589; other researchers have discovered pyramids erected on London's streets in 1603 to celebrate the coronation of James I. As these illustrations suggest, speculative dating can be used to support a hypothesis of early or late composition. The wary consensus of most scholars is that the sonnets were written over a number of years; a large number, certainly, before 1598, but some perhaps later and even up to the date of publication in 1609.

However fruitless this quest for nonexistent certainties, it does at least direct us to a meaningful critical question: should we expect sonnets of this "personal" nature to be at least partly autobiographical? Shakespeare's sonnets have struck many readers as cries from the heart, voicing at times fears of rejection, self-hatred, and humiliation, and at other times a serene gratitude for reciprocated affection. This power of expression may, however, be a tribute to Shakespeare's dramatic gift rather than evidence of personal involvement. Earlier sonnet sequences, both Elizabethan and pre-Elizabethan, had established a variety of artistic conventions that tended to displace biography. Petrarch's famous *Rime*, or sonnets, later collected in his *Canzoniere*, though addressed to Laura in two sequences (during her life and after her death), idealized her into the unapproachable lady worshiped by the self-abasing and miserable lover. Petrarch's imitators—Serafino Aquilano, Pietro Bembo, Ludovico Ariosto, and Torquato Tasso among the Italians, Clement Marot, Joachim du Bellay, Pierre de Ronsard, and Philippe Desportes among the French Pléiade—reworked these conventions in countless variations. In England, the fashion was taken up by Sir Thomas Wyatt, the Earl of Surrey, George Gascoigne, Thomas Watson, and others. Spenser's *Amoretti* and Sidney's *Astrophel and Stella*, though inspired at least in part by real women in the poets' lives, are also deeply concerned with theories of writing poetry. Rejection of the stereotyped attitudes and relationships that had come to dominate the typical Petrarchan sonnet sequence is evidence not of biographical literalism in art but of a new insistence on lifelike emotion in art; as Sidney's muse urges him, "look in thy heart and write." Thus, both the Petrarchan and the anti-Petrarchan schools avoid biographical writing for its own sake. This is essentially true of all Elizabethan sonneteering, from Drayton's serious pursuit of platonic abstraction in his *Idea's Mirror* to the facile chorusing of lesser sonnet writers about Diana, Phyllis, Zepheria, or Fidessa.

The "story" connecting the individual poems of an Elizabethan sonnet sequence is never very important or consistent, even when we can be sure of the order in which the sonnets were written. Dante had used prose links in his *La Vita Nuova* (c. 1282) to stress narrative continuity, and so had Petrarch, but this sturdy framework had been abandoned by the late sixteenth century. Rather than telling a chronological story, the typical Elizabethan sonnet sequence offers a thematically connected series of lyrical meditations, chiefly on love but also on poetic theory, the adversities of fortune, death, or what have you. The narrative events mentioned from time to time are not the substance of the sequence but the occasion for meditative reflection. Attitudes need not be consistent throughout, and the characters need not be consistently motivated like dramatis personae in a play.

Shakespeare's sonnet sequence retains these conventions of Elizabethan sonneteering and employs many archetypal situations and themes that had been explored by his predecessors and contemporaries. His emphasis on friendship seems new, for no other sequence addressed a majority of its sonnets to a friend rather than to a mistress, but even here the anti-Petrarchan quest for spontaneity and candor is in the best Elizabethan tradition of Sidney and Spenser. Besides, the exaltation of friendship over love was itself a widespread Neoplatonic commonplace recently popularized in the writings of John Lyly. Shakespeare's sequence makes use of the structural design found in contemporary models. Even though we cannot reconstruct a rigorously consistent chronological narrative from the sonnets, we can discern overall patterns out of which the poet's emotional crises arise and upon which he constructs his meditative lyrics. Certain groupings, such as the sonnets addressed to the "Dark Lady," 127–52, in which individually they comment on one another through reinforcement or antithetical design and are thus enhanced by their context, achieve a plausible cohesion; a case can be made, in other words, for the order of the poems as Thorpe printed them. Even the last two sonnets, 153 and 154, have their defenders (see Michael J. B. Allen's essay in *Shakespeare Survey*, 1978). Juxtaposition is a favorite technique in Shakespeare's plays, and we must remember that he alone among the major Elizabethan sonneteers wrote for the stage.

Taking note of such considerations, we can account for most of the situations portrayed in Shakespeare's sonnets by postulating four figures: the poet-speaker himself, his friend, his mistress, and a rival poet. The order of events in this tangled relationship is not what the poet wishes to describe; instead, he touches upon this situation from time to time as he explores his own reaction to love in its various aspects.

The poet's relationship to his friend is a vulnerable one. This friend to whom he writes is aristocratic, handsome, and younger than he is. The poet is beholden to this friend as a sponsor and must consider himself as subservient, no matter how deep their mutual affection. Even at its happiest, their relationship is hierarchical. The poet abases himself in order to extol his friend's beauty and virtues (sonnets 52–4, 105–6). He confesses that his love would be idolatry, except that the friend's goodness excels all poetic hyperbole. As the older of the two, the poet sententiously urges his young friend to marry and eternize his beauty through the engendering of children (sonnets 1–17). Such a course, he argues, is the surest way to conquer devouring Time, the enemy of all earthly beauty and love. Yet elsewhere the poet exalts his own art as the surest defense against Time (sonnets 55, 60, 63–5, etc.). These conclusions are nominally contradictory, offering procreation in one instance and poetry in another as the best hope for immortality, but thematically the two are obviously related. In even the happiest of the sonnets, such as those giving thanks for "the marriage of true minds" (116, 123), the consciousness of devouring Time is inescapable. If love and celebratory poetry can sometimes triumph over Time, the victory is all the more precious because it is achieved in the face of such odds.

Love and perfect friendship are a refuge for the poet faced with hostile fortune and an indifferent world. He is too often "in disgrace with fortune and men's eyes" (sonnet 29), oppressed by his own failings, saddened by the facile success of opportunists (sonnets 66–8), ashamed of having sold himself cheap in his own profession (sonnets 110–11). If taken biographically, this could mean that Shakespeare was not happy about his career as actor and playwright, but the motif makes complete sense in the sonnet sequence without resort to biography. A biographical reading also raises the question of homosexual attraction, as urged by Joseph Pequigney in his *Such Is My Love* (University of Chicago Press, 1985). The bawdy reference in sonnet 20.12 to the friend's possession of "one thing to my purpose nothing" would seem to militate against the idea of a consummated homosexual relationship, while conversely many sonnets (such as 138) do point to the poet's sexual consummation with his mistress. Still, the bond between poet and friend is extraordinarily strong, and certainly there is a danger that traditional scholarship has minimized the erotic bond between the poet and his friend out of a distaste for the idea. Occasional absences torture the poet with the physical separation, even though he realizes that pure love of the spirit ought not to be hampered by distance or time (sonnets 43–51). The absence is especially painful when the poet must confess his own disloyalty (sonnets 117–18). The chronology of these absences cannot be worked out satisfactorily, but the haunting theme of separation is incessant and overwhelming. By extension, it includes the fear of separation through death (sonnets 71–3, 126). The concern with absence is closely related to the poet's obsession with devouring Time.

All the poet's misfortunes would be bearable if love were constant, but his dependency on the aristocratic friend leaves him at the mercy of that friend's changeable moods. The poet must not complain when his wellborn friend entertains a rival poet (sonnets 78–86) or forms other emotional attachments, even with the poet's own mistress (sonnets 40–2). These disloyalties evoke outbursts of jealousy. The poet vacillates between forgiveness and recrimination. Sometimes even his forgiveness is self-loathing, in which the poet confesses he would take back the friend on any terms (sonnets 93–5). At times the poet grovels, conceding that he deserves no better treatment (sonnets 57–8), but at other times his stored-up resentment bursts forth (sonnets 93–5). The poet's fears, though presented in no clear chronological order, run the gamut from a fatalistic sense that rejection will come one day (sonnet 49) to an abject and bitter final farewell (sonnet 87). Sometimes he is tormented by jealousy (sonnet 61) and sometimes by self-hate (sonnets 88–9).

The sonnets addressed to the poet's mistress, the "Dark Lady," similarly convey fear, self-abasement, and a panicky awareness of loss of self-control. In rare moments of happiness, the poet praises her dark features as proof of her being a real woman, not a Petrarchan goddess (sonnet 130). Too often, however, her lack of ideal beauty reminds the poet of his irrational enchantment (sonnets 148–50). She is tyrannous, disdainful, spiteful, disloyal, a "female evil" (sonnet 144) who has tempted away from the poet his better self, his friend. The poet is distressed not so much by her perfidy as by his own self-betrayal; he sees bitterly that he offends his nobler reason by his attachment to the rebellious flesh. He worships what others abhor and perjures himself by swearing to what he knows to be false (sonnets 150–2). His only hope for escape is to punish his flesh and renounce the vanity of all worldly striving (sonnet 146), but this solution evades him as he plunges helplessly back into the perverse enslavement of a sickened appetite.

This sketch of only some themes of the sequence may suggest the range and yet the interconnection of Shakespeare's meditations on love, friendship, and poetry. Patterns are visible, even if the exact chronology (never important in the Elizabethan sonnet sequence) cannot be determined. The pattern suggests a pivotal role for the sonnets in Shakespeare's development, as Richard Wheeler has urged in his *Shakespeare's Development* (University of California Press, 1981): the early sonnets about love and marriage pursue relationships central to the comedies, whereas subsequent sonnets move with increasing intensity toward the portrayal of promiscuity and degradation in erotic love and toward new assaults upon the binding power of friendship in such a way as to anticipate the darker vision of the tragedies. The playful and unthreatening heroine of the comedies gives way to a dark lady who inspires in the poet a compulsive and humiliating self-hatred; mutuality in friendship finds itself threatened by a one-sided relationship in which the abasement of the poet is answered by the indifference and infidelity of the friend. It is as though in the sonnets Shakespeare opened the Pandora's box of hazardous erotic entanglements he was to dramatize in his late plays.

Shakespeare's concern with patterning is equally evident in matters of versification and imagery. The sonnets are written throughout in the "Shakespearean" or English form, *abab cdcd efef gg*. (Sonnet 126, written entirely in couplets, is an exception, perhaps because it was intended as the envoi to the series addressed to the poet's friend.) This familiar sonnet form, introduced by Wyatt, differs markedly from the octave-sestet division of the Petrarchan, or Italian, sonnet. The English form of three quatrains and a concluding couplet lends itself to a step-by-step development of idea and image, culminating in an epigrammatic two-line conclusion that may summarize the thought of the preceding twelve lines or give a sententious interpretation of the images developed up to this point. Sonnet 7 pursues the image of the sun at morning, noon, and evening through three quatrains, one for each phase of the day, and then in the couplet "applies" the image to the friend's unwillingness to beget children. Sonnet 29 moves from resentment of misfortune to a rejoicing in the friend's love and rhetorically mirrors this sudden elevation of mood in the image of the lark "at break of day arising / From sullen earth." Shakespeare's rhetorical and imagistic devices exploit the sonnet structure he inherited and perfected, and remind us again of the strong element of convention and artifice in these supremely "personal" sonnets. The recurring images—the canker on the rose, the pleading of a case at law, the seasonal rhythms of summer and winter, the alternations of day and night, the harmonies and dissonances of music—also testify to the artistic unity of the whole and to the artist's extraordinary discipline in evoking a sense of helpless loss of self-control.

# Sonnets

❧

*To the Only Begetter of These Ensuing Sonnets*

MR. W. H.

All Happiness and That Eternity Promised
    by Our Ever-living Poet
Wisheth the Well-wishing Adventurer in
    Setting Forth

                                        T. T.

## 1

From fairest creatures we desire increase,
That thereby beauty's rose might never die,
But as the riper should by time decease,                    3
His tender heir might bear his memory;                      4
But thou, contracted to thine own bright eyes,             5
Feed'st thy light's flame with self-substantial fuel,      6
Making a famine where abundance lies,
Thyself thy foe, to thy sweet self too cruel.
Thou that art now the world's fresh ornament
And only herald to the gaudy spring,                       10
Within thine own bud buriest thy content,                  11
And, tender churl, mak'st waste in niggarding.             12
    Pity the world, or else this glutton be:
    To eat the world's due, by the grave and thee.         14

## 2

When forty winters shall besiege thy brow
And dig deep trenches in thy beauty's field,               2

Thy youth's proud livery, so gazed on now,                 3
Will be a tattered weed, of small worth held.              4
Then being asked where all thy beauty lies,
Where all the treasure of thy lusty days,                  6
To say within thine own deep-sunken eyes
Were an all-eating shame and thriftless praise.            8
How much more praise deserved thy beauty's use             9
If thou couldst answer, "This fair child of mine
Shall sum my count and make my old excuse,"                11
Proving his beauty by succession thine.                    12
    This were to be new made when thou art old,            13
    And see thy blood warm when thou feel'st it cold.

## 3

Look in thy glass, and tell the face thou viewest          1
Now is the time that face should form another,
Whose fresh repair if now thou not renewest                3
Thou dost beguile the world, unless some mother.           4
For where is she so fair whose uneared womb                5
Disdains the tillage of thy husbandry?                     6
Or who is he so fond will be the tomb                      7
Of his self-love, to stop posterity?
Thou art thy mother's glass, and she in thee               9
Calls back the lovely April of her prime;
So thou through windows of thine age shalt see,            11
Despite of wrinkles, this thy golden time.                 12
    But if thou live remembered not to be,                 13
    Die single, and thine image dies with thee.

**3 proud livery** handsome garments   **4 weed** garment. (With a play
on a *weed* growing in *beauty's field*, line 2.)   **6 lusty** (1) vigorous
(2) lustful   **8 Were . . . praise** would be a shameful admission of gluttony and praise of idle extravagance.   **9 deserved . . . use** would
the proper investment and employment of your beauty deserve
**11 Shall . . . excuse** will balance my account and make amends in my
old age   **12 thine** derived from you.   **13 were** would be
**3.1 glass** mirror   **3 fresh repair** youthful condition   **4 beguile** cheat.
**unless some mother** withhold the happiness of childbearing from
some woman.   **5 uneared** untilled, uncultivated   **6 husbandry** cultivation. (With obvious suggestion of "playing the husband.")   **7 fond**
foolish, (self-)loving.   **will be** i.e., that he is willing to be   **9 thy
mother's glass** the image of your mother   **11–12 So . . . time** in just
the same way, you, looking through eyes dimmed by advancing
years, and despite your own wrinkles of age, will see in your child an
image of your own happy youth.   **13 remembered not to be** in such
a way as not to be remembered, without children

**1.1 increase** procreation   **3 as** just as, while.   **by** in   **4 His** its, the
ripening creation (including the young man).   **bear his memory**
i.e., immortalize it by bearing its features   **5 contracted** (1) engaged,
espoused (2) shrunk   **6 self-substantial** of your own substance
**10 only herald** to principal or unique messenger of   **11 thy content**
(1) that which is contained in you; potential fatherhood (2) your contentment   **12 mak'st . . . niggarding** squander your substance by
being miserly. (An oxymoron, like *tender churl*, "youthful old miser.")
**14 the world's due** i.e., the offspring you owe to posterity.   **by . . .
thee** (consumed) by death and by your willfully remaining childless.
**2.2 trenches** i.e., wrinkles.   **field** (1) meadow (2) battlefield
(3) heraldic background

## 4

Unthrifty loveliness, why dost thou spend                         1
Upon thyself thy beauty's legacy?                                 2
Nature's bequest gives nothing, but doth lend,
And being frank she lends to those are free.                      4
Then, beauteous niggard, why dost thou abuse
The bounteous largess given thee to give?
Profitless usurer, why dost thou use                              7
So great a sum of sums, yet canst not live?                       8
For having traffic with thyself alone,                            9
Thou of thyself thy sweet self dost deceive.                      10
Then how, when Nature calls thee to be gone,                      11
What acceptable audit canst thou leave?
    Thy unused beauty must be tombed with thee,   13
    Which, usèd, lives th'executor to be.           14

## 5

Those hours, that with gentle work did frame                      1
The lovely gaze where every eye doth dwell,                       2
Will play the tyrants to the very same                            3
And that unfair which fairly doth excel;                          4
For never-resting Time leads summer on                            5
To hideous winter and confounds him there,                       6
Sap checked with frost and lusty leaves quite gone,               7
Beauty o'ersnowed and bareness everywhere.
Then, were not summer's distillation left                         9
A liquid prisoner pent in walls of glass,                         10
Beauty's effect with beauty were bereft,                          11
Nor it nor no remembrance what it was.                            12
    But flowers distilled, though they with winter meet,
    Leese but their show; their substance still lives sweet.   14

## 6

Then let not winter's ragged hand deface                          1
In thee thy summer ere thou be distilled.
Make sweet some vial; treasure thou some place                    3
With beauty's treasure ere it be self-killed.
That use is not forbidden usury                                   5
Which happies those that pay the willing loan;                    6
That's for thyself to breed another thee,                         7

Or ten times happier, be it ten for one.                          8
Ten times thyself were happier than thou art,                     9
If ten of thine ten times refigured thee;                         10
Then what could death do, if thou shouldst depart,
Leaving thee living in posterity?
    Be not self-willed, for thou art much too fair   13
    To be death's conquest and make worms thine heir.

## 7

Lo, in the orient when the gracious light                         1
Lifts up his burning head, each under eye                         2
Doth homage to his new-appearing sight,
Serving with looks his sacred majesty;
And having climbed the steep-up heavenly hill,
Resembling strong youth in his middle age,
Yet mortal looks adore his beauty still,
Attending on his golden pilgrimage;
But when from highmost pitch, with weary car,                     9
Like feeble age, he reeleth from the day,
The eyes, 'fore duteous, now converted are                        11
From his low tract and look another way.                          12
    So thou, thyself outgoing in thy noon,
    Unlooked on diest, unless thou get a son.           14

## 8

Music to hear, why hear'st thou music sadly?                      1
Sweets with sweets war not, joy delights in joy.                  2
Why lov'st thou that which thou receiv'st not gladly,             3
Or else receiv'st with pleasure thine annoy?                      4
If the true concord of well-tunèd sounds,
By unions married, do offend thine ear,                           6
They do but sweetly chide thee, who confounds                     7
In singleness the parts that thou shouldst bear.                  8
Mark how one string, sweet husband to another,                   9
Strikes each in each by mutual ordering,                          10
Resembling sire and child and happy mother
Who, all in one, one pleasing note do sing;
    Whose speechless song, being many, seeming one,   13
    Sings this to thee: "Thou single wilt prove none."   14

---

**4.1 Unthrifty** (1) Prodigal (2) Unavailing   **2 thy beauty's legacy** the beauty you inherited (and should pass on to your children).   **4 frank** liberal, bounteous.   **are free** who are generous.   **7 use** (1) use up (2) fail to invest for profit. (See sonnet 6.5 and note.)   **8 live** (1) have a livelihood (2) live in your posterity.   **9 traffic** commerce. (The commercial and financial metaphor hints at sexual self-fascination.)   **10 deceive** cheat.   **11 when . . . gone** when you die   **13 unused** (1) unemployed (2) not invested for profit   **14 lives** would live (in your son)
**5.1 frame** make   **2 gaze** object of gazes   **3 play . . . to** oppress **4 that unfair** make that unlovely.   **fairly** (1) in beauty (2) truly, honestly   **5 leads summer on** (1) guides the steps of summer (2) lures summer   **6 confounds** destroys   **7 lusty** vigorous   **9 summer's distillation** distilled perfume of flowers   **10 walls of glass** glass containers   **11 Beauty's . . . bereft** the beauty distilled into perfume would be lost along with beauty itself   **12 Nor it nor no** (leaving behind) neither it (beauty) nor any   **14 Leese . . . show** lose only the outward appearance of beauty.   **still** (1) notwithstanding (2) always
**6.1 ragged** rough   **3 vial** (With suggestion of a womb.)   **treasure** enrich   **5 use** lending money at interest   **6 Which . . . loan** which makes happy those who are willing to repay the loan with interest (in the form of children)   **7 That's . . . thee** i.e., such would be the case if you were to sire a child like you

**8 Or . . . one** i.e., or indeed the happy mother (of line 6) would be ten times happier were she to bear you ten children instead of one. (*Ten for one* alludes to the highest legal rate of interest, one for ten.)
**9 Ten . . . art** i.e., Ten children of yours would be a tenfold blessing and would make you happier   **10 refigured** duplicated, copied (producing one hundred grandchildren)   **13 self-willed** (1) obstinate (2) bequeathed to self
**7.1 orient** east.   **light** i.e., sun   **2 under** earthly   **9 pitch** highest point (as of a falcon's flight before it attacks).   **car** chariot (of the sungod)   **11 converted** turned away   **12 tract** course   **14 get** beget
**8.1 Music to hear** i.e., You whom it is music to hear.   **2 Sweets** Sweet things   **3–4 Why . . . annoy?** Why do you not gladly love the sweet things you hear, or find irksome that which is pleasurable?   **6 By unions married** perfectly blended in harmonious chords   **7–8 who . . . bear** you who destroy, by playing a single part only, the harmony (i.e., marriage) that you should sustain.   **9 sweet husband** i.e., paired, as on the double strings of the lute, one string vibrating sympathetically to the other   **10 each in each** i.e., with double resonance, sounding mutually   **13 Whose** i.e., the strings'.   **being . . . one** i.e., making harmony out of several voices   **14 Thou . . . none** (Alludes to the proverb, "One is no number." The single person who dies without posterity leaves nothing of himself behind.)

## 9

Is it for fear to wet a widow's eye                                    1
That thou consum'st thyself in single life?
Ah, if thou issueless shalt hap to die,                               3
The world will wail thee like a makeless wife.                        4
The world will be thy widow and still weep                            5
That thou no form of thee hast left behind,
When every private widow well may keep,                               7
By children's eyes, her husband's shape in mind.                      8
Look what an unthrift in the world doth spend                         9
Shifts but his place, for still the world enjoys it;                  10
But beauty's waste hath in the world an end,
And, kept unused, the user so destroys it.                            12
    No love toward others in that bosom sits
    That on himself such murd'rous shame commits.

## 10

For shame, deny that thou bear'st love to any,
Who for thyself art so unprovident!
Grant, if thou wilt, thou art beloved of many,
But that thou none lov'st is most evident;
For thou art so possessed with murd'rous hate
That 'gainst thyself thou stick'st not to conspire,                   6
Seeking that beauteous roof to ruinate                                7
Which to repair should be thy chief desire.
Oh, change thy thought, that I may change my mind!                    9
Shall hate be fairer lodged than gentle love?
Be, as thy presence is, gracious and kind,                            11
Or to thyself at least kindhearted prove:
    Make thee another self, for love of me,
    That beauty still may live in thine or thee.

## 11

As fast as thou shalt wane, so fast thou grow'st                      1
In one of thine from that which thou departest;                       2
And that fresh blood which youngly thou bestow'st                     3
Thou mayst call thine when thou from youth convertest.                4
Herein lives wisdom, beauty, and increase;
Without this, folly, age, and cold decay.
If all were minded so, the times should cease                         7
And threescore year would make the world away.                        8
Let those whom Nature hath not made for store,                        9
Harsh, featureless, and rude, barrenly perish;                        10

Look whom she best endowed she gave the more,                         11
Which bounteous gift thou shouldst in bounty cherish.                 12
    She carved thee for her seal, and meant thereby                   13
    Thou shouldst print more, not let that copy die.

## 12

When I do count the clock that tells the time,                        1
And see the brave day sunk in hideous night;                          2
When I behold the violet past prime,
And sable curls all silvered o'er with white;                         4
When lofty trees I see barren of leaves
Which erst from heat did canopy the herd,                             6
And summer's green, all girded up in sheaves,                         7
Borne on the bier with white and bristly beard,                       8
Then of thy beauty do I question make                                 9
That thou among the wastes of time must go,
Since sweets and beauties do themselves forsake
And die as fast as they see others grow;
    And nothing 'gainst Time's scythe can make defense
    Save breed, to brave him when he takes thee hence.                14

## 13

Oh, that you were yourself! But, love, you are                        1
No longer yours than you yourself here live.                          2
Against this coming end you should prepare,                           3
And your sweet semblance to some other give.
So should that beauty which you hold in lease
Find no determination; then you were                                  6
Yourself again after your self's decease,
When your sweet issue your sweet form should bear.                    8
Who lets so fair a house fall to decay,
Which husbandry in honor might uphold                                 10
Against the stormy gusts of winter's day
And barren rage of death's eternal cold?
    Oh, none but unthrifts! Dear my love, you know                    13
    You had a father; let your son say so.

## 14

Not from the stars do I my judgment pluck,                            1
And yet methinks I have astronomy—                                    2
But not to tell of good or evil luck,
Of plagues, of dearths, or seasons' quality;                          4
Nor can I fortune to brief minutes tell,                              5
'Pointing to each his thunder, rain, and wind,                        6

---

**9.1 Is . . . eye** Is it for fear of eventually leaving some woman a grieving widow when you die   **3 issueless** without offspring   **4 makeless** mateless, widowed   **5 still** continually   **7 private** individual, as distinguished from the whole world   **8 By** by means of   **9 Look what** Whatever.   **unthrift** spendthrift   **10 his** its.   **enjoys** uses, keeps in circulation   **12 user** i.e., he who should use it. (With a suggestion of a *usurer* who is miserly.)
**10.6 thou stick'st** you scruple   **7 that . . . roof** i.e., your aristocratic family   **9 thought** intention.   **my mind** my opinion.   **11 presence** appearance, bearing
**11.1–2 thou grow'st . . . departest** i.e., you survive in a child of your own, though you leave the world behind   **3 youngly** in youth
**4 when thou . . . convertest** when you change from youth (to old age).
**7 minded so** sharing your intention (to have no children).   **times** succeeding generations   **8 year** years   **9 for store** for breeding
**10 Harsh . . . rude** ugly, lacking attractive features or appearance, and rudely fashioned

**11 Look . . . more** to whomever Nature endowed with the greatest gifts, she gave even more   **12 in bounty** abundantly   **13 seal** stamp of authority, stamp from which impressions are made
**12.1 tells** (1) announces (2) counts   **2 brave** splendid   **4 sable** black
**6 erst** formerly   **7 girded** bundled   **8 bier** i.e., harvest cart. (But with suggestion of funeral bier.)   **beard** i.e., the tufted grain. (But suggesting also a dead man laid out for burial.)   **9 do . . . make** I discuss with myself   **14 breed** begetting offspring.   **brave him** defy Time
**13.1 yourself** i.e., your eternal self, not vulnerable to Time's decay.
**2 here** i.e., here on earth   **3 Against** In anticipation of   **6 determination** end.   **were** would be   **8 issue** offspring   **10 husbandry** careful management. (With a pun on "being a husband.")   **in honor** honorably   **13 unthrifts** spendthrifts
**14.1 my judgment pluck** derive my conclusions   **2 have astronomy** am skilled in astrology   **4 seasons' quality** what the weather of the seasons will be like   **5 fortune . . . tell** foretell events to the precise minute
**6 'Pointing** appointing, assigning.   **each** each minute.   **his** its

Or say with princes if it shall go well          7
By oft predict that I in heaven find.          8
But from thine eyes my knowledge I derive,
And, constant stars, in them I read such art          10
As truth and beauty shall together thrive          11
If from thyself to store thou wouldst convert.          12
　　Or else of thee this I prognosticate:
　　Thy end is truth's and beauty's doom and date.          14

## 15

When I consider every thing that grows
Holds in perfection but a little moment,
That this huge stage presenteth naught but shows          2
Whereon the stars in secret influence comment;          3
When I perceive that men as plants increase,          5
Cheerèd and checked even by the selfsame sky,          6
Vaunt in their youthful sap, at height decrease,          7
And wear their brave state out of memory;          8
Then the conceit of this inconstant stay          9
Sets you most rich in youth before my sight,
Where wasteful Time debateth with Decay          11
To change your day of youth to sullied night;
　　And, all in war with Time for love of you,          13
　　As he takes from you I engraft you new.          14

## 16

But wherefore do not you a mightier way
Make war upon this bloody tyrant, Time,
And fortify yourself in your decay
With means more blessèd than my barren rhyme?          4
Now stand you on the top of happy hours,
And many maiden gardens yet unset          6
With virtuous wish would bear your living flowers,          7
Much liker than your painted counterfeit.          8
So should the lines of life that life repair          9
Which this time's pencil, or my pupil pen,          10
Neither in inward worth nor outward fair          11
Can make you live yourself in eyes of men.          12
　　To give away yourself keeps yourself still,          13
　　And you must live, drawn by your own sweet skill.          14

## 17

Who will believe my verse in time to come
If it were filled with your most high deserts?          2
Though yet, heaven knows, it is but as a tomb          3
Which hides your life and shows not half your parts.          4
If I could write the beauty of your eyes
And in fresh numbers number all your graces,          6
The age to come would say, "This poet lies;
Such heavenly touches ne'er touched earthly faces."          8
So should my papers, yellowed with their age,
Be scorned like old men of less truth than tongue,          10
And your true rights be termed a poet's rage          11
And stretchèd meter of an antique song.          12
　　But were some child of yours alive that time,
　　You should live twice, in it and in my rhyme.

## 18

Shall I compare thee to a summer's day?
Thou art more lovely and more temperate.
Rough winds do shake the darling buds of May,
And summer's lease hath all too short a date.          4
Sometime too hot the eye of heaven shines,          5
And often is his gold complexion dimmed;
And every fair from fair sometimes declines,          7
By chance or nature's changing course untrimmed.          8
But thy eternal summer shall not fade
Nor lose possession of that fair thou ow'st;          10
Nor shall Death brag thou wand'r'st in his shade,
When in eternal lines to time thou grow'st.          12
　　So long as men can breathe or eyes can see,
　　So long lives this, and this gives life to thee.          14

## 19

Devouring Time, blunt thou the lion's paws,
And make the earth devour her own sweet brood;
Pluck the keen teeth from the fierce tiger's jaws,
And burn the long-lived phoenix in her blood;          4
Make glad and sorry seasons as thou fleet'st,          5
And do whate'er thou wilt, swift-footed Time,
To the wide world and all her fading sweets.
But I forbid thee one most heinous crime:
Oh, carve not with thy hours my love's fair brow,
Nor draw no lines there with thine antique pen;          10
Him in thy course untainted do allow          11
For beauty's pattern to succeeding men.

---

7 **Or . . . well** or say if things will go well for certain rulers   8 **oft predict** frequent predictions   10–11 **read . . . As** gather such learning as, in effect, that   12 **store** replenishment (through the begetting of children).   **convert** turn.   14 **doom and date** limit of duration, destruction.
15.2 **Holds in perfection** maintains its prime   3 **stage** i.e., the world   5 **as** like   6 **Cheerèd and checked** (1) urged on, nourished, and held back, starved (2) applauded and hissed   7 **Vaunt** boast, exult.   **sap** vigor.   **at height decrease** i.e., no sooner reach full maturity but they (humans) start to decline   8 **brave** splendid.   **out of memory** until forgotten   9 **conceit** notion.   **inconstant stay** mutable brief time (on earth)   11 **debateth** competes   13 **all in war** I, fighting with might and main   14 **engraft you new** renew you by grafting, infusing new life into you (by means of my verse).
16.4 **barren** (1) unable to produce offspring (2) poetically sterile   6 **unset** (1) unplanted (2) unimpregnated   7 **virtuous wish** desire that is still chaste   8 **liker** more resembling you.   **painted** rendered by art (including poetry), artificial.   **counterfeit** portrait.   9 **lines of life** lineage, i.e., children (whose lineaments are more lifelike than lines of verse or of a portrait)   10 **this time's pencil** a portraiture done in this present age.   **pupil** apprenticed, inexpert   11 **fair** beauty   12 **live** survive as   13 **give away yourself** i.e., marry and beget children.   **keeps** preserves   14 **skill** i.e., artistry in reproducing yourself, mightier than the poet's pen.

17.2 **If** even if   3 **yet** as yet   4 **parts** qualities.   6 **numbers** verses   8 **Such . . . faces** i.e., the heavenly beauties celebrated in these poems are exaggerated; they never were actually to be seen in a human face.   10 **of . . . tongue** more garrulous than truthful   11 **And . . . rage** and what your beauty truly deserved would be dismissed as mere poetic effusion   12 **stretchèd meter** overstrained poetry, poetic license
18.4 **lease** allotted time.   **date** duration.   5 **eye** i.e., sun   7 **fair from fair** beautiful thing from beauty   8 **untrimmed** stripped of ornament and beauty.   10 **fair thou ow'st** beauty you own   12 **lines** i.e., of poetry.   **to . . . grow'st** you become incorporated into time, engrafted to it.   14 **this** i.e., this sonnet
19.4 **phoenix** legendary bird reputed to live for hundreds of years and then to be consumed alive (*in her blood*) in its own ashes, from which it is then reborn   5 **sorry** i.e., miserable, uncomfortable.   **thou fleet'st** you fleet, hurry   10 **antique** (1) old (2) antic, capricious, fantastic   11 **untainted** unsullied; uninjured

Yet, do thy worst, old Time. Despite thy wrong,
My love shall in my verse ever live young.                              14

## 20

A woman's face with Nature's own hand painted                          1
Hast thou, the master-mistress of my passion;                          2
A woman's gentle heart, but not acquainted
With shifting change, as is false women's fashion;                     4
An eye more bright than theirs, less false in rolling,                 5
Gilding the object whereupon it gazeth;                                6
A man in hue, all hues in his controlling,                             7
Which steals men's eyes and women's souls amazeth.
And for a woman wert thou first created,
Till Nature, as she wrought thee, fell a-doting,                       10
And by addition me of thee defeated,                                   11
By adding one thing to my purpose nothing.                             12
    But since she pricked thee out for women's pleasure,   13
    Mine be thy love and thy love's use their treasure.    14

## 21

So is it not with me as with that muse,                                1
Stirred by a painted beauty to his verse,                              2
Who heaven itself for ornament doth use                                3
And every fair with his fair doth rehearse,                            4
Making a couplement of proud compare                                   5
With sun and moon, with earth and sea's rich gems,
With April's firstborn flowers, and all things rare
That heaven's air in this huge rondure hems.                           8
Oh, let me, true in love, but truly write,
And then, believe me, my love is as fair
As any mother's child, though not so bright
As those gold candles fixed in heaven's air.                           12
    Let them say more that like of hearsay well;           13
    I will not praise that purpose not to sell.            14

## 22

My glass shall not persuade me I am old                                1
So long as youth and thou are of one date;                             2
But when in thee Time's furrows I behold,
Then look I death my days should expiate.                              4
For all that beauty that doth cover thee                               5
Is but the seemly raiment of my heart,                                 6
Which in thy breast doth live, as thine in me.                         7
How can I then be elder than thou art?
Oh, therefore, love, be of thyself so wary
As I, not for myself, but for thee will,                               10
Bearing thy heart, which I will keep so chary                          11
As tender nurse her babe from faring ill.
    Presume not on thy heart when mine is slain;           13
    Thou gav'st me thine, not to give back again.

## 23

As an unperfect actor on the stage                                     1
Who with his fear is put beside his part,                              2
Or some fierce thing replete with too much rage,                       3
Whose strength's abundance weakens his own heart,                      4
So I, for fear of trust, forget to say                                 5
The perfect ceremony of love's rite,
And in mine own love's strength seem to decay,
O'ercharged with burden of mine own love's might.
Oh, let my books be then the eloquence                                 9
And dumb presagers of my speaking breast,                              10
Who plead for love and look for recompense
More than that tongue that more hath more expressed.                   12
    Oh, learn to read what silent love hath writ.
    To hear with eyes belongs to love's fine wit.          14

## 24

Mine eye hath played the painter and hath stelled                      1
Thy beauty's form in table of my heart;                                2
My body is the frame wherein 'tis held,                                3
And perspective it is best painter's art.                              4
For through the painter must you see his skill                         5

14 **My love** (1) my beloved friend (2) my affection for him
**20.1 with . . . hand** i.e., naturally beautiful   **2 master-mistress** i.e.,
both master and mistress, male and female.   **passion** love   **4 as . . .
fashion** as is the way with women, who are false by nature   **5 rolling** i.e., roving   **6 Gilding** causing to shine brightly   **7 A man . . .
controlling** one who has a manly appearance encompassing and
surpassing all other forms. (Suggesting, too, that he captivates all
beholders and that his *hue* is womanly as well as manly.)   **10 fell
a-doting** fell infatuatedly in love with you and so went mildly
crazy   **11 by addition** by adding a new feature (namely, a penis).
**defeated** defrauded, deprived   **12 to my purpose nothing** out of line
with my wishes.   **13 pricked** designated. (With bawdy suggestion;
the *thing* in line 12 is a phallus.)   **for women's pleasure** to give (sexual and maternal) pleasure to women   **14 Mine . . . treasure** I will
have your love in the truest sense, while women will enjoy you sexually and bear you children. (Expressed as a metaphor of financial capital or principal, which belongs to the poet, versus the *use* or interest,
which belongs to women.)
**21.1 muse** i.e., poet   **2 Stirred** inspired.   **painted** artificial, created
by cosmetics   **3 Who . . . use** who does not scruple to invoke heaven
itself as an ornament of praise for his mistress   **4 every . . . rehearse**
compares his lady fair with every lovely thing   **5 Making . . . compare** joining (her) in proud comparison   **8 rondure** sphere.   **hems**
encloses, encircles.   **12 gold candles** i.e., stars. (The trite and exaggerated metaphor is of the sort the poet hopes to eschew.)   **13 like . . .
well** like to deal in secondhand or trite expressions   **14 I will . . . sell**
I, who do not intend to sell as a merchant might, will accordingly not
indulge in extravagant and empty praise.

**22.1 glass** mirror   **2 of one date** of an age, i.e., young   **4 look I** I
foresee that.   **expiate** end.   **5–7 For . . . me** Since my heart dwells in
your breast (and yours in me), your beauty is in effect a becoming
cover for my heart.   **10 will** i.e., will take wary care of myself for
your sake   **11 Bearing** since I bear.   **chary** carefully   **13 Presume . . .
slain** Do not expect to receive back your heart when mine is slain
(as would happen if you were to stop loving me)
**23.1 unperfect** one who has not learned his lines sufficiently   **2 is . . .
part** forgets his lines   **3 Or . . . rage** i.e., or some wild creature overfilled with ungovernable rage   **4 Whose . . . heart** whose excess of
emotion collapses on itself   **5 for . . . trust** mistrusting myself and
fearful of not being trusted.   **forget** forget how   **9 books** (Possibly
refers to the sonnets or to *Venus and Adonis* and *The Rape of Lucrece* or,
more generally, the works of the persona poet.)   **10 dumb presagers**
silent messengers or presenters   **12 that tongue** the tongue of some
rival speaker.   **more hath more expressed** has more often or more
fully said more.   **14 fine wit** sharp intelligence.
**24.1 played** acted the part of.   **stelled** fixed, installed; or perhaps steeled,
i.e., engraved. (The quarto reads "steeld.")   **2 table** tablet, wooden panel
used for painting   **3 frame** (1) picture frame (2) bodily frame   **4 perspective** an artist's method of producing a distorted picture that looks
right only from an oblique point of view; or, a painter's technique used to
produce the illusion of reality; or, the science of optics   **5 For . . . skill**
i.e., You must look through the eyes of me, the skillful painter

To find where your true image pictured lies,
Which in my bosom's shop is hanging still,  7
That hath his windows glazèd with thine eyes.  8
Now see what good turns eyes for eyes have done:
Mine eyes have drawn thy shape, and thine for me
Are windows to my breast, wherethrough the sun
Delights to peep, to gaze therein on thee.
    Yet eyes this cunning want to grace their art:  13
    They draw but what they see, know not the heart.  14

## 25

Let those who are in favor with their stars  1
Of public honor and proud titles boast,
Whilst I, whom fortune of such triumph bars,  3
Unlooked for joy in that I honor most.  4
Great princes' favorites their fair leaves spread  5
But as the marigold at the sun's eye,  6
And in themselves their pride lies burièd,  7
For at a frown they in their glory die.  8
The painful warrior famousèd for fight,  9
After a thousand victories once foiled
Is from the book of honor rasèd quite,  11
And all the rest forgot for which he toiled.  12
    Then happy I, that love and am beloved
    Where I may not remove nor be removed.  14

## 26

Lord of my love, to whom in vassalage  1
Thy merit hath my duty strongly knit,
To thee I send this written embassage
To witness duty, not to show my wit—  4
Duty so great, which wit so poor as mine  5
May make seem bare, in wanting words to show it,  6
But that I hope some good conceit of thine  7
In thy soul's thought, all naked, will bestow it;  8
Till whatsoever star that guides my moving  9
Points on me graciously with fair aspect,  10
And puts apparel on my tattered loving
To show me worthy of thy sweet respect.
    Then may I dare to boast how I do love thee;
    Till then not show my head where thou mayst prove
      me.  14

## 27

Weary with toil, I haste me to my bed,
The dear repose for limbs with travel tirèd;  2
But then begins a journey in my head,
To work my mind when body's work's expirèd.
For then my thoughts, from far where I abide,  5
Intend a zealous pilgrimage to thee,  6
And keep my drooping eyelids open wide,
Looking on darkness which the blind do see;  8
Save that my soul's imaginary sight  9
Presents thy shadow to my sightless view,  10
Which, like a jewel hung in ghastly night,
Makes black night beauteous and her old face new.
    Lo, thus by day my limbs, by night my mind,
    For thee and for myself no quiet find.  14

## 28

How can I then return in happy plight  1
That am debarred the benefit of rest?
When day's oppression is not eased by night,
But day by night, and night by day, oppressed?  4
And each, though enemies to either's reign,  5
Do in consent shake hands to torture me,  6
The one by toil, the other to complain  7
How far I toil, still farther off from thee.
I tell the day, to please him, thou art bright
And dost him grace when clouds do blot the heaven;  10
So flatter I the swart-complexioned night,  11
When sparkling stars twire not, thou gild'st th' even.  12
    But day doth daily draw my sorrows longer,  13
    And night doth nightly make grief's strength seem
      stronger.

## 29

When, in disgrace with fortune and men's eyes,
I all alone beweep my outcast state,
And trouble deaf heaven with my bootless cries,  3
And look upon myself and curse my fate,  4
Wishing me like to one more rich in hope,  5
Featured like him, like him with friends possessed,  6
Desiring this man's art and that man's scope,  7

---

7 **bosom's shop** i.e., heart  **8 his** its.  **glazèd** fitted with glass, paned. (The friend, looking into the poet's eyes where his own eyes are reflected, can see into the poet's heart.)  **13 this cunning want** lack this skill.  **grace** enhance  **14 know not** do not perceive the thoughts of
**25.1 who . . . stars** i.e., who are fortunate  **3 of** from  **4 Unlooked for** (1) unexpectedly (2) out of the public eye.  **that** that which  **5 their . . . spread** i.e., flourish, blossom, prosper  **6 But** only  **7 lies burièd** i.e., will die with the ending of their brief glory  **8 a frown** (1) a prince's frown (2) a cloud obscuring the sun  **9 painful** enduring much, striving.  **famousèd** renowned.  **fight** (Reads "worth" in the 1609 quarto; some editors retain and emend "quite" in line 11 to "forth." Other editors prefer "might.")  **11 rasèd** erased (or *razèd*, scraped out)  **12 the rest** i.e., his *thousand victories*  **14 remove** i.e., be unfaithful.  **removed** i.e., removed from favor.
**26.1 vassalage** feudal allegiance  **4 witness** bear witness to.  **wit** skill, literary ingenuity  **5 wit** intelligence and skill  **6 wanting** lacking  **7 good conceit** good conception, favorable opinion  **8 all naked** i.e., poor verse though it is.  **bestow** give lodging to  **9 moving** life and deeds  **10 Points on** directs its rays at.  **aspect** influence (as of a star or planet)  **14 prove** test

**27.2 travel** (With connotation also of *travail*; spelled "trauaill" in the quarto.)  **5 from far** i.e., far away from you  **6 Intend** (1) set out upon (2) have purposefully in mind  **8 Looking . . . see** while my thoughts try to peer (toward you) through the darkness, like the blind, who see only darkness  **9 Save** except  **10 thy shadow** the image of you  **14 For** on account of
**28.1 plight** condition  **4 But . . . oppressed** i.e., but experiencing sleeplessness at night and fatigue during the day.  **5 either's** each other's  **6 in . . . hands** i.e., come to a mutual agreement  **7 The one** the day.  **the other to complain** i.e., the night by causing me to complain  **10 And . . . heaven** i.e., and that you celebrate his beauty in place of the sun when the sun is overclouded  **11 So flatter I** similarly I gratify.  **swart** dark  **12 When . . . even** i.e., by saying that, when sparkling stars do not twinkle or peep out, you make bright the evening.  **13 draw . . . longer** lengthen my sorrow
**29.3 bootless** unavailing  **4 look upon myself** consider my predicament  **5 more rich in hope** with better prospects of success  **6 Featured** formed, i.e., having good looks.  **like him, like him** like a second man, like a third  **7 art** literary skill, learning.  **scope** range of powers

With what I most enjoy contented least; 8
Yet in these thoughts myself almost despising,
Haply I think on thee, and then my state, 10
Like to the lark at break of day arising
From sullen earth, sings hymns at heaven's gate;
　　For thy sweet love remembered such wealth brings
　　That then I scorn to change my state with kings. 14

## 30

When to the sessions of sweet silent thought 1
I summon up remembrance of things past,
I sigh the lack of many a thing I sought, 3
And with old woes new wail my dear time's waste. 4
Then can I drown an eye, unused to flow, 5
For precious friends hid in death's dateless night, 6
And weep afresh love's long-since-canceled woe, 7
And moan th'expense of many a vanished sight. 8
Then can I grieve at grievances foregone, 9
And heavily from woe to woe tell o'er 10
The sad account of fore-bemoanèd moan, 11
Which I new pay as if not paid before.
　　But if the while I think on thee, dear friend,
　　All losses are restored and sorrows end.

## 31

Thy bosom is endearèd with all hearts 1
Which I by lacking have supposèd dead, 2
And there reigns love and all love's loving parts, 3
And all those friends which I thought burièd.
How many a holy and obsequious tear 5
Hath dear religious love stol'n from mine eye 6
As interest of the dead, which now appear 7
But things removed that hidden in thee lie! 8
Thou art the grave where buried love doth live,
Hung with the trophies of my lovers gone, 10
Who all their parts of me to thee did give; 11
That due of many now is thine alone. 12
　　Their images I loved I view in thee, 13
　　And thou, all they, hast all the all of me. 14

## 32

If thou survive my well-contented day 1
When that churl Death my bones with dust shall cover,
And shalt by fortune once more re-survey 3
These poor rude lines of thy deceasèd lover, 4
Compare them with the bett'ring of the time, 5
And though they be outstripped by every pen,
Reserve them for my love, not for their rhyme, 7
Exceeded by the height of happier men. 8
Oh, then vouchsafe me but this loving thought: 9
"Had my friend's Muse grown with this growing age, 10
A dearer birth than this his love had brought 11
To march in ranks of better equipage; 12
　　But since he died and poets better prove, 13
　　Theirs for their style I'll read, his for his love."

## 33

Full many a glorious morning have I seen 1
Flatter the mountaintops with sovereign eye, 2
Kissing with golden face the meadows green,
Gilding pale streams with heavenly alchemy;
Anon permit the basest clouds to ride 5
With ugly rack on his celestial face, 6
And from the forlorn world his visage hide,
Stealing unseen to west with this disgrace.
Even so my sun one early morn did shine
With all-triumphant splendor on my brow.
But out, alack! He was but one hour mine; 11
The region cloud hath masked him from me now. 12
　　Yet him for this my love no whit disdaineth; 13
　　Suns of the world may stain when heaven's sun
　　　　staineth. 14

## 34

Why didst thou promise such a beauteous day
And make me travel forth without my cloak,
To let base clouds o'ertake me in my way, 3
Hiding thy brav'ry in their rotten smoke? 4
'Tis not enough that through the cloud thou break,
To dry the rain on my storm-beaten face, 6
For no man well of such a salve can speak
That heals the wound and cures not the disgrace. 8

8 **most enjoy** possess most securely and take greatest pleasure in
10 **Haply** perchance; happily. **state** state of mind. (Suggesting also
"fortunes.") 14 **change** exchange
30.1 **sessions** (The metaphor is that of a court of law, continued in
*summon up,* line 2.) 3 **sigh** sigh for 4 **new . . . waste** lament anew
the wasting of precious time or time's erosion of those things held
precious. 5 **unused to flow** not prone to weep 6 **dateless** endless 7 **canceled** paid in full (by grieving) 8 **th'expense** the loss,
expenditure, passing 9 **grievances foregone** sorrows past
10 **heavily** sadly. **tell** count 11 **account** (1) narrative (2) financial
reckoning. **fore-bemoanèd moan** previously uttered laments
31.1 **endearèd with all hearts** (1) beloved by all (2) made dear to me
by representing and including those I have loved 2 **lacking** not having
3 **parts** attributes 5 **obsequious** suitable to mourning 6 **religious**
dutiful, reverent 7 **interest of** that which is rightfully due to. **which**
who 8 **But . . . lie** i.e., no more than absent persons (now dead),
whose best qualities are to be found buried in you. 10 **Hung . . . gone**
festooned with symbolic memorials of my past loves 11 **parts**
shares 12 **That due of many** that which was both owed by, and paid
to, many 13 **I loved** which I loved
14 **all they** (you) who comprise all of them

32.1 **my . . . day** i.e., the day of my death, which will content me
well 3 **And . . . fortune** and if by chance you happen 4 **rude** unpolished. **lover** friend 5 **bett'ring** i.e., improved writing, greater cultural sophistication 7 **Reserve** preserve. **for my love** (1) out of love
for me (2) for the sake of my love for you. **rhyme** i.e., poetic skill
8 **height** superiority, highest achievement. **happier** more gifted or
fortunate 9 **vouchsafe me but** deign to bestow on me just
10 **grown** matured stylistically. **growing** increasingly sophisticated
11 **dearer birth** i.e., better poem, better artistic creation. **had** would
have 12 **better equipage** i.e., more finely wrought verse 13 **better
prove** turn out to be superior
33.1 **Full** Very 2 **sovereign eye** i.e., morning sunlight 5 **Anon** soon
afterward. **basest** darkest 6 **rack** mass of cloud scudding before
the wind 11 **out, alack!** (An expression of dismay.) 12 **region** of
the upper air 13 **Yet . . . disdaineth** Yet I love him no less for this
14 **Suns . . . staineth** i.e., as a mere mortal, I may suffer disgrace when
my friend and patron no longer shines on me.
34.3 **To** only to 4 **brav'ry** finery. **rotten smoke** foul vapors.
6 **To . . . face** i.e., trying to make amends for the way you have treated
me 8 **the disgrace** i.e., the scar, the disfigurement caused by his
friend's neglect or harsh treatment; the *loss* mentioned in line 10.

Nor can thy shame give physic to my grief;    9
Though thou repent, yet I have still the loss.
Th'offender's sorrow lends but weak relief
To him that bears the strong offense's cross.    12
    Ah, but those tears are pearl which thy love sheds,
    And they are rich, and ransom all ill deeds.    14

### 35

No more be grieved at that which thou hast done.
Roses have thorns, and silver fountains mud,
Clouds and eclipses stain both moon and sun,    3
And loathsome canker lives in sweetest bud.    4
All men make faults, and even I in this,
Authorizing thy trespass with compare,    6
Myself corrupting, salving thy amiss,    7
Excusing thy sins more than thy sins are.    8
For to thy sensual fault I bring in sense—    9
Thy adverse party is thy advocate—    10
And 'gainst myself a lawful plea commence.
Such civil war is in my love and hate
    That I an accessary needs must be    13
    To that sweet thief which sourly robs from me.

### 36

Let me confess that we two must be twain,    1
Although our undivided loves are one;    2
So shall those blots that do with me remain,    3
Without thy help, by me be borne alone.
In our two loves there is but one respect,    5
Though in our lives a separable spite,    6
Which, though it alter not love's sole effect,    7
Yet doth it steal sweet hours from love's delight.
I may not evermore acknowledge thee,    9
Lest my bewailèd guilt should do thee shame,
Nor thou with public kindness honor me
Unless thou take that honor from thy name.    12
    But do not so; I love thee in such sort    13
    As, thou being mine, mine is thy good report.    14

### 37

As a decrepit father takes delight
To see his active child do deeds of youth,

So I, made lame by Fortune's dearest spite,    3
Take all my comfort of thy worth and truth.    4
For whether beauty, birth, or wealth, or wit,    5
Or any of these all, or all, or more,
Entitled in thy parts do crownèd sit,    7
I make my love engrafted to this store.    8
So then I am not lame, poor, nor despised,
Whilst that this shadow doth such substance give    10
That I in thy abundance am sufficed
And by a part of all thy glory live.
    Look what is best, that best I wish in thee.    13
    This wish I have; then ten times happy me!    14

### 38

How can my Muse want subject to invent    1
While thou dost breathe, that pour'st into my verse    2
Thine own sweet argument, too excellent    3
For every vulgar paper to rehearse?    4
Oh, give thyself the thanks, if aught in me    5
Worthy perusal stand against thy sight,    6
For who's so dumb that cannot write to thee,    7
When thou thyself dost give invention light?    8
Be thou the tenth Muse, ten times more in worth
Than those old nine which rhymers invocate;
And he that calls on thee, let him bring forth
Eternal numbers to outlive long date.    12
    If my slight Muse do please these curious days,    13
    The pain be mine, but thine shall be the praise.    14

### 39

Oh, how thy worth with manners may I sing,    1
When thou art all the better part of me?
What can mine own praise to mine own self bring?    3
And what is't but mine own when I praise thee?    4
Even for this let us divided live,    5
And our dear love lose name of single one,    6
That by this separation I may give
That due to thee which thou deserv'st alone.
O absence, what a torment wouldst thou prove,
Were it not thy sour leisure gave sweet leave    10
To entertain the time with thoughts of love,    11
Which time and thoughts so sweetly doth deceive,    12

---

**9 thy shame** repentance for the wrong you've done to me.   **physic** remedy   **12 cross** affliction.   **14 ransom** atone for
**35.3 stain** dim, obscure   **4 canker** cankerworm   **6 Authorizing** sanctioning, justifying.   **compare** comparisons (as in this sonnet)   **7 Myself . . . amiss** excusing your misdeed, blaming myself   **8 Excusing . . . are** going further to excuse your sins than they warrant, or, excusing you for even worse sins than you have actually committed.   **9 For . . . sense** I reason away your fleshly offenses   **10 Thy . . . advocate** I who profess to be your accuser find myself, instead, pleading your case   **13 That . . . be** that I am compelled (by my love) to be a guilty accomplice
**36.1 twain** parted   **2 Although . . . one** although our souls remain inseparably united   **3 blots** defects, stains of dishonor   **5 but one respect** a mutual regard, singleness of attitude   **6 separable spite** vexing separation   **7 sole effect** unique effect (of making the two of us into one)   **9 acknowledge thee** publicly lay claim to your friendship   **12 Unless . . . from** without consequent loss of honor to   **13 in such sort** in such a way   **14 As . . . report** that since you are mine, your good reputation sustains me also.

**37.3 made lame** handicapped in life.   **dearest** most bitter   **4 of** in, from   **5 wit** intelligence   **7 Entitled . . . sit** enrolled among your qualities   **8 I make . . . store** I add my love to this abundance (and thereby flourish by drawing on their strength).   **10 Whilst that** while.   **shadow** idea (in the platonic sense).   **substance** actuality   **13 Look what** Whatever   **14 The pain be mine** let me take on the labor
**38.1 want . . . invent** lack something to write about   **2 that** you who   **3 Thine . . . argument** yourself as subject   **4 vulgar paper** common piece of writing.   **rehearse** recite, repeat.   **5–6 if . . . sight** if any of my writing strikes you as worthy of perusal   **7 dumb** silent, lacking in subject   **8 When . . . light** when you bring such a light of invention to yourself as poetic subject.   **12 numbers** verses.   **long date** even a very distant limit in time.   **13 curious** finicky   **14 The pain be mine** let me take on the labor
**39.1 with manners** decently, becomingly   **3–4 What . . . thee?** i.e., Since my better self is entirely yours, what can I gain from praising you but a kind of vainglorious self-praise?   **5 Even for** Precisely because of   **6 lose . . . one** lose the reputation of our being a unified single soul   **10 not** not that   **11 entertain** pass, occupy   **12 Which . . . deceive** (thoughts of love), which sweetly beguile away time and (sad) thoughts

And that thou teachest how to make one twain
By praising him here who doth hence remain! 14

### 40

Take all my loves, my love, yea, take them all; 1
What hast thou then more than thou hadst before?
No love, my love, that thou mayst true love call; 3
All mine was thine before thou hadst this more.
Then if for my love thou my love receivest, 5
I cannot blame thee for my love thou usest; 6
But yet be blamed if thou this self deceivest 7
By willful taste of what thyself refusest. 8
I do forgive thy robb'ry, gentle thief,
Although thou steal thee all my poverty; 10
And yet love knows it is a greater grief
To bear love's wrong than hate's known injury. 12
    Lascivious grace, in whom all ill well shows, 13
    Kill me with spites; yet we must not be foes. 14

### 41

Those pretty wrongs that liberty commits 1
When I am sometime absent from thy heart, 2
Thy beauty and thy years full well befits, 3
For still temptation follows where thou art. 4
Gentle thou art, and therefore to be won;
Beauteous thou art, therefore to be assailed;
And when a woman woos, what woman's son 7
Will sourly leave her till he have prevailed? 8
Ay me, but yet thou mightst my seat forbear, 9
And chide thy beauty and thy straying youth,
Who lead thee in their riot even there 11
Where thou art forced to break a twofold truth: 12
    Hers, by thy beauty tempting her to thee,
    Thine, by thy beauty being false to me.

### 42

That thou hast her, it is not all my grief,
And yet it may be said I loved her dearly;
That she hath thee is of my wailing chief, 3
A loss in love that touches me more nearly.
Loving offenders, thus I will excuse ye:

Thou dost love her because thou know'st I love her,
And for my sake even so doth she abuse me, 7
Suff'ring my friend for my sake to approve her. 8
If I lose thee, my loss is my love's gain, 9
And, losing her, my friend hath found that loss; 10
Both find each other, and I lose both twain,
And both for my sake lay on me this cross. 12
    But here's the joy: my friend and I are one.
    Sweet flattery! Then she loves but me alone. 14

### 43

When most I wink, then do mine eyes best see, 1
For all the day they view things unrespected; 2
But when I sleep, in dreams they look on thee,
And, darkly bright, are bright in dark directed. 4
Then thou, whose shadow shadows doth make bright, 5
How would thy shadow's form form happy show 6
To the clear day with thy much clearer light,
When to unseeing eyes thy shade shines so! 8
How would, I say, mine eyes be blessèd made
By looking on thee in the living day,
When in dead night thy fair imperfect shade 11
Through heavy sleep on sightless eyes doth stay! 12
    All days are nights to see till I see thee, 13
    And nights bright days when dreams do show thee
    me. 14

### 44

If the dull substance of my flesh were thought, 1
Injurious distance should not stop my way;
For then despite of space I would be brought,
From limits far remote, where thou dost stay. 4
No matter then although my foot did stand
Upon the farthest earth removed from thee; 6
For nimble thought can jump both sea and land
As soon as think the place where he would be. 8
But, ah, thought kills me that I am not thought, 9
To leap large lengths of miles when thou art gone,
But that, so much of earth and water wrought, 11
I must attend time's leisure with my moan, 12

14 **here** (1) here where I am (2) here in this poem.   **hence remain** dwell elsewhere.
**40.1 all my loves** (1) all those whom I love (2) all the love I have. (The young man addressed has taken away the poet's mistress.)   **3 No . . . call** i.e., Any love more than you had already—my complete affection—cannot be called true love   **5 my love . . . my love** love of me . . . her whom I love   **6 for** because.   **thou usest** you enjoy (sexually)   **7 this self** i.e., me, your other self. (Often emended to "thyself.")   **8 By . . . refusest** i.e., by tasting sexual pleasures that your best self would refuse.   **10 steal . . . poverty** take for your own the poor little that I have   **12 To . . . injury** to endure injuries arising out of a loving relationship than those stemming from calculated hatred.   **13 Lascivious grace** i.e., You who are gracious even in your lasciviousness.   **well shows** looks attractive   **14 spites** hurtful wrongs
**41.1 pretty** graciously committed, sportive.   **liberty** licentiousness   **2 thy heart** you whom I love   **3 befits** (The object is *wrongs*, line 1.)   **4 still** constantly   **7–8 And . . . prevailed** i.e., When a woman woos, what man can resist until he has scored? (*He* is sometimes emended to "she.")   **9 seat** place, that which belongs to me (i.e., my mistress)   **11 Who** which.   **riot** debauchery   **12 twofold truth** i.e., her plighted love to me and your plighted friendship to me
**42.3 is . . . chief** is chief cause of my lamentation

**7 abuse** betray, wrong   **8 Suff'ring** allowing.   **approve** try, test (in a sexual sense)   **9 my love's** hers whom I love, my mistress's   **10 losing her** i.e., I losing her   **12 for my sake** as though out of love for me.   **cross** torment.   **14 flattery** gratifying deception.
**43.1 wink** close my eyes in sleep   **2 unrespected** unnoticed, unregarded; not deserving notice   **4 And . . . directed** and, able to see in the darkness (though still shut), are directed toward your brightness in the dark.   **5 whose . . . bright** whose image makes darkness bright   **6 thy shadow's . . . show** the substance of the shadow, i.e., your presence, make a gladdening sight   **8 unseeing eyes** i.e., closed eyes of the dreamer   **11 imperfect** unsubstantial, indistinct as in a dream   **12 stay** linger, dwell.   **13 All . . . to see** All days are gloomy to behold   **14 thee me** you to me. (But also suggesting "me to you.")
**44.1 dull** heavy   **4 limits** regions, bounds.   **where** to the place where   **6 farthest earth removed** that part of the earth farthest removed   **8 he** thought   **9 ah, thought** ah, the thought   **11 so . . . wrought** i.e., I, compounded to such an extent of the heavier elements, earth and water. (The lighter elements are fire and air.)
**12 attend time's leisure** i.e., wait until time has leisure to reunite us

Receiving naught by elements so slow                13
But heavy tears, badges of either's woe.            14

### 45

The other two, slight air and purging fire,         1
Are both with thee, wherever I abide;
The first my thought, the other my desire,
These present-absent with swift motion slide.       4
For when these quicker elements are gone
In tender embassy of love to thee,
My life, being made of four, with two alone         7
Sinks down to death, oppressed with melancholy,     8
Until life's composition be recured                 9
By those swift messengers returned from thee,       10
Who even but now come back again, assured
Of thy fair health, recounting it to me.
     This told, I joy; but then no longer glad,
     I send them back again and straight grow sad.  14

### 46

Mine eye and heart are at a mortal war              1
How to divide the conquest of thy sight;            2
Mine eye my heart thy picture's sight would bar,    3
My heart mine eye the freedom of that right.        4
My heart doth plead that thou in him dost lie—
A closet never pierced with crystal eyes—
But the defendant doth that plea deny               6
And says in him thy fair appearance lies.           7
To 'cide this title is impanelèd                    9
A quest of thoughts, all tenants to the heart,      10
And by their verdict is determinèd
The clear eye's moiety and the dear heart's part,   12
     As thus: mine eye's due is thy outward part,   13
     And my heart's right thy inward love of heart.

### 47

Betwixt mine eye and heart a league is took,        1
And each doth good turns now unto the other.
When that mine eye is famished for a look,          3
Or heart in love with sighs himself doth smother,   4

With my love's picture then my eye doth feast,      5
And to the painted banquet bids my heart;           6
Another time mine eye is my heart's guest
And in his thoughts of love doth share a part.
So, either by thy picture or my love,
Thyself, away, are present still with me;
For thou no farther than my thoughts canst move,
And I am still with them and they with thee;        12
     Or, if they sleep, thy picture in my sight
     Awakes my heart to heart's and eye's delight.

### 48

How careful was I, when I took my way,              1
Each trifle under truest bars to thrust,            2
That to my use it might unusèd stay                 3
From hands of falsehood, in sure wards of trust!    4
But thou, to whom my jewels trifles are,            5
Most worthy comfort, now my greatest grief,         6
Thou best of dearest and mine only care,
Art left the prey of every vulgar thief.            8
Thee have I not locked up in any chest,
Save where thou art not—though I feel thou art—
Within the gentle closure of my breast,
From whence at pleasure thou mayst come and part;   12
     And even thence thou wilt be stol'n, I fear,
     For truth proves thievish for a prize so dear. 14

### 49

Against that time, if ever that time come,          1
When I shall see thee frown on my defects,
Whenas thy love hath cast his utmost sum,           3
Called to that audit by advised respects;           4
Against that time when thou shalt strangely pass    5
And scarcely greet me with that sun, thine eye,
When love, converted from the thing it was,
Shall reasons find of settled gravity—              8
Against that time do I ensconce me here             9
Within the knowledge of mine own desart,            10
And this my hand against myself uprear,             11
To guard the lawful reasons on thy part.            12
     To leave poor me thou hast the strength of laws,
     Since why to love I can allege no cause.       14

13 **by** from   14 **badges** signs, tokens.   **either's** (1) both earth's and water's, because the earth is heavy and the sea is salt and wet like tears (2) both your and my
45.1 **other two** (i.e., of the four elements discussed in sonnet 44).
**slight** insubstantial.   **purging** purifying   4 **present-absent** (1) now here and immediately gone (2) simultaneously both present and absent   7 **two alone** i.e., earth and water   8 **melancholy** a humor thought to be induced by an excess of earth and water   9 **composition** proper balance among the four elements.   **recured** restored
10 **swift messengers** i.e., fire and air, thought and desire   14 **straight** straightaway
46.1 **mortal** deadly   2 **How . . . sight** how to divide the spoils of war, namely, the sight of you   3–4 **Mine . . . right** my eye wishes to bar my heart from seeing your image (perhaps a painting), and conversely my heart would like to deny my eye the free enjoyment of that right.
6 **closet** (1) small private room (2) cabinet   7 **the defendant** the eye
9 **'cide** decide.   **impanelèd** convened   10 **quest** inquest, jury
12 **moiety** portion   13 **mine . . . part** i.e., the eye gets the outward appearance of you. (The jury, composed entirely of those who are loyal to the heart, being its *tenants*, awards true love to the heart.)
47.1 **a league is took** a truce is reached   3 **When that** When
4 **Or . . . smother** or when my loving heart smothers itself with sighs

5 **With** i.e., on   6 **painted** i.e., visually splendid but limited to outward show. (Perhaps an actual picture of the friend.)
12 **still** constantly
48.1 **took my way** set out on my journey   2 **truest** most trusty   3 **to my use** for my own use and profit   3–4 **stay . . . falsehood** remain out of the hands of thieves   5 **to** compared to   6 **worthy** valuable.
**grief** anxiety, cause of sorrow (i.e., because of your absence and likelihood of being stolen from me)   8 **vulgar** common   12 **part** depart
14 **truth** i.e., even honesty itself
49.1 **Against** In anticipation of   3 **Whenas** when.   **cast . . . sum** added up the sum total. (The metaphor is from closing accounts on a dissolution of partnership.)   4 **advised respects** careful consideration
5 **strangely** as a stranger   8 **of settled gravity** (1) for a dignified reserve or continued coldness (2) of sufficient weight   9 **ensconce me** fortify myself   10 **desart** i.e., deserving, such as it is. (This quarto spelling of desert, "desart," indicates the rhyme with *part*.)   11 **this . . . uprear** I raise my own hand (as a witness) against my own interest
12 **To . . . part** i.e., to testify in behalf of the lawful reasons on your side of the case.   14 **Since . . . cause** since I can urge no lawful cause why you should love me.

## 50

How heavy do I journey on the way,  1
When what I seek, my weary travel's end,  2
Doth teach that ease and that repose to say,  3
"Thus far the miles are measured from thy friend!"  4
The beast that bears me, tirèd with my woe,
Plods dully on, to bear that weight in me,
As if by some instinct the wretch did know
His rider loved not speed being made from thee.
The bloody spur cannot provoke him on
That sometimes anger thrusts into his hide,
Which heavily he answers with a groan,
More sharp to me than spurring to his side;
    For that same groan doth put this in my mind:
    My grief lies onward and my joy behind.

## 51

Thus can my love excuse the slow offense  1
Of my dull bearer when from thee I speed:  2
From where thou art why should I haste me thence?  3
Till I return, of posting is no need.  4
Oh, what excuse will my poor beast then find
When swift extremity can seem but slow?  6
Then should I spur, though mounted on the wind;
In wingèd speed no motion shall I know.  8
Then can no horse with my desire keep pace;
Therefore desire, of perfect'st love being made,
Shall neigh—no dull flesh—in his fiery race.  11
But love, for love, thus shall excuse my jade:  12
    Since from thee going he went willful slow,
    Towards thee I'll run, and give him leave to go.  14

## 52

So am I as the rich whose blessèd key  1
Can bring him to his sweet up-lockèd treasure,
The which he will not ev'ry hour survey,
For blunting the fine point of seldom pleasure.  4
Therefore are feasts so solemn and so rare,  5
Since, seldom coming, in the long year set,
Like stones of worth they thinly placèd are,
Or captain jewels in the carcanet.  8
So is the time that keeps you as my chest,  9
Or as the wardrobe which the robe doth hide,  10
To make some special instant special blest

By new unfolding his imprisoned pride.  12
    Blessèd are you whose worthiness gives scope,  13
    Being had, to triumph; being lacked, to hope.  14

## 53

What is your substance, whereof are you made,
That millions of strange shadows on you tend?  2
Since everyone hath, every one, one shade,  3
And you, but one, can every shadow lend.  4
Describe Adonis, and the counterfeit  5
Is poorly imitated after you;
On Helen's cheek all art of beauty set,  7
And you in Grecian tires are painted new.  8
Speak of the spring and foison of the year;  9
The one doth shadow of your beauty show,
The other as your bounty doth appear,
And you in every blessèd shape we know.  12
    In all external grace you have some part,
    But you like none, none you, for constant heart.  14

## 54

Oh, how much more doth beauty beauteous seem
By that sweet ornament which truth doth give!  2
The rose looks fair, but fairer we it deem
For that sweet odor which doth in it live.
The canker blooms have full as deep a dye  5
As the perfumèd tincture of the roses,
Hang on such thorns, and play as wantonly  7
When summer's breath their maskèd buds discloses;  8
But, for their virtue only is their show,  9
They live unwooed and unrespected fade,  10
Die to themselves. Sweet roses do not so;  11
Of their sweet deaths are sweetest odors made.  12
    And so of you, beauteous and lovely youth,  13
    When that shall vade, by verse distills your truth.  14

## 55

Not marble nor the gilded monuments
Of princes shall outlive this powerful rhyme,

**12 his** its.  **pride** splendor, proud treasure.  **13–14 gives . . . hope** gives me opportunity, when you are with me, to rejoice, and when you are away from me, to hope for reunion.
**53.2 strange** (1) exotic (2) not belonging to you.  **tend** attend.
**3 shade** shadow (as cast by the sun)  **4 And . . . lend** and yet you, being only one person, can cast all sorts of shadowy images or reflections (such as Adonis, Helen, etc.).  **5 Describe Adonis** Draw Adonis, the beautiful youth loved by Venus.  **counterfeit** likeness, portrait  **7–8 On . . . new** set forth the entire art used to beautify the cheek of Helen of Troy, and the result will be a portrait of you in Grecian attire or headdress.  **9 foison** abundance, i.e., autumn  **12 you . . . know** we recognize you in every beautiful image.
**14 But . . . heart** but in the matter of constancy you resemble no one and no one can resemble you.
**54.2 By** by means of.  **truth** (1) constancy (2) substance, integrity  **5 canker blooms** dog roses (outwardly attractive but not as sweetly scented as the damask rose).  **dye** tincture  **7 wantonly** sportively  **8 discloses** causes to open  **9 for** because.  **their show** in their appearance  **10 unrespected** unappreciated  **11 to themselves** i.e., alone and without profit to others.  **12 Of . . . made** i.e., perfumes are made from the crushed petals of these roses.  **13 of you** (1) distilled from you (2) with regard to you.  **lovely** (1) lovable (2) handsome  **14 When . . . truth** when your physical beauty fades, your true substance will be distilled and preserved by (my) verse. (See sonnet 5.)  **vade** (1) fade (2) go away

**50.1 heavy** sadly and slowly  **2–4 When . . . friend** when the ease and repose I seek at journey's end will merely remind me that I have gone so many miles from my friend.
**51.1 slow offense** offense consisting in slowness  **2 my dull bearer** i.e., the horse  **4 posting** riding swiftly  **6 swift extremity** extreme swiftness (in returning to you)  **8 In . . . know** even at the speed of flight I won't perceive the motion at all, won't feel as though I'm moving.  **11 Shall . . . race** i.e., will neigh proudly in its fire-swift race, since it, composed like fire of a lighter element, is not held back by the heavy flesh. (See sonnet 45.)
**12 for love** for love's sake.  **jade** nag  **14 Towards . . . go** i.e., my desire, not being inhibited by "dull flesh" (line 11), will speed toward you, while I allow my horse to travel at its own slow pace.
**52.1 as the rich** like the rich man  **4 For . . . pleasure** lest he blunt the delicacy of pleasure sparingly enjoyed.  **5 feasts** feast days.  **solemn** ceremonious, festive.  **rare** excellent; uncommon  **8 captain** principal.  **carcanet** necklace of jewels.  **9 keeps you** (1) watches over you (2) keeps you from me.  **as** like  **10 hide** conceal from view

But you shall shine more bright in these contents   3
Than unswept stone besmeared with sluttish time.   4
When wasteful war shall statues overturn,   5
And broils root out the work of masonry,   6
Nor Mars his sword nor war's quick fire shall burn   7
The living record of your memory.
'Gainst death and all-oblivious enmity   9
Shall you pace forth; your praise shall still find room
Even in the eyes of all posterity
That wear this world out to the ending doom.   12
    So, till the judgment that yourself arise,   13
    You live in this, and dwell in lovers' eyes.

## 56

Sweet love, renew thy force! Be it not said   1
Thy edge should blunter be than appetite,   2
Which but today by feeding is allayed,   3
Tomorrow sharpened in his former might.   4
So, love, be thou; although today thou fill
Thy hungry eyes even till they wink with fullness,   6
Tomorrow see again, and do not kill
The spirit of love with a perpetual dullness.
Let this sad int'rim like the ocean be   9
Which parts the shore where two contracted new   10
Come daily to the banks, that, when they see   11
Return of love, more blest may be the view;   12
    As call it winter, which being full of care   13
    Makes summer's welcome thrice more wished, more
      rare.   14

## 57

Being your slave, what should I do but tend   1
Upon the hours and times of your desire?
I have no precious time at all to spend,
Nor services to do, till you require.
Nor dare I chide the world-without-end hour   5
Whilst I, my sovereign, watch the clock for you,   6
Nor think the bitterness of absence sour   7
When you have bid your servant once adieu.   8
Nor dare I question with my jealous thought   9
Where you may be, or your affairs suppose,   10

But, like a sad slave, stay and think of naught
Save where you are how happy you make those.   12
    So true a fool is love that in your will,   13
    Though you do anything, he thinks no ill.

## 58

That god forbid, that made me first your slave,
I should in thought control your times of pleasure,
Or at your hand th'account of hours to crave,   3
Being your vassal, bound to stay your leisure!   4
Oh, let me suffer, being at your beck,   5
Th'imprisoned absence of your liberty,   6
And, patience-tame to sufferance, bide each check,   7
Without accusing you of injury.
Be where you list, your charter is so strong   9
That you yourself may privilege your time   10
To what you will; to you it doth belong
Yourself to pardon of self-doing crime.   12
    I am to wait, though waiting so be hell,   13
    Not blame your pleasure, be it ill or well.

## 59

If there be nothing new, but that which is   1
Hath been before, how are our brains beguiled,
Which, laboring for invention, bear amiss   3
The second burden of a former child!   4
Oh, that record could with a backward look,   5
Even of five hundred courses of the sun,   6
Show me your image in some antique book,
Since mind at first in character was done!   8
That I might see what the old world could say
To this composèd wonder of your frame;   10
Whether we are mended, or whe'er better they,   11
Or whether revolution be the same.   12
    Oh, sure I am the wits of former days   13
    To subjects worse have given admiring praise.

## 60

Like as the waves make towards the pebbled shore,   1
So do our minutes hasten to their end,
Each changing place with that which goes before,   3

---

**55.3 these contents** i.e., the contents of my poems written in praise of you   **4 Than unswept stone** than in a memorial stone that has been left unswept, unattended.   **sluttish** neglectful, slovenly, whorish   **5 wasteful** laying waste   **6 broils** uprisings, battles   **7 Nor Mars his sword** Neither Mars's sword (shall destroy)   **9 all-oblivious enmity** oblivion, at enmity with everything   **12 That . . . doom** that will last from now till doomsday. (*That* may refer to *eyes, praise,* or *posterity*.)   **13 till . . . arise** until the Judgment Day, when you will arise from the dead
**56.1 love** i.e., the spirit of love. (The friend is not directly mentioned in this sonnet.)   **1–2 Be . . . appetite** Let no one attempt to argue that true love should be any less sharp-edged in desire than sexual appetite   **3 but** only for   **4 his** its   **6 wink** shut   **9 sad int'rim** a period of love's abatement or absence   **10 parts the shore** separates the shores.   **contracted new** newly betrothed   **11 banks** shores   **12 love** the loved one   **13 As** just as appropriately   **14 rare** treasured.
**57.1 tend** attend   **5 world-without-end** interminable   **6 Whilst . . . you** while I count the minutes, my sovereign, waiting for your command   **7 Nor think** nor dare I think   **8 your servant** me, your humble servant   **9 question with** (1) debate with (2) seek to know by means of   **10 suppose** make conjectures about

**12 those** those persons where you are.   **13 true** (1) constant (2) utter. **in your will** with regard to your desire (with perhaps an allusion to "Will Shakespeare"; "will" is capitalized in the 1609 quarto, as in sonnet 135).
**58.3 th'account . . . crave** should crave an accounting of how you spend your time   **4 stay** wait upon   **5 beck** beck and call   **6 Th'imprisoned . . . liberty** the lack of freedom I suffer in being absent from you, arising from (*of*) your freedom and licentious behavior   **7 And . . . check** and, trained to endure any suffering, put up with each rebuke   **9 list** please.   **charter** privilege   **10 privilege** authorize, allocate   **12 self-doing** committed by yourself   **13 am to** must
**59.1 that** everything   **3–4 laboring . . . child** striving to give birth to a new creation, merely miscarry with the repetition of something created before.   **5 record** memory, especially memory preserved in writing   **6 courses . . . sun** years   **8 Since . . . done** since thought was first expressed in writing.   **10 composèd wonder** wonderful composition   **11 mended** improved.   **or . . . they** or whether poets saw things better in olden times   **12 revolution . . . same** the revolving of the ages brings only repetition.   **13 wits** discerning persons; poets
**60.1 Like . . . shore** Just as waves move up the shingle beach   **3 changing place with** replacing

In sequent toil all forwards do contend. 4
Nativity, once in the main of light, 5
Crawls to maturity, wherewith being crowned,
Crookèd eclipses 'gainst his glory fight, 7
And Time that gave doth now his gift confound. 8
Time doth transfix the flourish set on youth 9
And delves the parallels in beauty's brow, 10
Feeds on the rarities of nature's truth, 11
And nothing stands but for his scythe to mow. 12
    And yet to times in hope my verse shall stand, 13
    Praising thy worth despite his cruel hand.

## 61

Is it thy will thy image should keep open
My heavy eyelids to the weary night?
Dost thou desire my slumbers should be broken
While shadows like to thee do mock my sight? 4
Is it thy spirit that thou send'st from thee
So far from home into my deeds to pry,
To find out shames and idle hours in me, 7
The scope and tenor of thy jealousy? 8
Oh, no, thy love, though much, is not so great; 9
It is my love that keeps mine eye awake,
Mine own true love that doth my rest defeat,
To play the watchman ever for thy sake.
    For thee watch I whilst thou dost wake elsewhere, 13
    From me far off, with others all too near.

## 62

Sin of self-love possesseth all mine eye,
And all my soul, and all my every part;
And for this sin there is no remedy,
It is so grounded inward in my heart.
Methinks no face so gracious is as mine, 5
No shape so true, no truth of such account,
And for myself mine own worth do define 7
As I all other in all worths surmount. 8
But when my glass shows me myself indeed, 9
Beated and chapped with tanned antiquity, 10
Mine own self-love quite contrary I read;
Self so self-loving were iniquity. 12
    'Tis thee, my self, that for myself I praise, 13
    Painting my age with beauty of thy days. 14

## 63

Against my love shall be, as I am now, 1
With Time's injurious hand crushed and o'erworn; 2
When hours have drained his blood and filled his brow
With lines and wrinkles; when his youthful morn
Hath traveled on to age's steepy night, 5
And all those beauties whereof now he's king
Are vanishing or vanished out of sight,
Stealing away the treasure of his spring:
For such a time do I now fortify 9
Against confounding age's cruel knife, 10
That he shall never cut from memory 11
My sweet love's beauty, though my lover's life. 12
    His beauty shall in these black lines be seen, 13
    And they shall live, and he in them still green. 14

## 64

When I have seen by Time's fell hand defaced 1
The rich proud cost of outworn buried age; 2
When sometime lofty towers I see down-razed 3
And brass eternal slave to mortal rage; 4
When I have seen the hungry ocean gain
Advantage on the kingdom of the shore,
And the firm soil win of the wat'ry main, 7
Increasing store with loss and loss with store; 8
When I have seen such interchange of state, 9
Or state itself confounded to decay, 10
Ruin hath taught me thus to ruminate
That Time will come and take my love away. 12
    This thought is as a death, which cannot choose 13
    But weep to have that which it fears to lose. 14

## 65

Since brass, nor stone, nor earth, nor boundless sea 1
But sad mortality o'ersways their power,
How with this rage shall beauty hold a plea, 3
Whose action is no stronger than a flower? 4
Oh, how shall summer's honey breath hold out
Against the wrackful siege of batt'ring days, 6

4 In . . . contend one after another, all struggle onward.   5 Nativity . . . light The newborn infant, no sooner born into the broad expanse of this world and the light of day   7 Crookèd perverse, malignant   8 doth . . . confound now destroys beauty it gave.   9 doth . . . flourish pierces through and destroys the ornament, i.e., the physical beauty   10 delves the parallels digs the wrinkles, furrows   11 Feeds . . . truth consumes the most precious things created by the fidelity of nature   12 but . . . mow that can escape the mowing of Time's scythe.   13 times in hope times to come
61.4 shadows images. (But also suggesting spirits.)   7–8 To . . . jealousy to find out my shameful and lazy behavior that is the object and intent of your suspicion.   9 so great so great as to be that jealous   13 watch stay awake.   wake revel
62.5 Methinks It seems to me   7 for myself (1) by my own reckoning (2) for my own pleasure   8 As as if.   other others   9 glass mirror. indeed as I actually am   10 Beated battered, weather-beaten.   tanned antiquity i.e., leathery old age   12 Self . . . iniquity it would be wicked for the self to love such an aged and unattractive self.   13 thee, my self you, with whom I identify myself.   for as   14 days i.e., youth.

63.1 Against my love Anticipating the time when my beloved friend   2 crushed and o'erworn creased and worn threadbare (like a long-used garment)   5 traveled (1) journeyed (2) labored.   steepy precipitous, i.e., descending swiftly toward death   9 For such a time (Parallel in construction with Against in line 1.)   fortify raise works of defense   10 confounding destroying   11 That so that   12 though i.e., though he cut   13 black (1) inscribed in ink (2) the opposite of fair or beautiful   14 still (1) even in death (2) forever.   green i.e., as in springtime and youth.
64.1 fell cruel   2 The rich . . . age i.e., those monuments that were the product of proud wealth and magnificent outlay in times now past and forgotten   3 sometime formerly   4 brass . . . rage i.e., seemingly indestructible brass subdued by the destructive power of decay   7 of . . . main at the expense of the ocean   8 Increasing . . . store one gaining as the other loses, and losing as the other gains   9 state condition   10 state pomp, greatness; condition in the abstract.   confounded to decay destroyed to the point of being in ruins   12 love beloved friend   13 which cannot choose (Modifies thought.)   14 to have at having
65.1 Since i.e., Since there is neither   3 How . . . plea how against this destructive force can beauty hope to make its case   4 action (1) efficacy (2) case (in law)   6 wrackful destructive

When rocks impregnable are not so stout,  7
Nor gates of steel so strong, but Time decays?  8
Oh, fearful meditation! Where, alack,  9
Shall Time's best jewel from Time's chest lie hid?  10
Or what strong hand can hold his swift foot back?
Or who his spoil of beauty can forbid?  12
    Oh, none, unless this miracle have might,
    That in black ink my love may still shine bright.  14

### 66

Tired with all these, for restful death I cry:  1
As, to behold desert a beggar born,  2
And needy nothing trimmed in jollity,  3
And purest faith unhappily forsworn,  4
And gilded honor shamefully misplaced,  5
And maiden virtue rudely strumpeted,  6
And right perfection wrongfully disgraced,  7
And strength by limping sway disablèd,  8
And art made tongue-tied by authority,  9
And folly doctorlike controlling skill,  10
And simple truth miscalled simplicity,  11
And captive good attending captain ill.  12
    Tired with all these, from these would I be gone,
    Save that, to die, I leave my love alone.  14

### 67

Ah, wherefore with infection should he live,  1
And with his presence grace impiety,
That sin by him advantage should achieve  3
And lace itself with his society?  4
Why should false painting imitate his cheek
And steal dead seeming of his living hue?  6
Why should poor beauty indirectly seek  7
Roses of shadow, since his rose is true?  8

Why should he live, now Nature bankrupt is,  9
Beggared of blood to blush through lively veins,  10
For she hath no exchequer now but his,  11
And, proud of many, lives upon his gains?  12
    Oh, him she stores, to show what wealth she had  13
    In days long since, before these last so bad.  14

### 68

Thus is his cheek the map of days outworn,  1
When beauty lived and died as flowers do now,
Before these bastard signs of fair were born,  3
Or durst inhabit on a living brow;  4
Before the golden tresses of the dead,  5
The right of sepulchers, were shorn away  6
To live a second life on second head;  7
Ere beauty's dead fleece made another gay.  8
In him those holy antique hours are seen  9
Without all ornament, itself and true,  10
Making no summer of another's green,
Robbing no old to dress his beauty new;
    And him as for a map doth Nature store,  13
    To show false art what beauty was of yore.

### 69

Those parts of thee that the world's eye doth view
Want nothing that the thought of hearts can mend;  2
All tongues, the voice of souls, give thee that due,  3
Utt'ring bare truth even so as foes commend.  4
Thy outward thus with outward praise is crowned,  5
But those same tongues that give thee so thine own  6
In other accents do this praise confound  7
By seeing farther than the eye hath shown.
They look into the beauty of thy mind,
And that, in guess, they measure by thy deeds;  10
Then, churls, their thoughts, although their eyes were
    kind,  11
To thy fair flower add the rank smell of weeds.  12

---

**7 stout** sturdy, impregnable   **8 decays** brings about their decay.
**9–10 Where . . . hid?** Where, alas, shall the youth and beauty of my
friend (*Time's best jewel*) be hidden away from being deposited by
Time in its repository of forgetfulness?   **12 spoil** despoliation, ravag-
ing   **14 my love** (1) my beloved friend (2) the love I feel for him
**66.1 all these** i.e., the following   **2 As** for instance, namely. **desert**
one who is deserving   **3 And needy . . . jollity** and empty worthless-
ness adorned in finery   **4 unhappily forsworn** wretchedly and evilly
betrayed   **5 gilded** golden, splendid. (Not here suggesting mere
appearance of splendor.)   **6 strumpeted** accused of profligacy, or
violated   **7 right** true. **disgraced** banished from favor   **8 limping
sway** halting leadership   **9 And art . . . authority** and literature and
learning stifled by censorship   **10 doctorlike** assuming a learned
bearing. **controlling** dominating, curbing   **11 miscalled simplicity**
slandered as foolishness, naiveté   **12 attending** waiting on, subordinated to   **14 to die** in dying
**67.1 wherefore** why. **with infection** i.e., with the world's ills, as
enumerated in the preceding sonnet. **he** i.e., the poet's friend
**3 That . . . achieve** with the result that sin should flourish by being
associated with him   **4 lace . . . society** (1) adorn itself with his company (2) weave its way into his company.   **6 dead seeming of** lifeless
appearance from   **7 poor** inferior. **indirectly** imitatively, or,
falsely   **8 Roses of shadow** i.e., painted roses, cosmetically
applied. **since** (1) just because (2) since after all

**9–12 Why . . . gains?** Why should he continue to live in this bad
world, seeing that Nature has now squandered all her resources of
beauty on him, with no genuine way left to produce a natural blush
on the cheek, since she has no treasury of natural beauty other than
what is vested in him, and, though (falsely) taking pride in her abundance (of offspring), lives solely on the wealth (of beauty) that he
provides?   **13 stores** preserves, keeps in store   **14 last** i.e., recent
days, the present
**68.1 map** embodiment, image   **3 bastard . . . fair** i.e., cosmetics.
**born** (Suggesting also *borne*, "worn.")   **4 inhabit** dwell   **5–7 Before . . .
head** i.e., before the deplorable current fad of making wigs out of dead
persons' hair   **8 gay** lovely, gaudy.   **9 holy antique hours** blessed
ancient times   **10 all** any   **13 store** stock (with beauty) and preserve
**69.2 Want** lack. **mend** improve upon   **3–4 the voice . . . commend**
i.e., uttering heartfelt conviction, allow that as your due, thus saying
what even your enemies would concede to be the bare truth.
**5 outward praise** the kind of praise suited to mere outward qualities
**6 thine own** your due   **7 In other accents** in other terms and with
another emphasis. **confound** confute, undermine   **10 in guess**
reluctantly hazarding an opinion   **11 Then . . . kind** i.e., then,
finding themselves obliged churlishly to contradict the pleasurable
outward impression of you that they received from their eyes
**12 To . . . weeds** i.e., to the flower of your outward beauty, they
contrastingly suggest something putrid within.

But why thy odor matcheth not thy show, 13
The soil is this: that thou dost common grow. 14

## 70

That thou art blamed shall not be thy defect, 1
For slander's mark was ever yet the fair; 2
The ornament of beauty is suspect, 3
A crow that flies in heaven's sweetest air.
So thou be good, slander doth but approve 5
Thy worth the greater, being wooed of time, 6
For canker vice the sweetest buds doth love, 7
And thou present'st a pure unstainèd prime. 8
Thou hast passed by the ambush of young days, 9
Either not assailed, or victor being charged; 10
Yet this thy praise cannot be so thy praise 11
To tie up envy, evermore enlarged. 12
　　If some suspect of ill masked not thy show, 13
　　Then thou alone kingdoms of hearts shouldst owe. 14

## 71

No longer mourn for me when I am dead
Than you shall hear the surly sullen bell 2
Give warning to the world that I am fled
From this vile world, with vilest worms to dwell.
Nay, if you read this line, remember not
The hand that writ it, for I love you so
That I in your sweet thoughts would be forgot
If thinking on me then should make you woe. 8
Oh, if, I say, you look upon this verse
When I perhaps compounded am with clay, 10
Do not so much as my poor name rehearse, 11
But let your love even with my life decay, 12
　　Lest the wise world should look into your moan 13
　　And mock you with me after I am gone. 14

## 72

Oh, lest the world should task you to recite 1
What merit lived in me that you should love,

After my death, dear love, forget me quite;
For you in me can nothing worthy prove— 4
Unless you would devise some virtuous lie
To do more for me than mine own desert,
And hang more praise upon deceasèd I 7
Than niggard truth would willingly impart.
Oh, lest your true love may seem false in this,
That you for love speak well of me untrue, 10
My name be buried where my body is, 11
And live no more to shame nor me nor you. 12
　　For I am shamed by that which I bring forth, 13
　　And so should you, to love things nothing worth. 14

## 73

That time of year thou mayst in me behold
When yellow leaves, or none, or few, do hang
Upon those boughs which shake against the cold,
Bare ruined choirs where late the sweet birds sang. 4
In me thou see'st the twilight of such day
As after sunset fadeth in the west,
Which by and by black night doth take away,
Death's second self, that seals up all in rest. 8
In me thou see'st the glowing of such fire
That on the ashes of his youth doth lie 10
As the deathbed whereon it must expire,
Consumed with that which it was nourished by. 12
　　This thou perceiv'st, which makes thy love more strong,
　　To love that well which thou must leave ere long. 14

## 74

But be contented when that fell arrest 1
Without all bail shall carry me away;
My life hath in this line some interest, 3
Which for memorial still with thee shall stay. 4
When thou reviewest this, thou dost review 5
The very part was consecrate to thee. 6
The earth can have but earth, which is his due; 7
My spirit is thine, the better part of me.

**13–14 But . . . is this** The shameful reason why your reputation does not match your physical beauty is this.　**14 common** cheapened by being too familiar and available to all, inferior (like a weed)
**70.1 defect** fault　**2 mark** target　**3 The . . . suspect** i.e., Beauty is always attended by suspicion (*suspect*), as though suspicion were a necessary ornament to beauty　**5 So** Provided that.　**approve** prove　**6 being . . . time** i.e., being as you are courted by the world　**7 canker vice** i.e., slander, that is like the cankerworm
**8 unstainèd prime** unspotted youth (like the pure, unspoiled flower that attracts the cankerworm)　**9 ambush . . . days** temptations of youth　**10 being charged** when you were assailed　**11–12 Yet . . . enlarged** yet the praise you receive cannot be enough to silence malice, which is always at large to do its worst.　**13 If . . . show** If some suspicion (*suspect*) of ill doing did not partly obscure your outward attractiveness　**14 owe** own.
**71.2 bell** a passing bell for one who has died, rung once for each year of that person's life　**8 on** of, about.　**make you woe** cause you woe or make you woeful.　**10 compounded** mingled　**11 rehearse** repeat　**12 even with** at the same time as　**13 look . . . moan** investigate the cause of your sorrow　**14 with** because of; for loving; along with
**72.1 recite** tell, enumerate

**4 For . . . prove** for you would not be able to prove me worthy in any way　**7 hang** (as in hanging trophies on a funeral monument)
**10 of me untrue** (1) about me untruly (2) about me, flawed as I am
**11 My name be** let my name be　**12 nor . . . nor** neither . . . nor
**13 that . . . forth** (Perhaps a deprecatory reference to the author's acting and writing of plays, or to his verse and his written work generally.)
**14 should you** i.e., you ought to be ashamed
**73.4 Bare . . . sang** (In their arched shape, the bare trees resemble the church choir where the service is sung; with a hint of *quires*, gatherings of *leaves* [see line 2] in a book or manuscript, and evoking memories of church buildings left in ruins by the dissolution of the monasteries in the English Reformation. *Late* means "lately.")
**8 seals** closes　**10 That** as.　**his** its　**12 with** (1) by (2) along with. (The image in these lines is of the phoenix, a mythical bird imagined to have been reborn out of the fiery ashes in which it expired; see Sonnet 19.4.)　**14 that** (1) me, your beloved friend (2) youth and life itself.　**leave** i.e., lose by the speaker's death
**74.1 be contented . . . arrest** do not be distressed when that cruel arrest (carried out by Death)　**3 line** verse.　**interest** legal concern, right, or title　**4 still** (1) always (2) despite death　**5 reviewest this** see this again (and view it with a critical eye)　**6 part was consecrate** part (of me) that was dedicated solemnly (as in a religious service)
**7 but earth** i.e., my body.　**his** its

So then thou hast but lost the dregs of life,
The prey of worms, my body being dead,
The coward conquest of a wretch's knife,    11
Too base of thee to be rememberèd.    12
    The worth of that is that which it contains,    13
    And that is this, and this with thee remains.    14

### 75

So are you to my thoughts as food to life,    1
Or as sweet-seasoned showers are to the ground.    2
And for the peace of you I hold such strife    3
As twixt a miser and his wealth is found:
Now proud as an enjoyer, and anon    5
Doubting the filching age will steal his treasure;    6
Now counting best to be with you alone,    7
Then bettered that the world may see my pleasure;    8
Sometime all full with feasting on your sight,
And by and by clean starvèd for a look;    10
Possessing or pursuing no delight
Save what is had or must from you be took.    12
    Thus do I pine and surfeit day by day,    13
    Or gluttoning on all, or all away.    14

### 76

Why is my verse so barren of new pride?    1
So far from variation or quick change?    2
Why with the time do I not glance aside    3
To newfound methods and to compounds strange?    4
Why write I still all one, ever the same,    5
And keep invention in a noted weed,    6
That every word doth almost tell my name,
Showing their birth and where they did proceed?    8
Oh, know, sweet love, I always write of you,
And you and love are still my argument;    10
So all my best is dressing old words new,
Spending again what is already spent.
    For as the sun is daily new and old,    13
    So is my love still telling what is told.    14

### 77

Thy glass will show thee how thy beauties wear,    1
Thy dial how thy precious minutes waste;    2
The vacant leaves thy mind's imprint will bear,    3
And of this book this learning mayst thou taste:    4
The wrinkles which thy glass will truly show
Of mouthèd graves will give thee memory;    6
Thou by thy dial's shady stealth mayst know    7
Time's thievish progress to eternity.
Look what thy memory cannot contain    9
Commit to these waste blanks, and thou shalt find    10
Those children nursed, delivered from thy brain,    11
To take a new acquaintance of thy mind.    12
    These offices, so oft as thou wilt look,    13
    Shall profit thee and much enrich thy book.    14

### 78

So oft have I invoked thee for my Muse
And found such fair assistance in my verse    2
As every alien pen hath got my use    3
And under thee their poesy disperse.    4
Thine eyes, that taught the dumb on high to sing    5
And heavy ignorance aloft to fly,
Have added feathers to the learnèd's wing    7
And given grace a double majesty.    8
Yet be most proud of that which I compile,    9
Whose influence is thine and born of thee.    10
In others' works thou dost but mend the style,    11
And arts with thy sweet graces gracèd be;    12
    But thou art all my art, and dost advance    13
    As high as learning my rude ignorance.

### 79

Whilst I alone did call upon thy aid,
My verse alone had all thy gentle grace,    2
But now my gracious numbers are decayed,    3
And my sick Muse doth give another place.    4

11 **The coward . . . knife** i.e., the cowardly conquest that even such a poor wretch as Mortality, or Death, can make with his scythe    **12 of . . . rememberèd** to be remembered by you.    **13–14 The worth . . . remains** The only worth of my body is the spirit it contains, i.e., this verse, which will remain with you and endure through you.
**75.1 as food to life** what food is to life    **2 sweet-seasoned** of the sweet season, i.e., spring    **3 of you** to be found in loving you    **5 proud . . . enjoyer** proud to be wealthy    **6 Doubting** suspecting, fearing that.    **filching** thieving    **7 counting** (1) thinking it (2) reckoning, like a miser    **8 bettered** made happier, better pleased.    **see my pleasure** i.e., see me with you, enjoying your company    **10 clean** completely, absolutely.    **a look** (1) a glimpse of you (2) an exchange of glances    **12 Save . . . took** except what is had or must be received from you alone.    **13 pine and surfeit** starve and overeat    **14 Or . . . or** either . . . or.    **all away** i.e., deprived of all food.
**76.1 pride** ornament.    **2 quick change** fashionable innovation.    **3 time** way of the world, fashion    **4 compounds strange** literary inventions, or perhaps, compound words, neologisms.    **5 still all one** continually one way    **6 invention** literary creation.    **noted weed** familiar garment    **8 where** whence    **10 still** always.    **argument** subject, theme    **13 daily new and old** daily rising and setting    **14 telling** (1) retelling (2) counting over. (Continuing the financial wordplay of *Spending* and *spent* in line 12, and *counting* in 75.7.)

**77.1 glass** mirror.    **wear** wear away    **2 dial** sundial    **3 vacant leaves** blank pages. (Apparently these lines accompanied the gift of a book of blank pages, a memorandum book.)    **thy mind's imprint** i.e., your reflections and ideas, to be set down in the memorandum book    **4 this learning** i.e., mental profit derived from reflecting and keeping a journal, as explained in lines 9 ff.    **6 mouthèd** all-devouring, gaping.    **memory** reminder    **7 shady stealth** stealing shadow    **9 Look what** Whatever    **10 waste blanks** blank pages    **10–12 thou . . . mind** you will see those thoughts, the children of your brain, nursed to maturity and ready to be newly reencountered by your mind.    **13 offices** duties (of meditation and reflection)    **14 thy book** i.e., the memorandum book, where these reflections are to be set down.
**78.2 fair** favorable    **3 As** that.    **alien** belonging to others.    **got my use** adopted my practice    **4 under thee** i.e., with you as their muse or patron; under your influence.    **disperse** circulate.    **5 on high** aloud. (Also anticipating *aloft*.)    **7 added . . . wing** i.e., enabled learned poets to fly higher still. (A falconry metaphor; birds could be given extra wing feathers.)    **8 And . . . majesty** and have added to the majesty of poets already capable of it.    **9 compile** compose, write    **10 influence** inspiration. (With suggestion of astrological meaning.)    **11 mend the style** correct or improve the style. (Also with a suggestion of repairing the point of a writing quill or stylus, continuing the metaphor of *pen* and *feathers*.)    **12 arts** learning, literary culture    **13 advance** lift up
**79.2 had . . . grace** enjoyed your gracious endorsement    **3 my . . . decayed** my poetry is no longer in favor with you    **4 doth . . . place** yields place to another.

I grant, sweet love, thy lovely argument 5
Deserves the travail of a worthier pen, 6
Yet what of thee thy poet doth invent 7
He robs thee of and pays it thee again. 8
He lends thee virtue, and he stole that word
From thy behavior; beauty doth he give,
And found it in thy cheek; he can afford 11
No praise to thee but what in thee doth live.
  Then thank him not for that which he doth say,
  Since what he owes thee thou thyself dost pay.

## 80

Oh, how I faint when I of you do write, 1
Knowing a better spirit doth use your name, 2
And in the praise thereof spends all his might
To make me tongue-tied, speaking of your fame!
But since your worth, wide as the ocean is, 5
The humble as the proudest sail doth bear, 6
My saucy bark, inferior far to his, 7
On your broad main doth willfully appear. 8
Your shallowest help will hold me up afloat, 9
Whilst he upon your soundless deep doth ride; 10
Or, being wrecked, I am a worthless boat, 11
He of tall building and of goodly pride. 12
  Then if he thrive and I be cast away, 13
  The worst was this: my love was my decay.

## 81

Or I shall live your epitaph to make, 1
Or you survive when I in earth am rotten,
From hence your memory death cannot take, 3
Although in me each part will be forgotten. 4
Your name from hence immortal life shall have, 5
Though I, once gone, to all the world must die;
The earth can yield me but a common grave,
When you entombèd in men's eyes shall lie.
Your momument shall be my gentle verse,
Which eyes not yet created shall o'erread,
And tongues to be your being shall rehearse 11
When all the breathers of this world are dead. 12
  You still shall live—such virtue hath my pen— 13
  Where breath most breathes, even in the mouths of
   men. 14

## 82

I grant thou wert not married to my Muse,
And therefore mayst without attaint o'erlook 2
The dedicated words which writers use 3
Of their fair subject, blessing every book. 4
Thou art as fair in knowledge as in hue, 5
Finding thy worth a limit past my praise, 6
And therefore art enforced to seek anew
Some fresher stamp of these time-bettering days. 8
And do so, love; yet when they have devised
What strainèd touches rhetoric can lend,
Thou, truly fair, wert truly sympathized 11
In true plain words by thy true-telling friend;
  And their gross painting might be better used 13
  Where cheeks need blood; in thee it is abused. 14

## 83

I never saw that you did painting need, 1
And therefore to your fair no painting set; 2
I found, or thought I found, you did exceed
The barren tender of a poet's debt; 4
And therefore have I slept in your report, 5
That you yourself, being extant, well might show 6
How far a modern quill doth come too short, 7
Speaking of worth, what worth in you doth grow. 8
This silence for my sin you did impute, 9
Which shall be most my glory, being dumb; 10
For I impair not beauty, being mute, 11
When others would give life and bring a tomb. 12
  There lives more life in one of your fair eyes
  Than both your poets can in praise devise. 14

## 84

Who is it that says most which can say more 1
Than this rich praise: that you alone are you, 2
In whose confine immurèd is the store 3
Which should example where your equal grew? 4

5 **thy lovely argument** the theme of your lovable qualities   6 **travail** labor   7–8 **Yet . . . again** yet whatever a poet under your patronage discovers as a literary subject concerning you he merely robs from you and gives you back your own again.   11 **afford** furnish, extend 80.1 **faint** grow weak, falter   2 **better spirit** i.e., rival poet, whom the speaker admires   5 **wide . . . is** as wide as is the ocean   6 **The humble . . . bear** carries on its broad surface both the most humble and the proudest sail, i.e., provides patronage for writers of low and high abilities 7 **bark** ship   8 **main** ocean.   **willfully** perversely, audaciously 9 **Your . . . afloat** i.e., My slight genius can derive only a slight benefit from your support   10 **soundless** unfathomable   11 **wrecked** ship-wrecked   12 **He . . . building** whereas he is of sturdy construction. **pride** splendor.   13 **cast away** (1) shipwrecked (2) abandoned 81.1 **Or** Whether   3 **hence** (1) this poetry (2) the world   4 **in . . . part** every quality of mine (as distinguished from the poetry)   5 **from hence** (1) from this poetry (2) henceforth   11 **to be** i.e., of persons yet unborn.   **rehearse** recite   12 **breathers** living people.   **this world** this present time   13 **virtue** power   14 **even in the** in the very

82.2 **attaint** blame, discredit.   **o'erlook** look at, peruse   3 **dedicated** devoted. (With suggestion of "dedicatory.")   **writers** i.e., other writers 4 **blessing every book** i.e., you bestowing favor thus on the writings presented to you, or, writers commending their own work.   5 **hue** complexion, appearance   6 **a limit . . . praise** a region extending beyond the capacities of my praise   8 **Some . . . days** some more recently issued imprint or commendation of this culturally sophisti-cated age.   11 **wert truly sympathized** would be more faithfully described   13 **gross painting** flattery that is heavily laid on, like a cosmetic   14 **Where . . . blood** on pale cheeks in need of cosmetic reddening.   **abused** wrongly applied.
83.1 **painting** i.e., artificial enhancement of beauty   2 **fair** beauty. **set** applied   4 **The barren . . . debt** the worthless homage that a poet can offer you   5 **slept . . . report** been neglectful in writing praisingly of you   6 **That** so that.   **extant** still alive and much in the public eye   7 **modern** (1) commonplace (2) fashionable   7–8 **doth come . . . grow** comes too short, in describing your worth, of the actual worth that flourishes in you.   9–10 **This . . . dumb** You imputed my silence to willful failure when, in fact, it will prove most to my credit 11 **being mute** (Modifies *I*.)   12 **bring a tomb** i.e., instead, they bring forth an inadequate monument that conceals lifelessly rather than enhances.   14 **both your poets** i.e., (probably,) I and the rival poet 84.1–2 **Who . . . praise** What extravagant writer of praise can say more than this in way of praise   3–4 **In . . . grew** in whose person are contained all those rich qualities that would be needed as a model to produce again your equal in beauty.

Lean penury within that pen doth dwell                                    5
That to his subject lends not some small glory;                           6
But he that writes of you, if he can tell
That you are you, so dignifies his story.                                 8
Let him but copy what in you is writ,
Not making worse what nature made so clear,                              10
And such a counterpart shall fame his wit,                               11
Making his style admirèd everywhere.
    You to your beauteous blessings add a curse,                         13
    Being fond on praise, which makes your praises
        worse.                                                           14

### 85

My tongue-tied Muse in manners holds her still,                           1
While comments of your praise, richly compiled,                           2
Reserve thy character with golden quill                                   3
And precious phrase by all the Muses filed.                               4
I think good thoughts whilst other write good words,                      5
And like unlettered clerk still cry "Amen"                                6
To every hymn that able spirit affords                                    7
In polished form of well-refinèd pen.
Hearing you praised, I say "'Tis so, 'tis true,"
And to the most of praise add something more;                            10
But that is in my thought, whose love to you,                            11
Though words come hindmost, holds his rank before.                       12
    Then others for the breath of words respect,                         13
    Me for my dumb thoughts, speaking in effect.                         14

### 86

Was it the proud full sail of his great verse,                            1
Bound for the prize of all-too-precious you,                              2
That did my ripe thoughts in my brain inhearse,                           3
Making their tomb the womb wherein they grew?                             4
Was it his spirit, by spirits taught to write                             5
Above a mortal pitch, that struck me dead?                                6
No, neither he, nor his compeers by night                                 7
Giving him aid, my verse astonishèd.                                      8
He, nor that affable familiar ghost                                       9

Which nightly gulls him with intelligence,                               10
As victors, of my silence cannot boast;
I was not sick of any fear from thence.                                  12
    But when your countenance filled up his line,                        13
    Then lacked I matter; that enfeebled mine.                           14

### 87

Farewell! Thou art too dear for my possessing,                            1
And like enough thou know'st thy estimate.                                2
The charter of thy worth gives thee releasing;                            3
My bonds in thee are all determinate.                                     4
For how do I hold thee but by thy granting,
And for that riches where is my deserving?
The cause of this fair gift in me is wanting,                             7
And so my patent back again is swerving.                                  8
Thyself thou gav'st, thy own worth then not knowing,
Or me, to whom thou gav'st it, else mistaking;                           10
So thy great gift, upon misprision growing,                              11
Comes home again, on better judgment making.                             12
    Thus have I had thee as a dream doth flatter,                        13
    In sleep a king, but waking no such matter.

### 88

When thou shalt be disposed to set me light                               1
And place my merit in the eye of scorn,
Upon thy side against myself I'll fight                                    3
And prove thee virtuous, though thou art forsworn.
With mine own weakness being best acquainted,
Upon thy part I can set down a story
Of faults concealed, wherein I am attainted,                              7
That thou in losing me shall win much glory.                              8
And I by this will be a gainer too;
For, bending all my loving thoughts on thee,
The injuries that to myself I do,
Doing thee vantage, double-vantage me.                                   12
    Such is my love, to thee I so belong,
    That for thy right myself will bear all wrong.

### 89

Say that thou didst forsake me for some fault,                            1
And I will comment upon that offense;                                     2
Speak of my lameness, and I straight will halt,                           3

5–6 **Lean . . . glory** It is a poor piece of writing indeed that does not confer at least some glory on its subject    **8 so** sufficiently, thus    **10 clear** glorious, shining    **11 counterpart** copy, likeness.    **fame** endow with fame    **13 curse** (1) defect in character (2) burden for those seeking to praise you    **14 Being fond** doting.    **which . . . worse** (1) which encourages false flattery (2) which makes all praise seem inadequate in comparison to you.
**85.1 in . . . still** tactfully remains silent    **2 comments . . . compiled** eulogies of you composed in fine language    **3 Reserve thy character** store up praise of you in their writings.    **golden** aureate, affected    **4 precious** affected.    **filed** polished.    **5 other** others    **6–7 like . . . affords** like an illiterate assistant to a priest continually give my approval to every praising verse that the rival poet (and others like him) provides    **10 most** highmost    **11 that . . . thought** that which I add is added silently    **12 holds . . . before** is second to none in love.    **13 Then . . . respect** Then take notice of others for what they say    **14 speaking in effect** conveying what speech would say.
**86.1 his** i.e., an unidentified rival poet's    **2 prize** capture, booty (as in a seized cargo vessel)    **3 inhearse** coffin up    **4 Making . . . grew?** causing those thoughts to die unspoken where they began, in my brain?    **5 spirits** i.e., literary ancestors or contemporaries. (With a suggestion also of *daemons*, attendant spirits.)    **6 pitch** height. (A term from falconry.)    **dead** i.e., dumb, silent.    **7 compeers by night** spirits (see line 5) visiting and aiding the rival poet in his dreams or nighttime reading    **8 astonishèd** struck dumb.    **9 ghost** spirit (as in lines 5 and 7)

**10 gulls** misleads.    **intelligence** information, ideas    **12 of** with    **13 countenance filled up** (1) approval repaired any defect in (2) beauty served as subject for    **14 lacked I matter** I had nothing left to write about    **87.1 dear** precious    **2 like** likely, probably.    **estimate** value.    **3 charter of** privilege derived from.    **releasing** i.e., release from obligations of love    **4 determinate** ended, expired. (A legal term, as throughout this sonnet.)    **7 wanting** lacking    **8 my . . . swerving** my rights of possession revert to you.    **10 mistaking** i.e., overvaluing    **11 upon misprision growing** arising out of error    **12 on . . . making** on your forming a more accurate judgment.    **13 flatter** giving false hope    **88.1 set me light** make light of me, value me slightingly    **3 Upon thy side** supporting your case. (Also *Upon thy part* in line 6.)    **7 concealed** not publicly known.    **attainted** dishonored    **8 That** so that.    **losing** i.e., separating from. (With a suggestion of "loosing," "setting free," the quarto spelling.)    **12 vantage** advantage    **89.1 Say** Assert, claim    **2 comment** enlarge    **3 Speak . . . halt** i.e., if you ascribe to me any kind of handicap, I immediately will limp to show that you are right. (*Halt* also has the suggestion of ceasing to object, remaining silent.)

Against thy reasons making no defense.     4
Thou canst not, love, disgrace me half so ill,     5
To set a form upon desirèd change,     6
As I'll myself disgrace, knowing thy will.     7
I will acquaintance strangle and look strange,     8
Be absent from thy walks, and in my tongue     9
Thy sweet belovèd name no more shall dwell,
Lest I, too much profane, should do it wrong
And haply of our old acquaintance tell.     12
     For thee against myself I'll vow debate,     13
     For I must ne'er love him whom thou dost hate.

## 90

Then hate me when thou wilt; if ever, now;
Now, while the world is bent my deeds to cross,     2
Join with the spite of fortune, make me bow,
And do not drop in for an after-loss.     4
Ah, do not, when my heart hath scaped this sorrow,     5
Come in the rearward of a conquered woe;     6
Give not a windy night a rainy morrow,     7
To linger out a purposed overthrow.     8
If thou wilt leave me, do not leave me last,
When other petty griefs have done their spite,
But in the onset come; so shall I taste     11
At first the very worst of fortune's might,
     And other strains of woe, which now seem woe,     13
     Compared with loss of thee will not seem so.

## 91

Some glory in their birth, some in their skill,
Some in their wealth, some in their body's force,
Some in their garments, though newfangled ill,     3
Some in their hawks and hounds, some in their horse;     4
And every humor hath his adjunct pleasure,     5
Wherein it finds a joy above the rest.
But these particulars are not my measure;     7
All these I better in one general best.     8
Thy love is better than high birth to me,
Richer than wealth, prouder than garments' cost,     10
Of more delight than hawks or horses be;
And having thee, of all men's pride I boast—     12
     Wretched in this alone, that thou mayst take
     All this away and me most wretched make.

## 92

But do thy worst to steal thyself away,     1
For term of life thou art assurèd mine,     2
And life no longer than thy love will stay,     3
For it depends upon that love of thine.
Then need I not to fear the worst of wrongs,     5
When in the least of them my life hath end;     6
I see a better state to me belongs     7
Than that which on thy humor doth depend.     8
Thou canst not vex me with inconstant mind,
Since that my life on thy revolt doth lie.     10
Oh, what a happy title do I find,     11
Happy to have thy love, happy to die!     12
     But what's so blessèd-fair that fears no blot?     13
     Thou mayst be false, and yet I know it not.     14

## 93

So shall I live, supposing thou art true,     1
Like a deceivèd husband; so love's face     2
May still seem love to me, though altered new,     3
Thy looks with me, thy heart in other place.
For there can live no hatred in thine eye,     5
Therefore in that I cannot know thy change.     6
In many's looks the false heart's history
Is writ in moods and frowns and wrinkles strange,     8
But heaven in thy creation did decree
That in thy face sweet love should ever dwell;
Whate'er thy thoughts or thy heart's workings be,
Thy looks should nothing thence but sweetness tell.
     How like Eve's apple doth thy beauty grow,
     If thy sweet virtue answer not thy show!     14

## 94

They that have power to hurt and will do none,     1
That do not do the thing they most do show,     2
Who, moving others, are themselves as stone,
Unmovèd, cold, and to temptation slow,     4
They rightly do inherit heaven's graces     5
And husband nature's riches from expense;     6

---

**4 reasons** charges, arguments   **5 disgrace** discredit   **6 To . . . change** to provide a pretext for (in the interest of justifying) your change of affection and to set it in proper order   **7 As . . . disgrace** as I will disfigure and depreciate myself   **8 acquaintance strangle** put an end to familiarity (with you).   **look strange** act like a stranger   **9 walks** haunts   **12 haply** perchance   **13 vow debate** declare hostility, quarrel   **90.2 bent** determined.   **cross** thwart   **4 drop . . . after-loss** crushingly add to my sorrow.   **5–6 do not . . . woe** do not, when I have just recovered from my present grief, attack me from the rear   **7 windy, rainy** (Suggestive of sighs and tears.)   **8 linger out** protract.   **purposed** intended, inevitable   **11 in the onset** at the outset   **13 strains** (1) kinds (2) stresses   **91.3 newfangled ill** fashionably unattractive   **4 horse** horses   **5 humor** disposition, temperament.   **his adjunct** its corresponding   **7 measure** standard (of happiness); lot in life   **8 better** surpass, improve upon   **10 prouder** more splendid.   **garments' cost** costly garments   **12 of . . . boast** I boast of having the equivalent of everything that other men take pride in

**92.1 But do** i.e., But even if you do   **2 term of life** i.e., my lifetime   **3 And life . . . stay** i.e., I will live no longer if your love ceases   **5–6 Then . . . end** I need not fear what most people would call the worst of misfortunes, since the seemingly lesser misfortune—loss of your friendship—would prove fatal to me   **7–8 I see . . . depend** i.e., I see that I am happier than most people whose happiness ends when they are cast from favor, since my very existence will cease when I am cast from favor and thus will end my misery.   **humor** whim, fancy   **10 Since . . . lie** since if you desert me it will cost me my life.   **11 happy title** right to be thought happy; fortunate legal right of ownership   **12 happy to die** (if your love for me should cease).   **13 that fears** as to fear   **14 Thou . . . not** i.e., My worst fate would be to lose your affection without knowing it and thereby live on in an unloved state, unreleased by the death that certainty of your desertion would bring.   **93.1 So** (Continues the thought of sonnet 92.)   **supposing** I supposing (incorrectly)   **2 face** appearance   **3 new** to something new   **5 For** Since   **6 in . . . change** I won't be able to detect your changed affection from your eyes.   **8 moods** moody looks.   **strange** unfriendly   **14 answer . . . show** does not conform with your outward appearance.   **94.1 and . . . none** and do not willfully try to do hurt   **2 show** i.e., show themselves capable of and imply by their looks   **4 cold** dispassionate   **5 inherit** (1) receive through inheritance (2) enjoy, make use of   **6 husband** carefully manage, preserve.   **expense** waste, expenditure

They are the lords and owners of their faces, 7
Others but stewards of their excellence. 8
The summer's flower is to the summer sweet, 9
Though to itself it only live and die, 10
But if that flower with base infection meet,
The basest weed outbraves his dignity. 12
    For sweetest things turn sourest by their deeds;
    Lilies that fester smell far worse than weeds. 14

## 95

How sweet and lovely dost thou make the shame
Which, like a canker in the fragrant rose, 2
Doth spot the beauty of thy budding name! 3
Oh, in what sweets dost thou thy sins enclose!
That tongue that tells the story of thy days,
Making lascivious comments on thy sport, 6
Cannot dispraise, but, in a kind of praise,
Naming thy name, blesses an ill report. 8
Oh, what a mansion have those vices got
Which for their habitation chose out thee,
Where beauty's veil doth cover every blot,
And all things turns to fair that eyes can see! 12
    Take heed, dear heart, of this large privilege; 13
    The hardest knife ill used doth lose his edge. 14

## 96

Some say thy fault is youth, some wantonness; 1
Some say thy grace is youth and gentle sport; 2
Both grace and faults are loved of more and less; 3
Thou mak'st faults graces that to thee resort. 4
As on the finger of a thronèd queen
The basest jewel will be well esteemed,
So are those errors that in thee are seen
To truths translated and for true things deemed. 8
How many lambs might the stern wolf betray, 9
If like a lamb he could his looks translate! 10
How many gazers mightst thou lead away, 11
If thou wouldst use the strength of all thy state! 12
    But do not so; I love thee in such sort 13
    As, thou being mine, mine is thy good report. 14

## 97

How like a winter hath my absence been
From thee, the pleasure of the fleeting year!
What freezings have I felt, what dark days seen!
What old December's bareness everywhere!
And yet this time removed was summer's time, 5
The teeming autumn, big with rich increase, 6
Bearing the wanton burden of the prime, 7
Like widowed wombs after their lords' decease.
Yet this abundant issue seemed to me 9
But hope of orphans and unfathered fruit, 10
For summer and his pleasures wait on thee, 11
And, thou away, the very birds are mute;
    Or, if they sing, 'tis with so dull a cheer 13
    That leaves look pale, dreading the winter's near.

## 98

From you have I been absent in the spring,
When proud-pied April, dressed in all his trim, 2
Hath put a spirit of youth in everything,
That heavy Saturn laughed and leapt with him. 4
Yet nor the lays of birds nor the sweet smell 5
Of different flowers in odor and in hue 6
Could make me any summer's story tell, 7
Or from their proud lap pluck them where they grew. 8
Nor did I wonder at the lily's white,
Nor praise the deep vermilion in the rose;
They were but sweet, but figures of delight 11
Drawn after you, you pattern of all those. 12
    Yet seemed it winter still, and, you away,
    As with your shadow I with these did play. 14

## 99

The forward violet thus did I chide: 1
"Sweet thief, whence didst thou steal thy sweet that
    smells, 2
If not from my love's breath? The purple pride 3
Which on thy soft cheek for complexion dwells
In my love's veins thou hast too grossly dyed." 5
The lily I condemnèd for thy hand, 6
And buds of marjoram had stol'n thy hair; 7
The roses fearfully on thorns did stand, 8

**7 They . . . faces** they are completely masters of themselves and of the qualities that appear in them   **8 but stewards** are merely custodians or dispensers   **9–10 The summer's . . . die** i.e., Such self-contained persons may seem like flowers that live and die unto themselves, though having much sweetness and beauty to bestow   **12 outbraves his dignity** surpasses in show its worth.   **14 Lilies . . . weeds** (This line appears in the anonymous play *Edward III*, usually dated before 1595 and attributed in part by some editors to Shakespeare.)
**95.2 canker** cankerworm that destroys buds and leaves   **3 name** reputation.   **6 sport** amours   **8 blesses** graces   **12 all . . . fair** makes everything deceptively beautiful   **13 large** unlimited, licentious   **14 his** its
**96.1 wantonness** (1) exuberance (2) lechery   **2 gentle sport** gentlemanlike amorousness   **3 of more and less** by high and low   **4 Thou . . . resort** you convert into graces the faults that attend you.   **8 translated** transformed   **9 stern** cruel   **10 like** i.e., unto those of   **11 away** astray   **12 the strength . . . state** the full power at your command, i.e., your wealth, charm, and social rank.   **13–14 But . . . report** (The same couplet ends sonnet 36.)   **report** reputation.

**97.5 time removed** time of separation   **6 big** pregnant   **7 the wanton . . . prime** the fruit or offspring of wanton spring, i.e., the crops planted in springtime   **9 issue** offspring   **10 hope of orphans** orphaned hope   **11 his** its.   **wait on thee** attend on you, are at your disposal   **13 with . . . cheer** in so melancholy a fashion
**98.2 proud-pied** gorgeously multicolored.   **trim** finery   **4 That** so that even.   **Saturn** (A planet associated with melancholy, *heavy*.)   **5 nor the lays** neither the songs   **6 different flowers** flowers differing   **7 any summer's story** i.e., any pleasant story   **8 proud lap** i.e., the ground   **11 but sweet . . . delight** mere sweetness, mere delightful forms or emblems   **12 after** resembling   **14 shadow** image, portrait.   **these** i.e., the flowers
**99.1 forward** early and presumptuous. (This sonnet has fifteen lines, the first being introductory.)   **2 thy sweet** your scent   **3 pride** splendor   **5 grossly** obviously and heavily   **6 for thy hand** i.e., because it has stolen its whiteness from your hand   **7 And . . . hair** i.e., and I condemned the buds of marjoram for having stolen your hair.   **buds of marjoram** (These are dark purple-red or auburn, and it may be that the reference is to color, although marjoram is noted for its sweet scent.)   **8 on thorns did stand** grew on thorny stems. (With a suggestion of being apprehensive.)

One blushing shame, another white despair;   9
A third, nor red nor white, had stol'n of both   10
And to his robbery had annexed thy breath;   11
But, for his theft, in pride of all his growth   12
A vengeful canker ate him up to death.   13
> More flowers I noted, yet I none could see
> But sweet or color it had stol'n from thee.   15

## 100

Where art thou, Muse, that thou forget'st so long
To speak of that which gives thee all thy might?
Spend'st thou thy fury on some worthless song,   3
Dark'ning thy pow'r to lend base subjects light?   4
Return, forgetful Muse, and straight redeem   5
In gentle numbers time so idly spent;   6
Sing to the ear that doth thy lays esteem   7
And gives thy pen both skill and argument.   8
Rise, resty Muse, my love's sweet face survey   9
If Time have any wrinkle graven there;   10
If any, be a satire to decay,   11
And make Time's spoils despisèd everywhere.   12
> Give my love fame faster than Time wastes life;   13
> So thou prevent'st his scythe and crooked knife.   14

## 101

O truant Muse, what shall be thy amends   1
For thy neglect of truth in beauty dyed?   2
Both truth and beauty on my love depends;   3
So dost thou too, and therein dignified.   4
Make answer, Muse. Wilt thou not haply say,   5
"Truth needs no color with his color fixed,   6
Beauty no pencil, beauty's truth to lay,   7
But best is best, if never intermixed"?   8
Because he needs no praise, wilt thou be dumb?   9
Excuse not silence so, for't lies in thee
To make him much outlive a gilded tomb
And to be praised of ages yet to be.   12
> Then do thy office, Muse; I teach thee how   13
> To make him seem, long hence, as he shows now.   14

## 102

My love is strengthened, though more weak in seeming;   1
I love not less, though less the show appear.
That love is merchandized whose rich esteeming   3
The owner's tongue doth publish everywhere.   4
Our love was new and then but in the spring   5
When I was wont to greet it with my lays,   6
As Philomel in summer's front doth sing   7
And stops her pipe in growth of riper days—   8
Not that the summer is less pleasant now
Than when her mournful hymns did hush the night,
But that wild music burdens every bough   11
And sweets grown common lose their dear delight.
> Therefore like her I sometime hold my tongue,
> Because I would not dull you with my song.   14

## 103

Alack, what poverty my Muse brings forth,   1
That, having such a scope to show her pride,   2
The argument all bare is of more worth   3
Than when it hath my added praise beside.   4
Oh, blame me not if I no more can write!   5
Look in your glass, and there appears a face   6
That overgoes my blunt invention quite,   7
Dulling my lines and doing me disgrace.   8
Were it not sinful then, striving to mend,   9
To mar the subject that before was well?
For to no other pass my verses tend   11
Than of your graces and your gifts to tell;
> And more, much more, than in my verse can sit   13
> Your own glass shows you when you look in it.

## 104

To me, fair friend, you never can be old,
For, as you were when first your eye I eyed,
Such seems your beauty still. Three winters cold
Have from the forests shook three summers' pride,   4
Three beauteous springs to yellow autumn turned
In process of the seasons have I seen,   6
Three April perfumes in three hot Junes burned
Since first I saw you fresh, which yet are green.   8

9 **shame** i.e., red for shame   10 **nor red** neither (purely) red
11 **to . . . annexed** to this robbery had added the robbery of
12 **But, for** although, in punishment for.   **in pride . . . growth** in its
prime   13 **canker** cankerworm   15 **But . . . thee** that had not stolen
its sweet perfume (compare line 2) and color from you.
**100.3 fury** poetic inspiration   4 **Dark'ning** debasing   5 **straight**
straightaway   6 **gentle numbers** noble verses.   **idly** foolishly
7 **lays** songs   8 **argument** subject.   9 **resty** inactive, lazy   10 **If to**
see if   11 **If any** if there are any.   **satire to** satirist of, here one composing a satire on Time as a despoiler   12 **spoils** acts of destruction,
ravages   13 **faster** (1) more quickly (2) more firmly   14 **thou**
**prevent'st** you forestall, thwart.   **crooked knife** curved blade.
**101.1 what . . . amends** what reparation will you make   2 **truth . . .**
**dyed** truth made integrally a part of the beauty which it inhabits.
3–4 **Both . . . dignified** i.e., Both faith and beauty depend on my love
for their proper appreciation and recognition, and you, my Muse,
depend for your very office and dignity on that same function.
5 **haply** perhaps   6 **no . . . fixed** no artificial color (with suggestion of
*pretense*) added to his natural and permanent color or hue   7 **Beauty . . .**
**lay** beauty needs no paintbrush to apply artificial color to his true and
natural coloring   8 **intermixed** adulterated with cosmetics   9 **dumb**
silent.   12 **of** by   13 **office** function   14 **long hence** long in the
future.   **shows** appears

102.1 **seeming** outward appearance   3 **merchandized** degraded by
being treated as a thing for sale.   **esteeming** valuation   4 **publish**
announce, advertise   5 **in the spring** only just beginning   6 **wont . . .**
**lays** accustomed to salute it (our love) with my song   7 **Philomel** the
nightingale.   **front** forehead, beginning   8 **stops her pipe** stops
singing.   **riper** i.e., those of late summer and autumn   11 **But . . .**
**music** i.e., but because a profusion of wild birds' singing. (Refers to
other poets.)   **burdens** weighs down. (But with a musical sense as
well; a *burden* is a chorus.)   14 **dull** surfeit
103.1 **poverty** poor stuff   2 **pride** splendor   3–4 **The argument . . .**
**beside** the subject of your beauteous excellence is, all by itself, more
worthy than what my praise can add.   5 **no more can write** i.e., (1) am
silent (2) cannot go beyond what you yourself are, cannot excel my own
poverty of invention.   6 **glass** mirror   7 **That . . . quite** that entirely
surpasses anything my dull powers of poetic invention can achieve
8 **Dulling** i.e., making dull by comparison   9 **Were it not** would it not
be.   **mend** improve   11 **pass** purpose, issue   13 **sit** reside
104.4 **pride** splendor   6 **process** the progression   8 **which yet** who
still

Ah, yet doth beauty, like a dial hand,    9
Steal from his figure and no pace perceived.    10
So your sweet hue, which methinks still doth stand,    11
Hath motion, and mine eye may be deceived,
    For fear of which, hear this, thou age unbred:    13
    Ere you were born was beauty's summer dead.

## 105

Let not my love be called idolatry,
Nor my belovèd as an idol show,    2
Since all alike my songs and praises be
To one, of one, still such, and ever so.    4
Kind is my love today, tomorrow kind,
Still constant in a wondrous excellence;
Therefore my verse, to constancy confined,
One thing expressing, leaves out difference.    8
"Fair, kind, and true" is all my argument,
"Fair, kind, and true" varying to other words;
And in this change is my invention spent,    11
Three themes in one, which wondrous scope affords.
    Fair, kind, and true have often lived alone,    13
    Which three till now never kept seat in one.    14

## 106

When in the chronicle of wasted time    1
I see descriptions of the fairest wights,    2
And beauty making beautiful old rhyme    3
In praise of ladies dead and lovely knights,
Then, in the blazon of sweet beauty's best,    5
Of hand, of foot, of lip, of eye, of brow,
I see their antique pen would have expressed
Even such a beauty as you master now.
So all their praises are but prophecies    8
Of this our time, all you prefiguring;
And, for they looked but with divining eyes,    11
They had not skill enough your worth to sing.
    For we, which now behold these present days,    13
    Have eyes to wonder, but lack tongues to praise.    14

## 107

Not mine own fears nor the prophetic soul    1
Of the wide world dreaming on things to come    2
Can yet the lease of my true love control,    3
Supposed as forfeit to a confined doom.    4
The mortal moon hath her eclipse endured,    5
And the sad augurs mock their own presage;    6
Incertainties now crown themselves assured,    7
And peace proclaims olives of endless age.    8
Now with the drops of this most balmy time    9
My love looks fresh, and Death to me subscribes,    10
Since, spite of him, I'll live in this poor rhyme,
While he insults o'er dull and speechless tribes;    12
    And thou in this shalt find thy monument,
    When tyrants' crests and tombs of brass are spent.    14

## 108

What's in the brain that ink may character    1
Which hath not figured to thee my true spirit?    2
What's new to speak, what now to register,    3
That may express my love or thy dear merit?
Nothing, sweet boy; but yet, like prayers divine,
I must each day say o'er the very same,
Counting no old thing old—thou mine, I thine—    7
Even as when first I hallowed thy fair name.    8
So that eternal love in love's fresh case    9
Weighs not the dust and injury of age,    10
Nor gives to necessary wrinkles place,    11
But makes antiquity for aye his page,    12
    Finding the first conceit of love there bred    13
    Where time and outward form would show it dead.    14

## 109

Oh, never say that I was false of heart,
Though absence seemed my flame to qualify.    2

9–10 yet . . . perceived yet beauty slips almost imperceptibly away, like the dial hand of a watch making its stealthy progress from number to number on the dial face.    11 hue appearance, complexion. still doth stand remains seemingly unaltered    13 unbred not yet born 105.2 show appear    4 To . . . so (The poet loves his friend in phrases that recall the paradoxical and mysterious duality of two in one, as in "The Phoenix and Turtle." Such sacred love, by analogy, cannot be idolatry.)    8 difference diversity of theme and the seeming diversity of two persons (the poet and his friend) who are essentially one; also the seeming diversity of "Fair, kind, and true" which is also a variation on a single theme.    11 this change variations on this theme. invention inventiveness.    spent expended    13 alone separately (in different people)    14 kept seat resided; sat enthroned 106.1 wasted past, used up    2 wights persons    3 beauty (1) beauty of style and language (2) beauty of the persons described    5 blazon i.e., glorification, cataloguing of qualities. (A heraldic metaphor.) 8 master possess, control    11 for because.    divining guessing or predicting as to the future    13 For we For even we    14 praise i.e., praise you worthily, sufficiently.

107.1–2 soul . . . world collective consciousness of humanity 3–4 Can . . . doom can set a limit to the time allotted to me to love you, though imagined to be destined to expire after a limited term. 5 mortal moon (Probably a reference to Queen Elizabeth, ill or deceased, most probably to her death in 1603; she was known as Diana, Cynthia, etc.)    6 And . . . presage and the solemn prophets of disaster now mock their earlier predictions    7 Incertainties . . . assured uncertainties have triumphantly given way to certainties. (Probably a reference to the accession and coronation of King James VI of Scotland and I of England.)    8 olives (Conventionally associated with peace and probably pointing here to King James I's resolutions of war with Spain and strife in Ireland.)    of endless age without foreseen end.    9 with the drops i.e., healed as though by a balmy dew. (Balm was employed in the coronation ceremony for James in 1603, as in all such coronations.)    10 subscribes yields 12 insults . . . tribes triumphs scornfully over endless generations of dead who have no poet to celebrate them    14 crests trophies adorning a tomb.    spent expended, wasted away.
108.1 character write    2 figured revealed, represented.    true constant    3 register record    7 Counting . . . thine dismissing no old truth as out of date or shopworn, such as the truth that you are mine and I yours    8 hallowed (As in "hallowed be thy name" from the Lord's Prayer.)    9 fresh case new exterior and circumstance 10 Weighs not is unconcerned about    11 Nor . . . place nor yields priority to the inevitable wrinkles of old age    12–14 But . . . dead but makes old age forever the servant of eternal love (line 9), finding the first stirrings of love to have been generated in a place (i.e., in the old age of the speaker-poet and in his poetry) where conventionally one might expect to find love to be dead.
109.2 flame passion.    qualify temper, moderate, lessen.

As easy might I from myself depart
As from my soul, which in thy breast doth lie.
That is my home of love; if I have ranged,            5
Like him that travels I return again,
Just to the time, not with the time exchanged,        7
So that myself bring water for my stain.              8
Never believe, though in my nature reigned
All frailties that besiege all kinds of blood,        10
That it could so preposterously be stained
To leave for nothing all thy sum of good;             12
    For nothing this wide universe I call
    Save thou, my rose; in it thou art my all.

## 110

Alas, 'tis true, I have gone here and there
And made myself a motley to the view,                 2
Gored mine own thoughts, sold cheap what is most dear, 3
Made old offenses of affections new;                  4
Most true it is that I have looked on truth           5
Askance and strangely. But, by all above,            6
These blenches gave my heart another youth,           7
And worse essays proved thee my best of love.         8
Now all is done, have what shall have no end.         9
Mine appetite I never more will grind                 10
On newer proof, to try an older friend,               11
A god in love, to whom I am confined.
    Then give me welcome, next my heaven the best,  13
    Even to thy pure and most most loving breast.

## 111

Oh, for my sake do you with Fortune chide,            1
The guilty goddess of my harmful deeds,               2
That did not better for my life provide               3
Than public means which public manners breeds.        4
Thence comes it that my name receives a brand,        5
And almost thence my nature is subdued
To what it works in, like the dyer's hand.            7
Pity me then, and wish I were renewed,                8
Whilst, like a willing patient, I will drink

Potions of eisel 'gainst my strong infection;         10
No bitterness that I will bitter think,               11
Nor double penance, to correct correction.            12
    Pity me then, dear friend, and I assure ye
    Even that your pity is enough to cure me.      14

## 112

Your love and pity doth th'impression fill            1
Which vulgar scandal stamped upon my brow;            2
For what care I who calls me well or ill,
So you o'ergreen my bad, my good allow?               4
You are my all the world, and I must strive           5
To know my shames and praises from your tongue;
None else to me, nor I to none alive,                 7
That my steeled sense or changes, right or wrong.     8
In so profound abysm I throw all care                 9
Of others' voices that my adder's sense               10
To critic and to flatterer stoppèd are.               11
Mark how with my neglect I do dispense:               12
    You are so strongly in my purpose bred         13
    That all the world besides, methinks, are dead. 14

## 113

Since I left you, mine eye is in my mind,             1
And that which governs me to go about                 2
Doth part his function and is partly blind,           3
Seems seeing, but effectually is out;                 4
For it no form delivers to the heart                  5
Of bird, of flower, or shape which it doth latch;     6
Of his quick objects hath the mind no part,           7
Nor his own vision holds what it doth catch;          8
For if it see the rud'st or gentlest sight,           9
The most sweet-favor or deformd'st creature,          10
The mountain or the sea, the day or night,
The crow or dove, it shapes them to your feature.     12

10 **eisel** vinegar, used as an antiseptic against the plague and also as an agent for removing stains   11 **No bitterness** there is no bitterness   12 **Nor . . . correction** nor will I think it bitter to undertake a twofold penance in order to correct what must be doubly corrected. 14 **Even that your pity** that very pity of yours
112.1 **doth th'impression fill** effaces the scar   2 **vulgar scandal** notoriety (for being an actor?)   4 **So you o'ergreen** provided that you cover as with green growth. **allow** approve.   5 **my all the world** everything to me   7–8 **None . . . wrong** no one else but you affects my fixed and hardened sensibilities, whether for better or for worse.   9–11 **In . . . are** Into so deep an abyss do I throw all concern as to what others may think that, adderlike, my ears are deaf to critic and flatterer alike. (Adders were popularly supposed to have no sense of hearing.)   12 **Mark . . . dispense** See how I justify my disregard of the opinion of others   13 **You . . . bred** you are so nurtured in my thoughts and are such a powerful influence over my intentions   14 **That . . . dead** that all people except yourself might just as well not even exist, as far as I'm concerned.
113.1 **mine . . . mind** i.e., I'm guided by my mind's eye   2 **And . . . go about** and it's as though my physical sight, which should steer me on my path   3 **Doth . . . function** divides and abandons its (the eye's) function   4 **Seems . . . out** seems to be seeing, but in reality is blind   5 **heart** (Here portrayed as capable of receiving sense impressions and of consciousness, as in sonnet 47.)   6 **latch** catch or receive the sight of   7 **Of . . . part** i.e., the mind, attuned to its inner eye, takes no part in the fleeting and lively (*quick*) things seen by the physical sight   8 **Nor . . . holds** nor does the eye itself retain. **catch** see glimpsingly   9 **For . . . sight** for whether it see the most uncouth or most gracious sight   10 **sweet-favor** sweet-featured   12 **shapes . . . feature** makes them resemble you.

5 **ranged** traveled, wandered   7 **Just . . . exchanged** punctual to the minute, not changed by the period of separation   8 **water for my stain** i.e., repentant tears, to wash away the stain of my offending absence.   10 **blood** temperament, sensual nature   12 **for** in exchange for
110.2 **motley** jester, fool.   **to the view** in the eyes of the world   3 **Gored** wounded   4 **Made . . . new** i.e., repeated old offenses or made offense against old friendship in forming new attachments   5 **truth** constancy   6 **Askance and strangely** disdainfully, obliquely and at a distance.   **by all above** by heaven   7 **blenches** swervings. **another youth** i.e., a renewal of true friendship   8 **essays** experiments (in friendship)   9 **Now all** Now that all that.   **have what . . . end** take what is eternal (my friendship).   10 **grind** whet, sharpen   11 **newer proof** further experiment, experience.   **try** test   13 **next my heaven** you, who are to me second only to heaven itself
111.1 **do you** (A command: "Do")   2 **guilty goddess of** goddess responsible for   3 **life** livelihood   4 **Than . . . breeds** than providing me a means of livelihood that depends on catering to the public. (A probable reference to Shakespeare's career as an actor.)   5 **receives a brand** is disgraced (through prejudice against my occupation)   7 **like the dyer's hand** (The dyer's hand is stained by the dye it handles, just as the dramatist's or actor's nature is almost overpowered by the medium in which he works—the theater.)   8 **renewed** restored to what I was by nature, cleansed

Incapable of more, replete with you,
My most true mind thus maketh mine eye untrue.

## 114

Or whether doth my mind, being crowned with you,   1
Drink up the monarch's plague, this flattery?   2
Or whether shall I say mine eye saith true,   3
And that your love taught it this alchemy,   4
To make of monsters and things indigest   5
Such cherubins as your sweet self resemble,   6
Creating every bad a perfect best   7
As fast as objects to his beams assemble?   8
Oh, 'tis the first, 'tis flatt'ry in my seeing,   9
And my great mind most kingly drinks it up;   10
Mine eye well knows what with his gust is greeing,   11
And to his palate doth prepare the cup.   12
    If it be poisoned, 'tis the lesser sin   13
    That mine eye loves it and doth first begin.   14

## 115

Those lines that I before have writ do lie,
Even those that said I could not love you dearer;
Yet then my judgment knew no reason why
My most full flame should afterwards burn clearer.
But reckoning Time, whose millioned accidents   5
Creep in twixt vows and change decrees of kings,   6
Tan sacred beauty, blunt the sharp'st intents,   7
Divert strong minds to th' course of alt'ring things—   8
Alas, why, fearing of Time's tyranny,   9
Might I not then say, "Now I love you best,"   10
When I was certain o'er incertainty,   11
Crowning the present, doubting of the rest?   12
    Love is a babe; then might I not say so,   13
    To give full growth to that which still doth grow.   14

## 116

Let me not to the marriage of true minds
Admit impediments. Love is not love   2

Which alters when it alteration finds,   3
Or bends with the remover to remove.   4
Oh, no, it is an ever-fixèd mark   5
That looks on tempests and is never shaken;
It is the star to every wand'ring bark,   7
Whose worth's unknown, although his height be taken.   8
Love's not Time's fool, though rosy lips and cheeks   9
Within his bending sickle's compass come;   10
Love alters not with his brief hours and weeks,
But bears it out even to the edge of doom.   12
    If this be error and upon me proved,
    I never writ, nor no man ever loved.

## 117

Accuse me thus: that I have scanted all   1
Wherein I should your great deserts repay,
Forgot upon your dearest love to call,   3
Whereto all bonds do tie me day by day;
That I have frequent been with unknown minds,   5
And given to time your own dear-purchased right;   6
That I have hoisted sail to all the winds
Which should transport me farthest from your sight.   8
Book both my willfulness and errors down,   9
And on just proof surmise accumulate;   10
Bring me within the level of your frown,   11
But shoot not at me in your wakened hate,
    Since my appeal says I did strive to prove   13
    The constancy and virtue of your love.

## 118

Like as to make our appetites more keen   1
With eager compounds we our palate urge;   2
As to prevent our maladies unseen   3
We sicken to shun sickness when we purge:   4
Even so, being full of your ne'er-cloying sweetness,   5
To bitter sauces did I frame my feeding   6
And, sick of welfare, found a kind of meetness   7

**114.1, 3 Or whether** (Indicates alternative possibilities.)   **1 crowned with you** elevated by possession of you   **2 the monarch's . . . flattery** this pleasing delusion to which all monarchs are prone.   **4 your love** my love of you.  **alchemy** science of transmuting base metals into precious things   **5 indigest** chaotic, formless   **6 cherubins** angelic forms (suggesting the youth and beauty of the friend)   **7 Creating** creating out of   **8 his beams** its (the eye's) gaze   **9 'tis flatt'ry . . . seeing** my eye is flattering my mind (see lines 1–2)   **10 great** self-infatuated   **11 what . . . greeing** what agrees with the mind's taste   **12 to** to suit   **13–14 'tis . . . begin** it extenuates the eye's sinful deed (of misleading the mind) by tasting the poison first, like an official taster sampling food before it is given to the king.
**115.5 reckoning Time** (1) Time, which we reckon up (2) Time, which demands a reckoning and settles all accounts.  **millioned accidents** multitudinous unforeseen occurrences   **6 twixt vows** i.e., between the making of vows and their fulfillment   **7 Tan** darken, i.e., coarsen   **8 Divert . . . things** divert the most resolute of intentions into changing course   **9 fearing of** fearing   **10 Might . . . say** i.e., wasn't it understandable for me to say then, when I wrote *Those lines* (line 1)   **11 certain o'er incertainty** i.e., certain of my love's perfection then, as contrasted with the uncertainty of the future   **12 Crowning** exalting.  **doubting of** fearing   **13 then might . . . so** i.e., therefore I shouldn't have said, "Now I love you best" (line 10)   **14 To give** thereby giving
**116.2 Admit** concede that there might be, allow consideration of. (An echo of the marriage service.)

**3 alteration** i.e., in age, beauty, affection, health, circumstance   **4 Or . . . remove** or changes simply because there is change (by ill health, mental deterioration, death, absence, or inconstancy) in the person loved.   **5 mark** seamark, conspicuous object distinguishable at sea as an aid to navigation   **7 wand'ring bark** lost ship   **8 Whose . . . taken** whose value is beyond estimation, although its altitude above the horizon can be determined (for purposes of navigation).   **9 fool** plaything, laughingstock   **10 his** i.e., Time's. (Also in line 11.)  **bending** curved.  **compass** range   **12 bears . . . doom** endures or holds out to the eve of the Day of Judgment.
**117.1 scanted** come short in   **3 Forgot . . . call** forgot to invoke or call upon your most precious love   **5 frequent** familiar.  **unknown minds** strangers of no consequence   **6 And . . . right** and wasted time that should have been devoted to you, to which you had every right   **8 should** were likely to   **9 Book . . . down** Record both my willful faults and errors   **10 on . . . accumulate** to sure proof add surmise, suspicion   **11 level** point-blank range, aim   **13 appeal** legal appealing of the case.  **I . . . prove** my intention was to test
**118.1 Like as** Just as   **2 eager compounds** pungent, bitter concoctions.  **urge** stimulate   **3 As** just as.  **prevent** anticipate, forestall   **4 We . . . purge** we induce a kind of sickness through purging (i.e., evacuation of stomach or bowel), in order to ward off greater sickness   **5 Even so** in just the same way   **6 bitter sauces** i.e., other loves, undesirable in comparison with you.  **frame** adapt, direct   **7 sick of welfare** surfeited by health and happiness (in love).  **meetness** suitability

To be diseased ere that there was true needing.   8
Thus policy in love, t'anticipate   9
The ills that were not, grew to faults assured,   10
And brought to medicine a healthful state   11
Which, rank of goodness, would by ill be cured.   12
    But thence I learn, and find the lesson true:
    Drugs poison him that so fell sick of you.   14

## 119

What potions have I drunk of siren tears,   1
Distilled from limbecks foul as hell within,   2
Applying fears to hopes and hopes to fears,   3
Still losing when I saw myself to win!   4
What wretched errors hath my heart committed,
Whilst it hath thought itself so blessèd never!   6
How have mine eyes out of their spheres been fitted   7
In the distraction of this madding fever!   8
Oh, benefit of ill! Now I find true
That better is by evil still made better;
And ruined love, when it is built anew,
Grows fairer than at first, more strong, far greater.
    So I return rebuked to my content,
    And gain by ills thrice more than I have spent.

## 120

That you were once unkind befriends me now,   1
And for that sorrow which I then did feel   2
Needs must I under my transgression bow,   3
Unless my nerves were brass or hammered steel.   4
For if you were by my unkindness shaken
As I by yours, you've passed a hell of time,   6
And I, a tyrant, have no leisure taken   7
To weigh how once I suffered in your crime.   8
Oh, that our night of woe might have remembered   9
My deepest sense how hard true sorrow hits,   10
And soon to you, as you to me then, tendered   11

The humble salve which wounded bosoms fits!   12
    But that your trespass now becomes a fee;   13
    Mine ransoms yours, and yours must ransom me.   14

## 121

'Tis better to be vile than vile esteemed   1
When not to be receives reproach of being,   2
And the just pleasure lost which is so deemed   3
Not by our feeling but by others' seeing.   4
For why should others' false adulterate eyes   5
Give salutation to my sportive blood?   6
Or on my frailties why are frailer spies,   7
Which in their wills count bad what I think good?   8
No, I am that I am, and they that level   9
At my abuses reckon up their own.   10
I may be straight though they themselves be bevel.   11
By their rank thoughts my deeds must not be shown,   12
    Unless this general evil they maintain:
    All men are bad, and in their badness reign.   14

## 122

Thy gift, thy tables, are within my brain   1
Full charactered with lasting memory,   2
Which shall above that idle rank remain   3
Beyond all date, even to eternity—
Or at the least, so long as brain and heart
Have faculty by nature to subsist;   6
Till each to razed oblivion yield his part   7
Of thee, thy record never can be missed.   8
That poor retention could not so much hold,   9
Nor need I tallies thy dear love to score;   10
Therefore to give them from me was I bold,   11

**8 ere . . . needing** before there was any real necessity for it.   **9 policy** shortsighted calculation.   **t'anticipate** to forestall   **10 assured** sure to happen   **11 to medicine** into a state of needing medical care   **12 Which . . . cured** which, gorged with good health, sought to be cured by the very opposite of good health.   **14 Drugs . . . you** a rash and unnecessary course of treatment inflicted true sickness on one (myself) who had thought himself weary of your company.
**119.1 siren** i.e., deceitful. (The poet seems to speak of an affair.)
**2 limbecks** vessels used in distillation.   **foul as hell within** i.e., possessing an inner ugliness and evil contrasted with a beautiful and seductive appearance   **3 Applying . . . fears** trying vainly to control my wild hopes with a sense of fear and to assuage my fears with hope   **4 Still** always.   **saw myself** vainly expected   **6 so blessèd never** never before so fortunate.   **7 How . . . fitted** How my eyes have popped out in convulsive fit   **8 distraction** frenzy.   **madding fever** fever that drives me mad.
**120.1 befriends** benefits (by giving me perspective on what I now need to do)   **2–3 for . . . bow** i.e., realizing the sorrow I felt from your unkindness, I must now acknowledge my own guilt in being unkind to you   **4 nerves** sinews   **6 hell of** hellish   **7 have . . . taken** have not taken the opportunity   **8 weigh** consider.   **in your crime** i.e., from your unkindness; or, from erring as you did. (If I suffered so, I should realize you've suffered, too, from my unkindness.)   **9 that our night of woe** would that the dark and woeful time of our earlier estrangement.   **remembered** reminded   **10 sense** consciousness, apprehension   **11 And . . . tendered** i.e., and would that I had quickly offered to you, as you did to me

**12 humble salve** i.e., apology and remorse.   **which . . . fits** which is just what wounded hearts need.   **13 that your trespass** that unkindness of yours.   **fee** payment, compensation   **14 ransoms** redeems, excuses   **121.1 vile esteemed** (to be) considered vile   **2 When . . . being** when not to be vile receives the reproach of vileness. (It's even worse to be unjustly accused of wickedness than to be reproved when one's conduct is truly vile.)   **3–4 And . . . seeing** and to lose justifiable pleasure because its justification has to depend not on our feelings but on the censorious attitudes of others.   **5 false adulterate eyes** i.e., the eyes of those whose own wickedness prompts them to misconstrue my innocent love   **6 Give . . . blood** i.e., greet me, in my lusty merriment, with familiarity and with a knowing wink of the eye.   **7 Or . . . spies** Or why should there be persons more faulty than I spying on my fleshly indulgences   **8 Which in their wills** who by the measure of their prurient, licentious minds   **9 am that** am what.   **level** (1) aim (2) guess   **10 abuses** misdoings.   **reckon up their own** i.e., merely enumerate their own misdeeds.   **11 bevel** out of square, crooked.   **12 rank** ugly, foul.   **shown** viewed, interpreted   **14 reign** i.e., prosper. (Only a cynic would interpret my success in love as a paradoxical proof of my sharing in general human depravity.)
**122.1 tables** writing tablet, memorandum book   **2 charactered with** written by   **3 that idle rank** i.e., the relative unimportance of that memorandum book (as compared with the memory itself)   **6 faculty . . . subsist** natural power to survive   **7–8 Till . . . missed** until both heart and brain have given up their memory of you to the ravages of time, what you have written never can be lost. (Hence the memorandum book itself, which the poet has given away, is not essential.)   **9 retention** i.e., the book, an instrument for retaining memoranda.   **so much** i.e., as much as is in my memory   **10 tallies** sticks notched to serve for reckoning. (The notebook is such a mere *tally*.)   **score** reckon   **11 to . . . me** i.e., to give away the writing tablet.   **bold** i.e., bold in taking the liberty

To trust those tables that receive thee more.    12
    To keep an adjunct to remember thee    13
    Were to import forgetfulness in me.    14

### 123

No, Time, thou shalt not boast that I do change.
Thy pyramids built up with newer might    2
To me are nothing novel, nothing strange;    3
They are but dressings of a former sight.    4
Our dates are brief, and therefore we admire    5
What thou dost foist upon us that is old,
And rather make them born to our desire    7
Than think that we before have heard them told.    8
Thy registers and thee I both defy,    9
Not wond'ring at the present nor the past,    10
For thy records and what we see doth lie,    11
Made more or less by thy continual haste.    12
    This I do vow and this shall ever be:
    I will be true, despite thy scythe and thee.

### 124

If my dear love were but the child of state,    1
It might for Fortune's bastard be unfathered,    2
As subject to Time's love or to Time's hate,
Weeds among weeds, or flowers with flowers gathered.    4
No, it was builded far from accident;    5
It suffers not in smiling pomp, nor falls    6
Under the blow of thrallèd discontent,    7
Whereto th'inviting time our fashion calls.    8
It fears not Policy, that heretic,    9
Which works on leases of short-numbered hours,    10
But all alone stands hugely politic,    11
That it nor grows with heat nor drowns with showers.    12
    To this I witness call the fools of Time,    13
    Which die for goodness, who have lived for crime.    14

### 125

Were't aught to me I bore the canopy,    1
With my extern the outward honoring,    2
Or laid great bases for eternity    3
Which proves more short than waste or ruining?    4
Have I not seen dwellers on form and favor    5
Lose all, and more, by paying too much rent,    6
For compound sweet forgoing simple savor,    7
Pitiful thrivers, in their gazing spent?    8
No, let me be obsequious in thy heart,    9
And take thou my oblation, poor but free,    10
Which is not mixed with seconds, knows no art    11
But mutual render, only me for thee.    12
    Hence, thou suborned informer! A true soul    13
    When most impeached stands least in thy control.    14

### 126

O thou, my lovely boy, who in thy power    1
Dost hold Time's fickle glass, his sickle hour;    2
Who hast by waning grown, and therein show'st    3
Thy lovers withering as thy sweet self grow'st;    4
If Nature, sovereign mistress over wrack,    5
As thou goest onwards, still will pluck thee back,    6
She keeps thee to this purpose, that her skill    7
May Time disgrace and wretched minutes kill.    8
Yet fear her, O thou minion of her pleasure!    9
She may detain, but not still keep, her treasure.    10
Her audit, though delayed, answered must be,    11
And her quietus is to render thee.    12

---

12 **those tables** i.e., those of memory.    **receive thee more** retain more of you.    13 **adjunct** aid    14 **Were** would be.    **import** imply, impute
123.2 **pyramids** (May refer to obelisks or other structures erected in Rome in 1586 or in London in 1603.)    3 **nothing** not at all    4 **dressings . . . sight** reconstructions in new form of things from the past.    5 **dates** life spans    7 **make . . . desire** consider them newly created to our liking and reinvented by us    8 **told** reckoned, told about.    9 **registers** visual records, monuments    10 **wond'ring** marveling    11 **doth lie** deceives us    12 **Made . . . haste** i.e., raised one minute and ruined the next (by Time), and alternately overvalued and undervalued by us.
124.1–2 **If . . . unfathered** If my love for you were merely the product of circumstances and your high position, we might disavow it as nothing but the bastard child of Fortune    4 **Weeds . . . gathered** either despised as worthless like a weed or cherished like a flower as Fortune dictates.    5 **accident** chance, fortune    6–8 **It . . . calls** it does not change in response to the dictates of pomp and finery, nor does it weaken under the blows of slavish adversity, both of which the insidious mores of our present age tempt us to regard as fashionable.    9 **Policy, that heretic** cunning expediency, false to the spirit of love    10 **Which . . . hours** which thinks only shortsightedly of short-term gain and makes only short-term commitments    11 **hugely politic** prudent in a long-term sense    12 **That . . . showers** so that it neither pins its hopes unrealistically on rising fortunes nor grows desperate in times of adversity.    13–14 **To . . . crime** I call as witnesses those creatures of Time who succumb to the moral weaknesses described in this sonnet, and who repent their evil ways only after having lived corruptly.

125.1–4 **Were't . . . ruining?** Would it mean anything to me if I did public homage to great persons by carrying over their heads a cloth of state as they go in procession, thereby honoring what is external by means of a purely external action, or if I laid foundations for supposedly eternal monuments which then prove to last no longer than the forces of decay and ruin allow?    5 **dwellers . . . favor** those who depend on court etiquette and influence peddling; also, in figure and face    6 **by paying . . . rent** i.e., by overdoing flattery and depending too much on hopes of obtaining favor    7 **For . . . savor** i.e., foregoing wholesome sincerity for the sake of obsequious flattery    8 **Pitiful . . . spent** pitiful in their unsuccessful attempts, their means consumed in their ineffectual fawning on greatness.    9 **obsequious** (1) courtly (2) devoted    10 **And . . . free** and let you take the offering of my poor but freely offered love    11 **seconds** inferior matter, adulterants.    **art** artifice    12 **render** exchange    13 **suborned informer** perjured witness, the envious one who has charged the poet with self-interested flattery.    14 **impeached** accused
126.1 (This sonnet is made up of six couplets.)    2 **Time's . . . hour** Time's treacherous and inexorable hourglass, his reaping time    3 **Who . . . grown** you who have grown more youthfully beautiful as you have aged.    **show'st** show by way of contrast with yourself    4 **Thy lovers** (including the poet)    5 **wrack** ruin. (Nature is mistress over decay in that she decays and renews.)    6 **onwards** i.e., in life's journey, toward death.    **still** constantly    7 **to** for    8 **May . . . kill** may put Time to shame and render powerless the passing of the minutes.    9 **Yet . . . pleasure!** Yet fear Nature too, you who as her darling are subject to her will!    10 **She . . . treasure** i.e., Nature may keep and restore you for a time, but Time will ultimately triumph.    11 **Her audit** i.e., The proverbial paying of one's debt to Nature through death; also, Nature's account to Time.    **answered** paid    12 **quietus** discharge, quittance.    **render** surrender

## 127

In the old age black was not counted fair,    1
Or if it were, it bore not beauty's name;    2
But now is black beauty's successive heir,    3
And beauty slandered with a bastard shame.    4
For since each hand hath put on nature's power,    5
Fairing the foul with art's false borrowed face,    6
Sweet beauty hath no name, no holy bower,    7
But is profaned, if not lives in disgrace.    8
Therefore my mistress' eyes are raven black,
Her brows so suited, and they mourners seem    10
At such who, not born fair, no beauty lack,    11
Sland'ring creation with a false esteem.    12
    Yet so they mourn, becoming of their woe,    13
    That every tongue says beauty should look so.

## 128

How oft, when thou, my music, music play'st
Upon that blessèd wood whose motion sounds    2
With thy sweet fingers when thou gently sway'st    3
The wiry concord that mine ear confounds,    4
Do I envy those jacks that nimble leap    5
To kiss the tender inward of thy hand,
Whilst my poor lips, which should that harvest reap,
At the wood's boldness by thee blushing stand!    8
To be so tickled, they would change their state    9
And situation with those dancing chips
O'er whom thy fingers walk with gentle gait,
Making dead wood more blest than living lips.
    Since saucy jacks so happy are in this,    13
    Give them thy fingers, me thy lips to kiss.

## 129

Th'expense of spirit in a waste of shame    1
Is lust in action; and, till action, lust    2

Is perjured, murd'rous, bloody, full of blame,    3
Savage, extreme, rude, cruel, not to trust,    4
Enjoyed no sooner but despisèd straight,    5
Past reason hunted, and no sooner had    6
Past reason hated, as a swallowed bait
On purpose laid to make the taker mad;
Mad in pursuit, and in possession so;    9
Had, having, and in quest to have, extreme;
A bliss in proof, and proved, a very woe;    11
Before, a joy proposed; behind, a dream.    12
    All this the world well knows; yet none knows well
    To shun the heaven that leads men to this hell.    14

## 130

My mistress' eyes are nothing like the sun;    1
Coral is far more red than her lips' red;
If snow be white, why then her breasts are dun;    3
If hairs be wires, black wires grow on her head.    4
I have seen roses damasked, red and white,    5
But no such roses see I in her cheeks;
And in some perfumes is there more delight
Than in the breath that from my mistress reeks.    8
I love to hear her speak, yet well I know
That music hath a far more pleasing sound.
I grant I never saw a goddess go;    11
My mistress, when she walks, treads on the ground.
    And yet, by heaven, I think my love as rare    13
    As any she belied with false compare.    14

## 131

Thou art as tyrannous, so as thou art,    1
As those whose beauties proudly make them cruel;
For well thou know'st to my dear doting heart    3
Thou art the fairest and most precious jewel.
Yet, in good faith, some say that thee behold
Thy face hath not the power to make love groan;
To say they err I dare not be so bold,
Although I swear it to myself alone.
And, to be sure that is not false I swear,    9
A thousand groans, but thinking on thy face,    10
One on another's neck, do witness bear    11
Thy black is fairest in my judgment's place.    12
    In nothing art thou black save in thy deeds,
    And thence this slander, as I think, proceeds.    14

127.1 **old age** olden times.    **black** darkness of hair and eyes.    **fair** (1) beautiful (2) light-complexioned    **2 it bore . . . name** i.e., it was not called beautiful    **3 now . . . heir** nowadays black has been named lawful successor to the title of beauty    **4 beauty . . . shame** i.e., blonde beauty is declared illegitimate, created artificially by cosmetics.
**5 put on** assumed, usurped    **6 Fairing the foul** making the ugly beautiful.    **borrowed face** i.e., cosmetics    **7 no name . . . bower** no reputation or pride of family, and no sacred abode    **8 if not** or even    **10 so suited** decked out in the same color and for the same reason    **11 At** for.    **no beauty lack** i.e., nonetheless make themselves attractive    **12 Sland'ring . . . esteem** i.e., dishonoring nature by blurring the distinction between real and false beauty.    **13 so** in such a way.    **they** i.e., my mistress' eyes.    **becoming of** gracing or being graced by    **128.2 wood** keys of the spinet or virginal.    **motion** mechanism    **3 thou gently sway'st** you gently control    **4 wiry concord** harmony produced by strings.    **confounds** i.e., pleasurably overwhelms    **5 jacks** (Literally, upright pieces of wood fixed to the key lever and fitted with a quill that plucks the strings of the virginal; here used of the keys and with a pun on *jacks* in the sense of "common fellows," as in line 13.)    **8 by** beside, or, with. (The poet stands beside the lady as she plays, blushing to his very lips; he blushes in vexation at the *jacks'* boldness with her hand.)    **9 they** i.e., my lips    **13 jacks** (With a pun on "knaves, fellows," as in line 5.)
**129.1–2 Th'expense . . . in action** Lust being consummated is the expenditure or dissipation of vital energy in an orgy of shameful extravagance and guilt. (*Spirit* also suggests "sperm.")    **2 till action** until it achieves consummation

**3 blame** (1) guilt (2) recrimination    **4 rude** brutal.    **to trust** to be trusted    **5 straight** immediately    **6 Past reason** madly, intemperately    **9 so** i.e., mad    **11 in proof** while experienced.    **proved** i.e., afterward    **12 Before** in prospect    **14 the heaven** the seeming bliss of sexual consummation.    **hell** (Often equated imagistically with the vagina.)
**130.1 nothing** not at all    **3 dun** dull grayish brown, mouse-colored    **4 black wires** (not golden wires, as often described in Renaissance love poetry)    **5 damasked** mingled red and white    **8 reeks** emanates.    **11 go** walk    **13 rare** extraordinary and unique    **14 As . . . compare** as any woman misrepresented by false comparison.
**131.1 tyrannous** pitiless and domineering.    **so as thou art** just as you are (dark, not considered handsome)    **3 dear** fond    **9 to be sure** as proof.    **false I** false that I    **10 but thinking on** when I do no more than think of    **11 One . . . neck** one rapidly after another    **12 black** dark complexion.    **my judgment's place** my opinion.    **14 this slander** (See lines 5–6.)    **proceeds** originates.

## 132

Thine eyes I love, and they, as pitying me,                1
Knowing thy heart torment me with disdain,               2
Have put on black, and loving mourners be,
Looking with pretty ruth upon my pain.                   4
And truly not the morning sun of heaven
Better becomes the gray cheeks of the east,              6
Nor that full star that ushers in the even               7
Doth half that glory to the sober west                   8
As those two mourning eyes become thy face.              9
Oh, let it then as well beseem thy heart                 10
To mourn for me, since mourning doth thee grace,         11
And suit thy pity like in every part.                    12
      Then will I swear beauty herself is black,
      And all they foul that thy complexion lack.        14

## 133

Beshrew that heart that makes my heart to groan          1
For that deep wound it gives my friend and me!
Is't not enough to torture me alone,
But slave to slavery my sweet'st friend must be?         4
Me from myself thy cruel eye hath taken,                 5
And my next self thou harder hast engrossed.            6
Of him, myself, and thee I am forsaken—
A torment thrice threefold thus to be crossed.          8
Prison my heart in thy steel bosom's ward,               9
But then my friend's heart let my poor heart bail;       10
Whoe'er keeps me, let my heart be his guard;             11
Thou canst not then use rigor in my jail.                12
      And yet thou wilt; for I, being pent in thee,      13
      Perforce am thine, and all that is in me.          14

## 134

So, now I have confessed that he is thine,               1
And I myself am mortgaged to thy will,                   2
Myself I'll forfeit, so that other mine                  3
Thou wilt restore to be my comfort still.
But thou wilt not, nor he will not be free,              5
For thou art covetous and he is kind;

He learned but surety-like to write for me               7
Under that bond that him as fast doth bind.              8
The statute of thy beauty thou wilt take,                9
Thou usurer, that put'st forth all to use,               10
And sue a friend came debtor for my sake;                11
So him I lose through my unkind abuse.                   12
      Him have I lost; thou hast both him and me;
      He pays the whole, and yet am I not free.          14

## 135

Whoever hath her wish, thou hast thy Will,               1
And Will to boot, and Will in overplus;                  2
More than enough am I that vex thee still,               3
To thy sweet will making addition thus.
Wilt thou, whose will is large and spacious,             5
Not once vouchsafe to hide my will in thine?             6
Shall will in others seem right gracious,                7
And in my will no fair acceptance shine?
The sea, all water, yet receives rain still
And in abundance addeth to his store;                    10
So thou, being rich in Will, add to thy Will
One will of mine, to make thy large Will more.
      Let no unkind no fair beseechers kill;             13
      Think all but one, and me in that one Will.        14

## 136

If thy soul check thee that I come so near,              1
Swear to thy blind soul that I was thy Will,             2
And will, thy soul knows, is admitted there;             3
Thus far for love my love suit, sweet, fulfill.          4
Will will fulfill the treasure of thy love,              5
Ay, fill it full with wills, and my will one.            6
In things of great receipt with ease we prove            7
Among a number one is reckoned none.                     8
Then in the number let me pass untold,                   9

**7 surety-like** as security, as guarantor.   **write** sign the bond, endorse (suggesting that the friend has taken the poet's place with the mistress)   **8 Under . . . bind** under that mortgage or bond (of sexual enslavement) that now binds him as securely as it does me.   **9 statute** a usurer's security or amount of money secured under his bond.   **take** call in, invoke. (The lady will exact the full forfeiture specified in the mortgage as the amount to which her beauty entitles her.)   **10 that** you who.   **use** (1) usury (2) sexual pleasure   **11 sue** (With suggestion also of "woo.")   **came** i.e., who became   **12 So** thus.   **my unkind abuse** your ill usage and unkind deceiving (of me).   **14 pays** (With sexual suggestion.)
**135.1 Will** (This and the following sonnet and sonnet 143 ring changes on the word *will*—sexual desire, temper, passion, and the poet's name; possibly also the friend's name. The word can also suggest the sexual organs, male and female.)   **2 to boot** in addition   **3 vex** (by unwelcome wooing).   **still** continually   **5 whose . . . spacious** whose sexual appetite and anatomy are capacious   **6 hide . . . thine** (With sexual suggestion.)   **7 will in others** others' wills   **10 his** its   **13 Let . . . kill** Let no unkind word kill any who seek your favors, or, do not kill your wooers with the word *no*   **14 Think . . . Will** i.e., think all your wooers and their wills to be but one, all comprised in me.
**136.1 check** rebuke.   **come so near** i.e., come so near the truth about you (in my previous sonnet); with suggestion of physical nearness also   **2 blind** unperceptive; shut up in the body without sensory organs   **3 admitted** (1) acknowledged (2) granted sexual entry   **4 fulfill** grant.   **5 fulfill the treasure** fill full the treasury. (With suggestion of sexual entry.)   **6 my will** (Suggesting "my penis.")   **one** one of them.   **7 receipt** capacity. (Suggesting profligacy.)   **8 one . . . none** i.e., You have so many lovers that having one more (namely, me) shouldn't make a big difference. (A variant of the common saying "one is no number.")   **9 untold** uncounted

**132.1 as** as if   **2 Knowing . . . torment** knowing that your heart torments   **4 ruth** pity   **6 becomes** adorns.   **cheeks** i.e., clouds   **7 that full star** the evening star, Hesperus, i.e., Venus.   **even** evening   **8 Doth** i.e., lends.   **sober** somber, subdued in color   **9 mourning** black. (Spelled "morning" in the quarto, suggesting a pun on line 5.)   **10 beseem** suit   **11 since . . . grace** since you look very attractive in mourning black   **12 And suit . . . part** and dress your pity similarly, in your heart as well as eyes.   **14 And . . . that** and that all those are ugly who
**133.1 Beshrew** i.e., A plague upon   **4 slave to slavery** utterly enslaved   **5 Me . . . taken** Your cruel eye has turned me into someone I scarcely recognize   **6 And . . . engrossed** i.e., and you have put my dearest friend, my other self, under even greater restraint.   **engrossed** (1) driven into obsession (2) bought up wholesale.   **8 crossed** thwarted, afflicted.   **9 Prison** Imprison.   **thy . . . ward** the prison cell of your hard heart   **10 bail** set free by taking its place   **11 keeps** has custody of.   **his guard** my friend's prison   **12 rigor** harshness.   **my jail** i.e., my heart, where my friend is kept (and where I can protect him from your harsh authority).   **13 pent** shut up   **14 Perforce** necessarily.   **and all** along with everything (including my friend's heart)
**134.1 now** now that   **2 will** (1) wishes (2) fleshly desire   **3 so . . . mine** provided that my other self, my friend   **5 wilt not** does not wish to, won't

Though in thy store's account I one must be;    10
For nothing hold me, so it please thee hold    11
That nothing me, a something, sweet, to thee.    12
  Make but my name thy love, and love that still,    13
  And then thou lovest me for my name is Will.    14

## 137

Thou blind fool, Love, what dost thou to mine eyes    1
That they behold and see not what they see?    2
They know what beauty is, see where it lies,    3
Yet what the best is take the worst to be.    4
If eyes corrupt by overpartial looks    5
Be anchored in the bay where all men ride,    6
Why of eyes' falsehood hast thou forgèd hooks,    7
Whereto the judgment of my heart is tied?    8
Why should my heart think that a several plot    9
Which my heart knows the wide world's common place?    10
Or mine eyes seeing this, say this is not,    11
To put fair truth upon so foul a face?    12
  In things right true my heart and eyes have erred,    13
  And to this false plague are they now transferred.    14

## 138

When my love swears that she is made of truth    1
I do believe her, though I know she lies,    2
That she might think me some untutored youth,    3
Unlearnèd in the world's false subtleties.    4
Thus vainly thinking that she thinks me young,    5
Although she knows my days are past the best,    6
Simply I credit her false-speaking tongue;    7
On both sides thus is simple truth suppressed.    8
But wherefore says she not she is unjust?    9
And wherefore say not I that I am old?    10
Oh, love's best habit is in seeming trust,    11
And age in love loves not to have years told.    12

Therefore I lie with her, and she with me,    13
And in our faults by lies we flattered be.    14

## 139

Oh, call not me to justify the wrong    1
That thy unkindness lays upon my heart;    2
Wound me not with thine eye but with thy tongue;    3
Use power with power, and slay me not by art.    4
Tell me thou lov'st elsewhere, but in my sight,    5
Dear heart, forbear to glance thine eye aside;    6
What need'st thou wound with cunning when thy might    7
Is more than my o'erpressed defense can bide?    8
Let me excuse thee: "Ah, my love well knows    9
Her pretty looks have been mine enemies,    10
And therefore from my face she turns my foes,    11
That they elsewhere might dart their injuries."    12
  Yet do not so; but since I am near slain,    13
  Kill me outright with looks and rid my pain.    14

## 140

Be wise as thou art cruel; do not press    1
My tongue-tied patience with too much disdain,    2
Lest sorrow lend me words, and words express    3
The manner of my pity-wanting pain.    4
If I might teach thee wit, better it were,    5
Though not to love, yet, love, to tell me so,    6
As testy sick men, when their deaths be near,    7
No news but health from their physicians know.    8
For if I should despair, I should grow mad,    9
And in my madness might speak ill of thee.    10
Now this ill-wresting world is grown so bad,    11
Mad slanderers by mad ears believèd be.    12
  That I may not be so, nor thou belied,    13
  Bear thine eyes straight, though thy proud heart go
    wide.    14

## 141

In faith, I do not love thee with mine eyes,    1
For they in thee a thousand errors note;    2
But 'tis my heart that loves what they despise,    3
Who in despite of view is pleased to dote.    4
Nor are mine ears with thy tongue's tune delighted,    5

10 **Though . . . must be** although in your (huge) inventory (of lovers) you must reckon me as simply one among many    **11–12 For . . . thee** i.e., consider me too insignificant to think of, provided that you deign to hold insignificant me to you, my sweet, thereby making me something of worth. (*Something* is sexually suggestive of "some thing.")    **13 my name** i.e., "will," that is, desire.    **still** continually    **14 for** because

**137.1 Love** Cupid, portrayed as blind    **2 see not** do not comprehend    **3 lies** resides (and deceives through false appearance)    **4 Yet . . . be** yet take the worst for the best.    **5 corrupt by overpartial looks** corrupted by doting and frankly prejudiced gazing    **6 Be . . . ride** seek harbor where all men do so, i.e., *ride* in the arms and body of promiscuous women    **7 Why . . . hooks** why have you, Love, fashioned snares out of my eyes' delusion    **9 think . . . plot** think that to be a private field, i.e., that woman to be the exclusive property of one man    **10 knows** knows to be.    **common place** (1) a commons, a common pasture (2) a woman's body that is open, promiscuous.    **11 Or** Or why should.    **not** not so    **12 To put . . . face?** to conceal a face betokening sinfulness with a mask of seeming virtue    **14 false plague** (1) plague of judging falsely (2) false woman

**138.1** (A version of this sonnet appears in *The Passionate Pilgrim*.)    **truth** fidelity, constancy    **2 believe** i.e., pretend to believe    **5 vainly thinking** acting as though I thought    **7 Simply** (1) pretending to be foolish (2) naively.    **credit** give credence to    **9 unjust** unfaithful, deceitful.    **11 habit** demeanor. (With, however, a suggestion of *garb*, i.e., "something put on.")    **seeming trust** apparent fidelity    **12 age in love** an aging person in love, or, in matters of love.    **told** (1) counted (2) divulged.

**13 lie with** (1) deceive (2) have sex with    **14 And . . . be** and so by lies we flatteringly deceive ourselves about our moral lapses.
**139.1 call** ask.    **justify the wrong** i.e., condone something actually taking place under my very eyes    **2 unkindness** i.e., flagrant infidelity    **3 with thine eye** i.e., with a roving eye. (See lines 5–6.)    **4 with power** i.e., candidly, directly.    **art** artifice, cunning.    **7 What** why    **8 bide** endure, withstand.    **11 foes** i.e., the *pretty looks*, the beauty and wanton glances of line 10    **13 near** nearly    **14 rid** end. (*Rid my pain* also suggests "satiate my craving.")
**140.4 manner** substance.    **pity-wanting** (1) unpitied by you (2) pity-craving    **5 wit** wisdom, prudence    **5–6 better . . . so** (I would teach you that) even though you don't love me, yet, dear friend, it would be better to tell me that you do    **8 know** wish to learn.    **11 ill-wresting** misinterpreting in an evil sense    **12 Mad . . . be** that malicious slanderers are too easily believed by ears of persons who are inclined to believe the worst.    **13 so** i.e., a *mad slanderer* who is *believèd*.    **belied** slandered    **14 Bear . . . straight** keep your eyes on me.    **wide** astray.
**141.2 errors** flaws in beauty    **4 Who . . . view** which (i.e., the heart), in spite of what the eyes see.    **dote** love dotingly.

Nor tender feeling to base touches prone,                              6
Nor taste, nor smell, desire to be invited
To any sensual feast with thee alone.
But my five wits nor my five senses can                                9
Dissuade one foolish heart from serving thee,
Who leaves unswayed the likeness of a man,                             11
Thy proud heart's slave and vassal wretch to be.                       12
    Only my plague thus far I count my gain,        13
    That she that makes me sin awards me pain.      14

## 142

Love is my sin, and thy dear virtue hate,                              1
Hate of my sin, grounded on sinful loving.                             2
Oh, but with mine compare thou thine own state,
And thou shalt find it merits not reproving;                           4
Or, if it do, not from those lips of thine
That have profaned their scarlet ornaments                             6
And sealed false bonds of love as oft as mine,                         7
Robbed others' beds' revenues of their rents.                          8
Be it lawful I love thee as thou lov'st those                          9
Whom thine eyes woo as mine importune thee.                            10
Root pity in thy heart, that when it grows
Thy pity may deserve to pitied be.                                     12
    If thou dost seek to have what thou dost hide,  13
    By self-example mayst thou be denied.

## 143

Lo, as a careful huswife runs to catch                                 1
One of her feathered creatures broke away,                             2
Sets down her babe and makes all swift dispatch                        3
In pursuit of the thing she would have stay,
Whilst her neglected child holds her in chase,                         5
Cries to catch her whose busy care is bent
To follow that which flies before her face,                            7

Not prizing her poor infant's discontent:                              8
So run'st thou after that which flies from thee,
Whilst I, thy babe, chase thee afar behind;
But if thou catch thy hope, turn back to me,                           11
And play the mother's part: kiss me, be kind.
    So will I pray that thou mayst have thy Will,    13
    If thou turn back and my loud crying still.      14

## 144

Two loves I have, of comfort and despair,                              1
Which like two spirits do suggest me still:                            2
The better angel is a man right fair,                                  3
The worser spirit a woman colored ill.                                 4
To win me soon to hell, my female evil
Tempteth my better angel from my side,
And would corrupt my saint to be a devil,
Wooing his purity with her foul pride.
And whether that my angel be turned fiend
Suspect I may, yet not directly tell;
But being both from me, both to each friend,                           11
I guess one angel in another's hell.                                   12
    Yet this shall I ne'er know, but live in doubt
    Till my bad angel fire my good one out.           14

## 145

Those lips that Love's own hand did make                               1
Breathed forth the sound that said "I hate"
To me that languished for her sake;
But when she saw my woeful state,
Straight in her heart did mercy come,                                  5
Chiding that tongue that ever sweet
Was used in giving gentle doom,                                        7
And taught it thus anew to greet:
"I hate" she altered with an end,
That followed it as gentle day
Doth follow night, who like a fiend
From heaven to hell is flown away.
    "I hate" from hate away she threw,               13
    And saved my life, saying "not you."             14

**6 Nor . . . prone** nor (is) my delicate sense of touch inclined toward carnal contact (with you)   **9 my five wits** (neither) my five intellectual senses, i.e., the common sense, imagination, fancy, estimation (judgment), and memory.   **my five senses** i.e., sight, hearing, touch, taste, and smell, as enumerated in this sonnet   **11 Who . . . man** i.e., which heart abandons the proper government of my person, leaving me the mere likeness of a man   **12 to be** (The sense of this goes at the beginning of the line.)   **13 thus far** to the following extent   **14 That . . . pain** i.e., that the sin brings with it its own punishment and contrition, thus presumably shortening my torment after death. (With a suggestion in *pain* of "sexual pleasure"; see sonnet 139.)
**142.1–2 Love . . . loving** My sin is to love you, and your best virtue is to hate—hate that sin in me, but also because of your uncontrolled sexual longing for other men. (The bitter paradox here is that hatred of sin must be virtue, and yet the lady is herself deeply implicated in this sin; her hatred is more a disdainful rejection of the poet's love than a noble virtue.)   **4 it** i.e., my state   **6–7 That . . . mine** i.e., that have forsworn themselves in love as often as my lips have. (The *scarlet ornaments* are lips and also red wax used to seal documents; they *seal* with a kiss.)   **8 Robbed . . . rents** i.e., and committed adultery with other women's husbands. (The metaphor is of income-yielding estates, *revenues*, whose *rents* or payments made by tenants are not properly paid; the husband does not pay what is owed to the wife in terms of marital affection and the producing of children.)   **9–10 Be . . . thee** i.e., I am as justified in loving you and imploring you with my eyes as you are in pursuing other men. (*Be it lawful* is a legal phrase meaning "Let it be considered lawful that.")   **12 deserve** make you deserving   **13 what . . . hide** what you withhold, i.e., pity
**143.1 careful** distressed, full of cares, busy.   **huswife** housewife   **2 feathered . . . away** domestic fowl which has broken away, escaped   **3 makes . . . dispatch** hurries   **5 holds her in chase** chases after her   **7 flies** flees

**8 Not prizing** disregarding   **11 catch my hope** i.e., hear my cries of help   **13 Will** (See sonnets 135, 136.)   **14 still** hush, make quiet.
**144.1** (This sonnet appears, somewhat altered, in *The Passionate Pilgrim*.)   **2 suggest** urge, offer counsel, tempt.   **still** continually   **3 right fair** very handsome and blond   **4 ill** i.e., dark of complexion.   **11 from me** away from me. (The poet suspects they are together.)   **both . . . friend** friends to each other   **12 I . . . hell** I suspect that she (the evil angel) has him in her power (i.e., her sexual embracement; *hell* is slang for the vagina).   **14 fire . . . out** drives out my good angel, stops seeing him. (With the suggestion of driving him out of the lady's sexual body as one would use fire and smoke to drive an animal out of its burrow, and with the further suggestion that the *fire* is venereal disease. *Bad angel* also hints at bad coinage driving out good money.)
**145.1** (This sonnet is in eight-syllable meter.)   **5 Straight** at once   **7 used . . . doom** accustomed to passing a mild sentence   **13 "I hate" . . . threw** i.e., She separated the phrase "I hate" from the hatred I feared it expressed, from hateful meaning   **13–14 hate away . . . And** (Punning perhaps on the name of Shakespeare's wife, Anne Hathaway.)

## 146

Poor soul, the center of my sinful earth,                                          1
Thrall to these rebel powers that thee array,                                      2
Why dost thou pine within and suffer dearth,
Painting thy outward walls so costly gay?                                          4
Why so large cost, having so short a lease,                                        5
Dost thou upon thy fading mansion spend?                                           6
Shall worms, inheritors of this excess,
Eat up thy charge? Is this thy body's end?                                         8
Then, soul, live thou upon thy servant's loss,                                     9
And let that pine to aggravate thy store;                                          10
Buy terms divine in selling hours of dross;                                        11
Within be fed, without be rich no more.
    So shalt thou feed on Death, that feeds on men,
    And Death once dead, there's no more dying then.

## 147

My love is as a fever, longing still                                               1
For that which longer nurseth the disease,                                         2
Feeding on that which doth preserve the ill,                                       3
Th'uncertain sickly appetite to please.                                            4
My reason, the physician to my love,
Angry that his prescriptions are not kept,
Hath left me, and I desperate now approve                                          7
Desire is death, which physic did except.                                          8
Past cure I am, now reason is past care,                                           9
And frantic-mad with evermore unrest;                                             10
My thoughts and my discourse as madmen's are,                                     11
At random from the truth vainly expressed;                                        12
    For I have sworn thee fair and thought thee bright,
    Who art as black as hell, as dark as night.

## 148

Oh, me, what eyes hath love put in my head,
Which have no correspondence with true sight!
Or, if they have, where is my judgment fled,
That censures falsely what they see aright?                                         4
If that be fair whereon my false eyes dote,
What means the world to say it is not so?

If it be not, then love doth well denote                                           7
Love's eye is not so true as all men's "no."                                       8
How can it? Oh, how can love's eye be true,
That is so vexed with watching and with tears?                                    10
No marvel then though I mistake my view;                                          11
The sun itself sees not till heaven clears.                                       12
    O cunning love, with tears thou keep'st me blind,
    Lest eyes well-seeing thy foul faults should find!

## 149

Canst thou, O cruel, say I love thee not,
When I against myself with thee partake?                                           2
Do I not think on thee when I forgot                                               3
Am of myself, all tyrant for thy sake?                                             4
Who hateth thee that I do call my friend?
On whom frown'st thou that I do fawn upon?
Nay, if thou lour'st on me, do I not spend                                         7
Revenge upon myself with present moan?                                             8
What merit do I in myself respect                                                  9
That is so proud thy service to despise,                                          10
When all my best doth worship thy defect,                                         11
Commanded by the motion of thine eyes?
    But, love, hate on, for now I know thy mind:
    Those that can see thou lov'st, and I am blind.                               14

## 150

Oh, from what power hast thou this powerful might
With insufficiency my heart to sway?                                               2
To make me give the lie to my true sight                                           3
And swear that brightness doth not grace the day?                                  4
Whence hast thou this becoming of things ill,                                      5
That in the very refuse of thy deeds                                               6
There is such strength and warrantise of skill                                     7
That, in my mind, thy worst all best exceeds?                                      8
Who taught thee how to make me love thee more,
The more I hear and see just cause of hate?                                       10
Oh, though I love what others do abhor,
With others thou shouldst not abhor my state.                                     12
    If thy unworthiness raised love in me,                                        13
    More worthy I to be beloved of thee.                                          14

146.1 **sinful earth** body   2 **Thrall . . . array** made captive by the rebellious flesh that decks you in finery and lines you up in battle array. ("Thrall to" is one of several conjectures; the quarto repeats "My sinfull earth" from line 1.)   4 **outward walls** i.e., the body, decked out in finery, cosmetics, etc.   5 **having . . . lease** having so brief a period of living in this world   6 **mansion** dwelling, i.e., the body   8 **charge** expense, outlay.   **Is . . . end?** Is this what your body was intended to be used for?   9 **thy servant's** i.e., the body's   10 **let that . . . store** let the body starve to increase your stock of spiritual riches   11 **Buy . . . dross** i.e., purchase eternal life in return for giving up (selling) mere hours of wasteful pleasure—secure *terms* that only God can provide
147.1 **still** always   2 **nurseth** nourishes   3 **preserve the ill** sustain the illness   4 **Th'uncertain** the finicky   7–8 **and I . . . except** and I now, desperately sick and in desperation, discover by experience that desire, which rejected medicine (or, which medical advice warned against), is fatal.   9 **care** medical care. (The line is an inversion of the proverb, "things past cure are past care," i.e., don't worry about what can't be helped. Reason, the physician, has ceased to care for his patient.)   10 **evermore** constant and increasing   11–12 **as madman's . . . expressed** are like a madman's thoughts, departing disconnectedly from truth and expressed to no purpose
148.4 **censures** judges

7 **love** i.e., the self-deceiving nature of my love.   **denote** indicate, demonstrate (that)   8 **eye** (With a pun on "ay," yes.)   10 **vexed** troubled.   **watching** remaining awake   11 **I** (Punning on "eye.") **mistake my view** err in what I see   12 **till heaven clears** till the sky is clear of clouds.
149.2 **partake** take part (against myself).   3–4 **Do . . . sake?** Do I not put consideration of you foremost when I am tyrannously neglectful of, or oblivious of, myself and my best interests on your behalf? 7 **thou lour'st** you scowl.   **spend** vent   8 **present moan** immediate suffering and lamentation.   9 **respect** value   10 **thy . . . despise** as to think it demeaning to serve you   11 **When . . . defect** when all that is best in me worships you despite your faults   14 **Those . . . blind** i.e., you scorn one who loves you in a blind passion, in defiance of reason, and are drawn instead to those who know you for what you are.
150.2 **With insufficiency** despite all your shortcomings.   **sway** rule.
3 **give the lie to** accuse flatly of lying   4 **And . . . day** i.e., and swear that what is so is not so, that what is fair and beautiful is not fair and beautiful, since you are dark.   5 **becoming . . . ill** i.e., ability to show ill things in a becoming light   6 **in . . . deeds** in the most debased of your actions   7 **warrantise of skill** warrant or assurance of expertise 8 **That . . . exceeds?** that to my way of thinking your least attractive actions excel the very best efforts of others?   10 **The more** despite the more   12 **With others** joining with others.   **state** i.e., condition of being helplessly in love.   13–14 **If . . . of thee** If it's my unworthiness that you love me for, love me all the more; I am truly unworthy of you.

## 151

Love is too young to know what conscience is;                1
Yet who knows not conscience is born of love?              2
Then, gentle cheater, urge not my amiss,                        3
Lest guilty of my faults thy sweet self prove.                 4
For, thou betraying me, I do betray                                  5
My nobler part to my gross body's treason.                    6
My soul doth tell my body that he may                           7
Triumph in love; flesh stays no farther reason,           8
But, rising at thy name, doth point out thee                 9
As his triumphant prize. Proud of this pride,            10
He is contented thy poor drudge to be,
To stand in thy affairs, fall by thy side.                      12
    No want of conscience hold it that I call        13
    Her "love" for whose dear love I rise and fall.  14

## 152

In loving thee thou know'st I am forsworn,               1
But thou art twice forsworn, to me love swearing:    
In act thy bed-vow broke, and new faith torn           3
In vowing new hate after new love bearing.              4
But why of two oaths' breach do I accuse thee,
When I break twenty? I am perjured most,
For all my vows are oaths but to misuse thee,            7
And all my honest faith in thee is lost.
For I have sworn deep oaths of thy deep kindness,
Oaths of thy love, thy truth, thy constancy,
And, to enlighten thee, gave eyes to blindness,
Or made them swear against the thing they see;       11

For I have sworn thee fair. More perjured eye,          13
To swear against the truth so foul a lie!                      14

## 153

Cupid laid by his brand and fell asleep.                        1
A maid of Dian's this advantage found,                        2
And his love-kindling fire did quickly steep
In a cold valley-fountain of that ground,                     4
Which borrowed from this holy fire of Love
A dateless lively heat, still to endure,                            6
And grew a seething bath, which yet men prove        7
Against strange maladies a sovereign cure.                8
But at my mistress' eye Love's brand new-fired,        9
The boy for trial needs would touch my breast;       10
I, sick withal, the help of bath desired,                         11
And thither hied, a sad distempered guest,                12
    But found no cure. The bath for my help lies
    Where Cupid got new fire—my mistress' eyes.

## 154

The little love god lying once asleep
Laid by his side his heart-inflaming brand,               2
Whilst many nymphs that vowed chaste life to keep
Came tripping by; but in her maiden hand
The fairest votary took up that fire                                5
Which many legions of true hearts had warmed,
And so the general of hot desire                                     7
Was, sleeping, by a virgin hand disarmed.
This brand she quenchèd in a cool well by,                9
Which from Love's fire took heat perpetual,
Growing a bath and healthful remedy                        11
For men diseased; but I, my mistress' thrall,            12
    Came there for cure, and this by that I prove:      13
    Love's fire heats water, water cools not love.

151.1 **too young** (Love is personified as the young Cupid.) **2 conscience** guilty knowing, carnal knowledge. (Playing on *conscience*, "moral sense," in line 1.)   **3 cheater** i.e., the poet's faithless mistress.   **urge** stress, point out.   **amiss** sin   **4 Lest . . . prove** lest your sweet self turn out to be guilty of the very sins you upbraid me for.   **5–6 For . . . treason** For, if you undertake to castigate my sins, I will confirm your accusation by betraying my soul to the rebellion of the flesh.   **7–8 that . . . in love** that he, the soul, may triumph in virtuous love. (But ambiguously misinterpretable as conceding that the flash may triumph carnally.)   **8 flesh . . . reason** (but) my flesh waits no longer to hear reason's lecture   **9 rising** (With bawdy suggestion of erection, continued in *point, Proud, stand, fall*. Metaphors of conjuration and of the compass needle's point are also invoked.)   **10 triumphant prize** i.e., intended sexual conquest. (Literally, the spoils of war.)   **Proud of** Swelling with.   **pride** splendor; erection   **12 stand** (1) serve, undertake business (2) be erect.   **fall** (as in battle; with sexual suggestion of detumescence)   **13–14 No . . . fall** i.e., It is not lack of moral conscience prompting me to address by the name of "love" (whether noble love or else lust) the woman for whose dear sake I strive and sometimes fail (suggesting also erection and detumescence).
**152.1 forsworn** i.e., faithless to my vows of love (perhaps marriage vows)   **3 act** sexual act.   **bed-vow** marriage vows to your husband or lover   **3–4 and new . . . bearing** i.e., and your new promise of fidelity (to me) is torn up by your then vowing hatred for me as you enter into yet another new sexual relationship. (Or the *new faith* that is torn up may be that which the lady has sworn to the friend.)
**7 but to misuse** merely to deceive   **11 And . . . blindness** i.e., and, to invest you with beauty and truth, I made my eyes testify to things they did not see

**13 eye** (With a pun on "I.")
**153** (This sonnet and the following seemingly have no direct connection with those preceding. They are derived ultimately, through Renaissance adaptations, from an epigram by the fifth-century Byzantine poet Marianus Scholasticus in the Greek Anthology.)
**1 brand** torch. (With phallic suggestion.)   **2 maid** attendant virgin, votaress.   **Dian** Diana, goddess of chastity   **4 of that ground** i.e., nearby. (*Valley-fountain* suggests the female sexual anatomy; compare with 154.9.)   **6 dateless** endless, eternal.   **still** always   **7–8 And grew . . . cure** and became a spring of hot medicinal waters, which even today men discover to be an efficacious cure against strange maladies. (Syphilis was conventionally treated with hot medicinal baths.)   **9 new-fired** having been reignited   **10 for trial** by way of test   **11 withal** from it   **12 hied** hastened.   **distempered** sick. (The bath is suggestive again of the sweating cure for venereal disease.)
**154.2 brand** torch   **5 fairest** very handsome   **7 general** inspirer and commander, i.e., Cupid   **9 by** nearby   **11 Growing** becoming   **12 thrall** slave, bondman   **13 cure** (With suggestion of treatment for venereal disease, as in 153.7–14.)   **this** i.e., the following proposition.   **that** i.e., my coming, which failed to cure me

# Appendix 1

# Canon, Dates, and Early Texts

By "canon" we mean a listing of plays that can be ascribed to Shakespeare on the basis of reliable evidence. Such evidence is either "internal," derived from matters of style or poetics in the plays themselves (see General Introduction), or "external," derived from outside the play. The latter includes any reference by Shakespeare's contemporaries to his plays, any allusions in the plays themselves to contemporary events, the entering of Shakespeare's plays for publication in the Stationers' Register (S. R.), actual publication of the plays, and records of early performances. These matters of external evidence are also essential in attempting to date the plays.

The greatest single source of information is the First Folio text of Shakespeare's plays, sponsored by Shakespeare's fellow actors John Heminges and Henry Condell and published in 1623. It contains all the plays included in this present edition of Shakespeare and offers strong presumptive evidence of being a complete and accurate compilation of Shakespeare's work by men who knew him and cherished his memory. It provides the only texts we have for these eighteen plays: *The Comedy of Errors, The Two Gentlemen of Verona, The Taming of the Shrew, I Henry VI, King John, As You Like It, Twelfth Night, Julius Caesar, All's Well That Ends Well, Measure for Measure, Timon of Athens, Macbeth, Antony and Cleopatra, Coriolanus, Cymbeline, The Winter's Tale, The Tempest*, and *Henry VIII*. This includes nearly half the known canon of Shakespeare's plays. Our debt to the First Folio is incalculable and confirms our impression of its reliability.

The information of the First Folio is further confirmed by contemporary references. In 1598, a cleric and minor writer of the period named Francis Meres wrote in his *Palladis Tamia, Wit's Treasury*:

As the soul of Euphorbus was thought to live in Pythagoras, so the sweet, witty soul of Ovid lives in mellifluous and honey-tongued Shakespeare: witness his *Venus and Adonis*, his *Lucrece*, his sugared sonnets among his private friends, etc.

As Plautus and Seneca are accounted the best for comedy and tragedy among the Latins, so Shakespeare among the English is the most excellent in both kinds for the stage; for comedy, witness his *Gentlemen of Verona*, his *Errors*, his *Love's Labor's Lost*, his *Love's Labor's Won*, his *Midsummer's Night Dream*, and his *Merchant of Venice*; for tragedy his *Richard the II, Richard the III, Henry the IV, King John, Titus Andronicus* and his *Romeo and Juliet*.

Though this list was meant to offer praise, not to be an exhaustive catalogue, it is remarkably full. If the tantalizing *Love's Labor's Won* refers to *The Taming of the Shrew*, Meres's list of comedies is substantially complete down almost to 1598. It does not include the comedies that Shakespeare appears to have written around that date or soon afterward: *Much Ado About Nothing, The Merry Wives of Windsor, As You Like It*, and *Twelfth Night*. Meres correctly names all of Shakespeare's history plays except the *Henry VI* trilogy and of course the later histories, *Henry V* (1599) and *Henry VIII* (1613). He names both of Shakespeare's early tragedies that are not based on English history: *Titus Andronicus* and *Romeo and Juliet*. He tells us about the important nondramatic poems, which did not appear in the First Folio, since that volume is devoted exclusively to plays. Not much can be made of the order in which Meres names the plays, however, for we learn from other sources that *Richard III* clearly precedes *Richard II* in date of composition and that *King John* precedes the *Henry IV* plays.

Other writers of the 1590s add further confirming evidence. John Weever, in an epigram "*Ad Gulielmum Shakespeare*," published in 1599, refers to "Rose-cheeked Adonis" and "Fair fire-hot Venus," to "Chaste Lucretia" and "Proud lust-stung Tarquin," and to "*Romeo, Richard*—more whose names I know not." Richard Barnfield, in

*Poems in Divers Humors* (1598), praises Shakespeare for "*Venus*" and "*Lucrece.*" Both Thomas Nashe and Robert Greene seemingly refer to the *Henry VI* plays, missing from Meres's list. Nashe, in his *Pierce Penniless* (1592), speculates how it would "have joyed brave Talbot (the terror of the French) to think that after he had lain two hundred years in his tomb, he should triumph again on the stage." Talbot is the hero of *1 Henry VI*, and we know of no other play on the subject. Greene, in his *Greene's Groats-worth of Wit* (1592), lashes out at an "upstart crow, beautified with our feathers, that with his '*Tiger's heart wrapped in a player's hide*' supposes he is as well able to bombast out a blank verse as the best of you, and, being an absolute *Johannes Factotum*, is in his own conceit the only Shake-scene in a country." The line about "Tiger's heart" is deliberately misquoted from *3 Henry VI*, 1.4.137. (It is possible that this famous attack on Shakespeare was actually written not by Greene himself but by Henry Chettle, his literary executor.)

### The Taming of the Shrew (*c. 1590–1593*)

*The Taming of the Shrew* was not printed until the First Folio of 1623. Francis Meres does not mention the play in 1598 in his *Palladis Tamia*, unless it is the mysterious "*Loue labours wonne*" on his list. (Meres is not totally accurate, for he omits *Henry VI* from the history plays.) The play must have existed prior to 1598, however, for its style is comparable with that of *The Two Gentlemen of Verona* and other early comedies. Moreover, a play called *The Taming of a Shrew* appeared in print in 1594 (Stationers' Register, 1594). Four theories can be adduced to explain the problematic relationship of *A Shrew* to Shakespeare's play. The two least plausible theories are that Shakespeare, for some reason, reworked someone else's play shortly after its first performance or else wrote *A Shrew* himself as an early version. The third theory is that *A Shrew* represents an imitation of Shakespeare's play by some rival dramatist, who relied chiefly on his memory and who changed characters' names and the location to make the play seem his. Fourth and most plausibly, *A Shrew* may be a somewhat uncharacteristic kind of reported or memorially reconstructed quarto, "improved" upon by a writer who also borrowed admiringly from Christopher Marlowe and other Elizabethan dramatists. In either of the latter two scenarios, Shakespeare's play would have to be dated earlier than May 1594.

The title page of *A Shrew* proclaims that "it was sundry times acted by the *Right honorable the Earle of* Pembrook his seruants." Quite possibly this derivative version was merely trying to capitalize on the original's stage success and was, in fact, describing performances of Shakespeare's play. Theater owner and manager

Philip Henslowe's record of a performance of "*the Tamynge of A Shrowe*" in 1594 at Newington Butts, a mile south of London Bridge, may also refer to Shakespeare's play; certainly, the minute distinction between "A Shrew" and "The Shrew" is one that the official records of the time would overlook. The Admiral's Men and the Lord Chamberlain's Men, acting companies, were playing at Newington Butts at the time, either jointly or alternatingly. Since Shakespeare's company, the Lord Chamberlain's, later owned *The Shrew*, they may well have owned and acted it on this occasion in 1594, having obtained it from the Earl of Pembroke's Men when that company disbanded in 1593. Many of Pembroke's leading players joined the Lord Chamberlain's, Shakespeare being quite possibly among them. (The possibility that he came to the Lord Chamberlain's from Lord Strange's men seems less certain today than it once did.) Several echoes of Shakespeare's play in other plays of the early 1590s tend to confirm a date in or before 1593. It is entirely possible, then, that *The Shrew* was acted by Pembroke's Men in 1592–1593 and subsequently passed along to the Lord Chamberlain's.

The Folio text of this play is now generally thought to have been printed from Shakespeare's working manuscript or possibly from a transcript of his papers, with perhaps some theatrical annotations as well. Some signs of revision are discernible.

### A Midsummer Night's Dream (*c. 1595*)

*A Midsummer Night's Dream* was entered on the Stationers' Register, the official record book of the London Company of Stationers (booksellers and printers), by Thomas Fisher on October 8, 1600, and published by Richard Bradock that same year in quarto:

A Midsommer nights dreame. As it hath beene sundry times pub*lickely acted, by the Right honoura*ble, the Lord Chamberlaine his *seruants. Written by William Shakespeare*. Imprinted at London, for *Thomas Fisher*, and are to be soulde at his shoppe, at the Signe of the White Hart, in *Fleetestreete*. 1600.

This text appears to have been set from Shakespeare's working manuscript. Its inconsistencies in time scheme and other irregularities may reflect some revision, although the inconsistencies are not noticeable in performance. A second quarto appeared in 1619, though falsely dated 1600; it was a reprint of the first quarto, with some minor corrections and many new errors. A copy of this second quarto, evidently with some added stage directions and other minor changes from a theatrical manuscript in the company's possession, served as the basis for the First Folio text of 1623. Changes of speech assignment in the Folio text, especially in Act 5, may reflect a late revival over which Shakespeare had no control. Essentially, the first quarto remains the authoritative text.

Other than Francis Meres's listing of the play in 1598 in his *Palladis Tamia*, external clues as to date are elusive. Possibly the worry that a lion in a play might frighten the ladies (3.1.24–31) echoes published accounts of a baptismal feast at court in August 1594, when a blackamoor was chosen to draw in a chariot in place of a lion for fear of alarming nearby spectators. The description of unruly weather (2.1.88–114) has been related to the bad summer of 1594, but complaints about the weather are perennial. On the assumption that the play celebrates some noble wedding of the period, scholars have come up with a number of suitable marriages. Chief are those of Sir Thomas Heneage to Mary, Countess of Southampton, in 1594; of William Stanley, Earl of Derby, to Elizabeth Vere, daughter of the Earl of Oxford, in 1595; and of Thomas, son of Lord Berkeley, to Elizabeth, daughter of Lord Carey, in 1596. The Countess of Southampton was the widowed mother of the young Earl of Southampton, to whom Shakespeare had dedicated his *Venus and Adonis* and *The Rape of Lucrece*. No one has ever proved convincingly, however, that the play was written for any occasion other than commercial public performance. The play makes sense for a general audience and does not need to depend on references to a private marriage. Shakespeare was, after all, in the business of writing plays for his fellow actors, who earned their livelihood chiefly by public acting before large paying audiences. In any event, the search for a court marriage is a circular argument in terms of dating; suitable court marriages can be found for any year of the decade. In the last analysis, the play has to be dated on the basis of its stylistic affinity to plays like *Romeo and Juliet* and *Richard II*, works of the "lyric" mid-1590s. The "Pyramus and Thisbe" performance in *A Midsummer Night's Dream* would seem to bear an obvious relation to *Romeo and Juliet*, although no one can say for sure which came first.

## The Merchant of Venice (c. 1596–1597)

The Stationers' Register, the official record book of the London Company of Stationers (booksellers and printers), for July 22, 1598, contains an entry on behalf of the printer James Roberts for "a booke of the Marchaunt of Venyce, or otherwise called the Iewe of Venyce, Prouided, that yt bee not prynted by the said James Robertes or anye other whatsoeuer without lycence first had from the Right honorable the lord Chamberlen." Roberts evidently enjoyed a close connection with the Chamberlain's Men (Shakespeare's acting company) and seemingly was granted the special favor of registering the play at this time, even though the company did not wish to see the play published until later (or until they were paid). In 1600, at any rate, Roberts

transferred his rights as publisher to Thomas Heyes and printed the volume for him with the following title:

The most excellent Historie of the *Merchant of Venice*. With the extreame crueltie of *Shylocke* the Iewe towards the sayd Merchant, in cutting a iust pound of his flesh: and the obtayning of *Portia* by the choyse of three chests. *As it hath beene diuers times acted by the Lord Chamberlaine his Seruants*. Written by William Shakespeare. AT LONDON, Printed by *I. R.* [James Roberts] for Thomas Heyes, and are to be sold in Paules Church-yard, at the signe of the Greene Dragon. 1600.

The text of this 1600 quarto is generally a good one, based seemingly on an accurate copy of Shakespeare's papers by the dramatist himself or some reliable transcriber. It served as copy for the second quarto of 1619 (printed by William Jaggard for Thomas Pavier and fraudulently dated 1600) and for the First Folio of 1623. Although some theatrical manuscript seems also to have been consulted in preparation for the Folio text, the Folio variations appear to have little authority.

Francis Meres mentions the play in 1598 in his *Palladis Tamia*. Establishing an earlier limit for dating has proven not so easy. Many scholars have urged a connection with the Roderigo Lopez affair of 1594 (see the Introduction to the play). The supposed allusion to Lopez in the lines about "a wolf, who, hanged for human slaughter" (4.1.134) may simply indicate, however, that wolves were actually hanged for attacking men in Shakespeare's day (as dogs were for killing sheep). Besides, the Lopez case remained so notorious throughout the 1590s that even a proven allusion to it in *The Merchant* would not limit the play to 1594 or 1595. Christopher Marlowe's play, *The Jew of Malta*, was revived in 1594 to exploit anti-Lopez sentiment but was also revived in 1596. There may be, moreover, an allusion in 1.1.27 to the *St. Andrew*, a Spanish ship captured at Cadiz in 1596, and Shylock's allusion to Jacob and Laban (1.3.69–88) may well echo Miles Mosse's *The Arraignment and Conviction of Usury*, 1595. If so, the likeliest date is 1596–1597.

## Much Ado About Nothing (1598–1599)

"The Commedie of muche A doo about nothing a booke" was entered in the Stationers' Register, the official record book of the London Company of Stationers (booksellers and printers), on August 4, 1600, along with *As You Like It*, *Henry V*, and Ben Jonson's *Every Man in His Humor*, all marked as plays of "My lord chamberlens men" (Shakespeare's acting company) and all "to be staied"— that is, not published without further permission. Earlier in the same memorandum, written on a spare page in the Register, occurs the name of the printer James Roberts, whose registration of *The Merchant of Venice* in 1598 was similarly stayed, pending further permission to publish.

Evidently, the Chamberlain's Men were attempting to ensure that they were paid for any plays printed or else to prevent unauthorized publication of these very popular plays. If the latter was their motive, they were too late to forestall the appearance of an unauthorized quarto of *Henry V* in August 1600, but they did manage to control release of the others. *Much Ado About Nothing* appeared later that same year in a seemingly authorized version:

Much adoe about Nothing. *As it hath been sundrie times publikely* acted by the right honourable, the Lord Chamberlaine his seruants. *Written by William Shakespeare.* LONDON Printed by V. S. [Valentine Sims] for Andrew Wise, and William Aspley. 1600.

Once thought to have been set up from a theatrical play-book and then used itself in the theater as a playbook before serving as copy for the First Folio of 1623, this 1600 quarto text is now generally regarded as having been set from Shakespeare's own manuscript. The names of the actors Will Kempe and Richard Cowley appear among the speech prefixes in 4.2, indicating that Shakespeare had them in mind as he wrote; other irregularities in speech prefixes and scene headings (including "ghost" characters, such as Leonato's wife Innogen) read more like a manuscript in the last stages of revision than a playbook for a finished production. The Folio text was based on this 1600 quarto, lightly annotated with reference to the playbook but providing little in the way of new readings other than the correction of obvious error.

Francis Meres does not mention the play in September 1598 in his *Palladis Tamia*, unless (and this seems unlikely) it is his "*Loue labours wonne.*" Will Kempe, who played Dogberry, left the Chamberlain's Men early in 1599. The likeliest date, then, is the winter of 1598–1599, though publication was not until 1600.

### *As You Like It* (1598–1600)

"As you like yt, a booke" was entered in the Stationers' Register, the official record book of the London Company of Stationers (booksellers and printers), on August 4, 1600, along with *Much Ado About Nothing, Henry V*, and Ben Jonson's *Every Man in His Humor*, all labeled as "My lord chamberlens mens plaies" and all ordered "to be staied" from publication until further notice. Evidently, the Chamberlain's Men (Shakespeare's acting company) were anxious to ensure payment or otherwise protect their rights to these very popular plays. Despite their efforts, *Henry V* appeared in an unauthorized quarto that same month. *As You Like It* did not appear in print, however, until the First Folio of 1623. The Folio text is a good one, based seemingly on the theatrical playbook that still retained certain authorial features (conceivably, because an autograph fair copy served as the basis for it) or on a

literary transcript either of the playbook or of an authorial manuscript.

Francis Meres does not mention the play in September 1598 in his *Palladis Tamia*. However, the play contains an unusually clear allusion to Christopher Marlowe's *Hero and Leander* ("Who ever loved that loved not at first sight?" 3.5.82), of which the first extant edition appeared in 1598, although Shakespeare may well have known it earlier in manuscript or in some lost edition. Even so, other possible allusions, to the burning of satirical books in June 1599 (see 1.2.85–6) and to the new Globe Theater ("All the world's a stage," 2.7.138), point to a date between late 1598 and the summer of 1600, probably after *Much Ado About Nothing*.

### *Twelfth Night* (1600–1602)

*Twelfth Night* was registered with the London Company of Stationers (booksellers and printers) in 1623 and was first published in the First Folio of that year in a good text set up from what may have been a scribal transcript of Shakespeare's draft manuscript or possibly the playbook (assuming that the scribe might omit theatrical notations). There was a brief delay in printing *Twelfth Night* in the First Folio, possibly because a transcript was being prepared. The play was first mentioned, however, in the *Diary* of a Middle Temple law student or barrister named John Manningham, who describes the festivities for Candlemas Day, February 2, 1602, as follows:

At our feast wee had a play called "Twelue Night, or What you Will," much like the Commedy of Errores, or Menechmi in Plautus, but most like and neere to that in Italian called *Inganni*. A good practise in it to make the Steward beleeve his Lady widdowe was in love with him, by couterfeyting a letter as from his Lady in generall termes, telling him what shee liked best in him, and prescribing his gesture in smiling, his apparaile, & c., and then when he came to practise making him beleeue they tooke him to be mad.

This entry was once suspected to be a forgery perpetrated by John Payne Collier, who published the *Diary* in 1831, but its authenticity is now generally accepted. The date accords with several possible allusions in the play itself. When Fabian jokes about "a pension of thousands to be paid from the Sophy" (2.5.176–7), he seems to be recalling Sir Anthony Shirley's reception by the Shah of Persia (the Sophy) between the summer of 1598 and late 1601. An account of this visit was entered in the Stationers' Register in November 1601. Viola's description of Feste as "wise enough to play the fool" (3.1.60) may recall a poem beginning "True it is, he plays the fool indeed," published in 1600–1601 by Robert Armin (who had played the role of Feste). Maria's comparison of Malvolio's smiling face to "the new map with the augmentation of the Indies" (3.2.77–8) refers to new maps published in 1599 in which more was shown of the East Indies, including Japan, than had been mapped before. Fabian's reference to sailing north and to the icicle on a Dutchman's beard (3.2.25–6) sounds like an allusion to William Barentz's Arctic expedition, first described in English in an account entered in the Stationers' Register on June 13, 1598, though no edition survives before 1609. Leslie Hotson (*The First Night of Twelfth Night*, 1954) has argued for a first performance at court on Twelfth Night in January 1601, when Queen Elizabeth entertained Don Virginio Orsino, Duke of Bracciano, but this hypothesis has not gained general acceptance, partly because the role of Orsino in the play would scarcely flatter such a noble visitor and partly because there is no proof that any of Shakespeare's plays were originally commissioned for private performance. Nevertheless, the episode may have suggested to Shakespeare the name Orsino. All in all, a date between 1600 and early 1602 seems most likely. Francis Meres does not mention the play in 1598 in his *Palladis Tamia*.

## Measure for Measure (1603–1604)

*Measure for Measure* first appeared in the First Folio of 1623. The text was evidently set from scrivener Ralph Crane's copy, possibly of Shakespeare's own draft; the usual inconsistencies of composition have not yet been smoothed away by use in the theater. On the other hand, spellings tend to suggest that Crane was copying a transcript. A recent and controversial hypothesis is that Crane based his copy on a playbook in use after Shakespeare's death, which incorporated some theatrical adaptation by Thomas Middleton and some other reviser, including a song (4.1.1–6) that could have originated in *Rollo, Duke of Normandy* (c. 1617) by John Fletcher and others.

The first recorded performance (according to a Revels account document) was on December 26, 1604, St. Stephen's Night, when "a play Caled Mesur for Mesur" by "Shaxberd" was acted in the banqueting hall at Whitehall "by his Maiesties plaiers." Shakespeare's acting company, previously the Lord Chamberlain's Men, had become the King's Men after the accession to the throne of James I in 1603. Several allusions in the play seem to point to the summer of 1604, when the theaters, having been closed for a year because of the plague, were reopened. A reference to the King of Hungary (1.2.1–5) may reflect anxieties in England over James's negotiations for a settlement with Spain; censorship would forbid a direct mentioning of Spain. Mistress Overdone's complaint about the war, the "sweat" (plague), the "gallows" (public executions), and poverty (1.2.81–3) are all suggestive of events in 1603–1604, when war with Spain and the plague were still very much in evidence. Duke Vincentio's reticent habits

have been seen as a flattering reference to James's well-known dislike of crowds. Stylistically, the play is clearly later than *Twelfth Night* (1600–1602), so that a date close to the first recorded performance in 1604 is a necessity, even if we cannot be positive about all the supposed allusions to King James.

## Richard III (c. 1592–1594)

A quarto edition of *Richard III*, registered by Andrew Wise on October 20, 1597, appeared later that same year with the following title:

THE TRAGEDY of King Richard the third. Containing, His treacherous Plots against his brother Clarence: the pittiefull murther of his iunocent nephewes: his tyrannicall vsurpation: with the whole course of his detested life, and most deserued death. As it hath beene lately Acted by the Right honourable the Lord Chamberlaine his seruants. AT LONDON Printed by Valentine Sims, for Andrew Wise, dwelling in Paules Chu[r]ch-yard, at the Signe of the Angell. 1597.

This text, one of the most perplexing in all Shakespeare, is sometimes regarded as one that was created when the acting company banded together to reconstruct a play of which the copy was missing. The reconstructed version may have been cut, perhaps for provincial performance. This defective text was the basis of the 1597 quarto, which was reprinted in 1598, 1602, 1605, 1612, 1622, 1629, and 1634, each of which was successively more error-laden than the previous one. The First Folio text of 1623 seems to have been set mainly from copies of the third and sixth quartos (1602 and 1622), which had been sporadically but heavily corrected against an independent manuscript—possibly Shakespeare's own working manuscript or a copy of it. This manuscript source, some of which may have been interleaved into the printers' copy, represents a generally superior authority to that of the first quarto. Parts of the Folio text, however, were set from an uncorrected copy of the third quarto (1602), and for those passages (3.1.1–158 and 5.3.48 to end of play) the first quarto, from which the third quarto was derived, must serve as copy text. Otherwise, the Folio text is the most authoritative, though it must be approached with caution.

The situation is indeed fraught with unusual uncertainty, since there are many opportunities for the Folio to have perpetuated errors of the earlier quartos; moreover, its "improvements" over the readings of those quartos could in some instances be editorial sophistications. The first quarto offers some readings that demand serious attention. Especially when the Folio's reading differs from those of the first quarto and is instead derived from quartos two through six, the first quarto should be preferred unless it is manifestly wrong. At the same time, however, since the first quarto may reflect adaptation of the original acting text, its changes may not represent

Shakespeare's artistic intention either. For these reasons, one must be wary of the first quarto's assignment of speeches when they vary from the Folio's assignments and also of the first quarto's cuts, some of which are substantial.

The play is mentioned by Francis Meres in 1598 in his *Palladis Tamia*. John Weever names a *"Richard"* in his *Epigrams*, published in 1599. Most scholars date *Richard III* as 1592–1594, on the basis of its style and its close affinity to the *Henry VI* series (completed probably in 1591–1592). The play may have been influenced by the anonymous *The True Tragedy of Richard III*, registered in June 1594 but probably written in 1590–1592 or even earlier. Shakespeare's play may also have been influenced by Thomas Kyd's *The Spanish Tragedy* (c. 1587) and by Christopher Marlowe's dramas (he died in 1593).

## Richard II (c. 1595–1596)

On August 29, 1597, "The Tragedye of Richard the Second" was entered in the Stationers' Register, the official record book of the London Company of Stationers (booksellers and printers), by Andrew Wise, and was published by him later that same year:

THE Tragedie of King Richard the second. *As it hath beene publikely acted by the right Honourable the Lorde Chamberlaine his Seruants.* LONDON Printed by Valentine Simmes for Androw Wise, and are to be sold at his shop in Paules church yard at the signe of the Angel. 1597.

This is a good text, printed evidently from the author's papers or a nontheatrical transcript of them. Wise issued two more quartos of this popular play in 1598, each set from the previous quarto, and then in 1603 transferred his rights to the play to Matthew Law. This publisher issued in 1608 a fourth quarto "With new additions of the Parliament Sceane, and the deposing of King Richard" (according to the title page in some copies). The deposition scene has indeed been omitted from the earlier quartos, probably through censorship. A fifth quarto appeared in 1615, based on the fourth quarto. All the quartos after the first attribute the play to Shakespeare. The added deposition scene in quartos 4 and 5 seems to have been memorially reconstructed. The First Folio text of 1623 gives a better version of the deposition scene, seemingly because the printers of the Folio had access to the manuscript playbook for this portion of the text. (Some scholars maintain that the Folio text was derived from an earlier quarto or quartos that had been marked up and used as a playbook, but that case has been weakened by recent research.) Most of the Folio text was probably set from an annotated copy of the third quarto, and perhaps a leaf in Act 5 from the fifth quarto. The annotation was evidently quite uneven, and so the most authoritative text for all

but the deposition scene remains the first quarto; nevertheless, at certain points (especially the first 900 lines, part of 3.2, and much of Act 5), the annotation with reference to the playbook seems to have been more thorough. At such points, the Folio readings deserve serious attention, and the stage directions are often illuminating.

Francis Meres mentions the play in 1598 in his *Palladis Tamia*. Clearly it had been written and performed prior to the Stationers' Register entry in August 1597. Its earliest probable date is 1595, since the play seemingly is indebted to Samuel Daniel's poem, *The First Four Books of the Civil Wars*, published in that year. Shakespeare follows Daniel, for example, in increasing the Queen's age from eleven (according to the chronicles) to maturity, and in other significant details. On December 7, 1595, Sir Edward Hoby invited Sir Robert Cecil to his house in Cannon Row, "where as late as it shall please you a gate for your supper shall be open, and King Richard present himself to your view." Although it is by no means certain that this passage refers to a private performance of Shakespeare's play, stylistic considerations favor a date around 1595 rather than 1597. If, as some scholars contend, Daniel's *Civil Wars* was written after Shakespeare's play rather than before it, the date of *Richard II* might be as early as 1594.

## Henry IV, Part I (1596–1597)

On February 25, 1598, "The historye of Henry the IIIJth with his battaile of Shrewsburye against Henry Hottspurre of the Northe with the conceipted mirthe of Sir John Ffalstoff" was entered in the Stationers' Register, the official record book of the London Company of Stationers (booksellers and printers), by Andrew Wise. Later that year appeared the following quarto:

THE HISTORY OF HENRIE THE FOVRTH; With the battell at Shrewsburie, *betweene the King and Lord* Henry Percy, surnamed Henrie Hotspur of the North. *With the humorous conceits of Sir* Iohn Falstaffe. AT LONDON, Printed by P. S. [Peter Short] for *Andrew Wise*, dwelling in Paules Churchyard, at the signe of the Angell. 1598.

Actually this was not the first quarto, for an earlier fragment of eight pages has survived, part of a text that served as copy for the first complete extant quarto. Together, these quartos make up an excellent authoritative text, based seemingly on the author's papers or, more probably, a scribal transcript of them. Four more quartos appeared before the First Folio of 1623, each based on the previous quarto. The Folio itself was based on the last of these, perhaps with reference also to some kind of manuscript, although the number of authoritative readings that can be claimed for the Folio is small.

*1 Henry IV* shows signs of revision in the use of characters' names, most notably that of Falstaff. Plainly, the original version of the play called him Sir John Oldcastle, after one of the prince's companions in the anonymous *Famous Victories of Henry the Fifth* (c. 1588). The name "Oldcastle" was originally intended for *2 Henry IV* as well. The speech prefix "Old." is left standing at 1.2.119 in the quarto of *2 Henry IV*, one or two lines of verse in *1 Henry IV* are one syllable short, evidently because "Oldcastle" has been altered to "Falstaff," and Falstaff is jokingly referred to as "my old lad of the castle" (*1 Henry IV*, 1.2.41). Moreover, there are several contemporary allusions to a play about a fat knight named Oldcastle. Apparently, Henry Brooke, Lord Cobham, a living descendant of the Lollard martyr Oldcastle of Henry V's reign, took umbrage at the profane use Shakespeare had made of this revered name, whereupon Shakespeare's acting company shifted to another less controversial name from the chronicles, Sir John Fastolfe or Falstaff (called "Falstaffe" in the Folio text of Shakespeare's *1 Henry VI* and assigned a cowardly role in the French wars of that play). The revision also changed the names of Oldcastle's cronies from Harvey and Russell to Peto and Bardolph. This edition retains the name "Falstaff," since Shakespeare clearly accepted it as the new name of the character in all his "Falstaff" plays.

Cobham was Lord Chamberlain from July 1596 until his death in March 1597, during which interval Shakespeare's company bore the name of Lord Hunsdon's Men. Quite possibly, the difficulty over the name "Oldcastle" erupted during that period, for *1 Henry IV* seems to have been written and performed in late 1596 and early 1597, not long after Shakespeare had finished *Richard II* (c. 1595–1596).

Francis Meres, in his *Palladis Tamia*, 1598, refers to "*Henry the IV*" without specifying one or two parts. Publication of *1 Henry IV* in 1598 confirmed to the Elizabethan public that the changes in names to Falstaff, Peto, and Bardolph had taken place.

## Henry V (1599)

An entry in the Stationers' Register, the official record book of the London Company of Stationers (booksellers and printers), for August 4, 1600, provides that "Henry the fift" and three other plays belonging to the Lord Chamberlain's Men (Shakespeare's acting company) are "to be staied" from publication until further permission is granted. Evidently, the Chamberlain's Men were anxious to ensure they were paid or to prevent unauthorized publication. They did not succeed, in any event, in preventing the appearance of an unauthorized text of *Henry V*. An entry in the Stationers' Register for August 14 assigns to Thomas Pavier an already published work entitled "The historye of Henry the Vth with the battell of Agencourt." The quarto volume to which this entry refers is the following:

THE CHRONICLE History of Henry the fift, With his battell fought at *Agin Court* in *France*. Togither with *Auntient Pistoll*. As it hath bene sundry times playd by the Right honorable the Lord Chamberlaine his seruants. LONDON Printed by *Thomas Creede*, for Tho. Millington, and Iohn Busby. And are to be sold at his house in Carter Lane, next the Powle head. 1600.

The text of this play is manifestly corrupt. It is considerably shorter than the First Folio version and completely omits the choruses and three entire scenes (1.1, 3.1, and 4.2). The remainder seems to have been put together by memorial reconstruction. This unauthorized quarto served as the basis for a second quarto printed by Thomas Creede for Thomas Pavier in 1602 and a third printed by William Jaggard for Thomas Pavier in 1619 but fraudulently dated 1608. The Folio text was printed seemingly from an authorial manuscript, perhaps with occasional reference to the third quarto (which contains some potentially troublesome contamination). The Folio text is thus the most reliable version, though the first quarto is also an interesting witness, especially for visual effects recorded in its stage directions, for a few readings in the text, and for verse lineation of Pistol's speeches.

Francis Meres does not mention the play in 1598 in his *Palladis Tamia*, though he does mention "*Henry the IV*." The epilogue to *2 Henry IV* (written probably in 1597) promises that "our humble author will continue the story, with Sir John in it, and make you merry with fair Katharine of France"; since the prediction is not really accurate regarding Falstaff, we can be reasonably certain that Shakespeare had not yet begun *Henry V* in 1597. An allusion in the Chorus of Act 5 to "the General of our gracious Empress," who may in good time come home from Ireland with "rebellion broachèd on his sword," has been taken by virtually all editors to refer to the Earl of Essex, who left in March 1599 to quell the Irish rebellion headed by Tyrone. Although Essex returned on September 28 of that same year, having failed utterly in his assignment, the departure of such a charismatic figure could have inspired Shakespeare's praising remark. A minority view holds that the choruses (which do not appear in the unauthorized quarto of 1600) could have been written later in 1601 for Essex's far more victorious successor, Lord Mountjoy (see Warren D. Smith on *Henry V* in *JEGP*, 1954). Still, Essex was more prominent during those exciting years, more likely to have been the subject of adulation. In any case, the play itself must have been written before August 1600, most probably in 1599. The reference to "this wooden O" in the Chorus of Act 1 is often thought to be Shakespeare's compliment to the company's new theater, the Globe, which was ready for their use probably in 1599; but the play may have been produced at the Curtain instead.

## *Romeo and Juliet (1594–1596)*

A corrupt and unregistered quarto of *Romeo and Juliet* appeared in 1597 with the following title:

AN excellent conceited Tragedie OF Romeo and Iuliet, As it hath been often (with great applause) plaid publiquely, by the right Honourable t he L. of *Hunsdon* his Seruants. LONDON, Printed by Iohn Danter. 1597.

This edition, intended no doubt to capitalize on the play's great popularity, seems to have been memorially reconstructed by two or more actors (probably those playing Romeo and Paris), and possibly thereafter to have been used as a playbook. Its appearance seems to have caused the issuance two years later of a clearly authoritative version:

THE MOST Excellent and lamentable Tragedie, of Romeo and Iuliet. *Newly corrected, augmented, and amended*: As it hath bene sundry times publiquely acted, by the right Honourable the Lord Chamberlaine his Seruants. LONDON Printed by Thomas Creede, for Cuthbert Burby, and are to be sold at his shop neare the Exchange. 1599.

This text is some 800 lines longer than the first and corrects errors in that earlier version. It seems at one point, however, to have been contaminated by the first quarto, as though the manuscript source for the second quarto (probably the author's rough draft) was defective at some point. A passage from 1.2.53 to 1.3.34 was apparently set directly from the first quarto. (On this matter, see George W. Williams's old-spelling edition of the play, Duke Univ. Press, 1964.) Q1 may also have influenced Q2 in some other isolated instances. Despite this contamination, however, the second quarto is the authoritative text, except for the passage of direct indebtedness to Q1. Q2 served as the basis for the third quarto (1609), which in turn served as copy for the fourth quarto (undated, but placed in 1622) and the First Folio of 1623. A fifth quarto appeared in 1637. The Folio text may embody a few authoritative readings of its own, perhaps by way of reference to a theatrical manuscript.

Francis Meres, in his *Palladis Tamia*, 1598, assigns the play to Shakespeare. So does John Weever in his *Epigrams* of 1599. Internal evidence on dating is not reliable. The Nurse observes that "'Tis since the earthquake now eleven years" (1.3.24); however, it has been discovered that suitable earthquakes occurred in 1580, 1583, 1584, and 1585, giving us a wide choice of dates even if we accept the dubious proposition that the Nurse is speaking accurately. Astronomical reckoning of the position of the moon at the time the play purportedly takes place ("A fortnight and odd days" before Lammastide, August 1, 1.3.16) indicates the year 1596; again, however, we have no reason to assume Shakespeare cared about this sort of internal accuracy. More suggestive perhaps is the argument that Danter's unauthorized publication in 1597 was seeking to exploit a popular new play—one the acting company certainly did not yet wish to see published, since it was a moneymaker. Danter assigns the play to Lord Hunsdon's servants, a name that Shakespeare's company could have used only from July 22, 1596 (when the old Lord Chamberlain, Henry Carey, first Lord Hunsdon, died) to March 17, 1597 (when George Carey, second Lord Hunsdon, was appointed to his father's erstwhile position as Lord Chamberlain). Danter could simply have been using the name of the company at the time he obtained the play, but he may also have indicated performance in late 1596. Danter printed only the first four sheets, but he must have done so by February–March 1597, when his presses were seized. Stylistically, the play is clearly of the "lyric" period of *A Midsummer Night's Dream* and *Richard II*. There are also stylistic affinities to the sonnets and to the narrative poems of 1593–1594. A date between 1594 and 1596 is likely, especially toward the latter end of this period. Whether the play comes before or after *A Midsummer Night's Dream* is, however, a matter of conjecture.

## *Julius Caesar (1599)*

*Julius Caesar* was first published in the First Folio of 1623. The text is an excellent one, based evidently on a theater playbook or a transcript of it; some theatrical features, such as a provision for the doubling of Cassius and Caius Ligarius, appear to represent a staging configuration that Shakespeare had not anticipated. On the other hand, some stage directions sound authorial, as though Shakespeare's own words had survived into the playbook. Some confusions have survived as well, notably in the handling of Lucilius, Lucius, Titinius, and Pindarus in 4.2. In the Folio, the play is included among the tragedies and entitled *The Tragedy of Julius Caesar*, although the table of contents lists it as *The Life and death of Julius Caesar*.

The play's first performance must have occurred in 1599 or slightly earlier. On September 21, 1599, a Swiss visitor named Thomas Platter crossed the River Thames after lunch with a company of spectators to see "the tragedy of the first Emperor Julius Caesar" performed in a thatched-roofed building. The description fits the Globe, the Rose, and the Swan theaters, but the last of these was not in regular use. The Admiral's Men at the Rose are not known to have had a Caesar play, whereas the Chamberlain's Men certainly had Shakespeare's play about this time. They had only recently moved from their Theatre in the northeast suburbs of London to the Globe south of the river, and *Julius Caesar* was probably a new play for the occasion.

John Weever, in *The Mirror of Martyrs* (1601), is surely referring to Shakespeare's play when he describes "the many-headed multitude" listening first to "Brutus' speech, that Caesar was ambitious" and then to "eloquent Mark Antony." (The dedication to Weever's book claims he wrote it "some two years ago," in 1599; however, since this book has been shown to be heavily indebted to a work that first appeared in 1600, Weever's allusion is not as helpful in limiting the date as was once thought.) Ben Jonson's *Every Man in His Humor*, acted in 1599, may also contain allusions to Shakespeare's play. Francis Meres does not mention it in 1598 in his *Palladis Tamia*.

## Hamlet (c. 1600–1601)

Like everything else about *Hamlet*, the textual problem is complicated. On July 26, 1602, James Roberts entered in the Stationers' Register, the official record book of the London Company of Stationers (booksellers and printers), "A booke called the Revenge of Hamlett Prince Denmarke as yt was latelie Acted by the Lord Chamberleyne his servantes." For some reason, however, Roberts did not print his copy of *Hamlet* until 1604, by which time the following unauthorized edition had appeared:

THE Tragicall Historie of HAMLET *Prince of Denmarke* By William Shake-speare. As it hath beene diuerse times acted by his Highnesse seruants in the Cittie of London: as also in the two Vniuersities of Cambridge and Oxford, and else-where. At London printed for N. L. [Nicholas Ling] and Iohn Trundell. 1603.

This edition, the first quarto of *Hamlet*, seems to have been memorially reconstructed by actors who toured the provinces (note the references to Cambridge, Oxford, and so on), with some recollection of an earlier *Hamlet* play (the *Ur-Hamlet*) written before 1589 and acted during the 1590s. The actors seemingly had no recourse to an authoritative manuscript. One of these actors may have played Marcellus and possibly Lucianus and Voltimand. Their version appears to have been based on an adaptation of the company's original playbook, which itself stood once removed from Shakespeare's working papers by way of an intermediate manuscript. The resulting text is very corrupt, and yet it seems to have affected the more authentic text, because the compositors of the second quarto made use of it, especially when they typeset the first act.

The authorized quarto of *Hamlet* appeared in 1604. Roberts, the printer, seems to have reached some agreement with Ling, one of the publishers of the first quarto, for their initials are now paired on the title page:

THE Tragicall Historie of HAMLET, *Prince of Denmarke*. By William Shakespeare. Newly imprinted and enlarged to almost as much againe as it was, according to the true and perfect Coppie. AT LONDON, Printed by I. R. [James Roberts] for N. L. [Nicholas Ling] and are to be sold at his shoppe vnder Saint Dunstons Church in Fleetstreet. 1604.

Some copies of this edition are dated 1605. This text was based seemingly on Shakespeare's own papers, with bookkeeper's annotations, but is marred by printing errors and is at times contaminated by the first quarto—presumably, when the printers found Shakespeare's manuscript unreadable. This second quarto served as copy for a third quarto in 1611, Ling having meanwhile transferred his rights in the play to John Smethwick. A fourth quarto, undated but before 1623, was based on the third.

The First Folio text of 1623 omits more than two hundred lines found in the second quarto, yet it supplies some clearly authentic passages. It seems to derive from a transcript of Shakespeare's draft, in which cuts made by the author were observed—cuts made by Shakespeare quite possibly because he knew the draft to be too long for performance and which had either not been marked in the second quarto copy or had been ignored there by the compositors. The Folio also incorporates other alterations seemingly made for clarity or in anticipation of performance. To this theatrically motivated transcript, Shakespeare apparently contributed many revisions. Subsequently, this version evidently was copied again by a careless scribe who took many liberties with the text. Typesetting from this inferior manuscript, the Folio compositors occasionally consulted the fourth quarto, but not often enough. Thus, even though the Folio supplies many genuine readings, as does the first quarto when both the Folio and the second quarto are wrong, the second quarto remains the control text for this present edition.

Since the text of the second quarto is too long to be accommodated in the two hours' traffic of the stage and since it becomes even longer when the words found only in the Folio are added, Shakespeare must have known it would have to be cut for performance and probably marked at least some omissions himself. Since he may have consented to such cuts primarily because of the constraints of time, however, this present edition holds to the view that the passages in question should not be excised from the text we read. The *Hamlet* presented here is doubtless longer than any version ever acted in Shakespeare's day and thus does not represent a script for any actual performance, but it may well represent the play as Shakespeare wrote it and then expanded it somewhat while also including passages that he may reluctantly have consented to cut for performance. It is also possible that some cuts were artistically intended, but, in the face of real uncertainty in this matter, an editorial policy of inclusion gives to the reader those passages that would otherwise have to be excised or put in an appendix on questionable grounds of authorial "intent."

*Hamlet* must have been produced before the Stationers' Register entry of July 26, 1602. Francis Meres does not mention the play in 1598 in his *Palladis Tamia*. Gabriel Harvey attributes the "tragedy of Hamlet, Prince of Denmark" to Shakespeare in a marginal note in Harvey's copy of Speght's Chaucer; Harvey acquired the book in 1598, but he could have written the note any time between then and 1601, or even 1603. More helpful in dating is *Hamlet*'s clear reference to the so-called War of the Theaters, the rivalry between the adult actors and the boy actors whose companies had newly revived in 1598–1599 after nearly a decade of inactivity (see 2.2.337–62). The Children of the Chapel Royal began acting at Blackfriars in 1598 and provided such keen competition in 1599–1601 that the adult actors were at times forced to tour the provinces (see *Hamlet*, 2.2.332–62). *Hamlet*'s reference to the rivalry appears, however, only in the Folio text and could represent a late addition. The reference to an "inhibition" imposed on acting companies "by the means of the late innovation" (2.2.332–3), printed in the 1604 quarto, may possibly refer to the abortive uprising of the Earl of Essex on February 8, 1601, or to a decree issued by the Privy Council on June 22, 1600, restricting London companies to two performances a week in each of two playhouses. Revenge tragedy was also in fashion during these years: John Marston's *Antonio's Revenge*, for example, dates from 1599–1601, and *The Malcontent* is from about the same time or slightly later, though it is hard to tell who influenced whom. *Hamlet*'s apparent indebtedness to John Florio's translation of Montaigne suggests that Shakespeare had access to that work in manuscript before its publication in 1603; the Florio had been registered for publication in 1595 and 1600.

## Othello (*c. 1603–1604*)

On October 6, 1621, Thomas Walkley entered in the Stationers' Register, the official record book of the London Company of Stationers (booksellers and printers), "The Tragedie of Othello, the moore of Venice," and published the play in the following year:

THE Tragoedy of Othello, The Moore of Venice. *As it hath beene diuerse times acted at the* Globe, and at the Black-Friers, by *his Maiesties Seruants. Written by* VVilliam Shakespeare. LONDON, Printed by N. O. [Nicholas Okes] for *Thomas Walkley*, and are to be sold at his shop, at the Eagle and Child, in Brittans Bursse. 1622.

This text of this quarto is a good one, based probably on a scribal transcript of Shakespeare's working manuscript, although it is some one hundred and sixty lines shorter than the Folio text of 1623, mostly in scattered small omissions. The Folio text may have been derived (via an intermediate transcript) from a revision of the original authorial manuscript, in which Shakespeare himself copied over his work and made a large number of synonymous or nearly synonymous changes as he

did so. These papers, edited by someone else to remove profanity as required by law and introducing other stylistic changes in the process, seemingly became the basis of the playbook and also of the Folio text. E. A. J. Honigmann (*The Texts of "Othello" and Shakespearian Revision*, 1996) proposes that Ralph Crane prepared a transcript to serve as copy for the Folio text, though not all scholars have agreed.

The textual situation is thus complex. The Folio text appears to contain a significant number of authorial changes, but it was also worked on by one or more sophisticating scribes and by compositors whose changes are sometimes hard to distinguish from those of Shakespeare. The quarto text was printed by a printing establishment that was not known for careful work but does stand close in some ways to a Shakespearean original. Editorially, then, the Folio is the copy text, and its readings are to be preferred when the quarto is not clearly correct and especially when the Folio gives us genuinely new words, but the quarto's readings demand careful consideration when the Folio text may be suspected of mechanical error (e.g., the shortening of words in full lines) or compositorial substitution of alternative forms, normalizations, and easy adjustments of meter. There are times when the Folio's compositor may have been misled by nearby words or letters in his copy. And, because some of the Folio's stage directions are probably scribal, attention should be paid to those in the quarto.

According to a Revels account that was suspected of being a forgery soon after its publication in 1842 but is now generally accepted, the earliest mention of the play is on "Hallamas Day, being the first of Nouembar," 1604, when "the Kings Maiesties plaiers" performed "A Play in the Banketinge house att Whit Hall Called The Moor of Venis." Possible echoes of *Othello* in *The Honest Whore, Part I*, by Thomas Dekker and Thomas Middleton (1604) and in Richard Knolles's *History of the Turks* (1603) help fix a forward date of composition. Francis Meres does not list the play in 1598. On stylistic grounds, the play is usually dated in 1603 or 1604, although arguments are sometimes presented for a date as early as 1601 or 1602.

## King Lear (*c. 1605–1606*)

On November 26, 1607, Nathaniel Butter and John Busby entered in the Stationers' Register, the official record book of the London Company of Stationers (booksellers and printers), "A booke called. Master William Shakespeare his historye of Kinge Lear, as yt was played before the Kinges maiestie at Whitehall vppon Sainct Stephens night at Christmas Last, by his maiesties servantes playinge vsually at the Globe on the Banksyde." Next year appeared the following quarto:

M. William Shak-speare: HIS True Chronicle Historie of the life and death of King LEAR and his three Daughters. *With the vnfortunate life* of Edgar, *sonne* and heire to the Earle of Gloster, and his sullen and assumed humor of Tom of Bedlam: *As it was played before the Kings Maiestie at Whitehall vpon S.* Stephans *night in Christmas Hollidayes.* By his Maiesties seruants playing vsually at the Gloabe on the Bancke-side. LONDON, Printed for *Nathaniel Butter*, and are to be sold at his shop in *Pauls* Churchyard at the signe of the Pide Bull neere St. *Austins* Gate. 1608.

This quarto is often called the "Pied Bull" quarto in reference to its place of sale. Twelve copies exist today, in ten different "states," because proofreading was being carried on while the sheets were being run off in the press; the copies variously combine corrected and uncorrected sheets. A second quarto, printed in 1619 by William Jaggard for Thomas Pavier with the fraudulent date of 1608, was based on a copy of the first quarto, combining corrected and uncorrected sheets.

The First Folio text of 1623 may have been typeset from a playbook cut for performance or from a transcript of such a manuscript, and the playbook in its turn appears to have been based on Shakespeare's fair copy (with revisions) of his first draft. The Folio compositors also almost certainly consulted a copy of the second quarto from time to time or may have typeset directly from this quarto as annotated with reference to Shakespeare's fair copy. In writing the fair copy, Shakespeare may have marked some three hundred lines for deletion, but it is possible that he did so chiefly to shorten the time of performance. He also seems to have added some one hundred lines, an apparent contradiction in view of the need for cutting, but possibly dictated by Shakespeare's developing sense of his play. It is also possible that the cuts were carried out by someone else in the preparation of the playbook.

The first quarto, on the other hand, appears to have been printed from Shakespeare's unrevised and evidently untidy working papers. It is often corrupt, owing in part to type shortages, compositorial uncertainties with the manuscript, and other difficulties in Nicholas Okes's shop. Still, in some matters—especially variants indifferent in meaning (such as *an/if* or *thine/thy*)—the first quarto may be closer to Shakespeare's preferences than the Folio, behind which are several stages of transmission.

This edition agrees with most recent students of the *Lear* text that the Folio represents a theatrical revision, in which the cuts were devised for performance by Shakespeare's company and quite possibly by Shakespeare himself as a member of that company. The case for artistic preference in the making of those cuts, on the other hand, is less certain and may have been overstated. Many of the cuts have the effect of shortening scenes, especially in the latter half of the play. Some scenes, like 3.6, show open gaps as a result of the cutting: Lear's "Then let them anatomize Regan" (line 75) implies the trial of Goneril as it is dramatized in the first quarto but cut from the Folio.

Other omissions also read like expedients, although they can also be explained by a hypothesis of literary and theatrical rewriting; if Shakespeare himself undertook the cutting, he would presumably do so as expertly as possible. The fact that the Folio text gives almost no rewritten speeches may suggest that the large cuts were motivated by the need for shortening. This edition holds to the principle that it is unwise to omit the material cut from the Folio text, since we cannot be sure that Shakespeare would have shortened the text had there been no external constraints. At the same time, the added material in the Folio is clearly his and belongs in his conception of the play. The resulting text is a conflation, but one that avoids cutting material that Shakespeare may well have regretted having to excise.

The Stationers' Register entry for November 26, 1607, describes a performance at court on the previous St. Stephen's night, December 26, 1606. The title page of the first quarto confirms this performance on St. Stephen's night. Such a performance at court was not likely to have been the first, however. Shakespeare's repeated use of Samuel Harsnett's *Declaration of Egregious Popish Impostures*, registered on March 16, 1603, sets an early limit for composition of the play. Other circumstances point to composition of the quarto text in 1605 or 1606. In May 1605, an old play called *The True Chronicle History of King Leir* was entered in the Stationers' Register as a "Tragecall historie," a phrase possibly suggesting the influence of Shakespeare's play, since the old *King Leir* does not end tragically. Moreover, the title page of the old *King Leir*, issued in 1605, proclaims the text to be "as it hath bene diuers and sundry times lately acted." In view of the unlikelihood that such an old play (written before 1594) would be revived in 1605, scholars have suggested that the title page was the publisher's way of trying to capitalize on the recent popularity of Shakespeare's play. In this case, the likeliest date for the composition of Shakespeare's *King Lear* would be in the winter of 1604–1605. Shakespeare certainly used the old *King Leir* as a chief source, but he need not have waited for its publication in 1605 if, as seems perfectly plausible, his company owned the playbook. This hypothesis of the publication of the old *King Leir* after performances of Shakespeare's play must do battle, however, with indications that Shakespeare did not write *King Lear* until late 1605 or 1606. Gloucester's mentioning of "These late eclipses in the sun and moon" (1.2.106) seems to refer to an eclipse of the moon in September and of the sun in October 1605.

There may be echoes in the first quarto of *King Lear* of *Eastward Ho!* by George Chapman, Ben Jonson, and John Marston, written in early 1605, and *Miseries of Enforced Marriage*, written by mid-1605. *King Lear* may allude to concerns at court about the King's frequent absences for hunting, about monopolies, the giving away of knighthoods, the King's need of money, and the like, all of which would have seemed pertinent in 1605–1606. The Folio revisions may date from some time around 1610, according to the editors of the Oxford Shakespeare.

## Macbeth (c. 1606–1607)

*Macbeth* was first printed in the First Folio of 1623. It was set up from a playbook or a transcript of one. The text is unusually short and seems to have been cut for reasons of censorship or for some special performance. Moreover, all of 3.5 and parts of 4.1 (39–43, 125–32) appear to be interpolations, containing songs from Thomas Middleton's *The Witch* (c.1609–1616). Middleton may have been responsible for other alterations and additions.

Simon Forman, in his manuscript *The Book of Plays and Notes thereof per Formans for Common Policy*, records the first known performance of *Macbeth* on April 20, 1611, at the Globe Theatre. The play must have been in existence by 1607, however, for allusions to it seemingly occur in *Lingua* and *The Puritan* (both published in 1607) and in *The Knight of the Burning Pestle* (probably acted in 1607). On the other hand, the play itself seemingly alludes to James I's royal succession in 1603, to his touching for "the king's evil" (see 4.3.147), and to the trial of the notorious Gunpowder Plot conspirators in March 1606. The interpolations from Middleton's *The Witch* are probably from a later date, perhaps after 1613.

## Antony and Cleopatra (1606–1607)

On May 20, 1608, Edward Blount entered in the Stationers' Register, the official record book of the London Company of Stationers (booksellers and printers), "A booke Called. Anthony. and Cleopatra," along with "A booke called. The booke of Pericles prynce of Tyre." Blount was friendly with Shakespeare's company, and his entry may have been a "staying entry" designed to forestall unauthorized publication of these texts. If so, the tactic did not succeed with *Pericles*, issued in 1609 by another publisher, but it did succeed with *Antony and Cleopatra*. The play was first printed in the First Folio of 1623. It is a good text, set evidently from Shakespeare's own draft in a more finished state than most of his working papers, or possibly from a transcript of those papers, though not yet prepared to be a playbook.

The year 1608 is thus the latest possible date for *Antony and Cleopatra*. Evidently, it was written in 1606–1607, however, for a "newly altered" edition in 1607 of Samuel Daniel's play *Cleopatra* seems to have been influenced by Shakespeare's play. Shakespeare himself had probably consulted the original edition of *Cleopatra*, published in 1594, or the slightly revised edition of 1599, but Daniel's more thorough revision in 1607 shows signs of his

having seen Shakespeare's play in the interim. Also, a play by Barnabe Barnes called *The Devil's Charter* (1607) may contain a parody of Cleopatra's death by asps. Although the printed text of this play advertises corrections and augmentations that could postdate a court performance in February 1607, recent scholarship favors the likelihood that Barnes saw *Antony and Cleopatra* before that—perhaps in late 1606.

## The Winter's Tale (c. 1609–1611)

*The Winter's Tale* was first printed in the First Folio of 1623. Its text is a good one, taken evidently from Ralph Crane's transcript of Shakespeare's own well-finished draft or possibly the playbook. As in most other Crane transcriptions, the stage directions are sparse, and the characters' names are grouped at the beginning of each scene. The first recorded performance was on May 15, 1611, when Simon Forman saw the play at the Globe Theater and recorded a summary of it in his commonplace book. Another performance that year at court, on November 5, is recorded in the *Revels Account,* and still another during the winter of 1612–1613. Quite possibly the play was new at the time Forman saw it. It apparently contains an allusion to the dance of ten or twelve satyrs in Ben Jonson's *Masque of Oberon*, performed at court on January 1, 1611. A 1623 entry in the *Office book* of Sir Henry Herbert, Master of the Revels, refers to *The Winter's Tale* as "an old play . . . formerly allowed of by Sir George Bucke." Bucke (or Buc) was first appointed Master of the Revels in 1610 but had occasionally licensed plays before that date during his predecessor's illness, so that the backward limit of 1610 cannot be considered absolute. Still, matters of style confirm the likelihood that Forman was seeing a new play in 1611.

## The Tempest (c. 1611)

*The Tempest* was first printed in the First Folio of 1623. It occupies first place in the volume and is a scrupulously prepared text from a transcript by Ralph Crane of a theater playbook or of Shakespeare's draft after it had been annotated for production; or, Crane may have provided some of the elaboration of stage directions. Shakespeare's colleagues may have placed *The Tempest* first in the Folio because they considered it his most recent complete play. The first recorded performance was at court on November 1, 1611: "Hallomas nyght was presented att Whithall before ye kinges Maiestie a play Called the Tempest." The actors were "the Kings players" (*Revels Account*). The play was again presented at court during the winter of 1612–1613, this time "before the Princes Highnes the Lady Elizabeth and the Prince Pallatyne Elector." The festivities for this important betrothal and wedding were sumptuous and included at least thirteen other plays. Various arguments have been put forward that Shakespeare composed parts of *The Tempest*, especially the masque, for this occasion, but there is absolutely no evidence that the play was singled out for special prominence among the many plays presented, and the masque is integral to the play as it stands. Probably the 1611 production was of a fairly new play. Simon Forman, who saw *Cymbeline* and *The Winter's Tale* in 1611, does not mention *The Tempest*. He died in September 1611. According to every stylistic test, such as run-on and hypermetric lines, the play is very late. Shakespeare probably knew Sylvester Jourdain's *A Discovery of the Bermudas*, published in 1610, and William Strachey's *A True Reportory of the Wreck and Redemption*, dated July 1610, although not published until 1625.

## The Sonnets (*c. 1593–1603*)

On May 20, 1609, "Thomas Thorpe Entred for his copie vnder thandes of master Wilson and master Lownes Warden a Booke called Shakespeares sonnettes." In the same year appeared the following volume:

SHAKE-SPEARES SONNETS. Neuer before Imprinted. AT LONDON By *G. Eld* for *T. T.* [Thomas Thorpe] and are to be solde by *Iohn Wright*, dwelling at Christ Church gate. 1609.

Some copies of this same edition are marked to be sold by William Aspley rather than John Wright; evidently, Thorpe had set up two sellers to distribute the volume. The sonnets were not reprinted until John Benson's rearranged edition of 1640, possibly because the first edition had been suppressed or because sonnets were no longer in vogue. The 1609 edition may rest on a transcript of Shakespeare's sonnets by someone other than the author, and the edition itself is marred by misprints, though Thorpe was a reputable printer. Clearly, the collection was not supervised through the press as were *Venus and Adonis* and *The Rape of Lucrece*. All the evidence suggests that it was obtained without Shakespeare's permission from a manuscript that had been in private circulation (as we know from Francis Meres's 1598 allusion, in his *Palladis Tamia*, to Shakespeare's "sugared sonnets among his private friends"). Two sonnets, 138 and 144, had appeared in 1599 in *The Passionate Pilgrim*. On questions of dating and order of the sonnets, see the Introduction to *The Sonnets* in this volume.

# Appendix 2

# Sources

## *The Taming of the Shrew*

Scholars do not agree on the relationship of *The Taming of the Shrew* to the play called *The Taming of a Shrew,* published in 1594. *A Shrew* has been argued to be an earlier version of Shakespeare's play, or a memorial reconstruction of it, or derived from a common original. Some recent critics argue that the two versions should be treated as distinct texts. An often-held view is that *A Shrew* is derived from a now-lost earlier version of Shakespeare's play, to which the compiler added original material and borrowed or even plagiarized from other literary sources as well. If so, *A Shrew* would not appear to be a source for Shakespeare's play, as Geoffrey Bullough has argued in his *Narrative and Dramatic Sources of Shakespeare.* Apart from this question, all critics agree that Shakespeare's play consists of three elements, each with its own source: the romantic love plot of Lucentio and Bianca, the wife-taming plot of Petruchio and Kate, and the framing plot, or induction, of Christopher Sly.

The romantic love plot is derived from George Gascoigne's *Supposes*, a neoclassical comedy performed at Gray's Inn (one of the Inns of Court, where young men studied law in London) in 1566. Gascoigne's play was a rather close translation of Ludovico Ariosto's *I Suppositi* (1509), which in turn was based on two classical plays, Terence's *Eunuchus* and Plautus's *Captivi.* The heroine of Gascoigne's version (as of Ariosto's) is Polynesta, the resourceful daughter of Damon, a widower of Ferrara. Two suitors vie for Polynesta's hand: Dr. Cleander, an aged and miserly lawyer, and Erostrato, a Sicilian gentleman who has purportedly come to Ferrara to study. In fact, however, this "Erostrato" is the servant Dulippo in disguise, having changed places with his master. (These disguisings are the "supposes"

of the title.) As a servant in Damon's household, "Dulippo" has secretly become the lover of Polynesta and has made her pregnant. Balia, the nurse or duenna, is their go-between. Meanwhile, "Erostrato" takes great delight in outwitting Dr. Cleander and his unattractive parasite, Pasiphilo. The counterfeit Erostrato's ruse is to produce a rich father who will guarantee a handsome dowry and thereby outbid Cleander in the contest for Polynesta's hand. The "father" he produces, however, is actually an old Sienese stranger, who is persuaded that he is in danger in Ferrara unless he cloaks his identity. Complications arise when Damon learns of his daughter's affair and throws the lover, "Dulippo," into a dungeon. The crafty Pasiphilo overhears this compromising information and resolves to cause mischief for all the principals. Moreover, when Erostrato's real father, Philogano, arrives in Ferrara, he is barred from his son's house by the counterfeit Philogano and resolves to get help. His clever servant, Litio, suggests employing the famous lawyer, Cleander. All is happily resolved when the real Dulippo proves to be the son of Dr. Cleander and the real Erostrato is revealed to be rich and socially eligible for Polynesta's hand in marriage. Cleander is even reconciled to his parasite, Pasiphilo.

Shakespeare, in his play, has almost entirely eliminated the satire of the law that is in his source. Gremio is aged and wealthy, but no shyster. The lover is not imprisoned in a dungeon. The parasite is gone, as also in *The Comedy of Errors.* Bianca does not consummate her affair with Lucentio, as does Polynesta, and hence has no need for a go-between like Balia. Shakespeare adapts a sophisticated neoclassical comedy, racy and cosmopolitan, to the moral standards of his public theater. The witless

Hortensio, the tutoring in Latin, and the music lesson appear to be Shakespeare's inventions.

The wife-taming plot of Petruchio and Kate reflects an ancient comic misogynistic tradition, still extant today in the Scottish folksong "The Cooper of Fife" or "The Wife Wrapped in Wether's Skin" (Francis James Child, *The English and Scottish Popular Ballads* [1888–1898], 5:104). Richard Hosley has argued (in *Huntington Library Quarterly, 27*, 1964) that Shakespeare's likeliest source was *A Merry Jest of a Shrewd and Curst Wife Lapped in Morel's Skin, for her Good Behavior* (printed c. 1550). In this version, the husband beats his shrewish wife with birch rods until she bleeds and faints, whereupon he wraps her in the raw salted skin of an old plow-horse named Morel. Like Kate, this shrewish wife has a gentle younger sister who is their father's favorite. This father warns the man who proposes to marry his older daughter that she is shrewish, but the suitor goes ahead and subsequently tames his wife with Morel's skin. Thereafter, at a celebratory dinner, everyone is impressed by the thoroughness of the taming.

Shakespeare avoids the misogynistic extremes of this story, despite the similarity of the narrative. Instead, he seems to have had in mind the more humanistic spirit of Erasmus's *A Merry Dialogue Declaring the Properties of Shrewd Shrews and Honest Wives* (translated 1557) and Juan Luis Vives's *The Office and Duty of an Husband* (translated 1555). Specific elements of the wife-taming plot have been traced to other possible sources. The scolding of a tailor occurs in Gerard Legh's *Accidence of Armory* (1562); a wife agrees with her husband's assertion of a patent falsehood in Don Juan Manuel's *El Conde Lucanor* (1335); and three husbands wager on the obedience of their wives in *The Book of the Knight of La Tour-Landry* (printed 1484).

The induction story, of the beggar duped into believing himself a rich lord, is an old tale occurring in the *Arabian Nights*. An interesting analogue occurs in P. Heuterus's *De Rebus Burgundicis* (1584), translated into the French of S. Goulart (1606?) and thence into the English of Edward Crimeston (1607). According to Heuterus, in 1440, Philip the Good of Burgundy actually entertained a drunken beggar in his palace "to make trial of the vanity of our life," plying him with fine clothes, bed, a feast, and the performance of "a pleasant comedy."

## A Midsummer Night's Dream

No single source has been discovered that unites the various elements that we find in *A Midsummer Night's Dream*, but the four main strands of action can be individually discussed in terms of sources. The four strands are: (1) the marriage of Theseus (Duke of Athens) and Queen Hippolyta, (2) the romantic tribulations and triumphs of the four young lovers, (3) the quarrel of King Oberon and Queen Titania, together with the fairies' manipulations of human affairs, and (4) the "rude mechanicals" and their play of "Pyramus and Thisbe."

For his conception of Theseus, Shakespeare went chiefly to Geoffrey Chaucer's "The Knight's Tale" and to Thomas North's 1579 translation of "The Life of Theseus" in Plutarch's *Lives of the Noble Grecians and Romans*. Chaucer's Theseus is a duke of "wisdom" and "chivalrye," renowned for his conquest of the Amazons and his marriage to Hippolyta. Plutarch provides information concerning Theseus's other conquests (to which Oberon alludes in 2.1.77 ff.), including that of Antiopa. Shakespeare could have learned more about Theseus from Chaucer's *The Legend of Good Women* and from Ovid's *Metamorphoses*. He seems to have blended all or some of these impressions together with his own notion of a noble yet popular Renaissance ruler.

The romantic narrative of the four lovers appears to be original with Shakespeare, although one can find many analogous situations of misunderstanding and rivalry in love. Chaucer's "The Knight's Tale" tells of two friends battling over one woman. Shakespeare's own *The Two Gentlemen of Verona* gives us four lovers, properly matched at first until one of the men shifts his attentions to his friend's ladylove; eventually, all is righted when the false lover recovers his senses. Parallel situations arise in Sir Philip Sidney's *Arcadia* (1590) and in Jorge de Montemayor's *Diana Enamorada* (c. 1559), a source for *The Two Gentlemen*. What Shakespeare adds in *A Midsummer* is the intervention of the fairies in human love affairs.

Shakespeare's knowledge of fairy lore must have been extensive and is hard to trace exactly. Doubtless, much of it was from oral traditions about leprechauns, gremlins, and elves, who were thought to cause such mischief as spoiling fermentation or preventing milk from churning into butter; Puck's tricks mentioned in 2.1.34 ff. are derived from such lore. Some of the oral tales circulating about Robin Goodfellow later reached print, probably somewhat modified, in the prose pamphlet *Robin Good Fellow, His Mad Pranks and Merry Jests* (London, 1628) and a ballad, "The Mad Merry Pranks of Robbin Good-fellow" (c. 1600) in Roxburghe Ballads, vol. 2, ed. William Chappell (Hertford: Stephen Austin for the Ballad Society, 1872), p. 83. Shakespeare seems to have consulted literary sources as well. In Chaucer's "The Merchant's Tale," Pluto and Proserpina as King and Queen of the fairies intervene in the affairs of old January, his young wife May, and her lover Damyan. Fairies appear on stage in John Lyly's *Endymion* (1588), protecting true lovers and tormenting those who are morally tainted. Shakespeare later reflects this tradition in *The Merry Wives of Windsor* (1597–1601). The name Oberon probably comes from the French romance *Huon of Bordeaux* (translated by Lord Berners by about 1540), where Oberon is a dwarfish fairy King from the mysterious East who practices enchantment in a haunted wood. In Edmund Spenser's *The Faerie Queene*, Oberon is the Elfin father of Queen Gloriana (2.10. 75–6). Robert Greene's *James IV* (c. 1591) also features Oberon as the fairy King, and a lost play called *Huon of Bordeaux* was performed by Sussex's Men, an acting company, at about this same time. The name "Titania" comes from Ovid's *Metamorphoses*, where it is used as a synonym for both the enchantress Circe and the chaste goddess Diana. The name "Titania" does not appear in Arthur Golding's translation (1567), suggesting that Shakespeare found it in the Latin original. Puck, or Robin Goodfellow, is essentially the product of oral tradition, although Reginald Scot's *The Discovery of Witchcraft* (1584) discusses Robin in pejorative terms as an incubus or hobgoblin in whom intelligent people no longer believe.

Scot also reports the story of a man who finds an ass's head placed on his shoulders by enchantment. Similar legends of transformation occur in Apuleius's *The Golden Ass* (translated by William Adlington, 1566) and in the well-known story of the ass's ears bestowed by Phoebus Apollo on King Midas for his presumption. Perhaps the most suggestive possible source for Shakespeare's clownish actors, however, is Anthony Munday's play *John a Kent and John a Cumber* (c. 1587–1590). In it a group of rude artisans, led by the intrepid Turnop, stage a ludicrous interlude written by their churchwarden in praise of his millhorse. Turnop's prologue is a medley of lofty comparisons. The entertainment is presented before noble spectators, who are graciously amused. *John a Kent* also features a lot of magic trickery, a boy named Shrimp whose role is comparable to that of Puck, and a multiple love plot.

"Pyramus and Thisbe" itself is based on the *Metamorphoses* (4.55 ff.). Other versions that Shakespeare may have known include Chaucer's *The Legend of Good Women*, a poem by William Griffith in 1562, George Pettie's *A Petite Palace of Pettie His Pleasure* (1576), *A Gorgeous Gallery of Gallant Inventions* (1578), and "A New Sonnet of Pyramus and Thisbe" from Clement Robinson's *A Handful of Pleasant Delights* (1584). Several of these, especially the last three, are bad enough to have given Shakespeare materials to lampoon, though the sweep of his parody goes beyond the particular story of Pyramus and Thisbe. The occasionally stilted phraseology of Golding's translation of the *Metamorphoses* contributed to the fun. According to Kenneth Muir (*Shakespeare's Sources*, 1957), Shakespeare must also have known Thomas Mouffet's *Of the Silkworms and Their Flies* (published 1599, but possibly circulated earlier in manuscript), which contains perhaps the most ridiculous of all versions of the Pyramus and Thisbe story. Shakespeare also appears to have been spoofing the inept dramatic style and lame verse of English dramas of the 1560s, 1570s, and 1580s, especially

in their treatment of tragic sentiment and high emotion; *Cambises, Damon and Pythias*, and *Appius and Virginia* are examples.

## The Merchant of Venice

Shakespeare's probable chief source for *The Merchant of Venice* was the first story of the fourth day of *Il Pecorone (The Dunce)*, by Ser Giovanni Fiorentino. This collection of tales dates from the late fourteenth century but was first published in 1558 at Milan and was not published in English translation in Shakespeare's time. Shakespeare may have read it in the Italian, though he may conceivably have consulted a translation in some now-lost manuscript; such translations did sometimes circulate. Behind Ser Giovanni's story lies an old tradition of a bond given for human flesh, as found in Persia, India, and the Twelve Tables of Roman Law. This legend first appears in English in the thirteenth-century *Cursor Mundi*, with a Jew as the creditor. A thirteenth-century version of the *Gesta Romanorum* (a popular collection of stories in Latin) adds a romantic love plot; the evil moneylender in this story is not Jewish. The hero pawns his own flesh to a merchant in order to win a lady. He succeeds on his third attempt, having learned to avoid a magic spell that had previously put him to sleep and cost him a large number of florins. When he goes to pay his forfeit, the lady follows him disguised as a knight, and foils the evil merchant by pointing out a quibbling distinction between flesh and blood.

*Il Pecorone* provided Shakespeare with a number of essential elements, although not all that he has included. Ser Giovanni's story tells of Giannetto, the adventurous youngest son of a Florentine merchant, who goes to live with his father's dearest friend, Ansaldo, in Venice. This worthy merchant gives him money to seek his fortune at sea. Unbeknownst to Ansaldo, Giannetto twice risks everything to woo the lady of Belmont: if he can succeed in sleeping with her, he will win her and her country, but, if he fails, he loses all his wealth. Twice Giannetto is given a sleeping medicine and has to forfeit everything. Returning destitute to Venice twice, he is reunited each time with Ansaldo and given the means to seek his fortune again. For the third such voyage, however, Ansaldo is driven to borrow ten thousand florins from a Jew, using the forfeiture of a pound of flesh as a guarantee. This time, one of the lady's maids warns Giannetto not to drink his wine, and he finally possesses the lady as his wife. Sometime later, remembering that the day of Ansaldo's forfeiture has arrived, Giannetto explains the predicament to his wife and is sent by her to Venice with a hundred thousand florins, but he arrives after the forfeiture has fallen due. The lady, however, following after him in the disguise of a doctor of laws, decrees that the Jew may have no blood and must take no more or no less than one pound of flesh. The Jew is jeered at and receives no money. The "doctor of laws" refuses any payment other than the ring Giannetto was given by his lady. Giving it up unwillingly, he returns to Belmont, where his lady vexes him about the ring but finally relents and tells him all. Shakespeare could thus have found in one source the wooing, the borrowing from a Jewish moneylender, the pound of flesh, the trial, and the business of the rings. The story provides no casket episode, courtship of Nerissa by Gratiano, elopement of Jessica, or clowning of Lancelot Gobbo. The Jew's motive is not prompted by the way he has been treated.

Shakespeare may also have known "The Ballad of Gernutus," a popular English work that seems to be older than the play. It has no love plot but dwells on the unnatural cruelty of a Jewish Venetian usurer who takes a bond of flesh for "a merry jest." Anthony Munday's prose *Zelauto* (1580), though its villain is a Christian rather than a Jewish moneylender, also features a bond of this sort, taken purportedly as a mere sport but with hidden malice. Truculento, the villain, takes the bond of two young men, Rodolfo and his friend Strabino, as surety for a loan. If they forfeit the loan, the young men are to lose their lands and their right eyes as well. The villain has a daughter, Brisana, whom he permits to marry Rodolfo, since Truculento expects to marry Rodolfo's sister Cornelia himself. When Cornelia instead marries Strabino, Truculento angrily takes the young men to court to demand his bond. The two brides disguise themselves as scholars and go to court, where they appeal for mercy and then foil Truculento by means of the legal quibble about blood.

Another possible source for the courtroom scene is *The Orator*, translated into English in 1596 from the French of Alexandre Sylvain. An oration, entitled "Of a Jew, who would for his debt have a pound of the flesh of a Christian," uses many specious arguments also employed by Shylock, and is forthrightly confuted in "The Christian's Answer."

Shylock's relationship to his daughter finds obvious earlier parallels in *Zelauto* and in Christopher Marlowe's play, *The Jew of Malta* (c. 1589), in which Barabas's daughter Abigail loves a Christian and ultimately renounces her faith. The actual elopement, however, is closer to the fourteenth story in Masuccio of Salerno's fifteenth-century *Il Novellino* (not published in English translation in Shakespeare's day).

The casket-choosing episode, not found in *Il Pecorone*, was a widespread legend, occurring, for example, in the story of *Barlaam and Josaphat* (ninth-century Greek, translated into Latin by the thirteenth century), in Vincent of Beauvais's *Speculum Historiale*, in the *Legenda Aurea*, in Giovanni Boccaccio's *Decameron* (Day 10, Story 1), in John Gower's *Confessio Amantis*, and—closest to Shakespeare—in the *Gesta Romanorum* (translated into English

in 1577 by Richard Robinson and "bettered" by him in 1595). In this last account, the choice is between a gold, silver, and lead casket, each with its own inscription. The first two inscriptions are like Shakespeare's; the third reads, "Thei that chese me, shulle fynde [in] me that God hathe disposid." The chooser, however, is a maiden, and she is not preceded by other contestants.

An old play called *The Jew* is referred to by Stephen Gosson in 1579 as containing "the greediness of worldly choosers, and bloody minds of usurers." Scholars have speculated that this was a source play for Shakespeare, but actually we have too little to go on to make a reliable judgment. Gosson was surely not referring to Robert Wilson's *The Three Ladies of London* (c. 1581) in any case, even though it is sometimes suggested as an analogue to *The Merchant of Venice*, for its Jewish figure, named Gerontus (compare Gernutus in the ballad), is an exemplary person. Besides, the probable date of this play is later than Gosson's remark.

## Much Ado About Nothing

Shakespeare's probable chief source for the Hero-Claudio plot of *Much Ado* was the twenty-second story from the *Novelle* of Matteo Bandello (Lucca, 1554). A French translation by François de Belleforest, in his *Histoires Tragiques* (1569 edition), was available to Shakespeare, as was the Italian original. The story of the maiden falsely accused was, however, much older than the story by Bandello. Perhaps the earliest version that has been found is the Greek romance *Chaereas and Callirrhoe*, fourth or fifth century A.D., in which the hero Chaereas, warned by envious rivals of his wife's purported infidelity, watches at dusk while an elegantly attired stranger is admitted by the maid to the house where Callirrhoe lives. Chaereas rushes in and strikes mistakenly at his wife in the dark but is acquitted of murder when the maid confesses her part in a conspiracy to delude Chaereas. Callirrhoe is buried in a deathlike trance but awakens in time to be carried off by pirates. The story reappears in a fifteenth-century Spanish romance, *Tirante el Blanco*, in which the princess Blanche is courted seemingly by a repulsive black man. This Spanish version probably inspired the account in Canto 5 of Ludovico Ariosto's *Orlando Furioso* (1516), to which all subsequent Renaissance versions are ultimately indebted.

In Ariosto's account, as translated into English by Sir John Harington (1591), the narrator is Dalinda, maid to the virtuous Scottish princess Genevra. Dalinda tells how she has fallen guiltily in love with Polynesso, Duke of Albany, an evil man who often makes love to Dalinda in her mistress's rooms but who longs in fact to marry Genevra. Consequently, Polynesso arranges for Genevra's noble Italian suitor, Ariodante, and Ariodante's brother Lurcanio, to witness the Duke's ascent to Genevra's window by a rope ladder. The woman who admits the Duke is, of course, not Genevra but Dalinda disguised as her mistress, having been duped into believing that the Duke merely wishes to satisfy his craving for Genevra by making love to her image. Lurcanio publicly accuses the innocent Genevra and offers to fight anyone who defends her cause (compare Claudio's quarrel with Leonato). The evil Duke tries to get rid of Dalinda, but all is finally put to rights by Rinaldo (the hero of *Orlando Furioso*) and Ariodante. This account gives an unusually vivid motivation for the maid and the villain—a clearer motivation than in Shakespeare's play. A lost dramatic version, *Ariodante and Genevora*, was performed at the English court in 1583.

Shakespeare probably consulted not only Ariosto but also Edmund Spenser's *The Faerie Queene* (2.4), based on Ariosto. Spenser's emphasis is on the blind rage of Phedon, a young squire in love with Claribell. Phedon is tricked by his erstwhile friend Philemon and by Claribell's maid Pryene into believing Claribell false. Pryene's motive in dressing up as Claribell is to prove she is as beautiful as her mistress. When, after having slain Claribell for her supposed perfidy, Phedon learns the truth, he poisons Philemon and furiously pursues Pryene until he is utterly possessed by a mad frenzy.

Shakespeare's greatest debt is, however, to Bandello's story. In a number of details, the story is closer to Shakespeare's play than are those already discussed. Several names are substantially the same as in Shakespeare: the location is Messina, the father of the slandered bride is Lionato di' Lionati (compare Shakespeare's Leonato), and her lover is in the service of King Piero of Aragon (compare Don Pedro of Aragon). As in Shakespeare, a young knight (named Sir Timbreo) seeks the hand in marriage of his beloved (Fenicia) through the matchmaking offices of a noble emissary. The complication of this wooing is somewhat different in that Timbreo's friend Girondo also falls in love with Fenicia, but Girondo then plots with a mischief-loving courtier (resembling Shakespeare's Don John) to poison Timbreo's mind against Fenicia, and Girondo thereupon escorts Timbreo to a garden, where they see Girondo's servant, elegantly dressed, enter Fenicia's window. No maid takes part in the ruse, however, nor indeed is any woman seen at the window. When Fenicia is wrongly accused, she falls into a deathlike trance and is pronounced dead by a doctor, but she is revived. Her father, believing in her innocence, sends her off to a country retreat and circulates the report that she is, in fact, dead. Soon both Timbreo and Girondo are stricken with remorse, Timbreo magnanimously spares his friend's life, and both confess the truth to Fenicia's family. A year later, Timbreo marries a wife chosen for him by Lionato who turns out, of course, to be Fenicia. Girondo marries her sister Belfiore. This account does not provide any equivalent for Beatrice and Benedick. Shakespeare enhances the Friar's role and provides a brother for Leonato. Claudio and Leonato are of comparable social station in Shakespeare, whereas Bandello makes a point of Timbreo's superior social rank.

A lost play, *Panecia* (1574–1575), may have been based on Bandello's work. One other version Shakespeare may have known is George Whetstone's *The Rock of Regard* (1576), based on Ariosto and Bandello. It contains a suggestive parallel to Claudio's rejection of Hero in church. Various Italian plays in the tradition of Luigi Pasqualigo's *Il Fedele* (1579), and also a version perhaps by Anthony Munday, *Fedele and Fortunio* (published 1585), are analogous in situation, though Shakespeare need not have known any of them.

For the Beatrice-Benedick plot, no source has been discovered, apart from Shakespeare's own earlier fascination with wit-combat and candid wooing in *Love's Labor's Lost* and *The Taming of the Shrew*. Nor has a plausible source been found for Dogberry and the watch.

## As You Like It

Shakespeare's chief source for *As You Like It* was Thomas Lodge's graceful pastoral romance, *Rosalynde: Euphues' Golden Legacy* (1590). Lodge was indebted in turn to *The Tale of Gamelyn*, a fourteenth-century poem wrongly included by some medieval scribes as "The Cook's Tale" in Chaucer's *Canterbury Tales. Gamelyn* was not printed until 1721, but Lodge clearly had access to a manuscript of it. Although Shakespeare may not have known *Gamelyn* directly, his play still retains the hearty spirit of this Robin Hood legend. (In later Robin Hood ballads, Gamelyn or Gandelyn is identified with Will Scarlet, a member of Robin Hood's band.)

Even a brief account of *Gamelyn* suggests how greatly the original tale is inspired by Robin Hood legends of outlaws valiantly defying the corrupt social order presided over by the Sheriff and his henchmen. Gamelyn, the youngest of three brothers, is denied his inheritance by his churlish eldest brother John. When Gamelyn demands his rights, John orders his men to beat Gamelyn, but the young man arms himself with a pestle and proves to be a formidable fighter. After defeating the champion wrestler in a local wrestling match (a lower-class sport befitting the social milieu of this story), Gamelyn returns home to find himself locked out by his brother. He kills the porter, flings the man's body down a well, and feasts his companions day and night for a week. John feigns a reconciliation and slyly asks if he can bind Gamelyn hand and foot merely to satisfy an oath he has sworn over the death of the porter. Gamelyn trustingly agrees and is made prisoner. After his bonds have been secretly loosed by Adam the Spencer (the steward), Gamelyn pretends to remain bound until the propitious moment for revenge and escape. The moment arrives during a feast of monks who churlishly refuse to help Gamelyn. With

Adam's aid, he fells many of them, ties up his brother, and escapes to the woods, where he and Adam are rescued from hunger by a band of merry outlaws. As their chief, Gamelyn becomes a champion of the poor and an enemy of rich churchmen. His brother, now sheriff, brands Gamelyn an outlaw and manages to imprison him, but Gamelyn's second brother, Sir Ote, stands bail for him. On the day of the trial, Gamelyn frees Sir Ote and hangs the sheriff and the jury. Gamelyn finally obtains his inheritance and becomes chief officer of the King's royal forests. This story is uninfluenced by the pastoral tradition and contains no love plot. Its Robin Hood traditions are very much present, nonetheless, in Shakespeare's contrasting portrayal of a tyrannical court and of a just society in banishment.

Lodge retains the primitive vigor of *Gamelyn* but adds generous infusions of pastoral sentiment in the manner of Sir Philip Sidney's *Arcadia* (1590) and sententious moralizing in the manner of John Lyly's *Euphues* (1578). The pastoralism is presented in conventional terms, with none of the genial self-reflexive satire we find in Shakespeare. Psychological motive is intricate, often more so than in Shakespeare's play. The style is also heavily influenced by Lyly's exquisitely balanced, antithetical, and ornamented prose. For his pastoralism, Lodge was indebted not only to Sidney but also to the ancient pastoral tradition that included the Greek Theocritus and the Roman Virgil, the Italian Sannazaro (*Arcadia*), and the Portuguese Jorge de Montemayor (*Diana*). Pastoralism by Lodge's time had become thoroughly imbued with artificial conventions: abject lovers writing sonnets to their disdainful mistresses, princes and princesses in shepherds' disguise, idealized landscapes, stylized debate as to the relative merits of love and friendship, youth and age, city life and country life, and so on. Some of these conventions were derived also from the vogue of sonneteering pioneered by Francesco Petrarch and can thus be described as the stereotypes of "Petrarchism." Lodge accepts these conventions and gives us typical pastoral lovers even in his hero and heroine, although the elements he derived from *Gamelyn* certainly add a contrasting note of violence and danger.

Lodge's account begins much like that of *Gamelyn*. Saladyne, the envious eldest brother, bribes the champion wrestler to do away with Rosader (Orlando) in the wrestling match. Rosader succeeds instead in killing the wrestler and in winning the heart of Rosalynde, daughter of the banished King Gerismond. When she sends him a jewel, Rosader is not at all at a loss for words; indeed, he composes a Petrarchan sonnet on the spot. The usurping King Torismond (no relation to Gerismond), despite his evil nature, is impressed by Rosader's grace and martial prowess. Rosader returns home with friends, breaks open the door, and feasts his company. The wily Saladyne overwhelms Rosader in his sleep and binds him to a post,

but Rosader is untied by Adam and makes havoc among the eldest brother's guests, as in *Gamelyn*. In this case, however, the guests are Saladyne's kindred and allies, all of whom have refused to help Rosader. The sheriff tries to arrest Rosader and Adam, but they make good their escape to the Forest of Arden in France. They are saved from starvation by the kindly King Gerismond and his exiled followers. Rosalynde and King Torismond's daughter Alinda meanwhile have been banished from court and have taken abode in the forest under the names of Ganymede and Aliena. They befriend old Corydon (Corin) and young Montanus (Silvius), who is hopelessly in love with the haughty Phoebe. "Ganymede" poses as a woman to test Rosader in his wooing, and they are joined in a mock marriage. Saladyne, now repenting of his evil deeds, comes to the forest, is saved by his brother from a lion, and falls in love with Alinda (whom he helps to rescue from ruffians). The denouement is as in Shakespeare, although the triumphant return to society is more complete: King Torismond is slain, Gerismond is restored to his throne, Rosader is named heir-apparent, and all the friends are appropriately rewarded.

Despite Shakespeare's extensive indebtedness to this charming romance, there is a crucial difference: Lodge's pastoral world is never subjected to a wry or satirical exploration. Lodge offers no equivalent for Touchstone, the fool who sees the absurdity of both country and city; Jaques, the malcontent traveler; William and Audrey, the clownishly simple peasants; or Sir Oliver Martext, the ridiculous hedge-priest. Nor does Lodge tell of Le Beau, the court butterfly. Hymen is a Shakespearean addition, and the conversion of Duke Frederick by a hermit instead of his being overthrown and killed is a characteristically Shakespearean softening touch. Shakespeare's added characters are virtually all foils to the conventional pastoral vision he found in his source.

## Twelfth Night

John Manningham's description of a performance of *Twelfth Night* on February 2, 1602, at the Middle Temple (one of the Inns of Court, where young men studied law in London), compares the play to Plautus's *Menaechmi* and to an Italian play called *Inganni*. The comment offers a helpful hint on sources. The *Menaechmi* had been the chief source for Shakespeare's earlier play, *The Comedy of Errors*, and that farce of mistaken identity clearly resembles *Twelfth Night* in the hilarious mix-ups resulting from the confusion of two look-alike twins. Shakespeare certainly profited from his earlier experimenting with this sort of comedy. *Twelfth Night* is not necessarily directly indebted to the *Menaechmi*, however, for Renaissance Italian comedy offered many imitations of Plautus from which Shakespeare could have taken his *Twelfth Night* plot. These include *Gl'Inganni* (1562) by Nicolò Secchi, another *Gl'Inganni* (1592) by Curzio Gonzaga, and, most important, an anonymous *Gl'Ingannati* (published 1537). This last play was translated into French by Charles Estienne as *Les Abusés* (1543) and adapted into Spanish by Lope de Rueda in *Los Engaños* (1567). A Latin version, *Laelia,* based on the French, was performed at Cambridge in the 1590s but never printed. Obviously, *Gl'Ingannati* was widely known, and Manningham was probably referring to it in his diary. To trace Shakespeare's own reading in this matter is difficult, owing to the large number of versions available to him, but we can note the suggestive points of comparison in each.

Both *Inganni* plays feature a brother and a sister mistaken for one another. In the later play (by Gonzaga), the sister uses the disguise name of "Cesare." In Secchi's *Inganni,* the disguised sister is in love with her master, who is told that a woman the exact age of his supposed page is secretly in love with him. Another play by Secchi, *L'Interesse* (1581), has a comic duel involving a disguised heroine. Of the Italian plays considered here, however, *Gl'Ingannati* is closest to Shakespeare's play. A short prefatory entertainment included with it in most editions features the name Malevolti. In the play itself, the heroine, Lelia, disguises herself as a page in the service of Flaminio, whom she secretly loves, and is sent on embassies to Flaminio's disdainful mistress Isabella. This lady falls in love with "Fabio," as Lelia calls herself. Lelia's father, Virginio, learning of her disguise and resolving to marry her to old Gherardo (Isabella's father), seeks out Lelia but instead mistakenly arrests her long-lost twin brother, Fabrizio, who has just arrived in Modena. Fabrizio is locked up as a madman in Isabella's room, whereupon Isabella takes the opportunity to betroth herself to the person she mistakes for "Fabio." A recognition scene clears up everything and leads to the marriages of Fabrizio to Isabella and Flaminio to Lelia. This story lacks the subplot of Malvolio, Sir Toby, *et al*. Nor is there a shipwreck.

Matteo Bandello based one of the stories in his *Novelle* (1554) on *Gl'Ingannati,* and this prose version was then translated into French by François de Belleforest in his *Histoires Tragiques* (1579 edition). Shakespeare may well have read both, for he consulted these collections of stories in writing *Much Ado About Nothing.* His most direct source, however, seems to have been the story of "Apollonius and Silla" by Barnabe Riche (an English soldier and fiction writer), in *Riche His Farewell to Military Profession* (1581), which was derived from Belleforest. Riche involves his characters in more serious moral predicaments than Shakespeare allows in his festive comedy. The plot situation is much the same: Silla (the equivalent of Shakespeare's Viola) is washed ashore near Constantinople, where, disguised as "Silvio," she takes service with a duke, Apollonius (Shakespeare's Orsino), and goes on embassies to the wealthy widow Julina

(Shakespeare's Olivia), who proceeds at once to fall in love with "Silvio." When Silla's twin brother, the real Silvio, arrives, he is mistaken by Julina for his twin and is invited to a rendezvous, like Shakespeare's Sebastian. The differences at this point are marked, however, for Silvio becomes Julina's lover and leaves her pregnant when he departs the next day on his quest for Silla. Apollonius is understandably furious to learn of "Silvio's" apparent success with Julina and throws his page into prison. Julina is no less distressed when she learns that the supposed father of her child is in actuality a woman. Only Silvio's eventual return to marry Julina resolves these complications. Shakespeare eschews the pregnancy, the desertion, the imprisonment, and all of Riche's stern moralizing about the bestiality of lust that accompanies this lurid tale. Moreover, he adds the plot of Malvolio, for which Riche provides little suggestion. Shakespeare changes the location to Illyria, with its hint of delirium and illusion, and provides an English flavor in the comic scenes that intensifies the festive character of the play.

Shakespeare's reading may also have included the anonymous play *Sir Clyomon and Sir Clamydes* (c. 1570–1583), Sir Philip Sidney's *Arcadia* (1590), and Emmanuel Forde's prose romance *Parismus* (1598), in which one "Violetta" borrows the disguise of a page. Scholars have suggested that the Malvolio plot may reflect an incident at Queen Elizabeth's court in which the Comptroller of the Household, Sir William Knollys, interrupted a noisy late-night party dressed in only his nightshirt and a pair of spectacles, with a copy of the Italian pornographic writer Aretino's work in his hand. A similar confrontation between revelry and sobriety occurred in 1598: Ambrose Willoughby quieted a disturbance after the Queen had gone to bed and was afterward thanked by her for doing his duty. Such incidents were no doubt common, however, and there is no compelling reason to suppose Shakespeare was sketching from current court gossip.

## Measure for Measure

Stories about corrupt magistrates are ancient and universal, but Shakespeare's particular story in *Measure for Measure* seems to go back to an actual incident in the sixteenth-century Italian court of Don Ferdinando de Gonzaga. A Hungarian student named Joseph Macarius, writing from Vienna, tells about an Italian citizen accused of murder whose wife submitted to the embraces of the magistrate in hopes of saving her husband. When the magistrate executed her husband despite her having fulfilled her bargain, she appealed to the Duke, who ordered the magistrate to give her a dowry and marry her. Thereafter, the Duke ordered the magistrate to be executed. This incident seems to have inspired a Senecan drama by Claude

Rouillet called *Philanira* (1556), a French translation of this play (1563), a novella in the *Hecatommithi* of G. B. Giraldi Cinthio (1565), and a play by Cinthio called *Epitia* (posthumously published in 1583). Shakespeare may have known both the prose and the dramatic versions by Cinthio.

In Cinthio's story, the wise Emperor Maximian appoints his friend Juriste to govern Innsbruck, warning him to rule justly or expect no mercy from the Emperor. Juriste rules long and well, to the satisfaction of his master and the people of Innsbruck. When a young man named Vico is brought before him for ravishing a virgin, Juriste assigns the mandatory sentence of death. Vico's sister, Epitia, an extraordinarily beautiful virgin of eighteen, pleads for Vico's life, urging that his deed was one of passion and that he stands ready to marry the girl he forced. The judge, secretly inflamed with lust for Epitia, promises to consider the matter carefully. She reports this seemingly encouraging news to Vico, who urges her to persevere. When, however, the judge proposes to take her chastity in return for her brother's life, Epitia is mortified and refuses unless Juriste will marry her. During another interim in these negotiations, Vico begs his sister to save his life at any cost. She then submits to Juriste on the condition that he will both marry her and spare Vico. Next morning, however, the jailer brings her the body of her decapitated brother. She lays her complaint before the Emperor, who confronts Juriste with his guilt. Conscience-stricken, Juriste confesses and begs for mercy. At first, Epitia demands strict justice, but when the Emperor compels Juriste to marry her and then be beheaded, she reveals "her natural kindness" and begs successfully for the life of her wronger. There are several important differences between this account and Shakespeare's play: Vico is actually killed, unlike Claudio, and Epitia sleeps with Juriste and then is married to him. No equivalent to Mariana appears, or to Lucio, Pompey, Mistress Overdone, Elbow, and other characters in the comic scenes of Shakespeare's play. No duke oversees the career of Juriste and ensures that no fatal wrong will occur.

Shakespeare may also have consulted Cinthio's play *Epitia*, but his chief source was George Whetstone's two-part play *Promos and Cassandra* (1578) and a novella on the same subject. In the English play, the corrupt judge is Promos, administrator of the city of Julio under the King of Hungary. The law forbidding adultery has lain in abeyance for some years when a young gentleman named Andrugio is arrested and condemned for "incontinency." His sister Cassandra, like Epitia in Cinthio's play, lays down her precious chastity to Promos in response to her brother's piteous entreaties. Promos gives his assurance that he will marry her and save Andrugio's life. When Promos instead treacherously orders the execution of Andrugio, the jailer secretly substitutes the head of a felon, newly executed and so mutilated as to be unrecognizable even by Cassandra. (This rescue is seen as an intervention "by the providence of God.") The King sentences Promos, just as the Emperor sentences Juriste in Cinthio's play, but in Whetstone's play the King refuses Cassandra's pleas for the life of her new husband until Andrugio reveals himself to be still alive and offers to die for Promos. The King forgives Andrugio on condition that he marry Polina, whom he has wronged. The play also features a courtesan named Lamia and her man, Rosko, who ingratiate themselves with the corrupt officer (Phallax) in charge of investigating their case. Phallax is ultimately caught and dismissed from office while Lamia is publicly humiliated.

Whetstone wrote a prose novella of this same story in the *Heptameron of Civil Discourses* (1582). Shakespeare appears to have consulted it as well as the play, for the prose version mentions the names of Isabella (as the narrator of the story) and Crassus (compare *Measure for Measure*, 4.5.8), and the King's awarding of measure for measure in his sentencing of Promos—"You shall be measured with the grace you bestowed on Andrugio"—may have given Shakespeare an idea for the title of his play. Shakespeare was also indebted for a few details to a version in Thomas Lupton's *Too Good to Be True* (1581).

Even though Shakespeare's play is closely related to Whetstone's play and novella, Shakespeare has changed much. He adds the motif of the Duke's mysterious disguise. (A not very compelling analogue to this motif occurs in Sir Thomas Elyot's *The Image of Governance*, 1541.) Shakespeare introduces the use of the bed trick, found also in his presumably earlier play *All's Well That Ends Well*. Most important, Shakespeare stresses the moral and legal complexity of his story. Isabella is about to renounce the world by entering a convent. By contrast, Lucio, a Shakespearean addition, is an engaging cynic, hedonist, and slanderer. Claudio, although guilty of fornication, is only technically in violation of the laws against sexual license. Isabella does not surrender her chastity. Her breakdown in the scene with Claudio intensifies her emotional crisis and renders all the more triumphant her final ability to forgive Angelo. Angelo himself is made puritanical in temperament and is spared the actual consequences of his worst intentions so that he can be worthy of being forgiven. Isabella need not marry Angelo, since he has not actually seduced her; she is thus free to marry the Duke. No felon need be executed in Claudio's stead, for Providence provides a natural death in the prison. In the subplot, going well beyond the merest hints in Whetstone, Pompey is a brilliantly original innovation, Elbow a characteristically Shakespearean clown modeled on the earlier Dogberry of *Much Ado About Nothing*, and Escalus a significant spokesman for a moderate and practical course of equity in the law.

## Richard III

*Richard III*, like the *Henry VI* series, is based on Edward Hall's *The Union of the Two Noble and Illustre Families of Lancaster and York* (1542) and on the 1587 edition of Raphael Holinshed's *The Chronicles of England, Scotland, and Ireland*. Both of these historical compilations were deeply indebted for their hostile view of Richard III to Polydore Vergil and Thomas More. Vergil, a papal tax collector who came to England in 1501, spent many years under the patronage of Henry VII writing in Latin his *Anglica Historia* (first published in Basel, 1534). This work portrayed Richard negatively in order to glorify the claim of the Tudor monarch who had deposed Richard in 1485. Vergil argued that England's suffering was a divinely sent scourge, intended to cleanse England of rebelliousness and to prepare the English people for the providential reward of Tudor rule.

Thomas More's *The History of King Richard III*, left unfinished in 1513, was published in two slightly different versions: one in English (1557) and one in Latin (1566). Thomas More obtained much information and possibly an early draft of his narrative from Cardinal Morton, in whose household More lived as a youth. Morton had figured in the struggles of Richard III's reign—he was the Bishop of Ely from whom Richard requested the strawberries (3.4.32–3)—and had become a bitter enemy of the Yorkist king. Thomas More's own purpose in writing the life of Richard III was surely not to glorify Henry VII, with whom More had a strained relationship, but to characterize the evil of political opportunism. His portrait of Richard becomes that of the generic tyrant, behaving as such tyrants behaved in the various literary models from Renaissance Italy with which More was doubtless familiar. The result was, in any case, one-sided. The historical Richard seems to have been no worse than many another late medieval ruler and had indeed some admirable ideas on efficiency in government. More's blackened portrait, because it served the purposes of the Tudor state, became part of the legend and was available to Shakespeare in many versions. Holinshed incorporated verbatim a good deal of More's account.

Apart from Hall's and Holinshed's chronicles, those of Robert Fabyan (first published in 1516) and the *Annals* of John Stow (1580, 1592) may have provided Shakespeare with further details. Another possible source is *A Mirror for Magistrates* (first published in 1559), in which, for example, in "The Complaint of George, Duke of Clarence," we find the riddling prophecy about the letter G (see 1.1.39). A second edition of the *Mirror* (1563) contains the Complaints of Edward IV, Anthony Woodville (Lord Rivers), Hastings, Buckingham, Shore's wife, and others. Shakespeare's particular indebtedness to the *Mirror* is not great, though he certainly was familiar with it. The same is probably true of the Latin tragedy *Richardus Tertius* by Thomas Legge (1579) at Cambridge, which contains an interesting scene of Richard's wooing of the Lady Anne not reported in the chronicles. The anonymous *The True Tragedy of Richard III* (published 1594, written c. 1590–1592) may have been useful in its fusing of Senecan revenge motifs with English history and in its focus on the single figure of Richard. The Richard of this anonymous play is an overreacher, a worshiper of Fortune who meets his nemesis in the devoutly Christian Earl of Richmond. Opinion is divided as to whether Shakespeare actually used the play, chiefly because by 1590 he could have found the legend of Richard III set forth in so many works.

## Richard II

Shakespeare's primary source for *Richard II* was the 1587 edition of Raphael Holinshed's *Chronicles* covering the years 1398 to 1400. As in his earlier *Henry VI* plays and *Richard III*, Shakespeare departs from historical accuracy in the interests of artistic design. Queen Isabel's part is almost wholly invented, for historically she was a child of eleven at the time the events in this play occurred. Her "Garden Scene" (3.4) is a fine piece of invention, bringing together images of order and disorder that are found in the rest of the play. The Duchess of York's role is entirely original; Holinshed reports the scene in which York's son Aumerle (the Earl of Rutland) rides to the new king and begs for mercy while his father simultaneously denounces him as a traitor, but the Duchess is never mentioned. Shakespeare has added the poignant conflict between husband and wife. Northumberland's role as conspirator against Richard and as hatchet man for Bolingbroke is greatly enlarged; for example, Holinshed never names the persons who engage in the original plotting against Richard. Shakespeare's Bolingbroke returns to England on his own initiative, whereas in Holinshed he does so at the barons' invitation, a change that accentuates the puzzle of Bolingbroke's motive. Another invention is the meeting between John of Gaunt and the Duchess of Gloucester (1.2). In fact, most of Gaunt's character and behavior has no basis in Holinshed at all. Shakespeare creates him to fill the role of thoughtfully conservative statesman, agonized by his son's banishment but doggedly obedient to his monarch. Finally, and most important, Shakespeare has greatly enlarged the role and the poetic nature of King Richard, especially in the final two acts.

Many of these alterations are Shakespeare's own; others derive from his reading in other sources. Samuel Daniel's *The First Four Books of the Civil Wars* (1595) may have had an important influence. Although we cannot discount the possibility that Shakespeare's play may have been written first, the consensus today is that he knew Daniel's poem. It gave him the idea of the Queen's maturity and grief (although not the Garden Scene), and the final meeting of King and Queen. Daniel's Hotspur is unhistorically a young man, as in 2.3 of Shakespeare's play. Like Shakespeare, Daniel sees York as a man of "a mild temperateness." Daniel's Richard and Bolingbroke ride together into London, not separately as in Holinshed. In Daniel's poem, Bolingbroke's indirect manner of insinuating his desire for Richard's death ("And wished that some would so his life esteem/As rid him of these fears wherein he stood") is verbally close to Shakespeare's depiction of this scene. Richard's final soliloquies in these two works show an unmistakable similarity to one another.

Richard II's reign was a controversial subject in the 1590s and produced other plays of varying political coloration that Shakespeare must have known. *The Life and Death of Jack Straw* (anonymous, 1590–1593) distorts history in its friendly portrayal of Richard's role in the Peasants' Revolt of 1381 and whitewashes government policy. In contrast, the anonymous play *Thomas of Woodstock*, sometimes known as *1 Richard II* (1591–1595), is almost a call for open rebellion against tyranny. Many verbal similarities link this latter play with Shakespeare's *Richard II*, and, although scholars have difficulty in determining which was written first, the wary consensus is that Shakespeare borrowed from *Woodstock*. Such a hypothesis would explain some of the mysterious references to Woodstock's death in the first act of *Richard II*, since the anonymous play deals with historical events preceding those of Shakespeare's play. Shakespeare's debt to *Jack Straw*, on the other hand, is slight, even though he probably knew the play. Christopher Marlowe's *Edward II* (c. 1592), although dealing with another reign, probably taught Shakespeare much about constructing a play in which a weak king gains sympathy in his suffering, while his successor becomes morally tainted by the act of deposition.

Other sources have been proposed—so many, in fact, that Shakespeare's task of writing the play has been compared to that of a historical researcher. More probably he assimilated his wide and varied reading without any formal program of study. He had certainly read Edward Hall's *Union of the Two Noble and Illustre Families of Lancaster and York* (1542), a chief source for his earlier history plays, but in *Richard II* he seems to have recalled little more than its overall thematic pattern. Shakespeare must have known the Complaints of Mowbray and Richard in *A Mirror for Magistrates*, but the verbal echoes are slight in this case. The same is essentially true of *The Chronicles of England* by Jean Froissart, translated by Lord Berners (1525), and two French eyewitness accounts available to Shakespeare only in manuscript: the anonymous *Chronique de la Traïson et Mort de Richard Deux Roi d'Angleterre* and Jean Créton's *Histoire du Roi d'Angleterre Richard*. The Froissart *Chronicles* perhaps gave some hints

for Gaunt's refusal to avenge Gloucester's death, for Richard's insensitivity at Gaunt's death, and for Northumberland's role as conspirator. The *Traïson* is notably sympathetic to Richard in his decline, although Shakespeare might also have found this sympathy in Daniel's *Civil Wars*.

Shakespeare's second series of English history plays (*Richard II, 1* and *2 Henry IV, Henry V*) is even freer of the Tudor providential view of history than his first. The second series does not lead forward by any direct link to the reign of the Tudors, as does the first. Henry A. Kelly has shown (*Divine Providence in the England of Shakespeare's Histories*, 1970) that Shakespeare does not follow a single "Tudor myth" but allows spokesmen for both Richard II and his opponents to repeat arguments found in the various chronicles. This practice is especially evident in *Richard II*, in which some spokesmen eloquently warn of the disasters that will follow Bolingbroke's assumption of the throne, while other spokesmen are sympathetic to Bolingbroke's takeover as a political necessity.

## Henry IV, Part I

Shakespeare's chief historical source for *1 Henry IV* was the 1587 edition of Raphael Holinshed's *Chronicles*, but he also took some important ideas from Samuel Daniel's *The First Four Books of the Civil Wars* (1595). Following Daniel, Shakespeare readjusts the age of Hotspur (who was historically older than Henry IV) to match that of Prince Hal. Daniel's Hotspur is, like Shakespeare's, dauntless and stubborn, a turbulent yet noble spirit. The theme of a nemesis of rebellion afflicting Henry IV for his usurpation, only touched upon in Shakespeare's play, owes something to Daniel's presentation, although the idea of nemesis is to be found also in Holinshed. Both Holinshed and Daniel err in confusing the Edmund Mortimer whom Glendower captured with his nephew Edmund Mortimer, claimant to the throne; Shakespeare perpetuates this error. Hal's killing of Hotspur is unhistorical, since both Holinshed and Daniel report only that Hal bravely helped rescue his father from attack and that Hotspur was killed in the melee. Daniel does give prominence to Prince Henry in the battle, however, and implies that he and Hotspur will meet face-to-face. Shakespeare invents the scenes in which we see Mortimer as a devoted husband and Hotspur as a fond combatant in wit with his wife Kate; Holinshed merely informs us that these two men were married. Shakespeare greatly expands Glendower's fascination with magic and poetry, changing him from a ruthless barbarian (in Holinshed) into a cranky but charismatic Welshman. Hotspur, despite hints from Daniel and Holinshed, is chiefly Shakespeare's creation.

The most impressive transformations are those of Hal and Falstaff. Shakespeare knew many legends of Hal's wild youth: some from John Stow's *The Chronicles of England* (1580) and *The Annals of England* (1592); others from oral tradition. Many of these stories were also available in Holinshed. Shakespeare's readiest source, however, was a rowdy and chauvinistic play called *The Famous Victories of Henry the Fifth*, registered 1594 but usually ascribed to Richard Tarlton or Samuel Rowley around 1587 or 1588. This play covers all the events of the *Henry IV* plays and *Henry V* in one breathless sequence. Prince Hal has three companions, Sir John Oldcastle, Tom, and Ned (cf. Ned Poins), in whose company he robs the King's receivers of 1,000 pounds, visits the old tavern in Eastcheap, vexes his father, and strikes the Lord Chief Justice. A crucial difference is that this Hal is truly unregenerate. He not only chases after women and robs, but encourages his companions to look forward to unrestricted license when he is king. Hal seems consciously to desire his father's death. Yet he does reform and banishes his companions beyond a ten-mile limit with a promise to assist them if they amend their conduct. Although Hal's reform is crude and sudden, his popularity aids him when he goes to war against the French. He is followed by a comic crew of London artisans and thieves, who prove invincible against the effete enemy.

Shakespeare owes much to this unsophisticated, vibrant account of Hal's riotous youth, but he has transformed it to his own use. He limits himself in *1 Henry IV* to the action leading up to the Battle of Shrewsbury in order to focus on the coming of age of Prince Henry and the pairing and contrasting of Hotspur, Falstaff, and King Henry IV as alternative models for Hal's behavior. He invents unforgettable comic characters, such as Mistress Quickly, Francis, and Bardolph. Most of all, Shakespeare's portrayal of Falstaff is essentially his own. Sir John Oldcastle of the anonymous play is a minor character, not Hal's closest companion. Falstaff owes something to the tradition of the guileful and inventive Vice of the Tudor morality play (especially when Falstaff is called jestingly "that reverend Vice, that gray Iniquity," 2.4.448), but the influence of the morality play is general rather than specific. To label Falstaff a "Vice" is to reduce him to comic tempter and villain. Falstaff is in part an allowed fool, a parasite, and a *miles gloriosus* or braggart soldier, but he transcends all these conventionalized types with his own unique vitality.

*1 Henry IV* suggests some acquaintance with the anonymous play *Thomas of Woodstock* (c. 1591–1595), which Shakespeare may also have used for *Richard II*, and with the Complaints of Owen Glendower and Northumberland in *A Mirror for Magistrates* (1559). In neither case is the debt extensive. More suggestive as possible sources are events and social conditions in Shakespeare's England: the Northern Rebellion of 1569 against Queen Elizabeth's government, abuses of military authority by unscrupulous officers, the dangerous state of the highways, the raucous vitality of tavern life in Eastcheap, and the like.

## Henry V

Shakespeare's principal historical source for *Henry V*, as for *Richard II* and the *Henry IV* plays, was the 1587 edition of Raphael Holinshed's *Chronicles*. Holinshed's account of Henry V, however, depended so heavily on Edward Hall's *The Union of the Two Noble and Illustre Families of Lancaster and York* (1542) that we sometimes have difficulty knowing whether Shakespeare consulted Holinshed or Hall. He was certainly familiar with both. Shakespeare's sources all acclaim Henry V a hero-king. Samuel Daniel's *The First Four Books of the Civil Wars* (1595), which Shakespeare may have used for his account of the treasonous plot against Henry (2.2), also praises the King in encomiastic terms.

Shakespeare follows the order of events laid down in Holinshed and Hall: the personal rivalry between Henry and the French Dauphin, Henry's request for reassurance from the clergy as to the legitimacy of the war, the maneuvering of the clergy to forestall a bill in Parliament threatening to seize Church land, the foiling of a plot against Henry's life, the siege of Harfleur, and the glorious victory at Agincourt. Both Holinshed and Hall offer Shakespeare many particulars about the English claim to France: in both accounts, the Archbishop quotes Salic law—*In terram Salicam mulieres ne succedant*—and goes on at length about King Pharamond, the rivers Elbe and Saale, King Pepin, Hugh Capet, the Book of Numbers, and the rest. On the other hand, Shakespeare omits a three-year campaign that historically intervened between Agincourt and the peace treaty of Troyes. He passes over the Lollard controversy in England, with the execution of Sir John Oldcastle. And, of course, he adds unforgettable characters whom we do not find in the chronicles—Welshmen, Irishmen, Scots, common soldiers, thieves—who show the unity of the British nation under King Henry's charismatic leadership.

For many of his additions to the chronicles, Shakespeare was indebted to the anonymous *The Famous Victories of Henry the Fifth* (c. 1588), a work to which he had turned earlier in writing *1* and *2 Henry IV*. This old play, not registered until 1594 and not printed until 1598, exists today only in a corrupt text; quite possibly Shakespeare knew a fuller and more authentic version that would have given him still more material. Other plays may have existed on the subject, for the Admiral's Men (a rival acting company) acted a "harey the v" in 1595 and 1596 that may or may not have been *The Famous Victories*. In any event, the relationship between *Henry V* and *Famous Victories* is at times close. *Famous Victories* omits Henry's long campaign between Agincourt and the final peace treaty, as does Shakespeare's play. The Archbishop of *Famous*

*Victories* discusses the French claim just before the arrival of the French Ambassador with the tennis balls. (In Holinshed, the tennis-ball incident occurs first, at Kenilworth, whereas the Archbishop's lecture occurs sometime later at a meeting of Parliament in Leicester.) Henry assures the French ambassador that he has "free liberty and license to speak." To the Dauphin's insolent gift, taunting Henry about his wild youth, the King suavely replies that "My lord prince Dauphin is very pleasant with me" and promises to repay the insult with balls of brass and iron. (Holinshed mentions this apparently nonhistorical legend only briefly.) When the French noblemen assembled at the French court hear of Henry's arrival on their shores, they tremble with fear, even though the Dauphin recklessly scoffs at so young and prodigal a king. Henry is accompanied to France by a ludicrous assortment of London artisans and thieves, such as John Cobbler, who bids farewell to his wife in a comic scene similar to Pistol's parting from the Hostess, and Derick, who turns the tables on a French soldier much as Pistol deals with Monsieur le Fer. When King Henry woos Katharine of France, he protests to her that he cannot speak flatteringly because he is a plain soldier. She asks in return: "How should I love him, that hath dealt so hardly / With my father?" Despite these resemblances, however, Shakespeare's *Henry V* is incomparably superior to the old play and contains many original scenes and characters, such as King Henry's touring of his camp incognito before the battle, the quarrel between Henry and Williams, and above all the scenes involving Fluellen and his fellow captains.

Other possible sources include the *Henrici Quinti Angliae Regis Gesta*, written by a chaplain in Henry V's army; the *Vita et Gesta Henrici Quinti*, erroneously ascribed to Thomas Elmham; the *Vita Henrici Quinti* by "Titus Livius," translated in 1513 (in which the French brag about their horses and armor); a ballad called "The Battle of Agincourt" (c. 1530); and *The Annals of Cornelius Tacitus*, translated in 1598 (in which Germanicus walks disguised through his camp at night "to sound the soldiers' mind," and hears his leadership praised).

## *Romeo and Juliet*

Shakespeare's chief source for *Romeo and Juliet* was a long narrative poem by Arthur Brooke called *The Tragical History of Romeus and Juliet, written first in Italian by Bandell and now in English by Ar. Br.* (1562). Other English versions of this popular legend were available to Shakespeare, in particular William Painter's *The Palace of Pleasure* (1566), but Shakespeare shows only a passing indebtedness to it. Brooke mentions having seen (prior to 1562) a play about the two lovers, but such an old play is not likely to have been of much service to Shakespeare. Nor does he appear to have extensively consulted the various continental versions that lay behind Brooke's poem. Still, these versions help explain the genesis of the story.

The use of a sleeping potion to escape an unwelcome marriage goes back at least to the *Ephesiaca* of Xenophon of Ephesus (by the fifth century A.D.). Masuccio of Salerno, in his *Il Novellino* (1476), seems to have been the first to combine this sleeping potion story with an ironic aftermath of misunderstanding and suicide (as found in the Pyramus and Thisbe story of Ovid's *Metamorphoses*). In Masuccio's account, the lovers Mariotto and Giannozza of Siena are secretly married by a friar. When Mariotto kills a prominent citizen of Siena in a quarrel, he is banished to Alexandria. Giannozza, to avoid marriage with a suitor of her father's choosing, takes a sleeping potion given her by the friar and is buried as though dead. She is thereupon taken from the tomb by the friar and sent on her way to Alexandria. Mariotto, however, having failed to hear from her because the messenger is intercepted by pirates, returns in disguise to her tomb where he is discovered and executed. Giannozza, hearing this sad news, retires to a Sienese convent and dies of a broken heart.

In Luigi da Porto's *Historia novellamente ritrovata di due Nobili Amanti* (published c. 1530), based on Masuccio's account, the scene shifts to Verona. Despite the feuding of their two families, the Montecchi and the Cappelletti, Romeo and Guilietta meet and fall in love at a carnival ball. Romeo at once forgets his unrequited passion for a scornful lady. Friar Lorenzo, an experimenter in magic, secretly marries the lovers. Romeo tries to avoid brawling with the Cappelletti, but when some of his own kinsmen suffer defeat, he kills Theobaldo Cappelletti. After Romeo's departure for Mantua, Guilietta's family arranges a match for her with the Count of Lodrone. Friar Lorenzo gives Guilietta a sleeping potion and sends a letter to Romeo by a fellow friar, but this messenger is unable to find Romeo in Mantua. Romeo, hearing of Guilietta's supposed death from her servant Peter, returns to Verona with a poison he already possesses. Guilietta awakens in time to converse with Romeo before he dies. Then, refusing the Friar's advice to retire to a convent, she dies by stopping her own breath. This story provides no significant equivalents for Mercutio and the Nurse, although a young man named Marcuccio appears briefly at the Cappelletti's ball.

Da Porto's version inspired that of Matteo Bandello in his *Novelle* of 1554. Some details are added: Romeo goes to the ball in a vizard (mask), he has a servant named Pietro, a rope ladder is given to the Nurse enabling Romeo to visit Julietta's chamber before their marriage, Romeo obtains a poison from one Spolentino, and so on. The young man at the ball, Marcuccio, is now named Mercutio but is still a minor figure. This Bandello version was translated into French by Pierre Boaistuau in his *Histoires Tragiques* (1559); Boaistuau adds the Apothecary (who is racked and hanged for his part in the tragedy) and has Romeo die before Juliet awakens and slays herself with Romeo's dagger.

Despite Arthur Brooke's implication on the title page that his version is based on Bandello, the narrative poem *Romeus and Juliet* is taken from Boaistuau. Brooke's poem is a severely pious work written in "Poulter's Measure," couplets with alternating lines of six and seven feet. Brooke openly disapproves of the lovers' carnality and haste, although fortunately the story itself remains sympathetic to Romeus and Juliet. Brooke stresses star-crossed fortune and the antithesis of love and hate. He reduces Juliet's age from eighteen (as in Bandello) to sixteen. (Shakespeare further reduces her age to less than fourteen.) Brooke's narrative is generally close to Shakespeare's, though with important exceptions. Shakespeare compresses time from some nine months to a few days. In Brooke, for example, some two weeks elapse between the masked ball and Romeus's encounter with Juliet in her garden, and about two months elapse between the marriage and Tybalt's death. Shakespeare also unifies his play by such devices as introducing Tybalt and Paris early in the story; in Brooke's poem, Tybalt appears only at the time he is slain, and Juliet's proposed marriage to Count Paris emerges as a threat only after Romeus's banishment. Shakespeare's greatest transformation is of the characters. Brooke's Juliet is scheming. His Mercutio remains a shadowy figure, as in Bandello *et al*. Brooke's Nurse is unattractive, although she does occasionally hint at comic greatness: for example, she garrulously confides to Romeus the details of Juliet's infancy and then keeps Juliet on tenterhooks while she prates about Romeus's fine qualities (lines 631–714). Even if Shakespeare's play is incomparably superior to Brooke's drably versified poem, the indebtedness is extensive.

## Julius Caesar

*Julius Caesar* represents Shakespeare's first extensive use of the work of the first-century Greek biographer Plutarch, in Thomas North's translation (based on the French of Jacques Amyot) of *The Lives of the Noble Grecians and Romans* (1579 and 1595). Plutarch was to become Shakespeare's most often used source in the 1600s; prior to 1599 he had consulted it briefly on a number of other occasions. In *Julius Caesar*, he borrows details from three lives: Caesar, Brutus, and Antonius. He uses particular traits of character, such as Caesar's belief that it is "better to die once than always to be afraid of death," Brutus's determination to "frame his manners of life by the rules of virtue and study of philosophy," Cassius's choleric disposition and his "hating Caesar privately more than he did the tyranny openly," and Antonius's inclination to "rioting and banqueting."

The events of the play are substantially present in Plutarch, especially in "The Life of Julius Caesar."

Antonius runs the course on the Feast of Lupercal to cure barrenness and offers the diadem to Caesar. Flavius and Marullus despoil the images of Caesar. Caesar observes that he mistrusts pale and lean men such as Brutus and Cassius. Papers are thrown by the conspirators where Brutus can find them, proclaiming "Thou sleepest, Brutus, and art not Brutus indeed." Caesar's death is preceded by prodigies: a slave's hand burns but is unconsumed, a sacrificial beast is found to contain no heart. When Caesar encounters the soothsayer who previously had warned him of his fate and boasts that "the ides of March be come," the soothsayer has the last word: "So they be, but yet are they not past." Brutus's wife Portia complains to him of being treated "like a harlot," not like a partner. Brutus commits what Plutarch calls two serious errors when he forbids his fellow conspirators to kill Antonius and when he permits Antonius to speak at Caesar's funeral. Cinna the Poet is slain by an angry crowd mistaking him for Cinna the conspirator. A ghost appears to Brutus shortly before the last battle saying, "I am thy ill angel, Brutus, and thou shalt see me by the city of Phillippes," to which Brutus replies, "Well, I shall see thee then." Antonius says of the vanquished conspirators that "there was none but Brutus only that was moved to do it, as thinking the act commendable of itself: but that all the other conspirators did conspire his death for some private malice or envy." Shakespeare's debt to Plutarch is greater than these few examples can indicate.

Of course, Shakespeare reshapes and selects, as in his history plays. He compresses into one day Caesar's triumphant procession, the disrobing of the images, and the offer of the crown to Caesar on the Lupercal, when, in fact, these events were chronologically separate. Casca is by and large an invented character, and Octavius's role is considerably enlarged. Brutus's servant Lucius is a minor but effective addition, illustrating Brutus's capacity for warmth and humanity. Brutus's two speeches after the assassination (as mentioned by Plutarch) become one, and Antonius's speech is made to follow immediately after. (In Plutarch, Antonius speaks the following day, after the reading of the will.) Shakespeare accentuates the irrationality and vacillation of the mob, whereas in Plutarch the people are never much swayed by Brutus's rhetoric, even though they respectfully allow him to speak. The unforgettable speeches of both Brutus and Antonius are not set down at all in Plutarch. More compression of time occurs after the assassination: in Plutarch, Octavius does not arrive in Rome until some six weeks afterward and does not agree to the formation of the Triumvirate until more than a year of quarreling has taken place. The inexorable buildup of tension in Shakespeare's play is the result of careful selection from a vast amount of material. Shakespeare's borrowing from "The Life of Marcus Brutus" is no less extensive and is at the same time reshaped and given new emphasis.

Although Shakespeare depended heavily on Plutarch, he was also aware of later and conflicting traditions about Caesar. On the one hand, Dante's *Divine Comedy* (c. 1310–1321) consigns Brutus and Cassius to the lowest circle of hell, along with Judas Iscariot and other betrayers of their masters. Geoffrey Chaucer's "The Monk's Tale," from the *Canterbury Tales*, similarly portrays Caesar as the manly and uncorruptible victim of envious attackers. On the other hand, Montaigne stresses the hubris of Caesar in aspiring to divinity. (Shakespeare could have read Montaigne in the French original or, if he had access to a manuscript, in John Florio's English translation, published in 1603.) A pro-Brutus view could also be found in the Latin *Julius Caesar* of Marc-Antoine Muret (1553) and the French *César* of Jacques Grévin (1561). That Shakespeare knew these works is unlikely, but they kept alive a tradition with which he was certainly familiar. Possibly he knew such Roman works as Lucan's account of Caesar in the *Pharsalia* and Cicero's letters and orations, which were republican in tenor. Other possible sources include the *Chronicle of the Romans' Wars* by Appian of Alexandria (translated 1578), the anonymous play *Caesar's Revenge* (published 1606–1607, performed in the early 1590s at Oxford), and Thomas Kyd's *Cornelia* (translated from the French Senecan tragedy by Garnier). *Il Cesare* by Orlando Pescetti (1594) is now almost universally rejected as a possible source. The result of Shakespeare's acquaintance with both pro- and anti-Caesar traditions is that he subordinates his own political vision to a balanced presentation of history, showing the significant strengths and disabling weaknesses in both Caesar and the conspirators.

## Hamlet

The ultimate source of the *Hamlet* story is Saxo Grammaticus's *Historia Danica* (1180–1208), the saga of one Amlothi or (as Saxo calls him) Amlethus. The outline of the story is essentially that of Shakespeare's play, even though the emphasis of the Danish saga is overwhelmingly on cunning, brutality, and bloody revenge. Amlethus's father is Horwendil, a Governor of Jutland, who bravely kills the King of Norway in single combat and thereby wins the hand in marriage of Gerutha, daughter of the King of Denmark. This good fortune goads the envious Feng into slaying his brother Horwendil and marrying Gerutha, "capping unnatural murder with incest." Though the deed is known to everyone, Feng invents excuses and soon wins the approbation of the fawning courtiers. Young Amlethus vows revenge but, perceiving his uncle's cunning, feigns madness. His mingled words of craft and candor awaken suspicions that he may be playing a game of deception.

Two attempts are made to lure Amlethus into revealing that he is actually sane. The first plan is to tempt him into lechery, on the theory that one who lusts for women cannot be truly insane. Feng causes an attractive woman to be placed in a forest where Amlethus will meet her as though by chance; but Amlethus, secretly warned of the trap by a kindly foster brother, spirits the young lady off to a hideaway where they can make love unobserved by Feng's agents. She confesses the plot to Amlethus. In a second stratagem, a courtier who is reported to be "gifted with more assurance than judgment" hides himself under some straw in the Queen's chamber in order to overhear her private conversations with Amlethus. The hero, suspecting just such a trap, feigns madness and begins crowing like a noisy rooster, bouncing up and down on the straw until he finds the eavesdropper. Amlethus stabs the man to death, drags him forth, cuts the body into morsels, boils them, and flings the bits "through the mouth of an open sewer for the swine to eat." Thereupon he returns to his mother to accuse her of being an infamous harlot. He wins her over to repentant virtue and even cooperation. When Feng, returning from a journey, looks around for his counselor, Amlethus jestingly (but in part truly) suggests that the man went to the sewer and fell in.

Feng now sends Amlethus to the King of Britain with secret orders for his execution. However, Amlethus finds the letter to the British King in the coffers of the two unnamed retainers accompanying him on the journey and substitutes a new letter ordering their execution instead. The new letter, purportedly written and signed by Feng, goes on to urge that the King of Britain marry his daughter to a young Dane being sent from the Danish court. By this means, Amlethus gains an English wife and rids himself of the escorts. A year later Amlethus returns to Jutland, gets the entire court drunk, flings a tapestry (knitted for him by his mother) over the prostrate courtiers, secures the tapestry with stakes, and then sets fire to the palace. Feng escapes this holocaust, but Amlethus cuts him down with the King's own sword. (Amlethus exchanges swords because his own has been nailed fast into its scabbard by his enemies.) Subsequently, Amlethus convinces the people of the justice of his cause and is chosen King of Jutland. After ruling for several years, he returns to Britain, bigamously marries a Scottish Queen, fights a battle with his first father-in-law, is betrayed by his second wife, and is finally killed in battle.

In Saxo's account, we thus find the prototypes of Hamlet, Claudius, Gertrude, Polonius, Ophelia, Rosencrantz, and Guildenstern. Several episodes are close in narrative detail to Shakespeare's play: the original murder and incestuous marriage, the feigned madness, the woman used as a decoy, the eavesdropping counselor, and especially the trip to England. A translation of Saxo into French by François de Belleforest, in *Histoires Tragiques* (1576 edition), adds a few details, such as Gertrude's adultery before the murder and Hamlet's melancholy. Belleforest's version is longer than Saxo's, with more psychological and moral observation and more dialogue. Shakespeare probably consulted it.

Shakespeare need not have depended extensively on these older versions of his story, however. His main source was almost certainly an old play of *Hamlet*. Much evidence testifies to the existence of such a play. The *Diary* of Philip Henslowe, a theater owner and manager, records a performance, not marked as "new," of a *Hamlet* at Newington Butts on June 11, 1594, by "my Lord Admiral's Men" or "my Lord Chamberlain's Men," probably the latter. Thomas Lodge's pamphlet, *Wit's Misery, and the World's Madness* (1596), refers to "the visard of the ghost which cried so miserably at the theater, like an oyster wife, 'Hamlet, revenge!' " And Thomas Nashe, in his *Epistle* prefixed to Robert Greene's romance *Menaphon* (1589), offers the following observation:

It is a common practice nowadays amongst a sort of shifting companions, that run through every art and thrive by none, to leave the trade of noverint, whereto they were born, and busy themselves with the endeavors of art, that could scarcely Latinize their neck verse if they should have need; yet English Seneca read by candlelight yields many good sentences, as "Blood is a beggar," and so forth; and if you entreat him fair in a frosty morning, he will afford you whole *Hamlets*, I should say handfuls, of tragical speeches. But O grief! *Tempus edax rerum*, what's that will last always? The sea exhaled by drops will in continuance be dry, and Seneca, let blood line by line and page by page, at length must needs die to our stage; which makes his famished followers to imitate the Kid in Aesop, who, enamored with the Fox's newfangles, forsook all hopes of life to leap into a new occupation; and these men, renouncing all possibilities of credit or estimation, to intermeddle with Italian translations . . .

Nashe's testimonial describes a *Hamlet* play, written in the Senecan style by some person born to the trade of "noverint," or scrivener, who has turned to hack writing and translation. The description has often been fitted to Thomas Kyd, though this identification is not certain. (Nashe could be punning on Kyd's name when he refers to "the Kid in Aesop.") Certainly Thomas Kyd's *The Spanish Tragedy* (c. 1587) shows many affinities with Shakespeare's play and provides many Senecan ingredients missing from Saxo and Belleforest: the ghost, the difficulty in ascertaining whether the ghost's words are believable, the resulting need for delay and a feigning of madness, the moral perplexities afflicting a sensitive man called upon to revenge, the play within the play, the clever reversals and ironically caused deaths in the catastrophe, the rhetoric of tragic passion. Whether or not Kyd, in fact, wrote the *Ur-Hamlet*, his extant play enables us to see more clearly what that lost play must have contained. The unauthorized first quarto of *Hamlet* (1603) also offers a few seemingly authentic details that are not found in the authoritative second quarto but are found in

the earlier sources and may have been a part of the *Ur-Hamlet*. For example, after Hamlet has killed Corambis (corresponding to Polonius), the Queen vows to assist Hamlet in his strategies against the King; later, when Hamlet has returned to England, the Queen sends him a message by Horatio warning him to be careful.

One last document sheds light on the *Ur-Hamlet*. A German play, *Der bestrafte Brudermord (Fratricide Punished)*, from a now-lost manuscript dated 1710, seems to have been based on a text used by English actors traveling in Germany in 1586 and afterward. Though changed by translation and manuscript transmission, and too entirely different from Shakespeare's play to have been based on it, this German version may well have been based on Shakespeare's source-play. Polonius's name in this text, Corambus, is the Corambis of the first quarto of 1603. (The name may mean "cabbage cooked twice," from *coramblebis*, a proverbially dull dish.)

*Der bestrafte Brudermord* begins with a prologue in the Senecan manner, followed by the appearance of the ghost to Francisco, Horatio, and sentinels of the watch. Within the palace, meanwhile, the King carouses. Hamlet joins the watch, confiding to Horatio that he is "sick at heart" over his father's death and his mother's hasty remarriage. The ghost appears to Hamlet, tells him how the juice of hebona was poured into his ear, and urges revenge. When Hamlet swears Horatio and Francisco to silence, the ghost (now invisible) says several times "We swear," his voice following the men as they move from place to place. Hamlet reveals to Horatio the entire circumstance of the murder. Later, in a formal session of the court, the new King speaks hypocritically of his brother's death and explains the reasons for his marriage to the Queen. Hamlet is forbidden to return to Wittenberg, though Corambus's son Leonhardus has already set out for France.

Some time afterward, Corambus reports the news of Hamlet's madness to the King and Queen, and presumes on the basis of his own youthful passions to diagnose Hamlet's malady as lovesickness. Concealed, he and the King overhear Hamlet tell Ophelia to "go to a nunnery." When players arrive from Germany, Hamlet instructs them in the natural style of acting and then requests them to perform a play before the King about the murder of King Pyrrus by his brother. (Death is again inflicted by hebona poured in the ear.) After the King's guilty reaction to the play, Hamlet finds him alone at prayers but postpones the killing lest the King's soul be sent to heaven. Hamlet kills Corambus behind the tapestry in the Queen's chamber and is visited again by the ghost (who says nothing, however). Ophelia, her mind deranged, thinks herself in love with a court butterfly named Phantasmo. (This creature is also involved in a comic action to help the clown Jens with a tax problem.)

The King sends Hamlet to England with two unnamed courtiers who are instructed to kill Hamlet after their arrival. A contrary wind takes them instead to an island near Dover, where Hamlet foils his two enemies by kneeling between them and asking them to shoot him on signal; at the proper moment, he ducks and they shoot one another. He finishes them off with their own swords and discovers a letter on their persons ordering Hamlet's execution by the English King if the original plot should fail. When Hamlet returns to Denmark, the King arranges a duel between him and Corambus's son Leonhardus. If Leonhardus's poisoned dagger misses its mark, a beaker of wine containing finely ground oriental diamond dust is to do the rest. Hamlet is informed of the impending duel by Phantasmo (compare Osric), whom Hamlet taunts condescendingly and calls "Signora Phantasmo." Shortly before the duel takes place, Ophelia is reported to have thrown herself off a hill to her death. The other deaths occur much as in Shakespeare's play. The dying Hamlet bids that the crown be conveyed to his cousin, Duke Fortempras of Norway, of whom we have not heard earlier.

From the extensive similarities between *Hamlet* and this German play, we can see that Shakespeare inherited his narrative material almost intact, though in a jumble and so pitifully mangled that the modern reader can only laugh at the contrast. No source study in Shakespeare reveals so clearly the extent of Shakespeare's wholesale borrowing of plot and the incredible transformation he achieved in reordering his materials.

## Othello

Shakespeare's main source for *Othello* was the seventh story from the third decade of G. B. Giraldi Cinthio's *Hecatommithi* (1565). Cinthio was available in French but not in English translation during Shakespeare's lifetime. The verbal echoes in Shakespeare's play are usually closer to the Italian original than to Gabriel Chappuys's French version of 1584. Cinthio's account may have been based on an actual incident occurring in Venice around 1508.

Shakespeare is considerably indebted to Cinthio's story for the essentials of the narrative: the marriage of a Moorish captain to a Venetian lady, Disdemona, whose relatives wish her to marry someone else, the mutual attraction to noble qualities of mind in both husband and wife, their happiness together at first, the dispatching of the Moor to Cyprus to take charge of the garrison there, Disdemona's insistence on accompanying her husband through whatever dangers may occur (though the sea voyage, as it turns out, is a very calm one), the ensign's treachery and resolve to destroy the Moor's happiness with Disdemona, her begging her husband to reinstate the squadron leader whom the Moor has demoted for fighting on guard duty (although no mention is made of drunkenness or of the ensign's role in starting the trouble), the ensign's insinuations to the Moor that his wife is

cuckolding him because she is becoming weary of her marriage with a black man, the ensign's difficulty in providing ocular proof, his planting of Disdemona's handkerchief in the squadron leader's quarters and his showing the Moor that the handkerchief is now in the squadron leader's possession, his arranging for the Moor to witness at a distance a conversation between the ensign and squadron leader that is, in fact, not about Disdemona, Disdemona's confusion when she is asked to produce the handkerchief, the attack on the squadron leader in the dark, the murder of Disdemona in her bed, the Moor's deep regret at the loss of his wife, the eventual punishment of both the Moor and and the ensign, and the telling of the story publicly by the ensign's wife, who has heretofore kept silent because of her fear of her husband.

Although these correspondences in the story are many, Shakespeare has changed a great deal. He provides Disdemona with a caring and saddened father, Brabantio, out of Cinthio's brief suggestion of family opposition to her marriage, and adds the entire opening scene in which Iago arouses the prejudices of Brabantio. Roderigo is a brilliantly invented character used to reveal Iago's skill in manipulation. Cinthio's ensign, though thoroughly wicked, never expresses a resentment for the squadron leader's promotion and favored treatment by the Moor; instead, the ensign lusts for Disdemona and turns against her and the Moor only when his passion is unrequited. In his complex portrayal of a consuming and irrational jealousy in Iago, Shakespeare goes far beyond his source, making use as well of the inventive villainy of the Vice in the English late medieval morality play. In Cinthio's account, the ensign filches the handkerchief from Disdemona while she is hugging the ensign's three-year-old daughter; the ensign's wife is uninvolved in this mischief, though she does unwillingly learn of her husband's villainy (since he has an idea of using her in his plot) and later feels constrained to hold her tongue when Disdemona asks her if she knows why the Moor is behaving so strangely. As is usual in prose narrative, the passage of time is much more extended than in Shakespeare's play.

In the later portions of the story, the changes are more marked. Cinthio relates an episode in which the squadron leader, finding the handkerchief in his room, takes it back to Disdemona while the Moor is out but is interrupted by the Moor's unexpected return home; Shakespeare instead has Cassio approach Desdemona (earlier in the story) to beg her assistance in persuading Othello to reinstate him. Cinthio tells of a woman in the squadron leader's household who copies the embroidery of the handkerchief before it is returned and is seen with it at a window by the Moor; here, Shakespeare finds a suggestion for Bianca, but her role is considerably augmented, partly with the help of a passing remark in Cinthio's account that the squadron leader is attacked and wounded as he leaves the house of a courtesan with whom he occasionally takes his pleasure. In the absence of any character corresponding to Roderigo, the Cinthio narrative assigns to the ensign himself the role of wounding the squadron leader. The manner in which Disdemona is murdered is strikingly different. Cinthio has nothing equivalent to the tender scene between Desdemona and Emilia as Desdemona prepares to go to bed. Cinthio's Moor hides the ensign in a dressing room next to his bedroom and commissions the ensign to bludgeon her to death with a sand-filled stocking, after which the two murderers cause the ceiling of the room to collapse on her and create the impression that a rafter has smashed her skull.

Cinthio also treats the aftermath of the murder in a very different way. The Moor, distracted with grief, turns on the ensign and demotes him, whereupon the ensign persuades the squadron commander to take vengeance on the Moor as his attacker (according to the lying ensign) and killer of Disdemona. When the squadron commander accuses the Moor before the Seigniory, the Moor keeps silent but is banished and eventually killed by Desdemona's relatives. The ensign, returning to his own country, gets in trouble by making a false accusation and dies as the result of torture. Cinthio sees this as God's retribution. The ensign's wife lives to tell her story, unlike Shakespeare's Emilia.

The changed ending is essential to Shakespeare's play. Emilia becomes a more complex figure than the ensign's wife: Shakespeare implicates her in the stealing of the handkerchief but also accentuates her love for Desdemona and her brave denunciation of her husband when at last she knows the full truth. Othello's ritual slaying of Desdemona avoids the appalling butchery of the source story. Shakespeare's ending is more unified, and brings both Othello and Iago to account for the deeds they have committed in this play. Most important, Shakespeare transforms a sensational murder story into a moving tragedy of love.

## King Lear

The story of Lear goes back into ancient legend. The motif of two wicked sisters and a virtuous youngest sister reminds us of Cinderella. Lear himself appears to come from Celtic mythology. Geoffrey of Monmouth, a Welshman in close contact with Celtic legend, included a Lear or Leir as one of the pseudo-historical Kings in his *Historia Regum Britanniae* (c. 1136). This fanciful mixture of history and legend traces a supposed line of descent from Brut, great-grandson of Aeneas of Troy, through Locrine, Bladud, Leir, Gorboduc, Ferrex and Porrex, Lud, Cymbeline, Bonduca, Vortigern, Arthur, and so forth, to the historical Kings of England. The Tudor monarchs made much of their purported claim to such an ancient dynasty,

and in Shakespeare's day this mythology had a quasi-official status demanding a certain reverential suspension of disbelief.

King Leir, according to Geoffrey, is the father of three daughters, Gonorilla, Regan, and Cordeilla, among whom he intends to divide his kingdom. To determine who deserves most, he asks them who loves him most. The two eldest sisters protest undying devotion, but Cordeilla, perceiving how the others flatter and deceive him, renounces hyperbole and promises only to love him as a daughter should love a father. Furious, the King denies Cordeilla her third of the kingdom but permits her to marry Aganippus, King of the Franks, without dowry. Thereafter, Leir bestows his two eldest daughters on the Dukes of Albania and Cornubia (Albany and Cornwall), together with half the island during his lifetime and the possession of the remainder after his death. In due course, his two sons-in-law rebel against Leir and seize his power. Thereafter Maglaunus, Duke of Albania, agrees to maintain Leir with sixty retainers, but, after two years of chafing at this arrangement, Gonorilla insists that the number be reduced to thirty. Angrily, the King goes to Henvin, Duke of Cornubia, where all goes well for a time; within a year, however, Regan demands that Leir reduce his retinue to five knights. When Gonorilla refuses to take him back with more than one retainer, Leir crosses into France and is generously received by Cordeilla and Aganippus. An invasion restores Leir to his throne. Three years later, he and Aganippus die, after which Cordeilla rules successfully for five years until overthrown by the sons of Maglaunus and Henvin. In prison she commits suicide.

This story, as part of England's mythic genealogy, was repeated in various Tudor versions, such as *The First Part of the Mirror for Magistrates* (1574), William Warner's *Albion's England* (1586), and Raphael Holinshed's *Chronicles* (second edition, 1587). Warner refers to the King's sons-in-law as "the Prince of Albany" and "the Cornish prince"; Holinshed refers to them as "the Duke of Albania" and "the Duke of Cornwall" but reports that it is Cornwall who marries the eldest daughter Gonorilla. *The Mirror*, closer to Shakespeare in these details, speaks of "Gonerell" as married to "Albany" and of "Cordila" as married to "the King of France." Edmund Spenser's *The Faerie Queene* (2.10.27–32) reports that "Cordeill" or "Cordelia" ends her life by hanging herself. Other retellings appear in Gerard Legh's *Accidence of Armory* and William Camden's *Remains*. All of these accounts leave the story virtually unchanged.

Shakespeare's immediate source for *King Lear* was an old play called *The True Chronicle History of King Leir*. It was published in 1605 but plainly is much earlier in style. The Stationers' Register, the official record of the London Company of Stationers (booksellers and printers), for May 14, 1594, lists "A booke called the Tragecall historie of Kinge Leir and his Three Daughters &c.," and a short time earlier Philip Henslowe's *Diary* records the performance of a "Kinge Leare" at the Rose Theatre on April 6 and 8, 1594. The actors were either the Queen's or the Earl of Sussex's Men (two acting companies), probably the Queen's. The play may have been written as early as 1588. George Peele, Robert Greene, Thomas Lodge, and Thomas Kyd have all been suggested as possible authors. Shakespeare probably knew the play before its publication in 1605.

This play of *Leir* ends happily, with the restoration of Leir to his throne. Essentially, the play is a legendary history with a strong element of romance. The two wicked sisters are warned of the King's plans for dividing his kingdom by an obsequious courtier named Skalliger (compare Oswald). It is Skalliger, in fact, who proposes the idea of apportioning the Kingdom in accord with the lovingness of the daughters' responses. Cordella receives the ineffectual support of an honest courtier, Perillus (compare Kent) but is disinherited by her angry father. Trusting herself to God's mercy and setting forth alone to live by her own labor, Cordella is found by the Gallian King and his bluff companion Mumford, who have come to England disguised as palmers to see if the English King's daughters are as beautiful as reported. The King hears Cordella's sad story, falls in love with her, and woos her (still wearing his disguise) in the name of the Gallian King. When she virtuously suggests the palmer woo for himself, he throws off his disguise and marries her forthwith.

Meanwhile the other sons-in-law, Cornwall and Combria (compare Albany), draw lots for their shares of the kingdom. Leir announces that he will sojourn with Cornwall and Gonorill first. Cornwall treats the King with genuine solicitude, but Gonorill, abetted by Skalliger, tauntingly drives her father away. The King acknowledges to his loyal companion Perillus that he has wronged Cordella. Regan, who rules her mild husband as she pleases, receives the King with seeming tenderness but secretly hires an assassin to end his life. (Gonorill is partner in this plot.) The suborned agent, frightened into remorse by a providentially sent thunderstorm, shows his intended victim the letter ordering the assassination.

The Gallian King and Cordella, who have previously sent ambassadors to Leir urging him to come to France, now decide to journey with Mumford into Britain disguised as countryfolk. Before they can do so, however, Leir and Perillus arrive in France, in mariners' garb, where they encounter Cordella and her party dressed as country folk. Cordella recognizes Leir's voice, and father and daughter are tearfully reunited. The Gallian King invades England and restores Leir to his throne.

Shakespeare has changed much in the narrative of his source. He discards not only the happy ending but also the attempted assassination and the numerous romancelike uses of disguise (although Tom o' Bedlam, in an added plot, repeatedly uses disguise). Shakespeare eliminates the humorous Mumford and replaces Perillus with both Kent and the Fool. He turns Cornwall into a villain and Albany into a belated champion of justice. He creates the storm scene out of a mere suggestion of such an event, serving a very different purpose, in his source.

Most of all, he adds the parallel plot of Gloucester, Edgar, and Edmund. Here Shakespeare derived some of his material from Sir Philip Sidney's *Arcadia* (1590). In Book 2, chapter 10 of this greatest of Elizabethan prose romances, the two heroes, Pyrocles and Musidorus, encounter a son leading his blind old father. The old man tells his pitiful tale. He is the deposed King of Paphlagonia, father of a bastard son named Plexirtus who, he now bitterly realizes, turned the King against his true son Leonatus—the very son who is now his guide and guardian. The true son, having managed to escape his father's order of execution, has been forced to live poorly as a soldier, while the bastard son has proceeded to usurp his father's throne. In his wretchedness, the King has been succored by his forgiving true son and has been prevented from casting himself off the top of a hill. At the conclusion of this narrative, the villain Plexirtus arrives and attacks Leonatus; reinforcements arrive on both sides, but eventually Plexirtus is driven off, enabling the King to return to his court and bestow the crown on Leonatus. The old King thereupon dies, his heart having been stretched beyond the limits of endurance.

Other parts of the *Arcadia* may have given Shakespeare further suggestions; for example, the disguises adopted by Kent and Edgar are like those of Zelmane and Pyrocles in Sidney's prose work, and Albany's speeches about anarchy and the monstrosity that results from assaults on the rule of law recall one of Sidney's deepest concerns. Edmund is decidedly indebted to the allegorical Vice figure of the late medieval morality play tradition. For Tom o' Bedlam's mad language, Shakespeare consulted Samuel Harsnett's *Declaration of Egregious Popish Impostures*, 1603. (See Kenneth Muir's Arden edition of *King Lear*, pp. 253–6, for an extensive comparison.)

## Macbeth

Shakespeare's chief source for *Macbeth* was Raphael Holinshed's *Chronicles* (1587 edition). Holinshed had gone for most of his material to Hector Boece, *Scotorum Historiae* (1526–1527), who in turn was indebted to a fourteenth-century priest named John of Fordun and to a fifteenth-century chronicler, Andrew of Wyntoun. By the time Holinshed found it, the story of Macbeth had become more fiction than fact. The historical Macbeth, who ruled from 1040 to 1057, did take the throne by killing Duncan, but in a civil conflict between two clans contending for the kingship. Contemporary observers credit him with having been a good ruler. Although he was defeated by the Earl of Northumbria (the Siward of Shakespeare's play) at Birnam Wood in 1054, the Earl was forced by his own losses to retire, and Macbeth ruled three years longer before being slain by Duncan's son Malcolm. Banquo and Fleance are fictional characters apparently invented by Boece.

In Holinshed's telling of the story, Duncan is a King with a soft and gentle nature, negligent in punishing his enemies and thereby an unwitting encourager of sedition. It falls to his cousin, Macbeth, a critic of this soft line, and to Banquo, the Thane of Lochaber, to defend Scotland against her enemies: first against Macdowald (Macdonwald in Shakespeare), with his Irish kerns and gallowglasses, and then against Sueno, King of Norway. (Shakespeare fuses these battles into one.) Shortly thereafter, Macbeth and Banquo encounter "three women in strange and wild apparel, resembling creatures of elder world," who predict their futures as in the play. Although Macbeth and Banquo jest about the matter, common opinion later maintains that "these women were either the Weird Sisters, that is (as ye would say), the goddesses of destiny, or else some nymphs or fairies, endued with knowledge of prophecy." Certainly Macbeth soon becomes the Thane of Cawdor, whereupon, jestingly reminded of the three sisters' promise by Banquo, he resolves to seek the throne. His way is blocked, however, by Duncan's naming of his eldest but still underage son Malcolm to be Prince of Cumberland and heir to the throne. Macbeth's resentment at this is understandable, since Scottish law provides that, until the King's son is of age, the "next of blood unto him"—that is, Macbeth himself, as Duncan's cousin—should reign. Accordingly, Macbeth begins to plot with his associates how to usurp the kingdom by force. His "very ambitious" wife urges him on because of her "unquenchable desire" to be Queen. Banquo is one among many trusted friends with whose support Macbeth slays the King at Inverness or at Bothgowanan. (No mention is made of a visit to Macbeth's castle.) Malcolm and Donald Bane, the dead King's sons, fly for their safety to Cumberland, where Malcolm is well received by Edward the Confessor of England; Donald Bane proceeds on to Ireland.

Holinshed's Macbeth is at first no brutal tyrant, as in Shakespeare. For some ten years he rules well, using great liberality and correcting the laxity of his predecessor's reign. (Holinshed does suggest, to be sure, that his justice is only contrived to court popularity among his subjects.) Inevitably, however, the Weird Sisters' promise of a posterity to Banquo goads Macbeth into ordering the murder of his onetime companion. Fleance escapes Macbeth's henchmen in the dark and afterward founds the lineage of the Stuart Kings. (This genealogy is fictitious.) Macbeth's vain quest for absolute power further causes him to build Dunsinane fortress. When Macduff refuses to help, the King turns against him and would kill him except that "a certain witch, whom he had in great trust," tells the King he need never fear a man born of woman nor any vanquishment till Birnam Wood come to Dunsinane. Macduff flees for his safety into England and joins Malcolm, whereupon Macbeth's agents slaughter Macduff's wife and children at Fife. Malcolm, fearing that Macduff may be an agent of Macbeth, dissemblingly professes to be a voluptuary, miser, and tyrant, but, when Macduff responds as he should in righteous sorrow at Scotland's evil condition, Malcolm reveals his steadfast commitment to the cause of right. These leaders return to Scotland and defeat Macbeth at Birnam Wood, with their soldiers carrying branches before them. Macduff, proclaiming that he is a man born of no woman since he was "ripped out" of his mother's womb, slays Macbeth.

Despite extensive similarities, Shakespeare has made significant changes. Duncan is no longer an ineffectual king. Macbeth can no longer justify his claim to the throne. Most important, Banquo is no longer partner in a broadly based though secret conspiracy against Duncan. Banquo is, after all, ancestor of James I (at least according to this legendary history), and so his hands must be kept scrupulously clean; King James disapproved of all tyrannicides, whatever the circumstances. Macbeth is no longer a just lawgiver. The return of Banquo's ghost to Macbeth's banqueting table is an added scene. Macbeth hears the prophecy about Birnam Wood and Macduff from the Weird Sisters, not, as in Holinshed, from some witch. Lady Macbeth's role is considerably enhanced, and her sleepwalking scene is original. Shakespeare compresses time, as he usually does.

In making some of these alterations, Shakespeare turned to another story in Holinshed's chronicle of Scotland: the murder of King Duff by Donwald. King Duff, never suspecting any treachery in Donwald, often spends time at the castle of Forres, where Donwald is captain of the castle. On one occasion, Donwald's wife, bearing great malice toward the King, shows Donwald (who already bears a grudge against Duff) "the means whereby he might soonest accomplish" the murder. The husband and wife ply Duff's few chamberlains with much to eat and drink. Donwald abhors the act "greatly in heart" but perseveres "through instigation of his wife." Four of Donwald's servants actually commit the murder under his instruction. Next morning, Donwald breaks into the King's chamber and slays the chamberlains, as though believing them guilty. Donwald is so overzealous in his investigation of the murder that many lords begin to suspect him of having done it. For six months afterward, the sun refuses to appear by day and the moon by night.

The chronicle accounts in Holinshed of Malcolm and Edward the Confessor supplied Shakespeare with further details. A more important supplementary source may have been George Buchanan's *Rerum Scoticarum Historia* (1582), a Latin history not translated in Shakespeare's lifetime, presenting a more complex psychological portrait of the protagonist than in Holinshed. Finally, Shakespeare may have used King James I's *Daemonology* (1597), John Studley's early-seventeenth-century version of Seneca's *Medea*, Samuel Harsnett's *Declaration of Egregious Popish Impostures* (1603), and accounts of the Scottish witch trials published around 1590.

## Antony and Cleopatra

In writing *Antony* and *Cleopatra*, Shakespeare relied to an unusual extent on his chief source, "The Life of Marcus Antonius" in the first-century Greek biographer Plutarch's *The Lives of the Noble Grecians and Romans* (in an English version by Sir Thomas North, 1579). Perhaps the best-known example in all Shakespeare of his skillful use of source material is in 2.2.201–36, when Enobarbus describes the first meeting of Antony and Cleopatra on the river Cydnus. Plutarch reports the event as follows:

She disdained to set forward otherwise but to take her barge in the river of Cydnus, the poop whereof was of gold, the sails of purple, and the oars of silver, which kept stroke in rowing after the sound of the music of flutes, hautboys, citterns, viols, and such other instruments as they played upon in the barge. And now for the person of herself: she was laid under a pavilion of cloth of gold of tissue, appareled and attired like the goddess Venus, commonly drawn in picture; and hard by her, on either hand of her, pretty fair boys appareled as painters do set forth god Cupid, with little fans in their hands with the which they fanned wind upon her. Her ladies and gentlewomen also, the fairest of them, were appareled like the nymphs Nereides (which are the mermaids of the waters) and like the Graces, some steering the helm, others tending the tackle and ropes of the barge, out of the which there came a wonderful passing sweet savor of perfumes that perfumed the wharf's side, pestered with innumerable multitudes of people. Some of them followed the barge all alongst the river's side; others also ran out of the city to see her coming in. So that in the end, there ran such multitudes of people one after another to see her that Antonius was left post alone in the marketplace, in his imperial seat, to give audience.

Shakespeare retains virtually every detail describing Cleopatra's barge: the poop of gold, the sails of purple, the oars of silver, the flutes, the boys with fans, the gentlewomen like the Nereides, and so on. He borrows phrases and images virtually intact from North, as in the account of Cleopatra's own person. Yet Shakespeare also transforms this scene by putting the description in the mouth of Enobarbus, a largely invented character. Enobarbus's sardonic view derived from military experience, his wry but genuine admiration for Cleopatra, and the prurient curiosity of his Roman listeners—all combine to produce the paradox of cloying appetite and insatiable hunger that helps to define the unforgettable greatness of Cleopatra as a character.

Shakespeare turns to Plutarch for other fabulous stories as well: eight wild boars roasted whole for only twelve guests (2.2.189–90), Cleopatra teasing Antony by causing an old dried salt fish to be placed on his fishing line (2.5.15–18), Menas the pirate suggesting to Pompey that they cut the anchor cable with all their noble guests still aboard (2.7.62–85), Cleopatra's sudden changes from weeping to laughing, and her willingness to be flattered by those who tell her Antony has married Octavia solely out of necessity (3.3), Octavius's tenderness for his sister, the ill-omened nesting of swallows in Cleopatra's sails (4.12.3–4), Antony's disregarding the advice of a valiant captain not to fight at sea (3.7.62–71), Cleopatra's study of swift means of death (5.2.353–6), Antony's jealous reaction to the embassy of the young Thyreus, or Thidias (3.13.86–170), the suicide of Antony's servant Eros (4.14.85–97), Cleopatra's difficulty in lifting Antony up to her tomb or monument (4.15.30–8), his warning that she should trust none but Proculeius (4.15.50), Cleopatra's deception of Caesar through persuading him that she desires to live (5.2.110–90), the countryman with the basket of figs (5.2.233–5), Cleopatra's death "attired and arrayed in her royal robes" attended by Charmian and Iras, and much more.

Despite these extensive and detailed borrowings, Shakespeare is highly innovative in his use of his sources. He compresses time in order to give a sense of dramatic momentum to the events of many years. He creates vibrant characters like Enobarbus, Charmian, Iras, Mardian, the Soothsayer, Menas, Thidias, Dollabella, and many others for whom the historical sources provide only a sketchy impression or no information at all. In his characterization of the main figures as well, Shakespeare is not content to rely on Plutarch's estimate. To Plutarch, Antony is the tragic victim of infatuation. For all Cleopatra's cultivation and fascination—she knows several languages and rules her country with royal bearing—she is the source of Antony's downfall. Plutarch's attitude is, like Enobarbus's, admiring but ironic. "In the end," he writes, "the horse of the mind, as Plato termeth it, that is so hard of rein (I mean the unreined lust of concupiscence) did put out of Antonius's head all honest and commendable thoughts." This "Roman" view is present in *Antony and Cleopatra*, to be sure, but is counterbalanced by the "Egyptian" view that finds greatness in Antony and Cleopatra's capacity for love. Shakespeare's play sets up a debate among conflicting traditions, as found in various medieval and Renaissance treatments of this famous story. The moralistic perspective condemning vice was popular in medieval texts, such as *De Casibus Virorum Illustrium* and its continuation, John Lydgate's *The Fall of Princes*. The interpretation of Cleopatra as love's martyr was to be found in Geoffrey Chaucer's *The Legend of Good Women*.

And, finally, the view of Antony and Cleopatra as heroic protagonists rising above their guilt found expression in several neo-Senecan dramas of the later sixteenth century. Most important for Shakespeare were *The Tragedy of Antony*, translated from Robert Garnier's *Marc Antoine* by Mary Herbert, Countess of Pembroke, in about 1590 (published 1592 and 1595), and *The Tragedy of Cleopatra* by Samuel Daniel (1594), a companion play dealing mainly with the end of Cleopatra's life. Garnier's play had been based on Étienne Jodelle's *Cléopâtre Captive* (1552), the first regular French tragedy. Shakespeare certainly gained from such works as these a sense of tragic greatness in his protagonists. He seems also to have been aware of favorable and unfavorable historical appraisals of Octavius Caesar as both a great ruler and a ruthless and even treacherous politician. One influential work on the more critical side may have been the *Chronicle of the Romans' Wars* by Appian of Alexandria (translated 1578). Virgil's *Aeneid* gave Shakespeare a model for a drama of passion set in the context of Roman history.

## The Winter's Tale

Shakespeare based *The Winter's Tale* on Robert Greene's romantic novella called *Pandosto: The Triumph of Time* (1588), or *The History of Dorastus and Fawnia* in its running title. Shakespeare changes the names, reverses the two kingdoms of Sicilia and Bohemia, and alters the unhappy ending that afflicts King Pandosto and Queen Bellaria of Bohemia (Leontes and Hermione of Sicilia). Otherwise, the narrative outline remains intact. The story begins with the state visit of King Egistus of Sicilia (Polixenes of Bohemia) to his boyhood companion, King Pandosto of Bohemia. Queen Bellaria entertains their guest with such warmth, "oftentimes coming herself into his bedchamber to see that nothing should be amiss to mislike him," that Pandosto grows jealous. He commands his cupbearer Franion (Camillo) to murder Egistus, and the latter seems to agree but instead warns his victim to flee with him. Their hasty departure appears to confirm Pandosto's worst suspicions. He sends the guard to arrest Bellaria as she plays with her young son Garinter (Mamillius). When the Queen gives birth to a daughter in prison, the King orders the child destroyed, but he relents upon the insistence of his courtiers and causes the infant to be set adrift in a small boat. The Queen nobly defends herself at her trial (in language that Shakespeare has copied in some detail). She herself requests that the oracle at Delphos be consulted. The oracle replies in words that Shakespeare has altered only slightly: "Bellaria is chaste, Egistus blameless, Franion a true subject, Pandosto treacherous, his babe an innocent; and the King shall live without an heir if that which is lost be not found." Pandosto is immediately stricken with remorse, and, when Queen Bellaria

collapses at the news of her son Garinter's death, she is truly and irrecoverably dead.

A similarly close parallel in the narrative, along with telling changes in a number of details, characterizes the story's second half. The babe is conveyed by a tempest to the coast of Sicilia and is discovered by an impoverished shepherd named Porrus. He and his wife Mopsa adopt the child, naming her Fawnia. By the age of sixteen, Fawnia's natural beauty rivals that of the goddess Flora. At a meeting of the farmers' daughters of Sicilia, where she is chosen mistress of the feast, Fawnia is seen by the King's son Dorastus on his way home from hawking. She counters his importunate suit with the argument that she is too lowly a match for him, but he replies that the gods themselves sometimes take earthly lovers. Her foster father, distressed by the Prince's repeated visits (though he comes in shepherd's costume), resolves to carry the jewels he found with Fawnia to the King and reveal her story, thereby escaping blame for the goings-on. Dorastus escapes with Fawnia to a ship, aided by his servant Capnio (compare Camillo). Capnio also fulfills a role given by Shakespeare to Autolycus, for he manages to trick the shepherd Porrus into thinking he can see the King if he comes aboard Dorastus's ship. A storm drives these voyagers to Bohemia where, because of the ancient enmity between Egistus and Pandosto, they disguise themselves. Pandosto, happening to hear of Fawnia's beauty, orders her and the others to be arrested as spies and summoned to court, whereupon he falls incestuously in love with the disguised Fawnia. He promises to free the young man (who has taken the name of Meleagrus to conceal his identity) only if he will relinquish his claim to Fawnia. King Egistus meanwhile has discovered his son's whereabouts and sends ambassadors to Bohemia demanding the return of Dorastus and the execution of Fawnia, Capnio, and Porrus. Pandosto, his love for Fawnia having turned to hate, is about to comply when Porrus reveals the circumstances of Fawnia's infancy. Overjoyed to rediscover his daughter, Pandosto permits her to marry Dorastus but then falls into a melancholy fit and commits suicide.

Shakespeare has almost entirely created some characters, such as Paulina, Antigonus, the clownish shepherd's son, and Autolycus, though Capnio does perform one of Autolycus's functions by inveigling the old shepherd aboard ship. Antigonus's journey to the seacoast of Bohemia with the infant Perdita and his fatal exit *"pursued by a bear"* are Shakespearean additions. The character of Time is also added, and the shift in tone from tragedy to tragicomedy averts the catastrophe in Greene's novella (in which Pandosto commits suicide). The shepherdesses at the sheep-shearing are Shakespearean. The old shepherd has a more substantial and comic role; Camillo is a stronger person than Capnio. Greene's Mopsa, the shrewish wife of old Porrus, disappears from the play. Shakespeare omits the incestuous love of Pandosto for his daughter and brings Hermione back to life. (For this motif of a statue made to breathe, he may well have recalled Ovid's account of Pygmalion in Ovid's *Metamorphoses*, Book 10.) Shakespeare's Leontes is more irrationally jealous than in Greene's account. Leontes's purgative sorrow is more intense and also more restorative than in the source; he is a truly noble and tragicomic figure, the center of a play about forgiveness and renewal.

Shakespeare may also have known Francis Sabie's *The Fisherman's Tale* (1595) and its continuation, *Flora's Fortune* (1595). From Greene's pamphlets, describing in vividly colloquial detail the life of London's underworld, Shakespeare probably derived many of Autolycus's tricks.

## The Tempest

No direct literary source for the whole of *The Tempest* has been found. Shakespeare does seem to have drawn material from various accounts of the shipwreck of the *Sea Venture* in the Bermudas, in 1609, although the importance of these materials should not be overstated. Several of the survivors wrote narratives of the shipwreck itself and of their life on the islands for some nine months. Sylvester Jourdain, in *A Discovery of the Bermudas*, published 1610, speaks of miraculous preservation despite the island's reputation for being "a most prodigious and enchanted place." William Strachey's letter, written in July of 1610 and published much later (1625) as *A True Reportory of the Wreck and Redemption . . . from the Islands of the Bermudas*, describes the panic among the passengers and crew, the much feared reputation of the island as the habitation of devils and wicked spirits, the actual beauty and fertility of the place with its abundance of wild life (compare Caliban's descriptions), and the treachery of the Indians they later encounter in Virginia. Shakespeare seems to have read Strachey's letter in manuscript and may have been acquainted with him. The storm scene in Chapter 4 of Laurence Twine's *The Pattern of Painful Adventures*, a major source for *Pericles*, may also have given Shakespeare material for the first scene of *The Tempest*. Shakespeare also kept up with travel accounts of Sir Walter Ralegh and Thomas Harriot, and knew various classical evocations of a New World. The name "Setebos" came from Richard Eden's *History of Travel* (1577), translated from Peter Martyr's *De Novo Orbe* and from other travel accounts of the period. (See the Introduction to *The Tempest* for the potential relevance of various journals of the circumnavigation of the globe.) All these hints are indeed suggestive, but they are scattered and relate more to the setting and general circumstance of Shakespeare's play than to the plot.

Shakespeare certainly consulted Michel de Montaigne's essay "Of the Cannibals," as translated by John Florio in 1603. Gonzalo's reverie on an ideal commonwealth (2.1.150–71) contains many verbal echoes of the essay. Montaigne's point is that supposedly civilized men who condemn as barbarous any society not conforming with their own are simply refusing to examine their own shortcomings. A supposedly primitive society may well embody perfect religion, justice, and harmony; civilized art can never rival the achievements of nature. The ideal commonwealth has no need of magistrates, riches, poverty, and contracts, all of which breed dissimulation and covetousness. The significance of these ideas for *The Tempest* extends well beyond the particular passage in which they are found. And Caliban himself, whose name is an anagram of "cannibal," illustrates (even though he is not an eater of human flesh) the truth of Montaigne's observation apropos of the intense and wanton cruelty he finds so widespread in so-called Western civilization: "I think there is more barbarism in eating men alive than to feed upon them being dead."

Prospero's famous valedictory speech to "Ye elves of hills, brooks, standing lakes, and groves" (5.1.33–57) owes its origin to Medea's similar invocation in Ovid's *Metamorphoses* (Book 7), which Shakespeare knew both in the Latin original and in Golding's translation: "Ye airs and winds, ye elves of hills, of brooks, of woods alone, / Of standing lakes . . ." Medea also anticipates Shakespeare's Sycorax. Medea thus provides material for the representation of both black and white magic in *The Tempest*, so carefully differentiated by Shakespeare. Ariel is part English fairy, like Puck, and part daemon. The pastoral situation in *The Tempest* is perhaps derived from Edmund Spenser's *The Faerie Queene*, Book 6 (with its distinctions between savage lust and true courtesy, between nature and art). Italian pastoral drama as practiced by Guarini and (in England) by John Fletcher may also have been an influence. The masque element in *The Tempest*, prominent as in much late Shakespeare, bears the imprint of the courtly masque tradition of Ben Jonson, Francis Beaumont, and John Fletcher. Virgil's *Aeneid* may have provided Shakespeare with a more indirect source, with its story of wandering in the Mediterranean and storm at sea, love in Carthage, the intervention of the gods, and the fulfillment of destiny in Italy. Donna Hamilton (*Virgil and "The Tempest,"* 1990) contends that Shakespeare "imitated" Virgil so as to argue for a politics of retrenchment.

A German play, *Die Schöne Sidea* by Jacob Ayrer, written before 1605, was once thought to have been based on an earlier version of *The Tempest* as performed by English players traveling in Germany. Today, the similarities between the two plays are generally attributed to conventions found everywhere in romance.

## The Sonnets

See the Introduction to *The Sonnets* for a discussion of the sonnet vogue in England of the 1590s, and the previous history of the sonnet in England and on the Continent.

# Appendix 3

# Shakespeare in Performance

*Lois Potter, University of Delaware*

Although we know a good deal about the conditions of performance at the time Shakespeare's plays were first produced, much of this information (summarized in the Introduction, pp. I-37–46) raises as many questions as it answers. We know, for example, that Shakespeare wrote most of his plays for the Lord Chamberlain's Men, first formed in 1594 after a period of plague and theater closures, and that the company (officially servants of the courtier whose duties included supervising court entertainments) was honored with the title of the King's Men at the accession of James I in 1603. Elizabethan acting companies were all male, with boys or young men playing women's roles, but we know almost nothing about how they acted, or who played which parts. We know that the stages of the partially-roofed public playhouses jutted into the yard where the audience stood on three sides, looking up at the actors; the rest of the spectators sat in covered galleries, looking down on them. But we are not sure whether the gallery above the stage, pictured in the contemporary illustration of the Swan Theatre interior shown on page I-40, was meant for musicians, spectators, or both. (And of course we do not know how much the Globe's interior resembled the Swan's.) If, as appears from the illustrations of theater interiors on pages I-40 and I-41, some spectators normally watched the action from behind the stage, the actors would have had to move a great deal during a scene, as in modern theater-in-the-round productions, to make sure that they were visible and audible to all parts of their audience.

However much information we have, we still cannot know if aspects of the theater that were common then but unusual in our eyes were taken for granted by the spectators who watched the plays in the reigns of Elizabeth and James I. Did they think of the boy actresses as boys or believe in them as women? Those who had traveled to France and Italy would have known that women played women's parts in those countries and were often as famous as the male actors. What was the acting style for love scenes between a man and a cross-dressed boy, and what was the range of responses to it? The players in the open theaters performed by day (normally beginning at 2 P.M.), but used torches and candles to indicate when the action was supposed to be taking place at night. Did audiences find it difficult to accept a convention by which actors, fully visible to the audience, declare that they are unable to see anything? There is probably no single answer. It is likely that then, as always, audience members differed as to whether they preferred to believe in the performance or feel superior to it.

To the audiences of Shakespeare's time, the theaters were sumptuous and impressive buildings. Their wooden interiors were painted to look like marble, and the ceiling of the Globe was apparently decorated with the signs of the zodiac (perhaps, when Hamlet and Othello addressed the heavens, they looked at both a real and an artificial sky). Visitors from abroad were taken to see plays; actors traveled with them as far as Prague; versions of them were being translated into German as early as 1618. All this indicates how much English plays and players were respected. By about 1597, the company for which Shakespeare wrote was the one most frequently invited to perform at court, evidence that it was considered the best in London.

The theater in fact offered a great deal of visual and musical pleasure even for those who could not understand the language. Vast sums of money were spent on costumes. The most valuable surviving evidence, an account book of Philip Henslowe, manager of the Rose playhouse, shows that their bright or striking colors (often red and black, with silver and gold) allowed them to stand out on a stage that depended on daylight for most of its illumination. These were not "costumes" but clothes, sometimes bought in secondhand shops and sometimes donated or sold by gentlemen patrons. Characters normally wore contemporary dress, but with some indications of historical costume, like togas for classical characters (see the contemporary drawing, usually taken to be an illustration of *Titus Andronicus*, on p. I-55). Costumes and wigs, as well as false beards, were obviously important for a theater in which twelve to fourteen actors frequently doubled in as many as thirty roles. Music was frequently used in productions and a number of writers, including Shakespeare, incorporated popular contemporary songs into their plays. Robert Johnson, who is credited with the songs to a number of Jacobean plays, may have been the company's in-house composer. Some plays may have had as much music as a modern musical comedy, though very little of it has been identified.

Shakespeare's plays were designed to show off the actors' talents: singing, playing an instrument, dancing, and fencing. Most of his most popular plays end with either a dance or a fight, and nearly all of his tragic heroes (with the interesting exceptions of Othello and Antony) have at least one heroic fight scene. Since memorization and oratory were part of every grammar school education, audiences could recognize the superior memories of the actors who learned the long and complicated speeches that Shakespeare wrote for them. The combination of great actors and a dramatist who wrote great roles for them was attractive to other playwrights, and helped to ensure the company's continuing preeminence.

Shakespeare's practice of writing plays dominated by one very large starring role probably followed Richard Burbage's rise to stardom. Many contemporary references identify him with Richard III (see the anecdote on p. I-65), and he is also known to have played Romeo, Hamlet, Othello, and Lear. John Lowin, who joined the company in 1602–1603, seems to have partnered Burbage in plays with two substantial roles. Shakespeare was unusual in that he wrote equally well for tragic and comic actors, and for the company clown, a type of performer traditionally famous for his ad-libs. Will Kempe, the most famous comedian of his day, certainly created the role of Dogberry—his name accidentally replaces the character's in one quarto of the play. It is not absolutely certain that he played Falstaff, but his departure from the Lord Chamberlain's Men in 1599 is often linked with Shakespeare's writing the character out of *Henry V* after having apparently promised (at the end of *2 Henry IV*) to include him in the sequel. Those who think that Shakespeare was in agreement with Hamlet's advice to the players ("Let those that play your clowns speak no more than is set down for them") wonder whether Kempe's inability to refrain from "speaking" led to friction with his leading playwright. Kempe's

successor was Robert Armin, and it is often said that the more literary quality of Shakespeare's later fools resulted from their being tailored for the new actor.

Little is known about the other chief sharers in the company, though attempts have been made to identify them with, for example, references to exceptionally thin or exceptionally fat actors. It is not known whether any particular young actor inspired Shakespeare to write his best female roles, but many boys seem to have been good enough to have a personal following. A spectator who saw *Othello* in Oxford in 1610 mentions how moved the spectators were at the sight of Desdemona after her death.

It has often been suggested that Hamlet's insistence on naturalness, and the First Player's modest claim to have "reformed" the practice of overacting at least to some extent, reflect a perceived difference between the actors for whom Shakespeare wrote and the more melodramatic ones in the company led by Philip Henslowe and its leading actor Edward Alleyn. Yet Alleyn, who created the major Marlowe roles, was no less intelligent and talented than Burbage. It was Alleyn who retired early to live the life of a gentleman (in 1597, when he was only 31), with one brief comeback in 1601–1604. Burbage, on the other hand, went on acting up to his death at the age of 51, a fact that suggests a more theatrical personality than Alleyn's. If there was a movement toward greater naturalism in the 1590s, it probably resulted from greater professionalization and better training of actors, along with greater sophistication of the audiences themselves.

As the Lord Chamberlain's Men grew more successful, they looked for a more select location. In 1597 James Burbage, Richard's father, purchased part of the disused monastic site of Blackfriars in the City of London. Protests from the local residents forced him to rent out the building to boys' companies (which performed less frequently) until, early in the reign of James I, times became more favorable. Finally moving into the new premises, perhaps as late as 1610, the company was able to restrict its public to those who could afford the higher admission prices. In the indoor theaters, all the spectators were seated. Comfortable spectators cause less trouble than uncomfortable ones. The smaller size may have allowed for a more "realistic" style of playing. At the same time, the company continued to use the Globe throughout the period, as well as acting at court and elsewhere, so the actors must have been able to adapt their style to circumstances. In many ways, Shakespeare's last plays are his least "realistic," since they often involve magic, but the technology available in the Blackfriars playhouse may have made the magic convincing.

Besides, if realistic acting means acting that makes one forget that one is watching a play, it is unlikely that the drama was ever truly realistic. Other dramatists' allusions to Shakespeare are obviously meant to break the dramatic illusion: "What, Hamlet, are you mad?" asks a character in *Eastward Ho!* (1605), speaking to a servant who is named Hamlet only so that someone can ask him that question. Shakespeare himself also refers to his own plays. It is likely that the lovers' suicides in "Pyramus and Thisbe," performed at the end of *A Midsummer Night's Dream*, are meant as an absurd version of the end of *Romeo and Juliet*; Malvolio's madness, in *Twelfth Night*, probably parodies Hamlet's. Perhaps a comedy can make jokes about a tragedy without destroying the atmosphere, but *Hamlet* does the same thing. When Polonius tells Hamlet about playing Julius Caesar "at the university," and being killed by Brutus, many of their audience would remember that, not long before, the two actors speaking these lines had played Caesar and Brutus, respectively, in *Julius Caesar*.

The deaths of Shakespeare in 1616 and of Burbage in 1619 may have temporarily affected Shakespeare's theatrical popularity. Burbage was so much identified with the major roles that, according to one elegy, these characters seemed to have died with him. The Earl of Pembroke may have been typical when, in a letter, he expresses reluctance to go to the theater again. Joseph Taylor, who replaced Burbage in 1619, inherited a number of his roles. He and Lowin led the company for the next twenty years, with first John Fletcher and then Philip Massinger as their leading dramatist. The company had been called the King's Men since 1603, but the name was even more appropriate under Charles I than under his father, since the actors were much closer to the court. Taylor even served as acting coach to Queen Henrietta Maria and her ladies when they put on a pastoral tragicomedy in 1633.

Though not all Puritans or parliamentarians were hostile to the theater, and not all of Charles I's courtiers approved of it, the English civil war created a further association between theater and crown. Parliament closed the theaters at the start of the war in 1642, refusing to reopen them even when hostilities had ended. Performances continued nevertheless: professionals acted illegally in the theater buildings that were still usable, or, like amateurs, legally in private houses and inns. Some also went abroad and acted for English royalists in exile. Since the prohibition applied only to plays, scenes involving popular characters (Hamlet and the gravediggers, Falstaff, Bottom) were adapted and disguised as "drolls"—comic sketches—that could be performed in a mixed program of music, dance, and drama. The 1662 frontispiece to a collection of these drolls (p. I-58) shows how Falstaff and Mrs. Quickly were probably costumed in this period.

## The Restoration and the Eighteenth Century (1660–1776)

At the Restoration of 1660, one of Charles II's first acts was to establish two licensed acting companies, one patronized by him, the other by his brother the Duke of York. Each company was assigned a selection of plays from the prewar period. Shakespeare's were among the first to be revived; indeed, actors were already playing them in London before the new theaters had opened. Although one of the speakers in Dryden's dialogue on drama (*An Essay of Dramatic Poesy*, 1665) says that Beaumont and Fletcher's plays were more popular than Shakespeare's or Jonson's, the evidence indicates that Shakespeare went on being a frequently acted dramatist throughout this period. Since the King's company seems to have received preferential treatment, it is likely that the plays awarded to them—*1 Henry IV*, *The Merry Wives of Windsor*, and *Othello*—were the most popular of Shakespeare's works in 1660.

It was natural that Shakespeare's works would need updating; nearly fifty years after their author's death, their language, grammar, and jokes were already becoming obsolete. Audiences saw themselves as too refined for plays with clowns and devils. Both theater managers (Thomas Killigrew and William Davenant) had been playwrights before the war, and both produced the prewar drama with extensive alterations. *The Taming of the Shrew*, as produced in 1667 by the King's company under Killigrew, was called, improbably, *Sauny the Scot*, after the new comic servant who replaced Grumio; the actor John Lacy wrote the title role for himself, exploiting the anti-Scots feeling that had been exacerbated by the Civil War. "Scenes," or scenery, the norm in the theaters of France and Italy, had already been used in prewar masques, and in the 1630s Davenant had already been planning to open a theater equipped to use it for plays. As manager of the Duke's company, he set about revising old plays to create more possibilities for spectacle. His *The Law Against Lovers* (1662) conflated *Measure for Measure* and *Much Ado About Nothing*, neither of which was well known at the period. The result was an emphasis on the romantic part of both plays, as opposed to their low comedy. He added more music and scenery in his adaptations of *Macbeth* (1664) and *The Tempest* (1667); in later revivals, these two works became almost operatic. The new theaters were rather small, and actors still played at the front of the stage, with the wings and backdrop of the new scenery stretching away behind them. Scene changes could be made quickly by rolling away one sliding backdrop to reveal another one behind it, sometimes with a new set of characters already in place. The same painted wings and backdrop were expected to serve for a number of plays, acting as a kind of shorthand to distinguish indoor from outdoor settings. The idea that each play belonged to its own particular visual world did not gain currency until well into the nineteenth century.

Charles II had insisted, in his patent for the new theaters, that the custom of boy actors—unique to England—must end. Most of the women who became actresses during the early years of the Restoration were, inevitably, untrained. The famous Nell Gwyn, mistress of Charles II, was a star of the King's company. She was considered delightful in contemporary comedies, some of which were written especially for her; however, Pepys always insisted that she was disastrous in serious roles, and there is no record of her playing Shakespeare. The new actresses could exploit their natural gifts, their beauty, and their novelty, but no one wanted to see them in character parts, especially those of elderly women. As a result, roles like the witches in *Macbeth* were taken by men, often the company's low comedians, a practice that continued for centuries. The small number of parts for attractive young women in Shakespeare now became a problem. Davenant was skillful at multiplying them. He expanded the part of Lady Macduff; Miranda, no longer the only woman in *The Tempest*, acquired a naïve younger sister, while Caliban and Ariel were likewise paired off with a female monster and spirit respectively.

Some of these changes also had a moral purpose. Davenant balanced the wickedness of Macbeth and his Lady by developing the virtuous Macduffs as foils to them. He also gave Macbeth a death speech (only one line long) to show that the dying man recognized the vanity of his ambition. Later adaptations were still more concerned with "poetic justice." This term meant simply that art ought to reward virtue and punish vice, not because this is what happens in the real world, but because art's duty is to offer virtuous models whenever possible. John Dryden, who had worked with Davenant on *The Tempest*, later wrote free adaptations of both *Antony and Cleopatra* and *Troilus and Cressida*, in which the lovers, far from being unfaithful, are only sympathetic victims of misunderstanding. His version of *Antony and Cleopatra*, called *All for Love, or, the World Well Lost* (1677), largely replaced its model for much of the next century, and was often played under Shakespeare's title. Though Dryden claimed that he had made Antony's wife Octavia a virtuous foil to Cleopatra, the play's success was due less to its superior morality (indeed, its most popular scene was one in which the two women insult each other) than to its simplification of the structure, which subordinated political history to the love story. Shadwell's *Timon of Athens* (1678) provided a faithful woman as well as a faithful steward, to contrast with the mercenary friends and mistress who desert the hero. Thomas Otway's *Caius Marius* (1679) made the suicides of Romeo and Juliet more acceptable by locating them in a classical world. One of Otway's other innovations—letting the heroine revive in time to converse with the hero before they die—was to outlast the adaptation itself. Nahum Tate's *King Lear* (1681) made the virtuous Cordelia a large and dramatic role, worthy of a star actress. He also added a love interest between her and Edgar, and provided a happy ending in which Lear is restored to his throne. The adaptation remained in the repertory for 150 years, and Samuel Johnson defended it in 1765 on the grounds that, although the unjust tragic ending might be more true to life, "all reasonable beings naturally love justice." Tate's omission of the Fool, a character associated with old-fashioned theater, was not even noticed.

After 1679, the Popish Plot and uncertainty over the royal succession led to Shakespearean adaptations designed to score political points. In 1680, John Crowne wrote *The Miseries of Civil War* (1680), the first of two adaptations based on the *Henry VI* plays, while Tate's *The Sicilian Usurper*, adapted from *Richard II*, fell foul of the censor, even though its deposed ruler was more sympathetic than Shakespeare's. In the following year, Tate reversed the order of scenes in *King Lear*, beginning with Edmund's first soliloquy: a bastard son claiming his right to inherit was bound to be topical in the reign of a king who had no legitimate children and whose next heir was a Roman Catholic brother. The turbulent political climate kept audiences away, and the two companies amalgamated in 1682. Very few plays of any kind survive from the last years of Charles II's reign and the three years of James II's leading to the revolution of 1688. In the reign of William and Mary (James's daughter), *King Lear* was once again so topical that it could not be staged. Mary and her sister Anne looked all too much like Lear's daughters, especially since Tate's version ends with the king's abdication in favor of his daughter and son-in-law.

Colley Cibber's *Richard III* (1699), the most successful of all adaptations, benefited from the fact that a number of Shakespeare's history plays had dropped out of the repertory by the end of the century, thus providing a quarry from which the adapter could borrow. Feeling that he had a free hand, Cibber removed Queen Margaret and, since he intended to play Richard himself, gave him some good lines from other histories, including (from *2 Henry IV*) the death speech that Shakespeare had neglected to write for his hero. This Richard, literally an actor's dream, was more theatrically popular than Shakespeare's had been, a fact that kept the version alive well into the twentieth century (the Olivier film, which also cut Margaret's role, used two recognizable Cibber lines). Cibber had some difficulties with the licenser just before the first performance because it was feared that his opening scene, showing the deposed Henry VI in the Tower, would remind its audiences of the deposed James II. He made sure to show his loyalty later—*King John*, under the title *Papal Tyranny*, coincided with the threatened invasion, in 1745, of James II's exiled Catholic grandson. As one of the managers of Drury Lane, and as poet laureate (from 1730), Cibber became a popular target for satire, and he is best remembered for Pope's attacks on him in *The Dunciad* (1743). But his entertaining autobiography, *An Apology for the Life of Colley Cibber, Comedian* (1740), is still the best source of information on the early eighteenth-century theater.

Indeed, without Cibber's book, it would be difficult to say much about Shakespearean acting at the turn of the

SHAKESPEARE IN PERFORMANCE

eighteenth century. Though Thomas Betterton was recognized as the greatest actor of his age from the first years of the Restoration, those, like Samuel Pepys, who saw him at this time, praised him highly but in vague terms. Because of the division of the theatrical repertory, Betterton acquired some major Shakespearean roles, like Othello, only after the unification of the two companies in 1682, when senior actors of the King's company took the opportunity to retire. After this, he had virtually a monopoly, and went on playing a much-acclaimed Hamlet until he was seventy, as well as taking the role of Falstaff in what seems to have been his own adaptation of the *Henry IV* plays. Cibber's description of Betterton's Hamlet reacting to the first sight of his father's ghost became a point of comparison for later Hamlets well into the nineteenth century. It is clear that his effects had to do with "presence" rather than with movement—though, of course, Cibber was describing him in his last years, when he was presumably less active.

The early female performers are still more shadowy figures. Women had appeared on stage as singers, or singing actresses, in "operas" performed in the 1650s, and one of these, perhaps Margaret Hughes, may have been the first to play a Shakespearean role (probably Desdemona). Mary Sanderson, who became Mrs. Betterton, was the first Lady Macbeth. Her successor, Elizabeth Barry, was primarily a tragic actress. She is said to have owed her initial success to careful instruction by her lover, the Earl of Rochester, who recognized the importance of constant repetition and, like a modern director, insisted that she should rehearse in the dress that she was going to wear in performance. The best-loved comic actress of Cibber's youth, Anne Bracegirdle, played several Shakespearean comedy heroines alongside the Congreve roles for which she was famous. The popularity of *The Merry Wives of Windsor* may have been due not only to Betterton's playing of Falstaff but also to its two excellent roles for actresses past their first youth, probably the only women in the company experienced enough to do justice to Shakespearean comedy.

Though the history of Shakespeare editing begins in the early eighteenth century, the plays still belonged essentially to the theater; hence, the publication of acting editions, which allowed audiences to read what they were actually going to see in the theater, usually heavily cut and partially modernized. Even so, the first half of the century saw a steady return to original versions, as one role after another was suddenly revealed to be a superb vehicle for a particular actor. Shylock, for instance, had been a not-very-interesting comic miser in a not-very-interesting romantic comedy, often replaced by George Granville's adaptation, *The Jew of Venice* (1701). When Shakespeare's original was revived in 1741, Charles Macklin astonished his fellow-actors as much as the audience by emphasizing Shylock's terrifying malevolence.

Although later actors would play the character more sympathetically, Macklin made him what he has been ever since: a disturbing character who cannot be assimilated into a comic structure. Something of a theorist on acting, Macklin, in teaching other actors, insisted on clear and intelligent diction. Perhaps for that reason, his Iago was the most convincing of the period.

Richard III, in Cibber's version, was the role in which David Garrick made his London debut in 1741. The actor became famous almost instantly and went on to manage the Drury Lane Theatre from 1747 to 1776. Garrick was a self-proclaimed idolater of Shakespeare whose "Jubilee" at Stratford-upon-Avon in 1769 not only inaugurated the practice of celebrations and festivals but also led contemporaries to regard him as almost equal in importance with his author. Despite his reputation for restoring Shakespeare, Garrick was as much of an adapter as his famous predecessors, turning *The Taming of the Shrew* and the last part of *The Winter's Tale* into short three-act plays and making operas out of *A Midsummer Night's Dream* and *The Tempest*. His *Macbeth* had a death speech, much more dramatic and pathetic than the one-line moral that Davenant had given him. His *Romeo and Juliet* had a pathetic farewell scene based on the one in Otway's *Caius Marius*. In response to French criticisms, he even revised *Hamlet* in 1771, removing the low comedy of the gravediggers. Yet he also revived many plays not seen in their Shakespearean form since the Restoration, showing by his acting what superb roles they contained. He was equally gifted at comedy and tragedy. Two of his most popular roles were Benedick and (Tate's) King Lear. *Julius Caesar* and *Othello,* plays in which Betterton had been particularly successful, were better acted by Garrick's chief rival, Spranger Barry, a tall and handsome actor with a beautiful voice. Garrick, shorter and less romantic in appearance, was famous for his mobile and expressive features that allowed him to delineate the transitions between the "passions." It was this grasp of human psychology that he praised in Shakespeare and that others praised in him. His most significant leading lady, Hannah Pritchard, must have been equally versatile, since she was famous both as Rosalind and as Lady Macbeth. It was, however, characteristic of Garrick that he was able to form an excellent company around himself, including a number of fine actresses and low comedians. Without these conditions, it would have been impossible to revive so many of the comedies.

## The Romantic Period (1776–1850)

Between Garrick's retirement in 1776 and the end of the century, the theaters changed to the point where a rapid, subtle style like Garrick's was becoming almost impossible. The Licensing Act of 1737 had limited spoken drama to Drury Lane and Covent Garden, the descendents of the two London theaters licensed in 1660 by Charles II. The late eighteenth century saw the rapid growth of a London population in search of entertainment. The two theaters responded by increasing their audience capacity until, at the end of the century, Covent Garden held over 3,000 spectators, and Drury Lane 3,600. When much of the audience was too far from the stage to see facial expressions or hear the softer tones of an actor's voice, the most successful performers were those who could establish themselves through their volume or through visual effects. Two tall and statuesque actors, John Philip Kemble and his more gifted sister, Sarah Siddons, dominated the theater of this period. Siddons's Lady Macbeth was probably the finest performance of the age: when she said that she could smell blood, at least one contemporary spectator declared that he could smell it too. Her other finest Shakespearean roles were Isabella in *Measure for Measure* and Hermione in *The Winter's Tale*, both of them strong women whose sublime moral grandeur dwarfed everyone else. Kemble's attempt to impose greater discipline and unity on theatrical productions, with more historically "correct" sets and costumes, resulted in what must have been the most genuinely classical theater yet seen in Britain. *Coriolanus*, with Kemble in the title role and Siddons as a heroically obsessed Volumnia, was the triumph of their approach. It was ironic that it should have come in an age dominated by the spirit of revolution and of the complex attitudes that are summed up as Romanticism.

It was to this spirit that Edmund Kean appealed. Those who saw him make his famous London debut as Shylock in 1814, wearing a black wig instead of the traditional red one, would have realized at once that he was going to play, not a tragic villain, but a tragic victim. He had been a singer, dancer, and Harlequin before taking London by storm, and his acting benefited from these other skills. Unlike Kemble, who expressed authority and aristocratic dignity, he excelled as Shakespeare's outsiders and outlaws: the hunchbacked Richard III (still in Cibber's softened version), the Moor Othello, and the melancholy Hamlet. Knowing his gift for pathos, he starred in an adaptation of *3 Henry VI* (where York sobs over his murdered son) and attempted to bring back the original ending of *King Lear* (where Lear grieves over the dead Cordelia), but audiences were not yet ready for either. Those who saw him at his best never forgot his haunting delivery of Richard III's forebodings before Bosworth and Othello's farewell to arms, which provided the kind of appreciative, poetic commentary on Shakespeare that characterized the best contemporary criticism.

Kean's career was short, wrecked by drink and scandal. In 1833, just as he had reached his miserable end, another actor, using the stage name of Keane, made his Covent Garden debut in the role of Othello. Ira Aldridge, a black American, may have hoped to announce himself as Kean's successor, but racial prejudice in England prevented him from being accepted as a leading tragedian. He would, however, play Othello all over Europe, and especially in Russia, in bilingual productions with local casts. Like Kean, he sought out the roles of victims and social outcasts: Aaron in his own adaptation of *Titus Andronicus*, as well as (in white make-up) Macbeth, Shylock, and King Lear; like Kean, he was also capable of singing songs in dialect or even a Russian folksong. The excitement that German and Russian spectators felt at the sight of a black actor playing a black character would become an important part of theatrical experience a century later; at this point, it was a novelty. In the 1860s Aldridge finally acted in major London theaters and might have returned to the United States after the Civil War if he had not died unexpectedly while on tour in Poland.

Meanwhile, both of the unruly London theaters were managed, in turn, by William Macready, who, as his diary makes clear, took seriously his responsibility to a dramatist he worshipped. Still more than Kemble, he behaved like a modern director, with a vision of the production as a whole. His revivals of the history plays showed the possibilities of historical reconstruction. He is best known for restoring the Fool to *King Lear* in 1838, though he gave the role to a young woman to ensure that it would be played for pathos rather than low comic effects that might distract from his own scenes. A number of fine actresses played opposite him: Helen Faucit, young, fragile, refined, who would later write a perceptive if sentimental account of her approach to acting some of Shakespeare's female characters; Fanny Kemble, a member of the famous Kemble family, whose memoirs indicate the struggle involved for women in a star-dominated theater; Charlotte Cushman, a powerful visitor from America who also played Romeo and Hamlet. The plays were still heavily cut and showed the influence of earlier adaptations, but by the end of his career, Macready could fairly claim to have restored a good deal of Shakespeare's text and to have made the theater more respectable. The repeal of the Licensing Act in 1843, which allowed smaller theaters to cater to different publics, also encouraged gentrification. Samuel Phelps, who managed the working-class Sadler's Wells Theatre from 1844 to 1869, did still more than Macready, performing thirty-four of Shakespeare's plays; he even restored the original *Richard III*, though other actors continued to prefer the Cibber version. Charles Kean (son of Edmund), at the Princess's Theatre from 1850 to 1859, carried the historicizing process still further; his "archaeological" productions were likely to be accompanied by notes explaining the reason for the choice of period, costumes, and props.

Still, it was only rarely that anyone had the opportunity to impose a concept of Shakespearean production on an acting company in his own theater. Star actors tended to spend much of their time on tour, both in England and America, performing their favorite roles after perhaps one rehearsal with the resident company. Far from seeking new ways to interpret a play, these actors had to rely on standardized stage business (when Mr. Wopsle plays Hamlet in Dickens's *Great Expectations*, an unsympathetic audience comments loudly on each theatrical cliché as it occurs). They naturally tended to conceive of their characters in isolation and to favor tragedy over comedy, which requires ensemble playing. (Similarly, nineteenth-century critics usually focus on the analysis of individual characters.) A common practice was the pitting of one actor against another in a famous role, arguing over which one was the "true" Hamlet or Lear. In one case, the rivalry developed a nationalistic dimension. Macready's visit to America, in 1849, is notorious for the riot at Astor Place in New York, when soldiers fired on and killed some of the crowd outside the theater. The rioters had been trying to drown out Macready's performance of *Macbeth* out of a misguided loyalty to the American tragedian, Edwin Forrest. On a visit to Britain, Forrest had hissed Macready for some foppish business with a handkerchief that the actor, as Hamlet, had used to illustrate the phrase "I must be idle." Now his personal hostility became a quarrel about effete English acting versus the manly American tradition. In fact, the distinction was largely meaningless: many well-known American actors had begun their careers in England or Ireland. While some American Shakespeareans might have seen themselves as part of the Forrest tradition, and some (like the touring performers depicted by Mark Twain in *Huckleberry Finn*) were of no tradition at all, most American actors continued to look to Europe for models.

## The Victorian Era and the Early Twentieth Century (1850–1912)

The greatest American actor of the next generation, Edwin Booth, was a refined and melancholy figure whose readings of the great Shakespearean roles were psychological and poetic. Booth was the son of Junius Brutus Booth, who had acted in London opposite Edmund Kean, and the brother of John Wilkes Booth, the assassin of Abraham Lincoln. (Ironically, all three members of this acting family had once performed together in the great assassination play, *Julius Caesar*.) Though Booth briefly attempted theater management, he spent much of his time in the exhausting business of touring. He clearly thought deeply about his own roles, and about the moments when other characters interacted with him. His correspondence with the New Variorum Shakespeare

editor, H.H. Furness, is quoted in many notes of that edition—an early example of successful communication between the theater and the scholarly world. Yet when Booth was alternating the two leading roles of *Othello* with Henry Irving in 1881, he sent his servant to take notes at rehearsal for him. Nothing in his experience had prepared him for a theater in which the actor-manager expected everyone to fit into a total artistic conception.

It was Irving, the first actor to be knighted, who dominated English Shakespearean acting in the late Victorian era. His pictorial sense was even stronger than that of the actor-managers who preceded him, and the technical means at his disposal in the Lyceum Theatre, which he began to manage in 1878, were much better. The old system of sliding screens in grooves, flanked by a series of wings, had been replaced by the "box set," which was built like a piece of architecture, creating a complete environment. Electric lighting, introduced in the 1880s, provided new, subtle visual effects. The elaborate and beautiful sets often required interminable scene changes and, sometimes, rearrangement of the plays to accommodate them. Irving's own performances were usually controversial. His Malvolio, like his Shylock, was a tragic figure, while his Iago was so witty and likeable that, playing opposite Booth's Othello, he stole all the sympathy from the hero. His theater offered a beautiful dream for the spectator to share: if it also disturbed the spectator, it was through its revelation of the psychological depths of character, never through its comments on social and political issues. Irving's leading lady, Ellen Terry, was both beautiful and brilliant; in most productions she was allowed to be only the former. Bernard Shaw, longing for her to appear in plays about "grownup" topics, by himself or Henrik Ibsen, resented her imprisonment in Irving's world. For Shaw and other modern thinkers, Shakespeare was becoming synonymous with nostalgia and with the moralistic and idealistic thinking that the new drama regarded as a vice. The early twentieth-century theater was finally affected by these critical attempts to reform it, but two kinds of production coexisted for some time. At His Majesty's Theatre, Herbert Beerbohm Tree, like Irving, offered psychologically based character acting in a beautiful scenic environment, recreating Cleopatra's Egypt and Henry VIII's England; having seen his lavish production of *Macbeth*, one critic commented that "Nature put up a pretty feeble imitation of what several barrels of stones and a few sheets of tin could do in His Majesty's." At the Savoy, on the other hand, Harley Granville Barker, a disciple of Bernard Shaw, developed a decorative visual style that was not tied to a specific historical period.

Meanwhile, a more experimental approach to acting was being developed in Germany. The country's unusual political structure, with small dukedoms and cities sponsoring their own theaters, made it possible for the Duke of Saxe-Meiningen to sponsor his own company of players, sixty-six in all. His leading actors were unremarkable but, when he took them on tour in the 1880s, audiences were impressed by his handling of large groups. The Duke insisted that those who played major roles in one production should be walk-ons in another, so that crowds could be properly rehearsed instead of being assembled from those gathered around the stage door and drilled by the stage manager immediately before each performance.

Frank Benson, a young Oxford graduate, saw the Saxe-Meiningen company at Drury Lane in 1881, and was inspired to develop his own touring company—though, unlike the Duke, he acted in his own productions and consequently shaped them from a star's point of view. From 1886 on, the Bensonians became regular visitors at Stratford-upon-Avon. Shakespeare's birthplace had been briefly famous in 1769, the year of Garrick's Jubilee, but it was only in 1879, when the first Memorial Theatre was built, that tourists had any reason to visit for more than a few hours. Benson essentially created the first Stratford company, though it used the theater only during a short "Festival" season. Having a regular venue and a devoted audience enabled him to revive unusual works, if often drastically cut. In 1901 he inaugurated the new century with a "Grand Cycle" of Shakespeare's histories—the first English production of the plays as a group.

The desire to return to fuller texts and something like the original conditions of Shakespearean performance was initially associated with Germany and then with outsiders like William Poel, who founded the English Stage Society in 1894. Previously, Poel had given an experimental matinee of the first quarto Hamlet at St. George's Hall in 1881. More surprisingly (though his friendship with Bernard Shaw in part explains it), the popular London actor Johnston Forbes-Robertson played an unusually full text of Hamlet in 1897, with characters like Reynaldo and Fortinbras appearing for the first time in centuries. Then Benson's company played an uncut Hamlet in 1899 and 1900. Poel, who often worked with amateurs, using all-purpose curtains rather than scenery on what was meant to be an Elizabethan stage, revived works by Shakespeare's contemporaries and by Shakespeare himself that had previously been considered unperformable. For example, he gave the first important Troilus and Cressida to be seen in London since 1734, dressing it in Elizabethan rather than classical costume. It was 1912. He had discovered the play's antiwar potential.

## The Twentieth Century

World War I drastically curtailed many Shakespearean projects, including those for a gigantic celebration of the anniversary of his death in 1916, which at one point was intended to include the opening of a National Theatre. Although this theater did not come into existence until nearly 100 years after Irving had first suggested it, other developments were creating the conditions that would make Shakespeare plays, with their large casts, commercially viable.

One was the rise of repertory theaters, which could support a large company and a varied range of plays. The most famous of these was London's Royal Victoria, or "Old Vic," founded in 1914. Under a number of gifted directors (notably Robert Atkins, who had directed all the plays in the 1623 Folio by 1923, Harcourt Williams, and Tyrone Guthrie), it was the home to many legendary productions, including John Gielgud's first Hamlet (1929) and Laurence Olivier's first Hamlet (1937). At the Birmingham Repertory Theatre, Barry Jackson had already directed a modern-dress Hamlet in 1925. Modern dress had been common practice until the nineteenth century; it now seemed eccentric, but would by the end of the century become almost the norm. The Memorial Theatre at Stratford, after struggling to find its identity, saw some brilliant productions by Peter Brook in the 1940s and 1950s, including three plays traditionally considered minor: Love's Labor's Lost (1946), Measure for Measure (1948), and a Titus Andronicus (1955), starring Olivier, where audience members regularly fainted at what was then unusual stage violence: the amputation of the hero's hand and the cutting of the villains' throats. Stratford and the Old Vic were becoming rival Shakespeare companies and in the 1960s each achieved a new status. The Memorial Theatre was renamed the Royal Shakespeare Theatre in 1960, with Peter Hall as director, whereas the Old Vic was designated the National Theatre in 1963. Olivier directed its opening production of Hamlet, with Peter O'Toole in the title role, and played a famous Othello in 1964. The National Theatre eventually moved into new premises in an arts complex, with three stages, on the South Bank of the Thames.

In the United States, the most exciting Shakespeare productions also occurred during a period of government subsidy: it was depression-era financing that enabled Orson Welles to direct Shakespeare on radio, and, for the Mercury Theatre, his "voodoo" Macbeth (1938) with an all-black cast, his anti-Fascist Julius Caesar (1937), and his condensation of the major history plays, Five Kings, which, although unsuccessful, later influenced his Falstaff film, Chimes at Midnight (1966). The other significant development in North America was the growth of summer Shakespeare festivals at outdoor Elizabethan-style theaters, beginning with the Elizabethan Stage at Ashland, Oregon (founded 1935), and the Guthrie-designed Festival Theatre at Stratford, Ontario (1953). Festival seasons allowed juxtapositions of related plays and the yearly performance of successive plays in a history cycle.

It was the English Stratford-upon-Avon, however, that fully seized on the history plays, performing the *Richard II–Henry V* group in 1951, during the Festival of Britain that celebrated the country's emergence from wartime and postwar rationing. For the rest of the century, the "cycle" of history plays would be recognized as a national epic, to be performed for special occasions. For the new Royal Shakespeare Company, Peter Hall and John Barton produced the *Henry VI–Richard III* sequence rewritten, reduced to three plays, and called *The Wars of the Roses*. They revived these, along with the other *Henry* plays, for the Shakespeare quatercentenary in 1964. The histories were produced again in 1975 by Terry Hands, with Alan Howard playing all the kings except Henry IV; in 1982 the *Henry IV* plays opened the company's new London theater at the Barbican under Trevor Nunn; and the company, now under Adrian Noble, marked the arrival of the millennium with a freshly conceived production. Just as the 1951 production showed the influence of Tillyard's essays on the histories as a unified cycle, the plays of the year 2000, deliberately disparate in style and even venue, were the product of a critical movement that emphasized discontinuity and diversity.

The complete sequence of histories tends to be an ensemble work, viable only for a repertory company. The RSC's 2007 revival deliberately emphasized doubling, so as to suggest the haunting of figures in the present by those of the past. Richard II was dressed and made up to resemble Queen Elizabeth, who is supposed to have said "I am Richard II, know ye not that?" The eight plays, given in succession (as probably never happened in Shakespeare's lifetime), lend themselves to directorial statements about historical process or the state of England. Performed singly or as a sequence, the plays from *Richard II* to *Henry V* are more likely to emphasize the personal stories: Richard II's agonized transition from self-assured and tyrannical ruler to a bewildered prisoner in search of his identity; Prince Hal's growth into kingship through his relationships with his real father, Henry IV, and the substitute father, Falstaff. This is particularly true when the production has a charismatic Falstaff (Robert Stephens at the RSC, 1991; Roger Allam at Shakespeare's Globe, 2010; Antony Sher at the RSC, 2014–15). *Henry V* is now likely to be done in modern dress and to allude to contemporary conflicts: Michael Kahn's 1969 production was a comment on the Vietnam war, while in 1997 he directed it again with the Iraq war in mind (both productions were seen in Washington, D.C.), as did Nicholas Hytner at the National Theatre in 2003.

## Contemporary Critical Approaches

By now, productions might require as much interpretation as the plays themselves. In the last half of the twentieth century, the spread of school and university education had created a substantial population that had studied at least one Shakespeare play and a smaller population, including some theater practitioners, that had read not only the plays but also the criticism. Stratford's John Barton, a former Cambridge don, directed *Twelfth Night* (1969) as if it were by Chekhov, encouraging the audience to imagine the unspoken feelings of the characters—not only Viola (Judi Dench), smiling through heartbreak, but Maria, in her apparently hopeless love for Sir Toby, and Sir Andrew in his even more hopeless love for Olivia. This attention to character, often created out of masses of tiny realistic details, informed some of the theater's most highly praised productions. Barton's *Richard II* (1973) worked very differently, externalizing the play's images in ways that were clearly independent of the characters' awareness: for instance, a glimpse of a melting snowman echoed Richard's wish that he were "a mockery king of snow" and linked the fall and rise of kings to a natural cycle of dissolution and renewal.

Other major critical approaches, easier to categorize, quickly found their way onto the stage. Political readings, often influenced by a Brechtian production style, dominated the 1960s and 1970s. These were usually Marxist and anti-authority: lines in which characters expressed high moral sentiments might be juxtaposed (legitimately) with those in which they showed themselves less noble, or (illegitimately) by setting them in a context that undermined them, as when, in Peter Zadek's *Held Henry* (*Hero Henry*, 1965), Henry V delivers the St. Crispin's Day speech to his bored mistress. Even before its first English publication in 1964, *Shakespeare Our Contemporary*, by the Polish critic Jan Kott, had powerfully influenced theater with his comparison of *Hamlet* and the histories to life under a totalitarian regime, *King Lear* to Theater of the Absurd, and the comedies to a Freudian nightmare. Both Brecht and Kott could be recognized behind Peter Brook's *King Lear* (1962), which, in place of the traditional sympathy with the king, offered a frighteningly harsh Paul Scofield, emphasizing his and his followers' brutality toward Goneril's servants, and ruthlessly cutting anything that might be cathartic; the Dover cliff meeting between Lear and Gloucester frankly drew on the stage imagery of Samuel Beckett's *Waiting for Godot*. Brook's *A Midsummer Night's Dream* (1970), which based its erotic treatment of Titania and Bottom on Kott's work, found a purely theatrical language for the critical commonplaces about the play's metatheatricality. Without makeup, under bright light, in a white-walled gymnasium that replaced the traditional moonlit forest, Oberon and Puck sat on trapezes and passed the aphrodisiac "flower," a metal plate, from one spinning metallic wand to another. The fact that this operation could, and occasionally did, go wrong was the point: it reminded the audience that the real magic lay in its own willingness to trust the actors. Even the "Pyramus and Thisbe" actors in the final scene were treated as serious artists, representatives of working-class culture who deserved respect. For most of his later productions, Peter Brook went abroad in search of a multilingual, multiethnic cast, searching for ways of escaping the "easy" assumptions about Shakespeare.

It was in fact race and gender rather than class that dominated Shakespeare production in the last quarter of the century. The concern with race began with the great American theatrical event of the 1940s, Margaret Webster's production of *Othello* with the charismatic Paul Robeson in the title role. After the longest run of any Shakespeare play on Broadway, it was taken on tour all over America in 1945, playing only in desegregated theaters. Although Robeson had already played Othello in London (1930), and would do so again at Stratford-upon-Avon, England, in 1959, his long period of disgrace in the politically polarized United States of the 1950s delayed the movement toward race-based casting as a norm. After initial embarrassment about racist language in Shakespeare, the theater began deliberately to explore its implications, as race became a subject for academic study. The range of *Othello* videos available by the 1990s indicates the play's performance history: besides Orson Welles's film from 1952, these include the National Theatre production of 1964 starring Laurence Olivier and the BBC one with Antony Hopkins (1981), both with white actors in the title role; Trevor Nunn's Chekhovian version originally staged in 1989; the historic South African production by Janet Suzman, a political act at a time when apartheid still existed; and Oliver Parker's 1994 version, with Laurence Fishburne (opposite Kenneth Branagh's convincingly ordinary Iago), consciously conveying the concentrated power and sensuality associated with blackness. Confusion between "color-blind casting" (when the audience is supposed to ignore the race of both actor and character) and "race-based casting" (when the audience is being told something about race through the casting) was deliberately cultivated in Jude Kelly's *Othello* (Washington, D.C., 1997). This production enabled Patrick Stewart to achieve his otherwise unrealizable ambition of playing the title role by surrounding a white Othello with African American and Hispanic actors, yet with the play's racial references unaltered.

A different effect is created when Iago and Emilia are played by actors of color, as at the Shakespeare Theatre, Washington, D.C. (1990), and the RSC (2015). Many theatres now recognize the need to provide roles for actors of traditionally underrepresented groups. While all acting involves imitation, some kinds of imitation are now regarded as unacceptable, as when white actors are made up to resemble black or Asian characters, or when non-Jews play Shylock. *The Merchant of Venice* is frequently directed with emphasis on the Jewish setting of Shylock's house and the latent or actual homosexuality of Antonio's relation to Bassanio. The play's ending is often dark: at Shakespeare's Globe in 2015 an interpolated scene showed Shylock's forced conversion to Christianity (in this production, Shylock and Jessica were also a real father and daughter, Jonathan and Phoebe Pryce).

Just as some critics of racism felt that *Othello* and *The Merchant of Venice* had become theatrically unacceptable, some feminist responses to Shakespeare argued the same about *The Taming of the Shrew*, in which a female character is made to acquiesce in her humiliation by a husband who uses patriarchal arguments to justify his behavior. The play had usually been directed to soften its final moral, either by making it clear that the protagonists have fallen in love at first sight or by emphasizing its nature as a play within a play, safely distant from real life. A famous production by Michael Bogdanov (Royal Shakespeare Theatre, 1978) doubled the drunken tinker Sly with Petruchio and showed Kate being brutalized into a dazed submission that horrified even her husband. Obviously, the play in this version was no longer a comedy. A less obvious effect of feminism has been the increasing attention paid to Shakespeare's female characters. They tend now to be on stage more than the text directs, as when Ophelia stands appalled while her father reads Hamlet's love letters to the court or Gertrude enters in time to hear Claudius and Laertes plan to poison Hamlet, so that her decision to drink from the cup is recognized as an heroic attempt to save her son's life. The young Elizabeth of York, who does not appear in the text of *Richard III* although she is important to its plot, has frequently appeared in stage versions, as in the 1995 film by Richard Loncraine. The fact that women are often denied speech at crucial moments can be turned to an advantage, as when John Barton and a number of subsequent directors of *Measure for Measure* in the 1980s made Isabella silently refuse the Duke's proposal, which earlier actors and directors had assumed she would eagerly accept.

Still more important, in a theater in which women are far more likely than men to be underemployed, were devices that increased the number of Shakespearean roles for women. Cross-dressed performances, parallel to the productions focused on race, hovered between gender based and gender blind. Deborah Warner's *Richard II* in 1995, with Fiona Shaw as the title character (National Theatre, London), suggested a troubled and potentially erotic relationship between Richard and Bolingbroke without defining it further. Other notable appropriations of male roles have included Falstaff in *The Merry Wives*

(Pat Carroll, Washington, D.C., 1990), Kathryn Hunter as *Richard III* in an all-female production (Shakespeare's Globe, 2003) and King Lear (2004). London saw an all-female *Julius Caesar* and *1 Henry IV* in 2012 and 2014. Female Prosperos have been particularly common (e.g.,Vanessa Redgrave at Shakespeare's Globe in 2000 and Helen Mirren in Julie Taymor's film, 2014). In 2014–15 Maxine Peake played Hamlet in a Manchester production where women also appeared as Marcellus/Marcella, Polonius/Polonia, and Rose Crantz. In the all-male Cheek-by-Jowl production of *As You Like It* (1995), the audience was never certain whether it was meant to be thinking of Rosalind (Adrian Lester) as male or female. A similar confusion was exploited when Michael Kahn's *King Lear* (Washington, D.C., 1999) cast Cordelia as a deaf-mute, signing her lines, which were then interpreted by the Fool. This decision, which would have been meaningless if the audience had not known that the actress (Monique Holt) really was a deaf-mute, might be seen either as a return to the self-conscious theatricality of the Renaissance stage or as an example of identity politics.

## Shakespeare on Film

Of course, the sense of identity between actor and role is strongest in the cinema, where physical appearance matters more and where audiences are particularly likely to bring with them recollections of an actor's previous roles. Films of Shakespeare plays are as old as film itself. Their transfer to videotape and then laserdisc and DVD, a process that began in the 1970s, has given them a much wider circulation and canonized some performances: Olivier's Richard III, for instance, now has much the same iconic status that Cibber gave to Betterton's Hamlet. Orson Welles's film versions of *Macbeth* (1947) and *Othello* (1952), visually remarkable as they were, have benefited from remastering to make their soundtracks more intelligible. The BBC made-for-TV versions of Shakespeare, 1979–1985, often disappointed scholars of both film and Shakespeare, though for different reasons, but have been widely used in schools. Kenneth Branagh's films, including a remarkable four-hour uncut *Hamlet* (1996), have been surprisingly successful in making the plays accessible to a popular audience. His *Henry V* (1989) was unfairly praised for being more "real" than Olivier's; both films were star-centered, with Olivier playing a more controlled king, Branagh a more vulnerable one. Whereas Olivier began his film with a view of an idealized Elizabethan London, then of a playhouse viewed from a superior perspective as old-fashioned and in some ways comic, Branagh introduced his Chorus (Derek Jacobi) in a room full of movie cameras, though he later allowed him to move among the actors in the film. As often in films, the moments most remembered were visual: Henry's (Branagh's) grief when, in order to

enforce proper discipline, he is obliged to order the hanging of Bardolph, or the long shot, after the Battle of Agincourt, that shows Henry carrying the dead boy in a procession of English soldiers singing *Non nobis Domine*.

Branagh's youth was an asset in bringing Shakespeare to a young audience. Later filmmakers have aimed at a still younger group. *William Shakespeare's Romeo + Juliet* (directed by Baz Luhrmann, 1996), filled as it was with icons of contemporary youth culture, is perhaps the first of these, though it retains Shakespeare's language, juxtaposing it with contradictory images, so that it can be understood either as a complex visual-verbal experience or as a rather simple visual one. The *Hamlet* directed by Michael Almereyda (2000) represents its young characters as college students obsessed with modern technology: Hamlet (Ethan Hawke) is an amateur filmmaker and Ophelia is a photographer; "To be or not to be" is spoken in a video store against a background of videos labeled "Action." For students of the new field of Shakespeare in Popular Culture, Teenage Shakespeare, with the stories rewritten in contemporary language and settings, is becoming a genre in its own right. *10 Things I Hate About You* (directed by Gil Junger, 1999) and *O* (directed by Tim Blake Nelson, 2001) retell *The Taming of the Shrew* and *Othello* in American high school settings. *The Children's Midsummer Night's Dream* (directed by Christine Edzard, 2001) has a cast of primary school children.

While film adaptations of the most popular plays continue to proliferate, there have also been versions of less well known works like Taymor's *Titus* (1999) and Branagh's *Love's Labour's Lost* (2000), and the made-for-television adaptation of the second tetralogy as a miniseries called *The Hollow Crown* (2012). Among the most successful were Michael Radford's tragic *The Merchant of Venice* (2004), where the audience's last view of Shylock (Al Pacino) came as the doors of the synagogue were closed against him, and Joss Whedon's simple, modern, black-and-white *Much Ado About Nothing* (2010), deliberately contrasted with Branagh's spectacular costume drama of 1993. However, the boundaries between theatre and film are becoming blurred, as technology now allows the transmitting of live performances of plays to audiences in movie theatres. Increasingly, playing a major Shakespearean role on stage has become the climax of a film or television actor's career (as with the stage Hamlets of David Tennant and Benedict Cumberbatch). Al Pacino, having played Shylock on film, took up the role again in New York in 2010. Even the actor-audience boundary is proving permeable, since new apps on the electronic media allow individuals to perform Shakespeare roles opposite famous (prerecorded) actors. For anyone who wants simply to hear the words of a Shakespeare play intelligently and movingly spoken by good actors, the best option is the Arkangel series of audio-recordings directed by Clive

Brill. The plays are well-cast, performed uncut, and include the entire canon—even *The Two Noble Kinsmen*, which has so far been ignored by every other "complete" Shakespeare project.

## International Contexts and Contemporary Adaptations

Not only have the plays been adapted for every age group, they have turned out to speak an international language. This had not always been true, though English and French actors had visited each other's countries since the seventeenth century: in 1629 French actresses were booed by English audiences, still accustomed to an all-male stage; one group of English actors was booed in the Paris of 1818, but another visiting company in 1827 inspired French writers and actors to try to understand Shakespeare. English and American audiences saw *Othello* with new eyes when the Italian actor Tommaso Salvini, followed by several other famous Italians, performed on tour in the late nineteenth century. Along with the visit of the Berliner Ensemble to London in 1956, the most important influences in the late twentieth century came from Asian, especially Japanese, theater and from central and eastern Europe. Akiro Kurosawa's films, *Throne of Blood* (*Macbeth*, 1957) and *Ran* (*King Lear*, 1986), transpose Shakespearean plots into Japanese culture and images. Successful Russian films have ranged from the visually stunning colors of Yan Fried's *Twelfth Night* and Sergei Yutkevitch's *Othello* (both 1955) to Grigori Kozintsev's black-and-white *Hamlet* (1964) and *King Lear* (1971).

The opening up of contacts with central and eastern Europe after 1989 has resulted in visits from theater companies of the former eastern bloc countries. When London audiences in 1990 saw *Hamlet* by the Bulandra Theatre of Romania (directed by Alexander Tocilescu), they discovered that plays often regarded in Britain and America as "conservative" tools of the "establishment" had elsewhere been a powerful vehicle for the expression of political dissent. When first produced in 1985, Tocilescu's *Hamlet* was clearly understood to be equating the rottenness of Elsinore with the world created by Nicolae Ceaucescu, the dictator executed in 1989; Ion Caramitru, the actor who played Hamlet, had been one of the leaders of the revolution. In Czech productions of Shakespeare, similarly, actors and audience had gathered in a deliberate act of misreading directed at the occupying Russians: in *Love's Labor's Lost*, of all plays, the princess's suggestion that the courtiers disguised as Muscovites should "be gone" was the high point of the evening.

Subversive comedy can also be turned against the speakers of Shakespeare's language. For example, in a Philippine production of *The Taming of the Shrew* (2002)

a Filipina Kate and an American soldier Petruchio were the director's political comment on Americans who want not only to dominate but to be loved. In the Arab world, too, the plays have had a powerful political meaning, with *Hamlet,* for example, used to imply opposition to both local and foreign rulers.

Western directors have sometimes attempted to deal with a difficult text by interpreting it as "Other," particularly as Japanese: the samurai warrior culture was the background to Barry Kyle's *The Two Noble Kinsmen* (Swan Theatre, Stratford, 1986) and to David Farr's *Coriolanus* (Royal Shakespeare Theatre, 2002), whereas Ron Daniels's *Timon of Athens* (The Other Place, Stratford, 1980) drew on the concept of a society based on gift-giving. Conversely, Yukio Ninagawa's Japanese Shakespeare productions have combined Japanese costumes with a soundtrack of European music (*Macbeth*) and interpreted *The Tempest* through the story of the famous Japanese exile, Shunkan. Such cross-cultural borrowings have sometimes been denigrated as "cultural tourism," by which critics seem to mean that it is illegitimate to pick and choose among the aspects of a culture to which one does not belong.

Similarly, the reconstructed "Shakespeare's Globe" in London, which opened in 1997, was accused of attempting to appropriate the emotions of another historical period. Perhaps because the opening production was *Henry V*, the "groundlings" who stood in the yard for only £5 apiece seemed to be modeling themselves on their counterparts in the Globe sequence of Olivier's film, who boo when they hear that Falstaff has been banished. Their willingness to boo the French (and, in the next season, Shylock) at first shocked the critics, and it was suggested that this theater might be suited only to comedies and histories demanding a presentational style, but productions of *Hamlet* (2000) and *King Lear* (2001) showed that it was possible to control audience response to the tragedies. Mark Rylance's Hamlet skillfully played his line about groundlings "capable of nothing but inexplicable dumbshow," so that he could respond to their laughter by emphasizing "*and* noise." Whether or not the theater can really tell anyone anything about Elizabethan stage conventions and audience response, it has given considerable pleasure. Many early productions experimented with "original practices": authentic period costumes, often made by traditional methods; casting of men in women's roles (not boys, and so not really authentic); early modern music played on period instruments; and clowns who had an aggressive rapport with the audience. Later, the playhouse gave room to different directorial philosophies and a variety of experiments: all-male productions; all-female productions; actors on wires in a circus tent (*Timon of Athens,* 2008) or bulldozing through the groundlings on giant wheeled towers (*Titus Andronicus,* 2009 and 2014). Other

Globes, more and less historically based, have been created in several countries (the United States, Japan, Poland, and the Czech Republic, among others), while the open stage of Stratford, Canada, remains one of the most successful modifications of the Elizabethan model. In a reversal of the search for authenticity, the Shakespeare Theatre in Washington, D.C., abandoned its home in the reconstructed Fortune Theatre at the Folger Shakespeare Library for a purpose-built modern auditorium. In fact, the two kinds of theater can coexist. The well-established Shakespeare festivals of Stratford, Ontario; Ashland, Oregon; and Santa Cruz, California, have added well-equipped indoor theaters to their outdoor acting spaces, and an indoor auditorium is projected as an addition to Shakespeare's Globe in London. A reconstruction of the Blackfriars Playhouse opened in Staunton, Virginia, in 2001.

The fast-moving productions incorporate a good deal of music and comedy, with special emphasis on the actor-audience relationship. Spectators here can sit on the stage, where they are frequently and willingly dragged into the performance. The Sam Wanamaker Playhouse (2014), also modelled on the Jacobean indoor playhouse, does not usually have onstage spectators, but performances are given by candlelight and the theatre often experiments with early modern staging techniques.

Although it has been impossible to discuss the theatrical fortunes of every Shakespeare play, it may be interesting to end by reflecting how greatly these have fluctuated. If some plays, like *Hamlet* and *Macbeth*, have always been popular, the history of others is more checkered. Some of the comedies most popular today, such as *As You Like It* and *Twelfth Night*, were regarded as insipid in the eighteenth century, redeemed only by their scenes of low comedy and occasional sententious speeches. *The Merry Wives of Windsor* was the most popular comedy during the Restoration; *King John* and *Henry VIII* were more popular in the nineteenth century than *Richard II* (now a surprisingly frequent choice for star actors) or *2 Henry IV*. *Othello* was acted without the "willow scene" (4.3) for most of the eighteenth and nineteenth centuries, and *Troilus and Cressida* and *Titus Andronicus* were performed, if at all, only in heavily adapted versions. It is arguable that the attitude to Shakespeare that Bernard Shaw ridiculed as "Bardolatry" reached its height, not in the Victorian age, but at the end of the twentieth century, a time when any Shakespeare play, however minor, was likely to find a director and an audience. One reason might be that the subsidized theaters had been giving fewer controversial productions since 1980, emphasizing instead what the plays have in common with musical comedies and films. An important American contribution to Shakespeare in performance has taken the form of musicals like *The Boys from Syracuse* (1938), *Kiss Me, Kate* (1948), and *West Side Story* (1957), based respectively on *The Comedy of Errors*, *The Taming of the Shrew*, and *Romeo and Juliet*. Many productions of the comedies follow the Restoration practice of filling them with popular music. What was new was not the practice of adaptation but the attitude toward it. In the mid-twentieth century, the plays were taken to be fixed quantities: the job of the theater director, as of the critic, was to uncover the "real" work, whether through more authentic staging, a more accurate text, or a better understanding of its meaning. By the end of the millennium, when some theorists were insisting that the text itself was unknowable, there was a much greater tolerance for re-creations and explorations of the plays in other forms.

So the Shakespeare name is now likely to evoke his stories and characters rather than his words. Perhaps this has always been true, but the globalization of Shakespeare has inevitably led to the de-emphasis on his language. Any theatrical history will necessarily focus on theaters in the Anglophone world, dedicated chiefly to Shakespeare production, much of it now available in recorded form. But it is increasingly possible to see brilliant productions in other languages. In 2006–2007 the RSC's Complete Works Festival included all of Shakespeare's plays (if sometimes for only very brief runs) in performances by local and visiting companies, eleven of them in languages other than English. The Cultural Olympiad of 2012 (paralleling the London Olympics) involved the RSC, the Globe, and several other theatres, and brought seventy Shakespeare productions or adaptations to London, half of them in languages other than English. Some of these also toured to other countries. The 450th anniversary of Shakespeare's birth in 2014 and the 400th anniversary of his death in 2016 were also the occasions for large-scale Shakespeare celebrations. Commemorating both events, the Globe sent a production of *Hamlet* on a round-the-world tour between 23 April 2014 and 23 April 2016. It might seem that the present enthusiasm for Shakespeare in performance is bound to wane, yet the theater continues to invent experiences that audiences cannot easily find elsewhere. Besides those already mentioned, there are "site-specific" and "promenade" performances, where actors and audience move through a space that becomes part of the production, and occasional eccentricities like *King Lear with Sheep* (by Missouri Williams, at the Courtyard Theatre, Hoxton, 2015), a half-hour adaptation featuring one actor and nine sheep. If Shakespeare is sometimes only the excuse for theatrical experimentation, he has at any rate proved a powerful catalyst. And public demand for theater tickets remains high, especially for the combination of a famous Shakespeare role and a star performer.

# Appendix 4

# Films and Videos as a Guide to the Study of Shakespeare

*by David Bevington*

The general introduction to this volume makes the point that seeing a Shakespeare play in production is often a very good way to start with the study of that play. Aspects of Shakespeare that might seem daunting at first—the occasionally unfamiliar vocabulary and idiom, unusual Elizabethan grammatical constructions, and other difficulties of meaning—can disappear as a problem when good actors interpret for us. Watching a production can be fun and exciting. It erases much of the distance of time between Shakespeare's day and our own. And, since film and video versions are far more readily available than live stage performances, productions on screen are likely to be our best choice.

The choices are surprisingly numerous. One can find a worthwhile screen interpretation of virtually every play Shakespeare wrote. For the better known plays, multiple versions are available, so that comparisons can be made of varying styles and interpretations. What follows here is a brief history of Shakespeare on film and video, stressing the highlights, as a way of indicating what is available and what are perhaps the best choices today. This brief history is followed by a selective filmography—that is, a bibliography of film and video, listing the best and most available versions, play by play.

Silent film versions of Shakespeare's plays are numerous in the early twentieth century. They are, of course, of interest to the specialist, but are omitted here since this account is aimed at providing a practical listing of screen productions best suited to the reader wishing to gain a lively acquaintance with a play or plays. The story begins early in the days of talking movies.

Mary Pickford and Douglas Fairbanks Sr. starred as Kate and Petruchio in the first full-length talking film of any Shakespeare play, Sam Taylor's *The Taming of the Shrew*, 1929. *A Midsummer Night's Dream* enjoyed real box-office success in Max Reinhardt's 1935 film, starring a young Mickey Rooney as Puck, James Cagney as Bottom the Weaver, and Olivia de Havilland as Hermia, along with some other notable Hollywood favorites. Franco Zeffirelli scored a great hit with his film version of *The Taming* in 1967, starring Richard Burton and Elizabeth Taylor as Petruchio and Kate.

Laurence Olivier achieved an artistic breakthrough in 1944 with his full-length color film of *Henry V*, produced during World War II to keep up morale on the home front. Olivier's *Hamlet*, 1948, *Richard III*, 1955, and *Othello*, 1965, were similar triumphs. Orson Welles's *Macbeth*, 1948, and *Othello*, 1952, were conscious and serious attempts to show that the United States could challenge Olivier at his own game. Welles's *Chimes at Midnight* (1965), with himself in the role of Falstaff, combined elements of *1* and *2 Henry IV* and bits of *The Merry Wives of Windsor* into a moving account of the ultimate rejection of Falstaff by Prince Hal.

Another wave of film revivals of Shakespeare began in 1989 with Kenneth Branagh's highly successful *Henry V*. Young, brash, superbly self-confident, Branagh deliberately chose *Henry V* as a way of confronting the legendary Olivier on his own turf. Olivier's film had been patriotic and upbeat, albeit with an awareness of the grim aspects of war. Branagh's version, in the aftermath of Vietnam and the Falklands military engagement, was more wary of patriotic fervor. Branagh followed up this triumph in 1993 with *Much Ado About Nothing*, starring himself as Benedick and his then-wife Emma Thompson as Beatrice, along with Denzel Washington as Don Pedro, Keanu Reeves as Don John, and Michael Keaton as Dogberry. The age of star turns in Shakespeare films was by now in full swing. Branagh repeated this surefire box-office stratagem with his four-hour *Hamlet* in 1996, with himself as

Hamlet, Julie Christie as Gertrude, Kate Winslet as Ophelia, Derek Jacobi as Claudius, and a host of cameo appearances by Jack Lemmon (Marcellus), Gérard Depardieu (Reynaldo), Robin Williams (Osric), Billy Crystal (the Gravedigger), and Charlton Heston (the Player King).

Not to be outdone in this contest of the stars, Franco Zeffirelli had already cast Mel Gibson as Hamlet, Glenn Close as Gertrude, Helena Bonham Carter as Ophelia, Ian Holm as Polonius, Alan Bates as Claudius, and Paul Scofield as the Ghost in his 1990 Hamlet.

Zeffirelli had scored a great success earlier, in 1968, with his visually gorgeous Romeo and Juliet, starring Olivia Hussey as Juliet, Leonard Whiting as Romeo, and Michael York as Tybalt. With brief and tactful nudity, and a handsome couple in the title roles, this film could not fail. No less popular with the younger set particularly was Baz Luhrmann's Romeo + Juliet, 1996, starring Claire Danes and Leonardo DiCaprio. Filmed in Mexico City in such a way as to suggest a major U.S. sunbelt city like Miami or Los Angeles, this version updates its story with panache: Tybalt and his cohorts are Hispanic gang members, the Capulets are nouveau riche, and Friar Laurence is a New Age priest.

Many other Shakespeare films are eminently worth studying, with well-known stars in key roles. Julius Caesar, produced in 1953 by John Houseman with Joseph L. Mankiewicz as director, Marlon Brando as Mark Antony, James Mason as Brutus, John Gielgud as Cassius, Louis Calhern as Julius Caesar, Greer Garson as Calpurnia, and Deborah Kerr as Portia, is a Hollywood extravaganza, bringing together famous actors from the UK and the United States. Trevor Nunn's Twelfth Night, 1996, stars Imogen Stubbs as Viola, Helena Bonham Carter as Olivia, Nigel Hawthorne as Malvolio, and Ben Kingsley as Feste, along with some spectacularly handsome Cornish scenery. Ian McKellen and Judi Dench are outstanding in Trevor Nunn's Macbeth, 1979. Roman Polanski's film version of the same play in 1971, for Playboy Productions, is quirky but interesting. Al Pacino as Shylock, Jeremy Irons as Antonio, and Joseph Fiennes as Bassanio are admirable in Michael Radford's The Merchant of Venice, 2004. No less excellent are Laurence Olivier and Joan Plowright in Jonathan Sichel's 1969 film of this same play. Kenneth Branagh's recent As You Like It (2006), with Kevin Kline as Jaques, has some lively moments. Even some lesser plays occasionally get in on the act: Julie Taymor's film version of Titus Andronicus (1999) has excellent performances by Anthony Hopkins as Titus, Jessica Lange as Tamora, Harry Lennix as Aaron, and still others. Branagh's Love's Labour's Lost (2000) enlivens this little-known play by adapting some hit tunes by Irving Berlin, Jerome Kern, the Gershwins, and Cole Porter.

At least three film Othello are eminently worth watching, in addition to that of Laurence Olivier in 1965 mentioned above. Janet Suzman's film version is based on a stage production in Johannesburg, South Africa, in 1988, shortly before the end of Apartheid, with John Kani as Othello, Joanna Weinberg as Desdemona, and Richard Haddon Haines as Iago. Trevor Nunn's 1990 film stars Willard White as Othello, Imogen Stubbs as Desdemona, and Ian McKellen as Iago. Oliver Parker's 1995 Othello features notable performances by Laurence Fishburne as Othello, Kenneth Branagh as Iago, and Irène Jacob as Desdemona. The availability of several excellent films on a single play offers the opportunity for comparison and contrast of acting styles, interpretation, and filming techniques.

The same is even more true of Hamlet, where we have the versions discussed above by Olivier, Zeffirelli, and Branagh, along with Richard Burton as Hamlet in John Gielgud's 1964 film, a Russian Hamlet by Grigori Kozintsev in 1964, Nicol Williamson in the lead role in 1969 as directed by Tony Richardson, Richard Chamberlain in 1970 as directed by Peter Wood, and Kevin Kline in an especially intelligent production of 1990 as directed by Kirk Browning and Kevin Kline. Michael Almereyda's Hamlet (2000), set in midtown Manhattan at the turn of the twentieth century, stars Ethan Hawke as Hamlet, Diane Venora as Gertrude, Julia Stiles as Ophelia, Kyle MacLachlan as Claudius, Bill Murray as Polonius, and Sam Shepard as the Ghost. A film version of Hamlet filmed in 2009, based on an excellent Royal Shakespeare Company stage production directed by Gregory Doran, starred David Tennant (of "Doctor Who" fame) as Hamlet and Patrick Stewart as Claudius. A live video Hamlet 2010 was also based on a successful stage production, that of the National Theatre in London, directed by Nicholas Hytner in a modern police-state setting, with Rory Kinnear in the title role and Clare Higgins as Gertrude.

King Lear also affords several worthy film versions for comparison, notably Kozintsev's 1970 film with music by Dimitri Shostakovich, Peter Brook's starkly pessimistic version of 1971 with Paul Scofield in the title role, and Michael Elliott's version for Granada Television in 1983 starring Laurence Olivier. Richard III offers brilliant choices to compare, including the Olivier discussed above and Richard Loncraine's film version, 1995, set in 1930s London with Ian McKellen as Richard. Still other plays are available in multiple interpretations on film; see the selected filmography at the end of this essay.

Film adaptations attest no less eloquently to the popularity of Shakespeare today on film, stressing as they do the appeal of adapting the original to current mores and cultural preoccupations. Akira Kurosawa's black-and-white Throne of Blood, 1957, transfers the story of Macbeth to late medieval warlord Japan. His Ran, 1985, colorfully retells King Lear as a saga about an aging King and his three sons (rather than daughters). These are

FILMS AND VIDEOS A-51

among the finest films Kurosawa ever produced. *West Side Story* triumphantly entered the world of film in 1961, based on the stage musical adaptation of *Romeo and Juliet*, with Leonard Bernstein as the composer and Stephen Sondheim as lyricist. *Kiss Me, Kate*, 1953, has proven to be no less immortal in its reworking of *The Taming of the Shrew*. The same play was relocated to the world of high-school dating and jealous rivalries in Gil Junger's *10 Things I Hate About You*, 1999, with Julia Stiles as Katharine Stratford. *Othello* also has been resituated in a high-school setting in Tim Blake Nelson's *O*, 2001, with Julia Stiles this time as Desi Brable, the Desdemona equivalent. *Hamlet* has been given a modern twist in Kurosawa's *The Bad Sleep Well* (1960). *Shakespeare in Love* (1998), scripted by Tom Stoppard and Marc Norman, contains some radiant moments from *Romeo and Juliet*, with Gwyneth Paltrow as Juliet and Joseph Fiennes as Romeo.

## A Selected Filmography

(Compiled by David Bevington with special thanks to David Scott Kastan)

Here is a listing, play by play, of some interesting and generally successful film or video versions of Shakespeare's plays. Most are available in video and DVD. Comparison of one or more versions can offer invaluable insights into the potential range of various interpretations. Also included here are some adaptations and spin-offs. BBC/ Time-Life Television has produced videos of all the plays; those of special note are described here.

### ANTONY AND CLEOPATRA

A Royal Shakespeare Company/ITC production, 1974, directed by Trevor Nunn and Jon Scoffield, with Richard Johnson as Antony, Janet Suzman as Cleopatra, Patrick Stewart as Enobarbus, Corin Redgrave as Octavius, Rosemary McHale as Charmian, Raymond Westfall as Lepidus, Ben Kingsley as Thidias, Mary Rutherford as Octavia, and Tim Pigott-Smith as Proculeius. (Charlton Heston directed a film version in 1972, with himself as Antony and Hildegard Neil as Cleopatra, but it is generally accounted a failure.)

A Merchant-Ivory production, 1965, of *Shakespeare Wallah*, directed by James Ivory, with Felicity and Geoffrey Kendal. An adaptation, with scenes from *Antony and Cleopatra*.

### AS YOU LIKE IT

A Twentieth Century British Fox production, directed by Paul Czinner, 1936, with Laurence Olivier and Elisabeth Bergner as Orlando and Rosalind, Felix Aylmer as Duke Frederick, Sophie Stewart as Celia, John Laurie as Oliver, MacKenzie Ward as Touchstone, Leon Quartermaine as Jaques, Henry Ainley as Duke Senior, Dorice Fordred as

Audrey, and J. Fisher White as Adam. A flawed production, but notable for the casting of a very young Olivier.

A BBC-TV production with the Royal Shakespeare Company, 1963, directed by Ronald Eyre for TV, based on a stage production by Michael Elliott, with Patrick Allen and Vanessa Redgrave as Orlando and Rosalind, Tony Church as Duke Frederick, Paul Hardwick as Duke Senior, Patrick Wymark as Touchstone, Max Adrian as Jaques, Rosalind Knight as Celia, David Buck as Oliver, Russell Hunter as Corin, Peter Gill as Silvius, Jeanne Hepple as Phoebe, Gordon Gostelow as William, Patsy Byrne as Audrey, and Ian Richardson as Le Beau.

A BBC Shakespeare Collection television version of 1978, produced by Cedric Messina and directed by Basil Coleman, shot mostly on location and outdoors in Masterpiece Theatre style with stately aristocratic homes and leafy forests; with Helen Mirren as Rosalind, Angharad Rees as Celia, Brian Stirner as Orlando, Clive Francis as Oliver, Tony Church as Duke Senior, Richard Easton as Duke Frederick, John Quentin as Le Beau, James Bolan as Touchstone, Richard Pasco as Jaques, Maynard Williams as Silvius, Victoria Plucknett as Phoebe, Marilyn Le Conte as Audrey, David Lloyd Meredith as Corin, Arthur Hewlett as Adam, and Tom McDonnell as Amiens.

A Sands Films production, 1992, directed by Christine Edzard, modernized, with Andrew Tiernan and Emma Croft as Orlando and Rosalind, Celia Bannerman as Celia, James Fox as Jaques, Don Henderson as Duke Senior and Duke Frederick, Cyril Cusack as Adam, Valerie Gogan as Phoebe, Miriam Margolyes as Audrey, and Griff Rhys Jones as Touchstone.

An HBO production, 2006, directed by Kenneth Branagh, with Bryce Dallas Howard as Rosalind, David Oyelowo as Orlando, Alfred Molina as Touchstone, Kevin Kline as Jaques, Brian Blessed as Duke Senior and Duke Frederick, Romola Garai as Celia, Adrian Lester as Oliver, Richard Clifford as Le Beau, Richard Briers as Adam, Jimmy Yuill as Corin, Alex Wyndham as Silvius, Jade Jefferies as Phoebe, Paul Chan as William, and Janet McTeer as Audrey.

A film version, 2010, based on Thea Sharrock's London Globe Theatre production of 2009, with Naomi Frederick as Rosalind, Jack Laskey as Orlando, Dominic Rowan as Touchstone, Tim McMullan as Jaques, Philip Bird as Duke Senior, Trevor Martin as old Adam, Laura Rogers as Celia, Jamie Parker as Oliver, Brendon Hughes as Duke Frederick, Michael Benz as Silvius, Sophie Duval as Audrey, Gregory Dudgeon as Le Beau and William, Trevor Martin as Adam, and Jade Williams as Phoebe.

### HAMLET

A Two Cities Films production, 1948, directed by Laurence Olivier, with Olivier as Hamlet, Basil Sydney as Claudius, Eileen Herlie as Gertrude, Felix Aylmer as Polonius, Jean Simmons as Ophelia, Norman Wooland as Horatio, Terence Morgan as Laertes, and Stanley Holloway as the First Gravedigger.

A Classic Cinemas filming of a stage performance at the Lunt-Fontaine Theatre, 1964, directed by John Gielgud on stage and Bill Colleran on film, with Richard Burton as Hamlet, Alfred Drake as Claudius, Eileen Herlie as Gertrude, Hume Cronyn as Polonius, Linda Marsh as Ophelia, John Cullum as Laertes, Robert Milli as Horatio, and John Gielgud as the voice of the Ghost.

A Lenfilm production, 1964, in Russian with subtitles, directed by Grigori Kozintsev, with Innokenti Smoktunovsky as Hamlet, Mikhail Nazvanov as Claudius, Elza Radzina-Szolkonis as Gertrude, Yuri Tolubeyev as Polonius, Anastasia Vertinskaya as Ophelia, Stepan Oleksenko as Laertes, Vladimir Erenberg as Horatio, and V. Kolpakor as the Gravedigger.

A Woodfall Productions/Columbia Pictures production, 1969, directed by Tony Richardson, with Nicol Williamson as Hamlet, Anthony Hopkins as Claudius, Judy Parfitt as Gertrude, Mark Dignam as Polonius, Marianne Faithfull as Ophelia, Michael Pennington as Laertes, Gordon Jackson as Horatio, Roger Livesay as the First Player and the Gravedigger, Ben Aris as Rosencrantz, and Clive Graham as Guildenstern.

A Hallmark Hall of Fame production, 1970, directed by Peter Wood, with Richard Chamberlain as Hamlet, Richard Johnson as Claudius, Margaret Leighton as Gertrude, Michael Redgrave as Polonius, Ciaran Madden as Ophelia, Martin Shaw as Horatio, Nicholas Jones as Laertes, John Gielgud as the Ghost, and Alan Bennett as Osric.

A Warner Brothers production, 1990, directed by Franco Zeffirelli, with Mel Gibson as Hamlet, Alan Bates as Claudius, Glenn Close as Gertrude, Ian Holm as Polonius, Helena Bonham Carter as Ophelia, Nathaniel Parker as Laertes, Stephen Dillane as Horatio, Michael Maloney as Rosencrantz, Sean Murray as Guildenstern, Pete Postlethwaite as the Player King, John McEnery as Osric, and Paul Scofield as the Ghost.

A PBS Television Great Performances production, 1990, not shown in movie theaters, directed by Kirk Browning and Kevin Kline, with Kevin Kline as Hamlet, Brian Murray as Claudius, Dana Ivey as Gertrude, Michael Krumpsty as Laertes, Diane Venora as Ophelia, Peter Francis James as Horatio, Philip Goodwin as Rosencrantz, Reg E. Cathey as Guildenstern, Don Reilly as Fort-inbras, and Leo Burmester as Osric.

A Columbia production, 1996, four hours in length, essentially uncut, directed by Kenneth Branagh, with Kenneth Branagh as Hamlet, Derek Jacobi as Claudius, Julie Christie as Gertrude, Richard Briers as Polonius, Kate Winslet as Ophelia, Michael Maloney as Laertes, Nicholas Farrell as Horatio, Jack Lemmon as Marcellus, Gérard Depardieu as Reynaldo, Charlton Heston as the Player King, Robin Williams as Osric, Billy Crystal as the First Gravedigger, and Brian Blessed as the Ghost.

A Miramax production, 2000, directed by Michael Almereyda, with Ethan Hawke as Hamlet, Kyle MacLachlan as Claudius, Diane Venora as Gertrude, Bill Murray as Polonius, Julia Stiles as Ophelia, Liev Schreiber as Laertes, Karl Geary as Horatio, and Sam Shepard as the Ghost.

A Hallmark Entertainment production directed for TV by Campbell Scott and Eric Simonson in 2000, starring Campbell Scott as Hamlet, Jamey Sheridan as Claudius, Blair Brown as Gertrude, Roscoe Lee Browne as Polonius, LisaGay Hamilton as Ophelia, Roger Guenveur Smith as Laertes, John Benjamin Hickey as Horatio, Bill Buell as Bernardo, John Campion as Marcellus, David Debesse as Francisco, Marcus Giamatti as Guildenstern, Michael Imperioli as Rosencrantz, Lewis Arlt as Voltemand, Dan Moran as the Gravedigger, Denis O'Hare as Osric, Byron Jennings as the Ghost of Hamlet's father and First Player, and Sam Robards as Fortinbras.

A production by Bethan Jones, David Horn, Denise Wood, John Wyver, and Seb Grant, based on a highly praised stage production by the Royal Shakespeare Company as directed by Gregory Doran, filmed in 2009, with David Tennant as Hamlet, Patrick Stewart as Claudius, Penny Downie as Gertrude, Oliver Ford Davies as Polonius, Mariah Gale as Ophelia, Edward Bennett as Laertes, Peter De Jersey as Horatio, Sam Alexander as Rosencrantz and the Second Gravedigger, Tom Davey as Guildenstern, and Mark Hadfield as the Gravedigger.

A filming of 2010, based on the stage production at the National's Olivier Theatre in London, set in a modern police state, directed by Nicholas Hytner, starring Rory Kinnear as Hamlet, Clare Higgins as an alcoholic Gertrude, Patrick Malahide as a cold-blooded and ruthless Claudius, David Calder as Polonius, Ruth Negga as Ophelia, Alex Lanipekun as Laertes, and James Laurenson as the Ghost and Player King.

The much-acclaimed 2009 London production of *Hamlet* starring Jude Law appears to be included (in portions, at least) in the Video Library of the New York Times. An interview about it is available on British Universities Film.

Kurosawa Productions, 1960, of *The Bad Sleep Well*, directed by Akiria Kurosawa, with Toshiro Mifune as the Hamlet-like hero and Takeshi Kato as the Claudius-like villain. An adaptation.

A production of *Rosencrantz and Guildenstern Are Dead*, 1990, based on the stage play by Tom Stoppard, with Gary Oldman as Rosencrantz, Tim Roth as Guildenstern, Richard Dreyfuss as the Player, Iain Glen as Hamlet, Joanna Miles as Gertrude, Donald Sumpter as Claudius, Joanna Roth as Ophelia, and Ian Richardson as Polonius. A witty excursion into the world of *Hamlet* from the point of view of Hamlet's two youthful companions.

## HENRY IV PART I

An Internacional Films/Alpine Films production, *Chimes at Midnight*, 1966, directed by Orson Welles, with Welles as Falstaff, John Gielgud as King Henry IV, Keith Baxter as Prince Hal, Tony Beckley as Poins, Norman Rodway as Hotspur, Fernando Rey as Mortimer, Michael Aldridge as Pistol, Alan Webb as Justice Shallow, and Margaret Rutherford as Mistress Quickly. A synthesis of *1* and *2 Henry IV*, with parts of *The Merry Wives of Windsor*.

A BBC/Time-Life Television production, 1979-80, directed by David Giles, with David Gwillim as Prince Hal, Anthony Quayle as Falstaff, Jon Finch as King Henry IV, Tim Pigott-Smith as Hotspur, David Buck as Westmorland, Clive Percy as Worcester, Robert Brown as Blunt, Bruce Purchase as Northumberland, Robert Morris as the Earl of March, Michele Dotrice as Lady Percy, and Brenda Bruce as Mistress Quickly.

A New Line Cinema production, 1991, of *My Own Private Idaho*, directed by Gus Van Sant, with Keanu Reeves as the Hal-like Scott Favor, William Richert as the Falstaff-like Bob, and River Phoenix as Scott's friend Mike Waters. An adaptation of *1* and *2 Henry IV*.

A film version staged during a production at London's Globe Theatre, 2011 (in tandem with a production of *2 Henry IV*), directed by Dominic Dromgoole, with Roger Allam as Falstaff, Oliver Cotton as King Henry IV, Jamie Parker as Prince Hal, Sam Crane as Hotspur, William Gaunt as Worcester, Daon Broni as Mortimer, Christopher Godwin as Northumberland, Jason Baughan as Westmorland, Sean Kearns as Glendower, Barbara Marten as Mistress Quickly, Danny Lee Wynter as Poins, Paul Rider as Bardolph, Joseph Timms as Francis, Kevork Malikyan as Vernon, Lorna Stuart as Lady Percy, Jade Williams as Lady Mortimer, James Lalley as Mowbray and Gadshill, and Phil Cheadle as the Earl of Douglas.

## HENRY V

A Two Cities Films Ltd. production, directed by Laurence Olivier, 1944, with Olivier as King Henry, Renée Asherson as the Princess Katharine, Felix Aylmer as the Archbishop of Canterbury, Robert Helpmann as the Bishop of Ely, Nicholas Hannen as Exeter, Michael Shepley as Captain Gower, John Laurie as Captain Jamy, Niall MacGinnis as Captain MacMorris, Harcourt Williams as the French King, Max Adrian as the Dauphin, Leo Genn as the Constable of France, Francis Lister as the Duke of Orleans, Ralph Truman as Mountjoy, Valentine Dyall as the Duke of Burgundy, Esmond Knight as Fluellen, Robert Newton as Pistol, Roy Emmerton as Bardolph, Freda Jackson as Mistress Quickly, Ivy St. Helier as Alice, and Leslie Banks as the Chorus.

A BBC/Renaissance Films production, 1989, directed by Kenneth Branagh, with Branagh as King Henry, Derek Jacobi as the Chorus, Emma Thompson as the Princess Katharine, Brian Blessed as Exeter, Charles Kay as the Archbishop of Canterbury, Alec McCowen as the Bishop of Ely, Danny Webb as Captain Gower, Jimmy Yuill as Captain Jamy, John Sessions as Captain MacMorris, Paul Scofield as the French King, Michael Maloney as the Dauphin, Richard Easton as the Constable of France, Christopher Ravenscroft as Mountjoy, Ian Holm as Fluellen, Robert Stephens as Pistol, Richard Briers as Bardolph, Judi Dench as Mistress Quickly, and Geraldine McEwan as Alice.

## JULIUS CAESAR

An MGM John Houseman production, 1953, directed by Joseph L. Mankiewicz, with Marlon Brando as Mark Antony, James Mason as Brutus, John Gielgud as Cassius, Louis Calhern as Julius Caesar, Greer Garson as Calpurnia, Edmond O'Brien as Casca, Richard Hale as the Sooothsayer, and Deborah Kerr as Portia.

A production by Peter Snell, 1969–70, directed by Stuart Burge, with Charlton Heston as Mark Antony, Jason Robards as Brutus, Richard Johnson as Cassius, John Gielgud as Caesar, Richard Chamberlain as Octavius Caesar, Diana Rigg as Portia, Jill Bennett as Calpurnia, and Robert Vaughn as Casca.

## KING LEAR

A Lenfilm production, 1970, directed by Grigori Kozintsev, in Russian (*Karol Lir*), with subtitles, with Yuri Yarvet as Lear, Valentina Shendrikova as Cordelia, Elze Radzina as Goneril, Galina Volchek as Regan, Oleg Dal as the Fool, Vladimir Yemelyanov as Kent, Karl Sebris as Gloucester, Regimantas Adomaitis as Edmund, and Leonard Merzin as Edgar.

A Filmways production, 1971, directed by Peter Brook, with Paul Scofield as Lear, Anne-lise Gabold as Cordelia, Jack MacGowran as the Fool, Cyril Cusack as Albany, Irene Worth as Goneril, Susan Engel as Regan, Patrick Magee as Cornwall, Tom Fleming as Kent, Alan Webb as Gloucester, Ian Hogg as Edmund, and Robert Lloyd as Edgar.

A Granada Television production, 1983, directed by Michael Elliott, with Laurence Olivier as Lear, Anna Calder-Marshall as Cordelia, Dorothy Tutin as Goneril, Diana Rigg as Regan, John Hurt as the Fool, David Threlfall as Edgar, Robert Lindsay as Edmund, Colin Blakely as Kent, Robert Lang as Albany, Jeremy Kemp as Cornwall, and Leo McKern as Gloucester,

A Great Performances version, directed by Trevor Nunn in 2008 and based on a stage production by the Royal Shakespeare Company, with Ian McKellen as King Lear, William Gaunt as Gloucester, Philip

Winchester as Edmund, Ben Meyjes as Edgar, Frances Barber as Goneril, Monica Dolan as Regan, Romola Garai as Cordelia, Sylvester McCoy as the Fool, Jonathan Hyde as Kent, Guy Williams as Cornwall, Julian Harries as Albany, John Heffernan as Oswald, and Peter Hinton as Burgundy.

A film of the play called *The Dresser*, 1983–5, with Albert Finney as Sir and Tom Courtney as the Dresser (Norman). An adaptation, based loosely on the career of the Shakespearan actor-manager Donald Wolfit, with scenes from *King Lear*.

An Orion Classics production, 1985, directed by Akira Kurosawa, in Japanese (*Ran*), with subtitles. With Tatsuya Nakadai as the Lear-like Hidetora Ichimonji; his three sons Akira Terao as the Goneril-like Taro, Jinpachi Nezu as the Regan-like Jiro, and Daisuke Ryu as the Cordelia-like Saburo; Meiko Harada as the daunting Lady Kaede, wife of Taro; Peter as the Fool-like Kyoami; Masayuki Yui as the Kent-like Tango; Yoshiko Miyazaki as Lady Sue, the saintly wife of Jiro; and Takeshi Nomura as the Edgar- and Gloucester-like Tsurmaru, brother of Lady Sue. An adaptation.

## MACBETH

A Republic Pictures and Mercury Films production, 1948, directed by Orson Welles, with Welles as Macbeth, Jeanette Nolan as Lady Macbeth, Dan O'Herlihy as Macduff, Edgar Barrier as Banquo, Erskine Sanford as Duncan, and Roddy McDowall as Malcolm.

Playboy Productions and Columbia Pictures, 1971, directed by Roman Polanski, with Jon Finch as Macbeth, Francesca Annis as Lady Macbeth, Terence Bayler as Macduff, Martin Shaw as Banquo, Nicholas Selby as Duncan, Stephan Chase as Malcolm, Sydney Bromley as the Porter, Andrew Laurence as Lennox, Noel Davis as Seyton, and John Stride as Ross.

A Thames Television production, 1979, based on a Royal Shakespeare stage and then TV production of 1976, directed by Trevor Nunn on stage and Philip Casson on TV, with Ian McKellen as Macbeth, Judi Dench as Lady Macbeth, Bob Peck as Macduff, Griffith Jones as Duncan, Roger Rees as Malcolm, Ian McDiarmid as Ross and the Porter, and John Woodvine as Banquo.

A televised version, directed by Gregory Doran, based on a 2001 production by the Royal Shakespeare Company and shot in 2004 at London's Roundhouse, using edgy fly-on-the-wall documentary technique, starring Antony Sher as Macbeth, Harriet Walter as Lady Macbeth, Richard Armitage as Angus, Joseph O'Conor as Duncan, Ken Bones, and Nigel Cooke, with Noma Dumezweni, Polly Kemp, and Diane Beck as the three Weird Sisters.

A production (2011) directed by Rupert Goold, based on a stage production by the Royal Shakespeare Company, starring Patrick Stewart as Macbeth, Kate

Fleetwood as Lady Macbeth, Scott Handy, Martin Turner, and Oliver Burch.

A 2005 adaptation in the "Shakespeare Re-told" series, by screenwriter Peter Moffat, directed by Mark Brozel and set in a three-star London restaurant, with James McAvoy as Joe Macbeth, Keeley Hawes as his wife and scheming hostess Ella, Vincent Regan as Duncan Docherty the chief restauranteur (cf. Duncan), Joseph Millson as Billy (Banquo), Richard Armitage as Peter Macduff, and the avenging headwaiter Toby Kebbell as Malcolm.

A Toho Company Ltd. production of *Throne of Blood*, 1957, directed by Akira Kurosawa, with Toshiro Mifune as the Macbeth-like Washizu, Isuzu Yamada as the Lady Macbeth-like Asaji, Minoru Chiaki as the Banquo-like Miki, Takamaru Sasaki as the Duncan-like Tsuzuki, Takashi Shimura as the Macduff-like Noriyasu, Akira Kubo as the Fleance-like Yoshiteru, Yoichi Tachikawa as the Malcolm-like Kunimaru, and Chieko Naniwa as the Evil Spirit. An adaptation.

## MEASURE FOR MEASURE

A BBC/Time-Life Television production, 1979, directed by Desmond Davis, with Tim Pigott-Smith as Angelo, Kate Nelligan as Isabella, Kenneth Colley as Duke Vincentio, Christopher Strauli as Claudio, John McEnery as Lucio, Frank Middlemass as Pompey, Adrienne Corri as Mistress Overdone, Ellis Jones as Elbow, Alun Armstrong as the Provost, and Kevin Stoney as Escalus.

A contemporary adaptation, 1994–5, made for BBC's new TV Performance series, with considerable use of closed-circuit television, directed by David Thacker, with Tom Wilkinson as a dejected Duke watching (in the opening scene) a TV montage of Vienna in moral decline, Corin Redgrave as Angelo, Juliet Aubrey as Isabella, Ben Miles as Claudio, Rob Edwards as Lucio, Ian Bannen as the Provost, Sue Johnston as Mistress Overdone, and Henry Goodman as Pompey.

A 2006 adaptation, Lucky Strike Productions, in a script by Gian Carlo Rossi and others, set in a modern-day British army barracks, directed by Bob Komar; with Daniel Roberts as Angelo, Josephine Rogers as Isabella, Simon Phillips as the Duke, Kristopher Milnes as the Provost, Dawn Murphy as Escalus, Simon Brandon (Simon Nuckley) as Claudio, Emma Agerwal (Emma Ager) as Mariana, Robert Anderson as Froth, Leah Grayson as Pompey, Luke Leeves as Lucio, Piers Pereira as Elbow, Hanne Steen as Mistress Overdone, Kate Sullington as Juliet, and Roberto Argenti as a priest.

## THE MERCHANT OF VENICE

A Precision Video production, directed by John Sichel, based on a stage production directed by Jonathan Miller,

FILMS AND VIDEOS  A-55

1969 (1973–4 in the U.S.), with Laurence Olivier as Shylock, Joan Plowright as Portia, Jeremy Brett as Bassanio, Anthony Nicholls as Antonio, Michael Jayston as Gratiano, Anna Carteret as Nerissa, Louise Purnell as Jessica, and Malcolm Reid as Lorenzo.

A BBC Masterpiece Theatre television production by Chris Hunt, Andy Picheta, and Richard Price, directed by Trevor Nunn, based on the Royal National Theatre's Cottesloe production of 1999, which was then moved to the Olivier Theatre; then filmed by Chris Hunt and Trevor Nunn in 2001, with Henry Goodman as Shylock, Derbhle Crotty as Portia, Alex Kelly as Nerissa, Alexander Hanson as Bassanio, David Bamber as Antonio, Richard Henders as Gratiano, Peter De Jersey as Salerio, Mark Umbers as Solanio, Jack James as Lorenzo, Gabrielle Jourdan as Jessica, Andrew French as Launcelot Gobbo, Oscar James as Old Gobbo, Chu Omambala as the Prince of Morocco, and Raymon Coulthard as the Prince of Aragon.

An Arclight Films/Sony Picture Classics production, directed by Michael Radford, 2004, with Al Pacino as Shylock, Jeremy Irons as Antonio, Joseph Fiennes as Bassanio, Lynn Collins as Portia, Zuleikha Robinson as Jessica, Charlie Cox as Lorenzo, Mackenzie Crook as Launcelot Gobbo, Allan Corduner as Tubal, Kris Marshall as Gratiano, John Sessions as Salerio, and Gregor Fisher as Solanio.

A 2011 video recording of Rupert Goold's stage production for the Royal Shakespeare Company, set in modern-day Las Vegas, with Patrick Stewart as Shylock, Susannah Fielding as Portia in a Dolly Parton hairdo, Emily Plumtree as Nerissa, Scott Handy as Antonio (a homosexual professional gambler), Richard Riddell as Bassanio, Caroline Martin as Jessica, Daniel Percival as Lorenzo, Jamie Beamish (an Elvis Presley impersonator) as Launcelot Gobbo, Chris Jarman as the Prince of Morocco, Jason Morell as the Prince of Aragon, Howard Charles as Gratiano, Aidan Kelly as Solanio, and Steve Toussaint as Salerio.

A Grandfather Films adaptation, directed by Douglas Morse for the ADC Theatre at the University of Cambridge in 2008, somewhat in the style of Monty Python's Flying Circus, with Thomas Yarrow as Shylock, Lizzy Crarer as Portia, Natalie Kasterton as Nerissa, Edward Martineau as Bassanio, Molly Goyer Gorman as Gratiano, Mark Corbin as Lorenzo, Stephanie Bain as Jessica, James Everest as Launcelot Gobbo, and Dan Martin as the Princes of Morocco and Aragon.

## A MIDSUMMER NIGHT'S DREAM

A Warner Brothers production, 1935, directed by Max Reinhardt and William Dieterle, with Mickey Rooney as Puck, James Cagney as Bottom, Ian Hunter as Theseus, Verree Teasdale as Hippolyta, Dick Powell as Lysander, Ross Alexander as Demetrius, Olivia de Havilland as Hermia, Jean Muir as Helena, Victor Jory as Oberon, Anita Louise as Titania, and Joe E. Brown as Flute/Thisbe.

A Royal Shakespeare Enterprise production, 1969, directed by Peter Hall, with Derek Godfrey as Theseus, Barbara Jefford as Titania, Paul Rogers as Bottom, Helen Mirren as Hermia, Diana Rigg as Helena, Michael Jayston as Demetrius, David Warner as Lysander, Judi Dench as Titania, Ian Richardson as Oberon, Ian Holm as Puck, and Sebastian Shaw as Peter Quince.

A Lindsay Kemp/David Haughton counterculture production, 1984, directed by Celestino Coronado, with Lindsay Kemp as Puck, Jack Birkett (a.k.a. The Incredible Orlando) as Hippolyta and Titania in drag, François Testory as the Changeling Indian boy, and Michael Matou as Theseus and Oberon, and with an explicit rape of the Amazons by Theseus's soldiers. Some stunning effects in a mix of high camp and low burlesque.

A Fox Searchlight Pictures production, 1999, directed by Michael Hoffman, with David Strathairn as Theseus, Sophie Marceau as Hippolyta, Christian Bale as Demetrius, Dominic West as Lysander, Anna Friel as Hermia, Calista Flockhart as Helena, Stanley Tucci as Puck, Kevin Kline as Bottom, Michelle Pfeiffer as Titania, and Rupert Everett as Oberon.

A 1996 production directed by Adrian Noble for the Royal Shakespeare Company, with Alex Jennings as Theseus and Oberon, Lindsay Duncan as Hippolyta and Titania, Desmond Barrit as Bottom, Finbar Lynch as Puck and Philostrate, Emily Raymond as Helena, Monica Dolan as Hermia, Daniel Evans as Lysander, Kevin Doyle as Demetrius, Alfred Burke as Egeus, and Osheen Jones as the changeling boy.

An Oliver Stockman production, directed by Christine Edzard, of *The Children's Midsummer Night's Dream*, 2001, with Dominic Haywood-Benge as Oberon, Rajouana Zalal as Titania, Leane Lyson as Puck, Oliver Szczypka as Bottom, Danny Bishop as Lysander, John Heyfron as Demetrius, Jamie Peachey as Hermia, Jessica Fowler as Helena, David Joyce as Flute, Daniel Rouse as Quince, Hassan Lahrech as Snug, Jack Nottage as Snout, and Mathew Zelic as Starveling.

A 2006 updating in the "Shakespeare Re-told" series, scripted by Peter Bowker and directed by Ed Fraiman, with Bill Paterson and Imelda Staunton as Theo and Polly, hosts of a party in Dream Park to celebrate the engagement of their daughter Hermia (played by Zoë Tapper) to James (William Ash), until Xander (Rupert Evans), Hermia's preferred choice, shows up. With Sharon Small as Titania, Lennie James as Oberon, Dean Lennox Kelly as Puck, and Johnny Vegas as Bottom, a security guard at Dream Park.

A delightful filming of Benjamin Britten's operatic adaptation, with dialogue entirely from Shakespeare's play, available in DVD as conducted by Bernard Haitink and directed by Peter Hall for the Glyndebourne Festival, 1981, and filmed under Peter Hall's direction in 2004. With Ileanna Cotrubas, James Bowman, Curt Appelgren, Felicity Lott, and Isobel Buchanan.

## MUCH ADO ABOUT NOTHING

A New York Shakespeare Festival production, filming a stage production, 1973, directed by A. J. Antoon, with Sam Waterston and Kathleen Widdoes as Benedick and Beatrice, Barnard Hughes as Dogberry, Glenn Walken as Claudio, April Shawnhan as Hero, and Douglas Watson as Don Pedro.

A Samuel Goldwyn Company production, 1993, directed by Kenneth Branagh, with Branagh and Emma Thompson as Benedick and Beatrice, Denzel Washington as Don Pedro, Keanu Reeves as Don John, Michael Keaton as Dogberry, Richard Briers as Leonato, Robert Sean Leonard as Claudio, Kate Beckinsale as Hero, and Imelda Staunton as Margaret.

A 2005 modern adaptation, in the "Shakespeare Re-told" series, directed by Brian Percival, set in a television news studio, with Sarah Parish and Damian Lewis as Beatrice and Benedick, and with Billie Piper as Hero, Tom Ellis as Claude (Claudio), Martin Jarvis as Leonard (Leonardo), and Derek Riddell as Don (Don John). Adapted by screenwriter David Nicholls.

## OTHELLO

Film Marceau/Mercury Productions, 1952, directed by Orson Welles, with Welles as Othello, Suzanne Cloutier as Desdemona, Michael MacLiammóir as Iago, Michael Lawrence as Cassio, Fay Compton as Emilia, Robert Coote as Roderigo, Hilton Edwards as Brabantio, Nicholas Bruce as Lodovico, Doris Dowling as Bianca, Joseph Cotten as a Senator, and Joan Fontaine as a Page.

A Mosfilm production, in Russian, with subtitles, 1955, directed by Sergei Yutkevich, with Sergei Bondarchuk as Othello, Irina Skobtseva as Desdemona, Andrei Popov as Iago, Vladimir Soshalsky as Cassio, A. Maximova as Emilia, E. Vesnik as Roderigo, and E. Teterin as Brabantio.

A production by Anthony Havelock-Allan and John Brabourne, 1965, directed by Stuart Burge, based on the National Theatre's successful stage production of 1964 directed by John Dexter, with Laurence Olivier as Othello in blackface, Maggie Smith as Desdemona, Frank Finlay as Iago, Derek Jacobi as Cassio, Joyce Redman as Emilia, Robert Lang as Roderigo, Anthony Nicholls as Brabantio, and Sheila Reid as Bianca.

Othello Productions, Inc., 1988, adapted from a stage production at Market Place Theatre, Johannesburg, 1987, directed by Janet Suzman, with John Kani as Othello,

Joanna Weinberg as Desdemona, Richard Haddon Haines as Iago, Stuart Brown as Brabantio, Dorothy Gould as Emilia, Neil McCarthy as Cassio, Frantz Dobrowsky as Roderigo, and Gaynor Young as Bianca.

A production by Greg Smith, 1990, directed by Trevor Nunn, with Willard White as Othello, Imogen Stubbs as Desdemona, Ian McKellen as Iago, Zoë Wanamaker as Emilia, Sean Baker as Cassio, Michael Grandage as Roderigo, and Clive Swift as Brabantio, and Marsha Hunt as Bianca.

A Castle Rock production, 1995, directed by Oliver Parker, with Laurence Fishburne as Othello, Irène Jacob as Desdemona, Kenneth Branagh as Iago, Nathaniel Parker as Cassio, Anne Patrick as Emilia, Michael Maloney as Roderigo, and Pierre Vaneck as Brabantio.

A Merchant-Ivory production, 1965, of *Shakespeare Wallah*, directed by James Ivory, with Felicity Kendal. An adaptation, with scenes from *Othello*.

A production by Michael J. Levy and William Shively of *O*, 2001, with Mekhi Phifer as the Othello-like Odin James, Julia Stiles as the Desdemona-like Desi Brable, and Josh Hartnett as the Iago-like Hugo Goulding. An adaptation.

A 2001 British television adaptation, scripted by Andrew Davies (not using the language of Shakespeare's text) and directed by Geoffrey Sax, with Eamonn Walker as a black police officer in modern-day London named John Othello, Christopher Eccleston as Ben Jago, jealous of Othello's promotion to commissioner of his precinct, Keeley Hawes as Dessie Brabant (Desdemona), Richard Coyle as Michael Cass (Cassio), Rachael Stirling as Lulu (Emilia), Joss Ackland as James Brabant (Brabantio), and Bill Paterson as the London Metropolitan Police Commissioner Sinclair Carver (cf. the Duke of Venice).

A London Globe Theatre production, recorded for television in 2007 as directed by Wilson Milam, with Eamonn Walker as Othello, Tim McInnerny as Iago, Zoë Tapper as Desdemona, Sam Crane as Roderigo, Nick Barber as Cassio, Lorraine Burroughs as Emilia, Zawe Ashton as Bianca, John Stahl as Brabantio, Jonathan Newth as the Duke of Venice, Michael O'Hagan as Gratiano, Nigel Hastings as Montano, and Dickon Tyrrell as Lodovico.

A Canadian Broadcasting Corporation (CBC) television movie of 2008, directed by Zaib Shaikh, with Carlo Rota as Othello, Christine Horne as Desdemona, Matthew Deslippe as Iago, Graham Abbey as Cassio, Emma Campbell as Emilia, Ryan Hollyman as Roderigo, Peter Donaldson as Brabantio, Jonathan Goad as Montano, Nazneen Contractor as Bianca, and John Gilbert as the Duke of Venice.

A film of Verdi's opera, *Otello*, directed by Franco Zeffirelli, 1986, with Placido Domingo as Otello and Justino Diaz as Iago.

## RICHARD II

A BBC/Time-Life Television production, 1978–9, directed by David Giles, with Derek Jacobi as King Richard, Janet Maw as the Queen, Jon Finch as Bolingbroke, John Gielgud as John of Gaunt, Charles Gray as the Duke of York, David Swift as Northumberland, Wendy Hiller as the Duchess of York, and Mary Morris as the Duchess of Gloucester.

A BBC/The Globe Theatre production, 2003, in an all-male cast, directed by Tim Carroll, with Mark Rylance as King Richard, Liam Brennan as Bolingbroke, John McEnery as John of Gaunt, Michael Brown as the Queen, Terence McGinty as Mowbray, Chu Omambala as Aumerle, William Osbourne as the Duchess of Gloucester, and Bill Stewart as the Duke of York.

## RICHARD III

A London Films Productions, 1955, directed by Laurence Olivier, with Olivier as Richard, Claire Bloom as the Lady Anne, Cedric Hardwicke as King Edward IV, Ralph Richardson as the Duke of Buckingham, John Gielgud as the Duke of Clarence, Alec Clunes as Lord Hastings, Norman Wooland as Catesby, Esmond Knight as Ratcliffe, Mary Kerridge as Queen Elizabeth, Helen Haye as the Duchess of York, Pamela Brown as Jane Shore, Laurence Naismith as Lord Stanley, and Stanley Baker as the Earl of Richmond.

A Bayly-Paré Productions/United Artists production, 1995–6, directed by Richard Loncraine, with Ian Mc-Kellen as Richard, Kristin Scott Thomas as the Lady Anne, Jim Broadbent as the Duke of Buckingham, Nigel Hawthorne as the Duke of Clarence, John Wood as King Edward IV, Jim Carter as Hastings, Tim McInnerny as Catesby, Annette Bening as Queen Elizabeth, Maggie Smith as the Duchess of York, Robert Downey Jr. as Lord Rivers, Adrian Dunbar as Tyrell, Bill Patterson as Ratcliffe, Edward Harwicke as Stanley, Kate Stevenson-Payne as Princess Elizabeth of York, and Dominic West as the Earl of Richmond.

A Twentieth Century Fox production, *Looking for Richard*, 1996, directed by Al Pacino. A documentary about Pacino's stage interpretation of Richard. With Pacino as Richard, Winona Ryder as the Lady Anne, Kevin Spacey as the Duke of Buckingham, Alec Baldwin as Clarence, and Aidan Quinn as the Earl of Richmond.

## ROMEO AND JULIET

Verona Productions, 1954, directed by Renato Castallani, with John Gielgud as Chorus, Laurence Harvey and Susan Shentall as Romeo and Juliet, Ubaldo Zollo as Mercutio, Enzo Fiermonte as Tybalt, Flora Robson as the Nurse, Norman Wooland as Paris, Mervyn Johns as Friar Laurence, Bill Travers as Benvolio, Sebastian Cabot as Capulet, and Lydia Sherwood as Capulet's wife.

A Paramount production, 1968, directed by Franco Zeffirelli, with Leonard Whiting and Olivia Hussey as Romeo and Juliet, Michael York as Tybalt, John McEnery as Mercutio, Pat Heywood as the Nurse, Milo O'Shea as Friar Laurence, Bruce Robinson as Benvolio, Paul Hardwick as Capulet, Natasha Parry as Capulet's wife, Roberto Bisacco as Count Paris, and Robert Stephens as Prince Escalus.

A Twentieth Century Fox production, 1996, *Romeo + Juliet,* directed by Baz Luhrmann, with Leonardo DiCaprio and Claire Danes as Romeo and Juliet, Harold Perrineau as Mercutio, Miriam Margolyes as the Nurse, Pete Postlethwaite as Friar Laurence, John Leguizamo as Tybalt, Jesse Bradford as Benvolio, Paul Sorvino as Fulgencio Capulet, Diane Venora as Gloria Capulet, Paul Rudd as Dave Paris, Brian Dennehy as Ted Montague, and Vondie Curtis-Hall as the Prince.

A film version, based on a popular London Globe Theatre production directed by Dominic Dromgoole, 2009, with Adetomiwa Edun as Romeo, Ellie Kendrick as Juliet, Philip Cumbus as Mercutio, Jack Farthing as Benvolio, Ukweli Roach as Tybalt, Rawiri Paratene as Friar Laurence, Tom Stuart as Count Paris, Michael O'Hagan as Montague, Holly Atkins as Montague's wife, Ian Redford as Capulet, Miranda Foster as Capulet's wife, Penny Layden as the Nurse, Graham Vick as Abraham and the Apothecary, and Andrew Vincent as the Prince.

A United Artists production of *West Side Story,* 1961, directed by Jerome Robbins and Robert Wise, with Richard Beymer as Tony, Natalie Wood as Maria, George Chakiris as Bernardo, and Rita Moreno as Anita. An adaptation.

A production by David Parfitt, Marc Norman, and others, of *Shakespeare in Love,* 1998, directed by John Madden, with Joseph Fiennes as Shakespeare/Romeo, Gwyneth Paltrow as Viola de Lesseps/Thomas Kent/Juliet, Colin Firth as Lord Wessex, Imelda Staunton as the Nurse, Ben Affleck as Ned Alleyn, Geoffrey Rush as Philip Henslowe, Rupert Everett as Christopher Marlowe, Tom Wilkinson as Fennyman, Martin Clunes as Richard Burbage, and Judi Dench as Queen Elizabeth I. An adaptation by Tom Stoppard containing scenes from *Romeo and Juliet.*

## THE TAMING OF THE SHREW

A United Artists/Pickford Corporation production, 1929, directed by Sam Taylor, with Douglas Fairbanks Sr. and Mary Pickford as Petruchio and Kate, Edwin Maxwell as Baptista Minola, Dorothy Jordan as Bianca, Geoffrey Wardell as Hortensio, Joseph Cawthorn as Gremio, and Clyde Cook as Grumio.

A Royal Films International production, 1966–7, directed by Franco Zeffirelli, with Richard Burton and Elizabeth Taylor as Petruchio and Kate, Natasha Pyne as

Bianca, Michael Hordern as Baptista Minola, Michael York as Lucentio, Alfred Lynch as Tranio, Victor Spinetti as Hortensio, Alan Webb as Gremio, Cyril Cusack as Grumio, and Bice Valori as the Widow.

A NET/American Conservatory Theatre production, 1976, in commedia dell'arte style, directed by William Ball and Kirk Browning, with Marc Singer and Fredi Olster as Petruchio and Kate, Stephen St. Paul as Lucentio, Raye Birk as Gremio, Ronald Boussom as Grumio, Rick Hamilton as Tranio, William Paterson as Baptista Minola, and Sandra Shotwell as Bianca.

Bard Productions, 1983, directed by John Allison, with Franklyn Seales and Karen Austin as Petruchio and Kate, Larry Drake as Baptista Minola, Bruce Davison as Tranio, Jeremy Lawrence as Grumio, Kay E. Kuter as Gremio, Charles Berendt as Hortensio, and Kathryn Jonson as Bianca.

A Metro-Goldwyn-Mayer production of *Kiss Me, Kate*, 1953, directed by George Sidney, with Howard Keel as Fred Graham/Petruchio, Kathryn Grayson as Lili Vanessi/Kate, Ann Miller as Lois Lane/Bianca, Tommy Rall as Bill Calhoun/Lucentio, Ron Randell as Cole Porter, Keenan Wynn as Lippy, and James Whitmore as Slug. An adaptation.

A Jaret Entertainment production of *10 Things I Hate About You*, 1999, directed by Gil Junger, with Julia Stiles as Katharina 'Kat' Stratford, Heath Ledger as the Petruchio-like Patrick Verona, Larisa Oleynik as Bianca Stratford, Larry Miller as the girls' father (Dr. Walter Stratford), David Krumholtz as the Tranio-like Michael Eckman, Joseph Gordon-Leavitt as the Lucentio-like Cameron James, and Andrew Keegan as the Hortensio- and Grumio-like Joey Donner. An adaptation.

A 2005 modern adaptation, in the "Shakespeare Re-told" series, directed by David Richard, with Shirley Henderson as Katharine Minola, member of Parliament and aspiring prime minister, Jaime Murray as her sister and supermodel Bianca, Rufus Sewell as a spendthrift Petruchio, Stephen Tompkinson as Harry (cf. Hortensio), Twiggy as Kate and Bianca's mother (not in Shakespeare's play), and David Mitchell as Kate's hapless secretary, Tim. Adapted by screenwriter Sally Wainwright.

THE TEMPEST

A BBC/Time-Life Television production, 1981, directed by John Gorrie, with Michael Hordern as Prospero, Pippa Guard as Miranda, David Dixon as Ariel, Christopher Guard as Ferdinand, Derek Godfrey as Antonio, David Waller as Alonso, Warren Clarke as Caliban, Nigel Hawthorne as Stephano, and Andrew Sachs as Trinculo. Reviewers were generally disappointed; it is listed here in the absence of any other reliable "straight" interpretation of the play on film.

A Boyd's Company production, 1979–80, directed by Derek Jarman, with Heathcote Williams as Prospero, Toyah Willcox as Miranda, David Meyer as Ferdinand, Karl Johnson as Ariel, Jack Birkett (a.k.a. the Incredible Orlando) as Caliban, Christopher Biggins as Stephano, Peter Turner as Trinculo, Peter Bull as Alonso, Richard Warwick as Antonio, Neil Cunningham as Sebastian, Ken Campbell as Gonzalo, and Elisabeth Welch as a goddess singing "Stormy Weather." A starkly transgressive and postmodern film that some viewers find offensive, but compelling.

A production by Kees Kasander, 1991, *Prospero's Books*, directed by Peter Greenaway, in which John Gielgud as Prospero speaks most of the lines. With Isabelle Pasco as Miranda, Mark Rylance as Ferdinand, Michael Clark as Caliban, and several figures representing Ariel. Strange but fascinating.

A film adaptation of 2010, shot on the Hawaiian island of Lanai, directed by Julie Taymor, starring Helen Mirren as Prospera, the Duchess of Milan, with Felicity Jones as Miranda, Reeve Carney as Ferdinand, Djimon Hounsou as Caliban, Ben Whishaw as Ariel, Russell Brand as Trinculo, Alfred Molina as Stephano, Chris Cooper as Antonio, Alan Cumming as Sebastian, David Strathairn as Alonso, Tom Conti as Gonzalo, Jude Akuwudike as the Boatswain, and David Scott Klein as Prospera's husband.

A production by Nicholas Nayfack, 1956, of *Forbidden Planet*, an adaptation of *The Tempest* as a journey into space, directed by Fred McLeod Wilcox, with Walter Pidgeon as the Prospero-like Doctor Morbius, Anne Francis as the Miranda-like Altaira, Leslie Nielsen as the Ferdinand-like Commander J. J. Adams, and Robby the Robot as the Ariel-like servant to Doctor Morbius.

A Columbia Pictures production, 1982, an adaptation in a twentieth-century setting, with John Cassavetes as the Prospero-like Philip, Molly Ringwald as Miranda, Raul Julia as Kalianos, and Susan Sarandon as the Ariel-like Aretha.

TWELFTH NIGHT

An Incorporated Television Company production, 1970, directed by John Sichel, with Joan Plowright as Viola, Gary Raymond as Orsino, Adrienne Corri as Olivia, Alec Guinness as Malvolio, Tommy Steele as Feste, John Moffat as Sir Andrew Aguecheek, Ralph Richardson as Sir Toby Belch, and Sheila Reid as Maria.

A 1988 production directed by Kenneth Branagh for the Renaissance Theatre Company, with Richard Briers as Malvolio, Caroline Langrishe as Olivia, Frances Barber as Viola, Anton Lesser as Feste, Christopher Ravenscroft as Orsino, James Saxon as Sir Toby, James Simmons as Sir Andrew, Christopher Hollis as Sebastian and Curio, Tim Barker as Antonio and the Sea Captain, Abigail McKern as Maria, and Shaun Prendergast as Fabian. With original music by Paul McCartney and Pat Doyle.

A Renaissance Films/Summit Entertainment production, 1996, directed by Trevor Nunn, with Imogen Stubbs as Viola, Helena Bonham Carter as Olivia, Toby Stephens as Orsino, Ben Kingsley as Feste, Nigel Hawthorne as Malvolio, Imelda Staunton as Maria, Stephen Mackintosh as Sebastian, Mel Smith as Sir Toby Belch, Richard E. Grant as Sir Andrew Aguecheek, and Peter Gunn as Fabian.

## THE WINTER'S TALE
A BBC/Time-Life Television production, 1980–1, directed by Jane Howell, with Jeremy Kemp as Leontes, Anna Calder-Marshall as Hermione, Robert Stephens as Polixenes, Debbie Farrington as Perdita, Robin Kermode as Florizel, David Burke as Camillo, Margaret Tyzack as Paulina, Cyril Luckham as Antigonus, Rikki Fulton as Autolycus, and Paul Jesson as the Young Shepherd or Clown.

A version filmed for TV and based on the Royal Shakespeare Company's 1999 production at the Barbican Theatre, London, directed by Robin Lough and Gregory Doran, with Antony Sher as Leontes, Alexandra Gilbreath as Hermione, Emily Bruni as Perdita, Ryan McCluskey as Florizel, Estelle Kohler as Paulina, Jeffrey Wickham as Antigonus, Ken Bones as Polixenes, Geoffrey Freshwater as Camillo, Ian Hughes as Autolycus, James Hayes as the Old Shepherd, and Christopher Brand as the Young Shepherd.

# THE ROYAL GENEALOGY OF ENGLAND, 1154–1625

## THE PLANTAGENET KINGS

## THE LANCASTRIAN KINGS

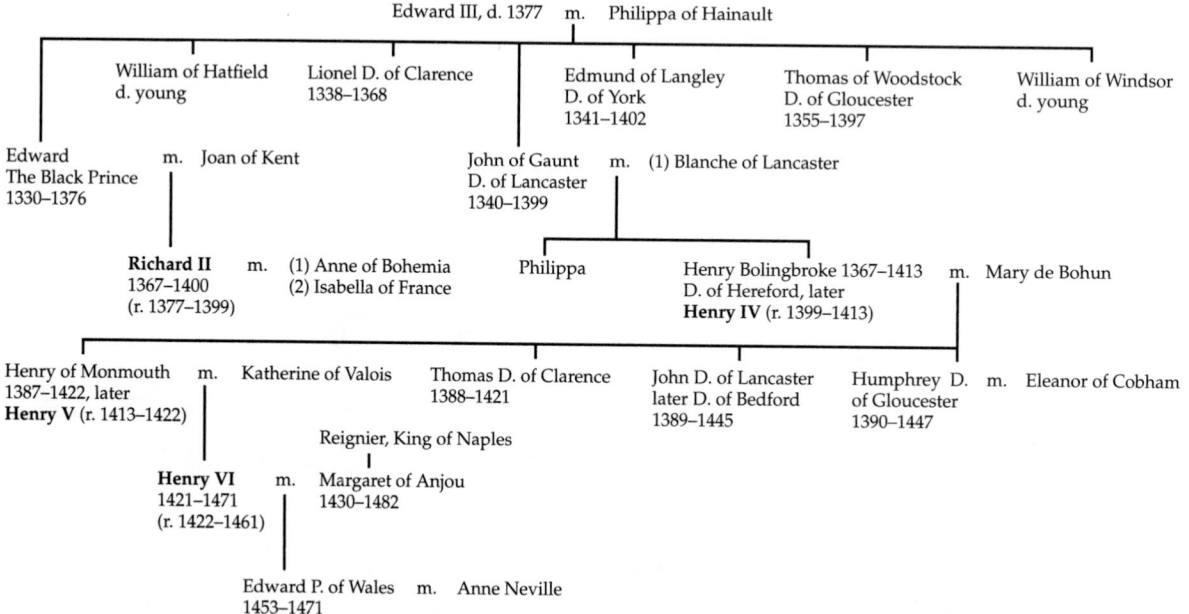

*In these diagrams, reigning dates are given in parentheses; other dates indicate life span. Abbreviations: P., Prince, D., Duke, E., Earl; b., born, d., died, m., married, r., reigned. English monarchs are printed in boldface type. The spatial arrangement of names in a family indicates order of birth.*

*In 1 Henry IV, Shakespeare confuses the Edmund Mortimer who married Glendower's daughter and died in 1409 with his nephew Edmund, fifth Earl of March, who asserted a claim to the English throne (see "The Yorkist Kings"). Shakespeare also refers to Henry Percy's (Hotspur's) wife as "Kate," though historically she was named Elizabeth.*

*Catherine Swynford, third wife of John of Gaunt (see "The Tudor Kings"), bore him children before their eventual marriage. These Beauforts, although later legitimized, were specifically barred from any claim to the English throne.*

# THE YORKIST KINGS

# THE TUDOR KINGS

# Maps

*A map of London* (below) *of Shakespeare's time shows the prominent landmarks, as well as the theaters and other places where plays were performed.*
*A map of England and western France* (opposite) *gives the locations for the scenes of Shakespeare's history plays.*

# ENGLAND AND WESTERN FRANCE

**IRELAND**

Dublin

Isle of Man

Carlisle

Berwick

**IRISH SEA**

**NORTH SEA**

Durham

Lancaster

Carnarvon · Conway

York
Towton
Pomfret
Wakefield

Chester

Doncaster

Derby
Nottingham
Lincoln
Ravenspur
Humber

Milford Haven
Pembroke

Shrewsbury

**ATLANTIC**

**OCEAN**

Bosworth
Worcester · Leicester
Coventry
Warwick
Hereford
Monmouth
Tewkesbury
Gloucester
Berkeley
Bristol

Northampton
Bedford

The Wash

Oxford

Ely · Norwich
Cambridge

Exeter

Plymouth

Salisbury

Weymouth
Winchester

St. Albans
Barnet
Guildford · LONDON
Southampton

Bury St. Edmunds
Ipswich

Rochester
Lewes
Canterbury
Dover

Isle of Wight

**ENGLISH CHANNEL**

Brest

Cherbourg

Boulogne
Calais
Flushing

Fécamp

Guines · Dunkirk

Dieppe

Agincourt
Ghent
Antwerp

St.-Lô

Harfleur

Crécy
Lille
Abbeville
Brussels

Caen

**BRITTANY**

Vannes · Rennes

**NORMANDY**

Rouen

Amiens

Évreux

Beauvais

**MAINE**

Alençon

Pontoise
Compiègne

Nantes

Le Mans

**ILE DE FRANCE**

PARIS
Meaux

Angiers

Chartres

Reims

**ANJOU**

Saumur

**BAY OF BISCAY**

**POITOU**

La Rochelle

Tours

Orleans

**BERRY**

**CHAMPAGNE**

Poitiers

Troyes

Cognac

Toul

**BOURBON**

Angoulême

Limoges

Nevers

**BURGUNDY**

Bordeaux

**LIMOUSIN**

Dijon

Perigueux

**AQUITAINE**

Bayonne

**GASCONY**

miles 0 50 100 150

R.J.B.

# Bibliography

**Abbreviations Used**

| | |
|---|---|
| *English Literary History* | *ELH* |
| *Publications of the Modern* | |
| *Language Association of America* | *PMLA* |
| *Shakespeare Quarterly* | *SQ* |
| *Shakespeare Studies* | *ShakS* |
| *Shakespeare Survey* | *ShS* |

## *Works of Reference*

Abbott, E. A. *A Shakespearian Grammar.* New ed., London, 1870.

Allen, Michael J. B., and Kenneth Muir, eds. *Shakespeare's Plays in Quarto.* Berkeley, 1981.

Bentley, G. E. *The Jacobean and Caroline Stage.* 7 vols. Oxford, 1941–1968.

Berger, Thomas L., William C. Bradford, and Sidney L. Sondergard, eds. *An Index of Characters in Early Modern English Drama: Printed Plays, 1500–1660.* Cambridge, Eng., 1998.

Bergeron, David M. *Shakespeare: A Study and Research Guide.* New York, 1975; 2nd ed., rev. David Bergeron and Geraldo de Sousa. Lawrence, Kans., 1987.

Bullough, Geoffrey, ed. *Narrative and Dramatic Sources of Shakespeare.* 8 vols. London, 1957–1975.

Chambers, E.K. *The Elizabethan Stage.* 4 vols. Oxford, 1923; rev., 1945.

———. *The Mediaeval Stage.* 2 vols. Oxford, 1903.

———. *William Shakespeare: A Study of Facts and Problems.* 2 vols. Oxford, 1930.

Dent, R. W. *Shakespeare's Proverbial Language: An Index.* Berkeley, 1981.

Edelman, Charles. *Shakespeare's Military Language: A Dictionary.* London and New Brunswick, 2000.

Garland Shakespeare Bibliographies, gen. ed. William Godshalk. Published in separate volumes for various plays, at varying dates. Garland: New York.

Gillespie, Stuart. *Shakespeare's Books: A Dictionary of Shakespeare's Resources.* London, 2001.

Greg, W. W. *A Bibliography of the English Printed Drama to the Restoration.* 4 vols. London, 1939–1959.

———, ed. *Shakespeare Quarto Facsimiles.* London, 1939–. (An incomplete set; Greg's work has been supplemented by Charlton Hinman.)

Harbage, Alfred. *Annals of English Drama, 975–1700.* Rev. S. Schoenbaum. Philadelphia, 1964; 3rd ed., Sylvia Stoler Wagonheim, 1989.

Hinman, Charlton, ed. *The Norton Facsimile: The First Folio of Shakespeare.* New York, 1968.

Hosley, Richard, ed. *Shakespeare's Holinshed.* New York, 1968.

Kökeritz, Helge. *Shakespeare's Names.* New Haven, 1959.

———. *Shakespeare's Pronunciation.* New Haven, 1953.

Long, John. *Shakespeare's Use of Music: Comedies.* Gainesville, Fla., 1955. *Final Comedies,* 1961; *Histories and Tragedies,* 1971.

McDonald, Russ. *The Bedford Companion to Shakespeare: An Introduction with Documents.* Boston, 1996; 2nd ed., 2001.

McManaway, James G., and Jeanne Addison Roberts, compilers. *A Selective Bibliography of Shakespeare.* Charlottesville, Va., 1975.

Muir, Kenneth. *Shakespeare's Sources.* 2 vols. London, 1957.

———, and S. Schoenbaum, eds. *A New Companion to Shakespeare Studies.* London and New York, 1971.

Munro, John, ed. *The Shakespeare Allusion Book.* 2 vols. London and New York, 1909; reissued 1932.

Naylor, Edward W. *Shakespeare and Music.* New ed., London, 1931.

Noble, Richmond. *Shakespeare's Biblical Knowledge and Use of the Book of Common Prayer.* London, 1935.

———. *Shakespeare's Use of Song.* London, 1923.

Onions, C. T. *A Shakespeare Glossary.* Rev. and enlgd. R. D. Eagleson. Oxford, 1986.

Pegasus Shakespeare Bibliographies. Annotated bibliographies of Shakespeare studies in a 12-volume series, gen. ed. Richard L. Nochimson, including *Love's Labor's Lost, A Midsummer Night's Dream,* and *The Merchant of Venice* (Clifford Chalmers Huffman), *Richard II, Henry IV, I and II,* and *Henry V* (Joseph Candido), *Hamlet* (Michael E. Mooney), *The Rape of Lucrece, Titus Andronicus, Julius Caesar, Antony and Cleopatra,* and *Coriolanus* (Clifford Chalmers Huffman and John W. Velz), *King Lear* and *Macbeth* (Rebecca W. Bushnell), and *Shakespeare and the Renaissance Stage to 1616* and *Shakespearean Stage History 1616 to 1998* (Hugh Macrae Richmond). Binghamton, N.Y., 1995, and Asheville, N.C., 1996—.

*Publications of the Modern Language Association of America (PMLA).* Annual Bibliography.

Rothwell, Kenneth S., and Annabelle Henkin Melzer. *Shakespeare on Screen: An International Filmography and Videography.* New York and London, 1990.

Schmidt, Alexander. *Shakespeare-Lexicon.* 5th ed. Berlin, 1962.

Seager, H. W. *Natural History in Shakespeare's Time.* London, 1896.

Seng, Peter J. *The Vocal Songs in the Plays of Shakespeare.* Cambridge, Mass., 1967.

Shaheen, Naseeb. *Biblical References in Shakespeare's Plays.* Newark, Del., and London, 1999.

*Shakespeare Bulletin.*

*Shakespeare-Jahrbuch.*

*Shakespeare Newsletter.*

*Shakespeare Quarterly.* Annual Bibliography.

*Shakespeare Studies.*

*Shakespeare Survey.*

Spencer, T. J. B., ed. *Shakespeare's Plutarch.* Harmondsworth, Eng., 1964.

Spevack, Marvin. *The Harvard Concordance to Shakespeare.* Cambridge, Mass., 1973.

Thomson, J. A. K. *Shakespeare and the Classics.* London, 1952.

Wells, Stanley, ed. *Shakespeare: Select Bibliographical Guides*. London, 1973.

———, ed. *The Cambridge Companion to Shakespeare Studies*. Cambridge, Eng., 1986.

## Life in Shakespeare's England

Allen, Don Cameron. *The Star-Crossed Renaissance*. Durham, N.C., 1941.

Appelbaum, Robert. *Aguecheek's Beef, Belch's Hiccup, and Other Gastronomic Interjections: Literature, Culture, and Food Among the Early Moderns*. Chicago, 2006.

Baker, Herschel. *The Image of Man: A Study of the Idea of Human Dignity in Classical Antiquity, the Middle Ages, and the Renaissance*. Cambridge, Mass., 1961. (First published in 1947 as *The Dignity of Man*.)

———. *The Wars of Truth: Studies in the Decay of Christian Humanism in the Earlier Seventeenth Century*. Cambridge, Mass., 1952.

Bakhtin, Mikhail M. *Rabelais and His World*, trans. H. Iswolsky. Cambridge, Mass., 1968.

Barkan, Leonard. *Nature's Work of Art: The Human Body as Image of the World*. New Haven, 1975.

———. *The Gods Made Flesh: Metamorphosis and the Pursuit of Paganism*. New Haven, 1986.

Barkan, Leonard, Bradin Cormack, and Sean Keilen, eds. *The Forms of Renaissance Thought: New Essays in Literature and Culture*. Basingstoke, Hampshire, 2009.

Barroll, J. Leeds. *Politics, Plague, and Shakespeare's Theater: The Stuart Years*. Ithaca, N.Y., 1991.

Bertram, Benjamin. *The Time Is Out of Joint: Skepticism in Shakespeare's England*. Newark, Del., and Cranbury, N.J., 2004.

Bindoff, S. T., et al., eds. *Elizabethan Government and Society*. Essays presented to Sir John Neale. London, 1961.

Bromley, James M. *Intimacy and Sexuality in the Age of Shakespeare*. Cambridge, Eng., 2012.

Brown, Georgia. *Redefining Elizabethan Literature*. Cambridge, Eng., 2004

Bush, Douglas. *The Renaissance and English Humanism*. Toronto, 1939.

Buxton, John. *Elizabethan Taste*. London, 1963.

Byrne, Muriel St. Clare. *Elizabethan Life in Town and Country*. 8th ed. London, 1970.

Camden, Carroll. *The Elizabethan Woman*. Houston, 1952.

Caspari, Fritz. *Humanism and the Social Order in Tudor England*. Chicago, 1954.

Cassirer, Ernst. *The Platonic Renaissance in England*, trans. J. E. Pettegrove. Austin, Tex., 1953.

Cefalu, Paul. *Moral Identity in Early Modern English Literature*. Cambridge, Eng., 2004.

Clark, Glenn, Judith Owens, and Greg T. Smith. *City Limits: Perspectives on the Historical European City*. Montreal, 2010.

Cormack, Bradin. *A Power to Do Justice: Jurisdiction, English Literature, and the Rise of Common Law, 1509–1625*. Chicago, 2007.

Crockett, Bryan. *The Play of Paradox: Stage and Sermon in Renaissance England*. Philadelphia, 1995.

Curran, Kevin. *Marriage, Performance, and Politics at the Jacobean Court*. Farnham, Surrey, 2009.

De Grazia, Margreta, Maureen Quilligan, and Peter Stallybrass, eds. *Subject and Object in Renaissance Culture*. Cambridge, Eng., 1996.

Dimmock, Matthew, and Andrew Hatfield, eds. *Literature and Popular Culture in Early Modern England*. Farnham, Eng., 2009.

Dobranski, Stephen B. *Readers and Authorship in Early Modern England*. Cambridge, Eng., 2005.

Dubrow, Heather, and Richard Strier, eds. *The Historical Renaissance: New Essays on Tudor and Stuart Literature and Culture*. Chicago, 1988.

Einstein, Lewis. *Tudor Ideals*. New York, 1921.

Elizabeth I. *Collected Works*, eds. Leah S. Marcus, Janel Mueller, and Mary Beth Rose. Chicago, 2000.

Elton, G. R. *The Tudor Revolution in Government*. Cambridge, Eng., 1959.

Fisher, Will. *Materializing Gender in Early Modern English Literature and Culture*. Cambridge, Eng., 2006.

Fumerton, Patricia, and Simon Hunt, eds. *Renaissance Culture and the Everyday*. Philadelphia, 1999.

Gallagher, Lowell. *Medusa's Gaze: Casuistry and Conscience in the Renaissance*. Stanford, 1991.

Hackel, Heidi Brayman. *Reading Material in Early Modern England: Print, Gender, and Literacy*. Cambridge, Eng., 2005.

Harrison, G. B. *An Elizabethan Journal*. London, 1928; supplements.

———. *A Jacobean Journal . . . 1603–1606*. London, 1941.

———. *A Second Jacobean Journal . . . 1607 to 1610*. Ann Arbor, Mich., 1958.

Haydn, Hiram. *The Counter-Renaissance*. New York, 1950.

Helgerson, Richard. *Forms of Nationhood: The Elizbethan Writing of England*. Chicago, 1992.

———. *Adulterous Alliances: Home, State, and History in Early Modern European Drama and Painting*. Chicago, 2000.

Heninger, S. K., Jr. *A Handbook of Renaissance Meteorology*. Durham, N.C., 1960.

Hirst, Derek. *Authority and Conflict: England, 1603–1658*. Cambridge, Mass., 1986.

Hirst, Derek, and Richard Strier, eds. *Writing and Political Engagement in Seventeenth-Century England*. Cambridge, Eng., 1999.

Huizinga, Johan. *The Waning of the Middle Ages*. London, 1924; Baltimore, 1955.

Hurstfield, Joel, *Elizabeth I and the Unity of England*. London, 1960.

Jones, Ann Rosalind, and Peter Stallybrass. *Renaissance Clothing and the Materials of Memory*. Cambridge, Eng., 2000.

Jordan, Constance. *Renaissance Feminism: Literary Texts and Political Models*. Ithaca, N.Y., 1990.

Judges, A. V., ed. *The Elizabethan Underworld*. London and New York, 1930. Rpt., London, 1965.

Kewes, Paulina, ed. *Plagiarism in Early Modern England*. Basingstoke, Hampshire, Eng., 2003.

Kingsley-Smith, Jane. *Cupid in Early Modern Literature and Culture*. Cambridge, Eng., 2010.

Knapp, Jeffrey. *Shakespeare's Tribe: Church, Nation, and Theater in Renaissance England*. Chicago, 2002.

Knights, L. C. *Drama and Society in the Age of Jonson*. London, 1937.

Kocher, Paul. *Science and Religion in Elizabethan England*. San Marino, Calif., 1953.

Landreth, David. *The Face of Mammon: The Matter of Money in English Renaissance Literature*. Oxford, 2012.

Lee, Morris. *Great Britain's Solomon: James VI and I in His Three Kingdoms*. Urbana, Ill., 1990.

Lemon, Rebecca. *Treason by Words: Literature, Law, and Rebellion in Shakespeare's England*. Ithaca, N.Y., 2006.

Leinwand, Theodore B. *Theatre, Finance and Society in Early Modern England*. Cambridge, Eng., 1999.

Lockey, Brian C. *Law and Empire in English Renaissance Literature*. Cambridge, Eng., 2006.

Loewenstein, David, and John Marshall, eds. *Heresy, Literature, and Politics in Early Modern English Culture*. Cambridge, Eng., 2006.

Longfellow, Erica. *Women and Religious Writing in Early Modern England*. Cambridge, Eng., 2004.

Lovejoy, A. O. *The Great Chain of Being*. Cambridge, Mass., 1936.

MacCaffrey, Wallace T. *The Shaping of the Elizabethan Regime*. Princeton, 1968.

MacFaul, Tom. *Poetry and Paternity in Renaissance England: Sidney, Spenser, Shakespeare, Donne, and Jonson*. Cambridge, Eng., 2010.

Maquerlot, Jean-Pierre, and Michéle Willems. *Travel and Drama in Shakespeare's Time*. Cambridge, Eng., 1996.

Marotti, Arthur F., ed. *Catholicism and Anti-Catholicism in Early Modern English Texts*. Basingstoke, Hampshire, Eng., 1999.

Matar, Nabil. *Turks, Moors, and Englishmen in the Age of Discovery*. New York, 1999.

Mattingly, Garrett. *The Armada*. Boston, 1959.

McEachern, Claire, and Debora Shuger, eds. *Religion and Culture in Renaissance England*. Cambridge, Eng., 1997.

McElwee, W. *The Wisest Fool in Christendom*. [About James VI and I.] New York, 1958.

McPeek, James A. S. *The Black Book of Knaves and Unthrifts in Shakespeare and Other Renaissance Authors*. Storrs, Conn., 1969.

Monta, Susannah Brietz. *Martyrdom and Literature in Early Modern England*. Cambridge, Eng., 2005.

Montrose, Louis. *The Subject of Elizabeth: Authority, Gender, and Representation*. Chicago, 2006.

Neale, John E. *Elizabeth I and Her Parliaments*. 2 vols. London and New York, 1953–1958.

———. *The Elizabethan House of Commons*. London, 1949.

———. *Queen Elizabeth I*. London, 1934; New York, 1957.

Nichols, John, ed. *The Progresses and Public Processions of Queen Elizabeth*. 3 vols. London, 1823.

Orlin, Lena Cowen, ed. *Material London, ca. 1600*. Philadelphia, 2000.

Osherow, Michele. *Biblical Women's Voices in Early Modern England*. Farnham, Eng., and Burlington, Vt., 2009.

Patterson, Annabel M. *Reading Holinshed's Chronicles*. Chicago, 1994.

Peck, Linda Levy. *Court Patronage and Corruption in Early Stuart England*. Boston, 1990.

Penrose, Boies. *Travel and Discovery in the Renaissance, 1420–1620*. Cambridge, Mass., 1955.

Perry, Curtis. *Literature and Favoritism in Early Modern England*. Cambridge, Eng., 2006.

Porter, Stephen. *Shakespeare's London: Everyday Life in London 1580–1616*. Stroud, Gloucestershire, 2009.

Quinones, Ricardo J. *The Renaissance Discovery of Time*. Cambridge, Mass., 1972.

Rivlin, Elizabeth. *The Aesthetics of Service in Early Modern England*. Evanston, Il., 2012.

Rowse, A. L. *The England of Elizabeth: The Structure of Society*. London, 1951.

Schwyzer, Philip. *Literature, Nationalism, and Memory in Early Modern England and Wales*. Cambridge, Eng., 2004.

Spiller, Elizabeth. *Science, Reading, and Renaissance Literature: The Art of Making Knowledge*. Cambridge, Eng., 2005.

Stallybrass, Peter, and Allon White. *The Politics and Poetics of Transgression*. Ithaca, N.Y., and London, 1986.

Stone, Lawrence. *The Crisis of the Aristocracy, 1558–1641*. Oxford, 1965.

———. *The Family, Sex and Marriage in England, 1500–1800*. London, 1977.

Stow, John. *Survey of London*, ed. C. L. Kingsford. Oxford, 1971.

Strier, Richard. *Resistant Structures: Particularity, Radicalism, and Renaissance Texts*. Berkeley, 1995.

———. *The Unrepentant Renaissance: From Petrarch to Shakespeare to Milton*. Chicago, 2011.

Swift, Daniel. *Shakespeare's Common Prayers: The Book of Common Prayer and the Elizabethan Age*. Oxford, 2012.

Targoff, Ramie. *Common Prayer: The Language of Public Devotion in Early Modern England*. Chicago, 2001.

Tawney, R. H. *Religion and the Rise of Capitalism*. New York, 1926, 1962.

Tillyard, E. M. W. *The Elizabethan World Picture*. London, 1943, 1967.

Trevor, Douglas. *The Poetics of Melancholy in Early Modern England*. Cambridge, Eng., 2004.

Underdown, David. *Revel, Riot, and Rebellion: Popular Politics and Culture in England, 1603–1660*. Oxford, 1985.

Whigham, Frank. *Ambition and Privilege: The Social Tropes of Elizabethan Courtesy Theory*. Berkeley, 1984.

Willson, David Harris. *King James VI & I*. New York, 1956.

Wilson, F. P. *Elizabethan and Jacobean*. Oxford, 1945.

Wilson, J. Dover, ed. *Life in Shakespeare's England*. Cambridge, Eng., 1911; 2nd ed., 1926.

Witmore, Michael. *Culture of Accidents: Unexpected Knowledges in Early Modern England*. Stanford, 2001.

Woodbridge, Linda. *Vagrancy, Homelessness, and English Renaissance Literature*. Urbana, Ill., 2001.

Wormerley, David. *Divinity and State*. Oxford, 2012.

Wright, Louis B. *Middle-Class Culture in Elizabethan England*. Chapel Hill, N.C., 1935.

Wrightson, Keith. *English Society, 1580–1680*. New Brunswick, N.J., 1982.

Wyatt, Michael. *The Italian Encounter with Tudor England: A Cultural Politics of Translation*. Cambridge, Eng., 2005.

Zeeveld, W. Gordon. *Foundations of Tudor Policy*. Cambridge, Mass., 1948.

## Shakespeare's Predecessors and Contemporaries

See also, under *Works of Reference*, Bentley, Chambers, Greg, and Harbage; under *London Theaters and Dramatic Companies*, McMillin and MacLean; under *Shakespeare Criticism Since 1980*, Dollimore, Garber (*Cannibals*), Goldberg, Greenblatt, Jardine, Loomba, Mullaney, Newman, and Skura; under *The Histories*, Ribner; and under *The Tragedies*, Bushnell.

Alford, John A. *From Page to Performance: Essays in Early English Drama*. East Lansing, Mich., 1995.

Altman, Joel B. *The Tudor Play of Mind: Rhetorical Inquiry and the Development of Elizabethan Drama*. Berkeley, 1978.

Bamford, Karen. *Sexual Violence on the Jacobean Stage*. New York, 2000.

Barber, C. L. *Creating Elizabethan Tragedy: The Theater of Kyd and Marlowe*. Chicago, 1988.

Bartels, Emily C. *Spectacles of Strangeness: Imperialism, Alienation, and Marlowe*. Philadelphia, 1993.

Bednarz, James P. *Shakespeare and the Poets' War*. New York, 2001.

Belsey, Catherine. *The Subject of Tragedy: Identity and Difference in Renaissance Drama*. London, 1985.

Bentley, G. E. *Shakespeare and Jonson: Their Reputations in the Seventeenth Century Compared*. 2 vols. Chicago, 1945.

Bergeron, David M. *Practicing Renaissance Scholarship Plays and Pageants, Patrons and Politics*. Pittsburgh, 2000.

Berry, Philippa. *Of Chastity and Power: Elizabethan Literature and the Unmarried Queen*. London and New York, 1989.

Bevington, David. *From "Mankind" to Marlowe: Growth of Structure in the Popular Drama of Tudor England*. Cambridge, Mass., 1962.

———. *Tudor Drama and Politics*. Cambridge, Mass., 1968.

———, and Peter Holbrook, eds. *The Politics of the Stuart Court Masque*. Cambridge, Eng., 1991.

———, Lars Engle, Katharine Eisaman Maus, and Eric Rasmussen, eds. *English Renaissance Drama: A Norton Anthology*. New York, 2002.

———, Martin Butler, and Ian Donaldson, gen. eds. *The Cambridge Edition of the Complete Works of Ben Jonson*. 7 vols. Cambridge, Eng., 2012.

Bowers, Fredson T. *Elizabethan Revenge Tragedy, 1587–1642*. Princeton, 1940.

Braden, Gordon. *Renaissance Tragedy and the Senecan Tradition*. New Haven, 1985.

Braunmuller, A. R., and Michael Hattaway, eds. *The Cambridge Companion to English Renaissance Drama*. Cambridge, Eng., 1990; 2nd ed., 2003.

Bristol, Michael D. *Carnival and Theater: Plebeian Culture and the Structure of Authority in Renaissance England*. London, 1985.

Bromley, James M. *Intimacy and Sexuality in the Age of Shakespeare*. Cambridge, Eng., 2012.

Brooke, C. F. Tucker, ed. *The Shakespeare Apocrypha*. Oxford, 1908.

Brooks, Douglas A. *From Playhouse to Printing House: Drama and Authorship in Early Modern England*. Cambridge, Eng., 2000.

Bruster, Douglas. *Drama and the Market in the Age of Shakespeare*. Cambridge, Eng., 1992.

Burt, Richard. *Licensed by Authority: Ben Jonson and the Discourses of Censorship*. Ithaca, N.Y., 1993.

Bushnell, Rebecca W. *Tragedies of Tyrants: Political Thought and Theater in the English Renaissance*. Ithaca, N.Y., 1990.

Butterworth, Philip. *Theatre of Fire: Special Effects in Early English and Scottish Theatre*. London, 1998.

Caputi, Anthony. *John Marston, Satirist*. Ithaca, N.Y., 1961.

Cohen, Walter. *Drama of a Nation: Public Theater in Renaissance England and Spain*. Ithaca, N.Y., 1985.

Comensoli, Viviana, and Anna Russell, eds. *Enacting Gender on the English Renaissance Stage*. Urbana, Ill., 1999.

Cousins, A. D., and Alison V. Scott, eds. *Ben Jonson and the Politics of Genre*. Cambridge, Eng., 2009.

Cox, John D. *The Devil and the Sacred in English Drama, 1350–1642*. Cambridge, Eng., 2000.

———, and David Scott Kastan, eds. *A New History of Early English Drama*. New York, 1997.

Craik, T. W. *The Tudor Interlude*. Leicester, 1958, 1962.

Curran, Kevin. *Marriage, Performance, and Politics at the Jacobean Court*. Farnham and Burlington, Vt., 2009.

Dawson, Anthony B., and Paul Yachnin. *The Culture of Playgoing in Shakespeare's England: A Collaborative Debate*. Cambridge, Eng., 2001.

Deats, Sara Munson. *Sex, Gender, and Desire in the Plays of Christopher Marlowe*. Newark, Del., 1997.

Dessen, Alan C. *Elizabethan Drama and the Viewer's Eye*. Chapel Hill, N.C., 1977.

Diehl, Huston. *Staging Reform, Reforming the Stage: Protestantism and Popular Theater in Early Modern England*. Ithaca, N.Y., 1997.

Dillon, Janette. *Theatre, Court and City, 1595–1610: Drama and Social Space in London*. Cambridge, Eng., 2000.

———. *The Cambridge Introduction to Early English Theatre*. Cambridge, Eng., 2006.

DiGangi, Mario. *The Homoerotics of Early Modern Drama*. Cambridge, Eng., 1997.

Dolan, Frances E. *Dangerous Familiars: Representations of Domestic Crime in England, 1550–1700*. Ithaca, N.Y., 1994.

Doran, Madeleine. *Endeavors of Art: A Study of Form in Elizabethan Drama*. Madison, Wis., 1954, 1972.

Engel, Lars, and Eric Rasmussen. *Studying Shakespeare's Contemporaries*. Oxford, 2014.

Erickson, Peter, and Clark Hulse, eds. *Early Modern Visual Culture: Representation, Race, and Empire in Renaissance England*. Philadelphia, 2000.

Erne, Lukas. *Beyond "The Spanish Tragedy": A Study of the Works of Thomas Kyd*. Manchester, 2001.

Esche, Edward J. *Shakespeare and His Contemporaries in Performance*. Aldershot, Hants., 2000.

Falco, Raphael. *Charismatic Authority in Early Modern English Tragedy*. Baltimore, 2000.

Farley-Hills, David. *Shakespeare and the Rival Playwrights, 1600–1606*. London, 1990.

Findlay, Alison. *A Feminist Perspective on Renaissance Drama*. Oxford, 1999.

———. *Illegitimate Power: Bastards in Renaissance Drama*. Manchester, Eng., 1994.

———. *Playing Spaces in Early Women's Drama*. Cambridge, Eng., 2006.

Finkelpearl, Philip. *John Marston of the Middle Temple*. Cambridge, Mass., 1969.

Freer, Coburn. *The Poetics of Jacobean Drama*. Baltimore, 1981.

Gardiner, H. C. *Mysteries' End*. New Haven, 1946.

Gibbons, Brian. *Jacobean City Comedy*. London, 1968.

Gossett, Suzanne, ed. *Thomas Middleton in Context*. Cambridge, Eng., 2011.

Griffin, Eric J. *English Renaissance Drama and the Specter of Spain: Ethnopoetics and Empire*. Philadelphia, 2009.

Hall, Kim F. *Things of Darkness: Economies of Race and Gender in Early Modern England*. Ithaca, N.Y., 1995.

Hardison, O. B., Jr. *Christian Rite and Christian Drama in the Middle Ages*. Baltimore, 1965.

Hart, Jonathan. *Shakespeare and His Contemporaries*. New York, 2010.

Hassel, R. Chris. *Renaissance Drama and the English Church Year*. Lincoln, Neb., 1979.

Hattaway, Michael. *Elizabethan Popular Theatre: Plays in Performance*. London, 1982.

Hawkins, Harriett. *Likenesses of Truth in Elizabethan and Restoration Drama*. Oxford, 1972.

Helgerson, Richard. *Adulterous Alliances: Home, State, and History in Early Modern European Drama and Painting*. Chicago, 2000.

Hendricks, Margo, and Patricia Parker, eds. *Women, "Race," and Writing in the Early Modern Period*. London and New York, 1994.

Hillman, Richard. S*hakespeare, Marlowe, and the Politics of France*. Houndmills, Eng., 2002.

Holbrook, Peter. *Literature and Degree in Renaissance England: Nashe, Bourgeois Tragedy, Shakespeare*. Newark, Del., 1994.

Honigmann, E. A. J., ed. *Shakespeare and His Contemporaries: Essays in Comparison*. Manchester, 1986.

Hopkins, Lisa. *The Cultural Uses of the Caesars on the English Renaissance Stage*. Aldershot, Eng., and Burlington, Vt., 2008.

Howard, Jean. *The Stage and Social Struggle in Early Modern England*. London and New York, 1994.

Hunter, G. K. *John Lyly: The Humanist as Courtier*. Cambridge, Mass., 1962.

Jankowski, Theodora A. *Pure Resistance: Queer Virginity in Early Modern English Drama*. Philadelphia, 2000.

Kastan, David Scott, and Peter Stallybrass, eds. *Staging the Renaissance: Reinterpretations of Elizabethan and Jacobean Drama*. New York and London, 1991.

Kermode, Lloyd Edward. *Aliens and Englishness in Elizabethan Drama*. Cambridge, Eng., 2009.

———, and Nova Myhill, eds. *Imagining the Audience in Early Modern Drama, 1558–1642*. New York, 2011.

Kernan, Alvin. *The Cankered Muse: Satire of the English Renaissance*. New Haven, 1959.

Kerrigan, John. *Revenge Tragedy: Aeschylus to Armageddon*. Oxford, 1998.

———. *Archipelagic English: Literature, History, and Politics, 1603–1707*. Oxford, 2008, 2010.

Kiefer, Frederick. *Writing on the Renaissance Stage: Written Words, Printed Pages, Metaphoric Books*. Newark, Del., 1996.

Kirsch, Arthur C. *Jacobean Dramatic Perspectives*. Charlottesville, Va., 1972.

Kitch, Aaron. *Political Economy and the States of Literature in Early Modern England*. Farnham, Surrey, 2009.

Knapp, Jeffrey. *Shakespeare's Tribe: Church, Nation, and Theater in Renaissance England*. Chicago, 2002.

Kolve, V. A. *The Play Called Corpus Christi*. Palo Alto and London, 1966.

Kuriyama, Constance Brown. *Christopher Marlowe: A Renaissance Life*. Ithaca, N.Y., 2002.

Leggatt, Alexander. *Citizen Comedy in the Age of Shakespeare*. Toronto, 1973.

———. *Introduction to English Renaissance Comedy*. Manchester, 1999.

———. *Jacobean Public Theatre*. London, 1992.

Leishman, J. B., ed. *The Three Parnassus Plays (1598–1601)*. London, 1949.

Lesser, Zachary. *Renaissance Drama and the Politics of Publication: Readings in the English Book Trade*. Cambridge, Eng., 2004.

Levin, Harry. *The Overreacher: A Study of Christopher Marlowe*. Cambridge, Mass., 1952, 1964.

Levin, Richard. *The Multiple Plot in English Renaissance Drama*. Chicago, 1971.

Liebler, Naomi Conn, ed. *The Female Tragic Hero in English Renaissance Drama*. New York and Basingstoke, Eng., 2002.

Limon, Jerzy, and Jay L. Halio, eds. *Shakespeare and His Contemporaries: Eastern and Central European Studies*. Newark, Del., 1993.

Logan, Robert P., and Denzell S. Smith. *The Predecessors of Shakespeare: A Survey and Bibliography of Recent Studies in English Renaissance Drama*. Lincoln, Neb., 1973.

Low, Jennifer. *Manhood and the Duel: Masculinity in Early Modern Drama and Culture*. New York and Basingstoke, Eng., 2003.

MacFoul, Thomas. *Male Friendship in Shakespeare and His Contemporaries*. Cambridge, Eng., 2007.

Maguire, Nancy Klein. *Renaissance Tragicomedy: Explorations in Genre and Politics*. New York, 1987.

Malay, Jessica L. *Prophecy and Sibylline Imagery in the Renaissance: Shakespeare's Sibyls*. New York, 2010.

Mann, David. *The Elizabethan Player: Contemporary Stage Representation*. London, 1991.

Mardock, James D. *Our Scene Is London: Ben Jonson's City and the Space of the Author*. New York and London, 2008.

Margeson, J. M. R. *The Origins of English Tragedy*. Oxford, 1967.

Marrapodi, Michele, ed., with A. J. Hoenselaars. *The Italian World of English Renaissance Drama: Cultural Exchange and Intertextuality*. Newark, Del., 1998.

Maul, Victoria. *Jonson, Horace, and the Classical Tradition*. Cambridge, Eng., 2010.

Maus, Katharine Eisaman. *Inwardness and Theater in the English Renaissance Drama*. Chicago, 1995.

McAlindon, T. *English Renaissance Tragedy*. London, 1986.

McDonald, Russ. *Shakespeare and Jonson, Jonson and Shakespeare*. Lincoln, Neb., 1988.

McInnis, David. *Mind-Travelling and Voyage Drama in Early Modern England*. Houndmills, Basingstoke, 2013.

McLuskie, Kathleen. *Renaissance Dramatists*. (Feminist Readings.) Atlantic Highlands, N.J., 1989.

McMahan, Chris. *Family and the State in Early Modern Revenge Drama*. New York, 2012.

McManus, Clare. *Women on the Renaissance Stage: Anna of Denmark and Female Masquing in the Stuart Court (1590–1619)*. Manchester, 2002.

McMillin, Scott, and Sally-Beth MacLean. *The Queen's Men and Their Plays*. Cambridge, Eng., 1998.

Mukherji, Subha. *Law and Representation in Early Modern Drama*. Cambridge, Eng., 2006.

Neill, Michael. *Putting History to the Question: Power, Politics, and Society in English Renaissance Drama*. New York, 2000.

Orgel, Stephen. *The Illusion of Power: Political Theater in the English Renaissance*. Berkeley, 1975.

———. *Impersonations: The Performance of Gender in Shakespeare's England*. Cambridge, Eng., 1996.

Orgel, Stephen, and Roy Strong. *Inigo Jones: The Theatre of the Stuart Court*. 2 vols. London and Berkeley, 1973.

Ornstein, Robert. *The Moral Vision of Jacobean Tragedy*. Madison, Wis., 1960.

Panek, Jennifer. *Widows and Suitors in Early Modern English Comedy*. Cambridge, Eng., 2004.

Rabkin, Norman, ed: *Reinterpretations of Elizabethan Drama*. New York, 1969.

Rasmussen, Mark David, ed. *Renaissance Literature and Its Formal Engagements*. Basingstoke, Hampshire, 2002.

Rose, Mary Beth. *The Expense of Spirit: Love and Sexuality in English Renaissance Drama*. Ithaca, N.Y., 1988.

———. *Gender and Heroism in Early Modern English Literature*. Chicago, 2002.

———. ed. *Renaissance Drama as Cultural History*. Evanston, Ill., 1990.

Sanders, Julie. *Ben Jonson in Context*. Cambridge, Eng., 2010.

Sanders, Wilbur. *The Dramatist and the Received Idea: Studies in the Plays of Marlowe and Shakespeare*. Cambridge, Eng., 1968.

Shannon, Laurie. *Sovereign Amity: Figures of Friendship in Shakespearean Contexts*. Chicago, 2002.

Shapiro, James. *Rival Playwrights: Marlowe, Jonson, Shakespeare*. New York, 1991.

Simon, Eckehard, ed. *The Theatre of Medieval Europe: New Research in Early Drama*. Cambridge, Eng., 1991.

Smith, Bruce R. *The Acoustic World of Early Modern England*. Chicago, 1999.

Smith, David L., Richard Strier, and David Bevington, eds. *The Theatrical City: Culture, Theatre and Politics in London, 1567–1649*. Cambridge, Eng., 1995.

Smith, Emma, and Garrett A. Sullivan, Jr. *The Cambridge Companion to English Renaissance Tragedy*. Cambridge, Eng., 2010.

Southern, Richard. *The Medieval Theatre in the Round*. London, 1957.

Spivack, Bernard. *Shakespeare and the Allegory of Evil*. New York, 1958.

Straznicky, Marta. *Privacy, Playreading, and Women's Closet Drama, 1550–1700*. Cambridge, Eng., 2004.

Sullivan, Jr., Garrett A. *Memory and Forgetting in English Renaissance Drama: Shakespeare, Marlowe, Webster*. Cambridge, Eng., 2005.

Traub, Valerie, M. Lindsay Kaplan, and Dympna C. Callaghan, eds. *Feminist Readings of Early Modern Culture: Emerging Subjects*. Cambridge, Eng., 1996.

Vickers, Brian. *"Counterfeiting" Shakespeare: Evidence, Authorship, and John Ford's "Funerall Elegye."* Cambridge, Eng., 2002.

Waith, Eugene M. *The Herculean Hero in Marlowe, Chapman, Shakespeare, and Dryden*. New York, 1962.

Wall, Wendy. *Staging Domesticity: Household Work and English Identity in Early Modern Drama*. Cambridge, Eng., 2002.

Wells, Stanley. *Shakespeare & Co.: Christopher Marlowe, Thomas Dekker, Ben Jonson, Thomas Middleton, John Fletcher, and the Other Players in His Story*. New York, 2007.

Whigham, Frank. *Seizures of the Will in Early Modern English Drama*. Cambridge, Eng., 1996.

White, Paul Whitfield. *Marlowe, History, and Sexuality: New Critical Essays on Christopher Marlowe*. New York, 1998.

———, *Theatre and Reformation: Protestantism, Patronage and Playing in Tudor England*. Cambridge, Eng., 1993.

Whitmore, Michael. *Pretty Creatures: Children and Fiction in the English Renaissance*. Ithaca, N.Y., 2007.

Whitney, Charles. *Early Responses to Renaissance Drama*. Cambridge, Eng., 2006.

Wickham, Glynne. *Early English Stages, 1300 to 1660*. 3 vols. London, 1959–1972.

Wiggins, Martin. *Shakespeare and the Drama of His Time*. Oxford, 2000.

———, and Catherine Richardson, compilers. *British Drama, 1533–1642: A Catalogue*. Vol. 1. Oxford, 2012.

Wilson, F. P. *Marlowe and the Early Shakespeare*. Oxford, 1953.

Wilson, Luke. *Theaters of Intention: Drama and the Law in Early Modern England*. Stanford, Calif., 2000.

Wong, Katrine K. *Music and Gender in English Renaissance Drama*. New York, 2012.

Woodbridge, Linda. *Women and the English Renaissance: Literature and the Nature of Womankind, 1540–1620*. Urbana, Ill., 1984.

———. *English Revenge Drama: Money, Resistance, Equality*. Cambridge, Eng., 2010.

Woolf, Rosemary. *The English Mystery Plays*. Berkeley and Los Angeles, 1972.

Yachnin, Paul. *Stage-Wrights: Shakespeare, Jonson, Middleton, and the Making of Theatrical Value*. Philadelphia, 1997.

Zimmerman, Susan, ed. *Erotic Politics: Desire on the Renaissance Stage*. London and New York, 1992.

Zucker, Adam. *The Places of Wit in Early Modern English Comedy*. Cambridge, Eng., 2011.

## London Theaters and Dramatic Companies

See also, under *Works of Reference*, Bentley, and Chambers (*Elizabethan Stage*).

Aaron, Melissa D. *Global Economics: A History of the Theater Business, the Chamberlain's/King's Men, and Their Plays, 1599–1642*. Newark, Del., 2005.

Astington, John H., ed. *The Development of Shakespeare's Theater*. New York, 1992.

Beckerman, Bernard. *Shakespeare at the Globe, 1599–1609*. New York, 1962, 1967.

Bentley, Gerald Eades. *The Profession of Dramatist in Shakespeare's Time, 1590–1642*. Princeton, 1971.

———. *The Profession of Player in Shakespeare's Time, 1590–1642*. Princeton, 1984.

Berry, Herbert. *Shakespeare's Playhouses*. New York, 1987.

Bradley, David. *From Text to Performance in the Elizabethan Theatre: Preparing the Play for the Stage*. Cambridge, Eng., 1992.

Clare, Janet. *"Art Made Tongue-Tied by Authority": Elizabethan and Jacobean Dramatic Censorship*. Manchester, 1990; 2nd ed., 1999.

Cook, Ann Jennalie. *The Privileged Playgoers of Shakespeare's London, 1576–1642*. Princeton, 1981.

Dillon, Janet. *The Language of Space in Court Performance, 1400–1625*. Cambridge, Eng., 2010.

Dutton, Richard. *Mastering the Revels: The Regulation and Censorship of English Renaissance Drama*. Iowa City, 1991.

———, ed. *The Oxford Handbook of Early Modern Theatre*. Oxford, 2012.

Feuillerat, Albert, ed. *Documents Relating to the Office of the Revels in the Time of Queen Elizabeth*. Louvain (Louven), Belgium, 1908.

Foakes, R. A., ed. *The Henslowe Papers: The Diary, Theatre Papers, and Bear Garden Papers*. In full and in facsimile. 3 vols. in 2. London, 1976.

Foakes, R. A., and R. T. Rickert, eds. *Henslowe's Diary*. London, 1961.

Gair, W. Reavley. *The Children of Paul's*. Cambridge, Eng., 1982.

Greg, W. W., ed. *Dramatic Documents from the Elizabethan Playhouses: Stage Plots; Actors' Parts; Prompt Books*. 2 vols. Oxford, 1931.

Gurr, Andrew. *Playgoing in Shakespeare's London*. Cambridge, Eng., 1987; 2nd ed., 1996.

———. *The Shakespeare Company, 1594–1642*. Cambridge, Eng., 2004.

———. *The Shakespearian Playing Companies*. Oxford, 1996.

———. *The Shakespearean Stage, 1574–1642*. Cambridge, Eng., 1970; 2nd ed., 1980.

———. *Shakespeare's Opposites: The Admiral's Company, 1594–1625*. Cambridge, Eng., 2009.

———, and John Orrell. *Rebuilding Shakespeare's Globe*. London and New York, 1989.

———, and Mariko Ichikawa. *Staging in Shakespeare's Theatres*. Oxford, 2000.

Harbage, Alfred. *Shakespeare's Audience*. New York, 1941.

Hill, Janet. *Stages and Playgoers: From Guild Plays to Shakespeare*. Montreal and Kingston, 2002.

Hodges, C. Walter. *The Globe Restored*. London, 1953; 2nd ed., New York, 1968.

Hosley, Richard. "Was There a Music-room in Shakespeare's Globe?" *ShS 13* (1960), 113–23.

Ingram, William. *The Business of Playing: The Beginnings of the Adult Professional Theater in Elizabethan London*. Ithaca, N.Y., 1992.

Jones, Ann Rosalind, and Peter Stallybrass. *Renaissance Clothing and the Materials of Memory*. Cambridge, Eng., 2000.

Kathman, David. "Grocers, Goldsmiths, and Drapers: Freemen and Apprentices in the Elizabethan Theater," *SQ* 55 (2004), 1–49.

King, T. J. *Casting Shakespeare's Plays: London Actors and Their Roles, 1590–1642*. Cambridge, Eng., 1992.

———. *Shakespearean Staging, 1599–1642*. Cambridge, Mass., 1971.

Knutson, Roslyn Lander. *The Repertory of Shakespeare's Company, 1594–1613*. Fayetteville, Ark., 1991.

———. *Playing Companies and Commerce in Shakespeare's Time*. Cambridge, Eng., 2001.

Linthicum, Marie C. *Costume in the Drama of Shakespeare and His Contemporaries*. Oxford, 1936.

Mackay, Ellen. *Persecution, Plague and Fire: Fugitive Histories of the Stage in Early Modern England*. Chicago, 2011.

Mann, David. *The Elizabethan Player: Contemporary Stage Representation*. London, 1991.

McMillin, Scott. *The Elizabethan Theatre and "The Book of Sir Thomas More."* Ithaca, N.Y., 1987.

McMillin, Scott, and Sally-Beth MacLean. *The Queen's Men and Their Plays*. Cambridge, Eng., 1998.

Munro, Lucy. *Children of the Queen's Revels: A Jacobean Theatre Repertory*. Cambridge, Eng., 2005.

Nelson, Alan H. *Early Cambridge Theatres: College, University, and Town Stages, 1464–1720*. Cambridge, Eng., 1994.

Nungezer, Edwin. *A Dictionary of Actors*. London and New Haven, 1929.

Ostovich, Helen, Holger Schott Syme, and Andrew Griffin, eds. *Locating the Queen's Men, 1583–1603: Material Practices and Conditions of Playing*. Farnham, Eng., 2009.

Schoone-Jongen, Terence G. *Shakespeare's Companies: William Shakespeare's Early Career and the Acting Companies, 1577–1594*. Farnham, Eng., and Burlington Vt., 2008.

Shapiro, Michael. *Children of the Revels: The Boys' Companies of Shakespeare's Time and Their Plays*. New York, 1977.

Turner, Henry S. *The English Renaissance Stage: Geometry, Poetics, and the Practical Spatial Arts*. Oxford, 2006.

Vaughan, Virginia Mason. *Performing Blackness on English Stages, 1500–1800*. Cambridge, Eng., 2005.

West, Russell. *Spatial Representations and the Jacobean Stage: From Shakespeare to Webster*. Basingstoke, Eng., and New York, 2002.

White, Paul Whitfield, and Suzanne R. Westfall, eds. *Shakespeare and Theatrical Patronage in Early Modern England*. Cambridge, Eng., 2002.

Wickham, Glynne. *Early English Stages, 1300 to 1660*. 3 vols. London, 1959–1972.

## Shakespeare's Life and Work

Alexander, Peter. *Shakespeare's Life and Art*. New ed., New York, 1961.

Baldwin, T. W. *William Shakspere's Small Latine and Lesse Greeke*. 2 vols. Urbana, Ill., 1944.

Bate, Jonathan. *Soul of the Age: A Biography of the Mind of William Shakespeare*. New York, 2009.

Bevington, David. *Shakespeare and Biography*. Oxford, 2010.

Chambers, E. K. *William Shakespeare: A Study of Facts and Problems*. 2 vols. Oxford, 1930.

Duncan-Jones, Katherine. *Ungentle Shakespeare: Scenes from His Life*. London, 2001.

———. *Shakespeare: Upstart Crow to Sweet Swan, 1592–1623*. London, 2011.

Eccles, Mark. *Shakespeare in Warwickshire*. Madison, Wis., 1961.

Ellis, David. *The Truth about William Shakespeare: Fact, Fiction, and Modern Biographies*. Edinburgh, 2012.

Greenblatt, Stephen. *Will in the World: How Shakespeare Became Shakespeare*. New York, 2004.

Greer, Germaine. *Shakespeare*. Oxford, 1986.

———. *Shakespeare's Wife*. London and New York, 2007.

Holderness, Graham. *Nine Lives of Shakespeare*. London, 2011.

Honan, Park. *Shakespeare: A Life*. Oxford, 1998.

Kay, Dennis. *Shakespeare: His Life, Work, and Era*. London and New York, 1992.

Matus, Irvin Leigh, *Shakespeare, In Fact*. New York, 1994.

McCrea, Scott. *The Case for Shakespeare: The End of the Authorship Question*. Westport, Conn., 2005.

Nicholl, Charles. *The Lodger Shakespeare: His Life on Silver Street*. New York, 2007.

Pogue, Kate Emery. *Shakespeare's Family*. Westport, Conn., and London, 2008.

Potter, Lois. *The Life of William Shakespeare*. Oxford, 2012.

Schoenbaum, S. *Shakespeare's Lives*. Oxford and New York, 1970.

———. *William Shakespeare: A Documentary Life*. Oxford, 1975. Also published with fewer illustrations and a slightly revised text as *A Compact Documentary Life*. 1977.

———. *William Shakespeare: Records and Images*. Oxford, 1981.

Shapiro, James S. *A Year in the Life of William Shakespeare, 1599*. New York, 2005.

———. *Contested Will: Who Wrote Shakespeare?* New York, 2010.

Thomas, Julia. *Shakespeare's Shrine: The Bard's Birthplace and the Invention of Stratford-upon-Avon*. Philadelphia, 2012.

Wells, Stanley. *Shakespeare: A Life in Drama*. New York and London, 1995.

———. *Shakespeare: For All Time*. Oxford, 2003.

———. *Is It True What They Say about Shakespeare?* Ebrington, Glos., 2007.

———. *Shakespeare and Co.* London, 2007.

Wheeler, Richard P. "Deaths in the Family: The Loss of a Son and the Rise of Shakespearean Comedy," *SQ* 51 (2000), 127–53.

## Shakespeare's Language: His Development as Poet and Dramatist

See also, under *Works of Reference*, Abbott, Onions, and Schmidt; and under *The Comedies*, Elam.

Adamson, Sylvia, Gavin Alexander, and Katrin Ettenhuber, eds. *Renaissance Figures of Speech*. Cambridge, Eng., 2007.

Alexander, Catherine M. S., ed. *Shakespeare and Language*. Cambridge, Eng., 2004.

Barton, Anne. "Shakespeare and the Limits of Language," *ShS* 24 (1971), 19–30.

Byrne, Muriel St. Clare. "The Foundations of Elizabethan Language," *ShS* 17 (1964), 223–39.

Cercignani, Fausto. *Shakespeare's Works and Elizabethan Pronunciation*. Oxford, 1981.

Charney, Maurice. *Shakespeare's Roman Plays: The Function of Imagery in the Drama*. Cambridge, Mass., 1961.

———. *Style in Hamlet*. Princeton, 1969.

Clemen, Wolfgang H. *The Development of Shakespeare's Imagery*. Cambridge, Mass., 1951.

Coleman, E. A. M. *The Dramatic Use of Bawdy in Shakespeare*. London, 1974.

Craig, Hugh. "Shakespeare's Vocabulary: Myth and Reality," *SQ* 62.1 (2011), 53–74.

Cruttwell, Patrick. *The Shakespearean Moment and Its Place in the Poetry of the Seventeenth Century*. London, 1954.

Crystal, David. *Pronouncing Shakespeare: The Globe Experiment*. Cambridge, Eng., 2005.

———, and Ben Crystal. *Shakespeare's Words: A Glossary and Language Companion*. London and New York, 2002.

Desmet, Christy. *Reading Shakespeare's Characters: Rhetoric, Ethics, and Identity*. Amherst, Mass., 1992.

Dobson, E. J. *English Pronunciation, 1500–1700*. 2 vols. 2nd ed. Oxford, 1968.

Donawerth, Jane. *Shakespeare and the Sixteenth-Century Study of Language*. Urbana, Ill., 1984.

Doran, Madeleine. *Shakespeare's Dramatic Language*. Madison, Wis., 1976.

Empson, William. *The Structure of Complex Words*. London, 1951; 3rd ed., 1977.

Enterline, Lynn. *Shakespeare's Classroom: Rhetoric, Discipline, Emotion*. Philadelphia, 2012.

Freedman, Penelope. *Power and Passion in Shakespeare's Pronouns: Interrogating "You" and "Thou."* Aldershot, Eng., and Burlington, Vt., 2007.

Hazard, Mary E. *Elizabethan Silent Language*. Lincoln, Neb., 2000.

Hirsch, James E. *Shakespeare and the History of Soliloquies*. Madison, N.J., and London, 2003.

Hoenselaars, Ton, ed. *Shakespeare and the Language of Translation*. London, 2004.

———. *Shakespeare's Grammar*. London, 2003.

Hope, Jonathan. *Shakespeare and Language: Reason, Eloquence, and Artifice in the Renaissance*. London, 2010.

———. *Shakespeare's Grammar*. London, 2003.

Hulme, Hilda M. *Explorations in Shakespeare's Language*. London, 1962.

Kermode, Frank. *Shakespeare's Language*. New York, 2000.

Kökeritz, Helge. *Shakespeare's Names*. New Haven, 1959.

———. *Shakespeare's Pronunciation*. New Haven, 1953.

Lanham, Richard A. *The Motives of Eloquence: Literary Rhetoric in the Renaissance*. New Haven, 1976.

Lloyd, Megan S. *"Speak It in Welsh": Wales and the Welsh Language in Shakespeare*. Lanham, Md., 2007.

Lyne, Raphael. *Shakespeare, Rhetoric, and Cognition*. Cambridge, Eng., 2011.

Magnussen, Lynne. *Shakespeare and Social Dialogue: Dramatic Language and Elizabethan Letters*. Cambridge, Eng., 1999.

Mahood, M. M. *Shakespeare's Wordplay*. London, 1957.

———. *Shakespeare and the Arts of Language*. Oxford, 2001.

McDonald, Russ. *Shakespeare's Late Style*. Cambridge, Eng., 2006.

Miriam Joseph, Sister. *Shakespeare's Use of the Arts of Language*. New York, 1947. Rpt. in part as *Rhetoric in Shakespeare's Time*. 1962.

Nares, Robert. *A Glossary . . . of Shakespeare and His Contemporaries*. New ed. J. O. Halliwell and Thomas Wright. 2 vols. London, 1859, 1905, Rpt. Detroit 1966.

Partridge, Eric. *Shakespeare's Bawdy*. London, 1947, 1955.

Perng, Ching-Hsi. *Dialogue with Monologue: A Study in Shakespearean Soliloquy*. Taiwan, 2011.

Pogue, Kate Emery. *Shakespeare's Figures of Speech: A Reader's Guide*. New York and Bloomington, Ind., 2009.

Rhodes, Neil. *Shakespeare and the Origins of English*. Oxford, 2004.

Siemon, James R. *Word Against Word: Shakespearian Utterance*. Amherst and Boston, 2002.

Sokol, B. J., and Mary Sokol. *Shakespeare's Legal Language: A Dictionary*. London and New Brunswick, N.J., 2000.

Spurgeon, Caroline. *Shakespeare's Imagery and What it Tells Us*. Cambridge, Eng., 1935.

Thompson, Ann and John O. *Shakespeare: Meaning and Metaphor*. Iowa City, 1987.

Thorne, Alison. *Vision and Rhetoric in Shakespeare: Looking Through Language*. Basingstoke and New York, 2000.

Trousdale, Marion. *Shakespeare and the Rhetoricians*. Chapel Hill, N.C., 1982.

Vickers, Brian. *The Artistry of Shakespeare's Prose*. London, 1968.

Willbern, David. *Poetic Will: Shakespeare and the Play of Language*. Philadelphia, 1997.

Willcock, Gladys D. "Shakespeare and Elizabethan English," *ShS* 7 (1954), 12–24.

———. *Shakespeare and Rhetoric*. Oxford, 1944.

Williams, Gordon. *A Dictionary of Sexual Language and Imagery in Shakespearean and Stuart Literature*. 3 vols. London, 1994.

Wright, George T. *Shakespeare's Metrical Art*. Berkeley, 1988.

## Textual Criticism and Bibliography

See also under *Shakespeare's Predecessors and Contemporaries*, Cox and Kastan (essay by Blayney); and, under *King Lear*, Urkowitz.

Alexander, Peter. *Shakespeare's "Henry VI" and "Richard III."* Cambridge, Eng., 1929.

Bergeron, David M. *Textual Patronage in English Drama, 1570–1640*. Aldershot, Eng., and Burlington, Vt., 2005.

Blayney, Peter W. M. *The First Folio of Shakespeare*. Washington D.C., 1991.

———. *The Texts of "King Lear" and Their Origins*. Vol. 1. Cambridge, Eng., 1982.

Bowers, Fredson. *Bibliography and Textual Criticism*. Oxford, 1964.

———. *On Editing Shakespeare*. Charlottesville, Va., 1966.

———. *Principles of Bibliographical Description*. Princeton, 1949.

———. *Textual and Literary Criticism*. Cambridge, Eng., 1959.

Brooks, Douglas A. *From Playhouse to Printing House: Drama and Authorship in Early Modern England*. Cambridge, Eng., 2000.

Chambers, E. K. *William Shakespeare: A Study of Facts and Problems*. 2 vols. Oxford, 1930.

Davidson, Adele. *Shakespeare in Shorthand: The Textual Mystery of "King Lear."* Newark, Del., 2009.

De Grazia, Margreta. *Shakespeare Verbatim: The Reproduction of Authenticity and the 1790 Apparatus*. Oxford, 1991.

Doran, Madeleine. *"Henry VI", Parts II and III: Their Relation to "The Contention" and "The True Tragedy."* Iowa City, 1928.

Duthie, G. I. *Elizabethan Shorthand and the First Quarto of "King Lear."* Oxford, 1949.

Egan, Gabriel. *The Struggle for Shakespeare's Text: Twentieth-Century Editorial Theory and Practice*. Cambridge, Eng., 2010.

Erne, Lukas. *Shakespeare as Literary Dramatist*. Cambridge, Eng., 2003.

———. "Shakespeare and the Publication of His Plays," *SQ* 53.1 (2002), 1–20.

———, ed. *Textual Performances: The Modern Reproduction of Shakespeare's Drama*. Cambridge, Eng., 2004.

———. *Shakespeare's Modern Collaborators*. London, 2008.

Gaskell, Philip. *A New Introduction to Bibliography*. New York and Oxford, 1972.

Gondris, Joanna, ed. *Reading Readings: Essays on Shakespeare Editing in the Eighteenth Century*. Madison, N.J., 1998.

Greg, W. W. *The Editorial Problem in Shakespeare*. 3rd ed. Oxford, 1954.

———. *Principles of Emendation in Shakespeare*. London, 1928.

———. *The Shakespeare First Folio: Its Bibliographical and Textual History*. Oxford, 1955.

Hart, Alfred. *Stolne and Surreptitious Copies: A Comparative Study of Shakespeare's Bad Quartos*. Melbourne and London, 1942.

Hinman, Charlton. *The Printing and Proof-Reading of the First Folio of Shakespeare*. 2 vols. Oxford, 1963.

Holland, Peter, ed. *Editing Shakespeare. Shakespeare Survey 59*. Cambridge, Eng., 2006.

Honigmann, E. A. J. *The Stability of Shakespeare's Text*. London and Lincoln, Neb., 1965.

Ioppolo, Grace. *Revising Shakespeare*. Cambridge, Mass., 1991.

Jowett, John. *Shakespeare and Text*. Oxford, 2007.

Long, William B. " 'A bed for woodstock': A Warning for the Unwary," *Medieval and Renaissance Drama in England* 2 (1985), 91–118.

Maguire, Laurie E., and Thomas L. Berger, eds. *Textual Formations and Reformations*. Newark, Del., 1998.

Massai, Sonia. *Shakespeare and the Rise of the Editor*. Cambridge, Eng., 2007.

Masten, Jeffrey. *Textual Intercourse: Collaboration, Authorship, and Sexualities in Renaissance Drama*. Cambridge, Eng., 1997.

Mays, Andrea. *The Millionaire and the Bard: Henry Folger's Obsessive Hunt for Shakespeare's First Folio*. New York, 2015.

McKerrow, Ronald B. *An Introduction to Bibliography for Literary Students*. Oxford, 1927.

———. *Prolegomena for the Oxford Shakespeare*. Oxford, 1939.

McLeod, Randall, ed. *Crisis in Editing: Texts of the English Renaissance*. New York, 1994.

McMillin, Scott, ed. *The First Quarto of "Othello."* Cambridge, Eng., 2001.

Mowat, Barbara, and Paul Werstine, eds. *The New Folger Library Shakespeare*. New York, 1992–.

Murphy, Andrew. *Shakespeare in Print: A History and Chronology of Shakespeare Publishing*. Cambridge, Eng., 2003.

Nosworthy, J. M. *Shakespeare's Occasional Plays: Their Origin and Transmission*. London and New York, 1965.

Pechter, Edward, ed. *Textual and Theatrical Shakespeare: Questions of Evidence*. Iowa City, 1996.

Peterson, Lene B. *Shakespeare's Errant Texts: Textual Form and Linguistic Style in Shakespeare's "Bad" Quartos and Co-authored Plays*. Cambridge, Eng., 2010.

Pollard, Alfred W. *Shakespeare Folios and Quartos: A Study in the Bibliography of Shakespeare's Plays, 1594–1685*. London, 1909.

———. *Shakespeare's Fight with the Pirates and the Problems of the Transmission of His Text*. Rev. ed. Cambridge, Eng., 1937.

Proudfoot, Richard. *Shakespeare: Text, Stage, and Canon*. London, 2001.

Richardson, Catherine. *Shakespeare's Stationers: Studies in Cultural Bibliography*. Philadelphia, 2013.

Sisson, C. J. *New Readings in Shakespeare.* 2 vols. Cambridge, Eng., 1956.

Straznicky, Marta. *The Book of the Play: Playwrights, Stationers, and Readers in Early Modern England.* Amherst, Mass., 2006.

Taylor, Gary. *Shakespeare Reshaped, 1606–1623.* Oxford, 1993.

———, and Michael Warren, eds. *The Division of the Kingdoms: Shakespeare's Two Versions of "King Lear."* Oxford, 1983.

Thompson, Ann, and others. *Which Shakespeare? A User's Guide to Editions.* Milton Keynes, Eng., 1992.

Vickers, Brian. *Appropriating Shakespeare: Contemporary Critical Quarrels.* New Haven, 1993.

———. *Shakespeare, Co-Author: A Historical Study of Five Collaborative Plays.* Oxford, 2002.

Walker, Alice. *Textual Problems of the First Folio.* Cambridge, Eng., 1953.

Wells, Stanley. *Re-editing Shakespeare for the Modern Reader.* Oxford, 1984.

Wells, Stanley, and Gary Taylor. *Modernizing Shakespeare's Spelling.* Oxford, 1979.

Werstine, Paul. "'Foul Papers' and 'Prompt-books': Printer's Copy for Shakespeare's *Comedy of Errors*," *Studies in Bibliography* 41 (1988), 232–46.

West, Anthony James. *The Shakespeare First Folio: The History of the Book.* Oxford, 2001.

### *Shakespeare Criticism to the 1930s*

Badawi, M. M. *Coleridge: Critic of Shakespeare.* Cambridge, Eng., 1973.

Bradby, Anne, ed. *Shakespeare Criticism, 1919–35.* London, 1936.

Coleridge, S. T. *Coleridge on Shakespeare: The Text of the Lectures of 1811–12,* ed. R. A. Foakes. Charlottesville, Va., 1971.

———. *Coleridge's Writings on Shakespeare,* ed. Terence Hawkes. New York, 1959.

Dowden, Edward. *Shakspere: A Critical Study of His Mind and Art.* 3rd ed. London, 1905.

Evans, G. Blakemore, ed. *Shakespeare: Aspects of Influence.* Cambridge, Mass., 1976.

Hazlitt, William. *Characters of Shakespear's Plays.* London, 1817.

Johnson, Samuel. *Johnson on Shakespeare,* ed. Arthur Sherbo. Vol. 7 of *The Yale Edition of the Works of Samuel Johnson.* New Haven, 1968.

Kermode, Frank, ed. *Four Centuries of Shakespearean Criticism.* New York, 1965.

Knight, G. Wilson. *The Shakespearian Tempest.* London, 1932, 1953.

Muir, Kenneth. "Fifty Years of Shakespearian Criticism: 1900–1950," *ShS* 4 (1951), 1–25.

Rabkin, Norman, ed. *Approaches to Shakespeare.* New York, 1964.

Ralli, Augustus. *A History of Shakespearian Criticism.* 2 vols. London, 1932.

Raysor, T. M., ed. *Samuel Taylor Coleridge: Shakespearean Criticism.* 2 vols. 2nd ed. London, 1960.

Schlegel, August Wilhelm. *Lectures on Dramatic Art and Literature,* trans. John Black, 1846. Rpt., New York, 1965.

Schücking, Levin L. *Character Problems in Shakespeare's Plays.* London, 1917; trans., 1922.

Shaw, G. B. *Shaw on Shakespeare,* ed. Edwin Wilson. New York, 1961.

Sherbo, Arthur. *Samuel Johnson, Editor of Shakespeare.* Urbana, Ill., 1956.

Smith, David Nichol, ed. *Shakespeare Criticism: A Selection.* World's Classics, Oxford, 1916.

———, ed. *Eighteenth Century Essays on Shakespeare.* 2nd ed. Oxford, 1963.

Stoll, E. E. *Art and Artifice in Shakespeare.* Cambridge, Eng., 1933, 1962.

Vickers, Brian, ed. *Shakespeare: The Critical Heritage.* Several volumes. London and Boston, 1974–.

Welsford, Enid. *The Fool: His Social and Literary History.* London, 1935; rpt. 1966.

Westfall, A. V. *American Shakespearean Criticism, 1607–1865.* New York, 1939.

### *Shakespeare Criticism from the 1940s to the 1970s*

Armstrong, Edward A. *Shakespeare's Imagination: A Study of the Psychology of Association and Inspiration.* London, 1946.

Barton, Anne. See Righter, Anne.

Bethell, S. L. *Shakespeare and the Popular Dramatic Tradition.* London and Durham, N.C., 1944.

Bevington, David, and Jay L. Halio, eds. *Shakespeare: Pattern of Excelling Nature.* Newark, Del., 1978.

Bloom, Allan, with Harry V. Jaffa. *Shakespeare's Politics.* New York and London, 1964.

Brown, John Russell. *Shakespeare's Plays in Performance.* London, 1966.

Bryant, J. A., Jr. *Hippolyta's View: Some Christian Aspects of Shakespeare's Plays.* Lexington, Ky., 1961.

Burckhardt, Sigurd. *Shakespearean Meanings.* Princeton, 1968.

Burke, Kenneth. *Language as Symbolic Action.* Berkeley, 1966.

Burke, Peter. *Popular Culture in Early Modern Europe.* New York, 1978.

Bush, Geoffrey. *Shakespeare and the Natural Condition.* Cambridge, Mass., 1956.

Calderwood, James L. *Shakespearean Metadrama.* Minneapolis, 1971.

Coghill, Neville. *Shakespeare's Professional Skills.* Cambridge, Eng., 1964.

Colie, Rosalie L. *Shakespeare's Living Art.* Princeton, 1974.

Council, Norman. *When Honour's at the Stake: Ideas of Honour in Shakespeare's Plays.* London, 1973.

Danby, John F. *Poets on Fortune's Hill: Studies in Sidney, Shakespeare, and Beaumont and Fletcher.* London, 1952.

Dean, Leonard F., ed. *Shakespeare: Modern Essays in Criticism.* New York, 1967.

Driver, Tom F. *The Sense of History in Greek and Shakespearean Drama.* New York, 1960.

Dusinberre, Juliet. *Shakespeare and the Nature of Women.* New York, 1975; 2nd ed., 1996.

Eagleton, Terence. *Shakespeare and Society.* New York and London, 1967.

Edwards, Philip. *Shakespeare and the Confines of Art.* London and New York, 1968.

Empson, William. *The Structure of Complex Words.* London, 1951.

Falconer, Alexander Frederick. *Shakespeare and the Sea.* London, 1964.

Fiedler, Leslie A. *The Stranger in Shakespeare.* New York, 1972.

Fly, Richard. *Shakespeare's Mediated World.* Amherst, Mass., 1976.

Frye, Roland M. *Shakespeare and Christian Doctrine.* Princeton, 1963.

Garber, Marjorie B. *Dream in Shakespeare: From Metaphor to Metamorphosis.* New Haven and London, 1974.

Goddard, Harold C. *The Meaning of Shakespeare.* Chicago, 1951.

Goldman, Michael. *Shakespeare and the Energies of Drama.* Princeton, 1972.

Granville-Barker, Harley. *Prefaces to Shakespeare.* 2 vols. Princeton, 1946–1947.

Harbage, Alfred. *As They Liked it.* New York, 1947.

———. *Shakespeare and the Rival Traditions.* New York, 1952.

Hawkes, Terence. *Shakespeare's Talking Animals: Language and Drama in Society.* London, 1973.

Hawkins, Harriett. *Poetic Freedom and Poetic Truth: Chaucer, Shakespeare, Marlowe, Milton.* Oxford, 1976.

Holland, Norman. *Psychoanalysis and Shakespeare.* New York, 1966.

———. *The Shakespearean Imagination.* New York, 1964.

Hunter, Robert Grams. *Shakespeare and the Mystery of God's Judgments.* Athens, Ga., 1976.

Jones, Emrys. *The Origins of Shakespeare.* Oxford, 1977.

Jorgensen, Paul A. *Shakespeare's Military World.* Berkeley and Los Angeles, 1956.

Kermode, Frank. *On Shakespeare's Learning.* Manchester, 1965, 2004.

Kernan, Alvin B. *The Playwright as Magician: Shakespeare's Image of the Poet in the English Public Theater.* New Haven, 1979.

———, ed. *Modern Shakespearean Criticism.* New York, 1970.

Kettle, Arnold, ed. *Shakespeare in a Changing World.* London and New York, 1964.

Knights, L. C. *Some Shakespearean Themes.* London, 1959.

Kott, Jan. *Shakespeare Our Contemporary.* New York, 1964.

Leavis, F. R. *The Common Pursuit.* London, 1952.

Levin, Harry. *Shakespeare and the Revolution of the Times: Perspectives and Commentaries.* Oxford, 1976.

Levin, Richard. *New Readings vs. Old Plays: Recent Trends in the Reinterpretation of English Renaissance Drama.* Chicago, 1979.

McAlindon, T. *Shakespeare and Decorum.* London and New York, 1973.

Rabkin, Norman. *Shakespeare and the Common Understanding*. New York, 1967.

Righter, Anne. *Shakespeare and the Idea of the Play*. London, 1962.

Rossiter, A. P. *Angel with Horns*. London, 1961.

Sanders, Wilbur. *The Dramatist and the Received Idea: Studies in the Plays of Marlowe and Shakespeare*. Cambridge, Eng., 1968.

Sewell, Arthur. *Character and Society in Shakespeare*. London, 1951.

Soellner, Rolf. *Shakespeare's Patterns of Self-Knowledge*. Columbus, Ohio, 1972.

Spencer, Theodore. *Shakespeare and the Nature of Man*. New York, 1942.

Spivack, Bernard. *Shakespeare and the Allegory of Evil*. New York, 1958.

Stewart, J. I. M. *Character and Motive in Shakespeare*. London, 1949.

Stirling, Brents. *The Populace in Shakespeare*. New York, 1949.

Traversi, Derek. *An Approach to Shakespeare*. 2 vols. Rev. ed. London, 1968.

Turner, Frederick. *Shakespeare and the Nature of Time: Moral and Philosophical Themes in Some Plays and Poems of William Shakespeare*. Oxford, 1971.

Van Laan, Thomas F. *Role-Playing in Shakespeare*. Toronto, 1978.

Vyvyan, John. *Shakespeare and the Rose of Love: A Study of the Early Plays in Relation to the Medieval Philosophy of Love*. London, 1960.

Watson, Curtis Brown. *Shakespeare and the Renaissance Concept of Honor*. Princeton, 1960.

Weimann, Robert. *Shakespeare and the Popular Tradition in the Theater*, ed. Robert Schwartz. Baltimore, 1978.

Whitaker, Virgil K. *Shakespeare's Use of Learning*. San Marino, Calif., 1953.

Zeeveld, W. Gordon. *The Temper of Shakespeare's Thought*. New Haven and London, 1974.

## *Shakespeare Criticism Since 1980, Including New Historicism, Gender Studies, and Poststructuralism*

See also, under *Shakespeare's Predecessors and Contemporaries*, Bednarz, Belsey, Braden, Bristol, Bruster, Cohen, Dolan, Farley-Hills, Findlay (two items), Freer, McLuskie, Orgel, Rasmussen, Rose, Shannon, Sullivan, and Vickers; and under *Shakespeare Criticism from the 1940s to the 1970s*, Weimann.

Adelman, Janet. *Suffocating Mothers: Fantasies of Maternal Origin in Shakespeare's Plays, "Hamlet" to "The Tempest."* Chicago, 1992.

Albanese, Denise. *Extramural Shakespeare*. New York, 2010.

Alexander, Catherine M. S., ed. *Shakespeare and Politics*. Cambridge, Eng., 2004.

———, and Stanley Wells, eds. *Shakespeare and Race*. Cambridge, Eng., 2000.

———, eds. *Shakespeare and Sexuality*. Cambridge, Eng., 2001.

Archer, John Michael. *Citizen Shakespeare: Freemen and Aliens in the Language of the Plays*. New York, 2005.

Aridge, Anthony. *Shakespeare and the Prince of Love: The Feast of Misrule in the Middle Temple*. London, 2000.

Armitage, David, Conal Condren, and Andrew Fitzmaurice, eds. *Shakespeare and Early Modern Political Thought*. Cambridge, 2009.

Armstrong, Philip. *Shakespeare in Psychoanalysis*. London and New York, 2001.

Atkins, G. Douglas, and David Bergeron, eds. *Shakespeare and Deconstruction*. New York, 1988.

Auden, W. H. *Lectures on Shakespeare*, ed. Arthur Kirsch. Princeton, 2000.

Bach, Rebecca Ann. *Shakespeare and Renaissance Literature before Heterosexuality*. New York, 2007.

Bache, William B., and Vernon P. Loggins. *Shakespeare's Deliberate Art*. Lanham, Md., 1996.

Bamber, Linda. *Comic Women, Tragic Men: A Study of Gender and Genre in Shakespeare*. Stanford, 1982.

Barber, C. L. *The Whole Journey: Shakespeare's Power of Development*. Berkeley, 1986.

Barroll, Leeds. *Politics, Plague, and Shakespeare's Theater: The Stuart Years*. Ithaca, N.Y., 1991.

Bate, Jonathan. *The Genius of Shakespeare*. Oxford, 1997.

———. *Shakespeare and Ovid*. Oxford, 1993.

———. *Shakespeare and the English Romantic Imagination*. Oxford, 1986, 1989.

———. *Shakespearean Constitutions: Politics, Theatre, Criticism, 1730–1830*. Oxford, 1989.

———, ed. *The Romantics on Shakespeare*. New York and London, 1992.

———, Jill L. Levenson, and Dieter Mehl, eds. *Shakespeare and the Twentieth Century: The Selected Proceedings of the International Shakespeare Association World Congress, Los Angeles, 1996*. Newark, Del., 1998.

Bates, Robin E. *Shakespeare and the Cultural Colonization of Ireland*. New York, 2008.

Beauregard, David N. *Catholic Theology in Shakespeare's Plays*. Newark, Del., 2008.

Beckwith, Sarah. *Shakespeare and the Grammar of Forgiveness*. Ithaca, N.Y., 2011.

Belsey, Catherine. *Shakespeare and the Loss of Eden: The Construction of Family Values in Early Modern Culture*. New Brunswick, N.J., 1999.

———. *Shakespeare in Theory and Practice*. Edinburgh, 2008.

Berger, Harry, Jr. *Making Trifles of Terrors: Redistributing Complicities in Shakespeare*. ed. Peter Erickson. Stanford, 1997.

Bergeron, David, ed. *Pageantry in the Shakespearean Theater*. Athens, Ga., 1985.

Berry, Edward. *Shakespeare and the Hunt: A Cultural and Social Study*. Cambridge, Eng., 2001.

Berryman, John. *Shakespeare*. New York, 1999.

Bevington, David. *How to Read a Shakespeare Play*. Oxford, 2006.

———. *Shakespeare: The Seven Ages of Human Experience*. Oxford, 2002, 2005.

———. *Shakespeare's Ideas: More Things in Heaven and Earth*. Oxford, 2008.

Blank, Paula. *Shakespeare and the Mismeasure of Renaissance Man*. Ithaca, N.Y., 2006.

Bloom, Allan David. *Shakespeare on Love and Friendship*. Chicago, 2000.

Bloom, Harold. *Shakespeare: The Invention of the Human*. New York, 1998.

Boehrer, Bruce Thomas. *Shakespeare among the Animals: Nature and Society in the Drama of Early Modern England*. New York, 2002.

Boose, Lynda E. "The Father and the Bride in Shakespeare," *PMLA* 97 (1982), 325–47.

Brayton, Dan, and Lynne Bruckner, eds. *Ecocritical Shakespeare*. Burlington, Vt., 2011.

Bretzius, Stephen. *Shakespeare in Theory: The Postmodern Academy and the Early Modern Theater*. Ann Arbor, Mich., 1997.

Bristol, Michael. *Shakespeare's America, America's Shakespeare*. London and New York, 1990.

———, ed. *Shakespeare and Moral Agency*. London and New York, 2009.

Brustein, Robert. *The Tainted Muse: Prejudice and Presumption in Shakespeare and His Time*. New Haven, 2009.

Bruster, Douglas. *Shakespeare and the Question of Culture: Early Modern Literature and the Cultural Turn*. New York, 2003.

Bulman, James C., ed. *Shakespeare, Theory, and Performance*. London and New York, 1996.

Burnett, Mark Thorton. *Constructing "Monsters" in Shakespearian Drama and Early Modern Culture*. Houndmills, Basingstoke, UK, and New York, 2002.

———, and Ramona Wray. *Shakespeare and Ireland: History, Politics, Culture*. New York, 1997.

Burrow, Colin. *Shakespeare and Classical Antiquity*. Oxford, 2013.

Burt, Richard. *Shakespeare and Mass Media*. New York and Basingstoke, Eng., 2002.

Caines, Michael. *Shakespeare and the Eighteenth Century*. Oxford, 2013.

Calderwood, James. *Shakespeare and the Denial of Death*. Amherst, Mass., 1987.

Callaghan, Dympna C. *Shakespeare Without Women: Representing Gender and Race on the Renaissance Stage*. London and New York, 2000.

———, ed. *A Feminist Companion to Shakespeare*. Oxford, 2000.

Callaghan, Dympna, Lorraine Helms, and Jyotsna Singh. *The Weyward Sisters: Shakespeare and Feminist Politics*. Cambridge, Eng., 1994.

Canino, Catherine Grace. *Shakespeare and the Nobility: The Negotiation of Lineage*. Cambridge, Eng., 2007.

Carey, John, ed. *English Renaissance Studies*. Oxford, 1980.

Cartelli, Thomas. *Repositioning Shakespeare: National Formations, Postcolonial Appropriations*. London and New York, 1999.

Cavell, Stanley. *Disowning Knowledge in Six Plays of Shakespeare*. Cambridge, Eng., 1987.

Charnes, Linda. *Notorious Identity: Materializing the Subject in Shakespeare*. Cambridge, Mass., 1993.

Chedgzoy, Kate, ed. *Shakespeare, Feminism, and Gender*. Basingstoke, Hants., New York, 2001.

———, Susanne Greenhaigh, and Robert Shaughnessy, eds. *Shakespeare and Childhood*. Cambridge, 2007.

Cheney, Patrick. *Shakespeare, National Poet-Playwright*. Cambridge, Eng., 2004.

———. *Shakespeare's Literary Authorship*. Cambridge, Eng., 2008.

Chernaik, Warren. *The Myth of Rome in Shakespeare and His Contemporaries*. Cambridge, Eng., 2011.

Clayton, Tom, Susan Brock, and Vincente Forés, eds. *Shakespeare and the Mediterranean: The Selected Proceedings of the International Shakespeare Association World Congress, Valencia, 2001*. Newark, Del., 2004.

Cohen, Adam Max. *Shakespeare and Technology: Dramatizing Early Modern Technological Revolutions*. New York, 2006.

Cohen, Adam Max, and others. *Wonder in Shakespeare*. New York, 2012.

Cohen, Stephen, ed. *Shakespeare and Historical Formalism*. Aldershot, Eng., 2007.

Cook, Amy. *Shakespearean Neuroplay: Reinvigorating the Study of Dramatic Texts through Cognitive Science*. New York, 2010.

Cook, Ann Jennalie. *Making a Match: Courtship in Shakespeare and His Society*. Princeton, 1991.

Cooper, Helen. *Shakespeare and the Medieval World*. London, 2010.

Corcoran, Neil. *Shakespeare and the Modern Poet*. Cambridge, Eng., 2010.

Cormack, Bradin, Martha C. Nussbaum, and Richard Strier, eds. *Shakespeare and the Law: A Conversation among Disciplines and Professions*. Chicago, 2013.

Cox, John D. *Shakespeare and the Dramaturgy of Power*. Princeton, 1989.

———. *Seeming Knowledge: Shakespeare and Skeptical Faith*. Waco, Tex., 2007.

Crane, Mary Thomas. *Shakespeare's Brain: Reading with Cognitive Theory*. Princeton, 2001.

Daileader, Celia R. *Eroticism on the Renaissance Stage: Transcendence, Desire, and the Limits of the Visible*. Cambridge, Eng., 1998.

Danson, Lawrence. *Shakespeare's Dramatic Genres*. Oxford, 2000.

Dawson, Anthony B. *Indirections: Shakespeare and the Art of Illusion*. Toronto, 1984.

Davis, Philip. *Shakespeare Thinking*. London, 2007.

De Cook, Travis, and Alan Galey, eds. *Shakespeare, the Bible, and the Form of the Book: Contested Scriptures*. New York, 2012.

Degenhardt, Jane Hwang, and Elizabeth Williamson. *Religion and Drama in Early Modern England: The Performance of Religion on the Renaissance Stage*. Farnham, Eng., and Burlington, Vt., 2011.

De Grazia, Margreta. *Shakespeare Verbatim: The Reproduction of Authenticity and the 1790 Apparatus*. Oxford, 1991.

———. Margreta, Maureen Quilligan, and Peter Stallybrass, eds. *Subject and Object in Renaissance Culture*. Cambridge, Eng., 1996.

———. Margreta, and Stanley Wells, eds. *The Cambridge Companion to Shakespeare*. Cambridge, Eng., 2nd ed., 2011.

Delabastita, Dirk, Jozef de Vos, and Paul Franssen, eds. *Shakespeare and European Politics*. Newark, Del., 2008.

Desmet, Christy. *Reading Shakespeare's Characters: Rhetoric, Ethics, and Identity*. Amherst, Mass., 1992.

Desmet, Christy, and Robert Sawyer, eds. *Shakespeare and Appropriation*. London and New York, 1999.

Desmet, Christy, and Anne Williams. Shakespearean *Gothic*. Cardiff, 2009.

DiPietro, Cary. *Shakespeare and Modernism*. Cambridge, Eng., 2006.

Dobsky, Bernard J., and Dustin Gish, eds. *Shakespeare and the Body Politic*. Lanham, Md., 2013.

Dobson, Michael. *The Making of the National Poet: Shakespeare, Adaptation, and Authorship, 1660–1769*. Oxford, 1992.

———, and Stanley Wells, eds. *The Oxford Companion to Shakespeare*. Oxford, 2001.

Dolan, Frances E. *Dangerous Familiars: Representations of Domestic Crime in England, 1550–1700*. Ithaca, N.Y., 1994.

Dollimore, Jonathan. *Radical Tragedy: Religion, Ideology and Power in the Drama of Shakespeare and His Contemporaries*. Chicago, 1984; New York, 1989.

Dollimore, Jonathan, and Alan Sinfield, eds. *Political Shakespeare: New Essays in Cultural Materialism*. Manchester, Eng., 1985.

Donaldson, E. Talbot. *The Swan at the Well: Shakespeare Reading Chaucer*. New Haven, 1985.

———, ed. *Alternative Shakespeares*. London, 1985.

Dorval, Patricia, ed. *Shakespeare et le Moyen-Âge*. Paris, 2002.

Dowd, Michelle M. "Shakespeare's Sleeping Workers," *ShakS* 41 (2013), 148–76.

Drakakis, John, and Dale Townshend. *Gothic Shakespeares*. New York, 2008.

Driver, Martha A., and Sid Ray, eds. *Shakespeare and the Middle Ages: Essays on the Performance and Adaptation of the Plays with Medieval Sources or Settings*. Jefferson, N.C., 2009.

Dubrow, Heather. *Shakespeare and Domestic Loss: Forms of Deprivation, Mourning, and Recuperation*. Cambridge, Eng., 1999 and 2004.

———, and Richard Strier, eds. *The Historical Renaissance: New Essays on Tudor and Stuart Literature and Culture*. Chicago, 1988.

Eagleton, Terence. *William Shakespeare*. Oxford, 1986.

Edmondson, Paul. *Shakespeare: Ideas in Profile*. Stratford-upon-Avon, 2015.

Edwards, Philip. *Shakespeare: A Writer's Progress*. Oxford, 1986.

———, et al., eds. *Shakespeare's Styles*. Cambridge, Eng., 1980.

Egan, Gabriel. *Shakespeare and Marx*. Oxford, 2004.

Engle, Lars. *Shakespearean Pragmatism: Market of His Time*. Chicago, 1993.

Enterline, Lynn. *The Rhetoric of the Body from Ovid to Shakespeare*. Cambridge, Eng., 2000.

Erickson, Peter. *Patriarchal Structures in Shakespeare's Drama*. Berkeley, 1985.

Erickson, Peter. *Rewriting Shakespeare, Rewriting Ourselves*. Berkeley, Cal., 1991.

Erickson, Peter, and Coppélia Kahn, eds. *Shakespeare's Rough Magic: Essays in Honor of C. L. Barber*. Newark, Del., 1985.

Erne, Lukas. *Shakespeare's Modern Collaborators*. London, 2008.

———. *Shakespeare as Literary Dramatist*. Cambridge, Eng., 2003.

Estok, Simon C. *Ecocriticism and Shakespeare: Reading Ecophobia*. New York, 2011.

Evett, David. *Discourses of Service in Shakespeare's England*. New York and Houndmills, Eng., 2005.

Fernie, Ewan. *Spiritual Shakespeare*. London and New York, 2005.

———. *Shame in Shakespeare*. London and New York, 2001.

Fitzpatrick, Joan. "Diet and Identity in Early Modern Dietaries and Shakespeare; The Inflections of Nationality, Gender, Social Rank, and Age," *ShakS* 42 (2014), 75–90.

Foakes, R. A. *Shakespeare and Violence*. Cambridge, Eng., 2003.

Frazer, Elizabeth. *Shakespeare and the Political Way*. London, 2007.

French, Marilyn. *Shakespeare's Division of Experience*. New York, 1981.

Frye, Northrop. *Northrop Frye on Shakespeare*, ed. Robert Sandler. New Haven, 1986.

Frye, Susan. *Pens and Needles: Women's Textualities in Early Modern England*. Philadelphia, 2010.

Fumerton, Patricia, and Simon Hunt, eds. *Renaissance Culture and the Everyday*. Philadelphia, 1999.

Gager, Valerie L. *Shakespeare and Dickens: The Dynamics of Influence*. Cambridge, Eng., 1996.

Gallagher, Lowell, and Shankar Raman. *Knowing Shakespeare: Senses, Embodiment and Cognition*. Basingstoke, Eng., and New York, 2010.

Garber, Marjorie. *Coming of Age in Shakespeare*. London, 1981.

———. *Shakespeare's Ghost Writers: Literature as Uncanny Causality*. London and New York, 1987.

———. *Shakespeare After All*. New York, 2004.

———, ed. *Cannibals, Witches, and Divorce: Estranging the Renaissance*. Baltimore, 1987.

———. *Profiling Shakespeare*. New York, 2008.

———. *Shakespeare and Modern Culture*. New York, 2008.

Garner, Shirley Nelson, Claire Kehane, and Madelon Sprengnether, eds. *The (M)other Tongue: Essays in Feminist Psychoanalytic Interpretation*. Ithaca, N.Y., 1985.

Ghose, Indira. *Shakespeare and Laughter: A Cultural History*. Manchester, 2008.

Gibbons, Brian. *Shakespeare and Multiplicity*. Cambridge, Eng., 1993.

Gillespie, Stuart, and Neil Rhodes. *Shakespeare and Elizabethan Popular Culture*. London, 2006.

Gillies, John. *Shakespeare and the Geography of Difference*. Cambridge, Eng., 1994.

Goldberg, Jonathan. *James I and the Politics of Literature: Jonson, Shakespeare, Donne, and Their Contemporaries*. Baltimore, 1983.

———. *Sodometries: Renaissance Texts, Modern Sexualities*. Stanford, 1992.

Gonzáles, José Manuel, and Holger Klein, eds. *Shakespeare and Spain*. Lewiston, Maine, 2002.

Grady, Hugh. *Shakespeare, Machiavelli, and Montaigne: Power and Subjectivity from "Richard II" to "Hamlet."* Oxford, 2002.

———, ed. *Shakespeare and Modernity: Early Modern to Millennium*. London and New York, 2000.

———. *Shakespeare's Universal Wolf: Postmodernist Studies in Early Modern Reification*. Oxford, 1996.

———. *The Modernist Shakespeare*. Oxford, 1991.

———. *Shakespeare and Impure Aesthetics*. Cambridge, 2009.

Graham, Kenneth J. E., and Philip D. Colington, eds. *Shakespeare and Religious Change*. Basingstoke, Hants., and New York, 2009.

Grav, Peter F. *Shakespeare and the Economic Imperative: What's Aught but as 'Tis Valued?* New York, 2008.

Greenblatt, Stephen. *Learning to Curse: Essays in Early Modern Culture*. London and New York, 1990.

———. *Marvelous Possessions: The Wonder of the New World*. Chicago, 1991.

———. *Renaissance Self-Fashioning: From More to Shakespeare*. Chicago, 1980.

———. *Shakespearean Negotiations: The Circulation of Social Energy in Renaissance England*. Berkeley, 1988.

———. *Shakespeare's Freedom*. Chicago, 2010.

———. *Will in the World: How Shakespeare Became Shakespeare*. New York, 2004.

Gross, Kenneth. *Shakespeare's Noise*. Chicago, 2001.

Groves, Beatrice. *Texts and Traditions: Religion in Shakespeare 1592–1604*. Oxford, 2007.

Guneratne, Anthony R. *Shakespeare and Genre: From Early Inheritances to Postmodern Legacies*. Basingstoke, Hants., and New York, 2011.

Habib, Imtiaz. *Shakespeare and Race: Postcolonial Praxis in the Early Modern Period*. Lanham and Oxford, 2000.

Hackett, Helen. *Shakespeare and Elizabeth: The Meeting of Two Myths*. Princeton, 2009.

Hadfield, Andrew. *Shakespeare and Republicanism*. Cambridge, Eng., 2004.

———. *Shakespeare and Renaissance Politics*. London, 2004.

———. *Shakespeare, Spenser, and the Matter of Britain*. Basingstoke, Hants, and New York, 2004.

———, and Paul Hammond, eds. *Shakespeare and Renaissance Europe*. London, 2004.

Hager, Alan. *Shakespeare's Political Animal: Schema and Schemata in the Canon*. Newark, Del., 1990.

Hall, Kim F. *Things of Darkness: Economies of Race and Gender in Early Modern England*. Ithaca, N.Y., 1994.

Hallett, Charles A. and Elaine S. *Analyzing Shakespeare's Action: Scene versus Sequence*. Cambridge, Eng., 1991.

Halpern, Richard. *Shakespeare Among the Moderns*. Ithaca, N.Y., 1997.

Hamilton, Donna B. *Shakespeare and the Politics of Protestant England*. Lexington, Ky., 1992.

Hamlin, William M. *The Image of America in Montaigne, Spenser, and Shakespeare: Renaissance Ethnography and Literary Tradition*. New York, 1995.

Hapgood, Robert. *Shakespeare the Theatre-Poet*. Oxford, 1991.

Hardy, Barbara. *Shakespeare's Storytellers: Dramatic Narration*. London and Chester Springs, 1997.

Harris, Jonathan Gil. *Shakespeare and Literary Theory*. Oxford, 2010.

———. *Sick Economics: Drama, Mercantilism, and Disease in Shakespeare's England*. Philadelphia, 2004.

———. *Untimely Matter in the Time of Shakespeare*. Philadelphia, 2010.

Hart, Jonathan. *Columbus, Shakespeare, and the Interpretation of the New World*. New York, 2003.

Hassel, R. Chris. *Shakespeare's Religious Language: A Dictionary*. London and New York, 2005.

Haverkamp, Anselm. *Shakespearean Genealogies of Power: A Whispering of Nothing in Hamlet, Richard II, Julius Caesar, Macbeth, The Merchant of Venice, and The Winter's Tale*. New York, 2011.

Hawkes, Terence. *Meaning by Shakespeare*. London and New York, 1992.

———, ed. *Alternative Shakespeares*. Vol. 2. London and New York, 1996.

Hawkins, Harriet. *The Devil's Party: Critical Counter-interpretations of Shakespearian Drama*. Oxford, 1985.

Henderson, Diana E. *Alternative Shakespeares 3*. London and New York, 2008.

———. *Collaborations with the Past: Reshaping Shakespeare across Time and Media*. Ithaca, N.Y., 2006.

Heller, Agnes. *Shakespeare as Philosopher of History*. Lanham, Md., 2002.

Hillman, David. *Shakespeare's Entrails: Belief, Scepticism and the Interior of the Body*. Houndmills, Eng., and New York, 2007.

Hillman, Richard. *Shakespeare, Marlowe, and the Politics of France*. Basingstoke, Hants., and New York, 2002.

Hofele, Andreas. *Stage, Stake, and Scaffold: Humans and Animals in Shakespeare's Theatre*. Oxford, 2011.

Holbrook, Peter. *Shakespeare's Individualism*. Cambridge, Eng., 2010.

Holderness, Graham. *Shakespeare and Venice*. Farnham, Surrey, Burlington, Vermont, 2010.

Holland, Norman, et al., eds. *Shakespeare's Personality*. Berkeley, 1989.

Holland, Peter. *Shakespeare and Narrative*. Cambridge, Eng., 2000.

Hopkins, Lisa. *Shakespeare on the Edge: Border-Crossing in the Tragedies and the Henriad*. Aldershot and Burlington, Vt., 2005.

Howard, Jean E. *Shakespeare's Art of Orchestration: Stage Technique and Audience Response*. Urbana, Ill., 1984.

———. *The Stage and Social Struggle in Early Modern England*. London, 1994.

———, and Marion F. O'Connor, eds. *Shakespeare Reproduced: The Text in History and Ideology*. London and New York, 1987.

———, and Scott Cutler Shershow, eds. *Marxist Shakespeares*. London and New York, 2001.

Huang, Alexander C. Y. *Chinese Shakespeares: Two Centuries of Cultural Exchange*. New York, 2009.

Hughes, Ted. *Shakespeare and the Goddess of Complete Being*. London, 1992.

Hulbert, Jennifer. *Shakespeare and Youth Culture*. New York, 2006.

Hunt, Maurice. *Shakespeare's Religious Allusiveness: Its Play and Tolerance*. Aldershot, Hampshire, and Burlington, Vt., 2004.

Iyengar, Sujata. *Shakespeare's Medical Language: A Dictionary*. New York, 2011.

Jackson, Ken, and Arthur F. Marotti. *Shakespeare and Religion: Early Modern and Postmodern Perspectives*. Notre Dame, Ind., 2011.

Jacobus, Lee A. *Shakespeare and the Dialectic of Certainty*. New York, 1992.

James, Heather. *Shakespeare's Troy: Drama, Politics, and the Translation of Empire*. Cambridge, Eng., 1997.

Jardine, Lisa. *Reading Shakespeare Historically*. London and New York, 1996.

———. *Still Harping on Daughters: Women and Drama in the Age of Shakespeare*. Sussex and Totowa, N.J., 1983; New York, 1989.

Johnson, David, ed. *Shakespeare and South Africa*. Oxford, 1996.

Jones, John. *Shakespeare at Work*. Oxford, 1995, 2000.

Joughlin, John J. *Shakespeare and National Culture*. Manchester, 1997.

Kahn, Coppélia. *Man's Estate: Masculine Identity in Shakespeare*. Berkeley, 1981.

———. *Roman Shakespeare: Warriors, Wounds, and Women*. London and New York, 1997.

Kamps, Ivo, ed. *Materialist Shakespeare: A History*. London, 1995.

———, ed. *Shakespeare Left and Right*. New York and London, 1991.

Karim-Cooper, Farah. *Cosmetics in Shakespeare and Renaissance Drama*. Edinburgh, 2006.

Kastan, David Scott. *Shakespeare After Theory*. London, 1999.

———. *Shakespeare and the Book*. Cambridge, Eng., 2001.

———. *Shakespeare and the Shapes of Time.* Hanover, N.H., 1982.

———, ed. *A Companion to Shakespeare.* Oxford, 1999.

Keevak, Michael. *Sexual Shakespeare: Forgery, Authorship, Portraiture.* Detroit, 2001.

Kehler, Dorothea. *Shakespeare's Widows.* New York, 2009.

Kendall, Gillian Murray, ed. *Shakespearean Power and Punishment: A Volume of Essays.* Madison, N.J., London, 1998.

Kernan, Alvin. *Shakespeare, the King's Playwright: Theater in the Stuart Court, 1603–1613.* New Haven, 1995.

Kerrigan, William. *Shakespeare's Promises.* Baltimore, 1999.

———. *On Shakespeare and Early Modern Literature: Essays.* Oxford, 2001.

Kidnie, Margaret Jane. *Shakespeare and the Problem of Adaptation.* Abingdon, Oxon., New York, 2009.

Kiefer, Frederick. *Shakespeare's Visual Theatre: Staging the Personified Characters.* Cambridge, Eng., 2003.

King, Ros, and Paul J. C. M. Fanssen. *Shakespeare and War.* Basingstoke, Hants., and New York, 2008.

Kinney, Arthur F. *Shakespeare and Cognition: Aristotle's Legacy and Shakespearean Drama.* New York, 2006.

———. *Shakespeare by Stages: An Historical Introduction.* Oxford, 2003.

———. *Shakespeare's Webs: Networks of Meaning in Renaissance Drama.* New York, 2004.

———, ed. *The Oxford Handbook of Shakespeare.* Oxford, 2012.

Kirsch, Arthur. *Shakespeare and the Experience of Love.* Cambridge, Eng., 1981.

Kishi, Tetsuo, and Graham Bradshaw. *Shakespeare in Japan.* London and New York, 2005.

Klein, Holger, and Jean-Marie Maguin. *Shakespeare and France.* Lewiston, N.Y., 1995.

———, and James L. Harner, eds. *Shakespeare and the Visual Arts.* Lewiston, Maine, 2000.

———. *Shakespeare Only.* Chicago, 2009.

Knapp, Robert S. *Shakespeare—The Theater and the Book.* Princeton, 1989.

———. *Shakespeare Only.* Chicago, 2009.

———. *Shakespeare's Tribe: Church, Nation, and Theater in Renaissance England.* Chicago, 2002.

Knowles, Richard, ed. *Shakespeare and Carnival: After Bakhtin.* London and New York, 1998.

Korda, Natasha. *Shakespeare's Domestic Economies: Gender and Property in Early Modern England.* Philadelphia, 2002.

———. *Labors Lost: Women's Work and the Early Modern English Stage.* Philadelphia, 2011.

Kosthová, Marcela. *Shakespeare in Transition: Political Appropriations in the Postcommunist Czech Republic.* Basingstoke, Hants., New York, 2010.

Krier, Theresa M. *Birth Passages: Maternity and Nostalgia, Antiquity to Shakespeare.* Ithaca, N.Y., 2001.

Lamb, Mary Ellen. *The Popular Culture of Shakespeare, Spenser, and Jonson.* London and New York, 2006.

Lander, Jesse M. *Inventing Polemic: Religion, Print, and Literary Culture in Early Modern England.* Cambridge, Eng., 2006.

Langley, Eric Francis. *Narcissism and Suicide in Shakespeare and His Contemporaries.* Oxford, 2009.

Lanier, Douglas. *Shakespeare and Modern Popular Culture.* Oxford, 2002.

Laoutaris, Chris. *Shakespearean Maternities: Crises of Conception in Early Modern England.* Edinburgh, 2008.

Lemon, Rebecca. *Treason by Words: Literature, Law, and Rebellion in Shakespeare's England.* Ithaca, N.Y., 2006.

Lenz, Carolyn, et al., eds. *The Woman's Part: Feminist Criticism of Shakespeare.* Urbana, Ill., 1980.

Lethbridge, J. B. *Shakespeare and Spenser: Attractive Opposites.* Manchester, 2008.

Levin, Carole, and John Watkins. *Shakespeare's Foreign Words: National and Transnational Identities in the Elizabethan Age.* Ithaca, N.Y., 2009.

Levin, Richard A. *Shakespeare's Secret Schemers: The Study of an Early Modern Dramatic Device.* Newark, Del., 2002.

Lindley, David. *Shakespeare and Music.* London, 2006.

Little, Arthur L., Jr. *Shakespeare Jungle Fever: National-Imperial Re-Visions of Race, Rape, and Sacrifice.* Stanford, 2000.

Loewenstain, David, and Michael Witmore, eds., *Shakespeare and Early Modern Religion.* Cambridge, 2015.

Loomba, Ania. *Gender, Race, Renaissance Drama.* Manchester, Eng., 1989.

———. *Shakespeare, Race, and Colonialism.* Oxford, 2002.

Loomba, Ania, and Martin Orkin, eds. *Post-colonial Shakespeares.* London and New York, 1998.

Loxley, James, and Mark Robson. *Shakespeare, Jonson, and the Claims of the Performative.* New York, 2012.

Lowenthal, David. *Shakespeare and the Good Life: Ethics and Politics in Dramatic Form.* Lanham, Md., 1997.

Lupton, Julia Reinhard. *Citizen-Saints: Shakespeare and Political Theology.* Chicago, 2005.

———. *Thinking with Shakespeare: Comparative and Interdisciplinary Essays for A. D. Nuttall.* London, 2007.

———. *Thinking with Shakespeare: Essays on Politics and Life.* Chicago, 2011.

MacFaul, Tom. *Male Friendship in Shakespeare and His Contemporaries.* Cambridge, Eng., 2007.

———. *Poetry and Paternity in Renaissance England: Sidney, Spenser, Shakespeare, Donne and Jonson.* Cambridge, Eng., 2010.

Maguire, Laurie E. *Shakespeare's Names.* Oxford, 2007.

———. *How to Do Things with Shakespeare: New Approaches, New Essays.* Oxford, 2008.

Mahon, John W., and Thomas A. Pendleton, eds. *"Fanned and Winnowed Opinion": Shakespearean Essays Presented to Harold Jenkins.* London, 1987.

Majeske, Andrew, and Emily Detmer-Goebel, eds. *Justice, Women, and Power in English Renaissance Drama.* Madison, N.J., 2009.

Makaryk, Irena R., and Joseph G. Price, eds. *Shakespeare and the Worlds of Communism and Socialism.* Toronto, 2006.

Maley, Willy, and Andrew Murphy, eds. *Shakespeare and Scotland.* Manchester, 2004.

———, and Philip Schwyer. *Shakespeare and Wales: From the Marches to the Assembly.* Farnham, Eng., and Burlington, Vermont, 2010.

Mallin, Eric. *Inscribing the Time: Shakespeare and the End of Elizabethan England.* Berkeley, 1995.

———. *Godless Shakespeare.* London, 2007.

Marcus, Leah. *Puzzling Shakespeare: Local Reading and its Discontents.* Berkeley, 1988.

Marrapodi, Michele, ed. *Shakespeare and Renaissance Literary Theories: Anglo-Italian Translations.* Aldershot, Eng., and Burlington, Vermont, 2010.

———, ed. *Shakespeare, Italy, and Intertextuality.* Manchester, 2004.

Marshall, Gail. *Shakespeare in the Nineteenth Century.* Cambridge, Eng., 2012.

———. *Shakespeare and Victorian Women.* Cambridge, Eng., 2009.

Martin, Christopher. *Constituting Old Age in Early Modern English Literature from Queen Elizabeth to King Lear.* Amherst, Mass., 2012.

Martindale, Charles, and A. B. Taylor, eds. *Shakespeare and the Classics.* Cambridge, Eng., 2004.

Martindale, Charles and Michelle. *Shakespeare and the Uses of Antiquity.* London and New York, 1990.

Marx, Steven. *Shakespeare and the Bible.* Oxford, 2000.

Matchett, William H. *Shakespeare and Forgiveness.* Santa Barbara, Cal., 2002.

Maus, Katharine Eisaman. *Being and Having in Shakespeare.* Oxford, 2013.

Mayer, Jean-Christophe. *Shakespeare's Hybrid Faith: History, Religion and the Stage.* Houndmills, Eng., and New York, 2006.

Mazzio, Carla, and Douglas Trevor, eds. *Historicism, Psychoanalysis, and Early Modern Culture.* London and New York, 2000.

McAlindon, T. *Shakespeare Minus "Theory."* Aldershot, Hants., and Burlington, Vermont, 2004.

McCoy, Richard C. *Faith in Shakespeare.* Oxford, 2013.

McDonald, Russ, ed. *Shakespeare Reread: The Texts in New Contexts.* Ithaca, N.Y., 1994.

———. *The Bedford Companion to Shakespeare: An Introduction with Documents.* Boston, 2001.

McMullan, Gordon, and Jonathan Hope, eds. *The Politics of Tragicomedy: Shakespeare and After.* London and New York, 1992.

McNeill, Fiona. *Poor Women in Shakespeare.* Cambridge, Eng., 2007.

McPherson, David C. *Shakespeare, Jonson, and the Myth of Venice.* Newark, Del., 1990.

Melchiori, Giorgio. *Shakespeare's Garter Plays: "Edward III" to "Merry Wives of Windsor."* Newark, Del., 1994.

Meron, Theodor. *Bloody Constraint: War, and Chivalry in Shakespeare.* Oxford, 1998.

———. *Henry's Wars and Shakespeare's Laws: Perspectives on the Law of War in the Later Middle Ages.* Oxford, 1994.

Milwes, Geoffrey. *Shakespeare and the Constant Romans.* Oxford, 1996.

Miola, Robert S. *Shakespeare's Reading.* Oxford and New York, 2000.

———. *Shakespeare's Rome.* Cambridge, Eng., 1983.

Moisan, Thomas, and Douglas Bruster, eds. *In the Company of Shakespeare: Essays on English Renaissance Literature in Honor of G. Blakemore Evans.* Madison, N.J., 2002.

Montrose, Louis. *The Purpose of Playing: Shakespeare and Cultural Politics of the Elizabethan Theatre.* Chicago, 1996.

———. *The Subject of Elizabeth: Authority, Gender, and Representation.* Chicago, 2006.

Mullaney, Steven. *The Place of the Stage: License, Play, and Power in Renaissance England.* Chicago, 1988.

Murphy, Andrew. *Shakespeare for the People: Working-Class Readers, 1800–1900.* Cambridge, Eng., 2008.

Nagarajan, S., and S. Viswanathan, eds. *Shakespeare in India.* Oxford, 1987.

Neely, Carol Thomas. *Broken Nuptials in Shakespeare's Plays.* New Haven, 1985.

Newman, Karen. *Fashioning Femininity and the English Renaissance Drama.* Chicago, 1991.

Nordlund, Marcus. *Shakespeare and the Nature of Love: Literature, Culture, Evolution.* Evanston, Ill., 2007.

Novy, Marianne. *Love's Argument: Gender Relations in Shakespeare.* Chapel Hill, N.C., 1984.

———, ed. *Women's Re-Visions of Shakespeare.* Urbana, Ill., 1990.

———, ed. *Transforming Shakespeare: Contemporary Women's Re-Visions in Literature and Performance.* New York, 1999.

Nuttall, A. D. *A New Mimesis: Shakespeare and the Representation of Reality.* London, 1983.

———. *Shakespeare the Thinker.* New Haven, 2007.

O'Neill, Stephen. *Staging Ireland: Representations in Shakespeare and Renaissance Drama.* Dublin, 2007.

Orgel, Stephen. *The Authentic Shakespeare and Other Problems of the Early Modern Stage.* London and New York, 2002.

———. *Imagining Shakespeare: A History of Texts and Visions.* Basingstoke, Eng., and New York, 2003.

———. *Spectacular Performances: Essays on Theatre, Imagery, Books and Selves in Early Modern England.* Manchester, 2011.

Orgel, Stephen, and Sean Keilen, eds. *Shakespeare and History; Post-modern Shakespeare; Shakespeare and the Interpretive Tradition; Shakespeare and the Literary Tradition; Shakespeare and Gender; Political Shakespeare; Shakespeare and the Arts, Shakespeare and the Editorial Tradition.* In separate volumes, New York, 1999.

Orkin, Martin. *Local Shakespeare: Proximations and Power.* London and New York, 2005.

Ortiz, Joseph M. *Shakespeare and the Politics of Music.* Ithaca, N.Y., 2011.

O'Rourke, James. *Retheorizing Shakespeare Through Presentist Readings.* New York, 2012.

Palfrey, Simon. *Shakespeare in Parts.* Oxford, 2007.

Parker, Patricia. *Shakespeare from the Margins: Language, Culture, Context.* Chicago, 1996.

———, and Geoffrey Hartman, eds. *Shakespeare and the Question of Theory.* London, 1985, 1990.

Paster, Gail Kern. *The Body Embarrassed: Drama and the Disciplines of Shame in Early Modern England.* Ithaca, N.Y., 1993.

———. *Humoring the Body: Emotions and the Renaissance Stage.* Chicago, 2004.

Patterson, Annabel. *Shakespeare and the Popular Voice.* Oxford, 1989.

Pechter, Edward. *Shakespeare Studies Today: Romanticism Lost.* Basingstoke, Hants., 2011.

Perry, Curtis, and John Watkins. *Shakespeare and the Middle Ages.* Oxford, 2009.

Pettigrew, Todd Howard James. *Shakespeare and the Practice of Physics: Medical Narratives on the Early Modern English Stage.* Newark, Del., 2007.

Pinciss, Gerald M. *Forbidden Matter: Religion and the Drama of Shakespeare and His Contemporaries.* Newark, Del., 2000.

Platt, Peter G. *Shakespeare and the Culture of Paradox.* Farnham, Eng., and Burlington, Vermont, 2009.

Polka, Brayton. *Shakespeare and Interpretation, or What You Will.* Newark, Del., 2011.

Poole, Kristen. *Radical Religion from Shakespeare to Milton.* Cambridge, Eng., 2000.

Poole, William, and Richard Scholar, eds. *Thinking with Shakespeare: Comparative and Interdisciplinary Essays.* London, 2007.

Pugliatti, Paola. *Shakespeare and the Just War Tradition.* Farnham, Eng., and Burlington, Vermont, 2010.

Pye, Christopher. *The Vanishing: Shakespeare, the Subject, and Early Modern Culture.* Durham, N.C., 2000.

Rabkin, Norman. *Shakespeare and the Problem of Meaning.* Chicago, 1981.

Rackin, Phyllis. *Shakespeare and Women.* Oxford, 2005.

Raffield, Paul, and Gary Watt, eds. *Shakespeare and the Law.* Oxford, 2008.

Rasmussen, Eric, and Aaron Santesso, eds. *Comparative Excellence: New Essays on Shakespeare and Johnson.* New York, 2007.

Richardson, Catherine. *Shakespeare and Material Culture.* Oxford, 2011.

———. *Political Shakespeare: New Essays in Cultural Materialism.* Ithaca, N.Y., 1985.

Ritchie, Fiona, and Peter Sabor, eds. *Shakespeare in the Eighteenth Century.* Cambridge, Eng., 2012.

Richmond, Velma Bourgeois. *Shakespeare, Catholicism, and Romance.* New York, 2000.

Roberts, Jeanne Addison. *Literary Criticism as Dream Analysis: Essays on Renaissance and Modern Writers.* Baltimore, 2009.

———. *The Shakespearean Will: Geography, Genus, and Gender.* Lincoln, Neb., 1991.

Roe, John. *Shakespeare and Machiavelli.* Cambridge, Eng., 2002.

Rozmovits, Linda. *Shakespeare and the Politics of Culture in Late Victorian England.* Baltimore, 1998.

Sabor, Peter, and Paul Yachnin. *Shakespeare and the Eighteenth Century.* Aldershot, Eng., and Burlington, Vermont, 2008.

Salingar, Leo. *Dramatic Form in Shakespeare and the Jacobeans.* Cambridge, Eng., 1986.

Sanders, Julie. *Shakespeare and Music: Afterlives and Borrowings.* Cambridge, Eng., and Malden, Mass., 2007.

Schalkwyk, David. *Shakespeare, Love, and Service.* Cambridge, Eng., 2008.

Schmidgall, Gary. *Shakespeare and Opera.* Oxford, 1990.

Schoch, Richard W. *Not Shakespeare: Bardolatry and Burlesque in the Nineteenth Century.* Cambridge, Eng., 2002.

Schreyer, Kurt A. *Shakespeare's Medieval Craft: Remnants of the Mysteries on the London Stage.* Ithaca, N.Y., 2014.

Schwartz, Murray, and Coppélia Kahn, eds. *Representing Shakespeare: New Psychoanalytic Essays.* Baltimore, 1980.

Scott, Charlotte. *Shakespeare and the Idea of the Book.* Oxford, 2007.

Scott, Michael. *Shakespeare and the Modern Dramatist.* New York, 1989.

Scott-Douglas, Amy. *Shakespeare Inside: The Bard Behind Bars.* London, 2007.

Shannon, Laurie. *Sovereign Amity: Figures of Friendship in Shakespeare's Contexts.* Chicago, 2002.

———. *The Accommodated Animal: Cosmopolity in Shakespeare's Locales.* Chicago, 2013.

Shapiro, James S. *Shakespeare and the Jews.* New York, 1996.

———. *A Year in the Life of William Shakespeare, 1599.* New York, 2005.

Shaughnessy, Robert, ed. *The Cambridge Companion to Shakespeare and Popular Culture.* Cambridge, Eng., 2007.

Shell, Alison. *Shakespeare and Religion.* London, 2005.

Sherman, Anita Gilman. *Skepticism and Memory in Shakespeare and Donne.* New York, 2007.

Shurbanov, Aleksandŭr. *Shakespeare's Lyricized Drama.* Newark, Del., 2010.

Siemon, James R. *Shakespearean Iconoclasm.* Berkeley, 1985.

Sillars, Suart. *Painting Shakespeare: The Artist as Critic, 1720–1820.* Cambridge, Eng., 2006.

Sinfield, Alan. *Faultlines: Cultural Materialism and the Politics of Dissident Reading.* Berkeley, 1992.

———. *Shakespeare, Authority, Sexuality: Unfinished Business in Cultural Materialism.* London and New York, 2006.

Skura, Meredith Anne. *The Literary Use of the Psychoanalytic Process.* New Haven, 1981.

———. *Shakespeare the Actor and the Purposes of Playing.* Chicago, 1993.

Slights, William W. E. *The Heart in the Age of Shakespeare.* Cambridge, Eng., 2008.

Spolsky, Ellen. *Word vs Image: Cognitive Hunger in Shakespeare's England.* Houndmills, Eng., 2007.

Smith, Bruce R. *Homosexual Desire in Shakespeare's England.* Chicago, 1991.

———. *Shakespeare and Masculinity.* Oxford, 2000.

Smith, Emma. *The Cambridge Shakespeare Guide.* Cambridge, 2012.

Snyder, Susan. *Shakespeare: A Wayward Journey.* Newark, Del., 2002.

Sokol, B. J. *Shakespeare and Tolerance.* Cambridge, Eng., 2008.

———, and Mary Sokol. *Shakespeare, Law, and Marriage.* Cambridge, Eng., 2003.

Stapleton, M. L. *Fated Sky: The "Femina Furens" in Shakespeare.* Newark, Del., and London, 2000.

Sterett, Joseph. *The Unheard Prayer: Religious Toleration in Shakespeare's Drama.* Leiden and Boston, 2012.

Stewart, Alan. *Shakespeare's Letters.* Oxford, 2008.

Stewart, Stanley. *Shakespeare and Philosophy.* New York, 2010.

Stockholder, Kay. *Dream Works: Lovers and Families in Shakespeare's Plays.* Toronto, 1987.

Stone, James W. *Crossing Gender in Shakespeare: Feminist Psychoanalysis and the Difference Within.* New York, 2010.

Streete, Adrian. *Protestantism and Drama in Early Modern England.* Cambridge, Eng., 2009.

Stríbrný, Zdeněk. *Shakespeare and Eastern Europe.* Oxford, 2000.

Strier, Richard. *The Unrepentant Renaissance: From Petrarch to Shakespeare to Milton.* Chicago, 2011.

Studing, Richard. *Shakespeare in American Painting: A Catalogue from the Late Eighteenth Century to the Present.* Rutherford, N.J., 1993.

Sturgess, Kim C. *Shakespeare and the American Nation.* Cambridge, Eng., 2004.

Tanner, Tony. *Prefaces to Shakespeare.* Cambridge, Mass., 2010.

Tassi, Marguerite A. *Women and Revenge in Shakespeare: Gender, Genre, and Ethics.* Selinsgrove, Pa., 2011.

Taylor, A. B. *Shakespeare's Ovid: The Metamorphoses in the Plays and Poems.* Cambridge, Eng., 2000.

Taylor, Dennis, and David Beauregard, eds. *Shakespeare and the Culture of Christianity in Early Modern England.* New York, 2003.

Taylor, Gary. *Reinventing Shakespeare: A Cultural History from the Restoration to the Present.* New York, 1989.

Taylor, Mark. *Shakespeare's Imitations.* Newark, Del., 2002.

Taylor, Michael. *Shakespeare Criticism in the Twentieth Century.* Oxford, 2001.

Tetsuo, Kiski, and Graham Bradshaw. *Shakespeare in Japan.* London, 2005.

Thompson, Ayanna. *Passing Strange: Shakespeare, Race, and Contemporary America.* Oxford, 2011.

———. *Colorblind Shakespeare: New Perspectives on Race and Performance.* New York and London, 2006.

Tigner, Amy L. *Literature and the Renaissance Garden from Elizabeth I to Charles II: England's Paradise.* Burlington, Vt., 2012.

Tobin, J. J. M. *Shakespeare's Favorite Novel: A Study of "The Golden Asse" as Prime Source.* Lanham, Md., 1984.

Traub, Valerie. *Desire and Anxiety: Circulations of Sexuality in Shakespearean Drama.* London, 1992.

Trawick, Buckner B. *Shakespeare and Alcohol.* Amsterdam, 1976.

Tribble, Evelyn G. *Cognition in the Globe: Attention and Memory in Shakespeare's Theatre.* New York and Houndmills, Eng., 2011.

Trivedi, Poonam, and David Bartholomeusz, eds. *India's Shakespeare: Translation, Interpretation, and Performance.* Newark, Del., 2005. Wells, Stanley. *Shakespeare, Sex, and Love.* Oxford, 2010.

Trudeau-Clayton, Margaret. *Jonson, Shakespeare, and Early Modern Virgil.* Cambridge, Eng., 1998.

Tucker, Kenneth. *Shakespeare and Jungian Typology: A Reading of the Plays.* Jefferson, N.C., 2003.

Turner, Henry. *Shakespeare's Double Helix.* London, 2007.

Usher, Peter D. *Shakespeare and the Dawn of Modern Science.* Amherst, N.Y., 2010.

Wagner, Matthew D. *Shakespeare, Theatre, and Time.* New York, 2012.

Ward, Ian. *Shakespeare and the Legal Imagination.* London, 1999.

Watson, Robert N. *The Rest is Silence: Death as Annihilation in the English Renaissance.* Berkeley, 1994.

———. *Shakespeare and the Hazards of Ambition.* Cambridge, Mass., 1984.

Wayne, Valerie, ed. *The Matter of Difference: Materialist Feminist Criticism of Shakespeare.* Ithaca, N.Y., 1991.

Weil, Judith. *Service and Dependency in Shakespeare's Plays.* Cambridge, Eng., 2005.

Weimann, Robert. *Author's Pen and Actor's Voice: Playing and Writing in Shakespeare's Theatre.* Cambridge, Eng., 2000.

Wells, Robin Headlam. *Shakespeare on Masculinity.* Cambridge, Eng., 2000.

———. *Shakespeare, Politics, and the State.* London, 1986.

———. *Shakespeare's Humanism.* Cambridge, Eng., 2005.

Wells, Stanley. *Shakespeare: For All Time.* Oxford, 2003.

———. *Shakespeare, Sex, and Love.* Oxford, 2010.

Wells, Stanley, and Lena Cowen Orlin, eds. *Shakespeare: An Oxford Guide.* Oxford, 2003.

Wheeler, Richard P. *Shakespeare's Development and the Problem Comedies: Turn and Counter-Turn.* Berkeley, 1981.

White, Paul Whitfield, and Suzanne R. Westfall, eds. *Shakespeare and Theatrical Patronage in Early Modern England.* Cambridge, Eng., 2002.

Wiggins, Martin. *Shakespeare and the Drama of His Time.* Oxford, 2000.

Williams, Gordon. *Shakespeare, Sex, and the Print Revolution.* London and Atlantic Highlands, N.J., 1996.

Wilson, Christopher. *Shakespeare's Musical Imagery.* London and New York, 2012.

Wilson, Richard. *Shakespeare in French Theory: King of Shadows.* London and New York, 2007.

Witmore, Michael. *Shakespearean Metaphysics.* London, 2007.

Woodbridge, Linda. *The Scythe of Saturn: Shakespeare and Magical Thinking.* Urbana, Ill., 1994.

Woodbridge, Linda, and Edward Berry, eds. *True Rites and Maimed Rites: Ritual and Anti-Ritual in Shakespeare and His Age.* Urbana, Ill., 1992.

Yachnin, Paul, and Jessica Sights, eds. *Shakespeare and Character: Theory, History, Performance, and Theatrical Persons.* New York, 2009.

———, and Patricia Badir, eds. *Shakespeare and the Culture of Performance.* Aldershot, Eng., and Burlington, Vermont, 2008.

Young, Alan R. *Hamlet and the Visual Arts, 1709–1900.* Newark, Del., and London, 2003.

Zamir, Tzachi. *Double Vision: Moral Philosophy and Shakespearean Drama.* Princeton, 2007.

Ziegler, Georgianna, ed. *Shakespeare's Unruly Women.* Washington, D.C., 1997.

Zurcher, Andrew. *Shakespeare and Law.* London, 2010.

## Shakespeare in Performance; Dramaturgy; Shakespeare in Film and Video

See also, under *Shakespeare Criticism from the 1940s to the 1970s,* Goldman and Granville-Barker; and under *Shakespeare Criticism Since 1980,* Weimann.

Aebischer, Pascale. *Shakespeare's Violated Bodies: Stage and Screen Performance.* Cambridge, Eng., 2004.

Anderson, Thomas P. *Performing Early Modern Trauma from Shakespeare to Milton.* Aldershot, Eng., 2006.

Astington, John. *Actors and Acting in Shakespeare's Time: The Art of Stage Playing.* Cambridge, Eng., 2010.

Bartholomeusz, Dennis. *Macbeth and the Players.* Cambridge, Eng., 1969.

Barton, John. *Playing Shakespeare*. London, 1984.

Bate, Jonathan, and Russell Jackson, eds. *Shakespeare: An Illustrated Stage History*. Oxford, 1996.

Beckerman, Bernard. *Shakespeare at the Globe, 1599–1609*. New York, 1962.

Berger, Harry. *Imaginary Audition: Shakespeare on Stage and Page*. Berkeley, 1989.

Bevington, David. *Action is Eloquence: Shakespeare's Language of Gesture*. Cambridge, Mass., 1984.

———. *This Wide and Universal Theater: Shakespeare in Performance Then and Now*. Chicago, 2007.

Bovilsky, Lara. *Barbarous Play: Race on the English Renaissance Stage*. Minneapolis, 2008.

Bristol, Michael, and Kathleen McLuskie, eds., with Christopher Holmes. *Shakespeare and Modern Theatre: The Performance of Modernity*. London and New York, 2001.

Brockbank, Philip, ed. *Players of Shakespeare*. Cambridge, Eng., 1985.

Brode, Douglas. *Shakespeare in the Movies: From the Silent Era to "Shakespeare in Love."* Oxford, 2000.

Brooks, Douglas A., and Lingui Yang, eds. *Shakespeare and Asia*. Lewiston, Maine, 2010.

Brown, Ivor. *Shakespeare and the Actors*. London, 1970.

Brown, John Russell. *Shakespeare's Plays in Performance*. London, 1966.

———. *Shakespeare's Dramatic Style*. London, 1970.

———. *Shakespeare and the Theatrical Event*. Basingstoke, Eng., and New York, 2002.

———. *Shakespeare Dancing: A Theatrical Study of the Plays*. Basingstoke, Hants., New York, 2005.

———. ed. *The Routledge Companion to Directors' Shakespeare*. New York, 2008.

———, and Kevin Ewart, eds. *The Routledge Companion to Actors' Shakespeare*. New York and Abingdon, Eng., 2012.

Brown, Pamela Allen, and Peter Parolin. *Women Players in England, 1500–1660: Beyond the All-Male Stage*. Aldershot, Eng., and Burlington, Vt., 2005.

Brydon, Diana, and Irena R. Makaryk, eds. *Shakespeare in Canada: A World Elsewhere*. Toronto, 2002.

Buchanan, Judith. *Shakespeare on Silent Film: An Excellent Dumb Discourse*. Cambridge, Eng., 2009.

Buhler, Stephen M. *Shakespeare in the Cinema: Ocular Proof*. Albany, N.Y., 2002.

Bulman, James C., ed. *Shakespeare Re-dressed: Cross-Gender Casting in Contemporary Performance*. Madison, N.J., 2008.

Bulman, J. C., and H. R. Coursen, eds. *Shakespeare on Television*. Hanover, N.H., 1988.

Burnet, Mark Thornton. *Filming Shakespeare in the Global Marketplace*. Basingstoke, Eng., and New York, 2007.

———, and Adrian Streete, eds. *Filming and Performing Renaissance History*. Houndmills, Eng., and New York, 2011.

———, and Ramona Wray, eds. *Screening Shakespeare in the Twenty-First Century*. Edinburgh, 2006.

Burt, Richard, and Lynda E. Boose, eds. *Shakespeare, the Movie, I and II: Popularizing the Plays on Film, TV, Video, and DVD*. London and New York, 1997 and 2003.

Cahill, Patricia A. *Unto the Breach: Martial Formations, Historical Trauma, and the Early Modern Stage*.

Carlisle, Carol Jones. *Shakespeare from the Greenroom: Actors' Criticisms of Four Major Tragedies*. Chapel Hill, N.C., 1969.

Cartelli, Thomas, and Katherine Rowe. *New Wave Shakespeare on Screen*. Cambridge, Mass., 2007.

Coghill, Nevill. *Shakespeare's Professional Skills*. Cambridge, Eng., 1964.

Cohen, Robert. *Acting Shakespeare*. Mountain View, Cal., 1991.

Cohn, Ruby. *Modern Shakespeare Offshoots*. Princeton, 1976.

Cook, Judith. *Shakespeare's Players*. London, 1983.

Coursen, Herbert R. *Shakespeare in Space: Recent Productions on Screen*. New York, 2002.

Cunningham, Vanessa. *Shakespeare and Garrick*. Cambridge, Eng., 2008.

D'Amico, Jack. *Shakespeare and Italy: The City and the Stage*. Gainesville, Fla., 2001.

Dash, Irene G. *Shakespeare and the American Musical*. Bloomington, In., 2010.

Davies, Anthony, and Stanley Wells, eds. *Shakespeare and the Moving Image: The Plays on Film and Television*. Cambridge, Eng., 1994.

Dessen, Alan C. *Recovering Shakespeare's Theatrical Vocabulary*. Cambridge, Eng., 1995.

———. *Rescripting Shakespeare: The Text, the Director, and Modern Productions*. Cambridge, Eng., 2002.

———, and Leslie Thomson. *A Dictionary of Stage Directions in English Drama, 1580–1642*. Cambridge, Eng., 1999.

Dobson, Michael. *Performing Shakespeare's Tragedies Today: The Actor's Perspective*. Cambridge, Eng., 2006.

———. *Shakespeare and Amateur Performance: A Cultural History*. Cambridge, Eng., 2011.

Donohue, Joseph W., Jr. *Dramatic Character in the English Romantic Age*. Princeton, 1970.

Downer, Alan S. *The Eminent Tragedian, William Charles Macready*. Cambridge, Mass., 1966.

Dymkowski, Christine, and Christie Carson, eds. *Shakespeare in Stages: New Theatre Histories*. Cambridge, Eng., 2010.

Edelman, Charles. *Brawl Ridiculous: Swordfighting in Shakespeare's Plays*. Manchester, Eng., 1992.

Escolme, Bridget. *Talking to the Audience: Shakespeare, Performance, Self*. Abingdon, Eng., 2005.

Falocco, Joe. *Reimagining Shakespeare's Playhouse: Early Modern Staging Conventions in the Twentieth Century*. Cambridge, Eng., 2010.

Fitter, Chris. *Radical Shakespeare: Politics and Stagecraft in the Early Career*. New York, 2012.

Flachmann, Michael. *Shakespeare in Performance: Inside the Creative Process*. Salt Lake City, Utah, 2011.

Fontane, Theodor. *Shakespeare in the London Theatre 1855–58*, trans. Russell Jackson. London, 1999.

Foulkes, Richard. *Performing Shakespeare in the Age of Empire*. Cambridge, Eng., 2002.

———, ed. *Shakespeare and the Victorian Age*. Cambridge, Eng., 1986.

Gregor, Keith. *Shakespeare in the Spanish Theatre: 1772 to the Present*. London, 2010.

Guneratne, Anthony R. *Shakespeare, Film Studies, and the Visual Cultures of Modernity*. New York, 2008.

Harris, Jonathan Gil, and Natasha Korda. *Staged Properties in Early Modern English Drama*. Cambridge, Eng., 2002.

Hatchuel, Sarah. *Shakespeare: From Stage to Screen*. Cambridge, Eng., 2004.

———, and Nathalie Vienne-Guerrin, eds. *Shakespeare on Screen: Television Shakespeare: Essays in Honour of Michele Willems*. Mont-Saint-Aignan, 2008.

Hattaway, Michael. *Elizabethan Popular Theatre: Plays in Performance*. London, 1982.

Hattaway, Michael, Boika Sokolova, and Derek Roper, eds. *Shakespeare in the New Europe*. Sheffield, Eng., 1994.

Hill, Errol. *Shakespeare in Sable: A History of Black Shakespearean Actors*. Amherst, Mass., 1984.

Hirrel, Michael J. "Duration of Performances and Length of Plays: How Shall We Beguile the Lazy Time?" *SQ* 61.2 (2010), 159–82.

Hodgdon, Barbara. *The Shakespeare Trade: Performances and Appropriations*. Philadelphia, 1998.

Höefle, Andreas. *Stage, Stake, and Scaffold: Humans and Animals in Shakespeare's Theatre*. Oxford, 2011.

Hogan, Charles B. *Shakespeare in the Theatre, 1701–1800*. 2 vols. Oxford, 1952–1957.

Holland, Peter. *Shakespeare, Memory, and Performance*. Cambridge, Eng., 2006.

———, ed. *Great Shakespeareans*, vol. 2: *Garrick, Siddons, Kean*. London and New York, 2010.

Huang, Alexander C. Y., and Charles S. Ross, eds. *Shakespeare in Hollywood, Asia, and Cyberspace*. West Lafayette, Ind., 2009.

Hunter, Lynette, and Peter Lichtenfels, eds. *Shakespeare, Language, and the Stage: The Fifth Wall, Approaches to Shakespeare from Criticism, Performance, and Theatre Studies*. London, 2005.

Jackson, Russell, ed. *The Cambridge Companion to Shakespeare on Film*. Cambridge, Eng., 2000.

———, *Shakespeare Films in the Making: Vision, Production, and Reception*. Cambridge, Eng., 2007.

———, and Robert Smallwood, eds. *Players of Shakespeare 2.* Cambridge, Eng., 1988. Followed by vols. 3 (1993); and 4, ed. Smallwood (1998).

Jones, Emrys. *Scenic Form in Shakespeare.* Oxford, 1971.

Jorgens, Jack L. *Shakespeare on Film.* Bloomington, Ind., 1977.

Kanelos, Peter, and Matt Kozusko, eds. *Thunder at a Playhouse: Essaying Shakespeare and the Early Modern Stage.* Selinsgrove, Penn., 2010.

Keegan, Daniel L. "Performing Prophecy: More Life on the Shakespearean Scene," *SQ* 62.3 (2011), 420–43.

Kennedy, Dennis, and Li Lan Yong, eds. *Shakespeare in Asia: Contemporary Performance.* Cambridge, Eng., 2010.

Kidnie, Margaret Jane. *Shakespeare and the Problem of Adaptation.* Milton Park, Abingdon, and New York, 2009.

Kiefer, Frederick. *Shakespeare's Visual Theatre: Staging the Personified Characters.* Cambridge, Eng., 2003.

Lehmann, Courtney. *Shakespeare Remains: Theater to Film, Early Modern to Postmodern.* Ithaca, N.Y., 2002.

Levith, Murray J. *Shakespeare in China.* London, 2004.

Lopez, Jeremy. *Theatrical Convention and Audience Response in Early Modern England.* Cambridge, Eng., 2003.

MacKay, Ellen. *Persecution, Plague, and Fire: Fugitive Histories of the Stage in Early Modern England.* Chicago, 2011.

Magnus, Laury, and Walter W. Cannon, eds. *Who Hears in Shakespeare? Auditory Worlds on Stage and Screen.* Madison, N.J., 2012.

Mann, David. *Shakespeare's Women: Performance and Conception.* Cambridge, Eng., 2008.

Manvell, Roger. *Shakespeare and the Film.* London and New York, 1971.

Massai, Sonia. *World-Wide Shakespeares: Local Appropriations in Film and Performance.* Abingdon, Eng., and New York, 2005.

McGuire, Philip C. *Speechless Dialect: Shakespeare's Open Silences.* Berkeley, 1985.

McGuire, Philip C., and David A. Samuelson. *Shakespeare: The Theatrical Dimension.* New York, 1979.

McLuskie, Kathleen, and Michael Bristol, with Christopher Holmes. *Shakespeare and Modern Theatre: The Performance of Modernity.* London and New York, 2001.

Meagher, John C. *Pursuing Shakespeare's Dramaturgy.* Madison, N.J., 2003.

Moncrief, Kathryn M., and Kathryn R. McPherson. *Performing Maternity in Early Modern England.* Aldershot, Eng., and Burlington, Vt., 2007.

Murray, Barbara A., ed. *Shakespeare Adaptations from the Restoration: Five Plays.* Madison, N.J., 2005.

Occhiogrosso, Frank, ed. *Shakespeare in Performance: A Collection of Essays.* Newark, Del., 2003.

———. *Shakespearean Performance: New Studies.* Madison, N.J., 2008.

Odell, George C. D. *Shakespeare from Betterton to Irving.* 2 vols. New York, 1920, 1966.

Orlin, Lena Cowen, and Miranda Johnson-Haddad, eds. *Staging Shakespeare: Essays in Honor of Alan C. Dessen.* Newark, Del., 2007.

Paulin, Roger, ed. *Great Shakespeareans*, vol. 3: *Voltaire, Goethe, Schlegel, Coleridge.* London and New York, 2010.

Poel, William. *Shakespeare in the Theatre.* London, 1913, 1968.

Poole, Adrian, ed. *Great Shakespeareans*, vol. 4: *Lamb, Hazlitt, Keats.* London and New York, 2010.

Pressly, William L. *The Artist as Original Genius: Shakespeare's "Fine Frenzy" in Late-Eighteenth-Century British Art.* Newark, Del., 2007.

Price, Joseph G., ed. *The Triple Bond: Plays, Mainly Shakespearean, in Performance.* University Park, Pa., 1975.

Quince, Rohan. *Shakespeare in South Africa: Stage Productions During the Apartheid Era.* New York, 2000.

Rawson, Claude, ed. *Great Shakespeareans*, vol. 1: *Dryden, Pope, Johnson, Malone.* London and New York, 2010.

Rhu, Lawrence F. *Stanley Cavell's American Dream: Shakespeare, Philosophy, and Hollywood Movies.* New York, 2006.

Rokison, Abigail. *Shakespearean Verse Speaking: Text and Theatre Practice.* Cambridge, Eng., 2009.

Rothwell, Kenneth S. *A History of Shakespeare on Screen: A Century of Film and Television.* Cambridge, Eng., 1999; 2nd ed., 2005.

———, and Annabella Hankin Melzer. *Shakespeare on Screen: An International Filmography and Videography.* New York, 1990.

Rutter, Carol Chillington. *Enter the Body: Women and Representation on Shakespeare's Stage.* London and New York, 2001.

———. *Shakespeare and Child's Play: Performing Lost Boys on Stage and Screen.* London and New York, 2007.

———, ed. *Documents of the Rose Playhouse.* Manchester, Eng., 1999.

———, et al. *Clamorous Voices: Shakespeare's Women Today.* New York, 1989.

Sammons, Eddie. *Shakespeare: A Hundred Years on Film.* Lanham, Md., 2004.

Samuelson, David A., ed. *Shakespeare: The Theatrical Dimension.* New York, 1959.

Sanders, Julie. *Shakespeare and Music: Afterlives and Borrowings.* Cambridge, Eng., 2007.

Sasayama, Takashi, J. R. Mulryne, and Margaret Shewring, eds. *Shakespeare and the Japanese Stage.* Cambridge, Eng., 1998.

Schalkwyk, David. *Speech and Performance in Shakespeare's Sonnets and Plays.* Cambridge, Eng., 2002.

Schoch, Richard W. *Shakespeare's Victorian Stage: Performing History in the Theatre of Charles Kean.* Cambridge, Eng., 1998.

Shapiro, Michael. *Gender in Play on the Shakespearean Stage: Boy Heroines and Female Pages.* Ann Arbor, Mich., 1994.

Shattuck, Charles H. *The Shakespeare Promptbooks: A Descriptive Catalogue.* Urbana, Ill., 1965.

———. *Shakespeare on the American Stage from the Hallams to Edwin Booth.* Washington, D.C., 1976; *from Booth and Barrett to Sothern and Marlowe*, Washington, D.C., 1987.

Shaughnessy, Robert. *Shakespeare in Performance.* New York, 2000.

Sheen, Erica. *Shakespeare and the Institution of Theatre: The Best in This Kind.* Basingstoke, Hants., and New York, 2009.

Slater, Ann Pasternak. *Shakespeare the Director.* Brighton, Sussex, and Totowa, N.J., 1982.

Speaight, Robert. *William Poel and the Elizabethan Revival.* London, 1954.

Spencer, Hazelton. *Shakespeare Improved: The Restoration Versions in Quarto and on the Stage.* Cambridge, Mass., 1927.

Sprague, Arthur Colby. *Shakespeare and the Actors.* Cambridge, Mass., 1944.

———. *Shakespearian Players and Performances.* Cambridge, Mass., 1953.

Styan, J. L. *Shakespeare's Stagecraft.* Cambridge, Eng., 1967.

Teague, Frances. *Shakespeare and the American Popular Stage.* Cambridge, Eng., 2006.

Thompson, Ayanna. *Performing Race and Torture on the Early Modern Stage.* New York and London, 2008.

Thompson, Marvin and Ruth, eds. *Shakespeare and the Sense of Performance: Essays in the Tradition of Performance Criticism in Honor of Bernard Beckerman.* Newark, Del., 1989.

Van Laan, Thomas F. *Role-Playing in Shakespeare.* Toronto, 1958.

Weimann, Robert. *Shakespeare and the Power of Performance: Stage and Page in Elizabethan Theatre.* Cambridge, Eng., 2008.

———, and Douglas Bruster. *Shakespeare and the Power of Performance: Stage and Page in the Elizabethan Theatre.* Cambridge, Eng., 2008.

Wells, Stanley. *Royal Shakespeare: Four Major Productions at Stratford-upon-Avon.* Manchester, Eng., 1977.

———, and Sarah Stanton, eds. *The Cambridge Companion to Shakespeare on Stage.* Cambridge, Eng., 2002.

Werner, Sarah. *Shakespeare and Feminist Performance: Ideology on Stage.* London and New York, 2001.

Wilder, Lina Perkins. *Shakespeare's Memory Theatre: Recollection, Properties, and Character.* Cambridge, Eng., 2010.

Wilson, Robert Frank. *Shakespeare in Hollywood.* Madison, N.J., and London, 2000.

Worthen, W. B. *Shakespeare and the Force of Modern Performance.* Cambridge, Eng., 2003.

## *The Comedies*

See also, under *Shakespeare Criticism Since 1980*, Drakakis (essay by Belsey), Erickson and Kahn (essay by Adelman), and Paster (Chapter 7).

Anderson, Linda. *A Kind of Wild Justice: Revenge in Shakespeare's Comedies*. Newark, Del., 1987.

Barber, C. L. *Shakespeare's Festive Comedy*. Princeton, 1959.

Barton, Anne. *The Names of Comedy*. Toronto, 1990.

Berry, Edward. *Shakespeare's Comic Rites*. Cambridge, Eng., 1984.

Berry, Ralph. *Shakespeare's Comedies: Explorations in Form*. Princeton, 1972.

———. *The Shakespearean Metaphor: Studies in Language and Form*. Totowa, N.J., 1978.

Bloom, Harold, ed., *William Shakespeare: Comedies and Romances*. New York, 1986.

Bradbury, Malcolm, and David Palmer, eds. *Shakespearian Comedy*. London, 1972.

Brown, John Russell. *Shakespeare and His Comedies*. London, 1957, 1968.

Brown, John Russell, and Bernard Harris, eds. *Early Shakespeare*. Stratford-upon-Avon Studies 3. London, 1961. (Including an essay by Frank Kermode on "The Mature Comedies.")

Bryant, J. A., Jr. *Shakespeare and the Uses of Comedy*. Lexington, Ky., 1986.

Burke, William Kenneth. *A New Approach to Shakespeare's Early Comedies: Theoretical Foundations*. New York, 1998.

Carroll, William C. *The Metamorphoses of Shakespearean Comedy*. Princeton, 1985.

Champion, Larry S. *The Evolution of Shakespeare's Comedy*. Cambridge, Mass., 1970.

Charlton, H. B. *Shakespearian Comedy*. London, 1938.

Charney, Maurice, ed. *Shakespearean Comedy*. New York, 1980.

Cody, Richard. *The Landscape of the Mind: Pastoralism and Platonic Theory in Tasso's "Aminta" and Shakespeare's Early Comedies*. Oxford, 1969.

Collins, Michael J., ed. *Shakespeare's Sweet Thunder: Essays on the Early Comedies*. Newark, Del., 1997.

Cook, Ann Jennalie. *Making a Match: Courtship in Shakespeare and His Society*. Princeton, 1991.

Cordner, Michael, Peter Holland, and John Kerrigan, eds. *English Comedy*. Cambridge, Eng., 1994.

Cox, Roger L. *Shakespeare's Comic Changes: The Time-Lapse Metaphor as Plot Device*. Athens, Ga., 1991.

Draper, Ronald P. *Shakespeare: The Comedies*. New York, 2000.

Dutton, Richard, and Jean E. Howard, eds. *A Companion to Shakespeare's Works*. Vol. 3, The Comedies. Oxford, 2003.

Elam, Keir. *Shakespeare's Universe of Discourse: Language-Games in the Comedies*. Cambridge, Eng., 1984.

Evans, Bertrand. *Shakespeare's Comedies*. Oxford, 1960.

Freedman, Barbara. *Staging the Gaze: Postmodernism, Psychoanalysis, and Shakespearean Comedy*. Ithaca, N. Y., 1991.

Friedman, Michael D. *"The World Must Be Peopled": Shakespeare's Comedies of Forgiveness*. Madison, N. J., and London, 2002.

Frye, Northrop. "The Argument of Comedy," *English Institute Essays 1948*. New York, 1949.

———. *A Natural Perspective: The Development of Shakespearean Comedy and Romance*. New York, 1965.

Gay, Penny. *The Cambridge Introduction to Shakespeare's Comedies*. Cambridge, Eng., 2008.

Hale, John K. *The Shakespeare of the Comedies: A Multiple Approach*. Bern, N.Y., 1996.

Hall, Jonathan. *Anxious Pleasures: Shakespearean Comedy and the Nation-State*. Madison, N. J., 1995.

Hamilton, A. C. *The Early Shakespeare*. San Marino, Calif., 1967.

Hassel, R. Chris. *Faith and Folly in Shakespeare's Romantic Comedies*. Athens, Ga., 1980.

Hawkins, Sherman H. "The Two Worlds of Shakespearean Comedy," *ShakS 3* (1967), 62–80.

Howard, Jean E. *Theater of a City: The Places of London Comedy, 1598–1642*. Philadelphia, 2007.

Hunter, Robert G. *Shakespeare and the Comedy of Forgiveness*. New York, 1965.

Huston, J. Dennis. *Shakespeare's Comedies of Play*. New York, 1981.

Jensen, Ejner J. *Shakespeare and the Ends of Comedy*. Bloomington, Ind., 1991.

Jensen, Eijner J. *Shakespeare and the Ends of Comedy*. Bloomington, Ind., 1991.

———. *Religion and Revelry in Shakespeare's Festive World*. Cambridge, Eng., 2008.

Leggatt, Alexander. *English Stage Comedy, 1490–1990: Five Centuries of a Genre*. London and New York, 1998.

———. *Shakespeare's Comedy of Love*. London and New York, 1974.

———, ed. *The Cambridge Companion to Shakespearean Comedy*. Cambridge, Eng., 2002.

Lerner, Laurence, ed. *Shakespeare's Comedies: An Anthology of Modern Criticism*. Baltimore, 1967.

Levin, Richard A. *Love and Society in Shakespearean Comedy: A Study of Dramatic Form and Content*. Newark, Del., 1985.

Maslen, R. W. *Shakespeare and Comedy*. London, 2005.

Miola, Robert S. *Shakespeare and Classical Comedy: The Influence of Plautus and Terence*. Oxford, 1994.

Nevo, Ruth. *Comic Transformations in Shakespeare*. London, 1980.

Newman, Karen. *Shakespeare's Rhetoric of Comic Character*. New York and London, 1985.

Palmer, David J., and Malcolm Bradbury, eds. *Shakespearian Comedy*. Statford-upon-Avon Studies 1. London, 1972.

Palmer, John. *Comic Characters of Shakespeare*. London, 1946.

Pettet, E. C. *Shakespeare and the Romance Tradition*. London, 1949.

Phialas, Peter G. *Shakespeare's Romantic Comedies*. Chapel Hill, N.C., 1966.

Richmond, Hugh M. *Shakespeare's Sexual Comedy*. Indianapolis, 1971.

Ryan, Keirnan. *Shakespeare's Comedies*. Basingstoke, Eng., and New York, 2009.

Salingar, Leo. *Shakespeare and the Traditions of Comedy*. Cambridge, Eng., 1974.

Shaheen, Naseeb. *Biblical References in Shakespeare's Comedies*. Newark, Del., 1993.

Smidt, Kristian. *Unconformities in Shakespeare's Early Comedies*. London, 1986.

Smith, Emma, ed. *Shakespeare's Comedies*. Malden, Mass., and Oxford, 2004.

Stevenson, David L. *The Love-Game Comedy*. New York, 1946.

Stockton, Will. *Playing Dirty: Sexuality and Waste in Early Modern Comedy*. Minneapolis, 2011.

Traversi, Derek. *Shakespeare: The Early Comedies*. London, 1960.

Turner, Robert Y. *Shakespeare's Apprenticeship*. Chicago, 1974.

Westlund, Joseph. *Shakespeare's Reparative Comedies: A Psychoanalytic View of the Middle Plays*. Chicago, 1984.

Wheeler, Richard P. "Deaths in the Family: The Loss of a Son and the Rise of Shakespearean Comedy," *SQ* 51 (2000), 127–53.

Williamson, Marilyn. *The Patriarchy of Shakespeare's Comedies*. Detroit, 1986.

## The Problem Plays

Bentley, Greg W. *Shakespeare and the New Disease: The Dramatic Function of Syphilis in "Troilus and Cressida," "Measure for Measure," and "Timon of Athens."* New York and Bern, 1989.

Campbell, Oscar James. *Shakespeare's Satire*. London and New York, 1943, 1963.

Clark, Ira. *Rhetorical Readings, Dark Comedies, and Shakespeare's Problem Plays*. Gainesville, Fla., 2007.

Dutton, Richard, and Jean E. Howard, eds. *A Companion to Shakespeare's Works*. Vol. 4, The Poems, Problem Comedies, Late Plays. Oxford, 2003.

Foakes, R. A. *Shakespeare, The Dark Comedies to the Last Plays: From Satire to Celebration*. Charlottesville, Va., 1971.

Frye, Northrop. *The Myth of Deliverance: Reflections on Shakespeare's Problem Comedies*. Toronto, 1983.

Hawkes, Terry. *Shakespeare and the Reason: A Study of the Tragedies and the Problem Plays*. London and New York, 1964.

Jamieson, Michael. "The Problem Plays, 1920–1970: A Retrospect," *ShS* 25 (1972), 1–10.

Lawrence, W. W. *Shakespeare's Problem Comedies*. New York, 1931, 1960.

Maquerlot, Jean-Pierre. *Shakespeare and the Mannerist Tradition: A Reading of Five Problem Plays*. Cambridge, Eng., 1995. (Includes consideration of *Julius Caesar* and *Hamlet*.)

McCandless, David. *Gender and Performance in Shakespeare's Problem Comedies*. Bloomington, Ind., 1997.

Muir, Kenneth, and Stanley Wells, eds. *Aspects of Shakespeare's "Problem Plays": Articles Reprinted from "Shakespeare Survey."* Cambridge, Eng., 1982.

Schanzer, Ernest. *The Problem Plays of Shakespeare.* New York, 1963.

Thomas, Vivian. *The Moral Universe of Shakespeare's Problem Plays.* New York, 1987.

Tillyard, E. M. W. *Shakespeare's Problem Plays.* Toronto, 1949.

Wheeler, Richard P. *Shakespeare's Development and the Problem Comedies: Turn and Counter-Turn.* Berkeley, 1981.

Ure, Peter. *William Shakespeare: The Problem Plays.* London, 1961.

## The Taming of the Shrew

See also, under *Shakespeare's Predecessors and Contemporaries*, Marrapodi (essay by Bevington); under *Shakespeare Criticism from the 1940s to the 1970s*, Garber; under *Shakespeare Criticism Since 1980*, Auden, Fumerton and Hunt (essay by Dolan), Kahn, Lenz et al. (essay by Bean), McDonald (essay by Boose), Novy (*Love's Argument*), and Parker and Hartman (essay by Fineman); under *Shakespeare in Performance*, Rutter; and under *The Comedies*, R. Berry, Charlton, Collins (essays by Dessen and Rutter), Evans, Hawkins, Huston, Leggatt, Nevo, and Stevenson.

Boose, Lynda E. " 'Scolding Brides and Bridling Scolds': Taming the Woman's Unruly Member," *SQ* 42 (1991), 179–213.

Brunvand, Jan Harold. "The Folktale Origin of *The Taming of the Shrew,*" *SQ* 17 (1966), 345–59.

Crocker, Holly A. "Performing Passivity and Playing A-Part in *The Taming of the Shrew,*" *SQ* 54 (2003), 142–59.

Dolan, Frances E., ed. *"The Taming of the Shrew": Text and Contexts.* New York, 1996.

Haring-Smith, Tori. *From Farce to Metadrama; A Stage History of "The Taming of the Shrew," 1594–1983.* Westport, Conn., 1985.

Hosley, Richard. "Was There a 'Dramatic Epilogue' to *The Taming of the Shrew?*" *Studies in English Literature* 1:2 (1961), 17–34.

Hutson, Lorna. *The Usurer's Daughter: Male Friendship and Fictions of Women in Sixteenth-Century England.* London and New York, 1994.

Jayne, Sears. "The Dreaming of *The Shrew,*" *SQ* 17 (1966), 41–56.

Korda, Natasha. "Household Kates: Domesticating Commodities in *The Taming of the Shrew,*" *SQ* 47 (1996), 109–31.

Maguire, Laurie E. "Cultural Control in *The Taming of the Shrew,*" *Renaissance Drama* n.s. 26 (1995), 83–104.

Marcus, Leah. "The Shakespearean Editor as Shrew-Tamer," *English Literary Rennaisance* 22 (1922), 177–200.

Marino, James J. "The Anachronistic Shrews," *SQ* 60.1 (2009), 25–46.

Newman, Karen. "Renaissance Family Politics and Shakespeare's *The Taming of the Shrew,*" *English Literary Renaissance* 16 (1986), 86–100.

Saccio, Peter. "Shrewd and Kindly Farce," *ShS* 37 (1984), 33–40.

Thompson, Ann, ed., *The Taming of the Shrew.* Cambridge, Eng., 1984.

Thorne, W. B. "Folk Elements in *The Taming of the Shrew,*" *Queen's Quarterly* 75 (1968), 482–96.

## A Midsummer Night's Dream

See also, under *Life in Shakespeare's England*, De Grazia, Quilligan, and Stallybrass (essay by Parker); under *Shakespeare Criticism from the 1940s to the 1970s*, Calderwood, Coghill, Garber, Granville-Barker, and Kott; under *Shakespeare Criticism Since 1980*, Callaghan (*A Feminist Companion*, essay by Loomba), Mazzio and Trevor (essay by Maus), Montrose, Parker, Paster, and Patterson (Chapter 3); and under *The Comedies*, Barber, Bloom (essay by Girard), Brown and Harris (essays by Kermode and Merchant), Carroll, Collins (essay by Halio), Evans, Huston, Leggatt, Lerner, Palmer and Bradbury (essay by Wells), and Smidt.

Arab, Ronda. *Manly Mechanicals on the Early Modern English Stage.* Selinsgrove, Pa., 2011.

Bevington, David. " 'But We Are Spirits of Another Sort': The Dark Side of Love and Magic in *A Midsummer Night's Dream,*" *Medieval and Renaissance Studies*, ed. Siegfried Wenzel. Chapel Hill, N.C., 1978.

Burke, Kenneth. "Why 'A Midsummer Night's Dream'?" *SQ* 57.3 (2006), 297–308.

Donaldson, E. Talbot. *The Swan at the Well: Shakespeare Reads Chaucer.* New Haven, 1985.

Garner, Shirley Nelson. "*A Midsummer Night's Dream*: 'Jack Shall Have Jill; Nought Shall Go Ill,' " *Women's Studies* 9 (1981), 47–63.

Girard, René. "Myth and Ritual in Shakespeare's *A Midsummer Night's Dream,*" *Textual Strategies: Perspectives in Post-Structuralist Criticism*, ed. Josué V. Harari. Ithaca, N.Y., 1979.

Herbert, T. Walter. *Oberon's Mazed World.* Baton Rouge, La., 1977.

Howard, Skiles. "Hands, Feet, and Bottoms: Decentering the Cosmic Dance in *A Midsummer Night's Dream,*" *SQ* 44 (1993), 325–42.

Lamb, Mary Ellen. "*A Midsummer Night's Dream*: The Myth of Theseus and the Minotaur," *Texas Studies in Literature and Language* 21 (1979), 478–91.

———. " 'Taken by the Fairies': Fairy Practices and the Production of Popular Culture in *A Midsummer Night's Dream,*" *SQ* 51 (2000), 277–312.

Montrose, Louis Adrian. " 'Shaping Fantasies': Figurations of Gender and Power in Elizabethan Culture," *Representations 2* (1.2, Spring 1983), 61–94.

Nuttall, A. D. "*A Midsummer Night's Dream*: Comedy as *Apotrope* of Myth," *ShS* 53 (2000), 49–59.

Olson, Paul A. "*A Midsummer Night's Dream* and the Meaning of Court Marriage," *ELH* 24 (1957), 95–119.

Ormerod, David. "*A Midsummer Night's Dream*: The Monster in the Labyrinth," *ShakS* 11 (1978), 39–52.

Sofer, Andrew. *Dark Matter: Invisibility in Drama, Theater, and Performance.* Ann Arbor, Mi., 2013.

Paster, Gail Kern, and Howard Skiles, eds. *A Midsummer Night's Dream: Texts and Contexts.* Boston and New York, 1999.

Pearson, D'Orsay W. " 'Unkinde' Theseus: A Study in Renaissance Mythography," *English Literary Renaissance* 4 (1974), 276–98.

Wall, Wendy. "Why Does Puck Sweep?: Fairylore, Merry Wives, and Social Struggle," *SQ* 52 (2001), 67–106.

Warren, Roger. "*A Midsummer Night's Dream*": Text and Performance. Text and Performance. London, 1983.

Williams, Gary Jay. *Our Moonlight Revels: "A Midsummer Night's Dream" in the Theatre.* Ames, Iowa, 1997.

Young, David P. *Something of Great Constancy: The Art of "A Midsummer Night's Dream."* New Haven, 1966.

## The Merchant of Venice

See also, under *Shakespeare's Predecessors and Contemporaries*, Rose (ed. *Renaissance Drama*, essay by Whigham); under *Shakespeare's Language*, Donawerth; under *Shakespeare Criticism from the 1940s to the 1970s*, Burkhardt, Fiedler, and Granville-Barker; under *Shakespeare Criticism Since 1980*, Auden, Callaghan (*A Feminist Companion*, essay by Singh), Dawson, Erickson and Kahn (essays by Kahn and Wheeler), Garber (*Cannibals*, essay by Mullaney), Grady (essays by Drakakis, Freinkel, and Mallin), Howard and O'Connor (essay by Moisan), Mazzio and Trevor (essay by Siemon), Novy (*Love's Argument*, Chapter 4), Rabkin, and Wayne (essay by Leventen); and under *The Comedies*, Barber, Bradbury and Palmer (essay by Palmer), Brown and Harris (essays by J. R. Brown and Kermode), Evans, Leggatt, Levin, Nevo, and Smidt.

Adelman, Janet. *Blood Relations: Christian and Jew in "The Merchant of Venice."* Chicago, 2008.

Ackermann, Zeno. "Performing Oblivion / Enacting Remembrance: The Merchant of Venice in West Germany, 1945 to 1961," *SQ* 62.1 (2011), 364–95.

Adelman, Janet. *Blood Relations: Christian and Jew in "The Merchant of Venice."* Chicago, 2008.

Auden, W. H. "Brothers and Others," *"The Dyer's Hand" and Other Essays.* New York, 1948.

Bailey, Amanda. "Shylock and the Slaves: Owing and Owning in *The Merchant of Venice*," *SQ* 62.1 (2011), 1–24.

Berger, Harry, Jr. "Marriage and Mercifixion in *The Merchant of Venice*: The Casket Scene Revisited," *SQ* 32 (1981), 155–62.

———. *A Fury in the Words: Love and Embarrassment in Shakespeare's Venice*. New York, 2012.

Bonnell, Andrew G. *Shylock in Germany: Antisemitism and the German Theatre from the Enlightenment to the Nazis*. London and New York, 2008.

Boose, Lynda E. "The Comic Contract and Portia's Golden Ring," *ShakS* 20 (1988), 241–54.

Bulman, James C. *The Merchant of Venice*. Shakespeare in Performance. Manchester, Eng., 1991.

Cohen, Walter. "*The Merchant of Venice* and the Possibilities of Historical Criticism," *ELH* 49 (1982), 765–89.

Daniel, Drew. "'Let me have judgment, and the Jew his will': Melancholy Epistemology and Masochieti Fantasy in *The Merchant of Venice*," *SQ* 61.2 (2010), 206–34.

Danson, Lawrence. *The Harmonies of "The Merchant of Venice."* New Haven and London, 1978.

Dessen, Alan C. "The Elizabethan Stage Jew and Christian Example: Gerontus, Barabas, and Shylock," *Modern Language Quarterly* 35 (1974), 231–45.

Edelman, Charles. "Which is the Jew that Shakespeare Knew? Shylock on the Elizabethan Stage," *ShS* 52 (1999), 99–106.

Engle, Lars. "'Thrift is Blessing': Exchange and Explanation in *The Merchant of Venice*," *SQ* 37 (1986), 20–37.

Freud, Sigmund. "The Theme of the Three Caskets," *Complete Psychological Works of Sigmund Freud*, trans. James Strachey et al. London, 1973–4.

Girard, René. "'To Entrap the Wisest': A Reading of *The Merchant of Venice*," *Literature and Society*. Selected Papers from the English Institute, 1978, ed. Edward W. Said. Baltimore, 1980.

Gross, Kenneth. *Shylock Is Shakespeare*. Chicago, 2006.

Hammill, Graham. "Converting Cruelty and Constituting Community in Shakespeare's Venice: A Response to Drew Daniel," *SQ* 61.2 (2010), 234–40.

Hutson, Lorna. *The Usurer's Daughter: Male Friendship and Fictions of Women in Sixteenth-Century England*. London and New York, 1994.

Jardine, Lisa. "Cultural Confusion and Shakespeare's Learned Heroines: 'These Are Old Paradoxes,'" *SQ* 38 (1987), 1–18.

Kaplan, Lindsay M. "Jessica's Mother: Medieval Constructions of Jewish Race and Gender in *The Merchant of Venice*," *SQ* 58 (2007), 1–30.

Kitch, Aaron. "Shylock's Sacred Nation," *SQ* 59.2 (2008), 131–55.

Korda, Natasha. "Dame Usury: Gender, Credit and (Ac)counting in the Sonnets and *The Merchant of Venice*." *SQ* 60.2 (2009), 129–53.

Lever, J. W. "Shylock, Portia, and the Values of Shakespearian Comedy," *SQ* 3 (1952), 383–6.

Lewalski, Barbara K. "Biblical Allusion and Allegory in *The Merchant of Venice*," *SQ* 13 (1962), 327–43.

MacKay, Maxine. "*The Merchant of Venice*: A Reflection of the Early Conflict Between Courts of Law and Courts of Equity," *SQ* 15:4 (1964), 371–5.

Mahon, John W., and Ellen MacLeod Mahon, eds. "*The Merchant of Venice*": *New Critical Essays*. London, 2002.

Moody, A. D. *Shakespeare: "The Merchant of Venice."* London, 1964.

Newman, Karen. "Portia's Ring: Unruly Women and Structures of Exchange in *The Merchant of Venice*," *SQ* 38 (1987), 19–33.

Normand, Lawrence. "Reading the Body in *The Merchant of Venice*," *Textual Practice* 5 (1991), 55–73.

Overton, Bill. "*The Merchant of Venice*": *Text and Performance*. Atlantic Highlands, N.J., 1987.

Parten, Anne. "Re-establishing Sexual Order: The Ring Episode in *The Merchant of Venice*," *Women's Studies* 9 (1982), 145–55.

Pettet, E. C. "*The Merchant of Venice* and the Problem of Usury," *English Association Essays and Studies* 31 (1945), 19–33.

Shapiro, James. *Shakespeare and the Jews*. New York, 1996.

Shapiro, Michael. *How Shylock Became Fagin's Cousin: The Jewish Old Clothes Man in Shakespeare, Dickens, and Victorian Burlesque Theatre*. Santa Cruz, Cal., 2009.

Smith, Emma. "Was Shylock Jewish?" *SQ* 64.2 (2013), 188–219.

Turner, Henry S. "The Problem of the More-Than-One: Friendship, Calculation, and Political Association in *The Merchant of Venice*," *SQ* 57 (2006), 413–42.

Whigham, Frank. "Ideology and Class Conduct in *The Merchant of Venice*," *Renaissance Drama* 10 (1979), 93–115.

Yaffe, Martin D. *Shylock and the Jewish Question*. Baltimore, 1997.

## Much Ado About Nothing

See also, under *Shakespeare's Predecessors and Contemporaries*, Marrapodi (essay by Salingar); under *The Comedies*, R. Berry, Brown, Cordner et al. (essay by Everett), Evans, Hunter, Huston, Leggatt, Levin, Nevo, Newman, Salingar, and Stevenson; under *Shakespeare Criticism from the 1940s to the 1970s*, Rossiter; and under *Shakespeare Criticism Since 1980*, Howard and O'Connor (essay by Howard), Kirsch, Lenz et al. (essay by Hays), and Neely.

Barish, Jonas A. "Pattern and Purpose in the Prose of Much Ado About Nothing," *Rice U. Studies* 60:2 (1974), 19–30.

Berger, Harry, Jr. "Against the Sink-a-Pace: Sexual and Family Politics in *Much Ado About Nothing*," *SQ* 33 (1982), 302–13.

Cook, Carol. "'The Sign and Semblance of Her Honor': Reading Gender Difference in *Much Ado about Nothing*," *PMLA* 101 (1986), 186–202.

Dawson, Anthony B. "Much Ado about Signifying," *Studies in English Literature* 22 (1982), 211–21.

Dusinberre, Juliet. "Much Ado about Lying," *Shakespeare Readers, Audiences, Players*, eds. R. S. White, Charles Edelman, and Christopher Wortham. Nedlands, Australia, 1998.

Everett, Barbara. "*Much Ado About Nothing*," *Critical Quarterly* 3 (1961), 319–35.

Friedman, Michael D. "Male Bonds and Marriage in *All's Well* and *Much Ado*," *Studies in English Literature* 35 (1995), 231–49.

Jorgensen, Paul A. "*Much Ado About Nothing*," *SQ* 5 (1954), 287–95. Rpt. in *Redeeming Shakespeare's Words*. Berkeley, 1962.

Lane, Robert. "'Foremost in report': Social Identity and Masculinity in *Much Ado About Nothing*," *Upstart Crow* 16 (1996), 31–47.

Lewalski, Barbara K. "Love, Appearance, and Reality: Much Ado About Something," *Studies in English Literature* 8 (1968), 235–51.

Mason, Pamela. "*Much Ado About Nothing*": *Text and Performance*. Basingstoke, 1992.

Ormerod, David. "Faith and Fashion in *Much Ado About Nothing*," *ShS* 25 (1972), 93–105.

Taylor, Michael. "*Much Ado About Nothing*: The Individual in Society," *Essays in Criticism* 23 (1973), 146–53.

## As You Like It

See also, under *The Comedies*, Barber, R. Berry, Bradbury and Palmer (essay by Anne Barton), Brown, Hunter, Leggatt, Nevo, and Salingar; and under *Shakespeare Criticism Since 1980*, Belsey, Callaghan (*A Feminist Companion*, essay by Neely), Erickson, Lenz et al. (essay by Park), Mahon and Pendleton (essay by Gibbons), and McDonald (essay by Wofford).

Alpers, Paul. *What Is Pastoral?* Chicago, 1996.

Barnet, Sylvan. "Strange Events: Improbability in *As You Like It*," *ShakS* 4 (1968), 119–31.

Bono, Barbara J. "Mixed Gender, Mixed Genre in Shakespeare's *As You Like It*," *Renaissance Genres: Essays on Theory, History, and Interpretation*, ed. Barbara Kiefer Lewalski. Cambridge, Mass., 1986.

Debax, Jean-Paul, and Yves Peyré, eds. "*As You Like It*": *Essais critiques*. Toulouse, 1998.

Doran, Madeleine. "'Yet Am I Inland Bred,'" *SQ* 15:2 (1964), 99–114.

Fortin, René E. "'Tongues in Trees': Symbolic Patterns in *As You Like it*," *Texas Studies in Literature and Language* 14 (1973), 569–82.

Gardner, Helen. "*As You Like It*," *More Talking of Shakespeare*, ed. John Garrett. London and New York, 1959.

Halio, Jay L. " 'No Clock in the Forest': Time in *As You Like It*," *Studies in English Literature* 2 (1962), 197–207.

Hattaway, Michael. "Dating *As You Like It*: Epilogues and Prayers, and the Problems of 'As the Dial Hand Tell's O'er,'" *SQ* 60.2 (2009), 154–67.

Hayles, Nancy K. "Sexual Disguise in *As You Like It* and *Twelfth Night*," *ShS* 32 (1979), 63–72.

Howard, Jean E. "Crossdressing, The Theatre, and Gender Struggle in Early Modern England," *SQ* 39 (1988), 418–40.

Kernan, Alvin B. *The Cankered Muse*. New Haven, 1959.

Knowles, Richard. "Myth and Type in *As You Like It*," *ELH* 33 (1966), 1–22.

Marcus, Leah S. "Anti-Conquest and *As You Like It*," *ShakS* 42 (2014), 170–95.

Marshall, Cynthia. "The Doubled Jaques and Constructions of Negation in *As You Like It*," *SQ* 49 (1998), 375–92.

———, ed. *Shakespeare in Production: "As You Like It."* Cambridge, Eng., 2004.

Montrose, Louis Adrian. " 'The Place of a Brother' in *As You Like It*: Social Process and Comic Form," *SQ* 32 (1981), 28–54.

Ronk, Martha. "Locating the Visual in *As You Like It*," *SQ* 52 (2001), 255–76.

Schleiner, Louise. "Voice, Ideology, and Gendered Subjects: The Case of *As You Like It* and *Two Gentlemen*," *SQ* 50 (1999), 285–309.

Young, David. *The Heart's Forest*. New Haven, 1972.

## Twelfth Night

See also, under *The Comedies*, Barber, E. Berry, Bradbury and Palmer (essay by Anne Barton), Brown, Brown and Harris (essay by Kermode), Hunter, Leggatt, Levin, Nevo, and Salingar; and under *Shakespeare Criticism Since 1980*, Callaghan (*A Feminist Companion*, essay by Neely), Erickson and Kahn (essay by Booth), Greenblatt (*Shakespearean Negotiations*, Chapter 3), Hamilton (Chapter 4), Hawkes (essay by Elam), Howard, and Parker and Hartman (essay by Hartman).

Arlidge, Anthony. *Shakespeare and the Prince of Love: The Feast of Misrule in the Middle Temple*. London, 2000.

Auden, W. H. "Music in Shakespeare," *"The Dyer's Hand" and Other Essays*. New York, 1948.

Bloom, Harold, ed. *Modern Critical Interpretations of "Twelfth Night."* New York, 1987.

Booth, Stephen. *Precious Nonsense: The Gettysburg Address, Ben Jonson's Epitaphs on His Children, and "Twelfth Night."* Berkeley, 1998.

Brown, John Russell. "Directions for *Twelfth Night*, or What You Will," *Tulane Drama Review* 5:4 (1961), 77–88.

Downer, Alan S. "Feste's Night," *College English* 13 (1952), 258–65.

Eagleton, Terence. "Language and Reality in *Twelfth Night*," *Critical Quarterly* 9 (1967), 217–28.

Elam, Keir. "The Fertile Eunuch: *Twelfth Night*, Early Modern Intercourse, and the Fruits of Castration," *SQ* 47 (1996), 1–36.

Hollander, John. "*Twelfth Night* and the Morality of Indulgence," *Sewanee Review* 67 (1959), 220–38.

Hutson, Lorna. "On Not Being Deceived: Rhetoric and the Body in *Twelfth Night*," *Texas Studies in Literature and Language* 38 (1996), 140–74.

Kerrigan, John. "Secrecy and Gossip in *Twelfth Night*," *ShS* 50 (1997), 65–80.

Leech, Clifford. *"Twelfth Night" and Shakespearian Comedy*. Toronto, 1965.

Lewalski, Barbara K. "Thematic Patterns in *Twelfth Night*," *ShakS* 1 (1965), 168–81.

Potter, Lois. *"Twelfth Night": Text and Performance*. London, 1985.

Salingar, L. D. "The Design of *Twelfth Night*," *SQ* 9 (1958), 117–39.

Schalkwyk, David. "Love and Service in *Twelfth Night* and the Sonnets," *SQ* 56 (2005), 76–100.

Schiffer, James, ed. *"Twelfth Night": New Critical Essays*. London and New York, 2011.

Shannon, Laurie J. "Nature's Bias: Renaissance Homonormativity and Elizabethan Likeness," *Modern Philology* 98 (2000), 183–210.

Wells, Stanley. *Royal Shakespeare*. Manchester, Eng., 1977. (Includes an account of John Barton's production of *Twelfth Night*.)

Welsford, Enid. *The Fool: His Social and Literary History*. London, 1935.

Williams, Porter, Jr. "Mistakes in *Twelfth Night* and Their Resolution," *PMLA* 76 (1961), 193–9.

## Measure for Measure

See also, under *The Comedies*, Hunter and Newman; under *The Problem Plays*, Frye, Schanzer, and Wheeler; under *Shakespeare Criticism from the 1940s to the 1970s*, Empson, Fly, Holland, Levin (pp. 171–93), and Sewell; and under *Shakespeare Criticism Since 1980*, Cox, Dollimore, Dollimore and Sinfield (essays by Dollimore and McLuskie), Drakakis (essay by Rose), Goldberg (Chapter 5), Grady (*Shakespeare and Modernity*, essay by Engle), Hamilton (Chapter 5), Holland et al. (essay by Adelman), Kirsch, Marcus, Mullaney (Chapter 4), and Skura (pp. 243–70).

Bennett, Josephine Waters. *"Measure for Measure" as Royal Entertainment*. New York, 1966.

Bennett, Robert B. *Romance and Reformation: The Erasmian Spirit of Shakespeare's "Measure for Measure."* Newark, Del., 2000.

Brown, Carolyn E. "The Wooing of Duke Vincentio and Isabella of *Measure for Measure*: 'The Image of It Gives [Them] Content,' " *ShakS* 22 (1994), 189–219.

Cacicedo, Alberto. " 'She is fast my wife': Sex, Marriage, and Ducal Authority in *Measure for Measure*," *ShakS* 23 (1995), 187–209.

Chamberlain, Stephanie. "Defrocking Ecclesiastical Authority: *Measure for Measure* and the Struggle for Matrimonial Reform in Early Modern England," *Ben Jonson Journal* 7 (2000), 115–28.

Chambers, R. W. "The Jacobean Shakespeare and *Measure for Measure*," *Proceedings of the British Academy* 23 (1937), 135–92.

Coghill, Nevill. "Comic Form in *Measure for Measure*," *ShS* 8 (1955), 14–27.

Desens, Marliss C. *The Bed-Trick in English Renaissance Drama: Explorations in Gender, Sexuality, and Power*. Newark, Del., 1994.

Fergusson, Francis. *The Human Image in Dramatic Literature*. Garden City, N.Y., 1957.

Gless, Darryl. *"Measure for Measure," the Law, and the Convent*. Princeton, 1979.

Gurnis, Musa. " 'Most ignorant of what he's most assured': The Hermeneutics of Predestination in *Measure for Measure*," *ShakS* 42 (2014), 141–69.

Lascelles, Mary. *Shakespeare's "Measure for Measure."* London, 1953.

Leavis, F. R. "The Greatness of *Measure for Measure*," *Scrutiny* 10 (1942), 234–47.

Leggatt, Alexander. "Substitution in *Measure for Measure*," *SQ* 39 (1988), 342–59.

Nagarajan, S. "*Measure for Measure* and Elizabethan Betrothals," *SQ* 14 (1963), 115–19.

Shell, Marc. *The End of Kinship: "Measure for Measure," Incest, and the Ideal of Universal Siblinghood*. Stanford, 1988.

Shuger, Debora Kuller. *Political Theologies in Shakespeare's England: The Sacred and the State in "Measure for Measure."* Basingstoke, Eng., and New York, 2001.

Stevenson, David L. *The Achievement of "Measure for Measure."* Ithaca, N.Y., 1966.

Wilson, Harold S. "Action and Symbol in *Measure for Measure* and *The Tempest*." *SQ* 4 (1953), 375–84.

Wood, Nigel. *"Measure for Measure."* Theory in Practice Series. Buckingham and Philadelphia, 1996.

## The Histories

See also, under *Shakespeare's Predecessors and Contemporaries*, Hillman.

Alexander, Peter. *Shakespeare's, "Henry VI" and "Richard III."* Cambridge, Eng., 1929.

Baldo, Jonathan. *Memory in Shakespeare's Histories: Stages of Forgetting in Early Modern England*. New York, 2012.

Berry, Edward I. *Patterns of Decay: Shakespeare's Early Histories*. Charlottesville, Va., 1975.

Blanpied, John W. *Time and the Artist in Shakespeare's English Histories*. Newark, Del., 1983.

Calderwood, James L. *Metadrama in Shakespeare's Henriad: "Richard II" to "Henry V."* Berkeley, 1979.

Campbell, Lily B. *Shakespeare's "Histories": Mirrors of Elizabethan Policy.* San Marino, Calif., 1947.

Cavanagh, Dermot, Stuart Hampton-Ross, and Stephen Longstaffe, eds. *Shakespeare's Histories and Counter-Histories.* Manchester, 2006.

Champion, Larry S. *"The Noise of Threatening Drum": Dramatic Strategy and Political Ideology in Shakespeare and the English Chronicle Plays.* Newark, Del., 1990.

———. *Perspective in Shakespeare's English Histories.* Athens, Ga., 1980.

Dillon, Janette. *Shakespeare and the Staging of English History.* Oxford, 2012.

Dorius, R. J. "A Little More Than a Little," *SQ* 11 (1960), 13–26.

Dutton, Richard, and Jean E. Howard, eds. *A Companion to Shakespeare's Works.* Vol. 2, The Histories. Oxford, 2003.

Edwards, Philip. "The Hidden King: Shakespeare's History Plays," *Threshold of a Nation: A Study in English and Irish Drama.* Cambridge, Eng., 1979.

Forker, Charles R. "Shakespeare's Chronicle Plays as Historical-Pastoral," *ShakS* 1 (1965), 85–104.

Goy-Blanquet, Dominique. *Shakespeare's Early History Plays.* Oxford, 2003.

Grene, Nicholas. *Shakespeare's Serial History Plays.* Cambridge, Eng., 2002.

Hattaway, Michael, ed. *The Cambridge Companion to Shakespeare's History Plays.* Cambridge, Eng., 2002.

Heller, Agnes. *The Time Is Out of Joint: Shakespeare as Philosopher of History.* Lanham, Md., 2002.

Hodgdon, Barbara. *The End Crowns All: Closure and Contradiction in Shakespeare's History.* Princeton, 1991.

Hoenselaars, Ton, ed. *Shakespeare's History Plays: Performance, Translation, and Adaptation in Britain and Abroad.* Cambridge, Eng., 2004.

Holderness, Graham. *Shakespeare's History.* New York, 1985. Largely reprinted in *Shakespeare Recycled: The Making of Historical Drama.* Hempstead, Eng., New York, 1992.

———. *Shakespeare—The Histories.* New York, 2000.

———, ed. *Shakespeare's History Plays: "Richard II" to "Henry V."* London, 1992.

Howard, Jean E., and Phyllis Rackin. *Engendering a Nation: A Feminist Account of Shakespeare's English Histories.* London and New York, 1997.

Jenkins, Harold. "Shakespeare's History Plays: 1900–1951," *ShS* 6 (1953), 1–15.

Jones, Robert C. *These Valiant Dead: Renewing the Past in Shakespeare's Histories.* Iowa City, 1991.

Jorgensen, Paul A. *Shakespeare's Military World.* Berkeley and Los Angeles, 1956.

Kantorowicz, Ernst. *The King's Two Bodies: A Study in Mediaeval Political Theology.* Princeton, 1957.

Kastan, David Scott. *Shakespeare and the Shapes of Time.* Hanover, N. H., 1982.

Kelly, Henry A. *Divine Providence in the England of Shakespeare's Histories.* Cambridge, Mass., 1970.

Knights, L. C. "Shakespeare's Politics: With Some Reflections on the Nature of Tradition," *Proceedings of the British Academy* 43 (1957), 115–32.

Knowles, Roland. *Shakespeare's Arguments with History.* Basingstoke, Eng., and New York, 2002.

Leggatt, Alexander. *Shakespeare's Political Drama: The History Plays and the Roman Plays.* London, 1988.

Levine, Nina S. *Women's Matters: Politics, Gender, and Nation in Shakespeare's Early History Plays.* Newark, Del., 1998.

Manheim, Michael. *The Weak King Dilemma in the Shakespearean History Play.* Syracuse, N.Y., 1973.

Mayer, Jean-Christophe. *Shakespeare's Hybrid Faith: Religion and the Stage.* Basingstoke, Hants., and New York, 2006.

McAlindon, Tom. *Shakespeare's Tudor History: A Study of Henry IV, Parts 1 and 2.* Aldershot, Eng., and Burlington, Vt., 2001.

Norwich, John Julius. *Shakespeare's Kings: The Great Plays and the History of England in the Middle Ages: 1337–1485.* London, 1999; New York, 2000.

Orgel, Stephen, and Sean Kellen, eds. *Shakespeare and History.* New York, 1999.

Ornstein, Robert. *A Kingdom for a Stage.* Cambridge, Mass., 1972.

Palmer, John. *Political Characters of Shakespeare.* London, 1945.

Paris, Bernard J. *Character as a Subversive Force in Shakespeare: The History and Roman Plays.* Rutherford, N.J., and London, 1991.

Patterson, Annabel. *Reading Holinshed's Chronicles.* Chicago, 1994.

Pierce, Robert B. *Shakespeare's History Plays: The Family and the State.* Columbus, Ohio, 1971.

Pilkington, Ace G. *Screening Shakespeare from "Richard II" to "Henry V."* Newark, Del., 1991.

Porter, Joseph. *The Drama of Speech Acts: Shakespeare's Lancastrian Tetralogy.* Berkeley, 1979.

Prior, Moody E. *The Drama of Power: Studies in Shakespeare's History Plays.* Evanston, Ill., 1973.

Pugliatti, Paola. *Shakespeare the Historian.* New York, 1996.

Pye, Christopher. *The Regal Phantasm: Shakespeare and the Politics of Spectacle.* London, 1990.

Rackin, Phyllis. "Anti-Historians: Women's Roles in Shakespeare's Histories," *Theatre Journal* 37 (1985), 329–44.

———. *Stages of History: Shakespeare's English Chronicles.* Ithaca, N.Y., 1990.

Raffield, Paul. *Shakespeare's Imaginary Constitution: Late Elizabethan Politics and the Theatre of Law.* Oxford, 2010.

Reese, M. M. *The Cease of Majesty.* London and New York, 1961.

Ribner, Irving. *The English History Play in the Age of Shakespeare,* Rev. ed., London, 1965.

Rossiter, A. P. "Ambivalence: The Dialectic of the Histories," *Talking of Shakespeare,* ed. John Garrett. London, 1954.

Saccio, Peter. *Shakespeare's English Kings: History, Chronicle, and Drama.* New York, 1977.

Shafer, Ronald G. *Shakespeare and English History: Interdisciplinary Perspectives.* Bloomington, Ind., 1976.

Shaheen, Naseeb. *Biblical References in Shakespeare's History Plays.* Newark, Del., 1989.

Smith, Emma, ed. *Shakespeare's Histories.* Malden, Mass., 2004.

Sprague, Arthur Colby. *Shakespeare's Histories: Plays for the Stage.* London, 1964.

Sterling, Eric. *The Movement Towards Subversion: The English History Play from Skelton to Shakespeare.* Lanham, Md., 1996.

Tillyard, E. M. W. *Shakespeare's History Plays.* London, 1944, 1961.

Traversi, Derek. *Shakespeare from "Richard II" to "Henry V."* London, 1957.

Velz, John W., ed. *Shakespeare's English Histories: A Quest for Form and Genre.* Binghamton, N.Y., 1996.

Walsh, Brian. *Shakespeare, the Queen's Men, and the Elizabethan Performance of History.* Cambridge, Eng., 2009.

Winny, James. *The Player King: A Theme of Shakespeare's Histories.* London, 1968.

Yeats, William Butler. "At Stratford-upon-Avon," *Ideas of Good and Evil.* London, 1903.

## *Richard III*

See also, under *The Histories,* Alexander, Berry, Campbell, Kelly, Ornstein, Prior, Ribner, and Saccio; under *Shakespeare's Predecessors and Contemporaries,* Sanders; under *Shakespeare Criticism from the 1940s to the 1970s,* Jones, Rossiter, and Spivack; under *Shakespeare Criticism since 1980,* Dubrow and Strier (essay by Garber), and Lenz et al. (essay by Miner); under *The Tragedies,* Garner and Sprengnether (essay by Rackin), and Hunter; and under *The Henry VI Plays,* Watson.

Anderson, Judith H. "Shakespeare's *Richard III:* The Metamorphosis of Biographical Truth to Fiction," *Biographical Truth: The Representation of Historical Persons in Tudor-Stuart Writing.* New Haven, 1984.

Bevington, David. " 'Why Should Calamity Be Full of Words?' The Efficacy of Cursing in *Richard III,*" *Iowa State Journal of Research* 56:1 (1981), 9–21.

Colley, Scott. *"Richard's Himself Again": A Stage History of "Richard III."* New York, 1992.

French, A. L. "The World of *Richard III*," *ShakS* 4 (1968), 25–39.

Hankey, Julie, ed. *Plays in Performance: "Richard III."* Bristol, 1981; 2nd ed., 1988.

Hassel, R. Chris, Jr. *Songs of Death: Performance, Interpretation, and the Text of "Richard III."* Lincoln, Neb., 1987.

Hunter, Robert G. *Shakespeare and the Mystery of God's Judgments.* Athens, Ga., 1976.

Kendall, Paul Murray. *Richard the Third.* New York and London, 1956.

Krieger, Murray. "The Dark Generations of *Richard III*," *Criticism* 1 (1959), 32–48.

Neill, Michael. "Shakespeare's Halle of Mirrors: Play, Politics, and Psychology in *Richard III*," *ShakS* 8 (1975), 99–129.

Schwyzer, Philip. "Trophies, Traces, Relics, and Props: The Untimely Objects of *Richard III*," *SQ* 63.3 (2912), 297–327.

Sher, Antony. *Year of the King: An Actor's Diary and Sketchbook.* London, 1985.

Torrey, Michael. " 'The plain devil and dissembling looks': Ambivalent Physiognomy and Shakespeare's *Richard III*," *English Literary Renaissance* 30 (2000), 123–53.

Wheeler, Richard P. "History, Character, and Conscience in *Richard III*," *Comparative Drama* 5 (1971–1972), 301–21.

## Richard II

See also, under *The Histories*, Calderwood, Campbell, Dorius, Forker, Ornstein, Palmer, Porter, Reese, Ribner, Saccio and Tillyard; under *Shakespeare's Predecessors and Contemporaries*, Sanders; under *Shakespeare's Language*, Mahood; under *Shakespeare Criticism to the 1930s*, Coleridge (*Coleridge's Writings*); under *Shakespeare Criticism from the 1940s to the 1970s*, Bryant, Calderwood, Hawkes, Kernan (essay on the "Major History Plays"), and Rabkin (pp. 81–98); under *Shakespeare Criticism Since 1980*, Bergeron (essay by Black), Parker and Hartman (essay by Berger), and Woodbridge and Berry (essay by Liebler); under *Shakespeare in Performance*, McGuire and Samuelson (essay by McGuire); and under *The Tragedies*, Nevo.

Barkan, Leonard. "The Theatrical Consistency of *Richard II*," *SQ* 29 (1978), 5–19.

Berger, Harry, Jr. "Textual Dramaturgy: Representing the Limits of Theatre in *Richard II*," *Theatre Journal* 39 (1987), 135–55.

Bergeron, David M. "*Richard II*: Internal and External Evidence," *Practicing Renaissance Scholarship: Plays and Pageants, Patrons and Politics.* Pittsburgh, Pa., 2000.

Dorius, R. J. "A Little More Than a Little," *SQ* 11 (1960), 13–26.

Doty, Jeffrey S. "Shakespeare's *Richard II*, 'Popularity,' and the Early Modern Public Sphere," *SQ* 61.2 (2010), 183–205.

Elliott, John R., Jr. "History and Tragedy in *Richard II*," *Studies in English Literature* 8 (1968), 253–71.

Forker, Charles. *Shakespeare: The Critical Tradition: Richard II.* London, 1998.

Gaudet, Paul. "The 'Parasitical' Counselors in Shakespeare's *Richard II*: A Problem in Dramatic Interpretation," *SQ* 33 (1982), 142–54.

Halvorson, John. "The Lamentable Comedy of *Richard II*," *English Literary Renaissance* 24 (1994), 343–69.

Hammer, E. J. "*Shakespeare's Richard II*, the Play of 7 February 1601, and the Essex Rising," *SQ* 59.1 (2008), 1–35.

Harris, Kathryn Montgomery. "Sun and Water Imagery in *Richard II*: Its Dramatic Function," *SQ* 21 (1970), 157–65.

Heninger, S. K., Jr. "The Sun-King Analogy in *Richard II*," *SQ* 11 (1960), 319–27.

Humphreys, A. R. *Shakespeare: "Richard II."* London, 1967.

Kantorowicz, Ernst H. *The King's Two Bodies: A Study in Medieval Political Theology.* Princeton, 1957.

Laroche, Rebecca, and Jennifer Munroe. "On a bank of rue; or, Material Ecofeminist Inquiry and the Garden of *Richard II*," *ShakS* 42 (2014), 42–50.

Lisak, Catherine. "In Search of *Richard II*: Shakespeare's Use of Eyewitness Accounts of the Revolution (1399–1400); Conflicting Tales and the Dramatic Structure of the Play," *Shakespeare et le Moyen-Âge*. Actes du colloque international de la Société française Shakespeare, gen. ed. Jean-Marie Maguin. Montpellier, France, 2002.

Lopez, Jeremy, ed. *"Richard II": New Critical Essays.* London and New York, 2012.

MacKenzie, Clayton G. "Paradise and Paradise Lost in *Richard II*," *SQ* 37 (1986), 318–39.

McMillin, Scott. "Shakespeare's *Richard II*: Eyes of Sorrow, Eyes of Desire," *SQ* 35 (1984), 40–52.

Page, Malcolm. *Text and Performance: "Richard II."* Atlantic Highlands, N.J., 1987.

Potter, Lois. "The Antic Disposition of Richard II," *ShS* 27 (1974), 33–41.

Schoenbaum, S. "*Richard II* and the Realities of Power," *ShS* 28 (1975), 1–13.

Shewring, Margaret. *Shakespeare in Performance: "King Richard II."* Manchester, 1996.

Siemon, James R. *Word Against Word: Shakespearean Utterance.* Amherst, Mass, 2002.

Stirling, Brents. "Bolingbroke's 'Decision,'" *SQ* 2 (1951), 27–34.

Syme, Holger Schott. *Theatre and Testimony in Shakespeare's England: A Culture of Mediation.* New York, 2012.

Yeats, W. B. "At Stratford-upon-Avon," *Ideas of Good and Evil*, collected in *Essays and Introductions.* New York, 1961.

Zitner, Sheldon P. "Aumerle's Conspiracy," *Studies in English Literature* 14 (1974), 239–57.

## Henry IV, Part I

See also, under *The Histories*, Blanpied, Calderwood, Campbell, Dorius, Kelly, Manheim, Ornstein, Palmer, Porter, Prior, Reese, Saccio, Sprague, Tillyard, and Velz (essay by Rumrich); under *Shakespeare Criticism to the 1930s*, Johnson and Smith (*Eighteenth Century*, essay by Morgann); under *Shakespeare Criticism from the 1940s to the 1970s*, Bevington and Halio (essay by R. G. Hunter), Bryant, Burckhardt, Council, Goldman, Kernan (essay on the "Major History Plays"), Spivack, and Stewart; and under *Shakespeare Criticism Since 1980*, Auden, Dollimore and Sinfield (essay by Greenblatt, originally published by *Glyph 8* and in *Shakespearean Negotiations*), Hopkins, Nuttall, and Watson; and under *The Comedies*, Barber.

Auden, W. H. "The Prince's Dog," *"The Dyer's Hand" and Other Essays.* New York, 1948.

Barber, C. L. "Rule and Misrule in *Henry IV*," *Shakespeare's Festive Comedy.* Princeton, 1959.

Barish, Jonas A. "The Turning Away of Prince Hal," *ShakS* 1 (1965), 9–17.

Barker, Roberta. "Tragical-Comical-Historical Hotspur," *SQ* 54 (2003), 288–307.

Bradley, A. C. "The Rejection of Falstaff," *Oxford Lectures on Poetry.* London, 1909, 1961.

Bryant, J. A., Jr., "Prince Hal and the Ephesians," *Sewanee Review* 67 (1959), 204–19.

Cohen, Derek. "The Rite of Violence in *1 Henry IV*," *ShS* 38 (1985), 77–84.

Dessen, Alan. "Dual Protagonists in *1 Henry IV*," *Shakespeare and the Late Moral Plays.* Lincoln, Neb., 1986.

Doran, Madeleine. "Imagery in *Richard II* and in *Henry IV*," *Modern Language Review* 37 (1942), 113–22.

Dorius, R. J., ed. *Twentieth Century Interpretations of "Henry IV Part I."* Englewood Cliffs, N.J., 1970.

Empson, William. "Falstaff and Mr. Dover Wilson," *Kenyon Review* 15 (1953), 213–62.

Everett, Barbara. "The Fatness of Falstaff: Shakespeare and Character," *Proceedings of the British Academy* 76 (1990), 109–28.

Gottschalk, Paul A. "Hal and the 'Play Extempore' in *1 Henry IV*," *Texas Studies in Literature and Language* 15 (1974), 605–14.

Hawkins, Sherman H. "Virtue and Kingship in Shakespeare's *Henry IV*," *English Literary Renaissance* 5 (1975), 313–43.

Hunter, G. K. "Shakespeare's Politics and the Rejection of Falstaff," *Critical Quarterly* 1 (1959), 229–36.

Jenkins, Harold. *The Structural Problem in Shakespeare's "Henry the Fourth."* London, 1956.

Kris, Ernst. "Prince Hal's Conflict," *Psychoanalytic Explorations in Art.* New York, 1964.

Levine, Nina. "Extending Credit in the *Henry IV* Plays," *SQ* 51 (2000), 403–31.

McAlindon, Tom. *Shakespeare's Tudor History: A Study of "Henry IV, Parts 1 and 2."* Aldershot, Eng., 2001.

McLuhan, Herbert Marshall. "*Henry IV*, A Mirror for Magistrates," *University of Toronto Quarterly* 17 (1947–1948), 152–60.

McMillin, Scott. *Shakespeare in Performance: "Henry IV, Part One."* Manchester, Eng., 1991.

Palmer, D. J. "Casting Off the Old Man: History and St. Paul in *Henry IV*," *Critical Quarterly* 12 (1970), 267–83.

Poole, Kristen. "Saints Alive! Falstaff, Martin Marprelate, and the Staging of Puritanism," *SQ* 46 (1995), 47–75.

Stewart, Alan. "Shakespeare and the Carriers," *SQ* 58.4 (2007), 431–64.

Toliver, Harold E. "Falstaff, the Prince, and the History Play," *SQ* 16 (1965), 63–80.

Wharton, T. F. *"Henry the Fourth, Parts 1 and 2": Text and Performance.* London, 1983.

Wilson, J. Dover. *The Fortunes of Falstaff.* Cambridge, Eng., 1943.

Womersley, David. "Why Is Falstaff Fat?" *Review of English Studies* n.s. 47 (1996), 1–22.

## Henry V

See also, under *The Histories*, Calderwood, Campbell, Jorgensen, Kastan, Ornstein, Porter, Prior, Reese, Ribner, Saccio, and Traversi; under *Shakespeare Criticism to the 1930s*, Hazlitt and Schlegel; under *Shakespeare Criticism from the 1940s to the 1970s*, Burckhardt, Goddard, Goldman, and Kernan (essay on the "Major History Plays"); under *Shakespeare Criticism Since 1980*, Dollimore and Sinfield (essays by Greenblatt and Tennenhouse), Drakakis (essay by Dollimore and Sinfield), Erickson, Mahon and Pendleton (essay by Hammond), Patterson (Chapter 4), and Rabkin (Chapter 2); and under *Shakespeare in Performance*, Price (essay by Barton).

Altman, Joel B. " 'Vile Participation': The Amplification of Violence in the Theater of *Henry V*," *SQ* 42 (1991), 1–32.

Beauman, Sally, ed. *"King Henry V": The Royal Shakespeare Company's Production of "Henry V" for the Centenary Season at the Royal Shakespeare Theatre.* Oxford, 1976. (Includes information on Terry Hands's *Henry V.*)

Cubeta, Paul M. "Falstaff and the Art of Dying," *Studies in English Literature* 27 (1987), 197–211.

Eggert, Katherine. "Nostalgia and the Not Yet Late Queen: Refusing Female Rule in *Henry V*," *ELH* 61 (1994), 523–50.

Granville-Barker, Harley. "From *Henry V* to *Hamlet*," *Proceedings of the British Academy* 11 (1925), 283–309.

Gurr, Andrew. "*Henry V* and the Bees' Commonwealth," *ShS* 30 (1977): 61–72.

Haber, Judith. " 'I cannot tell wat is like me': Simile, Paternity, and Identity in *Henry V*," *ShakS* 41 (2013), 127–47.

Levin, Richard. "Hazlitt on *Henry V*, and the Appropriation of Shakespeare," *SQ* 35 (1984), 134–41.

McEachern, Claire. *The Poetics of English Nationhood, 1590–1612.* Cambridge, Eng., 1996.

## The Tragedies

See also, under *Shakespeare's Predecessors and Contemporaries*, Belsey, Falco, and Liebler; and under *Shakespeare Criticism Since 1980*, Dollimore and Hopkins.

Alfar, Cristina León. *Fantasies of Female Evil: The Dynamics of Gender and Power in Shakespearean Tragedy.* Newark, Del., and London, 2003.

Armstrong, Philip. *Shakespeare's Visual Regime: Tragedy, Psychoanalysis, and the Gaze.* Basingstoke and New York, 2000.

Baldo, Jonathan. *The Unmasking of Drama: Contested Representation in Shakespeare's Tragedies.* Detroit, 1996.

Barker, Francis, ed. *The Culture of Violence: Essays on Tragedy and History.* Chicago, 1993.

Barroll, J. Leeds. *Artificial Persons: The Formation of Character in the Tragedies of Shakespeare.* Columbia, S. C., 1974.

Bayley, John. *Shakespeare and Tragedy.* London, 1981.

Bell, Millicent. *Shakespeare's Tragic Skepticism.* New Haven, 2002.

Berry, Philippa. *Shakespeare's Feminine Endings: Disfiguring Death in the Tragedies.* London and New York, 1999.

Berry, Ralph. *Tragic Instance: The Sequence of Shakespeare's Tragedies.* Newark, Del., 1999.

Bradley, A. C. *Shakespearean Tragedy.* London, 1904. *(Hamlet, Othello, King Lear, Macbeth.)*

Brooke, Nicholas. *Shakespeare's Early Tragedies.* London and New York, 1968.

Brown, John Russell. *Shakespeare: The Tragedies.* Houndmills, Basingstoke, 2001.

———, and Bernard Harris, eds. *Early Shakespeare.* London, 1961.

Bulman, James C. *The Heroic Idiom of Shakespearean Tragedy.* Newark, Del., 1985.

Bushnell, Rebecca. *Tragedies of Tyrants: Political Thought and Theater in the English Renaissance.* Ithaca, N.Y., 1990.

Campbell, Lily B. *Shakespeare's Tragic Heroes: Slaves of Passion.* Cambridge, Eng., 1930.

Champion, Larry S. *Shakespeare's Tragic Perspective.* Athens, Ga., 1976.

Charlton, H. B. *Shakespearian Tragedy.* Cambridge, Eng., 1948.

Cunningham, I. V. *Woe or Wonder: The Emotional Effect of Shakespearean Tragedy.* Denver, 1951. Rpt. in *Tradition and Poetic Structure.* Denver, 1960.

Danson, Lawrence. *Tragic Alphabet: Shakespeare's Drama of Language.* New Haven and London, 1974.

Dickey, Franklin M. *Not Wisely But Too Well: Shakespeare's Love Tragedies.* San Marino, Calif., 1957.

Dobson, Michael. *Performing Shakespeare's Tragedies Today: The Actor's Perspective.* Cambridge, Eng., 2006.

Dutton, Richard, and Jean E. Howard, eds. *A Companion to Shakespeare's Works.* Vol. 1, The Tragedies. Oxford, 2003.

Eliot, T. S. "Shakespeare and the Stoicism of Seneca," *Selected Essays, 1917–1932.* London, 1932.

Everett, Barbara. *Young Hamlet: Essays on Shakespeare's Tragedies.* Oxford, 1989.

Falco, Raphael. *Charismatic Authority in Early Modern English Tragedy.* Baltimore, 2000.

Farnham, Willard. *Shakespeare's Tragic Frontier.* Berkeley, 1950.

Frye, Northrop. *Fools of Time: Studies in Shakespearean Tragedy.* Toronto, 1967.

Gajowski, Evelyn. *The Art of Loving: Female Subjectivity and Male Discursive Traditions in Shakespeare's Tragedies.* Newark, Del., 1992.

Garner, Shirley Nelson, and Madelon Sprengnether, eds. *Shakespearean Tragedy and Gender.* Bloomington, Ind., 1996.

Goldman, Michael. *Acting and Action in Shakespearean Tragedy.* Princeton, 1985.

Goodland, Katharine. *Female Mourning and Tragedy in Medieval and Renaissance English Drama: From the Raising of Lazarus to King Lear.* Aldershot, Eng., and Burlington, Vt., 2005.

Grene, Nicholas. *Shakespeare's Tragic Imagination.* New York, 1992.

Hamlin, William M. *Tragedy and Scepticism in Shakespeare's England.* Houndmills, Eng., 2005.

Hammond, Paul. *The Strangeness of Tragedy.* Oxford, 2009.

Hawkes, Terence. *Shakespeare and the Reason: A Study of the Tragedies and the Problem Plays.* London, 1964.

Hays, Michael L. *Shakespearean Tragedy as Chivalric Romance: Rethinking Macbeth, Hamlet, Othello, and King Lear.* Cambridge, Eng., 2003.

Held, George F. *The Good That Lives After Them: A Pattern in Shakespeare's Tragedies.* Heidelberg, 1995.

Hillman, Richard. *French Origins of English Tragedy.* Manchester, 2010.

Holloway, John. *The Story of the Night: Studies in Shakespeare's Major Tragedies.* London and Lincoln, Neb., 1961.

Honigmann, E. A. J. *Myriad-Minded Shakespeare: Essays, Chiefly on the Tragedies and Problem Comedies.* New York, 1989.

———. *Shakespeare: Seven Tragedies Revisited: The Dramatist's Manipulation of Response.* London and New York, 1976; 2nd ed., 2002.

Hopkins, Lisa. *The Female Hero in English Renaissance Tragedy.* Basingstoke, Eng., and New York, 2002.

Hunter, Robert Grams. *Shakespeare and the Mystery of God's Judgments.* Athens, Ga., 1976.

Ide, Richard S. *Possessed with Greatness: The Heroic Tragedies of Chapman and Shakespeare.* Chapel Hill, N.C., 1980.

Kiefer, Frederick. *Fortune and Elizabethan Tragedy.* San Marino, Calif., 1983.

Kirsch, Arthur. *The Passions of Shakespeare's Tragic Heroes.* Charlottesville, Va., 1990.

Knight, G. Wilson. *The Wheel of Fire.* London, 1930, 1965.

Kottman, Paul A. *Tragic Conditions in Shakespeare: Disinheriting the Globe.* Baltimore, 2009.

Lawlor, John. *The Tragic Sense in Shakespeare.* London, 1960.

Leech, Clifford. *Shakespeare's Tragedies and Other Studies in Seventeenth-Century Drama.* London, 1950.

———, ed. *Shakespeare: The Tragedies.* Chicago, 1965.

Leggatt, Alexander. *Shakespeare's Tragedies: Violation and Identity.* Cambridge, Eng., 2005.

Liebler, Naomi Conn. *Shakespeare's Festive Tragedy: The Ritual Foundations of Genre.* London and New York, 1995.

Mack, Maynard. *Everybody's Shakespeare: Reflections Chiefly on the Tragedies.* Lincoln, Neb., 1993.

———. "The Jacobean Shakespeare: Some Observations on the Construction of the Tragedies," *Jacobean Theatre,* eds. John Russell Brown and Bernard Harris. Stratford-upon-Avon Studies 1. London, 1960.

Mack, Maynard, Jr. *Killing the King: Three Studies in Shakespeare's Tragic Structure.* New Haven and London, 1973.

Margolies, David. *Monsters of the Deep: Social Dissolution in Shakespeare's Tragedies.* Manchester, Eng., 1992.

McAlindon, T. *Shakespeare's Tragic Cosmos.* Cambridge, 1991.

McEachern, Claire, ed. *The Cambridge Companion to Shakespearean Tragedy.* Cambridge, Eng., 2002, 2013.

Miola, Robert S. *Shakespeare and Classical Tragedy: The Influence of Seneca.* Oxford, 1992.

Neill, Michael. *Issues of Death: Mortality and Identity in English Renaissance Tragedy.* Oxford, 1997.

Nevo, Ruth. *Tragic Form in Shakespeare.* Princeton, 1972.

Oya, Reiko. *Representing Shakespearean Tragedy: Garrick, the Kembles, and Kean.* Cambridge, Eng., 2007.

Proser, Matthew N. *The Heroic Image in Five Shakespearean Tragedies.* Princeton, 1965.

Rackin, Phyllis. *Shakespeare's Tragedies.* New York, 1978.

Reid, Robert Lanier. *Shakespeare's Tragic Form: Spirit in the Wheel.* Newark, Del., 2000.

Ribner, Irving. *Patterns in Shakespearean Tragedy.* New York, 1960.

Rosen, William. *Shakespeare and the Craft of Tragedy.* Cambridge, Mass., 1960.

Sanders, Wilbur, and Howard Jacobson. *Shakespeare's Magnanimity: Four Tragic Heroes, Their Friends and Families.* Oxford, 1978.

Shaheen, Naseeb. *Biblical References in Shakespeare's Tragedies.* Newark, Del., 1987.

Smith, Emma. *Shakespeare's Tragedies.* Malden, Mass., 2004.

Smith, Molly. *The Darker World Within: Evil in the Tragedies of Shakespeare and His Successors.* Newark, Del., 1991.

Snyder, Susan. *The Comic Matrix of Shakespeare's Tragedies.* Princeton, 1979.

Spivack, Bernard. *Shakespeare and the Allegory of Evil.* New York, 1958.

Sternfeld, Frederick W. *Music in Shakespearean Tragedy.* London, 1963, 1967.

Whitaker, Virgil. *The Mirror up to Nature.* San Marino, Calif., 1965.

Wilson, Harold S. *On the Design of Shakespearian Tragedy.* Toronto, 1957.

Young, David. *The Action to the Word: Structure and Style in Shakespearean Tragedy.* New Haven, 1990.

———, *Shakespeare's Middle Tragedies: A Collection of Critical Essays.* Englewood Cliffs, N.J., 1993.

## The Greek and Roman Tragedies

See also, under *Shakespeare Criticism Since 1980,* Paster (Chapter 3).

Brower, Reuben A. *Hero and Saint: Shakespeare and the Graeco-Roman Heroic Tradition.* New York and Oxford, 1971.

Cantor, Paul A. *Shakespeare's Rome: Republic and Empire.* Ithaca, N.Y., 1976.

Charney, Maurice, ed. *Discussions of Shakespeare's Roman Plays.* Boston, 1964.

———. *Shakespeare's Roman Plays: The Function of Imagery in the Drama.* Cambridge, Mass., 1961.

Knight, G. Wilson. *The Imperial Theme: Further Interpretations of Shakespeare's Tragedies Including the Roman Plays.* London, 1931, 1953.

Leggatt, Alexander. *Shakespeare's Political Drama: The History Plays and the Roman Plays.* London and New York, 1988.

MacCallum, M. W. *Shakespeare's Roman Plays and Their Background.* London, 1910.

Maxwell, J. C. "Shakespeare's Roman Plays: 1900–1956," *ShS* 10 (1957), 1–11.

Miles, Geoffrey. *Shakespeare and the Constant Romans.* Oxford, 1996.

Miola, Robert S. *Shakespeare's Rome.* Cambridge, Eng., 1983.

Nicoll, Allardyce, ed. *Shakespeare Survey 10* (1957).

Paris, Bernard J. *Character as a Subversive Force in Shakespeare: The History and Roman Plays.* Rutherford, N.J., and London, 1991.

Phillips, James E., Jr. *The State in Shakespeare's Greek and Roman Plays.* New York, 1940.

Simmons, J. L. *Shakespeare's Pagan World: The Roman Tragedies.* Charlottesville, Va., 1973.

Thomas, Vivian. *Shakespeare's Roman Worlds.* London, 1989.

Thomson, J. A. K. *Shakespeare and the Classics.* London, 1952.

Traversi, Derek. *Shakespeare: The Roman Plays.* Palo Alto, Calif., 1963.

Velz, John W. "The Ancient World in Shakespeare: Authenticity or Anachronism? A Retrospect," *ShS* 31 (1978), 1–12.

———. *Shakespeare and the Classical Tradition: A Critical Guide to Commentary, 1660–1960.* Minneapolis, 1968.

## Romeo and Juliet

See also, under *The Tragedies,* Brooke, Brown and Harris (essay by Lawlor), Charlton, Dickey, Nevo, Ribner, and Snyder; under *Shakespeare's Language,* Mahood; under *Shakespeare Criticism to the 1930s,* Hazlitt; under *Shakespeare Criticism from the 1940s to the 1970s,* Calderwood, Granville-Barker, and Rabkin (pp. 162–84); under *Shakespeare Criticism Since 1980,* Callaghan (*A Feminist Companion,* essay by Berry), Daileader, Edwards et al. (essay by Wells), Erickson and Kahn (essay by Snow), Lenz et al. (essay by Kahn), and Novy (*Love's Argument*); and under *Shakespeare in Performance,* Brockbank (essay by Brenda Bruce).

Appelbaum, Robert. " 'Standing to the wall': The Pressures of Masculinity in *Romeo and Juliet,*" *SQ* 48 (1997), 251–72.

Auden, W. H. "Commentary on the Poetry and Tragedy of *Romeo and Juliet.*" The Laurel Shakespeare, gen. ed. Francis Fergusson. New York, 1958.

Evans, Bertrand. "The Brevity of Friar Lawrence," *PMLA* 65 (1950), 841–65.

Evans, Robert O. *The Osier Cage: Rhetorical Devices in "Romeo and Juliet."* Lexington, Ky., 1966.

Everett, Barbara. "*Romeo and Juliet:* The Nurse's Story," *Critical Quarterly* 14 (1972), 129–39.

Halio, Jay, ed. *"Romeo and Juliet": Texts, Contexts, and Interpretation.* Newark, Del., 1995.

Hosley, Richard. "The Use of the Upper Stage in *Romeo and Juliet,*" *SQ* 5 (1954), 371–9.

Kottman, Paul. "Defying the Stars: Tragic Love as the Struggle for Freedom in *Romeo and Juliet,*" *SQ* 63.1 (2012), 1–38.

Levenson, Jill L. *Shakespeare in Performance: "Romeo and Juliet."* Manchester, Eng., 1987.

Melchiori, Giorgio. "Peter, Balthasar, and Shakespeare's Art of Doubling," *Modern Language Review* 78 (1983), 777–92.

Prunster, Nicole, trans. and ed. *Romeo and Juliet before Shakespeare: Four Early Stories of Star-Crossed Love.* Toronto, 2000.

Williams, George W., ed. *The Most Excellent and Lamentable Tragedie of Romeo and Juliet.* Durham, N.C., 1964.

## Julius Caesar

See also, under *The Greek and Roman Tragedies,* Brower, Charney (both titles), Knight, Miola, and Traversi; under *Shakespeare's Language,* Doran; under *Shakespeare Criticism to the 1930s,* Shaw; under *Shakespeare Criticism from the 1940s to the 1970s,* Burckhardt, Council, Goldman (Chapter 4), Granville-Barker, Kernan (essay by Mack), Rabkin (pp. 105–19), and Stirling; under *Shakespeare Criticism Since 1980,* Kahn; under *The Problem Plays,* Schanzer; and under *The Histories,* Palmer.

Blits, Jan H. *The End of the Ancient Republic: Essays on "Julius Caesar."* Durham, N.C., 1982.

Burke, Kenneth. "Antony in Behalf of the Play," *Southern Review* 1 (1935), 308–19. Rpt. in *The Philosophy of Literary Form*. Baton Rouge, La., 1941.

Knights, L. C. "Shakespeare and Political Wisdom: A Note on the Personalism of *Julius Caesar and Coriolanus*," *Sewanee Review* 61 (1953), 43–55.

Liebler, Naomi Conn. " 'Thou Bleeding Piece of Earth': The Ritual Ground of *Julius Caesar*," *ShakS* 14 (1981), 175–96.

Miola, Robert S. *"Julius Caesar* and the Tyrannicide Debate," *Renaissance Quarterly* 38 (1985), 271–89.

Ornstein, Robert. "Seneca and the Political Drama of *Julius Caesar*," *Journal of English and Germanic Philology* 57 (1958), 51–6.

Parker, Barbara L. " 'A Thing Unfirm': Plato's *Republic* and Shakespeare's *Julius Caesar*," *SQ* 44 (1993), 30–43.

Paster, Gail Kern. " 'In the spirit of men there is no blood': Blood as Trope of Gender in *Julius Caesar*," *SQ* 40 (1989), 284–98.

Ribner, Irving. "Political Issues in *Julius Caesar*," *Journal of English and Germanic Philology* 56 (1957), 10–22.

Ripley, John. *"Julius Caesar" on Stage in England and America, 1599–1973*. Cambridge, Eng., 1980.

Rose, Mark. "Conjuring Caesar: Ceremony, History, and Authority in 1599," *English Literary Renaissance* 19 (1989), 291–304.

Velz, John W. "Clemency, Will, and Just Cause in *Julius Caesar*," *ShS* 22 (1969), 109–18.

———. " 'If I Were Brutus Now … ': Role-Playing in *Julius Caesar*," *ShakS* 4 (1968), 149–59.

———. "Undular Structure in *Julius Caesar*," *Modern Language Review* 66 (1971), 21–30.

### Hamlet

See also, under *Shakespeare's Language*, Donawerth; under *The Tragedies*, Barker, Bradley, Brooke, Goldman, Holloway, Kirsch, Mack, Mack Jr., Rosen, and Whitaker; under *The Greek and Roman Tragedies*, Brower; under *Shakespeare's Predecessors and Contemporaries*, Bowers, and Rabkin (essay by Booth); under *Shakespeare Criticism to the 1930s*, Coleridge (*Coleridge's Writings*); under *Shakespeare Criticism from the 1940s to the 1970s*, Granville-Barker, Hawkes, and Righter; under *Shakespeare Criticism Since 1980*, Cavell (Chapter 5), Drakakis (essay by Rose), Erickson, Garber (*Shakespeare's Ghost Writers*, Chapter 6), Loomba and Orkin (essay by Bertoldi), Mazzio and Trevor (essays by De Grazia and Guillory), McDonald (essay by Parker), Parker and Hartman (essays by Weimann, Ferguson, and Hawkes), Patterson (Chapters 1 and 5), and Schwartz and Kahn (essays by Fineman and Leverenz); under *Shakespeare in Performance*, Bevington; and under *The Problem Plays*, Tillyard.

Attie, Katherine Bootie. "Passion Turned to Prettiness: Rhyme or Reason in *Hamlet*," *SQ* 63.3 (2012), 393–423.

———. "Tragic Proportions: The Art of Tyranny and the Politics of the Soul in *Hamlet*," *ELR* 44 (2014), 78–107.

Bertram, Paul, and Bernice W. Kliman, eds. *The Three-Text "Hamlet": Parallel Texts of the First and Second Quartos and First Folio*. New York, 1991.

Belsie, Catherine. "Shakespeare's Sad Tale for Winter: *Hamlet* and the Tradition of Fireside Ghost Stories," *SQ* 61.1 (2010), 1–27.

Bevington, David. *Murder Most Foul: Hamlet Through the Ages*. Oxford, 2011.

Bevington, David. *Murder Most Foul: Hamlet Through the Ages*. Oxford, 2011.

Bloom, Harold. *Hamlet: Poem Unlimited*. New York, 2003.

Bowers, Fredson T. "Hamlet as Minister and Scourge," *PMLA* 70 (1955), 740–9.

Bristol, Michael. "The Customary and the Ethical: Understanding Hamlet's Bad Habits," *ShakS* 40 (2012), 70–6.

Bruster, Douglas. *To Be or Not To Be*. London, 2007.

Calderwood, James L. *To Be and Not to Be: Negation and Metadrama in "Hamlet."* New York, 1983.

Charnes, Linda. *Hamlet's Heirs: Shakespeare and the Politics of a New Millennium*. New York and London, 2006.

Charney, Maurice. *Style in "Hamlet."* Princeton, 1969.

Clayton, Thomas, ed. *The "Hamlet" First Published (Q1, 1603): Origin, Form, Intertextualities*. Newark, Del., 1992.

Curran, John E., Jr. *"Hamlet," Protestantism, and the Mourning of Contingency: Not to Be."* Aldershot, Eng., and Burlington, Vt., 2006.

Cutrofello, Andrew. *All for Nothing: Hamlet's Negativity*. Cambridge, Mass., 2014.

Dawson, Anthony B. *Hamlet*. Shakespeare in Performance. Manchester, Eng., 1995.

De Grazia, Margreta. *"Hamlet" without Hamlet*. Cambridge, Eng., 2007.

Deutermann, Allison K. "'Caviare to the general'?: Taste, Hearing, and Genre in *Hamlet*," *SQ* 59.2 (2011), 230–55.

Engle, Lars. "Moral Agency in *Hamlet*," *ShakS* 40 (2012), 87–97.

Eliot, T. S. "Hamlet and His Problems," *Selected Essays, 1917–1932*. London and New York, 1932.

Erlich, Avi. *Hamlet's Absent Father*. Princeton, 1977.

Ewbank, Inga-Stina. "*Hamlet* and the Power of Words," *ShS* 30 (1977), 85–102.

Fergusson, Francis. *The Idea of a Theater*. Princeton, 1949.

Foakes, R. A. *"Hamlet" versus "Lear": Cultural Politics and Shakespeare's Art*. Cambridge, Eng., 1993.

Frye, Roland Mushat. *The Renaissance "Hamlet": Issues and Responses in 1600*. Princeton, 1984.

Gallagher, Catherine, and Stephen Greenblatt, "The Mousetrap," in *Practicing New Historicism*. Chicago, 2000.

Garber, Marjorie. "A Tale of Three *Hamlets* or Repetition and Revenge," *SQ* 61.1 (2010), 28–55.

Greenblatt, Stephen. *Hamlet in Purgatory*. Princeton, 2001.

Halpern, Richard. "Eclipse of Action: *Hamlet* and the Political Economy of Playing," *SQ* 59.4 (2008), 450–82.

Hanson, Elizabeth. "Fellow Students: Hamlet, Horatio, and the Early Modern University," *SQ* 62.2 (2011), 205–29.

Hatchuel, Sarah, and Nathalie Vienne-Guerrin, eds. *Shakespeare on Screen: "Hamlet."* Mont-Saint-Aignan, France, 2011.

Heilbrun, Carolyn G. *Hamlet's Mother and Other Women*. New York, 1990.

Hirschfeld, Heather Anne. "Hamlet's 'first corse': Repetition, Trauma, and the Displacement of Redemptive Typology," *SQ* 54 (2003), 424–48.

Howard, Tony. *Woman as Hamlet: Performance and Interpretation in Theatre, Film and Fiction*. Cambridge, Eng., 2007.

Hunt, Marvin W. *Looking for Hamlet*. New York, 2007.

James, D. G. *The Dream of Learning*. Oxford, 1951.

Jones, Ernest. *Hamlet and Oedipus*. Rev. ed. New York, 1949, 1954.

Joseph, Bertram. *Conscience and the King*. London, 1953.

Justice, Hilary Kovar. *A Groundling's Guide to Shakespeare's "Hamlet."* Cincinnati, 2014.

Kerrigan, William. *Hamlet's Perfection*. Baltimore, 1994.

Kinney, Arthur E., ed. *Hamlet: New Critical Essays*. New York and London, 2002.

Kitto, H. D. F. *Form and Meaning in Drama*. London, 1956.

Knights, L. C. *An Approach to Hamlet*. London, 1960.

Lacan, Jacques. "Desire and the Interpretation of Desire in *Hamlet*," *Yale French Studies* 55/56 (1977), 11–52.

Landau, Aaron. " 'Let Me Not Burst in Ignorance': Skepticism and Anxiety in *Hamlet*," *English Studies*, 82 (2001), 218–29.

Lee, John. *Shakespeare's "Hamlet" and the Controversies of Self*. Oxford, 2000.

Lesser, Zachary. *Hamlet after Q1: An Uncanny History of the Shakespearean Text*. Philadelphia, 2015.

Levin, Harry. *The Question of Hamlet*. New York and London, 1959.

Lewis, C. S. "Hamlet: The Prince or the Poem?" *Proceedings of the British Academy* 28 (1942), 139–54.

Litvin, Margaret. *Hamlet's Arab Journey: Shakespeare's Prince and Nasser's Ghost*. Princeton, 2011.

Long, Zackariah. *"The Spanish Tragedy* and *Hamlet*: Infernal Memory in English Renaissance Revenge Tragedy," *ELR* 44 (2014), 153–92.

Mack, Maynard. "The World of *Hamlet*," *Yale Review* 41 (1952), 502–23.

Marino, James J. "Burbage's Father's Ghost," *ELR* 44 (2014), 56–77.

McCoy, Richard C. "A Wedding and Four Funerals: Conjunction and Commemoration in *Hamlet*," *ShS* 54 (2001), 122–39.

McGee, Arthur. *The Elizabethan Hamlet*. New Haven, 1987.

Muir, Kenneth, and Stanley Wells, eds., *Aspects of "Hamlet": Articles Reprinted from "Shakespeare Survey."* Cambridge, Eng., 1979. (Especially essay by Inga-Stina Ewbank.)

Murray, Gilbert. *Hamlet and Orestes*. Annual Shakespeare Lecture for the British Academy, 1914. London, 1919.

Nicoll, Allardyce, ed. *Shakespeare Survey 9* (1956).

Nietzsche, Friedrich. "The Birth of Tragedy or: Hellenism and Pessimism" (1872), *The Birth of Tragedy and The Case of Wagner*, trans. Walter Kaufmann. New York, 1967.

Parris, Benjamin. "'The body is with the King, but the King is not with the body': Sovereign Sleep in *Hamlet* and *Macbeth*," *ShakS* 49 (2012), 101–42.

Rose, Mark. "*Hamlet* and the Shape of Revenge," *English Literary Renaissance* 1 (1971), 132–43.

Rosenberg, Marvin. *The Masks of "Hamlet."* Newark, Del., 1992.

Russell, John. *Hamlet and Narcissus*. Cranbury, N.J., 1995.

Skulsky, Harold. " 'I Know My Course': Hamlet's Confidence," *PMLA* 89 (1974), 477–86.

Smith, Emma. "'To buy, or not to boy': Hamlet and Consumer Culture." *ShakS* 39 (2011), 188–208.

Stallybrass, Peter. "Hamlet's Tables and the Technologies of Writing in Renaissance England," *SQ* 55 (2004), 379–419.

States, Bert O. "*Hamlet*" and the Concept of Character. Baltimore, 1992.

Tronch-Pérez, Jesús. *A Synoptic "Hamlet": A Critical-Synoptic Edition of the Second Quarto and First Folio Texts of "Hamlet."* Valencia, Spain, 2002.

Welsh, Alexander. *Hamlet in His Modern Guises*. Princeton, 2001.

Wilson, J. Dover. *What Happens in "Hamlet."* London and New York, 1935, 1951.

Wright, George T. "Hendiadys and *Hamlet*," *PMLA* 96 (1981), 168–93.

Young, David. "*Hamlet*, Son of Hamlet," *Perspectives on "Hamlet,"* eds. William G. Holzberger and Peter B. Waldock. Lewisburg, Pa., and London, 1975.

## Othello

See also, under *The Tragedies*, Philippa Berry, Bradley, Dickey, Garner and Sprengnether (essays by Orlin, Hendricks, and Rose), Goldman, Hawkes, Holloway, Knight, Snyder, and Spivack; under *Shakespeare's Language*, Doran; under *Shakespeare's Predecessors and Contemporaries*, Hendricks

and Parker (essays by Boose and Parker); under *Shakespeare Criticism to the 1930s*, Coleridge (*Coleridge's Writings*) and Johnson; under *Shakespeare Criticism from the 1940s to the 1970s*, Empson, Fiedler, Granville-Barker, and Sewell; and under *Shakespeare Criticism Since 1980*, Cavell (Chapter 3), Daileder, Erickson, Erickson and Kahn (essay by Wheeler), Greenblatt (*Renaissance Self-Fashioning*, Chapter 6), Howard and O'Connor (essay by Newman), Kirsch, Lenz et al. (essay by Neely), Loomba and Orkin (essay by Burton), McDonald (essay by Parker), Novy (*Love's Argument*, Chapter 7), and Parker and Hartman (essays by Parker and Showalter).

Adamson, Jane. "*Othello*" as Tragedy: Some Problems of Judgment and Feeling. Cambridge, Eng., 1980.

Altman, Joel B. " 'Preposterous Conclusions': Eros, *Enargeia*, and the Composition of *Othello*," *Representations* 18 (1987), 129–57.

———. *The Improbability of "Othello": Rhetorical Anthropology and Shakespearean Selfhood*. Chicago, 2010.

Bartels, Emily C. "Making More of the Moor: Aaron, Othello, and Renaissance Refashionings of Race," *SQ* 41 (1990), 433–54.

Bartels, Emily C. *Speaking of the Moor: From "Alcazar" to "Othello."* Philadelphia, 2008.

Bates, Catherine. "Weaving and Writing in *Othello*," *SQ* 46 (1995), 51–60.

Bayley, John. *The Characters of Love*. London, 1960.

Boose, Lynda E. "Othello's Handkerchief: 'The Recognizance and Pledge of Love,'" *English Literary Renaissance* 5 (1975), 360–74.

Calderwood, James L. *The Properties of "Othello."* Amherst, Mass., 1989.

Daileader, Celia R. *Racism, Misogyny, and the "Othello" Myth: Interracial Couples from Shakespeare to Spike Lee*. Cambridge, Eng., 2005.

Daileader, Celia R. *Racism, Misogyny, and the "Othello" Myth: Inter-Racial Couples from Shakespeare to Spike Lee*. Cambridge, Eng., 2005.

Dean, Leonard F., ed. *A Casebook on "Othello."* New York, 1961.

Evans, Robert C. "Friendship in Shakespeare's *Othello*," *Ben Jonson Journal* 6 (1999), 109–46.

Everett, Barbara. "Inside *Othello*." *ShS* 53 (2000), 184–95.

———. "Reflections on the Sentimentalist's *Othello*," *Critical Quarterly* 3 (1961), 127–39. (A comment on the Leavis article below.)

Garner, S. N. "Shakespeare's Desdemona," *ShakS* 9 (1976), 233–52.

Hankey, Julie, ed. *Plays in Performance: "Othello."* Bristol, 1987.

Heilman, Robert B. *Magic in the Web: Action and Language in "Othello."* Lexington, Ky., 1956.

Honigmann, E. A. J. *The Texts of "Othello" and Shakespearian Revision*. London, 1996.

Hyman, Stanley Edgar. *Iago: Some Approaches to the Illusion of His Motivation*. New York, 1970.

Jones, Eldred. *Othello's Countrymen: The African in English Renaissance Drama*. London, 1965.

Kolin, Philip C. *Othello: New Critical Essays*. New York and London, 2002.

Korda, Natasha. *Shakespeare's Domestic Economies: Gender and Property in Early Modern England*. Philadelphia, 2002 (Chapter 4).

Leavis, F. R. "Diabolic Intellect and the Noble Hero: Or The Sentimentalist's Othello," *The Common Pursuit*. London, 1952.

Muir, Kenneth, ed. *Shakespeare Survey 21* (1968).

Nowottny, Winifred M. T. "Justice and Love in *Othello*," *University of Toronto Quarterly* 21 (1952), 330–44.

Orkin, Martin. "Othello and the 'plain face' of Racism," *SQ* 38 (1987), 166–88.

Orlin, Lena Cowen. *Private Matters and Public Culture in Post-Reformation England*. Ithaca, N.Y., 1994.

Pechter, Edward. "*Othello*" and Interpretive Traditions. Iowa City, 1999.

Potter, Lois. *Shakespeare in Performance: "Othello."* Manchester, 2002.

Pye, Christopher. "To Throw out Our Eyes for Brave Othello': Shakespeare and Aesthetic Ideology," *SQ* 60.4 (2009), 425–47.

Raatzsch, Richard, trans. Ladislaus Löb. *The Apologetics of Evil: The Case of Iago*. Princeton, 2009.

Rosenberg, Marvin. *The Masks of "Othello."* Berkeley, 1961.

Saunders, Ben. "Iago's Clyster: Purgation, Anality, and the Civilizing Process," *SQ* 55 (2004), 148–76.

Seltzer, Daniel. "Elizabethan Acting in *Othello*," *SQ* 10 (1959), 201–10.

Snyder, Susan, ed. "*Othello*": Critical Essays. New York, 1988.

Stoll, E. E. "*Othello*": An Historical and Comparative Study. Minneapolis, 1915. Rpt. New York, 1964.

Vaughan, Virginia Mason. *Performing Blackness on English Stages, 1500–1800*. Cambridge, Eng., 2005.

Walen, Denise A. "Unpinning Desdemona," *SQ* 58.4 (2007), 487–508.

Wine, Martin L. "*Othello*": Text and Performance. London, 1984.

## King Lear

See also, under *Life in Shakespeare's England*, De Grazia, Quilligan, and Stallybrass (essay by De Grazia); under *The Tragedies*, Bradley, Cunningham, Frye, Goldman, Holloway, Hunter, Kirsch, Knight, and Rosen; under *The Greek and Roman Tragedies*, Brower; under *Textual Criticism and Bibliography*, Blayney, and Taylor and Warren; under *Shakespeare's Language*, Doran; under

*Shakespeare Criticism to the 1930s*, Hazlitt, Johnson, and Stoll; under *Shakespeare Criticism from the 1940s to the 1970s*, Bloom (essay by Jaffa), Burckhardt, Empson, Fly, Granville-Barker, Knights, Kott, and Sewell; under *Shakespeare Criticism Since 1980*, Auden, Boose, Cavell (Chapter 2, identical with the Cavell entry below), Dollimore, Dollimore and Sinfield (essay by McLuskie), Dubrow and Strier (essay by Strier), Erickson, Erickson and Kahn (essay by Berger), Garber (*Shakespeare's Ghost Writers*, Chapter 5), Greenblatt (*Shakespearean Negotiations*, Chapter 4), Loomba and Orkin (essay by Visser), Novy (*Love's Argument*), Patterson (Chapter 5), and Wayne (essay by Thompson); and under *The Romances*, Felperin and Young.

Alpers, Paul J. "*King Lear* and the Theory of the 'Sight Pattern,'" *In Defense of Reading*, ed. Reuben A. Brower and Richard Poirier. New York, 1962.

Berger, Harry, Jr. "*King Lear*": The Lear Family Romance," *Centennial Review* 23 (1979), 348–76.

Booth, Stephen. "*King Lear*," "*Macbeth*," *Indefinition, and Tragedy*, New Haven, 1983.

Brownlow, F. W. *Shakespeare, Harsnett, and the Devils of Denham*. Newark, Del., 1993.

Cavell, Stanley. "The Avoidance of Love: A Reading of *King Lear*," *Must We Mean What We Say?* New York, 1969. Rpt. in *Disowning Knowledge in Six Plays of Shakespeare*. Cambridge, Eng., 1987.

Colie, Rosalie L., and F. T. Flahiff, eds. *Some Facets of "King Lear."* Toronto, 1974.

Craig, Leon Harold. *Of Philosophers and Kings: Political Philosophy in Shakespeare's "Macbeth" and "King Lear."* Toronto, 2001.

Danby, John F. *Shakespeare's Doctrine of Nature: A Study of King Lear.* London, 1949.

Davidson, Adele. *Shakespeare in Shorthand: The Textual Mystery of "King Lear."* Newark, Del., 2009.

Delany, Paul. "*King Lear*" and the Decline of Feudalism," *PMLA* 92 (1977), 429–40.

Elton, William R. *King Lear and the Gods*. San Marino, Calif., 1966. Rpt. Lexington, Ky., 1988.

Everett, Barbara. "The New *King Lear*," *Critical Quarterly* 2 (1960), 325–39.

Foakes, R. A. "*Hamlet*" Versus "*Lear*": Cultural Politics and Shakespeare's Art. Cambridge, Eng., 1993.

Freud, Sigmund. "The Theme of the Three Caskets," *Complete Psychological Works of Sigmund Freud* 12 (1911–1913), pp. 291–301. London, 1958.

Goldberg, S. L. *An Essay on "King Lear."* Cambridge, Eng., 1974.

Graham, Kenneth J. E. " 'Without the form of justice': Plainness and the Performance of Love in *King Lear*," *SQ* 42 (1991), 438–61.

Halio, Jay L. *King Lear: A Guide to the Play.* Greenwood, Conn., 2001.

Hardison, O. B., Jr. "Myth and History in *King Lear*," *SQ* 26 (1975), 227–42.

Heilman, Robert B. *This Great Stage: Image and Structure in "King Lear."* Baton Rouge, La., 1948. Rpt. Seattle, 1963.

Heinemann, Margot. " 'Demystifying the Mystery of State': *King Lear* and the World Upside Down," *ShS* 44 (1992), 75–83.

James, D. G. *The Dream of Learning*. Oxford, 1951.

Jorgensen, Paul A. *Lear's Self-Discovery*, Berkeley, 1967.

Kahn, Coppélia. "The Absent Mother in *King Lear*," *Rewriting the Renaissance: The Discourses of Sexual Difference in Early Modern Europe*, eds. Margaret W. Ferguson et al. Chicago, 1986.

Kahn, Paul W. *Law and Love: The Trials of King Lear.* New Haven, 2000.

Kernan, Alvin. "Formalism and Realism in Elizabethan Drama: The Miracles in *King Lear*," *Renaissance Drama* 9 (1966), 59–66.

Kirsch, Arthur. "The Emotional Landscape of *King Lear*," *SQ* 39 (1988), 154–70.

Kronenfeld, Judy. *King Lear and the Naked Truth: Rethinking the Language of Religion and Resistance.* Durham, N.C., 1998.

Leggatt, Alexander. *King Lear.* Shakespeare in Performance. Manchester, Eng., 1991.

Lothian, J. M. "*King Lear*": A Tragic Reading of Life. Toronto, 1949.

Lusardi, James P., and June Schlueter. *Reading Shakespeare in Performance: "King Lear."* Rutherford, N.J., 1991.

Mack, Maynard. *King Lear in Our Time.* Berkeley, 1965.

Maclean, Norman. "Episode, Scene, Speech, and Word: The Madness of Lear," *Critics and Criticism*, ed. R. S. Crane. Chicago, 1952.

Maguire, Laurie. "Poor, Bare, Forked: Animal Sovereignty, Human Negative Exceptionalism, and the Natural History of *King Lear*," *SQ* 60.2 (2009), 168–96.

Matchett, William H. "Some Dramatic Techniques in *King Lear*," in *Shakespeare: The Theatrical Dimension*, eds. Philip G. McGuire and David A. Samuelson. New York, 1959.

Michie, Donald M., ed. *A Critical Edition of "The True Chronicle History of King Leir and His Three Daughters, Gonorill, Ragan and Cordella."* New York, 1991.

Murphy, John L. *Darkness and Devils: Exorcism and "King Lear."* Athens, Ohio, 1984.

Palfrey, Simon. *Poor Tom: Living "King Lear."* Chicago, 2014.

Reibetanz, John. *The "Lear" World: A Study of "King Lear" in Its Dramatic Context.* Toronto, 1977.

Rosenberg, Marvin. *The Masks of "King Lear."* Berkeley, 1972.

Scott, William O. "Contracts of Love and Affection: Lear, Old Age, and Kingship," *ShS* 55 (2002), 36–42.

Sewall, Richard B. *The Vision of Tragedy.* New Haven, 1959.

Snyder, Susan. "*King Lear* and the Psychology of Dying," *SQ* 33 (1982), 449–60.

Soellner, Rolf. "*King Lear* and the Magic of the Wheel," *SQ* 35 (1984), 274–89.

Tate, Nahum. *The History of King Lear* (1681), ed. James Black. Lincoln, Neb. 1975.

Taylor, Gary, and Michael Warren, eds. *The Division of the Kingdoms: Shakespeare's Two Versions of "King Lear."* Oxford, 1983.

Urkowitz, Steven. *Shakespeare's Revision of "King Lear."* Princeton, 1980.

Warren, Michael, preparer. *The Parallel "King Lear," 1608–1623: Parallel Texts of the First Quarto (1608) and the First Folio (1623).* Berkeley, 1989.

Wittreich, Joseph. "*Image of that Horror*": History, Prophecy, and Apocalypse in "*King Lear*." San Marino, Calif., 1984.

## *Macbeth*

See also, under *The Tragedies*, Berry, Bradley, Garner and Sprengnether (essay by Adelman), Goldman, Holloway, Hunter, Kirsch, Mack, Mack Jr., and Rosen; under *Shakespeare Criticism to the 1930s*, Smith (essay by De Quincey); under *Shakespeare Criticism from the 1940s to the 1970s*, Sanders and Sewell; under *Shakespeare Criticism Since 1980*, Garber (*Cannibals*, essay by Adelman), Howard and O'Connor (essay by Goldberg), Mullaney (Chapter 5), Schwartz and Kahn (essay by Gohlke), Watson, and Woodbridge and Berry (essay by Willis); and under *The Histories*, Pye.

Aitchison, Nick. *Macbeth: Man and Myth.* Stroud, Eng., 1999.

Bartholomeusz, Dennis. "*Macbeth*" and the Players. Cambridge, Eng., 1969.

Booth, Stephen. "*King Lear*," "*Macbeth*," *Indefinition, and Tragedy*. New Haven, 1983.

Brooks, Cleanth. "The Naked Babe and the Cloak of Manliness," *The Well Wrought Urn.* New York, 1947.

Calderwood, James L. *If It Were Done: "Macbeth" and Tragic Action*. Amherst, 1986.

Carroll, William C. *Macbeth: Texts and Contexts.* Boston and New York, 1999.

Craig, Leon Harold. *Of Philosophers and Kings: Political Philosophy in Shakespeare's "Macbeth" and "King Lear."* Toronto, 2001.

Driver, Tom. *The Sense of History in Greek and Shakespearean Drama.* New York, 1960.

Elliott, G. R. *Dramatic Providence in "Macbeth."* Princeton, 1958.

Fergusson, Francis. "*Macbeth* as the Imitation of an Action," *English Institute Essays 1951* (1952), 31–43.

Freud, Sigmund. "Some Character-Types Met with in Psycho-Analytic Work," trans. E. Cobern Mayne, *Collected Papers*. Vol. 4, pp. 326–32. London, 1925.

Gardner, Helen. "Milton's 'Satan' and the Theme of Damnation in Elizabethan Tragedy," *English Association Essays and Studies* n.s. 1 (1948), 46–66.

Harris, Jonathan Gil. "The Smell of *Macbeth*," *SQ* 58.4 (2007), 465–86.

Howell, Maria A. *Manhood and Masculine Identity in William Shakespeare's "Tragedy of Macbeth."* Lanham, Md., 2008.

Jorgensen, Paul A. *Our Naked Frailties: Sensational Art and Meaning in "Macbeth."* Berkeley, 1971.

Kinney, Arthur F. *Lies Like Truth: Shakespeare, Macbeth, and the Cultural Moment.* Detroit, 2001.

Kliman, Bernice W. *Macbeth.* Shakespeare in Performance. Manchester, Eng., 1992.

Knights, L. C. "How Many Children Had Lady Macbeth? An Essay in the Theory and Practice of Shakespeare Criticism," *Explorations.* London, 1946. Rpt. Westport, Conn., 1975.

Langis, Unhae. "Shakespeare and Prudential Psychology: Ambition and Akrasia in *Macbeth.*" *ShakS* 40 (2012), 44–52.

Newstok, Scott L., and Ayanna Thompson. *Weyward Macbeth: Intersections of Race and Performance.* Basingstoke, Eng., 2010.

Norbrook, David. "*Macbeth* and the Politics of Historiography," *Politics of Discourse: The Literature and History of Seventeenth-Century England,* eds. Kevin Sharpe and Steven Zwicker, pp. 78–116. Berkeley, 1987.

Orgel, Stephen. "Macbeth and the Antic Round," *ShS* 52 (1999), 143–53. Rpt. in Orgel, under *Shakespeare Criticism Since 1980.*

Parris, Benjamin. "'The body is with the King, but the King is not with the body': Sovereign Sleep in *Hamlet* and *Macbeth,*" *ShakS* 49 (2012), 101–42.

Paul, Henry N. *The Royal Play of Macbeth.* New York, 1950.

Purkiss, Diane. *The Witch in History: Early Modern and Twentieth-Century Representations.* London and New York, 1996.

Rosenberg, Marvin. *The Masks of "Macbeth."* Berkeley, 1978.

Sinfield, Alan. "*Macbeth*: History, Ideology and Intellectuals," *Critical Quarterly* 28 (1986), 63–77.

Spender, Stephen. "Time, Violence, and *Macbeth,*" *Penguin New Writing,* 3. London, 1940–1941.

Wilders, John, ed. *Shakespeare in Production: "Macbeth."* Cambridge, Eng., 2004.

Williams, Raymond. "Monologue in *Macbeth,*" *Teaching the Text,* eds. Susanne Kappeler and Norman Bryson. London, 1983.

Wills, Garry. *Witches and Jesuits: Shakespeare's "Macbeth."* Oxford, 1995.

Wilson, Luke. "Macbeth and the Contingency of Future Persons," *ShakS* 40 (2012), 53–62.

### *Antony and Cleopatra*

See also, under *The Tragedies,* Frye, Garner and Sprengnether (essays by Cook and Charnes), Goldman, Holloway, Mack, and Rosen; under *The Greek and Roman Tragedies,* Brower, Cantor, Charney, Miola, and Traversi; under *Shakespeare's Predecessors and Contemporaries,* Comensoli and Russell (essay by Adelman), and Waith; under *Shakespeare's Language,* Doran; under

*Shakespeare Criticism to the 1930s,* Coleridge (*Coleridge's Writings*); under *Shakespeare Criticism from the 1940s to the 1970s,* Bethell, Burke, Colie, Granville-Barker, Kettle (essay by Nandy), McAlindon, and Van Laan; under *Shakespeare Criticism Since 1980,* Auden, Bamber, Cavell (pp. 18–37), Charnes, Dollimore (*Radical Tragedy*), Edwards et al. (essay by Hibbard), Erickson (Chapter 4), Holland et al. (essay by Sprengnether), and Neely; under *The Problem Plays,* Schanzer; under *The Histories,* Palmer; and under *The Romances,* Brown and Harris (essay by Ornstein), Danby, and Felperin.

Adelman, Janet. *The Common Liar: An Essay on "Antony and Cleopatra."* New Haven, 1973.

Barroll, J. Leeds. *Shakespearean Tragedy: Genre, Tradition, and Change in "Antony and Cleopatra,"* Washington, D.C., 1984.

Bono, Barbara J. "The Shakespearean Synthesis: *Antony and Cleopatra,*" *Literary Transvaluation: From Vergilian Epic to Shakespearean Tragicomedy.* Berkeley, 1984.

Bradley, A. C. *Oxford Lectures on Poetry.* London, 1909, 1961.

Drakakis, John, ed. *"Antony and Cleopatra."* Basingstoke, 1994.

Fitz, L. T. [Linda Woodbridge], "Egyptian Queens and Male Reviewers: Sexist Attitudes in *Antony and Cleopatra* Criticism," *SQ* 28 (1977), 297–316.

Hatchuel, Sarah. *Shakespeare and the Cleopatra/Caesar Intertext: Sequel, Conflation, Remake.* Madison, N.J., and Lanham, Md., 2011.

Hillman, David. "'If it be love indeed': Transference, Love, and *Anthony and Cleopatra,*" *SQ* 64.3 (2013), 301–33.

Kaula, David. "The Time Sense of *Antony and Cleopatra,*" *SQ* 15:3 (1964), 211–23.

Knights, L. C. *Some Shakespearean Themes.* London, 1959.

Lamb, Margaret. *"Antony and Cleopatra" on the English Stage.* Rutherford, N.J., and London, 1980.

Leavis, F. R. "*Antony and Cleopatra* and *All for Love*: A Critical Exercise," *Scrutiny* 5 (1936–1937), 158–69.

Levine, Laura. *Men in Women's Clothing: Anti-Theatricality and Effeminization, 1579–1642.* Cambridge, Eng., 1994.

Lloyd, Michael. "Cleopatra as Isis," *ShS* 12 (1959), 88–94.

Mack, Maynard. "*Antony and Cleopatra*: The Stillness and the Dance," *Shakespeare's Art: Seven Essays,* ed. Milton Crane. Chicago, 1973.

Madelaine, Richard, ed. *Antony and Cleopatra.* Shakespeare in Production. Cambridge, Eng., 1998.

Markels, Julian. *The Pillar of the World: "Antony and Cleopatra" in Shakespeare's Development.* Columbus, Ohio, 1968.

Mayer, Jean-Christophe, ed. *Lectures de Shakespeare: "Antony and Cleopatra."* Rennes, France, 2000.

Rackin, Phyllis. "Shakespeare's Boy Cleopatra, the Decorum of Nature, and the Golden World of Poetry," *PMLA* 87 (1972), 201–12.

Reimer, A. P. *A Reading of Shakespeare's "Antony and Cleopatra."* Sydney, 1968.

Scott, Michael. *Antony and Cleopatra.* Text and Peformance. London, 1983.

Steppat, Michael. *The Critical Reception of Shakespeare's "Antony and Cleopatra" from 1607 to 1905.* Amsterdam, 1980.

Williamson, Marilyn L. *Infinite Variety: "Antony and Cleopatra" in Renaissance Drama and Earlier Tradition.* Mystic, Conn., 1974.

Wood, Nigel, ed. *"Antony and Cleopatra."* Theory in Practice. Buckingham and Philadelphia, 1996.

Yachnin, Paul. "Shakespeare's Politics of Loyalty: Sovereignty and Subjectivity in *Antony and Cleopatra,*" *Studies in English Literature* 33 (1993), 343–63.

### *The Romances*

See also, under *Shakespeare Criticism Since 1980,* McMullan and Hope.

Beckwith, Sarah. *Shakespeare and the Grammar of Forgiveness.* Ithaca, N.Y., 2011.

Bergeron, David M. *Shakespeare's Romances and the Royal Family.* Lawrence, Kans., 1985.

Bishop, T. G. *Shakespeare and the Theatre of Wonder.* Cambridge, Eng., 1996.

Brown, John Russell, and Bernard Harris, eds. *Later Shakespeare.* Stratford-upon-Avon Studies 8. London, 1966.

Cobb, Christopher J. *The Staging of Romance in Late Shakespeare: Text and Theatrical Technique.* Newark, Del., 2007.

Danby, John F. *Poets on Fortune's Hill.* London, 1952. Reprinted as *Elizabethan and Jacobean Poets.* London, 1964.

Dutton, Richard, and Jean E. Howard, eds. *A Companion to Shakespeare's Works.* Vol. 4, The Poems, Problem Comedies, Late Plays. Oxford, 2003.

Edwards, Philip. "Shakespeare's Romances: 1900–1957," *ShS* 11 (1958), 1–18. See also other articles in this issue.

Fawkner, H. W. *Shakespeare's Miracle Plays: "Pericles," "Cymbeline," and "The Winter's Tale."* Rutherford, N.J., 1992.

Felperin, Howard. *Shakespearean Romance.* Princeton, 1972.

Foakes, R. A. *Shakespeare: From the Dark Comedies to the Last Plays.* London and Charlottesville, Va., 1971.

Frye, Northrop. *Anatomy of Criticism.* Princeton, 1957.

———. *A Natural Perspective: The Development of Shakespearean Comedy and Romance.* New York, 1965.

———. *The Secular Scripture: A Study of the Structure of Romance.* Cambridge, Mass., 1976.

Gesner, Carol. *Shakespeare and the Greek Romance: A Study of Origins.* Lexington, Ky., 1970.

Hartwig, Joan. *Shakespeare's Tragicomic Vision.* Baton Rouge, La., 1972.

Hunter, Robert Grams. *Shakespeare and the Comedy of Forgiveness.* New York, 1965.

James, D. G. "The Failure of the Ballad-Makers," *Scepticism and Poetry.* London, 1937.

Jordan, Constance. *Shakespeare's Monarchies: Ruler and Subject in the Romances.* Ithaca, N.Y., 1997.

Kermode, Frank. *William Shakespeare: The Final Plays.* London, 1963.

Knight, G. Wilson. *The Crown of Life.* London, 1947, 1966.

———. *The Shakespearian Tempest.* London, 1932, 1953.

Leavis, F. R. "A Criticism of Shakespeare's Last Plays," *Scrutiny* 10 (1942), 339–45. Rpt. in *The Common Pursuit.* London, 1952.

Lyne, Raphael. *Shakespeare's Late Work.* Oxford, 2007.

Marsh, D. R. C. *The Recurring Miracle: A Study of "Cymbeline" and the Last Plays.* Pietermaritzburg, Natal, 1962, 1964.

Marshall, Cynthia. *Last Things and Last Plays: Shakespearean Eschatology.* Carbondale, Ill., 1991.

McDonald, Russ. *Shakespeare's Late Style.* Cambridge, Eng., 2006.

McMullan, Gordon. *Shakespeare and the Idea of Late Writing: Authorship in the Proximity of Death.* Cambridge, Eng., 2007.

Mincoff, Marco. *Things Supernatural and Causeless: Shakespearean Romance.* Newark, Del., 1992.

Mowat, Barbara A. *The Dramaturgy of Shakespeare's Romances.* Athens, Ga., 1976.

Nevo, Ruth. *Shakespeare's Other Language.* New York and London, 1987.

Palfrey, Simon. *Late Shakespeare: A New World of Words.* Oxford, 1997.

Peterson, Douglas L. *Time, Tide, and Tempest: A Study of Shakespeare's Romances.* San Marino, Calif., 1973.

Pettet, E. C. *Shakespeare and the Romance Tradition.* London, 1949.

Platt, Peter G. *Reason Diminished: Shakespeare and the Marvelous.* Lincoln, Neb., 1997.

Richards, Jennifer, and James Knowles, eds. *Shakespeare's Late Plays: New Readings.* Edinburgh, 1999.

Ryan, Kiernan, ed. *Shakespeare: The Late Plays.* New York, 1999.

Smith, Hallett. *Shakespeare's Romances.* San Marino, Calif., 1972.

Smith, Stephen W. *Shakespeare's Last Plays: Essays in Literature and Politics.* Lanham, Md., and Oxford, 2002.

Strachey, Lytton. "Shakespeare's Final Period," *Books and Characters.* London, 1922.

Tborne, Alison, ed. *Shakespeare's Romances.* Basingstoke, Eng., and New York, 2003.

Traversi, Derek. *Shakespeare: The Last Phase.* New York, 1954.

Yates, Frances A. *Shakespeare's Last Plays: A New Approach.* London, 1975.

Young, David. *The Heart's Forest: A Study of Shakespeare's Pastoral Plays.* New Haven and London, 1972.

## The Winter's Tale

See also, under *The Romances,* Felperin, Foakes, Hartwig, Hunter, Knight (*Crown of Life*), Mowat, and Young; and under *Shakespeare Criticism Since 1980,* Cavell (Chapter 6), Erickson, Neely, and Parker and Hartman (essay by Felperin).

Alpers, Paul. *What Is Pastoral?* Chicago, 1996.

Apfelbaum, Robert. "'Lawful as eating': Art, Life, and Magic in *The Winter's Tale,*" *ShakS* 42 (20124), 32–41.

Barber, C. L. "'Thou That Beget'st Him That Did Thee Beget': Transformation in *Pericles* and *The Winter's Tale,*" *ShS* 22 (1969), 59–67.

Bartholomeusz, Dennis. *"The Winter's Tale" in Performance in England and America, 1611–1976.* Cambridge, Eng., 1982.

Bethell, S. L. *The Winter's Tale: A Study.* London, 1947.

Bishop, T. G. *Shakespeare and the Theatre of Wonder.* Cambridge, Eng., 1996.

Coghill, Nevill. "Six Points of Stage-Craft in *The Winter's Tale,*" *ShS* 11 (1958), 31–41.

Draper, R. P. *"The Winter's Tale": Text and Performance.* London, 1985.

Ewbank, Inga-Stina. "The Triumph of Time in *The Winter's Tale,*" *Review of English Literature* 5:2 (1964), 83–100.

Frey, Charles. *Shakespeare's Vast Romance: A Study of "The Winter's Tale."* Columbia, Mo., 1980.

Frey, Northrop. "Recognition in *The Winter's Tale,*" *Essays on Shakespeare and Elizabethan Drama in Honor of Hardin Craig,* ed. R. Hosley, pp. 235–46. Columbia, Mo., 1962.

Jensen, Phebe. "Singing Psalms to Hornpipes: Festivity, Iconoclasm, and Catholicism in *The Winter's Tale,*" *SQ* 55 (2004), 279–306.

Kaplan, Lindsay M., and Katherine Eggert. "'Good queen, my lord, good queen': Sexual Slanders and the Trials of Female Authority in *The Winter's Tale,*" *Renaissance Drama* n.s. 25 (1994), 89–118.

Knapp, James A. "Visual and Ethical Truth in *The Winter's Tale,*" *SQ* 55 (2004), 253–78.

Lindenbaum, Peter. "Time, Sexual Love, and the Uses of Pastoral in *The Winter's Tale,*" *Modern Language Quarterly* 33 (1972), 3–22.

Matchett, William H. "Some Dramatic Techniques in *The Winter's Tale,*" *ShS* 22 (1969), 93–107.

Siemon, James Edward. " 'But It Appears She Lives': Iteration in *The Winter's Tale,*" *PMLA* 89 (1974), 10–16.

Snyder, Susan. "Mamillius and Gender Polarization in *The Winter's Tale,*" *SQ* 50 (1999), 1–8.

Sokol, B. J. *Art and Illusion in "The Winter's Tale."* Manchester, Eng., 1994.

Syme, Holger Schott. *Theatre and Testimony in Shakespeare's England: A Culture of Mediation.* Cambridge, Eng., 2012.

Tayler, Edward W. *Nature and Art in Renaissance Literature.* New York, 1964.

Wickham, Glynne. "Romance and Emblem: A Study in the Dramatic Structure of *The Winter's Tale," The Elizabethan Theatre III,* ed. David Galloway. Hamden, Conn., 1973.

Williams, John Anthony. *The Natural Work of Art: The Experience of Romance in Shakespeare's "Winter's Tale."* Cambridge, Mass., 1967.

## The Tempest

See also, under *The Romances,* Brown and Harris (essay by Brockbank), Felperin, Frye (*Natural Perspective*), Hartwig, Kermode, Mowat, Peterson, and Young; under *Shakespeare's Predecessors and Contemporaries,* Bevington and Holbrook (essay by Bevington); under *Shakespeare Criticism to the 1930s,* Coleridge (*Coleridge's Writings*); under *Shakespeare Criticism from the 1940s to the 1970s,* Fiedler, Kernan (*Playwright as Magician,* Chapter 6), and Kott; under *Shakespeare Criticism Since 1980,* Dollimore and Sinfield (essay by Brown), Drakakis (essay by Barker and Hulme), Garber (*Cannibals,* essay by Orgel), Greenblatt (*Shakespearean Negotiations,* Chapter 5), Hamlin, Howard and O'Connor (essay by Cartelli), Lenz et al. (essay by Leininger), Loomba and Orkin (essay by Brotton), McMullan and Hope (essay by Norbrook), and Schwartz and Kahn (essay by Sundelson); and under *The Comedies,* Palmer and Bradbury (essay by Wells).

Auden, W. H. "The Sea and the Mirror: A Commentary on Shakespeare's *The Tempest,*" *The Collected Poetry.* New York, 1945.

Berger, Harry, Jr. "Miraculous Harp: A Reading of Shakespeare's *Tempest,*" *ShakS* 5 (1969), 253–83.

Demaray, John G. *Shakespeare and the Spectacles of Strangeness: "The Tempest" and the Transformation of Renaissance Theatrical Forms.* Pittsburgh, Pa., 1998.

Frey, Charles. *"The Tempest* and the New World," *SQ* 30 (1979), 29–41.

Hamilton, Donna. *Virgil and "The Tempest": The Politics of Imitation.* Columbus, Ohio, 1990.

Hulme, Peter, and William H. Sherman, eds. *"The Tempest" and Its Travels.* Philadelphia, 2000.

James, D. G. *The Dream of Prospero.* Oxford, 1967.

James, Henry. "Introduction to *The Tempest.*" Rpt. in *Henry James: Selected Literary Criticism,* ed. Morris Shapiro. London, 1963.

Mebane, John S. *Renaissance Magic and the Return of the Golden Age: The Occult Tradition and Marlowe, Jonson, and Shakespeare.* Lincoln, Neb., 1989.

Mowat, Barbara A. "Prospero's Book," *SQ* 52 (2001), 1–33.

Neill, Michael. "'Noises, / Sounds, and Sweet Airs': The Burden of Shakespeare's *Tempest,*" *SQ,* 59.1 (2008), 36–59.

Orgel, Stephen. "New Uses of Adversity: Tragic Experience in *The Tempest*," *In Defense of Reading*, eds. Reuben A. Brower and Richard Poirier. New York, 1962.

———. "Prospero's Wife," *Representations* 8 (1984), 1–13. Rpt. in Orgel, under *Shakespeare Criticism Since 1980*.

Skura, Meredith Anne. "Discourse and the Individual: The Case of Colonialism in *The Tempest*," *SQ* 40 (1989), 42–69.

Strier, Richard. " 'I am Power': Normal and Magical Politics in *The Tempest*," in *Writing and Political Engagement in Seventeenth-Century England*, eds. Derek Hirst and Richard Strier. Cambridge, Eng., 1999.

Thompson, Ann. " 'Miranda, where's your sister?': Reading Shakespeare's *The Tempest*," *Feminist Criticism: Theory and Practice*, ed. Susan Sellers. New York, 1991.

Vaughan, Alden T. "Shakespeare's Indian: The Americanization of Caliban," *SQ* 39 (1988), 137–53.

Vaughan, Alden T., and Virginia Mason Vaughan. *Shakespeare's Caliban: A Cultural History*. Cambridge, Eng., 1991.

Vaughan, Virginia Mason, and Alden T. Vaughan, eds. *Critical Essays on Shakespeare's "The Tempest."* New York and London, 1998.

William, David. "*The Tempest* on the Stage," *Jacobean Theatre*, eds. John Russell Brown and Bernard Harris, pp. 133–57. Stratford-upon-Avon Studies 1. London, 1960.

Potter, Lois. "Topicality or Politics? *The Two Noble Kinsmen, 1613–34*," *The Politics of Tragicomedy: Shakespeare and After*, eds. Gordon McMullan and Jonathan Hope. London, 1992.

Shannon, Laurie J. "Emilia's Argument: Friendship and 'Human Title' in *The Two Noble Kinsmen*," *ELH* 64 (1997), 657–82.

Taylor, David Francis. "The Disenchanted Island: A Political History of *The Tempest*, 1760–1830," *SQ* 63.4 (2012), 487–517.

Waith, Eugene. "Shakespeare and Fletcher on Love and Friendship," *ShakS* 18 (1986), 235–49.


## The Poems

Cheney, Patrick, ed. *The Cambridge Companion to Shakespeare's Poetry*. Cambridge, Eng., 2007.

Dubrow, Heather. *Captive Victors: Shakespeare's Narrative Poems and Sonnets*. Ithaca, N.Y., 1987.

Hulse, Clarke. *Metamorphic Verse: The Elizabethan Minor Epic*. Princeton, 1981.

Schoenfeldt, Michael Carl. *The Cambridge Introduction to Shakespeare's Poetry*. Cambridge, Eng., 2010.

*Shakespeare Survey 15* (1962). Devoted chiefly to the poems and music, including the sonnets.

Vickers, Brian. *Counterfeiting Shakespeare: Evidence, Authorship, and John Ford's "Funerall Elegye."* Cambridge, Eng., 2002.


## Sonnets

See also, under *The Poems*, Dubrow; under *Shakespeare's Predecessors and Contemporaries*, Rasmussen (essay by Alpers); under *Shakespeare Criticism from the 1940s to the 1970s*, Colie, and Kernan (*Playwright as Magician*, Chapter 2); under *Shakespeare Criticism Since 1980*, Loomba and Orkin (essay by Hall), McDonald (essay by Vendler), Parker and Hartman (essay by Greene), and Wheeler (pp. 179–90); and, under *Twelfth Night*, Schalkwyk.

Allen, Michael J. B. "Shakespeare's Man Descending a Staircase: Sonnets 126 to 154," *ShS* 31 (1978), 127–38.

Booth, Stephen. *An Essay on Shakespeare's Sonnets*. New Haven, 1969.

———, ed. *Shakespeare's Sonnets, Edited with Analytic Commentary*. New Haven, 1977.

Boyd, Brian. *Why Lyrics Last: Evolution, Cognition, and Shakespeare's Sonnets*. Cambridge, Mass., 2012.

Bradley, A. C. *Oxford Lectures on Poetry*. London, 1909, 1961.

Brown, Richard Danson, and David Johnson, eds. *Cymbeline and The Sonnets*. New York, 2000.

Callaghan, Dympna. *Shakespeare's Sonnets*. Malden, Mass., 2007.

Cheney, Patrick. "'O, let my books be . . . dumb presagers': Poetry and Theater in Shakespeare's Sonnets," *SQ* 52 (2001), 222–54.

Clark, S. H. *Sordid Images: The Poetry of Masculine Desire*. London and New York, 1994.

Cousins, A. D. *Shakespeare's Sonnets and Narrative Poems*. Harlow, Eng., 2000.

De Grazia, Margreta. "The Scandal of Shakespeare's Sonnets," *ShS* 46 (1994), 35–49.

Dubrow, Heather. *Echoes of Desire: English Petrarchism and Its Counterdiscourses*. Ithaca, N.Y., 1995.

Edmundson, Paul, and Stanley Wells. *Shakespeare's Sonnets*. Oxford, 2004.

Fineman, Joel. *Shakespeare's Perjured Eye: The Invention of Poetic Subjectivity in the Sonnets*. Berkeley, 1986.

Giroux, Robert. *The Book Known as Q: A Consideration of Shakespeare's Sonnets*. New York, 1982.

Halpern, Richard. *Shakespeare's Perfume: Sodomy and Sublimity in the Sonnets, Wilde, Freud, and Lacan*. Philadelphia, 2002.

Healy, Margaret. *Shakespeare's Alchemy and the Creative Imagination: The Sonnets and "A Lover's Complaint."* Cambridge, Eng., 2011.

Hokama, Rhema. "Love's Rites: Performing Prayer in Shakespeare's Sonnets," *SQ* 63.2 (2012), 199–223.

Hopkins, Lisa. *Shakespeare's "The Tempest": The Relationship between Text and Film*. London, 2008.

Hubler, Edward, Northrop Frye, Leslie A. Fiedler, Stephen Spender, and R. P. Blackmur. *The Riddle of Shakespeare's Sonnets*. New York, 1962.

Ingram, W. G., and Theodore Redpath, eds. *Shakespeare's Sonnets*. London, 1964.

Innes, Paul. *Shakespeare and the English Renaissance Sonnet: Verses of Feigning Love*. Basingstoke and New York, 1997.

Knight, G. Wilson. *The Mutual Flame: On Shakespeare's Sonnets and "The Phoenix and the Turtle."* London, 1955.

Korda, Natasha. "Dame Usury: Gender, Credit and (Ac)counting in the Sonnets and *The Merchant of Venice*." *SQ* 60.2 (2009), 129–53.

Krieger, Murray. *A Window to Criticism: Shakespeare's Sonnets and Modern Poetics*. Princeton, 1964.

Landry, Hilton. *Interpretations in Shakespeare's Sonnets*. Berkeley, 1963.

———, ed. *New Essays on Shakespeare's Sonnets*. New York, 1976.

Leishman, J. B. *Themes and Variations in Shakespeare's Sonnets*. London, 1961.

Lever, J. W. *The Elizabethan Love Sonnet*. London, 1956.

Melchiori, Giorgio. *Shakespeare's Dramatic Meditations: An Experiment in Criticism*. Oxford, 1976.

Muir, Kenneth. *Shakespeare's Sonnets*. London, 1979.

Paterson, Don. *Reading Shakespeare's Sonnets: A New Commentary*. London, 2010.

Pequigney, Joseph. *Such is My Love: A Study of Shakespeare's Sonnets*. Chicago, 1985.

Ramsay, Paul. *The Fickle Glass: A Study of Shakespeare's Sonnets*. New York, 1979.

Ransom, John Crowe. *The World's Body*. New York and London, 1938, 1968.

Schalkwyk, David. *Speech and Performance in Shakespeare's Sonnets and Plays*. Cambridge, Eng., 2002.

Schiffer, James, ed. *Shakespeare's Sonnets: Critical Essays*. New York, 1999.

Schoenfeldt, Michael. *A Companion to Shakespeare's Sonnets*. Oxford, 2007.

Vendler, Helen. *The Art of Shakespeare's Sonnets*. Cambridge, Mass., 1997.

Warley, Christopher. *Sonnet Sequences and Social Distinction in Renaissance England*. Cambridge, Eng., 2005.

# Textual Notes

These textual notes do not offer an historical collation, either of the early quartos and folios or of more recent editions; they are simply a record of departures in this edition from the copy text. For most plays the notes give the adopted reading of this edition in bold face, followed by the rejected reading in the relevant copy text. Where two substantive early texts are involved, or where a reading from some other earlier edition has been adopted, the notes provide information on the source of the reading in square brackets. In a few texts, adopted readings of editions more recent than the First Folio are indicated by [eds.]. Alterations in lineation are not indicated, nor are some minor and obvious typographical errors; changes in punctuation are indicated when the resulting change in meaning is substantive.

Abbreviations used:
F The First Folio
Q quarto
O octavo
s.d. stage direction
s.p. speech prefix

## The Taming of the Shrew

Copy Text: The First Folio. The act and scene divisions are missing in the Folio except for Act 1 (before the first Induction), Act 3, Act 4 (at 4.3), and Act 5 (at 5.2).

**Ind.1. 0.1 Christopher Sly** [printed at the end of the s.d. in F as "Christophero Sly"] **1** [and elsewhere] SLY *Begger* **10–11 thirdborough** Headborough **16 Breathe** Brach **21** [and elsewhere] FIRST HUNTSMAN *Hunts.* **81 FIRST PLAYER** 2. *Player* **87 SECOND PLAYER** *Sincklo* **99 FIRST PLAYER** *Plai.* **134 peasant.** peasant,

**Ind. 2. 2 Lordship** Lord **18 Sly's** Sies **26** [and elsewhere] THIRD SERVINGMAN 3. *Man* **27** [and elsewhere] SECOND SERVINGMAN 2 *Man* **47** [and elsewhere] FIRST SERVINGMAN 1 *Man* **53 wi'th'** with **93 Greet** Greece **98 lose** loose **99** [and elsewhere] PAGE *Lady* **125 SERVINGMAN** *Mes.* **133 it. Is** it is

**1.1. 3 fore** for **13 Vincentio** *Vincentio's* **14 brought** brough **24 satiety** sacietie **25 Mi perdonate** *Me Pardonato* **33 Ovid be** *Ouid;* be **146 s.d. Manent** *Manet* **163 captum** captam **208 colored** Conlord **227 time.** time **244 your** you **248.2 speak** speakes

**1.2. 17.1 wrings** rings **18 masters** mistris **24 Con . . . trovato** Contutti le core bene trobatto **25 ben** bene **26 Molto** multo **onorato** honorata

**33 pip** peepe **45 this's** this **51 grows. But** growes but **few,** few. **72 me, were she** me. Were she is **119 me and other more,** me. Other more **170 help me** helpe one **188 Antonio's** Butonios **189 his** my **211 ours** yours **264 feat** seeke **279 ben** Been

**2.1. 8 thee tell** tel **75–6 wooing.—Neighbors,** wooing neighbors: **79 unto you** vnto **104 Pisa. By report** *Pisa* by report, **153 struck** stroke **157 rascal fiddler** Rascall, Fidler **168 s.d. Exeunt** *Exit* **186 bonny** bony **244 askance** a sconce **322 s.d. Exeunt** *Exit* **328 in me** in me **352 Valance** Vallens **355 pail** pale **373 Marseilles** Marcellus

**3.1. 28 Sigeia** *sigeria* [also at lines 33 and 42] **43 steterat** staterat **47** [*Aside*] *Luc.* **50 BIANCA** [not in F] **51 LUCENTIO** *Bian.* **53 BIANCA** *Hort.* **74 B mi** Beeme **76 clef** Cliffe **80 change** charge **odd** old **81 SERVANT** *Nicke*

**3.2. 13 behavior.** behauiour, **14 man;** man; **29 of thy** of **30 old news** newes **33 hear** heard **54 swayed** Waid **56 cheeked** chekt **60 velour** velure **128 to love** Loue **130 As I** As **150 e'er** ere **182 s.d. Music plays** [after line 183 in F] **199 GREMIO** *Gra.*

**4.1. 23 CURTIS** *Gru.* **59 Imprimis** Inprimis **81 sleekly** slickely **106 GRUMIO** *Gre.* **168.1 Curtis** *Curtis a Seruant* [after line 169 in F]

**4.2. 4 HORTENSIO** *Luc.* **6 LUCENTIO** *Hor.* [and at line 8] **7 you? First resolve** you first, resolue **8 read that I profess,** *The* reade, that I professe the **13 none** me **31 her** them **72 Take . . . alone** [assigned to "*Par.*" in F] **in me**

**4.[3]** [F has "*Actus Quartus. Scena Prima*" here] **48 to** too **62.1 Enter Haberdasher** [after 61 in F] **63 HABERDASHER** *Fel.* **81 is a** is **88 like a** like **146 where,** where **148 mete-yard** meat-yard **177 account'st** accountedst

**4.4. 0.2** [*booted*] [appears at line 18.2 in F] **1 Sir** Sirs **18.2 bareheaded booted and bare headed **68.1 Exit** [after line 67 in F; F also adds a s.d., "Enter Peter," after line 68] **78 he's** has **91 except** expect **93 solum** solem

**4.5. 14 An** And **18 is** in **35 make a** make the **37 Whither** Whether **where** whether **77 she be** she

**5.1. 4** [F has "*Exit*" here] **6 master's** mistris **42 brought** brough **50 master's** Mistris **62 copintank** copataine **104.1 Exeunt** Exit **139 No** Mo **143 than never** then ueuer

**5.[2]** [F has "*Actus Quintus*" here] **2 done** come **37 thee, lad** the lad **39 butt** But **40 butt! An** but an **45 bitter** better **two** too **52 TRANIO** *Tri.* **57 Oho** Oh, oh **62 two** too **65 for sir** **93.1 Enter Biondello** [after "Do what you can" in 93 in F] **132 a** fiue **136 you're** your **152 maintenance commits** maintenance. Commits

A-94

## A Midsummer Night's Dream

Copy text: the first quarto of 1600. The act and scene divisions are absent from the quarto; the Folio provides act divisions only.

**1.1. 4 wanes** waues **10 New** Now **19.1** *Lysander* Lysander *and Helena* **24 Stand forth, Demetrius** [printed as s.d. in Q] **26 Stand forth, Lysander** [printed as s.d. in Q] **74 their** there **114** [and elsewhere] **lose** loose **132 Ay** Eigh **133 hear** here **136 low** loue **187 Yours would** Your words **191 I'd** ile **216 sweet** sweld **219 stranger companies** strange companions **224 s.d.** *Exit Hermia* [after line 223 in Q]

**2.1. 1** [and elsewhere] PUCK *Robin* **61** [and elsewhere] TITANIA *Qu.* **61 Fairies** Fairy **79 Aegles** Eagles **109 thin** chinne **158 the west** west **183 off** of **190 slay** stay **slayeth** stayeth **194 thee** the **201 not nor** not, not **206 lose** loose **246.1** [after line 247 in Q]

**2.2. 4 leathern** lethren **9 FIRST FAIRY** [not in Q] **13 CHORUS** [not in Q; also at line 24] **44 comfort** comfor **45 Be** Bet **49 good** god **53 is it** 63 **human** humane **155 ate** eate

**3.1. 52 BOTTOM** *Cet.* **72 PUCK** *Ro.* **77 BOTTOM** *Pyra.* [also at lines 79 and 98] **78 Odors, odors** Odours, odorous **83 PUCK** *Quin.* **84 FLUTE** *Thys.* [also at lines 88 and 97] **120 ousel** Woosell **144 own** owe **156** [and elsewhere] **Mote** *Moth* **157–8 Ready . . . go** [assigned to FAIRIES in Q] **170 PEASEBLOSSOM** *1. Fai.* **171 COBWEB** [not in Q] **172 MOTE** *2. Fair.* **173 MUSTARDSEED** *3. Fai.* **190 you of** you **196.1** *Exeunt* Exit

**3.2. 0.1** [Q: *Enter King of* Fairies, *and* Robin goodfellow] **3.1** [See previous note.] **6–7 love. / Near . . . bower,** loue, / Neere . . . bower. **15–16 brake. / When . . . take,** brake, / When . . . take: **19 mimic** Minnick **38** [and elsewhere] PUCK *Rob.* **80 I so** I **85 sleep** slippe **213 like** life **215 rend** rent **220 passionate words** words **250 prayers** praise **260 off** of **299 gentlemen** gentleman **313 too** to **326 but** hut **344 s.d.** *Exit Exeunt* **406 Speak! In some bush?** Speake in some bush. **426 shalt** shat **451 To your** your

**4.1. 5** [and elsewhere] BOTTOM *Clown* **20 courtesy** curtsie **24 marvelous** maruailes **54 flowerets'** flouriets **64 off** of **72 o'er** or **81 five** fine **82 ho** howe **116 Seemed** Seeme **127 this is** this **132 rite** right **137.2 Wind . . . up** they all start vp. *Winde hornes* **171 saw** see **177 hear** here **190 found** fonnd **198 let us** lets **205 to expound** expound **208 a patched** patcht a **213 ballad** Ballet

**4.2. 0.1** [*Snout, and Starveling*] Thisby *and the rabble* **3 STARVELING** *Flut.* **5 FLUTE** *Thys.* [and at lines 9, 13, 19] **29 no** not **34 ribbons** ribands

**5.1. 34 our** Or **107** [and elsewhere] THESEUS *Duk* **122 his** this **150.1** *Exeunt* Exit [after line 153 in Q] **155 Snout** Flute **190 up in thee** now againe **193 love! Thou art my** loue thou art, my **205 mural down** Moon vsed **209** [and elsewhere] HIPPOLYTA *Dutch.* **216 beasts in, a** beasts, in a **265.1** *Enter Pyramus* [after 267 in Q] **270 gleams** beames **309 before** before? **315 mote** moth **317 war- rant** warnd **325 tomb** tumbe **347 BOTTOM** *Lyon* **363 gait** gate (also at 411) **366 lion** Lyons **367 behowls** beholds **414–15 And . . . rest** [these lines are transposed in Q]

## The Merchant of Venice

Copy text: the first quarto of 1600 [Q]. The act and scene divisions are absent from the quarto; the Folio provides act divisions only.

**1.1. 0.1** *Salerio* Salaryno [and also elsewhere *Salarino,* and abbreviated *Salar., Sala.,* and *Sal.*] *Solanio* Salanio [and abbreviated elsewhere *Sola.* and *Sol.*] **19 Peering** Piring **27 docked** docks **84 alabaster** Alablaster **85 jaundice** *laundies* **112 tongue** togue **113 Is** It is **128 off** of **151 back** bake

**1.2. 44 Palatine** Palentine [and at line 57] **53 Bone** *Boune* **58 throstle** Trassell **119.1** *Enter a Servingman* [after line 120 in Q]

**1.3. 28** [and elsewhere] SHYLOCK *lew* **76 compromised** compremyzd **82 peeled** pyld **110 spit** spet [also at lines 124 and 129] **125 day, another time** day another time,

**2.1. 0.2** *Morocco* Morochus **25 Sophy . . . prince,** Sophy, and a Persian Prince **31 thee** the **35 page** rage

**2.2. 1** [and elsewhere] LAUNCELOT *Clowne* **3** [and elsewhere in this scene] **Gobbo** *Iobbe* **42 By** Be **76 murder** muder **91 fill horse** philhorse **94 last** lost **165.1** *Exit Leonardo* [after line 164 in Q] **168 a suit** sute **180** [and elsewhere] **lose** loose

**2.3. 11 did** doe

**2.4. 8 o'clock** of clocke **9 s.d.** [after line 9 in Q] **14 Love news,** Loue, newes **20.1** *Exit clown* [after line 23 in Q] **39 s.d.** *Exeunt* Exit

**2.5. 44 Jewess'** Iewes

**2.6. 26 Ho! Who's** Howe whose **35 night, you** night you **59 gentlemen** gentleman **61 Who's** Whose

**2.7. 18 threatens.** Men threatens men **45 Spits** Spets **69 tombs** timber

**2.8. 8 gondola** Gondylo **39 Slubber** slumber

**2.9. 6 rites** rights **48 chaff** chaft **49 varnished** varnist **64 judgment** *iudement* **73** [Q provides a s.p.: *Arrag.*]

**3.1. 19** [and elsewhere] **lest** least **21.1** *Enter Shylock* [after line 22 in Q] **46 courtesy** cursie **70 MAN** [not in Q] **74.1** [Q repeats the s.d. "*Enter* Tuball"] **100 Heard** heere **114 turquoise** Turkies

**3.2. 23 eke** ech **61 live. With** liue with **67 eyes** *eye* **81 vice** voyce **84 stairs** stayers **99 Veiling** vailing **101 Therefore** Therefore then **110 shuddering** shyddring **117 whether** whither **199 loved; for intermission** lou'd for intermission, **204 roof** rough **217.1–2** [after line 219 in Q] **315 BASSANIO** [not in Q] **336 e'er** ere

**3.3. 0.1** *Solanio* Salerio **24 SOLANIO** *Sal.*

**3.4. 13 equal** egall **23 Hear other things:** heere other things **49 Padua** Mantua **50 cousin's** cosin **53 traject** Tranect **80 near** nere **81 my** my my

**3.5. 20 enough** enow **e'en** in **26 comes** come **74 merit it,** meane it, it **81 a wife** wife **85 howsome'er** how so mere **87 s.d.** *Exeunt* Exit

**4.1. 30 his state** this states **31 flint** flints **35** [and elsewhere in this scene] SHYLOCK *Iewe* **50 urine; for affection,** vrine for affection. **51 Mistress** Maisters **73 You may as well** well **74 Why he hath made the** the bleat bleake **75 pines** of Pines **81 more** moe **100 is** as **123 sole . . . soul** soule . . . soule **136 whilst** whilest **228 No, not** Not not **233 tenor** tenure **270 off** of **322 off** of **396 GRATIANO** *Shy.* **405.1** *Exeunt* Exit

**5.1. 26 STEPHANO** *Messen.* [also Mess. at lines 28 and 33] **41 Lorenzo** Lorenzo, & **49 Sweet soul** [assigned in Q to Lancelot] **51 Stephano** Stephen **62 choiring** quiring **87 Erebus** *Terebus* **106 wren** Renne **109 ho!** how **152 give it** giue **233 my** mine

## Much Ado About Nothing

Copy text: the quarto of 1600. The act and scene divisions are missing from the quarto; the Folio provides act divisions only.

**1.1. 0.1.** *Messina* Messina, *Innogen, his wife* **2 Pedro** Peter [also in line 9] **40 bird-bolt** Burbolt **84 Benedick** Benedict **141 all, Leonato.** Signor all: Leonato, signior **194.1** *Pedro* Pedro, *Iohn the bastard* **239** [and elsewhere] **lose** loose

**1.2. 3** [and elsewhere] ANTONIO *Old* **6 event** euents **24 skill** shill

**1.3. 46 brother's** bothers **70 s.d.** *Exeunt* exit

**2.1. 0.1** *Hero his wife,* Hero **0.3** *Ursula* [Q adds "*and a kinsman*"] **2** [and elsewhere] ANTONIO *brother* **37 bearward** Berrord **44 Peter, for the heavens;** Peter, for the heauens, **50, 53 curtsy** cursie **67 hear** here **79.3.** *and Don* or dumb **80 a bout** about **94 BALTHASAR** *Bene.* [also at lines 97 and 99] **187 drover** Drouier **201.2** *Leonato* Leonato, *Iohn and Borachio, and Conrade* **311** [and elsewhere] DON PEDRO *Prince* **369 s.d.** *Exeunt* exit

**2.3. 7 s.d.** [at line 5 in Q] **25 an** and **35.1** *Claudio* Claudio, *Musicke* **61 BALTHASAR** [not in Q] **73–6 but . . . nonny** &c. **84 lief** liue **91 s.d.** [after line 90 in Q] **139 us of** vs **171 doffed** daft

**3.1. 0.2.** *Ursula* Ursley **23 s.d.** [after line 25 in Q] **63 antic** antique **111 on; I** on I

**3.2. 27 can** cannot **51 DON PEDRO** *Bene.* **74** [and elsewhere] DON JOHN *Bastard* **75 e'en** den **91–2 manifest. For my brother, I . . . heart hath** manifest, for my brother (I . . . heart) hath **108 her then, tomorrow** her, then to morrow **118 her, tomorrow** her to morrow

**3.3. 17** SEACOAL *Watch* 2 [also at line 27] **87** SEACOAL *Watch* [also at lines 95, 105, 125] **134 reechy** rechie **161** SEACOAL *Watch* 1 [also at line 165] **162 FIRST WATCH** *Watch* 2 [also at line 168] **171** SEACOAL [missing in Q]

**3.4. 17 in** it

**3.5. 2** [and elsewhere] DOGBERRY *Const. Dog.* **7** [and elsewhere] VERGES *Headb.* **9 off** of **32 talking. As** talking as **50** [Q provides an "*exit*" at this point]

**4.1. 4** FRIAR *Fran.* **28** DON PEDRO *Princn* **167 tenor** tenure **202 princes** princesse

**4.2. 0.1–3** [Q reads "*Enter the Constables, Borachio, and the Towne clearke in gownes.*"] **1** DOGBERRY *Keeper* **2** [and elsewhere in this scene] VERGES *Cowley* **4** DOGBERRY *Andrew* **9** [and elsewhere in this scene] DOGBERRY *Kemp* **18** CONRADE, BORACHIO *Both* **39** SEACOAL *Watch* 1 [also at line 53] **47 FIRST WATCH** *Watch* 2 **51** VERGES *Const.* **67** [and elsewhere] DOGBERRY *Constable* **69** CONRADE [missing in Q] **Off** of **73** CONRADE *Couley* **86.1** *Exeunt exit*

**5.1. 16 Bid** And **97 anticly** antiquely, and **98 off** of **116 like** likt **167 there's** theirs **179 on** one **189 Lackbeard there, he** Lackebeard, there hee **201.1.2** [after line 197 in Q] **252** VERGES *Con.* 2

**5.2. 41.1** [after line 42 in Q] **81 myself. So** my self so **97 s.d.** *Exeunt exit*

**5.3. 2** A LORD *Lord* **3** CLAUDIO [missing in Q] **10 dumb** dead **11** [Q provides a s.p. "*Claudio*" here] **12** BALTHASAR [missing in Q] **23** CLAUDIO *Lo.* **24 rite** right **32 speed's** speeds

**5.4. 54** ANTONIO *Leo.* **97** BENEDICK *Leon.*


## As You Like It

Copy text: the First Folio. Act and scene divisions follow the Folio text throughout.

**1.1. 105 she** hee **154** OLIVER [not in F] **154 s.d.** *Exit* [at line 153 in F]

**1.2. 3 I were** were **51 goddesses and** goddesses **53** [and elsewhere] **whither** whether **55** [and elsewhere] TOUCHSTONE *Clow.* **56 father** farher **80** CELIA *Ros.* **88 Le** the **233 love** loue; **251.1** [at line 249 in F] **280** [and occasionally elsewhere] **Rosalind** *Rosaline*

**1.3. 55 likelihood** likelihoods **76 her** per **87.1** *with Lords &c* **124 be** by **129 travel** trauaile **131** [and elsewhere] **woo** woe **135 we in** in we

**2.1. 31 antique** anticke **49 much** must **50 friends** friend **59 of the** of

**2.3. 10 some** seeme **16** ORLANDO [not in F] **29** ORLANDO *Ad.* **71 seventeen** seauentie

**2.4. 1 weary** merry **42 thy wound** they would **65 you**, your

**2.5. 1** AMIENS [not in F; also at line 35] **38.1** *All together here* [before line 35 in F] **41–2 No . . . weather** *&c* **46** JAQUES *Amy.*

**2.7. 0.1** *Lords* Lord **38 brain** braiue **55 Not to seem** Seeme **87 comes** come **161 treble, pipes** trebble pipes, **174** AMIENS [not in F] **182 Then** *The* **190–3 heigh-ho . . . jolly** *&c.* **201 master** masters

**3.2. 26 good** pood **115 graft** graffe [twice] **123 a desert** *Desert* **143 her** *his* **190 whooping** hooping **234 such fruit** fruite **241 thy the** the **254** [and elsewhere] **b'wi'you** buy you **340 lectures** Lectors **354 deifying** defying **362 are** art

**3.3. 52–3 so. Poor men alone? No** so poore men alone: No **88** TOUCHSTONE *Ol.* **99 s.d.** *Exit Exeunt*

**3.4. 29 a lover** Louer **41 puny** puisny

**3.5. 11 pretty, sure** pretty sure **65 hear** here **105 erewhile** yere-while **128 I have** Haue

**4.1. 1 me be** me **18 my** by **27 travel** trauaile **36 gondola** Gundello **44 thousandth** thousand **72 warrant** warne **148 hyena** Hyen **202 it** in

**4.2. 2 FIRST LORD** *Lord* **7 SECOND LORD** *Lord* **10 SECOND LORD** [not in F]

**4.3. 5.1** [after line 3 in F] **8 bid** did bid **12 tenor** tenure **79–80 bottom;** bottom **104–5 itself:** it selfe **143 In** I **156 his** this

**5.1. 14 gi'** ye **37 sir** sit **56 policy** police

**5.2. 7 nor her** nor **31 overcame** ouercome

**5.3. 15 BOTH PAGES** [not in F] **18 In** *In the* **ring** *rang* **24–6 In . . . spring** *In spring time, &c* [also at lines 30–2 and 36–8] **33–8** [this stanza comes after line 20 in F]

**5.4. 25.1.** *Exeunt Exit* **34.1** [after line 33 in F] **80 so to** the so ro **113 her** *his* **150** JAQUES DE BOYS *2 Bro.* [also at line 182] **163 them** him **170 were** vvete **196 rites** rights **197 trust they'll end, in** trust, they'l end in **197.1** *Exeunt Exit*


## Twelfth Night

Copy text: the First Folio. Act and scene divisions follow the Folio text throughout.

**1.1. 1** [and throughout] ORSINO *Duke* **10 capacity** capacitie, **11 sea, naught** sea. Nought **22 s.d.** [after 22 in F]

**1.2. 15 Arion** Orion

**1.3. 51 SIR ANDREW** *Ma.* **54 Mary Accost** *Mary,* accost **96 curl by** coole my **98 me** we **132 dun** dam'd **set** sit **136 That's** That

**1.5. 5** [and throughout] FESTE *Clo.* **85 gagged** gag'd [also at 5.1. 376] **144 He's** Ha's **163.1** *Viola Uiolenta* **296 County's** Countes **306 s.d.** [F adds "*Finis, Actus primus*"]

**2.2. 20 That sure** That **31 our** O **32 made of, such** made, if such

**2.3. 2** *diluculo* Deliculo **25 leman** Lemon **39** FESTE **(sings)** *Clowne sings.* **119 stoop** stope **133 a nayword** an ayword

**2.4. 51** FESTE [not in F] **53 Fly . . . fly** *Fye . . . fie* **55 yew** Ew **88 I** It

**2.5. 14 metal** *Mettle* **112 staniel** stallion **118 portend?** portend, **142 born** become **achieve** atcheeues **156–7 Unhappy." Daylight** vnhappy daylight **173 dear** *deero* **203 s.d.** [F adds "*Finis Actus secundus*"]

**3.1. 8 king** Kings **68 wise men** wisemens **91 all ready** already **124 grece** grize

**3.2. 7 thee** the the **64 nine** mine

**3.4. 15.1–2 s.d.** [at line 14 in F, after "hither"] **25** OLIVIA *Mal.* **65.1** *Exeunt exit* **72 tang** langer **106 lose** loose **175 You** Yon **222 thee** the **228 sir. I am sure no** sir I am sure, no **249 competent** computent **397.1** *Exeunt Exit*

**4.1. 34 struck** stroke

**4.2. 6 in** in in **38 clerestories** cleere stores **71 sport to** sport **101 b'wi'** buy

**4.3. 1** SEBASTIAN [not in F] **35 s.d.** [F adds "*Finis Actus Quartus*"]

**5.1. 5 freight** fraught **141 Whither** Whether **173 He's** H'as **190.1** [after line 187 in F] **195 He's** has **200 pavane** panyn **205 help?** An helpe an **207 to** too **285 He's** has **389 tiny** tine **406 With hey** hey


## Measure for Measure

Copy text: the First Folio. Act and scene divisions are from the Folio except as indicated below.

**The Names of All the Actors** [at the end of the play in F]

**1.1. 76 s.d.** [at line 75 in F]

**1.2. 58** [and elsewhere] MISTRESS OVERDONE *Bawd* **83.1** [after line 84 in F] **85** [and elsewhere] POMPEY *Clo.* **115** [F begins "*Scena Tertia*" here] **134 morality** mortality

**1.3.** [F labels as "*Scena Quarta*"] **20 steeds** weedes **27 Becomes more** More **48** [and elsewhere] **More** Moe **54.1** *Exeunt Exit*

**1.4.** [F labels as "*Scena Quinta*"] **0.1** [and elsewhere] *Isabella Isabell* **2** [and throughout] FRANCISCA *Nun* **5 sisterhood** Sisterstood **17 stead** steed [also at 3.2. 252] **54 givings-out** giuing-out **61–2 mind, study, and fast. / He** minde: Studie, and fast / He **72 He's** Has **78** [and elsewhere] **lose** loose

**2.1. 12 your** our **39 breaks** brakes **90** [and elsewhere] **prunes** prewyns **139.1** [at line 138 in F]

**2.2. 63 back again** againe **104 ere** here

**2.3. 31 least** lest **41 law** Loue

**2.4. 9 sere** feard **17 s.d.** *Enter Servant* [after line 17 in F] **30 s.d.** *Enter Isabella* [after line 30 in F] **48 metal** mettle **53 or** and **75 craftily** crafty **76 me be** be **94 all-binding** all-building

**3.1. 29 thee sire,** thee, fire    **31 serpigo** Sapego    **52 me to hear them** them to heare me    **68 Though** Through    **91 enew** emmew    **96 damned'st** damnest    **131 penury** periury    **200 advisings. To . . . good a** aduisings, to . . . good; a    **216 by oath** oath
**3.2. 0** [not marked as a new scene in F]    **8 law a** Law; a    **9 on** and    **26 eat, array** eate away    **48 it clutched** clutch'd    **74–5 bondage. If . . . patiently, why** bondage if . . . patiently: Why    **109 ungenerative** generatiue    **147 dearer** deare    **214 See** Sea
**4.1. 1 BOY** [not in F]    **49.1** [after line 48 in F]    **61 quests** Quest    **64 s.d. Enter . . . Isabella** [after line 64 in F]
**4.2. 43–7 If . . . thief** [assigned in F to *Clo.*]    **58 yare** y'are    **60.1** [at line 59 in F]    **72 s.d. Enter Duke** [after line 72 in F]    **100 This . . . man** [assigned in F to *Duke*] **Lordship's** Lords    **101 DUKE** *Pro.*    **120 PROVOST** [not in F]
**4.3. 92.1** [at line 91 in F]    **93 Varrius** *Angelo*    **100 well** weale
**4.4. 6 redeliver** reliuer    **15–16 proclaimed. Betimes** proclaim'd betimes    **19 s.d.** [at line 18 in F]
**4.5. 6 Flavius'** *Flauia's*
**5.1. 14 me** we    **34 hear!** heere.    **173 s.d. Enter Mariana** [after line 173 in F]    **174 her face** your face    **226 promisèd** promis'd    **268 s.d.** [at line 267 in F]    **288.1** [after line 286 in F]    **407 s.d. Mariana** *Maria*    **431 confiscation** confutation    **488.2 Juliet** *Iulietta*    **550 that's** that

## Richard III

Copy text: the First Folio, except for two passages, 3.1.1–158 and 5.3.48 to end of play, for which Q1 is copy text. Unless otherwise indicated, the adopted readings are from the first quarto of 1597 [Q1]. Act and scene divisions are marked in the copy text except as indicated below.

**1.1. 1 RICHARD** [not in F]    **41.1 Enter . . . Brackenbury** [eds.] *Enter Clarence, and Brackenbury, guarded*    **45 the** th'    **52 for** but    **65 tempers him to this** tempts him to this harsh    **75 to her for his** for her    **88 An 't** and    **103 I** I do    **124 the** this    **133 prey** play
**1.2. 27 life** [eds.] death    **38 HALBERDIER** [eds.] *Gen.*    **39 stand** Stand'st    **78 of a** of    **80 t'accuse** [eds.] to curse    **94 hand** hands    **141 thee** the    **171 words** word    **204 RICHARD** [not in F]    **205** [not in F]    **227.1 Exeunt** [eds.] *Exit* [also at line 229]    **228 RICHARD Sirs . . . corpse** [not in F]    **229.1 Exeunt** *Exit*
**1.3. 17 come** comes    **lords** Lord    **19 [and elsewhere] STANLEY** *Der.*    **54 whom** who    **69** [not in F]    **109.1** [after line 110 in F]    **114** [not in F]    **155 Ah, little** A little    **160 of** off    **309 QUEEN ELIZABETH** *Mar.*    **342 FIRST MURDERER** *Vil.* [also at lines 350 and 355]    **351 doers. Be assured** dooers, be assur'd:
**1.4. 13 Thence** There    **22 waters** water    **22, 23 my** mine    **25 Ten** A    **39 seek** find    **41 Which** Who    **64 my lord** Lord    **99 s.d. Exit** [at line 97 in F]    **100 I** we    **122 Faith** [not in F]    **126 Zounds** Come    **147 Zounds** [not in F]    **152 Tut** [not in F]    **192 to have redemption** for any goodnesse    **193** [not in F]    **240** [not in F]    **242 of** on    **269** [in F, printed after line 263]    **272 s.d. Stabs him** [after line 272 in F]
**2.1. 0.3 Buckingham** [eds.] *Buckingham, Wooduill*    **5 in** to    **7 Rivers and Hastings** *Dorset* and *Riuers*    **39 God** heauen    **57 unwittingly** vnwillingly    **59 By** To    **68** [F follows with a line: "Of you Lord *Wooduill*, and Lord *Scales* of you"]    **93 but** and    **108 at** and
**2.2. 1 BOY** *Edw.*    **3 [and throughout scene] GIRL** [eds.] *Daugh.*    **3 do you** do    **26 his** a    **47 have I** haue    **83 weep** weepes    **84–5 Clarence . . . they** *Clarence* weep, so do not they    **87 Pour** Power    **142 Ludlow** London [also at line 154]    **145** [not in F]    **145.1 Manent** [eds.] *Manet*
**2.3. 44 Ensuing** Pursuing [but the catchword on page 184 in F is "Ensuing"]
**2.4. 1 hear** heard    **9 young** good    **21 ARCHBISHOP** *Car.* [Q1] *Yor.* [F]    **65 death** earth
**3.1. 1–158** [based on Q1 as copy text]    **2 [and elsewhere] RICHARD** *Glo.*    **60.1** [bracketed s.d. from F]    **111 With all** withall [Q1]    **150.1** [*A sen- net* ] [from F]    **150.2 Hastings** *Hast. Dors. Manent* [F2] *manet*
**3.2. 20 councils** Councell    **78 as you do** as

**3.3. 1** [not in F]
**3.4. 9 methinks** we thinke    **58** [not in F]    **79.1 Exeunt** [at line 78 in F] *Manent Manet*    **82 raze** rowse
**3.5. 4 wert** were    **20 innocence** Innocencie    **34 Look . . . Mayor** [not in F; after line 26 in Q1]    **56 we** I    **hear** heard    **66 cause** case    **74 meet'st advantage** meetest vantage    **104 Penker** [eds.] *Peuker*    **105.1. Exeunt** [eds.] *Exit*    **109 s.d. Exit** Exeunt
**3.7. 7 insatiate** vnsatiate    **20 mine** my    **33 spake** spoke    **40 wisdoms** wisdome    **43** [not in F]    **44 RICHARD** [not in F]    **54 we'll** we    **83 My lord** [not in F]    **125 her** his [also in lines 126 and 127]    **214 whe'er** where [also in line 229]    **219 Zounds! I'll** we will    **220** [not in F]    **224 stone** Stones    **240 Richard** King *Richard*    **241 MAYOR AND CITIZENS** *All*    **247 cousin** Cousins
**4.1. 0.1–5** [F: *Enter the Queene, Anne Duchesse of Gloucester, the Duchesse of Yorke, and Marquesse Dorset*]    **15 BRACKENBURY** *Lieu.* [and at lines 18 and 26]
**4.2. 36 My Lord** [not in F]    **72 there** then    **87 to** vnto    **90 Hereford** Hertford    **98–118 perhaps . . . today** [not in F]
**4.3. 0** [scene division not in F]    **4 whom** who    **5 ruthless** ruthfull    **13 Which** And    **15 once** one    **20 gone; with . . . remorse** gone with . . . Remorse,    **31 at** and    **33 thee** the    **40 Breton** Britaine    **53 leads** leds
**4.4. 0** [*Scena Tertia in* F]    **10 unblown** vnblowed    **39** [not in F]    **o'er** over [Q1]    **41 Harry** [eds.] Husband    **45 holp'st** hop'st    **52–3** [lines reversed in F]    **64 Thy** The    **112 weary** wearied    **118 nights . . . days** night . . . day    **128 intestate** intestine    **141 Where** Where't    **225 lanced** [eds.] lanch'd    **239 or** and    **268 would** I would    **284 This is** this    **324 Of ten** [eds.] Often    **364–5** [lines reversed in F, and the s.p. *Queen Elizabeth* is missing]    **366 KING RICHARD** [not in F]    **377 God** Heauen    **God's** Heanens    **392 in** with    **396 o'erpast** repast    **417 fond** found    **430.1 Exit Queen** [at line 429 in F]    **431.1 Enter Ratcliffe** [below line 432 in F]    **444 Ratcliffe** [eds.] *Catesby*    **498 FIRST MESSENGER** *Mess.*    **503 SECOND MESSENGER** *Mess.*    **506 THIRD MESSENGER** *Mess.* [also at lines 509 and 517]    **518 FOURTH MESSENGER** *Mess.*    **534 tidings** Newes, but
**4.5. 0** [*Scena Quarta in* F]
**5.1. 11 is, my lord** is
**5.2. 11 center** Centry    **12 Near** Ne're    **17 swords** men
**5.3. 0** [scene not marked in F]    **20 track** Tract    **28 you** [eds.] your    **48 ff.** [to the end of the play] [copy text is Q1]    **54 sentinels** [F] centinell [Q1]    **59 CATESBY** *Rat.*    **79 sit** [F] set [Q1; also at line 131]    **85 that. The** that the [Q1]    **100 sundered** sundried [Q1]    **107.1** [*Richmond remains*] [substantially from F]    **119 stabbed'st** stabst    **139 GHOST OF RIVERS** *King* [Q1]    **141 GHOST OF GREY** *Gray*    **142 GHOST OF VAUGHAN** *Vaugh.*    **145 Will** Wel [Q1]    **145.2–150** [after line 158 in Q1]    **151 GHOSTS** [F] *Ghost* [Q1]    **159 GHOST** [not in Q1]    **167 GHOST** [not in Q1]    **176 fall** [F] fals [Q1]    **183 am** and [Q1]    **209 My** Ratcliffe, my    **223 LORDS** *Lo.* [Q1]    **226, 235 A LORD** *Lo.* [Q1]    **243 Richard except**, Richard, except    **270.1 Ratcliffe** *Rat. & c.*    **299 main** [F] matne [Q1]    **301 boot** bootes [Q1]    **304 KING RICHARD** [at line 306 ("*King*") in Q1]    **324 Brittany** Brittaine    **351 them! Victory** them victorie [Q1]
**5.5. 13 STANLEY** [not in Q1]    **13 Ferrers** *Ferri* [Q1]    **15 becomes** become [Q1]    **41 s.d. Exeunt** [F; not in Q1]

## Richard II

Copy text: the first quarto of 1597 as press-corrected in all four extant copies [Q1]; and, for the deposition scene, 4.1. 155–321, the First Folio. Act and scene divisions, absent in Q1, are from F except that F provides no scene marking at 5.4 and labels 5.5 and 5.6 as "*Scoena Quarta*" and "*Scoena Quinta*," respectively.

**1.1. 15 presence. Face** presence face    **19.1 [and throughout]** *Bolingbroke Bullingbrooke*    **118 by my** [F] by    **139 But** Ah but    **152 gentlemen** [F] gentleman    **162–3 Harry, when? / Obedience bids** Harry? when obedience bids. / Obedience bids    **176 gage. My** gage, my    **178 reputation; that** Reputation that    **192 parle** parlee    **205.1 Exeunt** *Exit*

**1.2. 25 him. Thou** him, thou    **42 alas** [not in Q]    **47 sit** [F] set    **48 butcher** [Qb, F] butchers [Qa]    **58 it** [Q2–5, F] is    **59 empty** [Qb, F] emptines, [Qa]    **60 begun** begone    **70 hear** [F] cheere
**1.3. 15 thee** the    **33 comest** [Q5] comes    **58 thee** the    **104 FIRST HERALD** *Herald*    **108 his God** [F] God    **128 civil** [Qb, F] cruel [Qa]    **133 Draws** [Qb] Draw [Qa]    **136 wrathful iron** [F] harsh resounding [Qa]    **172 then but** [F] but    **180 you owe** [F] y'owe    **193 far** fare    **222 night** [Q4–5, F] nightes    **239 had it** had't    **241 sought** ought    **269 world** world:
**1.4. 0.1 Bagot** [F] *Bushie*    **20 our cousin,** [F] our Coosens    **23 Bagot here, and Green** [Q6; not in Q1]    **27 What** [Qb, F] With [Qa]    **47 hand. If** hand if    **52.1 Enter Bushy** [F] *Enter Bushie with newes*    **53 Bushy, what news** [F; not in Q1]    **65 ALL** [not in Q1]
**2.1. 15 life's** liues    **18 fond** found    **30 [and elsewhere] lose** loose    **48 as a** [Q4–5, F] as    **68.1–2** [after line 70 in Q1]    **70 reined** ragde    **102 encagèd** [F] inraged    **113 not** not, not    **124 brother** brothers    **156 kerns** [Qb, F] kerne    **161 coin** [Qb, F] coines [Qa]    **168 my** [Qb, F] mine    **177 the** [F] a    **209 seize** cease    **239 more** mo    **257 King's** [Q3–5, F] King    **277 Port le Blanc** le Port Blan    **278 Brittany** Brittaine [also in 285]    **284 Coint** Coines
**2.2. 19 Show** [Q6, F] Shows [Qa]    **31 though** [Q2–5, F] thought    **53 Harry** H.
**2.3. 9 Cotswold** Cotshall    **30 Lordship** Lo:    **36 Hereford** [Q3–5, F] Herefords    **75 raze** race    **99 the lord** [F] Lord    **164 [and elsewhere] Bristol** Bristow
**2.4. 1 WELSH CAPTAIN** *Welsh* [also at line 7]
**3.2. 32 succor** succors    **40 boldly** bouldy    **72 O'erthrows** [F] Ouerthrowes    **86 name! A** name a    **170 through** [Q2–5, F] thorough
**3.3. 13 brief with you** [F] briefe    **31 lord** [F] Lords    **59 rain** raigne.    **60 waters—on** water's on    **100 pastures'** pastors    **119 a prince and** princesse    **127 ourself** our selues
**3.4. 11 joy** griefe    **26 pins** [F] pines    **27 state, for** state for    **28 change; woe** change woe    **29 apricots** Aphricokes    **34 too** [F] two    **48 hath** htah    **55 seized** ceasde    **57 We at** at    **80 Cam'st** [Q2–5, F] Canst
**4.1. 23 him** [Q3–5, F] them    **44 Fitzwater** [F] Fitzwaters    **55 As** As it    **56 sun to sun** sinne to sinne    **63 true. You** true you    **77 my bond** [Q3–5, F] bond    **110 thee** [Q2–5, F] the    **146 you** yon    **155–321** [This deposition scene is based on the First Folio text; Q1 has only: "Let it be so, and loe on wednesday next, / We solemnly proclaime our Coronation, / Lords be ready all." Unless otherwise indicated all the departures in F from lines 155–321 are taken from Q4.]    **184 and on** on    **252 and** a    **256 Nor** No, nor    **297 manners** manner    **321.2 Carlisle** Caleil
**5.1.11 model** modle    **41 thee** [Q2–5, F] the    **84 NORTHUMBERLAND** [F] *King*
**5.2. 2 off** [F] of    **11 thee** [F] the [also at lines 17 and 94]    **78 my troth** by my troth    **94 thee** the    **116 And** An
**5.3. 0.1 King** the King    **10 While** Which    **31 the** my    **36 I may** [Q2–5, F] May    **68 And** An    **75 shrill-voiced** shril voice    **111 KING HENRY** yorke    **135–6 With . . . him** I pardon him with al my heart
**5.4. 0.1 Enter** [F] *Manet*    **Exton** Exton, etc.
**5.5. 20 through** [F] thorow    **22 cannot, die** cannot die    **27 sit** [Q3–5, F] set    **33 treason makes** treasons make    **55 sounds that tell** sound that telles    **56 that** which    **58 hours, and times** times, and houres
**5.6. 8 Salisbury, Spencer** [F] Oxford, Salisbury    **12.1 Fitzwater** *Fitzwaters*    **43 through the** [F] through ß

# 1 Henry IV

Copy text: the first complete quarto of 1598 [Q1]; and, for 1.3.201 through 2.2.110, the fragment of an earlier Quarto [Q0]. The act and scene divisions, missing in Q0 and Q1, are based on F except that F provides no break at 5.3.
**1.1. 22 levy** leauy    **39 Herdfordshire** Herdforshire    **62 a dear** deere    **69 blood, did** bloud. Did    **70 plains. Of** plaines, of    **76 In faith, it is** [assigned in Q1 to King]

**1.2. 16 king** a king    **33 proof, now:** proofe. Now    **78 similes** smiles    **154 thou** the    **158 Peto, Bardolph** Haruey, Rossill
**1.3. 12 too** to,    **137 [and throughout] Bolingbroke** Bullingbrooke    **194 good night** god-night    **201 HOTSPUR** [missing in Q0–Q4]    **222 holler** hollow    **238 whipped** [Q1] whip [Q0]
**2.1. 34 FIRST CARRIER** Car.    **48.1** [below line 47 in Q0]    **56 Weald** wild    **70 Trojans** Troyans
**2.2. 0.1 Poins, Peto, and** *Poines, and Peto &c*    **12 square** squire    **16 two-and-twenty** xxii:    **20 Bardolph** Bardol [and thus, or "Bardoll," throughout the play]    **34 mine** [Q1] my [Q0]    **42 Go hang** [F] Hang [Q0]    **51 BARDOLPH** What news [all assigned as continuation of Poins's speech in line 50]    **52 GADSHILL** Bar.    **78 FIRST TRAVELER** *Trauel.*    **82 TRAVELERS** *Trauel.*    **86 TRAVELERS** *Tra.*
**2.3. 1 HOTSPUR** [not in Q1]    **4 In** the in    **48 thee** the    **69 A roan** Roane
**2.4. 33 precedent** present    **36 POINS** *Prin.*    **121 sun's** soanes    **171 PRINCE** *Gad*    **172 GADSHILL** *Ross.* [also at lines 174 and 178]    **226 keech** catch    **242 eel-skin** elsskin    **322.1** [after line 321 in Q1]    **337 Owen** O    **390 tristful** trustfull    **398 yet** so    **468 lean** lane    **518 Good** God [also at line 519]    **526 s.d. pockets** pocket    **530 PETO** [not in Q1]    **535 PRINCE** [not in Q1]
**3.1. 55 coz** coose [also at line 75]    **97 cantle** scantle    **126 meter** miter    **129 on** an    **183 Loseth** Looseth    **261 hot Lord** Hot. Lord
**3.2. 32 Council** counsell    **59 won** wan    **84 gorged** gordge    **96 then** than    **145 northern** Northren    **161.1** [after line 162 in Q1]
**3.3. 35 that's** that    **57 tithe** tight    **119 no thing** nothing    **135 owed** ought    **173 guests** ghesse    **201 o'clock** of clocke
**4.1. 1 [and elsewhere] HOTSPUR** Per.    **20 lord** mind    **55 is** tis    **96 doffed** daft    **105 cuisses** cushes    **108 dropped** drop    **116 altar** altars    **123 ne'er** neare    **126 cannot** can    **127 yet** it    **134 merrily** merely
**4.2. 3 Coldfield** cop-hill    **15 yeomen's** Yeomans    **31 feazed** fazd    **33–4 tattered** tottered    **80 s.d. Exit** *Exeunt*
**4.3. 23 horse** horses    **74 heirs . . . followed** heires, as Pages followed    **84 country's** Countrey
**4.4. 0.1 [and throughout] Michael** *Mighell*    **18 o'erruled** ouerrulde    **36 not, ere** not ere    **37 power he** power, he
**5.1. 0.2 Lancaster** Lancaster, Earle of Westmerland    **2 bosky** bulky    **3 southern** Southren    **88 off** of    **138 will it** wil
**5.2. 3 undone** vnder one    **8 Suspicion** Supposition    **12 merrily** merely    **25.1 Hotspur** Percy    **79 FIRST MESSENGER** *Mes.*    **89 SECOND MESSENGER** *Mes.*    **94–5 withal / . . . day.** withall. / . . . day,
**5.3. 1 in** the in    **22 A** Ah    **35–6 ragamuffins** rag of Muffins
**5.4. 4 [and elsewhere] LANCASTER** *P. John*    **68 Nor** Now    **76.1 who** he    **92 enough. This** inough, this    **thee** the
**5.5. 36 bend you** bend, you

# Henry V

Copy text: the First Folio. Act and scene divisions are for the most part editorially supplied; F marks "*Actus Secundus*" at Act 3, "*Actus Tertius*" at Act 4, "*Actus Quartus*" at 4.7, and "*Actus Quintus*" at Act 5.
**Prologue. 1 CHORUS** [not in F, but is in prologues to other acts]
**1.2. 38 succedant** *succedaul*    **45 Elbe** Elue [also at line 52]    **76 [and elsewhere] Lewis** *Lewes*    **82 Ermengard** *Ermengare*    **90–1 day, / Howbeit** day. / Howbeit,    **115 ELY** *Bish.*    **131 blood** Bloods.    **163 her** their    **166 A LORD** *Bish. Ely*    **197 majesty** Maiesties    **212 End** [Q] And    **221 [and elsewhere] Dauphin** Dolphin    **237 FIRST AMBASSADOR** *Amb.* [also at line 245]    **310.1 Flourish** [at the beginning of 2.0 in F]
**2.1. 23 mare** [Q] name    **28 NYM** [Q; not in F]    **42, 43 Iceland** Island    **73 thee defy** [Q] defie thee    **80 enough** enough to    **83 you** your    **105–6** [Q; not in F]    **betting** [Q] beating    **116 that's** that
**2.2. 29 GREY** *Kni.*    **86 furnish him** [Q] furnish    **106 a** an    **107 whoop** hoope    **113 All** And    **138 mark the** make thee    **139 suspicion . . . thee;** suiption, . . . thee.    **146 Henry** [Q] *Thomas*    **147 Masham** [Q] *Marsham*    **158 Which I** Which    **175 have sought** [Q] sought    **180.1 Exeunt** Exit
**2.3. 16–17 'a babbled** a Table    **24 upward** vp-peer'd    **32 HOSTESS** *Woman*    **48 word** world

**2.4. 0.2** *Brittany* Britaine   **1** [and elsewhere] FRENCH KING *King*   **132 Louvre** Louer   **146.1** *Flourish* [at the beginning of 3.0 in F]

**3.0. 6 fanning** fayning   **17** [and elsewhere] **Harfleur** Harflew   **35 eke** eech

**3.1. 7 conjure** commune   **17 noblest** Noblish   **24 men** me   **32 Straining** Straying

**3.2. 25 runs** wins   **67** [and elsewhere in scene] FLUELLEN *Welch*   **82** [and elsewhere in scene] JAMY *Scot*   **87** [and elsewhere in scene] MACMORRIS *Irish*   **102 quite** quit   **112 Chrish** Christ

**3.3. 32 heady** headly   **35 Defile** Desire   **43** [here F has s.d. *"Enter Gouernour"*]   **54 all. For** all for

**3.4. 2 parles** *parlas* [throughout the play, the French has been somewhat modernized, besides the emendations listed here]   **7 Elle** *il*   **8 Et les doigts** [assigned to Alice in F]   **9** ALICE *Kat.*   **les doigts** *e doyt*   **10 souviendrai** *souemeray*   **12** KATHARINE *Alice*   **13 j'ai** *Kath. I'ay*   **14 les** *le*   **16 Nous** [not in F]   **40 pas déjà** *y desia*   **42 Non** *Nome*   **46 Sauf** *Sans*   **51 les** *le* [also in line 52]

**3.5. 11 de** du   **26 "Poor" may** Poore   **43 Vaudemont** *Vandemont*   **45 Foix . . . Boucicault** *Loys, Lestrale, Bouciquall*   **46 knights** Kings

**3.6. 31 her** [Q] his   **37 is make** [Q] makes   **110–11 lenity** Leuitie

**3.7. 12 pasterns** postures   **14** *qui a ches*   **59 lief** liue   **65** *et est*   **truie** *leuye*

**4.0. 16 name** nam'd   **20 cripple** creeple   **27 Presenteth** Presented

**4.1. 3 Good** God   **95 Thomas** *Iohn*   **158 deaths** [Q] death   **propose** purpose   **227 s.d.** *Exeunt Exit* [at line 222 in F]   **243 What is** What? is   **adoration** Odoration   **251 Think'st** Thinks   **273 Hyperion** *Hiperio*   **289 reck'ning, ere . . . numbers** reckning of . . . numbers:   **307 friends** friend

**4.2. 4 eaux** ewes   **6 Cieux** *Cein*   **11 dout** doubt   **47 drooping** dropping   **49 gimmaled** Iymold   **52 all impatient** all, impatient

**4.3. 12** [placed after line 14 in F]   **48** [Q; not in F]   **124 'em** vm

**4.4. 15 Or** for   **36 à cette heure** *asture*   **37 couper** *couppes*   **54 l'avez** *layt* a   **57 remercîments** *remercie*   **58 j'ai tombé** *Ie intombe*   **59 très-distinguè** *tres distinie*   **68 Suivez-vous** *Saaue vous*

**4.5. 2 perdu . . . perdu** *perdia . . . perdie*   **3 Mort de** *Mor Dieu*   **16 by a** [Q] a base   **24.1** *Exeunt Exit*

**4.6. 34 mistful** mixtfull   **38 s.d.** *Exeunt Exit*

**4.7. 22 e'en** in   **69** [and elsewhere in this scene] MONTJOY *Her.*   **77 the with** [Q] countryman   **109 countryman** Countrymen   **114 God** Good   **123 'a live** aliue   **126 'a lived** aliue   **161** [and elsewhere] **an't** and

**4.8. 77 Boucicault** *Bouchiquald*   **99 Foix** *Foyes*   **100 Vaudemont** *Vandemont*   **Lestrelles** *Lestrale*   **104 Keighley** *Ketly*   **110–11 loss / On . . . other?** losse? / On . . . other,   **113 we** me   **121 in my** [Q] my   **122 rites** Rights

**5.0. 29 but** but by

**5.1. 39 By Jesu** [Q] I say   **69 begun** began   **88 swear** swore

**5.2. 1** [and elsewhere] KING HENRY *King*   **12** [and throughout scene] QUEEN ISABEL *Quee.*   **12 England** Ireland   **21** [also elsewhere] KING HENRY *Eng.*   **45 fumitory** Femetary   **50 all** withall   **61 diffused** defus'd   **72 tenors** Tenures   **77 cursitory** curselarie   **93 Haply** Happily   **98 s.d.** *Manent Manet*   **114** [and elsewhere] ALICE *Lady*   **190 meilleur** *melieus*   **255 grandeur** *grandeus*   **261 noces** *nopcese*   **264 les** *le*   **265 baiser** *buisse*   **267 entend** *entendre*   **323 hath never** hath   **332 then** in in   **364 paction** Pation

**Epilogue** CHORUS [not in F]

## *Romeo and Juliet*

Copy text: the second quarto of 1599, except for 1.2.53–1.3.34, for which Q1 (the first quarto) is the prior authority. Act and scene divisions are absent from the second quarto and the Folio. The rejected readings in these notes are from Q2 unless otherwise indicated.

**1.1. 27 it in** [Q1] it   **38 side** sides   **73** CITIZENS *Offi.*   **76** CAPULET'S WIFE *Wife*   **92 Verona's** *Neronas*   **120 drave** driue   **147 his** is   **153 sun** same   **177 create** [Q1] created   **179 well-seeming** [Q1] welseeing   **189 grief to** [Q1] grief, too   **192 lovers'** louing   **202 Bid a** [Q1] A make** [Q1] makes   **206 markman** mark man   **211 unharmed** [Q1] vncharmd   **218 makes** make

**1.2. 14 The earth** Earth   **32 on** one   **38–9 written here** written. Here   **46 One** [Q1] on   **56 Good e'en** Goddess   **57 God gi' good e'en** Godgigoden   **70 and Livia** [Q1] Liuia [Q2]   **79 thee** [Q1] you [Q2]   **91 fires** fier [Q1]

**1.3. 12 an** [Q2] a [Q1]   **18 shall** [Q1] *stal* [Q2]   **33 wi' th'** [Q1: *with*] *with the* [Q2]   **50** [and elsewhere] WIFE *Old La.*   **66 disposition** [F] dispositions   **67, 68 honor** [Q1] houre   **100 it fly** [Q1] flie   **105** [and elsewhere] WIFE *Mo.*

**1.4. 7–8** [Q1; not in Q2]   **23** MERCUTIO *Horatio*   **31 quote** cote   **39 done** [Q1] dum   **42 Of** Or   **45 like lamps** [Q1] lights lights   **47 five** fine   **57 atomi** [Q1] ottamie   **59–61** [these lines follow line 69 in Q2]   **66 film** Philome   **69 maid** [Q1] man   **72 O'er** [Q1] On   **74 on** one   **76 breaths** [Q1] breath   **80 parson's** Persons   **81 dreams he** [Q1] he dreams   **90 elflocks** Elklocks   **111 forfeit** fofreit

**1.5. 0.1** [Q2 adds: *"Enter Romeo"*]   **1** FIRST SERVINGMAN *Ser.* [also at lines 6 and 12]   **3** SECOND SERVINGMAN 1   **7 court cupboard** Courtcubbert   **11** THIRD SERVINGMAN 2   **14** FOURTH SERVINGMAN 3   **15 longest** longer   **17** CAPULET 1. *Capu.* [also at lines 35 and 40]   **18 a bout** about   **57 antic** anticque   **96 ready** [Q1] did readie

**2.0. Chorus 1** CHORUS [not in Q2]   **4 matched** match

**2.1. 7 Nay . . . too** [assigned in Q2 to Benvolio]   **10 one** [Q1] on   **11 Pronounce** [Q1] prouaunt   **dove** [Q1] day   **13 heir** [Q1] her   **14 trim** [Q1] true   **39 open-arse, and** open, or   **pop'ring** Poprin

**2.2. 16 do** [Q1] to   **20 eyes** [Q1] eye   **26 slays** [Q1] staies   **41–2 nor any . . . name** ô be some other name / Belonging to a man   **45 were** [Q1] wene   **82 pilot** Pylat   **83 washed** [Q1] washeth   **92–3 false . . . They** false at louers periuries. / They   **99 havior** behauiour   **101 more cunning** coying   **110 circled** [Q1] circle   **146** [and elsewhere] **rite** right   **149, 151** NURSE [not in Q2]   **150, 151** JULIET [not in Q2]   **163 than mine** then   **168 nyas** Neece   **180 gyves** giues   **187 Sleep . . . breast** [Q1; assigned in Q2 to Juliet]   **189–90** [preceded in Q2 by an earlier version of lines 1–4 of the next scene, in which "fleckled darkness" reads "darknesse fleckted" and "and Titan's fiery wheels" reads "made by *Tytans* wheels"]

**2.3. 2 Check'ring** [Q1] Checking   **22 sometime's** sometime   **50 me** me:   **51 wounded. Both our** wounded both, our   **85 not. She whom** [Q1] me not, her

**2.4. 18** BENVOLIO [Q1] *Ro.*   **28 antic** antique   **28–9 phantasimes** phantacies   **33 pardon-me's** pardons mees   **40 but a** a   **68 Switch . . . switch** Swits . . . swits   **113–14 for himself** [Q1] himself   **205 dog's dog**   **212 s.d.** *Exeunt Exit*

**2.5. 11 three** there   **15 And** *M.* And   **26 I had** [Q1] I

**2.6. 18 gossamer** gossamours   **27 music's** musicke

**3.1. 2 Capels are** *Capels*   **67 injured** iniuried   **73 stoccada** stucatho   **90 your houses** houses   **107 soundly too. Your** soundly, to your   **121 Alive** He gan   **123 fire-eyed** [Q1] fier end   **136** FIRST CITIZEN *Citti.*   **138** FIRST CITIZEN *Citi.*   **141 all** all:   **165 agile** [Q1] aged   **183** MONTAGUE *Capu.*   **187 hate's** heart's   **191 I** [Q1] it   **196.1** *Exeunt Exit*

**3.2. 1** JULIET [nòt in Q2]   **9 By** And by   **12** [and elsewhere] **lose** loose   **15 grown** grow   **47 darting** arting   **49 shut** shot   **51 Brief sounds** Briefe, sounds,   **of my** my   **54** [and elsewhere] **corpse** coarse   **60 one** on   **72 It . . . day** it did [assigned in Q2 to Juliet]   **73 O . . . face** [assigned in Q2 to Nurse]   **76 Dove-feathered** Rauenous doue-featherd   **79 damnèd** dimme   **143.1** *Exeunt Exit*

**3.3. 0.1** [Q2 has *"Enter Friar and Romeo"*]   **39** [Q2 follows with a line: "This may flyes do, when I from this must flie"]   **43** [printed in Q2 before line 40]   **52 Thou** [Q1] Then   **61 madmen** [Q1] mad man   **70.1** *Knock Enter Nurse, and knocke*   **73 s.d.** *Knock They knocke*   **74 Who's** whose   **75.1** *Knock Slud knock*   **80.1** *Enter Nurse* [below line 78 in Q2]   **110 denote** [Q1] deuote   **117 lives** [Q1] lies   **144 pout'st upon** puts vp   **168 disguised** disguise

**3.4. 10** [and elsewhere] WIFE *La.*   **13 be** [Q1] me   **23 We'll keep** Well, keepe

**3.5. 13 exhaled** exhale   **19 the** the the   **31 changed** change   **36.1** *Enter Nurse Enter Madame and Nurse*   **54** JULIET *Ro.*   **67.1** [bracketed s.d. from Q1]   **82 pardon him** padon   **130–1 body . . . a bark** body? / Thou counterfeits. A Barke   **133–4 is, . . . flood;** is: . . . floud,

**139 gives** giue    **142 How? Will** How will    **151–2 proud . . . Thank** proud mistresse minion you? / Thanke    **160 [and elsewhere]** CAPULET *Fa.*    **172** CAPULET **Oh, God-i'-good-e'en** Father, Godigeden    **173** NURSE [not in Q2]    **181 liened** liand
**4.1. 7 talked** [Q1] talke    **45 cure** [Q1] care    **46 Ah** [Q1] O    **72 slay** [Q1] stay    **78 off** [Q1] of    **83 chopless** [Q1] chapels    **85 his tomb** his    **98 breath** [Q1] breast    **100 To wanny** Too many    **110 In** Is [Q2 follows with a line: "Be borne to buriall in thy kindreds graue"]    **111 shalt** shall    **115 and he** an he    **116 waking** walking    **126 s.d.** *Exeunt Exit*
**4.2. 3, 6** SERVINGMAN *Ser.*    **14 willed** wield    **26 becomèd** becomd    **38 [and elsewhere]** WIFE *Mo.*    **47.1** *Exeunt Exit*
**4.3. 20 vial** Violl    **49 wake** walke
**4.4. 1 [and elsewhere]** WIFE *La.*    **12.1** *Exeunt Exit*    **13.1–2** [after line 14 in Q2]    **15** FIRST SERVINGMAN *Fel.*    **18** SECOND SERVIN- GMAN *Fel.*    **21 Thou** Twou    **faith** father    **23 s.d.** [after line 21 in Q2]
**4.5. 40 all; life** all life    **41 long** [Q1] loue    **51 behold** bedold    **65 cure** care    **65–6 not . . . Heaven** not, / In these confusions heauen    **82 fond** some    **96** FIRST MUSICIAN *Musi.*    **98 s.d.** *Exit Exit omnes* [below line 99]    **99, 103** FIRST MUSICIAN *Fid.*    **99 by** [Q1] my    **99.1 Enter Peter** *Enter Will Kemp*    **107** FIRST MUSICIAN *Minstrels* [and subsequently in this scene indicated by *Minst.* or *Minstrel*]    **123 Then . . . wit** [assigned in Q2 to 2 *M*]    **127 And . . . oppress** [Q1; not in Q2]    **133, 136 Pretty** [Q1] *Prates*    **145 s.d.** *Exeunt Exit*
**5.1. 15 fares my** [Q1] doth my Lady    **17, 27, 32** BALTHASAR *Man*    **24 e'en** in    **defy** [Q1] denie    **33.1** [at line 32, after "good lord," in Q2]    **76 pay** [Q1] pray    **86 s.d.** *Exit Exeunt*
**5.3. 3 yew** [Q1] young    **21.2** [*Balthasar*] [Q1] Peter    **25 light. Upon** light vpon    **40, 43** BALTHASAR *Pet.*    **68 conjuration** commiration    **71** PAGE *Boy* [Q1; s.p. missing in Q2 and line treated as a s.d.]    **102 fair** faire? I will beleeue    **107 palace** pallat    **108** [Q2 has four undeleted lines here: "Depart againe, come lye thou in my arme; / Heer's to thy health, where ere thou tumblest in. / O true Appothecarie! / Thy drugs are quicke. Thus with a kisse I die."]    **123 [and elsewhere]** BALTHASAR *Man*    **137 yew** yong    **168** FIRST WATCH *Watch* [also at lines 172, 195, 199]    **171** PAGE *Watch boy*    **182** SECOND WATCH *Watch*    **183, 187** FIRST WATCH *Chief. watch*    **187 too** too too    **190 shrieked** shrike    **194 our** your    **199 slaughtered** Slaughter    **201** [Q2 has a s.d. here: "*Enter Capulet and his wife*"]    **209 more early** [Q1] now earling    **232 that** thats    **274–5 place . . . This** place. To this same monument / This    **281** PAGE *Boy*    **299 raise** raie

## *Julius Caesar*

Copy text: the First Folio. Act divisions are marked in the Folio; scene divisions are editorially supplied.

**1.1. 0.1 [and elsewhere]** *Marullus Murellus*    **37 Pompey? . . . oft** *Pompey* many a time and oft?    **61 [and elsewhere] whe'er** where
**1.2. 0.1 [and elsewhere]** *Calpurnia Calphurnia*    **24.1 Manent** *Manet*    **124 [and elsewhere] lose** loose    **254 like. He** like he    **301 digest** disgest
**1.3. 129 In favor's like** Is Fauors, like
**2.1. 28 [and elsewhere] lest** least    **40 ides** first    **67 of** of a    **83 put path** path    **122 women, then,** women. Then    **136 oath, when** Oath. When    **214 eighth** eight    **268 his** hit    **281 the** tho    **310.1 Enter Lucius and Ligarius** [after "with haste" in line 310 in F]    **314 [and through line 322]** LIGARIUS *Cai.*
**2.2. 23 did neigh** do neigh    **46 are** heare    **81 Of** And    **120 to blame** too blame
**2.3. 1** ARTEMIDORUS [not in F]
**3.1. 40 law** lane    **114 states** State    **116 lies** lye    **201 [and elsewhere] corpse** Coarse [also Course and Corpes]    **256** ANTONY [not in F]    **277.1** *Octavius' Octauio's* [also at 5.2.4]    **285 for** from
**3.2. 106 art** are    **205** ALL [not in F]    **222 wit** writ    **260 s.d.** *Exeunt Exit*    **262 s.d. Enter Servant** [after "fellow" in F]
**3.3. 6 Whither** Whether

**4.2. 34–6** FIRST, SECOND, THIRD SOLDIER [not in F]    **50 Lucius** *Lucillius*    **52 Lucilius** *Lucius*    **52.1 Manent** *Manet*
**4.3. 209–10 off / If** off. / If    **230 s.d. Enter Lucius** [before line 230 in F]    **244, 246 [and throughout]** *Claudius Claudio*    **246 [and throughout] Varro** *Varrus*    **252 will** will it    **303, 307** VARRO, CLAUDIUS *Both*
**5.1. 42 teeth** teethes    **67.1** *Exeunt Exit*    **70** [F has s.d.: "*Lucillius and Messala stand forth*"]    **71** LUCILIUS (**stands forth**) *Luc.*    **73** MESSALA (**stands forth**) *Messa.*    **99 rest** rests
**5.3. 99 fare** far    **104 Thasos** *Tharsus*    **108 Flavius** *Flauio*
**5.4. 7** LUCILIUS [not in F]    **9 O** *Luc.* O    **12, 15** FIRST SOLDIER *Sold.*    **16.1 Enter Antony** [before line 16 in F]    **17 the news** thee newes
**5.5. 33 too, Strato** to *Strato*    **77 With all** Withall

## *Hamlet*

Copy text: the second quarto of 1604–1605 [Q2]. The First Folio text also represents an independently authoritative text; although seemingly not the correct choice for copy text, the Folio text is considerably less marred by typographical errors than is Q2. The adopted readings in these notes are from F unless otherwise indicated; [eds.] means that the adopted reading was first proposed by some editor since the time of F. Some readings also are supplied from the first quarto of 1603 [Q1]. Act and scene divisions are missing in Q$_q$ 1–2; the Folio provides such markings only through 1.3 and at Act 2.

**1.1. 1 Who's** Whose    **19 soldier** [F, Q1] souldiers    **43.1 the Ghost** [F] *Ghost*    **44 off** [Q1] of    **47 it** [F] a    **48 harrows** horrowes    **49 Question** [F] Speake to it    **55 the Ghost** [F] *Ghost*    **67 sledded Polacks** [eds.] sleaded pollax    **77 why** [F, Q1] with    **cast** cost    **91 heraldry** [F, Q1] heraldy    **92 those** [F, Q1] these    **95 returned** returne    **97 cov'nant** comart    **98 designed** [eds.] desseigne    **102 landless** [F] lawlesse    **107 compulsative** [F] compulsatory    **112 e'en so** [eds.] enso    **116 mote** [eds.] moth    **119 tenantless** tennat-lesse    **125 feared** [eds.] feare    **129.1 Ghost again** [F] *Ghost*    **142 you** [F, Q1] your    **144 at it** it    **147 s.d. Exit Ghost** [F; not in Q2]    **166 The** [F] This    **167 can walk** [F] dare sturre    **181 conveniently** [F, Q1] conuenient
**1.2. 0.2 [and elsewhere]** *Gertrude Gertrad*    **1** KING *Claud.*    **11 one . . . one** [F] an . . . a    **41.1 Exeunt Voltemand and Cornelius (Exit)** [F; not in Q2]    **50 Dread my** [F] My dread    **67 so** [F] so much;    **i' th'** [F] in the    **77 good** coold    **82 shapes** [Q3] chapes    **83 denote** deuote    **85 passeth** [F] passes    **96 a** or    **105 corpse** [eds.] course    **112 you.** For you    **114 retrograde** retrogard    **127 heavens** [F] heauen    **129 solid** [F] sallied [Q2] sullied [eds.]    **132 self** seale    **133 weary** wary    **137 to this** thus    **140 satyr** [F4] satire    **143 would** [F, Q1] should    **149 even she** [F; not in Q2]    **170 have** [F] heare    **175 to drink deep** [F, Q1] for to drinke    **178 to see** [F, Q1] to    **185 Oh, where** [F] Where    **199 waste** [F2] wast [Q2, F]    **201 at all points** [F] at point    **206 jelly with . . . fear,** gelly, with . . . feare    **210 Where, as** [Q5] Whereas    **214 watched** [F] watch    **225 Indeed, indeed** [F, Q1] Indeede    **241 Very like, very like** [F, Q1] Very like    **242 hundred** hundreth    **243** MARCELLUS, BERNARDO [eds.] *Both*    **247 tonight** to nigh    **256 fare** farre    **257 eleven** a leauen    **259.1 Exeunt** [at line 258 in Q2]    **262 Foul** [F, Q1] fonde
**1.3. 3 convoy is** conuay, in    **12 bulk** bulkes    **18** [F; not in Q2]    **29 weigh** way    **49 Whilst like a** [F] Whiles a    **63 to** [F] vnto    **65 comrade** [F] courage    **74 Are of all** [eds.] Or of a [Q2] Are of a [F]    **75 be** boy    **76 loan** loue    **83 invites** [F] inuests    **106 I'll** [F] I will    **110 Running** [eds.] Wrong [Q2] Roaming [F]    **116 springes** springs    **121 daughter** [F; not in Q2]    **124 parley** [F] parle    **126 tether** tider    **130 implorators** imploratotors    **131 bawds** [eds.] bonds    **132 beguile** beguide
**1.4. 2 is a** is    **6.1 A flourish . . . goes off** [Q2; not in F]    **17 revel** [Q3] reueale    **19 clepe** clip    **27 the** [eds.] their [Q2]    **36 evil** [eds.] eale [Q2] ease [Q3]    **37 often dout** [eds.] of a doubt    **49 inurned** interr'd [Q2, Q1]    **58.1 Ghost beckons Hamlet** [F] *Beckins* [Q2]    **61, 79 wafts** waues    **80 off** of    **82 artery** arture    **86.1 Exeunt Exit**    **87 imagination** [F, Q1] imagion

**1.5. 1 Whither** [eds.] Whether   **20 on** [eds.] an   **21 fretful porcupine** [F, Q1] fearfull Porpentine   **23 List, Hamlet, oh, list** [F] list, list, ô list   **34 rots** [F] rootes   **44 wit** [eds.] wits   **48 what a** what   **56 lust** [F, Q1] but   **angel** Angle   **57 sate** [F] sort   **59 scent** [eds.] sent   **morning's** [F] morning   **68 alleys** [eds.] allies   **69 posset** possesse   **92 Hamlet !** [F] adiew   **96 stiffly** swiftly   **119 bird** and   **124 you'll** [F] you will   **128** HORATIO, MARCELLUS *Booth* [also at line 151]   **heaven, my lord** heauen   **129 ne'er** [F] neuer   **132 i th'** [F] in the   **135 desires** [F] desire   **138 Look you, I'll** I will   **157 s.d.** *cries Ghost cries*   **168-9 Never . . . heard / Swear by my sword** [F] Sweare . . . sword / Neuer . . . heard   **179 some'er** so mere   **185 Well** well, well [Q1, Q2]   **188 this not to do** [F] this doe sweare   **189 swear** [F; not in Q2]
**2.1 0.1 man** [eds.] *man or two*   **3 marvelous** meruiles   **29 Faith, no** Fayth   **41 warrant** wit   **42 sullies** sallies   **43 i' th'** [F] with   **60 o'ertook** or tooke   **64 takes** take   **76 s.d.** *Exit Reynaldo. Enter Ophelia* [after line 75 in Q2]   **77 Alas** [F] O my Lord   **79 chamber** [F] closset   **97 That** [F] As   **101 help** [F] helps   **107 passion** passions   **114 quoted** [eds.] coted
**2.2. 0.1 [and elsewhere]** *Rosencrantz* Rosencraus   **5 so I call** [F] so call   **6 Since not** [F] Sith nor   **12 since** [F] sith   **humor** [F] hauior   **16 occasions** [F] occasion   **43 Assure you** [F] I assure   **54 sweet queen, that** [F] deere *Gertrard*   **57 o'erhasty** hastie   **57.1–2** *Enter Polonius, Voltemand, and Cornelius* [F] *Enter Embassadors*   **73 three** [F, Q1] threescore   **78 his** [F] this   **90 since brevity** breuitie   **97 he is** [F] hee's   **106 whilst** [F] while   **112–13 hear. / These in** [F] heare: thus in   **125 This** [Q2 has a speech prefix: *Pol.* This]   **126 above** about   **137 winking** working   **142 precepts** [F] prescripts   **143 his** her   **146 repulsèd** [F] repell'd   **148 watch** wath   **149 to a** to   **151 'tis** [F, Q1; not in Q2]   **165.1** *reading on a book* [F; not in Q2]   **174 Excellent, excellent well. You're** [F] Excellent well, you are   **203 you** [F; not in A2]   **210 sanity** sanctity   **212–13 and suddenly . . . him** [F; not in Q2]   **213 honorable lord** Lord   **214 most humbly take** take   **215 cannot, sir** cannot   **216 more** not more   **224 excellent** extent   **226 ye** [F] you   **228–9 overhappy. / On** euer happy on   **229 cap** lap   **237 that** [F; not in Q2]   **240–70 Let . . . attended** [F; not in Q2]   **267** ROSENCRANTZ, GUILDENSTERN *Both* [F]   **273 even** euer   **276 Come** [F] come, come   **279 Why** [F; not in Q2]   **288 could** can   **292 off** of   **298 exercise** [F] exercises   **303 no other thing to me than** [F] nothing to me but   **304 What a** What   **306–7 admirable, in action how . . . angel, in** [F, subst.] admirable in action, how . . . Angell in   **310 no, nor** nor   **314 you** yee   **321 of** on   **324–5 the clown . . . sear** [F; not in Q2]   **tickle** [eds.] tickled [F]   **326 blank** black   **336 they are** [F] are they   **337–62 How . . . too** [F; not in Q2]   **342 berattle** [eds.] be-ratled [F]   **349 most like** [eds.] like most [F]   **364 mows** [eds.] mouths [Q2]   **368.1** *Flourish for the players* [F] *A Florish*   **371 come** [F] come then   **373 lest my** let me   **375 outward** [F] outwards   **381 too** to   **398–9 tragical-historical, tragical-comical-historical-pastoral** [F; not in Q2]   **401 light . . . these** [eds.] light for the lawe of writ, and the liberty: these   **420.1 four or five** [F] *the*   **422 my** [F; not in Q2]   **425 By'r** [F] by   **nearer** [F] nerer to   **429 e'en to 't** ento't   **French falconers** friendly Fankners   **433 [and elsewhere]** FIRST PLAYER *Player*   **436–7 caviare** cauiary   **443 affectation** affection   **446 tale** [F, Q1] talke   **447 where** [F] when   **454 the** [F] th'   **456 heraldry** [F, Q1] heraldy   **dismal. Head** dismall head   **460 and a** [F] and   **461 vile murders** [F] Lords murther   **474 Then senseless Ilium** [F; not in Q2]   **481 And, like** Like   **490 Mars his** [F] *Marses*   **495 fellies** [F4] follies [Q2] Fallies [F]   **502 oh, who** [F] ah woe   **504 "Moblèd queen" is good** [F; not in Q2; F reads "Inobled"]   **506 bisson** *Bison*   **509 th'** [F] the   **514 husband's** [F, Q1] husband   **519 whe'er** where   **523 ye** [F] you   **524 abstracts** [F] abstract   **529 bodikins** [F] bodkin   **530 should** [F] shall   **534** *Exit Polonius* [F; not in Q2]   **540 a** [F; not in Q2]   **541 or** [F, Q1] lines, or   **546 s.d.** *Exeunt players* [see textual note at line 548.1]   **547 till** tell   **548.1** *Exeunt* [F; Q2 has "*Exeunt Pol. and Players*" after line 547]   **549 God b 'wi' ye** [F God buy'ye] God buy to you   **553 whole** [F] owne   **554 his** the   **555 in's** [F] in his   **556 and** an   **559 to Hecuba** [F, Q1] to her   **561 the cue** that   **574 th'** [F] the   **582 Oh, vengeance** [F; not in Q2]   **584 father** [Q1, Q3, Q4; not in Q2, F]   **588 scullion** [F]

stallyon [Q2] scalion [Q1]   **598 but** [F] doe   **600 the devil** a deale **the devil** the deale
**3.1. 0.2 and lords** [F] *Lords*   **1 And** [F] An   **circumstance** [F] conference   **19 are about** [F] are heere about   **27 on to** [F] into   **28 too** two   **32 lawful espials** [F; not in Q2]   **33 Will** Wee'le   **46 loneliness** lowlines   **to** too   **56 Let's withdraw** with-draw   **56.2** *Enter Hamlet* [after line 55 in Q2]   **65 wished. To** wisht to   **73 disprized** despiz'd   **77 these** [F; not in Q2]   **84 of us all** [F, Q1; not in Q2]   **86 sicklied** sickled   **87 pith** [F] pitch   **93 well, well, well** well   **100 the** these   **108 your honesty** you   **119 inoculate** euocutat   **122 to a** to a   **129-30 heaven and earth** [F] earth and heauen   **130 knaves all** knaues   **139 go** [F; not in Q2]   **143 O** [F; not in Q2]   **144 paintings too** [Q1] paintings   **146 jig, you amble** gig & amble   **147 lisp** list   **148 your ignorance** [F, Q1] ignorance   **150 more marriages** [F] momarriage   **155 Th'expectancy** Th'expectation   **159 music** musickt   **160 that** what   **161 tune** time   **162 feature** stature   **164** [Q2 has "*Exit*" at the end of this line]   **170 to** [F] for to   **191 unwatched** vnmatcht
**3.2. 0.1 two or three** [F] *three*   **3 your** [F] our   **10 tatters** totters   **split** [F, Q1] spleet   **27 of the** of   **29 praise** praysd   **32 nor no man** [eds.] nor man [Q2] or Norman [F]   **37 sir** [F; not in Q2]   **45.1** *Enter . . . Rosencrantz* [after line 47 in Q2]   **68 commingled** [F] comedled   **88 detecting** detected   **88.1-4** *Enter King, Queen, Polonius, Ophelia, Rosencrantz, Guildenstern, and other lords attendant, with his guard carrying torches. Danish march. Sound a flourish* [F] *Enter Trumpets and Kettle Drummes, King, Queene, Polonius, Ophelia*   **96 now. My lord, now my Lord.**   **98 I did** [F] did I   **100 And what** [F] What   **107 [and elsewhere]** QUEEN *Ger.*   **112–13** [F; not in Q2]   **127 devil** deule [Q2] Diuel [F]   **133.1-16** [F and Q2 differ verbally but provide for similar action]   **133.1 sound** [eds.] *sounds*   **133.7** *Anon comes* anon come   **135 this is** [F] this   **miching** [F] munching   **140 keep counsel** [F, Q1] keepe   **152.1 his** [F; not in Q2]   **153 [and throughout scene]** PLAYER KING *King*   **154 orbèd** orb'd the   **159 [and throughout scene]** PLAYER QUEEN *Quee.*   **162 your** our   **164** [Q2 follows here with an extraneous unrhymed line: "For women feare too much, euen as they loue"]   **165 For** And   **holds** [F] hold   **166 In** Eyther none, in   **167 love** Lord   **179 Wormwood, wormwood** That's wormwood   **180** PLAYER QUEEN [not in Q2]   **188 like** the   **197 joys** joy   **217 An** And   **221 a widow** [F, Q1] I be a widow   **be** [F] be a   **226.1** *Exit* [F, Q1] *Exeunt*   **240 wince** [Q1] winch [Q2, F]   **241.1** [after line 242 in Q2]   **251 Pox** [F; not in Q2]   **254 Confederate** [F, Q1] Considerat   **256 infected** [F, Q1, Q4] inuected   **258 usurp** vsurps   **258.1** *Pours the poison in his ears* [F; not in Q2]   **264** [F; not in Q2]   **268** SH COURTIERS [F: *All*] Pol.   **274 with two** with   **288.1** [F; after line 293 in Q2]   **305 his** [F] the   **306 far** [F; not in Q2]   **308 start** stare   **317 of my** of   **319** SH GUILDENSTERN [F] *Ros.*   **334 So I** [F] And   **343.1** [after line 341 in Q2]   **357 thumb** the vmber   **366 to the top of** to   **370 can fret me** [F] fret me not [Q2] can fret me, yet [Q1]   **371.1** [after line 372 in Q2]   **385** POLONIUS [F; not in Q2]   **385 s.d.** *Exit* [F; not in Q2]   **386 Leave me, friends** [so F; Q2 places before "I will say so," and assigns both to Hamlet]   **388 breathes** breakes   **390 bitter . . . day** business as the bitter day   **395 daggers** [F, Q1] dagger
**3.3. 6 dangerous** [F] neer's   **7 lunacies** [F] browes   **15 cease** [F] cesse   **17 it. It** [F] it, or it   **19 huge** hough   **22 ruin** raine   **23 but with** but   **25 upon** [F] about   **26** SH ROSENCRANTZ AND GUILDENSTERN [F: *Both*] *Ros.*   **35.1** *Exit* [after "I know" in F]   **50 pardoned** pardon   **58 Offense's** [eds.] Offences   **shove** showe   **73 pat . . . a-praying** but now a is a praying   **75 revenged** reuendge   **79 hire and salary** base and silly   **81 With all** Withall   **91 At gaming, swearing** [F] At game a swearing
**3.4. 0.1** *Enter Queen* [F] *Enter Gertrard*   **5–6 with him . . . Mother, Mother, Mother** [F; not in Q2]   **7 warrant** wait   **8.1** *Enter Hamlet* [at line 5 in Q2]   **21 inmost** most   **23 Help, ho!** Helpe how   **24 Help, help, help!** [F] helpe   **43 off** of   **51 tristful** heated   **53** [assigned in Q2 to Hamlet]   **60 heaven-kissing** heaue, a kissing   **89 panders** pardons   **91 mine . . . soul** my very eyes into my soule   **92 grainèd** greeued   **93 not leave** leaue there   **100 tithe** kyth   **108 you** [F] your

146 **Ecstasy** [F; not in Q2]  150 **I the** the  165 **live** leaue
172 **Refrain tonight** to refraine night  176 **[in]** [eds.; not in Q2, F]
186 **Thus** [F] This  193 **ravel** rouell  205 **to breathe** [eds.] to breath
222 **a** [F, Q1] a most  224.1 *Exit Hamlet, tugging in Polonius* [F] *Exit*
**4.1.** 0.1 *Enter King [and Queen], with Rosencrantz and Guildenstern*
[eds.] *Enter King, and Queene, with Rosencraus and Guyldensterne* [Q2]
*Enter King* [F]  5 **my good** [F] mine owne  32.1 [at 31 in Q2]
37.1 *Exit Gentlemen* [F; not in Q2]  40 **So envious slander** [eds.; not
in Q1, Q2, F1]
**4.2.** 0.1 [Q2: "*Enter Hamlet, Rosencraus, and others.*"]  2–3 [F; not in Q2;
the s.p. in F is "*Gentlemen*"]  4 **HAMLET** [not in Q2]  5.1 [F; not in Q2]
7 **Compounded** Compound  18–19 **an ape** [not in Q2]  31–2 **Hide . . .
after** [F; not in Q2]
**4.3.** 0.1 *and two or three* [Q2; not in F]  15 **Ho, Guildenstern! Bring in
my** [F] How, bring in the  15.1 *Enter Hamlet and Guildenstern* [F]
*They enter*  41 **of thine** [F; not in Q2]  44 **With fiery quickness** [F;
not in Q2]  56 **and so** so  72 **were** will  **begun** begin
**4.4.** 20–1 **name. To** name To
**4.5.** 0.1 *Enter Queen and Horatio* [F] *Enter Horatio, Gertrard, and a
Gentleman*  1, 4 **SH HORATIO** [F] *Quee.*  14 **SH QUEEN** [F] *Hora.*
16 **Let . . . in** [assigned in Q2 to Horatio]  20.1 *Enter Ophelia distracted, playing on a lute, and her hair down, singing* [Q1] *Enter
Ophelia* [Q2, after line 16] *Enter Ophelia distracted* [F]  38 **with all**
with  39 **grave** [F] ground  46 **you** [F; not in Q2]  52 **clothes**
close  57 **Indeed, la** Indeede  62 **to** too  83 **in their** in  98 [F; not in
Q2]  100.1 [below line 97 in Q2]  103 **impetuous** [Q3, F2] impituous
[Q2] impittious [F]  109 **They** The  146 **swoopstake** [eds.] soopstake
[Q1 reads "Swoop-stake-like"]  157 **VOICES WITHIN Let her come in!**
[F, "*Let her come in*" printed as s.d.; not in Q2]  158 **Let her come in**
[assigned in Q2 to Laertes and placed before "How now, what noyse
is that?"]  s.d. *Enter Ophelia* [after line 157 in Q2]  162 **Till Tell turns**
[F] turne  165 **an old** [F, Q1] a poore  166–8, 170 [F; not in Q2]
171 **on** [F] in  186 **Oh, you** [F] you  **must** [F, Q1] may  191 **affliction**
[F, Q1] afflictions  199 **All flaxen** Flaxen  203 **Christian** [F] Christians
**souls, I pray God** [F, Q1] soules  203.1 *Exeunt Ophelia* [F; not in Q2]
204 **you see** you  216 **burial** [F] funeral  217 **trophy, sword** trophe
sword
**4.6.** 0.1 *with an Attendant* [F] *and others*  2 **SERVINGMAN Sailors** [F: *Ser.*
Saylors] *Gent.* Sea-faring men  6.1 *Sailors* [Q2] *Saylor* [F]  9 **an't**
and  10 **comes** [F] came  13 **(reads the letter)** [F; not in Q2]
22 **good turn** turne  23 **haste** [F] speede  26 **bore** bord  30 **He** *So*
31 **will give** will
**4.7.** 6 **proceeded** proceede  7 **crimeful** criminall  15 **She's** [F] She is
**conjunctive** concliue  21 **Would** [F] Worke  22 **gyves** Giues  23 **loud
a wind** loued Arm'd  25 **had** haue  37 **How . . . Hamlet** [F; not in
Q2]  38 **This** These  43 s.d. *Exit Messenger* [F; not in Q2]  46–7 **your
pardon** you pardon  48 **and more strange** [F; not in Q2]  **Hamlet** [F;
not in Q2]  53 **advise** deuise  56 **shall live** [F, Q1] liue  57 **diddest**
[F] didst  60 **If so you'll** [F] so you will  62 **checking** the King
78 **ribbon** [eds.] ribaud  86 **into** [F] vnto  89 **passed my** [F] topt me
100 **especially** [F] especiall  101 **escrimers** [eds.] Scrimures  106 **him** [F]
you  116 **wick** [eds.] weeke  123 **spendthrift's** [Q2: spend thrifts; not
in F] spendthrift [Q5]  135 **on** ore  139 **pass** pace  141 **for that**
for  151 **shape. If** shape if  155 **should** [F] did  157 **ha 't** hate
160 **prepared** prefard  163 **How [now] sweet queen** [F: how sweet
Queene] but stay, what noyse [Q2]  167 **aslant a** [F] ascaunt the
168 **hoar** horry  172 **cold** cull-cold  192 **douts** [F "doubts"] drownes
**5.1.** 1 **[and throughout] FIRST CLOWN** *Clowne*  1 **that** when she  3 **[and
throughout] SECOND CLOWN** *Other*  9 **se offendendo** so offended
12 **and to** to  **Argal** or all  34–7 **SECOND CLOWN: Why . . . arms?** [F; not
in Q2]  43 **that frame** that  55.1 *afar off* [F] not in Q2's entry s.d. at
line 64.1  59 **that** [F; not in Q2]  60 **to Johan. Fetch** [F: to *Yaughan*,
fetch] in, and fetch  **stoup** scoope  65 **that** [F; not in Q2]  70 **daintier** dintier  73 **intil** [F] into  79 **o'er-offices** [F] ore-reaches
83 **good lord** [F] sweet lord  85 **meant** [F, Q1, Q3] went  89 **mazard**
massene  98 **might** [F] may  99–100 **quillets** [F] quillites  101 **rude**
[F] madde  106–7 **Is . . . recoveries** [F; not in Q2]  107–8 **Will his**

will  109 **double ones too** doubles  111 **hardly** [F] scarcely  120 **Oh**
or  121 [F; not in Q2]  139 **these** [F] this  **taken** [F] tooke  143 **Of all**
Of  147 **the** [F] that  164 **I'faith** [F] Fayth  165 **nowadays** [F; not in
Q2]  170–1 **now: this skull** [F] now  171 **lain** [F] lyen you  180 **was**
[F] was sir  183 **Let me see** [F; not in Q2]  185 **borne** [F] bore  192
**chamber** [F, Q1] table  208–9 **As thus** [F; not in Q2]  210 **into** [F]
to  213 **Imperial** [F] Imperious  216 **winter's** waters  217 **aside** [F]
awhile  218 **this** [F] that  226, 235 **PRIEST** *Doct.*  227 **warrantise** [F:
warrantis] warrantie  231 **Shards, flints** Flints  237 **sage** [F] a
246 **t' have** haue  247 **treble** double  250.1 *leaps in the grave* [F; not
in Q2]  262 **and rash** rash  263 **something in me** [F] in me something
264 **wiseness fear. Away** [F] wisedom feare; hold off  280 **thou** [F;
not in Q2]  288 **thus** this  295.1 *Exit Hamlet* [F: *Exit*] *Exit Hamlet and
Horatio*  296 **you** [F] thee  301 **shortly** there-by  302 **Till** Tell
**5.2.** 1 **let me see** [F] shall you see  5 **Methought** my thought  6 **bilboes**
bilbo  9 **pall** fall  17 **unseal** vnfold  19 **Oh** [F] A  27 **me** [F] now
29 **villainies** villaines  30 **Ere** Or  43 **"as"es** as sir  46 **the** [F] those
52 **Subscribed** Subscribe  57, 68–80 [F; not in Q2]  63 **think'st** [F]
thinke  78 **court** [eds.] count [F]  80.1 *young Osric* [F] *a Courtier* [Q2]
81 **[and throughout] OSRIC** *Cour.*  82 **humbly** humble  93 **Put your**
your  98 **sultry** sully  **for** or  101 **But, my** [F] my  107 **gentleman**
[eds.] gentlemen  109 **feelingly** [Q4] fellingly  114 **dazzle** [eds.]
dazzie  **yaw** [eds.] raw  141 **his** [eds.] this  142 **him by them,** him,
by them  149 **hangers** [F] hanger  **or so** [F] and so  155 **margin**
[eds.] margent [Q2; not in F]  156 **carriages** carriage  158 **cannon** [F]
a cannon  159 **might be** be might  162 **impawned, as** [eds.] all [Q2]
impon'd, as [F]  165 **on't** [F] on  174 **purpose, I** purpose; I  177 **re-deliver
you e'en** so [F] deliuer you so  181–2 **Yours, yours. 'A does** Yours
doo's  186 **comply** so sir  187 **bevy** [F: Beauy] breede  190 **yeasty**
histy  191 **fanned** [eds.] prophane [Q2] fond [F]  **winnowed**
trennowed  208 **this wager** [F; not in Q2]  210 **But thou** thou
217 **There's a** [F] there is  218 **be now** be  220 **will come** well come
222.1–4 *Trumpets . . . wine on it* [F] *A table prepard, Trumpets, Drums
and officers with Cushions, King, Queene, and all the state, Foiles,
daggers, and Laertes*  238 [F; not in Q2]  248 **To keep** To  **till** all
250 **I do** [F] I  252 **foils. Come on** foiles.  255 **off** of  261 **bettered**
better  263.1 *prepare to play* [F; not in Q2]  270 **union** Vnice ["Onixe"
in some copies]  279 s.d. *They play* [F; not in Q2]  285.1 *Trumpets
sound . . . goes off* [F] *Drum, trumpets, and shot. Florish, a peece goes off*
288 **A touch, a touch, I** I  302 **afeard** sure  303 s.d. *play* [F; not in Q2]
305.1–2 *in scuffling, they change rapiers* [F; not in Q2]  316 **Hamlet.**
Hamlet *Hamlet*  318 **hour of** [F] houres  319 **thy** [F, Q1] my
327 **murderous** [F; not in Q2]  328 **off of**  **thy union** [F, Q1] the Onixe
329 s.d. *King dies* [F; not in Q2]  333 s.d. *dies* [F; not in Q2]  345 **ha 't**
[eds.] hate [Q2] have 't [F]  347 **live** [F] leaue  362 s.d. *dies* [F; not in
Q2]  365.1–2 *Enter Fortinbras . . . Attendants* [F] *Enter Fortenbrasse,
with the Embassadors*  366 **proud** prou'd  369 **FIRST AMBASSADOR**
*Embas.*  381 **th' yet** yet  385 **forced** for no  394 **on** no  405 **body** [F]
bodies  407.1–2 *Exeunt . . . off* [F] *Exeunt*

Passages contained only in F and omitted from Q2 are noted in the
textual notes above. Listed below are the more important instances
in which Q2 contains words, lines, and passages omitted in F.
**1.1.** 112–29 **BERNARDO I think . . . countrymen**
**1.2.** 58–60 **wrung . . . consent**
**1.3.** 9 **perfume and**
**1.4.** 6.1 *A flourish of trumpets, and two pieces goes off*  17–38 **This heavy-
headed . . . scandal**  75–8 **The very . . . beneath**
**2.1.** 122 **Come**
**2.2.** 17 **Whether . . . thus**  217 **except my life**  363 **very**  366 **'Sblood**
(and some other profanity passim)  371 **then**  444–5 **as wholesome
. . . fine**  465 **So proceed you**  521–2 **of this**  589 **Hum**
**3.2.** 169–70 **Where . . . there**  216–17 **To . . . shape**  385 s.d. *Exit*
**3.4.** 72–2 **Sense . . . difference**  79–82 **Eyes . . . mope**  168–72 **That
monster . . . put on**  174–7 **the next . . . potency**  187 **One word . . .
lady**  209–17 **There's . . . meet**
**4.1.** 4 **Bestow . . . while**  41–4 **Whose . . . air**

**4.2. 4** But soft

**4.3. 26–9** KING Alas . . . worm

**4.4. 9.1–67** *Enter Hamlet, Rosencrantz, etc. . . . be nothing worth*

**4.5. 33** Oho   **76–8** Oh, this is . . . Gertrude, Gertrude

**4.7. 68–82** LAERTES My lord . . . graveness   **101–3** Th' escrimers . . . them   **115–24** There . . . ulcer

**5.1. 154** There

**5.2. 106–42** here is . . . unfellowed (replaced in F by "you are not ignorant of what excellence *Laertes* is at his weapon")   **154–5** HORATIO [*to Hamlet*] I knew . . . done   **193.1–206** *Enter a Lord . . . instructs me*   **193–207** *Enter a Lord… lose, my lord* (replaced in F by "*Hor* You will lose this wager, my Lord")   **222** Let be   **276.1** *Trumpets the while*


## *Othello*

Copy text: the First Folio. The adopted readings are from the quarto of 1622 [Q1], unless otherwise indicated; [eds.] means that the adopted reading was first proposed by some editor subsequent to the First Folio. Act and scene divisions are marked in the Folio with the exception of 2.3.

**1.1. 1 Tush, never** Neuer   **4 'Sblood, but** But   **16 And, in conclusion** [Q1; not in F]   **26 togaed** Tongued   **30 other** others   **34 God bless** blesse   **68 full** fall   **thick-lips** Thicks-lips   **74 changes** chances   **75 [and elsewhere] lose** [eds.] loose   **81 Thieves, thieves, thieves** Theeues, Theeues   **83.1** *Brabantio above* [in F, printed as a speech prefix to line 84]   **88 Zounds, sir** Sir [also at line 111]   **103 bravery** knauerie   **119 are now** are   **158 pains** apines   **161 sign. That** [eds.] signe) that   **186 night** might

**1.2. 34 Duke** Dukes   **50 carrack** Carract   **64 her!** [eds.] her   **69 darlings** Deareling   **89 I do** do

**1.3. 1 There is** There's   **these** this   **61 DUKE AND SENATORS** [*All* Q1] *Sen.*   **101 maimed** main'd   **108 upon** vp on   **DUKE** [Q1; not in F]   **109 overt** ouer   **112 [and elsewhere] FIRST SENATOR** *Sen.*   **124 till** tell   **132 battles** Battaile   **fortunes** Fortune   **141 travels'** Trauellours   **143 rocks, and** Rocks   **heads** head   **145 other** others   **146 Anthropophagi** *Antropophague*   **147 Do grow** Grew   **149 thence** hence   **157 intentively** instinctiuely   **161 sighs** kisses   **203 grece** grise   **204 Into your favor** [Q1; not in F]   **222 piercèd** pierc'd   **ear** eares   **227 sovereign** more soueraigne   **233 couch** [eds.] Coach [F] Cooch [Q1]   **237 These** [eds.] This   **244 Nor I. I would not** Nor would I   **251 did love** loue   **267 me** [eds.] my   **273 instruments** Instrument   **281 DESDEMONA Tonight, my lord?** DUKE This night [Q1; not in F]   **285 With** And   **294 FIRST SENATOR** *Sen.*   **296.1** *Exeunt Exit*   **302 matters** matter   **303 the** the the   **329 beam** [eds.] braine [F] ballance [Q1]   **333–4 our unbitted** or vnbitted   **335 scion** [eds.] Seyen [F] syen [Q1]   **353 error** errors   **354 She . . . she must** [Q1; not in F]   **358 a supersubtle** super-subtle   **378–82 RODERIGO What . . . purse** [Q1; not in F]   **386 a snipe** Snpe   **389 He's** [Ha's Q1] She ha's   **396 ear** eares

**2.1. 35 prays** praye   **36 heaven** Heauens   **42 THIRD GENTLEMAN** *Gent.*   **44 arrivance** Arriuancie   **45 this** the   **58 SECOND GENTLEMAN** *Gent.* [also at lines 61, 68, and 95]   **72 clog** enclogge   **84 And . . . comfort** [Q1; not in F]   **90 tell me** tell   **94 the sea** Sea   **96 their** this   **107 list** leaue   **111 doors** doore   **156 [and elsewhere] ne'er** neu'r   **158 such wight** *such wightes*   **170 gyve** [eds.] giue   **174 An** and   **175 courtesy** Curtsie   **176 clyster pipes** Cluster-pipes   **214.1** *Exeunt* [eds.] *Exit*   **217 hither** thither   **230 again** a game   **240 fortune** Forune   **242–3 compassing** compasse   **244–5 finder out** finder   **245 occasions** occasion   **has** he's   **264 mutualities** mutabilities   **299 inwards** [F] innards [eds.]   **301 for wife** for wift   **308 rank** right   **309 nightcap** Night-Cape

**2.2. 6 addiction** [eds.] addition   **10 Heaven bless** Blesse

**2.3. 27 stoup** [eds.] stope   **38 unfortunate** infortunate   **52 lads** else   **57 to put** put to   **61, 71 God** heauen   **76 Englishman** Englishmen   **91 Then . . . auld** [*Then . . . owd* Q1] *And take thy awl'd*   **93 'Fore God** Why   **97 God's** heau'ns   **106 God forgive** Forgiue   **110 speak**

**I speake**   **123 the** his   **138 s.d.** *Cry within*: **Help! Help!** [from Q1: "Helpe, helpe, within"]   **139 Zounds, you** You   **152 God's will** Alas   **153 Montano—sir** *Montano*   **156 God's will, Lieutenant, hold** Fie, fie Lieutenant   **158 Zounds, I** I   **161 sense of place** [eds.] place of sense   **184 wont be** wont to be   **201 Zounds, if I** If I once   **212 leagued** [eds.] league   **218 Thus** This   **227 the** then   **246 well now** well   **250 vile** vil'd   **255 God** Heauen   **260 thought** had thought   **283 Oh, God** Oh   **308 I'll** I   **311 denotement** [eds.] deuotement   **325–6 me here** me   **337 were't** were   **356 s.d.** *Enter Roderigo* [after line 356 in F]   **369 hast** hath   **372 By the Mass** Introth   **378 on;** [on Q1]   **379 the while** [eds.] a while

**3.1. 1** *Musicians* [eds.] *Musicians, and Clowne*   **5 [and at lines 7, 9, and 15]** A MUSICIAN *Mus.*   **21 s.d.** *Exeunt* [eds.] *Exit*   **22 hear** heare me   **26 General's wife** Generall   **31 CASSIO Do, good my friend** [Q1; not in F]   **42 s.d.** *Exit* [at line 41 in F]   **52 To . . . front** [Q1; not in F]

**3.3. 16 circumstance** Circumstances   **41 you** your   **55 Yes, faith** I sooth   **66 or** on   **80 By'r Lady** Trust me   **103 you** he   **118 By heaven** Alas   **124 In** Of   **148 that all** that: All   **free to free** some   **152 But some** Wherein   **160 oft** of   **161 wisdom then** wisdome   **175 By heaven, I'll** Ile   **183 fondly** [eds.] soundly [F] strongly [Q1]   **188 God** Heauen   **194 Is once** Is   **196 blowed** [F] blown [Q1]   **199 dances well** Dances   **216 God** Heauen   **218 keep't** [eds.] keepe [Q1] kept [F]   **225 [and elsewhere] to** too   **230 I'faith** Trust me   **232 my** your   **249 disproportion** disproportions   **264 to hold to** qualities   **275 qualities** Quantities   **276 human** humane   **289 of** to   **294 oh, then heaven mocks** Heauen mock'd   **301 Faith** Why   **305.1** *Exit* [at line 304 in F]   **328 faith** but   **345 s.d.** *Enter Othello* [after "I did say so" in F]   **354 of her** in her   **385 remorse;** [remorce. Q1] remorse   **407 see, sir** see   **411 supervisor** super-vision   **439 then** laid   laid   **440 Over** ore   **sighed** sigh   **kissed** kisse   **441 Cried** cry   **455 any that was** [eds.] any, it was   **468 mind perhaps** minde   **471 Ne'er** [eds.] Neu'r [F]   **keeps** [F] knows [eds.]

**3.4. 23 that** the   **37 It yet** It   **56 faith** indeed   **77 I'faith** Indeed   **79 God** Heauen   **83 Heaven bless** Blesse   **88 can, sir** can   **94–5 DESDEMONA I pray . . . Cassio.** OTHELLO The handkerchief! [Q1; not in F]   **99 I'faith** Insooth   **100 Zounds** Away   **142 s.d.** *Exit* [after line 141 in F]   **164 that** the   **169.1** *Exit* [after line 168 in F]   **172 I'faith** Indeed   **182 friend.** [eds.] Friend,   **183 absence** [eds.] absence, [Q1] Absence: [F]   **188 by my faith** in good troth

**4.1. 32 Faith** Why   **36 Zounds, that's** that's   **45 work** workes   **52 No, forbear** [Q1; not in F]   **72 couch** [Coach Q1] Cowch;   **79 unsuiting** [Q1 corrected] vnfitting [Q1 uncorrected] resulting [F]   **81 'scuse** scuses   **97 clothes** Cloath   **103 conster** conserue   **105 you now** you   **109 power** dowre   **113 a woman** woman   **114 i'faith** indeed   **121 Do you triumph, Roman?** Do ye triumph, Romaine?   **122 marry her** marry   **125 win** winnes   **126 Faith** Why   **shall marry** marry   **133 beckons** becomes   **138 by this hand, she** [Q1; not in F]   **166 Faith, I** I   **168 Faith** Yes   **215.1** [after line 212 in F]   **218 God save** Saue   **241 By my troth** Trust me   **254 Truly, an** Truely   **287 denote** deonte [F uncorrected] deuote [F corrected]

**4.2. 32 Nay** May   **33 knees** knee   **35 But not the words** [Q1; not in F]   **49 God** Heauen   **50 He** they   **51 kinds** kind   **56 A** The   **66 Ay, there** [eds.] I heere   **71 ne'er** neuer   **83 Impudent strumpet** [Q1; not in F]   **96 keep** [eds.] keepes   s.d. *Enter Emilia* [after line 94 in F]   **148 heaven** Heauens   **155 O God** Alas   **162 them in** [eds.] them: or   **174 And . . . you** [Q1; not in F]   **177 you to** to   **190 Faith, I** I   **for** and   **201 By this hand** Nay   **232 takes** taketh   **236 of** [Q1; not in F]

**4.3. 10.1** *Exit* [after line 9 in F]   **22 favor in them** fauour   **25 faith** Father   **26 before thee** before   **35 Barbary** *Braberie*   **43 sighing** [eds.] *singing* [F corrected] *sining* [F uncorrected]   **73 Good troth** Introth   **74 By my troth** Introth   **78 Uds pity** why   **107 God** Heauen

**5.1. 1 bulk** Barke   **22 Be't** But   **hear** heard   **36 Forth** For   **50 Did** Do   **91 Oh, heaven** Yes, 'tis   **106 out o'** o'   **113 'Las, what's . . .** What's   Alas, what is . . . What is   **116 dead** quite dead   **126 Faugh!** Fie   Fie

**5.2. 34 heaven** Heauens   **37 say so** say   **56 Yes, presently** Presently   **61 Then Lord** O Heauen   **96 high** [F] here [Q1]   **104 Should** Did   **108 s.d.** *Enter Emilia* [after line 108 in F]   **121 Oh, Lord** Alas

131 heard heare   148 Nay, had had   225 Oh, God! Oh, heavenly God Oh Heauen! oh heauenly Powres   226 Zounds Come   248 have here haue   317 not. Here [not: here Q1] not) heere   357 Indian Iudean

## King Lear

Copy text: the First Folio, except for those 300 or so lines found only in the first quarto of 1608 [Q1]. Unless otherwise indicated, adopted readings are from the corrected state (Qb) of Q1. A few readings are supplied from the second quarto of 1619 [Q2]. All readings subsequent to 1619 are marked as supplied by "eds." Act and scene divisions are as marked in F, except that F does not mark 2.3 and 2.4, and omits 4.3 entirely, so that 4.4 is marked "*Scena Tertia*" and similarly with 4.5 and 4.6 (though 4.7 is marked "*Scena Septima*").

1.1. 5 equalities qualities   20–2 account . . . yet [eds.] account, though . . . for: yet   35 liege Lord   55 words word   66 issue issues   68 Speak [Q1; not in F]   69 Sir, I I   74 possesses professes   85 interested [eds.] interest   104 [Q1; not in F]   110 mysteries [eds.] miseries [F] mistresse [Q1]   135 turns turne   136 additions addition   150 Reserve thy state [F] Reverse thy doom [Q1]   156 as a as   157 nor nere   161 LEAR *Kear*   162 KENT *Lent*   165 CORNWALL [eds.] *Cor.*   166 Do, kill Kill the thy   167 gift [F] doom [Q1]   171 Since That   173 sentence sentences   191 GLOUCESTER *Cor.*   217 best object obiect   219 Most best, most The best, the   229 well will   252 respects of fortune respect and Fortunes   272 Ye [eds.] The   285 shame them with shame   286.1 *Exeunt* [eds.] *Exit*   293 hath not hath   306 hit sit

1.2. 1 [and elsewhere] EDMUND *Bast.*   21 top [eds.] to'   the legitimate th' legitimate   56 waked wake   59 this to you? you to this?   97–9 EDMUND Nor . . . earth [Q1; not in F]   122 surfeit surfeits   124 and the stars and stars   villains by villains on   130 disposition to disposition on   134 Fut, I I   136 Edgar [Q1; not in F]   137 and pat [eds.] Pat [F] and out [Q1]   147–55 as . . . come, [Q1; not in F]   182 s.d. [at line 181 in F]

1.3. 3 [and elsewhere] OSWALD [eds.] *Ste.*   15 distaste [F] dislike [Q1]   17–21 [Q1; not in F]   26–7 I would . . . speak [Q1; not in F]   28 very [Q1; not in F]

1.4. 1 well will   31 canst thou [F] canst [Q1]   43.1 *Enter steward* [eds.; after line 44 in F]   50 daughter Daughters   76.1 *Enter steward* [eds.; after line 77 in F]   96 KENT *Lear*   Fool my Boy   110 Lady the Brach the Lady Brach   135 Dost thou Do'st thou   138–53 That . . . snatching [Q1; not in F]   158 crown Crownes   170 mother mothers   175 fools Foole   195 nor crumb not crum   214 it had it's had   216–17 Come, sir, / I would I would   223 Doth Do's   224 Doth Do's   229–32 [Q1; not in F]   242 Make Makes   255 Oh . . . come [Q1; not in F]   290 more of it [F] the cause [Q1]   303 Yea . . . this [Q1; not in F]   304 Let . . . a daughter Ha! Let it be so. I have another daughter   343 You are [F] Your are [Q1]   attaxed [eds.] at task [F]

1.5. 0.1 Kent Kent, Gentleman   11 ne'er not   17 What . . . boy? [F] What canst thou tell, my boy? [Q1]   51 s.d. *Exit Exeunt*

2.1. 2 you your   8 ear-bussing ear-kissing   19.1 [after line 18 in F]   39 stand 's stand   61 caitiff Coward   69 I should should I   70 ay, though though   76 strong strange   78 I never got him [Q1; not in F]   78 s.d. [at line 76 in F, after "seeke it"]   79 why wher   87 strange news strangenesse   95 tend tended   100 spoil wast   106 'Twas It was   122 poise prize   132 *Flourish. Exeunt* [eds.] Exeunt. Flourish

2.2. 22 clamorous clamours   44 Part [F; not in Q1]   45 an if   52 What's What is   59 Ay, a tailor A Taylor   60 he they   61 at the [Q1] oth' [F]   66 you'll you will   78 Bring . . . their Being . . . the   79 Renege Reuenge   80 gale gall   83 Smile Smoile   84 an if   90 What is his fault [F] What's his offense? [Q1]   101 take't take it   109 flick-ering flicking   119 conjunct compact   124 dread dead   127 their there   132 respect respects   142.1 [at line 140 in F]   144–8 His . . . with [Q1; not in F]   146 contemned'st [eds.] temnest [Q1]   148 King King his Master, needs   153 [Q1; not in F]   154 Come . . . away [assigned in F to Cornwall] good [Q1; not in F]   154.1 *Exeunt* [eds.] *Exit*   155 Duke's Duke

2.3. 15 bare [Q1; not in F]   18 sheepcotes Sheeps-Coates

2.4. 2 messenger Messengers   9 man's man   18–19 [Q1; not in F]   30 panting painting   33 whose those   56 *Hysterica* [eds.] *Historica*   62 the the the   74 have hause   128 you your   130 mother's Mother   168 blister [F] blast her pride [Q1]   183 s.d. [after line 182 in F]   185.1 [at line 183 in F, after "Stockes"]   187 fickle fickly   190 s.d. [after line 188 in F]   213 hot-blooded hot-bloodied   285 s.d. [after "weeping" in line 286 in F]   297 s.d. [after line 296 in F]   298 Whither Whether [also in line 299]   302 bleak high

3.1. 7–15 tears . . . all [Q1; not in F]   10 outstorm [eds.] outscorne [Q1]   30–42 [Q1; not in F]

3.2. 3 drowned drown   9 make makes   12 ask [F] and ask [Q1]   38.1 [after line 36 in F]   50 pother pudder   85–6 [these lines follow line 92 in F]

3.3. 17 for 't for it

3.4. 7 skin. So 'tis skinso: 'tis   10 thy they   12 This the   27 s.d. [at line 26 in F]   31 looped lop'd   38.1 *Enter Fool* [F, after line 36: "*Enter Edgar, and Foole*"]   44.1 [after line 36 in F]   46 blows the cold wind blow the windes   51 through fire though Fire   52 ford Sword   57, 58 Bless Blisse   90 deeply deerely   99 sessa [eds.] *Sesey*   112.1 [after line 108 in F]   114 fiend [Q1; not in F]   115 till the at   116 squinnies [eds.] squints [F] squemes [Q1]   134 stock-punished stockt, punish'd   hath had hath   147 To obey T'obey   160 to unsettle t'unsettle   173 in th' into th'

3.5. 11 he which hee   26 dearer deere

3.6. 5.1 *Exit* [at line 3 in F]   17–55 [Q1; not in F]   21 justicer [eds.] Iustice [Q1]   22 Now [Q2] no [Q1]   24 eyes at trial, madam? eyes, at tral madam   25 burn [eds.] broome [Q1]   34 cushions [eds.] cushings [Q1]   36 robèd robbed   51 joint [eds.] ioyne [Q1]   53 on [eds.] an [Q1]   67 mongrel grim Mongrill, Grim   68 lym [eds.] Hym   69 Bobtail tike or trundle-tail Or Bobtaile tight, or Troudle taile   73 Sessa sese   76 makes make   83 So, so, so So, so   85.1 [after line 80 in F]   97–101 KENT Oppressèd . . . behind [Q1; not in F]   101 GLOUCESTER [not in F]   102–15 [Q1; not in F]

3.7. 3 traitor [F] villain [Q1]   10 festinate [eds.] festiuate   18 lord's dependents Lords, dependents   23 s.d. *Exeunt* [eds.] *Exit* [at line 22 in F]   61 stick [F] rash [Q1]   66 dern sterne   75 FIRST SERVANT *Seru.* [also Seru. or Ser. at lines 79, 82, 84]   83 [F provides a stage direction: "*Killes him*"]   102–10 [Q1; not in F]   102 SECOND SERVANT *Seruant* [and called "1 Ser" at line 106 in Q1]   103 THIRD SERVANT 2 *Seruant* [Q1]   107 roguish [Qa; not in Qb]   109 THIRD SERVANT 2 *Ser.*   110.1 *Exeunt Exit*

4.1. 2 flattered. To be worst flattered to be worst,   41 Then . . . gone Get thee away   45 Who Which   57–62 Five . . . master [Q1; not in F]   60 Flibbertigibbet [eds.] *Stiberdigebit* [Q1]   60–1 mopping and mowing [eds.] Mobing, & *Mohing* [Q1]

4.2. 0.1 *Bastard Bastard, and Steward*   2 s.d. *steward* [Q1; placed at scene beginning in F]   17 arms names   30 whistling whistle   32–51 I fear . . . deep [Q1; not in F]   33 it [Q1; not in F] its [eds.]   48 these [eds.] this [Q1]   54–60 that . . . so [Q1; not in F]   58 to threat threat [Q1 corrected]   61 shows seemes   63–9, 70 [Q1; not in F]   76 threat enraged threat-enrag'd   80 justicers [Q1 corrected] Iustices

4.3. 1–57 [scene omitted in F]   11 sir [eds.] say [Q1]   16 strove [eds.] streme [Q1]   20 seemed [eds.] seeme [Q1]   22 dropped. In dropt in   32 then her, then   44 benediction, turned her benediction turnd her,   57 s.d. *Exeunt* [eds.] *Exit* [Q1]

4.4 [F reads "*Scena Tertia*"]   0.2 *Doctor Gentleman*   3 fumiter [eds.] femiter [Q1] Fenitar [F]   6 century Centery   11 SH DOCTOR *Gent.*   18 distress desires   28 right Rite

4.5 [F reads "*Scena Quarta*"]   8 letter [F] letters [Q1]   23 Something Some things   27 oeillades [eds.] Eliads   41 meet him meet

4.6 [F reads "*Scena Quinta*"]   17 walk walk'd   32 you ye   57 summit Somnet   66–7 strangeness. / Upon . . . cliff what [eds.] strangenesse, / Vpon . . . Cliffe. What   71 enridgèd enraged   83 coining crying   97 white the white   124 they are they're   131 to sweeten sweeten   161 thine thy   164 Through Thorough   small great   165 Plate sin [eds.] Place sinnes

**197 Ay, and . . . dust. / GENTLEMAN Good sir–** [Q1; not in F]
**202 Nay, an** Come, an  **205 one** a  **218.1 Exit** [after "moved on" in line 218 in F]  **235 Dar'st** [F] Durst [Q1]  **238 'cagion** 'casion
**263–4 not. / To** not / To  **269 done if . . . conqueror. Then** [eds.] *done. If . . . Conqueror then* [Q1]  **274 and . . . venture** [Q1; not in F]
**275 indistinguished** indinguish'd  **288 s.d. Drum afar off** [after line 286 in F]
**4.7. 13, 18, 22, 26, 44, 52, 82 SH DOCTOR Gent.**  **25 doubt not** doubt
**25–6 CORDELIA Very . . . there** [Q1; not in F]  **32 Had challenged** Did challenge  **33 warring** iarring  **34–7 To stand . . . helm** [Q1; not in F]
**59 hands** hand  **60 No, sir** [Q1; not in F]  **83–4 and . . . lost** [Q1; not in F]  **91–103** [Q1; not in F]
**5.1. 12–14** [Q1; not in F]  **18 me not** not  **19–20** [Q1; not in F]  **22 hear** heard  **24–9 Where . . . nobly** [Q1; not in F]  **26 touches** [Q1] toucheth [eds.]  **35** [Q1; not in F]  **41 s.d. Exeunt . . . armies** [after line 39 in F]  **48 love** loues
**5.3. 13 and hear poor rogues** and heare (poore Rogues)  **39–40** [Q1; not in F]  **49 and appointed guard** [Q1 corrected; not in F]  **56–61 At . . . place** [Q1; not in F]  **57 We** [Q1 corrected] mee [Q1 uncorrected]
**59 sharpness** [Q1 corrected] sharpes [Q1 uncorrected]  **72 GONERIL Alb.**  **85 attaint** arrest  **86 sister** Sisters  **87 bar** [eds.] bare  **100 he is** hes  **105 EDMUND A herald, ho, a herald** [Q1; not in F]  **105.1 Enter a Herald** [after line 104 in F]  **106 ALBANY** [not in F]  **112 CAPTAIN Sound, trumpet** [Q1; not in F]  **118 EDMUND Sound** [Q1; not in F]  **124–5 lost, / By . . . canker-bit.** lost / By Treasons tooth: bare-gnawne, and Canker-bit,  **132 the** my priuiledge, The  **135 Despite** Despise  **146 tongue some say of** tongue (some say) of  **149 those** these  **151 scarcely** scarcely  **153.1 Fight** [eds.] Fights. ["Alarums. Fights" is opposite "Saue him, saue him," in line 154 in F.]  **155 arms** Warre  **158 stopple** stop  **163 GONERIL Bast.**  **163 s.d. Exit** [at line 162 after " for 't" in F]  **208–25 This . . . slave** [Q1; not in F]  **217 him** [eds.] me [Q1]
**241.1** [after line 234 in F]  **255 The captain** [Q1; not in F]  **262 you** your  **280 CAPTAIN Gent.**  **282 them** him  **294 You are** [eds.] Your are [F] You'r [Q1]  **298 it is** is it  **299.1 Captain Messenger** [after "to him" in line 299 in F]  **300 SH CAPTAIN Mess.**  **320 rack** wracke

The above textual notes list all instances in which material not in F is included from Q1. To enable the reader to compare further the F and Q1 texts, a list is provided here of material not in Q1 that is to be found in F. There are some 100 lines in all.
**1.1. 40–5** while . . . now  **49–50** Since . . . state  **64–5** and . . . rivers  **83–5** to whose . . . interested  **88–9** LEAR Nothing? CORDELIA Nothing  **165** ALBANY, CORNWALL Dear sir, forbear.
**1.2. 112–17** This . . . graves  **169–75** I pray . . . brother
**1.4. 260** ALBANY Pray . . . patient  **273** Of . . . you  **321–33** This . . . unfitness
**2.4. 6** KENT No, my lord  **21** KENT By Juno . . . ay  **45–54** FOOL Winter's . . . year  **96–7** GLOUCESTER Well . . . man  **101–2** Are they . . . Fiery? The  **139–44** LEAR Say . . . blame  **298–9** CORNWALL Whither . . . horse
**3.1. 22–9** Who . . . furnishings
**3.2. 79–96** FOOL This . . . time. Exit
**3.4. 17–18** In . . . endure  **26–7** In . . . sleep  **37–8** Fathom . . . Tom
**3.6. 12–14** FOOL No . . . him  **85** FOOL And . . . noon
**4.1. 6–9** Welcome . . . blasts
**4.2. 26** Oh, the . . . man
**4.6. 165–70** Plate . . . lips
**5.2. 11** GLOUCESTER And . . . too
**5.3. 78** Dispose . . . thine  **91** GONERIL An interlude  **147** What . . . delay  **226** ALBANY Speak, man  **316–17** Do you . . . look there

## Macbeth

Copy text: the First Folio. Act and scene divisions follow the Folio text, except that 5.8 is not marked in the Folio.
**1.1. 9 SECOND WITCH All**  **10 THIRD WITCH** [not in F]  **11 ALL** [at line 9 in F]
**1.2. 1 [and elsewhere] DUNCAN King**  **13 gallowglasses** Gallowgrosses  **14 quarrel** Quarry  **21 ne'er** neu'r  **26 thunders break** Thunders

**1.3. 32 Weird** weyward [elsewhere in F spelled "weyard"]  **39 Forres** Soris  **97 death. As** death, as  **98 Came** Can  **111 lose** loose
**1.4. 1 Are** Or
**1.5. 1 [and elsewhere] LADY MACBETH Lady**  **12 lose** loose  **47 it** hit
**1.6. 4 martlet** Barlet  **9 most** must
**1.7. 6 shoal** Schoole  **48 do** no
**2.1. 56 strides** sides  **57 sure** sowre  **58 way they** they may
**2.2. 13.1** [at line 8 in F, after "die"]
**2.3. 41.1** [after line 40 in F]  **142 nea'er** neere
**3.1. 76 MURDERERS Murth.**  **116 BOTH MURDERERS Murth.** [also at line 141]  **142.1 Exeunt** [at line 144 in F]
**3.3. 7 and** end
**3.4. 79 time** times  **122.1 Exeunt Exit**
**3.6. 24 son** Sonnes  **38 the** their
**4.1. 34 cauldron** Cawdron  **38.1 to** and  **59 germens** Germaine  **93 Dunsinane** Dunsmane  **94 s.d. Descends Descend**  **98 Birnam** Byrnan [also spelled "Byrnam" at line 93 and "Birnan," "Byrnane," and "Birnane" in Act 5]  **119 eight** eight
**4.2. 1 [and throughout] LADY MACDUFF Wife**  **22 none** moue  **70–1 ones . . . methinks, ones** / To fright you thus. Me thinkes  **80 s.d. Enter Murderers** [after "What are these faces" in F]  **81 [and throughout scene] FIRST MURDERER Mur.**  **84 shag-haired** shagge-ear'd
**4.3. 4 downfall'n** downfall  **15 deserve** discerne  **35 Fare** Far  **108 accurst** accust  **124 detraction, here** detraction. Heere  **134 thy** they  **144 essay** assay  **146.1** [after "amend" in F]  **161 not** nor  **237 tune** time
**5.1. 38 fear who** feare? who
**5.3. 41 Cure her** Cure  **54 pristine** pristiue  **57 senna** Cyme  **62.1 Exeunt** [at line 64 in F]
**5.4. 16 SIWARD Sey.**

## Antony and Cleopatra

Copy text: the First Folio. Act and scene divisions, missing in the Folio, are editorially supplied.
**1.1. 41 On** One  **52 whose** who
**1.2. 4 charge** change  **41 fertile** fore-tell  **64 Alexas** [printed in F as s.p.]  **83 Saw** Saue  **90 Alexas Alexias**  **93 [and through line 118] FIRST MESSENGER Messen.** (or Mess.)  **116 minds** windes  **119 ho** how  **120 SECOND MESSENGER 1. Mes.**  **121 THIRD MESSENGER 2. Mes.**  **124 FOURTH MESSENGER 3. Mes.**  **126 FOURTH MESSENGER Mes.**  **137.1 Enter Enobarbus** [after "hatch," line 137, in F]  **144 occasion** an occasion  **162 travel** Trauaile  **186 leave** loue  **191 Hath** Haue  **200 hair** heire  **202 place is** places  **requires** require
**1.3. 2 who's** Whose  **20 What, says** What sayes  **43 services** Seruicles  **63 vials** Violles  **80 blood. No more.** blood no more?  **82 by my** by
**1.4. 3 Our** One  **8 Vouchsafed** vouchsafe  **9 abstract** abstracts  **34 FIRST MESSENGER Mes.**  **44 deared** fear'd  **46 lackeying** lacking  **48 SECOND MESSENGER Mes.**  **57 wassails** Vassailes  **58 Modena** Medena  **59 Pansa Pausa**  **77 we** me
**1.5. 3 mandragora Mandragoru**  **5 time** time:  **35.1 Alexas Alexas from Caesar**  **52 dumbed** dumbe  **53, What, was** What was  **64 man** mans
**2.1. 2 [and throughout scene] MENAS Mene.**  **22 joined** ioyne  **39 ne'er** neere  **42 warred** wan'd  **44–5 greater.... all,** greater, . . . all:
**2.2. 77 Alexandria; you** Alexandria you  **113 soldier only. Speak** Souldier, onely speak  **128 so say** so  **129 reproof** proofe  **180.1 Exeunt Exit omnes Manent Manet**  **204 lovesick . . . The** Loue-sicke. With them the  **214 glow** gloue  **216 gentlewomen** Gentlewoman  **233 heard** hard
**2.3. 23 afeard** a feare  **25 thee; . . . to thee.** thee no more but: when to thee,  **31 away** alway  **32 [and elsewhere] Ventidius Ventigius**  **41 s.d. Enter Ventidius** [after "Ventigius," line 41, in F]
**2.4. 6 th' Mount** Mount  **9 MAECENAS, AGRIPPA Both**

**2.5. 2** ALL *Omnes*    **10 river. There** Riuer there    **11 off, I** off. I    **12 finned** fine    **23 s.d.** *Enter a Messenger* [after "Italy," line 23, in F]    **28 him, there** him. / There    **44 is** 'tis    **85 s.d.** *Enter . . . again* [after "sir" line 85, in F]

**2.6. 0.1** *Menas* [listed after *Agrippa* in F]    **16 th'all-honored** all-honor'd    **19 is** his    **39** CAESAR, ANTONY, LEPIDUS *Omnes*    **42–3 impatience. Though . . . telling,** impatience: though . . . telling.    **58 composition** composition    **67 meanings** meaning    **71 more of** more    **83** CAESAR, ANTONY, LEPIDUS *All*    **83.1** *Manent Manet*

**2.7. 1 their** th'their    **4 colored** Conlord    **39 s.d.** *whispers in 's ear* [at line 41 in F]    **93 is he** is    **101 grows** grow    **113 bear** beate    **115** BOY [not in F]    **119** ALL [not in F]    **122 off. Our** of our    **126 Splits** Spleet's    **130 father's** Father    **132** MENAS [not in F]

**3.1. 5 [and throughout scene]** SILIUS *Romaine*    **8 [and elsewhere] whither** whether

**3.2. 10** AGRIPPA *Ant.*    **16 figures** Figure    **49 full** the full    **60 wept** weepe

**3.3. 2 s.d.** *Enter . . . before* [after "sir," line 2, in F]    **19 looked'st** look'st

**3.4. 8 them,** then    **9 took't** look't    **24 yours** your    **30 Your** You    **38 has** he's

**3.5. 13 world** would    **hast** hadst    **chops** chaps    **15 grind the one** grind

**3.6. 13 he there** hither    **the kings** the King    **30 being, that** being that,    **62 obstruct** abstract    **73 Adallas** *Adullas*    **74 Manchus** *Mauchus*    **76 Comagene** Comageat    **Polemon** *Polemen*    **77 Lycaonia** Licoania

**3.7. 4 it is** it it    **14 Photinus, an** *Photinus an*    **19 s.d.** *Canidius Camidias* [also spelled "Camidius" in this scene and elsewhere]    **21 Brundusium** Brandusium    **23 Toryne** Troine    **29 [and elsewhere]** CANIDIUS *Cam.*    **36 muleteers** Militers    **52 Actium** Action    **57 impossible;** impossible    **67.1** *Exeunt exit*    **70 leader's** led Leaders leade    **73** CANIDIUS *Ven.*    **80 Well I** Well, I    **82 in** with

**3.8. 6 s.d.** *Exeunt exit*

**3.9. 4 s.d.** *Exeunt exit*

**3.10. 0.5.** *Enobarbus Enobarbus and Scarus*    **14 June** Inne    **28 he** his

**3.11. 6** ALL *Omnes*    **19 that** them    **46 seize** cease    **50 led** lead    **57 tow** stowe    **58 Thy** The

**3.12. 0.1.** *Dolabella Dollabello*    **13 lessens** Lessons

**3.13. 26 caparisons** Comparisons    **34 alike. That** alike, that    **55 Caesar** *Caesars*    **74 deputation** disputation    **76 kneel / Till** kneele. / Tell him,    **94 s.d.** *Enter a Servant* [after "him," in line 94, in F]    **104 This** the    **114–15 eyes, / In . . . filth** eyes / In . . . filth,    **133 s.d.** *Enter . . . Thidias* [after "whipped," in line 133, in F]    **140 whipped . . . Henceforth** whipt. For following him, henceforth    **165 smite** smile    **168 discandying** discandering    **171 sits** sets    **202 on** in    **204 s.d.** *Exit Exeunt*

**4.2. 1 Domitius** *Domitian*    **20** ALL *Omnes*

**4.3. 8** THIRD 1    **25, 31** ALL *Omnes*

**4.4. 5 too** too, *Anthony*    **6** ANTONY [not in F, or mistakenly placed in line 5 as part of Cleopatra's speech]    **8** CLEOPATRA [not in F]    **24** CAPTAIN *Alex.*    **32–3 compliment . . . Now** Complement, Ile leaue thee. / Now

**4.5. 1, 3, 6** SOLDIER *Eros*    **17 Dispatch.—Enobarbus** Dispatch *Enobarbus*    **17.1** *Exeunt Exit*

**4.6. 37–8 do 't.** I doo't. I feele / I

**4.7** **3 s.d.** *Exeunt Exit*    **8 s.d.** [after "heads," line 6, in F]

**4.8. 2 gests** guests    **18 My** Mine    **23 favoring** sauouring

**4.12. 3 s.d.** *Alarum . . . fight* [at 0.1 in F]    **4 augurers** Auguries    **21 spanieled** pannelled

**4.13. 10 death. To** death to'

**4.14. 4 towered** toward    **10 dislimns** dislimes    **19 Caesar** *Caesars*    **104 ho** how    **119** DERCETUS *Decre.*    **145.1** *Exeunt Exit*

**4.15. 26–7 me. If . . . operation,** me, if . . . operation.    **56 lived the** liued. The    **78 e'en** in    **96.1** *off of*

**5.1 0.1** *Maecenas Menas*    **3.1** *Dercetus Decretas*    **5, 13, 19** DERCETUS *Dec.*    **5 Dercetus** *Decretas*    **26 you sad, friends?** you sad Friends,    **28, 31** AGRIPPA *Dol.*    **48.1** [after "says," line 51, in F]    **54 intents desires** intents, desires,    **59 live** leaue

**5.2. 26 dependency** dependacie    **35** [F repeats s.p. *Pro.*]    **55 varletry** Varlotarie    **69.1** [after "to him" in F]    **80 O, the o'th'** 'twas *Anthony* it was    **102 success but** successe: But    **103 smites suites** suites    **144 seal** seele    **156 soulless villain** Soule-lesse, Villain    **178 merits in our name,** merits, in our name    **207 s.d.** *Exit* [at line 206 in F]    **216 Ballad** Ballads    **223 my** mine    **228 Cydnus** *Cidrus*    **318 awry** away    **319.1** *in in, and Dolabella*    **342–3 diadem . . . mistress;** Diadem; . . . Mistris

## The Winter's Tale

Copy text: the First Folio. Characters' names are groups at the heads of scenes throughout the play. Act and scene divisions are as marked in the Folio.

**The Names of the Actors** [printed in F at the end of the play]    ARCHIDAMUS [after *Autoclycus* in F]

**1.1. 9 us, we** vs: we

**1.2. 104 And** A    **121 hast** has't    **137–8 be?—/ Affection, thy** be / Affection? thy    **148 What . . . brother** [assigned in F to Leontes]    **151–3 its folly, . . . Its tenderness, . . . bosoms!** it's folly? . . . It's tendernesse? . . . bosomes?    **158 do** do's    **202–3 powerful, think it, . . . south. Be** powreful: thinke it: . . . South, be    **208 you, they** you    **253 forth. In . . . lord,** forth in . . . (my Lord.)    **275 hobbyhorse** Holy-Horse    **386 How? Caught** How caught    **461 off. Hence!** off, hence:

**2.1. 2 [and throughout scene]** FIRST LADY *Lady*    **91 fedarie** Federarie

**2.2. 32–3 me. / If . . . blister** me, / If . . . blister.

**2.3. 2 thus, mere weakness. If** thus: meere weaknesse, if    **39 What Who** **61 good, so** good so,

**3.2. 10 Silence** [printed in F as a s.d.]    **10.1–2 Hermione, as to her trial . . . Ladies** [at start of scene in F, as generally with the s.d. in this play]    **33 Who** Whom    **99 Starred** Star'd    **156 woo** woe

**3.3. 64 scar'd** scarr'd    **116 made** mad

**4.2. 13 thee. Thou,** thee, thou

**4.3. 1** AUTOLYCUS [not in F]    **7 on** an    **10 With heigh, with heigh** *With heigh*    **38 currants** Currence

**4.4. 12 Digest it** Digest    **13 swoon** sworne    **60 a fire** o'fire    **83 bastards. Of** bastards) of    **93 scion** Sien    **98 your** you    **160 out on't    218** AUTOLYCUS [not in F]    **244 kilnhole** kill-hole    **297** AUTOLYCUS [in F, appears at line 298]    **299 Whither** Whether [and similarly throughout song]    **310 gentleman** Gent.    **316 cape** Crpe    **339 square squire    355 reply, at least** reply at least,    **361 who** whom    **421 acknowledged** acknowledge    **425 who** whom    **430 see** neuer see    **441 hoop** hope    **470 your** my    **473 sight as yet, I fear.** sight, as yet I feare;    **485–6 fancy. If . . . obedient, I** fancie, if . . . obedient: I    **503 our** her    **614 could** would    **filed** fill'd    **off** of    **644 flayed** fled    v**708 know not** know    **738 to** at    **833 s.d.** *Exeunt* [at 845 in F]

**5.1. 6 Whilst** Whilest [also at line 169]    **59 Where . . . appear** (Where we Offendors now appeare)    **61 just** just such    **75 I have done** [assigned in F to Cleomenes]    **84 s.d.** *Gentleman Seruant*    **85 [and through line 110]** GENTLEMAN, *Ser.*    **114 s.d.** *Exit* [after "us" in line 115 in F]    **160 his, parting** his parting

**5.2. 113 s.d.** *Exeunt Exit*

**5.3. 18 Lonely** Louely    **67 fixture** fixure

## The Tempest

Copy text: the First Folio. Characters' names are grouped at the heads of scenes throughout. Act and scene divisions are as marked in the Folio.

**Names of the Actors** [printed in F at the end of the play]

**1.1. 8.1 Ferdinand** Ferdinando    **34 s.d.** *Exeunt Exit*    **36 [and elsewhere] wi' the** with    **38.1** [at line 37 in F]

**1.2. 99 exact, like** exact. Like    **166 steaded much.** steeded much,    **174 princes** Princesse    **201 bowsprit** Bore-spritt    **213 me. The** me the    **230 Bermudas** *Bermoothes*    **284 she** he    **288 service. Thou** service, thou    **330 forth at** for that    **377.5, 399.1** *Ariel's* Ariel (or Ariell)

**385 s.d.** *Burden, dispersedly* [before "Hark, hark!" in line 384 in F]
**387** [F provides a speech prefix, *Ar.*]   **400** ARIEL [not in F]
**2.1. 38** ANTONIO *Seb.*   **39** SEBASTIAN *Ant.*   **183 mettle** mettal   **232 throes** throwes
**2.2. 9 mow** moe   **116 spirits** sprights
**3.1. 2 sets** set
**3.2. 51–2 isle; / From me he** Isle / From me, he   **122 scout** *cout*
**3.3. 15 travel** trauaile   **17.1–2** *Solemn . . . invisible* [after "they are fresh" in F, and followed by the s.d. at line 19, *Enter . . . depart*]   **28 me** me?
**29 islanders?** Islands;   **33 human** humaine   **65 plume** plumbe
**4.1. 9 off** of   **13 gift** guest   **25 love as 'tis now, the** loue, as 'tis now the   **61 vetches** Fetches   **68 poll-clipped** pole-clipt   **74 Her** here   **110** CERES [not in F]   **124.1–2** [after line 127 in F]   **163.1** *Exeunt Exit*   **193 s.d.** *Enter Ariel . . . etc.* [after "on this line" in F, and followed by *Enter* Caliban . . . *all wet*]   **193 them on** on them
**232 Let't** let's
**5.1. 16 run** runs   **60 boiled** boile   **72 Didst** Did   **75 entertained** entertaine   **82 lies** ly   **88** ARIEL [not in F]   **111 Whe'er** Where   **236 horrible,** horrible.   **238 her** our   **249 business.** At businesse, at   **250 Which . . . single** (Which shall be shortly single)   **260** *coraggio Corasio*

## The Sonnets

Copy text: the quarto of 1609 [Q].
**2.4 tattered** totter'd [also at 26.11]   **2.14 cold** could   **6.4 beauty's** beau-tits   **8.10 Strikes** Strike [in some copies]   **12.4 all** or   **13.7 Yourself** You selfe   **15.8 wear** were   **17.12 meter** miter   **17.14 twice, in it and** twise in it, and   **18.10 [and elsewhere] lose** loose   **19.3 jaws** yawes   **20.2 Hast** Haste   **22.3 furrows** forrwes   **23.6 rite** right   **23.14 with wit** wit wiht   **24.1 stelled** steeld   **25.9 fight** worth   **26.12 thy** their [also at 27.10, 35.8 (twice), 37.7, 43.11, 45.12, 46.3, 46.8, 46.13, 46.14, 69.5, 70.6, 85.3, 128.11, 128.14]   **27.2 travel** trauaill   **28.12 gild'st** guil'st   **28.14 strength** length   **31.8 thee** there   **34.2 travel** trauaile   **34.12 cross** losse   **34.13 sheds** sheeds   **38.2 pour'st** poor'st   **38.3 too to** 39.12 doth** dost   **41.7 woos** woes   **42.10 losing** loosing   **44.12 attend time's** attend, times   **44.13 naught** naughts   **45.9 life's** liues   **46.9 'cide** side   **46.12 the** he [in some copies]   **47.2 other.** other,   **47.4 smother,** smother;   **47.11 no** nor   **50.6 dully** duly   **51.10 perfect'st** perfects   **55.1 monuments** monument   **56.3 [and elsewhere] today** too daie   **58.7 patience-tame to suffrance,** patience tame, to sufferance   **59.6 hundred** hundreth   **59.11 whe'er** where   **61.14 off** of   **too to** 62.10 chapped** chopt   **63.5 traveled** trauaild   **65.12 of** or   **67.6 seeming** seeing   **69.3 due** end   **69.14 soil** solye   **71.13 Lest** Least [also at 72.1, 72.9, and elsewhere]   **73.4 ruined** rn'wd   **choirs** quiers   **76.7 tell** fel   **77.1 wear** were   **77.10 blanks** blacks   **82.8 these** the   **83.7 too** to   **88.8 losing** loosing   **90.11 shall** stall   **91.9 better** bitter   **93.5 there** their   **98.11 were** weare   **99.4 dwells** dwells?   **99.9 One** Our   **99.13 ate** eate   **102.8 her** his   **106.12 skill** still   **111.1 with** wish   **112.14 are** y'are   **113.6 latch** lack   **113.13 more, replete with** more repleat, with   **113.14 mine eye** mine   **116** [numbered 119 in Q]   **117.10 surmise accumulate;** surmise, accumulate   **118.5 ne'er-cloying** nere cloying   **118.10 were not, grew** were, not grew   **119.4 losing** loosing   **121.11 bevel.** beuel   **125.6 rent,** rent   **125.7 sweet forgoing** sweet; Forgoing   **126.2 sickle hour;** sickle, hower;   **126.8 minutes** mynuit   **127.2 were** weare   **127.10 brows** eyes   **129.9 Mad** Made   **129.10 quest to have,** quest, to haue   **129.11 proved, a** proud and   **132.6 the east** th' East   **132.9 mourning** morning   **138.12 to have** t' haue   **140.5 were** weare   **144.6 side** [adopted from *The Passionate Pilgrim*] sight   **144.9 fiend** [adopted from *The Passionate Pilgrim*] finde   **146.2 Thrall to** My sinfull earth   **147.7 approve** approoue.   **153.14 eyes** eye

# Index

Page ranges in **bold** indicate the page range for the entire play.
Page references followed by *n* indicate a footnote.

Index-21